In celebration of the diverse cultures represented in Kirszner & Mandell's fourth edition of *Literature: Reading, Reacting, Writing,* textile artist Greta Vaught designed this quilt.

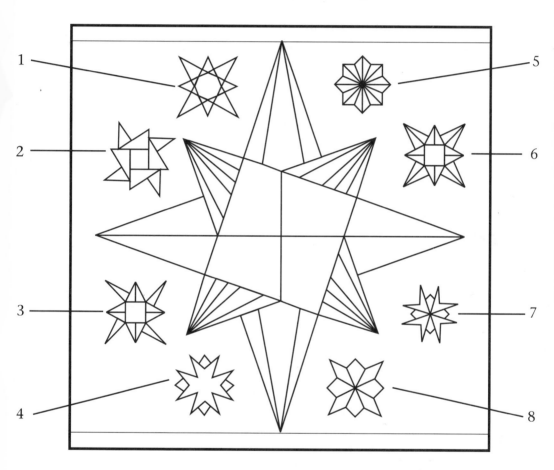

1	*Newfoundland Snowflake*	*Banbridge Star*	5
2	*Morumbi Wheel*	*Hedland Star*	6
3	*Kobe Pinwheel*	*Cape Star*	7
4	*Absaroka Trail*	*Roman Pinwheel*	8

LITERATURE

READING ◆ REACTING ◆ WRITING

FOURTH EDITION

LAURIE G. KIRSZNER
University of the Sciences in Philadelphia

STEPHEN R. MANDELL
Drexel University

HARCOURT COLLEGE PUBLISHERS

Fort Worth   Philadelphia   San Diego   New York   Orlando   Austin   San Antonio
Toronto   Montreal   London   Sydney   Tokyo

Publisher	Earl McPeek
Acquisitions Editor	Bill Hoffman
Market Strategist	John Meyers
Developmental Editor	Camille Adkins
Project Editor	Jon Davies
Art Director	Sue Hart
Production Manager	Cindy Young

ISBN: 0-15-507350-8
Library of Congress Catalog Card Number: 00-102493

Address for Domestic Orders
Harcourt, Inc., 6277 Sea Harbor Drive, Orlando, FL 32887-6777
800-782-4479

Address for International Orders
International Customer Service
Harcourt, Inc., 6277 Sea Harbor Drive, Orlando, FL 32887-6777
407-345-3800
(fax) 407-345-4060
(e-mail) hbintl@harcourtbrace.com

Address for Editorial Correspondence
Harcourt College Publishers, 301 Commerce Street, Suite 3700, Fort Worth, TX 76102

Web Site Address
http://www.harcourtcollege.com

Harcourt College Publishers will provide complimentary supplements or supplement packages to those adopters qualified under our adoption policy. Please contact your sales representative to learn how to qualify. If as an adopter or potential user you receive supplements you do not need, please return them to your sales representative or send them to: Attn: Returns Department, Troy Warehouse, 465 South Lincoln Drive, Troy, MO 63379.

Printed in the United States of America

1 2 3 4 5 6 7 8 9   039   9 8 7 6 5 4 3

Harcourt College Publishers

Preface

In Susan Glaspell's *Trifles* (p. 1163), two women try to understand the emotional pain of a third by studying a quilt she is making. In this sense, the pieces of the quilt are also pieces of a puzzle they (and the audience) must assemble, and the process of creating a quilt becomes a metaphor for piecing together scraps of meaning to discover truth. In Alice Walker's "Everyday Use" (p. 324), two sisters compete for possession of two quilts that have been in their family for years. At the end of the story, the narrator's description of the two quilts suggests their significance—as a link between the old and the new, between what was and what is:

> One was in the Lone Star pattern. The other was Walk Around the Mountain. In both of them were scraps of dresses that Grandma Dee had worn fifty and more years ago. Bits and pieces of Grandpa Jarrell's Paisley shirts. And one teeny faded blue piece, about the size of a penny matchbox, that was from Great Grandpa Ezra's uniform that he wore in the Civil War. (329)

During the time we were writing the first edition of *Literature: Reading, Reacting, Writing,* we came to see the book as a kind of literary quilt, one that placed nontraditional works alongside classics, integrated the familiar with the unfamiliar, and invited students to see well-known works in new contexts. Because a quilt is made of many different pieces, with the whole adding up to more than the sum of its parts, it is consistent with one of our primary goals—to include works that represent various voices and viewpoints and to weave together old and new, past and present. To help us convey this message, Harcourt College Publishers commissioned a hand-made quilt by textile artist Greta Vaught for the cover of our first edition—and a new one for each subsequent edition.

READING SELECTIONS

Our goal in this fourth edition has remained what it has been from the start: to expand the personal literary boundaries of both students and instructors. In order to further this purpose, we have fine-tuned the reading selections in response to thoughtful comments from our reviewers and from our students.

In fiction, we continue to include a wide range of stories. Some—like "The Lottery," "A Rose for Emily," "The Story of an Hour," and (new to this edition) "Bartleby, the Scrivener"—are perennial favorites; others are stories we introduced readers to in the first edition, such as David Michael Kaplan's "Doe Season," Anne Tyler's "Teenage Wasteland," and Charles Baxter's "Gryphon." In this edition, we have added several seldom-anthologized stories—for example, Gary Gildner's "Sleepy Time Gal," Grace Coates's "Wild Plums," Chitra Banerjee Divakaruni's "The Disappearance," and Carol Shields's "Fifteen Minutes in the Life of Larry Weller." We have also added works so that we now have pairs of stories by seven authors: Nathaniel Hawthorne ("Young Goodman Brown" and "The Birthmark"), Flannery O'Connor ("A Good Man Is Hard to Find" and "A Late Encounter with the Enemy"), Joyce Carol Oates ("Shopping" and "Where Are You Going, Where Have You Been?"), and Shirley Jackson ("The Lottery" and "The Possibility of Evil"), in addition to William Faulkner, James Joyce, and Edgar Allan Poe.

In the poetry section, we have maintained the balance between old and new with works by classic poets like Robert Frost and Emily Dickinson placed alongside works by more contemporary poets like Linda Pastan, Sherman Alexie, Marge Piercy, and Michael Ondaatje. The poetry section also includes "An Album of Fifty Poets," which contains photos and brief biographies of fifty of the poets represented in the text. New to this edition are an expanded "Discovering Themes in Poetry" section that contains three groups of poems—"Poems about Parents," "Poems about Love," and "Poems about War"—and a new casebook showcasing the poetry of Langston Hughes.

The drama section also juxtaposes classic and contemporary works, with selections retained from previous editions ranging from Shakespeare's *Hamlet* to August Wilson's *Fences* to Milcha Sanchez-Scott's *The Cuban Swimmer*. Six plays are new to this edition: August Strindberg's classic two-character play *The Stronger*, Shakespeare's comedy *A Midsummer Night's Dream*, Wendy Wasserstein's moving short play *Tender Offer*, Alice Childress's understated and provocative *Florence*, Paddy Chayefsky's 1950's television drama *Marty*, and Marsha Norman's powerful *'night Mother*.

PEDAGOGICAL FEATURES
◇ ◇ ◇

Literature: Reading, Reacting, Writing, Fourth Edition, is designed to demystify the study of literature and to prepare students to explore the literary works collected in this anthology.

◇ **Chapter 1, "Understanding Literature"**—This introductory chapter introduces students to some of the most important issues surrounding the study of literature, acquainting students with traditional literary themes as well as with the concept of the canon. The chapter also lays the groundwork for students' independent exploration of literary texts by discussing the processes of interpreting and evaluating literature, placing special emphasis on how readers' personal experiences affect meaning. Finally, the chapter examines the role of literary criticism and considers how critics' interpretations can help students expand their literary horizons.

◇ **Four full chapters of writing instruction**—To help students see writing about literature as a process of discovering and testing ideas, writing instruction is presented in four full chapters. Chapter 2, "Reading and Writing about Literature," discusses and illustrates the process of planning, drafting, and revising essays about literary works, concluding with an exercise juxtaposing two student papers (one effective and one less effective) that examine the same three short stories. Three additional chapters, "Reading and Writing about Fiction" (Chapter 3), "Reading and Writing about Poetry" (Chapter 12), and "Reading and Writing about Drama" (Chapter 21), follow the writing process of students as they write about each genre: Alberto Alvaro Ríos's short story "The Secret Lion" (p. 49); two poems, Seamus Heaney's "Digging" (p. 679) and Robert Hayden's "Those Winter Sundays" (p. 678); and Susan Glaspell's one-act play *Trifles* (p. 1163).

◇ **Eight model student papers**—The text includes eight model student papers, five of which are source based (the other three are shown in multiple drafts, along with annotations and commentary).

◇ **Three casebooks**—Three separate casebooks—one for Joyce Carol Oates's "Where Are You Going, Where Have You Been?," one for a selection of poems by Langston Hughes, and one for Tennessee Williams's play *The Glass Menagerie*—present articles by literary critics, biographical essays, and other useful material, including a list of relevant Internet sites. Students can use these casebooks to supplement their reading or as source material for a research project. A model student paper at the end of each casebook shows students how they can use sources (including Internet sources) in their writing. By gathering research materials in a convenient, accessible format, these casebooks offer students a controlled, self-contained introduction to source-based writing.

◇ **Checklists**—Most chapter introductions end with a checklist designed to help students measure their understanding of concepts introduced in the chapter and to support students as they generate, explore, focus, and organize ideas for writing about works of literature.

◇ **Reading and Reacting questions**—Reading and Reacting questions, including journal prompts, follow many selections throughout the text. These questions ask students to interpret and evaluate what they have read, sometimes encouraging them to make connections between the literary work being studied and other works in the text.

◊ **Related Works**—A Related Works section following the Reading and Reacting questions lists works linked (by theme, author, or genre) to the particular work under study. This feature encourages students to see connections between works by different writers, between works in different genres, or between two themes— connections they can explore in class discussion or in writing.

◊ **Authors represented by multiple works**—Many writers have more than one work in the text, and a number of these writers are represented by works in more than one literary genre. A listing of all such works follows the book's table of contents (p. xli), giving students an opportunity to see how a particular writer explores different themes, styles, and genres.

◊ **Writing Suggestions**—Suggestions for paper topics are included at the end of each chapter. New to this edition are writing suggestions in each chapter linked directly to the Harcourt Web site.

◊ **Critical Perspectives**—Most chapters open with a group of quotations that provide a thought-provoking yet accessible introduction to the words of literary critics on a particular aspect of literature, such as point of view or language. In addition, Critical Perspective questions (included in most sets of Reading and Reacting questions) ask students to respond to analytical, interpretive, or evaluative comments critics have made about the work. This feature encourages students to apply their own critical-thinking skills to literary criticism as well as to literature itself.

◊ **Four helpful appendixes**—The text also includes four appendixes. Appendix A, "Writing a Research Paper," takes students through the process of writing a paper on Eudora Welty's "A Worn Path," explaining and illustrating MLA-style documentation (including the most up-to-date guidelines on documenting electronic sources). This appendix includes two source-based student papers. One, on "A Worn Path," uses conventional print sources; the other, on John Updike's "A&P," uses a variety of electronic sources, including an e-mail communication and a magazine article accessed through an online database. In addition, each paper cites a filmed interview with the story's author. Appendix B, "Literary History: Aristotle to the Twentieth Century," and Appendix C, "Twentieth-Century Literary Theories," provide a critical context for the articles in the casebooks as well as useful background information for students' own writing. Appendix D—new to this edition—provides useful guidelines for writing an essay exam about literature.

◇ **Full-color reproductions of fine art works**—The poetry section includes a four-page color insert reproducing fine art linked to various poems in the text: W. H. Auden's "Musée des Beaux Arts," Jane Flanders's "Cloud Painter," William Carlos Williams's "The Great Figure," Robert Hayden's "Monet's Waterlillies," Delmore Schwartz's "The True-Blue American," and the poetry in the Langston Hughes casebook. These color plates are intended to enhance students' understanding and enjoyment of the poems to which they are linked as well as to introduce them to another medium of artistic expression.

◇ **Cultural Contexts**—A Cultural Context entry has been added to each author headnote in fiction and drama, providing vital background about the social and historical climate in which a work was written.

◇ **Web Activities**—A Web Activity has been added to every set of Writing Suggestions.

Each of the pedagogical features described above encourages students both to appreciate works representing diverse literary subjects, styles, and perspectives and to develop their own critical abilities by reading, reacting to, and writing about these works. If this anthology can encourage students to respond enthusiastically to what they read and to see their responses as part of an ongoing dialogue with their peers, with critics, with their instructors, with themselves, and with the work itself—then it will have accomplished its purpose.

ANCILLARIES
◇ ◇ ◇

To support users of the fourth edition of *Literature: Reading, Reacting, Writing,* the following ancillary materials are available from Harcourt:

Instructor's Resource Guide—discussion and activities for every story, poem, and play in the anthology; thematic table of contents; semester and quarter syllabi; articles on the evolution of the literary canon and reader-response theory.

The Harcourt Brace Casebook Series in Literature—ten complete casebooks, each providing in one convenient location all the materials a college student needs to complete a literary research paper.

FICTION

"A Rose for Emily" by William Faulkner

"The Yellow Wall-Paper" by Charlotte Perkins Gilman

"A Good Man Is Hard to Fine" by Flannery O'Connor

"A&P" by John Updike

"A Worn Path" by Eudora Welty

POETRY

A Collection of Poems by Emily Dickinson

A Collection of Poems by Langston Hughes

A Collection of Poems by Walt Whitman

DRAMA

"Master Harold" . . . *and the Boys* by Athol Fugard

Hamlet by William Shakespeare

The Harcourt Brace Original Film Series in Literature— film adaptations of Eudora Welty's "A Worn Path" and John Updike's "A&P." Each film lasts thirty minutes or less and includes an interview with the author.

Additional Videos—fourteen videos, including adaptations of plays in the fourth edition and films to accompany each casebook in the text.

ACKNOWLEDGMENTS
◊ ◊ ◊

From start to finish, this text has been a true collaboration for us, not only with each other, but also with our students and colleagues. We have worked hard on the book, and many people at Harcourt have worked along with us. As always, the credit for the endless day-to-day coordination of people and pages goes to our smart, funny, and incredibly patient developmental editor, Camille Adkins. Bill Hoffman, acquisitions editor, has worked hard to make good things happen, and Jon Davies, project editor, has guided the manuscript through production with patience and skill. David Day oversaw the creation of yet another beautiful design, and Cindy Young managed the book's production with professionalism and ease. We also thank Laura Mandell Zaidman of the University of South Carolina— Sumter for coordinating the revision of the Instructor's Resource Guide, with contributions from Cheryl Carvajal of Coker College, Lois Rauch Gibson of Coker College, and Sandy Richardson of Central Carolina Technical College. We are especially grateful to Laura Mandell Zaidman for her work on the Album of Fifty Poets and to Deborah P. Barberousse for her work on the Cultural Contexts and Web Activities.

We would like to thank the following reviewers of the fourth edition: Crystal V. Bacon, Glouchester County College; Gwen Barklay-Toy, North Carolina State University; Eric Birdsall, University of Akron; John Doyle, Quinnipiac College; David Fear, Valencia Community College; Elizabeth Keats Flores, College of Lake Country; Linda Gruber, Kishwaukee College; Lynn Hildenbrand, Chesapeake College; Teresa Kennedy, Mary Washington College; Michael Kraus, Marian College of Fond du Lac; Teri Maddox, Jackson State Community College; Judith P. Moray, Moraine Valley Community College; Mary Beth Namm, North Carolina State University; Rodney D. Newton, Central Texas College; Monte Prater, Tulsa Community College—Northeast; Gail Rung, Black Hawk College; Robert M. Temple, Manatee Community College; Maria W. Warren, University of West Florida; Donnie Yeilding, Central Texas College; and Laura Mandell Zaidman, University of South Carolina—Sumter.

We would also like to thank all the reviewers who made valuable contributions to the third edition: Ben Accardi, University of Kansas; Thomas Bailey, Western Michigan University; John Bails, University of Sioux Falls; Leigh Boyd, Temple Junior College; Cathy Cowan, Cabrillo College; Pat Cowart, Frostburg State University; Kitty Dean, Nassau Community College; Jo Devine, University of Alaska—Southeast; Jack Doyle, University of South Carolina—Sumter; Lynn Fauth, Oxnard College; David Fear, Valencia Community College; Mary Fleming, Jackson State Community College; Ann Fogg, University of Maine; Wayne Gilbert, Community College of Aurora; Shain Graham, Orange Coast College; Linda Gruber, Kishwaukee College; Chris Hacskaylo, University of Alaska—Ketchikan; Richard Hascal, Contra Costa College; Gwen Hauk, Temple Junior College; Michael Herzog, Gonzaga University; Andrew Kelly, Jackson State Community College; Benna Kime, Jackson State Community College; Amy Sparks Kolker, University of Kansas; Michael Kraus, Marian College of Fond du Lac; Heidi Ledett, Ulster County Community College; Teri Maddox, Jackson State Community College; Jeanne Mauzy, Valencia Community College; Fred Milley, Anderson University; Robert Milliken, University of Southern Maine; Andrew Moody, University of Kansas; Paul Perry, Palo Alto Community College; Angela Rapkin, Manatee Community College; Jean Reynolds, Polk Community College; Ellen Robbins, Ulster County Community College; Paul Rogalus, Plymouth State College; Neil Sebacher, Valencia Community College; Larry Severeid, College of Eastern Utah; Sharon Small, Des Moines Area Community College; Virginia Streamer, Dundalk Community College; Robert Temple, Manatee Community College; Margie Whelan, Mt. San Antonio College; Mike White, Odessa College; Rebecca Yancey, Jackson State Community College; Donnie Yielding, Central Texas College; and Martha Zamorano, Miami Dade–Kendall Campus.

Reviewers of the second edition were Deborah Barberousse, Horry-Georgetown Technical College; Bob Mayberry, University of Nevada—Las

Vegas; Shireen Carroll, University of Miami; Stephen Wright, Seminole Community College; Robert Dees, Orange Coast College; Larry Gray, Southeastern Louisiana University; Nancy Rayl, Cypress College; James Clemmer, Austin Peay State University; Roberta Kramer, Nassau Community College.

Reviewers of the first edition included Anne Agee, Anne Arundel Community College; Lucien Agosta, California State University—Sacramento; Diana Austin, University of New Brunswick; Judith Bechtel, Northern Kentucky University; Laureen Belmont, North Idaho College; Vivian Brown, Laredo Junior College; Rebecca Butler, Dalton Junior College; Susan Coffey, Central Virginia Community College; Douglas Crowell, Texas Tech University; Shirley Ann Curtis, Polk Community College; Kitty Dean, Nassau Community College; Robert Dees, Orange Coast College; Joyce Dempsey, Arkansas Tech University; Mindy Doyle, Orange County Community College; James Egan, University of Akron; Susan Fenyves, University of North Carolina—Charlotte; Marvin Garrett, University of Cincinnati; Ann Gebhard, State University of New York—Cortland; Emma Givaltney, Arkansas Tech University; Corrinne Hales, California State University—Fresno; Gary Hall, North Harris County College; Iris Hart, Santa Fe Community College; James Helvey, Davidson County Community College; Chris Henson, California State University—Fresno; Gloria Hochstein, University of Wisconsin—Eau Claire; Angela Ingram, Southwest Texas State University; John Iorio, University of South Florida; George Ives, North Idaho College; Lavinia Jennings, University of North Carolina—Chapel Hill; Judy Kidd, North Carolina State University; Leonard Leff, Oklahoma State University; Michael Matthews, Tarrant County Junior College—Northeast; Craig McLuckie, Okanagan College; Candy Meier, Des Moines Area Community College; Judith Michna, DeKalb College—North; Christopher O'Hearn, Los Angeles Harbor College; James O'Neil, Edison Community College; Melissa Pennell, University of Lowell; Sam Phillips, Gaston College; Robbie Pinter, Belmont College; Joseph Sternberg, Harper College; Kathleen Tickner, Brevard Community College; Betty Wells, Central Virginia Community College; Susan Yaeger, Monroe Business Institute.

We would also like to thank our families—Mark, Adam, and Rebecca Kirszner and Demi, David, and Sarah Mandell—for being there when we needed them. And finally, we each thank the person on the other side of the ampersand for making our collaboration work one more time.

Brief Contents

Detailed Contents

Fiction

◈ Chapter 3   Reading and Writing about Fiction   44

◆ **CHAPTER 4**   PLOT   72

◆ **CHAPTER 5**   CHARACTER   108

◆ **Fiction Casebook**   **612**

POETRY

◆ **Chapter 16 Figures of Speech 806**

◆ **An Album of Fifty Poets**   **1015**

◆ **Poetry Casebook**   **1040**

DRAMA

◊ CHAPTER 22   PLOT   1157

◊ CHAPTER 23   CHARACTER   1253

◊ Chapter 24   Staging 1488

◊ Chapter 25   Theme 1617

◈ DRAMA CASEBOOK   1803

◈ APPENDIX A WRITING A RESEARCH PAPER   1901

◆ ◆ ◆

Authors Represented by Multiple Works

CHAPTER 1

Understanding Literature

WHAT IS LITERATURE?

IMAGINATIVE LITERATURE

Imaginative literature begins with a writer's need to convey a personal vision to readers. Even when writers use factual material—historical documents, newspaper stories, or personal experience, for example—their primary purpose is to present a unique view of experience, one that has significance beyond the moment. (As the poet Ezra Pound said, "Literature is the news that *stays* news.") To convey their views of experience, writers of imaginative literature often manipulate facts—changing dates, inventing characters, and putting words into their mouths. For example, when Herman Melville wrote his novella *Benito Cereno,* he drew many of his facts from an account of an actual slave revolt. In his story he reproduces court records and plot details from this primary source, but he leaves out incidents, and he adds material of his own. The result is an original work of literature that serves the author's purpose. Wanting to do more than retell the original story, Melville used the factual material as "a skeleton of actual reality" upon which he built a story that attacked the institution of slavery and examined the nature of truth.

Imaginative literature is more likely than other types of writing to include words chosen not only because they communicate the writer's ideas, but also because they are memorable. Using vivid imagery and evocative comparisons, writers of imaginative literature often stretch language to its limits. By relying on the multiple connotations of words and images, a work of imaginative literature encourages readers to see the possibilities of language and to move beyond the factual details of an event. Consider, for example, how William Wordsworth uses language in the following lines from his poem "Composed upon Westminster Bridge, September 3, 1802" (p. 1008):

1

> This City now doth, like a garment, wear
> The beauty of the morning; silent, bare,
> Ships, towers, domes, theatres, and temples lie
> Open unto the fields, and to the sky;
>   All bright and glittering in the smokeless air.

Wordsworth does not try to present a picture of London that is topographically or sociologically accurate. Instead, by comparing the city at dawn to a person wearing a beautiful garment, Wordsworth creates a striking picture that has its own kind of truth. By using a vivid, original comparison, the poet is able to suggest the oneness of the city, nature, and himself—an idea that is not easily communicated.

Even though imaginative literature can be divided into types called **genres**—fiction, poetry, and drama—the nature of literary genres varies from culture to culture. In fact, some literary forms that Western readers take for granted are alien to other literary traditions. For example, the sonnet, although fairly common in the West, is not a conventional literary form in Chinese or Arabic poetry. Similarly, the most popular theatrical entertainment in Japan since the mid-seventeenth century, the kabuki play, has no exact counterpart in the West. (In a kabuki play, which includes stories, scenes, dances, music, acrobatics, and elaborate costumes and stage settings, all of the actors are men, some of whom play the parts of females. Many of the kabuki plays have little plot and seem to be primarily concerned with spectacle. One feature of this form of drama is a walkway that extends from the stage through the audience to the back of the theater.)

Conventions of narrative organization and character development can also vary considerably from culture to culture, especially in literature derived from oral traditions. For example, narrative organization in some Native American stories (and, even more commonly, in some African stories) can be very different from what contemporary Western readers are accustomed to. Events may be arranged spatially instead of chronologically: first a story presents all the events that happened in one place, then it presents everything that happened in another location, and so on. Character development is also much less important in some traditional African and Native American stories than it is in modern short fiction. In fact, a character's name, description, and personality can change dramatically (and without warning) during the course of a story.

Despite such differences, the imaginative literature of all cultures can have similar effects on readers: memorable characters, vivid descriptions, imaginative use of language, and intricately developed plots can fascinate and delight. Literature can take readers where they have never been before and, in so doing, can create a sense of wonder and adventure.

At another level, however, readers can find more than just pleasure or escape in literature. Beyond transporting readers out of their lives and times, literature can enable readers to see their lives and times more clearly. Whether a work of imaginative literature depicts a young girl as she experiences the disillusionment of adulthood for the first time, as in David Michael Kaplan's "Doe Season" (p. 349), or examines the effect of discrimination on a black African who is looking for an apartment, as in Wole Soyinka's "Telephone Conversation" (p. 6), it can help readers to understand their own experiences and the experiences of others. In this sense, literature offers readers increased insight and awareness. As the Chilean poet Pablo Neruda said, works of imaginative literature fulfill "the most ancient rites of our conscience in the awareness of being human and of believing in a common destiny."

CONVENTIONAL THEMES

The **theme** of a work of literature is its central or dominant idea. This idea is seldom stated explicitly. Instead, it is conveyed through the selection and arrangement of details; through the emphasis of certain words, events, or images; and through the actions and reactions of characters.

Although one central theme may dominate a literary work, most works explore a number of different themes or ideas. For example, the central theme of Mark Twain's *Adventures of Huckleberry Finn* might be the idea that an individual's innate sense of right and wrong is superior to society's artificial and sometimes unnatural values. The main character, Huck, gains a growing awareness of this idea by witnessing feuds, duels, and all manner of human folly. As a result, he makes a decision to help his friend Jim escape from slavery despite the fact that society, as well as his own conscience, condemns this action. However, *Huckleberry Finn* also examines other themes. Throughout his novel Twain criticizes many of the ideas that prevailed in the pre–Civil War South, such as the racism and religious hypocrisy that pervaded the towns along the Mississippi.

A literary work can explore any theme, but certain themes have recurred so frequently over the years that they have become **conventions.** One theme frequently explored in literature, a character's loss of innocence, appears in the biblical story of Adam and Eve and later finds its way into works such as Nathaniel Hawthorne's 1835 short story "Young Goodman Brown" (p. 304) and James Joyce's 1914 short story "Araby" (p. 254). Another conventional theme—the conflict between an individual's values and the values of society—is examined in the ancient Greek play *Antigone* by Sophocles. Almost two thousand years later, Norwegian playwright Henrik Ibsen deals with the same theme in *A Doll House* (p. 1196).

Other conventional themes examined in literary works include the individual's quest for spiritual enlightenment, the *carpe diem* ("seize the day") theme, the making of the artist, the nostalgia for a vanished past, the disillusionment of adulthood, the pain of love, the struggle of women for equality, the conflict between parents and children, the clash between civilization and the wilderness, the evils of unchecked ambition, the inevitability of fate, the impact of the past on the present, the conflict between human beings and machines, and the tension between the ideal and the actual realms of experience.

Nearly every culture explores similar themes, but writers from different cultures may develop these themes differently. A culture's history, a particular region's geography, or a country's social structure can suggest unique ways of developing conventional themes. In addition, the assumptions, concerns, values, ideals, and beliefs of a particular country or society—or of a particular group within that society—can help to determine the themes writers choose to explore and the manner in which they do so.

In American literature, for instance, familiar themes include the loss of innocence, rites of passage, childhood epiphanies, and the ability (or inability) to form relationships. American writers of color, in addition to exploring these themes, may also express their frustration with racism or celebrate their cultural identities. Even when they explore conventional themes, writers of color in America may choose to do so in the context of their own experience. For example, the theme of loss of innocence may be presented as a first encounter with racial prejudice; a conflict between the individual and society may be presented as a conflict between a minority view and the values of the dominant group; and the theme of failure or aborted relationships may be explored in a work about cultural misunderstandings.

Finally, modern works of literature sometimes treat conventional themes in new ways. For example, in *1984* George Orwell explores the negative consequences of unchecked power by creating a nightmare world in which technology controls and dehumanizes a population. Even though Orwell's novel is set in an imaginary future (it was written in 1948), its theme echoes ideas frequently examined in the plays of both Sophocles and Shakespeare.

THE LITERARY CANON

Originally the term *canon* referred to the authoritative or accepted list of books that made up the Christian Bible. Recently, the term **literary canon** has come to denote a group of works generally agreed upon by writers, teachers, and critics to be worth reading and studying. Over the years, as standards have changed, the definition of "good" literature has also changed, and the literary canon has been modified accordingly. For example, at various times, critics have characterized Shakespeare's plays as mundane, immoral, commonplace, and brilliant. The eighteenth-century critic Samuel Johnson said of Shakespeare that "in his comick scenes he is seldom very successful" and in tragedy "his performance seems constantly to be worse, as his labor is more." Many people find it difficult to believe that a writer whose name today is synonymous with great literature could ever have been judged so harshly. But like all aesthetic works, the plays of Shakespeare affect individuals in different periods of history or in different societies in different ways.

Lately, educators and literary scholars have charged that the traditional literary canon, like a restricted club, admits some authors and excludes all others. This fact is borne out, they say, by an examination of the literature curriculum that until recently was standard at many North American universities. This curriculum typically began with Homer, Plato, Dante, and Chaucer, progressed to Shakespeare, Milton, the eighteenth-century novel, the Romantics, and the Victorians, and ended with some of the "classics" of modern British and American literature. Most of the authors of these works are white and male, and their writing for the most part reflects Western values.

Missing from the literature courses in North American universities for many years were South American, African, and Asian writers. Students of American literature were not encouraged to consider the perspectives of women or of Latinos, Native Americans, or other ethnic or racial groups. During the past two decades, however, many universities have sought to expand the traditional canon by including more works by women, people of color, and writers from a variety of cultures. These additional works, studied alongside those representing the traditional canon, have opened up the curriculum and redefined the standards by which literature is judged.

One example of a literary work that challenges the traditional canon is "All about Suicide" by Luisa Valenzuela, an Argentinean writer. An experimental story, moving freely in time, bending the facts, and speaking directly to readers, "All about Suicide" is part of a large and growing genre of literature that purposely violates standard literary expectations to make its point—in this case, a point about the political realities of Argentina in the 1960s.

◊ ◊ ◊

LUISA VALENZUELA
(1938–   )

All about Suicide
(1967)

Translated by Helen Lane

Ismael grabbed the gun and slowly rubbed it across his face. Then he pulled the trigger and there was a shot. Bang. One more person dead in the city. It's getting to be a vice. First he grabbed the revolver that was in a desk drawer, rubbed it gently across his face, put it to his temple, and pulled the trigger. Without saying a word. Bang. Dead.

Let's recapitulate: the office is grand, fit for a minister. The desk is ministerial too, and covered with a glass that must have reflected the scene, the shock. Ismael knew where the gun was, he'd hidden it there himself. So he didn't lose any time, all he had to do was open the right-hand drawer and stick his hand in. Then he got a good hold on it and rubbed it over his face with a certain pleasure before putting it to his temple and pulling the trigger. It was something almost sensual and quite unexpected. He hadn't even had time to think about it. A trivial gesture, and the gun had fired.

There's something missing: Ismael in the bar with a glass in his hand thinking over his future act and its possible consequences.

We must go back farther if we want to get at the truth: Ismael in the cradle crying because his diapers are dirty and nobody is changing him.

5   Not that far.

Ismael in the first grade fighting with a classmate who'll one day become a minister, his friend, a traitor.

No, Ismael in the ministry without being able to tell what he knew, forced to be silent. Ismael in the bar with the glass (his third) in his hand, and the irrevocable decision: better death.

Ismael pushing the revolving door at the entrance to the building, pushing the swinging door leading to the office section, saying good morning to the guard, opening the door of his office. Once in his office, seven steps to his desk. Terror, the act of opening the drawer, taking out the revolver, and rubbing it across his face, almost a single gesture and very quick. The act of putting it to his temple and pulling the trigger—another act, immediately following the previous one. Bang. Dead. And Ismael coming out of his office (the other man's office, the minister's) almost relieved, even though he can predict what awaits him.

The Nigerian poet and playwright Wole Soyinka is another writer whose works are not part of the traditional canon. The subject of the following poem may not seem "relevant" to European audiences, and the language ("pillar-box," "omnibus") may not be clear to Americans. Still, as a reading of the poem demonstrates, Soyinka's work makes a compelling plea for individual rights and self-determination—a theme that transcends the boundaries of time and place.

◈ ◈ ◈

WOLE SOYINKA
(1934–   )

Telephone Conversation
(1962)

The price seemed reasonable, location
Indifferent. The landlady swore she lived
Off premises. Nothing remained
But self-confession. "Madam," I warned
5 "I hate a wasted journey—I am—African."
Silence. Silenced transmission of
Pressurized good-breeding. Voice, when it came,

Lip-stick coated, long gold-rolled
Cigarette-holder pipped. Caught I was, foully.
10 "HOW DARK?" . . . I had not misheard . . .
     "ARE YOU LIGHT
OR VERY DARK?" Button B. Button A. Stench
Of rancid breath of public-hide-and-speak.
Red booth. Red pillar-box. Red double-tiered
15 Omnibus squelching tar. It *was* real! Shamed
By ill-mannered silence, surrender
Pushed dumbfoundment to beg simplification.
Considerate she was, varying the emphasis—
"ARE YOU DARK? OR VERY LIGHT?" Revelation came.
20 "You mean—like plain or milk chocolate?"
Her assent was clinical, crushing in its light,
Impersonality. Rapidly, wave-length adjusted,
I chose, "West African sepia"—and as an afterthought,
"Down in my passport." Silence for spectroscopic
25 Flight of fancy, till truthfulness clanged her accent
Hard on the mouthpiece. "WHAT'S THAT?" conceding
"DON'T KNOW WHAT THAT IS." "Like brunette."
"THAT'S DARK, ISN'T IT?" "Not altogether.
Facially, I am brunette, but madam, you should see
30 The rest of me. Palm of my hand, soles of my feet
Are a peroxide blond. Friction, caused—
Foolishly madam—by sitting down, has turned
My bottom raven black—One moment madam!"—sensing
Her receiver rearing on the thunder clap
35 About my ears—"Madam," I pleaded, "Wouldn't you rather
See for yourself?"

Certainly canon revision is not without problems—for example, the possibility of including a work more for political or sociological reasons than for literary merit. Nevertheless, if the debate about the literary canon has accomplished anything, it has revealed that the canon is not fixed and that many works formerly excluded—African-American slave narratives and eighteenth-century women's diaries, for example—deserve to be read.

THINKING CRITICALLY
◆ ◆ ◆

INTERPRETING LITERATURE

When you *interpret* a literary work, you explore its possible meanings. One commonly held idea about reading a literary work is that its meaning lies buried somewhere within it, waiting to be unearthed. This reasoning suggests that a clever reader has only to discover the author's intent to find out what a story or poem means, and that the one actual meaning of a work is hidden between the lines, unaffected by a reader's experiences or interpretations. More recently, however, a different model of the reading process—one that takes into consideration the reader as well as the work he or she is interpreting—has emerged.

Many contemporary critics see the reading process as *interactive.* In other words, meaning is created through the reader's interaction with a text. The meaning of a particular work comes alive in the imagination of an individual reader, and no reader can determine a work's meaning without considering his or her own reaction to the text. Meaning, therefore, is created partly by what is supplied by a work and partly by what is supplied by the reader.

The most obvious meaning a work supplies is factual, the information that enables a reader to follow the plot of a story, the action of a play, or the development of a poem. For instance, the work itself will provide factual details about the setting; the characters' names, ages, and appearances; the sequence of events; and the emotions and attitudes of a poem's speaker, a story's narrator, or the characters in a play or story. This factual information cannot be ignored: if a play's stage directions identify its setting as nineteenth-century Norway or the forest of Arden, that is where it is set.

In addition to facts, a work also conveys the social, political, class, and gender attitudes of the writer. Thus, a work may have an overt feminist or working-class bias or a subtle political agenda; it may confirm or challenge contemporary attitudes; it may communicate a writer's nostalgia for a vanished past or his or her outrage at a corrupt present; it may take an elitist, distant view of characters and events or present a sympathetic perspective. A reader's understanding of these attitudes will contribute to his or her interpretation of the work.

Finally, a work also includes assumptions about literary conventions. A poet, for example, may have definite ideas about whether a poem should be rhymed or unrhymed or about whether a particular subject is appropriate or inappropriate for poetic treatment. Therefore, a knowledge of the literary conventions of a particular period or the preferences of a particular writer can provide a starting point for your interpretation of literature.

As a reader you also bring to a work your own personal perspectives. Your experiences, your beliefs, your ideas about the issues discussed in the work, and your assumptions about literature color your interpretations. In fact, virtually every literary work has somewhat different meanings to different people, depending on their age, gender, nationality, political and religious beliefs, ethnic background, social and economic class, education, knowledge, and experiences. Depending on your religious beliefs, for instance, you can react to a passage from the Old Testament as literal truth, symbolic truth, or fiction. Depending on your race, where you live, your biases, and the nature of your experience, a story about racial discrimination can strike you as accurate and realistic, exaggerated and unrealistic, or understated and restrained.

In a sense, then, the process of determining meaning is like a conversation, one in which both you and the text have a voice. Sometimes, by clearly dictating the terms of the discussion, the text determines the direction of the conversation; at other times, by using your knowledge and experience to interpret the text, you dominate. Thus, because every reading of a literary work is actually an interpretation, it is a mistake to look for a single "correct" reading.

The 1923 poem "Stopping by Woods on a Snowy Evening" (p. 960), by the American poet Robert Frost, illustrates how a single work can have more than one interpretation. Readers may interpret the poem as being about the inevitability of death; as suggesting that the poet is tired or world weary; or as making a comment about duty and the need to persevere or about the conflicting pulls of life and art. Beyond these possibilities, readers' own associations of snow with quiet and sadness could lead them to define the mood of the poem as sorrowful or melancholy. Information about Robert Frost's life or his ideas about poetry could add to readers' appreciation of the poem, and they might even develop ideas about the poem that are quite different from the poet's. In fact, on several occasions, Frost himself gave strikingly different—even contradictory—interpretations of "Stopping by Woods on a Snowy Evening," sometimes insisting that the poem had no hidden meaning and at other times saying that it required a good deal of explication. (Literary critics also disagree about its meaning.) When reading a work of literature, then, keep in mind that the meaning of the text is not fixed. Your best strategy is to open yourself up to the text's many possibilities and explore the full range of your responses.

Although no single reading of a literary work is "correct," some readings are more defensible than others. Like a scientific theory, a literary interpretation must have a basis in fact, and the text supplies the facts against which your interpretation should be judged. For example, after you read Shirley Jackson's "The Lottery" (p. 315), a 1948 short story in which a randomly chosen victim is stoned to death by her neighbors, it would be reasonable for you to conclude that the ceremonial aspects of the lottery suggest a pagan ritual. Your understanding of what a pagan ritual is, combined with your observation that a number of details in the text suggest ancient fertility rites, might lead you to this conclusion. Another possibility is that "The Lottery" provides a commentary on mob psychology. The way characters reinforce one another's violent tendencies lends support to this interpretation. However, the interpretation that the ritual of the lottery is a thinly veiled attack on the death penalty would be difficult to support. Certainly a character in the story is killed, but she is not accused of a crime, nor is she tried or convicted; in fact, the killing is random and seemingly without motivation. Still, although seeing "The

Lottery" as a comment on the death penalty may be far-fetched, this interpretation is a reasonable starting point. A second, closer reading of the story will allow you to explore other, more plausible, interpretations.

As you read, do not be afraid to take chances and develop unusual or creative interpretations of a work. A "safe" reading of a work is likely to result in a dull paper that simply states the obvious, but an aggressive or "strong" reading of a work—one that challenges generally held assumptions—can lead to interesting and intellectually challenging conclusions. Even if your reading differs from established critics' interpretations, you should not automatically assume it has no merit. Your own special knowledge of the material discussed in the text—a regional practice, an ethnic custom, an attitude toward gender—may give you a unique perspective from which to view the work. Whatever interpretation you make, be sure that you support it with specific references to the text. If your interpretation is based on your own experiences, explain those experiences and relate them clearly to the work you are discussing. As long as you can make a reasonable case, you have the right (and perhaps the obligation) to present your ideas. By doing so, you may provide your fellow students and your instructor with new insight into the work.

Remember, however, that some interpretations are *not* reasonable. You may contribute ideas based on your own perspectives, but you cannot ignore or contradict evidence in the text to suit your own biases. As you read and reread a text, continue to question and reexamine your judgments. The conversation between you and the text should be a dialogue, not a monologue or a shouting match.

EVALUATING LITERATURE

When you *evaluate* a work of literature, you do more than interpret it; you make a judgment about it. You reach conclusions—not simply about whether the work is good or bad, but also about how effectively the work presents itself to you, the reader. To evaluate a work, you *analyze* it, breaking it apart and considering its individual elements. As you evaluate a work of literature, remember that different works are designed to fulfill different needs—entertainment, education, or enlightenment, for example. Before you begin to evaluate a work, be sure you understand its purpose; then, follow these guidelines:

Begin your evaluation by considering how various literary elements function within a work. Fiction may be divided into chapters and use flashbacks and foreshadowing; plays may be divided into scenes and acts and include dialogue and special staging techniques; poems may be arranged in regularly ordered groups of lines and use poetic devices such as rhyme and meter. Understanding the choices writers make about these and other literary elements can help you form judgments about a work. For example, why does Alberto Alvaro Ríos use a first-person narrator (*I* and *we*) in his story "The

Secret Lion" (p. 49)? Would the story have been different had it been told in the third person *(they)* by a narrator who was not a character in the story? How does unusual staging contribute to the effect Edward Albee achieves in his play *The Sandbox* (p. 1610)? How would a more realistic setting change the play? Naturally, you cannot focus on every aspect of a particular story, poem, or play. But you can and should focus on those that play a major role in determining your responses to a work. For this reason the unusual stanzaic form in E. E. Cummings's poem "Buffalo Bill's" (p. 939) or the very specific stage directions in Arthur Miller's *Death of a Salesman* (p. 1410) should be of special interest to you.

As you read, then, you should ask questions. Do the characters in a short story seem real, or do they seem like cardboard cutouts? Are the images in a poem original and thought-provoking, or are they clichéd? Are the stage directions of a play sketchy or very detailed? The answers to these questions will help you to shape your response.

As you continue your evaluation, decide whether or not the literary elements of a work interact to achieve a common goal.   Well-crafted literary works are aesthetically pleasing, fitting together in a way that conceals the craft of the writer. Good writers are like master cabinetmakers; their skill disguises the actual work that has gone into the process of creation. Consider the following stanza from the 1862 poem "Echo" by Christina Rossetti:

> Come to me in the silence of the night;
>> Come to me in the speaking silence of a dream;
> Come with soft round cheeks and eyes as bright
>> As sunlight on a stream;
>>> Come back in tears,
> O memory, hope, love of finished years.

Throughout this stanza Rossetti repeats words (<u>Come</u> to me. . . . / <u>Come</u> with soft. . . . / <u>Come</u> back. . . .) and initial consonants (<u>s</u>peaking <u>s</u>ilence / <u>s</u>unlight on a <u>s</u>tream) to create an almost hypnotic mood. The rhyme scheme *(night/bright, dream/stream,* and *tears/years)* reinforces the mood by creating a musical undercurrent that extends throughout the poem. Thus, this stanza is effective because its repeated words and sounds work together to create a single lyrical effect.

The chorus in *Antigone* by Sophocles (p. 1631) also illustrates how the elements of a well-crafted work of literature function together. In ancient Greece plays were performed by masked male actors who played both male and female roles. A chorus of fifteen men would remain in a central circle called the *orchestra* and comment on and react to the action taking place around them. The chorus expresses the judgment of the community and acts as a moral guide for the audience. Once modern audiences grow accustomed to the presence of the chorus, it becomes an integral part of the play. It neither distracts the audience nor intrudes upon the action. In fact, eliminating the chorus would diminish the impact of the play.

Next, consider whether a work reinforces or calls into question your ideas about the world. The 1985 short story "Gryphon" by Charles Baxter (p. 134) is one that may lead readers to question their assumptions. It presents a boy in a rural town whose ailing teacher is temporarily replaced by an eccentric substitute. In her idiosyncratic way, the substitute introduces the boy to a whole new range of intellectual possibilities. Because we, like the children in the story, have learned to expect substitute teachers to be dull and conventional, the story challenges our basic assumptions about substitute teachers and, by extension, about education itself.

Works of popular fiction—those aimed at a mass audience—usually do little more than reassure readers that what they believe is correct. Catering to people's prejudices, or to their desires (for wealth or success, for example), or to their fears, these works serve as escapes from life. Serious fiction, however, often goes against the grain, challenging cherished beliefs and leading readers to reexamine long-held assumptions. For instance, in the 1957 short story "Big Black Good Man" (p. 207) Richard Wright's protagonist, a night porter at a hotel, struggles with his consuming yet irrational fear of a "big black" sailor and with his inability to see beyond the sailor's size and color. Only at the end of the story do many readers see that they, like the night porter, have stereotyped and dehumanized the sailor.

Then, consider whether or not a work is intellectually challenging. The extended comparison between a draftsperson's compass and two people in love in "A Valediction: Forbidding Mourning" by the seventeenth-century English poet John Donne (p. 816) illustrates how effectively an image can communicate complex ideas to a reader. Compressed into this comparison are ideas about the perfection of love, the pain of enforced separation, and the difference between sexual and spiritual love. As intellectually challenging as the extended comparison is, it is nonetheless accessible to the careful reader. After all, many people have used a compass to draw a circle and, therefore, are able to understand the relationship between the two points of the compass and the two lovers.

A fine line exists, however, between works that are intellectually challenging and those that are simply obscure. An *intellectually challenging* work requires effort on the part of readers to unlock ideas that enrich and expand their understanding of themselves and the world. Although complex, the work gives readers a sense that they have gained something by putting forth the effort to interpret it. An *obscure* work, however, exists solely to display a writer's erudition or intellectual idiosyncrasies. Allusions to other works and events are so numerous and confusing that the work may seem more like a private code than an effort to enlighten readers. Consider the following excerpt from "Canto LXXVI" by the twentieth-century American poet Ezra Pound:

> Le Paradis n'est pas artificiel
>   States of mind are inexplicable to us.
>   δακρύων δακρύων δακρύων
> L.   P. gli onesti
>   J'ai eu pitié des autres
> probablement pas assez, and at moments that suited my own
>   convenience
>   Le paradis n'est pas artificiel,
>   l'enfer non plus.
> Came Eurus as comforter
> and at sunset la pastorella dei suini
>   driving the pigs home, benecomata dea
>   under the two-winged cloud
>   as of less and more than a day

This passage contains lines in French, Greek, and Italian; a reference to Eurus, the ancient Greek personification of the east wind; and the initials L.P. (Loomis Pound?). Admittedly, it demands a lot from readers; the question is whether the reward is worth the effort.

No hard and fast rule exists for determining whether a work is intellectually challenging or simply obscure. Just as a poem has no fixed meaning, it also has no fixed value. Some readers would say that the passage above is good, even great, poetry. Others would argue that these lines do not yield enough pleasure and insight to justify the work needed to analyze them. As a reader, you must draw your own conclusions and justify them in a clear and reasonable way. Do not assume that just because a work is difficult, it is obscure. (Nor should you assume that all difficult works are great literature or that all accessible literature is trivial.) Some of the most beautiful and inspiring literary works demand a great deal of effort. Most readers would agree, however, that the time spent exploring such works yields tremendous rewards.

Finally, consider whether a work gives you pleasure. One of the primary reasons that literature endures is that it gives readers enjoyment. As subjective as this assessment is, it is a starting point for critical judgment. When readers ask themselves what they liked about a work, why they liked it, or what they learned, they begin the process of evaluation. Although this process is largely uncritical, it can lead to an involvement with the work and to a critical response. When you encounter great literature, with all its complexities, you may lose sight of the idea of literature as a source of pleasure. But literature should touch you on a deep emotional or intellectual level, and if it does not—despite its technical perfection—it fails to achieve one of its primary aims.

THE FUNCTION OF LITERARY CRITICISM

Sometimes your personal reactions and knowledge cannot give you enough insight into a literary work. For example, archaic language, obscure references, historical allusions, and textual inconsistencies can make reading a work particularly difficult. Similarly, an intellectual or philosophical movement such as Darwinism, Marxism, naturalism, structuralism, or feminism may influence a work, and if this is the case, you will need some knowledge of the movement before you can interpret the work (see Appendix C, Twentiety-Century Literary Theories). In addition, you may not have the background to appreciate the technical or historical dimension of a work. To widen the context of your reading, you may choose to read **literary criticism**—books and journal articles written by experts who describe, analyze, interpret, or evaluate a work of literature. Reading literary criticism enables you to expand your knowledge of a particular work and to participate in the public dialogue about literature. In a sense, you become part of a community of scholars who share their ideas and who are connected to one another through their writing.

Literary criticism is written by experts, but this does not mean you must always accept it. You have to evaluate literary criticism just as you would any new opinion that you encounter. Not all criticism is sound, timely, or responsible (and not all literary criticism is pertinent to your assignment or useful for your purposes). Some critical comments will strike you as plausible, whereas others will seem unfounded or biased. Quite often two critics will reach strikingly different conclusions about the quality or significance of the same work or writer or will interpret a character, a symbol, or even the entire work quite differently.

The Fiction Casebook that begins on page 612 includes articles in which critics disagree in just this fashion. In "In Fairyland, without a Map: Connie's Exploration Inward in Joyce Carol Oates' 'Where Are You Going, Where Have You Been?'" Gretchen Schulz and R. J. R. Rockwood examine the parallels between a character, Arnold Friend, and a real-life psychopathic killer. They see Arnold in mythological terms and conclude that he is the "exact transpositional counterpart of the real-life Pied Piper of Tucson." In Mike Tierce and John Michael Crafton's "Connie's Tambourine Man: A New Reading of Arnold Friend," however, the authors explicitly reject this suggestion as well as other critical interpretations, concluding instead that "The key question . . . is who is this musical messiah, and the key to the answer is the dedication 'For Bob Dylan.'"

Although critics may disagree, even conflicting ideas can help you to reach your own conclusions about a work. It is up to you to sort out the various opinions and decide which have merit and which do not.

Checklist: Evaluating Literary Criticism

✓ What is the main point of the book or article you are reading?

✓ Does the critic supply enough examples to support his or her conclusions?

✓ Does the critic acknowledge and refute the most obvious arguments against his or her position?

✓ Does the critic ignore any information in the text that might call his or her conclusions into question?

✓ Does the critic present historical information? Biographical information? Literary information? How does this information shed light on the work or works being discussed?

✓ Does the critic hold any beliefs that might interfere with his or her critical judgment?

✓ Does the critic slant the facts or read the text critically and objectively?

✓ Does the critic support conclusions with references to other sources? Does the critic provide documentation and a list of works cited?

✓ Do other critics mention the critical book or article you are reading? Do they agree or disagree with its conclusions?

With your instructor's help, you might also try to answer these questions:

✓ Does the critic identify with a particular critical school of thought—deconstruction or Marxism, for example? What perspective does this school of thought provide?

✓ Is the critic well known and respected or unknown?

✓ Does the critic take into consideration the most important critical books and articles on his or her subject? Are there works that should have been mentioned but were not? Do these omissions cast doubts on the critic's conclusions?

✓ Is the critical work's publication date of any significance?

CHAPTER 2

Reading and Writing about Literature

READING LITERATURE
◇ ◇ ◇

The process of writing about literature starts the moment you begin to read, when you begin interacting with a work and start to discover ideas about it. This process of **active reading** helps you to interpret what you read and, eventually, to develop your ideas into a clear and logical paper.

Most readers are passive; that is, they expect the text to give them everything they need, and they don't expect to contribute much to the reading process. Active readers, however, participate in the reading process—thinking about what they read, asking questions, and challenging ideas. Active reading is excellent preparation for the discussion and writing you will do in college literature classes. And, because it helps you understand and appreciate the works you read, active reading will continue to be of value to you long after your formal classroom study of literature has ended.

Three strategies in particular—*previewing, highlighting,* and *annotating*—will help you to become a more effective reader. Remember, though, that reading and responding to what you read is not an orderly process—or even a sequential one. You will most likely find yourself doing more than one thing at a time—annotating at the same time you highlight, for example. For the sake of clarity, however, we discuss each active reading strategy separately in the pages that follow.

PREVIEWING

You begin the active reading process by **previewing** a work to get a general idea of what to look for later, when you read it more carefully.

Start with the work's most obvious physical characteristics. For example, how long is a short story? How many acts and scenes does a play have?

Is a poem divided into stanzas? The answers to these and similar questions will help you begin to notice more subtle aspects of the work's form. For example, previewing may reveal that a contemporary short story is presented entirely in a question-and-answer format, that it is organized as diary entries, or that it is divided into sections by headings. Previewing may identify poems that seem to lack formal structure, such as E. E. Cummings's unconventional "l(a" (p. 670); those written in traditional forms (such as sonnets) or in experimental forms, such as the numbered list of questions and answers in Denise Levertov's "What Were They Like?" (p. 695); or concrete poems such as George Herbert's "Easter Wings" (p. 892). Your awareness of these and other distinctive features at this point may help you gain insight into a work later on.

Perhaps the most physically distinctive element of a work is its title. Not only can the title give you a general idea of what the work is about, as straightforward titles like "Miss Brill" and "The Cask of Amontillado" do, but it can also isolate (and thus call attention to) a word or phrase that emphasizes an important idea. For example, the title of Amy Tan's short story "Two Kinds" (p. 594) refers to two kinds of daughters—Chinese and American—suggesting the two perspectives that create the story's conflict. A title can also be an allusion to another work. Thus, *The Sound and the Fury,* the title of a novel by William Faulkner, alludes to a speech from Shakespeare's *Macbeth* that reinforces the major theme of the novel. Finally, a title can introduce a symbol that will gain meaning in the course of a work—as the image of a shroud does in Ann Petry's story "Like a Winding Sheet" (p. 125).

Other physical elements—such as paragraphing, capitalization, italics, and punctuation—can also provide clues about how to read a work. In William Faulkner's short story "Barn Burning" (p. 226), for instance, previewing would help you to notice passages in italic type, indicating the protagonist's thoughts, which occasionally interrupt the narrator's story.

Finally, previewing can enable you to see some of the more obvious stylistic and structural features of a work—the point of view used in a story, how many characters a play has and where it is set, or the repetition of certain words or lines in a poem, for example. Such features may or may not be important; at this stage, your goal is to observe, not to analyze or evaluate.

Previewing is a useful strategy not because it provides answers but because it suggests questions to ask later, as you read more closely. For instance, *why* does Faulkner use italics in "Barn Burning," and *why* does Herbert shape his poem on the page as he does? Elements such as those described may be noticeable as you preview, but they will gain significance as you read more carefully and review your notes.

HIGHLIGHTING

When you go on to read a work closely, you will notice additional, sometimes more subtle, elements that you may want to examine further. At this point, you should begin **highlighting**—physically marking the text to identify key details and to note relationships among ideas.

What should you highlight? As you read, ask yourself whether repeated words or phrases form a pattern, as they do in Ernest Hemingway's short story "A Clean, Well-Lighted Place" (p. 261), in which the Spanish word *nada* ("nothing") appears again and again. Because this word appears so frequently, and because it appears at key points in the story, it helps to reinforce the story's pessimistic theme—that all human experience amounts to *nada,* or nothingness. Repeated words and phrases are particularly important in poetry. In Dylan Thomas's "Do Not Go Gentle into That Good Night" (p. 677), for example, the repetition of two of the poem's nineteen lines four times each enhances the poem's rhythmic, almost monotonous, cadence. As you read, highlight your text to identify such repeated words and phrases. Later on, you can consider *why* they are repeated.

During the highlighting stage, also pay particular attention to images that occur repeatedly in a work, keeping in mind that such repeated images may form patterns that can help you to interpret the work. When you reread the work, you can begin to determine what pattern the images form and perhaps decide how this pattern enhances the work's ideas. When highlighting Robert Frost's "Stopping by Woods on a Snowy Evening" (p. 960), for instance, you might identify the related images of silence, cold, and darkness. Later, you can consider their significance.

✴ CHECKLIST: USING HIGHLIGHTING SYMBOLS

- ✓ Underline important ideas that you should read again.
- ✓ Box or circle repeated words, phrases, or images.
- ✓ Put question marks beside confusing passages, unfamiliar references, or words that need to be defined.
- ✓ Draw lines or arrows to connect related ideas or images.
- ✓ Number incidents that occur in sequence.
- ✓ Set off a long portion of the text with a vertical line in the margin.
- ✓ Place stars beside particularly important ideas.

The following poem by Maya Angelou has been highlighted by a student preparing to write about it. Notice how the student uses highlighting symbols to help him identify stylistic features, key points, and patterns of repetition that he may want to examine later.

◇ ◇ ◇ ◇
MAYA ANGELOU
(1928–   )

My Arkansas
(1978)

There is a deep brooding
in Arkansas.
Old crimes like moss pend
from poplar trees.
5 The sullen earth
is much too
red for comfort.

Sunrise seems to hesitate
and in that second
10 lose its
incandescent aim, and
dusk no more shadows
than the noon.
The past is brighter yet.

15 Old hates and
ante-bellum lace are rent
but not discarded.
Today is yet to come
in Arkansas.
20 It writhes. It writhes in awful
waves of brooding.

This student identifies repeated words and phases ("brooding"; "it writhes") and places question marks beside the two words ("pend" and "rent") that he plans to look up in a dictionary. He also boxes two phrases—"old crimes" and "ante-bellum lace"—that he needs to think more about. Finally, he stars what he tentatively identifies as the poem's key ideas. When he rereads the poem, his highlighting will make it easier for him to react to and interpret the writer's ideas.

ANNOTATING

At the same time you highlight a text, you also **annotate** it, recording your reactions as marginal notes. In these notes you may define new words, identify allusions, identify patterns of language or imagery, summarize plot relationships, list a work's possible themes, suggest a character's motivation, examine the possible significance of particular images or symbols, or record questions that occur to you as you read. Ideally, your annotations will help you find ideas to write about.

The following paragraph from John Updike's 1961 short story "A&P" (p. 113) was highlighted and annotated by a student in an introduction to literature course who was writing an essay in response to the question "Why does Sammy quit his job?":

> Lengel sighs and begins to look very patient and old and gray. He's
> *Action* been a friend of my parents for years. "Sammy, you don't want to do
> *doesn't* this to your Mom and Dad," he tells me. It's true, I don't. But it seems
> *seem* to me that once you begin a gesture it's fatal not to go through with ✳
> *to be* it. I fold the apron, "Sammy" stitched in red on the pocket, and put it
> *the* on the counter, and drop the bow tie on top of it. The bow tie is
> *result* theirs, if you've ever wondered. "You'll feel this for the rest of your ✳
> *of* life," Lengel says, and I know that's true, too, but remembering how
> *thought.* he made the pretty girl blush makes me so scrunchy inside I punch
> *Sammy* the No Sale tab and the machine whirs "pee-pul" and the drawer
> *reacts* splats out. One advantage to this scene taking place in summer, I can   ✳ Need
> *to the* follow this up with a clean exit, there's no fumbling around getting   for a
> *girl's* your coat and galoshes, I just saunter into the electric eye in my white   clean
> *embar-* shirt that my mother ironed the night before, and the door heaves it-   exit—
> *rassment.* self open, and outside the sunshine is skating around on the asphalt.   reinforces
>   immature
>   romantic
>   ideas.

Romantic cowboy, but his mother irons his shirt. Irony.

Because the instructor had discussed the story in class and given the class a specific assignment, the student's annotations are quite focused. In addition to highlighting important information, she notes her reactions to the story and tries to interpret Sammy's actions. Sometimes, however, you annotate a work before you have decided on a topic—in fact, the process of reading and responding to your text can help you to focus on a topic. In the absence of a topic, your annotations are likely to be less focused, so you will probably need to repeat the process when your paper's direction is clearer.

WRITING ABOUT LITERATURE
◆ ◆ ◆

Writing about literature—or about anything else, for that matter—is an idiosyncratic process during which many activities occur at once: as you write, you think of ideas; as you think of ideas, you clarify the focus of your essay; and as you clarify your focus, you reshape your paragraphs and sentences and refine your word choice. Even though this process sounds chaotic, it has three stages: *planning, drafting,* and *revising and editing.*

PLANNING AN ESSAY

Considering Your Audience

Sometimes—for example, in a journal entry—you write primarily for yourself. At other times, however, you write for others. As you write an essay, you should consider the special requirements of that **audience.** Is your audience your classmates or your instructor? Can you assume your readers are familiar with your paper's topic and with any technical terms you will use, or will they need brief plot summaries or definitions of key terms? If your audience is your instructor, remember that he or she is a representative of a larger academic audience and therefore expects accurate information; standard English; correct grammar, mechanics, and spelling; logical arguments; and a certain degree of stylistic fluency. In addition, your instructor expects you to support your statements with specific information, to express yourself clearly and explicitly, and to document your sources. In short, your instructor wants to see how clearly you think and whether you are able to arrange your ideas into a well-organized, coherent essay.

In addition to being a member of a general academic audience, your instructor is also a member of a particular community of scholars—in this case, those who study literature. By writing about literature, you engage in a dialogue with this community. For this reason, you should adhere to the specific **conventions**—procedures that by habitual use have become accepted practice—its members follow. Many of the conventions that apply specifically to writing about literature—matters of style, format, and the like—will be discussed in this book. (The checklist on page 35 addresses some of these conventions.)

Understanding Your Purpose

Sometimes you write with a single **purpose** in mind; at other times, a writing assignment may suggest more than one purpose. In general terms, you may write for any of the following reasons:

Writing to Respond When you write to *respond,* your goal is to discover and express your reactions to a work. To record your responses you engage in relatively informal activities, such as brainstorming, listing, and journal writing (see pp. 24–26). As you write, you explore your own ideas, forming and reforming your impressions of the work.

Writing to Interpret When you write to *interpret,* your aim is to explain a work's possible meanings. To do so, you may summarize, give examples, or compare and contrast the work to other works or to your own experiences. Then, you may go on to analyze the work, studying each of its elements in turn, putting complex statements in your own words, defining difficult concepts, or placing ideas in context.

Writing to Evaluate When you write to *evaluate,* your purpose is to assess a work's literary merits. You may consider not only its aesthetic appeal, but also its ability to retain that appeal over time and across national or cultural boundaries. As you write, you use your own critical sense and the opinions of experts in the field to help you make judgments about the work.

Choosing a Topic

When you write an essay about literature, you develop and support an idea about a literary work or works. Before you begin your writing, you should make certain that you understand your assignment. Do you know how much time you have to complete your essay? Are you expected to rely on your own ideas, or are you able to consult outside sources? Is your essay to focus on a specific work or on a particular element of literature? Do you have to write on an assigned topic, or are you free to choose a topic? About how long should your essay be? Do you understand exactly what the assignment is asking you to do?

Sometimes your assignment limits your options by telling you what you should discuss:

◊ Write an essay in which you analyze Thomas Hardy's use of irony in his poem "The Man He Killed."

◊ Discuss Hawthorne's use of allegory in his short story "Young Goodman Brown."

◊ Write a short essay in which you explain Nora's actions at the end of Ibsen's *A Doll House.*

At other times, however, your instructor will give you few guidelines other than a paper's length and format. In such situations, where you must choose a topic on your own, you can often find a topic by brainstorming or by writing journal entries. As you engage in these activities, however, keep in mind that you have many options for writing papers about literature:

◇ You can compare two works of literature. ("Related Works" listed at the end of each set of "Reading and Reacting" questions in the text suggest possible connections.)

◇ You can compare two characters or discuss some trait those characters share.

◇ You can trace a common theme—jealousy, revenge, power, coming of age—in several works.

◇ You can consider how a common subject—war, love, nature—is treated in several works.

◇ You can examine a single element in one or more works—for instance, plot, point of view, or character development.

◇ You can focus on a single aspect of that element, such as the use of flashbacks, the effect of a shifting narrative perspective, or the role of a minor character.

◇ You can apply a critical theory to a work of literature—for instance, apply a feminist perspective to Tillie Olsen's "I Stand Here Ironing."

◇ You can examine connections between an issue treated in a work of literature—for instance, spousal abuse in Ann Petry's "Like a Winding Sheet"—and that same issue as it is treated in sociological or psychological journals or in the popular press.

◇ You can examine some aspect of history or biography and consider its impact on a literary work—for instance, the influence of World War I on Wilfred Owen's poems.

◇ You can explore a problem within a work and propose a possible solution—for example, consider Montresor's actual reason for killing Fortunato in Edgar Allan Poe's "The Cask of Amontillado."

Any of the preceding options may lead you to an interesting topic. Remember, however, that you will still have to narrow the scope of your topic so that it fits within the limits of your assignment.

Finding Something to Say

Once you have a topic, you have to find something to say about it. The information you collected when you highlighted and annotated will help you formulate the statement that will be the central idea of your essay and find ideas that can support that statement.

You can use a variety of different strategies to find supporting material:

◇ You can discuss ideas with others—friends, classmates, instructors, or parents, for example.

◇ You can ask questions.

◇ You can do research, either in the library or on the Internet.

◇ You can *freewrite*—that is, keep writing on your topic for a given period of time without pausing to consider style, structure, or content.

Three additional strategies—*brainstorming, keeping a journal,* and *listing*—are especially helpful.

Brainstorming   When you **brainstorm,** you record ideas—single words, phrases, or sentences; statements or questions; quotations, paraphrases, summaries, or your own ideas—as they occur to you, moving as quickly as possible. Your starting point may be a general assignment, a particular work (or works) of literature, a specific topic, or even a thesis statement; in fact, you can brainstorm at any stage of the writing process (alone or in a group), and you can repeat this activity as often as you like.

The brainstorming notes that follow were made by a student preparing to write a paper on the relationships between children and parents in four poems. She began by brainstorming about each poem and went on to consider thematic relationships among the poems. These notes are her preliminary reactions to one of the four poems she planned to study, Adrienne Rich's "A Woman Mourned by Daughters" (p. 673):

Memory: then and now

Then: leaf, straw, dead insect (= light); ignored

Now: swollen, puffed up, weight (= heavy); focus of

attention. controls their movements.

＊Kitchen = a "universe"

Teaspoons, goblets, etc. = concrete representations

of mother; also = obligations, responsibilities

(like plants and father)

(weigh on them, keep

them under her spell)

Milestones of past: weddings, being fed as children

"You breathe upon us now"

PARADOX? (Dead, she breathes, has weight, fills house

and sky. Alive, she was a dead insect, no one paid

attention to her.)

Keeping a Journal A journal can be a notebook, a small notepad, or a computer file. You can use a journal to find ideas—and, later, to help you to find a topic or a thesis. In a **journal** you expand your marginal annotations, recording your responses to works you have read, noting questions, exploring emerging ideas, experimenting with possible paper topics, trying to paraphrase or summarize difficult concepts, or speculating about a work's ambiguities. A journal is the place to take chances, to try out ideas that may initially seem frivolous or irrelevant; here you can think on paper (or on a computer screen) until connections become clear or ideas crystallize. You can also use your journal as a convenient place to collect your brainstorming notes and, later, your lists of related ideas.

As he prepared to write a paper analyzing the role of Jim, the "gentleman caller" in Tennessee Williams's play *The Glass Menagerie* (p. 1805), a student explored ideas in the following journal entry:

> When he tells Laura that being disappointed is not
> the same as being discouraged, and that he's disappointed
> but not discouraged, Jim reveals his role as a symbol
> of the power of newness and change--a "bulldozer" that
> will clear out whatever is in its path, even delicate
> people like Laura. But the fact that he is disappointed
> shows Jim's human side. He has run into problems since
> high school, and these problems have blocked his pro-
> gress toward a successful future. Working at the ware-
> house, Jim needs Tom's friendship to remind him of what
> he used to be (and what he still can be?), and this
> shows his insecurity. He isn't as sure of himself as
> he seems to be.

This journal entry, which represents the student's preliminary explorations, can help him to decide on a specific direction for his essay.

Seeing Connections

Listing After you have actively read a work, you should have a good many underlinings and marginal notes. Some of this material will be useful, and some will be irrelevant. **Listing** is the process of reviewing your notes, deciding which ideas are most interesting, and arranging related ideas into lists. Listing enables you to discover patterns: to see repeated images, similar characters, recurring words and phrases, and interrelated themes or ideas. Identifying these patterns can help you to decide which points to make in your paper and what information you will use to support these points. A student preparing a paper about D. H. Lawrence's short story "The Rocking-Horse Winner" (p. 362) made the following list of related details:

<u>Secrets</u>
    Mother can't feel love
    Paul gambles
    Paul gives mother money
    Family lives beyond means
    Paul gets information from horse
<u>Religion</u>
    Gambling becomes like a religion
    They all worship money
    Specific references: "serious as a church"; "It's as
    if he had it from heaven"; "secret, religious voice"
<u>Luck</u>
    Father is unlucky
    Mother is desperate for luck
    Paul is lucky (ironic)

This kind of listing can be a very helpful preliminary organizing strategy, but remember that the lists you make now do not necessarily reflect the order or emphasis of ideas in your paper. As your thoughts become more focused, you will add, delete, and rearrange material.

Deciding on a Thesis

Whenever you are ready, you should try to express the main idea of your emerging essay in a tentative **thesis statement**—an idea, often expressed in a single sentence, that the rest of your essay supports. This idea should emerge logically out of your highlighting, annotating, brainstorming notes, journal entries, and lists. Eventually, you will write a **thesis-and-support** paper: stating your thesis in your introduction, supporting the thesis in the body paragraphs of your essay, and reinforcing the thesis or summarizing your points in your conclusion.

An effective thesis statement tells readers what your essay will discuss and how you will approach your material. Consequently, it should be precisely worded, making its point clear to your readers, and it should contain no vague words or inexact diction that will make it difficult for readers to follow your discussion. Although the statement "The use of sound in Tennyson's poem 'The Eagle' is interesting" is accurate, it does not convey a precise idea to your readers because the words *sound* and *interesting* are not specific. A more effective thesis statement would be "Unity in 'The Eagle' is achieved by Tennyson's use of alliteration, assonance, and rhyme throughout the poem." In addition to being specific, your thesis statement should give your readers an accurate sense of the scope and direction of your essay. It should not make promises that you do not intend to fulfill or contain extraneous details that might confuse your readers. If, for example, you are going to write a paper about the dominant image in a poem, your thesis should not imply that you will focus on the poem's setting or tone.

Remember that as you organize your ideas and as you write, you will probably modify and sharpen your tentative thesis. Sometimes you will even begin planning your essay with one thesis in mind and end it with an entirely different idea. If this happens, be sure to revise your support paragraphs so that they are consistent with your changes and so that the points you include support your new thesis. If you find that your thoughts about your topic are changing, don't be concerned; remember that this is how the writing process works.

Preparing an Outline

Once you have decided on a tentative thesis and have some idea of how you will support it, you can begin to plan your essay's structure. Quite often, an outline can help you to shape your essay. Not all writers outline, but many do because it helps them to clarify their ideas and the relationship of these ideas to one another. Realizing, however, that they will discover many new ideas as they write, these writers seldom take the time to prepare a detailed formal outline, preferring instead to make a scratch outline that lists just the major points they plan to discuss.

A **scratch outline** is perhaps the most useful kind of outline for a short paper. An informal list of the main points you will discuss in your essay, a scratch outline is more focused than a simple list of related points because it presents ideas in the order in which they will be introduced. As its name implies, however, a scratch outline lacks the detail and the degree of organization of a more formal outline. The main purpose of a scratch outline is to give you a sense of the shape and order of your paper and thus enable you to begin writing. A student writing a short essay on Edwin Arlington Robinson's use of irony in his poem "Miniver Cheevy" (p. 985) used the following scratch outline as a guide:

Speaker's Attitude
    Ironic
    Cynical
    Critical
Use of Diction
    Formal
    Detached
Use of Allusions
    Thebes
    Camelot
    Priam
    Medici
Use of Repetition
    "Miniver"
    "thought"
    regular rhyme scheme

Once this outline was complete, the student was ready to write a first draft.

DRAFTING AN ESSAY

Your first draft is a preliminary version of your paper, something to react to and revise. Still, before you actually begin drafting your paper, you should review the material you have collected to support your thesis.

First, make sure you have collected enough information to support your thesis.   The points you make are only as convincing as the evidence you present to support them. As you read and took notes, you collected examples from the work or works about which you are writing—summaries, paraphrases, or quoted lines of narrative, verse, or dialogue—to back up your statements. Just how many of these examples you need to use in your draft depends on the breadth of your thesis and how skeptical you believe your audience to be. In general, the more inclusive your thesis, the more material you need to support it. For example, if you were supporting the rather narrow thesis that the speech of a certain character in the second scene of a play was wooden or awkward, only a few examples would be needed. However, if you wanted to support the inclusive thesis that Nora and Torvald Helmer in Henrik Ibsen's 1879 play *A Doll House* (p. 1196) are trapped in their roles, you would need to present a wide range of examples.

Second, see if the work includes any details that contradict your thesis.   Before you begin writing, you should test the validity of your thesis by looking for details that contradict it. For example, if you plan to support the thesis that in *A Doll House* Ibsen makes a strong case for the rights of women, you should look for counterexamples. Can you find subtle hints in the play that suggest women should remain locked in their traditional roles and continue to defer to their fathers and husbands? If so, you will want to modify your thesis accordingly.

Finally, consider whether you need to use literary criticism to help you support your thesis. You could, for example, strengthen the thesis that *A Doll House* challenged contemporary attitudes about marriage by including the information that when the play first opened, Ibsen was convinced by an apprehensive theater manager to write another ending. In the new ending, Ibsen had Nora decide, after she stopped briefly to look in at her sleeping children, that she could not leave her family. Sometimes information from another source can even lead you to change your thesis. For example, after reading *A Doll House,* you might have decided that Ibsen's purpose was to make a strong case for the rights of women. In class, however, you might learn that Ibsen repeatedly said that his play was about the rights of all human beings, not just of women. This information could lead you to a thesis that suggests Torvald is just as trapped in his role as Nora is in hers. Naturally, Ibsen's interpretation of his work does not invalidate your first judgment, but it does suggest another conclusion that is worth investigating.

After you have carefully evaluated the completeness, relevance, and validity of your supporting material, you can begin drafting your essay, using your scratch outline as your guide. Your goal is to get your ideas down on paper, so you should write quickly. Once you have a draft, you will be able to examine the connections among ideas and to evaluate preliminary versions of your paragraphs and sentences. Your focus in this draft should be on the body of your essay; this is not the time to worry about constructing the "perfect" introduction and conclusion. In fact, many writers, knowing that their ideas will change as they write, postpone writing these paragraphs until a later draft, preferring instead to begin with just their tentative thesis. As you write, remember that your first draft is naturally going to be rough and will probably not be as clear as you would like it to be; still, it will enable you to see the ideas you have outlined begin to take shape.

REVISING AND EDITING AN ESSAY

As soon as you begin to draft your essay, you begin the process of revision. When you **revise,** you literally "re-see" your draft and, in many cases, you go on to reorder and rewrite substantial portions of your essay. Before you are satisfied with your essay, you will probably write several drafts, each more closely focused and more coherent than the previous one.

Strategies for Revision

Two strategies can help you to revise your drafts: *peer review* and *a dialogue with your instructor.*

Peer review is a process in which students assess each other's work-in-progress. This activity may be carried out in informal sessions, during which one student comments on another's draft, or it may be a formal process in which a student responds to specific questions on a form supplied by the instructor. In either case, one student's reactions can help another student revise.

A **dialogue with your instructor**—in conference or by e-mail—can give you a sense of how to proceed with your revision. Establishing such an oral or written dialogue can help you learn how to respond critically to your own writing, and your reactions to your instructor's comments on any draft can help you to clarify your essay's goals. (If your instructor is not available, try to schedule a conference with a writing center tutor, if your school offers this service.) Using your own responses as well as those of your classmates and your instructor, you can write drafts that are increasingly more consistent with these goals.

The Revision Process

As you move through successive drafts, the task of revising your essay will be easier if you follow a systematic process. As you read and react to your essay, begin by assessing the effectiveness of the larger elements—thesis and support, for instance—and proceed to examine increasingly smaller elements.

Thesis Statement First, reconsider your **thesis statement.** Is it carefully and precisely worded? Does it provide a realistic idea of what your essay will cover? Does it make a point that is worth supporting? It is not enough, for instance, to base an essay about literature on a vague thesis.

> **Vague:** Many important reasons exist to explain why Margot Macomber's shooting of her husband was probably intentional.
>
> **Vague:** Dickens's characters are a lot like those of Addison and Steele.

To give focus and direction to your essay, a thesis statement must be more pointed and more specific:

> **Revised:** Although Hemingway's text states that Margot Macomber "shot at the buffalo," a careful analysis of her relationship with her husband suggests that in fact she intended to kill him.
>
> **Revised:** With their extremely familiar, almost caricature-like physical and moral traits, many of Charles Dickens's minor characters reveal that he owes a debt to the "characters" created by the seventeenth-century essayists Joseph Addison and Richard Steele for the newspaper The Spectator.

Support Next, assess the appropriateness of your **supporting ideas** and consider whether you present enough support for your thesis and whether all the details you include are relevant to that thesis. Make sure you have supported all points with specific, concrete examples from the work or works you are discussing, briefly summarizing key events, quoting dialogue or description, describing characters or settings, or paraphrasing important ideas. Make certain, however, that your own ideas control the essay and that you have not substituted plot summary for analysis and interpretation. Your goal is to draw a conclusion about one or more works and to support that conclusion with pertinent details. If a plot detail supports a point you wish to make, include a *brief* summary of the event or series of events, showing its relevance by explicitly connecting the summary to the point you are making. In the following excerpt from a paper on a short story by James Joyce, the first sentence summarizes a key event and the second sentence explains its significance:

> At the end of "Counterparts," when Farrington returns home after a day of frustration and abuse at work, his reaction is to strike out at his son Tom. This act shows that although he and his son are similarly victimized, Farrington is also the counterpart of his tyrannical boss.

Topic Sentences   Now, turn your attention to the **topic sentences** that present the main idea of each body paragraph, making sure that they are clearly worded and that they communicate the direction of your ideas and the precise relationships of ideas to one another.

Be especially careful to avoid abstractions and vague generalities in topic sentences:

> **Vague:**   One similarity revolves around the dominance of the men by women. *(What exactly is the similarity?)*
>
> **Revised:**   In both stories, a man is dominated by a woman.
>
> **Vague:**   There is one reason for the fact that Jay Gatsby remains a mystery. *(What is the reason?)*
>
> **Revised:**   Because The Great Gatsby is narrated by the outsider Nick Carraway, Jay Gatsby himself remains a mystery.

When revising topic sentences that are intended to move readers from one point (or section of your paper) to another, be sure the relationship between the ideas they link is clear:

> **Relationship between ideas unclear:**   Now the poem's imagery will be discussed.
>
> **Revised:**   Another reason for the poem's effectiveness is its unusual imagery.
>
> **Relationship between ideas unclear:**   The sheriff's wife is another interesting character.
>
> **Revised:**   Like her friend Mrs. Hale, the sheriff's wife has mixed feelings about what Mrs. Wright has done.

Introductions and Conclusions   When you are satisfied with the body of your essay, you can go on to examine your paper's *introduction* and *conclusion*.

The **introduction** of an essay about literature should identify the works to be discussed and indicate the emphasis of the discussion to follow. Depending on your purpose and on your paper's topic, you may want to provide some historical background or biographical information or to briefly discuss the work in relation to other, similar works. Like all introductions, the one you write for an essay about literature should create interest in your topic and include a clear thesis statement.

The following introduction, although adequate for a first draft, is in need of revision:

> Revenge, which is defined as "the chance to retaliate, get satisfaction, take vengeance, or inflict damage or injury in return for an injury, insult, etc.," is a major component in many of the stories we have read. The stories that will be discussed here deal with a variety of ways to seek revenge. In my essay, I will show some of these differences.

Although the student clearly identifies her paper's topic, she does not identify the works she will discuss or the particular point she will make about revenge. Her tired opening strategy, a dictionary definition, is not likely to create interest in her topic, and her announcement of her intention in the last sentence is awkward and unnecessary. The following revision is much more effective:

> In Edgar Allan Poe's "The Cask of Amontillado" Montresor vows revenge on Fortunato for an unspecified "insult"; in Ring Lardner's "Haircut" Paul, a young retarded man, gets even with a cruel practical joker who has taunted him for years. Both of these stories present characters who seek revenge, and both stories end in murder. However, the murderers' motivations are presented very differently. In "Haircut" the unreliable narrator is unaware of the significance of many events, and his ignorance helps to create sympathy for the murderer. In "The Cask of Amontillado," where the untrustworthy narrator is the murderer himself, Montresor's inability to offer a convincing motive turns the reader against him.

In your **conclusion** you restate your thesis or sum up your essay's main points; then, you make a graceful exit.

The concluding paragraph that follows is acceptable for a first draft, but it communicates little information:

> Although the characters of Montresor and Paul were created by different authors at different times, they do have similar motives and goals. However, they are portrayed very differently.

The following revision reinforces the essay's main point, effectively incorporating a brief quotation from "The Cask of Amontillado" (p. 000):

> In fact, then, what is significant is not whether or not each murderer's act is justified, but rather how each murderer, and each victim, is portrayed by the narrator. Montresor--driven by a thirst to avenge "a thousand injuries" as well as a final insult--is shown to be sadistic and unrepentant; in "Haircut" it is Jim, the victim, whose sadism and lack of remorse are revealed to the reader.

Sentences and Words   Now, focus on the individual sentences and words of your essay. Begin by evaluating your **transitions,** the words and phrases that link sentences and paragraphs. Be sure that every necessary transitional element has been supplied and that each word or phrase you have selected accurately conveys the exact relationship (sequence, contradiction, and so on) between ideas. When you are satisfied with the clarity and appropriateness of your paper's transitions, consider sentence variety and word choice.

First, be sure you have varied your sentence structure. You will bore your readers if all your sentences begin the same way ("The story. . . . "; "The story. . . . "), or if they are all about the same length. In addition, make sure that all the words you select accurately communicate your ideas and that you have not used vague, inexact diction. For example, saying that a character is *bad* is a lot less effective than characterizing him or her as *ruthless, conniving,* or *malicious.* Finally, eliminate subjective expressions, such as *I think, in my opinion, I believe, it seems to me,* and *I feel.* These phrases weaken your essay by suggesting that its ideas are "only" opinions and have no objective validity.

Using and Documenting Sources   Make certain that all references to sources are integrated smoothly and documented appropriately (see pages 1903–05 and 1908–18 of Appendix A, "Writing a Research Paper").

✳ Checklist: Using Sources

✓ Acknowledge all sources, including the work or works under discussion, using the documentation style of the Modern Language Association (MLA).

✓ Combine paraphrases, summaries, and quotations with your own interpretations, weaving quotations smoothly into your paper. Introduce the words or ideas of others with a phrase that identifies their source ("According to Richard Wright's biographer, . . . "), and end with appropriate parenthetical documentation.

✓ Use quotations *only* when something vital would be lost if you did not reproduce the author's exact words.

✓ Integrate short quotations (four lines or less of prose or three lines or less of poetry) smoothly into your paper. (Use a slash to separate lines of poetry.) Be sure that you enclose quotations in quotation marks.

✓ Set off quotations of more than four lines of prose or three lines of poetry by indenting ten spaces (approximately one inch) from the left-hand margin. Double-space, and do not use quotation marks. If you are quoting a single paragraph, do not indent the first line.

✓ Use ellipses—three spaced periods—and square brackets to indicate material omitted within a quotation ("Miller revised his play often [. . .] that summer."). Use ellipses and brackets followed by end punctuation to indicate an omission at the end of a sentence ("He frequently spent days without writing [. . .]. "). Use a single line of periods surrounded by brackets to indicate that you have omitted a line of poetry.

✓ Use brackets to indicate that you have added words to a quotation ("[Willie] is a modern-day Everyman."). Use brackets to alter a quotation so that it fits grammatically into your sentence (Wilson says that Miller "offer[s] audiences a dark view of the present.").

✓ Place commas and periods *inside* the quotation marks (According to Robert Coles, the child "could make others smile.").

✓ Place punctuation marks other than commas and periods *outside* the quotation marks (What does Frost mean when he says "a poem must ride on its own melting"?). If the punctuation marks are part of the quoted material, place them inside the quotation marks (In "Mending Wall," Frost asks, "*Why* do they make good neighbors?").

✓ When citing a part of a short story or novel, supply the page number (143); for a poem, supply the line numbers (3–5); for a play, supply the act, scene, and line numbers (2.2.17–22).

✓ Include a Works Cited list (unless your instructor tells you otherwise).

Editing

Once you have finished revising, you **edit**—that is, you make certain that your paper's grammar, punctuation, spelling, and mechanics are correct. Always run a spell check—but remember that you still have to proofread carefully for errors that the spell checker will not identify. These include homophones (*brake* incorrectly used instead of *break*), typos that create correctly spelled words (*work* instead of *word*), and proper nouns that may not be in your computer's dictionary. If you use a grammar checker, remember that grammar programs may identify potential problems—long sentences, for example—but may not be able to determine whether or not a particular long sentence is grammatically correct (let alone stylistically pleasing). Always keep a style handbook as well as a dictionary nearby so that you can double check any problems a spell checker or grammar checker highlights in your writing.

As you edit, pay particular attention to the mechanical conventions of literary essays, some of which are addressed in the checklist below. When your editing is complete, give your essay a descriptive title; before you retype or reprint it, be sure that its format conforms to your instructor's requirements.

CHECKLIST: CONVENTIONS OF WRITING ABOUT LITERATURE

- ✓ Use present-tense verbs when discussing works of literature: "The character of Mrs. Mallard's husband *is* not developed. . . . "
- ✓ Use past-tense verbs only when discussing historical events ("Owen's poem conveys the destructiveness of World War I, which at the time the poem *was* written *was* considered to be . . ."), when presenting historical or biographical data ("Her first novel which *was* published in 1811 when Austen *was* thirty-six, . . ."), or when identifying events that occurred prior to the time of the story's main action ("Miss Emily is a recluse; since her father *died* she has lived alone except for a servant").
- ✓ Support all points with specific, concrete examples from the work you are discussing, briefly summarizing key events, quoting dialogue or description, describing characters or setting, or paraphrasing ideas.
- ✓ Avoid unnecessary plot summary. Your goal is to draw a conclusion about one or more works and to support that conclusion with pertinent details. If a plot detail supports a point you wish to make, a *brief* summary is acceptable. But plot summary is no substitute for analysis.

✓ Use *literary terms* accurately. For example, be careful not to confuse *narrator* or *speaker* with *author;* feelings or opinions expressed by a narrator or character do not necessarily represent those of the author. You should not say, "In the poem's last stanza, *Frost* expresses his indecision" when you mean that the poem's *speaker* is indecisive.

✓ Underline titles of novels and plays; place titles of short stories and poems within quotation marks.

✓ Refer to authors of literary works by their full names *(Edgar Allan Poe)* in your first reference to them and by their last names *(Poe)* in subsequent references. Never refer to authors by their first names, and never use titles that indicate marital status *(Flannery O'Connor* or *O'Connor,* never *Flannery* or *Miss O'Connor).*

Exercise: Two Student Papers

The following student papers, "Initiation into Adulthood" and "Hard Choices," were written for the same introduction to literature class. Both consider the initiation theme in the same three short stories: James Joyce's "Eveline" (p. 470), John Updike's "A&P" (p. 113), and William Faulkner's "Barn Burning" (p. 226). However, while "Hard Choices" conforms to the conventions of writing about literature discussed in this chapter, "Initiation into Adulthood" does not.

Read the two essays. Then, guided by this chapter's discussion of writing about literature and by the checklists on pages 34 and 35, identify the features that make "Hard Choices" the more effective essay, and decide where "Initiation into Adulthood" needs further revision. Finally, suggest some possible revisions for "Hard Choices."

Initiation into Adulthood

At an early age, the main focus in a child's life is his parents. But as this child grows, he begins to get his own view of life which may be, and usually is, different from that of his parents. Sooner or later there will come a time in this child's life when he must stand up for what he truly believes in. At this point in his life, he can no longer be called a child and he becomes part of the adult world. In literature, many stories--such as James Joyce's "Eveline," John Updike's "A&P," and William Faulkner's "Barn Burning"-- focus on this initiation into adulthood.

James Joyce's "Eveline" is a story that de-scribes a major turning point in a woman's life. At home, Eveline's life was very hard. She was responsi-ble for keeping the house together and caring for the younger children left to her after her mother's death. Unfortunately, the only thoughts that ran through her mind were thoughts of escape, of leaving her unhappy life and beginning a new life of her own. The night before she was to secretly leave with Frank on a boat to Buenos Ayres, a street organ playing re-minded her of her promise to her dying mother to keep the home together as long as she could. She was now forced to make a decision between life with Frank and her present life, which didn't look wholly undesir-able now that she was about to leave. The next night, just as she was about to step on the boat, she real-ized she could not leave. The making of this decision was in essence Eveline's initiation into adulthood.

Introduction

Thesis statement

Discussion of first story: "Eveline"

Discussion of
second story:
"A & P"

John Updike's "A&P" presented the brief infatuation of a young boy, Sammy, and the consequences that followed. Sammy's home was a small quiet town a few miles from the shore. He worked in the local A&P as a cashier, a job his father had gotten for him. One day, three girls in nothing but bathing suits walked through the front door. Immediately they caught Sammy's eye, especially the leader, the one he nicknamed "Queenie." After prancing through the store, eventually they came to Sammy's checkout with an unusual order. It was not long before they caught the attention of Mr. Lengel, the manager. Unpleasant words were exchanged between the manager and Queenie pertaining to their inappropriate shopping attire. Before the girls left the store, Sammy told Lengel that he quit, hoping they would stop and watch their unsuspected hero. But they kept walking, and Sammy was faced with the decision of whether or not to follow through with his gesture. Knowing that it is "fatal" not to follow through with a gesture once you've started, he removed his apron and bow tie and walked out the door, realizing how hard the world was going to be to him hereafter. The making of this decision, to leave the mundane life of the A&P and enter the harsh world, was in essence Sammy's initiation into adulthood.

Discussion of
third story:
"Barn
Burning"

William Faulkner's "Barn Burning" is a story about Sarty Snopes, an innocent young boy who must make a decision between his family and his honor. Because Abner Snopes, Sarty's father, had so little, he tried to hurt those who had more than he had--often by burning their barns. These acts forced the Snopes family to move around quite a bit. The last time Snopes burned a barn, he did it without warning his victim, making Sarty realize how cruel and dishonest he really was. Because of this realization, Sarty decided to leave his family. This decision of Sarty's not to stick to his own blood was his initiation into adulthood.

"Eveline," "A&P," and "Barn Burning" all deal with a youth maturing to adulthood in the process of deciding whether to stay unhappy or to go and seek a better life. Sammy and Sarty leave their unpleasant situations because of something done unfairly. Eveline, on the other hand, decides to stay, remembering a responsibility to her mother. The decisions of these characters presented in their respective stories are focal points in the literary works and pertain to initiation into adulthood. Conclusion

Hard Choices

Introduction

Although William Faulkner's "Barn Burning" focuses on a young boy in the American South, John Updike's "A&P" on a teenager in a town north of Boston, and James Joyce's "Eveline" on a young woman in Dublin, each of the three stories revolves around a decision the central character must make. These decisions are not easy ones; in all three cases, family loyalty competes with a desire for individual freedom.

Thesis statement

However, the difficult decision-making process helps each character to mature, and in this sense, all three works are initiation stories.

Discussion of first story: "Barn Burning"

For Sarty Snopes in "Barn Burning," initiation into adulthood means coming to terms with his father's concept of revenge. Mr. Snopes believes that a person should take revenge into his own hands if he cannot get justice in court. Revenge, for this bitter man, means burning down barns. Sarty knows that his father is doing wrong, but Mr. Snopes drills into his son's mind the idea that "You got to learn to stick to your own blood or you ain't going to have any blood to stick to you" (Faulkner 229), and for a long time Sarty believes him. Naturally, this blood tie makes Sarty's decision to leave his family extremely difficult. In the end, though, Sarty decides to reject his father's values and remain behind when his family moves.

Discussion of second story: "A & P"

In a similar manner, Sammy must choose between his values and his parents' values (reflected in his job at the supermarket). While Sammy is working in the A&P, he notices how "sheep-like" people are. Most customers have a routine life that they never consider changing, and Sammy does not want to wind up like them. When three seemingly carefree girls enter the store and exhibit nonconformist behavior--such as going against the flow of people in the aisles, not having a grocery list, and wearing bathing suits-- Sammy sees them as rebels, and he longs to escape through them from his humdrum world. In the end, he chooses to defend the girls and quit the job his parents helped him to get.

Likewise, Eveline has to decide between a new life with her boyfriend, Frank, in South America and her dull, hard life at home with her father. The new life offers change and freedom, while her life at home is spent working and keeping house. Still, when given the chance to leave, she declines because she has promised her dying mother to keep the house as long as she could.

Discussion of third story: "Eveline"

All three characters enter adulthood by making difficult decisions. Sarty realizes that in order for him to grow, he must repudiate his father's wrongdoings. He stands up for his values and rejects his "blood." Sammy makes the same decision, although with less extreme consequences: knowing that he will have to confront his parents, he defends the three girls and stands up to his boss, rejecting a life of conformity and security. Unlike the other two, Eveline does not reject her parents' values. Instead, she decides to sacrifice her own future by remaining with her father. She keeps her promise to her mother and places

Comparative analysis of the three stories

her father before herself because she knows that caring for him is her duty.

Further analysis of the three stories

Each of the three characters confronts a challenging future. Sarty must support himself and make a new life. Because he is the youngest and because he has no one to help him, his future is the most uncertain of the three. Unlike Sammy and Eveline, who still have homes, Sarty has only his judgment and his values to guide him. Sammy's future is less bleak but still unpredictable: He knows that the world will be a harder place for him from now on (Updike 118) because now he is a man of principle. Unlike the other two, Eveline knows exactly what her future holds: work, pain, and boredom. She has no fear of uncertainty--but no hope for a better tomorrow either.

Conclusion

"Barn Burning," "A&P," and "Eveline" are stories of initiation in which the main characters struggle with decisions that help them to grow up. All three consider giving up the known for the unknown, challenging their parents and becoming truly themselves, but only Sarty and Sammy do so. Both boys defy their parents and trade difficult lives for uncertain ones. Eveline, however, chooses to stay on in her familiar life, choosing the known--however deadening--over the unknown. Still, all three, in confronting hard choices and deciding to do what their values tell them they must do, experience an initiation into adulthood.

FICTION

CHAPTER 3

Reading and Writing about Fiction

UNDERSTANDING FICTION

❖ ❖ ❖

A **narrative** tells a story by presenting events in some logical or orderly way. Works of narrative fiction originate in the imagination of the author, not in history or fact. Certainly some fiction—historical or autobiographical fiction, for example—focuses on real people and actual events, but the way the characters interact and how the plot unfolds are the author's invention.

Even before they know how to read, most people have learned how narratives are structured. Once children can tell a story, they also know how to exaggerate, how to add or delete details, how to rearrange events, and how to bend facts—in other words, how to fictionalize a narrative to achieve a desired effect. This kind of informal, personal narrative is similar in many ways to the more structured literary narratives included in this anthology.

Our earliest examples of narrative fiction are stories and songs that came out of a prehistoric oral tradition. These stories, embellished with each telling, were often quite long, embodying the history, the central myths, and the religious beliefs of the cultures in which they originated. Eventually transcribed, these extended narratives became **epics**—long narrative poems about heroic figures whose actions determine the fate of a nation or an entire race. Homer's *Iliad* and *Odyssey,* the ancient Babylonian *Epic of Gilgamesh,* the Hindu *Bhagavad Gita,* and the Anglo-Saxon *Beowulf* are examples. Many of the tales of the Old Testament also came out of this tradition. The setting of an epic is vast—sometimes worldwide or cosmic, including heaven and hell—and the action commonly involves a battle or a perilous journey. Quite often divine beings participate in the action and influence the outcome of events, as they do in the Trojan War in the *Iliad* and in the founding of Rome in Vergil's *Aeneid.*

Folktales and **fairy tales** also come out of an oral tradition. These tales, which developed along with other narrative forms, have influenced works as diverse as Chaucer's *The Canterbury Tales* and D. H. Lawrence's "The Rocking-Horse Winner" (p. 362). The folktales and fairy tales that survive (such as "Cinderella" and Aesop's *Fables*) are contemporary versions of old, even ancient, tales that can be traced back centuries through many different cultures. Folktales and fairy tales share several characteristics. First, they feature simple characters who illustrate a quality or trait that can be summed up in a few words. Much of the appeal of "Cinderella," for example, depends on the contrast between the selfish, sadistic stepsisters and poor, gentle, victimized Cinderella. In addition, the folktale or fairy tale has an obvious theme or moral—good triumphing over evil, for instance. The stories move directly to their conclusions, never interrupted by ingenious or unexpected twists of plot. (Love is temporarily thwarted, but the prince eventually finds Cinderella and marries her.) Finally, these tales are anchored not in specific times or places but in "Once upon a time" settings, green worlds of prehistory filled with royalty, talking animals, and magic.

During the Middle Ages, the **romance** supplanted the epic. Written initially in verse but later in prose, the romance replaced the epic's gods, goddesses, and central heroic figures with knights, kings, and damsels in distress. Events were controlled by enchantments rather than by the will of divine beings. *Sir Gawain and the Green Knight* and other tales of King Arthur and the Knights of the Round Table are examples of romances. Eventually the romance gave way to other types of narratives. Short prose tales, such as those collected in Giovanni Boccaccio's *The Decameron*, originated in fourteenth-century Italy, and the **picaresque,** an episodic, often satirical work about a rogue or rascal, such as Miguel de Cervantes's *Don Quixote,* emerged in seventeenth-century Spain. The **pastoral romance,** a prose tale set in an idealized rural world, and the **character,** a brief satirical sketch illustrating a type of personality, both became popular in Renaissance England.

From these diverse sources emerged the **novel.** The English writer Daniel Defoe is commonly given credit for writing the first novel in 1719. His *Robinson Crusoe* is an episodic narrative similar to a picaresque but unified by a single setting as well as by a central character. By the nineteenth century, the novel reached a high point in its development, replacing other kinds of extended narratives. Because of its ability to present a wide range of characters in realistic settings and to develop them in depth, the novel appealed to members of the rising middle class, who seemed to have an insatiable desire to see themselves portrayed. Writers such as George Eliot, Charles Dickens, William Thackeray, and Charlotte and Emily Brontë appealed to this desire by creating large fictional worlds populated by many different characters who reflected the complexity—and at times the melodrama—of Victorian society. From these roots, the novel as a literary form continued to develop throughout the twentieth century.

THE SHORT STORY

Like the novel, the short story evolved from the various forms of narrative discussed earlier. Because the short story comes from so many different sources from all over the world, it is difficult to determine where it originated. We can say with certainty, however, that in the United States during the nineteenth century a group of writers—in particular Nathaniel Hawthorne and Edgar Allan Poe—took it seriously and exploited its fictional possibilities. Because the short story was embraced so readily and developed so quickly in the United States, it is commonly, although not quite accurately, thought of as an American literary form.

Whereas the novel is an extended piece of narrative fiction, the **short story** is limited in length and scope. These limitations account for the characteristics that distinguish the short story from longer prose forms. Unlike the novelist, the short story writer cannot devote a great deal of space to developing a highly complex plot or a large number of characters. As a result, the short story begins close to or at the height of action and develops only one character in depth. Usually concentrating on a single incident, the writer develops a character by showing his or her responses to events. (This attention to character development, as well as its detailed description of setting, is what distinguishes the short story from earlier short narrative forms, such as folktales and fairy tales.) In many contemporary stories, a character experiences an **epiphany,** a moment of illumination in which something hidden or not understood becomes immediately clear. Examples of epiphany are found in this anthology in James Joyce's "Araby," John Updike's "A&P," and David Michael Kaplan's "Doe Season."

Today the term *short story* is applied to a wide variety of prose narratives: short stories such as Charles Baxter's "Gryphon" (p. 134), which runs about twelve pages; **short short stories,** such as Luisa Valenzuela's "All about Suicide" (p. 5), which are under five pages in length; and long stories, such as Franz Kafka's "The Metamorphosis" (p. 474) and Herman Melville's "Bartleby" (p. 520), which may more accurately be called short novels or **novellas.**

As the selections in this anthology show, the possibilities of the short story are infinite. A short story may be comic or tragic; its subject may be growing up, marriage, crime and punishment, war, sexual awakening, death, or any number of other human concerns. The setting can be an imaginary world, the old West, rural America, the jungles of Uruguay, nineteenth-century Russia, pre-communist China, or modern Egypt. The story may have a conventional form, with a definite beginning, middle, and end, or it may be structured as a letter, as a diary entry, or even as a collection of random notes. The narrator of a story may be trustworthy or unreliable, involved in the action or a disinterested observer, sympathetic or deserving of scorn, extremely ignorant or highly insightful, limited in vision or able to see inside the minds of all the characters.

READING FICTION

◊ ◊ ◊

As you read more works of short fiction, you will begin paying careful attention to elements such as plot; character; setting; point of view; style, tone, and language; symbol and allegory; and theme. The following guidelines, designed to help you explore works of fiction, focus on issues that will be examined in depth in chapters to come.

◇ Look at the **plot** of the story. How do the events in the story relate to one another, and how do they relate to the story as a whole? What conflicts occur in the story, and how are these conflicts developed or resolved? Does the story include any noteworthy plot devices, such as flashbacks or foreshadowing? (See Chapter 4.)

◇ Analyze the **characters** of the story. What are their most striking traits? How do these individuals interact with one another? What motivates them? Are the characters fully developed, or are they stereotypes whose sole purpose is to express a single trait (good, evil, generosity) or to move the plot along? (See Chapter 5.)

◇ Identify the **setting** of the story. At what time period and in what geographic location does the action of the story occur? How does the setting affect the characters of the story? How does it determine the relationships among the characters? How does the setting affect the plot? Does the setting create a mood for the story? In what way does the setting reinforce the central ideas that the story examines? (See Chapter 6.)

◇ Examine the narrative **point of view** of the story. What person or persons are telling the story? Is the story told in the first person (*I* or *we*) or in the third person (*he, she,* or *they*)? Does the narrator see from various perspectives, or is the story restricted to the perspective of one person—a major character, a minor character, or just an observer? How much does the narrator know about the events in the story? Does the narrator present an accurate or inaccurate picture of events? Does the narrator understand the full significance of the story he or she is telling? (See Chapter 7.)

◇ Analyze the **style, tone,** and **language** of the story. Does the writer make any unusual use of diction or syntax? Does the writer use imaginative figures of speech? Patterns of imagery? What styles or levels of speech are associated with particular characters? What words or phrases are repeated throughout the work? Is the story's style plain or elaborate? Does the narrator's tone reveal his or her attitude toward characters or events? Are there any discrepancies between the narrator's attitude and the attitude of the author? Is the tone of the story playful, humorous, ironic, satirical, serious, somber, solemn, bitter, condescending, formal, informal—or does the tone suggest some other attitude? (See Chapter 8.)

◇ Focus on **symbolism** and **allegory.** Does the author use any objects or ideas symbolically? What characters or objects in the story are part of an *allegorical framework?* How does an object establish its symbolic or allegorical significance in the story? Does the same object have different meanings at different places in the story? Are the symbols or *allegorical figures* conventional or unusual? At what points in the story do symbols or allegorical figures appear? (See Chapter 9.)

◇ Identify the **themes** of the story. What is the central theme? How is this idea or concept expressed in the work? What elements of the story develop the central theme? How do character, plot, setting, point of view, and symbols reinforce the central theme? How does the title of the story contribute to readers' understanding of the central theme? What other themes are explored? (See Chapter 10.)

ACTIVE READING

John Frei, a student in an introduction to literature course, was assigned to write a two- to three-page essay on a topic of his choice, focusing on any short story in this literature anthology, without consulting outside sources. After considering a number of possible choices, John selected Alberto Alvaro Ríos's "The Secret Lion," which appears on the pages that follow.

◇ **ALBERTO ALVARO RÍOS** (1952–   ) was born and raised in the border town of Nogales, Arizona, the son of a Mexican father and an English mother. He has published many poems and short stories, including the poetry collections *Teodora Luna's Two Kisses* (1990); *The Warring Poems* (1989); *The Lime Orchard Woman* (1988); and *Whispering to Fool the Wind* (1982), which won the American Academy of Poets Walt Whitman Award; and the short story collections *Pig Cookies and Other Stories* (1995) and *The Iguana Killer: Twelve Stories of the Heart* (1984), from which "The Secret Lion" is drawn. Ríos lives in Chandler, Arizona, and teaches at Arizona State University in Tempe.

Reviewer Mary Logue, writing in the October 1982 *Village Voice Literary Supplement,* says that Ríos's writings "carry the feel of another world. . . . Ríos's tongue is both foreign and familiar," reflecting an upbringing "where one is neither in this country nor the other." In many of his stories, Ríos expresses the seeming "other-ness" of Anglo culture as seen through the eyes of Chicano children: a little boy frightened by the sight of his first snowfall, or (as in "The Secret Lion") boys amazed by the otherworldly sight of "heaven." Through Ríos's children, we see our own world with new eyes.

Cultural Context ◇   When Ríos was a boy, he and his friends were told that they could no longer speak Spanish in school, even though it was their first language. Some of the children were even punished for speaking Spanish on the playground. As a result, Ríos began to equate Spanish with something bad, a perception that he says took years to overcome.

◇ ◇ ◇

ALBERTO ALVARO RÍOS

The Secret Lion
(1984)

I was twelve and in junior high school and something happened that we didn't have a name for, but it was there nonetheless like a lion, and roaring, roaring that way the biggest things do. Everything changed. Just that. Like the rug, the one that gets pulled—or better, like the tablecloth those magicians pull where the stuff on the table stays the same but the gasp! from the audience makes the staying-the-same part not matter. Like that.

What happened was there were teachers now, not just one teacher, teach-erz, and we felt personally abandoned somehow. When a person had all these teachers now, he didn't get taken care of the same way, even though six was more than one. Arithmetic went out the door when we walked in. And we saw girls now, but they weren't the same girls we used to know because we couldn't talk to them anymore, not the same way we used to, certainly not to Sandy, even though she was my neighbor, too. Not even to her. She just played the piano all the time. And there were words, oh there were words in junior high school, and we wanted to know what they were, and how a person did them—that's what school was supposed to be for. Only, in junior high school, school wasn't school, everything was backward-like. If you went up to a teacher and said the word to try and find out what it meant you got in trouble for saying it. So we didn't. And we figured it must have been that way about other stuff, too, so we never said anything about anything—we weren't stupid.

But my friend Sergio and I, we solved junior high school. We would come home from school on the bus, put our books away, change shoes, and go across the highway to the arroyo. It was the one place we were not supposed to go. So we did. This was, after all, what junior high had at least shown us. It was our river, though, our personal Mississippi, our friend from long back, and it was full of stories and all the branch forts we had built in it when we were still the Vikings of America, with our own symbol, which we had carved everywhere, even in the sand, which let the water take it. That was good, we had decided; whoever was at the end of this river would know about us.

At the very very top of our growing lungs, what we would do down there was shout every dirty word we could think of, in every combination we could come up with, and we would yell about girls, and all the things we wanted to do with them, as loud as we could—we didn't know what we wanted to do with them, just things—and we would yell about teachers, and how we loved some of them, like Miss Crevelone, and how we wanted to dissect some of them, making signs of the cross, like priests, and we would yell this stuff over and over because it felt good, we couldn't explain why, it just felt good and for the first time in our lives there was nobody to tell us we couldn't. So we did.

5   One Thursday we were walking along shouting this way, and the railroad, the Southern Pacific, which ran above and along the far side of the arroyo, had dropped a grinding ball down there, which was, we found out later, a cannonball thing used in mining. A bunch of them were put in a big vat which turned around and crushed the ore. One had been dropped, or thrown—what do caboose men do when they get bored—but it got down there regardless and as we were walking along yelling about one girl or another, a particular Claudia, we found it, one of these things, looked at it, picked it up, and got very very excited, and held it and passed it back and forth, and we were saying "Guythisis, this is, geeGuythis . . .": we had this perception about nature then, that nature is imperfect and that round things are perfect: we said "GuyGodthis is perfect, thisisthis is perfect, it's round, round and heavy, it'sit's the best thing we'veeverseen. Whatisit?" We didn't know. We just knew it was great. We just, whatever, we played with it, held it some more.

And then we had to decide what to do with it. We knew, because of a lot of things, that if we were going to take this and show it to anybody, this discovery, this best thing, was going to be taken away from us. That's the way it works with little kids, like all the polished quartz, the tons of it we had collected piece by piece over the years. Junior high kids too. If we took it home, my mother, we knew, was going to look at it and say "throw that dirty thing in the, get rid of it." Simple like, like that. "But ma it's the best thing I" "Getridofit." Simple.

So we didn't. Take it home. Instead, we came up with the answer. We dug a hole and buried it. And we marked it secretly. Lots of secret signs. And came back the next week to dig it up and, we didn't know, pass it around some more or something, but we didn't find it. We dug up that whole bank, and we never found it again. We tried.

Sergio and I talked about that ball or whatever it was when we couldn't find it. All we used were small words, neat, good. Kid words. What we were really saying, but didn't know the words, was how much that ball was like that place, that whole arroyo: couldn't tell anybody about it, didn't understand what it was, didn't have a name for it. It just felt good. It was just perfect in the way it was that place, that whole going to that place, that whole junior high school lion. It was just iron-heavy, it had no name, it felt good or not, we couldn't take it home to show our mothers, and once we buried it, it was gone forever.

The ball was gone, like the first reasons we had come to that arroyo years earlier, like the first time we had seen the arroyo, it was gone like everything else that had been taken away. This was not our first lesson. We stopped going to the arroyo after not finding the thing, the same way we had stopped going there years earlier and headed for the mountains. Nature seemed to keep pushing us around one way or another, teaching us the same thing every place we ended up. Nature's gang was tough that way, teaching us stuff.

10   When we were young we moved away from town, me and my family. Sergio's was already out there. Out in the wilds. Or at least the new place seemed like the wilds since everything looks bigger the smaller a man is. I was five, I guess, and we had moved three miles north of Nogales where we had lived, three miles north of the Mexican border. We looked across the highway in one direction and there was the arroyo; hills stood up in the other direction. Mountains, for a small man.

When the first summer came the very first place we went to was of course the one place we weren't supposed to go, the arroyo. We went down in there and found water running, summer rain water mostly, and we went swimming. But every third or fourth or fifth day, the sewage treatment plant that was, we found out, upstream, would release whatever it was that it released, and we would never know exactly what day that was, and a person really couldn't tell right off by looking at the water, not every time, not so a person could get out in time. So, we went swimming that summer and some days we had a lot of fun. Some days we didn't. We found a thousand ways to explain what happened on those other days, constructing elaborate stories about the neighborhood dogs, and hadn't she, my mother, miscalculated her step before, too? But she knew something was up because we'd come running into the house those days, wanting to take a shower, even—if this can be imagined—in the middle of the day.

That was the first time we stopped going to the arroyo. It taught us to look the other way. We decided, as the second side of summer came, we wanted to go into the mountains. They were still mountains then. We went running in one summer Thursday morning, my friend Sergio and I, into my mother's kitchen, and said, well, what'zin, what'zin those hills over there—we used her word so she'd understand us—and she said nothingdon'tworryaboutit. So we went out, and we weren't dumb, we thought with our eyes to each other, ohhoshe'stryingtokeepsomethingfromus. We knew adults.

We had read the books, after all; we knew about bridges and castles and wildtreacherousraging alligatormouth rivers. We wanted them. So we were going to go out and get them. We went back that morning into that kitchen and we said, "We're going out there, we're going into the hills, we're going away for three days, don't worry." She said, "All right."

"You know," I said to Sergio, "if we're going to go away for three days, well, we ought to at least pack a lunch."

15   But we were two young boys with no patience for what we thought at the time was mom-stuff: making sa-and-wiches. My mother didn't offer. So we got out little kid knapsacks that my mother had sewn for us, and into them we put the jar of mustard. A loaf of bread. Knivesforksplates, bottles of Coke, a can opener. This was lunch for the two of us. And we were weighed down, humped over to be strong enough to carry this stuff. But we started walking anyway, into the hills. We were going to eat berries and stuff otherwise. "Goodbye." My mom said that.

After the first hill we were dead. But we walked. My mother could still see us. And we kept walking. We walked until we got to where the sun is straight overhead, noon. That place. Where that is doesn't matter; it's time to eat. The truth is we weren't anywhere close to that place. We just agreed that the sun was overhead and that it was time to eat, and by tilting our heads a little we could make that the truth.

"We really ought to start looking for a place to eat."

"Yeah. Let's look for a good place to eat." We went back and forth saying that for fifteen minutes, making it lunchtime because that's what we always said back and forth before lunchtimes at home. "Yeah, I'm hungry all right." I nodded my head. "Yeah, I'm hungry all right too. I'm hungry." He nodded his head. I nodded my head back. After a good deal more nodding, we were ready, just as we came over a little hill. We hadn't found the mountains yet. This was a little hill.

And on the other side of this hill we found heaven.

20   It was just what we thought it would be.

Perfect. Heaven was green, like nothing else in Arizona. And it wasn't a cemetery or like that because we had seen cemeteries and they had gravestones and stuff and this didn't. This was perfect, had trees, lots of trees, had birds, like we had never seen before. It was like "The Wizard of Oz," like when they got to Oz and everything was so green, so emerald, they had to wear those glasses, and we ran just like them, laughing, laughing that way we did that moment, and we went running down to this clearing in it all, hitting each other that good way we did.

We got down there, we kept laughing, we kept hitting each other, we unpacked our stuff, and we started acting "rich." We knew all about how to do that, like blowing on our nails, then rubbing them on our chests for the shine. We made our sandwiches, opened our Cokes, got out the rest of the stuff, the salt and pepper shakers. I found this particular hole and I put my Coke right into it, a perfect fit, and I called it my Coke-holder. I got down next to it on my back, because everyone knows that rich people eat lying down, and I got my sandwich in one hand and put my other arm around the Coke in its holder. When I wanted a drink, I lifted my neck a little, put out my lips, and tipped my Coke a little with the crook of my elbow. Ah.

We were there, lying down, eating our sandwiches, laughing, throwing bread at each other and out for the birds. This was heaven. We were laughing and we couldn't believe it. My mother was keeping something from us, ah ha, but we had found her out. We even found water over at the side of the clearing to wash our plates with—we had brought plates. Sergio started washing his plates when he was done, and I was being rich with my Coke, and this day in summer was right.

When suddenly these two men came, from around a corner of trees and the tallest grass we had ever seen. They had bags on their backs, leather bags, bags and sticks.

25   We didn't know what clubs were, but I learned later, like I learned about the grinding balls. The two men yelled at us. Most specifically, one wanted me to take my Coke out of my Coke-holder so he could sink his golf ball into it.

Something got taken away from us that moment. Heaven. We grew up a little bit, and couldn't go backward. We learned. No one had ever told us about golf. They had told us about heaven. And it went away. We got golf in exchange.

We went back to the arroyo for the rest of that summer, and tried to have fun the best we could. We learned to be ready for finding the grinding ball. We loved it, and when we buried it we knew what would happen. The truth is, we didn't look so hard for it. We were two boys and twelve summers then, and not stupid. Things get taken away.

We buried it because it was perfect. We didn't tell my mother, but together it was all we talked about, till we forgot. It was the lion.

◆

Previewing

John Frei began the reading process by previewing his text. A quick glance at the story showed him that it was quite short (under five pages), that it was written in the first person ("I was twelve"), that it included dialogue as well as narrative, and that it had a provocative title.

Previewing "The Secret Lion" prepared John to read it more closely and, eventually, to write about it. In preparation for writing, he read and reread the story, highlighting and annotating it as he went along.

Highlighting and Annotating

As he reread the story, John highlighted words and ideas that he thought might be useful to him, indicated possible connections among ideas, and noted questions and comments as they occurred to him. During this process, he considered the meaning of the term *secret lion,* and he paid close attention to the narrator's voice. The highlighted and annotated passage that follows illustrates his responses to the last five paragraphs of the story:

When suddenly these two men came, from around a corner of trees

and the tallest grass we had ever seen. They had bags on their backs,

leather bags, bags and sticks.

We didn't know what clubs were, but I learned later, like I learned   *pt. of view*

about the grinding balls. The two men yelled at us. Most specifically,

one wanted me to take my Coke out of my Coke-holder so he could

sink his golf ball into it.

Something got taken away from us that moment. Heaven. We grew   *Heaven = innocence*

up a little bit, and couldn't go backward. We learned. No one had

ever told us about golf. They had told us about heaven. And it went   *Golf = adulthood*

away. We got golf in exchange.

We went back to the arroyo for the rest of that summer, and tried   *Things lose*

to have fun the best we could. We learned to be ready for finding the   *their magic + specialness.*

grinding ball. We loved it, and when we buried it we knew what   *Also— loss*

would happen. The truth is, we didn't look so hard for it. We were   *of innocence, trust, belief*

two boys and twelve summers then, and not stupid. Things get taken   *in things being*

away.   *perfect.*

5   We buried it because it was perfect. We didn't tell my mother, but   *ball?*

together it was all we talked about, till we forgot. It was the lion.

Lion = knowledge that growing up = loss? or is lion growing up itself?

John's highlighting and annotations suggested a number of interesting possibilities for his paper. First, John noticed that the story reveals both the narrator's childhood innocence and his adult knowledge. John's highlighting also identified some unusual stylistic features, such as words run together ("Getridofit") and repetition of words like *neat* and *perfect.* Finally, John noticed that four items—the arroyo, the grinding ball, the golf course, and the lion—are mentioned again and again. This emphasis led him to suspect that one or more of these items—particularly the secret lion, prominently mentioned in the story's title—had symbolic significance.

WRITING ABOUT FICTION

◈ ◈ ◈

PLANNING AN ESSAY

At this stage, John had not thought of a topic; he knew only that he would be writing a paper on "The Secret Lion." However, his previewing, highlighting, and annotations had revealed some interesting ideas about style and point of view—and, possibly, about symbolism. Now, because his paper was to be no more than three pages long, he decided to select just one element on which to concentrate.

Choosing a Topic

John decided to explore possible topics in his journal. His journal entry on the story's style and point of view follows:

> Style--Style is informal, with lots of contractions
> and slang terms like "neat." Words are run together. Most
> of the time, the boys combine words to indicate something
> unimportant to them. When they're packing the lunch, they
> include "knivesforksplates." They're not interested in
> packing the lunch--they just want to get to the
> "mountains." Packing lunches is very important to the
> mother, so she does the opposite of combining words: she
> breaks them down ("sa-and-wiches"). Maybe the words
> running together are supposed to suggest the days of a
> child, especially in the summer, when days just blend
> together. This style gets pretty annoying after a while,
> though--it's too cute.
>
> Point of view--We see the story through the eyes of
> the narrator, who is a character in the story. Sergio is
> developed along with the narrator as part of a "we." It's
> unusual that the characters are not really individuals--
> they function as "we" for most of the story, and nothing
> is done to give them separate voices. We don't see into
> the minds of the boys to any greater extent than what the
> narrator tells us, but the narrator has a double
> perspective: he takes the reader back to childhood, and
> this helps us understand the boys' excitement and

disappointment, but he also shows us how much more he
knows now, so we know that too.

John had no trouble writing paragraphs on style and point of view in
his journal, but he ran out of ideas quickly; he knew that he did not have
enough material to write a paper about either of these two possible topics.
When he started to write a journal entry about the symbolic significance
of certain elements in the story, however, he found that he had a lot to say.
As a result, he chose "Symbols in 'The Secret Lion'" as his paper's topic.
His journal entry on symbolism appears below:

> <u>Symbolism</u>--The arroyo, the grinding ball, the golf
> course, and of course the secret lion all seem to mean
> something beyond their literal meanings as objects and
> places. (Maybe the "mountains" do too.) For one thing,
> they're all repeated over and over again. Also, they
> all seem to be related somehow to magic and perfection
> and surprise and expectation and idealism (and, later,
> to disillusionment and disappointment). If this is a
> story about growing up, these things could be related
> somehow to that theme.

Finding Something to Say

Brainstorming   Once he had decided to write about symbolism, John moved
on to brainstorm about his topic, focusing on what he considered the
story's most important—and most obvious—symbol: the secret lion itself.
He wrote:

(Lion)= "roaring, roaring that way the biggest things do"

EVERYTHING CHANGED   (= secret because it's

something they have to find

out on their own, not from

adults?)

(Tablecloth)-rug (= magic).   "Staying-the-same part" is

most important--why?

(Arroyo:) not supposed to go (= rebellion)--Mississippi, "friend

from long back"; freedom. Place that doesn't change.

(Grinding ball)-Perfection in imperfect world, innocence in adult

world. "Nature = imperfect," but "round things = perfect"
--"the best thing." ("That ball was like that place, that
whole arroyo")

    Buried and "gone forever"--"taken away" (like arroyo)
Mountains: "everything looks bigger the smaller a man is";
hills = "Mountains for a small man." (Mother calls them hills)
Arroyo = polluted with sewage (never know when it's
    coming)--went to mts.
On other side of hills = golf course (= heaven)--perfect "perfect"
x3
                    *Like Oz—green, emerald
                    *Place to act "rich"
                    *Men with clubs = reality,
                    future--they go back to arroyo
                    (= end of innocence)
"Things get taken away" (heaven, ball--something buried and
lost--arroyo)
"We buried it because it was perfect. [. . .] It was the lion."
Lion = secret place inside us that still craves childhood (as
adults, we learn we have to keep it buried, like ball).
How can a roaring lion be secret?

Seeing Connections

Listing   When he looked over his brainstorming notes in search of an organizing scheme for his paper, John saw that he had plenty of information
about the secret lion, the arroyo, the grinding ball, and the golf course. His
most obvious option was to discuss one item at a time. But he knew that
he needed to find a common element among the four separate items, a
thematic connection that would relate them to one another. When he noticed that each item seemed to have different meanings at different periods of the boys' lives, he realized that his essay could discuss the changes
in meaning that occurred as the boys move from childhood to adolescence
to adulthood. He experimented with this possibility in the following lists
of related details:

The secret lion
Beginning: "raging beast" inside of them (6th grade
class) = frustration, puberty

```
Beginning: "roaring, roaring that way the biggest things do"
Middle: "that whole junior high school lion"
End: Lion = greatness, something important (also = puberty?)
Also = great discoveries they expect to make in their lives.
End: "It was the lion."
Arroyo
Place that doesn't change (= childhood); constant in
changing lives. (But it changes too)
Mississippi--horizons
Freedom of childhood
Waste dump
Grinding ball
Perfection (in imperfect world)
Childhood innocence (in adult world)
Undiscovered knowledge?
Secrets of childhood (buried)
Something lost: "Things get taken away"
Golf course
Heaven--knowledge that there is no heaven, that it's a
fraud, like the Wizard of Oz.
Adulthood--men with clubs
Scene of remembered humiliation
End of innocence (realization that it's just a golf
course)
```

John's lists confirmed that the meanings of the four items did seem to change as the boys grew up. To the boys, the arroyo, the grinding ball, and the golf course were magical, but when the boys grew up, all three lost their magic and became ordinary. The secret lion, however, seemed more complex than the other three, and John knew that he would have to develop his ideas further before he could show how the lion's meaning changes and how these changes affect the story as a whole.

Deciding on a Thesis

With his ideas organized into lists that clarified some possible relationships among them, John began to see a central idea for his essay. He expressed this idea in a tentative thesis, a sentence that he could use to guide his essay's first draft (for a full discussion of this stage of the writing process, see "Deciding on a Thesis," p. 26, in Chapter 2):

```
The meanings of the story's key symbols change as the boys
move from childhood to adolescence to adulthood; these
```

changes reveal corresponding changes in the boys' view of the world from idealism to frustration to resignation.

Preparing an Outline

Even though his essay was to be short, John prepared a scratch outline that mapped out an arrangement for his ideas. He decided to discuss the four key symbols one by one, tracing each through the boys' childhood, adolescence, and adulthood. He planned to discuss the lion last because he saw it as the story's most important symbol. Looking back over all his notes, and paying close attention to his thesis statement, John constructed the following scratch outline:

```
Arroyo
        Mississippi
        Rebellion
        Waste dump
Grinding ball
        [Not yet discovered]
        Lost perfection
        "Things get taken away."
Golf course
        Heaven
        Humiliation
        Golf course
Lion
        [Not yet discovered]
        "roaring"; "raging beast"
        Just the lion
```

DRAFTING AN ESSAY

Guided by his scratch outline, his thesis statement, and his notes, John wrote the following first draft. Because his notes included many ideas not included on his scratch outline, and because he discovered new ideas and connections among ideas as he wrote, the draft does not follow the scratch outline exactly.

Symbols in "The Secret Lion"

first draft

"The Secret Lion" is a story that is rich in symbols. It is also a story about change. The meanings of the story's key symbols change as the boys move from childhood to adolescence to adulthood; these changes reveal corresponding changes in the boys' view of the world from idealism to frustration to resignation.

The arroyo, a dry gulch that can fill up with water, is special to the narrator and his friend Sergio when they are boys. Literally, it is a place to play. Symbolically, it is a place to rebel (they're not supposed to be there; they yell forbidden words). It could also symbolize the continuum of discoveries they will make before they are completely grown up. To the young boys, the arroyo symbolizes a retreat from the disappointment of the golf course; it is their second choice. Later, it represented adventure, the uncertainty and unpredictability of adolescence, as illustrated by the fact that they cannot tell just by looking at it from the riverside whether the river was going to be tainted with sewage. When they are children, it is their Mississippi. When they are adolescents, it is a place to hang out and a symbol of adolescent rebellion; as an adult, the narrator looks back at it for what it was: an ordinary river polluted by sewage. The arroyo doesn't change, but the boys' view of it changes as they change.

At first, when they find the grinding ball, it stands for everything that is perfect and fascinating (and therefore forbidden and unattainable) in life. Like a child's life, it is perfect. They knew they

couldn't keep it forever, just as they couldn't be
children forever, so they buried it. When they tried
to look for it again, they couldn't find it. They
admit later that they don't look very hard. (People
always wish they can find youth again, but they
can't.) The ball represents perfection in an imperfect
world, childhood innocence in an adult world. They
hide it from their mother because they know she won't
see it as perfect; she'll make them "getridofit" (50).
They hide it because they want to retain the excitement of the undiscovered, but once they've used it and
seen it and buried it, it's not new anymore. Even if
they'd been able to find it, it would still be lost.
To the adult narrator, it's just an ordinary object
used in mining.

The golf course, which they wander into at age
five, is, for a short period of time, "heaven" (52).
It is lush and green and carefully cared for, and it
is the opposite of the polluted arroyo. It is also another world, as mysterious as the Land of Oz. With the
realization that it is not heaven to the golfers, the
boys see what outsiders they really are. They may
start "acting 'rich'" (52), but it will be just an
act. There are no Coke-holders, no Oz, no heaven. The
adolescents see the golf course as a scene of defeat
and embarrassment, the setting for the confrontation
that sent them back to the arroyo. To the adult, the
golf course is just a golf course.

The secret lion is the most complex symbol in the
story. In a sense it stands for the innocence of
childhood, something we lose when we learn more. The

lion symbolizes a great "roaring" disturbance (49). It is a change that unsettles everything for a brief time and then passes, leaving everything changed in irrevocable, indescribable ways. It symbolizes the boys' growing up: they are changed, but still the same people. The "secret lion" is that thing that changes little boys into men. It is secret because no one notices it happening; before it is noticed, the change has occurred, and the little boy is gone forever. It is a lion because it "roars" through the boy like a storm and makes all of the growing-up changes, which can be "the biggest things" (49). In a more specific sense, the lion stands for puberty, reflected in their rage and frustration when they shout profanity. In the beginning of the story, the lion is rage (puberty, adolescence); in the middle, it suggests greatness (passing through adolescence into manhood); at the end it's just the lion--"It was the lion" (53)--without any symbolic significance.

By the time they bury the ball, they have already learned one lesson, and the force of adulthood is pushing childhood aside. The golf course changes from heaven to shame to golf course; the ball changes from a special, perfect thing to something ordinary; the arroyo changes from grand river to polluted stream. Maybe it is the knowledge that life is not perfect, the knowledge that comes from growing up, that is the secret lion.

First Draft: Commentary

As John reviewed his first draft, he made a number of changes in content, style, and organization. He deleted wordiness and repetition; added more specific references, including quotations, from the story; sharpened transitions and added clearer topic sentences; and reorganized paragraphs to make logical and causal connections more obvious.

Discussions with classmates in a peer review group and with his instructor gave him some additional insights. The students' major criticism was that John's thesis seemed to make a complicated claim he could not support: that the development of all four symbols follows the three stages of the boys' lives. One student pointed out that two of the four symbols (the grinding ball and the secret lion) do not even enter the boys' lives until adolescence and that John's treatment of the story's most prominent symbol—the lion—does not show it to change in any significant way. The group agreed that he should simplify his thesis, focusing on the way the four symbols all reflect the story's theme about the inevitability of change.

John also discussed his draft with his instructor, who helped him with the arrangement of his essay, suggesting that he discuss the golf course first because it is the setting for the event that occurred first in time and because the disillusionment associated with it influences the subsequent events. John and his instructor also explored ideas for his introduction and conclusion, deciding to use these paragraphs to stress the common theme that all four symbols convey instead of focusing on the different ways in which each of the four separate symbols changes.

Finally, John's instructor expressed his concern about John's tendency to engage in "symbol hunting." He suggested that rather than focusing on finding equivalents for each of the four items ("the ball represents perfection," "the lion stands for puberty," and so on), John should consider how the use of these symbols opens up the story, how they work together to communicate the story's theme. His instructor pointed out that in looking for neat equivalent values for each symbol, John was oversimplifying very complex, suggestive symbols. And, as John's own draft indicated, the symbols seem to suggest different things at different stages in the boys' lives.

REVISING AND EDITING AN ESSAY

The revisions John decided to make are reflected in his second draft.

(second draft)

Symbols in "The Secret Lion"

"The Secret Lion" is a story about change. The first paragraph of the story gives a twelve-year-old's view of growing up: everything changes. When the child watches the magician, he is amazed at the "staying-the-same part" (49); adults focus on the tablecloth. As adults, we lose the ability to see the world through innocent eyes. We have the benefit of experience, confident the trick will work as long as the magician pulls the tablecloth in the proper way. The "staying-the-same part" is less important than the technique. In a story full of prominent symbols, the magician's trick does not seem very important, but all the key symbols, like the sleight of hand, are about change. In fact, each of the story's key symbols highlights the theme of the inevitability of change that permeates the lives of the narrator and his friend Sergio.

The golf course is one such symbol. When the boys first see it, it is "heaven" (52). Lush and green and carefully cared for, it is completely different from the dry brown Arizona countryside and the polluted arroyo. In fact, to the boys it is another world, as mysterious as Oz--and just as unreal. Almost at once, the Emerald City becomes black and white again, the "Coke-holders" disappear, and the boys stop "acting 'rich'" (52). Heaven becomes a golf course, and the boys are changed forever.

The arroyo, a dry gulch that can fill up with water, is another symbol that reinforces the theme of the inevitability of change. It is a special place for the boys--a place to rebel, to shout forbidden words, to swim in waters polluted by a sewage treatment plant. Although it represents a retreat from the disillusionment of the golf course, clearly second choice, it is the boys' "personal Mississippi" (50), full of possibilities. Eventually, though, the arroyo too disappoints the boys, and they stop going there. "Nature seemed to keep pushing us around one way or another, teaching us the same thing every place we ended up" (51). The lesson they keep learning is that nothing is permanent.

The grinding ball, round and perfect, seems to suggest permanence and stability. But when the boys find it, they realize at once that they cannot keep it forever, just as they cannot remain children forever. Like a child's life, it is perfect--but temporary. Burying it is their futile attempt to make time stand still, to preserve perfection in an imperfect world, innocence in an adult world, and they have already learned Nature's lesson well enough to know that this is not possible. They do not look very hard for the ball, but even if they'd been able to find it, the perfection and the innocence it represents would still be unattainable.

The secret lion, the most complex symbol, suggests the most profound kind of change: moving from innocence to experience, from childhood to adulthood. When the narrator is twelve, he says, "something happened that we didn't have a name for, but it was there nonetheless like a lion, and roaring, roaring that way the biggest things do. Everything changed" (49). School is different, girls are different, language is different. Innocence was lost. The lion is associated with a great "roaring" disturbance, a change that unsettles everything for a brief time and then passes, leaving everything changed in irrevocable, indescribable ways. The secret lion is the thing that changes little boys into men. It is a lion because it "roars" through the boys like a storm; everything changes.

In an attempt to make things stay the same, to make time stand still, the boys bury the grinding ball "because it was perfect. [. . .] It was the lion" (53). The grinding ball is "like that place, that whole arroyo" (51): secret and perfect. In other words, the ball and the arroyo and the lion are all tightly connected. By the time the boys bury the ball, they have already learned one sad lesson and are already on their way to adulthood. Heaven is just a golf course; the round, perfect object is only "a cannonball thing used in mining" (50); the arroyo is no Mississippi but only a polluted stream; and childhood does not last forever. "Things get taken away" (53), and this knowledge that things do not last is the secret lion.

Second Draft: Commentary

John felt satisfied with his second draft. His revised thesis statement was clearer and simpler than the one in his first draft; it was also convincingly supported, with clearly worded topic sentences that introduced support paragraphs and connected them to the thesis statement. The second draft was also a good deal less wordy and more focused than the first, notably in the paragraphs about the arroyo and the grinding ball, and the introduction and conclusion were more fully developed. Moreover, he had given up his search for the one true "meaning" of each symbol, focusing instead on the many possibilities of each.

Now, John felt ready to turn his attention to smaller items, such as style, grammar, mechanics, punctuation, and format. For instance, he planned to eliminate contractions, to check all verb tenses carefully, to work quotations into his text more smoothly, to make his thesis statement more precise and his title more interesting, and to revise the language of his introduction and conclusion further. As he made his revisions, he planned to scrutinize this draft carefully, aiming to make his final paper even more concise.

Frei 1

John Frei

Professor Nyysola

English 102

14 April 2000

"The Secret Lion": Everything Changes

Opening paragraph identifies work and author. Parenthetical documentation identifies source of quotation.

The first paragraph of Alberto Alvaro Ríos's "The Secret Lion" presents a twelve-year-old's view of growing up: everything changes. When the magician pulls a tablecloth out from under a pile of dishes, the child is amazed at the "staying-the-same part" (49); adults focus on the tablecloth. As adults, we have the benefit of experience; we know the trick will work as long as the technique is correct. We gain confidence, but we lose our innocence, and we lose our sense of wonder. The price we pay for knowledge is a

Thesis statement

permanent sense of loss, and this tradeoff is central to "The Secret Lion," a story whose key symbols reinforce its central theme: that change is inevitable and that change is always accompanied by loss.

Topic sentence identifies one key symbol.

The golf course is one symbol that helps to convey this theme. When the boys first see the golf course, it is "heaven" (52). Lush and green and carefully tended, it is the antithesis of the dry, brown Arizona landscape and the polluted arroyo. In fact, to the boys it is another world, as exotic as Oz and ultimately as unreal. Before long, the Emerald City becomes black and white again. They learn that there is no such thing as a "Coke-holder," that their "acting 'rich'" is just an act, and that their heaven is only a golf course (52). As the narrator acknowledges,

Frei 2

"Something got taken away from us that moment. Heaven"
(53).

The arroyo, a dry gulch that can fill up with
water, is another symbol that reflects the idea of the
inevitability of change and of the loss that accompanies change. It is a special, Edenlike place for the
boys--a place where they can rebel by shouting forbidden words and by swimming in forbidden waters. Although it is a retreat from the disillusionment of the
golf course, it is still their "personal Mississippi"
(50), full of possibilities. Eventually, though, the
arroyo too disappoints the boys, and they stop going
there. As the narrator says, "Nature seemed to keep
pushing us around one way or another, teaching us the
same thing every place we ended up" (51). The lesson
they keep learning is that nothing is permanent.

The grinding ball, round and perfect, suggests
permanence and stability. But when the boys find it,
they realize at once that they cannot keep it forever,
just as they cannot remain balanced forever between
childhood and adulthood. Like a child's life, the
ball is perfect--but temporary. Burying it is their
desperate attempt to stop time, to preserve perfection in an imperfect world, innocence in an adult
world. But the boys are already twelve years old, and
they have learned nature's lesson well enough to
know that this action will not work. Even if they
had been able to find the ball, the perfection and
the innocence it suggests to them would still be unattainable. Perhaps that is why they do not try very
hard to find it.

Topic
sentence
identifies
another key
symbol.

Topic
sentence
identifies
another key
symbol.

Topic sentence identifies final (and most important) symbol.

Like the story's other symbols, the secret lion itself suggests the most profound kind of change: the movement from innocence to experience, from childhood to adulthood, from expectation to disappointment to resignation. The narrator explains that when he was twelve, "something happened that we didn't have a name for, but it was there nonetheless like a lion, and roaring, roaring that way the biggest things do. Everything changed" (49). School was different, girls were different, language was different. Despite its loud roar, the lion remained paradoxically "secret," unnoticed until it passed. Like adolescence, the secret lion is a roaring disturbance that unsettles everything for a brief time and then passes, leaving everything changed.

Conclusion

In an attempt to make things stay the same, to make time stand still, the boys bury the grinding ball "because it was perfect. [. . .] It was the lion" (53). The grinding ball is "like that place, that whole arroyo" (51): secret and perfect. The ball and the arroyo and the lion are all perfect, but all, ironically, are temporary. The first paragraph of "The Secret Lion" tells us "Everything changed" (49); by the last paragraph we learn what this change means: "Things get taken away" (53). In other words, change implies loss. Heaven turns out to be just a golf course; the round, perfect object only "a cannonball thing used in mining" (50); the arroyo just a polluted stream; and childhood just a phase. "Things get taken away," and this knowledge that things do not last is the lion, secret yet roaring.

Final Draft: Commentary

As he revised and edited his second draft, John made many changes in word choice and sentence structure. He also changed his title, edited to eliminate errors in mechanics and punctuation, and ran a spell check. In this final draft he made his thesis statement even more precise than it was in the previous draft, to communicate the idea of the relationship between change and loss that is central to the essay. In addition, he worked all quoted material smoothly into his discussion, taking care to use quotations only when the author's words added something vital to the paper. (Because students in John's class were permitted to write papers only about works in this anthology, his instructor did not require a Works Cited page.) Finally, John checked all his references to page numbers in the story, so readers would be able to return to his source if necessary to check the accuracy and appropriateness of his quotations.

CHAPTER 4

Plot

◇ ◇ ◇

It's a truism that there are only two basic plots in fiction: one, somebody takes a trip; two, a stranger comes to town.

LEE SMITH, *New York Times Book Review*

The beginning of an action always presents us with a situation in which there is some element of instability, some conflict; in the middle of an action there is a period of readjustment of forces in the process of seeking a new kind of stability; in the end of an action, some point of stability is reached, the forces that have been brought into play have been resolved.

CLEANTH BROOKS AND ROBERT PENN WARREN, *Understanding Fiction*

The simplest way to tell a story, equally favoured by tribal bards and parents at bedtime, is to begin at the beginning, and go on until you reach the end, or your audience falls asleep. But even in antiquity, storytellers perceived the interesting effects that could be obtained by deviating from chronological order. [. . .] A shift of narrative focus back in time may change our interpretation of something which happened much later in the chronology of the story, but which we have already experienced as readers of the text. This is a familiar device of cinema, the flashback.

DAVID LODGE, *The Art of Fiction*

So much for endings. Beginnings are always more fun. True connoisseurs, however, are known to favor the stretch in between, since it's the hardest to do anything with.

That's about all that can be said for plots, which anyway are just one thing after another, a what and a what and a what.

Now try How and Why.

MARGARET ATWOOD, "Happy Endings"

I like stories that end rather than merely stop, stories that somehow assure me that their stopping point is the best moment for all progress to cease.

RICHARD FORD (quoted in *New York Times Book Review*)

◇ ◇ ◇

Alfred Hitchcock's 1951 film *Strangers on a Train,* based on a suspense novel by Patricia Highsmith, offers an intriguing premise: two men, strangers, each can murder someone the other wishes dead; because they have no apparent connection to their victims, both can escape suspicion. Many people would describe this ingenious scheme as the film's "plot," but in fact it is simply the gimmick around which the complex plot revolves. Certainly a clever twist can be an important ingredient of a story's plot, but plot is more than "what happens"; it is how what happens is presented. **Plot** is the way in which a story's events are arranged; it is shaped by causal connections—historical, social, and personal—by the interaction between characters, and by the juxtaposition of events. In *Strangers on a Train,* as in many well-developed works of fiction, the plot that unfolds is complex, with one character directing the events and determining their order while the other character is drawn into the action against his will. The same elements that enrich the plot of the film—unexpected events, conflict, suspense, flashbacks, foreshadowing—can also enrich the plot of a work of short fiction.

CONFLICT

◊ ◊ ◊

Readers' interest and involvement are heightened by a story's **conflict,** the struggle between opposing forces that emerges as the action develops. This conflict is a clash between the **protagonist,** a story's principal character, and an **antagonist,** someone or something presented in opposition to the protagonist. Sometimes the antagonist is a villain; more often, he or she simply represents a conflicting point of view or advocates a course of action different from the one the protagonist follows. Sometimes the antagonist is not a character at all but a situation (for instance, war or poverty) or an event (a natural disaster, such as a flood or a storm, for example) that challenges the protagonist. In other stories, the protagonist may struggle against a supernatural force, or the conflict may occur within a character's mind. It may, for example, be a struggle between two moral choices, such as whether to stay at home and care for an aging parent or to leave and make a new life.

STAGES OF PLOT

◊ ◊ ◊

A work's plot explores one or more conflicts, moving from *exposition* through a series of *complications* to a *climax* and, finally, to a *resolution.*

In a story's **exposition** the writer presents the basic information readers need to understand the events that follow. Typically, the exposition sets the story in motion: it establishes the scene, introduces the major characters, and perhaps suggests the major events or conflicts to come. Sometimes a single sentence can present exposition clearly and economically, giving readers information vital to their understanding of the plot that will unfold. For example, the opening sentence of Amy Tan's "Two Kinds" (p. 594)—"My mother believed you could be anything you wanted to be in America"—establishes an important fact about a central character. Similarly, the opening sentence of Shirley Jackson's "The Lottery" (p. 315)—"The morning of June 27th was clear and sunny, with the fresh warmth of a full-summer day; the flowers were blossoming profusely and the grass was richly green"—introduces the picture-perfect setting that is essential to the story's irony. At other times, as in John Updike's "A&P" (p. 113), a more fully developed exposition section establishes the story's setting, introduces the main characters, and suggests possible conflicts. In some experimental stories a distinct exposition component may be absent, as it is in Luisa Valenzuela's "All about Suicide" (p. 5) and Lorrie Moore's "How to Talk to Your Mother (Notes)" (p. 96).

As the plot progresses, the story's conflict unfolds through a series of complications that will eventually lead readers to the story's climax. The action may include several crises. A **crisis** is a peak in the story's action, a moment of considerable tension or importance; the **climax** is the point of greatest tension or importance, the scene that presents a story's decisive action or event.

The final stage of plot, the **resolution,** or **denouement** (French for "untying of the knot"), draws the action to a close and accounts for all remaining loose ends. Sometimes this resolution is achieved with the help of a **deus ex machina** (Latin for "a god from a machine"), an intervention of some force or agent previously extraneous to the story—for example, the appearance of a long-lost relative or a fortuitous inheritance, the discovery of a character's true identity, a last-minute rescue by a character not previously introduced. Usually, however, the resolution is more plausible: all the events lead logically and convincingly (although not necessarily predictably) to the resolution. Sometimes the ending of a story is indefinite—that is, readers are not quite sure what the protagonist will do, or what will happen next. This kind of resolution, although it may leave some readers feeling cheated, has its advantages: it mirrors the complexity of life, where closure rarely occurs, and it can draw readers into the action as they try to understand the significance of the story's ending or to decide how conflicts should have been resolved.

ORDER AND SEQUENCE
◊ ◊ ◊

A writer may present a story's events in strict chronological order, with each event presented in the sequence in which it actually took place. More often, however, especially in relatively modern fiction, writers do not present events chronologically. Instead, they present incidents out of expected order, or in no apparent order. For example, a writer may choose to begin **in medias res** (Latin for "in the midst of things"), starting with a key event and later going back in time to explain events that preceded it, as Tillie Olsen does in "I Stand Here Ironing" (p. 160). Or, a writer can decide to begin a work of fiction at the end and then move back to reconstruct events that led up to the final outcome, as William Faulkner does in "A Rose for Emily" (p. 87). Many sequences are possible as the writer manipulates events to create interest, suspense, confusion, wonder, or some other effect.

Writers who wish to depart from strict chronological order use *flashbacks* and *foreshadowing*. A **flashback** moves out of sequence to examine an event or situation that occurred before the time in which the story's action takes place. A character can remember an earlier event, or a story's narrator can re-create an earlier situation. For example, in Alberto Alvaro Ríos's "The Secret Lion" (p. 49), the adult narrator looks back at events that occurred when he was twelve years old—and then moves further back in time to consider related events that occurred when he was five. In Edgar Allan Poe's "The Cask of Amontillado" (p. 219), the entire story is told as a flashback. Flashbacks are valuable because they can substitute for or supplement formal exposition by presenting background vital to the readers' understanding of a story's events. One disadvantage of flashbacks is that, because they interrupt the natural flow of events, they may be intrusive or distracting. Such distractions, however, can be an advantage if the writer wishes to reveal events gradually and subtly or to obscure causal links.

Foreshadowing is the introduction early in a story of situations, events, characters, or objects that hint at things to come. A chance remark, a natural occurrence, or a seemingly trivial event is eventually revealed to have great significance. For example, a dark cloud passing across the sky can foreshadow future problems. In this way, foreshadowing allows a writer to hint provocatively at what is to come, so that readers only gradually become aware of a particular detail's role in a story. Thus, foreshadowing helps readers sense what will occur and grow increasingly involved as they see the likelihood (or even the inevitability) of a particular outcome.

In addition to employing conventional techniques like flashbacks and foreshadowing, writers may experiment with sequence by substantially tampering with—or even dispensing with—chronological order. An example is the scrambled chronology of "A Rose for Emily." In such instances the experimental form enhances interest and encourages readers to become involved with the story as they work to untangle or reorder the events and determine their logical and causal connections.

A FINAL NOTE

◊ ◊ ◊

In popular fiction, plot is likely to dominate the story, as it does, for example, in mystery or adventure stories, which tend to lack fully developed characters, complex themes, and elaborately described settings. In richer, more complicated works of fiction, however, plot is often more complex and less obvious.

CHECKLIST: WRITING ABOUT PLOT

✓ What happens in the story?

✓ Where does the story's formal exposition section end? What do readers learn about characters in this section? What do readers learn about setting? What possible conflicts are suggested here?

✓ What is the story's central conflict? What other conflicts are presented? Who is the protagonist? Who (or what) serves as the antagonist?

✓ Identify the story's crisis or crises.

✓ Identify the story's climax.

✓ How is the story's central conflict resolved? Is this resolution plausible? Satisfying?

✓ Which portion of the story constitutes the resolution? Do any problems remain unresolved? Does any uncertainty remain? If so, does this uncertainty strengthen or weaken the story? Would another ending be more effective?

✓ How are the story's events arranged? Are they presented in chronological order? What events are presented out of logical sequence? Does the story use foreshadowing? Flashbacks? Are the causal connections between events clear? Logical? If not, can you explain why?

◆ **KATE CHOPIN** (1851–1904) must, in a sense, be considered a contemporary writer. Her honest, sexually frank stories (many of which had been out of print for more than half a century) were rediscovered in the 1960s and 1970s, influencing a new generation of writers. Though she was a popular contributor of stories and sketches to the magazines of her day, Chopin scandalized many critics with her outspoken novel *The Awakening* (1899), in which a woman seeks sexual and emotional fulfillment with a man who is not her husband. The book was removed from the shelves of the public library in St. Louis, where Chopin was born.

Chopin was born Katherine O'Flaherty, the daughter of a wealthy Irish-born merchant and his aristocratic Creole wife. Educated at convent schools, she was married at nineteen to Oscar Chopin, a Louisiana cotton broker, who took her to live first in New Orleans and later on a plantation at Cloutierville, near Natchitoches, in central Louisiana, where it is said that she offended members of polite society by drinking beer and crossing her legs—at the knees. Chopin's representations of the Cane River region and its people in two volumes of short stories—*Bayou Folk* (1894) and *A Night in Arcadie* (1897)—are the foundation of her reputation as a local colorist. Resemblances have been noted between these stories and certain works of Guy de Maupassant, which Chopin had translated from French to English.

A busy wife and mother, Chopin seems to have begun writing only after she returned to St. Louis following her husband's sudden death in 1883. "The Story of an Hour" depicts a brief event in a woman's life, but in this single hour, Chopin reveals both a lifetime's emotional torment and the momentary joy of freedom.

CULTURAL CONTEXT ◊   Louisiana, where Chopin grew up, has a different legal system from the rest of the country. Louisiana is the only civil-law state in the United States; the legal systems of all other states are based on common law. The civil code of Louisiana is closely connected with the Napoleonic Code, the French civil code enacted in France in 1804. Under the Napoleonic Code, married women had no control over their property and men were the only ones allowed to request a divorce. (These laws were in force until 1980.)

◊ ◊ ◊

KATE CHOPIN

The Story of an Hour
(1894)

Knowing that Mrs. Mallard was afflicted with a heart trouble, great care was taken to break to her as gently as possible the news of her husband's death.

It was her sister Josephine who told her, in broken sentences, veiled hints that revealed in half concealing. Her husband's friend Richards was there, too, near her. It was he who had been in the newspaper office when intelligence of the railroad disaster was received, with Brently Mallard's name leading the list of "killed." He had only taken the time to assure himself of its truth by a second telegram, and had hastened to forestall any less careful, less tender friend in bearing the sad message.

She did not hear the story as many women have heard the same, with a paralyzed inability to accept its significance. She wept at once, with sudden, wild abandonment, in her sister's arms. When the storm of grief had spent itself she went away to her room alone. She would have no one follow her.

There stood, facing the open window, a comfortable, roomy armchair. Into this she sank, pressed down by a physical exhaustion that haunted her body and seemed to reach into her soul.

5   She could see in the open square before her house the tops of trees that were all aquiver with the new spring life. The delicious breath of rain was in the air. In the street below a peddler was crying his wares. The notes of a distant song which some one was singing reached her faintly, and countless sparrows were twittering in the eaves.

There were patches of blue sky showing here and there through the clouds that had met and piled one above the other in the west facing her window.

She sat with her head thrown back upon the cushion of the chair, quite motionless, except when a sob came up into her throat and shook her, as a child who has cried itself to sleep continues to sob in its dreams.

She was young, with a fair, calm face, whose lines bespoke repression and even a certain strength. But now there was a dull stare in her eyes, whose gaze was fixed away off yonder on one of those patches of blue sky. It was not a glance of reflection, but rather indicated a suspension of intelligent thought.

There was something coming to her and she was waiting for it, fearfully. What was it? She did not know; it was too subtle and elusive to name. But she felt it, creeping out of the sky, reaching toward her through the sounds, the scents, the color that filled the air.

10   Now her bosom rose and fell tumultuously. She was beginning to recognize this thing that was approaching to possess her, and she was striving to beat it back with her will—as powerless as her two white slender hands would have been.

When she abandoned herself a little whispered word escaped her slightly parted lips. She said it over and over under her breath: "Free, free, free!" The vacant stare and the look of terror that had followed it went from her eyes. They stayed keen and bright. Her pulses beat fast, and the coursing blood warmed and relaxed every inch of her body.

She did not stop to ask if it were not a monstrous joy that held her. A clear and exalted perception enabled her to dismiss the suggestion as trivial.

She knew that she would weep again when she saw the kind, tender hands folded in death; the face that had never looked save with love upon her, fixed and gray and dead. But she saw beyond that bitter moment a long procession of years to come that would belong to her absolutely. And she opened and spread her arms out to them in welcome.

There would be no one to live for during those coming years; she would live for herself. There would be no powerful will bending her in that blind persistence with which men and women believe they have a right to impose a private will upon a fellow creature. A kind intention or a cruel intention made the act seem no less a crime as she looked upon it in that brief moment of illumination.

15   And yet she had loved him—sometimes. Often she had not. What did it matter! What could love, the unsolved mystery, count for in face of this possession of self-assertion which she suddenly recognized as the strongest impulse of her being.

"Free! Body and soul free!" she kept whispering.

Josephine was kneeling before the closed door with her lips to the key-hole, imploring for admission. "Louise, open the door! I beg; open the door—you will make yourself ill. What are you doing, Louise? For heaven's sake open the door."

"Go away. I am not making myself ill." No; she was drinking in a very elixir of life through that open window.

Her fancy was running riot along those days ahead of her. Spring days, and summer days, and all sorts of days that would be her own. She breathed a quick prayer that life might be long. It was only yesterday she had thought with a shudder that life might be long.

20   She arose at length and opened the door to her sister's importunities. There as a feverish triumph in her eyes, and she carried herself unwittingly like a goddess of Victory. She clasped her sister's waist, and together they descended the stairs. Richards stood waiting for them at the bottom.

Some one was opening the front door with a latchkey. It was Brently Mallard who entered, a little travel-stained, composedly carrying his gripsack and umbrella. He had been far from the scene of the accident, and did not even know there had been one. He stood amazed at Josephine's piercing cry; at Richards' quick motion to screen him from the view of his wife.

But Richards was too late.

When the doctors came they said she had died of heart disease—of joy that kills.

READING AND REACTING

1. The story's basic exposition is presented in its first two paragraphs. What additional information about character or setting would you like to know? Why do you suppose the writer does not supply this information?

2. "The Story of an Hour" is a very economical story, with little action or dialogue. Is this a strength or a weakness? Explain.

3. When "The Story of an Hour" was first published in *Vogue* magazine in 1894, the magazine's editors titled it "The Dream of an Hour." A film version, echoing the last words of the story, is called *The Joy That Kills*. Which of the three titles do you believe most accurately represents what happens in the story?

4. Did Brently Mallard abuse his wife? Did he love her? Did she love him? Exactly why was she so relieved to be rid of him? Can you answer any of these questions with certainty?

5. What is the nature of the conflict in this story? Who, or what, do you see as Mrs. Mallard's antagonist?

6. What emotions does Mrs. Mallard experience during the hour she spends alone in her room? What events do you imagine take place during this same period outside her room? Outside her house?

7. Do you find the story's ending satisfying? Believable? Contrived?

8. Was the story's ending unexpected, or were you prepared for it? What elements foreshadowed this ending?

9. **JOURNAL ENTRY** Rewrite the story's ending, substituting a few paragraphs of your own for the last three paragraphs of the story.

10. **CRITICAL PERSPECTIVE** Writing in the *Southern Literary Journal,* Cynthia Griffin Wolff observes that before the 1960s, many critics had a "tendency to dismiss Chopin's fiction as little more than local color," viewing her as essentially a regional writer. Accordingly, they saw her major contribution to literature as the accurate depiction of setting, customs, and manners in the Louisiana bayou. Other critics, according to Wolff, believe Chopin's major contribution is her surprise or "trick" conclusions, endings that are not what readers expect.

Which do you see as more important to "The Story of an Hour," the setting or the ending? Do you believe that the story has something to offer beyond these two elements, or do you agree with those critics who would see Chopin as "only" a local colorist or the creator of clever plot twists?

Related Works: "The Storm" (p. 154), "The Yellow Wall-Paper" (p. 168), "The Disappearance" (p. 419), "Women" (p. 891), *A Doll House* (p. 1196)

◊ **NADINE GORDIMER** (1923–   ), winner of the 1991 Nobel Prize in literature, has been publishing short stories, essays, and novels about South Africa, her native country, since she was fifteen. Gordimer once explained that after growing up as a middle-class child of Jewish immigrants, becoming a politically aware writer in South Africa was like "peeling an onion. You're sloughing off all the conditioning that you've had since you were a child." The prevailing attitude of her extensive work has evolved from cautious optimism to pessimism in accord with the changing nature of Africa in her lifetime. *New York Times* book critic Michiko Kakutani suggests that in the attempt to illustrate that apartheid debases the lives of both blacks and whites, "she has mapped out the social, political and emotional geography of that troubled land with extraordinary passion and precision." Though Gordimer's work was often banned in her own country because of its condemnation of apartheid, she continues to live in Johannesburg.

Gordimer's novels include *The Lying Days* (1953), *A Guest of Honor* (1970), *Burger's Daughter* (1979), *July's People* (1981), and *None to Accompany Me* (1994). Her short stories have been collected in such volumes as *Face to Face* (1949), *Jump and Other Stories* (1991), and *Why Haven't You Written?* (1992).

CULTURAL CONTEXT ◈   Under apartheid (1948–1991), racial categories regulated where citizens of South Africa could live, what kind of work they could do, what kind of education they could receive, who they could marry, and what political rights they had. Apartheid governed relations between South Africa's white minority and nonwhite majority and sanctioned racial segregation and political and economic discrimination against nonwhites; during apartheid, over eleven million people were arrested for violations against racial regulations.

◈ ◈ ◈

NADINE GORDIMER

Once upon a Time
(1991)

Someone has written to ask me to contribute to an anthology of stories for children. I reply that I don't write children's stories; and he writes back that at a recent congress/book fair/seminar a certain novelist said every writer ought to write at least one story for children. I think of sending a postcard saying I don't accept that I 'ought' to write anything.

And then last night I woke up—or rather was wakened without knowing what had roused me.

A voice in the echo-chamber of the subconscious?

A sound.

5   A creaking of the kind made by the weight carried by one foot after another along a wooden floor. I listened. I felt the apertures of my ears distend with concentration. Again: the creaking. I was waiting for it; waiting to hear if it indicated that feet were moving from room to room, coming up the passage—to my door. I have no burglar bars, no gun under the pillow, but I have the same fears as people who do take these precautions, and my windowpanes are thin as rime, could shatter like a wineglass. A woman was murdered (how do they put it) in broad daylight in a house two blocks away, last year, and the fierce dogs who guarded an old widower and his collection of antique clocks were strangled before he was knifed by a casual labourer he had dismissed without pay.

I was staring at the door, making it out in my mind rather than seeing it, in the dark. I lay quite still—a victim already—but the arrhythmia of my heart was fleeing, knocking this way and that against its body-cage. How finely tuned the senses are, just out of rest, sleep! I could never listen intently as that in the distractions of the day; I was reading every faintest sound, identifying and classifying its possible threat.

But I learned that I was to be neither threatened nor spared. There was no human weight pressing on the boards, the creaking was a buckling, an epicentre of stress. I was in it. The house that surrounds me while I sleep is built on undermined ground; far beneath my bed, the floor, the house's foundations, the stopes and passages of gold mines have hollowed the rock, and when some face trembles, detaches and falls, three thousand feet below, the whole house shifts slightly, bringing uneasy strain to the balance and counterbalance of brick, cement, wood and glass that hold it as a structure around me. The misbeats of my heart tailed off like the last muffled flourishes on one of the wooden xylophones made by the Chopi and Tsonga migrant miners who might have been down there, under me in the earth at that moment. The stope where the fall was could have been disused, dripping water from its ruptured veins; or men might now be interred there in the most profound of tombs.

I couldn't find a position in which my mind would let go of my body—release me to sleep again. So I began to tell myself a story; a bedtime story.

In a house, in a suburb, in a city, there were a man and his wife who loved each other very much and were living happily ever after. They had a little boy, and they loved him very much. They had a cat and a dog that the little boy loved very much. They had a car and a caravan trailer for holidays, and a swimming-pool which was fenced so that the little boy and his playmates would not fall in and drown. They had a housemaid who was absolutely trustworthy and an itinerant gardener who was highly recommended by the neighbours. For when they began to live happily ever after they were warned, by that wise old witch, the husband's mother, not to take on anyone off the street. They were inscribed in a medical benefit society, their pet dog was licensed, they were insured against fire, flood damage and theft, and subscribed to the local Neighbourhood Watch, which supplied them with a plaque for their gates lettered YOU HAVE BEEN WARNED over the silhouette of a would-be intruder. He was masked; it could not be said if he was black or white, and therefore proved the property owner was no racist.

10   It was not possible to insure the house, the swimming pool or the car against riot damage. There were riots, but these were outside the city, where people of another colour were quartered. These people were not allowed into the suburb except as reliable housemaids and gardeners, so there was nothing to fear, the husband told the wife. Yet she was afraid that some day such people might come up the street and tear off the plaque YOU HAVE BEEN WARNED and open the gates and stream in . . . Nonsense, my dear, said the husband, there are police and soldiers and tear-gas and guns to keep them away. But to please her—for he loved her very much and buses were being burned, cars stoned, and schoolchildren shot by the police in those quarters out of sight and hearing of the suburb—he had electronically-controlled gates fitted. Anyone who pulled off the sign YOU HAVE BEEN WARNED and tried to open the gates would have to announce his intentions by pressing a button and speaking into a receiver relayed to the house. The little boy was fascinated by the device and used it as a walkie-talkie in cops and robbers play with his small friends.

The riots were suppressed, but there were many burglaries in the suburb and somebody's trusted housemaid was tied up and shut in a cupboard by thieves while she was in charge of her employers' house. The trusted house-maid of the man and wife and little boy was so upset by this misfortune befalling a friend left, as she herself often was, with responsibility for the possessions of the man and his wife and the little boy that she implored her employers to have burglar bars attached to the doors and windows of the house, and an alarm system installed. The wife said, She is right, let us take heed to her advice. So from every window and door in the house where they were living happily ever after they now saw the trees and sky through bars, and when the little boy's pet cat tried to climb in by the fanlight to keep him company in his little bed at night, as it customarily had done, it set off the alarm keening through the house.

The alarm was often answered—it seemed—by other burglar alarms, in other houses, that had been triggered by pet cats or nibbling mice. The alarms called to one another across the gardens in shrills and bleats and wails that everyone soon became accustomed to, so that the din roused the inhabitants of the suburb no more than the croak of frogs and musical grat-ing of cicadas' legs. Under cover of the electronic harpies' discourse intrud-ers sawed the iron bars and broke into homes, taking away hi-fi equipment, television sets, cassette players, cameras and radios, jewellery and clothing, and sometimes were hungry enough to devour everything in the refrigera-tor or paused audaciously to drink the whisky in the cabinets or patio bars. Insurance companies paid no compensation for single malt, a loss made keener by the property owner's knowledge that the thieves wouldn't even have been able to appreciate what it was they were drinking.

Then the time came when many of the people who were not trusted housemaids and gardeners hung about the suburb because they were un-employed. Some importuned for a job: weeding or painting a roof; any-thing, *baas,* madam. But the man and his wife remembered the warning about taking on anyone off the street. Some drank liquor and fouled the street with discarded bottles. Some begged, waiting for the man or his wife to drive the car out of the electronically-operated gates. They sat about with their feet in the gutters, under the jacaranda trees that made a green tunnel of the street—for it was a beautiful suburb, spoilt only by their presence—and sometimes they fell asleep lying right before the gates in the midday sun. The wife could never see anyone go hungry. She sent the trusted housemaid out with bread and tea, but the trusted housemaid said these were loafers and *tsotsis,*[1] who would come and tie her up and shut her in a cupboard. The husband said, She's right. Take heed of her ad-vice. You only encourage them with your bread and tea. They are looking for their chance . . . And he brought the little boy's tricycle from the gar-den into the house every night, because if the house was surely secure, once locked and with the alarm set, someone might still be able to climb over the wall or the electronically-closed gates into the garden.

You are right, said the wife, then the wall should be higher. And the wise old witch, the husband's mother, paid for the extra bricks as her

---

[1] Criminals.

Christmas present to her son and his wife—the little boy got a Space Man outfit and a book of fairy tales.

15   But every week there were more reports of intrusion: in broad daylight and the dead of night, in the early hours of the morning, and even in the lovely summer twilight—a certain family was at dinner while the bedrooms were being ransacked upstairs. The man and his wife, talking of the latest armed robbery in the suburb, were distracted by the sight of the little boy's pet cat effortlessly arriving over the seven-foot wall, descending first with a rapid bracing of extended forepaws down on the sheer vertical surface, and then a graceful launch, landing with swishing tail within the property. The whitewashed wall was marked with the cat's comings and goings; and on the street side of the wall there were larger red-earth smudges that could have been made by the kind of broken running shoes, seen on the feet of unemployed loiterers, that had no innocent destination.

When the man and wife and little boy took the pet dog for its walk round the neighbourhood streets they no longer paused to admire this show of roses or that perfect lawn; these were hidden behind an array of different varieties of security fences, walls and devices. The man, wife, little boy and dog passed a remarkable choice: there was the low-cost option of pieces of broken glass embedded in cement along the top of walls, there were iron grilles ending in lance-points, there were attempts at reconciling the aesthetics of prison architecture with the Spanish Villa style (spikes painted pink) and with the plaster urns of neoclassical façades (twelve-inch pikes finned like zigzags of lightning and painted pure white). Some walls had a small board affixed, giving the name and telephone number of the firm responsible for the installation of the devices. While the little boy and the pet dog raced ahead, the husband and wife found themselves comparing the possible effectiveness of each style against its appearance; and after several weeks when they paused before this barricade or that without needing to speak, both came out with the conclusion that only one was worth considering. It was the ugliest but the most honest in its suggestion of the pure concentration-camp style, no frills, all evident efficacy. Placed the length of walls, it consisted of a continuous coil of stiff and shining metal serrated into jagged blades, so that there would be no way of climbing over it and no way through its tunnel without getting entangled in its fangs. There would be no way out, only a struggle getting bloodier and bloodier, a deeper and sharper hooking and tearing of flesh. The wife shuddered to look at it. You're right, said the husband, anyone would think twice . . . And they took heed of the advice on a small board fixed to the wall: Consult DRAGON'S TEETH The People for Total Security.

Next day a gang of workmen came and stretched the razor-bladed coils all round the walls of the house where the husband and wife and little boy and pet dog and cat were living happily ever after. The sunlight flashed and slashed, off the serrations, the cornice of razor thorns encircled the home, shining. The husband said, Never mind. It will weather. The wife said, You're wrong. They guarantee it's rust-proof. And she waited until the little boy had run off to play before she said, I hope the cat will take heed . . . The husband said, Don't worry, my dear, cats always look before they leap. And it was true that from that day on the cat slept in the little boy's bed and kept to the garden, never risking a try at breaching security.

One evening, the mother read the little boy to sleep with a fairy story from the book the wise old witch had given him at Christmas. Next day he pretended to be the Prince who braves the terrible thicket of thorns to enter the palace and kiss the Sleeping Beauty back to life: he dragged a ladder to the wall, the shining coiled tunnel was just wide enough for his little body to creep in, and with the first fixing of its razor-teeth in his knees and hands and head he screamed and struggled deeper into its tangle. The trusted housemaid and the itinerant gardener, whose 'day' it was, came running, the first to see and to scream with him, and the itinerant gardener tore his hands trying to get at the little boy. Then the man and his wife burst wildly into the garden and for some reason (the cat, probably) the alarm set up wailing against the screams while the bleeding mass of the little boy was hacked out of the security coil with saws, wire-cutters, choppers, and they carried it—the man, the wife, the hysterical trusted housemaid and the weeping gardener—into the house.

READING AND REACTING

1. How is the introduction—paragraphs 1 through 8—related thematically to the fairy tale the narrator tells? What specific plot elements do they share?

2. In what respects is the story that begins with paragraph 9 of "Once upon a Time" similar to a fairy tale? In what respects is it different? Would the story be more or less effective without the narrator's introduction?

3. In paragraph 8, the narrator characterizes the paragraphs that follow as a "bedtime story." How does her tale differ from your idea of a bedtime story?

4. The story's events are presented in strict chronological order. Give some examples of words and phrases that move readers from one time period to another. Why is chronological order so important?

5. Imagine Gordimer's fairy tale dramatized, perhaps as a television documentary. Where would you interrupt the story to provide commercial breaks or station identification? How would you present the introduction? Explain your decisions.

6. Throughout the fairy tale, various objects and events (and even specific warnings) foreshadow the grim ending. Give several examples of such hints, and explain how each anticipates the ending.

7. Which characters are in conflict in the fairy tale? Does the story have a hero? A villain? What larger forces are in conflict? Are the conflicts between these forces resolved at the end? Explain.

8. What tendencies in her society do you think the author of "Once upon a Time" means to criticize? Do you agree that these tendencies are dangerous?

9. **JOURNAL ENTRY** "Once upon a Time" is set in South Africa. Could it have been set in the United States?

10. **CRITICAL PERSPECTIVE** In an interview conducted in the early 1980s, Gordimer spoke about her education and about the town in which she lived:

> When I got to university, it was through mixing with other people who were writing or painting that I got to know black people as equals. In a general and inclusive, nonracial way, I met people who lived in the world of ideas, in the world that interested me passionately.
>
> In the town where I lived, there was no mental food of this kind at all. I'm often amazed to think how they live, those people, and what an oppressed life it must be, because human beings *must* live in the world of ideas. This dimension in the human psyche is very important. It was there, but they didn't know how to express it. Conversation consisted of trivialities. For women, household matters, problems with children. The men would talk about golf or business or horseracing or whatever their practical interests were. Nobody ever talked about, or even around, the big things—life and death.

Focusing on Gordimer's characterization of the conversation in her town as consisting of "trivialities" rather than of "the big things," consider how her description of that town might apply to "Once upon a Time." How, for example, might the family's self-exclusion from what Gordimer calls "the world of ideas" have contributed to the story's tragic outcome?

Related Works: "The Rocking-Horse Winner" (p. 362), "Gretel in Darkness" (p. 724), "Cinderella" (p. 751), "The Chimney Sweeper" (p. 928)

◊ **WILLIAM FAULKNER** (1897–1962), winner of the 1949 Nobel Prize in literature and the 1955 and 1963 Pulitzer prizes for fiction, was an unabashedly "Southern" writer whose work continues to transcend the regional label. His nineteen novels, notably *The Sound and the Fury* (1929), *As I Lay Dying* (1930), *Light in August* (1932), *Absalom, Absalom!* (1936), and *The Reivers* (1962), explore a wide range of human experience—from high comedy to tragedy—as seen in the life of one community, Faulkner's fictional "Yoknapatawpha County" (modeled on the area around Faulkner's own hometown of Oxford, Mississippi). Faulkner's Yoknapatawpha stories—a fascinating blend of complex Latinate prose and primitive Southern dialect—paint an extraordinary portrait of a community bound together by ties of blood, by a shared belief in moral "verities," and by an old grief (the Civil War). Faulkner's grandfather raised "Billy" on Civil War tales and local legends, including many about the "Old Colonel," the writer's great-grandfather, who was a colorful Confederate officer. But Faulkner was no Margaret Mitchell. Like Mitchell's *Gone with the Wind,* his stories elegize the agrarian virtues of the Old South, but they look unflinchingly at that world's tragic flaw: the "peculiar institution" of slavery.

Local legends and gossip frequently served as the spark for Faulkner's stories. As John B. Cullen, writing in *Old Times in Faulkner Country,* notes, "A Rose for Emily," Faulkner's first nationally published short story, was based on the tale of Oxford's aristocratic "Miss Mary" Neilson, who married Captain Jack Hume, the charming Yankee foreman of a street-paving crew, over her family's shocked protests. But Hume didn't meet the fate of "Miss Emily's" lover. He lived on to a ripe old age and lovingly cared for his wife during her final illness. According to Cullen, one of Faulkner's neighbors said he created his story "out of fears and rumors"—the dire predictions of what *might* happen if Mary Neilson married her Yankee.

CULTURAL CONTEXT ❖   The United States Civil War (1861–1865) began less than one year after Abraham Lincoln was elected president. His election, combined with disagreements about slavery and states' rights, resulted in South Carolina's secession from the Union, followed by six other Southern states. The government set up by the seceded states was named the Confederate States of America. The Confederacy's constitution resembled the United States' constitution, but it included provisions for states' rights and slavery.

❖ ❖ ❖

WILLIAM FAULKNER

A Rose for Emily
(1930)

I

When Miss Emily Grierson died, our whole town went to her funeral: the men through a sort of respectful affection for a fallen monument, the women mostly out of curiosity to see the inside of her house, which no one save an old manservant—a combined gardener and cook—had seen in at least ten years.

It was a big, squarish frame house that had once been white, decorated with cupolas and spires and scrolled balconies in the heavily lightsome style of the seventies, set on what had once been our most select street. But garages and cotton gins had encroached and obliterated even the august names of that neighborhood; only Miss Emily's house was left, lifting its stubborn and coquettish decay above the cotton wagons and the gasoline pumps—an eyesore among eyesores. And now Miss Emily had gone to join the representatives of those august names where they lay in the cedar-bemused cemetery among the ranked and anonymous graves of Union and Confederate soldiers who fell at the battle of Jefferson.

Alive, Miss Emily had been a tradition, a duty, and a care; a sort of hereditary obligation upon the town, dating from that day in 1894 when Colonel Sartoris, the mayor—he who fathered the edict that no Negro woman should appear on the streets without an apron—remitted her taxes, the dispensation dating from the death of her father on into perpetuity. Not that Miss Emily would have accepted charity. Colonel Sartoris invented an involved tale to the effect that Miss Emily's father had loaned money to the town, which the town, as a matter of business, preferred this way of repaying. Only a man of Colonel Sartoris' generation and thought could have invented it, and only a woman could have believed it.

When the next generation, with its more modern ideas, became mayors and aldermen, this arrangement created some little dissatisfaction. On the first of the year they mailed her a tax notice. February came, and there was no reply. They wrote her a formal letter, asking her to call at the sheriff's office at her convenience. A week later the mayor wrote her himself, offering to call or to send his car for her, and received in reply a note on paper of an archaic shape, in a thin, flowing calligraphy in faded ink, to the effect that she no longer went out at all. The tax notice was also enclosed, without comment.

5   They called a special meeting of the Board of Aldermen. A deputation waited upon her, knocked at the door through which no visitor had passed since she ceased giving china-painting lessons eight or ten years earlier. They were admitted by the old Negro into a dim hall from which a stairway mounted into still more shadow. It smelled of dust and disuse—a close, dank smell. The Negro led them into the parlor. It was furnished in heavy, leather-covered furniture. When the Negro opened the blinds of one window, they could see that the leather was cracked; and when they sat down, a faint dust rose sluggishly about their thighs, spinning with slow motes in the single sun-ray. On a tarnished gilt easel before the fireplace stood a crayon portrait of Miss Emily's father.

They rose when she entered—a small, fat woman in black, with a thin gold chain descending to her waist and vanishing into her belt, leaning on an ebony cane with a tarnished gold head. Her skeleton was small and spare; perhaps that was why what would have been merely plumpness in another was obesity in her. She looked bloated, like a body long submerged in motionless water, and of that pallid hue. Her eyes, lost in the fatty ridges of her face, looked like two small pieces of coal pressed into a lump of dough as they moved from one face to another while the visitors stated their errand.

She did not ask them to sit. She just stood in the door and listened quietly until the spokesman came to a stumbling halt. Then they could hear the invisible watch ticking at the end of the gold chain.

Her voice was dry and cold. "I have no taxes in Jefferson. Colonel Sartoris explained it to me. Perhaps one of you can gain access to the city records and satisfy yourselves."

"But we have. We are the city authorities, Miss Emily. Didn't you get a notice from the sheriff, signed by him?"

10 "I received a paper, yes," Miss Emily said. "Perhaps he considers himself the sheriff . . . I have no taxes in Jefferson."

"But there is nothing on the books to show that, you see. We must go by the—"

"See Colonel Sartoris. I have no taxes in Jefferson."

"But, Miss Emily—"

"See Colonel Sartoris." (Colonel Sartoris had been dead almost ten years.) "I have no taxes in Jefferson. Tobe!" The Negro appeared. "Show these gentlemen out."

II

15 So she vanquished them, horse and foot, just as she had vanquished their fathers thirty years before about the smell. That was two years after her father's death and a short time after her sweetheart—the one we believed would marry her—had deserted her. After her father's death she went out very little; after her sweetheart went away, people hardly saw her at all. A few of the ladies had the temerity to call, but were not received, and the only sign of life about the place was the Negro man—a young man then— going in and out with a market basket.

"Just as if a man—any man—could keep a kitchen properly," the ladies said; so they were not surprised when the smell developed. It was another link between the gross, teeming world and the high and mighty Griersons.

A neighbor, a woman, complained to the mayor, Judge Stevens, eighty years old.

"But what will you have me do about it, madam?" he said.

"Why, send her word to stop it," the woman said. "Isn't there a law?"

20 "I'm sure that won't be necessary," Judge Stevens said. "It's probably just a snake or a rat that nigger of hers killed in the yard. I'll speak to him about it."

The next day he received two more complaints, one from a man who came in diffident deprecation. "We really must do something about it, Judge. I'd be the last one in the world to bother Miss Emily, but we've got to do something." That night the Board of Aldermen met—three graybeards and one younger man, a member of the rising generation.

"It's simple enough," he said. "Send her word to have her place cleaned up. Give her a certain time to do it in, and if she don't . . ."

"Dammit, sir," Judge Stevens said, "will you accuse a lady to her face of smelling bad?"

So the next night, after midnight, four men crossed Miss Emily's lawn and slunk about the house like burglars, sniffing along the base of the brickwork and at the cellar openings while one of them performed a regular sowing motion with his hand out of a sack slung from his shoulder. They broke open the cellar door and sprinkled lime there, and in all the outbuildings. As they recrossed the lawn, a window that had been dark was lighted and Miss Emily sat in it, the light behind her, and her upright torso motionless as that of an idol. They crept quietly across the lawn and into the shadow of the locusts that lined the street. After a week or two the smell went away.

25   That was when people had begun to feel really sorry for her. People in our town, remembering how old lady Wyatt, her great-aunt, had gone completely crazy at last, believed that the Griersons held themselves a little too high for what they really were. None of the young men were quite good enough for Miss Emily and such. We had long thought of them as a tableau, Miss Emily a slender figure in white in the background, her father a spraddled silhouette in the foreground, his back to her and clutching a horsewhip, the two of them framed by the back-flung front door. So when she got to be thirty and was still single, we were not pleased exactly, but vindicated; even with insanity in the family she wouldn't have turned down all of her chances if they had really materialized.

When her father died, it got about that the house was all that was left to her; and in a way, people were glad. At last they could pity Miss Emily. Being left alone, and a pauper, she had become humanized. Now she too would know the old thrill and the old despair of a penny more or less.

The day after his death all the ladies prepared to call at the house and offer condolence and aid, as is our custom. Miss Emily met them at the door, dressed as usual and with no trace of grief on her face. She told them that her father was not dead. She did that for three days, with the ministers calling on her, and the doctors, trying to persuade her to let them dispose of the body. Just as they were about to resort to law and force, she broke down, and they buried her father quickly.

We did not say she was crazy then. We believed she had to do that. We remembered all the young men her father had driven away, and we knew that with nothing left, she would have to cling to that which had robbed her, as people will.

III

She was sick for a long time. When we saw her again, her hair was cut short, making her look like a girl, with a vague resemblance to those angels in colored church windows—sort of tragic and serene.

30   The town had just let the contracts for paving the sidewalks, and in the summer after her father's death they began the work. The construction company came with niggers and mules and machinery, and a foreman named Homer Barron, a Yankee—a big, dark, ready man, with a big voice and eyes lighter than his face. The little boys would follow in groups to hear him cuss the niggers, and the niggers singing in time to the rise and fall of picks. Pretty soon he knew everybody in town. Whenever you heard a lot of laughing anywhere about the square, Homer Barron would be in

the center of the group. Presently we began to see him and Miss Emily on Sunday afternoons driving in the yellow-wheeled buggy and the matched team of bays from the livery stable.

At first we were glad that Miss Emily would have an interest, because the ladies all said, "Of course a Grierson would not think seriously of a Northerner, a day laborer." But there were still others, older people, who said that even grief could not cause a real lady to forget *noblesse oblige*[1]— without calling it *noblesse oblige*. They just said, "Poor Emily. Her kinsfolk should come to her." She had some kin in Alabama; but years ago her father had fallen out with them over the estate of old lady Wyatt, the crazy woman, and there was no communication between the two families. They had not even been represented at the funeral.

And as soon as the old people said, "Poor Emily," the whispering began. "Do you suppose it's really so?" they said to one another. "Of course it is. What else could . . ." This behind their hands; rustling of craned silk and satin behind jalousies closed upon the sun of Sunday afternoon as the thin, swift clop-clop-clop of the matched team passed: "Poor Emily."

She carried her head high enough—even when we believed that she was fallen. It was as if she demanded more than ever the recognition of her dignity as the last Grierson; as if it had wanted that touch of earthiness to reaffirm her imperviousness. Like when she bought the rat poison, the arsenic. That was over a year after they had begun to say "Poor Emily," and while the two female cousins were visiting her.

"I want some poison," she said to the druggist. She was over thirty then, still a slight woman, though thinner than usual, with cold, haughty black eyes in a face the flesh of which was strained across the temples and about the eye-sockets as you imagine a lighthouse-keeper's face ought to look. "I want some poison," she said.

35   "Yes, Miss Emily. What kind? For rats and such? I'd recom—"

"I want the best you have. I don't care what kind."

The druggist named several. "They'll kill anything up to an elephant. But what you want is—"

"Arsenic," Miss Emily said. "Is that a good one?"

"Is . . . arsenic? Yes, ma'am. But what you want—"

40   "I want arsenic."

The druggist looked down at her. She looked back at him, erect, her face like a strained flag. "Why, of course," the druggist said. "If that's what you want. But the law requires you to tell what you are going to use it for."

Miss Emily just stared at him, her head tilted back in order to look him eye for eye, until he looked away and went and got the arsenic and wrapped it up. The Negro delivery boy brought her the package; the druggist didn't come back. When she opened the package at home there was written on the box, under the skull and bones: "For rats."

---

[1] The obligation of those of high birth or rank to behave in an honorable fashion.

IV

So the next day we all said, "She will kill herself"; and we said it would be the best thing. When she had first begun to be seen with Homer Barron, we had said, "She will marry him." Then we said, "She will persuade him yet," because Homer himself had remarked—he liked men, and it was known that he drank with the younger men in the Elks' Club—that he was not a marrying man. Later we said, "Poor Emily" behind the jalousies as they passed on Sunday afternoon in the glittering buggy, Miss Emily with her head high and Homer Barron with his hat cocked and a cigar in his teeth, reins and whip in a yellow glove.

Then some of the ladies began to say that it was a disgrace to the town and a bad example to the young people. The men did not want to interfere, but at last the ladies forced the Baptist minister—Miss Emily's people were Episcopal—to call upon her. He would never divulge what happened during that interview, but he refused to go back again. The next Sunday they again drove about the streets, and the following day the minister's wife wrote to Miss Emily's relations in Alabama.

45   So she had blood-kin under her roof again and we sat back to watch developments. At first nothing happened. Then we were sure that they were to be married. We learned that Miss Emily had been to the jeweler's and ordered a man's toilet set in silver, with the letters H. B. on each piece. Two days later we learned that she had bought a complete outfit of men's clothing, including a nightshirt, and we said, "They are married." We were really glad. We were glad because the two female cousins were even more Grierson than Miss Emily had ever been.

So we were not surprised when Homer Barron—the streets had been finished some time since—was gone. We were a little disappointed that there was not a public blowing-off, but we believed that he had gone on to prepare for Miss Emily's coming, or to give her a chance to get rid of the cousins. (By that time it was a cabal, and we were all Miss Emily's allies to help circumvent the cousins.) Sure enough, after another week they departed. And, as we had expected all along, within three days Homer Barron was back in town. A neighbor saw the Negro man admit him at the kitchen door at dusk one evening.

And that was the last we saw of Homer Barron. And of Miss Emily for some time. The Negro man went in and out with the market basket, but the front door remained closed. Now and then we would see her at a window for a moment, as the men did that night when they sprinkled the lime, but for almost six months she did not appear on the streets. Then we knew that this was to be expected too; as if that quality of her father which had thwarted her woman's life so many times had been too virulent and too furious to die.

When we next saw Miss Emily, she had grown fat and her hair was turning gray. During the next few years it grew grayer and grayer until it attained an even pepper-and-salt iron-gray, when it ceased turning. Up to the day of her death at seventy-four it was still that vigorous iron-gray, like the hair of an active man.

From that time on her front door remained closed, save for a period of six or seven years, when she was about forty, during which she gave lessons in china-painting. She fitted up a studio in one of the downstairs rooms, where the daughters and granddaughters of Colonel Sartoris' contemporaries were sent to her with the same regularity and in the same spirit that they were sent to church on Sundays with a twenty-five-cent piece for the collection plate. Meanwhile her taxes had been remitted.

50   Then the newer generation became the backbone and the spirit of the town, and the painting pupils grew up and fell away and did not send their children to her with boxes of color and tedious brushes and pictures cut from the ladies' magazines. The front door closed upon the last one and remained closed for good. When the town got free postal delivery, Miss Emily alone refused to let them fasten the metal numbers above her door and attach a mailbox to it. She would not listen to them.

Daily, monthly, yearly we watched the Negro grow grayer and more stooped, going in and out with the market basket. Each December we sent her a tax notice, which would be returned by the post office a week later, unclaimed. Now and then we would see her in one of the downstairs windows—she had evidently shut up the top floor of the house—like the carven torso of an idol in a niche, looking or not looking at us, we could never tell which. Thus she passed from generation to generation—dear, inescapable, impervious, tranquil, and perverse.

And so she died. Fell ill in the house filled with dust and shadows, with only a doddering Negro man to wait on her. We did not even know she was sick; we had long since given up trying to get any information from the Negro. He talked to no one, probably not even to her, for his voice had grown harsh and rusty, as if from disuse.

She died in one of the downstairs rooms, in a heavy walnut bed with a curtain, her gray head propped on a pillow yellow and moldy with age and lack of sunlight.

V

The Negro met the first of the ladies at the front door and let them in, with their hushed, sibilant voices and their quick, curious glances, and then he disappeared. He walked right through the house and out the back and was not seen again.

55   The two female cousins came at once. They held the funeral on the second day, with the town coming to look at Miss Emily beneath a mass of bought flowers, with the crayon face of her father musing profoundly above the bier and the ladies sibilant and macabre; and the very old men—some in their brushed Confederate uniforms—on the porch and the lawn, talking of Miss Emily as if she had been a contemporary of theirs, believing that they had danced with her and courted her perhaps, confusing time with its mathematical progression, as the old do, to whom all the past is not a diminishing road but, instead, a huge meadow which no winter ever quite touches, divided from them now by the narrow bottle-neck of the most recent decade of years.

Already we knew that there was one room in that region above stairs which no one had seen in forty years, and which would have to be forced. They waited until Miss Emily was decently in the ground before they opened it.

The violence of breaking down the door seemed to fill this room with pervading dust. A thin, acrid pall as of the tomb seemed to lie everywhere upon this room decked and furnished as for a bridal: upon the valance curtains of faded rose color, upon the rose-shaded lights, upon the dressing table, upon the delicate array of crystal and the man's toilet things backed with tarnished silver, silver so tarnished that the monogram was obscured. Among them lay collar and tie, as if they had just been removed, which, lifted, left upon the surface a pale crescent in the dust. Upon a chair hung the suit, carefully folded; beneath it the two mute shoes and the discarded socks.

The man himself lay in the bed.

For a long while we just stood there, looking down at the profound and fleshless grin. The body had apparently once lain in the attitude of an embrace, but now the long sleep that outlasts love, that conquers even the grimace of love, had cuckolded him. What was left of him, rotted beneath what was left of the nightshirt, had become inextricable from the bed in which he lay; and upon him and upon the pillow beside him lay that even coating of the patient and biding dust.

60   Then we noticed that in the second pillow was the indentation of a head. One of us lifted something from it, and leaning forward, that faint and invisible dust dry and acrid in the nostrils, we saw a long strand of iron-gray hair.

READING AND REACTING

1. Arrange these events in the sequence in which they actually occur: Homer's arrival in town, the aldermen's visit, Emily's purchase of poison, Colonel Sartoris's decision to remit Emily's taxes, the development of the odor around Emily's house, Emily's father's death, the arrival of Emily's relatives, Homer's disappearance. Then, list the events in the sequence in which they are presented in the story. Why do you suppose Faulkner presents these events out of their actual chronological order?

2. Despite the story's confusing sequence, many events are foreshadowed. Give some examples of this technique. How does foreshadowing enrich the story?

3. Where does the exposition end and the movement toward the story's climax begin? Where does the resolution stage begin?

4. Emily is clearly the story's protagonist. In the sense that he opposes her wishes, Homer is the antagonist. What other characters—or what larger forces—are in conflict with Emily?

5. Explain how each of these phrases moves the story's plot along: "So she vanquished them, horse and foot . . ." (15); "After a week or two the smell went away" (24); "And that was the last we saw of Homer Barron" (47); "And so she died" (52); "The man himself lay in the bed" (58).

6. The narrator of the story is an observer, not a participant. Who might this narrator be? How do you suppose the narrator might know so much about Emily? Why do you think the narrator uses *we* instead of *I?*

7. The original version of "A Rose for Emily" included a two-page deathbed scene in which Emily tells a servant that Homer's body lies upstairs. Why do you think Faulkner deleted this scene? Do you think he made the right decision?

8. Some critics have suggested that Miss Emily Grierson is a kind of symbol of the Old South, the last defender of its outdated ideas of chivalry, formal manners, and tradition. Do you think this interpretation is justified? Would you characterize Miss Emily as a champion or a victim of the values her town tries to preserve?

9. **JOURNAL ENTRY** When asked at a seminar at the University of Virginia about the meaning of the title "A Rose for Emily," Faulkner replied, "Oh, it's simply the poor woman had no life at all. Her father had kept her more or less locked up and then she had a lover who was about to quit her, she had to murder him. It was just 'A Rose for Emily'—that's all." In another interview, asked the same question, he replied, "I pitied her and this was a salute, just as if you were to make a gesture, a salute, to anyone; to a woman you would hand a rose, as you would lift a cup of *sake* to a man." What do you make of Faulkner's responses? Can you offer other possible interpretations of the title's significance?

10. **CRITICAL PERSPECTIVE** In his essay "William Faulkner: An American Dickens," literary critic Leslie A. Fiedler characterizes Faulkner as "primarily [. . .] a sentimental writer; not a writer with the occasional vice of sentimentality, but one whose basic mode of experience is sentimental." He continues, "In a writer whose very method is self-indulgence, that sentimentality becomes sometimes downright embarrassing." Fiedler also notes Faulkner's "excesses of maudlin feelings and absurd indulgences in overripe rhetoric."

    Do you think these criticisms apply to "A Rose for Emily"? If so, does the "vice of sentimentality" diminish the story, or do you agree with Fiedler—who calls Faulkner a "supereminently good 'bad' writer"—that the author is able to surmount these excesses?

Related Works: "Miss Brill" (p. 119), "The Possibility of Evil" (p. 463), "The German Refugee" (p. 511), "Porphyria's Lover" (p. 745), *Trifles* (p. 1163)

◊ **LORRIE MOORE** (1957–   )   gives this advice in her story "How to Become a Writer": "First, try to become something, anything, else. A movie star/astronaut. A movie star/missionary. A movie star/kindergarten teacher. President of the World. Fail miserably." Born in Glens Falls, New York, Moore was educated at St. Lawrence University and at Cornell University. Her first book was *Self-Help* (1985), a collection of short stories—including "How to Talk to Your Mother (Notes)," which rated an enthusiastic front-page review in the *New York Times Book Review.* More recent works include *Anagrams* (1986), *The Forgotten Helper* (1987), *Like Life* (1990), and *Who Will Run the Frog Hospital?* (1994). Moore divides her time between New York City and her teaching position at the University of Wisconsin, Madison.

Of the origins of her writing career, Moore is typically humorous. In a 1985 interview printed in the magazine *Vanity Fair* she explains, "I signed up for a course called 'The Romance and Reality of Words' in high school and got put in the creative writing class by mistake." Her voice is what *New York Times* reviewer Michiko Kakutani describes as the "wry, crackly" and vulnerable voice of the women in her stories: women who fend off anxiety with irreverent, self-bolstering humor. The stories of *Self-Help* are, according to Moore's comments in *Contemporary Authors,* "second person, mock-imperative narratives [. . .] what happens when one appropriates the 'how-to' form for a fiction, for an irony, for a 'how-not-to.' "

CULTURAL CONTEXT ◊   The modern "women's movement" in the United States began in the 1960s, when women leaders pushed for equal rights in employment, greater educational opportunity, and more influence in national politics. It was a time in which the generation gap widened between mothers and daughters, as young women searched for a new collective identity with greater freedoms than those afforded their mothers.

◊ ◊ ◊

LORRIE MOORE

How to Talk to Your Mother (Notes)
(1985)

1982 Without her, for years now, murmur at the defrosting refrigerator, "What?" "Huh?" "Shush now," as it creaks, aches, groans, until the final ice block drops from the ceiling of the freezer like something vanquished.

Dream, and in your dreams babies with the personalities of dachshunds, fat as Macy balloons, float by the treetops.

The first permanent polyurethane heart is surgically implanted.[1]

Someone upstairs is playing "You'll Never Walk Alone" on the recorder. Now it's "Oklahoma!" They must have a Rodgers and Hammerstein book.[2]

5 *1981* On public transportation, mothers with soft, soapy, corduroyed seraphs glance at you, their faces dominoes of compassion. Their seraphs are small and quiet or else restlessly counting bus-seat colors: "Blue-blue-blue, red-red-red, lullow-lullow-lullow." The mothers see you eyeing their children. They smile sympathetically. They believe you envy them. They believe you are childless. They believe they know why. Look quickly away, out the smudge of the window.

1980 The hum, rush, clack of things in the kitchen. These are some of the sounds that organize your life. The clink of the silverware inside the drawer, piled like bones in a mass grave. Your similes grow grim, grow tired.

Reagan is elected President, though you distributed donuts and brochures for Carter.

Date an Italian. He rubs your stomach and says, "These are marks of stretch, no? Marks of stretch?" and in your dizzy mind you think: Marks of Harpo, Ideas of Marx, Ides of March, Beware.[3] He plants kisses on the sloping ramp of your neck, and you fall asleep against him, your underpants peeled and rolled around one thigh like a bride's garter.

1979 Once in a while take evening trips past the old unsold house you grew up in, that haunted rural crossroads two hours from where you now live. It is like Halloween: the raked, moonlit lawn, the mammoth, tumid trees, arms and fingers raised into the starless wipe of sky like burns, cracks, map rivers. Their black shadows rock against the side of the east porch. There are dream shadows, other lives here. Turn the corner slowly but continue to stare from the car window. This house is embedded in you deep, something still here you know, you think you know, a voice at the top of those stairs, perhaps, a figure on the porch, an odd apron caught high in the twigs, in the too-warm-for-a-fall-night breeze, something not right, that turret window you can still see from here, from outside, but which can't be reached from within. (The ghostly brag of your childhood:

---

[1] The Jarvik-7, created by Robert K. Jarvik, was implanted in Barney Clark by Dr. William C. DeVries on December 2, 1982.

[2] The American songwriting team of composer Richard Rodgers (1902–1979) and lyricist Oscar Hammerstein II (1895–1960) created many modern classics, including "You'll Never Walk Alone" (from *Carousel*) and "Oklahoma!" (from the musical of the same name).

[3] The narrator's "free association," prompted by "marks of stretch" (stretch marks) alludes to comedian Arthur 'Harpo' Marx (1893–1964), philosopher Karl Marx (1818–1883), and the warning the soothsayer issues ("Beware the Ides of March") in Shakespeare's *Julius Caesar*.

"We have a mystery room. The window shows from the front, but you can't go in, there's no door. A doctor lived there years ago and gave secret operations, and now it's blocked off.") The window sits like a dead eye in the turret.

10   You see a ghost, something like a spinning statue by a shrub.

1978 Bury her in the cold south sideyard of that Halloweenish house. Your brother and his kids are there. Hug. The minister in a tweed sports-coat, the neighborless fields, the crossroads, are all like some stark Kansas. There is praying, then someone shoveling. People walk toward the cars and hug again. Get inside your car with your niece. Wait. Look up through the windshield. In the November sky a wedge of wrens moves south, the lines of their formation, the very sides and vertices mysteriously choreographed, shifting, flowing, crossing like a skater's legs. "They'll descend instinc-tively upon a tree somewhere," you say, "but not for miles yet." You mar-vel, watch, until, amoeba-slow, they are dark, faraway stitches in the horizon. You do not start the car. The quiet niece next to you finally speaks: "Aunt Ginnie, are we going to the restaurant with the others?" Look at her. Recognize her: nine in a pile parka. Smile and start the car.

1977 She ages, rocks in your rocker, noiseless as wind. The front strands of her white hair dangle yellow at her eyes from too many cigarettes. She smokes even now, her voice husky with phlegm. Sometimes at dinner in your tiny kitchen she will simply stare, rheumy-eyed, at you, then burst into a fit of coughing that racks her small old man's body like a storm.

        Stop eating your baked potato. Ask if she is all right.

        She will croak: "Do you remember, Ginnie, your father used to say that one day, with these cigarettes, I was going to have to 'face the mucus'?" At this she chuckles, chokes, gasps again.

15   Make her stand up.

        Lean her against you.

        Slap her lightly on the curved mound of her back.

        Ask her for chrissakes to stop smoking.

        She will smile and say: "For chrissakes? Is that any way to talk to your mother?"

20   At night go in and check on her. She lies there awake, her lips apart, open and drying. Bring her some juice. She murmurs, "Thank you, honey." Her mouth smells, swells like a grave.

1976 The Bicentennial. In the laundromat, you wait for the time on your coins to run out. Through the porthole of the dryer, you watch your be-deviled towels and sheets leap and fall. The radio station piped in from the ceiling plays slow, sad Motown; it encircles you with the desperate hope-fulness of a boy at a dance, and it makes you cry. When you get back to your apartment, dump everything on your bed. Your mother is knitting crookedly: red, white, and blue. Kiss her hello. Say: "Sure was warm in that place." She will seem not to hear you.

1975 Attend poetry readings alone at the local library. Find you don't really listen well. Stare at your crossed thighs. Think about your mother. Sometimes you confuse her with the first man you ever loved, who ever loved you, who buried his head in the pills of your sweater and said magnificent things like "Oh god, oh god," who loved you unconditionally, terrifically, like a mother.

The poet loses his nerve for a second, a red flush through his neck and ears, but he regains his composure. When he is finished, people clap. There is wine and cheese.

Leave alone, walk home alone. The downtown streets are corridors of light holding you, holding you, past the church, past the community center. March, like Stella Dallas,[4] spine straight, through the melodrama of street lamps, phone posts, toward the green house past Borealis Avenue, toward the rear apartment with the tilt and the squash on the stove.

25   Your horoscope says: Be kind, be brief.

You are pregnant again. Decide what you must do.

1974 She will have bouts with a mad sort of senility. She calls you at work. "There's no food here! Help me! I'm starving!" although you just bought forty dollars' worth of groceries yesterday. "Mom, there is too food there!"

When you get home the refrigerator is mostly empty. "Mom, where did you put all the milk and cheese and stuff?" Your mother stares at you from where she is sitting in front of the TV set. She has tears leaking out of her eyes. "There's no food here, Ginnie."

There is a rustling, scratching noise in the dishwasher. You open it up, and the eyes of a small rodent glint back at you. It scrambles out, off to the baseboards behind the refrigerator. Your mother, apparently, has put all the groceries inside the dishwasher. The milk is spilled, a white pool against blue, and things like cheese and bologna and apples have been nibbled at.

30 *1973* At a party when a woman tells you where she bought some wonderful pair of shoes, say that you believe shopping for clothes is like masturbation—everyone does it, but it isn't very interesting and therefore should be done alone, in an embarrassed fashion, and never be the topic of party conversation. The woman will tighten her lips and eyebrows and say, "Oh,

---

[4] Originally introduced in Olive Higgins Prouty's novel *Stella Dallas;* also the main character in the radio show of the same name, which the announcer introduced as a "world famous drama of mother love and sacrifice." *Stella Dallas* was filmed three times, in 1926 (with Belle Bennett), 1937 (with Barbara Stanwyck), and 1990 (with Bette Midler).

I suppose you have something more fascinating to talk about." Grow clumsy and uneasy. Say, "No," and head for the ginger ale. Tell the person next to you that your insides feel sort of sinking and vinyl like a Claes Oldenburg toilet.[5] They will say, "Oh?" and point out that the print on your dress is one of paisleys impregnating paisleys. Pour yourself more ginger ale.

1972 Nixon wins by a landslide.

Sometimes your mother calls you by her sister's name. Say, "No, Mom, it's me. Virginia." Learn to repeat things. Learn that you have a way of knowing each other which somehow slips out and beyond the ways you have of not knowing each other at all.

Make apple crisp for the first time.

1971 Go for long walks to get away from her. Walk through wooded areas; there is a life there you have forgotten. The smells and sounds seem sudden, unchanged, exact, the papery crunch of the leaves, the mouldering sachet of the mud. The trees are crooked as backs, the fence posts splintered, trusting and precarious in their solid grasp of arms, the asters spindly, dry, white, havishammed (Havishammed!)[6] by frost. Find a beautiful reddish stone and bring it home for your mother. Kiss her. Say: "This is for you." She grasps it and smiles. "You were always such a sensitive child," she says.

35   Say: "Yeah, I know."

1970 You are pregnant again. Try to decide what you should do.

Get your hair chopped, short as a boy's.

1969 Mankind leaps upon the moon.

Disposable diapers are first sold in supermarkets.

40   Have occasional affairs with absurd, silly men who tell you to grow your hair to your waist and who, when you are sad, tickle your ribs to cheer you up. Moonlight through the blinds stripes you like zebras. You laugh. You never marry.

1968 Do not resent her. Think about the situation, for instance, when you take the last trash bag from its box: you must throw out the box by putting it in that very trash bag. What was once contained, now must contain. The container, then, becomes the contained, the enveloped, the held. Find more and more that you like to muse over things like this.

---

[5] Claes Oldenburg (1929–   )—American artist noted for his oversized soft sculptures of everyday objects, made from such materials as canvas and vinyl.

[6] Miss Havisham, in Charles Dickens's *Great Expectations,* is an elderly recluse who lives surrounded by the decaying remnants of her aborted wedding, called off years earlier by her fiancé.

1967   Your mother is sick and comes to live with you. There is no place else for her to go. You feel many different emptinesses.

The first successful heart transplant is performed in South Africa.[7]

1966   You confuse lovers, mix up who had what scar, what car, what mother.

45   *1965*   Smoke marijuana. Try to figure out what has made your life go wrong. It is like trying to figure out what is stinking up the refrigerator. It could be anything. The lid off the mayonnaise, Uncle Ron's honey wine four years in the left corner. Broccoli yellowing, flowering fast. They are all metaphors. They are all problems. Your horoscope says: Speak gently to a loved one.

1964   Your mother calls long distance and asks whether you are coming home for Thanksgiving, your brother and the baby will be there. Make excuses.

"As a mother gets older," your mother says, "these sorts of holidays become increasingly important."

Say: "I'm sorry, Mom."

1963   Wake up one morning with a man you had thought you'd spend your life with, and realize, a rock in your gut, that you don't even like him. Spend a weepy afternoon in his bathroom, not coming out when he knocks. You can no longer trust your affections. People and places you think you love may be people and places you hate.

50   Kennedy is shot.

Someone invents a temporary artificial heart, for use during operations.

1962   Eat Chinese food for the first time, with a lawyer from California. He will show you how to hold the chopsticks. He will pat your leg. Attack his profession. Ask him whether he feels the law makes large spokes out of the short stakes of men.

1961   Grandma Moses dies.[8]

You are a zoo of insecurities. You take to putting brandy in your morning coffee and to falling in love too easily. You have an abortion.

55   *1960*   There is money from your father's will and his life insurance. You buy a car and a green velvet dress you don't need. You drive two hours to meet your mother for lunch on Saturdays. She suggests things for you to

---

[7] By Dr. Christiaan Barnard (1923–   ).

[8] Grandma Moses (Anna Mary Robertson Moses, 1860–1961)—American artist, famous for her "primitive" paintings depicting rural life. Completely self-taught, she did not begin painting seriously until the age of 67.

write about, things she's heard on the radio: a woman with telepathic twins, a woman with no feet.

1959   At the funeral she says: "He had his problems, but he was a generous man," though you know he was tight as a scout knot, couldn't listen to anyone, the only time you remember loving him being that once when he got the punchline of one of your jokes before your mom did and looked up from his science journal and guffawed loud as a giant, the two of you, for one split moment, communing like angels in the middle of that room, in that warm, shared light of mind.

Say: "He was okay."

"You shouldn't be bitter," your mother snaps. "He financed you and your brother's college educations." She buttons her coat. "He was also the first man to isolate a particular isotope of helium, I forget the name, but he should have won the Nobel Prize." She dabs at her nose.

Say: "Yeah, Mom."

60 *1958*   At your brother's wedding, your father is taken away in an ambulance. A tiny cousin whispers loudly to her mother, "Did Uncle Will have a hard attack?" For seven straight days say things to your mother like: "I'm sure it'll be okay," and "I'll stay here, why don't you go home and get some sleep."

1957   Dance the calypso with boys from a different college. Get looped on New York State burgundy, lose your virginity, and buy one of the first portable electric typewriters.

1956   Tell your mother about all the books you are reading at college. This will please her.

1955   Do a paint-by-numbers of Elvis Presley. Tell your mother you are in love with him. She will shake her head.

1954   Shoplift a cashmere sweater.

65 *1953*   Smoke a cigarette with Hillary Swedelson. Tell each other your crushes. Become blood sisters.

1952   When your mother asks you if there are any nice boys in junior high, ask her how on earth would you ever know, having to come in at nine! every night. Her eyebrows will lift like theater curtains. "You poor, abused thing," she will say.

Say, "Don't I know it," and slam the door.

1951   Your mother tells you about menstruation. The following day you promptly menstruate, your body only waiting for permission, for a signal. You wake up in the morning and feel embarrassed.

1949   You learn how to blow gum bubbles and to add negative numbers.

70 *1947*   The Dead Sea Scrolls are discovered.[9]

You have seen too many Hollywood musicals. You have seen too many people singing in public places and you assume you can do it, too. Practice. Your teacher asks you a question. You warble back: "The answer to number two is twelve." Most of the class laughs at you, though some stare, eyes jewel-still, fascinated. At home your mother asks you to dust your dresser. Work up a vibrato you could drive a truck through. Sing: "Why do I have to do it now?" and tap your way through the dining room. Your mother requests that you calm down and go take a nap. Shout: "You don't care about me! You don't care about me at all!"

1946   Your brother plays "Shoofly Pie" all day long on the Victrola.

Ask your mother if you can go to Ellen's for supper. She will say, "Go ask your father," and you, pulling at your fingers, walk out to the living room and whimper by his chair. He is reading. Tap his arm. "Dad? Daddy? Dad?" He continues reading his science journal. Pull harder on your fingers and run back to the kitchen to tell your mother, who storms into the living room, saying, "Why don't you ever listen to your children when they try to talk to you?" You hear them arguing. Press your face into a kitchen towel, ashamed, the hum of the refrigerator motor, the drip in the sink scaring you.

1945   Your father comes home from his war work. He gives you a piggyback ride around the broad yellow thatch of your yard, the dead window in the turret, dark as a wound, watching you. He gives you wordless pushes on the swing.

75   Your brother has new friends, acts older and distant, even while you wait for the school bus together.

You spend too much time alone. You tell your mother that when you grow up you will bring your babies to Australia to see the kangaroos.

Forty thousand people are killed in Nagasaki.

1944   Dress and cuddle a tiny babydoll you have named "the Sue." Bring her everywhere. Get lost in the Wilson Creek fruit market, and call softly, "Mom, where are you?" Watch other children picking grapes, but never dare yourself. Your eyes are small, dark throats, your hand clutches the Sue.

1943   Ask your mother about babies. Have her read to you only the stories about babies. Ask her if she is going to have a baby. Ask her about the baby that died. Cry into her arm.

---

[9] Parchment scrolls containing Hebrew and Aramaic scriptural texts, as well as communal writings. Generally dated from 100 B.C. to A.D. 100, they were discovered in a cave near the Dead Sea, between Israel and Jordan.

80 *1940*   Clutch her hair in your fist. Rub it against your cheek.

1939   As through a helix, as through an ear, it is here you are nearer the dream flashes, the other lives.

There is a tent of legs, a sundering of selves, as you both gasp blindly for breath. Across the bright and cold, she knows it when you try to talk to her, though this is something you never really manage to understand.

Germany invades Poland.

The year's big song is "Three Little Fishies" and someone, somewhere, is playing it.

READING AND REACTING

1. What do you think the word *notes* in the story's title means?
2. Who is the story's protagonist? With whom (or what) is the protagonist in conflict? Explain the nature of this conflict.
3. What does the writer gain by arranging the story's events in reverse chronological order? What, if anything, does she lose?
4. What do the dates and the references to historical events contribute to the story?
5. Despite its unconventional sequence of events, does the story contain any foreshadowing? Explain.
6. A student, encountering this story for the first time, commented, "It's hard to follow because it has no plot." Do you agree with this student's assessment? Does this story include any of the conventional stages of plot (exposition, resolution, and so on)? If so, where? Identify several crises (peaks of tension). Does the story have a climax? Explain.
7. Moore says that in the stories in *Self-Help* she is "telling a how-to that is, of course, a how-not-to." What do you think she means? What does the narrator in this story want to teach her readers?
8. What is the effect of the narrator's use of the second person, as in the title and in phrases like "The mothers see you eyeing their children"? Explain the impact of "notes" like "Date an Italian."
9. **JOURNAL ENTRY** Although the story's title is "How to Talk to Your Mother (Notes)," the narrator actually does *not* talk to her mother. What do you think she wants to tell her mother? What stops her?
10. **CRITICAL PERSPECTIVE** When *Self-Help*, the collection in which "How to Talk to Your Mother (Notes)" appeared, was published in 1985, reviews were mixed. For example, the *Kirkus Reviews* called the book a "flimsy, strained collection" that relied on "a single gimmick and two limited situations. The gimmick? Stories in the form of self-help/instruction manuals. [. . .] The situations: a young woman caught in an unhappy no-win romantic

relationship; and a young woman's recollections of her unhappy, unstable mother [. . .]." The reviewer concluded by characterizing the book as "maudlin/juvenile work overall: boutique fiction at its most cutesy-poo." Other critics disagreed. Jay McInerney, writing in the *New York Times Book Review,* called "How to Talk to Your Mother (Notes)" a "splendid" story and saw the "complex puzzle of maternal love" as "haunting the quests" of many of Moore's narrators. Ray Olson's review in *Booklist,* although it expressed disappointment with the way the distant narrative voice robbed the stories of emotion, nevertheless called the book "absorbing," and the critic commented that it contained "many funny and sharp lines and effects."

How can you account for such different opinions of Moore's work? With which evaluation do you agree?

Related Works: "Everyday Use" (p. 324), "Shopping" (p. 559), "Two Kinds" (p. 594), "Those Winter Sundays" (p. 678), *'night, Mother* (p. 1708), *The Glass Menagerie* (p. 1805)

◆ WRITING SUGGESTIONS: PLOT

1. Write a sequel to "The Story of an Hour," telling the story in the voice of Brently Mallard. Use flashbacks to provide information about his view of the Mallards' marriage.
2. Write your own life story, imitating the style and structure of "How to Talk to Your Mother (Notes)." That is, use reverse chronology, use *you* instead of *I,* and divide your story into sections according to year. Be sure to include mentions of world events, song titles, and the like, as well as recurring themes in your life, to provide continuity and to unify your "notes" into a story.
3. Locate a newspaper story that you find disturbing. Then, write a "once upon a time" story like Gordimer's in which you retell the story's events in a detached tone without adding analysis or commentary.
4. "The Story of an Hour" includes a *deus ex machina,* an outside force or agent that suddenly appears to change the course of events. Consider the possible effects of a *deus ex machina* on the other two stories in this chapter. What might this outside force be in each story? How might it change the story's action? How plausible would such a dramatic turn of events be in each case?
5. Like Emily in "A Rose for Emily," the narrator of "The Yellow Wall-Paper" (Chapter 6) is a privileged, protected woman driven to the edge of madness by events she cannot control. Despite similarities in the two women's situations, however, their tragic stories are resolved in very different ways. What factors account for the two stories' different outcomes?

6. Read the article below from the January 30, 1987, *Philadelphia Inquirer*. After listing some similarities and differences between the events in the article's story and those in "A Rose for Emily," write an essay in which you discuss how the presentation of events differs. Can you draw any conclusions about journalistic and fictional treatments of similar incidents?

◇ ◇ ◇

A Woman's Wintry Death Leads to a Long-Dead Friend

DICK POTHIER AND THOMAS J. GIBBONS, JR.

For more than two years, Frances Dawson Hamilton lived with the body of her long-time companion, draping his skeletonized remains with palm fronds and rosary beads.

Yesterday, the 70-year-old woman was found frozen to death in the home in the 4500 block of Higbee Street where she had lived all her life—the last year without heat or hot water. Her body was found by police accompanying a city social worker who came bearing an order to have her taken to a hospital.

Police investigators said the body of Bernard J. Kelly, 84, was found in an upstairs bedroom of the two-story brick home in the Wissinoming section, on the twin bed where he apparently died at least two years ago.

Two beds had been pushed together, and Hamilton apparently had been sleeping beside Kelly's remains since he died of unknown causes, police said.

Kelly's remains were clothed in long johns and socks, investigators said. The body was draped with rosary beads and palm fronds, and on the bed near his body were two boxes of Valentine's Day candy.

"It was basically a funeral—we've seen it before in such cases," said one investigator who was at the scene but declined to be identified.

Neighbors and investigators said Hamilton and Kelly had lived together in the house for at least 15 years. Several neighbors said Hamilton came from an affluent family, was educated in Europe, and lived on a trust fund until a year or so ago.

Last winter, said John Wasniewski, Hamilton's next-door neighbor, the basement of the home was flooded and the heater destroyed. "There was no heat in that house last winter or this winter," he said.

An autopsy will be performed on Hamilton today, but she apparently froze to death sometime since Monday, when a friend spoke to her on the telephone, investigators said.

Over the last two years, neighbors said, Hamilton had become increasingly reclusive and irrational. Just last week, a city social worker summoned by a friend arranged for a Philadelphia Gas Works team to visit the home and try to repair the furnace—but she refused to let them in.

The friend was James Phillips, 44, of Horsham, a salesman for Apex Electric in Souderton.

In October 1985, he said, Hamilton visited the Frankford Avenue electrical shop where he was then working, told him that she had an electrical problem in her house and had no lights, and asked whether he could help.

Phillips said he visited the house, fixed the problem and gave her some light bulbs.

"She was really paranoid," Phillips said. "She believed that all her problems were from people doing things to her. For some reason or other, she took to me."

Phillips said that he began visiting her, taking her shopping and doing some shopping for her. But, he said, he never saw the body on the second floor.

Hamilton told him there was a man up there. "I thought it was a story she was telling to protect herself," Phillips said.

He provided her with electric heaters and also contacted a caseworker with the city's Department of Human Services whom Phillips identified as Albert Zbik.

Between the two of them, he said, "we got her through last winter." Phillips said Zbik helped her obtain food stamps and Social Security assistance.

When the snowstorm hit last week, Phillips became concerned because he knew Hamilton would have

trouble getting food. On Saturday, he took her a plate of hot food and bought more food from a local store.

On Monday, she telephoned him. "I didn't like the way she sounded," he said. He called Zbik and told him he felt it was time that they forced her to go to a hospital.

Phillips said Zbik went to her home yesterday, carrying a form authorizing an involuntary admission to a hospital for observation or required medical treatment.

Phillips told police that he was never allowed above the first floor and was often told by Hamilton that "Bernie is not feeling well today."

Neighbors and police investigators said Kelly was last seen alive about two years ago, and appeared to be quite ill at the time.

"As recently as last month, I asked Frances how Bernard was and whether she should get a doctor, and she said it wasn't necessary. She said 'He's sick, but I'm taking care of him—I'm feeding him with an eyedropper,'" Wasniewski said.

"I told her in December that if he was that sick, she should call a doctor, but she'd say she was taking care of him very well," Wasniewski said.

7. **WEB ACTIVITY** The following Web site contains information about Kate Chopin:

http://falcon.jmu.edu/~ramseyil/chopin.html

From that site, follow the link under "Reviews" to "Southern Women Writers." After reading the article "Southern Literature: Women Writers" by Patricia Evans, write an essay discussing Chopin's role as a Southern woman writer and, in particular, her role in the Southern Renaissance. Use Chopin's stories "The Story of an Hour" (p. 77) and "The Storm" (p. 154) as the basis for your essay.

CHAPTER 5

Character

◊ ◊ ◊

New writers think the way to begin a piece of fiction is to invent the most original plot possible. It is the way I myself was taught in college and too many classes still use that approach. Think up a plot, think up some characters, think up a conflict and suspense, pigeonhole them into the plot. *Voilà*, a story! Baloney. Every real writer I ever knew, and I have known many both in Europe and in this country, starts with people and their emotions and actions and lets them make their own stories. A woman once applied for one of my classes when I was teaching at Columbia University. "I want to be a writer," she told me, "so I can be like God and make people do what I want them to do." I had to tell her it was just the opposite. Characters make the author do what they want him to do.

MARTHA FOLEY, *Best American Short Stories* (Foreword)

Making false biography, false history, concocting a half-imaginary existence out of the actual drama of my life *is* my life. There has to be some pleasure in this job, and that's it. To go around in disguise. To act a character. To pass oneself off as what one is not. To *pretend*. [. . .] You don't necessarily, as a writer, have to abandon your biography completely to engage in an act of impersonation. It may be more intriguing when you don't.

PHILIP ROTH, *Writers at Work*, 7th ed.

Much of what a writer learns he learns simply by imitation. Making up a scene, he asks himself at every step. "Would she really say that?" or "Would he really throw the shoe?" He plays the scene through in his imagination, taking all the parts, being absolutely fair to everyone involved (mimicking each in turn, as Aristotle pointed out, and never sinking to stereotype for even the most minor characters), and when he finishes the scene he understands by sympathetic imitation what each character has done throughout and why the fight, or accident, or whatever, developed as it did.

JOHN GARDNER, *On Moral Fiction*

◊ ◊ ◊

A **character** is a fictional representation of a person—usually (but not necessarily) a psychologically realistic depiction. **Characterization** is the way writers develop characters and reveal those characters' traits to readers. Writers may portray characters through their actions, through their reactions to situations or to other characters, through their physical appearance, through their speech and gestures and expressions, and even through their names.

Generally speaking, characters are developed in two ways. First, readers can be *told* about characters. Third-person narrators can give us information about what characters are doing and thinking, what experiences they have had, what they look like, how they are dressed, and so on. Sometimes they also offer analysis of and judgments about a character's behavior. Similarly, first-person narrators can tell us about themselves or about other characters. Thus, Sammy in John Updike's "A&P" (p. 113) tells us that he lives with his parents and that he disapproves of the supermarket's customers. He also tells us what various characters are wearing and describes their actions, attitudes, and gestures. (For more information about first-person narrators, see Chapter 7, "Point of View.")

Alternatively, a character's personality traits and motivation may be *revealed* through actions, dialogue, or thoughts. For instance, Sammy's vivid fantasies and his disapproval of his customers' lives suggest to readers that he is something of a nonconformist; however, Sammy himself does not actually tell us this information.

Round and Flat Characters

◇ ◇ ◇

In his influential 1927 work *Aspects of the Novel,* English novelist E. M. Forster classifies characters as **round** (well developed, closely involved in and responsive to the action) or **flat** (barely developed or stereotypical). In an effective story, the major characters will usually be complex and fully developed; if they are not, readers will not care what happens to them. In much fiction, readers are encouraged to become involved with the characters, even to identify with them. This empathy is possible only when we know something about the characters—their strengths and weaknesses, for example, or their likes and dislikes. We must know at least enough to understand why characters act the way they do. In some cases, of course, a story can be effective even when its central characters are not well developed. Sometimes, in fact, a story's effectiveness is enhanced by an *absence* of character development, as in Shirley Jackson's "The Lottery" (p. 315).

Readers often expect characters to behave as "real people" in their situation might behave. Real people are not perfect, and realistic characters cannot be perfect either. The flaws that are revealed as round characters are developed—greed, gullibility, naïveté, shyness, a quick temper, or a lack of insight or judgment or tolerance or even intelligence—make them believable. In modern fiction, the protagonist is seldom if ever the noble "hero"; more often, he or she is at least partly a victim, someone to whom some unpleasant things happen, and someone who is sometimes ill-equipped to cope with events.

Unlike major characters, minor characters are frequently not well developed. Often they are flat, perhaps acting as *foils* for the protagonist. A **foil** is a supporting character whose role in the story is to highlight a major character by presenting a contrast with him or her. For instance, in "A&P," Stokesie, another young checkout clerk, is a foil for Sammy. Because he is a little older than Sammy and shows none of Sammy's imagination, restlessness, or nonconformity, Stokesie suggests what Sammy might become if he were to continue to work at the A&P. Some flat characters are **stock characters,** easily identifiable types who behave so consistently that readers can readily recognize them. The kindly old priest, the tough young bully, the ruthless business executive, and the reckless adventurer are all stock characters. Some flat characters can even be **caricatures,** characterized by a single dominant trait, such as miserliness, or even by one physical trait, such as nearsightedness.

DYNAMIC AND STATIC CHARACTERS
◈ ◈ ◈

Characters may also be classified as either *dynamic* or *static*. **Dynamic** characters grow and change in the course of a story, developing as they react to events and to other characters. In "A&P," for instance, Sammy's decision to speak out in defense of the girls—as well as the events that lead him to do so—changes him. His view of the world has changed at the end of the story, and as a result his position in the world will change too. A **static** character may face the same challenges a dynamic character might face but will remain essentially unchanged: a static character who was selfish and arrogant will remain selfish and arrogant, regardless of the nature of the story's conflict. In the fairy tale "Cinderella," for example, the title character is as sweet and good-natured at the end of the story—despite her mistreatment by her family—as she is at the beginning. Her situation may have changed, but her character has not.

Whereas round characters tend to be dynamic, flat characters tend to be static. But even a very complex, well-developed major character may be static; sometimes, in fact, the point of a story may hinge on a character's inability to change. A familiar example is the title character in William Faulkner's "A Rose for Emily" (p. 87), who lives a wasted, empty life, at least in part because she is unwilling or unable to accept that the world around her and the people in it have changed.

A story's minor characters are often static; their growth is not usually relevant to the story's development. Moreover, we usually do not learn enough about a minor character's traits, thoughts, actions, or motivation to determine whether or not the character changes significantly.

MOTIVATION

◆ ◆ ◆

Because round characters are complex, they are not always easy to understand. They may act differently in similar situations, just as real people do. They wrestle with decisions, resist or succumb to temptation, make mistakes, ask questions, search for answers, hope and dream, rejoice and despair. What is important is not whether we approve of a character's actions but whether those actions are *plausible*—whether the actions make sense in light of what we know about the character. We need to see a character's **motivation**—the reasons behind his or her behavior—or we will not believe or accept that behavior. For instance, given Sammy's age, his dissatisfaction with his job, and his desire to impress the young woman he calls Queenie, the decision he makes at the end of the story is perfectly plausible. Without having established his motivation, Updike could not have expected readers to accept Sammy's actions.

Even when readers get to know a character, they still are not able to predict how a complex, round character will behave in a given situation; only a flat character is predictable. The tension that develops as readers wait to see how a character will act or react, and thus how a story's conflict will be resolved, is what holds readers' interest and keeps them involved as a story's action unfolds.

✳ CHECKLIST: WRITING ABOUT CHARACTER

- ✓ Who is the story's protagonist? Who is the antagonist? Who are the other major characters?
- ✓ Who are the minor characters? What roles do they play in the story? How would the story be different without them?
- ✓ What do the major characters look like? Is their physical appearance important?
- ✓ What are the major characters' most noticeable traits?
- ✓ What are the major characters' likes and dislikes? Their strengths and weaknesses?
- ✓ What are we told about the major characters' backgrounds and prior experiences? What can we infer?

✓ Are characters developed for the most part through the narrator's comments and descriptions or through the characters' actions and dialogue?

✓ Are the characters round or flat?

✓ Are the characters dynamic or static?

✓ Does the story include any stock characters? Any caricatures? Does any character serve as a foil?

✓ Do the characters act in a way that is consistent with how readers expect them to act?

✓ With which characters are readers likely to be most (and least) sympathetic?

◈ **John Updike** (1932–   ) is a prolific writer of novels, short stories, essays, poems, plays, and children's tales. Updike's earliest ambition was to be a cartoonist for *The New Yorker*. He attended Harvard hoping to draw cartoons for *The Lampoon*, studied drawing and fine art at Oxford, and in 1955 went to work for *The New Yorker*—not as a cartoonist, but as a "Talk of the Town" reporter. Updike left *The New Yorker* after three years to write full-time but (over thirty years later) is still contributing stories, reviews, and essays to the magazine. Among his novels are *Rabbit, Run* (1960), *The Centaur* (1963), *Rabbit Redux* (1971), *Rabbit Is Rich* (1981), *The Witches of Eastwick* (1985), *Rabbit at Rest* (1990), *Memories of the Ford Administration* (1992), *Brazil* (1994), *In the Beauty of the Lilies* (1996), and *Toward the End of Time* (1997). His most recent novel is *Bech at Bay: A Quasi-Novel* (1998). Updike has also published *Collected Poems 1953–1993* (1993) and a collection of essays titled *The Afterlife and Other Stories* (1994).

In early stories such as "A&P" (1961), Updike draws on memories of his childhood and teenage years for the sort of "small" scenes and stories for which he quickly became famous. "There is a great deal to be said about almost anything," Updike comments in an interview in *Contemporary Authors*. "All people can be equally interesting. [. . .] Now either nobody is a hero or everybody is. I vote for everybody. My subject is the American Protestant small-town middle class. I like middles. It is in middles that extremes clash [. . .]. "

"What John Updike does for a living," writes John Romano in the *New York Times Book Review*, "is remind us of the human costliness of an everyday situation." In "A&P," there is cost, and a small triumph—and a young man's growing awareness of the "hard" world ahead.

CULTURAL CONTEXT ◆ Nineteen sixty-one, the year "A&P" was first published, was considered a watershed year in the United States. It was the year that John F. Kennedy, the youngest president ever elected, was inaugurated as the thirty-fifth president of the United States and the year that Alan Shepard made the first U.S. space flight. John Updike, noted for his realistic portrayal of American life, depicts a watershed event in the life of a small-town boy in "A&P," a coming-of-age story dealing with change, responsibility, and disillusionment.

◆ ◆ ◆

JOHN UPDIKE

A&P
(1961)

In walks these three girls in nothing but bathing suits. I'm in the third check-out slot, with my back to the door, so I don't see them until they're over by the bread. The one that caught my eye first was the one in the plaid green two-piece. She was a chunky kid, with a good tan and a sweet broad soft-looking can with those two crescents of white just under it, where the sun never seems to hit, at the top of the backs of her legs. I stood there with my hand on a box of HiHo crackers trying to remember if I rang it up or not. I ring it up again and the customer starts giving me hell. She's one of these cash-register-watchers, a witch about fifty with rouge on her cheekbones and no eyebrows, and I know it made her day to trip me up. She'd been watching cash registers for fifty years and probably never seen a mistake before.

By the time I got her feathers smoothed and her goodies into a bag—she gives me a little snort in passing, if she'd been born at the right time they would have burned her over in Salem—by the time I get her on her way the girls had circled around the bread and were coming back, without a push-cart, back my way along the counters, in the aisle between the check-outs and the Special bins. They didn't even have shoes on. There was this chunky one, with the two-piece—it was bright green and the seams on the bra were still sharp and her belly was still pretty pale so I guessed she just got it (the suit)—there was this one, with one of those chubby berry-faces, the lips all bunched together under her nose, this one, and a tall one, with black hair that hadn't quite frizzed right, and one of these sunburns right across under the eyes, and a chin that was too long—you know, the kind of girl other girls think is very "striking" and "attractive" but never quite makes it, as they very well know, which is why they like her so much—and then the third one, that wasn't quite so tall. She was the queen. She kind of led them, the other two peeking around and making their shoulders round. She didn't look around, not this queen, she just walked straight on slowly, on these long white prima-donna legs. She came down a little hard on her heels, as if she didn't walk in her bare feet that much, putting down her heels and then letting the weight move along to her toes as if she was testing the floor with every step, putting a little deliberate extra action into it. You never know for sure how girls' minds work (do you really think it's a mind in there or just a little buzz like a bee in a glass jar?) but you got the idea she had talked the other two into coming in here with her, and now she was showing them how to do it, walk slow and hold yourself straight.

She had on a kind of dirty-pink—beige maybe, I don't know—bathing suit with a little nubble all over it and, what got me, the straps were down. They were off her shoulders looped loose around the cool tops of her arms, and I guess as a result the suit had slipped a little on her, so all around the top of the cloth there was this shining rim. If it hadn't been there you wouldn't have known there could have been anything whiter than those shoulders. With the straps pushed off, there was nothing between the top of the suit and the top of her head except just *her,* this clean bare plane of the top of her chest down from the shoulder bones like a dented sheet of metal tilted in the light. I mean, it was more than pretty.

She had sort of oaky hair that the sun and salt had bleached, done up in a bun that was unravelling, and a kind of prim face. Walking into the A&P with your straps down, I suppose it's the only kind of face you *can* have. She held her head so high her neck, coming up out of those white shoulders, looked kind of stretched, but I didn't mind. The longer her neck was, the more of her there was.

5   She must have felt in the corner of her eye me and over my shoulder Stokesie in the second slot watching, but she didn't tip. Not this queen. She kept her eyes moving across the racks, and stopped, and turned so slow it made my stomach rub the inside of my apron, and buzzed to the other two, who kind of huddled against her for relief, and they all three of them went up the cat-and-dog-food-breakfast-cereal-macaroni-rice-raisins-seasonings-spreads-spaghetti-soft-drinks-crackers-and-cookies aisle. From the third slot I look straight up this aisle to the meat counter, and I watched them all the way. The fat one with the tan sort of fumbled with the cookies, but on second thought she put the packages back. The sheep pushing their carts down the aisle—the girls were walking against the usual traffic (not that we have one-way signs or anything)—were pretty hilarious. You could see them, when Queenie's white shoulders dawned on them, kind of jerk, or hop, or hiccup, but their eyes snapped back to their own baskets and on they pushed. I bet you could set off dynamite in an A&P and the people would by and large keep reaching and checking oatmeal off their lists and muttering "Let me see, there was a third thing, began with A, asparagus, no, ah, yes, applesauce!" or whatever it is they do mutter. But there was no doubt, this jiggled them. A few houseslaves in pin curlers even looked around after pushing their carts past to make sure what they had seen was correct.

You know, it's one thing to have a girl in a bathing suit down on the beach, where what with the glare nobody can look at each other much anyway, and another thing in the cool of the A&P, under the fluorescent lights, against all those stacked packages, with her feet paddling along naked over our checkerboard green-and-cream rubber-tile floor.

"Oh Daddy," Stokesie said beside me. "I feel so faint."

"Darling," I said. "Hold me tight." Stokesie's married, with two babies chalked up on his fuselage already, but as far as I can tell that's the only difference. He's twenty-two, and I was nineteen this April.

"Is it done?" he asks, the responsible married man finding his voice. I forgot to say he thinks he's going to be manager some sunny day, maybe in 1990 when it's called the Great Alexandrov and Petrooshki Tea Company or something.

10   What he meant was, our town is five miles from a beach, with a big summer colony out on the Point, but we're right in the middle of town, and the women generally put on a shirt or shorts or something before they get out of the car into the street. And anyway these are usually women with six children and varicose veins mapping their legs and no-body, including them, could care less. As I say, we're right in the middle of town, and if you stand at our front doors you can see two banks and the Congregational church and the newspaper store and three real-estate offices and about twenty-seven old freeloaders tearing up Central Street because the sewer broke again. It's not as if we're on the Cape; we're north of Boston and there's people in this town haven't seen the ocean for twenty years.

The girls had reached the meat counter and were asking McMahon something. He pointed, they pointed, and they shuffled out of sight be-hind a pyramid of Diet Delight peaches. All that was left for us to see was old McMahon patting his mouth and looking after them sizing up their joints. Poor kids, I began to feel sorry for them, they couldn't help it.

Now here comes the sad part of the story, at least my family says it's sad but I don't think it's sad myself. The store's pretty empty, it being Thursday afternoon, so there was nothing much to do except lean on the register and wait for the girls to show up again. The whole store was like a pinball machine and I didn't know which tunnel they'd come out of. After a while they come around out of the far aisle, around the light bulbs, records at discount of the Caribbean Six or Tony Martin Sings or some such gunk you wonder they waste the wax on, sixpacks of candy bars, and plastic toys done up in cellophane that fall apart when a kid looks at them anyway. Around they come, Queenie still leading the way, and holding a little gray jar in her hand. Slots Three through Seven are unmanned and I could see her wondering between Stokes and me, but Stokesie with his usual luck draws an old party in baggy gray pants who stumbles up with four giant cans of pineapple juice (what do these bums *do* with all that pineapple juice? I've often asked myself) so the girls come to me. Queenie puts down the jar and I take it into my fingers icy cold. Kingfish Fancy Herring Snacks in Pure Sour Cream: 49. Now her hands are empty, not a ring or a bracelet, bare as God made them, and I wonder where the money's coming from. Still with that prim look she lifts a folded dollar bill out of the hollow at the center of her nubbled pink top. The jar went heavy in my hand. Really, I thought that was so cute.

Then everybody's luck begins to run out. Lengel comes in from haggling with a truck full of cabbages on the lot and is about to scuttle into that door marked MANAGER behind which he hides all day when the girls touch his eye. Lengel's pretty dreary, teaches Sunday school and the rest, but he doesn't miss that much. He comes over and says, "Girls, this isn't the beach."

Queenie blushes, though maybe it's just a brush of sunburn I was noticing for the first time, now that she was so close. "My mother asked me to pick up a jar of herring snacks." Her voice kind of startled me, the way voices do when you see the people first, coming out so flat and dumb yet kind of tony, too, the way it ticked over "pick up" and "snacks." All of a sudden I slid right down her voice into her living room. Her father and the other men were standing around in ice-cream coats and bow ties and the women were in sandals picking up herring snacks on toothpicks off a big plate and they were all holding drinks the color of water with olives and sprigs of mint in them. When my parents have somebody over they get lemonade and if it's a real racy affair Schlitz in tall glasses with "They'll Do It Every Time" cartoons stencilled on.

15   "That's all right," Lengel said. "But this isn't the beach." His repeating this struck me as funny, as if it had just occurred to him, and he had been thinking all these years the A&P was a great big dune and he was the head lifeguard. He didn't like my smiling—as I say he doesn't miss much—but he concentrates on giving the girls that sad Sunday-school-superintendent stare.

Queenie's blush is no sunburn now, and the plump one in plaid, that I liked better from the back—a really sweet can—pipes up, "We weren't doing any shopping. We just came in for the one thing."

"That makes no difference," Lengel tells her, and I could see from the way his eyes went that he hadn't noticed she was wearing a two-piece before. "We want you decently dressed when you come in here."

"We *are* decent," Queenie says suddenly, her lower lip pushing, getting sore now that she remembers her place, a place from which the crowd that runs the A&P must look pretty crummy. Fancy Herring Snacks flashed in her very blue eyes.

"Girls, I don't want to argue with you. After this come in here with your shoulders covered. It's our policy." He turns his back. That's policy for you. Policy is what the kingpins want. What the others want is juvenile delinquency.

20   All this while, the customers had been showing up with their carts but, you know, sheep, seeing a scene, they had all bunched up on Stokesie, who shook open a paper bag as gently as peeling a peach, not wanting to miss a word. I could feel in the silence everybody getting nervous, most of all Lengel, who asks me, "Sammy, have you rung up this purchase?"

I thought and said "No" but it wasn't about that I was thinking. I go through the punches, 4, 9, GROC, TOT—it's more complicated than you think, and after you do it often enough, it begins to make a little song, that you hear words to, in my case "Hello *(bing)* there, you *(gung)* hap-py pee-pul *(splat)*!"—the *splat* being the drawer flying out. I uncrease the bill, tenderly as you may imagine, it just having come from between the two smoothest scoops of vanilla I had ever known were there, and pass a half and a penny into her narrow pink palm, and nestle the herrings in a bag and twist its neck and hand it over, all the time thinking.

The girls, and who'd blame them, are in a hurry to get out, so I say "I quit" to Lengel quick enough for them to hear, hoping they'll stop and watch me, their unsuspected hero. They keep right on going, into the electric eye; the door flies open and they flicker across the lot to their car, Queenie and Plaid and Big Tall Goony-Goony (not that as raw material she was so bad), leaving me with Lengel and a kink in his eyebrow.

"Did you say something, Sammy?"

"I said I quit."

25 "I thought you did."

"You didn't have to embarrass them."

"It was they who were embarrassing us."

I started to say something that came out "Fiddle-de-doo." It's a saying of my grandmother's, and I know she would have been pleased.

"I don't think you know what you're saying," Lengel said.

30 "I know you don't," I said. "But I do." I pull the bow at the back of my apron and start shrugging it off my shoulders. A couple customers that had been heading for my slot begin to knock against each other, like scared pigs in a chute.

Lengel sighs and begins to look very patient and old and gray. He's been a friend of my parents for years. "Sammy, you don't want to do this to your Mom and Dad," he tells me. It's true, I don't. But it seems to me that once you begin a gesture it's fatal not to go through with it. I fold the apron, "Sammy" stitched in red on the pocket, and put it on the counter, and drop the bow tie on top of it. The bow tie is theirs, if you've ever wondered. "You'll feel this for the rest of your life," Lengel says, and I know that's true, too, but remembering how he made that pretty girl blush makes me so scrunchy inside I punch the No Sale tab and the machine whirs "pee-pul" and the drawer splats out. One advantage to this scene taking place in summer, I can follow this up with a clean exit, there's no fumbling around getting your coat and galoshes, I just saunter into the electric eye in my white shirt that my mother ironed the night before, and the door heaves itself open, and outside the sunshine is skating around the asphalt.

I look around for my girls, but they're gone, of course. There wasn't anybody but some young married screaming with her children about some candy they didn't get by the door of a powder-blue Falcon station wagon. Looking back in the big windows, over the bags of peat moss and aluminum lawn furniture stacked on the pavement, I could see Lengel in my place in the slot, checking the sheep through. His face was dark gray and his back stiff, as if he'd just had an injection of iron, and my stomach kind of fell as I felt how hard the world was going to be to me hereafter.

READING AND REACTING

1. Summarize the information Sammy gives readers about his tastes and background. Why is this exposition vital to the story's development?
2. List some of the most obvious physical characteristics of the A&P's customers. How do these characteristics make them foils for Queenie and her friends?
3. What is it about Queenie and her friends that appeals to Sammy?
4. Is Queenie a stock character? Explain.
5. What rules and conventions are customers expected to follow in a supermarket? How does the behavior of Queenie and her friends violate these conventions?
6. Is the supermarket setting vital to the story? Could the story have been set in a car wash? In a fast-food restaurant?
7. How accurate are Sammy's judgments about the other characters? How might the characters be portrayed if the story were told by Lengel?
8. Given what you learn about Sammy during the course of the story, what do you see as his *primary* motivation for quitting his job? What other factors motivate him?
9. **JOURNAL ENTRY** Where do you think Sammy will find himself in ten years? Why?
10. **CRITICAL PERSPECTIVE** In her 1976 book *The Necessary Blackness,* critic Mary Allen observes, "Updike's most tender reverence is reserved for women's bodies. The elegant style with which he describes female anatomy often becomes overwrought, as his descriptions do generally. But it always conveys wonder."

    In what passages in "A&P" does Updike (through Sammy) convey this sense of wonder? Do you think today's audience, reading the story nearly forty years after Updike wrote it, and more than twenty years after Allen's essay was published, would still see such passages as conveying "tender reverence"? Or do you think readers might now see Sammy (and, indeed, Updike) as sexist? How do you see these passages?

Related Works: "Araby" (p. 254), "Bartleby the Scrivener" (p. 520), "Boys and Girls" (p. 548), "Ex-Basketball Player" (p. 813), "The Road Not Taken" (p. 959)

◆ **KATHERINE MANSFIELD** (1888–1923), one of the pioneers of the modern short story, was born in New Zealand and educated in England. Very much a "modern young woman," she began living on her own in London at the age of nineteen, soon publishing stories and book reviews in many of the most influential literary magazines of the day. One of these she edited with critic John Middleton Murry, whom she married in 1918.

A short story writer of great versatility, Mansfield produced sparkling social comedies for popular consumption as well as more intellectually and technically complex works intended for "perceptive readers." According to one critic, her best works "[w]ith delicate plainness . . . present elusive moments of decision, defeat, and small triumph." Her last two story collections—*Bliss and Other Stories* (1920) and *The Garden Party and Other Stories* (1922)—were met with immediate critical acclaim, but Mansfield's career was cut short in 1923 when she died of complications from tuberculosis at the age of thirty-five.

One notable theme in Mansfield's work is the *dame seule,* the "woman alone," which provides the basis for the poignant "Miss Brill."

CULTURAL CONTEXT ◆   Katherine Mansfield is believed to have been greatly influenced as a writer by Anton Chekhov (1860–1904), a Russian writer who gained a reputation as a master of the short story. His stories, like Mansfield's, emphasize characterization and mood, rather than plot, and focus on the tragicomic aspects of ordinary and seemingly trite events.

◇ ◇ ◇

KATHERINE MANSFIELD

Miss Brill
(1922)

Although it was so brilliantly fine—the blue sky powdered with gold and great spots of light like white wine splashed over the Jardins Publiques[1]— Miss Brill was glad that she had decided on her fur. The air was motionless, but when you opened your mouth there was just a faint chill, like a chill from a glass of iced water before you sip, and now and again a leaf came drifting—from nowhere, from the sky. Miss Brill put up her hand and touched her fur. Dear little thing! It was nice to feel it again. She had taken it out of its box that afternoon, shaken out the moth-powder, given it a good brush, and rubbed the life back into the dim little eyes. "What has been happening to me?" said the sad little eyes. Oh, how sweet it was to

---

[1] Public Gardens (French).

see them snap at her again from the red eiderdown! . . . But the nose, which was of some black composition, wasn't at all firm. It must have had a knock, somehow. Never mind—a little dab of black sealing-wax when the time came—when it was absolutely necessary. . . . Little rogue! Yes, she really felt like that about it. Little rogue biting its tail just by her left ear. She could have taken it off and laid in on her lap and stroked it. She felt a tingling in her hands and arms, but that came from walking, she supposed. And when she breathed, something light and sad—no, not sad, exactly— something gentle seemed to move in her bosom.

There were a number of people out this afternoon, far more than last Sunday. And the band sounded louder and gayer. That was because the Season had begun. For although the band played all year round on Sundays, out of season it was never the same. It was like some one playing with only the family to listen; it didn't care how it played if there weren't any strangers present. Wasn't the conductor wearing a new coat, too? She was sure it was new. He scraped with his foot and flapped his arms like a rooster about to crow, and the bandsmen sitting in the green rotunda blew out their cheeks and glared at the music. Now there came a little "flutey" bit—very pretty!—a little chain of bright drops. She was sure it would be repeated. It was; she lifted her head and smiled.

Only two people shared her "special" seat: a fine old man in a velvet coat, his hands clasped over a huge carved walking-stick, and a big old woman, sitting upright, with a roll of knitting on her embroidered apron. They did not speak. This was disappointing, for Miss Brill always looked forward to the conversation. She had become really quite expert, she thought, at listening as though she didn't listen, at sitting in other people's lives just for a minute while they talked round her.

She glanced, sideways, at the old couple. Perhaps they would go soon. Last Sunday, too, hadn't been as interesting as usual. An Englishman and his wife, he wearing a dreadful Panama hat and she button boots. And she'd gone on the whole time about how she ought to wear spectacles; she knew she needed them; but that it was no good getting any; they'd be sure to break and they'd never keep on. And he'd been so patient. He'd suggested everything—gold rims, the kind that curved round your ears, little pads inside the bridge. No, nothing would please her. "They'll always be sliding down my nose!" Miss Brill wanted to shake her.

5   The old people sat on the bench, still as statues. Never mind, there was always the crowd to watch. To and fro, in front of the flower-beds and the band rotunda, the couples and groups paraded, stopped to talk, to greet, to buy a handful of flowers from the old beggar who had his tray fixed to the railings. Little children ran among them, swooping and laughing; little boys with big white silk bows under their chins, little girls, little French dolls, dressed up in velvet and lace. And sometimes a tiny staggerer came suddenly rocking into the open from under the trees, stopped, stared, as suddenly sat down "flop," until its small high-stepping mother, like a young hen, rushed scolding to its rescue. Other people sat on the benches

and green chairs, but they were nearly always the same, Sunday after Sunday, and—Miss Brill had often noticed—there was something funny about nearly all of them. They were odd, silent, nearly all old, and from the way they stared they looked as though they'd just come from dark little rooms or even—even cupboards!

Behind the rotunda the slender trees with yellow leaves down drooping, and through them just a line of sea, and beyond the blue sky with gold-veined clouds.

Tum-tum-tum tiddle-um! tiddle-um! tum tiddley-um tum ta! blew the band.

Two young girls in red came by and two young soldiers in blue met them, and they laughed and paired and went off arm-in-arm. Two peasant women with funny straw hats passed, gravely, leading beautiful smoke-colored donkeys. A cold, pale nun hurried by. A beautiful woman came along and dropped her bunch of violets, and a little boy ran after to hand them to her, and she took them and threw them away as if they'd been poisoned. Dear me! Miss Brill didn't know whether to admire that or not! And now an ermine toque[2] and a gentleman in grey met just in front of her. He was tall, stiff, dignified, and she was wearing the ermine toque she'd bought when her hair was yellow. Now everything, her hair, her face, even her eyes, was the same color as the shabby ermine, and her hand, in its cleaned glove, lifted to dab her lips, was a tiny yellowish paw. Oh, she was so pleased to see him—delighted! She rather thought they were going to meet that afternoon. She described where she'd been—everywhere, here, there, along by the sea. The day was so charming—didn't he agree? And wouldn't he, perhaps? . . . But he shook his head, lighted a cigarette, slowly breathed a great deep puff into her face, and, even while she was still talking and laughing, flicked the match away and walked on. The ermine toque was alone; she smiled more brightly than ever. But even the band seemed to know what she was feeling and played more softly, played tenderly, and the drum beat, "The Brute! The Brute!" over and over. What would she do? What was going to happen now? But as Miss Brill wondered, the ermine toque turned, raised her hand as though she'd seen some one else, much nicer, just over there, and pattered away. And the band changed again and played more quickly, more gaily than ever, and the old couple on Miss Brill's seat got up and marched away, and such a funny old man with long whiskers hobbled along in time to the music and was nearly knocked over by four girls walking abreast.

Oh, how fascinating it was! How she enjoyed it! How she loved sitting here, watching it all! It was like a play. It was exactly like a play. Who could believe the sky at the back wasn't painted? But it wasn't till a little brown dog trotted on solemn and then slowly trotted off, like a little "theatre" dog, a little dog that had been drugged, that Miss Brill discovered what it was that made it so exciting. They were all on the stage. They

---

[2] Small, close-fitting woman's hat.

weren't only the audience, not only looking on; they were acting. Even she had a part and came every Sunday. No doubt somebody would have noticed if she hadn't been there; she was part of the performance after all. How strange she'd never thought of it like that before! And yet it explained why she made such a point of starting from home at just the same time each week—so as not to be late for the performance—and it also explained why she had quite a queer, shy feeling at telling her English pupils how she spent her Sunday afternoons. No wonder! Miss Brill nearly laughed out loud. She was on the stage. She thought of the old invalid gentleman to whom she read the newspaper four afternoons a week while he slept in the garden. She had got quite used to the frail head on the cotton pillow, the hollowed eyes, the open mouth and the high pinched nose. If he'd been dead she mightn't have noticed for weeks; she wouldn't have minded. But suddenly he knew he was having the paper read to him by an actress! "An actress!" The old head lifted; two points of light quivered in the old eyes. "An actress—are ye?" And Miss Brill smoothed the newspaper as though it were the manuscript of her part and said gently: "Yes, I have been an actress for a long time."

10   The band had been having a rest. Now they started again. And what they played was warm, sunny, yet there was just a faint chill—a something, what was it?—not sadness—no, not sadness—a something that made you want to sing. The tune lifted, lifted, the light shone; and it seemed to Miss Brill that in another moment all of them, all the whole company, would begin singing. The young ones, the laughing ones who were moving together, they would begin, and the men's voices, very resolute and brave, would join them. And then she too, she too, and the others on the benches—they would come in with a kind of accompaniment—something low, that scarcely rose or fell, something so beautiful—moving. . . . And Miss Brill's eyes filled with tears and she looked smiling at all the other members of the company. Yes, we understand, we understand, she thought—though what they understood she didn't know.

Just at that moment a boy and a girl came and sat down where the old couple had been. They were beautifully dressed; they were in love. The hero and heroine, of course, just arrived from his father's yacht. And still soundlessly singing, still with that trembling smile, Miss Brill prepared to listen.

"No, not now," said the girl. "Not here, I can't."

"But why? Because of that stupid old thing at the end there?" asked the boy. "Why does she come here at all—who wants her? Why doesn't she keep her silly old mug at home?"

"It's her fu-fur which is so funny," giggled the girl. "It's exactly like a fried whiting."[3]

---

[3] Food fish related to the cod.

15   "Ah, be off with you!" said the boy in an angry whisper. Then: "Tell me, my petite chérie—"[4]

"No, not here," said the girl. "Not *yet*."

On her way home she usually bought a slice of honeycake at the baker's. It was her Sunday treat. Sometimes there was an almond in her slice, sometimes not. It made a great difference. If there was an almond it was like carrying home a tiny present—a surprise—something that might very well not have been there. She hurried on the almond Sundays and struck the match for the kettle in quite a dashing way.

But to-day she passed the baker's boy, climbed the stairs, went into the little dark room—her room like a cupboard—and sat down on the red eiderdown. She sat there for a long time. The box that the fur came out of was on the bed. She unclasped the necklet quickly; quickly, without looking, laid it inside. But when she put the lid on she thought she heard something crying.

READING AND REACTING

1. What specific details can you infer about Miss Brill's character (and, perhaps, about her life) from this statement: "She had become really quite expert, she thought, at listening as though she didn't listen, at sitting in other people's lives just for a minute while they talked round her" (3)?
2. How do Miss Brill's observations of the people around her give us insight into her own character? Why do you suppose she doesn't interact with any of the people she observes?
3. In paragraph 9, Miss Brill realizes that the scene she observes is "exactly like a play" and that "even she had a part and came every Sunday." What part does Miss Brill play? Is she a stock character in this play, or is she a three-dimensional character? Does she play a lead role or a supporting role?
4. What do you think Miss Brill means when she says, "I have been an actress for a long time" (9)? What does this comment reveal about how Miss Brill sees herself? Is her view of herself similar to or different from the view the other characters have of her?
5. What role does Miss Brill's fur piece play in the story? In what sense, if any, does it function as a character?
6. What happens in paragraphs 11–16 to break Miss Brill's mood? Why is the scene she observes so upsetting to her?
7. At the end of the story, has Miss Brill changed as a result of what she has overheard, or is she the same person she was at the beginning? Do you think she will return to the park the following Sunday?

---

[4] Little darling (French).

8. The story's last paragraph describes Miss Brill's room as being "like a cupboard." Where else has this image appeared in the story? What does its repetition in the conclusion tell us?

9. **Journal Entry** Write a character sketch of Miss Brill, inventing a plausible family and personal history that might help to explain the character you see in the story.

10. **Critical Perspective** Critic Gillian Boddy, in *Katherine Mansfield: The Woman, The Writer,* offers the following analysis of Mansfield's fiction:

> The story evolves through the characters' minds. The external narrator is almost eliminated. As so often in her work, the reader is dropped into the story and simply confronted by a particular situation. There is no preliminary establishing and identification of time and place. The reader is immediately involved; it is assumed that he or she has any necessary prerequisite knowledge and is, in a sense, part of the story too.

Do you see this absence of conventional exposition as a problem in "Miss Brill"? Do you think the story would be more effective if Mansfield had supplied more preliminary information about setting and character? Or do you believe that what Boddy calls Mansfield's "concentration on a moment or episode" is a satisfactory substitute for the missing exposition, effectively shifting interest from "what *happens*" to "*why* it happens"?

Related Works: "A Clean, Well-Lighted Place" (p. 261), "Rooming Houses Are Old Women" (p. 811), "After Great Pain, a Formal Feeling Comes" (p. 940), "Acquainted with the Night" (p. 955)

◆ **Ann Petry** (1908–1997) was born in Old Saybrook, Connecticut, the daughter of a pharmacist and a businesswoman. She later studied pharmacy herself and between 1931 and 1938 worked as a pharmacist in her hometown. In 1938, she moved to New York City to pursue a writing career, attending Columbia University and working for the *Amsterdam News*, a newspaper geared to the city's African-American residents. She also worked as a teacher and as an actress with the American Negro Theatre.

Petry's early short stories appeared in various magazines, but it was with the publication of her first novel, *The Street* (1946), that she was recognized as an important talent. The first novel by an African-American woman to focus on the prejudice and economic difficulties facing poor urban blacks, *The Street* was also the first best-seller by an African-American woman. It is still in print today. Petry has published just two other novels—*Country Place* (1947) and *The Narrows* (1953)—in addition to a number of books aimed at young people, including a biography of Harriet Tubman.

"Like a Winding Sheet," which appears in her 1945 collection *Miss Muriel and Other Stories,* is a grim reminder of how the insult of injustice can fester into anger and blind violence.

CULTURAL CONTEXT ◆ After World War II, African-Americans fleeing the racism and poverty of the South migrated to northern cities. It is in this context of difficult conditions for poor, urban blacks in the 1940s that the story "Like a Winding Sheet" takes place. Ann Petry was the first black female author to address the problems of African women as they struggled to cope with inner city life.

◆ ◇ ◆

ANN PETRY

Like a Winding Sheet
(1945)

He had planned to get up before Mae did and surprise her by fixing breakfast. Instead he went back to sleep and she got out of bed so quietly he didn't know she wasn't there beside him until he woke up and heard the queer soft gurgle of water running out of the sink in the bathroom.

He knew he ought to get up but instead he put his arms across his forehead to shut the afternoon sunlight out of his eyes, pulled his legs up close to his body, testing them to see if the ache was still in them.

Mae had finished in the bathroom. He could tell because she never closed the door when she was in there and now the sweet smell of talcum powder was drifting down the hall and into the bedroom. Then he heard her coming down the hall.

"Hi, babe," she said affectionately.

5   "Hum," he grunted, and moved his arms away from his head, opened one eye.

"It's a nice morning."

"Yeah." He rolled over and the sheet twisted around him, outlining his thighs, his chest. "You mean afternoon, don't ya?"

Mae looked at the twisted sheet and giggled. "Looks like a winding sheet," she said. "A shroud—"[1] Laughter tangled with her words and she had to pause for a moment before she could continue. "You look like a huckleberry—in a winding sheet—"

"That's no way to talk. Early in the day like this," he protested.

---

[1] Cloth wrapped around a corpse; a winding sheet.

10   He looked at his arms silhouetted against the white of the sheets. They were inky black by contrast and he had to smile in spite of himself and he lay there smiling and savoring the sweet sound of Mae's giggling.

"Early?" She pointed a finger at the alarm clock on the table near the bed and giggled again. "It's almost four o'clock. And if you don't spring up out of there, you're going to be late again."

"What do you mean 'again'?"

"Twice last week. Three times the week before. And once the week before and—"

"I can't get used to sleeping in the daytime," he said fretfully. He pushed his legs out from under the covers experimentally. Some of the ache had gone out of them but they weren't really rested yet. "It's too light for good sleeping. And all that standing beats the hell out of my legs."

15   "After two years you oughta be used to it," Mae said.

He watched her as she fixed her hair, powdered her face, slipped into a pair of blue denim overalls. She moved quickly and yet she didn't seem to hurry.

"You look like you'd had plenty of sleep," he said lazily. He had to get up but he kept putting the moment off, not wanting to move, yet he didn't dare let his legs go completely limp because if he did he'd go back to sleep. It was getting later and later but the thought of putting his weight on his legs kept him lying there.

When he finally got up he had to hurry, and he gulped his breakfast so fast that he wondered if his stomach could possibly use food thrown at it at such a rate of speed. He was still wondering about it as he and Mae were putting their coats on in the hall.

Mae paused to look at the calendar. "It's the thirteenth," she said. Then a faint excitement in her voice. "Why, it's Friday the thirteenth." She had one arm in her coat sleeve and she held it there while she stared at the calendar. "I oughta stay home," she said. "I shouldn't go outa the house."

20   "Aw, don't be a fool," he said. "Today's payday. And payday is a good luck day everywhere, any way you look at it." And as she stood hesitating he said, "Aw, come on."

And he was late for work again because they spent fifteen minutes arguing before he could convince her she ought to go to work just the same. He had to talk persuasively, urging her gently, and it took time. But he couldn't bring himself to talk to her roughly or threaten to strike her like a lot of men might have done. He wasn't made that way.

So when he reached the plant he was late and he had to wait to punch the time clock because the day-shift workers were streaming out in long lines, in groups and bunches that impeded his progress.

Even now just starting his workday his legs ached. He had to force himself to struggle past the outgoing workers, punch the time clock, and get the little cart he pushed around all night, because he kept toying with the idea of going home and getting back in bed.

He pushed the cart out on the concrete floor, thinking that if this was his plant he'd make a lot of changes in it. There were too many standing-up jobs for one thing. He'd figure out some way most of 'em could be done sitting down and he'd put a lot more benches around. And this job he had—this job that forced him to walk ten hours a night, pushing this little cart, well, he'd turn it into a sitting-down job. One of those little trucks they used around railroad stations would be good for a job like this. Guys sat on a seat and the thing moved easily, taking up little room and turning in hardly any space at all like on a dime.

25   He pushed the car near the foreman. He never could remember to refer to her as the forelady even in his mind. It was funny to have a white woman for a boss in a plant like this one.

She was sore about something. He could tell by the way her face was red and her eyes were half-shut until they were slits. Probably been out late and didn't get enough sleep. He avoided looking at her and hurried a little, head down, as he passed her though he couldn't resist stealing a glance at her out of the corner of his eye. He saw the edge of the light-colored slacks she wore and the tip end of a big tan shoe.

"Hey, Johnson!" the woman said.

The machines had started full blast. The whirr and the grinding made the building shake, made it impossible to hear conversations. The men and women at the machines talked to each other but looking at them from just a little distance away, they appeared to be simply moving their lips be-cause you couldn't hear what they were saying. Yet the woman's voice cut across the machine sounds—harsh, angry.

He turned his head slowly. "Good evenin', Mrs. Scott," he said, and waited.

30   "You're late again."

"That's right. My legs were bothering me."

The woman's face grew redder, angrier looking. "Half this shift comes in late," she said. "And you're the worst one of all. You're always late. Whatsa matter with ya?"

"It's my legs," he said. "Somehow they don't ever get rested. I don't seem to get used to sleeping days. And I just can't get started."

"Excuses. You guys always got excuses," her anger grew and spread. "Every guy comes in here late always has an excuse. His wife's sick or his grandmother died or somebody in the family had to go to the hospital," she paused, drew a deep breath. "And the niggers is the worse. I don't care what's wrong with your legs. You get in here on time. I'm sick of you niggers—"

35   "You got the right to get mad," he interrupted softly. "You got the right to cuss me four ways to Sunday but I ain't letting nobody call me a nigger."

He stepped closer to her. His fists were doubled. His lips were drawn back in a thin narrow line. A vein in his forehead stood out swollen, thick.

And the woman backed away from him, not hurriedly but slowly—two, three steps back.

"Aw, forget it," she said. "I didn't mean nothing by it. It slipped out. It was an accident." The red of her face deepened until the small blood vessels in her cheeks were purple. "Go on and get to work," she urged. And she took three more slow backward steps.

He stood motionless for a moment and then turned away from the sight of the red lipstick on her mouth that made him remember that the foreman was a woman. And he couldn't bring himself to hit a woman. He felt a curious tingling in his fingers and he looked down at his hands. They were clenched tight, hard, ready to smash some of those small purple veins in her face.

40   He pushed the cart ahead of him, walking slowly. When he turned his head, she was staring in his direction, mopping her forehead with a dark blue handkerchief. Their eyes met and then they both looked away.

He didn't glance in her direction again but moved past the long work benches, carefully collecting the finished parts, going slowly and steadily up and down, and back and forth the length of the building, and as he walked he forced himself to swallow his anger, get rid of it.

And he succeeded so that he was able to think about what had happened without getting upset about it. An hour went by but the tension stayed in his hands. They were clenched and knotted on the handles of the cart as though ready to aim a blow.

And he thought he should have hit her anyway, smacked her hard in the face, felt the soft flesh of her face give under the hardness of his hands. He tried to make his hands relax by offering them a description of what it would have been like to strike her because he had the queer feeling that his hands were not exactly a part of him anymore—they had developed a separate life of their own over which he had no control. So he dwelt on the pleasure his hands would have felt—both of them cracking at her, first one and then the other. If he had done that his hands would have felt good now—relaxed, rested.

And he decided that even if he'd lost his job for it, he should have let her have it and it would have been a long time, maybe the rest of her life, before she called anybody else a nigger.

45   The only trouble was he couldn't hit a woman. A woman couldn't hit back the same way a man did. But it would have been a deeply satisfying thing to have cracked her narrow lips wide open with just one blow, beautifully timed and with all his weight in back of it. That way he would have gotten rid of all the energy and tension his anger had created in him. He kept remembering how his heart had started pumping blood so fast he had felt it tingle even in the tips of his fingers.

With the approach of night, fatigue nibbled at him. The corners of his mouth drooped, the frown between his eyes deepened, his shoulders sagged; but his hands stayed tight and tense. As the hours dragged by he noticed that the women workers had started to snap and snarl at each other. He couldn't hear what they said because of the sound of machines but he could see the quick lip movements that sent words tumbling from the sides of their mouths. They gestured irritably with their hands and scowled as their mouths moved.

Their violent jerky motions told him that it was getting close on to quitting time but somehow he felt that the night still stretched ahead of him, composed of endless hours of steady walking on his aching legs. When the whistle finally blew he went on pushing the cart, unable to believe that it had sounded. The whirring of the machines died away to a murmur and he knew then that he'd really heard the whistle. He stood still for a moment, filled with a relief that made him sigh.

Then he moved briskly, putting the cart in the storeroom, hurrying to take his place in the line forming before the paymaster. That was another thing he'd change, he thought. He'd have the pay envelopes handed to the people right at their benches so there wouldn't be ten or fifteen minutes lost waiting for the pay. He always got home about fifteen minutes late on payday. They did it better in the plant where Mae worked, brought the money right to them at their benches.

He stuck his pay envelope in his pants' pocket and followed the line of workers heading for the subway in a slow-moving stream. He glanced up at the sky. It was a nice night, the sky looked packed full to running over with stars. And he thought if he and Mae would go right to bed when they got home from work they'd catch a few hours of darkness for sleeping. But they never did. They fooled around—cooking and eating and listening to the radio and he always stayed in a big chair in the living room and went almost but not quite to sleep and when they finally got to bed it was five or six in the morning and daylight was already seeping around the edges of the sky.

50   He walked slowly, putting off the moment when he would have to plunge into the crowd hurrying toward the subway. It was a long ride to Harlem and tonight the thought of it appalled him. He paused outside an all-night restaurant to kill time, so that some of the first rush of workers would be gone when he reached the subway.

The lights in the restaurant were brilliant, enticing. There was life and motion inside. And as he looked through the window he thought that everything within range of his eyes gleamed—the long imitation marble counter, the tall stools, the white porcelain-topped tables and especially the big metal coffee urn right near the window. Steam issued from its top and a gas flame flickered under it—a lively, dancing, blue flame.

A lot of the workers from his shift—men and women—were lining up near the coffee urn. He watched them walk to the porcelain-topped tables carrying steaming cups of coffee and he saw that just the smell of the coffee lessened the fatigue lines in their faces. After the first sip their faces softened, they smiled, they began to talk and laugh.

On a sudden impulse he shoved the door open and joined the line in front of the coffee urn. The line moved slowly. And as he stood there the smell of the coffee, the sound of the laughter and the voices, helped dull the sharp ache in his legs.

He didn't pay any attention to the white girl who was serving the coffee at the urn. He kept looking at the cups in the hands of the men who had been ahead of him. Each time a man stepped out of the line with one of the thick white cups the fragrant steam got in his nostrils. He saw that they walked carefully so as not to spill a single drop. There was a froth of bubbles at the top of each cup and he thought about how he would let the bubbles break against his lips before he actually took a big deep swallow.

55   Then it was his turn. "A cup of coffee," he said, just as he had heard the others say.

The white girl looked past him, put her hands up to her head and gently lifted her hair away from the back of her neck, tossing her head back a little. "No more coffee for a while," she said.

He wasn't certain he'd heard her correctly and he said "What?" blankly.

"No more coffee for a while," she repeated.

There was silence behind him and then uneasy movement. He thought someone would say something, ask why or protest, but there was only silence and then a faint shuffling sound as though the men standing behind him had simultaneously shifted their weight from one foot to the other.

60   He looked at the girl without saying anything. He felt his hands begin to tingle and the tingling went all the way down to his finger tips so that he glanced down at them. They were clenched tight, hard, into fists. Then he looked at the girl again. What he wanted to do was hit her so hard that the scarlet lipstick on her mouth would smear and spread over her nose, her chin, out toward her cheeks, so hard that she would never toss her head again and refuse a man a cup of coffee because he was black.

He estimated the distance across the counter and reached forward, balancing his weight on the balls of his feet, ready to let the blow go. And then his hands fell back down to his sides because he forced himself to lower them, to unclench them and make them dangle loose. The effort took his breath away because his hands fought against him. But he couldn't hit her. He couldn't even now bring himself to hit a woman, not even this one, who had refused him a cup of coffee with a toss of her head. He kept seeing the gesture with which she had lifted the length of her blond hair from the back of her neck as expressive of her contempt for him.

When he went out the door he didn't look back. If he had he would have seen the flickering blue flame under the shiny coffee urn being extinguished. The line of men who had stood behind him lingered a moment to watch the people drinking coffee at the tables and then they left just as he had without having had the coffee they wanted so badly. The girl behind the counter poured water in the urn and swabbed it out and as she waited for the water to run out, she lifted her hair gently from the back of her neck and tossed her head before she began making a fresh pot of coffee.

• • •

But he had walked away without a backward look, his head down, his hands in his pockets, raging at himself and whatever it was inside of him that had forced him to stand quiet and still when he wanted to strike out.

The subway was crowded and he had to stand. He tried grasping an overhead strap and his hands were too tense to grip it. So he moved near the train door and stood there swaying back and forth with the rocking of the train. The roar of the train beat inside his head, making it ache and throb, and the pain in his legs clawed up into his groin so that he seemed to be bursting with pain and he told himself that it was due to all that anger-born energy that had piled up in him and not been used and so it had spread through him like a poison—from his feet and legs all the way up to his head.

65   Mae was in the house before he was. He knew she was home before he put the key in the door of the apartment. The radio was going. She had it turned up loud and she was singing along with it.

"Hello, babe," she called out, as soon as he opened the door.

He tried to say "hello" and it came out half grunt and half sigh.

"You sure sound cheerful," she said.

She was in the bedroom and he went and leaned against the doorjamb. The denim overalls she wore to work were carefully draped over the back of a chair by the bed. She was standing in front of the dresser, tying the sash of a yellow housecoat around her waist and chewing gum vigorously as she admired her reflection in the mirror over the dresser.

70   "Whatsa matter?" she said. "You get bawled out by the boss or somep'n?"

"Just tired," he said slowly. "For God's sake, do you have to crack that gum like that?"

"You don't have to lissen to me," she said complacently. She patted a curl in place near the side of her head and then lifted her hair away from the back of her neck, ducking her head forward and then back.

He winced away from the gesture. "What you got to be always fooling with your hair for?" he protested.

"Say, what's the matter with you anyway?" She turned away from the mirror to face him, put her hands on her hips. "You ain't been in the house two minutes and you're picking on me."

75   He didn't answer her because her eyes were angry and he didn't want to quarrel with her. They'd been married too long and got along too well and so he walked all the way into the room and sat down in the chair by the bed and stretched his legs out in front of him, putting his weight on the heels of his shoes, leaning way back in the chair, not saying anything.

"Lissen," she said sharply. "I've got to wear those overalls again tomorrow. You're going to get them all wrinkled up leaning against them like that."

He didn't move. He was too tired and his legs were throbbing now that he had sat down. Besides the overalls were already wrinkled and dirty, he thought. They couldn't help but be for she'd worn them all week. He leaned farther back in the chair.

"Come on, get up," she ordered.

"Oh, what the hell," he said wearily, and got up from the chair. "I'd just as soon live in a subway. There'd be just as much place to sit down."

80   He saw that her sense of humor was struggling with her anger. But her sense of humor won because she giggled.

"Aw, come on and eat," she said. There was a coaxing note in her voice. "You're nothing but an old hungry nigger trying to act tough and—" she paused to giggle and then continued, "You—"

He had always found her giggling pleasant and deliberately said things that might amuse her and then waited, listening for the delicate sound to emerge from her throat. This time he didn't even hear the giggle. He didn't let her finish what she was saying. She was standing close to him and that funny tingling started in his finger tips, went fast up his arms and sent his fist shooting straight for her face.

There was the smacking sound of soft flesh being struck by a hard object and it wasn't until she screamed that he realized he had hit her in the mouth—so hard that the dark red lipstick had blurred and spread over her full lips, reaching up toward the tip of her nose, down toward her chin, out toward her cheeks.

The knowledge that he had struck her seeped through him slowly and he was appalled but he couldn't drag his hands away from her face. He kept striking her and he thought with horror that something inside him was holding him, binding him to this act, wrapping and twisting about him so that he had to continue it. He had lost all control over his hands. And he groped for a phrase, a word, something to describe what this thing was like that was happening to him and he thought it was like being enmeshed in a winding sheet—that was it—like a winding sheet. And even as the thought formed in his mind, his hands reached for her face again and yet again.

READING AND REACTING

1. This story appeared in a 1945 collection of Petry's stories. What information does this date suggest about the characters' experiences prior to the beginning of the story? Does the date help in any way to explain Johnson's character? His motivation?

2. Johnson is portrayed as exhausted, frustrated, and tense with rage. How are these character traits communicated to readers?

3. When the forelady calls Johnson a nigger, he speaks up to her quietly yet firmly, and she backs off. Given what we know about Johnson, is his action plausible? Is it consistent with his other actions?

4. How do Johnson's physical ailments help to develop his character? How do they help to explain his motivation? Do you think they in any way mitigate his final act?

5. What do readers really know about Mae besides the facts that she wears overalls to work, sings along with the radio, wears red lipstick, and chews gum? Do we really *need* to know anything else? Would the story have a different impact if Mae's character were as fully developed as Johnson's?

6. What function is served by Johnson's boss, Mrs. Scott? By the woman at the coffee urn? Are both minor characters necessary to the story? Is it essential or incidental that both are women?

7. What finally causes Johnson to snap? Why does he lose his temper at this point? Why do you think he doesn't lose it earlier?

8. Do you see the story's outcome as inevitable? How is this outcome foreshadowed?

9. **JOURNAL ENTRY** Whom do you blame for Johnson's violent act? Is he alone to blame, or should someone—or something—else also be held responsible? Could you argue that Johnson is as much a victim as Mae is?

10. **CRITICAL PERSPECTIVE** In *From the Dark Tower: Afro-American Writers 1900–1960,* Arthur P. Davis focuses on Petry's short fiction:

> The short stories of Ann Petry show a great sensitivity. They tend to deal with those subtle aspects of racial hurt which are not always understood by non-blacks. [. . .] Petry's voice is low when she speaks of the tragedy of ghetto living in these stories—the broken homes, the deserted children, the faithless wives, the young girls going on the street—and it is more effective than shouting.

In his discussion, Davis uses "Like a Winding Sheet" as one example to support his assertions. Do you agree with him that the muted voice Petry uses in this story is "more effective than shouting," or do you believe that "shouting" would have conveyed Petry's point more effectively? How might she have "shouted" in this story?

Related Works: "Barn Burning" (p. 226), "Fleur" (p. 426), "Bartleby the Scrivener" (p. 520), "Harlem" (p. 808), *Trifles* (p. 1163), *Florence* (p. 1183)

◆ **CHARLES BAXTER** (1947–   ) was born in Minneapolis and educated at Macalester College and at the State University of New York, Buffalo. He is currently a professor of English at the University of Michigan. Baxter is the author of three critically praised collections of short stories: *Harmony of the World* (1984), *Through the Safety Net* (1985), and *A Relative Stranger: Stories* (1990). His most recent collection of short fiction is *Believers: A Novella and*

Stories (1997). He is the author of two novels, *First Light* (1987) and *Shadow Play* (1993), and one book of poetry, *Imaginary Paintings and Other Poems* (1989). Baxter has also written a book of nonfiction, *Burning Down the House* (1997), a collection of essays on fiction.

Baxter's critics often mention the compassion he shows in writing about his fictional characters: a couple who lose their child, a hospital worker who wants to be famous, a tired businessman who really wants to paint. In many of the short stories in *Through the Safety Net* (from which "Gryphon" is taken), unexpected events jar Baxter's characters out of their routines—forcing them to consider different choices, to call on inner strength, or to swim against the tide of "middle America's" conventions.

Cultural Context ◈   The tarot, a system of interpreting symbols on seventy-eight cards in relation to the future or current life influences, has its roots in ancient sacred rituals. References to tarot cards appear in European history from the mid-1300s (as well as in "Gryphon," where they are important to the plot). The skeletal figure on card 13, the "Death card," represents a transition to a new state, a death—not necessarily a physical death—in order to give birth to the new.

◈ ◈ ◈

CHARLES BAXTER

Gryphon
(1985)

On Wednesday afternoon, between the geography lesson on ancient Egypt's hand-operated irrigation system and an art project that involved drawing a model city next to a mountain, our fourth-grade teacher, Mr. Hibler, developed a cough. This cough began with a series of muffled throat clearings and progressed to propulsive noises contained within Mr. Hibler's closed mouth. "Listen to him," Carol Peterson whispered to me. "He's gonna blow up." Mr. Hibler's laughter—dazed and infrequent— sounded a bit like his cough, but as we worked on our model cities we would look up, thinking he was enjoying a joke, and see Mr. Hibler's face turning red, his cheeks puffed out. This was not laughter. Twice he bent over, and his loose tie, like a plumb line, hung down straight from his neck as he exploded himself into a Kleenex. He would excuse himself, then go on coughing. "I'll bet you a dime," Carol Peterson whispered, "we get a substitute tomorrow."

Carol sat at the desk in front of mine and was a bad person—when she thought no one was looking she would blow her nose on notebook paper, then crumble it up and throw it into the wastebasket—but at times of crisis she spoke the truth. I knew I'd lose the dime.

"No deal," I said.

When Mr. Hibler stood us up in formation at the door just prior to the final bell, he was almost incapable of speech. "I'm sorry, boys and girls," he said. "I seem to be coming down with something."

5   "I hope you feel better tomorrow, Mr. Hibler," Bobby Kryzanowicz, the faultless brown-noser said, and I heard Carol Peterson's evil giggle. Then Mr. Hibler opened the door and we walked out to the buses, a clique of us starting noisily to hawk and cough as soon as we thought we were a few feet beyond Mr. Hibler's earshot.

Five Oaks being a rural community, and in Michigan, the supply of substitute teachers was limited to the town's unemployed community college graduates, a pool of about four mothers. These ladies fluttered, provided easeful class days, and nervously covered material we had mastered weeks earlier. Therefore it was a surprise when a woman we had never seen came into the class the next day, carrying a purple purse, a checkerboard lunchbox, and a few books. She put the books on one side of Mr. Hibler's desk and the lunchbox on the other, next to the Voice of Music phonograph. Three of us in the back of the room were playing with Heever, the chameleon that lived in the terrarium and on one of the plastic drapes, when she walked in.

She clapped her hands at us. "Little boys," she said, "why are you bent over together like that?" She didn't wait for us to answer. "Are you tormenting an animal? Put it back. Please sit down at your desks. I want no cabals this time of the day." We just stared at her. "Boys," she repeated, "I asked you to sit down."

I put the chameleon in his terrarium and felt my way to my desk, never taking my eyes off the woman. With white and green chalk, she had started to draw a tree on the left side of the blackboard. She didn't look usual. Furthermore, her tree was outsized, disproportionate, for some reason.

"This room needs a tree," she said, with one line drawing the suggestion of a leaf. "A large, leafy, shady, deciduous . . . oak."

10   Her fine, light hair had been done up in what I would learn years later was called a chignon, and she wore gold-rimmed glasses whose lenses seemed to have the faintest blue tint. Harold Knardahl, who sat across from me, whispered "Mars," and I nodded slowly, savoring the imminent weirdness of the day. The substitute drew another branch with an extravagant arm gesture, then turned around and said, "Good morning. I don't believe I said good morning to all you yet."

Facing us, she was no special age—an adult is an adult—but her face had two prominent lines, descending vertically from the sides of her mouth to her chin. I knew where I had seen those lines before: *Pinocchio*. They were marionette lines. "You may stare at me," she said to us, as a few more kids from the last bus came into the room, their eyes fixed on her, "for a few more seconds, until the bell rings. Then I will permit no more staring. Looking I will permit. Staring, no. It is impolite to stare, and a sign of bad breeding. You cannot make a social effort while staring."

Harold Knardahl did not glance at me, or nudge, but I heard him whisper "Mars" again, trying to get more mileage out of his single joke with the kids who had just come in.

When everyone was seated, the substitute teacher finished her tree, put down her chalk fastidiously on the phonograph, brushed her hands, and faced us. "Good morning," she said. "I am Miss Ferenczi, your teacher for the day. I am fairly new to your community, and I don't believe any of you know me. I will therefore start by telling you a story about myself."

While we settled back, she launched into her tale. She said her grandfather had been a Hungarian prince; her mother had been born in some place called Flanders, had been a pianist, and had played concerts for people Miss Ferenczi referred to as "crowned heads." She gave us a knowing look. "Grieg," she said, "the Norwegian master, wrote a concerto for piano that was," she paused, "my mother's triumph at her debut concert in London." Her eyes searched the ceiling. Our eyes followed. Nothing up there but ceiling tile. "For reasons that I shall not go into, my family's fortunes took us to Detroit, then north to dreadful Saginaw, and now here I am in Five Oaks, as your substitute teacher, for today, Thursday, October the eleventh. I believe it will be a good day: All the forecasts coincide. We shall start with your reading lesson. Take out your reading book. I believe it is called *Broad Horizons,* or something along those lines."

15   Jeannie Vermeesch raised her hand. Miss Ferenczi nodded at her. "Mr. Hibler always starts the day with the Pledge of Allegiance," Jeannie whined.

"Oh, does he? In that case," Miss Ferenczi said, "you must know it *very* well by now, and we certainly need not spend our time on it. No, no allegiance pledging on the premises today, by my reckoning. Not with so much sunlight coming into the room. A pledge does not suit my mood." She glanced at her watch. "Time *is* flying. Take out *Broad Horizons.*"

She disappointed us by giving us an ordinary lesson, complete with vocabulary word drills, comprehension questions, and recitation. She didn't seem to care for the material, however. She sighed every few minutes and rubbed her glasses with a frilly perfumed handkerchief that she withdrew, magician style, from her left sleeve.

After reading we moved on to arithmetic. It was my favorite time of the morning, when the lazy autumn sunlight dazzled its way through ribbons of clouds past the windows on the east side of the classroom, and crept across the linoleum floor. On the playground the first group of children, the kindergartners, were running on the quack grass just beyond the monkey bars. We were doing multiplication tables. Miss Ferenczi had made John Wazny stand up at his desk in the front row. He was supposed to go through the tables of six. From where I was sitting, I could smell the Vitalis soaked into John's plastered hair. He was doing fine until he came to six times eleven and six times twelve. "Six times eleven," he said, "is sixty-eight. Six times twelve is . . . ." He put his fingers to his head, quickly and secretly sniffed his fingertips, and said, "seventy-two." Then he sat down.

"Fine," Miss Ferenczi said. "Well now. That was very good."

20 "Miss Ferenczi!" One of the Eddy twins was waving her hand desperately in the air. "Miss Ferenczi! Miss Ferenczi!"

"Yes?"

"John said that six times eleven is sixty-eight and you said he was right!"

"*Did* I?" She gazed at the class with a jolly look breaking across her marionette's face. "Did I say that? Well, what *is* six times eleven?"

"It's sixty-six!"

25 She nodded. "Yes. So it is. But, and I know some people will not entirely agree with me, at some times it is sixty-eight."

"When? When is it sixty-eight?"

We were all waiting.

"In higher mathematics, which you children do not yet understand, six times eleven can be considered to be sixty-eight." She laughed through her nose. "In higher mathematics numbers are . . . more fluid. The only thing a number does is contain a certain amount of something. Think of water. A cup is not the only way to measure a certain amount of water, is it?" We were staring, shaking our heads. "You could use saucepans or thimbles. In either case, the water *would be the same*. Perhaps," she started again, "it would be better for you to think that six times eleven is sixty-eight only when I am in the room."

"Why is it sixty-eight," Mark Poole asked, "when you're in the room?"

30 "Because it's more interesting that way," she said, smiling very rapidly behind her blue-tinted glasses. "Besides, I'm your substitute teacher, am I not?" We all nodded. "Well, then, think of six times eleven equals sixty-eight as a substitute fact."

"A substitute fact?"

"Yes." Then she looked at us carefully. "Do you think," she asked, "that anyone is going to be hurt by a substitute fact?"

We looked back at her.

"Will the plants on the windowsill be hurt?" We glanced at them. There were sensitive plants thriving in a green plastic tray, and several wilted ferns in small clay pots. "Your dogs and cats, or your moms and dads?" She waited. "So," she concluded, "what's the problem?"

35 "But it's wrong," Janice Weber said, "isn't it?"

"What's your name, young lady?"

"Janice Weber."

"And you think it's wrong, Janice?"

"I was just asking."

40 "Well, all right. You were just asking. I think we've spent enough time on this matter by now, don't you, class? You are free to think what you like. When your teacher, Mr. Hibler, returns, six times eleven will be sixty-six again, you can rest assured. And it will be that for the rest of your

lives in Five Oaks. Too bad, eh?" She raised her eyebrows and glinted her-self at us. "But for now, it wasn't. So much for that. Let us go to your as-signed problems for today, as painstakingly outlined, I see, in Mr. Hibler's lesson plan. Take out a sheet of paper and write your names in the upper left-hand corner."

For the next half hour we did the rest of our arithmetic problems. We handed them in and went on to spelling, my worst subject. Spelling always came before lunch. We were taking spelling dictation and looking at the clock. "Thorough," Miss Ferenczi said. "Boundary." She walked in the aisles between the desks, holding the spelling book open and looking down at our papers. "Balcony." I clutched my pencil. Somehow, the way she said those words, they seemed foreign, Hungarian, mis-voweled and mis-consonanted. I stared down at what I had spelled. *Balconie.* I turned my pencil upside down and erased my mistake. *Balconey.* That looked bet-ter, but still incorrect. I cursed the world of spelling and tried erasing it again and saw the paper beginning to wear away. *Balkony.* Suddenly I felt a hand on my shoulder.

"I don't like that word either," Miss Ferenczi whispered, bent over, her mouth near my ear. "It's ugly. My feeling is, if you don't like a word, you don't have to use it." She straightened up, leaving behind a slight odor of Clorets.

At lunchtime we went out to get our trays of sloppy joes, peaches in heavy syrup, coconut cookies, and milk, and brought them back to the classroom, where Miss Ferenczi was sitting at the desk, eating a brown sticky thing she had unwrapped from tightly rubber-banded wax paper. "Miss Ferenczi," I said, raising my hand. "You don't have to eat with us. You can eat with the other teachers. There's a teachers' lounge," I ended up, "next to the principal's office."

"No, thank you," she said. "I prefer it here."

45   "We've got a room monitor," I said. "Mrs. Eddy." I pointed to where Mrs. Eddy, Joyce and Judy's mother, sat silently at the back of the room, doing her knitting.

"That's fine," Miss Ferenczi said. "But I shall continue to eat here, with you children. I prefer it," she repeated.

"How come?" Wayne Razmer asked without raising his hand.

"I talked with the other teachers before class this morning," Miss Fer-enczi said, biting into her brown food. "There was a great rattling of the words for the fewness of ideas. I didn't care for their brand of hilarity. I don't like ditto machine jokes."

"Oh," Wayne said.

50   "What's that you're eating?" Maxine Sylvester asked, twitching her nose. "Is it food?"

"It most certainly *is* food. It's a stuffed fig. I had to drive almost down to Detroit to get it. I also bought some smoked sturgeon. And this," she said, lifting some green leaves out of her lunchbox, "is raw spinach, cleaned this morning before I came out here to the Garfield-Murry school."

"Why're you eating raw spinach?" Maxine asked.

"It's good for you," Miss Ferenczi said. "More stimulating than soda pop or smelling salts." I bit into my sloppy joe and stared blankly out the window. An almost invisible moon was faintly silvered in the daytime autumn sky. "As far as food is concerned," Miss Ferenczi was saying, "you have to shuffle the pack. Mix it up. Too many people eat . . . well, never mind."

"Miss Ferenczi," Carol Peterson said, "what are we going to do this afternoon?"

55   "Well," she said, looking down at Mr. Hibler's lesson plan, "I see that your teacher, Mr. Hibler, has you scheduled for a unit on the Egyptians." Carol groaned. "Yessss," Miss Ferenczi continued, "that is what we will do: the Egyptians. A remarkable people. Almost as remarkable as the Americans. But not quite." She lowered her head, did her quick smile, and went back to eating her spinach.

After noon recess we came back into the classroom and saw that Miss Ferenczi had drawn a pyramid on the blackboard, close to her oak tree. Some of us who had been playing baseball were messing around in the back of the room, dropping the bats and the gloves into the playground box, and I think that Ray Schontzeler had just slugged me when I heard Miss Ferenczi's high-pitched voice quavering with emotion. "Boys," she said, "come to order right this minute and take your seats. I do not wish to waste a minute of class time. Take out your geography books." We trudged to our desks and, still sweating, pulled out *Distant Lands and Their People.* "Turn to page forty-two." She waited for thirty seconds, then looked over at Kelly Munger. "Young man," she said, "why are you still fossicking in your desk?"

Kelly looked as if his foot had been stepped on. "Why am I what?"

"Why are you . . . burrowing in your desk like that?"

"I'm lookin' for the book, Miss Ferenczi."

60   Bobby Kryzanowicz, the faultless brown-noser who sat in the first row by choice, softly said, "His name is Kelly Munger. He can't ever find his stuff. He always does that."

"I don't care what his name is, especially after lunch," Miss Ferenczi said. *"Where is your book?"*

"I just found it." Kelly was peering into his desk and with both hands pulled at the book, shoveling along in front of it several pencils and crayons, which fell into his lap and then to the floor.

"I hate a mess," Miss Ferenczi said. "I hate a mess in a desk or a mind. It's . . . unsanitary. You wouldn't want your house at home to look like your desk at school, now, would you?" She didn't wait for an answer. "I should think not. A house at home should be as neat as human hands can make it. What were we talking about? Egypt. Page forty-two. I note from Mr. Hibler's lesson plan that you have been discussing the modes of Egyptian irrigation. Interesting, in my view, but not so interesting as what we are about to cover. The pyramids and Egyptian slave labor. A plus on one side, a minus on the other." We had our books open to page forty-two, where there was a picture of a pyramid, but Miss Ferenczi wasn't looking at the book. Instead, she was staring at some object just outside the window.

"Pyramids," Miss Ferenczi said, still looking past the window. "I want you to think about the pyramids. And what was inside. The bodies of the pharaohs, of course, and their attendant treasures. Scrolls. Perhaps," Miss Ferenczi said, with something gleeful but unsmiling in her face, "these scrolls were novels for the pharaohs, helping them to pass the time in their long voyage through the centuries. But then, I am joking." I was looking at the lines on Miss Ferenczi's face. "Pyramids," Miss Ferenczi went on, "were the repositories of special cosmic powers. The nature of a pyramid is to guide cosmic energy forces into a concentrated point. The Egyptians knew that; we have generally forgotten it. Did you know," she asked, walking to the side of the room so that she was standing by the coat closet, "that George Washington had Egyptian blood, from his grandmother? Certain features of the Constitution of the United States are notable for their Egyptian ideas."

65   Without glancing down at the book, she began to talk about the movement of souls in Egyptian religion. She said that when people die, their souls return to Earth in the form of carpenter ants or walnut trees, depending on how they behaved—"well or ill"—in life. She said that the Egyptians believed that people act the way they do because of magnetism produced by tidal forces in the solar system, forces produced by the sun and by its "planetary ally," Jupiter. Jupiter, she said, was a planet, as we had been told, but had "certain properties of stars." She was speaking very fast. She said that the Egyptians were great explorers and conquerors. She said that the greatest of all the conquerors, Genghis Khan, had had forty horses and forty young women killed on the site of his grave. We listened. No one tried to stop her. "I myself have been in Egypt," she said, "and have witnessed much dust and many brutalities." She said that an old man in Egypt who worked for a circus had personally shown her an animal in a cage, a monster, half bird and half lion. She said that this monster was called a gryphon and that she had heard about them but never seen them until she traveled to the outskirts of Cairo. She said that Egyptian astronomers had discovered the planet Saturn, but had not seen its rings. She said that the Egyptians were the first to discover that dogs, when they are ill, will not drink from rivers, but wait for rain, and hold their jaws open to catch it.

"She lies."

We were on the school bus home. I was sitting next to Carl Whiteside, who had bad breath and a huge collection of marbles. We were arguing. Carl thought she was lying. I said she wasn't, probably.

"I didn't believe that stuff about the bird," Carl said, "and what she told us about the pyramids? I didn't believe that either. She didn't know what she was talking about."

"Oh yeah?" I had liked her. She was strange. I thought I could nail him. "If she was lying," I said, "what'd she say that was a lie?"

70 "Six times eleven isn't sixty-eight. It isn't ever. It's sixty-six, I know for a fact."

"She said so. She admitted it. What else did she lie about?"

"I don't know," he said. "Stuff."

"What stuff?"

"Well." He swung his legs back and forth. "You ever see an animal that was half lion and half bird?" He crossed his arms. "It sounded real fakey to me."

75 "It could happen," I said. I had to improvise, to outrage him. "I read in this newspaper my mom bought in the IGA about this scientist, this mad scientist in the Swiss Alps, and he's been putting genes and chromosomes and stuff together in test tubes, and he combined a human being and a hamster." I waited, for effect. "It's called a humster."

"You never." Carl was staring at me, his mouth open, his terrible bad breath making its way toward me. "What newspaper was it?"

"The *National Enquirer*," I said, "that they sell next to the cash registers." When I saw his look of recognition, I knew I had bested him. "And this mad scientist," I said, "his name was, um, Dr. Frankenbush." I realized belatedly that this name was a mistake and waited for Carl to notice its resemblance to the name of the other famous mad master of permutations, but he only sat there.

"A man and a hamster?" He was staring at me, squinting, his mouth opening in distaste. "Jeez. What'd it look like?"

When the bus reached my stop, I took off down our dirt road and ran up through the back yard, kicking the tire swing for good luck. I dropped my books on the back steps so I could hug and kiss our dog, Mr. Selby. Then I hurried inside. I could smell Brussels sprouts cooking, my unfavorite vegetable. My mother was washing other vegetables in the kitchen sink, and my baby brother was hollering in his yellow playpen on the kitchen floor.

80 "Hi, Mom," I said, hopping around the playpen to kiss her, "Guess what?"

"I have no idea."

"We had this substitute today, Miss Ferenczi, and I'd never seen her before, and she had all these stories and ideas and stuff."

"Well. That's good." My mother looked out the window behind the sink, her eyes on the pine woods west of our house. Her face and hairstyle always reminded other people of Betty Crocker, whose picture was framed inside a gigantic spoon on the side of the Bisquick box; to me, though, my mother's face just looked white. "Listen, Tommy," she said, "go upstairs and pick your clothes off the bathroom floor, then go outside to the shed and put the shovel and ax away that your father left outside this morning."

"She said that six times eleven was sometimes sixty-eight!" I said. "And she said she once saw a monster that was half lion and half bird." I waited. "In Egypt, she said."

85 "Did you hear me?" my mother asked, raising her arm to wipe her forehead with the back of her hand. "You have chores to do."

"I know," I said. "I was just telling you about the substitute."

"It's very interesting," my mother said, quickly glancing down at me, "and we can talk about it later when your father gets home. But right now you have some work to do."

"Okay, Mom." I took a cookie out of the jar on the counter and was about to go outside when I had a thought. I ran into the living room, pulled out a dictionary next to the TV stand, and opened it to the G's. *Gryphon:* "variant of griffin." *Griffin:* "a fabulous beast with the head and wings of an eagle and the body of a lion." Fabulous was right. I shouted with triumph and ran outside to put my father's tools back in their place.

Miss Ferenczi was back the next day, slightly altered. She had pulled her hair down and twisted it into pigtails, with red rubber bands holding them tight one inch from the ends. She was wearing a green blouse and pink scarf, making her difficult to look at for a full class day. This time there was no pretense of doing a reading lesson or moving on to arithmetic. As soon as the bell rang, she simply began to talk.

90 She talked for forty minutes straight. There seemed to be less connection between her ideas, but the ideas themselves were, as the dictionary would say, fabulous. She said she had heard of a huge jewel, in what she called the Antipodes, that was so brilliant that when the light shone into it at a certain angle it would blind whoever was looking at its center. She said that the biggest diamond in the world was cursed and had killed everyone who owned it, and that by a trick of fate it was called the Hope diamond. Diamonds are magic, she said, and this is why women wear them on their fingers, as a sign of the magic of womanhood. Men have strength, Miss Ferenczi said, but no true magic. That is why men fall in love with women but women do not fall in love with men; they just love being loved. George Washington had died because of a mistake he made about a diamond. Washington was not the first *true* President, but she did not say who was. In some places in the world, she said, men and women still live in the trees and eat monkeys for breakfast. Their doctors are magicians. At the bottom of the sea are creatures thin as pancakes which have never been studied by scientists because when you take them up to the air, the fish explode.

There was not a sound in the classroom, except for Miss Ferenczi's voice, and Donna DeShano's coughing. No one even went to the bathroom.

Beethoven, she said, had not been deaf; it was a trick to make himself famous, and it worked. As she talked, Miss Ferenczi's pigtails swung back and forth. There are trees in the world, she said, that eat meat: their leaves are sticky and close up on bugs like hands. She lifted her hands and brought them together, palm to palm. Venus, which most people think is the next closest planet to the sun, is not always closer, and, besides, it is the planet of greatest mystery because of its thick cloud cover. "I know what lies underneath those clouds," Miss Ferenczi said, and waited. After the silence, she said, "Angels. Angels live under those clouds." She said that angels were not invisible to everyone and were in fact smarter than most people. They did not dress in robes as was often claimed but instead wore formal evening clothes, as if they were about to attend a concert. Often angels *do* attend concerts and sit in the aisles where, she said, most people pay no attention to them. She said the most terrible angel had the shape of the Sphinx. "There is no running away from that one," she said. She said that unquenchable fires burn just under the surface of the earth in Ohio, and that the baby Mozart fainted dead away in his cradle when he first heard the sound of a trumpet. She said that someone named Narzim al Harrardim was the greatest writer who ever lived. She said that planets control behavior, and anyone conceived during a solar eclipse would be born with webbed feet.

"I know you children like to hear these things," she said, "these secrets, and that is why I am telling you all this." We nodded. It was better than doing comprehension questions for the readings in *Broad Horizons*.

"I will tell you one more story," she said, "and then we will have to do arithmetic." She leaned over, and her voice grew soft. "There is no death," she said. "You must never be afraid. Never. That which is, cannot die. It will change into different earthly and unearthly elements, but I know this as sure as I stand here in front of you, and I swear it: you must not be afraid. I have seen this truth with these eyes. I know it because in a dream God kissed me. Here." And she pointed with her right index finger to the side of her head, below the mouth, where the vertical lines were carved into her skin.

95 Absent-mindedly we all did our arithmetic problems. At recess the class was out on the playground, but no one was playing. We were all standing in small groups, talking about Miss Ferenczi. We didn't know if she was crazy, or what. I looked out beyond the playground, at the rusted cars piled in a small heap behind a clump of sumac, and I wanted to see shapes there, approaching me.

On the way home, Carl sat next to me again. He didn't say much, and I didn't either. At last he turned to me. "You know what she said about the leaves that close up on bugs?"

"Huh?"

"The leaves," Carl insisted. "The meat-eating plants. I know it's true. I saw it on television. The leaves have this icky glue that the plants have got smeared all over them and the insects can't get off 'cause they're stuck. I saw it." He seemed demoralized. "She's tellin' the truth."

"Yeah."

100   "You think she's seen all those angels?"

I shrugged.

"I don't think she has," Carl informed me. "I think she made that part up."

"There's a tree," I suddenly said. I was looking out the window at the farms along County Road H. I knew every barn, every broken windmill, every fence, every anhydrous ammonia tank, by heart. "There's a tree that's . . . that I've seen . . ."

"Don't you try to do it," Carl said. "You'll just sound like a jerk."

105   I kissed my mother. She was standing in front of the stove. "How was your day?" she asked.

"Fine."

"Did you have Miss Ferenczi again?"

"Yeah."

"Well?"

110   "She was fine. Mom," I asked, "can I go to my room?"

"No," she said, "not until you've gone out to the vegetable garden and picked me a few tomatoes." She glanced at the sky. "I think it's going to rain. Skedaddle and do it now. Then you come back inside and watch your brother for a few minutes while I go upstairs. I need to clean up before dinner." She looked down at me. "You're looking a little pale, Tommy." She touched the back of her hand to my forehead and I felt her diamond ring against my skin. "Do you feel all right?"

"I'm fine," I said, and went out to pick the tomatoes.

Coughing mutedly, Mr. Hibler was back the next day, slipping lozenges into his mouth when his back was turned at forty-five minute intervals and asking us how much of the prepared lesson plan Miss Ferenczi had followed. Edith Atwater took the responsibility for the class of explaining to Mr. Hibler that the substitute hadn't always done exactly what he would have done, but we had worked hard even though she talked a lot. About what? he asked. All kinds of things, Edith said. I sort of forgot. To our relief, Mr. Hibler seemed not at all interested in what Miss Ferenczi had said to fill the day. He probably thought it was woman's talk; unserious and not suited for school. It was enough that he had a pile of arithmetic problems from us to correct.

For the next month, the sumac turned a distracting red in the field, and the sun traveled toward the southern sky, so that its rays reached Mr. Hibler's Halloween display on the bulletin board in the back of the room, fading the scarecrow with a pumpkin head from orange to tan. Every three days I measured how much farther the sun had moved toward the southern horizon by making small marks with my black Crayola on the north wall, ant-sized marks only I knew were there, inching west.

115   And then in early December, four days after the first permanent snowfall, she appeared again in our classroom. The minute she came in the door, I felt my heart begin to pound. Once again, she was different: this time, her

hair hung straight down and seemed hardly to have been combed. She hadn't brought her lunchbox with her, but she was carrying what seemed to be a small box. She greeted all of us and talked about the weather. Donna DeShano had to remind her to take her overcoat off.

When the bell to start the day finally rang, Miss Ferenczi looked out at all of us and said, "Children, I have enjoyed your company in the past, and today I am going to reward you." She held up the small box. "Do you know what this is?" She waited. "Of course you don't. It is a tarot pack."

Edith Atwater raised her hand. "What's a tarot pack, Miss Ferenczi?"

"It is used to tell fortunes," she said. "And that is what I shall do this morning. I shall tell your fortunes, as I have been taught to do."

"What's fortune?" Bobby Kryzanowicz asked.

120   "The future, young man. I shall tell you what your future will be. I can't do your whole future, of course. I shall have to limit myself to the five-card system, the wands, cups, swords, pentacles, and the higher arcanes. Now who wants to be first?"

There was a long silence. Then Carol Peterson raised her hand.

"All right," Miss Ferenczi said. She divided the pack into five smaller packs and walked back to Carol's desk, in front of mine. "Pick one card from each of these packs," she said. I saw that Carol had a four of cups, a six of swords, but I couldn't see the other cards. Miss Ferenczi studied the cards on Carol's desk for a minute. "Not bad," she said. "I do not see much higher education. Probably an early marriage. Many children. There's something bleak and dreary here, but I can't tell what. Perhaps just the tasks of a housewife life. I think you'll do very well, for the most part." She smiled at Carol, a smile with a certain lack of interest. "Who wants to be next?"

Carl Whiteside raised his hand slowly.

"Yes," Miss Ferenczi said, "let's do a boy." She walked over to where Carl sat. After he picked his five cards, she gazed at them for a long time. "Travel," she said. "Much distant travel. You might go into the Army. Not too much romantic interest here. A late marriage, if at all. Squabbles. But the Sun is in your major arcana, here, yes, that's a very good card." She giggled. "Maybe a good life."

125   Next I raised my hand, and she told me my future. She did the same with Bobby Kryzanowicz. Kelly Munger, Edith Atwater, and Kim Foor. Then she came to Wayne Razmer. He picked his five cards, and I could see that the Death card was one of them.

"What's your name?" Miss Ferenczi asked.

"Wayne."

"Well, Wayne," she said, you will undergo a *great* metamorphosis, the greatest, before you become an adult. Your earthly element will leap away, into thin air, you sweet boy. This card, this nine of swords here, tells of suffering and desolation. And this ten of wands, well, that's certainly a heavy load."

"What about this one?" Wayne pointed to the Death card.

130 "That one? That one means you will die soon, my dear." She gathered
up the cards. We were all looking at Wayne. "But do not fear," she said.
"It's not really death, so much as change." She put the cards on Mr. Hibler's desk. "And now, let's do some arithmetic."

At lunchtime Wayne went to Mr. Faegre, the principal, and told him
what Miss Ferenczi had done. During the noon recess, we saw Miss Ferenczi
drive out of the parking lot in her green Rambler. I stood under the slide,
listening to the other kids coasting down and landing in the little depres-
sive bowl at the bottom. I was kicking stones and tugging at my hair right
up to the moment when I saw Wayne come out to the playground. He
smiled, the dead fool, and with the fingers of his right hand he was showing everyone how he had told on Miss Ferenczi.

I made my way toward Wayne, pushing myself past two girls from another class. He was watching me with his little pinhead eyes.

"You told," I shouted at him. "She was just kidding."

"She shouldn't have," he shouted back. "We were supposed to be doing
arithmetic."

135 "She just scared you," I said. "You're a chicken. You're a chicken,
Wayne. You are. Scared of a little card," I singsonged.

Wayne fell at me, his two fists hammering down on my nose. I gave
him a good one in the stomach and then I tried for his head. Aiming my
fist, I saw that he was crying. I slugged him.

"She was right," I yelled. "She was always right! She told the truth!"
Other kids were whooping. "You were just scared, that's all!"

And then large hands pulled at us, and it was my turn to speak to
Mr. Faegre.

In the afternoon Miss Ferenczi was gone, and my nose was stuffed
with cotton clotted with blood, and my lip had swelled, and our class had
been combined with Mrs. Mantei's sixth-grade class for a crowded afternoon science unit on insect life in ditches and swamps. I knew where Mrs.
Mantei lived: she had a new house trailer just down the road from us, at
the Clearwater Park. She was no mystery. Somehow she and Mr. Bodine,
the other fourth-grade teacher, had managed to fit forty-five desks into
the room. Kelly Munger asked if Miss Ferenczi had been arrested, and Mrs.
Mantei said no, of course not. All that afternoon, until the buses came to
pick us up, we learned about field crickets and two-striped grasshoppers,
water bugs, cicadas, mosquitoes, flies, and moths. We learned about insects' hard outer shell, the exoskeleton, and the usual parts of the mouth,
including the labrum, mandible, maxilla, and glossa. We learned about
compound eyes and the four-stage metamorphosis from egg to larva to
pupa to adult. We learned something, but not much, about mating. Mrs.
Mantei drew, very skillfully, the internal anatomy of the grasshopper on
the blackboard. We learned about the dance of the honeybee, directing
other bees in the hive to pollen. We found out about which insects were
pests to man, and which were not. On lined white pieces of paper we made

lists of insects we might actually see, then a list of insects too small to be clearly visible, such as fleas; Mrs. Mantei said that our assignment would be to memorize these lists for the next day, when Mr. Hibler would certainly return and test us on our knowledge.

READING AND REACTING

1. In classical mythology a gryphon (also spelled *griffin*) is a monster that has the head and wings of an eagle and the body of a lion. Why is this story called "Gryphon"?
2. Describe Miss Ferenczi's physical appearance. Why is her appearance important to the story? How does it change as the story progresses?
3. How is Miss Ferenczi different from other teachers? From other substitute teachers? From other people in general? How is her differentness communicated to her pupils? To the story's readers?
4. What is the significance of the narrator's comment, in paragraph 11, that the lines on Miss Ferenczi's face remind him of Pinocchio?
5. Is Miss Ferenczi a round or a flat character? Explain.
6. In what sense is the narrator's mother a foil for Miss Ferenczi?
7. Why does the narrator defend Miss Ferenczi, first in his argument with Carl Whiteside and later on the playground? What does his attitude toward Miss Ferenczi reveal about his character?
8. Are all of Miss Ferenczi's "substitute facts" lies, or is there some truth in what she says? Is she correct when she says that substitute facts cannot hurt anyone? Could it be argued that much of what is taught in schools today could be viewed as "substitute facts"? Explain.
9. **JOURNAL ENTRY** Is Miss Ferenczi a good teacher? Why or why not?
10. **CRITICAL PERSPECTIVE** Writing in the *New York Times Book Review*, critic William Ferguson characterizes *A Relative Stranger*, a more recent collection of Baxter's short stories than the one in which "Gryphon" appeared, as follows:

    > The thirteen stories in *A Relative Stranger*, all quietly accomplished, suggest a mysterious yet fundamental marriage of despair and joy. Though in one way or another each story ends in disillusionment, the road that leads to that dismal state is so richly peopled, so finely drawn, that the effect is oddly reassuring.

    Do you think this characterization of Baxter's work in *A Relative Stranger* applies to "Gryphon" as well? For example, how are despair and joy joined? Do you find the story reassuring in any way, or does it convey only the sense of disillusionment?

Related Works: "The Secret Lion" (p. 49), "A&P" (p. 113), "A Worn Path" (p. 388), "When I Heard the Learn'd Astronomer" (p. 762), "On First Looking into Chapman's Homer" (p. 868)

◆ WRITING SUGGESTIONS: CHARACTER

1. Focusing on an unconventional character in a conventional setting, "Gryphon" explores the question of what constitutes a good education. Taking into account your own school experiences as well as those of the students in the story, write an essay in which you discuss what you believe the purpose of education should (and should not) be.

2. In "A&P," "Like a Winding Sheet," and "Gryphon," characters struggle against rules, authority figures, and inflexible social systems. Choose two of these stories, and compare and contrast the struggles in which the characters are engaged.

3. Write an essay in which you contrast the character of Miss Brill with the character of Phoenix Jackson in "A Worn Path" (Chapter 10). Consider how each character interacts with those around her as well as how each seems to see her role or mission in the world.

4. Write a letter from Mae to Johnson in which you reveal information about her character that does not appear in "Like a Winding Sheet." What is her typical day like? What frustrations does *she* experience? Does she too feel a sense of rage? Conclude the letter by explaining what she plans to do now, as she recovers physically and emotionally. Will she leave Johnson or stay with him?

5. Sammy, Miss Brill, and Miss Ferenczi all use their active imaginations to create scenarios that help get them through the day. None of them is able to sustain the illusion, however. As a result, all three find out how harsh reality can be. What steps could these three characters take to fit more comfortably into the worlds they inhabit? *Should* they take such steps? Are they able to do so?

6. **WEB ACTIVITY** The following Web site contains information about Ann Petry:

   http://voices.cla.umn.edu/authors/AnnPetry.html

   After reading the excerpt from Petry's novel *The Street* reprinted on that Web page, write an essay in which you examine how Petry portrays the tensions that result between black men and women who endure prejudice and discrimination. Use Petry's story "Like a Winding Sheet" and the excerpt from *The Street* as support as you discuss how Petry illustrates the effect of racism on male-female relationships. Consider both the alienation depicted in the excerpt and the violence shown in the short story.

CHAPTER 6

Setting

◇ ◇ ◇

Many authors find it hard to write about new environments that they did
not know in childhood. The voices reheard from childhood have a truer
pitch. And the foliage—the trees of childhood—are remembered more
exactly. When I work from within a different locale from the South, I have
to wonder what time the flowers are in bloom—and what flowers? I hardly
let characters speak unless they are Southern.

    CARSON MCCULLERS, "The Flowering Dream"

I think that the sense of place is extremely important to most writers.
Certainly it is to me. I identify very strongly with places where I have lived,
where I have been, where I have invested some part of my being. . . . The
earth was here before I was. When I came, I simply identified place by living
in it or looking at it. One does create place in the same way that the
storyteller creates himself, creates his listener. The writer creates a place.

    N. SCOTT MOMADAY, *Ancestral Voices*

We all know that the weather affects our moods. The [writer] is in the happy
position of being able to invent whatever weather is appropriate to the mood
he or she wants to evoke.
    Weather is therefore frequently a trigger for the effect John Ruskin called
the pathetic fallacy, the projection of human emotions onto phenomena in
the natural world. "All violent feelings [. . .] produce in us a falseness in our
impressions of external things, which I would generally characterize as the
pathetic fallacy," he wrote. As the name implies, Ruskin thought it was a bad
thing, a symptom of the decadence of modern (as compared to classical)
art and literature, and it is indeed often the occasion of overblown,
self-indulgent writing. But used with intelligence and discretion it is a
rhetorical device capable of moving and powerful effects, without which
fiction would be much the poorer.

    DAVID LODGE, *The Art of Fiction*

◇ ◇ ◇

The **setting** of a work of fiction establishes its historical, geographical, and physical location. *Where* a work is set—on a tropical island, in a dungeon, at a crowded party, in a tent in the woods—influences our interpretation of the story's events and characters. *When* a work takes place—during the French Revolution, during the Vietnam War, today, or in the future—is equally important. Setting, however, is more than just the approximate time and place in which the work is set; setting also encompasses a wide variety of physical and cultural elements.

Clearly, setting is more important in some works than in others. In some stories, no particular time or place is specified, or even suggested, perhaps because the writer does not consider a specific setting to be important or because the writer wishes the story's events to seem timeless and universal. In Nadine Gordimer's "Once upon a Time" (p. 81), for example, the writer follows the conventions of fairy tales, which are set in unidentified, faraway places. In other stories, a writer may provide only minimal information about setting, telling readers little more than where and when the action takes place. Sometimes, however, a particular setting may be vital to the story, perhaps influencing characters' behavior, as it does in Charlotte Perkins Gilman's "The Yellow Wall-Paper" (p. 168). In such cases, of course, setting must be fully described.

Sometimes a story's central conflict is between the protagonist and the setting—for example, Alice in Wonderland; a northerner in the South; a naive, unsophisticated American tourist in an old European city; a sane person in a mental hospital; a moral person in a corrupt environment; an immigrant in a new world; or a city dweller in the country. This conflict helps to define the characters as well as drive the plot. (A conflict between events and setting—for example, the intrusion of nuclear war into a typical suburban neighborhood, the intrusion of modern social ideas into an old-fashioned world, or the intrusion of a brutal, senseless murder into a peaceful English village—can also enrich a story.)

HISTORICAL SETTING
◊ ◊ ◊

A particular historical period, and the events associated with it, can be important in a story; therefore, some familiarity with a period can be useful (or even essential) to readers who wish to understand a story fully. Historical context establishes a social, cultural, economic, and political environment. Knowing, for instance, that "The Yellow Wall-Paper" was written in the late nineteenth century, when doctors treated women as delicate and dependent creatures, helps to explain the narrator's emotional state. Likewise, it may be important to know that a story is set during a particularly volatile (or static) political era, during a time of permissive (or repressive) attitudes toward sex, during a war, or during a period of economic prosperity or recession. Any one of these factors may determine—or help to explain—characters' actions. Historical events or cultural norms may, for instance, limit or expand a character's options, and our knowledge of history may reveal to us a character's incompatibility with his or her milieu. In F. Scott Fitzgerald's "Bernice Bobs Her Hair," set in the 1920s in a midwestern town, a young girl is goaded into cutting her long hair. To understand the significance of Bernice's act— and to understand the reactions of others to that act—readers must know that during that era only racy "society vampires," not nice girls from good families, bobbed their hair.

Knowing the approximate year or historical period during which a story takes place can explain forces that act on characters, help to account for their behavior, clarify circumstances that influence the story's action, and help to justify a writer's use of plot devices that might otherwise seem improbable. For instance, stories set before the development of modern transportation and communication systems may hinge on plot devices readers would not accept in a modern story. Thus, in "Paul's Case," a 1904 story by Willa Cather, a young man who steals a large sum of money in Pittsburgh is able to spend several days enjoying it before the news of the theft reaches New York, where he has fled. In other stories we see such outdated plot devices as characters threatened by diseases that have now been eradicated (and subjected to outdated medical or psychiatric treatment). In addition, characters may be constrained by social conventions different from those that operate in our own society.

GEOGRAPHICAL SETTING
❖ ❖ ❖

In addition to knowing when a work takes place, readers need to know *where* it takes place. Knowing whether a story is set in the United States, in Europe, or in a developing nation can help to explain anything from why language and customs are unfamiliar to us to why characters act in ways we find improbable. Even in stories set in our own country, regional differences may account for differences in plot development and characters' motivation. For example, knowing that William Faulkner's "A Rose for Emily" (p. 87) is set in the post–Civil War American South helps to explain why the townspeople are so chivalrously protective of Miss Emily. Similarly, the fact that Bret Harte's "The Outcasts of Poker Flat" is set in the American West accounts for its unusual cast of characters—including a gambler, a prostitute, and a traveling salesman.

The size of the town or city in which a story takes place may also be important. In a small town, for example, a character's problems are more likely to be subject to intense scrutiny by other characters, as they are in stories of small-town life such as those in Sherwood Anderson's *Winesburg, Ohio*. In a large city, characters may be more likely to be isolated and anonymous, like Mrs. Miller in Truman Capote's "Miriam," who is so lonely that she creates an imaginary companion. Characters may also be alienated by their big-city surroundings, as Gregor Samsa is in Franz Kafka's "The Metamorphosis" (p. 474).

Of course, a story may not have a recognizable geographical setting; its location may not be specified, and it may even be set in a fantasy world. Such settings may free writers from the constraints placed on them by familiar environments, allowing them to experiment with situations and characters, unaffected by readers' expectations or associations with familiar settings.

PHYSICAL SETTING

◊ ◊ ◊

The *time of day* can clearly influence a story's mood as well as its development. The gruesome murder described in Edgar Allan Poe's "The Cask of Amontillado" (p. 219) takes place in an appropriate setting: not just underground, but in the darkness of night. Conversely, the horrifying events of Shirley Jackson's "The Lottery" (p. 315) take place in broad daylight, contrasting dramatically with the darkness of the society that permits— and even participates in—such events. Many stories, of course, move through several time periods as the action unfolds, and changes in time may also be important. For instance, the approach of evening, or of dawn, can signal the end of a crisis in the plot.

Whether a story is set primarily *inside* or *out-of-doors* may also be significant. The characters may be physically constrained by a closed-in setting or liberated by an expansive landscape. Some interior settings may be psychologically limiting. For instance, the narrator in "The Yellow Wall-Paper" feels suffocated by her room, whose ugly wallpaper comes to haunt her. In many of Poe's stories, the central character is trapped, physically or psychologically, in a confined, suffocating space. In other stories, an interior setting may serve a symbolic function. For instance, in "A Rose for Emily" the house is for Miss Emily a symbol of the South's past glory as well as a refuge, a fortress, and a hiding place. Similarly, a building or house may represent society, with its rules and norms and limitations. In John Updike's "A&P" (p. 113), for instance, the supermarket establishes social as well as physical limits. This is also the case in Katherine Mansfield's "Her First Ball," where a ballroom serves as the setting for a young girl's initiation into the rules and realities of adult society.

Conversely, an outdoor setting can free a character from social norms of behavior, as it does for Ernest Hemingway's Nick Adams, a war veteran who, in "Big Two-Hearted River," finds order, comfort, and peace only when he is away from civilization. An outdoor setting can also expose characters to physical dangers, such as untamed wilderness, uncharted seas, and frighteningly empty open spaces.

Weather can be another important aspect of setting. A storm can threaten a character's life or just make the character—and readers—*think* danger is present, distracting us from other, more subtle threats. Extreme weather conditions can make characters act irrationally or uncharacteristically, as in Kate Chopin's "The Storm" (p. 154), where a storm provides the complication and determines the characters' actions. In numerous stories set in hostile landscapes, where extremes of heat and cold influence the action, weather may pose a test for characters, as in Jack London's "To Build a Fire," in which the main character struggles unsuccessfully against a brutally cold, hostile environment.

The various physical attributes of setting combine to create a story's **atmosphere** or **mood.** In "The Cask of Amontillado," for example, several factors work together to create the eerie, intense atmosphere appropriate to the story's events: it is nighttime; it is the hectic carnival season; and the catacombs are dark, damp, and filled with the bones of the narrator's ancestors. The atmosphere that is created in a story can reflect a character's mental state—for example, darkness and isolation can reflect a character's depression, whereas an idyllic, peaceful atmosphere can express a character's joy. A story's atmosphere may also *influence* the characters' reactions or state of mind, causing them to react one way in a crowded, busy, hectic atmosphere but to react very differently in a peaceful rural atmosphere. At the same time, the mood or atmosphere that is created often helps to convey a story's central theme—as the ironic contrast between the pleasant atmosphere and the horrible events that unfold communicates the theme of "The Lottery."

 # CHECKLIST: WRITING ABOUT SETTING

- ✓ Is the setting specified or unidentified? Is it fully described or just sketched in?
- ✓ Is the setting just background, or is it a key force in the story?
- ✓ How does the setting influence the characters? Does it affect (or reflect) their emotional state? Does it help to explain their motivation?
- ✓ Are any characters in conflict with their environment?
- ✓ Are any situations set in sharp contrast to the setting?
- ✓ How does the setting influence the story's plot? Does it cause characters to act?
- ✓ Does the setting add irony to the story?
- ✓ In what time period does the story take place? How can you tell? What social, political, or economic characteristics of the historical period might influence the story?
- ✓ In what geographical location is the story set? Is this location important to the story?

✓ At what time of day is the story set? Is time important to the development of the story?

✓ Is the story set primarily indoors or out-of-doors? What role does this aspect of the setting play in the story?

✓ What role do weather conditions play in the story?

✓ Is the story's general atmosphere dark or bright? Clear or murky? Tumultuous or calm? Gloomy or cheerful?

✓ Does the atmosphere change as the story progresses? Is this change significant?

◇ **KATE CHOPIN** (1851–1904) (picture and biography on p. 76) Chopin's style is realistic yet infused with a dense, sensual texture that is perhaps, in part, Chopin's artistic response to her memories of the exotic Louisiana bayou country. Like her contemporary Gustave Flaubert (Chopin's short novel *The Awakening* has often been called a "Creole *Bovary*"), Chopin used the physical world—as in the charged atmosphere of "The Storm"—to symbolize the inner truths of her characters' minds and hearts. Unlike Flaubert, however, she depicts sex not as a frantic and destructive force, but as a joyous, elemental part of life. Apparently Kate Chopin knew how daring "The Storm" was: she never submitted it for publication.

CULTURAL CONTEXT ◇   "The Storm" was not published until well after Chopin's death. Her novel *The Awakening* created such controversy that Chopin had trouble publishing afterward. Her editors even reversed their acceptance of her third collection of stories, *A Vocation and a Voice*, which was not published until 1991.

◇ ◇ ◇

KATE CHOPIN

The Storm
(c. 1899)

I

The leaves were so still that even Bibi thought it was going to rain. Bobinôt, who was accustomed to converse on terms of perfect equality with his little son, called the child's attention to certain sombre clouds that were rolling with sinister intention from the west, accompanied by a sullen, threatening roar. They were at Friedheimer's store and decided to remain there till the storm had passed. They sat within the door on two empty kegs. Bibi was four years old and looked very wise.

"Mama'll be 'fraid, yes," he suggested with blinking eyes.

"She'll shut the house. Maybe she got Sylvie helpin' her this evenin'," Bobinôt responded reassuringly.

"No; she ent got Sylvie. Sylvie was helpin' her yistiday," piped Bibi.

5   Bobinôt arose and going across to the counter purchased a can of shrimps, of which Calixta was very fond. Then he returned to his perch on the keg and sat stolidly holding the can of shrimps while the storm burst. It shook the wooden store and seemed to be ripping great furrows in the distant field. Bibi laid his little hand on his father's knee and was not afraid.

II

Calixta, at home, felt no uneasiness for their safety. She sat at a side window sewing furiously on a sewing machine. She was greatly occupied and did not notice the approaching storm. But she felt very warm and often stopped to mop her face on which the perspiration gathered in beads. She unfastened her white sacque at the throat. It began to grow dark, and suddenly realizing the situation she got up hurriedly and went about closing windows and doors.

Out on the small front gallery she had hung Bobinôt's Sunday clothes to air and she hastened out to gather them before the rain fell. As she stepped outside, Alcée Laballière rode in at the gate. She had not seen him very often since her marriage, and never alone. She stood there with Bobinôt's coat in her hands, and the big rain drops began to fall. Alcée rode his horse under the shelter of a side projection where the chickens had huddled and there were plows and a harrow piled up in the corner.

"May I come and wait on your gallery till the storm is over, Calixta?" he asked.

"Come 'long in, M'sieur Alcée."

10   His voice and her own startled her as if from a trance, and she seized Bobinôt's vest. Alcée, mounting to the porch, grabbed the trousers and snatched Bibi's braided jacket that was about to be carried away by a sudden gust of wind. He expressed an intention to remain outside, but it was soon apparent that he might as well have been out in the open: the water beat in upon the boards in driving sheets, and he went inside, closing the door after him. It was even necessary to put something beneath the door to keep the water out.

"My! what a rain! It's good two years since it rain' like that," exclaimed Calixta as she rolled up a piece of bagging and Alcée helped her to thrust it beneath the crack.

She was a little fuller of figure than five years before when she married; but she had lost nothing of her vivacity. Her blue eyes still retained their melting quality; and her yellow hair, dishevelled by the wind and rain, kinked more stubbornly than ever about her ears and temples.

The rain beat upon the low, shingled roof with a force and clatter that threatened to break an entrance and deluge them there. They were in the dining room—the sitting room—the general utility room. Adjoining was her bed room, with Bibi's couch along side her own. The door stood open, and the room with its white, monumental bed, its closed shutters, looked dim and mysterious.

Alcée flung himself into a rocker and Calixta nervously began to gather up from the floor the lengths of a cotton sheet which she had been sewing.

15   "If this keeps up, *Dieu sait*[1] if the levees[2] goin' to stan' it!" she exclaimed.

"What have you got to do with the levees?"

"I got enough to do! An' there's Bobinôt with Bibi out in that storm— if he only didn't left Friedheimer's!"

"Let us hope, Calixta, that Bobinôt's got sense enough to come in out of a cyclone."

She went and stood at the window with a greatly disturbed look on her face. She wiped the frame that was clouded with moisture. It was stiflingly hot. Alcée got up and joined her at the window, looking over her shoulder. The rain was coming down in sheets obscuring the view of far-off cabins and enveloping the distant wood in a gray mist. The playing of the lightning was incessant. A bolt struck a tall chinaberry tree at the edge of the field. It filled all visible space with a blinding glare and the crash seemed to invade the very boards they stood upon.

20   Calixta put her hands to her eyes, and with a cry, staggered backward. Alcée's arm encircled her, and for an instant he drew her close and spasmodically to him.

"*Bonté!*"[3] she cried, releasing herself from his encircling arm and retreating from the window, "the house'll go next! If I only knew w'ere Bibi was!" She would not compose herself; she would not be seated. Alcée clasped her shoulders and looked into her face. The contact of her warm, palpitating body when he had unthinkingly drawn her into his arms, had aroused all the old-time infatuation and desire for her flesh.

"Calixta," he said, "don't be frightened. Nothing can happen. The house is too low to be struck, with so many tall trees standing about. There! aren't you going to be quiet? say, aren't you?" He pushed her hair back from her face that was warm and steaming. Her lips were as red and moist as pomegranate seed. Her white neck and a glimpse of her full, firm bosom disturbed him powerfully. As she glanced up at him the fear in her liquid blue eyes had given place to a drowsy gleam that unconsciously betrayed a sensuous desire. He looked down into her eyes and there was nothing for him to do but to gather her lips in a kiss. It reminded him of Assumption.

"Do you remember—in Assumption, Calixta?" he asked in a low voice broken by passion. Oh! she remembered; for in Assumption he had kissed

---

[1] God knows.

[2] A raised embankment designed to keep a river from overflowing.

[3] "Goodness!"

her and kissed and kissed her; until his senses would well nigh fail, and to save her he would resort to a desperate flight. If she was not an immaculate dove in those days, she was still inviolate; a passionate creature whose very defenselessness had made her defense, against which his honor forbade him to prevail. Now—well, now—her lips seemed in a manner free to be tasted, as well as her round, white throat and her whiter breasts.

They did not heed the crashing torrents, and the roar of the elements made her laugh as she lay in his arms. She was a revelation in that dim, mysterious chamber; as white as the couch she lay upon. Her firm, elastic flesh that was knowing for the first time its birthright, was like a creamy lily that the sun invites to contribute its breath and perfume to the undying life of the world.

25   The generous abundance of her passion, without guile or trickery, was like a white flame which penetrated and found response in depths of his own sensuous nature that had never yet been reached.

When he touched her breasts they gave themselves up in quivering ecstasy, inviting his lips. Her mouth was a fountain of delight. And when he possessed her, they seemed to swoon together at the very borderland of life's mystery.

He stayed cushioned upon her, breathless, dazed, enervated, with his heart beating like a hammer upon her. With one hand she clasped his head, her lips lightly touching his forehead. The other hand stroked with a soothing rhythm his muscular shoulders.

The growl of the thunder was distant and passing away. The rain beat softly upon the shingles, inviting them to drowsiness and sleep. But they dared not yield.

The rain was over; and the sun was turning the glistening green world into a palace of gems. Calixta, on the gallery, watched Alcée ride away. He turned and smiled at her with a beaming face; and she lifted her pretty chin in the air and laughed aloud.

III

30 Bobinôt and Bibi, trudging home, stopped without at the cistern to make themselves presentable.

"My! Bibi, w'at will yo' mama say! You ought to be ashame'. You oughtn' put on those good pants. Look at 'em! An' that mud on yo' collar! How you got that mud on yo' collar, Bibi? I never saw such a boy!" Bibi was the picture of pathetic resignation. Bobinôt was the embodiment of serious solicitude as he strove to remove from his own person and his son's the signs of their tramp over heavy roads and through wet fields. He scraped the mud off Bibi's bare legs and feet with a stick and carefully removed all traces from his heavy brogans. Then, prepared for the worst— the meeting with an over-scrupulous housewife, they entered cautiously at the back door.

Calixta was preparing supper. She had set the table and was dripping coffee at the hearth. She sprang up as they came in.

"Oh, Bobinôt! You back! My! but I was uneasy. W'ere you been during the rain? An' Bibi? he ain't wet? he ain't hurt?" She had clasped Bibi and was kissing him effusively. Bobinôt's explanations and apologies which he had been composing all along the way, died on his lips as Calixta felt him to see if he were dry, and seemed to express nothing but satisfaction at their safe return.

"I brought you some shrimps, Calixta," offered Bobinôt, hauling the can from his ample side pocket and laying it on the table.

35   "Shrimps! Oh, Bobinôt! you too good fo' anything!" and she gave him a smacking kiss on the cheek that resounded. "*J'vous réponds,*[4] we'll have a feas' tonight! umph-umph!"

Bobinôt and Bibi began to relax and enjoy themselves, and when the three seated themselves at table they laughed much and so loud that anyone might have heard them as far away as Laballière's.

IV

Alcée Laballière wrote to his wife, Clarisse, that night. It was a loving letter, full of tender solicitude. He told her not to hurry back, but if she and the babies liked it at Biloxi, to stay a month longer. He was getting on nicely; and though he missed them, he was willing to bear the separation a while longer—realizing that their health and pleasure were the first things to be considered.

V

As for Clarisse, she was charmed upon receiving her husband's letter. She and the babies were doing well. The society was agreeable; many of her old friends and acquaintances were at the bay. And the first free breath since her marriage seemed to restore the pleasant liberty of her maiden days. Devoted as she was to her husband, their intimate conjugal life was something which she was more than willing to forego for a while.

So the storm passed and everyone was happy.

READING AND REACTING

1. Trace the progress of the storm through the five parts of the story. Then, trace the stages of the story's plot. How does the progress of the storm parallel the developing plot?
2. How does the weather help to create the story's atmosphere? How would you characterize this atmosphere?
3. In Part I the "sombre clouds . . . rolling with sinister intention" introduce the storm. In what sense does this description introduce the story's action as well?
4. In what ways does the storm *cause* the action of the story? List specific events that occur because of the storm. Is the presence of the storm essential to the story? Explain.

---

[4] "I tell you."

5. In what sense could the storm be considered a character in the story?

6. The weather is the most obvious element of the story's setting. What other aspects of setting are important to the story?

7. After Part II the storm is not mentioned again until the last line of the story. What signs of the storm remain in Parts III, IV, and V?

8. Besides denoting the weather, what else might the title suggest?

9. **JOURNAL ENTRY** The storm sets in motion the chain of events that leads to the characters' adultery. Do you think the storm excuses the characters in any way from responsibility for their actions?

10. **CRITICAL PERSPECTIVE** In his discussion of "The Storm," Donald F. Larsson focuses on the story's ending:

> While the storm mirrors the physical passion of the couple, neither it nor the passion itself is destructive. Where one would expect some retribution for this infidelity in a story, the results are only beneficial: Calixta, physically fulfilled, happily welcomes back her returning husband and son; Alcée writes to Clarisse, off visiting relatives, that he does not need her back right away; and Clarisse, enjoying "the first free breath since her marriage," is content to stay where she is for the time. Even today, Chopin's ending seems audacious: "So the storm passed and every one was happy."

Do you agree that the ending is "audacious"? What do you think should have happened at the end of the story?

Related Works: "What Lips My Lips Have Kissed" (p. 686), "The Faithful Wife" (p. 776), "Wild Nights—Wild Nights!" (p. 944), *The Stronger* (p. 1177)

◊ **TILLIE OLSEN** (1912 or 1913–   ) is known for her works of fiction about working-class Americans. Her short stories and one novel are inhabited by those she called the "despised people"—coal miners, farm laborers, packinghouse butchers, and housewives. Olsen was born in Nebraska into a working-class family. Though she has been described as a Depression-era dropout, Olsen has observed that she educated herself, with libraries as her college. According to an account in her nonfiction work *Silences* (1978), Olsen was at age fifteen inspired to write about working-class people when she read Rebecca Harding Davis's *Life in the Iron Mills,* a tale of the effects of industrialization upon workers, in an 1861 issue of *Atlantic Monthly* bought for ten cents in a junk shop.

Shortly after she left high school, she was jailed for helping to organize packinghouse workers. Motivated by her experiences, she began to write a novel, *Yonnondio*. Under her maiden name, Tillie Lerner, she published two poems, a short story, and part of her novel in the 1930s. After her marriage, she did not publish again for twenty-two years, spending her time raising four children and working at a variety of jobs. The collection of short stories *Tell Me a Riddle* (1961), which includes "I Stand Here Ironing" (originally titled "Help Her to Believe"), was published when she was fifty. Her only other work of fiction is *Yonnondio* (1974), which she pieced together from drafts she wrote in the 1930s and edited for publication in 1974.

Because she believed her own career was "ruined" by the passage of time when she could not write because of other responsibilities, she focuses on encouraging young writers by lecturing or reading her own works to writers' groups and holding writer-in-residency or visiting professorships at several major universities. She is also known for her efforts to rediscover long-forgotten works by other working-class women. In 1984, she edited *Mother to Daughter, Daughter to Mother: Mothers on Mothering*, a collection of poems, letters, short fiction, and diary excerpts written by famous and not-so-famous women. Olsen lives in San Francisco.

Cultural Context ◇   During the Great Depression of the 1930s in the United States, jobs were scarce, and many people who had jobs were forced to take pay cuts. Many Americans suffered harsh deprivation and struggled daily for survival in the "prerelief" years before the Social Security Act of 1935 established public assistance, unemployment insurance, and social security.

◇ ◇ ◇

TILLIE OLSEN

I Stand Here Ironing
(1961)

I stand here ironing, and what you asked me moves tormented back and forth with the iron.

"I wish you would manage the time to come and talk with me about your daughter. I'm sure you can help me understand her. She's a youngster who needs help and whom I'm deeply interested in helping."

"Who needs help." . . . Even if I came, what good would it do? You think because I am her mother I have a key, or that in some way you could use me as a key? She has lived for nineteen years. There is all that life that has happened outside of me, beyond me.

And when is there time to remember, to sift, to weigh, to estimate, to total? I will start and there will be an interruption and I will have to gather it all together again. Or I will become engulfed with all I did or did not do, with what should have been and what cannot be helped.

5   She was a beautiful baby. The first and only one of our five that was beautiful at birth. You do not guess how new and uneasy her tenancy in her now-loveliness. You did not know her all those years she was thought

homely, or see her poring over her baby pictures, making me tell her over and over how beautiful she had been—and would be, I would tell her—and was now, to the seeing eye. But the seeing eyes were few or nonexistent. Including mine.

I nursed her. They feel that's important nowadays. I nursed all the children, but with her, with all the fierce rigidity of first motherhood, I did like the books then said. Though her cries battered me to trembling and my breasts ached with swollenness, I waited till the clock decreed.

Why do I put that first? I do not even know if it matters, or if it explains anything.

She was a beautiful baby. She blew shining bubbles of sound. She loved motion, loved light, loved color and music and textures. She would lie on the floor in her blue overalls patting the surface so hard in ecstasy her hands and feet would blur. She was a miracle to me, but when she was eight months old I had to leave her daytimes with the woman downstairs to whom she was no miracle at all, for I worked or looked for work and for Emily's father, who "could no longer endure" (he wrote in his good-bye note) "sharing want with us."

I was nineteen. It was the pre-relief, pre-WPA[1] world of the depression. I would start running as soon as I got off the streetcar, running up the stairs, the place smelling sour, and awake or asleep to startle awake, when she saw me she would break into a clogged weeping that could not be comforted, a weeping I can hear yet.

10   After a while I found a job hashing at night so I could be with her days, and it was better. But it came to where I had to bring her to his family and leave her.

It took a long time to raise the money for her fare back. Then she got chicken pox and I had to wait longer. When she finally came, I hardly knew her, walking quick and nervous like her father, looking like her father, thin, and dressed in a shoddy red that yellowed her skin and glared at the pockmarks. All the baby loveliness gone.

She was two. Old enough for nursery school they said, and I did not know then what I know now—the fatigue of the long day, and the lacerations of group life in the kinds of nurseries that are only parking places for children.

Except that it would have made no difference if I had known. It was the only place there was. It was the only way we could be together, the only way I could hold a job.

And even without knowing, I knew. I knew the teacher that was evil because all these years it has curdled into my memory, the little boy hunched in the corner, her rasp, "why aren't you outside, because Alvin hits you? that's no reason, go out, scaredy." I knew Emily hated it even if

---

[1] Works Progress Administration, created in 1935 as part of President Franklin D. Roosevelt's New Deal program. The purpose of the WPA (renamed the Works Projects Administration in 1939) was to provide jobs for the unemployed during the Great Depression.

she did not clutch and implore "don't go Mommy" like the other children, mornings.

15   She always had a reason why we should stay home. Momma, you look sick. Momma, I feel sick. Momma, the teachers aren't there today, they're sick. Momma, we can't go, there was a fire there last night. Momma, it's a holiday today, no school, they told me.

But never a direct protest, never rebellion. I think of our others in their three-, four-year-oldness—the explosions, the tempers, the denunciations, the demands—and I feel suddenly ill. I put the iron down. What in me demanded that goodness in her? And what was the cost, the cost to her of such goodness?

The old man living in the back once said in his gentle way: "You should smile at Emily more when you look at her." What *was* in my face when I looked at her? I loved her. There were all the acts of love.

It was only with the others I remembered what he said, and it was the face of joy, and not of care or tightness or worry I turned to them—too late for Emily. She does not smile easily, let alone almost always as her brothers and sisters do. Her face is closed and sombre, but when she wants, how fluid. You must have seen it in her pantomimes, you spoke of her rare gift for comedy on the stage that rouses laughter out of the audience so dear they applaud and applaud and do not want to let her go.

Where does it come from, that comedy? There was none of it in her when she came back to me that second time, after I had had to send her away again. She had a new daddy now to learn to love, and I think perhaps it was a better time.

20   Except when we left her alone nights, telling ourselves she was old enough.

"Can't you go some other time, Mommy, like tomorrow?" she would ask. "Will it be just a little while you'll be gone? Do you promise?"

The time we came back, the front door open, the clock on the floor in the hall. She rigid awake. "It wasn't just a little while. I didn't cry. Three times I called you, just three times, and then I ran downstairs to open the door so you could come faster. The clock talked loud. I threw it away, it scared me what it talked."

She said the clock talked loud again that night I went to the hospital to have Susan. She was delirious with the fever that comes before red measles, but she was fully conscious all the week I was gone and the week after we were home when she could not come near the new baby or me.

She did not get well. She stayed skeleton thin, not wanting to eat, and night after night she had nightmares. She would call for me, and I would rouse from exhaustion to sleepily call back: "You're all right, darling, go to sleep, it's just a dream," and if she still called, in a sterner voice, "now go to sleep, Emily, there's nothing to hurt you." Twice, only twice, when I had to get up for Susan anyhow, I went in to sit with her.

25   Now when it is too late (as if she would let me hold and comfort her like I do the others) I get up and go to her at once at her moan or restless stirring. "Are you awake, Emily? Can I get you something?" And

the answer is always the same: "No, I'm all right, go back to sleep, Mother."

They persuaded me at the clinic to send her away to a convalescent home in the country where "she can have the kind of food and care you can't manage for her, and you'll be free to concentrate on the new baby." They still send children to that place. I see pictures on the society page of sleek young women planning affairs to raise money for it, or dancing at the affairs, or decorating Easter eggs or filling Christmas stockings for the children.

They never have a picture of the children so I do not know if the girls still wear those gigantic red bows and the ravaged looks on the every other Sunday when parents can come to visit "unless otherwise notified"—as we were notified the first six weeks.

Oh it is a handsome place, green lawns and tall trees and fluted flower beds. High up on the balconies of each cottage the children stand, the girls in their red bows and white dresses, the boys in white suits and giant red ties. The parents stand below shrieking up to be heard and the children shriek down to be heard, and between them the invisible wall: "Not to Be Contaminated by Parental Germs or Physical Affection."

There was a tiny girl who always stood hand in hand with Emily. Her parents never came. One visit she was gone. "They moved her to Rose Cottage," Emily shouted in explanation. "They don't like you to love anybody here."

30   She wrote once a week, the labored writing of a seven-year-old. "I am fine. How is the baby. If I write my leter nicly I will have a star. Love." There never was a star. We wrote every other day, letters she could never hold or keep but only hear read—once. "We simply do not have room for children to keep any personal possessions," they patiently explained when we pieced one Sunday's shrieking together to plead how much it would mean to Emily, who loved so to keep things, to be allowed to keep her letters and cards.

Each visit she looked frailer. "She isn't eating," they told us.

(They had runny eggs for breakfast or mush with lumps, Emily said later, I'd hold it in my mouth and not swallow. Nothing ever tasted good, just when they had chicken.)

It took us eight months to get her released home, and only the fact that she gained back so little of her seven lost pounds convinced the social worker.

I used to try to hold and love her after she came back, but her body would stay stiff, and after a while she'd push away. She ate little. Food sickened her, and I think much of life too. Oh she had physical lightness and brightness, twinkling by on skates, bouncing like a ball up and down up and down over the jump rope, skimming over the hill; but these were momentary.

35   She fretted about her appearance, thin and dark and foreign-looking at a time when every little girl was supposed to look or thought she should look a chubby blonde replica of Shirley Temple. The doorbell sometimes

rang for her, but no one seemed to come and play in the house or be a best friend. Maybe because we moved so much.

There was a boy she loved painfully through two school semesters. Months later she told me how she had taken pennies from my purse to buy him candy. "Licorice was his favorite and I brought him some every day, but he still liked Jennifer better'n me. Why, Mommy?" The kind of question for which there is no answer.

School was a worry to her. She was not glib or quick in a world where glibness and quickness were easily confused with ability to learn. To her overworked and exasperated teachers she was an overconscientious "slow learner" who kept trying to catch up and was absent entirely too often.

I let her be absent, though sometimes the illness was imaginary. How different from my now-strictness about attendance with the others. I wasn't working. We had a new baby, I was home anyhow. Sometimes, after Susan grew old enough, I would keep her home from school, too, to have them all together.

Mostly Emily had asthma, and her breathing, harsh and labored, would fill the house with a curiously tranquil sound. I would bring the two old dresser mirrors and her boxes of collections to her bed. She would select beads and single earrings, bottle tops and shells, dried flowers and pebbles, old postcards and scraps, all sorts of oddments; then she and Susan would play Kingdom, setting up landscapes and furniture, peopling them with action.

40 Those were the only times of peaceful companionship between her and Susan. I have edged away from it, that poisonous feeling between them, that terrible balancing of hurts and needs I had to do between the two, and did so badly, those earlier years.

Oh there are conflicts between the others too, each one human, needing, demanding, hurting, taking—but only between Emily and Susan, no, Emily toward Susan that corroding resentment. It seems so obvious on the surface, yet it is not obvious. Susan, the second child, Susan, golden- and curly-haired and chubby, quick and articulate and assured, everything in appearance and manner Emily was not; Susan, not able to resist Emily's precious things, losing or sometimes clumsily breaking them; Susan telling jokes and riddles to company for applause while Emily sat silent (to say to me later: that was *my* riddle, Mother, I told it to Susan); Susan, who for all the five years' difference in age was just a year behind Emily in developing physically.

I am glad for that slow physical development that widened the difference between her and her contemporaries, though she suffered over it. She was too vulnerable for that terrible world of youthful competition, of preening and parading, of constant measuring of yourself against every other, of envy, "If I had that copper hair," "If I had that skin. . . . " She tormented herself enough about not looking like the others, there was enough of the unsureness, the having to be conscious of words before you speak, the constant caring—what are they thinking of me? without having it all magnified by the merciless physical drives.

Ronnie is calling. He is wet and I change him. It is rare there is such a cry now. That time of motherhood is almost behind me when the ear is not one's own but must always be racked and listening for the child cry, the child call. We sit for a while and I hold him, looking out over the city spread in charcoal with its soft aisles of light. *"Shoogily,"* he breathes and curls closer. I carry him back to bed, asleep. *Shoogily.* A funny word, a family word, inherited from Emily, invented by her to say: *comfort.*

In this and other ways she leaves her seal, I say aloud. And startle at my saying it. What do I mean? What did I start to gather together, to try and make coherent? I was at the terrible, growing years. War years. I do not remember them well. I was working, there were four smaller ones now, there was not time for her. She had to help be a mother, and housekeeper, and shopper. She had to set her seal. Mornings of crisis and near hysteria trying to get lunches packed, hair combed, coats and shoes found, everyone to school or Child Care on time, the baby ready for transportation. And always the paper scribbled on by a smaller one, the book looked at by Susan then mislaid, the homework not done. Running out to that huge school where she was one, she was lost, she was a drop; suffering over the unpreparedness, stammering and unsure in her classes.

45   There was so little time left at night after the kids were bedded down. She would struggle over books, always eating (it was in those years she developed her enormous appetite that is legendary in our family) and I would be ironing, or preparing food for the next day, or writing V-mail[3] to Bill, or tending the baby. Sometimes, to make me laugh, or out of her despair, she would imitate happenings or types at school.

I think I said once: "Why don't you do something like this in the school amateur show?" One morning she phoned me at work, hardly understandable through the weeping: "Mother, I did it. I won, I won; they gave me first prize; they clapped and clapped and wouldn't let me go."

Now suddenly she was Somebody, and as imprisoned in her difference as she had been in anonymity.

She began to be asked to perform at other high schools, even in colleges, then at city and statewide affairs. The first one we went to, I only recognized her that first moment when thin, shy, she almost drowned herself into the curtains. Then: Was this Emily? The control, the command, the convulsing and deadly clowning, the spell, then the roaring, stamping audience, unwilling to let this rare and precious laughter out of their lives.

Afterwards: You ought to do something about her with a gift like that—but without money or knowing how, what does one do? We have left it all to her, and the gift has as often eddied inside, clogged and clotted, as been used and growing.

50   She is coming. She runs up the stairs two at a time with her light graceful step, and I know she is happy tonight. Whatever it was that occasioned your call did not happen today.

---

[3] Mail sent to or from members of the armed forces during World War II. Letters were reduced onto microfilm and enlarged and printed out at their destination.

"Aren't you ever going to finish the ironing, Mother? Whistler painted his mother in a rocker. I'd have to paint mine standing over an ironing board." This is one of her communicative nights and she tells me everything and nothing as she fixes herself a plate of food out of the icebox.

She is so lovely. Why did you want me to come in at all? Why were you concerned? She will find her way.

She starts up the stairs to bed. "Don't get me up with the rest in the morning." "But I thought you were having midterms." "Oh, those," she comes back in, kisses me, and says quite lightly, "in a couple of years when we'll all be atom-dead they won't matter a bit."

She has said it before. She *believes* it. But because I have been dredging the past, and all that compounds a human being is so heavy and meaningful in me, I cannot endure it tonight.

55   I will never total it all. I will never come in to say: She was a child seldom smiled at. Her father left me before she was a year old. I had to work her first six years when there was work, or I sent her home and to his relatives. There were years she had care she hated. She was dark and thin and foreign-looking in a world where the prestige went to blondeness and curly hair and dimples, she was slow where glibness was prized. She was a child of anxious, not proud, love. We were poor and could not afford for her the soil of easy growth. I was a young mother, I was a distracted mother. There were other children pushing up, demanding. Her younger sister seemed all that she was not. There were years she did not want me to touch her. She kept too much in herself, her life was such she had to keep too much in herself. My wisdom came too late. She has much to her and probably little will come of it. She is a child of her age, of depression, of war, of fear.

Let her be. So all that is in her will not bloom—but in how many does it? There is still enough left to live by. Only help her to know—help make it so there is cause for her to know—that she is more than this dress on the ironing board, helpless before the iron.

READING AND REACTING

1. "I Stand Here Ironing" focuses on incidents that took place in the "pre-relief, pre-WPA world" of the Depression (9). In light of social, political, and economic changes that have occurred since the 1930s, do you think the events the story presents could occur today? Explain.
2. In what sense is the image of a mother at an ironing board appropriate for this story?
3. The narrator is overwhelmed by guilt. What does she believe she has done wrong? What, if anything, do *you* think she has done wrong? Do you think she has been a good mother? Why or why not?
4. Who, or what, do you blame for the narrator's problems? For example, do you blame Emily's father? The Depression? The social institutions and "experts" to which the narrator turns?

5. Do you see the narrator as a victim limited by the times in which she lives? Do you agree with the narrator that Emily is "a child of her age, of depression, of war, of fear"? Or do you believe both women have some control over their own destinies, regardless of the story's historical setting?
6. What do you think the narrator wants for her daughter? Do you think her goals for Emily are realistic ones?
7. Paragraph 28 describes the physical setting of the convalescent home to which Emily was sent. What does this description add to the story? Why do you suppose there is no physical description of the apartment in which Emily lived as a child? How do you picture this apartment?
8. To whom do you think the mother is speaking in this story?
9. **JOURNAL ENTRY** Put yourself in Emily's position. What do you think she would like to tell her mother?
10. **CRITICAL PERSPECTIVE** Writing in *The Red Wheelbarrow*, psychologist Robert Coles discusses the complex family relationships depicted in "I Stand Here Ironing" and reaches an optimistic conclusion:

   > But the child did not grow to be a mere victim of the kind so many of us these days are rather eager to recognize—a hopeless tangle of psychopathology. The growing child, even in her troubled moments, revealed herself to be persistent, demanding, and observant. In the complaints we make, in the "symptoms" we develop, we reveal our strengths as well as our weaknesses. The hurt child could summon her intelligence, exercise her will, smile and make others smile.

   Do you agree with Coles's psychological evaluation of Emily? Do you find the story's ending as essentially uplifting as he seems to? Why or why not?

Related Works: "How to Talk to Your Mother (Notes)" (p. 96), "Everyday Use" (p. 324), "Seventeen Syllables" (p. 376), "Those Winter Sundays" (p. 678), *'night, Mother* (p. 1708), *The Glass Menagerie* (p. 1805)

◇ **CHARLOTTE PERKINS GILMAN** (1860–1935) was a prominent feminist and social thinker at the turn of the century. Her essays, lectures, and nonfiction works—such as *Women and Economics* (1898), *Concerning Children* (1900), and *The Man-Made World* (1911)—are forceful statements of Gilman's opinions on women's need for economic independence and social equality. In the main, Gilman's fiction is a didactic expression of her social views. She is probably best known for three utopian feminist novels: *Moving the*

Mountain (1911), *Herland* (1915; unpublished until 1978), and *With Her in Ourland* (1916). Gilman's fictional works are full of humor and satire: In *Herland,* for instance, a male sociologist (wandering in by accident from the outside world) is chagrined to find that the women of "Herland" want him for a friend, not a lover.

Although "The Yellow Wall-Paper" (1892) is not typical of Gilman's other fiction, it is considered her artistic masterpiece. The terse, clinical precision of the writing, conveying the tightly wound and distraught mental state of the narrator, is particularly chilling when it is read with a knowledge of Gilman's personal history. In the 1880s, she met and married a young artist, Charles Walter Stetson. Following the birth of their daughter, she grew increasingly depressed and turned to a noted Philadelphia neurologist for help. Following the traditions of the time, he prescribed complete bed rest and mental inactivity—a treatment that, Gilman said later, drove her "so near the borderline of utter mental ruin that I could see over." "The Yellow Wall-Paper" is not simply a psychological study. Like most of Gilman's work, it makes a point—this time about the dangers of women's utter dependence on a male interpretation of their needs.

CULTURAL CONTEXT ◊   Until the eighteenth century, mental illness was believed to be caused by demonic possession. Eventually it came to be considered a sickness requiring treatment. Much of modern psychiatry developed from the efforts of Philippe Pinel in France and J. Connolly in England, both of whom advocated a more humane approach to mental illness. By the nineteenth century, research and treatment of mental illness evolved from its origins in spiritual healing, and by the twentieth century, behavior therapies were developed.

◊   ◊   ◊

CHARLOTTE PERKINS GILMAN

The Yellow Wall-Paper
(1892)

It is very seldom that mere ordinary people like John and myself secure ancestral halls for the summer.

A colonial mansion, a hereditary estate, I would say a haunted house, and reach the height of romantic felicity—but that would be asking too much of fate!

Still I will proudly declare that there is something queer about it.

Else, why should it be let so cheaply? And why have stood so long untenanted?

5   John laughs at me, of course, but one expects that in marriage.

John is practical in the extreme. He has no patience with faith, an intense horror of superstition, and he scoffs openly at any talk of things not to be felt and seen and put down in figures.

John is a physician, and *perhaps*—(I would not say it to a living soul, of course, but this is dead paper and a great relief to my mind—) *perhaps* that is one reason I do not get well faster.

You see he does not believe I am sick!

And what can one do?

10   If a physician of high standing, and one's own husband, assures friends and relatives that there is really nothing the matter with one but temporary nervous depression—a slight hysterical tendency—what is one to do?

My brother is also a physician, and also of high standing, and he says the same thing.

So I take phosphates or phosphites[1]—whichever it is, and tonics, and journeys, and air, and exercise, and am absolutely forbidden to "work" until I am well again.

Personally, I disagree with their ideas.

Personally, I believe that congenial work, with excitement and change, would do me good.

15   But what is one to do?

I did write for a while in spite of them; but it *does* exhaust me a good deal—having to be so sly about it, or else meet with heavy opposition.

I sometimes fancy that in my condition if I had less opposition and more society and stimulus—but John says the very worst thing I can do is to think about my condition, and I confess it always makes me feel bad.

So I will let it alone and talk about the house.

The most beautiful place! It is quite alone, standing well back from the road, quite three miles from the village. It makes me think of English places that you read about, for there are hedges and walls and gates that lock, and lots of separate little houses for the gardeners and people.

20   There is a *delicious* garden! I never saw such a garden—large and shady, full of box-bordered paths, and lined with long grape-covered arbors with seats under them.

There were greenhouses, too, but they are all broken now.

There was some legal trouble, I believe, something about the heirs and co-heirs; anyhow, the place has been empty for years.

That spoils my ghostliness, I am afraid, but I don't care—there is something strange about the house—I can feel it.

I even said so to John one moonlight evening, but he said what I felt was a *draught,* and shut the window.

25   I get unreasonably angry with John sometimes. I'm sure I never used to be so sensitive. I think it is due to this nervous condition.

---

[1] Both terms refer to salts of phosphorous acid. The narrator, however, means "phosphate," a carbonated beverage of water, flavoring, and a small amount of phosphoric acid.

But John says if I feel so, I shall neglect proper self-control; so I take pains to control myself—before him, at least, and that makes me very tired.

I don't like our room a bit. I wanted one downstairs that opened on the piazza and had roses all over the window, and such pretty old-fashioned chintz hangings! But John would not hear of it.

He said there was only one window and not room for two beds, and no near room for him if he took another.

He is very careful and loving, and hardly lets me stir without special direction.

30   I have a schedule prescription for each hour in the day; he takes all care from me, and so I feel basely ungrateful not to value it more.

He said we came here solely on my account, that I was to have perfect rest and all the air I could get. "Your exercise depends on your strength, my dear," said he, "and your food somewhat on your appetite; but air you can absorb all the time." So we took the nursery at the top of the house.

It is a big, airy room, the whole floor nearly, with windows that look all ways, and air and sunshine galore. It was nursery first and then play-room and gymnasium, I should judge; for the windows are barred for little children, and there are rings and things in the walls.

The paint and paper look as if a boys' school had used it. It is stripped off—the paper—in great patches all around the head of my bed, about as far as I can reach, and in a great place on the other side of the room low down. I never saw a worse paper in my life.

One of those sprawling flamboyant patterns committing every artistic sin.

35   It is dull enough to confuse the eye in following, pronounced enough to constantly irritate and provoke study, and when you follow the lame uncertain curves for a little distance they suddenly commit suicide—plunge off at outrageous angles, destroy themselves in unheard of contradictions.

The color is repellent, almost revolting; a smouldering unclean yellow, strangely faded by the slow-turning sunlight.

It is a dull yet lurid orange in some places, a sickly sulphur tint in others.

No wonder the children hated it! I should hate it myself if I had to live in this room long.

There comes John, and I must put this away,—he hates to have me write a word.

40   We have been here two weeks, and I haven't felt like writing before, since that first day.

I am sitting by the window now, up in this atrocious nursery, and there is nothing to hinder my writing as much as I please, save lack of strength.

John is away all day, and even some nights when his cases are serious.
I am glad my case is not serious!

But these nervous troubles are dreadfully depressing.

45   John does not know how much I really suffer. He knows there is no *reason* to suffer, and that satisfies him.

Of course it is only nervousness. It does weigh on me so not to do my duty in any way!

I meant to be such a help to John, such a real rest and comfort, and here I am a comparative burden already!

Nobody would believe what an effort it is to do what little I am able,—to dress and entertain, and order things.

It is fortunate Mary is so good with the baby. Such a dear baby!

50   And yet I *cannot* be with him, it makes me so nervous.

I suppose John never was nervous in his life. He laughs at me so about this wall-paper!

At first he meant to repaper the room, but afterwards he said that I was letting it get the better of me, and that nothing was worse for a nervous patient than to give way to such fancies.

He said that after the wall-paper was changed it would be the heavy bedstead, and then the barred windows, and then that gate at the head of the stairs, and so on.

"You know the place is doing you good," he said, "and really, dear, I don't care to renovate the house just for a three months' rental."

55   "Then do let us go downstairs," I said, "there are such pretty rooms there."

Then he took me in his arms and called me a blessed little goose, and said he would go down cellar, if I wished, and have it whitewashed into the bargain.

But he is right enough about the beds and windows and things.

It is an airy and comfortable room as any one need wish, and, of course, I would not be so silly as to make him uncomfortable just for a whim.

I'm really getting quite fond of the big room, all but that horrid paper.

60   Out of one window I can see the garden, those mysterious deep-shaded arbors, the riotous old-fashioned flowers, and bushes and gnarly trees.

Out of another I get a lovely view of the bay and a little private wharf belonging to the estate. There is a beautiful shaded lane that runs down there from the house. I always fancy I see people walking in these numerous paths and arbors, but John has cautioned me not to give way to fancy in the least. He says that with my imaginative power and habit of story-making, a nervous weakness like mine is sure to lead to all manner of excited fancies, and that I ought to use my will and good sense to check the tendency. So I try.

I think sometimes that if I were only well enough to write a little it would relieve the press of ideas and rest me.

But I find I get pretty tired when I try.

It is so discouraging not to have any advice and companionship about my work. When I get really well, John says we will ask Cousin Henry and Julia down for a long visit; but he says he would as soon put fireworks in my pillow-case as to let me have those stimulating people about now.

65 I wish I could get well faster.

But I must not think about that. This paper looks to me as if it *knew* what a vicious influence it had!

There is a recurrent spot where the pattern lolls like a broken neck and two bulbous eyes stare at you upside down.

I get positively angry with the impertinence of it and the everlastingness. Up and down and sideways they crawl, and those absurd, unblinking eyes are everywhere. There is one place where two breadths didn't match, and the eyes go all up and down the line, one a little higher than the other.

I never saw so much expression in an inanimate thing before, and we all know how much expression they have! I used to lie awake as a child and get more entertainment and terror out of blank walls and plain furniture than most children could find in a toy-store.

70 I remember what a kindly wink the knobs of our big, old bureau used to have, and there was one chair that always seemed like a strong friend.

I used to feel that if any of the other things looked too fierce I could always hop into that chair and be safe.

The furniture in this room is no worse than inharmonious, however, for we had to bring it all from downstairs. I suppose when this was used as a playroom they had to take the nursery things out, and no wonder! I never saw such ravages as the children have made here.

The wall-paper, as I said before, is torn off in spots, and it sticketh closer than a brother—they must have had perseverance as well as hatred.

Then the floor is scratched and gouged and splintered, the plaster itself is dug out here and there, and this great heavy bed which is all we found in the room, looks as if it had been through the wars.

75 But I don't mind it a bit—only the paper.

There comes John's sister. Such a dear girl as she is, and so careful of me! I must not let her find me writing.

She is a perfect and enthusiastic housekeeper, and hopes for no better profession. I verily believe she thinks it is the writing which made me sick!

But I can write when she is out, and see her a long way off from these windows.

There is one that commands the road, a lovely shaded winding road, and one that just looks off over the country. A lovely country, too, full of great elms and velvet meadows.

80 This wall-paper has a kind of sub-pattern in a different shade, a particularly irritating one, for you can only see it in certain lights, and not clearly then.

But in the places where it isn't faded and where the sun is just so—I can see a strange, provoking, formless sort of figure, that seems to skulk about behind that silly and conspicuous front design.

There's sister on the stairs!

Well, the Fourth of July is over! The people are all gone and I am tired out. John thought it might do me good to see a little company, so we just had mother and Nellie and the children down for a week.

Of course I didn't do a thing. Jennie sees to everything now.

85 But it tired me all the same.

John says if I don't pick up faster he shall send me to Weir Mitchell[2] in the fall.

But I don't want to go there at all. I had a friend who was in his hands once, and she says he is just like John and my brother, only more so!

Besides, it is such an undertaking to go so far.

I don't feel as if it was worth while to turn my hand over for anything, and I'm getting dreadfully fretful and querulous.

90 I cry at nothing, and cry most of the time.

Of course I don't when John is here, or anybody else, but when I am alone.

And I am alone a good deal just now. John is kept in town very often by serious cases, and Jennie is good and lets me alone when I want her to.

So I walk a little in the garden or down that lovely lane, sit on the porch under the roses, and lie down up here a good deal.

I'm getting really fond of the room in spite of the wall-paper. Perhaps *because* of the wall-paper.

95 It dwells in my mind so!

I lie here on this great immovable bed—it is nailed down, I believe—and follow that pattern about by the hour. It is as good as gymnastics, I assure you. I start, we'll say, at the bottom, down in the corner over there where it has not been touched, and I determine for the thousandth time that I *will* follow that pointless pattern to some sort of a conclusion.

I know a little of the principle of design, and I know this thing was not arranged on any laws of radiation, or alternation, or repetition, or symmetry, or anything else that I ever heard of.

It is repeated, of course, by the breadths, but not otherwise.

Looked at in one way each breadth stands alone, the bloated curves and flourishes—a kind of "debased Romanesque" with *delirium tremens*[3] go waddling up and down in isolated columns of fatuity.

---

[2] Silas Weir Mitchell (1829–1914)—a Philadelphia neurologist-psychologist who introduced the "rest cure" for nervous diseases.

[3] Mental confusion caused by alcohol poisoning and characterized by physical tremors and hallucinations.

100 But, on the other hand, they connect diagonally, and the sprawling outlines run off in great slanting waves of optic horror, like a lot of wallowing seaweeds in full chase.

The whole thing goes horizontally, too, at least it seems so, and I exhaust myself in trying to distinguish the order of its going in that direction.

They have used a horizontal breadth for a frieze, and that adds wonderfully to the confusion.

There is one end of the room where it is almost intact, and there, when the crosslights fade and the low sun shines directly upon it, I can almost fancy radiation after all,—the interminable grotesque seems to form around a common center and rush off in headlong plunges of equal distraction.

It makes me tired to follow it. I will take a nap I guess.

105 I don't know why I should write this.

I don't want to.

I don't feel able.

And I know John would think it absurd. But I *must* say what I feel and think in some way—it is such a relief!

But the effort is getting to be greater than the relief.

110 Half the time now I am awfully lazy, and lie down ever so much.

John says I mustn't lose my strength, and has me take cod liver oil and lots of tonics and things, to say nothing of ale and wine and rare meat.

Dear John! He loves me very dearly, and hates to have me sick. I tried to have a real earnest reasonable talk with him the other day, and tell him how I wish he would let me go and make a visit to Cousin Henry and Julia.

But he said I wasn't able to go, nor able to stand it after I got there; and I did not make out a very good case for myself, for I was crying before I had finished.

It is getting to be a great effort for me to think straight. Just this nervous weakness I suppose.

115 And dear John gathered me up in his arms, and just carried me upstairs and laid me on the bed, and sat by me and read to me till it tired my head.

He said I was his darling and his comfort and all he had, and that I must take care of myself for his sake, and keep well.

He says no one but myself can help me out of it, that I must use my will and self-control and not let any silly fancies run away with me.

There's one comfort, the baby is well and happy, and does not have to occupy this nursery with the horrid wall-paper.

If we had not used it, that blessed child would have! What a fortunate escape! Why, I wouldn't have a child of mine, an impressionable little thing, live in such a room for worlds.

120 I never thought of it before, but it is lucky that John kept me here after all, I can stand it so much easier than a baby, you see.

Of course I never mention it to them any more—I am too wise,—but I keep watch of it all the same.

There are things in that paper that nobody knows but me, or ever will.

Behind that outside pattern the dim shapes get clearer every day.

It is always the same shape, only very numerous.

125   And it is like a woman stooping down and creeping about behind that pattern. I don't like it a bit. I wonder—I begin to think—I wish John would take me away from here!

It is so hard to talk with John about my case, because he is so wise, and because he loves me so.

But I tried it last night.

It was moonlight. The moon shines in all around just as the sun does.

I hate to see it sometimes, it creeps so slowly, and always comes in by one window or another.

130   John was asleep and I hated to waken him, so I kept still and watched the moonlight on that undulating wall-paper till I felt creepy.

The faint figure behind seemed to shake the pattern, just as if she wanted to get out.

I got up softly and went to feel and see if the paper *did* move, and when I came back John was awake.

"What is it, little girl?" he said. "Don't go walking about like that— you'll get cold."

I thought it was a good time to talk, so I told him that I really was not gaining here, and that I wished he would take me away.

135   "Why, darling!" said he, "our lease will be up in three weeks, and I can't see how to leave before.

"The repairs are not done at home, and I cannot possibly leave town just now. Of course if you were in any danger, I could and would, but you really are better, dear, whether you can see it or not. I am a doctor, dear, and I know. You are gaining flesh and color, your appetite is better, I feel really much easier about you."

"I don't weigh a bit more," said I, "nor as much; and my appetite may be better in the evening when you are here, but it is worse in the morning when you are away!"

"Bless her little heart!" said he with a big hug, "she shall be as sick as she pleases! But now let's improve the shining hours by going to sleep, and talk about it in the morning!"

"And you won't go away?" I asked gloomily.

140   "Why, how can I, dear? It is only three weeks more and then we will take a nice little trip of a few days while Jennie is getting the house ready. Really dear you are better!"

"Better in body perhaps—" I began, and stopped short, for he sat up straight and looked at me with such a stern, reproachful look that I could not say another word.

"My darling," said he, "I beg of you, for my sake and for our child's sake, as well as for your own, that you will never for one instant let that idea enter your mind! There is nothing so dangerous, so fascinating, to a temperament like yours. It is a false and foolish fancy. Can you not trust me as a physician when I tell you so?"

So of course I said no more on that score, and we went to sleep before long. He thought I was asleep first, but I wasn't, and lay there for hours trying to decide whether that front pattern and the back pattern really did move together or separately.

On a pattern like this, by daylight, there is a lack of sequence, a defiance of law, that is a constant irritant to a normal mind.

145 The color is hideous enough, and unreliable enough, and infuriating enough, but the pattern is torturing.

You think you have mastered it, but just as you get well underway in following, it turns back-somersault and there you are. It slaps you in the face, knocks you down, and tramples upon you. It is like a bad dream.

The outside pattern is a florid arabesque, reminding one of a fungus. If you can imagine a toadstool in joints, an interminable string of toadstools, budding and sprouting in endless convolutions—why, that is something like it.

That is, sometimes!

There is one marked peculiarity about this paper, a thing nobody seems to notice but myself, and that is that it changes as the light changes.

150 When the sun shoots in through the east window—I always watch for that first long, straight ray—it changes so quickly that I never can quite believe it.

That is why I watch it always.

By moonlight—the moon shines in all night when there is a moon—I wouldn't know it was the same paper.

At night in any kind of light, in twilight, candlelight, lamplight, and worst of all by moonlight, it becomes bars! The outside pattern I mean, and the woman behind it is as plain as can be.

I didn't realize for a long time what the thing was that showed behind, that dim sub-pattern, but now I am quite sure it is a woman.

155 By daylight she is subdued, quiet. I fancy it is the pattern that keeps her so still. It is so puzzling. It keeps me quiet by the hour.

I lie down ever so much now. John says it is good for me, and to sleep all I can.

Indeed he started the habit by making me lie down for an hour after each meal.

It is a very bad habit I am convinced, for you see I don't sleep.

And that cultivates deceit, for I don't tell them I'm awake—O no!

160 The fact is I am getting a little afraid of John.

He seems very queer sometimes, and even Jennie has an inexplicable look.

It strikes me occasionally, just as a scientific hypothesis,—that perhaps it is the paper!

I have watched John when he did not know I was looking, and come into the room suddenly on the most innocent excuses, and I've caught him several times *looking at the paper!* And Jennie too. I caught Jennie with her hand on it once.

She didn't know I was in the room, and when I asked her in a quiet, a very quiet voice, with the most restrained manner possible, what she was doing with the paper—she turned around as if she had been caught stealing, and looked quite angry—asked me why I should frighten her so!

165   Then she said that the paper stained everything it touched, that she had found yellow smooches on all my clothes and John's, and she wished we would be more careful!

Did not that sound innocent? But I know she was studying that pattern, and I am determined that nobody shall find it out but myself!

Life is very much more exciting now than it used to be. You see I have something more to expect, to look forward to, to watch. I really do eat better, and am more quiet than I was.

John is so pleased to see me improve! He laughed a little the other day, and said I seemed to be flourishing in spite of my wall-paper.

I turned it off with a laugh. I had no intention of telling him it was *because* of the wall-paper—he would make fun of me. He might even want to take me away.

170   I don't want to leave now until I have found it out. There is a week more, and I think that will be enough.

I'm feeling ever so much better! I don't sleep much at night, for it is so interesting to watch developments; but I sleep a good deal in the daytime.

In the daytime it is tiresome and perplexing.

There are always new shoots on the fungus, and new shades of yellow all over it. I cannot keep count of them, though I have tried conscientiously.

It is the strangest yellow, that wall-paper! It makes me think of all the yellow things I ever saw—not beautiful ones like buttercups, but old foul, bad yellow things.

175   But there is something else about that paper—the smell! I noticed it the moment we came into the room, but with so much air and sun it was not bad. Now we have had a week of fog and rain, and whether the windows are open or not, the smell is here.

It creeps all over the house.

I find it hovering in the dining-room, skulking in the parlor, hiding in the hall, lying in wait for me on the stairs.

It gets into my hair.

Even when I go to ride, if I turn my head suddenly and surprise it—there is that smell!

180   Such a peculiar odor, too! I have spent hours in trying to analyze it, to find what it smelled like.

It is not bad—at first, and very gentle, but quite the subtlest, most enduring odor I ever met.

In this damp weather it is awful, I wake up in the night and find it hanging over me.

It used to disturb me at first. I thought seriously of burning the house—to reach the smell.

But now I am used to it. The only thing I can think of that it is like is the *color* of the paper! A yellow smell.

185   There is a very funny mark on this wall, low down, near the mopboard. A streak that runs round the room. It goes behind every piece of furniture, except the bed, a long, straight, even *smooch,* as if it had been rubbed over and over.

I wonder how it was done and who did it, and what they did it for. Round and round and round—round and round and round!—it makes me dizzy!

I really have discovered something at last.

Through watching so much at night, when it changes so, I have finally found out.

The front pattern *does* move—and no wonder! The woman behind shakes it!

190   Sometimes I think there are a great many women behind, and sometimes only one, and she crawls around fast, and her crawling shakes it all over.

Then in the very bright spots she keeps still, and in the very shady spots she just takes hold of the bars and shakes them hard.

And she is all the time trying to climb through. But nobody could climb through that pattern—it strangles so; I think that is why it has so many heads.

They get through, and then the pattern strangles them off and turns them upside down, and makes their eyes white!

If those heads were covered or taken off it would not be half so bad.

195   I think that woman gets out in the daytime!

And I'll tell you why—privately—I've seen her!

I can see her out of every one of my windows!

It is the same woman, I know, for she is always creeping, and most women do not creep by daylight.

I see her in that long shaded lane, creeping up and down. I see her in those dark grape arbors, creeping all around the garden.

200   I see her on that long road under the trees, creeping along, and when a carriage comes she hides under the blackberry vines.

I don't blame her a bit. It must be very humiliating to be caught creeping by daylight!

I always lock the door when I creep by daylight. I can't do it at night, for I know John would suspect something at once.

And John is so queer now, that I don't want to irritate him. I wish he would take another room! Besides, I don't want anybody to get that woman out at night but myself.

I often wonder if I could see her out of all the windows at once.

205   But, turn as fast as I can, I can only see out of one at one time.

And though I always see her, she *may* be able to creep faster than I can turn!

I have watched her sometimes away off in the open country, creeping as fast as a cloud shadow in a high wind.

If only that top pattern could be gotten off from the under one! I mean to try it, little by little.

I have found out another funny thing, but I shan't tell it this time! It does not do to trust people too much.

210   There are only two more days to get this paper off, and I believe John is beginning to notice. I don't like the look in his eyes.

And I heard him ask Jennie a lot of professional questions about me. She had a very good report to give.

She said I slept a good deal in the daytime.

John knows I don't sleep very well at night, for all I'm so quiet!

He asked me all sorts of questions, too, and pretended to be very loving and kind.

215   As if I couldn't see through him!

Still, I don't wonder he acts so, sleeping under this paper for three months.

It only interests me, but I feel sure John and Jennie are secretly affected by it.

Hurrah! This is the last day, but it is enough. John to stay in town over night, and won't be out until this evening.

Jennie wanted to sleep with me—the sly thing! But I told her I should undoubtedly rest better for a night all alone.

220   That was clever, for really I wasn't alone a bit! As soon as it was moonlight and that poor thing began to crawl and shake the pattern, I got up and ran to help her.

I pulled and she shook, I shook and she pulled, and before morning we had peeled off yards of that paper.

A strip about as high as my head and half around the room.

And then when the sun came and that awful pattern began to laugh at me, I declared I would finish it to-day!

We go away to-morrow, and they are moving all my furniture down again to leave things as they were before.

225   Jennie looked at the wall in amazement, but I told her merrily that I did it out of pure spite at the vicious thing.

She laughed and said she wouldn't mind doing it herself, but I must not get tired.

How she betrayed herself that time!

But I am here, and no person touches this paper but me,—not *alive!*

She tried to get me out of the room—it was too patent! But I said it was so quiet and empty and clean now that I believed I would lie down again and sleep all I could; and not to wake me even for dinner—I would call when I woke.

230   So now she is gone, and the servants are gone, and the things are gone, and there is nothing left but that great bedstead nailed down, with the canvas mattress we found on it.

We shall sleep downstairs to-night, and take the boat home tomorrow.

I quite enjoy the room, now it is bare again.

How those children did tear about here!

This bedstead is fairly gnawed!

235   But I must get to work.

I have locked the door and thrown the key down into the front path.

I don't want to go out, and I don't want to have anybody come in, till John comes.

I want to astonish him.

I've got a rope up here that even Jennie did not find. If that woman does get out, and tries to get away, I can tie her!

240   But I forgot I could not reach far without anything to stand on!

This bed will *not* move!

I tried to lift and push it until I was lame, and then I got so angry I bit off a little piece at one corner—but it hurt my teeth.

Then I peeled off all the paper I could reach standing on the floor. It sticks horribly and the pattern just enjoys it! All those strangled heads and bulbous eyes and waddling fungus growths just shriek with derision!

I am getting angry enough to do something desperate. To jump out of the window would be admirable exercise, but the bars are too strong even to try.

245   Besides I wouldn't do it. Of course not. I know well enough that a step like that is improper and might be misconstrued.

I don't like to *look* out of the windows even—there are so many of those creeping women, and they creep so fast.

I wonder if they all come out of that wall-paper as I did?

But I am securely fastened now by my well-hidden rope—you don't get *me* out in the road there!

I suppose I shall have to get back behind the pattern when it comes night, and that is hard!

250   It is so pleasant to be out in this great room and creep around as I please!

I don't want to go outside. I won't, even if Jennie asks me to.

For outside you have to creep on the ground, and everything is green instead of yellow.

But here I can creep smoothly on the floor, and my shoulder just fits in that long smooch around the wall, so I cannot lose my way.

Why there's John at the door!
255   It is no use, young man, you can't open it!
How he does call and pound!
Now he's crying for an axe.
It would be a shame to break down that beautiful door!
"John dear!" said I in the gentlest voice, "the key is down by the front steps, under a plantain leaf!"
260   That silenced him for a few moments.
Then he said—very quietly indeed, "Open the door, my darling!"
"I can't," said I. "The key is down by the front door under a plantain leaf!"
And then I said it again, several times, very gently and slowly, and said it so often that he had to go and see, and he got it of course, and came in. He stopped short by the door.
"What is the matter?" he cried. "For God's sake, what are you doing!"
265   I kept on creeping just the same, but I looked at him over my shoulder.
"I've got out at last," said I, "in spite of you and Jane. And I've pulled off most of the paper, so you can't put me back!"
Now why should that man have fainted? But he did, and right across my path by the wall, so that I had to creep over him every time!

READING AND REACTING

1. The story's narrator, who has recently given birth, is suffering from what her husband, a doctor, calls "temporary nervous depression—a slight hysterical tendency" (10). What is the relationship between this depression and the story's setting?

2. Describe the house and grounds. How do they affect the narrator's mood?

3. What aspects of the room in which the narrator lives upset her? Why?

4. Describe the wallpaper. What does the narrator actually see in it, and what does she imagine? How can you tell the difference?

5. What do the following comments reveal about the narrator's situation: "John laughs at me, of course, but one expects that in marriage" (5); "I must put this away,—he hates to have me write a word" (39); "He laughs at me so about this wall-paper" (51); "Then he took me in his arms and called me a blessed little goose" (56)?

6. What has probably caused the narrator's depression? What factors aggravate it? How much insight does the narrator seem to have into her situation?

7. How does the narrator's mood change as the story progresses? How do her descriptions of her setting change?

8. Aside from the physical setting—the room, the house, and the garden—what other aspects of the story's setting are important?

9. **JOURNAL ENTRY** Do you think a present-day physician or psychiatrist would give the narrator different advice? Do you think a present-day woman would respond differently to advice from her husband or doctor? Explain.

10. **CRITICAL PERSPECTIVE** "The Yellow Wall-Paper" was originally seen by some as a ghost story, and even anthologized as such. More recently, critics have tended to interpret the story from a feminist perspective, focusing on the way in which the nameless narrator is victimized by the men around her and by the values of the Victorian society which they uphold. In the essay "An Unnecessary Maze of Sign-Reading," Mary Jacobus concludes that the overwhelmingly feminist perspective of recent criticism, although certainly valuable and enlightening, has overlooked other promising critical possibilities—for example, "the Gothic and uncanny elements present in the text."

If you were teaching "The Yellow Wall-Paper," would you present it as a feminist story or as a chilling Gothic ghost story? Do you think interpreting the story as a Gothic horror tale precludes a feminist reading, or do you see the two interpretations as compatible?

Related Works: "The Story of an Hour" (p. 77), "The Disappearance" (p. 419), "Barbie Doll" (p. 980), *A Doll House* (p. 1196)

 ◇ **SHERMAN ALEXIE** (1966–   ), a highly praised young Native American writer, was born in Spokane, Washington, of Spokane and Coeur d'Alene heritage. He attended Pullman State University with plans to become a doctor but changed his mind after attending a poetry workshop; by the time he left school, he had already written over two hundred poems. Since then his work has appeared in various magazines and journals, and he has published three poetry collections—*The Business of Fancydancing* (1992), *I Would Steal Anything* (1992), and *Old Shirts and New Skins* (1993)—as well as a collection of short stories, *The Lone Ranger and Tonto Fistfight in Heaven* (1993), which was adapted for the screen in the 1997 film *Smoke Signals,* and a well-received novel, *Reservation Blues* (1995).

Of Native American culture Alexie has said, "One of the biggest misconceptions about Indians is that we're stoic, but humor is an essential part of our culture." "This Is What It Means to Say Phoenix, Arizona" (from *The Lone Ranger and Tonto Fistfight in Heaven*) demonstrates this unique use of humor to transcend the harsh realities of life on the reservation and the struggle to adapt to contemporary American life.

CULTURAL CONTEXT ◊   When the Coeur d'Alene Indians were first noticed by American explorers Lewis and Clark in 1805, they were a tribe of wanderers who lived in communal houses. In 1841, a Jesuit priest established the Sacred Heart mission among the Coeur d'Alene. Within ten years, the tribe had largely converted to Christianity and adopted the traditions and lifestyle introduced by the missionaries.

◊ ◊ ◊

S H E R M A N   A L E X I E

This Is What It Means to Say
Phoenix, Arizona
(1993)

Just after Victor lost his job at the Bureau of Indian Affairs,[1] he also found out that his father had died of a heart attack in Phoenix, Arizona. Victor hadn't seen his father in a few years, had only talked to him on the telephone once or twice, but there still was a genetic pain, which was as real and immediate as a broken bone. Victor didn't have any money. Who does have money on a reservation, except the cigarette and fireworks salespeople? His father had a savings account waiting to be claimed, but Victor needed to find a way to get from Spokane to Phoenix. Victor's mother was just as poor as he was, and the rest of his family didn't have any use at all for him. So Victor called the tribal council.

"Listen," Victor said. "My father just died. I need some money to get to Phoenix to make arrangements."

"Now Victor," the council said, "you know we're having a difficult time financially."

"But I thought the council had special funds set aside for stuff like this."

5   "Now, Victor, we do have some money available for the proper return of tribal members' bodies. But I don't think we have enough to bring your father all the way back from Phoenix."

"Well," Victor said. "It ain't going to cost all that much. He had to be cremated. Things were kind of ugly. He died of a heart attack in his trailer and nobody found him for a week. It was really hot, too. You get the picture."

"Now, Victor, we're sorry for your loss and the circumstances. But we can really only afford to give you one hundred dollars."

"That's not even enough for a plane ticket."

"Well, you might consider driving down to Phoenix."

---

[1] Division of the U.S. Department of the Interior that manages Native American matters; operated by government officials, not tribal leaders.

10   "I don't have a car. Besides, I was going to drive my father's pickup back up here."

"Now, Victor," the council said, "we're sure there is somebody who could drive you to Phoenix. Or could anybody lend you the rest of the money?"

"You know there ain't nobody around with that kind of money."

"Well, we're sorry, Victor, but that's the best we can do."

Victor accepted the tribal council's offer. What else could he do? So he signed the proper papers, picked up his check, and walked over to the Trading Post to cash it.

15   While Victor stood in line, he watched Thomas Builds-the-Fire standing near the magazine rack talking to himself. Like he always did. Thomas was a storyteller whom nobody wanted to listen to. That's like being a dentist in a town where everybody has false teeth.

Victor and Thomas Builds-the-Fire were the same age, had grown up and played in the dirt together. Ever since Victor could remember, it was Thomas who had always had something to say.

Once, when they were seven years old, when Victor's father still lived with the family, Thomas closed his eyes and told Victor this story: "Your father's heart is weak. He is afraid of his own family. He is afraid of you. Late at night, he sits in the dark. Watches the television until there's nothing but that white noise. Sometimes he feels like he wants to buy a motorcycle and ride away. He wants to run and hide. He doesn't want to be found."

Thomas Builds-the-Fire had known that Victor's father was going to leave, known it before anyone. Now Victor stood in the Trading Post with a one-hundred-dollar check in his hand, wondering if Thomas knew that Victor's father was dead, if he knew what was going to happen next.

Just then, Thomas looked at Victor, smiled, and walked over to him.

20   "Victor, I'm sorry about your father," Thomas said.

"How did you know about it?" Victor asked.

"I heard it on the wind. I heard it from the birds. I felt it in the sunlight. Also, your mother was just in here crying."

"Oh," Victor said and looked around the Trading Post. All the other Indians stared, surprised that Victor was even talking to Thomas. Nobody talked to Thomas anymore because he told the same damn stories over and over again. Victor was embarrassed, but he thought that Thomas might be able to help him. Victor felt a sudden need for tradition.

"I can lend you the money you need," Thomas said suddenly. "But you have to take me with you."

25   "I can't take your money," Victor said. "I mean, I haven't hardly talked to you in years. We're not really friends anymore."

"I didn't say we were friends. I said you had to take me with you."

"Let me think about it."

Victor went home with his one hundred dollars and sat at the kitchen table. He held his head in his hands and thought about Thomas

Builds-the-Fire, remembered little details, tears and scars, the bicycle they shared for a summer, so many stories.

Thomas Builds-the-Fire sat on the bicycle, waiting in Victor's yard. He was ten years old and skinny. His hair was dirty because it was the Fourth of July.

30   "Victor," Thomas yelled. "Hurry up. We're going to miss the fireworks."

After a few minutes, Victor ran out of his family's house, vaulted over the porch railing, and landed gracefully on the sidewalk.

Thomas gave him the bike and they headed for the fireworks. It was nearly dark and the fireworks were about to start.

"You know," Thomas said, "it's strange how us Indians celebrate the Fourth of July. It ain't like it was our independence everybody was fighting for."

"You think about things too much," Victor said. "It's just supposed to be fun. Maybe Junior will be there."

35   "Which Junior? Everybody on this reservation is named Junior."

The fireworks were small, hardly more than a few bottle rockets and a fountain. But it was enough for two Indian boys. Years later, they would need much more.

Afterward, sitting in the dark, fighting off mosquitoes, Victor turned to Thomas Builds-the-Fire.

"Hey," Victor said. "Tell me a story."

Thomas closed his eyes and told this story: "There were these two Indian boys who wanted to be warriors. But it was too late to be warriors in the old way. All the horses were gone. So the two Indian boys stole a car and drove to the city. They parked the stolen car in the front of the police station and then hitchhiked back home to the reservation. When they got back, all their friends cheered and their parents' eyes shone with pride. 'You were very brave,' everybody said to the two Indian boys. 'Very brave.'"

40   "Ya-hey," Victor said. "That's a good one. I wish I could be a warrior."

"Me too," Thomas said.

Victor sat at his kitchen table. He counted his one hundred dollars again and again. He knew he needed more to make it to Phoenix and back. He knew he needed Thomas Builds-the-Fire. So he put his money in his wallet and opened the front door to find Thomas on the porch.

"Ya-hey, Victor," Thomas said. "I knew you'd call me."

Thomas walked into the living room and sat down in Victor's favorite chair.

45   "I've got some money saved up," Thomas said. "It's enough to get us down there, but you have to get us back."

"I've got this hundred dollars," Victor said. "And my dad had a savings account I'm going to claim."

"How much in your dad's account?"

"Enough. A few hundred."

"Sounds good. When we leaving?"

50   When they were fifteen and had long since stopped being friends, Victor and Thomas got into a fistfight. That is, Victor was really drunk and beat Thomas up for no reason at all. All the other Indian boys stood around and watched it happen. Junior was there and so were Lester, Seymour, and a lot of others.

The beating might have gone on until Thomas was dead if Norma Many Horses hadn't come along and stopped it.

"Hey, you boys," Norma yelled and jumped out of her car. "Leave him alone."

If it had been someone else, even another man, the Indian boys would've just ignored the warnings. But Norma was a warrior. She was powerful. She could have picked up any two of the boys and smashed their skulls together. But worse than that, she would have dragged them all over to some tepee and made them listen to some elder tell a dusty old story.

The Indian boys scattered, and Norma walked over to Thomas and picked him up.

55   "Hey, little man, are you O.K.?" she asked.

Thomas gave her a thumbs-up.

"Why they always picking on you?"

Thomas shook his head, closed his eyes, but no stories came to him, no words or music. He just wanted to go home, to lie in his bed and let his dreams tell the stories for him.

Thomas Builds-the-Fire and Victor sat next to each other in the airplane, coach section. A tiny white woman had the window seat. She was busy twisting her body into pretzels. She was flexible.

60   "I have to ask," Thomas said, and Victor closed his eyes in embarrassment.

"Don't," Victor said.

"Excuse me, miss," Thomas asked. "Are you a gymnast or something?"

"There's no something about it," she said. "I was first alternate on the 1980 Olympic team."

"Really?" Thomas asked.

65   "Really."

"I mean, you used to be a world-class athlete?" Thomas asked.

"My husband thinks I still am."

Thomas Builds-the-Fire smiled. She was a mental gymnast too. She pulled her leg straight up against her body so that she could've kissed her kneecap.

"I wish I could do that," Thomas said.

70   Victor was ready to jump out of the plane. Thomas, that crazy Indian storyteller with ratty old braids and broken teeth, was flirting with a

beautiful Olympic gymnast. Nobody back home on the reservation would ever believe it.

"Well," the gymnast said. "It's easy. Try it."

Thomas grabbed at his leg and tried to pull it up into the same position as the gymnast's. He couldn't even come close, which made Victor and the gymnast laugh.

"Hey," she asked. "You two are Indian, right?"

"Full-blood," Victor said.

75   "Not me," Thomas said. "I'm half magician on my mother's side and half clown on my father's."

They all laughed.

"What are your names?" she asked.

"Victor and Thomas."

"Mine is Cathy. Pleased to meet you all."

80   The three of them talked for the duration of the flight. Cathy the gymnast complained about the government, how they screwed the 1980 Olympic team by boycotting the games.

"Sounds like you all got a lot in common with Indians," Thomas said.

Nobody laughed.

After the plane landed in Phoenix and they had all found their way to the terminal, Cathy the gymnast smiled and waved goodbye.

"She was really nice," Thomas said.

85   "Yeah, but everybody talks to everybody on airplanes," Victor said.

"You always used to tell me I think too much," Thomas said. "Now it sounds like you do."

"Maybe I caught it from you."

"Yeah."

Thomas and Victor rode in a taxi to the trailer where Victor's father had died.

90   "Listen," Victor said as they stopped in front of the trailer. "I never told you I was sorry for beating you up that time."

"Oh, it was nothing. We were just kids and you were drunk."

"Yeah, but I'm still sorry."

"That's all right."

Victor paid for the taxi, and the two of them stood in the hot Phoenix summer. They could smell the trailer.

95   "This ain't going to be nice," Victor said. "You don't have to go in."

"You're going to need help."

Victor walked to the front door and opened it. The stink rolled out and made them both gag. Victor's father had lain in that trailer for a week in hundred-degree temperatures before anyone had found him. And the only reason anyone found him was the smell. They needed dental records to identify him. That's exactly what the coroner said. They needed dental records.

"Oh, man," Victor said. "I don't know if I can do this."

"Well, then don't."

100   "But there might be something valuable in there."

"I thought his money was in the bank."

"It is: I was talking about pictures and letters and stuff like that."

"Oh," Thomas said as he held his breath and followed Victor into the trailer.

When Victor was twelve, he stepped into an underground wasps' nest. His foot was caught in the hole and no matter how hard he struggled, Victor couldn't pull free. He might have died there, stung a thousand times, if Thomas Builds-the-Fire had not come by.

105   "Run," Thomas yelled and pulled Victor's foot from the hole. They ran then, hard as they ever had, faster than Billy Mills, faster than Jim Thorpe, faster than the wasps could fly.

Victor and Thomas ran until they couldn't breathe, ran until it was cold and dark outside, ran until they were lost and it took hours to find their way home. All the way back, Victor counted his stings.

"Seven," Victor said. "My lucky number."

Victor didn't find much to keep in the trailer. Only a photo album and a stereo. Everything else had that smell stuck in it or was useless anyway. "I guess this is all," Victor said. "It ain't much."

"Better than nothing," Thomas said.

110   "Yeah, and I do have the pickup."

"Yeah," Thomas said. "It's in good shape."

"Dad was good about that stuff."

"Yeah, I remember your dad."

"Really?" Victor asked. "What do you remember?"

115   Thomas Builds-the-Fire closed his eyes and told this story: "I remember when I had this dream that told me to go to Spokane, to stand by the falls in the middle of the city and wait for a sign. I knew I had to go there but I didn't have a car. Didn't have a license. I was only thirteen. So I walked all the way, took me all day, and I finally made it to the falls. I stood there for an hour waiting. Then your dad came walking up. 'What the hell are you doing here?' he asked me. I said, 'Waiting for a vision.' Then your father said, 'All you're going to get here is mugged.' So he drove me over to Denny's, bought me dinner, and then drove me home to the reservation. For a long time, I was mad because I thought my dreams had lied to me. But they hadn't. Your dad was my vision. *Take care of each other* is what my dreams were saying. *Take care of each other.*"

Victor was quiet for a long time. He searched his mind for memories of his father, found the good ones, found a few bad ones, added it all up, and smiled.

"My father never told me about finding you in Spokane," Victor said.

"He said he wouldn't tell anybody. Didn't want me to get in trouble. But he said I had to watch out for you as part of the deal."

"Really?"

120   "Really. Your father said you would need the help. He was right."

"That's why you came down here with me, isn't it?" Victor asked.

"I came because of your father."

Victor and Thomas climbed into the pickup, drove over to the bank, and claimed the three hundred dollars in the savings account.

Thomas Builds-the-Fire could fly.

125   Once, he jumped off the roof of the tribal school and flapped his arms like a crazy eagle. And he flew. For a second he hovered, suspended above all the other Indian boys, who were too smart or too scared to jump too.

"He's flying," Junior yelled, and Seymour was busy looking for the trick wires or mirrors. But it was real. As real as the dirt when Thomas lost altitude and crashed to the ground.

He broke his arm in two places.

"He broke his wing, he broke his wing, he broke his wing," all the Indian boys chanted as they ran off, flapping their wings, wishing they could fly too. They hated Thomas for his courage, his brief moment as a bird. Everybody has dreams about flying. Thomas flew.

One of his dreams came true for just a second, just enough to make it real.

130   Victor's father, his ashes, fit in one wooden box with enough left over to fill a cardboard box.

"He always was a big man," Thomas said.

Victor carried part of his father out to the pickup, and Thomas carried the rest. They set him down carefully behind the seats, put a cowboy hat on the wooden box and a Dodgers cap on the cardboard box. That was the way it was supposed to be.

"Ready to head back home?" Victor asked.

"It's going to be a long drive."

135   "Yeah, take a couple days, maybe."

"We can take turns," Thomas said.

"O.K.," Victor said, but they didn't take turns. Victor drove for sixteen hours straight north, made it halfway up Nevada toward home before he finally pulled over.

"Hey, Thomas," Victor said. "You got to drive for a while."

"O.K."

140   Thomas Builds-the-Fire slid behind the wheel and started off down the road. All through Nevada, Thomas and Victor had been amazed at the lack of animal life, at the absence of water, of movement.

"Where is everything?" Victor had asked more than once.

Now, when Thomas was finally driving, they saw the first animal, maybe the only animal in Nevada. It was a long-eared jackrabbit.

"Look," Victor yelled. "It's alive."

Thomas and Victor were busy congratulating themselves on their discovery when the jackrabbit darted out into the road and under the wheels
of the pickup.

145   "Stop the goddamn car," Victor yelled, and Thomas did stop and
backed the pickup to the dead jackrabbit.

"Oh, man, he's dead," Victor said as he looked at the squashed animal.
"Really dead."

"The only thing alive in this whole state and we just killed it."

"I don't know," Thomas said. "I think it was suicide."

150   Victor looked around the desert, sniffed the air, felt the emptiness and
loneliness, and nodded his head.

"Yeah," Victor said. "It had to be suicide."

"I can't believe this," Thomas said. "You drive for a thousand miles
and there ain't even any bugs smashed on the windshield. I drive for ten
seconds and kill the only living thing in Nevada."

"Yeah," Victor said. "Maybe I should drive."

"Maybe you should."

155   Thomas Builds-the-Fire walked through the corridors of the tribal
school by himself. Nobody wanted to be anywhere near him because of all
those stories. Story after story.

Thomas closed his eyes and this story came to him: "We are all
given one thing by which our lives are measured, one determination.
Mine are the stories that can change or not change the world. It doesn't
matter which, as long as I continue to tell the stories. My father, he died
on Okinawa[2] in World War II, died fighting for this country, which had
tried to kill him for years. My mother, she died giving birth to me, died
while I was still inside her. She pushed me out into the world with her
last breath. I have no brothers or sisters. I have only my stories, which
came to me before I even had the words to speak. I learned a thousand
stories before I took my first thousand steps. They are all I have. It's all I
can do."

Thomas Builds-the-Fire told his stories to all those who would stop and
listen. He kept telling them long after people had stopped listening.

Victor and Thomas made it back to the reservation just as the sun was
rising. It was the beginning of a new day on earth, but the same old shit
on the reservation.

"Good morning," Thomas said.

160   "Good morning."

The tribe was waking up, ready for work, eating breakfast, reading the
newspaper, just like everybody else does. Willene LeBret was out in her
garden, wearing a bathrobe. She waved when Thomas and Victor drove by.

_____

[2] Largest island of the Ryukus, a chain of Japanese islands in the Western Pacific
Ocean.

"Crazy Indians made it," she said to herself and went back to her roses.

Victor stopped the pickup in front of Thomas Builds-the-Fire's HUD[3] house. They both yawned, stretched a little, shook dust from their bodies.

"I'm tired," Victor said.

165 "Of everything," Thomas added.

They both searched for words to end the journey. Victor needed to thank Thomas for his help and for the money, and to make the promise to pay it all back.

"Don't worry about the money," Thomas said. "It don't make any difference anyhow."

"Probably not, enit?"

"Nope."

170 Victor knew that Thomas would remain the crazy storyteller who talked to dogs and cars, who listened to the wind and pine trees. Victor knew that he couldn't really be friends with Thomas, even after all that had happened. It was cruel but it was real. As real as the ash, as Victor's father, sitting behind the seats.

"I know how it is," Thomas said. "I know you ain't going to treat me any better than you did before. I know your friends would give you too much shit about it."

Victor was ashamed of himself. Whatever happened to the tribal ties, the sense of community? The only real thing he shared with anybody was a bottle and broken dreams. He owed Thomas something, anything.

"Listen," Victor said and handed Thomas the cardboard box that contained half of his father. "I want you to have this."

Thomas took the ashes and smiled, closed his eyes, and told this story: "I'm going to travel to Spokane Falls one last time and toss these ashes into the water. And your father will rise like a salmon, leap over the bridge, over me, and find his way home. It will be beautiful. His teeth will shine like silver, like a rainbow. He will rise, Victor, he will rise."

175 Victor smiled.

"I was planning on doing the same thing with my half," Victor said. "But I didn't imagine my father looking anything like a salmon. I thought it'd be like cleaning the attic or something. Like letting things go after they've stopped having any use."

"Nothing stops, cousin," Thomas said. "Nothing stops."

Thomas Builds-the-Fire got out of the pickup and walked up his driveway. Victor started the pickup and began the drive home.

"Wait," Thomas yelled suddenly from his porch. "I just got to ask one favor."

180 Victor stopped the pickup, leaned out the window, and shouted back.

"What do you want?" he asked.

"Just one time when I'm telling a story somewhere, why don't you stop and listen?" Thomas asked.

---

[3] The U.S. Department of Housing and Urban Development.

"Just once?"

"Just once."

185   Victor waved his arms to let Thomas know that the deal was good. It was a fair trade. That's all Thomas had ever wanted from his whole life. So Victor drove his father's pickup toward home while Thomas went into his house, closed the door behind him, and heard a new story come to him in the silence afterward.

Reading and Reacting

1. In paragraph 1 readers are told that Victor lives on an Indian reservation. What details elsewhere in the story establish this setting? What associations does this setting have for you? Do you think the story could take place anywhere else?

2. In addition to various locations on the reservation, the story's settings include an airplane, a trailer in Phoenix, and a road through Nevada. What does each of these settings contribute to the story's plot?

3. Is the scene on the plane necessary? Intrusive? Distracting? Farfetched?

4. How would you characterize the story's mood or atmosphere? How do Thomas's stories help to create this mood? How do they help to establish his character? Do you think Alexie should have included more of these stories?

5. Why do you suppose Victor and Thomas cannot be friends when they get back to the reservation? Why can they be friends when they are traveling to Phoenix?

6. Do the flashbacks to the two men's childhood add something vital to the story? What purpose do these flashbacks serve?

7. In Native American culture the storyteller holds an important position, telling tales that transmit and preserve the tribe's basic beliefs. Do you think Thomas's stories serve such a function? Or is he, as Victor characterizes him near the end of the story, simply "the crazy storyteller who talked to dogs and cars, who listened to the wind and pine trees" (170)?

8. What do you think the story's title means?

9. **Journal Entry** At the end of the story, when Thomas returns home, he hears "a new story come to him in the silence" after he closes the door. What kind of story do you think comes to him at this point? Why do you think so?

10. **Critical Perspective** In the introduction to a collection of Native American literature, Clifford E. Trafzer, the collection's editor, discusses the unique characteristics of Native American writers:

    > Due to their grounding in the oral tradition of their people, Native American writers do not follow the literary canon of

the dominant society in their approach to short stories. Rather than focusing on one theme or character in a brief time frame, or using one geographical area, they often use multiple themes and characters with few boundaries of time or place. Their stories do not always follow a linear and clear path, and frequently the past and present, real and mythic, and conscious and unconscious are not distinguishable. Multidimensional characters are common, and involved stories usually lack absolute conclusions. Native American writers may also play tricks with language, deliberately misusing grammar, syntax, and spelling—sometimes in defiance of the dominant culture—in order to make English reflect the language of their peoples.

Do you think "This Is What It Means to Say Phoenix, Arizona" has the characteristics Trafzer associates with Native American writers?

Related Works: "Sleepy Time Gal" (p. 242), "The Rotifer" (p. 441), "My Father's Song" (p. 680), "Defending Walt Whitman" (p. 922), *The Glass Menagerie* (p. 1805)

◊ WRITING SUGGESTIONS: SETTING

1. Write the story of the trip to Phoenix as Thomas-Builds-the-Fire ("This Is What It Means to Say Phoenix, Arizona") might tell it.
2. In the first three of the four stories in this chapter, social constraints determined by the story's historical setting limit a woman's options. Explore the options each woman might reasonably exercise in order to break free of the limits that social institutions impose on her.
3. Write an essay in which you consider how any one of the four stories in this chapter would be different if its historical, geographical, or physical setting were changed to a setting of your choice. In your essay, examine the changes (in plot development as well as in the characters' conflicts, reactions, and motivation) that might be caused by the change in setting.
4. Select a story from another chapter, and write an essay in which you consider how setting affects its plot—for example, how it creates conflict or crisis, how it forces characters to act, or how it determines how the plot is resolved.
5. Both "The Storm" and "The Yellow Wall-Paper" use rich language to create a mood that dominates the story. Analyze this use of language in one of the two stories—or compare two short passages, one from eaach story. How does language create and enrich each story's setting?
6. **WEB ACTIVITY** The following Web site contains information about Tillie Olsen:

http://mockingbird.creighton.edu/NCW/olsen.htm

From the Tillie Olsen Web page, link to "Commentary" and then to "Tell Me a Riddle." One of the reviewers states the following about Olsen:

> [She] writes about those people who, because of their class, sex, or race, have been denied the opportunity to express and develop themselves. In a strongly emotional style, she tells of their dreams and failures, of what she calls "the unnatural thwarting of what struggles to come into being but cannot."

Now link to "Selection" from the Olsen page and read "These Things Shall Be." Then, write an essay discussing how "These Things Shall Be" and "I Stand Here Ironing," are about people who "have been denied the opportunity to express and develop themselves." In your essay, you may want to focus on the mother in "I Stand Here Ironing" and the father in "These Things Shall Be." Consider how both have been denied the opportunity for self-expression because of what others have expected of them.

CHAPTER 7

Point of View

◊ ◊ ◊

In dealing with point-of-view the [writer] must always deal with the
individual work: which particular character shall tell this particular story, or
part of a story, with what precise degree of reliability, privilege, freedom to
comment, and so on. [. . .] Even if the [writer] has decided on a narrator who
will fit one of the critic's classifications—"omniscient," "first-person,"
"limited omniscient," "objective," [. . .] and so on—his troubles have just
begun. He simply cannot find answers to his immediate, precise, practical
problems by referring to statements that the "omniscient is the most flexible
method," or "the objective the most rapid or vivid," or whatever. Even the
soundest of generalizations at this level will be of little use to him.

WAYNE C. BOOTH, "Distance and Point of View"

For reasons that should not need explanation here, until very recently, and
regardless of the race of the author, the readers of virtually all of American
fiction have been positioned as white. I am interested to know what that
assumption has meant to the literary imagination. [. . .] What happens to the
writerly imagination of a black author who is at some level *always* conscious
of representing one's own race to, or in spite of, a race of readers that
understands itself to be "universal" or race-free? In other words, how is
"literary whiteness" and "literary blackness" made, and what is the
consequence of that construction?

TONI MORRISON, *Playing in the Dark*

Tied to issues of gender, social stratification, racial oppression, and the need
to restore the foundations of our history and culture, the most recurrent
theme in our writing is what I call claiming America for Asian Americans.
That does not mean disappearing like raindrops in the ocean of white
America, fighting to become "normal," losing ourselves in the process. It
means inventing a new identity, defining ourselves according to the truth
instead of a racial fantasy, so that we can be reconciled with one another in
order to celebrate our marginality.

ELAINE H. KIM, "Defining Asian American Realities through Literature"

◊ ◊ ◊

All stories are told, or narrated, by someone, and one of the first choices writers make is who tells the story. This choice determines the story's **point of view**—the vantage point from which events are presented. The implications of this choice are far reaching. Consider for a moment the following scenario. Five people witness a crime and are questioned by the police. Their stories agree on certain points: a crime was committed, a body was found, and the crime occurred at noon. But in other ways their stories are different. The man who fled the scene was either tall or of average height; his hair was either dark or light; he either was carrying an object or was empty handed. The events that led up to the crime and even the description of the crime itself are markedly different depending on who tells the story. Thus, the perspective from which a story is told determines what details are included in the story and how they are arranged—in short, the plot. In addition, the perspective of the narrator affects the story's style, language, and themes.

The narrator of a work of fiction is not the same as the writer—even when a writer uses the first-person *I*. Writers create narrators, often with personalities and opinions far different from theirs, to tell their stories. (The term **persona**—which literally means "mask"—is used for this narrator.) By assuming this mask, a writer expands the creative possibilities of a work.

When deciding on a point of view for a work of fiction, a writer can choose to tell the story either in the *first person* or in the *third person*.

FIRST-PERSON NARRATOR
♦ ♦ ♦

Sometimes the narrator is a character who uses the **first person** *I* (or sometimes *we*) to tell the story. Often this narrator is a major character—Sammy in John Updike's "A&P" (p. 113) and the boy in James Joyce's "Araby" (p. 254), for example—who tells his or her own story and is the focus of that story. Sometimes, however, a first-person narrator may tell a story that is primarily about someone else. Such a narrator may be a minor character who plays a relatively small part in the story or simply an observer who reports events experienced or related by others. The narrator of William Faulkner's "A Rose for Emily" (p. 87), for example, is an unidentified witness to the story's events. By using *we* instead of *I*, this narrator speaks on behalf of all the town's residents, expressing their shared views of their neighbor, Emily Grierson:

> We did not say she was crazy then. We believed she had to do that.
> We remembered all the young men her father had driven away, and
> we knew that with nothing left, she would have to cling to that which
> had robbed her, as people will.

Writers gain a number of advantages when they use a first-person narrator. First, they are able to present incidents very convincingly. Readers are more willing to accept a statement like "My sister changed a lot after that day" than they are to accept the impersonal observations of a third-person narrator. The first-person narrator also simplifies a writer's task of selecting details. Only the events and details that the narrator could actually have seen or experienced can be introduced into the story.

Another major advantage of first-person narrators is that their restricted view can create **irony**—a discrepancy between what is said and what readers believe to be true. Irony may be *dramatic, situational,* or *verbal.* **Dramatic irony** occurs when a narrator or character perceives less than readers do; **situational irony** occurs when what happens is at odds with what readers are led to expect; **verbal irony** occurs when the narrator says one thing but actually means another.

"Gryphon," by Charles Baxter (p. 134), illustrates all three kinds of irony. Baxter creates *dramatic irony* when he has his main character see less than readers do. For example, at the end of the story, the young boy does not yet realize what readers already know—that he has learned more from Miss Ferenczi's way of teaching than from Mr. Hibler's. The setting of the story—a conventional school—creates *situational irony* because it contrasts with the unexpected events that unfold there. In addition, many of the narrator's comments create *verbal irony* because they mean something different from what they seem to mean. At the end of the story, for example, after the substitute, Miss Ferenczi, has been fired, the narrator relates another teacher's comment that life will now return to "normal" and that their regular teacher will soon return to test them on their "knowledge." This comment is ironic in light of all Miss Ferenczi has done to redefine her students' ideas about "normal" education.

UNRELIABLE NARRATORS

Sometimes first-person narrators may be self-serving, mistaken, confused, unstable, or even mad. These **unreliable narrators,** whether intentionally or unintentionally, misrepresent events and misdirect readers. In Edgar Allan Poe's "The Cask of Amontillado" (p. 219), for example, the narrator, Montresor, tells his story to justify a crime he committed fifty years before. Montresor's version of what happened is not accurate, and perceptive readers know it: his obvious self-deception, his sadistic manipulation of Fortunato, his detached description of the cold-blooded murder, and his lack of remorse lead readers to question his sanity (and, therefore, to distrust his version of events). This distrust creates an ironic distance between readers and narrator.

The narrator of Charlotte Perkins Gilman's "The Yellow Wall-Paper" (p. 168) is also an unreliable narrator. Suffering from "nervous depression," she unintentionally distorts the facts when she says that the shapes in the wallpaper of her bedroom are changing and moving. Moreover, she does not realize what is wrong with her or why, or how her husband's "good intentions" are hurting her. Readers, however, see the disparity between the narrator's interpretation of events and their own, and this irony enriches their understanding of the story.

Some narrators are unreliable because they are naive. Because they are immature, sheltered, or innocent of evil, these narrators may not be aware of the full significance of the events they are relating. Having the benefit of experience, readers interpret events differently from the way these narrators do. When we read a passage by a child narrator—such as the following from J. D. Salinger's novel *The Catcher in the Rye*—we are aware of the narrator's innocence, and we know his interpretation of events is flawed:

> Anyway, I keep picturing all these little kids playing some game in this big field of rye and all. Thousands of little kids, and nobody's around—nobody big, I mean—except me. And I'm standing on the edge of some crazy cliff. What I have to do, I have to catch everybody if they start to go over the cliff—I mean if they're running and they don't look where they're going I have to come out from somewhere and catch them. I'd just be the catcher in the rye. . . .

The irony in the preceding passage comes from our knowledge that the naive narrator, Holden Caulfield, cannot stop children from growing up. Ultimately, they all fall off the "crazy cliff" and mature into adults. Although he is not aware of the futility of trying to protect children from the dangers of adulthood, readers know that his efforts are doomed from the start.

A naive narrator's background can also limit his or her ability to understand a situation. The narrator in Sherwood Anderson's short story "I'm a Fool," for example, lies to impress a rich girl he meets at a race track. At the end of the story the boy laments the fact that he lied, believing that if he had told the truth, he could have seen the girl again. The reader knows, however, that the narrator is deceiving himself because the social gap that separates the narrator and the girl could never be bridged.

Keep in mind that there is a difference between an unreliable narrator and a narrator whose perspective is limited. All first-person narrators are, by definition, limited because they present a situation as only one person sees it. "In a Grove," by Ryūnosuke Akutagawa (p. 398), illustrates this idea. In this story, seven characters act as narrators and give different accounts of a murder. Some of the characters seem to be lying or bending the facts to suit their own needs, but others simply have an incomplete or mistaken understanding of the event. No character, of course, has all the information the story's author has.

As a reader focusing on a story's point of view, you should look for discrepancies between a narrator's view of events and your own. Discovering that a story has an unreliable narrator enables you not only to question the truth of the narrative but also to recognize the irony in the narrator's version of events. By doing so, you gain insight into the story and learn something about the writer's purpose.

THIRD-PERSON NARRATOR
◇ ◇ ◇

Writers can also use **third-person** narrators, who are not characters in the story. These narrators fall into three categories.

OMNISCIENT

Some third-person narrators are **omniscient** (all-knowing) narrators, moving at will from one character's mind to another. One advantage of omniscient narrators is that they are objective; they have none of the naïveté, dishonesty, gullibility, or mental instability that can characterize first-person narrators. In addition, because omniscient narrators are not characters in the story, their perception is not limited to what any one character can observe or comprehend. As a result, they can present a more inclusive overview of events and characters than first-person narrators can. In short, omniscient narrators are reliable; they maintain an objective distance from events, giving readers an accurate version of what happened, as the omniscient narrator of Nadine Gordimer's "Once upon a Time" (p. 81) does:

> In a house, in a suburb, in a city, there were a man and his wife who loved each other very much and were living happily ever after. They had a little boy, and they loved him very much. They had a cat and a dog that the little boy loved very much. They had a car and a caravan trailer for holidays, and a swimming-pool which was fenced so that the little boy and his playmates would not fall in and drown. They had a housemaid who was absolutely trustworthy and an itinerant gardener who was highly recommended by the neighbours. For when they began to live happily ever after they were warned, by that wise old witch, the husband's mother, not to take anyone off the street.

Occasionally, omniscient narrators move not only in and out of the minds of the characters but also in and out of a persona (representing the voice of the author) that speaks directly to readers. This experimental narrative technique was popular with writers during the eighteenth century, when the novel was a new literary form. It permitted writers to present themselves as masters of artifice, able to know and control all aspects of experience. Few contemporary writers would give themselves the license that Henry Fielding does in the following passage from *Tom Jones:*

> And true it was that [Mr. Alworthy] did many of these things; but had he done nothing more I should have left him to have recorded his own merit on some fair freestone over the door of that hospital. Matters of a much more extraordinary kind are to be the subject of this history, or I should grossly misspend my time in writing so voluminous a work; and you my sagacious friend, might with equal profit and pleasure travel through some pages which certain droll authors have been facetiously pleased to call *The History of England.*

A contemporary example of this type of omniscient point of view occurs in Ursula K. LeGuin's "The Ones Who Walk Away from Omelas." This story presents a description of a city that in the narrator's words is "like a city in a fairy tale." As the story proceeds, however, the description of Omelas changes, and the narrator's tone changes as well: "Do you believe? Do you accept the festival, the city, the joy? No? Then let me describe one more thing." By undercutting her own narrative, the narrator underscores the ironic theme of the story, which suggests the impossibility of human beings ever achieving an ideal society.

Limited Omniscient

Third-person narrators can have **limited omniscience,** focusing on only what a single character experiences. In other words, events are limited to one character's perspective, and nothing is revealed that the character does not see, hear, feel, or think. Andy in David Michael Kaplan's "Doe Season" (p. 349) is just such a limited-focus character. Limited omniscient narrators, like all third-person narrators, have certain advantages over first-person narrators. When a writer uses a first-person narrator, the narrator's personality and speech color the story, creating a personal or even idiosyncratic narrative. Also, the first-person narrator's character flaws or lack of knowledge may limit his or her awareness of the significance of events. Limited omniscient narrators are more flexible: they take readers into a particular character's mind just as a first-person narrator does, but without the first-person narrator's subjectivity, self-deception, or naiveté. In the following example from Anne Tyler's "Teenage Wasteland" (p. 603), the limited omniscient narrator presents the story from the point of view of a single character, Daisy:

> Daisy and Matt sat silent, shocked. Matt rubbed his forehead with his fingertips. Imagine, Daisy thought, how they must look to Mr. Lanham: an overweight housewife in a cotton dress and a too-tall, too-thin insurance agent in a baggy, frayed suit. Failures, both of them—the kind of people who are hurrying to catch up, missing the

point of things that everyone else grasps at once. She wished she'd worn nylons instead of knee socks.

Here the narrative point of view gives readers the impression that they are standing off to the side watching Daisy and her husband Matt. At the same time we have the advantage of this objective view, however, we are also able to see into the mind of one character.

OBJECTIVE

Finally, third-person narrators can tell a story from an **objective** (or *dramatic*) point of view, remaining entirely outside the characters' minds. With objective narrators, events unfold the way they would in a play or a movie: narrators tell the story only by presenting dialogue and recounting events; they do not reveal the characters' thoughts or explain their motivation. Thus, they allow readers to interpret the actions of the characters without any interference. Ernest Hemingway uses the objective point of view in his short story "A Clean, Well-Lighted Place" (p. 261):

> The waiter took the brandy bottle and another saucer from the counter inside the café and marched out to the old man's table. He put down the saucer and poured the glass full of brandy.
> "You should have killed yourself last week," he said to the deaf man. The old man motioned with his finger. "A little more," he said. The waiter poured on into the glass so that the brandy slopped over and ran down the stem into the top saucer of the pile. "Thank you," the old man said. The waiter took the bottle back inside the café. He sat down at the table with his colleague again.

The story's narrator is distant, seemingly emotionless, and this perspective is consistent with the author's purpose: for Hemingway, the attitude of the narrator reflects the stunned, almost anesthetized condition of people in the post–World War I world.

SELECTING AN APPROPRIATE POINT OF VIEW

◇ ◇ ◇

Writers of short stories often maintain a consistent point of view, but there is no rule that says they must. Although one point of view may be dominant, writers of fiction frequently introduce additional points of view to achieve complexity and depth. The main criterion writers use when they decide on a point of view is how the distance they maintain from their material will affect their narrative. For example, consider the following passage from "Doe Season":

Limited Omniscient Point of View

They were always the same woods, she thought sleepily as they drove through the early morning darkness—deep and immense, covered with yesterday's snowfall, which had frozen overnight. They were the same woods that lay behind her house, *and they stretch all the way to here,* she thought, *for miles and miles, longer than I could walk in a day, or a week even, but they are still the same woods.* The thought made her feel good: it was like thinking of God; it was like thinking of the space between here and the moon; it was like thinking of all the foreign countries from her geography book where even now, Andy knew, people were going to bed, while they—she and her father and Charlie Spoon and Mac, Charlie's eleven-year-old son—were driving deeper into the Pennsylvania countryside, to go hunting.

They had risen before dawn. Her mother, yawning and not trying to hide her sleepiness, cooked them eggs and French toast. Her father smoked a cigarette and flicked ashes into his saucer while Andy listened, wondering *Why doesn't he come?* and *Won't he ever come?* until at last a car pulled into the graveled drive and honked. "That will be Charlie Spoon," her father said; he always said "Charlie Spoon," even though his real name was Spreun, because Charlie was, in a sense, shaped like a spoon, with a large head and a narrow waist and chest.

In the preceding passage, David Michael Kaplan uses a third-person limited omniscient narrator to tell the story of Andy, a nine-year-old girl who is going hunting with her father for the first time. This point of view has the advantage of allowing the narrator to focus on the thoughts, fears, and reactions of the child while at the same time giving readers information about Andy that she herself is too immature or unsophisticated to know. Rather than simply presenting the thoughts of the child (represented in the story by italics), the third-person narrator makes connections between ideas and offers a level of language and a degree of insight that readers would not accept from Andy as a first-person narrator. In addition, the limited omniscient perspective enables the narrator to maintain some distance. Consider how different the passage would be if it were narrated by nine-year-old Andy.

First-Person Point of View (Child)

"I like the woods," I thought. "They're big and scary. I wonder if they're the same woods that are behind my house. They go on for miles. They're bigger than I could walk in a day, or a week even." It was neat to think that while we were driving into the woods people were going to bed in other countries.

When I woke up this morning, I couldn't wait to go hunting. My mother was cooking breakfast, but all I could think of was, "When will he come?" and "Won't he ever come?" Finally, I heard a car honk. "That will be Charlie Spoon," my father said. I think he called him "Charlie Spoon" because he thought Charlie was shaped like a big spoon.

As a first-person narrator, nine-year-old Andy must have the voice of a child; moreover, she is restricted to only those observations that a nine-year-old could reasonably make. Because of these limitations, the passage lacks the level of vocabulary, syntax, and insight necessary to develop the central character and the themes of the story. This point of view could succeed only if Andy's words established an ironic contrast between her naive sensibility and the reality of the situation.

Kaplan could have avoided these problems and still gained the advantages of using a first-person narrator by having Andy tell her story as an adult looking back on a childhood experience. (This technique is used by James Joyce in "Araby," p. 254; Charles Baxter in "Gryphon," p. 134; and Alberto Alvaro Ríos in "The Secret Lion," p. 49.)

FIRST-PERSON POINT OF VIEW (ADULT)

"They are always the same woods," I thought sleepily as we drove through the early morning darkness—deep and immense, covered with yesterday's snowfall, which had frozen overnight. "They're the same woods that lie behind my house, and they stretch all the way to here," I thought. I knew that they stretched for miles and miles, longer than I could walk in a day, or even in a week but that they were still the same woods. Knowing this made me feel good: I thought it was like thinking of God; it was like thinking of the space between that place and the moon; it was like thinking of all the foreign countries from my geography book where even then, I knew, people were going to bed, while we—my father and I and Charlie Spoon and Mac, Charlie's eleven-year-old son—were driving deeper into the Pennsylvania countryside, to go hunting.

We had risen before dawn. My mother, who was yawning and not trying to hide her sleepiness, cooked us eggs and French toast. My father smoked a cigarette and flicked ashes into his saucer while I listened, wondering, "Why doesn't he come?" and "Won't he ever come?" until at last a car pulled into our driveway and honked. "That will be Charlie Spoon," my father said. He always said "Charlie Spoon," even though his real name was Spreun, because Charlie was, in a sense, shaped like a spoon, with a large head and a narrow waist and chest.

Although this passage presents the child's point of view, it does not use a child's voice; the language and scope of the passage are too sophisticated for a child. By using a mature style, the adult narrator is able to consider ideas that a child could not possibly understand, such as the symbolic significance of the woods. By doing so, however, he sacrifices the ironic detachment that characterizes the narrator of the original story.

Kaplan had other options as well. For example, he could have used an omniscient narrator to tell his story. In this case, the narrator would be free to reveal and comment not only on Andy's thoughts but also on those of her father, and possibly even on the thoughts of her mother and Charlie

Spoon. In the following passage, the omniscient narrator interprets the behavior of the characters and tells what each one is thinking.

Omniscient Point of View

They were always the same woods, she thought sleepily as they drove through the early morning darkness—deep and immense, covered with yesterday's snowfall, which had frozen overnight. They were the same woods that lay behind her house, and they stretch all the way to here, she thought, for miles and miles, longer than I could walk in a day, or a week even, but they are still the same woods.

They had risen before dawn. The mother, yawning and not trying to hide her sleepiness, cooked them eggs and French toast. She looked at her husband and her daughter and wondered if she was doing the right thing by allowing them to go hunting together. "After all," she thought, "he's not the most careful person. Will he watch her? Make sure that no harm comes to her?"

The father smoked a cigarette and flicked ashes into his saucer. He was listening to the sounds of the early morning. "I know everything will be all right," he thought. "It's about time Andy went hunting. When I was her age. . . ." Andy listened, wondering Why doesn't he come? and Won't he ever come? until at last a car pulled into the graveled drive and honked. Suddenly the father cocked his head and said, "That will be Charlie Spoon."

Andy thought it was funny that her father called Charlie "Spoon" even though his real name was Spreun, because Charlie was, in a sense, shaped like a spoon, with a large head and a narrow waist and chest.

Certainly this point of view has its advantages; for example, the wide scope of this perspective provides a great deal of information about the characters. However, the use of an omniscient point of view deprives the story of its focus on Andy.

Finally, Kaplan could have used an objective narrator. This point of view would eliminate all interpretation by the narrator and force readers to make judgments solely on the basis of what the characters say and do. Here is an example of the passage from "Doe Season" presented from this point of view.

Objective Point of View

Andy sat sleepily staring into her cereal. She played with the dry flakes of bran as they floated in the surface of the milk.

Andy's mother, yawning, cooked them eggs and French toast. She looked at her husband and her daughter, paused for a second, and then went about what she was doing.

Andy's father smoked a cigarette and flicked ashes into his saucer. He looked out the window and said, "I wonder where Charlie Spoon is?"

Andy squirmed restlessly and repeatedly looked up at the clock that hung above the stove.

The disadvantage of this point of view is that it creates a great deal of distance between the characters and the readers. Instead of gaining the intimate knowledge of Andy that the limited omniscient point of view provides—knowledge even greater than she herself has—readers must infer what she thinks and feels without any help from the narrator.

As the preceding examples illustrate, writers choose the point of view that best enables them to achieve their objectives. If they want to create an intimate, subjective portrait of a character, they will employ a first-person narrator. If they want to have a great deal of freedom in telling their story, they will use an omniscient narrator. A limited omniscient narrator enables writers to maintain the focus on a single individual while commenting on the action. And finally, the objective point of view allows writers to remove the narrator from the story and present events in a distant, emotionless way.

SELECTING AN APPROPRIATE POINT OF VIEW: REVIEW

FIRST-PERSON NARRATOR (*I* OR *WE*)

◊ *Major character telling his or her own story* "Every morning I lay on the floor in the front parlour watching her door." (James Joyce, "Araby")

◊ *Minor character as witness or nonparticipant* "And so she died. . . . We did not even know she was sick; we had long since given up trying to get information. . . . " (William Faulkner, "A Rose for Emily")

THIRD-PERSON NARRATOR (*HE, SHE, IT,* OR *THEY*)

◊ *Omniscient—able to move at will from character to character and comment about them* "In a house, in a suburb, in a city, there were a man and his wife who loved each other very much. . . . " (Nadine Gordimer, "Once upon a Time")

◊ *Limited Omniscient—restricts focus to a single character* "The wagon went on. He did not know where they were going." (William Faulkner, "Barn Burning")

◊ *Objective (Dramatic)—simply reports the dialogue and the actions of characters* "'You'll be drunk,' the waiter said. The old man looked at him. The waiter went away." (Ernest Hemingway, "A Clean, Well-Lighted Place")

✴ CHECKLIST: WRITING ABOUT POINT OF VIEW

✓ What is the dominant point of view from which the story is told?

✓ Is the narrator a character in the story? If so, is he or she a participant in the story's events or just a witness?

✓ Does the story's point of view create irony?

✓ If the story has a first-person narrator, is the narrator reliable or unreliable? Are there any inconsistencies in the narrator's presentation of the story?

✓ If the story has a third-person narrator, is he or she omniscient? Does he or she have limited omniscience? Is the narrator objective?

✓ What are the advantages of the story's point of view? How does the point of view accomplish the author's purpose?

✓ Does the point of view remain consistent throughout the story, or does it shift?

✓ How might a different point of view change the story?

◈ **RICHARD WRIGHT** (1908–1960) was born near Natchez, Mississippi, the son of sharecroppers. He had little formal schooling but as a young man was a voracious reader, attracted particularly to naturalistic fiction. Relocating to Chicago in the late 1920s, Wright worked as a postal clerk until 1935, when he joined the Federal Writers' Project, an association that took him to New York City soon after. Deeply troubled by the economic and social oppression suffered by fellow African-Americans, Wright joined the Communist Party in 1932, and his early poems and stories reflect a distinctly Marxist perspective. However, he broke with the party in 1944 because of its stifling effect on "new ideas, new facts, [. . .] new hints at ways to live."

Wright began to reach a mainstream audience when a group of four long stories on the theme of racial oppression and violence was judged best manuscript in a contest sponsored by *Story* magazine; these stories were published as *Uncle Tom's Children* in 1938. Two years later Wright published his most famous work, *Native Son,* an angry and brutal novel exploring the moral devastation wrought by a racist society. The autobiographical *Black Boy* was published in 1945. In later years, Wright abandoned the United

States for Paris in protest against the treatment of blacks in his native country and focused his work on reports about national independence movements in Africa and elsewhere in the third world.

The following story, published in the posthumous collection *Eight Men* (1961), is uncharacteristic of Wright's work in a number of ways—not least of which is that it is told through the eyes of a white protagonist.

CULTURAL CONTEXT ◊ In 1957, the year "Big Black Good Man" was written, President Eisenhower sent paratroopers to Little Rock, Arkansas, to forestall violence over desegregation in the schools. The crisis began on September 2, when Governor Orval Faubus ordered the Arkansas National Guard to blockade Little Rock Central High School to prevent the entrance of the nine black students who were to begin classes there. The United States Federal Court ordered the troops removed, and on September 25, the students entered the school, escorted by members of the 101st Airborne Division of the United States Army.

◊   ◊   ◊

R I C H A R D   W R I G H T

Big Black Good Man
(1957)

Through the open window Olaf Jenson could smell the sea and hear the occasional foghorn of a freighter; outside, rain pelted down through an August night, drumming softly upon the pavements of Copenhagen,[1] inducing drowsiness, bringing dreamy memory, relaxing the tired muscles of his work-wracked body. He sat slumped in a swivel chair with his legs outstretched and his feet propped atop an edge of his desk. An inch of white ash tipped the end of his brown cigar and now and then he inserted the end of the stogie[2] into his mouth and drew gently upon it, letting wisps of blue smoke eddy from the corners of his wide, thin lips. The watery gray irises behind the thick lenses of his eyeglasses gave him a look of abstraction, of absentmindedness, of an almost genial idiocy. He sighed, reached for his half-empty bottle of beer, and drained it into his glass and downed it with a long slow gulp, then licked his lips. Replacing the cigar, he slapped his right palm against his thigh and said half aloud:

"Well, I'll be sixty tomorrow. I'm not rich, but I'm not poor either . . . Really, I can't complain. Got good health. Traveled all over the world and had my share of girls when I was young . . . And my Karen's a good wife. I own my home. Got no debts. And I love digging in my garden in the spring . . . Grew the biggest carrots of anybody last year. Ain't saved

---

[1] The capital of Denmark.
[2] Cheap cigar.

much money, but what the hell . . . Money ain't everything. Got a good job. Night portering ain't too bad." He shook his head and yawned. "Karen and I could of had some children, though. Would of been good company . . . 'Specially for Karen. And I could of taught 'em languages . . . English, French, German, Danish, Dutch, Swedish, Norwegian, and Spanish . . ." He took the cigar out of his mouth and eyed the white ash critically. "Hell of a lot of good language learning did me . . . Never got anything out of it. But those ten years in New York were fun . . . Maybe I could of got rich if I'd stayed in America . . . Maybe. But I'm satisfied. You can't have everything."

Behind him the office door opened and a young man, a medical student occupying room number nine, entered.

"Good evening," the student said.

5 "Good evening," Olaf said, turning.

The student went to the keyboard and took hold of the round, brown knob that anchored his key.

"Rain, rain, rain," the student said.

"That's Denmark for you," Olaf smiled at him.

"This dampness keeps me clogged up like a drainpipe," the student complained.

10 "That's Denmark for you," Olaf repeated with a smile.

"Good night," the student said.

"Good night, son," Olaf sighed, watching the door close.

Well, my tenants are my children, Olaf told himself. Almost all of his children were in their rooms now . . . Only seventy-two and forty-four were missing . . . Seventy-two might've gone to Sweden . . . And forty-four was maybe staying at his girl's place tonight, like he sometimes did . . . He studied the pear-shaped blobs of hard rubber, reddish brown like ripe fruit, that hung from the keyboard, then glanced at his watch. Only room thirty, eighty-one, and one hundred and one were empty . . . And it was almost midnight. In a few moments he could take a nap. Nobody hardly ever came looking for accommodations after midnight, unless a stray freighter came in, bringing thirsty, women-hungry sailors. Olaf chuckled softly. Why in hell was I ever a sailor? The whole time I was at sea I was thinking and dreaming about women. Then why didn't I stay on land where women could be had? Hunh? Sailors are crazy . . .

But he liked sailors. They reminded him of his youth, and there was something so direct, simple, and childlike about them. They always said straight out what they wanted, and what they wanted was almost always women and whisky . . . "Well, there's no harm in that . . . Nothing could be more natural," Olaf sighed, looking thirstily at his empty beer bottle. No; he'd not drink any more tonight; he'd had enough; he'd go to sleep . . .

15 He was bending forward and loosening his shoelaces when he heard the office door crack open. He lifted his eyes, then sucked in his breath. He did not straighten; he just stared up and around at the huge black thing that filled the doorway. His reflexes refused to function; it was not fear; it

was just simple astonishment. He was staring at the biggest, strangest, and blackest man he'd ever seen in all his life.

"Good evening," the black giant said in a voice that filled the small office. "Say, you got a room?"

Olaf sat up slowly, not to answer but to look at this brooding black vision; it towered darkly some six and a half feet into the air, almost touching the ceiling, and its skin was so black that it had a bluish tint. And the sheer bulk of the man! . . . His chest bulged like a barrel; his rocklike and humped shoulders hinted of mountain ridges; the stomach ballooned like a threatening stone; and the legs were like telephone poles . . . The big black cloud of a man now lumbered into the office, bending to get its buffalolike head under the door frame, then advanced slowly upon Olaf, like a stormy sky descending.

"You got a room?" the big black man asked again in a resounding voice.

Olaf now noticed that the ebony giant was well dressed, carried a wonderful new suitcase, and wore black shoes that gleamed despite the raindrops that peppered their toes.

20   "You're American?" Olaf asked him.

"Yeah, man; sure," the black giant answered.

"Sailor?"

"Yeah. American Continental Lines."

Olaf had not answered the black man's question. It was not that the hotel did not admit men of color; Olaf took in all comers—blacks, yellows, whites, and browns . . . To Olaf, men were men, and, in his day, he'd worked and eaten and slept and fought with all kinds of men. But this particular black man . . . Well, he didn't seem human. Too big, too black, too loud, too direct, and probably too violent to boot . . . Olaf's five feet seven inches scarcely reached the black giant's shoulder and his frail body weighed less, perhaps, than one of the man's gigantic legs . . . There was something about the man's intense blackness and ungainly bigness that frightened and insulted Olaf; he felt as though this man had come here expressly to remind him how puny, how tiny, and how weak and how white he was. Olaf knew, while registering his reactions, that he was being irrational and foolish; yet, for the first time in his life, he was emotionally determined to refuse a man a room solely on the basis of the man's size and color . . . Olaf's lips parted as he groped for the right words in which to couch his refusal, but the black giant bent forward and boomed:

25   "I asked you if you got a room. I got to put up somewhere tonight, man."

"Yes, we got a room," Olaf murmured.

And at once he was ashamed and confused. Sheer fear had made him yield. And he seethed against himself for his involuntary weakness. Well, he'd look over his book and pretend that he'd made a mistake; he'd tell this hunk of blackness that there was really no free room in the hotel, and that he was so sorry . . . Then, just as he took out the hotel register to make believe that he was poring over it, a thick roll of American bank notes, crisp and green, was thrust under his nose.

"Keep this for me, will you?" the black giant commanded. "Cause I'm gonna get drunk tonight and I don't wanna lose it."

Olaf stared at the roll; it was huge, in denominations of fifties and hundreds. Olaf's eyes widened.

30   "How much is there?" he asked.

"Two thousand six hundred," the giant said. "Just put it into an enve-lope and write 'Jim' on it and lock it in your safe, hunh?"

The black mass of man had spoken in a manner that indicated that it was taking it for granted that Olaf would obey. Olaf was licked. Resent-ment clogged the pores of his wrinkled white skin. His hands trembled as he picked up the money. No; he couldn't refuse this man . . . The impulse to deny him was strong, but each time he was about to act upon it some-thing thwarted him, made him shy off. He clutched about desperately for an idea. Oh yes, he could say that if he planned to stay for only one night, then he could not have the room, for it was against the policy of the hotel to rent rooms for only one night . . .

"How long are you staying? Just tonight?" Olaf asked.

"Naw. I'll be here for five or six days, I reckon," the giant answered offhandedly.

35   "You take room number thirty," Olaf heard himself saying. "It's forty kroner a day."

"That's all right with me," the giant said.

With slow, stiff movements, Olaf put the money in the safe and then turned and stared helplessly up into the living, breathing blackness loom-ing above him. Suddenly he became conscious of the outstretched palm of the black giant; he was silently demanding the key to the room. His eyes downcast, Olaf surrendered the key, marveling at the black man's tremen-dous hands . . . He could kill me with one blow, Olaf told himself in fear.

Feeling himself beaten, Olaf reached for the suitcase, but the black hand of the giant whisked it out of his grasp.

"That's too heavy for you, big boy; I'll take it," the giant said.

40   Olaf let him. He thinks I'm nothing . . . He led the way down the cor-ridor, sensing the giant's lumbering presence behind him. Olaf opened the door of number thirty and stood politely to one side, allowing the black giant to enter. At once the room seemed like a doll's house, so dwarfed and filled and tiny it was with a great living blackness . . . Fling-ing his suitcase upon a chair, the giant turned. The two men looked di-rectly at each other now. Olaf saw that the giant's eyes were tiny and red, buried, it seemed, in muscle and fat. Black cheeks spread, flat and broad, topping the wide and flaring nostrils. The mouth was the biggest that Olaf had ever seen on a human face; the lips were thick, pursed, parted, show-ing snow-white teeth. The black neck was like a bull's . . The giant ad-vanced upon Olaf and stood over him.

"I want a bottle of whiskey and a woman," he said. "Can you fix me up?"

"Yes," Olaf whispered, wild with anger and insult.

But what was he angry about? He'd had requests like this every night from all sorts of men and he was used to fulfilling them; he was a night porter in a cheap, water-front Copenhagen hotel that catered to sailors and students. Yes, men needed women, but this man, Olaf felt, ought to have a special sort of woman. He felt a deep and strange reluctance to phone any of the women whom he habitually sent to men. Yet he had promised. Could he lie and say that none was available? No. That sounded too fishy. The black giant sat upon the bed, staring straight before him. Olaf moved about quickly, pulling down the window shades, taking the pink coverlet off the bed, nudging the giant with his elbow to make him move as he did so . . . That's the way to treat 'im . . . Show 'im I ain't scared of 'im . . . But he was still seeking for an excuse to refuse. And he could think of nothing. He felt hypnotized, mentally immobilized. He stood hesitantly at the door.

"You send the whiskey and the woman quick, pal?" the black giant asked, rousing himself from a brooding stare.

45   "Yes," Olaf grunted, shutting the door.

Goddamn, Olaf sighed. He sat in his office at his desk before the phone. Why did *he* have to come here? . . . I'm not prejudiced . . . No, not at all . . . But . . . He couldn't think any more. God oughtn't make men as big and black as that . . . But what the hell was he worrying about? He'd sent women of all races to men of all colors . . . So why not a woman to the black giant? Oh, only if the man were small, brown, and intelligent-looking . . . Olaf felt trapped.

With a reflex movement of his hand, he picked up the phone and dialed Lena. She was big and strong and always cut him in for fifteen per cent instead of the usual ten per cent. Lena had four small children to feed and clothe. Lena was willing; she was, she said, coming over right now. She didn't give a good goddamn about how big and black the man was . . .

"Why you ask me that?" Lena wanted to know over the phone. "You never asked that before . . ."

"But this one is *big*," Olaf found himself saying.

50   "He's just a man," Lena told him, her voice singing stridently, laughingly over the wire. "You just leave that to me. You don't have to do anything. *I'll* handle 'im."

Lena had a key to the hotel door downstairs, but tonight Olaf stayed awake. He wanted to see her. Why? He didn't know. He stretched out on the sofa in his office, but sleep was far from him. When Lena arrived, he told her again how big and black the man was.

"You told me that over the phone," Lena reminded him.

Olaf said nothing. Lena flounced off on her errand of mercy. Olaf shut the office door, then opened it and left it ajar. But why? He didn't know. He lay upon the sofa and stared at the ceiling. He glanced at his watch; it was almost two o'clock . . . She's staying in there a long time . . . Ah, God, but he could do with a drink . . . Why was he so damned worked up and nervous about a nigger and a white whore? . . . He'd never been so upset in all his life. Before he knew it, he had drifted off to sleep. Then he heard the office door swinging creakingly open on its rusty hinges. Lena stood in it, grim and businesslike, her face scrubbed free of powder and rouge. Olaf scrambled to his feet, adjusting his eyeglasses, blinking.

"How was it?" he asked her in a confidential whisper.

55   Lena's eyes blazed.

"What the hell's that to you?" she snapped. "There's your cut," she said, flinging him his money, tossing it upon the covers of the sofa. "You're sure nosy tonight. You wanna take over my work?"

Olaf's pasty cheeks burned red.

"You go to hell," he said, slamming the door.

"I'll meet you there!" Lena's shouting voice reached him dimly.

60   He was being a fool; there was no doubt about it. But, try as he might, he could not shake off a primitive hate for that black mountain of energy, of muscle, of bone; he envied the easy manner in which it moved with such a creeping and powerful motion; he winced at the booming and commanding voice that came to him when the tiny little eyes were not even looking at him; he shivered at the sight of those vast and clawlike hands that seemed always to hint of death . . .

Olaf kept his counsel. He never spoke to Karen about the sordid doings at the hotel. Such things were not for women like Karen. He knew instinctively that Karen would have been amazed had he told her that he was worried sick about a nigger and a blonde whore . . . No; he couldn't talk to anybody about it, not even the hard-bitten[3] old bitch who owned the hotel. She was concerned only about money; she didn't give a damn about how big and how black a client was as long as he paid his room rent.

Next evening, when Olaf arrived for duty, there was no sight or sound of the black giant. A little later after one o'clock in the morning he appeared, left his key, and went out wordlessly. A few moments past two the giant returned, took his key from the board, and paused.

"I want that Lena again tonight. And another bottle of whiskey," he said boomingly.

"I'll call her and see if she's in," Olaf said.

65   "Do that," the black giant said and was gone.

He thinks he's God, Olaf fumed. He picked up the phone and ordered Lena and a bottle of whiskey, and there was a taste of ashes in his mouth. On the third night came the same request: Lena and whiskey. When the black giant appeared on the fifth night, Olaf was about to make a sarcastic remark to the effect that maybe he ought to marry Lena, but he checked it in time . . . After all, he could kill me with one hand, he told himself.

---

[3] Stubborn, tough.

Olaf was nervous and angry with himself for being nervous. Other black sailors came and asked for girls and Olaf sent them, but with none of the fear and loathing that he sent Lena and a bottle of whiskey to the giant . . . All right, the black giant's stay was almost up. He'd said that he was staying for five or six nights; tomorrow night was the sixth night and that ought to be the end of this nameless terror.

On the sixth night Olaf sat in his swivel chair with his bottle of beer and waited, his teeth on edge, his fingers drumming the desk. But what the hell am I fretting for? . . . The hell with 'im . . . Olaf sat and dozed. Occasionally he'd awaken and listen to the foghorns of freighters sounding as ships came and went in the misty Copenhagen harbor. He was half asleep when he felt a rough hand on his shoulder. He blinked his eyes open. The giant, black and vast and powerful, all but blotted out his vision.

"What I owe you, man?" the giant demanded. "And I want my money."

70   "Sure," Olaf said, relieved, but filled as always with fear of this living wall of black flesh.

With fumbling hands, he made out the bill and received payment, then gave the giant his roll of money, laying it on the desk so as not to let his hands touch the flesh of the black mountain. Well, his ordeal was over. It was past two o'clock in the morning. Olaf even managed a wry smile and muttered a guttural "Thanks" for the generous tip that the giant tossed him.

Then a strange tension entered the office. The office door was shut and Olaf was alone with the black mass of power, yearning for it to leave. But the black mass of power stood still, immobile, looking down at Olaf. And Olaf could not, for the life of him, guess at what was transpiring in that mysterious black mind. The two of them simply stared at each other for a full two minutes, the giant's tiny little beady eyes blinking slowly as they seemed to measure and search Olaf's face. Olaf's vision dimmed for a second as terror seized him and he could feel a flush of heat overspread his body. Then Olaf sucked in his breath as the devil of blackness commanded:

"Stand up!"

Olaf was paralyzed. Sweat broke on his face. His worst premonitions about this black beast were coming true. This evil blackness was about to attack him, maybe kill him . . . Slowly Olaf shook his head, his terror permitting him to breathe:

75   "What're you talking about?"

"Stand up, I say!" the black giant bellowed.

As though hypnotized, Olaf tried to rise; then he felt the black paw of the beast helping him roughly to his feet.

They stood an inch apart. Olaf's pasty-white features were glued to the giant's swollen black face. The ebony ensemble of eyes and nose and mouth and cheeks looked down at Olaf, silently; then, with a slow and deliberate movement of his gorillalike arms, he lifted his mammoth hands to Olaf's throat. Olaf had long known and felt that this dreadful moment was coming; he felt trapped in a nightmare. He could not move. He wanted to scream, but could find no words. His lips refused to open; his tongue felt icy and inert. Then he knew that his end had come when the giant's black fingers slowly, softly encircled his throat while a horrible grin of delight broke out on the sooty face . . . Olaf lost control of the reflexes of his body and he felt a hot stickiness flooding his underwear . . . He stared without breathing, gazing into the grinning blackness of the face that was bent over him, feeling the black fingers caressing his throat and waiting to feel the sharp, stinging ache and pain of the bones in his neck being snapped, crushed . . . He knew all along that I hated 'im . . . Yes, and now he's going to kill me for it, Olaf told himself with despair.

The black fingers still circled Olaf's neck, not closing, but gently massaging it, as it were, moving to and fro, while the obscene face grinned into his. Olaf could feel the giant's warm breath blowing on his eyelashes and he felt like a chicken about to have its neck wrung and its body tossed to flip and flap dyingly in the dust of the barnyard . . . Then suddenly the black giant withdrew his fingers from Olaf's neck and stepped back a pace, still grinning. Olaf sighed, trembling, his body seeming to shrink; he waited. Shame sheeted him for the hot wetness that was in his trousers. Oh, God, he's teasing me . . . He's showing me how easily he can kill me . . . He swallowed, waiting, his eyes stones of gray.

80   The giant's barrel-like chest gave forth a low, rumbling chuckle of delight.

"You laugh?" Olaf asked whimperingly.

"Sure I laugh," the giant shouted.

"Please don't hurt me," Olaf managed to say.

"I wouldn't hurt you, boy," the giant said in a tone of mockery. "So long."

85   And he was gone. Olaf fell limply into the swivel chair and fought off losing consciousness. Then he wept. He was showing me how easily he could kill me . . . He made me shake with terror and then laughed and left . . . Slowly, Olaf recovered, stood, then gave vent to a string of curses:

"Goddamn 'im! My gun's right there in the desk drawer; I should of shot 'im. Jesus, I hope the ship he's on sinks . . . I hope he drowns and the sharks eat 'im . . ."

Later, he thought of going to the police, but sheer shame kept him back; and, anyway, the giant was probably on board his ship by now. And he had to get home and clean himself. Oh, Lord, what could he tell Karen? Yes, he would say that his stomach had been upset . . . He'd change clothes and return to work. He phoned the hotel owner that he was ill and wanted an hour off; the old bitch said that she was coming right over and that poor Olaf could have the evening off.

Olaf went home and lied to Karen. Then he lay awake the rest of the night dreaming of revenge. He saw that freighter on which the giant was sailing; he saw it springing a dangerous leak and saw a torrent of sea water flooding, gushing into all the compartments of the ship until it found the bunk in which the black giant slept. Ah, yes, the foamy, surging waters would surprise that sleeping black bastard of a giant and he would drown, gasping and choking like a trapped rat, his tiny eyes bulging until they glittered red, the bitter water of the sea pounding his lungs until they ached and finally burst . . . The ship would sink slowly to the bottom of the cold, black, silent depths of the sea and a shark, a *white* one, would glide aimlessly about the shut portholes until it found an open one and it would slither inside and nose about until it found that swollen, rotting, stinking carcass of the black beast and it would then begin to nibble at the decomposing mass of tarlike flesh, eating the bones clean . . . Olaf always pictured the giant's bones as being jet black and shining.

Once or twice, during these fantasies of cannibalistic revenge, Olaf felt a little guilty about all the many innocent people, women and children, all white and blonde, who would have to go down into watery graves in order that that white shark could devour the evil giant's black flesh . . . But, despite feelings of remorse, the fantasy lived persistently on, and when Olaf found himself alone, it would crowd and cloud his mind to the exclusion of all else, affording him the only revenge he knew. To make me suffer just for the pleasure of it, he fumed. Just to show me how strong he was . . . Olaf learned how to hate, and got pleasure out of it.

90   Summer fled on wings of rain. Autumn flooded Denmark with color. Winter made rain and snow fall on Copenhagen. Finally spring came, bringing violets and roses. Olaf kept to his job. For many months he feared the return of the black giant. But when a year had passed and the giant had not put in an appearance, Olaf allowed his revenge fantasy to peter out, indulging in it only when recalling the shame that the black monster had made him feel.

Then one rainy August night, a year later, Olaf sat drowsing at his desk, his bottle of beer before him, tilting back in his swivel chair, his feet resting atop a corner of his desk, his mind mulling over the more pleasant aspects of his life. The office door cracked open. Olaf glanced boredly up and around. His heart jumped and skipped a beat. The black nightmare of terror and shame that he had hoped that he had lost forever was again upon him . . . Resplendently dressed, suitcase in hand, the black looming mountain filled the doorway. Olaf's thin lips parted and a silent moan, half a curse, escaped them.

"Hi," the black giant boomed from the doorway.

Olaf could not reply. But a sudden resolve swept him: this time he would even the score. If this black beast came within so much as three feet of him, he would snatch his gun out of the drawer and shoot him dead, so help him God . . .

"No rooms tonight," Olaf heard himself announcing in a determined voice.

95   The black giant grinned; it was the same infernal grimace of delight and triumph that he had had when his damnable black fingers had been around his throat . . .

"Don't want no room tonight," the giant announced.

"Then what are you doing here?" Olaf asked in a loud but tremulous voice.

The giant swept toward Olaf and stood over him; and Olaf could not move, despite his oath to kill him . . .

"What do you want then?" Olaf demanded once more, ashamed that he could not lift his voice above a whisper.

100   The giant still grinned, then tossed what seemed the same suitcase upon Olaf's sofa and bent over it; he zippered it open with a sweep of his clawlike hand and rummaged in it, drawing forth a flat, gleaming white object done up in glowing cellophane. Olaf watched with lowered lids, wondering what trick was now being played on him. Then, before he could defend himself, the giant had whirled and again long, black, snakelike fingers were encircling Olaf's throat . . . Olaf stiffened, his right hand clawing blindly for the drawer where the gun was kept. But the giant was quick.

"Wait," he bellowed, pushing Olaf back from the desk.

The giant turned quickly to the sofa and, still holding his fingers in a wide circle that seemed a noose for Olaf's neck, he inserted the rounded fingers into the top of the flat, gleaming object. Olaf had the drawer open and his sweaty fingers were now touching the gun, but something made him freeze. The flat, gleaming object was a shirt and the black giant's circled fingers were fitting themselves into its neck . . .

"A perfect fit!" the giant shouted.

Olaf stared, trying to understand. His fingers loosened about the gun. A mixture of a laugh and a curse struggled in him. He watched the giant plunge his hands into the suitcase and pull out other flat, gleaming shirts.

105   "One, two, three, four, five, six," the black giant intoned, his voice crisp and businesslike. "Six nylon shirts. And they're all yours. One shirt for each time Lena came . . . See, Daddy-O?"

The black, cupped hands, filled with billowing nylon whiteness, were extended under Olaf's nose. Olaf eased his damp fingers from his gun and pushed the drawer closed, staring at the shirts and then at the black giant's grinning face.

"Don't you like 'em?" the giant asked.

Olaf began to laugh hysterically, then suddenly he was crying, his eyes so flooded with tears that the pile of dazzling nylon looked like snow in the dead of winter. Was this true? Could he believe it? Maybe this too was a trick? But, no. There were six shirts, all nylon, and the black giant had had Lena six nights.

"What's the matter with you, Daddy-O?" the giant asked. "You blowing your top? Laughing and crying . . ."

110   Olaf swallowed, dabbed his withered fists at his dimmed eyes; then he realized that he had his glasses on. He took them off and dried his eyes

and sat up. He sighed, the tension and shame and fear and haunting dread of his fantasy went from him, and he leaned limply back in his chair . . .

"Try one on," the giant ordered.

Olaf fumbled with the buttons of his shirt, let down his suspenders, and pulled the shirt off. He donned a gleaming nylon one and the giant began buttoning it for him.

"Perfect, Daddy-O," the giant said.

His spectacled face framed in sparkling nylon, Olaf sat with trembling lips. So he'd not been trying to kill me after all.

115   "You want Lena, don't you?" he asked the giant in a soft whisper. "But I don't know where she is. She never came back here after you left—"

"I know where Lena is," the giant told him. "We been writing to each other. I'm going to her house. And, Daddy-O, I'm late." The giant zippered the suitcase shut and stood a moment gazing down at Olaf, his tiny little red eyes blinking slowly. Then Olaf realized that there was a compassion in that stare that he had never seen before.

"And I thought you wanted to kill me," Olaf told him. "I was scared of you . . ."

"Me? Kill you?" the giant blinked. "When?"

"That night when you put your fingers around my throat—"

120   "What?" the giant asked, then roared with laughter. "Daddy-O, you're a funny little man. I wouldn't hurt you. I like you. You a *good* man. You helped me."

Olaf smiled, clutching the pile of nylon shirts in his arms.

"You're a good man too," Olaf murmured. Then loudly, "You're a big black good man."

"Daddy-O, you're crazy," the giant said.

He swept his suitcase from the sofa, spun on his heel, and was at the door in one stride.

125   "Thanks!" Olaf cried after him.

The black giant paused, turned his vast black head, and flashed a grin.

"Daddy-O, drop dead," he said and was gone.

READING AND REACTING

1. Why do you suppose Wright has his third-person narrator see events through Olaf's eyes? How would the story be different if the sailor told it?

2. This story was published in 1957. What attitudes about race does Wright expect his American readers to have? Do these attitudes predispose readers to identify with the sailor or with Olaf? Explain.

3. Why does Olaf dislike the sailor? What does the narrator mean in paragraph 24 when he says that the sailor's "intense blackness and ungainly bigness [. . .] frightened and insulted Olaf"?

4. In what ways do the sailor's words and actions contribute to Olaf's fears? Do you think Olaf's reactions are reasonable, or do you believe he is overreacting?

5. The sailor's name is Jim, but this name is almost never used in the story. Why not? List some words used to describe Jim. Why are they used? How do they affect your reaction to Jim?

6. Do you think the story's title is ironic? In what other respects is the story ironic?

7. How would "Big Black Good Man" be different if Jim were white? Would there even *be* a story?

8. Why do you think Wright set the story in Copenhagen? Could it have been set in the United States in 1957?

9. **JOURNAL ENTRY** What do you think Jim thinks of Olaf? Do you suppose he realizes the effect he has on him? How do you explain his last comment?

10. **CRITICAL PERSPECTIVE** In his 1982 article "The Short Stories: *Uncle Tom's Children, Eight Men,*" Edward Margolies notes that "Big Black Good Man" was somewhat of a departure for Wright:

> "Big Black Good Man," which first appeared in *Esquire* in 1957, is the last short story Wright published in his lifetime. Possibly it is the last he ever wrote. In any event it represents a more traditional approach to storytelling in that Wright here avoids confining himself exclusively to dialogue. On the other hand, "Big Black Good Man" deviates from the usual Wright short story. For one thing, the narrative, by Wright's standards at least, is practically pointless. Scarcely anything "happens." There is no violence, practically no external narrative action, and no change of milieu.

Do you agree that the story is "practically pointless"? If not, what point do you think the story makes?

Related Works: "The Cask of Amontillado" (p. 219), "Girl" (p. 509), "We Wear the Mask" (p. 949), *The Brute* (p. 1266)

◆ **EDGAR ALLAN POE** (1809–1849) profoundly influenced many corners of the literary world. His tales of psychological terror and the macabre, his hauntingly musical lyric poems, and his writings on the craft of poetry and short-story writing affected the development of symbolic fiction, the modern detective story, and the Gothic horror tale. In most of Poe's horror tales (as in "The Cask of Amontillado"), readers vicariously "live" the story through the first-person narrator who tells the tale.

Poe was born in 1809, the son of a talented English-born actress who, deserted by her actor husband, died of tuberculosis before her son's third birthday. Though Poe was raised in material comfort by foster parents in Richmond, Virginia, his life was increasingly uncertain: his foster mother loved him, but her husband became antagonistic. He kept the young Poe so short of money at the University of Virginia (and later at West Point) that Poe resorted to gambling to raise money for food and clothing. Finally, debt-ridden, he left school altogether.

Poe found work as a magazine editor, gaining recognition as a perceptive (if sometimes vitriolic) literary critic. In 1836, he married his frail thirteen-year-old cousin, Virginia Clemm. Poe produced many of his most famous stories and poems in the next few years, working feverishly to support his tubercular wife; but although his stories were widely admired, financial success never came. His wife died in 1847. Less than two years after her death, Poe was found barely conscious in a Baltimore street after a mysterious disappearance; three days later, he was dead at age forty.

CULTURAL CONTEXT ◊ Throughout antiquity, catacombs were used to bury the dead. Catacombs, such as those in Poe's story "The Cask of Amontillado," are subterranean cemeteries composed of passages with side recesses for tombs. The early Christian catacombs of Rome, consisting of approximately forty known chambers located in a rough circle about three miles from the center of the city, are the most extensive of all known catacombs. Funeral feasts were often celebrated in family vaults on the day of burial and on anniversary dates of the deaths of loved ones.

◊   ◊   ◊

EDGAR ALLAN POE

The Cask of Amontillado
(1846)

The thousand injuries of Fortunato I had borne as I best could, but when he ventured upon insult I vowed revenge. You, who so well know the nature of my soul, will not suppose, however, that I gave utterance to a threat. *At length* I would be avenged; this was a point definitely settled— but the very definitiveness with which it was resolved precluded the idea of risk. I must not only punish but punish with impunity. A wrong is unredressed when retribution overtakes its redresser. It is equally unredressed when the avenger fails to make himself felt as such to him who has done the wrong.

It must be understood that neither by word nor deed had I given Fortunato cause to doubt my good will. I continued, as was my wont, to smile in his face, and he did not perceive that my smile *now* was at the thought of his immolation.

He had a weak point—this Fortunato—although in other regards he was a man to be respected and even feared. He prided himself on his connoisseurship in wine. Few Italians have the true virtuoso spirit. For the most part their enthusiasm is adopted to suit the time and opportunity, to practise imposture upon the British and Austrian *millionaires.* In painting and gemmary, Fortunato, like his countrymen, was a quack, but in the matter of old wines he was sincere. In this respect I did not differ from him materially;—I was skillful in the Italian vintages myself, and bought largely whenever I could.

It was about dusk, one evening during the supreme madness of the carnival season, that I encountered my friend. He accosted me with excessive warmth, for he had been drinking much. The man wore motley.[1] He had on a tight-fitting parti-striped dress, and his head was surmounted by the conical cap and bells. I was so pleased to see him that I thought I should never have done wringing his hand.

5   I said to him—"My dear Fortunato, you are luckily met. How remarkably well you are looking to-day. But I have received a pipe[2] of what passes for Amontillado,[3] and I have my doubts."

"How?" said he. "Amontillado? A pipe? Impossible! And in the middle of the carnival!"

"I have my doubts," I replied; "and I was silly enough to pay the full Amontillado price without consulting you in the matter. You were not to be found, and I was fearful of losing a bargain."

"Amontillado!"

"I have my doubts."

10   "Amontillado!"

"And I must satisfy them."

"Amontillado!"

"As you are engaged, I am on my way to Luchresi. If any one has a critical turn it is he. He will tell me—"

"Luchresi cannot tell Amontillado from Sherry."

15   "And yet some fools will have it that his taste is a match for your own."

"Come, let us go."

"Whither?"

"To your vaults."

"My friend, no; I will not impose upon your good nature. I perceive you have an engagement. Luchresi—"

20   "I have no engagement;—come."

"My friend, no. It is not the engagement, but the severe cold with which I perceive you are afflicted. The vaults are insufferably damp. They are encrusted with nitre."[4]

"Let us go, nevertheless. The cold is merely nothing. Amontillado! You have been imposed upon. And as for Luchresi, he cannot distinguish Sherry from Amontillado."

---

[1] The many-colored attire of a court jester.

[2] In the United States and England, a cask containing a volume equal to 126 gallons.

[3] A pale, dry sherry; literally, a wine "from Montilla" (Spain).

[4] Mineral deposits.

Thus speaking, Fortunato possessed himself of my arm; and putting on a mask of black silk and drawing a *roquelaire*[5] closely about my person, I suffered him to hurry me to my palazzo.

There were no attendants at home; they had absconded to make merry in honor of the time. I had told them that I should not return until the morning, and had given them explicit orders not to stir from the house. These orders were sufficient, I well knew, to insure their immediate disappearance, one and all, as soon as my back was turned.

25   I took from their sconces two flambeaux, and giving one to Fortunato, bowed him through several suites of rooms to the archway that led into the vaults. I passed down a long and winding staircase, requesting him to be cautious as he followed. We came at length to the foot of the descent, and stood together upon the damp ground of the catacombs of the Montresors.

The gait of my friend was unsteady, and the bells upon his cap jingled as he strode.

"The pipe," he said.

"It is farther on," said I; "but observe the white web-work which gleams from these cavern walls."

He turned towards me, and looked into my eyes with two filmy orbs that distilled the rheum of intoxication.

30   "Nitre?" he asked at length.

"Nitre," I replied. "How long have you had that cough?"

"Ugh! ugh! ugh!—ugh! ugh! ugh!—ugh! ugh! ugh!—ugh! ugh! ugh!— ugh! ugh! ugh!"

My poor friend found it impossible to reply for many minutes.

"It is nothing," he said at last.

35   "Come," I said, with decision, "we will go back; your health is precious. You are rich, respected, admired, beloved; you are happy, as once I was. You are a man to be missed. For me it is no matter. We will go back; you will be ill, and I cannot be responsible. Besides, there is Luchresi—"

"Enough," he said; "the cough is a mere nothing; it will not kill me. I shall not die of a cough."

"True—true," I replied; "and, indeed, I had no intention of alarming you unnecessarily—but you should use all proper caution. A draught of this Médoc[6] will defend us from the damps."

Here I knocked off the neck of a bottle which I drew from a long row of its fellows that lay upon the mould.

"Drink," I said, presenting him the wine.

40   He raised it to his lips with a leer. He paused and nodded to me familiarly, while his bells jingled.

"I drink," he said, "to the buried that repose around us."

"And I to your long life."

---

[5] A short cloak.
[6] A claret from the Médoc, near Bordeaux, France.

He again took my arm, and we proceeded.

"These vaults," he said, "are extensive."

45   "The Montresors," I replied, "were a great and numerous family."

"I forget your arms."

"A huge human foot d'or, in a field azure; the foot crushes a serpent rampant whose fangs are imbedded in the heel."

"And the motto?"

"Nemo me impune lacessit."[7]

50   "Good!" he said.

The wine sparkled in his eyes and the bells jingled. My own fancy grew warm with the Médoc. We had passed through long walls of piled skeletons, with casks and puncheons[8] intermingling, into the inmost recesses of the catacombs. I paused again, and this time I made bold to seize Fortunato by an arm above the elbow.

"The nitre!" I said; "see, it increases. It hangs like moss upon the vaults. We are below the river's bed. The drops of moisture trickle among the bones. Come, we will go back ere it is too late. Your cough—"

"It is nothing," he said; "let us go on. But first, another draught of the Médoc."

I broke and reached him a flagon of De Grâve.[9] He emptied it at a breath. His eyes flashed with a fierce light. He laughed and threw the bottle upwards with a gesticulation I did not understand.

55   I looked at him in surprise. He repeated the movement—a grotesque one.

"You do not comprehend?" he said.

"Not I," I replied.

"Then you are not of the brotherhood."

"How?"

60   "You are not of the masons."[10]

"Yes, yes," I said; "yes, yes."

"You? Impossible! A mason?"

"A mason," I replied.

"A sign," he said, "a sign."

65   "It is this," I answered, producing from beneath the folds of my *roquelaire* a trowel.

"You jest," he exclaimed, recoiling a few paces. "But let us proceed to the Amontillado."

"Be it so," I said, replacing the tool beneath the cloak and again offering him my arm. He leaned upon it heavily. We continued our route in search of the Amontillado. We passed through a range of low arches,

---

[7] "No one insults me with impunity"; this is the legend of the royal arms of Scotland.

[8] Barrel.

[9] Correctly, "Gráves," a light wine from the Bordeaux area.

[10] Freemasons (members of a secret fraternity). The trowel is a symbol of their alleged origin as a guild of stonemasons.

descended, passed on, and descending again, arrived at a deep crypt, in which the foulness of the air caused our flambeaux rather to glow than flame.

At the most remote end of the crypt there appeared another less spacious. Its walls had been lined with human remains, piled to the vault overhead, in the fashion of the great catacombs of Paris. Three sides of this interior crypt were still ornamented in this manner. From the fourth side the bones had been thrown down, and lay promiscuously upon the earth, forming at one point a mound of some size. Within the wall thus exposed by the displacing of the bones, we perceived a still interior crypt or recess, in depth about four feet, in width three, in height six or seven. It seemed to have been constructed for no especial use within itself, but formed merely the interval between two of the colossal supports of the roof of the catacombs, and was backed by one of their circumscribing walls of solid granite.

It was in vain that Fortunato, uplifting his dull torch, endeavored to pry into the depth of the recess. Its termination the feeble light did not enable us to see.

70   "Proceed," I said; "herein is the Amontillado. As for Luchresi—"

"He is an ignoramus," interrupted my friend, as he stepped unsteadily forward, while I followed immediately at his heels. In an instant he had reached the extremity of the niche, and finding his progress arrested by the rock, stood stupidly bewildered. A moment more and I had fettered him to the granite. In its surface were two iron staples, distant from each other about two feet, horizontally. From one of these depended a short chain, from the other a padlock. Throwing the links about his waist, it was but the work of a few seconds to secure it. He was too much astounded to resist. Withdrawing the key I stepped back from the recess.

"Pass your hand," I said, "over the wall; you cannot help feeling the nitre. Indeed, it is *very* damp. Once more let me *implore* you to return. No? Then I must positively leave you. But I must first render you all the little attentions in my power."

"The Amontillado!" ejaculated my friend, not yet recovered from his astonishment.

"True," I replied; "the Amontillado."

75   As I said these words I busied myself among the pile of bones of which I have before spoken. Throwing them aside, I soon uncovered a quantity of building stone and mortar. With these materials and with the aid of my trowel, I began vigorously to wall up the entrance of the niche.

I had scarcely laid the first tier of the masonry when I discovered that the intoxication of Fortunato had in a great measure worn off. The earliest indication I had of this was a low moaning cry from the depth of the recess. It was *not* the cry of a drunken man. There was a long and obstinate silence. I laid the second tier, and the third, and the fourth; and then I heard the furious vibrations of the chain. The noise lasted for several minutes, during which, that I might hearken to it with the more satisfaction, I ceased my labors and sat down upon the bones. When at last the clanking subsided, I resumed the trowel, and finished without interruption the fifth, the sixth, and the seventh tier. The wall was now nearly upon a level with my breast. I again paused, and holding the flambeaux over the mason-work, threw a few feeble rays upon the figure within.

A succession of loud and shrill screams, bursting suddenly from the throat of the chained form, seemed to thrust me violently back. For a brief moment I hesitated, I trembled. Unsheathing my rapier, I began to grope with it about the recess; but the thought of an instant reassured me. I placed my hand upon the solid fabric of the catacombs, and felt satisfied. I reapproached the wall; I replied to the yells of him who clamoured. I re-echoed, I aided, I surpassed them in volume and in strength. I did this, and the clamourer grew still.

It was now midnight, and my task was drawing to a close. I had completed the eighth, the ninth and the tenth tier. I had finished a portion of the last and the eleventh; there remained but a single stone to be fitted and plastered in. I struggled with its weight; I placed it partially in its destined position. But now there came from out the niche a low laugh that erected the hairs upon my head. It was succeeded by a sad voice, which I had difficulty in recognizing as that of the noble Fortunato. The voice said—

"Ha! ha! ha!—he! he! he!—a very good joke, indeed—an excellent jest. We will have many a rich laugh about it at the palazzo—he! he! he!—over our wine—he! he! he!"

80   "The Amontillado!" I said.

"He! he! he!—he! he! he!—yes, the Amontillado. But is it not getting late? Will not they be awaiting us at the palazzo, the Lady Fortunato and the rest? Let us be gone."

"Yes," I said, "let us be gone."

"For the love of God, Montresor!"

"Yes," I said, "for the love of God."

85   But to these words I hearkened in vain for a reply. I grew impatient. I called aloud—

"Fortunato!"

No answer. I called again—

"Fortunato!"

No answer still. I thrust a torch through the remaining aperture and let it fall within. There came forth in return only a jingling of the bells. My heart grew sick; it was the dampness of the catacombs that made it so. I hastened to make an end of my labour. I forced the last stone into its position; I plastered it up. Against the new masonry I re-erected the old rampart of bones. For the half of a century no mortal has disturbed them. *In pace requiescat!*[11]

---

[11] "May he rest in peace."

READING AND REACTING

1. Montresor cites a "thousand injuries" and an "insult" as his motivation for murdering Fortunato. Given what you learn about the two men during the course of the story, what do you suppose the "injuries" and "insult" might be?
2. Do you find Montresor to be a reliable narrator? If not, what makes you question his version of events?
3. What is Montresor's concept of personal honor? Is it consistent or inconsistent with the values of contemporary American society? How relevant are the story's ideas about revenge and guilt to present-day society? Explain.
4. Does Fortunato ever understand why Montresor hates him? What is Fortunato's attitude toward Montresor?
5. What is the significance of Montresor's family coat of arms and motto? What is the significance of Fortunato's costume?
6. In what ways does Montresor manipulate Fortunato? What weaknesses does Montresor exploit?
7. Why does Montresor wait fifty years to tell his story? How might the story be different if he had told it the next morning?
8. Why does Montresor wait for a reply before he puts the last stone in position? What do you think he wants Fortunato to say?
9. **JOURNAL ENTRY** Do you think the use of a first-person point of view makes you more sympathetic toward Montresor than you would be if his story were told by a third-person narrator? Why or why not?
10. **CRITICAL PERSPECTIVE** In his discussion of this story in *Edgar Allan Poe: A Study of the Short Fiction,* Charles E. May says, "We can legitimately hypothesize that the listener is a priest and that Montresor is an old man who is dying and making final confession [. . .]."

    Do you agree or disagree with May's hypothesis? Do you think that Montresor has atoned for his sin? Who else could be listening to Montresor's story?

Related Works: "A Rose for Emily" (p. 87), "The Love Song of J. Alfred Prufrock" (p. 950), *Trifles* (p. 1163)

◆ **WILLIAM FAULKNER** (1897–1962) (picture and biography on p. 00) "Barn Burning" (1939) marks the first appearance of the Snopes clan in Faulkner's fiction. These crafty and unappealing tenant farmers and traders run roughshod over the aristocratic families of Yoknapatawpha County in three Faulkner novels: *The Hamlet* (1940), *The Town* (1957), and *The Mansion* (1959). According to Ben Wasson in *Count No 'Count,* Faulkner once told a friend that "somebody said I was a genius writer. The only thing I'd claim genius for is thinking up that name *Snopes*." In

Southern literary circles, at least, the name "Snopes" still serves as a short-hand term for the graceless and greedy (but frequently successful) opportunists of the "New South."

CULTURAL CONTEXT ◈   Tenant farming is a system of agriculture in which landowners contribute their land while tenants contribute labor. One form of tenant farming known as sharecropping requires the landowner to furnish all the capital and usually the food, clothing, and shelter to the tenant in return for labor. The sharecropper was lucky to end the year without owing money to the landowner. In "Barn Burning," Abner Snopes is a poor sharecropper who takes out his frustrations against the post–Civil War aristocracy of landowners.

◈ ◈ ◈

WILLIAM FAULKNER

Barn Burning
(1939)

The store in which the Justice of the Peace's court was sitting smelled of cheese. The boy, crouched on his nail keg at the back of the crowded room, knew he smelled cheese, and more: from where he sat he could see the ranked shelves close-packed with the solid, squat, dynamic shapes of tin cans whose labels his stomach read, not from the lettering which meant nothing to his mind but from the scarlet devils and the silver curve of fish—this, the cheese which he knew he smelled and the hermetic meat[1] which his intestines believed he smelled coming in intermittent gusts momentary and brief between the other constant one, the smell and sense just a little of fear because mostly of despair and grief, the old fierce pull of blood. He could not see the table where the Justice sat and before which his father and his father's enemy (*our enemy* he thought in that despair; *ourn! mine and hisn both! He's my father!*) stood, but he could hear them, the two of them that is, because his father had said no word yet:

"But what proof have you, Mr. Harris?"

"I told you. The hog got into my corn. I caught it up and sent it back to him. He had no fence that would hold it. I told him so, warned him. The next time I put the hog in my pen. When he came to get it I gave him enough wire to patch up his pen. The next time I put the hog up and kept it. I rode down to his house and saw the wire I gave him still rolled on to the spool in his yard. I told him he could have the hog when he paid me a dollar pound fee. That evening a nigger came with the dollar and got the hog. He was a strange nigger. He said, 'He say to tell you wood and hay kin burn.' I said, 'What?' 'That whut he say to tell you,' the nigger said. 'Wood and hay kin burn.' That night my barn burned. I got the stock out but I lost the barn."

---

[1] Canned meat.

"Where is the nigger? Have you got him?"

5   "He was a strange nigger, I tell you. I don't know what became of him."

"But that's not proof. Don't you see that's not proof?"

"Get that boy up here. He knows." For a moment the boy thought too that the man meant his older brother until Harris said, "Not him. The little one. The boy," and, crouching, small for his age, small and wiry like his father, in patched and faded jeans even too small for him, with straight, uncombed, brown hair and eyes gray and wild as storm scud, he saw the men between himself and the table part and become a lane of grim faces, at the end of which he saw the Justice, a shabby, collarless, graying man in spectacles, beckoning him. He felt no floor under his bare feet; he seemed to walk beneath the palpable weight of the grim turning faces. His father, stiff in his black Sunday coat donned not for the trial but for the moving, did not even look at him. *He aims for me to lie,* he thought, again with that frantic grief and despair. *And I will have to do hit.*

"What's your name, boy?" the Justice said.

"Colonel Sartoris Snopes," the boy whispered.

10   "Hey?" the Justice said. "Talk louder. Colonel Sartoris? I reckon anybody named for Colonel Sartoris in this country can't help but tell the truth, can they?" The boy said nothing. *Enemy! Enemy!* he thought; for a moment he could not even see, could not see that the Justice's face was kindly nor discern that his voice was troubled when he spoke to the man named Harris: "Do you want me to question this boy?" But he could hear, and during those subsequent long seconds while there was absolutely no sound in the crowded little room save that of quiet and intent breathing it was as if he had swung outward at the end of a grape vine, over a ravine, and at the top of the swing had been caught in a prolonged instant of mesmerized gravity, weightless in time.

"No!" Harris said violently, explosively. "Damnation! Send him out of here!" Now time, the fluid world, rushed beneath him again, the voices coming to him again through the smell of cheese and sealed meat, the fear and despair and the old grief of blood:

"This case is closed. I can't find against you, Snopes, but I can give you advice. Leave this country and don't come back to it."

His father spoke for the first time, his voice cold and harsh, level, without emphasis: "I aim to. I don't figure to stay in a country among people who . . ." he said something unprintable and vile, addressed to no one.

"That'll do," the Justice said. "Take your wagon and get out of this country before dark. Case dismissed."

15   His father turned, and he followed the stiff black coat, the wiry figure walking a little stiffly from where a Confederate provost's man's[2] musket ball had taken him in the heel on a stolen horse thirty years ago, followed the two backs now, since his older brother had appeared from somewhere in the crowd, no taller than the father but thicker, chewing tobacco

---

[2] Military policeman.

steadily, between the two lines of grim-faced men and out of the store and across the worn gallery and down the sagging steps and among the dogs and half-grown boys in the mild May dust, where as he passed a voice hissed:

"Barn burner!"

Again he could not see, whirling; there was a face in a red haze, moon-like, bigger than the full moon, the owner of it half again his size, he leaping in the red haze toward the face, feeling no blow, feeling no shock when his head struck the earth, scrabbling up and leaping again, feeling no blow this time either and tasting no blood, scrabbling up to see the other boy in full flight and himself already leaping into pursuit as his father's hand jerked him back, the harsh, cold voice speaking above him: "Go get in the wagon."

It stood in a grove of locusts and mulberries across the road. His two hulking sisters in their Sunday dresses and his mother and her sister in calico and sunbonnets were already in it, sitting on and among the sorry residue of the dozen and more movings which even the boy could remember—the battered stove, the broken beds and chairs, the clock inlaid with mother-of-pearl, which would not run, stopped at some fourteen minutes past two o'clock of a dead and forgotten day and time, which had been his mother's dowry. She was crying, though when she saw him she drew her sleeve across her face and began to descend from the wagon. "Get back," the father said.

"He's hurt. I got to get some water and wash his . . ."

20   "Get back in the wagon," his father said. He got in too, over the tailgate. His father mounted to the seat where the older brother already sat and struck the gaunt mules two savage blows with the peeled willow, but without heat. It was not even sadistic; it was exactly that same quality which in later years would cause his descendants to overrun the engine before putting a motor car into motion, striking and reining back in the same movement. The wagon went on, the store with its quiet crowd of grimly watching men dropped behind; a curve in the road hid it. *Forever* he thought. *Maybe he's done satisfied now, now that he has . . .* stopping himself, not to say it aloud even to himself. His mother's hand touched his shoulder.

"Does hit hurt?" she said.

"Naw," he said. "Hit don't hurt. Lemme be."

"Can't you wipe some of the blood off before hit dries?"

"I'll wash to-night," he said. "Lemme be, I tell you."

25   The wagon went on. He did not know where they were going. None of them ever did or ever asked, because it was always somewhere, always a house of sorts waiting for them a day or two days or even three days away. Likely his father had already arranged to make a crop on another farm before he . . . Again he had to stop himself. He (the father) always did. There was something about his wolf-like independence and even courage when the advantage was at least neutral which impressed strangers, as if they got

from his latent ravening ferocity not so much a sense of dependability as a feeling that his ferocious conviction in the rightness of his own actions would be of advantage to all whose interest lay with his.

That night they camped, in a grove of oaks and beeches where a spring ran. The nights were still cool and they had a fire against it, of a rail lifted from a nearby fence and cut into lengths—a small fire, neat, niggard almost, a shrewd fire; such fires were his father's habit and custom always, even in freezing weather. Older, the boy might have remarked this and wondered why not a big one; why should not a man who had not only seen the waste and extravagance of war, but who had in his blood an inherent voracious prodigality with material not his own, have burned everything in sight? Then he might have gone a step farther and thought that that was the reason: that niggard blaze was the living fruit of nights passed during those four years in the woods hiding from all men, blue or gray, with his strings of horses (captured horses, he called them). And older still, he might have divined the true reason: that the element of fire spoke to some deep mainspring of his father's being, as the element of steel or of powder spoke to other men, as the one weapon for the preservation of integrity, else breath were not worth the breathing, and hence to be regarded with respect and used with discretion.

But he did not think this now and he had seen those same niggard blazes all his life. He merely ate his supper beside it and was already half asleep over his iron plate when his father called him, and once more he followed the stiff back, the stiff and ruthless limp, up the slope and on to the starlit road where, turning, he could see his father against the stars but without face or depth—a shape black, flat, and bloodless as though cut from tin in the iron folds of the frockcoat which had not been made for him, the voice harsh like tin and without heat like tin:

"You were fixing to tell them. You would have told him." He didn't answer. His father struck him with the flat of his hand on the side of the head, hard but without heat, exactly as he had struck the two mules at the store, exactly as he would strike either of them with any stick in order to kill a horse fly, his voice still without fear or anger: "You're getting to be a man. You got to learn. You got to learn to stick to your own blood or you ain't going to have any blood to stick to you. Do you think either of them, any man there this morning, would? Don't you know all they wanted was a chance to get at me because they knew I had them beat? Eh?" Later, twenty years later, he was to tell himself, "If I had said they wanted only truth, justice, he would have hit me again." But now he said nothing. He was not crying. He just stood there. "Answer me," his father said.

"Yes," he whispered. His father turned.

30   "Get on to bed. We'll be there tomorrow."

Tomorrow they were there. In the early afternoon the wagon stopped before a paintless two-room house identical almost with the dozen others it had stopped before even in the boy's ten years, and again, as on the other dozen occasions, his mother and aunt got down and began to unload the wagon, although his two sisters and his father and brother had not moved.

"Likely hit ain't fitten for hawgs," one of the sisters said.

"Nevertheless, fit it will and you'll hog it and like it," his father said. "Get out of them chairs and help your Ma unload."

The two sisters got down, big, bovine, in a flutter of cheap ribbons; one of them drew from the jumbled wagon bed a battered lantern, the other a worn broom. His father handed the reins to the older son and began to climb stiffly over the wheel. "When they get unloaded, take the team to the barn and feed them." Then he said, and at first the boy thought he was still speaking to his brother: "Come with me."

35   "Me?" he said.

"Yes," his father said. "You."

"Abner," his mother said. His father paused and looked back—the harsh level stare beneath the shaggy, graying, irascible brows.

"I reckon I'll have a word with the man that aims to begin tomorrow owning me body and soul for the next eight months."

They went back up the road. A week ago—or before last night, that is—he would have asked where they were going, but not now. His father had struck him before last night but never before had he paused afterward to explain why; it was as if the blow and the following calm, outrageous voice still rang, repercussed, divulging nothing to him save the terrible handicap of being young, the light weight of his few years, just heavy enough to prevent his soaring free of the world as it seemed to be ordered but not heavy enough to keep him footed solid in it, to resist it and try to change the course of its events.

40   Presently he could see the grove of oaks and cedars and the other flowering trees and shrubs, where the house would be, though not the house yet. They walked beside a fence massed with honeysuckle and Cherokee roses and came to a gate swinging open between two brick pillars, and now, beyond a sweep of drive, he saw the house for the first time and at that instant he forgot his father and the terror and despair both, and even when he remembered his father again (who had not stopped) the terror and despair did not return. Because, for all the twelve movings, they had sojourned until now in a poor country, a land of small farms and fields and houses, and he had never seen a house like this before. *Hit's big as a courthouse* he thought quietly, with a surge of peace and joy whose reason he could not have thought into words, being too young for that: *They are safe from him. People whose lives are a part of this peace and dignity are beyond his touch, he no more to them than a buzzing wasp: capable of stinging for a little moment but that's all; the spell of this peace and dignity rendering even the barns and stable and cribs which belong to it impervious to the puny flames he might contrive* . . . this, the peace and joy, ebbing for an instant as he looked again at the stiff black back, the stiff and implacable limp of the figure which was not dwarfed by the house, for the reason that it had never looked big anywhere and which now, against the serene columned

backdrop, had more than ever that impervious quality of something cut ruthlessly from tin, depthless, as though, sidewise to the sun, it would cast no shadow. Watching him, the boy remarked the absolutely undeviating course which his father held and saw the stiff foot come squarely down in a pile of fresh droppings where a horse had stood in the drive and which his father could have avoided by a simple change of stride. But it ebbed only for a moment, though he could not have thought this into words either, walking on in the spell of the house, which he could even want but without envy, without sorrow, certainly never with that ravening and jealous rage which unknown to him walked in the ironlike black coat before him: *Maybe he will feel it too. Maybe it will even change him now from what maybe he couldn't help but be.*

They crossed the portico. Now he could hear his father's stiff foot as it came down on the boards with clocklike finality, a sound out of all proportion to the displacement of the body it bore and which was not dwarfed either by the white door before it, as though it had attained to a sort of vicious and ravening minimum not to be dwarfed by anything—the flat, wide, black hat, the formal coat of broadcloth which had once been black but which had now that friction-glazed greenish cast of the bodies of old house flies, the lifted sleeve which was too large, the lifted hand like a curled claw. The door opened so promptly that the boy knew the Negro must have been watching them all the time, an old man with neat grizzled hair, in a linen jacket, who stood barring the door with his body, saying, "Wipe yo foots, white man, fo you come in here. Major ain't home nohow."

"Get out of my way, nigger," his father said, without heat too, flinging the door back and the Negro also and entering, his hat still on his head. And now the boy saw the prints of the stiff foot on the doorjamb and saw them appear on the pale rug behind the machinelike deliberation of the foot which seemed to bear (or transmit) twice the weight which the body compassed. The Negro was shouting "Miss Lula! Miss Lula!" somewhere behind them, then the boy, deluged as though by a warm wave by a suave turn of carpeted stair and a pendant glitter of chandeliers and a mute gleam of gold frames, heard the swift feet and saw her too, a lady—perhaps he had never seen her like before either—in a gray, smooth gown with lace at the throat and an apron tied at the waist and the sleeves turned back, wiping cake or biscuit dough from her hands with a towel as she came up the hall, looking not at his father at all but at the tracks on the blond rug with an expression of incredulous amazement.

"I tried," the Negro cried, "I tole him to . . ."

"Will you please go away?" she said in a shaking voice. "Major de Spain is not at home. Will you please go away?"

45 His father had not spoken again. He did not speak again. He did not even look at her. He just stood stiff in the center of the rug, in his hat, the shaggy iron-gray brows twitching slightly above the pebble-colored eyes as he appeared to examine the house with brief deliberation. Then with the

same deliberation he turned; the boy watched him pivot on the good leg and saw the stiff foot drag round the arc of the turning, leaving a final long and fading smear. His father never looked at it, he never once looked down at the rug. The Negro held the door. It closed behind them, upon the hysteric and indistinguishable woman-wail. His father stopped at the top of the steps and scraped his boot clean on the edge of it. At the gate he stopped again. He stood for a moment, planted stiffly on the stiff foot, looking back at the house. "Pretty and white, ain't it?" he said. "That's sweat. Nigger sweat. Maybe it ain't white enough yet to suit him. Maybe he wants to mix some white sweat with it."

Two hours later the boy was chopping wood behind the house within which his mother and aunt and the two sisters (the mother and aunt, not the two girls, he knew that; even at this distance and muffled by walls the flat loud voices of the two girls emanated an incorrigible idle inertia) were setting up the stove to prepare a meal, when he heard the hooves and saw the linen-clad man on a fine sorrel mare, whom he recognized even before he saw the rolled rug in front of the Negro youth following on a fat bay carriage horse—a suffused, angry face vanishing, still at full gallop, beyond the corner of the house where his father and brother were sitting in the two tilted chairs; and a moment later, almost before he could have put the axe down, he heard the hooves again and watched the sorrel mare go back out of the yard, already galloping again. Then his father began to shout one of the sisters' names, who presently emerged backward from the kitchen door dragging the rolled rug along the ground by one end while the other sister walked behind it.

"If you ain't going to tote, go on and set up the wash pot," the first said.

"You, Sarty!" the second shouted. "Set up the wash pot!" His father appeared at the door, framed against that shabbiness, as he had been against that other bland perfection, impervious to either, the mother's anxious face at his shoulder.

"Go on," the father said. "Pick it up." The two sisters stooped, broad, lethargic; stooping, they presented an incredible expanse of pale cloth and a flutter of tawdry ribbons.

50 "If I thought enough of a rug to have to git hit all the way from France I wouldn't keep hit where folks coming in would have to tromp on hit," the first said. They raised the rug.

"Abner," the mother said. "Let me do it."

"You go back and git dinner," his father said. "I'll tend to this."

From the woodpile through the rest of the afternoon the boy watched them, the rug spread flat in the dust beside the bubbling wash-pot, the two sisters stooping over it with that profound and lethargic reluctance, while the father stood over them in turn, implacable and grim, driving them though never raising his voice again. He could smell the harsh homemade lye[3] they were using; he saw his mother come to the door once and look

---

[3] A soap made from wood ashes and water, unsuitable for washing fine fabrics.

toward them with an expression not anxious now but very like despair; he saw his father turn, and he fell to with the axe and saw from the corner of his eye his father raise from the ground a flattish fragment of field stone and examine it and return to the pot, and this time his mother actually spoke: "Abner. Abner. Please don't. Please, Abner."

Then he was done too. It was dusk; the whippoorwills had already begun. He could smell coffee from the room where they would presently eat the cold food remaining from the mid-afternoon meal, though when he entered the house he realized they were having coffee again probably because there was a fire on the hearth, before which the rug now lay spread over the backs of the two chairs. The tracks of his father's foot were gone. Where they had been were now long, water-cloudy scoriations resembling the sporadic course of a Lilliputian mowing machine.

55   It still hung there while they ate the cold food and then went to bed, scattered without order or claim up and down the two rooms, his mother in one bed, where his father would later lie, the older brother in the other, himself, the aunt, and the two sisters on pallets on the floor. But his father was not in bed yet. The last thing the boy remembered was the depthless, harsh silhouette of the hat and coat bending over the rug and it seemed to him that he had not even closed his eyes when the silhouette was standing over him, the fire almost dead behind it, the stiff foot prodding him awake. "Catch up the mule," his father said.

When he returned with the mule his father was standing in the black door, the rolled rug over his shoulder. "Ain't you going to ride?" he said.

"No. Give me your foot."

He bent his knee into his father's hand, the wiry, surprising power flowed smoothly, rising, he rising with it, on to the mule's bare back (they had owned a saddle once; the boy could remember it though not when or where) and with the same effortlessness his father swung the rug up in front of him. Now in the starlight they retraced the after-noon's path, up the dusty road rife with honeysuckle, through the gate and up the black tunnel to the drive to the lightless house, where he sat on the mule and felt the rough warp of the rug drag across his thighs and vanish.

"Don't you want me to help?" he whispered. His father did not answer and now he heard again that stiff foot striking the hollow portico with that wooden and clocklike deliberation, that outrageous overstatement of the weight it carried. The rug, hunched, not flung (the boy could tell that even in the darkness) from his father's shoulder struck the angle of wall and floor with a sound unbelievably loud, thunderous, then the foot again, unhurried and enormous; a light came on in the house and the boy sat, tense, breathing steadily and quietly and just a little fast, though the foot itself did not increase its beat at all, descending the steps now; now the boy could see him.

60   "Don't you want to ride now?" he whispered. "We kin both ride now," the light within the house altering now, flaring up and sinking. *He's coming down the stairs now,* he thought. He had already ridden the

mule up beside the horse block; presently his father was up behind him and he doubled the reins over and slashed the mule across the neck, but before the animal could begin to trot the hard, thin arm came round him, the hard, knotted hand jerking the mule back to a walk.

In the first red rays of the sun they were in the lot, putting plow gear on the mules. This time the sorrel mare was in the lot before he heard it at all, the rider collarless and even bareheaded, trembling, speaking in a shaking voice as the woman in the house had done, his father merely looking up once before stooping again to the hame[4] he was buckling, so that the man on the mare spoke to his stooping back:

"You must realize you have ruined that rug. Wasn't there anybody here, any of your women . . ." he ceased, shaking, the boy watching him, the older brother leaning now in the stable door, chewing, blinking slowly and steadily at nothing apparently. "It cost a hundred dollars. But you never had a hundred dollars. You never will. So I'm going to charge you twenty bushels of corn against your crop. I'll add it in your contract and when you come to the commissary you can sign it. That won't keep Mrs. de Spain quiet but maybe it will teach you to wipe your feet off before you enter her house again."

Then he was gone. The boy looked at his father, who still had not spoken or even looked up again, who was now adjusting the loggerhead in the hame.

"Pap," he said. His father looked at him—the inscrutable face, the shaggy brows beneath which the gray eyes glinted coldly. Suddenly the boy went toward him, fast, stopping as suddenly. "You done the best you could!" he cried. "If he wanted hit done different why didn't he wait and tell you how? He won't git no twenty bushels! He won't git none! We'll gether hit and hide hit! I kin watch . . ."

65   "Did you put the cutter back in that straight stock like I told you?"

"No, sir," he said.

"Then go do it."

That was Wednesday. During the rest of that week he worked steadily, at what was within his scope and some which was beyond it, with an industry that did not need to be driven nor even commanded twice; he had this from his mother, with the difference that some at least of what he did he liked to do, such as splitting wood with the half-size axe which his mother and aunt had earned, or saved money somehow, to present him with at Christmas. In company with the two older women (and on one afternoon, even one of the sisters), he built pens for the shoat and the cow which were a part of his father's contract with the landlord, and one afternoon, his father being absent, gone somewhere on one of the mules, he went to the field.

They were running a middle buster now, his brother holding the plow straight while he handled the reins, and walking beside the straining mule,

---

[4] Harness.

the rich black soil shearing cool and damp against his bare ankles, he thought *Maybe this is the end of it. Maybe even that twenty bushels that seems hard to have to pay for just a rug will be a cheap price for him to stop forever and always from being what he used to be;* thinking, dreaming now, so that his brother had to speak sharply to him to mind the mule: *Maybe he even won't collect the twenty bushels. Maybe it will all add up and balance and vanish—corn, rug, fire; the terror and grief, the being pulled two ways like between two teams of horses—gone, done with for ever and ever.*

70 Then it was Saturday; he looked up from beneath the mule he was harnessing and saw his father in the black coat and hat. "Not that," his father said. "The wagon gear." And then, two hours later, sitting in the wagon bed behind his father and brother on the seat, the wagon accomplished a final curve, and he saw the weathered paintless store with its tattered tobacco- and patent-medicine posters and the tethered wagons and saddle animals below the gallery. He mounted the gnawed steps behind his father and brother, and there again was the lane of quiet, watching faces for the three of them to walk through. He saw the man in spectacles sitting at the plank table and he did not need to be told this was a Justice of the Peace; he sent one glare of fierce, exultant, partisan defiance at the man in collar and cravat now, whom he had seen but twice before in his life, and that on a galloping horse, who now wore on his face an expression not of rage but of amazed unbelief which the boy could not have known was at the incredible circumstance of being sued by one of his own tenants, and came and stood against his father and cried at the Justice: "He ain't done it! He ain't burnt . . ."

"Go back to the wagon," his father said.

"Burnt?" the Justice said. "Do I understand this rug was burned too?"

"Does anybody here claim it was?" his father said. "Go back to the wagon." But he did not, he merely retreated to the rear of the room, crowded as that other had been, but not to sit down this time, instead, to stand pressing among the motionless bodies, listening to the voices:

"And you claim twenty bushels of corn is too high for the damage you did to the rug?"

75 "He brought the rug to me and said he wanted the tracks washed out of it. I washed the tracks out and took the rug back to him."

"But you didn't carry the rug back to him in the same condition it was in before you made the tracks on it."

His father did not answer, and now for perhaps half a minute there was no sound at all save that of breathing, the faint, steady suspiration of complete and intent listening.

"You decline to answer that, Mr. Snopes?" Again his father did not answer. "I'm going to find against you, Mr. Snopes. I'm going to find that you were responsible for the injury to Major de Spain's rug and hold you liable for it. But twenty bushels of corn seems a little high for a man in your circumstances to have to pay. Major de Spain claims it cost a hundred dollars. October corn will be worth about fifty cents. I figure that if Major de Spain can stand a ninety-five dollar loss on something he paid cash for, you can stand a five-dollar loss you haven't earned yet. I hold you in damages to Major de Spain to the amount of ten bushels of corn over and above your contract with him, to be paid to him out of your crop at gathering time. Court adjourned."

It had taken no time hardly, the morning was but half begun. He thought they would return home and perhaps back to the field, since they were late, far behind all other farmers. But instead his father passed on behind the wagon, merely indicating with his hand for the older brother to follow with it, and crossed the road toward the blacksmith shop opposite, pressing on after his father, overtaking him, speaking, whispering up at the harsh, calm face beneath the weathered hat: "He won't git no ten bushels neither. He won't git one. We'll . . ." until his father glanced for an instant down at him, the face absolutely calm, the grizzled eyebrows tangled above the cold eyes, the voice almost pleasant, almost gentle:

80   "You think so? Well, we'll wait till October anyway."

The matter of the wagon—the setting of a spoke or two and the tightening of the tires—did not take long either, the business of the tires accomplished by driving the wagon into the spring branch behind the shop and letting it stand there, the mules nuzzling into the water from time to time, and the boy on the seat with the idle reins, looking up the slope and through the sooty tunnel of the shed where the slow hammer rang and where his father sat on an upended cypress bolt, easily, either talking or listening, still sitting there when the boy brought the dripping wagon up out of the branch and halted it before the door.

"Take them on to the shade and hitch," his father said. He did so and returned. His father and the smith and a third man squatting on his heels inside the door were talking, about crops and animals; the boy, squatting too in the ammoniac dust and hoof-parings and scales of rust, heard his father tell a long and unhurried story out of the time before the birth of the older brother even when he had been a professional horse-trader. And then his father came up beside him where he stood before a tattered last year's circus poster on the other side of the store, gazing rapt and quiet at the scarlet horses, the incredible poisings and convolutions of tulle and tights and the painted leers of comedians, and said, "It's time to eat."

But not at home. Squatting beside his brother against the front wall, he watched his father emerge from the store and produce from a paper sack a segment of cheese and divide it carefully and deliberately into three with his pocket knife and produce crackers from the same sack. They all three squatted on the gallery and ate, slowly, without talking; then in the store again, they drank from a tin dipper tepid water smelling of the cedar bucket and of living beech trees. And still they did not go home. It was a horse lot this time, a tall rail fence upon and along which men stood and sat and out of which one by one horses were led, to be walked and trotted and then cantered back and forth along the road while the slow swapping and buying went on and the sun began to slant westward, they—the three of them—watching and listening, the older brother with his muddy eyes and his steady, inevitable tobacco, the father commenting now and then on certain of the animals, to no one in particular.

It was after sundown when they reached home. They ate supper by lamplight, then, sitting on the doorstep, the boy watched the night fully accomplish, listening to the whippoorwills and the frogs, when he heard his mother's voice: "Abner! No! No! Oh, God. Oh, God. Abner!" and he rose, whirled, and saw the altered light through the door where a candle stub now burned in a bottle neck on the table and his father, still in the hat and coat, at once formal and burlesque as though dressed carefully for some shabby and ceremonial violence, emptying the reservoir of the lamp back into the five-gallon kerosene can from which it had been filled, while the mother tugged at his arm until he shifted the lamp to the other hand and flung her back, not savagely or viciously, just hard, into the wall, her hands flung out against the wall for balance, her mouth open and in her face the same quality of hopeless despair as had been in her voice. Then his father saw him standing in the door.

85   "Go to the barn and get that can of oil we were oiling the wagon with," he said. The boy did not move. Then he could speak.

"What . . ." he cried. "What are you . . ."

"Go get that oil," his father said. "Go."

Then he was moving, running, outside the house, toward the stable: this the old habit, the old blood which he had not been permitted to choose for himself, which had been bequeathed him willy nilly and which had run for so long (and who knew where, battening on what of outrage and savagery and lust) before it came to him. *I could keep on,* he thought. *I could run on and on and never look back, never need to see his face again. Only I can't. I can't,* the rusted can in his hand now, the liquid sploshing in it as he ran back to the house and into it, into the sound of his mother's weeping in the next room, and handed the can to his father.

"Ain't you going to even send a nigger?" he cried. "At least you sent a nigger before!"

90   This time his father didn't strike him. The hand came even faster than the blow had, the same hand which had set the can on the table with almost excruciating care flashing from the can toward him too quick for him to follow it, gripping him by the back of his shirt and on to tiptoe before he had seen it quit the can, the face stooping at him in breathless and frozen ferocity, the cold, dead voice speaking over him to the older brother who leaned against the table, chewing with that steady, curious, sidewise motion of cows:

"Empty the can into the big one and go on. I'll catch up with you."

"Better tie him to the bedpost," the brother said.

"Do like I told you," the father said. Then the boy was moving, his bunched shirt and the hard, bony hand between his shoulderblades, his toes just touching the floor, across the room and into the other one, past the sisters sitting with spread heavy thighs in the two chairs over the cold hearth, and to where his mother and aunt sat side by side on the bed, the aunt's arms about his mother's shoulders.

"Hold him," the father said. The aunt made a startled movement. "Not you," the father said. "Lennie. Take hold of him. I want to see you do it." His mother took him by the wrist. "You'll hold him better than that. If he gets loose don't you know what he is going to do? He will go up yonder." He jerked his head toward the road. "Maybe I'd better tie him."

95 "I'll hold him," his mother whispered.

"See you do then." Then his father was gone, the stiff foot heavy and measured upon the boards, ceasing at last.

Then he began to struggle. His mother caught him in both arms, he jerking and wrenching at them. He would be stronger in the end, he knew that. But he had no time to wait for it. "Lemme go!" he cried. "I don't want to have to hit you!"

"Let him go!" the aunt said. "If he don't go, before God, I am going up there myself!"

"Don't you see I can't?" his mother cried. "Sarty! Sarty! No! No! Help me, Lizzie!"

100 Then he was free. His aunt grasped at him but it was too late. He whirled, running, his mother stumbled forward on to her knees behind him, crying to the nearest sister: "Catch him, Net! Catch him!" But that was too late too, the sister (the sisters were twins, born at the same time, yet either of them now gave the impression of being, encompassing as much living meat and volume and weight as any other two of the family) not yet having begun to rise from the chair, her head, face, alone merely turned, presenting to him in the flying instant an astonishing expanse of young female features untroubled by any surprise even, wearing only an expression of bovine interest. Then he was out of the room, out of the house, in the mild dust of the starlit road and the heavy rifeness of honeysuckle, the pale ribbon unspooling with terrific slowness under his running feet, reaching the gate at last and turning in, running, his heart and lungs drumming, on up the drive toward the lighted house, the lighted door. He did not knock, he burst in, sobbing for breath, incapable for the moment of speech; he saw the astonished face of the Negro in the linen jacket without knowing when the Negro had appeared.

"De Spain!" he cried, panted. "Where's . . ." then he saw the white man too emerging from a white door down the hall. "Barn!" he cried. "Barn!"

"What?" the white man said. "Barn?"

"Yes!" the boy cried. "Barn!"

"Catch him!" the white man shouted.

105 But it was too late this time too. The Negro grasped his shirt, but the entire sleeve, rotten with washing, carried away, and he was out that door too and in the drive again, and had actually never ceased to run even while he was screaming into the white man's face.

Behind him the white man was shouting, "My horse! Fetch my horse!" and he thought for an instant of cutting across the park and climbing the fence into the road, but he did not know the park nor how high the vine-massed fence might be and he dared not risk it. So he ran on down the drive, blood and breath roaring; presently he was in the road again though he could not see it. He could not hear either: the galloping mare was almost upon him before he heard her, and even then he held his course, as if the very urgency of his wild grief and need must in a moment more find him wings, waiting until the ultimate instant to hurl himself aside and into the weed-choked roadside ditch as the horse thundered past and on, for an instant in furious silhouette against the stars, the tranquil early summer night sky which, even before the shape of the horse and rider vanished, stained abruptly and violently upward: a long, swirling roar incredible and soundless, blotting the stars, and he springing up and into the road again, running again, knowing it was too late yet still running even after he heard the shot and, an instant later, two shots, pausing now without knowing he had ceased to run, crying "Pap! Pap!", running again before he knew he had begun to run, stumbling, tripping over something and scrabbling up again without ceasing to run, looking backward over his shoulder at the glare as he got up, running on among the invisible trees, panting, sobbing, "Father! Father!"

At midnight he was sitting on the crest of a hill. He did not know it was midnight and he did not know how far he had come. But there was no glare behind him now and he sat now, his back toward what he had called home for four days anyhow, his face toward the dark woods which he would enter when breath was strong again, small, shaking steadily in the chill darkness, hugging himself into the remainder of his thin, rotten shirt, the grief and despair now no longer terror and fear but just grief and despair. *Father. My father,* he thought. "He was brave!" he cried suddenly, aloud but not loud, no more than a whisper: "He was! He was in the war! He was in Colonel Sartoris' cav'ry!" not knowing that his father had gone to that war a private in the fine old European sense, wearing no uniform, admitting the authority of and giving fidelity to no man or army or flag, going to war as Malbrouck[5] himself did: for booty—it meant nothing and less than nothing to him if it were enemy booty or his own.

The slow constellations wheeled on. It would be dawn and then sunup after a while and he would be hungry. But that would be tomorrow and now he was only cold, and walking would cure that. His breathing was easier now and he decided to get up and go on, and then he found that he had been asleep because he knew it was almost dawn, the night almost over. He could tell that from the whippoorwills. They were everywhere now among the dark trees below him, constant and inflectioned and ceaseless, so that, as the instant for giving over to the day birds drew nearer and nearer, there was no interval at all between them.

---

[5] A character in a popular eighteenth-century nursery rhyme about a famous warrior.

He got up. He was a little stiff, but walking would cure that too as it would the cold, and soon there would be the sun. He went on down the hill, toward the dark woods within which the liquid silver voices of the birds called unceasing—the rapid and urgent beating of the urgent and quiring heart of the late spring night. He did not look back.

READING AND REACTING

1. Is the third-person narrator of "Barn Burning" omniscient, or is his omniscience limited? Explain.

2. What is the point of view of the italicized passages? What do we learn from them? Do they create irony? How would the story have been different without these passages?

3. "Barn Burning" includes a great deal of dialogue. How would you characterize the **level of diction** of this dialogue? What information about various characters does it provide?

4. What conflicts are presented in "Barn Burning"? Which, if any, are resolved in the story? Are the conflicts avoidable? Explain.

5. Why does Ab Snopes burn barns? Do you think his actions are justified? Explain your reasoning.

6. What role does the Civil War play in "Barn Burning"? What does Abner Snopes's behavior during the war tell readers about his character?

7. In Books 1 and 2 of Samuel in the Old Testament, Abner was a relative of King Saul and commander in chief of his armies. Abner supported King Saul against David and was killed as a result of his own jealousy and rage. What, if any, significance is there in the fact that Faulkner names Ab Snopes, loyal to no man, fighter "for booty, and father of the Snopes clan," after this mighty biblical leader?

8. Why does Sarty Snopes insist that his father was brave? How does your knowledge of events unknown to the boy affect your reactions to this statement?

9. **JOURNAL ENTRY** How would the story be different if it were told from Ab's point of view? From Sarty's? From the point of view of Ab's wife? From the point of view of a member of a community in which the Snopeses have lived?

10. **CRITICAL PERSPECTIVE** Critic Edmond L. Volpe argues in his article "'Barn Burning': A Definition of Evil" that "Barn Burning" is not really about the class conflict between the sharecropping Snopeses and landowners like the de Spains:

   > The story is centered upon Sarty's emotional dilemma. His conflict would not have been altered in any way if the person

whose barn Ab burns had been a simple poor farmer, rather than an aristocratic plantation owner. [. . .] Sarty's struggle is against the repressive and divisive force his father represents. The boy's anxiety is created by his awakening sense of his own individuality. Torn between strong emotional attachment to the parent and his growing need to assert his own identity, Sarty's crisis is psychological and his battle is being waged far below the level of his intellectual and moral awareness.

Do you believe "Barn Burning" is, as Volpe suggests, essentially a coming-of-age story, or do you believe it is about something else—class conflict, for example?

Related Works: "A Worn Path" (p. 388), "Eveline" (p. 470), "Child's Grave, Hale County, Alabama" (p. 899), "The Satisfaction Coal Company" (p. 948), *Fences* (p. 1745)

◊ **GARY GILDNER** (1938–) is an award-winning writer living in Idaho with his wife and daughter. His work includes *Blue Like the Heavens: New and Selected Poems* (1984), *Clackamas* (1991), and *The Swing* (1996), as well as a novel, *The Second Bridge* (1987), and two collections of stories, The *Crush* (1983) and *A Week in South Dakota* (1987). His popular memoir *The Warsaw Sparks* (1990) recounts his experiences as a baseball coach in Warsaw, Poland.

One of Gildner's most acclaimed collections of poetry, *The Bunker in the Parsley Fields* (1997), won the Iowa poetry prize. Most of the poems in the award-winning collection are based on the experiences Gildner and his wife shared while living in Slovakia during 1992–93, when Czechoslovakia split in two. They lived, like thousands around them, in cramped quarters in a cement flat above an abondoned bunker not far from the Tatra Mountains.

In his short story "Sleepy Time Gal," Gildner writes of love and loss in a small town during the Depression. The narrator attempts to tell a simple story without intruding, but his perspective, as well as the perspective of others in the story, makes it clear that stories of love and loss are never simple.

CULTURAL CONTEXT ◊ "Sleepy Time Gal" is the actual name of a blues song first published in 1925. The blues is a form of secular folk music with its origins among Southern blacks in the early 20th century. Its simple but expressive style makes the blues an important influence on popular music in the United States.

◇ ◇ ◇

GARY GILDNER

Sleepy Time Gal
(1979)

In the small town in northern Michigan where my father lived as a young man, he had an Italian friend who worked in a restaurant. I will call his friend Phil. Phil's job in the restaurant was as ordinary as you can imagine—from making coffee in the morning to sweeping up at night. But what was not ordinary about Phil was his piano playing. On Saturday nights my father and Phil and their girlfriends would drive ten or fifteen miles to a roadhouse by a lake where they would drink beer from schooners and dance and Phil would play an old beat-up piano. He could play any song you named, my father said, but the song everyone waited for was the one he wrote, which he would always play at the end before they left to go back to the town. And everyone knew of course that he had written the song for his girl, who was as pretty as she was rich. Her father was the banker in their town, and he was a tough old German, and he didn't like Phil going around with his daughter.

My father, when he told the story, which was not often, would tell it in an offhand way and emphasize the Depression and not having much, instead of the important parts. I will try to tell it the way he did, if I can.

So they would go to the roadhouse by the lake, and finally Phil would play his song, and everyone would say, Phil, that's a great song, you could make a lot of money from it. But Phil would only shake his head and smile and look at his girl. I have to break in here and say that my father, a gentle but practical man, was not inclined to emphasize the part about Phil looking at his girl. It was my mother who said the girl would rest her head on Phil's shoulder while he played, and that he got the idea for the song from the pretty way she looked when she got sleepy. My mother was not part of the story, but she had heard it when she and my father were younger and therefore had that information. I would like to intrude further and add something about Phil writing the song, maybe show him whistling the tune and going over the words slowly and carefully to get the best ones, while peeling onions or potatoes in the restaurant; but my father is already driving them home from the roadhouse, and saying how patched up his tires were, and how his car's engine was a gingerbread of parts from different makes, and some parts were his own invention as well. And my mother is saying that the old German had made his daughter promise not to get involved with any man until after college, and they couldn't be late. Also my mother likes the sad parts and is eager to get to their last night before the girl goes away to college.

So they all went out to the roadhouse, and it was sad. The women got tears in their eyes when Phil played her song, my mother said. My father said that Phil spent his week's pay on a new shirt and tie, the first tie he ever owned, and people kidded him. Somebody piped up and said, Phil, you ought to take that song down to Bay City—which was like saying New York City to them, only more realistic—and sell it and take the money and go to college too. Which was not meant to be cruel, but that was the result because Phil had never even got to high school. But you can see people were trying to cheer him up, my mother said.

5   Well, she'd come home for Thanksgiving and Christmas and Easter and they'd all sneak out to the roadhouse and drink beer from schooners and dance and everything would be like always. And of course there were the summers. And everyone knew Phil and the girl would get married after she made good her promise to her father because you could see it in their eyes when he sat at the old beat-up piano and played her song.

That last part about their eyes was not, of course, in my father's telling, but I couldn't help putting it in there even though I know it is making some of you impatient. Remember that this happened many years ago in the woods by a lake in northern Michigan, before television. I wish I could put more in, especially about the song and how it felt to Phil to sing it and how the girl felt when hearing it and knowing it was hers, but I've already intruded too much in a simple story that isn't even mine.

Well, here's the kicker part. Probably by now many of you have guessed that one vacation near the end she doesn't come home to see Phil, because she meets some guy at college who is good-looking and as rich as she is and, because her father knew about Phil all along and was pressuring her into forgetting about him, she gives in to this new guy and goes to his hometown during the vacation and falls in love with him. That's how the people in town figured it, because after she graduates they turn up, already married, and right away he takes over the old German's bank—and buys a new Pontiac at the place where my father is the mechanic and pays cash for it. The paying cash always made my father pause and shake his head and mention again that times were tough, but here comes this guy in a spiffy white shirt (with French cuffs, my mother said) and pays the full price in cash.

And this made my father shake his head too: Phil took the song down to Bay City and sold it for twenty-five dollars, the only money he ever got for it. It was the same song we'd just heard on the radio and which reminded my father of the story I just told you. What happened to Phil? Well, he stayed in Bay City and got a job managing a movie theater. My father saw him there after the Depression when he was on his way to Detroit to work for Ford. He stopped and Phil gave him a box of popcorn. The song he wrote for the girl has sold many millions of records, and if I told you the name of it you could probably sing it, or at least whistle the tune. I wonder what the girl thinks when she hears it. Oh yes, my father met Phil's wife too. She worked in the movie theater with him, selling tickets and cleaning the carpet after the show with one of those sweepers you push. She was also big and loud and nothing like the other one, my mother said.

Reading and Reacting

1. What are the advantages of using a first-person narrator in this story? How might a third-person omniscient narrator change the story?
2. How does Gildner introduce other points of view into the story? What do these different perspectives contribute to the narrative?
3. In paragraph 2, the narrator says that when his father told the story about Phil, he emphasized the Depression "instead of the important parts." What does the narrator mean? In your opinion, what are the "important parts" of the story?
4. What facts does the narrator's mother emphasize? How is her view of the story different from her husband's?
5. The narrator describes Phil as a person who is "as ordinary as you can imagine" (1). What attracts the girl—whose father is the town banker—to Phil?
6. Why does Phil write the song? Why does he sell it for so little money?
7. In paragraph 6, the narrator says, "I've already intruded too much in a simple story that isn't even mine." How has he intruded? Whose story is it?
8. How does the story's setting—a small town in northern Michigan during the Depression—affect the story?
9. **Journal Entry** What do you think attracts Phil to the girl? Her money? Her good looks? Something else? Explain.
10. **Critical Perspective** Gary Gildner says of his writing technique: "I write, I work, I do with a pencil. I like how the words come out of my head and travel down my arm to that sharp point. I like holding a pencil. Also a baseball, a smooth stone fresh from the river, a walking stick, my daughter's hand. So I write everything in pencil first."

    The first-person narration in "Sleepy Time Gal" follows the sometimes circuitous route of memory despite the narrator's determination not to intrude in the story. How is Gildner's narrative style in the story consistent with his technique of writing in pencil first? Would a more careful, revised version of the story be more effective?

Related Works: "Once upon a Time" (p. 81), "In a Grove" (p. 398), "Fifteen Minutes in the Life of Larry Weller" (p. 587), "Poetry" (p. 664), "Nothing Gold Can Stay" (p. 800), *The Stronger* (p. 1177)

◆ Writing Suggestions: Point of View

1. How would Poe's "The Cask of Amontillado" be different if it were told by a minor character who observed the events? Rewrite the

story from this point of view—or tell the story that precedes the story, explaining the thousand injuries and the insult.

2. Assume that you are the sailor in "Big Black Good Man" and that you are keeping a journal of your travels. Write the journal entries for the time you spent in Copenhagen. Include your impressions of Olaf, Lena, the hotel, and anything else that caught your attention. Make sure you present your version of the key events described in the story—especially Olaf's reaction to you.

3. Both "The Cask of Amontillado" and "Barn Burning" deal with crimes that essentially go unpunished and with the emotions that accompany these crimes. In what sense does each story's use of point of view shape its treatment of the crime in question? For instance, how does point of view determine how much readers know about the motives for the crime, the crime's basic circumstances, and the extent to which the crime is justified?

4. Tell the story in "Sleepy Time Gal" entirely from Phil's point of view, filling in the gaps in the story. For example, explain why Phil wrote the song and why he sold it for twenty-five dollars.

5. "Barn Burning" is, among other things, a story about a child's conflict with his parent's values. Write an essay in which you compare "Barn Burning" with another work that explores this theme—for example, "Digging" (p. 679) or *The Glass Menagerie* (p. 1805).

6. **WEB ACTIVITY** The following Web site contains information about Richard Wright:

http://www.pbs.org/rwbb/rwtoc.html

Read the "Overview" section, making note of the biographical details and the introduction of themes in Wright's work. Focusing on Wright's experiences with prejudice as he was growing up, write an essay discussing how his story "Big Black Good Man" expresses his "deep interest in the large questions of authority, power, and freedom." Concentrate in particular on the relationship between the white protagonist and the title character in the story as representative of Wright's own struggle against oppression.

CHAPTER 8

Style, Tone, and Language

◇ ◇ ◇

A word is intrinsically powerful. If you believe in the power of words, you can bring about physical change in the universe. This is a notion of language that is ancient and it is valid to me. For example, the words of a charm or a spell are formulaic. They are meant to bring about physical change. The person who utters such a formula believes beyond any shadow of doubt that his utterance is going to have this or that actual effect. Because he believes in it and because words are what they are, it is true. It is true. [. . .] Every day we produce magical results with words.

N. Scott Momaday, *Ancestral Voices*

INTERVIEWER: You describe seemingly fantastic events in such minute detail that it gives them their own reality. Is this something you have picked up from journalism?

García Márquez: That's a journalistic trick which you can also apply to literature. For example, if you say that there are elephants flying in the sky, people are not going to believe you. But if you say that there are four hundred and twenty-five elephants in the sky, people will probably believe you. [. . .] I remember particularly the story about the character who is surrounded by yellow butterflies. [. . .] I discovered that if I didn't say the butterflies were yellow, people would not believe it. [. . .] The problem for every writer is credibility. Anybody can write anything so long as it's believed.

Gabriel García Márquez, *Writers at Work*, 6th ed.

When a writer starts in very young, his problems apart from his story are those of technique, of words, of rhythms, of story methods, of transition, of characterization, of ways of creating effects. But after years of trial and error most of these things are solved and one gets what is called a style. It is then that a story conceived falls into place neatly and is written down having the indelible personal hallmark of the writer.

John Steinbeck, Letter

◇ ◇ ◇

One of the qualities that gives a work of literature its individual personality is its **style,** the way in which a writer selects and arranges words to say what he or she wants to say. Style encompasses elements such as word choice; syntax; sentence length and structure; and the presence, frequency, and prominence of imagery and figures of speech. Closely related to style is **tone,** the attitude of the narrator or author of a work toward the subject matter, characters, or audience. Word choice and sentence structure help to create a work's tone, which may be intimate or distant, bitter or affectionate, straightforward or cautious, supportive or critical, respectful or condescending. (Tone may also be **ironic;** see Chapter 7, "Point of View," for a discussion of irony.)

Style offers almost limitless possibilities to a writer. Creative use of language (unusual word choice, word order, or sentence structure, for instance) can enrich a story and add to its overall effect. Sometimes style can help to create an atmosphere that enhances the setting or communicates the story's theme. In other cases, style can reveal a character's mental state. For instance, the breathless, disjointed style of Edgar Allan Poe's "The Tell-Tale Heart" (p. 576) suggests the narrator's increasing emotional instability: "Was it possible they heard not? Almighty God!—no, no! They heard!—they suspected!—they *knew!*—they were making a mockery of my horror!" In his short story "Big Two-Hearted River," Ernest Hemingway strings sentences together without transitions to create a flat, emotionless prose style that reveals his character's alienation and fragility as he struggles to maintain control: "Now things were done. There had been this to do. Now it was done. It had been a hard trip. He was very tired. That was done. He had made his camp. He was settled. Nothing could touch him." Finally, style can expand a story's possibilities through its very inventiveness. For example, James Joyce's innovative **stream-of-consciousness** style mimics thought, allowing ideas to run into one another as random associations are made, so that readers may follow and participate in the thought processes of the narrator. Here is a stream-of-consciousness passage from Joyce's experimental novel *Ulysses:*

> frseeeeeeeefronnnng train somewhere whistling the strength those engines have in them like big giants and the water rolling all over and out of them all sides like the end of Loves old sweet sonnnng the poor men that have to be out all the night from their wives and families in those roasting engines stifling it was today [. . .].

The following passage from Alberto Alvaro Ríos's story "The Secret Lion" (p. 49) illustrates the power of creative language to enrich a story:

> We had read the books, after all; we knew about bridges and castles and wildtreacherousraging alligatormouth rivers. We wanted them. So we were going to go out and get them. We went back that morning into that kitchen and we said, "We're going out there, we're going

into the hills, we're going away for three days, don't worry." She said, "All right."

"You know," I said to Sergio, "if we're going to go away for three days, well, we ought to at least pack a lunch."

But we were two young boys with no patience for what we thought at the time was mom-stuff: making sa-and-wiches. My mother didn't offer. So we got out little kid knapsacks that my mother had sewn for us, and into them we put the jar of mustard. A loaf of bread. Knivesforksplates, bottles of Coke, a can opener. This was lunch for the two of us. And we were weighed down, humped over to be strong enough to carry this stuff. But we started walking anyway, into the hills. We were going to eat berries and stuff otherwise. "Goodbye." My mom said that.

Through language, the adult narrator of the preceding paragraphs recaptures the bravado of the boys in search of "wildtreacherousraging alligatormouth rivers" even as he suggests to readers that the boys are not going far. The story's use of language is original and inventive: words are blended together ("getridofit," "knivesforksplates"), linked to form new language ("mom-stuff"), and drawn out ("sa-and-wiches") to mimic speech. These experiments with language show the narrator's willingness to move back into a child's frame of reference while maintaining the advantage of distance. The adult narrator uses sentence fragments ("A loaf of bread."), colloquialisms ("kid," "mom," "stuff"), and contractions. He also includes conversational elements such as *you know* and *well* in the dialogue, accurately re-creating the childhood scene at the same time he sees its folly and remains aware of the disillusionment that awaits him. Thus, the unique style permits the narrator to bring readers with him into the child's world even as he maintains his adult stance: "But we were two young boys with no patience for what we thought at the time was mom-stuff [. . .]."

Use of stylistic devices that place emphasis on the sounds and rhythm of words and sentences also enriches works of fiction. Consider the use of such techniques in the following sentence from James Joyce's "Araby" (p. 254):

The light from the lamp opposite our door caught the white curve of her neck, lit up her hair that rested there and, falling, lit up the hand upon the railing.

Here the narrator is describing his first conversation with a girl who fascinates him, and the lush, lyrical, almost musical language reflects his enchantment. Note in particular the **alliteration** (light/lamp; caught/curve; hair/hand), the repetition (lit up/lit up), and the rhyme (lit up her *hair*/that rested *there*) and **near rhyme** (falling/railing); these poetic devices connect the words of the sentence into a smooth, rhythmic whole. Another example of this emphasis on sound may be found in the measured **parallelism** of this sentence from Nathaniel Hawthorne's "The Birthmark" (p. 450):

> He had left his laboratory to the care of an assistant, cleared his fine countenance from the furnace smoke, washed the stain of acids from his fingers, and persuaded a beautiful woman to become his wife.

The style of the preceding sentence, conveying methodical precision and order, reflects the compulsive personality of the character being described.

Although many stylistic options are available to writers, style must be consistent with the writer's purpose and with the effect he or she hopes to create. Just as writers may experiment with point of view or manipulate events to create a complex plot, so they can adjust style to suit particular narrators, characters, settings, or themes. Two elements with which writers frequently experiment are *level of diction,* and *imagery* and *figurative language.*

LEVEL OF DICTION

◊ ◊ ◊

The level of diction—how formal or informal a story's language is—can suggest a good deal about those who use the language, thus providing insights into the story's theme.

FORMAL DICTION

Formal diction is characterized by elaborate, complex sentences; a learned vocabulary; and a serious, objective, detached tone. The speaker avoids contractions, shortened word forms (like *phone*), regional expressions, and slang, and he or she may use *one* or *we* in place of *I*. At its most extreme, formal language may be stiff and stilted, far removed from everyday speech.

Formal diction, whether used by a narrator or by a character, may indicate erudition, a high educational level, a superior social or professional position, or emotional detachment. When one character's language is significantly more formal than others', he or she may seem old-fashioned or stuffy; when language is inappropriately elevated or complex, it may reveal the character to be pompous or ridiculous; when a narrator's language is noticeably more formal than that of the characters, the narrator may seem superior or even condescending. Thus, level of diction reveals a good deal about characters and about the narrator's attitude toward them.

The following passage from "The Birthmark" illustrates formal style:

> In the latter part of the last century there lived a man of science, an eminent proficient in every branch of natural philosophy, who not long before our story opens had made experience of a spiritual affinity more attractive than any chemical one. He had left his laboratory to the care of an assistant, cleared his fine countenance from the furnace smoke, washed the stain of acids from his fingers, and persuaded a beautiful woman to become his wife. In those days when the comparatively recent discovery of electricity and other kindred mysteries of Nature seemed to open paths into the region of miracle, it was not unusual for the love of science to rival the love of woman in its depth and absorbing energy. The higher intellect, the imagination, the spirit, and even the heart might all find their congenial ailment in pursuits which, as some of their ardent votaries believed, would ascend from one step of powerful intelligence to another, until the philosopher should lay his hand on the secret of creative force and perhaps make new worlds for himself.

The long, complex sentences; learned vocabulary ("countenance," "ailment," "votaries"); and absence of colloquialisms suit Hawthorne's purpose well, re-creating the formal language of the earlier era in which his story is set. The omniscient narrator, despite his use of the first person in "our story," is aloof and controlled.

INFORMAL DICTION

Informal diction, consistent with everyday speech, is characterized by slang, contractions, colloquial expressions like *you know* and *I mean*, shortened word forms, incomplete sentences, and a casual, conversational tone. A first-person narrator may use informal style, or characters may speak informally; in either case, informal style tends to narrow the distance between readers and text.

Informal language can range from the straightforward contemporary style of Cal's dialogue in "Teenage Wasteland" ("'I think this kid is hurting. You know?'") to the regionalisms and dialect employed in Flannery O'Connor's "A Good Man Is Hard to Find" ("aloose"; "you all"; "britches"). In "Teenage Wasteland" (p. 603), Cal's self-consciously slangy, conversational style tells readers a good deal about his motives and his method of operating; in "A Good Man Is Hard to Find" (p. 266), the characters' speech patterns and diction reveal the region in which they live and their social class. In other stories, a character's use of obscenities may suggest his or her crudeness or adolescent bravado, and use of racial or ethnic slurs suggests that a character is insensitive and bigoted.

The following passage from John Updike's "A&P" (p. 113) illustrates informal style:

> She had sort of oaky hair that the sun and salt had bleached, done up in a bun that was unravelling, and a kind of prim face. Walking into

the A&P with your straps down, I suppose it's the only kind of face you *can* have. She held her head so high her neck, coming out of those white shoulders, looked kind of stretched, but I didn't mind. The longer her neck was, the more of her there was.

In the preceding passage, the first-person narrator uses a conversational style, including colloquialisms ("sort of," "I suppose," "kind of"), contractions ("it's," "didn't"), and the imprecise, informal *you* ("Walking into the A&P with *your* straps down [. . .]."). The narrator uses neither elaborate sentences nor learned diction.

IMAGERY AND FIGURATIVE LANGUAGE

◇ ◇ ◇

IMAGERY

Imagery—words and phrases that describe what is seen, heard, smelled, tasted, or touched—can have a significant impact in a story. A pattern of repeated imagery can help to convey a particular impression about a character or situation, or a writer may use such a pattern to communicate or reinforce a story's theme. For example, the theme of newly discovered sexuality can be conveyed through repeated use of words and phrases suggesting blooming or ripening.

In T. Coraghessan Boyle's "Greasy Lake" (p. 404), the narrator's vivid description of Greasy Lake itself uses rich visual imagery to evoke a scene:

> Through the center of town, up the strip, past the housing developments and shopping malls, street lights giving way to the thin streaming illumination of the headlights, trees crowding the asphalt in a black unbroken wall: that was the way out to Greasy Lake. The Indians had called it Wakan, a reference to the clarity of its waters. Now it was fetid and murky, the mud banks glittering with broken glass and strewn with beer cans and the charred remains of bonfires. There was a single ravaged island a hundred yards from shore, so stripped of vegetation it looked as if the air force had strafed it. We went up to the lake because everyone went there, because we wanted to snuff the rich scent of possibility on the breeze, watch a girl take off her clothes and plunge into the festering murk, drink beer, smoke pot, howl at the stars, savor the incongruous full-throated roar of rock and roll against the primeval susurrus of frogs and crickets. This was nature.

By characterizing a natural setting with surprising words like "fetid," "murky," and "greasy" and unpleasant images such as the "glittering of broken glass," the "ravaged island," and the "charred remains of bonfires,"

Boyle creates a picture that is completely at odds with a traditional pastoral view of nature. The incongruous images are nevertheless perfectly consistent with the sordid events that take place at Greasy Lake.

FIGURATIVE LANGUAGE

Figures of speech—such as *similes, metaphors,* and *personification*—can enrich a story, subtly revealing information about characters and themes. (See Chapter 16 for more information about figures of speech.)

By using **metaphors** and **similes**—figures of speech that compare two dissimilar items—writers can indicate a particular attitude toward characters and events. Thus, Flannery O'Connor's many grotesque similes in "A Good Man Is Hard to Find" help to dehumanize her characters; the children's mother, for instance, has a face "as broad and innocent as a cabbage." In Tillie Olsen's "I Stand Here Ironing" (p. 160), an extended metaphor in which a mother compares her daughter to a dress waiting to be ironed expresses the mother's attitude toward her daughter, effectively suggesting to readers the daughter's vulnerability. Similes and metaphors are used freely in Kate Chopin's "The Storm" (p. 154). In a scene of sexual awakening, Calixta's skin is "like a creamy lily," her passion is "like a white flame," and her mouth is "a fountain of delight"; these figures of speech add a lushness and sensuality to the story.

Personification—a figure of speech, closely related to metaphor, that endows inanimate objects or abstract ideas with life or with human characteristics—is used in "Araby" (p. 254), where houses, "conscious of decent lives within them, gazed at one another with brown imperturbable faces." This use of figurative language expands readers' vision of the story's setting and gives a dreamlike quality to the passage. (Other figures of speech, such as **hyperbole** and **understatement,** can also enrich works of fiction. See Chapter 16, "Figures of Speech," for further information.)

Allusions—references to familiar historical or literary personages or events—may also expand readers' understanding and appreciation of a work. An allusion widens a work's context by bringing it into the context of a related subject or idea. For instance, Wole Soyinka's frequent references to political figures and events in "Future Plans" (p. 908) enable readers who recognize the references to gain a deeper understanding of the speaker's position on various political and social issues. Literary and biblical allusions may be used in much the same way.

A FINAL NOTE
◈ ◈ ◈

In analyzing the use of language in a work of fiction, you may occasionally encounter obscure allusions, foreign words and phrases, unusual comparisons, and unfamiliar regional expressions—particularly in works treating cultures and historical periods other than your own. Frequently such language will be clarified by the context, or by explanatory notes in your text; when it is not, you should consult a dictionary, encyclopedia, or other reference work.

✴ CHECKLIST: WRITING ABOUT STYLE, TONE, AND LANGUAGE

✓ Is the story's tone intimate? Distant? Ironic? How does the tone advance the writer's purpose?

✓ Does the writer make any unusual creative use of diction, word order, or sentence structure?

✓ Does the style emphasize the sound and rhythm of language? For example, does the writer use alliteration and assonance? Repetition and parallelism? What do such techniques add to the story?

✓ Is the level of diction generally formal, informal, or somewhere in between?

✓ Is there a difference between the style of the narrator and the style of the characters' speech? If so, what is the effect of this difference?

✓ Do any of the story's characters use regionalisms, colloquial language, or nonstandard speech? If so, what effect does this language have?

✓ What do different characters' levels of diction reveal about them?

✓ What kind of imagery predominates? Where, and why, is imagery used?

✓ Does the story develop a pattern of imagery? How does this pattern of imagery relate to the story's themes?

✓ Does the story use simile and metaphor? Personification? What is the effect of these figures of speech?

✓ Do figures of speech reinforce the story's themes? Reveal details about characters?

✓ Does the story make any historical, literary, or biblical allusions? What do these allusions contribute to the story?

✓ What unfamiliar, obscure, or foreign words, phrases, or images are used in the story? What is the effect of these words or expressions?

◊ **James Joyce** (1884–1941) was born in Dublin but lived his entire adult life in self-imposed exile from his native Ireland. Though his parents sent him to schools that trained young men for the priesthood, Joyce saw himself as a religious and artistic rebel, and he fled to Paris soon after graduation in 1902. Recalled briefly to Dublin by his mother's fatal illness, Joyce returned to the Continent in 1904, taking with him an uneducated Irish country girl named Nora Barnacle, who became his wife in 1931. In dreary quarters in Trieste, Zurich, and Paris, Joyce struggled to support a growing family, sometimes teaching classes in Berlitz language schools.

Though Joyce never again lived in Ireland, he continued to write about Dublin. Publication of *Dubliners* (1914), a collection of short stories that included "Araby," was delayed for seven years because the Irish publisher feared libel suits from local citizens who were thinly disguised as characters in the stories. Joyce's autobiographical *Portrait of the Artist as a Young Man* (1916) tells of a young writer's rejection of family, church, and country. *Ulysses* (1922), the comic tale of eighteen hours in the life of a wandering Dublin advertising salesman, was banned when the U.S. Post Office brought charges of obscenity against the book, and it remained banned in the United States and England for more than a decade. In *Ulysses,* Joyce begins a revolutionary journey away from traditional techniques of plot and characterization to the interior monologues and stream-of-consciousness style that mark his last great novel, *Finnegans Wake* (1939).

Cultural Context ◊ In the years between the Great Famine of the 1840s and World War I, Ireland experienced a severe decline in living standards, and the resulting emigration led to a reduction in population by almost one third. It is against the background of these harsh economic conditions that Joyce juxtaposes a young boy's idealism with the conditions of his day-to-day life in "Araby."

◊ ◊ ◊

JAMES JOYCE

Araby
(1914)

North Richmond Street, being blind,[1] was a quiet street except at the hour when the Christian Brothers' School set the boys free. An uninhabited house of two storeys stood at the blind end, detached from its neighbours in a square ground. The other houses of the street, conscious of decent lives within them, gazed at one another with brown imperturbable faces.

---

[1] A dead-end street.

The former tenant of our house, a priest, had died in the back drawing-room. Air, musty from having been long enclosed, hung in all the rooms, and the waste room behind the kitchen was littered with old useless papers. Among these I found a few paper-covered books, the pages of which were curled and damp: *The Abbot,* by Walter Scott, *The Devout Communicant* and *The Memoirs of Vidocq.*[2] I liked the last best because its leaves were yellow. The wild garden behind the house contained a central apple-tree and a few straggling bushes under one of which I found the late tenant's rusty bicycle-pump. He had been a very charitable priest; in his will he had left all his money to institutions and the furniture of his house to his sister.

When the short days of winter came dusk fell before we had well eaten our dinners. When we met in the street the houses had grown sombre. The space of sky above us was the colour of ever-changing violet and towards it the lamps of the street lifted their feeble lanterns. The cold air stung us and we played till our bodies glowed. Our shouts echoed in the silent street. The career of our play brought us through the dark muddy lanes behind the houses where we ran the gauntlet of the rough tribes from the cottages, to the back doors of the dark dripping gardens where odours arose from the ashpits, to the dark odorous stables where a coachman smoothed and combed the horse or shook music from the buckled harness. When we returned to the street light from the kitchen windows had filled the areas. If my uncle was seen turning the corner we hid in the shadow until we had seen him safely housed. Or if Mangan's sister came out on the doorstep to call her brother in to his tea we watched her from our shadow peer up and down the street. We waited to see whether she would remain or go in and, if she remained, we left our shadow and walked up to Mangan's steps resignedly. She was waiting for us, her figure defined by the light from the half-opened door. Her brother always teased her before he obeyed and I stood by the railings looking at her. Her dress swung as she moved her body and the soft rope of her hair tossed from side to side.

Every morning I lay on the floor in the front parlour watching her door. The blind was pulled down to within an inch of the sash so that I could not be seen. When she came out on the doorstep my heart leaped. I ran to the hall, seized my books and followed her. I kept her brown figure always in my eye and, when we came near the point at which our ways diverged, I quickened my pace and passed her. This happened morning after morning. I had never spoken to her, except for a few casual words, and yet her name was like a summons to all my foolish blood.

5   Her image accompanied me even in places the most hostile to romance. On Saturday evenings when my aunt went marketing I had to go

---

[2] Sir Walter Scott (1771–1832)—an English Romantic novelist; *The Devout Communicant*—a variant title for *Pious Meditations,* written by an eighteenth-century English Franciscan friar, Pacifus Baker; *The Memoirs of Vidocq*—an autobiography of François-Jules Vidocq (1775–1857), a French soldier of fortune turned police agent.

to carry some of the parcels. We walked through the flaring streets, jostled by drunken men and bargaining women, amid the curses of labourers, the shrill litanies of shop-boys who stood on guard by the barrels of pigs' cheeks, the nasal chanting of street-singers, who sang a *come-all-you* about O'Donovan Rossa,[3] or a ballad about the troubles in our native land. These noises converged in a single sensation of life for me: I imagined that I bore my chalice safely through a throng of foes. Her name sprang to my lips at moments in strange prayers and praises which I myself did not understand. My eyes were often full of tears (I could not tell why) and at times a flood from my heart seemed to pour itself out into my bosom. I thought little of the future. I did not know whether I would ever speak to her or not or, if I spoke to her, how I could tell her of my confused adoration. But my body was like a harp and her words and gestures were like fingers running upon the wires.

One evening I went into the back drawing-room in which the priest had died. It was a dark rainy evening and there was no sound in the house. Through one of the broken panes I heard the rain impinge upon the earth, the fine incessant needles of water playing in the sodden beds. Some distant lamp or lighted window gleamed below me. I was thankful that I could see so little. All my senses seemed to desire to veil themselves and, feeling that I was about to slip from them, I pressed the palms of my hands together until they trembled, murmuring: *"O love! O love!"* many times.

At last she spoke to me. When she addressed the first words to me I was so confused that I did not know what to answer. She asked me was I going to *Araby*. I forgot whether I answered yes or no. It would be a splendid bazaar, she said she would love to go.

"And why can't you?" I asked.

While she spoke she turned a silver bracelet round and round her wrist. She could not go, she said, because there would be a retreat that week in her convent.[4] Her brother and two other boys were fighting for their caps and I was alone at the railings. She held one of the spikes, bowing her head towards me. The light from the lamp opposite our door caught the white curve of her neck, lit up her hair that rested there and, falling, lit up the hand upon the railing. It fell over one side of her dress and caught the white border of a petticoat, just visible as she stood at ease.

10   "It's well for you," she said.

"If I go," I said, "I will bring you something."

What innumerable follies laid waste my waking and sleeping thoughts after that evening! I wished to annihilate the tedious intervening days. I chafed against the work of school. At night in my bedroom and by day in the classroom her image came between me and the page I strove

---

[3] Any popular song beginning "Come all you gallant Irishmen . . ."; O'Donovan Rossa was an Irish nationalist who was banished in 1870 for advocating violent rebellion against the British.

[4] A week devoted to prayer and meditation in her convent school.

to read. The syllables of the word *Araby* were called to me through the silence in which my soul luxuriated and cast an Eastern enchantment over
me. I asked for leave to go to the bazaar on Saturday night. My aunt was
surprised and hoped it was not some Freemason[5] affair. I answered few
questions in class. I watched my master's face pass from amiability to
sternness; he hoped I was not beginning to idle. I could not call my wandering thoughts together. I had hardly any patience with the serious work
of life which, now that it stood between me and my desire, seemed to me
child's play, ugly monotonous child's play.

On Saturday morning I reminded my uncle that I wished to go to the
bazaar in the evening. He was fussing at the hallstand, looking for the hat-
brush, and answered me curtly:

"Yes, boy, I know."

15   As he was in the hall I could not go into the front parlour and lie at the
window. I left the house in bad humour and walked slowly towards the
school. The air was pitilessly raw and already my heart misgave me.

When I came home to dinner my uncle had not yet been home. Still it
was early. I sat staring at the clock for some time and, when its ticking
began to irritate me, I left the room. I mounted the staircase and gained
the upper part of the house. The high cold empty gloomy rooms liberated
me and I went from room to room singing. From the front window I saw
my companions playing below in the street. Their cries reached me weakened and indistinct and, leaning my forehead against the cool glass, I
looked over at the dark house where she lived. I may have stood there for
an hour, seeing nothing but the brown-clad figure cast by my imagination, touched discreetly by the lamplight at the curved neck, at the hand
upon the railings and at the border below the dress.

When I came downstairs again I found Mrs. Mercer sitting at the fire.
She was an old garrulous woman, a pawnbroker's widow, who collected
used stamps for some pious purpose. I had to endure the gossip of the tea-
table. The meal was prolonged beyond an hour and still my uncle did not
come. Mrs. Mercer stood up to go: she was sorry she couldn't wait any
longer, but it was after eight o'clock and she did not like to be out late, as
the night air was bad for her. When she had gone I began to walk up and
down the room, clenching my fists. My aunt said:

"I'm afraid you may put off your bazaar for this night of Our Lord."

At nine o'clock I heard my uncle's latchkey in the halldoor. I heard
him talking to himself and heard the hallstand rocking when it had received the weight of his overcoat. I could interpret these signs. When he
was midway through his dinner I asked him to give me the money to go to
the bazaar. He had forgotten.

20   "The people are in bed and after their first sleep now," he said.

I did not smile. My aunt said to him energetically:

---

[5] At the time the story takes place, Catholics in Ireland thought the Masonic Order was
a threat to the church.

"Can't you give him the money and let him go? You've kept him late enough as it is."

My uncle said he was very sorry he had forgotten. He said he believed in the old saying: "All work and no play makes Jack a dull boy." He asked me where I was going and, when I had told him a second time he asked me did I know *The Arab's Farewell to his Steed*.[6] When I left the kitchen he was about to recite the opening lines of the piece to my aunt.

I held a florin tightly in my hand as I strode down Buckingham Street towards the station. The sight of the streets thronged with buyers and glaring with gas recalled to me the purpose of my journey. I took my seat in a third-class carriage of a deserted train. After an intolerable delay the train moved out of the station slowly. It crept onward among ruinous houses and over the twinkling river. At Westland Row Station a crowd of people pressed to the carriage doors; but the porters moved them back, saying that it was a special train for the bazaar. I remained alone in the bare carriage. In a few minutes the train drew up beside an improvised wooden platform. I passed out on to the road and saw by the lighted dial of a clock that it was ten minutes to ten. In front of me was a large building which displayed the magical name.

25   I could not find any sixpenny entrance and, fearing that the bazaar would be closed, I passed in quickly through a turnstile, handing a shilling to a weary-looking man. I found myself in a big hall girdled at half its height by a gallery. Nearly all the stalls were closed and the greater part of the hall was in darkness. I recognised a silence like that which pervades a church after a service. I walked into the centre of the bazaar timidly. A few people were gathered about the stalls which were still open. Before a curtain, over which the words *Café Chantant*[7] were written in coloured lamps, two men were counting money on a salver. I listened to the fall of the coins.

Remembering with difficulty why I had come I went over to one of the stalls and examined porcelain vases and flowered tea-sets. At the door of the stall a young lady was talking and laughing with two young gentlemen. I remarked their English accents and listened vaguely to their conversation.

"O, I never said such a thing!"

"O, but you did!"

"O, but I didn't!"

30   "Didn't she say that?"

"Yes. I heard her."

"O, there's a . . . fib!"

Observing me the young lady came over and asked me did I wish to buy anything. The tone of her voice was not encouraging; she seemed to

---

[6] A sentimental poem by Caroline Norton (1808–1877) that tells the story of a nomad's heartbreak after selling his much-loved horse.

[7] A Paris café featuring musical entertainment.

have spoken to me out of a sense of duty. I looked humbly at the great jars that stood like eastern guards at either side of the dark entrance to the stall and murmured:

"No, thank you."

35   The young lady changed the position of one of the vases and went back to the two young men. They began to talk of the same subject. Once or twice the young lady glanced at me over her shoulder.

I lingered before her stall, though I knew my stay was useless, to make my interest in her wares seem the more real. Then I turned away slowly and walked down the middle of the bazaar. I allowed the two pennies to fall against the sixpence in my pocket. I heard a voice call from one end of the gallery that the light was out. The upper part of the hall was now completely dark.

Gazing up into the darkness I saw myself as a creature driven and derided by vanity; and my eyes burned with anguish and anger.

READING AND REACTING

1. How would you characterize the story's level of diction? Is this level appropriate for a story about a young boy's experiences? Explain.

2. Identify several examples of figurative language in the story. Where is Joyce most likely to use this kind of language? Why?

3. What words and phrases express the boy's extreme idealism and romantic view of the world? In what way does such language help to communicate the story's major theme?

4. In paragraph 4, the narrator says, "her name was like a summons to all my foolish blood." In the story's last sentence he sees himself as "a creature driven and derided by vanity." What other expressions does he use to describe his feelings? How would you characterize these feelings?

5. How does word choice illustrate the contrast between the narrator's day-to-day life and the exotic promise of the bazaar?

6. What does each of the italicized words suggest: "We walked through the *flaring* streets" (5); "I heard the rain *impinge* upon the earth" (6); "I *chafed* against the work of school" (12); "I found myself in a big hall *girdled* at half its height by a gallery" (25)? What other examples of unusual word choice can you identify in the story?

7. What is it about the events in this story that causes the narrator to remember them years later?

8. Identify words and phrases in the story that are associated with religion. What purpose do these references to religion serve?

9. **JOURNAL ENTRY** Rewrite a brief passage from this story in the voice of the young boy. Use informal style, simple figures of speech, and vocabulary appropriate for a child.

10. **CRITICAL PERSPECTIVE** In *Notes on the American Short Story Today,* Richard Kostelanetz discusses the epiphany, one of Joyce's most significant contributions to literature:

> In Joyce's pervasively influential theory of the short story we remember, the fiction turned upon an epiphany, a moment of revelation in which, in [critic] Harry Levin's words, "amid the most encumbered circumstances it suddenly happens that the veil is lifted, the [. . .] mystery laid bare, and the ultimate secret of things made manifest." The epiphany, then, became a technique for jelling the narrative and locking the story's import into place. [. . .] What made this method revolutionary was the shifting of the focal point of the story from its end [. . .] to a spot within the body of the text, usually near (but not at) the end.

Where in "Araby" does the story's epiphany occur? Does it do all that Kostelanetz believes an epiphany should do? Or do you think that, at least in the case of "Araby," the epiphany may not be as significant a force as Kostelanetz suggests?

Related Works: "A&P" (p. 113), "Gryphon" (p. 134), "Doe Season" (p. 349), "Shall I Compare Thee to a Summer's Day?" (p. 807)

◆ **ERNEST HEMINGWAY** (1898–1961) grew up in Oak Park, Illinois, and after high school graduation began his writing career as a cub reporter on the *Kansas City Star.* While working as a volunteer ambulance driver in World War I, eighteen-year-old Hemingway was wounded. As Hemingway himself told the story, he was hit by machine-gun fire while carrying an Italian soldier to safety. (Hemingway biographer Michael Reynolds, however, reports that Hemingway was wounded when a mortar shell fell and killed the man next to him.) In 1922, Hemingway and his first wife (he married four times) moved to Paris, where he taught Ezra Pound how to box, let Gertrude Stein mind the baby, and talked literary shop with expatriate writers F. Scott Fitzgerald and James Joyce. He was, said Joyce, "a big, powerful peasant, as strong as a buffalo [. . .] and ready to live the life he writes about." In fact, this public image of the "man's man"—the war correspondent, the deep-sea fisherman, the hunter on safari—was one Hemingway carefully created for himself.

Success came early, with publication of the short story collection *In Our Time* (1925) and his first and most acclaimed novel, *The Sun Also Rises* (1926), a portrait of a postwar "lost generation" of Americans adrift in Europe. Hemingway's novels make fiction and art out of the reality of his own life. *A Farewell to Arms* (1929) harks back to his war experiences; *For*

Whom the Bell Tolls (1940) emerged out of his experiences as a journalist in Spain during the Spanish Civil War. Late in life, he made his home in Key West, Florida, and then in Cuba, where he wrote *The Old Man and the Sea* (1952). Hemingway's heroes embody the writer's own belief that although life may be followed by *nada*, or nothingness, strong individuals can embrace life and live it with dignity and honor. In 1961, plagued by poor health and mental illness—and perhaps by the difficulty of living up to his own image—Hemingway took his own life.

According to novelist and critic Anthony Burgess, Hemingway changed the sound of English prose by struggling to write a "true simple declarative sentence." His spare, unadorned style "sounds easy now, chiefly because Hemingway has shown us how to do it, but it was not easy at a time when 'literature' still meant fine writing in the Victorian sense [. . .]." Hemingway was awarded the 1954 Nobel Prize in literature.

CULTURAL CONTEXT ❖   Ernest Hemingway's granddaughter, Margaux Hemingway, who died in 1996, was the fifth Hemingway to commit suicide. Ernest Hemingway himself committed suicide in 1961, and his father, brother, and sister also died at their own hands.

❖ ❖ ❖

ERNEST HEMINGWAY

A Clean, Well-Lighted Place
(1933)

It was late and every one had left the café except an old man who sat in the shadow the leaves of the tree made against the electric light. In the day time the street was dusty, but at night the dew settled the dust and the old man liked to sit late because he was deaf and now at night it was quiet and he felt the difference. The two waiters inside the café knew that the old man was a little drunk, and while he was a good client they knew that if he became too drunk he would leave without paying, so they kept watch on him.

"Last week he tried to commit suicide," one waiter said.

"Why?"

"He was in despair."

5   'What about?"

"Nothing."

"How do you know it was nothing?"

"He has plenty of money."

They sat together at a table that was close against the wall near the door of the café and looked at the terrace where the tables were all empty except where the old man sat in the shadow of the leaves of the tree that moved slightly in the wind. A girl and a soldier went by in the street. The street light shone on the brass number on his collar. The girl wore no head covering and hurried beside him.

10   "The guard will pick him up," one waiter said.

"What does it matter if he gets what he's after?"

"He had better get off the street now. The guard will get him. They went by five minutes ago."

The old man sitting in the shadow rapped on his saucer with his glass. The younger waiter went over to him.

"What do you want?"

15   The old man looked at him. "Another brandy," he said.

"You'll be drunk," the waiter said. The old man looked at him. The waiter went away.

"He'll stay all night," he said to his colleague. "I'm sleepy now. I never get into bed before three o'clock. He should have killed himself last week."

The waiter took the brandy bottle and another saucer from the counter inside the café and marched out to the old man's table. He put down the saucer and poured the glass full of brandy.

"You should have killed yourself last week," he said to the deaf man. The old man motioned with his finger. "A little more," he said. The waiter poured on into the glass so that the brandy slopped over and ran down the stem into the top saucer of the pile. "Thank you," the old man said. The waiter took the bottle back inside the café. He sat down at the table with his colleague again.

20   "He's drunk now," he said.

"He's drunk every night."

"What did he want to kill himself for?"

"How should I know."

"How did he do it?"

25   "He hung himself with a rope."

"Who cut him down?"

"His niece."

"Why did they do it?"

"Fear for his soul."

30   "How much money has he got?"

"He's got plenty."

"He must be eighty years old."

"Anyway I should say he was eighty."

"I wish he would go home. I never get to bed before three o'clock. What kind of hour is that to go to bed?"

35   "He stays up because he likes it."

"He's lonely. I'm not lonely. I have a wife waiting in bed for me."

"He had a wife once too."

"A wife would be no good to him now."

"You can't tell. He might be better with a wife."

40   "His niece lookes after him. You said she cut him down."

"I know."

"I wouldn't want to be that old. An old man is a nasty thing."

"Not always. This old man is clean. He drinks without spilling. Even now, drunk. Look at him."

"I don't want to look at him. I wish he would go home. He has no regard for those who must work."

45   The old man looked from his glass across the square, then over at the waiters.

"Another brandy," he said, pointing to his glass. The waiter who was in a hurry came over.

"Finished," he said, speaking with that omission of syntax stupid people employ when talking to drunken people or foreigners. "No more tonight. Close now."

"Another," said the old man.

"No. Finished." The waiter wiped the edge of the table with a towel and shook his head.

50   The old man stood up, slowly counted the saucers, took a leather coin purse from his pocket and paid for the drinks, leaving half a peseta tip.

The waiter watched him go down the street, a very old man walking unsteadily but with dignity.

"Why didn't you let him stay and drink?" the unhurried waiter asked. They were putting up the shutters. "It is not half-past two."

"I want to go home to bed."

"What is an hour?"

55   "More to me than to him."

"An hour is the same."

"You talk like an old man yourself. He can buy a bottle and drink at home."

"It's not the same."

"No, it is not," agreed the waiter with a wife. He did not wish to be unjust. He was only in a hurry.

60   "And you? You have no fear of going home before your usual hour?"

"Are you trying to insult me?"

"No, hombre, only to make a joke."

"No," the waiter who was in a hurry said, rising from pulling down the metal shutters. "I have confidence. I am all confidence."

"You have youth, confidence, and a job," the older waiter said. "You have everything."

65   "And what do you lack?"

"Everything but work."

"You have everything I have."

"No. I have never had confidence and I am not young."

"Come on. Stop talking nonsense and lock up."

70   "I am of those who like to stay late at the café," the older waiter said. "With all those who do not want to go to bed. With all those who need a light for the night."

"I want to go home and into bed."

"We are of two different kinds," the older waiter said. He was now dressed to go home. "It is not only a question of youth and confidence although those things are very beautiful. Each night I am reluctant to close up because there may be some one who needs the café."

"Hombre, there are bodegas[1] open all night long."

"You do not understand. This is a clean and pleasant café. It is well lighted. The light is very good and also, now, there are shadows of the leaves."

75   "Good night," said the younger waiter.

"Good night," the other said. Turning off the electric light he continued the conversation with himself. It is the light of course but it is necessary that the place be clean and pleasant. You do not want music. Certainly you do not want music. Nor can you stand before a bar with dignity although that is all that is provided for these hours. What did he fear? It was not fear or dread. It was a nothing that he knew too well. It was all a nothing and a man was nothing too. It was only that and light was all it needed and a certain cleanness and order. Some lived in it and never felt it but he knew it all was nada y pues nada y nada y pues nada.[2] Our nada who art in nada, nada be thy name thy kingdom nada thy will be nada in nada as it is in nada. Give us this nada our daily nada and nada us our nada as we nada our nadas and nada us not into nada but deliver us from nada; pues nada. Hail nothing full of nothing, nothing is with thee. He smiled and stood before a bar with a shining steam pressure coffee machine.

"What's yours?" asked the barman.

"Nada."

"Otro loco más[3]," said the barman and turned away.

80   "A little cup," said the waiter.

The barman poured it for him.

"The light is very bright and pleasant but the bar is unpolished," the waiter said.

The barman looked at him but did not answer. It was too late at night for conversation.

"You want another copita[4]?" the barman asked.

85   "No, thank you," said the waiter and went out. He disliked bars and bodegas. A clean, well-lighted café was a very different thing. Now, without thinking further, he would go home to his room. He would lie in the bed and finally, with daylight, he would go to sleep. After all, he said to himself, it is probably only insomnia. Many must have it.

Reading and Reacting

1. Throughout the story certain words—*nada,* for example—are repeated. Identify as many of these repeated words as you can. What do you think such repetition achieves?
2. The story's dialogue is presented in alternating exchanges of very brief sentences. What is the effect of these clipped exchanges?

---

[1] Small grocery stores, sometimes combined with wineshops.
[2] Nothing and then nothing and nothing and then nothing.
[3] Another lunatic.
[4] Little cup.

3. Characterize the tone of the story.

4. Does the story present the human condition in optimistic or pessimistic terms? In what sense are the story's style and tone well suited to this worldview?

5. The story is set in Spain, yet Hemingway uses only a few Spanish words. Why does he use these words? Would the impact of the prayer be different if it had been spoken in English? Explain.

6. The café is described as "clean" and "pleasant." Why is this description a key element of the story? In what sense, if any, is this description ironic?

7. The story's primary **point of view** is objective. At times, however, a limited omniscient point of view is used. Identify such instances, and try to explain the reason for each shift in point of view.

8. Identify examples of figurative language used in the story. How does the presence (or absence) of such language help to convey the story's theme?

9. **JOURNAL ENTRY** Rewrite about half a page of the story, supplying logical transitions between sentences. How does your editing change the passage? Do your changes improve the story or take something away?

10. **CRITICAL PERSPECTIVE** In *The Writer's Art of Self-Defense,* Jackson J. Benson states, "Blindness versus awareness is Hemingway's most pervasive theme, and it is borne on a rippling wave of irony into almost everything he writes."

    How do the contrasting perspectives of the two waiters in "A Clean, Well-Lighted Place" express this theme? Which one is "blind," and which one is "aware"? How do their words reveal their knowledge or lack of knowledge?

Related Works: "Dreams of Suicide" (p. 910), "Dover Beach" (p. 926), "The Love Song of J. Alfred Prufrock" (p. 950), "Desert Places" (p. 957), "Not Waving but Drowning" (p. 992), *'night, Mother* (p. 1708)

◆ **(MARY) FLANNERY O'CONNOR** (1925–1964) was born to a prosperous Catholic family in Savannah, Georgia, and spent most of her adult life on a farm near the town of Milledgeville. She left the South to study writing at the University of Iowa, moving to New York to work on her first novel, *Wise Blood* (1952). On a train going south for Christmas, O'Connor fell desperately ill; she was diagnosed as having lupus, the immune system disease that killed her father and would cause O'Connor's death when she was only thirty-nine years old.

While her mother ran the farm, O'Connor spent mornings writing and afternoons wandering the fields with cane or crutches. Her short story collection *A Good Man Is Hard to Find* (1955) and an excellent French translation of *Wise Blood* established her international reputation, which was solidified with the publication of a second novel, *The Violent Bear It Away* (1960), and a posthumously published book of short stories, *Everything That Rises Must Converge* (1965).

O'Connor delighted in local reaction to her grotesque, often grisly stories: "Ask her," the men at the hardware store prodded her uncle, "why she don't write about some nice people." O'Connor, said a friend, believed that an artist "should face all the truth down to the worst of it." Yet however dark, O'Connor's stories are infused with grim humor and a fierce belief in the possibility of spiritual redemption, even for her most tortured characters. A line from her short story "A Good Man Is Hard to Find" says much about what O'Connor perceived about both natural things and her characters: "The trees were full of silver-white sunlight and the meanest of them sparkled." In O'Connor's work, the "meanest" things and people can sparkle, touched by a kind of holy madness and beauty.

CULTURAL CONTEXT ◊   Some critics consider O'Connor a Christian writer. O'Connor once said that "virtue can believably triumph only in completely drawn characters and against a backdrop whose roots are recognized to be in original sin." The theological concepts of sin, redemption, and free will are viable in much of O'Connor's work, and in "A Good Man Is Hard to Find," her characters avoid confronting their weaknesses until the necessity for salvation and grace is directly upon them. (On the other hand, when asked why the misfit wears a hat, O'Connor answered, "To cover his head.")

◊ ◊ ◊

FLANNERY O'CONNOR

A Good Man Is Hard to Find
(1955)

The grandmother didn't want to go to Florida. She wanted to visit some of her connections in east Tennessee and she was seizing at every chance to change Bailey's mind. Bailey was the son she lived with, her only boy. He was sitting on the edge of his chair at the table, bent over the orange sports section of the *Journal*. "Now look here, Bailey," she said, "see here, read this," and she stood with one hand on her thin hip and the other rattling the newspaper at his bald head. "Here this fellow that calls himself The Misfit is aloose from the Federal Pen and headed toward Florida and you read here what it says he did to these people. Just you read it. I wouldn't take my children in any direction with a criminal like that aloose in it. I couldn't answer to my conscience if I did."

Bailey didn't look up from his reading so she wheeled around then and faced the children's mother, a young woman in slacks, whose face was as broad and innocent as a cabbage and was tied around with a green head-kerchief that had two points on the top like a rabbit's ears. She was sitting on the sofa, feeding the baby his apricots out of a jar. "The children have been to Florida before," the old lady said. "You all ought to take them somewhere else for a change so they would see different parts of the world and be broad. They never have been to east Tennessee."

The children's mother didn't seem to hear her but the eight-year-old boy, John Wesley, a stocky child with glasses, said, "If you don't want to go to Florida, why dontcha stay at home?" He and the little girl, June Star, were reading the funny papers on the floor.

"She wouldn't stay at home to be queen for a day," June Star said without raising her yellow head.

5   "Yes and what would you do if this fellow, the Misfit, caught you?" the grandmother asked.

"I'd smack his face," John Wesley said.

"She wouldn't stay at home for a million bucks," June Star said. "Afraid she'd miss something. She has to go everywhere we go."

"All right, Miss," the grandmother said. "Just remember that the next time you want me to curl your hair."

June Star said her hair was naturally curly.

10   The next morning the grandmother was the first one in the car, ready to go. She had her big black valise that looked like the head of a hippopotamus in one corner, and underneath it she was hiding a basket with Pitty Sing, the cat, in it. She didn't intend for the cat to be left alone in the house for three days because he would miss her too much and she was afraid he might brush against one of the gas burners and ac-cidentally asphyxiate himself. Her son, Bailey, didn't like to arrive at a motel with a cat.

She sat in the middle of the back seat with John Wesley and June Star on either side of her. Bailey and the children's mother and the baby sat in front and they left Atlanta at eight forty-five with the mileage on the car at 55890. The grandmother wrote this down because she thought it would be interesting to say how many miles they had been when they got back. It took them twenty minutes to reach the outskirts of the city.

The old lady settled herself comfortably, removing her white cotton gloves and putting them up with her purse on the shelf in front of the back window. The children's mother still had on slacks and still had her head tied up in a green kerchief, but the grandmother had on a navy blue straw sailor hat with a bunch of white violets on the brim and a navy blue dress with a small white dot in the print. Her collars and cuffs were white organdy trimmed with lace and at her neckline she had pinned a purple spray of cloth violets containing a sachet. In case of an accident, anyone seeing her dead on the highway would know at once that she was a lady.

She said she thought it was going to be a good day for driving, neither too hot nor too cold, and she cautioned Bailey that the speed limit was fifty-five miles an hour and that the patrolmen hid themselves behind billboards and small clumps of trees and sped out after you before you had a chance to slow down. She pointed out interesting details of the scenery: Stone Mountain; the blue granite that in some places came up to both sides of the highway; the brilliant red clay banks slightly streaked with purple; and the various crops that made rows of green lace-work on the ground. The trees were full of silver-white sunlight and the meanest of them sparkled. The children were reading comic magazines and their mother had gone back to sleep.

"Let's go through Georgia fast so we won't have to look at it much," John Wesley said.

15 "If I were a little boy," said the grandmother, "I wouldn't talk about my native state that way. Tennessee has the mountains and Georgia has the hills."

"Tennessee is just a hillbilly dumping ground," John Wesley said, "and Georgia is a lousy state too."

"You said it," June Star said.

"In my time," said the grandmother, folding her thin veined fingers, "children were more respectful of their native states and their parents and everything else. People did right then. Oh look at the cute little pickaninny!" she said and pointed to a Negro child standing in the door of a shack. "Wouldn't that make a picture, now?" she asked and they all turned and looked at the little Negro out of the back window. He waved.

"He didn't have any britches on," June Star said.

20 "He probably didn't have any," the grandmother explained. "Little niggers in the country don't have things like we do. If I could paint, I'd paint that picture," she said.

The children exchanged comic books.

The grandmother offered to hold the baby and the children's mother passed him over the front seat to her. She set him on her knee and bounced him and told him about the things they were passing. She rolled her eyes and screwed up her mouth and stuck her leathery thin face into his smooth bland one. Occasionally he gave her a faraway smile. They passed a large cotton field with five or six graves fenced in the middle of it, like a small island. "Look at the graveyard!" the grandmother said, pointing it out. "That was the old family burying ground. That belonged to the plantation."

"Where's the plantation?" John Wesley asked.

"Gone With the Wind," said the grandmother. "Ha. Ha."

25 When the children finished all the comic books they had brought, they opened the lunch and ate it. The grandmother ate a peanut butter sandwich and an olive and would not let the children throw the box and the paper napkins out the window. When there was nothing else to do they played a game by choosing a cloud and making the other two guess what shape it suggested. John Wesley took one the shape of a cow and June Star guessed a cow and John Wesley said, no, an automobile, and June Star said he didn't play fair, and they began to slap each other over the grandmother.

The grandmother said she would tell them a story if they would keep quiet. When she told a story, she rolled her eyes and waved her head and was very dramatic. She said once when she was a maiden lady she had been courted by a Mr. Edgar Atkins Teagarden from Jasper, Georgia. She said he was a very good-looking man and a gentleman and that he brought her a watermelon every Saturday afternoon with his initials cut in it, E. A. T. Well, one Saturday, she said, Mr. Teagarden brought the watermelon and there was nobody at home and he left it on the front porch and returned in his buggy to Jasper, but she never got the watermelon, she said, because a nigger boy ate it when he saw the initials, E. A. T.! This story tickled John Wesley's funny bone and he giggled and giggled but June Star didn't think it was any good. She said she wouldn't marry a man that just brought her a watermelon on Saturday. The grandmother said she would have done well to marry Mr. Teagarden because he was a gentleman and had bought Coca-Cola stock when it first came out and that he died only a few years ago, a very wealthy man.

They stopped at The Tower for barbecued sandwiches. The Tower was a part stucco and part wood filling station and dance hall set in a clearing outside of Timothy. A fat man named Red Sammy Butts ran it and there were signs stuck here and there on the building and for miles up and down the highway saying, TRY RED SAMMY'S FAMOUS BARBECUE. NONE LIKE FAMOUS RED SAMMY'S! RED SAM! THE FAT BOY WITH THE HAPPY LAUGH. A VETERAN! RED SAMMY'S YOUR MAN!

Red Sammy was lying on the bare ground outside The Tower with his head under a truck while a gray monkey about a foot high, chained to a small chinaberry tree, chattered nearby. The monkey sprang back into the tree and got on the highest limb as soon as he saw the children jump out of the car and run toward him.

Inside, The Tower was a long dark room with a counter at one end and tables at the other and dancing space in the middle. They all sat down at a board table next to the nickelodeon and Red Sam's wife, a tall burnt-brown woman with hair and eyes lighter than her skin, came and took their order. The children's mother put a dime in the machine and played "The Tennessee Waltz," and the grandmother said that tune always made her want to dance. She asked Bailey if he would like to dance but he only glared at her. He didn't have a naturally sweet disposition like she did and trips made him nervous. The grandmother's brown eyes were very bright. She swayed her head from side to side and pretended she was dancing in her chair. June Star said play something she could tap to so the children's mother put in another dime and played a fast number and June Star stepped out onto the dance floor and did her tap routine.

30   "Ain't she cute?" Red Sam's wife said, leaning over the counter. "Would you like to come be my little girl?"

"No I certainly wouldn't," June Star said. "I wouldn't live in a broken-down place like this for a million bucks!" and she ran back to the table.

"Ain't she cute?" the woman repeated, stretching her mouth politely.

"Aren't you ashamed?" hissed the grandmother.

Red Sam came in and told his wife to quit lounging on the counter and hurry up with these people's order. His khaki trousers reached just to his hip bones and his stomach hung over them like a sack of meal swaying under his shirt. He came over and sat down at a table nearby and let out a combination sigh and yodel. "You can't win," he said. "You can't win," and he wiped his sweating red face off with a gray handkerchief. "These days you don't know who to trust," he said. "Ain't that the truth?"

35   "People are certainly not nice like they used to be," said the grandmother.

"Two fellers come in here last week," Red Sammy said, "driving a Chrysler. It was a old beat-up car but it was a good one and these boys looked all right to me. Said they worked at the mill and you know I let them fellers charge the gas they bought? Now why did I do that?"

"Because you're a good man!" the grandmother said at once.

"Yes'm, I suppose so," Red Sam said as if he were struck with this answer.

His wife brought the orders, carrying the five plates all at once without a tray, two in each hand and one balanced on her arm. "It isn't a soul in this green world of God's that you can trust," she said. "And I don't count nobody out of that, not nobody," she repeated, looking at Red Sammy.

40   "Did you read about that criminal, The Misfit, that's escaped?" asked the grandmother.

"I wouldn't be a bit surprised if he didn't attact this place right here," said the woman. "If he hears about it being here, I wouldn't be none surprised to see him. If he hears it's two cent in the cash register, I wouldn't be at all surprised if he . . ."

"That'll do," Red Sam said. "Go bring these people their Co'-Colas," and the woman went off to get the rest of the order.

"A good man is hard to find," Red Sammy said. "Everything is getting terrible. I remember the day you could go off and leave your screen door unlatched. Not no more."

He and the grandmother discussed better times. The old lady said that in her opinion Europe was entirely to blame for the way things were now. She said the way Europe acted you would think we were made of money and Red Sam said it was no use talking about it, she was exactly right. The children ran outside into the white sunlight and looked at the monkey in the lacy chinaberry tree. He was busy catching fleas on himself and biting each one carefully between his teeth as if it were a delicacy.

45   They drove off again into the hot afternoon. The grandmother took cat naps and woke up every few minutes with her own snoring. Outside of Toombsboro she woke up and recalled an old plantation that she had visited in this neighborhood once when she was a young lady. She said the house had six white columns across the front and that there was an avenue of oaks leading up to it and two little wooden trellis arbors on either side in front where you sat down with your suitor after a stroll in the garden. She recalled exactly which road to turn off to get to it. She knew that

Bailey would not be willing to lose any time looking at an old house, but the more she talked about it, the more she wanted to see it once again and find out if the little twin arbors were still standing. "There was a secret panel in this house," she said craftily, not telling the truth but wishing that she were, "and the story went that all the family silver was hidden in it when Sherman came through but it was never found . . ."

"Hey!" John Wesley said. "Let's go see it! We'll find it! We'll poke all the woodwork and find it! Who lives there? Where do you turn off at? Hey Pop, can't we turn off there?"

"We never have seen a house with a secret panel!" June Star shrieked. "Let's go to the house with the secret panel! Hey Pop, can't we go see the house with the secret panel!"

"It's not far from here, I know," the grandmother said. "It wouldn't take over twenty minutes."

Bailey was looking straight ahead. His jaw was as rigid as a horseshoe. "No," he said.

50   The children began to yell and scream that they wanted to see the house with the secret panel. John Wesley kicked the back of the front seat and June Star hung over her mother's shoulder and whined desperately into her ear that they never had any fun even on their vacation, that they could never do what THEY wanted to do. The baby began to scream and John Wesley kicked the back of the seat so hard that his father could feel the blows in his kidney.

"All right!" he shouted and drew the car to a stop at the side of the road. "Will you all shut up? Will you all just shut up for one second? If you don't shut up, we won't go anywhere."

"It would be very educational for them," the grandmother murmured.

"All right," Bailey said, "but get this: this is the only time we're going to stop for anything like this. This is the one and only time."

"The dirt road that you have to turn down is about a mile back," the grandmother directed. "I marked it when we passed."

55   "A dirt road," Bailey groaned.

After they had turned around and were headed toward the dirt road, the grandmother recalled other points about the house, the beautiful glass over the front doorway and the candle-lamp in the hall. John Wesley said that the secret panel was probably in the fireplace.

"You can't go inside this house," Bailey said. "You don't know who lives there."

"While you all talk to the people in front, I'll run around behind and get in a window," John Wesley suggested.

"We'll all stay in the car," his mother said.

60   They turned onto the dirt road and the car raced roughly along in a swirl of pink dust. The grandmother recalled the times when there were no paved roads and thirty miles was a day's journey. The dirt road was hilly and there were sudden washes in it and sharp curves on dangerous embankments. All at once they would be on a hill, looking down over the

blue tops of trees for miles around, then the next minute, they would be in a red depression with the dust-coated trees looking down on them.

"This place had better turn up in a minute," Bailey said, "or I'm going to turn around."

The road looked as if no one had traveled on it in months.

"It's not much farther," the grandmother said and just as she said it, a horrible thought came to her. The thought was so embarrassing that she turned red in the face and her eyes dilated and her feet jumped up, upsetting her valise in the corner. The instant the valise moved, the newspaper top she had over the basket under it rose with a snarl and Pitty Sing, the cat, sprang onto Bailey's shoulder.

The children were thrown to the floor and their mother, clutching the baby, was thrown out the door onto the ground; the old lady was thrown into the front seat. The car turned over once and landed right-side-up in a gulch off the side of the road. Bailey remained in the driver's seat with the cat—gray-striped with a broad white face and an orange nose—clinging to his neck like a caterpillar.

65   As soon as the children saw they could move their arms and legs, they scrambled out of the car, shouting, "We've had an ACCIDENT!" The grandmother was curled up under the dashboard, hoping she was injured so that Bailey's wrath would not come down on her all at once. The horrible thought she had had before the accident was that the house she had remembered so vividly was not in Georgia but in Tennessee.

Bailey removed the cat from his neck with both hands and flung it out the window against the side of a pine tree. Then he got out of the car and started looking for the children's mother. She was sitting against the side of the red gutted ditch, holding the screaming baby, but she only had a cut down her face and a broken shoulder. "We've had an ACCIDENT!" the children screamed in a frenzy of delight.

"But nobody's killed," June Star said with disappointment as the grandmother limped out of the car, her hat still pinned to her head but the broken front brim standing up at a jaunty angle and the violet spray hanging off the side. They all sat down in the ditch, except the children, to recover from the shock. They were all shaking.

"Maybe a car will come along," said the children's mother hoarsely.

"I believe I have injured an organ," said the grandmother, pressing her side, but no one answered her. Bailey's teeth were clattering. He had on a yellow sport shirt with bright blue parrots designed in it and his face was as yellow as the shirt. The grandmother decided that she would not mention that the house was in Tennessee.

70   The road was about ten feet above and they could see only the tops of the trees on the other side of it. Behind the ditch they were sitting in there were more woods, tall and dark and deep. In a few minutes they saw a car some distance away on top of a hill, coming slowly as if the occupants were watching them. The grandmother stood up and waved both arms

dramatically to attract their attention. The car continued to come on slowly, disappeared around a bend and appeared again, moving even slower, on top of the hill they had gone over. It was a big black battered hearse-like automobile. There were three men in it.

It came to a stop just over them and for some minutes, the driver looked down with a steady expressionless gaze to where they were sitting, and didn't speak. Then he turned his head and muttered something to the other two and they got out. One was a fat boy in black trousers and a red sweat shirt with a silver stallion embossed on the front of it. He moved around on the right side of them and stood staring, his mouth partly open in a kind of loose grin. The other had on khaki pants and a blue striped coat and a gray hat pulled down very low, hiding most of his face. He came around slowly on the left side. Neither spoke.

The driver got out of the car and stood by the side of it, looking down at them. He was an older man than the other two. His hair was just beginning to gray and he wore silver-rimmed spectacles that gave him a scholarly look. He had a long creased face and didn't have on any shirt or undershirt. He had on blue jeans that were too tight for him and was holding a black hat and a gun. The two boys also had guns.

"We've had an ACCIDENT!" the children screamed.

The grandmother had the peculiar feeling that the bespectacled man was someone she knew. His face was as familiar to her as if she had known him all her life but she could not recall who he was. He moved away from the car and began to come down the embankment, placing his feet carefully so that he wouldn't slip. He had on tan and white shoes and no socks, and his ankles were red and thin. "Good afternoon," he said. "I see you all had you a little spill."

75   "We turned over twice!" said the grandmother.

"Oncet," he corrected. "We seen it happen. Try their car and see will it run, Hiram," he said quietly to the boy with the gray hat.

"What you got that gun for?" John Wesley asked. "Watcha gonna do with that gun?"

"Lady," the man said to the children's mother, "would you mind calling them children to sit down by you? Children make me nervous. I want all you all to sit down right together there where you're at."

"What are you telling US what to do for?" June Star asked.

80   Behind them the line of woods gaped like a dark open mouth. "Come here," said their mother.

"Look here now," Bailey began suddenly, "we're in a predicament! We're in . . ."

The grandmother shrieked. She scrambled to her feet and stood staring. "You're The Misfit!" she said. "I recognized you at once!"

"Yes'm," the man said, smiling slightly as if he were pleased in spite of himself to be known, "but it would have been better for all of you, lady, if you hadn't of reckernized me."

Bailey turned his head sharply and said something to his mother that shocked even the children. The old lady began to cry and The Misfit reddened.

85   "Lady," he said, "don't you get upset. Sometimes a man says things he don't mean. I don't reckon he meant to talk to you thataway."

"You wouldn't shoot a lady, would you?" the grandmother said and removed a clean handkerchief from her cuff and began to slap at her eyes with it.

The Misfit pointed the toe of his shoe into the ground and made a little hole and then covered it up again. "I would hate to have to," he said.

"Listen," the grandmother almost screamed, "I know you're a good man. You don't look a bit like you have common blood. I know you must come from nice people!"

"Yes mam," he said, "finest people in the world." When he smiled he showed a row of strong white teeth. "God never made a finer woman than my mother and my daddy's heart was pure gold," he said. The boy with the red sweat shirt had come around behind them and was standing with his gun at his hip. The Misfit squatted down on the ground. "Watch them children, Bobby Lee," he said. "You know they make me nervous." He looked at the six of them huddled together in front of him and he seemed to be embarrassed as if he couldn't think of anything to say. "Ain't a cloud in the sky," he remarked, looking up at it. "Don't see no sun but don't see no cloud neither."

90   "Yes, it's a beautiful day," said the grandmother. "Listen," she said, "you shouldn't call yourself The Misfit because I know you're a good man at heart. I can just look at you and tell."

"Hush!" Bailey yelled. "Hush! Everybody shut up and let me handle this!" He was squatting in the position of a runner about to sprint forward but he didn't move.

"I pre-chate that, lady," The Misfit said and drew a little circle in the ground with the butt of his gun.

"It'll take a half a hour to fix this here car," Hiram called, looking over the raised hood of it.

"Well, first you and Bobby Lee get him and that little boy to step over yonder with you," The Misfit said, pointing to Bailey and John Wesley. "The boys want to ast you something," he said to Bailey. "Would you mind stepping back in them woods there with them?"

95   "Listen," Bailey began, "we're in a terrible predicament! Nobody realizes what this is," and his voice cracked. His eyes were as blue and intense as the parrots in his shirt and he remained perfectly still.

The grandmother reached up to adjust her hat brim as if she were going to the woods with him but it came off in her hand. She stood staring at it and after a second she let it fall on the ground. Hiram pulled Bailey up by the arm as if he were assisting an old man. John Wesley caught hold of his father's hand and Bobby Lee followed. They went off toward the woods and just as they reached the dark edge, Bailey turned and supporting himself against a gray naked pine trunk, he shouted, "I'll be back in a minute, Mamma, wait on me!"

"Come back this instant!" his mother shrilled but they all disappeared into the woods.

"Bailey Boy!" the grandmother called in a tragic voice but she found she was looking at The Misfit squatting on the ground in front of her. "I just know you're a good man," she said desperately. "You're not a bit common!"

"Nome, I ain't a good man," The Misfit said after a second as if he had considered her statement carefully, "but I ain't the worst in the world neither. My daddy said I was a different breed of dog from my brothers and sisters. 'You know,' Daddy said, 'it's some that can live their whole life out without asking about it and it's others has to know why it is, and this boy is one of the latters. He's going to be into everything!'" He put on his black hat and looked up suddenly and then away deep into the woods as if he were embarrassed again. "I'm sorry I don't have on a shirt before you ladies," he said, hunching his shoulders slightly. "We buried our clothes that we had on when we escaped and we're just making do until we can get better. We borrowed these from some folks we met," he explained.

100   "That's perfectly all right," the grandmother said. "Maybe Bailey has an extra shirt in his suitcase."

"I'll look and see terrectly," The Misfit said.

"Where are they taking him?" the children's mother screamed.

"Daddy was a card himself," The Misfit said. "You couldn't put anything over on him. He never got in trouble with the Authorities though. Just had the knack of handling them."

"You could be honest too if you'd only try," said the grandmother. "Think how wonderful it would be to settle down and live a comfortable life and not have to think about somebody chasing you all the time."

105   The Misfit kept scratching in the ground with the butt of his gun as if he were thinking about it. "Yes'm, somebody is always after you," he murmured.

The grandmother noticed how thin his shoulder blades were just behind his hat because she was standing up looking down on him. "Do you ever pray?" she asked.

He shook his head. All she saw was the black hat wiggle between his shoulder blades. "Nome," he said.

There was a pistol shot from the woods, followed closely by another. Then silence. The old lady's head jerked around. She could hear the wind move through the tree tops like a long satisfied insuck of breath. "Bailey Boy!" she called.

"I was a gospel singer for a while," The Misfit said. "I been most everything. Been in the arm service, both land and sea, at home and abroad, been twict married, been an undertaker, been with the railroads, plowed Mother Earth, been in a tornado, seen a man burnt alive oncet," and he looked up at the children's mother and the little girl who were sitting close together, their faces white and their eyes glassy; "I even seen a woman flogged," he said.

110   "Pray, pray," the grandmother began, "pray, pray . . ."

"I never was a bad boy that I remember of," The Misfit said in an almost dreamy voice, "but somewheres along the line I done something wrong and got sent to the penitentiary. I was buried alive," and he looked up and held her attention to him by a steady stare.

"That's when you should have started to pray," she said. "What did you do to get sent to the penitentiary that first time?"

"Turn to the right, it was a wall," The Misfit said, looking up again at the cloudless sky. "Turn to the left, it was a wall. Look up it was a ceiling, look down it was a floor. I forget what I done, lady. I set there and set there, trying to remember what it was I done and I ain't recalled it to this day. Oncet in a while, I would think it was coming to me, but it never come."

"Maybe they put you in by mistake," the old lady said vaguely.

115   "Nome," he said. "It wasn't no mistake. They had the papers on me."

"You must have stolen something," she said.

The Misfit sneered slightly. "Nobody had nothing I wanted," he said. "It was a head-doctor at the penitentiary said what I had done was kill my daddy but I known that for a lie. My daddy died in nineteen ought nineteen of the epidemic flu and I never had a thing to do with it. He was buried in the Mount Hopewell Baptist churchyard and you can go there and see for yourself."

"If you would pray," the old lady said, "Jesus would help you."

"That's right," The Misfit said.

120   "Well then, why don't you pray?" she asked trembling with delight suddenly.

"I don't want no hep," he said. "I'm doing all right by myself."

Bobby Lee and Hiram came ambling back from the woods. Bobby Lee was dragging a yellow shirt with bright blue parrots in it.

"Thow me that shirt, Bobby Lee," The Misfit said. The shirt came flying at him and landed on his shoulder and he put it on. The grandmother couldn't name what the shirt reminded her of. "No, lady," The Misfit said while he was buttoning it up, "I found out the crime don't matter. You can do one thing or you can do another, kill a man or take a tire off his car, because sooner or later you're going to forget what it was you done and just be punished for it."

The children's mother had begun to make heaving noises as if she couldn't get her breath. "Lady," he asked, "would you and that little girl like to step off yonder with Bobby Lee and Hiram and join your husband?"

125   "Yes, thank you," the mother said faintly. Her left arm dangled helplessly and she was holding the baby, who had gone to sleep, in the other. "Hep that lady up, Hiram," The Misfit said as she struggled to climb out of the ditch, "and Bobby Lee, you hold onto that little girl's hand."

"I don't want to hold hands with him," June Star said. "He reminds me of a pig."

The fat boy blushed and laughed and caught her by the arm and pulled her off into the woods after Hiram and her mother.

Alone with The Misfit, the grandmother found that she had lost her voice. There was not a cloud in the sky nor any sun. There was nothing around her but woods. She wanted to tell him that he must pray. She opened and closed her mouth several times before anything came out. Finally she found herself saying, "Jesus, Jesus," meaning, Jesus will help you, but the way she was saying it, it sounded as if she might be cursing.

"Yes'm," The Misfit said as if he agreed. "Jesus thown everything off balance. It was the same case with Him as with me except He hadn't committed any crime and they could prove I had committed one because they had the papers on me. Of course," he said, "they never shown me my papers. That's why I sign myself now. I said long ago, you get you a signature and sign everything you do and keep a copy of it. Then you'll know what you done and you can hold up the crime to the punishment and see do they match and in the end you'll have something to prove you ain't been treated right. I call myself The Misfit," he said, "because I can't make what all I done wrong fit what all I gone through in punishment."

130   There was a piercing scream from the woods, followed closely by a pistol report. "Does it seem right to you, lady, that one is punished a heap and another ain't punished at all?"

"Jesus!" the old lady cried. "You've got good blood! I know you wouldn't shoot a lady! I know you come from nice people! Pray! Jesus, you ought not to shoot a lady. I'll give you all the money I've got!"

"Lady," The Misfit said, looking beyond her far into the woods, "there never was a body that give the undertaker a tip."

There were two more pistol reports and the grandmother raised her head like a parched old turkey hen crying for water and called, "Bailey Boy, Bailey Boy!" as if her heart would break.

"Jesus was the only One that ever raised the dead," The Misfit continued, "and He shouldn't have done it. He thown everything off balance. If He did what He said, then it's nothing for you to do but thow away everything and follow Him, and if He didn't, then it's nothing for you to do but enjoy the few minutes you got left the best way you can—by killing somebody or burning down his house or doing some other meanness to him. No pleasure but meanness," he said and his voice became almost a snarl.

135   "Maybe He didn't raise the dead," the old lady mumbled, not knowing what she was saying and feeling so dizzy that she sank down in the ditch with her legs twisted under her.

"I wasn't there so I can't say He didn't," The Misfit said. "I wisht I had of been there," he said, hitting the ground with his fist. "It ain't right I wasn't there because if I had of been there I would of known. Listen, lady," he said in a high voice, "if I had of been there I would of known and I wouldn't be like I am now." His voice seemed about to crack and the grandmother's head cleared for an instant. She saw the man's face twisted close to her own as if he were going to cry and she murmured, "Why you're one of my babies. You're one of my own children!" She reached out and touched him on the shoulder. The Misfit sprang back as if a snake had bitten him and shot her three times through the chest. Then he put his gun down on the ground and took off his glasses and began to clean them.

Hiram and Bobby Lee returned from the woods and stood over the ditch, looking down at the grandmother who half sat and half lay in a puddle of blood with her legs crossed under her like a child's and her face smiling up at the cloudless sky.

Without his glasses, The Misfit's eyes were red-rimmed and pale and defenseless-looking. "Take her off and thow her where you thown the others," he said, picking up the cat that was rubbing itself against his leg.

"She was a talker, wasn't she?" Bobby Lee said, sliding down the ditch with a yodel.

140 "She would of been a good woman," The Misfit said, "if it had been somebody there to shoot her every minute of her life."

"Some fun!" Bobby Lee said.

"Shut up, Bobby Lee," The Misfit said. "It's no real pleasure in life."

Reading and Reacting

1. How are the style and tone of the narrator's voice different from those of the characters? What, if anything, is the significance of this difference?
2. Figurative language in this story sometimes creates unflattering, even grotesque, pictures of the characters. Find several examples of such negative figures of speech. Why do you think the author uses them?
3. What does the grandmother's use of the words *pickaninny* and *nigger* reveal about her? How are readers expected to reconcile this language with her very proper appearance and her preoccupation with manners? How does her use of these words affect your reaction to her?
4. Explain the **irony** in this statement: "In case of an accident, anyone seeing her dead on the highway would know at once that she was a lady" (12).
5. How does The Misfit's dialect characterize him?
6. What does the allusion to *Gone with the Wind* (24) contribute to the story?
7. How do the style and tone of the two-paragraph description of the three men in the car (71–72) help to prepare readers for the events that follow?
8. When The Misfit tells the grandmother about his life, his language takes on a measured, rhythmic quality: "Been in the arm service, both land and sea, at home and abroad, been twict married, been an undertaker, been with the railroads, plowed

Mother Earth, been in a tornado, seen a man burnt alive oncet, [. . .]" (109). Find other examples of parallelism and rhythmic repetition in this character's speech. How does this style help to develop The Misfit's character?

9. **JOURNAL ENTRY** Why do you think the grandmother tells The Misfit she recognizes him? Why does she fail to realize the danger of her remark?

10. **CRITICAL PERSPECTIVE** In a discussion of "A Good Man Is Hard to Find," Martha Stephens is critical of the story's ending, commenting that "the failure of the final scene—and hence of the story—seems to result from the fact that a tonal shift that occurs midway through the story finally runs out of control." The "tonal shift" to which she refers is the abrupt movement from grotesque comedy to senseless, shocking tragedy. Stephens asks:

> What *is* the reader to think or feel about anything in the massacre scene? There is pain and shock but much that mocks that pain and shock—the heavy comedy, for instance, indeed one might say the almost burlesque treatment, of the three killers. There is the feeling that though we cannot help but pity the tormented family, the story continues to demand our contempt for them. One feels that somehow the central experience of the story—in spite of the affecting, the chilling details surrounding these deaths, in spite even of the not altogether abusive treatment of the grandmother in Part One—will elude anyone who gives way to these feelings of pain and pity. If the writer's task is, as Conrad said, to make us "see," what is here to be seen? Surely not that life is wholly senseless and contemptible and that our fitting end is in senseless pain.

Do you agree that the story's ending is unsatisfactory? Does the violence "make us 'see,'" or is it just gratuitous? Explain.

Related Works: "The Lottery" (p. 315), "A Late Encounter with the Enemy" (p. 568), "Where Are You Going, Where Have You Been?" (p. 614)

◊ **TIM O'BRIEN** (1946–   ) is sometimes described as a writer whose books are on the shortlist of essential fiction about the Vietnam War. His plots focus on danger, violence, courage, endurance, despair, and other topics often associated with war fiction, but O'Brien treats these topics with an emphasis on the contemporary dilemmas faced by those who may be unwilling participants in an unpopular war. O'Brien calls *If I Die in a Combat Zone, Box Me Up and Ship Me Home* (1979) a memoir because it relates his war experiences as a naive young college graduate who suddenly finds himself facing bullets and land mines rather than sitting behind a desk. *Northern Lights* (1975) concentrates on the wilderness survival experiences of two brothers, one of whom has just returned from the Vietnam War. A fantastic daydream of an American soldier, *Going After Cacciato* (1978), which has been compared to *Catch 22,* won a National Book Award. *The Things They Carried* (1990) is a quasi-fictional collection of interrelated stories that deal with a single platoon; some stories involve a young soldier named Tim O'Brien, and some a forty-three-year-old writer named Tim O'Brien who writes about his memories. *The Vietnam in Me* (1994) emphasizes the destructive effects of war upon a soldier, even after he has returned home. *In the Lake of the Woods* (1994) tells a dramatic story of a couple missing in Minnesota.

After graduating summa cum laude from Macalester College in 1968, O'Brien was immediately drafted into the U.S. Army and sent to Vietnam, where he served with the 198th Infantry Brigade. He was promoted to sergeant and awarded a Purple Heart after receiving a shrapnel wound in a battle near My Lai. In 1970, after discharge from the army, he attended Harvard graduate school to study government. He worked as a reporter for the *Washington Post* before pursuing a full-time career as a writer. Currently, O'Brien lives in Cambridge, Massachusetts.

CULTURAL CONTEXT ◇ Although the United States did not become involved until the early 1960s, the Vietnam War actually lasted for twenty years. (The French were involved in Vietnam as early as 1954.) By the war's end, more than 47,000 Americans had been killed in action, nearly 11,000 had died of other causes, and more than 303,000 had been wounded in the war. Estimates of casualties of the Army of the Republic of Vietnam range from 185,000 to 225,000 killed and 500,000 to 570,000 wounded. The North Vietnamese and Viet Cong, the guerrilla force that fought against South Vietnam and the United States, lost about 900,000 troops. In addition, more than 1,000,000 North and South Vietnamese civilians were killed during the war.

◇ ◇ ◇

TIM O'BRIEN

The Things They Carried
(1986)

First Lieutenant Jimmy Cross carried letters from a girl named Martha, a junior at Mount Sebastian College in New Jersey. They were not love letters, but Lieutenant Cross was hoping, so he kept them folded in plastic at the bottom of his rucksack. In the late afternoon, after a day's march, he would dig his foxhole, wash his hands under a canteen, unwrap the letters, hold them with the tips of his fingers, and spend the last hour of light pretending. He would imagine romantic camping trips into the White Mountains in New Hampshire. He would sometimes taste the envelope flaps, knowing her tongue had been there. More than anything, he wanted Martha to love him as he loved her, but the letters were mostly chatty, elusive on the matter of love. She was a virgin, he was almost sure. She was an English major at Mount Sebastian, and she wrote beautifully about her professors and roommates and midterm exams, about her respect for Chaucer and her great affection for Virginia Woolf. She often quoted lines of poetry; she never mentioned the war, except to say, Jimmy, take care of yourself. The letters weighed ten ounces. They were signed "Love, Martha," but Lieutenant Cross understood that "Love" was only a way of signing and did not mean what he sometimes pretended it meant. At dusk, he would carefully return the letters to his rucksack. Slowly, a bit distracted, he would get up and move among his men, checking the perimeter, then at full dark he would return to his hole and watch the night and wonder if Martha was a virgin.

The things they carried were largely determined by necessity. Among the necessities or near necessities were P-38 can openers, pocket knives, heat tabs, wrist watches, dog tags, mosquito repellent, chewing gum, candy, cigarettes, salt tablets, packets of Kool-Aid, lighters, matches, sewing kits, Military Payment Certificates, C rations, and two or three canteens of water. Together, these items weighed between fifteen and twenty pounds, depending upon a man's habits or rate of metabolism. Henry Dobbins, who was a big man, carried extra rations; he was especially fond of canned peaches in heavy syrup over pound cake. Dave Jensen, who practiced field hygiene, carried a toothbrush, dental floss, and several hotel-size bars of soap he'd stolen on R&R in Sydney, Australia. Ted Lavender, who was scared, carried tranquilizers until he was shot in the head outside the village of Than Khe in mid-April. By necessity, and because it was SOP, they all carried steel helmets that weighed five pounds including the liner and camouflage cover. They carried the standard fatigue jackets and trousers. Very few carried underwear. On their feet they carried jungle boots—2.1 pounds—and Dave Jensen carried three pairs of socks and a can of Dr. Scholl's foot powder as a precaution against trench foot. Until he was shot, Ted Lavender carried six or seven ounces of premium dope, which for him was a necessity. Mitchell Sanders, the RTO, carried condoms. Norman Bowker carried a diary. Rat Kiley carried comic books. Kiowa, a devout Baptist, carried an illustrated New Testament that had been presented to him by his father, who taught Sunday school in Oklahoma City, Oklahoma. As a hedge against bad times, however, Kiowa also carried his grandmother's distrust of the white man, his grandfather's old hunting hatchet. Necessity dictated. Because the land was mined and booby-trapped, it was SOP for each man to carry a steel-centered, nylon-covered flak jacket, which weighed 6.7 pounds, but which on hot days seemed much heavier. Because you could die so quickly, each man carried at least one large compress bandage, usually in the helmet band for easy access. Because the nights were cold, and because the monsoons were wet, each carried a green plastic poncho that could be used as a raincoat or ground sheet or makeshift tent. With its quilted liner, the poncho weighed almost two pounds, but it was worth every ounce. In April, for instance, when Ted Lavender was shot, they used his poncho to wrap him up, then to carry him across the paddy, then to lift him into the chopper that took him away.

They were called legs or grunts.

To carry something was to "hump" it, as when Lieutenant Jimmy Cross humped his love for Martha up the hills and through the swamps. In its intransitive form, "to hump" meant "to walk," or "to march," but it implied burdens far beyond the intransitive.

5   Almost everyone humped photographs. In his wallet, Lieutenant Cross carried two photographs of Martha. The first was a Kodachrome snapshot signed "Love," though he knew better. She stood against a brick wall. Her eyes were gray and neutral, her lips slightly open as she stared straight-on at the camera. At night, sometimes, Lieutenant Cross wondered who had taken the picture, because he knew she had boyfriends, because he loved her so much, and because he could see the shadow of the picture taker spreading out against the brick wall. The second photograph had been clipped from the 1968 Mount Sebastian yearbook. It was an action shot— women's volleyball—and Martha was bent horizontal to the floor, reaching, the palms of her hands in sharp focus, the tongue taut, the expression frank and competitive. There was no visible sweat. She wore white gym shorts. Her legs, he thought, were almost certainly the legs of a virgin, dry and without hair, the left knee cocked and carrying her entire weight, which was just over one hundred pounds. Lieutenant Cross remembered touching that left knee. A dark theater, he remembered, and the movie was *Bonnie and Clyde,* and Martha wore a tweed skirt, and during the final scene, when he touched her knee, she turned and looked at him in a sad, sober way that made him pull his hand back, but he would always remember the feel of the tweed skirt and the knee beneath it and the sound of the gunfire that killed Bonnie and Clyde, how embarrassing it was, how slow and oppressive. He remembered kissing her good night at the dorm door. Right then, he thought, he should've done something brave. He should've carried her up the stairs to her room and tied her to the bed and touched that left knee all night long. He should've risked it. Whenever he looked at the photographs, he thought of new things he should've done.

What they carried was partly a function of rank, partly of field specialty.

As a first lieutenant and platoon leader, Jimmy Cross carried a compass, maps, code books, binoculars, and a .45-caliber pistol that weighed 2.9 pounds fully loaded. He carried a strobe light and the responsibility for the lives of his men.

As an RTO, Mitchell Sanders carried the PRC-25 radio, a killer, twenty-six pounds with its battery.

As a medic, Rat Kiley carried a canvas satchel filled with morphine and plasma and malaria tablets and surgical tape and comic books and all the things a medic must carry, including M&M's for especially bad wounds, for a total weight of nearly twenty pounds.

10 As a big man, therefore a machine gunner, Henry Dobbins carried the M-60, which weighed twenty-three pounds unloaded, but which was almost always loaded. In addition, Dobbins carried between ten and fifteen pounds of ammunition draped in belts across his chest and shoulders.

As PFCs or Spec 4s, most of them were common grunts and carried the standard M-16 gas-operated assault rifle. The weapon weighed 7.5 pounds unloaded, 8.2 pounds with its full twenty-round magazine. Depending on numerous factors, such as topography and psychology, the riflemen carried anywhere from twelve to twenty magazines, usually in cloth bandoliers, adding on another 8.4 pounds at minimum, fourteen pounds at maximum. When it was available, they also carried M-16 maintenance gear—rods and steel brushes and swabs and tubes of LSA oil—all of which weighed about a pound. Among the grunts, some carried the M-79 grenade launcher, 5.9 pounds unloaded, a reasonably light weapon except for the ammunition, which was heavy. A single round weighed ten ounces. The typical load was twenty-five rounds. But Ted Lavender, who was scared, carried thirty-four rounds when he was shot and killed outside Than Khe, and he went down under an exceptional burden, more than twenty pounds of ammunition, plus the flak jacket and helmet and rations and water and toilet paper and tranquilizers and all the rest, plus the unweighed fear. He was dead weight. There was no twitching or flopping. Kiowa, who saw it happen, said it was like watching a rock fall, or a big sandbag or something—just boom, then down—not like the movies where the dead guy rolls around and does fancy spins and goes ass over teakettle—not like that, Kiowa said, the poor bastard just flat-fuck fell. Boom. Down. Nothing else. It was a bright morning in mid-April. Lieutenant Cross felt the pain. He blamed himself. They stripped off Lavender's canteens and ammo, all the heavy things, and Rat Kiley said the obvious, the guy's dead, and Mitchell Sanders used his radio to report one U.S. KIA and to request a chopper. Then they wrapped Lavender in his poncho. They carried him out to a dry paddy, established security, and sat smoking the dead man's dope until the chopper came. Lieutenant Cross kept to himself. He pictured Martha's smooth young face, thinking he loved her more than anything, more than his men, and now Ted Lavender was dead because he loved her so much and could not stop thinking about her. When the dust-off arrived, they carried Lavender aboard. Afterward they burned Than Khe. They marched until dusk, then dug their holes, and that night Kiowa kept explaining how you had to be there, how fast it was, how the poor guy just dropped like so much concrete. Boom-down, he said. Like cement.

• • •

In addition to the three standard weapons—the M-60, M-16, and M-79—they carried whatever presented itself, or whatever seemed appropriate as a means of killing or staying alive. They carried catch-as-catch-can. At various times, in various situations, they carried M-14s and CAR-15s and Swedish Ks and grease guns and captured AK-47s and Chi-Coms and RPGs and Simonov carbines and black-market Uzis and .38-caliber Smith & Wesson handguns and 66 mm LAWs and shotguns and silencers and blackjacks and bayonets and C-4 plastic explosives. Lee Strunk carried a slingshot; a weapon of last resort, he called it. Mitchell Sanders carried brass knuckles. Kiowa carried his grandfather's feathered hatchet. Every third or fourth man carried a Claymore antipersonnel mine—3.5 pounds with its firing device. They all carried fragmentation grenades—fourteen ounces each. They all carried at least one M-18 colored smoke grenade—twenty-four ounces. Some carried CS or tear-gas grenades. Some carried white-phosphorus grenades. They carried all they could bear, and then some, including a silent awe for the terrible power of the things they carried.

In the first week of April, before Lavender died, Lieutenant Jimmy Cross received a good-luck charm from Martha. It was a simple pebble, an ounce at most. Smooth to the touch, it was a milky-white color with flecks of orange and violet, oval-shaped, like a miniature egg. In the accompanying letter, Martha wrote that she had found the pebble on the Jersey shoreline, precisely where the land touched water at high tide, where things came together but also separated. It was this separate-but-together quality, she wrote, that had inspired her to pick up the pebble and to carry it in her breast pocket for several days, where it seemed weightless, and then to send it through the mail, by air, as a token of her truest feelings for him. Lieutenant Cross found this romantic. But he wondered what her truest feelings were, exactly, and what she meant by separate-but-together. He wondered how the tides and waves had come into play on that afternoon along the Jersey shoreline when Martha saw the pebble and bent down to rescue it from geology. He imagined bare feet. Martha was a poet, with the poet's sensibilities, and her feet would be brown and bare, the toenails unpainted, the eyes chilly and somber like the ocean in March, and though it was painful, he wondered who had been with her that afternoon. He imagined a pair of shadows moving along the strip of sand where things came together but also separated. It was phantom jealousy, he knew, but he couldn't help himself. He loved her so much. On the march, through the hot days of early April, he carried the pebble in his mouth, turning it with his tongue, tasting sea salts and moisture. His mind wandered. He had difficulty keeping his attention on the war. On occasion he would yell at his men to spread out the column, to keep their eyes open, but then he would slip away into daydreams, just pretending, walking barefoot along the

Jersey shore, with Martha, carrying nothing. He would feel himself rising. Sun and waves and gentle winds, all love and lightness.

What they carried varied by mission.

15   When a mission took them to the mountains, they carried mosquito netting, machetes, canvas tarps, and extra bug juice.

If a mission seemed especially hazardous, or if it involved a place they knew to be bad, they carried everything they could. In certain heavily mined AOs, where the land was dense with Toe Poppers and Bouncing Betties, they took turns humping a twenty-eight-pound mine detector. With its headphones and big sensing plate, the equipment was a stress on the lower back and shoulders, awkward to handle, often useless because of the shrapnel in the earth, but they carried it anyway, partly for safety, partly for the illusion of safety.

On ambush, or other night missions, they carried peculiar little odds and ends. Kiowa always took along his New Testament and a pair of moccasins for silence. Dave Jensen carried night-sight vitamins high in carotin. Lee Strunk carried his slingshot; ammo, he claimed, would never be a problem. Rat Kiley carried brandy and M&M's. Until he was shot, Ted Lavender carried the starlight scope, which weighed 6.3 pounds with its aluminum carrying case. Henry Dobbins carried his girlfriend's pantyhose wrapped around his neck as a comforter. They all carried ghosts. When dark came, they would move out single file across the meadows and paddies to their ambush coordinates, where they would quietly set up the Claymores and lie down and spend the night waiting.

Other missions were more complicated and required special equipment. In mid-April, it was their mission to search out and destroy the elaborate tunnel complexes in the Than Khe area south of Chu Lai. To blow the tunnels, they carried one-pound blocks of pentrite high explosives, four blocks to a man, sixty-eight pounds in all. They carried wiring, detonators, and battery-powered clackers. Dave Jensen carried earplugs. Most often, before blowing the tunnels, they were ordered by higher command to search them, which was considered bad news, but by and large they just shrugged and carried out orders. Because he was a big man, Henry Dobbins was excused from tunnel duty. The others would draw numbers. Before Lavender died there were seventeen men in the platoon, and whoever drew the number seventeen would strip off his gear and crawl in head first with a flashlight and Lieutenant Cross's .45-caliber pistol. The rest of them would fan out as security. They would sit down or kneel, not facing the hole, listening to the ground beneath them, imagining cobwebs and ghosts, whatever was down there—the tunnel walls squeezing in—how the flashlight seemed impossibly heavy in the hand and how it was tunnel vision in the very strictest sense, compression in all ways, even time, and how you had to wiggle in—ass and elbows—a swallowed-up feeling—and how you found yourself worrying about odd things—will your flashlight go dead? Do rats carry rabies? If you screamed, how far would the sound carry? Would your buddies hear it? Would they have the courage to drag you out? In some respects, though not many, the waiting was worse than the tunnel itself. Imagination was a killer.

On April 16, when Lee Strunk drew the number seventeen, he laughed and muttered something and went down quickly. The morning was hot and very still. Not good, Kiowa said. He looked at the tunnel opening, then out across a dry paddy toward the village of Than Khe. Nothing moved. No clouds or birds or people. As they waited, the men smoked and drank Kool-Aid, not talking much, feeling sympathy for Lee Strunk but also feeling the luck of the draw. You win some, you lose some, said Mitchell Sanders, and sometimes you settle for a rain check. It was a tired line and no one laughed.

20 Henry Dobbins ate a tropical chocolate bar. Ted Lavender popped a tranquilizer and went off to pee.

After five minutes, Lieutenant Jimmy Cross moved to the tunnel, leaned down, and examined the darkness. Trouble, he thought—a cave-in maybe. And then suddenly, without willing it, he was thinking about Martha. The stresses and fractures, the quick collapse, the two of them buried alive under all that weight. Dense, crushing love. Kneeling, watching the hole, he tried to concentrate on Lee Strunk and the war, all the dangers, but his love was too much for him, he felt paralyzed, he wanted to sleep inside her lungs and breathe her blood and be smothered. He wanted her to be a virgin and not a virgin, all at once. He wanted to know her. Intimate secrets—why poetry? Why so sad? Why that grayness in her eyes? Why so alone? Not lonely, just alone—riding her bike across campus or sitting off by herself in the cafeteria. Even dancing, she danced alone— and it was the aloneness that filled him with love. He remembered telling her that one evening. How she nodded and looked away. And how, later, when he kissed her, she received the kiss without returning it, her eyes wide open, not afraid, not a virgin's eyes, just flat and uninvolved.

Lieutenant Cross gazed at the tunnel. But he was not there. He was buried with Martha under the white sand at the Jersey shore. They were pressed together, and the pebble in his mouth was her tongue. He was smiling. Vaguely, he was aware of how quiet the day was, the sullen paddies, yet he could not bring himself to worry about matters of security. He was beyond that. He was just a kid at war, in love. He was twenty-two years old. He couldn't help it.

A few moments later Lee Strunk crawled out of the tunnel. He came up grinning, filthy but alive. Lieutenant Cross nodded and closed his eyes while the others clapped Strunk on the back and made jokes about rising from the dead.

Worms, Rat Kiley said. Right out of the grave. Fuckin' zombie.

25 The men laughed. They all felt great relief.

Spook City, said Mitchell Sanders.

Lee Strunk made a funny ghost sound, a kind of moaning, yet very happy, and right then, when Strunk made that high happy moaning sound, when he went *Ahhooooo*, right then Ted Lavender was shot in the head on his way back from peeing. He lay with his mouth open. The teeth were broken. There was a swollen black bruise under his left eye. The cheekbone was gone. Oh shit, Rat Kiley said, the guy's dead. The guy's dead, he kept saying, which seemed profound—the guy's dead. I mean really.

The things they carried were determined to some extent by superstition. Lieutenant Cross carried his good-luck pebble. Dave Jensen carried a rabbit's foot. Norman Bowker, otherwise a very gentle person, carried a thumb that had been presented to him as a gift by Mitchell Sanders. The thumb was dark brown, rubbery to the touch, and weighed four ounces at most. It had been cut from a VC corpse, a boy of fifteen or sixteen. They'd found him at the bottom of an irrigation ditch, badly burned, flies in his mouth and eyes. The boy wore black shorts and sandals. At the time of his death he had been carrying a pouch of rice, a rifle, and three magazines of ammunition.

You want my opinion, Mitchell Sanders said, there's a definite moral here.

30 He put his hand on the dead boy's wrist. He was quiet for a time, as if counting a pulse, then he patted the stomach, almost affectionately, and used Kiowa's hunting hatchet to remove the thumb.

Henry Dobbins asked what the moral was.

Moral?

You know. *Moral.*

Sanders wrapped the thumb in toilet paper and handed it across to Norman Bowker. There was no blood. Smiling, he kicked the boy's head, watched the flies scatter, and said, It's like with that old TV show—Paladin. Have gun, will travel.

35 Henry Dobbins thought about it.

Yeah, well, he finally said. I don't see no moral.

There it *is,* man.

Fuck off.

They carried USO stationery and pencils and pens. They carried Sterno, safety pins, trip flares, signal flares, spools of wire, razor blades, chewing tobacco, liberated joss sticks and statuettes of the smiling Buddha, candles, grease pencils, *The Stars and Stripes,* fingernail clippers, Psy Ops leaflets, bush hats, bolos, and much more. Twice a week, when the resupply choppers came in, they carried hot chow in green Mermite cans and large canvas bags filled with iced beer and soda pop. They carried plastic water containers, each with a two-gallon capacity. Mitchell Sanders carried a set of starched tiger fatigues for special occasions. Henry Dobbins carried Black Flag insecticide. Dave Jensen carried empty sandbags that could be filled at night for added protection. Lee Strunk carried tanning lotion. Some things they carried in common. Taking turns, they carried the big PRC-77 scrambler radio, which weighed thirty pounds with its battery. They shared the weight of memory. They took up what others could no longer bear. Often, they carried each other, the wounded or weak. They carried infections. They carried chess sets, basketballs, Viet-namese-English dictionaries, insignia of rank, Bronze Stars and Purple Hearts, plastic cards imprinted with the Code of Conduct. They carried diseases, among them malaria and dysentery. They carried lice and ring-worm and leeches and paddy algae and various rots and molds. They car-ried the land itself—Vietnam, the place, the soil—a powdery orange-red dust that covered their boots and fatigues and faces. They carried the sky. The whole atmosphere, they carried it, the humidity, the monsoons, the stink of fungus and decay, all of it, they carried gravity. They moved like mules. By daylight they took sniper fire, at night they were mortared, but it was not battle, it was just the endless march, village to village, without purpose, nothing won or lost. They marched for the sake of the march. They plodded along slowly, dumbly, leaning forward against the heat, un-thinking, all blood and bone, simple grunts, soldiering with their legs, toiling up the hills and down into the paddies and across the rivers and up again and down, just humping, one step and then the next and then an-other, but no volition, no will, because it was automatic, it was anatomy, and the war was entirely a matter of posture and carriage, the hump was everything, a kind of inertia, a kind of emptiness, a dullness of desire and intellect and conscience and hope and human sensibility. Their principles were in their feet. Their calculations were biological. They had no sense of strategy or mission. They searched the villages without knowing what to look for, not caring, kicking over jars of rice, frisking children and old men, blowing tunnels, sometimes setting fires and sometimes not, then forming up and moving on to the next village, then other villages, where it would always be the same. They carried their own lives. The pressures were enormous. In the heat of early afternoon, they would remove their helmets and flak jackets, walking bare, which was dangerous but which helped ease the strain. They would often discard things along the route of march. Purely for comfort, they would throw away rations, blow their Claymores and grenades, no matter, because by nightfall the resupply choppers would arrive with more of the same, then a day or two later still more, fresh watermelons and crates of ammunition and sunglasses and woolen sweaters—the resources were stunning—sparklers for the Fourth of July, colored eggs for Easter. It was the great American war chest—the fruits of science, the smokestacks, the canneries, the arsenals at Hartford, the Minnesota forests, the machine shops, the vast fields of corn and wheat—they carried like freight trains; they carried it on their backs and shoulders—and for all the ambiguities of Vietnam, all the mysteries and unknowns, there was at least the single abiding certainty that they would never be at a loss for things to carry.

● ● ●

40   After the chopper took Lavender away, Lieutenant Jimmy Cross led his men into the village of Than Khe. They burned everything. They shot chickens and dogs, they trashed the village well, they called in artillery and watched the wreckage, then they marched for several hours through the hot afternoon, and then at dusk, while Kiowa explained how Lavender died, Lieutenant Cross found himself trembling.

He tried not to cry. With his entrenching tool, which weighed five pounds, he began digging a hole in the earth.

He felt shame. He hated himself. He had loved Martha more than his men, and as a consequence Lavender was now dead, and this was something he would have to carry like a stone in his stomach for the rest of the war.

All he could do was dig. He used his entrenching tool like an ax, slashing, feeling both love and hate, and then later, when it was full dark, he sat at the bottom of his foxhole and wept. It went on for a long while. In part, he was grieving for Ted Lavender, but mostly it was for Martha, and for himself, because she belonged to another world, which was not quite real, and because she was a junior at Mount Sebastian College in New Jersey, a poet and a virgin and uninvolved, and because he realized she did not love him and never would.

Like cement, Kiowa whispered in the dark. I swear to God—boom-down. Not a word.

45   I've heard this, said Norman Bowker.

A pisser, you know? Still zipping himself up. Zapped while zipping.

All right, fine. That's enough.

Yeah, but you had to see it, the guy just—

I *heard,* man. Cement. So why not shut the fuck *up?*

50   Kiowa shook his head sadly and glanced over at the hole where Lieutenant Jimmy Cross sat watching the night. The air was thick and wet. A warm, dense fog had settled over the paddies and there was the stillness that precedes rain.

After a time Kiowa sighed.

One thing for sure, he said. The Lieutenant's in some deep hurt. I mean that crying jag—the way he was carrying on—it wasn't fake or anything, it was real heavy-duty hurt. The man cares.

Sure, Norman Bowker said.

Say what you want, the man does care.

55   We all got problems.

Not Lavender.

No, I guess not, Bowker said. Do me a favor, though.

Shut up?

That's a smart Indian. Shut up.

60   Shrugging, Kiowa pulled off his boots. He wanted to say more, just to lighten up his sleep, but instead he opened his New Testament and arranged it beneath his head as a pillow. The fog made things seem hollow

and unattached. He tried not to think about Ted Lavender, but then he was thinking how fast it was, no drama, down and dead, and how it was hard to feel anything except surprise. It seemed un-Christian. He wished he could find some great sadness, or even anger, but the emotion wasn't there and he couldn't make it happen. Mostly he felt pleased to be alive. He liked the smell of the New Testament under his cheek, the leather and ink and paper and glue, whatever the chemicals were. He liked hearing the sounds of night. Even his fatigue, it felt fine, the stiff muscles and the prickly awareness of his own body, a floating feeling. He enjoyed not being dead. Lying there, Kiowa admired Lieutenant Jimmy Cross's capacity for grief. He wanted to share the man's pain, he wanted to care as Jimmy Cross cared. And yet when he closed his eyes, all he could think was Boom-down, and all he could feel was the pleasure of having his boots off and the fog curling in around him and the damp soil and the Bible smells and the plush comfort of night.

After a moment Norman Bowker sat up in the dark.

What the hell, he said. You want to talk, *talk*. Tell it to me.

Forget it.

No, man, go on. One thing I hate, it's a silent Indian.

65   For the most part they carried themselves with poise, a kind of dignity. Now and then, however, there were times of panic, when they squealed or wanted to squeal but couldn't, when they twitched and made moaning sounds and covered their heads and said Dear Jesus and flopped around on the earth and fired their weapons blindly and cringed and sobbed and begged for the noise to stop and went wild and made stupid promises to themselves and to God and to their mothers and fathers, hoping not to die. In different ways, it happened to all of them. Afterward, when the firing ended, they would blink and peek up. They would touch their bodies, feeling shame, then quickly hiding it. They would force themselves to stand. As if in slow motion, frame by frame, the world would take on the old logic—absolute silence, then the wind, then sunlight, then voices. It was the burden of being alive. Awkwardly, the men would reassemble themselves, first in private, then in groups, becoming soldiers again. They would repair the leaks in their eyes. They would check for casualties, call in dust-offs, light cigarettes, try to smile, clear their throats and spit and begin cleaning their weapons. After a time someone would shake his head and say, No lie, I almost shit my pants, and someone else would laugh, which meant it was bad, yes, but the guy had obviously not shit his pants, it wasn't that bad, and in any case nobody would ever do such a thing and then go ahead and talk about it. They would squint into the dense, oppressive sunlight. For a few moments, perhaps, they would fall silent, lighting a joint and tracking its passage from man to man, inhaling, holding in the humiliation. Scary stuff, one of them might say. But then someone else would grin or flick his eyebrows and say, Roger-dodger, almost cut me a new asshole, *almost*.

There were numerous such poses. Some carried themselves with a sort of wistful resignation, others with pride or stiff soldierly discipline or good humor or macho zeal. They were afraid of dying but they were even more afraid to show it.

They found jokes to tell.

They used a hard vocabulary to contain the terrible softness. *Greased,* they'd say. *Offed, lit up, zapped while zipping.*[1] It wasn't cruelty, just stage presence. They were actors and the war came at them in 3-D. When someone died, it wasn't quite dying, because in a curious way it seemed scripted, and because they had their lines mostly memorized, irony mixed with tragedy, and because they called it by other names, as if to encyst and destroy the reality of death itself. They kicked corpses. They cut off thumbs. They talked grunt lingo. They told stories about Ted Lavender's supply of tranquilizers, how the poor guy didn't feel a thing, how incredibly tranquil he was.

There's a moral here, said Mitchell Sanders.

70   They were waiting for Lavender's chopper, smoking the dead man's dope.

The moral's pretty obvious. Sanders said, and winked. Stay away from drugs. No joke, they'll ruin your day every time.

Cute, said Henry Dobbins.

Mind-blower, get it? Talk about wiggy—nothing left, just blood and brains.

They made themselves laugh.

75   There it is, they'd say, over and over, as if the repetition itself were an act of poise, a balance between crazy and almost crazy, knowing without going. There it is, which meant be cool, let it ride, because oh yeah, man, you can't change what can't be changed, there it is, there it absolutely and positively and fucking well *is.*

They were tough.

They carried all the emotional baggage of men who might die. Grief, terror, love, longing—these were intangibles, but the intangibles had their own mass and specific gravity, they had tangible weight. They carried shameful memories. They carried the common secret of cowardice barely restrained, the instinct to run or freeze or hide, and in many respects this was the heaviest burden of all, for it could never be put down, it required perfect balance and perfect posture. They carried their reputations. They carried the soldier's greatest fear, which was the fear of blushing. Men killed, and died, because they were embarrassed not to. It was what had brought them to the war in the first place, nothing positive, no dreams of glory or honor, just to avoid the blush of dishonor. They died so as not to die of embarrassment. They crawled into tunnels and walked point and advanced under fire. Each morning, despite the unknowns, they made their legs move. They endured. They kept humping. They did not submit

---

[1] Offed, lit up—killed; zapped while zipping—killed while urinating.

to the obvious alternative, which was simply to close the eyes and fall. So easy, really. Go limp and tumble to the ground and let the muscles unwind and not speak and not budge until your buddies picked you up and lifted you into the chopper that would roar and dip its nose and carry you off to the world. A mere matter of falling, yet no one ever fell. It was not courage, exactly; the object was not valor. Rather, they were too frightened to be cowards.

By and large they carried these things inside, maintaining the masks of composure. They sneered at sick call. They spoke bitterly about guys who had found release by shooting off their own toes or fingers. Pussies, they'd say. Candyasses. It was fierce, mocking talk, with only a trace of envy or awe, but even so, the image played itself out behind their eyes.

They imagined the muzzle against flesh. They imagined the quick, sweet pain, then the evacuation to Japan, then a hospital with warm beds and cute geisha nurses.

80   They dreamed of freedom birds.

At night, on guard, staring into the dark, they were carried away by jumbo jets. They felt the rush of takeoff. *Gone!* they yelled. And then velocity, wings and engines, a smiling stewardess—but it was more than a plane, it was a real bird, a big sleek silver bird with feathers and talons and high screeching. They were flying. The weights fell off, there was nothing to bear. They laughed and held on tight, feeling the cold slap of wind and altitude, soaring, thinking *It's over, I'm gone!*—they were naked, they were light and free—it was all lightness, bright and fast and buoyant, light as light, a helium buzz in the brain, a giddy bubbling in the lungs as they were taken up over the clouds and the war, beyond duty, beyond gravity and mortification and global entanglements—*Sin loi!* they yelled, *I'm sorry, motherfuckers, but I'm out of it, I'm goofed, I'm on a space cruise, I'm gone!*—and it was a restful, disencumbered sensation, just riding the light waves, sailing that big silver freedom bird over the mountains and oceans, over America, over the farms and great sleeping cities and cemeteries and highways and the golden arches of McDonald's. It was flight, a kind of fleeing, a kind of falling, falling higher and higher, spinning off the edge of the earth and beyond the sun and through the vast, silent vacuum where there were no burdens and where everything weighed exactly nothing. *Gone!* they screamed, *I'm sorry but I'm gone!* And so at night, not quite dreaming, they gave themselves over to lightness, they were carried, they were purely borne.

On the morning after Ted Lavender died, First Lieutenant Jimmy Cross crouched at the bottom of his foxhole and burned Martha's letters. Then he burned the two photographs. There was a steady rain falling, which made it difficult, but he used heat tabs and Sterno to build a small fire, screening it with his body, holding the photographs over the tight blue flame with the tips of his fingers.

He realized it was only a gesture. Stupid, he thought. Sentimental, too, but mostly just stupid.

Lavender was dead. You couldn't burn the blame.

85   Besides, the letters were in his head. And even now, without photographs, Lieutenant Cross could see Martha playing volleyball in her white gym shorts and yellow T-shirt. He could see her moving in the rain.

When the fire died out, Lieutenant Cross pulled his poncho over his shoulders and ate breakfast from a can.

There was no great mystery, he decided.

In those burned letters Martha had never mentioned the war, except to say, Jimmy, take care of yourself. She wasn't involved. She signed the letters "Love," but it wasn't love, and all the fine lines and technicalities did not matter.

The morning came up wet and blurry. Everything seemed part of everything else, the fog and Martha and the deepening rain.

90   It was a war, after all.

Half smiling, Lieutenant Jimmy Cross took out his maps. He shook his head hard, as if to clear it, then bent forward and began planning the day's march. In ten minutes, or maybe twenty, he would rouse the men and they would pack up and head west, where the maps showed the country to be green and inviting. They would do what they had always done. The rain might add some weight, but otherwise it would be one more day layered upon all the other days.

He was realistic about it. There was that new hardness in his stomach.

No more fantasies, he told himself.

Henceforth, when he thought about Martha, it would be only to think that she belonged elsewhere. He would shut down the daydreams. This was not Mount Sebastian, it was another world, where there were no pretty poems or midterm exams, a place where men died because of carelessness and gross stupidity. Kiowa was right. Boom-down, and you were dead, never partly dead.

95   Briefly, in the rain, Lieutenant Cross saw Martha's gray eyes gazing back at him.

He understood.

It was very sad, he thought. The things men carried inside. The things men did or felt they had to do.

He almost nodded at her, but didn't.

Instead he went back to his maps. He was now determined to perform his duties firmly and without negligence. It wouldn't help Lavender, he knew that, but from this point on he would comport himself as a soldier. He would dispose of his good-luck pebble. Swallow it, maybe, or use Lee Strunk's slingshot, or just drop it along the trail. On the march he would impose strict field discipline. He would be careful to send out flank security, to prevent straggling or bunching up, to keep his troops moving at the proper pace and at the proper interval. He would insist on clean weapons. He would confiscate the remainder of Lavender's dope. Later in the day, perhaps, he would call the men together and speak to them plainly. He would accept the blame for what had happened to Ted Lavender. He would be a man about it. He would look them in the eyes, keeping his chin level, and he would issue the new SOPs in a calm, impersonal tone of voice, an officer's voice, leaving no room for argument or discussion. Commencing immediately, he'd tell them, they would no longer abandon equipment along the route of march. They would police up their acts. They would get their shit together, and keep it together, and maintain it neatly and in good working order.

100   He would not tolerate laxity. He would show strength, distancing himself.

Among the men there would be grumbling, of course, and maybe worse, because their days would seem longer and their loads heavier, but Lieutenant Cross reminded himself that his obligation was not to be loved but to lead. He would dispense with love; it was not now a factor. And if anyone quarreled or complained, he would simply tighten his lips and arrange his shoulders in the correct command posture. He might give a curt little nod. Or he might not. He might just shrug and say Carry on, then they would saddle up and form into a column and move out toward the villages west of Than Khe.

Reading and Reacting

1. Although the setting and the events described in "The Things They Carried" are dramatic and moving, its tone is often flat and emotionless. How is this tone created? Why do you think the narrator adopts this kind of tone?

2. Consider the different meanings of the word *carry*, which can refer to burdens abstract or concrete and to things carried physically or emotionally, actively or passively. Give several examples of the different senses in which O'Brien uses the word. How does his use of the word enhance the story?

3. A striking characteristic of the story's style is its thorough catalogs of the concrete, tangible "things" the soldiers carry. Why do you suppose such detailed lists are included? What does what each man carries tell you about him? In a less literal, more abstract sense, what else do these men "carry"?

4. One stylistic technique O'Brien uses is intentional repetition—of phrases ("they carried"); people's names and identifying details (Martha's virginity, for example); and pieces of equipment. What effect do you think O'Brien hopes to achieve through such repetition? Is he successful?

5. Interspersed among long paragraphs crammed with detail are short one- or two-sentence paragraphs. What function do these brief paragraphs serve?

6. What function does Martha serve in the story? Why does Lieutenant Cross burn her letters?

7. In paragraph 68 the narrator says of the soldiers, "They used a hard vocabulary to contain the terrible softness." What do you

think he means by this? Do you think this "hard vocabulary" is necessary? How does it affect your reaction to the story?

8. Describing Lieutenant Cross's new sense of purpose in the story's final paragraph, the narrator uses the phrase "Carry on." Do you think this phrase is linked in any way to the story's other uses of the word *carry,* or do you believe it is unrelated? Explain.

9. **JOURNAL ENTRY** "The Things They Carried" is a story about war. Do you think it is an antiwar story? Why or why not?

10. **CRITICAL PERSPECTIVE** In an essay about war memoirs, Clayton W. Lewis questions O'Brien's decision to present "the nightmare [he] faced in a Vietnam rice paddy" as fiction. Lewis believes that some of O'Brien's stories "dissolve into clever artifice" and, therefore, are not as effective as actual memoirs of the Vietnam experience would be. He concludes that "for all its brilliance and emotional grounding, [the stories do not] satisfy one's appetite to hear what happened rendered as it was experienced and remembered."

    Do you think Lewis has a point? Or do you think O'Brien's "artifice" communicates his emotions and experiences more effectively than a straightforward memoir could? Explain your position.

Related Works: "Goodnight Saigon" (p. 698), "Facing It" (p. 699), "Dulce et Decorum Est" (p. 802)

◆ WRITING SUGGESTIONS: STYLE, TONE, AND LANGUAGE

1. "A Clean, Well-Lighted Place" does not have a conventional plot in which characters grow and change and conflicts are resolved. For this reason, it might be argued that in this story language takes on more of a central role than it plays in other stories. Write an essay in which you examine this idea as it applies to "A Clean, Well-Lighted Place" and to any other story in this text.

2. Several of the stories in this chapter present characters who are outsiders or misfits in their social milieus. Choose two or three characters, and explain why each is estranged from others and what efforts, if any, each makes to reconcile himself with society. Be sure to show how language helps to convey each character's alienation.

3. In "A Clean, Well-Lighted Place," two waiters discuss an old man, but readers do not really learn what the old man is thinking or feeling. Write a letter (or a suicide note) from the old man to a friend or family member in which you reveal his thoughts about his life and try to account for his despair. Be sure the tone of your letter is consistent with his feelings of sadness.

4. Imagine The Misfit in a prison cell, relating the violent incident at the end of "A Good Man Is Hard to Find" to another prisoner—or to a member of the clergy. Would his tone be boastful? Regretful? Apologetic? Defiant? Would he use the elaborate poetic style he sometimes uses in the story or more straightforward language? Tell his version of the incident in his own words.

5. Both "Araby" and "The Things They Carried" deal, at least in part, with infatuation. Compare and contrast the infatuations described in the two stories. How do the kinds of language used by the narrators in the two stories communicate the two character's fascination and subsequent disillusionment?

6. **WEB ACTIVITY** The following Web site contains information about Tim O'Brien:

http://www.illyria.com/tobhp.html

From that Web page, read several excerpts from various O'Brien works. Then link to the O'Brien interview under "Miscellany." Based on what you have discovered about O'Brien from these sites, write an essay discussing how O'Brien's themes in "The Things They Carried" are consistent with the overall themes in his other work. Consider his use of language and tone to express his themes, and consider the perspective he uses in telling his stories.

CHAPTER 9

Symbol and Allegory

◊ ◊ ◊

Symbols and metaphors share several qualities, but they are far from being synonymous. Both are figurative expressions that transcend literal language. Both rely heavily on implication and suggestion. Both present the abstract in concrete terms, and both can be interpreted with varying degrees of openness or specificity. They differ, however, in important ways. A symbol expands language by substitution, a metaphor by comparison and interaction. A symbol does not ask a reader to merge two concepts but rather to let one thing suggest another. A symbol derives its meaning through development and consensus, a metaphor through invention and originality. A symbol is strengthened by repetition, but a metaphor is destroyed by it.

ROLAND BARTEL, *Metaphors and Symbols*

Symbols have to spring from the work direct, and stay alive. Symbols for the sake of symbols are counterfeit, and were they all stamped on the page in red they couldn't any more quickly give themselves away. So are symbols failing their purpose when they don't keep to proportion in the book. However alive they are, they should never call for an emphasis greater than the emotional reality they serve, in their moment, to illuminate.

EUDORA WELTY, "Words into Fiction"

The truth is, I do indeed include images in my work, but I don't think of them as symbols, [. . .] To me, symbols are stand-in's for abstract ideas. They belong to the High School of Hidden Meanings: vases symbolize female orifices, broken vases symbolize a loss of virginity and innocence. Heavy stuff. I prefer using images. My writing tends toward the Elementary School of Word Pictures: the accidental shattering of a vase in an empty room changes the emotions of a scene from sanity to uneasiness, perhaps even to dread. The point is, if there are symbols in my work they exist largely by accident or through someone else's interpretive design.

AMY TAN, *The Threepenny Review*

◊ ◊ ◊

A **symbol** is a person, object, action, place, or event that, in addition to its literal meaning, suggests a more complex meaning or range of meanings. **Universal** or **archetypal symbols,** such as the Old Man, the Mother, or the Grim Reaper, are so much a part of human experience that they suggest much the same thing to most people. **Conventional symbols** are also likely to suggest the same thing to most people, provided the people have common cultural and social assumptions (a rose suggests love, a skull and crossbones denotes poison). Such symbols are often used as a kind of shorthand in films, popular literature, and advertising, where they encourage automatic responses.

Conventional symbols such as the stars and stripes of the American flag can evoke powerful feelings of pride and patriotism in a group of people who share the same orientation toward it, just as the maple leaf and the Union Jack can. Symbols used in works of literature can function in much the same way, enabling writers to convey particular emotions or messages with a high degree of predictability. Thus, spring can be expected to suggest rebirth and promise; autumn, declining years and powers; summer, youth and beauty. Because a writer expects a dark forest to evoke fear, or a rainbow to communicate hope, he or she can be quite confident in using such an image to convey a particular idea or mood (provided the audience shares the writer's frame of reference).

Many symbols, however, suggest different things to different people. (For one thing, different cultures may react differently to the same symbols. In the United States, for example, an owl suggests wisdom; in India it suggests just the opposite.) Thus, symbols enrich meaning, expanding the possibilities for interpretation and for reader interaction with the text. Because they are so potentially rich, symbols have the power to open up a work of literature.

LITERARY SYMBOLS
◊ ◊ ◊

Both universal and conventional symbols can function as **literary symbols** that take on additional meanings in particular works. For instance, a watch or clock denotes time; as a conventional symbol, it suggests the passing of time; as a literary symbol in a particular work, it might also convey anything from a character's inability to recapture the past to the idea of time running out—or, it might suggest more than one of these ideas.

Considering an object's possible symbolic significance can suggest a variety of ways to interpret a text. For instance, William Faulkner focuses attention on an unseen watch in a pivotal scene in "A Rose for Emily" (p. 87). The narrator first describes Emily Grierson as "a small, fat woman in black, with a thin gold chain descending to her waist and vanishing into her belt." Several sentences later, the narrator returns to the watch, noting that Emily's visitors "could hear the invisible watch ticking at the end of the gold chain." Like these visitors, readers are drawn to the unseen watch as it ticks away. Because Emily is portrayed as a woman living in the past, readers can assume that the watch is intended to reinforce the impression that she cannot see that time (the watch) has moved on. The vivid picture of the pale, plump woman in the musty room with the watch invisibly ticking does indeed suggest both that she has been left back in time and that she remains unaware of the progress around her. Thus, the symbol enriches both the depiction of character and the story's theme.

In "Barn Burning" (p. 226), another Faulkner story, the clock is a more complex symbol. The itinerant Snopes family is without financial security and apparently without a future. The clock the mother carries from shack to shack—"The clock inlaid with mother-of-pearl, which would not run, stopped at some fourteen minutes past two o'clock of a dead and forgotten day and time, which had been [Sarty's] mother's dowry"—is their only possession of value. The fact that the clock no longer works seems at first to suggest that time has run out for the family. On another level, the clock stands in pathetic contrast to Major de Spain's grand home, with its gold and glitter and Oriental rugs. Knowing that the clock was part of the mother's dowry, and that a dowry suggests a promise, readers may decide that the broken clock symbolizes lost hope; the fact that the mother still clings to the clock, however, could suggest just the opposite: her refusal to give up.

As you read, you should not try to find the one exact equivalent for each symbol; in fact, this kind of search is very limiting and not very productive. Instead, consider the different meanings a symbol might suggest. Then, consider how these various interpretations enrich other elements of the story and the work as a whole.

RECOGNIZING SYMBOLS

When is a clock just a clock, and when is it also a symbol with a meaning or meanings beyond its literal significance? If a character waiting for a friend glances once at his or her watch to verify the time, there is probably nothing symbolic about the watch or about the act of looking at it. If, however, the watch keeps appearing again and again in the story, at key moments; if the narrator devotes a good deal of time to describing it; if it is placed in a conspicuous physical location; if characters keep noticing it and commenting on its presence; if it is lost (or found) at a critical moment; if its function in some way parallels the development of plot or character (for instance, if it stops as a relationship ends or as a character dies); if the story's opening or closing paragraph focuses on the timepiece; or if the story is called "The Watch"—the watch most likely has symbolic significance. In other words, considering how an image is used, how often it is used, and when it appears will help you to determine whether or not it functions as a symbol.

THE PURPOSE OF SYMBOLS

Symbols expand the possible meanings of a story, thereby heightening interest and actively involving readers in the text. In "The Lottery" (p. 315), for example, the mysterious black box has symbolic significance. It is mentioned prominently and repeatedly, and it plays a pivotal role in the story's action. Of course, the black box is important on a purely literal level: it functions as a key component of the lottery. But the box has other associations as well, and it is these associations that suggest what its symbolic significance might be.

The black wooden box is very old, a relic of many past lotteries; the narrator observes that it represents tradition. It is also closed and closely guarded, suggesting mystery and uncertainty. It is shabby, "splintered badly along one side [. . .] and in places faded or stained," and this state of disrepair could suggest that the ritual it is part of has also deteriorated or that tradition itself has deteriorated. The box is also simple in construction and design, suggesting the primitive (and therefore perhaps outdated) nature of the ritual. Thus, this symbol encourages readers to probe the story for values and ideas, to consider and weigh the suitability of a variety of interpretations. It serves as a "hot spot" that invites questions, and the answers to these questions reinforce and enrich the story's theme.

ALLEGORY

✧ ✧ ✧

An **allegory** communicates a doctrine, message, or moral principle by making it into a narrative in which the characters personify ideas, concepts, qualities, or other abstractions. Thus, an allegory is a story with two parallel and consistent levels of meaning—one literal and one figurative. The figurative level, which offers some moral or political lesson, is the story's main concern. The allegorical figures are significant only because they represent something beyond their literal meaning in a fixed system.

Whereas a symbol has multiple symbolic associations as well as a literal meaning, an **allegorical figure**—a character, object, place, or event in the allegory—has just one meaning within an **allegorical framework,** the set of ideas that conveys the allegory's message. (At the simplest level, for instance, one character can stand for good and another can stand for evil.) For this reason, allegorical figures do not open up a text to various interpretations the way symbols do. Because the purpose of allegory is to communicate a particular lesson, readers are not encouraged to speculate about the allegory's possible meanings; each element has only one equivalent, which readers must discover if they are to make sense of the story.

Naturally, the better a reader understands the political, religious, and literary assumptions of a writer, the easier it will be to recognize the allegorical significance of his or her work. John Bunyan's *The Pilgrim's Progress*, for example, is a famous seventeenth-century allegory based on the Christian doctrine of salvation. In order to appreciate the complexity of Bunyan's work, you would have to familiarize yourself with this doctrine—possibly by consulting an encyclopedia or a reference work such as *The Oxford Companion to English Literature*.

One type of allegory, called a **beast fable,** is a short tale, usually including a moral, in which animals assume human characteristics. Aesop's fables are the best-known examples of beast fables. More recently, contemporary writers have used beast fables to satirize the political and social conditions of our time. In one such tale, "The Gentlemen of the Jungle" by the Kenyan writer Jomo Kenyatta, an elephant is allowed to put his trunk inside a man's hut during a rainstorm. Not content with keeping his trunk dry, the elephant pushes his entire body inside the hut, displacing the man. When the man protests, the elephant takes the matter to the lion, who appoints a Commission of Enquiry to settle the matter. Eventually the man is forced not only to abandon his hut to the elephant, but also to build new huts for all the animals in the Commission. Even so, the jealous animals occupy the man's new hut and begin fighting for space; while they are arguing, the man burns down the hut, animals and all. Like the tales told by Aesop, "The Gentlemen of the Jungle" has a moral: "Peace is costly," says the man as he walks away happily, "but it's worth the expense." The following passage from "The Gentlemen of the Jungle" reveals how the allegorical figures work within the framework of the allegory:

> The elephant, obeying the command of his master (the lion), got busy with the other ministers to appoint a Commission of Enquiry. The following elders of the jungle were appointed to sit in the Commission: (1) Mr. Rhinoceros; (2) Mr. Buffalo; (3) Mr. Alligator; (4) The Rt. Hon. Mr. Fox to act as chairman; and (5) Mr. Leopard to act as Secretary of the Commission. On seeing the personnel, the man protested and asked if it was not necessary to include in this Commission a member from his side. But he was told that it was impossible, since no one from his side was well enough educated to understand the intricacy of jungle law.

From this excerpt we can see that each character represents a particular idea. For example, the members of the Commission stand for bureaucratic smugness and inequity, and the man stands for the citizens who are victimized by the government. In order to fully understand the allegorical significance of each figure in this story, of course, readers would have to know something about government bureaucracies, colonialism in Africa, and possibly a specific historical event in Kenya.

Some works contain both symbolic elements *and* allegorical elements, as Nathaniel Hawthorne's "Young Goodman Brown" (p. 304) does. The names of the story's two main characters, "Goodman" and "Faith," suggest that they fit within an allegorical system of some sort: Young Goodman Brown represents a good person who, despite his best efforts, strays from the path of righteousness; his wife, Faith, represents the quality he must hold on to in order to avoid temptation. As characters, they have no significance outside of their allegorical functions. Other elements of the story, however, are not so clear-cut. The older man whom Young Goodman Brown meets in the woods carries a staff that has carved on it "the likeness of a great black snake, so curiously wrought, that it might almost be seen to twist and wriggle itself like a living serpent." This staff, carried by a Satanic figure who represents evil and temptation, suggests the snake in the Garden of Eden, an association that neatly fits into the allegorical context of the story. Alternately, however, the staff could suggest the "slippery," ever-changing nature of sin, the difficulty people have in perceiving sin, or sexuality (which may explain Young Goodman Brown's susceptibility to temptation). This range of possible meanings suggests that the staff functions as a symbol that enriches Hawthorne's allegory.

Other stories work entirely on a symbolic level and contain no allegorical figures. "The Lottery," despite its moral overtones, is not an allegory because its characters, events, and objects are not arranged to serve one rigid, didactic purpose. In fact, many different interpretations have been suggested for this story. When it was first published in June 1948 in *The New Yorker*, some readers believed it to be a story about an actual custom or ritual. As Shirley Jackson reports in her essay "Biography of a Story," even those who recognized it as fiction speculated about its meaning, seeing it as (among other things) an attack on prejudice, a criticism of society's need for a scapegoat, or a treatise on witchcraft, Christian martyrdom, or village gossip. Various critics have argued that "The Lottery" is a story about the evils of violence, mob psychology, or Nazi Germany. The fact is that no single allegorical interpretation will account for every major character, object, and event in the story.

✳ Checklist: Writing about Symbol and Allegory

✓ Are any universal symbols used in the work? Any conventional symbols? What is their function?

✓ Is any character, place, action, event, or object given unusual prominence or emphasis in the story? If so, does this element seem to have symbolic as well as literal value?

✓ What possible meanings does each symbol suggest?

✓ How do symbols help to depict the story's characters?

✓ How do symbols help to characterize the story's setting?

✓ How do symbols help to advance the story's plot?

✓ Are any of the symbols related? Taken together, do they seem to support a common theme?

✓ Does the story have a moral or didactic purpose? What is the message, idea, or moral principle the story seeks to convey?

✓ What equivalent may be assigned to each allegorical figure in the story?

✓ Does the story combine allegorical figures and symbols? How do they work together in the story?

◆ **NATHANIEL HAWTHORNE** (1804–1864) was born in Salem, Massachusetts, the great-great-grandson of a judge who presided over the infamous Salem witch trials. After his sea captain father was killed on a voyage when Hawthorne was four years old, his childhood was one of genteel poverty. An uncle paid for his education at Bowdoin College in Maine, where Hawthorne's friends included a future president of the United States, Franklin Pierce, who in 1853 would appoint him U.S. consul in Liverpool, England. Hawthorne published four novels—*The Scarlet Letter* (1850), *The House of the Seven Gables* (1851), *The Blithedale Romance* (1852), and *The Marble Faun* (1860)—and more than one hundred short stories and sketches.

Hawthorne referred to his own work as *romance*. He used this term to mean not an escape from reality, but rather a method of confronting "the depths of our common nature" and "the truth of the heart." His stories probe the dark side of human nature and frequently paint a world that is virtuous on the surface but (as young Goodman Brown comes to believe) "one stain of guilt, one mighty blood spot" beneath. Hawthorne's stories often emphasize the ambiguity of human experience. For example, the reader is left to wonder whether Goodman Brown actually saw a witch's coven or dreamed a dream. For Hawthorne, what is important is Brown's recognition that evil may be found everywhere. "Young Goodman Brown," as Hawthorne's neighbor and friend Herman Melville once said, is a tale "as deep as Dante."

CULTURAL CONTEXT ◆ During the five months of the Salem witch trials of 1692, a total of nineteen women and men accused of being witches were put to death by hanging. The accusations began when a few young girls claimed they were possessed by the devil and subsequently accused three Salem women of witchcraft. As the hysteria grew throughout Massachusetts, the list of the accused grew as well. Eventually 150 people were imprisoned before the governor dismissed the special witchcraft court and released the remaining prisoners. It is in this historical setting that "Young Goodman Brown" takes place.

◊ ◊ ◊

NATHANIEL HAWTHORNE

Young Goodman[1] Brown
(1835)

Young Goodman Brown came forth at sunset, into the street of Salem village, but put his head back, after crossing the threshold, to exchange a parting kiss with his young wife. And Faith, as the wife was aptly named, thrust her own pretty head into the street, letting the wind play with the pink ribbons of her cap, while she called to Goodman Brown.

"Dearest heart," whispered she, softly and rather sadly, when her lips were close to his ear, "prithee, put off your journey until sunrise, and sleep in your own bed to-night. A lone woman is troubled with such dreams and such thoughts, that she's afeard of herself, sometimes. Pray, tarry with me this night, dear husband, of all nights in the year!"

"My love and my Faith," replied young Goodman Brown, "of all nights in the year, this one night must I tarry away from thee. My journey, as thou callest it, forth and back again, must needs be done 'twixt now and sunrise. What, my sweet, pretty wife, dost thou doubt me already, and we but three months married!"

"Then God bless you!" said Faith with the pink ribbons, "and may you find all well, when you come back."

5   "Amen!" cried Goodman Brown. "Say thy prayers, dear Faith, and go to bed at dusk, and no harm will come to thee."

So they parted; and the young man pursued his way, until, being about to turn the corner by the meeting-house, he looked back and saw the head of Faith still peeping after him, with a melancholy air, in spite of her pink ribbons.

"Poor little Faith!" thought he, for his heart smote him. "What a wretch am I, to leave her on such an errand! She talks of dreams, too. Methought, as she spoke, there was trouble in her face, as if a dream had warned her what work is to be done to-night. But no, no! 't would kill her to think it. Well; she's a blessed angel on earth; and after this one night, I'll cling to her skirts and follow her to Heaven."

With this excellent resolve for the future, Goodman Brown felt himself justified in making more haste on his present evil purpose. He had taken a dreary road, darkened by all the gloomiest trees of the forest, which barely

---

[1] A form of address, similar to Mr., meaning "husband."

stood aside to let the narrow path creep through, and closed immediately behind. It was as lonely as could be; and there is this peculiarity in such a solitude, that the traveller knows not who may be concealed by the innumerable trunks and the thick boughs overhead; so that, with lonely footsteps, he may yet be passing through an unseen multitude.

"There may be a devilish Indian behind every tree," said Goodman Brown to himself; and he glanced fearfully behind him, as he added, "What if the devil himself should be at my very elbow!"

10   His head being turned back, he passed a crook of the road, and looking forward again, beheld the figure of a man, in grave and decent attire, seated at the foot of an old tree. He arose at Goodman Brown's approach, and walked onward, side by side with him.

"You are late, Goodman Brown," said he. "The clock of the Old South[2] was striking, as I came through Boston; and that is full fifteen minutes agone."

"Faith kept me back awhile," replied the young man, with a tremor in his voice, caused by the sudden appearance of his companion, though not wholly unexpected.

It was now deep dusk in the forest, and deepest in that part of it where these two were journeying. As nearly as could be discerned, the second traveller was about fifty years old, apparently in the same rank of life as Goodman Brown, and bearing a considerable resemblance to him, though perhaps more in expression than features. Still, they might have been taken for father and son. And yet, though the elder person was as simply clad as the younger, and as simple in manner too, he had an indescribable air of one who knew the world, and would not have felt abashed at the governor's dinner-table, or in King William's court,[3] were it possible that his affairs should call him thither. But the only thing about him that could be fixed upon as remarkable, was his staff, which bore the likeness of a great black snake, so curiously wrought, that it might almost be seen to twist and wriggle itself like a living serpent. This, of course, must have been an ocular deception, assisted by the uncertain light.

"Come, Goodman Brown!" cried his fellow-traveller, "this is a dull pace for the beginning of a journey. Take my staff, if you are so soon weary."

15   "Friend," said the other, exchanging his slow pace for a full stop, "having kept covenant by meeting thee here, it is my purpose now to return whence I came. I have scruples, touching the matter thou wot'st of."

"Sayest thou so?" replied he of the serpent, smiling apart. "Let us walk on, nevertheless, reasoning as we go, and if I convince thee not, thou shalt turn back. We are but a little way in the forest, yet."

"Too far, too far!" exclaimed the goodman, unconsciously resuming his walk. "My father never went into the woods on such an errand, nor his father before him. We have been a race of honest men and good Christians,

---

[2] Old South Church, Boston, renowned meeting place for American patriots during the Revolution.

[3] William III, king of England from 1689 to 1702.

since the days of the martyrs. And shall I be the first of the name of Brown that ever took this path and kept—"

"Such company, thou wouldst say," observed the elder person, interrupting his pause. "Well said, Goodman Brown! I have been as well acquainted with your family as with ever a one among the Puritans; and that's no trifle to say. I helped your grandfather, the constable, when he lashed the Quaker woman so smartly through the streets of Salem. And it was I that brought your father a pitch-pine knot, kindled at my own hearth, to set fire to an Indian village, in King Philip's war.[4] They were my good friends, both; and many a pleasant walk have we had along this path, and returned merrily after midnight. I would fain be friends with you, for their sake."

"If it be as thou sayest," replied Goodman Brown, "I marvel they never spoke of these matters. Or, verily, I marvel not, seeing that the least rumor of the sort would have driven them from New England. We are a people of prayer, and good works to boot, and abide no such wickedness."

20   "Wickedness or not," said the traveller with the twisted staff, "I have a very general acquaintance here in New England. The deacons of many a church have drunk the communion wine with me; the selectmen, of divers towns, make me their chairman; and a majority of the Great and General Court are firm supporters of my interest. The governor and I, too—but these are state secrets."

"Can this be so!" cried Goodman Brown, with a stare of amazement at his undisturbed companion. "Howbeit, I have nothing to do with the governor and council; they have their own ways, and are no rule for a simple husbandman like me. But, were I to go on with thee, how should I meet the eye of that good old man, our minister, at Salem village? Oh, his voice would make me tremble, both Sabbath-day and lecture-day!"[5]

Thus far, the elder traveller had listened with due gravity, but now burst into a fit of irrepressible mirth, shaking himself so violently, that his snakelike staff actually seemed to wriggle in sympathy.

"Ha, ha, ha!" shouted he, again and again; then composing himself, "Well, go on, Goodman Brown, go on; but, prithee, don't kill me with laughing!"

"Well, then, to end the matter at once," said Goodman Brown, considerably nettled, "there is my wife, Faith. It would break her dear little heart; and I'd rather break my own!"

25   "Nay, if that be the case," answered the other, "e'en go thy ways, Goodman Brown. I would not, for twenty old women like the one hobbling before us, that Faith should come to any harm."

---

[4] A war of Indian resistance, led by King Philip, or Metacomet, of the Wampanoags. The war, intended to halt expansion of English settlers in Massachusetts, collapsed after King Philip's death in August 1676.

[5] The day of the midweek sermon, usually Thursday.

As he spoke, he pointed his staff at a female figure on the path, in whom Goodman Brown recognized a very pious and exemplary dame, who had taught him his catechism in youth, and was still his moral and spiritual adviser, jointly with the minister and Deacon Gookin.

"A marvel, truly, that Goody[6] Cloyse should be so far in the wilderness, at nightfall!" said he. "But, with your leave, friend, I shall take a cut through the woods, until we have left this Christian woman behind. Being a stranger to you, she might ask whom I was consorting with, and whither I was going."

"Be it so," said his fellow-traveller. "Betake you to the woods, and let me keep the path."

Accordingly, the young man turned aside, but took care to watch his companion, who advanced softly along the road, until he had come within a staff's length of the old dame. She, meanwhile, was making the best of her way, with singular speed for so aged a woman, and mumbling some indistinct words, a prayer, doubtless, as she went. The traveller put forth his staff, and touched her withered neck with what seemed the serpent's tail.

30   "The devil!" screamed the pious old lady.

"Then Goody Cloyse knows her old friend?" observed the traveller, confronting her, and leaning on his writhing stick.

"Ah, forsooth, and is it your worship, indeed?" cried the good dame. "Yea, truly is it, and in the very image of my old gossip, Goodman Brown, the grandfather of the silly fellow that now is. But, would your worship believe it? my broomstick hath strangely disappeared, stolen, as I suspect, by that unhanged witch, Goody Cory, and that, too, when I was all anointed with the juice of smallage and cinque-foil and wolf's bane—"[7]

"Mingled with fine wheat and the fat of a new-born babe," said the shape of old Goodman Brown.

"Ah, your worship knows the recipe," cried the old lady, cackling aloud. "So, as I was saying, being all ready for the meeting, and no horse to ride on, I made up my mind to foot it; for they tell me there is a nice young man to be taken into communion to-night. But now your good worship will lend me your arm, and we shall be there in a twinkling."

35   "That can hardly be," answered her friend. "I may not spare you my arm, Goody Cloyse, but here is my staff, if you will."

So saying, he threw it down at her feet, where, perhaps, it assumed life, being one of the rods which its owner had formerly lent to the Egyptian Magi. Of this fact, however, Goodman Brown could not take cognizance. He had cast his eyes in astonishment, and looking down again,

---

[6] A contraction of "Goodwife," a term of politeness used in addressing a woman of humble station. Goody Cloyse, like Goody Cory and Martha Carrier, who appear later in the story, was one of the Salem "witches" sentenced in 1692.

[7] All plants believed to have magical powers. "Smallage" is wild celery.

beheld neither Goody Cloyse nor the serpentine staff, but his fellow-traveller alone, who waited for him as calmly as if nothing had happened.

"That old woman taught me my catechism!" said the young man; and there was a world of meaning in this simple comment.

They continued to walk onward, while the elder traveller exhorted his companion to make good speed and persevere in the path, discoursing so aptly, that his arguments seemed rather to spring up in the bosom of his auditor, than to be suggested by himself. As they went he plucked a branch of maple, to serve for a walking-stick, and began to strip it of the twigs and little boughs, which were wet with evening dew. The moment his fingers touched them, they became strangely withered and dried up, as with a week's sunshine. Thus the pair proceeded, at a good free pace, until suddenly, in a gloomy hollow of the road, Goodman Brown sat himself down on the stump of a tree, and refused to go any farther.

"Friend," said he, stubbornly, "my mind is made up. Not another step will I budge on this errand. What if a wretched old woman do choose to go to the devil, when I thought she was going to Heaven! Is that any reason why I should quit my dear Faith, and go after her?"

40   "You will think better of this by and by," said his acquaintance, composedly. "Sit here and rest yourself awhile; and when you feel like moving again, there is my staff to help you along."

Without more words, he threw his companion the maple stick, and was as speedily out of sight as if he had vanished into the deepening gloom. The young man sat a few moments by the roadside, applauding himself greatly, and thinking with how clear a conscience he should meet the minister, in his morning walk, nor shrink from the eye of good old Deacon Gookin. And what calm sleep would be his, that very night, which was to have been spent so wickedly, but purely and sweetly now, in the arms of Faith! Amidst these pleasant and praiseworthy meditations, Goodman Brown heard the tramp of horses along the road, and deemed it advisable to conceal himself within the verge of the forest, conscious of the guilty purpose that had brought him thither, though now so happily turned from it.

On came the hoof-tramps and the voices of the riders, two grave old voices, conversing soberly as they drew near. These mingled sounds appeared to pass along the road, within a few yards of the young man's hiding-place; but owing, doubtless, to the depth of the gloom, at that particular spot, neither the travellers nor their steeds were visible. Though their figures brushed the small boughs by the wayside, it could not be seen that they intercepted, even for a moment, the faint gleam from the strip of bright sky, athwart which they must have passed. Goodman Brown alternately crouched and stood on tiptoe, pulling aside the branches, and thrusting forth his head as far as he durst, without discerning so much as a shadow. It vexed him the more, because he could have sworn, were such a thing possible, that he recognized the voices of the minister and Deacon Gookin, jogging along quietly, as they were wont to do, when bound to some ordination or ecclesiastical council. While yet within hearing, one of the riders stopped to pluck a switch.

"Of the two, reverend Sir," said the voice like the deacon's, "I had rather miss an ordination dinner than to-night's meeting. They tell me that some of our community are to be here from Falmouth and beyond, and others from Connecticut and Rhode Island; besides several of the Indian powwows, who, after their fashion, know almost as much deviltry as the best of us. Moreover, there is a goodly young woman to be taken into communion."

"Mighty well, Deacon Gookin!" replied the solemn old tones of the minister. "Spur up, or we shall be late. Nothing can be done, you know, until I get on the ground."

45   The hoofs clattered again, and the voices, talking so strangely in the empty air, passed on through the forest, where no church had ever been gathered, nor solitary Christian prayed. Whither, then, could these holy men be journeying, so deep into the heathen wilderness? Young Goodman Brown caught hold of a tree, for support, being ready to sink down on the ground, faint and over-burthened with the heavy sickness of his heart. He looked up to the sky, doubting whether there really was a Heaven above him. Yet, there was the blue arch, and the stars brightening in it.

"With Heaven above, and Faith below, I will yet stand firm against the devil!" cried Goodman Brown.

While he still gazed upward, into the deep arch of the firmament, and had lifted his hands to pray, a cloud, though no wind was stirring, hurried across the zenith, and hid the brightening stars. The blue sky was still visible, except directly overhead, where this black mass of cloud was sweeping swiftly northward. Aloft in the air, as if from the depths of the cloud, came a confused and doubtful sound of voices. Once, the listener fancied that he could distinguish the accents of townspeople of his own, men and women, both pious and ungodly, many of whom he had met at the communion-table, and had seen others rioting at the tavern. The next moment, so indistinct were the sounds, he doubted whether he had heard aught but the murmur of the old forest, whispering without a wind. Then came a stronger swell of those familiar tones, heard daily in the sunshine, at Salem village, but never, until now, from a cloud at night. There was one voice, of a young woman, uttering lamentations, yet with an uncertain sorrow, and entreating for some favor, which, perhaps, it would grieve her to obtain. And all the unseen multitude, both saints and sinners, seemed to encourage her onward.

"Faith!" shouted Goodman Brown, in a voice of agony and desperation; and the echoes of the forest mocked him, crying—"Faith! Faith!" as if bewildered wretches were seeking her, all through the wilderness.

The cry of grief, rage, and terror was yet piercing the night, when the unhappy husband held his breath for a response. There was a scream, drowned immediately in a louder murmur of voices fading into far-off laughter, as the dark cloud swept away, leaving the clear and silent sky above Goodman Brown. But something fluttered lightly down through the air, and caught on the branch of a tree. The young man seized it and beheld a pink ribbon.

50 "My Faith is gone!" cried he, after one stupefied moment. "There is no good on earth, and sin is but a name. Come, devil! for to thee is this world given."

And maddened with despair, so that he laughed loud and long, did Goodman Brown grasp his staff and set forth again, at such a rate, that he seemed to fly along the forest path, rather than to walk or run. The road grew wilder and drearier, and more faintly traced, and vanished at length, leaving him in the heart of the dark wilderness, still rushing onward, with the instinct that guides mortal man to evil. The whole forest was peopled with frightful sounds: the creaking of the trees, the howling of wild beasts, and the yell of Indians; while, sometimes, the wind tolled like a distant church bell, and sometimes gave a broad roar around the traveller, as if all Nature was laughing him to scorn. But he was himself the chief horror of the scene, and shrank not from its other horrors.

"Ha! ha! ha!" roared Goodman Brown, when the wind laughed at him. "Let us hear which will laugh loudest! Think not to frighten me with your deviltry! Come witch, come wizard, come Indian powwow, come devil himself! and here comes Goodman Brown. You may as well fear him as he fear you!"

In truth, all through the haunted forest, there could be nothing more frightful than the figure of Goodman Brown. On he flew, among the black pines, brandishing his staff with frenzied gestures, now giving vent to an inspiration of horrid blasphemy, and now shouting forth such laughter, as set all the echoes of the forest laughing like demons around him. The fiend in his own shape is less hideous, than when he rages in the breast of man. Thus sped the demoniac on his course, until, quivering among the trees, he saw a red light before him, as when the felled trunks and branches of a clearing have been set on fire, and throw up their lurid blaze against the sky, at the hour of midnight. He paused, in a lull of the tempest that had driven him onward, and heard the swell of what seemed a hymn, rolling solemnly from a distance, with the weight of many voices. He knew the tune. It was a familiar one in the choir of the village meeting-house. The verse died heavily away, and was lengthened by a chorus, not of human voices, but of all the sounds of the benighted wilderness, pealing in awful harmony together. Goodman Brown cried out; and his cry was lost to his own ear, by its unison with the cry of the desert.

In the interval of silence, he stole forward, until the light glared full upon his eyes. At one extremity of an open space, hemmed in by the dark wall of the forest, arose a rock, bearing some rude, natural resemblance either to an altar or a pulpit, and surrounded by four blazing pines, their tops aflame, their stems untouched, like candles at an evening meeting. The mass of foliage, that had overgrown the summit of the rock, was all on fire, blazing high into the night, and fitfully illuminating the whole field. Each pendent twig and leafy festoon was in a blaze. As the red light arose and fell, a numerous congregation alternately shone forth, then disappeared in shadow, and again grew, as it were, out of the darkness, peopling the heart of the solitary woods at once.

55   "A grave and dark-clad company!" quoth Goodman Brown.

In truth, they were such. Among them, quivering to-and-fro, between gloom and splendor, appeared faces that would be seen, next day, at the council-board of the province, and others which, Sabbath after Sabbath, looked devoutly heavenward, and benignantly over the crowded pews, from the holiest pulpits in the land. Some affirm, that the lady of the governor was there. At least, there were high dames well known to her, and wives of honored husbands, and widows a great multitude, and ancient maidens, all of excellent repute, and fair young girls, who trembled lest their mothers should espy them. Either the sudden gleams of light, flashing over the obscure field, bedazzled Goodman Brown, or he recognized a score of the church members of Salem village, famous for their especial sanctity. Good old Deacon Gookin had arrived, and waited at the skirts of that venerable saint, his reverend pastor. But, irreverently consorting with these grave, reputable, and pious people, these elders of the church, these chaste dames and dewy virgins, there were men of dissolute lives and women of spotted fame, wretches given over to all mean and filthy vice, and suspected even of horrid crimes. It was strange to see, that the good shrank not from the wicked, nor were the sinners abashed by the saints. Scattered, also, among their pale-faced enemies, were the Indian priests, or powwows, who had often scared their native forest with more hideous incantations than any known to English witchcraft.

"But, where is Faith?" thought Goodman Brown; and, as hope came into his heart, he trembled.

Another verse of the hymn arose, a slow and mournful strain, such as the pious love, but joined to words which expressed all that our nature can conceive of sin, and darkly hinted at far more. Unfathomable to mere mortals is the lore of fiends. Verse after verse was sung, and still the chorus of the desert swelled between, like the deepest tone of a mighty organ. And, with the final peal of that dreadful anthem, there came a sound, as if the roaring wind, the rushing streams, the howling beasts, and every other voice of the unconverted wilderness were mingling and according with the voice of guilty man, in homage to the prince of all. The four blazing pines threw up a loftier flame, and obscurely discovered shapes and visages of horror on the smoke-wreaths, above the impious assembly. At the same moment, the fire on the rock shot redly forth, and formed a glowing arch above its base, where now appeared a figure. With reverence be it spoken, the apparition bore no slight similitude, both in garb and manner, to some grave divine of the New England churches.

"Bring forth the converts!" cried a voice, that echoed through the field and rolled into the forest.

60   At the word, Goodman Brown stepped forth from the shadow of the trees, and approached the congregation, with whom he felt a loathful brotherhood, by the sympathy of all that was wicked in his heart. He could

have well-nigh sworn, that the shape of his own dead father beckoned him to advance, looking downward from a smoke-wreath, while a woman, with dim features of despair, threw out her hand to warn him back. Was it his mother? But he had no power to retreat one step, nor to resist, even in thought, when the minister and good old Deacon Gookin seized his arms, and led him to the blazing rock. Thither came also the slender form of a veiled female, led between Goody Cloyse, that pious teacher of the catechism, and Martha Carrier, who had received the devil's promise to be queen of hell. A rampant hag was she! And there stood the proselytes, beneath the canopy of fire.

"Welcome, my children," said the dark figure, "to the communion of your race! Ye have found, thus young, your nature and your destiny. My children, look behind you!"

They turned; and flashing forth, as it were, in a sheet of flame, the fiend-worshippers were seen; the smile of welcome gleamed darkly on every visage.

"There," resumed the sable form, "are all whom ye have reverenced from youth. Ye deemed them holier than yourselves, and shrank from your own sin, contrasting it with their lives of righteousness and prayerful aspirations heavenward. Yet, here are they all, in my worshipping assembly! This night it shall be granted you to know their secret deeds; how hoary-bearded elders of the church have whispered wanton words to the young maids of their households; how many a woman, eager for widow's weeds, has given her husband a drink at bedtime, and let him sleep his last sleep in her bosom; how beardless youths have made haste to inherit their father's wealth; and how fair damsels—blush not, sweet ones!—have dug little graves in the garden, and bidden me, the sole guest, to an infant's funeral. By the sympathy of your human hearts for sin, ye shall scent out all the places—whether in church, bedchamber, street, field, or forest—where crime has been committed, and shall exult to behold the whole earth one stain of guilt, one mighty blood-spot. Far more than this! It shall be yours to penetrate, in every bosom, the deep mystery of sin, the fountain of all wicked arts, and which inexhaustibly supplies more evil impulses than human power—than my power, at its utmost!—can make manifest in deeds. And now, my children, look upon each other."

They did so; and, by the blaze of the hell-kindled torches, the wretched man beheld his Faith, and the wife her husband, trembling before that unhallowed altar.

65 "Lo! there ye stand, my children," said the figure, in a deep and solemn tone, almost sad, with its despairing awfulness, as if his once angelic nature could yet mourn for our miserable race. "Depending upon one another's hearts, ye had still hoped that virtue were not all a dream! Now are ye undeceived!—Evil is the nature of mankind. Evil must be your only happiness. Welcome, again, my children, to the communion of your race!"

"Welcome!" repeated the fiend-worshippers, in one cry of despair and triumph.

And there they stood, the only pair, as it seemed, who were yet hesitating on the verge of wickedness, in this dark world. A basin was hollowed, naturally, in the rock. Did it contain water, reddened by the lurid light? or was it blood? or, perchance, a liquid flame? Herein did the Shape of Evil dip his hand, and prepare to lay the mark of baptism upon their foreheads, that they might be partakers of the mystery of sin, more conscious of the secret guilt of others, both in deed and thought, than they could now be of their own. The husband cast one look at his pale wife, and Faith at him. What polluted wretches would the next glance show them to each other, shuddering alike at what they disclosed and what they saw!

"Faith! Faith!" cried the husband. "Look up to Heaven, and resist the Wicked One!"

Whether Faith obeyed, he knew not. Hardly had he spoken, when he found himself amid calm night and solitude, listening to a roar of the wind, which died heavily away through the forest. He staggered against the rock, and felt it chill and damp, while a hanging twig, that had been all on fire, besprinkled his cheek with the coldest dew.

70   The next morning, young Goodman Brown came slowly into the street of Salem village staring around him like a bewildered man. The good old minister was taking a walk along the grave-yard, to get an appetite for breakfast and meditate his sermon, and bestowed a blessing, as he passed, on Goodman Brown. He shrank from the venerable saint, as if to avoid an anathema. Old Deacon Gookin was at domestic worship, and the holy words of his prayer were heard through the open window. "What God doth the wizard pray to?" quoth Goodman Brown. Goody Cloyse, that excellent old Christian, stood in the early sunshine, at her own lattice, catechising a little girl, who had brought her a pint of morning's milk. Goodman Brown snatched away the child, as from the grasp of the fiend himself. Turning the corner by the meeting-house, he spied the head of Faith, with the pink ribbons, gazing anxiously forth, and bursting into such joy at sight of him that she skipt along the street, and almost kissed her husband before the whole village. But Goodman Brown looked sternly and sadly into her face, and passed on without a greeting.

Had Goodman Brown fallen asleep in the forest, and only dreamed a wild dream of a witch-meeting?

Be it so, if you will. But, alas! it was a dream of evil omen for young Goodman Brown. A stern, a sad, a darkly meditative, a distrustful, if not a desperate man did he become, from the night of that fearful dream. On the Sabbath day, when the congregation were singing a holy psalm, he could not listen, because an anthem of sin rushed loudly upon his ear, and drowned all the blessed strain. When the minister spoke from the pulpit, with power and fervid eloquence, and with his hand on the open Bible, of the sacred truths of our religion, and of saint-like lives and triumphant deaths, and of future bliss or misery unutterable, then did Goodman Brown turn pale, dreading lest the roof should thunder down upon the gray blasphemer and his hearers. Often, awaking suddenly at midnight, he shrank from the bosom of Faith, and at morning or eventide, when the family knelt down at prayer, he scowled, and muttered to himself, and gazed sternly at his wife, and turned away. And when he had lived long, and was borne to his grave, a hoary corpse, followed by Faith, an aged woman, and children and grand-children, a goodly procession, besides neighbors not a few, they carved no hopeful verse upon his tombstone; for his dying hour was gloom.

READING AND REACTING

1. Who is the narrator of "Young Goodman Brown"? What advantages does the narrative point of view give the author?
2. What does young Goodman Brown mean when he says "of all nights in the year, this one must I tarry away from thee" (3)? What is important about *this* night, and why does Goodman Brown believe he must journey "'twixt now and sunrise"?
3. Is Goodman Brown surprised to encounter the second traveler on the road, or does he seem to expect him? What is the significance of their encounter? What do you make of the fact that the stranger bears a strong resemblance to young Goodman Brown?
4. What sins are the various characters Goodman Brown meets in the woods guilty of committing?
5. "Young Goodman Brown" has two distinct settings: Salem and the woods. What are the differences between these settings? What significance does each have in the story?
6. Which figures in the story are allegorical, and which are symbols? On what evidence do you base your conclusions?
7. Why do the people gather in the woods? Why do they attend the ceremony?
8. Explain the change that takes place in young Goodman Brown at the end of the story. Why can he not listen to the singing of holy psalms or to the minister's sermons? What causes him to turn away from Faith and die in gloom?
9. **JOURNAL ENTRY** At the end of the story the narrator suggests that Goodman Brown might have fallen asleep and imagined his encounter with the witches. Do you think the events are all a dream?
10. **CRITICAL PERSPECTIVE** In *The Power of Blackness*, his classic study of nineteenth-century American writers, Harry Levin observes that Hawthorne had doubts about conventional religion. This, Levin believes, is why all efforts to read an enlightening theological message into Hawthorne's works are "doomed to failure."

    What comment do you think Hawthorne is making in "Young Goodman Brown" about religious faith?

Related Works: "Once upon a Time" (p. 81), "Where Are You Going, Where Have You Been?" (p. 614), "We Wear the Mask" (p. 949), "La Belle Dame sans Merci: A Ballad" (p. 969)

◆ **SHIRLEY JACKSON** (1916–1965) is best known for her restrained tales of horror and the supernatural, most notably her novel *The Haunting of Hill House* (1959) and the short story "The Lottery" (1948). Among her other works are two novels dealing with divided personalities—*The Bird's Nest* (1954) and *We Have Always Lived in the Castle* (1962)—and two collections of comic tales about her children and family life, *Life among the Savages* (1953) and *Raising Demons* (1957). A posthumous collection of stories, *Just an Ordinary Day* (1997), was published after the discovery of a box of some of Jackson's unpublished papers in a Vermont barn and her heirs' subsequent search for her other uncollected works.

Jackson was an intense, self-destructive, contradictory personality: a witty hostess to crowds of literary friends; a self-described witch, clairvoyant, and student of magic; a cookie-baking "Mom" who wrote chilling tales between loads of laundry. With her husband, literary critic Stanley Edgar Hyman, she settled in the small town of Bennington, Vermont, but was never accepted by the townspeople. "The Lottery" is set in much the same kind of small, hidebound town. The story's publication in *The New Yorker* magazine provoked a torrent of letters from enraged and horrified readers. Americans of the post–World War II era saw themselves as "good guys" defending the world against foreign evils. Jackson's story, written scarcely three years after the liberation of Auschwitz, told Americans something they did not want to hear—that the face of human evil could look just like their next-door neighbor. Horror master Stephen King dedicated his book *Firestarter* "to Shirley Jackson, who never had to raise her voice."

CULTURAL CONTEXT ◆ "The Lottery" is sometimes seen as a protest against totalitarianism, a form of authoritarian government that permits no individual freedom. In *Eichmann in Jerusalem* (1963), political scientist Hannah Arendt (1906–1975) wrote about totalitarianism as it pertained to Nazi Germany and the Holocaust. Here, she introduced the concept of "the banality of evil," the potential in ordinary people to do evil things.

◆ ◆ ◆

SHIRLEY JACKSON

The Lottery
(1948)

The morning of June 27th was clear and sunny, with the fresh warmth of a full-summer day; the flowers were blossoming profusely and the grass was richly green. The people of the village began to gather in the square, between the post office and the bank, around ten o'clock; in some towns there were so many people that the lottery took two days and had to be started on June 26th, but in this village, where there were only about three hundred people, the whole lottery took less than two hours, so it could begin at ten o'clock in the morning and still be through in time to allow the villagers to get home for noon dinner.

The children assembled first, of course. School was recently over for the summer, and the feeling of liberty sat uneasily on most of them; they tended to gather together quietly for a while before they broke into boisterous play, and their talk was still of the classroom and the teacher, of books and reprimands. Bobby Martin had already stuffed his pockets full of stones, and the other boys soon followed his example, selecting the smoothest and roundest stones; Bobby and Harry Jones and Dickie Delacroix—the villagers pronounced this name "Dellacroy"—eventually made a great pile of stones in one corner of the square and guarded it against the raids of the other boys. The girls stood aside, talking among themselves, looking over their shoulders at the boys, and the very small children rolled in the dust or clung to the hands of their older brothers or sisters.

Soon the men began to gather, surveying their own children, speaking of planting and rain, tractors and taxes. They stood together, away from the pile of stones in the corner, and their jokes were quiet and they smiled rather than laughed. The women, wearing faded house dresses and sweaters, came shortly after their menfolk. They greeted one another and exchanged bits of gossip as they went to join their husbands. Soon the women, standing by their husbands, began to call to their children, and the children came reluctantly, having to be called four or five times. Bobby Martin ducked under his mother's grasping hand and ran, laughing, back to the pile of stones. His father spoke up sharply, and Bobby came quickly and took his place between his father and his oldest brother.

The lottery was conducted—as were the square dances, the teen-age club, the Halloween program—by Mr. Summers, who had time and energy to devote to civic activities. He was a round-faced, jovial man and he ran the coal business, and people were sorry for him, because he had no children and his wife was a scold. When he arrived in the square, carrying the black wooden box, there was a murmur of conversation among the villagers, and he waved and called, "Little late today, folks." The postmaster, Mr. Graves, followed him, carrying a three-legged stool, and the stool was put in the center of the square and Mr. Summers set the black box down on it. The villagers kept their distance, leaving a space between themselves and the stool, and when Mr. Summers said, "Some of you fellows want to give me a hand?" there was a hesitation before two men, Mr. Martin and his oldest son, Baxter, came forward to hold the box steady on the stool while Mr. Summers stirred up the papers inside it.

5   The original paraphernalia for the lottery had been lost long ago, and the black box now resting on the stool had been put into use even before

Old Man Warner, the oldest man in town, was born. Mr. Summers spoke frequently to the villagers about making a new box, but no one liked to upset even as much tradition as was represented by the black box. There was a story that the present box had been made with some pieces of the box that had preceded it, the one that had been constructed when the first people settled down to make a village here. Every year, after the lottery, Mr. Summers began talking again about a new box, but every year the subject was allowed to fade off without anything's being done. The black box grew shabbier each year; by now it was no longer completely black but splintered badly along one side to show the original wood color, and in some places faded or stained.

Mr. Martin and his oldest son, Baxter, held the black box securely on the stool until Mr. Summers had stirred the papers thoroughly with his hand. Because so much of the ritual had been forgotten or discarded, Mr. Summers had been successful in having slips of paper substituted for the chips of wood that had been used for generations. Chips of wood, Mr. Summers had argued, had been all very well when the village was tiny, but now that the population was more than three hundred and likely to keep on growing, it was necessary to use something that would fit more easily into the black box. The night before the lottery, Mr. Summers and Mr. Graves made up the slips of paper and put them in the box, and it was then taken to the safe of Mr. Summers's coal company and locked up until Mr. Summers was ready to take it to the square next morning. The rest of the year, the box was put away, sometimes one place, sometimes another; it had spent one year in Mr. Graves's barn and another year underfoot in the post office, and sometimes it was set on a shelf in the Martin grocery and left there.

There was a great deal of fussing to be done before Mr. Summers declared the lottery open. There were the lists to make up—of heads of families, heads of households in each family, members of each household in each family. There was the proper swearing-in of Mr. Summers by the postmaster, as the official of the lottery; at one time, some people remembered, there had been a recital of some sort, performed by the official of the lottery, a perfunctory, tuneless chant that had been rattled off duly each year; some people believed that the official of the lottery used to stand just so when he said or sang it, others believed that he was supposed to walk among the people, but years and years ago this part of the ritual had been allowed to lapse. There had been, also, a ritual salute, which the official of the lottery had had to use in addressing each person who came up to draw from the box, but this also had changed with time, until now it was felt necessary only for the official to speak to each person approaching. Mr. Summers was very good at all this; in his clean white shirt and blue jeans, with one hand resting carelessly on the black box, he seemed very proper and important as he talked interminably to Mr. Graves and the Martins.

Just as Mr. Summers finally left off talking and turned to the assembled villagers, Mrs. Hutchinson came hurriedly along the path to the square, her sweater thrown over her shoulders, and slid into place in the back of the crowd. "Clean forgot what day it was," she said to Mrs. Delacroix, who stood next to her, and they both laughed softly. "Thought my old man was out back stacking wood," Mrs. Hutchinson went on, "and then I looked out the window and the kids was gone, and then I remembered it was the twenty-seventh and came a-running." She dried her hands on her apron, and Mrs. Delacroix said, "You're in time, though. They're still talking away up there."

Mrs. Hutchinson craned her neck to see through the crowd and found her husband and children standing near the front. She tapped Mrs. Delacroix on the arm as a farewell and began to make her way through the crowd. The people separated good-humoredly to let her through; two or three people said, in voices just loud enough to be heard across the crowd, "Here comes your Missus, Hutchinson," and "Bill, she made it after all." Mrs. Hutchinson reached her husband, and Mr. Summers, who had been waiting, said cheerfully, "Thought we were going to have to get on without you, Tessie." Mrs. Hutchinson said, grinning, "Wouldn't have me leave m'dishes in the sink, now, would you, Joe?," and soft laughter ran through the crowd as the people stirred back into position after Mrs. Hutchinson's arrival.

10 "Well, now," Mr. Summers said soberly, "guess we better get started, get this over with, so's we can go back to work. Anybody ain't here?"

"Dunbar," several people said. "Dunbar, Dunbar."

Mr. Summers consulted his list. "Clyde Dunbar," he said. "That's right. He's broke his leg, hasn't he? Who's drawing for him?"

"Me, I guess," a woman said, and Mr. Summers turned to look at her. "Wife draws for her husband," Mr. Summers said. "Don't you have a grown boy to do it for you, Janey?" Although Mr. Summers and everyone else in the village knew the answer perfectly well, it was the business of the official of the lottery to ask such questions formally. Mr. Summers waited with an expression of polite interest while Mrs. Dunbar answered.

"Horace's not but sixteen yet," Mrs. Dunbar said regretfully. "Guess I gotta fill in for the old man this year."

15 "Right," Mr. Summers said. He made a note on the list he was holding. Then he asked, "Watson boy drawing this year?"

A tall boy in the crowd raised his hand. "Here," he said. "I'm drawing for m'mother and me." He blinked his eyes nervously and ducked his head as several voices in the crowd said things like "Good fellow, Jack," and "Glad to see your mother's got a man to do it."

"Well," Mr. Summers said, "guess that's everyone. Old Man Warner make it?"

"Here," a voice said, and Mr. Summers nodded.

A sudden hush fell on the crowd as Mr. Summers cleared his throat and looked at the list. "All ready?" he called. "Now, I'll read the names—heads of families first—and the men come up and take a paper out of the box. Keep the paper folded in your hand without looking at it until everyone has had a turn. Everything clear?"

20   The people had done it so many times that they only half listened to the directions; most of them were quiet, wetting their lips, not looking around. Then Mr. Summers raised one hand high and said, "Adams." A man disengaged himself from the crowd and came forward. "Hi, Steve," Mr. Summers said, and Mr. Adams said, "Hi, Joe." They grinned at one another humorlessly and nervously. Then Mr. Adams reached into the black box and took out a folded paper. He held it firmly by one corner as he turned and went hastily back to his place in the crowd, where he stood a little apart from his family, not looking down at his hand.

"Allen," Mr. Summers said. "Anderson. . . . Bentham."

"Seems like there's no time at all between lotteries any more," Mrs. Delacroix said to Mrs. Graves in the back row. "Seems like we got through with the last one only last week."

"Time sure goes fast," Mrs. Graves said.

"Clark. . . . Delacroix."

25   "There goes my old man," Mrs. Delacroix said. She held her breath while her husband went forward.

"Dunbar," Mr. Summers said, and Mrs. Dunbar went steadily to the box while one of the women said, "Go on, Janey," and another said, "There she goes."

"We're next," Mrs. Graves said. She watched while Mr. Graves came around from the side of the box, greeted Mr. Summers gravely, and selected a slip of paper from the box. By now, all through the crowd there were men holding the small folded papers in their large hands, turning them over and over nervously. Mrs. Dunbar and her two sons stood together, Mrs. Dunbar holding the slip of paper.

"Harburt. . . . Hutchinson."

"Get up there, Bill," Mrs. Hutchinson said, and the people near her laughed.

30   "Jones."

"They do say," Mr. Adams said to Old Man Warner, who stood next to him, "that over in the north village they're talking of giving up the lottery."

Old Man Warner snorted. "Pack of crazy fools," he said. "Listening to the young folks, nothing's good enough for *them*. Next thing you know, they'll be wanting to go back to living in caves, nobody work any more, live *that* way for a while. Used to be a saying about 'Lottery in June, corn be heavy soon.' First thing you know, we'd all be eating stewed chickweed and acorns. There's *always* been a lottery," he added petulantly. "Bad enough to see young Joe Summers up there joking with everybody."

"Some places have already quit lotteries," Mrs. Adams said.

"Nothing but trouble in *that*," Old Man Warner said stoutly. "Pack of young fools."

35   "Martin." And Bobby Martin watched his father go forward. "Overdyke. . . . Percy."

"I wish they'd hurry," Mrs. Dunbar said to her older son. "I wish they'd hurry."

"They're almost through," her son said.

"You get ready to run tell Dad," Mrs. Dunbar said.

Mr. Summers called his own name and then stepped forward precisely and selected a slip from the box. Then he called, "Warner."

40 "Seventy-seventh year I been in the lottery," Old Man Warner said as he went through the crowd. "Seventy-seventh time."

"Watson." The tall boy came awkwardly through the crowd. Someone said, "Don't be nervous, Jack," and Mr. Summers said, "Take your time, son."

"Zanini."

After that, there was a long pause, a breathless pause, until Mr. Summers, holding his slip of paper in the air, said, "All right, fellows." For a minute, no one moved, and then all the slips of paper were opened. Suddenly, all the women began to speak at once, saying, "Who is it?," "Who's got it?," "Is it the Dunbars?," "Is it the Watsons?" Then the voices began to say, "It's Hutchinson. It's Bill," "Bill Hutchinson's got it."

"Go tell your father," Mrs. Dunbar said to her older son.

45 People began to look around to see the Hutchinsons. Bill Hutchinson was standing quiet, staring down at the paper in his hand. Suddenly, Tessie Hutchinson shouted to Mr. Summers, "You didn't give him time enough to take any paper he wanted. I saw you. It wasn't fair!"

"Be a good sport, Tessie," Mrs. Delacroix called, and Mrs. Graves said, "All of us took the same chance."

"Shut up, Tessie," Bill Hutchinson said.

"Well, everyone," Mr. Summers said, "that was done pretty fast, and now we've got to be hurrying a little more to get done in time." He consulted his next list. "Bill," he said, "you draw for the Hutchinson family. You got any other households in the Hutchinsons?"

"There's Don and Eva," Mrs. Hutchinson yelled, "Make *them* take their chance!"

50 "Daughters draw with their husbands' families, Tessie," Mr. Summers said gently. "You know that as well as anyone else."

"It wasn't *fair*," Tessie said.

"I guess not, Joe," Bill Hutchinson said regretfully. "My daughter draws with her husband's family, that's only fair. And I've got no other family except the kids."

"Then, as far as drawing for families is concerned, it's you," Mr. Summers said in explanation, "and as far as drawing for households is concerned, that's you, too. Right?"

"Right," Bill Hutchinson said.

55 "How many kids, Bill?" Mr. Summers asked formally.

"Three," Bill Hutchinson said. "There's Bill, Jr., and Nancy, and little Dave. And Tessie and me."

"All right, then," Mr. Summers said. "Harry, you got their tickets back?"

Mr. Graves nodded and held up the slips of paper. "Put them in the box, then," Mr. Summers directed. "Take Bill's and put it in."

"I think we ought to start over," Mrs. Hutchinson said, as quietly as she could. "I tell you it wasn't *fair*. You didn't give him time enough to choose. *Every*body saw that."

60 Mr. Graves had selected the five slips and put them in the box, and he dropped all the papers but those onto the ground, where the breeze caught them and lifted them off.

"Listen, everybody," Mrs. Hutchinson was saying to the people around her.

"Ready, Bill?" Mr. Summers asked, and Bill Hutchinson, with one quick glance around at his wife and children, nodded.

"Remember," Mr. Summers said, "take the slips and keep them folded until each person has taken one. Harry, you help little Dave." Mr. Graves took the hand of the little boy, who came willingly with him up to the box. "Take a paper out of the box, Davy," Mr. Summers said. Davy put his hand into the box and laughed. "Take just *one* paper," Mr. Summers said. "Harry, you hold it for him." Mr. Graves took the child's hand and removed the folded paper from the tight fist and held it while little Dave stood next to him and looked at him wonderingly.

"Nancy next," Mr. Summers said. Nancy was twelve, and her school friends breathed heavily as she went forward, switching her skirt, and took a slip daintily from the box. "Bill, Jr.," Mr. Summers said, and Billy, his face red and his feet overlarge, nearly knocked the box over as he got a paper out. "Tessie," Mr. Summers said. She hesitated for a minute, looking around defiantly, and then set her lips and went up to the box. She snatched a paper out and held it behind her.

65 "Bill," Mr. Summers said, and Bill Hutchinson reached into the box and felt around, bringing his hand out at last with the slip of paper in it.

The crowd was quiet. A girl whispered, "I hope it's not Nancy," and the sound of the whisper reached the edges of the crowd.

"It's not the way it used to be," Old Man Warner said clearly. "People ain't the way they used to be."

"All right," Mr. Summers said. "Open the papers. Harry, you open little Dave's."

Mr. Graves opened the slip of paper and there was a general sigh through the crowd as he held it up and everyone could see that it was blank. Nancy and Bill, Jr., opened theirs at the same time, and both beamed and laughed, turning around to the crowd and holding their slips of paper above their heads.

70 "Tessie," Mr. Summers said. There was a pause, and then Mr. Summers looked at Bill Hutchinson, and Bill unfolded his paper and showed it. It was blank.

"It's Tessie," Mr. Summers said, and his voice was hushed. "Show us her paper, Bill."

Bill Hutchinson went over to his wife and forced the slip of paper out of her hand. It had a black spot on it, the black spot Mr. Summers had made the night before with the heavy pencil in the coal-company office. Bill Hutchinson held it up, and there was a stir in the crowd.

"All right, folks," Mr. Summers said. "Let's finish quickly."

Although the villagers had forgotten the ritual and lost the original black box, they still remembered to use stones. The pile of stones the boys had made earlier was ready; there were stones on the ground with the blowing scraps of paper that had come out of the box. Mrs. Delacroix selected a stone so large she had to pick it up with both hands and turned to Mrs. Dunbar. "Come on," she said. "Hurry up."

75 Mrs. Dunbar had small stones in both hands, and she said, gasping for breath, "I can't run at all. You'll have to go ahead and I'll catch up with you."

The children had stones already, and someone gave little Davy Hutchinson a few pebbles.

Tessie Hutchinson was in the center of a cleared space by now, and she held her hands out desperately as the villagers moved in on her. "It isn't fair," she said. A stone hit her on the side of the head.

Old Man Warner was saying, "Come on, come on, everyone." Steve Adams was in the front of the crowd of villagers, with Mrs. Graves beside him.

"It isn't fair, it isn't right," Mrs. Hutchinson screamed, and then they were upon her.

READING AND REACTING

1. What possible significance, beyond their literal meaning, might each of these items have: the village square, Mrs. Hutchinson's apron, Old Man Warner, the slips of paper, the black spot?

2. "The Lottery" takes place in summer, a conventional symbol that has a positive connotation. What does this setting contribute to the story's plot? To its atmosphere?

3. What, if anything, might the names *Graves, Adams, Summers,* and *Delacroix* signify in the context of this story? Do you think these names are intended to have any special significance? Why or why not?

4. What role do the children play in the ritual? How can you explain their presence in the story? Do they have any symbolic role?

5. What symbolic significance might be found in the way the characters are dressed? In their conversation?

6. In what sense is the story's title ironic?

7. Throughout the story there is a general atmosphere of excitement. What indication is there of nervousness or apprehension?

8. Early in the story, the boys stuff their pockets with stones, foreshadowing the attack in the story's conclusion. What other examples of foreshadowing can you identify?

9. **JOURNAL ENTRY** How can a ritual like the lottery continue to be held year after year? Why does no one move to end it? Can you think of a modern-day counterpart to this lottery—a situation in which people continue to act in ways they know to be wrong rather than challenge the status quo? How can you account for such behavior?

10. **CRITICAL PERSPECTIVE** When "The Lottery" was published in the June 26, 1948, issue of *The New Yorker,* its effect was immediate. The story, as the critic Judy Oppenheimer notes in her book *Private Demons: The Life of Shirley Jackson,* "provoked an unprecedented outpouring of fury, horror, rage, disgust, and intense fascination." As a result, Jackson received hundreds of letters, which contained (among others) the following interpretations of the story:

◇ The story is an attack on small-town America.

◇ The story is a parable about the perversion of democracy.

◇ The story is a criticism of prejudice, particularly anti-Semitism.

◇ The story has no point at all.

How plausible do you think each of these interpretations is? Which comes closest to your interpretation of the story? Why?

Related Works: "Like a Winding Sheet" (p. 125), "Where Are You Going, Where Have You Been?" (p. 614), "Patterns" (p. 737), "The Colonel" (p. 889)

◈ **ALICE WALKER** (1944–   ) is an accomplished writer of poetry, fiction, and criticism. Her characters are mainly rural African-Americans, often living in her native Georgia, who struggle to survive in hostile environments. Her writing displays a particular sensitivity to the emotions of people who suffer physical or psychological harm in their efforts to assert their own identities.

Walker was the youngest of eight children born to Willie Lee and Minnie Tallulah Grant Walker, sharecroppers who raised cotton. She left the rural South to attend Atlanta's Spelman College (1961–1963) and Sarah Lawrence College in Bronxville, New York (1963–1965).

In 1967, Walker moved to Mississippi, where she was supported in the writing of her first novel, *The Third Life of Grange Copeland* (1970), by a

National Endowment for the Arts grant. Her short story "Everyday Use" was included in *Best American Short Stories 1973.* Other novels and short story collections followed, including *In Love and Trouble: Stories of Black Women* (1973), *Meridian* (1976), *You Can't Keep a Good Woman Down* (short stories, 1981), *The Temple of My Familiar* (1989), *Possessing the Secret of Joy* (1993), *The Complete Stories* (short stories, 1994), and *By the Light of My Father's Smile* (1998). Walker's third novel, *The Color Purple* (1982), won the American Book Award and a Pulitzer Prize.

In the third year of her marriage, Walker took back her maiden name because she wanted to honor her great-great-great-grandmother who walked, carrying her two children, from Virginia to Georgia. Walker's renaming is consistent with one of her goals in writing, which is to further the process of reconnecting people to their ancestors. She has said that "it is fatal to see yourself as separate" and that if people can reaffirm the past, they can "make a different future."

Cultural Context ◊ Quilting attained the status of art in Europe in the fourteenth century. It was in North America, however, that quilting reached its fullest development. By the end of the eighteenth century, the American quilt had taken on unique and distinctive features separating it from the craft in other parts of the world. Today, quilting reflects a heritage passed down through generations.

◊ ◊ ◊

A L I C E   W A L K E R

Everyday Use
(1973)

for your grandma

I will wait for her in the yard that Maggie and I made so clean and wavy yesterday afternoon. A yard like this is more comfortable than most people know. It is not just a yard. It is like an extended living room. When the hard clay is swept clean as a floor and the fine sand around the edges lined with tiny, irregular grooves, anyone can come and sit and look up into the elm tree and wait for the breezes that never come inside the house.

Maggie will be nervous until after her sister goes: she will stand hopelessly in corners, homely and ashamed of the burn scars down her arms and legs, eying her sister with a mixture of envy and awe. She thinks her sister has held life always in the palm of one hand, that "no" is a word the world never learned to say to her.

You've no doubt seen those TV shows where the child who has "made it" is confronted, as a surprise, by her own mother and father, tottering in weakly from backstage. (A pleasant surprise, of course: What would they do if parent and child came on the show only to curse out and insult each other?) On TV mother and child embrace and smile into each other's faces. Sometimes the mother and father weep, the child wraps them in her arms and leans across the table to tell how she would not have made it without their help. I have seen these programs.

Sometimes I dream a dream in which Dee and I are suddenly brought together on a TV program of this sort. Out of a dark and soft-seated limousine I am ushered into a bright room filled with many people. There I meet a smiling, gray, sporty man like Johnny Carson who shakes my hand and tells me what a fine girl I have. Then we are on the stage and Dee is embracing me with tears in her eyes. She pins on my dress a large orchid, even though she has told me once that she thinks orchids are tacky flowers.

5   In real life I am a large, big-boned woman with rough, man-working hands. In the winter I wear flannel nightgowns to bed and overalls during the day. I can kill and clean a hog as mercilessly as a man. My fat keeps me hot in zero weather. I can work outside all day, breaking ice to get water for washing; I can eat pork liver cooked over the open fire minutes after it comes steaming from the hog. One winter I knocked a bull calf straight in the brain between the eyes with a sledge hammer and had the meat hung up to chill before nightfall. But of course all this does not show on television. I am the way my daughter would want me to be: a hundred pounds lighter, my skin like an uncooked barley pancake. My hair glistens in the hot bright lights. Johnny Carson has much to do to keep up with my quick and witty tongue.

But that is a mistake. I know even before I wake up. Who ever knew a Johnson with a quick tongue? Who can even imagine me looking a strange white man in the eye? It seems to me I have talked to them always with one foot raised in flight, with my head turned in whichever way is farthest from them. Dee, though. She would always look anyone in the eye. Hesitation was no part of her nature.

"How do I look, Mama?" Maggie says, showing just enough of her thin body enveloped in pink skirt and red blouse for me to know she's there, almost hidden by the door.

"Come out into the yard," I say.

Have you ever seen a lame animal, perhaps a dog run over by some careless person rich enough to own a car, sidle up to someone who is ignorant enough to be kind to him? That is the way my Maggie walks. She has been like this, chin on chest, eyes on ground, feet in shuffle, ever since the fire that burned the other house to the ground.

10   Dee is lighter than Maggie, with nicer hair and a fuller figure. She's a woman now, though sometimes I forget. How long ago was it that the other house burned? Ten, twelve years? Sometimes I can still hear the flames and feel Maggie's arms sticking to me, her hair smoking and her dress falling off her in little black papery flakes. Her eyes seemed stretched open, blazed open by the flames reflected in them. And Dee. I see her

standing off under the sweet gum tree she used to dig gum out of; a look of concentration on her face as she watched the last dingy gray board of the house fall in toward the red-hot brick chimney. Why don't you do a dance around the ashes? I'd wanted to ask her. She had hated the house that much.

I used to think she hated Maggie, too. But that was before we raised the money, the church and me, to send her to Augusta to school. She used to read to us without pity; forcing words, lies, other folks' habits, whole lives upon us two, sitting trapped and ignorant underneath her voice. She washed us in a river of make-believe, burned us with a lot of knowledge we didn't necessarily need to know. Pressed us to her with the serious way she read, to shove us away at just the moment, like dimwits, we seemed about to understand.

Dee wanted nice things. A yellow organdy dress to wear to her graduation from high school; black pumps to match a green suit she'd made from an old suit somebody gave me. She was determined to stare down any disaster in her efforts. Her eyelids would not flicker for minutes at a time. Often I fought off the temptation to shake her. At sixteen she had a style of her own, and knew what style was.

I never had an education myself. After second grade the school was closed down. Don't ask me why: in 1927 colored asked fewer questions than they do now. Sometimes Maggie reads to me. She stumbles along good-naturedly but can't see well. She knows she is not bright. Like good looks and money, quickness passed her by. She will marry John Thomas (who has mossy teeth in an earnest face) and then I'll be free to sit here and I guess just sing church songs to myself. Although I never was a good singer. Never could carry a tune. I was always better at a man's job. I used to love to milk till I was hooked in the side in '49. Cows are soothing and slow and don't bother you, unless you try to milk them the wrong way.

I have deliberately turned my back on the house. It is three rooms, just like the one that burned, except the roof is tin; they don't make shingle roofs any more. There are no real windows, just some holes cut in the sides, like the portholes in a ship, but not round and not square, with rawhide holding the shutters up on the outside. This house is in a pasture, too, like the other one. No doubt when Dee sees it she will want to tear it down. She wrote me once that no matter where we "choose" to live, she will manage to come see us. But she will never bring her friends. Maggie and I thought about this and Maggie asked me, "Mama, when did Dee ever *have* any friends?"

15   She had a few. Furtive boys in pink shirts hanging about on washday after school. Nervous girls who never laughed. Impressed with her they worshiped the well-turned phrase, the cute shape, the scalding humor that erupted like bubbles in lye. She read to them.

When she was courting Jimmy T she didn't have much time to pay to us, but turned all her faultfinding power on him. He *flew* to marry a cheap city girl from a family of ignorant flashy people. She hardly had time to recompose herself.

When she comes I will meet—but there they are!

Maggie attempts to make a dash for the house, in her shuffling way, but I stay her with my hand. "Come back here," I say. And she stops and tries to dig a well in the sand with her toe.

It is hard to see them clearly through the strong sun. But even the first glimpse of leg out of the car tells me it is Dee. Her feet were always neat-looking, as if God himself had shaped them with a certain style. From the other side of the car comes a short, stocky man. Hair is all over his head a foot long and hanging from his chin like a kinky mule tail. I hear Maggie suck in her breath. "Uhnnnh," is what it sounds like. Like when you see the wriggling end of a snake just in front of your foot on the road. "Uhnnnh."

20   Dee next. A dress down to the ground, in this hot weather. A dress so loud it hurts my eyes. There are yellows and oranges enough to throw back the light of the sun. I feel my whole face warming from the heat waves it throws out. Earrings gold, too, and hanging down to her shoulders. Bracelets dangling and making noises when she moves her arm up to shake the folds of the dress out of her armpits. The dress is loose and flows, and as she walks closer, I like it. I hear Maggie go "Uhnnnh" again. It is her sister's hair. It stands straight up like the wool on a sheep. It is black as night and around the edges are two long pigtails that rope about like small lizards disappearing behind her ears.

"Wa-su-zo-Tean-o!"[1] she says, coming on in that gliding way the dress makes her move. The short stocky fellow with the hair to his navel is all grinning and he follows up with "Asalamalakim,[2] my mother and sister!" He moves to hug Maggie but she falls back, right up against the back of my chair. I feel her trembling there and when I look up I see the perspiration falling off her chin.

"Don't get up," says Dee. Since I am stout it takes something of a push. You can see me trying to move a second or two before I make it. She turns, showing white heels through her sandals, and goes back to the car. Out she peeks next with a Polaroid. She stoops down quickly and lines up picture after picture of me sitting there in front of the house with Maggie cowering behind me. She never takes a shot without making sure the house is included. When a cow comes nibbling around the edge of the yard she snaps it and me and Maggie *and* the house. Then she puts the Polaroid in the back seat of the car, and comes up and kisses me on the forehead.

Meanwhile Asalamalakim is going through motions with Maggie's hand. Maggie's hand is as limp as a fish, and probably as cold, despite the sweat, and she keeps trying to pull it back. It looks like Asalamalakim

---

[1] Greeting in Swahili; Dee sounds it out one syllable at a time.
[2] Greeting in Arabic: "Peace be upon you."

wants to shake hands but wants to do it fancy. Or maybe he don't know how people shake hands. Anyhow, he soon gives up on Maggie.

"Well," I say. "Dee."

25 "No, Mama," she says. "Not 'Dee,' Wangero Leewanika Kemanjo!"

"What happened to 'Dee'?" I wanted to know.

"She's dead," Wangero said. "I couldn't bear it any longer, being named after the people who oppress me."

"You know as well as me you was named after your aunt Dicie," I said. Dicie is my sister. She named Dee. We called her "Big Dee" after Dee was born.

"But who was *she* named after?" asked Wangero.

30 "I guess after Grandma Dee," I said.

"And who was she named after?" asked Wangero.

"Her mother," I said, and saw Wangero was getting tired. "That's about as far back as I can trace it," I said. Though, in fact, I probably could have carried it back beyond the Civil War through the branches.

"Well," said Asalamalakim, "there you are."

"Uhnnnh," I heard Maggie say.

35 "There I was not," I said, "before 'Dicie' cropped up in our family, so why should I try to trace it that far back?"

He just stood there grinning, looking down on me like somebody inspecting a Model A car. Every once in a while he and Wangero sent eye signals over my head.

"How do you pronounce this name?" I asked.

"You don't have to call me by it if you don't want to," said Wangero.

"Why shouldn't I?" I asked. "If that's what you want us to call you, we'll call you."

40 "I know it might sound awkward at first," said Wangero.

"I'll get used to it," I said. "Ream it out again."

Well, soon we got the name out of the way. Asalamalakim had a name twice as long and three times as hard. After I tripped over it two or three times he told me to just call him Hakim-a-barber. I wanted to ask him was he a barber, but I didn't really think he was, so I didn't ask.

"You must belong to those beef-cattle peoples down the road," I said. They said "Asalamalakim" when they met you, too, but they didn't shake hands. Always too busy: feeding the cattle, fixing the fences, putting up salt-lick shelters, throwing down hay. When the white folks poisoned some of the herd the men stayed up all night with rifles in their hands. I walked a mile and a half just to see the sight.

Hakim-a-barber said, "I accept some of their doctrines, but farming and raising cattle is not my style." (They didn't tell me, and I didn't ask, whether Wangero [Dee] had really gone and married him.)

45 We sat down to eat and right away he said he didn't eat collards and pork was unclean. Wangero, though, went on through the chitlins and corn bread, the greens and everything else. She talked a blue streak over the sweet potatoes. Everything delighted her. Even the fact that we still

used the benches her daddy made for the table when we couldn't afford to buy chairs.

"Oh, Mama!" she cried. Then turned to Hakim-a-barber. "I never knew how lovely these benches are. You can feel the rump prints," she said, running her hands underneath her and along the bench. Then she gave a sigh and her hand closed over Grandma Dee's butter dish. "That's it!" she said. "I knew there was something I wanted to ask you if I could have." She jumped up from the table and went over in the corner where the churn stood, the milk in it clabber by now. She looked at the churn and looked at it.

"This churn top is what I need," she said. "Didn't Uncle Buddy whittle it out of a tree you all used to have?"

"Yes," I said.

"Uh huh," she said happily. "And I want the dasher, too."

50   "Uncle Buddy whittle that, too?" asked the barber.

Dee (Wangero) looked up at me.

"Aunt Dee's first husband whittled the dash," said Maggie so low you almost couldn't hear her. "His name was Henry, but they called him Stash."

"Maggie's brain is like an elephant's," Wangero said, laughing. "I can use the churn top as a centerpiece for the alcove table," she said, sliding a plate over the churn, "and I'll think of something artistic to do with the dasher."

When she finished wrapping the dasher the handle stuck out. I took it for a moment in my hands. You didn't even have to look close to see where hands pushing the dasher up and down to make butter had left a kind of sink in the wood. In fact, there were a lot of small sinks; you could see where thumb and fingers had sunk into the wood. It was beautiful light yellow wood, from a tree that grew in the yard where Big Dee and Stash had lived.

55   After dinner Dee (Wangero) went to the trunk at the foot of my bed and started rifling through it. Maggie hung back in the kitchen over the dishpan. Out came Wangero with two quilts. They had been pieced by Grandma Dee and then Big Dee and me had hung them on the quilt frames on the front porch and quilted them. One was in the Lone Star pattern. The other was Walk Around the Mountain. In both of them were scraps of dresses Grandma Dee had worn fifty and more years ago. Bits and pieces of Grandpa Jarrell's Paisley shirts. And one teeny faded blue piece, about the size of a penny matchbox, that was from Great Grandpa Ezra's uniform that he wore in the Civil War.

"Mama," Wangero said sweet as a bird. "Can I have these old quilts?"

I heard something fall in the kitchen, and a minute later the kitchen door slammed.

"Why don't you take one or two of the others?" I asked. "These old things was just done by me and Big Dee from some tops your grandma pieced before she died."

"No," said Wangero. "I don't want those. They are stitched around the borders by machine."

60 "That'll make them last better," I said.

"That's not the point," said Wangero. "These are all pieces of dresses Grandma used to wear. She did all this stitching by hand. Imagine!" She held the quilts securely in her arms, stroking them.

"Some of the pieces, like those lavender ones, come from old clothes her mother handed down to her," I said, moving up to touch the quilts. Dee (Wangero) moved back just enough so that I couldn't reach the quilts. They already belonged to her.

"Imagine!" she breathed again, clutching them closely to her bosom.

"The truth is," I said, "I promised to give them quilts to Maggie, for when she marries John Thomas."

65 She gasped like a bee had stung her. "Maggie can't appreciate these quilts!" she said. "She'd probably be backward enough to put them to everyday use."

"I reckon she would," I said. "God knows I been saving 'em for long enough with nobody using 'em. I hope she will!" I didn't want to bring up how I had offered Dee (Wangero) a quilt when she went away to college. Then she had told me they were old-fashioned, out of style.

"But, they're *priceless!*" she was saying now, furiously; for she has a temper. "Maggie would put them on the bed and in five years they'd be in rags. Less than that!"

"She can always make some more," I said. "Maggie knows how to quilt."

Dee (Wangero) looked at me with hatred. "You just will not understand. The point is these quilts, *these* quilts!"

70 "Well," I said, stumped. "What would *you* do with them?"

"Hang them," she said. As if that was the only thing you *could* do with quilts.

Maggie by now was standing in the door. I could almost hear the sound her feet made as they scraped over each other.

"She can have them, Mama," she said, like somebody used to never winning anything, or having anything reserved for her. "I can 'member Grandma Dee without the quilts."

I looked at her hard. She had filled her bottom lip with checkerberry snuff and it gave her face a kind of dopey, hangdog look. It was Grandma Dee and Big Dee who taught her how to quilt herself. She stood there with her scarred hands hidden in the folds of her skirt. She looked at her sister with something like fear but she wasn't mad at her. This was Maggie's portion. This was the way she knew God to work.

75 When I looked at her like that something hit me in the top of my head and ran down to the soles of my feet. Just like when I'm in church and the spirit of God touches me and I get happy and shout. I did something I never had done before: hugged Maggie to me, then dragged her

on into the room, snatched the quilts out of Miss Wangero's hands and dumped them into Maggie's lap. Maggie just sat there on my bed with her mouth open.

"Take one or two of the others," I said to Dee.

But she turned without a word and went out to Hakim-a-barber.

"You just don't understand," she said, as Maggie and I came out to the car.

"What don't I understand?" I wanted to know.

80   "Your heritage," she said. And then she turned to Maggie, kissed her, and said, "You ought to try to make something of yourself, too, Maggie. It's really a new day for us. But from the way you and Mama still live you'd never know it."

She put on some sunglasses that hid everything above the tip of her nose and her chin.

Maggie smiled; maybe at the sunglasses. But a real smile, not scared. After we watched the car dust settle I asked Maggie to bring me a dip of snuff. And then the two of us sat there just enjoying, until it was time to go in the house and go to bed.

READING AND REACTING

1. In American culture, what does a patchwork quilt symbolize?
2. What is the *literal* meaning of the two quilts to Maggie and her mother? To Dee? Beyond this literal meaning, what symbolic meaning, if any, do they have to Maggie and her mother? Do the quilts have any symbolic meaning to Dee?
3. How does the contrast between the two sisters' appearances, personalities, lifestyles, and feelings about the quilts help to convey the story's theme?
4. What does the name *Wangero* signify to Dee? To her mother and sister? Could the name be considered a symbol? Why or why not?
5. Why do you think Maggie relinquishes the quilts to her sister?
6. What is Dee's opinion of her mother and sister? Do you agree with her assessment?
7. What does the story's title suggest to you? Is it ironic? What other titles would be effective?
8. What possible meanings, aside from their literal meanings, might each of the following suggest: the family's yard, Maggie's burn scars, the trunk in which the quilts are kept, Dee's Polaroid camera? What symbolic functions, if any, do these items serve in the story?
9. **JOURNAL ENTRY** What objects have the kind of symbolic value to you that the quilts have to Maggie? What gives these objects this value?

10. **Critical Perspective** In her article "The Black Woman Artist as Wayward," critic Barbara Christian characterizes "Everyday Use" as a story in which Alice Walker examines the "creative legacy" of ordinary African-American women. According to Christian, the story "is about the use and misuse of the concept of heritage. The mother of two daughters, one selfish and stylish, the other scarred and caring, passes on to us its true definition."

What definition of heritage does the mother attempt to pass on to her children? How is this definition like or unlike Dee's definition?

Related Works: "Two Kinds" (p. 594), "Digging" (p. 679), "Aunt Jennifer's Tigers" (p. 843), *Trifles* (p. 1163), *Fences* (p. 1745)

 ◆ **John Steinbeck** (1902–1968), winner of the 1962 Nobel Prize in literature, is noted for his sympathetic portraits of hardscrabble working people, particularly farm laborers, and for his evocation of rural landscapes that reflect the geography of the Salinas Valley in California, where he grew up. After attending Stanford University, Steinbeck worked as a journalist before publishing his first novel, *Cup of Gold* (1929), an adventure story, followed by *Tortilla Flat* (1935), about a poor Mexican-American community in Monterey, and *In Dubious Battle* (1936), about a farmworkers' strike. After the success of *Of Mice and Men* (1937), his tragic story set among migrant farmworkers, Steinbeck traveled with a group of farmers migrating to the "paradise" of California from the dust bowl of Oklahoma, an experience that provided the basis for his most enduring work, *The Grapes of Wrath* (1939), winner of a Pulitzer Prize. Other well-known Steinbeck novels include *Cannery Row* (1945), *East of Eden* (1952), and *The Winter of Our Discontent* (1961). A number of Steinbeck's works have been adapted for the stage and for film.

"The Chrysanthemums," from the collection *The Long Valley,* is not set in the social milieu generally associated with Steinbeck's work, but it has been hailed as containing one of his richest character studies.

Cultural Context ◆ California's Salinas Valley, where "The Chrysanthemums" is set and where Steinbeck grew up, is known as the "Salad Bowl of the Nation." The Salinas Valley parallels the Santa Lucia Mountain Range. The city of Salinas, Steinbeck's birthplace, lies in the Salinas Valley just east of Monterey Bay at a crossroads on the old Spanish trail between San Diego and San Francisco.

◇ ◇ ◇

JOHN STEINBECK

The Chrysanthemums
(1937)

The high grey-flannel fog of winter closed off the Salinas Valley from the sky and from all the rest of the world. On every side it sat like a lid on the mountains and made of the great valley a closed pot. On the broad, level land floor the gang plows bit deep and left the black earth shining like metal where the shares had cut. On the foothill ranches across the Salinas River, the yellow stubble fields seemed to be bathed in pale cold sunshine, but there was no sunshine in the valley now in December. The thick willow scrub along the river flamed with sharp and positive yellow leaves.

It was a game of quiet and of waiting. The air was cold and tender. A light wind blew up from the southwest so that the farmers were mildly hopeful of a good rain before long; but fog and rain do not go together.

Across the river, on Henry Allen's foothill ranch there was little work to be done, for the hay was cut and stored and the orchards were plowed up to receive the rain deeply when it should come. The cattle on the higher slopes were becoming shaggy and rough-coated.

Elisa Allen, working in her flower garden, looked down across the yard and saw Henry, her husband, talking to two men in business suits. The three of them stood by the tractor shed, each man with one foot on the side of the little Fordson. They smoked cigarettes and studied the machine as they talked.

5   Elisa watched them for a moment and then went back to her work. She was thirty-five. Her face was lean and strong and her eyes were as clear as water. Her figure looked blocked and heavy in her gardening costume, a man's black hat pulled low down over her eyes, clod-hopper shoes,[1] a figured print dress almost completely covered by a big corduroy apron with four big pockets to hold the snips, the trowel and scratcher, the seeds and the knife she worked with. She wore heavy leather gloves to protect her hands while she worked.

She was cutting down the old year's chrysanthemum stalks with a pair of short and powerful scissors. She looked down toward the men by the tractor shed now and then. Her face was eager and mature and handsome; even her work with the scissors was over-eager, over-powerful. The chrysanthemum stems seemed too small and easy for her energy.

She brushed a cloud of hair out of her eyes with the back of her glove, and left a smudge of earth on her cheek in doing it. Behind her stood the neat white farm house with red geraniums close-banked around it as high

---

[1] Heavy shoes, such as the ones that might be worn by a plowman.

as the windows. It was a hard-swept looking little house with hard-polished windows, and a clean mud-mat on the front steps.

Elisa cast another glance toward the tractor shed. The strangers were getting into their Ford coupe. She took off a glove and put her strong fingers down into the forest of new green chrysanthemum sprouts that were growing around the old roots. She spread the leaves and looked down among the close-growing stems. No aphids were there, no sowbugs or snails or cutworms. Her terrier fingers destroyed such pests before they could get started.

Elisa started at the sound of her husband's voice. He had come near quietly, and he leaned over the wire fence that protected her flower garden from cattle and dogs and chickens.

10   "At it again," he said. "You've got a strong new crop coming."

Elisa straightened her back and pulled on the gardening glove again. "Yes. They'll be strong this coming year." In her tone and on her face there was a little smugness.

"You've got a gift with things," Henry observed. "Some of those yellow chrysanthemums you had this year were ten inches across. I wish you'd work out in the orchard and raise some apples that big."

Her eyes sharpened. "Maybe I could do it, too. I've a gift with things, all right. My mother had it. She could stick anything in the ground and make it grow. She said it was having planters' hands that knew how to do it."

"Well, it sure works with flowers," he said.

15   "Henry, who were those men you were talking to?"

"Why, sure, that's what I came to tell you. They were from the Western Meat Company. I sold those thirty head of three-year-old steers. Got nearly my own price, too."

"Good," she said. "Good for you."

"And I thought," he continued, "I thought how it's Saturday afternoon, and we might go into Salinas for dinner at a restaurant, and then to a picture show—to celebrate, you see."

"Good," she repeated. "Oh, yes. That will be good."

20   Henry put on his joking tone. "There's fights tonight. How'd you like to go to the fights?"

"Oh, no," she said breathlessly. "No, I wouldn't like fights."

"Just fooling, Elisa. We'll go to a movie. Let's see. It's two now. I'm going to take Scotty and bring down those steers from the hill. It'll take us maybe two hours. We'll go in town about five and have dinner at the Cominos Hotel. Like that?"

"Of course I'll like it. It's good to eat away from home."

"All right, then. I'll go get up a couple of horses."

25   She said, "I'll have plenty of time to transplant some of these sets, I guess."

She heard her husband calling Scotty down by the barn. And a little later she saw the two men ride up the pale yellow hillside in search of the steers.

There was a little square sandy bed kept for rooting the chrysanthemums. With her trowel she turned the soil over and over, and smoothed it
and patted it firm. Then she dug ten parallel trenches to receive the sets.
Back at the chrysanthemum bed she pulled out the little crisp shoots,
trimmed off the leaves of each one with her scissors and laid it on a small
orderly pile.

A squeak of wheels and plod of hoofs came from the road. Elisa looked
up. The country road ran along the dense bank of willows and cotton-
woods that bordered the river, and up this road came a curious vehicle, curiously drawn. It was an old spring-wagon, with a round canvas top on it
like the cover of a prairie schooner.[2] It was drawn by an old bay horse and
a little grey-and-white burro. A big stubble-bearded man sat between the
cover flaps and drove the crawling team. Underneath the wagon, between
the hind wheels, a lean and rangy mongrel dog walked sedately. Words
were printed on the canvas, in clumsy, crooked letters. "Pots, pans, knives,
sisors, lawn mores, Fixed." Two rows of articles, and the triumphantly definitive "Fixed" below. The black paint had run down in little sharp points
beneath each letter.

Elisa, squatting on the ground, watched to see the crazy, loose-jointed
wagon pass by. But it didn't pass. It turned into the farm road in front of
her house, crooked old wheels skirling and squeaking. The rangy dog
darted from between the wheels and ran ahead. Instantly the two ranch
shepherds flew out at him. Then all three stopped, and with stiff and quivering tails, with taut straight legs, with ambassadorial dignity, they slowly
circled, sniffing daintily. The caravan pulled up to Elisa's wire fence and
stopped. Now the newcomer dog, feeling outnumbered, lowered his tail
and retired under the wagon with raised hackles and bared teeth.

30   The man on the wagon seat called out, "That's a bad dog in a fight
when he gets started."

Elisa laughed. "I see he is. How soon does he generally get started?"

The man caught up her laughter and echoed it heartily. "Sometimes
not for weeks and weeks," he said. He climbed stiffly down, over the
wheel. The horse and the donkey drooped like unwatered flowers.

Elisa saw that he was a very big man. Although his hair and beard were
greying, he did not look old. His worn black suit was wrinkled and spotted
with grease. The laughter had disappeared from his face and eyes the moment his laughing voice ceased. His eyes were dark, and they were full of
the brooding that gets in the eyes of teamsters and of sailors. The cal-
loused hands he rested on the wire fence were cracked, and every crack was
a black line. He took off his battered hat.

"I'm off my general road, ma'am," he said. "Does this dirt road cut
over across the river to the Los Angeles highway?"

---

[2] Covered wagon used by American pioneers.

35   Elisa stood up and shoved the thick scissors in her apron pocket. "Well, yes, it does, but it winds around and then fords the river. I don't think your team could pull through the sand."

He replied with some asperity. "It might surprise you what them beasts can pull through."

"When they get started?" she asked.

He smiled for a second. "Yes. When they get started."

"Well," said Elisa, "I think you'll save time if you go back to the Salinas road and pick up the highway there."

40   He drew a big finger down the chicken wire and made it sing. "I ain't in any hurry, ma'am. I go from Seattle to San Diego and back every year. Takes all my time. About six months each way. I aim to follow nice weather."

Elisa took off her gloves and stuffed them in the apron pocket with the scissors. She touched the under edge of her man's hat, searching for fugitive hairs. "That sounds like a nice kind of a way to live," she said.

He leaned confidentially over the fence. "Maybe you noticed the writing on my wagon. I mend pots and sharpen knives and scissors. You got any of them things to do?"

"Oh, no," she said quickly. "Nothing like that." Her eyes hardened with resistance.

"Scissors is the worst thing," he explained. "Most people just ruin scissors trying to sharpen 'em, but I know how. I got a special tool. It's a little bobbit kind of thing, and patented. But it sure does the trick."

45   "No. My scissors are all sharp."

"All right, then. Take a pot," he continued earnestly, "a bent pot, or a pot with a hole. I can make it like new so you don't have to buy no new ones. That's a saving for you."

"No," she said shortly. "I tell you I have nothing like that for you to do."

His face fell to an exaggerated sadness. His voice took on a whining undertone. "I ain't had a thing to do today. Maybe I won't have no supper tonight. You see I'm off my regular road. I know folks on the highway clear from Seattle to San Diego. They save their things for me to sharpen up because they know I do it so good and save them money."

"I'm sorry," Elisa said irritably. "I haven't anything for you to do."

50   His eyes left her face and fell to searching the ground. They roamed about until they came to the chrysanthemum bed where she had been working. "What's them plants, ma'am?"

The irritation and resistance melted from Elisa's face. "Oh, those are chrysanthemums, giant whites and yellows. I raise them every year, bigger than anybody around here."

"Kind of a long-stemmed flower? Looks like a quick puff of colored smoke?" he asked.

"That's it. What a nice way to describe them."

"They smell kind of nasty till you get used to them," he said.

55   "It's a good bitter smell," she retorted, "not nasty at all."

He changed his tone quickly. "I like the smell myself."

"I had ten-inch blooms this year," she said.

The man leaned farther over the fence. "Look. I know a lady down the road a piece, has got the nicest garden you ever seen. Got nearly every kind of flower but no chrysanthemums. Last time I was mending a copper-bottom washtub for her (that's a hard job but I do it good), she said to me, 'If you ever run acrost some nice chrysanthemums I wish you'd try to get me a few seeds.' That's what she told me."

Elisa's eyes grew alert and eager. "She couldn't have known much about chrysanthemums. You *can* raise them from seed, but it's much easier to root the little sprouts you see there."

60   "Oh," he said. "I s'pose I can't take none to her, then."

"Why yes you can," Elisa cried. "I can put some in damp sand, and you can carry them right along with you. They'll take root in the pot if you keep them damp. And then she can transplant them."

"She'd sure like to have some, ma'am. You say they're nice ones?"

"Beautiful," she said. "Oh, beautiful." Her eyes shone. She tore off the battered hat and shook out her dark pretty hair. "I'll put them in a flower pot, and you can take them right with you. Come into the yard."

While the man came through the picket gate Elisa ran excitedly along the geranium-bordered path to the back of the house. And she returned carrying a big red flower pot. The gloves were forgotten now. She kneeled on the ground by the starting bed and dug up the sandy soil with her fingers and scooped it into the bright new flower pot. Then she picked up the little pile of shoots she had prepared. With her strong fingers she pressed them into the sand and tamped around them with her knuckles. The man stood over her. "I'll tell you what to do," she said. "You remember so you can tell the lady."

65   "Yes, I'll try to remember."

"Well, look. These will take root in about a month. Then she must set them out, about a foot apart in good rich earth like this, see?" She lifted a handful of dark soil for him to look at. "They'll grow fast and tall. Now remember this: In July tell her to cut them down, about eight inches from the ground."

"Before they bloom?" he asked.

"Yes, before they bloom." Her face was tight with eagerness. "They'll grow right up again. About the last of September the buds will start."

She stopped and seemed perplexed. "It's the budding that takes the most care," she said hesitantly. "I don't know how to tell you." She looked deep into his eyes, searchingly. Her mouth opened a little, and she seemed to be listening. "I'll try to tell you," she said. "Did you ever hear of planting hands?"

70   "Can't say I have, ma'am."

"Well, I can only tell you what it feels like. It's when you're picking off the buds you don't want. Everything goes right down into your fingertips.

You watch your fingers work. They do it themselves. You can feel how it is. They pick and pick the buds. They never make a mistake. They're with the plant. Do you see? Your fingers and the plant. You can feel that, right up your arm. They know. They never make a mistake. You can feel it. When you're like that you can't do anything wrong. Do you see that? Can you understand that?"

She was kneeling on the ground looking up at him. Her breast swelled passionately.

The man's eyes narrowed. He looked away self-consciously. "Maybe I know," he said. "Sometimes in the night in the wagon there—"

Elisa's voice grew husky. She broke in on him, "I've never lived as you do, but I know what you mean. When the night is dark—why, the stars are sharp-pointed, and there's quiet. Why, you rise up and up! Every pointed star gets driven into your body. It's like that. Hot and sharp and—lovely."

75 Kneeling there, her hand went out toward his legs in the greasy black trousers. Her hesitant fingers almost touched the cloth. Then her hand dropped to the ground. She crouched low like a fawning dog.

He said, "It's nice, just like you say. Only when you don't have no dinner, it ain't."

She stood up then, very straight, and her face was ashamed. She held the flower pot out to him and placed it gently in his arms. "Here. Put it in your wagon, on the seat, where you can watch it. Maybe I can find something for you to do."

At the back of the house she dug in the can pile and found two old and battered aluminum saucepans. She carried them back and gave them to him. "Here, maybe you can fix these."

His manner changed. He became professional. "Good as new I can fix them." At the back of his wagon he sat a little anvil, and out of an oily tool box dug a small machine hammer. Elisa came through the gate to watch him while he pounded out the dents in the kettles. His mouth grew sure and knowing. At a difficult part of the work he sucked his under-lip.

80 "You sleep right in the wagon?" Elisa asked.

"Right in the wagon, ma'am. Rain or shine I'm dry as a cow in there."

"It must be nice," she said. "It must be very nice. I wish women could do such things."

"It ain't the right kind of a life for a woman."

Her upper lip raised a little, showing her teeth. "How do you know? How can you tell?" she said.

85 "I don't know, ma'am," he protested. "Of course I don't know. Now here's your kettles, done. You don't have to buy no new ones."

"How much?"

"Oh, fifty cents'll do. I keep my prices down and my work good. That's why I have all them satisfied customers up and down the highway."

Elisa brought him a fifty-cent piece from the house and dropped it in his hand. "You might be surprised to have a rival some time. I can sharpen scissors, too. And I can beat the dents out of little pots. I could show you what a woman might do."

He put his hammer back in the oily box and shoved the little anvil out of sight. "It would be a lonely life for a woman, ma'am, and a scarey life, too, with animals creeping under the wagon all night." He climbed over the singletree,[3] steadying himself with a hand on the burro's white rump. He settled himself in the seat, picked up the lines. "Thank you kindly, ma'am," he said. "I'll do like you told me; I'll go back and catch the Salinas road."

90   "Mind," she called, "if you're long in getting there, keep the sand damp."

"Sand, ma'am? . . . Sand? Oh, sure. You mean around the chrysanthemums. Sure I will." He clucked his tongue. The beasts leaned luxuriously into their collars. The mongrel dog took his place between the back wheels. The wagon turned and crawled out the entrance road and back the way it had come, along the river.

Elisa stood in front of her wire fence watching the slow progress of the caravan. Her shoulders were straight, her head thrown back, her eyes half-closed, so that the scene came vaguely into them. Her lips moved silently, forming the words "Good-bye—good-bye." Then she whispered, "That's a bright direction. There's a glowing there." The sound of her whisper startled her. She shook herself free and looked about to see whether anyone had been listening. Only the dogs had heard. They lifted their heads toward her from their sleeping in the dust, and then stretched out their chins and settled asleep again. Elisa turned and ran hurriedly into the house.

In the kitchen she reached behind the stove and felt the water tank. It was full of hot water from the noonday cooking. In the bathroom she tore off her soiled clothes and flung them into the corner. And then she scrubbed herself with a little block of pumice, legs and thighs, loins and chest and arms, until her skin was scratched and red. When she had dried herself she stood in front of a mirror in her bedroom and looked at her body. She tightened her stomach and threw out her chest. She turned and looked over her shoulder at her back.

After a while she began to dress, slowly. She put on her newest under-clothing and her nicest stockings and the dress which was the symbol of her prettiness. She worked carefully on her hair, penciled her eyebrows and rouged her lips.

95   Before she was finished she heard the little thunder of hoofs and the shouts of Henry and his helper as they drove the red steers into the corral. She heard the gate bang shut and set herself for Henry's arrival.

His step sounded on the porch. He entered the house calling, "Elisa, where are you?"

"In my room, dressing. I'm not ready. There's hot water for your bath. Hurry up. It's getting late."

When she heard him splashing in the tub, Elisa laid his dark suit on the bed, and shirt and socks and tie beside it. She stood his polished shoes

---

[3] A wooden bar that connects a wagon to the horses' harnesses.

on the floor beside the bed. Then she went to the porch and sat primly and stiffly down. She looked toward the river road where the willow-line was still yellow with frosted leaves so that under the high grey fog they seemed a thin band of sunshine. This was the only color in the grey afternoon. She sat unmoving for a long time. Her eyes blinked rarely.

Henry came banging out of the door, shoving his tie inside his vest as he came. Elisa stiffened and her face grew tight. Henry stopped short and looked at her. "Why—why, Elisa. You look so nice!"

100 "Nice? You think I look nice? What do you mean by 'nice'?"

Henry blundered on. "I don't know. I mean you look different, strong and happy."

"I am strong? Yes, strong. What do you mean 'strong'?"

He looked bewildered. "You're playing some kind of a game," he said helplessly. "It's a kind of a play. You look strong enough to break a calf over your knee, happy enough to eat it like a watermelon."

For a second she lost her rigidity. "Henry! Don't talk like that. You didn't know what you said." She grew complete again. "I'm strong," she boasted. "I never knew before how strong."

105 Henry looked down toward the tractor shed, and when he brought his eyes back to her, they were his own again. "I'll get out the car. You can put on your coat while I'm starting."

Elisa went into the house. She heard him drive to the gate and idle down his motor, and then she took a long time to put on her hat. She pulled it here and pressed it there. When Henry turned the motor off she slipped into her coat and went out.

The little roadster[4] bounced along on the dirt road by the river, raising the birds and driving the rabbits into the brush. Two cranes flapped heavily over the willow-line and dropped into the river-bed.

Far ahead on the road Elisa saw a dark speck. She knew.

She tried not to look as they passed it, but her eyes would not obey. She whispered to herself sadly, "He might have thrown them off the road. That wouldn't have been much trouble, not very much. But he kept the pot," she explained. "He had to keep the pot. That's why he couldn't get them off the road."

110 The roadster turned a bend and she saw the caravan ahead. She swung full around toward her husband so she could not see the little covered wagon and the mismatched team as the car passed them.

In a moment it was over. The thing was done. She did not look back.

She said loudly, to be heard above the motor, "It will be good, tonight, a good dinner."

"Now you're changed again," Henry complained. He took one hand from the wheel and patted her knee. "I ought to take you in to dinner oftener. It would be good for both of us. We get so heavy out on the ranch."

"Henry," she asked, "could we have wine at dinner?"

---

[4] An early roofless automobile, with a single seat for two or three passengers.

115   "Sure we could. Say! That will be fine."

She was silent for a while; then she said, "Henry, at those prize fights, do the men hurt each other very much?"

"Sometimes a little, not often. Why?"

"Well, I've read how they break noses, and blood runs down their chests. I've read how the fighting gloves get heavy and soggy with blood."

He looked around at her. "What's the matter, Elisa? I didn't know you read things like that." He brought the car to a stop, then turned to the right over the Salinas River bridge.

120   "Do any women ever go to the fights?" she asked.

"Oh, sure, some. What's the matter, Elisa? Do you want to go? I don't think you'd like it, but I'll take you if you really want to go."

She relaxed limply in the seat. "Oh, no. No. I don't want to go. I'm sure I don't." Her face was turned away from him. "It will be enough if we can have wine. It will be plenty." She turned up her coat collar so he could not see that she was crying weakly—like an old woman.

READING AND REACTING

1. The first few paragraphs establish the setting of the story. What details does Steinbeck choose to emphasize? Why?

2. What symbolic significance does the image of the pot have at various points in the story? (Notice that in paragraph 1, the valley where Elisa and Henry Allen live is described as a "closed pot.")

3. Throughout the story Mrs. Allen says she has a gift. What is her gift? How is her gift important to the story?

4. What effect does the man in the wagon have on Mrs. Allen? What does he symbolize to her?

5. What do the chrysanthemums mean to Mrs. Allen? To the man in the wagon? Why do you think the man in the wagon takes such an interest in Mrs. Allen's chrysanthemums?

6. In paragraphs 64 through 71, Steinbeck describes Mrs. Allen's planting of the chrysanthemums; in paragraphs 93 and 94, he describes her preparation for her night out with her husband. Why does he dwell on these details? What do they tell readers about her?

7. Why do you think the man in the wagon throws away the chrysanthemum shoots? Why does Mrs. Allen react the way she does when she sees the chrysanthemums in the road? When she passes the wagon?

8. Why is Mrs. Allen so insistent on ordering wine with dinner? Why does she ask about the prize fights? Do you see these actions as symbolic? Explain.

9. **JOURNAL ENTRY** Do you think Mrs. Allen is as trapped as she thinks she is? What, if anything, could she do to improve her situation?

10. **Critical Perspective** In her article "Steinbeck's Strong Women in Short Stories," critic Marilyn L. Mitchell points out that Elisa feels frustrated by the fact that she and her work are not taken seriously by the men around her. According to Mitchell, Elisa is frustrated "in her role as a rancher's wife; and part of Elisa's sense of frustration stems from the fact that her work, even the dirty work of gardening, remains 'woman's work.'"

Are there any hints in the story that the men, like Elisa, are also frustrated and victimized?

Related Works: "The Story of an Hour" (p. 77), "Araby" (p. 254), "Wild Plums" (p. 415), "My Mama Moved among the Days" (p. 678), *Trifles* (p. 1163)

◆ Writing Suggestions: Symbol and Allegory

1. Select a story from anywhere in this text, and discuss its use of symbols.
2. Strangers figure prominently in "Young Goodman Brown" and "The Chrysanthemums." Write an essay in which you discuss the possible symbolic significance of strangers in each story. If you like, you can also discuss Arnold Friend in "Where Are You Going, Where Have You Been?" (p. 614).
3. Write an essay in which you discuss the conflicts present in "Young Goodman Brown," showing how the allegorical elements in the story reflect and reinforce these conflicts.
4. If Shirley Jackson had wished to write "The Lottery" as an allegory whose purpose was to expose the evils of Nazi Germany, what revisions would she have had to make to convey the dangers of blind obedience to authority? Consider the story's symbols, the characters (and their names), and the setting.
5. In a number of works in this anthology, prized possessions function as symbols—for example, the quilt in "Everyday Use," the grinding ball in "The Secret Lion," the clock and de Spain's rug in "Barn Burning," and the glass animals in *The Glass Menagerie.* Write an essay in which you discuss the symbolic significance of a prized possession in any two works in this text.
6. **Web Activity** The following Web site contains information about Nathaniel Hawthorne:

   http://www.cwrl.utexas.edu/%7Edaniel/amlit/goodman/goodman.html

   From that site, read "A View of Young Goodman Brown" by Bert A. Mikosh, and consider what the article says about Puritanism. Then write an essay applying Mikosh's ideas to the theme of good versus evil in "Young Goodman Brown," focusing on the portrait of Puritanism that emerges from the story and on the Puritans' difficulty in dealing with the issue of good versus evil.

CHAPTER 10

Theme

◆ ◆ ◆

The truth about any subject only comes when all the sides of the story are put together, and all their different meanings make one new meaning.

ALICE WALKER, *Discovering Fiction*

I think a writer's job is to provoke questions. I like to think that if someone's read a book of mine, they've had—I don't know—the literary equivalent of a shower. Something that would start them thinking in a slightly different way perhaps. That's what I think writers are for.

DORIS LESSING, *Writers at Work,* 9th ed.

A work of art encountered as a work of art is an experience, not a statement or an answer to a question. Art is not only about something; it is something. A work of art is a thing in the world, not just a text or commentary on the world.

SUSAN SONTAG, "On Style" in *Against Interpretation*

One of the most difficult things is the first paragraph. I have spent many months on a first paragraph, and once I get it, the rest just comes out very easily. In the first paragraph you solve most of the problems with your book. The theme is defined, the style, the tone. At least in my case, the first paragraph is a kind of sample of what the rest of the book is going to be. That's why writing a book of short stories is much more difficult than writing a novel. Every time you write a short story, you have to begin all over again.

GABRIEL GARCÍA MÁRQUEZ, *Writers at Work,* 6th ed.

The concepts of beauty and ugliness are mysterious to me. Many people write about them. In mulling over them, I try to get underneath them and see what they mean, undersand the impact they have on what people do. I also write about love and death. The problem I face as a writer is to make my stories mean something.

TONI MORRISON, *Discovering Fiction*

◆ ◆ ◆

The **theme** of a work of literature is its central or dominant idea. *Theme* is not the same as *plot* or *subject,* two terms with which it is sometimes confused. A simple *plot summary* of Tadeusz Borowski's "Silence," a story about survivors of the Holocaust, could be "Prisoners are liberated from a concentration camp and, despite the warnings of the American officer, they kill a captured German guard." The statement " 'Silence' is about freed prisoners and a guard" could define the *subject* of the story. A statement of the *theme* of "Silence," however, would have to do more than summarize its plot or identify its subject; it would have to convey the values and ideas expressed by the story. Many effective stories are complex, expressing more than one theme, and "Silence" is no exception. You could say, for example, that "Silence" suggests that human beings have a need for vengeance. You could also say the story demonstrates that silence is sometimes the only response possible when one is confronting unspeakable horrors. Although both these themes—and others—are expressed in the story, one theme seems to dominate—the idea that under extreme conditions the oppressed can become as morally bankrupt as their oppressors.

When you write about theme, you need to do more than tell what happens in the story. The theme you identify should be a general idea that extends beyond the story and applies to the world outside fiction. Compare these two statements about Edgar Allan Poe's "The Cask of Amontillado" (p. 219):

> Poe's "The Cask of Amontillado" is about a man who loses his humanity because of his obsessive desire to avenge himself on Fortunato.

> Poe's "The Cask of Amontillado" suggests that when the desire for revenge becomes obsessive, it can deprive individuals of all that makes them human.

The first statement merely tells what the story is about; the second statement identifies the story's theme, a general observation about humanity.

Granted, some short works (fairy tales or fables, for example) have themes that can be summed up as *clichés*—overused phrases or expressions—or as *morals*—lessons dramatized by the work. The fairy tale "Cinderella," for example, expresses the clichéd theme that a virtuous girl who endures misfortune will eventually achieve her just reward; the fable "The Tortoise and the Hare" illustrates the moral "Slow and steady wins the race." Like "The Cask of Amontillado," however, the stories in this anthology have themes that are more complex than clichés or morals.

INTERPRETING THEMES

◇ ◇ ◇

Contemporary critical theory holds that the theme of a work of fiction is as much the creation of readers as of the writer. The readers' backgrounds, knowledge, values, and beliefs all play a part in determining the theme or themes they will identify in a work. Most readers, for example, will realize that David Michael Kaplan's story "Doe Season" (p. 349)—in which the main character goes hunting, kills her first deer, and is forced to confront suffering and death—expresses a conventional **initiation theme,** revealing growing up to be a disillusioning and painful process. Still, different readers bring different perspectives to the story and, in some cases, see different themes.

During a classroom discussion of "Doe Season," a student familiar with hunting saw more than his classmates did in the story's conventional initiation theme. He knew that in many states there really is a doe season, which lasts approximately three days. Shorter than the ten-day buck season, its purpose is to enable hunters to control the size of the deer herd by killing females. This knowledge enabled the student to conclude that by the end of the story the female child's innocence must inevitably be destroyed, just as the doe must be.

Another student pointed out that the participation of Andy—a female who uses a male name—in hunting, a traditional male rite of passage, leads to her killing the deer and to her subsequent disillusionment. It also leads to her decision to abandon her nickname. By contrasting "Andrea" with "Andy," the story reveals the inner conflict between her "female" nature (illustrated by her compassion) and her desire to emulate the men to whom killing is a sport. This interpretation led the student to conclude that the theme of "Doe Season" is that males and females have very different outlooks on life.

Other students did not accept the negative characterization of the story's male characters that the above interpretation implies. They pointed out that the father is a sympathetic figure who is extremely supportive; he encourages and defends his daughter. He takes her hunting because he loves her, not because he wants to initiate her into life or to hurt her. One student mentioned that Andy's reaction (called *buck fever*) when she sees the doe is common in children who kill their first deer. In light of this information, several students thought that far from being about irreconcilable male and female perspectives, "Doe Season" makes a statement about a young girl who is hunting for her own identity and who in the process discovers her own mortality. Her father is therefore the agent who enables her to confront the inevitability of death, a fact she must accept if she is going to take her place in the adult world. In this sense, the theme of the story is the idea that in order to mature, a child must come to terms with the reality of death.

Different readers may see different themes in a story, but any interpretation of a theme must make sense in light of what is actually in the story. Evidence from the work, not just your own feelings or assumptions, must support your interpretation, and a single symbol or one statement by a character is not enough in itself to reveal a story's theme. Therefore, you must identify a cross section of examples from the text to support your interpretation of the story's theme. If you say that the theme of James Joyce's "Araby" (p. 254) is that an innocent idealist is inevitably doomed to disillusionment, you have to find examples from the text to support your statement. You could begin with the title, concluding that the word *Araby* suggests dreams of exotic beauty that the boy tries to find when he goes to the bazaar. You could reinforce your idea about the elusiveness of beauty by pointing out that Mangan's unattainable sister is a symbol of this beauty that the boy wants so desperately to find. Finally, you could show how idealism is ultimately crushed by society: at the end of the story, the boy stands alone in the darkness and realizes that his dreams of beauty are childish fantasies. Although other readers may have different responses to "Araby," they should find your interpretation reasonable if you support it with enough examples.

IDENTIFYING THEMES
◆ ◆ ◆

Every element of a story can shed light on its themes. As you analyze a short story, look for features that reveal and reinforce what you perceive to be the story's most important ideas.

The *title* of a story can often provide insight into the theme or themes of a story. The title of an F. Scott Fitzgerald story, "Babylon Revisited," emphasizes a major idea in the story—that Paris of the 1920s is like Babylon, the ancient city the Bible singles out as the epitome of evil and corruption. The story's protagonist, Charlie Wales, comes to realize that no matter how much money he lost after the stock market crash, he lost more—his wife and his daughter—during the boom, when he was in Paris. Charlie's search through his past—his return to "Babylon"—provides new meaning to his life and offers at least a small bit of hope for the future.

Sometimes a *narrator's or character's statement* can reveal a theme. For example, at the beginning of Alberto Alvaro Ríos's "The Secret Lion" (p. 49), the first-person narrator says, "I was twelve and in junior high school and something happened that we didn't have a name for, but it was there nonetheless like a lion, and roaring, roaring that way the biggest things do. Everything changed." Although the narrator does not directly announce the story's theme, he does suggest that the story will convey the idea that the price children pay for growing up is realizing that everything changes, that nothing stays the way it is.

The *arrangement of events* in a story can suggest a story's theme, as it does in an Ernest Hemingway story, "The Short Happy Life of Francis Macomber." At the beginning of the story, the title character is a coward who is stuck in an unhappy marriage. As the story progresses, he gradually learns the nature of courage and, finally, finds it in himself. At the moment of his triumph, however, Francis is killed; his "happy life" is short indeed. The way the events of the story are presented, through foreshadowing and flashbacks, reveals the connection between Macomber's marriage and his behavior as a hunter, and this connection in turn helps to reveal a possible theme: that sometimes courage can be more important than life itself.

A story's *conflict* can offer clues to its theme. In "Araby" the young boy believes that his society neglects art and beauty and glorifies the mundane. This conflict between the boy's idealism and his world can help readers understand why the boy isolates himself in his room reading books and why he retreats into dreams of idealized love. A major theme of the story—that growing up leads to the loss of youthful idealism—is revealed by this central conflict.

Similarly, the main character in "The Yellow Wall-Paper" (p. 168), a woman who has recently had a baby, is in conflict with the nineteenth-century society in which she lives. She is suffering from "temporary nervous depression," what doctors today recognize as postpartum depression. Following the practice of the time, her physician has ordered complete bed rest and has instructed her husband to deprive her of all mental and physical stimulation. This harsh treatment leads the narrator to lose her grasp on reality; eventually, she begins to hallucinate. The central conflict of the story is clearly between the woman and her society, controlled by men. This conflict communicates the theme: that in nineteenth-century America, women are controlled not just by their husbands and the male medical establishment, but also by society as a whole.

The *point of view* of a story can also help shed light on theme. For instance, a writer's use of an unreliable first-person narrator can help to communicate the theme of a story. Thus, Montresor's self-serving first-person account of his crime in "The Cask of Amontillado"—and his convincing attempts to justify these actions—enable readers to understand the dangers of irrational anger and misplaced ideas about honor. The voice of a third-person narrator can also help to convey a story's theme. For example, the detachment of the narrator in Stephen Crane's Civil War novel *The Red Badge of Courage* reinforces the theme of the novel: that bravery, cowardice, battle, and even life itself are insignificant when set beside the indifference of the universe.

Quite often a story will give names, places, and objects symbolic significance. These *symbols* can not only enrich the story, but also help to convey a central theme. For example, the rocking horse in D. H. Lawrence's "The Rocking-Horse Winner" (p. 362) can be seen as a symbol of the boy's desperate desire to remain a child. Interpreted in this way, it reinforces the theme that innocence cannot survive when it confronts greed and selfishness. Similarly, Hawthorne's "Young Goodman Brown" (p. 304) uses symbols such as the walking stick, the woods, sunset and night, and the vague shadows to develop one of its central themes: that once a person strays from the path of faith, evil is everywhere.

Finally, *changes in a character* can shed light on the theme or themes of the story. The main character in Charles Baxter's "Gryphon" (p. 134), for example, eventually comes to realize that the "lies" Miss Ferenczi tells may be closer to the truth than the "facts" his teachers present, and his changing attitude toward Miss Ferenczi helps to communicate the story's central theme about the nature of truth.

✷ CHECKLIST: WRITING ABOUT THEME

✓ What is the central theme of the story?

✓ What other themes can you identify?

✓ Does the title of the story suggest a theme?

✓ Does the narrator, or any character, make statements that express or imply a theme?

✓ In what way does the arrangement of events in the story suggest a theme?

✓ In what way does the central conflict of the story suggest a theme?

✓ How does the point of view shed light on the story's central theme?

✓ Do any symbols suggest a theme?

✓ Do any characters in the story change in any significant way? Do their changes convey a particular theme?

✓ Have you clearly identified the story's central theme, rather than just summarized the plot or stated the subject?

✓ Does your statement of the story's central theme make a general observation that has an application beyond the story itself?

◈ **DAVID MICHAEL KAPLAN** (1946–   ) is one of a group of American writers who, along with South American writers such as Gabriel García Márquez of Colombia, are called "magic realists." Magic realists work outside of the "hobbits and wizards" borders of traditional fantasy writing, seamlessly interweaving magical elements with detailed, realistically drawn "everyday" settings. These elements, says a reviewer of Kaplan's work, are invoked "to illuminate and underscore heightened moments of reality." The story "Doe Season," which appears in Kaplan's debut short story collection, *Comfort* (1987), was included in *Best American Short Stories 1985*. Kaplan's first novel, *Skating in the Dark,* was published in 1991.

Interestingly, the stories in *Comfort* break from classic "first-time author" tradition by sidestepping the autobiographical, young-man-comes-of-age theme. Instead, these stories are about young girls—or young women—coming to grips with parents (present or absent) and with loss and searching for ways to resolve their ambivalence about becoming women. In "Doe Season" Andy's surreal encounter with the doe may be a dream, but the beauty and horror of their meeting will affect the rest of her life.

CULTURAL CONTEXT ◊   When European settlers came to America, deer roamed freely from coast to coast, and the pioneers hunted deer to put meat on the table. It wasn't until after the end of the nineteenth century that deer hunting became less a means of survival than a sport. Regardless of the purpose, however, deer hunting has long been viewed as a coming-of-age ritual for young men. In fact, even today, a boy's first hunting trip is symbolic of his first step into adulthood.

◊ ◊ ◊

DAVID MICHAEL KAPLAN

Doe Season
(1985)

They were always the same woods, she thought sleepily as they drove through the early morning darkness—deep and immense, covered with yesterday's snowfall, which had frozen overnight. They were the same woods that lay behind her house, *and they stretch all the way to here*, she thought, *for miles and miles, longer than I could walk in a day, or a week even, but they are still the same woods*. The thought made her feel good: it was like thinking of God; it was like thinking of the space between here and the moon; it was like thinking of all the foreign countries from her geography book where even now, Andy knew, people were going to bed, while they—she and her father and Charlie Spoon and Mac, Charlie's eleven-year-old son—were driving deeper into the Pennsylvania country-side, to go hunting.

They had risen long before dawn. Her mother, yawning and not trying to hide her sleepiness, cooked them eggs and French toast. Her father smoked a cigarette and flicked ashes into his saucer while Andy listened, wondering *Why doesn't he come?* and *Won't he ever come?* until at last a car pulled into the graveled drive and honked. "That will be Charlie Spoon," her father said; he always said "Charlie Spoon," even though his real name was Spreun, because Charlie was, in a sense, shaped like a spoon, with a large head and a narrow waist and chest.

Andy's mother kissed her and her father and said, "Well, have a good time" and "Be careful." Soon they were outside in the bitter dark, loading gear by the back-porch light, their breath steaming. The woods behind the house were then only a black streak against the wash of night.

Andy dozed in the car and woke to find that it was half light. Mac—also sleeping—had slid against her. She pushed him away and looked out the window. Her breath clouded the glass, and she was cold; the car's heater didn't work right. They were riding over gentle hills, the woods on both sides now—the same woods, she knew, because she had been watching the whole way, even while she slept. They had been in her dreams, and she had never lost sight of them.

5   Charlie Spoon was driving. "I don't understand why she's coming," he said to her father. "How old is she anyway—eight?"

"Nine," her father replied. "She's small for her age."

"So—nine. What's the difference? She'll just add to the noise and get tired besides."

"No, she won't," her father said. "She can walk me to death. And she'll bring good luck, you'll see. Animals—I don't know how she does it, but they come right up to her. We go walking in the woods, and we'll spot more raccoons and possums and such than I ever see when I'm alone."

Charlie grunted.

10   "Besides, she's not a bad little shot, even if she doesn't hunt yet. She shoots the .22 real good."

"Popgun," Charlie said, and snorted. "And target shooting ain't deer hunting."

"Well, she's not gonna be shooting anyway, Charlie," her father said. "Don't worry. She'll be no bother."

"I still don't know why she's coming," Charlie said.

"Because she wants to, and I want her to. Just like you and Mac. No difference."

15   Charlie turned onto a side road and after a mile or so slowed down. "That's it!" he cried. He stopped, backed up, and entered a narrow dirt road almost hidden by trees. Five hundred yards down, the road ran parallel to a fenced-in field. Charlie parked in a cleared area deeply rutted by frozen tractor tracks. The gate was locked. *In the spring,* Andy thought, *there will be cows here, and a dog that chases them,* but now the field was unmarked and bare.

"This is it," Charlie Spoon declared. "Me and Mac was up here just two weeks ago, scouting it out, and there's deer. Mac saw the tracks."

"That's right," Mac said.

"Well, we'll just see about that," her father said, putting on his gloves. He turned to Andy. "How you doing, honeybun?"

"Just fine," she said.

20   Andy shivered and stamped as they unloaded: first the rifles, which they unsheathed and checked, sliding the bolts, sighting through scopes, adjusting the slings; then the gear, their food and tents and sleeping bags and stove stored in four backpacks—three big ones for Charlie Spoon and her father and Mac, and a day pack for her.

"That's about your size," Mac said, to tease her.

She reddened and said, "Mac, I can carry a pack big as yours any day." He laughed and pressed his knee against the back of hers, so that her leg buckled. "Cut it out," she said. She wanted to make an iceball and throw it at him, but she knew that her father and Charlie were anxious to get going, and she didn't want to displease them.

Mac slid under the gate, and they handed the packs over to him. Then they slid under and began walking across the field toward the same woods that ran all the way back to her home, where even now her mother was probably rising again to wash their breakfast dishes and make herself a fresh pot of coffee. *She is there, and we are here:* the thought satisfied Andy. There was no place else she would rather be.

Mac came up beside her. "Over there's Canada," he said, nodding toward the woods.

25 "Huh!" she said. "Not likely."

"I don't mean *right* over there. I mean farther up north. You think I'm dumb?"

Dumb as your father, she thought.

"Look at that," Mac said, pointing to a piece of cow dung lying on a spot scraped bare of snow. "A frozen meadow muffin." He picked it up and sailed it at her. "Catch!"

"Mac!" she yelled. His laugh was as gawky as he was. She walked faster. He seemed different today somehow, bundled in his yellow-and-black-checkered coat, a rifle in hand, his silly floppy hat not quite covering his ears. They all seemed different as she watched them trudge through the snow—Mac and her father and Charlie Spoon—bigger, maybe, as if the cold landscape enlarged rather than diminished them, so that they, the only figures in that landscape, took on size and meaning just by being there. If they weren't there, everything would be quieter, and the woods would be the same as before. *But they are here,* Andy thought, looking behind her at the boot prints in the snow, *and I am too, and so it's all different.*

30 "We'll go down to the cut where we found those deer tracks," Charlie said as they entered the woods. "Maybe we'll get lucky and get a late one coming through."

The woods descended into a gully. The snow was softer and deeper here, so that often Andy sank to her knees. Charlie and Mac worked the top of the gully while she and her father walked along the base some thirty yards behind them. "If they miss the first shot, we'll get the second," her father said, and she nodded as if she had known this all the time. She listened to the crunch of their boots, their breathing, and the drumming of a distant woodpecker. And the crackling. In winter the woods crackled as if everything were straining, ready to snap like dried chicken bones.

We are hunting, Andy thought. The cold air burned her nostrils.

They stopped to make lunch by a rock outcropping that protected them from the wind. Her father heated the bean soup her mother had made for them, and they ate it with bread already stiff from the cold. He and Charlie took a few pulls from a flask of Jim Beam while she scoured the plates with snow and repacked them. Then they all had coffee with sugar and powdered milk, and her father poured her a cup too. "We won't tell your momma," he said, and Mac laughed. Andy held the cup the way her father did, not by the handle but around the rim. The coffee tasted smoky. She felt a little queasy, but she drank it all.

Charlie Spoon picked his teeth with a fingernail. "Now, you might've noticed one thing," he said.

35 "What's that?" her father asked.

"You might've noticed you don't hear no rifles. That's because there ain't no other hunters here. We've got the whole damn woods to ourselves. Now, I ask you—do I know how to find 'em?"

"We haven't seen deer yet, neither."

"Oh, we will," Charlie said, "but not for a while now." He leaned back against the rock. "Deer're sleeping, resting up for the evening feed."

"I seen a deer behind our house once, and it was afternoon," Andy said.

40 "Yeah, honey, but that was *before* deer season," Charlie said, grinning. "They know something now. They're smart that way."

"That's right," Mac said.

Andy looked at her father—had she said something stupid?

"Well, Charlie," he said, "if they know so much, how come so many get themselves shot?"

"Them's the ones that don't *believe* what they know," Charlie replied. The men laughed. Andy hesitated, and then laughed with them.

45 They moved on, as much to keep warm as to find a deer. The wind became even stronger. Blowing through the treetops, it sounded like the ocean, and once Andy thought she could smell salt air. But that was impossible; the ocean was *hundreds* of miles away, farther than Canada even. She and her parents had gone last summer to stay for a week at a motel on the New Jersey shore. That was the first time she'd seen the ocean, and it frightened her. It was huge and empty, yet always moving. Everything lay hidden. If you walked in it, you couldn't see how deep it was or what might be below; if you swam, something could pull you under and you'd never be seen again. Its musky, rank smell made her think of things dying. Her mother had floated beyond the breakers, calling to her to come in, but Andy wouldn't go farther than a few feet into the surf. Her mother swam and splashed with animal-like delight while her father, smiling shyly, held his white arms above the waist-deep water as if afraid to get them wet. Once a comber rolled over and sent them both tossing, and when her mother tried to stand up, the surf receding behind, Andy saw that her mother's swimsuit top had come off, so that her breasts swayed free, her nipples like two dark eyes. Embarrassed, Andy looked around: except for two women under a yellow umbrella farther up, the beach was empty. Her mother stood up unsteadily, regained her footing. Taking what seemed the longest time, she calmly refixed her top. Andy lay on the beach towel and closed her eyes. The sound of the surf made her head ache.

And now it was winter; the sky was already dimming, not just with the absence of light but with a mist that clung to the hunters' faces like cobwebs. They made camp early. Andy was chilled. When she stood still, she kept wiggling her toes to make sure they were there. Her father rubbed her arms and held her to him briefly, and that felt better. She unpacked the food while the others put up the tents.

"How about rounding us up some firewood, Mac?" Charlie asked.

"I'll do it," Andy said. Charlie looked at her thoughtfully and then handed her the canvas carrier.

There wasn't much wood on the ground, so it took her a while to get a good load. She was about a hundred yards from camp, near a cluster of high, lichen-covered boulders, when she saw through a crack in the rock a buck and two does walking gingerly, almost daintily, through the alder trees. She tried to hush her breathing as they passed not more than twenty yards away. There was nothing she could do. If she yelled, they'd be gone; by the time she got back to camp, they'd be gone. The buck stopped, nostrils quivering, tail up and alert. He looked directly at her. Still she didn't move, not one muscle. He was a beautiful buck, the color of late-turned maple leaves. Unafraid, he lowered his tail, and he and his does silently merged into the trees. Andy walked back to camp and dropped the firewood.

50 "I saw three deer," she said. "A buck and two does."

"Where?" Charlie Spoon cried, looking behind her as if they might have followed her into camp.

"In the woods yonder. They're gone now."

"Well, hell!" Charlie banged his coffee cup against his knee.

"Didn't I say she could find animals?" her father said, grinning.

55 "Too late to go after them," Charlie muttered. "It'll be dark in a quarter hour. Damn!"

"Damn," Mac echoed.

"They just walk right up to her," her father said.

"Well, leastwise this proves there's deer here." Charlie began snapping long branches into shorter ones. "You know, I think I'll stick with you," he told Andy, "since you're so good at finding deer and all. How'd that be?"

"Okay, I guess," Andy murmured. She hoped he was kidding; no way did she want to hunt with Charlie Spoon. Still, she was pleased he had said it.

60 Her father and Charlie took one tent, she and Mac the other. When they were in their sleeping bags, Mac said in the darkness, "I bet you really didn't see no deer, did you?"

She sighed. "I did, Mac. Why would I lie?"

"How big was the buck?"

"Four point. I counted."

Mac snorted.

65 "You just believe what you want, Mac," she said testily.

"Too bad it ain't buck season," he said. "Well, I got to go pee."

"So pee."

She heard him turn in his bag. "You ever see it?" he asked.

"It? What's 'it'?"

70 "It. A pecker."

"Sure," she lied.

"Whose? Your father's?"

She was uncomfortable. "No," she said.

"Well, whose then?"

75 "Oh I don't know! Leave me be, why don't you?"

"Didn't see a deer, didn't see a pecker," Mac said teasingly.

She didn't answer right away. Then she said, "My cousin Lewis. I saw his."

"Well, how old's he?"

"One and a half."

80 "Ha! A baby! A baby's is like a little worm. It ain't a real one at all."

If he says he'll show me his, she thought, *I'll kick him. I'll just get out of my bag and kick him.*

"I went hunting with my daddy and Versh and Danny Simmons last year in buck season," Mac said, "and we got ourselves one. And we hog-dressed the thing. You know what that is, don't you?"

"No," she said. She was confused. What was he talking about now?

"That's when you cut him open and take out all his guts, so the meat don't spoil. Makes him lighter to pack out, too."

85 She tried to imagine what the deer's guts might look like, pulled from the gaping hole. "What do you do with them?" she said. "The guts?"

"Oh, just leave 'em for the bears."

She ran her finger like a knife blade along her belly.

"When we left them on the ground," Mac said, "they smoked. Like they were cooking."

"Huh," she said.

90 "They cut off the deer's pecker, too, you know."

Andy imagined Lewis's pecker and shuddered. "Mac, you're disgusting."

He laughed. "Well, I gotta go pee." She heard him rustle out of his bag. "Broo!" he cried, flapping his arms. "It's cold!"

He makes so much noise, she thought, *just noise and more noise.*

Her father woke them before first light. He warned them to talk softly and said that they were going to the place where Andy had seen the deer, to try to cut them off on their way back from their night feeding. Andy couldn't shake off her sleep. Stuffing her sleeping bag into its sack seemed to take an hour, and tying her boots was the strangest thing she'd ever done. Charlie Spoon made hot chocolate and oatmeal with raisins. Andy closed her eyes and, between beats of her heart, listened to the breathing of the forest. *When I open my eyes, it will be lighter,* she decided. But when she did, it was still just as dark, except for the swaths of their flashlights and the hissing blue flame of the stove. *There has to be just one moment when it all changes from dark to light,* Andy thought. She had missed it yesterday, in the car; today she would watch more closely.

95 But when she remembered again, it was already first light and they had moved to the rocks by the deer trail and had set up shooting positions—Mac and Charlie Spoon on the up-trail side, she and her father behind them, some six feet up on a ledge. The day became brighter, the sun piercing the tall pines, raking the hunters, yet providing little warmth. Andy now smelled alder and pine and the slightly rotten odor of rock

lichen. She rubbed her hand over the stone and considered that it must be very old, had probably been here before the giant pines, *before anyone was in these woods at all.* A chipmunk sniffed on a nearby branch. She aimed an imaginary rifle and pressed the trigger. The chipmunk froze, then scurried away. Her legs were cramping on the narrow ledge. Her father seemed to doze, one hand in his parka, the other cupped lightly around the rifle. She could smell his scent of old wool and leather. His cheeks were speckled with gray-black whiskers, and he worked his jaws slightly, as if chewing a small piece of gum.

Please let us get a deer, she prayed.

A branch snapped on the other side of the rock face. Her father's hand stiffened on the rifle, startling her—*He hasn't been sleeping at all,* she marveled—and then his jaw relaxed, as did the lines around his eyes, and she heard Charlie Spoon call, "Yo, don't shoot, it's us." He and Mac appeared from around the rock. They stopped beneath the ledge. Charlie solemnly crossed his arms.

"I don't believe we're gonna get any deer here," he said drily.

Andy's father lowered his rifle to Charlie and jumped down from the ledge. Then he reached up for Andy. She dropped into his arms and he set her gently on the ground.

100   Mac sidled up to her. "I knew you didn't see no deer," he said.

"Just because they don't come when you want 'em to don't mean she didn't see them," her father said.

Still, she felt bad. Her telling about the deer had caused them to spend the morning there, cold and expectant, with nothing to show for it.

They tramped through the woods for another two hours, not caring much about noise. Mac found some deer tracks, and they argued about how old they were. They split up for a while and then rejoined at an old logging road that deer might use, and followed it. The road crossed a stream, which had mostly frozen over but in a few spots still caught leaves and twigs in an icy swirl. They forded it by jumping from rock to rock. The road narrowed after that, and the woods thickened.

They stopped for lunch, heating up Charlie's wife's corn chowder. Andy's father cut squares of applesauce cake with his hunting knife and handed them to her and Mac, who ate his almost daintily. Andy could faintly taste knife oil on the cake. She was tired. She stretched her leg; the muscle that had cramped on the rock still ached.

105   "Might as well relax," her father said, as if reading her thoughts. "We won't find deer till suppertime."

Charlie Spoon leaned back against his pack and folded his hands across his stomach. "Well, even if we don't get a deer," he said expansively, "it's still great to be out here, breathe some fresh air, clomp around a bit. Get away from the house and the old lady." He winked at Mac, who looked away.

"That's what the woods are all about, anyway," Charlie said. "It's where the women don't want to go." He bowed his head toward Andy.

"With your exception, of course, little lady." He helped himself to another piece of applesauce cake.

"She ain't a woman," Mac said.

"Well, she damn well's gonna be," Charlie said. He grinned at her. "Or will you? You're half a boy anyway. You go by a boy's name. What's your real name? Andrea, ain't it?"

110   "That's right," she said. She hoped that if she didn't look at him, Charlie would stop.

"Well, which do you like? Andy or Andrea?"

"Don't matter," she mumbled. "Either."

"She's always been Andy to me," her father said.

Charlie Spoon was still grinning. "So what are you gonna be, Andrea? A boy or a girl?"

115   "I'm a girl," she said.

"But you want to go hunting and fishing and everything, huh?"

"She can do whatever she likes," her father said.

"Hell, you might as well have just had a boy and be done with it!" Charlie exclaimed.

"That's funny," her father said, and chuckled. "That's just what her momma tells me."

120   They were looking at her, and she wanted to get away from them all, even from her father, who chose to joke with them.

"I'm going to walk a bit," she said.

She heard them laughing as she walked down the logging trail. She flapped her arms; she whistled. *I don't care how much noise I make,* she thought. Two grouse flew from the underbrush, startling her. A little farther down, the trail ended in a clearing that enlarged into a frozen meadow; beyond it the woods began again. A few moldering posts were all that was left of a fence that had once enclosed the field. The low afternoon sunlight reflected brightly off the snow, so that Andy's eyes hurt. She squinted hard. A gust of wind blew across the field, stinging her face. And then, as if it had been waiting for her, the doe emerged from the trees opposite and stepped cautiously into the field. Andy watched: it stopped and stood quietly for what seemed a long time and then ambled across. It stopped again about seventy yards away and began to browse in a patch of sugar grass uncovered by the wind. Carefully, slowly, never taking her eyes from the doe, Andy walked backward, trying to step into the boot prints she'd already made. When she was far enough back into the woods, she turned and walked faster, her heart racing. *Please let it stay,* she prayed.

"There's doe in the field yonder," she told them.

They got their rifles and hurried down the trail.

125   "No use," her father said. "We're making too much noise any way you look at it."

"At least we got us the wind in our favor," Charlie Spoon said, breathing heavily.

But the doe was still there, grazing.

"Good Lord," Charlie whispered. He looked at her father. "Well, whose shot?"

"Andy spotted it," her father said in a low voice. "Let her shoot it."

130   "What!" Charlie's eyes widened.

Andy couldn't believe what her father had just said. She'd only shot tin cans and targets; she'd never even fired her father's .30-.30, and she'd never killed anything.

"I can't," she whispered.

"That's right, she can't," Charlie Spoon insisted. "She's not old enough and she don't have a license even if she was!"

"Well, who's to tell?" her father said in a low voice. "Nobody's going to know but us." He looked at her. "Do you want to shoot it, punkin?"

135   *Why doesn't it hear us?* she wondered. *Why doesn't it run away?* "I don't know," she said.

"Well, I'm sure as hell gonna shoot it," Charlie said. Her father grasped Charlie's rifle barrel and held it. His voice was steady.

"Andy's a good shot. It's her deer. She found it, not you. You'd still be sitting on your ass back in camp." He turned to her again. "Now—do you want to shoot it, Andy? Yes or no."

He was looking at her; they were all looking at her. Suddenly she was angry at the deer, who refused to hear them, who wouldn't run away even when it could. "I'll shoot it," she said. Charlie turned away in disgust.

She lay on the ground and pressed the rifle stock against her shoulder bone. The snow was cold through her parka; she smelled oil and wax and damp earth. She pulled off one glove with her teeth. "It sights just like the .22," her father said gently. "Cartridge's already chambered." As she had done so many times before, she sighted down the scope; now the doe was in the reticle. She moved the barrel until the cross hairs lined up. Her father was breathing beside her.

140   "Aim where the chest and legs meet, or a little above, punkin," he was saying calmly. "That's the killing shot."

But now, seeing it in the scope, Andy was hesitant. Her finger weakened on the trigger. Still, she nodded at what her father said and sighted again, the cross hairs lining up in exactly the same spot—the doe had hardly moved, its brownish-gray body outlined starkly against the blue-backed snow. *It doesn't know,* Andy thought. *It just doesn't know.* And as she looked, deer and snow and faraway trees flattened within the circular frame to become like a picture on a calendar, not real, and she felt calm, as if she had been dreaming everything—the day, the deer, the hunt itself. And she, finger on trigger, was only a part of that dream.

"Shoot!" Charlie hissed.

Through the scope she saw the deer look up, ears high and straining.

Charlie groaned, and just as he did, and just at the moment when Andy knew—*knew*—the doe would bound away, as if she could feel its haunches tensing and gathering power, she pulled the trigger. Later she would think, *I felt the recoil, I smelled the smoke, but I don't remember pulling the trigger.* Through the scope the deer seemed to shrink into itself, and then slowly knelt, hind legs first, head raised as if to cry out. It trembled, still straining to keep its head high, as if that alone would save it; failing, it collapsed, shuddered, and lay still.

145 "Whoee!" Mac cried.

"One shot! One shot!" her father yelled, clapping her on the back. Charlie Spoon was shaking his head and smiling dumbly.

"I told you she was a great little shot!" her father said. "I told you!" Mac danced and clapped his hands. She was dazed, not quite understanding what had happened. And then they were crossing the field toward the fallen doe, she walking dreamlike, the men laughing and joking, released now from the tension of silence and anticipation. Suddenly Mac pointed and cried out, "Look at that!"

The doe was rising, legs unsteady. They stared at it, unable to comprehend, and in that moment the doe regained its feet and looked at them, as if it too were trying to understand. Her father whistled softly. Charlie Spoon unslung his rifle and raised it to his shoulder, but the doe was already bounding away. His hurried shot missed, and the deer disappeared into the woods.

"Damn, damn, damn," he moaned.

150 "I don't believe it," her father said. "That deer was dead."

"Dead, hell!" Charlie yelled. "It was gutshot, that's all. Stunned and gutshot. Clean shot, my ass!"

What have I done? Andy thought.

Her father slung his rifle over his shoulder. "Well, let's go. It can't get too far."

"Hell, I've seen deer run ten miles gutshot," Charlie said. He waved his arms. "We may never find her!"

155 As they crossed the field, Mac came up to her and said in a low voice, "Gutshoot a deer, you'll go to hell."

"Shut up, Mac," she said, her voice cracking. It was a terrible thing she had done, she knew. She couldn't bear to think of the doe in pain and frightened. *Please let it die,* she prayed.

But though they searched all the last hour of daylight, so that they had to recross the field and go up the logging trail in a twilight made even deeper by thick, smoky clouds, they didn't find the doe. They lost its trail almost immediately in the dense stands of alderberry and larch.

"I am cold, and I am tired," Charlie Spoon declared. "And if you ask me, that deer's in another county already."

"No one's asking you, Charlie," her father said.

160 They had a supper of hard salami and ham, bread, and the rest of the applesauce cake. It seemed a bother to heat the coffee, so they had cold chocolate instead. Everyone turned in early.

"We'll find it in the morning, honeybun," her father said, as she went to her tent.

"I don't like to think of it suffering." She was almost in tears.

"It's dead already, punkin. Don't even think about it." He kissed her, his breath sour and his beard rough against her cheek.

Andy was sure she wouldn't get to sleep; the image of the doe falling, falling, then rising again, repeated itself whenever she closed her eyes. Then she heard an owl hoot and realized that it had awakened her, so she must have been asleep after all. She hoped the owl would hush, but instead it hooted louder. She wished her father or Charlie Spoon would wake up and do something about it, but no one moved in the other tent, and suddenly she was afraid that they had all decamped, wanting nothing more to do with her. She whispered, "Mac, Mac," to the sleeping bag where he should be, but no one answered. She tried to find the flashlight she always kept by her side, but couldn't, and she cried in panic, "Mac, are you there?" He mumbled something, and immediately she felt foolish and hoped he wouldn't reply.

165   When she awoke again, everything had changed. The owl was gone, the woods were still, and she sensed light, blue and pale, light where before there had been none. *The moon must have come out,* she thought. And it was warm, too, warmer than it should have been. She got out of her sleeping bag and took off her parka—it was that warm. Mac was asleep, wheezing like an old man. She unzipped the tent and stepped outside.

The woods were more beautiful than she had ever seen them. The moon made everything ice-rimmed glimmer with a crystallized, immanent light, while underneath that ice the branches of trees were as stark as skeletons. She heard a crunching in the snow, the one sound in all that silence, and there, walking down the logging trail into their camp, was the doe. Its body, like everything around her, was silvered with frost and moonlight. It walked past the tent where her father and Charlie Spoon were sleeping and stopped no more than six feet from her. Andy saw that she had shot it, yes, had shot it cleanly, just where she thought she had, the wound a jagged, bloody hole in the doe's chest.

A heart shot, she thought.

The doe stepped closer, so that Andy, if she wished, could have reached out and touched it. It looked at her as if expecting her to do this, and so she did, running her hand, slowly at first, along the rough, matted fur, then down to the edge of the wound, where she stopped. The doe stood still. Hesitantly, Andy felt the edge of the wound. The torn flesh was sticky and warm. The wound parted under her touch. And then, almost without her knowing it, her fingers were within, probing, yet still the doe didn't move. Andy pressed deeper, through flesh and muscle and sinew, until her whole hand and more was inside the wound and she had found the doe's heart, warm and beating. She cupped it gently in her hand. *Alive,* she marveled. *Alive.*

The heart quickened under her touch, becoming warmer and warmer until it was hot enough to burn. In pain, Andy tried to remove her hand, but the wound closed about it and held her fast. Her hand was burning. She cried out in agony, sure they would all hear and come help, but they didn't.

And then her hand pulled free, followed by a steaming rush of blood, more blood than she ever could have imagined—it covered her hand and arm, and she saw to her horror that her hand was steaming. She moaned and fell to her knees and plunged her hand into the snow. The doe looked at her gently and then turned and walked back up the trail.

170   In the morning, when she woke, Andy could still smell the blood, but she felt no pain. She looked at her hand. Even though it appeared unscathed, it felt weak and withered. She couldn't move it freely and was afraid the others would notice. *I will hide it in my jacket pocket,* she decided, *so nobody can see.* She ate the oatmeal that her father cooked and stayed apart from them all. No one spoke to her, and that suited her. A light snow began to fall. It was the last day of their hunting trip. She wanted to be home.

    Her father dumped the dregs of his coffee. "Well, let's go look for her," he said.

    Again they crossed the field. Andy lagged behind. She averted her eyes from the spot where the doe had fallen, already filling up with snow. Mac and Charlie entered the woods first, followed by her father. Andy remained in the field and considered the smear of gray sky, the nearby flock of crows pecking at unyielding stubble. *I will stay here,* she thought, *and not move for a long while.* But now someone—Mac—was yelling. Her father appeared at the woods' edge and waved for her to come. She ran and pushed through a brake of alderberry and larch. The thick underbrush scratched her face. For a moment she felt lost and looked wildly about. Then, where the brush thinned, she saw them standing quietly in the falling snow. They were staring down at the dead doe. A film covered its upturned eye, and its body was lightly dusted with snow.

    "I told you she wouldn't get too far," Andy's father said triumphantly. "We must've just missed her yesterday. Too blind to see."

    "We're just damn lucky no animal got to her last night," Charlie muttered.

175   Her father lifted the doe's foreleg. The wound was blood-clotted, brown, and caked like frozen mud. "Clean shot," he said to Charlie. He grinned. "My little girl."

    Then he pulled out his knife, the blade gray as the morning. Mac whispered to Andy, "Now watch this," while Charlie Spoon lifted the doe from behind by its forelegs so that its head rested between his knees, its underside exposed. Her father's knife sliced thickly from chest to belly to crotch, and Andy was running from them, back to the field and across, scattering the crows who cawed and circled angrily. And now they were all calling to her—Charlie Spoon and Mac and her father—crying *Andy, Andy* (but that wasn't her name, she would no longer be called that); yet louder than any of them was the wind blowing through the treetops, like the ocean where her mother floated in green water, also calling *Come in, come in,* while all around her roared the mocking of the terrible, now inevitable, sea.

READING AND REACTING

1. The initiation of a child into adulthood is a very common literary theme. In this story, hunting is presented as an initiation rite. In what way is hunting an appropriate coming-of-age ritual?
2. Which characters are in conflict in this story? What ideas are in conflict? How do these conflicts help to communicate the story's initiation theme?
3. In the story's opening paragraph and elsewhere, Andy finds comfort and reassurance in the idea that the woods are "always the same"; later in the story, she remembers the ocean, "huge and empty, yet always moving. Everything lay hidden . . ." (45). How does the contrast between the woods and the ocean suggest the transition she must make from childhood to adulthood?
4. How are the references to blood consistent with the story's initiation theme? Do they suggest another theme as well?
5. Throughout the story, references are made to Andy's ability to inspire the trust of animals. As her father says, "I don't know how she does it, but they come right up to her" (8). How does his comment foreshadow later events?
6. Why do you think Andy prays that she and the others will get a deer? What makes her change her mind? How does the change in Andy's character help to convey the story's theme?
7. Andy's mother is not an active participant in the story's events. Still, her presence is important to the story. *Why* is it important? How does paragraph 45 reveal the importance of the mother's role?
8. What has Andy learned as a result of her experience? What else do you think she has to learn?
9. **JOURNAL ENTRY** How would the story be different if Andy were a boy? What would be the same?
10. **CRITICAL PERSPECTIVE** In a review of *Comfort,* the book in which "Doe Season" appears, Susan Wood makes the following observation:

> The dozen or so stories in David Michael Kaplan's affecting first collection share a common focus on the extraordinary moments of recognition in ordinary lives. He is at his best suggesting how such moments may alter, for better or for worse, our relationships with those to whom we are most deeply bound—children, parents, lovers—in love and guilt.

At what point does "the extraordinary moment of recognition" occur in "Doe Season"? How does this moment alter Andy's relationship with both her parents?

Related Works: "A&P" (p. 113), "Boys and Girls" (p. 548), "Traveling through the Dark" (p. 997), *Tender Offer* (p. 1623)

◆ **DAVID HERBERT LAWRENCE** (1885–1930) was born in Nottinghamshire, England, the son of a coal miner and a schoolteacher. Determined to escape the devastation of the mines, Lawrence taught for several years after graduating from high school. However, he soon began writing fiction and established himself in London literary circles. He married a German aristo-crat, Frieda von Richthofen, in 1912.

During World War I, Lawrence and his wife were suspected of treason because of his pacifism and her connection to German aristocracy. Because Lawrence suffered from tuber-culosis, he and his wife left England after the armistice in search of a healthier climate. They traveled in Australia, France, Italy, Mexico, and the United States throughout their lives.

Lawrence is recognized for his impassioned portrayal of our unconscious and instinctive natures. In his novel *Lady Chatterley's Lover* (1928), he at-tempted to restore explicit sexuality to English fiction, and the book was banned for years in Britain and the United States. His other novels include *Sons and Lovers* (1913), *The Rainbow* (1915), *Women in Love* (1921), and *The Plumed Serpent* (1926). Lawrence was also a gifted poet, essayist, travel writer, and short story writer, and his work and personal magnetism had a strong influence on other writers.

Lawrence's fascination with the struggle between the unconscious and the intellect is revealed in his short story "The Rocking-Horse Winner" (1920). Lawrence sets his story in a house full of secrets and weaves sym-bolism with elements of the fairy tale and the gothic to produce a tale that is often the subject of literary debate.

CULTURAL CONTEXT ◆ The concepts of superstition and luck as de-picted in "The Rocking-Horse Winner" have been influential in almost all cultures throughout history. Many superstitions can be traced to Roman and Anglo-Saxon times, others to Victorian rhymes, and still others to folklore that has been passed down generation after generation. Even today, many individuals admit to holding irrational beliefs concerning what brings good and bad fortune.

◆ ◆ ◆
D. H. LAWRENCE

The Rocking-Horse Winner
(1920)

There was a woman who was beautiful, who started with all the advan-tages, yet she had no luck. She married for love, and the love turned to dust. She had bonny children, yet she felt they had been thrust upon her, and she could not love them. They looked at her coldly, as if they were finding fault with her. And hurriedly she felt she must cover up some fault in herself. Yet what it was that she must cover up she never knew. Nevertheless, when her children were present, she always felt the centre of her heart go hard. This troubled her, and in her manner she was all the more gentle and anxious for her children, as if she loved them very much. Only she herself knew that at the centre of her heart was a hard little place that could not feel love, no, not for anybody. Everybody else said of her: "She is such a good mother. She adores her children." Only she herself, and her children themselves, knew it was not so. They read it in each other's eyes.

There were a boy and two little girls. They lived in a pleasant house, with a garden, and they had discreet servants, and felt themselves superior to anyone in the neighbourhood.

Although they lived in style, they felt always an anxiety in the house. There was never enough money. The mother had a small income, and the father had a small income, but not nearly enough for the social position which they had to keep up. The father went into town to some office. But though he had good prospects, these prospects never materialised. There was always the grinding sense of the shortage of money, though the style was always kept up.

At last the mother said: "I will see if *I* can't make something." But she did not know where to begin. She racked her brains, and tried this thing and the other, but could not find anything successful. The failure made deep lines come into her face. Her children were growing up, they would have to go to school. There must be more money, there must be more money. The father, who was always very handsome and expensive in his tastes, seemed as if he never *would* be able to do anything worth doing. And the mother, who had a great belief in herself, did not succeed any better, and her tastes were just as expensive.

5   And so the house came to be haunted by the unspoken phrase: *There must be more money! There must be more money!* The children could hear it all the time, though nobody said it aloud. They heard it at Christmas, when the expensive and splendid toys filled the nursery. Behind the shining modern rocking-horse, behind the smart doll's house, a voice would start whispering: "There *must* be more money! There *must* be more money!" And the children would stop playing, to listen for a moment. They would look into each other's eyes, to see if they had all heard. And each one saw in the eyes of the other two that they too had heard. "There *must* be more money! There *must* be more money!"

It came whispering from the springs of the still-swaying rocking-horse, and even the horse, bending his wooden, champing head, heard it. The big doll, sitting so pink and smirking in her new pram, could hear it quite plainly, and seemed to be smirking all the more self-consciously because of it. The foolish puppy, too, that took the place of the teddybear, he was looking so extraordinarily foolish for no other reason but that he heard the secret whisper all over the house: "There *must* be more money!"

Yet nobody ever said it aloud. The whisper was everywhere, and therefore no one spoke it. Just as no one ever says: "We are breathing!" in spite of the fact that breath is coming and going all the time.

"Mother," said the boy Paul one day, "why don't we keep a car of our own? Why do we always use uncle's, or else a taxi?"

"Because we're the poor members of the family," said the mother.

10 "But why *are* we, mother?"

"Well—I suppose," she said slowly and bitterly, "it's because your father has no luck."

The boy was silent for some time.

"Is luck money, mother?" he asked, rather timidly.

"No, Paul. Not quite. It's what causes you to have money."

15 "Oh!" said Paul vaguely. "I thought when Uncle Oscar said *filthy lucker,* it meant money."

"*Filthy lucre* does mean money," said the mother. "But it's lucre, not luck."

"Oh!" said the boy. "Then what *is* luck, mother?"

"It's what causes you to have money. If you're lucky you have money. That's why it's better to be born lucky than rich. If you're rich, you may lose your money. But if you're lucky, you will always get more money."

"Oh! Will you? And is father not lucky?"

20 "Very unlucky, I should say," she said bitterly.

The boy watched her with unsure eyes.

"Why?" he asked.

"I don't know. Nobody ever knows why one person is lucky and another unlucky."

"Don't they? Nobody at all? Does *nobody* know?"

25 "Perhaps God. But He never tells."

"He ought to, then. And aren't you lucky either, mother?"

"I can't be, if I married an unlucky husband."

"But by yourself, aren't you?"

"I used to think I was, before I married. Now I think I am very unlucky indeed."

30 "Why?"

"Well—never mind! Perhaps I'm not really," she said.

The child looked at her to see if she meant it. But he saw, by the lines of her mouth, that she was only trying to hide something from him.

"Well, anyhow," he said stoutly, "I'm a lucky person."

"Why?" said his mother, with a sudden laugh.

35 He stared at her. He didn't even know why he had said it.

"God told me," he asserted, brazening it out.

"I hope He did, dear!" she said, again with a laugh, but rather bitter.

"He did, mother!"

"Excellent!" said the mother, using one of her husband's exclamations.

40 The boy saw she did not believe him; or rather, that she paid no attention to his assertion. This angered him somewhat, and made him want to compel her attention.

He went off by himself, vaguely, in a childish way, seeking for the clue to "luck." Absorbed, taking no heed of other people, he went about with a sort of stealth, seeking inwardly for luck. He wanted luck, he wanted it, he wanted it. When the two girls were playing dolls in the nursery, he would sit on his big rocking-horse, charging madly into space, with a frenzy that made the little girls peer at him uneasily. Wildly the horse careered, the waving dark hair of the boy tossed, his eyes had a strange glare in them. The little girls dared not speak to him.

When he had ridden to the end of his mad little journey, he climbed down and stood in front of his rocking-horse, staring fixedly into its lowered face. Its red mouth was slightly open, its big eye was wide and glassy-bright.

"Now!" he would silently command the snorting steed. "Now, take me to where there is luck! Now take me!"

And he would slash the horse on the neck with the little whip he had asked Uncle Oscar for. He *knew* the horse could take him to where there was luck, if only he forced it. So he would mount again and start on his furious ride, hoping at last to get there. He knew he could get there.

45   "You'll break your horse, Paul!" said the nurse.

"He's always riding like that! I wish he'd leave off!" said his elder sister Joan.

But he only glared down on them in silence. Nurse gave him up. She could make nothing of him. Anyhow, he was growing beyond her.

One day his mother and his Uncle Oscar came in when he was on one of his furious rides. He did not speak to them.

"Hallo, you young jockey! Riding a winner?" said his uncle.

50   "Aren't you growing too big for a rocking-horse? You're not a very little boy any longer, you know," said his mother.

But Paul only gave a blue glare from his big, rather close-set eyes. He would speak to nobody when he was in full tilt. His mother watched him with an anxious expression on her face.

At last he suddenly stopped forcing his horse into the mechanical gallop and slid down.

"Well, I got there!" he announced fiercely, his blue eyes still flaring, and his sturdy long legs straddling apart.

"Where did you get to?" asked his mother.

55   "Where I wanted to go," he flared back at her.

"That's right, son!" said Uncle Oscar. "Don't you stop till you get there. What's the horse's name?"

"He doesn't have a name," said the boy.

"Gets on without all right?" asked the uncle.

"Well, he has different names. He was called Sansovino last week."

60   "Sansovino, eh? Won the Ascot.[1] How did you know this name?"

"He always talks about horse-races with Bassett," said Joan.

---

[1] The annual horse race at Ascot Heath in England.

The uncle was delighted to find that his small nephew was posted with all the racing news. Bassett, the young gardener, who had been wounded in the left foot in the war and had got his present job through Oscar Cresswell, whose batman[2] he had been, was a perfect blade of the "turf." He lived in the racing events, and the small boy lived with him.

Oscar Cresswell got it all from Bassett.

"Master Paul comes and asks me, so I can't do more than tell him, sir," said Bassett, his face terribly serious, as if he were speaking of religious matters.

65 "And does he ever put anything on a horse he fancies?"

"Well—I don't want to give him away—he's a young sport, a fine sport, sir. Would you mind asking him himself? He sort of takes a pleasure in it, and perhaps he'd feel I was giving him away, sir, if you don't mind."

Bassett was serious as a church.

The uncle went back to his nephew and took him off for a ride in the car.

"Say, Paul, old man, do you ever put anything on a horse?" the uncle asked.

70 The boy watched the handsome man closely.

"Why, do you think I oughtn't to?" he parried.

"Not a bit of it! I thought perhaps you might give me a tip for the Lincoln."[3]

The car sped on into the country, going down to Uncle Oscar's place in Hampshire.

"Honour bright?" said the nephew.

75 "Honour bright, son!" said the uncle.

"Well, then, Daffodil."

"Daffodil! I doubt it, sonny. What about Mirza?"

"I only know the winner," said the boy. "That's Daffodil."

"Daffodil, eh?"

80 There was a pause. Daffodil was an obscure horse comparatively.

"Uncle!"

"Yes, son?"

"You won't let it go any further, will you? I promised Bassett."

"Bassett be damned, old man! What's he got to do with it?"

85 "We're partners. We've been partners from the first. Uncle, he lent me my first five shillings, which I lost. I promised him, honour bright, it was only between me and him; only you gave me that ten-shilling note I started winning with, so I thought you were lucky. You won't let it go any further, will you?"

The boy gazed at his uncle from those big, hot, blue eyes, set rather close together. The uncle stirred and laughed uneasily.

---

[2] A British military officer's personal assistant.

[3] The Lincolnshire Handicap.

"Right you are, son! I'll keep your tip private. Daffodil, eh? How much are you putting on him?"

"All except twenty pounds," said the boy. "I keep that in reserve."

The uncle thought it a good joke.

90 "You keep twenty pounds in reserve, do you, you young romancer? What are you betting, then?"

"I'm betting three hundred," said the boy gravely. "But it's between you and me, Uncle Oscar! Honour bright?"

The uncle burst into a roar of laughter.

"It's between you and me all right, you young Nat Gould,"[4] he said, laughing. "But where's your three hundred?"

"Bassett keeps it for me. We're partners."

95 "You are, are you! And what is Bassett putting on Daffodil?"

"He won't go quite as high as I do, I expect. Perhaps he'll go a hundred and fifty."

"What, pennies?" laughed the uncle.

"Pounds," said the child, with a surprised look at his uncle. "Bassett keeps a bigger reserve than I do."

Between wonder and amusement Uncle Oscar was silent. He pursued the matter no further, but he determined to take his nephew with him to the Lincoln races.

100 "Now, son," he said, "I'm putting twenty on Mirza, and I'll put five on for you on any horse you fancy. What's your pick?"

"Daffodil, uncle."

"No, not the fiver on Daffodil!"

"I should if it was my own fiver," said the child.

"Good! Good! Right you are! A fiver for me and a fiver for you on Daffodil."

105 The child had never been to a race-meeting before, and his eyes were blue fire. He pursed his mouth tight and watched. A Frenchman just in front had put his money on Lancelot. Wild with excitement, he flayed his arms up and down, yelling *"Lancelot! Lancelot!"* in his French accent.

Daffodil came in first, Lancelot second, Mirza third. The child, flushed and with eyes blazing, was curiously serene. His uncle brought him four five-pound notes, four to one.

"What am I to do with these?" he cried, waving them before the boy's eyes.

"I suppose we'll talk to Bassett," said the boy. "I expect I have fifteen hundred now; and twenty in reserve; and this twenty."

His uncle studied him for some moments.

110 "Look here, son!" he said. "You're not serious about Bassett and that fifteen hundred, are you?"

"Yes, I am. But it's between you and me, uncle. Honour bright?"

---

[4] Nathaniel Gould (1857–1919), British journalist and writer known for his stories about horse racing.

"Honour bright all right, son! But I must talk to Bassett."

"If you'd like to be a partner, uncle, with Bassett and me, we could all be partners. Only, you'd have to promise, honour bright, uncle, not to let it go beyond us three. Bassett and I are lucky, and you must be lucky, because it was your ten shillings I started winning with. . . . ."

Uncle Oscar took both Bassett and Paul into Richmond Park for an afternoon, and there they talked.

115   "It's like this, you see, sir," Bassett said. "Master Paul would get me talking about racing events, spinning yarns, you know, sir. And he was always keen on knowing if I'd made or if I'd lost. It's about a year since, now, that I put five shillings on Blush of Dawn for him: and we lost. Then the luck turned, with that ten shillings he had from you: that we put on Singhalese. And since that time, it's been pretty steady, all things considering. What do you say, Master Paul?"

"We're all right when we're sure," said Paul. "It's when we're not quite sure that we go down."

"Oh, but we're careful then," said Bassett.

"But when are you *sure*?" smiled Uncle Oscar.

"It's Master Paul, sir," said Bassett in a secret, religious voice. "It's as if he had it from heaven. Like Daffodil, now, for the Lincoln. That was as sure as eggs."

120   "Did you put anything on Daffodil?" asked Oscar Cresswell.

"Yes, sir. I made my bit."

"And my nephew?"

Bassett was obstinately silent, looking at Paul.

"I made twelve hundred, didn't I, Bassett? I told uncle I was putting three hundred on Daffodil."

125   "That's right," said Bassett, nodding.

"But where's the money?" asked the uncle.

"I keep it safe locked up, sir. Master Paul can have it any minute he likes to ask for it."

"What, fifteen hundred pounds?"

"And twenty! And *forty*, that is, with the twenty he made on the course."

130   "It's amazing!" said the uncle.

"If Master Paul offers you to be partners, sir, I would, if I were you: if you'll excuse me," said Bassett.

Oscar Cresswell thought about it.

"I'll see the money," he said.

They drove home again, and, sure enough, Bassett came round to the garden-house with fifteen hundred pounds in notes. The twenty pounds reserve was left with Joe Glee, in the Turf Commission deposit.

135   "You see, it's all right, uncle, when I'm *sure!* Then we go strong, for all we're worth. Don't we, Bassett?"

"We do that, Master Paul."

"And when are you sure?" said the uncle, laughing.

"Oh, well, sometimes I'm *absolutely* sure, like about Daffodil," said the boy; "and sometimes I have an idea; and sometimes I haven't even an idea, have I, Bassett? Then we're careful, because we mostly go down."

"You do, do you! And when you're sure, like about Daffodil, what makes you sure, sonny?"

140   "Oh, well, I don't know," said the boy uneasily. "I'm sure, you know, uncle; that's all."

"It's as if he had it from heaven, sir," Bassett reiterated.

"I should say so!" said the uncle.

But he became a partner. And when the Leger[5] was coming on Paul was "sure" about Lively Spark, which was a quite inconsiderable horse. The boy insisted on putting a thousand on the horse, Bassett went for five hundred, and Oscar Cresswell two hundred. Lively Spark came in first, and the betting had been ten to one against him. Paul had made ten thousand.

"You see," he said, "I was absolutely sure of him."

145   Even Oscar Cresswell had cleared two thousand.

"Look here, son," he said, "this sort of thing makes me nervous."

"It needn't, uncle! Perhaps I shan't be sure again for a long time."

"But what are you going to do with your money?" asked the uncle.

"Of course," said the boy, "I started it for mother. She said she had no luck, because father is unlucky, so I thought if *I* was lucky, it might stop whispering."

150   "What might stop whispering?"

"Our house. I *hate* our house for whispering."

"What does it whisper?"

"Why—why"—the boy fidgeted—"why, I don't know. But it's always short of money, you know, uncle."

"I know it, son, I know it."

155   "You know people send mother writs,[6] don't you, uncle?"

"I'm afraid I do," said the uncle.

"And then the house whispers, like people laughing at you behind your back. It's awful, that is! I thought if I was lucky . . . "

"You might stop it," added the uncle.

The boy watched him with big blue eyes, that had an uncanny cold fire in them, and he said never a word.

160   "Well, then!" said the uncle. "What are we doing?"

"I shouldn't like mother to know I was lucky," said the boy.

"Why not, son?"

---

[5] The St. Leger Stakes.
[6] Letters from creditors requesting payment.

"She'd stop me."

"I don't think she would."

165   "Oh!"—and the boy writhed in an odd way—"I *don't* want her to know, uncle."

"All right, son! We'll manage it without her knowing."

They managed it very easily. Paul, at the other's suggestion, handed over five thousand pounds to his uncle, who deposited it with the family lawyer, who was then to inform Paul's mother that a relative had put five thousand pounds into his hands, which sum was to be paid out a thousand pounds at a time, on the mother's birthday, for the next five years.

"So she'll have a birthday present of a thousand pounds for five successive years," said Uncle Oscar. "I hope it won't make it all the harder for her later."

Paul's mother had her birthday in November. The house had been "whispering" worse than ever lately, and, even in spite of his luck, Paul could not bear up against it. He was very anxious to see the effect of the birthday letter, telling his mother about the thousand pounds.

170   When there were no visitors, Paul now took his meals with his parents, as he was beyond the nursery control. His mother went into town nearly every day. She had discovered that she had an odd knack of sketching furs and dress materials, so she worked secretly in the studio of a friend who was the chief "artist" for the leading drapers. She drew the figures of ladies in furs and ladies in silk and sequins for the newspaper advertisements. This young woman artist earned several thousand pounds a year, but Paul's mother only made several hundreds, and she was again dissatisfied. She so wanted to be first in something, and she did not succeed, even in making sketches for drapery advertisements.

She was down to breakfast on the morning of her birthday. Paul watched her face as she read her letters. He knew the lawyer's letter. As his mother read it, her face hardened and became more expressionless. Then a cold, determined look came on her mouth. She hid the letter under the pile of others, and said not a word about it.

"Didn't you have anything nice in the post for your birthday, mother?" said Paul.

"Quite moderately nice," she said, her voice cold and absent.

She went away to town without saying more.

175   But in the afternoon Uncle Oscar appeared. He said Paul's mother had had a long interview with the lawyer, asking if the whole five thousand could not be advanced at once, as she was in debt.

"What do you think, uncle?" asked the boy.

"I leave it to you, son."

"Oh, let her have it, then! We can get some more with the other," said the boy.

"A bird in the hand is worth two in the bush, laddie!" said Uncle Oscar.

180   "But I'm sure to *know* for the Grand National; or the Lincolnshire; or else the Derby.[7] I'm sure to know for *one* of them," said Paul.

So Uncle Oscar signed the agreement, and Paul's mother touched the whole five thousand. Then something very curious happened. The voices in the house suddenly went mad, like a chorus of frogs on a spring evening. There was certain new furnishings, and Paul had a tutor. He was *really* going to Eton, his father's school, in the following autumn. There were flowers in the winter, and a blossoming of the luxury Paul's mother had been used to. And yet the voices in the house, behind the sprays of mimosa and almond-blossom, and from under the piles of iridescent cushions, simply trilled and screamed in a sort of ecstasy: "There *must* be more money! Oh-h-h; there *must* be more money. Oh, now, now-w! Now-w-w-w—there *must* be more money!—more than ever! More than ever!"

It frightened Paul terribly. He studied away at his Latin and Greek with his tutor. But his intense hours were spent with Bassett. The Grand National had gone by: he had not "known," and had lost a hundred pounds. Summer was at hand. He was in agony for the Lincoln. But even for the Lincoln he didn't "know," and he lost fifty pounds. He became wild-eyed and strange, as if something were going to explode in him.

"Let it alone, son! Don't you bother about it!" urged Uncle Oscar. But it was as if the boy couldn't really hear what his uncle was saying.

"I've got to know for the Derby! I've got to know for the Derby!" the child reiterated, his big blue eyes blazing with a sort of madness.

185   His mother noticed how overwrought he was.

"You'd better go to the seaside. Wouldn't you like to go now to the seaside, instead of waiting? I think you'd better," she said, looking down at him anxiously, her heart curiously heavy because of him.

But the child lifted his uncanny blue eyes.

"I couldn't possibly go before the Derby, mother!" he said. "I couldn't possibly!"

"Why not?" she said, her voice becoming heavy when she was opposed. "Why not? You can still go from the seaside to see the Derby with your Uncle Oscar, if that's what you wish. No need for you to wait here. Besides, I think you care too much about these races. It's a bad sign. My family has been a gambling family, and you won't know till you grow up how much damage it has done. But it has done damage. I shall have to send Bassett away, and ask Uncle Oscar not to talk racing to you, unless you promise to be reasonable about it: go away to the seaside and forget it. You're all nerves!"

190   "I'll do what you like, mother, so long as you don't send me away till after the Derby," the boy said.

---

[7] Famous British horse races. The Grand National is run at Aintree, the Derby at Epsom Downs.

"Send you away from where? Just from this house?"

"Yes," he said, gazing at her.

"Why, you curious child, what makes you care about this house so much, suddenly? I never knew you loved it."

He gazed at her without speaking. He had a secret within a secret, something he had not divulged, even to Bassett or to his Uncle Oscar.

195 But his mother, after standing undecided and a little bit sullen for some moments, said:

"Very well, then! Don't go to the seaside till after the Derby, if you don't wish it. But promise me you won't let your nerves go to pieces. Promise you won't think so much about horse-racing and *events,* as you call them!"

"Oh no," said the boy casually. "I won't think much about them, mother. You needn't worry. I wouldn't worry, mother, if I were you."

"If you were me and I were you," said his mother, "I wonder what we *should* do!"

"But you know you needn't worry, mother, don't you?" the boy repeated.

200 "I should be awfully glad to know it," she said wearily.

"Oh, well, you *can,* you know. I mean, you *ought* to know you needn't worry," he insisted.

"Ought I? Then I'll see about it," she said.

Paul's secret of secrets was his wooden horse, that which had no name. Since he was emancipated from a nurse and a nursery-governess, he had had his rocking-horse removed to his own bedroom at the top of the house.

"Surely you're too big for a rocking-horse!" his mother had remonstrated.

205 "Well, you see, mother, till I can have a *real* horse, I like to have *some* sort of animal about," had been his quaint answer.

"Do you feel he keeps you company?" she laughed.

"Oh yes! He's very good, he always keeps me company, when I'm there," said Paul.

So the horse, rather shabby, stood in an arrested prance in the boy's bedroom.

The Derby was drawing near, and the boy grew more and more tense. He hardly heard what was spoken to him, he was very frail, and his eyes were really uncanny. His mother had sudden strange seizures of uneasiness about him. Sometimes, for half an hour, she would feel a sudden anxiety about him that was almost anguish. She wanted to rush to him at once, and know he was safe.

210 Two nights before the Derby, she was at a big party in town, when one of her rushes of anxiety about her boy, her firstborn, gripped her heart till she could hardly speak. She fought with the feeling, might and main, for she believed in common sense. But it was too strong. She had to leave the dance and go downstairs to telephone to the country. The children's

nursery-governess was terribly surprised and startled at being rung up in the night.

"Are the children all right, Miss Wilmot?"

"Oh yes, they are quite all right."

"Master Paul? Is he all right?"

"He went to bed as right as a trivet. Shall I run up and look at him?"

215   "No," said Paul's mother reluctantly. "No! Don't trouble. It's all right. Don't sit up. We shall be home fairly soon." She did not want her son's privacy intruded upon.

"Very good," said the governess.

It was about one o'clock when Paul's mother and father drove up to their house. All was still. Paul's mother went to her room and slipped off her white fur cloak. She had told her maid not to wait up for her. She heard her husband downstairs, mixing a whisky and soda.

And then, because of the strange anxiety at her heart, she stole upstairs to her son's room. Noiselessly she went along the upper corridor. Was there a faint noise? What was it?

She stood, with arrested muscles, outside his door, listening. There was a strange, heavy, and yet not loud noise. Her heart stood still. It was a soundless noise, yet rushing and powerful. Something huge, in violent, hushed motion. What was it? What in God's name was it? She ought to know. She felt that she knew the noise. She knew what it was.

220   Yet she could not place it. She couldn't say what it was. And on and on it went, like a madness.

Softly, frozen with anxiety and fear, she turned the door-handle.

The room was dark. Yet in the space near the window, she heard and saw something plunging to and fro. She gazed in fear and amazement.

Then suddenly she switched on the light, and saw her son, in his green pyjamas, madly surging on the rocking-horse. The blaze of light suddenly lit him up, as he urged the wooden horse, and lit her up, as she stood, blonde, in her dress of pale green and crystal, in the doorway.

"Paul!" she cried. "Whatever are you doing?"

225   "It's Malabar!" he screamed in a powerful, strange voice. "It's Malabar!"

His eyes blazed at her for one strange and senseless second, as he ceased urging his wooden horse. Then he fell with a crash to the ground, and she, all her tormented motherhood flooding upon her, rushed to gather him up.

But he was unconscious, and unconscious he remained, with some brain-fever. He talked and tossed, and his mother sat stonily by his side.

"Malabar! It's Malabar! Bassett, Bassett, I *know!* It's Malabar!"

So the child cried, trying to get up and urge the rocking-horse that gave him his inspiration.

230   "What does he mean by Malabar?" asked the heart-frozen mother.

"I don't know," said the father stonily.

"What does he mean by Malabar?" she asked her brother Oscar.

"It's one of the horses running for the Derby," was the answer.

And, in spite of himself, Oscar Cresswell spoke to Bassett, and himself put a thousand on Malabar: at fourteen to one.

235   The third day of the illness was critical: they were waiting for a change. The boy, with his rather long, curly hair, was tossing ceaselessly on the pillow. He neither slept nor regained consciousness, and his eyes were like blue stones. His mother sat, feeling her heart had gone, turned actually into a stone.

In the evening, Oscar Cresswell did not come, but Bassett sent a message, saying could he come up for one moment, just one moment? Paul's mother was very angry at the intrusion, but on second thought she agreed. The boy was the same. Perhaps Bassett might bring him to consciousness.

The gardener, a shortish fellow with a little brown moustache and sharp little brown eyes, tiptoed into the room, touched his imaginary cap to Paul's mother, and stole to the bedside, staring with glittering, smallish eyes at the tossing, dying child.

"Master Paul!" he whispered. "Master Paul! Malabar came in first all right, a clean win. I did as you told me. You've made over seventy thousand pounds, you have; you've got over eighty thousand. Malabar came in all right, Master Paul."

"Malabar! Malabar! Did I say Malabar, mother? Did I say Malabar? Do you think I'm lucky, mother? I knew Malabar, didn't I? Over eighty thousand pounds! I call that lucky, don't you, mother? Over eighty thousand pounds! I knew, didn't I know I knew? Malabar came in all right. If I ride my horse till I'm sure, then I tell you, Bassett, you can go as high as you like. Did you go for all you were worth, Bassett?"

240   "I went a thousand on it, Master Paul."

"I never told you, mother, that if I can ride my horse, and *get there,* then I'm absolutely sure—oh, absolutely! Mother, did I ever tell you? I *am* lucky!"

"No, you never did," said his mother.

But the boy died in the night.

And even as he lay dead, his mother heard her brother's voice saying to her: "My God, Hester, you're eighty-odd thousand to the good, and a poor devil of a son to the bad. But, poor devil, poor devil, he's best gone out of a life where he rides his rocking-horse to find a winner."

READING AND REACTING

1. From what point of view is "The Rocking-Horse Winner" told? How does this point of view help to communicate the story's theme?

2. In what respects is "The Rocking-Horse Winner" like a fairy tale? How is it different?

3. Many fairy tales involve a hero who goes on a journey to search for something of great value. What journey does Paul go on? What does he search for? Is he successful?

4. In paragraph 5, the narrator says that the house is "haunted by the unspoken phrase 'There must be more money.'" In what way does the phrase "haunt" the house?

5. How would you characterize Paul's parents? His uncle? Bassett? Are they weak? Evil? What motivates them?

6. Beginning with paragraph 10, Paul's mother attempts to define the word *luck*. According to her definition, does she consider Paul lucky? Do you agree?

7. In what ways does Paul behave like other children? In what ways is he different? How do you account for these differences? How old do you think Paul is? Why is his age significant?

8. The rocking horse is an important literary symbol in the story. What possible meanings might the rocking horse suggest? In what ways does this symbol reinforce the story's theme?

9. What secrets do the various characters keep from one another? Why do they keep them? How do these secrets relate to the story's theme?

10. How does Paul know who the winners will be? Does the rocking horse really tell him? Does he get his information "from heaven" as Bassett suggests? Or, does he just guess?

11. **JOURNAL ENTRY** In your opinion, who or what is responsible for Paul's death?

12. **CRITICAL PERSPECTIVE** In a letter dated January 17, 1913, Lawrence wrote:

> My great religion is a belief in the blood, the flesh, as being wiser than the intellect. We can go wrong in our minds. But what our blood feels and believes and says, is always true. The intellect is only a bit and a bridle. What do I care about knowledge. All I want is to answer to my blood, direct, without fribbling intervention of mind, or moral, or what-not.

How does Lawrence's portrayal of Paul in "The Rocking-Horse Winner" support his belief in "the blood . . . being wiser than the intellect"? How does Lawrence remain true in this story to his metaphor of the intellect as bit and bridle?

Related Works: "Once upon a Time" (p. 81), "Teenage Wasteland" (p. 603), "Gretel in Darkness" (p. 724), "Suicide Note" (p. 733), "The Chimney Sweeper" (p. 928), *A Doll House* (p. 1196)

♦ **HISAYE YAMAMOTO** (1921–   ) was born in Redondo Beach, California, the daughter of emigrants from Kuamamota, Japan, and studied languages at Compton Junior College. She began writing as a teenager, contributing to columns in the English sections of Japanese-language newspapers. Forced by the U.S. government to relocate with her family to an internment camp in Poston, Arizona, during World War II, Yamamoto authored the camp newsletter, *The Poston Chronicle,* as well as a mystery serial, "Death Rides the Rails to Poston."

After her release, Yamamoto worked from 1945 to 1948 as a columnist for the *Los Angeles Tribune.* At the same time, she was submitting short stories about Japanese-American life to literary magazines such as *Partisan Review,* which in 1949 published "Seventeen Syllables." Yamamoto's output has been very small but nonetheless influential. She was, according to one editor, "one of the first Japanese-American writers to gain national recognition after the war, at a time when anti-Japanese sentiment was still rampant," and her story "Yoneko's Earthquake" was included in *Best American Short Stories 1952.*

Of the widely anthologized "Seventeen Syllables," Yamamoto has said that although the incidents are invented, it is the story of her mother.

CULTURAL CONTEXT ♦ During World War II, more than 100,000 Japanese and Japanese-Americans living in the United States were taken into custody and placed in internment camps. During the spring, summer, and fall of 1942, those of Japanese ancestry—including many American citizens—up and down the West Coast were removed from their homes on the basis of "Civilian Exclusion Orders" and taken to detention camps.

♦ ♦ ♦

HISAYE YAMAMOTO

Seventeen Syllables
(1949)

The first Rosie knew that her mother had taken to writing poems was one evening when she finished one and read it aloud for her daughter's approval. It was about cats, and Rosie pretended to understand it thoroughly and appreciate it no end, partly because she hesitated to disillusion her mother about the quantity and quality of Japanese she had learned in all the years now that she had been going to Japanese school every Saturday (and Wednesday, too, in the summer). Even so, her mother must have been skeptical about the depth of Rosie's understanding, because she explained afterwards about the kind of poem she was trying to write.

See, Rosie, she said, it was a *haiku*,[1] a poem in which she must pack all her meaning into seventeen syllables only, which were divided into three lines of five, seven, and five syllables. In the one she had just read, she had tried to capture the charm of a kitten, as well as comment on the superstition that owning a cat of three colors meant good luck.

"Yes, yes, I understand. How utterly lovely," Rosie said, and her mother, either satisfied or seeing through the deception and resigned, went back to composing.

The truth was that Rosie was lazy; English lay ready on the tongue but Japanese had to be searched for and examined, and even then put forth tentatively (probably to meet with laughter). It was so much easier to say yes, yes, even when one meant no, no. Besides, this was what was in her mind to say: I was looking through one of your magazines from Japan last night, Mother, and toward the back I found some *haiku* in English that delighted me. There was one that made me giggle off and on until I fell asleep—

It is morning, and lo!
I lie awake, comme il faut,
sighing for some dough.

5   Now, how to reach her mother, how to communicate the melancholy song? Rosie knew formal Japanese by fits and starts, her mother had even less English, no French. It was much more possible to say yes, yes.

It developed that her mother was writing the *haiku* for a daily newspaper, the *Mainichi Shimbun,* that was published in San Francisco. Los Angeles, to be sure, was closer to the farming community in which the Hayashi family lived and several Japanese vernaculars[2] were printed there, but Rosie's parents said they preferred the tone of the northern paper. Once a week, the *Mainichi* would have a section devoted to *haiku,* and her mother became an extravagant contributor, taking for herself the blossoming pen name, Ume Hanazono.

So Rosie and her father lived for a while with two women, her mother and Ume Hanazono. Her mother (Tome Hayashi by name) kept house, cooked, washed, and, along with her husband and the Carrascos, the Mexican family hired for the harvest, did her ample share of picking tomatoes out in the sweltering fields and boxing them in tidy strata in the cool packing shed. Ume Hanazono, who came to life after the dinner dishes were done, was an earnest, muttering stranger who often neglected speaking when spoken to and stayed busy at the parlor table as late as midnight scribbling with pencil on scratch paper or carefully copying characters on good paper with her fat, pale-green Parker.

---

[1] A classical Japanese poetical form.

[2] Dialects, usually associated with particular regions.

The new interest had some repercussions on the household routine. Before, Rosie had been accustomed to her parents and herself taking their hot baths early and going to bed almost immediately afterwards, unless her parents challenged each other to a game of flower cards or unless company dropped in. Now if her father wanted to play cards, he had to resort to solitaire (at which he always cheated fearlessly), and if a group of friends came over, it was bound to contain someone who was also writing *haiku,* and the small assemblage would be split in two, her father entertaining the non-literary members and her mother comparing ecstatic notes with the visiting poet.

If they went out, it was more of the same thing. But Ume Hanazono's life span, even for a poet's, was very brief—perhaps three months at most.

10   One night they went over to see the Hayano family in the neighboring town to the west, an adventure both painful and attractive to Rosie. It was attractive because there were four Hayano girls, all lovely and each one named after a season of the year (Haru, Natsu, Aki, Fuyu), painful because something had been wrong with Mrs. Hayano ever since the birth of her first child. Rosie would sometimes watch Mrs. Hayano, reputed to have been the belle of her native village, making her way about a room, stooped, slowly shuffling, violently trembling (*always* trembling), and she would be reminded that this woman, in this same condition, had carried and given issue to three babies. She would look wonderingly at Mr. Hayano, handsome, tall, and strong, and she would look at her four pretty friends. But it was not a matter she could come to any decision about.

On this visit, however, Mrs. Hayano sat all evening in the rocker, as motionless and unobtrusive as it was possible for her to be, and Rosie found the greater part of the evening practically anaesthetic. Too, Rosie spent most of it in the girls' room, because Haru, the garrulous one, said almost as soon as the bows and other greetings were over, "Oh, you must see my new coat!"

It was a pale plaid of grey, sand, and blue, with an enormous collar, and Rosie, seeing nothing special in it, said, "Gee, how nice."

"Nice?" said Haru, indignantly. "Is that all you can say about it? It's gorgeous! And so cheap, too. Only seventeen ninety-eight, because it was a sale. The saleslady said it was twenty-five dollars regular."

"Gee," said Rosie. Natsu, who never said much and when she said anything said it shyly, fingered the coat covetously and Haru pulled it away.

15   "Mine," she said, putting it on. She minced in the aisle between the two large beds and smiled happily. "Let's see how your mother likes it."

She broke into the front room and the adult conversation and went to stand in front of Rosie's mother, while the rest watched from the door. Rosie's mother was properly envious. "May I inherit it when you're through with it?"

Haru, pleased, giggled, and said yes, she could, but Natsu reminded gravely from the door, "You promised me, Haru."

Everyone laughed but Natsu, who shamefacedly retreated into the bedroom. Haru came in laughing, taking off the coat. "We were only kidding, Natsu," she said. "Here, you try it on now."

After Natsu buttoned herself into the coat, inspected herself solemnly in the bureau mirror, and reluctantly shed it, Rosie, Aki, and Fuyu got their turns, and Fuyu, who was eight, drowned in it while her sisters and Rosie doubled up in amusement. They all went into the front room later, because Haru's mother quaveringly called to her to fix the tea and rice cakes and open a can of sliced peaches for everybody. Rosie noticed that her mother and Mr. Hayano were talking together at the little table—they were discussing a *haiku* that Mr. Hayano was planning to send to the *Mainichi*, while her father was sitting at one end of the sofa looking through a copy of *Life*, the new picture magazine. Occasionally, her father would comment on a photograph, holding it toward Mrs. Hayano and speaking to her as he always did—loudly, as though he thought someone such as she must surely be at least a trifle deaf also.

20   The five girls had their refreshments at the kitchen table, and it was while Rosie was showing the sisters her trick of swallowing peach slices without chewing (she chased each slippery crescent down with a swig of tea) that her father brought his empty teacup and untouched saucer to the sink and said, "Come on, Rosie, we're going home now."

"Already?" asked Rosie.

"Work tomorrow," he said.

He sounded irritated, and Rosie, puzzled, gulped one last yellow slice and stood up to go, while the sisters began protesting, as was their wont.

"We have to get up at five-thirty," he told them, going into the front room quickly, so that they did not have their usual chance to hang onto his hands and plead for an extension of time.

25   Rosie, following, saw that her mother and Mr. Hayano were sipping tea and still talking together, while Mrs. Hayano concentrated, quivering, on raising the handleless Japanese cup to her lips with both her hands and lowering it back to her lap. Her father, saying nothing, went out the door, onto the bright porch, and down the steps. Her mother looked up and asked, "Where is he going?"

"Where is he going?" Rosie said. "He said we were going home now."

"Going home?" Her mother looked with embarrassment at Mr. Hayano and his absorbed wife and then forced a smile. "He must be tired," she said.

Haru was not giving up yet. "May Rosie stay overnight?" she asked, and Natsu, Aki, and Fuyu came to reinforce their sister's plea by helping her make a circle around Rosie's mother. Rosie, for once having no desire to stay, was relieved when her mother, apologizing to the perturbed Mr. and Mrs. Hayano for her father's abruptness at the same time, managed to shake her head no at the quartet, kindly but adamant, so that they broke their circle and let her go.

Rosie's father looked ahead into the windshield as the two joined him. "I'm sorry," her mother said. "You must be tired." Her father, stepping on the starter, said nothing. "You know how I get when it's *haiku*," she continued, "I forget what time it is." He only grunted.

30   As they rode homeward silently, Rosie, sitting between, felt a rush of hate for both—for her mother for begging, for her father for denying her mother. I wish this old Ford would crash, right now, she thought, then immediately, no, no, I wish my father would laugh, but it was too late: already the vision had passed through her mind of the green pick-up crumpled in the dark against one of the mighty eucalyptus trees they were just riding past, of the three contorted, bleeding bodies, one of them hers.

Rosie ran between two patches of tomatoes, her heart working more rambunctiously than she had ever known it to. How lucky it was that Aunt Taka and Uncle Gimpachi had come tonight, though, how very lucky. Otherwise she might not have really kept her half-promise to meet Jesus Carrasco. Jesus was going to be a senior in September at the same school she went to, and his parents were the ones helping with the tomatoes this year. She and Jesus, who hardly remembered seeing each other at Cleveland High where there were so many other people and two whole grades between them, had become great friends this summer—he always had a joke for her when he periodically drove the loaded pick-up up from the fields to the shed where she was usually sorting while her mother and father did the packing, and they laughed a great deal together over infinitesimal repartee[3] during the afternoon break for chilled watermelon or ice cream in the shade of the shed.

What she enjoyed most was racing him to see which could finish picking a double row first. He, who could work faster, would tease her by slowing down until she thought she would surely pass him this time, then speeding up furiously to leave her several sprawling vines behind. Once he had made her screech hideously by crossing over, while her back was turned, to place atop the tomatoes in her green-stained bucket a truly monstrous, pale green worm (it had looked more like an infant snake). And it was when they had finished a contest this morning, after she had pantingly pointed a green finger at the immature tomatoes evident in the lugs[4] at the end of his row and he had returned the accusation (with justice), that he had startlingly brought up the matter of their possibly meeting outside the range of both their parents' dubious eyes.

"What for?" she had asked.

"I've got a secret I want to tell you," he said.

---

[3] Witty conversation.

[4] Shallow boxes in which produce is shipped to market.

35 "Tell me now," she demanded.

"It won't be ready till tonight," he said.

She laughed. "Tell me tomorrow then."

"It'll be gone tomorrow," he threatened.

"Well, for seven hakes, what is it?" she had asked, more than twice, and when he had suggested that the packing shed would be an appropriate place to find out, she had cautiously answered maybe. She had not been certain she was going to keep the appointment until the arrival of mother's sister and her husband. Their coming seemed a sort of signal of permission, of grace, and she had definitely made up her mind to lie and leave as she was bowing them welcome.

40 So as soon as everyone appeared settled back for the evening, she announced loudly that she was going to the privy[5] outside, "I'm going to the *benjo!*"[6] and slipped out the door. And now that she was actually on her way, her heart pumped in such an undisciplined way that she could hear it with her ears. It's because I'm running, she told herself, slowing to a walk. The shed was up ahead, one more patch away, in the middle of the fields. Its bulk, looming in the dimness, took on a sinisterness that was funny when Rosie reminded herself that it was only a wooden frame with a canvas roof and three canvas walls that made a slapping noise on breezy days.

Jesus was sitting on the narrow plank that was the sorting platform and she went around to the other side and jumped backwards to seat herself on the rim of a packing stand. "Well, tell me," she said without greeting, thinking her voice sounded reassuringly familiar.

"I saw you coming out the door," Jesus said. "I heard you running part of the way, too."

"Uh-huh," Rosie said. "Now tell me the secret."

"I was afraid you wouldn't come," he said.

45 Rosie delved around on the chicken-wire bottom of the stall for number two tomatoes, ripe, which she was sitting beside, and came up with a left-over that felt edible. She bit into it and began sucking out the pulp and seeds. "I'm here," she pointed out.

"Rosie, are you sorry you came?"

"Sorry? What for?" she said. "You said you were going to tell me something."

"I will, I will," Jesus said, but his voice contained disappointment, and Rosie fleetingly felt the older of the two, realizing a brand-new power which vanished without category under her recognition.

"I have to go back in a minute," she said. "My aunt and uncle are here from Wintersburg. I told them I was going to the privy."

50 Jesus laughed. "You funny thing," he said. "You slay[7] me!"

---

[5] Outbuilding containing a toilet.

[6] A lavatory with a flush toilet (Japanese).

[7] Amuse, delight (slang).

"Just because you have a bathroom *inside*," Rosie said. "Come on, tell me."

Chuckling, Jesus came around to lean on the stand facing her. They still could not see each other very clearly, but Rosie noticed that Jesus became very sober again as he took the hollow tomato from her hand and dropped it back into the stall. When he took hold of her empty hand, she could find no words to protest; her vocabulary had become distressingly constricted and she thought desperately that all that remained intact now was yes and no and oh, and even these few sounds would not easily come out. Thus, kissed by Jesus, Rosie fell for the first time entirely victim to a helplessness delectable beyond speech. But the terrible, beautiful sensation lasted no more than a second, and the reality of Jesus' lips and tongue and teeth and hands made her pull away with such strength that she nearly tumbled.

Rosie stopped running as she approached the lights from the windows of home. How long since she had left? She could not guess, but gasping yet, she went to the privy in back and locked herself in. Her own breathing deafened her in the dark, close space, and she sat and waited until she could hear at last the nightly calling of the frogs and crickets. Even then, all she could think to say was oh, my, and the pressure of Jesus' face against her face would not leave.

No one had missed her in the parlor, however, and Rosie walked in and through quickly, announcing that she was next going to take a bath. "Your father's in the bathhouse," her mother said, and Rosie, in her room, recalled that she had not seen him when she entered. There had been only Aunt Taka and Uncle Gimpachi with her mother at the table, drinking tea. She got her robe and straw sandals and crossed the parlor again to go outside. Her mother was telling them about the *haiku* competition in the *Mainichi* and the poem she had entered.

55   Rosie met her father coming out of the bathhouse. "Are you through, Father?" she asked. "I was going to ask you to scrub my back."

"Scrub your own back," he said shortly, going toward the main house.

"What have I done now?" she yelled after him. She suddenly felt like doing a lot of yelling. But he did not answer, and she went into the bathhouse. Turning on the dangling light, she removed her denims and T-shirt and threw them in the big carton for dirty clothes standing next to the washing machine. Her other things she took with her into the bath compartment to wash after her bath. After she had scooped a basin of hot water from the square wooden tub, she sat on the grey cement of the floor and soaped herself at exaggerated leisure, singing "Red Sails in the Sunset" at the top of her voice and using da-da-da where she suspected her words. Then, standing up, still singing, for she was possessed by the notion that any attempt now to analyze would result in spoilage and she believed that the larger her volume the less she would be able to hear herself think, she obtained more hot water and poured it on until she was free of lather.

Only then did she allow herself to step into the steaming vat, one leg first, then the remainder of her body inch by inch until the water no longer stung and she could move around at will.

She took a long time soaking, afterwards remembering to go around outside to stoke the embers of the tin-lined fireplace beneath the tub and to throw on a few more sticks so that the water might keep its heat for her mother, and when she finally returned to the parlor, she found her mother still talking *haiku* with her aunt and uncle, the three of them on another round of tea. Her father was nowhere in sight.

At Japanese school the next day (Wednesday it was), Rosie was grave and giddy by turns. Preoccupied at her desk in the row for students on Book Eight, she made up for it at recess by performing wild mimicry for the benefit of her friend Chizuko. She held her nose and whined a witticism or two in what she considered was the manner of Fred Allen;[8] she assumed intoxication and a British accent to go over the climax of the Rudy Vallee[9] recording of the pub conversation about William Ewart Gladstone;[10] she was the child Shirley Temple[11] piping, "On the Good Ship Lollipop"; she was the gentleman soprano of the Four Inkspots trilling, "If I Didn't Care." And she felt reasonably satisfied when Chizuko wept and gasped, "Oh, Rosie, you ought to be in the movies!"

60 Her father came after her at noon, bringing her sandwiches of minced ham and two nectarines to eat while she rode, so that she could pitch right into the sorting when they got home. The lugs were piling up, he said, and the ripe tomatoes in them would probably have to be taken to the cannery tomorrow if they were not ready for the produce haulers tonight. "This heat's not doing them any good. And we've got no time for a break today."

It *was* hot, probably the hottest day of the year, and Rosie's blouse stuck damply to her back even under the protection of the canvas. But she worked as efficiently as a flawless machine and kept the stalls heaped, with one part of her mind listening in to the parental murmuring about the heat and the tomatoes and with another part planning the exact words she would say to Jesus when he drove up with the first load of the afternoon. But when at last she saw that the pick-up was coming, her hands went berserk and the tomatoes started falling in the wrong stalls, and her father said, "Hey, hey! Rosie, watch what you're doing!"

"Well, I have to go to the *benjo*," she said, hiding panic.

"Go in the weeds over there," he said, only half-joking.

"Oh, Father!" she protested.

65 "Oh, go on home," her mother said. "We'll make out for awhile."

---

[8] American humorist (1894–1956) and radio personality.

[9] American singer (1901–1986), stage, radio, and movie personality.

[10] English politician (1809–1902) and reformer.

[11] Child actress (1928–   ) of the 1930s, known for her ringlets and dimples.

In the privy Rosie peered through a knothole toward the fields, watching as much as she could of Jesus. Happily she thought she saw him look in the direction of the house from time to time before he finished unloading and went back toward the patch where his mother and father worked. As she was heading for the shed, a very presentable black car purred up the dirt driveway to the house and its driver motioned to her. Was this the Hayashi home, he wanted to know. She nodded. Was she a Hayashi? Yes, she said, thinking that he was a good-looking man. He got out of the car with a huge, flat package and she saw that he warmly wore a business suit. "I have something here for your mother then," he said, in a more elegant Japanese than she was used to.

She told him where her mother was and he came along with her, patting his face with an immaculate white handkerchief and saying something about the coolness of San Francisco. To her surprised mother and father, he bowed and introduced himself as, among other things, the *haiku* editor of the *Mainichi Shimbun,* saying that since he had been coming as far as Los Angeles anyway, he had decided to bring her the first prize she had won in the recent contest.

"First prize?" her mother echoed, believing and not believing, pleased and overwhelmed. Handed the package with a bow, she bobbed her head up and down numerous times to express her utter gratitude.

"It is nothing much," he added, "but I hope it will serve as a token of our great appreciation for your contributions and our great admiration of your considerable talent."

70 "I am not worthy," she said, falling easily into his style. "It is I who should make some sign of my humble thanks for being permitted to contribute."

"No, no, to the contrary," he said, bowing again.

But Rosie's mother insisted, and then saying that she knew she was being unorthodox, she asked if she might open the package because her curiosity was so great. Certainly she might. In fact, he would like her reaction to it, for personally, it was one of his favorite *Hiroshiges.*

Rosie thought it was a pleasant picture, which looked to have been sketched with delicate quickness. There were pink clouds, containing some graceful calligraphy,[12] and a sea that was a pale blue except at the edges, containing four sampans[13] with indications of people in them. Pines edged the water and on the far-off beach there was a cluster of thatched huts towered over by pine-dotted mountains of grey and blue. The frame was scalloped and gilt.

After Rosie's mother pronounced it without peer and somewhat prodded her father into nodding agreement, she said Mr. Kuroda must at least have a cup of tea after coming all this way, and although Mr. Kuroda did

---

[12] Graceful or artistic handwriting.
[13] Flatbottomed Asian boats.

not want to impose, he soon agreed that a cup of tea would be refreshing and went along with her to the house, carrying the picture for her.

75 "Ha, your mother's crazy!" Rosie's father said, and Rosie laughed uneasily as she resumed judgment on the tomatoes. She had emptied six lugs when he broke into an imaginary conversation with Jesus to tell her to go and remind her mother of the tomatoes, and she went slowly.

Mr. Kuroda was in his shirtsleeves expounding some *haiku* theory as he munched a rice cake, and her mother was rapt. Abashed in the great man's presence, Rosie stood next to her mother's chair until her mother looked up inquiringly, and then she started to whisper the message, but her mother pushed her gently away and reproached, "You are not being very polite to our guest."

"Father says the tomatoes . . ." Rosie said aloud, smiling foolishly.

"Tell him I shall only be a minute," her mother said, speaking the language of Mr. Kuroda.

When Rosie carried the reply to her father, he did not seem to hear and she said again, "Mother says she'll be back in a minute."

80 "All right, all right," he nodded, and they worked again in silence. But suddenly, her father uttered an incredible noise, exactly like the cork of a bottle popping, and the next Rosie knew, he was stalking angrily toward the house, almost running in fact, and she chased after him crying, "Father! Father! What are you going to do?"

He stopped long enough to order her back to the shed. "Never mind!" he shouted. "Get on with the sorting!"

And from the place in the fields where she stood, frightened and vacillating, Rosie saw her father enter the house. Soon Mr. Kuroda came out alone, putting on his coat. Mr. Kuroda got into his car and backed out down the driveway onto the highway. Next her father emerged, also alone, something in his arms (it was the picture, she realized), and, going over to the bathhouse woodpile, he threw the picture on the ground and picked up the axe. Smashing the picture, glass and all (she heard the explosion faintly), he reached over for the kerosene that was used to encourage the bath fire and poured it over the wreckage. I am dreaming, Rosie said to herself, I am dreaming, but her father, having made sure that his act of cremation was irrevocable, was even then returning to the fields.

Rosie ran past him and toward the house. What had become of her mother? She burst into the parlor and found her mother at the back window watching the dying fire. They watched together until there remained only a feeble smoke under the blazing sun. Her mother was very calm.

"Do you know why I married your father?" she said without turning.

85 "No," said Rosie. It was the most frightening question she had ever been called upon to answer. Don't tell me now, she wanted to say, tell me tomorrow, tell me next week, don't tell me today. But she knew she would be told now, that the telling would combine with the other violence of the hot afternoon to level her life, her world to the very ground.

It was like a story out of the magazines illustrated in sepia,[14] which she had consumed so greedily for a period until the information had somehow reached her that those wretchedly unhappy autobiographies, offered to her as the testimonials of living men and women, were largely inventions: Her mother, at nineteen, had come to America and married her father as an alternative to suicide.

At eighteen she had been in love with the first son of one of the well-to-do families in her village. The two had met whenever and wherever they could, secretly, because it would not have done for his family to see him favor her—her father had no money; he was a drunkard and a gambler besides. She had learned she was with child; an excellent match had already been arranged for her lover. Despised by her family, she had given premature birth to a stillborn son, who would be seventeen now. Her family did not turn her out, but she could no longer project herself in any direction without refreshing in them the memory of her indiscretion. She wrote to Aunt Taka, her favorite sister in America, threatening to kill herself if Aunt Taka would not send for her. Aunt Taka hastily arranged a marriage with a young man of whom she knew, but lately arrived from Japan, a young man of simple mind, it was said, but of kindly heart. The young man was never told why his unseen betrothed was so eager to hasten the day of meeting.

The story was told perfectly, with neither groping for words nor untoward passion. It was as though her mother had memorized it by heart, reciting it to herself so many times over that its nagging vileness had long since gone.

"I had a brother then?" Rosie asked, for this was what seemed to matter now; she would think about the other later, she assured herself, pushing back the illumination which threatened all that darkness that had hitherto been merely mysterious or even glamorous. "A half-brother?"

90   "Yes."

"I would have liked a brother," she said.

Suddenly, her mother knelt on the floor and took her by the wrists. "Rosie," she said urgently, "promise me you will never marry!" Shocked more by the request than the revelation, Rosie stared at her mother's face. Jesus, Jesus, she called silently, not certain whether she was invoking the help of the son of the Carrascos or of God, until there returned sweetly the memory of Jesus' hand, how it had touched her and where. Still her mother waited for an answer, holding her wrists so tightly that her hands were going numb. She tried to pull free. Promise, her mother whispered fiercely, promise. Yes, yes, I promise, Rosie said. But for an instant she turned away, and her mother, hearing the familiar glib agreement, released her. Oh, you, you, you, her eyes and twisted mouth said, you fool. Rosie, covering her face, began at last to cry, and the embrace and consoling hand came much later than she expected.

---

[14] Dark brown ink or pigment.

READING AND REACTING

1. Why do you think Rosie's mother begins writing *haiku?* Why does she stop?
2. What does the narrator mean when she says, "So Rosie and her father lived for a while with two women, her mother and Ume Hanazono" (7)? How are these two women different?
3. How does the fact that the mother writes *haiku* reveal the differences between Rosie's mother and father? Why does Rosie's father destroy his wife's prize? Do you think his actions are understandable? Do you think they are justified?
4. What role does Mrs. Hayano play in the story? How does she shed light on Rosie's mother's life and on her motivation?
5. Explain how the conflict between each of the following contributes to your understanding of the story: husband and wife, mother and daughter, Japanese and American cultures, Rosie's mother and Ume Hanazono, farm work and poetry.
6. Who is the story's main character? Explain.
7. What is the story really about? Creativity? Communication? Culture? Tradition? Work? Gender roles? Something else?
8. How would you sum up the story's major theme? In what way does the title express that theme?
9. **JOURNAL ENTRY** In paragraphs 84 through 88, Rosie's mother tells her daughter the story of her life. What is the significance of this story? In what sense is this tale—"told perfectly"—the heart of the story?
10. **CRITICAL PERSPECTIVE** In his article "The *Issei* Father in the Fiction of Hisaye Yamamoto," Charles Crow observes that Yamamoto's stories deal with the disruptions of Japanese-American life caused by the Second World War. Parents, who in many cases were born in Japan, came into conflict with children, who had assimilated into the American mainstream. "Like most Japanese-American authors," says Crow, "Yamamoto explores the frustrated relationship between these two generations—a relationship which changed abruptly and forever in the relocation centers during the war."

    In what sense is "Seventeen Syllables" about the struggle between two generations of Japanese-Americans? How do the different perspectives of the two generations frustrate their attempts to communicate with each other? Is this generational struggle the story's primary focus, or is it really about something else?

Related Works: "The Chrysanthemums" (p. 333), "Shopping" (p. 559), "Two Kinds" (p. 594), "Four Haiku" (p. 798), "Lineage" (p. 1003), *A Doll House* (p. 1196)

◆ **EUDORA WELTY** (1909–   ) was born and raised in Jackson, Mississippi, where she still lives in her family's home. After attending the Mississippi College for Women, the University of Wisconsin, and Columbia University (where she studied advertising), she returned to Jackson to pursue her long career as a writer, beginning as a journalist. In 1936, she wrote the first of her many short stories, which are gathered in *Collected Stories* (1980). Welty has also authored several novels, including *Delta Wedding* (1946), *Losing Battles* (1970), and the Pulitzer Prize-winning *The Optimist's Daughter* (1972). Her volume of memoirs, *One Writer's Beginnings* (1984), was a best-seller.

One of the country's most accomplished writers, Welty has focused much of her fiction on life in Southern towns and villages peopled with dreamers, eccentrics, and close-knit families. Her sharply observed characters are sometimes presented with great humor, sometimes with poignant lyricism, but always with clarity and sympathy. "Of course any writer is in part all of his characters," she has written. "How otherwise would they be known to him, occur to him, become what they are?" In "A Worn Path," Welty creates a particularly memorable character in the tenacious Phoenix Jackson and explores a theme that transcends race and region.

CULTURAL CONTEXT ◆   Eudora Welty is not only a writer but also a photographer. In 1989, she published *Eudora Welty Photographs,* a collection of black and white photographs, most of which depict black people in the South. Another collection of her photographs, *One Time One Place: Mississippi in the Depression: A Snapshot Album,* was published in 1996. The duotone pictures in this collection are from her travels in Mississippi during the Great Depression.

◇ ◇ ◇

E U D O R A   W E L T Y

A Worn Path
(1940)

It was December—a bright frozen day in the early morning. Far out in the country there was an old Negro woman with her head tied in a red rag, coming along a path through the pinewoods. Her name was Phoenix Jackson. She was very old and small and she walked slowly in the dark pine shadows, moving a little from side to side in her steps, with the balanced heaviness and lightness of a pendulum in a grandfather clock. She carried a thin, small cane made from an umbrella, and with this she kept tapping the frozen earth in front of her. This made a grave and persistent noise in the still air, that seemed meditative like the chirping of a solitary little bird.

She wore a dark striped dress reaching down to her shoe tops, and an equally long apron of bleached sugar sacks, with a full pocket: all neat and tidy, but every time she took a step she might have fallen over her shoelaces, which dragged from her unlaced shoes. She looked straight ahead. Her eyes were blue with age. Her skin had a pattern all its own of numberless branching wrinkles and as though a whole little tree stood in the middle of her forehead, but a golden color ran underneath, and the two knobs of her cheeks were illumined by a yellow burning under the dark. Under the red rag her hair came down on her neck in the frailest of ringlets, still black, and with an odor like copper.

Now and then there was a quivering in the thicket. Old Phoenix said, "Out of my way, all you foxes, owls, beetles, jack rabbits, coons and wild animals! . . . Keep out from under these feet, little bob-whites. . . . Keep the big wild hogs out of my path. Don't let none of those come running my direction. I got a long way." Under her small black-freckled hand her cane, limber as a buggy whip, would switch at the brush as if to rouse up any hiding things.

On she went. The woods were deep and still. The sun made the pine needles almost too bright to look at, up where the wind rocked. The cones dropped as light as feathers. Down in the hollow was the mourning dove— it was not too late for him.

5   The path ran up a hill. "Seem like there is chains about my feet, time I get this far," she said, in the voice of argument old people keep to use with themselves. "Something always take a hold of me on this hill—pleads I should stay."

After she got to the top she turned and gave a full, severe look behind her where she had come. "Up through pines," she said at length. "Now down through oaks."

Her eyes opened their widest, and she started down gently. But before she got to the bottom of the hill a bush caught her dress.

Her fingers were busy and intent, but her skirts were full and long, so that before she could pull them free in one place they were caught in another. It was not possible to allow the dress to tear. "I in the thorny bush," she said. "Thorns, you doing your appointed work. Never want to let folks pass, no sir. Old eyes thought you was a pretty little *green* bush."

Finally, trembling all over, she stood free, and after a moment dared to stoop for her cane.

10   "Sun so high!" she cried, leaning back and looking, while the thick tears went over her eyes. "The time getting all gone here."

At the foot of this hill was a place where a log was laid across the creek.

"Now comes the trial," said Phoenix.

Putting her right foot out, she mounted the log and shut her eyes. Lifting her skirt, leveling her cane fiercely before her, like a festival figure in some parade, she began to march across. Then she opened her eyes and she was safe on the other side.

"I wasn't as old as I thought," she said.

15   But she sat down to rest. She spread her skirts on the bank around her and folded her hands over her knees. Up above her was a tree in a pearly cloud of mistletoe. She did not dare to close her eyes, and when a little boy brought her a plate with a slice of marble-cake on it she spoke to him. "That would be acceptable," she said. But when she went to take it there was just her own hand in the air.

So she left that tree, and had to go through a barbed-wire fence. There she had to creep and crawl, spreading her knees and stretching her fingers like a baby trying to climb the steps. But she talked loudly to herself: she could not let her dress be torn now, so late in the day, and she could not pay for having her arm or her leg sawed off if she got caught fast where she was.

At last she was safe through the fence and risen up out in the clearing. Big dead trees, like black men with one arm, were standing in the purple stalks of the withered cotton field. There sat a buzzard.

"Who you watching?"

In the furrow she made her way along.

20   "Glad this not the season for bulls," she said, looking sideways, "and the good Lord made his snakes to curl up and sleep in the winter. A pleasure I don't see no two-headed snake coming around that tree, where it come once. It took a while to get by him, back in the summer."

She passed through the old cotton and went into a field of dead corn. It whispered and shook and was taller than her head. "Through the maze now," she said, for there was no path.

Then there was something tall, black, and skinny there, moving before her.

At first she took it for a man. It could have been a man dancing in the field. But she stood still and listened, and it did not make a sound. It was as silent as a ghost.

"Ghost," she said sharply, "who be you the ghost of? For I have heard of nary death close by."

25   But there was no answer—only the ragged dancing in the wind.

She shut her eyes, reached out her hand, and touched a sleeve. She found a coat and inside that an emptiness, cold as ice.

"You scarecrow," she said. Her face lighted. "I ought to be shut up for good," she said with laughter. "My senses is gone. I too old. I the oldest people I ever know. Dance, old scarecrow," she said, "while I dancing with you."

She kicked her foot over the furrow, and with mouth drawn down, shook her head once or twice in a little strutting way. Some husks blew down and whirled in streamers about her skirts.

Then she went on, parting her way from side to side with the cane, through the whispering field. At last she came to the end, to a wagon track where the silver grass blew between the red ruts. The quail were walking around like pullets, seeming all dainty and unseen.

30   "Walk pretty," she said. "This is the easy place. This the easy going."

She followed the track, swaying through the quiet bare fields, through the little strings of trees silver in their dead leaves, past cabins silver from weather, with the doors and windows boarded shut, all like old women under a spell sitting there. "I walking in their sleep," she said, nodding her head vigorously.

In a ravine she went where a spring was silently flowing through a hollow log. Old Phoenix bent and drank. "Sweet-gum makes the water sweet," she said, and drank more. "Nobody know who made this well, for it was here when I was born."

The track crossed a swampy part where the moss hung as white as lace from every limb. "Sleep on, alligators, and blow your bubbles." Then the track went into the road.

Deep, deep the road went down between the high green-colored banks. Overhead the live-oaks met, and it was as dark as a cave.

35   A black dog with a lolling tongue came up out of the weeds by the ditch. She was meditating, and not ready, and when he came at her she only hit him a little with her cane. Over she went in the ditch, like a little puff of milkweed.

Down there, her senses drifted away. A dream visited her, and she reached her hand up, but nothing reached down and gave her a pull. So she lay there and presently went to talking. "Old woman," she said to herself, "that black dog come up out of the weeds to stall you off, and now there he sitting on his fine tail, smiling at you."

A white man finally came along and found her—a hunter, a young man, with his dog on a chain.

"Well, Granny!" he laughed. "What are you doing there?"

"Lying on my back like a June-bug waiting to be turned over, mister," she said, reaching up her hand.

40   He lifted her up, gave her a swing in the air, and set her down. "Anything broken, Granny?"

"No sir, them old dead weeds is springy enough," said Phoenix, when she had got her breath. "I thank you for your trouble."

"Where do you live, Granny?" he asked, while the two dogs were growling at each other.

"Away back yonder, sir, behind the ridge. You can't even see it from here."

"On your way home?"

45   "No sir, I going to town."

"Why, that's too far! That's as far as I walk when I come out myself, and I get something for my trouble." He patted the stuffed bag he carried, and there hung down a little closed claw. It was one of the bob-whites, with its beak hooked bitterly to show it was dead. "Now you go on home, Granny!"

"I bound to go to town, mister," said Phoenix. "The time come around."

He gave another laugh, filling the whole landscape. "I know you old colored people! Wouldn't miss going to town to see Santa Claus!"

But something held old Phoenix very still. The deep lines in her face went into a fierce and different radiation. Without warning, she had seen with her own eyes a flashing nickel fall out of the man's pocket onto the ground.

50 "How old are you, Granny?" he was saying.

"There is no telling, mister," she said, "no telling."

Then she gave a little cry and clapped her hands and said, "Git on away from here, dog! Look! Look at that dog!" She laughed as if in admiration. "He ain't scared of nobody. He a big black dog." She whispered, "Sic him!"

"Watch me get rid of that cur," said the man. "Sic him, Pete! Sic him!"

Phoenix heard the dogs fighting, and heard the man running and throwing sticks. She even heard a gunshot. But she was slowly bending forward by that time, further and further forward, the lid stretched down over her eyes, as if she were doing this in her sleep. Her chin was lowered almost to her knees. The yellow palm of her hand came out from the fold of her apron. Her fingers slid down and along the ground under the piece of money with the grace and care they would have in lifting an egg from under a setting hen. Then she slowly straightened up, she stood erect, and the nickel was in her apron pocket. A bird flew by. Her lips moved. "God watching me the whole time. I come to stealing."

55 The man came back, and his own dog panted about them. "Well, I scared him off that time," he said, and then he laughed and lifted his gun and pointed it at Phoenix.

She stood straight and faced him.

"Doesn't the gun scare you?" he said, still pointing it.

"No, sir, I seen plenty go off closer by, in my day, and for less than what I done," she said, holding utterly still.

He smiled, and shouldered the gun. "Well, Granny," he said, "you must be a hundred years old, and scared of nothing. I'd give you a dime if I had any money with me. But you take my advice and stay home, and nothing will happen to you."

60 "I bound to go on my way, mister," said Phoenix. She inclined her head in the red rag. Then they went in different directions, but she could hear the gun shooting again and again over the hill.

She walked on. The shadows hung from the oak trees to the road like curtains. Then she smelled wood-smoke, and smelled the river, and she saw a steeple and the cabins on their steep steps. Dozens of little black children whirled around her. There ahead was Natchez shining. Bells were ringing. She walked on.

In the paved city it was Christmas time. There were red and green electric lights strung and crisscrossed everywhere, and all turned on in the daytime. Old Phoenix would have been lost if she had not distrusted her eyesight and depended on her feet to know where to take her.

She paused quietly on the sidewalk where people were passing by. A lady came along in the crowd, carrying an armful of red-, green- and silver-wrapped presents; she gave off perfume like the red roses in hot summer, and Phoenix stopped her.

"Please, missy, will you lace up my shoe?" She held up her foot.

65   "What do you want, Grandma?"

"See my shoe," said Phoenix. "Do all right for out in the country, but wouldn't look right to go in a big building."

"Stand still then, Grandma," said the lady. She put her packages down on the sidewalk beside her and laced and tied both shoes tightly.

"Can't lace 'em with a cane," said Phoenix. "Thank you, missy. I doesn't mind asking a nice lady to tie up my shoe, when I gets out on the street."

Moving slowly and from side to side, she went into the big building, and into a tower of steps, where she walked up and around and around until her feet knew to stop.

70   She entered a door, and there she saw nailed up on the wall the document that had been stamped with the gold seal and framed in the gold frame, which matched the dream that was hung up in her head.

"Here I be," she said. There was a fixed and ceremonial stiffness over her body.

"A charity case, I suppose," said an attendant who sat at the desk before her.

But Phoenix only looked above her head. There was sweat on her face, the wrinkles in her face shone like a bright net.

"Speak up, Grandma," the woman said. "What's your name? We must have your history, you know. Have you been here before? What seems to be the trouble with you?"

75   Old Phoenix only gave a twitch to her face as if a fly were bothering her.

"Are you deaf?" cried the attendant.

But then the nurse came in.

"Oh, that's just old Aunt Phoenix," she said. "She doesn't come for herself—she has a little grandson. She makes these trips just as regular as clockwork. She lives away back off the Old Natchez Trace." She bent down. "Well, Aunt Phoenix, why don't you just take a seat? We won't keep you standing after your long trip." She pointed.

The old woman sat down, bolt upright in the chair.

80   "Now, how is the boy?" asked the nurse.

Old Phoenix did not speak.

"I said, how is the boy?"

But Phoenix only waited and stared straight ahead, her face very solemn and withdrawn into rigidity.

"Is his throat any better?" asked the nurse. "Aunt Phoenix, don't you hear me? Is your grandson's throat any better since the last time you came for the medicine?"

85   With her hands on her knees, the old woman waited, silent, erect and motionless, just as if she were in armor.

"You mustn't take up our time this way, Aunt Phoenix," the nurse said. "Tell us quickly about your grandson, and get it over. He isn't dead, is he?"

At last there came a flicker and then a flame of comprehension across her face, and she spoke.

"My grandson. It was my memory had left me. There I sat and forgot why I made my long trip."

"Forgot?" The nurse frowned. "After you came so far?"

90   Then Phoenix was like an old woman begging a dignified forgiveness for waking up frightened in the night. "I never did go to school, I was too old at the Surrender,"[1] she said in a soft voice. "I'm an old woman without an education. It was my memory fail me. My little grandson, he is just the same, and I forgot it in the coming."

"Throat never heals, does it?" said the nurse, speaking in a loud, sure voice to old Phoenix. By now she had a card with something written on it, a little list. "Yes. Swallowed lye. When was it?—January—two–three years ago—"

Phoenix spoke unasked now. "No, missy, he not dead, he just the same. Every little while his throat begin to close up again, and he not able to swallow. He not get his breath. He not able to help himself. So the time come around, and I go on another trip for the soothing medicine."

"All right. The doctor said as long as you came to get it, you could have it," said the nurse. "But it's an obstinate case."

"My little grandson, he sit up there in the house all wrapped up, waiting by himself," Phoenix went on. "We is the only two left in the world. He suffer and it don't seem to put him back at all. He got a sweet look. He going to last. He wear a little patch quilt and peep out holding his mouth open like a little bird. I remembers so plain now. I not going to forget him again, no, the whole enduring time. I could tell him from all the others in creation."

95   "All right." The nurse was trying to hush her now. She brought her a bottle of medicine. "Charity," she said, making a check mark in a book.

Old Phoenix held the bottle close to her eyes, and then carefully put it into her pocket.

"I thank you," she said.

"It's Christmas time, Grandma," said the attendant. "Could I give you a few pennies out of my purse?"

"Five pennies is a nickel," said Phoenix stiffly.

100   "Here's a nickel," said the attendant.

---

[1] Of General Robert E. Lee to General Ulysses S. Grant at the end of the Civil War, April 9, 1865.

Phoenix rose carefully and held out her hand. She received the nickel and then fished the other nickel out of her pocket and laid it beside the new one. She stared at her palm closely, with her head on one side.

Then she gave a tap with her cane on the floor.

"This is what come to me to do," she said. "I going to the store and buy my child a little windmill they sells, made out of paper. He going to find it hard to believe there such a thing in the world. I'll march myself back where he waiting, holding it straight up in this hand."

She lifted her free hand, gave a little nod, turned around, and walked out of the doctor's office. Then her slow step began on the stairs, going down.

READING AND REACTING

1. How does the first paragraph set the scene for the story? How does it foreshadow the events that will take place later on?

2. Traditionally, a quest is a journey in which a knight overcomes a series of obstacles in order to perform a prescribed feat. In what way is Phoenix's journey like a quest? What obstacles does she face? What feat must she perform?

3. Because Phoenix is so old, she has trouble seeing. What things does she have difficulty seeing? How do her mistakes shed light on her character? How do they contribute to the impact of the story?

4. What is the major theme of this story? What other themes are expressed?

5. A phoenix is a mythical bird that would live for five hundred years, be consumed by fire, and then rise from its own ashes. In what way is this name appropriate for the main character of this story?

6. Phoenix is not intimidated by the man with the gun and has no difficulty asking a white woman to tie her shoe. In spite of this nobility of character, however, Phoenix has no qualms about stealing a nickel or taking charity from the doctor. How do you account for this apparent contradiction?

7. How do the various people Phoenix encounters react to her? Do they treat her with respect? With disdain? Why do you think they react the way they do?

8. In paragraph 90, Phoenix says that she is an old woman without an education. Does she nevertheless seem to have any knowledge that the other characters lack?

9. **JOURNAL ENTRY** Could "A Worn Path" be an **allegory?** If so, what might each of the characters represent?

10. **CRITICAL PERSPECTIVE** Writing about "A Worn Path," Eudora Welty says that the question she is asked most frequently by both students and teachers is whether Phoenix Jackson's grandson is actually dead. Here she attempts to answer this question:

> I had not meant to mystify readers by withholding any fact; it is not a writer's business to tease. The story is told through Phoenix's mind and she undertakes her errand. As the author at one with the character as I tell it, I must assume that the boy is alive. As the reader, you are free to think as you like, of course; the story invites you to believe that no matter what happens, Phoenix for as long as she is able to walk and can hold to her purpose will make her journey.

Do you think Phoenix's grandson is alive or dead? Why?

Related Works: "Miss Brill" (p. 119), "Araby" (p. 254), "Reapers" (p. 801), *The Cuban Swimmer* (p. 1495)

◆ WRITING SUGGESTIONS: THEME

1. In both "Doe Season" and "Seventeen Syllables," a young girl learns a hard lesson. Write an essay in which you compare the lessons that Andy and Rosie learn and discuss the effects the knowledge they gain has on them.
2. Two of this chapter's stories deal with the importance of patience and persistence. Write an essay in which you examine the value of enduring despite difficulties, citing the main characters in "Seventeen Syllables" and "A Worn Path." Which character is more successful? How do you explain their relative degrees of success?
3. Both "Seventeen Syllables" and "The Chrysanthemums" are about farm wives. In what ways are these wives similar? How are they different? What comment do these stories make on the condition of women in general and of rural women in particular? If you like, you may also discuss the narrator's mother in Alice Munro's "Boys and Girls" (p. 548).
4. Both "The Rocking-Horse Winner" and "A Worn Path" deal with characters who make journeys. What is the significance of each journey? How do the protagonists of these two stories overcome the obstacles they encounter? In what sense are these journeys symbolic as well as actual?
5. Like "Doe Season," the following poem focuses on a child's experience with hunting. Write an essay in which you contrast its central theme with the central theme of "Doe Season."

> > ◇

ROBERT HUFF
(1924–1993)

Rainbow[1]

After the shot the driven feathers rock
In the air and are by sunlight trapped.
Their moment of descent is eloquent.
It is the rainbow echo of a bird
5 Whose thunder, stopped, puts in my daughter's eyes
A question mark. She does not see the rainbow,
And the folding bird-fall was for her too quick.
It is about the stillness of the bird
Her eyes are asking. She is three years old;
10 Has cut her fingers; found blood tastes of salt;
But she has never witnessed quiet blood,
Nor ever seen before the peace of death.
I say: "The feathers—Look!" but she is torn
And wretched and draws back. And I am glad
15 That I have wounded her, have winged her heart,
And that she goes beyond my fathering.

6. **WEB ACTIVITY** The following Web site contains excerpts from
D. H. Lawrence's letters:

    http://www.wmich.edu/english/tchg/lit/pms/dhl.letters.html

After reading the excerpt from January 17, 1933, write an essay
discussing how Lawrence portrays his belief "in the blood, the
flesh [. . .] being wiser than the intellect." Consider Lawrence's use
of Paul, the youthful protagonist in "The Rocking-Horse Winner,"
to carry out his theme and explain why Paul's youthful perspective
is superior to the rationality of the mature characters.

---

[1] Publication date is not available.

FICTION

FOR FURTHER READING

◇ ◇ ◇

RYŪNOSUKE AKUTAGAWA
(1892–1927)

In a Grove
(1952)

THE TESTIMONY OF A WOODCUTTER
QUESTIONED BY A HIGH POLICE COMMISSIONER

Yes, sir. Certainly, it was I who found the body. This morning, as usual, I went to cut my daily quota of cedars, when I found the body in a grove in a hollow in the mountains. The exact location? About 150 meters off the Yamashina stage road.[1] It's an out-of-the-way grove of bamboo and cedars.

The body was lying flat on its back dressed in a bluish silk kimono and a wrinkled head-dress of the Kyoto style. A single sword-stroke had pierced the breast. The fallen bamboo-blades around it were stained with bloody blossoms. No, the blood was no longer running. The wound had dried up, I believe. And also, a gad-fly was stuck fast there, hardly noticing my footsteps.

You ask me if I saw a sword or any such thing?

No, nothing, sir. I found only a rope at the root of a cedar near by. And . . . well, in addition to a rope, I found a comb. That was all. Apparently he must have made a battle of it before he was murdered, because the grass and fallen bamboo-blades had been trampled down all around.

5   "A horse was near by?"

No, sir. It's hard enough for a man to enter, let alone a horse.

THE TESTIMONY OF A TRAVELING BUDDHIST PRIEST
QUESTIONED BY A HIGH POLICE COMMISSIONER

The time? Certainly, it was about noon yesterday, sir. The unfortunate man was on the road from Sekiyama to Yamashina. He was walking toward

---

[1] Near Kyoto, the capital of Japan until 1868.

Sekiyama with a woman accompanying him on horseback, who I have since learned was his wife. A scarf hanging from her head hid her face from view. All I saw was the color of her clothes, a lilac-colored suit. Her horse was a sorrel with a fine mane. The lady's height? Oh, about four feet five inches. Since I am a Buddhist priest, I took little notice about her details. Well, the man was armed with a sword as well as a bow and arrows. And I remember that he carried some twenty odd arrows in his quiver.

Little did I expect that he would meet such a fate. Truly human life is as evanescent as the morning dew or a flash of lightning. My words are inadequate to express my sympathy for him.

THE TESTIMONY OF A POLICEMAN
QUESTIONED BY A HIGH POLICE COMMISSIONER

The man that I arrested? He is a notorious brigand called Tajomaru. When I arrested him, he had fallen off his horse. He was groaning on the bridge at Awataguchi. The time? It was in the early hours of last night. For the record, I might say that the other day I tried to arrest him, but unfortunately he escaped. He was wearing a dark blue silk kimono and a large plain sword. And, as you see, he got a bow and arrows somewhere. You say that this bow and these arrows look like the ones owned by the dead man? Then Tajomaru must be the murderer. The bow wound with leather strips, the black lacquered quiver, the seventeen arrows with hawk feathers— these were all in his possession I believe. Yes, sir, the horse is, as you say, a sorrel with a fine mane. A little beyond the stone bridge I found the horse grazing by the roadside, with his long rein dangling. Surely there is some providence in his having been thrown by the horse.

10   Of all the robbers prowling around Kyoto, this Tajomaru has given the most grief to the women in town. Last autumn a wife who came to the mountain back of the Pindora of the Toribe Temple, presumably to pay a visit, was murdered, along with a girl. It has been suspected that it was his doing. If this criminal murdered the man, you cannot tell what he may have done with the man's wife. May it please your honor to look into this problem as well.

THE TESTIMONY OF AN OLD WOMAN
QUESTIONED BY A HIGH POLICE COMMISSIONER

Yes, sir, that corpse is the man who married my daughter. He does not come from Kyoto. He was a samurai in the town of Kokufu in the province of Wakasa. His name was Kanazawa no Takehiko, and his age was twenty-six. He was of a gentle disposition, so I am sure he did nothing to provoke the anger of others.

My daughter? Her name is Masago, and her age is nineteen. She is a spirited, fun-loving girl, but I am sure she has never known any man except Takehiko. She has a small, oval, dark-complected face with a mole at the corner of her left eye.

Yesterday Takehiko left for Wakasa with my daughter. What bad luck it is that things should have come to such a sad end! What has become of my daughter? I am resigned to giving up my son-in-law as lost, but the fate of my daughter worries me sick. For heaven's sake leave no stone unturned to find her. I hate that robber Tajomaru, or whatever his name is. Not only my son-in-law, but my daughter . . . (Her later words were drowned in tears.)

TAJOMARU'S CONFESSION

I killed him, but not her. Where's she gone? I can't tell. Oh, wait a minute. No torture can make me confess what I don't know. Now things have come to such a head, I won't keep anything from you.

15   Yesterday a little past noon I met that couple. Just then a puff of wind blew, and raised her hanging scarf, so that I caught a glimpse of her face. Instantly it was again covered from my view. That may have been one reason; she looked like a Bodhisattva.[2] At that moment I made up my mind to capture her even if I had to kill her man.

Why? To me killing isn't a matter of such great consequence as you might think. When a woman is captured, her man has to be killed anyway. In killing, I use the sword I wear at my side. Am I the only one who kills people? You, you don't use your swords. You kill people with your power, with your money. Sometimes you kill them on the pretext of working for their good. It's true they don't bleed. They are in the best of health, but all the same you've killed them. It's hard to say who is a greater sinner, you or me. (An ironical smile.)

But it would be good if I could capture a woman without killing her man. So, I made up my mind to capture her, and do my best not to kill him. But it's out of the question on the Yamashina stage road. So I managed to lure the couple into the mountains.

It was quite easy. I became their traveling companion, and I told them there was an old mound in the mountain over there, and that I had dug it open and found many mirrors and swords. I went on to tell them I'd buried the things in a grove behind the mountain, and that I'd like to sell them at a low price to anyone who would care to have them. Then . . . you see, isn't greed terrible? He was beginning to be moved by my talk before he knew it. In less than half an hour they were driving their horse toward the mountain with me.

When he came in front of the grove, I told them that the treasures were buried in it, and I asked them to come and see. The man had no objection—he was blinded by greed. The woman said she would wait on horseback. It was natural for her to say so, at the sight of a thick grove. To tell you the truth, my plan worked just as I wished, so I went into the grove with him, leaving her behind alone.

---

[2] A Buddhist holy person, mediator between man and the Buddha.

20   The grove is only bamboo for some distance. About fifty yards ahead there's a rather open clump of cedars. It was a convenient spot for my purpose. Pushing my way through the grove, I told him a plausible lie that the treasures were buried under the cedars. When I told him this, he pushed his laborious way toward the slender cedar visible through the grove. After a while the bamboo thinned out, and we came to where a number of cedars grew in a row. As soon as we got there, I seized him from behind. Because he was a trained, sword-bearing warrior, he was quite strong, but he was taken by surprise, so there was no help for him. I soon tied him up to the root of a cedar. Where did I get a rope? Thank heaven, being a robber, I had a rope with me, since I might have to scale a wall at any moment. Of course it was easy to stop him from calling out by gagging his mouth with fallen bamboo leaves.

When I disposed of him, I went to his woman and asked her to come and see him, because he seemed to have been suddenly taken sick. It's needless to say that this plan also worked well. The woman, her sedge hat off, came into the depths of the grove, where I led her by the hand. The instant she caught sight of her husband, she drew a small sword. I've never seen a woman of such violent temper. If I'd been off guard, I'd have got a thrust in my side. I dodged, but she kept on slashing at me. She might have wounded me deeply or killed me. But I'm Tajomaru. I managed to strike down her small sword without drawing my own. The most spirited woman is defenseless without a weapon. At least I could satisfy my desire for her without taking her husband's life.

Yes, . . . without taking his life. I had no wish to kill him. I was about to run away from the grove, leaving the woman behind in tears, when she frantically clung to my arm. In broken fragments of words, she asked that either her husband or I die. She said it was more trying than death to have her shame known to two men. She gasped out that she wanted to be the wife of whichever survived. Then a furious desire to kill him seized me. (Gloomy excitement.)

Telling you in this way, no doubt I seem a crueler man than you. But that's because you didn't see her face. Especially her burning eyes at that moment. As I saw her eye to eye, I wanted to make her my wife even if I were to be struck by lightning. I wanted to make her my wife . . . this single desire filled my mind. This was not only lust, as you might think. At that time if I'd had no other desire than lust, I'd surely not have minded knocking her down and running away. Then I wouldn't have stained my sword with his blood. But the moment I gazed at her face in the dark grove, I decided not to leave there without killing him.

But I didn't like to resort to unfair means to kill him. I untied him and told him to cross swords with me. (The rope that was found at the root of the cedar is the rope I dropped at the time.) Furious with anger, he drew his thick sword. And quick as thought, he sprang at me ferociously, without speaking a word. I needn't tell you how our fight turned out. The twenty-third stroke . . . please remember this. I'm impressed with this fact still. Nobody under the sun has ever clashed swords with me twenty strokes. (A cheerful smile.)

25   When he fell, I turned toward her, lowering my blood-stained sword. But to my great astonishment she was gone. I wondered to where she had run away. I looked for her in the clump of cedars. I listened, but heard only a groaning sound from the throat of the dying man.

As soon as we started to cross swords, she may have run away through the grove to call for help. When I thought of that, I decided it was a matter of life and death to me. So, robbing him of his sword, and bow and arrows, I ran out to the mountain road. There I found her horse still grazing quietly. It would be a mere waste of words to tell you the later details, but before I entered town I had already parted with the sword. That's all my confession. I know that my head will be hung in chains anyway, so put me down for the maximum penalty. (A defiant attitude.)

THE CONFESSION OF A WOMAN WHO HAS COME TO THE *SHIMIZU* TEMPLE

That man in the blue silk kimono, after forcing me to yield to him, laughed mockingly as he looked at my bound husband. How horrified my husband must have been! But no matter how hard he struggled in agony, the rope cut into him all the more tightly. In spite of myself I ran stumblingly toward his side. Or rather I tried to run toward him, but the man instantly knocked me down. Just at that moment I saw an indescribable light in my husband's eyes. Something beyond expression . . . his eyes make me shudder even now. That instantaneous look of my husband, who couldn't speak a word, told me all his heart. The flash in his eyes was neither anger nor sorrow . . . only a cold light, a look of loathing. More struck by the look in his eyes than by the blow of the thief, I called out in spite of myself and fell unconscious.

In the course of time I came to, and found that the man in blue silk was gone. I saw only my husband still bound to the root of the cedar. I raised myself from the bamboo-blades with difficulty, and looked into his face; but the expression in his eyes was just the same as before.

Beneath the cold contempt in his eyes, there was hatred. Shame, grief, and anger . . . I didn't know how to express my heart at that time. Reeling to my feet, I went up to my husband.

30   "Takejiro," I said to him, "since things have come to this pass, I cannot live with you. I'm determined to die, . . . but you must die, too. You saw my shame. I can't leave you alive as you are."

This was all I could say. Still he went on gazing at me with loathing and contempt. My heart breaking, I looked for his sword. It must have been taken by the robber. Neither his sword nor his bow and arrows were to be seen in the grove. But fortunately my small sword was lying at my feet. Raising it over head, once more I said, "Now give me your life. I'll follow you right away."

When he heard these words, he moved his lips with difficulty. Since his mouth was stuffed with leaves, of course his voice could not be heard at all. But at a glance I understood his words. Despising me, his look said only, "Kill me." Neither conscious nor unconscious, I stabbed the small sword through the lilac-colored kimono into his breast.

Again at this time I must have fainted. By the time I managed to look up, he had already breathed his last—still in bonds. A streak of sinking sunlight streamed through the clump of cedars and bamboos, and shone on his pale face. Gulping down my sobs, I untied the rope from his dead body. And . . . and what has become of me since I have no more strength to tell you. Anyway I hadn't the strength to die. I stabbed my own throat with the small sword, I threw myself into a pond at the foot of the mountain, and I tried to kill myself in many ways. Unable to end my life, I am still living in dishonor. (A lonely smile.) Worthless as I am, I must have been forsaken even by the most merciful Kwannon.[3] I killed my own husband. I was violated by the robber. Whatever can I do? Whatever can I . . . I . . . (Gradually, violent sobbing.)

The Story of the Murdered Man,
as Told through a Medium

After violating my wife, the robber, sitting there, began to speak comforting words to her. Of course I couldn't speak. My whole body was tied fast to the root of a cedar. But meanwhile I winked at her many times, as much as to say "Don't believe the robber." I wanted to convey some such meaning to her. But my wife, sitting dejectedly on the bamboo leaves, was looking hard at her lap. To all appearances, she was listening to his words. I was agonized by jealousy. In the meantime the robber went on with his clever talk, from one subject to another. The robber finally made his bold, brazen proposal. "Once your virtue is stained, you won't get along well with your husband, so won't you be my wife instead? It's my love for you that made me be violent toward you."

35   While the criminal talked, my wife raised her face as if in a trance. She had never looked so beautiful as at that moment. What did my beautiful wife say in answer to him while I was sitting bound there? I am lost in space, but I have never thought of her answer without burning with anger and jealousy. Truly she said, . . . "Then take me away with you wherever you go."

This is not the whole of her sin. If that were all, I would not be tormented so much in the dark. When she was going out of the grove as if in a dream, her hand in the robber's, she suddenly turned pale, and pointed at me tied to the root of the cedar, and said, "Kill him! I cannot marry you as long as he lives." "Kill him!" she cried many times, as if she had gone crazy. Even now these words threaten to blow me headlong into the

---

[3] The Buddhist goddess of mercy.

bottomless abyss of darkness. Has such a hateful thing come out of a human mouth ever before? Have such cursed words ever struck a human ear, even once? Even once such a . . . (A sudden cry of scorn.) At these words the robber himself turned pale. "Kill him," she cried, clinging to his arms. Looking hard at her, he answered neither yes or no . . . but hardly had I thought about his answer before she had been knocked down into the bamboo leaves. (Again a cry of scorn.) Quietly folding his arms, he looked at me and said, "What will you do with her? Kill her or save her? You have only to nod. Kill her?" For these words alone I would like to pardon his crime.

While I hesitated, she shrieked and ran into the depths of the grove. The robber instantly snatched at her, but he failed even to grasp her sleeve.

After she ran away, he took up my sword, and my bow and arrows. With a single stroke he cut one of my bonds. I remember his mumbling, "My fate is next." Then he disappeared from the grove. All was silent after that. No, I heard someone crying. Untying the rest of my bonds, I listened carefully, and I noticed that it was my own crying. (Long silence.)

I raised my exhausted body from the root of the cedar. In front of me there was shining the small sword which my wife had dropped. I took it up and stabbed in into my breast. A bloody lump rose to my mouth, but I didn't feel any pain. When my breast grew cold, everything was as silent as the dead in their graves. What profound silence! Not a single bird-note was heard in the sky over this grave in the hollow of the mountains. Only a lonely light lingered on the cedars and mountains. By and by the light gradually grew fainter, till the cedars and bamboo were lost to view. Lying there, I was enveloped in deep silence.

40   Then someone crept up to me. I tried to see who it was. But darkness had already been gathering round me. Someone . . . that someone drew the small sword softly out of my breast in its invisible hand. At the same time once more blood flowed into my mouth. And once and for all I sank down into the darkness of space.

◇ ◇ ◇

T. CORAGHESSAN BOYLE
(1948–   )

Greasy Lake
(1985)

It's about a mile down on the dark side of Route 88.

BRUCE SPRINGSTEEN

There was a time when courtesy and winning ways went out of style, when it was good to be bad, when you cultivated decadence like a taste. We were all dangerous characters then. We wore torn-up leather jackets, slouched around with toothpicks in our mouths, sniffed glue and ether and what somebody claimed was cocaine. When we wheeled our parents' whining station wagons out into the street we left a patch of rubber half a block long. We drank gin and grape juice, Tango, Thunderbird, and Bali Hai. We were nineteen. We were bad. We read André Gide[1] and struck elaborate poses to show that we didn't give a shit about anything. At night, we went up to Greasy Lake.

Through the center of town, up the strip, past the housing developments and shopping malls, street lights giving way to the thin streaming illumination of the headlights, trees crowding the asphalt in a black unbroken wall: that was the way out to Greasy Lake. The Indians had called it Wakan, a reference to the clarity of its waters. Now it was fetid and murky, the mud banks glittering with broken glass and strewn with beer cans and the charred remains of bonfires. There was a single ravaged island a hundred yards from shore, so stripped of vegetation it looked as if the air force had strafed it. We went up to the lake because everyone went there, because we wanted to snuff the rich scent of possibility on the breeze, watch a girl take off her clothes and plunge into the festering murk, drink beer, smoke pot, howl at the stars, savor the incongruous full-throated roar of rock and roll against the primeval susurrus[2] of frogs and crickets. This was nature.

I was there one night, late, in the company of two dangerous characters. Digby wore a gold star in his right ear and allowed his father to pay his tuition at Cornell; Jeff was thinking of quitting school to become a painter/musician/head-shop proprietor. They were both expert in the social graces, quick with a sneer, able to manage a Ford with lousy shocks over a rutted and gutted blacktop road at eighty-five while rolling a joint as compact as a Tootsie Roll Pop stick. They could lounge against a bank of booming speakers and trade "man"s with the best of them or roll out across the dance floor as if their joints worked on bearings. They were slick and quick and they wore their mirror shades at breakfast and dinner, in the shower, in closets and caves. In short, they were bad.

I drove. Digby pounded the dashboard and shouted along with Toots & the Maytals while Jeff hung his head out the window and streaked the side of my mother's Bel Air with vomit. It was early June, the air soft as a hand on your cheek, the third night of summer vacation. The first two nights we'd been out till dawn, looking for something we never found. On this, the third night, we'd cruised the strip sixty-seven times, been in and out of every bar and club we could think of in a twenty-mile radius, stopped twice for bucket chicken and forty-cent hamburgers, debated going to a party at the house of a girl Jeff's sister knew, and chucked two dozen raw

---

[1] André Gide (1869–1951). French novelist and critic whose work—much of it semi-autobiographical—examines the conflict between desire and discipline and shows individuals battling conventional morality.

[2] A whispering or rustling sound.

eggs at mailboxes and hitchhikers. It was 2:00 A.M.; the bars were closing. There was nothing to do but take a bottle of lemon-flavored gin up to Greasy Lake.

5   The taillights of a single car winked at us as we swung into the dirt lot with its tufts of weed and washboard corrugations; '57 Chevy, mint, metallic blue. On the far side of the lot, like the exoskeleton of some gaunt chrome insect, a chopper leaned against its kickstand. And that was it for excitement: some junkie half-wit biker and a car freak pumping his girl-friend. Whatever it was we were looking for, we weren't about to find it at Greasy Lake. Not that night.

But then all of a sudden Digby was fighting for the wheel. "Hey, that's Tony Lovett's car! Hey!" he shouted, while I stabbed at the brake pedal and the Bel Air nosed up to the gleaming bumper of the parked Chevy. Digby leaned on the horn, laughing, and instructed me to put my brights on. I flicked on the brights. This was hilarious. A joke. Tony would experience premature withdrawal and expect to be confronted by grim-looking state troopers with flashlights. We hit the horn, strobed the lights, and then jumped out of the car to press our witty faces to Tony's windows; for all we knew we might even catch a glimpse of some little fox's tit, and then we could slap backs with red-faced Tony, roughhouse a little, and go on to new heights of adventure and daring.

The first mistake, the one that opened the whole floodgate, was losing my grip on the keys. In the excitement, leaping from the car with the gin in one hand and a roach clip in the other, I spilled them in the grass—in the dark, rank, mysterious nighttime grass of Greasy Lake. This was a tac-tical error, as damaging and irreversible in its way as Westmoreland's deci-sion to dig in at Khe Sanh.[3] I felt it like a jab of intuition, and I stopped there by the open door, peering vaguely into the night that puddled up round my feet.

The second mistake—and this was inextricably bound up with the first—was identifying the car as Tony Lovett's. Even before the very bad character in greasy jeans and engineer boots ripped out of the driver's door, I began to realize that this chrome blue was much lighter than the robin's-egg of Tony's car, and that Tony's car didn't have rear-mounted speakers. Judging from their expressions, Digby and Jeff were privately groping toward the same inevitable and unsettling conclusion as I was.

In any case, there was no reasoning with this bad greasy character—clearly he was a man of action. The first lusty Rockette[4] kick of his steel-toed boot caught me under the chin, chipped my favorite tooth, and left me sprawled in the dirt. Like a fool, I'd gone down on one knee to comb the stiff hacked grass for the keys, my mind making connections in the

---

[3] In late 1967 North Vietnamese and Viet Cong forces mounted a strong attack against American troops at Khe Sanh, thereby causing General William C. Westmoreland, commander of U.S. forces in Vietnam, to "dig in" to defend an area of relatively lit-tle tactical importance.

[4] Famed dancing troupe at New York's Radio City Music Hall, noted for their precision and can-can-like high kicks.

most dragged-out, testudineous[5] way, knowing that things had gone wrong, that I was in a lot of trouble, and that the lost ignition key was my grail and my salvation. The three or four succeeding blows were mainly absorbed by my right buttock and the tough piece of bone at the base of my spine.

10   Meanwhile, Digby vaulted the kissing bumpers and delivered a savage kung-fu blow to the greasy character's collarbone. Digby had just finished a course in martial arts for phys-ed credit and had spent the better part of the past two nights telling us apocryphal tales of Bruce Lee types and of the raw power invested in lightning blows shot from coiled wrists, ankles, and elbows. The greasy character was unimpressed. He merely backed off a step, his face like a Toltec mask, and laid Digby out with a single whistling roundhouse blow . . . but by now Jeff had got into the act, and I was beginning to extricate myself from the dirt, a tinny compound of shock, rage, and impotence wadded in my throat.

Jeff was on the guy's back, biting at his ear. Digby was on the ground, cursing. I went for the tire iron I kept under the driver's seat. I kept it there because bad characters always keep tire irons under the driver's seat, for just such an occasion as this. Never mind that I hadn't been involved in a fight since sixth grade, when a kid with a sleepy eye and two streams of mucus depending from his nostrils hit me in the knee with a Louisville slugger,[6] never mind that I'd touched the tire iron exactly twice before, to change tires: it was there. And I went for it.

I was terrified. Blood was beating in my ears, my hands were shaking, my heart turning over like a dirtbike in the wrong gear. My antagonist was shirtless, and a single cord of muscle flashed across his chest as he bent forward to peel Jeff from his back like a wet overcoat. "Motherfucker," he spat, over and over, and I was aware in that instant that all four of us— Digby, Jeff, and myself included—were chanting "motherfucker, motherfucker," as if it were a battle cry. (What happened next? the detective asks the murderer from beneath the turned-down brim of his porkpie hat. I don't know, the murderer says, something came over me. Exactly.)

Digby poked the flat of his hand in the bad character's face and I came at him like a kamikaze, mindless, raging, stung with humiliation—the whole thing, from the initial boot in the chin to this murderous primal instant involving no more than sixty hyperventilating, gland-flooding seconds—I came at him and brought the tire iron down across his ear. The effect was instantaneous, astonishing. He was a stunt man and this was Hollywood, he was a big grimacing toothy balloon and I was a man with a straight pin. He collapsed. Wet his pants. Went loose in his boots.

A single second, big as a zeppelin, floated by. We were standing over him in a circle, gritting our teeth, jerking our necks, our limbs and hands and feet twitching with glandular discharges. No one said anything. We just stared down at the guy, the car freak, the lover, the bad greasy character laid

---

[5] Slow, like the pace of a tortoise.
[6] A popular brand of baseball bat.

low. Digby looked at me; so did Jeff. I was still holding the tire iron, a tuft of hair clinging to the crook like dandelion fluff, like down. Rattled, I dropped it in the dirt, already envisioning the headlines, the pitted faces of the police inquisitors, the gleam of handcuffs, clank of bars, the big black shadows rising from the back of the cell . . . when suddenly a raw torn shriek cut through me like all the juice in all the electric chairs in the country.

15   It was the fox. She was short, barefoot, dressed in panties and a man's shirt. "Animals!" she screamed, running at us with her fists clenched and wisps of blow-dried hair in her face. There was a silver chain round her ankle, and her toenails flashed in the glare of the headlights. I think it was the toenails that did it. Sure, the gin and the cannabis and even the Kentucky Fried may have had a hand in it, but it was the sight of those flaming toes that set us off—the toad emerging from the loaf in *Virgin Spring,*[7] lipstick smeared on a child: she was already tainted. We were on her like Bergman's deranged brothers—see no evil, hear none, speak none—panting, wheezing, tearing at her clothes, grabbing for flesh. We were bad characters, and we were scared and hot and three steps over the line—anything could have happened.

It didn't.

Before we could pin her to the hood of the car, our eyes masked with lust and greed and the purest primal badness, a pair of headlights swung into the lot. There we were, dirty, bloody, guilty, dissociated from humanity and civilization, the first of the Ur-crimes[8] behind us, the second in progress, shreds of nylon panty and spandex brassiere dangling from our fingers, our flies open, lips licked—there we were, caught in the spotlight. Nailed.

We bolted. First for the car, and then, realizing we had no way of starting it, for the woods. I thought nothing. I thought escape. The headlights came at me like accusing fingers. I was gone.

Ram-bam-bam, across the parking lot, past the chopper and into the feculent undergrowth at the lake's edge, insects flying up in my face, weeds whipping, frogs and snakes and red-eyed turtles splashing off into the night: I was already ankle-deep in muck and tepid water and still going strong. Behind me, the girl's screams rose in intensity, disconsolate, incriminating, the screams of the Sabine women,[9] the Christian martyrs, Anne Frank[10] dragged from the garret. I kept going, pursued by those cries,

---

[7] Film by Swedish director Ingmar Bergman.

[8] Primitive crimes.

[9] According to legend, members of an ancient Italian tribe abducted by Romans who took them for wives. The "Rape of the Sabine Women" has been depicted by various artists, most notably by seventeenth-century French painter Nicolas Poussin.

[10] Anne Frank (1929–1945), German Jewish girl whose family was forced to hide in an attic in Amsterdam during the Nazi occupation of the Netherlands. Frank, who along with her family was discovered by storm troopers and sent to die at the concentration camp at Belsen, is famous for her diary, which recounts her days in hiding. A new version of the diary containing five missing pages that surfaced in 1998 is awaiting publication.

imagining cops and bloodhounds. The water was up to my knees when I
realized what I was doing: I was going to swim for it. Swim the breadth of
Greasy Lake and hide myself in the thick clot of woods on the far side.
They'd never find me there.

20   I was breathing in sobs, in gasps. The water lapped at my waist as I
looked out over the moon-burnished ripples, the mats of algae that clung to
the surface like scabs. Digby and Jeff had vanished. I paused. Listened. The
girl was quieter now, screams tapering to sobs, but there were male voices,
angry, excited, and the high-pitched ticking of the second car's engine. I
waded deeper, stealthy, hunted, the ooze sucking at my sneakers. As I was
about to take the plunge—at the very instant I dropped my shoulder for the
first slashing stroke—I blundered into something. Something unspeakable,
obscene, something soft, wet, moss-grown. A patch of weed? A log? When I
reached out to touch it, it gave like a rubber duck, it gave like flesh.

In one of those nasty little epiphanies for which we are prepared by
films and TV and childhood visits to the funeral home to ponder the
shrunken painted forms of dead grandparents, I understood what it was
that bobbed there so inadmissibly in the dark. Understood, and stumbled
back in horror and revulsion, my mind yanked in six different directions
(I was nineteen, a mere child, an infant, and here in the space of five minutes I'd struck down one greasy character and blundered into the water-
logged carcass of a second), thinking, The keys, the keys, why did I have to
go and lose the keys? I stumbled back, but the muck took hold of my
feet—a sneaker snagged, balance lost—and suddenly I was pitching face
forward into the buoyant black mass, throwing out my hands in desperation while simultaneously conjuring the image of reeking frogs and
muskrats revolving in slicks of their own deliquescing juices. AAAAArrrgh!
I shot from the water like a torpedo, the dead man rotating to expose a
mossy beard and eyes cold as the moon. I must have shouted out, thrash-
ing around in the weeds, because the voices behind me suddenly became
animated.

"What was that?"

"It's them, it's them: they tried to, tried to . . . *rape* me!" Sobs.

A man's voice, flat Midwestern accent. "You sons a bitches, we'll kill
you!"

25   Frogs, crickets.

Then another voice, harsh, *r*-less, Lower East Side: "Motherfucker!" I
recognized the verbal virtuosity of the bad greasy character in the engineer boots. Tooth chipped, sneakers gone, coated in mud and slime and
worse, crouching breathless in the weeds waiting to have my ass thoroughly and definitively kicked and fresh from the hideous stinking embrace of a three-days-dead-corpse, I suddenly felt a rush of joy and
vindication: the son of a bitch was alive! Just as quickly, my bowels turned
to ice. "Come on out of there, you pansy mothers!" the bad greasy character was screaming. He shouted curses till he was out of breath.

The crickets started up again, then the frogs. I held my breath. All at
once there was a sound in the reeds, a swishing, a splash: thunk-a-thunk.

They were throwing rocks. The frogs fell silent. I cradled my head. Swish, swish, thunk-a-thunk. A wedge of feldspar the size of a cue ball glanced off my knee. I bit my finger.

It was then that they turned to the car. I heard a door slam, a curse, and then the sound of the headlights shattering—almost a good-natured sound, celebratory, like corks popping from the necks of bottles. This was succeeded by the dull booming of the fenders, metal on metal, and then the icy crash of the windshield. I inched forward, elbows and knees, my belly pressed to the muck, thinking of guerrillas and commandos and *The Naked and the Dead*.[11] I parted the weeds and squinted the length of the parking lot.

The second car—it was a Trans-Am—was still running, its high beams washing the scene in a lurid stagy light. Tire iron flailing, the greasy bad character was laying into the side of my mother's Bel Air like an avenging demon, his shadow riding up the trunks of the trees. Whomp. Whomp. Whomp-whomp. The other two guys—blond types, in fraternity jackets—were helping out with tree branches and skull-sized boulders. One of them was gathering up bottles, rocks, muck, candy wrappers, used condoms, pop-tops, and other refuse and pitching it through the window on the driver's side. I could see the fox, a white bulb behind the windshield of the '57 Chevy. "Bobbie," she whined over the thumping, "come *on*." The greasy character paused a moment, took one good swipe at the left tail-light, and then heaved the tire iron halfway across the lake. Then he fired up the '57 and was gone.

30   Blond head nodded at blond head. One said something to the other, too low for me to catch. They were no doubt thinking that in helping to annihilate my mother's car they'd committed a fairly rash act, and thinking too that there were three bad characters connected with that very car watching them from the woods. Perhaps other possibilities occurred to them as well—police, jail cells, justices of the peace, reparations, lawyers, irate parents, fraternal censure. Whatever they were thinking, they suddenly dropped branches, bottles, and rocks and sprang for their car in unison, as if they'd choreographed it. Five seconds. That's all it took. The engine shrieked, the tires squealed, a cloud of dust rose from the rutted lot and then settled back on darkness.

I don't know how long I lay there, the bad breath of decay all around me, my jacket heavy as a bear, the primordial ooze subtly reconstituting itself to accommodate my upper thighs and testicles. My jaws ached, my knee throbbed, my coccyx was on fire. I contemplated suicide, wondered if I'd need bridgework, scraped the recesses of my brain for some sort of excuse to give my parents—a tree had fallen on the car, I was blindsided by a bread truck, hit and run, vandals had got to it while we were playing

---

[11] A popular and critically successful 1948 novel by Norman Mailer, depicting U.S. Army life during World War II.

chess at Digby's. Then I thought of the dead man. He was probably the only person on the planet worse off than I was. I thought about him, fog on the lake, insects chirring eerily, and felt the tug of fear, felt the darkness opening up inside me like a set of jaws. Who was he, I wondered, this victim of time and circumstance bobbing sorrowfully in the lake at my back. The owner of the chopper, no doubt, a bad older character come to this. Shot during a murky drug deal, drowned while drunkenly frolicking in the lake. Another headline. My car was wrecked; he was dead.

When the eastern half of the sky went from black to cobalt and the trees began to separate themselves from the shadows, I pushed myself up from the mud and stepped out into the open. By now the birds had begun to take over for the crickets, and dew lay slick on the leaves. There was a smell in the air, raw and sweet at the same time, the smell of the sun firing buds and opening blossoms. I contemplated the car. It lay there like a wreck along the highway, like a steel sculpture left over from a vanished civilization. Everything was still. This was nature.

I was circling the car, as dazed and bedraggled as the sole survivor of an air blitz, when Digby and Jeff emerged from the trees behind me. Digby's face was crosshatched with smears of dirt; Jeff's jacket was gone and his shirt was torn across the shoulder. They slouched across the lot, looking sheepish, and silently came up beside me to gape at the ravaged automobile. No one said a word. After a while Jeff swung open the driver's door and began to scoop the broken glass and garbage off the seat. I looked at Digby. He shrugged. "At least they didn't slash the tires," he said.

It was true: the tires were intact. There was no windshield, the headlights were staved in, and the body looked as if it had been sledgehammered for a quarter a shot at the county fair, but the tires were inflated to regulation pressure. The car was drivable. In silence, all three of us bent to scrape the mud and shattered glass from the interior. I said nothing about the biker. When we were finished, I reached in my pocket for the keys, experienced a nasty stab of recollection, cursed myself, and turned to search the grass. I spotted them almost immediately, no more than five feet from the open door, glinting like jewels in the first tapering shaft of sunlight. There was no reason to get philosophical about it: I eased into the seat and turned the engine over.

35   It was at that precise moment that the silver Mustang with the flame decals rumbled into the lot. All three of us froze; then Digby and Jeff slid into the car and slammed the door. We watched as the Mustang rocked and bobbed across the ruts and finally jerked to a halt beside the forlorn chopper at the far end of the lot. "Let's go," Digby said. I hesitated, the Bel Air wheezing beneath me.

Two girls emerged from the Mustang. Tight jeans, stiletto heels, hair like frozen fur. They bent over the motorcycle, paced back and forth aimlessly, glanced once or twice at us, and then ambled over to where the reeds sprang up in a green fence round the perimeter of the lake. One of them cupped her hands to her mouth. "Al," she called, "Hey, Al!"

"Come on," Digby hissed. "Let's get out of here."

But it was too late. The second girl was picking her way across the lot, unsteady on her heels, looking up at us and then away. She was older—twenty-five or -six—and as she came closer we could see there was something wrong with her: she was stoned or drunk, lurching now and waving her arms for balance. I gripped the steering wheel as if it were the ejection lever of a flaming jet, and Digby spat out my name, twice, terse and impatient.

"Hi," the girl said.

40   We looked at her like zombies, like war veterans, like deaf-and-dumb pencil peddlers.

She smiled, her lips cracked and dry. "Listen," she said, bending from the waist to look in the window, "you guys seen Al?" Her pupils were pinpoints, her eyes glass. She jerked her neck. "That's his bike over there—Al's. You seen him?"

Al. I didn't know what to say. I wanted to get out of the car and retch, I wanted to go home to my parents' house and crawl into bed. Digby poked me in the ribs. "We haven't seen anybody," I said.

The girl seemed to consider this, reaching out a slim veiny arm to brace herself against the car. "No matter," she said, slurring the *t*'s, "he'll turn up." And then, as if she'd just taken stock of the whole scene—the ravaged car and our battered faces, the desolation of the place—she said: "Hey, you guys look like some pretty bad characters—been fightin', huh?" We stared straight ahead, rigid as catatonics. She was fumbling in her pocket and muttering something. Finally she held out a handful of tablets in glassine wrappers: "Hey, you want to party, you want to do some of these with me and Sarah?"

I just looked at her. I thought I was going to cry. Digby broke the silence. "No, thanks," he said, leaning over me. "Some other time."

45   I put the car in gear and it inched forward with a groan, shaking off pellets of glass like an old dog shedding water after a bath, heaving over the ruts on its worn springs, creeping toward the highway. There was a sheen of sun on the lake. I looked back. The girl was still standing there, watching us, her shoulders slumped, hand outstretched.

⋄ ⋄ ⋄

RAYMOND CARVER
(1938–1988)

Popular Mechanics
(1981)

Early that day the weather turned and the snow was melting into dirty water. Streaks of it ran down from the little shoulder-high window that faced the backyard. Cars slushed by on the street outside, where it was getting dark. But it was getting dark on the inside too.

He was in the bedroom pushing clothes into a suitcase when she came to the door.

I'm glad you're leaving! I'm glad you're leaving! she said. Do you hear?

He kept on putting his things into the suitcase.

5 Son of a bitch! I'm so glad you're leaving! She began to cry. You can't even look me in the face, can you?

Then she noticed the baby's picture on the bed and picked it up.

He looked at her and she wiped her eyes and stared at him before turning and going back to the living room.

Bring that back, he said.

Just get your things and get out, she said.

10 He did not answer. He fastened the suitcase, put on his coat, looked around the bedroom before turning off the light. Then he went out to the living room.

She stood in the doorway of the little kitchen, holding the baby.

I want the baby, he said.

Are you crazy?

No, but I want the baby. I'll get someone to come by for his things.

15 You're not touching this baby, she said.

The baby had begun to cry and she uncovered the blanket from around his head.

Oh, oh, she said, looking at the baby.

He moved toward her.

For God's sake! she said. She took a step back into the kitchen.

20 I want the baby.

Get out of here!

She turned and tried to hold the baby over in a corner behind the stove.

But he came up. He reached across the stove and tightened his hands on the baby.

Let go of him, he said.

25 Get away, get away! she cried.

The baby was red-faced and screaming. In the scuffle they knocked down a flowerpot that hung behind the stove.

He crowded her into the wall then, trying to break her grip. He held on to the baby and pushed with all his weight.

Let go of him, he said.

Don't, she said. You're hurting the baby, she said.

30 I'm not hurting the baby, he said.

The kitchen window gave no light. In the near-dark he worked on her fisted fingers with one hand and with the other hand he gripped the screaming baby up under an arm near the shoulder.

She felt her fingers being forced open. She felt the baby going from her.

No! she screamed just as her hands came loose.

She would have it, this baby. She grabbed for the baby's other arm. She caught the baby around the wrist and leaned back.

35   But he would not let go. He felt the baby slipping out of his hands and he pulled back very hard.

In this manner, the issue was decided.

◊ ◊ ◊

SANDRA CISNEROS
(1954–   )

Barbie-Q
(1991)

Yours is the one with mean eyes and a ponytail. Striped swimsuit, stilettos,[1] sunglasses, and gold hoop earrings. Mine is the one with bubble hair. Red swimsuit, stilettos, pearl earrings, and a wire stand. But that's all we can afford, besides one extra outfit apiece. Yours, "Red Flair," sophisticated A-line coatdress with a Jackie Kennedy pillbox hat, white gloves, handbag, and heels included. Mine, "Solo in the Spotlight," evening elegance in black glitter strapless gown with a puffy skirt at the bottom like a mermaid tail, formal-length gloves, pink chiffon scarf, and mike included. From so much dressing and undressing, the black glitter wears off where her titties stick out. This and a dress invented from an old sock where we cut holes here and here and here, the cuff rolled over for the glamorous, fancy-free, off-the-shoulder look.

Every time the same story. Your Barbie is roommates with my Barbie, and my Barbie's boyfriend comes over and your Barbie steals him, okay? Kiss kiss kiss. Then the two Barbies fight. You dumbbell! He's mine. Oh no he's not, you stinky! Only Ken's invisible, right? Because we don't have money for a stupid-looking boy doll when we'd both rather ask for a new Barbie outfit next Christmas. We have to make do with your mean-eyed Barbie and my bubblehead Barbie and our one outfit apiece not including the sock dress.

Until next Sunday when we are walking through the flea market on Maxwell Street and *there!* Lying on the street next to some tool bits, and platform shoes with the heels all squashed, and a fluorescent green wicker wastebasket, and aluminum foil, and hubcaps, and a pink shag rug, and windshield wiper blades, and dusty mason jars, and a coffee can full of rusty nails. *There!* Where? Two Mattel boxes. One with the "Career Gal" ensemble, snappy black-and-white business suit, three-quarter-length sleeve jacket with kick-pleat skirt, red sleeveless shell, gloves, pumps, and matching hat included. The other, "Sweet Dreams," dreamy pink-and-white plaid

---

[1] Women's shoes with a thin high heel that is narrower than a spike heel.

nightgown and matching robe, lace-trimmed slippers, hairbrush and hand mirror included. How much? Please, please, please, please, please, please, please, until they say okay.

On the outside you and me skipping and humming but inside we are doing loopity-loops and pirouetting. Until at the next vendor's stand, next to boxed pies, and bright orange toilet brushes, and rubber gloves, and wrench sets, and bouquets of feather flowers, and glass towel racks, and steel wool, and Alvin and the Chipmunks records, *there!* And *there!* And *there!* And *there!* and *there!* and *there!* and *there!* Bendable Legs Barbie with her new page-boy hairdo. Midge, Barbie's best friend. Ken, Barbie's boyfriend. Skipper, Barbie's little sister. Tutti and Todd, Barbie and Skipper's tiny twin sister and brother. Skipper's friends, Scooter and Ricky. Alan, Ken's buddy. And Francie, Barbie's MOD'ern cousin.

5   Everybody today selling toys, all of them damaged with water and smelling of smoke. Because a big toy warehouse on Halsted Street burned down yesterday—see there?—the smoke still rising and drifting across the Dan Ryan expressway. And now there is a big fire sale at Maxwell Street, today only.

So what if we didn't get our new Bendable Legs Barbie and Midge and Ken and Skipper and Tutti and Todd and Scooter and Ricky and Alan and Francie in nice clean boxes and had to buy them on Maxwell Street, all water-soaked and sooty. So what if our Barbies smell like smoke when you hold them up to your nose even after you wash and wash and wash them. And if the prettiest doll, Barbie's MOD'ern cousin Francie with real eyelashes, eyelash brush included, has a left foot that's melted a little—so? If you dress her in her new "Prom Pinks" outfit, satin splendor with matching coat, gold belt, clutch, and hair bow included, so long as you don't lift her dress, right?—who's to know.

◆ ◆ ◆

GRACE STONE COATES
(1881–1976)

Wild Plums
(1929)

I knew about wild plums twice before I tasted any.

The first time was when the Sunday school women were going plumming; Father hunched his shoulders and laughed without making any sound. He said wild plums were small and inferior, and told us of fruits he had eaten in Italy.

Mother and father were surprised that Mrs. Guare and the school teacher would go with Mrs. Slump to gather plums. I knew it was not nice to go plumming, but I didn't know why. I wanted to go once, so that I would understand. The women stopped at the house to invite mother. She explained that we did not care for wild plums; but father said we feared to taste the sacred seed lest we be constrained to dwell forever in the nether regions.

Mrs. Slump said, "Huh? You don't eat the pits. You spit 'em out," and father hunched his shoulders and laughed the noiseless laugh that bothered mother.

5   When father talked to people he didn't like he sorted his words, and used only the smooth, best ones. Mother explained to me it was because he had spoken only German when he was little.

After the women had gone mother and father quarreled. They spoke low so I would not hear them. Just before mother sent me out to play she said that even wild plums might give savor to the dry bread of monotony.

The second time I knew about plums was at Mrs. Slump's house when she was making plum butter. She said she couldn't ask us in because the floor was dirty from stirring jam. The Slumps didn't use chairs. They had boxes to sit on, and the children sat on the floor with the dogs. They were the only people I knew who had hounds. I wanted to go in. We never had visited them. We were at their house now because father needed to take home a plow they had borrowed. Father didn't like to have his machinery stand outdoors. He had a shed where he kept plows when he was not using them, but the Slumps left theirs where they unhitched.

Mrs. Slump was standing in the door with her back towards us when we drove up. She was fat, and wore wrappers. Her wrapper was torn down the back.

Mr. Slump came out, and father talked to him. He was tall and lean. Mrs. Slump came and stood by the buggy, too. Mother and father sat on the front seat of the buggy, and Teressa and I on the back seat. Teressa was older than I, and had longer legs. When she stretched her feet straight out she could touch the front seat with her toes, and I couldn't. She bumped the seat behind mother, and mother turned around and told her to stop. My feet didn't touch father's seat, so I wasn't doing anything and didn't have to stop it. Teressa pinched me.

10   I climbed out of the buggy without asking if I might. Teressa started to tell mother I was getting out, but waited to see what I intended to do. I was going to walk around behind Mrs. Slump. She had no stockings on, and the Sunday school women said she didn't wear underclothes. I wanted to see if this was so.

Mother called me back. Sometimes mother knew what I was thinking about without asking me. She took hold of my arm, hard, as I climbed onto the buggy step, and said under her breath, "I'd be ashamed! I'd be ashamed!" Her face was twisted because she tried not to stop smiling at Mrs. Slump while she shook my arm. I kept trying to explain, but she wouldn't let me. Her stopping me made me want to say the thing she thought I was going to, but I didn't dare.

Mr. Slump said he would bring the plow back in the morning. Father wanted to take it home himself, then; but Mr. Slump said he wouldn't hear to it, being as how he had borrowed it and all. He would bring it behind the lumber wagon the next day, and leave it in the road. They were going after more plums and would be passing the house anyway.

The next morning after breakfast, father, mother, and I were in the kitchen. Teressa had scraped the plates and gone to feed the chickens. She did not like to sit still while people talked. She liked to do things that made her move around. Mother and father were talking, and I was looking out of the window. If I looked at the sun and then away, it made enormous morning-glories float over the yard. Father had told me they were in my eyes and not in the air, so I didn't call him to look at them. While I was watching them, Clubby Slump came up the lane in the middle of a lavender one. Clubby was bigger than I, and stupider. When any one spoke to him, he stood with his mouth open and didn't answer. His hair needed combing, and he didn't use a handkerchief. Mother said good morning to him. He pointed to a wagon at the end of the lane. He said, "Plums!" and ran back down the path.

Mother and father started toward the road, and I went ahead of them. The wagon had stopped at the foot of the cottonwood lane. Mr. Slump sat on the high board seat, holding the reins. Mrs. Slump was beside him, with the baby on her lap. Liney Slump was between them. On the seat behind were Mrs. Guare and two women I didn't know. The rest of the wagon was full of children. Mr. Slump had forgotten the plow.

15 "All you'uns pile in," Mrs. Slump called to us. "We're goin' plummin' on the Niniscaw and stay all night. The younguns can go wadin'. There ain't no work drivin' you this time a' year, so just pile in. We got beddin' for everybody."

Mr. Slump sat looking at the horses' ears. Whenever Mrs. Slump stopped talking he would say, "I *tole* you they'all wouldn't go, but you *would* stop," and Mrs. Slump would answer, "There now, Paw, you hush!"

I had not known one could live so long without breathing as I lived while Mrs. Slump was asking us to go. I could see my heart-beats shaking my collar—a lace collar that was hanging by one end down my chest; I had forgotten to put it on right.

I waited for mother to lift her foot and plant it on the wagon hub, ready for "pilin' in"; for father to take her elbow, and lift. Every one would laugh a little, and talk loud. They always did when women got into wagons. I had never seen mother climb into a wagon, but I knew how it would be. I wondered if father would jump in without tossing me up first. Father got into wagons quick, without laughing or joking. I wondered if he would forget me. The children would see me, and lean over the end-board, and dangle me up by one arm. I thought frantically of Teressa.

Then father was speaking, and my breath came back.

20 He was saying, "If you happen on a plum thicket, an outcome highly unlikely, you still face the uncertainty of finding plums. The season has been too dry. And should you find them, they will prove acrid and unfit for human consumption."

My collar hung limp and motionless. My heart was dead. Father was spoiling things again.

Mrs. Slump said, "They make fine jell," and Mr. Slump repeated, "I *tole* you they-all wouldn't go, but you *would* stop." He was gathering up the lines.

I hated to see mother's face, feeling the stricken look it would have. But I knew I must smile at her not to care. Strangely enough, she had a polite look on her face. It was the look that made my fingers think of glass. My mind slipped off from it without knowing what it meant. She was smiling.

"Really, it isn't possible for us to go with you to-day," she said. "It was kind of you to ask us. I hope you will have a lovely outing, and find lots of plums."

25   As she spoke she glanced at me. She moved closer, and took my hand. Mrs. Slump looked down at me, too, and said, "Can't the kids go? Kids like bein' out."

Mother's hand closed firmly on mine. "I'm afraid not, without me. Besides," with a severe look at my collar, "she isn't properly dressed."

Oh, we kin wait while she takes off that purty dress," Mrs. Slump suggested comfortably; but mother flushed and shook her head.

Mr. Slump was twitching at the lines and clucking to the horses. His last "I tole you" was drowned in shouted good-bys, and the wagon clattered down the road.

Mother walked back to the house still holding my hand. Once inside, she turned to me. "Would you really have gone with those—" She hesitated, and finished, "with those persons?"

30   "They were going to sleep outdoors all night," I said.

Mother shuddered. "Would you have gone with them?"

"Mrs. Guare was with them," I parried, knowing all she did not say.

"Would you have gone?"

"Yes."

35   She stood for a long time looking out of the window at the prairie horizon, then searched my face curiously. "It might have been as well," she said. "It might be as well," and turning, she began to clear the breakfast table.

The next day I played in the road. Usually I spent the afternoons under the box-elder trees, or by the ditch behind the machine-sheds, where dragon-flies and pale blue moths circled just out of reach. But this day I spent beside the road. Mother called me to the house to bring cobs, and called me again to gather eggs in the middle of the afternoon. She called me a third time. Her face looked uncomfortable.

She said, "If the Slumps go by, do not ask them for any plums."

Mother knew I would not ask.

"If they offer any, do not take them."

40   "What shall I say?"

"Say we do not care for them."

"If they make me take them?"

"Refuse them."

When the Slumps came in sight the horses were walking. The Ninis-caw was fifteen miles away, and the team was tired. I thought I could talk to the children as the wagon passed, but just before it reached me, Mr. Slump hit the horses twice with a willow branch. They trotted, and the wagon rattled by.

45   The children on the last seat were facing toward me. They laughed and waved their arms. Clubby leaned backward and caught up a handful of plums. The wagon bed must have been half filled. He flung them toward me; and then another handful. They fell, scattering, in the thick dust, which curled around them in little eddies, almost hiding them before I could catch them up.

The plums were small and red. They felt warm to my fingers. I wiped them on the front of my dress, and dropped them in my apron. I waited only for one secret rite, before I ran, heart pounding, to tell my mother what I had discovered.

She interrupted me, "Did they see you picking them up?"

I thought of myself standing like Clubby Slump, mouth open, without moving. I laughed till two plums rolled out of my apron. "Oh, yes! I had them picked up almost before the dust stopped wriggling. I called, 'Thank you.'"

Still mother was not pleased. "Throw them away," she said. "Surely you would not care to eat something flung to you in the road."

50   It was hard to speak. I moved close to her and whispered, "Can't I keep them?"

Mother left the room. It seemed long before she came back. She put her arm around me and said, "Take them to the pump and wash them thoroughly. Eat them slowly, and do not swallow the skins. You will not want many of them, for you will find them bitter and not fit to eat."

I went out quietly, knowing I would never tell her that they were strange on my tongue as wild honey, holding the warmth of sand that sun had fingered, and the mystery of water under leaning boughs.

For I had eaten one at the road.

◇ ◇ ◇

CHITRA BANERJEE DIVAKARUNI
(1956–   )

The Disappearance
(1995)

At first when they heard about the disappearance, people didn't believe it.

Why, we saw her just yesterday at the Ram Ratan Indian Grocery, friends said, picking out radishes for pickling. And wasn't she at the Mountain View park with her little boy last week, remember, we waved from our car and she waved back, she was in that blue *salwaar-kameez*, yes, she never did wear American clothes. And the boy waved too, he must be, what, two and a half? Looks just like her with those big black eyes, that dimple. What a shame, they said, it's getting so that you aren't safe anywhere in this country nowadays.

Because that's what everyone suspected, including the husband. Crime. Otherwise, he said to the investigating policeman (he had called the police that very night), how could a young Indian woman wearing a yellow-flowered *kurta* and Nike walking shoes just *disappear*? She'd been out for her evening walk, she took one every day after he got back from the office. Yes, yes, always alone, she said that was her time for herself. (He didn't quite understand that, but he was happy to watch his little boy, play ball with him, perhaps, until she returned to serve them dinner.)

Did you folks have a quarrel, asked the policeman, looking up from his notepad with a frown, and the husband looked directly back into his eyes and said, No, of course we didn't.

5   Later he would think about what the policeman had asked, while he sat in front of his computer in his office, or while he lay in the bed which still seemed to smell of her. (But surely that was his imagination—the linen had been washed already.) He *had* told the truth about them not having a quarrel, hadn't he? (He prided himself on being an honest man, he often told his son how important it was not to lie, see what happened to Pinocchio's nose. And even now when the boy asked him where Mama was, he didn't say she had gone on a trip, as some of his friends' wives had advised him. I don't know, he said. And when the boy's thin face would crumple, want Mama, when she coming back, he held him in his lap awkwardly and tried to stroke his hair, like he had seen his wife do, but he couldn't bring himself to say what the boy needed to hear, *soon-soon*. I don't know, he said over and over.)

They hadn't really had a fight. She wasn't, thank God, the quarrelsome type, like some of his friends' wives. Quiet. That's how she was, at least around him, although sometimes when he came home unexpectedly he would hear her singing to her son, her voice slightly off-key but full and confident. Or laughing as she chased him around the family room, Mama's going to get you, get you, both of them shrieking with delight until they saw him. Hush now, she would tell the boy, settle down, and they would walk over sedately to give him his welcome-home kiss.

He couldn't complain, though. Wasn't that what he had specified when his mother started asking, When are you getting married, I'm getting old, I want to see a grandson before I die.

If you can find me a quiet, pretty girl, he wrote, not brash, like Calcutta girls are nowadays, not with too many western ideas. Someone who would be relieved to have her husband make the major decisions. But she had to be smart, at least a year of college, someone he could introduce to his friends with pride.

He'd flown to Calcutta to view several suitable girls that his mother had picked out. But now, thinking back, he can only remember her. She had sat, head bowed, jasmine plaited into her hair, silk sari draped modestly over her shoulders, just like all the other prospective brides he'd seen. Nervous, he'd thought, yearning to be chosen. But when she'd glanced up there had been a cool, considering look in her eyes. Almost disinterested, almost as though *she* were wondering if he would make a suitable spouse. He had wanted her then, had married her within the week in spite of his mother's protests (had she caught that same look?) that something about the girl just didn't feel *right*.

10   He was a good husband. No one could deny it. He let her have her way, indulged her, even. When the kitchen was remodeled, for example, and she wanted pink and gray tiles even though he preferred white. Or when she wanted to go to Yosemite Park instead of Reno, although he knew he would be dreadfully bored among all those bearshit-filled trails and dried-up waterfalls. Once in a while, of course, he had to put his foot down, like when she wanted to get a job or go back to school or buy American clothes. But he always softened his no's with a remark like, What for, I'm here to take care of you, or, You look so much prettier in your Indian clothes, so much more feminine. He would pull her onto his lap and give her a kiss and a cuddle which usually ended with him taking her to the bedroom.

That was another area where he'd had to be firm. Sex. She was always saying, Please, not tonight, I don't feel up to it. He didn't mind that. She was, after all, a well-bred Indian girl. He didn't expect her to behave like those American women he sometimes watched on X-rated videos, screaming and biting and doing other things he grew hot just thinking about. But her reluctance went beyond womanly modesty. After dinner for instance she would start on the most elaborate household projects, soaping down the floors, changing the liners in cabinets. The night before she disappeared she'd started cleaning windows, taken out the Windex and the rags as soon as she'd put the boy to bed, even though he said, Let's go. Surely he couldn't be blamed for raising his voice at those times (though never so much as to wake his son), or for grabbing her by the elbow and pulling her to the bed, like he did that last night. He was always careful not to hurt her, he prided himself on that. Not even a little slap, not like some of the men he'd known growing up, or even some of his friends now. And he always told himself he'd stop if she really begged him, if she cried. After some time, though, she would quit struggling and let him do what he wanted. But that was nothing new. That could have nothing to do with the disappearance.

Two weeks passed and there was no news of the woman, even though the husband had put a notice in the *San Jose Mercury* as well as a half-page ad in *India West,* which he photocopied and taped to neighborhood lampposts. The ad had a photo of her, a close-up taken in too-bright sunlight where she gazed gravely at something beyond the camera. WOMAN MISSING, read the ad. REWARD $100,000. (How on earth would he come up with that kind of money, asked his friends. The husband confessed that it would be difficult, but he'd manage somehow. His wife was more important to him, after all, than all the money in the world. And to prove it he went to the bank the very same day and brought home a sheaf of forms to fill so that he could take out a second mortgage on the house.) He kept calling the police station, too, but the police weren't much help. They were working on it, they said. They'd checked the local hospitals and morgues, the shelters. They'd even sent her description to other states. But there were no leads. It didn't look very hopeful.

So finally he called India and over a faulty long-distance connection that made his voice echo eerily in his ear told his mother what had happened. My poor boy, she cried, left all alone (the word flickered unpleasantly across his brain, *left, left*), how can you possibly cope with the household and a child as well. And when he admitted that yes, it was very difficult, could she perhaps come and help out for a while if it wasn't too much trouble, she had replied that of course she would come right away and stay as long as he needed her, and what was all this American nonsense about too much trouble, he was her only son, wasn't he. She would contact the wife's family too, she ended, so he wouldn't have to deal with that awkwardness.

Within a week she had closed up the little flat she had lived in since her husband's death, got hold of a special family emergency visa, and was on her way. Almost as though she'd been waiting for something like this to happen, said some of the women spitefully. (These were his wife's friends, though maybe acquaintances would be a more accurate word. His wife had liked to keep to herself, which had been just fine with him. He was glad, he'd told her several times, that she didn't spend hours chattering on the phone like the other Indian wives.)

15   He was angry when this gossip reached him (perhaps because he'd had the same insidious thought for a moment when, at the airport, he noticed how happy his mother looked, her flushed excited face appearing suddenly young). Really, he said to his friends, some people see only what they *want* to see. Didn't *they* think it was a good thing she'd come over? Oh yes, said his friends. Look how well the household was running now, the furniture dusted daily, laundry folded and put into drawers (his mother, a smart woman, had figured out the washing machine in no time at all). She cooked all his favorite dishes, which his wife had never managed to learn quite right, and she took *such* good care of the little boy, walking him to the park each afternoon, bringing him into her bed when he woke up crying at night. (He'd told her once or twice that his wife had never done that, she had this idea about the boy needing to be independent. What nonsense, said his mother.) Lucky man, a couple of his friends added and he silently agreed, although later he thought it was ironic that they would say that about a man whose wife had disappeared.

As the year went on, the husband stopped thinking as much about the wife. It wasn't that he loved her any less, or that the shock of her disappearance was less acute. It was just that it wasn't on his mind all the time. There would be stretches of time—when he was on the phone with an important client, or when he was watching after-dinner TV or driving his son to kiddie gym class—when he would forget that his wife was gone, that he had had a wife at all. And even when he remembered that he had forgotten, he would experience only a slight twinge, similar to what he felt in his teeth when he drank something too cold too fast. The boy, too, didn't ask as often about his mother. He was sleeping through the nights again, he had put on a few pounds (because he was finally being fed right, said the grandmother), and he had started calling her "Ma," just like his father did.

So it seemed quite natural for the husband to, one day, remove the photographs of his wife from the frames that sat on the mantelpiece and replace them with pictures of himself and his little boy that friends had taken on a recent trip to Great America, and also one of the boy on his grandma's lap, holding a red birthday balloon, smiling (she said) exactly like his father used to at that age. He put the old pictures into a manila envelope and slid them to the back of a drawer, intending to show them to his son when he grew up. The next time his mother asked (as she had been doing ever since she got there), shall I put away all those saris and *kameezes*, it'll give you more space in the closet, he said, if you like. When she said, it's now over a year since the tragedy, shouldn't we have a prayer service done at the temple, he said OK. And when she told him, you really should think about getting married again, you're still young, and besides, the boy needs a mother, shall I contact second aunt back home, he remained silent but didn't disagree.

Then one night while cooking cauliflower curry, her specialty, his mother ran out of *hing*, which was, she insisted, essential to the recipe. The Indian grocery was closed, but the husband remembered that sometimes his wife used to keep extra spices on the top shelf. So he climbed on a chair to look. There were no extra spices, but he did find something he had forgotten about, an old tea tin in which he'd asked her to hide her jewelry in case the house ever got burgled. Nothing major was ever kept there. The expensive wedding items were all stored in a vault. Still, the husband thought it would be a good idea to take them into the bank in the morning.

But when he picked up the tin it felt surprisingly light, and when he opened it, there were only empty pink nests of tissue inside.

20   He stood there holding the tin for a moment, not breathing. Then he reminded himself that his wife had been a careless woman. He'd often had to speak to her about leaving things lying around. The pieces could be anywhere—pushed to the back of her makeup drawer or forgotten under a pile of books in the spare room where she used to spend inordinate amounts of time reading. Nevertheless he was not himself the rest of the evening, so much so that his mother said, What happened, you're awfully

quiet, are you all right, your face looks funny. He told her he was fine, just a little pain in the chest area. Yes, he would make an appointment with the doctor tomorrow, no, he wouldn't forget, now could she please leave him alone for a while.

The next day he took the afternoon off from work, but he didn't go to the doctor. He went to the bank. In a small stuffy cubicle that smelled faintly of mold, he opened his safety deposit box to find that all her jewelry was gone. She hadn't taken any of the other valuables.

The edges of the cubicle seemed to fade and darken at the same time, as though the husband had stared at a lightbulb for too long. He ground his fists into his eyes and tried to imagine her on that last morning, putting the boy in his stroller and walking the twenty minutes to the bank (they only had one car, which he took to work; they could have afforded another, but why, he said to his friends, when she didn't even know how to drive). Maybe she had sat in this very cubicle and lifted out the emerald earrings, the pearl choker, the long gold chain. He imagined her wrapping the pieces carefully in plastic bags, the thin, clear kind one got at the grocery for vegetables, then slipping them into her purse. Or did she just throw them in anyhow, the strands of the necklace tangling, the brilliant green stones clicking against each other in the darkness inside the handbag, the boy laughing and clapping his hands at this new game.

At home that night he couldn't eat any dinner, and before he went to bed he did thirty minutes on the dusty exercise bike that sat in the corner of the family room. Have you gone crazy, asked his mother. He didn't answer. When he finally lay down, the tiredness did not put him to sleep as he had hoped. His calves ached from the unaccustomed strain, his head throbbed from the images that would not stop coming, and the bedclothes, when he pulled them up to his neck, smelled again of his wife's hair.

Where was she now? And with whom? Because surely she couldn't manage on her own. He'd always thought her to be like the delicate purple passion-flower vines that they'd put up on trellises along their back fence, and once, early in the marriage, had presented her with a poem he'd written about this. He remembered how, when he held out the sheet to her, she'd stared at him for a long moment and a look he couldn't quite read had flickered in her eyes. Then she'd taken the poem with a small smile. He went over and over all the men she might have known, but they (mostly his Indian friends) were safely married and still at home, every one.

25 The bed felt hot and lumpy. He tossed his feverish body around like a caught animal, punched the pillow, threw the blanket to the floor. Even thought, for a wild moment, of shaking the boy awake and asking him, *Who did your mama see?* And as though he had an inbuilt antenna that picked up his father's agitation, in the next room the boy started crying (which he hadn't done for months), shrill screams that left him breathless. And when his father and grandmother rushed to see what the problem

was, he pushed them from him with all the strength in his small arms, saying, Go way, don't want you, want Mama, want Mama.

After the boy had been dosed with gripe water and settled in bed again, the husband sat alone in the family room with a glass of brandy. He wasn't a drinker. He believed that alcohol was for weak men. But somehow he couldn't face the rumpled bed just yet, the pillows wrested onto the floor. The unknown areas of his wife's existence yawning blackly around him like chasms. Should he tell the police, he wondered, would it do any good? What if somehow his friends came to know? *Didn't I tell you, right from the first,* his mother would say. And anyway it was possible she was already dead, killed by a stranger from whom she'd hitched a ride, or by a violent, jealous lover. He felt a small, bitter pleasure at the thought, and then a pang of shame.

Nevertheless he made his way to the dark bedroom (a trifle unsteadily; the drink had made him light-headed) and groped in the bottom drawer beneath his underwear until he felt the course manila envelope with her photos. He drew it out and, without looking at them, tore the pictures into tiny pieces. Then he took them over to the kitchen, where the trash compactor was.

The roar of the compactor seemed to shake the entire house. He stiffened, afraid his mother would wake and ask what was going on, but she didn't. When the machine ground to a halt, he took a long breath. Finished, he thought. Finished. Tomorrow he would contact a lawyer, find out the legal procedure for remarriage. Over dinner he would mention to his mother, casually, that it was OK with him if she wanted to contact second aunt. Only this time he didn't want a college-educated woman. Even good looks weren't that important. A simple girl, maybe from their ancestral village. Someone whose family wasn't well off, who would be suitably appreciative of the comforts he could provide. Someone who would be a real mother to his boy.

He didn't know then that it wasn't finished. That even as he made love to his new wife (a plump, cheerful girl, good-hearted, if slightly unimaginative), or helped his daughters with their homework, or disciplined his increasingly rebellious son, he would wonder about *her*. Was she alive? Was she happy? With a sudden anger that he knew to be irrational, he would try to imagine her body tangled in swaying kelp at the bottom of the ocean where it had been flung. Bloated. Eaten by fish. But all he could conjure up was the intent look on her face when she rocked her son back and forth, singing a children's rhyme in Bengali, *Khoka jabe biye korte, shonge chhasho dhol, my little boy is going to be married, six hundred drummers.* Years later, when he was an old man living in a home for seniors (his second wife dead, his daughters moved away to distant towns, his son not on speaking terms with him), he would continue to be dazzled by that brief unguarded joy in her face, would say to himself, again, how much she must have hated me to choose to give *that* up.

30   But he had no inkling of any of this yet. So he switched off the trash compactor with a satisfied click, the sense of a job well done and, after taking a shower (long and very hot, the way he liked it, the hard jets of water turning the skin of his chest a dull red), went to bed and fell immediately into a deep, dreamless sleep.

◇ ◇ ◇

LOUISE ERDRICH

(1954–   )

Fleur
(1986)

The first time she drowned in the cold and glassy waters of Lake Turcot, Fleur Pillager was only a girl. Two men saw the boat tip, saw her struggle in the waves. They rowed over to the place she went down, and jumped in. When they dragged her over the gunwales, she was cold to the touch and stiff, so they slapped her face, shook her by the heels, worked her arms back and forth, and pounded her back until she coughed up lake water. She shivered all over like a dog, then took a breath. But it wasn't long afterward that those two men disappeared. The first wandered off, and the other, Jean Hat, got himself run over by a cart.

It went to show, my grandma said. It figured to her, all right. By saving Fleur Pillager, those two men had lost themselves.

The next time she fell in the lake, Fleur Pillager was twenty years old and no one touched her. She washed onshore, her skin a dull dead gray, but when George Many Women bent to look closer, he saw her chest move. Then her eyes spun open, sharp black riprock, and she looked at him. "You'll take my place," she hissed. Everybody scattered and left her there, so no one knows how she dragged herself home. Soon after that we noticed Many Women changed, grew afraid, wouldn't leave his house, and would not be forced to go near water. For his caution, he lived until the day that his sons brought him a new tin bathtub. Then the first time he used the tub he slipped, got knocked out, and breathed water while his wife stood in the other room frying breakfast.

Men stayed clear of Fleur Pillager after the second drowning. Even though she was good-looking, nobody dared to court her because it was clear that Misshepeshu, the waterman, the monster, wanted her for himself. He's a devil, that one, love-hungry with desire and maddened for the touch of young girls, the strong and daring especially, the ones like Fleur.

5   Our mothers warn us that we'll think he's handsome, for he appears with green eyes, copper skin, a mouth tender as a child's. But if you fall into his arms, he sprouts horns, fangs, claws, fins. His feet are joined as one and his skin, brass scales, rings to the touch. You're fascinated, cannot move. He casts a shell necklace at your feet, weeps gleaming chips that harden into mica on your breasts. He holds you under. Then he takes the

body of a lion or a fat brown worm. He's made of gold. He's made of beach moss. He's a thing of dry foam, a thing of death by drowning, the death a Chippewa cannot survive.

Unless you are Fleur Pillager. We all knew she couldn't swim. After the first time, we thought she'd never go back to Lake Turcot. We thought she'd keep to herself, live quiet, stop killing men off by drowning in the lake. After the first time, we thought she'd keep the good ways. But then, after the second drowning, we knew that we were dealing with something much more serious. She was haywire, out of control. She messed with evil, laughed at the old women's advice, and dressed like a man. She got herself into some half-forgotten medicine, studied ways we shouldn't talk about. Some say she kept the finger of a child in her pocket and a powder of unborn rabbits in a leather thong around her neck. She laid the heart of an owl on her tongue so she could see at night, and went out, hunting, not even in her own body. We know for sure because the next morning, in the snow or dust, we followed the tracks of her bare feet and saw where they changed, where the claws sprang out, the pad broadened and pressed into the dirt. By night we heard her chuffing cough, the bear cough. By day her silence and the wide grin she threw to bring down our guard made us frightened. Some thought that Fleur Pillager should be driven off the reservation, but not a single person who spoke like this had the nerve. And finally, when people were just about to get together and throw her out, she left on her own and didn't come back all summer. That's what this story is about.

During that summer, when she lived a few miles south in Argus, things happened. She almost destroyed that town.

When she got down to Argus in the year of 1920, it was just a small grid of six streets on either side of the railroad depot. There were two elevators, one central, the other a few miles west. Two stores competed for the trade of the three hundred citizens, and three churches quarreled with one another for their souls. There was a frame building for Lutherans, a heavy brick one for Episcopalians, and a long narrow shingled Catholic church. This last had a tall slender steeple, twice as high as any building or tree.

No doubt, across the low, flat wheat, watching from the road as she came near Argus on foot, Fleur saw that steeple rise, a shadow thin as a needle. Maybe in that raw space it drew her the way a lone tree draws lightning. Maybe, in the end, the Catholics are to blame. For if she hadn't seen that sign of pride, that slim prayer, that marker, maybe she would have kept walking.

10   But Fleur Pillager turned, and the first place she went once she came into town was to the back door of the priest's residence attached to the landmark church. She didn't go there for a handout, although she got that, but to ask for work. She got that too, or the town got her. It's hard to tell which came out worse, her or the men or the town, although the upshot of it all was that Fleur lived.

The four men who worked at the butcher's had carved up about a thousand carcasses between them, maybe half of that steers and the other half pigs, sheep, and game animals like deer, elk, and bear. That's not even mentioning the chickens, which were beyond counting. Pete Kozka owned the place, and employed Lily Veddar, Tor Grunewald, and my stepfather, Dutch James, who had brought my mother down from the reservation the year before she disappointed him by dying. Dutch took me out of school to take her place. I kept house half the time and worked the other in the butcher shop, sweeping floors, putting sawdust down, running a hambone across the street to a customer's bean pot or a package of sausage to the corner. I was a good one to have around because until they needed me, I was invisible. I blended into the stained brown walls, a skinny, big-nosed girl with staring eyes. Because I could fade into a corner or squeeze beneath a shelf, I knew everything, what the men said when no one was around, and what they did to Fleur.

Kozka's Meats served farmers for a fifty-mile area, both to slaughter, for it had a stock pen and chute, and to cure the meat by smoking it or spicing it in sausage. The storage locker was a marvel, made of many thicknesses of brick, earth insulation, and Minnesota timber, lined inside with sawdust and vast blocks of ice cut from Lake Turcot, hauled down from home each winter by horse and sledge.

A ramshackle board building, part slaughterhouse, part store, was fixed to the low, thick square of the lockers. That's where Fleur worked. Kozka hired her for her strength. She could lift a haunch or carry a pole of sausages without stumbling, and she soon learned cutting from Pete's wife, a string-thin blonde who chain-smoked and handled the razor-sharp knives with nerveless precision, slicing close to her stained fingers. Fleur and Fritzie Kozka worked afternoons, wrapping their cuts in paper, and Fleur hauled the packages to the lockers. The meat was left outside the heavy oak doors that were only opened at 5:00 each afternoon, before the men ate supper.

Sometimes Dutch, Tor, and Lily ate at the lockers, and when they did I stayed too, cleaned floors, restoked the fires in the front smokehouses, while the men sat around the squat cast-iron stove spearing slats of herring onto hardtack bread. They played long games of poker or cribbage on a board made from the planed end of a salt crate. They talked and I listened, although there wasn't much to hear since almost nothing ever happened in Argus. Tor was married, Dutch had lost my mother, and Lily read circulars. They mainly discussed about the auctions to come, equipment, or women.

15   Every so often, Pete Kozka came out front to make a whist, leaving Fritzie to smoke cigarettes and fry raised doughnuts in the back room. He sat and played a few rounds but kept his thoughts to himself. Fritzie did not tolerate him talking behind her back, and the one book he read was the New Testament. If he said something, it concerned weather or a surplus of sheep stomachs, a ham that smoked green or the markets for corn and

what. He had a good-luck talisman, the opal-white lens of a cow's eye. Playing cards, he rubbed it between his fingers. That soft sound and the slap of cards was about the only conversation.

Fleur finally gave them a subject.

Her cheeks were wide and flat, her hands large, chapped, muscular. Fleur's shoulders were broad as beams, her hips fishlike, slippery, narrow. An old green dress clung to her waist, worn thin where she sat. Her braids were thick like the tails of animals, and swung against her when she moved, deliberately, slowly in her work, held in and half-tamed, but only half. I could tell, but the others never saw. They never looked into her sly brown eyes or noticed her teeth, strong and curved and very white. Her legs were bare, and since she padded around in beadwork moccasins they never saw that her fifth toes were missing. They never knew she'd drowned. They were blinded, they were stupid, they only saw her in the flesh.

And yet it wasn't just that she was a Chippewa, or even that she was a woman, it wasn't that she was good-looking or even that she was alone that made their brains hum. It was how she played cards.

Women didn't usually play with men, so the evening that Fleur drew a chair up to the men's table without being so much as asked, there was a shock of surprise.

20 "What's this," said Lily. He was fat, with a snake's cold pale eyes and precious skin, smooth and lily-white, which is how he got his name. Lily had a dog, a stumpy mean little bull of a thing with a belly drum-tight from eating pork rinds. The dog liked to play cards just like Lily, and straddled his barrel thighs through games of stud, rum poker, vingt-un.[1] The dog snapped at Fleur's arm that first night, but cringed back, its snarl frozen, when she took her place.

"I thought," she said, her voice soft and stroking, "you might deal me in."

There was a space between the heavy bin of spiced flour and the wall where I just fit. I hunkered down there, kept my eyes open, saw her black hair swing over the chair, her feet solid on the wood floor. I couldn't see up on the table where the cards slapped down, so after they were deep in their game I raised myself up in the shadows, and crouched on a sill of wood.

I watched Fleur's hands stack and ruffle, divide the cards, spill them to each player in a blur, rake them up and shuffle again. Tor, short and scrappy, shut one eye and squinted the other at Fleur. Dutch screwed his lips around a wet cigar.

"Gotta see a man," he mumbled, getting up to go out back to the privy. The others broke, put their cards down, and Fleur sat alone in the lamplight that glowed in a sheen across the push of her breasts. I watched her closely, then she paid me a beam of notice for the first time. She

---

[1] Twenty-one, a card game.

turned, looked straight at me, and grinned the white wolf grin a Pillager turns on its victims, except that she wasn't after me.

25   "Pauline there," she said, "how much money you got?"

We'd all been paid for the week that day. Eight cents was in my pocket.

"Stake me," she said, holding out her long fingers. I put the coins in her palm and then I melted back to nothing, part of the walls and tables. It was a long time before I understood that the men would not have seen me no matter what I did, how I moved. I wasn't anything like Fleur. My dress hung loose and my back was already curved, an old woman's. Work had roughened me, reading made my eyes sore, caring for my mother before she died had hardened my face. I was not much to look at, so they never saw me.

When the men came back and sat around the table, they had drawn together. They shot each other small glances, stuck their tongues in their cheeks, burst out laughing at odd moments, to rattle Fleur. But she never minded. They played their vingt-un, staying even as Fleur slowly gained. Those pennies I had given her drew nickels and attracted dimes until there was a small pile in front of her.

Then she hooked them with five-card draw, nothing wild. She dealt, discarded, drew, and then she sighed and her cards gave a little shiver. Tor's eye gleamed, and Dutch straightened in his seat.

30   "I'll pay to see that hand," said Lily Veddar.

Fleur showed, and she had nothing there, nothing at all.

Tor's thin smile cracked open, and he threw his hand in too.

"Well, we know one thing," he said, leaning back in his chair, "the squaw can't bluff."

With that I lowered myself into a mound of swept sawdust and slept. I woke up during the night, but none of them had moved yet, so I couldn't either. Still later, the men must have gone out again, or Fritzie come out to break the game, because I was lifted, soothed, cradled in a woman's arms and rocked so quiet that I kept my eyes shut while Fleur rolled me into a closet of grimy ledgers, oiled paper, balls of string, and thick files that fit beneath me like a mattress.

35   The game went on after work the next evening. I got my eight cents back five times over, and Fleur kept the rest of the dollar she'd won for a stake. This time they didn't play so late, but they played regular, and then kept going at it night after night. They played poker now, or variations, for one week straight, and each time Fleur won exactly one dollar, no more and no less, too consistent for luck.

By this time, Lily and the other men were so lit with suspense that they got Pete to join the game with them. They concentrated, the fat dog sitting tense in Lily Veddar's lap, Tor suspicious, Dutch stroking his huge square brow, Pete steady. It wasn't that Fleur won that hooked them in so, because she lost hands too. It was rather that she never had a freak hand or even anything above a straight. She only took on her low cards, which didn't sit right. By chance, Fleur should have gotten a full or flush by now.

The irritating thing was she beat with pairs and never bluffed, because she couldn't, and still she ended up each night with exactly one dollar. Lily couldn't believe, first of all, that a woman could be smart enough to play cards, but even if she was, that she would then be stupid enough to cheat for a dollar a night. By day I watched him turn the problem over, his hard white face dull, small fingers probing at his knuckles, until he finally thought he had Fleur figured out as a bit-time player, caution her game. Raising the stakes would throw her.

More than anything now, he wanted Fleur to come away with something but a dollar. Two bits less or ten more, the sum didn't matter, just so he broke her streak.

Night after night she played, won her dollar, and left to stay in a place that just Fritzie and I knew about. Fleur bathed in the slaughtering tub, then slept in the unused brick smokehouse behind the lockers, a window-less place tarred on the inside with scorched fats. When I brushed against her skin I noticed that she smelled of the walls, rich and woody, slightly burnt. Since that night she put me in the closet I was no longer afraid of her, but followed her close, stayed with her, became her moving shadow that the men never noticed, the shadow that could have saved her.

August, the month that bears fruit, closed around the shop, and Pete and Fritzie left for Minnesota to escape the heat. Night by night, running, Fleur had won thirty dollars, and only Pete's presence had kept Lily at bay. But Pete was gone now, and one payday, with the heat so bad no one could move but Fleur, the men sat and played and waited while she finished work. The cards sweat, limp in their fingers, the table was slick with grease, and even the walls were warm to the touch. The air was motionless. Fleur was in the next room boiling heads.

40   Her green dress, drenched, wrapped her like a transparent sheet. A skin of lakeweed. Black snarls of veining clung to her arms. Her braids were loose, half-unraveled, tied behind her neck in a thick loop. She stood in steam, turning skulls through a vat with a wooden paddle. When scraps boiled to the surface, she bent with a round tin sieve and scooped them out. She'd filled two dishpans.

"Ain't that enough now?" called Lily. "We're waiting." The stump of a dog trembled in his lap, alive with rage. It never smelled me or noticed me above Fleur's smoky skin. The air was heavy in my corner, and pressed me down. Fleur sat with them.

"Now what do you say?" Lily asked the dog. It barked. That was the signal for the real game to start.

"Let's up the ante," said Lily, who had been stalking this night all month. He had a roll of money in his pocket. Fleur had five bills in her dress. The men had each saved their full pay.

"Ante a dollar then," said Fleur, and pitched hers in. She lost, but they let her scrape along, cent by cent. And then she won some. She played un-evenly, as if chance was all she had. She reeled them in. The game went on.

The dog was stiff now, poised on Lily's knees, a ball of vicious muscle with its yellow eyes slit in concentration. It gave advice, seemed to sniff the lay of Fleur's cards, twitched and nudged. Fleur was up, then down, saved by a scratch. Tor dealt seven cards, three down. The pot grew, round by round, until it held all the money. Nobody folded. Then it all rode on one last card and they went silent. Fleur picked hers up and blew a long breath. The heat lowered like a bell. Her card shook, but she stayed in.

45   Lily smiled and took the dog's head tenderly between his palms.

"Say, Fatso," he said, crooning the words, "you reckon that girl's bluffing?"

The dog whined and Lily laughed. "Me too," he said, "let's show." He swept his bills and coins into the pot and then they turned their cards over.

Lily looked once, looked again, then he squeezed the dog up like a fist of dough and slammed it on the table.

Fleur threw her arms out and drew the money over, grinning that same wolf grin that she'd used on me, the grin that had them. She jammed the bills in her dress, scooped the coins up in waxed white paper that she tied with string.

50   "Let's go another round," said Lily, his voice choked with burrs. But Fleur opened her mouth and yawned, then walked out back to gather slops for the one big hog that was waiting in the stock pen to be killed.

The men sat still as rocks, their hands spread on the oiled wood table. Dutch had chewed his cigar to damp shreds, Tor's eye was dull. Lily's gaze was the only one to follow Fleur. I didn't move. I felt them gathering, saw my stepfather's veins, the ones in his forehead that stood out in anger. The dog had rolled off the table and curled in a knot below the counter, where none of the men could touch it.

Lily rose and stepped out back to the closet of ledgers where Pete kept his private stock. He brought back a bottle, uncorked and tipped it between his fingers. The lump in his throat moved, then he passed it on. They drank, quickly felt the whiskey's fire, and planned with their eyes things they couldn't say out loud.

When they left, I followed. I hid out back in the clutter of broken boards and chicken crates beside the stock pen, where they waited. Fleur could not be seen at first, and then the moon broke and showed her, slipping cautiously along the rough board chute with a bucket in her hand. Her hair fell, wild and coarse, to her waist, and her dress was a floating patch in the dark. She made a pig-calling sound, rang the tin pail lightly against the wood, froze suspiciously. But too late. In the sound of the ring Lily moved, fat and nimble, stepped right behind Fleur and put out his creamy hands. At his first touch, she whirled and doused him with the bucket of sour slops. He pushed her against the big fence and the package of coins split, went clinking and jumping, winked against the wood. Fleur rolled over once and vanished in the yard.

The moon fell behind a curtain of ragged clouds, and Lily followed into the dark muck. But he tripped, pitched over the huge flank of the pig, who lay mired to the snout, heavily snoring. I sprang out of the weeds and climbed the side of the pen, stuck like glue. I saw the sow rise to her neat, knobby knees, gain her balance, and sway, curious, as Lily stumbled forward. Fleur had backed into the angle of rough wood just beyond, and when Lily tried to jostle past, the sow tipped up on her hind legs and struck, quick and hard as a snake. She plunged her head into Lily's thick side and snatched a mouthful of his shirt. She lunged again, caught him lower, so that he grunted in pained surprise. He seemed to ponder, breathing deep. Then he launched his huge body in a swimmer's dive.

55   The sow screamed as his body smacked over hers. She rolled, striking out with her knife-sharp hooves, and Lily gathered himself upon her, took her foot-long face by the ears and scraped her snout and cheeks against the trestles of the pen. He hurled the sow's tight skull against an iron post, but instead of knocking her dead, he merely woke her from her dream.

She reared, shrieked, drew him with her so that they posed standing upright. They bowed jerkily to each other, as if to begin. Then his arms swung and flailed. She sank her black fangs into his shoulder, clasping him, dancing him forward and backward through the pen. Their steps picked up pace, went wild. The two dipped as one, box-stepped, tripped each other. She ran her split foot through his hair. He grabbed her kinked tail. They went down and came up, the same shape and then the same color, until the men couldn't tell one from the other in that light and Fleur was able to launch herself over the gates, swing down, hit gravel.

The men saw, yelled, and chased her at a dead run to the smokehouse. And Lily too, once the sow gave up in disgust and freed him. That is where I should have gone to Fleur, saved her, thrown myself on Dutch. But I went stiff with fear and couldn't unlatch myself from the trestles or move at all. I closed my eyes and put my head in my arms, tried to hide, so there is nothing to describe but what I couldn't block out, Fleur's hoarse breath, so loud it filled me, her cry in the old language, and my name repeated over and over among the words.

The heat was still dense the next morning when I came back to work. Fleur was gone but the men were there, slack-faced, hung over. Lily was paler and softer than ever, as if his flesh had steamed on his bones. They smoked, took pulls off a bottle. It wasn't noon yet. I worked awhile, waiting shop and sharpening steel. But I was sick, I was smothered, I was sweating so hard that my hands slipped on the knives, and I wiped my fingers clean of the greasy touch of the customers' coins. Lily opened his mouth and roared once, not in anger. There was no meaning to the sound. His boxer dog, sprawled limp beside his foot, never lifted its head. Nor did the other men.

They didn't notice when I stepped outside, hoping for a clear breath. And then I forgot them because I knew that we were all balanced, ready to tip, to fly, to be crushed as soon as the weather broke. The sky was so low that I felt the weight of it like a yoke. Clouds hung down, witch teats, a tornado's green-brown cones, and as I watched one flicked out and became a delicate probing thumb. Even as I picked up my heels and ran back inside, the wind blew suddenly, cold, and then came rain.

60   Inside, the men had disappeared already and the whole place was trembling as if a huge hand was pinched at the rafters, shaking it. I ran straight through, screaming for Dutch or for any of them, and then I stopped at the heavy doors of the lockers, where they had surely taken shelter. I stood there a moment. Everything went still. Then I heard a cry building in the wind, faint at first, a whistle and then a shrill scream that tore through the walls and gathered around me, spoke plain so I understood that I should move, put my arms out, and slam down the great iron bar that fit across the hasp and lock.

Outside, the wind was stronger, like a hand held against me. I struggled forward. The bushes tossed, the awnings flapped off storefronts, the rails of porches rattled. The odd cloud became a fat snout that nosed along the earth and sniffled, jabbed, picked at things, sucked them up, blew them apart, rooted around as if it was following a certain scent, then stopped behind me at the butcher shop and bored down like a drill.

I went flying, landed somewhere in a ball. When I opened my eyes and looked, stranger things were happening.

A herd of cattle flew through the air like giant birds, dropping dung, their mouths opened in stunned bellows. A candle, still lighted, blew past, and tables, napkins, garden tools, a whole school of drifting eyeglasses, jackets on hangers, hams, a checkerboard, a lampshade, and at last the sow from behind the lockers, on the run, her hooves a blur, set free, swooping, diving, screaming as everything in Argus fell apart and got turned upside down, smashed, and thoroughly wrecked.

Days passed before the town went looking for the men. They were bachelors, after all, except for Tor, whose wife had suffered a blow to the head that made her forgetful. Everyone was occupied with digging out, in high relief because even though the Catholic steeple had been torn off like a peaked cap and sent across five fields, those huddled in the cellar were unhurt. Walls had fallen, windows were demolished, but the stores were intact and so were the bankers and shop owners who had taken refuge in their safes or beneath their cash registers. It was a fair-minded disaster, no one could be said to have suffered much more than the next, at least not until Fritzie and Pete came home.

65   Of all the businesses in Argus, Kozka's Meats had suffered worst. The boards of the front building had been split to kindling, piled in a huge pyramid, and the shop equipment was blasted far and wide. Pete paced off the distance the iron bathtub had been flung—a hundred feet. The glass candy case went fifty, and landed without so much as a cracked pane. There were other surprises as well, for the back rooms where Fritzie and Pete lived were undisturbed. Fritzie said the dust still coated her china

figures, and upon her kitchen table, in the ashtray, perched the last cigarette she'd put out in haste. She lit it up and finished it, looking through the window. From there, she could see that the old smokehouse Fleur had slept in was crushed to a reddish sand and the stock pens were completely torn apart, the rails stacked helter-skelter. Fritzie asked for Fleur. People shrugged. Then she asked about the others and, suddenly, the town understood that three men were missing.

There was a rally of help, a gathering of shovels and volunteers. We passed boards from hand to hand, stacked them, uncovered what lay beneath the pile of jagged splinters. The lockers, full of the meat that was Pete and Fritzie's investment, slowly came into sight, still intact. When enough room was made for a man to stand on the roof, there were calls, a general urge to hack through and see what lay below. But Fritzie shouted that she wouldn't allow it because the meat would spoil. And so the work continued, board by board, until at last the heavy oak doors of the freezer were revealed and people pressed to the entry. Everyone wanted to be the first, but since it was my stepfather lost, I was let go in when Pete and Fritzie wedged through into the sudden icy air.

Pete scraped a match on his boot, lit the lamp Fritzie held, and then the three of us stood still in its circle. Light glared off the skinned and hanging carcasses, the crates of wrapped sausages, the bright and cloudy blocks of lake ice, pure as winter. The cold bit into us, pleasant at first, then numbing. We must have stood there a couple of minutes before we saw the men, or more rightly, the humps of fur, the iced and shaggy hides they wore, the bearskins they had taken down and wrapped around themselves. We stepped closer and tilted the lantern beneath the flaps of fur into their faces. The dog was there, perched among them, heavy as a doorstop. The three had hunched around a barrel where the game was still laid out, and a dead lantern and an empty bottle, too. But they had thrown down their last hands and hunkered tight, clutching one another, knuckles raw from beating at the door they had also attacked with hooks. Frost stars gleamed off their eyelashes and the stubble of their beards. Their faces were set in concentration, mouths open as if to speak some careful thought, some agreement they'd come to in each other's arms.

* * *

Power travels in the bloodlines, handed out before birth. It comes down through the hands, which in the Pillagers were strong and knotted, big, spidery, and rough, with sensitive fingertips good at dealing cards. It comes through the eyes, too, belligerent, darkest brown, the eyes of those in the bear clan, impolite as they gaze directly at a person.

In my dreams, I look straight back at Fleur, at the men. I am no longer the watcher on the dark sill, the skinny girl.

70   The blood draws us back, as if it runs through a vein of earth. I've come home and, except for talking to my cousins, live a quiet life. Fleur lives quiet too, down on Lake Turcot with her boat. Some say she's married

to the waterman, Misshepeshu, or that she's living in shame with white men or windigos, or that she's killed them all. I'm about the only one here who ever goes to visit her. Last winter, I went to help out in her cabin when she bore the child, whose green eyes and skin the color of an old penny made more talk, as no one could decide if the child was mixed blood or what, fathered in a smokehouse, or by a man with brass scales, or by the lake. The girl is bold, smiling in her sleep, as if she knows what people wonder, as if she hears the old men talk, turning the story over. It comes up different every time and has no ending, no beginning. They get the middle wrong too. They only know that they don't know anything.

⋄ ⋄ ⋄ ⋄

GABRIEL GARCÍA MÁRQUEZ
(1928–   )

A Very Old Man with Enormous Wings
A TALE FOR CHILDREN
(1968)

Translated from the Spanish by Gregory Rabassa

On the third day of rain they had killed so many crabs inside the house that Pelayo had to cross his drenched courtyard and throw them into the sea, because the newborn child had a temperature all night and they thought it was due to the stench. The world had been sad since Tuesday. Sea and sky were a single ash-gray thing and the sands of the beach, which on March nights glimmered like powdered light, had become a stew of mud and rotten shellfish. The light was so weak at noon that when Pelayo was coming back to the house after throwing away the crabs, it was hard for him to see what it was that was moving and groaning in the rear of the courtyard. He had to go very close to see that it was an old man, a very old man, lying face down in the mud, who, in spite of his tremendous efforts, couldn't get up, impeded by his enormous wings.

Frightened by that nightmare, Pelayo ran to get Elisenda, his wife, who was putting compresses on the sick child, and he took her to the rear of the courtyard. They both looked at the fallen body with mute stupor. He was dressed like a ragpicker.[1] There were only a few faded hairs left on his bald skull and very few teeth in his mouth, and his pitiful condition of a drenched great-grandfather had taken away any sense of grandeur he might have had. His huge buzzard wings, dirty and half-plucked, were forever entangled in the mud. They looked at him so long and so closely that Pelayo and Elisenda very soon overcame their surprise and in the end found him familiar. Then they dared speak to him, and he answered in an incomprehensible dialect with a strong sailor's voice. That was

---

[1] Someone who makes a living collecting rags and other refuse.

how they skipped over the inconvenience of the wings and quite intelligently concluded that he was a lonely castaway from some foreign ship wrecked by the storm. And yet, they called in a neighbor woman who knew everything about life and death to see him, and all she needed was one look to show them their mistake.

"He's an angel," she told them. "He must have been coming for the child, but the poor fellow is so old that the rain knocked him down."

On the following day everyone knew that a flesh-and-blood angel was held captive in Pelayo's house. Against the judgment of the wise neighbor woman, for whom angels in those times were the fugitive survivors of a celestial conspiracy, they did not have the heart to club him to death. Pelayo watched over him all afternoon from the kitchen, armed with his bailiff's club, and before going to bed he dragged him out of the mud and locked him up with the hens in the wire chicken coop. In the middle of the night, when the rain stopped, Pelayo and Elisenda were still killing crabs. A short time afterward the child woke up without a fever and with a desire to eat. Then they felt magnanimous and decided to put the angel on a raft with fresh water and provisions for three days and leave him to his fate on the high seas. But when they went out into the courtyard with the first light of dawn, they found the whole neighborhood in front of the chicken coop having fun with the angel, without the slightest reverence, tossing him things to eat through the openings in the wire as if he weren't a supernatural creature but a circus animal.

5   Father Gonzaga arrived before seven o'clock, alarmed by the strange news. By that time onlookers less frivolous than those at dawn had already arrived and they were making all kinds of conjectures concerning the captive's future. The simplest among them thought that he should be named mayor of the world. Others of sterner mind felt that he should be promoted to the rank of five-star general in order to win all wars. Some visionaries hoped that he could be put to stud in order to implant on earth a race of winged wise men who could take charge of the universe. But Father Gonzaga, before becoming a priest, had been a robust woodcutter. Standing by the wire, he reviewed his catechism[2] in an instant and asked them to open the door so that he could take a close look at that pitiful man who looked more like a huge decrepit hen among the fascinated chickens. He was lying in a corner drying his open wings in the sunlight among the fruit peels and breakfast leftovers that the early risers had thrown him. Alien to the impertinences of the world, he only lifted his antiquarian[3] eyes and murmured something in his dialect when Father Gonzaga went into the chicken coop and said good morning to him in Latin. The parish priest had his first suspicion of an imposter when he saw that he did not understand the language of God or know how to greet His ministers.

---

[2] A book that summarizes the doctrines of Roman Catholicism in question-and-answer form.

[3] Refers to someone who studies antiquities, particularly old books.

Then he noticed that seen close up he was much too human; he had an unbearable smell of the outdoors, the back side of his wings was strewn with parasites and his main feathers had been mistreated by terrestrial winds, and nothing about him measured up to the proud dignity of angels. Then he came out of the chicken coop and in a brief sermon warned the curious against the risks of being ingenuous. He reminded them that the devil had the bad habit of making use of carnival tricks in order to confuse the unwary. He argued that if wings were not the essential element in determining the difference between a hawk and an airplane, they were even less so in the recognition of angels. Nevertheless, he promised to write a letter to his bishop so that the latter would write to his primate so that the latter would write to the Supreme Pontiff[4] in order to get the final verdict from the highest courts.

His prudence fell on sterile hearts. The news of the captive angel spread with such rapidity that after a few hours the courtyard had the bustle of a marketplace and they had to call in troops with fixed bayonets to disperse the mob that was about to knock the house down. Elisenda, her spine all twisted from sweeping up so much marketplace trash, then got the idea of fencing in the yard and charging five cents admission to see the angel.

The curious came from far away. A traveling carnival arrived with a flying acrobat who buzzed over the crowd several times, but no one paid any attention to him because his wings were not those of an angel but, rather, those of a sidereal[5] bat. The most unfortunate invalids on earth came in search of health: a poor woman who since childhood had been counting her heartbeats and had run out of numbers; a Portuguese man who couldn't sleep because the noise of the stars disturbed him; a sleepwalker who got up at night to undo the things he had done while awake; and many others with less serious ailments. In the midst of that shipwreck disorder that made the earth tremble, Pelayo and Elisenda were happy with fatigue, for in less than a week they had crammed their rooms with money and the line of pilgrims waiting their turn to enter still reached beyond the horizon.

The angel was the only one who took no part in his own act. He spent his time trying to get comfortable in his borrowed nest, befuddled by the hellish heat of the oil lamps and sacramental candles that had been placed along the wire. At first they tried to make him eat some mothballs, which, according to the wisdom of the wise neighbor woman, were the food prescribed for angels. But he turned them down, just as he turned down the papal lunches that the penitents brought him, and they never found out whether it was because he was an angel or because he was an old man that in the end he ate nothing but eggplant mush. His only supernatural virtue seemed to be patience. Especially during the first days, when the hens

---

[4] The Pope.
[5] Relating to the stars.

pecked at him, searching for the stellar parasites that proliferated in his wings, and the cripples pulled out feathers to touch their defective parts with, and even the most merciful threw stones at him, trying to get him to rise so they could see him standing. The only time they succeeded in arousing him was when they burned his side with an iron for branding steers, for he had been motionless for so many hours that they thought he was dead. He awoke with a start, ranting in his hermetic[6] language and with tears in his eyes, and he flapped his wings a couple of times, which brought on a whirlwind of chicken dung and lunar dust and a gale of panic that did not seem to be of this world. Although many thought that his reaction had been one not of rage but of pain, from then on they were careful not to annoy him, because the majority understood that his passivity was not that of a hero taking his ease but that of a cataclysm in repose.

Father Gonzaga held back the crowd's frivolity with formulas of maidservant inspiration while awaiting the arrival of a final judgment on the nature of the captive. But the mail from Rome showed no sense of urgency. They spent their time finding out if the prisoner had a navel, if his dialect had any connection with Aramaic,[7] how many times he could fit on the head of a pin, or whether he wasn't just a Norwegian with wings. Those meager letters might have come and gone until the end of time if a providential event had not put an end to the priest's tribulations.

10   It so happened that during those days, among so many other carnival attractions, there arrived in town the traveling show of the woman who had been changed into a spider for having disobeyed her parents. The admission to see her was not only less than the admission to see the angel, but people were permitted to ask her all manner of questions about her absurd state and to examine her up and down so that no one would ever doubt the truth of her horror. She was a frightful tarantula the size of a ram and with the head of a sad maiden. What was most heart-rending, however, was not her outlandish shape but the sincere affliction with which she recounted the details of her misfortune. While still practically a child she had sneaked out of her parents' house to go to a dance, and while she was coming back through the woods after having danced all night without permission, a fearful thunderclap rent the sky in two and through the crack came the lightning bolt of brimstone that changed her into a spider. Her only nourishment came from the meatballs that charitable souls chose to toss into her mouth. A spectacle like that, full of so much human truth and with such a fearful lesson, was bound to defeat without even trying that of a haughty angel who scarcely deigned to look at mortals. Besides, the few miracles attributed to the angel showed a certain mental disorder, like the blind man who didn't recover his sight but grew

---

[6] Occult, magical.

[7] An ancient Middle Eastern language, believed to have been the language spoken by Jesus.

three new teeth, or the paralytic who didn't get to walk but almost won the lottery, and the leper whose sores sprouted sunflowers. Those consolation miracles, which were more like mocking fun, had already ruined the angel's reputation when the woman who had been changed into a spider finally crushed him completely. That was how Father Gonzaga was cured forever of his insomnia and Pelayo's courtyard went back to being as empty as during the time it had rained for three days and crabs walked through the bedrooms.

The owners of the house had no reason to lament. With the money they saved they built a two-story mansion with balconies and gardens and high netting so that crabs wouldn't get in during the winter, and with iron bars on the windows so that angels wouldn't get in. Pelayo also set up a rabbit warren close to town and gave up his job as bailiff for good, and Elisenda bought some satin pumps with high heels and many dresses of iridescent silk, the kind worn on Sunday by the most desirable women in those times. The chicken coop was the only thing that didn't receive any attention. If they washed it down with creolin[8] and burned tears of myrrh[9] inside it every so often, it was not in homage to the angel but to drive away the dungheap stench that still hung everywhere like a ghost and was turning the new house into an old one. At first, when the child learned to walk, they were careful that he not get too close to the chicken coop. But then they began to lose their fears and got used to the smell, and before the child got his second teeth he'd gone inside the chicken coop to play, where the wires were falling apart. The angel was no less standoffish with him than with other mortals, but he tolerated the most ingenious infamies with the patience of a dog who had no illusions. They both came down with chicken pox at the same time. The doctor who took care of the child couldn't resist the temptation to listen to the angel's heart, and he found so much whistling in the heart and so many sounds in his kidneys that it seemed impossible for him to be alive. What surprised him most, however, was the logic of his wings. They seemed so natural on that completely human organism that he couldn't understand why other men didn't have them too.

When the child began school it had been some time since the sun and rain had caused the collapse of the chicken coop. The angel went dragging himself about here and there like a stray dying man. They would drive him out of the bedroom with a broom and a moment later find him in the kitchen. He seemed to be in so many places at the same time that they grew to think that he'd been duplicated, that he was reproducing himself all through the house, and the exasperated and unhinged Elisenda shouted that it was awful living in that hell full of angels. He could scarcely eat and his antiquarian eyes had also become so foggy that he went about

---

[8] A disinfectant.
[9] A type of incense.

bumping into posts. All he had left were the bare cannulae[10] of his last feathers. Pelayo threw a blanket over him and extended him the charity of letting him sleep in the shed, and only then did they notice that he had a temperature at night, and was delirious with the tongue twisters of an old Norwegian. That was one of the few times they became alarmed, for they thought he was going to die and not even the wise neighbor woman had been able to tell them what to do with dead angels.

And yet he not only survived his worst winter, but seemed improved with the first sunny days. He remained motionless for several days in the farthest corner of the courtyard, where no one would see him, and at the beginning of December some large, stiff feathers began to grow on his wings, the feathers of a scarecrow, which looked more like another misfortune of decrepitude. But he must have known the reason for those changes, for he was quite careful that no one should notice them, that no one should hear the sea chanteys that he sometimes sang under the stars. One morning Elisenda was cutting some bunches of onions for lunch when a wind that seemed to come from the high seas blew into the kitchen. Then she went to the window and caught the angel in his first attempt at flight. They were so clumsy that his fingernails opened a furrow in the vegetable patch and he was on the point of knocking the shed down with the ungainly flapping that slipped on the light and couldn't get a grip on the air. But he did manage to gain altitude. Elisenda let out a sigh of relief, for herself and for him, when she saw him pass over the last houses, holding himself up in some way with the risky flapping of a senile vulture. She kept watching him even when she was through cutting the onions and she kept on watching until it was no longer possible for her to see him, because then he was no longer an annoyance in her life but an imaginary dot on the horizon of the sea.

◊ ◊ ◊

MARY LADD GAVELL
(1919–1967)

The Rotifer
(1968)

Though I sit hunched studiously over my microscope, I am gazing dreamily past it and out the open window, at the lazy afternoon campus. But the lab instructor, a graduate student who stutters a little and dreams of the day when he will be an assistant professor, comes hovering down the row of tables, and I return to my microscope. I do not plan to become a biologist. Two sciences are required, and I regard with detachment the sophomores' frogs' legs and sheep's livers, each with a name tag attached, which float in the barrel of formaldehyde in the corner. It gives off a technical,

---

[10] Tubes at the base of feathers.

advanced, arcane smell, but it does not stir me. Next year I shall be off to another lab and another science and shall putter about with Bunsen burners or magnetic fields.

It is late in the fall, although it is still warm here in Texas, and the faint sounds of football practice drift in through the open window. We forty freshmen in this room have, since our arrival at the state university from the sleepy cactusy towns and the raw cities and the piny woods and the plains, been learning of the protozoa, the one-celled creatures who simply divide when they want to become two, and are not always sure whether they are plants or animals. The lab instructor has hovered over us yearningly, wanting us to get a *good* view of the amoeba, to really *appreciate* the spyrogyra.

But today, as he gives each of us a glass slide with a drop of pond water on it, he tells us that we are leaving the protozoa and beginning the long evolutionary climb. Today we shall see the rotifers, who belong to the metazoa. We too, at the other end of the microscope, are metazoa; the rotifer, like us, has a brain, a nervous system, and a stomach.

I am fairly good, by this time, at adjusting my microscope. I know that those long, waving fronds are reflections of my own eyelashes, and I recognize algae when I see it, greenish leafy stuff rather like the broccoli on a dormitory dinner plate. Soon I find the rotifers—furiously alive, almost transparent little animals, churning powerfully along in their native ocean.

5   Watching, I am a witness to a crisis in the life of a rotifer. He is entangled in a snarl of algae, and he can't get loose. His transparent little body chugs this way and that, but the fence of algae seems impenetrable. He turns, wriggles, oscillates, but he is caught. *Rest a moment,* I whisper to him, *lie still and catch your breath and then give a good heave to the left.* But he is in a wild panic, beyond any reasonable course of action. It seems to me that his movements are slowing down, as if he is becoming exhausted.

Maybe I can help him. Perhaps I can put my finger on the edge of the glass slide and tip it ever so slightly, tilt it just enough so that the water will wash him over the barrier. Cautiously, gently, I touch the slide.

But the result is a violent revolution in the whole rotifer universe! My rotifer and his algae prison wash recklessly out of sight, and whole other worlds of rotifers and algae and amoebae and miscellaneous creatures of the deep reel by, spinning on the waves of a cataclysm. My rotifer is gone, lost to me. Huge and clumsy, more gargantuan than any Gulliver, I am separated from him forever by my monstrous size, and there is no way I can get through from my dimension to his.

The bell rings; lab is over. I take my slide out from under my microscope; there on it is the merest drop of water, and I look at it uncertainly. I start to wipe it off, to put the slide away, but I hesitate and look at it again. The lab instructor, seeing me still standing there, hurries over. "Did you get a *good* conception of the ciliary movement?" he asks me anxiously.

"I guess so," I answer, and I polish the slide until it is dry and shiny and put it away.

10   Like that earnest young man, the lab instructor, I became, for a little while a few years later, an intellectual sharecropper, as we called young graduate students who had various ill-defined and ill-paid functions around the university. During this period I was for some reason handed the job of going through the papers of the Benton family, which a descendant, looking for something suitable to do with them, had turned over to the university. The Bentons had been a moderately prominent family who had moved from the East to Tennessee in the 1790's, and then, thirty or so years later, to the Southwest. They were notable for having been respectable, prosperous, God-fearing and right-doing lawyers and landowners, and they were also notable for having saved most of the papers that came into their hands. All these qualities had culminated in Josiah Benton, who had been State Treasurer in the 1840's and had saved every paper he got his hands on.

So for weeks and weeks, I sat in a corner of the archives library and turned through fragile and yellowed papers, making out the dim and faded handwriting of Benton love letters, lists of Benton expenditures for curtain material and camisoles, reports and complaints to various Bentons from their tenants, letters to traveling Benton husbands from Benton wives, bills of sale for Benton slaves, political gossip from Benton cronies and domestic gossip from Benton relatives, diaries begun and never finished, and a few state papers filched by Josiah, like many another bureaucrat after him, from the official files.

It was impossible not to become interested in the Bentons. I sat down with those boxes of ancient gossip and circumstance more eagerly than I asked a friend, what's new? Lydia May Benton feuded with her sister-in-law Sally, and the mysterious trouble about Jonathan Bentley, it turned out, was that he *drank*. Aunt Millie Benton's letters to her traveling husband began and ended with protestations of devotion and obedience, but in between she told him what to do and when to do it. But if Josiah's wife Lizzi had ever had an opinion, it went unrecorded; when she was mentioned at all, it was to say how dear, sweet, good, and ailing poor Lizzie was. Josiah emerged like a rock; he was honest, he was rigid, he was determined, and he carried through what he began. But it was his son, little Robert Josiah Benton, who interested me most.

There was little said about Robert Josiah before 1832, when at ten he was sent away to a school in Massachusetts. There had, of course, been a few references to him earlier. When he was born, Josiah, whose first two children had been girls, wrote proudly to his brother, "My Lizzie was delivered of a fine eight-pound boy this morning. I shall make of him, God willing, a Scholar and a Gentleman." Later on, in one of the few letters that Lizzie seemed to have received, her sister, who had recently been to visit them, exclaimed over what a "Beautiful and Clever child your Robert

Josiah is." And once, when Robert Josiah must have been about eight, Josiah's list of expenditures included, "To roan horse for my Son."

Robert Josiah was sent to Massachusetts to be made into a scholar and a gentleman, as Josiah had probably written the headmaster of the school. "According to your instructions," the headmaster replied, "your son will be given a thorough grounding in Mathematics and Latin, with somewhat subordinate attention given to French and to those Sports which befit a Gentleman. You will receive Quarterly Reports from me as to the progress of your Son, and the Rules of our School require that each Scholar shall write his Father fortnightly so that you shall be well inform'd concerning his Welfare. I personally supervise the writing of these letters, ascertaining that they contain no misleading statements, as the inexperience and frivolity of Youth might give them a tendency to do, so that you shall at all times have a True and Correct account."

15   Robert Josiah went away to school at the end of the summer, and in the fall and winter months the fortnightly letters appeared, painfully neat, carefully spelled, stiff little letters, beginning, "My Dear and Respected Father"—Lizzie was not addressed, although somewhere in the letter Robert Josiah would say, "Give my Dear Love to my Mother." The letters always ended "Your obedient Son." He would report that he was well and that he was studying hard in order to gain the full benefits of the advantages that his father was so generously providing for him, that he was treated with the utmost consideration by the professors and by the headmaster, and that he hoped the headmaster's reports of him would be found to be satisfactory. Once he said that he found Latin very difficult, but he hastened to add, "Do not believe, Dear Father, that I question on this account your Wisdom in desiring me to study it or that I shall Neglect it." Sometimes he apologized for the shortness of a letter by saying, "I am allow'd only one Candle and it is almost finished."

At Christmas he went so far as to say, "I miss my Dear Mother and you Very much, and my Sisters also, but I shall try to overcome it and to Devote my Attention more fully to my Studies." Often he would inquire about his horse, whose name was Jupiter, and about Nero, his dog. "Does Timothy take good care of Jupiter and of Nero?" he would ask.

And so the letters continued—stiff, polite, adult little notes. But sometimes a barely wistful, faintly childish sound crept into them; once in a while it became perfectly clear that Robert Josiah wanted to come home. In January he failed to write, and instead the headmaster wrote that Robert Josiah was ill with a mild attack of the "Grippe," but felt confident that he would soon be fully recovered. And apparently he was, for two weeks later his letters resumed. But now he wrote once, "I wish I could see my Dear Mother."

Then a letter appeared from John Benton, an older cousin of Robert Josiah's, who was attending Harvard College, and who had had an occasion, on returning to college from a short vacation, to stop by Robert Josiah's school.

"My Dear Uncle," he wrote, "I trust that you will forgive the extreme liberty which I am taking in addressing you regarding my recent visit with your Son Robert Josiah. Your Son looks very thin, as a result of his recent bout with the Grippe, and I think perhaps he is studying too hard. I have no doubt that the Headmaster of the School is an extremely Fine and Conscientious Scholar and that his School is an excellent one, but his regime is most Rigorous, and while some boys no doubt profit greatly from this, I think it may be too severe at this stage for Robert Josiah, who is perhaps of delicate constitution and of course of still tender years. I beg to assure you that the attitude of Robert Josiah is one of loving obedience to your wishes, and I trust that you will forgive, my Dear Uncle, this intrusion of mine into your Family Affairs, since I am confident of your Excellent Judgment in all matters. Your respectful Nephew, John Benton."

20   Well, it was a good thing that somebody had looked in on little Robert Josiah to see how he really was, but the question was, would anyone as determined as Josiah listen?

Apparently not. The weeks passed, and the stiff little letters kept coming from Robert Josiah. But they were more openly homesick now, and once or twice he wandered curiously from the subject as he was writing. Probably John's letter had merely rubbed Josiah the wrong way; he was, after all, only a young upstart of a nephew. Somebody else would have to try to make Josiah understand that Robert Josiah needed to come home—and there was no relying on Lizzie, poor, pale, ailing little thing, probably worried sick but unable to have an opinion about anything. But somebody had to do something! Josiah was not mean; he was just rigid, opinionated, and ambitious; he could be made to understand. Frantically I searched in my mind for the right tack to take with Josiah, the best way to put it to him.

But then something happened—maybe a student going out of the library banged a door—and past and present whirled around me in waves and washed me up at a library table, well into the second half of the twentieth century, with yellow old papers stacked around me. It had all happened in 1832; they were all dead and gone. There was nothing I could do for little Robert Josiah; I could hold in my hand the letters that he had written, and read the words he had put down there, but I was far, far away, separated from him by more than a century. There was nothing I could tell his father; there was no way I could get through from my dimension to his.

Rather halfheartedly I looked for the rest of the letters. There were just two or three more from little Robert Josiah, and then they stopped. There was nothing more. There were accounts, bills, business letters, and, later on, more personal letters to Josiah, but there was nothing mentioning Robert Josiah. I read through thirty or forty more years of Benton papers, but I never saw another word about a son of Josiah Benton's.

My cousin Leah and I grew up in different parts of the country and never knew each other well. When she came to live in the city where I now worked, we felt an obligation to be friendly, but the friendliness was a trifle forced, weighted down by our families' expectations that we would have a great deal to say to each other and the inescapable fact that we did not. We rang each other up from time to time to chat and exchange family news, and since she was new to the city I introduced her to my friends. But she was six years younger than I, and the people I knew seemed jaded to her. They were not really jaded at all, but then almost anybody seemed a little battered beside Leah.

25   Leah's father, my uncle, was old when she was born. His first wife had died, leaving four sons already grown, and eventually he married again, a gentle girl who gave him one daughter and died shortly afterward. People wondered how that stern, hard old man was going to manage with a little girl, but he managed very well. A tender fatherliness flowered in him which his sons had never known. He and Leah were always together; they rode horseback over his farms together, and supervised the haying together, and went shopping for her clothes together, the old man looking as out of place as possible, but calm in the conviction that here, as everywhere else in the world, all you had to do was make it plain what was wanted and be able to pay for it. My uncle was a rich man—not a private-yacht kind of rich, but a Midwest-farming kind of rich, a turn-out-the-lights-when-you're-finished-with-them and don't-dip-into-your-principal kind of rich. When Leah got into her teens and began to be beautiful, he sent her to the best girls' school he could get her into, because he figured their reputation might not mean much, but it was all he had to go on. But first he asked them what they had to teach her that she could earn her living by.

She became a commercial artist, and eventually she came to the city and got a job. The best word I can think of to describe her when I first encountered her, twenty-one, all grown-up and on her own, is dazzling. She was radiant; she twinkled and glittered and dazzled like a diamond, yet her strange, pure, golden-brown eyes looked out at the world with the simplicity and delight of a child.

She saw the best in everyone. She met a notorious misogynist and thought him *so* sweet and shy; and she was introduced to a celebrated old lecher and reported that he was so *good* all through that he reminded her a lot of her Daddy. She made me nervous. But she was sharing an apartment with two former schoolmates, and the three of them—all as lovely and charming and gay as if they had been turned out by some heavenly production line, giggling and putting up each other's hair and wearing each other's clothes, living off peanut butter sandwiches and chewing over their combined worldly wisdom like so many puppies with a shoe—presented themselves in an invincible girls'-dormitory armor to the world. And I was, after all, young myself and in no mood to worry, in love with the city, with my job in an international organization, and, as I recall it, with the Third Executive Assistant of the British Delegation.

Then she called me up one night to say that she was engaged and was going to be married right away. He was a junior associate in the well-known law firm of Judd, Parker, and Avery, and his credentials of age, height, education, and background seemed to be impeccable. I felt that she emphasized his suitability a trifle for my benefit; she put me in the older-relative category. Her father was not too well; he had recently had an operation, and she was planning to go home to see him, and so they had decided to be married here the following Sunday and to go home together. On Saturday night her roommates were throwing a little party for them at the apartment, and would I come and meet Dick then? I said I'd love to, and I wished her all the happiness in the world.

That was Monday night, and I had such a busy week that I didn't have much time to think about Leah. A series of international meetings kept me working late every night. On Wednesday I didn't get away until almost midnight, and I was exhausted when I finally caught a cab. I sank back and wiggled out of my high-heeled shoes in the dark. The cab driver had a girl friend with him in the front seat; I suppose it's lonely work, cruising the night streets. She leaned against his shoulder, and when he stopped at a red light, he rested his head companionably against her; he said something monosyllabic, and she laughed. I thought wisely, looking at the backs of their heads, that they were too comfortable in their closeness to be a young dating pair, but were old lovers, or married. When we got to my address he turned on the light for a moment to make change. I saw that he was good-looking and probably in his late twenties, and that she was about the same age, pretty, with a mop of blond hair, and in blue jeans.

30   I must pause here to explain that I am a recognizer of people. I am a sort of Paganini, or Escoffier, of recognizing. People who say, "I remember faces but I just can't remember names," are amateurs; I remember thousands of faces for which I have never known a name. The streets swarm with them: People who once did my hair or sold me shoes, stood next to me in elevators, in ticket lines, or at fires, gave me a new blouse in exchange for one that didn't fit, or four words at a cocktail party in exchange for four of mine. I remember them all; but they cut me dead.

The first time I ever set forth on the streets of Paris, I was with a friend, a woman who occupied a high position in the international organization for which I worked, and who had, as it happened, been mainly responsible for the firing from that organization, a year or so before, of a Frenchman named Charpentier, the reason being general quarrelsomeness, I think. No doubt his side of the story was different; I never knew all the ins and outs of it. He returned to the French civil service, from whence he had come, but not before delivering some fairly painful parting shots.

My friend and I stopped from the boat train out into the spring morning sunshine of Paris, bent on none but pleasant errands, and at once I recognized M. Charpentier on the street. I was used to domestic recognizing; at home I damped down the recognizing smile on my face as automatically as I glanced at the traffic lights; but I lost my head at such a stunning foreign success and cried out, "Monsieur Charpentier!" He stopped, we stopped, and the shock turned both their faces to concrete. He gave a short, savage jerk of a bow, and her teeth met like gears as she ground out a greeting between them. It had been the dearest wish of both their hearts never to see each other again. As the hostess, so to speak, in the situation, I babbled something like, "How nice once more to see you again, and how beautiful is your city!" speaking pidgin English, although his own was perfect. He looked at me with a mixture of loathing and bewilderment. We had known each other only slightly a year or more before, and he did not recognize me. My friend and I proceeded on our way, but a shadow had settled over the day. She was rather silent, and I smiled, whenever I caught her eye, Uriah Heepishly. Paris has never been the magic city to me that it is to some.

On Saturday night I went to my cousin's apartment and met her fiancé. He was a good-looking young man in his late twenties, with a conservative tie, a direct eye, and a firm handshake. He greeted me with a special, cousinly warmth, and his manner toward Leah was a charming mixture of serious protectiveness and teasing adoration. And of course he didn't recognize me; there was not the faintest cloud in his clear young gaze. My cousin was radiant; she flitted among the guests like a sprite. "Tell me, Mary," she whispered when she alighted near me for a moment, "what do you think of him? Isn't he *wonderful? Isn't* he?"

"He's very handsome and very charming," I said.

35 "Oh, I'm *so* glad you like him," she cried, and she gave me a hug. "You and Dad are the people I want to like him—I don't care about anybody else!" And she was off.

Well, I suppose that more than one struggling young professional man has driven a cab at nights to make a little extra. And surely many a young man has an auld luve to be off wi' before he be on wi' the new—and if the timetable's a bit crowded, it's not a hanging offense. I'm as broad-minded as the next, and yet—and yet—this was my little cousin Leah, my beautiful, shining little cousin, with whom I had not a blessed thing in common, who thought all the world loved her as well as her Daddy did. I looked at the young man again, and I imagined that his neatly cut face was clearly sinister and that his every word and gesture was plainly false. Was he really a lawyer with Judd, Parker, and Avery? It would be possible to find out; I could, in fact, simply call them up and ask, on some pretext or other. But it was Saturday night, and the wedding was Sunday, and on Monday I wouldn't want to know.

Or I could, then and there, look him right in the sincere blue eye and tell him I had seen him driving a cab last Wednesday night with a blond young woman under circumstances suggestive of considerable intimacy, and what, as a promising young lawyer on the eve of marriage to my cousin, did he have to say about it? But how in the name of heaven could I say that? It was melodramatic. It was a line to be delivered by an outraged father, back to the fireplace, or perhaps by a worldly, erect old aunt in her parlor, shooting a severe glance past her teacup. I simply couldn't manage it; I was only a cousin, about his own age and considerably less self-assured than he looked, spectacles slipping woefully down my nose, licensed in neither duenna nor private eye, nervous of making a fool of myself and showing it, in the crush of a large party in a small apartment, where it took a shout to be heard at all, and elbows jostled into conversations from all sides. And, after all, what if I were mistaken? I may be a Paganini, I may be an Escoffier, but the possibility had to be granted, and it would not make a very auspicious beginning for us all. And anyway, it was too late. The chapel was reserved, the wedding dress hung on its satin hanger in the closet, and the organist was instructed to play "I Love You Truly."

When I left that night, I suddenly at the door, without intending to at all, threw my arms around Leah and held her tight. There she was, my little cousin, my equal, my contemporary, within the circle of my arms; but I was separated from her forever by all the complexities of what I did not know and could not do. Our lives carried us on in our own dimensions, like people passing on different escalators, headlong to meet whatever harm or good was to come our way. And so I left her awkwardly, and I smiled jerkily at the bridegroom, who gave me a cousinly peck on the cheek, and we all said something about seeing each other the next day.

I had dinner with them a couple of months later, after they had returned to the city. They seemed very happy, and the stars shone in Leah's eyes as brightly as ever. I couldn't say I liked him; but there was, as I looked him over, this time more quietly and leisurely, something reassuring about his very ordinariness. He simply didn't have the stuff in him to be a Bluebeard or a Landru. He was a bright enough, nice enough young man, who, I surmised, thought his ways to be a little more winning, and other people a little more simple, than they were, and whose eye was firmly fixed on the main chance. But that was the worst I could think of him, and I was glad I hadn't tried to confront him with my silly cab-riding story; it wouldn't have done anyone any good, and perhaps it was all a mistake, anyway. They left the city shortly afterward; Leah called to tell me that an opportunity had opened up for Dick out in the Midwest, and he was leaving Judd, Parker, and Avery. She was glad because she would be nearer her father.

40   They were divorced about a year later, very shortly after her father died, and my cousin is back in the city, with a job doing fashion-ad illustrations. I assumed she was working just to keep herself busy, but a newsy old aunt of mine who was through town recently tells me that's not so. Leah will be a rich woman, one day, but at present she has to make her living, for her father, just before he died, changed his will so as to tie up the money very securely for a good while to come. I don't know why the divorce, of course—mental cruelty, or something, I suppose; it's nothing I can ask Leah about unless she wants to talk about it. Dick immediately got

married again, to a cheap, fuzzy-headed little blond, as my aunt puts it. Leah's still a handsome woman, but the dazzle is gone, and she looks tired around the eyes. But so do I; so, in time, does everybody.

◇ ◇ ◇

NATHANIEL HAWTHORNE
(1804–1864)

The Birthmark
(1843)

In the latter part of the last century there lived a man of science, an eminent proficient in every branch of natural philosophy, who not long before our story opens had made experience of a spiritual affinity more attractive than any chemical one. He had left his laboratory to the care of an assistant, cleared his fine countenance from the furnace smoke, washed the stain of acids from his fingers, and persuaded a beautiful woman to become his wife. In those days when the comparatively recent discovery of electricity and other kindred mysteries of Nature seemed to open paths into the region of miracle, it was not unusual for the love of science to rival the love of woman in its depth and absorbing energy. The higher intellect, the imagination, the spirit, and even the heart might all find their congenial ailment in pursuits which, as some of their ardent votaries believed, would ascend from one step of powerful intelligence to another, until the philosopher should lay his hand on the secret of creative force and perhaps make new worlds for himself. We know not whether Aylmer possessed this degree of faith in man's ultimate control over Nature. He had devoted himself, however, too unreservedly to scientific studies ever to be weaned from them by any second passion. His love for his young wife might prove the stronger of the two; but it could only be by intertwining itself with his love of science, and uniting the strength of the latter to his own.

Such a union accordingly took place, and was attended with truly remarkable consequences and a deeply impressive moral. One day, very soon after their marriage, Aylmer sat gazing at his wife with a trouble in his countenance that grew stronger until he spoke.

"Georgiana," said he, "has it ever occurred to you that the mark upon your cheek might be removed?"

"No, indeed," said she, smiling; but perceiving the seriousness of his manner, she blushed deeply. "To tell you the truth it has been so often called a charm that I was simple enough to imagine it might be so."

5   "Ah, upon another face perhaps it might," replied her husband; "but never on yours. No, dearest Georgiana, you came so nearly perfect from the hand of Nature that this slightest possible defect, which we hesitate whether to term a defect or a beauty, shocks me, as being the visible mark of earthly imperfection."

"Shocks you, my husband!" cried Georgiana, deeply hurt; at first reddening with momentary anger, but then bursting into tears. "Then why did you take me from my mother's side? You cannot love what shocks you!"

To explain this conversation it must be mentioned that in the center of Georgiana's left cheek there was a singular mark, deeply interwoven, as it were, with the texture and substance of her face. In the usual state of her complexion—a healthy though delicate bloom—the mark wore a tint of deeper crimson, which imperfectly defined its shape amid the surrounding rosiness. When she blushed it gradually became more indistinct, and finally vanished amid the triumphant rush of blood that bathed the whole cheek with its brilliant glow. But if any shifting motion caused her to turn pale, there was the mark again, a crimson stain upon the snow, in what Aylmer sometimes deemed an almost fearful distinctness. Its shape bore not a little similarity to the human hand, though of the smallest pygmy size. Georgiana's lovers were wont to say that some fairy at her birth hour had laid her tiny hand upon the infant's cheek, and left this impress there in token of the magic endowments that were to give her such sway over all hearts. Many a desperate swain would have risked life for the privilege of pressing his lips to the mysterious hand. It must not be concealed, however, that the impression wrought by this fairy sign manual varied exceedingly, according to the difference of temperament in the beholders. Some fastidious persons—but they were exclusively of her own sex—affirmed that the bloody hand, as they chose to call it, quite destroyed the effect of Georgiana's beauty, and rendered her countenance even hideous. But it would be as reasonable to say that one of those small blue stains which sometimes occur in the purest statuary marble would convert the Eve of Powers[1] to a monster. Masculine observers, if the birthmark did not heighten their admiration, contented themselves with wishing it away, that the world might possess one living specimen of ideal loveliness without the semblance of a flaw. After his marriage,—for he thought little or nothing of the matter before,—Aylmer discovered that this was the case with himself.

Had she been less beautiful,—if Envy's self could have found aught else to sneer at,—he might have felt his affection heightened by the prettiness of this mimic hand, now vaguely portrayed, now lost, now stealing forth again and glimmering to and fro with every pulse of emotion that throbbed within her heart; but seeing her otherwise so perfect, he found this one defect grow more and more intolerable with every moment of their united lives. It was the fatal flaw of humanity which Nature, in one shape or another, stamps ineffaceably on all her productions, either to imply that they are temporary and finite, or that their perfection must be wrought by toil and pain. The crimson hand expressed the ineludible

---

[1] A statue, *Eve before the Fall*, by Hiram Powers (1805–1873), a sculptor known for his idealized portraits of feminine purity.

gripe[2] in which mortality clutches the highest and purest of earthly mold, degrading them into kindred with the lowest, and even with the very brutes, like whom their visible frames return to dust. In this manner, selecting it as the symbol of his wife's liability to sin, sorrow, decay, and death, Aylmer's somber imagination was not long in rendering the birthmark a frightful object, causing him more trouble and horror than ever Georgiana's beauty, whether of soul or sense, had given him delight.

At all the seasons which should have been their happiest, he invariably and without intending it, nay, in spite of a purpose to the contrary, reverted to this one disastrous topic. Trifling as it at first appeared, it so connected itself with innumerable trains of thought and modes of feeling that it became the central point of all. With the morning twilight Aylmer opened his eyes upon his wife's face and recognized the symbol of imperfection; and when they sat together at the evening hearth his eyes wandered stealthily to her cheek, and beheld, flickering with the blaze of the wood fire, the spectral hand that wrote mortality where he would fain have worshiped. Georgiana soon learned to shudder at his gaze. It needed but a glance with the peculiar expression that his face often wore to change the roses of her cheek into a deathlike paleness, amid which the crimson hand was brought strongly out, like a bas-relief of ruby on the whitest marble.

10   Late one night when the lights were growing dim, so as hardly to betray the stain on the poor wife's cheek, she herself, for the first time, voluntarily took up the subject.

"Do you remember, my dear Aylmer," said she, with a feeble attempt at a smile, "have you any recollection of a dream last night about this odious hand?"

"None! none whatever!" replied Aylmer, starting; but then he added, in a dry, cold tone, affected for the sake of concealing the real depth of his emotion, "I might well dream of it; for before I fell asleep it had taken a pretty firm hold of my fancy."

"And you did dream of it?" continued Georgiana hastily, for she dreaded lest a gush of tears should interrupt what she had to say. "A terrible dream! I wonder that you can forget it. Is it possible to forget this one expression?—'It is in her heart now; we must have it out!' Reflect, my husband; for by all means I would have you recall that dream."

The mind is in a sad state when Sleep, the all-involving, cannot confine her specters within the dim region of her sway, but suffers them to break forth, affrighting this actual life with secrets that perchance belong to a deeper one. Aylmer now remembered his dream. He had fancied himself with his servant Aminadab, attempting an operation for the removal of the birthmark; but the deeper went the knife, the deeper sank the hand, until at length its tiny grasp appeared to have caught hold of Georgiana's

---

[2] Grip.

heart; whence, however, her husband was inexorably resolved to cut or wrench it away.

15   When the dream had shaped itself perfectly in his memory, Aylmer sat in his wife's presence with a guilty feeling. Truth often finds its way to the mind close muffled in robes of sleep, and then speaks with uncompromising directness of matters in regard to which we practice an unconscious self-deception during our waking moments. Until now he had not been aware of the tyrannizing influence acquired by one idea over his mind, and of the lengths which he might find in his heart to go for the sake of giving himself peace.

"Aylmer," resumed Georgiana solemnly, "I know not what may be the cost to both of us to rid me of this fatal birthmark. Perhaps its removal may cause cureless deformity; or it may be the stain goes as deep as life itself. Again: do we know that there is a possibility, on any terms, of unclasping the firm grip of this little hand which was laid upon me before I came into the world?"

"Dearest Georgiana, I have spent much thought upon the subject," hastily interrupted Aylmer. "I am convinced of the perfect practicability of its removal."

"If there be the remotest possibility of it," continued Georgiana, "let the attempt be made at whatever risk. Danger is nothing to me; for life, while this hateful mark makes me the object of your horror and disgust,— life is a burden which I would fling down with joy. Either remove this dreadful hand, or take my wretched life! You have deep science. All the world bears witness of it. You have achieved great wonders. Cannot you remove this little, little mark, which I cover with the tips of two small fingers? Is this beyond your power, for the sake of your own peace, and to save your poor wife from madness?"

"Noblest, dearest, tenderest wife," cried Aylmer rapturously, "doubt not my power. I have already given this matter the deepest thought— thought which might almost have enlightened me to create a being less perfect than yourself. Georgiana, you have led me deeper than ever into the heart of science. I feel myself fully competent to render this dear cheek as faultless as its fellow; and then, most beloved, what will be my triumph when I shall have corrected what Nature left imperfect in her fairest work! Even Pygmalion,[3] when his sculptured woman assumed life, felt not greater ecstasy than mine will be."

20   "It is resolved, then," said Georgiana, faintly smiling. "And, Aylmer, spare me not, though you should find the birthmark take refuge in my heart at last."

Her husband tenderly kissed her cheek—her right cheek—not that which bore the impress of the crimson hand.

---

[3] The king of Cyprus in Greek mythology, who fell in love with a statue he had sculpted. Aphrodite, the goddess of love, brought the statue to life for him.

The next day Aylmer apprised his wife of a plan that he had formed whereby he might have opportunity for the intense thought and constant watchfulness which the proposed operation would require; while Georgiana, likewise, would enjoy the perfect repose essential to its success. They were to seclude themselves in the extensive apartments occupied by Aylmer as a laboratory, and where, during his toilsome youth, he had made discoveries in the elemental powers of Nature that had roused the admiration of all the learned societies in Europe. Seated calmly in this laboratory, the pale philosopher had investigated the secrets of the highest cloud region and of the profoundest mines; he had satisfied himself of the causes that kindled and kept alive the fires of the volcano; and had explained the mystery of fountains, and how it is that they gush forth, some so bright and pure, and others with such rich medicinal virtues, from the dark bosom of the earth. Here, too, at an earlier period, he had studied the wonders of the human frame, and attempted to fathom the very process by which Nature assimilates all her precious influences from earth and air, and from the spiritual world, to create and foster man, her masterpiece. The latter pursuit, however, Aylmer had long laid aside in unwilling recognition of the truth—against which all seekers sooner or later stumble— that our great creative Mother, while she amuses us with apparently working in the broadest sunshine, is yet severely careful to keep her own secrets, and, in spite of her pretended openness, shows us nothing but results. She permits us, indeed, to mar, but seldom to mend, and, like a jealous patentee, on no account to make. Now, however, Aylmer resumed these half-forgotten investigations,—not, of course, with such hopes or wishes as first suggested them, but because they involved much physiological truth and lay in the path of his proposed scheme for the treatment of Georgiana.

As he led her over the threshold of the laboratory, Georgiana was cold and tremulous. Aylmer looked cheerfully into her face, with intent to reassure her, but was so startled with the intense glow of the birthmark upon the whiteness of her cheek that he could not restrain a strong convulsive shudder. His wife fainted.

"AminadabAminadab!" shouted Aylmer, stamping violently on the floor.

25   Forthwith there issued from an inner apartment a man of low stature, but bulky frame, with shaggy hair hanging about his visage, which was grimed with the vapors of the furnace. This personage had been Aylmer's underworker during his whole scientific career, and was admirably fitted for that office by his great mechanical readiness, and the skill with which, while incapable of comprehending a single principle, he executed all the details of his master's experiments. With his vast strength, his shaggy hair, his smoky aspect, and the indescribable earthiness that encrusted him, he seemed to represent man's physical nature; while Aylmer's slender figure, and pale, intellectual face, were no less apt a type of the spiritual element.

"Throw open the door of the boudoir, Aminadab," said Aylmer, "and burn a pastille."[4]

"Yes, master," answered Aminadab, looking intently at the lifeless form of Georgiana; and then he muttered to himself, "If she were my wife, I'd never part with that birthmark."

When Georgiana recovered consciousness she found herself breathing an atmosphere of penetrating fragrance, the gentle potency of which had recalled her from her deathlike faintness. The scene around her looked like enchantment. Aylmer had converted those smoky, dingy, somber rooms, where he had spent his brightest years in recondite pursuits, into a series of beautiful apartments not unfit to be the secluded abode of a lovely woman. The walls were hung with gorgeous curtains, which imparted the combination of grandeur and grace that no other species of adornment can achieve; and as they fell from the ceiling to the floor, their rich and ponderous folds, concealing all angles and straight lines, appeared to shut in the scene from infinite space. For aught Georgiana knew, it might be a pavilion among the clouds. And Aylmer, excluding the sunshine, which would have interfered with his chemical processes, had supplied its place with perfumed lamps, emitting flames of various hue, but all uniting in a soft, empurpled radiance. He now knelt by his wife's side, watching her earnestly, but without alarm; for he was confident in his science, and felt that he could draw a magic circle round her within which no evil might intrude.

"Where am I? Ah, I remember," said Georgiana faintly; and she placed her hand over her cheek to hide the terrible mark from her husband's eyes.

30   "Fear not, dearest!" exclaimed he. "Do not shrink from me! Believe me, Georgiana, I even rejoice in this single imperfection, since it will be such a rapture to remove it."

"Oh, spare me!" sadly replied his wife. "Pray do not look at it again. I never can forget that convulsive shudder."

In order to soothe Georgiana, and, as it were, to release her mind from the burden of actual things, Aylmer now put in practice some of the light and playful secrets which science had taught him among its profounder lore. Airy figures, absolutely bodiless ideas, and forms of unsubstantial beauty came and danced before her, imprinting their momentary footsteps on beams of light. Though she had some indistinct idea of the method of these optical phenomena, still the illusion was almost perfect enough to warrant the belief that her husband possessed sway over the spiritual world. Then again, when she felt a wish to look forth from her seclusion, immediately, as if her thoughts were answered, the procession of external existence flitted across a screen. The scenery and the figures of actual life were perfectly represented, but with that bewitching, yet indescribable difference which always makes a picture, an image, or a shadow so much more attractive than the original. When wearied of this, Aylmer bade her

---

[4] Incense.

cast her eyes upon a vessel containing a quantity of earth. She did so, with little interest at first; but was soon startled to perceive the germ of a plant shooting upward from the soil. Then came the slender stalk; the leaves gradually unfolded themselves; and amid them was a perfect and lovely flower.

"It is magical!" cried Georgiana. "I dare not touch it."

"Nay, pluck it," answered Aylmer: "pluck it, and inhale its brief perfume while you may. The flower will wither in a few moments and leave nothing save its brown seed vessels; but thence may be perpetuated a race as ephemeral as itself."

35   But Georgiana had no sooner touched the flower than the whole plant suffered a blight, its leaves turning coal-black as if by the agency of fire.

"There was too powerful a stimulus," said Aylmer thoughtfully.

To make up for this abortive experiment, he proposed to take her portrait by a scientific process of his own invention. It was to be effected by rays of light striking upon a polished plate of metal. Georgiana assented; but, on looking at the result, was affrighted to find the features of the portrait blurred and indefinable; while the minute figure of a hand appeared where the cheek should have been. Aylmer snatched the metallic plate and threw it into a jar of corrosive acid.

Soon, however, he forgot these mortifying failures. In the intervals of study and chemical experiment he came to her flushed and exhausted, but seemed invigorated by her presence, and spoke in glowing language of the resources of his art. He gave a history of the long dynasty of the alchemists,[5] who spent so many ages in quest of the universal solvent by which the golden principle might be elicited from all things vile and base. Aylmer appeared to believe that, by the plainest scientific logic, it was altogether within the limits of possibility to discover this long-sought medium; "but," he added, "a philosopher who should go deep enough to acquire the power would attain too lofty a wisdom to stoop to the exercise of it." Not less singular were his opinions in regard to the elixir vitae. He more than intimated that it was at his option to concoct a liquid that should prolong life for years, perhaps interminably; but that it would produce a discord in Nature which all the world, and chiefly the quaffer of the immortal nostrum, would find cause to curse.

"Aylmer, are you in earnest?" asked Georgiana, looking at him with amazement and fear. "It is terrible to possess such power, or even to dream of possessing it."

40   "Oh, do not tremble, my love," said her husband. "I would not wrong either you or myself by working such inharmonious effects upon our lives; but I would have you consider how trifling, in comparison, is the skill requisite to remove this little hand."

---

[5] Medieval scientists who attempted to create an elixir that would prolong life indefinitely.

At the mention of the birthmark, Georgiana, as usual, shrank as if a red-hot iron had touched her cheek.

Again Aylmer applied himself to his labors. She could hear his voice in the distant furnace-room giving directions to Aminadab, whose harsh, uncouth, misshapen tones were audible in response, more like the grunt or growl of a brute than human speech. After hours of absence, Aylmer reappeared and proposed that she should now examine his cabinet of chemical products and natural treasures of the earth. Among the former he showed her a small vial, in which, he remarked, was contained a gentle yet most powerful fragrance, capable of impregnating all the breezes that blow across a kingdom. They were of inestimable value, the contents of that little vial; and, as he said so, he threw some of the perfume into the air and filled the room with piercing and invigorating delight.

"And what is this?" asked Georgiana, pointing to a small crystal globe containing a gold-colored liquid. "It is so beautiful to the eye that I could imagine it the elixir of life."

"In one sense it is," replied Aylmer; "or rather, the elixir of immortality. It is the most precious poison that ever was concocted in this world. By its aid I could apportion the lifetime of any mortal at whom you might point your finger. The strength of the dose would determine whether he were to linger out years, or drop dead in the midst of a breath. No king on his guarded throne could keep his life if I, in my private station, should deem that the welfare of millions justified me in depriving him of it."

45   "Why do you keep such a terrific drug?" inquired Georgiana in horror.

"Do not mistrust me, dearest," said her husband, smiling; "its virtuous potency is yet greater than its harmful one. But see! here is a powerful cosmetic. With a few drops of this in a vase of water, freckles may be washed away as easily as the hands are cleansed. A stronger infusion would take the blood out of the cheek, and leave the rosiest beauty a pale ghost."

"Is it with this lotion that you intend to bathe my cheek?" asked Georgiana, anxiously.

"Oh, no," hastily replied her husband; "this is merely superficial. Your case demands a remedy that shall go deeper."

In his interviews with Georgiana, Aylmer generally made minute inquiries as to her sensations and whether the confinement of the rooms and the temperature of the atmosphere agreed with her. These questions had such a particular drift that Georgiana began to conjecture that she was already subjected to certain physical influences, either breathed in with the fragrant air or taken with her food. She fancied likewise, but it might be altogether fancy, that there was a stirring up of her system—a strange, indefinite sensation creeping through her veins, and tingling, half painfully, half pleasurably, at her heart. Still, whenever she dared to look into the mirror, there she beheld herself pale as a white rose and with the crimson birthmark stamped upon her cheek. Not even Aylmer now hated it so much as she.

50   To dispel the tedium of the hours which her husband found it necessary to devote to the processes of combination and analysis, Georgiana turned over the volumes of his scientific library. In many dark old tomes she met with chapters full of romance and poetry. They were the works of the philosophers of the middle ages, such as Albertus Magnus, Cornelius Agrippa, Paracelsus, and the famous friar who created the prophetic Brazen Head.[6] All these antique naturalists stood in advance of their centuries, yet were imbued with some of their credulity, and therefore were believed, and perhaps imagined themselves to have acquired from the investigation of Nature a power above Nature, and from physics a sway over the spiritual world. Hardly less curious and imaginative were the early volumes of the Transactions of the Royal Society, in which the members, knowing little of the limits of natural possibility, were continually recording wonders or proposing methods whereby wonders might be wrought.

But to Georgiana the most engrossing volume was a large folio from her husband's own hand, in which he had recorded every experiment of his scientific career, its original aim, the methods adopted for its development, and its final success or failure, with the circumstances to which either event was attributable. The book, in truth, was both the history and emblem of his ardent, ambitious, imaginative, yet practical and laborious life. He handled physical details as if there were nothing beyond them; yet spiritualized them all, and redeemed himself from materialism by his strong and eager aspiration towards the infinite. In his grasp the veriest clod of earth assumed a soul. Georgiana, as she read, reverenced Aylmer and loved him more profoundly than ever, but with a less entire dependence on his judgment than heretofore. Much as he had accomplished, she could not but observe that his most splendid successes were almost invariably failures, if compared with the ideal at which he aimed. His brightest diamonds were the merest pebbles, and felt to be so by himself, in comparison with the inestimable gems which lay hidden beyond his reach. The volume, rich with achievements that had won renown for its author, was yet as melancholy a record as ever mortal hand had penned. It was the sad confession and continual exemplification of the shortcomings of the composite man, the spirit burdened with clay and working in matter, and of the despair that assails the higher nature of finding itself so miserably thwarted by the earthly part. Perhaps every man of genius in whatever sphere might recognize the image of his own experience in Aylmer's journal.

So deeply did these reflections affect Georgiana that she laid her face upon the open volume and burst into tears. In this situation she was found by her husband.

"It is dangerous to read in a sorcerer's books," said he with a smile, though his countenance was uneasy and displeased. "Georgiana, there are

---

[6] An English scientist and philosopher, Friar Roger Bacon, was reputed to have created a brass head that could speak.

pages in that volume which I can scarcely glance over and keep my senses. Take heed lest it prove as detrimental to you."

"It has made me worship you more than ever," said she.

55   "Ah, wait for this one success," rejoined he, "then worship me if you will. I shall deem myself hardly unworthy of it. But come, I have sought you for the luxury of your voice. Sing to me, dearest."

So she poured out the liquid music of her voice to quench the thirst of his spirit. He then took his leave with a boyish exuberance of gaiety, assuring her that her seclusion would endure but a little longer, and that the result was already certain. Scarcely had he departed when Georgiana felt irresistibly impelled to follow him. She had forgotten to inform Aylmer of a symptom which for two or three hours past had begun to excite her attention. It was a sensation in the fatal birthmark, not painful, but which induced a restlessness throughout her system. Hastening after her husband, she intruded for the first time into the laboratory.

The first thing that struck her eye was the furnace, that hot and feverish worker, with the intense glow of its fire, which by the quantities of soot clustered above it seemed to have been burning for ages. There was a distilling apparatus in full operation. Around the room were retorts, tubes, cylinders, crucibles, and other apparatus of chemical research. An electrical machine stood ready for immediate use. The atmosphere felt oppressively close, and was tainted with gaseous odors which had been tormented forth by the process of science. The severe and homely simplicity of the apartment, with its naked walls and brick pavement, looked strange, accustomed as Georgiana had become to the fantastic elegance of her boudoir. But what chiefly, indeed almost solely, drew her attention, was the aspect of Aylmer himself.

He was pale as death, anxious and absorbed, and hung over the furnace as if it depended upon his utmost watchfulness whether the liquid which it was distilling should be the draught of immortal happiness or misery. How different from the sanguine and joyous mien that he had assumed for Georgiana's encouragement!

"Carefully now, Aminadab; carefully, thou human machine; carefully, thou man of clay!" muttered Aylmer, more to himself than his assistant. "Now, if there be a thought too much or too little, it is all over."

60   "Ho! ho!" mumbled Aminadab. "Look, master! look!"

Aylmer raised his eyes hastily, and at first reddened, then grew paler than ever, on beholding Georgiana. He rushed towards her and seized her arm with a gripe that left the print of his fingers upon it.

"Why do you come hither? Have you no trust in your husband?" cried he impetuously. "Would you throw the blight of that fatal birthmark over my labors? It is not well done. Go, prying woman, go!"

"Nay, Aylmer," said Georgiana with the firmness of which she possessed no stinted endowment, "it is not you that have a right to complain. You mistrust your wife; you have concealed the anxiety with which you watch the development of this experiment. Think not so unworthily of me, my husband. Tell me all the risk we run, and fear not that I shall shrink; for my share in it is far less than your own."

"No, no, Georgiana!" said Aylmer impatiently; "it must not be."

65 "I submit," replied she calmly. "And, Aylmer, I shall quaff whatever draught you bring me; but it will be on the same principle that would induce me to take a dose of poison if offered by your hand."

"My noble wife," said Aylmer, deeply moved, "I knew not the height and depth of your nature until now. Nothing shall be concealed. Know, then, that this crimson hand, superficial as it seems, has clutched its grasp into your being with a strength of which I had no previous conception. I have already administered agents powerful enough to do aught except to change your entire physical system. Only one thing remains to be tried. If that fails us we are ruined."

"Why did you hesitate to tell me this?" asked she.

"Because, Georgiana," said Aylmer in a low voice, "there is danger."

"Danger? There is but one danger—that this horrible stigma shall be left upon my cheek!" cried Georgiana. "Remove it, remove it, whatever be the cost, or we shall both go mad!"

70 "Heaven knows your words are too true," said Aylmer sadly. "And now, dearest, return to your boudoir. In a little while all will be tested."

He conducted her back and took leave of her with a solemn tenderness which spoke far more than his words how much was now at stake. After his departure Georgiana became rapt in musings. She considered the character of Aylmer, and did it completer justice than at any previous moment. Her heart exulted, while it trembled, at his honorable love—so pure and lofty that it would accept nothing less than perfection nor miserably make itself contented with an earthlier nature than he had dreamed of. She felt how much more precious was such a sentiment than that meaner kind which would have borne with the imperfection for her sake, and have been guilty of treason to holy love by degrading its perfect idea to the level of the actual; and with her whole spirit she prayed that, for a single moment, she might satisfy his highest and deepest conception. Longer than one moment she well knew it could not be; for his spirit was ever on the march, ever ascending, and each instant required something that was beyond the scope of the instant before.

The sound of her husband's footsteps aroused her. He bore a crystal goblet containing a liquor colorless as water, but bright enough to be the draught of immortality. Aylmer was pale; but it seemed rather the consequence of a highly wrought state of mind and tension of spirit than of fear or doubt.

"The concoction of the draught has been perfect," said he, in answer to Georgiana's look. "Unless all my science have deceived me, it cannot fail."

"Save on your account, my dearest Aylmer," observed his wife, "I might wish to put off this birthmark of mortality by relinquishing mortality itself in preference to any other mode. Life is but a sad possession to those who have attained precisely the degree of moral advancement at which I stand. Were I weaker and blinder it might be happiness. Were I stronger, it might be endured hopefully. But, being what I find myself, methinks I am of all mortals the most fit to die."

75   "You are fit for heaven without tasting death!" replied her husband. "But why do we speak of dying? The draught cannot fail. Behold its effect upon this plant."

On the window seat there stood a geranium diseased with yellow blotches, which had overspread all its leaves. Aylmer poured a small quantity of the liquid upon the soil in which it grew. In a little time, when the roots of the plant had taken up the moisture, the unsightly blotches began to be extinguished in a living verdure.

"There needed no proof," said Georgiana quietly. "Give me the goblet. I joyfully stake all upon your word."

"Drink, then, thou lofty creature!" exclaimed Aylmer, with fervid admiration. "There is no taint of imperfection on thy spirit. Thy sensible frame, too, shall soon be all perfect."

She quaffed the liquid and returned the goblet to his hand.

80   "It is grateful," said she, with a placid smile. "Methinks it is like water from a heavenly fountain; for it contains I know not what of unobtrusive fragrance and deliciousness. It allays a feverish thirst that had parched me for many days. Now, dearest, let me sleep. My earthly senses are closing over my spirit like the leaves around the heart of a rose at sunset."

She spoke the last words with a gentle reluctance, as if it required almost more energy than she could command to pronounce the faint and lingering syllables. Scarcely had they loitered through her lips ere she was lost in slumber. Aylmer sat by her side, watching her aspect with the emotions proper to a man the whole value of whose existence was involved in the process now to be tested. Mingled with this mood, however, was the philosophic investigation characteristic of the man of science. Not the minutest symptom escaped him. A heightened flush of the cheek, a slight irregularity of breath, a quiver of the eyelid, a hardly perceptible tremor through the frame,—such were the details which, as the moments passed, he wrote down in his folio volume. Intense thought had set its stamp upon every previous page of that volume, but the thoughts of years were all concentrated upon the last.

While thus employed, he failed not to gaze often at the fatal hand, and not without a shudder. Yet once, by a strange and unaccountable impulse, he pressed it with his lips. His spirit recoiled, however, in the very act; and Georgiana, out of the midst of her deep sleep, moved uneasily and murmured as if in remonstrance. Again Aylmer resumed his watch. Nor was it without avail. The crimson hand, which at first had been strongly visible upon the marble paleness of Georgiana's cheek, now grew more faintly outlined. She remained not less pale than ever; but the birthmark, with every breath that came and went, lost somewhat of its former distinctness. Its presence had been awful; its departure was more awful still. Watch the stain of the rainbow fading out of the sky, and you will know how that mysterious symbol passed away.

"By Heaven! it is well-nigh gone!" said Aylmer to himself, in almost irrepressible ecstasy. "I can scarcely trace it now. Success! success! And now it is like the faintest rose color. The lightest flush of blood across her cheek would overcome it. But she is so pale!"

He drew aside the window curtain and suffered the light of natural day to fall into the room and rest upon her cheek. At the same time he heard a gross, hoarse chuckle, which he had long known as his servant Aminadab's expression of delight.

85   "Ah, clod! ah, earthly mass!" cried Aylmer, laughing in a sort of frenzy, "you have served me well! Matter and spirit—earth and heaven— have both done their part in this! Laugh, thing of the senses! You have earned the right to laugh."

These exclamations broke Georgiana's sleep. She slowly unclosed her eyes and gazed into the mirror which her husband had arranged for that purpose. A faint smile flitted over her lips when she recognized how barely perceptible was now that crimson hand which had once blazed forth with such disastrous brilliancy as to scare away all their happiness. But then her eyes sought Aylmer's face with a trouble and anxiety that he could by no means account for.

"My poor Aylmer!" murmured she.

"Poor? Nay, richest, happiest, most favored!" exclaimed he. "My peerless bride, it is successful! You are perfect!"

"My poor Aylmer," she repeated, with a more than human tenderness, "you have aimed loftily; you have done nobly. Do not repent that with so high and pure a feeling, you have rejected the best the earth could offer. Aylmer, dearest Aylmer, I am dying!"

90   Alas! it was too true! The fatal hand had grappled with the mystery of life, and was the bond by which an angelic spirit kept itself in union with a mortal frame. As the last crimson tint of the birthmark—that sole token of human imperfection—faded from her cheek, the parting breath of the now perfect woman passed into the atmosphere, and her soul, lingering a moment near her husband, took its heavenward flight. Then a hoarse, chuckling laugh was heard again! Thus ever does the gross fatality of earth exult in its invariable triumph over the immortal essence which, in this dim sphere of half development, demands the completeness of a higher state. Yet, had Aylmer reached a profounder wisdom, he need not thus have flung away the happiness which would have woven his mortal life of the selfsame texture with the celestial. The momentary circumstance was too strong for him; he failed to look beyond the shadowy scope of time, and, living once for all in eternity, to find the perfect future in the present.

◇ ◇ ◇

SHIRLEY JACKSON
(1916–1965)

The Possibility of Evil
(1968)

Miss Adela Strangeworth stepped daintily along Main Street on her way to the grocery. The sun was shining, the air was fresh and clear after the night's heavy rain, and everything in Miss Strangeworth's little town looked washed and bright. Miss Strangeworth took deep breaths, and thought that there was nothing in the world like a fragrant summer day.

She knew everyone in town, of course; she was fond of telling strangers—tourists who sometimes passed through the town and stopped to admire Miss Strangeworth's roses—that she had never spent more than a day outside this town in all her long life. She was seventy-one, Miss Strangeworth told the tourists, with a pretty little dimple showing by her lip, and she sometimes found herself thinking that the town belonged to her. "My grandfather built the first house on Pleasant Street," she would say, opening her blue eyes wide with the wonder of it. "This house, right here. My family has lived here for better than a hundred years. My grandmother planted these roses, and my mother tended them, just as I do. I've watched my town grow; I can remember when Mr. Lewis, Senior, opened the grocery store, and the year the river flooded out the shanties on the low road, and the excitement when some young folks wanted to move the park over to the space in front of where the new post office is today. They wanted to put up a statue of Ethan Allen"—Miss Strangeworth would frown a little and sound stern—"but it should have been a statue of my grandfather. There wouldn't have been a town here at all if it hadn't been for my grandfather and the lumber mill."

Miss Strangeworth never gave away any of her roses, although the tourists often asked her. The roses belonged on Pleasant Street, and it bothered Miss Strangeworth to think of people wanting to carry them away, to take them into strange towns and down strange streets. When the new minister came, and the ladies were gathering flowers to decorate the church, Miss Strangeworth sent over a great basket of gladioli; when she picked the roses at all, she set them in bowls and vases around the inside of the house her grandfather had built.

Walking down Main Street on a summer morning, Miss Strangeworth had to stop every minute or so to say good morning to someone or to ask after someone's health. When she came into the grocery, half a dozen people turned away from the shelves and the counters to wave at her or call out good morning.

5   "And good morning to you, too, Mr. Lewis," Miss Strangeworth said at last. The Lewis family had been in the town almost as long as the

Strangeworths; but the day young Lewis left high school and went to work in the grocery, Miss Strangeworth had stopped calling him Tommy and started calling him Mr. Lewis, and he had stopped calling her Addie and started calling her Miss Strangeworth. They had been in high school together, and had gone to picnics together, and to high school dances and basketball games; but now Mr. Lewis was behind the counter in the grocery, and Miss Strangeworth was living alone in the Strangeworth house on Pleasant Street.

"Good morning," Mr. Lewis said, and added politely, "lovely day."

"It is a very nice day," Miss Strangeworth said as though she had only just decided that it would do after all. "I would like a chop, please, Mr. Lewis, a small, lean veal chop. Are those strawberries from Arthur Parker's garden? They're early this year."

"He brought them in this morning," Mr. Lewis said.

"I shall have a box," Miss Strangeworth said. Mr. Lewis looked worried, she thought, and for a minute she hesitated, but then she decided that he surely could not be worried over the strawberries. He looked very tired indeed. He was usually so chipper, Miss Strangeworth thought, and almost commented, but it was far too personal a subject to be introduced to Mr. Lewis, the grocer, so she only said, "And a can of cat food and, I think, a tomato."

10   Silently, Mr. Lewis assembled her order on the counter and waited. Miss Strangeworth looked at him curiously and then said, "It's Tuesday, Mr. Lewis. You forgot to remind me."

"Did I? Sorry."

"Imagine your forgetting that I always buy my tea on Tuesday," Miss Strangeworth said gently. "A quarter pound of tea, please, Mr. Lewis."

"Is that all, Miss Strangeworth?"

"Yes, thank you, Mr. Lewis. Such a lovely day, isn't it?"

15   "Lovely," Mr. Lewis said.

Miss Strangeworth moved slightly to make room for Mrs. Harper at the counter. "Morning, Adela," Mrs. Harper said, and Miss Strangeworth said, "Good morning, Martha."

"Lovely day," Mrs. Harper said, and Miss Strangeworth said, "Yes, lovely," and Mr. Lewis, under Mrs. Harper's glance, nodded.

"Run out of sugar for my cake frosting," Mrs. Harper explained. Her hand shook slightly as she opened her pocketbook. Miss Strangeworth wondered, glancing at her quickly, if she had been taking proper care of herself. Martha Harper was not as young as she used to be, Miss Strangeworth thought. She probably could use a good, strong tonic.

"Martha," she said, "you don't look well."

20   "I'm perfectly all right," Mrs. Harper said shortly. She handed her money to Mr. Lewis, took her change and her sugar, and went out without speaking again. Looking after her, Miss Strangeworth shook her head slightly. Martha definitely did *not* look well.

Carrying her little bag of groceries, Miss Strangeworth came out of the store into the bright sunlight and stopped to smile down on the Crane baby. Don and Helen Crane were really the two most infatuated young parents she had ever known, she thought indulgently, looking at the delicately embroidered baby cap and the lace-edged carriage cover.

"That little girl is going to grow up expecting luxury all her life," she said to Helen Crane.

Helen laughed. "That's the way we want her to feel," she said. "Like a princess."

"A princess can be a lot of trouble sometimes," Miss Strangeworth said dryly. "How old is her highness now?"

25 "Six months next Tuesday," Helen Crane said, looking down with rapt wonder at her child. "I've been worrying, though, about her. Don't you think she ought to move around more? Try to sit up, for instance?"

"For plain and fancy worrying," Miss Strangeworth said, amused, "give me a new mother every time."

"She just seems—slow," Helen Crane said.

"Nonsense. All babies are different. Some of them develop much more quickly than others."

"That's what my mother says." Helen Crane laughed, looking a little bit ashamed.

30 "I suppose you've got young Don all upset about the fact that his daughter is already six months old and hasn't yet begun to learn to dance?"

"I haven't mentioned it to him. I suppose she's just so precious that I worry about her all the time."

"Well, apologize to her right now," Miss Strangeworth said. "*She* is probably worrying about why you keep jumping around all the time." Smiling to herself and shaking her old head, she went on down the sunny street, stopping once to ask little Billy Moore why he wasn't out riding in his daddy's shiny new car, and talking for a few minutes outside the library with Miss Chandler, the librarian, about the new novels to be ordered, and paid for by the annual library appropriation. Miss Chandler seemed absentminded and very much as though she was thinking about something else. Miss Strangeworth noticed that Miss Chandler had not taken much trouble with her hair that morning, and sighed. Miss Strangeworth hated sloppiness.

Many people seemed disturbed recently, Miss Strangeworth thought. Only yesterday the Stewarts' fifteen-year-old Linda had run crying down her own front walk and all the way to school, not caring who saw her. People around town thought she might have had a fight with the Harris boy, but they showed up together at the soda shop after school as usual, both of them looking grim and bleak. Trouble at home, people concluded, and sighed over the problems of trying to raise kids right these days.

From halfway down the block Miss Strangeworth could catch the heavy accent of her roses, and she moved a little more quickly. The perfume of roses meant home, and home meant the Strangeworth House on Pleasant Street. Miss Strangeworth stopped at her own front gate, as she always did, and looked with deep pleasure at her house, with the red and pink and white roses massed along the narrow lawn, and the rambler going up along the porch; and the neat, the unbelievably trim lines of the house itself, with its slimness and its washed white look. Every window sparkled, every curtain hung stiff and straight, and even the stones of the front walk were swept and clear. People around town wondered how old Miss Strangeworth managed to keep the house looking the way it did, and there was a legend about a tourist once mistaking it for the local museum and going all through the place without finding out about his mistake. But the town was proud of Miss Strangeworth and her roses and her house. They had all grown together. Miss Strangeworth went up her front steps, unlocked her front door with her key, and went into the kitchen to put away her groceries. She debated having a cup of tea and then decided that it was too close to midday dinnertime; she would not have the appetite for her little chop if she had tea now. Instead she went into the light, lovely sitting room, which still glowed from the hands of her mother and her grandmother, who had covered the chairs with bright chintz and hung the curtains. All the furniture was spare and shining, and the round hooked rugs on the floor had been the work of Miss Strangeworth's grandmother and her mother. Miss Strangeworth had put a bowl of her red roses on the low table before the window, and the room was full of their scent.

35   Miss Strangeworth went to the narrow desk in the corner, and unlocked it with her key. She never knew when she might feel like writing letters, so she kept her notepaper inside, and the desk locked. Miss Strangeworth's usual stationery was heavy and cream-colored, with "Strangeworth House" engraved across the top, but, when she felt like writing her other letters, Miss Strangeworth used a pad of various-colored paper, bought from the local newspaper shop. It was almost a town joke, that colored paper, layered in pink and green and blue and yellow; everyone in town bought it and used it for odd, informal notes and shopping lists. It was usual to remark, upon receiving a note written on a blue page, that so-and-so would be needing a new pad soon—here she was, down to the blue already. Everyone used the matching envelopes for tucking away recipes, or keeping odd little things in, or even to hold cookies in the school lunch boxes. Mr. Lewis sometimes gave them to the children for carrying home penny candy.

Although Miss Strangeworth's desk held a trimmed quill pen, which had belonged to her grandfather, and a gold-frost fountain pen, which had belonged to her father, Miss Strangeworth always used a dull stub of pencil when she wrote her letters, and she printed them in a childish block print. After thinking for a minute, although she had been phrasing the letter in the back of her mind all the way home, she wrote on a pink sheet: *Didn't you ever see an idiot child before? Some people just shouldn't have children, should they?*

She was pleased with the letter. She was fond of doing things exactly right. When she made a mistake, as she sometimes did, or when the letters were not spaced nicely on the page, she had to take the discarded page to the kitchen stove and burn it at once. Miss Strangeworth never delayed when things had to be done.

After thinking for a minute, she decided that she would like to write another letter, perhaps to go to Mrs. Harper, to follow up the ones she had already mailed. She selected a green sheet this time and wrote quickly: *Have you found out yet what they were all laughing about after you left the bridge club on Thursday? Or is the wife really always the last one to know?*

Miss Strangeworth never concerned herself with facts; her letters all dealt with the more negotiable stuff of suspicion. Mr. Lewis would never have imagined for a minute that his grandson might be lifting petty cash from the store register if he had not had one of Miss Strangeworth's letters. Miss Chandler, the librarian, and Linda Stewart's parents would have gone unsuspectingly ahead with their lives, never aware of possible evil lurking nearby, if Miss Strangeworth had not sent letters to open their eyes. Miss Strangeworth would have been genuinely shocked if there *had* been anything between Linda Stewart and the Harris boy, but, as long as evil existed unchecked in the world, it was Miss Strangeworth's duty to keep her town alert to it. It was far more sensible for Miss Chandler to wonder what Mr. Shelley's first wife had really died of than to take a chance on not knowing. There were so many wicked people in the world and only one Strangeworth left in town. Besides, Miss Strangeworth liked writing her letters.

40   She addressed an envelope to Don Crane after a moment's thought, wondering curiously if he would show the letter to his wife, and using a pink envelope to match the pink paper. Then she addressed a second envelope, green, to Mrs. Harper. Then an idea came to her and she selected a blue sheet and wrote: *You never know about doctors. Remember they're only human and need money like the rest of us. Suppose the knife slipped accidentally. Would Doctor Burns get his fee and a little extra from that nephew of yours?*

She addressed the blue envelope to old Mrs. Foster, who was having an operation next month. She had thought of writing one more letter, to the head of the school board, asking how a chemistry teacher like Billy Moore's father could afford a new convertible, but all at once she was tired of writing letters. The three she had done would do for one day. She could write more tomorrow; it was not as though they all had to be done at once.

She had been writing her letters—sometimes two or three every day for a week, sometimes no more than one in a month—for the past year. She never got any answers, of course, because she never signed her name. If she had been asked, she would have said that her name, Adela Strangeworth, a name honored in the town for so many years, did not belong on such trash. The town where she lived had to be kept clean and sweet, but people everywhere were lustful and evil and degraded, and needed to be watched; the world was so large, and there was only one Strangeworth left in it. Miss Strangeworth sighed, locked her desk, and put the letters into her big, black leather pocketbook, to be mailed when she took her evening walk.

She broiled her little chop nicely, and had a sliced tomato and good cup of tea ready when she sat down to her midday dinner at the table in her dining room, which could be opened to seat twenty-two, with a second table, if necessary, in the hall. Sitting in the warm sunlight that came through the tall windows of the dining room, seeing her roses massed outside, handling the heavy, old silverware and the fine, translucent china, Miss Strangeworth was pleased; she would not have cared to be doing anything else. People must live graciously, after all, she thought, and sipped her tea. Afterward, when her plate and cup and saucer were washed and dried and put back onto the shelves where they belonged, and her silverware was back in the mahogany silver chest, Miss Strangeworth went up the graceful staircase and into her bedroom, which was the front room overlooking the roses, and had been her mother's and her grandmother's. Their Crown Derby dresser set and furs had been kept here, their fans and silver-backed brushes and their own bowls of roses; Miss Strangeworth kept a bowl of white roses on the bed table.

She drew the shades, took the rose-satin spread from the bed, slipped out of her dress and her shoes, and lay down tiredly. She knew that no doorbell or phone would ring; no one in town would dare to disturb Miss Strangeworth during her afternoon nap. She slept, deep in the rich smell of roses.

45   After her nap she worked in her garden for a little while, sparing herself because of the heat; then she went in to her supper. She ate asparagus from her own garden, with sweet-butter sauce, and a soft-boiled egg, and, while she had her supper, she listened to a late-evening news broadcast and then to a program of classical music on her small radio. After her dishes were done and her kitchen set in order, she took up her hat—Miss Strangeworth's hats were proverbial in the town; people believed that she had inherited them from her mother and her grandmother—and, locking the front door of her house behind her, set off on her evening walk, pocketbook under her arm. She nodded to Linda Stewart's father, who was washing his car in the pleasantly cool evening. She thought that he looked troubled.

There was only one place in town where she could mail her letters, and that was the new post office, shiny with red brick and silver letters. Although Miss Strangeworth had never given the matter any particular thought, she had always made a point of mailing her letters very secretly; it would, of course, not have been wise to let anyone see her mail them. Consequently, she timed her walk so she could reach the post office just as darkness was starting to dim the outlines of the trees and the shapes of people's faces, although no one could ever mistake Miss Strangeworth, with her dainty walk and her rustling skirts.

There was always a group of young people around the post office, the very youngest roller-skating upon its driveway, which went all the way around the building and was the only smooth road in town; and the slightly older ones already knowing how to gather in small groups and chatter and laugh and make great, excited plans for going across the street to the soda shop in a minute or two. Miss Strangeworth had never had any self-consciousness before the children. She did not feel that any of them were staring at her unduly or longing to laugh at her; it would have been most reprehensible for their parents to permit their children to mock Miss Strangeworth of Pleasant Street. Most of the children stood back respectfully as Miss Strangeworth passed, silenced briefly in her presence, and some of the older children greeted her, saying soberly, "Hello, Miss Strangeworth."

Miss Strangeworth smiled at them and quickly went on. It had been a long time since she had known the name of every child in town. The mail slot was in the door of the post office. The children stood away as Miss Strangeworth approached it, seemingly surprised that anyone should want to use the post office after it had been officially closed up for the night and turned over to the children. Miss Strangeworth stood by the door, opening her black pocketbook to take out the letters, and heard a voice which she knew at once to be Linda Stewart's. Poor little Linda was crying again, and Miss Strangeworth listened carefully. This was, after all, her town, and these were her people; if one of them was in trouble, she ought to know about it.

"I can't tell you, Dave," Linda was saying—so she *was* talking to the Harris boy, as Miss Strangeworth had supposed—"I just *can't*. It's just *nasty*."

50 "But why won't your father let me come around anymore? What on earth did I do?"

"I can't tell you. I just wouldn't tell you for *any*thing. You've got to have a dirty dirty mind for things like that."

"But something's happened. You've been crying and crying, and your father is all upset. Why can't *I* know about it, too? Aren't I like one of the family?"

"Not anymore, Dave, not anymore. You're not to come near our house again; my father said so. He said he'd horsewhip you. That's all I can tell you: You're not to come near our house anymore."

"But I didn't *do* anything."

55 "Just the same, my father said . . ."

Miss Strangeworth sighed and turned away. There was so much evil in people. Even in a charming little town like this one, there was still so much evil in people.

She slipped her letters into the slot, and two of them fell inside. The third caught on the edge and fell outside, onto the ground at Miss Strangeworth's feet. She did not notice it because she was wondering whether a letter to the Harris boy's father might not be of some service in wiping out this potential badness. Wearily Miss Strangeworth turned to go home to her quiet bed in her lovely house, and never the Harris boy calling to her to say that she had dropped something.

"Old lady Strangeworth's getting deaf," he said, looking after her and holding in his hand the letter he had picked up.

"Well, who cares?" Linda said. "Who cares anymore, anyway?"

60   "It's for Don Crane," the Harris boy said, "this letter. She dropped a letter addressed to Don Crane. Might as well take it on over. We pass his house anyway." He laughed. "Maybe it's got a check or something in it and he'd be just as glad to get it tonight instead of tomorrow."

"Catch old lady Strangeworth sending anybody a check," Linda said. "Throw it in the post office. Why do anyone a favor?" She sniffed. "Doesn't seem to me anybody around here cares about us," she said. "Why should we care about them?"

"I'll take it over, anyway," the Harris boy said. "Maybe it's good news for them. Maybe they need something happy tonight, too. Like us."

Sadly, holding hands, they wandered off down the dark street, the Harris boy carrying Miss Strangeworth's pink envelope in his hand.

Miss Strangeworth awakened the next morning with a feeling of intense happiness and, for a minute, wondered why, and then remembered that this morning three people would open her letters. Harsh, perhaps, at first, but wickedness was never easily banished, and a clean heart was a scoured heart. She washed her soft, old face and brushed her teeth, still sound in spite of her seventy-one years, and dressed herself carefully in her sweet, soft clothes and buttoned shoes. Then, going downstairs, reflecting that perhaps a little waffle would be agreeable for breakfast in the sunny dining room, she found the mail on the hall floor, and bent to pick it up. A bill, the morning paper, a letter in a green envelope that looked oddly familiar. Miss Strangeworth stood perfectly still for a minute, looking down at the green envelope with the penciled printing, and thought: It looks like one of my letters. Was one of my letters sent back? No, because no one would know where to send it. How did this get here?

65   Miss Strangeworth was a Strangeworth of Pleasant Street. Her hand did not shake as she opened the envelope and unfolded the sheet of green paper inside. She began to cry silently for the wickedness of the world when she read the words: *Look out at what used to be your roses.*

◇ ◇ ◇

JAMES JOYCE
(1884–1941)

Eveline
(1914)

She sat at the window watching the evening invade the avenue. Her head was leaned against the window curtains and in her nostrils was the odor of dusty cretonne.[1] She was tired.

Few people passed. The man out of the last house passed on his way home; she heard his footsteps clacking along the concrete pavement and

---

[1] Heavy cloth used for curtains and upholstery.

afterwards crunching on the cinder path before the new red houses. One time there used to be a field there in which they used to play every evening with other people's children. Then a man from Belfast[2] bought the field and built houses in it—not like their little brown houses but bright brick houses with shining roofs. The children of the avenue used to play together in that field—the Devines, the Waters, the Dunns, little Keogh the cripple, she and her brothers and sisters. Ernest, however, never played: he was too grown up. Her father used often to hunt them in out of the field with his blackthorn stick; but usually little Keogh used to keep *nix*[3] and call out when he saw her father coming. Still they seemed to have been rather happy then. Her father was not so bad then; and besides, her mother was alive. That was a long time ago; she and her brothers and sisters were all grown up; her mother was dead. Tizzie Dunn was dead, too, and the Waters had gone back to England. Everything changes. Now she was going to go away like the others, to leave her home.

Home! She looked around the room, reviewing all its familiar objects which she had dusted once a week for so many years, wondering where on earth all the dust came from. Perhaps she would never see again those familiar objects from which she had never dreamed of being divided. And yet during all those years she had never found out the name of the priest whose yellowing photograph hung on the wall above the broken harmonium beside the colored print of the promises made to Blessed Margaret Mary Alacoque. He had been a school friend of her father. Whenever he showed the photograph to a visitor her father used to pass it with a casual word:

"He is in Melbourne now."

5   She had consented to go away, to leave her home. Was that wise? She tried to weigh each side of the question. In her home anyway she had shelter and food; she had those whom she had known all her life about her. Of course she had to work hard both in the house and at business. What would they say of her in the Stores when they found out that she had run away with a fellow? Say she was a fool, perhaps; and her place would be filled up by advertisement. Miss Gavan would be glad. She had always had an edge on her, especially whenever there were people listening.

"Miss Hill, don't you see these ladies are waiting?"

"Look lively, Miss Hill, please."

She would not cry many tears at leaving the Stores.

But in her new home, in a distant unknown country, it would not be like that. Then she would be married—she, Eveline. People would treat her with respect then. She would not be treated as her mother had been. Even now, though she was over nineteen, she sometimes felt herself in danger of her father's violence. She knew it was that that had given her the palpitations.

---

[2] Capital of present-day Northern Ireland. This story refers to a time before the Partition of Ireland.

[3] Keep watch (slang).

When they were growing up he had never gone for her, like he used to go for Harry and Ernest, because she was a girl; but latterly he had begun to threaten her and say what he would do to her only for her dead mother's sake. And now she had nobody to protect her. Ernest was dead and Harry, who was in the church decorating business, was nearly always down somewhere in the country. Besides, the invariable squabble for money on Saturday nights had begun to weary her unspeakably. She always gave her entire wages—seven shillings—and Harry always sent up what he could but the trouble was to get any money from her father. He said she used to squander the money, that she had no head, that he wasn't going to give her his hard-earned money to throw about the streets, and much more, for he was usually fairly bad of a Saturday night. In the end he would give her the money and ask her had she any intention of buying Sunday dinner. Then she had to rush out as quickly as she could and do her marketing, holding her black leather purse tightly in her hand as she elbowed her way through the crowds and returning home late under her load of provisions. She had hard work to keep the house together and to see that the two young children, who had been left to her charge went to school regularly and got their meals regularly. It was hard work—a hard life—but now that she was about to leave it she did not find it a wholly undesirable life.

10   She was about to explore another life with Frank. Frank was very kind, manly, open-hearted. She was to go away with him by the night-boat to be his wife and to live with him in Buenos Aires where he had a home waiting for her. How well she remembered the first time she had seen him; he was lodging in a house on the main road where she used to visit. It seemed a few weeks ago. He was standing at the gate, his peaked cap pushed back on his head and his hair tumbled forward over a face of bronze. Then they had come to know each other. He used to meet her outside the Stores every evening and see her home. He took her to see *The Bohemian Girl* and she felt elated as she sat in an unaccustomed part of the theater with him. He was awfully fond of music and sang a little. People knew that they were courting and, when he sang about the lass that loves a sailor, she always felt pleasantly confused. He used to call her Poppens out of fun. First of all it had been an excitement for her to have a fellow and then she had begun to like him. He had tales of distant countries. He had started as a deck boy at a pound a month on a ship of the Allan Line going out to Canada. He told her the names of the ships he had been on and the names of the different services. He had sailed through the Straits of Magellan[4] and he told her stories of the terrible Patagonians.[5] He had fallen on his feet in Buenos Aires, he said, and had come over to the old country just for a holiday. Of course, her father had found out the affair and had forbidden her to have anything to say to him.

---

[4] Sea channel at the southern tip of South America.
[5] People from Patagonia, a tableland region in southern Argentina and Chile.

"I know these sailor chaps," he said.

One day he had quarreled with Frank and after that she had to meet her lover secretly.

The evening deepened in the avenue. The white of two letters in her lap grew indistinct. One was to Harry; the other was to her father. Ernest had been her favorite but she liked Harry too. Her father was becoming old lately, she noticed; he would miss her. Sometimes he could be very nice. Not long before, when she had been laid up for a day, he had read her out a ghost story and made toast for her at the fire. Another day, when their mother was alive, they had all gone for a picnic to the Hill of Howth. She remembered her father putting on her mother's bonnet to make the children laugh.

Her time was running out but she continued to sit by the window, leaning her head against the window curtain, inhaling the odor of dusty cretonne. Down far in the avenue she could hear a street organ playing. She knew the air. Strange that it should come that very night to remind her of the promise to her mother, her promise to keep the home together as long as she could. She remembered the last night of her mother's illness; she was again in the close dark room at the other side of the hall and outside she heard a melancholy air of Italy. The organ player had been ordered to go away and given sixpence. She remembered her father strutting back into the sickroom saying:

15   "Damned Italians! coming over here!"

As she mused the pitiful vision of her mother's life laid its spell on the very quick of her being—that life of commonplace sacrifices closing in final craziness. She trembled as she heard again her mother's voice saying constantly with foolish insistence:

"Derevaun Seraun! Derevaun Seraun!"[6]

She stood up in a sudden impulse of terror. Escape! She must escape! Frank would save her. He would give her life, perhaps love, too. But she wanted to live. Why should she be unhappy? She had a right to happiness. Frank would take her in his arms, fold her in his arms. He would save her.

She stood among the swaying crowd in the station at the North Wall. He held her hand and she knew that he was speaking to her, saying something about the passage over and over again. The station was full of soldiers with brown baggages. Through the wide doors of the sheds she caught a glimpse of the black mass of the boat, lying in beside the quay[7] wall, with illumined portholes. She answered nothing. She felt her cheek pale and cold and, out of a maze of distress, she prayed to God to direct her, to show her what was her duty. The boat blew a long mournful whistle into the mist. If she went, tomorrow she would be on the sea with

---

[6] "The end of pleasure is pain!" (Irish).

[7] A paved stretch of shoreline facing navigable water, used for loading and unloading ships.

Frank, steaming toward Buenos Aires. Their passage had been booked. Could she still draw back after all he had done for her? Her distress awoke a nausea in her body and she kept moving her lips in silent, fervent prayer.

20   A bell clanged upon her heart. She felt him seize her hand:

"Come!"

All the seas of the world tumbled about her heart. He was drawing her into them: he would drown her. She gripped with both hands at the iron railing.

"Come!"

No! No! No! It was impossible. Her hands clutched the iron in frenzy. Amid the seas she sent a cry of anguish!

25   "Eveline! Evvy!"

He rushed beyond the barrier and called to her to follow. He was shouted at to go on but he still called to her. She set her white face to him, passive, like a helpless animal. Her eyes gave him no sign of love or farewell or recognition.

◇ ◇ ◇

FRANZ KAFKA
(1883–1924)

The Metamorphosis
(1915)

I

As Gregor Samsa awoke one morning from uneasy dreams he found himself transformed in his bed into a gigantic insect. He was lying on his hard, as it were armor-plated, back and when he lifted his head a little he could see his dome-like brown belly divided into stiff arched segments on top of which the bed quilt could hardly keep in position and was about to slide off completely. His numerous legs, which were pitifully thin compared to the rest of his bulk, waved helplessly before his eyes.

What has happened to me? he thought. It was no dream. His room, a regular human bedroom, only rather too small, lay quiet between the four familiar walls. Above the table on which a collection of cloth samples was unpacked and spread out—Samsa was a commercial traveler—hung the picture which he had recently cut out of an illustrated magazine and put into a pretty gilt frame. It showed a lady, with a fur cap on and a fur stole, sitting upright and holding out to the spectator a huge fur muff into which the whole of her forearm had vanished!

Gregor's eyes turned next to the window, and the overcast sky—one could hear rain drops beating on the window gutter—made him quite melancholy. What about sleeping a little longer and forgetting all this nonsense, he thought, but it could not be done, for he was accustomed to sleep on his right side and in his present condition he could not turn himself over. However violently he forced himself towards his right side he always rolled on to his back again. He tried it at least a hundred times, shutting his eyes to keep from seeing his struggling legs, and only desisted when he began to feel in his side a faint dull ache he had never experienced before.

Oh God, he thought, what an exhausting job I've picked on! Traveling about day in, day out. It's much more irritating work than doing the actual business in the office, and on top of that there's the trouble of constant traveling, of worrying about train connections, the bed and irregular meals, casual acquaintances that are always new and never become intimate friends. The devil take it all! He felt a slight itching up on his belly; slowly pushed himself on his back nearer to the top of the bed so that he could lift his head more easily; identified the itching place which was surrounded by many small white spots the nature of which he could not understand and made to touch it with a leg, but drew the leg back immediately, for the contact made a cold shiver run through him.

5   He slid down again into his former position. This getting up early, he thought, makes one quite stupid. A man needs his sleep. Other commercials live like harem women. For instance, when I come back to the hotel of a morning to write up the orders I've got, these others are only sitting down to breakfast. Let me just try that with my chief; I'd be sacked on the spot. Anyhow, that might be quite a good thing for me, who can tell? If I didn't have to hold my hand because of my parents I'd have given notice long ago, I'd have gone to the chief and told him exactly what I think of him. That would knock him endways from his desk! It's a queer way of doing, too, this sitting on high at a desk and talking down to employees, especially when they have to come quite near because the chief is hard of hearing. Well, there's still hope; once I've saved enough money to pay back my parents' debts to him—that should take another five or six years—I'll do it without fail. I'll cut myself completely loose then. For the moment, though, I'd better get up, since my train goes at five.

He looked at the alarm clock ticking on the chest. Heavenly Father! he thought. It was half-past six o'clock and the hands were quietly moving on, it was even past the half-hour, it was getting on toward a quarter to seven. Had the alarm clock not gone off? From the bed one could see that it had been properly set for four o'clock; of course it must have gone off. Yes, but was it possible to sleep quietly through that ear-splitting noise? Well, he had not slept quietly, yet apparently all the more soundly for that. But what was he to do now? The next train went at seven o'clock; to catch that he would need to hurry like mad and his samples weren't even packed up, and he himself wasn't feeling particularly fresh and active. And even if he did catch the train he wouldn't avoid a row with the chief, since the firm's porter would have been waiting for the five o'clock train and would have long since reported his failure to turn up. The porter was a creature of the chief's, spineless and stupid. Well, supposing he were to say he was sick? But that would be most unpleasant and would look suspicious, since during his five years' employment he had not been ill once. The chief himself would be sure to come with the sick-insurance doctor, would reproach his parents with their son's laziness and would cut all excuses short by referring to the insurance doctor, who of course regarded all mankind as perfectly healthy malingerers. And would he be so far wrong on this occasion? Gregor really felt quite well, apart from a drowsiness that was utterly superfluous after such a long sleep, and he was even unusually hungry.

As all this was running through his mind at top speed without his being able to decide to leave his bed—the alarm clock had just struck a quarter to seven—there came a cautious tap at the door behind the head of his bed. "Gregor," said a voice—it was his mother's—"it's a quarter to seven. Hadn't you a train to catch?" That gentle voice! Gregor had a shock as he heard his own voice answering hers, unmistakably his own voice, it was true, but with a persistent horrible twittering squeak behind it like an undertone, that left the words in their clear shape only for the first moment and then rose up reverberating round them to destroy their sense, so that one could not be sure one had heard them rightly. Gregor wanted to answer at length and explain everything, but in the circumstances he confined himself to saying: "Yes, yes, thank you, Mother, I'm getting up now." The wooden door between them must have kept the change in his voice from being noticeable outside, for his mother contented herself with this statement and shuffled away. Yet this brief exchange of words had made the other members of the family aware that Gregor was still in the house, as they had not expected, and at one of the side doors his father was already knocking, gently, yet with his fist. "Gregor, Gregor," he called, "what's the matter with you?" And after a little while he called again in a deeper voice: "Gregor! Gregor!" At the other side door his sister was saying in a low, plaintive tone: "Gregor? Aren't you well? Are you needing anything?" He answered them both at once: "I'm just ready," and did his best to make his voice sound as normal as possible by enunciating the words very clearly and leaving long pauses between them. So his father went back to his breakfast, but his sister whispered: "Gregor, open the door, do." However, he was not thinking of opening the door, and felt thankful for the prudent habit he had acquired in traveling of locking all doors during the night, even at home.

His immediate intention was to get up quietly without being disturbed, to put on his clothes and above all eat his breakfast, and only then to consider what else was to be done, since in bed, he was well aware, his meditations would come to no sensible conclusion. He remembered that often enough in bed he had felt small aches and pains, probably caused by awkward postures, which had proved purely imaginary once he got up, and he looked forward eagerly to seeing this morning's delusions gradually fall away. That the change in his voice was nothing but the precursor of a severe chill, a standing ailment of commercial travelers, he had not the least possible doubt.

To get rid of the quilt was quite easy; he had only to inflate himself a little and it fell off by itself. But the next move was difficult, especially because he was so uncommonly broad. He would have needed arms and hands to hoist himself up; instead he had only the numerous little legs which never stopped waving in all directions and which he could not control in the least. When he tried to bend one of them it was the first to stretch itself straight; and did he succeed at last in making it do what he wanted, all the other legs meanwhile waved the more wildly in a high degree of unpleasant agitation. "But what's the use of lying idle in bed," said Gregor to himself.

10   He thought that he might get out of bed with the lower part of his body first, but this lower part, which he had not yet seen and of which he could form no clear conception, proved too difficult to move; it shifted so slowly; and when finally, almost wild with annoyance, he gathered his forces together and thrust out recklessly, he had miscalculated the direction and bumped heavily against the lower end of the bed, and the stinging pain he felt informed him that precisely this lower part of his body was at the moment probably the most sensitive.

So he tried to get the top part of himself out first, and cautiously moved his head towards the edge of the bed. That proved easy enough, and despite its breadth and mass the bulk of his body at last slowly followed the movement of his head. Still, when he finally got his head free over the edge of the bed he felt too scared to go on advancing, for after all if he let himself fall in this way it would take a miracle to keep his head from being injured. And at all costs he must not lose consciousness now, precisely now; he would rather stay in bed.

But when after a repetition of the same efforts he lay in his former position again, sighing, and watched his little legs struggling against each other more wildly than ever, if that were possible, and saw no way of bringing any order into this arbitrary confusion, he told himself again that it was impossible to stay in bed and that the most sensible course was to risk everything for the smallest hope of getting away from it. At the same time he did not forget meanwhile to remind himself that cool reflection, the coolest possible, was much better than desperate resolves. In such moments he focused his eyes as sharply as possible on the window, but, unfortunately, the prospect of the morning fog, which muffled even the other side of the narrow street, brought him little encouragement and comfort. "Seven o'clock already," he said to himself when the alarm clock chimed again, "seven o'clock already and still such a thick fog." And for a little while he lay quiet, breathing lightly, as if perhaps expecting such complete repose to restore all things to their real and normal condition.

But then he said to himself: "Before it strikes a quarter past seven I must be quite out of this bed, without fail. Anyhow, by that time someone will have come from the office to ask for me, since it opens before seven." And he set himself to rocking his whole body at once in a regular rhythm, with the idea of swinging it out of the bed. If he tipped himself out in that way he could keep his head from injury by lifting it at an acute angle when he fell. His back seemed to be hard and was not likely to suffer from a fall on the carpet. His biggest worry was the loud crash he would not be able to help making, which would probably cause anxiety, if not terror, behind all the doors. Still, he must take the risk.

When he was already half out of the bed—the new method was more a game than an effort, for he needed only to hitch himself across by rocking to and fro—it struck him how simple it would be if he could get help. Two strong people—he thought of his father and the servant girl—would be amply sufficient; they would only have to thrust their arms under his convex back, lever him out of the bed, bend down with their burden and then be patient enough to let him turn himself right over on to the floor, where it was to be hoped his legs would then find their proper function. Well, ignoring the fact that the doors were all locked, ought he really to call for help? In spite of his misery he could not suppress a smile at the very idea of it.

15　He had got so far that he could barely keep his equilibrium when he rocked himself strongly, and he would have to nerve himself very soon for the final decision since in five minutes' time it would be a quarter past seven—when the front door bell rang. "That's someone from the office," he said to himself, and grew almost rigid, while his little legs only jigged about all the faster. For a moment everything stayed quiet. "They're not going to open the door," said Gregor to himself, catching at some kind of irrational hope. But then of course the servant girl went as usual to the door with her heavy tread and opened it. Gregor needed only to hear the first good morning of the visitor to know immediately who it was—the chief clerk himself. What a fate, to be condemned to work for a firm where the smallest omission at once gave rise to the gravest suspicion! Were all employees in a body nothing but scoundrels, was there not among them one single loyal devoted man who, had he wasted only an hour or so of the firm's time in a morning, was so tormented by conscience as to be driven out of his mind and actually incapable of leaving his bed? Wouldn't it really have been sufficient to send an apprentice to inquire—if any inquiry were necessary at all—did the chief clerk himself have to come and thus indicate to the entire family, an innocent family, that this suspicious circumstance could be investigated by no one less versed in affairs than himself? And more through the agitation caused by these reflections than through any act of will Gregor swung himself out of bed with all his strength. There was a loud thump, but it was not really a crash. His fall was broken to some extent by the carpet, his back, too, was less stiff than he thought, and so there was merely a dull thud, not so very startling. Only he had not lifted his head carefully enough and had hit it; he turned it and rubbed it on the carpet in pain and irritation.

"That was something falling down in there," said the chief clerk in the next room to the left. Gregor tried to suppose to himself that something like what had happened to him today might some day happen to the chief clerk; one really could not deny that it was possible. But as if in brusque reply to this supposition the chief clerk took a couple of firm steps in the next-door room and his patent leather boots creaked. From the right-hand room his sister was whispering to inform him of the situation: "Gregor, the chief clerk's here." "I know," muttered Gregor to himself; but he didn't dare to make his voice loud enough for his sister to hear it.

"Gregor," said his father now from the left-hand room, "the chief clerk has come and wants to know why you didn't catch the early train. We don't know what to say to him. Besides, he wants to talk to you in person. So open the door, please. He will be good enough to excuse the untidiness of your room." "Good morning, Mr. Samsa," the chief clerk was calling amiably meanwhile. "He's not well," said his mother to the visitor, while his father was still speaking through the door, "he's not well, sir, believe me. What else would make him miss a train! The boy thinks about nothing but his work. It makes me almost cross the way he never goes out in the evenings; he's been here the last eight days and has stayed at home every single evening. He just sits there quietly at the table reading a newspaper or looking through railway timetables. The only amusement he gets is doing fretwork. For instance, he spent two or three evenings cutting out a little picture frame; you would be surprised to see how pretty it is; it's hanging in his room; you'll see it in a minute when Gregor opens the door. I must say I'm glad you've come, sir; we should never have got him to unlock the door by ourselves; he's so obstinate; and I'm sure he's unwell, though he wouldn't have it to be so this morning." "I'm just coming," said Gregor slowly and carefully, not moving an inch for fear of losing one word of the conversation. "I can't think of any other explanation, madam," said the chief clerk, "I hope it's nothing serious. Although on the other hand I must say that we men of business—fortunately or unfortunately—very often simply have to ignore any slight indisposition, since business must be attended to." "Well, can the chief clerk come in now?" asked Gregor's father impatiently, again knocking on the door. "No," said Gregor. In the left-hand room a painful silence followed this refusal, in the right-hand room his sister began to sob.

Why didn't his sister join the others? She was probably newly out of bed and hadn't even begun to put on her clothes yet. Well, why was she crying? Because he wouldn't get up and let the chief clerk in, because he was in danger of losing his job, and because the chief would begin dunning his parents again for the old debts? Surely these were things one didn't need to worry about for the present. Gregor was still at home and not in the least thinking of deserting the family. At the moment, true, he was lying on the carpet and no one who knew the condition he was in could seriously expect him to admit the chief clerk. But for such a small discourtesy, which could plausibly be explained away somehow later on, Gregor could hardly be dismissed on the spot. And it seemed to Gregor that it would be much more sensible to leave him in peace for the present than to trouble him with tears and entreaties. Still, of course, their uncertainty bewildered them all and excused their behavior.

"Mr. Samsa," the chief clerk called now in a louder voice, "what's the matter with you? Here you are, barricading yourself in your room, giving only 'yes' and 'no' for answers, causing your parents a lot of unnecessary trouble and neglecting—I mention this only in passing—neglecting your business duties in an incredible fashion. I am speaking here in the name of your parents and of your chief, and I beg you quite seriously to give me an immediate and precise explanation. You amaze me, you amaze me. I thought you were a quiet, dependable person, and now all at once you seem bent on making a disgraceful exhibition of yourself. The chief did hint to me early this morning a possible explanation for your disappearance—with reference to the cash payments that were entrusted to you recently—but I almost pledged my solemn word of honor that this could not be so. But now that I see how incredibly obstinate you are, I no longer have the slightest desire to take your part at all. And your position in the firm is not so unassailable. I came with the intention of telling you all this in private, but since you are wasting my time so needlessly I don't see why your parents shouldn't hear it too. For some time past your work has been most unsatisfactory; this is not the season of the year for a business boom, of course, we admit that, but a season of the year for doing no business at all, that does not exist, Mr. Samsa, must not exist."

20   "But, sir," cried Gregor, beside himself and in his agitation forgetting everything else, "I'm just going to open the door this very minute. A slight illness, an attack of giddiness, has kept me from getting up. I'm still lying in bed. But I feel all right again. I'm getting out of bed now. Just give me a moment or two longer! I'm not quite so well as I thought. But I'm all right, really. How a thing like that can suddenly strike one down! Only last night I was quite well, my parents can tell you, or rather I did have a slight presentiment. I must have showed some sign of it. Why didn't I report it at the office! But one always thinks that an indisposition can be got over without staying in the house. Oh sir, do spare my parents! All that you're reproaching me with now has no foundation; no one has ever said a word to me about it. Perhaps you haven't looked at the last orders I sent in. Anyhow, I can still catch the eight o'clock train, I'm much the better for my few hours' rest. Don't let me detain you here, sir; I'll be attending to business very soon, and do be good enough to tell the chief so and to make my excuses to him!"

And while all this was tumbling out pell-mell and Gregor hardly knew what he was saying, he had reached the chest quite easily, perhaps because of the practice he had had in bed, and was now trying to lever himself upright by means of it. He meant actually to open the door, actually to show himself and speak to the chief clerk; he was eager to find out what the others, after all their insistence, would say at the sight of him. If they were horrified then the responsibility was no longer his and he could stay quiet. But if they took it calmly, then he had no reason either to be upset, and could really get to the station for the eight o'clock train if he hurried. At first he slipped down a few times from the polished surface of the chest, but at length with a last heave he stood upright; he paid no more attention to the pains in the lower part of his body, however they smarted. Then he let himself fall against the back of a near-by chair, and clung with his little legs to the edges of it. That brought him into control of himself again and he stopped speaking, for now he could listen to what the chief clerk was saying.

"Did you understand a word of it?" the chief clerk was asking; "surely he can't be trying to make fools of us?" "Oh dear," cried his mother, in tears, "perhaps he's terribly ill and we're tormenting him. Grete! Grete!" she called out then. "Yes Mother?" called his sister from the other side. They were calling to each other across Gregor's room. "You must go this minute for the doctor. Gregor is ill. Go for the doctor, quick. Did you hear how he was speaking?" "That was no human voice," said the chief clerk in a voice noticeably low beside the shrillness of the mother's. "Anna! Anna!" his father was calling through the hall to the kitchen, clapping his hands, "get a locksmith at once!" And the two girls were already running through the hall with a swish of skirts—how could his sister have got dressed so quickly?—and were tearing the front door open. There was no sound of its closing again; they had evidently left it open, as one does in houses where some great misfortune has happened.

But Gregor was now much calmer. The words he uttered were no longer understandable, apparently, although they seemed clear enough to him, even clearer than before, perhaps because his ear had grown accustomed to the sound of them. Yet at any rate people now believed that something was wrong with him, and were ready to help him. The positive certainty with which these first measures had been taken comforted him. He felt himself drawn once more into the human circle and hoped for great and remarkable results from both the doctor and the locksmith, without really distinguishing precisely between them. To make his voice as clear as possible for the decisive conversation that was now imminent he coughed a little, as quietly as he could, of course, since this noise too might not sound like a human cough for all he was able to judge. In the next room meanwhile there was complete silence. Perhaps his parents were sitting at the table with the chief clerk, whispering, perhaps they were all leaning against the door and listening.

Slowly Gregor pushed the chair towards the door, then let go of it, caught hold of the door for support—the soles at the end of his little legs were somewhat sticky—and rested against it for a moment after his efforts. Then he set himself to turning the key in the lock with his mouth. It seemed, unhappily, that he hadn't really any teeth—what could he grip the key with?—but on the other hand his jaws were certainly very strong; with their help he did manage to set the key in motion, heedless of the fact that he was undoubtedly damaging them somewhere, since a brown fluid issued from his mouth, flowed over the key and dripped on the floor. "Just listen to that," said the chief clerk next door; "he's turning the key." That was a great encouragement to Gregor; but they should all have shouted encouragement to him, his father and mother too: "Go on, Gregor," they should have called out, "keep going, hold on to that key!" And in the belief that they were all following his efforts intently, he clenched his jaws recklessly on the key with all the force at his command. As the turning of the key progressed he circled round the lock, holding on now only with his mouth, pushing on the key, as required, or pulling it down again with all the weight of his body. The louder click of the finally yielding lock literally quickened Gregor. With a deep breath of relief he said to himself: "So I didn't need the locksmith," and laid his head on the handle to open the door wide.

25   Since he had to pull the door towards him, he was still invisible when it was really wide open. He had to edge himself slowly round the near half of the double door, and to do it very carefully if he was not to fall plump upon his back just on the threshold. He was still carrying out this difficult manoeuvre, with no time to observe anything else, when he heard the chief clerk utter a loud "Oh!"—it sounded like a gust of wind—and now he could see the man, standing as he was nearest to the door, clapping one hand before his open mouth and slowly backing away as if driven by some invisible steady pressure. His mother—in spite of the chief clerk's being there her hair was still undone and sticking up in all directions—first clasped her hands and looked at his father, then took two steps towards Gregor and fell on the floor among her outspread skirts, her face quite hidden on her breast. His father knotted his fist with a fierce expression on his face as if he meant to knock Gregor back into his room, then looked uncertainly round the living room, covered his eyes with his hands and wept till his great chest heaved.

Gregor did not go now into the living room, but leaned against the inside of the firmly shut wing of the door, so that only half his body was visible and his head above it bending sideways to look at the others. The light had meanwhile strengthened; on the other side of the street one could see clearly a section of the endlessly long, dark gray building opposite—it was a hospital—abruptly punctuated by its row of regular windows; the rain was still falling, but only in large singly discernible and literally singly splashing drops. The breakfast dishes were set out on the table lavishly, for breakfast was the most important meal of the day to Gregor's father, who lingered it out for hours over various newspapers. Right opposite Gregor on the wall hung a photograph of himself on military service, as a lieutenant, hand on sword, a carefree smile on his face, inviting one to respect his uniform and military bearing. The door leading to the hall was open, and one could see that the front door stood open too, showing the landing beyond and the beginning of the stairs going down.

"Well," said Gregor, knowing perfectly that he was the only one who had retained any composure, "I'll put my clothes on at once, pack up my samples and start off. Will you only let me go? You see, sir, I'm not obstinate, and I'm willing to work; traveling is a hard life, but I couldn't live without it. Where are you going, sir? To the office? Yes? Will you give a true account of all this? One can be temporarily incapacitated, but that's just the moment for remembering former services and bearing in mind that later on, when the incapacity has been got over, one will certainly work with all the more industry and concentration. I'm loyally bound to serve the chief, you know that very well. Besides, I have to provide for my parents and my sister. I'm in great difficulties, but I'll get out of them again. Don't make things any worse for me than they are. Stand up for me in the firm. Travelers are not popular there, I know. People think they earn sacks of money and just have a good time. A prejudice there's no particular reason for revising. But you, sir, have a more comprehensive view of affairs than the rest of the staff, yes, let me tell you in confidence, a more comprehensive view than the chief himself, who, being the owner, lets his judgment easily be swayed against one of his employees. And you know very well that the traveler, who is never seen in the office almost the whole year round, can so easily fall a victim to gossip and ill luck and unfounded complaints, which he mostly knows nothing about, except when he comes back exhausted from his rounds, and only then suffers in person from their evil consequences, which he can no longer trace back to the original causes. Sir, sir, don't go away without a word to me to show that you think me in the right at least to some extent!"

But at Gregor's very first words the chief clerk had already backed away and only stared at him with parted lips over one twitching shoulder. And while Gregor was speaking he did not stand still one moment but stole away towards the door, without taking his eyes off Gregor, yet only an inch at a time, as if obeying some secret injunction to leave the room. He was already at the hall, and the suddenness with which he took his last step out of the living room would have made one believe he had burned the sole of his foot. Once in the hall he stretched his right arm before him towards the staircase, as if some supernatural power were waiting there to deliver him.

Gregor perceived that the chief clerk must on no account be allowed to go away in this frame of mind if his position in the firm were not to be endangered to the utmost. His parents did not understand this so well; they had convinced themselves in the course of years that Gregor was settled for life in this firm, and besides they were so occupied with their immediate troubles that all foresight had forsaken them. Yet Gregor had this foresight. The chief clerk must be detained, soothed, persuaded and finally won over; the whole future of Gregor and his family depended on it! If only his sister had been there! She was intelligent; she had begun to cry while Gregor was still lying quietly on his back. And no doubt the chief clerk, so partial to ladies, would have been guided by her; she would have shut the door of the flat and in the hall talked him out of his horror. But she was not there, and Gregor would have to handle the situation himself. And without remembering that he was still unaware what powers of movement he possessed, without even remembering that his words in all possibility, indeed in all likelihood, would again be unintelligible, he let go the

wing of the door, pushed himself through the opening, started to walk towards the chief clerk, who was already ridiculously clinging with both
hands to the railing on the landing; but immediately, as he was feeling for
a support, he fell down with a little cry upon all his numerous legs. Hardly
was he down when he experienced for the first time this morning a sense
of physical comfort; his legs had firm ground under them; they were completely obedient, as he noted with joy; they even strove to carry him forward in whatever direction he chose; and he was inclined to believe that a
final relief from all his sufferings was at hand. But in the same moment as
he found himself on the floor, rocking with suppressed eagerness to move,
not far from his mother, indeed just in front of her, she, who had seemed
so completely crushed, sprang all at once to her feet, her arms and fingers
outspread, cried: "Help, for God's sake, help!" bent her head down as if to
see Gregor better, yet on the contrary kept backing senselessly away; had
quite forgotten that the laden table stood behind her; sat upon it hastily,
as if in absence of mind, when she bumped into it; and seemed altogether
unaware that the big coffee pot beside her was upset and pouring coffee in
a flood over the carpet.

30   "Mother, Mother," said Gregor in a low voice, and looked up at her.
The chief clerk, for the moment, had quite slipped from his mind; instead,
he could not resist snapping his jaws together at the sight of the streaming
coffee. That made his mother scream again, she fled from the table and fell
into the arms of his father, who hastened to catch her. But Gregor had now
no time to spare for his parents; the chief clerk was already on the stairs;
with his chin on the banisters he was taking one last backward look. Gregor made a spring, to be as sure as possible of overtaking him; the chief
clerk must have divined his intention, for he leaped down several steps
and vanished; he was still yelling "Ugh!" and it echoed through the whole
staircase.

Unfortunately, the flight of the chief clerk seemed completely to upset
Gregor's father, who had remained relatively calm until now, for instead
of running after the man himself, or at least not hindering Gregor in his
pursuit, he seized in his right hand the walking stick which the chief clerk
had left behind on a chair, together with a hat and greatcoat, snatched in
his left hand a large newspaper from the table and began stamping his feet
and flourishing the stick and the newspaper to drive Gregor back into his
room. No entreaty of Gregor's availed, indeed no entreaty was even understood, however humbly he bent his head his father only stamped on the
floor the more loudly. Behind his father his mother had torn open a window, despite the cold weather, and was leaning far out of it with her face in
her hands. A strong draught set in from the street to the staircase, the window curtains blew in, the newspapers on the table fluttered, stray pages
whisked over the floor. Pitilessly Gregor's father drove him back, hissing
and crying "Shoo!" like a savage. But Gregor was quite unpracticed in
walking backwards, it really was a slow business. If he only had a chance
to turn around he could get back to his room at once, but he was afraid of

exasperating his father by the slowness of such a rotation and at any moment the stick in his father's hand might hit him a fatal blow on the back
or on the head. In the end, however, nothing else was left for him to do
since to his horror he observed that in moving backwards he could not
even control the direction he took; and so, keeping an anxious eye on his
father all the time over his shoulder, he began to turn round as quickly as
he could, which was in reality very slowly. Perhaps his father noted his
good intentions, for he did not interfere except every now and then to
help him in the manoeuvre from a distance with the point of the stick. If
only he would have stopped making that unbearable hissing noise! It made
Gregor quite lose his head. He had turned almost completely round when
the hissing noise so distracted him that he even turned a little the wrong
way again. But when at last his head was fortunately right in front of the
doorway, it appeared that his body was too broad simply to get through
the opening. His father, of course, in his present mood was far from thinking of such a thing as opening the other half of the door, to let Gregor
have enough space. He had merely the fixed idea of driving Gregor back
into his room as quickly as possible. He would never have suffered Gregor
to make the circumstantial preparations for standing up on end and perhaps slipping his way through the door. Maybe he was now making more
noise than ever to urge Gregor forward, as if no obstacle impeded him; to
Gregor, anyhow, the noise in his rear sounded no longer like the voice of
one single father; this was really no joke, and Gregor thrust himself—come
what might—into the doorway. One side of his body rose up, he was tilted
at an angle in the doorway, his flank was quite bruised, horrid blotches
stained the white door, soon he was stuck fast and, left to himself, could
not have moved at all, his legs on one side fluttered trembling to the air,
those on the other were crushed painfully to the floor—when from behind
his father gave him a strong push which was literally a deliverance and he
flew far into the room, bleeding freely. The door was slammed behind him
with the stick, and then at last there was silence.

II

Not until it was twilight did Gregor awake out of a deep sleep, more like a
swoon than a sleep. He would certainly have waked up of his own accord
not much later, for he felt himself sufficiently rested and well-slept, but it
seemed to him as if a fleeting step and a cautious shutting of the door
leading into the hall had aroused him. The electric lights in the street cast
a pale sheen here and there on the ceiling and the upper surfaces of the
furniture, but down below, where he lay, it was dark. Slowly, awkwardly
trying out his feelers, which he now first learned to appreciate, he pushed
his way to the door to see what had been happening there. His left side felt
like one single long, unpleasantly tense scar, and he had actually to limp
on his two rows of legs. One little leg, moreover, had been severely damaged in the course of that morning's events—it was almost a miracle that
only one had been damaged—and trailed uselessly behind him.

He had reached the door before he discovered what had really drawn him to it: the smell of food. For there stood a basin filled with fresh milk in which floated little sops of white bread. He could almost have laughed with joy, since he was now still hungrier than in the morning, and he dipped his head almost over the eyes straight into the milk. But soon in disappointment he withdrew it again; not only did he find it difficult to feed because of his tender left side—and he could only feed with the palpitating collaboration of his whole body—he did not like the milk either, although milk had been his favorite drink and that was certainly why his sister had set it there for him, indeed it was almost with repulsion that he turned away from the basin and crawled back to the middle of the room.

He could see through the crack of the door that the gas was turned on in the living room, but while usually at this time his father made a habit of reading the afternoon newspaper in a loud voice to his mother and occasionally to his sister as well, not a sound was now to be heard. Well, perhaps his father had recently given up this habit of reading aloud, which his sister had mentioned so often in conversation and in her letters. But there was the same silence all around, although the flat was certainly not empty of occupants. "What a quiet life our family has been leading," said Gregor to himself, and as he sat there motionless staring into the darkness he felt great pride in the fact that he had been able to provide such a life for his parents and sister in such a fine flat. But what if all the quiet, the comfort, the contentment were now to end in horror? To keep himself from being lost in such thoughts Gregor took refuge in movement and crawled up and down the room.

35   Once during the long evening one of the side doors was opened a little and quickly shut again, later the other side door too; someone had apparently wanted to come in and then thought better of it. Gregor now stationed himself immediately before the living room door, determined to persuade any hesitating visitor to come in or at least to discover who it might be; but the door was not opened again and he waited in vain. In the early morning, when the doors were locked, they had all wanted to come in, now that he had opened one door and the other had apparently been opened during the day, no one came in and even the keys were on the other side of the doors.

It was late at night before the gas went out in the living room, and Gregor could easily tell that his parents and his sister had all stayed awake until then, for he could clearly hear the three of them stealing away on tiptoe. No one was likely to visit him, not until the morning, that was certain; so he had plenty of time to meditate at his leisure on how he was to arrange his life afresh. But the lofty, empty room in which he had to lie flat on the floor filled him with an apprehension he could not account for, since it had been his very own room for the past five years—and with a half-unconscious action, not without a slight feeling of shame, he scuttled under the sofa, where he felt comfortable at once, although his back was a little cramped and he could not lift his head up, and his only regret was that his body was too broad to get the whole of it under the sofa.

He stayed there all night, spending the time partly in a light slumber, from which his hunger kept waking him up with a start, and partly in worrying and sketching vague hopes, which all led to the same conclusion, that he must lie low for the present and, by exercising patience and the utmost consideration, help the family to bear the inconvenience he was bound to cause them in his present condition.

Very early in the morning, it was still almost night, Gregor had the chance to test the strength of his new resolutions, for his sister, nearly fully dressed, opened the door from the hall and peered in. She did not see him at once, yet when she caught sight of him under the sofa—well, he had to be somewhere, he couldn't have flown away, could he?—she was so startled that without being able to help it she slammed the door shut again. But as if regretting her behavior she opened the door again immediately and came in on tiptoe, as if she were visiting an invalid or even a stranger. Gregor had pushed his head forward to the very edge of the sofa and watched her. Would she notice that he had left the milk standing, and not for lack of hunger, and would she bring in some other kind of food more to his taste? If she did not do it of her own accord, he would rather starve than draw her attention to the fact, although he felt a wild impulse to dart out from under the sofa, throw himself at her feet and beg her for something to eat. But his sister at once noticed, with surprise, that the basin was still full, except for a little milk that had been spilt all around it, she lifted it immediately, not with her bare hands, true, but with a cloth and carried it away. Gregor was wildly curious to know what she would bring instead, and made various speculations about it. Yet what she actually did next, in the goodness of her heart, he could never have guessed at. To find out what he liked she brought him a whole selection of food, all set out on an old newspaper. There were old, half-decayed vegetables, bones from last night's supper covered with a white sauce that had thickened; some raisins and almonds; a piece of cheese that Gregor would have called uneatable two days ago; a dry roll of bread, a buttered roll, and a roll both buttered and salted. Besides all that, she set down again the same basin, into which she had poured some water, and which was apparently to be reserved for his exclusive use. And with fine tact, knowing that Gregor would not eat in her presence, she withdrew quickly and even turned the key, to let him understand that he could take his ease as much as he liked. Gregor's legs all whizzed towards the food. His wounds must have healed completely, moreover, for he felt no disability, which amazed him and made him reflect how more than a month ago he had cut one finger a little with a knife and had still suffered pain from the wound only the day before yesterday. Am I less sensitive now? he thought, and sucked greedily at the cheese, which above all the other edibles attracted him at once and strongly. One after another and with tears of satisfaction in his eyes he quickly devoured the cheese, the vegetables and the sauce; the fresh food, on the other hand, had no charms for him, he could not even stand the smell of it and actually dragged away to some little distance the things he could eat. He had long finished his meal and was only lying lazily on the same spot when his sister turned the key slowly as a sign for him to retreat. That roused him at once, although he was nearly asleep, and he hurried under the sofa again. But it took considerable self-control for him to stay under the sofa, even for the short time his sister was in the room, since the large meal had swollen his body somewhat and he was so cramped he could hardly breathe. Slight attacks of breathlessness afflicted him and his eyes were starting a little out of his head as he watched his unsuspecting sister sweeping together with a broom not only the remains of what he had eaten but even the things he had not touched, as if these were now of no use to anyone, and hastily shoveling it all into a bucket, which she covered with a wooden lid and carried away. Hardly had she turned her back when Gregor came from under the sofa and stretched and puffed himself out.

In this manner Gregor was fed, once in the early morning while his parents and the servant girl were still asleep, and a second time after they had all had their midday dinner, for then his parents took a short nap and the servant girl could be sent out on some errand or other by his sister. Not that they would have wanted him to starve, of course, but perhaps they could not have borne to know more about his feeding than from hearsay, perhaps too his sister wanted to spare them such little anxieties wherever possible, since they had quite enough to bear as it was.

40　　Under what pretext the doctor and the locksmith had been got rid of on that first morning Gregor could not discover, for since what he said was not understood by the others it never struck any of them, not even his sister, that he could understand what they said, and so whenever his sister came into his room he had to content himself with hearing her utter only a sigh now and then and an occasional appeal to the saints. Later on, when she had got a little used to the situation—of course she could never get completely used to it—she sometimes threw out a remark which was kindly meant or could be so interpreted. "Well, he liked his dinner today," she would say when Gregor had made a good clearance of his food; and when he had not eaten, which gradually happened more and more often, she would say almost sadly: "Everything's been left standing again."

But although Gregor could get no news directly, he overheard a lot from the neighboring rooms, and as soon as voices were audible, he would run to the door of the room concerned and press his whole body against it. In the first few days especially there was no conversation that did not refer to him somehow, even if only indirectly. For two whole days there were family consultations at every mealtime about what should be done; but also between meals the same subject was discussed, for there were always at least two members of the family at home, since no one wanted to be alone in the flat and to leave it quite empty was unthinkable. And on the very first of these days the household cook—it was not quite clear what and how much she knew of the situation—went down on her knees to his mother and begged leave to go, and when she departed, a quarter of an hour later, gave thanks for her dismissal with tears in her eyes as if for the greatest benefit that could have been conferred on her, and without any prompting swore a solemn oath that she would never say a single word to anyone about what had happened.

Now Gregor's sister had to cook too, helping her mother; true, the cooking did not amount to much, for they ate scarcely anything. Gregor was always hearing one of the family vainly urging another to eat and getting no answer but: "Thanks, I've had all I want," or something similar. Perhaps they drank nothing either. Time and again his sister kept asking his father if he wouldn't like some beer and offered kindly to go and fetch it herself, and when he made no answer suggested that she could ask the concierge to fetch it, so that he need feel no sense of obligation, but then a round "No" came from his father and no more was said about it.

In the course of that very first day Gregor's father explained the family's financial position and prospects to both his mother and his sister. Now and then he rose from the table to get some voucher or memorandum out of the small safe he had rescued from the collapse of his business five years earlier. One could hear him opening the complicated lock and rustling papers out and shutting it again. This statement made by his father was the first cheerful information Gregor had heard since his imprisonment. He had been of the opinion that nothing at all was left over from his father's business, at least his father had never said anything to the contrary, and of course he had not asked him directly. At that time Gregor's sole desire was to do his utmost to help the family to forget as soon as possible the catastrophe which had overwhelmed the business and thrown them all into a state of complete despair. And so he had set to work with unusual ardor and almost overnight had become a commercial traveler instead of a little clerk, with of course much greater chances of earning money, and his success was immediately translated into good round coin which he could lay on the table for his amazed and happy family. These had been fine times, and they had never recurred, at least not with the same sense of glory, although later on Gregor had earned so much money that he was able to meet the expenses of the whole household and did so. They had simply got used to it, both the family and Gregor; the money was gratefully accepted and gladly given, but there was no special uprush of warm feeling. With his sister alone had he remained intimate, and it was a secret plan of his that she, who loved music, unlike himself, and could play movingly on the violin, should be sent next year to study at the Conservatorium, despite the great expense that would entail, which must be made up in some other way. During his brief visits home the Conservatorium was often mentioned in the talks he had with his sister, but always merely as a beautiful dream which could never come true, and his parents discouraged even these innocent references to it; yet Gregor had made up his mind firmly about it and meant to announce the fact with due solemnity on Christmas Day.

Such were the thoughts, completely futile in his present condition, that went through his head as he stood clinging upright to the door and listening. Sometimes out of sheer weariness he had to give up listening and let his head fall negligently against the door, but he always had to pull himself together again at once, for even the slight sound his head made was audible next door and brought all conversation to a stop. "What can he be doing now?" his father would say after a while, obviously turning towards the door, and only then would the interrupted conversation gradually be set going again.

45   Gregor was now informed as amply as he could wish—for his father tended to repeat himself in his explanations, partly because it was a long time since he had handled such matters and partly because his mother could not always grasp things at once—that a certain amount of investments, a very small amount it was true, had survived the wreck of their fortunes and had even increased a little because the dividends had not been touched meanwhile. And besides that, the money Gregor brought home every month—he had kept only a few dollars for himself—had never been quite used up and now amounted to a small capital sum. Behind the door Gregor nodded his head eagerly, rejoiced at this evidence of unexpected thrift and foresight. True, he could really have paid off some more of his father's debts to the chief with his extra money, and so brought much nearer the day on which he could quit his job, but doubtless it was better the way his father had arranged it.

Yet this capital was by no means sufficient to let the family live on the interest of it; for one year, perhaps, or at the most two, they could live on the principal, that was all. It was simply a sum that ought not to be touched and should be kept for a rainy day; money for living expenses would have to be earned. Now his father was still hale enough but an old man, and he had done no work for the past five years and could not be expected to do much; during these five years, the first years of leisure in his laborious though unsuccessful life, he had grown rather fat and become sluggish. And Gregor's old mother, how was she to earn a living with her asthma, which troubled her even when she walked through the flat and kept her lying on a sofa every other day panting for breath beside an open window? And was his sister to earn her bread, she who was still a child of seventeen and whose life hitherto had been so pleasant, consisting as it did in dressing herself nicely, sleeping long, helping in the housekeeping, going out to a few modest entertainments and above all playing the violin? At first whenever the need for earning money was mentioned Gregor let go his hold on the door and threw himself down on the cool leather sofa beside it, he felt so hot with shame and grief.

Often he just lay there the long nights through without sleeping at all, scrabbling for hours on the leather. Or he nerved himself to the great effort of pushing an armchair to the window, then crawled up over the window sill and, braced against the chair, leaned against the window panes, obviously in some recollection of the sense of freedom that looking out of a window always used to give him. For in reality day by day things that were even a little way off were growing dimmer to his sight; the hospital across the street, which he used to execrate for being all too often before his eyes, was now quite beyond his range of vision, and if he had not known that he lived in Charlotte Street, a quiet street but still a city street, he might have believed that his window gave on a desert waste where gray sky and gray land blended indistinguishably into each other. His quick-witted sister only needed to observe twice that the armchair stood by the window; after that whenever she had tidied the room she always pushed the chair back to the same place at the window and even left the inner casements open.

If he could have spoken to her and thanked her for all she had to do for him, he could have borne her ministrations better; as it was, they oppressed him. She certainly tried to make as light as possible of whatever was disagreeable in her task, and as time went on she succeeded, of course, more and more, but time brought more enlightenment to Gregor too. The very way she came in distressed him. Hardly was she in the room when she rushed to the window, without even taking time to shut the door, careful as she was usually to shield the sight of Gregor's room from the others, and as if she were almost suffocating tore the casements open with hasty fingers, standing then in the open draught for a while even in the bitterest cold and drawing deep breaths. This noisy scurry of hers upset Gregor twice a day; he would crouch trembling under the sofa all the time, knowing quite well that she would certainly have spared him such a disturbance had she found it at all possible to stay in his presence without opening a window.

On one occasion, about a month after Gregor's metamorphosis, when there was surely no reason for her to be still startled at his appearance, she came a little earlier than usual and found him gazing out of the window, quite motionless, and thus well placed to look like a bogey. Gregor would not have been surprised had she not come in at all, for she could not immediately open the window while he was there, but not only did she retreat, she jumped back as if in alarm and banged the door shut; a stranger might well have thought that he had been lying in wait for her there meaning to bite her. Of course he hid himself under the sofa at once, but he had to wait until midday before she came again, and she seemed more ill at ease than usual. This made him realize how repulsive the sight of him still was to her, and that it was bound to go on being repulsive, and what an effort it must cost her not to run away even from the sight of the small portion of his body that stuck out from under the sofa. In order to spare her that, therefore, one day he carried a sheet on his back to the sofa—it cost him four hours' labor—and arranged it there in such a way as to hide him completely, so that even if she were to bend down she could not see him. Had she considered the sheet unnecessary, she would certainly have stripped it off the sofa again, for it was clear enough that this curtaining and confining of himself was not likely to conduce Gregor's comfort, but she left it where it was, and Gregor even fancied that he caught a thankful glance from her eye when he lifted the sheet carefully a very little with his head to see how she was taking the new arrangement.

50   For the first fortnight his parents could not bring themselves to the point of entering his room, and he often heard them expressing their appreciation of his sister's activities, whereas formerly they had frequently scolded her for being as they thought a somewhat useless daughter. But now, both of them often waited outside the door, his father and his mother, while his sister tidied his room, and as soon as she came out she had to tell them exactly how things were in the room, what Gregor had eaten, how he had conducted himself this time and whether there was not perhaps some slight improvement in his condition. His mother, moreover, began relatively soon to want to visit him, but his father and sister dissuaded her at first with arguments which Gregor listened to very attentively and altogether approved. Later, however, she had to be held back by main force, and when she cried out: "Do let me in to Gregor, he is my unfortunate son! Can't you understand that I must go to him?" Gregor thought it might be well to have her come in, not every day, of course, but perhaps once a week; she understood things, after all, much better than his sister, who was only a child despite the efforts she was making and had perhaps taken on so difficult a task merely out of childish thoughtlessness.

Gregor's desire to see his mother was soon fulfilled. During the daytime he did not want to show himself at the window, out of consideration for his parents, but he could not crawl very far around the few square yards of floor space he had, nor could he bear lying quietly at rest all during the night, while he was fast losing any interest he had ever taken in food, so that for mere recreation he had formed the habit of crawling crisscross over the walls and ceiling. He especially enjoyed hanging suspended from the ceiling; it was much better than lying on the floor; one could breathe more freely; one's body swung and rocked lightly; and in the almost blissful absorption induced by this suspension it could happen to his own surprise that he let go and fell plump on the floor. Yet he now had his body much better under control than formerly, and even such a big fall did him no harm. His sister at once remarked the new distraction Gregor had found for himself—he left traces behind him of the sticky stuff on his soles wherever he crawled—and she got the idea in her head of giving him as wide a field as possible to crawl in and of removing the pieces of furniture that hindered him, above all the chest of drawers and the writing desk. But that was more than she could manage all by herself; she did not dare ask her father to help her; and as for the servant girl, a young creature of sixteen who had had the courage to stay on after the cook's departure, she could not be asked to help, for she had begged as an especial favor that she might keep the kitchen door locked and open it only on a definite summons; so there was nothing left but to apply to her mother at an hour when her father was out. And the old lady did come, with exclamations of joyful eagerness, which, however, died away at the door of Gregor's room. Gregor's sister, of course, went in first, to see that everything was in order before letting his mother enter. In great haste Gregor pulled the sheet lower and rucked it more in folds so that it really looked as if it had been thrown accidentally over the sofa. And this time he did not peer out from under it; he renounced the pleasure of seeing his mother on this occasion and was only glad that she had come at all. "Come in, he's out of sight," said his sister, obviously leading her mother in by the hand. Gregor could now hear the two women struggling to shift the heavy old chest from its place, and his sister claiming the greater part of the labor for herself, without listening to the admonitions of her mother who feared she might overstrain herself. It took a long time. After at least a quarter of an hour's tugging his mother objected that the chest had better be left where it was, for in the first place it was too heavy and could never be got out before his father came home, and standing in the middle of the room like that it would only hamper Gregor's movements, while in the second place it was not at all certain that removing the furniture would be doing a service to Gregor. She was inclined to think to the contrary; the sight of the naked walls made her own heart heavy, and why shouldn't Gregor have the same feeling, considering that he had been used to his furniture for so long and might feel forlorn without it. "And doesn't it look," she concluded in a low voice—in fact she had been almost whispering all the time as if to avoid letting Gregor, whose exact whereabouts she did not know, hear even the tones of her voice, for she was convinced that he could not understand her words—"doesn't it look as if we were showing him, by taking away his furniture, that we have given up hope of his ever getting better and are just leaving him coldly to himself? I think it would be best to keep his room exactly as it has always been, so that when he comes back to us he will find everything unchanged and be able all the more easily to forget what has happened in between."

On hearing these words from his mother Gregor realized that the lack of all direct human speech for the past two months together with the monotony of family life must have confused his mind, otherwise he could not account for the fact that he had quite earnestly looked forward to having his room emptied of furnishing. Did he really want his warm room, so comfortably fitted with old family furniture, to be turned into a naked den in which he would certainly be able to crawl unhampered in all directions but at the price of shedding simultaneously all recollection of his human background? He had indeed been so near the brink of forgetfulness that only the voice of his mother, which he had not heard for so long, had drawn him back from it. Nothing should be taken out of his room; everything must stay as it was; he could not dispense with the good influence of the furniture on his state of mind; and even if the furniture did hamper him in his senseless crawling round and round, that was no drawback but a great advantage.

Unfortunately his sister was of the contrary opinion; she had grown accustomed, and not without reason, to consider herself an expert in Gregor's affairs as against her parents, and so her mother's advice was now enough to make her determined on the removal not only of the chest and the writing desk, which had been her first intention, but of all the furniture except the

indispensable sofa. This determination was not, of course, merely the outcome of childish recalcitrance and of the self-confidence she had recently
developed so unexpectedly and at such cost; she had in fact perceived that
Gregor needed a lot of space to crawl about in, while on the other hand he
never used the furniture at all, so far as could be seen. Another factor
might have been also the enthusiastic temperament of an adolescent girl,
which seeks to indulge itself on every opportunity and which now
tempted Grete to exaggerate the horror of her brother's circumstances in
order that she might do all the more for him. In a room where Gregor
lorded it all alone over empty walls no one save herself was likely ever to
set foot.

And so she was not to be moved from her resolve by her mother who
seemed moreover to be ill at ease in Gregor's room and therefore unsure of
herself, was soon reduced to silence and helped her daughter as best she
could to push the chest outside. Now, Gregor could do without the chest, if
need be, but the writing desk he must retain. As soon as the two women
had got the chest out of his room, groaning as they pushed it, Gregor stuck
his head out from under the sofa to see how he might intervene as kindly
and cautiously as possible. But as bad luck would have it, his mother was
the first to return, leaving Grete clasping the chest in the room next door
where she was trying to shift it all by herself, without of course moving
it from the spot. His mother however was not accustomed to the sight of
him, it might sicken her and so in alarm Gregor backed quickly to the
other end of the sofa, yet could not prevent the sheet from swaying a little
in front. That was enough to put her on the alert. She paused, stood still
for a moment and then went back to Grete.

55   Although Gregor kept reassuring himself that nothing out of the way
was happening, but only a few bits of furniture were being changed
round, he soon had to admit that all this trotting to and fro of the two
women, their little ejaculations and the scraping of furniture along the
floor affected him like a vast disturbance coming from all sides at once,
and however much he tucked in his head and legs and cowered to the very
floor he was bound to confess that he would not be able to stand it for
long. They were clearing his room out; taking away everything he loved;
the chest in which he kept his fret saw and other tools was already dragged
off; they were now loosening the writing desk which had almost sunk into
the floor, the desk at which he had done all his homework when he was at
the commercial academy, at the grammar school before that, and, yes,
even at the primary school—he had no more time to waste in weighing the
good intentions of the two women, whose existence he had by now almost
forgotten, for they were so exhausted that they were laboring in silence
and nothing could be heard but the heavy scuffling of their feet.

And so he rushed out—the women were just leaning against the writing desk in the next room to give themselves a breather—and four times
changed his direction, since he really did not know what to rescue first,
then on the wall opposite, which was already otherwise cleared, he was

struck by the picture of the lady muffled in so much fur and quickly crawled up to it and pressed himself to the glass, which was a good surface to hold on to and comforted his hot belly. This picture at least,which was entirely hidden beneath him, was going to be removed by nobody. He turned his head towards the door of the living room so as to observe the women when they came back.

They had not allowed themselves much of a rest and were already coming; Grete had twined her arm round her mother and was almost supporting her. "Well, what shall we take now?" said Grete, looking round. Her eyes met Gregor's from the wall. She kept her composure, presumably because of her mother, bent her head down to her mother, to keep her from looking up, and said, although in a fluttering, unpremeditated voice: "Come, hadn't we better go back to the living room for a moment?" Her intentions were clear enough to Gregor, she wanted to bestow her mother in safety and then chase him down from the wall. Well, just let her try it! He clung to his picture and would not give it up. He would rather fly in Grete's face.

But Grete's words had succeeded in disquieting her mother, who took a step to one side, caught sight of the huge brown mass on the flowered wallpaper, and before she was really conscious that what she saw was Gregor screamed in a loud, hoarse voice: "Oh God, oh God!" fell with outspread arms over the sofa as if giving up and did not move. "Gregor!" cried his sister, shaking her fist and glaring at him. This was the first time she had directly addressed him since his metamorphosis. She ran into the next room for some aromatic essence with which to rouse her mother from her fainting fit. Gregor wanted to help too—there was still time to rescue the picture—but he was stuck fast to the glass and had to tear himself loose; he then ran after his sister into the next room as if he could advise her, as he used to do; but then had to stand helplessly behind her; she meanwhile searched among various small bottles and when she turned round started in alarm at the sight of him; one bottle fell on the floor and broke; a splinter of glass cut Gregor's face and some kind of corrosive medicine splashed him; without pausing a moment longer Grete gathered up all the bottles she could carry and ran to her mother with them; she banged the door shut with her foot. Gregor was now cut off from his mother, who was perhaps nearly dying because of him; he dared not open the door for fear of frightening away his sister, who had to stay with her mother; there was nothing he could do but wait; and harassed by self-reproach and worry he began now to crawl to and fro, over everything, walls, furniture and ceiling, and finally in his despair, when the whole room seemed to be reeling round him, fell down on to the middle of the big table.

A little while elapsed, Gregor was still lying there feebly and all around was quiet, perhaps that was a good omen. Then the doorbell rang. The servant girl was of course locked in her kitchen, and Grete would have to open the door. It was his father. "What's been happening?" were his first words; Grete's face must have told him everything. Grete answered in a muffled voice, apparently hiding her head on his breast: "Mother has been fainting, but she's better now. Gregor's broken loose." "Just what I expected," said his father, "just what I've been telling you, but you women would never listen." It was clear to Gregor that his father had taken the worst interpretation of Grete's all too brief statement and was assuming that Gregor had been guilty of some violent act. Therefore Gregor must now try to propitiate his father, since he had neither time nor means for an explanation. And so he fled to the door of his own room and crouched against it, to let his father see as soon as he came in from the hall that his son had the good intention of getting back into his room immediately and that it was not necessary to drive him there, but that if only the door were opened he would disappear at once.

60   Yet his father was not in the mood to perceive such fine distinctions. "Ah!" he cried as soon as he appeared, in a tone which sounded at once angry and exultant. Gregor drew his head back from the door and lifted it to look at his father. Truly, this was not the father he had imagined to himself; admittedly he had been too absorbed of late in his new recreation of crawling over the ceiling to take the same interest as before in what was happening elsewhere in the flat, and he ought really to be prepared for some changes. And yet, and yet, could that be his father? The man who used to lie wearily sunk in bed whenever Gregor set out on a business journey; who welcomed him back of an evening lying in a long chair in a dressing gown; who could not really rise to his feet but only lifted his arms in greeting, and on the rare occasions when he did go out with his family, on one or two Sundays a year and on high holidays, walked between Gregor and his mother, who were slow walkers anyhow, even more slowly than they did, muffled in his old greatcoat, shuffling laboriously forward with the help of his crookhandled stick which he set down most cautiously at every step and, whenever he wanted to say anything, nearly always came to a full stop and gathered his escort around him? Now he was standing there in fine shape; dressed in a smart blue uniform with gold buttons, such as bank messengers wear; his strong double chin bulged over the stiff high collar of his jacket; from under his bushy eyebrows his black eyes darted fresh and penetrating glances; his onetime tangled white hair had been combed flat on either side of a shining and carefully exact parting. He pitched his cap, which bore a gold monogram, probably the badge of some bank, in a wide sweep across the whole room on to a sofa and with the tail-ends of his jacket thrown back, his hands in his trouser pockets, advanced with a grim visage towards Gregor. Likely enough he did not himself know what he meant to do; at any rate he lifted his feet uncommonly high, and Gregor was dumbfounded at the enormous size of his shoe soles. But Gregor could not risk standing up to him, aware as he had been from the very first day of his new life that his father believed only the severest measures suitable for dealing with him. And so he ran before his father, stopping when he stopped and scuttling forward again when his father made any kind of move. In this way they circled the room

several times without anything decisive happening; indeed the whole operation did not even look like a pursuit because it was carried out so slowly. And so Gregor did not leave the floor, for he feared that his father might take as a piece of peculiar wickedness any excursion of his over the walls or the ceiling. All the same, he could not stay this course much longer, for while his father took one step he had to carry out a whole series of movements. He was already beginning to feel breathless, just as in his former life his lungs had not been very dependable. As he was staggering along, trying to concentrate his energy on running, hardly keeping his eyes open; in his dazed state never even thinking of any other escape than simply going forward; and having almost forgotten that the walls were free to him, which in this room were well provided with finely carved pieces of furniture full of knobs and crevices—suddenly something lightly flung landed close behind him and rolled before him. It was an apple; a second apple followed immediately; Gregor came to a stop in alarm; there was no point in running on, for his father was determined to bombard him. He had filled his pockets with fruit from the dish on the sideboard and was now shying apple after apple, without taking particularly good aim for the moment. The small red apples rolled about the floor as if magnetized and cannoned into each other. An apple thrown without much force grazed Gregor's back and glanced off harmlessly. But another following immediately landed right on his back and sank in; Gregor wanted to drag himself forward, as if this startling, incredible pain could be left behind him: but he felt as if nailed to the spot and flattened himself out in a complete derangement of all his senses. With his last conscious look he saw the door of his room being torn open and his mother rushing out ahead of his screaming sister, in her underbodice, for her daughter had loosened her clothing to let her breathe more freely and recover from her swoon, he saw his mother rushing towards his father, leaving one after another behind her on the floor her loosened petticoats, stumbling over her petticoats straight to his father and embracing him, in complete union with him—but here Gregor's sight began to fail—with her hands clasped round his father's neck as she begged for her son's life.

III

The serious injury done to Gregor, which disabled him for more than a month—the apple went on sticking in his body as a visible reminder, since no one ventured to remove it—seemed to have made even his father recollect that Gregor was a member of the family, despite his present unfortunate and repulsive shape, and ought not to be treated as an enemy, that, on the contrary, family duty required the suppression of disgust and the exercise of patience, nothing but patience.

And although his injury had impaired, probably for ever, his power of movement, and for the time being it took him long, long minutes to creep across his room like an old invalid—there was no question now of crawling up the wall—yet in his own opinion he was sufficiently compensated for this worsening of his condition by the fact that towards evening the living-room door, which he used to watch intently for an hour or two beforehand, was always thrown open, so that lying in the darkness of his room, invisible to the family, he could see them all at the lamp-lit table and listen to their talk, by general consent as it were, very different from his earlier eavesdropping.

True, their intercourse lacked the lively character of former times, which he had always called to mind with a certain wistfulness in the small hotel bedrooms where he had been wont to throw himself down, tired out, on damp bedding. They were now mostly very silent. Soon after supper his father would fall asleep in his armchair; his mother and sister would admonish each other to be silent; his mother, bending low over the lamp, stitched at fine sewing for an underwear firm; his sister, who had taken a job as a salesgirl, was learning shorthand and French in the evenings on the chance of bettering herself. Sometimes his father woke up, and as if quite unaware that he had been sleeping said to his mother: "What a lot of sewing you're doing today!" and at once fell asleep again, while the two women exchanged a tired smile.

With a kind of mulishness his father persisted in keeping his uniform on even in the house; his dressing gown hung uselessly on its peg and he slept fully dressed where he sat, as if he were ready for service at any moment and even here only at the beck and call of his superior. As a result, his uniform, which was not brand-new to start with, began to look dirty, despite all the loving care of the mother and sister to keep it clean, and Gregor often spent whole evenings gazing at the many greasy spots on the garment, gleaming with gold buttons always in a high state of polish, in which the old man sat sleeping in extreme discomfort and yet quite peacefully.

65 As soon as the clock struck ten his mother tried to rouse his father with gentle words and to persuade him after that to get into bed, for sitting there he could not have a proper sleep and that was what he needed most, since he had to go to duty at six. But with the mulishness that had obsessed him since he became a bank messenger he always insisted on staying longer at the table, although he regularly fell asleep again and in the end only with the greatest trouble could be got out of his armchair and into his bed. However insistently Gregor's mother and sister kept urging him with gentle reminders, he would go on slowly shaking his head for a quarter of an hour, keeping his eyes shut, and refuse to get to his feet. The mother plucked at his sleeve, whispering endearments in his ear, the sister left her lessons to come to her mother's help, but Gregor's father was not to be caught. He would only sink down deeper in his chair. Not until the two women hoisted him up by the armpits did he open his eyes and look at them both, one after the other, usually with the remark: "This is a life. This is the peace and quiet of my old age." And leaning on the two of them he would heave himself up, with difficulty, as if he were a great burden to himself, suffer them to lead him as far as the door and then wave them off and go on alone, while the mother abandoned her needlework and the sister her pen in order to run after him and help him farther.

Who could find time, in this overworked and tired-out family, to bother about Gregor more than was absolutely needful? The household was reduced more and more; the servant girl was turned off; a gigantic bony charwoman with white hair flying round her head came in morning and evening to do the rough work; everything else was done by Gregor's mother, as well as great piles of sewing. Even various family ornaments, which his mother and sister used to wear with pride at parties and celebrations, had to be sold, as Gregor discovered of an evening from hearing them all discuss the prices obtained. But what they lamented most was the fact that they could not leave the flat which was much too big for their present circumstances, because they could not think of any way to shift Gregor. Yet Gregor saw well enough that consideration for him was not the main difficulty preventing the removal, for they could have easily shifted him in some suitable box with a few air holes in it; what really kept them from moving into another flat was rather their own complete hopelessness and the belief that they had been singled out for a misfortune such as had never happened to any of their relations or acquaintances. They fulfilled to the uttermost all that the world demands of poor people, the father fetched breakfast for the small clerks in the bank, the mother devoted her energy to making underwear for strangers, the sister trotted to and fro behind the counter at the behest of customers, but more than this they had not the strength to do. And the wound in Gregor's back began to nag at him afresh when his mother and sister, after getting his father into bed came back again, left their work lying, drew close to each other and sat cheek by cheek; when his mother, pointing towards his room, said: "Shut that door now, Grete," and he was left again in darkness, while next door the women mingled their tears or perhaps sat dry-eyed staring at the table.

Gregor hardly slept at all by night or by day. He was often haunted by the idea that next time the door opened he would take the family's affairs in hand again just as he used to do; once more, after this long interval, there appeared in his thoughts the figures of the chief and the chief clerk, the commercial travelers and the apprentices, the porter who was so dull-witted, two or three friends in other firms, a chambermaid in one of the rural hotels, a sweet and fleeting memory, a cashier in a milliner's shop, whom he had wooed earnestly but too slowly—they all appeared, together with strangers or people he had quite forgotten, but instead of helping him and his family they were one and all unapproachable and he was glad when they vanished. At other times he would not be in the mood to bother about his family, he was only filled with rage at the way they were neglecting him, and although he had no clear idea of what he might care to eat he would make plans for getting into the larder to take the food that was after all his due, even if he were not hungry. His sister no longer took thought to bring him what might especially please him, but in the morning and at noon before she went to business hurriedly pushed into his room with her foot any food that was available, and in the evening cleared it out again with one sweep of the broom, heedless of whether it had been merely tasted, or—as most frequently happened—left untouched. The cleaning of his room, which she now did always in the evenings, could not have been more hastily done. Streaks of dirt stretched along the walls, here and there lay balls of dust and filth. At first Gregor used to station himself in some particularly filthy corner when his sister arrived, in order to reproach her with it, so to speak. But he could have sat there for weeks without getting her to make any improvements; she could see the dirt as well as he did, but she had simply made up her mind to leave it alone. And yet, with a touchiness that was new to her, which seemed anyhow to have infected the whole family, she jealously guarded her claim to be the sole caretaker of Gregor's room. His mother once subjected his room to a thorough cleaning, which was achieved only by means of several buckets of water—all this dampness of course upset Gregor too and he lay widespread, sulky and motionless on the sofa—but she was well punished for it. Hardly had his sister noticed the changed aspect of his room that evening than she rushed in high dudgeon into the living room and, despite the imploringly raised hands of her mother, burst into a storm of weeping, while her parents—her father had of course been startled out of his chair—looked on at first in helpless amazement; then they too began to go into action; the father reproached the mother on his right for not having left the cleaning of Gregor's room to his sister; shrieked at the sister on his left that never again was she to be allowed to clean Gregor's room; while the mother tried to pull the father into his bedroom, since he was beyond himself with agitation; the sister, shaken with sobs, then beat upon the table with her small fists; and Gregor hissed loudly with rage because not one of them thought of shutting the door to spare him such a spectacle and so much noise.

Still, even if the sister, exhausted by her daily work, had grown tired of looking after Gregor as she did formerly, there was no need for his mother's intervention or for Gregor's being neglected at all. The charwoman was there. This old widow, whose strong bony frame had enabled her to survive the worst a long life could offer, by no means recoiled from Gregor. Without being in the least curious she had once by chance opened the door of his room and at the sight of Gregor, who, taken by surprise, began to rush to and fro although no one was chasing him, merely stood there with her arms folded. From that time she never failed to open his door a little for a moment, morning and evening, to have a look at him. At first she even used to call him to her, with words which apparently she took to be friendly, such as: "Come along, then, you old dung beetle!" or "Look at the old dung beetle, then!" To such allocutions Gregor made no answer, but stayed motionless where he was, as if the door had never been opened. Instead of being allowed to disturb him so senselessly whenever the whim took her, she should rather have been ordered to clean out his room daily, that charwoman! Once, early in the morning—heavy rain was lashing on the windowpanes, perhaps a sign that spring was on the way—Gregor was so exasperated when she began addressing him again that he ran at her, as if to attack her, although slowly and feebly enough. But the charwoman instead of showing fright merely lifted high a chair that happened to be beside the door, and as she stood there with her mouth wide open it was clear that she meant to shut it only when she brought the chair down on Gregor's back. "So you're not coming any nearer?" she asked, as Gregor turned away again, and quietly put the chair back into the corner.

Gregor was now eating hardly anything. Only when he happened to pass the food laid out for him did he take a bit of something in his mouth as a pastime, kept it there for an hour at a time and usually spat it out again. At first he thought it was chagrin over the state of his room that prevented him from eating, yet he soon got used to the various changes in his room. It had become a habit in the family to push into his room things there was no room for elsewhere, and there were plenty of these now, since one of the rooms had been let to three lodgers. These serious gentlemen—all three of them with full beards, as Gregor once observed through a crack in the door—had a passion for order, not only in their own room but, since they were now members of the household, in all its arrangements, especially in the kitchen. Superfluous, not to say dirty, objects they could not bear. Besides, they had brought with them most of the furnishings they needed. For this reason many things could be dispensed with that it was no use trying to sell but that should not be thrown away either. All of them found their way into Gregor's room. The ash can likewise and the kitchen garbage can. Anything that was not needed for the moment was simply flung into Gregor's room by the charwoman, who did everything in a hurry; fortunately Gregor usually saw only the object, whatever it was, and the hand that held it. Perhaps she intended to take the things away again as time and opportunity offered, or to collect them until she could throw them all out in a heap, but in fact they just lay wherever she happened to throw them, except when Gregor pushed his way through the junk heap and shifted it somewhat, at first out of necessity, because he had not room enough to crawl, but later with increasing enjoyment, although after such excursions, being sad and weary to death, he would lie motionless for hours. And since the lodgers often ate their supper at home in the common living room, the living-room door stayed shut many an evening, yet Gregor reconciled himself quite easily to the shutting of the door, for often enough on evenings when it was opened he had disregarded it entirely and lain in the darkest corner of his room, quite unnoticed by the family. But on one occasion the charwoman left the door open a little and it stayed ajar even when the lodgers came in for supper and the lamp was lit. They set themselves at the top end of the table where formerly Gregor and his father and mother had eaten their meals, unfolded their napkins and took knife and fork in hand. At once his mother appeared in the other doorway with a dish of meat and close behind her his sister with a dish of potatoes piled high. The food steamed with a thick vapor. The lodgers bent over the food set before them as if to scrutinize it before eating, in fact the man in the middle, who seemed to pass for an authority with the other two, cut a piece of meat as it lay on the dish, obviously to discover if it were tender or should be sent back to the kitchen. He showed satisfaction, and Gregor's mother and sister, who had been watching anxiously, breathed freely and began to smile.

70   The family itself took its meals in the kitchen. Nonetheless, Gregor's father came into the living room before going into the kitchen and with one prolonged bow, cap in hand, made a round of the table. The lodgers all stood up and murmured something in their beards. When they were alone again they ate their food in almost complete silence. It seemed remarkable to Gregor that among the various noises coming from the table he could always distinguish the sound of their masticating teeth, as if this were a sign to Gregor that one needed teeth in order to eat, and that with toothless jaws even of the finest make one could do nothing. "I'm hungry enough," said Gregor sadly to himself, "But not for that kind of food. How these lodgers are stuffing themselves, and here am I dying of starvation!"

On that very evening—during the whole of his time there Gregor could not remember ever having heard the violin—the sound of violin-playing came from the kitchen. The lodgers had already finished their supper, the one in the middle had brought out a newspaper and given the other two a page apiece, and now they were leaning back at ease reading and smoking. When the violin began to play they pricked up their ears, got to their feet, and went on tiptoe to the hall door where they stood huddled together. Their movements must have been heard in the kitchen, for Gregor's father called out: "Is the violin-playing disturbing you, gentlemen? It can be stopped at once." "On the contrary," said the middle lodger, "could not Fräulein Samsa come and play in this room, beside us, where it is much more convenient and comfortable?" "Oh certainly," cried Gregor's father, as if he were the violin-player. The lodgers came back into the living room and waited. Presently Gregor's father arrived with the music stand, his mother carrying the music and his sister with the violin. His sister quietly made everything ready to start playing; his parents, who had never let rooms before and so had an exaggerated idea of the courtesy due to lodgers, did not venture to sit down on their own chairs; his father leaned against the door, the right hand thrust between two buttons of his livery coat, which was formally buttoned up; but his mother was offered a chair by one of the lodgers and, since she left the chair just where he had happened to put it, sat down in a corner to one side.

Gregor's sister began to play; the father and mother, from either side, intently watched the movements of her hands. Gregor, attracted by the playing, ventured to move forward a little until his head was actually inside the living room. He felt hardly any surprise at his growing lack of consideration for the others; there had been a time when he prided himself on being considerate. And yet just on this occasion he had more reason than ever to hide himself, since owing to the amount of dust which lay thick in his room and rose into the air at the slightest movement, he too was covered with dust; fluff and hair and remnants of food trailed with him, caught on his back and along his sides; his indifference to everything was much too great for him to turn on his back and scrape himself clean on the carpet, as once he had done several times a day. And in spite of his condition, no shame deterred him from advancing a little over the spotless floor of the living room.

To be sure, no one was aware of him. The family was entirely absorbed in the violin-playing; the lodgers, however, who first of all had stationed themselves, hands in pockets, much too close behind the music stand so that they could all have read the music, which must have bothered his sister, had soon retreated to the window, half-whispering with downbent heads, and stayed there while his father turned an anxious eye on them. Indeed, they were making it more than obvious that they had been disappointed in their expectation of hearing good or enjoyable violin-playing, that they had had more than enough of the performance and only out of courtesy suffered a continued disturbance of their peace. From the way they all kept blowing the smoke of their cigars high in the air through nose and mouth one could divine their irritation. And yet Gregor's sister was playing so beautifully. Her face leaned sideways, intently and sadly her eyes followed the notes of music. Gregor crawled a little farther forward and lowered his head to the ground so that it might be possible for his eyes to meet hers. Was he an animal, that music had such an effect upon him? He felt as if the way were opening before him to the unknown nourishment he craved. He was determined to push forward till he reached his sister, to pull at her skirt and so let her know that she was to come into his room with her violin, for no one here appreciated her playing as he would appreciate it. He would never let her out of his room, at least, not so long as he lived; his frightful appearance would become, for the first time, useful to him; he would watch all the doors of his room at once and spit at intruders; but his sister should need no constraint, she should stay with him of her own free will; she should sit beside him on the sofa, bend down her ear to him and hear him confide that he had had the firm intention of sending her to the Conservatorium, and that, but for his mishap, last Christmas—surely Christmas was long past?—he would have announced it to everybody without allowing a single objection. After this confession his sister would be so touched that she would burst into tears, and Gregor would then raise himself to her shoulder and kiss her on the neck, which, now that she went to business, she kept free of any ribbon or collar.

"Mr. Samsa!" cried the middle lodger, to Gregor's father, and pointed, without wasting any more words, at Gregor, now working himself slowly forwards. The violin fell silent, the middle lodger first smiled to his friends with a shake of the head and then looked at Gregor again. Instead of driving Gregor out, his father seemed to think it more needful to begin by soothing down the lodgers, although they were not at all agitated and apparently found Gregor more entertaining than the violin-playing. He hurried toward them and, spreading out his arms, tried to urge them back into their own room and at the same time to block their view of Gregor.

They now began to be really a little angry, one could not tell whether because of the old man's behavior or because it had just dawned on them that all unwittingly they had such a neighbor as Gregor next door. They demanded explanations of his father, they waved their arms like him, tugged uneasily at their beards, and only with reluctance backed towards their room. Meanwhile Gregor's sister, who stood there as if lost when her playing was so abruptly broken off, came to life again, pulled herself together all at once after standing for a while holding violin and bow in nervelessly hanging hands and staring at her music, pushed her violin into the lap of her mother, who was still sitting in her chair fighting asthmatically for breath, and ran into the lodgers' room to which they were now being shepherded by her father rather more quickly than before. One could see the pillows and blankets on the beds flying under her accustomed fingers and being laid in order. Before the lodgers had actually reached their room she had finished making the beds and slipped out.

75   The old man seemed once more to be so possessed by his mulish self-assertiveness that he was forgetting all the respect he should show to his lodgers. He kept driving them on and driving them on until in the very door of the bedroom the middle lodger stamped his foot loudly on the floor and so brought him to a halt. "I beg to announce," said the lodger, lifting one hand and looking also at Gregor's mother and sister, "that because of the disgusting conditions prevailing in this household and family"—here he spat on the floor with emphatic brevity—"I give you notice on the spot. Naturally I won't pay you a penny for the days I have lived here, on the contrary I shall consider bringing an action for damages against you, based on claims—believe me—that will be easily susceptible of proof." He ceased and stared straight in front of him, as if he expected something. In fact his two friends at once rushed into the breach with these words: "And we too give notice on the spot." On that he seized the door-handle and shut the door with a slam.

Gregor's father, groping with his hands, staggered forward and fell into his chair; it looked as if he were stretching himself there for his ordinary evening nap, but the marked jerkings of his head, which was as if uncontrollable, showed that he was far from asleep. Gregor had simply stayed quietly all the time on the spot where the lodgers had espied him. Disappointment at the failure of his plan, perhaps also the weakness arising from extreme hunger, made it impossible for him to move. He feared, with a fair degree of certainty, that at any moment the general tension would discharge itself in a combined attack upon him, and he lay waiting. He did not react even to the noise made by the violin as it fell off his mother's lap from under her trembling fingers and gave out a resonant note.

"My dear parents," said his sister, slapping her hand on the table by way of introduction, "things can't go on like this. Perhaps you don't realize that, but I do. I won't utter my brother's name in the presence of this creature, and so all I say is: we must try to get rid of it. We've tried to look after it and to put up with it as far as is humanly possible, and I don't think anyone could reproach us in the slightest."

"She is more than right," said Gregor's father to himself. His mother, who was still choking for lack of breath, began to cough hollowly into her hand with a wild look in her eyes.

His sister rushed over to her and held her forehead. His father's thoughts seemed to have lost their vagueness at Grete's words, he sat more upright, fingering his service cap that lay among the plates still lying on the table from the lodgers' supper, and from time to time looked at the still form of Gregor.

80 "We must try to get rid of it," his sister now said explicitly to her father, since her mother was coughing too much to hear a word, "it will be the death of both of you, I can see that coming. When one has to work as hard as we do, all of us, one can't stand this continual torment at home on top of it. At least I can't stand it any longer." And she burst into such a passion of sobbing that her tears dropped on her mother's face, where she wiped them off mechanically.

"My dear," said the old man sympathetically, and with evident understanding, "but what can we do?"

Gregor's sister merely shrugged her shoulders to indicate the feeling of helplessness that had now overmastered her during her weeping fit, in contrast to her former confidence.

"If he could understand us," said her father, half questioningly; Grete, still sobbing, vehemently waved a hand to show how unthinkable that was.

"If he could understand us," repeated the old man, shutting his eyes to consider his daughter's conviction that understanding was impossible, "then perhaps we might come to some agreement with him. But as it is—"

85 "He must go," cried Gregor's sister, "That's the only solution, Father. You must try to get rid of the idea that this is Gregor. The fact that we've believed it for so long is the root of all our trouble. But how can it be Gregor? If this were Gregor, he would have realized long ago that human beings can't live with such a creature, and he'd have gone away on his own accord. Then we wouldn't have any brother, but we'd be able to go on living and keep his memory in honor. As it is, this creature persecutes us, drives away our lodgers, obviously wants the whole apartment to himself and would have us all sleep in the gutter. Just look, Father," she shrieked all at once, "he's at it again!" And in an access of panic that was quite incomprehensible to Gregor she even quitted her mother, literally thrusting the chair from her as if she would rather sacrifice her mother than stay so near to Gregor, and rushed behind her father, who also rose up, being simply upset by her agitation, and half-spread his arms out as if to protect her.

Yet Gregor had not the slightest intention of frightening anyone, far less his sister. He had only begun to turn round in order to crawl back to his room, but it was certainly a startling operation to watch, since because of his disabled condition he could not execute the difficult turning movements except by lifting his head and then bracing it against the floor over and over again. He paused and looked round. His good intentions seemed to have been recognized; the alarm had only been momentary. Now they were all watching him in melancholy silence. His mother lay in her chair, her legs stiffly outstretched and pressed together, her eyes almost closing for sheer weariness; his father and his sister were sitting beside each other, his sister's arm around the old man's neck.

Perhaps I can go on turning round now, thought Gregor, and began his labors again. He could not stop himself from panting with the effort, and had to pause now and then to take breath. Nor did anyone harass him, he was left entirely to himself. When he had completed the turn-round he began at once to crawl straight back. He was amazed at the distance separating him from his room and could not understand how in his weak state he had managed to accomplish the same journey so recently, almost without remarking it. Intent on crawling as fast as possible, he barely noticed that not a single word, not an ejaculation from his family, interfered with his progress. Only when he was already in the doorway did he turn his head round, not completely, for his neck muscles were getting stiff, but enough to see that nothing had changed behind him except that his sister had risen to her feet. His last glance fell on his mother, who was not quite overcome by sleep.

Hardly was he well inside his room when the door was hastily pushed shut, bolted and locked. The sudden noise in his rear startled him so much that his little legs gave beneath him. It was his sister who had shown such haste. She had been standing ready waiting and made a light spring forward, Gregor had not even heard her coming, and she cried "At last!" to her parents as she turned the key in the lock.

"And what now?" said Gregor to himself, looking round in the darkness. Soon he made the discovery that he was now unable to stir a limb. This did not surprise him, rather it seemed unnatural that he should ever actually have been able to move on these feeble little legs. Otherwise he felt relatively comfortable. True, his whole body was aching, but it seemed that the pain was gradually growing less and would finally pass away. The rotting apple in his back and the inflamed area around it, all covered with soft dust, already hardly troubled him. He thought of his family with tenderness and love. The decision that he must disappear was one that he held to even more strongly than his sister, if that were possible. In this state of vacant and peaceful meditation he remained until the tower clock struck three in the morning. The first broadening of light in the world outside the window entered his consciousness once more. Then his head sank to the floor of its own accord and from his nostrils came the last faint flicker of his breath.

90   When the charwoman arrived early in the morning—what between her strength and her impatience she slammed all the doors so loudly, never mind how often she had been begged not to do so, that no one in the whole apartment could enjoy any quiet sleep after her arrival—she noticed nothing unusual as she took her customary peep into Gregor's room. She thought he was lying motionless on purpose, pretending to be in the sulks; she credited him with every kind of intelligence. Since she

happened to have the longhanded broom in her hand she tried to tickle him up with it from the doorway. When that too produced no reaction she felt provoked and poked at him a little harder, and only when she had pushed him along the floor without meeting any resistance was her attention aroused. It did not take her long to establish the truth of the matter, and her eyes widened, she let out a whistle, yet did not waste much time over it but tore open the door of the Samsas' bedroom and yelled into the darkness at the top of her voice: "Just look at this, it's dead; it's lying here dead and done for!"

Mr. and Mrs. Samsa started up in their double bed and before they realized the nature of the charwoman's announcement had some difficulty in overcoming the shock of it. But then they got out of bed quickly, one on either side, Mr. Samsa throwing a blanket over his shoulders, Mrs. Samsa in nothing but her nightgown; in this array they entered Gregor's room. Meanwhile the door of the living room opened, too, where Grete had been sleeping since the advent of the lodgers; she was completely dressed as if she had not been to bed, which seemed to be confirmed also by the paleness of her face. "Dead?" said Mrs. Samsa, looking questioningly at the charwoman, although she could have investigated for herself, and the fact was obvious enough without investigation. "I should say so," said the charwoman, proving her words by pushing Gregor's corpse a long way to one side with her broomstick. Mrs. Samsa made a movement as if to stop her, but checked it. "Well," said Mr. Samsa, "now thanks be to God." He crossed himself, and the three women followed his example. Grete, whose eyes never left the corpse, said: "Just see how thin he was. It's such a long time since he's eaten anything. The food came out again just as it went in." Indeed, Gregor's body was completely flat and dry, as could only now be seen when it was no longer supported by the legs and nothing prevented one from looking closely at it.

"Come in beside us, Grete, for a little while," said Mrs. Samsa with a tremulous smile, and Grete, not without looking back at the corpse, followed her parents into their bedroom. The charwoman shut the door and opened the window wide. Although it was so early in the morning a certain softness was perceptible in the fresh air. After all, it was already the end of March.

The three lodgers emerged from their room and were surprised to see no breakfast; they had been forgotten. "Where's our breakfast?" said the middle lodger peevishly to the charwoman. But she put her finger to her lips and hastily, without a word, indicated by gestures that they should go into Gregor's room. They did so and stood, their hands in the pockets of their somewhat shabby coats, around Gregor's corpse in the room where it was now fully light.

At that the door of the Samsas' bedroom opened and Mr. Samsa appeared in his uniform, his wife on one arm, his daughter on the other. They all looked a little as if they had been crying; from time to time Grete hid her face on her father's arm.

95   "Leave my house at once!" said Mr. Samsa, and pointed to the door without disengaging himself from the women. "What do you mean by that?" said the middle lodger, taken somewhat aback, with a feeble smile. The two others put their hands behind them and kept rubbing them together, as if in gleeful expectation of a fine set-to in which they were bound to come off the winners. "I mean just what I say," answered Mr. Samsa, and advanced in a straight line with his two companions towards the lodger. He stood his ground at first quietly, looking at the floor as if his thoughts were taking a new pattern in his head. "Then let us go, by all means," he said, and looked up at Mr. Samsa as if in a sudden access of humility he were expecting some renewed sanction for this decision. Mr. Samsa merely nodded briefly once or twice with meaning eyes. Upon that the lodger really did go with long strides into the hall, his two friends had been listening and had quite stopped rubbing their hands for some moments and now went scuttling after him as if afraid that Mr. Samsa might get into the hall before them and cut them off from their leader. In the hall they all three took their hats from the rack, their sticks from the umbrella stand, bowed in silence and quitted the apartment. With a suspiciousness which proved quite unfounded Mr. Samsa and the two women followed them out to the landing; leaning over the banister they watched the three figures slowly but surely going down the long stairs, vanishing from sight at a certain turn of the staircase on every floor and coming into view again after a moment or so; the more they dwindled, the more the Samsa family's interest in them dwindled, and when a butcher's boy met them and passed them on the stairs coming up proudly with a tray on his head, Mr. Samsa and the two women soon left the landing and as if a burden had been lifted from them went back into their apartment.

They decided to spend this day in resting and going for a stroll; they had not only deserved such a respite from work, but absolutely needed it. And so they sat down at the table and wrote three notes of excuse, Mr. Samsa to his board of management, Mrs. Samsa to her employer and Grete to the head of her firm. While they were writing, the charwoman came in to say that she was going now, since her morning's work was finished. At first they only nodded without looking up, but as she kept hovering there they eyed her irritably. "Well?" said Mr. Samsa. The charwoman stood grinning in the doorway as if she had good news to impart to the family but meant not to say a word unless properly questioned. The small ostrich feather standing upright on her hat, which had annoyed Mr. Samsa ever since she was engaged, was waving gaily in all directions. "Well, what is it then?" asked Mrs. Samsa, who obtained more respect from the charwoman than the others. "Oh," said the charwoman, giggling so amiably that she could not at once continue, "just this, you don't need to bother about how to get rid of the thing next door. It's been seen to already." Mrs. Samsa and Grete bent over their letters again, as if preoccupied; Mr. Samsa, who perceived that she was eager to begin describing it all in detail, stopped her with a decisive hand. But since she was not allowed to tell her story, she remembered the great hurry she was in, being obviously deeply huffed: "Bye, everybody," she said, whirling off violently, and departed with a frightful slamming of doors.

"She'll be given notice tonight," said Mr. Samsa, but neither from his wife nor his daughter did he get any answer, for the charwoman seemed to have shattered again the composure they had barely achieved. They rose, went to the window and stayed there, clasping each other tight. Mr. Samsa turned to his chair to look at them and quietly observed them for a little. Then he called out: "Come along, now, do. Let bygones be bygones. And you might have some consideration for me." The two of them complied at once, hastened to him, caressed him and quickly finished their letters.

Then they all three left the apartment together, which was more than they had done for months, and went by tram into the open country outside the town. The tram, in which they were the only passengers, was filled with warm sunshine. Leaning comfortably back in their seats they canvassed their prospects for the future, and it appeared on closer inspection that these were not at all bad, for the jobs they had got, which so far they had never really discussed with each other, were all three admirable and likely to lead to better things later on. The greatest immediate improvement in their condition would of course arise from moving to another house; they wanted to take a smaller and cheaper but also better situated and more easily run apartment than the one they had, which Gregor had selected. While they were thus conversing, it struck both Mr. and Mrs. Samsa, almost at the same moment, as they became aware of their daughter's increasing vivacity, that in spite of all the sorrow of recent times, which had made her cheeks pale, she had bloomed into a pretty girl with a good figure. They grew quieter and half unconsciously exchanged glances of complete agreement, having come to the conclusion that it would soon be time to find a good husband for her. And it was like a confirmation of their new dreams and excellent intentions that at the end of their journey their daughter sprang to her feet first and stretched her young body.

◊ ◊ ◊

JAMAICA KINCAID
(1949–   )

Girl
(1984)

Wash the white clothes on Monday and put them on the stone heap; wash the color clothes on Tuesday and put them on the clothesline to dry; don't walk barehead in the hot sun; cook pumpkin fritters in very hot sweet oil; soak your little clothes right after you take them off; when buying cotton to make yourself a nice blouse, be sure that it doesn't have gum on it, because that way it won't hold up well after a wash; soak salt fish overnight before you cook it; is it true that you sing benna[1] in Sunday School?; always eat your food in such a way that it won't turn someone else's stomach; on Sundays try to walk like a lady and not like the slut you are so bent on becoming; don't sing benna in Sunday School; you mustn't speak to wharf-rat boys, not even to give directions; don't eat fruits on the street—flies will follow you; *but I don't sing benna on Sundays at all and never in Sunday school;* this is how to sew on a button; this is how to make a buttonhole for the button you have just sewed on; this is how to hem a dress when you see the hem coming down and so to prevent yourself from looking like the slut I know you are so bent on becoming; this is how you iron your father's khaki shirt so that it doesn't have a crease; this is how you iron your father's khaki pants so that they don't have a crease; this is how you grow okra—far from the house, because okra tree harbors red ants; when you are growing dasheen, make sure it gets plenty of water or else it makes your throat itch when you are eating it; this is how you sweep a corner; this is how you sweep a whole house; this is how you sweep a yard; this is how you smile to someone you don't like too much; this is how you smile to someone you don't like at all; this is how you smile to someone you like completely; this is how you set a table for tea; this is how you set a table for dinner; this is how you set a table for dinner with an important guest; this is how you set a table for lunch; this is how you set a table for breakfast; this is how to behave in the presence of men who don't know you very well, and this way they won't recognize immediately the slut I have warned you against becoming; be sure to wash every day, even if it is with your own spit; don't squat down to play marbles—you are not a boy, you know; don't pick people's flowers—you might catch something; don't throw stones at blackbirds, because it might not be a blackbird at all; this is how to make a bread pudding; this is how to make doukona;[2] this is how to make pepper pot; this is how to make a good medicine for a cold; this is how to make a good medicine to throw away a child before it even becomes a child; this is how to catch a fish; this is how to throw back a fish you don't like, and that way something bad won't fall on you; this is how to bully a man; this is how a man bullies you; this is how to love a man, and if this doesn't work there are other ways, and if they don't work don't feel too bad about giving up; this is how to spit up in the air if you feel like it, and this is how to move quick so that it doesn't fall on you; this is how to make ends meet; always squeeze bread to make sure it's fresh; *but what if the baker won't let me feel the bread?;* you mean to say that after all you are really going to be the kind of woman who the baker won't let near the bread?

---

[1] Calypso music.

[2] Spicy plantain pudding.

◊ ◊ ◊

BERNARD MALAMUD
(1914–1986)

The German Refugee
(1964)

Oskar Gassner sits in his cotton-mesh undershirt and summer bathrobe at the window of his stuffy, hot, dark hotel room on West Tenth Street while I cautiously knock. Outside, across the sky, a late-June green twilight fades in darkness. The refugee fumbles for the light and stares at me, hiding despair but not pain.

I was in those days a poor student and would brashly attempt to teach anybody anything for a buck an hour, although I have since learned better. Mostly I gave English lessons to recently arrived refugees. The college sent me; I had acquired a little experience. Already a few of my students were trying their broken English, theirs and mine, in the American marketplace. I was then just twenty, on my way into my senior year in college, a skinny, life-hungry kid, eating himself waiting for the next world war to start. It was a goddamn cheat. Here I was palpitating to get going, and across the ocean Adolf Hitler, in black boots and a square mustache, was tearing up all the flowers. Will I ever forget what went on with Danzig that summer?

Times were still hard from the depression but anyway I made a little living from the poor refugees. They were all over uptown Broadway in 1939. I had four I tutored—Karl Otto Alp, the former film star; Wolfgang Novak, once a brilliant economist; Friedrich Wilhelm Wolff, who had taught medieval history at Heidelberg; and, after that night I met him in his disordered cheap hotel room, Oskar Gassner, the Berlin critic and journalist, at one time on the *Acht Uhr Abendblatt*. They were accomplished men. I had my nerve associating with them, but that's what a world crisis does for people—they get educated.

Oskar was maybe fifty, his thick hair turning gray. He had a big face and heavy hands. His shoulders sagged. His eyes, too, were heavy, a clouded blue; and as he stared at me after I had identified myself, doubt spread in them like underwater currents. It was as if, on seeing me, he had again been defeated. I stayed at the door in silence. In such cases I would rather be elsewhere, but I had to make a living. Finally he opened the door and I entered. Rather he released it and I was in. *"Bitte . . ."* He offered me a seat and didn't know where to sit himself. He would attempt to say something and then stop, as though it could not possibly be said. The room was cluttered with clothing, boxes of books he had managed to get out of Germany and some paintings. Oskar sat on a box and attempted to fan himself with his meaty hand. "Zis heat," he muttered, forcing his mind to the deed. "Impozzible. I do not know such heat." It was bad enough for me but terrible for him. He had difficulty breathing. He tried again to speak, lifted a hand and let it drop like a dead duck. He breathed as though he were fighting a battle; and maybe he won because after ten minutes we sat and slowly talked.

5   Like most educated Germans Oskar had at one time studied English. Although he was certain he couldn't say a word, he managed sometimes to put together a fairly decent, if rather comical, English sentence. He misplaced consonants, mixed up nouns and verbs and mangled idioms, yet we were able at once to communicate. We conversed mostly in English, with an occasional assist by me in pidgin-German or Yiddish, what he called "Jiddish." He had been to America before—last year for a short visit. He had come a month before *Kristallnacht*, when the Nazis shattered the Jewish store windows and burned all the synagogues, to see if he could find a job for himself; he had no relatives in America, and getting a job would permit him quickly to enter the country. He had been promised something, not in journalism but with the help of a foundation, as a lecturer. Then he had returned to Berlin, and after a frightening delay of six months was permitted to emigrate. He had sold whatever he could, managed to get some paintings, gifts of Bauhaus friends, and some boxes of books out by bribing two Nazi border guards; he had said goodbye to his wife and left the accursed country. He gazed at me with cloudy eyes. "We parted amicably," he said in German. "My wife was gentile. Her mother was an appalling anti-Semite. They returned to live in Stettin." I asked no questions. Gentile is gentile, Germany is Germany.

His new job was in the Institute for Public Studies here in New York. He was to give a lecture a week in the fall term, and during next spring, a course, in English translation, on "The Literature of the Weimar Republic." He had never taught before and was afraid to. He was in that way to be introduced to the public, but the thought of giving the lecture in English just about paralyzed him. He didn't see how he could do it. "How is it pozzible? I cannot say two words. I cannot pronounziate. I will make a fool of myself." His melancholy deepened. Already in the two months since his arrival, and after a round of diminishingly expensive hotel rooms, he had had two English tutors, and I was the third. The others had given him up, he said, because his progress was so poor, and he thought also that he depressed them. He asked me whether I felt I could do something for him, or should he go to a speech specialist—someone, say, who charged five dollars an hour—and beg his assistance? "You could try him," I said, "and then come back to me." In those days I figured what I knew, I knew. At that he managed a smile. Still I wanted him to make up his mind, or it would be no confidence down the line. He said, after a while, that he would stay with me. If he went to the five-dollar professor it might help his tongue but not his stomach. He would have no money left to eat with. The institute had paid him in advance for the summer, but it was only three hundred dollars and all he had.

He looked at me dully. *"Ich weiss nicht wie ich weiter machen soll."*

I figured it was time to move past the first step. Either we did that quickly or it would be like drilling rock for a long time. "Let's stand at the mirror," I said.

He rose with a sigh and stood there beside me: I thin, elongated, red-headed, praying for success, his and mine; Oskar uneasy, fearful, finding it hard to face either of us in the faded round glass above his dresser.

10   "Please," I said to him, "could you say 'right'?"

"Ghight," he gargled.

"No. 'Right.' You put your tongue here." I showed him where. As he tensely watched the mirror, I tensely watched him. "The tip of it curls behind the ridge on top, like this."

He placed his tongue where I showed him.

"Please," I said, "now say 'right.'"

15   Oskar's tongue fluttered, "Rright."

"That's good. Now say 'treasure'—that's harder."

"Tgheasure."

"The tongue goes up in front, not in the back of the mouth. Look."

He tried, his brow wet, eyes straining. "Trreasure."

20   "That's it."

"A miracle," Oskar murmured.

I said that if he had done that he could do the rest.

We went for a bus ride up Fifth Avenue and then walked for a while around Central Park Lake. He had put on his German hat, with its hatband bow at the back, a broad-lapeled wool suit, a necktie twice as wide as the one I was wearing, and walked with a small-footed waddle. The night wasn't bad; it had got a bit cooler. There were a few large stars in the sky and they made me sad.

"Do you sink I will succezz?"

25   "Why not?" I asked.

Later he bought me a bottle of beer.

To many of these people, articulate as they were, the great loss was the loss of language—that they could no longer say what was in them to say. They could, of course, manage to communicate, but just to communicate was frustrating. As Karl Otto Alp, the ex-film star who became a buyer for Macy's, put it years later, "I felt like a child, or worse, often like a moron. I am left with myself unexpressed. What I knew, indeed, what I am, becomes to me a burden. My tongue hangs useless." The same with Oskar it figures. There was a terrible sense of useless tongue, and I think the reason for his trouble with his other tutors was that to keep from drowning in things unsaid he wanted to swallow the ocean in a gulp: Today he would learn English and tomorrow wow them with an impeccable Fourth of July speech, followed by a successful lecture at the Institute for Public Studies.

We performed our lessons slowly, step by step, everything in its place. After Oskar moved to a two-room apartment in a house on West

Eighty-fifth Street, near the Drive, we met three times a week at four-thirty, work an hour and a half; then, since it was too hot to cook, had supper at the Seventy-second Street automat and conversed on my time. The lessons we divided into three parts: diction exercises and reading aloud, then grammar, because Oskar felt the necessity of it, and composition correction; with conversation, as I said, thrown in at supper. So far as I could see, he was coming along. None of these exercises was giving him as much trouble as they apparently had in the past. He seemed to be learning and his mood lightened. There were moments of elation as he heard this accent flying off. For instance, when "sink" became "think." He stopped calling himself "hopelezz."

Neither of us said much about the lecture he had to give early in October, and I kept my fingers crossed. It was somehow to come out of what we were doing daily, I think I felt, but exactly *how,* I had no idea; and to tell the truth, although I didn't say so to Oskar, the lecture frightened me. That and the ten more to follow during the fall term. Later when I learned that he had been attempting, with the help of the dictionary, to write in English, and had produced "a complete disahster," I suggested maybe he ought to stick to German and we could afterward both try to put it into passable English. I was cheating when I said that, because my German is meager. Anyway the idea was to get Oskar into production and worry about translating later. He sweated, from enervating morning to exhausted night, but no matter what language he tried, though he had been a professional writer for most of his life and knew his subject cold, the lecture refused to move past page one.

30   It was a sticky, hot July and the heat didn't help at all.

I had met Oskar at the end of June, and by the seventeenth of July we were no longer doing lessons. They had foundered on the "impozzible" lecture. He had worked on it each day in frenzy and growing despair. After writing more than a hundred opening pages, he furiously flung his pen against the wall, shouting he could no longer write in that filthy tongue. He cursed the German language. He hated the damned country and the damned people. After that, what was bad became worse. When he gave up attempting to write the lecture, he stopped making progress in English. He seemed to forget what he already knew. His tongue thickened and the accent returned in all its fruitiness. The little he had to say was in handcuffed and tortured English. The only German I heard him speak was in a whisper to himself. I doubt he knew he was talking it. That ended our formal work together, though I did drop in every other day or so to sit with him. For hours he sat motionless in a large green velours armchair, hot enough to broil in, and through the tall windows stared at the colorless sky above Eighty-fifth Street, with a wet depressed eye.

Then once he said to me, "If I do not this legture prepare, I will take my life."

"Let's begin again, Oskar," I said. "You dictate and I'll write. The ideas count, not the spelling."

He didn't answer so I stopped talking.

35   He had plunged into an involved melancholy. We sat for hours, often in profound silence. This was alarming to me, though I had already had some experience with such depression. Wolfgang Novak, the economist, though English came more easily to him, was another. His problems arose mainly, I think, from physical illness. And he felt a greater sense of the lost country than Oskar. Sometimes in the early evening I persuaded Oskar to come with me for a short walk on the Drive. The tail end of sunsets over the Palisades seemed to appeal to him. At least he looked. He would put on full regalia—hat, suit coat, tie, no matter how hot—and we went slowly down the stairs, I wondering whether he would ever make it to the bottom. He seemed to me always suspended between two floors.

We walked slowly uptown, stopping to sit on a bench and watch night rise above the Hudson. When we returned to his room, if I sensed he had loosened up a bit, we listened to music on the radio; but if I tried to sneak in a news broadcast, he said to me, "Please I can not more stand of world misery." I shut off the radio. He was right, it was a time of no good news. I squeezed my brain. What could I tell him? Was it good news to be alive? Who could argue the point? Sometimes I read aloud to him—I remember he liked the first part of *Life on the Mississippi.* We still went to the Automat once or twice a week; he perhaps out of habit, because he didn't feel like going anywhere, and I to get him out of his room. Oskar ate little, he toyed with a spoon. His dull eyes looked as though they had been squirted with a dark dye.

Once after a momentary cooling rainstorm we sat on newspapers on a wet bench overlooking the river, and Oskar at last began to talk. In tormented English he conveyed his intense and everlasting hatred of the Nazis for destroying his career, uprooting his life after half a century and flinging him like a piece of bleeding meat to hawks. He cursed them thickly, the German nation, as an inhuman, conscienceless, merciless people. "They are pigs mazquerading as peacogs," he said. "I feel certain that my wife, in her heart, was a Jew hater." It was a terrible bitterness, an eloquence almost without vocabulary. He became silent again. I hoped to hear more about his wife but decided not to ask.

Afterwards, in the dark Oskar confessed that he had attempted suicide during his first week in America. He was living, at the end of May, in a small hotel, and had filled himself with barbiturates one night, but his phone had fallen off the table and the hotel operator had sent up the elevator boy, who found him unconscious and called the police. He was revived in the hospital.

"I did not mean to do it," he said. "It was a mistage."

40   "Don't ever think of it again," I said. "It's total defeat."

"I don't," he said wearily, "because it is so arduouz to come back to life."

"Please, for any reason whatever."

Later, when we were walking, he surprised me by saying, "Maybe we ought to try now the legture onze more."

We trudged back to the house and he sat at his hot desk, I trying to read as he slowly began to reconstruct the first page of his lecture. He wrote, of course, in German.

45 He got nowhere. We were back to nothing, to sitting in silence in the heat. Sometimes after a few minutes I had to take off before his mood overcame mine. One afternoon I came unwillingly up the stairs—there were times I felt momentary surges of irritation with him—and was frightened to find Oskar's door ajar. When I knocked, no one answered. As I stood there, chilled down the spine, I realized I was thinking about the possibility of his attempting suicide again. "Oskar?" I went into the apartment, looked into both rooms and the bathroom, but he wasn't there. I thought he might have drifted out to get something from a store, and took the opportunity to look quickly around. There was nothing startling in the medicine chest, no pills but aspirin, no iodine. Thinking, for some reason, of a gun, I searched his desk drawer. In it I found a thin-paper airmail letter from Germany. Even if I had wanted to, I couldn't have read the handwriting, but as I held the thin paper in my hand I did make out one sentence: *"Ich bin dir siebenundzwanzig Jahre treu gewesen."* Twenty-seven years is a long time, I thought. There was no gun in the drawer. I shut it and stopped looking. It had occurred to me that if you want to kill yourself, all you need is a straight pin. When Oskar returned he said he had been sitting in the public library, unable to read.

Now we are once more enacting the changeless scene, curtain rising on two speechless characters in a furnished apartment, I in a straight-back chair, Oskar in the velours armchair that smothered rather than supported him, his flesh gray, the big gray face, unfocused, sagging. I reached over to switch on the radio, but he looked at me in a way that begged no. I then got up to leave, but Oskar, clearing his throat, thickly asked me to stay. I stayed, thinking, was there more to this than I could see into? His problems, God knows, were real enough, but could there be something more than a refugee's displacement, alienation, financial insecurity, being in a strange land without friends or a speakable tongue? My speculation was the old one: Not all drown in this ocean, why does he? After a while I shaped the thought and asked him was there something below the surface, invisible? I was full of this thing from college, and wondered if there mightn't be some unknown quantity in his depression that a psychiatrist maybe might help him with, enough to get him started on his lecture.

He meditated on this, and after a few minutes haltingly said he had been psychoanalyzed in Vienna as a young man. "Just the jusual *drek*," he said, "fears and fantazies that afterwaards no longer bothered me."

"They don't now?"

"Not."

50 "You've written many articles and lectures before," I said. "What I can't understand, though I know how hard the situation is, is why you can never get past page one."

He half lifted his hand. "It is a paralyzis of my will. The whole legture is clear in my mind, but the minute I write down a single word—or in English or in German—I have a terrible fear I will not be able to write the negst. As though someone has thrown a stone at a window and the whole house—the whole idea—zmashes. This repeats until I am dezperate."

He said the fear grew as he worked that he would die before he completed the lecture, or if not that, that he would write it so disgracefully he would wish for death. The fear immobilized him.

"I have lozt faith. I do not—not longer possezz my former value of myself. In my life there has been too much illusion."

I tried to believe what I was saying: "Have confidence, the feeling will pass."

55 "Confidenze I have not. For this, and alzo whatever elze I have lozt, I thank the Nazis."

It was by then mid-August and things were growing steadily worse wherever one looked. The Poles were mobilizing for war. Oskar hardly moved. I was full of worries though I pretended calm weather.

He sat in his massive armchair with sick eyes, breathing like a wounded animal.

"Who can write about Walt Whitman in such terrible times?"

"Why don't you change the subject?"

60 "It mages no differenze what is the subject. It is all uzelezz."

I came every day to see him, neglecting my other students and therefore my livelihood. I had a panicky feeling that if things went on as they were going, they would end in Oskar's suicide; and I felt a frenzied desire to prevent that. What's more, I was sometimes afraid I was myself becoming melancholy, a new talent, call it, of taking less pleasure in my little pleasures. And the heat continued, oppressive, relentless. We thought of escape into the country, but neither of us had the money. One day I bought Oskar a secondhand fan—wondering why we hadn't thought of that before—and he sat in the breeze for hours each day until after a week, shortly after the Soviet-Nazi nonaggression pact was signed, the motor gave out. He could not sleep at night and sat at his desk with a wet towel on his head, still attempting to write his lecture. He wrote reams on a treadmill; it came out nothing. When he did sleep, out of exhaustion, he had fantastic frightening dreams of the Nazis inflicting tortures on him, sometimes forcing him to look upon the corpses of those they had slain. In one dream he told me about, he had gone back to Germany to visit his wife. She wasn't home and he had been directed to a cemetery. There, though the tombstone read another name, her blood seeped out of the earth above her shallow grave. He groaned at the memory of the dream.

Afterwards, he told me something about her. They had met as students, lived together, and were married at twenty-three. It wasn't a very happy marriage. She had turned into a sickly woman, physically unable to have children. "Something was wrong with her interior strugture."

Though I asked no questions, Oskar said, "I offered her to come with me here but she refused this."

"For what reason?"

65 "She did not think I wished her to come."

"Did you?" I asked.

"Not," he said.

He explained he had lived with her for almost twenty-seven years under difficult circumstances. She had been ambivalent about their Jewish friends and his relatives, though outwardly she seemed not a prejudiced person. But her mother was always a violent anti-Semite.

"I have nothing to blame myself," Oskar said.

70 He took to his bed. I took to the New York Public Library. I read some of the German poets he was trying to write about, in English translation. Then I read *Leaves of Grass* and wrote down what I thought one or two of them had got from Whitman. One day toward the end of August I brought Oskar what I had written. It was in good part guessing, but my idea wasn't to write the lecture for him. He lay on his back, motionless, and listened utterly sadly to what I had written. Then he said, no, it wasn't the love of death they had got from Whitman—that ran through German poetry— but it was most of all his feeling for *Brudermensch,* his humanity.

"But this does not grow long on German earth," he said, "and is soon deztroyed."

I said I was sorry I had got it wrong, but he thanked me anyway.

I left defeated, and as I was going down the stairs, heard someone sobbing. I will quit this, I thought. It has gotten to be too much for me. I can't drown with him.

I stayed home the next day, tasting a new kind of private misery too old for somebody my age, but that same night Oskar called me on the phone, blessing me wildly for having read those notes to him. He had got up to write me a letter to say what I had missed, and it ended by his having written half the lecture. He had slept all day and tonight intended to finish it up.

75 "I thank you," he said, "for much, alzo including your faith in me."

"Thank God," I said, not telling him I had just about lost it.

Oskar completed his lecture—wrote and rewrote it—during the first week in September. The Nazis had invaded Poland, and though we were greatly troubled, there was some sense of release; maybe the brave Poles would beat them. It took another week to translate the lecture, but here we had the assistance of Friedrich Wilhelm Wolff, the historian, a gentle, erudite man, who liked translating and promised his help with future lectures. We then had about two weeks to work on Oskar's delivery. The weather had changed, and so, slowly, had he. He had awakened from defeat, battered, after a wearying battle. He had lost close to twenty pounds. His complexion was still gray; when I looked at his face I expected to see scars, but it had lost its flabby unfocused quality. His blue eyes had returned to life and he walked with quick steps, as though to pick up a few for all the steps he hadn't taken during those long, hot days he had lain torpid in his room.

We went back to our former routine, meeting three late afternoons a week for diction, grammar and the other exercises. I taught him the phonetic alphabet and transcribed long lists of words he was mispronouncing. He worked many hours trying to fit each sound into place, holding half a matchstick between his teeth to keep his jaws apart as he exercised his tongue. All this can be a dreadfully boring business unless you think you have a future. Looking at him I realized what's meant when somebody is called "another man."

The lecture, which I now knew by heart, went off well. The director of the institute had invited a number of prominent people. Oskar was the first refugee they had employed, and there was a move to make the public cognizant of what was then a new ingredient in American life. Two reporters had come with a lady photographer. The auditorium was crowded. I sat in the last row, promising to put up my hand if he couldn't be heard, but it wasn't necessary. Oskar, in a blue suit, his hair cut, was of course nervous, but you couldn't see it unless you studied him. When he stepped up to the lectern, spread out his manuscript and spoke his first English sentence in public, my heart hesitated; only he and I, of all the people there, had any idea of the anguish he had been through. His enunciation wasn't at all bad—a few s's for *th*'s, and he once said "bag" for "back," but otherwise he did all right. He read poetry well—in both languages—and though Walt Whitman, in his mouth, sounded a little as though he had come to the shores of Long Island as a German immigrant, still the poetry read as poetry:

> And I know that the spirit of God is the brother of my own,
> And that all the men ever born are also my brothers, and the women my
>   sisters and lovers,
> And that a kelson of creation is love. . .

80   Oskar read it as though he believed it. Warsaw had fallen but the verses were somehow protective. I sat back, conscious of two things: how easy it is to hide the deepest wounds; and the pride I felt in the job I had done.

Two days later I came up the stairs into Oskar's apartment to find a crowd there. The refugee, his face beet red, lips bluish, a trace of froth in the corners of his mouth, lay on the floor in his limp pajamas, two firemen on their knees, working over him with an inhalator. The windows were open and the air stank of gas.

A policeman asked me who I was and I could only answer, "No, oh no."

I said no, but it was unchangeably yes. He had taken his life—gas—I hadn't even thought of the stove in the kitchen.

"Why?" I asked myself. "Why did he do it?" Maybe it was the fate of Poland on top of everything else, but the only answer anyone could come up with was Oskar's scribbled note that he was not well, and that he left Martin Goldberg all his possessions. I am Martin Goldberg.

85   I was sick for a week, had no desire either to inherit or investigate, but I thought I ought to look through his things before the court impounded them, so I spent a morning sitting in the depths of Oskar's velours arm-chair, trying to read his correspondence. I had found in the top drawer of his desk a thin packet of letters from his wife and an airmail letter of recent date from his anti-Semitic mother-in-law.

     She writes, in a tight script it takes me hours to decipher, that her daughter, after Oskar abandons her, against her own mother's fervent pleas and anguish, is converted to Judaism by a vengeful rabbi. One night the Brown Shirts appear, and though the mother wildly waves her bronze crucifix in their faces, they drag Frau Gassner, together with the other Jews, out of the apartment house, and transport them in lorries to a small border town in conquered Poland. There, it is rumored, she is shot in the head and topples into an open tank ditch, with the naked Jewish men, their wives and children, some Polish soldiers and a handful of gypsies.

◊ ◊ ◊

HERMAN MELVILLE
(1819–1891)

Bartleby, the Scrivener[1]
A STORY OF WALL STREET
(1853)

I am a rather elderly man. The nature of my avocations, for the last thirty years, has brought me into more than ordinary contact with what would seem an interesting and somewhat singular set of men, of whom, as yet, nothing, that I know of, has ever been written—I mean, the law-copyists, or scriveners. I have known very many of them, professionally and privately, and, if I pleased, could relate divers histories, at which good-natured gentlemen might smile, and sentimental souls might weep. But I waive the biographies of all other scriveners, for a few passages in the life of Bartleby, who was a scrivener, the strangest I ever saw, or heard of. While, of other law-copyists, I might write the complete life, of Bartleby nothing of that sort can be done. I believe that no materials exist, for a full and satisfactory biography of this man. It is an irreparable loss to literature. Bartleby was one of those beings of whom nothing is ascertainable, except from the original sources, and, in his case, those are very small. What my own astonished eyes saw of Bartleby, *that* is all I know of him, except, indeed, one vague report, which will appear in the sequel.

     Ere introducing the scrivener, as he first appeared to me, it is fit I make some mention of myself, my *employés,* my business, my chambers,

---

[1] A copyist—prior to the photocopy and mimeograph, copies had to be created by a scribe.

and general surroundings, because some such description is indispensable to an adequate understanding of the chief character about to be presented. Imprimis:[2] I am a man who, from his youth upwards, has been filled with a profound conviction that the easiest way of life is the best. Hence, though I belong to a profession proverbially energetic and nervous, even to turbulence, at times, yet nothing of that sort have I ever suffered to invade my peace. I am one of those unambitious lawyers who never address a jury, or in any way draw down public applause; but, in the cool tranquillity of a snug retreat, do a snug business among rich men's bonds, and mortgages, and title-deeds. All who know me, consider me an eminently *safe* man. The late John Jacob Astor,[3] a personage little given to poetic enthusiasm, had no hestitation in pronouncing my first grand point to be prudence; my next, method. I do not speak it in vanity, but simply record the fact, that I was not unemployed in my profession by the late John Jacob Astor; a name which, I admit, I love to repeat; for it hath a rounded and orbicular sound to it, and rings like unto bullion. I will freely add, that I was not insensible to the late John Jacob Astor's good opinion.

Some time prior to the period at which this little history begins, my avocations had been largely increased. The good old office, now extinct in the State of New York, of a Master in Chancery, had been conferred upon me. It was not a very arduous office, but very pleasantly remunerative. I seldom lose my temper; much more seldom indulge in dangerous indignation at wrongs and outrages; but I must be permitted to be rash here and declare, that I consider the sudden and violent abrogation of the office of Master in Chancery, by the new Constitution, as a——premature act; inasmuch as I had counted upon a life-lease of the profits, whereas I only received those of a few short years. But this is by the way.

My chambers were up stairs, at No.—Wall Street. At one end, they looked upon the white wall of the interior of a spacious skylight shaft, penetrating the building from top to bottom.

5   This view might have been considered rather tame than otherwise, deficient in what landscape painters call "life." But, if so, the view from the other end of my chambers offered, at least, a contrast, if nothing more. In that direction, my windows commanded an unobstructed view of a lofty brick wall, black by age and everlasting shade; which wall required no spyglass to bring out its lurking beauties, but, for the benefit of all nearsighted spectators, was pushed up to within ten feet of my window-panes. Owing to the great height of the surrounding buildings, and my chambers being on the second floor, the interval between this wall and mine not a little resembled a huge square cistern.

At the period just preceding the advent of Bartleby, I had two persons as copyists in my employment, and a promising lad as an office-boy. First, Turkey; second, Nippers; third, Ginger Nut. These may seem names, the

---

[2] In the first place.
[3] American capitalist (1763–1848) who made his first fortune in the fur trade.

like of which are not usually found in the Directory. In truth, they were nicknames, mutually conferred upon each other by my three clerks, and were deemed expressive of their respective persons or characters. Turkey was a short, pursy[4] Englishman, of about my own age—that is, somewhere not far from sixty. In the morning, one might say, his face was of a fine florid hue, but after twelve o'clock, meridian[5]—his dinner hour—it blazed like a grate full of Christmas coals; and continued blazing—but, as it were, with a gradual wane—till six o'clock, P.M., or thereabouts; after which, I saw no more of the proprietor of the face, which, gaining its meridian with the sun, seemed to set with it, to rise, culminate, and decline the following day, with the like regularity and undiminished glory. There are many singular coincidences I have known in the course of my life, not the least among which was the fact, that, exactly when Turkey displayed his fullest beams from his red and radiant countenance, just then, too, at that critical moment, began the daily period when I considered his business capacities as seriously disturbed for the remainder of the twenty-four hours. Not that he was absolutely idle, or averse to business then; far from it. The difficulty was, he was apt to be altogether too energetic. There was a strange, inflamed, flurried, flighty recklessness of activity about him. He would be incautious in dipping his pen into his inkstand. All his blots upon my documents were dropped there after twelve o'clock, meridian. Indeed, not only would he be reckless, and sadly given to making blots in the afternoon, but, some days, he went further, and was rather noisy. At such times, too, his face flamed with augmented blazonry, as if cannel coal had been heaped on anthracite. He made an unpleasant racket with his chair; spilled his sand-box; in mending his pens, impatiently split them all to pieces, and threw them on the floor in a sudden passion; stood up, and leaned over his table, boxing his papers about in a most indecorous manner, very sad to behold in an elderly man like him. Nevertheless, as he was in many ways a most valuable person to me, and all the time before twelve o'clock, meridian, was the quickest, steadiest creature, too, accomplishing a great deal of work in a style not easily to be matched—for these reasons, I was willing to overlook his eccentricities, though, indeed, occasionally, I remonstrated with him. I did this very gently, however, because, though the civilest, nay, the blandest and most reverential of men in the morning, yet, in the afternoon, he was disposed, upon provocation, to be slightly rash with his tongue—in fact, insolent. Now, valuing his morning services as I did, and resolved not to lose them—yet, at the same time, made uncomfortable by his inflamed ways after twelve o'clock—and being a man of peace, unwilling by my admonitions to call forth unseemly retorts from him, I took upon me, one Saturday noon (he was always worse on Saturdays) to hint to him, very kindly, that, perhaps, now that he was growing old, it might be well to abridge his labors; in short, he need not come to my chambers after twelve o'clock, but, dinner over, had best go home to

---

[4] Overweight.
[5] Noon.

his lodgings, and rest himself till tea-time. But no; he insisted upon his afternoon devotions. His countenance became intolerably fervid, as he oratorically assured me—gesticulating with a long ruler at the other end of the room—that if his services in the morning were useful, how indispensable, then, in the afternoon?

"With submission, sir," said Turkey, on this occasion, "I consider myself your right-hand man. In the morning I but marshal and deploy my columns; but in the afternoon I put myself at their head, and gallantly charge the foe, thus"—and he made a violent thrust with the ruler.

"But the blots, Turkey," intimated I.

"True; but, with submission, sir, behold these hairs! I am getting old. Surely, sir, a blot or two of a warm afternoon is not to be severely urged against gray hairs. Old age—even if it blot the page—is honorable. With submission, sir, we *both* are getting old."

10 This appeal to my fellow-feeling was hardly to be resisted. At all events, I saw that go he would not. So, I made up my mind to let him stay, resolving, nevertheless, to see to it that, during the afternoon, he had to do with my less important papers.

Nippers, the second on my list, was a whiskered, sallow, and, upon the whole, rather piratical-looking young man, of about five-and-twenty. I always deemed him the victim of two evil powers—ambition and indigestion. The ambition was evinced by a certain impatience of the duties of a mere copyist, an unwarrantable usurpation of strictly professional affairs such as the original drawing up of legal documents. The indigestion seemed betokened in an occasional nervous testiness and grinning irritability, causing the teeth to audibly grind together over mistakes committed in copying; unnecessary maledictions, hissed, rather than spoken, in the heat of business; and especially by a continual discontent with the height of the table where he worked. Though of a very ingenious mechanical turn, Nippers could never get this table to suit him. He put chips under it, blocks of various sorts, bits of pasteboard, and at last went so far as to attempt an exquisite adjustment, by final pieces of folded blotting-paper. But no invention would answer. If, for the sake of easing his back, he brought the table-lid at a sharp angle well up towards his chin, and wrote there like a man using the steep roof of a Dutch house for his desk, then he declared that it stopped the circulation in his arms. If now he lowered the table to his waistbands, and stooped over it in writing, then there was a sore aching in his back. In short, the truth of the matter was, Nippers knew not what he wanted. Or, if he wanted anything, it was to be rid of a scrivener's table altogether. Among the manifestations of his diseased ambition was a fondness he had for receiving visits from certain ambiguous-looking fellows in seedy coats, whom he called his clients. Indeed, I was aware that not only was he, at times, considerable of a ward-politician, but he occasionally did a little business at the justices' courts, and was not unknown on the steps of the Tombs.[6] I have good reason to

---

[6] A jail in New York city.

believe, however, that one individual who called upon him at my chambers, and who, with a grand air, he insisted was his client, was no other than a dun,[7] and the alleged title-deed, a bill. But, with all his failings, and the annoyances he caused me, Nippers, like his compatriot Turkey, was a very useful man to me; wrote a neat, swift hand; and, when he chose, was not deficient in a gentlemanly sort of deportment. Added to this, he always dressed in a gentlemanly sort of way; and so, incidentally, reflected credit upon my chambers. Whereas, with respect to Turkey, I had much ado to keep him from being a reproach to me. His clothes were apt to look oily, a smell of eating-houses. He wore his pantaloons very loose and baggy in summer. His coats were execrable, his hat not to be handled. But while the hat was a thing of indifference to me, inasmuch as his natural civility and deference, as a dependent Englishman, always led him to doff it the moment he entered the room, yet his coat was another matter. Concerning his coats, I reasoned with him; but with no effect. The truth was, I suppose, that a man with so small an income could not afford to sport such a lustrous face and a lustrous coat at one and the same time. As Nippers once observed, Turkey's money went chiefly for red ink. One winter day, I presented Turkey with a highly respectable-looking coat of my own—a padded gray coat, of a most comfortable warmth, and which buttoned straight up from the knee to the neck. I thought Turkey would appreciate the favor, and abate his rashness and obstreperousness of afternoons. But no; I verily believe that buttoning himself up in so downy and blanket-like a coat had a pernicious effect upon him—upon the same principle that too much oats are bad for horses. In fact, precisely as a rash, restive horse is said to feel his oats, so Turkey felt his coat. It made him insolent. He was a man whom prosperity harmed.

Though, concerning the self-indulgent habits of Turkey, I had my own private surmises, yet, touching Nippers, I was well persuaded that, whatever might be his faults in other respects, he was, at least, a temperate young man. But indeed, nature herself seemed to have been his vintner, and, at his birth, charged him so thoroughly with an irritable, brandy-like disposition, that all subsequent potations were needless. When I consider how, amid the stillness of my chambers, Nippers would sometimes impatiently rise from his seat, and stooping over his table, spread his arms wide apart, seize the whole desk, and move it, and jerk it, with a grim, grinding motion on the floor, as if the table were a perverse voluntary agent, intent on thwarting and vexing him, I plainly perceive that, for Nippers, brandy-and-water were altogether superfluous.

It was fortunate for me that, owing to its peculiar cause—indigestion—the irritability and consequent nervousness of Nippers were mainly observable in the morning, while in the afternoon he was comparatively mild. So that, Turkey's paroxysms only coming on about twelve o'clock, I never had to do with their eccentricities at one time. Their fits relieved

---

[7] Bill collector.

each other, like guards. When Nippers' was on, Turkey's was off; and *vice versa*. This was a good natural arrangement, under the circumstances.

Ginger Nut, the third on my list, was a lad, some twelve years old. His father was a carman, ambitious of seeing his son on the bench instead of a cart, before he died. So he sent him to my office, as student at law, errand-boy, cleaner, and sweeper, at the rate of one dollar a week. He had a little desk to himself, but he did not use it much. Upon inspection, the drawer exhibited a great array of the shells of various sorts of nuts. Indeed, to this quick-witted youth, the whole noble science of the law was contained in a nutshell. Not the least among the employments of Ginger Nut, as well as one which he discharged with the most alacrity, was his duty as cake and apple purveyor for Turkey and Nippers. Copying lawpapers being proverbially a dry, husky sort of business, my two scriveners were fain[8] to moisten their mouths very often with Spitzenbergs,[9] to be had at the numerous stalls nigh the Custom House and Post Office. Also, they sent Ginger Nut very frequently for that peculiar cake—small, flat, round, and very spicy—after which he had been named by them. Of a cold morning, when business was but dull, Turkey would gobble up scores of these cakes, as if they were mere wafers—indeed, they sell them at the rate of six or eight for a penny—the scrape of his pen blending with the crunching of the crisp particles in his mouth. Of all the fiery afternoon blunders and flurried rashness of Turkey, was his once moistening a ginger-cake between his lips, and clapping it on to a mortgage, for a seal. I came within an ace of dismissing him then. But he mollified me by making an oriental bow, and saying—

15 "With submission, sir, it was generous of me to find you in stationery on my own account."

Now my original business—that of a conveyancer and title hunter, and drawer-up of recondite documents of all sorts—was considerably increased by receiving the Master's office. There was now great work for scriveners. Not only must I push the clerks already with me, but I must have additional help.

In answer to my advertisement, a motionless young man one morning stood upon my office threshold, the door being open, for it was summer. I can see that figure now—pallidly neat, pitiably respectable, incurably forlorn! It was Bartleby.

After a few words touching his qualifications, I engaged him, glad to have among my corps of copyists a man of so singularly sedate an aspect, which I thought might operate beneficially upon the flighty temper of Turkey, and the fiery one of Nippers.

I should have stated before that ground-glass folding-doors divided my premises into two parts, one of which was occupied by my scriveners, the other by myself. According to my humor, I threw open these doors, or

---

[8] Inclined, desirous.

[9] New York variety of apple.

closed them. I resolved to assign Bartleby a corner by the folding-doors, but on my side of them, so as to have this quiet man within easy call, in case any trifling thing was to be done. I placed his desk close up to a small side-window in that part of the room, a window which originally had afforded a lateral view of certain grimy brickyards and bricks, but which, owing to subsequent erections, commanded at present no view at all, though it gave some light. Within three feet of the panes was a wall, and the light came down from far above, between two lofty buildings, as from a very small opening in a dome. Still further to a satisfactory arrangement, I procured a high green folding screen, which might entirely isolate Bartleby from my sight, though not remove him from my voice. And thus, in a manner, privacy and society were conjoined.

20   At first, Bartleby did an extraordinary quantity of writing. As if long famishing for something to copy, he seemed to gorge himself on my documents. There was no pause for digestion. He ran a day and night line, copying by sunlight and by candle-light. I should have been quite delighted with his application, had he been cheerfully industrious. But he wrote on silently, palely, mechanically.

    It is, of course, an indispensable part of a scrivener's business to verify the accuracy of his copy, word by word. Where there are two or more scriveners in an office, they assist each other in this examination, one reading from the copy, the other holding the original. It is a very dull, wearisome, and lethargic affair. I can readily imagine that, to some sanguine temperaments, it would be altogether intolerable. For example, I cannot credit that the mettlesome poet, Byron, would have contentedly sat down with Bartleby to examine a law document of, say five hundred pages, closely written in a crimpy hand.

    Now and then, in the haste of business, it had been my habit to assist in comparing some brief document myself, calling Turkey or Nippers for this purpose. One object I had, in placing Bartleby so handy to me behind the screen, was, to avail myself of his services on such trivial occasions. It was on the third day, I think, of his being with me, and before any necessity had arisen for having his own writing examined, that, being much hurried to complete a small affair I had in hand, I abruptly called to Bartleby. In my haste and natural expectancy of instant compliance, I sat with my head bent over the original on my desk, and my right hand sideways, and somewhat nervously extended with the copy, so that, immediately upon emerging from his retreat, Bartleby might snatch it and proceed to business without the least delay.

    In this very attitude did I sit when I called to him, rapidly stating what it was I wanted him to do—namely, to examine a small paper with me. Imagine my surprise, nay, my consternation, when, without moving from his privacy, Bartleby, in a singularly mild, firm voice, replied, "I would prefer not to."

    I sat awhile in perfect silence, rallying my stunned faculties. Immediately it occurred to me that my ears had deceived me, or Bartleby had entirely misunderstood my meaning. I repeated my request in the clearest tone I could assume; but in quite as clear a one came the previous reply, "I would prefer not to."

25   "Prefer not to," echoed I, rising in high excitement, and crossing the room with a stride. "What do you mean? Are you moonstruck? I want you to help me compare this sheet here—take it," and I thrust it towards him.

"I would prefer not to," said he.

I looked at him steadfastly. His face was leanly composed; his gray eye dimly calm. Not a wrinkle of agitation rippled him. Had there been the least uneasiness, anger, impatience, or impertinence in his manner; in other words, had there been anything ordinarily human about him, doubtless I should have violently dismissed him from the premises. But as it was, I should have as soon thought of turning my pale plaster-of-paris bust of Cicero out of doors. I stood gazing at him awhile, as he went on with his own writing, and then reseated myself at my desk. This is very strange, thought I. What had one best do? But my business hurried me. I concluded to forget the matter for the present, reserving it for my future leisure. So, calling Nippers from the other room, the paper was speedily examined.

A few days after this, Bartleby concluded four lengthy documents, being quadruplicates of a week's testimony taken before me in my High Court of Chancery. It became necessary to examine them. It was an important suit, and great accuracy was imperative. Having all things arranged, I called Turkey, Nippers, and Ginger Nut, from the next room, meaning to place the four copies in the hands of my four clerks, while I should read from the original. Accordingly, Turkey, Nippers, and Ginger Nut had taken their seats in a row, each with his document in his hand, when I called to Bartleby to joint this interesting group.

"Bartleby! quick, I am waiting."

30   I heard a slow scrape of his chair legs on the uncarpeted floor, and soon he appeared standing at the entrance of his hermitage.

"What is wanted?" said he, mildly.

"The copies, the copies," said I, hurriedly. "We are going to examine them. There"—and I held towards him the fourth quadruplicate.

"I would prefer not to," he said, and gently disappeared behind the screen.

For a few moments I was turned into a pillar of salt, standing at the head of my seated column of clerks. Recovering myself, I advanced towards the screen, and demanded the reason for such extraordinary conduct.

35   "*Why* do you refuse?"

"I would prefer not to."

With any other man I should have flown outright into a dreadful passion, scorned all further words, and thrust him ignominiously from my presence. But there was something about Bartleby that not only strangely disarmed me, but, in a wonderful manner, touched and disconcerted me. I began to reason with him.

"These are your own copies we are about to examine. It is labor saving to you, because one examination will answer for your four papers. It is common usage. Every copyist is bound to help examine his copy. Is it not so? Will you not speak? Answer!"

"I prefer not to," he replied in a flute-like tone. It seemed to me that, while I had been addressing him, he carefully revolved every statement that I made; fully comprehended the meaning; could not gainsay the irresistible conclusion; but, at the same time, some paramount consideration prevailed with him to reply as he did.

40 "You are decided, then, not to comply with my request—a request made according to common usage and common sense?"

He briefly gave me to understand, that on that point my judgment was sound. Yes: his decision was irreversible.

It is not seldom the case that, when a man is browbeaten in some unprecedented and violently unreasonable way, he begins to stagger in his own plainest faith. He begins, as it were, vaguely to surmise that, wonderful as it may be, all the justice and all the reason is on the other side. Accordingly, if any disinterested persons are present, he turns to them for some reinforcement for his own faltering mind.

"Turkey," said I, "what do you think of this? Am I not right?"

"With submission, sir," said Turkey, in his blandest tone, "I think that you are."

45 "Nippers," said I, "what do *you* think of it?"

"I think I should kick him out of the office."

(The reader of nice perceptions will have perceived that, it being morning, Turkey's answer is couched in polite and tranquil terms, but Nippers replies in ill-tempered ones. Or, to repeat a previous sentence, Nippers' ugly mood was on duty, and Turkey's off.)

"Ginger Nut," said I, willing to enlist the smallest suffrage in my behalf, "what do *you* think of it?"

"I think, sir, he's a little *luny,*" replied Ginger Nut, with a grin.

50 "You hear what they say," said I, turning towards the screen, "come forth and do your duty."

But he vouchsafed no reply. I pondered a moment in sore perplexity. But once more business hurried me. I determined again to postpone the consideration of this dilemma to my future leisure. With a little trouble we made out to examine the papers without Bartleby, though at every page or two Turkey deferentially dropped his opinion, that this proceeding was quite out of the common; while Nippers, twitching in his chair with a dyspeptic nervousness, ground out, between his set teeth, occasional hissing maledictions against the stubborn oaf behind the screen. And for his (Nippers') part, this was the first and the last time he would do another man's business without pay.

Meanwhile Bartleby sat in his hermitage, oblivious to everything but his own peculiar business there.

Some days passed, the scrivener being employed upon another lengthy work. His late remarkable conduct led me to regard his ways narrowly. I observed that he never went to dinner; indeed, that he never went anywhere. As yet I had never, of my personal knowledge, known him to be outside of my office. He was a perpetual sentry in the corner. At about eleven o'clock though, in the morning, I noticed that Ginger Nut would advance toward the opening in Bartleby's screen, as if silently beckoned thither by a gesture invisible to me where I sat. The boy would then leave the office, jingling a few pence, and reappear with a handful of gingernuts, which he delivered in the hermitage, receiving two of the cakes for his trouble.

He lives, then, on ginger-nuts, thought I; never eats a dinner, properly speaking; he must be a vegetarian, then, but no; he never eats even vegetables, he eats nothing but ginger-nuts. My mind then ran on in reveries concerning the probable effects upon the human constitution of living entirely on ginger-nuts. Ginger-nuts are so called, because they contain ginger as one of their peculiar constituents, and the final flavoring one. Now, what was ginger? A hot, spicy thing. Was Bartleby hot and spicy? Not at all. Ginger, then, had no effect upon Bartleby. Probably he preferred it should have none.

55   Nothing so aggravates an earnest person as a passive resistance. If the individual so resisted be of a not inhumane temper, and the resisting one perfectly harmless in his passivity, then, in the better moods of the former, he will endeavor charitably to construe to his imagination what proves impossible to be solved by his judgment. Even so, for the most part, I regarded Bartleby and his ways. Poor fellow! thought I, he means no mischief; it is plain he intends no insolence; his aspect sufficiently evinces that his eccentricities are involuntary. He is useful to me. I can get along with him. If I turn him away, the chances are he will fall in with some less indulgent employer, and then he will be rudely treated, and perhaps driven forth miserably to starve. Yes. Here I can cheaply purchase a delicious self-approval. To befriend Bartleby; to humor him in his strange wilfulness, will cost me little or nothing, while I lay up in my soul what will eventually prove a sweet morsel for my conscience. But this mood was not invariable with me. The passiveness of Bartleby sometimes irritated me. I felt strangely goaded on to encounter him in new opposition—to elicit some angry spark from him answerable to my own. But, indeed, I might as well have essayed to strike fire with my knuckles against a bit of Windsor soap. But one afternoon the evil impulse in me mastered me, and the following little scene ensued:

"Bartleby," said I, "when those papers are all copied, I will compare them with you."

"I would prefer not to."

"How? Surely you do not mean to persist in that mulish vagary?"

No answer.

60   I threw open the folding-doors nearby, and turning upon Turkey and Nippers, exclaimed:

"Bartleby a second time says, he won't examine his papers. What do you think of it, Turkey?"

It was afternoon, be it remembered. Turkey sat glowing like a brass boiler; his bald head steaming; his hands reeling among his blotted papers.

"Think of it?" roared Turkey. "I think I'll just step behind his screen, and black his eyes for him!"

So saying, Turkey rose to his feet and threw his arms into a pugilistic position. He was hurrying away to make good his promise, when I detained him, alarmed at the effect of incautiously rousing Turkey's combativeness after dinner.

65 "Sit down, Turkey," said I, "and hear what Nippers has to say. What do you think of it, Nippers? Would I not be justified in immediately dismissing Bartleby?"

"Excuse me, that is for you to decide, sir. I think his conduct quite unusual, and, indeed, unjust, as regards Turkey and myself. But it may only be a passing whim."

"Ah," exclaimed I, "you have strangely changed your mind, then—you speak very gently of him now."

"All beer," cried Turkey; "gentleness is effects of beer—Nippers and I dined together to-day. You see how gentle *I* am, sir. Shall I go and black his eyes?"

"You refer to Bartleby, I suppose. No, not to-day, Turkey," I replied; "pray, put up your fists."

70 I closed the doors, and again advanced towards Bartleby. I felt additional incentives tempting me to my fate. I burned to be rebelled against again. I remembered that Bartleby never left the office.

"Bartleby," said I, "Ginger Nut is away; just step around to the Post Office, won't you?" (it was but a three minutes' walk) "and see if there is anything for me."

"I would prefer not to."

"You *will* not?"

"I *prefer* not."

75 I staggered to my desk, and sat there in a deep study. My blind inveteracy returned. Was there any other thing in which I could procure myself to be ignominiously repulsed by this lean, penniless wight?—my hired clerk? What added thing is there, perfectly reasonable, that he will be sure to refuse to do?

"Bartleby!"

No answer.

"Bartleby," in a louder tone.

No answer.

80 "Bartleby," I roared.

Like a very ghost, agreeably to the laws of magical invocation, at the third summons, he appeared at the entrance of his hermitage.

"Go to the next room, and tell Nippers to come to me."

"I prefer not to," he respectfully and slowly said, and mildly disappeared.

"Very good, Bartleby," said I, in a quiet sort of serenely-severe self-possessed tone, intimating the unalterable purpose of some terrible retribution very close at hand. At the moment I half intended something of the kind. But upon the whole, as it was drawing towards my dinner-hour, I thought it best to put on my hat and walk home for the day, suffering much from perplexity and distress of mind.

85   Shall I acknowledge it? The conclusion of this whole business was, that it soon became a fixed fact of my chambers, that a pale young scrivener, by the name of Bartleby, had a desk there; that he copied for me at the usual rate of four cents a folio (one hundred words); but he was permanently exempt from examining the work done by him, that duty being transferred to Turkey and Nippers, out of compliment, doubtless, to their superior acuteness; moreover, said Bartleby was never, on any account, to be dispatched on the most trivial errand of any sort; and that even if entreated to take upon him such a matter, it was generally understood that he would "prefer not to"—in other words, that he would refuse point-blank.

As days passed on, I became considerably reconciled to Bartleby. His steadiness, his freedom from all dissipation, his incessant industry (except when he chose to throw himself into a standing revery behind his screen), his great stillness, his unalterableness of demeanor under all circumstances, made him a valuable acquisition. One prime thing was this—*he was always there*—first in the morning, continually through the day, and the last at night. I had a singular confidence in his honesty. I felt my most precious papers perfectly safe in his hands. Sometimes, to be sure, I could not, for the very soul of me, avoid falling into sudden spasmodic passions with him. For it was exceeding difficult to bear in mind all the time those strange peculiarities, privileges, and unheard-of exemptions, forming the tacit stipulations on Bartleby's part under which he remained in my office. Now and then, in the eagerness of dispatching pressing business, I would inadvertently summon Bartleby, in a short, rapid tone, to put his finger, say, on the incipient tie of a bit of red tape with which I was about compressing some papers. Of course, from behind the screen the usual answer, "I prefer not to," was sure to come; and then, how could a human creature, with the common infirmities of our nature, refrain from bitterly exclaiming upon such perverseness—such unreasonableness? However, every added repulse of this sort which I received only tended to lessen the probability of my repeating the inadvertence.

Here it must be said, that, according to the custom of most legal gentlemen occupying chambers in densely populated law buildings, there were several keys to my door. One was kept by a woman residing in the attic, which person weekly scrubbed and daily swept and dusted my apartments. Another was kept by Turkey for convenience sake. The third I sometimes carried in my own pocket. The fourth I knew not who had.

Now, one Sunday morning I happened to go to Trinity Church, to hear a celebrated preacher, and finding myself rather early on the ground I thought I would walk round to my chambers for a while. Luckily I had my key with me; but upon applying it to the lock, I found it resisted by something inserted from the inside. Quite surprised, I called out; when to my consternation a key was turned from within; and thrusting his lean visage at me, and holding the door ajar, the apparition of Bartleby appeared, in his shirt-sleeves, and otherwise in a strangely tattered *deshabille*,[10] saying quietly that he was sorry, but he was deeply engaged just then, and—preferred not admitting me at present. In a brief word or two, he moreover added, that perhaps I had better walk round the block two or three times, and by that time he would probably have concluded his affairs.

Now, the utterly unsurmised appearance of Bartleby, tenanting my law-chambers of a Sunday morning, with his cadaverously gentlemanly *nonchalance,* yet withal firm and self-possessed, had such a strange effect upon me, that incontinently I slunk away from my own door, and did as desired. But not without sundry twinges of impotent rebellion against the mild effrontery of this unaccountable scrivener. Indeed, it was his wonderful mildness chiefly, which not only disarmed me, but unmanned me, as it were. For I consider that one, for the time, is sort of unmanned when he tranquilly permits his hired clerk to dictate to him, and order him away from his own premises. Furthermore, I was full of uneasiness as to what Bartleby could possibly be doing in my office in his shirt-sleeves, and in an otherwise dismantled condition of a Sunday morning. Was anything amiss going on? Nay, that was out of the question. It was not to be thought of for a moment that Bartleby was an immoral person. But what could he be doing there?—copying? Nay again, whatever might be his eccentricities, Bartleby was an eminently decorous person. He would be the last man to sit down to his desk in any state approaching to nudity. Besides, it was Sunday; and there was something about Bartleby that forbade the supposition that he would by any secular occupation violate the proprieties of the day.

90   Nevertheless, my mind was not pacified; and full of a restless curiosity, at last I returned to the door. Without hindrance I inserted my key, opened it, and entered. Bartleby was not to be seen. I looked round anxiously, peeped behind his screen; but it was very plain that he was gone. Upon more closely examining the place, I surmised that for an indefinite period Bartleby must have ate, dressed, and slept in my office, and that too without plate, mirror, or bed. The cushioned seat of a rickety old sofa in one corner bore the faint impress of a lean, reclining form. Rolled away under his desk, I found a blanket; under the empty grate, a blacking box and brush; on a chair, a tin basin, with soap and a ragged towel; in a newspaper a few crumbs of ginger-nuts and a morsel of cheese. Yes, thought I, it is evident enough that Bartleby has been making his home here, keeping bachelor's hall all by himself. Immediately then the thought came sweeping across me, what miserable friendlessness and loneliness are here revealed! His poverty is great; but his solitude, how horrible! Think of it. Of

---

[10] Careless dress.

a Sunday, Wall Street is deserted as Petra;[11] and every night of every day it is an emptiness. This building, too, which of week-days hums with industry and life, at nightfall echoes with sheer vacancy, and all through Sunday is forlorn. And here Bartleby makes his home; sole spectator of a solitude which he has seen all populous—a sort of innocent and transformed Marius brooding among the ruins of Carthage?[12]

For the first time in my life a feeling of overpowering stinging melancholy seized me. Before, I had never experienced aught but a not unpleasing sadness. The bond of a common humanity now drew me irresistibly to gloom. A fraternal melancholy! For both I and Bartleby were sons of Adam. I remembered the bright silks and sparkling faces I had seen that day, in gala trim, swan-like sailing down the Mississippi of Broadway; and I contrasted them with the pallid copyist, and thought to myself, Ah, happiness courts the light, so we deem the world is gay; but misery hides aloof, so we deem that misery there is none. These sad fancyings—chimeras, doubtless, of a sick and silly brain—led on to other and more special thoughts, concerning the eccentricities of Bartleby. Presentiments of strange discoveries hovered round me. The scrivener's pale form appeared to me laid out, among uncaring strangers, in its shivering winding-sheet.

Suddenly I was attracted by Bartleby's closed desk, the key in open sight left in the lock.

I mean no mischief, seek the gratification of no heartless curiosity, thought I; besides, the desk is mine, and its contents, too, so I will make bold to look within. Everything was methodically arranged, the papers smoothly placed. The pigeon-holes were deep, and removing the files of documents, I groped into their recesses. Presently I felt something there, and dragged it out. It was an old bandanna handkerchief, heavy and knotted. I opened it, and saw it was a saving's bank.

I now recalled all the quiet mysteries which I had noted in the man. I remembered that he never spoke but to answer; that, though at intervals he had considerable time to himself, yet I had never seen him reading— no, not even a newspaper; that for long periods he would stand looking out, at his pale window behind the screen, upon the dead brick wall; I was quite sure he never visited any refectory or eating-house; while his pale face clearly indicated that he never drank beer like Turkey; or tea and coffee even, like other men; that he never went anywhere in particular that I could learn; never went out for a walk, unless, indeed, that was the case at present; that he had declined telling who he was, or whence he came, or whether he had any relatives in the world; that though so thin and pale, he never complained of ill-health. And more than all, I remembered a certain

---

[11] Ancient ruined city of northwest Arabia, once capital of the Edomites and Nabataeans.

[12] Gaius Marius (157–86 B.C.) was a Roman general who sought refuge in the city of Carthage after he was exiled. The Romans later destroyed Carthage.

unconscious air of pallid—how shall I call it?—of pallid haughtiness, say, or rather an austere reserve about him, which had positively awed me into my tame compliance with his eccentricities, when I had feared to ask him to do the slightest incidental thing for me, even though I might know, from his long-continued motionlessness, that behind his screen he must be standing in one of those dead-wall reveries of his.

95   Revolving all these things, and coupling them with the recently discovered fact, that he made my office his constant abiding place and home, and not forgetful of his morbid moodiness; revolving all these things, a prudential feeling began to steal over me. My first emotions had been those of pure melancholy and sincerest pity; but just in proportion as the forlornness of Bartleby grew and grew to my imagination, did that same melancholy merge into fear, that pity into repulsion. So true it is, and so terrible, too, that up to a certain point the thought or sight of misery enlists our best affections; but, in certain special cases, beyond that point it does not. They err who would assert that invariably this is owing to the inherent selfishness of the human heart. It rather proceeds from a certain hopelessness of remedying excessive and organic ill. To a sensitive being, pity is not seldom pain. And when at last it is perceived that such pity cannot lead to effectual succor, common sense bids the soul be rid of it. What I saw that morning persuaded me that the scrivener was the victim of innate and incurable disorder. I might give alms to his body; but his body did not pain him; it was his soul that suffered, and his soul I could not reach.

    I did not accomplish the purpose of going to Trinity Church that morning. Somehow, the things I had seen disqualified me for the time from churchgoing. I walked homeward, thinking what I would do with Bartleby. Finally, I resolved upon this—I would put certain calm questions to him the next morning, touching his history, etc., and if he declined to answer them openly and unreservedly (and I supposed he would prefer not), then to give him a twenty dollar bill over and above whatever I might owe him, and tell him his services were no longer required; but that if in any other way I could assist him, I would be happy to do so, especially if he desired to return to his native place, wherever that might be, I would willingly help to defray the expenses. Moreover, if, after reaching home, he found himself at any time in want of aid, a letter from him would be sure of a reply.

    The next morning came.

    "Bartleby," said I, gently calling to him behind his screen.

    No reply.

100   "Bartleby," said I, in a still gentler tone, "come here; I am not going to ask you to do anything you would prefer not to do—I simply wish to speak to you."

    Upon this he noiselessly slid into view.

    "Will you tell me, Bartleby, where you were born?"

    "I would prefer not to."

"Will you tell me *anything* about yourself?"

105   "I would prefer not to."

"But what reasonable objection can you have to speak to me? I feel friendly towards you."

He did not look at me while I spoke, but kept his glance fixed upon my bust of Cicero, which, as I then sat, was directly behind me, some six inches above my head.

"What is your answer, Bartleby?" said I, after waiting a considerable time for a reply, during which his countenance remained immovable, only there was the faintest conceivable tremor of the white attenuated mouth.

"At present I prefer to give no answer," he said, and retired into his hermitage.

110   It was rather weak in me I confess, but his manner, on this occasion, nettled me. Not only did there seem to lurk in it a certain calm disdain, but his perverseness seemed ungrateful, considering the undeniable good usage and indulgence he had received from me.

Again I sat ruminating what I should do. Mortified as I was at his behavior, and resolved as I had been to dismiss him when I entered my office, nevertheless I strangely felt something superstitious knocking at my heart, and forbidding me to carry out my purpose, and denouncing me for a villain if I dared to breathe one bitter word against this forlornest of mankind. At last, familiarly drawing my chair behind his screen, I sat down and said: "Bartleby, never mind, then, about revealing your history; but let me entreat you, as a friend, to comply as far as may be with the usages of this office. Say now, you will help to examine papers tomorrow or next day: in short, say now, that in a day or two you will begin to be a little reasonable:—say so, Bartleby."

"At present I would prefer not to be a little reasonable," was his mildly cadaverous reply.

Just then the folding-doors opened, and Nippers approached. He seemed suffering from an unusually bad night's rest, induced by severer indigestion than common. He overheard those final words of Bartleby.

"*Prefer not*, eh?" gritted Nippers—"I'd *prefer* him, if I were you, sir," addressing me—"I'd *prefer* him; I'd give him preferences, the stubborn mule! What is it, sir, pray, that he *prefers* not to do now?"

115   Bartleby moved not a limb.

"Mr. Nippers," said I, "I'd prefer that you would withdraw for the present."

Somehow, of late, I had got into the way of involuntarily using this word "prefer" upon all sorts of not exactly suitable occasions. And I trembled to think that my contact with the scrivener had already and seriously affected me in a mental way. And what further and deeper aberration might is not yet produce? This apprehension had not been without efficacy in determining me to summary measures.

As Nippers, looking very sour and sulky, was departing, Turkey blandly and deferentially approached.

"With submission, sir," said he, "yesterday I was thinking about Bartleby here, and I think that if he would but prefer to take a quart of good ale every day, it would do much towards mending him, and enabling him to assist in examining his papers."

120 "So you have got the word, too," said I, slightly excited.

"With submission, what word, sir?" asked Turkey, respectfully crowding himself into the contracted space behind the screen, and by so doing, making me jostle the scrivener. "What word, sir?"

"I would prefer to be left alone here," said Bartleby, as if offended at being mobbed in his privacy.

"*That's* the word, Turkey," said I—*that's* it."

"Oh, *prefer?* of yes—queer word. I never use it myself. But, sir, as I was saying, if he would but prefer—"

125 "Turkey," interrupted I, "you will please withdraw."

"Oh certainly, sir, if you prefer that I should."

As he opened the folding door to retire, Nippers at his desk caught a glimpse of me, and asked whether I would prefer to have a certain paper copied on blue paper or white. He did not in the least roguishly accent the word "prefer." It was plain that it involuntarily rolled from his tongue. I thought to myself, surely I must get rid of a demented man, who already has in some degree turned the tongues, if not the heads of myself and clerks. But I thought it prudent not to break the dismission at once.

The next day I noticed that Bartleby did nothing but stand at his window in his dead-wall revery. Upon asking him why he did not write, he said that he had decided upon doing no more writing.

"Why, how now? what next?" exclaimed I, "do no more writing?"

130 "No more."

"And what is the reason?"

"Do you not see the reason for yourself?" he indifferently replied.

I looked steadfastly at him, and perceived that his eyes looked dull and glazed. Instantly it occurred to me, that his unexampled diligence in copying by his dim window for the first few weeks of his stay with me might have temporarily impaired his vision.

I was touched. I said something in condolence with him. I hinted that of course he did wisely in abstaining from writing for a while; and urged him to embrace that opportunity of taking wholesome exercise in the open air. This, however, he did not do. A few days after this, my other clerks being absent, and being in a great hurry to dispatch certain letters by the mail, I thought that, having nothing else earthly to do, Bartleby would surely be less inflexible than usual, and carry these letters to the Post Office. But he blankly declined. So, much to my inconvenience, I went myself.

125 Still added days went by. Whether Bartleby's eyes improved or not, I could not say. To all appearance, I thought they did. But when I asked him if they did, he vouchsafed no answer. At all events, he would do no copying.

At last, in replying to my urgings, he informed me that he had permanently given up copying.

"What!" exclaimed I; "suppose your eyes should get entirely well—better than ever before—would you not copy then?"

"I have given up copying," he answered, and slid aside.

He remained as ever, a fixture in my chamber. Nay—if that were possible—he became still more of a fixture than before. What was to be done? He would do nothing in the office; why should he stay there? In plain fact, he had now become a millstone to me, not only useless as a necklace, but afflictive to bear. Yet I was sorry for him. I speak less than truth when I say that, on his own account, he occasioned me uneasiness. If he would but have earned a single relative or friend, I would instantly have written, and urged their taking the poor fellow away to some convenient retreat. But he seemed alone, absolutely alone in the universe. A bit of wreck in the mid-Atlantic. At length, necessities connected with my business tyrannized over all other considerations. Decently as I could, I told Bartleby that in six days' time he must unconditionally leave the office. I warned him to take measures, in the interval, for procuring some other abode. I offered to assist him in this endeavor, if he himself would but take the first step towards a removal. "And when you finally quit me, Bartleby," added I, "I shall see that you go not away entirely unprovided. Six days from this hour, remember."

At the expiration of that period, I peeped behind the screen, and lo! Bartleby was there.

140 I buttoned up my coat, balanced myself; advanced slowly towards him, touched his shoulder, and said, "The time has come; you must quit this place; I am sorry for you; here is money; but you must go."

"I would prefer not," he replied, with his back still towards me.

"You *must.*"

He remained silent.

Now I had an unbounded confidence in this man's common honesty. He had frequently restored to me sixpences and shillings carelessly dropped upon the floor, for I am apt to be very reckless in such shirt-button affairs. The proceeding, then, which followed will not be deemed extraordinary.

145 "Bartleby," said I, "I owe you twelve dollars on account; here are thirty-two, the odd twenty are yours—Will you take it?" and I handed the bills towards him.

But he made no motion.

"I will leave them here, then," putting them under a weight on the table. Then taking my hat and cane and going to the door, I tranquilly turned and added—"After you have removed your things from these offices, Bartleby, you will of course lock the door—since every one is now gone for the day but you—and if you please, slip your key underneath the mat, so that I may have it in the morning. I shall not see you again; so good-bye to you. If, hereafter, in your new place of abode, I can be of any service to you, do not fail to advise me by letter. Good-bye, Bartleby, and fare you well."

But he answered not a word; like the last column of some ruined temple, he remained standing mute and solitary in the middle of the otherwise deserted room.

As I walked home in a pensive mood, my vanity got the better of my pity. I could not but highly plume myself on my masterly management in getting rid of Bartleby. Masterly I call it, and such it must appear to any dispassionate thinker. The beauty of my procedure seemed to consist in its perfect quietness. There was no vulgar bullying, no bravado of any sort, no choleric hectoring, and striding to and fro across the apartment, jerking out vehement commands for Bartleby to bundle himself off with his beggarly traps. Nothing of the kind. Without loudly bidding Bartleby depart—as an inferior genius might have done—I *assumed* the ground that depart he must; and upon that assumption built all I had to say. The more I thought over my procedure, the more I was charmed with it. Nevertheless, next morning, upon awakening, I had my doubts—I had somehow slept off the fumes of vanity. One of the coolest and wisest hours a man has, is just after he awakes in the morning. My procedure seemed as sagacious as ever—but only in theory. How it would prove in practice—there was the rub. It was truly a beautiful thought to have assumed Bartleby's departure; but, after all, that assumption was simply my own, and none of Bartleby's. The great point was, not whether I had assumed that he would quit me, but whether he would prefer to do so. He was more a man of preferences than assumptions.

150   After breakfast, I walked down town, arguing the probabilities *pro* and *con*. One moment I thought it would prove a miserable failure, and Bartleby would be found all alive at my office as usual; the next moment it seemed certain that I should find his chair empty. And so I kept veering about. At the corner of Broadway and Canal Street, I saw quite an excited group of people standing in earnest conversation.

"I'll take odds he doesn't," said a voice as I passed.

"Doesn't go?—done!" said I, "put up your money."

I was instinctively putting my hand in my pocket to produce my own, when I remembered that this was an election day. The words I had overheard bore no reference to Bartleby, but to the success or non-success of some candidate for the mayoralty. In my intent frame of mind, I had, as it were, imagined that all Broadway shared in my excitement, and were debating the same question with me. I passed on, very thankful that the uproar of the street screened my momentary absent-mindedness.

As I had intended, I was earlier than usual at my office door. I stood listening for a moment. All was still. He must be gone. I tried the knob. The door was locked. Yes, my procedure had worked to a charm; he indeed must be vanished. Yet a certain melancholy mixed with this: I was almost sorry for my brilliant success. I was fumbling under the door mat for the key, which Bartleby was to have left there for me, when accidentally my knee knocked against a panel, producing a summoning sound, and in response a voice came to me from within—"Not yet; I am occupied."

155   It was Bartleby.

I was thunderstruck. For an instant I stood like the man who, pipe in mouth, was killed one cloudless afternoon long ago in Virginia, by summer lightning; at his own warm open window he was killed, and remained leaning out there upon the dreamy afternoon, till some one touched him, when he fell.

"Not gone!" I murmured at last. But again obeying that wondrous ascendancy which the inscrutable scrivener had over me, and from which ascendancy, for all my chafing, I could not completely escape, I slowly went down stairs and out into the street, and while walking round the block, considered what I should next do in this unheard-of perplexity. Turn the man out by an actual thrusting I could not; to drive him away by calling him hard names would not do; calling in the police was an unpleasant idea; and yet, permit him to enjoy his cadaverous triumph over me—this, too, I could not think of. What was to be done? or, if nothing could be done, was there anything further that I could *assume* in the matter? Yes, as before I had prospectively assumed that Bartleby would depart, so now I might retrospectively assume that departed he was. In the legitimate carrying out of this assumption, I might enter my office in a great hurry, and pretending not to see Bartleby at all, walk straight against him as if he were air. Such a proceeding would in a singular degree have the appearance of a home-thrust. It was hardly possible that Bartleby could withstand such an application of the doctrine of assumption. But upon second thoughts the success of the plan seemed rather dubious. I resolved to argue the matter over with him again.

"Bartleby," said I, entering the office, with a quietly severe expression, "I am seriously displeased. I am pained, Bartleby. I had thought better of you. I had imagined you of such a gentlemanly organization, that in any delicate dilemma a slight hint would suffice—in short, an assumption. But it appears I am deceived. Why," I added, unaffectedly starting, "you have not even touched that money yet," pointing to it, just where I had left it the evening previous.

He answered nothing.

160   "Will you, or will you not, quit me?" I now demanded in a sudden passion, advancing close to him.

"I would prefer *not* to quit you," he replied, gently emphasizing the *not*.

"What earthly right have you to stay here? Do you pay any rent? Do you pay my taxes? Or is this property yours?"

He answered nothing.

"Are you ready to go on and write now? Are your eyes recovered? Could you copy a small paper for me this morning? or help examine a few lines? or step round to the Post Office? In a word, will you do anything at all, to give a coloring to your refusal to depart the premises?"

165   He silently retired into his hermitage.

    I was now in such a state of nervous resentment that I thought it but prudent to check myself at present from further demonstrations. Bartleby and I were alone. I remembered the tragedy of the unfortunate Adams and the still more unfortunate Colt[13] in the solitary office of the latter; and how poor Colt, being dreadfully incensed by Adams, and imprudently permitting himself to get wildly excited, was at unawares hurried into his fatal act—an act which certainly no man could possibly deplore more than the actor himself. Often it had occurred to me in my ponderings upon the subject that had that altercation taken place in the public street, or at a private residence, it would not have terminated as it did. It was the circumstance of being alone in a solitary office, up stairs, of a building entirely unhallowed by humanizing domestic associations—an uncarpeted floor, doubtless, of a dusty, haggard sort of appearance—this it must have been, which greatly helped to enhance the irritable desperation of the hapless Colt.

    But when this old Adam of resentment rose in me and tempted me concerning Bartleby, I grappled him and threw him. How? Why, simply by recalling the divine injunction: "A new commandment give I unto you, that ye love one another." Yes, this it was that saved me. Aside from higher considerations, charity often operates as a vastly wise and prudent principle—a great safeguard to its possessor. Men have committed murder for jealousy's sake, and anger's sake, and hatred's sake, and selfishness' sake, and spiritual pride's sake; but no man, that ever I heard of, ever committed a diabolical murder for sweet charity's sake. Mere self-interest, then, if no better motive can be enlisted, should, especially with high-tempered men, prompt all beings to charity and philanthropy. At any rate, upon the occasion in question, I strove to drown my exasperated feelings towards the scrivener by benevolently construing his conduct. Poor fellow, poor fellow! thought I, he don't mean anything; and besides, he has seen hard times, and ought to be indulged.

    I endeavored, also, immediately to occupy myself, and at the same time to comfort my despondency. I tried to fancy, that in the course of the morning, at such time as might prove agreeable to him, Bartleby, of his own free accord, would emerge from his hermitage and take up some decided line of march in the direction of the door. But no. Half-past twelve o'clock came; Turkey began to glow in the face, overturn his inkstand, and become generally obstreperous; Nippers abated down into quietude and courtesy; Ginger Nut munched his noon apple; and Bartleby remained standing at his window in one of his profoundest dead-wall reveries. Will it be credited? Ought I to acknowledge it? That afternoon I left the office without saying one further word to him.

---

[13] During a fight in 1842, Samuel Adams was killed by John C. Colt, brother of the Colt gun maker. Colt was tried and sentenced to hang, but he committed suicide just before the sentence was to be carried out.

Some days now passed, during which, at leisure intervals I looked a little into "Edwards on the Will," and "Priestley on Necessity."[14] Under the circumstances, those books induced a salutary feeling. Gradually I slid into the persuasion that these troubles of mine, touching the scrivener, had been all predestined from eternity, and Bartleby was billeted upon me for some mysterious purpose of an all-wise Providence, which it was not for a mere mortal like me to fathom. Yes, Bartleby, stay there behind your screen, thought I; I shall persecute you no more; you are harmless and noiseless as any of these old chairs; in short, I never feel so private as when I know you are here. At last I see it, I feel it; I penetrate to the predestined purpose of my life. I am content. Others may have loftier parts to enact; but my mission in this world, Bartleby, is to furnish you with office-room for such period as you may see fit to remain.

170   I believe that this wise and blessed frame of mind would have continued with me, had it not been for the unsolicited and uncharitable remarks obtruded upon me by my professional friends who visited the rooms. But thus it often is, that the constant friction of illiberal minds wears out at last the best resolves of the more generous. Though to be sure, when I reflected upon it, it was not strange that people entering my office should be struck by the peculiar aspect of the unaccountable Bartleby, and so be tempted to throw out some sinister observations concerning him. Sometimes an attorney, having business with me, and calling at my office, and finding no one but the scrivener there, would undertake to obtain some sort of precise information from him touching my whereabouts; but without heeding his idle talk, Bartleby would remain standing immovable in the middle of the room. So after contemplating him in that position for a time, the attorney would depart, no wiser than he came.

Also, when a reference was going on, and the room full of lawyers and witnesses, and business driving fast, some deeply-occupied legal gentleman present, seeing Bartleby wholly unemployed, would request him to run around to his (the legal gentleman's) office and fetch some papers for him. Thereupon, Bartleby would tranquilly decline, and yet remain idle as before. Then the lawyer would give a great stare, and turn to me. And what could I say? At last I was made aware that all through the circle of my professional acquaintance, a whisper of wonder was running round, having reference to the strange creature I kept at my office. This worried me very much. And as the idea came upon me of his possibly turning out a long-lived man, and keeping occupying my chambers, and denying my authority; and perplexing my visitors; and scandalizing my professional reputation; and casting a general gloom over the premises; keeping soul and body together to the last upon his savings (for doubtless he spent but half a dime a day), and in the end perhaps outlive me, and claim possession of

---

[14] Philosophical treatises of the time that argued the absence of free will—Jonathan Edwards's *Freedom of Will* (1754) and Joseph Priestley's *Doctrine of Philosophical Necessity* (1777).

my office by right of his perpetual occupancy: as all these dark anticipations crowded upon me more and more, and my friends continually intruded their relentless remarks upon the apparition in my room; a great change was wrought in me. I resolved to gather all my faculties together, and forever rid me of this intolerable incubus.

Ere revolving any complicated project, however, adapted to this end, I first simply suggested to Bartleby the propriety of his permanent departure. In a calm and serious tone, I commended the idea to his careful and mature consideration. But, having taken three days to meditate upon it, he apprised me, that his original determination remained the same; in short, that he still preferred to abide with me.

What shall I do? I now said to myself, buttoning up my coat to the last button. What shall I do? what ought I to do? what does conscience say I *should* do with this man, or, rather, ghost. Rid myself of him, I must; go, he shall. But how? You will not thrust him, the poor, pale, passive mortal—you will not thrust such a helpless creature out of your door? you will not dishonor yourself by such cruelty? No, I will not, I cannot do that. Rather would I let him live and die here, and then mason up his remains in the wall. What, then, will you do? For all your coaxing, he will not budge. Bribes he leaves under your own paper-weight on your table; in short, it is quite plain that he prefers to cling to you.

Then something severe, something unusual must be done. What! surely you will not have him collared by a constable, and commit his innocent pallor to the common jail? And upon what ground could you procure such a thing to be done?—a vagrant, is he? What! he a vagrant, a wanderer, who refuses to budge? It is because he will *not* be a vagrant, then, that you seek to count him *as* a vagrant. That is too absurd. No visible means of support: there I have him. Wrong again: for indubitably he *does* support himself, and that is the only unanswerable proof that any man can show of his possessing the means so to do. No more, then. Since he will not quit me, I must quit him. I will change my offices; I will move elsewhere, and give him fair notice, that if I find him on my new premises I will then proceed against him as a common trespasser.

175   Acting accordingly, next day I thus addressed him: "I find these chambers too far from the City Hall; the air is unwholesome. In a word, I propose to remove my offices next week, and shall no longer require your services. I tell you this now, in order that you may seek another place."

He made no reply, and nothing more was said.

On the appointed day I engaged carts and men, proceeded to my chambers, and having but little furniture, everything was removed in a few hours. Throughout, the scrivener remained standing behind the screen, which I directed to be removed the last thing. It was withdrawn; and, being folded up like a huge folio, left him the motionless occupant of a naked room. I stood in the entry watching him a moment, while something from within me upbraided me.

I re-entered, with my hand in my pocket—and—and my heart in my mouth.

"Good-bye, Bartleby; I am going—good-bye, and God some way bless you; and take that," slipping something in his hand. But it dropped upon the floor, and then—strange to say—I tore myself from him whom I had so longed to be rid of.

180   Established in my new quarters, for a day or two I kept the door locked, and started at every footfall in the passages. When I returned to my rooms, after any little absence, I would pause at the threshold for an instant, and attentively listen, ere applying my key. But these fears were needless. Bartleby never came nigh me.

I thought all was going well, when a perturbed-looking stranger visited me, inquiring whether I was the person who had recently occupied rooms at No.—Wall Street.

Full of forebodings, I replied that I was.

"Then, sir," said the stranger, who proved a lawyer, "you are responsible for the man you left there. He refuses to do any copying; he refuses to do anything; he says he prefers not to; and he refuses to quit the premises."

"I am very sorry, sir," said I, with assumed tranquillity, but an inward tremor, "but, really, the man you allude to is nothing to me—he is no relation or apprentice of mine, that you should hold me responsible for him."

185   "In mercy's name, who is he?"

"I certainly cannot inform you. I know nothing about him. Formerly I employed him as a copyist; but he has done nothing for me now for some time past."

"I shall settle him, then—good morning, sir."

Several days passed, and I heard nothing more; and, though I often felt a charitable prompting to call at the place and see poor Bartleby, yet a certain squeamishness, of I know not what, withheld me.

All is over with him, by this time, thought I, at last, when, through another week, no further intelligence reached me. But, coming to my room the day after, I found several persons waiting at my door in a high state of nervous excitement.

190   "That's the man—here he comes," cried the foremost one, whom I recognized as the lawyer who had previously called upon me alone.

"You must take him away, sir, at once," cried a portly person among them, advancing upon me, and whom I knew to be the landlord of No.—Wall Street. "These gentlemen, my tenants, cannot stand it any longer; Mr. B——," pointing to the lawyer, "has turned him out of his room, and he now persists in haunting the building generally, sitting upon the banisters of the stairs by day, and sleeping in the entry by night. Everybody is concerned; clients are leaving the offices; some fears are entertained of a mob; something you must do, and that without delay."

Aghast at this torrent, I fell back before it, and would fain have locked myself in my new quarters. In vain I persisted that Bartleby was nothing to me—no more than to any one else. In vain—I was the last person known to have anything to do with him, and they held me to the terrible account. Fearful, then, of being exposed in the papers (as one person present obscurely threatened), I considered the matter, and, at length, said, that if the lawyer would give me a confidential interview with the scrivener, in his (the lawyer's) own room, I would, that afternoon, strive my best to rid them of the nuisance they complained of.

Going up stairs to my old haunt, there was Bartleby silently sitting upon the banister at the landing.

"What are you doing here, Bartleby?" said I.

195   "Sitting upon the banister," he mildly replied.

I motioned him into the lawyer's room, who then left us.

"Bartleby," said I, "are you aware that you are the cause of great tribulation to me, by persisting in occupying the entry after being dismissed from the office?"

No answer.

"Now one of two things must take place. Either you must do something, or something must be done to you. Now what sort of business would you like to engage in? Would you like to re-engage in copying for some one?"

200   "No; I would prefer not to make any change."

"Would you like a clerkship in a dry-goods store?"

"There is too much confinement about that. No, I would not like a clerkship; but I am not particular."

"Too much confinement," I cried, "why, you keep yourself confined all the time!"

"I would prefer not to take a clerkship," he rejoined, as if to settle that little item at once.

205   "How would a bar-tender's business suit you? There is no trying of the eye-sight in that."

I would not like it at all; though, as I said before, I am not particular."

His unwonted wordiness inspirited me. I returned to the charge.

"Well, then, would you like to travel through the country collecting bills for the merchants? That would improve your health."

"No, I would prefer to be doing something else."

210   "How, then, would going as a companion to Europe, to entertain some young gentleman with your conversation—how would that suit you?"

"Not at all. It does not strike me that there is anything definite about that. I like to be stationary. But I am not particular."

"Stationary you shall be, then," I cried, now losing all patience, and, for the first time in all my exasperating connection with him, fairly flying into a passion. "If you do not go away from these premises before night, I shall feel bound—indeed, I *am* bound—to—to quit the premises myself!" I rather absurdly concluded, knowing not with what possible threat to try to frighten his immobility into compliance. Despairing of all further efforts, I was precipitately leaving him, when a final thought occurred to me—one which had not been wholly unindulged before.

"Bartleby," said I, in the kindest tone I could assume under such exciting circumstances, "will you go home with me now—not to my office, but my dwelling—and remain there till we can conclude upon some convenient arrangement for you at our leisure? Come, let us start now, right away."

"No: at present I would prefer not to make any change at all."

215 I answered nothing; but, effectually dodging every one by the suddenness and rapidity of my flight; rushed from the building, ran up Wall Street towards Broadway, and, jumping into the first omnibus, was soon removed from pursuit. As soon as tranquillity returned, I distinctly perceived that I had now done all that I possibly could, both in respect to the demands of the landlord and his tenants, and with regard to my own desire and sense of duty, to benefit Bartleby, and shield him from rude persecution. I now strove to be entirely carefree and quiescent; and my conscience justified me in the attempt; though, indeed, it was not so successful as I could have wished. So fearful was I of being again hunted out by the incensed landlord and his exasperated tenants, that, surrendering my business to Nippers, for a few days, I drove about the upper part of the town and through the suburbs, in my rockaway;[15] crossed over to Jersey City and Hoboken, and paid fugitive visits to Manhattanville and Astoria. In fact, I almost lived in my rockaway for the time.

When again I entered my office, lo, a note from the landlord lay upon the desk. I opened it with trembling hands. It informed me that the writer had sent to the police, and had Bartleby removed to the Tombs as a vagrant. Moreover, since I knew more about him than any one else, he wished me to appear at that place, and make a suitable statement of the facts. These tidings had a conflicting effect upon me. At first I was indignant; but, at last, almost approved. The landlord's energetic, summary disposition, had led him to adopt a procedure which I do not think I would have decided upon myself; and yet, as a last resort, under such peculiar circumstances, it seemed the only plan.

As I afterwards learned, the poor scrivener, when told that he must be conducted to the Tombs, offered not the slightest obstacle, but, in his pale, unmoving way, silently acquiesced.

Some of the compassionate and curious by-standers joined the party; and headed by one of the constables arm-in-arm with Bartleby, the silent procession filed its way through all the noise, and heat, and joy of the roaring thoroughfares at noon.

The same day I received the note, I went to the Tombs, or, to speak more properly, the Halls of Justice. Seeking the right officer, I stated the purpose of my call, and was informed that the individual I described was,

---

[15] Carriage.

indeed, within. I then assured the functionary that Bartleby was a perfectly honest man, and greatly to be compassionated, however unaccountably eccentric. I narrated all I knew, and closed by suggesting the idea of letting him remain in as indulgent confinement as possible, till something less harsh might be done—though, indeed, I hardly knew what. At all events, if nothing else could be decided upon, the almshouse must receive him. I then begged to have an interview.

220   Being under no disgraceful charge, and quite serene and harmless in all his ways, they had permitted him freely to wander about the prison, and, especially, in the inclosed grass-platted yards thereof. And so I found him there, standing all alone in the quietest of the yards, his face towards a high wall, while all around, from the narrow slits of the jail windows, I thought I saw peering out upon him the eyes of murderers and thieves.

"Bartleby!"

"I know you," he said, without looking round—"and I want nothing to say to you."

"It was not I that brought you here, Bartleby," said I, keenly pained at his implied suspicion. "And to you, this should not be so vile a place. Nothing reproachful attaches to you by being here. And see, it is not so sad a place as one might think. Look, there is the sky, and here is the grass."

"I know where I am," he replied, but would say nothing more, and so I left him.

225   As I entered the corridor again, a broad meat-like man, in an apron, accosted me, and, jerking his thumb over his shoulder, said—"Is that your friend?"

"Yes."

"Does he want to starve? If he does, let him live on the prison fare, that's all."

"Who are you?" asked I, not knowing what to make of such an unofficially speaking person in such a place.

"I am the grub-man. Such gentlemen as have friends here, hire me to provide them with something good to eat."

230   "Is this so?" said I, turning the turnkey.

He said it was.

"Well, then," said I, slipping some silver into the grub-man's hands (for so they called him), "I want you to give particular attention to my friend there; let him have the best dinner you can get. And you must be as polite to him as possible."

"Introduce me, will you?" said the grub-man, looking at me with an expression which seemed to say he was all impatience for an opportunity to give a specimen of his breeding.

Thinking it would prove of benefit to the scrivener, I acquiesced; and, asking the grub-man his name, went up with him to Bartleby.

235   "Bartleby, this is a friend; you will find him very useful to you."

"Your sarvant, sir, your sarvant," said the grub-man, making a low salutation behind his apron. "Hope you find it pleasant here, sir; nice grounds—cool apartments—hope you'll stay with us some time—try to make it agreeable. What will you have for dinner to-day?"

"I prefer not to dine to-day," said Bartleby, turning away. "It would disagree with me; I am unused to dinners." So saying, he slowly moved to the other side of the inclosure, and took up a position fronting the deadwall.

"How's this?" said the grub-man, addressing me with a stare of astonishment. "He's odd, ain't he?"

"I think he is a little deranged," said I, sadly.

240　　"Deranged? deranged is it? Well, now, upon my word, I thought that friend of yourn was a gentleman forger; they are always pale and genteel-like, them forgers. I can't help pity 'em—can't help it, sir. Did you know Monroe Edwards?" he added, touchingly, and paused. Then, laying his hand piteously on my shoulder, sighed, "he died of consumption at Sing-Sing. So you weren't acquainted with Monroe?"

"No, I was never socially acquainted with any forgers. But I cannot stop longer. Look to my friend yonder. You will not lose by it. I will see you again."

Some few days after this, I again obtained admission to the Tombs, and went through the corridors in quest of Bartleby; but without finding him.

"I saw him coming from his cell not long ago," said a turnkey, "may be he's gone to loiter in the yards."

So I went in that direction.

245　　"Are you looking for the silent man?" said another turnkey, passing me. "Yonder he lies—sleeping in the yard there. 'Tis not twenty minutes since I saw him lie down."

The yard was entirely quiet. It was not accessible to the common prisoners. The surrounding walls, of amazing thickness, kept off all sounds behind them. The Egyptian character of the masonry weighed upon me with its gloom. But a soft imprisoned turf grew under foot. The heart of the eternal pyramids, it seemed, wherein, by some strange magic, through the clefts, grassseed, dropped by birds, had sprung.

Strangely huddled at the base of the wall, his knees drawn up, and lying on his side, his head touching the cold stones, I saw the wasted Bartleby. But nothing stirred. I paused; then went close up to him; stooped over, and saw that his dim eyes were open; otherwise he seemed profoundly sleeping. Something prompted me to touch him. I felt his hand, when a tingling shiver ran up my arm and down my spine to my feet.

The round face of the grub-man peered upon me now. "His dinner is ready. Won't he dine to-day, either? Or does he live without dining?"

"Lives without dining," said I, and closed the eyes.

250　　"Eh!—He's asleep, ain't he?"

"With kings and counselors,"[16] murmured I.

---

[16] Reference to the Bible, Job 3:13–14—in death, Bartleby is now "at rest, / With kings and counselors of the earth [. . .]"

There would seem little need for proceeding further in this history. Imagination will readily supply the meagre recital of poor Bartleby's interment. But, ere parting with the reader, let me say, that if this little narrative has sufficiently interested him, to awaken curiosity as to who Bartleby was, and what manner of life he led prior to the present narrator's making his acquaintance, I can only reply, that in such curiosity I fully share, but am wholly unable to gratify it. Yet here I hardly know whether I should divulge one little item of rumor, which came to my ear a few months after the scrivener's decease. Upon what basis it rested, I could never ascertain; and hence, how true it is I cannot now tell. But, inasmuch as this vague report has not been without a certain suggestive interest to me, however sad, it may prove the same with some others; and so I will briefly mention it. The report was this: that Bartleby had been a subordinate clerk in the Dead Letter Office at Washington, from which he had been suddenly removed by a change in the administration. When I think over this rumor, hardly can I express the emotions which seize me. Dead letters! does it not sound like dead men? Conceive a man by nature and misfortune prone to a pallid hopelessness, can any business seem more fitted to heighten it than that of continually handling these dead letters, and assorting them for the flames? For by the cart-load they are annually burned. Sometimes from out the folded paper the pale clerk takes a ring— the finger it was meant for, perhaps, moulders in the grave; a bank-note sent in swiftest charity—he whom it would relieve, nor eats nor hungers any more; pardon for those who died despairing; hope for those who died unhoping; good tidings for those who died stifled by unrelieved calamities. On errands of life, these letters speed to death.

Ah, Bartleby! Ah, humanity!

◇ ◇ ◇

ALICE MUNRO
(1931–   )

Boys and Girls
(1968)

My father was a fox farmer. That is, he raised silver foxes, in pens; and in the fall and early winter, when their fur was prime, he killed them and skinned them and sold their pelts to the Hudson's Bay Company or the Montreal Fur Traders. These companies supplied us with heroic calendars to hang, one on each side of the kitchen door. Against a background of cold blue sky and black pine forests and treacherous northern rivers, plumed adventurers planted the flags of England or of France; magnificent savages bent their backs to the portage.[1]

---

[1] Carrying boats or goods overland from one body of water to another or around an obstacle such as rapids.

For several weeks before Christmas, my father worked after supper in the cellar of our house. The cellar was whitewashed, and lit by a hundred-watt bulb over the worktable. My brother Laird and I sat on the top step and watched. My father removed the pelt inside-out from the body of the fox, which looked surprisingly small, mean and rat-like, deprived of its arrogant weight of fur. The naked, slippery bodies were collected in a sack and buried at the dump. One time the hired man, Henry Bailey, had taken a swipe at me with this sack, saying, "Christmas present!" My mother thought that was not funny. In fact she disliked the whole pelting operation—that was what the killing, skinning, and preparation of the furs was called—and wished it did not have to take place in the house. There was the smell. After the pelt had been stretched inside-out on a long board my father scraped away delicately, removing the little clotted webs of blood vessels, the bubbles of fat; the smell of blood and animal fat, with the strong primitive odour of the fox itself, penetrated all parts of the house. I found it reassuringly seasonal, like the smell of oranges and pine needles.

Henry Bailey suffered from bronchial troubles. He would cough and cough until his narrow face turned scarlet, and his light blue, derisive eyes filled up with tears; then he took the lid off the stove, and, standing well back, shot out a great clot of phlegm—hsss—straight into the heart of the flames. We admired him for his performance and for his ability to make his stomach growl at will, and for his laughter, which was full of high whistlings and gurglings and involved the whole faulty machinery of his chest. It was sometimes hard to tell what he was laughing at, and always possible that it might be us.

After we had been sent to bed we could still smell fox and still hear Henry's laugh, but these things, reminders of the warm, safe, brightly lit downstairs world, seemed lost and diminished, floating on the stale cold air upstairs. We were afraid at night in the winter. We were not afraid of *outside* though this was the time of year when snowdrifts curled around our house like sleeping whales and the wind harassed us all night, coming up from the buried fields, the frozen swamp, with its old bugbear chorus of threats and misery. We were afraid of *inside*, the room where we slept. At this time the upstairs of our house was not finished. A brick chimney went up one wall. In the middle of the floor was a square hole, with a wooden railing around it; that was where the stairs came up. On the other side of the stairwell were the things that nobody had any use for any more—a soldiery roll of linoleum, standing on end, a wicker baby carriage, a fern basket, china jugs and basins with cracks in them, a picture of the Battle of Balaclava, very sad to look at. I had told Laird, as soon as he was old enough to understand such things, that bats and skeletons lived over there; whenever a man escaped from the county jail, twenty miles away, I imagined that he had somehow let himself in the window and was hiding behind the linoleum. But we had rules to keep us safe. When the light was on, we were safe as long as we did not step off the square of worn carpet which defined our bedroom-space; when the light was off no place was

safe but the beds themselves. I had to turn out the light kneeling on the
end of my bed, and stretching as far as I could to reach the cord.

5   In the dark we lay on our beds, our narrow life rafts, and fixed our
eyes on the faint light coming up the stairwell, and sang songs. Laird sang
"Jingle Bells," which he would sing any time, whether it was Christmas or
not, and I sang "Danny Boy." I love the sound of my own voice, frail and
supplicating, rising in the dark. We could make out the tall frosted shapes
of the windows now, gloomy and white. When I came to the part, *When I
am dead, as dead I well may be*—a fit of shivering caused not by the cold
sheets but by pleasurable emotion almost silenced me. *You'll kneel and say,
an Ave there above me*—What was an Ave? Every day I forgot to find out.

Laird went straight from singing to sleep. I could hear his long, satisfied, bubbly breaths. Now for the time that remained to me, the most perfectly private and perhaps the best time of the whole day, I arranged
myself tightly under the covers and went on with one of the stories I was
telling myself from night to night. These stories were about myself, when
I had grown a little older; they took place in a world that was recognizably
mine, yet one that presented opportunities for courage, boldness and self-
sacrifice, as mine never did. I rescued people from a bombed building (it
discouraged me that the real war had gone on so far away from Jubilee). I
shot two rabid wolves who were menacing the schoolyard (the teachers
cowered terrified at my back). I rode a fine horse spiritedly down the main
street of Jubilee, acknowledging the towns-people's gratitude for some yet-
to-be-worked-out piece of heroism (nobody ever rode a horse there, except
King Billy in the Orangemen's Day parade). There was always riding and
shooting in these stories, though I had only been on a horse twice—bare-
back because we did not own a saddle—and the second time I had slid
right around and dropped under the horse's feet; it had stepped placidly
over me. I really was learning to shoot, but I could not hit anything yet,
not even tin cans on fence posts.

Alive, the foxes inhabited a world my father made for them. It was surrounded by a high guard fence, like a medieval town, with a gate that was
padlocked at night. Along the streets of this town were ranged large,
sturdy pens. Each of them had a real door that a man could go through, a
wooden ramp along the wire, for the foxes to run up and down on, and a
kennel—something like a clothes chest with airholes—where they slept
and stayed in winter and had their young. There were feeding and watering dishes attached to the wire in such a way that they could be emptied
and cleaned from the outside. The dishes were made of old tin cans, and
the ramps and kennels of odds and ends of old lumber. Everything was
tidy and ingenious; my father was tirelessly inventive and his favourite
book in the world was *Robinson Crusoe*. He had fitted a tin drum on a
wheelbarrow, for bringing water down to the pens. This was my job in
summer, when the foxes had to have water twice a day. Between nine and
ten o'clock in the morning, and again after supper, I filled the drum at the

pump and trundled it down through the barnyard to the pens, where I parked it, and filled my watering can and went along the streets. Laird came too, with his little cream and green gardening can, filled too full and knocking against his legs and slopping water on his canvas shoes. I had the real watering can, my father's, though I could only carry it three-quarters full.

The foxes all had names, which were printed on a tin plate and hung beside their doors. They were not named when they were born, but when they survived the first year's pelting and were added to the breeding stock. Those my father had named were called names like Prince, Bob, Wally and Betty. Those I had named were called Star or Turk, or Maureen or Diana. Laird named one Maud after a hired girl we had when he was little, one Harold after a boy at school, and one Mexico, he did not say why.

Naming them did not make pets out of them, or anything like it. Nobody but my father ever went into the pens, and he had twice had blood-poisoning from bites. When I was bringing them their water they prowled up and down on the paths they had made inside their pens, barking seldom—they saved that for nighttime, when they might get up a chorus of community frenzy—but always watching me, their eyes burning, clear gold, in their pointed, malevolent faces. They were beautiful for their delicate legs and heavy, aristocratic tails and the bright fur sprinkled on dark down their backs—which gave them their name—but especially for their faces, drawn exquisitely sharp in pure hostility, and their golden eyes.

10   Besides carrying water I helped my father when he cut the long grass, and the lamb's quarter and flowering money-musk, that grew between the pens. He cut with the scythe and I raked into piles. Then he took a pitchfork and threw fresh-cut grass all over the top of the pens, to keep the foxes cooler and shade their coats, which were browned by too much sun. My father did not talk to me unless it was about the job we were doing. In this he was quite different from my mother, who, if she was feeling cheerful, would tell me all sorts of things—the name of a dog she had had when she was a little girl, the names of boys she had gone out with later on when she was grown up, and what certain dresses of hers had looked like—she could not imagine now what had become of them. Whatever thoughts and stories my father had were private, and I was shy of him and would never ask him questions. Nevertheless I worked willingly under his eyes, and with a feeling of pride. One time a feed salesman came down into the pens to talk to him and my father said, "Like to have you meet my new hired man." I turned away and raked furiously, red in the face with pleasure.

"Could of fooled me," said the salesman. "I thought it was only a girl."

After the grass was cut, it seemed suddenly much later in the year. I walked on stubble in the earlier evening, aware of the reddening skies, the entering silences, of fall. When I wheeled the tank out of the gate and put the padlock on, it was almost dark. One night at this time I saw my mother and father standing talking on the little rise of ground we called the gangway, in front of the barn. My father had just come from the meathouse; he had his stiff bloody apron on, and a pail of cut-up meat in his hand.

It was an odd thing to see my mother down at the barn. She did not often come out of the house unless it was to do something—hang out the wash or dig potatoes in the garden. She looked out of place, with her bare lumpy legs, not touched by the sun, her apron still on and damp across the stomach from the supper dishes. Her hair was tied up in a kerchief, wisps of it falling out. She would tie her hair up like this in the morning, saying she did not have time to do it properly, and it would stay tied up all day. It was true, too; she really did not have time. These days our back porch was piled with baskets of peaches and grapes and pears, bought in town, and onions and tomatoes and cucumbers grown at home, all waiting to be made into jelly and jam and preserves, pickles and chili sauce. In the kitchen there was a fire in the stove all day, jars clinked in boiling water, sometimes a cheesecloth bag was strung on a pole between two chairs, straining blue-black grape pulp for jelly. I was given jobs to do and I would sit at the table peeling peaches that had been soaked in the hot water, or cutting up onions, my eyes smarting and streaming. As soon as I was done I ran out of the house, trying to get out of earshot before my mother thought of what she wanted me to do next. I hated the hot dark kitchen in summer, the green blinds and the flypapers, the same old oilcloth table and wavy mirror and bumpy linoleum. My mother was too tired and preoccupied to talk to me, she had no heart to tell about the Normal School Graduation Dance; sweat trickled over her face and she was always counting under her breath, pointing at jars, dumping cups of sugar. It seemed to me that work in the house was endless, dreary and peculiarly depressing; work done out of doors, and in my father's service, was ritualistically important.

I wheeled the tank up to the barn, where it was kept, and I heard my mother saying, "Wait till Laird gets a little bigger, then you'll have a real help."

15   What my father said I did not hear. I was pleased by the way he stood listening, politely as he would to a salesman or a stranger, but with an air of wanting to get on with his real work. I felt my mother had no business down here and I wanted him to feel the same way. What did she mean about Laird? He was no help to anybody. Where was he now? Swinging himself sick on the swing, going around in circles, or trying to catch caterpillars. He never once stayed with me till I was finished.

"And then I can use her more in the house," I heard my mother say. She had a dead-quiet, regretful way of talking about me that always made me uneasy. "I just get my back turned and she runs off. It's not like I had a girl in the family at all."

I went and sat on a feedbag in the corner of the barn, not wanting to appear when this conversation was going on. My mother, I felt, was not to be trusted. She was kinder than my father and more easily fooled, but you could not depend on her, and the real reasons for the things she said and did were not to be known. She loved me, and she sat up late at night making a dress of the difficult style I wanted, for me to wear when school started, but she was also my enemy. She was always plotting. She was plotting now to get me to stay in the house more, although she knew I hated it (*because* she knew I hated it) and keep me from working for my father. It seemed to me she would do this simply out of perversity, and to try her power. It did not occur to me that she could be lonely, or jealous. No grown-up could be; they were too fortunate. I sat and kicked my heels monotonously against a feed-bag, raising dust, and did not come out till she was gone.

At any rate, I did not expect my father to pay any attention to what she said. Who could imagine Laird doing my work—Laird remembering the padlock and cleaning out the watering-dishes with a leaf on the end of a stick, or even wheeling the tank without it tumbling over? It showed how little my mother knew about the way things really were.

I have forgotten to say what the foxes were fed. My father's bloody apron reminded me. They were fed horsemeat. At this time most farmers still kept horses, and when a horse got too old to work, or broke a leg or got down and would not get up, as they sometimes did, the owner would call my father, and he and Henry went out to the farm in the truck. Usually they shot and butchered the horse there, paying the farmer from five to twelve dollars. If they had already too much meat on hand, they would bring the horse back alive, and keep it for a few days or weeks in our stable, until the meat was needed. After the war the farmers were buying tractors and gradually getting rid of horses altogether, so it sometimes happened that we got a good healthy horse, that there was just no use for any more. If this happened in the winter we might keep the horse in our stable till spring, for we had plenty of hay and if there was a lot of snow—and the plow did not always get our road cleared—it was convenient to be able to go to town with a horse and cutter.

20   The winter I was eleven years old we had two horses in the stable. We did not know what names they had had before, so we called them Mack and Flora. Mack was an old black workhorse, sooty and indifferent. Flora was a sorrel mare, a driver. We took them both out in the cutter. Mack was slow and easy to handle. Flora was given to fits of violent alarm, veering at cars and even at other horses, but we loved her speed and high-stepping, her general air of gallantry and abandon. On Saturdays we went down to the stable and as soon as we opened the door on its cosy, animal-smelling darkness Flora threw up her head, rolled her eyes, whinnied despairingly and pulled herself through a crisis of nerves on the spot. It was not safe to go into her stall; she would kick.

This winter also I began to hear a great deal more on the theme my mother had sounded when she had been talking in front of the barn. I no longer felt safe. It seemed that in the minds of the people around me there was a steady undercurrent of thought, not to be deflected, on this one subject. The word *girl* had formerly seemed to me innocent and unburdened, like the word *child;* now it appeared that it was no such thing. A girl was not, as I had supposed, simply what I was; it was what I had to become. It was a definition, always touched with emphasis, with reproach and disappointment. Also it was a joke on me. Once Laird and I were fighting, and for the first time ever I had to use all my strength against him; even so, he caught and pinned my arm for a moment, really hurting me. Henry saw this, and laughed, saying, "Oh, that there Laird's gonna show you, one of these days!" Laird was getting a lot bigger. But I was getting bigger too.

My grandmother came to stay with us for a few weeks and I heard other things. "Girls don't slam doors like that." "Girls keep their knees together when they sit down." And worse still, when I asked some questions, "That's none of girls' business." I continued to slam the doors and sit as awkwardly as possible, thinking that by such measures I kept myself free.

When spring came, the horses were let out in the barnyard. Mack stood against the barn wall trying to scratch his neck and haunches, but Flora trotted up and down and reared at the fences, clattering her hooves against the rails. Snow drifts dwindled quickly, revealing the hard grey and brown earth, the familiar rise and fall of the ground, plain and bare after the fantastic landscape of winter. There was a great feeling of opening-out, of release. We just wore rubbers now, over our shoes; our feet felt ridiculously light. One Saturday we went out to the stable and found all the doors open, letting in the unaccustomed sunlight and fresh air. Henry was there, just idling around looking at his collection of calendars which were tacked up behind the stalls in a part of the stable my mother had probably never seen.

"Come to say goodbye to your old friend Mack?" Henry said. "Here, you give him a taste of oats." He poured some oats into Laird's cupped hands and Laird went to feed Mack. Mack's teeth were in bad shape. He ate very slowly, patiently shifting the oats around in his mouth, trying to find a stump of a molar to grind it on. "Poor old Mack," said Henry mournfully. "When a horse's teeth's gone, he's gone. That's about the way."

25   "Are you going to shoot him today?" I said. Mack and Flora had been in the stable so long I had almost forgotten they were going to be shot.

Henry didn't answer me. Instead he started to sing in a high, trembly, mocking-sorrowful voice, *Oh, there's no more work, for poor Uncle Ned, he's gone where the good darkies go.* Mack's thick, blackish tongue worked diligently at Laird's hand. I went out before the song was ended and sat down on the gangway.

I had never seen them shoot a horse, but I knew where it was done. Last summer Laird and I had come upon a horse's entrails before they were buried. We had thought it was a big black snake, coiled up in the sun. That was around in the field that ran up beside the barn. I thought that if we went inside the barn, and found a wide crack or a knothole to look through, we would be able to see them do it. It was not something I wanted to see; just the same, if a thing really happened, it was better to see it, and know.

My father came down from the house, carrying the gun.

"What are you doing here?" he said.

30   "Nothing."

"Go on up and play around the house."

He sent Laird out of the stable. I said to Laird, "Do you want to see them shoot Mack?" and without waiting for an answer led him around to the front door of the barn, opened it carefully, and went in. "Be quiet or they'll hear us," I said. We could hear Henry and my father talking in the stable, then the heavy, shuffling steps of Mack being backed out of his stall.

In the loft it was cold and dark. Thin, crisscrossed beams of sunlight fell through the cracks. The hay was low. It was a rolling country, hills and hollows, slipping under our feet. About four feet up was a beam going around the walls. We piled hay up in one corner and I boosted Laird up and hoisted myself. The beam was not very wide; we crept along it with our hands flat on the barn walls. There were plenty of knotholes, and I found one that gave me the view I wanted—a corner of the barnyard, the gate, part of the field. Laird did not have a knothole and began to complain.

I showed him a widened crack between two boards. "Be quiet and wait. If they hear you you'll get us in trouble."

35   My father came in sight carrying the gun. Henry was leading Mack by the halter. He dropped it and took out his cigarette papers and tobacco; he rolled cigarettes for my father and himself. While this was going on Mack nosed around in the old, dead grass along the fence. Then my father opened the gate and they took Mack through. Henry led Mack away from the path to a patch of ground and they talked together, not loud enough for us to hear. Mack again began searching for a mouthful of fresh grass, which was not to be found. My father walked away in a straight line, and stopped short at a distance which seemed to suit him. Henry was walking away from Mack too, but sideways, still negligently holding on to the halter. My father raised the gun and Mack looked up as if he had noticed something and my father shot him.

Mack did not collapse at once but swayed, lurched sideways and fell, first on his side; then he rolled over on his back and, amazingly, kicked his legs for a few seconds in the air. At this Henry laughed, as if Mack had done a trick for him. Laird, who had drawn a long, groaning breath of surprise when the shot was fired, said out loud, "He's not dead." And it seemed to me it might be true. But his legs stopped, he rolled on his side again, his muscles quivered and sank. The two men walked over and looked at him in a businesslike way; they bent down and examined his forehead where the bullet had gone in, and now I saw his blood on the brown grass.

"Now they just skin him and cut him up," I said. "Let's go." My legs were a little shaky and I jumped gratefully down into the hay. "Now you've seen how they shoot a horse," I said in a congratulatory way, as if I had seen it many times before. "Let's see if any barn cat's had kittens in the hay." Laird jumped. He seemed young and obedient again. Suddenly I remembered how, when he was little, I had brought him into the barn and told him to climb the ladder to the top beam. That was in the spring, too, when the hay was low. I had done it out of a need for excitement, a desire for something to happen so that I could tell about it. He was wearing a little bulky brown and white checked coat, made down from one of mine. He went all the way up, just as I told him, and sat down on the top beam with the hay far below him on one side, and the barn floor and some old machinery on the other. Then I ran screaming to my father, "Laird's up on the top beam!" My father came, my mother came, my father went up the ladder talking very quietly and brought Laird down under his arm, at which my mother leaned against the ladder and began to cry. They said to me, "Why weren't you watching him?" but nobody ever knew the truth. Laird did not know enough to tell. But whenever I saw the brown and white checked coat hanging in the closet, or at the bottom of the rag bag, which was where it ended up, I felt a weight in my stomach, the sadness of unexorcized guilt.

I looked at Laird who did not even remember this, and I did not like the look on his thin, winter-pale face. His expression was not frightened or upset, but remote, concentrating. "Listen," I said, in an unusually bright and friendly voice, "you aren't going to tell, are you?"

"No," he said absently.

40   "Promise."

"Promise," he said. I grabbed the hand behind his back to make sure he was not crossing his fingers. Even so, he might have a nightmare; it might come out that way. I decided I had better work hard to get all thoughts of what he had seen out of his mind—which, it seemed to me, could not hold very many things at a time. I got some money I had saved and that afternoon we went into Jubilee and saw a show, with Judy Canova, at which we both laughed a great deal. After that I thought it would be all right.

Two weeks later I knew they were going to shoot Flora. I knew from the night before, when I heard my mother ask if the hay was holding out all right, and my father said, "Well, after to-morrow there'll just be the cow, and we should be able to put her out to grass in another week." So I knew it was Flora's turn in the morning.

This time I didn't think of watching it. That was something to see just one time. I had not thought about it very often since, but sometimes when I was busy, working at school, or standing in front of the mirror combing my hair and wondering if I would be pretty when I grew up, the whole scene would flash into my mind: I would see the easy, practised way my father raised the gun, and hear Henry laughing when Mack kicked his legs in the air. I did not have any great feeling of horror and opposition, such as a city child might have had; I was too used to seeing the death of animals as a necessity by which we lived. Yet I felt a little ashamed, and there was a new wariness, a sense of holding-off, in my attitude to my father and his work.

It was a fine day, and we were going around the yard picking up tree branches that had been torn off in winter storms. This was something we had been told to do, and also we wanted to use them to make a teepee. We heard Flora whinny, and then my father's voice and Henry's shouting, and we ran down to the barnyard to see what was going on.

45   The stable door was open. Henry had just brought Flora out, and she had broken away from him. She was running free in the barnyard, from one end to the other. We climbed up on the fence. It was exciting to see her running, whinnying, going up on her hind legs, prancing and threatening like a horse in a Western movie, an unbroken ranch horse, though she was just an old driver, an old sorrel mare. My father and Henry ran after her and tried to grab the dangling halter. They tried to work her into a corner, and they had almost succeeded when she made a run between them, wild-eyed, and disappeared around the corner of the barn. We heard the rails clatter down as she got over the fence, and Henry yelled, "She's into the field now!"

That meant she was in the long L-shaped field that ran up by the house. If she got around the center, heading towards the lane, the gate was open; the truck had been driven into the field this morning. My father shouted to me, because I was on the other side of the fence, nearest the lane, "Go shut the gate!"

I could run very fast. I ran across the garden, past the tree where our swing was hung, and jumped across a ditch into the lane. There was the open gate. She had not got out, I could not see her up on the road; she must have run to the other end of the field. The gate was heavy. I lifted it out of the gravel and carried it across the roadway. I had it half-way across when she came in sight, galloping straight towards me. There was just time to get the chain on. Laird came scrambling through the ditch to help me.

Instead of shutting the gate, I opened it as wide as I could. I did not make any decision to do this, it was just what I did. Flora never slowed down; she galloped straight past me, and Laird jumped up and down, yelling, "Shut it, shut it!" even after it was too late. My father and Henry appeared in the field a moment too late to see what I had done. They only saw Flora heading for the township road. They would think I had not got there in time.

They did not waste any time asking about it. They went back to the barn and got the gun and the knives they used, and put these in the truck; then they turned the truck around and came bouncing up the field toward us. Laird called to them, "Let me go too, let me go too!" and Henry stopped the truck and they took him in. I shut the gate after they were all gone.

50   I supposed Laird would tell. I wondered what would happen to me. I had never disobeyed my father before, and I could not understand why I had done it. Flora would not really get away. They would catch up with her in the truck. Or if they did not catch her this morning somebody would see her and telephone us this afternoon or tomorrow. There was no wild country here for her to run to, only farms. What was more, my father had

paid for her, we needed the meat to feed the foxes, we needed the foxes to make our living. All I had done was make more work for my father who worked hard enough already. And when my father found out about it he was not going to trust me any more; he would know that I was not entirely on his side. I was on Flora's side, and that made me no use to anybody, not even to her. Just the same, I did not regret it; when she came running at me and I held the gate open, that was the only thing I could do.

I went back to the house, and my mother said, "What's all the commotion?" I told her that Flora had kicked down the fence and got away. "Your poor father," she said, "now he'll have to go chasing over the countryside. Well, there isn't any use planning dinner before one." She put up the ironing board. I wanted to tell her, but thought better of it and went upstairs and sat on my bed.

Lately I had been trying to make my part of the room fancy, spreading the bed with old lace curtains, and fixing myself a dressing-table with some leftovers of cretonne for a skirt. I planned to put up some kind of barricade between my bed and Laird's, to keep my section separate from his. In the sunlight, the lace curtains were just dusty rags. We did not sing at night any more. One night when I was singing Laird said, "You sound silly," and I went right on but the next night I did not start. There was not so much need to anyway, we were no longer afraid. We knew it was just old furniture over there, old jumble and confusion. We did not keep to the rules. I still stayed awake after Laird was asleep and told myself stories, but even in these stories something different was happening, mysterious alterations took place. A story might start off in the old way, with a spectacular danger, a fire or wild animals, and for a while I might rescue people; then things would change around, and instead, somebody would be rescuing me. It might be a boy from our class at school, or even Mr. Campbell, our teacher, who tickled girls under the arms. And at this point the story concerned itself at great length with what I looked like—how long my hair was, and what kind of dress I had on; by the time I had these details worked out the real excitement of the story was lost.

It was later than one o'clock when the truck came back. The tarpaulin was over the back, which meant there was meat in it. My mother had to heat dinner up all over again. Henry and my father had changed from their bloody overalls into ordinary working overalls in the barn, and they washed their arms and necks and faces at the sink, and splashed water on their hair and combed it. Laird lifted his arm to show off a streak of blood. "We shot old Flora," he said, "and cut her up in fifty pieces."

"Well, I don't want to hear about it," my mother said. "And don't come to my table like that."

55   My family made him go and wash the blood off.

We sat down and my father said grace and Henry pasted his chewing-gum on the end of his fork, the way he always did; when he took it off he would have us admire the pattern. We began to pass the bowls of steaming, overcooked vegetables. Laird looked across the table at me and said proudly, distinctly, "Anyway it was her fault Flora got away."

"What?" my father said.

"She could of shut the gate and she didn't. She just open' it up and Flora run out."

"Is that right?" my father said.

60   Everybody at the table was looking at me. I nodded, swallowing food with great difficulty. To my shame, tears flooded my eyes.

My father made a curt sound of disgust. "What did you do that for?"

I did not answer. I put down my fork and waited to be sent from the table, still not looking up.

But this did not happen. For some time nobody said anything, then Laird said matter-of-factly, "She's crying."

"Never mind," my father said. He spoke with resignation, even good humour, the words which absolved and dismissed me for good. "She's only a girl," he said.

65   I didn't protest that, even in my heart. Maybe it was true.

◈ ◈ ◈

JOYCE CAROL OATES
(1938–   )

Shopping
(1987)

An old ritual, Saturday morning shopping. Mother and daughter. Mrs. Dietrich and Nola. Shops in the village, stores and boutiques at the splendid Livingstone Mall on Route 12. Bloomingdale's, Saks, Lord & Taylor, Bonwit's, Neiman-Marcus: and the rest. Mrs. Dietrich would know her way around the stores blindfolded but there is always the surprise of lavish seasonal displays, extraordinary holiday sales, the openings of new stores at the Mall like Laura Ashley, Paraphernalia. On one of their Mall days Mrs. Dietrich and Nola would try to get there at midmorning, have lunch around 1 P.M. at one or another of their favorite restaurants, shop for perhaps an hour after lunch, then come home. Sometimes the shopping trips were more successful than at other times but you have to have faith, Mrs. Dietrich tells herself. Her interior voice is calm, neutral, free of irony. Ever since her divorce her interior voice has been free of irony. You have to have faith.

Tomorrow morning Nola returns to school in Maine; today will be a day at the Mall. Mrs. Dietrich has planned it for days. At the Mall, in such crowds of shoppers, moments of intimacy are possible as they rarely are at home. (Seventeen-year-old Nola, home on spring break for a brief eight days, seems always to be *busy,* always out with her *friends*—the trip to the Mall has been postponed twice.) But Saturday, 10:30 A.M., they are in the car at last headed south on Route 12, a bleak March morning following a night of freezing rain, there's a metallic cast to the air and no sun anywhere in the sky but the light hurts Mrs. Dietrich's eyes just the same. "Does it seem as if spring will ever come?—it must be twenty degrees colder up in Maine," she says. Driving in heavy traffic always makes Mrs. Dietrich nervous and she is overly sensitive to her daughter's silence, which seems deliberate, perverse, when they have so little time remaining together—not even a full day.

Nola asks politely if Mrs. Dietrich would like her to drive and Mrs. Dietrich says no, of course not, she's fine, it's only a few more miles and maybe traffic will lighten. Nola seems about to say something more, then thinks better of it. So much between them that is precarious, chancy—but they've been kind to each other these past seven days. Mrs. Dietrich loves Nola with a fierce unreasoned passion stronger than any she felt for the man who had been her husband for thirteen years, certainly far stronger than any she ever felt for her own mother. Sometimes in weak despondent moods, alone, lonely, self-pitying, when she has had too much to drink, Mrs. Dietrich thinks she is in love with her daughter—but this is a thought she can't contemplate for long. And how Nola would snort in amused contempt, incredulous, mocking—"Oh *Mother!*"—if she were told.

Mrs. Dietrich tries to engage her daughter in conversation of a harmless sort but Nola answers in monosyllables, Nola is rather tired from so many nights of partying with her friends, some of whom attend the local high school, some of whom are home for spring break from prep schools—Exeter, Lawrenceville, Concord, Andover, Portland. Late nights, but Mrs. Dietrich doesn't consciously lie awake waiting for Nola to come home: they've been through all that before. Now Nola sits beside her mother looking wan, subdued, rather melancholy. Thinking her private thoughts. She is wearing a bulky quilted jacket Mrs. Dietrich has never liked, the usual blue jeans, black calfskin boots zippered tightly to mid-calf. Mrs. Dietrich must resist the temptation to ask, "Why are you so quiet, Nola? What are you thinking?" They've been through all that before.

5 Route 12 has become a jumble of small industrial parks, high-rise office and apartment buildings, torn-up landscapes—mountains of raw earth, uprooted trees, ruts and ditches filled with muddy water. There is no natural sequence to what you see—buildings, construction work, leveled woods, the lavish grounds owned by Squibb. Though she has driven this route countless times, Mrs. Dietrich is never quite certain where the Mall is and must be prepared for a sudden exit. She remembers getting lost the first several times, remembers the excitement she and her friends felt about the grand opening of the Mall, stores worthy of serious shopping at last. Today is much the same. No, today is worse. Like Christmas when she was a small child, Mrs. Dietrich thinks. She'd hoped so badly to be happy she'd felt actual pain, a constriction in her throat like crying.

"*Are* you all right, Nola?—you've been so quiet all morning," Mrs. Dietrich asks, half-scolding. Nola stirs from her reverie, says she's fine, a just perceptible edge to her reply, and for the remainder of the drive there's some stiffness between them. Mrs. Dietrich chooses to ignore it. In any case she is fully absorbed in driving—negotiating a tricky exit across two lanes of traffic, then the hairpin curve of the ramp, the numerous looping drives of the Mall. Then the enormous parking lot, daunting to the inexperienced, but Mrs. Dietrich always heads for the area behind Lord & Taylor on the far side of the Mall, Lot D; her luck holds and she finds a space close in. "Well—we made it," she says, smiling happily at Nola. Nola laughs in reply—what does a seventeen-year-old's laughter *mean?*—but she remembers, getting out, to lock both doors on her side of the car. The smile Nola gives Mrs. Dietrich across the car's roof is careless and beautiful and takes Mrs. Dietrich's breath away.

The March morning tastes of grit with an undercurrent of something acrid, chemical; inside the Mall, beneath the first of the elegant brass-buttressed glass domes, the air is fresh and tonic, circulating from invisible vents. The Mall is crowded, rather noisy—it *is* Saturday morning—but a feast for the eyes after that long trip on Route 12. Tall slender trees grow out of the mosaic-tiled pavement, there are beds of Easter lilies, daffodils, jonquils, tulips of all colors. Mrs. Dietrich smiles with relief. She senses that Nola too is relieved, cheered. It's like coming home.

The shopping excursions began when Nola was a small child but did not acquire their special significance until she was twelve or thirteen years old and capable of serious, sustained shopping with her mother. This was about the time when Mr. Dietrich moved out of the house and back into their old apartment in the city—a separation, he'd called it initially, to give them perspective—though Mrs. Dietrich had no illusions about what "perspective" would turn out to entail—so the shopping trips were all the more significant. Not that Mrs. Dietrich and Nola spent very much money—they really didn't, *really* they didn't, when compared to friends and neighbors.

At seventeen Nola is shrewd and discerning as a shopper, not easy to please, knowledgeable as a mature woman about certain aspects of fashion, quality merchandise, good stores. Her closets, like Mrs. Dietrich's, are crammed, but she rarely buys anything that Mrs. Dietrich thinks shoddy or merely faddish. Up in Portland, at the Academy, she hasn't as much time to shop but when she is home in Livingstone it isn't unusual for her and her girlfriends to shop nearly every day. Like all her friends she has charge accounts at the better stores, her own credit cards, a reasonable allowance. At the time of their settlement Mr. Dietrich said guiltily that it was the least he could do for them—if Mrs. Dietrich wanted to work part-time, she could (she was trained, more or less, in public relations of a small-scale sort); if not, not. Mrs. Dietrich thought, It's the most you can do for us too.

10   Near Bloomingdale's entrance mother and daughter see a disheveled woman sitting by herself on one of the benches. Without seeming to look at her, shoppers are making a discreet berth around her, a stream following a natural course. Nola, taken by surprise, stares. Mrs. Dietrich has seen the woman from time to time at the Mall, always alone, smirking and talking

to herself, frizzed gray hair in a tangle, puckered mouth. Always wearing the same black wool coat, a garment of fairly good quality but shapeless, rumpled, stained, as if she sleeps in it. She might be anywhere from forty to sixty years of age. Once Mrs. Dietrich saw her make menacing gestures at children who were teasing her, another time she'd seen the woman staring belligerently at *her*. A white paste had gathered in the corners of her mouth. . . . "My God, that poor woman," Nola says. "I didn't think there were people like her here—I mean, I didn't think they would allow it."

"She doesn't seem to cause any disturbance," Mrs. Dietrich says. "She just sits—Don't stare, Nola, she'll see you."

"You've seen her here before? Here?"

"A few times this winter."

"Is she always like that?"

15 "I'm sure she's harmless, Nola. She just *sits*."

Nola is incensed, her pale blue eyes like washed glass. "I'm sure *she's* harmless, Mother. It's the harm the poor woman has to endure that is the tragedy."

Mrs. Dietrich is surprised and a little offended by her daughter's passionate tone but she knows enough not to argue. They enter Bloomingdale's, taking their habitual route. So many shoppers!—so much merchandise! Nola speaks of the tragedy of women like that woman—the tragedy of the homeless, the mentally disturbed—bag ladies out on the street—outcasts of an affluent society—but she's soon distracted by the busyness on all sides, the attractive items for sale. They take the escalator up to the third floor, to the Juniors department where Nola often buys things. From there they will move on to Young Collector, then to New Impressions, then to Petites, then one or another boutique and designer—Liz Claiborne, Christian Dior, Calvin Klein, Carlos Falchi, and the rest. And after Bloomingdale's the other stores await, to be visited each in turn. Mrs. Dietrich checks her watch and sees with satisfaction that there's just enough time before lunch but not *too* much time. She gets ravenously hungry, shopping at the Mall.

Nola is efficient and matter-of-fact about shopping, though she acts solely upon instinct. Mrs. Dietrich likes to watch her at a short distance— holding items of clothing up to herself in the three-way mirrors, modeling things she thinks especially promising. A twill blazer with rounded shoulders and blouson jacket, a funky zippered jumpsuit in white sailcloth, a pair of straight-leg Evan-Picone pants, a green leather vest: Mrs. Dietrich watches her covertly. At such times Nola is perfectly content, fully absorbed in the task at hand; Mrs. Dietrich knows she isn't thinking about anything that would distress her. (Like Mr. Dietrich's betrayal. Like Nola's difficulties with her friends. Like her difficulties at school—as much as Mrs. Dietrich knows of them.) Once, at the Mall, perhaps in this very store in this very department, Nola saw Mrs. Dietrich watching her and walked away angrily and when Mrs. Dietrich caught up with her she said, "I can't stand it, Mother." Her voice was choked and harsh, a vein prominent in her forehead. "Let me go. For Christ's sake will you let me go." Mrs. Dietrich didn't dare touch her though she could see Nola was trembling. For a long terrible moment mother and daughter stood side by side near a display of bright brash Catalina beachwear while Nola whispered, "Let me go. *Let me go.*"

Difficult to believe that girl standing so poised and self-assured in front of the three-way mirror was once a plain, rather chunky, unhappy child. She'd been unpopular at school. Overly serious. Anxious. Quick to tears. Aged eleven she hid herself away in her room for hours at a time, reading, drawing pictures, writing little stories she could sometimes be prevailed upon to read aloud to her mother, sometimes even to her father, though she dreaded his judgment. She went through a "scientific" phase a while later—Mrs. Dietrich remembers an ambitious bas-relief map of North America, meticulous illustrations for "photosynthesis," a pastel drawing of an eerie ball of fire labeled "Red Giant" (a dying star?) which won a prize in a state competition for junior high students. Then for a season it was stray facts Nola confronted them with, often at the dinner table. Interrupting her parents' conversation to say brightly: "Did you know that Nero's favorite color was green?—he carried a giant emerald and held it up to his eye to watch Christians being devoured by lions." And once at a large family gathering: "Did you know that last week downtown a little baby's nose was chewed off by rats in his crib?—a little *black* baby?" Nola meant only to call attention to herself but you couldn't blame her listeners for being offended. They stared at her, not knowing what to say. What a strange child! What queer glassy-pale eyes! Mr. Dietrich told her curtly to leave the table—he'd had enough of the game she was playing and so had everyone else.

20   Nola stared at him, her eyes filling with tears. Game?

When they were alone Mr. Dietrich said angrily to Mrs. Dietrich: "Can't you control her in front of other people, at least?" Mrs. Dietrich was angry too, and frightened. She said "I *try.*"

They sent her off aged fourteen to the Portland Academy up in Maine and without their help she matured into a girl of considerable beauty. A heart-shaped face, delicate features, glossy red-brown hair scissor-cut to her shoulders. Five feet seven inches tall, weighing less than one hundred pounds—the result of constant savage dieting. (Mrs. Dietrich, who has weight problems herself, doesn't dare to inquire as to details. They've been through that already.) Thirty days after they'd left her at the Portland Academy Nola telephoned home at 11:00 *p.m.* one Sunday giggly and high telling Mrs. Dietrich she adored the school she adored her suite mates she adored most of her teachers particularly her riding instructor Terri, Terri the Terrier they called the woman because she was so fierce, such a character, eyes that bore right through your skull, wore belts with the most amazing silver buckles! Nola loved Terri but she wasn't *in* love—there's a difference!

Mrs. Dietrich broke down weeping, *that* time.

Now of course Nola has boyfriends. Mrs. Dietrich has long since given up trying to keep track of their names. There is even one "boy"—or young man—who seems to be married: who seems to be, in fact, one of the junior instructors at the school. (Mrs. Dietrich does not eavesdrop on her daughter's telephone conversations but there are things she cannot help overhearing.) Is your daughter on the Pill? the women in Mrs. Dietrich's circle asked one another for a while, guiltily, surreptitiously. Now they no longer ask.

25   But Nola has announced recently that she loathes boys—she's fed up.

She's never going to get married. She'll study languages in college, French, Italian, something exotic like Arabic, go to work for the American foreign service. Unless she drops out of school altogether to become a model.

"Do you think I'm fat, Mother?" she asks frequently, worriedly, standing in front of the mirror twisted at the waist to reveal her small round belly which, it seems, can't help being round: she bloats herself on diet Cokes all day long. "Do you think it *shows?*"

When Mrs. Dietrich was pregnant with Nola she'd been twenty-nine years old and she and Mr. Dietrich had tried to have a baby for nearly five years. She'd lost hope, begun to despise herself, then suddenly it happened: like grace. Like happiness swelling so powerfully it can barely be contained. I can hear its heartbeat! her husband exclaimed. He'd been her lover then, young, vigorous, dreamy. Caressing the rock-hard belly, splendid white tight-stretched skin. Mr. Dietrich gave Mrs. Dietrich a reproduction on still glossy paper of Dante Gabriel Rossetti's *Beata Beatrix*, embarrassed, apologetic, knowing it was sentimental and perhaps a little silly but that was how he thought of her—so beautiful, rapturous, pregnant with their child. She told no one but she knew the baby was to be a girl. It would be herself again, reborn and this time perfect.

"Oh, Mother—isn't it *beautiful?*" Nola exclaims.

30   It is past noon. Past twelve-thirty. Mrs. Dietrich and Nola have made the rounds of a half-dozen stores, traveled countless escalators, one clothing department has blended into the next and the chic smiling saleswomen have become indistinguishable and Mrs. Dietrich is beginning to feel the urgent need for a glass of white wine. Just a glass. "Isn't it beautiful?—it's *perfect,*" Nola says. Her eyes glow with pleasure, her smooth skin is radiant. As Nola models in the three-way mirror a queer little yellow-and-black striped sweater with a ribbed waist, punk style, mock-cheap, Mrs. Dietrich feels the motherly obligation to register a mild protest, knowing that Nola will not hear. She must have it and will have it. She'll wear it a few times, then retire it to the bottom of a drawer with so many other novelty sweaters, accumulated since sixth grade. (She's like her mother in that regard—can't bear to throw anything away.)

"*Isn't* it beautiful?" Nola demands, studying her reflection in the mirror.

Mrs. Dietrich pays for the sweater on her charge account.

Next, they buy Nola a good pair of shoes. And a handbag to go with them. In Paraphernalia, where rock music blasts overhead and Mrs. Dietrich stands to one side, rather miserable, Nola chats companionably with two girls—tall, pretty, cutely made up—she'd gone to public school in Livingstone with, says afterward with an upward rolling of her eyes, "God, I was afraid they'd latch on to us!" Mrs. Dietrich has seen women friends and acquaintances of her own in the Mall this morning but has shrunk from being noticed, not wanting to share her daughter with anyone. She has a sense of time passing ever more swiftly, cruelly.

She watches Nola preening in a mirror, watches other shoppers watching her. My daughter. Mine. But of course there is no connection between them—they don't even resemble each other. A seventeen-year-old, a forty-seven-year-old. When Nola is away she seems to forget her mother entirely—doesn't telephone, certainly doesn't write. It's the way all their daughters are, Mrs. Dietrich's friends tell her. It doesn't *mean* anything. Mrs. Dietrich thinks how when she was carrying Nola, those nine long months, they'd been completely happy—not an instant's doubt or hesitation. The singular weight of the body. A trancelike state you are tempted to mistake for happiness because the body is incapable of thinking, therefore incapable of anticipating change. Hot rhythmic blood, organs, packed tight and moist, the baby upside down in her sac in her mother's belly, always present tense, always *now*. It was a shock when the end came so abruptly but everyone told Mrs. Dietrich she was a natural mother, praised and pampered her. For a while. Then of course she'd had her baby, her Nola. Even now Mrs. Dietrich can't really comprehend the experience. *Giving birth. Had a baby. Was born.* Mere words, absurdly inadequate. She knows no more of how love ends than she knew as a child, she nows only of how love begins—in the belly, in the womb, where it is always present tense.

35   The morning's shopping has been quite successful but lunch at La Crêperie doesn't go well for some reason. La Crêperie is Nola's favorite Mall restaurant—always amiably crowded, bustling, a simulated sidewalk café with red-striped umbrellas, wrought-iron tables and chairs, menus in French, music piped in overhead. Mrs. Dietrich's nerves are chafed by the pretense of gaiety, the noise, the openness onto one of the Mall's busy promenades where at any minute a familiar face might emerge, but she is grateful for her glass of chilled white wine. She orders a small tossed salad and a creamed-chicken crepe and devours it hungrily—she *is* hungry. While Nola picks at her seafood crepe with a disdainful look. A familiar scene: mother watching while daughter pushes food around on her plate. Suddenly Nola is tense, moody, corners of her mouth downturned. Mrs. Dietrich wants to ask, What's wrong? She wants to ask, Why are you unhappy? She wants to smooth Nola's hair back from her forehead, check to see if her forehead is overly warm, wants to hug her close, hard. Why, why? What did I do wrong? Why do you hate me?

Calling the Portland Academy a few weeks ago Mrs. Dietrich suddenly lost control, began crying. She hadn't been drinking and she hadn't known she was upset. A girl unknown to her, one of Nola's suite mates, was saying, "Please, Mrs. Dietrich, it's all right, I'm sure Nola will call you back later tonight, or tomorrow, Mrs. Dietrich?—I'll tell her you called, all right?— Mrs. Dietrich?" as embarrassed as if Mrs. Dietrich had been her own mother.

How love begins. How love ends.

Mrs. Dietrich orders a third glass of wine. This is a celebration of sorts isn't it?—their last shopping trip for a long time. But Nola resists, Nola isn't sentimental. In casual defiance of Mrs. Dietrich she lights up a ciga-rette—yes, Mother, Nola has said ironically, since *you* stopped smoking *everybody* is supposed to stop—and sits with her arms crossed, watching streams of shoppers pass. Mrs. Dietrich speaks lightly of practical matters, tomorrow morning's drive to the airport, and will Nola telephone when she gets to Portland to let Mrs. Dietrich know she has arrived safely?

Then with no warning—though of course she'd been planning this all along—Nola brings up the subject of a semester in France, in Paris and Rouen, the fall semester of her senior year it would be; she has put in her application, she says, and is waiting to hear if she's been accepted. She smokes her cigarette calmly, expelling smoke from her nostrils in a way Mrs. Dietrich thinks particularly coarse. Mrs. Dietrich, who believed that particular topic was finished, takes care to speak without emotion. "I just don't think it's a very practical idea right now, Nola," she says. "We've been through it haven't we? I—"

40 "I'm going," Nola says.

"The extra expense, for one thing. Your father—"

"If I get accepted, I'm going."

"Your father—"

"The hell with him too."

45 Mrs. Dietrich would like to slap her daughter's face. Bring tears to those steely eyes. But she sits stiff, turning her wine glass between her fin-gers, patient, calm, she's heard all this before; she says, "Surely this isn't the best time to discuss it, Nola."

Mrs. Dietrich is afraid her daughter will leave the restaurant, simply walk away, that has happened before and if it happens today she doesn't know what she will do. But Nola sits unmoving; her faced closed, impas-sive. Mrs. Dietrich feels her quickened heartbeat. Once after one of their quarrels Mrs. Dietrich told a friend of hers, the mother too of a teenage daughter, "I just don't know her any longer, how can you keep living with someone you don't know?" and the woman said, "Eventually you can't."

Nola says, not looking at Mrs. Dietrich: "Why don't we talk about it, Mother?"

"Talk about what?" Mrs. Dietrich asks.

"You know."

50 "The semester in France? Again?"

"No."

"What, then?"

"You *know*."

"I don't know, really. Really!" Mrs. Dietrich smiles, baffled. She feels the corners of her eyes pucker white with strain.

55 Nola says, sighing, "How exhausting it is."

"How *what*?"

"How exhausting it is."

"What is?"

"You and me—"

60 "What?"

"Being together—"

"Being together how—?"

"The two of us, like this—"

"But we're hardly ever together, Nola," Mrs. Dietrich says.

65 Her expression is calm but her voice is shaking. Nola turns away, covering her face with a hand, for a moment she looks years older than her age—in fact exhausted. Mrs. Dietrich sees with pity that her daughter's skin is fair and thin and dry—unlike her own, which tends to be oily—it will wear out before she's forty. Mrs. Dietrich reaches over to squeeze her hand. The fingers are limp, ungiving. "You're going back to school tomorrow, Nola," she says. "You won't come home again until June 12. And you probably will go to France—if your father consents."

Nola gets to her feet, drops her cigarette to the flagstone terrace and grinds it beneath her boot. A dirty thing to do, Mrs. Dietrich thinks, considering there's an ashtray right on the table, but she says nothing. She dislikes La Crêperie anyway.

Nola laughs, showing her lovely white teeth. "Oh, the hell with him," she says. "Fuck Daddy, right?"

They separate for an hour, Mrs. Dietrich to Neiman-Marcus to buy a birthday gift for her elderly aunt, Nola to the trendy new boutique Pour Vous. By the time Mrs. Dietrich rejoins her daughter she's quite angry, blood beating hot and hard and measured in resentment, she has had time to relive old quarrels between them, old exchanges, stray humiliating memories of her marriage as well, these last-hour disagreements are the cruelest and they are Nola's specialty. She locates Nola in the rear of the boutique amid blaring rock music, flashing neon lights, chrome-edged mirrors, her face still hard, closed, prim, pale. She stands beside another teenage girl looking in a desultory way through a rack of blouses, shoving the hangers roughly along, taking no care when a blouse falls to the floor. As Nola glances up, startled, not prepared to see her mother in front of her, their eyes lock for an instant and Mrs. Dietrich stares at her with hatred. Cold calm clear unmistakable hatred. She is thinking, Who are *you*? What have I to do with *you*? I don't know *you*, I don't love *you*, why should I?

Has Nola seen, heard?—she turns aside as if wincing, gives the blouses a final dismissive shove. Her eyes look tired, the corners of her mouth downturned. Anxious, immediately repentant, Mrs. Dietrich asks if she has found anything worth trying on. Nola says with a shrug, "Not a thing, Mother."

70   On their way out of the Mall Mrs. Dietrich and Nola see the disheveled woman in the black coat again, this time sitting prominently on a concrete ledge in front of Lord & Taylor's busy main entrance. Shopping bag at her feet, shabby purse on the ledge beside her. She is shaking her head in a series of annoyed twitches as if arguing with someone but her hands are loose, palms up, in her lap. Her posture is unfortunate—she sits with her knees parted, inner thighs revealed, fatty, dead white, the tops of cotton stockings rolled tight cutting into the flesh. Again, streams of shoppers are making a careful berth around her. Alone among them Nola hesitates, seems about to approach the woman—Please don't, Nola! please! Mrs. Dietrich thinks—then changes her mind and keeps on walking. Mrs. Dietrich murmurs isn't it a pity, poor thing, don't you wonder where she lives, who her family is, but Nola doesn't reply. Her pace through the first door of Lord & Taylor is so rapid that Mrs. Dietrich can barely keep up.

But Nola's upset. Strangely upset. As soon as they are in the car, packages and bags in the backseat, she begins crying.

It's childish helpless crying, as though her heart is broken. But Mrs. Dietrich knows it isn't broken, she has heard these very sobs before. Many times before. Still she comforts her daughter, embraces her, hugs her hard, hard. A sudden fierce passion. Vehemence. "Nola honey. Nola dear, what's wrong, dear, everything will be all right, dear," she says, close to weeping herself. She would embrace Nola even more tightly except for the girl's quilted jacket, that bulky L. L. Bean thing she has never liked, and Nola's stubborn lowered head. Nola has always been ashamed, crying, frantic to hide her face. Strangers are passing close by the car, curious, staring. Mrs. Dietrich wishes she had a cloak to draw over her daughter and herself, so that no one else would see.

◇ ◇ ◇

FLANNERY O'CONNOR
(1925–1964)

A Late Encounter with the Enemy
(1953)

General Sash was a hundred and four years old. He lived with his granddaughter, Sally Poker Sash, who was sixty-two years old and who prayed every night on her knees that he would live until her graduation from college. The General didn't give two slaps for her graduation but he never doubted he would live for it. Living had got to be such a habit with him that he couldn't conceive of any other condition. A graduation exercise was not exactly his idea of a good time, even if, as she said, he would be expected to sit on the stage in his uniform. She said there would be a long procession of teachers and students in their robes but that there wouldn't be anything to equal *him* in his uniform. He knew this well enough without her telling him, and as for the damn procession, it could march to hell and back and not cause him a quiver. He liked parades with floats full of Miss Americas and Miss Daytona Beaches and Miss Queen Cotton Products. He didn't have any use for processions and a procession full of school-teachers was about as deadly as the River Styx[1] to his way of thinking. However, he was willing to sit on the stage in his uniform so that they could see him.

Sally Poker was not as sure as he was that he would live until her graduation. There had not been any perceptible change in him for the last five years, but she had the sense that she might be cheated out of her triumph because she so often was. She had been going to summer school every year for the past twenty because when she started teaching, there were no such things as degrees. In those times, she said, everything was normal but nothing had been normal since she was sixteen, and for the past twenty summers, when she should have been resting, she had had to take a trunk in the burning heat to the state teacher's college; and though when she returned in the fall, she always taught in the exact way she had been taught not to teach, this was a mild revenge that didn't satisfy her sense of justice. She wanted the General at her graduation because she wanted to show what she stood for, or, as she said, "what all was behind her," and was not behind them. This *them* was not anybody in particular. It was just all the upstarts who had turned the world on its head and unsettled the ways of decent living.

She meant to stand on that platform in August with the General sitting in his wheel chair on the stage behind her and she meant to hold her head very high as if she were saying, "See him! See him! My kin, all you upstarts! Glorious upright old man standing for the old traditions! Dignity! Honor! Courage! See him!" One night in her sleep she screamed, "See him! See him!" and turned her head and found him sitting in his wheel chair behind her with a terrible expression on his face and with all his clothes off except the general's hat and she had waked up and had not dared to go back to sleep again that night.

For his part, the General would not have consented even to attend her graduation, if she had not promised to see to it that he sit on the stage. He liked to sit on any stage. He considered that he was still a very handsome man. When he had been able to stand up, he had measured five feet four inches of pure game cock. He had white hair that reached to his shoulders

---

[1] In Greek mythology, the river forming the border of Hades, the Underworld. According to mythology, the dead congregated on the shore of the river Styx seeking passage on the ferry. If they presented a bribe to the ferryman, they were allowed to cross the river; if not, they roamed the shore for eternity.

behind and he would not wear teeth because he thought his profile was more striking without them. When he put on his full-dress general's uniform, he knew well enough that there was nothing to match him anywhere.

5   This was not the same uniform he had worn in the War between the States. He had not actually been a general in that war. He had probably been a foot soldier; he didn't remember what he had been; in fact, he didn't remember that war at all. It was like his feet, which hung down now shriveled at the very end of him, without feeling, covered with a blue-gray afghan that Sally Poker had crocheted when she was a little girl. He didn't remember the Spanish-American War in which he had lost a son; he didn't even remember the son. He didn't have any use for history because he never expected to meet it again. To his mind, history was connected with processions and life with parades and he liked parades. People were always asking him if he remembered this or that—a dreary black procession of questions about the past. There was only one event in the past that had any significance for him and that he cared to talk about: that was twelve years ago when he had received the general's uniform and had been in the premiere.

"I was in that preemy they had in Atlanta," he would tell visitors sitting on his front porch. "Surrounded by beautiful guls. It wasn't a thing local about it. It was nothing local about it. Listen here. It was a nashnul event and they had me in it—up onto the stage. There was no bob-tails at it. Every person at it had paid ten dollars to get in and had to wear his tuxseeder. I was in this uniform. A beautiful gul presented me with it that afternoon in a hotel room."

"It was in a suite in the hotel and I was in it too, Papa," Sally Poker would say, winking at the visitors. "You weren't alone with any young lady in a hotel room."

"Was, I'd a known what to do," the old General would say with a sharp look and the visitors would scream with laughter. "This was a Hollywood, California, gul," he'd continue. "She was from Hollywood, California, and didn't have any part in the pitcher. Out there they have so many beautiful guls that they don't need that they call them a extra and they don't use them for nothing but presenting people with things and having their pitchers taken. They took my pitcher with her. No, it was two of them. One on either side and me in the middle with my arms around each of them's waist and their waist ain't any bigger than a half a dollar."

Sally Poker would interrupt again. "It was Mr. Govisky that gave you the uniform, Papa, and he gave me the most exquisite corsage. Really, I wish you could have seen it. It was made with gladiola petals taken off and painted gold and put back together to look like a rose. It was exquisite. I wish you could have seen it, it was . . ."

10   "It was as big as her head," the General would snarl. "I was tellin it. They gimme this uniform and they gimme this soward and they say, 'Now General, we don't want you to start a war on us. All we want you to do is march right up on that stage when you're innerduced tonight and answer

a few questions. Think you can do that?' 'Think I can do it!' I say. 'Listen here. I was doing things before you were born,' and they hollered."

"He was the hit of the show," Sally Poker would say, but she didn't much like to remember the premiere on account of what had happened to her feet at it. She had bought a new dress for the occasion—a long black crepe dinner dress with a rhinestone buckle and a bolero—and a pair of silver slippers to wear with it, because she was supposed to go up on the stage with him to keep him from falling. Everything was arranged for them. A real limousine came at ten minutes to eight and took them to the theater. It drew up under the marquee at exactly the right time, after the big stars and the director and the author and the governor and the mayor and some less important stars. The police kept traffic from jamming and there were ropes to keep the people off who couldn't go. All the people who couldn't go watched them step out of the limousine into the lights. Then they walked down the red and gold foyer and an usherette in a Confederate cap and little short skirt conducted them to their special seats. The audience was already there and a group of UDC members began to clap when they saw the General in his uniform and that started everybody to clap. A few more celebrities came after them and then the doors closed and the lights went down.

A young man with blond wavy hair who said he represented the motion-picture industry came out and began to introduce everybody and each one who was introduced walked up on the stage and said how really happy he was to be here for this great event. The General and his granddaughter were introduced sixteenth on the program. He was introduced as General Tennessee Flintrock Sash of the Confederacy, though Sally Poker had told Mr. Govisky that his name was George Poker Sash and that he had only been a major. She helped him up from his seat but her heart was beating so fast she didn't know whether she'd make it herself.

The old man walked up the aisle slowly with his fierce white head high and his hat held over his heart. The orchestra began to play the Confederate Battle Hymn very softly and the UDC members rose as a group and did not sit down again until the General was on the stage. When he reached the center of the stage with Sally Poker just behind him guiding his elbow, the orchestra burst out in a loud rendition of the Battle Hymn and the old man, with real stage presence, gave a vigorous trembling salute and stood at attention until the last blast had died away. Two of the usherettes in Confederate caps and short skirts held a Confederate and a Union flag crossed behind them.

The General stood in the exact center of the spotlight and it caught a weird moon-shaped slice of Sally Poker—the corsage, the rhinestone buckle and one hand clenched around a white glove and handkerchief. The young man with the blond wavy hair inserted himself into the circle of light and said he was *really* happy to have here tonight for this great event, one, he said, who had fought and bled in the battles they would soon see daringly reacted on the screen, and "Tell me, General," he asked, "how old are you?"

15   "Niiiiiinnttty-two!" the General screamed.

The young man looked as if this were just about the most impressive thing that had been said all evening. "Ladies and gentlemen," he said, "let's give the General the biggest hand we've got!" and there was applause immediately and the young man indicated to Sally Poker with a motion of his thumb that she could take the old man back to his seat now so that the next person could be introduced; but the General had not finished. He stood immovable in the exact center of the spotlight, his neck thrust forward, his mouth slightly open, and his voracious gray eyes drinking in the glare and the applause. He elbowed his granddaughter roughly away. "How I keep so young," he screeched, "I kiss all the pretty guls!"

This was met with a great din of spontaneous applause and it was at just that instant that Sally Poker looked down at her feet and discovered that in the excitement of getting ready she had forgotten to change her shoes: two brown Girl Scout oxfords protruded from the bottom of her dress. She gave the General a yank and almost ran with him off the stage. He was very angry that he had not got to say how glad he was to be here for this event and on the way back to his seat, he kept saying as loud as he could, "I'm glad to be here at this preemy with all these beautiful guls!" but there was another celebrity going up the other aisle and nobody paid any attention to him. He slept through the picture, muttering fiercely every now and then in his sleep.

Since then, his life had not been very interesting. His feet were completely dead now, his knees worked like old hinges, his kidneys functioned when they would, but his heart persisted doggedly to beat. The past and the future were the same thing to him, one forgotten and the other not remembered; he had no more notion of dying than a cat. Every year on Confederate Memorial Day, he was bundled up and lent to the Capitol City Museum where he was displayed from one to four in a musty room full of old photographs, old uniforms, old artillery, and historic documents. All these were carefully preserved in glass cases so that children would not put their hands on them. He wore his general's uniform from the premiere and sat, with a fixed scowl, inside a small roped area. There was nothing about him to indicate that he was alive except an occasional movement in his milky gray eyes, but once when a bold child touched his sword, his arm shot forward and slapped the hand off in an instant. In the spring when the old homes were opened for pilgrimages, he was invited to wear his uniform and sit in some conspicuous spot and lend atmosphere to the scene. Some of these times he only snarled at the visitors but sometimes he told about the premiere and the beautiful girls.

If he had died before Sally Poker's graduation, she thought she would have died herself. At the beginning of the summer term, even before she knew if she would pass, she told the Dean that her grandfather, General Tennessee Flintrock Sash of the Confederacy, would attend her graduation and that he was a hundred and four years old and that his mind was still clear as a bell. Distinguished visitors were always welcome and could sit on the stage and be introduced. She made arrangements with her nephew, John Wesley Poker Sash, a Boy Scout, to come wheel the General's chair. She thought how sweet it would be to see the old man in his courageous gray and the young boy in his clean khaki—the old and the new, she thought appropriately—they would be behind her on the stage when she received her degree.

20   Everything went almost exactly as she had planned. In the summer while she was away at school, the General stayed with other relatives and they brought him and John Wesley, the Boy Scout, down to the graduation. A reporter came to the hotel where they stayed and took the General's picture with Sally Poker on one side of him and John Wesley on the other. The General, who had had his picture taken with beautiful girls, didn't think much of this. He had forgotten precisely what kind of event this was he was going to attend but he remembered that he was to wear his uniform and carry the sword.

On the morning of the graduation, Sally Poker had to line up in the academic procession with the B.S.'s in Elementary Education and she couldn't see to getting him on the stage herself—but John Wesley, a fat blond boy of ten with an executive expression, guaranteed to take care of everything. She came in her academic gown to the hotel and dressed the old man in his uniform. He was as frail as a dried spider. "Aren't you just thrilled, Papa?" she asked. "I'm just thrilled to death!"

"Put the soward across my lap, damm you," the old man said, "where it'll shine."

She put it there and then stood back looking at him. "You look just grand," she said.

"God damm it," the old man said in a slow monotonous certain tone as if he were saying it to the beating of his heart. "God damm every goddam thing to hell."

25   "Now, now," she said and left happily to join the procession.

The graduates were lined up behind the Science building and she found her place just as the line started to move. She had not slept much the night before and when she had, she had dreamed of the exercises, murmuring, "See him, see him?" in her sleep but waking up every time just before she turned her head to look at him behind her. The graduates had to walk three blocks in the hot sun in their black wool robes and as she plodded stolidly along she thought that if anyone considered this academic procession something impressive to behold, they need only wait until they saw that old General in his courageous gray and that clean young Boy Scout stoutly wheeling his chair across the stage with the sunlight catching the sword. She imagined that John Wesley had the old man ready now behind the stage.

The black procession wound its way up the two blocks and started on the main walk leading to the auditorium. The visitors stood on the grass, picking out their graduates. Men were pushing back their hats and wiping their foreheads and women were lifting their dresses slightly from the shoulders to keep them from sticking to their backs. The graduates in their heavy robes looked as if the last beads of ignorance were being sweated out of them. The sun blazed off the fenders of automobiles and beat from the columns of the buildings and pulled the eye from one spot of glare to another. It pulled Sally Poker's toward the big red Coca-Cola machine that had been set up by the side of the auditorium. Here she saw the General parked, scowling and hatless in his chair in the blazing sun while John Wesley, his blouse loose behind, his hip and cheek pressed to the red machine, was drinking a Coca-Cola. She broke from the line and galloped to them and snatched the bottle away. She shook the boy and thrust in his blouse and put the hat on the old man's head. "Now get him in there!" she said, pointing one rigid finger to the side door of the building.

For his part the General felt as if there were a little hole beginning to widen in the top of his head. The boy wheeled him rapidly down a walk and up a ramp and into a building and bumped him over the stage entrance and into position where he had been told and the General glared in front of him at heads that all seemed to flow together and eyes that moved from one face to another. Several figures in black robes came and picked up his hand and shook it. A black procession was flowing up each aisle and forming to stately music in a pool in front of him. The music seemed to be entering his head through the little hole and he thought for a second that the procession would try to enter it too.

He didn't know what procession this was but there was something familiar about it. It must be familiar to him since it had come to meet him, but he didn't like a black procession. Any procession that came to meet him, he thought irritably, ought to have floats with beautiful guls on them like the floats before the preemy. It must be something connected with history like they were always having. He had no use for any of it. What happened then wasn't anything to a man living now and he was living now.

30   When all the procession had flowed into the black pool, a black figure began orating in front of it. The figure was telling something about history and the General made up his mind he wouldn't listen, but the words kept seeping in through the little hole in his head. He heard his own name mentioned and his chair was shuttled forward roughly and the Boy Scout took a big bow. They called his name and the fat brat bowed. Goddam you, the old man tried to say, get out of my way, I can stand up!—but he was jerked back again before he could get up and take the bow. He supposed the noise they made was for him. If he was over, he didn't intend to listen to any more of it. If it hadn't been for the little hole in the top of his head, none of the words would have got to him. He thought of putting his finger up there into the hole to block them but the hole was a little wider than his finger and it felt as if it were getting deeper.

Another black robe had taken the place of the first one and was talking now and he heard his name mentioned again but they were not talking about him, they were still talking about history. "If we forget our past," the speaker was saying, "we won't remember our future and it will be as well for we won't have one." The General heard some of these words gradually. He had forgotten history and he didn't intend to remember it again. He had forgotten the name and face of his wife and the names and faces of his children or even if he had a wife and children, and he had forgotten the names of places and the places themselves and what had happened at them.

He was considerably irked by the hole in his head. He had not expected to have a hole in his head at this event. It was the slow black music that had put it there and though most of the music had stopped outside, there was still a little of it in the hole, going deeper and moving around in his thoughts, letting the words he heard into the dark places of his brain. He heard the words, Chickamauga, Shiloh, Johnston, Lee, and he knew he was inspiring all these words that meant nothing to him. He wondered if he had been a general at Chickamauga or at Lee. Then he tried to see himself and the horse mounted in the middle of a float full of beautiful girls, being driven slowly through downtown Atlanta. Instead, the old words began to stir in his head as if they were trying to wrench themselves out of place and come to life.

The speaker was through with that war and had gone on to the next one and now he was approaching another and all his words, like the black procession, were vaguely familiar and irritating. There was a long finger of music in the General's head, probing various spots that were words, letting in a little light on the words and helping them to live. The words began to come toward him and he said, Dammit! I ain't going to have it! and he started edging backwards to get out of the way. Then he saw the figure in the black robe sit down and there was a noise and the black pool in front of him began to rumble and to flow toward him from either side to the black slow music, and he said, Stop dammit! I can't do but one thing at a time! He couldn't protect himself from the words and attend to the procession too and the words were coming at him fast. He felt that he was running backwards and the words were coming at him like musket fire, just escaping him but getting nearer and nearer. He turned around and began to run as fast as he could but he found himself running toward the words. He was running into a regular volley of them and meeting them with quick curses. As the music swelled toward him, the entire past opened up on him out of nowhere and he felt his body riddled in a hundred places with sharp stabs of pain and he fell down, returning a curse for every hit. He saw his wife's narrow face looking at him critically through her round gold-rimmed glasses; he saw one of his squinting bald-headed sons; and his mother ran toward him with an anxious look; then a succession of places—Chickamauga, Shiloh, Marthasville—rushed at him as if the past were the only future now and he had to endure it. Then suddenly he saw that the black procession was almost on him. He recognized it, for it had been dogging all his days. He made such a desperate effort to see over it and find out what comes after the past that his hand clenched the sword until the blade touched bone.

The graduates were crossing the stage in a long file to receive their scrolls and shake the president's hand. As Sally Poker, who was near the end, crossed, she glanced at the General and saw him sitting fixed and fierce, his eyes wide open, and she turned her head forward again and held it a perceptible degree higher and received her scroll. Once it was all over and she was out of the auditorium in the sun again, she located her kin and they waited together on a bench in the shade for John Wesley to wheel the old man out. That crafty scout had bumped him out the back way and rolled him at high speed down a flagstone path and was waiting now, with the corpse, in the long line at the Coca-Cola machine.

◇　◇　◇

EDGAR ALLAN POE
(1809–1849)

The Tell-Tale Heart
(1850)

True!—nervous—very, very dreadfully nervous I had been and am; but why *will* you say that I am mad? The disease had sharpened my senses—not destroyed—not dulled them. Above all was the sense of hearing acute. I heard all things in the heaven and in the earth. I heard many things in hell. How, then, am I mad? Hearken! and observe how healthily—how calmly I can tell you the whole story.

It is impossible to say how first the idea entered my brain; but once conceived, it haunted me day and night. Object there was none. Passion there was none. I loved the old man. He had never wronged me. He had never given me insult. For his gold I had no desire. I think it was his eye! yes, it was this! One of his eyes resembled that of a vulture—a pale blue eye, with a film over it. Whenever it fell upon me, my blood ran cold; and so by degrees—very gradually—I made up my mind to take the life of the old man, and thus rid myself of the eye for ever.

Now this is the point. You fancy me mad. Madmen know nothing. But you should have seen *me*. You should have seen how wisely I proceeded—with what caution—with what foresight—with what dissimulation I went to work! I was never kinder to the old man than during the whole week before I killed him. And every night, about midnight, I turned the latch of his door and opened it—oh, so gently! And then, when I had made an opening sufficient for my head, I put in a dark lantern, all closed, closed, so that no light shone out, and then I thrust in my head. Oh, you would have laughed to see how cunningly I thrust it in! I moved it slowly—very, very slowly, so that I might not disturb the old man's sleep. It took me an hour to place my whole head within the opening so far that I could see him as he lay upon his bed. Ha!—would a madman have been so wise as this? And then, when my head was well in the room, I undid the lantern cautiously—oh, so cautiously—cautiously (for the hinges creaked)—I undid it just so much that a single thin ray fell upon the vulture eye. And this I did for seven long nights—every night just at midnight—but I found the eye always closed; and so it was impossible to do the work; for it was not the old man who vexed me, but his Evil Eye. And every morning, when the day broke, I went boldly into the chamber, and spoke courageously to him, calling him by name in a hearty tone, and inquiring how he had passed the night. So you see he would have been a very profound old man, indeed, to suspect that every night, just at twelve, I looked in upon him while he slept.

Upon the eighth night I was more than usually cautious in opening the door. A watch's minute hand moves more quickly than did mine. Never before that night had I *felt* the extent of my own powers—of my sagacity. I could scarcely contain my feelings of triumph. To think that there I was, opening the door, little by little, and he not even to dream of my secret deeds or thoughts. I fairly chuckled at the idea; and perhaps he heard me; for he moved on the bed suddenly, as if startled. Now you may think that I drew back—but no. His room was as black as pitch with the thick darkness (for the shutters were close fastened, through fear of robbers), and so I knew that he could not see the opening of the door, and I kept pushing it on steadily, steadily.

5   I had my head in, and was about to open the lantern, when my thumb slipped upon the tin fastening, and the old man sprang up in the bed, crying out—"Who's there?"

I kept quite still and said nothing. For a whole hour I did not move a muscle, and in the meantime I did not hear him lie down. He was still sitting up in the bed listening;—just as I have done, night after night, hearkening to the death watches[1] in the wall.

Presently I heard a slight groan, and I knew it was the groan of mortal terror. It was not a groan of pain or of grief—oh, no!—it was the low stifled sound that arises from the bottom of the soul when overcharged with awe. I knew the sound well. Many a night, just at midnight, when all the world slept, it has welled up from my own bosom, deepening, with its dreadful echo, the terrors that distracted me. I say I knew it well. I knew what the old man felt, and pitied him, although I chuckled at heart. I knew that he had been lying awake ever since the first slight noise, when he had turned in the bed. His fears had been ever since growing upon him. He had been trying to fancy them causeless, but could not. He had been saying to himself—"It is nothing but the wind in the chimney—it is only a mouse crossing the floor," or "it is merely a cricket which has made a single chirp." Yes, he had been trying to comfort himself with these suppositions; but he

---

[1] Beetles that infest timbers. Their clicking sound was thought to be an omen of death.

had found all in vain. *All in vain;* because Death, in approaching him, had stalked with his black shadow before him, and enveloped the victim. And it was the mournful influence of the unperceived shadow that caused him to feel—although he neither saw nor heard—to *feel* the presence of my head within the room.

When I had waited a long time, very patiently, without hearing him lie down, I resolved to open a little—a very, very little crevice in the lantern. So I opened it—you cannot imagine how stealthily, stealthily—until, at length, a single dim ray, like the thread of the spider, shot from out the crevice and full upon the vulture eye.

It was open—wide, wide open—and I grew furious as I gazed upon it. I saw it with perfect distinctness—all a dull blue, with a hideous veil over it that chilled the very marrow in my bones; but I could see nothing else of the old man's face or person: for I had directed the ray as if by instinct, precisely upon the damned spot.

10   And now have I not told you that what you mistake for madness is but over-acuteness of the senses?—now, I say, there came to my ears a low, dull, quick sound, such as a watch makes when enveloped in cotton. I knew *that* sound well too. It was the beating of the old man's heart. It increased my fury, as the beating of a drum stimulates the soldier into courage.

But even yet I refrained and kept still. I scarcely breathed. I held the lantern motionless. I tried how steadily I could maintain the ray upon the eye. Meantime the hellish tattoo of the heart increased. It grew quicker and quicker, and louder and louder every instant. The old man's terror *must* have been extreme! It grew louder, I say, louder every moment!—do you mark me well? I have told you that I am nervous: so I am. And now at the dead hour of the night, amid the dreadful silence of that old house, so strange a noise as this excited me to uncontrollable terror. Yet, for some minutes longer I refrained and stood still. But the beating grew louder, louder! I thought the heart must burst. And now a new anxiety seized me—the sound would be heard by a neighbor! The old man's hour had come! With a loud yell, I threw open the lantern and leaped into the room. He shrieked once—once only. In an instant I dragged him to the floor, and pulled the heavy bed over him. I then smiled gaily, to find the deed so far done. But, for many minutes, the heart beat on with a muffled sound. This, however, did not vex me; it would not be heard through the wall. At length it ceased. The old man was dead. I removed the bed and examined the corpse. Yes, he was stone, stone dead. I placed my hand upon the heart and held it there many minutes. There was no pulsation. He was stone dead. His eye would trouble me no more.

If still you think me mad, you will think so no longer when I describe the wise precautions I took for the concealment of the body. The night waned, and I worked hastily, but in silence. First of all I dismembered the corpse. I cut off the head and the arms and the legs.

I then took up three planks from the flooring of the chamber, and deposited all between the scantlings. I then replaced the boards so cleverly, so cunningly, that no human eye—not even *his*—could have detected anything wrong. There was nothing to wash out—no stain of any kind—no blood-spot whatever. I had been too wary for that. A tub had caught all—ha! ha!

When I had made an end of these labors, it was four o'clock—still dark as midnight. As the bell sounded the hour, there came a knocking at the street door. I went down to open it with a light heart,—for what had I *now* to fear? There entered three men, who introduced themselves, with perfect suavity, as officers of the police. A shriek had been heard by a neighbor during the night; suspicion of foul play had been aroused; information had been lodged at the police office, and they (the officers) had been deputed to search the premises.

15   I smiled,—for *what* had I to fear? I bade the gentlemen welcome. The shriek, I said, was my own in a dream. The old man, I mentioned, was absent in the country. I took my visitors all over the house. I bade them search—search *well*. I led them, at length, to *his* chamber. I showed them his treasures, secure, undisturbed. In the enthusiasm of my confidence, I brought chairs into the room, and desired them *here* to rest from their fatigues, while I myself, in the wild audacity of my perfect triumph, placed my own seat upon the very spot beneath which reposed the corpse of the victim.

The officers were satisfied. My *manner* had convinced them. I was singularly at ease. They sat, and while I answered cheerily, they chatted familiar things. But, ere long, I felt myself getting pale and wished them gone. My head ached, and I fancied a ringing in my ears: but still they sat and still chatted. The ringing became more distinct:—it continued and became more distinct: I talked more freely to get rid of the feeling: but it continued and gained definitiveness—until, at length, I found that the noise was *not* within my ears.

No doubt I now grew *very* pale:—but I talked more fluently, and with a heightened voice. Yet the sound increased—and what could I do? It was *a low, dull, quick sound—much such a sound as a watch makes when enveloped in cotton.* I gasped for breath—and yet the officers heard it not. I talked more quickly—more vehemently; but the noise steadily increased. I arose and argued about trifles, in a high key and with violent gesticulations, but the noise steadily increased. Why *would* they not be gone? I paced the floor to and fro with heavy strides, as if excited to fury by the observation of the men—but the noise steadily increased. On God! what *could* I do? I foamed—I raved—I swore! I swung the chair upon which I had been sitting, and grated it upon the boards, but the noise arose over all and continually increased. It grew louder—louder—*louder!* And still the men chatted pleasantly, and smiled. Was it possible they heard not? Almighty God!—no, no! They heard!—they suspected!—they *knew!*—they were making a mockery of my horror!—this I thought, and this I think. But any thing was better than this agony! Any thing was more tolerable than this derision! I could bear those hypocritical smiles no longer! I felt that I must scream or die!—and now—again!—hark! louder! louder! louder! *louder!*—

"Villains!" I shrieked, "dissemble no more! I admit the deed!—tear up the planks!—here, here!—it is the beating of his hideous heart!"

◇ ◇ ◇

KATHERINE ANNE PORTER
(1890–1980)

The Jilting of Granny Weatherall
(1930)

She flicked her wrist neatly out of Doctor Harry's pudgy careful fingers and pulled the sheet up to her chin. The brat ought to be in knee breeches. Doctoring around the country with spectacles on his nose! "Get along now, take your schoolbooks and go. There's nothing wrong with me."

Doctor Harry spread a warm paw like a cushion on her forehead where the forked green vein danced and made her eyelids twitch. "Now, now, be a good girl, and we'll have you up in no time."

"That's no way to speak to a woman nearly eighty years old just because she's down. I'd have you respect your elders, young man."

"Well, Missy, excuse me." Doctor Harry patted her cheek. "But I've got to warn you, haven't I? You're a marvel, but you must be careful or you're going to be good and sorry."

5 "Don't tell me what I'm going to be. I'm on my feet now, morally speaking. It's Cornelia. I had to go to bed to get rid of her."

Her bones felt loose, and floated around in her skin, and Doctor Harry floated like a balloon around the foot of the bed. He floated and pulled down his waistcoat and swung his glasses on a cord. "Well, stay where you are, it certainly can't hurt you."

"Get along and doctor your sick," said Granny Weatherall. "Leave a well woman alone. I'll call for you when I want you. . . . Where were you forty years ago when I pulled through milk-leg and double pneumonia? You weren't even born. Don't let Cornelia lead you on," she shouted, because Doctor Harry appeared to float up to the ceiling and out. "I pay my own bills, and I don't throw my money away on nonsense!"

She meant to wave good-by, but it was too much trouble. Her eyes closed of themselves, it was like a dark curtain drawn around the bed. The pillow rose and floated under her, pleasant as a hammock in a light wind. She listened to the leaves rustling outside the window. No, somebody was swishing newspapers: no, Cornelia and Doctor Harry were whispering together. She leaped broad awake, thinking they whispered in her ear.

"She was never like this, *never* like this!" "Well, what can we expect?" "Yes, eighty years old. . . ."

10 Well, and what if she was? She still had ears. It was like Cornelia to whisper around doors. She always kept things secret in such a public way.

She was always being tactful and kind. Cornelia was dutiful; that was the trouble with her. Dutiful and good: "So good and dutiful," said Granny, "that I'd like to spank her." She saw herself spanking Cornelia and making a fine job of it.

"What'd you say, Mother?"

Granny felt her face tying up in hard knots.

"Can't a body think, I'd like to know?"

"I thought you might want something."

15   "I do. I want a lot of things. First off, go away and don't whisper."

She lay and drowsed, hoping in her sleep that the children would keep out and let her rest a minute. It had been a long day. Not that she was tired. It was always pleasant to snatch a minute now and then. There was always so much to be done, let me see: tomorrow.

Tomorrow was far away and there was nothing to trouble about. Things were finished somehow when the time came; thank God there was always a little margin over for peace: then a person could spread out the plan of life and tuck in the edges orderly. It was good to have everything clean and folded away, with the hair brushes and tonic bottles sitting straight on the white embroidered linen: the day started without fuss and the pantry shelves laid out with rows of jelly glasses and brown jugs and white stone-china jars with blue whirligigs and words painted on them: coffee, tea, sugar, ginger, cinnamon, allspice: and the bronze clock with the lion on top nicely dusted off. The dust that lion could collect in twenty-four hours! The box in the attic with all those letters tied up, well, she'd have to go through that tomorrow. All those letters—George's letters and John's letters and her letters to them both—lying around for the children to find afterwards made her uneasy. Yes, that would be tomorrow's business. No use to let them know how silly she had been once.

While she was rummaging around she found death in her mind and it felt clammy and unfamiliar. She had spent so much time preparing for death there was no need for bringing it up again. Let it take care of itself now. When she was sixty she had felt very old, finished, and went around making farewell trips to see her children and grandchildren, with a secret in her mind: This is the very last of your mother, children! Then she made her will and came down with a long fever. That was all just a notion like a lot of other things, but it was lucky too, for she had once and for all got over the idea of dying for a long time. Now she couldn't be worried. She hoped she had better sense now. Her father had lived to be one hundred and two years old and had drunk a noggin of strong hot toddy on his last birthday. He told the reporters it was his daily habit, and he owed his long life to that. He had made quite a scandal and was very pleased about it. She believed she'd just plague Cornelia a little.

"Cornelia! Cornelia!" No footsteps, but a sudden hand on her cheek. "Bless you, where have you been?"

20   "Here, Mother."

"Well, Cornelia, I want a noggin of hot toddy."

"Are you cold, darling?"

"I'm chilly, Cornelia. Lying in bed stops the circulation. I must have told you that a thousand times."

Well, she could just hear Cornelia telling her husband that Mother was getting a little childish and they'd have to humor her. The thing that most annoyed her was that Cornelia thought she was deaf, dumb, and blind. Little hasty glances and tiny gestures tossed around her and over her head saying, "Don't cross her, let her have her way, she's eighty years old," and she sitting there as if she lived in a thin glass cage. Sometimes Granny almost made up her mind to pack up and move back to her own house where nobody could remind her every minute that she was old. Wait, wait, Cornelia, till your own children whisper behind your back!

25   In her day she had kept a better house and had got more work done. She wasn't too old yet for Lydia to be driving eighty miles for advice when one of the children jumped the track, and Jimmy still dropped in and talked things over: "Now, Mammy, you've a good business head, I want to know what you think of this? . . ." Old. Cornelia couldn't change the furniture around without asking. Little things, little things! They had been so sweet when they were little. Granny wished the old days were back again with the children young and everything to be done over. It had been a hard pull, but not too much for her. When she thought of all the food she had cooked, and all the clothes she had cut and sewed, and all the gardens she had made—well, the children showed it. There they were, made out of her, and they couldn't get away from that. Sometimes she wanted to see John again and point to them and say, Well, I didn't do so badly, did I? But that would have to wait. That was for tomorrow. She used to think of him as a man, but now all the children were older than their father, and he would be a child beside her if she saw him now. It seemed strange and there was something wrong in the idea. Why, he couldn't possibly recognize her. She had fenced in a hundred acres once, digging the post holes herself and clamping the wires with just a negro boy to help. That changed a woman. John would be looking for a young woman with the peaked Spanish comb in her hair and the painted fan. Digging post holes changed a woman. Riding country roads in the winter when women had their babies was another thing: sitting up nights with sick horses and sick negroes and sick children and hardly ever losing one. John, I hardly ever lost one of them! John would see that in a minute, that would be something he could understand, she wouldn't have to explain anything!

It made her feel like rolling up her sleeves and putting the whole place to rights again. No matter if Cornelia was determined to be everywhere at once, there were a great many things left undone on this place. She would start tomorrow and do them. It was good to be strong enough for everything, even if all you made melted and changed and slipped under your hands, so that by the time you finished you almost forgot what you were working for. What was it I set out to do? she asked herself intently, but she could not remember. A fog rose over the valley, she saw it marching across the creek swallowing the trees and moving up the hill like an army of ghosts. Soon it would be at the near edge of the orchard, and then it was time to go in and light the lamps. Come in, children, don't stay out in the night air.

Lighting the lamps had been beautiful. The children huddled up to her and breathed like little calves waiting at the bars in the twilight. Their eyes followed the match and watched the flame rise and settle in a blue curve, then they moved away from her. The lamp was lit, they didn't have to be scared and hang on to mother any more. Never, never, never more. God, for all my life I thank Thee. Without Thee, my God, I could never have done it. Hail, Mary, full of grace.

I want you to pick all the fruit this year and see that nothing is wasted. There's always someone who can use it. Don't let good things rot for want of using. You waste life when you waste good food. Don't let things get lost. It's bitter to lose things. Now, don't let me get to thinking, not when I am tired and taking a little nap before supper. . . .

The pillow rose about her shoulders and pressed against her heart and the memory was being squeezed out of it: oh, push down the pillow, somebody: it would smother her if she tried to hold it. Such a fresh breeze blowing and such a green day with no threats in it. But he had not come, just the same. What does a woman do when she has put on the white veil and set out the white cake for a man and he doesn't come? She tried to remember. No, I swear he never harmed me but in that. He never harmed me but in that . . . and what if he did? There was the day, the day, but a whirl of dark smoke rose and covered it, crept up and over into the bright field where everything was planted so carefully in orderly rows. That was hell, she knew hell when she saw it. For sixty years she had prayed against remembering him and against losing her soul in the deep pit of hell, and now the two things were mingled in one and the thought of him was a smoky cloud from hell that moved and crept in her head when she had just got rid of Doctor Harry and was trying to rest a minute. Wounded vanity, Ellen, said a sharp voice in the top of her mind. Don't let your wounded vanity get the upper hand of you. Plenty of girls get jilted. You were jilted, weren't you? Then stand up to it. Her eyelids wavered and let in streamers of blue-gray light like tissue paper over her eyes. She must get up and pull the shades down or she'd never sleep. She was in bed again and the shades were not down. How could that happen? Better turn over, hide from the light, sleeping in the light gave you nightmares. "Mother, how do you feel now?" and a stinging wetness on her forehead. But I don't like having my face washed in cold water!

30   Hapsy? George? Lydia? Jimmy? No, Cornelia, and her features were swollen and full of little puddles. "They're coming, darling, they'll all be here soon." Go wash your face, child, you look funny.

Instead of obeying, Cornelia knelt down and put her head on the pillow. She seemed to be talking but there was no sound. "Well, are you tongue-tied? Whose birthday is it? Are you going to give a party?"

Cornelia's mouth moved urgently in strange shapes. "Don't do that, you bother me, daughter."

"O, no, Mother. Oh, no. . . . "

Nonsense. It was strange about children. They disputed your every word. "No what, Cornelia?"

35 "Here's Doctor Harry."

"I won't see that boy again. He just left five minutes ago."

"That was this morning, Mother. It's night now. Here's the nurse."

"This is Doctor Harry, Mrs. Weatherall. I never saw you look so young and happy!"

"Ah, I'll never be young again—but I'd be happy if they'd let me lie in peace and get rested."

40 She thought she spoke up loudly, but no one answered. A warm weight on her forehead, a warm bracelet on her wrist, and a breeze went on whispering, trying to tell her something. A shuffle of leaves in the everlasting hand of God. He blew on them and they danced and rattled. "Mother, don't mind, we're going to give you a little hypodermic." "Look here, daughter, how do ants get in this bed? I saw sugar ants yesterday." Did you send for Hapsy too?

It was Hapsy she really wanted. She had to go a long way back through a great many rooms to find Hapsy standing with a baby on her arm. She seemed to herself to be Hapsy also, and the baby on Hapsy's arm was Hapsy and himself and herself, all at once, and there was no surprise in the meeting. Then Hapsy melted from within and turned flimsy as gray gauze and the baby was a gauzy shadow, and Hapsy came up close and said, "I thought you'd never come," and looked at her very searchingly and said, "You haven't changed a bit!" They leaned forward to kiss, when Cornelia began whispering from a long way off, "Oh, is there anything you want to tell me? Is there anything I can do for you?"

Yes, she had changed her mind after sixty years and she would like to see George. I want you to find George. Find him and be sure to tell him I forgot him. I want him to know I had my husband just the same and my children and my house like any other woman. A good house too and a good husband that I loved and fine children out of him. Better than I hoped for even. Tell him I was given back everything he took away and more. Oh, no, oh, God, no, there was something else besides the house and the man and the children. Oh, surely they were not all? What was it? Something not given back. . . . Her breath crowded down under her ribs and grew into a monstrous frightening shape with cutting edges; it bored up into her head, and the agony was unbelievable: Yes, John, get the Doctor now, no more talk, my time has come.

When this one was born it should be the last. The last. It should have been born first, for it was the one she had truly wanted. Everything came in good time. Nothing left out, left over. She was strong, in three days she would be as well as ever. Better. A woman needed milk in her to have her full health.

"Mother, do you hear me?"

45   "I've been telling you—"

"Mother, Father Connolly's here."

"I went to Holy Communion last week. Tell him I'm not so sinful as all that."

"Father just wants to speak to you."

He could speak as much as he pleased. It was like him to drop in and inquire about her soul as if it were a teething baby, and then stay on for a cup of tea and a round of cards and gossip. He always had a funny story of some sort, usually about an Irishman who made his little mistakes and confessed them, and the point lay in some absurd thing he would blurt out in the confessional showing his struggles between native piety and original sin. Granny felt easy about her soul. Cornelia, where are your manners? Give Father Connolly a chair. She had her secret comfortable understanding with a few favorite saints who cleared a straight road to God for her. All as surely signed and sealed as the papers for the new Forty Acres. Forever . . . heirs and assigns forever. Since the day the wedding cake was not cut, but thrown out and wasted. The whole bottom dropped out of the world, and there she was blind and sweating with nothing under her feet and the walls falling away. His hand had caught her under the breast, she had not fallen, there was the freshly polished floor with the green rug on it, just as before. He had cursed like a sailor's parrot and said, "I'll kill him for you." Don't lay a hand on him, for my sake leave something to God. "Now, Ellen, you must believe what I tell you. . . . "

50   So there was nothing, nothing to worry about any more, except sometimes in the night one of the children screamed in a nightmare, and they both hustled out shaking and hunting for the matches and calling, "There, wait a minute, here we are!" John, get the doctor now, Hapsy's time has come. But there was Hapsy standing by the bed in a white cap. "Cornelia, tell Hapsy to take off her cap. I can't see her plain."

Her eyes opened very wide and the room stood out like a picture she had seen somewhere. Dark colors with the shadows rising towards the ceiling in long angles. The tall black dresser gleamed with nothing on it but John's picture, enlarged from a little one, with John's eyes very black when they should have been blue. You never saw him, so how do you know how he looked? But the man insisted the copy was perfect, it was very rich and handsome. For a picture, yes, but it's not my husband. The table by the bed had a linen cover and a candle and a crucifix. The light was blue from Cornelia's silk lampshades. No sort of light at all, just frippery. You had to live forty years with kerosene lamps to appreciate honest electricity. She felt very strong and she saw Doctor Harry with a rosy nimbus around him.

"You look like a saint, Doctor Harry, and I vow that's as near as you'll ever come to it."

"She's saying something."

"I heard you, Cornelia. What's all this carrying-on?"

55 "Father Connolly's saying—"

Cornelia's voice staggered and bumped like a cart in a bad road. It rounded corners and turned back again and arrived nowhere. Granny stepped up in the cart very lightly and reached for the reins, but a man sat beside her and she knew him by his hands, driving the cart. She did not look in his face, for she knew without seeing, but looked instead down the road where the trees leaned over and bowed to each other and a thousand birds were singing a Mass. She felt like singing too, but she put her hand in the bosom of her dress and pulled out a rosary, and Father Connolly murmured Latin in a very solemn voice and tickled her feet. My God, will you stop that nonsense? I'm a married woman. What if he did run away and leave me to face the priest by myself? I found another a whole world better. I wouldn't have exchanged my husband for anybody except St. Michael himself, and you may tell him that for me with a thank you in the bargain.

Light flashed on her closed eyelids, and a deep roaring shook her. Cornelia, is that lightning? I hear thunder. There's going to be a storm. Close all the windows. Call the children in. . . . "Mother, here we are, all of us." "Is that you, Hapsy?" "Oh, no, I'm Lydia. We drove as fast as we could." Their faces drifted above her, drifted away. The rosary fell out of her hands and Lydia put it back. Jimmy tried to help, their hands fumbled together, and Granny closed two fingers around Jimmy's thumb. Beads wouldn't do, it must be something alive. She was so amazed her thoughts ran round and round. So, my dear Lord, this is my death and I wasn't even thinking about it. My children have come to see me die. But I can't, it's not time. Oh, I always hated surprises. I wanted to give Cornelia the amethyst set— Cornelia, you're to have the amethyst set, but Hapsy's to wear it when she wants, and, Doctor Harry, do shut up. Nobody sent for you. Oh, my dear Lord, do wait a minute. I meant to do something about the Forty Acres, Jimmy doesn't need it and Lydia will later on, with that worthless husband of hers. I meant to finish the altar cloth and send six bottles of wine to Sister Borgia for her dyspepsia. I want to send six bottles of wine to Sister Borgia, Father Connolly, now don't let me forget.

Cornelia's voice made short turns and tilted over and crashed. "Oh, Mother, oh, Mother, oh, Mother. . . . "

"I'm not going, Cornelia. I'm taken by surprise. I can't go."

60 You'll see Hapsy again. What about her? "I thought you'd never come." Granny made a long journey outward, looking for Hapsy. What if I don't find her? What then? Her heart sank down and down, there was no bottom to death, she couldn't come to the end of it. The blue light from Cornelia's lampshade drew into a tiny point in the center of her brain, it flickered and winked like an eye, quietly it fluttered and dwindled. Granny lay curled down within herself, amazed and watchful, staring at the point of light that was herself; her body was now only a deeper mass of shadow in an endless darkness and this darkness would curl around the light and swallow it up. God, give a sign!

For the second time there was no sign. Again no bridegroom and the priest in the house. She could not remember any other sorrow because this grief wiped them all away. Oh, no, there's nothing more cruel than this— I'll never forgive it. She stretched herself with a deep breath and blew out the light.

◇ ◇ ◇

CAROL SHIELDS
(1935–   )

Fifteen Minutes in the Life of Larry Weller
(1997)

By mistake Larry Weller took someone else's Harris tweed jacket instead of his own, and it wasn't till he jammed his hand in the pocket that he knew something was wrong.

His hand was traveling straight into a silky void. His five fingers pushed down, looking for the balled-up Kleenex from his own familiar worn-out pocket, the nickels and dimes, the ticket receipts from all the movies he and Dorrie had been seeing lately. Also those hard little bits of lint, like meteor grit, that never seem to lose themselves once they've worked into the seams.

This pocket—today's pocket—was different. Clean, a slippery valley. The stitches he touched at the bottom weren't his stitches. His fingertips glided now on a sweet little sea of lining. He grabbed for the buttons. Leather, the real thing. And something else—the sleeves were a good half inch longer than they should have been.

This jacket was twice the value of his own. The texture, the seams. You could see it got sent all the time to the cleaners. Another thing, you could tell by the way the shoulders sprang out that this jacket got parked on a thick wooden hanger at night. Above a row of polished shoes. Refilling its tweedy warp and woof with oxygenated air.

5   He should have run back to the coffee shop to see if his own jacket was still scrunched there on the back of his chair, but it was already quarter to six, and Dorrie was expecting him at six sharp, and it was rush hour and he wasn't anywhere near the bus stop.

And—the thought came to him—what's the point? A jacket's a jacket. A person who patronizes a place like Cafe Capri is almost asking to get his jacket copped. This way all that's happened is a kind of exchange.

Forget the bus, he decided. He'd walk. He'd stroll. In his hot new Harris tweed apparel. He'd push his shoulders along, letting them roll loose in their sockets. Forward with the right shoulder, bam, then the left shoulder coming up from behind. He'd let his arms swing wide. Fan his fingers out. Here comes the Big Guy, watch out for the Big Guy.

The sleeves rubbed light across the back of his hands, scratchy but not *too* scratchy.

And then he saw that the cuff buttons were leather too, a smaller-size version of the main buttons, but the same design, a sort of cross-pattern like a pecan pie cut in quarters, only the slices overlapped this little bit. You could feel the raised design with your finger, the way the four quadrants of leather crossed over and over each other, their edges cut wavy on the inside margin. These waves intersected in the middle, dived down there in a dark center and disappeared. A black hole in the button universe. Zero.

10   *Quadrant* was a word Larry hadn't even thought of for about ten years, not since geometry class, grade eleven.

The color of the jacket was mixed shades of brown, a strong background of freckled tobacco tones with subtle orange flecks. Very subtle. No one would say: hey, here comes this person with orange flecks distributed across his jacket. You'd have to be one inch away before you took in those flecks.

Orange wasn't Larry's favorite color, at least not in the clothing line. He remembered he'd had orange swim trunks back in high school, MacDonald Secondary, probably about two sizes too big, since he was always worrying at that time in his life about his bulge showing, which was exactly the opposite of most guys, who made a big point of showing what they had. Modesty ran in his family, his mum, his dad, his sister, Midge, and once modesty gets into your veins you're stuck with it. Dorrie, on the other hand, doesn't even shut the bathroom door when she's in there, going. A different kind of family altogether.

He'd had orange socks once too, neon orange. That didn't last too long. Pretty soon he was back to white socks. Sports socks. You got a choice between a red stripe around the top, a blue stripe, or no stripe at all. Even geeks like Larry and his friend Bill Herschel, who didn't go in for sports, they still wore those thick cotton sports socks every single day. You bought them three in a pack and they lasted about a week before they fell into holes. You always thought, hey, what a bargain, three pairs of socks at this fantastic price!

White socks went on for a long time in Larry's life. A whole era.

15   Usually he didn't button a jacket, but it just came to him as he was walking along that he wanted to do up one of those leather buttons, the middle one. It felt good, not too tight over the gut. The guy must be about his own size, 40 medium, which is lucky for him. If, for example, he'd picked up Larry's old jacket, he could throw it in the garbage tomorrow, but at least he wasn't walking around Winnipeg with just his shirt on his back. The nights got cool this time of year. Rain was forecast too.

A lot of people don't know that Harris tweed is virtually waterproof. You'd think cloth this thick and woolly would soak up water like a sponge, but, in actual fact, rain slides right off the surface. This was explained to Larry by a knowledgeable old guy who worked in menswear at Hector's.

That would be, what, nine, ten years ago, before Hector's went out of business. Larry could tell that this wasn't just a sales pitch. The guy—he wore a lapel button that said "Salesman of the Year"—talked about how the sheep they've got over there are covered with special long oily hair that repels water. This made sense to Larry, a sheep standing out in the rain day and night. This was his protection.

Dorrie kept wanting him to buy a khaki trenchcoat, but he doesn't need one, not with his Harris tweed. You don't want bulk when you're walking along. He walks a lot. It's when he does his thinking. He hums his thoughts out on the air like music; they've got a disco beat: My name is Larry Weller. I'm a floral designer, twenty-six years old, and I'm walking down Notre Dame Avenue, in the city of Winnipeg, in the country of Canada, in the month of April, in the year 1977, and I'm thinking hard. About being hungry, about being late, about having sex later on tonight. About how great I feel in this other guy's Harris tweed jacket.

Cars were zipping along, horns honking, trucks going by every couple of seconds, people yelling at each other. Not a quiet neighborhood. But even with all the noise blaring out, Larry kept hearing this tiny slidey little underneath noise. He'd been hearing it for the last couple of minutes. Whoosh, wash, whoosh, wash. It was coming out of the body of Larry J. Weller. It wasn't that he found it objectionable. He liked it, as a matter of fact, but he just wanted to know what it was.

He whooshed past the Triple Value Store, past the Portuguese Funeral Home, past Big Mike's where they had their windows full of ski equipment on sale. The store was packed with people wearing spring clothes, denim jackets, super-flare pants, and so on, but they were already thinking ahead to next winter. They had snow in their heads instead of a nice hot beach. That's one thing Larry appreciates about Dorrie. She lives in the moment. When it's snowing she thinks about snow. When it's spring, like right now, she's thinking about getting some new sandals. That's what she's doing this very minute; buying sandals at Shoes Express, their two-for-one sale. Larry knows she's probably made up her mind already, but she told him she'd wait till he got to the store before buying. She wants to make sure Larry likes what she decides on, even though sandals are just sandals to him. Just a bunch of straps.

20   Dorrie knows how to stretch money. She saves the fifty-cents-off coupons from Ponderosa—which'll give you a rib eye steak, baked potato and salad, all for $1.69. Or she'll hear a rumor that next week shoe prices are going to get slashed double. So she'll say to the guy at Shoes Express, "Look, can you hold these for me till next Wednesday or Thursday or whatever, so I can get in on the sales price?"

It comes to Larry, what the noise is. It's the lining of his jacket moving back and forth across his shoulders as he strolls along, also the lining material sliding up and down against his shirt-sleeves. He can make it softer if he slows down. Or louder if he lifts his arm and waves at that guy across the street that he doesn't even know. The guy's waving back, he's trying to figure out who Larry is—*hey, who's that man striding along over there, that man in the very top-line Harris tweed jacket?*

Actually no one wears Harris tweed much anymore. In fact, they never did, no one Larry ever knew. It's vintage almost, like a costume. What happened was, Larry was about to graduate from Red River College (Floral Arts Diploma), just two guys and twenty-four girls. The ceremony was in the cafeteria instead of the general-purpose room, and dress was supposed to be informal. So what's informal? Suits or what? The girls ended up wearing just regular dresses, and the two guys opted for jackets and dress pants.

Larry and his mother went to Hector's, which she swears by, and that's where they found the Harris tweed, this nubby-dubby wool cloth, smooth and rough at the same time, heavy but also light, with the look of money and the feel of a grain sack, and everywhere these soft little hairs riding on top of the weave. The salesman said: "Hey, you could wear that jacket to a do at the Prime Minister's." Larry had never heard of Harris tweed, but the salesman said it was a classic. That it would never go out of style. That it would wear like iron. Then his mother chimed in about how it wouldn't show the dirt, and the salesman said he'd try real hard to get them twenty percent off, and that clinched it.

Larry wears the Harris tweed to Flowerfolks almost every day over a pair of jeans, and it's hardly worn out at all. It never looks wrinkled or dirty. Or at least it didn't until today when Larry put on this other jacket by mistake. So! There's Harris tweed and Harris tweed, uh-*huh*.

25   It was an accident how Larry got into floral design. A fluke. He'd been out of school for a few weeks, just goofing off, and finally his mother phoned Red River College one day and asked them to mail out their brochure on the Furnace Repair course. She figured everyone's got a furnace, so even with the economy up and down, furnaces were a good thing to get into. Well, someone must have been sleeping at the switch, because along came a pamphlet from Floral Arts, flowers instead of furnaces. Larry's mother, Dot, sat right down in the breakfast nook and read it straight through, tapping her foot as she turned the pages, and nodding her head at the ivy wallpaper as if she was saying, yes, yes, floral design really is the future.

Larry's father, though, wasn't too overwhelmed. Larry could tell he was thinking that flowers were for girls, not boys. Like maybe his only son was a homo and it was just starting to show. In the end, he did come to Larry's graduation in the cafeteria but he didn't know where to look. Even when Mrs. Starr presented Larry with the Rose Wreath for having the top point average, Larry's father just sat there with his chin scraping the floor.

Larry was offered a job right off at Flowerfolks, and he's been there ever since. Last October he got to do the centerpieces for the mayor's banquet. It was even on television, Channel 13. You saw the mayor standing up to give his speech and there were these sprays of wheat, eucalyptus branches, and baby orchids right there on the table. Orchids! So much for your average taxpayer. But Flowerfolks has a policy of delivering their flowers to hospital wards if their clients don't want them afterwards, so it's really not a waste. They're a chain with a social conscience, and also an emphasis on professionalism. They like the employees to look good. Shoulder-length hair's okay for male staff, but not a quarter inch longer. A tie's optional, but jackets are required. That's where the Harris tweed comes in.

Larry can't help thinking how this new, new jacket will knock their eyebrows off down at work.

Or maybe not, maybe they won't even notice. He hadn't noticed himself when he picked it up, so why should they? What happened was he went up to the counter to order his cappuccino. Not that he had to order it. He takes the same thing every day, a double cappuccino. He used to go to a bar for a few beers after work, but Dorrie got worried about all the booze he was soaking up. She was convinced his brain cells were getting killed off. One by one they were going out, like Christmas lights on a string, only there weren't any replacements available.

30 "Why don't you switch to coffee?" she said, and that's when Larry started dropping into Cafe Capri, which is just around the corner from Flowerfolks. A nothing place, but they've brought cappuccino to this town. Nobody knew what it was at first, and some people, like Larry's folks, still don't. Larry's tried it, and now he's on a streak with double cappuccinos. They start making it when they see him come through the door at five-thirty.

He likes to put on his own cinnamon. He likes it spread out thin across the entire foam area, not just sitting in a wet clump in the middle. You take the shaker, hold it sideways about two inches to the right of the cup and tap it twice, lightly. A soft little cinnamon cloud forms in the air—you can almost see it hanging there—and then the little grains drift down evenly into the cup. Total coverage. Like the dust storm in Winnipeg last summer, how it coated every ledge and leaf and petunia petal with this beautiful, evenly distributed layer of powdery dust.

Lots of coffee places have switched over to disposable plastic, but Cafe Capri still uses those old white cups and saucers with the green rims. You put one of those cups up to your mouth and the thickness feels exactly right, the same dimensions as your own tongue and lips. You and your cup melt together, it's like a kiss. Customers appreciate that. They're so grateful for regular cups and saucers that they carry their own empties up to the counter on their way out. That's what Larry must have done. Taken his cup back up, put his fifty-five cents by the cash, and picked up a jacket from the chair. Only it was someone else's chair. Or maybe the other guy had already made off with Larry's jacket at that point. A mistake can work both ways. Larry was probably busy thinking about meeting Dorrie, about the movie they were going to see that night, *Marathon Man*, their third time, and then coming back to her place after, his prick stirring at the thought.

When they first started going together they'd be lying there on top of her bed and she'd say, "Let's fuck and fuck and fuck forever."

"Do you have to say that?" Larry said to her after he'd known her a couple of months. "Can't you just say 'making love'?"

35   She got her hurt look. Parts of her face tended to lose their shape, especially around her mouth. "You say 'fuck,'" she said to Larry. "You say it all the time."

"No, I don't."

"Come off it. You're always saying 'fuck this' and 'fuck that.'"

"Maybe. Maybe I do. But I don't say it literally."

"What?" She looked baffled.

40   "Not *literally.*"

"There you go again," she said, "with those college words."

Larry stared at her. She actually thinks *flower* college is *college.*

It was sort of a mistake the way they got together. Larry had taken another girl to a Halloween party at St. Anthony's Hall. She, the other girl, had a pirate suit on, with a patch over the eye, a sword, the whole thing. And she'd made herself a moustache with an eyebrow pencil or something. That bothered Larry, turning his head around quick, and looking into the face of a girl wearing a moustache. A costume is supposed to change you, but you can go too far. Larry was a clown that night. He had the floppy shoes and the hat and the white paint on his face, but he'd skipped the red nose. Who's going to score points with a red nose? There was another girl, Dorrie, at the table who'd come with her girlfriends. She was dressed like a Martian, but only a little bit like a Martian. You got the general idea, but you didn't think when you were dancing with her that she was some weird extraterrestrial. She was just this skinny, swervy, good-looking girl who happened to be wearing a rented Martian suit.

"You in love with this Dorrie?" That's what Larry's father asked him a couple of months ago. They were sitting there in the stands. As usual the Jets were winning. Everyone around them was cheering like crazy, and Larry's father said to Larry, not quite turning his face: "So, you in love with this girl? This Dorrie person?"

45   "What?" Larry said. He had his eyes on the goalie all alone out there on the ice, big as a Japanese wrestler in his mask and shin pads, putting on a tap-dance show while the puck was coming down the ice.

"Love," Larry's father said. "You heard me."

"I like her," Larry said after a few seconds. He didn't know what else to say. The question set a flange around his thoughts, holding back his recent worrying days and nights, keeping them separate from right-now time.

"But you're not in love?"

"I guess not."

50   "You just like her?"

"Yes. But a lot."

"You're twenty-six years old," Larry's father said. "I married Mum when I was twenty-five."

Like a deadline's been missed, that was his tone of voice.

"Yeah," Larry said. "Twenty-six years old, and the kid's still living at home!"

55   He felt his bony face fall into confusion. And yet he loved this confusion, it was so unexpected, so full of thrill and danger. Love, love.

"Nothing wrong with living at home," Larry's father said, huffing a little, looking off sideways. "Did you say there was anything wrong with that?"

Larry was running this conversation through his head while he walked along Notre Dame Avenue in his stolen Harris tweed jacket, seeing himself in his self's silver mirror. The fabric swayed around him, shifting and reshifting on his shoulders with every step he took. It seemed like something alive. Inside him, and outside him too. It was like an apartment. He could move into this jacket and live there. Take up residence, get himself a new phone number and a set of cereal bowls.

That's when he realized he was in love with dopey smart Dorrie. In love. He was. He really was. Knowing it was like running into a wall of heat, his head and hands pushing right through it. This surprised him, but not completely. You can fall in love all by yourself. You don't have to be standing next to the person; you can do it alone, walking down a street with the wind blowing in your face, a whole lot of people you don't even know going by and they're kind of half bumping into you but you don't notice because you're in a trancelike state. He forgot, suddenly, how Dorrie had this too-little face with too much hair around it and how he always used to get turned on by girls with bigger faces and just average hair size.

He looked at his watch, worried. He knew she'd still be standing there, though, next to the cash with her arms full of shoes and she'd be pissed off for about two seconds and then she'd get an eyeful of Larry's jacket and before you knew it she'd be rubbing her hands up and down the cloth and fingering the buttons.

60   The problem, though, was tomorrow. Larry and his new jacket weren't going to make it tomorrow. He could go to work in this jacket, but no way could he go back to the Capri at five o'clock. They'd grab him the minute he walked in. *Hey, buddy, there's a call out for that jacket. That jacket's been reported.*

Wait a minute, it's all a mistake.

A mistake that led to another mistake that led to another. People make mistakes all the time, so many mistakes that they aren't mistakes anymore, they're just positive and negative charges shooting back and forth and moving you along. Like good luck and bad luck. Like a tunnel you're walking through, with all your pores wide open. When it turns, you turn too.

Larry remembers seeing a patient in the Winnipeg Chronic Care Unit when he delivered the flowers after the mayor's banquet. This guy didn't have any arms or legs, just little buds growing out of his body. He was one bad mistake, like a human salt shaker perched there on the edge of a bed.

Larry, set the flowers down on the table next to him, and the guy leaned over a couple of inches and brushed them with his forehead, then he smelled them, then he stuck his tongue out and licked the leaves and petals, all the while giving Larry a look, almost a wink but not quite. Larry took a lick too, lightly. What he found was, eucalyptus tastes like horse medicine. And orchids don't taste at all.

The sun was dipping low, and Larry was at the corner now, only half a block from Shoes Express. There was great big rubbish receptacle standing there with a sign on it: Help Keep Our City Clean.

65   Larry unbuttoned the Harris tweed jacket, slipped it off fast and rolled it up in a sweet little ball. He stuffed it into the rubbish bin. He had to cram it in. He didn't know if he was making a mistake or not, getting rid of that jacket, and he didn't care. The jacket had to go.

And that's when he really knew how cold the wind had got. It puffed his shirt-sleeves up like a couple of balloons, so that all of a sudden he had these huge brand-new muscles. Superman. Then it shifted around quick, and there he was with his shirt pressed flat against his arms and chest, puny and shrunk-up. The next minute he was inflated again. Then it all got sucked out. In and out, in and out. The windiest city in the country, in North America. It really was.

There were plenty of eyes on him, he could feel them boring through to his skin. In about two minutes some guy was going to pull that Harris tweed jacket out of the garbage and put it on. But by that time Larry would be around the corner, walking straight toward the next thing that was going to happen to him.

◇ ◇ ◇

A M Y   T A N
(1952–   )

<h1 style="text-align:center">Two Kinds</h1>
(1989)

My mother believed you could be anything you wanted to be in America. You could open a restaurant. You could work for the government and get good retirement. You could buy a house with almost no money down. You could become rich. You could become instantly famous.

"Of course you can be prodigy, too," my mother told me when I was nine. "You can be best anything. What does Auntie Lindo know? Her daughter, she is only best tricky."

America was where all my mother's hopes lay. She had come here in 1949 after losing everything in China: her mother and father, her family home, her first husband, and two daughters, twin baby girls. But she never looked back with regret. There were so many ways for things to get better.

• • •

We didn't immediately pick the right kind of prodigy. At first my mother thought I could be a Chinese Shirley Temple. We'd watch Shirley's old movies on TV as though they were training films. My mother would poke my arm and say, *"Ni kan"*—You watch. And I would see Shirley tapping her feet, or singing a sailor song, or pursing her lips into a very round O while saying, "Oh my goodness."

5   *"Ni kan,"* said my mother as Shirley's eyes flooded with tears. "You already know how. Don't need talent for crying!"

Soon after my mother got this idea about Shirley Temple, she took me to a beauty training school in the Mission district and put me in the hands of a student who could barely hold the scissors without shaking. Instead of getting big fat curls, I emerged with an uneven mass of crinkly black fuzz. My mother dragged me off to the bathroom and tried to wet down my hair.

"You look like Negro Chinese," she lamented, as if I had done this on purpose.

The instructor of the beauty training school had to lop off these soggy clumps to make my hair even again. "Peter Pan is very popular these days," the instructor assured my mother. I now had hair the length of a boy's, with straight-across bangs that hung at a slant two inches above my eyebrows. I liked the haircut and it made me actually look forward to my future fame.

In fact, in the beginning, I was just as excited as my mother, maybe even more so. I pictured this prodigy part of me as many different images, trying each one on for size. I was a dainty ballerina girl standing by the curtains, waiting to hear the right music that would send me floating on my tiptoes. I was like the Christ child lifted out of the straw manger, crying with holy indignity. I was Cinderella stepping from her pumpkin carriage with sparkly cartoon music filling the air.

10   In all of my imaginings, I was filled with a sense that I would soon become *perfect.* My mother and father would adore me. I would be beyond reproach. I would never feel the need to sulk for anything.

But sometimes the prodigy in me became impatient. "If you don't hurry up and get me out of here, I'm disappearing for good," it warned. "And then you'll always be nothing."

Every night after dinner, my mother and I would sit at the Formica kitchen table. She would present new tests, taking her examples from stories of amazing children she had read in *Ripley's Believe It or Not,* or *Good Housekeeping, Reader's Digest,* and a dozen other magazines she kept in a pile in our bathroom. My mother got these magazines from people whose houses she cleaned. And since she cleaned many houses each week, we had a great assortment. She would look through them all, searching for stories about remarkable children.

The first night she brought out a story about a three-year-old boy who knew the capitals of all the states and even most of the European countries.

A teacher was quoted as saying the little boy could also pronounce the names of the foreign cities correctly.

"What's the capital of Finland?" my mother asked me, looking at the magazine story.

15   All I knew was the capital of California, because Sacramento was the name of the street we lived on in Chinatown. "Nairobi!" I guessed, saying the most foreign word I could think of. She checked to see if that was possibly one way to pronounce "Helsinki" before showing me the answer.

The tests got harder—multiplying numbers in my head, finding the queen of hearts in a deck of cards, trying to stand on my head without using my hands, predicting the daily temperatures in Los Angeles, New York, and London.

One night I had to look at a page from the Bible for three minutes and then report everything I could remember. "Now Jehoshaphat had riches and honor in abundance and . . . that's all I remember, Ma," I said.

And after seeing my mother's disappointed face once again, something inside of me began to die. I hated the tests, the raised hopes and failed expectations. Before going to bed that night, I looked in the mirror above the bathroom sink and when I saw only my face staring back—and that it would always be this ordinary face—I began to cry. Such a sad, ugly girl! I made high-pitched noises like a crazed animal, trying to scratch out the face in the mirror.

And then I saw what seemed to be the prodigy side of me—because I had never seen that face before. I looked at my reflection, blinking so I could see more clearly. The girl staring back at me was angry, powerful. This girl and I were the same. I had new thoughts, willful thoughts, or rather thoughts filled with lots of won'ts. I won't let her change me, I promised myself. I won't be what I'm not.

20   So now on nights when my mother presented her tests, I performed listlessly, my head propped on one arm. I pretended to be bored. And I was. I got so bored I started counting the bellows of the foghorns out on the bay while my mother drilled me in other areas. The sound was comforting and reminded me of the cow jumping over the moon. And the next day, I played a game with myself, seeing if my mother would give up on me before eight bellows. After a while I usually counted only one, maybe two bellows at most. At last she was beginning to give up hope.

Two or three months had gone by without any mention of my being a prodigy again. And then one day my mother was watching *The Ed Sullivan Show* on TV. The TV was old and the sound kept shorting out. Every time my mother got halfway up from the sofa to adjust the set, the sound would go back on and Ed would be talking. As soon as she sat down, Ed would go silent again. She got up, the TV broke into loud piano music. She sat down. Silence. Up and down, back and forth, quiet and loud. It was like a stiff embraceless dance between her and the TV set. Finally she stood by the set with her hand on the sound dial.

She seemed entranced by the music, a little frenzied piano piece with this mesmerizing quality, sort of quick passages and then teasing lilting ones before it returned to the quick playful parts.

"*Ni kan,*" my mother said, calling me over with hurried hand gestures, "Look here."

I could see why my mother was fascinated by the music. It was being pounded out by a little Chinese girl, about nine years old, with a Peter Pan haircut. The girl had the sauciness of a Shirley Temple. She was proudly modest like a proper Chinese child. And she also did this fancy sweep of a curtsy, so that the fluffy skirt of her white dress cascaded slowly to the floor like the petals of a large carnation.

25   In spite of these warning signs, I wasn't worried. Our family had no piano and we couldn't afford to buy one, let alone reams of sheet music and piano lessons. So I could be generous in my comments when my mother bad-mouthed the little girl on TV.

"Play note right, but doesn't sound good! No singing sound," complained my mother.

"What are you picking on her for?" I said carelessly. "She's pretty good. Maybe she's not the best, but she's trying hard." I knew almost immediately I would be sorry I said that.

"Just like you," she said. "Not the best. Because you not trying." She gave a little huff as she let go of the sound dial and sat down on the sofa.

The little Chinese girl sat down also to play an encore of "Anitra's Dance" by Grieg. I remember the song, because later on I had to learn how to play it.

30   Three days after watching *The Ed Sullivan Show,* my mother told me what my schedule would be for piano lessons and piano practice. She had talked to Mr. Chong, who lived on the first floor of our apartment building. Mr. Chong was a retired piano teacher and my mother had traded housecleaning services for weekly lessons and a piano for me to practice on every day, two hours a day, from four until six.

When my mother told me this, I felt as though I had been sent to hell. I whined and then kicked my foot a little when I couldn't stand it anymore.

"Why don't you like me the way I am? I'm *not* a genius! I can't play the piano. And even if I could, I wouldn't go on TV if you paid me a million dollars!" I cried.

My mother slapped me. "Who ask you be genius?" she shouted. "Only ask you be your best. For you sake. You think I want you be genius? Hnnh! What for! Who ask you!"

"So ungrateful," I heard her mutter in Chinese. "If she had as much talent as she has temper, she would be famous now."

35   Mr. Chong, whom I secretly nicknamed Old Chong, was very strange, always tapping his fingers to the silent music of an invisible orchestra. He

looked ancient in my eyes. He had lost most of the hair on top of his head and he wore thick glasses and had eyes that always looked tired and sleepy. But he must have been younger than I thought, since he lived with his mother and was not yet married.

I met Old Lady Chong once and that was enough. She had this peculiar smell like a baby that had done something in its pants. And her fingers felt like a dead person's, like an old peach I once found in the back of the refrigerator; the skin just slid off the meat when I picked it up.

I soon found out why Old Chong had retired from teaching piano. He was deaf. "Like Beethoven!" he shouted to me. "We're both listening only in our head!" And he would start to conduct his frantic silent sonatas.

Our lessons went like this. He would open the book and point to different things, explaining their purpose: "Key! Treble! Bass! No sharps or flats! So this is C major! Listen now and play after me!"

And then he would play the C scale a few times, a simple chord, and then, as if inspired by an old, unreachable itch, he gradually added more notes and running trills and a pounding bass until the music was really something quite grand.

40 I would play after him, the simple scale, the simple chord, and then I just played some nonsense that sounded like a cat running up and down on top of garbage cans. Old Chong smiled and applauded and then said, "Very good! But now you must learn to keep time!"

So that's how I discovered that Old Chong's eyes were too slow to keep up with the wrong notes I was playing. He went through the motions in half-time. To help me keep rhythm, he stood behind me, pushing down on my right shoulder for every beat. He balanced pennies on top of my wrists so I would keep them still as I slowly played scales and arpeggios. He had me curve my hand around an apple and keep that shape when playing chords. He marched stiffly to show me how to make each finger dance up and down, staccato like an obedient little soldier.

He taught me all these things, and that was how I also learned I could be lazy and get away with mistakes, lots of mistakes. If I hit the wrong notes because I hadn't practiced enough, I never corrected myself. I just kept playing in rhythm. And Old Chong kept conducting his own private reverie.

So maybe I never really gave myself a fair chance. I did pick up the basics pretty quickly, and I might have become a good pianist at that young age. But I was so determined not to try, not to be anybody different that I learned to play only the most ear-splitting preludes, the most discordant hymns.

Over the next year, I practiced like this, dutifully in my own way. And then one day I heard my mother and her friend Lindo Jong both talking in a loud bragging tone of voice so others could hear. It was after church, and I was leaning against the brick wall wearing a dress with stiff white petticoats. Auntie Lindo's daughter, Waverly, who was about my age, was standing farther down the wall about five feet away. We had grown up together and shared all the closeness of two sisters squabbling over crayons and dolls. In other words, for the most part, we hated each other. I thought she was snotty. Waverly Jong had gained a certain amount of fame as "Chinatown's Littlest Chinese Chess Champion."

45   "She bring home too many trophy," lamented Auntie Lindo that Sunday. "All day she play chess. All day I have no time do nothing but dust off her winnings." She threw a scolding look at Waverly, who pretended not to see her.

"You lucky you don't have this problem," said Auntie Lindo with a sigh to my mother.

And my mother squared her shoulders and bragged: "Our problem worser than yours. If we ask Jing-mei wash dish, she hear nothing but music. It's like you can't stop this natural talent."

And right then, I was determined to put a stop to her foolish pride.

A few weeks later, Old Chong and my mother conspired to have me play in a talent show which would be held in the church hall. By then, my parents had saved up enough to buy me a secondhand piano, a black Wurlitzer spinet with a scarred bench. It was the showpiece of our living room.

50   For the talent show, I was to play a piece called "Pleading Child" from Schumann's *Scenes from Childhood*. It was a simple, moody piece that sounded more difficult than it was. I was supposed to memorize the whole thing, playing the repeat parts twice to make the piece sound longer. But I dawdled over it, playing a few bars and then cheating, looking up to see what notes followed. I never really listened to what I was playing. I daydreamed about being somewhere else, about being someone else.

The part I liked to practice best was the fancy curtsy: right foot out, touch the rose on the carpet with a pointed foot, sweep to the side, left leg bends, look up and smile.

My parents invited all the couples from the Joy Luck Club[1] to witness my debut. Auntie Lindo and Uncle Tin were there. Waverly and her two older brothers had also come. The first two rows were filled with children both younger and older than I was. The littlest ones got to go first. They recited simple nursery rhymes, squawked out tunes on miniature violins, twirled Hula Hoops, pranced in pink ballet tutus, and when they bowed or curtsied, the audience would sigh in unison, "Awww," and then clap enthusiastically.

When my turn came, I was very confident. I remember my childish excitement. It was as if I knew, without a doubt, that the prodigy side of me really did exist. I had no fear whatsoever, no nervousness. I remember thinking to myself, This is it! This is it! I looked out over the audience, at my mother's blank face, my father's yawn, Auntie Lindo's stiff-lipped smile, Waverly's sulky expression. I had on a white dress layered with

---

[1] A name denoting the mother's circle of friends, all of whom were Chinese immigrants to the United States.

sheets of lace, and a pink bow in my Peter Pan haircut. As I sat down I envisioned people jumping to their feet and Ed Sullivan rushing up to introduce me to everyone on TV.

And I started to play. It was so beautiful. I was so caught up in how lovely I looked that at first I didn't worry how I would sound. So it was a surprise to me when I hit the first wrong note and I realized something didn't sound quite right. And then I hit another and another followed that. A chill started at the top of my head and began to trickle down. Yet I couldn't stop playing, as though my hands were bewitched. I kept thinking my fingers would adjust themselves back, like a train switching to the right track. I played this strange jumble through two repeats, the sour notes staying with me all the way to the end.

55   When I stood up, I discovered my legs were shaking. Maybe I had just been nervous and the audience, like Old Chong, had seen me go through the right motions and had not heard anything wrong at all. I swept my right foot out, went down on my knee, looked up and smiled. The room was quiet, except for Old Chong, who was beaming and shouting, "Bravo! Bravo! Well done!" But then I saw my mother's face, her stricken face. The audience clapped weakly, and as I walked back to my chair, with my whole face quivering as I tried not to cry, I heard a little boy whisper loudly to his mother, "That was awful," and the mother whispered back, "Well, she certainly tried."

And now I realized how many people were in the audience, the whole world it seemed. I was aware of eyes burning into my back. I felt the shame of my mother and father as they sat stiffly throughout the rest of the show.

We could have escaped during intermission. Pride and some strange sense of honor must have anchored my parents to their chairs. And so we watched it all: the eighteen-year-old boy with a fake mustache who did a magic show and juggled flaming hoops while riding a unicycle. The breasted girl with white makeup who sang from *Madama Butterfly* and got honorable mention. And the eleven-year-old boy who won first prize playing a tricky violin song that sounded like a busy bee.

After the show, the Hsus, the Jongs, and the St. Clairs from the Joy Luck Club came up to my mother and father.

"Lots of talented kids," Auntie Lindo said vaguely, smiling broadly.

60   "That was somethin' else," said my father, and I wondered if he was referring to me in a humorous way, or whether he even remembered what I had done.

Waverly looked at me and shrugged her shoulders. "You aren't a genius like me," she said matter-of-factly. And if I hadn't felt so bad, I would have pulled her braids and punched her stomach.

But my mother's expression was what devastated me: a quiet, blank look that said she had lost everything. I felt the same way, and it seemed as if everybody were now coming up, like gawkers at the scene of an accident, to see what parts were actually missing. When we got on the bus to go home, my father was humming the busy-bee tune and my mother was silent. I kept thinking she wanted to wait until we got home before shouting at me. But when my father unlocked the door to our apartment, my mother walked in and then went to the back, into the bedroom. No accusations. No blame. And in a way, I felt disappointed. I had been waiting for her to start shouting, so I could shout back and cry and blame her for all my misery.

I assumed my talent-show fiasco meant I never had to play the piano again. But two days later, after school, my mother came out of the kitchen and saw me watching TV.

"Four clock," she reminded me as if it were any other day. I was stunned, as though she were asking me to go through the talent-show torture again. I wedged myself more tightly in front of the TV.

65   "Turn off TV," she called from the kitchen five minutes later.

I didn't budge. And then I decided. I didn't have to do what my mother said anymore. I wasn't her slave. This wasn't China. I had listened to her before and look what happened. She was the stupid one.

She came out from the kitchen and stood in the arched entryway of the living room. "Four clock," she said once again, louder.

"I'm not going to play anymore," I said nonchalantly. "Why should I? I'm not a genius."

She walked over and stood in front of the TV. I saw her chest was heaving up and down in an angry way.

70   "No!" I said, and I now felt stronger, as if my true self had finally emerged. So this was what had been inside me all along.

"No! I won't!" I screamed.

She yanked me by the arm, pulled me off the floor, snapped off the TV. She was frighteningly strong, half pulling, half carrying me toward the piano as I kicked the throw rugs under my feet. She lifted me up and onto the hard bench. I was sobbing by now, looking at her bitterly. Her chest was heaving even more and her mouth was open, smiling crazily as if she were pleased I was crying.

"You want me to be someone that I'm not!" I sobbed. "I'll never be the kind of daughter you want me to be!"

"Only two kinds of daughters," she shouted in Chinese. "Those who are obedient and those who follow their own mind! Only one kind of daughter can live in this house. Obedient daughter!"

75   "Then I wish I wasn't your daughter. I wish you weren't my mother," I shouted. As I said these things I got scared. It felt like worms and toads and slimy things crawling out of my chest, but it also felt good, as if this awful side of me had surfaced, at last.

"Too late change this," said my mother shrilly.

And I could sense her anger rising to its breaking point. I wanted to see it spill over. And that's when I remembered the babies she had lost in China, the ones we never talked about. "Then I wish I'd never been born!" I shouted. "I wish I were dead! Like them."

It was as if I had said the magic words. Alakazam!—and her face went blank, her mouth closed, her arms went slack, and she backed out of the room, stunned, as if she were blowing away like a small brown leaf, thin, brittle, lifeless.

It was not the only disappointment my mother felt in me. In the years that followed, I failed her so many times, each time asserting my own will, my right to fall short of expectations. I didn't get straight As. I didn't become class president. I didn't get into Stanford. I dropped out of college.

80 For unlike my mother, I did not believe I could be anything I wanted to be. I could only be me.

And for all those years, we never talked about the disaster at the recital or my terrible accusations afterward at the piano bench. All that remained unchecked, like a betrayal that was now unspeakable. So I never found a way to ask her why she had hoped for something so large that failure was inevitable.

And even worse, I never asked her what frightened me the most: Why had she given up hope?

For after our struggle at the piano, she never mentioned my playing again. The lessons stopped. The lid to the piano was closed, shutting out the dust, my misery, and her dreams.

So she surprised me. A few years ago, she offered to give me the piano, for my thirtieth birthday. I had not played in all those years. I saw the offer as a sign of forgiveness, a tremendous burden removed.

85 "Are you sure?" I asked shyly. "I mean, won't you and Dad miss it?"

"No, this your piano," she said firmly. "Always your piano. You only one can play."

"Well, I probably can't play anymore," I said. "It's been years."

"You pick up fast," said my mother, as if she knew this was certain. "You have natural talent. You could been genius if you want to."

"No I couldn't."

90 "You just not trying," said my mother. And she was neither angry nor sad. She said it as if to announce a fact that could never be disproved. "Take it," she said.

But I didn't at first. It was enough that she had offered it to me. And after that, every time I saw it in my parents' living room, standing in front of the bay windows, it made me feel proud, as if it were a shiny trophy I had won back.

Last week I sent a tuner over to my parents' apartment and had the piano reconditioned, for purely sentimental reasons. My mother had died a few months before and I had been getting things in order for my father, a little bit at a time. I put the jewelry in special silk pouches. The sweaters she had knitted in yellow, pink, bright orange—all the colors I hated—I put those in moth-proof boxes. I found some old Chinese silk dresses, the kind with little slits up the sides. I rubbed the old silk against my skin, then wrapped them in tissue and decided to take them home with me.

After I had the piano tuned, I opened the lid and touched the keys. It sounded even richer than I remembered. Really, it was a very good piano. Inside the bench were the same exercise notes with handwritten scales, the same secondhand music books with their covers held together with yellow tape.

I opened up the Schumann book to the dark little piece I had played at the recital. It was on the left-hand side of the page, "Pleading Child." It looked more difficult than I remembered. I played a few bars, surprised at how easily the notes came back to me.

95   And for the first time, or so it seemed, I noticed the piece on the right-hand side. It was called "Perfectly Contented." I tried to play this one as well. It had a lighter melody but the same flowing rhythm and turned out to be quite easy. "Pleading Child" was shorter but slower; "Perfectly Contented" was longer, but faster. And after I played them both a few times, I realized they were two halves of the same song.

◇ ◇ ◇

ANNE TYLER
(1941–   )

Teenage Wasteland
(1984)

He used to have very blond hair—almost white—cut shorter than other children's so that on his crown a little cowlick always stood up to catch the light. But this was when he was small. As he grew older, his hair grew darker, and he wore it longer—past his collar even. It hung in lank, taffy-colored ropes around his face, which was still an endearing face, fine-featured, the eyes an unusual aqua blue. But his cheeks, of course, were no longer round, and a sharp new Adam's apple jogged in his throat when he talked.

In October, they called from the private school he attended to request a conference with his parents. Daisy went alone; her husband was at work. Clutching her purse, she sat on the principal's couch and learned that Donny was noisy, lazy, and disruptive; always fooling around with his friends, and he wouldn't respond in class.

In the past, before her children were born, Daisy had been a fourth-grade teacher. It shamed her now to sit before this principal as a parent, a delinquent parent, a parent who struck Mr. Lanham, no doubt, as unseeing or uncaring. "It isn't that we're not concerned," she said. "Both of us are. And we've done what we could, whatever we could think of. We don't let him watch TV on school nights. We don't let him talk on the phone till he's finished his homework. But he tells us he doesn't *have* any homework or he did it all in study hall. How are we to know what to believe?"

From early October through November, at Mr. Lanham's suggestion, Daisy checked Donny's assignments every day. She sat next to him as he worked, trying to be encouraging, sagging inwardly as she saw the poor quality of everything he did—the sloppy mistakes in math, the illogical leaps in his English themes, the history questions left blank if they required any research.

5   Daisy was often late starting supper, and she couldn't give as much attention to Donny's younger sister. "You'll never guess what happened at . . ." Amanda would begin, and Daisy would have to tell her, "Not now, honey."

By the time her husband, Matt, came home, she'd be snappish. She would recite the day's hardships—the fuzzy instructions in English, the botched history map, the morass of unsolvable algebra equations. Matt would look surprised and confused, and Daisy would gradually wind down. There was no way, really, to convey how exhausting all this was.

In December, the school called again. This time, they wanted Matt to come as well. She and Matt had to sit on Mr. Lanham's couch like two bad children and listen to the news: Donny had improved only slightly, raising a D in history to a C, and a C in algebra to a B-minus. What was worse, he had developed new problems. He had cut classes on at least three occasions. Smoked in the furnace room. Helped Sonny Barnett break into a freshman's locker. And last week, during athletics, he and three friends had been seen off the school grounds; when they returned, the coach had smelled beer on their breath.

Daisy and Matt sat silent, shocked. Matt rubbed his forehead with his fingertips. Imagine, Daisy thought, how they must look to Mr. Lanham: an overweight housewife in a cotton dress and a too-tall, too-thin insurance agent in a baggy, frayed suit. Failures, both of them—the kind of people who are always hurrying to catch up, missing the point of things that everyone else grasps at once. She wished she'd worn nylons instead of knee socks.

It was arranged that Donny would visit a psychologist for testing. Mr. Lanham knew just the person. He would set this boy straight, he said.

10   When they stood to leave, Daisy held her stomach in and gave Mr. Lanham a firm, responsible handshake.

Donny said the psychologist was a jackass and the tests were really dumb; but he kept all three of his appointments, and when it was time for the follow-up conference with the psychologist and both parents, Donny combed his hair and seemed unusually sober and subdued. The psychologist said Donny had no serious emotional problems. He was merely going through a difficult period in his life. He required some academic help and a better sense of self-worth. For this reason, he was suggesting a man named Calvin Beadle, a tutor with considerable psychological training.

In the car going home, Donny said he'd be damned if he'd let them drag him to some stupid fairy tutor. His father told him to watch his language in front of his mother.

That night, Daisy lay awake pondering the term "self-worth." She had always been free with her praise. She had always told Donny he had talent, was smart, was good with his hands. She had made a big to-do over every little gift he gave her. In fact, maybe she had gone too far, although, Lord knows, she had meant every word. Was that his trouble?

She remembered when Amanda was born. Donny had acted lost and bewildered. Daisy had been alert to that, of course, but still, a new baby keeps you so busy. Had she really done all she could have? She longed—she ached—for a time machine. Given one more chance, she'd do it perfectly— hug him more, praise him more, or perhaps praise him less. Oh, who can say . . .

15   The tutor told Donny to call him Cal. All his kids did, he said. Daisy thought for a second that he meant his own children, then realized her mistake. He seemed too young, anyhow, to be a family man. He wore a heavy brown handlebar mustache. His hair was as long and stringy as Donny's, and his jeans as faded. Wire-rimmed spectacles slid down his nose. He lounged in a canvas director's chair with his fingers laced across his chest, and he casually, amiably questioned Donny, who sat upright and glaring in an armchair.

"So they're getting on your back at school," said Cal. "Making a big deal about anything you do wrong."

"Right," said Donny.

"Any idea why that would be?"

"Oh, well, you know, stuff like homework and all," Donny said.

20   "You don't do your homework?"

"Oh, well, I might do it sometimes but not just exactly like they want it." Donny sat forward and said, "It's like a prison there, you know? You've got to go to every class, you can never step off the school grounds."

"You cut classes sometimes?"

"Sometimes," Donny said, with a glance at his parents.

Cal didn't seem perturbed. "Well," he said, "I'll tell you what. Let's you and me try working together three nights a week. Think you can handle that? We'll see if we can show that school of yours a thing or two. Give it a month; then if you don't like it, we'll stop. If *I* don't like it, we'll stop. I mean, some-times people just don't get along, right? What do you say to that?"

25   "Okay," Donny said. He seemed pleased.

"Make it seven o'clock till eight, Monday, Wednesday, and Friday," Cal told Matt and Daisy. They nodded. Cal shambled to his feet, gave them a little salute, and showed them to the door.

This was where he lived as well as worked, evidently. The interview had taken place in the dining room, which had been transformed into a kind of office. Passing the living room, Daisy winced at the rock music she had been hearing, without registering it, ever since she had entered the house. She looked in and saw a boy about Donny's age lying on a sofa with a book. Another boy and a girl were playing Ping-Pong in front of the fire-place. "You have several here together?" Daisy asked Cal.

"Oh, sometimes they stay on after their sessions, just to rap. They're a pretty sociable group, all in all. Plenty of goof-offs like young Donny here."

He cuffed Donny's shoulder playfully. Donny flushed and grinned.

30 Climbing into the car, Daisy asked Donny, "Well? What do you think?"

But Donny had returned to his old evasive self. He jerked his chin toward the garage. "Look," he said. "He's got a basketball net."

Now on Mondays, Wednesdays, and Fridays, they had supper early—the instant Matt came home. Sometimes, they had to leave before they were really finished. Amanda would still be eating her dessert. "Bye, honey. Sorry," Daisy would tell her.

Cal's first bill sent a flutter of panic through Daisy's chest, but it was worth it, of course. Just look at Donny's face when they picked him up: alight and full of interest. The principal telephoned Daisy to tell her how Donny had improved. "Of course, it hasn't shown up in his grades yet, but several of the teachers have noticed how his attitude's changed. Yes, sir, I think we're onto something here."

At home, Donny didn't act much different. He still seemed to have a low opinion of his parents. But Daisy supposed that was unavoidable—part of being fifteen. He said his parents were too "controlling"—a word that made Daisy give him a sudden look. He said they acted like wardens. On weekends, they enforced a curfew. And any time he went to a party, they always telephoned first to see if adults would be supervising. "For God's sake!" he said. "Don't you trust me?"

35 "It isn't a matter of trust, honey . . ." But there was no explaining to him.

His tutor called one afternoon. "I get the sense," he said, "that this kid's feeling . . . underestimated, you know? Like you folks expect the worst of him. I'm thinking we ought to give him more rope."

"But see, he's still so suggestible," Daisy said. "When his friends suggest some mischief—smoking or drinking or such—why, he just finds it hard not to go along with them."

"Mrs. Coble," the tutor said, "I think this kid is hurting. You know? Here's a serious, sensitive kid, telling you he'd like to take on some grown-up challenges, and you're giving him the message that he can't be trusted. Don't you understand how that hurts?"

"Oh," said Daisy.

40 "It undermines his self-esteem—don't you realize that?"

"Well, I guess you're right," said Daisy. She saw Donny suddenly from a whole new angle: his pathetically poor posture, that slouch so forlorn that his shoulders seemed about to meet his chin . . . oh, wasn't it awful being young? She'd had a miserable adolescence herself and had always sworn no child of hers would ever be that unhappy.

They let Donny stay out later, they didn't call ahead to see if the parties were supervised, and they were careful not to grill him about his evening. The tutor had set down so many rules! They were not allowed any questions at all about any aspect of school, nor were they to speak with his teachers. If a teacher had some complaint, she should phone Cal. Only one teacher disobeyed—the history teacher, Miss Evans. She called one morning in February. "I'm a little concerned about Donny, Mrs. Coble."

"Oh, I'm sorry, Miss Evans, but Donny's tutor handles these things now . . ."

"I always deal directly with the parents. You are the parent," Miss Evans said, speaking very slowly and distinctly. "Now, here is the problem. Back when you were helping Donny with his homework, his grades rose from a D to a C, but now they've slipped back, and they're closer to an F."

45   "They are?"

"I think you should start overseeing his homework again."

"But Donny's tutor says . . ."

"It's nice that Donny has a tutor, but you should still be in charge of his homework. With you, he learned it. Then he passed his tests. With the tutor, well, it seems the tutor is more of a crutch. 'Donny,' I say, 'a quiz is coming up on Friday. Hadn't you better be listening instead of talking?' 'That's okay, Miss Evans,' he says. 'I have a tutor now.' Like a talisman! I really think you ought to take over, Mrs. Coble."

"I see," said Daisy. "Well, I'll think about that. Thank you for calling."

50   Hanging up, she felt a rush of anger at Donny. A talisman! For a talisman, she'd given up all luxuries, all that time with her daughter, her evenings at home!

She dialed Cal's number. He sounded muzzy. "I'm sorry if I woke you," she told him, "but Donny's history teacher just called. She says he isn't doing well."

"She should have dealt with me."

"She wants me to start supervising his homework again. His grades are slipping."

"Yes," said the tutor, "but you and I both know there's more to it than mere grades, don't we? I care about the *whole* child—his happiness, his self-esteem. The grades will come. Just give them time."

55   When she hung up, it was Miss Evans she was angry at. What a narrow woman!

It was Cal this, Cal that, Cal says this, Cal and I did that. Cal lent Donny an album by The Who. He took Donny and two other pupils to a rock concert. In March, when Donny began to talk endlessly on the phone with a girl named Miriam, Cal even let Miriam come to one of the tutoring sessions. Daisy was touched that Cal would grow so involved in Donny's life, but she was also a little hurt, because she had offered to have Miriam to dinner and Donny had refused. Now he asked them to drive her to Cal's house without a qualm.

This Miriam was an unappealing girl with blurry lipstick and masses of rough red hair. She wore a short, bulky jacket that would not have been out of place on a motorcycle. During the trip to Cal's she was silent, but coming back, she was more talkative. "What a neat guy, and what a house! All those kids hanging out, like a club. And the stereo playing rock . . . gosh, he's not like a grown-up at all! Married and divorced and everything, but you'd think he was our own age."

"Mr. Beadle was married?" Daisy asked.

"Yeah, to this really controlling lady. She didn't understand him a bit."

60   "No, I guess not," Daisy said.

Spring came, and the students who hung around at Cal's drifted out to the basketball net above the garage. Sometimes, when Daisy and Matt arrived to pick up Donny, they'd find him there with the others—spiky and excited, jittering on his toes beneath the backboard. It was staying light much longer now, and the neighboring fence cast narrow bars across the bright grass. Loud music would be spilling from Cal's windows. Once it was The Who, which Daisy recognized from the time that Donny had borrowed the album. *"Teenage Wasteland,"*[1] she said aloud, identifying the song, and Matt gave a short, dry laugh. "It certainly is," he said. He'd misunderstood; he thought she was commenting on the scene spread before them. In fact, she might have been. The players looked like hoodlums, even her son. Why, one of Cal's students had recently been knifed in a tavern. One had been shipped off to boarding school in midterm; two had been withdrawn by their parents. On the other hand, Donny had mentioned someone who'd been studying with Cal for five years. "Five years!" said Daisy. "Doesn't anyone ever stop needing him?"

Donny looked at her. Lately, whatever she said about Cal was read as criticism. "You're just feeling competitive," he said. "And controlling."

She bit her lip and said no more.

In April, the principal called to tell her that Donny had been expelled. There had been a locker check, and in Donny's locker they found five cans of beer and half a pack of cigarettes. With Donny's previous record, his offense meant expulsion.

65   Daisy gripped the receiver tightly and said, "Well, where is he now?"

"We've sent him home," said Mr. Lanham. "He's packed up all his belongings, and he's coming home on foot."

Daisy wondered what she would say to him. She felt him looming closer and closer, bringing this brand-new situation that no one had prepared her to handle. What other place would take him? Could they enter him in public school? What were the rules? She stood at the living room window, waiting for him to show up. Gradually, she realized that he was taking too long. She checked the clock. She stared up the street again.

When an hour had passed, she phoned the school. Mr. Lanham's secretary answered and told her in a grave, sympathetic voice that yes, Donny

---

[1] The song is actually "Baba O'Riley," from the band's *Who's Next* album.

Coble had most definitely gone home. Daisy called her husband. He was out of the office. She went back to the window and thought awhile, and then she called Donny's tutor.

"Donny's been expelled from school," she said, "and now I don't know where he's gone. I wonder if you've heard from him?"

70 There was a long silence. "Donny's with me, Mrs. Coble," he finally said.

"With you? How'd he get there?"

"He hailed a cab, and I paid the driver."

"Could I speak to him, please?"

There was another silence. "Maybe it'd be better if we had a conference," Cal said.

75 "I don't *want* a conference. I've been standing at the window picturing him dead or kidnapped or something, and now you tell me you want a—"

"Donny is very, very upset. Understandably so," said Cal. "Believe me, Mrs. Coble, this is not what it seems. Have you asked Donny's side of the story?"

"Well, of course not, how could I? He went running off to you instead."

"Because he didn't feel he'd be listened to."

"But I haven't even—"

80 "Why don't you come out and talk? The three of us," said Cal, "will try to get this thing in perspective."

"Well, all right," Daisy said. But she wasn't as reluctant as she sounded. Already, she felt soothed by the calm way Cal was taking this.

Cal answered the doorbell at once. He said, "Hi, there," and led her into the dining room. Donny sat slumped in a chair, chewing the knuckle of one thumb. "Hello, Donny," Daisy said. He flicked his eyes in her direction.

"Sit here, Mrs. Coble," said Cal, placing her opposite Donny. He himself remained standing, restlessly pacing. "So," he said.

Daisy stole a look at Donny. His lips were swollen, as if he'd been crying.

85 "You know," Cal told Daisy, "I kind of expected something like this. That's a very punitive school you've got him in—you realize that. And any half-decent lawyer will tell you they've violated his civil rights. Locker checks! Where's their search warrant?"

"But if the rule is—" Daisy said.

"Well, anyhow, let him tell you his side."

She looked at Donny. He said, "It wasn't my fault. I promise."

"They said your locker was full of beer."

90 "It was a put-up job! See, there's this guy that doesn't like me. He put all these beers in my locker and started a rumor going, so Mr. Lanham ordered a locker check."

"What was the boy's name?" Daisy asked.

"Huh?"

"Mrs. Coble, take my word, the situation is not so unusual," Cal said. "You can't imagine how vindictive kids can be sometimes."

"What was the boy's *name*," said Daisy, "so that I can ask Mr. Lanham if that's who suggested he run a locker check."

95   "You don't believe me," Donny said.

"And how'd this boy get your combination in the first place?"

"Frankly," said Cal, "I wouldn't be surprised to learn the school was in on it. Any kid that marches to a different drummer, why, they'd just love an excuse to get rid of him. The school is where I lay the blame."

"Doesn't *Donny* ever get blamed?"

"Now, Mrs. Coble, you heard what he—"

100   "Forget it," Donny told Cal. "You can see she doesn't trust me."

Daisy drew in a breath to say that of course she trusted him—a reflex. But she knew that bold-faced, wide-eyed look of Donny's. He had worn that look when he was small, denying some petty misdeed with the evidence plain as day all around him. Still, it was hard for her to accuse him outright. She temporized and said, "The only thing I'm sure of is that they've kicked you out of school, and now I don't know what we're going to do."

"We'll fight it," said Cal.

"We can't. Even you must see we can't."

"I could apply to Brantly," Donny said.

105   Cal stopped his pacing to beam down at him. "Brantly! Yes. They're really onto where a kid is coming from, at Brantly. Why, *I* could get you into Brantly. I work with a lot of their students."

Daisy had never heard of Brantly, but already she didn't like it. And she didn't like Cal's smile, which struck her now as feverish and avid—a smile of hunger.

On the fifteenth of April, they entered Donny in a public school, and they stopped his tutoring sessions. Donny fought both decisions bitterly. Cal, surprisingly enough, did not object. He admitted he'd made no headway with Donny and said it was because Donny was emotionally disturbed.

Donny went to his new school every morning, plodding off alone with his head down. He did his assignments, and he earned average grades, but he gathered no friends, joined no clubs. There was something exhausted and defeated about him.

The first week in June, during final exams, Donny vanished. He simply didn't come home one afternoon, and no one at school remembered seeing him. The police were reassuring, and for the first few days, they worked hard. They combed Donny's sad, messy room for clues; they visited Miriam and Cal. But then they started talking about the number of kids who ran away every year. Hundreds, just in this city. "He'll show up, if he wants to," they said. "If he doesn't, he won't."

110   Evidently, Donny didn't want to.

It's been three months now and still no word. Matt and Daisy still look for him in every crowd of awkward, heartbreaking teenage boys. Every time the phone rings, they imagine it might be Donny. Both parents have aged. Donny's sister seems to be staying away from home as much as possible.

At night, Daisy lies awake and goes over Donny's life. She is trying to figure out what went wrong, where they made their first mistake. Often, she finds herself blaming Cal, although she knows he didn't begin it. Then at other times she excuses him, for without him, Donny might have left earlier. Who really knows? In the end, she can only sigh and search for a cooler spot on the pillow. As she falls asleep, she occasionally glimpses something in the corner of her vision. It's something fleet and round, a ball—a basketball. It flies up, it sinks through the hoop, descends, lands in a yard littered with last year's leaves and striped with bars of sunlight as white as bones, bleached and parched and cleanly picked.

Fiction Casebook

This section contains the 1966 short story "Where Are You Going, Where Have You Been?" by Joyce Carol Oates, a collection of source materials,* questions to stimulate discussion and writing, and a student paper.

SOURCE MATERIALS

◊ ◊ ◊

Each of these sources provides insights (sometimes contradictory ones) into the short story "Where Are You Going, Where Have You Been?" Other kinds of sources can also enrich your understanding of the work—for instance, other stories by Oates, biographical data about the author, or

---

*Note that some of the critical articles in this Casebook were written before the current MLA documentation style was adopted. See Appendix A for current MLA format. Page references to specific editions of the Oates story have been deleted to avoid confusion.

stories by other writers dealing with similar themes. In addition, nonprint sources—such as the film *Smooth Talk*—and Web sites devoted to Oates and her work can offer insight into the story. Several interesting Web sites on Oates are as follows: <<http://www.kutztown.edu/faculty/reagan/oates.html>>; <<http://storm.usfca.edu/~southerr/jco.html>>; <<http://www.annonline.com/interviews/981013/biography.html>>; <<http://www.cis.yale.edu/ydn/paper/4.20/4.20.95storyno.AB.html>>; <<http://hs1.hst.msu.edu/cal/celeb/oates.html>>. Although no analytical or biographical source—not even the author's comments—can give you a magical key that will unlock a story's secrets, such sources can enhance your enjoyment and aid in your understanding of a work; they can also suggest topics that you can explore in writing.

In preparation for writing an essay on a topic of your choice about the story "Where Are You Going, Where Have You Been?" read the story and the accompanying source materials carefully. Then, consider the Reading and Reacting questions at the end of this Casebook (p. 652) in light of what you have read, and use your responses to help you find a topic you can develop in a three- to six-page essay. Be sure to document any words or ideas borrowed from the story or from another source, and remember to enclose words that are not your own in quotation marks. (For guidelines on evaluating literary criticism, see page 15; for guidelines on using source materials, see the Appendix.)

A complete student paper, "Mesmerizing Men and Vulnerable Teens: Power Relationships in 'Where Are You Going, Where Have You Been?' and 'Teenage Wasteland,'" based on the source materials in this Casebook, begins on page 655.

◆ **JOYCE CAROL OATES** (1938–   ) is one of contemporary America's most prolific novelists and short story writers. Born and raised in rural Erie County, New York, Oates first gained prominence in the 1960s with publication of *A Garden of Earthly Delights* (1967), *Expensive People* (1968), and *them* (1969), which won the National Book Award. In these and other works, Oates began to explore the multilayered nature of American society—writing about urban slums, decaying rural communities, and exclusive suburbs in a dense and compellingly realistic prose style. In some of her more recent

Photo of Joyce Carol Oates reprinted by permission of the author and Blanche C. Gregory, Inc.

novels, including *Bellefleur* (1980) and *Mysteries of Winterthurn* (1984), Oates reveals her deep fascination with the traditions of nineteenth-century gothic writers—Edgar Allan Poe, Fyodor Dostoevski, Mary Shelley, and others. Oates's recent works include *Lock My Door upon Myself* (1990), *The Rise of Life on Earth* (1991), *Black Water* (1992), *Foxfire* (1993), *What I Lived For* (1994), *Haunted* (1994), *Zombie* (1995), *First Love* (1996), and *My Heart Laid Bare* (1998).

Oates, wrote *Washington Post* critic Susan Wood, "attempts more than most of our writers [. . .] to explore the profound issues of evil and innocence, betrayal and revenge and atonement, as they are manifest in contemporary American experience [. . .]." Although Oates frequently centers her novels on larger issues and moral questions, she can also focus on the private worlds of her characters, as in *Black Water* (1992).

Critics responding to Oates's work have called it violent, lurid, even depraved. Yet, asks Laura Z. Hobson in a review of Oates's 1981 novel, *Angel of Light,* "Would there be such a hullabaloo about the violence in her books if they had been written by a man? From her earliest books onward, reviewers too often struck an insulting tone of surprise: *What's a nice girl like you doing in a place like this?* [. . . Oates] replies that in these violent times only tales of violence have reality. Well, maybe. But the critics' preoccupation with a single facet of her work ignores everything else: her inventiveness, her insider's knowledge of college life, her evocations of nature [. . .] her ability to tell a story, to write a spellbinder [. . .]."

◆ ◆ ◆

JOYCE CAROL OATES

Where Are You Going, Where Have You Been?
(1966)

For Bob Dylan

Her name was Connie. She was fifteen and she had a quick nervous giggling habit of craning her neck to glance into mirrors, or checking other people's faces to make sure her own was all right. Her mother, who noticed everything and knew everything and who hadn't much reason any longer to look at her own face, always scolded Connie about it. "Stop gawking at yourself, who are you? You think you're so pretty?" she would say. Connie would raise her eye-brows at these familiar complaints and look right through her mother, into a shadowy vision of herself as she was right at that moment: she knew she was pretty and that was everything. Her mother had been pretty once too, if you could believe those old snapshots in the album, but now her looks were gone and that was why she was always after Connie.

"Why don't you keep your room clean like your sister? How've you got your hair fixed—what the hell stinks? Hair spray? You don't see your sister using that junk."

Her sister June was twenty-four and still lived at home. She was a secretary in the high school Connie attended, and if that wasn't bad enough—with her in the same building—she was so plain and chunky and steady that Connie had to hear her praised all the time by her mother and her mother's sisters. June did this, June did that, she saved money and helped clean the house and cooked and Connie couldn't do a thing, her mind was all filled with trashy daydreams. Their father was away at work most of the time and when he came home he wanted supper and he read the newspaper at supper and after supper he went to bed. He didn't bother talking much to them, but around his bent head Connie's mother kept picking at her until Connie wished her mother was dead and she herself was dead and it was all over. "She makes me want to throw up sometimes," she complained to her friends. She had a high, breathless, amused voice which made everything she said sound a little forced, whether it was sincere or not.

There was one good thing: June went places with girl friends of hers, girls who were just as plain and steady as she, and so when Connie wanted to do that her mother had no objections. The father of Connie's best girl friend drove the girls the three miles to town and left them off at a shopping plaza, so that they could walk through the stores or go to a movie, and when he came to pick them up again at eleven he never bothered to ask what they had done.

5   They must have been familiar sights, walking around that shopping plaza in their shorts and flat ballerina slippers that always scuffed the sidewalk, with charm bracelets jingling on their thin wrists; they would lean together to whisper and laugh secretly if someone passed by who amused or interested them. Connie had long dark blond hair that drew anyone's eye to it, and she wore part of it pulled up on her head and puffed out and the rest of it she let fall down her back. She wore a pull-over jersey blouse that looked one way when she was at home and another way when she was away from home. Everything about her had two sides to it, one for home and one for anywhere that was not home: her walk that could be childlike and bobbing, or languid enough to make anyone think she was hearing music in her head, her mouth which was pale and smirking most of the time, but bright and pink on these evenings out, her laugh which was cynical and drawling at home—"Ha, ha, very funny"—but high-pitched and nervous anywhere else, like the jingling of the charms on her bracelet.

Sometimes they did go shopping or to a movie, but sometimes they went across the highway, ducking fast across the busy road, to a drive-in restaurant where older kids hung out. The restaurant was shaped like a big bottle, though squatter than a real bottle, and on its cap was a revolving figure of a grinning boy who held a hamburger aloft. One night in mid-summer they ran across, breathless with daring, and right away someone leaned out a car window and invited them over, but it was just a boy from high school they didn't like. It made them feel good to be able to ignore him. They went up through the maze of parked and cruising cars to the bright-lit, fly-infested restaurant, their faces pleased and expectant as if they were entering a sacred building that loomed out of the night to give them what haven and what blessing they yearned for. They sat at the counter and crossed their legs at the ankles, their thin shoulders rigid with excitement, and listened to the music that made everything so good: the music was always in the background like music at a church service, it was something to depend upon.

A boy named Eddie came in to talk with them. He sat backwards on his stool, turning himself jerkily around in semi-circles and then stopping and turning again, and after a while he asked Connie if she would like something to eat. She said she did and so she tapped her friend's arm on her way out— her friend pulled her face up into a brave droll look—and Connie said she would meet her at eleven, across the way. "I just hate to leave her like that," Connie said earnestly, but the boy said that she wouldn't be alone for long. So they went out to his car and on the way Connie couldn't help but let her eyes wander over the windshields and faces all around her, her face gleaming with a joy that had nothing to do with Eddie or even this place; it might have been the music. She drew her shoulders up and sucked in her breath with the pure pleasure of being alive, and just at that moment she happened to glance at a face just a few feet from hers. It was a boy with shaggy black hair, in a convertible jalopy painted gold. He stared at her and then his lips widened into a grin. Connie slit her eyes at him and turned away, but she couldn't help glancing back and there he was still watching her. He wagged a finger and laughed and said, "Gonna get you, baby," and Connie turned away again without Eddie noticing anything.

She spent three hours with him, at the restaurant where they ate hamburgers and drank Cokes in wax cups that were always sweating, and then down an alley a mile or so away, and when he left her off at five to eleven only the movie house was still open at the plaza. Her girl friend was there, talking with a boy. When Connie came up the two girls smiled at each other and Connie said, "How was the movie?" and the girl said, "*You* should know." They rode off with the girl's father, sleepy and pleased, and Connie couldn't help but look at the darkened shopping plaza with its big empty parking lot and its signs that were faded and ghostly now, and over at the drive-in restaurant where cars were still circling tirelessly. She couldn't hear the music at this distance.

Next morning June asked her how the movie was and Connie said, "So-so."

10   She and that girl and occasionally another girl went out several times a week that way, and the rest of the time Connie spent around the house—it was summer vacation—getting in her mother's way and thinking, dreaming, about the boys she met. But all the boys fell back and dissolved into a single face that was not even a face, but an idea, a feeling, mixed up with the urgent insistent pounding of the music and the humid night air of July. Connie's mother kept dragging her back to the daylight by finding things for her to do or saying, suddenly, "What's this about the Pettinger girl?"

And Connie would say nervously, "Oh, her. That dope." She always drew thick clear lines between herself and such girls, and her mother was simple and kindly enough to believe her. Her mother was so simple, Connie thought, that it was maybe cruel to fool her so much. Her mother went scuffling around the house in old bedroom slippers and complained over the telephone to one sister about the other, then the other called up and the two of them complained about the third one. If June's name was mentioned her mother's tone was approving, and if Connie's name was mentioned it was disapproving. This did not really mean she disliked Connie and actually Connie thought that her mother preferred her to June because she was prettier, but the two of them kept up a pretense of exasperation, a sense that they were tugging and struggling over something of little value to either of them. Sometimes, over coffee, they were almost friends, but something would come up—some vexation that was like a fly buzzing suddenly around their heads—and their faces went hard with contempt.

One Sunday Connie got up at eleven—none of them bothered with church—and washed her hair so that it could dry all day long, in the sun. Her parents and sister were going to a barbecue at an aunt's house and Connie said no, she wasn't interested, rolling her eyes to let her mother know just what she thought of it. "Stay home alone then," her mother said sharply. Connie sat out back in a lawn chair and watched them drive away, her father quiet and bald, hunched around so that he could back the car out, her mother with a look that was still angry and not at all softened through the windshield, and in the back seat poor old June all dressed up as if she didn't know what a barbecue was, with all the running yelling kids and the flies. Connie sat with her eyes closed in the sun, dreaming and dazed with the warmth about her as if this were a kind of love, the caresses of love, and her mind slipped over onto thoughts of the boy she had been with the night before and how nice he had been, how sweet it always was, not the way someone like June would suppose but sweet, gentle, the way it was in movies and promised in songs; and when she opened her eyes she hardly knew where she was, the back yard ran off into weeds and a fence-line of trees and behind it the sky was perfectly blue and still. The asbestos "ranch house" that was now three years old startled her—it looked small. She shook her head as if to get awake.

It was too hot. She went inside the house and turned on the radio to drown out the quiet. She sat on the edge of her bed, barefoot, and listened for an hour and a half to a program called *XYZ* Sunday Jamboree, record after record of hard, fast, shrieking songs she sang along with, interspersed by exclamations from "Bobby King": "An' look here you girls at Napoleon's—Son and Charley want you to pay real close attention to this song coming up!"

And Connie paid close attention herself, bathed in a glow of slow-pulsed joy that seemed to rise mysteriously out of the music itself and lay languidly about the airless little room, breathed in and breathed out with each gentle rise and fall of her chest.

15 After a while she heard a car coming up the drive. She sat up at once, startled, because it couldn't be her father so soon. The gravel kept crunching all the way in from the road—the driveway was long—and Connie ran to the window. It was a car she didn't know. It was an open jalopy, painted a bright gold that caught the sunlight opaquely. Her heart began to pound and her fingers snatched at her hair, checking it, and she whispered "Christ. Christ," wondering how bad she looked. The car came to a stop at the side door and the horn sounded four short taps as if this were a signal Connie knew.

She went into the kitchen and approached the door slowly, then hung out the screen door, her bare toes curling down off the step. There were two boys in the car and now she recognized the driver: he had shaggy, shabby black hair that looked crazy as a wig and he was grinning at her.

"I ain't late, am I?" he said.

"Who the hell do you think you are?" Connie said.

"Toldja I'd be out, didn't I?"

20 "I don't even know who you are."

She spoke sullenly, careful to show no interest or pleasure, and he spoke in a fast bright monotone. Connie looked past him to the other boy, taking her time. He had fair brown hair, with a lock that fell onto his forehead. His side-burns gave him a fierce, embarrassed look, but so far he hadn't even bothered to glance at her. Both boys wore sunglasses. The driver's glasses were metallic and mirrored everything in miniature.

"You wanta come for a ride?" he said.

Connie smirked and let her hair fall loose over one shoulder.

"Don'tcha like my car? New paint job," he said. "Hey."

25 "What?"

"You're cute."

She pretended to fidget, chasing flies away from the door.

"Don'tcha believe me, or what?" he said.

"Look, I don't even know who you are," Connie said in disgust.

30 "Hey, Ellie's got a radio, see. Mine's broke down." He lifted his friend's arm and showed her the little transistor the boy was holding, and now Connie began to hear the music. It was the same program that was playing inside the house.

"Bobby King?" she said.

"I listen to him all the time. I think he's great."

"He's kind of great," Connie said reluctantly.

"Listen, that guy's *great*. He knows where the action is."

35 Connie blushed a little, because the glasses made it impossible for her to see just what this boy was looking at. She couldn't decide if she liked him or if he was just a jerk, and so she dawdled in the doorway and wouldn't come down or go back inside. She said, "What's all that stuff painted on your car?"

"Can'tcha read it?" He opened the door very carefully, as if he was afraid it might fall off. He slid out just as carefully, planting his feet firmly on the ground, the tiny metallic world in his glasses slowing down like gelatine hardening and in the midst of it Connie's bright green blouse. "This here is my name, to begin with," he said. ARNOLD FRIEND was written in tarlike black letters on the side, with a drawing of a round grinning face that reminded Connie of a pumpkin, except it wore sunglasses. "I wanta introduce myself, I'm Arnold Friend and that's my real name and I'm gonna be your friend, honey, and inside the car's Ellie Oscar, he's kinda shy." Ellie brought his transistor radio up to his shoulder and balanced it there. "Now these numbers are a secret code, honey," Arnold Friend explained. He read off the numbers 33, 19, 17 and raised his eyebrows at her to see what she thought of that, but she didn't think much of it. The left rear fender had been smashed and around it was written, on the gleaming gold background: DONE BY CRAZY WOMAN DRIVER. Connie had to laugh at that.

Arnold Friend was pleased at her laughter and looked up at her. "Around the other side's a lot more—you wanta come and see them?"

"No."

"Why not?"

"Why should I?"

40   "Don'tcha wanta see what's on the car? Don'tcha wanta go for a ride?"

"I don't know."

"Why not?"

"I got things to do."

"Like what?"

45   "Things."

He laughed as if she had said something funny. He slapped his thighs. He was standing in a strange way, leaning back against the car as if he were balancing himself. He wasn't tall, only an inch or so taller than she would be if she came down to him. Connie liked the way he was dressed, which was the way all of them dressed: tight faded jeans stuffed into black, scuffed boots, a belt that pulled his waist in and showed how lean he was, and a white pull-over shirt that was a little soiled and showed the hard small muscles of his arms and shoulders. He looked as if he probably did hard work, lifting and carrying things. Even his neck looked muscular. And his face was a familiar face, somehow: the jaw and chin and cheeks slightly darkened, because he hadn't shaved for a day or two, and the nose long and hawk-like, sniffing as if she were a treat he was going to gobble up and it was all a joke.

"Connie, you ain't telling the truth. This is your day set aside for a ride with me and you know it," he said, still laughing. The way he straightened and recovered from his fit of laughing showed that it had been all fake.

"How do you know what my name is?" she said suspiciously.

"It's Connie."

50   "Maybe and maybe not."

"I know my Connie," he said, wagging his finger. Now she remembered him even better, back at the restaurant, and her cheeks warmed at the thought of how she sucked in her breath just at the moment she passed him—how she must have looked to him. And he had remembered her. "Ellie and I come out here especially for you," he said. "Ellie can sit in back. How about it?"

"Where?"

"Where what?"

"Where're we going?"

55   He looked at her. He took off the sunglasses and she saw how pale the skin around his eyes was, like holes that were not in shadow but instead in light. His eyes were chips of broken glass that catch the light in an amiable way. He smiled. It was as if the idea of going for a ride somewhere, to some place, was a new idea to him.

"Just for a ride, Connie sweetheart."

"I never said my name was Connie," she said.

"But I know what it is. I know your name and all about you, lots of things," Arnold Friend said. He had not moved yet but stood still leaning back against the side of his jalopy. "I took a special interest in you, such a pretty girl, and

found out all about you like I know your parents and sister are gone somewheres and I know where and how long they're going to be gone, and I know
who you were with last night, and your best girl friend's name is Betty. Right?"

He spoke in a simple lilting voice, exactly as if he were reciting the words to
a song. His smile assured her that everything was fine. In the car Ellie turned up
the volume on his radio and did not bother to look around at them.

60   "Ellie can sit in the back seat," Arnold Friend said. He indicated his friend
with a casual jerk of his chin, as if Ellie did not count and she should not bother
with him.

"How'd you find out all that stuff?" Connie said.

"Listen: Betty Schultz and Tony Fitch and Jimmy Pettinger and Nancy Pettinger," he said, in a chant. "Raymond Stanley and Bob Hutter—"

"Do you know all those kids?"

"I know everybody."

65   "Look, you're kidding. You're not from around here."

"Sure."

"But—how come we never saw you before?"

"Sure you saw me before," he said. He looked down at his boots, as if he
were a little offended. "You just don't remember."

"I guess I'd remember you," Connie said.

70   "Yeah?" He looked up at this, beaming. He was pleased. He began to mark
time with the music from Ellie's radio, tapping his fists lightly together. Connie
looked away from his smile to the car, which was painted so bright it almost
hurt her eyes to look at it. She looked at that name, ARNOLD FRIEND. And up
at the front fender was an expression that was familiar—MAN THE FLYING
SAUCERS. It was an expression kids had used the year before, but didn't use this
year. She looked at it for a while as if the words meant something to her that
she did not yet know.

"What're you thinking about? Huh?" Arnold Friend demanded. "Not worried about your hair blowing around in the car, are you?"

"No."

"Think I maybe can't drive good?"

"How do I know?"

75   "You're a hard girl to handle. How come?" he said. "Don't you know I'm
your friend? Didn't you see me put my sign in the air when you walked by?"

"What sign?"

"My sign." And he drew an X in the air, leaning out toward her. They were
maybe ten feet apart. After his hand fell back to his side the X was still in the air,
almost visible. Connie let the screen door close and stood perfectly still inside it,
listening to the music from her radio and the boy's blend together. She stared at
Arnold Friend. He stood there so stiffly relaxed, pretending to be relaxed, with
one hand idly on the door handle as if he were keeping himself up that way and
had no intention of ever moving again. She recognized most things about him,
the tight jeans that showed his thighs and buttocks and the greasy leather boots
and the tight shirt, and even that slippery friendly smile of his, that sleepy
dreamy smile that all the boys used to get across ideas they didn't want to put

into words. She recognized all this and also the singsong way he talked, slightly mocking, kidding, but serious and a little melancholy, and she recognized the way he tapped one fist against the other in homage to the perpetual music behind him. But all these things did not come together.

She said suddenly, "Hey, how old are you?"

His smile faded. She could see then that he wasn't a kid, he was much older—thirty, maybe more. At this knowledge her heart began to pound faster.

80   "That's a crazy thing to ask. Can'tcha see I'm your own age?"

"Like hell you are."

"Or maybe a coupla years older, I'm eighteen."

"Eighteen?" she said doubtfully.

He grinned to reassure her and lines appeared at the corners of his mouth. His teeth were big and white. He grinned so broadly his eyes became slits and she saw how thick the lashes were, thick and black as if painted with a black tar-like material. Then he seemed to become embarrassed, abruptly, and looked over his shoulder at Ellie. "*Him,* he's crazy," he said. "Ain't he a riot, he's a nut, a real character." Ellie was still listening to the music. His sunglasses told nothing about what he was thinking. He wore a bright orange shirt unbuttoned halfway to show his chest, which was a pale, bluish chest and not muscular like Arnold Friend's. His shirt collar was turned up all around and the very tips of the collar pointed out past his chin as if they were protecting him. He was pressing the transistor radio up against his ear and sat there in a kind of daze, right in the sun.

85   "He's kinda strange," Connie said.

"Hey, she says you're kinda strange! Kinda strange!" Arnold Friend cried. He pounded on the car to get Ellie's attention. Ellie turned for the first time and Connie saw with shock that he wasn't a kid either—he had a fair, hairless face, cheeks reddened slightly as if the veins grew too close to the surface of his skin, the face of a forty-year-old baby. Connie felt a wave of dizziness rise in her at this sight and she stared at him as if waiting for something to change the shock of the moment, make it all right again. Ellie's lips kept shaping words, mumbling along with the words blasting in his ear.

"Maybe you two better go away," Connie said faintly.

"What? How come?" Arnold Friend cried. "We come out here to take you for a ride. It's Sunday." He had the voice of the man on the radio now. It was the same voice, Connie thought. "Don'tcha know it's Sunday all day and honey, no matter who you were with last night today you're with Arnold Friend and don't you forget it!—Maybe you better step out here," he said, and this last was in a different voice. It was a little flatter, as if the heat was finally getting to him.

"No. I got things to do."

90   "Hey."

"You two better leave."

"We ain't leaving until you come with us."

"Like hell I am—"

"Connie, don't fool around with me. I mean, I mean, don't fool *around,*" he said, shaking his head. He laughed incredulously. He placed his sunglasses on top of his head, carefully, as if he were indeed wearing a wig, and brought the stems down behind his ears. Connie stared at him, another wave of dizziness and fear rising in her so that for a moment he wasn't even in focus but was just a blur, standing there against his gold car, and she had the idea that he had driven up the driveway all right but had come from nowhere before that and belonged nowhere and that everything about him and even about the music that was so familiar to her was only half real.

95   "If my father comes and sees you—"

"He ain't coming. He's at a barbecue."

"How do you know that?"

"Aunt Tillie's. Right now they're—uh—they're drinking. Sitting around," he said vaguely, squinting as if he were staring all the way to town and over to Aunt Tillie's backyard. Then the vision seemed to get clear and he nodded energetically. "Yeah. Sitting around. There's your sister in a blue dress, huh? And high heels, the poor sad bitch—nothing like you sweetheart! And your mother's helping some fat woman with the corn, they're cleaning the corn—husking the corn—"

"What fat woman?" Connie cried.

100   "How do I know what fat woman. I don't know every goddam fat woman in the world!" Arnold Friend laughed.

"Oh, that's Mrs. Hornby. . . . Who invited her?" Connie said. She felt a little light-headed. Her breath was coming quickly.

"She's too fat. I don't like them fat. I like them the way you are, honey," he said, smiling sleepily at her. They stared at each other for a while, through the screen door. He said softly, "Now what you're going to do is this: you're going to come out that door. You're going to sit up front with me and Ellie's going to sit in the back, the hell with Ellie, right? This isn't Ellie's date. You're my date. I'm your lover, honey."

"What? You're crazy—"

"Yes, I'm your lover. You don't know what that is but you will," he said. "I know that too. I know all about you. But look: it's real nice and you couldn't ask for nobody better than me, or more polite. I always keep my word. I'll tell you how it is, I'm always nice at first, the first time. I'll hold you so tight you won't think you have to try to get away or pretend anything because you'll know you can't. And I'll come inside you where it's all secret and you'll give in to me and you'll love me—"

105   "Shut up! You're crazy!" Connie said. She backed away from the door. She put her hands against her ears as if she'd heard something terrible, something not meant for her. "People don't talk like that, you're crazy," she muttered. Her heart was almost too big now for her chest and its pumping made sweat break out all over her. She looked out to see Arnold Friend pause and then take a step toward the porch lurching. He almost fell. But, like a clever drunken man, he managed to catch his balance. He wobbled in his high boots and grabbed hold of one of the porch posts.

"Honey?" he said. "You still listening?"

"Get the hell out of here!"

"Be nice, honey. Listen."

"I'm going to call the police—"

110 He wobbled again and out of the side of his mouth came a fast spat curse, an aside not meant for her to hear. But even this "Christ!" sounded forced. Then he began to smile again. She watched this smile come, awkward as if he were smiling from inside a mask. His whole face was a mask, she thought wildly, tanned down onto his throat but then running out as if he had plastered make-up on his face but had forgotten about his throat.

"Honey—? Listen, here's how it is. I always tell the truth and I promise you this: I ain't coming in that house after you."

"You better not! I'm going to call the police if you—if you don't—"

"Honey," he said, talking right through her voice, "honey, I'm not coming in there but you are coming out here. You know why?"

She was panting. The kitchen looked like a place she had never seen before, some room she had run inside but which wasn't good enough, wasn't going to help her. The kitchen window had never had a curtain, after three years, and there were dishes in the sink for her to do—probably—and if you ran your hand across the table you'd probably feel something sticky there.

115 "You listening, honey? Hey?"

"—going to call the police—"

"Soon as you touch the phone I don't need to keep my promise and can come inside. You won't want that."

She rushed forward and tried to lock the door. Her fingers were shaking. "But why lock it," Arnold Friend said gently, talking right into her face. "It's just a screen door. It's just nothing." One of his boots was at a strange angle, as if his foot wasn't in it. It pointed out to the left, bent at the ankle. "I mean, anybody can break through a screen door and glass and wood and iron or anything else if he needs to, anybody at all and specially Arnold Friend. If the place got lit up with a fire honey you'd come running out into my arms, right into my arms and safe at home—like you knew I was your lover and'd stopped fooling around. I don't mind a nice shy girl but I don't like no fooling around." Part of those words were spoken with a slight rhythmic lilt, and Connie somehow recognized them—the echo of a song from last year, about a girl rushing into her boy friend's arms and coming home again—

Connie stood barefoot on the linoleum floor, staring at him. "What do you want?" she whispered.

120 "I want you," he said.

"What?"

"Seen you that night and thought, that's the one, yes sir. I never needed to look any more."

"But my father's coming back. He's coming to get me. I had to wash my hair first—" She spoke in a dry, rapid voice, hardly raising it for him to hear.

"No, your daddy is not coming and yes, you had to wash your hair and you washed it for me. It's nice and shining and all for me, I thank you, sweetheart," he said, with a mock bow, but again he almost lost his balance. He had to bend and adjust his boots. Evidently his feet did not go all the way down; the boots must have been stuffed with something so that he would seem taller. Connie stared out at him and behind him Ellie in the car, who seemed to be looking off toward Connie's right, into nothing. This Ellie said, pulling the words out of the air one after another as if he were just discovering them, "You want me to pull out the phone?"

125   "Shut your mouth and keep it shut," Arnold Friend said, his face red from bending over or maybe from embarrassment because Connie had seen his boots. "This ain't none of your business."

"What—what are you doing? What do you want?" Connie said. "If I call the police they'll get you, they'll arrest you—"

"Promise was not to come in unless you touch that phone, and I'll keep that promise," he said. He resumed his erect position and tried to force his shoulders back. He sounded like a hero in a movie, declaring something important. He spoke too loudly and it was as if he were speaking to someone behind Connie. "I ain't made plans for coming in that house where I don't belong but just for you to come out to me, the way you should. Don't you know who I am?"

"You're crazy," she whispered. She backed away from the door but did not want to go into another part of the house, as if this would give him permission to come through the door. "What do you. . . . You're crazy, you . . ."

"Huh? What're you saying, honey?"

130   Her eyes darted everywhere in the kitchen. She could not remember what it was, this room.

"This is how it is, honey: you come out and we'll drive away, have a nice ride. But if you don't come out we're gonna wait till your people come home and then they're all going to get it."

"You want that telephone pulled out?" Ellie said. He held the radio away from his ear and grimaced, as if without the radio the air was too much for him.

"I toldja shut up, Ellie," Arnold Friend said, "you're deaf, get a hearing aid, right? Fix yourself up. This little girl's no trouble and's gonna be nice to me, so Ellie keep to yourself, this ain't your date—right? Don't hem in on me. Don't hog. Don't crush. Don't bird dog. Don't trail me," he said in a rapid meaningless voice, as if he were running through all the expressions he'd learned but was no longer sure which one of them was in style, then rushing on to new ones, making them up with his eyes closed, "Don't crawl under my fence, don't squeeze in my chipmunk hole, don't sniff my glue, suck my popsicle, keep your own greasy fingers on yourself!" He shaded his eyes and peered in at Connie, who was backed against the kitchen table. "Don't mind him honey he's just a creep. He's a dope. Right? I'm the boy for you and like I said you come out here nice like a lady and give me your hand, and nobody else gets hurt, I mean, your nice old bald-headed daddy and your mummy and your sister in her high heels. Because listen: why bring them in this?"

"Leave me alone," Connie whispered.

135   "Hey, you know that old woman down the road, the one with the chickens and stuff—you know her?"

"She's dead!"

"Dead? What? You know her?" Arnold Friend said.

"She's dead—"

"Don't you like her?"

140 "She's dead—she's—she isn't here any more—"

"But don't you like her, I mean, you got something against her? Some grudge or something?" Then his voice dipped as if he were conscious of a rudeness. He touched the sunglasses perched on top of his head as if to make sure they were still there. "Now you be a good girl."

"What are you going to do?"

"Just two things, or maybe three," Arnold Friend said. "But I promise it won't last long and you'll like me that way you get to like people you're close to. You will. It's all over for you here, so come on out. You don't want your people in any trouble, do you?"

She turned and bumped against a chair or something, hurting her leg, but she ran into the back room and picked up the telephone. Something roared in her ear, a tiny roaring, and she was so sick with fear that she could do nothing but listen to it—the telephone was clammy and very heavy and her fingers groped down to the dial but were too weak to touch it. She began to scream into the phone, into the roaring. She cried out, she cried for her mother, she felt her breath start jerking back and forth in her lungs as if it were something Arnold Friend were stabbing her with again and again with no tenderness. A noisy sorrowful wailing rose all about her and she was locked inside it the way she was locked inside the house.

145 After a while she could hear again. She was sitting on the floor with her wet back against the wall.

Arnold Friend was saying from the door, "That's a good girl. Put the phone back."

She kicked the phone away from her.

"No, honey. Pick it up. Put it back right."

She picked it up and put it back. The dial tone stopped.

150 "That's a good girl. Now you come outside."

She was hollow with what had been fear, but what was now just an emptiness. All that screaming had blasted it out of her. She sat, one leg cramped under her, and deep inside her brain was something like a pinpoint of light that kept going and would not let her relax. She thought, I'm not going to see my mother again. She thought, I'm not going to sleep in my bed again. Her bright green blouse was all wet.

Arnold Friend said, in a gentle-loud voice that was like a stage voice, "The place where you came from ain't there any more, and where you had in mind to go is cancelled out. This place you are now—inside your daddy's house—is nothing but a cardboard box I can knock down any time. You know that and always did know it. You hear me?"

She thought, I have got to think. I have to know what to do.

"We'll go out to a nice field, out in the country here where it smells so nice and it's sunny," Arnold Friend said. "I'll have my arms around you so you won't need to try to get away and I'll show you what love is like, what it does. The hell with this house! It looks solid all right," he said. He ran a fingernail down the screen and the noise did not make Connie shiver, as it would have the day before. "Now put your hand on your heart, honey. Feel that? That feels solid too but we know better, be nice to me, be sweet like you can because what else is there for a girl like you but to be sweet and pretty and give in?—and get away before her people come back?"

155   She felt her pounding heart. Her hand seemed to enclose it. She thought for the first time in her life that it was nothing that was hers, that belonged to her, but just a pounding, living thing inside this body that wasn't really hers either.

"You don't want them to get hurt," Arnold Friend went on. "Now get up, honey. Get up all by yourself."

She stood.

"Now turn this way. That's right. Come over here to me—Ellie, put that away, didn't I tell you? You dope. You miserable creepy dope," Arnold Friend said. His words were not angry but only part of an incantation. The incantation was kindly. "Now come out through the kitchen to me honey and let's see a smile, try it, you're a brave sweet little girl and now they're eating corn and hot-dogs cooked to bursting over an outdoor fire, and they don't know one thing about you and never did and honey you're better than them because not a one of them would have done this for you."

Connie felt the linoleum under her feet; it was cool. She brushed her hair back out of her eyes. Arnold Friend let go of the post tentatively and opened his arms for her, his elbows pointing in toward each other and his wrists limp, to show that this was an embarrassed embrace and a little mocking, he didn't want to make her self-conscious.

160   She put out her hand against the screen. She watched herself push the door slowly open as if she were safe back somewhere in the other doorway, watching this body and this head of long hair moving out into the sunlight where Arnold Friend waited.

"My sweet little blue-eyed girl," he said, in a half-sung sigh that had nothing to do with her brown eyes but was taken up just the same by the vast sunlit reaches of the land behind him and on all sides of him, so much land that Connie had never seen before and did not recognize except to know that she was going to it.

◆ ◆ ◆

When Characters from the Page Are Made Flesh on the Screen

JOYCE CAROL OATES

Some years ago in the American Southwest there surfaced a tabloid psychopath known as "The Pied Piper of Tucson." I have forgotten his name but his specialty was the seduction and occasional murder of teen-age girls. He may or may not have had actual accomplices, but his bizarre activities were known among a circle of teen-agers in the Tucson area; for some reason they kept his secrets, deliberately did not inform parents or police. It was this fact, not the fact of the mass murderer himself, that struck me at the time. And this was a pre-Manson time, this was early or mid-1960's.

The "Pied Piper" mimicked teen-agers in their talk, dress and behavior, but he was not a teen-ager— he was a man in his early 30's. Rather short, he stuffed rags in his leather boots to give himself height. (And sometimes walked unsteadily as a consequence: did none among his admiring constituency notice?) He charmed his victims, to the bewilderment of others who fancy themselves free of all lunatic attractions. "The Pied Piper of Tucson": a trashy dream, a tabloid archetype, sheer artifice, comedy, cartoon—surrounded, however improbably, and finally tragically, by real people. You think that, if you look twice, he won't be there. But there he is.

I don't remember any longer where I first read about "The Pied Piper"— very likely in *Life* magazine. I do recall deliberately not reading the full article because I didn't want to be distracted by too much detail. It was not after all the mass murderer himself who intrigued me, but the disturbing fact that a number of teen-agers— from "good" families—aided and abetted his crimes. This is the sort of thing authorities and responsible citizens invariably call "inexplicable" because they can't find explanations for it. *They* would not have fallen under this maniac's spell, after all.

An early draft of my short story "Where Are You Going, Where Have You Been?"—from which the current film "Smooth Talk" has been adapted by Joyce Chopra and Tom Cole—had the rather too explicit title "Death and the Maiden." It was cast in a mode of fiction to which I am still partial—indeed, every third or fourth story of mine is probably in this mode—"realistic allegory," it might be called. It is Hawthornian, romantic, shading into

parable. Like the medieval German engraving from which my title was taken the story was minutely detailed yet clearly an allegory of the fatal attractions of death (or the devil). An innocent young girl is seduced by way of her own vanity; she mistakes death for erotic romance of a particularly American/trashy sort.

In subsequent drafts the story changed its tone, its focus, its language, its title. It became "Where Are You Going, Where Have You Been?" Written at a time when the author was intrigued by the music of Bob Dylan, particularly the hauntingly elegiac song "It's All Over Now, Baby Blue," it was dedicated to Bob Dylan. The charismatic mass murderer drops into the background and his innocent victim, a 15-year-old, moves into the foreground. She becomes the true protagonist of the tale, courting and being courted by her fate, a self-styled 1950's pop figure, alternately absurd and winning.

There is no suggestion in the published story that "Arnold Friend" has seduced and murdered other young girls, or even that he necessarily intends to murder Connie. Is his interest "merely" sexual? (Nor is there anything about the complicity of other teen-agers. I saved that yet more provocative note for a current story, "Testimony.") Connie is shallow, vain, silly, hopeful, doomed—perhaps as I saw, and still see, myself?—but capable nonetheless of an unexpected gesture of heroism at the story's end.

Her smooth-talking seducer, who cannot lie, promises her that her family will be unharmed if she gives herself to him; and so she does. The story ends abruptly at the point of her "crossing over." We don't know the nature of her sacrifice, only that she is generous enough to make it.

In adapting a narrative so spare and thematically foreshortened as

"Where Are You Going, Where Have You Been?" film director Joyce Chopra and screenwriter Tom Cole were required to do a good deal of filling in, expanding, inventing. Connie's story becomes lavishly, and lovingly, textured; she is not an allegorical figure so much as a "typical" teen-age girl (if Laura Dern, spectacularly good-looking, can be so defined).

Joyce Chopra, who has done documentary films on contemporary teen-age culture, and, yet more authoritatively, has an adolescent daughter of her own, creates in "Smooth Talk" a believable world for Connie to inhabit. Or worlds: as in the original story there is Connie-at-home, and there is Connie-with-her-friends. Two 15-year-old girls, two finely honed styles, two voices, sometimes but not often overlapping. It is one of the marvelous visual features of the film that we *see* Connie and her friends transform themselves, once they are safely free of parental observation. What freedom, what joy! The girls claim their true identities in the neighborhood shopping mall!

"Smooth Talk" is, in a way, as much Connie's mother's story as it is Connie's; its center of gravity, its emotional nexus, is frequently with the mother—played by Mary Kay Place. (Though the mother's sexual jealousy of her daughter is slighted in the film.) Connie's ambiguous relationship with her affable, somewhat mysterious father (played by Levon Helm) is an excellent touch: I had thought, subsequent to the story's publication, that I should have built up the father, suggesting, as subtly as I could, an attraction there paralleling the attraction Connie feels for her seducer Arnold Friend.

Treat Williams impersonates Arnold Friend as Arnold Friend impersonates—is it James Dean? James Dean

regarding himself in mirrors, doing James Dean impersonations? Laura Dern is so right as "my" Connie that I may come to think I modeled the fictitious girl on her, in the way that writers frequently delude themselves about notions of causality.

My difficulties with "Smooth Talk" have primarily to do with my chronic hesitation—a justifiable shyness, I'm sure—about seeing/hearing work of mine abstracted from its contexture of language. All writers know that language is their subject; quirky word choices, patterns of rhythm, enigmatic pauses, punctuation marks. Where the quick-scanner sees "quick" writing, the writer conceals nine-tenths of his iceberg.

Of course we all have "real" subjects, and we will fight to the death to defend these subjects, but beneath the tale-telling it is the tale-telling that grips us so very fiercely: "the soul at the *white heat*" in Emily Dickinson's words. Because of this it is always an eerie experience for me, as a writer, to hear "my" dialogue floating back to me from the external world; particularly when it is surrounded, as of course it must be, by "other" dialogue I seem not to recall having written. Perhaps a panic reaction sets in—perhaps I worry that I might be responsible for knowing what "I" meant, in writing things "I" didn't write? Like a student who has handed in work not entirely his own, and dreads interrogation from his teacher?

It is startling too to *see* fictitious characters inhabiting, with such seeming aplomb, roles that until now seemed private, flat on the page. (I don't, like many of my writing colleagues, feel affronted, thinking, "*That* isn't how he/she looks!" I think instead, guiltily, "Is *that* how he/she really looks?")

I have also had a number of plays produced and so characteristically doubtful am I about intruding into my directors' territories that I nearly always abrogate my authority to them. The writer works in a single dimension, the director works in three. I assume that they are professionals to their fingertips; authorities in their medium as I am an authority (if I am) in mine. I would fiercely defend the placement of a semicolon in one of my novels, but I would probably have deferred fairly quickly to Joyce Chopra's decision to reverse the story's ending, turn it upside-down, in a sense, so that the film ends not with death, not with a sleepwalker's crossing-over to her fate, but upon a sense of reconciliation, rejuvenation. Laura Dern's Connie is no longer "my" Connie at the film's conclusion; she is very much alive, assertive, strong-willed—a girl, perhaps, of the mid-1980's, and not of the mid-1960's.

A girl's loss of virginity, bittersweet but not necessarily tragic. Not today. A girl's coming of age that involves her succumbing to, but then rejecting, the "trashy dreams" of her pop teen-age culture. "Where Are You Going, Where Have You Been?" deliberately betrays itself as allegorical in its conclusion: Death and Death's chariot (a funky souped-up convertible) have come for the Maiden. Awakening is, in the story's final lines, moving out into the sunlight where Arnold Friend waits:

> "My sweet little blue-eyed girl," he said in a half-sung sigh that had nothing to do with (Connie's) brown eyes but was taken up just the same by the vast sunlit reaches of the land behind him and on all sides of him—so much land that Connie had never seen before and did not recognize except to know that she was going to it.

I quite understand that this is an unfilmable conclusion, and "Where Are You Going, Where Have You Been?" is in fact an unfilmable short story. But Joyce Chopra's "Smooth Talk" is an accomplished and sophisticated movie that attempts to do just that.

◈ ◈ ◈

In Fairyland, without a Map: Connie's Exploration Inward in Joyce Carol Oates' "Where Are You Going, Where Have You Been?"

GRETCHEN SCHULZ AND R. J. R. ROCKWOOD

Joyce Carol Oates has stated that her prize-winning story *Where Are You Going, Where Have You Been?* (Fall, 1966) came to her "more or less in a piece" after hearing Bob Dylan's song *It's All Over Now, Baby Blue,* and then reading about a "killer in some Southwestern state," and thinking about "the old legends and folk songs of Death and the Maiden."[1] The "killer" that Miss Oates had in mind, the one on whom her character Arnold Friend is modeled, was twenty-three-year-old Charles Schmid of Tucson, Arizona. Schmid had been charged with the murders of three teen-age girls, and was the subject of a lengthy article in the March 4, 1966, issue of *Life* magazine. It is not surprising that this account should have generated mythic musings in Miss Oates—musings that culminated in a short story which has depths as mythic as any of the "old legends and folk songs." The *Life* reporter, Don Moser, himself had found in this raw material such an abundance of the reality which is the stuff of myth, that he entitled his article "The Pied Piper of Tucson."

The article states that Schmid—or "Smitty," as he was called—had sought deliberately "to create an exalted, heroic image of himself." To the teen-agers in Smitty's crowd, who "had little to do but look each other over," their leader was a "folk hero . . . more dramatic, more theatrical, more *interesting* than anyone else in their lives," and seemed to embody the very lyrics of a then popular song: "Hey, c'mon babe, follow me,/ I'm the Pied Piper, follow me,/ I'm the Pied Piper, And I'll show you where it's at." With a face which was "his own creation: the hair dyed raven black, the skin darkened to a deep tan with pancake make-up, the lips whitened, the whole effect heightened by a mole he had painted on one cheek," Smitty would cruise "in a golden car," haunting "all the teen-age hangouts," looking for pretty girls, especially ones with long blond hair. Because he was only five-foot-three, Smitty "habitually stuffed three or four inches of old rags and tin cans into the bottoms of his high-topped boots to make himself taller," even though the price he paid for that extra height was an awkward, stumbling walk that made people think he had "wooden feet."[2]

In his transformation into the Arnold Friend of *Where Are You Going, Where Have You Been?*, Smitty underwent the kind of apotheosis[3] which he had tried, by means of bizarre theatrics, to achieve in actuality, for Arnold is the exact transpersonal[4] counterpart of the real-life "Pied Piper of Tucson." Thus, although Arnold is a "realistic" figure, drawn from the life of a specific psychopathic killer, that superficial realism is only incidental to the more essential realism of the mythic characteristics—the archetypal qualities—he shares with the man who was his model. Asked to comment on Arnold, Miss Oates reveals that, to her, the character is *truly* mythological. No longer quite human, he functions as a personified subjective factor: "Arnold Friend," she says, "is a fantastic figure: he is Death, he is the 'elf-[king]' of the ballads, he is the Imagination, he is a Dream, he is a Lover, a Demon, *and all that.*"[5]

If '*Where Are You Going, Where Have You Been?*' is a "portrait of a psychopathic killer masquerading as a teenager,"[6] it is clear that this portrait is created in the mind of Connie, the teen-age protagonist of the story, and that it exists *there only.* It is thus Connie's inner world that determines how Arnold is, or has to be, at least in her eyes, for her personal problems are so compelling that they effectively rearrange and remodel the world of objective reality. Arnold Friend's own part in the creation of his image—whether he deliberately set about to become the "fantastic" figure he is, or seems to be, as his model, Smitty, did—Miss Oates ignores altogether. She is interested only in Connie, Arnold's young victim, and in how Connie's psychological state shapes her perceptions. We find—as we might expect with a writer who characterizes the mode in which she writes as "psychological realism"[7]—that the "fantastic" or mythological qualities of Arnold Friend (and of all those in the story) are presented as subjective rather than objective facts, aspects of the transpersonal psyche projected outward, products of the unconscious mental processes of a troubled adolescent girl.

Toward Arnold Friend, and what he represents, Connie is ambivalent: she is both fascinated and frightened. She is, after all, at that confusing age when a girl feels, thinks, and acts both like a child, put off by a possible lover, and like a woman, attracted to him. Uncertain how to bridge the chasm between "home" and "anywhere that was not home," she stands—or wavers—at the boundary between childhood and adulthood, hesitant and yet anxious to enter the new world of experience which is opening before her:

> Everything about her had two sides to it, one for home and one for anywhere that was not home: her walk, which could be childlike and bobbing, or languid enough to make anyone think she was hearing music in her head; her mouth, which was pale and smirking most of the time, but bright and pink on these evenings out; her laugh, which was cynical and drawling at home—"Ha, ha, very funny,"—but high-pitched and nervous anywhere else, like the jingling of the charms on her bracelet.[8]

That her laugh is "high-pitched and nervous" when she is "anywhere that was not home" betrays the fact that Connie, like all young people, needs help as she begins to move from the past to the future, as she begins the perilous inward journey towards maturity. This journey is an essential part of the adolescent's search for personal identity, and though it is a quest that he must undertake by himself, traditionally it has been the responsibility of culture to help by providing symbolic maps of the territory through which he will travel, territory that lies on the other side of consciousness.

Such models of behavior and maps of the unknown are generally provided by the products of fantasy—myth, legend, and folklore. Folk fairy tales have been especially useful in this way. In his book, *The Uses of Enchantment: The Meaning and Importance of Fairy Tales* (1976), Bruno Bettelheim argues that children's fairy tales offer "symbolic images" that suggest "happy solutions"[9] to the problems of adolescence. Indeed, Joyce Carol Oates herself has Hugh Petrie, the caricaturist in her novel *The Assassins* (1975) observe that "fairy tales are analogous to life as it is lived in the family."[10] In her fiction both short and long Miss Oates makes frequent use of fairy tale material. Again and again she presents characters and situations which parallel corresponding motifs from the world of folk fantasy. And never is this more true than in the present story—never in all the eight novels and eleven collections of short stories which she has written at last count. Woven into the complex texture of *Where Are You Going, Where Have You Been?* are motifs from such tales as *The Spirit in the Bottle, Snow White, Cinderella, Sleeping Beauty, Rapunzel, Little Red Riding Hood,* and *The Three Little Pigs.*[11] *The Pied Piper of Hamelin,* which ends tragically and so according to Bettelheim does not qualify as a proper fairy tale,[12] serves as the "frame device" that contains all the other tales.

There is a terrible irony here, for although the story is full of fairy tales, Connie, its protagonist, is not. Connie represents an entire generation of young people who have grown up—or tried to—without the help of those bedtime stories which not only entertain the child, but also enable him vicariously to experience and work through problems which he will encounter in adolescence. The only "stories" Connie knows are those of the sexually provocative but superficial lyrics of the popular songs she loves or of the equally insubstantial movies she attends. Such songs and movies provide either no models of behavior for her to imitate, or dangerously inappropriate ones. Connie has thus been led to believe that life and, in particular, love will be "sweet, gentle, the way it was in the movies and promised in songs." She has no idea that life actually can be just as grim as in folk fairy tales. The society that is depicted in *Where Are You Going, Where Have You Been*? has failed to make available to children like Connie maps of the unconscious such as fairy tales provide, because it has failed to recognize that in the unconscious past and future coalesce,[13] and that, psychologically, where the child is going is where he has already been. Since Connie has been left—in the words of yet another of the popular songs—to "wander through that wonderland alone"—it is small wonder, considering her lack of spiritual preparation, that Connie's journey there soon becomes a terrifying schizophrenic separation from reality, with prognosis for recovery extremely poor.

The fact that the Oates story, like the magazine article which inspired it, is framed around the motif of the Pied Piper is significant, for this device serves to fix blame for the catastrophe which the story describes. The motif suggests that the adults of Connie's world have made the same mistake as the Burghers[14] of Hamelin seven centuries before: having failed to live up to their moral obligations by refusing to "pay the piper," they themselves—albeit unknowingly—have unleashed the very force which will prove destructive to their children. What kind of force this is, and its particular implications for Con-

nie, we can understand more clearly by interpreting the symbolism underlying the fate of the legendary children of Hamelin: led outside the comfortable sanity of their walled city, the children disappear into that emblem of the devouring unconscious, the Koppenberg . . . victims, we would say, of an acute, collective psychosis. Assuming that the eternal patterns recur, each time as though for the first and last time, then this will be Connie's fate too, and her own psychosis will likewise have no remission. Certainly Arnold Friend is such that Connie cannot keep from following him, perhaps because in following him she is following the popular music she loves, music with which he is not only closely identified, but of which he is the personification. Thus, when Connie, "hearing music in her head," wanders into the bottle-shaped drive-in restaurant, charmed by "the music that made everything so good: the music . . . always in the background, like music at a church service," it is there that she first sees him. He later arrives at her house with a transistor radio which is playing "the same program that was playing inside the house," a program which leaves Connie feeling "bathed in a glow of slow-pulsed joy that seemed to rise mysteriously out of the music itself." Arnold even talks in a "simple lilting voice, exactly as if he were reciting the words to a song." There are many more passages of this kind, but let these suffice to show that Arnold is, indeed, depicted as a Pied Piper, incarnated by society's refusal to live up to its cultural obligation to provide what is needed to help the adolescent make it safely through to adulthood.

The help provided by fairy tales proper is such that a child can learn to compensate even when adult society makes errors of the gravest sort, capping with a happy ending a situation which might otherwise prove tragic for the child. Accordingly, the force which lures all save one of the unwitting children of Hamelin to their psychological death in the Koppenberg[15] is identical to that which the child is taught to tame in the fairy tale *Spirit in the Bottle*. For Connie, the "bottle" is the drive-in restaurant where the teen-agers hang out, a restaurant "shaped like a big bottle, though squatter than a real bottle . . . [and] on its cap a revolving figure of a grinning boy holding a hamburger aloft." The boy on the bottle-cap reminds us of "the boy named Eddie" inside the restaurant who, appropriately, sits *eddying* on his stool, "turning himself jerkily around in semi-circles and then stopping and turning back again," motion which suggests that bottled up sexual pressures are building, ever more insistent in their demand for release. Eddie takes Connie off for some petting, some rubbing that arouses her sexuality, too, until in her mind his face dissolves "into a single face that was not even a face but an idea, a feeling, mixed up with the urgent insistent pounding of the music and the humid night air of July." On this same visit to the restaurant Connie arouses Arnold Friend, who wags his finger at her, laughs, and says, "'Gonna get you, baby'," and who at this moment reveals that he is not only the Pied Piper, but also that hostile spirit in the bottle which is described in the fairy tale.

When the woodcutter's son discovers *his* mysterious bottle and releases a spirit which likewise threatens to destroy *him*, he manages to entrap the spirit once again, agreeing to release it only when it agrees to share its special powers with him, powers which enable the boy to become the "greatest physician in the land." As in the fairy tale, Connie has uncorked the bottle, but because she is unacquainted with this part of the psyche, she is not equipped to recognize the grinning boy atop the bottle-cap or the laughing Arnold Friend as a potentially destructive force which must be controlled if it is to make a positive contribution to her personality. What complicates the attempt to control this force is that it disguises itself as mere sexuality, as is evident from the fairy tale in the fact that the bottle is clearly phallic and the boy's handling of it masturbatory: if we consider that what leads to the boy's taking flight and finding the bottle is his father's belittling him for incompetence at chopping wood, we can say that, psychologically, the boy is seeking compensation in an eroticised flood of negative content from the unconscious. Bettelheim points out that a fairy tale like *Spirit in the Bottle* deals with two problems that confront the child as he struggles to establish a sense of identity: parental belittlement, and integration of a divided personality.[16] In Connie's case, her mother's belittling remarks that "Connie couldn't do a thing, her mind was all filled with trashy daydreams," certainly have contributed to Connie's two-sidedness, with her one personality "for home" and another for "anywhere that was not home," a division also apparent in the relationship between Connie and the "girl friend" who accompanies her to the bottle-shaped restaurant— the two are so poorly differentiated as to suggest a mere *doubling* of Connie, rather than two separate individuals. While such personality division may at first glance seem pathological, it is not, according to Bettelheim, necessarily abnormal, since "the manner in which the child can bring some order into his world view is by dividing everything into opposites," and that "in the later oedipal[17] and post oedipal ages, this splitting extends to the child himself."[18] In *Spirit in the Bottle,* the degraded hero, reacting to the anguish of being regarded by his parent as stupid and incompetent, withdraws into himself, undergoes a split into positive and negative aspects, de-energizes the negative (as represented by the spirit that comes out of the bottle), and then successfully reintegrates his personality, achieving a durable and socially productive synthesis. Had Connie been familiar with this fairy tale, she would have known that however deplorable her situation might seem at a given moment, the means toward an eventual happy solution is in learning to interact with the unconscious in such a way as to emulate the woodcutter's son, who, *by asserting rational control over the terms of the spirit's release into consciousness,* is able to demonstrate to himself and the world that he is not only wiser and better than his parent, but positively the "greatest physician in the land."

Knowledge of this tale alone, however, would not suffice, for it is merely a beginning: to be assured of safe passage through what Bettelheim terms "that thorniest of thickets, the oedipal period,"[19] a child like Connie would need to have absorbed the wisdom of the other fairy tales to which Miss Oates alludes, tales such as *Snow White, Cinderella, Rapunzel,* and *Little Red Riding Hood.* By their applicability to Connie's situation, these tales reveal that at its deepest level Connie's most compelling psychological problem is *unresolved oedipal conflict, aggravated by sibling rivalry.*

Suggestive of *Snow White* is Connie's "habit of craning her neck to glance into mirrors, or checking other people's faces to make sure her own was all right" (as though other people's faces were mirrors, too); and we are told also that her mother, "who noticed everything and knew everything"—as though with the wicked queen's magic power—"hadn't much reason any longer to look at her own face," and so was jealous of her daughter's beauty and "always after Connie." Arnold Friend's sunglasses also mirror everything, which means that, in this instance, he personifies the Magic Mirror, and, of course, he finds Connie the fairest one of all. In his words, "Seen you that night and thought, that's the one, yes sir, I never needed to look anymore." Though he thus serves as Prince, there is a hint of the dwarf motif in Arnold's short stature and obvious phallicism; and most particularly is this true of his friend, Ellie Oscar, a case of arrested development, whose face is that of a "forty-year-old baby." Connie's "Someday My Prince Will Come" daydreams, plus the many references to how dazed and sleepy she always is, especially the day Arnold comes for her, when she "lay languidly about the airless little room" and "breathed in and breathed out with each gentle rise and fall of her chest"—these, too, suggest *Snow White* and, for that matter, *Sleeping Beauty,* whose heroine in the Brothers Grimm is, like Connie, fifteen.

The oedipal implications of *Snow White* are evident in the fact that, as Bettelheim points out, the queen's Magic Mirror speaks not with the mother's but the daughter's voice, revealing the jealous child's own sense of inferiority and frustration projected onto her mother. The father's romantic feelings for the daughter are never at issue in such a fairy tale, and he is generally depicted as weak, ineffectual, and oblivious to the struggle that ensues between mother and daughter[20]—exactly as in Miss Oates' story:

Their father was away at work most of the time and when he came home he wanted supper and he read the newspaper at supper and after supper he went to bed. He didn't bother talking much to them, but around his bent head Connie's mother kept picking at her until Connie wished her mother was dead and she herself was dead and it was all over.

It would be difficult to find a more striking emblem of mother-daughter oedipal conflict than in this passage, where the second death wish serves as punishment for the first.

Bettelheim observes that whenever the child's feeling of "degradation" is the result of "oedipal entanglement of father and daughter," the "Cinderella" theme emerges.[21] Unlike *Snow White,* however, *Cinderella* centers on the "agonies and hopes which form the essential content of sibling rivalry . . . [since] 'having lived among the ashes' was a symbol of being debased in comparison to one's siblings."[22] In this case, the relationship between Connie and her sister June is a classical statement of the pattern:

Her sister June was twenty-four and still lived at home. She was a secretary in the high school Connie attended, and if that wasn't bad enough—with her in the same building—she was so plain and chunky and steady that Connie had to hear her praised all the time by her mother and her mother's sisters. June did this, June did that. . . .

Although grown up, June has not only not left home, but, in a sense, she is still in high school: this suggests that June is an even greater victim of oedipal entanglement than Connie—or, to put it another way, that June is Connie projected nine years into the future. What we have is

thus a feminine version of the tale *Two Brothers* in which the personality is split between "striving for independence and self-assertion" (Connie) and "the opposite tendency to remain safely home, tied to the parents" (June).[23] Implied also is the dichotomy underlying *Sinbad the Seaman and Sinbad the Porter,* in which the former character represents the "pleasure-oriented id" (Connie) and the latter the "reality-oriented ego" (June).[24] In this instance the ego is oriented toward the reality of permanent oedipal fixation, and therefore constitutes a negative personality, conforming to the Jungian concept of the *shadow.*[25] Perhaps the saddest commentary on the situation in Miss Oates' story is the fact that the personality receiving positive reinforcement is Connie's shadow: "If June's name was mentioned her mother's tone was approving, and if Connie's name was mentioned it was disapproving."

The theme of debasement with respect to one's siblings is, of course, not the only link between this story and *Cinderella.* Connie, with her other personality for "anywhere that was not home," suggests *Cinderella,* too, especially in the magical transformation from child to woman which she undergoes on her nights out. The description of the drive-in restaurant, with its music, and the boys with whom the girls pair up, and their feeling that the event is a wonderful experience which must end too soon—all of this brings to mind Cinderella's ball, particularly since it is here that Connie meets Arnold Friend, her "Prince Charming." And it is this meeting which sends him seeking her out and finding her, barefoot, in the kitchen. Certainly the "convertible jalopy painted gold" suggests *Cinderella,* though in the fairy tale it is Cinderella herself who has the "convertible" vehicle. This gold-painted car reminds us of a royal chariot, too, especially with the horn sounding as though to announce the arrival of royalty when the car comes up Connie's drive. Still more obvious in its reference to the fairy tale is the drawing on the car of "a round, grinning face that reminded Connie of a pumpkin, except it wore sunglasses" and was signed "ARNOLD FRIEND." It is also pertinent that Arnold proclaims that he has come to take her away, and that, as he talks, Connie notices "He had the voice of the man on the radio now," a man who has been mentioned several times, whose name suggests royalty epitomized, a man called "Bobby King."

If Connie is Cinderella, she is also, by virtue of her "long dark blond hair that drew anyone's eye to it," Rapunzel. On the day of Arnold's arrival, Connie "washed her hair so that it could dry all day long in the sun." At the first sound of the car, "her fingers snatched at her hair, checking it, and she whispered, 'Christ. Christ,' wondering how she looked." While she talks with Arnold, she makes the most of her hair: "Connie smirked and let her hair fall loose over one shoulder." Later, frightened by the desire she has aroused in him, she argues that her father is coming back to the house for her, that she has had to wash her hair in preparation for his return, but Arnold says, "No, your daddy is not coming and yes, you had to wash your hair and you washed it for me. It's nice and shining and all for me. I thank you sweetheart." Again, at the very end of the story, Connie watches "this body and this head of long hair moving out into the sunlight where Arnold Friend waited." It is obvious that Connie's *crowning glory* is, indeed, her hair, that she uses it to draw boys to her, among them Arnold Friend, and that

Arnold, like the Prince in the fairy tale, takes her away from a place where she feels "locked inside." The fact that in the fairy tale the Prince is temporarily blinded by thorns when he falls from the tower where Rapunzel is locked is perhaps echoed in Arnold's peculiar eyes, "like holes . . . like chips of broken glass," which he covers with those dark glasses.

Why Arnold Friend is conjured up when it is, as she claims, her father that Connie is waiting for, becomes clear if we consider that Arnold, the Prince of *Snow White, Sleeping Beauty, Cinderella,* and *Rapunzel,* is also the Big Bad Wolf of *Little Red Riding Hood,* a tale which, according to Bettelheim, "deals with the daughter's unconscious wish to be seduced by her father (the wolf)."[26] If Arnold represents an erotic transformation of Connie's father, then this suggests that Connie's oedipal death wish for her mother has undergone psychological realization. This in turn sheds light on that curious conversation between Arnold and Connie concerning "that old woman down the road" whom Connie insists is dead ("'She's dead—she's—she isn't here any more—'"), but about whom Arnold says "'But don't you like her, I mean, you got something against her? Some grudge or something?'" Connie's overreaction, so revealing in its guilt and terror, tells us that she has displaced onto the "old woman" the homicidal impulses unconsciously intended for her mother, an indiscretion for which she is already punishing herself through Arnold Friend. Bettelheim observes that when Little Red Riding Hood is swallowed up by the wolf, she is being "punished for arranging for the wolf to do away with a mother figure."[27]

Since one of Arnold's more lupine[28] characteristics is his *hairiness,* it is odd, though appropriate psychologically, considering that Arnold is experienced as a transformation of her "nice old bald-headed daddy," that Connie cannot keep from seeing "as a wig" Arnold's "shaggy, shabby, black hair." But Arnold's hairiness is not the only sign that Connie's daddy-substitute is wolvish. He also has trouble standing and moving about, which suggests a four-footed animal masquerading as a man. When he first gets out of his car, he moves "carefully, planting his feet firmly on the ground." Later, he stands "in a strange way, leaning back against the car as if he were balancing himself." Later still, "He wobble[s] in his high boots and grab[s] hold of one of the porch posts." No wonder Connie has the uneasy feeling that "his feet do not go all the way down" into those boots as they should. Then, of course, there are Arnold's teeth, so "big and white," and his way of "sniffing" at Connie as though "she were a treat he was going to gobble up." What could be more reminiscent of the Wolf in *Little Red Riding Hood*? And we should add that Arnold's talk of tearing Connie's house down reminds us of the Wolf in *The Three Little Pigs*, also. When Connie tries to lock the screen, Arnold says:

> "But why lock it . . . It's just a screen door. It's just nothing . . . I mean, anybody can break through a screen door and glass and wood and iron or anything else if he needs to, anybody at all, and specially Arnold Friend. If the place got lit up with a fire, honey, you'd come runnin' out into my arms."

Later, in a statement that accurately epitomizes Connie's entire situation, he says: " 'This place you are now—inside your daddy's house—is nothing but a cardboard box I can knock down any time. You know that and always did know it'."

If the structure of Connie's life—and of her psyche—were not, indeed, as flimsy as cardboard, she might be able to deal with Arnold Friend even as Beauty deals with the Beast who is *her* daddy-substitute; she might learn to love him for himself and so transform him into a Prince again. But Connie lacks the familial and psychic strength which allows Beauty and her love to mature.[29] She is still just as "little" as Little Red Riding Hood. And, as we shall see, her confrontation with "the Beast"—with the wolvish Arnold Friend—makes her more childlike, not less; she regresses to what Bettelheim describes as a "more primitive, earlier form of existence,"[30] as Red Riding Hood does under similar circumstances. Of course, "in typical fairy-story fashion" Red Riding Hood's regression is "impressively exaggerated." She goes all the way back to "the pre-birth existence in the womb" when she is swallowed by the Wolf (an act which has sexual significance, too). And she must then be cut from that "womb" by the Woodcutter, to emerge as a "born again" Red Riding Hood, a child who has learned that she is a child and still too young to deal with the Wolf.[31] Miss Oates is not free to exaggerate so fantastically, but she can and does suggest that Connie's psychological experience parallels Red Riding Hood's—in all respects save one. In Connie's case, Arnold Friend is the Woodcutter as well as the Wolf.

Connie begins to regress to a more childlike state as soon as she realizes that Arnold is more Wolf than Prince, more interested in animal sex than happy-ever-after romance. When he suddenly announces, " 'I'm your lover. You don't know what that is yet but you will'," she is frightened, and when he proceeds to explain "what that is" in some detail, she is more frightened still. Her flirtatious words and gestures give way to the frantic words and gestures of a child—and a very young child at that: "'Shut up! You're crazy!' Connie said. . . . She put her hands up against her ears as if she'd heard something terrible, something not meant for her. 'People don't talk like that, you're crazy,' she muttered." Furthermore, while she is saying this, she "back[s] away from the door," and so backs away from that symbolic threshold between "home" and "not home," childhood and womanhood, where she has been hovering ever since Arnold arrived. She has not locked the door, though, and when she remembers that fact and tries to do so, with fingers clumsy as a child's, she fails. A "wave of dizziness and fear" has left her sweating, "panting," "shaking"—utterly unable to save herself from the Wolf. Of course, we must not forget that this Wolf actually embodies Connie's own sexual impulses, a fact which implies that her childlike inability to save herself from him is complicated by a womanly desire to give herself to him. And, indeed, the very portions of the text which suggest that Connie is feeling like a terrified child simultaneously suggest that she is feeling like a woman thoroughly aroused by Arnold Friend and the sex he offers. The "wave of dizziness," the sweating, "panting," and "shaking" all characterize a woman well on the way to orgasm.

Connie's progression towards orgasm and her regression towards the womb both reach their climax in that decidedly schizophrenic moment when she tries to call her mother on the telephone. Miss Oates describes it thus:

> . . . she ran into the back room and picked up the telephone. Something roared in her ear, a tiny roaring, and she was so sick with fear that she could do nothing but listen to it— the telephone was clammy and very heavy and her fingers groped down

to the dial but were too weak to touch it. She began to scream into the phone, into the roaring. She cried out, she cried for her mother, she felt her breath start jerking back and forth in her lungs as if it were something Arnold Friend was stabbing her with again and again with no tenderness. A noisy sorrowful wailing rose all about her and she was locked inside it the way she was locked inside this house.

> After a while she could hear again. She was sitting on the floor with her wet back against the wall.

If the spasms which set Connie's "breath . . . jerking back and forth" as if Arnold were "stabbing her . . . again and again" suggest that she is experiencing something like the moment of climax in the sexual act, they also indicate that she is succumbing to sexual appetite exactly as Red Riding Hood does when she climbs into bed with the Wolf. Of course, Red Riding Hood is seeking the safety of a mother-figure's arms, the safety of a womb, not sex. This is true of Connie, too. The little girl in her is acting littler all the time, and now, more like a baby than a child, she is crying for her mother, trying to reach her mother through the umbilical-like cord on a phone she has forgotten how to use. She cannot reach her mother, but she does manage to reach the momentary safety of a womb of sorts. The lines which suggest that she is experiencing something like orgasm also suggest that she is experiencing something like birth—but in reverse. The description of the "breath . . . jerking back and forth in her lungs" in spasms that set her "wailing" reminds us of the moment of birth; and it is followed by a description that makes Connie sound like an unborn baby (rather than a newborn one), for she collapses into an unconscious and embryonic heap on the floor of the house where she feels "locked inside," even as a baby is "locked inside" a womb.

Connie does not stay in that "womb," however. The child in Connie may want to stay there, but the woman in Connie wants to be born. And the same spasms that suggest a birth-in-reverse suggest a birth-in-progress, too, a birth in which the two Connies who have thus far existed together in the one Connie, with the woman "locked inside" the womb of the child, are finally torn apart. As the story moves towards its conclusion, we note that the child who has thus become mother of the woman feels "hollow." She feels as if her "heart" and "body" are not "really hers" any more. They belong to that womanly part of her which now seems to be someone else entirely— someone who pushes her way out of the womb-like house where she has spent her formative years even as she has pushed her way out of the womb of the child:

> She put out her hand against the screen. She watched herself push the door slowly open as if she were back safe somewhere inside the house . . . watching this body and this head of long hair moving out into the sunlight where Arnold Friend waited.

Arnold Friend has not had to pull Connie out of the womb with the physical force which the Woodcutter uses in the fairy tale. We should remember that he has threatened to use such physical force if necessary, but his psychological force (as an embodiment of Connie's own impulses) proves to be more than sufficient to ensure that the birth takes place, whether the embryonic woman is really ready to be born or not.

Of course she is not ready to be born—despite the fact that it is only as a newborn that brown-eyed Connie can be Arnold's "sweet little blue-eyed girl." Connie has not developed enough to survive in the world outside the womb—in the world outside the conscious personality—and it is not surprising that she gazes upon this world in utter bewilderment: "—so much land that Connie had never seen before and did not recognize except to know that she was going to it."[32] Had she been nurtured on fairy tales instead of popular songs and movies she would not feel at such a loss; she would have "been" to this world before, through the vicarious experience offered by fairy tales, and she would have some sense of how to survive there now. Connie lacks the benefit of such experience, however, and even Arnold Friend appears to realize how that lack has hampered her development. He certainly speaks to the supposed woman as though she were still a child: "'Now, turn this way. That's right. Come over here to me. . . . and let's see a smile, try it, you're a brave, sweet little girl'." How fatherly he sounds. And how like the Woodcutter. But we know that he is still the Wolf, and that he still intends to "gobble up" this "little girl" as soon as he gets the chance. Connie is not going to live happily ever after. Indeed, it would seem that she is not going to live at all. She simply does not know how. She is stranded in Fairyland, without a map.[33]

NOTES

[1] "Interview with Joyce Carol Oates about Where Are You Going, Where Have You Been?" in *Mirrors: An Introduction to Literature,* ed. John R. Knott, Jr., and Christopher R. Keaske, 2nd ed. (San Francisco: Canfield Press, 1975), pp. 18–19.

[2] Don Moser, "The Pied Piper of Tucson," *Life,* 60, no. 9 (March 4, 1966), 18–19, 22–24, 80c–d.

[3] The raising of a human to divine status—Ed.

[4] Going beyond the individual or personal—Ed.

[5] Interview in *Mirrors,* p. 19. For a perceptive analysis of Arnold Friend as a demonic figure, a subject which will not be developed here, see Joyce M. Wegs, "'Don't You Know Who I Am?' The Grotesque in Oates's 'Where Are You Going, Where Have You Been?'," *The Journal of Narrative Technique,* 5 (January 1975), pp. 66–72.

[6] Wegs, p. 69.

[7] Joyce Carol Oates, "Preface," *Where Are You Going, Where Have You Been?: Stories of Young America* (Greenwich, CT: Fawcett Publications, 1974), p. 10.

[8] Joyce Carol Oates, "Where Are You Going, Where Have You Been?," *Where Are You Going, Where Have You Been?: Stories of Young America* (Greenwich, CT: Fawcett Publications, 1974), p. 13. All further references are to this edition of the story and will appear in the text of the essay. The story was originally published in *Epoch,* Fall 1966. It has since been included in *Prize Stories: The O. Henry Awards 1968;* in *The Best American Short Stories of 1967;* and in a collection of Oates' stories, *The Wheel of Love* (New York: Vanguard Press, 1970; Greenwich, CT: Fawcett Publications, 1972). The story is also being anthologized with increasing frequency in collections intended for use in the classroom, such as Donald McQuade and Robert Atwan, *Popular Writing in America: The Interaction of Style and Audience* (New York: Oxford University Press, 1974).

[9] Bruno Bettelheim, *The Uses of Enchantment: The Meaning and Importance of Fairy Tales* (New York: Alfred A. Knopf, 1976), p. 39.

[10] Joyce Carol Oates, *The Assassins* (New York: Vanguard Press, 1975), p. 378.

[11] At the MLA convention in New York, on December 26, 1976, I got a chance to ask Joyce Carol Oates if the many allusions to various fairy tales in "Where Are You Going, Where Have You Been?" were intentional. She replied that they were. (Gretchen Schulz)

[12] Bettelheim, n. 34, p. 316.

[13] Grow together; unite—Ed.

[14] Townspeople—Ed.

[15] According to the legend, one of the children of Hamelin does survive, though against his will. He is a lame boy who falls so far behind the other children that before he can reach the opening into the Koppenberg, it closes, swallowing all but himself. Psychologically, the boy's "lameness" can be interpreted as an unconscious protective mechanism which is capable of thwarting the boy's conscious will, thus saving him from destruction. This is protection exactly of the sort that properly internalized fairy tales provide, and its chief advantage is that it is not subject to the ego's often erring judgment, since it operates beyond the effective jurisdiction of consciousness.

[16] Bettelheim, pp. 66 ff.; n. 6, pp. 311–312; and passim.

[17] Refers to ages from about 3 to 6 when a child often has sexual feelings toward the parent of the opposite sex, while fearing the parent of the same sex as a rival—Ed.

[18] Bettelheim, p. 74.

[19] Bettelheim, p. 73.

[20] Bettelheim, pp. 207, 114.

[21] Bettelheim, p. 245.

[22] Bettelheim, p. 236.

[23] Bettelheim, p. 91.

[24] Bettelheim, p. 85.

[25] C. G. Jung, *The Archetypes and the Collective Unconscious,* 2nd ed., and *Aion,* 2nd ed., *Collected Works of C. G. Jung,* Vol. IX, pts. I & II (Princeton, NJ: Princeton University Press, 1968), passim.

[26] Bettelheim, p. 175.

[27] Bettelheim, p. 172.

[28] Wolfish.

[29] Bettelheim, pp. 303–309, passim.

[30] Bettelheim, p. 180.

[31] Bettelheim, p. 180.

[32] There is a fascinating and, it seems, rather significant echo between this line and the passage in Hemingway's "The Snows of Kilimanjaro," where at the moment of his death from gangrene, Harry imagines that the overdue plane that was to take him to the hospital in Arusha arrives, and shortly after taking off with Harry aboard, turns to the left (away from Arusha), and heads instead for the summit of Mt. Kilimanjaro: "Then they began to climb and they were going to the East it seemed, and then it darkened and they were in a storm, the rain so thick it seemed like flying through a waterfall, and then they were out and Compie [the pilot] turned his head and grinned and pointed and there, ahead, all he could see, as wide as all the world, great, high, and unbelievably white in the sun, was the square top of Kilimanjaro. *And then he knew that there was where he was going* [italics mine]." Ernest Hemingway, "The Snows of Kilimanjaro," *The Fifth Column and the First Forty-Nine Stories* (New York: Charles Scribner's Sons, 1938), p. 174.

[33] Concerning the plight of the Connies of the world, Bettelheim states thus: "unfed by our common fantasy heritage, the folk fairy tale, the child cannot invent stories on his own which help him cope with life's problems. All the stories he can invent are just expressions of his own wishes and anxieties. Relying on his own resources, all the child can imagine are elaborations of where he presently is, since he cannot know where he needs to go, or how to go about getting there" (pp. 121–122).

◇ ◇ ◇

Connie's Tambourine Man: A New Reading of Arnold Friend

MIKE TIERCE AND JOHN MICHEAL CRAFTON

The critical reception of Joyce Carol Oates' "Where Are You Going, Where Have You Been?" reveals a consistent pattern for reducing the text to a manageable, univocal[1] reading. Generally, this pattern involves two assumptions: Arnold *must* symbolize Satan and Connie *must* be raped and murdered. No critic has yet questioned Joyce Wegs' assertion that "Arnold is clearly a symbolic Satan."[2] Marie Urbanski argues that Arnold's "feet resemble the devil's cloven hoofs," Joan Winslow calls the story "an encounter with the devil," Tom Quirk maintains the story describes a "demoniac character," and Christina Marsden Gillis refers to "the satanic visitor's incantation."[3] Wegs' assertion that Arnold is "a criminal with plans to rape and probably murder Connie"[4] is also accepted at face value. Gillis assumes that Arnold "leads his victim . . . to a quick and violent sexual assault,"[5] and Quirk refers to "the rape and subsequent murder of Connie."[6] Even though Gretchen Schulz and R. J. R. Rockwood correctly claim that the portrait of Arnold "is created in the mind of Connie . . . and that it exists *there only*," they still persist in having Arnold as a demon and Connie as doomed: "But we know that he is still the Wolf, and that he still intends to 'gobble up' this 'little girl' as soon as he gets the chance. Connie is not going to live happily ever after. Indeed, it would seem that she is not going to live at all."[7]

While all of these critics insist on seeing satanic traces in Arnold, they refuse, on the other hand, to see that these traces are only part of a much more complex, more dynamic symbol. There are indeed diabolic shades to Arnold, but just as Blake and Shelley could see in Milton's Satan[8] a positive, attractive symbol of the poet, the rebellious embodiment of creative energy, so we should also be sensitive to Arnold's multifaceted and creative nature. Within the frame of the story, the fiction of Arnold burns in the day as the embodiment of poetic energy. The story is dedicated to Bob Dylan, the troubadour, the artist. Friend is the artist, the actor, the rhetorician, the teacher, all symbolized by Connie's overheated imagination. We should not assume that Arnold is completely evil because she is afraid of him. Her limited perceptions remind us of Blake's questioner in "The Tyger" who begins to perceive the frightening element of the experiential world but also is rather duped into his fear by his own limitations. Like the figure in Blake, Connie is the framer, the story creator—and the diabolic traces in her fiction frighten her not because they are the manifestations of an outside evil but because they are the symbolic extrapolations of her own psyche.

If the adamant insistence that Arnold Friend is Satan is rejected, then who is this intriguing mysterious visitor? In *Enter Mysterious Stranger: American Cloistral Fiction,* Roy Male asserts that many mysterious intruders throughout American literature "are almost always potential saviors, destroyers, or ambiguous combinations of both, and their initial entrance, however much it may be displaced toward realism, amounts to the entrance of God or the devil on a machine."[9] And if Arnold Friend is *not* satanic, then his arrival could be that of a savior. This possibility moreover is suggested by Connie's whispering "Christ. Christ"[10] when Arnold first arrives in his golden "machine." Not only is "33" part of Arnold's "secret code" of numbers, but his sign, an "X" that seems to hover in the air, is also one of the symbols for Christ. Because music is closely associated with religion—"the music was always in the background, like music at a church service"—it also adds a religious element to Arnold's arrival. The key question then is who is this musical messiah, and the key to the answer is the dedication "For Bob Dylan"—the element of the story so unsatisfactorily accounted for by our predecessors. Not only does the description of Arnold Friend also fit Bob Dylan—a type of rock-and-roll messiah—but three of Dylan's songs (popular when the story was written) are very similar to the story itself.

In the mid-sixties Bob Dylan's followers perceived him to be a messiah. According to his biographer, Dylan was "a rock-and-roll king."[11] It is no wonder then that Arnold speaks with "the voice of the man on the radio," the disc jockey whose name, Bobby King, is a reference to "Bobby" Dylan, the "king" of rock-and-roll. Dylan was more than just a "friend" to his listeners; he was "Christ revisited," "the prophet leading [his followers] into [a new] Consciousness."[12] In fact, "people were making him an idol; . . . thousands of men and women, young and old, felt their lives entwined with his because they saw him as a mystic, a messiah who would lead them to salvation."[13]

That Oates consciously associates Arnold Friend with Bob Dylan is clearly suggested by the similarities of their physical descriptions. Arnold's "shaggy, shabby black hair that looked crazy as a wig," his "long and hawk-like" nose, his unshavened face, his "big and white" teeth, his lashes, "thick and black as if painted with a black tarlike material" and his size ("only an inch or so taller than Connie") are all characteristic of Bob Dylan. Even Arnold's "fast, bright monotone voice" is suggestive of Dylan, especially since he speaks "in a simple lilting voice, exactly as if he were reciting the words to a song."

Dylan then provides a physical model for Arnold's appearance and a historical referent for Arnold's existence. Yet more profoundly, the myth of Dylan's being organized or somehow controlled by his music is reflected by Connie, Arnold, and Ellie being organized or perhaps even unified by the almost mystical music heard throughout the story. Connie, for example, notices the way Arnold "tapped one fist against another in homage to the perpetual music behind him." Since this "perpetual music" is the one thing that Connie can "depend upon," it even becomes her breath of life; she is "bathed in a glow of slow-pulsed joy that seemed to rise mysteriously out of the music itself, . . . breathed in and breathed out with each gentle rise of her chest." Paying "close attention" to the words and singing along with the songs played on the "*XYZ* Sunday Jamboree," Connie spends her Sunday afternoon worshiping "the music that made everything so good." And when her two visitors arrive, "the same program . . . playing inside the house" is also playing on Ellie Oscar's radio. In fact, "the music from [Connie's] radio and [Ellie's] blend together." Ellie is so closely associated with the radio that without it pressed up against his ear, he grimaces "as if . . . the air was too much for him." Both Ellie's and Arnold's existences seem to depend completely on the

"perpetual music"; consequently, Oates appears to be suggesting that they are not literally present. They are instead part of Connie's musically induced fantasy—another of her so-called "trashy daydreams."

Oates points out that Connie spends her summer "thinking, dreaming of the boys she met." But because of Connie's gradually changing desires, "all the boys fell back and dissolved into a single face that was not even a face but an idea, a feeling, mixed up with the urgent insistent pounding of the music." This "urgent" feeling reflects Connie's desire for something more sexually stimulating than the kissing sessions she spends with "boys" like Eddie. As Freud points out, "the motive forces of phantasies are unsatisfied wishes, and every single phantasy is the fulfillment of a wish, a correlation of unsatisfying reality. . . . In young women the erotic wishes predominate almost exclusively."[14] Although we acknowledge the sexist nature of Freud's generalization, his point seems to apply to Connie. Furthermore, Roy Male suggests that even though "there is no logical reason for the entrance of a stranger, it is equally true that he comes as if in answer to some unuttered call." Arnold is described as "talking right through Connie's voice" because that is the only voice he has. His arrival is the answer to Connie's "unuttered" call and to her "erotic" desires. Arnold's "face" is therefore "familiar" because it is the "face" that replaces the "boys" in her fantasies. Not only is the emphasis placed on Arnold's face reinforced by "a drawing of a round grinning face" on his car, but when Connie first encounters Arnold at Napoleon's drive-in restaurant, he is described as "a face just a few feet from hers"—perhaps her own distorted reflection in a car windshield.

Connie not only turns away from Arnold's face "without Eddie noticing anything," but many other elements in the story suggest that Arnold is just another "shadowy vision of [Connie] herself." For example, Arnold is described as being "just a blur . . . that . . . had come from nowhere . . . and belonged nowhere and that everything about him . . . was only half real." His "fake" laughter suggests that his threatening presence is "all a joke." He opens the door to his car carefully because it might fall off, he cannot walk without stumbling, his feet seem not to be in his boots, and he wears a mask and make-up. He even touches his sunglasses "as if to make sure they were still there." He also magically knows Connie's name, her best friend's name, her other friends' names, and where her parents are and when they will return. Part of the action that takes place also suggests a dream-like experience. Arnold's asking Connie if she has something against a dead woman, Connie's inability to dial the telephone, and Arnold's promise not to come into the house are all tinged with a sense of unreality. Even the fact that the phrase "as if" is used over thirty times suggests that there is something dubious about Connie's experience.

In order to reinforce the idea that Arnold's visit is another fantasy, Oates parallels the actual description of one of Connie's other daydreams to the description of her finally joining Arnold Friend at the story's end:

> Connie sat with her eyes closed in the sun, dreaming and dazed with the warmth about her as if this were a kind of love, the caresses of love, and her mind slipped over onto thoughts of the boy she had been with the night before and how nice he had been, how sweet it always was, not the way someone like June would suppose but sweet, gentle, the way it was in movies and promised in songs; and when she opened her eyes she hardly knew where she was, the back yard ran off into weeds and a fence-like line of trees and behind it the sky was perfectly blue and still. The asbestos "ranch house" that was now three years old startled her—it looked small. She shook her head as if to get awake. . . .
>
> "My sweet little blue-eyed girl," he said in a half-sung sigh that had nothing to do with her brown eyes but was taken up just the same by the vast sunlit reaches of the land behind him and on all sides of him—so much land that Connie had never seen before and did not recognize except to know that she was going to it.

The fence-like line of trees is replaced by "the vast sunlit reaches of the land" surrounding Arnold Friend. Through her encounter with this mysterious stranger, Connie frees herself from the sense of confinement she feels in her father's house. As Roy Male so aptly explains it, the "mysterious strangers who are potential saviors" force the "insider" to undergo a transformation, which "may involve the effort of the insider to break out of his fixed orientation."[15] The Dylanesque music initiates such a breakthrough for Connie. She no longer has to "dawdle in the doorway." As Dylan suggests in "Mister Tambourine Man," once she answers the call by forcing open the screen door, "there are no fences facin'" her any longer. She broadens her horizons to include the "vast sunlit reaches of the land" all around her.

The reference to "Mister Tambourine Man" implies another connection between the story and Dylan.

A few of his song lyrics are very similar to the story itself. Oates herself suggests that part of the story's inspiration was "hearing for some weeks Dylan's song 'It's All Over Now, Baby Blue.'"[16] Such lines as "you must leave now," "something calls for you," "the vagabond who's rapping at your door," and "go start anew" are suggestive of the impending change awaiting Connie. Two other Dylan songs are equally as applicable though. The following lines from "Like a Rolling Stone"—the second most popular song of 1965 (the story was first published in 1966)—are also very similar to Connie's situation at the end of the story:

> You used to be so amused
> At Napoleon in rags and the
>   language that he used
> Go to him now, he calls you, you
>   can't refuse
> When you got nothing, you got
>   nothing to lose
> You're invisible now, you got no
>   secrets to conceal.

But Dylan's "Mr. Tambourine Man" —the number ten song in 1965—is even more similar. The following stanza establishes the notion of using music to rouse one's imagination into a blissful fantasy world:

> Take me on a trip upon your magic
>   swirlin' ship,

My senses have been stripped,
My hands can't feel to grip,
My toes too numb to step,
Wait only for my boot heels to be
  wanderin'.
I'm ready to go anywhere,
I'm ready for to fade
Into my own parade.
Cast your dancin' spell my way,
I promise to go under it.
Hey, Mister Tambourine Man, play a
  song for me,
I'm not sleepy and there ain't no
  place I'm going to.
Hey, Mister Tambourine Man, play a
  song for me.
In the jingle, jangle morning I'll
  come followin' you.

Arnold Friend's car—complete with the phrase "MAN THE FLYING SAUCERS"—is just such "a magic swirlin' ship." Arnold is the personification of popular music, particularly Bob Dylan's music; and as such, Connie's interaction with him is a musically induced fantasy, a kind of "magic carpet ride" in "a convertible jalopy painted gold." Rising out of Connie's radio, Arnold Friend/Bob Dylan is a magical, musical messiah; he persuades Connie to abandon her father's house. As a manifestation of her own desires, he frees her from the limitations of a fifteen-year-old girl, assisting her maturation by stripping her of her childlike vision.

NOTES

[1] Having only one meaning.

[2] Joyce M. Wegs, "'Don't You Know Who I Am?' The Grotesque in Oates's, 'Where Are You Going, Where Have You Been?'" in *Critical Essays on Joyce Carol Oates*, ed. Linda W. Wagner (Boston: G. K. Hall, 1979), p. 90. First printed in *Journal of Narrative Technique*, 5 (1975), pp. 66–72.

[3] Marie Urbanski, "Existential Allegory: Joyce Carol Oates' 'Where Are You Going, Where Have You Been?'" *Studies in Short Fiction*, 15 (1978), p. 202; Joan Winslow, "The Stranger Within: Two Stories by Oates and Hawthorne," *Studies in Short Fiction*, 17 (1980), p. 264; Tom Quirk, "A Source for 'Where Are You Going, Where Have You Been?'" *Studies in Short Fiction*, 18 (1981), p. 416; Christina Marsden Gillis, "'Where

Are You Going, Where Have You Been?': Seduction, Space, and a Fictional Mode," *Studies in Short Fiction*, 18 (1981), p. 70.

[4] Wegs, p. 89.

[5] Gillis, p. 65.

[6] Quirk, p. 416.

[7] Gretchen Schulz and R. J. R. Rockwood, "In Fairyland, without a Map: Connie's Exploration Inward in Joyce Carol Oates' 'Where Are You Going, Where Have You Been?'" *Literature and Psychology,* 30 (1980), pp. 156, 165, & 166, respectively.

[8] In *Paradise Lost,* Milton clearly intends Satan to be a symbol of archetypal evil. Blake and Shelley, as true Romantics, saw in their predecessor's portrait of Lucifer a duality that embodied positive as well as negative traits.

[9] Roy Male, *Enter Mysterious Stranger: American Cloistral Fiction* (Norman: University of Oklahoma Press, 1979), p. 21.

[10] Joyce Carol Oates, "Where Are You Going, Where Have You Been?" in *The Wheel of Love* (New York: Vanguard Press, 1970), p. 40. Hereafter cited parenthetically within the text.

[11] Anthony Scaduto, *Bob Dylan* (New York: Grosset and Dunlop. 1971), p. 222.

[12] Scaduto, p. 274.

[13] Scaduto, p. 229.

[14] Sigmund Freud, "Creative Writers and Day-Dreamers," in *Criticism: The Major Statements,* ed. Charles Kaplan (New York: St. Martin's Press, 1975), p. 468.

[15] Male, p. 10.

[16] "Interview with Joyce Carol Oates about 'Where Are You Going, Where Have You Been?'" in *Mirrors: An Introduction to Literature,* eds. John R. Knott, Jr., and Christopher R. Keaske, 2nd ed. (San Francisco: Canfield Press, 1975), pp. 18–19.

◈ ◈ ◈

It's All Over Now, Baby Blue

BOB DYLAN

You must leave now, take what you need you think will last
But whatever you wish to keep, you better grab it fast
Yonder stands your orphan with his gun
Crying like a fire in the sun.
Look out, the saints are comin' through
And it's all over now, baby blue.

The highway is for gamblers, better use your sins
Take what you have gathered from coincidence
The empty-handed painter from your streets
Is drawing crazy patterns on your sheets
This sky too is folding under you
And it's all over now, baby blue.

All your seasick sailors they are rowing home
Your empty-handed army men are going home
The lover who has just walked out your door
Has taken all his blankets from the floor
The carpet too is moving under you
And it's all over now, baby blue.

Leave your stepping stones behind, something calls for you
Forget the dead you've left, they will not follow you
The vagabond who's rapping at your door
Is standing in the clothes that you once wore
Strike another match, go start anew
And it's all over now, baby blue.

◊ ◊ ◊

"Don't You Know Who I Am?" The Grotesque in Oates's "Where Are You Going, Where Have You Been?"

JOYCE M. WEGS

Joyce Carol Oates's ability to absorb and then to transmit in her fiction the terror which is often a part of living in America today has been frequently noted and admired. For instance, Walter Sullivan praises her skill by noting that "horror resides in the transformation of what we know best, the intimate and comfortable details of our lives made suddenly threatening."[1] Although he does not identify it as such, Sullivan's comment aptly describes a classic instance of a grotesque intrusion: a familiar world suddenly appears alien. Oates frequently evokes the grotesque in her fiction, drawing upon both its traditional or demonic and its contemporary or psychological manifestations.[2] In the prize-winning short story, "Where Are You Going, Where Have You Been?", Oates utilizes the grotesque in many of its forms to achieve a highly skillful integration of the multiple levels of the story and, in so doing, to suggest a transcendent reality which reaches beyond surface realism to evoke the simultaneous mystery and reality of the contradictions of the human heart. Full of puzzling and perverse longings, the heart persists in mixing lust and love, life and death, good and evil. Oates's teenage

protagonist, Connie, discovers that her dream love-god also wears the face of lust, evil and death.

Centering the narrative on the world of popular teenage music and culture, Oates depicts the tawdry world of drive-in restaurants and shopping plazas blaring with music with a careful eye for authentic surface detail. However, her use of popular music as a thematic referent is typical also of her frequent illumination of the illusions and grotesquely false values which may arise from excessive devotion to such aspects of popular culture as rock music, movies, and romance magazines. In all of her fiction as in this story, she frequently employs a debased religious imagery to suggest the gods which modern society has substituted for conventional religion. Oates delineates the moral poverty of Connie, her fifteen-year-old protagonist, by imaging a typical evening Connie spends at a drive-in restaurant as a grotesquely parodied religious pilgrimage. Left by her friend's father to stroll at the shopping center or go to a movie, Connie and her girlfriend immediately cross the highway to the restaurant frequented by older teenagers. A grotesque parody of a church, the building is bottle-shaped and has a grinning boy holding a hamburger aloft on top of it. Unconscious of any ludicrousness, Connie and her friend enter it as if going into a "sacred building"[3] which will give them "what haven and blessing they yearned for." It is the music which is "always in the background, like music at a church service" that has invested this "bright-lit, fly-infested" place with such significance. Indeed, throughout the story the music is given an almost mystical character, for it evokes in Connie a mysterious pleasure, a "glow of slow-pulsed joy that seemed to rise mysteriously out of the music itself."

Although the story undoubtedly has a moral dimension,[4] Oates does not take a judgmental attitude toward Connie. In fact, much of the terror of the story comes from the recognition that there must be thousands of Connies. By carefully including telltale phrases, Oates demonstrates in an understated fashion why Connies exist. Connie's parents, who seem quite typical, have disqualified themselves as moral guides for her. At first reading, the reader may believe Connie's mother to be concerned about her daughter's habits, views, and friends; but basically their arguments are little more than a "pretense of exasperation, a sense that they . . . [are] tugging and struggling over something of little value to either of them." Connie herself is uncertain of her mother's motives for constantly picking at her; she alternates between a view that her mother's harping proceeds from jealousy of Connie's good looks now that her own have faded and a feeling that her mother really prefers her over her plain older sister June because she is prettier. In other words, to Connie and her mother, real value lies in beauty. Connie's father plays a small role in her life, but by paralleling repeated phrases, Oates

suggests that this is precisely the problem. Because he does not "bother talking much" to his family, he can hardly ask the crucial parental questions, "Where are you going?" or "Where have you been?" The moral indifference of the entire adult society is underscored by Oates's parallel description of the father of Connie's friend, who also "never . . . [bothers] to ask" what they did when he picks up the pair at the end of one of their evenings out. Similarly, on Sunday morning, "none of them bothered with church," not even that supposed paragon, June.

Since her elders do not bother about her, Connie is left defenseless against the temptations represented by Arnold Friend. A repeated key phrase emphasizes her helplessness. As she walks through the parking lot of the restaurant with Eddie, she can not "help but" look about happily, full of joy in a life characterized by casual pickups and constant music. When she sees Arnold in a nearby car, she looks away, but her instinctive flirtatiousness triumphs and she can not "help but" look back. Later, like Lot's wife leaving Sodom and Gomorrah,[5] she cannot "help but look back" at the plaza and drive-in as her friend's father drives them home. In Connie's case, the consequences of the actions she can not seem to help are less biblically swift to occur and can not be simply labeled divine retribution.

Since music is Connie's religion, its values are hers also. Oates does not include the lyrics to any popular songs here, for any observer of contemporary America could surely discern the obvious link between Connie's high esteem for romantic love and youthful beauty and the lyrics of scores of hit tunes. The superficiality of Connie's values becomes terrifyingly apparent when

Arnold Friend, the external embodiment of the teenage ideal celebrated in popular songs, appears at Connie's home in the country one Sunday afternoon when she is home alone, listening to music and drying her hair. It is no accident that Arnold's clothes, car, speech, and taste in music reflect current teenage chic almost exactly, for they constitute part of a careful disguise intended to reflect Arnold's self-image as an accomplished youthful lover.

Suspense mounts in the story as the reader realizes along with Connie that Arnold is not a teenager and is really thirty or more. Each part of his disguise is gradually revealed to be grotesquely distorted in some way. His shaggy black hair, "crazy as a wig," is evidently really a wig. The mask-like appearance of his face has been created by applying a thick coat of makeup; however, he has carelessly omitted his throat. Even his eyelashes appear to be made-up, but with some tarlike material. In his clothing, his disguise appears more successful, for Connie approves of the way he dresses, as "all of them dressed," in tight jeans, boots, and pullover. When he walks, however, Connie realizes that the runty Arnold, conscious that the ideal teenage dream lover is tall, has stuffed his boots; the result is, however, that he can hardly walk and staggers ludicrously. Attempting to bow, he almost falls. Similarly, the gold jalopy covered with teenage slang phrases seems authentic until Connie notices that one of them is no longer in vogue. Even his speech is not his own, for it recalls lines borrowed from disc jockeys, teenage slang, and lines from popular songs. Arnold's strange companion, Ellie Oscar, is just as grotesque as Arnold. Almost totally absorbed in listening to music and interrupting this activity only

to offer threatening assistance to Arnold, Ellie is no youth either; he has the "face of a forty-year-old baby." Although Arnold has worked out his disguise with great care, he soon loses all subtlety in letting Connie know of his evil intentions; he is not simply crazy but a criminal with plans to rape and probably to murder Connie.

However, Arnold is far more than a grotesque portrait of a psychopathic killer masquerading as a teenager; he also has all the traditional sinister traits of that arch-deceiver and source of grotesque terror, the devil. As is usual with Satan, he is in disguise; the distortions in his appearance and behavior suggest not only that his identity is faked but also hint at his real self. Equating Arnold and Satan is not simply a gratuitous connection designed to exploit traditional demonic terror, for the early pages of the story explicitly prepare for this linking by portraying popular music and its values as Connie's perverted version of religion. When Arnold comes up the drive, her first glance makes Connie believe that a teenage boy with his jalopy, the central figure of her religion, has arrived; therefore, she murmurs "Christ. Christ" as she wonders about how her newly-washed hair looks. When the car—a parodied golden chariot?—stops, a horn sounds "as if this were a signal Connie knew." On one level, the horn honks to announce the "second coming" of Arnold, a demonic Day of Judgment.[6] Although Connie never specifically recognizes Arnold as Satan, her first comment to him both hints at his infernal origins and faithfully reproduces teenage idiom: "Who the *hell* do you think you are?" (emphasis mine). When he introduces himself, his name too hints at his identity, for "friend" is uncomfortably close to "fiend"; his initials could well stand for Arch Fiend. The frightened Connie sees Arnold as "only half real": he "had driven up her driveway all right but had come from nowhere before that and belonged nowhere." Especially supernatural is his mysterious knowledge about her, her family, and her friends. At one point, he even seems to be able to see all the way to the barbecue which Connie's family is attending and to get a clear vision of what all the guests are doing. Typical of his ambiguous roles is his hint that he had something to do with the death of the old woman who lived down the road. It is never clear whether Arnold has killed her, has simply heard of her death, or knows about it in his devil role of having come to take her away to hell. Although Arnold has come to take Connie away, in his traditional role as evil spirit, he may not cross a threshold uninvited; he repeatedly mentions that he is not going to come in after Connie, and he never does. Instead, he lures Connie out to him. Part of his success may be attributed to his black magic in having put his sign on her—X for victim. Because the devil is not a mortal being, existing as he does in all ages, it is not surprising that he slips in remembering what slang terms are in vogue. Similarly, his foolish attempt at a bow may result from a mixup in temporal concepts of the ideal lover. In addition, his clumsy bow may be due to the fact that it must be difficult to manipulate boots if one has cloven feet!

Although Oates attempts to explain the existence of Connie, she makes no similar effort to explain the existence of Arnold, for that would constitute an answer to the timeless and insoluble problem of evil in the world. As this story shows, Oates would agree with Pope Paul VI's recent commentary on the "terrible reality" of evil in the world, but she would not, I feel sure, endorse his view of this evil as being literally embodied in a specific being. Pope Paul describes evil as "not merely a lack of something, but an effective agent, a living spiritual being, perverted and perverting. A terrible reality. Mysterious and frightening."[7] Oates's description of her own views on religion is in terms strikingly similar to the language used by Pope Paul. To her, religion is a "kind of psychological manifestation of deep powers, deep imaginative, mysterious powers, which are always with us, and what has in the past been called supernatural I would prefer simply to call natural. However, though these things are natural, they are still inaccessible and cannot be understood, cannot be controlled."[8] Thus, although Arnold is clearly a symbolic Satan, he also functions on a psychological level.

On this level, Arnold Friend is the incarnation of Connie's unconscious erotic desires and dreams, but in uncontrollable nightmare form. When she first sees Arnold in the drive-in, she instinctively senses his sinister attraction, for she cannot "help glancing back" at him. Her "trashy daydreams" are largely filled with blurred recollections of the caresses of the many boys she has dated. That her dreams are a kind of generalized sexual desire—although Connie does not consciously identify them as such—is made evident by Oates's description of Connie's summer dreams: "But all the boys fell back and dissolved into a single face that was not even a face but an idea, a feeling, mixed up with the urgent insistent pounding of the music and the humid night air of July." What is frightening about Arnold is that he voices and makes explicit her own sexual desires; teenage boys more usually project their similar message with "that sleepy dreamy smile that all the boys used to get across ideas they didn't want to put into words." Connie's reaction to his bluntness is one of horror: "People don't talk like that, you're crazy."

Connie's fear drives her into a grotesque separation of mind from body in which her unconscious self takes over and betrays her. Terror-stricken, she cannot even make her weak fingers dial the police; she can only scream into the phone. In the same way that she is Arnold's prisoner, locked inside the house he alternately threatens to knock down or burn down, she is also a prisoner of her own body: "A noisy sorrowful wailing rose all about her and she was locked inside it the way she was locked inside this house." Finally, her conscious mind rejects any connection with her body and its impulses; her heart seems "nothing that was hers" "but just a pounding, living thing inside this body that wasn't really hers either." In a sense, her body with its puzzling desires "decides" to go with Arnold although her rational self is terrified of him: "She watched herself push the door slowly open as if she were back safe somewhere in the other doorway, watching this body and this head of long hair moving out into the sunlight where Arnold Friend waited."

Oates encourages the reader to look for multiple levels in this story and to consider Arnold and Connie at more than face value by her repeated emphasis on the question of identity. The opening of the story introduces the concept to which both Connie and her mother seem to subscribe—being pretty means being someone. In fact, her mother's acid questions as she sees Connie at her favorite activity of mirror-gazing—"Who are you? You think you're so pretty?"—also

introduce the converse of this idea, namely, that those who lack physical beauty have no identity. As does almost everything in the story, everything about Connie has "two sides to it." However, Connie's nature, one for at home and one for "anywhere that was not home," is simple in comparison to that of Arnold. Connie's puzzled questions at first query what role Arnold thinks he is playing: "Who the hell do you think you are?" Then she realizes that he sees himself all too literally as the man of her dreams, and she becomes more concerned about knowing his real identity. By the time that Arnold asks, "Don't you know who I am?" Connie realizes that it is no longer a simple question of whether he is a "jerk" or someone worth her attention but of just how crazy he is. By the end she knows him to be a murderer, for she realizes that she will never see her family again. However, only the reader sees Arnold's Satan identity. Connie's gradual realization of Arnold's identity brings with it a recognition of the actual significance of physical beauty: Arnold is indeed someone to be concerned about, even if he is no handsome youth. At the conclusion Connie has lost all identity except that of victim, for Arnold's half-sung sigh about her blue eyes ignores the reality of her brown ones. In Arnold's view, Connie's personal identity is totally unimportant.

Dedicated to contemporary balladeer Bob Dylan, this story in a sense represents Oates's updated prose version of a ballad in which a demon lover carries away his helpless victim. By adding modern psychological insights, she succeeds in revealing the complex nature of the victim of a grotesque intrusion by an alien force; on one level, the victim actually welcomes and invites this demonic visitation. Like Bob Dylan, she grafts onto the ballad tradition a moral commentary which explores but does not solve the problems of the evils of our contemporary society; an analogous Dylan ballad is his "It's a Hard Rain's a Gonna' Fall." Even the title records not only the ritual parental questions but also suggests that there is a moral connection between the two questions: where Connie goes is related to where she has been. Oates does not judge Connie in making this link, however; Connie is clearly not in complete control over where she has been. The forces of her society, her family, and her self combine to make her fate inescapable.

NOTES

[1] Walter Sullivan, "The Artificial Demon: Joyce Carol Oates and the Dimensions of the Real," *The Hollins Critic,* 9, No. 4 (Dec., 1972), p. 2.

[2] Joyce Markert Wegs, "The Grotesque in Some American Novels of the Nineteen-Sixties: Ken Kesey, Joyce Carol Oates, Sylvia Plath," Diss., University of Illinois, 1973.

[3] Joyce Carol Oates, "Where Are You Going, Where Have You Been?" *The Wheel of Love* (1970; rpt. Greenwich, CT: Fawcett, 1972), p. 31. All subsequent references to the story appear within parentheses in the text.

[4] See Walter Sullivan, "Where Have All the Flowers Gone?: The Short Story in Search of Itself," *Sewanee Review,* 78, No. 3 (Summer, 1970), p. 537.

[5] Lot and his family were spared when God destroyed the wicked cities of Sodom and Gomorrah, but Lot's wife was turned into a pillar of salt when she disobeyed God's injunction not to look back at the cities. See Genesis 19:24–26.

[6] The time of Christ's return; when all people on earth will be judged.

[7] Andrew M. Greeley, "The Devil, You Say," *The New York Times Magazine,* 4 Feb., 1973, p. 26, quotes an address by Pope Paul on 15 Nov., 1972, as reported in the Vatican newspaper.

[8] Linda Kuehl, "An Interview with Joyce Carol Oates," *Commonweal,* 91 (5 Dec., 1969), p. 308.

READING AND REACTING

◆ ◆ ◆

1. How is "Where Are You Going, Where Have You Been?" similar to and different from Anne Tyler's "Teenage Wasteland" (p. 603)?

2. Is Arnold Friend meant to be the devil? Is he an antisocial hoodlum? Is he a rapist and murderer (see the March 4, 1966, *Life* magazine article "The Pied Piper of Tucson" and "Killing for Kicks" in the March 14, 1966, issue of *Newsweek*)? Is he actually Bob Dylan (as Tierce and Crafton suggest in their article)? Or is he just a misunderstood social misfit who terrifies Connie more because of her innocence than because of his evil?

3. In a note accompanying the article she coauthored, Gretchen Schulz says that Oates told her the allusions to fairy tales in the

story are intentional. Do you think Oates's comment is accurate? Does it matter whether or not the allusions are intentional?

4. Many critical articles see "Where Are You Going, Where Have You Been?" as heavily symbolic, even allegorical, with elements of myth, dream, and fairy tale woven throughout. Is this analysis necessary, or could the story be seen in much simpler terms?

5. Who is the story's central character, Arnold Friend or Connie?

6. Dark undertones aside, in what sense is this story simply about the coming of age of a typical 1960s teenager?

7. What do music, sex, the weather, contemporary slang, and physical appearance contribute to the story?

8. Why do members of Connie's family play such minor roles in the story? How would expanding their roles change the story?

9. Which aspects of teenage culture have changed in the more than thirty years since Oates wrote the story? Which have stayed the same? Given the scope of the changes, is the story dated?

10. Most critics (like Oates herself) see the end of the story as alarmingly negative, suggesting rape and even murder. Do you see it this way?

11. Feminist critics might see this story as a familiar tale of a man who uses threats of physical violence to coerce a young woman into giving in to him. In what sense is this a story of male power and female powerlessness?

12. Do you agree with Oates that the differences in the endings of the film and the story are justified by the differences between the 1960s and the 1980s?

13. **JOURNAL ENTRY** How is the generation gap—the failure of one generation to understand another's culture, customs, and heroes—important to the story?

14. **CRITICAL PERSPECTIVE** According to *New York Times* book critic Michiko Kakutani, Joyce Carol Oates has several "fictional trademarks":

> [She has] a penchant for mixing the mundane and Gothic, the ordinary and sensationalistic; a fascination with the dark un-dercurrents of violence, eroticism and emotional chaos in American life, and a tendency to divide her characters' lives into a Before and After with one "unspeakable turn of destiny."

Do Kakutani's remarks apply to "Where Are You Going, Where Have You Been?"? Do you see a fascination with "the dark undercurrents of [. . .] life" in this story? What is the "unspeakable turn of destiny" that divides Connie's life into a "Before and After"?

Related Works: "A&P" (p. 113), "Young Goodman Brown" (p. 304), "The Lottery" (p. 315), "The German Refugee" (p. 511), "Shopping," (p. 559), *Hamlet* (p. 1307)

Research Questions

◆ ◆ ◆

1. Oates typically makes her readers look at a familiar reality from a new, and sometimes disturbing, perspective. In the essay in this casebook "In Fairyland, without a Map: Connie's Exploration Inward in Joyce Carol Oates's 'Where Are You Going, Where Have You Been?'" Oates's use of this kind of "psychological realism" is discussed. How does the unconscious mental process of a troubled adolescent girl in the story help to create such a perspective?

2. Although most noted for her fiction, Oates is also a prolific essayist. One of her essays is included in this casebook. Do some research to find other essays by Oates that discuss artistic creation. A good example is her essay "Against Nature." According to Oates, how do conscious and unconscious elements affect the process of the creative act?

3. In her article "When Characters from the Page Are Made Flesh on the Screen," included in this casebook, Oates refers to her own use of "realistic allegory" as a mode of fiction. She states that it is a mode of fiction that is "Hawthornian [. . .] shading into parable." Research Hawthorne's views on allegory by reading one of Hawthorne's many essays on the subject, such as "The Custom House." How can Oates's story "Where Are You Going, Where Have You Been?" be compared to Hawthorne's "Young Goodman Brown" in terms of its portrayal of good, evil, and innocence? Can elements in Oates's story be considered allegorical in the Hawthornian sense?

4. Oates's characters are often defined more by what they are not, rather than by what they are. Find another Oates story and analyze Oates's use of characterization in it. Can the characters in "Where Are You Going, Where Have You Been?," in "Shopping" (p. 559), and in the other Oates story be analyzed, at least in part, by what they are not?

5. Oates has been described as a modern realist, and she herself uses terms such as "realistic allegory" and "psychological realism" to describe her work. Research the history and emergence of literary realism in American literature. What elements of realism as it first appeared in literature at the end of the 19th century and the beginning of the 20th century are found in Oates's work?

6. Critics often see Oates's short stories as gothic. Research the term *gothic* as it applies to works of literature. Then, write a paper in which you make the case for three of her stories, including "Where Are You Going, Where Have You Been?," as gothic works.

Michele Olivari

Professor Biemiller

English 102

8 March 1999

Mesmerizing Men and Vulnerable Teens:

Power Relationships in "Where Are You Going,

Where Have You Been?" and "Teenage Wasteland"

Both Joyce Carol Oates's "Where Are You Going, Where Have You Been?" (1966) and Anne Tyler's "Teenage Wasteland" (1984) feature adolescents in conflict with their parents. Both stories are set in "teenage waste-lands" in which the protagonists ignore limits estab-lished by authority figures and avoid making decisions or finding a direction for their lives. The most striking similarity between the two stories, however, is the presence of a hypnotic older man--one who ex-erts enormous influence over the teenagers, pushing them out of their passive states and causing them to take action. Ironically, the actions in both cases, although decisive, have terrifying consequences.

Arnold Friend, the mysterious loner who pursues Connie in "Where Are You Going, Where Have You Been?," is characterized by Gretchen Schulz and R. J. R. Rock-wood as the fairy tale wolf who "intends to 'gobble up' this 'little girl' as soon as he gets the chance" (639). Many other critics, as Mike Tierce and John Micheal Crafton point out, see Arnold as the devil; Tierce and Crafton, however, prefer to see him as a Bob Dylan figure "--a type of rock and roll messiah--" (642). Oates herself, in stating that Arnold is based on a "charismatic mass murderer" (627), acknowledges both the threat he poses and his seductive powers. Regardless of whether Arnold is murderer, devil, wolf, or musical messiah, it is clear that he is a strong, controlling personality who has an unnaturally powerful hold over Connie. In a less dramatic way, Cal, the tutor in "Teenage Wasteland," has just such a hold over Donny. Both men, supported by background music, use their power to mesmerize young people, separating them from home and family and seducing them into following different—and dangerous—paths. In both stories, it is the adolescents' tendency to drift without an anchor that makes them vulnerable.

Both Connie and Donny are passive dreamers, stuck in numbing adolescence, waiting for something to happen. Meanwhile, both break the rules set by their parents. Connie is fifteen, and her mind is "all filled with trashy daydreams" (615). At night she sneaks out to forbidden hangouts, lying to her parents about where she is going. As she drifts through her unstructured summer days, she is "dazed with the warmth about her" (617) and caught up in the music she listens to and in her romantic fantasies. Donny is also stalled, caught in a cycle of failure and defeat, "noisy, lazy, and disruptive" (603) and unresponsive in school, cutting classes, smoking, and drinking beer.

Both Connie and Donny are emotionally separated from their parents. Connie's mother constantly nags her and compares her unfavorably to her sister June; her father does not even talk, choosing instead to

Olivari 3

read his newspaper and avoid conflict. In "Teenage Wasteland," Daisy's primary attitude toward her son Donny is disappointment. Ignoring his potential, she sees only "his pathetically poor posture, that slouch so forlorn that his shoulders [seem] about to meet his chin" (606). She feels sorry for him, but she is helpless to rescue him, let alone give him the emotional support he needs. Like Connie's mother, she clearly disapproves of her child's behavior. Despite her efforts to defend and encourage him, she is ashamed of his failures and upset at how they reflect upon her as a parent. Both Connie and Donny are unconnected to people or social institutions, and both are allowed to remain unconnected by weak, ineffective parents whom they neither respect nor admire. Both Connie and Donny, therefore, are vulnerable to the seductive power of a hypnotic older man.

Arnold Friend, a strange-looking man who acts like a teenager, has great power over Connie. Initially, she is drawn to him by how he looks and dresses and because of the music they share; later, his claims to know all about her, to know what she wants (which she herself does not know), draw her closer to him. Although she begins by flirting with him as she does with other boys, she soon realizes that he is different. At first "his face [is] a familiar face, somehow" (619), and "she recognize[s] most things about him" (620), but her confidence turns to fear when she realizes that he is older than he appears (621). By now, though, she is under his spell.

Olivari 4

Little by little, things that have been comforting and
familiar--the music, Arnold's clothing and mannerisms, even Connie's own kitchen--become "only half
real" (622), as Arnold himself is. As Arnold becomes
more and more threatening, Connie becomes more and
more helpless; toward the end of the story, cut off
from everything she has known, she is "hollow with
what had been fear, but what [is] now an emptiness"
(625). Totally in Arnold's power, she crosses the line
into uncertainty--and, perhaps, death.

Cal Beadle, Donny's tutor, has none of the
frightening mannerisms of Arnold Friend, and he has no
sinister intentions. Nevertheless, he is also a controlling figure. Like Arnold, Cal is an older man who
dresses and acts as adolescents do and listens to the
music they like. He immediately sides with Donny, setting himself in opposition to authority figures and
social institutions, such as school and the family.
This attitude makes it possible--and even acceptable--
for Donny to do the same thing. Never blaming or even
criticizing Donny, Cal suggests that Donny's parents
are too controlling and advises that they "give him
more rope" (606). But many of Cal's "kids," like
Donny, are allowed to continue their antisocial and
self-destructive patterns of behavior and remain under
Cal's loose supervision for years. Cal does not help
Donny to function in his world; he shelters him from
it. Still, Donny sides with Cal, adopting his attitudes and expressions: it becomes "Cal this, Cal that,
Cal says this, Cal and I did that" (607).

Olivari 5

Eventually, Cal becomes the role model Donny's own parents have failed to provide. Donny comes to depend on Cal, even going straight to Cal's house when he is expelled from school, and Cal comes to enjoy this dependence. But Cal does not necessarily have Donny's best interests at heart. Daisy, who despite her own failures with Donny seems to know him (and Cal) well, sees Cal as predatory and controlling, characterizing his smile as "feverish and avid--a smile of hunger" (610). Although Cal does not cause Donny to leave home, he makes it impossible for him to stay. Once he has convinced Donny that it is acceptable to reject the values established by his parents and teachers, Donny's departure becomes inevitable. Having removed all Donny's anchors, Cal then removes himself from Donny's life, deciding the teenager is "emotionally disturbed" (610) and thus absolving himself of blame. At this point, Donny, "exhausted and defeated" (610), has no real choice but to disappear.

Both Arnold Friend and Cal Beadle--Arnold odd-looking and out of date, Cal estranged from his "controlling" wife and surrounded by teenagers--seem to exist outside the adult world and its rules and values. Perhaps as a result, each has a need for power, a desire to control. Each selects someone weaker, less confident, and more confused than himself, a teenager with strained family relationships and no focused goals. Clearly, critics' characterizations of Arnold Friend, and the hypnotic power those characterizations suggest, apply not just to Arnold but also to Cal.

Even though Cal means Donny no harm, his casual dismissal of him after he has separated the boy from all that is familiar to him pushes Donny from the known and safe to the unknown and dangerous. It is to this uncertain world that Connie too is driven: a place she "[does] not recognize except to know that she [is] going to it" (626).

Olivari 7

Works Cited

Kirszner, Laurie G., and Stephen R. Mandell, eds. <u>Lit-</u><u>erature: Reading, Reacting, Writing</u>. 4th ed. Fort Worth: Harcourt Brace, 2001.

Oates, Joyce Carol. "When Characters from the Page Are Made Flesh on the Screen." Kirszner and Mandell 626–29.

---. "Where Are You Going, Where Have You Been?" Kirszner and Mandell 614–26.

Schulz, Gretchen, and R. J. R. Rockwood. "In Fairy-land, without a Map: Connie's Exploration Inward in Joyce Carol Oates' 'Where Are You Going, Where Have You Been?'" Kirszner and Mandell 629–41.

Tierce, Mike, and John Micheal Crafton. "Connie's Tam-bourine Man: A New Reading of Arnold Friend." Kirszner and Mandell 641–46.

Tyler, Anne. "Teenage Wasteland." Kirszner and Mandell 603–11.

POETRY

CHAPTER 11

Understanding Poetry

⬦ ⬦ ⬦

NIKKI GIOVANNI
(1943–   )

Poetry
(1975)

poetry is motion graceful
as a fawn
gentle as a teardrop
strong like the eye
5 finding peace in a crowded room
we poets tend to think
our words are golden
though emotion speaks too
loudly to be defined
10 by silence

sometimes after midnight or just before
the dawn
we sit typewriter in hand
pulling loneliness around us
15 forgetting our lovers or children
who are sleeping
ignoring the weary wariness
of our own logic
to compose a poem

20   no one understands it
it never says "love me" for poets are
beyond love
it never says "accept me" for poems seek not

acceptance but controversy
25 it only says "i am" and therefore
i concede that you are too
a poem is pure energy
horizontally contained
between the mind
30 of the poet and the ear of the reader
if it does not sing discard the ear
for poetry is song
if it does not delight discard
the heart for poetry is joy
35 if it does not inform then close
off the brain for it is dead
if it cannot heed the insistent message
that life is precious

which is all we poets
40 wrapped in our loneliness
are trying to say

◊ ◊ ◊

ARCHIBALD MACLEISH
(1892–1982)

Ars Poetica[1]
(1926)

A poem should be palpable and mute
As a globed fruit,

Dumb
As old medallions to the thumb,

5 Silent as the sleeve-worn stone
Of casement ledges where the moss has grown—

A poem should be wordless
As the flight of birds.

＊

A poem should be motionless in time
10 As the moon climbs,

---

[1] Art of Poetry.

Leaving, as the moon releases
Twig by twig the night-entangled trees,

Leaving, as the moon behind the winter leaves,
Memory by memory the mind—

15 A poem should be motionless in time
As the moon climbs.

*

A poem should be equal to:
Not true.

For all the history of grief
20 An empty doorway and a maple leaf.

For love
The leaning grasses and two lights above the sea—

A poem should not mean
But be.

◇ ◇ ◇

M A R I A N N E   M O O R E
(1887–1972)

Poetry
(1921)

I, too, dislike it: there are things that are important beyond all this
    fiddle.
    Reading it, however, with a perfect contempt for it, one discovers
    in it after all, a place for the genuine.
        Hands that can grasp, eyes
5   that can dilate, hair that can rise
            if it must, these things are important not because a

high-sounding interpretation can be put upon them but because they are
    useful. When they become so derivative as to become unintelligible,
    the same thing may be said for all of us, that we
10   do not admire what
        we cannot understand: the bat
            holding on upside down or in quest of something to

eat, elephants pushing, a wild horse taking a roll, a tireless wolf under
    a tree, the immovable critic twitching his skin like a horse that
       feels a flea, the base-
15   ball fan, the statistician—
       nor is it valid
          to discriminate against "business documents and

school-books";[1] all these phenomena are important. One must make a
    distinction
      however: when dragged into prominence by half poets, the result is
      not poetry,
20   nor till the poets among us can be
       "literalists of
       the imagination"[2]—above
         insolence and triviality and can present

for inspection, "imaginary gardens with real toads in them," shall
    we have
25   it. In the meantime, if you demand on the one hand,
    the raw material of poetry in
      all its rawness and
      that which is on the other hand
        genuine, you are interested in poetry.

DEFINING POETRY

◇ ◇ ◇

Throughout history and across various national and cultural boundaries,
poetry has held an important place. In ancient China and Japan, for example, poetry was prized above all else. One story tells of a samurai warrior who, when defeated, asked for a pen and paper. Thinking that he

---

[1] Moore quotes the *Diaries of Tolstoy* (New York, 1917): "Where the boundary between
prose and poetry lies, I shall never be able to understand. [. . .] Poetry is verse; prose
is not verse. Or else poetry is everything with the exception of business documents
and school books."

[2] A reference (given by Moore) to W. B. Yeats's "William Blake and His Illustrations"
(in *Ideas of Good and Evil*, 1903): "The limitation of his view was from the very intensity of his vision; he was a too literal realist of the imagination as others are of
nature; and because he believed that the figures seen by the mind's eye, when exalted by inspiration, were 'external existences,' symbols of divine essences, he hated
every grace of style that might obscure their lineaments."

wanted to write a will before being executed, his captor granted his wish. Instead of writing a will, however, the warrior wrote a farewell poem that so moved his captor that he immediately released him.

To the ancient Greeks and Romans, poetry was the medium of spiritual and philosophical expression. Epics such as the *Iliad* and the *Aeneid* are written in verse, and so are dramas such as *Oedipus the King* (p. 1509) and *Antigone* (p. 1631). Passages of the Bible, the Koran, and the Hindu holy books are also written in poetry. Today, throughout the world, poetry continues to delight and to inspire. For many people, in many places, poetry is the language of the emotions, the medium of expression they use when they speak from the heart.

Despite the longstanding place of poetry in our lives, however, many people—including poets themselves—have difficulty deciding just what poetry is. Is a poem "pure energy / horizontally contained / between the mind / of the poet and the ear of the reader," as Nikki Giovanni describes it? Or is a poem, as Archibald MacLeish says, "Dumb," "Silent," "wordless," and "motionless in time"? Or is it simply what Marianne Moore calls "all this fiddle"?

One way of defining poetry is to say that it uses language to condense experience into an intensely concentrated package, with each sound, each word, each image, and each line carrying great weight. But beyond this, it is difficult to pin down what makes a particular arrangement of words or lines a poem. Part of the problem is that poetry has many guises: a poem may be short or long, accessible or obscure; it may express a mood or tell a story; it may conform to a familiar poetic form—a sonnet, a couplet, a haiku—or follow no conventional pattern; it may or may not have a regular, identifiable meter or a rhyme scheme; it may depend heavily on elaborate imagery, figures of speech, irony, complex allusions or symbols, or repeated sounds—or it may include none of these features conventionally associated with poetry.

To further complicate the issue, different readers, different poets, different generations of readers and poets, and different cultures may have different expectations about poetry. As a result, they have different assumptions about poetry, and these different assumptions raise questions. Must poetry be written to delight or inspire, or can a poem have a political or social message? And must this message be conveyed subtly, embellished with imaginatively chosen sounds and words, or can it be explicit and straightforward? These questions, which have been debated by literary critics as well as by poets for many years, have no easy answers—and perhaps no answers at all. A haiku—short, rich in imagery, adhering to a rigid formal structure—is certainly poetry, and so is a political poem like Wole Soyinka's "Telephone Conversation" (p. 6). To some Western readers, however, a haiku might seem too plain and understated to be poetic, and Soyinka's poem might seem to be a political tract masquerading as poetry. Still, most of these readers would agree that the following lines qualify as poetry.

◈ ◈ ◈

WILLIAM SHAKESPEARE
(1564–1616)

That Time of Year Thou Mayst in Me Behold
(1609)

That time of year thou mayst in me behold
When yellow leaves, or none, or few, do hang
Upon those boughs which shake against the cold,
Bare ruined choirs, where late the sweet birds sang.
5 In me thou see'st the twilight of such day
As after sunset fadeth in the west,
Which by and by black night doth take away,
Death's second self that seals up all in rest.
In me thou see'st the glowing of such fire,
10 That on the ashes of his youth doth lie,
As the deathbed whereon it must expire,
Consumed with that which it was nourished by
    This thou perceiv'st, which makes thy love more strong,
    To love that well which thou must leave ere long.

This poem possesses many of the characteristics that Western readers associate with poetry. For instance, its lines have a regular pattern of rhyme and meter that identifies it as a **sonnet.** The poem also includes a complex network of related imagery and figurative language that compares the lost youth of the aging speaker to the sunset and to autumn. Finally, the pair of rhyming lines at the end of the poem states a familiar poetic theme: the lovers' knowledge that they must eventually die makes their love stronger.

    Even though the next poem is quite different from the preceding sonnet, most readers would probably agree that it too is a poem.

◈ ◈ ◈

LOUIS ZUKOFSKY
(1904–1978)

I Walk in the Old Street
(1944)

I walk in the old street
to hear the beloved songs

afresh
this spring night.

5 Like the leaves—my loves wake—
not to be the same
or look tireless to the stars
and a ripped doorbell.

Unlike Shakespeare's sonnet, Zukofsky's poem does not have a regular metrical pattern or rhyme scheme. Its diction is more conversational than poetic, and one of its images—a "ripped doorbell"—stands in stark contrast to the other, more conventionally "poetic" images. Nevertheless, the subject—love—is a traditional one; in fact, Zukofsky's poem echoes some of the sentiments of the Shakespeare sonnet. Finally, the poem's division into two four-line stanzas and its use of figurative language ("Like the leaves—my loves wake—") are unmistakably poetic.

Although the two preceding works can easily be classified as poems, readers might have trouble with the following lines.

◈ ◈ ◈

E. E. CUMMINGS
(1894–1962)

l(a
(1923)

l(a

le
af
fa

5 ll

s)
one
l

iness

Unlike the preceding two poems, "l(a" does not seem to have any of the characteristics normally associated with poetry. It has no meter, rhyme, or imagery. It has no repeated sounds, no figures of speech, no symbols. It cannot even be read aloud because its "lines" are fragments of words. In spite of its odd appearance, however, "l(a" does present an idea that is poetic. Reconstructed, the words Cummings broke apart—"l (a leaf falls) one l iness"—express a conventional poetic theme: the loneliness and isolation of the individual, as reflected in nature. Like Shakespeare and Zukofsky in the two previous poems, Cummings uses the image of a leaf to express his ideas about life and human experience. At the same time, by breaking words into bits and pieces, Cummings suggests the flexibility of language and conveys the need to break out of customary ways of using words to define experience.

As the preceding discussion illustrates, defining what a poem is (and is not) is almost impossible. It is true that most poems, particularly those divided into stanzas, look like poems, and it is also true that poems tend to use compressed language. Beyond this, however, what makes a poem a poem is more a matter of degree than a question of whether or not it conforms to a strict set of rules. A poem is likely to use *more* imagery, figurative language, rhyme, and so on than a prose piece—but, then again, it may not.

READING POETRY
◊ ◊ ◊

Some readers say they do not like poetry because they find it obscure or intimidating. One reason some people have difficulty reading poetry is that it tends to present information in subtle (and therefore potentially confusing) ways; it does not immediately "get to the point" as journalistic articles or business letters do. One could certainly argue that by concentrating experience, poetry actually "gets to the point" in ways—and to degrees—that other kinds of writing do not. Even so, some readers see poetry as an alien form. They have the misconception that poetry is always filled with obscure allusions, complex metrical schemes, and flowery diction. Others, feeling excluded from what they see as its secret language and mysterious structure, approach poetry as something that must be deciphered. Certainly, reading poetry often requires hard work and concentration. Because it is compressed, poetry often omits exposition and explanation; consequently, readers must be willing to take the time to read closely—to interpret ideas and supply missing connections. Many readers are simply not motivated to dig deeply for what they perceive to be uncertain rewards. But not all poems are difficult, and even those that are difficult are often well worth the effort. (For specific suggestions about how to read poetry, see Chapter 12.)

RECOGNIZING KINDS OF POETRY
◊ ◊ ◊

Most poems are either *narrative* poems, which recount a story, or *lyric* poems, which communicate a speaker's mood, feelings, or state of mind.

NARRATIVE POETRY

Although any brief poem that tells a story, such as Edwin Arlington Robinson's "Richard Cory" (p. 986), may be considered a narrative poem, the two most familiar forms of narrative poetry are the *epic* and the *ballad*.

Epic poems recount the accomplishments of heroic figures, typically including expansive settings, superhuman feats, and gods and supernatural beings. The language of epic poems tends to be formal, even elevated, and often quite elaborate. Epics span many cultures—from the *Odyssey* (Greek) to *Beowulf* (Anglo-Saxon) to *The Epic of Gilgamesh* (Babylonian). In ancient times, epics were handed down orally; more recently, poets have written literary epics, such as John Milton's 1667 *Paradise Lost* and Nobel Prize–winning poet Derek Walcott's 1990 *Omeros*, which follow many of the same conventions.

The **ballad** is another type of narrative poetry with roots in an oral tradition. Originally intended to be sung, a ballad uses repeated words and phrases, including a refrain, to advance its story. Some—but not all— ballads use the **ballad stanza.** For examples of traditional ballads in this text, see "Bonny Barbara Allen" (p. 924) and "Western Wind" (p. 926). Dudley Randall's "Ballad of Birmingham" (p. 755) and Gwendolyn Brooks's "The Ballad of Rudolph Reed" (p. 932) are examples of contemporary ballads.

LYRIC POETRY

Like narrative poems, lyric poems take various forms.

An **elegy** is a poem in which a poet mourns the death of a specific person, as in Robert Hayden's "Homage to the Empress of the Blues" (p. 965), about the singer Bessie Smith. Another example of this type of elegy is A. E. Housman's "To an Athlete Dying Young" (p. 786).

An **ode** is a long lyric poem, formal and serious in style, tone, and subject matter. An ode typically has a fairly complex stanzaic pattern, such as the **terza rima** used by Percy Bysshe Shelley in "Ode to the West Wind" (p. 990). Another ode in this text is "Ode on a Grecian Urn" (p. 971).

An **aubade** is a poem about morning, usually celebrating the coming of dawn. An example is Philip Larkin's "Aubade" (p. 973).

An **occasional poem** is written to celebrate a particular event or occasion. An example is Miller Williams's poem for President Clinton's second inaugural in 1997.

A **meditation** is a lyric poem that focuses on a physical object, using this object as a vehicle for considering larger issues. Edmund Waller's "Go, Lovely Rose" (p. 1004) is a meditation.

A **pastoral**—for example, Christopher Marlowe's "The Passionate Shepherd to His Love" (p. 682)—is a lyric poem that celebrates the simple, idyllic pleasures of country life.

Finally, a **dramatic monologue** is a poem whose speaker addresses one or more silent listeners, often revealing much more than he or she intends. Robert Browning's "My Last Duchess" (p. 729) and "Porphyria's

Lover" (p. 745) and Alfred, Lord Tennyson's "Ulysses" (p. 999) are three
dramatic monologues that appear in this text.

DISCOVERING THEMES IN POETRY
◇ ◇ ◇

A poem can be about anything, from the mysteries of the universe to poetry itself. Although no subject is really inappropriate for poetic treatment, certain conventional subjects recur frequently. For example, poets
often write about love, war, nature, death, family, the folly of human desires, and the inevitability of growing old.

A poem's **theme,** however, is more than its general subject. It denotes
the ideas the poet explores, the concerns the poem examines. More specifically, a poem's theme is its main point or idea. Poems "about nature," for
instance, may praise the beauty of nature, assert the superiority of its simplest creatures over humans, consider its evanescence, or mourn its destruction. Similarly, poems "about death" may examine the difficulty of
facing one's own mortality, eulogize a friend, assert the need for the acceptance of life's cycles, cry out against death's inevitability, or explore
the **carpe diem** theme ("life is brief, so let us seize the day").

In order to discover the theme of a poem, readers consider its form, its
voice, its language, its images, its allusions, its sound—all of its individual
elements. Together, these elements convey the ideas that are important in
the poem. (Of course, a poem may not communicate the same meaning to
every reader. Different readers bring different backgrounds, attitudes, and
experiences to a poem and therefore see different things and give weight
to different ideas.)

The following poem is rich enough in language and content to suggest
a variety of different interpretations.

◇ ◇ ◇

ADRIENNE RICH
(1929–   )

A Woman Mourned by Daughters
(1984)

> Now, not a tear begun,
> we sit here in your kitchen,
> spent, you see, already.
> You are swollen till you strain
> 5 this house and the whole sky.
> You, whom we so often

succeeded in ignoring!
You are puffed up in death
like a corpse pulled from the sea;
10 we groan beneath your weight.
And yet you were a leaf,
a straw blown on the bed,
you had long since become
crisp as a dead insect.
15 What is it, if not you,
that settles on us now
like satins you pulled down
over our bridal heads?
What rises in our throats
20 like food you prodded in?
Nothing could be enough.
You breathe upon us now
through solid assertions
of yourself: teaspoons, goblets,
25 seas of carpet, a forest
of old plants to be watered,
an old man in an adjoining
room to be touched and fed.
And all this universe
30 dares us to lay a finger
anywhere, save exactly
as you would wish it done.

In general terms, "A Woman Mourned by Daughters" is, of course, about the speaker's mother. More specifically, this poem explores a number of different ideas: the passing of time; the relationships between mother and daughters, father and daughters, husband and wife; the power of memory. Its central theme, however, may be expressed as a **paradox:** "In death, a person may be a stronger presence than she was when she was alive."

Many different elements in the poem suggest this interpretation. The poem's speaker directly addresses her mother. Her voice is searching, questioning, and the poem's unpoetic diction ("You, whom we so often / succeeded in ignoring") and metrical irregularities give it a halting, uncertain quality. The words, images, and figurative language work together to establish the central idea: alive, the mother was light as a leaf or a straw or a dead insect; dead, she seems "swollen" and "puffed up," and the daughters feel crushed by her weight. The concrete details of her life—"teaspoons, goblets, / seas of carpet [. . .]"—weigh on her survivors and keep them under her spell. In her kitchen, her memory is alive; in death, she has tremendous power over her daughters.

Like most complex poems, this one supports several alternate readings. Some readers will focus on the negative language used to describe the mother; others might emphasize the images of domesticity; still others might concentrate on the role of the sisters and the almost-absent father. Any of these focuses can lead to a redefinition of the poem's theme.

The following poem is also about a parent who inspires ambivalent feelings in a child.

❖ ❖ ❖

RAYMOND CARVER
(1938–1988)

Photograph of My Father in His Twenty-Second Year
(1983)

October. Here in this dank, unfamiliar kitchen
I study my father's embarrassed young man's face.
Sheepish grin, he holds in one hand a string
of spiny yellow perch, in the other
5 a bottle of Carlsbad beer.

In jeans and denim shirt, he leans
against the front fender of a 1934 Ford.
He would like to pose bluff and hearty for his posterity,
wear his old hat cocked over his ear.
10 All his life my father wanted to be bold.

But the eyes give him away, and the hands
that limply offer the string of dead perch
and the bottle of beer. Father, I love you,
yet how can I say thank you, I who can't hold my liquor either,
15 and don't even know the places to fish?

Like Rich's speaker, Carver's is in a kitchen. Studying a photograph, this speaker sees through his father's façade. Instead of seeing the "bold," "bluff and hearty" young man his father wanted to be, he sees him as he was: "embarrassed" and "sheepish," with limp hands. In the last three lines of the poem, the speaker addresses his father directly, comparing his father's shortcomings and his own. This frank acknowledgment of his own vulnerability and the explicit link between father and son suggest that the poem has more to do with the speaker than with his father. Still, it is clear that the poem has something universal to say about parents and children—specifically, about the ambivalent feelings that children have for parents whose faults and failings they may have inherited.

The following poem also looks back on a parent, but here the adult speaker assumes a child's point of view.

◈   ◈   ◈

JUDITH ORTIZ COFER
(1952–   )

My Father in the Navy:
A Childhood Memory
(1982)

Stiff and immaculate
in the white cloth of his uniform
and a round cap on his head like a halo,
he was an apparition on leave from a shadow-world
5 and only flesh and blood when he rose from below
the waterline where he kept watch over the engines
and dials making sure the ship parted the waters
on a straight course.
Mother, brother and I kept vigil
10 on the nights and dawns of his arrivals,
watching the corner beyond the neon sign of a quasar
for the flash of white our father like an angel
heralding a new day.
His homecomings were the verses
15 we composed over the years making up
the siren's song that kept him coming back
from the bellies of iron whales
and into our nights
like the evening prayer.

Even as an adult, the speaker seems still not to know her father, whom she remembers as "stiff and immaculate," dressed in white, "an apparition on leave from a shadow-world." She remembers him as being "like an angel," wearing his cap "like a halo." In lines 14–16, the speaker associates her father with the long-missing, long-awaited wanderer Odysseus, hero of Homer's *Odyssey*. The reference to the "siren's song" in line 16, also an allusion to the *Odyssey*, suggests the adult speaker's realization that the father is drawn back—perhaps against his will—to the family. Together, the poem's tone and imagery convey the child's view of the father as elusive and unreal—an impression the adult speaker neither confirms nor corrects. The poem seems to suggest that the speaker is still struggling to understand her father's complex role in her life; perhaps too it suggests the universal difficulty of a child's trying to understand a parent.

❖ Poems for Further Reading: Poems about Parents

◇ ◇ ◇

THEODORE ROETHKE
(1908–1963)

My Papa's Waltz
(1948)

The whiskey on your breath
Could make a small boy dizzy;
But I hung on like death:
Such waltzing was not easy.

5 We romped until the pans
Slid from the kitchen shelf;
My mother's countenance
Could not unfrown itself.

The hand that held my wrist
10 Was battered on one knuckle;
At every step you missed
My right ear scraped a buckle.

You beat time on my head
With a palm caked hard by dirt,
15 Then waltzed me off to bed
Still clinging to your shirt.

◇ ◇ ◇

DYLAN THOMAS
(1914–1953)

Do Not Go Gentle into That Good Night[1]
(1952)

Do not go gentle into that good night,
Old age should burn and rave at close of day;
Rage, rage against the dying of the light.

---

[1] This poem was written during the last illness of the poet's father, D. J. Thomas.

Though wise men at their end know dark is right,
5 Because their words had forked no lightning they
Do not go gentle into that good night.

Good men, the last wave by, crying how bright
Their frail deeds might have danced in a green bay,
Rage, rage against the dying of the light.

10 Wild men who caught and sang the sun in flight,
And learn, too late, they grieved it on its way,
Do not go gentle into that good night.

Grave men, near death, who see with blinding sight
Blind eyes could blaze like meteors and be gay,
15 Rage, rage against the dying of the light.

And you, my father, there on the sad height,
Curse, bless, me now with your fierce tears, I pray,
Do not go gentle into that good night.
Rage, rage against the dying of the light.

◊ ◊ ◊

LUCILLE CLIFTON
(1936–   )

My Mama Moved among the Days
(1969)

My Mama moved among the days
like a dreamwalker in a field;
seemed like what she touched was hers
seemed like what touched her couldn't hold,
5 she got us almost through the high grass
then seemed like she turned around and ran
right back in
right back on in

◊ ◊ ◊

ROBERT HAYDEN
(1913–1980)

Those Winter Sundays
(1962)

Sundays too my father got up early
and put his clothes on in the blueblack cold,
then with cracked hands that ached
from labor in the weekday weather made
5 banked fires blaze. No one ever thanked him.

I'd wake and hear the cold splintering, breaking.
When the rooms were warm, he'd call,
and slowly I would rise and dress,
fearing the chronic angers of that house,

10 Speaking indifferently to him,
who had driven out the cold
and polished my good shoes as well.
What did I know, what did I know
of love's austere and lonely offices?

◊   ◊   ◊

SEAMUS HEANEY[1]
(1939–   )

Digging
(1966)

Between my finger and my thumb
The squat pen rests; snug as a gun.

Under my window, a clean rasping sound
When the spade sinks into gravelly ground:
5 My father, digging. I look down

Till his straining rump among the flowerbeds
Bends low, comes up twenty years away
Stooping in rhythm through potato drills
Where he was digging.

10 The coarse boot nestled on the lug, the shaft
Against the inside knee was levered firmly.
He rooted out tall tops, buried the bright edge deep
To scatter new potatoes that we picked
Loving their cool hardness in our hands.
15 By God, the old man could handle a spade.
Just like his old man.

My grandfather cut more turf in a day
Than any other man on Toner's bog.
Once I carried him milk in a bottle
20 Corked sloppily with paper. He straightened up
To drink it, then fell to right away

---

[1] Winner of the 1995 Nobel Prize in Literature.

Nicking and slicing neatly, heaving sods
Over his shoulder, going down and down
For the good turf. Digging.

25 The cold smell of potato mould, the squelch and slap
Of soggy peat, the curt cuts of an edge
Through living roots awaken in my head.
But I've no spade to follow men like them.

Between my finger and my thumb
30 The squat pen rests.
I'll dig with it.

◆ ◆ ◆

SIMON J. ORTIZ
(1941–   )

My Father's Song
(1976)

Wanting to say things,
I miss my father tonight.
His voice, the slight catch,
the depth from his thin chest,
5 the tremble of emotion
in something he has just said
to his son, his song:

We planted corn one Spring at Acu—
we planted several times
10 but this one particular time
I remember the soft damp sand
in my hand.

My father had stopped at one point
to show me an overturned furrow;
15 the plowshare had unearthed
the burrow nest of a mouse
in the soft moist sand.

Very gently, he scooped tiny pink animals
into the palm of his hand
20 and told me to touch them.
We took them to the edge
of the field and put them in the shade
of a sand moist clod.

I remember the very softness
25 of cool and warm sand and tiny alive mice
and my father saying things.

◊   ◊   ◊
COLLEEN J. MCELROY
(1935–   )

My Father's Wars
(1984)

Once he followed simple rules
of casual strength,
summoned violence with the flick
of combat ribbon or hash mark;
5 now he forces a pulse into treasonous muscles
and commands soap opera villains.
He is camped in a world regimented
by glowing tubes,
his olive-black skin begging for the fire
10 of unlimited color.
In towns where he can follow
the orders of silence,
gunfights are replayed
in thirty-minute intervals
15 familiar as his stiff right arm
or the steel brace scaffolding his leg.

By midday the room is filled
with game shows and private eyes hurling
questions against all those who swear
20 their innocence;
his wife is in full retreat
and jumps when he answers in half-formed words
of single grunts deadly as shrapnel.
He need not remind her
25 he is always the hero;
the palms of his hands
are muddy with old battle lines.
He has fallen
heir to brutal days where he moves
30 battalions of enemies;
his mornings are shattered with harsh echoes
of their electronic voices.

Here he is on neutral ground
and need not struggle to capture words
35 he can no longer force his brain to master;
he plans his roster
and does not attend to his wife's
rapid-fire review of the neighbor's behavior.
He recalls too clearly the demarcation of blacks,

40 of Buffalo Soldier and 93rd Division.
By late afternoon he is seen rigidly
polishing his car in broad one-arm swipes,
its side windows and bumpers emblazoned
with stickers: US ARMY RETIRED REGULAR

READING AND REACTING: POEMS ABOUT PARENTS

1. What is each speaker's attitude toward his or her parent?
2. Which words and images suggest positive associations? Which help to create a negative impression?
3. How would you characterize each poem's tone? For example, is the poem sentimental, humorous, angry, resentful, or regretful?
4. What ideas about parent-child relationships are explored in each poem? What is the poem's central theme?
5. What does each poem say about the parent? What does it reveal about the speaker?

Related Works: "How to Talk to Your Mother (Notes)" (p. 96), "Sleepy Time Gal" (p. 242), "Seventeen Syllables" (p. 376), "Two Kinds" (p. 594), "Daddy" (p. 818), *'night, Mother* (p. 1708)

❖ POEMS FOR FURTHER READING: POEMS ABOUT LOVE

◇ ◇ ◇

CHRISTOPHER MARLOWE
(1564–1593)

The Passionate Shepherd
to His Love
(1600)

Come live with me and be my love,
And we will all the pleasures prove
That valleys, groves, hills, and fields,
Woods, or steepy mountain yields.

5 And we will sit upon the rocks,
Seeing the shepherds feed their flocks
By shallow rivers, to whose falls
Melodious birds sing madrigals.

And I will make thee beds of roses
10 And a thousand fragrant posies,
A cap of flowers and a kirtle[1]
Embroidered all with leaves of myrtle;

---

[1] Skirt.

A gown made of the finest wool
Which from our pretty lambs we pull;
15 Fair-linèd slippers for the cold,
With buckles of the purest gold;

A belt of straw and ivy buds,
With coral clasps and amber studs.
And if these pleasures may thee move,
20 Come live with me and be my love.

The shepherds' swains shall dance and sing
For thy delight each May morning.
If these delights thy mind may move,
Then live with me and be my love.

◆ ◆ ◆

SIR WALTER RALEIGH
(1552?–1618)

The Nymph's Reply
to the Shepherd
(1600)

If all the world and love were young,
And truth in every shepherd's tongue,
These pretty pleasures might me move
To live with thee and be thy love.

5 Time drives the flocks from field to fold,
When rivers rage and rocks grow cold;
And Philomel[1] becometh dumb;
The rest complains of cares to come.

The flowers do fade, and wanton fields
10 To wayward winter reckoning yields:
A honey tongue, a heart of gall,
Is fancy's spring, but sorrow's fall.

Thy gowns, thy shoes, thy beds of roses,
Thy cap, thy kirtle, and thy posies
15 Soon break, soon wither, soon forgotten,
In folly ripe, in reason rotten.

Thy belt of straw and ivy buds,
Thy coral clasps and amber studs.
All these in me no means can move
20 To come to thee and be thy love.

---

[1] The nightingale.

But could youth last, and love still breed,
Had joys no date, nor age no need,
Then these delights my mind might move
To live with thee and be thy love.

◇ ◇ ◇

THOMAS CAMPION
(1567–1620)

There Is a Garden in Her Face
(1617)

There is a garden in her face
Where roses and white lilies grow;
   A heav'nly paradise is that place
Wherein all pleasant fruits do flow.
5   There cherries grow which none may buy
   Till "Cherry-ripe" themselves do cry.

Those cherries fairly do enclose
Of orient pearl a double row,
   Which when her lovely laughter shows,
10 They look like rose-buds filled with snow;
    Yet them nor peer nor prince can buy,
   Till "Cherry-ripe" themselves do cry.

Her eyes like angels watch them still;
Her brows like bended bows do stand,
15   Threat'ning with piercing frowns to kill
All that attempt, with eye or hand
   Those sacred cherries to come nigh
   Till "Cherry-ripe" themselves do cry.

◇ ◇ ◇

WILLIAM SHAKESPEARE
(1564–1616)

My Mistress' Eyes Are
Nothing like the Sun
(1609)

My mistress' eyes are nothing like the sun;
Coral is far more red than her lips' red;
If snow be white, why then her breasts are dun;
If hairs be wires, black wires grow on her head.

5 I have seen roses damasked red and white,
But no such roses see I in her cheeks;
And in some perfumes is there more delight
Than in the breath that from my mistress reeks.
I love to hear her speak, yet well I know
10 That music hath a far more pleasing sound;
I grant I never saw a goddess go:
My mistress, when she walks, treads on the ground.
    And yet, by heaven, I think my love as rare
    As any she, belied with false compare.

◊ ◊ ◊

ROBERT BROWNING
(1812–1889)

Meeting at Night
(1845)

The gray sea and the long black land;
And the yellow half-moon large and low;
And the startled little waves that leap
In fiery ringlets from their sleep,
5 As I gain the cove with pushing prow,
And quench its speed i' the slushy sand.

Then a mile of warm sea-scented beach;
Three fields to cross till a farm appears;
A tap at the pane, the quick sharp scratch
10 And blue spurt of a lighted match,
And a voice less loud, through its joys and fears,
Than the two hearts beating each to each!

Parting at Morning
(1845)

Round the cape of a sudden came the sea,
And the sun looked over the mountain's rim:
And straight was a path of gold for him,
And the need of a world of men for me.

◇ ◇ ◇

ELIZABETH BARRETT BROWNING
(1806–1861)

How Do I Love Thee?[1]
(1850)

How do I love thee? Let me count the ways.
I love thee to the depth and breadth and height
My soul can reach, when feeling out of sight
For the ends of being and ideal grace.
5 I love thee to the level of every day's
Most quiet need, by sun and candle-light.
I love thee freely, as men strive for right.
I love thee purely, as they turn from praise.
I love thee with the passion put to use
10 In my old griefs, and with my childhood's faith.
I love thee with a love I seemed to lose
With my lost saints. I love thee with the breath,
Smiles, tears, of all my life; and, if God choose,
I shall but love thee better after death.

◇ ◇ ◇

EDNA ST. VINCENT MILLAY
(1892–1950)

What Lips My Lips Have Kissed
(1923)

What lips my lips have kissed, and where, and why,
I have forgotten, and what arms have lain
Under my head till morning; but the rain
Is full of ghosts tonight, that tap and sigh
5 Upon the glass and listen for reply,
And in my heart there stirs a quiet pain
For unremembered lads that not again
Will turn to me at midnight with a cry.
Thus in the winter stands the lonely tree,
10 Nor knows what birds have vanished one by one,
Yet knows its boughs more silent than before:
I cannot say what loves have come and gone,
I only know that summer sang in me
A little while, that in me sings no more.

---

[1] Elizabeth Barrett Browning's "Sonnets from the Portuguese" was originally published in 1850 in a two volume publication titled *Poems*. "How Do I Love Thee?" is sonnet number XLIII from that work.

◆ ◆ ◆

W. H. AUDEN
(1907–1973)

Stop All the Clocks,
Cut Off the Telephone[1]
(1936)

Stop all the clocks, cut off the telephone,
Prevent the dog from barking with a juicy bone,
Silence the pianos and with muffled drum
Bring out the coffin, let the mourners come.

5 Let aeroplanes circle moaning overhead
Scribbling on the sky the message He Is Dead,
Put the crepe bows round the white necks of the public doves,
Let the traffic policemen wear black cotton gloves.

He was my North, my South, my East and West,
10 My working week and my Sunday rest,
My noon, my midnight, my talk, my song;
I thought that love would last for ever. I was wrong.

The stars are not wanted now: put out every one;
Pack up the moon and dismantle the sun;
15 Pour away the ocean and sweep up the wood.
For nothing now can ever come to any good.

◆ ◆ ◆

DOROTHY PARKER
(1893–1967)

General Review of
the Sex Situation
(1933)

Woman wants monogamy;
Man delights in novelty.
Love is woman's moon and sun;
Man has other forms of fun.

---

[1] This poem was featured in the 1994 movie *Four Weddings and a Funeral*. The poem was originally titled "Funeral Blues," and Auden wrote it for the London production of his play *The Ascent of F6*. In his poem, Auden laments the death of love in whatever form. "Funeral Blues" reappeared substantially changed in *Another Time*, a 1940 Random House collection of Auden's poems.

5 Woman lives but in her lord;
    Count to ten, and man is bored.
    With this the gist and sum of it,
    What earthly good can come of it?

◆ ◆ ◆

SYLVIA PLATH
(1932–1963)

Wreath for a Bridal
(1956)

What though green leaves only witness
Such pact as is made once only; what matter
That owl voice sole 'yes', while cows utter
Low moos of approve; let sun surpliced in brightness
5 Stand stock still to laud these mated ones
Whose stark act all coming double luck joins.

Couched daylong in cloisters of stinging nettle
They lie, cut-grass assaulting each separate sense
With savor; coupled so, pure paragons of constance,
10 This pair seek single state from that dual battle.
Now speak some sacrament to parry scruple
For wedlock wrought within love's proper chapel.

Call here with flying colors all watchful birds
To people the twigged aisles; lead babel tongues
15 Of animals to choir: 'Look what thresh of wings
Wields guard of honor over these!' Starred with words
Let night bless that luck-rotted mead of clover
Where, bedded like angels, two burn one in fever.

From this holy day on, all pollen blown
20 Shall strew broadcast so rare a seed on wind
That every breath, thus teeming, set the land
Sprouting fruit, flowers, children most fair in legion
To slay spawn of dragon's teeth: speaking this promise,
Let flesh be knit, and each step hence go famous.

◆ ◆ ◆

TED HUGHES
(1930–1998)

A Pink Wool Knitted Dress
(1996)

In your pink wool knitted dress
Before anything had smudged anything
You stood at the altar. Bloomsday.

Rain—so that a just-bought umbrella
5 Was the only furnishing about me
Newer than three years inured.
My tie—sole, drab, veteran RAF black—
Was the used-up symbol of a tie.
My cord jacket—thrice-dyed black, exhausted,
10 Just hanging on to itself.

I was a post-war, utility son-in-law!
Not quite the Frog-Prince. Maybe the Swineherd
Stealing this daughter's pedigree dreams
From under her watchtowered searchlit future.

15 No ceremony could conscript me
Out of my uniform. I wore my whole wardrobe—
Except for the odd, spare, identical item.
My wedding, like Nature, wanted to hide.
However—if we were going to be married
20 It had better be Westminster Abbey. Why not?
The Dean told us why not. That is how
I learned that I had a Parish Church.
St George of the Chimney Sweeps.
So we squeezed into marriage finally.
25 Your mother, brave even in this
US Foreign Affairs gamble,
Acted all bridesmaids and all guests,
Even—magnanimity—represented
My family
30 Who had heard nothing about it.
I had invited only their ancestors.
I had not even confided my theft of you
To a closest friend. For Best Man—my squire
To hold the meanwhile rings—
35 We requisitioned the sexton. Twist of the outrage:
He was packing children into a bus,
Taking them to the Zoo—in that downpour!
All the prison animals had to be patient
While we married.
40   You were transfigured.
So slender and new and naked,
A nodding spray of wet lilac.
You shook, you sobbed with joy, you were ocean depth
Brimming with God.
45 You said you saw the heavens open
And how riches, ready to drop upon us.
Levitated beside you, I stood subjected
To a strange tense: the spellbound future.

In that echo-gaunt, weekday chancel
50 I see you
Wrestling to contain your flames
In your pink wool knitted dress
And in your eye-pupils—great cut jewels
Jostling their tear-flames, truly like big jewels
55 Shaken in a dice-cup and held up to me.

READING AND REACTING: POEMS ABOUT LOVE

1. What conventional images does each speaker use to express love?
2. Does the speaker use any images that are unexpected or shocking?
3. What ideas about love are expressed by each poem?
4. What is the tone of each poem? Is it happy? Sad? Celebratory? Regretful?
5. What does each poem reveal about the speaker? About the person to whom the poem is addressed?

Related Works: "Living in Sin" (p. 767), "I Knew a Woman" (p. 770), "The Faithful Wife" (p. 776), "A Valediction: Forbidding Mourning" (p. 816), "To My Dear and Loving Husband" (p. 823), "You Fit into Me" (p. 828), *The Brute* (p. 1266)

❖ POEMS FOR FURTHER READING: POEMS ABOUT WAR

◇ ◇ ◇

R U P E R T   B R O O K E
(1887–1915)

The Soldier[1]
(1915)

If I should die, think only this of me;
    That there's some corner of a foreign field
That is for ever England. There shall be
    In that rich earth a richer dust concealed;
5 A dust whom England bore, shaped, made aware,
    Gave, once, her flowers to love, her ways to roam,
A body of England's breathing English air,
    Washed by the rivers, blest by suns of home.

---

[1] Brooke's poem "The Soldier" appeared in 1915 in a posthumously published collection of his work titled *1914 and Other Poems*.

And think, this heart, all evil shed away,
10   A pulse in the eternal mind, no less
           Gives somewhere back the thoughts by England given;
Her sights and sounds; dreams happy as her day;
And laughter, learnt of friends; and gentleness,
           In hearts at peace, under an English heaven.

◇ ◇ ◇

WILFRED OWEN
(1893–1918)

Anthem for Doomed Youth
(1917?)

What passing-bells for these who die as cattle?
     Only the monstrous anger of the guns.
Only the stuttering rifles' rapid rattle
Can patter out their hasty orisons.[1]
5 No mockeries now for them; no prayers nor bells,
     Nor any voice of mourning save the choirs,—
The shrill, demented choirs of wailing shells;
     And bugles calling for them from sad shires.

What candles may be held to speed them all?
10   Not in the hands of boys, but in their eyes
     Shall shine the holy glimmers of good-byes.
The pallor of girls' brows shall be their pall;
Their flowers the tenderness of patient minds,
And each slow dusk a drawing-down of blinds.

◇ ◇ ◇

WILLIAM BUTLER YEATS
(1865–1939)

An Irish Airman
Foresees His Death
(1919)

I know that I shall meet my fate
Somewhere among the clouds above;
Those that I fight I do not hate,
Those that I guard I do not love;
5 My country is Kiltartan Cross
My countrymen Kiltartan's poor,

---

[1] Prayers.

No likely end could bring them loss
Or leave them happier than before.
Nor law, nor duty bade me fight,
10   Nor public men, nor cheering crowds,
A lonely impulse of delight
Drove to this tumult in the clouds;
I balanced all, brought all to mind,
The years to come seemed waste of breath,
15   A waste of breath the years behind
In balance with this life, this death.

◈ ◈ ◈

W. H. AUDEN
(1907–1973)

The Shield of Achilles[1]
(1955)

She looked over his shoulder
For vines and olive trees,
Marble well-governed cities,
And ships upon untamed seas,
5   But there on the shining metal
His hands had put instead
An artificial wilderness
And a sky like lead.

A plain without a feature, bare and brown,
10   No blade of grass, no sign of neighborhood,
Nothing to eat and nowhere to sit down,
Yet, congregated on its blankness, stood
An unintelligible multitude.
A million eyes, a million boots in line,
15   Without expression, waiting for a sign.

Out of the air a voice without a face
Proved by statistics that some cause was just
In tones as dry and level as the place:
No one was cheered and nothing was discussed;
20   Column by column in a cloud of dust
They marched away enduring a belief
Whose logic brought them, somewhere else, to grief.

---

[1] In Greek mythology, Achilles was a fierce warrior who was the epitome of great warriors and was noted for his pride and honor. In Homer's *The Iliad*, the pictures on the shield of Achilles represent the city at war and the city at peace. The city at peace depicts prosperity and life in perfect balance while the city at war depicts death, destruction, and chaos.

❖ | ❖ | ❖

ROBERT LOWELL
(1917–1977)

For the Union Dead
(1959)

"Relinquunt omnia servare rem publicam."[1]

The old South Boston Aquarium stands
in a Sahara of snow now. Its broken windows are boarded.
The bronze weathervane cod has lost half its scales.
The airy tanks are dry.

5 Once my nose crawled like a snail on the glass;
my hand tingled
to burst the bubbles
drifting from the noses of the cowed, compliant fish.

My hand draws back. I often sigh still
10 for the dark downward and vegetating kingdom
of the fish and reptile. One morning last March,
I pressed against the new barbed and galvanized

fence on the Boston Common. Behind their cage,
yellow dinosaur steamshovels were grunting
15 as they cropped up tons of mush and grass
to gouge their underworld garage.

Parking spaces luxuriate like civic
sandpiles in the heart of Boston.
A girdle of orange, Puritan-pumpkin colored girders
20 braces the tingling Statehouse,

shaking over the excavations, as it faces Colonel Shaw
and his bell-cheeked Negro infantry
on St. Gauden's shaking Civil War relief,
propped by a plant splint against the garage's earthquake.

25 Two months after marching through Boston,
half the regiment was dead;
at the dedication,
William James[2] could almost hear the bronze Negroes breathe.

---

[1] "They gave up everything to preserve the Republic." A monument in Boston Common bears a similar form of this quotation. Designed by Augustus Saint-Gaudens, the monument is dedicated to Colonel Robert Gould Shaw and the African-American troops he commanded during a Civil War battle at Fort Wagner, South Carolina, on July 18, 1863.

[2] Harvard psychologist and philosopher (1842–1910).

Their monument sticks like a fishbone
30 in the city's throat.
Its Colonel is as lean
as a compass-needle.

He has an angry wrenlike vigilance,
a greyhound's gentle tautness;
35 he seems to wince at pleasure,
and suffocate for privacy.

He is out of bounds now. He rejoices in man's lovely,
peculiar power to choose life and death—
when he leads his black soldiers to death,
40 he cannot bend his back.

On a thousand small town New England greens,
the old white churches hold their air
of sparse, sincere rebellion; frayed flags
quilt the graveyards of the Grand Army of the Republic.

45 The stone statues of the abstract Union Soldier
grow slimmer and younger each year—
wasp-waisted, they doze over muskets
and muse through their sideburns . . .

Shaw's father wanted no monument
50 except the ditch,
where his son's body was thrown
and lost with his "niggers."

The ditch is nearer.
There are no statues for the last war here;
55 on Boylston Street, a commercial photograph
shows Hiroshima boiling

over a Mosler Safe,[3] the "Rock of Ages"
that survived the blast. Space is nearer.
When I crouch to my television set,
60 the drained faces of Negro school-children rise like balloons.

Colonel Shaw
is riding on his bubble,
he waits
for the blessed break.

---

[3] A brand of safe known for being especially strong.

65 The Aquarium is gone. Everywhere,
  giant finned cars nose forward like fish;
  a savage servility
  slides by on grease.

◊ ◊ ◊

DENISE LEVERTOV
(1923–1997)

What Were They Like?
(1966)

1) Did the people of Viet Nam
   use lanterns of stone?
2) Did they hold ceremonies
   to reverence the opening of buds?
5 3) Were they inclined to rippling laughter?
4) Did they use bone and ivory,
   jade and silver, for ornament?
5) Had they an epic poem?
6) Did they distinguish between speech and singing?

10 1) Sir, their light hearts turned to stone.
   It is not remembered whether in gardens
   stone lanterns illumined pleasant ways.
2) Perhaps they gathered once to delight in blossom,
   but after the children were killed
15 there were no more buds.
3) Sir, laughter is bitter to the burned mouth.
4) A dream ago, perhaps. Ornament is for joy.
   All the bones were charred.
5) It is not remembered. Remember,
20 most were peasants; their life
   was in rice and bamboo.
   When peaceful clouds were reflected in the paddies
   and the water buffalo stepped surely along terraces,
   maybe fathers told their sons old tales.
25 When bombs smashed the mirrors
   there was time only to scream.
6) There is an echo yet, it is said,
   of their speech which was like a song.
   It is reported their singing resembled
30 the flight of moths in moonlight.
   Who can say? It is silent now.

◊ ◊ ◊

ANDREW SUKNASKI
(1942–   )

The Bitter Word
(1976)

from fort walsh
colonel irvine brings the bitter word
to sitting bull at wood mountain
makes clear the government welcomes the teton—
5 yet they must not expect provisions
or food from canada

sitting bull proudly replies:
when did i ever ask you for provisions?
before I beg
10 *i will cut willows for my young men to use*
while killing mice to survive

in the spring of 1881
sitting bull gathers his remaining 1200 sioux
and treks to fort qu'appelle to make
15 the final request for a reservation—
inspector sam steele tells them
the great white mother wishes them to return
to their own country
(a rather curious view of a people
20 whose meaning of country changes with
the migrations of tatanka)[1]
steele politely refuses the request
and supplies enough provisions for the return
to wood mountain
25 death by summer is certain
while irvine makes sure
provisions and seed never arrive
seeing the migrating game
sitting bull knew the tatanka
30 would never return
though his people dreamed of white tatanka rising
from the subterranean meadows others fled to
(hideous shrieks of red river carts grating in
their ears)
35 he must have sensed the hunger to follow
which was exactly what the authorities hoped for
on both sides of the border

---

[1] A Lakota-Nakota (Sioux) word meaning "god-animal" and referring to the buffalo.

◆ ◆ ◆

BORIS SLUTSKY[1]

How Did They Kill
My Grandmother?

Translated by Elaine Feinstein

How did they kill my grandmother?
I'll tell you how they killed her.
One morning a tank rolled up to
a building where
5 the hundred and fifty Jews of our town who,
weightless
       from a year's starvation,
and white
       with the knowledge of death,
10 were gathered holding their bundles.
And the German polizei[2] were
herding the old people briskly;
and their tin mugs clanked as
the young men led them away
15   far away.

But my small grandmother
my seventy-year-old grandmother
began to curse and
scream at the Germans;
20 shouting that I was a soldier.
She yelled at them: My grandson
is off at the front fighting!
Don't you dare
touch me!
25 Listen, you
      can hear our guns!

Even as she went off, my grandmother
cried abuse,
      starting all over again
30 with her curses.
From every window then
Ivanovnas and Andreyevnas
Sidorovnas and Petrovnas
sobbed: You tell them, Polina

---

[1] Birth date of author and publication date of poem are not available.
[2] Police.

35 Matveyevna, keep it up!
They all yelled together:
   "What can we do against
this enemy, the Hun?"
Which was why the Germans chose
40 to kill her inside the town.

A bullet struck her hair
and kicked her grey plait down.
My grandmother fell to the ground.
That is how she died there.

◇   ◇   ◇

BILLY JOEL
(1949–)

Goodnight Saigon
(1982)

We met as soul mates
On Parris Island
We left as inmates
From an asylum
5 And we were sharp
As sharp as knives
And we were so gung ho
To lay down our lives
We came in spastic
10 Like tameless horses
We left in plastic
As numbered corpses
And we learned fast
To travel light
15 Our arms were heavy
But our bellies were tight
We had no home front
We had no soft soap
They sent us Playboy
20 They gave us Bob Hope
We dug in deep
And shot on sight
And prayed to Jesus Christ
With all our might
25 We had no cameras
To shoot the landscape
We passed the hash pipe

And played our Doors tapes
And it was dark
30 So dark at night
And we held on to each other
Like brother to brother
We promised our mothers we'd write
And we would all go down together
35 We said we'd all go down together
Remember Charlie
Remember Baker
They left their childhood
On every acre
40 And who was wrong?
And who was right?
It didn't matter in the thick of the fight
We held the day
In the palm
45 Of our hand
They ruled the night
And the night
Seemed to last as long as six weeks
On Parris Island
50 We held the coastline
They held the highlands
And they were sharp
As sharp as knives
They heard the hum of our motors
55 They counted the rotors
And waited for us to arrive
And we would all go down together
We said we'd all go down together
Yes we would all go down together

❖ ❖ ❖

YUSEF KOMUNYAKAA
(1947–   )

Facing It
(1988)

My black face fades,
hiding inside the black granite.
I said I wouldn't,
dammit: No tears.
5 I'm stone. I'm flesh.
My clouded reflection eyes me

like a bird of prey, the profile of night
slanted against morning. I turn
this way—the stone lets me go.
10 I turn that way—I'm inside
the Vietnam Veterans Memorial
again, depending on the light
to make a difference.
I go down the 58,022 names,
15 half-expecting to find
my own in letters like smoke.
I touch the name Andrew Johnson;
I see the booby trap's white flash.
Names shimmer on a woman's blouse
20 but when she walks away
the names stay on the wall.
Brushstrokes flash, a red bird's
wings cutting across my stare.
The sky. A plane in the sky.
25 A white vet's images floats
closer to me, then his pale eyes
look through mine. I'm a window.
He's lost his right arm
inside the stone. In the black mirror
30 a woman's trying to erase names:
No, she's brushing a boy's hair.

Reading and Reacting: Poems about War

1. What is each speaker's attitude toward war?
2. What conventional images does each poem use to express its ideas about war?
3. Do any of the poems use unusual, unexpected, or shocking images?
4. How would you describe each poem's tone? Angry? Cynical? Sad? Disillusioned? Resigned?
5. What does each poem reveal about the speaker?
6. What is the central theme of each poem?

Related Works: "The Things They Carried" (p. 280), "The Man He Killed" (p. 736), "Patterns" (p. 737), "The Death of the Ball Turret Gunner" (p. 814), "Naming of Parts" (p. 984)

CHAPTER 12

Reading and Writing about Poetry

READING POETRY

◊ ◊ ◊

Sometimes readers approach poetry purely for pleasure. At other times, reading a poem is the first step toward writing about it. The following guidelines, which focus on issues discussed elsewhere in this section of the text, may help direct your reading.

◊ Rephrase the poem in your own words. What does your paraphrase reveal about the poem's subject and central concerns? What is lost or gained in your paraphrase of the poem?

◊ Consider the poem's **voice.** Who is the poem's persona or speaker? How would you characterize the poem's tone? Is the poem ironic? (See Chapter 13.)

◊ Study the poem's **diction** and look up unfamiliar words in a dictionary. How does word choice affect your reaction to the poem? What do the connotations of words reveal about the poem? What level of diction is used? Is dialect used? Is word order unusual or unexpected? How does the arrangement of words contribute to your understanding of the poem? (See Chapter 14.)

◊ Examine the poem's **imagery.** What kind of imagery predominates? What specific images are used? Is a pattern of imagery present? How does imagery enrich the poem? (See Chapter 15.)

◊ Identify the poem's **figures of speech.** Does the poet use metaphor? Simile? Personification? Hyperbole? Understatement?

Metonymy or synecdoche? Apostrophe? How do figures of speech affect your reading of the poem? (See Chapter 16.)

◇ Listen to the **sound** of the poem. Are rhythm and meter regular or irregular? How do rhythm and meter reinforce the poem's central concerns? Does the poem use alliteration? Assonance? Rhyme? How do these elements enhance the poem? (See Chapter 17.)

◇ Look at the poem's **form.** Is the poem written in closed or open form? Is the poem constructed as a sonnet? A sestina? A villanelle? An epigram? A haiku? Is the poem an example of concrete poetry? How does the poem's form reinforce its ideas? (See Chapter 18.)

◇ Consider the poem's use of **symbol, allegory, allusion,** or **myth.** Does the poem make use of symbols? Allusions? How do symbols or allusions support its theme? Is the poem an allegory? Does the poem retell or interpret a myth? (See Chapter 19.)

◇ Identify the poem's **theme.** What central theme or themes does the poem explore? How are the themes expressed? (See Chapter 11.)

ACTIVE READING

When you approach a poem that you plan to write about, you engage in the same active reading strategies you use when you read a short story or a play. When you finish recording your reactions to the poem, you focus on a topic, develop ideas about that topic, decide on a thesis, prepare an outline, and draft and revise your essay.

Catherine Whittaker, a student in an introduction to literature course, was asked to write a three- to five-page essay comparing any two of the seven poems about parents that appear in Chapter 11 (pp. 677–82). Her instructor told the class that the essay should reflect students' own reactions to the poems, not the opinions of literary critics. As Catherine planned and wrote her paper, she was guided by the process described in Chapter 2, "Reading and Writing about Literature."

Previewing

Catherine began her work by previewing the poems, eliminating those she considered obscure or difficult and those whose portrait of the speaker's parent did not seem sympathetic.

This process helped Catherine to narrow down her choices. As she looked through "Those Winter Sundays," she was struck by words in the opening lines ("Sundays too [. . .]"; "blueblack cold"). She had the same re-action to "The squat pen rests; snug as a gun" in line 2 of "Digging." In each case, the words made Catherine want to examine the poem further.

She noticed too that both poems were divided into stanzas of varying lengths and that both focused on fathers. Keeping these features in mind, Catherine began a close reading of each poem.

Highlighting and Annotating

As Catherine read and reread "Those Winter Sundays" and "Digging," she recorded her comments and questions. The highlighted and annotated poems follow.

◇ ◇ ◇

ROBERT HAYDEN
(1913–1980)

Those Winter Sundays
(1962)

Were there many Sundays like these? ←

Sundays [too] my father got up early — *Like all other days of the week?*

and put his clothes on in the blueblack cold, *Why did he get up before dawn?*

then with cracked hands that ached

from labor in the weekday weather made *What kind of job did the father have?*

5   banked fires blaze. No one ever thanked him. ↳ *Was there a large family?*

I'd wake and hear the cold splintering, breaking.

When the rooms were warm, he'd call,

and slowly I would rise and dress,

fearing the chronic angers of that house, ↳ *Were there problems in the family?*

10   Speaking indifferently to him,

who had driven out the cold

and polished my good shoes as well. *Was there a mother around?*

What did I know, what did I know

of love's austere and lonely offices? → *offices = duties or functions assigned to someone*

austere = without adornment or ornamentation, simple, bare — simple without luxury, harsh

◆ ◆ ◆

SEAMUS HEANEY
(1939–   )

Digging
(1966)

Between my finger and my thumb

The squat pen rests; snug as a gun.

[handwritten: gun = snug?]

[handwritten: Why a "squat" pen?]

Under my window, a clean rasping sound

When the spade sinks into gravelly ground:

5   My father, digging. I look down

Till his straining rump among the flowerbeds

Bends low, comes up twenty years away

[handwritten: Is he thinking about the past?]

Stooping in rhythm through potato drills

Where he was digging.

[handwritten: Like the poet's pen?]

10   The coarse boot nestled on the lug, the shaft

Against the inside knee was levered firmly.

He rooted out tall tops, buried the bright edge deep

To scatter new potatoes that we picked

[handwritten: Was this a family task?]

Loving their cool hardness in our hands.

15   By God, the old man could handle a spade.

Just like his old man.

[handwritten: Two generations could "handle a spade." Can the poet dig?]

My grandfather cut more turf in a day

Than any other man on Toner's bog.

Once I carried him milk in a bottle

20   Corked sloppily with paper. He straightened up

To drink it, then fell to right away

[handwritten: The grandfather was a hard worker.]

Nicking and slicing neatly, heaving sods   *Almost like an art of digging?*

Over his shoulder, going down and down

For the good turf. Digging.

25 The cold smell of potato mould, the squelch and slap

Of soggy peat, the curt cuts of an edge   *→ What does it make him remember?*

Through living roots awaken in my head.

But I've no spade to follow men like them.   *→ What are "men like them" like?*

Between my finger and my thumb

Same as first 2 lines { 30 The squat pen rests.   *→ Why is this repeated?*

I'll dig with it.

↳ Dig for what?

Catherine found the language of both poems appealing, and she believed her highlighting and annotating had given her some valuable insights. For example, she noticed some parallels between the two poems: both focus on the past, both portray fathers as hard workers, and neither mentions a mother.

WRITING ABOUT POETRY

◊ ◊ ◊

PLANNING AN ESSAY

Even though Catherine still had to find a specific topic for her paper, her preliminary work suggested some interesting possibilities. She was especially intrigued by the way both poems depict fathers as actively engaged in physical tasks.

Choosing a Topic

One idea Catherine thought she might want to write about was the significance of the sons' attitudes toward their fathers: although both see their fathers as hard workers, the son in "Those Winter Sundays" seems to have mixed feelings about his father's devotion to his family, whereas the son in "Digging" is more appreciative. Catherine explored this idea in the two journal entries that follow:

"Those Winter Sundays"

Why did the father get up early every morning? One could imagine that he had a large family and little money. There is no mention of a mother. Images are created of the utter coldness and "chronic angers" of the house. The father not only made fires to warm the house but also polished his child's (or children's) shoes--maybe for church. And yet, the child seems not to care about or appreciate the father's efforts. Is he too young to say thank you, or are there other problems in the house for which the child blames the father?

"Digging"

In the poem, the poet seems to be contemplating the subject about which to write when the sounds of digging capture his attention. He remembers the steady, artful rhythm of his father's digging of the potatoes and how they (probably the poet and his brothers and sisters) picked out the cool potatoes. His memories appear to be entirely appreciative of his father's and grandfather's hard work and skill. He does, however, feel regret that he is not like these dedicated men. Even though he cannot use a shovel, he hopes to use his pen in order to make his own contributions as a writer.

When Catherine reread her journal entries, she thought she was close to a specific topic for her paper. The more she reviewed the two poems, the more confident she felt exploring their similar views of the fathers' roles and their contrasting attitudes toward these fathers. (In fact, she had so many ideas that she did not feel she had to brainstorm to generate more material.) Before she could write a draft of her paper, however, Catherine needed to identify specific similarities and differences between the two poems.

Seeing Connections

Listing Catherine returned to the highlighted and annotated poems in order to compile the following lists:

Differences

"Those Winter Sundays"	"Digging"
--memories of family problems	--only happy memories are involved

--the child acts
  ambivalently toward his
  father
--atmosphere of tension

--the child admires his
  father

--atmosphere of happiness and
  togetherness

Similarities

--the fathers are hard workers
--the fathers appear to love their children
--similar time--impression that the events happened years
  ago
--children, now grown, appreciate their fathers'
  dedication
--children, now grown, are inspired by their fathers'
  determination

At this point, Catherine reviewed her notes carefully. As connections between the two poems came into focus, she was able to decide on a tentative thesis and on a possible order for her ideas.

Deciding on a Thesis

The more Catherine thought about the two poems, the more she focused on their similarities. She expressed a possible main idea for her paper in the following tentative thesis statement:

Although their family backgrounds are different, both now-
grown poets realize the determination and dedication of
their fathers and are consequently impassioned in their
writing.

Preparing an Outline

Catherine reviewed her notes to identify the specific ideas she wanted to address in her first draft. Then she arranged those ideas in a logical order in a scratch outline:

"Those Winter Sundays"
    Poet reflects back on childhood
        --father's hard work
        --his misunderstanding and lack of appreciation
          for everything his father did

Family setting in childhood
    --tension in the house
    --no mother mentioned in the poem
Poet's realization of father's love and dedication

"Digging"

    Poet reminisces
        --father's skill and hard work
        --grandfather's steady heaving of sods
        --children's participation and acceptance
    Happiness of the family

    The desire for the poet to continue the tradition

DRAFTING AN ESSAY

With a thesis statement and scratch outline to guide her, Catherine wrote the following first draft of her essay. Her instructor's comments appear in the margins and at the end of the paper.

(first draft)

A Comparison of Two Poems about Fathers

Robert Hayden's "Those Winter Sundays" and "Digging" by Seamus Heaney are poems that were inspired by fathers and composed as tributes to fathers. Although their family backgrounds are different, both now-grown poets realize the determination and dedication of their fathers and are consequently impassioned in their writing.

In "Those Winter Sundays," Hayden reflects back on his childhood. He remembers the many Sundays when his father got up early to start the fires to make the house warm for his children's awakening. The poet pictures his father's hands made rough by his weekday work. These same hands not only made the fires on Sunday but also polished his son's good shoes, in preparation, no doubt, for church.

Hayden also quite clearly remembers that his father was never thanked for his work. The reader imagines that the father had many children and may have been poor. There were inner tensions in the house and, quite noticeably, there is no mention of a mother.

Looking back, the poet now realizes the love and dedication with which his father took care of the family. As a child, he never thanked his father, but now, as an adult, the poet seems to appreciate the simple kindness of his father.

In a similar sense, Seamus Heaney writes "Digging" as a tribute to his father and grandfather. He also reminisces about his father and remembers with clarity the skill with which his father dug potatoes. The grandfather too is remembered, as is his technique

Careful! You're confusing poet and speaker.

Good detail— but quotations would be helpful.

Here two quotations from the poem would strengthen your discussion.

add line number in parentheses; →

for "heaving sods." There is an atmosphere of happiness in this poem. With the children helping the father harvest the potatoes, a sense of family togetherness is created. The reader feels that this family is a hard-working, but nevertheless happy, one.

As the poet reminisces about his childhood, he realizes that, unlike his father and grandfather, he will never be a master of digging or a person who uses physical strength to earn a living. He wishes to be like his father before him, desiring to accomplish and contribute. However, for the poet, any "digging" to be done will be by his pen, in the form of literature.

To conclude, the fathers in these poets' pasts inspire them to write. An appreciation for their fathers' dedication is achieved only after the children mature into adults. It is then that the fathers' impact on their children's lives is realized for its true importance.

Good start! When you revise, focus on the following:
– Edit use of "poet" and "speaker" carefully. You can't assume that these poems reflect the poets' own lives or attitudes toward their fathers.
– Add more specific references to the poems, particularly quotations. (Don't forget to give line numbers.)
– Consider adding brief references to other poems about parents. (Check the text.)
– Consider rearranging your material into a point-by-point comparison, which will make the specific points of similarity and differences clearer.
Let's discuss this draft in a conference.

First Draft: Commentary

After submitting her first draft, Catherine met with her instructor. Together, they reviewed not only her first draft but also her annotations, journal entries, lists of similarities and differences, and scratch outline. During the conference, her instructor explained his marginal comments and, building on Catherine's own ideas, helped her develop a plan for revision.

Catherine's instructor agreed that the poems' similarities were worth exploring in detail. He thought, however, that her references to the poems' language and ideas needed to be much more specific and that her paper's structure—discussing "Those Winter Sundays" first and then moving on to consider "Digging"—made the specific similarities between the two poems difficult to see.

Because the class had studied other poems in which speakers try to resolve their ambivalent feelings toward their parents, Catherine's instructor also suggested that she mention these poems to provide a wider context for her ideas. Finally, he explained the difference between the perspective of the poet and that of the **speaker,** a persona the poet creates, encouraging her to edit with this difference in mind.

As she reexamined her ideas in light of her discussion with her instructor, Catherine looked again at both the annotated poems and her notes about them. She then recorded her thoughts about her progress in an additional journal entry:

> After reviewing the poems again and talking to Professor Jackson, I discovered some additional points that I want to include in my next draft. The connection between the poet's pen and the shovel is evident in "Digging," and so is the link between the cold and the tensions in the house in "Those Winter Sundays." The tone of each poem should also be discussed. Specifically, I think that the poet's choice of <u>austere</u> in "Those Winter Sundays" has significance and should be included. In my next draft, I'll expand my first draft--hopefully, without reading into the poems too much. I also need to reorganize my ideas so parallels between the two poems will be clearer.

Because this journal entry suggested a new arrangement for her ideas, Catherine prepared a new scratch outline to guide her revision:

> Reflections on their fathers
>> Both poems
>>> --fathers' dedication and hard work

Family similarities and differences
　　"Digging"
　　　　--loving and caring
　　"Those Winter Sundays"
　　　　--family problems (tone of the poem)
Lessons learned from father
　　"Digging"
　　　　--inspiration (images of pen and shovel)
　　　　--realization of father's inner strength
　　"Those Winter Sundays"
　　　　--realization of father's inner strength
　　　　--"austere" caring (images of cold)
Brief discussion of other poems about fathers

Revising and Editing an Essay

After once again reviewing all the material she had accumulated, Catherine wrote a second draft.

(second draft)

A Comparison of Two Poems about Fathers

Robert Hayden's "Those Winter Sundays" and Seamus Heaney's "Digging" are two literary pieces that are tributes to the speakers' fathers. The inspiration and admiration the speakers feel are evident in each poem. Although the nature of the two family relationships may differ, the common thread of the love of fathers for their children weaves through each poem.

Reflections on one's childhood can bring assorted memories to light. Presumably, the speakers are now adults and reminisce on their childhood with a mature sense of enlightenment not found in childhood. Both speakers describe their fathers' hard work and dedication to their families. Hayden's speaker remembers that even after working hard all week, his father would get up early on Sunday to warm the house in preparation for his children's rising. The speaker vividly portrays his father's hands, describing "cracked hands that ached from labor in the weekday weather" (3–4). And yet, these same hands not only built the fires that drove out the cold but also polished his children's good shoes.

In a similar way, Heaney's speaker reminisces about his father's and grandfather's digging of soil and sod, elaborating on their skill and dedication to their task.

The fathers in these poems appear to be the hardest of workers, laborers who sought to support their families. Not only did they have a dedication to their work, but they also cared about and undoubtedly loved their children. Looking back, Hayden's speaker realizes that, although his childhood may not have been perfect nor his family life entirely without problems, his father loved him. Heaney's description of the potato picking makes us imagine a loving family led by a father and grandfather who worked together and included the children in both work and celebration. Heaney's speaker grows to become a man who has nothing but respect for his father and grandfather, wishing to be like them and somehow follow their greatness.

Although some similarities exist between the sons and fathers in the poems, the family life differs between the two. Perhaps it is the tone of the poems that best typifies the family atmosphere. The tone of "Digging" is wholesome, earthy, natural, and happy, emphasizing the healthy and caring nature of the poet's childhood. In reminiscing, Heaney's speaker seems to have no bad memories concerning his father or family. In contrast, the tone of Hayden's poem is very much like the coldness of the Sunday mornings. Even though the father warmed the house, the "chronic angers of that house" (9) did not leave with the cold. The speaker, as a child, seems full of resentment toward the father, no doubt blaming him for the family problems. (Curiously, it is the father and not the mother who polishes the children's good shoes. Was there no mother?) The reader senses that the father-son communication evident in Heaney's family is missing in Hayden's.

There are many other poets who have written about their fathers. Simon J. Ortiz in "My Father's Song" writes a touching tribute to his father, who taught him to respect and care for the lives of animals and to appreciate earthly wonders. In other poems, such as Theodore Roethke's "My Papa's Waltz" and Colleen J. McElroy's "My Father's Wars," the fathers are depicted as imperfect, vulnerable people who try to cope with life as well as possible.

"Digging" and "Those Winter Sundays" are poems written from the inspirations of sons, admiring and appreciating their fathers. Childhood memories act not only as images of the past but also as aids for the speakers' self-realization and enlightenment. Even after childhood, the fathers' influence over their sons is evident; only now do the speakers appreciate its true importance.

Second Draft: Commentary

When she reread her second draft, Catherine thought she had accomplished some of what she had set out to do. She had, for example, tightened her thesis statement, rearranged her discussion, added specific details, and changed *poet* to *speaker* where necessary. However, she still was not satisfied with her analysis of the poem's language and tone (she had not, for example, considered the importance of the word *austere* or examined the significance of Heaney's equation of *spade* and *pen*). She also thought that the material in paragraph 5 about other poems, although interesting, was distracting, so she decided to try to relocate it. Finally, she planned to edit and proofread carefully as she prepared her final draft.

Whittaker 1

Catherine Whittaker
Professor Jackson
English 102
5 March 2000

Digging for Memories

Robert Hayden's "Those Winter Sundays" and Seamus Heaney's "Digging" are two literary pieces that
are tributes to the speakers' fathers. Although the
depiction of the families and the tones of the two
poems are different, the common thread of love between
fathers and children extends through the two poems,
and each speaker is inspired by his father's example.

Many other poets have written about children and
their fathers. Simon J. Ortiz in "My Father's Song"
writes a touching tribute to a father who taught the
speaker to respect and care for the lives of animals
and to appreciate earthly wonders. In other poems,
such as Theodore Roethke's "My Papa's Waltz" and
Colleen J. McElroy's "My Father's Wars," fathers are
depicted as imperfect, vulnerable people who try to
cope with life as well as possible.

As all these poems reveal, reflections on childhood can bring complex memories to light, as they do
for Hayden's and Heaney's speakers. Now adults, they
reminisce about their childhoods with a mature sense
of enlightenment not found in childhood. Both speakers
describe their fathers' hard work and dedication to
their families. Hayden's speaker remembers that even
after working hard all week, his father would get up
early on Sunday to warm the house in preparation for

*Thesis
statement*

*¶ 5 from
second draft
has been
relocated.
References to
poems in
Chapter 11 of
this text
include
complete
authors'
names and
titles.*

his sleeping children. The speaker vividly portrays his father's hands, describing "cracked hands that ached from labor in the weekday weather" (3-4). And yet, these same hands not only built the fires that drove out the cold, but also polished his children's good shoes. In a similar way, Heaney's speaker reminisces about his father's and grandfather's digging of soil and sod, pointing out their skill and their dedication to their tasks.

The fathers in these poems appear to be hard workers, laborers who struggled to support their families. Not only were they dedicated to their work, but they also loved their children. Looking back, Hayden's speaker realizes that, although his childhood may not have been perfect and his family life was not entirely without problems, his father loved him. Heaney's description of the potato picking makes us imagine a loving family led by a father and grandfather who worked together and included the children in both work and celebration. Heaney's speaker grows into a man who has nothing but respect for his father and grandfather, wishing to be like them and to somehow fill their shoes.

Although some similarities exist between the sons and fathers in the poems, the family life the two poems depict is very different. Perhaps it is the tone of the poems that best reveals the family atmosphere. The tone of "Digging" is wholesome, earthy, natural, and happy, emphasizing the healthy and caring nature of the speaker's childhood. Heaney's speaker seems to

Parenthetical reference cites line numbers.

Whittaker 3

have no bad memories of his father or family. In contrast, the tone of Hayden's poem is very much like the
coldness of the Sunday mornings. Even though the father warmed the house, the "chronic angers of that
house" (9) did not leave with the cold. The speaker, as
a child, seems to have resented his father, no doubt
blaming him for the family's problems. The reader
senses that the warm relationship between the father
and the son in Heaney's poem is absent in Hayden's.

In spite of these differences, the reader cannot
go away from either poem without the impression that
both speakers learned important lessons from their fathers. Both fathers had a great amount of inner
strength and dedication to their families. As the
years pass, Hayden's speaker has come to realize the
depth of his father's devotion to his family. He uses
the image of the "blueblack cold" (2) that was splintered and broken by the fires lovingly prepared by his
father to suggest the father's efforts to keep his
family free from harm. The cold suggests the tensions
of the family that the father is determined to force
out of the house through his "austere and lonely offices" (14).

In Heaney's poem, the father and grandfather also
had a profound impact on the young speaker. As the
memories come pouring back, the speaker's admiration
for the men who came before him forces him to reflect
on his own life and work. He realizes that he will
never have the ability (or the desire) to do the physical labor of his relatives: "I've no spade to follow

> Topic
> sentence
> stresses
> paper's
> emphasis on
> similarities.

men like them" (28). However, just as the spade was the tool of his father and grandfather, the pen will be the tool with which the speaker will work. The shovel suggests the hard work, effort, and determination of the men who came before him, and the pen is the literary equivalent of the shovel. Heaney's speaker has been inspired by his father and grandfather and hopes to accomplish with a pen in the world of literature what they accomplished with a shovel on the land.

Conclusion reinforces thesis.

"Digging" and "Those Winter Sundays" are poems written from the perspective of sons, admiring and appreciating their fathers. Childhood memories not only act as images of the past but also evoke the speakers' self-realization and enlightenment. Even after childhood, the fathers' influence over their sons is evident; only now, however, do the speakers appreciate its true importance.

Final Draft: Commentary

As she wrote her final draft, Catherine expanded her analysis, looking more closely at the language and tone of the two poems. To support and clarify her points, she added more direct quotations, taking care to reproduce words and punctuation marks accurately and to cite line numbers in parentheses after each quotation. (Because all the students in Catherine's class had to select poems from Chapter 11 of this anthology, their instructor did not require a Works Cited page.) She also moved her discussion of other poems to paragraph 2, where it provides a smooth transition from her introduction to her discussion of Hayden and Heaney.

Chapter 13

Voice

◇ ◇ ◇

What makes a poem significant? What makes it memorable? Passion and thought, emotionally charged language, fresh imagery, surprising use of metaphor [. . .] yes. But also, I think, the very sure sense that the moment we enter the world of the poem we are participating in another episode of the myth-journey of humankind; that a voice has taken up the tale once more. The individual experience as related or presented in the poem renews our deep, implicit faith in that greater experience. A poem remains with us to the extent that it allows us to feel that we are listening to a voice at once contemporary and ancient. This makes all the difference.

JOHN HAINES, "The Hole in the Bucket"

I have been ruminating about "personal poems"—I am inclined to agree that one turns back to less personal poems yet you surely would not remove Shakespeare's sonnets, all of Donne, much of Yeats, all of Emily Dickinson, Sappho, Millay, Wylie (or most), Wyatt from the canon, would you? The trouble is that one does not choose what one is to write about: poetry is a seizure, and not done on will. The point is I think that a "personal" poem has to go deep enough to touch the *universal:* the "I" is only a device like any other. This is not to argue—as I agree that it would be better if the muse provided more *less* personal poems.

MAY SARTON, "Among the Visual Days"

Someone writing a poem believes in a reader, in readers, of that poem. The "who" of that reader quivers like a jellyfish. Self-reference is always possible: that my "I" is a universal "we," that the reader is my clone. That sending letters to myself is enough for attention to be paid. That my chip of mirror contains the world.

But most often someone writing a poem believes in, depends on, a delicate, vibrating range of difference, that an "I" can become a "we" without extinguishing others, that a partly common language exists to which strangers can bring their own heartbeat, memories, images. A language that itself has learned from the heartbeat, memories, images of strangers.

ADRIENNE RICH, *What Is Found There*

◇ ◇ ◇

◊ ◊ ◊
EMILY DICKINSON
(1830–1886)

I'm Nobody! Who Are You?
(1891)

I'm Nobody! Who are you?
Are you—Nobody—Too?
Then there's a pair of us?
Don't tell! they'd advertise—you know!

5 How dreary—to be—Somebody!
How public—like a Frog—
To tell one's name—the livelong June—
To an admiring Bog!

THE SPEAKER IN THE POEM
◊ ◊ ◊

In fiction, the author's careful choice and arrangement of words enable readers to form an impression of the narrator and to decide whether he or she is sophisticated or unsophisticated, trustworthy or untrustworthy, innocent or experienced. Like fiction, poetry depends on a **speaker** who describes events, feelings, and ideas to readers. Finding out as much as possible about this speaker can help readers to interpret the poem. For example, the speaker in Emily Dickinson's "I'm Nobody! Who Are You?" seems at once shy and playful. The first stanza of the poem suggests that the speaker is a private person, perhaps with little self-esteem. As the poem continues, however, the voice becomes almost defiant. In a sense, the speaker's two voices represent two ways of relating to the world. The first voice expresses the private self—internal, isolated, and revealed through poetry; the second expresses the public self—external, self-centered, and inevitably superficial. Far from being defeated by shyness, the speaker claims to have chosen her status as "nobody."

One question readers might ask about "I'm Nobody! Who Are You?" is how close the speaker's voice is to the poet's. Readers who conclude that the poem is about the conflict between a poet's public and private responsibilities may be tempted to see the speaker and the poet as one. But this is not necessarily the case. Like the narrator of a short story, the speaker of a poem is a **persona,** or mask, that the poet assumes. Granted, in some poems little distance exists between the poet and the speaker. Without hard evidence to support a link between speaker and poet, however, readers should not assume they are one and the same.

In most cases, the speaker is quite different from the poet. And even when the speaker's voice conveys the attitude of the poet, it may do so only indirectly. In "The Chimney Sweeper" (p. 928), for example, William Blake assumes the voice of a child to criticize the system of child labor that existed in eighteenth-century England. Even though the child speaker does not understand the conditions that cause his misery, readers sense the poet's anger as the trusting speaker describes the conditions under which he works. The poet's indignation is especially apparent in the biting irony of the last line, in which the victimized speaker innocently assures readers that if all people do their duty, "they need not fear harm."

Sometimes the poem's speaker is anonymous. In this case—as in William Carlos Williams's "Red Wheelbarrow" (p. 794), for instance— the first-person voice is absent and the speaker remains outside the poem. At other times, the speaker has a set identity—a king, a beggar, a high-wayman, a sheriff, a husband, a wife, a rich man, a chimney sweep, a child, a mythical figure, an explorer, a teacher, a faithless lover, a saint, or even a flower, an animal, or a clod of earth. Whatever the case, the speaker is not the poet, but rather a creation that the poet uses to convey his or her ideas. (For this reason, poems by a single poet may have very different voices. See Sylvia Plath's "Daddy" [p. 818] and "Morning Song" [p. 742], for example.)

In the following poem, the poet assumes the mask of a fictional character, Gretel from the fairy tale "Hansel and Gretel."

◆ ◆ ◆

LOUISE GLÜCK
(1943–)

Gretel in Darkness
(1971)

This is the world we wanted. All who would have seen us dead
Are dead. I hear the witch's cry
Break in the moonlight through a sheet of sugar: God rewards.
Her tongue shrivels into gas. . . .

5   Now, far from women's arms
And memory of women, in our father's hut
We sleep, are never hungry.
Why do I not forget?
My father bars the door, bars harm
10 From this house, and it is years.

No one remembers. Even you, my brother.
Summer afternoons you look at me as though you meant
To leave, as though it never happened. But I killed for you.
I see armed firs, the spires of that gleaming kiln come back, come
    back—

15 Nights I turn to you to hold me but you are not there.
   Am I alone? Spies
   Hiss in the stillness, Hansel we are there still, and it is real, real,
   That black forest, and the fire in earnest.

The speaker in this poem comments on her life after her encounter with the witch in the forest. Speaking to her brother, Gretel observes that they now live in the world they wanted: they live with their father in his hut, and the witch and the wicked stepmother are dead. Even so, the memory of the events in the forest haunt Gretel and make it impossible for her to live "happily ever after." The "armed firs," the "gleaming kiln," and "the black forest" break through the "sheet of sugar" that her life has become.

By assuming the persona of Gretel, Glück is able to convey some interesting and complex ideas. On one level, Gretel represents any person who has lived through a traumatic experience. Memories of the event keep breaking through into the present, frustrating her attempts to reestablish her belief in the goodness of the world. The voice we hear is sad, alone, and frightened: "Nights I turn to you to hold me," she says, "but you are not there." Although the murder Gretel committed for her brother was justified, it seems to haunt her. "No one remembers," laments Gretel, not even her brother. At some level, she realizes that by killing the witch she has killed a part of herself, perhaps the part of women that men fear and consequently transform into witches and wicked stepmothers. The world that is left after the killing is the father's and the brother's, not hers, and she is now alone in a dark world haunted by the memories of the black forest. In this sense, Gretel—"Now, far from women's arms / And memory of women"—may be the voice of all victimized women who, because of men, act against their own best interests—and regret it.

As "Gretel in Darkness" illustrates, a title can identify a poem's speaker, but the speaker's own words can provide much more information. This is the case in the following poem, where Spanish words help to establish the poem's frame of reference and to characterize the speaker.

◊ ◊ ◊

LEONARD ADAMÉ
(1947–   )

My Grandmother Would Rock Quietly and Hum
(1973)

in her house
she would rock quietly and hum

until her swelled hands
calmed

5 in summer
she wore thick stockings
sweaters
and grey braids

(when "el cheque"[1] came
10 we went to Payless
and I laughed greedily
when given a quarter)

mornings,
sunlight barely lit
15 the kitchen
and where
there were shadows
it was not cold

she quietly rolled
20 flour tortillas—
the "papas"[2]
cracking in hot lard
would wake me

she had lost her teeth
25 and when we ate
she had bread
soaked in "café"[3]

always her eyes
were clear
30 and she could see
as I cannot yet see—
through her eyes
she gave me herself

she would sit
35 and talk
of her girlhood—
of things strange to me:
    México
    epidemics

---

[1] The check.
[2] Potatoes.
[3] Coffee.

40   relatives shot
     her father's hopes
     of this country—
     how they sank
     with cement dust
45   to his insides

     now
     when I go
     to the old house
     the worn spots
50   by the stove
     echo of her shuffling
     and
     México
     still hangs in her
55   fading
     calendar pictures

In this poem, the speaker is an adult recalling childhood memories of his grandmother. Spanish words—*el cheque, tortillas, papas,* and *café*—identify the speaker as Latino. His easy use of English, his comment that talk of Mexico is strange to him, and his observation that he cannot yet see through his grandmother's eyes suggest, however, that he is not in touch with his ethnic identity. At one level, the grandmother evokes nostalgic memories of the speaker's youth. At another level, she is a living symbol of his ties with Mexico, connecting him to the ethnic culture he is trying to recover. The poem ends on an ambivalent note: even though the speaker is able to return to "the old house," the pictures of Mexico are fading, perhaps suggesting the speaker's assimilation into mainstream American culture.

Direct statements by the speaker can also help to characterize him. In the poem that follows, the first line of each stanza establishes the identity of the speaker—and defines his perspective.

◊ ◊ ◊

LANGSTON HUGHES
(1902–1967)

Negro
(1926)

I am a Negro:
    Black as the night is black,
    Black like the depths of my Africa.

I've been a slave:
5   Caesar told me to keep his door-steps clean.
I brushed the boots of Washington.

I've been a worker:
Under my hand the pyramids arose.
I made mortar for the Woolworth Building.

10 I've been a singer:
All the way from Africa to Georgia
I carried my sorrow songs.
I made ragtime.

I've been a victim:
15   The Belgians cut off my hands in the Congo.
They lynch me still in Mississippi.

I am a Negro:
Black as the night is black,
Black like the depths of my Africa.

Here the speaker, identifying himself as "a Negro," assumes each of the roles African-Americans have historically played in Western society—slave, worker, singer, and victim. By so doing, he gives voice to his ancestors who, by being forced to serve others, were deprived of their identities. By presenting not just their suffering, but also their accomplishments, the speaker asserts his pride in being black. The speaker also implies that the suffering of black people has been caused by economic exploitation: Romans, Egyptians, Belgians, and Americans all used black labor to help build their societies. In this context, the speaker's implied warning is clear: except for the United States, all the societies that have exploited blacks have declined, and long after these empires have fallen, black people still endure.

In each of the preceding poems, the speaker is alone. The following poem, a **dramatic monologue,** presents a more complex situation in which the poet creates a complete dramatic scene. The speaker is developed as a character whose distinctive personality is revealed through his words as he addresses a silent listener.

◊ ◊ ◊

ROBERT BROWNING
(1812–1889)

My Last Duchess
(1842)

Ferrara

That's my last Duchess painted on the wall,
Looking as if she were alive. I call
That piece a wonder, now: Frà Pandolf's[1] hands
Worked busily a day, and there she stands.
5 Will't please you sit and look at her? I said
"Frà Pandolf" by design, for never read
Strangers like you that pictured countenance,
The depth and passion of its earnest glance,
But to myself they turned (since none puts by
10 The curtain I have drawn for you, but I)
And seemed as they would ask me, if they durst,
How such a glance came there; so, not the first
Are you to turn and ask thus. Sir, 'twas not
Her husband's presence only, called that spot
15 Of joy into the Duchess' cheek: perhaps
Frà Pandolf chanced to say "Her mantle laps
Over my lady's wrist too much," or "Paint
Must never hope to reproduce the faint
Half-flush that dies along her throat": such stuff
20 Was courtesy, she thought, and cause enough
For calling up that spot of joy. She had
A heart—how shall I say?—too soon made glad,
Too easily impressed; she liked whate'er
She looked on, and her looks went everywhere.
25 Sir, 'twas all one! My favor at her breast,
The dropping of the daylight in the West,
The bough of cherries some officious fool
Broke in the orchard for her, the white mule
She rode with round the terrace—all and each
30 Would draw from her alike the approving speech,
Or blush, at least. She thanked men—good! but thanked
Somehow—I know not how—as if she ranked
My gift of a nine-hundred-years-old name
With anybody's gift. Who'd stoop to blame

---

[1] "Brother" Pandolf, a fictive painter.

35 This sort of trifling? Even had you skill
In speech—(which I have not)—to make your will
Quite clear to such an one, and say, "Just this
Or that in you disgusts me; here you miss,
Or there exceed the mark"—and if she let
40 Herself be lessoned so, nor plainly set
Her wits to yours, forsooth, and made excuse
—E'en then would be some stooping; and I choose
Never to stoop. Oh sir, she smiled, no doubt,
Whene'er I passed her; but who passed without
45 Much the same smile? This grew; I gave commands;
Then all smiles stopped together. There she stands
As if alive. Will't please you rise? We'll meet
The company below, then. I repeat,
The Count your master's known munificence
50 Is ample warrant that no just pretense
Of mine for dowry will be disallowed;
Though his fair daughter's self, as I avowed
At starting, is my object. Nay, we'll go
Together down, sir. Notice Neptune,[2] though,
55 Taming a sea horse, thought a rarity,
Which Claus of Innsbruck[3] cast in bronze for me!

The speaker is probably Alfonso II, duke of Ferrara, Italy, whose young wife, Lucrezia, died in 1561 after only three years of marriage. Shortly after her death, the duke began negotiations to marry again. When the poem opens, the duke is showing a portrait of his late wife to an emissary of an unnamed count who is there to arrange a marriage between the duke and the count's daughter. The duke remarks that the artist, Frà Pandolf, has caught a certain look upon the duchess's face. This look aroused the jealousy of the duke, who thought that it should have been for him alone. According to the duke, the duchess's crime was to have a heart "too soon made glad," "Too easily impressed." Eventually the duke could stand the situation no longer; he "gave commands," and "all smiles stopped together."

Much of what readers learn about the duke's state of mind comes from what is implied by his words. As he discusses the painting, the duke unintentionally reveals himself to be obsessively possessive and jealous, referring to "*my* last Duchess," "*my* favor at her breast," and "*my* gift of a nine-hundred-years-old name." He keeps the portrait of his late wife well

---

[2] God of the sea.
[3] An imaginary—or unidentified—sculptor. The count of Tyrol's capital was at Innsbrück, Austria.

hidden behind a curtain that no one draws except him. His interest in the picture has little to do with the memory of his wife, however. In death, the duchess has become just what the duke always wanted her to be: a personal possession that reflects his good taste.

The listener plays a subtle but important role in the poem: his presence establishes the dramatic situation that allows the character of the duke to be revealed. The purpose of the story is to communicate to the emissary exactly what the duke expects from his prospective bride and from her father. As he speaks, the duke conveys only the information that he wants the emissary to take back to his master, the count. Although he appears vain and superficial, the duke is actually extraordinarily shrewd. Throughout the poem, he turns the conversation to his own ends and gains the advantage through flattery and false modesty. Notice, for example, that he claims he has little skill in speaking when actually he is cleverly manipulating the conversation. The success of the poem lies in the poet's ability to develop the voice of this complex character, who embodies both superficial elegance and shocking cruelty.

❖ POEMS FOR FURTHER READING: THE SPEAKER IN THE POEM

◊ ◊ ◊

LESLIE MARMON SILKO
(1948–   )

Where Mountain Lion Lay Down with Deer
(1973)

I climb the black rock mountain
   stepping from day to day
         silently.
I smell the wind for my ancestors
5   pale blue leaves
      crushed wild mountain smell.
Returning
   up the gray stone cliff
   where I descended
10   a thousand years ago.
Returning to faded black stone.
   where mountain lion lay down with deer.
It is better to stay up here
        watching wind's reflection
15   in tall yellow flowers.

The old ones who remember me are gone
     the old songs are all forgotten
and the story of my birth.
How I danced in snow-frost moonlight
20   distant stars to the end of the Earth,
How I swam away
          in freezing mountain water
          narrow mossy canyon tumbling down
           out of the mountain
25   out of the deep canyon stone
      down
        the memory
          spilling out
          into the world.

Reading and Reacting

1. Who is speaking in line 4? In line 9? Can you explain this shift?
2. From where is the speaker returning? What is she trying to recover?
3. **Journal Entry** Is it important for you to know that the poet is of Native American descent? How does this information affect your interpretation of the poem?
4. **Critical Perspective** In her 1983 essay "Answering the Deer," Native American poet and critic Paula Gunn Allen observes that the possibility of cultural extinction is a basic reality Native Americans must face. Native American women writers, says Allen, face this fact directly, but with a kind of hope:

> The sense of hope . . . comes about when one has faced ultimate disaster time and time again over the ages and has emerged . . . stronger and more certain of the endurance of the people, the spirits, and the land from which they both arise and which informs both with life. Transformation, or more directly, metamorphosis, is the oldest tribal ceremonial theme. . . . And it comes once again into use within American Indian poetry of extinction and regeneration that is ultimately the only poetry any contemporary Indian woman can write.

Does Silko's poem address the issue of cultural extinction and the possibility of regeneration or metamorphosis? How?

Related Works: "Two Kinds" (p. 594), "Windigo" (p. 915), "Nikki-Rosa" (p. 961), *Fences* (p. 1745)

◆ ◆ ◆

JANICE MIRIKITANI
(1942–   )

Suicide Note
(1987)

*. . . An Asian-American college student was reported to have jumped to her death
from her dormitory window. Her body was found two days later under a deep
cover of snow. Her suicide note contained an apology to her parents for having received less than a perfect four point grade average. . . .*

How many notes written . . .
ink smeared like birdprints in snow.

    not good enough   not pretty enough   not smart enough
dear mother and father.
5 I apologize
for disappointing you.
I've worked very hard,
        not good enough
harder, perhaps to please you.
10 If only I were a son, shoulders broad
as the sunset threading through pine,
I would see the light in my mother's
eyes, or the golden pride reflected
in my father's dream
15 of my wide, male hands worthy of work
and comfort.
I would swagger through life
muscled and bold and assured,
drawing praises to me
20 like currents in the bed of wind, virile
with confidence.
    not good enough   not strong enough   not good enough

I apologize.
Tasks do not come easily.
25 Each failure, a glacier.
Each disapproval, a bootprint.
Each disappointment,
ice above my river.
So I have worked hard.
30   not good enough
My sacrifice I will drop
bone by bone, perched

on the ledge of my womanhood,
fragile as wings.
35   not strong enough
It is snowing steadily
surely not good weather
for flying—this sparrow
sillied and dizzied by the wind
40 on the edge.
              not smart enough
I make this ledge my altar
to offer penance.
This air will not hold me,
45 the snow burdens my crippled wings,
my tears drop like bitter cloth
softly into the gutter below.
         not good enough   not strong enough   not smart enough
              Choices thin as shaved
50   ice. Notes shredded
              drift like snow
on my broken body,
cover me like whispers
of sorries
55 sorries.
Perhaps when they find me
they will bury
my bird bones beneath
a sturdy pine
60 and scatter my feathers like
unspoken song
over this white and cold and silent
breast of earth.

READING AND REACTING

1. This poem is a suicide note that contains an apology. Why does the speaker feel she must apologize?
2. What attitude does the speaker convey toward her parents?
3. **JOURNAL ENTRY** Is the college student who speaks in this poem a stranger to you? Or is her voice in any way like that of students you know?

Related Works: "The Rocking-Horse Winner" (p. 362), "Teenage Wasteland" (p. 603), *The Cuban Swimmer* (p. 1495), *'night Mother* (p. 1708)

THE TONE OF THE POEM

◊ ◊ ◊

The **tone** of a poem conveys the speaker's attitude toward his or her subject or audience. In speech, this attitude can be conveyed easily: stressing a word in a sentence can modify or color a statement, drastically affecting the meaning of a sentence. For example, the statement "Of course, you would want to go to that restaurant" is quite straightforward, but changing the emphasis to "Of course *you* would want to go to *that* restaurant" transforms a neutral statement into a sarcastic one. For poets, however, conveying a particular tone to readers represents a challenge because readers rarely hear their spoken voices. Instead, poets indicate tone by using techniques such as rhyme, meter, word choice, sentence structure, figures of speech, and imagery.

The range of possible tones is wide. For example, a poem's speaker may be joyful, sad, playful, serious, comic, intimate, formal, relaxed, condescending, or ironic. The detached tone of the following poem conveys the speaker's attitude toward his subject.

◊ ◊ ◊

ROBERT FROST
(1874–1963)

Fire and Ice
(1923)

Some say the world will end in fire,
Some say in ice.
From what I've tasted of desire
I hold with those who favor fire.
5 But if it had to perish twice,
I think I know enough of hate
To say that for destruction ice
Is also great
And would suffice.

Here the speaker uses word choice, rhyme, and understatement to comment on the human condition. The conciseness and the simple, regular meter and rhyme suggest an **epigram**—a short poem that makes a pointed comment in an unusually clear, and often witty, manner. This pointedness is consistent with the speaker's glib, unemotional tone, as is the last line's wry understatement that ice "would suffice." The contrast between the poem's serious message—that active hatred and indifference are equally destructive—and its informal style and offhand tone is consistent with the speaker's detached, almost smug, posture.

Sometimes shifts in tone reveal changes in the speaker's attitude. In the following poem, changes in tone reveal a shift in the speaker's attitude toward war.

⬦ ⬦ ⬦

THOMAS HARDY
(1840–1928)

The Man He Killed
(1902)

"Had he and I but met
By some old ancient inn,
We should have sat us down to wet
Right many a nipperkin![1]

5 "But ranged as infantry,
And staring face to face,
I shot at him as he at me,
And killed him in his place.

"I shot him dead because—
10 Because he was my foe,
Just so: my foe of course he was;
That's clear enough; although

"He thought he'd 'list,[2] perhaps,
Off-hand-like—just as I—
15 Was out of work—had sold his traps—
No other reason why.

"Yes; quaint and curious war is!
You shoot a fellow down
You'd treat if met where any bar is,
20 Or help to half-a-crown."

The speaker in this poem is a soldier relating his wartime experiences. Quotation marks indicate that he is engaged in conversation—perhaps in a pub—and his dialect indicates that he is probably of the English working class. For him, at least at first, the object of war is simple: kill or be killed. To Hardy, this speaker represents all men who are thrust into a war

---

[1] A small container of liquor.
[2] Enlist.

without understanding its underlying social, economic, or ideological causes. In this sense, the speaker and his enemy are both victims of forces beyond their comprehension or control.

The tone of "The Man He Killed" changes as the speaker tells his story. As the poem unfolds, its sentence structure deteriorates, and this in turn helps to convey the speaker's changing attitude toward the war in which he has fought. In the first two stanzas of the poem, sentences are smooth and unbroken, establishing the speaker's matter-of-fact tone and reflecting his confidence that he has done what he had to do. In the third and fourth stanzas, however, broken syntax reflects the narrator's increasingly disturbed state of mind as he tells about the man he killed. The poem's singsong meter and regular rhyme scheme *(met/wet, inn/nipperkin)* suggest that the speaker is trying hard to maintain his composure; the smooth sentence structure of the last stanza and the use of a cliché ("Yes; quaint and curious war is!") show the speaker's efforts to trivialize the incident.

Sometimes a poem's tone can establish an ironic contrast between the speaker and his or her subject. In the next poem, the speaker's abrupt change of tone at the end of the poem establishes just such a contrast.

◇ ◇ ◇

AMY LOWELL
(1874–1925)

Patterns
(1915)

I walk down the garden-paths,
And all the daffodils
Are blowing, and the bright blue squills.
I walk down the patterned garden-paths
5 In my stiff, brocaded gown.
With my powdered hair and jewelled fan,
I too am a rare
Pattern. As I wander down
The garden-paths.

10 My dress is richly figured,
And the train
Makes a pink and silver stain
On the gravel, and the thrift
Of the borders.
15 Just a plate of current fashion
Tripping by in high-heeled, ribboned shoes.

Not a softness anywhere about me,
Only whalebone[1] and brocade.
And I sink on a seat in the shade
20 Of a lime tree. For my passion
Wars against the stiff brocade.
The daffodils and squills
Flutter in the breeze
As they please.
25 And I weep;
For the lime-tree is in blossom
And one small flower has dropped upon my bosom.
And the plashing of waterdrops
In the marble fountain
30 Comes down the garden-paths.
The dripping never stops.
Underneath my stiffened gown
Is the softness of a woman bathing in a marble basin,
A basin in the midst of hedges grown
35 So thick, she cannot see her lover hiding,
But she guesses he is near,
And the sliding of the water
Seems the stroking of a dear
Hand upon her.
40 What is Summer in a fine brocaded gown!
I should like to see it lying in a heap upon the ground.
All the pink and silver crumpled up on the ground.

I would be the pink and silver as I ran along the paths,
And he would stumble after,
45 Bewildered by my laughter.
I should see the sun flashing from his sword-hilt and buckles
    on his shoes.
I would choose
To lead him in a maze along the patterned paths,
A bright and laughing maze for my heavy-booted lover.
50 Till he caught me in the shade,
And the buttons of his waistcoat bruised my body as he clasped me,
Aching, melting, unafraid.
With the shadows of the leaves and the sundrops,
And the plopping of the waterdrops,
55 All about us in the open afternoon—
I am very like to swoon
    With the weight of this brocade,
    For the sun sifts through the shade.

---

[1] Used in making corsets.

Underneath the fallen blossom
60 In my bosom,
Is a letter I have hid.
It was brought to me this morning by a rider from the Duke.
Madam, we regret to inform you that Lord Hartwell
Died in action Thursday se'nnight.[2]
65 As I read it in the white, morning sunlight,
The letters squirmed like snakes.
"Any answer, Madam," said my footman.
"No," I told him.
"See that the messenger takes some refreshment.
70 No, no answer."
And I walked into the garden,
Up and down the patterned paths,
In my stiff, correct brocade.
The blue and yellow flowers stood up proudly in the sun,
75 Each one.
I stood upright too,
Held rigid to the pattern
By the stiffness of my gown.
Up and down I walked.
80 Up and down.

In a month he would have been my husband.
In a month, here, underneath this lime,
We would have broken the pattern;
He for me, and I for him,
85 He as Colonel, I as Lady,
On this shady seat.
He had a whim
That sunlight carried blessing.
And I answered, "It shall be as you have said."
90 Now he is dead.

In Summer and in Winter I shall walk
Up and down
The patterned garden-paths
In my stiff, brocaded gown.
95 The squills and daffodils
Will give place to pillared roses, and to asters, and to snow.
I shall go
Up and down,
In my gown.

---

[2] "Seven night," or a week ago Thursday.

100 　Gorgeously arrayed,
　　　Boned and stayed.
　　　And the softness of my body will be guarded from embrace
　　　By each button, hook, and lace.
　　　For the man who should loose me is dead,
105 　Fighting with the Duke in Flanders,[3]
　　　In a pattern called a war.
　　　Christ! What are patterns for?

The speaker begins by describing herself walking down garden paths. She wears a stiff brocaded gown, has powdered hair, and carries a jewelled fan. By her own admission she is "a plate of current fashion." Although her tone is controlled, she is preoccupied by sensual thoughts. Beneath her "stiffened gown" is the "softness of a woman bathing in a marble basin," and the "sliding of the water" in a fountain reminds the speaker of the stroking of her lover's hand. She imagines herself shedding her brocaded gown and running with her lover along the maze of "patterned paths." The sensuality of the speaker's thoughts stands in ironic contrast to the images of stiffness and control that dominate the poem; her passion "wars against the stiff brocade." She is also full of repressed rage. After all, she knows that her lover has been killed, and she realizes the meaninglessness of the patterns of her life, patterns to which she has conformed, just as her lover has conformed by going to war and doing what he was supposed to do. Throughout the poem, the speaker's tone reflects her barely contained anger and frustration. In the last line of the poem, when she finally lets out her rage, the poem's point about the senselessness of war becomes apparent.

❖ POEMS FOR FURTHER READING: THE TONE OF THE POEM

◇ ◇ ◇

WILLIAM WORDSWORTH
(1770–1850)

The World Is Too Much with Us
(1807)

　　　The world is too much with us; late and soon,
　　　Getting and spending, we lay waste our powers;
　　　Little we see in Nature that is ours;
　　　We have given our hearts away, a sordid boon!

---

[3] Region in northwestern Europe, including part of northern France and western Belgium. Flanders was the site of a historic World War I battle.

5 This Sea that bares her bosom to the moon;
The winds that will be howling at all hours,
And are up-gathered now like sleeping flowers;
For this, for everything, we are out of tune;
It moves us not. Great God! I'd rather be
10 A Pagan suckled in a creed outworn;
So might I, standing on this pleasant lea,
Have glimpses that would make me less forlorn;
Have sight of Proteus[1] rising from the sea;
Or hear old Triton[2] blow his wreathèd horn.

READING AND REACTING

1. What is the speaker's attitude toward the contemporary world? How is this attitude revealed through the poem's tone?
2. This poem is a **sonnet,** a highly structured traditional form. How do the rhyme scheme and the regular meter establish the poem's tone?
3. **JOURNAL ENTRY** Imagine you are a modern-day environmentalist, labor organizer, or corporate executive. Write a response to the sentiments expressed in this poem.
4. **CRITICAL PERSPECTIVE** According to M. H. Abrams in his 1972 essay "Two Roads to Wordsworth," critics have tended to follow one of two different paths to the poet, and these approaches have yielded two different versions of the poet:

> One Wordsworth is simple, elemental, forthright, the other is complex, paradoxical, problematic; one is an affirmative poet of life, love, and joy, the other is an equivocal or self-divided poet whose affirmations are implicitly qualified . . . by a pervasive sense of morality and an ever-incipient despair of life; . . . one is the Wordsworth of light, the other the Wordsworth of [shadow], or even darkness.

Does your reading of "The World Is Too Much with Us" support one of these versions of Wordsworth over the other? Which one? Why?

Related Works: "The Rocking-Horse Winner" (p. 362), "Dover Beach" (p. 926), "She Dwelt among the Untrodden Ways" (p. 1009), "The Lake Isle of Innisfree" (p. 1012)

---

[1] Sometimes said to be Poseidon's son, this Greek sea god had the ability to change shapes at will and to tell the future.

[2] The trumpeter of the sea, this sea god is usually pictured blowing on a conch shell. Triton was the son of Poseidon, ruler of the sea.

◈ ◈ ◈

SYLVIA PLATH
(1932–1963)

Morning Song
(1962)

Love set you going like a fat gold watch.
The midwife slapped your footsoles, and your bald cry
Took its place among the elements.

Our voices echo, magnifying your arrival. New statue.
5 In a drafty museum, your nakedness
Shadows our safety. We stand round blankly as walls.

I'm no more your mother
Than the cloud that distills a mirror to reflect its own slow
Effacement at the wind's hand.

10 All night your moth-breath
Flickers among the flat pink roses. I wake to listen:
A far sea moves in my ear.

One cry, and I stumble from bed, cow-heavy and floral
In my Victorian nightgown.
15 Your mouth opens clean as a cat's. The window square

Whitens and swallows its dull stars. And now you try
Your handful of notes;
The clear vowels rise like balloons.

READING AND REACTING

1. Who is the speaker? To whom is she speaking? What does the poem reveal about her?
2. What is the poem's subject? What attitudes about her subject do you suppose the poet expects her readers to have?
3. How is the tone of the first stanza different from that of the third? How does the tone reflect the content of each stanza?
4. **JOURNAL ENTRY** In what sense does this poem reinforce traditional ideas about motherhood? How does it undercut them?
5. **CRITICAL PERSPECTIVE** Sylvia Plath's life, which ended in suicide, was marked by emotional turbulence and instability. According to Anne Stevenson in *Bitter Fame,* her 1988 biography of Plath, in the weeks immediately preceding the composition of

"Morning Song" a fit of rage over her husband's supposed infidelity caused Plath to destroy many of his books and poetic works in progress. Then, only a few days later, she suffered a miscarriage. According to Stevenson, "Morning Song" is about sleepless nights and surely reflects Plath's depression. However, in a 1991 biography, *Rough Magic*, Paul Alexander says, "Beautiful, simple, touching, 'Morning Song' was Plath's—then—definitive statement of motherhood."

Which biographer's assessment of the poem do you think makes more sense? Why?

Related Works: "The Yellow Wall-Paper" (p. 168), "Those Winter Sundays" (p. 678), "My Son, My Executioner" (p. 827)

❖ ❖ ❖

ROBERT HERRICK
(1591–1674)

To the Virgins, to Make Much of Time
(1646)

Gather ye rosebuds while ye may,
Old Time is still a-flying;
And this same flower that smiles today,
Tomorrow will be dying.

5 The glorious lamp of heaven, the sun,
The higher he's a-getting,
The sooner will his race be run,
And nearer he's to setting.

That age is best which is the first,
10 When youth and blood are warmer;
But being spent, the worse, and worst
Times still succeed the former.

Then be not coy, but use your time,
And while ye may, go marry;
15 For having lost but once your prime,
You may forever tarry.

Reading and Reacting

1. How would you characterize the speaker? Do you think he expects his listeners to share his views? How might his expectations affect his tone?
2. This poem is developed like an argument. What is the speaker's main point? How does he support it?
3. What effect does the poem's use of rhyme have on its tone?
4. **Journal Entry** Whose side are you on—the speaker's or those he addresses?

Related Works: "Where Are You Going, Where Have You Been?" (p. 614), "The Passionate Shepherd to His Love" (p. 682), "Cinderella" (p. 751), *The Brute* (p. 1266)

Irony

◆ ◆ ◆

Just as in fiction and drama, **irony** in poetry occurs when a discrepancy exists between two levels of meaning or experience. Consider the tone of the following lines by Stephen Crane:

> Do not weep, maiden, for war is kind.
> Because your lover threw wild hands toward the sky
> And the afrightened steed ran on alone,
> Do not weep.
> War is kind.

How can war be "kind"? Isn't war exactly the opposite of "kind"? Surely the speaker does not intend his words to be taken literally. By making this ironic statement, the speaker actually conveys the opposite idea: war is a cruel, mindless exercise of violence.

Skillfully used, irony enables a poet to make a pointed comment about a situation or to manipulate a reader's emotions. Implicit in irony is the writer's assumption that readers will not be misled by the literal meaning of a statement. In order for irony to work, readers must recognize the disparity between what is said and what is meant, or between what a character or speaker thinks is occurring and what readers know to be occurring.

One kind of irony that appears in poetry is **dramatic irony,** which occurs when a speaker believes one thing and readers realize something else. In the following poem, the poet uses a deranged speaker to tell a story that is filled with irony.

◊ ◊ ◊

ROBERT BROWNING
(1812–1889)

Porphyria's Lover
(1836)

The rain set early in to-night,
    The sullen wind was soon awake,
It tore the elm-tops down for spite,
    And did its worst to vex the lake:
5   I listened with heart fit to break.
When glided in Porphyria; straight
    She shut the cold out and the storm,
And kneeled and made the cheerless grate
    Blaze up, and all the cottage warm;
10   Which done, she rose, and from her form
Withdrew the dripping cloak and shawl,
    And laid her soiled gloves by, untied
Her hat and let the damp hair fall,
    And, last, she sat down by my side
15   And called me. When no voice replied,
She put my arm about her waist,
    And made her smooth white shoulder bare,
And all her yellow hair displaced,
    And, stooping, made my cheek lie there,
20   And spread, o'er all, her yellow hair,
Murmuring how she loved me—she
    Too weak, for all her heart's endeavour,
To set its struggling passion free
    From pride, and vainer ties dissever,
25   And give herself to me for ever.
But passion sometimes would prevail,
    Nor could to-night's gay feast restrain
A sudden thought of one so pale
    For love of her, and all in vain:
30 So, she was come through wind and rain.
Be sure I looked up at her eyes
    Happy and proud; at last I knew
Porphyria worshipped me; surprise
    Made my heart swell, and still it grew
35   While I debated what to do.
That moment she was mine, mine, fair,
    Perfectly pure and good: I found
A thing to do, and all her hair
    In one long yellow string I wound

40 Three times her little throat around,
  And strangled her. No pain felt she;
   I am quite sure she felt no pain.
  As a shut bud that holds a bee,
   I warily oped her lids: again
45 Laughed the blue eyes without a stain.
  And I untightened next the tress
   About her neck; her cheek once more
  Blushed bright beneath my burning kiss:
   I propped her head up as before,
50 Only, this time my shoulder bore
  Her head, which droops upon it still:
   The smiling rosy little head,
  So glad it has its utmost will,
   That all it scorned at once is fled,
55 And I, its love, am gained instead!
  Porphyria's love: she guessed not how
   Her darling one wish would be heard.
  And thus we sit together now,
   And all night long we have not stirred,
60 And yet God has not said a word!

Like Browning's "My Last Duchess" (p. 729) this poem is a **dramatic monologue.** The speaker recounts his story in a straightforward manner, seemingly unaware of the horror of his tale. In fact, much of the effect of this poem comes from the speaker's telling his tale of murder in a flat, unemotional tone—and from readers' gradual realization that the speaker is mad.

  The irony of the poem, and of its title, becomes apparent as the monologue progresses. At first, the speaker fears that Porphyria is too weak to free herself from pride and vanity to love him. As he looks into her eyes, however, he comes to believe that she worships him. To preserve the perfection of Porphyria's love, the speaker strangles her with her own hair. He assures his silent listener, "I am quite sure she felt no pain." Like many of Browning's narrators, the speaker in this poem exhibits a selfish and perverse need to possess another person totally. The moment the speaker realizes that Porphyria loves him, he feels compelled to kill her and keep her his forever. According to him, she is at this point "mine, mine, fair, / Perfectly pure and good," and he believes that by murdering her, he actually fulfills "Her darling one wish"—to stay with him forever. As he attempts to justify his actions, the speaker reveals himself to be a deluded psychopathic killer.

  Another kind of irony is **situational irony,** which occurs when the situation itself contradicts readers' expectations. For example, in "Porphyria's Lover" the meeting of two lovers results not in joy and passion but in murder. In the next poem the situation also creates irony.

◈ ◈ ◈

PERCY BYSSHE SHELLEY
(1792–1822)

Ozymandias
(1818)

I met a traveler from an antique land
Who said: Two vast and trunkless legs of stone
Stand in the desert. Near them, on the sand,
Half sunk, a shattered visage lies, whose frown,
5 And wrinkled lip, and sneer of cold command,
Tell that its sculptor well those passions read
Which yet survive, stamped on these lifeless things,
The hand that mocked them, and the heart that fed;
And on the pedestal these words appear:
10 "My name is Ozymandias,[1] king of kings:
Look on my works, ye Mighty, and despair!"
Nothing beside remains. Round the decay
Of that colossal wreck, boundless and bare
The lone and level sands stretch far away.

The speaker tells a tale about a colossal statue that lies shattered in the desert. Its head lies separated from the trunk, and the face has a wrinkled lip and a "sneer of cold command." On the pedestal of the monument are words exhorting all those who pass: "Look on my works, ye Mighty, and despair!" The situational irony of the poem has its source in the contrast between the "colossal wreck" and the boastful inscription on its base. To the speaker, Ozymandias stands for the vanity of those who mistakenly think they can withstand the ravages of time.

Perhaps the most common kind of irony found in poetry is **verbal irony,** which is created when words say one thing but mean another, often exactly the opposite. When verbal irony is particularly biting, it is called **sarcasm**—for example, Stephen Crane's use of the word *kind* in his antiwar poem "War Is Kind." In speech, verbal irony is easy to detect through the speaker's change in tone or emphasis. In writing, when these signals are absent, verbal irony becomes more difficult to convey. Poets must depend on the context of a remark or on the contrast between a word and other images in the poem to create irony.

Consider how verbal irony is established in the following poem.

---

[1] The Greek name for Ramses II, ruler of Egypt in the thirteenth century B.C.

◈ ◈ ◈

ARIEL DORFMAN
(1942–   )

Hope
(1988)

Translated by Edith Grossman with the author

My son has been
missing
since May 8
of last year.

5   They took him
just for a few hours
they said
just for some routine
questioning.

10 After the car left,
the car with no license plate,
we couldn't

        find out
anything else
15 about him.
But now things have changed.
We heard from a compañero
who just got out
that five months later
20 they were torturing him
in Villa Grimaldi,
at the end of September
they were questioning him
in the red house
25 that belonged to the Grimaldis.

        They say they recognized
his voice his screams
they say.

        Somebody tell me frankly
30 what times are these
what kind of world
what country?
What I'm asking is
how can it be

35 that a father's
joy
a mother's
joy
is knowing
40 that they
that they are still
torturing
their son?
Which means
45 that he was alive
five months later
and our greatest
hope
will be to find out
50 next year
that they're still torturing him
eight months later

and he may   might   could
still be alive.

Although it is not necessary to know the background of the poet to appreciate this poem, it does help to know that Ariel Dorfman is a native of Chile. After the assassination of Salvador Allende, Chile's elected socialist president, in September 1973, the civilian government was replaced by a military dictatorship. Civil rights were suspended, and activists, students, and members of opposition parties were arrested and often detained indefinitely; sometimes they simply disappeared. The irony of this poem originates in the discrepancy between the way the word *hope* is used in the poem and the way it is usually used. For most people, hope has positive connotations, but in this poem it takes on a different meaning. This irony is not lost on the speaker.

❖ Poems for Further Reading: Irony

❖ ❖ ❖

W. H. AUDEN
(1907–1973)

The Unknown Citizen
(1939)

(To JS/07/M/378
This Marble Monument Is Erected by the State)

He was found by the Bureau of Statistics to be
One against whom there was no official complaint,
And all the reports on his conduct agree
That, in the modern sense of an old-fashioned word, he was a saint,
5 For in everything he did he served the Greater Community.
Except for the War till the day he retired
He worked in a factory and never got fired,
But satisfied his employers, Fudge Motors Inc.
Yet he wasn't a scab or odd in his views,
10 For his Union reports that he paid his dues,
(Our report on his Union shows it was sound)
And our Social Psychology workers found
That he was popular with his mates and liked a drink.
The Press are convinced that he bought a paper every day
15 And that his reactions to advertisements were normal in every way.
Policies taken out in his name prove that he was fully insured,
And his Health-card shows he was once in hospital but left it cured.
Both Producers Research and High-Grade Living declare
He was fully sensible to the advantages of the Installment Plan
20 And had everything necessary to the Modern Man,
A phonograph, a radio, a car and a frigidaire.
Our researchers into Public Opinion are content
That he held the proper opinions for the time of year;
When there was peace, he was for peace; when there was war, he went.
25 He was married and added five children to the population,
Which our Eugenist[1] says was the right number for a parent of his
    generation,
And our teachers report that he never interfered with their education.
Was he free? Was he happy? The question is absurd:
Had anything been wrong, we should certainly have heard.

---

[1] One who studies the science of human improvement, especially through genetic
control.

READING AND REACTING

1. The "unknown citizen" represents modern citizens, who, according to the poem, are programmed like machines. How does the title help to establish the tone of the poem? How does the inscription on the monument also help to establish the tone?
2. Who is the speaker? What is his attitude toward the unknown citizen? How can you tell?
3. What kinds of irony are present in the poem? Identify several examples.
4. **JOURNAL ENTRY** This poem was written in 1939. Does its message apply to contemporary society, or does the poem seem dated?
5. **CRITICAL PERSPECTIVE** In 1939, the same year this poem was published, Auden argued in his essay "The Public vs. The Late Mr. William Butler Yeats" that poetry can never really change anything. He reiterated this point as late as 1971 in his biographical *A Certain World:*

> By all means let a poet, if he wants to, write poems [. . . that protest] against this or that political evil or social injustice. But let him remember this. The only person who will benefit from them is himself; they will enhance his literary reputation among those who feel as he does. The evil or injustice, however, will remain exactly what it would have been if he had kept his mouth shut.

Do you believe that poetry—or any kind of literature—has the power to combat "evil or injustice" in the world? Do you consider "The Unknown Citizen" a political poem? How might this poem effect positive social or political change?

Related Works: "A&P" (p. 113), "The Metamorphosis" (p. 474), "The Man He Killed" (p. 736), "next to of course god america i" (p. 939), *A Doll House* (p. 1196)

◊   ◊   ◊

ANNE SEXTON
(1928–1974)

Cinderella
(1970)

You always read about it:
the plumber with twelve children
who wins the Irish Sweepstakes.
From toilets to riches.
5   That story.

Or the nursemaid,
some luscious sweet from Denmark
who captures the oldest son's heart.
From diapers to Dior.[1]
10 That story.

Or a milkman who serves the wealthy,
eggs, cream, butter, yogurt, milk,
the white truck like an ambulance
who goes into real estate
15 and makes a pile.
From homogenized to martinis at lunch.

Or the charwoman
who is on the bus when it cracks up
and collects enough from the insurance.
20 From mops to Bonwit Teller.[2]
That story.

Once
the wife of a rich man was on her deathbed
and she said to her daughter Cinderella:
25 Be devout. Be good. Then I will smile
down from heaven in the seam of a cloud.
The man took another wife who had
two daughters, pretty enough
but with hearts like blackjacks.
30 Cinderella was their maid.
She slept on the sooty hearth each night
and walked around looking like Al Jolson.[3]
Her father brought presents home from town,
jewels and gowns for the other women
35 but the twig of a tree for Cinderella.
She planted that twig on her mother's grave
and it grew to a tree where a white dove sat.
Whenever she wished for anything the dove
would drop it like an egg upon the ground.
40 The bird is important, my dears, so heed him.

Next came the ball, as you all know.
It was a marriage market.
The prince was looking for a wife.

---

[1] Fashion designer Christian Dior.

[2] Exclusive department store.

[3] Al Jolson (Asa Yoelson; 1886–1950)—American singer and songwriter, famous for his "black-face" minstrel performances.

All but Cinderella were preparing
45 and gussying up for the big event.
Cinderella begged to go too.
Her stepmother threw a dish of lentils
into the cinders and said: Pick them
up in an hour and you shall go.
50 The white dove brought all his friends;
all the warm wings of the fatherland came,
and picked up the lentils in a jiffy.
No, Cinderella, said the stepmother,
you have no clothes and cannot dance.
55 That's the way with stepmothers.

Cinderella went to the tree at the grave
and cried forth like a gospel singer:
Mama! Mama! My turtledove,
send me to the prince's ball!
60 The bird dropped down a golden dress
and delicate little gold slippers.
Rather a large package for a simple bird.
So she went. Which is no surprise.
Her stepmother and sisters didn't
65 recognize her without her cinder face
and the prince took her hand on the spot
and danced with no other the whole day.

As nightfall came she thought she'd better
get home. The prince walked her home
70 and she disappeared into the pigeon house
and although the prince took an axe and broke
it open she was gone. Back to her cinders.
These events repeated themselves for three days.
However on the third day the prince
75 covered the palace steps with cobbler's wax
and Cinderella's gold shoe stuck upon it.
Now he would find whom the shoe fit
and find his strange dancing girl for keeps.
He went to their house and the two sisters
80 were delighted because they had lovely feet.
The eldest went into a room to try the slipper on
but her big toe got in the way so she simply
sliced it off and put on the slipper.
The prince rode away with her until the white dove
85 told him to look at the blood pouring forth.
That is the way with amputations.
They don't just heal up like a wish.
The other sister cut off her heel

but the blood told as blood will.
90 The prince was getting tired.
He began to feel like a shoe salesman.
But he gave it one last try.
This time Cinderella fit into the shoe
like a love letter into its envelope.

95 At the wedding ceremony
the two sisters came to curry favor
and the white dove pecked their eyes out.
Two hollow spots were left
like soup spoons.

100 Cinderella and the prince
lived, they say, happily ever after,
like two dolls in a museum case
never bothered by diapers or dust,
never arguing over the timing of an egg,
105 never telling the same story twice,
never getting a middle-aged spread,
their darling smiles pasted on for eternity
Regular Bobbsey Twins.[4]
That story.

READING AND REACTING

1. The first twenty-one lines of the poem act as a prelude. How does this prelude help to establish the speaker's ironic tone?
2. At times the speaker talks directly to readers. What effect do these statements have on you? Would the poem be stronger without them?
3. Throughout the poem, the speaker mixes contemporary colloquial expressions with the conventional diction of a fairy tale. Find examples of these two kinds of language. How does the juxtaposition of these different kinds of diction create irony?
4. **JOURNAL ENTRY** What details of the Cinderella fairy tale does Sexton change in her poem? Why do you think she makes these changes?
5. **CRITICAL PERSPECTIVE** In his 1973 book *Confessional Poets*, Robert Phillips comments on Anne Sexton's use of the Grimm Brothers' fairy tales in her book *Transformations*. According to Phillips, by transforming the Grimms' stories into symbols of our own time, Sexton "has managed to offer us understandable images of the world around us":

---

[4] The two sets of twins—Nan and Bert, Flossie and Freddie—in a popular series of early twentieth-century children's books. They led an idealized, problem-free life.

["Cinderella"] she takes to be a prototype of the old rags to riches theme ("From diapers to Dior. / That story."). Cinderella is said to have slept on the sooty hearth each night and "walked around looking like Al Jolson"—a comparison indicative of the level of invention and humor in the book. At the end, when Cinderella marries the handsome prince to live happily ever after, [. . .] Sexton pulls a double whammy and reveals that the ending, in itself, is another fairy tale within a fairy tale, totally unreal and unlikely.

Is the poem "Cinderella," written in 1970, still a "symbol of our own time"? In what way does it offer us "understandable images of the world around us"?

Related Works: "The Story of an Hour" (p. 77), "Once upon a Time" (p. 81), "The Jilting of Granny Weatherall" (p. 580), "The Faithful Wife" (p. 776)

◆ ◆ ◆

DUDLEY RANDALL
(1914–   )

Ballad of Birmingham
(1969)

(On the bombing of a church in Birmingham, Alabama, 1963)

"Mother dear, may I go downtown
Instead of out to play,
And march the streets of Birmingham
In a Freedom March today?"

5 "No, baby, no, you may not go,
For the dogs are fierce and wild,
And clubs and hoses, guns and jails
Aren't good for a little child."

"But, mother, I won't be alone.
10 Other children will go with me,
And march the streets of Birmingham
To make our country free."

"No, baby, no, you may not go,
For I fear those guns will fire.
15 But you may go to church instead
And sing in the children's choir."

She has combed and brushed her night-dark hair,
And bathed rose petal sweet,
And drawn white gloves on her small brown hands,
20 And white shoes on her feet.

The mother smiled to know her child
Was in the sacred place,
But that smile was the last smile
To come upon her face.

25 For when she heard the explosion,
Her eyes grew wet and wild.
She raced through the streets of Birmingham
Calling for her child.

She clawed through bits of glass and brick,
30 Then lifted out a shoe.
"O, here's the shoe my baby wore,
But, baby, where are you?"

READING AND REACTING

1. Who are the two speakers in the poem? How do their attitudes differ? How does the tone of the poem convey their attitudes?
2. What kinds of irony are present in the poem? Give examples of each kind you identify.
3. This poem is a **ballad,** a form of poetry traditionally written to be sung or recited. Ballads typically repeat words and phrases and have regular meter and rhyme. How do the regular rhyme, repeated words, and singsong meter affect the poem's tone?
4. **JOURNAL ENTRY** This poem was written in response to the 1963 bombing of the 16th Street Baptist Church in Birmingham, Alabama, a bombing that killed four African-American children. How does this historical background help you to understand the irony of the poem?

Related Works: "Once upon a Time" (p. 81), "Bonny Barbara Allan" (p. 924), "The Ballad of Rudolph Reed" (p. 932), "Emmett Till" (p. 954), "If We Must Die" (p. 975), *Fences* (p. 1745)

 CHECKLIST: WRITING ABOUT VOICE

THE SPEAKER IN THE POEM

✓ What do we know about the speaker?

✓ Is the speaker anonymous, or does he or she have a particular identity?

✓ How does assuming a particular persona help the poet to convey his or her ideas?

✓ Does the title give information about the speaker's identity?

✓ In what way does word choice provide information about the speaker?

✓ Does the speaker make any direct statements that help you to establish his or her identity or character?

✓ Does the speaker address anyone? How can you tell? Does the presence of a listener seem to affect the speaker?

THE TONE OF THE POEM

✓ What is the speaker's attitude toward his or her subject?

✓ How do word choice, rhyme, meter, sentence structure, figures of speech, and imagery help to convey the attitude of the speaker?

✓ Is the tone of the poem consistent? How do shifts in tone reflect the changing mood or attitude of the speaker?

IRONY

✓ Does any dramatic irony exist in the poem?

✓ Does the poem include situational irony?

✓ Does verbal irony appear in the poem?

◆ WRITING SUGGESTIONS: VOICE

1. Poet Robert Frost once said that he wanted to write "poetry that talked." According to Frost, "whenever I write a line it is because that line has already been spoken clearly by a voice with my mind, an audible voice." Choose some poems in this chapter (or elsewhere in the book) that you consider "talking poems." Then, write an essay about how successful they are in communicating "an audible voice."

2. Compare the women's voices in "Cinderella" (p. 751) and "Gretel in Darkness" (p. 724). In what way are their attitudes toward men similar? In what way are they different?

3. The theme of Herrick's poem "To the Virgins, to Make Much of Time" (p. 743) is known as **carpe diem** or "seize the day." Read Andrew Marvell's "To His Coy Mistress" (p. 824), which has the same theme, and compare its tone with that of "To the Virgins, to Make Much of Time."

4. Read the following poem, and compare the speaker's use of the word *hope* with the way the speaker uses the word in Ariel Dorfman's "Hope" (p. 748).

◇ ◇ ◇

EMILY DICKINSON
(1830–1886)

"Hope" Is the Thing with Feathers
(1861)

"Hope" is the thing with feathers—
That perches in the soul—
And sings the tune without the words—
And never stops—at all—

5 And sweetest—in the Gale—is heard—
And sore must be the storm—
That could abash the little Bird—
That kept so many warm—

I've heard it in the chillest land—
10 And on the strangest Sea—
Yet, never, in Extremity,
It asked a crumb—of Me.

5. Because the speaker and the poet are not the same, poems by the same author can have different voices. Compare the voices of several poems by Sylvia Plath, W. H. Auden, William Blake, or any poet in this anthology.

6. **WEB ACTIVITY** According to Adrienne Rich, "Someone writing a poem believes in a reader, in readers, of that poem. The 'who' of that reader quivers like a jellyfish. Self-reference is always possible." Go to the Academy of American Poets Exhibit on Adrienne Rich at

http://www.wnet.org/archive/lol/rich.html

Read "Miracle Ice Cream" or "In These Years" or any other of Rich's poems that is addressed to a person referred to as "you." Speculate about the relationship between that person and the speaker in the poem.

CHAPTER 14

Word Choice, Word Order

◊ ◊ ◊

The poet's love of language must, if language is to reward him with unlooked-for miracles, that is, with poetry, amount to a passion. The passion for the things of the world and the passion for naming them must be in him indistinguishable.

DENISE LEVERTOV, "Origins of a Poem"

What is known in a poem is its language, that is, the words it uses. Yet those words seem different in a poem. Even the most familiar will seem strange. In a poem, each word, being equally important, exists in absolute focus, having a weight it rarely achieves in fiction. [. . .] Words in a novel are subordinate to broad slices of action or characterization that push the plot forward. In a poem, they *are* the action.

MARK STRAND, Introduction to *Best American Poems of 1991*

I like *mountain* and *prairie* and *sky*. When I write poetry, I use such words and I also use abstract words. But it is difficult to give you a list of favorite words because words become vital—they come alive—within a certain context. A given word is extremely important and vital in one context and not very interesting in another. It depends upon what's around the word. The environment. Although some words are naturally interesting, in my opinion. Like some creatures. The fox, I think, is a creature of almost immediate interest to most people. Other words are not as immediately interesting, or are even negatively received. Like some other creatures. The lizard, for example, is a creature most people wouldn't ordinarily care about. But in its natural habitat and in its dimension of wilderness, the lizard can be seen as a beautiful thing. Its movements are very wonderful to watch. Similarly, you can take almost any word and make it interesting by the way in which you use it.

N. SCOTT MOMADAY, in *Ancestral Voices*

◊ ◊ ◊

◆   ◆   ◆

SIPHO SEPAMLA

(1932–   )

Words, Words, Words[1]

We don't speak of tribal wars anymore
we say simple faction fights
there are no tribes around here
only nations
5   it makes sense you see
'cause from there
one moves to multinational
it makes sense you get me
'cause from there
10   one gets one's homeland
which is a reasonable idea
'cause from there
one can dabble with independence
which deserves warm applause
15   —the bloodless revolution

we are talking of words
words tossed around as if
denied location by the wind
we mean those words some spit
20   others grab
dress them up for the occasion
fling them on the lap of an audience
we are talking of those words
that stalk our lives like policemen
25   words no dictionary can embrace
words that change sooner than seasons
we mean words
that spell out our lives
words, words, words
30   for there's a kind of poetic licence
doing the rounds in these parts

Words identify and name, characterize and distinguish, compare and
contrast. Words describe, limit, and embellish; words locate and measure.

---

[1] Publication date is not available. This title is possibly an allusion to *Hamlet* 2.2.189.

Without words, there cannot be a poem. Even though words may be elusive and uncertain and changeable, "tossed around as if / denied location by the wind" and "can change sooner than seasons," they still can "stalk our lives like policemen." In poetry, as in love and in politics, words matter.

Beyond the quantitative—how many words, how many letters and syllables—is one much more important consideration: the *quality* of words. Which are chosen, and why? Why are certain words placed next to others? What does a word suggest in a particular context? How are the words arranged? What exactly constitutes the right word?

WORD CHOICE
◊ ◊ ◊

In poetry, even more than in fiction or drama, words tend to become the focus—sometimes even the true subject—of a work. For this reason, the choice of one word over another can be crucial. Because poems are brief, they must compress many ideas into a few lines; poets know how much weight each individual word carries, and so they choose with great care, trying to select words that imply more than they state.

A poet may choose a word because of its sound. For instance, a word may echo another word's sound, and such repetition may place emphasis on both words; it may rhyme with another word and therefore be needed to preserve the poem's rhyme scheme; or, it may have a certain combination of stressed and unstressed syllables needed to maintain the poem's metrical pattern. Occasionally, a poet may even choose a word because of how it looks on the page. Most often, though, poets select words because they help to communicate their ideas.

At the same time, poets may choose words for their degree of concreteness or abstraction, specificity or generality. A *concrete* word refers to an item that is a perceivable, tangible entity—for example, a kiss or a flag. An *abstract* word refers to an intangible idea, condition, or quality, something that cannot be perceived by the senses—love, patriotism, and so on. *Specific* words refer to particular items; *general* words refer to entire classes or groups of items. As the following example illustrates, whether a word is specific or general is relative; its degree of specificity or generality depends on its relationship to other words:

Poem → closed form poem → sonnet → seventeenth-century sonnet → Elizabethan sonnet → sonnet by Shakespeare → "My Mistress' Eyes Are Nothing Like the Sun"

Sometimes a poet wants a precise word, one that is both specific and concrete. At other times, however, a poet might prefer general or abstract language, which may allow for more subtlety—or even for intentional ambiguity.

Finally, a word may be chosen for its **connotation**—what it suggests. Every word has one or more **denotations**—what it signifies without emotional associations, judgments, or opinions. The word *family*, for example, denotes "a group of related things or people." Connotation is a more complex matter, however, because a single word may have many different associations. In general terms, a word may have a connotation that is positive, neutral, or negative. Thus, *family* may have a positive connotation when it describes a group of loving relatives, a neutral connotation when it describes a biological category, and an ironically negative connotation when it describes an organized crime family. Beyond this distinction, *family*, like any other word, may have a variety of emotional and social associations, suggesting loyalty, warmth, home, security, or duty. In fact, many words have somewhat different meanings in different contexts. When poets choose words, then, they must consider what a particular word may suggest to readers as well as what it denotes.

In the poem that follows, the poet chooses words for their sounds, their relationships to other words, and their connotations.

◇ ◇ ◇

WALT WHITMAN
(1819–1892)

When I Heard the Learn'd Astronomer
(1865)

When I heard the learn'd astronomer,
When the proofs, the figures, were ranged in columns before me,
When I was shown the charts and diagrams, to add, divide, and
    measure them,
When I sitting heard the astronomer where he lectured with much
    applause in the lecture-room,
5 How soon unaccountable I became tired and sick,
Till rising and gliding out I wander'd off by myself,
In the mystical moist night-air, and from time to time,
Look'd up in perfect silence at the stars.

This poem might be paraphrased as follows: "When I grew restless listening to an astronomy lecture, I went outside, where I found I learned more just by looking at the stars than I had learned inside." But the paraphrase is obviously neither as rich nor as complex as the poem. Through careful use of diction, Whitman establishes a dichotomy that supports the poem's central theme about the relative merits of two ways of learning.

The poem can be divided into two groups of four lines. The first four lines, unified by the repetition of "When," introduce the astronomer and his tools: "proofs," "figures," and "charts and diagrams" to be added, divided, and measured. In this section of the poem, the speaker is passive: he sits and listens ("I heard"; "I was shown"; "I sitting heard"). The repetition of "When" reinforces the dry monotony of the lecture. In the next four lines, the choice of words signals the change in the speaker's actions and reactions. The confined lecture hall is replaced by "the mystical moist night-air," and the dry lecture and automatic applause give way to "perfect silence"; instead of sitting passively, the speaker becomes active (he rises, glides, wanders); instead of listening, he looks. The mood of the first half of the poem is restrained: the language is concrete and physical, and the speaker is studying, receiving information from a "learn'd" authority. The rest of the poem, celebrating intuitive knowledge and feelings, is more abstract, freer. Throughout the poem, the lecture hall contrasts sharply with the natural world outside its walls.

After considering the poem as a whole, readers should not find it hard to understand why the poet selected certain words. Whitman's use of "lectured" in line 4 rather than a more neutral word like "spoke" is appropriate both because it suggests formality and distance and because it echoes "lecture-room" in the same line. The word "sick" in line 5 is striking because it connotes physical as well as emotional distress, more effectively conveying the extent of the speaker's discomfort than "bored" or "restless" would. "Rising" and "gliding" (6) are used rather than "standing" and "walking out" both because of the way their stressed vowel sounds echo each other (and echo "time to time" in the next line) and because of their connotation of dreaminess, which is consistent with "wander'd" (6) and "mystical" (7). The word "moist" (7) is chosen not only because its consonant sounds echo the *m* and *st* sounds in "mystical," but also because it establishes a contrast with the dry, airless lecture hall. Finally, line 8's "perfect silence" is a better choice than a reasonable substitute like "complete silence" or "total silence," either of which would suggest the degree of the silence but not its quality.

In the next poem, the poet also pays careful attention to word choice.

◊ ◊ ◊

WILLIAM STAFFORD
(1914–1993)

For the Grave of Daniel Boone
(1957)

The farther he went the farther home grew.
Kentucky became another room;
the mansion arched over the Mississippi;
flowers were spread all over the floor.
5 He traced ahead a deepening home,
and better, with goldenrod:

Leaving the snakeskin of place after place,
going on—after the trees
the grass, a bird flying after a song.
10 Rifle so level, sighting so well
his picture freezes down to now,
a story-picture for children.

They go over the velvet falls
into the tapestry of his time,
15 heirs to the landscape, feeling no jar:
it is like evening; they are the quail
surrounding his fire, coming in for the kill;
their little feet move sacred sand.

Children, we live in a barbwire time
20 but like to follow the old hands back—
the ring in the light, the knuckle, the palm,
all the way to Daniel Boone,
hunting our own kind of deepening home.
From the land that was his I heft this rock.

25 Here on his grave I put it down.

A number of words in "For the Grave of Daniel Boone" are noteworthy for their multiple denotations and connotations. In the first stanza, for example, "home" does not mean Boone's residence; it connotes an abstract state, a dynamic concept that grows and deepens, encompassing states and rivers while becoming paradoxically more and more elusive. In literal terms, Boone's "home" at the poem's end is a narrow, confined space: his grave. In a wider sense, his home is the United States, particularly the natural landscape he explored. Thus, the word "home" comes to have a variety of associations to readers beyond its denotative meaning, suggesting both the infinite possibilities beyond the frontier and the realities of civilization's walls and fences.

The word "snakeskin" denotes "the skin of a snake"; its most immediate connotations are smoothness and slipperiness. In this poem, however, the snakeskin signifies more, because it is Daniel Boone who is "leaving the snakeskin of place after place." Like a snake, Boone belongs to the natural world—and, like a snake, he wanders from place to place, shedding his skin as he goes. Thus, the word "snakeskin," with its connotation of rebirth and its links to nature, passing time, and the inevitability of change, is consistent with the image of Boone as both a man of nature and a restless wanderer, "a bird flying after a song."

In the poem's third stanza, the phrases "velvet falls" and "tapestry of time" seem at first to have been selected solely for their pleasing repetition of sounds ("ve<u>l</u>vet fa<u>ll</u>s"; "<u>t</u>apestry of <u>t</u>ime"). But both of these paradoxical phrases also support the poem's theme. Alive, Boone was in constant movement; he was also larger than life. Now he has been reduced; "his picture freezes down to [. . .] / a story-picture for children" (11–12), and he is as static and inorganic as velvet or tapestry—no longer dynamic, like "falls" and "time."

The word "barbwire" (in line 19's phrase "barbwire time") is another word whose multiple meanings enrich the poem's theme. In the simplest terms, "barbwire" denotes a metal fencing material. In light of the poem's concern with space and distance, however, "barbwire" (with its connotations of sharpness, danger, and confinement) is also the antithesis of Boone's free or peaceful wilderness, evoking images of prisons and concentration camps and reinforcing the poem's central dichotomy between past freedom and present restriction.

The phrase "old hands" (20) might also have multiple meanings in the context of the poem. On one level, the hands could belong to an elderly person holding a storybook; on another level, "old hands" could refer to those with considerable life experience—like Boone, who was an "old hand" at scouting. On still another level, given the poem's concern with time, "old hands" could suggest the hands of a clock.

Through what it says literally and through what its words suggest, "For the Grave of Daniel Boone" communicates a good deal about the speaker's identification with Daniel Boone and with the nation he called home. Boone's horizons, his concept of "home," expanded as he wandered. Now, when he is frozen in time and space, a character in a child's picture book, a body in a grave, we are still "hunting our own kind of deepening home," but our horizons, like Boone's, have narrowed in this "barbwire time."

❖ Poems for Further Reading: Word Choice

◆ ◆ ◆

JAMES WRIGHT
(1927–1980)

Autumn Begins in Martins Ferry, Ohio
(1963)

In the Shreve High football stadium,
I think of Polacks nursing long beers in Tiltonsville,
And gray faces of Negroes in the blast furnace at Benwood,
And the ruptured night watchman of Wheeling Steel,
5 Dreaming of heroes.

All the proud fathers are ashamed to go home.
Their women cluck like starved pullets,
Dying for love.

Therefore,
10 Their sons grow suicidally beautiful
At the beginning of October,
And gallop terribly against each other's bodies.

READING AND REACTING

1. Evaluate Wright's decision to use each of the following words: "Polacks" (2), "ruptured" (4), "pullets" (7), "suicidally" (10), "gallop" (12). Do any of these words seem unexpected, even unsettling, in the context in which he uses them? Can you explain why each is used instead of a more conventional word?

2. What thematic relationship, if any, do you see between line 5 ("Dreaming of heroes") and line 8 ("Dying for love")? What do these lines reveal about the people who live in Martins Ferry?

3. **JOURNAL ENTRY** What comment does this poem seem to be making about small towns? About high school football?

4. **CRITICAL PERSPECTIVE** In her 1980 essay "James Wright: Returning to the Heartland," Bonnie Costello discusses the poet's complex relationship to place and its effect on "Autumn Begins in Martins Ferry, Ohio," characterizing Wright as a kind of "fugitive" or "exile" from the past his poems reveal:

   James Wright was an elegiac poet of place. Place names echo through his lines as through deserted villages and wintry valleys, for Martins Ferry, Ohio; Fargo, North Dakota; Wheeling, West Virginia, are all dying. While he admired D. H.

Lawrence's essay "The Spirit of Place" and tried to follow its guidelines, his own subject raised a special problem since it was the departure of spirit that he best portrayed. Wright tried repeatedly to call his spirit back, but his finest poems are those which catch it crossing the last hill crest or disappearing into the mist. One might argue that there is, indeed, a spirit in this place, one hopeless, ignorant, and long suffering, nonetheless beautiful and mysterious.

How does "Autumn Begins in Martins Ferry, Ohio" convey the elegiac sense of place Costello describes?

Related Works: "To an Athlete Dying Young" (p. 786), "Ex-Basketball Player" (p. 813), *Fences* (p. 1745)

◊ ◊ ◊

A D R I E N N E   R I C H
(1929–   )

Living in Sin
(1955)

She had thought the studio would keep itself,
no dust upon the furniture of love.
Half heresy, to wish the taps less vocal,
the panes relieved of grime. A plate of pears,
5 a piano with a Persian shawl, a cat
stalking the picturesque amusing mouse
had risen at his urging.
Not that at five each separate stair would writhe
under the milkman's tramp; that morning light
10 so coldly would delineate the scraps
of last night's cheese and three sepulchral bottles;
that on the kitchen shelf among the saucers
a pair of beetle-eyes would fix her own—
envoy from some black village in the mouldings . . .
15 Meanwhile, he, with a yawn,
sounded a dozen notes upon the keyboard,
declared it out of tune, shrugged at the mirror,
rubbed at his beard, went out for cigarettes;
while she, jeered by the minor demons,
20 pulled back the sheets and made the bed and found
a towel to dust the table-top,
and let the coffee-pot boil over on the stove.
By evening she was back in love again,
though not so wholly but throughout the night
25 she woke sometimes to feel the daylight coming
like a relentless milkman up the stairs.

READING AND REACTING

1. How might the poem's impact change if each of these words were deleted: "Persian" (5), "picturesque" (6), "sepulchral" (11), "minor" (19), "sometimes" (25)?

2. What words in the poem have strongly negative connotations? What do these words suggest about the relationship the poem describes? How does the image of the "relentless milkman" (26) sum up this relationship?

3. This poem, about a woman in love, uses very few words conventionally associated with love poems. Instead, many of its words denote the everyday routine of housekeeping. Give examples of such words. Why do you think they are used?

4. **JOURNAL ENTRY** What connotations does the title have? What other phrases have similar denotative meanings? How do their connotations differ? Why do you think Rich chose the title she did?

5. **CRITICAL PERSPECTIVE** In "Her Cargo: Adrienne Rich and the Common Language," a 1979 essay examining the poet's work over almost thirty years, Alicia Ostriker notes that early poems by Rich, including "Living in Sin," reflect popular male poets' "resigned sense of life as a diminished thing" and only "tremble on the brink of indignation":

> They seem about to state explicitly [. . .] a connection between feminine subordination in male-dominated middle-class relationships, and emotionally lethal inarticulateness for both sexes. But the poetry [. . .] is minor because it is polite. It illustrates symptoms but does not probe sources. There is no disputing the ideas of the predecessors, and Adrienne Rich at this point is a cautious good poet in the sense of being a good girl, a quality noted with approval by her reviewers.

Does your reading of "Living in Sin" support Ostriker's characterization of the poem as "resigned," "polite," and "cautious"? Do you think Rich is "being a good girl"?

Related Works: "The Storm" (p. 154), "The Faithful Wife" (p. 776), *The Stronger* (p. 1177)

◊ ◊ ◊
E. E. CUMMINGS
(1894–1962)

in Just-[1]
(1923)

in Just-
spring   when the world is mud-
luscious the little
lame balloonman

5 whistles   far   and wee

and eddieandbill come
running from marbles and
piracies and it's
spring

10 when the world is puddle-wonderful
the queer
old balloonman whistles
far   and   wee
and bettyandisbel come dancing

15 from hop-scotch and jump-rope and
it's
spring
and
        the

20   goat-footed

balloonMan   whistles
far
and
wee

READING AND REACTING

1. In this poem, Cummings coins a number of words that he uses to modify other words. Identify these coinages. What other, more conventional, words could be used in their place? What does Cummings accomplish by using the coined words instead?
2. What do you think Cummings means by "far and wee" in lines 5, 13, and 22–24? Why do you think he arranges the three words in a different way each time he uses them?

---

[1] Also known as "Chansons Innocentes I."

3. **JOURNAL ENTRY** Evaluate this poem. Do you like it? Is it memorable or moving—or just clever?

4. **CRITICAL PERSPECTIVE** In "Latter-Day Notes on E. E. Cummings' Language" (1955), Robert E. Maurer suggests that Cummings often coined new words in the same way that children do: for example, "by adding the normal *-er* or *-est* (*beautifuler, chiefest*), or stepping up the power of a word such as *last,* which is already superlative, and saying *lastest,*" creating words such as *givingest* and *whirlingest.* In addition to "combining two or more words to form a single new one . . . to give an effect of wholeness, of one quality" (for example, *yellowgreen*), "in the simplest of his word coinages, he merely creates a new word by analogy as a child would without adding any shade of meaning other than that inherent in the prefix or suffix he utilizes, as in the words *unstrength* and *untimid* [. . .]." Many early reviewers, Maurer notes, criticized such coinages because they "convey a thrill but not a precise impression," a criticism also leveled at Cummings's poetry more broadly.

    Consider the coinages in "in Just-." Do you agree that many do not add "shades of meaning" or provide a "precise impression"? Or, do you find that the coinages contribute to the whole in a meaningful way?

Related Works: "The Secret Lion" (p. 49), "anyone lived in a pretty how town" (p. 785), "Constantly Risking Absurdity" (p. 809), "Jabberwocky" (p. 856), "the sky was can dy" (p. 883)

◇   ◇   ◇

THEODORE ROETHKE
(1908–1963)

I Knew a Woman
(1958)

I knew a woman, lovely in her bones,
When small birds sighed, she would sigh back at them;
Ah, when she moved, she moved more ways than one:
The shapes a bright container can contain!
5 Of her choice virtues only gods should speak,
Or English poets who grew up on Greek
(I'd have them sing in chorus, cheek to cheek).

How well her wishes went! She stroked my chin,
She taught me Turn, and Counter-turn, and Stand;
10 She taught me Touch, that undulant white skin;
I nibbled meekly from her proffered hand;
She was the sickle; I, poor I, the rake,

Coming behind her for her pretty sake
(But what prodigious mowing we did make).

15 Love likes a gander, and adores a goose:
Her full lips pursed, the errant note to seize;
She played it quick, she played it light and loose;
My eyes, they dazzled at her flowing knees;
Her several parts could keep a pure repose,
20 Or one hip quiver with a mobile nose
(She moved in circles, and those circles moved).

Let seed be grass, and grass turn into hay:
I'm martyr to a motion not my own;
What's freedom for? To know eternity.
25 I swear she cast a shadow white as stone.
But who would count eternity in days?
These old bones live to learn her wanton ways:
(I measure time by how a body sways).

READING AND REACTING

1. Many of the words in Roethke's poem have double meanings—for example, "gander" and "goose" in line 15. Identify other words that have more than one meaning, and consider the function these multiple meanings serve.
2. The poem's language contains many surprises; often, the word we expect is not the one we get. For example, "container" in line 4 is not a conventional means of describing a woman. What other words are used in unusual ways? What does Roethke achieve by choosing such words?
3. Is there a difference between the denotation or connotation of the word "bones" in the phrases "lovely in her bones" (1) and "These old bones" (27)? Explain.
4. **JOURNAL ENTRY** How does this poem differ from your idea of what a love poem should be?

Related Works: "My Mistress' Eyes Are Nothing like the Sun" (p. 684), "Oh, My Love Is like a Red, Red Rose" (p. 812), "She Walks in Beauty" (p. 937)

LEVELS OF DICTION
◊ ◊ ◊

Like other writers, poets use various levels of diction to convey their ideas. The diction of a poem may be formal or informal or fall anywhere in between, depending on the identity of the speaker and on the speaker's attitude toward the reader and toward his or her subject. At one extreme, very formal poems can be far removed in style and vocabulary from everyday speech. At the other extreme, highly informal poems can be full of jargon, regionalisms, and slang. Many poems, of course, use language that falls somewhere between formal and informal diction.

FORMAL DICTION

Formal diction is characterized by a learned vocabulary and grammatically correct forms. In general, formal diction does not include colloquialisms, such as contractions and shortened word forms (*phone* for *telephone*). As the following poem illustrates, a speaker who uses formal diction can sound aloof and impersonal.

◇ ◇ ◇

MARGARET ATWOOD
(1939–   )

The City Planners
(1966)

Cruising these residential Sunday
streets in dry August sunlight:
what offends us is
the sanities:
5 the houses in pedantic rows, the planted
sanitary trees, assert
levelness of surface like a rebuke
to the dent in our car door.
No shouting here, or
10 shatter of glass; nothing more abrupt
than the rational whine of a power mower
cutting a straight swath in the discouraged grass.

But though the driveways neatly
sidestep hysteria
15 by being even, the roofs all display
the same slant of avoidance to the hot sky,
certain things:
the smell of spilled oil a faint

sickness lingering in the garages,
20 a splash of paint on brick surprising as a bruise,
a plastic hose poised in a vicious
coil; even the too-fixed stare of the wide windows

give momentary access to
the landscape behind or under
25 the future cracks in the plaster

when the houses, capsized, will slide
obliquely into the clay seas, gradual as glaciers
that right now nobody notices.

That is where the City Planners
30 with the insane faces of political conspirators
are scattered over unsurveyed
territories, concealed from each other,
each in his own private blizzard;

guessing directions, they sketch
35 transitory lines rigid as wooden borders
on a wall in the white vanishing air

tracing the panic of suburb
order in a bland madness of snows.

Atwood's speaker is clearly concerned about the poem's central issue, but rather than use *I*, the poem uses the first-person plural (*us*) to maintain distance and to convey emotional detachment. Although phrases such as "sickness lingering in the garages" and "insane faces of political conspirators" communicate the speaker's disapproval, formal words—"pedantic," "rebuke," "display," "poised," "obliquely," "conspirators," "transitory"— help her to maintain her distance. Both the speaker herself and her attack on the misguided city planners gain credibility through her balanced, measured tone and through the use of language that is as formal and "professional" as theirs, with no slang, nonstandard diction, or colloquialisms.

INFORMAL DICTION

Informal diction is the language closest to everyday conversation. It includes colloquialisms—contractions, shortened word forms, and the like— and may also include slang, regional expressions, and even nonstandard words.

In the poem that follows, the speaker uses informal diction to highlight the contrast between James Baca, a law student speaking to the graduating class of his old high school, and the graduating seniors.

◆ ◆ ◆

JIM SAGEL
(1947–   )

Baca Grande[1]
(1982)

Una vaca se topó con un ratón y le dice:
"Tú—¿tan chiquito y con bigote?" Y le responde el ratón:
"Y tú tan grandota—¿y sin brassiere?"[2]

It was nearly a miracle
James Baca remembered anyone at all
from the old hometown gang
having been two years at Yale
5   no less
and halfway through law school
at the University of California at Irvine
They hardly recognized him either
in his three-piece grey business suit
10   and surfer-swirl haircut
with just the menacing hint
of a tightly trimmed Zapata moustache
        for cultural balance
and relevance

15   He had come to deliver the keynote address
to the graduating class of 80
at his old alma mater
and show off his well-trained lips
which laboriously parted
20   each Kennedyish "R"
and drilled the first person pronoun
through the microphone
like an oil bit
with the slick, elegantly honed phrases
25   that slid so smoothly
off his meticulously bleached
        tongue
He talked Big Bucks
with astronautish fervor and if he
30   the former bootstrapless James A. Baca

---

[1] *Baca* is both a phonetic spelling of the Spanish word "vaca" (cow) and the last name of one of the poem's characters. *Grande* means "large."

[2] A cow ran into a rat and said: "You—so small and with a moustache?" The rat responded: "And you—so big and without a bra?"

could dazzle the ass
off the universe
then even you
    yes you
35 Joey Martinez toying with your yellow
    tassle
and staring dumbly into space
could emulate Mr. Baca someday
    possibly
40 well
there was of course
such a thing
as being an outrageously successful
gas station attendant too
45   let us never forget
it doesn't really matter what you do
so long as you excel
    James said
never believing a word
50 of it
for he had already risen
    as high as they go

Wasn't nobody else
from this deprived environment
55 who'd ever jumped
    straight out of college
into the Governor's office
and maybe one day
he'd sit in that big chair
60   himself
and when he did
he'd forget this damned town
and all the petty little people
in it
65 once and for all

    That much he promised himself

"Baca Grande" uses numerous colloquialisms, including contractions; conversational placeholders, such as "no less" and "well"; shortened word forms, such as "gas"; slang terms, such as "Big Bucks"; whimsical coinages ("Kennedyish," "astronautish," "bootstrapless"); nonstandard grammatical constructions, such as "Wasn't nobody else"; and even profanity. The level of language is perfectly appropriate for the students Baca addresses—suspicious, streetwise, and unimpressed by Baca's "three-piece grey business suit" and "surfer-swirl haircut." In fact, the informal diction is a key element in the poem, expressing the gap between the slick James Baca, with "his well-trained lips / which laboriously parted / each Kennedyish 'R'" and members of his audience, with their unpretentious, forthright speech. In this sense "Baca Grande" is as much a linguistic commentary as a social one.

❖ POEMS FOR FURTHER READING: LEVELS OF DICTION

◊ ◊ ◊

BARBARA L. GREENBERG
(1932–   )

The Faithful Wife
(1978)

But if I *were* to have a lover, it would be someone
who could take nothing from you. I would, in conscience,
not dishonor you. He and I would eat at Howard Johnson's

which you and I do not enjoy. With him I would go
5 fishing because it is not your sport. He would wear blue
which is your worst color; he would have none of your virtues.

Not strong, not proud, not just, not provident, my lover
would blame me for his heart's distress, which you would never
think to do. He and I would drink too much and weep together

10 and I would bruise his face as I would not bruise your face
even in my dreams. Yes I would dance with him, but to a music
you and I would never choose to hear, and in a place

where you and I would never wish to be. He and I would speak
Spanish, which is not your tongue, and we would take
15 long walks in fields of burdock, to which you are allergic.

We would make love only in the morning. It would be
altogether different. I would know him with my other body,
the one that you have never asked to see.

READING AND REACTING

1. In what respect does this poem sound like everyday speech? What colloquial elements usually present in conversation are absent here?

2. The speaker seems to be addressing her husband. What words or phrases in the poem sound out of place given the identities of the participants in the conversation?
3. **JOURNAL ENTRY** How do you interpret the poem's title? In what sense is it ironic? In what sense is it not?

Related Works: "The Storm" (p. 154), "The Nymph's Reply to the Shepherd" (p. 683), "You Fit into Me" (p. 828), *A Doll House* (p. 1196)

◆ ◆ ◆

RICHARD WILBUR
(1921–)

For the Student Strikers
(1970)

Go talk with those who are rumored to be unlike you,
And whom, it is said, you are so unlike.
Stand on the stoops of their houses and tell them why
You are out on strike.

5 It is not yet time for the rock, the bullet, the blunt
Slogan that fuddles the mind toward force.
Let the new sound in our streets be the patient sound
Of your discourse.

Doors will be shut in your faces, I do not doubt.
10 Yet here or there, it may be, there will start,
Much as the lights blink on in a block at evening,
Changes of heart.

They are your houses; the people are not unlike you;
Talk with them, then, and let it be done
15 Even for the grey wife of your nightmare sheriff
And the guardsman's son.

READING AND REACTING

1. Is this poem's diction primarily formal or informal? List the words that support your conclusion.
2. Besides its vocabulary, what elements in the poem might lead you to characterize it as formal or informal?
3. **JOURNAL ENTRY** This poem is an *exhortation,* a form of discourse intended to incite or encourage listeners to take action. Given the speaker's audience and subject matter, is its level of diction appropriate? Explain.

Related Works: "The *Chicago Defender* Sends a Man to Little Rock" (p. 933), *Another Antigone* (p. 1663)

◇ ◇ ◇

CHARLES BUKOWSKI
(1920–1994)

Dog Fight
(1984)

he draws up against my rear bumper in the fast lane,
I can see his head in the rear view mirror, his eyes
are blue and he sucks upon a dead cigar.
I pull over. he passes, then slows. I don't like
5 this.
I pull back into the fast lane, engage myself upon
his rear bumper. we are as a team passing through
Compton.
I turn the radio on and light a cigarette.
10 he ups it 5 mph, I do likewise. we are as a team
entering Inglewood.
he pulls out of the fast lane and I drive past.
then I slow. when I check the rear view he is
upon my bumper again.
15 he has almost made me miss my turnoff at Century.
I hit the blinker and fire across 3 lanes of
traffic, just make the off-ramp ...
blazing past the front of an inflammable tanker.
blue eyes comes down from behind the tanker and
20 we veer down the ramp in separate lanes to the signal
and we sit there side by side, not looking at each
other.
I am caught behind an empty school bus as he idles
behind a Mercedes.
25 the signal switches and he is gone. I cut to the
inner lane behind him, then I see that the parking
lane is open and I flash by inside of him and the
Mercedes, turn up the radio, make the green as the
Mercedes and blue eyes run the yellow into the red.
30 they make it as I power it and switch back ahead of
them in their lane in order to miss a parked vegetable
truck.
now we are running 1-2-3, not a cop in sight, we are
moving through a 1980 California July
35 we are driving with skillful nonchalance
we are moving in perfect anger

we are as a team
approaching LAX:[1]
1-2-3
40   2-3-1
3-2-1.

READING AND REACTING

1. "Dog Fight" describes a car race from the emotionally charged perspective of a driver. Given this persona, comment on the appropriateness of the level of diction of the following words: "likewise" (10), "upon" (14), "nonchalance" (35), "perfect" (36).

2. Many of the words in the poem are **jargon**—specialized language associated with a particular trade or profession. In this case, Bukowski uses automotive terms and the action words and phrases that typically describe driving maneuvers. Would you characterize these words as formal, informal, or neither? Explain.

3. What colloquialisms are present in the poem? Could noncolloquial expressions be substituted for any of them? How would such substitutions change the poem?

4. **JOURNAL ENTRY** Look up the phrase *dog fight* in a dictionary. What meanings are listed? Which one do you think Bukowski had in mind? Why?

5. **CRITICAL PERSPECTIVE** In a 1978 review in the *Village Voice*, critic Michael Lally defended Bukowski's poetry:

> Despite what some criticize as prose in Bukowski's poetry, there is in much of his work a poetic sensibility that, though arrogantly smart-ass and self-protective as well as self-promotional (he's the granddaddy of "punk" sensibility for sure), is also sometimes poignant, emotionally revealing, uniquely "American" [. . .].

Is "Dog Fight" prose, or do you see in it a "poetic sensibility"? In what sense, if any, do you find it "uniquely 'American'"? Give examples from the poem to support your conclusions.

Related Works: "Popular Mechanics" (p. 412), "Chicago" (p. 880), *The Cuban Swimmer* (p. 1495)

DIALECT

Dialect denotes a regional variety of language, which may differ from the most widely used standard spoken or written language in its pronunciation, grammar, or vocabulary. (Dialect is different from *slang*, which tends

---

[1] Los Angeles International Airport.

to be associated with groups determined by age or special interest rather than by region. In addition, slang is calculated to call attention to itself and its user, whereas dialect is not.) Dialect is generally used in poetry to suggest an authentic, unedited voice. Because it is associated with a particular region, dialect can also create a sense of place.

The poem that follows is told in the voice of a rural mountain woman.

◆ ◆ ◆

FAYE KICKNOSWAY
(1939–   )

Gracie
(1986)

I mean, I'm a no shoes hillbilly an' home
is deeper in the map than Kentucky or Tennessee an'
all I been raised to do is walk the chicken
yard, spillin' grain from ma's
5 apron, maybe once a week wear a bonnet
into town. I have red hair an' white skin;

men lean on their elbows lookin' at me. Ma's
voice tells me, "Don't breathe so deep," an'
the preacher says how happy I'll be when I'm dead. Skin
10 touchin' skin is evil. I'm to keep inside the chicken
yard, no eye's to see beneath my bonnet.
Farm boys suck their cheeks an' call, "Come home

with me, I'll give you your own chicken
yard an' take you proudly once a week to town." Home
15 ain't enough. As I spill grain from ma's
apron, I see city streets hung with lights an'
a dark room with a window lookin' on the bonnet
of the sky. Voices stroke at my skin

through its walls. When the grain's gone from ma's
20 apron, I hang it on its hook by her bonnet.
I figure to be my own fare North an' leave home.
My legs are crossed under a counter. I smell chicken
fry. A man leans on his elbows; his eyes drink my skin.
In a dark room, my dress undoes my body an'

25 I lie with him. His hot mouth comes home
on mine. I expect to hear the preacher's or ma's
voice yellin' at me, but the only voices in the wall's
                        skin
are strange an' soft. I have beer an' chicken
30 for breakfast. All day I wear his body like a bonnet.

My stockins are run. The streets are hung with lights an'
he sleeps. I stand by the window an'
look into the night's skin, fancy home an' the chicken
yard, ma's apron an' my head cool in its bonnet.

"Gracie" juxtaposes nonstandard grammatical forms such as "I been,"
"ain't," and "My stockins are run" with rich, understated figurative language such as "the bonnet / of the sky" and "Voices stroke at my skin."
The speaker uses contractions; shortened word forms ("ma"); colloquialisms, such as "I mean," "a no shoes hillbilly," "deep" (for "deeply"), and
"I figure"; and regionalisms, such as "chicken fry" and "I [. . .] fancy."
Apostrophes indicate conversational pronunciation in words such as "an',"
"touchin'," and "lookin'." The natural, colorful diction reveals the
speaker's personality, and the apparent guilelessness of the dialect gives a
sense of authenticity and directness to her voice.

❖ POEMS FOR FURTHER READING: DIALECT

◇ ◇ ◇

ROBERT BURNS
(1759–1796)

John Anderson My Jo
(1790)

> John Anderson my jo,[1] John,
>   When we were first acquent,[2]
> Your locks were like the raven,
>   Your bonny brow was brent;[3]
> 5 But now your brow is beld,[4] John,
>   Your locks are like the snaw;
> But blessings on your frosty pow,[5]
> John Anderson my jo.
>
> John Anderson my jo, John,
> 10   We clamb the hill thegither;
> And mony a canty[6] day, John,

---

[1] Dear.
[2] Acquainted.
[3] Unwrinkled.
[4] Bald.
[5] Head.
[6] Happy.

We've had wi' ane anither:
Now we maun[7] totter down, John,
And hand in hand we'll go,
15 And sleep thegither at the foot,
John Anderson my jo.

READING AND REACTING

1. Reread the definition of dialect on page 779. In what respects do the words in Burns's poem conform to this definition?
2. **JOURNAL ENTRY** "Translate" the poem into modern colloquial English prose. What is gained and lost in this "translation"?

Related Works: "That Time of Year Thou Mayst in Me Behold" (p. 669), "Nothing Gold Can Stay" (p. 800)

◊ ◊ ◊

GWENDOLYN BROOKS
(1917–   )

We Real Cool
(1960)

The Pool Players.
Seven at the Golden Shovel.

We real cool. We
Left School. We

Lurk late. We
Strike straight. We

5 Sing sin. We
Thin gin. We

Jazz June. We
Die soon.

READING AND REACTING

1. What elements identify the poem's level of diction as dialect rather than simply informal?
2. How does the poem's use of dialect affect your attitude toward the speaker?
3. **JOURNAL ENTRY** Write a prose version of this poem, adding words, phrases, or sentences to expand the poem into a paragraph.

---

[7] Must.

4. **CRITICAL PERSPECTIVE** In *Gwendolyn Brooks: Poetry and the Heroic Voice,* critic D. H. Malhem writes of "We Real Cool," "Despite presentation in the voice of the gang, this is a maternal poem, gently scolding yet deeply sorrowing for the hopelessness of the boys." Do you agree?

Related Works: "Greasy Lake" (p. 404), "Teenage Wasteland" (p. 603), "Where Are You Going, Where Have You Been?" (p. 614)

WORD ORDER

◆ ◆ ◆

The order in which words are arranged in a poem is just as important as the choice of words. Because English sentences nearly always have a subject-verb-object sequence, with adjectives preceding the nouns they modify, a departure from this order calls attention to itself. Thus, poets can use readers' expectations about word order to their advantage. Poets often manipulate word order in order to place emphasis on a word. Sometimes they achieve this emphasis by using a very unconventional sequence; sometimes they simply place the word first or last in a line or place it in a stressed position in the line. Poets may also choose a particular word order to make two related—or startlingly unrelated—words fall in adjacent or parallel position, calling attention to the similarity (or the difference) between them. In other cases, poets may manipulate syntax to preserve a poem's rhyme or meter or highlight sound correspondences that might otherwise not be noticeable. Finally, irregular syntax may be used throughout a poem to reveal a speaker's mood—for example, to give a playful quality to a poem or to suggest a speaker's disoriented state.

In the poem that follows, the placement of many words departs from conventional English syntax.

◆ ◆ ◆

EDMUND SPENSER
(1552–1599)

One Day I Wrote Her Name
upon the Strand
(1595)

One day I wrote her name upon the strand,[1]
But came the waves and washed it away:
Again I wrote it with a second hand,

---

[1] Beach.

But came the tide and made my pains his prey.
5 "Vain man," said she, "that doest in vain assay,
A mortal thing so to immortalize,
For I myself shall like to this decay,
And eek[2] my name be wiped out likewise."
"Not so," quod[3] I, "let baser things devise,
10 To die in dust, but you shall live by fame:
My verse your virtues rare shall eternize,
And in the heavens write your glorious name.
Where whenas death shall all the world subdue,
Our love shall live, and later life renew."

"One Day I Wrote Her Name upon the Strand," a sonnet, has a fixed metrical pattern and rhyme scheme. To accommodate the sonnet's rhyme and meter, Spenser makes a number of adjustments in syntax. For example, to make sure certain rhyming words fall at the ends of lines, the poet sometimes moves words out of their conventional order, as the following three comparisons illustrate.

Conventional Word Order	Inverted Sequence
"'Vain man,' she said, 'that doest *assay in vain.'*"	"'Vain man,' said she, 'that doest *in vain assay.'*" ("Assay" appears at end of line 5, to rhyme with line 7's "decay.")
"My verse shall *eternize your rare virtues.*"	"My verse *your virtues rare shall eternize.*" ("Eternize" appears at end of line 11 to rhyme with line 9's "devise.")
"Where whenas death shall *subdue all the world,* / Our love shall live, and *later renew life.*"	"Where whenas death shall *all the world subdue,* / Our love shall live, and *later life renew.*" (Rhyming words "subdue" and "renew" are placed at ends of lines.)

To make sure the metrical pattern stresses certain words, the poet occasionally moves a word out of order so it will fall on a stressed syllable. The following comparison illustrates this technique.

Conventional Word Order	Inverted Sequence
"But *the waves came* and washed it away."	"But *came the waves* and washed it away." (Stress in line 2 falls on "waves" rather than on "the.")

---

[2] Also, indeed.
[3] Said.

As the comparisons show, Spenser's adjustments in syntax are motivated at least in part by a desire to preserve the sonnet's rhyme and meter.

The following poem does more than simply invert words; it presents an intentionally disordered syntax.

◊ ◊ ◊

E. E. CUMMINGS
(1894–1962)

anyone lived in a
pretty how town
(1940)

anyone lived in a pretty how town
(with up so floating many bells down)
spring summer autumn winter
he sang his didn't he danced his did.

5 Women and men (both little and small)
cared for anyone not at all
they sowed their isn't they reaped their same
sun moon stars rain

children guessed (but only a few
10 and down they forgot as up they grew
autumn winter spring summer)
that noone loved him more by more

when by now and tree by leaf
she laughed his joy she cried his grief
15 bird by snow and stir by still
anyone's any was all to her

someones married their everyones
laughed their cryings and did their dance
(sleep wake hope and then) they
20 said their nevers they slept their dream

stars rain sun moon
(and only the snow can begin to explain
how children are apt to forget to remember
with up so floating many bells down)

25 one day anyone died i guess
(and noone stooped to kiss his face)
busy folk buried them side by side
little by little and was by was

all by all and deep by deep
30 and more by more they dream their sleep
noone and anyone earth by april
wish by spirit and if by yes.

Women and men (both dong and ding)
summer autumn winter spring
35 reaped their sowing and went their came
sun moon stars rain

At times Cummings, like Spenser, manipulates syntax in response to the demands of rhyme and meter—for example, in line 10. But Cummings goes much further, using unconventional syntax as part of a scheme that encompasses other unusual elements of the poem, such as its unexpected departures from the musical metrical pattern (for example, in line 3 and line 8) and from the rhyme scheme (for example, in lines 3 and 4), and its use of parts of speech in unfamiliar contexts. Together, these techniques give the poem a playful quality. The refreshing disorder of the syntax (for instance, in lines 1–2, line 10, and line 24) adds to the poem's whimsical effect.

❖ Poems for Further Reading: Word Order

◇ ◇ ◇

A. E. HOUSMAN
(1859–1936)

To an Athlete Dying Young
(1896)

The time you won your town the race
We chaired you through the market-place;
Man and boy stood cheering by,
And home we brought you shoulder-high.

5 Today, the road all runners come,
Shoulder-high we bring you home,
And set you at your threshold down,
Townsman of a stiller town.

Smart lad, to slip betimes away
10 From fields where glory does not stay,
And early though the laurel grows
It withers quicker than the rose.

Eyes the shady night has shut
Cannot see the record cut,
15 And silence sounds no worse than cheers
After earth has stopped the ears.

Now you will not swell the rout
Of lads that wore their honors out,
Runners whom renown outran
20 And the name died before the man.

So set, before its echoes fade,
The fleet foot on the sill of shade,
And hold to the low lintel up
The still-defended challenge-cup.

25 And round that early-laureled head
Will flock to gaze the strengthless dead,
And find unwithered on its curls
The garland briefer than a girl's.

READING AND REACTING

1. Where does the poem's meter or rhyme scheme require the poet to depart from conventional syntax?
2. Reword the poem using conventional word order. Do your changes improve the poem?
3. **JOURNAL ENTRY** Who do you think the speaker is? What is his relationship to the athlete?

Related Works: "Anthem for Doomed Youth" (p. 691), "Nothing Gold Can Stay" (p. 800), "Ex-Basketball Player" (p. 813)

◇ ◇ ◇

EMILY DICKINSON
(1830–1886)

My Life Had Stood— A Loaded Gun
(c. 1863)

My Life had stood—a Loaded Gun—
In Corners—till a Day
The Owner passed—identified—
And carried Me away—

5 And now We roam in Sovereign Woods—
And now We hunt the Doe—

And every time I speak for Him—
The Mountains straight reply—

And do I smile, such cordial light
10 Upon the Valley glow—
It is as a Vesuvian[1] face
Had let its pleasure through—

And when at Night—Our good Day done—
I guard My Master's Head—
15 'Tis better than the Eider-Duck's[2]
Deep Pillow—to have shared—

To foe of His—I'm deadly foe—
None stir the second time—
On whom I lay a Yellow Eye—
20 Or an emphatic Thumb—

Though I than He—may longer live
He longer must—than I—
For I have but the power to kill,
Without—the power to die—

READING AND REACTING

1. Identify lines in which word order departs from conventional
   English syntax. Can you explain in each case why the word order
   has been manipulated?
2. Do any words gain added emphasis by virtue of their unexpected
   position? Which ones? How are these words important to the
   poem's meaning?
3. **JOURNAL ENTRY** Why do you think the speaker might be
   comparing her life to a loaded gun?
4. **CRITICAL PERSPECTIVE** Writing in the *New York Times*,
   Elizabeth Schmidt offers this evaluation of Dickinson's poetry:

   > Her formal discipline—the economy of her language and her
   > elaborate, idiosyncratic metrical schemes—turns out to be
   > anything but off-putting. She chose forms that readers could
   > learn by heart, creating one of literature's great, and most un-
   > likely, combinations of style and content. Her poems are often
   > conceptually difficult, and yet they are also surprisingly invit-
   > ing, whether they coax you to guess a riddle or carry you along
   > to the beat of a familiar tune.

---

[1] Refers to Mount Vesuvius, a volcano that erupted in 79 A.D., destroying the city of
Pompeii.

[2] Refers to the duck that produces eiderdown, used for stuffing pillows.

Do you find Dickinson's poetry as inviting as Schmidt does, or do you think a poem like "My Life Had Stood—A Loaded Gun" *is* "off-putting"?

Related Works: "Because I Could Not Stop for Death" (p. 940), "I Heard a Fly Buzz—When I Died" (p. 941), "I Taste a Liquor Never Brewed" (p. 942)

CHECKLIST: WRITING ABOUT WORD CHOICE AND WORD ORDER

WORD CHOICE

✓ Which words are of key importance in the poem?

✓ What is the denotative meaning of each of these key words?

✓ Why is each word chosen instead of a synonym? (For example, is the word chosen for its sound? Its connotation? Its relationship to other words in the poem? Its contribution to the poem's metrical pattern?)

✓ What other words could be effectively used in place of words now in the poem?

✓ How would substitutions change the poem's meaning?

✓ Which key words have neutral connotations? Which have negative connotations? Which have positive connotations? Beyond its literal meaning, what does each word suggest?

✓ Are any words repeated? Why?

LEVELS OF DICTION

✓ How would you characterize the poem's level of diction? Why is this level of diction used? Is it effective?

✓ Does the poem mix different levels of diction? To what end?

✓ Does the poem use dialect? For what purpose?

WORD ORDER

✓ Is the poem's syntax conventional, or are words arranged in unexpected order?

✓ Which phrases represent departures from conventional syntax?

✓ What is the purpose of the unusual syntax? (For example, does it preserve the poem's meter or rhyme scheme? Does it highlight particular sound correspondences? Does it place emphasis on a particular word or phrase? Does it reflect the speaker's mood?)

✓ How would the poem's impact change if conventional syntax were used?

◆ Writing Suggestions: Word Choice, Word Order

1. Reread the two poems by E. E. Cummings—"in Just-" (p. 769) and "anyone lived in a pretty how town" (p. 785)—in this chapter. If you like, you may also read one or two additional poems in this text by Cummings. Do you believe Cummings chose words primarily for their sound? For their appearance on the page? What other factors might have influenced his choices?

2. The tone of "We Real Cool" (p. 782) is flat and unemotional; the problem on which it focuses, however, is a serious one. Expand this concise poem into an essay or story that uses more detailed, more emotional language to communicate the speaker's hopeless situation.

3. Reread "Gracie" (p. 780), and choose another poem in the text whose speaker is a woman. Compare the two speakers' levels of diction and choice of words. What does their speech reveal about their lives?

4. Reread "For the Grave of Daniel Boone" (p. 764) alongside Delmore Schwartz's "The True-Blue American" (p. 911). What does each poem's choice of words reveal about the speaker's attitude toward his subject?

5. Analyze the choice of words and the level of diction in Margaret Atwood's "The City Planners" (p. 772), William Blake's "London" (p. 929), and Denise Levertov's "What Were They Like?" (p. 695). Pay particular attention to each poem's use of language to express social or political criticism.

6. **Web Activity** The following Web site contains information about Charles Bukowski:

   http://www.charm.net/~brooklyn/buk.html

In the second paragraph on the Bukowski Web page, the author writes:

> Bukowski is generally considered to be an honorary "beat writer," although he was never actually associated with Jack Kerouac, Allen Ginsberg, and the other bona fide beat writers. His style, which exhibits a strong sense of immediacy and a refusal to embrace standard formal structure, has earned him a place in the hearts of beat generation readers.

Locate a Web site (or Web sites) that will tell you about the Beat Generation and its major literary figures—Jack Kerouac, Allen Ginsberg, and William S. Burroughs. Write an essay that identifies the "beat" characteristics of Bukowski's poem "Dog Fight" by drawing parallels between Bukowski's language and imagery and that of the other "beat" writers.

CHAPTER 15

Imagery

◇ ◇ ◇

Images are probably the most important part of the poem. First of all, you want to tell a story, but images are what are going to shore it up and get to the heart of the matter. [. . .] If they're not coming, I'm not even writing a poem, it's pointless.

ANNE SEXTON, *Writers at Work,* 4th ed.

The difference between a literature that includes the image, and a literature that excludes the image (such as the newspaper or the scientific Newtonian essay) is that the first helps us to bridge the gap between ourselves and nature, and the second encourages us to remain isolated, living despairingly in the gap. Many philosophers and critics urge us to remain in the gap, and let the world of nature and the world of men fall further and further apart. We can do that; or a human being can reach out with his right hand to the natural world, and with his left hand to the world of human intelligence, and touch both at the same moment. Apparently no one but human beings can do this.

ROBERT BLY, "What the Image Can Do"

The poet sits before a blank piece of paper with a need to say many things in the small space of the poem. The world is huge, the poet is alone, and the poem is just a bit of language, a few scratchings of a pen surrounded by the silence of the night.

It could be that the poet wishes to tell you about his or her life. A few images of some fleeting moment when one was happy or exceptionally lucid. The secret wish of poetry is to stop time. The poet wants to retrieve a face, a mood, a cloud in the sky, a tree in the wind, and take a kind of mental photograph of that moment in which you as a reader recognize yourself. Poems are other people's snapshots in which we recognize ourselves.

CHARLES SIMIC, Introduction to *Best American Poetry, 1992*

It is better to present one Image in a lifetime than to produce voluminous works.

EZRA POUND, "A Retrospect"

◇ ◇ ◇

◊ ◊ ◊

JANE FLANDERS
(1940–   )

Cloud Painter
(1984)

Suggested by the life and art of John Constable[1]

At first, as you know, the sky is incidental—
a drape, a backdrop for trees and steeples.
Here an oak clutches a rock (already he works outdoors),
a wall buckles but does not break,
5 water pearls through a lock, a haywain[2] trembles.

The pleasures of landscape are endless. What we see
around us should be enough.
Horizons are typically high and far away.

Still, clouds let us drift and remember. He is, after all,
10 a miller's son, used to trying
to read the future in the sky, seeing instead
ships, horses, instruments of flight.
Is that his mother's wash flapping on the line?
His schoolbook, smudged, illegible?

15 In this period the sky becomes significant.
Cloud forms are technically correct—mares' tails,
sheep-in-the-meadow, thunderheads.
You can almost tell which scenes have been interrupted
by summer showers.

20 Now his young wife dies.
His landscapes achieve belated success.
He is invited to join the Academy. I forget
whether he accepts or not.

In any case, the literal forms give way
25 to something spectral, nameless. His palette shrinks
to gray, blue, white—the colors of charity.
Horizons sink and fade,
trees draw back till they are little more than frames,
then they too disappear.

---

[1] John Constable (1776–1837)—British painter noted for his landscapes.
[2] An open horse-drawn wagon for carrying hay.

30 Finally the canvas itself begins to vibrate
with waning light,
as if the wind could paint.
And we too, at last, stare into a space
which tell us nothing,
35 except that the world can vanish along with our need for it.

Because the purpose of poetry—and, for that matter, of all literature—is to expand the perception of readers, poets appeal to the senses. In "Cloud Painter," for example, Jane Flanders uses details, such as the mother's wash on the line and the smudged schoolbook, to enable readers to visualize particular scenes in John Constable's early work (see *Landscape, Noon, the Haywain* in the color insert). Clouds are described so readers can picture them—"mares' tails, / sheep-in-the-meadow, thunderheads." Thus, "Cloud Painter" is not just about the work of John Constable; it is also about the ability of an artist—poet or painter—to call up images in the minds of an audience. To achieve this end, a poet uses **imagery,** language that evokes a physical sensation produced by one of the five senses—sight, hearing, taste, touch, or smell.

Although the effect can be quite complex, the way images work is simple: when you read the word *red,* your memory of the various red things that you have seen determines how you picture the image. In addition, the word *red* may have emotional associations, or **connotations,** that define your response. A red sunset, for example, can have a positive connotation or a negative one depending on whether it is associated with the end of a perfect day or with air pollution. By choosing an image carefully, then, poets not only create pictures in a reader's mind, but also suggest a great number of imaginative associations. These associations help poets to establish the **atmosphere** or **mood** of the poem. The image of softly falling snow in "Stopping by Woods on a Snowy Evening" (p. 960), for example, creates a quiet, almost mystical mood.

Readers come to a poem with their own unique experiences, so an image in a poem does not always suggest the same thing to all readers. In "Cloud Painter," for example, the poet presents the image of an oak tree clutching a rock. Although most readers will probably see a picture that is consistent with the one the poet sees, no two images will be identical. Every reader will have his or her own distinct mental image of a tree clinging to a rock; some images will be remembered experiences, whereas others will be imaginative creations. Some readers may even be familiar enough with the work of the painter John Constable to visualize a particular tree clinging to a particular rock in one of his paintings.

By conveying what the poet sees and imagines, images open readers' minds and enrich their reading with perceptions and associations different from—and possibly more original and complex than—their own.

One advantage of imagery is its extreme economy. Just a few words enable poets to evoke a range of emotions and reactions. In the following poem, just a few visual images are enough to create a picture.

◇ ◇ ◇

WILLIAM CARLOS WILLIAMS
(1883–1963)

Red Wheelbarrow
(1923)

so much depends
upon

a red wheel
barrow

5 glazed with rain
water

beside the white
chickens

"Red Wheelbarrow" asks readers to pause to consider the uniqueness and mystery of everyday objects. What is immediately apparent is the poem's verbal economy. The poet does not tell readers what the barnyard smells like or what sounds the animals make. In fact, he does not even paint a detailed picture of the scene. How large is the wheelbarrow? In what condition is it? How many chickens are in the barnyard? In this poem, the answers to these questions are not important. Even without answering these questions, the poet is able to use simple imagery to create a scene upon which, he says, "so much depends."

The wheelbarrow establishes a momentary connection between the poet and his world. Like a still-life painting, the red wheelbarrow beside the white chickens gives order to a world that is full of seemingly unrelated objects. By asserting the importance of the objects in the poem, the poet suggests that our ability to perceive the objects of this world gives our lives meaning and that our ability to convey our perceptions to others is central to our lives as well as to art.

Images enable poets to present ideas that would be difficult to convey in any other way. Just one look at a dictionary will illustrate that concepts such as *beauty* and *mystery* are so abstract that they are difficult to define, let alone to discuss in specific terms. By choosing an image or series of images to embody these ideas, however, poets can effectively make their feelings known, as Ezra Pound does in the brief poem that follows.

◇ ◇ ◇

EZRA POUND
(1885–1972)

In a Station of the Metro
(1916)

The apparition of these faces in the crowd;
Petals on a wet, black bough.

This poem is almost impossible to paraphrase because the information it communicates is less important than the feelings associated with this information. The poem's title indicates that the first line is meant to suggest a group of people gathered in a station of the Paris subway. The scene, however, is presented not as a clear picture but as an "apparition," suggesting that it is unexpected or even dreamlike. In contrast with the image of the subway platform is the image of the people's faces as flower petals on the dark branch of a tree. Thus, the subway platform—dark, cold, wet, subterranean (associated with baseness, death, and hell)—is juxtaposed with white flowers—delicate, pale, radiant, lovely (associated with the ideal, life, and heaven). These contrasting images, presented without comment, bear the entire weight of the poem.

Although images can be strikingly visual, they can also appeal to the senses of hearing, smell, taste, and touch. The following poem uses images of sound and taste as well as visual images.

◇ ◇ ◇

GARY SNYDER
(1930–   )

Some Good Things to Be Said for the Iron Age
(1970)

A ringing tire iron
    dropped on the pavement
Whang of a saw
    brusht on limbs
5 the taste
    of rust

Here Snyder presents two commonplace aural images: the ringing of a tire iron and the sound of a saw. These somewhat ordinary images gain power, however, through their visual isolation in the poem. Together they produce a harsh and jarring chord that in turn creates a sense of uneasiness in the reader. This poem does more than present sensory images, though. It also conveys the speaker's interpretations of these images. The last two lines of the poem imply not only that the time in which we live (the Iron Age) is base and mundane, but also that it is declining, decaying into an age of rust. This idea is reinforced by the repeated consonant sounds in *taste* and *rust,* which encourage readers to hold the final image of the poem on their tongues. The title of the poem makes an ironic comment, suggesting that compared to the time that is approaching, the age of iron may be "good." Thus, in the mind of the poet, ordinary events gain added significance, and images that spring from everyday experience become sources of enlightenment and insight.

In shorter poems, such as most of those discussed earlier, one or two images may serve as focal points. A longer poem may introduce a cluster of related images, creating a more complex tapestry of sensory impressions—as in the following poem, where several related images are woven together.

◊ ◊ ◊

SUZANNE E. BERGER
(1944–   )

The Meal
(1984)

They have washed their faces until they are pale,
their homework is beautifully complete.
They wait for the adults to lean towards each other.
The hands of the children are oval
5 and smooth as pine-nuts.

The girls have braided and rebraided their hair,
and tied ribbons without a single mistake.
The boy has put away his coin collection.
They are waiting for the mother to straighten her lipstick,
10 and for the father to speak.

They gather around the table, carefully
as constellations waiting to be named.
Their minds shift and ready, like dunes.
It is so quiet, all waiting stars and dunes.

15 Their forks move across their plates without scraping,
they wait for the milk and the gravy
at the table with its forgotten spices.
They are waiting for a happiness to lift their eyes,
like sudden light flaring in the trees outside.

20 The white miles of the meal continue,
   the figures still travel across a screen:
   the father carving the Sunday roast,
   her mouth uneven as a torn hibiscus,
   their braids still gleaming in the silence.

"The Meal" presents related images that together evoke silence, order, and emptiness. It begins with the image of faces washed "until they are pale" and goes on to describe the children's oval hands as "smooth as pine-nuts." Forks move across plates "without scraping," and the table hints at the memory of "forgotten spices." Despite the poem's title, these children are emotionally starved. The attentive, well-scrubbed children sit at a table where, neither eating nor speaking, they wait for "the milk and the gravy" and for happiness that never comes. The "white miles of the meal" seem to go on forever, reinforcing the sterility and emptiness of the Sunday ritual. Suggesting an absence of sensation or feeling, a kind of paralysis, the poem's images challenge conventional assumptions about the family and its rituals.

    Much visual imagery is **static,** freezing the moment and thereby giving it the timeless quality of painting or sculpture. ("The Meal" presents just such a tableau, and so do "Red Wheelbarrow" and "In a Station of the Metro.") Some imagery, however, is **kinetic,** conveying a sense of motion or change.

◊ ◊ ◊

WILLIAM CARLOS WILLIAMS
(1883–1963)

The Great Figure
(1938)

    Among the rain
    and lights
    I saw the figure 5
    in gold
5 on a red
    firetruck
    moving
    tense
    unheeded
10 to gong clangs
    siren howls
    and wheels rumbling
    through the dark city.

Commenting on "The Great Figure" in his autobiography, Williams explains that while walking in New York, he heard the sound of a fire engine. As he turned the corner, he saw a golden figure 5 on a red background speed by. The impression was so forceful that he immediately jotted down a poem about it. In the poem, Williams attempts to re-create the sensation the figure 5 made as it moved into his consciousness, presenting the image as if it were a picture taken by a camera with a high-speed shutter. The poet presents images in the order in which he perceived them: first the 5 and then the red fire truck howling and clanging into the darkness. Thus, "The Great Figure" uses images of sight, sound, and movement to re-create for readers the poet's experience. The American painter Charles Demuth was fascinated by the kinetic quality of the poem. Working closely with his friend Williams, he attempted to capture the stop-action feature of the poem in the painting reproduced in the color insert.

A special use of imagery, called **synesthesia,** occurs when one sense is described in a way that is more appropriate for another—for instance, when a sound is described with color. When people say they are feeling *blue* or describe music as *hot,* they are using synesthesia. The poet John Keats uses this technique in the following lines from "Ode to a Nightingale":

> O, for a draught of vintage! that hath been
>   Cool'd a long age in the deep-delvéd earth,
> Tasting of Flora and the country green,
>   Dance and Provençal song, and sunburnt mirth!

In these lines, the speaker describes the taste of wine in terms of images that appeal to a variety of senses: flowers, a grassy field, dance, song, and sun.

❖ POEMS FOR FURTHER READING: IMAGERY

◆ ◆ ◆

MATSUO BASHO
(1644?–1694)

Four Haiku[1]

Translated by Geoffrey Bownas and Anthony Thwaite

Spring:
A hill without a name
Veiled in morning mist.

The beginning of autumn:

---
[1] Publication date is not available.

5 Sea and emerald paddy
Both the same green.

The winds of autumn
Blow: yet still green
The chestnut husks.

10 A flash of lightning:
Into the gloom
Goes the heron's cry.

READING AND REACTING

1. A **haiku** is a three-line Japanese poem that traditionally has
seventeen syllables. Haiku are admired for their extreme economy
and their striking images. What are the central images in each of
Basho's haiku? To what senses do these images appeal?
2. In another poem, Basho says that art begins with "The depths of
the country / and a rice-planting song." What do you think he
means? In what way do the preceding poems exemplify this idea?
3. Do you think the conciseness of these poems increases or decreases
the impact of their images?
4. **JOURNAL ENTRY** "In a Station of the Metro" (p. 795) is Ezra
Pound's version of a haiku. How successful do you think Pound
was? Do you think a longer poem could have conveyed the images
more effectively?

Related Works: "Seventeen Syllables" (p. 376), "Hokku Poems" (p. 878),
"the sky was can dy" (p. 883), "Birches" (p. 956)

◊ ◊ ◊

CAROLYN KIZER
(1925–   )

After Basho
(1984)

Tentatively, you
slip onstage this evening,
pallid, famous moon.

READING AND REACTING

1. What possible meanings might the word "After" have in the title?
What does the title tell readers about the writer's purpose?

2. What visual picture does the poem suggest? What mood does the poem's central image create?
3. What is the impact of "tentatively" in the first line and "famous" in the last line? How do the connotations of these words affect the image of the moon?

Related Works: "Photograph of My Father in His Twenty-Second Year" (p. 675), "Widow's Lament" (p. 877), "Homage to the Empress of the Blues" (p. 965).

◇ ◇ ◇

RICHARD WILBUR
(1921–   )

Sleepless at Crown Point
(1973)

> All night, this headland
> Lunges into the rumpling
> Capework of the wind.

READING AND REACTING

1. What scene is the speaker describing?
2. What is the significance of the title?
3. What are the poem's central images? How do the words "lunges" and "capework" help to establish these images?

Related Works: "The Story of an Hour" (p. 77), "Fog" (p. 986), "The Dance" (p. 1007).

◇ ◇ ◇

ROBERT FROST
(1874–1963)

Nothing Gold Can Stay
(1923)

> Nature's first green is gold,
> Her hardest hue to hold.
> Her early leaf's a flower;
> But only so an hour.
> 5 Then leaf subsides to leaf.
> So Eden sank to grief.
> So dawn goes down to day.
> Nothing gold can stay.

READING AND REACTING

1. What central idea does this poem express?
2. What do you think the first line of the poem means? In what sense is this line ironic?
3. What is the significance of the colors green and gold in this poem? What do these colors have to do with "Eden" and "dawn"?
4. **JOURNAL ENTRY** How do the various images in the poem prepare readers for the last line?
5. **CRITICAL PERSPECTIVE** In "The Figure a Poem Means," the introduction to the first edition of his *Collected Poems* (1930), Frost laid out a theory of poetry:

> It begins in delight, it inclines to the impulse, it assumes direction with the first line laid down, it runs a course of lucky events, and ends in a clarification of life—not necessarily a great clarification [. . .] but a momentary stay against confusion. [. . .] Like a piece of ice on a hot stove the poem must ride on its own melting. [. . .] Read it a hundred times: it will forever keep its freshness as a metal keeps its fragrance. It can never lose its sense of a meaning that once unfolded by surprise as it went.

Can you apply Frost's remarks to "Nothing Gold Can Stay"?

Related Works: "The Secret Lion" (p. 49), "Shall I Compare Thee to a Summer's Day?" (p. 807), "God's Grandeur" (p. 966)

◊ ◊ ◊

JEAN TOOMER
(1894–1967)

Reapers
(1923)

Black reapers with the sound of steel on stones
Are sharpening scythes. I see them place the hones[1]
In their hip-pockets as a thing that's done,
And start their silent swinging, one by one.
5 Black horses drive a mower through the weeds,
And there, a field rat, startled, squealing bleeds,
His belly close to ground. I see the blade,
Blood-stained, continue cutting weeds and shade.

---

[1] Stones used to sharpen cutting instruments.

READING AND REACTING

1. What determines the order in which the speaker arranges the images in this poem? At what point does he comment on these images?
2. The first four lines of the poem seem to suggest that the workers are content. What image contradicts this impression? How does it do so?
3. What ideas are traditionally associated with the image of the reaper? The scythe? The harvest? (You may want to consult a reference work, such as *A Dictionary of Symbols* by J. E. Cirlot.) In what way does the speaker rely on these conventional associations to help him convey his ideas? Can you appreciate the poem without understanding these associations?
4. **CRITICAL PERSPECTIVE** As Brian Joseph Benson and Mabel Mayle Dillard point out in their 1980 study *Jean Toomer,* the poet disagreed with some other artists of the Harlem Renaissance, choosing not to focus on "Negro" themes for a primarily black audience, but rather to try to make his work universal in scope.

   Do you think he has achieved this goal in "Reapers"?

Related Works: "A Worn Path" (p. 388), "Lineage" (p. 1003), "The Solitary Reaper" (p. 1010).

◆ ◆ ◆

WILFRED OWEN
(1893–1918)

Dulce et Decorum Est[1]
(1920)

Bent double, like old beggars under sacks,
Knock-kneed, coughing like hags, we cursed through sludge,
Till on the haunting flares we turned our backs
And towards our distant rest began to trudge.
5 Men marched asleep. Many had lost their boots
But limped on, blood-shod. All went lame; all blind;
Drunk with fatigue; deaf even to the hoots
Of tired, outstripped Five-Nines[2] that dropped behind.

---

[1] The title and last lines are from Horace, *Odes* 3.2: "Sweet and fitting it is to die for one's country."

[2] Shells that explode on impact and release poison gas.

Gas! Gas! Quick, boys!—An ecstasy of fumbling,
10 Fitting the clumsy helmets just in time;
But someone still was yelling out and stumbling
And flound'ring like a man in fire or lime . . .
Dim, through the misty panes and thick green light,
As under a green sea, I saw him drowning.
15 In all my dreams, before my helpless sight,
He plunges at me, guttering, choking, drowning.

If in some smothering dreams you too could pace
Behind the wagon that we flung him in,
And watch the white eyes writhing in his face,
20 His hanging face, like a devil's sick of sin;
If you could hear, at every jolt, the blood
Come gargling from the froth-corrupted lungs,
Obscene as cancer, bitter as the cud
Of vile, incurable sores on innocent tongues,—
25 My friend, you would not tell with such high zest
To children ardent for some desperate glory,
The old Lie: Dulce et decorum est
Pro patria mori.

READING AND REACTING

1. Who is the speaker in this poem? What is his attitude toward his subject?
2. What images are traditionally associated with soldiers? How do the images in this poem depart from these associations? Why do you think Owen selected such images?
3. To what senses (other than sight) does the poem appeal to? Is any of the imagery kinetic?
4. **JOURNAL ENTRY** Does the knowledge that Owen died in World War I change your reaction to the poem, or are the poem's images compelling enough to eliminate the need for biographical background?
5. **CRITICAL PERSPECTIVE** Like many other British poets who experienced fighting in the European trenches during World War I, Owen struggled to find a new poetic idiom to describe the horrors of this new kind of war. In his 1986 biography *Owen the Poet*, Dominic Hibberd praises the "controlled and powerful anger in 'Dulce et Decorum Est' which for some readers will be the poem's most valuable quality" and goes on to note that the "organization and clarity of the first half is replaced [beginning at line 15] by confused, choking syntax and a vocabulary of sickness and disgust, matching the nightmare which is in progress."

Give some examples to support Hibberd's statements. How do the images in the poem help establish the movement from control to confusion?

Related Works: "The Things They Carried" (p. 280), "Anthem for Doomed Youth" (p. 691)

Checklist: Writing about Imagery

✓ Do the images in the poem appeal to the sense of sight, touch, hearing, smell, or taste?

✓ Does the poem depend on a single image or on a variety of different images?

✓ Does the poem depend on a cluster of related images?

✓ What details make the images memorable?

✓ What mood do the images create?

✓ Are the images static or kinetic? Are there any examples of synesthesia?

✓ How do the poem's images help to convey its theme?

✓ How effective are the images? In what way do the images enhance your enjoyment of the poem?

◊ Writing Suggestions: Imagery

1. How are short poems such as "Some Good Things to Be Said for the Iron Age" (p. 795) and "In a Station of the Metro" (p. 795) like and unlike haiku?

2. Reread "Cloud Painter" (p. 792) and "The Great Figure" (p. 797), and read "Musée des Beaux Arts" (p. 919), and study the corresponding paintings in the color insert (*Landscape, Noon, the Haywain; The Figure 5 in Gold;* and *Landscape with the Fall of Icarus,* respectively). Then, write a paper in which you draw some conclusions about the differences between artistic and poetic images.

3. Reread "The Meal" (p. 796) and the discussion that accompanies it. Then, analyze the role of imagery in the depiction of the parent/child relationships in "My Papa's Waltz" (p. 677) and "My Father's Wars" (p. 681). How does each poem's imagery convey the nature of the relationship it describes?

4. Write an essay in which you discuss the color imagery in "Nothing Gold Can Stay" (p. 800), "Reapers" (p. 801), and "The Yellow

Wall-Paper" (p. 168). In what way does color reinforce the themes of these works?

5. Sometimes imagery can be used to make a comment about the society in which a scene takes place. Choose two poems in which imagery functions in this way—"For the Union Dead" (p. 693), "The Colonel" (p. 889), or "The *Chicago Defender* Sends a Man to Little Rock" (p. 933), for example—and discuss how the images chosen reinforce the social statement each poem makes.

6. **WEB ACTIVITY** The following Web site contains information about Wilfred Owen:

> http://www.emory.edu/ENGLISH/LostPoets/Owen2.html

On the Owen Web page, the biography includes the following statement by Owen about his decision to fight in World War I:

> I came out in order to help these boys—directly by leading them as well as an officer can; indirectly, by watching their sufferings that I may speak of them as well as a pleader can. I have done the first.

Read the biographical material, and then write an essay discussing to what degree Owen accomplished his second goal to be a "pleader" in "Dulce et Decorum Est" (p. 802). Consider in particular his use of imagery in his descriptions of the soldiers' suffering as well as in his characterization of those who witness such suffering. In what sense does he plead for peace as well as for the men?

CHAPTER 16

Figures of Speech

◇ ◇ ◇

The metaphor is probably the most fertile power possessed by man.

José Ortega y Gasset

Poetry is made of comparisons, simple or complex, open or concealed. The richness of poetry is obtained by mixing or interweaving or juxtaposing these comparisons. The mixture is either a mechanical mixture or a chemical mixture: when the mechanical becomes chemical the explosion takes place. That is the difference between prose and poetry. In prose all comparisons are simple and uncompounded. In poetry all metaphors are mixed metaphors.

J. Isaacs, *The Background of Modern Poetry*

I suppose we shall never be able to distinguish absolutely and with a hard edge the image from the metaphor, any more than anyone has so distinguished prose from poetry. [. . .] We shall very often be able to tell, just as we can very often tell the difference between snow and rain; but there are some weathers which are either-neither, and so here there is an area where our differences will mingle. If the poet says, simply, "The red bird," we shall probably take that as an image. But as soon as we read the rest of the line—"The red bird flies across the golden floor"—there arise obscure thoughts of relationships that lead in the direction of parable: the line alone is not, strictly, a metaphor, but its resonances take it prospectively beyond a pure perception. [. . .] Metaphor stands somewhat as a mediating term squarely between a thing and a thought, which may be why it is so likely to compose itself about a word of sense and a word of thought, as in this example of a common Shakespearean formula: "Even to the teeth and forehead of my fault."

Howard Nemerov, "On Metaphor"

Metaphor is not to be considered, [. . .] as the alternative of the poet, which he may elect to use or not, since he may state the matter directly and straightforwardly if he chooses. It is frequently the only means available if he is to write at all [. . .].

Cleanth Brooks, "Metaphor and the Tradition"

◇ ◇ ◇

◊ ◊ ◊

WILLIAM SHAKESPEARE
(1564–1616)

Shall I Compare Thee to a Summer's Day?
(1609)

Shall I compare thee to a summer's day?
Thou art more lovely and more temperate.
Rough winds do shake the darling buds of May,
And summer's lease hath all too short a date.
5 Sometime too hot the eye of heaven shines,
And often is his gold complexion dimmed;
And every fair from fair sometimes declines,
By chance, or nature's changing course, untrimmed.
But thy eternal summer shall not fade,
10 Nor lose possession of that fair thou ow'st;[1]
Nor shall death brag thou wand'rest in his shade,
When in eternal lines to time thou grow'st.
    So long as men can breathe or eyes can see,
    So long lives this, and this gives life to thee.

Although figurative language is used in all kinds of writing, poets in particular recognize the power of a figure of speech to take readers beyond the literal meaning of a word. For this reason, **figures of speech**—expressions that use words to achieve effects beyond the power of ordinary language—are more prominent in poetry than in other kinds of writing. For example, the preceding sonnet by Shakespeare compares a loved one to a summer's day in order to make the point that, unlike the fleeting summer, the loved one will—within the poem—remain forever young. But this sonnet goes beyond the obvious equation (loved one = summer's day); the speaker's assertion that his loved one will live forever in his poem actually says more about his confidence in his own talent and reputation (and about the power of figurative language) than about the loved one's beauty.

SIMILE, METAPHOR, AND PERSONIFICATION
◊ ◊ ◊

When William Wordsworth opens a poem with "I wandered lonely as a cloud" (p. 1008), he conveys a good deal more than he would if he simply

---

[1] Beauty you possess.

said "I wandered, lonely." By comparing himself in his loneliness to a cloud, he suggests that like the cloud he is a part of nature and that he too is drifting, passive, blown by winds, and lacking will or substance. Thus, by using a figure of speech, the poet can suggest a wide variety of feelings and associations in very few words. The phrase "I wandered lonely as a cloud" is a **simile**, a comparison between two unlike items that includes *like* or *as*. When an imaginative comparison between two unlike items does not include *like* or *as*—that is, when it says "a is b" rather than "a is like b"—it is a **metaphor.**

Accordingly, when the speaker in Adrienne Rich's "Living in Sin" (p. 767) speaks of "daylight coming / like a relentless milkman up the stairs," she is using a strikingly original simile to suggest that daylight brings not the conventional associations of promise and awakening, but rather a stale, never-ending routine that is greeted without enthusiasm. This idea is consistent with the rest of the poem, an account of an unhappy relationship. However, when the speaker in Audre Lorde's poem says "Rooming houses are old women" (p. 811), she uses a metaphor, equating two elements to stress their common associations with emptiness, transience, and hopelessness. In addition, by identifying rooming houses as old women, Lorde is using **personification,** a special kind of comparison, closely related to metaphor, that gives life or human characteristics to inanimate objects or abstract ideas.

Sometimes, as in Wordsworth's "I wandered lonely as a cloud," a single brief simile or metaphor can be appreciated for what it communicates on its own. At other times, however, a simile or metaphor may be one of several related figures of speech that work together to communicate a poem's meaning. The following poem, for example, presents a series of related similes. Together, they suggest the depth of the problem the poem explores in a manner that each individual simile could not do alone.

◇ ◇ ◇

LANGSTON HUGHES
(1902–1967)

Harlem
(1951)

What happens to a dream deferred?

Does it dry up
like a raisin in the sun?
Or fester like a sore—
5   And then run?
Does it stink like rotten meat?

Or crust and sugar over—
like a syrupy sweet?

Maybe it just sags
10   like a heavy load.

Or does it explode?

The dream to which Hughes alludes in his 1951 poem is the dream of racial equality. It is also the American Dream—or, by extension, any important unrealized dream. His speaker offers six tentative answers to the question asked in the poem's first line, and five of the six are presented as similes. As the poem unfolds, the speaker considers different alternatives: The dream can shrivel up and die, fester, decay, crust over—or just sag under the weight of the burden those who hold the dream must carry. In each case, the speaker transforms an abstract entity—a dream—into a concrete item—a raisin in the sun, a sore, rotten meat, syrupy candy, a heavy load. The final line of the poem, italicized for emphasis, gains power less from what it says than from what it leaves unsaid. Unlike the other alternatives explored in the poem, *"Or does it explode?"* is not presented as a simile. Nevertheless, because of the pattern of figurative language the poem has established, readers supply the other, unspoken half of the comparison: ". . . like a bomb."

Sometimes a single *extended simile* or *extended metaphor* is developed throughout a poem. The poem that follows, for example, develops an extended simile, comparing a poet to an acrobat.

◆ ◆ ◆

LAWRENCE FERLINGHETTI
(1919–)

Constantly Risking Absurdity
(1958)

Constantly risking absurdity
                    and death
        whenever he performs
                    above the heads
5   of his audience
        the poet like an acrobat
                    climbs on rime
                            to a high wire of his own making
        and balancing on eyebeams
10   above a sea of faces
                paces his way

> to the other side of day
> performing entrechats
> and sleight-of-foot tricks
> 15 and other high theatrics
> and all without mistaking
> any thing
> for what it may not be
>
> For he's the super realist
> 20 who must perforce perceive
> taut truth
> before the taking of each stance or step
> in his supposed advance
> toward that still higher perch
> 25 where Beauty stands and waits
> with gravity
> to start her death-defying leap
>
> And he
> a little charleychaplin man
> 30 who may or may not catch
> her fair eternal form
> spreadeagled in the empty air
> of existence

In his extended comparison between a poet and an acrobat, Ferlinghetti characterizes the poet as a kind of all-purpose circus performer, at once swinging recklessly on a trapeze and balancing carefully on a tightrope.

What the poem suggests is that the poet, like an acrobat, works hard at his craft but manages to make it all look easy. Something of an exhibitionist, the poet is innovative and creative, taking impossible chances yet also building on traditional skills in his quest for truth and beauty. Moreover, like an acrobat, the poet is balanced "on eyebeams / above a sea of faces," for he too depends on audience reaction to help him keep his performance focused. The poet may be "the super realist," but he also has plenty of playful tricks up his sleeve: "entrechats / and sleight-of-foot tricks / and other high theatrics," including puns ("above the heads / of his audience"), unexpected rhyme ("climbs on rime"), alliteration ("taut truth"), coinages ("a little charleychaplin man"), and all the other linguistic acrobatics available to poets. (Even the arrangement of the poem's lines on the page suggests the acrobatics it describes.) Like these tricks, the poem's central simile is a whimsical one, perhaps suggesting that Ferlinghetti is poking fun at poets who take their craft too seriously. In any case, the simile helps him to illustrate the acrobatic possibilities of language in a fresh and original manner.

The following poem develops an extended metaphor, personifying rooming houses as old women.

◊   ◊   ◊

AUDRE LORDE
(1934–1992)

Rooming Houses Are Old Women
(1968)

Rooming houses are old women
rocking dark windows into their whens
waiting incomplete circles
rocking
5 rent office to stoop to
community bathrooms to gas rings and
under-bed boxes of once useful garbage
city issued with a twice monthly check
and the young men next door
10 with their loud midnight parties
and fishy rings left in the bathtub
no longer arouse them
from midnight to mealtime no stops inbetween
light breaking to pass through jumbled up windows
15 and who was it who married the widow that Buzzie's son messed with?

To Welfare and insult form the slow shuffle
from dayswork to shopping bags
heavy with leftovers
Rooming houses
20 are old women waiting
searching
through darkening windows
the end or beginning of agony
old women seen through half-ajar doors
25 hoping
they are not waiting
but being
the entrance to somewhere
unknown and desired
30 but not new.

So closely does Lorde equate rooming houses and women in this poem that at times it is difficult to tell which of the two is actually the poem's subject. Despite the poem's assertion, rooming houses are *not* old women; however, they are *comparable to* the old women who live there, because their walls enclose a lifetime of disappointments as well as the physical detritus of life. Like the old women, rooming houses are in decline, rocking away their remaining years. Like the houses they inhabit, these women's boundaries are fixed—"rent office to stoop to / community bathrooms to gas rings"—and their hopes and expectations are few. They are surrounded by other people's loud parties, but their own lives have been reduced to a "slow shuffle" to nowhere, a hopeless, frightened—and perhaps point-less—"waiting / searching." Over time, the women and the places in which they live have become one. By using an unexpected comparison be-tween two seemingly unrelated entities, the poem illuminates both the essence of the rooming houses and the essence of their elderly occupants.

❖ POEMS FOR FURTHER READING: SIMILE, METAPHOR, AND PERSONIFICATION

◆ ◆ ◆

ROBERT BURNS
(1759–1796)

Oh, My Love Is like a Red, Red Rose
(1796)

Oh, my love is like a red, red rose
    That's newly sprung in June;
My love is like the melody
    That's sweetly played in tune.

5 So fair art thou, my bonny lass,
    So deep in love am I;
And I will love thee still, my dear,
    Till a' the seas gang[1] dry.

Till a' the seas gang dry, my dear,
10   And the rocks melt wi' the sun;
And I will love thee still, my dear,
    While the sands o' life shall run.

And fare thee weel, my only love!
    And fare thee weel awhile!
15 And I will come again, my love
    Though it were ten thousand mile.

READING AND REACTING

1. Why does the speaker compare his love to a rose? What other simile is used in the poem? For what purpose is it used?
2. Why do you suppose Burns begins his poem with similes? Would moving them to the end change the poem's impact?

---

[1] Go.

3. Where does the speaker seem to exaggerate the extent of his love? Why does he exaggerate? Do you think this exaggeration weakens the effectiveness of the poem? Explain.

Related Works: "Araby" (p. 254), "My Mistress' Eyes Are Nothing Like the Sun" (p. 684), "To His Coy Mistress" (p. 824)

◇ ◇ ◇

JOHN UPDIKE
(1932–   )

Ex-Basketball Player
(1958)

Pearl Avenue runs past the high-school lot,
Bends with the trolley tracks, and stops, cut off
Before it has a chance to go two blocks,
At Colonel McComsky Plaza. Berth's Garage
5 Is on the corner facing west, and there,
Most days, you'll find Flick Webb, who helps Berth out.

Flick stands tall among the idiot pumps—
Five on a side, the old bubble-head style,
Their rubber elbows hanging loose and low.
10 One's nostrils are two S's, and his eyes
An E and O. And one is squat, without
A head at all—more of a football type.

Once Flick played for the high-school team, the Wizards.
He was good: in fact, the best. In '46
15 He bucketed three hundred ninety points,
A county record still. The ball loved Flick.
I saw him rack up thirty-eight or forty
In one home game. His hands were like wild birds.

He never learned a trade, he just sells gas,
20 Checks oil, and changes flats. Once in a while,
As a gag, he dribbles an inner tube,
But most of us remember anyway.
His hands are fine and nervous on the lug wrench.
It makes no difference to the lug wrench, though.

25 Off work, he hangs around Mae's luncheonette.
Grease-gray and kind of coiled, he plays pinball,
Smokes those thin cigars, nurses lemon phosphates.
Flick seldom says a word to Mae, just nods
Beyond her face toward bright applauding tiers
30 Of Necco Wafers, Nibs, and Juju Beads.

READING AND REACTING

1. Explain the use of personification in the second stanza and in the poem's last two lines. What two elements make up each figure of speech? How are the two elements in each pair alike?
2. What kind of figure of speech is each of the following: "His hands were like wild birds" (18); "Grease-gray and kind of coiled" (26)? What other figures of speech can you identify in the poem?
3. **JOURNAL ENTRY** Who do you think this poem's speaker might be? What is his attitude toward Flick Webb? Do you think Flick himself shares this assessment? Explain.

Related Works: "Miss Brill" (p. 119), "Sadie and Maud" (p. 835), *Death of a Salesman* (p. 1410)

◊　◊　◊

RANDALL JARRELL
(1914–1965)

The Death of the Ball Turret Gunner
(1945)

From my mother's sleep I fell into the State
And I hunched in its belly till my wet fur froze.
Six miles from earth, loosed from its dream of life,
I woke to black flak and the nightmare fighters.
5 When I died they washed me out of the turret with a hose.

READING AND REACTING

1. Who is the speaker? To what does he compare himself in the poem's first two lines? What words establish this comparison?
2. Contrast the speaker's actual identity with the one he creates for himself in lines 1–2. What elements of his actual situation do you think lead him to characterize himself as he does in these lines?
3. **JOURNAL ENTRY** Both this poem and "Dulce et Decorum Est" (p. 802) use figurative language to describe the horrors of war. Which poem has a greater impact on you? How does the poem's figurative language contribute to this impact?
4. **CRITICAL PERSPECTIVE** In a 1974 article, Frances Ferguson criticizes "The Death of the Ball Turret Gunner," arguing that the poem "thoroughly manifests the lack of a middle between the gunner's birth and his death. [. . .] Because the poem presents a man who seems to have lived in order to die, we forget the fiction that he must have lived." However, in a 1978 explication, Patrick

J. Horner writes that the "manipulation of time reveals the stunning brevity of the gunner's waking life and the State's total disregard for that phenomenon. [. . .] Because of the telescoping of time, [. . . the poem] resonates with powerful feeling."

With which critic do you agree? That is, do you see the "lack of a middle" as a positive or negative quality of this poem?

Related Works: "The Things They Carried" (p. 280), "An Irish Airman Foresees His Death" (p. 691), "Goodnight Saigon" (p. 698), "Dulce et Decorum Est" (p. 802)

◊ ◊ ◊

MARGE PIERCY
(1934–   )

The Secretary Chant
(1973)

My hips are a desk.
From my ears hang
chains of paper clips.
Rubber bands form my hair.
5 My breasts are wells of mimeograph ink.
My feet bear casters.
Buzz. Click.
My head is a badly organized file.
My head is a switchboard
10 where crossed lines crackle.
Press my fingers
and in my eyes appear
credit and debit.
Zing. Tinkle.
15 My navel is a reject button.
From my mouth issue canceled reams.
Swollen, heavy, rectangular
I am about to be delivered
of a baby
20 Xerox machine.
File me under W
because I wonce
was
a woman.

READING AND REACTING

1. Examine each of the poem's figures of speech. Do they all make reasonable comparisons, or are some far-fetched or hard to

visualize? Explain the relationship between the secretary and each item with which she is compared.

2. **JOURNAL ENTRY**   Using as many metaphors and similes as you can, write a "chant" about a job you have held.

3. **CRITICAL PERSPECTIVE**   In a review of a recent collection of Piercy's poetry, feminist critic Sandra Gilbert notes instances of "a kind of bombast" (pompous language) and remarks, "As most poets realize, political verse is almost the hardest kind to write."

In what sense can "The Secretary Chant" be seen as "political verse"? Do you think Piercy successfully achieves her political purpose, or does she undercut it with "bombast"?

Related Works: "Like a Winding Sheet" (p. 125), "Barbie-Q" (p. 414), "The Metamorphosis" (p. 474), "Girl" (p. 509), "Women" (p. 891), "Metaphors" (p. 981)

◊ ◊ ◊

JOHN DONNE
(1572–1631)

A Valediction: Forbidding Mourning
(1611)

As virtuous men pass mildly away,
  And whisper to their souls to go,
Whilst some of their sad friends do say
  The breath goes now, and some say no:

5 So let us melt, and make no noise,
  No tear-floods, nor sigh-tempests move;
'Twere profanation of our joys
  To tell the laity[1] our love.

Moving of th' earth brings harms and fears;
10   Men reckon what it did and meant;
But trepidation of the spheres,
  Though greater far, is innocent.

Dull sublunary lovers' love
  (Whose soul is sense) cannot admit
15 Absence, because it doth remove
  Those things which elemented it.

----

[1] Here, "common people."

Charles Henry Demuth (1883–1935). *The Figure 5 in Gold*.
Oil on composition board, 36 × 29¾ in. THE METROPOLITAN MUSEUM OF ART,
THE ALFRED STEIGLITZ COLLECTION, 1949. (49.59.1)
Photograph © The Metropolitan Museum of Art.

John Constable (1776–1837). *Landscape, Noon, The Haywain*. 1821.
Oil on canvas, 130½ × 185½ cm.
LONDON, NATIONAL GALLERY.

Brueghel, Pieter the Elder (1525?–1569). *Landscape with the Fall of Icarus*.
MUSÉE ROYAUX DES BEAUX-ARTS.
Scala/Art Resource, N.Y.

Claude Monet (1840–1926).
Water Lilies. 1820–1821.
Oil on canvas.
THE CARNEGIE MUSEUM OF ART,
Pittsburgh
(acquired through the generosity of
Mrs. Alan M. Scaife, 1962).

Aaron Douglas
(1898–1979).
Aspects of Negro Life. 1934.
Mural at the
HARLEM BRANCH OF THE
NEW YORK PUBLIC LIBRARY.
Arts and Artifact
Division,
Schomburg Center for Re-
search in Black
Culture, the New York
Public Library.
Astor, Lenox and
Tilden Foudations.

Fritz Scholder (1937–   ). *American Indian No. 4.* 1972.
Courtesy of Fritz Scholder.

But we, by a love so much refined
 That ourselves know not what it is,
Inter-assurèd of the mind,
20 Care less, eyes, lips, and hands to miss.

Our two souls, therefore, which are one,
 Though I must go, endure not yet
A breach, but an expansion,
 Like gold to airy thinness beat.

25 If they be two, they are two so
 As stiff twin compasses[2] are two:
Thy soul, the fixed foot, makes no show
 To move, but doth, if th' other do.

And though it in the center sit,
30 Yet when the other far doth roam,
It leans and harkens after it,
 And grows erect as that comes home.

Such wilt thou be to me, who must,
 Like th' other foot, obliquely run;
35 Thy firmness makes my circle just,[3]
 And makes me end where I begun.

READING AND REACTING

1. Beginning with line 25, the poem develops an extended metaphor, called a **conceit,** which compares the speaker and his loved one to "twin compasses" (26), attached and yet separate. Why is the compass an especially apt metaphor? What qualities of the compass does the poet emphasize?

2. The poem uses other figures of speech to characterize both the lovers' union and their separation. To what other events does the speaker compare his separation from his loved one? To what other elements does he compare their attachment? Do you think these comparisons are effective?

3. **JOURNAL ENTRY** To what other object could Donne have compared his loved one and himself? Explain the logic of the extended metaphor you suggest.

4. **CRITICAL PERSPECTIVE** In *John Donne and the Metaphysical Poets* (1970), Judah Stampfer writes of this poem's "thin, dry texture, its stanzas of pinched music," noting that its form "has too clipped a brevity to qualify as a song" and that its "music

---

[2] The reference here is to the V-shaped instrument used to draw circles, not to the device used to determine direction.

[3] Perfect.

wobbles on a dry, measured beat." Yet, he argues, "the poem comes choked with emotional power" because "the speaker reads as a naturally reticent man, leaving his beloved in uncertainty and deep trouble." Stampfer concludes, "Easy self-expression here would be self-indulgent, if not reprehensible. [. . .] For all his careful dignity, we feel a heart is breaking here."

Do you find such emotional power in this highly intellectual poem?

Related Works: "How Do I Love Thee?" (p. 686), "To My Dear and Loving Husband" (p. 823), "The Silken Tent" (p. 960), *A Doll House* (p. 1196)

HYPERBOLE AND UNDERSTATEMENT
◊ ◊ ◊

Two additional kinds of figurative language, *hyperbole* and *understatement*, also give poets opportunities to suggest meaning beyond the literal level of language.

Hyperbole is intentional exaggeration—saying more than is actually meant. In the poem "Oh, My Love Is like a Red, Red Rose" (p. 812), when the speaker says that he will love his lady until all the seas go dry, he is using hyperbole. **Understatement** is just the opposite—saying less than is meant. When the speaker in the poem "Fire and Ice" (p. 735), weighing two equally grim alternatives for the end of the world, says that "for destruction ice / Is also great / And would suffice," he is using understatement. In both cases, poets rely on their readers to understand that their words are not to be taken literally.

By using hyperbole and understatement, poets attract readers' attention. For example, poets can use hyperbole to convey exaggerated anger or graphic images of horror—and to ridicule and satirize as well as to inflame and shock. With understatement, poets can convey the same kind of powerful emotions subtly, without artifice or embellishment, thereby leading readers to look more closely than they would otherwise do.

The emotionally charged poem that follows uses hyperbole to attract attention, conveying anger and bitterness that seem almost beyond the power of words.

◊ ◊ ◊

SYLVIA PLATH
(1932–1963)

Daddy
(1965)

You do not do, you do not do
Any more, black shoe
In which I have lived like a foot

For thirty years, poor and white,
5 Barely daring to breathe or Achoo.

Daddy, I have had to kill you.
You died before I had time—
Marble-heavy, a bag full of God,
Ghastly statue with one grey toe
10 Big as a Frisco seal

And a head in the freakish Atlantic
Where it pours bean green over blue
In the waters off beautiful Nauset.
I used to pray to recover you.
15 Ach, du.[1]

In the German tongue, in the Polish town[2]
Scraped flat by the roller
Of wars, wars, wars.
But the name of the town is common.
20 My Polack friend

Says there are a dozen or two.
So I never could tell where you
Put your foot, your root,
I never could talk to you.
25 The tongue stuck in my jaw.

It stuck in a barb wire snare.
Ich, ich, ich, ich,[3]
I could hardly speak.
I thought every German was you.
30 And the language obscene

An engine, an engine
Chuffing me off like a Jew.
A Jew to Dachau, Auschwitz, Belsen.[4]
I began to talk like a Jew.
35 I think I may well be a Jew.

The snows of the Tyrol, the clear beer of Vienna
Are not very pure or true.
With my gypsy ancestress and my weird luck
And my Taroc pack and my Taroc pack
40 I may be a bit of a Jew.

---

[1] Ah, you. (German)
[2] Grabôw, where Plath's father was born.
[3] I. (German)
[4] Nazi concentration camps.

I have always been scared of *you*,
With your Luftwaffe,[5] your gobbledygoo.
And your neat moustache
And your Aryan eye, bright blue.
45 Panzer[6]-man, panzer-man, O You—

Not God but a swastika
So black no sky could squeak through.
Every woman adores a Fascist,
The boot in the face, the brute
50 Brute heart of a brute like you.

You stand at the blackboard, daddy,
In the picture I have of you,
A cleft in your chin instead of your foot
But no less a devil for that, no not
55 Any less the black man who

Bit my pretty red heart in two.
I was ten when they buried you.
At twenty I tried to die
And get back, back, back to you.
60 I thought even the bones would do.

But they pulled me out of the sack,
And they stuck me together with glue.
And then I knew what to do.
I made a model of you,
65 A man in black with a Meinkampf[7] look

And a love of the rack and the screw.
And I said I do, I do.
So daddy, I'm finally through.
The black telephone's off at the root,
70 The voices just can't worm through.

If I've killed one man, I've killed two—
The vampire who said he was you
And drank my blood for a year,
Seven years, if you want to know.
75 Daddy, you can lie back now.

---

[5] The German air force.
[6] Protected by armor. The Panzer division was the German armored division.
[7] *Mein Kampf* (My Struggle) is Adolf Hitler's autobiography.

There's a stake in your fat black heart
And the villagers never liked you.
They are dancing and stamping on you.
They always *knew* it was you.
80 Daddy, daddy, you bastard, I'm through.

In her anger and frustration, the speaker sees herself as a helpless victim—
a foot entrapped in a shoe, a Jew in a concentration camp—of her father's
(and, later, her husband's) absolute tyranny. Thus, her hated father is characterized as a "black shoe," "a bag full of God," a "ghastly statue," and,
eventually, a Nazi, a torturer, the devil, a vampire. The poem "Daddy" is
widely accepted by scholars as autobiographical, and the fact that Plath's
own father was actually neither a Nazi nor a sadist (nor, obviously, the
devil or a vampire) makes it clear that the figurative comparisons in the
poem are wildly exaggerated. Even so, they may convey the poet's true
feelings toward her father—and, perhaps, toward the patriarchal society in
which she lived.

Plath uses hyperbole as the medium through which to communicate
these emotions to readers who she knows cannot possibly feel the way she
does. Her purpose, therefore, is not just to shock but also to enlighten, to
persuade, and perhaps even to empower her readers. Throughout the
poem, the inflammatory language is set in ironic opposition to the childish, affectionate term "Daddy"—most strikingly in the last line's choked
out "Daddy, daddy, you bastard, I'm through." The result of the exaggerated rhetoric is a poem that is vivid and shocking. And, although some
might believe that Plath's almost wild exaggeration undermines the
poem's impact, others would argue that the powerful figurative language
is necessary to convey the extent of the speaker's rage.

Like "Daddy," the next poem presents a situation whose emotional
impact is devastating. In this case, however, the poet does not use emotional language; instead, he uses understatement, presenting the events
without embellishment.

◆ ◆ ◆

DAVID HUDDLE
(1942–   )

Holes Commence Falling
(1979)

The lead & zinc company
owned the mineral rights
to the whole town anyway,
and after drilling holes

5 for 3 or 4 years,
they finally found the right
place and sunk a mine shaft.
We were proud
of all that digging,
10 even though nobody from
town got hired. They
were going to dig right
under New River and hook up
with the mine at Austinville.
15 Then people's wells
started drying up just like
somebody'd shut off a faucet,
and holes commenced falling,
big chunks of people's yards
20 would drop 5 or 6 feet,
houses would shift and crack.
Now and then the company'd
pay out a little money
in damages; they got a truck
25 to haul water and sell it
to the people whose wells
had dried up, but most
everybody agreed the
situation wasn't
30 serious.

Although "Holes Commence Falling" relates a tragic sequence of events, the tone of the poem is matter-of-fact and the language is understated. Certainly the speaker could have overdramatized the events, using inflated rhetoric to denounce big business and to predict disastrous events for the future. At the very least, he could have colored the events with realistic emotions, assigning blame to the lead and zinc company with justifiable anger. Instead, the speaker is so restrained, so nonchalant, so passive that readers must supply the missing emotions themselves—realizing, for example, that when the speaker concludes "everybody agreed the / situation wasn't / serious," he means just the opposite.

Throughout the poem, unpleasant events are presented without comment or emotion. As it proceeds, the poem traces the high and low points in the town's fortunes, but for every hope ("We were proud / of all that digging") there is a disappointment ("even though nobody from / town got hired"). The lead and zinc company offers some compensation for the damage it does, but never enough. The present tense verb of the poem's title indicates that the problems the town faces—wells drying up, yards dropping, houses shifting and cracking—are regular occurrences.

Eventually, readers come to see that what is not expressed, what lurks just below the surface—anger, powerlessness, resentment, hopelessness—is the poem's real subject. The speaker's laconic speech and flat tone seem to suggest an attitude of resignation, but the obvious contrast between the understated tone and the seriousness of the problem creates a sense of irony that makes the speaker's real attitude toward the lead and zinc company clear.

❖ POEMS FOR FURTHER READING: HYPERBOLE
   AND UNDERSTATEMENT

❖ ❖ ❖

ANNE BRADSTREET
(1612?–1672)

To My Dear and Loving Husband
(1678)

If ever two were one, then surely we.
If ever man were lov'd by wife, then thee;
If ever wife was happy in a man,
Compare with me ye women if you can.
5 I prize thy love more than whole Mines of gold,
Or all the riches that the East doth hold.
My love is such that Rivers cannot quench,
Nor ought but love from thee, give recompense.
Thy love is such I can no way repay,
10 The heavens reward thee manifold I pray.
Then while we live, in love let's so persever,
That when we live no more, we may live ever.

READING AND REACTING

1. Review the claims the poem's speaker makes about her husband in lines 5–8. Are such exaggerated declarations of love necessary, or would the rest of the poem be sufficient to convey the extent of her devotion to her husband?
2. **JOURNAL ENTRY** Compare this poem's declarations of love to those of John Donne's speaker in "A Valediction: Forbidding Mourning" (p. 816). Which speaker do you believe is more convincing? Why?

Related Works: "A Rose for Emily" (p. 87), "Bright Star! Would I Were Steadfast as Thou Art" (p. 971)

◊ ◊ ◊
ANDREW MARVELL
(1621–1678)

To His Coy Mistress
(1681)

Had we but world enough and time,
This coyness, lady, were no crime.
We would sit down and think which way
To walk, and pass our long love's day.
5 Thou by the Indian Ganges' side
Should'st rubies find; I by the tide
Of Humber[1] would complain. I would
Love you ten years before the Flood,
And you should, if you please, refuse
10 Till the conversion of the Jews.
My vegetable love should grow
Vaster than empires, and more slow.
An hundred years should go to praise
Thine eyes, and on thy forehead gaze,
15 Two hundred to adore each breast,
But thirty thousand to the rest.
An age at least to every part,
And the last age should show your heart.
For, lady, you deserve this state,
20 Nor would I love at lower rate.
    But at my back I always hear
Time's wingèd chariot hurrying near,
And yonder all before us lie
Deserts of vast eternity.
25 Thy beauty shall no more be found,
Nor in thy marble vault shall sound
My echoing song; then worms shall try
That long preserved virginity,
And your quaint honor turn to dust,
30 And into ashes all my lust.
The grave's a fine and private place,
But none, I think, do there embrace.
    Now therefore, while the youthful hue
Sits on thy skin like morning glew[2]
35 And while thy willing soul transpires
At every pore with instant fires,

---

[1] An estuary in the east coast of England.
[2] Dew.

Now let us sport us while we may;
And now, like amorous birds of prey,
Rather at once our time devour
40 Than languish in his slow-chapped[3] power.
Let us roll all our strength and all
Our sweetness up into one ball
And tear our pleasures with rough strife
Thorough the iron gates of life.
45 Thus, though we cannot make our sun
Stand still, yet we will make him run.

READING AND REACTING

1. In this poem, Marvell's speaker sets out to convince a reluctant woman to become his lover. In order to make his case more convincing, he uses hyperbole, exaggerating time periods, sizes, spaces, and the possible fate of the woman, should she refuse him. Identify as many examples of hyperbole as you can.

2. The tone of "To His Coy Mistress" is more whimsical than serious. Given this tone, what do you see as the purpose of Marvell's use of hyperbole?

3. **JOURNAL ENTRY** Using contemporary prose, paraphrase the first four lines of the poem. Then, beginning with the word *But*, write a few additional sentences, continuing the argument Marvell's speaker makes.

4. **CRITICAL PERSPECTIVE** In his poem "The Definition of Love," Marvell laments love that is kept apart by fate. He writes:

> For Fate with jealous eye does see
> Two perfect loves, nor lets them close;
> Their union would her ruin be,
> And her tyrannic pow'r depose.

How does Marvell propose to compensate for Fate's determination to keep true love apart in "To His Coy Mistress"?

Related Works: "Where Are You Going, Where Have You Been?" (p. 614), "The Passionate Shepherd to His Love" (p. 682), "To the Virgins, to Make Much of Time" (p. 743), *The Brute* (p. 1266)

---

[3] Slowly crushing.

◊ ◊ ◊

ROBERT FROST
(1874–1963)

"Out, Out—"
(1916)

The buzz saw snarled and rattled in the yard
And made dust and dropped stove-length sticks of wood,
Sweet-scented stuff when the breeze drew across it.
And from there those that lifted eyes could count
5 Five mountain ranges one behind the other
Under the sunset far into Vermont.
And the saw snarled and rattled, snarled and rattled,
As it ran light, or had to bear a load.
And nothing happened: day was all but done.
10 Call it a day, I wish they might have said
To please the boy by giving him the half hour
That a boy counts so much when saved from work.
His sister stood beside them in her apron
To tell them "Supper." At the word, the saw,
15 As if to prove saws knew what supper meant,
Leaped out at the boy's hand, or seemed to leap—
He must have given the hand. However it was,
Neither refused the meeting. But the hand!
The boy's first outcry was a rueful laugh,
20 As he swung toward them holding up the hand
Half in appeal, but half as if to keep
The life from spilling. Then the boy saw all—
Since he was old enough to know, big boy
Doing a man's work, though a child at heart—
25 He saw all spoiled. "Don't let him cut my hand off—
The doctor, when he comes. Don't let him, sister!"
So. But the hand was gone already.
The doctor put him in the dark of ether.
He lay and puffed his lips out with his breath.
30 And then—the watcher at his pulse took fright.
No one believed. They listened at his heart.
Little—less—nothing!—and that ended it.
No more to build on there. And they, since they
Were not the one dead, turned to their affairs.

READING AND REACTING

1. The poem's title is an **allusion** to a passage in Shakespeare's *Macbeth* (5.5.23–28) that attacks the brevity and meaninglessness of life in very emotional terms:

"Out, out brief candle!
Life's but a walking shadow, a poor player,
That struts and frets his hour upon the stage
And then is heard no more. It is a tale
Told by an idiot, full of sound and fury,
Signifying nothing."

What idea do you think Frost wants to convey through the title "Out, Out—"?

2. Explain why each of the following qualifies as understatement:

"Neither refused the meeting." (18)

"He saw all spoiled." (25)

"[. . .] that ended it." (32)

"No more to build on there." (33)

Can you identify any other examples of understatement in the poem?

3. **JOURNAL ENTRY** Do you think the poem's impact is strengthened or weakened by its understated tone? Why?

4. **CRITICAL PERSPECTIVE** In an essay on Frost in his 1985 book *Affirming Limits,* Robert Pack focuses on the single word "So" in line 27 of "Out, Out—":

For a moment, his narration is reduced to the impotent word "So," and in that minimal word all his restrained grief is held. [. . .] That "So" is the narrator's cry of bearing witness to a story that must be what it is in a scene he cannot enter. He cannot rescue or protect the boy. [. . .] In the poem's sense of human helplessness in an indifferent universe, we are all "watchers," and what we see is death without redemption, "signifying nothing." So. So? So! How shall we read that enigmatic word?

How do you read this "enigmatic word" in the poem?

Related Works: "The Lottery" (p. 315), "What Were They Like?" (p. 695), "Hope" (p. 748), "The Death of the Ball Turret Gunner" (p. 814)

◇ ◇ ◇

DONALD HALL
(1928–   )

My Son, My Executioner
(1955)

My son, my executioner,
    I take you in my arms,
Quiet and small and just astir,
    And whom my body warms.

5 Sweet death, small son, our instrument
　　Of immortality,
　Your cries and hungers document
　　Our bodily decay.

　We twenty-five and twenty-two,
10 　　Who seemed to live forever,
　Observe enduring life in you
　　And start to die together.

READING AND REACTING

1. Because the speaker is a young man holding his newborn son in his arms, the equation in line 1 comes as a shock. What is Hall's purpose in opening with such a startling statement?
2. In what sense is the comparison between baby and executioner a valid one? Could you argue that, given the underlying similarities between the two, Hall is *not* using hyperbole? Explain.

Related Works: "Doe Season" (p. 349), "That Time of Year Thou Mayst in Me Behold" (p. 669), "Morning Song" (p. 742), "Sailing to Byzantium" (p. 1012)

◊　◊◊◊

MARGARET ATWOOD
(1939–　　)

You Fit into Me
(1971)

you fit into me
like a hook into an eye

a fish hook
an open eye

READING AND REACTING

1. What connotations does Atwood expect readers to associate with the phrase "you fit into me"? What does the speaker seem at first to mean by "like a hook into an eye" in line 2?
2. The speaker's shift to the brutal suggestions of lines 3 and 4 is calculated to shock readers. Does the use of hyperbole here have another purpose in the context of the poem? Explain.

Related Works: "Popular Mechanics" (p. 412), "Daddy" (p. 818), *A Doll House* (p. 1196)

METONYMY AND SYNECDOCHE
◆ ◆ ◆

Metonymy and synecdoche are two related figures of speech. **Metonymy** is the substitution of the name of one thing for the name of another thing that most readers associate with the first—for example, using *hired gun* to mean "paid assassin" or *suits* to mean "business executives." A specific kind of metonymy, called **synecdoche,** is the substitution of a part for the whole (for example, using *bread*—as in "Give us this day our daily bread"—to mean "food") or the whole for a part (for example, saying "You can take the boy out of Brooklyn, but you can't take Brooklyn [meaning its distinctive traits] out of the boy"). With metonymy and synecdoche, instead of describing something by saying it is like something else (as in simile) or by equating it with something else (as in metaphor), writers can characterize an object or concept by using a term that evokes it. The following poem illustrates the use of synecdoche.

◆ ◆ ◆

RICHARD LOVELACE
(1618–1658)

To Lucasta Going to the Wars
(1649)

Tell me not, Sweet, I am unkind
    That from the nunnery
Of thy chaste breast and quiet mind,
    To war and arms I fly.

5 True, a new mistress now I chase,
    The first foe in the field;
And with a stronger faith embrace
    A sword, a horse, a shield.

Yet this inconstancy is such
10   As you too shall adore;
I could not love thee, Dear, so much,
    Loved I not Honor more.

Here, Lovelace's use of synecdoche allows him to condense a number of complex ideas into a very few words. In line 3, when the speaker says that he is flying from his loved one's "chaste breast and quiet mind," he is using "breast" and "mind" to stand for all his loved one's physical and intellectual attributes. In line 8, when he says that he is embracing "A sword, a horse, a shield," he is using these three items to represent all the trappings of war—and, thus, to represent war itself.

APOSTROPHE

◊ ◊ ◊

With **apostrophe,** a poem's speaker addresses an absent person or thing—for example, a historical or literary figure or even an inanimate object or an abstract concept.

In the following poem, the speaker addresses Vincent Van Gogh.

◊ ◊ ◊

SONIA SANCHEZ
(1934–   )

On Passing thru Morgantown, Pa.
(1984)

> i saw you
> vincent van
> gogh perched
> on those pennsylvania
> 5 cornfields communing
> amid secret black
> bird societies. yes.
> i'm sure that was
> you exploding your
> 10 fantastic delirium
> while in the
> distance
> red indian
> hills beckoned.

Expecting her readers to be aware that van Gogh is a Dutch postimpressionist painter known for his mental instability as well as for his art, Sanchez is able to give added meaning to a phrase such as "fantastic delirium" as well as to the poem's visual images. The speaker sees van Gogh perched like a black bird on a fence, and at the same time she also sees what he sees. Like van Gogh, then, the speaker sees the Pennsylvania cornfields as both a natural landscape and an "exploding" work of art.

✴ CHECKLIST: WRITING ABOUT FIGURES OF SPEECH

> ✓ Are any figures of speech present in the poem? Identify each example of simile, metaphor, personification, hyperbole, understatement, metonymy, synecdoche, and apostrophe.

✓ What two elements are being compared in each use of simile, metaphor, and personification? Is the comparison logical? What characteristics are shared by the two items being compared?

✓ How do figures of speech contribute to the impact of the poem as a whole?

✓ Does the poet use hyperbole? Why? For example, is it used to move or to shock readers, or is its use intended to produce a humorous or satirical effect?

✓ Does the poet use understatement? For what purpose? Would more straightforward language be more effective?

✓ In metonymy and synecdoche, what item is being substituted for another? What purpose does the substitution serve?

✓ If the poem includes apostrophe, whom or what does the speaker address? What is accomplished through the use of apostrophe?

❖ WRITING SUGGESTIONS: FIGURES OF SPEECH

1. Various figures of speech are often used to portray characters in a poem. Choose two or three poems that focus on a single character—for example, "Ex-Basketball Player" (p. 813), "Richard Cory" (p. 986), or "Gracie" (p. 780)—and explain how figures of speech are used to characterize each poem's central figure. If you like, you may write about poems that focus on real (rather than fictional) people—for example, "Emmett Till" (p. 954) or "Medgar Evers" (p. 935).

2. Write an essay in which you discuss the different ways poets use figures of speech to examine the nature of poetry itself. What kinds of figures of speech do poets use to describe their craft? (You might begin by reading the three poems about poetry that open Chapter 11.)

3. Write a letter replying to the speaker in a poem by Marvell, Bradstreet, Donne, or Burns that appears in this chapter. Use figurative language to express the depth of your love and the extent of your devotion.

4. Choose two or three poems that have a common subject—for example, love, nature, war, art, or mortality—and write a paper in which you draw some general conclusions about the relative effectiveness of the poems' use of figurative language to examine that subject. (If you like, you may focus on the poems clustered under the heads "Poems about Love," "Poems about War," and "Poems about Parents" in Chapter 11.)

5. Select a poem and a short story that treat the same subject matter, and write a paper in which you compare their use of figures of speech.

6. **WEB ACTIVITY** The following Web site contains information about Marge Piercy:

http://www.capecod.net/~timpiercy/

Read a sampling of the poems, interviews, reviews, and essays available at this site. Using the information you gather at the site, write an essay about how the figures of speech in Piercy's poetry reflect society's expectations of women and how those expectations can shape and limit women's lives.

CHAPTER 17

Sound

◊ ◊ ◊

A primary pleasure in poetry is [. . .] the pleasure of saying something over for its own sweet sake and because it sounds just right. For myself, [. . .] the thing said over will not necessarily be A Great Thought, though great thoughts are not necessarily excluded either; it may be as near as not to meaningless, especially if one says it without much attention to its context. For instance, a riddling song has the refrain: Sing ninety-nine and ninety. I can remember being charmed enough with that to say it over and over to myself for days, without ever having a single thought about its meaning except for a certain bemused wonder about how different it was from singing a hundred and eighty-nine.

HOWARD NEMEROV, "Poetry and Meaning"

I've never taught a poetry writing class that has not suffered my reiteration of Duke Ellington's line: "It don't mean a thing if it ain't got that swing." How can you describe the feeling of reading a Roethke poem, [. . .] when the rhythm is so palpable it is as if the poem could be cupped in your hands? Those poems move great distances in meaning between sentences and yet they hold together, largely because of the sound. The same thing is operating in a song that makes you want to get up and dance.

MICHAEL RYAN, "On the Nature of Poetry"

The most obvious function of the line-break is rhythmic: it can record the slight (but meaningful) hesitations between word and word that are characteristic of the mind's dance among perceptions but which are not noted by grammatical punctuation. Regular punctuation is a part of regular sentence structure, that is, of the expression of completed thoughts; and this expression is typical of prose, even though prose is not at all times bound by its logic. But in poems one has the opportunity not only, as in expressive prose, to depart from the syntactic norm, but [. . .] to present the dynamics of perception *along with* its arrival at full expression. The line-break is a form of punctuation *additional* to the punctuation that forms part of the logic of completed thoughts.

DENISE LEVERTOV, "On the Function of Line"

◊ ◊ ◊

◊ ◊ ◊

WALT WHITMAN
(1819–1892)

Had I the Choice[1]

Had I the choice to tally greatest bards,
To limn[2] their portraits, stately, beautiful, and emulate at will,
Homer with all his wars and warriors—Hector, Achilles, Ajax,
Or Shakespeare's woe-entangled Hamlet, Lear, Othello—Tennyson's
    fair ladies,
5 Meter or wit the best, or choice conceit to wield in perfect rhyme,
    delight of singers;
These, these, O sea, all these I'd gladly barter,
Would you the undulation of one wave, its trick to me transfer,
Or breathe one breath of yours upon my verse,
And leave its odor there.

RHYTHM

◊ ◊ ◊

Rhythm—the regular recurrence of sounds—is at the heart of all natural
phenomena: the beating of a heart, the lapping of waves against the shore,
the croaking of frogs on a summer's night, the whispering of wheat swaying in the wind. In fact, even mechanical phenomena, such as the movement of rush-hour traffic through a city's streets, have a kind of rhythm.
Poetry, which explores these phenomena, often tries to reflect the same
rhythms. Walt Whitman makes this point in "Had I the Choice" when he
says that he would gladly trade the "perfect rhyme" of Shakespeare for the
ability to reproduce "the undulation of one wave" in his verse.

    Effective public speakers frequently repeat key words and phrases to
create rhythm. In his speech "I Have a Dream," for example, Martin
Luther King, Jr., repeats the phrase "I have a dream" to create a cadence
that ties the central section of the speech together:

    I say to you today, my friends, even though we face the difficulties of
    today and tomorrow, *I still have a dream.* It is a dream deeply rooted

---

[1] Publication date is not available.
[2] To describe, depict.

in the American dream. *I have a dream* that one day this nation will rise up and live out the true meaning of its creed: "We hold these truths to be self-evident, that all men are created equal." *I have a dream* that one day, on the red hills of Georgia, sons of former slaves and the sons of former slave owners will be able to sit down together at the table of brotherhood. *I have a dream* that one day even the state of Mississippi, a state sweltering with the heat of injustice, sweltering with the heat of oppression, will be transformed into an oasis of freedom and justice. *I have a dream* that my four little children will one day live in a nation where they will not be judged by the color of their skin, but by the content of their character.

Poets too create rhythm by using repeated words and phrases, as Gwendolyn Brooks does in the poem that follows.

◇ ◇ ◇

GWENDOLYN BROOKS
(1917–   )

Sadie and Maud
(1945)

Maud went to college.
Sadie stayed at home.
Sadie scraped life
With a fine-tooth comb.

5 She didn't leave a tangle in.
Her comb found every strand.
Sadie was one of the livingest chits
In all the land.

Sadie bore two babies
10 Under her maiden name.
Maud and Ma and Papa
Nearly died of shame.

When Sadie said her last so-long
Her girls struck out from home.
15 (Sadie had left as heritage
Her fine-tooth comb.)

Maud, who went to college,
Is a thin brown mouse.
She is living all alone
20 In this old house.

Much of the force of this poem comes from its balanced structure and regular rhyme and meter, underscored by the repeated words "Sadie" and "Maud," which shift the focus from one subject to the other and back again ("Maud went to college / Sadie stayed home"). The poem's singsong rhythm recalls the rhymes children recite when jumping rope. This evocation of carefree childhood ironically contrasts with the adult realities that both Sadie and Maud face as they grow up: Sadie stays at home and has two children out of wedlock; Maud goes to college and ends up "a thin brown mouse." The speaker implies that the alternatives Sadie and Maud represent are both undesirable. Although Sadie "scraped life / with a fine-tooth comb," she dies young and leaves nothing to her girls but her desire to experience life. Maud, who graduated from college, shuts out life and cuts herself off from her roots.

Just as the repetition of words and phrases can create rhythm, so can the distribution of words among the lines of a poem—and even the appearance of words on a printed page. How a poem looks is especially important in **open form** poetry (see p. 879), which dispenses with traditional patterns of versification. In the following excerpt from a poem by E. E. Cummings, for example, an unusual arrangement of words forces readers to slow down and then to speed up, creating a rhythm that emphasizes a key phrase—"The / lily":

> the moon is hiding
> in her hair.
> The
> lily
> of heaven
> full of all dreams,
> draws down.

Poetic rhythm—the repetition of stresses and pauses—is an essential element in poetry. Rhythm helps to establish a poem's mood, and, in combination with other poetic elements, it conveys the poet's emphasis and helps communicate the poem's meaning. Although rhythm can be affected by the regular repetition of words and phrases or by the arrangement of words into lines, poetic rhythm is largely created by **meter,** the recurrence of regular units of stressed and unstressed syllables.

METER
◆ ◆ ◆

A **stress** (or accent) occurs when one syllable is emphasized more than another, unstressed, syllable: *fór • ceps, bá • sic, il • lú • sion, ma • lár • i • a.* In a poem, even one-syllable words can be stressed to create a particular effect.

For example, in Elizabeth Barrett Browning's line "How do I love thee? Let me count the ways," the metrical pattern that places stress on "love" creates one meaning; stressing "I" would create another.

Scansion is the process of analyzing patterns of stressed and unstressed syllables within a line. The most common method of poetic notation involves indicating stressed syllables with a ˈ and unstressed syllables with a �‿. Although scanning lines gives readers the "beat" of the poem, scansion only approximates the sound of spoken language, which contains an infinite variety of stresses. By providing a graphic representation of the stressed and unstressed syllables of a poem, scansion aids understanding, but it is no substitute for reading the poem aloud and experimenting with various patterns of emphasis.

The basic unit of meter is a **foot**—a group of syllables with a fixed pattern of stressed and unstressed syllables. The following chart illustrates the most common types of metrical feet in English and American verse.

FOOT	STRESS PATTERN	EXAMPLE
Iamb	‿ ˈ	They pace | in sleek | chi val|ric cer|tain ty (Adrienne Rich)
Trochee	ˈ ‿	Thou, when | thou re|turn'st, wilt | tell me. (John Donne)
Anapest	‿ ‿ ˈ	With a hey, | and a ho, | and a hey | nonino (William Shakespeare)
Dactyl	ˈ ‿ ‿	Constantly | risking ab|surdity (Lawrence Ferlinghetti)

Iambic and *anapestic* meters are called *rising meters* because they progress from unstressed to stressed syllables. *Trochaic* and *dactylic* meters are called *falling meters* because they progress from stressed to unstressed syllables.

The following types of metrical feet, less common than those listed above, are used to emphasize or to provide variety rather than to create the dominant meter of a poem.

Spondee	˙ ˙	Pomp, pride | and circumstance of glorious war! (William Shakespeare)
Pyrrhic	⌣ ⌣	A horse! a horse! My king|dom for | a horse! (William Shakespeare)

A metric line of poetry is measured by the number of feet it contains.

monometer one foot
dimeter two feet
trimeter three feet
tetrameter four feet

pentameter five feet
hexameter six feet
heptameter seven feet
octameter eight feet

The name for a metrical pattern of a line of verse identifies the name of the foot used and the number of feet the line contains. For example, the most common foot in English poetry is the **iamb,** most often occurring in lines of three or five feet.

Eight hun\|dred of \| the brave
(William Cowper)

Iambic trimeter

O, how \| much more \| doth
beau\|ty beau\|teous seem
(William Shakespeare)

Iambic pentameter

Because **iambic pentameter** is so well suited to the rhythms of English speech, writers frequently use it in plays and poems. Shakespeare's plays, for example, are written in unrhymed lines of iambic pentameter called **blank verse** (see p. 863).

Many other material combinations are also possible; a few are illustrated here:

Like a | high-born | maiden   Trochaic trimeter

(Percy Bysshe Shelley)

The As sy|rian came down | Anapestic tetrameter

like the wolf | on the fold

(Lord Byron)

Maid en most | beau ti ful | Dactylic hexameter

mother most | boun ti ful, | la

dy of | lands, (A. C. Swinburne)

The yel|low fog | that rubs | its   Iambic heptameter

back | upon | the win |

dow-panes (T. S. Eliot)

Scansion can be an extremely technical process, and when readers become bogged down with anapests and dactyls, they can easily forget that poetic meter is not an end in itself. Meter should be appropriate for the ideas expressed by the poem, and it should help to create a suitable tone. A light, skipping rhythm, for example, would be inappropriate for an **elegy,** and a slow, heavy rhythm would surely be out of place in an **epigram** or a limerick. The following lines of a poem by Samuel Taylor Coleridge illustrate the different types of metrical feet:

Trochee trips from long to short;

From long to long in solemn sort

Slow Spondee stalks; strong foot! yet ill able

Ever to come up with Dactyl trisyllable.

Iambics march from short to long—

With a leap and a bound the swift Anapests throng;

One syllable long, with one short at each side,

Amphibrachys hastes with a stately stride—

First and last being long, middle short, Amphimacer

Strikes his thundering hoofs like a proud high-bred Racer.

A poet may use one kind of meter—iambic meter, for example—throughout a poem. Even so, the poet may vary line length to relieve monotony or to accommodate the demands of meaning or emphasis. In the following poem, the poet uses iambic lines of different lengths.

◇ ◇ ◇

EMILY DICKINSON
(1830–1886)

I Like to See It Lap the Miles
(1891)

I like to see it lap the Miles—
And lick the Valleys up—
And stop to feed itself at Tanks—
And then—prodigious step

5 Around a Pile of Mountains—
And supercilious peer
In Shanties—by the sides of Roads—
And then a Quarry pare

To fit its Ribs
10 And crawl between
Complaining all the while
In horrid—hooting stanza—
Then chase itself down Hill—

And neigh like Boanerges[1]—
15 Then—punctual as a Star
Stop—docile and omnipotent
At its own stable door—

This poem is a single sentence that, except for some short pauses, stretches unbroken from beginning to end. Iambic lines of varying lengths actually suggest the movements of the train that the poet describes. Lines of iambic tetrameter, such as the first, give readers a sense of the train's steady, rhythmic movement across a flat landscape, and shorter lines ("To fit its Ribs / And crawl between") suggest the train's slowing motion. Beginning with two iambic dimeter lines and progressing to iambic trimeter lines, the third stanza increases in speed just like the train that is racing downhill "In horrid—hooting stanza—."

---

[1] A vociferous preacher and orator. Also, the name, meaning "son of thunder," Jesus gave to apostles John and James because of their fiery zeal.

A poet can also use more than one type of metrical foot. Any variation in a metrical pattern—the substitution of a trochee for an iamb, for instance—immediately calls attention to itself. Poets are aware of this fact and use it to their advantage. For example, in line 16 of "I Like to See It Lap the Miles," the poet departs from iambic meter by placing unexpected stress on the first word, *stop*. By emphasizing this word, the poet brings the flow of the poem to an abrupt halt, suggesting the jolt riders experience when a train comes to a stop. In the following segment from "The Rime of the Ancient Mariner," Samuel Taylor Coleridge also departs from his poem's dominant meter:

> The ship | was cheered, | the har|bor cleared,
>
> Merri|ly did | we drop
>
> Below | the kirk, | below | the hill,
>
> Below | the light|house top.

Although these lines are arranged in iambic tetrameter, the poet uses a trochee in the second line, breaking the meter in order to accommodate the natural pronunciation of "merrily" as well as to place stress on the word.

Another way of varying the meter is to introduce a pause in the rhythm known as a **caesura**—a Latin word meaning "a cutting"—within a line. When scanning a poem, you indicate a caesura with two parallel lines: ‖. Unless a line of poetry is extremely short, it probably will contain a caesura.

A caesura occurs after a punctuation mark or at a natural break in phrasing:

> How do I love thee? ‖ Let me count the ways.
> **ELIZABETH BARRETT BROWNING**

> Two loves I have ‖ of comfort and despair.
> **WILLIAM SHAKESPEARE**

> High on a throne of royal state, ‖ which far
> Outshone the wealth of Ormus ‖ and of Ind
> **JOHN MILTON**

Sometimes, more than one caesura occurs in a single line:

> 'Tis good. ‖ Go to the gate. ‖ Somebody knocks.
> **WILLIAM SHAKESPEARE**

Although the end of a line may mark the end of a metrical unit, it does not always coincide with the end of a sentence. Poets may choose to indicate a pause at this point, or they may continue, without a break, to the next line. Lines that have distinct pauses at the end—usually signaled by punctuation—are called **end-stopped lines.** Lines that do not end with strong pauses are called **run-on lines.** (Sometimes the term **enjambment** is used to describe this type of line.) End-stopped lines can seem formal, or even forced, because their length is rigidly dictated by the poem's meter, rhythm, and rhyme scheme. In the following excerpt from John Keats's "La Belle Dame sans Merci" (p. 969), for example, rhythm, meter, and rhyme dictate the pauses that occur at the ends of the lines:

> O, what can ail thee, knight-at-arms,
>   Alone and palely loitering?
> The sedge has withered from the lake,
>   And no birds sing.

In contrast to end-stopped lines, run-on lines seem more natural. Because their ending points are determined by the rhythms of speech and by the meaning and emphasis the poet wishes to convey rather than by meter and rhyme, run-on lines are suited to the open form of much modern poetry. In the following lines from the 1967 poem "We Have Come Home," by the poet Lenrie Peters, run-on lines give readers the sense of spoken language:

> We have come home
> From the bloodless war
> With sunken hearts
> Our boots full of pride—
> From the true massacre of the soul
> When we have asked
> 'What does it cost
> To be loved and left alone?'

Rather than relying exclusively on end-stopped or run-on lines, poets often use a combination of the two to produce the effects they want. In the following lines from "Pot Roast" by Mark Strand, for example, the juxtaposition of end-stopped and run-on lines controls the rhythm:

> I gaze upon the roast,
> that is sliced and laid out
> on my plate
> and over it
> I spoon the juices
> of carrot and onion.
> And for once I do not regret
> the passage of time.

❖ POEMS FOR FURTHER READING: RHYTHM AND METER

◇ ◇ ◇

ADRIENNE RICH
(1929–   )

Aunt Jennifer's Tigers
(1951)

Aunt Jennifer's tigers prance across a screen,
Bright topaz denizens of a world of green.
They do not fear the men beneath the tree;
They pace in sleek chivalric certainty.

5 Aunt Jennifer's fingers fluttering through her wool
Find even the ivory needle hard to pull.
The massive weight of Uncle's wedding band
Sits heavily upon Aunt Jennifer's hand.

When Aunt is dead, her terrified hands will lie
10 Still ringed with ordeals she was mastered by.
The tigers in the panel that she made
Will go on prancing, proud and unafraid.

READING AND REACTING

1. What is the dominant metrical pattern of the poem? In what way does the meter enhance the contrast the poem develops?
2. The lines in the first stanza are end-stopped, and those in the second and third stanzas combine end-stopped and run-on lines. What does the poet achieve by varying the rhythm?
3. What ideas do the caesuras in the first and fourth lines of the last stanza emphasize?
4. **JOURNAL ENTRY** What is the speaker's opinion of Aunt Jennifer's marriage? Do you think she is commenting on this particular marriage or on marriage in general?
5. **CRITICAL PERSPECTIVE** In her 1986 study of Rich's work, *The Aesthetics of Power,* Claire Keyes writes of this poem that although it is formally beautiful, almost perfect, its voice creates problems:

> [T]he tone seldom approaches intimacy, the speaker seeming fairly detached from the fate of Aunt Jennifer. [. . .] The dominant voice of the poem asserts the traditional theme that art outlives the person who produces it. [. . .] The speaker is almost callous in her disregard for Aunt's death. [. . .] Who cares that Aunt Jennifer dies? The speaker does not seem to; she gets

caught up in those gorgeous tigers. [. . .] Here lies the dominant voice: Aunt is not compelling; her creation is.

Do you agree with Keyes's interpretation of the poem?

Related Works: "Miss Brill" (p. 119), "Everyday Use" (p. 324), "Rooming
Houses Are Old Women" (p. 811), "Ethics" (p. 979)

◈ ◈ ◈

ETHERIDGE KNIGHT
(1931–1991)

For Malcolm,[1] a Year After
(1986)

Compose for Red[2] a proper verse;
Adhere to foot and strict iamb;
Control the burst of angry words
Or they might boil and break the dam.
5 Or they might boil and overflow
And drench me, drown me, drive me mad.
So swear no oath, so shed no tear,
And sing no song blue Baptist sad.
Evoke no image, stir no flame,
10 And spin no yarn across the air.
Make empty anglo tea lace words—
Make them dead white and dry bone bare.

Compose a verse for Malcolm man,
And make it rime and make it prim.
15 The verse will die—as all men do—
But not the memory of him!
Death might come singing sweet like C,
Or knocking like the old folk say,
The moon and stars may pass away,
20 But not the anger of that day.

READING AND REACTING

1. Why do you think Knight chooses to write a "proper verse" in
   "strict iamb"? Do you think this meter is an appropriate choice for
   his subject?

---

[1] Malcolm X.
[2] Malcolm X's nickname when he was a young man.

2. What sounds and words are repeated in this poem? How does this repetition enhance the poem's rhythm?
3. Where in the poem does Knight use caesuras? Why does he use this device in each instance?
4. **JOURNAL ENTRY** How would you describe the mood of the speaker? Is the poem's meter consistent with his mood or in conflict with it? Explain.

Related Works: "To an Athlete Dying Young" (p. 786), "In Memory of Donald A. Stauffer" (p. 875), "Medgar Evers" (p. 935), "If We Must Die" (p. 975)

ALLITERATION AND ASSONANCE
◇ ◇ ◇

Just as poetry depends on rhythm, it also depends on the sounds of individual words. An effect pleasing to the ear, such as "Did he who made the Lamb make thee?" from William Blake's "The Tyger" (p. 930), is called **euphony.** A jarring or discordant effect, such as "The vorpal blade went snicker-snack!" from Lewis Carroll's "Jabberwocky" (p. 856), is called **cacophony.**

One of the earliest, and perhaps the most primitive, methods of enhancing sound is **onomatopoeia,** which occurs when the sound of a word echoes its meaning, as it does in common words such as *bang, crash,* and *hiss.* Poets make broad application of this technique by using combinations of words that suggest a correspondence between sound and meaning, as Edgar Allan Poe does in the following lines from his poem "The Bells":

> Yet the ear, it fully knows,
>> By the twanging
>> And the clanging,
> How the danger ebbs and flows;
> Yet the ear distinctly tells,
>> In the jangling
>> And the wrangling
> How the danger sinks and swells
> By the sinking or the swelling in the anger of the bells—
>> Of the bells,—
> Of the bells, bells, bells, bells [. . .].

Poe's primary objective in this poem is to re-create the sound of ringing bells. Although he succeeds, the poem (113 lines long in its entirety) is extremely tedious. A more subtle use of onomatopoetic words appears in the following passage from *An Essay on Criticism* by Alexander Pope:

Soft is the strain when Zephyr gently blows,
And the smooth stream in smoother numbers flows;
But when the loud surges lash the sounding shore,
The hoarse, rough verse should like the torrent roar:
When Ajax strives some rock's vast weight to throw,
The line too Labors, and the words move slow.

After earlier admonishing readers that sound must echo sense, Pope uses onomatopoetic words such as *lash* and *roar* to convey the fury of the sea, and he uses repeated consonants to echo the sounds these words suggest. Notice, for example, how the *s* and *m* sounds suggest the gently blowing Zephyr and the flowing of the smooth stream and how the series of *r* sounds echoes the torrent's roar.

Alliteration—the repetition of consonant sounds in consecutive or neighboring words, usually at the beginning of words—is another device used to enhance sound in a poem. Both Poe ("sinks and swells") and Pope ("smooth stream") make use of alliteration in the preceding excerpts, and so does Alfred, Lord Tennyson in the following poem.

◆ ◆ ◆

ALFRED, LORD TENNYSON
(1809–1892)

The Eagle
(1851)

He clasps the crag with crooked hands;
Close to the sun in lonely lands,
Ringed with the azure world, he stands.

The wrinkled sea beneath him crawls:
5 He watches from his mountain walls,
And like a thunderbolt he falls.

Throughout the poem, *c*, *l*, and *w* sounds occur repeatedly. The poem is drawn together by the recurrence of these sounds and, as a result, it flows smoothly from beginning to end.

The following poem also uses alliteration to create special aural effects.

◈ ◈ ◈
N. SCOTT MOMADAY
(1934–   )

Comparatives
(1976)

Sunlit sea,
the drift of fronds,
and banners
of bobbing boats—
5 the seaside
upon the planks,
the coil and
crescent of flesh
extending
10 just into death.

Even so,
in the distant,
inland sea,
a shadow runs,
15 radiant,
rude in the rock:
fossil fish,
fissure of bone
forever.
20 It is perhaps
the same thing,
an agony
twice perceived.

It is most like
25 wind on waves—
mere commotion,
mute and mean,
perceptible—
that is all.

Throughout the poem, Momaday uses alliteration to create a pleasing effect and to link certain words and ideas. Each stanza of the poem has its
own alliterative pattern: the first stanza contains repeated *s* and *b* sounds,
the second stanza contains repeated *r* and *f* sounds, and the third stanza
contains repeated *w* and *m* sounds. Not only does this use of alliteration
create a pleasing effect, but also it reinforces the development of the
poem's theme from stanza to stanza.

Assonance—the repetition of the same or similar vowel sounds, especially in stressed syllables—can also enrich a poem. When used solely to produce aural effects, assonance can be distracting. Consider, for example, the clumsiness of the repeated vowel sounds in Tennyson's "Many a morning on the moorland did we hear the copses ring [. . .]." When used more subtly, however, assonance can enhance a poem's effectiveness.

Assonance can also unify an entire poem. In the following poem, assonance emphasizes the thematic connections among words and thus unifies the poem's ideas.

◇ ◇ ◇

R O B E R T   H E R R I C K
(1591–1674)

Delight in Disorder
(1648)

A sweet disorder in the dress
Kindles in clothes a wantonness.
A lawn[1] about the shoulders thrown
Into a fine distractión;
5 An erring lace, which here and there
Enthralls the crimson stomacher;[2]
A cuff neglectful, and thereby
Ribbons to flow confusedly;
A winning wave, deserving note,
10 In the tempestuous petticoat;
A careless shoestring, in whose tie
I see a wild civility;
Do more bewitch me than when art
Is too precise in every part.

Repeated vowel sounds extend throughout this poem—for instance, "sh*ou*lders" and "thr*ow*n" in line 3; and "t*ie*," "w*i*ld," and "prec*i*se" in lines 11, 12, and 14. Using alliteration as well as assonance, Herrick subtly links certain words—"*t*em*p*es*t*uous *p*e*tt*icoat," for example. By connecting these words, he calls attention to the pattern of imagery that helps to convey the poem's theme.

---

[1] A shawl made of fine fabric.
[2] A heavily embroidered garment worn by females over the chest and stomach.

RHYME

◊ ◊ ◊

In addition to alliteration and assonance, poets create sound patterns with **rhyme**—the use of matching sounds in two or more words: "tight" and "might"; "born" and "horn"; "sleep" and "deep." For a rhyme to be **perfect,** final vowel and consonant sounds must be the same, as they are in each of the preceding examples. **Imperfect rhyme** (also called *near rhyme, slant rhyme, approximate rhyme,* or *consonance*) occurs when the final consonant sounds in two words are the same but vowel sounds are different—"learn/barn" or "pads/lids," for example. William Stafford uses imperfect rhyme in "Traveling through the Dark" (p. 997) when he rhymes "road" with "dead." Finally, **eye rhyme** occurs when two words look as if they should rhyme but do not—for example, "watch" and "catch."

Rhyme can also be classified according to the position of the rhyming syllables in a line of verse. The most common type of rhyme is **end rhyme,** which occurs at the end of a line:

Tyger! Tyger! burning <u>bright</u>
In the forests of the <u>night</u>
WILLIAM BLAKE, "The Tyger"

Internal rhyme occurs within a line:

The Sun came up upon the left,
Out of the <u>sea</u> came <u>he</u>!
And he shone <u>bright</u> and on the <u>right</u>
Went down into the sea.
SAMUEL TAYLOR COLERIDGE, "The Rime of the Ancient Mariner"

Beginning rhyme occurs at the beginning of a line:

Red River, red river,
<u>Slow</u> flow heat is silence
<u>No</u> will is still as a river
Still. Will heat move
T. S. ELIOT, "Virginia"

Rhyme can also be classified according to the number of corresponding syllables. **Masculine rhyme** (also called **rising rhyme**) occurs when single syllables correspond ("can"/"ran"; "descend"/"contend"). **Feminine rhyme** (also called **double rhyme** or **falling rhyme**) occurs when two syllables, a stressed one followed by an unstressed one, correspond ("ocean"/"motion"; "leaping"/"sleeping"). Finally, **triple rhyme** occurs when three syllables correspond. Less common than the other two, triple rhyme is often used for humorous or satiric purposes, as in the following lines from the long poem *Don Juan* by Lord Byron:

Sagest of women, even of widows, she
  Resolved that Juan should be quite a <u>paragon</u>,
And worthy of the noblest pedigree:
  (His sire of Castile, his dam from <u>Aragon</u>).

In some cases—for example, when it is overused or used in unexpected places—rhyme can create unusual and even comic effects. In the following poem, humor is created by the incongruous connections established by rhymes such as "priest"/"beast" and "pajama"/"lllama."

◆ ◆ ◆

OGDEN NASH
(1902–1971)

The Lama
(1931)

The one-l lama
He's a priest.
The two-l llama,
He's a beast.
5 And I will bet
A silk pajama
There isn't any
Three-l lllama.

The conventional way to describe a poem's rhyme scheme is to chart rhyming sounds that appear at the ends of lines. The sound that ends the first line is designated *a,* and all subsequent lines that end in that sound are also labeled *a.* The next sound to appear at the end of a line is designated *b,* and all other lines whose last sounds rhyme with it are also designated *b*—and so on through the alphabet. The lines of the poem that follows have been labeled in this manner.

◆ ◆ ◆

RICHARD WILBUR
(1921–   )

A Sketch
(1975)

Into the lower right   *a*
Square of the window frame   *b*
There came   *b*
    with scalloped flight   *a*

5 A goldfinch, lit upon   *c*
The dead branch of a pine,   *d*
Shining,   *d*
      and then was gone,   *c*

Tossed in a double arc   *e*
10 Upward into the thatched   *f*
And cross-hatched   *f*
      pine-needle dark.   *e*

Briefly, as fresh drafts stirred   *g*
The tree, he dulled and gleamed   *h*
15 And seemed   *h*
      more coal than bird,   *g*

Then, dodging down, returned   *i*
In a new light, his perch   *j*
A birch—   *j*
20   twig, where he burned   *i*

In the sun's broadside ray,   *k*
Some seed pinched in his bill.   *l*
Yet still   *l*
      he did not stay,   *k*

25 But into a leaf-choken pane,   *m*
Changeful as even in heaven,   *n*
Even   *n*
      in Saturn's reign,   *m*

Tunneled away and hid.   *o*
30 And then? But I cannot well   *p*
Tell   *p*
      you all that he did.   *o*

It was like glancing at rough   *q*
Sketches tacked on a wall,   *r*
35 And all   *r*
      so less than enough   *q*

Of gold on beaten wing,   *s*
I could not choose that one   *t*
Be done   *t*
40   as the finished thing.   *s*

Although the rhyme scheme of this poem (*abba, cddc,* and so on) is regular, it is hardly noticeable until it is charted. Despite its subtlety, however, the rhyme scheme is not unimportant. In fact, it reinforces the poem's meaning and binds lines into structural units, connecting the first and fourth as well as the second and third lines of each stanza. In stanza 1, "right" and "flight" draw lines 1 and 4 of the stanza together, enclosing "fame" and "came" in lines 2 and 3. The pattern begins again with the next stanza and continues through the rest of the poem. Like the elusive goldfinch the poet describes, the rhymes are difficult to follow with the eye. In this sense, the rhyme reflects the central theme of the poem: the difficulty of capturing in words a reality which, like the goldfinch, is forever shifting.

Naturally, rhyme does not have to be subtle to enrich a poem. An obvious rhyme scheme can communicate meaning by connecting ideas that are not normally linked. Notice how Alexander Pope uses this technique in the following excerpt from *An Essay on Man:*

> Honour and shame from no condition rise;
> Act well your part, there all the honour lies.
> Fortune in men has some small diff'rence made,
> One flaunts in rags, one flutters in brocade;
> The cobbler aproned, and the parson gowned,
> The friar hooded, and the monarch crowned.
> "What differ more (you cry) than crown and cowl?"
> I'll tell you, friend; a wise man and a fool.
>
> You'll find, if once the monarch acts the monk,
> Or, cobbler-like, the parson will be drunk,
> Worth makes the man, and want of it, the fellow;
> The rest is all but leather or prunella.[1]
> Stuck o'er with titles and hung round with strings,
> That thou mayest be by kings, or whores of kings.
> Boast the pure blood of an illustrious race,
> In quiet flow from Lucrece[2] to Lucrece;
> But by your fathers' worth if yours you rate,
> Count me those only who were good and great.

This poem is written in **heroic couplets,** paired iambic pentameter lines with a rhyme scheme of *aa, bb, cc, dd,* and so on. In heroic couplets, greater stress falls on the second line of each pair, usually on the last word of the line. Coming at the end of the line, this word receives double emphasis: it is strengthened both because of its position in the line and because it is rhymed with the last word of the couplet's first line. In some cases, rhyme joins opposing ideas, thereby reinforcing a theme that runs through the passage: the contrast between the high and the low, the virtuous and the immoral. For example, "gowned" and "crowned" in lines 5

---

[1] Heavy cloth the color of prunes.

[2] In Roman legend, she stabbed herself after being defiled by Sextus Tarquinius.

and 6 convey the opposite conditions of the parson and the monarch and exemplify the idea expressed in lines 3 and 4 that fortune, not virtue, determines one's station.

❖ POEMS FOR FURTHER READING: ALLITERATION, ASSONANCE, AND RHYME

◇ ◇ ◇

GERARD MANLEY HOPKINS
(1844–1889)

Pied Beauty
(1918)

Glory be to God for dappled things—
 For skies of couple-color as a brinded[1] cow;
  For rose-moles all in stipple upon trout that swim;
Fresh-firecoal chestnut-falls; finches' wings;
5 Landscape plotted and pieced—fold, fallow, and plow;
  And áll trádes, their gear and tackle and trim.[2]

All things counter, original, spare, strange;
 Whatever is fickle, freckled (who knows how?)
  With swift, slow; sweet, sour; adazzle, dim;
10 He fathers-forth whose beauty is past change:
  Praise him.

READING AND REACTING

1. Identify examples of onomatopoeia, alliteration, assonance, imperfect rhyme, and perfect rhyme. Do you think all these techniques are essential to the poem? Are any of them annoying or distracting?
2. What is the central idea of this poem? In what way do the sounds of the poem help to communicate this idea?
3. Identify examples of masculine and feminine rhyme.
4. **JOURNAL ENTRY** Hopkins uses both pleasing and discordant sounds in his poem. Identify uses of euphony and cacophony, and explain how these techniques affect your reactions to the poem.

Related Works: "Women" (p. 891), "I Never Saw a Moor" (p. 942), "Batter My Heart, Three-Personed God" (p. 946)

---

[1] Brindled (streaked).
[2] Equipment.

◇ ◇ ◇

W. H. AUDEN
(1907–1973)

As I Walked Out One Evening
(1940)

As I walked out one evening,
    Walking down Bristol Street,
The crowds upon the pavement
    Were fields of harvest wheat.

5 And down by the brimming river
    I heard a lover sing
Under an arch of the railway:
    "Love has no ending.

"I'll love you, dear, I'll love you
10   Till China and Africa meet,
And the river jumps over the mountain
    And the salmon sing in the street,

"I'll love you till the ocean
    Is folded and hung up to dry,
15 And the seven stars go squawking
    Like geese about the sky.

"The years shall run like rabbits,
    For in my arms I hold
The Flower of the Ages,
20   And the first love of the world."

But all the clocks in the city
    Began to whirr and chime:
"O let not Time deceive you,
    You cannot conquer Time.

25 "In the burrows of the Nightmare
    Where Justice naked is,
Time watches from the shadow
    And coughs when you would kiss.

"In headaches and in worry
30   Vaguely life leaks away,
And Time will have his fancy
    Tomorrow or today.

"Into many a green valley
    Drifts the appalling snow;
35 Time breaks the threaded dances
    And the diver's brilliant bow.

"O plunge your hands in water,
　　Plunge them in up to the wrist;
Stare, stare in the basin
40　　And wonder what you've missed.

"The glacier knocks in the cupboard,
　　The desert sighs in the bed,
And the crack in the teacup opens
　　A lane to the land of the dead.

45 "Where the beggars raffle the banknotes
　　And the Giant is enchanting to Jack,
And the Lily-white Boy is a Roarer,
　　And Jill goes down on her back.

"O look, look in the mirror,
50　　O look in your distress;
Life remains a blessing
　　Although you cannot bless.

"O stand, stand at the window
　　As the tears scald and start;
55 You shall love your crooked neighbor
　　With your crooked heart."

It was late, late in the evening,
　　The lovers they were gone;
The clocks had ceased their chiming,
60　　And the deep river ran on.

READING AND REACTING

1. In lines 2 and 4 of almost every stanza, Auden uses perfect end rhyme. In stanzas 5 and 7, however, he uses imperfect rhyme. Should he have been more consistent in his use of rhyme? Would the poetic effect have been better had he consistently used perfect rhyme?
2. Chart the poem's rhyme scheme. Does Auden use internal rhyme? Where does he use alliteration and assonance? In what other ways does he use sound?
3. Does Auden's use of sound reinforce the poem's content or undercut it? Explain.
4. **JOURNAL ENTRY** Could this poem be considered a love poem? How are its sentiments about love different from those conventionally expressed in poems about love?
5. **CRITICAL PERSPECTIVE** In a 1940 British review of Auden's work, T. C. Worlsey made the following comments about this poem:

> There is no technical reason why such a poem as [this] should not be popular; the metre and the rhythm are easy and helpful, and the symbols have reference to a world of experience common to every inhabitant of these islands. Here [. . .] the poet has gone as far as he can along the road to creating a popular poetry.

Does Auden's poem strike you as a model for "popular" poetry— that is, poetry for people who don't usually read poetry?

Related Works: "Araby" (p. 254), "Oh, My Love Is like a Red, Red Rose" (p. 812), "To His Coy Mistress" (p. 824), "Not Marble nor the Gilded Monuments" (p. 989)

◊ ◊ ◊

LEWIS CARROLL
(1832–1898)

Jabberwocky
(1871)

'Twas brillig, and the slithy toves
    Did gyre and gimble in the wabe:
All mimsy were the borogoves,
    And the mome raths outgrabe.

5 "Beware the Jabberwock, my son!
    The jaws that bite, the claws that catch!
Beware the Jubjub bird, and shun
    The frumious Bandersnatch!"

He took his vorpal sword in hand;
10   Long time the manxome foe he sought—
So rested he by the Tumtum tree
    And stood awhile in thought.

And, as in uffish thought he stood,
    The Jabberwock, with eyes of flame,
15 Came whiffling through the tulgey wood,
    And burbled as it came!

One, two! One, two! And through and through
    The vorpal blade went snicker-snack!
He left it dead, and with its head
20   He went galumphing back.

"And hast thou slain the Jabberwock?
    Come to my arms, my beamish boy!
O frabjous day! Callooh, Callay!"
    He chortled in his joy.

25 'Twas brillig, and the slithy toves
    Did gyre and gimble in the wabe:
All mimsy were the borogoves,
    And the mome raths outgrabe.

READING AND REACTING

1. Many words in this poem may be unfamiliar to you. Are they actual words? Use a dictionary to check before you dismiss any. Do some words seem to have meaning in the context of the poem regardless of whether or not they appear in the dictionary? Explain.
2. This poem contains many examples of onomatopoeia. What ideas do the various words' sounds suggest?
3. **JOURNAL ENTRY** Summarize the story the poem tells. In what sense is this poem a story of a young man's initiation into adulthood?
4. **CRITICAL PERSPECTIVE** According to Humpty Dumpty in Carroll's *Alice in Wonderland,* the nonsense words in the poem are *portmanteau words* (that is, words whose form and meaning are derived from two other distinct words—as *smog* is a portmanteau of *smoke* and *fog*). Critic Elizabeth Sewell, however, rejects this explanation: "*[F]rumious,* for instance, is not a word, and does not have two meanings packed up in it; it is a group of letters without any meaning at all. [. . .]t looks like other words, and almost certainly more than two."

    Which nonsense words in the poem seem to you to be portmanteau words, and which do not? Can you suggest possible sources for those words that are not portmanteau words?

Related Works: "A&P" (p. 113), "Gryphon" (p. 134), "Rite of Passage" (p. 977), *The Cuban Swimmer* (p. 1495)

CHECKLIST: WRITING ABOUT SOUND

RHYTHM AND METER

✓ Does the poem contain repeated words and phrases? If so, how do they help to create rhythm?

✓ Does the poem have one kind of meter, or does the meter vary from line to line?

✓ How does the meter contribute to the overall effect of the poem?

✓ Which lines of the poem contain caesuras? What effect do they have?

✓ Are the lines of the poem end-stopped, run-on, or a combination of the two? What effects are produced by the presence or absence of pauses at the ends of lines?

ALLITERATION, ASSONANCE, AND RHYME

✓ Does the poem contain any examples of onomatopoeia?

✓ Are there any examples of alliteration or assonance?

✓ Does the poem have a regular rhyme scheme?

✓ Does the poem use internal rhyme? Beginning rhyme?

✓ Does the poem include examples of masculine, feminine, or triple rhyme?

✓ In what ways does rhyme unify the poem?

✓ How does rhyme reinforce the poem's ideas?

◈ WRITING SUGGESTIONS: SOUND

1. William Blake's "The Tyger" appeared in a collection entitled *Songs of Experience*. Compare this poem (p. 930) to "The Lamb" (p. 929), which appeared in a collection called *Songs of Innocence*. In what way are the speakers in these two poems relatively "innocent" or "experienced"? How does sound help to convey the voice of the speakers in these two poems?

2. "Sadie and Maud" (p. 835), like "The Faithful Wife" (p. 776), "My Papa's Waltz" (p. 677), and "Daddy" (p. 818), communicates attitudes toward home and family. How does the presence or absence of rhyme in these poems help to reinforce their themes?

3. Robert Frost once said that writing poems that have no fixed metrical pattern is like playing tennis without a net. What do you think he meant? Do you agree? After reading "Out, Out—" (p. 826), "Stopping by Woods on a Snowy Evening" (p. 960), and "The Road Not Taken" (p. 959), write an essay in which you discuss Frost's use of meter.

4. Select two or three contemporary poems that have no end rhyme. Write an essay in which you discuss what these poets gain and lose by not using rhyme.

5. Prose writers as well as poets use techniques such as assonance and alliteration. Choose a passage of prose—from "Araby" (p. 254), "A Clean, Well-Lighted Place" (p. 261), or "Barn Burning" (p. 226), for example—and discuss its use of assonance and alliteration. Where do assonance and alliteration occur? How do these techniques help the writer make his or her point?

6. **WEB ACTIVITY** The following Web site contains information about N. Scott Momaday:

http://www.achievement.org/autodoc/page/mom0pro-1

Read the profile on Momaday on this Web page. Note that the author states that Momaday "celebrates" western landscapes. Write an essay that provides evidence of Momaday's "celebration" of landscape in "Comparatives" (p. 847), focusing on how he juxtaposes images of beauty and death.

CHAPTER 18

Form

◇ ◇ ◇

Dryden chose the couplet because he thought it the plainest mode available, the verse "nearest prose," and he chose it in conscious reaction against the artificial stanzaic modes that had dominated English poetry during most of the sixteenth and seventeenth centuries. In short, he and his followers thought they were liberating poetry, just as Coleridge and Wordsworth liberated it a hundred years later, or Pound and Williams a hundred years after that. The history of poetry is a continual fixing and freeing of conventions.

HAYDEN CARRUTH, "The Question of Poetic Form"

Yeats said that the finished poem made a sound like the click of the lid on a perfectly made box. One-hundred-and-forty syllables, organized into a sonnet, do not necessarily make a click; the same number of syllables, dispersed in asymmetric lines of free verse, will click like a lid if the poem is good. In the sonnet and in the free verse poem, the poet improvises toward that click, and achieves his resolution in unpredictable ways. The rhymes and line lengths of the sonnet are too gross to contribute greatly to that sense of resolution. The click is our sense of lyric *form*.

DONALD HALL, "Goatfoot, Milktongue, Twinbird"

No verse can be free; it must be governed by some measure, but not by the old measure.

WILLIAM CARLOS WILLIAMS, "On Measure"

Poetic forms—meters, rhyming patterns, the shaping of poems into symmetrical blocks of lines called couplets or stanzas—have existed since poetry was an oral activity. Such forms can easily become format, of course, where the dynamics of experience and desire are forced to fit a pattern to which they have no organic relationship. People are often taught in school to confuse closed poetic forms (or formulas) with poetry itself [. . .] It's a struggle not to let the form take over, lapse into format, assimilate the poetry; and that very struggle can produce a movement, a music, of its own.

ADRIENNE RICH, "What Is Found There"

◇ ◇ ◇

◊ ◊ ◊

JOHN KEATS
(1795–1821)

On the Sonnet
(1819)

If by dull rhymes our English must be chained,
And like Andromeda,[1] the sonnet sweet
Fettered, in spite of painéd loveliness,
Let us find, if we must be constrained,
5 Sandals more interwoven and complete
To fit the naked foot of Poesy:
Let us inspect the lyre, and weigh the stress
Of every chord, and see what may be gained
By ear industrious, and attention meet;
10 Misers of sound and syllable, no less
Than Midas[2] of his coinage, let us be
Jealous of dead leaves in the bay-wreath crown;
So, if we may not let the Muse be free,
She will be bound with garlands of her own.

The **form** of a literary work is its structure or shape, the way its parts fit together to form a whole; **poetic form** is the design of a poem described in terms of rhyme, meter, and stanzaic pattern.

Until the twentieth century, most poetry was written in **closed form** (sometimes called **fixed form**), characterized by regular patterns of meter, rhyme, line length, and stanzaic divisions. Early poems that were passed down orally—epics and ballads, for example—relied on regular form to facilitate memorization. Even after poems began to be written down, poets tended to favor regular patterns. In fact, until relatively recently, regular form was what distinguished poetry from prose. Of course, strict adherence to regular patterns sometimes produced poems that were, in John Keats's words, "chained" by "dull rhymes" and "fettered" by the rules governing a particular form. But rather than feeling "constrained" by form, many poets experimented with imagery, figures of speech, allusion, and other techniques—stretching closed form to its limits.

As they sought new ways in which to express themselves, poets also used forms from other cultures, adapting them to the demands of their own languages. English and American poets, for example, adopted (and still use) early French forms, such as the villanelle and the sestina, and

---

[1] In Greek mythology, Andromeda was chained to a rock to appease a sea monster.
[2] King Midas was granted his wish that all he touched would turn to gold.

early Italian forms, such as the Petrarchan sonnet and terza rima. More recently, the nineteenth-century American poet Henry Wadsworth Longfellow studied Icelandic epics; the twentieth-century poet Ezra Pound studied the works of French troubadours; and Pound and other twentieth-century American poets, such as Richard Wright and Carolyn Kizer, were inspired by Japanese haiku. Other American poets, such as Vachel Lindsay, Langston Hughes, and Maya Angelou, looked closer to home—to the rhythms of blues, jazz, and spirituals—for inspiration.

As time went on, more and more poets moved away from closed form to experiment with **open form** poetry (sometimes called **free verse** or *vers libre*), varying line length within a poem, dispensing with stanzaic divisions, breaking lines in unexpected places, and even abandoning any semblance of formal structure. In English, nineteenth-century poets—such as William Blake and Matthew Arnold—experimented with lines of irregular meter and length, and Walt Whitman wrote **prose poems,** open form poems whose long lines made them look like prose. (Well before this time, Asian poetry and some biblical passages had used a type of free verse.) In nineteenth-century France, Symbolist poets such as Baudelaire, Rimbaud, Verlaine, and Mallarmé also used free verse. Later, in the early twentieth century, a group of American poets including Ezra Pound, William Carlos Williams, and Amy Lowell, who were associated with a movement known as **imagism,** wrote poetry that dispensed with traditional principles of English versification, creating new rhythms and meters.

Although much contemporary English and American poetry is composed in open form, many poets also write in closed form—even in very traditional, highly structured patterns. Still, new forms, and new variations of old forms, are being created all the time. And, because contemporary poets do not necessarily feel bound by rules or restrictions about what constitutes "acceptable" poetic form, they experiment freely, trying to discover the form that best suits the poem's purpose, subject, language, and theme.

CLOSED FORM
◊ ◊ ◊

A **closed form** (or *fixed form*) poem looks symmetrical; it has an identifiable, repeated pattern, with lines of similar length arranged in groups of two, three, four, or more. Such poems also tend to rely on regular metrical patterns and rhyme schemes.

Despite what its name suggests, closed form poetry does not have to be confining or conservative. In fact, sometimes contemporary poets experiment by using characteristics of open form poetry (such as lines of varying length) within a closed form, or by moving back and forth within a single poem from open to closed to open form. Sometimes they (like their eighteenth-century counterparts) experiment with closed form by combining different stanzaic forms (stanzas of two and three lines, for example) within a single poem.

Even when poets work within a traditional closed form, such as a *sonnet, sestina,* or *villanelle,* they can break new ground. For example, they can create a sonnet with an unexpected meter or rhyme scheme, add an extra line or even extra stanzas to a traditional sonnet form, combine two different traditional sonnet forms in a single poem, or write an abbreviated version of a sestina or villanelle. (See the sections on traditional closed forms in this chapter for examples of such experiments.) In other words, poets can use traditional forms as building blocks, combining them in innovative ways to create new patterns and new forms.

Sometimes a pattern (such as *blank verse*) simply determines the meter of a poem's individual lines. At other times, the pattern extends to the level of the *stanza*, with lines arranged into groups (*couplets, quatrains,* and so on). At still other times, as in the case of traditional closed forms like sonnets, a poetic pattern gives shape to an entire poem.

BLANK VERSE

Blank verse is unrhymed poetry with each line written in a set pattern of five stressed and five unstressed syllables called **iambic pentameter** (see p. 838). Many passages from Shakespeare's plays, such as the following lines from *Hamlet* (p. 1307), are written in blank verse:

> To sleep, perchance to dream, ay there's the rub,
> For in that sleep of death what dreams may come
> When we have shuffled off this mortal coil
> Must give us pause—there's the respect
> That makes calamity of so long life:

For a contemporary use of blank verse, see John Updike's "Ex-Basketball Player" (p. 813).

STANZA

A **stanza** is a group of two or more lines with the same metrical pattern—and often with a regular rhyme scheme as well—separated by blank space from other such groups of lines. The stanza in poetry is like the paragraph in prose: it groups related thoughts into units.

A two-line stanza with rhyming lines of similar length and meter is called a **couplet.** The **heroic couplet,** first used by Chaucer and especially popular throughout the eighteenth century, consists of two rhymed lines of iambic pentameter, with a weak pause after the first line and a strong pause after the second. The following example, from Alexander Pope's *An Essay on Criticism,* is a heroic couplet:

> True ease in writing comes from art, not chance,
> As those move easiest who have learned to dance.

A three-line stanza with lines of similar length and a set rhyme scheme is called a **tercet.** Percy Bysshe Shelley's "Ode to the West Wind" (p. 990) is built largely of tercets:

> O wild West Wind, thou breath of Autumn's being,
> Thou, from whose unseen presence the leaves dead
> Are driven, like ghosts from an enchanter fleeing,
>
> Yellow, and black, and pale, and hectic red,
> Pestilence-stricken multitudes: O Thou,
> Who chariotest to their dark wintry bed

Although in many tercets all three lines rhyme, "Ode to the West Wind" uses a special rhyme scheme, also used by Dante, called **terza rima.** This rhyme scheme (*aba, bcb, cdc, ded,* and so on) creates an interlocking series of stanzas. Line 2's *dead* looks ahead to the rhyming words *red* and *bed,* which close lines 4 and 6, and the pattern continues throughout the poem.

A four-line stanza with lines of similar length and a set rhyme scheme is called a **quatrain.** The quatrain, the most widely used and versatile unit in English and American poetry, is used by William Wordsworth in the following excerpt from "She Dwelt among the Untrodden Ways" (p. 1009):

> A violet by a mossy stone
>   Half hidden from the eye!
> Fair as a star, when only one
>   Is shining in the sky.

Quatrains are frequently used by contemporary poets as well—for instance, in Theodore Roethke's "My Papa's Waltz" (p. 677), Adrienne Rich's "Aunt Jennifer's Tigers" (p. 843), and William Stafford's "Traveling through the Dark" (p. 997).

One special kind of quatrain, called the **ballad stanza,** alternates lines of eight and six syllables; typically, only the second and fourth lines rhyme. The following lines from the traditional Scottish ballad "Sir Patrick Spence" illustrate the ballad stanza:

> The king sits in Dumferling toune,
>   Drinking the blude-reid wine:
> "O whar will I get guid sailor
>   To sail this schip of mine?"

Common measure, a four-line stanzaic pattern closely related to the ballad stanza, is used in hymns as well as in poetry. It differs from the ballad stanza in that its rhyme scheme is *abab* rather than *abcb*. This pattern appears in Donald Hall's 1955 poem "My Son, My Executioner" (p. 827).

Other stanzaic forms include **rhyme royal,** a seven-line stanza *(ababbcc)* set in iambic pentameter, used in Sir Thomas Wyatt's sixteenth-century poem "They Flee from Me That Sometimes Did Me Seke" as well as in Theodore Roethke's twentieth-century "I Knew a Woman" (p. 770); **ottava rima,** an eight-line stanza *(abababcc)* set in iambic pentameter; and the Spenserian stanza, a nine-line form *(ababbcbcc)* whose first eight lines are set in iambic pentameter and whose last line is in iambic hexameter. The Romantic poets John Keats and Percy Bysshe Shelley were among those who used this form. (See Chapter 17 for definitions and examples of various metrical patterns.)

THE SONNET

Perhaps the most familiar kind of traditional closed form poem written in English is the **sonnet,** a fourteen-line poem with a distinctive rhyme scheme and metrical pattern. The English or **Shakespearean sonnet,** which consists of fourteen lines divided into three quatrains and a concluding couplet, is written in iambic pentameter and follows the rhyme scheme *abab cdcd efef gg.* The **Petrarchan sonnet,** popularized in the fourteenth century by the Italian poet Francesco Petrarch, also consists of fourteen lines of iambic pentameter, but these lines are divided into an eight-line unit called an **octave** and a six-line unit (composed of two tercets) called a **sestet.** The rhyme scheme of the octave is *abba abba;* the rhyme scheme of the sestet is *cde cde.*

The conventional structures of these sonnet forms reflect the arrangement of ideas within a poem. In the Shakespearean sonnet, the poet typically presents three "paragraphs" of related thoughts, introducing an idea in the first quatrain, developing it in the two remaining quatrains, and summing up in a succinct closing couplet. In the Petrarchan sonnet, the octave introduces a problem that is resolved in the sestet. (Many Shakespearean sonnets also have a problem-solution structure.) Some poets vary the traditional patterns somewhat to suit the poem's language or ideas. For example, they may depart from the pattern to sidestep a forced rhyme or unnatural stress on a syllable, or they may not place the problem-solution break between octave and sestet.

The following poem follows the form of a traditional English sonnet.

◆ ◆ ◆

WILLIAM SHAKESPEARE
(1564–1616)

When, in Disgrace with Fortune and Men's Eyes
(1609)

When, in disgrace with Fortune and men's eyes,
I all alone beweep my outcast state,
And trouble deaf heaven with my bootless[1] cries,
And look upon myself and curse my fate,
5 Wishing me like to one more rich in hope,
Featured like him, like him with friends possessed,
Desiring this man's art, and that man's scope,
With what I most enjoy contented least,
Yet in these thoughts myself almost despising,
10 Haply[2] I think on thee, and then my state,
Like to the lark at break of day arising
From sullen earth, sings hymns at heaven's gate;
⠀⠀⠀For thy sweet love rememb'red such wealth brings
⠀⠀⠀That then I scorn to change my state with kings.

This sonnet is written in iambic pentameter and has a conventional rhyme scheme: *abab* (eyes-state-cries-fate), *cdcd* (hope-possessed-scope-least), *efef* (despising-state-arising-gate), *gg* (brings-kings). In this poem, in which the speaker explains how thoughts of his loved one can rescue him from despair, each quatrain is unified by rhyme as well as by subject. In the first quatrain, the speaker presents his problem: he is down on his luck and out of favor with his peers, isolated in self-pity and cursing his fate. In the second quatrain, he develops this idea further: he is envious of others and dissatisfied with things that usually please him. In the third quatrain, the focus shifts. Although the first two quatrains develop a dependent clause ("When [. . .]") that introduces a problem, line 9 begins to present the resolution. In the third quatrain the speaker explains how, in the midst of his despair and self-hatred, he thinks of his loved one, and his spirits soar. The closing couplet sums up the mood transformation the poem describes and explains its significance: when the speaker realizes the emotional riches his loved one gives him, he is no longer envious of others.

---

[1] Futile.
[2] Luckily.

❖ POEMS FOR FURTHER READING: THE SONNET

◊ ◊ ◊

CLAUDE MCKAY
(1890–1948)

The White City
(1922)

I will not toy with it nor bend an inch.
Deep in the secret chambers of my heart
I muse my life-long hate, and without flinch
I bear it nobly as I live my part.
5 My being would be a skeleton, a shell,
If this dark Passion that fills my every mood,
And makes my heaven in the white world's hell,
Did not forever feed me vital blood.
I see the mighty city through a mist—
10 The strident trains that speed the goaded mass,
The poles and spires and towers vapor-kissed,
The fortressed port through which the great ships pass,
The tides, the wharves, the dens I contemplate,
Are sweet like wanton loves because I hate.

READING AND REACTING

1. In what sense is the speaker's mood similar to that of the speaker in "When, in Disgrace with Fortune and Men's Eyes" (p. 866)? How is it different?
2. How is the speaker's description of the city in the third quatrain consistent with the emotions he expresses in lines 1–8?
3. The closing couplet of a Shakespearean sonnet traditionally sums up the sonnet's concerns. Is this true here? Explain.
4. **JOURNAL ENTRY** What possible meanings does the phrase "the white world's hell" (7) have? How does it express the poem's main idea?
5. **CRITICAL PERSPECTIVE** According to Tyrone Tillery's 1992 biography of McKay, the poet chose the sonnet form because "he found [it] admirable for a moment's thought. He understood that he had a tendency to be diffuse and repetitive, and he felt that tight rhythmic and metric forms helped him check these faults." Critic Onwuchekwa Jemie, in a 1973 survey of Harlem Renaissance poets, saw a paradox in McKay's use of the "old-fashioned" sonnet form to contain "venom and rage." Noting that "[e]ach of his protest sonnets just about explodes from the page," Jemie observes

that "McKay's attacks on the white world are carried out in one of that culture's most entrenched and conservative poetic forms. McKay's words deny the white world, but his form, style, language, and poetic attitude tend to affirm it." Jemie concludes, "It is the mark of his achievement that he is able to work that fragile sonnet frame into a vehicle of dynamite."

How do these observations help you to understand why McKay chose to express his ideas in a sonnet? Do you think he made the right choice?

Related Works: "Like a Winding Sheet" (p. 125), "The Man He Killed" (p. 736), "For Malcolm, a Year After" (p. 844), "We Wear the Mask" (p. 949), "If We Must Die" (p. 975)

◈ ◈ ◈

JOHN KEATS
(1795–1821)

On First Looking into Chapman's Homer[1]
(1816)

Much have I traveled in the realms of gold,
   And many goodly states and kingdoms seen;
   Round many western islands have I been
Which bards in fealty to Apollo[2] hold.
5 Oft of one wide expanse had I been told
   That deep-browed Homer ruled as his demesne;[3]
   Yet did I never breathe its pure serene[4]
Till I heard Chapman speak out loud and bold.
Then felt I like some watcher of the skies
10   When a new planet swims into his ken;
Or like stout Cortez[5] when with eagle eyes
   He stared at the Pacific—and all his men
Looked at each other with a wild surmise—
   Silent, upon a peak in Darien.[6]

---

[1] The translation of Homer by Elizabethan poet George Chapman.
[2] Greek god of light, truth, reason, male beauty; associated with music and poetry.
[3] Realm, domain.
[4] Air, atmosphere.
[5] It was Vasco de Balboa (not Hernando Cortez as Keats suggests) who first saw the Pacific Ocean, from "a peak in Darien."
[6] Former name of the Isthmus of Panama.

READING AND REACTING

1. Is this a Petrarchan or a Shakespearean sonnet? Explain your conclusion.

2. **JOURNAL ENTRY** The sestet's change of focus is introduced with the word "Then" in line 9. How does the mood of the sestet differ from the mood of the octave? How does the language differ?

3. **CRITICAL PERSPECTIVE** Biographer Aileen Ward offers an interesting explanation to suggest the reason for the excitement Keats felt "On First Looking into Chapman's Homer." Homer's epic tales of gods and heroes were known to most readers of Keats's day only in a very formal eighteenth-century translation by Alexander Pope. For instance, this is Pope's description of Ulysses escaping from a shipwreck:

> his knees no more
> Perform'd their office, or his weight upheld:
> His swoln heart heav'd, his bloated body swell'd:
> From mouth to nose the briny torrent ran,
> And lost in lassitude lay all the man,
> Deprived of voice, of motion, and of breath,
> The soul scarce waking in the arms of death [. . .]

In a rare 1616 edition of Chapman's translation, Keats discovered a very different poem:

> both knees falt'ring, both
> His strong hands hanging down, and all with froth
> His cheeks and nostrils flowing, voice and breath
> Spent to all use, and down he sank to death.
> The sea had soak'd his heart through [. . .].

This, as Ward notes, was "poetry of a kind that had not been written in England for two hundred years."

Can you understand why Keats was so moved by Chapman's translation? Do you think Keats's own poem seems closer in its form and language to Pope or to Chapman?

Related Works: "Gryphon" (p. 134), "Araby" (p. 254), "When I Heard the Learn'd Astronomer" (p. 762)

◇ ◇ ◇
GWENDOLYN BROOKS
(1917–   )

First Fight. Then Fiddle
(1949)

First fight. Then fiddle. Ply the slipping string
With feathery sorcery; muzzle the note
With hurting love; the music that they wrote
Bewitch, bewilder. Qualify to sing
5 Threadwise. Devise no salt, no hempen thing
For the dear instrument to bear. Devote
The bow to silks and honey. Be remote
A while from malice and from murdering.
But first to arms, to armor. Carry hate
10 In front of you and harmony behind.
Be deaf to music and to beauty blind.
Win war. Rise bloody, maybe not too late
For having first to civilize a space
Wherein to play your violin with grace.

READING AND REACTING

1. What is the subject of Brooks's poem? What do you think she
   means by "fight" and "fiddle"?
2. What is the poem's rhyme scheme? Is it an essential element of the
   poem? Would the poem be equally effective if it did not include
   end rhyme? Explain your position.
3. Study the poem's use of capitalization and punctuation carefully.
   Why do you think Brooks chooses to end many of her sentences in
   midline? How do her choices determine how you read the poem?

Related Works: "The Soldier" (p. 690), "The White City" (p. 867), "The
Chicago Defender Sends a Man to Little Rock" (p. 933)

THE SESTINA

The **sestina,** introduced in thirteenth-century France, is composed of six
six-line stanzas and a three-line conclusion called an **envoi.** Although the
sestina does not require end rhyme, it does require that each line end with
one of six key words, which are repeated throughout the poem in a fixed
order. The alternation of these six words in different positions—but always
at the ends of lines—in each of the poem's six stanzas creates a rhythmic
verbal pattern that unifies the poem, as the key words do in the poem that
follows.

◊ ◊ ◊

ALBERTO ALVARO RÍOS
(1952–   )

Nani
(1982)

Sitting at her table, she serves
the sopa de arroz[1] to me
instinctively, and I watch her,
the absolute mamá, and eat words
5 I might have had to say more
out of embarrassment. To speak,
now-foreign words I used to speak,
too, dribble down her mouth as she serves
me albóndigas.[2] No more
10 than a third are easy to me.
By the stove she does something with words
and looks at me only with her
back. I am full. I tell her
I taste the mint, and watch her speak
15 smiles at the stove. All my words
make her smile. Nani never serves
herself, she only watches me
with her skin, her hair. I ask for more.

I watch the mamá warming more
20 tortillas for me. I watch her
fingers in the flame for me.
Near her mouth, I see a wrinkle speak
of a man whose body serves
the ants like she serves me, then more words
25 from more wrinkles about children, words
about this and that, flowing more
easily from these other mouths. Each serves
as a tremendous string around her,
holding her together. They speak
30 nani was this and that to me
and I wonder just how much of me
will die with her, what were the words
I could have been, was. Her insides speak

---

[1] Rice soup.
[2] Meatballs.

through a hundred wrinkles, now, more
35 than she can bear, steel around her,
shouting, then, What is this thing she serves?

She asks me if I want more.
I own no words to stop her.
Even before I speak, she serves.

In many respects Ríos's poem closely follows the form of the traditional sestina. For instance, it interweaves six key words—"serves," "me," "her," "words," "more," and "speak"—through six groups of six lines each, rearranging the order in which the words appear so that the first line of each group of six lines ends with the key word that closed the preceding group of lines. The poem repeats the key words in exactly the order prescribed: *abcdef, faebdc, cfdabe,* and so on. In addition, the sestina closes with a three-line envoi that includes all six of the poem's key words, three at the ends of lines and three within the lines. However, Ríos departs from the sestina form by grouping his six sets of six lines not into six separate stanzas but rather into two eighteen-line stanzas.

The sestina form suits Ríos's subject matter. The focus of the poem, on the verbal and nonverbal interaction between the poem's "me" and "her," is reinforced by each of the related words. "Nani" is a poem about communication, and the key words return to probe this theme again and again. Throughout the poem these repeated words help to create a fluid, melodic, and tightly woven work.

❖ Poem for Further Reading: The Sestina

◇ ◇ ◇

ELIZABETH BISHOP
(1911–1979)

Sestina
(1965)

September rain falls on the house.
In the failing light, the old grandmother
sits in the kitchen with the child
beside the Little Marvel Stove,
5 reading the jokes from the almanac,
laughing and talking to hide her tears.

She thinks that her equinoctial tears
and the rain that beats on the roof of the house
were both foretold by the almanac,

10 but only known to a grandmother.
The iron kettle sings on the stove.
She cuts some bread and says to the child,

It's time for tea now; but the child
is watching the teakettle's small hard tears
15 dance like mad on the hot black stove,
the way the rain must dance on the house.
Tidying up, the old grandmother
hangs up the clever almanac

on its string. Birdlike, the almanac
20 hovers half open above the child,
hovers above the old grandmother
and her teacup full of dark brown tears.
She shivers and says she thinks the house
feels chilly, and puts more wood in the stove.

25 *It was to be,* says the Marvel Stove.
I know what I know, says the almanac.
With crayons the child draws a rigid house
and a winding pathway. Then the child
puts in a man with buttons like tears
30 and shows it proudly to the grandmother.

But secretly, while the grandmother
busies herself about the stove,
the little moons fall down like tears
from between the pages of the almanac
35 into the flower bed the child
has carefully placed in the front of the house.

Time to plant tears, says the almanac.
The grandmother sings to the marvellous stove
and the child draws another inscrutable house.

READING AND REACTING

1. Does the poet's adherence to a traditional form create any problems? For example, do you think the syntax is strained at any point? Explain.
2. How does this sestina use sound—meter, rhyme, alliteration, assonance, and so on? Could sound have been used more effectively? How?
3. **JOURNAL ENTRY** How are the six key words related to the poem's theme?

Related Works: "My Papa's Waltz" (p. 677), "The Meal" (p. 796), "Nani" (p. 871)

THE VILLANELLE

The **villanelle,** first introduced in France in the Middle Ages, is a nine-teen-line poem composed of five tercets and a concluding quatrain; its rhyme scheme is *aba aba aba aba aba abaa.* Two different lines are system-atically repeated in the poem: line 1 appears again in lines 6, 12, and 18, and line 3 reappears as lines 9, 15, and 19. Thus, each tercet concludes with an exact (or close) duplication of either line 1 or line 3, and the final quatrain concludes by repeating both line 1 and line 3.

◊ ◊ ◊

THEODORE ROETHKE
(1908–1963)

The Waking
(1953)

I wake to sleep, and take my waking slow.
I feel my fate in what I cannot fear.
I learn by going where I have to go.

We think by feeling. What is there to know?
5 I hear my being dance from ear to ear.
I wake to sleep, and take my waking slow.

Of those so close beside me, which are you?
God bless the Ground! I shall walk softly there,
And learn by going where I have to go.

10 Light takes the Tree; but who can tell us how?
The lowly worm climbs up a winding stair;
I wake to sleep, and take my waking slow.

Great Nature has another thing to do
To you and me; so take the lively air,
15 And, lovely, learn by going where to go.

This shaking keeps me steady. I should know.
What falls away is always. And is near.
I wake to sleep, and take my waking slow.
I learn by going where I have to go.

"The Waking," like all villanelles, closely intertwines threads of sounds and words. The repeated lines and the very regular rhyme and meter give the poem a monotonous, almost hypnotic, rhythm. This poem uses end rhyme and repeats entire lines. It also makes extensive use of alliteration (I feel my fate in what I cannot fear") and internal rhyme ("I hear my being dance from ear to ear"; "I wake to sleep and take my waking slow"). The result is a tightly constructed poem of overlapping sounds and images. (For another well-known example of a villanelle, see Dylan Thomas's "Do Not Go Gentle into That Good Night," p. 677.)

❖ POEM FOR FURTHER READING: THE VILLANELLE

◊ ◊ ◊

WILLIAM MEREDITH
(1919–   )

In Memory of Donald A. Stauffer
(1987)

Armed with an indiscriminate delight
His ghost left Oxford five summers ago,
Still on the sweet, obvious side of right.

How many friends and students talked all night
5 With this remarkable teacher? How many go
Still armed with his indiscriminate delight?

He liked, but often could not reach, the bright:
Young people sometimes prefer not to know
About the sweet or obvious sides of right.

10 But how all arrogance involves a slight
To knowledge, his humility would show
Them, and his indiscriminate delight

In what was true. This was why he could write
Commonplace books: his patience lingered so
15 Fondly on the sweet, obvious side of right.

What rare anthology of ghosts sits till first light
In the understanding air where he talks now,
Armed with his indiscriminate delight
There on the sweet and obvious side of right?

READING AND REACTING

1. Review the definition of *villanelle,* and explain how Meredith's poem expands the possibilities of the traditional villanelle.
2. Try to make the changes you believe are necessary to make Meredith's poem absolutely consistent with the traditional villanelle form. How does your editing change the poem?
3. **JOURNAL ENTRY** What kinds of subjects do you think would be most appropriate for villanelles? Why? What subjects, if any, do you think would not be appropriate? Explain.

Related Works: "Do Not Go Gentle into That Good Night" (p. 677), "The Waking" (p. 874)

THE EPIGRAM

Originally, an epigram was an inscription carved in stone on a monument or statue. As a literary form, an **epigram** is a very brief poem that makes a pointed, often sarcastic, comment in a surprising twist at the end. In a sense, it is a poem with a punch line. Although some epigrams rhyme, others do not. Many are only two lines long, but others are somewhat longer. What they have in common is their economy of language and their tone. One of the briefest of epigrams, written by Ogden Nash, appeared in *The New Yorker* magazine in 1931:

> The Bronx?
> No thonx.

In just four words, Nash manages to convey the unexpected, using rhyme and creative spelling to convey his assessment of a borough of New York City. The poem's two lines are perfectly balanced, making the contrast between the noncommittal tone of the first and the negative tone of the second quite striking.

❖ POEMS FOR FURTHER READING: THE EPIGRAM

◊ ◊ ◊

SAMUEL TAYLOR COLERIDGE
(1772–1834)

What Is an Epigram?
(1802)

> What is an epigram? a dwarfish whole,
> Its body brevity, and wit its soul.

◊ ◊ ◊

WILLIAM BLAKE
(1757–1827)

Her Whole Life Is an Epigram
(c. 1793–1811)

> Her whole life is an epigram: smack, smooth & neatly penned,
> Platted[1] quite neat to catch applause, with a sliding noose at the end.

---

[1] Braided.

READING AND REACTING

1. Read the two preceding epigrams, and explain the point each one makes.
2. Evaluate each poem. What qualities do you conclude make an epigram effective?

Related Works: "Popular Mechanics" (p. 412), "General Review of the Sex Situation" (p. 687), "Fire and Ice" (p. 735), "You Fit into Me" (p. 828)

HAIKU

Like an epigram, a haiku compresses words into a very small package. Unlike an epigram, however, a haiku focuses on an image, not an idea. A traditional Japanese form, the **haiku** is a brief unrhymed poem that presents the essence of some aspect of nature, concentrating a vivid image in just three lines. Although in the strictest sense a haiku consists of seventeen syllables divided into lines of five, seven, and five syllables, respectively, not all poets conform to this rigid form.

The following poem is a translation of a classic Japanese haiku by Matsuo Basho:

> Silent and still: then
> Even sinking into the rocks,
> The cicada's screech.

Notice that this poem conforms to the haiku's three-line structure and traditional subject matter, vividly depicting a natural scene without comment or analysis.

As the next poem illustrates, haiku in English is not always consistent with the traditional haiku in form or subject matter.

◊ ◊ ◊

RICHARD BRAUTIGAN
(1935–1984)

Widow's Lament[1]

> It's not quite cold enough
> to go borrow some firewood
> from the neighbors.

Brautigan's haiku adheres to the traditional pattern's number of lines and syllables, and its central idea is expressed in very concentrated terms. The

---

[1] Publication date is not available.

poem's focus, however, is not the natural world but human psychology. Moreover, without the title, the poem would be so ambiguous as to be meaningless. In this sense, the poet "cheats" the form, depending on the title's four syllables as well as on the seventeen of the poem itself to convey his ideas.

❖ POEMS FOR FURTHER READING: HAIKU

◊ ◊ ◊

RICHARD WRIGHT
(1908–1960)

Hokku Poems
(1960)

I am nobody
A red sinking autumn sun
Took my name away

*

Make up your mind snail!
You are half inside your house
And halfway out!

*

In the falling snow
A laughing boy holds out his palms
Until they are white

*

Keep straight down this block
Then turn right where you will find
A peach tree blooming

*

With a twitching nose
A dog reads a telegram
On a wet tree trunk

*

The spring lingers on
In the scent of a damp log
Rotting in the sun

*

Whose town did you leave
O wild and drowning spring rain
And where do you go?

*

The crow flew so fast
That he left his lonely caw
Behind in the fields

READING AND REACTING

1. The poems in this group of modern English haiku differ in several respects from the traditional Japanese form. Consider the form and subject matter of each haiku carefully, and explain how they are like and unlike classic haiku.
2. **JOURNAL ENTRY** Referring to the additional haiku poems in Chapter 15 as well as to those in this chapter, write a broad definition of *haiku* that applies to all of them.

Related Works: "Seventeen Syllables" (p. 376), "Fog" (p. 986), "I Wandered Lonely as a Cloud" (p. 1008)

OPEN FORM
◇ ◇ ◇

An **open form** poem (sometimes called **free verse** or *vers libre*) makes occasional use of rhyme and meter, but it has no easily identifiable pattern or design—that is, it has no conventional stanzaic divisions, no consistent metrical pattern, and no repeated rhyme scheme. Still, although open form poetry has no distinguishable pattern of meter, rhyme, or line length, it is not necessarily shapeless, untidy, or randomly ordered. All poems have form, and the form of a poem may be determined by factors such as the appearance of words on the printed page or pauses in natural speech as well as by conventional metrical patterns or rhyme schemes.

Open form poetry invites readers to participate in the creative process, to discover the relationship between form and meaning. Some modern poets believe that only open form offers them freedom to express their ideas or that the subject matter or mood of their poetry demands a relaxed, experimental approach to form. For example, when Lawrence Ferlinghetti portrays the poet as an acrobat who "climbs on rime" (p. 809), he constructs his poem in a way that is consistent with the poet/acrobat's willingness to take risks. Thus, the poem's idiosyncratic form supports its ideas about the possibilities of poetry and the poet as experimenter.

Without a predetermined pattern, however, poets must create forms that suit their needs, and they must continue to shape and reshape the look of the poem on the page as they revise its words. Thus, open form represents a challenge, a way to experiment with fresh arrangements of words and new juxtapositions of ideas.

For some poets, such as Carl Sandburg, open form provides an opportunity to create **prose poems.**

◊ ◊ ◊

CARL SANDBURG
(1878–1967)

Chicago
(1914)

Hog Butcher for the World,
Tool Maker, Stacker of Wheat,
Player with Railroads and the Nation's Freight Handler;
Stormy, husky, brawling,
5   City of the Big Shoulders:

They tell me you are wicked and I believe them, for I have seen
    your painted women under the gas lamps luring the farm boys.
And they tell me you are crooked and I answer: Yes, it is true I
    have seen the gunman kill and go free to kill again.
And they tell me you are brutal and my reply is: On the faces of
    women and children I have seen the marks of wanton hunger.
And having answered so I turn once more to those who sneer at this
    my city, and I give them back the sneer and say to them:
10 Come and show me another city with lifted head singing so proud
    to be alive and coarse and strong and cunning.
Flinging magnetic curses amid the toil of piling job on job, here is a
    tall bold slugger set vivid against the little soft cities;
Fierce as a dog with tongue lapping for action, cunning as a savage
    pitted against the wilderness,
        Bareheaded,
        Shoveling,
15   Wrecking,
        Planning,
        Building, breaking, rebuilding,
Under the smoke, dust all over his mouth, laughing with white teeth,
Under the terrible burden of destiny laughing as a young man laughs,
20 Laughing even as an ignorant fighter laughs who has never lost a battle,
Bragging and laughing that under his wrist is the pulse, and under his
    ribs the heart of the people,

Laughing!
Laughing the stormy, husky, brawling laughter of Youth, half-naked,
sweating, proud to be Hog Butcher, Tool Maker, Stacker of
Wheat, Player with railroads and Freight Handler to the Nation.

"Chicago" uses capitalization and punctuation conventionally, and it generally (although not always) divides words into lines consistent with the natural divisions of phrases and sentences. However, the poem is not divided into stanzas, and its lines vary widely in length—from a single word isolated on a line to a line crowded with words—and follow no particular metrical pattern. Instead, its form is created through its pattern of alternating sections of long and short lines; through its repeated words and phrases ("They tell me" in lines 6–8, "under" in lines 18–19, and "laughing" in lines 18–23, for example); through alliteration (for instance, "slugger set vivid against the little soft cities" in line 11); and, most of all, through the piling up of words into catalogs in lines 1–5, 13–17, and 23.

In order to understand Sandburg's reasons for choosing such a form, we must consider the poem's subject matter and theme. "Chicago" celebrates the scope and power of a "stormy, husky, brawling" city, one that is exuberant and outgoing, not sedate and civilized. Chicago the city does not follow anyone else's rules; it is, after all, "Bareheaded, / Shoveling, / Wrecking, / Planning, / Building, breaking," constantly active, in flux, on the move, "proud to be alive." "Fierce as a dog [. . .] cunning as a savage," the city is characterized as, among other things, a worker, a fighter, and a harborer of "painted women" and killers and hungry women and children. Just as Chicago itself does not conform to the rules, the poem clearly demands a departure from the orderly confines of stanzaic form and measured rhyme and meter, a kind of form better suited to "the little soft cities" than to the "tall / bold slugger" that is Chicago.

Of course, open form poetry does not have to look like Sandburg's prose poem. The following poem experiments with a different kind of open form.

✧ ✧ ✧
LOUISE GLÜCK
(1943–   )

Life Is a Nice Place
(1966)

Life is a nice place (They change
the decorations

every season; and the music,

my dear, is just too

5   marvellous, they play you

anything from birds to Bach. And

every day the Host

arranges for some clever sort

of contest and they give

10   the most

fantastic prizes; I go absolutely

green. Of course, celebrities abound;

I've even seen Love waltzing around

in amusing disguises.) to

15   visit. But

I wouldn't want to live there.

Glück's poem includes several end rhymes ("too"/"you"; "Host"/"most"; "abound"/"around"). It also forms a recognizable pattern on the page, broadening and narrowing with some regularity. Moreover, it has a clear syntactical structure, with one main sentence interrupted by parenthetical comments, and it follows the conventions of capitalization and punctuation. The poem clearly has a form, but its idiosyncratic, stanzaic divisions and uneven patterns of rhyme and meter mark it as fresh and original.

The poem's unusual form suits both its subject and its sarcastic tone. It is divided into five sentences, but only the final sentence ends at the end of a line. Moreover, the first sentence ("Life is a nice place [. . .] to visit") begins in line 1 but does not conclude until the end of the poem. The long parenthetical intrusion, unusual in itself, keeps readers from seeing at first that the poem is a grim new twist on an old cliché: "Life is a nice place [. . .] / to visit. But / I wouldn't want to live there."

The poem's first line is ironic, because the life the speaker presents is shallow, false, and ultimately meaningless. It is a cross between a stage set and a cocktail party, where love is elusive ("waltzing around / in amusing disguises") and nature is artificially re-created by piped-in music and painted backdrops. Although a traditional structure and regular rhyme and meter could, through their contrast with the subject matter, create ironic tension, Glück chooses an unconventional form that visually reinforces the empty cycles of the life the poem describes. Breaks in lines are determined not by conventional phrasing or punctuation but largely by the poem's shape; the result is unusual word groups such as "every season; and the music, [. . .] is just too" and "fantastic prizes; I go absolutely." These odd juxtapositions suggest the random quality of the speaker's encounters and, perhaps, the unpredictability of her life.

The poem that follows, an extreme example of open form, looks almost as if it has spilled out of a box of words.

◊ ◊ ◊
E. E. CUMMINGS
(1894–1962)

the sky was can dy
(1925)

the
    sky
        was
    can   dy lu
5 minous
        edible
spry
      pinks shy
lemons
10 greens   coo l choc
olate
s.

    un   der,
     a lo
15 co
mo
    tive   s pout
         ing
         vi
20   o
         lets

Like many of Cummings's poems, this one seems ready to skip off the page. Its irregular line length and its unconventional capitalization, punctuation, and word divisions immediately draw readers' attention to its form. Despite these oddities, and despite the absence of orderly rhyme and meter, the poem does have its conventional elements. A closer examination reveals that the poem's theme—the beauty of the sky—is quite conventional; that the poem is divided, although somewhat crudely, into two sections; and that the poet does use some rhyme—"spry" and "shy," for example. However, Cummings's sky is described not in traditional terms, but rather as something "edible," not only in terms of color but of flavor as well. The breaks within words ("can dy lu / minous"; "coo l choc / olate / s") seem to expand each word's possibilities, visually stretching them to the limit, extending their taste and visual image over several lines and, in the case of the last two words, visually reinforcing the picture the words describe. In addition, the isolation of syllables exposes hidden rhyme, as in "lo / co / mo" and "lu" / "coo." By using open form, Cummings makes a clear statement about the capacity of a poem to move beyond the traditional boundaries set by words and lines.

❖ Poems for Further Reading: Open Form

◇ ◇ ◇

WALT WHITMAN
(1819–1892)

from "Out of the Cradle Endlessly Rocking"
(1881)

Out of the cradle endlessly rocking,
Out of the mocking-bird's throat, the musical shuttle,
Out of the Ninth-month[1] midnight,
Over the sterile sands and the fields beyond, where the child leaving
    his bed wander'd alone, bareheaded, barefoot,
5 Down from the shower'd halo,
Up from the mystic play of shadows twining and twisting as if they
    were alive,
Out from the patches of briers and blackberries,
From the memories of the bird that chanted to me,
From your memories sad brother, from the fitful risings and fallings
    I heard,
10 From under that yellow half-moon late-risen and swollen as if with
    tears,
From those beginning notes of yearning and love there in the mist,
From the thousand responses of my heart never to cease,
From the myriad thence-arous'd words,
From the word stronger and more delicious than any,
15 From such as now they start the scene revisiting,
As a flock, twittering, rising, or overhead passing,
Borne hither, ere all eludes me, hurriedly,
A man, yet by these tears a little boy again,
Throwing myself on the sand, confronting the waves,
20 I, chanter of pains and joys, uniter of here and hereafter,
Taking all hints to use them, but swiftly leaping beyond them,
A reminiscence sing.

Reading and Reacting

    1. This excerpt, the first twenty-two lines of a poem nearly two
       hundred lines long, has no regular metrical pattern or rhyme
       scheme. What gives it form?

---

[1] The Quaker designation for September. In context, an allusion to the human birth
cycle.

2. How might you explain why the poem's lines vary in length?
3. **JOURNAL ENTRY** Compare this excerpt with the excerpt from Whitman's "Song of Myself" (p. 1006). In what respects are the forms of the two poems similar?
4. **CRITICAL PERSPECTIVE** Reviewing a recent biography of Whitman, Geoffrey O'Brien writes of a paradox in Whitman's poetry:

> [N]either fiction nor verse as they then existed could provide Whitman with what he needed, so he invented out of necessity his own form, a reversion to what he conceived of as the most archaic bardic impulses, representing itself as the poetry of the future.

Can you see the form of "Out of the Cradle" as both "archaic" and "of the future"?

Related Works: "Chicago" (p. 880), "Defending Walt Whitman" (p. 922), "Song of Myself" (p. 1006)

◊ ◊ ◊

DIANE WAKOSKI
(1937–   )

Sleep
(1966)

The mole
lifting snouts—
full of strained black dirt
    —his perfect tunnel
5   sculptured
      to fit
      the fat
      body. Sleep
  fits tight
10 —must keep bringing out.
the fine grit
to keep size
for even one day.

READING AND REACTING

1. This poem's form seems to be in direct conflict with the logical divisions its syntax and punctuation suggest. For instance, the words in lines 4–9 are set between dashes, indicating a parenthetical comment, yet only lines 4–8 are visually aligned. Also, line 10 ends with a period, but lines 11–13 are clearly part of

the same sentence as line 10. How can you account for such discrepancies?

2. How might the poem's discussion of the mole's constant search for the perfect-size tunnel have suggested the form of the poem?

3. **JOURNAL ENTRY** Why do you believe the poet placed the words "Sleep / fits tight" (8–9) where she did? Could—or should—these words be relocated? If so, where could they be placed, and what changes in form or punctuation would then have to be made?

Related Works: "Red Wheelbarrow" (p. 794), "Reapers" (p. 801)

◆ ◆ ◆

ROBERT HAYDEN
(1913–   )

Monet's "Waterlilies"[1]
(1966)

(for Bill and Sonja)

Today as the news from Selma[2] and Saigon[3]
poisons the air like fallout,
    I come again to see
the serene great picture that I love.
5 Here space and time exist in light
the eye like the eye of faith believes.
    The seen, the known
dissolve in irridescence, become
illusive flesh of light
10   that was not, was, forever is.

O light beheld as through refracting tears.
Here is the aura of that world
    each of us has lost.
Here is the shadow of its joy.

---

[1] Claude Monet (1840–1926), French impressionist painter. The poet's description of the painter's use of light in this particular painting is equally applicable to most of Monet's work.

[2] Selma, a city in central Alabama. In 1965, peaceful demonstrations in support of voting rights for blacks were brutally broken up by the Selma police. Two civil rights supporters were killed: one, minister James Reeb, was beaten to death on a town street; the other, homemaker Viola Liuzzo, was shot by Ku Klux Klansmen as she was driving along a highway.

[3] Saigon, the capital of the former South Vietnam, now known as Ho Chi Minh City. All news of the Vietnam War was cleared through Saigon by U.S. authorities.

READING AND REACTING

1. The speaker stands before Monet's *Waterlilies,* where he takes temporary refuge from the turbulent world. Why do you suppose Hayden chose not to use the soothing rhythms and comforting shape of closed form to convey the serenity of the moment? Do you think he made the right choice?
2. Hayden indents lines 3, 7, 10, and 13. What purpose, if any, do these indentations serve?
3. Why do you think the last four lines are separated from the rest of the poem?

Related Works: "Facing It" (p. 699), "The World Is Too Much with Us" (p. 740), "Cloud Painter" (p. 792), "Dover Beach" (p. 926), "Ethics" (p. 979), *Water Lilies* (color insert)

WILLIAM CARLOS WILLIAMS
(1883–1963)

Spring and All
(1923)

By the road to the contagious hospital
under the surge of the blue
mottled clouds driven from the
northeast—a cold wind. Beyond, the
5 waste of broad, muddy fields
brown with dried weeds, standing and fallen

patches of standing water
the scattering of tall trees

All along the road the reddish
10 purplish, forked, upstanding, twiggy
stuff of bushes and small trees
with dead, brown leaves under them
leafless vines—

Lifeless in appearance, sluggish
15 dazed spring approaches—

They enter the new world naked,
cold, uncertain of all
save that they enter. All about them
the cold, familiar wind—

20 Now the grass, tomorrow
the stiff curl of wildcarrot leaf
One by one objects are defined—
It quickens: clarity, outline of leaf

But now the stark dignity of
25 entrance—Still, the profound change
has come upon them: rooted, they
grip down and begin to awaken

Reading and Reacting

1. What elements of traditional closed form poems are present in "Spring and All"? What elements are absent?
2. What does Williams accomplish by isolating two sets of two lines each (7–8; 14–15)?
3. "Spring and All" uses assonance, alliteration, and repetition. Give several examples of each technique, and explain what each adds to the poem.
4. **Journal Entry** "Spring and All" includes only two periods. Elsewhere, where readers might expect to find end punctuation, the poet uses colons, dashes, or no punctuation at all. Why do you think the poet made these decisions about the use of punctuation?
5. **Critical Perspective** In the book *Spring and All,* in which this poem appeared, Williams claimed to be staking out a "new world" of poetry addressed "to the imagination." However, in *Lives of the Modern Poets* (1980), William H. Pritchard challenges this claim:

> [T]o believe that Williams's talk about the Imagination, the "new world," points to some radical way in which this poem is in advance of more traditional versifiers seems to me mistaken. Consider the last five lines of a poem [Robert] Frost had written, in conventional meters, a few years before:
>
> How Love burns through the Putting in the Seed
> On through the watching for that early birth
> When, just as the soil tarnishes with weed,
> The sturdy seedling with arched body comes
> Shouldering its way and shedding the earth crumbs.
>
> This birth is every bit as imaginative, every bit as much of a new world, as anything in ["Spring and All"].

What do you think of Pritchard's evaluation of Williams's poem?

Related Works: "Comparatives" (p. 847), "Pied Beauty" (p. 853)

◆ ◆ ◆
CAROLYN FORCHÉ
(1950–   )

The Colonel
(1978)

What you have heard is true. I was in his house. His wife carried
a tray of coffee and sugar. His daughter filed her nails, his son went
out for the night. There were daily papers, pet dogs, a pistol on the
cushion beside him. The moon swung bare on its black cord over
5 the house. On the television was a cop show. It was in English.
Broken bottles were embedded in the walls around the house to
scoop the kneecaps from a man's legs or cut his hands to lace. On
the windows there were gratings like those in liquor stores. We had
dinner, rack of lamb, good wine, a gold bell was on the table for
10 calling the maid. The maid brought green mangoes, salt, a type of
bread. I was asked how I enjoyed the country. There was a brief
commercial in Spanish. His wife took everything away. There was
some talk then of how difficult it had become to govern. The parrot
said hello on the terrace. The colonel told it to shut up, and pushed
15 himself from the table. My friend said to me with his eyes: say
nothing. The colonel returned with a sack used to bring groceries
home. He spilled many human ears on the table. They were like
dried peach halves. There is no other way to say this. He took one
of them in his hands, shook it in our faces, dropped it into a water
20 glass. It came alive there. I am tired of fooling around he said. As
for the rights of anyone, tell your people they can go fuck themselves. He swept the ears to the floor with his arm and held the last
of his wine in the air. Something for your poetry, no? he said. Some
of the ears on the floor caught this scrap of his voice. Some of the
25 ears on the floor were pressed to the ground.

READING AND REACTING

1. Treating Forché's prose poem as prose rather than poetry, try
   dividing it into paragraphs. What determines where you make your
   divisions?
2. If you were to reshape "The Colonel" into a more conventional-
   looking poem, what options might you have? Rewrite the poem so
   it "looks like poetry," and compare your revision to the original.
   Which version do you find more effective? Why?
3. What is the main point of "The Colonel"? How does the form help
   Forché to communicate this point?

4. **JOURNAL ENTRY** Do you think "The Colonel" is poetry or prose? Consider its subject matter and language as well as its form.

5. **Critical Pespective**   Writing in the *New York Times Book Review,* critic Katha Pollitt focuses on "poetic clichés," which, she says, are "attempts to energize the poem by annexing a subject that is guaranteed to produce a knee-jerk response in the reader. This saves a lot of bother all around, and enables poet and reader to drowse together in a warm bath of mutual admiration for each other's capacity for deep feeling and right thinking." Among these poetic clichés is something she calls "the CNN poem, which retells in overheated free verse a prominent news story involving war, famine, torture, child abuse or murder."

   Do you think "The Colonel" is a "CNN poem," or do you see it as something more than just a "poetic cliché"?

Related Works: "All about Suicide" (p. 5), "Once upon a Time" (p. 81), "Hope" (p. 748)

CONCRETE POETRY

◊ ◊ ◊

With roots in the ancient Greek *pattern poems* and the sixteenth- and seventeenth-century *emblem poems,* contemporary **concrete poetry** uses words—and, sometimes, different fonts and type sizes—to shape a picture on the page. The form of a concrete poem is not something that emerges from the poem's words and images, but rather something predetermined by the visual image the poet has decided to create. Although some concrete poems are little more than novelties, others—like the poem that follows—can be original and enlightening.

◇ ◇ ◇

MAY SWENSON
(1913–1989)

Women
(1970)

Women	Or they
should be	should be
pedestals	little horses
moving	those wooden
5 pedestals	sweet
moving	oldfashioned
to the	painted
motions	rocking
of men	horses

10   the gladdest things in the toyroom

The	feelingly
pegs	and then
of their	unfeelingly
ears	To be
15 so familiar	joyfully
and dear	ridden
to the trusting	rockingly
fists	ridden until
To be chafed	the restored

20 egos dismount and the legs stride away

Immobile	willing
sweetlipped	to be set
sturdy	into motion
and smiling	Women
25 women	should be
should always	pedestals
be waiting	to men

The curved shape of the poem immediately reinforces its title, and the arrangement of words on the page suggests a variety of visual directions readers might follow. The two columns seem at first to suggest two alternatives: "Women should be [. . .]" / "Or they should be [. . .]." A closer look, however, reveals that the poem's central figures of speech, such as woman as rocking horse and woman as pedestal, move back and forth between the two columns of images. This exchange of positions might suggest that the two possibilities are really just two ways of looking at one limited role. Thus, the experimental form of the poem visually challenges the apparent complacency of its words, suggesting that women, like words, need not fall into traditional roles or satisfy conventional expectations.

❖ POEM FOR FURTHER READING: CONCRETE POETRY

◊ ◊ ◊

GEORGE HERBERT
(1593–1633)

Easter Wings
(1633)

Lord, who createdst man in wealth and store,
Though foolishly he lost the same,
Decaying more and more,
Till he became
Most poor,
With thee
Oh, let me rise
As larks, harmoniously,
And sing this day thy victories;
Then shall the fall further the flight in me.

My tender age in sorrow did begin;
And still with sicknesses and shame
Thou didst so punish sin,
That I became
Most thin.
With thee
Let me combine,
And feel this day thy victory;
For if I imp my wing on thine,
Affliction shall advance the flight in me.

READING AND REACTING

1. In this example of an **emblem poem,** lines are arranged so that shape and language reinforce each other. Explain how this is accomplished. (For example, how does line length support the poem's images and ideas?)
2. This poem has a definite rhyme scheme. How would you describe it? What relationship do you see between the rhyme scheme and the poem's visual divisions?

Related Works: "l(a" (p. 670), "A Valediction Forbidding Mourning" (p. 816), "Because I Could Not Stop for Death" (p. 940)

✴ CHECKLIST: WRITING ABOUT FORM

✓ Is the poem written in open or closed form? On what characteristics do you base your conclusion?

✓ Why did the poet choose open or closed form? For example, is the poem's form consistent with its subject matter, tone, or theme? Is it determined by the conventions of the historical period in which it was written?

✓ If the poem is arranged in closed form, does the pattern apply to single lines, to groups of lines, or to the entire poem? What factors determine the breaks between groups of lines?

✓ Is the poem a sonnet? A sestina? A villanelle? An epigram? A haiku? How do the traditional form's conventions suit the poet's language and theme? Is the poem consistent with the requirements of the form at all times, or does it break any new ground?

✓ If the poem is arranged in open form, what determines the breaks at the ends of lines?

✓ Are certain words or phrases isolated on lines? Why?

✓ How do elements such as assonance, alliteration, rhyme, and repetition of words give the poem form?

✓ What use does the poet make of punctuation and capitalization? Of white space on the page?

✓ Is the poem a prose poem? How does this form support the poem's subject matter?

✓ Is the poem a concrete poem? How does the poet use the visual shape of the poem to convey meaning?

◆ WRITING SUGGESTIONS: FORM

1. Reread the definitions of *closed form* and *open form* in this chapter. Do you consider concrete poetry "open" or "closed"? Explain your position in a short essay, supporting your conclusion with specific references to the three concrete poems in this chapter.

2. Some poets—for example, Emily Dickinson and Robert Frost— write both open and closed form poems. Choose one open and one closed form poem by a single poet, and explain the poet's possible reasons for choosing each type of form. In your analysis of the two poems, defend the poet's choices if you can.

3. Do you see complex forms, such as the villanelle and the sestina, as just exercises, or even merely opportunities for poets to show off their skills, or do you believe the special demands of the forms add something valuable to the poem? To help you answer this question, read "Do Not Go Gentle into That Good Night" (p. 677), and analyze Dylan Thomas's use of the villanelle's structure to enhance his poem's theme. Or, study Elizabeth Bishop's "Sestina" (p. 872), and consider how her use of the sestina's form helps her to convey her ideas.

4. The following open form poem is an alternate version of May Swenson's "Women" (p. 891). Read the two versions carefully, and write an essay in which you compare them. What differences do you notice? Which do you think was written first? Why? Do the two poems make the same point? Which makes the point with less ambiguity? Which is more effective? Why?

◊ ◊ ◊

Women Should Be Pedestals

Women should be pedestals
moving pedestals
moving to the motions of men
Or they should be little horses
5 those wooden sweet oldfashioned painted rocking horses
the gladdest things in the toyroom
The pegs of their ears so familiar and dear
to the trusting fists
To be chafed feelingly
10 and then unfeelingly
To be joyfully ridden
until the restored egos dismount and the legs stride away
Immobile sweetlipped sturdy and smiling
women should always be waiting
15 willing to be set into motion
Women should be pedestals to men

5. Look through the "Poetry for Further Reading" section that follows Chapter 19 of this text, and identify one or two **prose poems.** Write an essay in which you consider why the form seems suitable for the poem or poems you have chosen. Is there a particular kind of subject matter that seems especially appropriate for a prose poem?

6. **WEB ACTIVITY** The following Web site contains information about William Carlos Williams:

http://www.learner.org/collections/multimedia/literature/
vvseries/vvspot/williams.html

William Carlos Williams is well known for his innovations in poetic form. View the video clip of "the Great Figure." (The text of this poem appears on page 797 of this book, and a painting based on the poem appears in the color insert.) Then, read the article on "the Poetry/Art Connection." Open the sections on Cubism and Dadaism. After reading several other Williams poems from the Web site, write an essay on the connection between visual images and the form of Williams's poetry.

CHAPTER 19

Symbol, Allegory, Allusion, Myth

◇ ◇ ◇

What the reader gets from a symbol depends not only upon what the author has put into it but upon the reader's sensitivity and his consequent apprehension of what is there. The feeling of profundity that accompanies it comes from a gradual but never final penetration of the form.

WILLIAM YORK TINDALL, "Excellent Dumb Discourse"

Myth is an expression of "primitive" people. People in the process of making what we call civilization, and its purpose is to explain and support them against darkness. [. . .] Myth is also a counter against morality in a world in which life is "solitary, nasty, poor, brutish, and short." [. . .] Myths are also composed—if they are "composed" and not built by accretion, like deltas— by anonymous authors. It would never occur to us to wonder, for example, who wrote about Demeter and Persephone. Nobody wrote it. Everybody did. It doesn't matter.

ADRIÀN OKTENBERG, *From the Bottom Up*

A myth is not "a large controlling image." The future of mythical poetry does not depend upon reconciling poetry with an image. It depends rather upon making of poetry something it is always striving against human bias and superficiality to become. The poetical imagination when it attains any consistent fire and efficacy is always displacing the texture of the mind into the external world so that it becomes a theater of preternatural forces. A certain control and direction given the poetical emotions, and poetry, as it always has, becomes mythical.

RICHARD CHASE, "Notes on the Study of Myth"

◇ ◇ ◇

⬦ ⬦ ⬦

WILLIAM BLAKE
(1757–1827)

The Sick Rose
(1794)

O Rose thou art sick.
The invisible worm
That flies in the night,
In the howling storm:

5 Has found out thy bed
Of crimson joy:
And his dark secret love
Does thy life destroy.

SYMBOL

⬦ ⬦ ⬦

As in fiction and drama, symbols in poetry function as a kind of short-hand, as a subtle way of introducing a significant idea or attitude. A **symbol** is an idea or image that suggests something else—but not in the simple way that a dollar sign stands for money or a flag represents a country. A symbol is an image that transcends its literal, or denotative, meaning in a complex way. For instance, if someone gives a rose to a loved one, it could simply be a sign of love. But in the poem "The Sick Rose," the rose has a range of contradictory and complementary meanings. For what does the rose stand? Beauty? Perfection? Passion? Something else? As this poem illustrates, the distinctive trait of a symbol is that its meaning cannot easily be pinned down or defined.

Such ambiguity can be frustrating, but it is precisely this characteristic of a symbol that enables it to enrich a work and to give it additional layers of meaning. As Robert Frost has said, a symbol is a little thing that touches a larger thing. In the poem of his that follows, the central symbol does just this.

⬦ ⬦ ⬦

ROBERT FROST
(1874–1963)

For Once, Then, Something
(1923)

Others taunt me with having knelt at well-curbs
Always wrong to the light, so never seeing

Deeper down in the well than where the water
Gives me back in a shining surface picture
5 Me myself in the summer heaven, godlike,
Looking out of a wreath of fern and cloud puffs.
Once, when trying with chin against a well-curb,
I discerned, as I thought, beyond the picture,
Through the picture, a something white, uncertain,
10 Something more of the depths—and then I lost it.
Water came to rebuke the too clear water.
One drop fell from a fern, and lo, a ripple
Shook whatever it was lay there at bottom,
Blurred it, blotted it out. What was that whiteness?
15 Truth? A pebble of quartz? For once, then, something.

The central symbol in this poem is the "something" that the speaker thinks he discerns at the bottom of a well. Traditionally, the act of looking down a well suggests a search for truth. In this poem, the speaker remarks that he always seems to look down the well at the wrong angle, so that all he can see is his own reflection—the surface, not the depths. Once, the speaker tells us, he thought he saw something "beyond the picture," something "white, uncertain," but the image remained indistinct, disappearing when a drop of water from a fern caused the water to ripple. The poem ends with the speaker questioning the significance of what he saw. Like a reader encountering a symbol, the speaker is left trying to come to terms with images that cannot be clearly perceived and suggestions that cannot be readily understood. In light of the elusive nature of truth, all the speaker can do is ask questions that have no definite answers.

Symbols that appear in works of poetry can be *conventional* or *universal*. **Conventional symbols** are those recognized by people who share certain cultural and social assumptions. National flags, for example, evoke a general and agreed-upon response in most people of a particular country and, for better or for worse, American children have for years perceived the golden arches of McDonald's as a symbol of food and fun. **Universal symbols** are those likely to be recognized by people regardless of their culture. In 1890, the noted Scottish anthropologist Sir James George Frazer wrote the first version of his work *The Golden Bough,* in which he showed parallels between the rites and beliefs of early cultures and those of Christianity. Fascinated by Frazer's work, the psychologist Carl Jung sought to explain these parallels by formulating a theory of **archetypes,** which held that certain images or ideas reside in the subconscious of all people. According to Jung, archetypal, or universal, symbols include water, symbolizing rebirth; spring, symbolizing growth; and winter, symbolizing death.

Sometimes symbols that appear in poems can be obscure or highly idiosyncratic. The works of William Blake and W. B. Yeats, for example, combine symbols from different cultural, theological, and philosophical sources to form complex networks of symbolic associations. To Blake, for example, the scientist Isaac Newton represents the tendency of scientists to quantify experience while ignoring the beauty and mystery of nature. Readers cannot begin to understand Blake's use of Newton as a symbol until they have read a number of his more difficult poems.

Most often, however, symbols in poems are not this challenging. In the following poem, for instance, the poet introduces a cross—a symbol that has specific associations to those familiar with Christianity—and makes his own use of it.

◊ ◊ ◊

JIM SIMMERMAN[1]

Child's Grave, Hale County, Alabama
(1983)

Someone drove a two-by-four
through the heart of this hard land
that even in a good year
will notch a plow blade worthless,
5 snap the head off a shovel,
or bow a stubborn back.
He'd have had to steal
the wood from a local mill
or steal, by starlight, across
10 his landlord's farm, to worry
a fencepost out of its well
and lug it the three miles home.
He'd have had to leave his wife
asleep on a corn shuck mat,
15 leave his broken brogans[2]
by the stove, to slip outside,
quiet as sin, with the child
bundled in a burlap sack.
What a thing to have to do
20 on a cold night in December,

---

[1] Birth date is not available.
[2] Sturdy, heavy work shoes, frequently ankle high.

     1936, alone
     but for a raspy wind
     and the red, rock-ridden dirt
     things come down to in the end.
   25 Whoever it was pounded
     this shabby half-cross
     into the ground must have toiled
     all night to root it so:
     five feet buried with the child
   30 for the foot of it that shows.
     And as there are no words
     carved here, it's likely that
     the man was illiterate,
     or addled with fatigue,
   35 or wrenched simple-minded
     by the one simple fact.
     Or else the unscored lumber
     driven deep into the land
     and the hump of busted rock
   40 spoke too plainly of his grief:
     forty years layed by and still
     there are no words for this.

Even in non-Christian cultures, the cross on a grave is a readily identifiable symbol of death and rebirth. In this poem, however, the cross is not simply presented as a conventional Christian symbol; it is also associated with the tenant farmer's hard work and difficult life. In this sense, the cross also suggests the poverty that helped bring about the death of the child and the social conditions that existed during the Depression. These associations take readers through many layers of meaning, so that the cross may ultimately stand for the tenant farmer's whole life (the cross *he* has to bear), not just for the death of the child. This interpretation by no means exhausts the possible symbolic significance of the cross in the poem. For example, the "shabby half-cross" might also suggest the rage and grief of the individual who made it, or it might call to mind the poor who live and die in anonymity. Certainly the poet could have assigned a fixed meaning to the cross that marks the child's grave, but he chose instead, by suggesting various ideas through a single powerful symbol, to let readers arrive at their own conclusions.

  How do you know when an idea or image in a poem is a symbol? At what point do you decide that a particular object or idea goes beyond the literal level and takes on symbolic significance? When, that is, is a rose more than a rose or a cross more than a cross? Frequently you can recognize a symbol by its prominence or repetition. In "Child's Grave, Hale County, Alabama," for example, the cross is introduced in the first line of the poem, and it is the focal point of the poem; in "The Sick Rose," the importance of the rose is emphasized by the title.

It is not enough, however, to identify an image or idea that seems to suggest something else. Your decision that a particular item has some symbolic significance must be supported by the details of the poem and make sense within the context of the ideas developed in the poem. Moreover, the symbol must support the poem's ideas. In the following poem, the image of the volcano helps readers to understand the poem's central theme.

✧ ✧ ✧

EMILY DICKINSON
(1830–1886)

Volcanoes Be in Sicily
(1914)

Volcanoes be in Sicily
And South America
I judge from my Geography—
Volcanoes nearer here
5   A Lava step at any time
Am I inclined to climb—
A Crater I may contemplate
Vesuvius at Home.

This poem opens with a statement of fact: volcanoes are located in Sicily and South America. In lines 3 and 4, however, the speaker makes the improbable observation that volcanoes are located near where she is at the moment. Readers familiar with Dickinson know that her poems are highly autobiographical and that she lived in Amherst, Massachusetts, a town with no volcanoes. This information leads readers to suspect that they should not take the speaker's observation literally and that in the context of the poem volcanoes may have symbolic significance. But what do volcanoes suggest here? On the one hand, volcanoes represent the awesome creative power of nature; on the other hand, they suggest its destructiveness. The speaker's contemplation of the crater of Vesuvius—the volcano that buried the ancient Roman city of Pompeii in A.D. 79—is therefore filled with contradictory associations. Because Dickinson was a recluse, volcanoes—active, destructive, unpredictable, and dangerous—may be seen as symbolic of everything she fears in the outside world and, perhaps, within herself. Or, volcanoes may even suggest her own creative power, which, like a volcano, is something to be feared as well as contemplated. She has a voyeur's attraction to danger and power, but she is also afraid of them. For this reason she (and her speaker) may feel safer contemplating

Vesuvius at home—not experiencing exotic lands, but simply reading a geography book.

❖ POEMS FOR FURTHER READING: SYMBOL

◇ ◇ ◇

LANGSTON HUGHES
(1902–1967)

Island
(1951)

Wave of sorrow,
Do not drown me now:

I see the island
Still ahead somehow.

5 I see the island
And its sands are fair:

Wave of sorrow,
Take me there.

READING AND REACTING

1. What makes you suspect that the island has symbolic significance in this poem? Explain your answer.
2. Is the "wave of sorrow" also a symbol?
3. **JOURNAL ENTRY** Beyond its literal meaning, what might the island in this poem suggest? Consider several possibilities.
4. **CRITICAL PERSPECTIVE** In *Langston Hughes,* a 1973 study of the poet's work, Onwuchekwa Jemie writes that "the black writer's problem is . . . how to actualize the oral tradition in written form":

> The black writer [. . .] has no long written tradition of his own to emulate; and for him to abandon the effort to translate into written form that oral medium which is the full reservoir of his culture would be to annihilate his identity and become a zombie, a programmed vehicle for "the message of another people."

Do you think "Island" successfully "actualizes the oral tradition in written form"? What elements help it to qualify as "oral" poetry?

Related Works: "A Worn Path" (p. 388), "Sea Grapes" (p. 917)

⬦ ⬦ ⬦

THEODORE ROETHKE
(1908–1963)

Night Crow
(1944)

When I saw that clumsy crow
Flap from a wasted tree,
Over the gulfs of dream
Flew a tremendous bird
5   Further and further away
Into a moonless black,
Deep in the brain, far back.

READING AND REACTING

1. What does the title suggest? How does it help you to interpret the symbolic significance of the crow?
2. How is the "clumsy crow" different from the crow "Deep in the brain"? What visual image does each suggest?
3. **JOURNAL ENTRY** It has been suggested that "Night Crow" is a commentary on the difference between reality and imagination. Does the poem's use of symbol support such an interpretation? Explain.

Related Works: "The Cask of Amontillado" (p. 219), "The Tyger" (p. 930), "The Windhover" (p. 966)

ALLEGORY
⬦ ⬦ ⬦

Allegory is a form of narrative that conveys a message or doctrine by using people, places, or things to stand for abstract ideas. **Allegorical figures,** each with a strict equivalent, form an **allegorical framework,** a set of ideas that conveys the allegory's message or lesson. Thus, the allegory takes place on two levels: a literal level that tells a story and a figurative level where the allegorical figures in the story stand for ideas, concepts, and other qualities. Like symbols, allegory uses things to suggest other things. But unlike symbols, which have a range of possible meanings, allegorical figures can always be assigned specific meanings. (Because writers use allegory to instruct, they gain nothing by hiding its significance.) Thus, symbols open up possibilities for interpretation, whereas allegories tend to restrict possibilities.

Quite often an allegory involves a journey or an adventure, as in the case of Dante's *Divine Comedy,* which traces a journey through Hell, Purgatory, and Heaven. Within an allegory, everything can have meaning: the road upon which the characters walk, the people they encounter, or a phrase that one of them repeats throughout the journey. Once you understand the allegorical framework, your main task is to see how the various elements fit within this system. Some allegorical poems can be relatively straightforward, but others can be so complicated that it takes a great deal of time and effort to unlock their meaning. In the following poem, a journey is central to the allegory.

◊   ◊   ◊

CHRISTINA ROSSETTI
(1830–1894)

Uphill
(1861)

Does the road wind uphill all the way?
    Yes, to the very end.
Will the day's journey take the whole long day?
    From morn to night, my friend.

5 But is there for the night a resting-place?
    A roof for when the slow dark hours begin.
May not the darkness hide it from my face?
    You cannot miss that inn.

Shall I meet other wayfarers at night?
10   Those who have gone before.
Then must I knock, or call when just in sight?
    They will not keep you standing at that door.

Shall I find comfort, travel-sore and weak?
    Of labor you shall find the sum.
15 Will there be beds for me and all who seek?
    Yea, beds for all who come.

"Uphill" uses a question-and-answer structure to describe a journey along an uphill road. Like the one described in John Bunyan's seventeenth-century allegory *The Pilgrim's Progress,* this is a spiritual journey, one that suggests the challenges a person faces throughout life. The day-and-night duration of the journey stands for life and death, and the inn at the end of the road stands for the grave, the final resting place.

❖ POEM FOR FURTHER READING: ALLEGORY

⬧ ⬧ ⬧

ADRIENNE RICH
(1929–   )

Diving into the Wreck
(1973)

First having read the book of myths,
and loaded the camera,
and checked the edge of the knife-blade,
I put on
5   the body-armor of black rubber
the absurd flippers
the grave and awkward mask.
I am having to do this
not like Cousteau with his
10   assiduous team
aboard the sun-flooded schooner
but here alone.

There is a ladder.
The ladder is always there
15   hanging innocently
close to the side of the schooner.
We know what it is for,
we who have used it.
Otherwise
20   it's a piece of maritime floss
some sundry equipment.

I go down.
Rung after rung and still
the oxygen immerses me
25   the blue light
the clear atoms
of our human air.
I go down.
My flippers cripple me,
30   I crawl like an insect down the ladder
and there is no one
to tell me when the ocean
will begin.

First the air is blue and then
35   it is bluer and then green and then

black I am blacking out and yet
my mask is powerful
it pumps my blood with power
the sea is another story
40 the sea is not a question of power
I have to learn alone
to turn my body without force
in the deep element.

And now: it is easy to forget
45 what I came for
among so many who have always
lived here
swaying their crenellated fans
between the reefs
50 and besides
you breathe differently down here.

I came to explore the wreck.
The words are purposes.
The words are maps.
55 I came to see the damage that was done
and the treasures that prevail.
I stroke the beam of my lamp
slowly along the flank
of something more permanent
60 than fish or weed

the thing I came for:
the wreck and not the story of the wreck
the thing itself and not the myth
the drowned face always staring
65 toward the sun
the evidence of damage
worn by salt and sway into this threadbare beauty
the ribs of the disaster
curving their assertion
70 among the tentative haunters.

This is the place.
And I am here, the mermaid whose dark hair
streams black, the merman in his armored body
We circle silently
75 about the wreck
we dive into the hold.
I am she: I am he

whose drowned face sleeps with open eyes
whose breasts still bear the stress
80 whose silver, copper, vermeil cargo lies
obscurely inside barrels
half-wedged and left to rot
we are the half-destroyed instruments
that once held to a course
85 the water-eaten log
the fouled compass

We are, I am, you are
by cowardice or courage
the one who finds our way
90 back to this scene
carrying a knife, a camera
a book of myths
in which
our names do not appear.

READING AND REACTING

1. On one level, this poem is about a deep-sea diver's exploration of a wrecked ship. What details suggest that the poet wants you to see something more?
2. Explain the allegorical figures presented in the poem. What, for example, might the diver and the wreck represent?
3. Does the poem contain any symbols? How can you tell they are symbols and not allegorical figures?
4. **JOURNAL ENTRY** In lines 62–63, the speaker says that she came for "the wreck and not the story of the wreck / the thing itself and not the myth." What do you think the speaker is really looking for?
5. **CRITICAL PERSPECTIVE** A number of critics have seen "Diving into the Wreck" as an attempt by Rich to reimagine or reinvent the myths of Western culture. Rachel Blau DuPlessis makes this observation:

> In this poem of journey and transformation Rich is tapping the energies and plots of myth, while re-envisioning the content. While there is a hero, a quest, and a buried treasure, the hero is a woman; the quest is a critique of old myths; the treasure is knowledge [. . .].

Why do you suppose Rich decided to "reinvent" myth?

Related Works: "Once upon a Time" (p. 81), "Young Goodman Brown" (p. 304), "The Love Song of J. Alfred Prufrock" (p. 950)

ALLUSION

◈ ◈ ◈

An **allusion** is a brief reference to a person, place, or event (fictional or actual) that readers are expected to recognize. Like symbols and allegories, allusions enrich a work by introducing associations and attitudes from another context.

When poets use allusions, they assume that they and their readers have a common body of knowledge. If, when reading a poem, you come across a reference with which you are not familiar, take the time to look it up in a dictionary or an encyclopedia. As you have probably realized by now, your understanding of a poem may depend on your ability to interpret an unfamiliar reference.

Although most poets expect readers to recognize their references, some use allusions to exclude certain readers from their work. In his 1922 poem "The Waste Land," for example, T. S. Eliot makes allusions to historical events, ancient languages, and obscure literary works. He even includes a set of notes to accompany his poem, but they do little more than complicate an already difficult text. (As you might expect, critical response to this poem was mixed, with some critics saying that it was a work of genius and others saying that it was pretentious.)

Allusions can come from any source: history, the arts, other works of literature, the Bible, current events, or even the personal life of the poet. In the following poem, the Nigerian poet and playwright Wole Soyinka alludes to several contemporary political figures.

◈ ◈ ◈

WOLE SOYINKA
(1934–   )

Future Plans
(1972)

The meeting is called
To odium: Forgers, framers
Fabricators Inter-
national. Chairman,
5 A dark horse, a circus nag turned blinkered sprinter

Mach Three
We rate him—one for the Knife
Two for 'iavelli, Three—
Breaking speed
10 Of the truth barrier by a swooping detention decree

Projects in view:
Mao Tse Tung in league
With Chiang Kai. Nkrumah
Makes a secret
15 Pact with Verwood, sworn by Hastings Banda.
Proven: Arafat
In flagrante cum
Golda Meir. Castro drunk
With Richard Nixon
20 Contraceptives stacked beneath the papal bunk . . .
. . . *and more to come*

This poem is structured like an agenda for a meeting. From the moment it announces that a meeting has been called "To odium" (a pun on "to order"), it is clear that the poem will be a bitter political satire. Those in attendance are "Forgers, framers / Fabricators." The second stanza contains three allusions that shed light on the character of the chairman. The first is to Mack the Knife, a petty criminal in Bertolt Brecht and Kurt Weill's 1933 *Threepenny Opera*. The second is to Niccolò Machiavelli, whose 1532 book *The Prince* advocates the use of unscrupulous means to strengthen the State. The last is to the term *mach*, which denotes the speed of an airplane in relation to the speed of sound—mach one, two, three, and so on. By means of these allusions, the poem implies that the meeting's chairman has been chosen for his ability to engage in violence, to be ruthless, and to break the "truth barrier"—that is, to lie.

The rest of the poem alludes to individuals involved in global politics—specifically, the politics of developing nations. According to the speaker, instead of fighting for the rights of the oppressed, these people consolidate their own political power by collaborating with those who oppose their positions. Thus, Mao Tse-tung, the former communist leader of China, is "in league with" Chiang Kai-shek, his old Nationalist Chinese enemy; Yassir Arafat, the leader of the Palestine Liberation Organization, is linked with Golda Meir, the former prime minister of Israel; Kwame Nkrumah, the first president of Ghana, conspires with Hendrick Verwoerd, the former prime minister of South Africa, assassinated in 1966; and former President Richard Nixon gets drunk with Cuba's communist leader, Fidel Castro. These allusions suggest the self-serving nature of political alliances and the extreme disorder of world politics. The ideological juxtapositions show the interchangeability of various political philosophies, none of which has the answer to the world's problems. Whether the poem is satirizing the United Nations and its idealistic agenda, criticizing the tendency of politics to make strange bedfellows, or showing how corrupt all politicians are, its allusions enable the poet to broaden his frame of reference and thus make the poem more meaningful to readers.

The following poem uses allusions to writers, as well as to a myth, to develop its theme.

◆ ◆ ◆

WILLIAM MEREDITH
(1919–   )

Dreams of Suicide
(1980)

(in sorrowful memory of Ernest Hemingway, Sylvia Plath, and John Berryman)

I

I reach for the awkward shotgun not to disarm
you, but to feel the metal horn,
furred with the downy membrane of dream.
More surely than the unicorn,
5   you are the mythical beast.

II

Or I am sniffing an oven. On all fours
I am imitating a totemic animal
but she is not my totem or the totem
of my people, this is not my magic oven.

III

10   If I hold you tight by the ankles,
still you fly upward from the iron railing.
Your father made these wings,
after he made his own, and now from beyond
he tells you *fly down*, in the voice
15   my own father might say *walk, boy*.

This poem is dedicated to the memory of three writers who committed suicide. In each stanza, the speaker envisions in a dream the death of one of the writers. In the first stanza, he dreams of Ernest Hemingway, who killed himself with a shotgun. The speaker grasps the "metal horn" of Hemingway's shotgun and transforms him into a mythical beast who, like a unicorn, represents the rare, unique talent of the artist. In the second stanza, the speaker dreams of Sylvia Plath, who asphyxiated herself in a gas oven. He sees himself, like Plath, on his knees imitating an animal sniffing an oven. Finally, in the third stanza, the speaker dreams of John Berryman, who leaped to his death. Berryman is characterized as Icarus, a mythological figure who, along with his father Daedalus, fled Crete by building wings made of feathers and wax. Together they flew away, but, ignoring his father's warning, Icarus flew too close to the sun and, when the wax melted, fell to his death in the sea. Like Icarus, Berryman ignores the warning of his father and, like Daedalus, the speaker tries to stop Berryman. In this poem, then, the speaker uses allusions to make a point about the difficult lives of writers—and, perhaps, to convey his own empathy for those who could not survive the struggle to reconcile art and life.

❖ POEM FOR FURTHER READING: ALLUSION

❖ ❖ ❖

DELMORE SCHWARTZ
(1913–1966)

The True-Blue American
(1959)

Jeremiah Dickson was a true-blue American,
For he was a little boy who understood America, for he felt that he
    must
Think about *everything;* because that's *all* there is to think about,
Knowing immediately the intimacy of truth and comedy,
5 Knowing intuitively how a sense of humor was a necessity
For one and for all who live in America. Thus, natively, and
Naturally when on an April Sunday in an ice cream parlor Jeremiah
Was requested to choose between a chocolate sundae and a banana
    split
He answered unhesitatingly, having no need to think of it
10 Being a true-blue American, determined to continue as he began:
Rejecting the either-or of Kierkegaard,[1] and many another European;
Refusing to accept alternatives, refusing to believe the choice of
    between;
Rejecting selection; denying dilemma; electing absolute affirmation:
    knowing
15   in his breast
            The infinite and the gold
            Of the endless frontier, the deathless West.
"Both: I will have them both!" declared this true-blue American
In Cambridge, Massachusetts, on an April Sunday, instructed
20   By the great department stores, by the Five-and-Ten,
Taught by Christmas, by the circus, by the vulgarity and grandeur of
        Niagara Falls and the Grand Canyon,
Tutored by the grandeur, vulgarity, and infinite appetite gratified and
        Shining in the darkness, of the light
25 On Saturdays at the double bills of the moon pictures,
The consummation of the advertisements of the imagination of the
    light
Which is as it was—the infinite belief in infinite hope—of Columbus,
    Barnum, Edison, and Jeremiah Dickson.

---

[1] Søren Kierkegaard (1813–1855)—Danish philosopher who greatly influenced twentieth-century existentialism. *Either-Or* (1841) is one of his best-known works.

READING AND REACTING

1. To what does the poem's title refer? Do you think this title has meaning beyond its identification of Jeremiah Dickson?
2. Read an encyclopedia article about Kierkegaard. Why do you suppose Schwartz alludes to him in line 11?
3. What do you think the significance of the name Jeremiah Dickson might be? Is it an allusion?
4. What is the significance of the allusions to places in lines 19–22 and to individuals in lines 27 and 28?
5. **JOURNAL ENTRY** How do you define a "true-blue" American? How do you think the poem's speaker would define this term?
6. **CRITICAL PERSPECTIVE** In his 1977 biography of Schwartz, James Atlas remarks on the poet's affinity with mass culture:

> Delmore's interest in the products of the popular mind, while in part motivated by a desire to ally himself with a wider public than was ordinarily available to poets, had none of the moralizing condescension [of other 1950s intellectuals]; it was a natural expression of his own affinities with all that was American, affinities derived from his early infatuation with baseball, tabloids, the movies, and whatever else he thought animated the drama of history. [. . .] He was genuinely democratic [. . .].

Do you see "The True-Blue American" as a celebration of mass culture? If not, what do you think Schwartz's purpose might have been?

Related Works: "The Secret Lion" (p. 49), "Chicago" (p. 880), "next to of course god america i" (p. 939), "The United Fruit Co." (p. 976), *The Glass Menagerie* (p. 1805), *American Indian No. 4* (color insert)

MYTH
◆ ◆ ◆

A **myth** is a narrative that embodies—and in some cases helps to explain—the religious, philosophical, moral, and political values of a culture. Using gods and supernatural beings, myths try to make sense of occurrences in the natural world. (The term *myth* can also refer to a private belief system invented by an individual poet as well as to any fully realized fictitious setting in which a literary work takes place, such as the myths of William Faulkner's Yoknapatawpha County or Lawrence Durrell's Alexandria.) Contrary to popular usage, *myth* is not the same as *falsehood*. In the broadest sense, myths are stories—usually whole groups of stories—that can be true or partly true as well as false; regardless of their degree of accuracy, however, myths frequently express the deepest beliefs of a culture. According to this definition, then, the *Iliad* and the

Odyssey, the Koran, and the Old and New Testaments can all be regarded as myths.

According to the mythologist Joseph Campbell, myths contain truths that link people together, whether they live today or lived 2,500 years ago. Myths do, after all, attempt to explain phenomena that human beings care about regardless of when and where they live. It is not surprising, then, that myths frequently contain archetypal images that cut across cultural and racial boundaries and touch us on a very deep level. Many Greek myths illustrate this power. For example, when Orpheus descends into Hades to rescue his wife, Eurydice, he acts out the human desire to transcend death; and when Telemachus sets out in search of his father, Odysseus, he reminds readers that we all are lost children searching for parents. When Icarus ignores his father and flies too near the sun and when Pandora cannot resist looking into a box that she has been told not to open, we are reminded of the human weaknesses we all share.

When poets use myths, they are actually making allusions. They expect readers to bring to the poem the cultural, emotional, and ethical context of the myths to which they are alluding. At one time, when all educated individuals studied the Greek and Latin classics as well as the Bible, poets could be reasonably sure that readers would recognize the mythological allusions they made. Many contemporary readers, however, are unable to understand the full significance of an allusion or its application within the poem. Although many of the poems in this anthology are accompanied by notes, these notes may not provide all the information you will need to understand each mythological allusion and to determine its significance within a poem. Occasionally, you may have to look for answers beyond this text, in dictionaries, encyclopedias, or collections of myths, such as the *New Larousse Encyclopedia of Mythology* or *Bulfinch's Mythology,* for example.

Sometimes a poet will allude to a myth in a title; sometimes references to various myths will appear throughout a poem; at other times, an entire poem will focus on a single myth. In each case, as in the following poem, the use of myth helps to communicate the poem's theme.

◇ ◇ ◇

COUNTEE CULLEN
(1903–1946)

Yet Do I Marvel
(1925)

I doubt not God is good, well-meaning, kind,
And did He stoop to quibble could tell why
The little buried mole continues blind,

Why flesh that mirrors Him must some day die,
5 Make plain the reason tortured Tantalus
Is baited by the fickle fruit, declare
If merely brute caprice dooms Sisyphus
To struggle up a never-ending stair.
Inscrutable His ways are, and immune
10 To catechism by a mind too strewn
With petty cares to slightly understand
What awful brain compels His awful hand.
Yet do I marvel at this curious thing:
To make a poet black, and bid him sing!

The speaker in this poem begins by affirming his belief in the benevolence of God, but he then goes on to question why God engages in what appear to be capricious acts. As part of his catalog of questions, the speaker mentions Tantalus and Sisyphus, two figures from Greek mythology. Tantalus was a king who was admitted to the society of the gods. Because he behaved so badly, he was condemned to Hades and forced to stand up to his chin in a pool of water over which hung a branch laden with fruit. When he got thirsty and tried to drink, the level of the water would drop, and when he got hungry and reached for fruit, it would move just out of his grasp. Thus, Tantalus was doomed to be near what he most desired, but forever unable to obtain it. Like Tantalus, Sisyphus was also condemned to Hades. For his disrespect to Zeus, he was sentenced to endless toil. Every day, Sisyphus would push a gigantic boulder up a steep hill. As he neared the top, the boulder would slip down the hill, and he would have to begin again. Like Tantalus, the speaker cannot have what he wants; like Sisyphus, he is forced to toil in vain. He wonders why a well-meaning God would "make a poet black, and bid him sing" in a racist society that does not listen to his voice. Thus, the poet's two allusions to Greek mythology enrich the poem by connecting the suffering of the speaker to a universal drama that has been acted out again and again.

❖ **POEMS FOR FURTHER READING: MYTH**

◊ ◊ ◊

LOUISE ERDRICH
(1954–   )

Windigo
(1984)

For Angela

The Windigo is a flesh-eating, wintry demon with a man buried deep inside of it.
In some Chippewa stories, a young girl vanquishes this monster by forcing boiling
lard down its throat, thereby releasing the human at the core of ice.

You knew I was coming for you, little one,
when the kettle jumped into the fire.
Towels flapped on the hooks,
and the dog crept off, groaning,
5 to the deepest part of the woods.

In the hackles of dry brush a thin laughter started up.
Mother scolded the food warm and smooth in the pot
and called you to eat.
But I spoke in the cold trees:
10 *New one, I have come for you, child hide and lie still.*

The sumac pushed sour red cones through the air.
Copper burned in the raw wood.
You saw me drag toward you.
Oh touch me, I murmured, and licked the soles of your feet.
15 You dug your hands into my pale, melting fur.

I stole you off, a huge thing in my bristling armor.
Steam rolled from my wintry arms, each leaf shivered
from the bushes we passed
until they stood, naked, spread like the cleaned spines of fish.

20 Then your warm hands hummed over and shoveled themselves full
of the ice and the snow. I would darken and spill
all night running, until at last morning broke the cold earth
and I carried you home,
a river shaking in the sun.

READING AND REACTING

1. Because Erdrich writes for a diverse audience, she cannot
   reasonably expect all her readers to be familiar with the Native

American myth in the poem. Does her epigraph provide enough information for those who are not?

2. Who is the speaker in the poem? How would you characterize the speaker? What advantage does Erdrich gain by assuming this persona?

3. What is the major theme of this poem? How does the myth of the Windigo express this theme?

4. **JOURNAL ENTRY** How is the Windigo described in the epigraph like and unlike the one portrayed in the poem?

5. **CRITICAL PERSPECTIVE** In her 1987 examination of various emerging American literatures, "The Bones of This Body Say, Dance," Lynda Koolish discusses Native American poetry:

> Earlier historical periods of Native American culture provide images of vision and power for many American Indian writers. Poetry, like prayers, chants, the telling of dreams, folktales, tribal lore, or oral history, is an essential part of the spiritual and aesthetic survival of American Indian people. [. . .] Like myth or folklore, legend or dream, poetry makes the unknowable intelligible. In Native American poetry, as in all these language art forms, access is provided to the mysterious and creative powers of the universe and thus to one's own inner power.

Does "Windigo" offer this kind of access to you? Why or why not?

Related Works: "Where Are You Going, Where Have You Been?" (p. 614), "Gretel in Darkness" (p. 724), "Fire and Ice" (p. 735), "Leda and the Swan" (p. 916)

◇　◇　◇

WILLIAM BUTLER YEATS
(1865–1939)

Leda and the Swan
(1924)

A sudden blow: the great wings beating still
Above the staggering girl, her thighs caressed
By the dark webs, her nape caught in his bill,
He holds her helpless breast upon his breast.

5 How can those terrified vague fingers push
The feathered glory from her loosening thighs?
And how can body, laid in that white rush,
But feel the strange heart beating where it lies?

A shudder in the loins engenders there
10 The broken wall, the burning roof and tower
And Agamemnon dead.

Being so caught up,
So mastered by the brute blood of the air,
Did she put on his knowledge with his power
15 Before the indifferent beak could let her drop?

READING AND REACTING

1. Look up the myth of Leda in an encyclopedia. What event is described in this poem? What is the mythological significance of the event?
2. How is Leda portrayed? Why is the swan described as a "feathered glory" (6)? Why in the poem's last line is Leda dropped by his "indifferent beak"?
3. The third stanza refers to the Trojan War, which was indirectly caused by the event described in the poem. How does the allusion to the Trojan War help develop the theme of the poem?
4. **JOURNAL ENTRY** Does the poem answer the question asked in its last two lines? Explain.
5. **CRITICAL PERSPECTIVE** According to Richard Ellmann this poem deals with "transcendence of opposites." The bird's "rape of the human, the coupling of god and woman, the moment at which one epoch ended and another began [. . .] in the act which included all these Yeats had the violent symbol for the transcendence of opposites which he needed."

   What opposite or contrary forces exist in the myth of Leda and the swan? Do you think the poem implies that these forces can be reconciled?

Related Works: "The Birthmark" (p. 450), "The Second Coming" (p. 1013)

◊ ◊ ◊

DEREK WALCOTT[1]
(1930–   )

Sea Grapes[2]
(1971)

That sail which leans on light,
    tired of islands,
    a schooner beating up the Caribbean

    for home, could be Odysseus,
5 home-bound on the Aegean;
    that father and husband's

---

[1] Winner of the 1992 Nobel Prize in literature.
[2] Small trees found on tropical sandy beaches.

longing, under gnarled sour grapes, is
like the adulterer hearing Nausicaa's[3] name
in every gull's outcry.

10 This brings nobody peace. The ancient war
between obsession and responsibility
will never finish and has been the same

for the sea-wanderer or the one on shore
now wriggling on his sandals to walk home,
15 since Troy sighed its last flame,

and the blind giant's boulder heaved the trough
from whose ground-swell the great hexameters come
to the conclusions of exhausted surf.

The classics can console. But not enough.

READING AND REACTING

1. Read a plot summary of the *Odyssey* in an encyclopedia. In the context of the myth of Odysseus, what is the "ancient war / between obsession and responsibility" (10–11) to which the speaker refers? Does this conflict have a wider application in the context of the poem? Explain.
2. Consider the following lines from the poem: "and the blind giant's boulder heaved the trough / from whose ground-swell the great hexameters come / to the conclusions of exhausted surf" (16–18). In what sense does the blind giant's boulder create the "great hexameters"? In what way does the trough end up as "exhausted surf"?
3. **JOURNAL ENTRY** This poem includes many references to Homer's *Odyssey*. Could you have appreciated it if you had not read a plot summary of the *Odyssey*?
4. **CRITICAL PERSPECTIVE** Asked in an interview about the final line of "Sea Grapes," Derek Walcott made the following comments:

> All of us have been to the point where, in extreme agony and distress, you turn to a book, and look for parallels, and you look for a greater grief than maybe your own. [. . .] But the truth of human agony is that a book does not assuage a toothache. It isn't that things don't pass and heal. Perhaps the only privilege that a poet has is that, in that agony, whatever chafes and hurts, if the person survives, [he] produces something that is hopefully lasting and moral from the experience.

How do Walcott's remarks help to explain the poem's last line?

---

[3] A young woman who befriended Odysseus.

Related Works: "Sleepy Time Gal" (p. 242), "My Father in the Navy: A Childhood Memory" (p. 676), "Dover Beach" (p. 926)

◆ ◆ ◆

W. H. AUDEN
(1907–1973)

Musée des Beaux Arts
(1940)

About suffering they were never wrong,
The Old Masters: how well they understood
Its human position; how it takes place
While someone else is eating or opening a window or just walking
    dully along
5 How, when the aged are reverently, passionately waiting
For the miraculous birth, there always must be
Children who did not specially want it to happen, skating
On a pond at the edge of the wood:
They never forgot
10 That even the dreadful martyrdom must run its course
Anyhow in a corner, some untidy spot
Where the dogs go on with their doggy life and the torturer's horse
Scratches its innocent behind on a tree.
In Brueghel's *Icarus,* for instance: how everything turns away
15 Quite leisurely from the disaster; the ploughman may
Have heard the splash, the forsaken cry,
But for him it was not an important failure; the sun shone
As it had to on the white legs disappearing into the green
Water; and the expensive delicate ship that must have seen
20 Something amazing, a boy falling out of the sky,
Had somewhere to get to and sailed calmly on.

READING AND REACTING

1. Reread the summary of the myth of Icarus on page 910. Is Auden's allusion to the myth essential to the poem?
2. What point does the poet make by referring to the "Old Masters" (2)?
3. **JOURNAL ENTRY** Look at Brueghel's painting *Landscape with the Fall of Icarus* in the color insert. How does looking at it help you to understand the poem? To what specific details in the painting does the poet refer?

Related Works: "The Lottery" (p. 315), "One Day I Wrote Her Name upon the Strand" (p. 783), "Shall I Compare Thee to a Summer's Day?" (p. 807), "Ethics" (p. 979), "Not Waving but Drowning" (p. 992)

✴ CHECKLIST: WRITING ABOUT SYMBOL, ALLEGORY, ALLUSION, MYTH

SYMBOL

- ✓ Are there any symbols in the poem? What leads you to believe they are symbols?
- ✓ Are these symbols conventional?
- ✓ Are they universal or archetypal?
- ✓ Are any symbols obscure or highly idiosyncratic?
- ✓ What is the literal meaning of each symbol in the context of the poem?
- ✓ Beyond its literal meaning, what else could each symbol suggest?
- ✓ How does your interpretation of each symbol enhance your understanding of the poem?

ALLEGORY

- ✓ Is the poem an allegory?
- ✓ Are there any allegorical figures within the poem? How can you tell?
- ✓ What do the allegorical figures signify on a literal level?
- ✓ What lesson does the allegory illustrate?

ALLUSION

- ✓ Are there any allusions in the poem?
- ✓ Do you recognize the names, places, historical events, or literary works to which the poet alludes?
- ✓ What does each allusion add to the poem? In what way does each deepen the poem's meaning? Does any allusion interfere with your understanding or enjoyment of the poem? If so, how?
- ✓ Would the poem be more effective without a particular allusion?

MYTH

- ✓ What myths or mythological figures are alluded to?
- ✓ How does the poem use myth to convey its meaning?
- ✓ How faithful is the poem to the myth? Does the poet add material to the myth? Are any details from the original myth omitted? Is any information distorted? Why?

◈ Writing Suggestions: Symbol, Allegory, Allusion, Myth

1. Read "Aunt Jennifer's Tigers" (p. 843) and "Diving into the Wreck" (p. 905) by Adrienne Rich. Then, write an essay in which you discuss similarities and differences in Rich's use of symbols in the two poems.
2. Many popular songs make use of allusion. Choose one or two popular songs that you know well, and analyze their use of allusion, paying particular attention to whether the allusions expand the impact and meaning of the song or create barriers to your understanding.
3. Read the Emily Dickinson poem "Because I Could Not Stop for Death" (p. 940), and then write an interpretation of the poem, identifying the allegorical figures in the poem.
4. What applications do the lessons of myth have for twentieth-century life? Choose two or three poems from the section on myth, and consider how you can use myth to make generalizations about your own life.
5. Both Judith Ortiz Cofer's "My Father in the Navy: A Childhood Memory" (p. 676) and Derek Walcott's "Sea Grapes" (p. 917) allude to Homer's *Odyssey*. Read a summary of the *Odyssey* in an encyclopedia or other reference book, and then write an essay in which you discuss the poets' treatments of Homer's tale. What specific use does each poet make of the story?
6. **Web Activity** The following Web site contains information about Christina Rossetti:

   http://landow.stg.brown.edu/victorian/crossetti/crov.html

   From the Rossetti Web page, link to "Themes" and read "Death As Release From Pain in Christina Rossetti's Works" by Hoxie Neal Fairchild. Then, write an essay applying Fairchild's thesis to Rossetti's poem "Uphill" (p. 904). Consider how Rossetti treats the theme of death in her poem and her use of sometimes ambiguous images of death. Does the poem imply that death offers rest after the "uphill" struggle of life?

POETRY

FOR FURTHER READING

◇ ◇ ◇

SHERMAN ALEXIE
(1966–   )

Defending Walt Whitman
(1996)

Basketball is like this for young Indian boys, all arms and legs
and serious stomach muscles. Every body is brown!
These are the twentieth-century warriors who will never kill,
although a few sat quietly in the deserts of Kuwait,
5 waiting for orders to do something, do something.

God, there is nothing as beautiful as a jump shot
on a reservation summer basketball court
where the ball is moist with sweat
and makes a sound when it swishes through the net
10 that causes Walt Whitman to weep because it is so perfect.

There are veterans of foreign wars here,
whose bodies are still dominated
by collarbones and knees, whose bodies still respond
in the ways that bodies are supposed to respond when we are young.
15 Every body is brown! Look there, that boy can run
up and down this court forever. He can leap for a rebound
with his back arched like a salmon, all meat and bone
synchronized, magnetic, as if the court were a river,
as if the rim were a dam, as if the air were a ladder
20 leading the Indian boy toward home.

Some of the Indian boys still wear their military haircuts
while a few have let their hair grow back.
It will never be the same as it was before!
One Indian boy has never cut his hair, not once, and he braids it

25 into wild patterns that do not measure anything.
He is just a boy with too much time on his hands.
Look at him. He wants to play this game in bare feet.

God, the sun is so bright! There is no place like this.
Walt Whitman stretches his calf muscles
30 on the sidelines. He has the next game.
His huge beard is ridiculous on the reservation.
Some body throws a crazy pass and Walt Whitman catches it with
        quick hands.
He brings the ball close to his nose
and breathes in all of its smells: leather, brown skin, sweat, black hair,
35 burning oil, twisted ankle, long drink of warm water,
gunpowder, pine tree. Walt Whitman squeezes the ball tightly.
He wants to run. He hardly has the patience to wait for his turn.
"What's the score?" he asks. He asks, "What's the score?"

Basketball is like this for Walt Whitman. He watches these Indian boys
40 as if they were the last bodies on earth. Every body is brown!
Walt Whitman shakes because he believes in God.
Walt Whitman dreams of the Indian boy who will defend him,
trapping him in the corner, all flailing arms and legs
and legendary stomach muscles. Walt Whitman shakes
45 because he believes in God. Walt Whitman dreams
of the first jump shot he will take, the ball arcing clumsily
from his fingers, striking the rim so hard that it sparks.
Walt Whitman shakes because he believes in God.
Walt Whitman closes his eyes. He is a small man and his beard
50 is ludicrous on the reservation, absolutely insane.
His beard makes the Indian boys laugh righteously. His beard
        frightens
the smallest Indian boys. His beard tickles the skin
of the Indian boys who dribble past him. His beard, his beard!

God, there is beauty in every body. Walt Whitman stands
55 at center court while the Indian boys run from basket to basket.
Walt Whitman cannot tell the difference between
offense and defense. He does not care if he touches the ball.
Half of the Indian boys wear T-shirts damp with sweat
and the other half are barebacked, skin slick and shiny.
60 There is no place like this. Walt Whitman smiles.
Walt Whitman shakes. This game belongs to him.

◇ ◇ ◇

MAYA ANGELOU
(1928–   )

Africa
(1975)

Thus she had lain
sugar cane sweet

deserts her hair
golden her feet
5 mountains her breasts
two Niles[1] her tears
Thus she has lain
Black through the years.

Over the white seas
10 rime white and cold
brigands ungentled
icicle bold
took her young daughters
sold her strong sons
15 churched her with Jesus
bled her with guns.
Thus she has lain.

Now she is rising
remember her pain
20 remember the losses
her screams loud and vain
remember her riches
her history slain
now she is striding
25 although she had lain.

◇ ◇ ◇

ANONYMOUS

Bonny Barbara Allan

(traditional Scottish ballad)

It was in and about the Martinmas[1] time,
    When the green leaves were afalling,
That Sir John Graeme, in the West Country,
    Fell in love with Barbara Allan.

---

[1] The Nile, an ancient African river.

---

[1] Saint Martin's Day, November 11.

5 He sent his men down through the town,
　　　To the place where she was dwelling;
　　"O haste and come to my master dear,
　　　Gin² ye be Barbara Allan."

　　O hooly,³ hooly rose she up,
10　　　To the place where he was lying,
　　And when she drew the curtain by:
　　　"Young man, I think you're dying."

　　"O it's I'm sick, and very, very sick,
　　　And 'tis a' for Barbara Allan."—
15 "O the better for me ye's never be,
　　　Tho your heart's blood were aspilling.

　　"O dinna ye mind,⁴ young man," said she,
　　　"When ye was in the tavern adrinking,
　　That ye made the health gae round and round,
20　　　And slighted Barbara Allan?"

　　He turned his face unto the wall,
　　　And death was with him dealing:
　　"Adieu, adieu, my dear friends all,
　　　And be kind to Barbara Allan."

25 And slowly, slowly raise she up,
　　　And slowly, slowly left him,
　　And sighing said she could not stay,
　　　Since death of life had reft him.

　　She had not gane a mile but twa,⁵
30　　　When she heard the dead-bell ringing,
　　And every jow⁶ that the dead-bell geid,
　　　It cried, "Woe to Barbara Allan!"

　　"O mother, mother, make my bed!
　　　O make it saft and narrow!
35 Since my love died for me today,
　　　I'll die for him tomorrow."

---

² If.
³ Slowly.
⁴ Don't you remember.
⁵ Two.
⁶ Stroke.

Western Wind

(English lyric)

Western wind, when wilt thou blow,
The[1] small rain down can rain?
Christ, if my love were in my arms,
And I in my bed again!

◊ ◊ ◊

MATTHEW ARNOLD
(1822–1888)

Dover Beach
(1867)

The sea is calm tonight.
The tide is full, the moon lies fair
Upon the straits;—on the French coast the light
Gleams and is gone; the cliffs of England stand,
5 Glimmering and vast, out in the tranquil bay.
Come to the window, sweet is the night-air!
Only, from the long line of spray
Where the sea meets the moon-blanched[1] land,
Listen! you hear the grating roar
10 Of pebbles which the waves draw back, and fling,
At their return, up the high strand,[2]
Begin, and cease, and then again begin,
With tremulous cadence slow, and bring
The eternal note of sadness in.

15 Sophocles[3] long ago
Heard it on the Aegean,[4] and it brought
Into his mind the turbid ebb and flow
Of human misery; we
Find also in the sound a thought,
20 Hearing it by this distant northern sea.

---

[1] [So that] the.

[1] Whitened by the moon.
[2] Beach.
[3] Greek playwright (496–406 B.C.), author of tragedies including *Oedipus Rex* and *Antigone*.
[4] Sea between Greece and Turkey.

The Sea of Faith
Was once, too, at the full, and round earth's shore
Lay like the folds of a bright girdle furled.
But now I only hear
25 Its melancholy, long, withdrawing roar,
Retreating, to the breath
Of the night-wind, down the vast edges drear
And naked shingles[5] of the world.

Ah, love, let us be true
30 To one another! for the world, which seems
To lie before us like a land of dreams,
So various, so beautiful, so new,
Hath really neither joy, nor love, nor light,
Nor certitude, nor peace, nor help for pain;
35 And we are here as on a darkling[6] plain
Swept with confused alarms of struggle and flight,
Where ignorant armies clash by night.

◇ ◇ ◇

MARGARET ATWOOD
(1939–   )

This Is a Photograph of Me
(1966)

It was taken some time ago.
At first it seems to be
a smeared
print: blurred lines and grey flecks
5 blended with the paper;

then, as you scan
it, you see in the left-hand corner
a thing that is like a branch: part of a tree
(balsam or spruce) emerging
10 and, to the right, halfway up
what ought to be a gentle
slope, a small frame house.

In the background there is a lake,
and beyond that, some low hills.

---

[5] Gravel beaches.
[6] Darkening.

15 (The photograph was taken
the day after I drowned.

I am in the lake, in the center
of the picture, just under the surface.

It is difficult to say where
20 precisely, or to say
how large or small I am:
the effect of water
on light is a distortion

but if you look long enough,
25 eventually
you will be able to see me.)

◇ ◇ ◇

WILLIAM BLAKE
(1757–1827)

The Chimney Sweeper
(1789)

When my mother died I was very young,
And my father sold me while yet my tongue
Could scarcely cry "'weep! 'weep! 'weep! 'weep!"
So your chimneys I sweep, and in soot I sleep.

5 There's little Tom Dacre, who cried when his head,
That curled like a lamb's back, was shaved: so I said
"Hush, Tom! never mind it, for when your head's bare
You know that the soot cannot spoil your white hair."

And so he was quiet, and that very night,
10 As Tom was a-sleeping, he had such a sight!
That thousands of sweepers, Dick, Joe, Ned, and Jack,
Were all of them locked up in coffins of black.

And by came an Angel who had a bright key,
And he opened the coffins and set them all free;
15 Then down a green plain leaping, laughing, they run,
And wash in a river, and shine in the sun.

Then naked and white, all their bags left behind,
They rise upon clouds and sport in the wind;

And the Angel told Tom, if he'd be a good boy,
20 He'd have God for his father, and never want joy.

And so Tom awoke; and we rose in the dark,
And got with our bags and our brushes to work.
Though the morning was cold, Tom was happy and warm;
So if all do their duty they need not fear harm.

The Lamb
(1789)

Little Lamb, who made thee?
Dost thou know who made thee?
Gave thee life & bid thee feed,
By the stream & o'er the mead;
5 Gave thee clothing of delight,
Softest clothing wooly bright;
Gave thee such a tender voice,
Making all the vales rejoice!
Little Lamb who made thee?
10 Dost thou know who made thee?

Little Lamb I'll tell thee,
Little Lamb I'll tell thee!
He is calléd by thy name,
For he calls himself a Lamb:
15 He is meek & he is mild,
He became a little child:
I a child & thou a lamb,
We are calléd by his name.
Little Lamb God bless thee.
20 Little Lamb God bless thee.

London
(1794)

I wander through each chartered street,
Near where the chartered Thames does flow,
And mark in every face I meet
Marks of weakness, marks of woe.

5 In every cry of every man,
In every infant's cry of fear,
In every voice, in every ban,
The mind-forged manacles I hear.

How the chimney-sweeper's cry
10 Every black'ning church appalls;
And the hapless soldier's sigh
Runs in blood down palace walls.

But most through midnight streets I hear
How the youthful harlot's curse
15 Blasts the new born infant's tear,
And blights with plagues the marriage hearse.

The Tyger
(1794)

Tyger! Tyger! burning bright
In the forests of the night,
What immortal hand or eye
Could frame thy fearful symmetry?

5 In what distant deeps or skies
Burnt the fire of thine eyes?
On what wings dare he aspire?
What the hand dare seize the fire?

And what shoulder, and what art,
10 Could twist the sinews of thy heart?
And when thy heart began to beat,
What dread hand? and what dread feet?

What the hammer? what the chain?
In what furnace was thy brain?
15 What the anvil? what dread grasp
Dare its deadly terrors clasp?

When the stars threw down their spears,
And watered heaven with their tears,
Did he smile his work to see?
20 Did he who made the Lamb make thee?

Tyger! Tyger! burning bright
In the forests of the night,
What immortal hand or eye
Dare frame thy fearful symmetry?

◊ ◊ ◊

ANNE BRADSTREET
(1612?–1672)

The Author to Her Book[1]
(1678)

Thou ill-formed offspring of my feeble brain,
Who after birth did'st by my side remain,
Till snatched from thence by friends, less wise than true,
Who thee abroad exposed to public view;
5 Made thee in rags, halting, to the press to trudge,
Where errors were not lessened, all may judge.
At thy return my blushing was not small,
My rambling brat (in print) should mother call;
I cast thee by as one unfit for light,
10 Thy visage was so irksome in my sight;
Yet being mine own, at length affection would
Thy blemishes amend, if so I could:
I washed thy face, but more defects I saw,
And rubbing off a spot, still made a flaw.
15 I stretched thy joints to make thee even feet,[2]
Yet still thou run'st more hobbling than is meet;[3]
In better dress to trim thee was my mind,
But nought save homespun cloth in the house I find.
In this array, 'mongst vulgars[4] may'st thou roam;
20 In critics' hands beware thou dost not come;
And take thy way where yet thou are not known.
If for thy Father asked, say thou had'st none;
And for thy Mother, she alas is poor,
Which caused her thus to send thee out of door.

---

[1] Bradstreet addresses *The Tenth Muse,* a collection of her poetry, which was published without her consent in 1650.
[2] Metrical feet.
[3] Appropriate or decorous.
[4] Common people.

◇ ◇ ◇
GWENDOLYN BROOKS
(1917–   )

The Ballad of Rudolph Reed
(1960)

Rudolph Reed was oaken.
His wife was oaken too.
And his two girls and his good little man
Oakened as they grew.

5 "I am not hungry for berries.
I am not hungry for bread.
But hungry hungry for a house
Where at night a man in bed

"May never hear the plaster
10 Stir as if in pain.
May never hear the roaches
Falling like fat rain.

"Where never wife and children need
Go blinking through the gloom.
15 Where every room of many rooms
Will be full of room.

"Oh my home may have its east or west
Or north or south behind it.
All I know is I shall know it,
20 And fight for it when I find it."

It was in a street of bitter white
That he made his application.
For Rudolph Reed was oakener
Than others in the nation.

25 The agent's steep and steady stare
Corroded to a grin.
Why, you black old, tough old hell of a man,
Move your family in!

Nary a grin grinned Rudolph Reed,
30 Nary a curse cursed he,
But moved in his House. With his dark little wife,
And his dark little children three.

A neighbor would *look*, with a yawning eye
That squeezed into a slit.
35 But the Rudolph Reeds and the children three
Were too joyous to notice it.

For were they not firm in a home of their own
With windows everywhere
And a beautiful banistered stair
40 And a front yard for flowers and a back yard for grass?

The first night, a rock, big as two fists.
The second, a rock big as three.
But nary a curse cursed Rudolph Reed.
(Though oaken as man could be.)

45 The third night, a silvery ring of glass.
Patience ached to endure.
But he looked, and lo! small Mabel's blood
Was staining her gaze so pure.

Then up did rise our Rudolph Reed
50 And pressed the hand of his wife,
And went to the door with a thirty-four
And a beastly butcher knife.

He ran like a mad thing into the night.
And the words in his mouth were stinking.
55 By the time he had hurt his first white man
He was no longer thinking.

By the time he had hurt his fourth white man
Rudolph Reed was dead.
His neighbors gathered and kicked his corpse.
60 "Nigger—" his neighbors said.

Small Mabel whimpered all night long,
For calling herself the cause.
Her oak-eyed mother did no thing
But change the bloody gauze.

The *Chicago Defender*[1] Sends a Man to Little Rock
(1960)

Fall, 1957[2]

In Little Rock the people bear
Babes, and comb and part their hair
And watch the want ads, put repair

---

[1] A weekly newspaper for African-American readers.
[2] When black students first entered the high school in Little Rock, Arkansas, in 1957, the city erupted in race riots protesting desegregation.

To roof and latch. While wheat toast burns
5 A woman waters multiferns.

Time upholds or overturns
The many, tight, and small concerns.

In Little Rock the people sing
Sunday hymns like anything,
10 Through Sunday pomp and polishing.

And after testament and tunes,
Some soften Sunday afternoons
With lemon tea and Lorna Doones.

I forecast
15 And I believe
Come Christmas Little Rock will cleave
To Christmas tree and trifle, weave,
From laugh and tinsel, texture fast.

In Little Rock is baseball; Barcarolle.[3]
20 That hotness in July . . . the uniformed figures raw and implacable
And not intellectual,
Batting the hotness or clawing the suffering dust.
The Open Air Concert, on the special twilight green. . . .
When Beethoven is brutal or whispers to lady-like air.
25 Blanket-sitters are solemn, as Johann troubles to lean
To tell them what to mean. . . .

There is love, too, in Little Rock. Soft women softly
Opening themselves in kindness,
Or, pitying one's blindness,
30 Awaiting one's pleasure
In azure
Glory with anguished rose at the root. . . .
To wash away old semi-discomfitures.
They re-teach purple and unsullen blue.
35 The wispy soils go. And uncertain
Half-havings have they clarified to sures.

In Little Rock they know
Not answering the telephone is a way of rejecting life,
That it is our business to be bothered, is our business
40 To cherish bores or boredom, be polite
To lies and love and many-faceted fuzziness.
I scratch my head, massage the hate-I-had.
I blink across my prim and pencilled pad.
The saga I was sent for is not down.

---

[3] A Venetian gondolier's song, or one suggesting the rhythm of rowing.

45 Because there is a puzzle in this town.
The biggest News I do not dare
Telegraph to the Editor's chair:
"They are like people everywhere."

The angry Editor would reply
50 In hundred harryings of Why.

And true, they are hurling spittle, rock,
Garbage and fruit in Little Rock.
And I saw coiling storm a-writhe
On bright madonnas. And a scythe
55 Of men harassing brownish girls.
(The bows and barrettes in the curls
And braids declined away from joy.)

I saw a bleeding brownish boy. . . .

The lariat lynch-wish I deplored.

60 The loveliest lynchee was our Lord.

Medgar Evers[1]
(1964)

For Charles Evers[2]

The man whose height his fear improved he
arranged to fear no further. The raw
intoxicated time was time for better birth or a final death.

Old styles, old tempos, all the engagement of
5 the day—the sedate, the regulated fray—
the antique light, the Moral rose, old gusts,
tight whistlings from the past, the mothballs
in the Love at last our man forswore.

Medgar Evers annoyed confetti and assorted
10 brands of businessmen's eyes.

The shows came down: to maxims and surprise.
And palsy.

Roaring no rapt arise-ye to the dead, he
leaned across tomorrow. People said that
15 he was holding clean globes in his hands.

---

[1] African-American civil rights leader who was killed by a sniper in 1963.
[2] Medgar Evers's brother.

◊ ◊ ◊

JOSEPH BRUCHAC
(1942–   )

Ellis Island
(1979)

Beyond the red brick of Ellis Island
where the two Slovak children
who became my grandparents
waited the long days of quarantine,
5 after leaving the sickness,
the old Empires of Europe,
a Circle Line ship[1] slips easily
on its way to the island
of the tall woman,[2] green
10 as dreams of forests and meadows
waiting for those who'd worked
a thousand years
yet never owned their own.

Like millions of others,
15 I too come to this island,
nine decades the answerer
of dreams.

Yet only one part of my blood[3] loves that memory.
Another voice speaks
20 of native lands
within this nation.
Lands invaded
when the earth became owned.
Lands of those who followed
25 the changing Moon,
knowledge of the seasons
in their veins.

---

[1] A tour boat that circles Manhattan Island.
[2] The Statue of Liberty.
[3] Bruchac is part Slovakian and part Native American.

◊ ◊ ◊

GEORGE GORDON, LORD BYRON
(1788–1824)

She Walks in Beauty
(1815)

1

She walks in beauty, like the night
    Of cloudless climes and starry skies;
And all that's best of dark and bright
    Meet in her aspect and her eyes:
5 Thus mellowed to that tender light
    Which heaven to gaudy day denies.

2

One shade the more, one ray the less,
    Had half impaired the nameless grace
Which waves in every raven tress,
10   Or softly lightens o'er her face;
Where thoughts serenely sweet express
    How pure, how dear their dwelling place.

3

And on that cheek, and o'er that brow,
    So soft, so calm, yet eloquent,
15 The smiles that win, the tints that glow,
    But tell of days in goodness spent,
A mind at peace with all below,
    A heart whose love is innocent!

◊ ◊ ◊

SAMUEL TAYLOR COLERIDGE
(1772–1834)

Kubla Khan[1]
(1797, 1798)

Or, a Vision in a Dream. A Fragment.

In Xanadu did Kubla Khan
A stately pleasure-dome decree:
Where Alph,[2] the sacred river, ran

---

[1] Coleridge mythologizes the actual Kublai Khan, a thirteenth-century Mongol emperor, as well as the Chinese city of Xanadu.

[2] Probably derived from the Greek river Alpheus, whose waters, according to legend, rose from the Ionian Sea in Sicily as the fountain of Arethusa.

Through caverns measureless to man
5 Down to a sunless sea.
So twice five miles of fertile ground
With walls and towers were girdled round;
And there were gardens bright with sinuous rills,
Where blossomed many an incense-bearing tree;
10 And here were forests ancient as the hills,
Enfolding sunny spots of greenery.

But oh! that deep romantic chasm which slanted
Down the green hill athwart a cedarn cover!
A savage place! as holy and enchanted
15 As e'er beneath a waning moon was haunted
By woman wailing for her demon-lover!
And from this chasm, with ceaseless turmoil seething,
As if this earth in fast thick pants were breathing,
A mighty fountain momently was forced:
20 Amid whose swift half-intermitted burst
Huge fragments vaulted like rebounding hail,
Or chaffy grain beneath the thresher's flail:
And 'mid these dancing rocks at once and ever
It flung up momently the sacred river.
25 Five miles meandering with a mazy motion
Through wood and dale the sacred river ran,
Then reached the caverns measureless to man,
And sank in tumult to a lifeless ocean:
And 'mid this tumult Kubla heard from far
30 Ancestral voices prophesying war!

The shadow of the dome of pleasure
Floated midway on the waves;
Where was heard the mingled measure
From the fountain and the caves.
35 It was a miracle of rare device,
A sunny pleasure-dome with caves of ice!

A damsel with a dulcimer
In a vision once I saw:
It was an Abyssinian maid,
40 And on her dulcimer she played,
Singing of Mount Abora.[3]
Could I revive within me
Her symphony and song,
To such a deep delight 'twould win me,

---

[3] Some scholars see a reminiscence here of John Milton's *Paradise Lost 4.* 280–82: "where Abassin kings their issue guard / Mount Amara, though this by some supposed / True Paradise under the Ethiop Line."

45 That with music loud and long,
 I would build that dome in air,
 That sunny dome! those caves of ice!
 And all who heard should see them there,
 And all should cry, Beware! Beware!
50 His flashing eyes, his floating hair!
 Weave a circle round him thrice,[4]
 And close your eyes with holy dread,
 For he on honey-dew hath fed,
 And drunk the milk of Paradise.

◊   ◊   ◊

E. E. CUMMINGS
(1894–1962)

Buffalo Bill's
(1923)

Buffalo Bill's
defunct
   who used to
   ride a watersmooth-silver
5   stallion
and break onetwothreefourfive pigeonsjustlikethat
             Jesus

he was a handsome man
       and what i want to know is
10 how do you like your blueeyed boy
Mister Death

next to of course god america i
(1926)

"next to of course god america i
love you land of the pilgrims' and so forth oh
say can you see by the dawn's early my
country 'tis of centuries come and go
5 and are no more what of it we should worry
in every language even deafanddumb
thy sons acclaim your glorious name by gorry
by jingo by gee by gosh by gum
why talk of beauty what could be more beaut-
10 iful than these heroic happy dead

---

[4] A magic ritual, to keep away intruding spirits.

who rushed like lions to the roaring slaughter
they did not stop to think they died instead
then shall the voice of liberty be mute?"

He spoke. And drank rapidly a glass of water

◊ ◊ ◊

EMILY DICKINSON
(1830–1886)

After Great Pain, a Formal Feeling Comes
(c. 1862)

After great pain, a formal feeling comes—
The Nerves sit ceremonious, like Tombs—
The stiff Heart questions was it He, that bore,
And Yesterday, or Centuries before?

5 The Feet, mechanical, go round—
Of Ground, or Air, or Ought—
A Wooden way
Regardless grown,
A Quartz contentment, like a stone—

10 This is the Hour of Lead—
Remembered, if outlived,
As Freezing persons, recollect the Snow—
First—Chill—then Stupor—then the letting go—

Because I Could Not Stop for Death
(1863)

Because I could not stop for Death—
He kindly stopped for me—
The Carriage held but just Ourselves—
And Immortality.

5 We slowly drove—He knew no haste
And I had put away
My labor and my leisure too,
For His Civility—

We passed the School, where Children strove
10 At Recess—in the Ring—
We passed the Fields of Gazing Grain—

We passed the Setting Sun—
Or rather—He passed Us—
The Dews drew quivering and chill—
15 For only Gossamer, my Gown—
My Tippet[1]—only Tulle—

We paused before a House that seemed
A Swelling of the Ground—
The Roof was scarcely visible—
20 The Cornice—in the Ground—

Since then—'tis Centuries—and yet
Feels shorter than the Day
I first surmised the Horses' Heads
Were toward Eternity—

The Brain—Is Wider Than the Sky
(c. 1862)

The Brain—is wider than the Sky—
For—put them side by side—
The one the other will contain
With ease—and You—beside—

5 The Brain is deeper than the sea—
For—hold them—Blue to Blue—
The one the other will absorb—
As Sponges—Buckets—do—

The Brain is just the weight of God—
10 For—Heft them—Pound for Pound—
And they will differ—if they do—
As Syllable from Sound—

I Heard a Fly Buzz—When I Died
(c. 1862)

I heard a Fly buzz—when I died—
The Stillness in the Room
Was like the Stillness in the Air—
Between the Heaves of Storm—

---

[1] Cape.

5 The Eyes around—had wrung them dry—
And Breaths were gathering firm
For that last Onset—when the King
Be witnessed—in the Room—

I willed my Keepsakes—Signed away
10 What portion of me be
Assignable—and then it was
There interposed a Fly—

With Blue—uncertain stumbling Buzz—
Between the light—and me—
15 And then the Windows failed—and then
I could not see to see—

I Never Saw a Moor
(c. 1865)

I never saw a Moor—
I never saw the Sea—
Yet know I how the Heather looks
And what a Billow be.

5 I never spoke with God
Nor visited in Heaven—
Yet certain am I of the spot
As if the Checks were given—

I Taste a Liquor Never Brewed
(1861)

I taste a liquor never brewed—
From Tankards scooped in Pearl—
Not all the Frankfort Berries[1]
Yield such an Alcohol!

5 Inebriate of Air—am I—
And Debauchee of Dew—
Reeling—thro endless summer days—
From inns of Molten Blue—

---

[1] This line is a variant reading for the usually accepted "Not all the Vats upon the Rhine." In both cases, the poet refers to German wine.

When "Landlords" turn the drunken Bee
10 Out of the Foxglove's door—
When Butterflies—renounce their "drams"—
I shall but drink the more!

Till Seraphs swing their snowy Hats—
And Saints—to windows run—
15 To see the little Tippler
From Manzanilla[2] come!

Much Madness Is Divinest Sense
(c. 1862)

Much Madness is divinest Sense—
To a discerning Eye—
Much Sense—the starkest Madness—
'Tis the Majority
5 In this, as All, prevail—
Assent—and you are sane—
Demur—you're straightway dangerous—
And handled with a Chain—

The Soul Selects Her Own Society
(1862)

The Soul selects her own Society—
Then—shuts the Door—
To her divine Majority—
Present no more—

5 Unmoved—she notes the Chariots—pausing—
At her low Gate—
Unmoved—an Emperor be kneeling
Upon her Mat—

---

[2] A pale Spanish sherry.

I've known her—from an ample nation—
10 Choose One—
Then—close the Valves of her attention—
Like Stone—

There's a Certain Slant of Light
(c. 1861)

There's a certain Slant of light,
Winter Afternoons—
That oppresses, like the Heft
Of Cathedral Tunes—

5 Heavenly Hurt, it gives us—
We can find no scar,
But internal difference,
Where the Meanings, are—

None may teach it—Any—
10 'Tis the Seal Despair—
An imperial affliction
Sent us of the Air—

When it comes, the Landscape listens—
Shadows—hold their breath—
15 When it goes, 'tis like the Distance
On the look of Death—

Wild Nights–Wild Nights!
(1890, c. 1861)

Wild Nights—Wild Nights!
Were I with thee
Wild Nights should be
Our luxury!

5 Futile—the Winds—
To a Heart in port—
Done with the Compass—
Done with the Chart!

Rowing in Eden—
10 Ah, the Sea!
Might I but moor—Tonight—
In Thee!

◈ ◈ ◈

CHITRA BANERJEE DIVAKARUNI
(1956–   )

The Brides Come to Yuba City[1]
(1977)

The sky is hot and yellow, filled
with blue screaming birds. The train
heaved us from its belly
and vanished in shrill smoke.
5 Now only the tracks
gleam dull in the heavy air,
a ladder to eternity, each receding rung
cleaved from our husbands' ribs.
Mica-flecked, the platform dazzles, burns up
10 through thin *chappal* soles, lurches like
the ship's dark hold,
blurred month of nights, smell of vomit,
a porthole like the bleached iris
of a giant unseeing eye.

15 Red-veiled, we lean into each other,
press damp palms, try
broken smiles. The man who met us at the ship
whistles a restless *Angrezi* tune
and scans the fields. Behind us,
20 the black wedding trunks, sharp-edged,
shiny, stenciled with strange men-names
our bodies do not fit into:
Mrs. Baldev Johl, Mrs. Kanwal Bains.
Inside, bright *salwar-kameezes* scented
25 with sandalwood. For the men,
kurtas and thin white gauze
to wrap their long hair.
Laddus from Jullundhur, sugar-crusted,
six kinds of lentils, a small bag
30 of bajra flour. Labeled in our mothers' hesitant hands,
packets of seeds—*methi, karela, saag*—
to burst from this new soil
like green stars.

He gives a shout, waves at the men, their slow,
35 uneven approach. We crease our eyes

---

[1] Because of immigration restrictions, the wives of many Sikhs who emigrated from India to Yuba City, California, in the 1900s had to remain in India until the 1940s.

through the veils' red film, cannot breathe. Thirty years
since we saw them. Or never,
like Harvinder, married last year at Hoshiarpur
to her husband's photo,
40 which she clutches tight to her
to stop the shaking. He is fifty-two,
she sixteen. Tonight—like us all—
she will open her legs to him.

The platform is endless-wide.
45 The men walk and walk
without advancing. Their lined,
wavering mouths, their eyes like drowning lights.
We cannot recognize a single face.

◇ ◇ ◇

JOHN DONNE
(1572–1631)

Batter My Heart, Three-Personed God
(c. 1610)

Batter my heart, three-personed God, for You
As yet but knock, breathe, shine, and seek to mend.
That I may rise and stand, o'erthrow me, and bend
Your force to break, blow, burn, and make me new.
5 I, like an usurped town to another due,
Labor to admit You, but Oh! to no end.
Reason, Your viceroy in me, me should defend,
But is captived, and proves weak or untrue.
Yet dearly I love You, and would be lovèd fain,
10 But am betrothed unto Your enemy;
Divorce me, untie or break that knot again;
Take me to You, imprison me, for I,
Except You enthrall me, never shall be free,
Nor ever chaste, except You ravish me.

Death Be Not Proud
(c. 1610)

Death be not proud, though some have callèd thee
Mighty and dreadful, for thou art not so;
For those whom thou think'st thou dost overthrow
Die not, poor death, nor yet canst thou kill me.

5 From rest and sleep, which but thy pictures be,
Much pleasure, then from thee much more must flow,
And soonest our best men with thee do go,
Rest of their bones, and soul's delivery.
Thou art slave to fate, chance, kings, and desperate men,
10 And dost with poison, war, and sickness dwell,
And poppy, or charms can make us sleep as well,
And better than thy stroke; why swell'st thou then?
One short sleep past, we wake eternally,
And death shall be no more; death, thou shalt die.

Song
(1633)

Go and catch a falling star,
    Get with child a mandrake root,[1]
Tell me where all past years are,
    Or who cleft the Devil's foot,
5 Teach me to hear mermaids singing,
    Or to keep off envy's stinging,
        And find
        What wind
Serves to advance an honest mind.

10 If thou be'st borne to strange sights,
    Things invisible to see,
Ride ten thousand days and nights,
    Till age snow white hairs on thee,
Thou, when thou return'st, wilt tell me
15   All strange wonders that befell thee,
        And swear
        Nowhere
Lives a woman true, and fair.

If thou findst one, let me know,
20   Such a pilgrimage were sweet—
Yet do not, I would not go,
    Though at next door we might meet;
Though she were true, when you met her,
    And last, till you write your letter,
25   Yet she
        Will be
False, ere I come, to two, or three.

---

[1] The mandrake root (or mandragora), which is forked and resembles the lower part of the human body, was thought to be an aphrodisiac.

◇ ◇ ◇ ◇

RITA DOVE

(1952–)

The Satisfaction Coal Company

(1986)

1

What to do with a day.
Leaf through *Jet*. Watch T.V.
Freezing on the porch
but he goes anyhow, snow too high
5 for a walk, the ice treacherous.
Inside, the gas heater takes care of itself;
he doesn't even notice being warm.

Everyone says he looks great.
Across the street a drunk stands smiling
10 at something carved in a tree.
The new neighbor with the floating hips
scoots out to get the mail
and waves once, brightly,
storm door clipping her heel on the way in.

2

15 Twice a week he had taken the bus down Glendale hill
to the corner of Market. Slipped through
the alley by the canal and let himself in.
Started to sweep
with terrible care, like a woman
20 brushing shine into her hair,
same motion, same lullaby.
No curtains—the cop on the beat
stopped outside once in the hour
to swing his billy club and glare.

25 It was better on Saturdays
when the children came along:
he mopped while they emptied
ashtrays, clang of glass on metal
then a dry scutter. Next they counted
30 nailheads studding the leather cushions.
Thirty-four! they shouted,
that was the year and
they found it mighty amusing.

But during the week he noticed more—
35 lights when they gushed or dimmed
at the Portage Hotel, the 10:32
picking up speed past the B & O switchyard,
floorboards trembling and the explosive
kachook kachook kachook kachook
40 and the oiled rails ticking underneath.

3

They were poor then but everyone had been poor.
He hadn't minded the sweeping,
just the thought of it—like now
when people ask him what he's thinking
45 and he says *I'm listening.*

Those nights walking home alone,
the bucket of coal scraps banging his knee,
he'd hear a roaring furnace
with its dry, familiar heat. Now the nights
50 take care of themselves—as for the days,
there is the canary's sweet curdled song,
the wino smiling through his dribble.
Past the hill, past the gorge
choked with wild sumac in summer,
55 the corner has been upgraded.
Still, he'd like to go down there someday
to stand for a while, and get warm.

◊ ◊ ◊

PAUL LAURENCE DUNBAR
(1872–1906)

We Wear the Mask
(1913)

We wear the mask that grins and lies,
It hides our cheeks and shades our eyes—
This debt we pay to human guile;
With torn and bleeding hearts we smile,
5 And mouth with myriad subtleties.

Why should the world be over-wise,
In counting all our tears and sighs?
Nay, let them only see us, while
We wear the mask.

10 We smile, but, O great Christ, our cries
To thee from tortured souls arise.
We sing, but oh the clay is vile
Beneath our feet, and long the mile;
But let the world dream otherwise,
15   We wear the mask!

◊ ◊ ◊

T. S. ELIOT
(1888–1965)

The Love Song of
J. Alfred Prufrock
(1917)

S'io credessi che mia risposta fosse
A persona che mai tornasse al mondo,
Questa fiamma staria senza piu scosse.
Ma perciocche giammai di questo fondo
Non torno vivo alcun, s'i'odo il vero,
Senza tema d'infamia ti rispondo.[1]

Let us go then, you and I,
When the evening is spread out against the sky
Like a patient etherized upon a table;
Let us go, through certain half-deserted streets,
5 The muttering retreats
Of restless nights in one-night cheap hotels
And sawdust restaurants with oyster-shells:
Streets that follow like a tedious argument
Of insidious intent
10 To lead you to an overwhelming question . . .
Oh, do not ask, "What is it?"
Let us go and make our visit.

In the room the women come and go
Talking of Michelangelo.

---

[1] The epigraph is from Dante's *Inferno*, Canto 27. In response to the poet's question about his identity, Guido da Montefelto, who for his sin of fraud must spend eternity wrapped in flames, replies: "If I thought that I was speaking to someone who could go back to the world, this flame would shake me no more. But since from this place nobody ever returns alive, if what I hear is true, I answer you without fear of infamy."

15 The yellow fog that rubs its back upon the window-panes,
The yellow smoke that rubs its muzzle on the window-panes
Licked its tongue into the corners of the evening,
Lingered upon the pools that stand in drains,
Let fall upon its back the soot that falls from chimneys,
20 Slipped by the terrace, made a sudden leap,
And seeing that it was a soft October night,
Curled once about the house, and fell asleep.

And indeed there will be time
For the yellow smoke that slides along the street,
25 Rubbing its back upon the window-panes;
There will be time, there will be time
To prepare a face to meet the faces that you meet;
There will be time to murder and create,
And time for all the works and days^2 of hands
30 That lift and drop a question on your plate;
Time for you and time for me,
And time yet for a hundred indecisions,
And for a hundred visions and revisions,
Before the taking of a toast and tea.

35 In the room the women come and go
Talking of Michelangelo.

And indeed there will be time
To wonder, "Do I dare?" and, "Do I dare?"
Time to turn back and descend the stair,
40 With a bald spot in the middle of my hair—
(They will say: "How his hair is growing thin!")
My morning coat, my collar mounting firmly to the chin,
My necktie rich and modest, but asserted by a simple pin—
(They will say: "But how his arms and legs are thin!")
45 Do I dare
Disturb the universe?
In a minute there is time
For decisions and revisions which a minute will reverse.

For I have known them all already, known them all—
50 Have known the evenings, mornings, afternoons,
I have measured out my life with coffee spoons;
I know the voices dying with a dying fall^3

---

2 "Works and Days" is the title of a work by the eighth-century B.C. Greek Hesiod, whose poem celebrates farmwork.
3 Allusion to Orsino's speech in *Twelfth Night* (1.1), "That strain again! It had a dying fall."

Beneath the music from a farther room.
So how should I presume?

55 And I have known the eyes already, known them all—
The eyes that fix you in a formulated phrase,
And when I am formulated, sprawling on a pin,
When I am pinned and wriggling on the wall,
Then how should I begin
60 To spit out all the butt-ends of my days and ways?
And how should I presume?

And I have known the arms already, known them all—
Arms that are braceleted and white and bare
(But in the lamplight, downed with light brown hair!)
65 Is it perfume from a dress
That makes me so digress?
Arms that lie along a table, or wrap about a shawl.
And should I then presume?
And how should I begin?

* * *

70 Shall I say, I have gone at dusk through narrow streets
And watched the smoke that rises from the pipes
Of lonely men in shirt-sleeves, leaning out of windows? . . .

I should have been a pair of ragged claws
Scuttling across the floors of silent seas.

* * *

75 And the afternoon, the evening, sleeps so peacefully!
Smoothed by long fingers,
Asleep . . . tired . . . or it malingers,
Stretched on the floor, here beside you and me.
Should I, after tea and cakes and ices,
80 Have the strength to force the moment to its crisis?
But though I have wept and fasted, wept and prayed,
Though I have seen my head (grown slightly bald) brought in
upon a platter,[4]
I am no prophet—and here's no great matter;
I have seen the moment of my greatness flicker,
85 And I have seen the eternal Footman[5] hold my coat, and snicker,
And in short, I was afraid.

---

[4] Like John the Baptist, who was beheaded by King Herod (see Matthew 14:3–11).
[5] Perhaps death, or fate.

And would it have been worth it, after all,
After the cups, the marmalade, the tea,
Among the porcelain, among some talk of you and me,
90 Would it have been worth while,
To have bitten off the matter with a smile,
To have squeezed the universe into a ball
To roll it toward some overwhelming question,
To say: "I am Lazarus,[6] come from the dead,
95 Come back to tell you all, I shall tell you all"—
If one, settling a pillow by her head,
    Should say: "That is not what I meant at all.
    That is not it, at all."

And would it have been worth it, after all,
100 Would it have been worth while,
After the sunsets and the dooryards and the sprinkled streets,
After the novels, after the teacups, after the skirts that trail along
    the floor—
And this, and so much more?—
It is impossible to say just what I mean!
105 But as if a magic lantern threw the nerves in patterns on a screen:
Would it have been worth while
If one, settling a pillow or throwing off a shawl,
And turning toward the window, should say:
    "That is not it at all,
110   That is not what I meant, at all."

        * * *

No! I am not Prince Hamlet, nor was meant to be;
Am an attendant lord, one that will do
To swell a progress,[7] start a scene or two,
Advise the prince; no doubt, an easy tool,
115 Deferential, glad to be of use,
Politic, cautious, and meticulous;
Full of high sentence,[8] but a bit obtuse;
At times, indeed, almost ridiculous—
Almost, at times, the Fool.

120 I grow old . . . I grow old . . .
I shall wear the bottoms of my trousers rolled.

---

[6] Lazarus was raised from the dead by Christ (see John 11:1–44).
[7] Here, in the Elizabethan sense of a royal journey.
[8] Opinions.

Shall I part my hair behind? Do I dare to eat a peach?
I shall wear white flannel trousers, and walk upon the beach.
I have heard the mermaids singing, each to each.

125 I do not think that they will sing to me.

I have seen them riding seaward on the waves
Combing the white hair of the waves blown back
When the wind blows the water white and black.

We have lingered in the chambers of the sea
130 By sea-girls wreathed with seaweed red and brown
Till human voices wake us, and we drown.

◆ ◆ ◆

JAMES A. EMANUEL
(1921–   )

Emmett Till[1]
(1968)

I hear a whistling
Through the water.
Little Emmett
Won't be still.
5 He keeps floating
Round the darkness,
Edging through
The silent chill.
Tell me, please,
10 That bedtime story
Of the fairy
River Boy
Who swims forever,
Deep in treasures,
15 Necklaced in
A coral toy.

---

[1] Emmett Till, a fourteen-year-old African-American from Chicago, was visiting relatives in Mississippi in 1955 when he made what he thought was an innocent remark to a white woman. Several days later his body was found in the river with a heavy cotton gin fan tied around his neck with barbed wire.

◊ ◊ ◊

LOUISE ERDRICH
(1954–   )

Indian Boarding School:
The Runaways
(1984)

Home's the place we head for in our sleep.
Boxcars stumbling north in dreams
don't wait for us. We catch them on the run.
The rails, old lacerations that we love,
5   shoot parallel across the face and break
just under Turtle Mountains.[1] Riding scars
you can't get lost. Home is the place they cross.

The lame guard strikes a match and makes the dark
less tolerant. We watch through cracks in boards
10 as the land starts rolling, rolling till it hurts
to be here, cold in regulation clothes.
We know the sheriff's waiting at midrun
to take us back. His car is dumb and warm.
The highway doesn't rock, it only hums
15 like a wing of long insults. The worn-down welts
of ancient punishments lead back and forth.

All runaways wear dresses, long green ones,
the color you would think shame was. We scrub
the sidewalks down because it's shameful work.
20 Our brushes cut the stone in watered arcs
and in the soak frail outlines shiver clear
a moment, things us kids pressed on the dark
face before it hardened, pale, remembering
delicate old injuries, the spines of names and leaves.

◊ ◊ ◊

ROBERT FROST
(1874–1963)

Acquainted with the Night
(1928)

I have been one acquainted with the night.
I have walked out in rain—and back in rain.
I have outwalked the furthest city light.

---

[1] Erdrich is a descendent of the Turtle Mountain Band of the Chippewa.

I have looked down the saddest city lane.
5 I have passed by the watchman on his beat
And dropped my eyes, unwilling to explain.

I have stood still and stopped the sound of feet
When far away an interrupted cry
Came over houses from another street,

10 But not to call me back or say good-by;
And further still at an unearthly height,
One luminary clock against the sky

Proclaimed the time was neither wrong nor right.
I have been one acquainted with the night.

Birches

(1915)

When I see birches bend to left and right
Across the lines of straighter darker trees,
I like to think some boy's been swinging them.
But swinging doesn't bend them down to stay
5 As ice-storms do. Often you must have seen them
Loaded with ice a sunny winter morning
After a rain. They click upon themselves
As the breeze rises, and turn many-colored
As the stir cracks and crazes their enamel.
10 Soon the sun's warmth makes them shed crystal shells
Shattering and avalanching on the snow-crust—
Such heaps of broken glass to sweep away
You'd think the inner dome of heaven had fallen.
They are dragged to the withered bracken by the load,
15 And they seem not to break; though once they are bowed
So low for long, they never right themselves:
You may see their trunks arching in the woods
Years afterwards, trailing their leaves on the ground
Like girls on hands and knees that throw their hair
20 Before them over their heads to dry in the sun.
But I was going to say when Truth broke in
With all her matter-of-fact about the ice-storm
I should prefer to have some boy bend them
As he went out and in to fetch the cows—
25 Some boy too far from town to learn baseball,
Whose only play was what he found himself,
Summer or winter, and could play alone.
One by one he subdued his father's trees

By riding them down over and over again
30 Until he took the stiffness out of them,
And not one but hung limp, not one was left
For him to conquer. He learned all there was
To learn about not launching out too soon
And so not carrying the tree away
35 Clear to the ground. He always kept his poise
To the top branches, climbing carefully
With the same pains you use to fill a cup
Up to the brim, and even above the brim.
Then he flung outward, feet first, with a swish,
40 Kicking his way down through the air to the ground.
So was I once myself a swinger of birches.
And so I dream of going back to be.
It's when I'm weary of considerations,
And life is too much like a pathless wood
45 Where your face burns and tickles with the cobwebs
Broken across it, and one eye is weeping
From a twig's having lashed across it open.
I'd like to get away from earth awhile
And then come back to it and begin over.
50 May no fate willfully misunderstand me
And half grant what I wish and snatch me away
Not to return. Earth's the right place for love:
I don't know where it's likely to go better.
I'd like to go by climbing a birch tree,
55 And climb black branches up a snow-white trunk
Toward Heaven, till the tree could bear no more,
But dipped its top and set me down again.
That would be good both going and coming back.
One could do worse than be a swinger of birches.

Desert Places
(1936)

Snow falling and night falling fast, oh, fast
In a field I looked into going past,
And the ground almost covered smooth in snow,
But a few weeds and stubble showing last.

5 The woods around it have it—it is theirs.
All animals are smothered in their lairs,
I am too absent-spirited to count;
The loneliness includes me unawares.

And lonely as it is, that loneliness
10 Will be more lonely ere it will be less—
A blanker whiteness of benighted snow
With no expression, nothing to express.

They cannot scare me with their empty spaces
Between stars—on stars where no human race is.
15 I have it in me so much nearer home
To scare myself with my own desert places.

Mending Wall
(1914)

Something there is that doesn't love a wall,
That sends the frozen-ground-swell under it,
And spills the upper boulders in the sun;
And makes gaps even two can pass abreast.
5 The work of hunters is another thing:
I have come after them and made repair
Where they have left not one stone on a stone,
But they would have the rabbit out of hiding,
To please the yelping dogs. The gaps I mean,
10 No one has seen them made or heard them made,
But at spring mending-time we find them there.
I let my neighbor know beyond the hill;
And on a day we meet to walk the line
And set the wall between us once again.
15 We keep the wall between us as we go.
To each the boulders that have fallen to each.
And some are loaves and some so nearly balls
We have to use a spell to make them balance:
"Stay where you are until our backs are turned!"
20 We wear our fingers rough with handling them.
Oh, just another kind of outdoor game,
One on a side. It comes to little more:
There where it is we do not need the wall:
He is all pine and I am apple orchard.
25 My apple trees will never get across
And eat the cones under his pines, I tell him.
He only says, "Good fences make good neighbors."
Spring is the mischief in me, and I wonder
If I could put a notion in his head:

30 "*Why* do they make good neighbors? Isn't it
   Where there are cows? But here there are no cows.
   Before I built a wall I'd ask to know
   What I was walling in or walling out,
   And to whom I was like to give offense.
35 Something there is that doesn't love a wall,
   That wants it down." I could say "Elves" to him,
   But it's not elves exactly, and I'd rather
   He said it for himself. I see him there
   Bringing a stone grasped firmly by the top
40 In each hand, like an old-stone savage armed.
   He moves in darkness as it seems to me,
   Not of woods only and the shade of trees.
   He will not go behind his father's saying,
   And he likes having thought of it so well
45 He says again, "Good fences make good neighbors."

The Road Not Taken
(1915)

Two roads diverged in a yellow wood,
And sorry I could not travel both
And be one traveler, long I stood
And looked down one as far as I could
5 To where it bent in the undergrowth;

Then took the other, as just as fair,
And having perhaps the better claim,
Because it was grassy and wanted wear;
Though as for that the passing there
10 Had worn them really about the same,

And both that morning equally lay
In leaves no step had trodden black.
Oh, I kept the first for another day!
Yet knowing how way leads on to way,
15 I doubted if I should ever come back.

I shall be telling this with a sigh
Somewhere ages and ages hence:
Two roads diverged in a wood, and I—
I took the one less traveled by,
20 And that has made all the difference.

The Silken Tent
(1942)

She is as in a field a silken tent
At midday when a sunny summer breeze
Has dried the dew and all its ropes relent,
So that in guys[1] it gently sways at ease,
5 And its supporting central cedar pole,
That is its pinnacle to heavenward
And signifies the sureness of the soul,
Seems to owe naught to any single cord,
But strictly held by none, is loosely bound
10 By countless silken ties of love and thought
To everything on earth the compass round,
And only by one's going slightly taut
In the capriciousness of summer air
Is of the slightest bondage made aware.

Stopping by Woods on a Snowy Evening
(1923)

Whose woods these are I think I know.
His house is in the village though;
He will not see me stopping here
To watch his woods fill up with snow.

5 My little horse must think it queer
To stop without a farmhouse near
Between the woods and frozen lake
The darkest evening of the year.

He gives his harness bells a shake
10 To ask if there is some mistake.
The only other sound's the sweep
Of easy wind and downy flake.

The woods are lovely, dark and deep,
But I have promises to keep,
15 And miles to go before I sleep,
And miles to go before I sleep.

---

[1] A rope or cable used to secure something.

◇ ◇ ◇

NIKKI GIOVANNI
(1943–)

Nikki-Rosa
(1968)

childhood remembrances are always a drag
if you're Black
you always remember things like living in Woodlawn[1]
with no inside toilet
5 and if you become famous or something
they never talk about how happy you were to have your mother
all to yourself and
how good the water felt when you got your bath from one of those
big tubs that folk in chicago barbecue in
10 and somehow when you talk about home
it never gets across how much you
understood their feelings
as the whole family attended meetings about Hollydale
and even though you remember
15 your biographers never understand
your father's pain as he sells his stock
and another dream goes
and though you're poor it isn't poverty that
concerns you
20 and though they fought a lot
it isn't your father's drinking that makes any difference
but only that everybody is together and you
and your sister have happy birthdays and very good christmasses
and I really hope no white person ever has cause to write about me
25 because they never understand Black love is Black wealth and they'll
probably talk about my hard childhood and never understand that
all the while I was quite happy

◇ ◇ ◇

H. D. (HILDA DOOLITTLE)
(1886–1961)

Heat
(1916)

O wind, rend open the heat,
cut apart the heat,
rend it to tatters.

---

[1] A predominantly black suburb of Cincinnati, Ohio.

Fruit cannot drop
5 through this thick air—
fruit cannot fall into heat
that presses up and blunts
the points of pears
and rounds the grapes.

10 Cut the heat—
plough through it,
turning it on either side
of your path.

Helen[1]
(1924)

All Greece hates
the still eyes in the white face,
the lustre as of olives
where she stands,
5 and the white hands.

All Greece reviles
the wan face when she smiles,
hating it deeper still
when it grows wan and white,
10 remembering past enchantments
and past ills.

Greece sees unmoved,
God's daughter, born of love,
the beauty of cool feet
15 and slenderest knees,
could love indeed the maid,
only if she were laid,
white ash amid funereal cypresses.

---

[1] In greek mythology, Helen was the most beautiful of all women. She was the daughter of the Greek god Zeus and the mortal Leda. After a decade or so of marriage to Menelaus, Helen was abducted by, or ran off with, Paris, the son of King Priam of Troy. Menelaus enlisted an army to recapture her in what would become known as the Trojan War, a portion of which is recounted in Homer's epic poem, *The Iliad*.

◊ ◊ ◊
THOMAS HARDY
(1840–1928)

The Convergence of the Twain
(1912)

(Lines on the loss of the 'Titanic')

I

In a solitude of the sea
Deep from human vanity,
And the Pride of Life that planned her, stilly couches she.

II

Steel chambers, late the pyres[1]
5   Of her salamandrine fires,[2]
Cold currents thrid,[3] and turn to rhythmic tidal lyres.

III

Over the mirrors meant
To glass the opulent
The sea-worm crawls—grotesque, slimed, dumb, indifferent.

IV

10   Jewels in joy designed
To ravish the sensuous mind
Lie lightless, all their sparkles bleared and black and blind.

V

Dim moon-eyed fishes near
Gaze at the gilded gear
15 And query: "What does this vaingloriousness down here?" . . .

VI

Well: while was fashioning
This creature of cleaving wing,
The Immanent[4] Will that stirs and urges everything

---

[1] Funeral pyres; piles of wood on which corpses were burned in ancient rites.
[2] Refers to the old belief that salamanders could live in fire.
[3] Thread (archaic verb form).
[4] Inherent, dwelling within.

VII

Prepared a sinister mate
20   For her—so gaily great—
A Shape of Ice, for the time far and dissociate.

VIII

And as the smart ship grew
In stature, grace, and hue,
In shadowy silent distance grew the Iceberg too.

IX

25   Alien they seemed to be:
No mortal eye could see
The intimate welding of their later history,

X

Or sign that they were bent
By paths coincident
30 On being anon[5] twin halves of one august[6] event,

XI

Till the Spinner of the Years
Said "Now!" And each one hears,
And consummation comes, and jars two hemispheres.

Hap
(1866)

If but some vengeful god would call to me
From up the sky, and laugh: "Thou suffering thing,
Know that thy sorrow is my ecstasy,
That thy love's loss is my hate's profiting!"

5 Then would I bear it, clench myself, and die,
Steeled by the sense of ire unmerited;
Half-eased in that a Powerfuller than I
Had willed and meted me the tears I shed.

But not so. How arrives it joy lies slain,
10 And why unblooms the best hope ever sown?
—Crass Casualty obstructs the sun and rain,
And dicing Time for gladness casts a moan. . . .
These purblind Doomsters had as readily strown
Blisses about my pilgrimage as pain.

---

[5] Soon.
[6] Awe-inspiring, majestic.

◊ ◊ ◊

ROBERT HAYDEN
(1913–   )

Homage to the Empress
of the Blues[1]
(1966)

Because there was a man somewhere in a candystripe silk shirt,
gracile and dangerous as a jaguar and because a woman moaned
for him in sixty-watt gloom and mourned him Faithless Love
Twotiming Love Oh Love Oh Careless Aggravating Love,

5   She came out on the stage in yards of pearls, emerging like
       a favorite scenic view, flashed her golden smile and sang.

Because grey laths began somewhere to show from underneath
torn hurdygurdy lithographs of dollfaced heaven;
and because there were those who feared alarming fists of snow
10 on the door and those who feared the riot-squad of statistics,

       She came out on the stage in ostrich feathers, beaded satin,
       and shone that smile on us and sang.

◊ ◊ ◊

SEAMUS HEANEY
(1939–   )

Lightenings viii
(1995)

The annals[1] say: when the monks of Clonmacnoise[2]
Were all at prayers inside the oratory
A ship appeared above them in the air.

The anchor dragged along behind so deep
5 It hooked itself into the altar rails
And then, as the big hull[3] rocked to a standstill,

A crewman shinned and grappled down a rope
And struggled to release it. But in vain.
"This man can't bear our life here and will drown,"

---

[1] An epitaph for Bessie Smith, American jazz singer, 1894–1937.

---

[1] Journals containing yearly records.
[2] An Irish abbey founded in 541, destroyed by the English in 1552.
[3] The frame or body of a ship.

10 The abbot[4] said, "Unless we help him." So
They did, the freed ship sailed and the man climbed back
Out of the marvelous as he had known it.

◇ ◇ ◇

GERARD MANLEY HOPKINS
(1844–1889)

God's Grandeur
(1877)

The world is charged with the grandeur of God.
    It will flame out, like shining from shook foil;
    It gathers to a greatness, like the ooze of oil
Crushed. Why do men then now not reck his rod?
5 Generations have trod, have trod, have trod;
    And all is seared with trade; bleared, smeared with toil;
    And wears man's smudge and shares man's smell: the soil
Is bare now, nor can foot feel, being shod.
And for all this, nature is never spent;
10   There lives the dearest freshness deep down things;
    And though the last lights off the black West went
    Oh, morning, at the brown brink eastward, springs—
Because the Holy Ghost over the bent
    World broods with warm breast and with ah! bright wings.

The Windhover[1]
(1877)

To Christ Our Lord

I caught this morning morning's minion,[2] king-
    dom of daylight's dauphin, dapple-dawn-drawn Falcon, in his riding
    Of the rolling level underneath him steady air, and striding
High there, how he rung upon the rein[3] of a wimpling[4] wing
5 In his ecstasy! then off, off forth on swing,

---

[4] The monk in authority over a community of monks.

---

[1] The kestrel, a European falcon, so called for its ability to hover in the air with its head to the wind.
[2] Favorite.
[3] A horse is "rung upon the rein" when it circles at the end of a long rein held by the trainer.
[4] Rippling.

As a skate's heel sweeps smooth on a bow-bend: the hurl and
gliding
Rebuffed the big wind. My heart in hiding
Stirred for a bird,—the achieve of, the mastery of the thing!
Brute beauty and valor and act, oh, air, pride, plume, here
10　　Buckle! and the fire that breaks from thee then, a billion
Times told lovelier, more dangerous, O my chevalier!
　　No wonder of it: shéer plód, makes plow down sillion[5]
Shine, and blue-bleak embers, ah my dear,
　　Fall, gall themselves, and gash gold-vermilion.

◊　◊　◊

TED HUGHES
(1930–1998)

Visit
(1998)

Lucas, my friend, one
Among those three or four who stay unchanged
Like a separate self,
A stone in the bed of the river
5　Under every change, became your friend.
I heard of it, alerted. I was sitting
Youth away in an office near Slough,
Morning and evening between Slough and Holborn,
Hoarding wage to fund a leap to freedom
10　And the other side of the earth—a free-fall
To strip my chrysalis off me in the slipstream.
Weekends I recidived
Into Alma Mater. Girl-friend
Shared a supervisor and weekly session
15　With your American rival and you.
She detested you. She fed snapshots
Of you and she did not know what
Inflammable celluloid into my silent
Insatiable future, my blind-man's-buff
20　Internal torch of search. With my friend,
After midnight, I stood in a garden
Lobbing soil-clods up at a dark window.

Drunk, he was certain it was yours.
Half as drunk, I did not know he was wrong.

---

[5] The ridge between two furrows.

25 Nor did I know I was being auditioned
   For the male lead in your drama,
   Miming through the first easy movements
   As if with eyes closed, feeling for the role.
   As if a puppet were being tried on its strings,
30 Or a dead frog's legs touched by electrodes.
   I jigged through those gestures—watched and judged
   Only by starry darkness and a shadow.
   Unknown to you and not knowing you.
   Aiming to find you, and missing, and again missing.
35 Flinging earth at a glass that could not protect you
   Because you were not there.

   Ten years after your death
   I meet on a page of your journal, as never before,
   The shock of your joy
40 When you heard of that. Then the shock
   Of your prayers. And under those prayers your panic
   That prayers might not create the miracle,
   Then, under the panic, the nightmare
   That came rolling to crush you:
45 Your alternative—the unthinkable
   Old despair and the new agony
   Melting into one familiar hell.

   Suddenly I read all this—
   Your actual words, as they floated
50 Out through your throat and tongue and onto your page—
   Just as when your daughter, years ago now,
   Drifting in, gazing up into my face,
   Mystified,
   Where I worked alone
55 In the silent house, asked, suddenly:
   'Daddy, where's Mummy?' The freezing soil
   Of the garden, as I clawed it.
   All round me that midnight's
   Giant clock of frost. And somewhere
60 Inside it, wanting to feel nothing,
   A pulse of fever. Somewhere
   Inside that numbness of the earth
   Our future trying to happen.
   I look up—as if to meet your voice
65 With all its urgent future
   That has burst in on me. Then look back
   At the book of the printed words.
   You are ten years dead. It is only a story.
   Your story. My story.

◊ ◊ ◊

JOHN KEATS
(1795–1821)

La Belle Dame sans Merci: A Ballad[1]
(1819, 1820)

1

O what can ail thee, knight at arms,
    Alone and palely loitering?
The sedge has wither'd from the lake,
    And no birds sing.

2

5 O what can ail thee, knight at arms,
    So haggard and so woe-begone?
The squirrel's granary is full,
    And the harvest's done.

3

I see a lily on thy brow
10   With anguish moist and fever dew,
And on thy cheeks a fading rose
    Fast withereth too.

4

I met a lady in the meads,
    Full beautiful, a fairy's child;
15 Her hair was long, her foot was light,
    And her eyes were wild.

5

I made a garland for her head,
    And bracelets too, and fragrant zone;[2]
She look'd at me as she did love,
20   And made sweet moan.

---

[1] The title, which means "The Lovely Lady without Pity," was taken from a medieval poem by Alain Chartier.
[2] Belt.

6

I set her on my pacing steed,
    And nothing else saw all day long,
For sidelong would she bend, and sing
    A fairy's song.

7

25 She found me roots of relish sweet,
    And honey wild, and manna dew,
And sure in language strange she said—
    I love thee true.

8

She took me to her elfin grot,[3]
30   And there she wept, and sigh'd full sore,
And there I shut her wild wild eyes
    With kisses four.

9

And there she lullèd me asleep,
    And there I dream'd—Ah! woe betide!
35 The latest[4] dream I ever dream'd
    On the cold hill's side.

10

I saw pale kings, and princes too,
    Pale warriors, death pale were they all;
They cried—"La belle dame sans merci
40   Hath thee in thrall!"

11

I saw their starv'd lips in the gloam[5]
    With horrid warning gapèd wide,
And I awoke and found me here
    On the cold hill's side.

12

45 And this is why I sojourn here,
    Alone and palely loitering,
Though the sedge is wither'd from the lake,
    And no birds sing.

---

[3] Grotto.
[4] Last.
[5] Twilight.

Bright Star! Would I Were Steadfast as Thou Art
(1819)

Bright star! would I were steadfast as thou art—
　　Not in lone splendor hung aloft the night,
And watching, with eternal lids apart,
　　Like nature's patient, sleepless Eremite[1]
5　The moving waters at their priest-like task
　　　Of pure ablution[2] round earth's human shores,
Or gazing on the new soft-fallen mask
　　Of snow upon the mountains and the moors—
No—yet still steadfast, still unchangeable,
10　　　Pillowed upon my fair love's ripening breast,
To feel for ever its soft fall and swell,
　　Awake for ever in a sweet unrest,
Still, still to hear her tender-taken breath,
And so live ever—or else swoon to death.

Ode on a Grecian Urn[1]
(1819)

1

Thou still unravish'd bride of quietness,
　　Thou foster-child of silence and slow time,
Sylvan[2] historian, who canst thus express
A flowery tale more sweetly than our rhyme:
5　What leaf-fring'd legend haunts about thy shape
　　　Of deities or mortals, or of both,
　　　　In Tempe[3] or the dales of Arcady?[4]
　　What men or gods are these? What maidens loth?
What mad pursuit? What struggle to escape?
10　　　What pipes and timbrels? What wild ecstasy?

---

[1] Hermit, religious recluse.

[2] Washing, cleansing.

---

[1] Though many urns similar to the one Keats describes actually exist, the subject of the poem is purely imaginary.

[2] Pertaining to woods or forests.

[3] A beautiful valley in Greece.

[4] The valleys of Arcadia, a mountainous region on the Greek peninsula. Like Tempe, they represent a rustic pastoral ideal.

2

Heard melodies are sweet, but those unheard
 Are sweeter; therefore, ye soft pipes, play on;
Not to the sensual ear, but, more endear'd,
 Pipe to the spirit ditties of no tone:
15 Fair youth, beneath the trees, thou canst not leave
 Thy song, nor ever can those trees be bare;
  Bold lover, never, never canst thou kiss,
Though winning near the goal—yet, do not grieve;
  She cannot fade, though thou hast not thy bliss,
20 For ever wilt thou love, and she be fair!

3

Ah, happy, happy boughs! that cannot shed
 Your leaves, nor ever bid the spring adieu;
And, happy melodist, unwearied,
 For ever piping songs for ever new;
25 More happy love! more happy, happy love!
 For ever warm and still to be enjoy'd,
  For ever panting, and for ever young;
All breathing human passion far above,
 That leaves a heart high-sorrowful and cloy'd,
30   A burning forehead, and a parching tongue.

4

Who are these coming to the sacrifice?
 To what green altar, O mysterious priest,
Lead'st thou that heifer lowing at the skies,
 And all her silken flanks with garlands drest?
35 What little town by river or sea shore,
 Or mountain-built with peaceful citadel,
  Is emptied of this folk, this pious morn?
And, little town, thy streets for evermore
 Will silent be; and not a soul to tell
40   Why thou art desolate, can e'er return.

5

O Attic[5] shape! Fair attitude! with brede[6]
 Of marble men and maidens overwrought,[7]
With forest branches and the trodden weed;

---

[5] Characteristic of Athens or Athenians.
[6] Braid.
[7] Elaborately ornamented.

Thou, silent form, dost tease us out of thought
45 As doth eternity: Cold Pastoral!
    When old age shall this generation waste,
        Thou shalt remain, in midst of other woe
Than ours, a friend to man, to whom thou say'st,
"Beauty is truth, truth beauty,"—that is all
50   Ye know on earth, and all ye need to know.

When I Have Fears
(1818)

When I have fears that I may cease to be
    Before my pen has gleaned my teeming brain,
Before high-piléd books, in charact'ry,[1]
    Hold like rich garners the full-ripened grain;
5 When I behold, upon the night's starred face,
    Huge cloudy symbols of a high romance,
And think that I may never live to trace
    Their shadows, with the magic hand of chance;
And when I feel, fair creature of an hour,
10   That I shall never look upon thee more,
Never have relish in the faery power
    Of unreflecting love!—then on the shore
Of the wide world I stand alone, and think
Till Love and Fame to nothingness do sink.

◊ ◊ ◊

PHILIP LARKIN
(1922–1985)

Aubade
(1977)

I work all day, and get half-drunk at night.
Waking at four to soundless dark, I stare.
In time the curtain-edges will grow light.
Till then I see what's really always there:
5 Unresting death, a whole day nearer now,
Making all thought impossible but how

---

[1] Print.

And where and when I shall myself die.
Arid interrogation: yet the dread
Of dying, and being dead,
10 Flashes afresh to hold and horrify.

The mind blanks at the glare. Not in remorse
—The good not done, the love not given, time
Torn off unused—nor wretchedly because
An only life can take so long to climb
15 Clear of its wrong beginnings, and may never;
But at the total emptiness for ever,
The sure extinction that we travel to
And shall be lost in always. Not to be here,
Not to be anywhere,
20 And soon; nothing more terrible, nothing more true.

This is a special way of being afraid
No trick dispels. Religion used to try,
That vast moth-eaten musical brocade
Created to pretend we never die,
25 And specious stuff that says *No rational being*
Can fear a thing it will not feel, not seeing
That this is what we fear—no sight, no sound,
No touch or taste or smell, nothing to think with,
Nothing to love or link with,
30 The anaesthetic from which none come round.

And so it stays just on the edge of vision,
A small unfocused blur, a standing chill
That slows each impulse down to indecision.
Most things may never happen: this one will,
35 And realization of it rages out
In furnace-fear when we are caught without
People or drink. Courage is no good:
It means not scaring others. Being brave
Lets no one off the grave.
40 Death is no different whined at than withstood.

Slowly light strengthens, and the room takes shape.
It stands plain as a wardrobe, what we know,
Have always known, know that we can't escape,
Yet can't accept. One side will have to go.
45 Meanwhile telephones crouch, getting ready to ring
In locked-up offices, and all the uncaring
Intricate rented world begins to rouse.
The sky is white as clay, with no sun.
Work has to be done.
50 Postmen like doctors go from house to house.

◊ ◊ ◊

CLAUDE MCKAY
(1890–1948)

If We Must Die
(1922)

If we must die, let it not be like hogs
Hunted and penned in an inglorious spot,
While round us bark the mad and hungry dogs,
Making their mock at our accursed lot.
5 If we must die, O let us nobly die,
So that our precious blood may not be shed
In vain; then even the monsters we defy
Shall be constrained to honor us though dead!
O kinsmen! we must meet the common foe!
10 Though far outnumbered let us show us brave,
And for their thousand blows deal one deathblow!
What though before us lies the open grave?
Like men we'll face the murderous, cowardly pack,
Pressed to the wall, dying, but fighting back!

◊ ◊ ◊

JOHN MILTON
(1608–1674)

When I Consider How
My Light Is Spent[1]
(1655?)

When I consider how my light is spent,
 Ere half my days in this dark world and wide,
 And that one talent[2] which is death to hide
Lodged with me useless, though my soul more bent
5 To serve therewith my Maker, and present
 My true account, lest He returning chide;
 "Doth God exact day-labor, light denied?"
I fondly[3] ask. But Patience, to prevent
That murmur, soon replies, "God doth not need
10 Either man's work or His own gifts. Who best
 Bear His mild yoke, they serve Him best. His state
Is kingly: thousands at His bidding speed,

---

[1] A meditation on his blindness.
[2] See Jesus' parable of the talents in Matthew 25:14–30.
[3] Foolishly.

And post o'er land and ocean without rest;
They also serve who only stand and wait."

◇ ◇ ◇

PABLO NERUDA
(1904–1973)

The United Fruit Co.[1]
(1950)

Translated by Robert Bly

When the trumpet sounded, it was
all prepared on the earth,
and Jehovah parceled out the earth
to Coca-Cola, Inc., Anaconda,
5   Ford Motors, and other entities:
The Fruit Company, Inc.
reserved for itself the most succulent,
the central coast of my own land,
the delicate waist of America.
10   It rechristened its territories
as the "Banana Republics"
and over the sleeping dead,
over the restless heroes
who brought about the greatness,
15   the liberty and the flags,
it established the comic opera:
abolished the independencies,
presented crowns of Caesar,
unsheathed envy, attracted
20   the dictatorship of the flies,
Trujillo flies, Tacho flies,
Carias flies, Martinez flies,
Ubico flies,[2] damp flies
of modest blood and marmalade,
25   drunken flies who zoom
over the ordinary graves,
circus flies, wise flies
well trained in tyranny.

---

[1] Incorporated in New Jersey in 1899 by Andrew Preston and Minor C. Keith, United Fruit became the major force in growing, transporting, and merchandising Latin American produce, especially bananas. The company is also notorious for its involvement in politics and is a symbol for many people of "Yankee" imperialism and oppression.

[2] Trujillo, Tacho, Carias, Martinez, and Ubico are all political dictators.

Among the bloodthirsty flies
30 the Fruit Company lands its ships,
taking off the coffee and the fruit;
the treasure of our submerged
territories flows as though
on plates into the ships.

35 Meanwhile Indians are falling
into the sugared chasms
of the harbors, wrapped
for burial in the mist of the dawn:
a body rolls, a thing
40 that has no name, a fallen cipher,
a cluster of dead fruit
thrown down on the dump.

◊ ◊ ◊

SHARON OLDS
(1942–   )

Rite of Passage
(1983)

As the guests arrive at my son's party
they gather in the living room—
short men, men in first grade
with smooth jaws and chins.
5 Hands in pockets, they stand around
jostling, jockeying for place, small fights
breaking out and calming. One says to another
How old are you? Six. I'm seven. So?
They eye each other, seeing themselves
10 tiny in the other's pupils. They clear their
throats a lot, a room of small bankers,
they fold their arms and frown. *I could beat you
up,* a seven says to a six,
the dark cake, round and heavy as a
15 turret, behind them on the table. My son,
freckles like specks of nutmeg on his cheeks,
chest narrow as the balsa[1] keel[2] of a
model boat, long hands
cool and thin as the day they guided him
20 out of me, speaks up as a host
for the sake of the group.

---

[1] A lightweight wood.
[2] The piece of wood that runs lengthwise along the center of a ship's bottom.

We could easily kill a two-year-old,
he says in his clear voice. The other
men agree, they clear their throats
25 like Generals, they relax and get down to
playing war, celebrating my son's life.

◊ ◊ ◊

MICHAEL ONDAATJE
(1943–   )

Dates[1]

It becomes apparent that I miss great occasions.
My birth was heralded by nothing
but the anniversary of Winston Churchill's marriage.
No monuments bled, no instruments
5 agreed on a specific weather.
It was a seasonal insignificance.

I console myself with my mother's eighth month.
While she sweated out her pregnancy in Ceylon[2]
a servant ambling over the lawn
10 with a tray of iced drinks,
a few friends visiting her
to placate her shape, and I
drinking the life lines,
Wallace Stevens sat down in Connecticut
15 a glass of orange juice at his table
so hot he wore only shorts
and on the back of a letter
began to write "The Well Dressed Man with a Beard."

That night while my mother slept
20 her significant belly cooled
by the bedroom fan
Stevens put words together
that grew to sentences
and shaved them clean and
25 shaped them, the page suddenly
becoming thought where nothing had been,
his head making his hand
move where he wanted

---

[1] Publication date is not available.
[2] Now known as Sri Lanka.

and he saw his hand was saying
30 the mind is never finished, no, never
and I in my mother's stomach was growing
as were the flowers outside the Connecticut windows.

◇ ◇ ◇

LINDA PASTAN
(1932–   )

Ethics
(1980)

In ethics class so many years ago
our teacher asked this question every fall:
if there were a fire in a museum
which would you save, a Rembrandt painting
5 or an old woman who hadn't many
years left anyhow? Restless on hard chairs
caring little for pictures or old age
we'd opt one year for life, the next for art
and always half-heartedly. Sometimes
10 the woman borrowed my grandmother's face
leaving her usual kitchen to wander
some drafty, half imagined museum.
One year, feeling clever, I replied
why not let the woman decide herself?
15 Linda, the teacher would report, eschews
the burdens of responsibility.
This fall in a real museum I stand
before a real Rembrandt, old woman,
or nearly so, myself. The colors
20 within this frame are darker than autumn,
darker even than winter—the browns of earth,
though earth's most radiant elements burn
through the canvas. I know now that woman
and painting and season are almost one
25 and all beyond saving by children.

Marks
(1978)

My husband gives me an A
for last night's supper,
an incomplete for my ironing,
a B plus in bed.

5 My son says I am average,
an average mother, but if
I put my mind to it
I could improve.
My daughter believes
10 in Pass/Fail and tells me
I pass. Wait 'til they learn
I'm dropping out.

◆ ◆ ◆

MARGE PIERCY
(1934–   )

Barbie Doll
(1973)

This girlchild was born as usual
and presented dolls that did pee-pee
and miniature GE stoves and irons
and wee lipsticks the color of cherry candy.
5 Then in the magic of puberty, a classmate said:
You have a great big nose and fat legs.

She was healthy, tested intelligent,
possessed strong arms and back,
abundant sexual drive and manual dexterity.
10 She went to and fro apologizing.
Everyone saw a fat nose on thick legs.

She was advised to play coy,
exhorted to come on hearty,
exercise, diet, smile and wheedle.
15 Her good nature wore out
like a fan belt.
So she cut off her nose and her legs
and offered them up.
In the casket displayed on satin she lay
20 with the undertaker's cosmetics painted on,
a turned-up putty nose,
dressed in a pink and white nightie.
Doesn't she look pretty? everyone said.
Consummation at last.
25 To every woman a happy ending.

The Friend
(1969)

We sat across the table.
He said, cut off your hands.
They are always poking at things.
They might touch me.
5 I said yes.

Food grew cold on the table.
He said, burn your body.
It is not clean and smells like sex.
It rubs my mind sore.
10 I said yes.

I love you, I said.
that's very nice, he said
I like to be loved,
that makes me happy.
15 Have you cut off your hands yet?

◆ ◆ ◆

SYLVIA PLATH
(1932–1963)

Metaphors
(1960)

I'm a riddle in nine syllables,
An elephant, a ponderous house,
A melon strolling on two tendrils.
O red fruit, ivory, fine timbers!
5 This loaf's big with its yeasty rising.
Money's new-minted in this fat purse.
I'm a means, a stage, a cow in calf.
I've eaten a bag of green apples,
Boarded the train there's no getting off.

Mirror
(1963)

I am silver and exact. I have no preconceptions.
Whatever I see I swallow immediately
Just as it is, unmisted by love or dislike.
I am not cruel, only truthful—
5 The eye of a little god, four-cornered.

Most of the time I meditate on the opposite wall.
It is pink, with speckles. I have looked at it so long
I think it is a part of my heart. But it flickers.
Faces and darkness separate us over and over.

10 Now I am a lake. A woman bends over me,
Searching my reaches for what she really is.
Then she turns to those liars, the candles or the moon.
I see her back, and reflect it faithfully.
She rewards me with tears and an agitation of hands.

15 I am important to her. She comes and goes.
Each morning it is her face that replaces the darkness.
In me she has drowned a young girl, and in me an old woman
Rises toward her day after day, like a terrible fish.

◊ ◊ ◊

E Z R A   P O U N D
(1885–1972)

The River-Merchant's Wife: A Letter[1]
(1515)

While my hair was still cut straight across my forehead
I played about the front gate, pulling flowers.
You came by on bamboo stilts, playing horse,
You walked about my seat, playing with blue plums.
5 And we went on living in the village of Chokan:[2]
Two small people, without dislike or suspicion.

At fourteen I married My Lord you.
I never laughed, being bashful.
Lowering my head, I looked at the wall.
10 Called to, a thousand times, I never looked back.

At fifteen I stopped scowling,
I desired my dust to be mingled with yours
Forever and forever and forever.
Why should I climb the lookout?

15 At sixteen you departed,
You went into far Ku-to-yen,[3] by the river of swirling eddies,
And you have been gone five months.
The monkeys make sorrowful noise overhead.

---

[1] This is one of the many translations Pound made of Chinese poems. The poem is a free translation of Li Po's (701–762) "Two Letters from Chang-Kan."
[2] Chang-Kan.
[3] An island in the river Ch'ū-t'ang.

You dragged your feet when you went out.
20 By the gate now, the moss is grown, the different mosses,
Too deep to clear them away!
The leaves fall early this autumn, in wind.
The paired butterflies are already yellow with August
Over the grass in the West garden;
25 They hurt me. I grow older.
If you are coming down through the narrows of the river Kiang,[4]
Please let me know beforehand,
And I will come out to meet you
    As far as Cho-fu-sa.[5]

❖ ❖ ❖

JOHN CROWE RANSOM
(1888–1974)

Bells for John Whiteside's Daughter
(1924)

There was such speed in her little body,
And such lightness in her footfall,
It is no wonder her brown study
Astonishes us all.

5 Her wars were bruited in our high window.
We looked among orchard trees and beyond,
Where she took arms against her shadow,
Or harried unto the pond

The lazy geese, like a snow cloud
10 Dripping their snow on the green grass,
Tricking and stopping, sleepy and proud,
Who cried in goose, Alas,

For the tireless heart within the little
Lady with rod that made them rise
15 From their noon apple-dreams, and scuttle
Goose-fashion under the skies!

But now go the bells, and we are ready;
In one house we are sternly stopped
To say we are vexed at her brown study,
20 Lying so primly propped.

---

[4] The Japanese name for the river Ch'ū-t'ang (see note 3). Pound's translations are based on commentaries derived from Japanese scholars; therefore, he usually uses Japanese instead of Chinese names.
[5] A beach several hundred miles upstream of Nanking.

◇ ◇ ◇

HENRY REED
(1914–1986)

Naming of Parts
(1946)

Today we have naming of parts. Yesterday,
We had daily cleaning. And tomorrow morning,
We shall have what to do after firing. But today,
Today we have naming of parts. Japonica[1]
5 Glistens like coral in all of the neighboring gardens,
    And today we have naming of parts.

This is the lower sling swivel. And this
Is the upper sling swivel, whose use you will see,
When you are given your slings. And this is the piling swivel,
10 Which in your case you have not got. The branches
Hold in the gardens their silent, eloquent gestures,
    Which in our case we have not got.

This is the safety-catch, which is always released
With an easy flick of the thumb. And please do not let me
15 See anyone using his finger. You can do it quite easy
If you have any strength in your thumb. The blossoms
Are fragile and motionless, never letting anyone see
    Any of them using their finger.

And this you can see is the bolt. The purpose of this
20 Is to open the breech, as you see. We can slide it
Rapidly backwards and forwards: we call this
Easing the spring. And rapidly backwards and forwards
The early bees are assaulting and fumbling the flowers:
    They call it easing the Spring.

25 They call it easing the Spring: it is perfectly easy
If you have any strength in your thumb: like the bolt,
And the breech, and the cocking-piece, and the point of balance,
Which in our case we have not got; and the almond-blossom
Silent in all of the gardens and the bees going backwards and
      forwards,
30   For today we have the naming of parts.

---

[1] A shrub having waxy flowers in a variety of colors.

◊ ◊ ◊

EDWIN ARLINGTON ROBINSON
(1869–1935)

Miniver Cheevy
(1910)

Miniver Cheevy, child of scorn,
    Grew lean while he assailed the seasons;
He wept that he was ever born,
    And he had reasons.

5 Miniver loved the days of old
    When swords were bright and steeds were prancing;
The vision of a warrior bold
    Would set him dancing.

Miniver sighed for what was not,
10   And dreamed, and rested from his labors;
He dreamed of Thebes[1] and Camelot,[2]
    And Priam's[3] neighbors.

Miniver mourned the ripe renown
    That made so many a name so fragrant;
15 He mourned Romance, now on the town,
    And Art, a vagrant.

Miniver loved the Medici,[4]
    Albeit he had never seen one;
He would have sinned incessantly
20   Could he have been one.

Miniver cursed the commonplace
    And eyed a khaki suit with loathing;
He missed the medieval grace
    Of iron clothing.

25 Miniver scorned the gold he sought,
    But sore annoyed was he without it;
Miniver thought, and thought, and thought,
    And thought about it.

---

[1] The setting of many Greek legends, including that of Oedipus.
[2] The legendary site of King Arthur's court.
[3] Priam was the last King of Troy; his "neighbors" included Helen, Aeneas, and Hector.
[4] Rulers of Florence, Italy, from the fifteenth through the eighteenth centuries. During the Renaissance, Lorenzo de Medici was a renowned patron of the arts.

Miniver Cheevy, born too late,
30   Scratched his head and kept on thinking;
Miniver coughed, and called it fate,
      And kept on drinking.

Richard Cory
(1897)

Whenever Richard Cory went down town,
We people on the pavement looked at him:
He was a gentleman from sole to crown,
Clean favored, and imperially slim.

5 And he was always quietly arrayed,
And he was always human when he talked;
But still he fluttered pulses when he said,
"Good-morning," and he glittered when he walked.

And he was rich—yes, richer than a king—
10 And admirably schooled in every grace:
In fine, we thought that he was everything
To make us wish that we were in his place.

So on we worked, and waited for the light,
And went without the meat, and cursed the bread;
15 And Richard Cory, one calm summer night,
Went home and put a bullet through his head.

◊ ◊ ◊

CARL SANDBURG
(1878–1967)

Fog
(1916)

The fog comes
on little cat feet.
It sits looking
over harbor and city
5 on silent haunches
and then moves on.

◇ ◇ ◇

ANNE SEXTON
(1928–1974)

Sylvia's Death[1]
(1966)

for Sylvia Plath

O Sylvia, Sylvia,
with a dead box of stones and spoons,

with two children, two meteors
wandering loose in the tiny playroom,

5 with your mouth into the sheet,
into the roofbeam, into the dumb prayer,

(Sylvia, Sylvia,
where did you go
after you wrote me
10 from Devonshire
about raising potatoes
and keeping bees?)

what did you stand by,
just how did you lie down into?

15 Thief!—
how did you crawl into,

crawl down alone
into the death I wanted so badly and for so long,

the death we said we both outgrew,
20 the one we wore on our skinny breasts,

the one we talked of so often each time
we downed three extra dry martinis in Boston,

the death that talked of analysts and cures,
the death that talked like brides with plots,

25 the death we drank to,
the motives and then the quiet deed?

---

[1] Poet Sylvia Plath, who committed suicide in 1963 (see p. 1030).

(In Boston
the dying
ride in cabs,
30 yes death again,
that ride home
with *our* boy.)

O Sylvia, I remember the sleepy drummer
who beat on our eyes with an old story,

35 how we wanted to let him come
like a sadist or a New York fairy

to do his job,
a necessity, a window in a wall or a crib,

and since that time he waited
40 under our heart, our cupboard,

and I see now that we store him up
year after year, old suicides

and I know at the news of your death,
a terrible taste for it, like salt.

45 (And me,
me too.
And now, Sylvia,
you again
with death again,
50 that ride home
with *our* boy.)

And I say only
with my arms stretched out into that stone place,

what is your death
55 but an old belonging,

a mole that fell out
of one of your poems?

(O friend,
while the moon's bad,
60 and the king's gone,
and the queen's at her wit's end
the bar fly ought to sing!)

O tiny mother,
you too!
65 O funny duchess!
O blonde thing!

◊ ◊ ◊

WILLIAM SHAKESPEARE
(1564–1616)

Let Me Not to the Marriage of True Minds
(1609)

Let me not to the marriage of true minds
Admit impediments.[1] Love is not love
Which alters when it alteration finds,
Or bends with the remover to remove:
5 Oh, no! it is an ever-fixéd mark,
That looks on tempests and is never shaken;
It is the star to every wandering bark,
Whose worth's unknown, although his height[2] be taken.
Love's not Time's fool,[3] though rosy lips and cheeks
10 Within his bending sickle's compass come;
Love alters not with his brief hours and weeks,
But bears it out even to the edge of doom.[4]
    If this be error and upon me proved,
    I never writ, nor no man ever loved.

Not Marble, nor the Gilded Monuments
(1609)

Not marble, nor the gilded monuments
Of princes, shall outlive this powerful rhyme;
But you shall shine more bright in these contents
Than unswept stone, besmeared with sluttish time.
5 When wasteful war shall statues overturn,
And broils root out the work of masonry,
Nor Mars[1] his sword nor war's quick fire shall burn
The living record of your memory.
'Gainst death and all-oblivious enmity

---

[1] A reference to "The Order of Solemnization of Matrimony" in the Anglican *Book of Common Prayer:* "I require that if either of you know any impediments why ye may not be lawfully joined together in Matrimony, ye do now confess it."

[2] Although the altitude of a star may be measured, its worth is unknowable.

[3] That is, mocked by Time.

[4] Doomsday.

---

[1] God of War.

10 Shall you pace forth; your praise shall still find room
   Even in the eyes of all posterity
   That wear this world out to the ending doom.
      So, till the judgment that yourself arise,
      You live in this, and dwell in lovers' eyes.

◊ ◊ ◊

PERCY BYSSHE SHELLEY
(1792–1822)

Ode to the West Wind
(1820)

I

O wild West Wind, thou breath of Autumn's being,
Thou, from whose unseen presence the leaves dead
Are driven, like ghosts from an enchanter fleeing,

Yellow, and black, and pale, and hectic[1] red,
5 Pestilence-stricken multitudes: O Thou,
Who chariotest to their dark wintry bed

The winged seeds, where they lie cold and low,
Each like a corpse within its grave, until
Thine azure sister of the Spring[2] shall blow

10 Her clarion o'er the dreaming earth, and fill
   (Driving sweet buds like flocks to feed in air)
   With living hues and odours plain and hill:

Wild Spirit, which art moving everywhere;
Destroyer and Preserver; hear, O hear!

II

15 Thou on whose stream, mid the steep sky's commotion,
   Loose clouds like Earth's decaying leaves are shed,
   Shook from the tangled boughs of Heaven and Ocean,

Angels of rain and lightning: there are spread
On the blue surface of thine aery surge,
20 Like the bright hair uplifted from the head
   Of some fierce Maenad,[3] even from the dim verge

---

[1] Reference to a tubercular fever that produces flushed cheeks.

[2] The west wind of the spring.

[3] A female votary who danced wildly in ceremonies for Dionysus (or Bacchus), Greek god of wine and vegetation, who according to legend died in the fall and was reborn in the spring.

Of the horizon to the zenith's height,
The locks of the approaching storm. Thou Dirge

Of the dying year, to which this closing night
25 Will be the dome of a vast sepulchre,
Vaulted with all thy congregated might

Of vapours, from whose solid atmosphere
Black rain and fire and hail will burst: O hear!

III

Thou who didst waken from his summer dreams
30 The blue Mediterranean, where he lay,
Lulled by the coil of his crystalline streams,

Beside a pumice isle in Baiae's bay,[4]
And saw in sleep old palaces and towers
Quivering within the wave's intenser day,

35 All overgrown with azure moss and flowers
So sweet, the sense faints picturing them! Thou
For whose path the Atlantic's level powers

Cleave themselves into chasms, while far below
The sea-blooms and the oozy woods which wear
40 The sapless foliage of the ocean, know

Thy voice, and suddenly grow grey with fear,
And tremble and despoil themselves: O hear!

IV

If I were a dead leaf thou mightest bear;
If I were a swift cloud to fly with thee;
45 A wave to pant beneath thy power, and share

The impulse of thy strength, only less free
Than thou, O Uncontrollable! If even
I were as in my boyhood, and could be

The comrade of thy wanderings over Heaven,
50 As then, when to outstrip thy skiey speed
Scarce seemed a vision; I would ne'er have striven

As thus with thee in prayer in my sore need,
Oh! lift me as a wave, a leaf, a cloud!
I fall upon the thorns of life! I bleed!

---

[4] A bay in the Mediterranean Sea, west of Naples. It was known for the opulent villas
built by Roman emperors along its shores.

55 A heavy weight of hours has chained and bowed
One too like thee: tameless, and swift, and proud.

V

Make me thy lyre,[5] even as the forest is:
What if my leaves are falling like its own!
The tumult of thy mighty harmonies

60 Will take from both a deep, autumnal tone,
Sweet though in sadness. Be thou, Spirit fierce,
My spirit! Be thou me, impetuous one!

Drive my dead thoughts over the universe
Like withered leaves to quicken a new birth!
65 And, by the incantation of this verse,

Scatter, as from an unextinguished hearth
Ashes and sparks, my words among mankind!
Be through my lips to unawakened Earth

The trumpet of a prophecy! O Wind,
70 If Winter comes, can Spring be far behind?

◊　◊　◊

STEVIE SMITH
(1902–1971)

Not Waving but Drowning
(1957)

Nobody heard him, the dead man,
But still he lay moaning:
I was much further out than you thought
And not waving but drowning.

5 Poor chap, he always loved larking
And now he's dead
It must have been too cold for him his heart gave way,
They said.

Oh, no no no, it was too cold always
10 (Still the dead one lay moaning)
I was much too far out all my life
And not waving but drowning.

---

[5] An Aeolian harp, a stringed instrument that produces musical sounds when exposed
to the wind.

◇ ◇ ◇

CATHY SONG
(1955–   )

Lost Sister
(1983)

1

In China,
even the peasants
named their first daughters
Jade—
5 the stone that in the far fields
could moisten the dry season,
could make men move mountains
for the healing green of the inner hills
glistening like slices of winter melon.

10 And the daughters were grateful:
they never left home.
To move freely was a luxury
stolen from them at birth.
Instead, they gathered patience,
15 learning to walk in shoes
the size of teacups,[1]
without breaking—
the arc of their movements
as dormant as the rooted willow,
20 as redundant as the farmyard hens.
But they traveled far
in surviving,
learning to stretch the family rice,
to quiet the demons,
25 the noisy stomachs.

2

There is a sister
across the ocean,
who relinquished her name,
diluting jade green
30 with the blue of the Pacific.
Rising with a tide of locusts,

---

[1] A reference to the practice of binding young girls' feet so that they remain small. This practice, which crippled women, was common in China until the communist revolution.

she swarmed with others
to inundate another shore.
In America,
35 there are many roads
and women can stride along with men.

But in another wilderness,
the possibilities,
the loneliness,
40 can strangulate like jungle vines.
The meager provisions and sentiments
of once belonging—
fermented roots, Mah-Jongg[2] tiles and firecrackers—
set but a flimsy household
45 in a forest of nightless cities.
A giant snake rattles above,
spewing black clouds into your kitchen.
Dough-faced landlords
slip in and out of your keyholes,
50 making claims you don't understand,
tapping into your communication systems
of laundry lines and restaurant chains.

You find you need China:
your one fragile identification,
55 a jade link
handcuffed to your wrist.
You remember your mother
who walked for centuries,
footless—
60 and like her,
you have left no footprints,
but only because
there is an ocean in between,
the unremitting space of your rebellion.

---

[2] Or mahjong, an ancient Chinese game played with dice and tiles.

⬦ ⬦ ⬦
GARY SOTO
(1952–   )

Black Hair
(1985)

At eight I was brilliant with my body.
In July, that ring of heat
We all jumped through, I sat in the bleachers
Of Romain Playground, in the lengthening
5 Shade that rose from our dirty feet.
The game before us was more than baseball.
It was a figure—Hector Moreno
Quick and hard with turned muscles,
His crouch the one I assumed before an altar
10 Of worn baseball cards, in my room.
I came here because I was Mexican, a stick
Of brown light in love with those
Who could do it—the triple and hard slide,
The gloves eating balls into double plays.
15 What could I do with 50 pounds, my shyness,
My black torch of hair, about to go out?
Father was dead, his face no longer
Hanging over the table or our sleep,
And mother was the terror of mouths
20 Twisting hurt by butter knives.

In the bleachers I was brilliant with my body,
Waving players in and stomping my feet,
Growing sweaty in the presence of white shirts.
I chewed sunflower seeds. I drank water
25 And bit my arm through the late innings.
When Hector lined balls into deep
Center, in my mind I rounded the bases
With him, my face flared, my hair lifting
Beautifully, because we were coming home
30 To the arms of brown people.

◇ ◇ ◇

ERIC SPRADO[1]

Wait 'til You Become a Man

I remember seeing men
Who lost their farms in the thirties—
Deep lines and haunted looks
Carved into those faces.

5 Why do those men look angry and sad?
I asked as a little boy.
You're too young to understand, son;
Wait 'til you're a man.

I grew up and forgot that look.
10 Good times were here to stay.
Drifting around, having fun,
Still, putting money away.

Finally, my dream come true.
A ranch of my own.

15 In harsh sagebrush country,
Hot in the summer, cold in the winter,
A country that makes you feel big and small,
Covered with alkali dust, I could
Break off a piece of sagebrush and say,
20   "I love you."

Herding cows in a blizzard, I could
Lay back my head and
     Laugh like a madman.

Now it's gone.
25 The deep, deep lines and haunted look
I think I understand.
Maybe I've become a man.

---

[1] Life dates of author and publication date of poem are not available.

◊ ◊ ◊

WILLIAM STAFFORD
(1914–1993)

Traveling through the Dark
(1962)

Traveling through the dark I found a deer
dead on the edge of the Wilson River road.
It is usually best to roll them into the canyon:
that road is narrow; to swerve might make more dead.

5 By glow of the tail-light I stumbled back of the car
and stood by the heap, a doe, a recent killing;
she had stiffened already, almost cold.
I dragged her off; she was large in the belly.

My fingers touching her side brought me the reason—
10 her side was warm; her fawn lay there waiting,
alive, still, never to be born.
Beside that mountain road I hesitated.

The car aimed ahead its lowered parking lights;
under the hood purred the steady engine.
15 I stood in the glare of the warm exhaust turning red;
around our group I could hear the wilderness listen.

I thought hard for us all—my only swerving—
then pushed her over the edge into the river.

◊ ◊ ◊

WALLACE STEVENS
(1879–1955)

Anecdote of the Jar
(1923)

I placed a jar in Tennessee,
And round it was, upon a hill.
It made the slovenly wilderness
Surround that hill.

5 The wilderness rose up to it,
And sprawled around, no longer wild.
The jar was round upon the ground
And tall and of a port in air.

It took dominion everywhere.
10 The jar was gray and bare.
It did not give of bird or bush,
Like nothing else in Tennessee.

The Emperor of Ice-Cream
(1923)

Call the roller of big cigars,
The muscular one, and bid him whip
In kitchen cups concupiscent curds.
Let the wenches dawdle in such dress
5 As they are used to wear, and let the boys
Bring flowers in last month's newspapers.
Let be be finale of seem.
The only emperor is the emperor of ice-cream.

Take from the dresser of deal,[1]
10 Lacking the three glass knobs, that sheet
On which she embroidered fantails[2] once
And spread it so as to cover her face.
If her horny feet protrude, they come
To show how cold she is, and dumb.
15 Let the lamp affix its beam.
The only emperor is the emperor of ice-cream.

◇ ◇ ◇

COLEN H. SWEETEN, JR.[1]

Hailstorm

I remember the deafening roar,
The wavering fields of wheat,
The huddled family—
A sudden chilling of the July heat,
5 And fear in my father's eyes—
My father who kicked badgers
And laughed at broncos!
Mother quietly put her arm around him
As if she feared he might rush,
10 Bare-fisted, to battle the icy pellets.

---

[1] Fir or pine wood.
[2] According to Stevens, "the word fantails does not mean fans, but fantail pigeons."

---

[1] Life dates of author and publication date of poem are not available.

I remember my father's eyes, filled
With tears as big as toadstools.
Icy tears which just hung there.
There was too much pride to fall,
15 And too much hurt to retreat.
And then our harvest was over.
Our valley was still, oh, so still.

Soon the hurt was healing.
There was no bitterness.
20 There was no blame.
I knew my parents still trusted God.

Now, in the quiet of my own silent hailstorms,
When I alone am aware of the roar,
I feel a strength from that old scar,
25 And find courage born of faith,
Not of understanding.

◊ ◊ ◊

ALFRED, LORD TENNYSON
(1809–1892)

Ulysses[1]
(1833)

It little profits that an idle king,
By this still hearth, among these barren crags,
Matched with an agèd wife, I mete and dole
Unequal laws unto a savage race
5 That hoard, and sleep, and feed, and know not me.
I cannot rest from travel; I will drink
Life to the lees. All times I have enjoyed
Greatly, have suffered greatly, both with those
That loved me, and alone; on shore, and when
10 Through scudding drifts the rainy Hyades[2]
Vexed the dim sea. I am become a name;
For always roaming with a hungry heart
Much have I seen and known—cities of men
And manners, climates, councils, governments,

---

[1] A legendary Greek king of Ithaca and hero of Homer's *Odyssey*, Ulysses (or Odysseus) is noted for his daring and cunning. After his many adventures—including encounters with the Cyclops, the cannibalistic Laestrygones, and the enchantress Circe—Ulysses returned home to his faithful wife, Penelope. Tennyson portrays an older Ulysses pondering his situation.
[2] A group of stars whose rising was supposedly followed by rain, and hence stormy seas.

15 Myself not least, but honored of them all—
And drunk delight of battle with my peers,
Far on the ringing plains of windy Troy.[3]
I am a part of all that I have met;
Yet all experience is an arch wherethrough
20 Gleams that untraveled world whose margin fades
Forever and forever when I move.
How dull it is to pause, to make an end,
To rust unburnished, not to shine in use!
As though to breathe were life! Life piled on life
25 Were all too little, and of one to me
Little remains; but every hour is saved
From that eternal silence, something more,
A bringer of new things; and vile it were
For some three suns to store and hoard myself,
30 And this grey spirit yearning in desire
To follow knowledge like a sinking star,
Beyond the utmost bound of human thought.

    This is my son, mine own Telemachus,
To whom I leave the scepter and the isle—
35 Well-loved of me, discerning to fulfill
This labor, by slow prudence to make mild
A rugged people, and through soft degrees
Subdue them to the useful and the good.
Most blameless is he, centered in the sphere
40 Of common duties, decent not to fail
In offices of tenderness, and pay
Meet adoration to my household gods,
When I am gone. He works his work, I mine.

    There lies the port; the vessel puffs her sail;
45 There gloom the dark, broad seas. My mariners,
Souls that have toiled, and wrought, and thought with me—
That ever with a frolic welcome took
The thunder and the sunshine, and opposed
Free hearts, free foreheads—you and I are old;
50 Old age hath yet his honor and his toil.
Death closes all; but something ere the end,
Some work of noble note, may yet be done,
Not unbecoming men that strove with Gods.
The lights begin to twinkle from the rocks;
55 The long day wanes; the low moon climbs; the deep
Moans round with many voices. Come, my friends,

---

[3] An ancient city in Asia Minor. According to legend, Paris, King of Troy, abducted Helen, initiating the famed Trojan War, in which numerous Greek heroes, including Ulysses, fought.

'Tis not too late to seek a newer world.
Push off, and sitting well in order smite
The sounding furrows; for my purpose holds
60 To sail beyond the sunset, and the baths
Of all the western stars, until I die.
It may be that the gulfs will wash us down;
It may be we shall touch the Happy Isles,[4]
And see the great Achilles,[5] whom we knew.
65 Though much is taken, much abides; and though
We are not now that strength which in old days
Moved earth and heaven, that which we are, we are—
One equal temper of heroic hearts,
Made weak by time and fate, but strong in will
70 To strive, to seek, to find, and not to yield.

◇   ◇   ◇

DYLAN THOMAS
(1914–1953)

Fern Hill
(1946)

Now as I was young and easy under the apple boughs
About the lilting house and happy as the grass was green,
    The night above the dingle[1] starry,
        Time let me hail and climb
5   Golden in the heydays of his eyes,
And honored among wagons I was prince of the apple towns
And once below a time I lordly had the trees and leaves
            Trail with daisies and barley
        Down the rivers of the windfall light.

10 And as I was green and carefree, famous among the barns
About the happy yard and singing as the farm was home,
    In the sun that is young once only,
        Time let me play and be
        Golden in the mercy of his means,
15 And green and golden I was huntsman and herdsman, the calves
Sang to my horn, the foxes on the hills barked clear and cold,
            And the sabbath rang slowly
        In the pebbles of the holy streams.

---

[4] Elysium, or Paradise, believed to be in the far western ocean.
[5] Famed Greek hero of the Trojan War.

---

[1] Wooded valley.

All the sun long it was running, it was lovely, the hay
20 Fields high as the house, the tunes from the chimneys, it was air
    And playing, lovely and watery
        And fire green as grass.
    And nightly under the simple stars
    As I rode to sleep the owls were bearing the farm away,
25 All the moon long I heard, blessed among stables, the nightjars
    Flying with the ricks, and the horses
        Flashing into the dark.

And then to awake, and the farm, like a wanderer white
With the dew, come back, the cock on his shoulder: it was all
30   Shining, it was Adam and maiden,
        The sky gathered again
    And the sun grew round that very day.
So it must have been after the birth of the simple light
In the first, spinning place, the spellbound horses walking warm
35   Out of the whinnying green stable
        On to the fields of praise.

And honored among foxes and pheasants by the gay house
Under the new made clouds and happy as the heart was long,
    In the sun born over and over,
40   I ran my heedless ways,
    My wishes raced through the house high hay
And nothing I cared, at my sky blue trades, that time allows
    In all his tuneful turning so few and such morning songs
    Before the children green and golden
45   Follow him out of grace,

Nothing I cared, in the lamb white days, that time would take me
Up to the swallow thronged loft by the shadow of my hand,
    In the moon that is always rising,
        Nor that riding to sleep
50   I should hear him fly with the high fields
And wake to the farm forever fled from the childless land.
Oh as I was young and easy in the mercy of his means,
    Time held me green and dying
    Though I sang in my chains like the sea.

◊ ◊ ◊

GINA VALDES
(1943–   )

My Mother Sews Blouses
(1986)

My mother sews blouses
for a dollar a piece.
They must be working on
black cloth again, I see
5 her fingers sliding on her eyelids.

Six months ago she went
to the old oculist, the
one who "knows all about
eyes," who turned her
10 eyelids inside out and
scraped them with a tiny
knife to get the black
lint out.

Her eyes were bright and
15 clear for a few months.
She's blinking now,
talking about night
school.

◊ ◊ ◊

MARGARET WALKER
(1915–   )

Lineage
(1942)

My grandmothers were strong.
They followed plows and bent to toil.
They moved through fields sowing seed.
They touched earth and grain grew.
5 They were full of sturdiness and singing.
My grandmothers were strong.

My grandmothers are full of memories
Smelling of soap and onions and wet clay
With veins rolling roughly over quick hands
10 They have many clean words to say.
My grandmothers were strong.
Why am I not as they?

◊ ◊ ◊

EDMUND WALLER
(1606–1687)

Go, Lovely Rose
(1645)

Go, lovely rose,
Tell her that wastes her time and me
That now she knows,
When I resemble her to thee,
5 How sweet and fair she seems to be.

Tell her that's young
And shuns to have her graces spied,
That hadst thou sprung
In deserts where no men abide,
10 Thou must have uncommended died.

Small is the worth
Of beauty from the light retired:
Bid her come forth,
Suffer herself to be desired,
15 And not blush so to be admired.

Then die, that she
The common fate of all things rare
May read in thee,
How small a part of time they share
20 That are so wondrous sweet and fair.

◊ ◊ ◊

JAMES WELCH
(1940–   )

The Man from Washington
(1976)

The end came easy for most of us.
Packed away in our crude beginnings
in some far corner of a flat world,
we didn't expect much more
5 than firewood and buffalo robes
to keep us warm. The man came down,
a slouching dwarf with rainwater eyes,

and spoke to us. He promised
that life would go on as usual,
10 that treaties would be signed, and everyone—
man, woman and child—would be inoculated
against a world in which we had no part,
a world of money, promise and disease.

◊ ◊ ◊

PHILLIS WHEATLEY
(1754–1784)

On Being Brought from Africa to America
(1773)

'Twas mercy brought me from my *Pagan* land,
Taught my benighted soul to understand
That there's a God, that there's a *Saviour* too:
Once I redemption neither sought nor knew.
5 Some view our sable race with scornful eye,
"Their colour is a diabolic die."
Remember, *Christians, Negroes,* black as *Cain,*
May be refin'd, and join th' angelic train.

◊ ◊ ◊

WALT WHITMAN
(1819–1892)

A Noiseless Patient Spider
(1881)

A noiseless patient spider,
I mark'd where on a little promontory it stood isolated,
Mark'd how to explore the vacant vast surrounding,
It launch'd forth filament, filament, filament, out of itself,
5 Ever unreeling them, ever tirelessly speeding them.

And you O my soul where you stand,
Surrounded, detached, in measureless oceans of space,
Ceaselessly musing, venturing, throwing, seeking the spheres to
connect them,
Till the bridge you will need be form'd, till the ductile anchor hold,
10 Till the gossamer thread you fling catch somewhere, O my soul.

from "Song of Myself"
(1855)

1

I celebrate myself, and sing myself,
And what I assume you shall assume,
For every atom belonging to me as good belongs to you.

I loafe and invite my soul,
5 I lean and loafe at my ease observing a spear of summer grass.

My tongue, every atom of my blood, form'd from this soil, this air,
Born here of parents born here from parents the same, and their
     parents the same,
I, now thirty-seven years old in perfect health begin,
Hoping to cease not till death.

10 Creeds and schools in abeyance,
Retiring back a while sufficed at what they are, but never forgotten,
I harbor for good or bad, I permit to speak at every hazard,
Nature without check with original energy.

2

Houses and rooms are full of perfumes, the shelves are crowded with
     perfumes,
15 I breathe the fragrance myself and know it and like it,
The distillation would intoxicate me also, but I shall not let it.

The atmosphere is not a perfume, it has no taste of the distillation,
     it is odorless,
It is for my mouth forever, I am in love with it,
I will go to the bank by the wood and become undisguised and naked,
20 I am mad for it to be in contact with me.

The smoke of my own breath,
Echoes, ripples, buzz'd whispers, love-root, silk-thread, crotch and
     vine,
My respiration and inspiration, the beating of my heart, the passing
     of blood and air through my lungs,
The sniff of green leaves and dry leaves, and of the shore and dark-
     color'd sea-rocks, and of hay in the barn,
25 The sound of the belch'd words of my voice loos'd to the eddies of
     the wind,
A few light kisses, a few embraces, a reaching around of arms,
The play of shine and shade on the trees as the supple boughs wag,
The delight alone or in the rush of the streets, or along the fields and
     hill-sides,

The feeling of health, the full-noon trill, the song of me rising from
    bed and meeting the sun.

30 Have you reckon'd a thousand acres much? have you reckon'd the
    earth much?
Have you practis'd so long to learn to read?
Have you felt so proud to get at the meaning of poems?

Stop this day and night with me and you shall possess the origin of
    all poems,
You shall possess the good of the earth and sun, (there are millions
    of suns left,)
35 You shall no longer take things at second or third hand, nor look
    through the eyes of the dead, nor feed on the spectres in books,
You shall not look through my eyes either, nor take things from me,
You shall listen to all sides and filter them from your self.

◇ ◇ ◇

WILLIAM CARLOS WILLIAMS
(1883–1963)

The Dance
(1944)

    In Breughel's[1] great picture, The Kermess,[2]
    the dancers go round, they go round and
    around, the squeal and the blare and the
    tweedle of bagpipes, a bugle and fiddles
  5 tipping their bellies (round as the thick-
    sided glasses whose wash they impound)
    their hips and their bellies off balance
    to turn them. Kicking and rolling about
    the Fair Grounds, swinging their butts, those
 10 shanks must be sound to bear up under such
    rollicking measures, prance as the dance
    in Breughel's great picture, The Kermess.

---

[1] Refers to the Flemish painter Peter Breughel (1525–1569).
[2] The Church Mass; Breughel's painting (1567) of peasants dancing at a church
festival.

WILLIAM WORDSWORTH
(1770–1850)

Composed upon Westminster Bridge, September 3, 1802
(1807)

Earth has not anything to show more fair:
Dull would he be of soul who could pass by
A sight so touching in its majesty:
This City now doth, like a garment, wear
5 The beauty of the morning; silent, bare,
Ships, towers, domes, theatres, and temples lie
Open unto the fields, and to the sky;
All bright and glittering in the smokeless air.
Never did sun more beautifully steep
10 In his first splendor, valley, rock, or hill;
Ne'er saw I, never felt, a calm so deep!
The river glideth at his own sweet will:
Dear God! the very houses seem asleep;
And all that mighty heart is lying still!

I Wandered Lonely as a Cloud
(1807)

I wandered lonely as a cloud
    That floats on high o'er vales and hills,
When all at once I saw a crowd,
    A host, of golden daffodils,
5 Beside the lake, beneath the trees,
Fluttering and dancing in the breeze.

Continuous as the stars that shine
    And twinkle on the milky way,
They stretched in never-ending line
10   Along the margin of a bay:
Ten thousand saw I at a glance,
Tossing their heads in sprightly dance.

The waves beside them danced; but they
    Out-did the sparkling waves in glee;
15 A poet could not but be gay,
    In such a jocund company;
I gazed—and gazed—but little thought
What wealth the show to me had brought:

For oft, when on my couch I lie
20   In vacant or in pensive mood,
They flash upon that inward eye
    Which is the bliss of solitude;
And then my heart with pleasure fills,
And dances with the daffodils.

My Heart Leaps Up
When I Behold
(1807)

My heart leaps up when I behold
    A rainbow in the sky:
So was it when my life began;
So is it now I am a man;
5 So be it when I shall grow old,
    Or let me die!
The Child is father of the Man;
And I could wish my days to be
Bound each to each by natural piety.

She Dwelt among the
Untrodden Ways
(1800)

She dwelt among the untrodden ways
    Beside the springs of Dove,[1]
A Maid whom there were none to praise
    And very few to love:

5 A violet by a mossy stone
    Half hidden from the eye!
—Fair as a star, when only one
    Is shining in the sky.

She lived unknown, and few could know
10   When Lucy ceased to be;
But she is in her grave, and, oh,
    The difference to me!

---

[1] River in the Lake District of England.

The Solitary Reaper[1]
(1807)

Behold her, single in the field,
Yon solitary Highland lass!
Reaping and singing by herself;
Stop here, or gently pass!
5 Alone she cuts and binds the grain,
And sings a melancholy strain;
O listen! for the vale profound
Is overflowing with the sound.

No nightingale did ever chaunt
10 More welcome notes to weary bands
Of travelers in some shady haunt
Among Arabian sands.
A voice so thrilling ne'er was heard
In springtime from the cuckoo-bird,
15 Breaking the silence of the seas
Among the farthest Hebrides.[2]

Will no one tell me what she sings?—
Perhaps the plaintive numbers flow
For old, unhappy, far-off things,
20 And battles long ago.
Or is it some more humble lay,
Familiar matter of today?
Some natural sorrow, loss, or pain,
That has been, and may be again?

25 Whate'er the theme, the maiden sang
As if her song could have no ending;
I saw her singing at her work,
And o'er the sickle[3] bending—
I listened, motionless and still;
30 And, as I mounted up the hill,
The music in my heart I bore
Long after it was heard no more.

---

[1] A person who harvests grain.
[2] A group of islands off the west coast of Scotland.
[3] A curved blade used for harvesting grain or cutting grass.

◆ ◆ ◆

JAMES WRIGHT
(1927–1980)

A Blessing
(1961)

Just off the highway to Rochester, Minnesota,
Twilight bounds softly forth on the grass.
And the eyes of those two Indian ponies
Darken with kindness.
5 They have come gladly out of the willows
To welcome my friend and me.
We step over the barbed wire into the pasture
Where they have been grazing all day, alone.
They ripple tensely, they can hardly contain their happiness
10 That we have come.
They bow shyly as wet swans. They love each other.
There is no loneliness like theirs.
At home once more,
They begin munching the young tufts of spring in the darkness.
15 I would like to hold the slenderer one in my arms,
For she has walked over to me
And nuzzled my left hand.
She is black and white,
Her mane falls wild on her forehead,
20 And the light breeze moves me to caress her long ear
That is delicate as the skin over a girl's wrist.
Suddenly I realize
That if I stepped out of my body I would break
Into blossom.

◆ ◆ ◆

WILLIAM BUTLER YEATS
(1865–1939)

Crazy Jane Talks with the Bishop
(1933)

I met the Bishop on the road
And much said he and I.
"Those breasts are flat and fallen now,
Those veins must soon be dry;
5 Live in a heavenly mansion,
Not in some foul sty."

"Fair and foul are near of kin,
And fair needs foul," I cried.
"My friends are gone, but that's a truth
10 Nor grave nor bed denied,
Learned in bodily lowliness
And in the heart's pride.

"A woman can be proud and stiff
When on love intent;
15 But Love has pitched his mansion in
The place of excrement;
For nothing can be sole or whole
That has not been rent."

The Lake Isle of Innisfree
(1892)

I will arise and go now, and go to Innisfree,[1]
And a small cabin build there, of clay and wattles[2] made:
Nine bean-rows will I have there, a hive for the honey-bee,
And live alone in the bee-loud glade.

5 And I shall have some peace there, for peace comes dropping slow,
Dropping from the veils of the morning to where the cricket sings;
There midnight's all a glimmer, and noon a purple glow,
And evening full of the linnet's wings.

I will arise and go now, for always night and day
10 I hear lake water lapping with low sounds by the shore;
While I stand on the roadway, or on the pavements grey,
I hear it in the deep heart's core.

Sailing to Byzantium
(1927)

That is no country for old men. The young
In one another's arms, birds in the trees
—Those dying generations—at their song,
The salmon-falls, the mackerel-crowded seas,
5 Fish, flesh, or fowl, commend all summer long
Whatever is begotten, born, and dies.
Caught in that sensual music all neglect
Monuments of unaging intellect.

---

[1] An island in Lough (Lake) Gill, County Sligo, in Ireland.
[2] Stakes interwoven with twigs or branches, used for walls and roofing.

An aged man is but a paltry thing,
10 A tattered coat upon a stick, unless
Soul clap its hands and sing, and louder sing
For every tatter in its mortal dress,
Nor is there singing school but studying
Monuments of its own magnificence;
15 And therefore I have sailed the seas and come
To the holy city of Byzantium.

O sages standing in God's holy fire
As in the gold mosaic of a wall,
Come from the holy fire, perne in a gyre,
20 And be the singing-masters of my soul.
Consume my heart away; sick with desire
And fastened to a dying animal
It knows not what it is; and gather me
Into the artifice of eternity.

25 Once out of nature I shall never take
My bodily form from any natural thing,
But such a form as Grecian goldsmiths make
Of hammered gold and gold enameling
To keep a drowsy Emperor awake;
30 Or set upon a golden bough to sing
To lords and ladies of Byzantium
Of what is past, or passing, or to come.

The Second Coming[1]
(1921)

Turning and turning in the widening gyre[2]
The falcon cannot hear the falconer;
Things fall apart; the center cannot hold;
Mere anarchy is loosed upon the world,
5 The blood-dimmed tide is loosed, and everywhere
The ceremony of innocence is drowned;
The best lack all conviction, while the worst
Are full of passionate intensity.[3]

---

[1] The Second Coming usually refers to the return of Christ. Yeats theorized cycles of history, much like the turning of a wheel. Here he offers a poetic comment on his view of the dissolution of civilization at the end of one such cycle.

[2] Spiral.

[3] Lines 4–8 refer to the Russian Revolution (1917).

Surely some revelation is at hand;
10 Surely the Second Coming is at hand;
The Second Coming! Hardly are those words out
When a vast image out of *Spiritus Mundi*[4]
Troubles my sight: somewhere in sands of the desert
A shape with lion body and the head of a man,
15 A gaze blank and pitiless as the sun,
Is moving its slow thighs, while all about it
Reel shadows of the indignant desert birds.
The darkness drops again; but now I know
That twenty centuries[5] of stony sleep
20 Were vexed to nightmare by a rocking cradle,
And what rough beast, its hour come round at last,
Slouches towards Bethlehem to be born?

---

[4] The Spirit of the World. Yeats believed all souls to be connected by a "Great Memory."

[5] The centuries since the birth of Christ.

An Album of Fifty Poets

◆ **MAYA ANGELOU** (1928–   ), born Marguerite Johnson in St. Louis, lived with her grandmother in Stamps, Arkansas, where she graduated from Lafayette County Training School. She has worked as a cook, streetcar conductor, screenwriter, singer, dancer, and actress. *I Know Why the Caged Bird Sings* (1970) and *Gather Together in My Name* (1974) include accounts of her rape at seven and her struggle for self-esteem in a hostile society. Professor of American Studies at Wake Forest University (Winston-Salem, North Carolina), Angelou has been nominated for the National Book Award (for *I Know Why the Caged Bird Sings*) and the Pulitzer Prize (for *Just Give Me a Cool Drink of Water 'Fore I Diiie*, 1974). She won an Emmy for her role in *Roots* (1977) and a Grammy for an album of her poem "On the Pulse of Morning," which she read at the 1993 inauguration of President Bill Clinton. Critic Carol E. Neubauer notes that "through all of her verse, Angelou reaches out to touch the lives of others and to offer them hope and confidence in place of humiliation and despair." Angelou summarizes her work in this way: "I speak to the black experience, but I am always talking about the human condition—about what we can endure, dream, fail at, and still survive."

◆ **MARGARET ATWOOD** (1939–   ) was born in Ottawa, Canada, and grew up in Toronto. She received her bachelor's degree from the University of Toronto and her master's from Radcliffe. Following her first book of poetry, *Double Persephone* (1962), she published *The Circle Game* (1966), winner of Canada's highest literary honor, the Governor General's Award. She has gained even greater prominence with novels—*The Handmaid's Tale* (1985, which was made into a movie), *Cat's Eye* (1988), and *The Robber Bride*

(1993); as well as, other volumes of poetry, short stories, critical essays, radio and television scripts, and children's books. She teaches at the University of British Columbia at Vancouver. Critic Carolyn Allen compares her to feminist writers Marge Piercy, Alice Munro, and Adrienne Rich, noting that "Atwood's increasingly unmistakable voice comes in part from her willingness to create women who attempt transformations and almost—but not quite—become trees, roots, foxes. By failing to change themselves into what they cannot be, they become instead what they most truly are." As Atwood has explained in an interview with critic Linda Sandler, "You can't write poetry unless you're willing to immerse yourself in language—not just in words, but in words of a certain potency. It's like learning a foreign language."

◈ **W(ystan) H(ugh) Auden** (1907–1973), son of an English physician, earned a scholarship to Oxford University, where he studied T. S. Eliot's poetry. He and his writer friends—Stephen Spender, Cecil Day-Lewis, Christopher Isherwood, and Louis MacNeice (called "The Auden Generation") exerted a considerable influence on modern literature. Auden left England in 1939 and became an American citizen in 1946. Among his many works probing the mysteries of religion, psychology, and politics are *The Double Man* (1941); *The Age of Anxiety*, winner of the Pulitzer Prize (1947); and *The Shield of Achilles*, winner of the National Book Award (1956). Seamus Heaney, noted critic and Nobel Prize-winning poet, has described Auden as "an epoch-making poet on public themes, the register of a new sensibility, a great sonneteer, a writer of perfect light verse, a prospector of literature at its most illiterate roots and a dandy of lexicography at its most extravagant reaches." As Auden commented in a 1971 interview with Daniel Halpern, "Truth in poetry is very important to me. I think you must feel, when you read a poem, that it says something about life which you recognize to be true."

◈ **Gwendolyn Brooks** (1917–   ) currently poet Laureate of Illinois, was, in 1950, the first African-American to win a Pulitzer Prize (for her second book of poems, *Annie Allen*). Born in Topeka, Kansas, Brooks was raised in a section of Chicago called "Bronzeville," which provided the setting for her first published poetry collection, *A Street in Bronzeville* (1945). Other collections include *The Bean Eaters* (1960), *In the Mecca* (1968), and *The World of Gwendolyn Brooks* (1971). Brooks has also published a novel, *Maud Martha* (1953), and *Report from Part One: An Autobiography* (1972).

In a review of *Annie Allen,* Langston Hughes, prominent poet of the Harlem Renaissance, noted that "the people and the poems in Gwendolyn Brooks's book are alive, reaching and very much of today." Brooks's desire to reach all African-American people is revealed in a 1974 interview in which she explained that she wanted "to develop a style that will appeal to black people in taverns, black people in gutters, schools, offices, factories, prisons, the consulate; I wish to reach black people in pulpits, black people in mines, on farms, on thrones."

◊ **RAYMOND CARVER** (1938–1988), born in Clatskanie, Oregon, and raised in Yakima, Washington, was inspired to become a writer as he listened to his father's stories. In 1963 Carver received a B.A. degree in creative writing at Humboldt State College (now California State University, Humboldt), and the University of Iowa (M.F.A., 1966). Recognized as an important innovator of minimalist fiction, he often wrote about poor working people in his native Pacific Northwest region. His short story "Will You Please Be Quiet, Please?" appeared in *The Best American Short Stories of 1967;* and his short-story collection *Cathedral* (1984) received Pulitzer Prize and National Book Critics Circle Award nominations. Among his works of poetry are his first book, *Near Klamath* (1968), and his posthumous collection, *A New Path to the Waterfall* (1989). According to critic Ted Solotaroff, Carver has "the kind of gift that travels: the common touch raised to the next power, the power of art, that can be conveyed intact to his readers and bring out [. . .] the giftedness in them [. . .]." In a *Paris Review* interview Carver stated that the writer must "be immensely daring, very skilled and imaginative and willing to tell everything on yourself. [. . .] What do you know better than your own secrets?"

◊ **LUCILLE CLIFTON** (1936–   ), born in Depew, New York, attended Howard University and graduated from Fredonia State Teachers College. She recalls her childhood fondly, especially listening to her parents' poems and stories. Named the Poet Laureate of Maryland, Clifton has been nominated for the Pulitzer Prize and has won two National Endowment for the Arts grants (1969, 1973). The *New York Times* named her book *Good Times* one of the best of 1969. Her more recent poetry collections include *Quilting: Poems 1987–1990* (1991), *The Book of Light* (1993), and *Blessing the Boats: New and*

Selected Poems 1988–2000 (forthcoming, 2000). Among her many children's books are the popular Everett Anderson series and *The Palm of My Heart: Poetry by African American Children* (1996). Critic Haki Madhubti has called Clifton "a poet of *mean* talent who has not let her gifts separate her from the work at hand. She is a teacher and an example. To read her is to give birth to bright seasons." Clifton has described her style as follows: "I use a simple language. [. . .] I am not interested if anyone knows whether or not I am familiar with big words; I am interested in trying to render big ideas in a simple way. I am interested in being understood, not admired. I wish to celebrate and not be celebrated."

◆ **E(DWARD) E(STLIN) CUMMINGS** (1894–1962), born in Cambridge, Massachusetts, completed his undergraduate and graduate degrees at Harvard. He served as an ambulance driver during World War I and then spent several years studying art in Paris. *Tulips and Chimneys* (1923), his first book of poems, received both praise and criticism for its idiosyncratic capitalization (such as using only lowercase letters in his name), diction, punctuation, and typography. The publication of his *Complete Poems: 1904–1962* (1994), a collection of his twelve volumes of verse, affirms his lasting literary reputation. Although best known as an experimental poet, the versatile Cummings was also a talented painter, prose writer, translator, and playwright. He won two Guggenheim fellowships (1933, 1951), a special citation from the National Book Awards (1955), and the Bollingen Prize in Poetry (1957). According to critic Malcolm Cowley, Cummings "suffers from comparison with those who built on a larger scale [. . .] but still he is unsurpassed in his field." Noted poet Randall Jarrell has concluded, "No one else [. . .] has ever made avant-garde, experimental poems so attractive to the general and special reader."

◆ **EMILY DICKINSON** (1830–1886), born into a prominent Amherst, Massachusetts, family, attended Amherst Academy and Mount Holyoke Female Seminary. She rarely left her hometown, and after 1862, she seldom left her home. In her lifetime, Dickinson published anonymously only seven of her poems, and most of these had been edited to make them more conventional. In 1955 Thomas H. Johnson edited the definitive Dickinson canon of 1,775 poems. He attributes her obscurity during the nineteenth century to her experimentation "in meters, rhyme, capitals, grammar, and punctuation." Noted writer Joyce Carol Oates calls her "the most paradoxical of poets" because, despite "the extraordinary intimacy of her poetry," her voice has "a tone of the purest anonymity." Oates considers Dickinson a "poet of the soul"—indeed, "our most endlessly fascinating American poet." Fascinating, indeed, is the way Dickinson saw poetry as a moment of great intensity. As she told her literary adviser Thomas Wentworth Higginson, "If I read a book and it makes my whole body so cold no fire can warm me, I know *that* is poetry. If I feel physically as if the top of my head were taken off, I know *that* is poetry."

◈ **RITA DOVE** (1952–   ), born and raised in Akron, Ohio, earned her bachelor's degree at Miami University of Ohio in 1973, studied in Germany on a Fulbright scholarship in 1974, and then did graduate work at the University of Iowa Writers' Workshop. In 1993 she became the first African-American, the second woman, and the youngest person named Poet Laureate of the United States; she also served as Consultant in Poetry at the Library of Congress. She presently teaches at the University of Virginia. Her volumes of poetry include *The Yellow House on the Corner* (1980); *Thomas and Beulah*, winner of the 1987 Pulitzer Prize; *Grace Notes: Poems* (1991); and *On the Bus with Rosa Parks: Poems* (1999). Critic Arnold Rampersad has observed that Dove's brilliance is reinforced by extensive reading, yet when she writes of the "black experience," it is "in the course of 'ordinary' things" and situations "almost always very close to the poet's private experience, part of her personal and family history[. . .]." As Dove has explained, her themes transcend racial boundaries: "Obviously, as a black woman, I am concerned with race. [. . .] But certainly not every poem of mine mentions the fact of being black. They are poems about humanity, and sometimes humanity happens to be black."

◈ **T(HOMAS) S(TEARNS) ELIOT** (1888–1965), born in St. Louis, received his undergraduate, master's, and doctoral degrees from Harvard. Then he emigrated to London, where he worked as a bank clerk and book editor. In 1927 he became a British citizen and declared himself an "Anglo-Catholic in religion, royalist in politics, and classicist in literature." He won prestigious professorships at Cambridge and Harvard, the Nobel Prize for Literature (1948), the British Order of Merit, the Emerson-Thoreau Medal from the American Academy of Arts and Sciences (1959), and the U.S. Medal of Freedom (1964). His best-known works of poetry include "The Love Song of J. Alfred Prufrock" (1917), *The Waste Land* (1922), *The Four Quartets*

(1943), and *Old Possum's Book of Practical Cats* (1939), the basis for the long-running musical *Cats*. His friend Ezra Pound, upon reading the manuscript of *The Waste Land,* suggested revisions but immediately recognized it as a work of genius, saying that Eliot's poem was enough "to make the rest of us shut up shop." To those who called this work social criticism, Eliot modestly replied that it was merely "the relief of a personal and wholly insignificant grouse against life [. . .] just a piece of rhythmical grumbling."

◊ **Louise Erdrich** (1954–   ), born in Little Falls, Minnesota, to a German-American father and a Chippewa mother, is a member of the Turtle Mountain Band of the Chippewa people. She graduated from Dartmouth College (B.A., 1976) and Johns Hopkins University (M.A., 1977). Her first novel, *Love Medicine* (1984), winner of the National Book Critics Circle Award, begins a saga that also includes *The Beet Queen* (1986), *Tracks* (1988), and *The Bingo Palace* (1994). Recent works are the nonfiction *The Blue Jay's Dance: A Birth Year* (1995), the novel *The Antelope Wife* (1998), and the children's book *The Birchbark House* (1999). Erdrich credits her family for teaching her to tell stories about strong females: "Everybody in my family is a storyteller . . . whether a liar or a storyteller—whatever." She recalls her father giving her a nickel for each story she wrote and her mother stapling them into book cover—"At an early age I felt myself to be a published author earning substantial royalties." Critic Carolyne Wright praises *Jacklight,* Erdrich's first volume of poetry, for its use of family and tribal history and for attaining "the enduring and universal via the minute particulars of individual and community experience [which] has been a stated aim of poetry written in English since Wordsworth's Preface to the *Lyrical Ballads.*"

◊ **Lawrence Ferlinghetti** (1919–   ), born in Yonkers, New York, and raised in France, attended the University of North Carolina at Chapel Hill, Columbia University, and the Sorbonne. This most scholarly writer of the 1950s Beat Generation began his literary career as a book reviewer for the San Francisco *Chronicle* and as a writer for Peter Martin's *City Lights*. In 1953 Martin and he established the avant-garde bookstore City Lights, which published his first book of poetry, *Pictures of the Gone World* (1955). In 1956 police arrested him for obscenity because he published Allen Ginsberg's controversial *Howl.* Ironically, the national publicity generated from this arrest helped to make a bestseller of Ferlinghetti's *A Coney Island of the Mind: Poems* (1958). Ginsberg has stated that Ferlinghetti "ought to receive some sort of Pulitzer Prize" for publishing so many important anti-establishment writers. *European Poems and Transitions: Over All the Obscene Boundaries* (1988) and *These Are My Rivers: New and Selected Poems 1955–1993* (1993) are among his more recent works. Ferlinghetti has expressed his belief in an ideal community, transcending nationalism: "Under it all, after all, all colors of skin at length blended into one skin with one tongue."

◇ **ROBERT FROST** (1874–1963) moved to New England from his birthplace of San Francisco and attended Dartmouth College and Harvard without taking a degree. In 1900 he settled on a New Hampshire dairy farm, writing many of his works there. Twenty years later he helped to establish the Bread Loaf School of English at Middlebury College, Vermont. Frost enjoyed enormous popularity as a revered poet, receiving honorary degrees from prestigious universities and winning major prizes, including the Pulitzer for *New Hampshire, Collected Poems, A Further Range,* and *Witness Tree.* He became the unofficial poet laureate of America when he was named Consultant in Poetry for the Library of Congress. In 1961 at the inauguration of President John F. Kennedy he recited from memory his poem "The Gift Outright," because poor eyesight at age eighty-seven prevented him from reading. "Stopping by Woods on a Snowy Evening," observes critic Donald J. Greiner, "has immortality written all over it" and "deserves its place alongside the many novels and stories that ponder the fate of those who dare to plunge beyond the safety of the clearing to the darkness of the woods." Frost himself, in a letter to poet-critic Louis Untermeyer in 1923, called this poem his "best bid for remembrance."

◇ **LOUISE GLÜCK** (1943–   ), born in New York City, attended Sarah Lawrence College and Columbia University and then taught at the University of North Carolina at Greensboro, the University of Virginia, the University of Iowa, and the University of Cincinnati. Among her many awards and honors are Columbia University's Academy of American Poets Prize (1967), a Rockefeller Foundation grant (1968), a National Endowment for the Arts grant (1969–1970), and a Guggenheim Fellowship (1975–1976). Glück's first collection of poetry, *First Born,* appeared in 1968, followed in 1975 by *The House on Marshland,* which brought her national recognition. She won the American Academy Award in 1981 and the National Book Critics Circle Award in 1985 for *The Triumph of Achilles.* Her most recent collection is *Meadowlands* (1996). Critic Deno Trakis suggests that although the world of Glück's poems is "bleak"—portraying people "isolated from family, or bitter from rejected love, or disappointed with what life has to offer"—it is "depicted with a lyrical grace, and her poems are attractive if disturbing." Perhaps Glück's outlook on her career is expressed by her persona in "To Autumn": "I am no longer young. What / of it? Summer approaches and the long / decaying days of autumn when I shall begin / the great poems of my middle period."

◆ **H(ilda) D(oolittle)** (1886–1961), born in Bethlehem, Pennsylvania, attended Bryn Mawr College briefly. Her first love, Ezra Pound, considered her an "imagist" poet, a label she never escaped. During her five-decade-long literary career, H. D. wrote prodigiously but published modestly and diversely. Besides her poetry, she wrote translations, a screenplay, verse drama, short prose, autobiographical novels, and a children's novel. In 1916 she published her first book of poems, *Sea Garden,* followed by *Hymen* (1921), *Heliodora and Other Poems* (1924), and *Collected Poems of H. D.* (1924). In 1960 she received the Award of Merit Medal for Poetry from the American Academy of Arts and Letters. Not until after her death did her long poems surface and thus provide readers with insights from another perspective. Critic Susan Stanford Friedman considers H. D. "a major poet belonging both to the modernist mainstream and the tradition of women's writing"—indeed, a "poet's poet." Recounting her steady, disciplined routine of writing, H. D. told a friend in the 1920s, "I sit at my typewriter until I drop. I have, in some way, to justify my existence."

◆ **Thomas Hardy** (1840–1928), born in Dorsetshire, England, became a full-time writer after working as an architect in London. This most versatile writer published fourteen novels, eight volumes of poetry, four short-story collections, two plays, and a variety of essays, prefaces, and other nonfiction prose. His best-known novels are *Far from the Madding Crowd* (1874), *The Return of the Native* (1878), *The Mayor of Casterbridge* (1886), *Tess of the D'Urbervilles* (1891), and *Jude the Obscure* (1896). Recipient of many honors, Hardy became the last great Victorian poet in the early twentieth century. Poet John Crowe Ransom connected Hardy to the succeeding generation "by reason of his naturalism and rebellion against the dogma," and Ezra Pound, W. H. Auden, and D. H. Lawrence—prominent poets of this next generation—acknowledged Hardy's influence on them. Often called a pessimist, Hardy regarded himself instead as a "meliorist"— one who believes the world can be improved by human effort. In his preface to *Late Lyrics and Earlier* (1922), Hardy wrote that pain "shall be kept down to a minimum by loving kindness, operating through scientific knowledge, and actuated by the modicum of free will [. . .]."

◆ **ROBERT HAYDEN** (1913–1980), born Asa Bundy Sheffey in Detroit, was renamed by his adoptive parents. Following his studies at Detroit City College (now Wayne State University) and the University of Michigan, Hayden taught at Fisk University and the University of Michigan. He published four significant volumes of poetry and in 1966 gained international recognition by winning the Grand Prize for Poetry in English at the First World Festival of Negro Arts in Dakar, Senegal, for *A Ballad of Remembrance*. Elected in 1975 to the Academy of American Poets, Hayden became the first African-American appointed Poetry Consultant at the Library of Congress (1976). His *Collected Poems,* reissued in 1995 with an introduction by noted scholar Arnold Rampersad, reaffirms his literary reputation. Critic Wilbur Williams notes that "Hayden's characteristically soft-spoken and fluid voice derives much of its power from the evident contrast between the maelstrom of anguish [from] which it originates and the quiet reflecting pool of talk into which it is inevitably channeled." Hayden has stated that he experiments with new forms and techniques "to arrive at something really my own, something patterned, wild, and free."

◆ **SEAMUS HEANEY** (1939–   ) comes from a Roman Catholic family in the predominantly Protestant town of Mossbawn, County Derry, Northern Ireland. After attending Queen's University, Belfast, and St. Joseph's College of Education, he left Northern Ireland in 1972 and eventually settled in Dublin in the Irish Republic. This influential contemporary Irish poet has received most of the literary prizes awarded in Ireland and England as well as the 1995 Nobel Prize in Literature—the third Irish writer to receive this award, joining W. B. Yeats (1923) and Samuel Beckett (1969). Heaney's translation of *Beowulf* was awarded the 1999 Whitbread Prize for Poetry and was dedicated to his friend, British poet Ted Hughes. Heaney's works include *Crediting Poetry: The Nobel Lecture* (1996) and *Open Ground: Selected Poems 1966–1996* (1998). Heaney's poetry, William Grimes observes, "is rooted in the Irish soil [. . .] as though Ireland's wet peat were a storehouse of images and memories. At the same time [he] moves easily from the homely images of farm and village to larger issues of history, language, and national identity." Nobel Prize-winning poet Derek Walcott calls Heaney "the guardian spirit of Irish poetry." Heaney metaphorically depicts the hard, patient work of poetry in "Digging," the first poem in his first book, *Death of a Naturalist* (1966): "Between my fingers and my thumb / The squat pen rests. / I'll dig with it."

◊ **GERARD MANLEY HOPKINS** (1844–1889), born into a cultivated London family, attended Oxford, where the renowned aesthetic critic Walter Pater and the Anglican High Church movement leader Cardinal John Henry Newman influenced him. As a result, Hopkins converted to Roman Catholicism and became a Jesuit priest. His long poem *The Wreck of the Deutschland* appeared in 1875; his shorter, more accessible nature poems came out in 1918. "The Windhover," his most famous sonnet with a typically religious theme, explores ways to praise, revere, and serve God. Hopkins is best known for his unusual metrical system, which he named "sprung rhythm." Stylistically, his poems boldly experiment with imagery, syntax, and rhythm. Thematically, they connect nature and Christianity with passionate, sometimes anguished, intensity. Critic Jerome Bump has suggested that because of this "idiosyncratic creativity" making Hopkins's style "so radically different from that of his contemporaries," his best work appeared only after his death, when readers then fully recognized his achievements. Hopkins believed that nature, like the Bible, offers moral instruction: "This world is word, expression, news of God" and "it is a book he has written [. . .] a poem of beauty [. . .]."

◊ **A(LFRED) E(DWARD) HOUSMAN** (1859–1936), born in Shropshire, England, studied at Oxford but did not graduate. After establishing himself as an independent Latin scholar, he won in 1911 an appointment as Professor of Latin at Cambridge, where he spent the rest of his life. He refused numerous honors, including the prestigious Royal Order of Merit because, according to critic William G. Holzberger, "he would be condescended to by no one, not even by the King." Besides two slim volumes of poetry—*A Shropshire Lad* (1896) and *Last Poems* (1922)—he published a collection of criticism, *The Name and Nature of Poetry* (1933). Influenced by classical Greek and Latin lyrics as well as English ballads, his best works express melancholy over the brevity of youth, beauty, and love. Holzberger calls Housman's treatment of nature "basically romantic," yet not quite "romantic worship of nature"; he finds Housman to be classical "in terms of conciseness and economy of language, precision of form, and in the Epicurean stoicism [. . .]." Housman described the process of creating his poetry as one of intuition from inexplicable sources, such as the time he enjoyed an especially creative spell in 1895, which he called a period of "continuous excitement."

◊ **TED HUGHES** (1930–1998), born in Mytholmroyd, Yorkshire, England, served in the Royal Air Force and studied at Cambridge. In 1956 he married poet Sylvia Plath, who committed suicide shortly after they separated. Hughes served as Britain's poet laureate from 1984 until his death. Two-time winner of the prestigious Whitbread Book Award, Hughes uses symbolic, often violent animal imagery in works such as *The Hawk in the Rain* (1957), *Wolfwatching* (1991) and the series of Crow poems, published in five volumes (1970–1971). Nonetheless, this versatile poet, translator of classical writers, radio playwright, and short-story writer has often been shadowed by Plath's ghost. He edited her collected poems and journals— yet he destroyed her final journals, saying he did so for the sake of their children. Hughes responded to Plath's own mythologizing with his final work *Birthday Letters* (1998), chronicling their relationship from first seeing her in a photograph of Fulbright scholars to imagining a reunion for her sixtieth birthday. Reviewer Sarah Maguire praises this "stunning literary sensation," calling it a work "full of tenderness and anger, warmth and despair"; *New York Times* reviewer Michiko Kakutani concurs, finding this poetry collection Hughes's "strongest, most emotionally tactile work."

◊ **ROBERT LOWELL** (1917–1977) came from a famous Boston family that included distinguished poets James Russell Lowell and Amy Lowell. He studied at Harvard and then at Kenyon College, where well-known poet-critics John Crowe Ransom and Allen Tate influenced him. Besides serving as Consultant in Poetry to the Library of Congress, Lowell won acclaim with the Pulitzer Prize (1947) for *Lord Weary's Castle;* the National Book Award (1960) for his autobiographical *Life Studies;* and the Bollingen

Poetry Translation Prize (1962) for Racine's *Phaedra*. Critic Ashley Brown notes that in *For the Union Dead* (1964), personal emotion merges magnificently with public themes. In 1965 Lowell made a public statement of protest against America's involvement in Vietnam by rejecting President Lyndon Johnson's invitation to the White House Festival of the Arts. Lowell told novelist V. S. Naipaul in 1969 that America is "beyond any country, it's an empire. I feel very bitter about it, but pious, and baffled by it." Lowell's poetry covers a wide range of topics in history and personal experience, including his own recurring mental illness. In the Afterthought to *Notebook 1967–68*, Lowell has written that "in truth I seem to have felt mostly the joys of living; in remembering, in recording, thanks to the gift of the Muse, it is the pain."

◊ **Claude McKay** (1890–1948), born in Jamaica, received part of his education from a well-read older brother. Two early volumes of poetry won him an award and stipend from the Jamaican Institute of Arts and Sciences to study at the Tuskeegee Institute and at Kansas State College. In 1914 he traveled to New York City and his works *Harlem Shadows* (1922) and *Home to Harlem* (1927) established him as an important writer of the Harlem Renaissance. His best work is collected in *The Passion of Claude McKay: Selected Poetry and Prose, 1912–1948*. Written in traditional meter and rhyme, his poetry expresses powerful, compressed passion about topics that are both personal and social. His elegant control disguises his anger, as seen in his descriptions of the New York City that he both loved and hated. According to critic Arthur D. Prayton, "McKay does not seek to hide his bitterness, but having preserved his vision as a poet and his status as a human being, he can transcend bitterness." Something of this transcendence appears in McKay's "If We Must Die": "Like men will face the murderous, cowardly push. / Press to the wall, dying, but fighting back."

◊ **Janice Mirikitani** (1942–   ) was a third-generation Japanese-American, born in Stockton, California; however, with America's distrust of all Japanese people after the attack on Pearl Harbor, she and her family were imprisoned in an internment camp from 1942 to 1945. She attended the University of California at both Los Angeles and Berkeley. Inspired by a student strike for Asian-American and Ethnic Studies, she became an activist and editor. In 1970 she founded the first Asian-American literary journal, *Aion*. Mirikitani also edited *Ayumi: A Japanese-American Anthology* (1980) and *Making Waves: An Anthology of Writings by and about Asian-American Women* (1989). Her incarceration experience informs her own poetry and prose in *Awake in the River* (1978) and *Shedding the Silence* (1987). Critic Russell C. Leong credits her for enlightening readers to "Third World communities, cultures, and conflicts as transformed through the visions and writing of women." Inspired by her mother, who broke four decades of silence by testifying during the 1981–82 U.S. Congressional hearings about her wartime internment camp experiences, Mirikitani writes that her mother "called us to history, memory and an inner anger that gave us new voice to unearth injustices."

◊ **N(AVARRE) SCOTT MOMADAY** (1934–   ) was born in Lawton, Oklahoma, and studied at the University of New Mexico and Stanford University, where he received his Ph.D. in 1963. In 1969 he became the first Native American writer to win a Pulitzer Prize, which was awarded to his first novel, *House Made of Dawn* (1968). His autobiographical work *The Names: A Memoir* (1976) recounts his growing up in New Mexico. His other publications include volumes of poetry—*Angle of Geese and Other Poems* (1974) and *Gourd Dancer* (1976); and *The Way to Rainy Mountain* (1969), a collection of personal and historical narratives interwoven with tales from Kiowa mythology. He also wrote a novel, *The Ancient Child* (1989), and a collection of poems and narratives he has illustrated, *In the Presence of Sun* (1992). Critic Roger Dickinson-Brown has referred to Momaday's work as "a fusion of alien cultures and [. . .] extraordinary experiments in different literary forms." Momaday, who considers himself primarily a poet, has stated that he returns again and again to his Kiowa culture for inspiration because it has "a certain strength and beauty I find missing in the modern world."

◊ **MARIANNE MOORE** (1887–1972) was born in St. Louis and educated at Bryn Mawr. Having been a teacher of stenography and a librarian, she worked as an editor at *Dial*, an influential literary magazine from 1925 to 1929. Her Pulitzer Prize-winning *Collected Poems* (1951) was followed by more than a dozen volumes of poetry, all collected in her *Complete Poems* (1981). Famous for her originality of style and format, Moore composed elaborate poems with complex line lengths. She considers hundreds of apparent "curiosities" as her subjects, her most typical being strange animals. Poet James Dickey has praised the way she remakes "our world from particulars that we have never adequately understood on our own." John Ashberry, another well-known poet-critic, has considered her the greatest poet of her time, outranking contemporaries William Carlos Williams and Wallace Stevens—both established poets of "obvious grandeur." Her poetry deceptively resembles prose, yet it has a remarkably daring metaphorical quality. An often-quoted line from her work "Poetry" epitomizes what she says all poetry should be: "imaginary gardens with real toads in them."

◊ **Sharon Olds** (1942–   ), born in San Francisco, attended Stanford and Columbia, where she received her Ph.D. degree in 1972. Her poetry collections include *The Dead and the Living* (1983), winner of both the Lamont Poetry Award and the National Book Critics Circle Award; *The Gold Cell* (1987); *The Father* (1992); and *The Wellspring* (1995). She received major grants from New York state, the National Endowment for the Arts, and the Guggenheim Foundation. Because she so graphically details personal traumas, some critics place her in the confessional tradition of Sylvia Plath. However, Olds's poems have a less tormented tone and are more easily understood. She celebrates and explores family life, erotic experience, and feminist topics in her work. Moreover, her style combines grotesque humor and straightforward reporting in a manner that *Poetry* magazine critic Lisel Mueller has called "a proud, urgent human voice." This persona is well illustrated in these lines from Olds's poem "35/10," published just a few years after Olds turned thirty-five: "Brushing out my daughter's dark / silken hair before the mirror / I see the grey gleaming on my head, / [. . .] it's an old / story—the oldest we have on our planet— / the story of replacement."

◊ **Simon J. Ortiz** (1941–   ), son of a Native American potter from the Acoma Pueblo, was born in Albuquerque. He attended Ft. Lewis College, the University of New Mexico, and the University of Iowa in the 1960s; he served in the U.S. Army from 1963 to 1966. His poetry collections include *Naked in the Wind* (1971), *Going for the Rain* (1976), *From Sand Creek: Rising in This Heart Which Is Our America* (1981), *After and Before the Lightning* (1991), and *Woven Stone* (1992). Ortiz has edited *Earth Power Coming: Short Fiction in Native American Literature* (1983) and *Speaking for*

the Generations (1998), a collection which includes Leslie Marmon Silko's essay about Native American art and culture. Among the critics who have applauded his optimism for the survival of mankind and nature is Harold Jaffe, who finds his work "not of gloom and despair, but of a renewed faith in the prospect of relationship with the land and solidarity among the dispossessed." Reflecting on how his community and his homeland inform his writing, Ortiz has said, "I've tried to consider most importantly my life as a Native American who is absolutely related to the land and all that that means culturally, politically, personally."

◊ **WILDRED OWEN** (1893–1918) was born in Plas Wilmot, near Oswestry, Shropshire, England, where his father worked on the railway. Owen was educated at the Birkenhead Institute and the Shrewsbury Technical School. Unable to afford the University of London, he joined the army in 1915. After he was injured, he recuperated at a hospital near Edinburgh, where he wrote most of his poems. Owen returned to battle in France and won the Military Cross for bravery. He died one week before the Armistice, having published only five poems in periodicals. His friend and fellow World War I "trench poet" Siegfried Sassoon published Owen's *Poems* in 1920, another collection, with Edmund Blunden's memoir, appeared in 1931. *Collected Poems,* edited by Cecil Day-Lewis, was published in 1963. Owens's elegies for the war dead, such as "Arms and the Boy," "Anthem for Doomed Youth," and "Dulce Et Decorum Est" all graphically detail the horrors of war. According to S.R. Welland, Owen's work had a special influence on the 1930s poets, because it is "a powerfully realistic poetry of social protest charged with pity for human suffering." Owen has portrayed himself as "a conscientious objector with a very seared conscience," a label reflecting his intense hatred of war and his sympathy for its victims.

◊ **LINDA PASTAN** (1932–   ), born in the Bronx, New York, received her B.A. from Radcliffe College, her M.L.S. from Simmons College, and her M.A. from Brandeis University. Her publications include *A Perfect Circle of Sun* (1971); *On the Way to the Zoo* (1975); *Aspects of Eve* (1977); *The Five Stages of Grief* (1978), winner of the Poetry Society of America award; *PM/AM: New and Selected Poems* (1983), American Book Award nominee; *The Imperfect Paradise* (1988); *Heroes in Disguise* (1991); and *An Early Afterlife* (1995). She has received fellowships from the Bread Loaf Writers' Conference and the

National Endowment for the Arts. According to prominent feminist critic Sandra M. Gilbert, Pastan "broods on the rewards as well as the risks of domesticity" because she's "quite self-consciously a *woman* poet" who "austerely ordains the necessity of acquiescence in the ordinary." Pastan has explained how she writes poetry: "By allowing myself to follow a poem wherever it wants to take me, I find that I often stumble upon truths about myself, my world, that I scarcely suspected I knew"; she then compares the writing process to "following the thread through the labyrinth, trying at all costs to avoid the minotaur."

◊ **Marge Piercy** (1936–   ) grew up poor and white in a predominantly black neighborhood in Detroit. She received a bachelor's degree from the University of Michigan in 1957 and a master's degree from Northwestern University in 1958. Her publications include *Hard Loving* (1969), *Living in the Open* (1976), *Woman on the Edge of Time* (1976), *The Moon Is Always Female* (1980), *Parti-Colored Blocks for a Quilt: Poets on Poetry* (1982), *Circles on the Water* (1982), *Braided Lives* (1982), *My Mother's Body* (1985), and *The Longings of Women* (1994). She has received the Shaeffer-Eaton-PEN New England award (1989) and the Shalom Center award (1992). Her fifteenth volume of poetry, *The Art of Blessing the Day: Poems with a Jewish Theme* (1999), celebrates the traditions of her religion. Author Erica Jong has called the often-controversial Piercy "an immensely gifted poet and novelist whose range and versatility have made it hard for her talents to be adequately appreciated critically." Piercy has said that she wants her writing to be "useful" so "readers will find poems that speak to and for them, will take those poems into their lives and say them to each other and put them up on the bathroom wall and remember bits and pieces of them in stressful or quiet moments."

◊ **Sylvia Plath** (1932–1963) was born in Boston to Polish-German parents who taught at Boston University. She graduated from Smith College (1955) then won a Fulbright Fellowship to Cambridge University (M.A., 1957), where she met and married poet Ted Hughes. Having won a *Mademoiselle* magazine prize (1953), an award from *Poetry* magazine (1957), and a Yaddo writers' colony fellowship (1959), she began a promising career. After *A Winter Ship* came *The Colossus and Other Poems* (1962) and *The Bell Jar* (1963). Plath committed suicide at thirty-one, soon after her seven year marriage to Hughes ended. Posthumous works are *Ariel* (1965), *Crossing the*

Water (1971), *Winter Trees* (1971), *Letters Home by Sylvia Plath: Correspondence 1950–1963* (1975), *Johnny Panic and the Bible of Dreams and Other Prose Writings* and her *Collected Poems,* a 1982 Pulitzer Prize winner. In the introduction to *Ariel,* Robert Lowell has praised her as "one of those superreal, hypnotic, great classical heroines." In a 1958 journal entry, Plath had prophesied: "coming again to make and make in the face of the flux; making of the moment something of permanence. That is the lifework. [. . .] My life, I feel, will not be lived until there are books and stories which relive it perpetually in time."

◊ **EZRA POUND** (1885–1972), born in Hailey, Idaho, spent his childhood near Philadelphia. He graduated from Hamilton College (Ph.B., 1905) and the University of Pennsylvania (M.A., 1906). After his first volume, *A Lume Spento* (1908), he published *Personae and Exultations of Ezra Pound* (1913), *Homage to Sextus Propertius* (1919), and *Hugh Selwyn Mauberley* (1920). In 1917 he began his best-known work—a series of cantos that eventually included *The Pisan Cantos* (1948) and *Thrones: Cantos 96–109* (1959). During World War II Pound fervently supported Mussolini and broadcast Fascist propaganda over Italian radio. After the war he was arrested for treason and incarcerated in a mental hospital from 1946 to 1958. A motivating force behind modern poetry, Pound won the Bollingen–Library of Congress Award in 1948. However, critic Robert Hillyer protested bitterly that Pound's Fascist and anti-Semitic poems "are the vehicle of contempt for America," and that the prize-winning *Pisan Cantos* themselves are a "ruthless mockery" of America's war dead. Leader of the Imagist poets, Pound experimented with poetic images to express "an intellectual and emotional complex in an instant of time." He once told an interviewer, "You cannot have literature without curiosity and when a writer's curiosity dries out he is finished."

◊ **ADRIENNE RICH** (1929–   ), born and raised in Baltimore, began her prolific publishing career during her senior year at Radcliffe when her first book, *A Change of World,* was published by W. H. Auden in the Yale Series of Younger Poets. After graduating in 1951, she studied at Oxford. She has received Guggenheim fellowships, a Poetry Society of America award, National Institute of Arts and Letters award, Bollingen Foundation grant, and a National Endowment for the Arts grant. Rich writes about feminist issues in her many poetry collections, including *Twenty-one Love Poems*

(1976), *The Dream of a Common Language, Poems 1974–1977* (1978), *The Fact of a Doorframe: Poems Selected and New 1950–1984* (1985), *Dark Fields of the Republic: Poems, 1991–1995* (1995). *Time's Power: Poems, 1985–88* (1989), and *Midnight Salvage: Poems, 1995–1998. The Diamond Cutters and Other Poems* (1955) won the Poetry Society of America award, and *Diving into the Wreck: Poems 1971–1972* (1973) won the 1974 National Book Award. William Heyen has noted that her work describes years of conflict as woman, wife, mother, and poet. As Rich once commented, "Instead of poems *about* experiences I am getting poems that *are* experiences, that contribute to my knowledge and my emotional life even while they reflect and assimilate it."

◆ **Edwin Arlington Robinson** (1869–1935), a descendant of the Puritan poet Anne Bradstreet, was born in Head Tide, Maine, where his father had a grain and lumber business. He grew up in Gardiner, Maine (the inspiration for his fictitious Tilbury Town) and then studied for two years at Harvard before his family's financial difficulties halted his education. He published *The Torrent and the Night Before* (1896), *The Children of the Night* (1897), and *Captain Craig* (1902). In 1916 *The Man Against the Sky* confirmed his reputation as a major poet. Pulitzer Prizes were awarded to his *Collected Poems* (1921), *The Man Who Died Twice* (1924), and *Tristam* (1927). Robert Frost, in his introduction to Robinson's posthumous *King Jasper* (1935), characterizes Robinson as a poet who "stayed content with the old-fashioned way to be new," unlike contemporary experimentalists who used poetry for their grievances against society; he praises Robinson's skillful blending of playful humor and profound melancholy. Robinson commented in a 1916 interview with poet Joyce Kilmer that poetry is both "undefinable" and "unmistakable: a language which tells us, through a more or less emotional experience, something that cannot be said."

◆ **Theodore Roethke** (1908–1963) was born and grew up in Saginaw, Michigan, where his father owned a twenty-five-acre greenhouse complex that inspired much of his symbolism. After completing his education at Michigan University and Harvard, he taught English at Lafayette College and became poet-in-residence at the University of Washington a year before he died. He won the Pulitzer Prize (1954) and two National Book Awards (1959 and 1965) for *Words for the Wind* (1958) and *The Far Field*, respectively. Critic Stanley Kunitz has praised his rare gifts as a writer: "The ferocity of Roethke's imagination makes most contemporary poetry seem pale and tepid in contrast. Even his wit is murderous. [. . .] What Roethke brings us is news of the root, of the minimal, of the primordial. The sub-human is given tongue; and the tongue proclaims the agony of coming alive, the painful miracle of growth." Roethke once explained that he writes about "trivial and vulgar" details "as barely and honestly as possible, symbolically, what few nuggets of observation and, let us hope, spiritual wisdom I have managed to seize upon in the course of a conventional albeit sometimes disordered existence."

◆ **SONIA SANCHEZ** (1934–   ) moved from her birthplace of Birmingham, Alabama, to New York City, where she later studied political science and poetry at Hunter College (B.A., 1955) and New York University. Her publications include *Homecoming* (1969), *It's a New Day: Poems for Young Brothas and Sistuhs* (1971), *A Blues Book for Blue Black Magical Women* (1973), *I'm Black When I'm Singing, I'm Blue When I Ain't* (1982), *homegirls & handgrenades* (1984), *Like the Singing Coming Off the Drums: Love Poems* (1998), and *Shake Loose My Skin: New and Selected Poems* (1999). She has received grants from the National Institute of Arts and Letters and the National Endowment for the Arts, and the American Book Award. Critic C.W.E. Bigsby finds her work distinguished by "language which catches the nuance of the spoken word, the rhythms of the street, and of a music which is partly jazz and partly a lyricism which underlies ordinary conversation." As a strong black feminist advocate, Sanchez supports change, not through rage, violence, or substance abuse but through political astuteness, moral power, and strong family relationships. Sanchez has declared, "I recognize that my writing must serve a dual purpose. It must be a clarion call to the values of change while it also speaks to the beauty of a nonexploitative age."

◆ **CARL SANDBURG** (1878–1967) was born in Galesburg, Illinois, to Swedish immigrant parents. He studied at Lombard College and later wrote for *Poetry* magazine. His volumes of verse, often about industrialized America, include *Chicago Poems* (1915), *Corn Huskers* (1918), *Smoke and Steel* (1920), and *Good Morning, America* (1928); in 1951 he won the Pulitzer Prize for his *Complete Poems*. He also wrote prose works, such as *Abraham Lincoln: The Prairie Years* (1926) and *Abraham Lincoln: The War Years* (1940). On his seventy-fifth birthday in 1953, Governor Adlai

Stevenson proclaimed Carl Sandburg Day in Illinois, and a representative of King Gustav VI of Sweden decorated him with the Commander Order of the Northern Star. According to critic Henry Steele Commager, Sandburg "celebrates what is best in us, and recalls us to our heritage and our humanity." In his notes to his *Complete Poems,* Sandburg has affirmed his purpose as a poet "of streets and struggles, of dust and combat, of violence wanton or justified, of plain folk living close to a hard earth." On his eighty-fifth birthday in 1963, when he published his final book, *Honey and Salt,* Sandburg confessed, "Being a poet is a damn dangerous business."

❖ **Leslie Marmon Silko** (1948–   ) describes her ancestry as Native American, Mexican, and Anglo. Born in Albuquerque, she grew up on the Laguna Pueblo Reservation and went to the Bureau of Indian Affairs school. She graduated from the University of New Mexico, attended law school, and completed graduate work in English. Then she taught writing at Navajo Community College and the University of Arizona. In 1981 Silko received a MacArthur Foundation fellowship granting her five years of financial support to pursue her creative endeavors. Her works include *Laguna Woman* (1974), *Ceremony* (1977), *Storyteller* (1981), *Almanac of the Dead* (1991), and *Gardens in the Dunes* (1999). Critic Edith Blicksilver notes Silko's "imaginative richness and beauty of tribal folk tales. The relationships between people and natural forces, the animal and vegetable kingdoms, are the subject of a series of poems describing different types of love relationships." Having listened as a child to her family's retelling of folklore, such as trickster Coyote's misadventures and accounts of Apache and Navajo raids upon the Pueblo, Silko affirms that stories define her culture's traditions and ceremonies: "There have to be stories. It's stories that make this a community."

❖ **Gary Soto** (1952–   ), born in Fresno, California, worked in the fields, as did his Mexican American parents and grandparents. He attended Fresno City College and California State University, and earned an M.F.A. in creative writing from the University of California at Irvine. He recreates the Fresno barrios in his poetry, short stories, and young adult fiction. His works include *The Elements of San Joaquin* (1977), *The Tale of Sunlight* (1978), *Where Sparrows Work Hard* (1981), *Home Course in Religion: New Poems* (1991), *Neighborhood Odes* (1992), *New and Selected Poems* (1995), *Junior College: Poems* (1997), and *Buried Onions* (1997). Soto has received awards from the Academy of American Poets (1975), the International Poetry

Forum (1976), and the American Library Association (1990), as well as Guggenheim and National Endowment for the Arts fellowships. Critic Maeve Visser Knoth has commented that his "simple poems of childhood, adolescence, and adulthood [. . . are] about ordinary events and emotions made remarkable by Soto's skilled use of words and images." Explains Soto, "I like the youth in my poetry, sort of a craziness. For me that's really important. I don't want to take a dreary look at the world [. . .]."

◇ **(Akinwande Oluwole) Wole Soyinka** (1934–   ) was born in western Nigeria; his parents were both educators. He has written about growing up under colonial rule in *Aké: The Years of Childhood* (1989). Soyinka attended the University College of Ibadan and the University of Leeds. His *Collected Plays,* along with major works such as *Death and the King's Horseman* and *The Interpreters,* led to his winning the Nobel Prize in Literature in 1986. The Swedish Academy described him as "a writer who in a wide cultural perspective and with poetic overtures fashions the drama of existence." In addition to his analytical work *Myth, Literature, and the African World,* he has published two volumes based on lectures at the W. E. B. Dubois Institute at Harvard: *Open Sore of a Continent: A Personal Narrative of the Nigerian Crisis* (1996) and *The Burden of Memory, the Muse of Forgiveness* (1998). A deeply committed political writer and activist, Soyinka endured repeated imprisonment for his outspoken beliefs. Despite this persecution, in 1999 he returned to his homeland after a long absence. Soyinka has explained, "I would be frankly ill at ease with myself if I failed to call attention to the public for [. . .] its [. . .] abdication of basic rights to official crooks, thugs, touts and other [. . .] scum of society."

◇ **Wallace Stevens** (1879–1955) was born in Reading, Pennsylvania, son of a prominent attorney and a schoolteacher. He attended Harvard and the New York Law School. In 1916 he took a job with the Hartford Accident and Indemnity Company that afforded him and his family a prosperous life. Stevens continued writing poetry, which he had begun at Harvard. For his life's work, he was awarded the Bollingen Prize in 1949, and in 1955 he won both the Pulitzer Prize and the National Book Award for his *Collected Poems.* As critic Richard Gray has noted, Stevens's poems fuse elements of the ancient, the Romantic, and the American poet. "Stevens returned the poet to his ancient role of bard or myth-maker, offering purpose and a sense of meaning to his tribe. And to this he added another more peculiarly Romantic and American dimension, which was that of hero." His poem "Of Modern Poetry" defines "the poem of the act of the mind." In a letter to his wife, Stevens wrote, "The priest in me worshipped one God at one shrine; the poet another God at another shrine. The priest worshipped Mercy and Love; the poet Beauty and Might."

◊ **Dylan Thomas** (1914–1953) was born in Swansea, Wales, to an indulgent mother and an atheistic father, who was a schoolmaster in English. Thomas benefited from his father's dramatic readings of Shakespeare and an extensive library of modern and nineteenth-century poets. In 1931 he became a copyreader and then reporter for the South Wales *Evening Post*. Besides winning many poetry prizes, he established a popular reputation through poetry readings on the radio in England and on college campuses in America. His collected work, as found in *The Poems of Dylan Thomas* (1952), is marked by passion and mysticism. His death at thirty-nine has been attributed to alcoholism and lung disease. Assessing Thomas's brief literary career, poet Karl Shapiro has called him "the first modern romantic you could put your finger on, the first whose journeys and itineraries became part of his own mythology, the first who offered himself up as a public, not a private sacrifice." Reflecting on his own work, Thomas asserted, "My poetry is, or should be, useful to me for one reason: it is the record of my individual struggle from darkness toward some measure of light."

◊ **Margaret Walker** (1915–1998), born in Birmingham, Alabama, graduated from Northwestern University (B.A., 1935) and the University of Iowa (M.A., 1940; Ph.D., 1965). In 1942 her first and most influential collection of poetry, *For My People*, won the prestigious Yale Series of Younger Poets Award. It was followed by *Prophets for a New Day* (1970) and *October Journey* (1973), both of which include ballads and sonnets about the struggle for civil rights. Her 1966 historical novel *Jubilee*—winner of the Houghton Mifflin Literary Fellowship—uses slave narrative to celebrate a heroic woman's journey to freedom. She also published *The Daemonic Genius of Richard Wright* (1987), *On Being Female, Black and Free* (1997), and *Moral Understanding: A Feminist Study in Ethics* (1998). Critic Theodore Hudson has described Walker's poetry as "insightful, compassionate, and sincere." Walker sought to capture in her work the strength of African-American women. In her 1942 poem "Lineage" she writes, "My mothers were strong. / Why am I not as they?" Her dedication to *For My People* acknowledges her indebtedness to and responsibility for "my people everywhere singing their slave songs repeatedly: their dirges and their ditties and their blues and jubilees."

❖ **JAMES WELCH** (1940–) was born in Browning, Montana, and educated in Blackfeet and Ft. Belknap reservation schools and at the University of Montana. As one of the best known contemporary Native American writers, he often focuses on the Native American experience, especially its emphasis on consciousness of nature and the earth. His publications include the poetry collection *Riding the Earthboy 40* (1971) and four novels—*Winter in the Blood* (1974), *The Death of Jim Loney* (1979), *Fools Crow* (1986), and *The Indian Lawyer* (1990). In 1994 he published the nonfiction work *Killing Custer: The Battle of the Little Bighorn and the Fate of the Plains Indians,* and in 1995 he contributed to *Sweet Medicine: Sites of Indian Massacres, Battlefields, and Treaties.* Joseph Bruchac has described Welch's poems as "always memorable and, in some cases, close to great. It seems he will continue to be a vital force in American writing." The closing lines of "Never Give a Bum an Even Break" (the final poem in *Riding the Earthboy 40*) suggests the purpose of Welch's writing: "Any day we will crawl out to settle / old scores or create new roles / our mask glittering in a comic rain."

❖ **WALT WHITMAN** (1819–1892) was born in West Hills, Long Island, New York. After only six years of formal education, he left school and eventually became a newspaper reporter and editor. He was a part-time carpenter while writing his major work *Leaves of Grass,* which he continued to revise and expand until his death. During the Civil War when his brother was wounded, Whitman went to Washington in 1862 to work as a hospital nurse volunteer, an experience that led to *Drum-Taps* (1865); a later edition of this volume included "When Lilacs Last in the Door-Yard Bloom'd." "Whitman has been an inescapable influence not only for most significant American poets after him," critic Harold Bloom has concluded, "but also for the most gifted writers of narrative fiction." Justifying the validity of the nontraditional forms of poetry he created, Whitman has asserted, "The rhyme and conformity of perfect poems show the free growth of metrical laws and bud from them as unerringly and loosely as lilacs or roses on a bush, and take shapes as compact as the shapes of chestnuts and oranges and melons and peas, and shed the perfume impalpable to form."

✧ **Richard Wilbur** (1921–   ), was born in New York City and grew up on a farm in North Caldwell, New Jersey. He graduated from Amherst in 1942, served in the infantry during World War II, and received his M.A. from Harvard in 1947. He began writing poetry in the army, and he has taught at Harvard, Wellesley, and Wesleyan. He won the Pulitzer Prize, the Edna St. Vincent Millay Memorial Award, and the National Book Award in 1957 for *Things of This World* (1956). Other works include *The Beautiful Changes and Other Poems* (1947); *Ceremony and Other Poems* (1950); *Poems, 1943–1956* (1957), *The Poems of Richard Wilbur* (1963), and *New and Collected Poems* (1989). Named Poet Laureate of the United States in 1987, Wilbur also has written translations, nonfiction, and operetta lyrics. Poet and critic Donald Hall has praised Wilbur's "capacity for drawing sympathetically on the world of the past without getting out of touch with the present." Wilbur advocates a "strictness of form" to structure his poetry because the "strength of the genie," he believes, "comes of his being confined in a bottle." Beyond his scholarly life, Wilbur seeks "non-verbal" activities because, as he has explained, it is "good for a writer to move into words out of silence as much as he can."

✧ **William Carlos Williams** (1883–1963) was born in Rutherford, New Jersey, to a British father and a mother of French, Dutch, and Spanish ancestry. He read the classics at home, attended private schools in Geneva and Paris, and then attended high school in New York City. Having studied medicine at the University of Pennsylvania (M.D., 1906) Williams was a pediatric doctor for over forty years. He published widely in several genres—poetry, fiction, autobiography, essays, and drama. His many honors include the National Book Award (1950), the Bollingen Prize in Poetry (1952), and a posthumous Pulitzer Prize (1963) for *Pictures from Brueghel and Other Poems*. Perhaps his best-known work is *Paterson* (1946–1958). Williams's poetry, according to poet Randall Jarrell, "is more remarkable for its empathy, sympathy, its muscular and emotional identification with its subjects, than any other modern poetry except Rilke's." Reflecting on the origins of modern poetry and of his own work, Williams has speculated that "it was the French painters rather than the writers who influenced us, and their influence was very great;

they created an atmosphere of release, color-release, from stereotypical forms, trite subjects."

◆ **JAMES WRIGHT** (1927–1980), a native of Martins Ferry, Ohio, served in the U.S. Army in Japan during World War II, and graduated from Kenyon College, where he won the Robert Frost Poetry Prize. He then earned his M.A. and Ph.D. from the University of Washington at Seattle. Describing himself as a "bookish man," Wright has taught at several colleges. His works of poetry include *The Green Wall* (1956), *Saint Judas* (1959), *The Branch Will Not Break* (1963), *Shall We Gather at the River* (1968), and the Pulitzer Prize-winning *Collected Poems* (1971). Other honors include awards from *Poetry* magazine, the *Kenyon Review* Poetry Fellowship, a Fulbright Fellowship, and a Guggenheim Fellowship. He has collaborated with poet Robert Bly for translations of the works of poets Cesar Vallejo (1963) and Pablo Neruda (1966). Critic Keith Walters has observed that "Wright was always haunted by human suffering, not only his own, but also the suffering of the social outcast—the murderer, the rapist, the untrue lover, the Judas." In a 1975 *Paris Review* interview Wright commented, "I do not have a talent for happiness [. . .] I tried to come to terms with that in the clearest and most ferociously perfect form that I could find and in all the traditional ways."

◆ **WILLIAM BUTLER YEATS** (1865–1939) came from an upper-middle-class Anglo-Irish family in Dublin. He was educated in London and Dublin, where he attended the Metropolitan School of Art from 1884 to 1886. In 1923 he won the Nobel Prize for Literature in recognition not only of his achievements as a poet but also of his tireless efforts to promote Irish Literature. As leader of the Celtic Renaissance in Ireland, Yeats celebrated nationalism in his early poetry, such as *The Wanderings of Oislin* (1889), based on Irish legend. However, his later poems, often mystical and deeply symbolic, reflect more expansive universal themes. Besides his highly regarded volumes of poetry, such as *The Wild Swans at Coole* (1917), *The Tower* (1928), and *The Winding Stair and Other Poems* (1929), his legacy also includes his plays and essays. Renowned poet and critic T. S. Eliot has praised Yeats for being among the few poets "whose history was the history of our own time, who are part of the consciousness of our age, which cannot be understood without them." Yeats's *Autobiographies* contains the following comment on the connection between art and artist: "When great artists were at their most creative the result was not simply a work of art, but rather the 're-creation of the man through that art.'"

Poetry Casebook

This Casebook contains eight poems by Langston Hughes, a collection of source materials,* questions to stimulate discussion and writing, and a student paper.

POEMS
◇ ◇ ◇

Other poems by Hughes included elsewhere in this text are "Negro" (p. 727), "Harlem" (p. 808), and "Island" (p. 902).

SOURCE MATERIALS
◇ ◇ ◇

---

* Note that the articles in this Casebook do not use current MLA documentation style. See Appendix A for current MLA style.

Each of the sources above provides insights into the poems in this Casebook. Other kinds of sources can also enrich your understanding of Hughes's accomplishments—for example, other poems by Hughes, biographical data about the author, or works of imaginative literature by other writers dealing with similar themes. In addition, the following Web sites devoted to Hughes can offer insights into his work: <http://www.csustan.edu/english/reuben/pal/chap9/hughes.html>; <http://www.tsa.si.edu/disctheater/sweet/tss03.htm>; http://www.poets.org/lit/poet/lhughfst.htm>; <http://www.library.vanderbilt.edu/central/afam.html>.

In preparation for writing an essay on the topic of your choice, read the poems carefully. Then consider the Reading and Reacting questions at the end of this Casebook (p. 1107) in light of what you have read, and use your responses to help you find a topic you can develop in a three- to six-page essay. Be sure to document any words or ideas borrowed from your sources, and remember to enclose words that are not your own in quotation marks. (For guidelines on evaluating literary criticism, see page 15; for guidelines on using source materials, see page 34.)

A complete student paper, "Challenging the Father/Challenging the Self: Langston Hughes's 'The Negro Speaks of Rivers,'" which uses some of the sources included in this Casebook, begins on page 1111.

◆ **Langston Hughes** (1902–1967) is often referred to as the most accomplished African-American poet of the twentieth century. He was also a skilled fiction writer, playwright, autobiographer, and essayist. Although most people associate him with the Harlem Renaissance, he wrote significant works of literature for close to half a century.

Born in Joplin, Missouri, Hughes was reared throughout the Midwest. His formal education included time spent at Columbia University and the historically black Lincoln University, from which he graduated in 1929. Perhaps more important than his formal education, however, were the years he spent working on a ship traveling to Europe and Africa, and his visits to Mexico, to the Soviet Union, to Europe on the eve of the Second World War—and, late in life, once again to Africa. Hughes opened African-American poetry to everyday speech, popular art forms, and spirituality—what contemporary critics sometimes call "the vernacular." Most important was the attention he paid to the multiple forms of African-influenced music in the United States: spirituals, blues, gospel, and jazz. Hughes discovered in this music not only a great reservoir of themes and characters for his poetry, but also a new approach to poetic diction and form.

Influenced by Walt Whitman, Carl Sandburg, and Paul Laurence Dunbar, Hughes's poetry is radically democratic, celebrating the great diversity of American and African-American cultures. Perhaps more than any other American poet of his stature, Hughes sought to address the widest possible audience. He wrote children's books, plays and musicals for the Broadway stage, and a widely syndicated column for the African-American newspaper the *Chicago Defender.*

For much of Hughes's life, his commitment to a democratic art was combined with a willingness and zeal to confront racism and economic inequality directly. Hughes always wrote as if there were no question about the possibility of art to transform society.

◊ ◊ ◊

The Negro Speaks of Rivers
(1925)

I've known rivers:
I've known rivers ancient as the world and older than the flow of
    human blood in human veins.

My soul has grown deep like the rivers.

5 I bathed in the Euphrates[1] when dawns were young.
I built my hut near the Congo[2] and it lulled me to sleep.
I looked upon the Nile and raised the pyramids above it.
I heard the singing of the Mississippi when Abe Lincoln went
    down to New Orleans, and I've seen its muddy bosom turn
    all golden in the sunset.

I've known rivers:
10 Ancient, dusky rivers.

My soul has grown deep like the rivers.

◊ ◊ ◊

The Weary Blues
(1925)

Droning a drowsy syncopated tune,
Rocking back and forth to a mellow croon,
    I heard a Negro play.
Down on Lenox Avenue[1] the other night
5 By the pale dull pallor of an old gas light
    He did a lazy sway . . .
    He did a lazy sway . . .
To the tune o' those Weary Blues.
With his ebony hands on each ivory key

---

[1] Major river of southwest Asia; with the Tigris, the Euphrates forms a valley sometimes referred to as the "cradle of civilization."

[2] River in equatorial Africa, the continent's second longest.

---

[1] Street in Harlem, noted for nightlife and music during the 1920s.

10 He made that poor piano moan with melody.
    O Blues!
Swaying to and fro on his rickety stool
He played that sad raggy tune like a musical fool.
    Sweet Blues!
15 Coming from a black man's soul.
    O Blues!
In a deep song voice with a melancholy tone
I heard that Negro sing, that old piano moan—
    "Ain't got nobody in all this world,
20   Ain't got nobody but ma self.
    I's gwine to quit ma frownin'
    And put ma troubles on the shelf."
Thump, thump, thump, went his foot on the floor.
He played a few chords then he sang some more—
25   "I got the Weary Blues
    And I can't be satisfied.
    Got the Weary Blues
    And can't be satisfied—
    I ain't happy no mo'
30   And I wish that I had died."
And far into the night he crooned that tune.
The stars went out and so did the moon.
The singer stopped playing and went to bed
While the Weary Blues echoed through his head.
35 He slept like a rock or a man that's dead.

◊ ◊ ◊

I, Too

(1925)

I, too, sing America.

I am the darker brother.
They send me to eat in the kitchen
When company comes,
5 But I laugh,
And eat well,
And grow strong.

Tomorrow,
I'll be at the table
10 When company comes.
Nobody'll dare
Say to me,
"Eat in the kitchen,"
Then.

15 Besides,
They'll see how beautiful I am
And be ashamed—

I, too, am America.

◇ ◇ ◇

Let America Be America Again
(1936)

Let America be America again.
Let it be the dream it used to be.
Let it be the pioneer on the plain
Seeking a home where he himself is free.

5 (America never was America to me.)

Let America be the dream the dreamers dreamed—
Let it be that great strong land of love
Where never kings connive nor tyrants scheme
That any man be crushed by one above.

10 (It never was America to me.)

O, let my land be a land where Liberty
Is crowned with no false patriotic wreath,
But opportunity is real, and life is free,
Equality is in the air we breathe.

15 (There's never been equality for me,
Nor freedom in this "homeland of the free.")

Say, who are you that mumbles in the dark?
And who are you that draws your veil across the stars?

I am the poor white, fooled and pushed apart,
20 I am the Negro bearing slavery's scars.
I am the red man driven from the land,
I am the immigrant clutching the hope I seek—
And finding only the same old stupid plan
Of dog eat dog, of mighty crush the weak.

25 I am the young man, full of strength and hope,
Tangled in that ancient endless chain
Of profit, power, gain, of grab the land!
Of grab the gold! Of grab the ways of satisfying need!
Of work the men! Of take the pay!
30 Of owning everything for one's own greed!

I am the farmer, bondsman to the soil.
I am the worker sold to the machine.

I am the Negro, servant to you all.
I am the people, humble, hungry, mean—
35 Hungry yet today despite the dream.
Beaten yet today—O, Pioneers!
I am the man who never got ahead,
The poorest worker bartered through the years.

Yet I'm the one who dreamt our basic dream
40 In that Old World while still a serf of kings,
Who dreamt a dream so strong, so brave, so true,
That even yet its mighty daring sings
In every brick and stone, in every furrow turned
That's made America the land it has become.
45 O, I'm the man who sailed those early seas
In search of what I meant to be my home—
For I'm the one who left dark Ireland's shore,
And Poland's plain, and England's grassy lea,
And torn from Black Africa's strand I came
50 To build a "homeland of the free."

The free?

Who said the free? Not me?
Surely not me? The millions on relief today?
The millions shot down when we strike?
55 The millions who have nothing for our pay?
For all the dreams we've dreamed
And all the songs we've sung
And all the hopes we've held
And all the flags we've hung,
60 The millions who have nothing for our pay—
Except the dream that's almost dead today.

O, let America be America again—
The land that never has been yet—
And yet must be—the land where *every* man is free.
65 The land that's mine—the poor man's, Indian's, Negro's, ME—
Who made America,
Whose sweat and blood, whose faith and pain,
Whose hand at the foundry, whose plow in the rain,
Must bring back our mighty dream again.

70 Sure, call me any ugly name you choose—
The steel of freedom does not stain.
From those who live like leeches on the people's lives,
We must take back our land again,
America!
75 O, yes,

I say it plain,
America never was America to me,
And yet I swear this oath—
America will be!

80 Out of the rack and ruin of our gangster death,
The rape and rot of graft, and stealth, and lies,
We, the people, must redeem
The land, the mines, the plants, the rivers.
The mountains and the endless plain—
85 All, all the stretch of these great green states—
And make America again!

◆ ◆ ◆

Ballad of the Landlord
(1940)

Landlord, landlord,
My roof has sprung a leak.
Don't you 'member I told you about it
Way last week?

5 Landlord, landlord,
These steps is broken down.
When you come up yourself
It's a wonder you don't fall down.

Ten Bucks you say I owe you?
10 Ten Bucks you say is due?
Well, that's Ten Bucks more'n I'll pay you
Till you fix this house up new.

What? You gonna get eviction orders?
You gonna cut off my heat?
15 You gonna take my furniture and
Throw it in the street?

Um-huh! You talking high and mighty.
Talk on—till you get through.
You ain't gonna be able to say a word
20 If I land my fist on you.

Police! Police!
Come and get this man!
He's trying to ruin the government
And overturn the land!

25 Copper's whistle!
Patrol bell!
Arrest.

Precinct Station.
Iron cell.
30 Headlines in press:

MAN THREATENS LANDLORD

.

. .

TENANT HELD NO BAIL

.

. .

JUDGE GIVES NEGRO 90 DAYS IN COUNTY JAIL

❖ ❖ ❖

Theme for English B
(1949)

The instructor said,

    Go home and write
    a page tonight.
    And let that page come out of you—
5   *Then, it will be true.*

I wonder if it's that simple?
I am twenty-two, colored, born in Winston-Salem.
I went to school there, then Durham, then here
to this college on the hill above Harlem.
10 I am the only colored student in my class.
The steps from the hill lead down into Harlem,
through a park, then I cross St. Nicholas,
Eighth Avenue, Seventh, and I come to the Y,
the Harlem Branch Y, where I take the elevator
15 up to my room, sit down and write this page:

It's not easy to know what is true for you or me
at twenty-two, my age. But I guess I'm what
I feel and see and hear, Harlem, I hear you:
hear you, hear me—we two—you, me, talk on this page.
20 (I hear New York, too) Me—who?
Well, I like to eat, sleep, drink, and be in love.
I like to work, read, learn, and understand life.
I like a pipe for a Christmas present,

or records—Bessie,[1] bop,[2] or Bach.
25 I guess being colored doesn't make me *not* like
the same things other folks like who are other races.
So will my page be colored that I write?
Being me, it will not be white.
But it will be
30 a part of you, instructor.
You are white—
yet a part of me, as I am a part of you.
That's American.
Sometimes perhaps you don't want to be a part of me.
35 Nor do I often want to be a part of you.
But we are, that's true!
As I learn from you,
I guess you learn from me—
although you're older—and white—
40 and somewhat more free.

This is my page for English B.

◇ ◇ ◇

Dream Boogie
(1951)

Good morning, daddy!
Ain't you heard
The boogie-woogie[1] rumble
Of a dream deferred?

5 Listen closely:
You'll hear their feet
Beating out and beating out a—

You think
It's a happy beat?

10 Listen to it closely:
Ain't you heard
something underneath
like a—

---

[1] Bessie Smith, blues singer, 1894–1937.
[2] Short for "bebop," a jazz style developed in the early 1940s by Charlie Parker, Dizzy Gillespie, and others.

---

[1] A popular black musical style with variants in both blues and jazz; more specifically, a vigorous piano style marked by heavy and repeated bass figures. Some commentators have also suggested that it was slang for syphilis.

What did I say?

15 Sure,
I'm happy!
Take it away!

Hey, pop!
Re-bop!
20 *Mop!*

Y-e-a-h!

❖ ❖ ❖

Birmingham Sunday
(September 15, 1963)[1]
(1967)

Four little girls
Who went to Sunday School that day
And never came back home at all
But left instead
5 Their blood upon the wall
With spattered flesh
And bloodied Sunday dresses
Torn to shreds by dynamite
That China made aeons ago—
10 Did not know
That what China made
Before China was ever Red at all
Would redden with their blood
This Birmingham-on-Sunday wall.

15 Four tiny girls
Who left their blood upon that wall,
In little graves today await
The dynamite that might ignite
The fuse of centuries of Dragon Kings[1]
20 Whose tomorrow sings a hymn
The missionaries never taught Chinese

---

[1] On this date, only weeks after Martin Luther King, Jr.'s historic March on Washington, DC, four young African-American girls were killed at their Sunday School in Birmingham, Alabama, by a bomb, likely in response to recent Civil Rights organizing in the area. The case has never been fully solved.

[2] In Chinese myth and lore, the dragon is a beneficent force that dispenses blessings in both the natural and supernatural worlds. Eventually the dragon became a symbol of imperial China. Ironically, the dragon has also been utilized in the mythology of white supremacist groups like the Ku Klux Klan.

In Christian Sunday School
To implement the Golden Rule.

    Four little girls
25 Might be awakened someday soon
By songs upon the breeze
As yet unfelt among magnolia trees.

◇ ◇ ◇

The Negro Artist and the Racial Mountain

LANGSTON HUGHES

One of the most promising of the young Negro poets said to me once, "I want to be a poet—not a Negro poet," meaning, I believe, "I want to write like a white poet": meaning subconsciously, "I would like to be a white poet," meaning behind that, "I would like to be white." And I was sorry the young man said that, for no great poet has ever been afraid of being himself. And I doubted then that, with his desire to run away spiritually from his race, this boy would ever be a great poet. But this is the mountain standing in the way of any true Negro art in America—this urge within the race toward whiteness, the desire to pour racial individuality into the mold of American standardization, and to be as little Negro and as much American as possible.

But let us look at the immediate background of this young poet. His family is of what I suppose one would call the Negro middle class: people who are by no means rich yet never uncomfortable nor hungry—smug, contented, respectable folk, members of the Baptist church. The father goes to work every morning. He is a chief steward at a large white club. The mother sometimes does fancy sewing or supervises parties for the rich families of the town. The children go to a mixed school. In the home they read white papers and magazines. And the mother often says, "Don't be like niggers" when the children are bad. A frequent phrase from the father is, "Look how well a white man does things." And so the word white comes to be unconsciously a symbol of all the virtues. It holds for the children beauty, morality, and money. The whisper of "I want to be white" runs silently through their minds. This young poet's home is, I believe, a fairly typical home of the colored middle class. One sees immediately how difficult it would be for an artist born in such a home to interest himself in interpreting the beauty of his own people. He is never taught to see that beauty. He is taught rather not to see it, or if he does, to be ashamed of it when it is not according to Caucasian patterns.

For racial culture the home of a self-styled "high-class" Negro has nothing better to offer. Instead there will perhaps be more aping of things white than in a less cultured or less wealthy home. The father is perhaps a doctor, lawyer, landowner, or politician. The mother may be a social worker, or a teacher, or she may do nothing and have a maid. Father is often dark but he has usually married the lightest woman he could find. The family attend a fashionable church where few really colored faces are to be found. And they themselves draw a color line. In the North they go to white theaters and white movies. And in the South they have at least two cars and a house "like white folks." Nordic manners, Nordic faces, Nordic hair, Nordic art (if any), and an Episcopal heaven. A very high mountain indeed for the would-be racial artist to climb in order to discover himself and his people.

But then there are the low-down folks, the so-called common element, and they are the majority—may the Lord be praised! The people who have their nip of gin on Saturday nights are not too important to themselves or the community, or too well fed, or too learned to watch the lazy world go round. They live on Seventh Street in Washington or State Street in Chicago and they do not particularly care whether they are like white folks or anybody else. Their joy runs, bang! into ecstasy. Their religion soars to a shout. Work maybe a little today, rest a little tomorrow. Play awhile. Sing awhile. O, let's dance! These common people are not afraid of spirituals, as for a long time their more intellectual brethren were, and jazz is their child. They furnish a wealth of colorful, distinctive material for any artist because they still hold their own individuality in the face of American standardizations. And perhaps these common people will give to the world its truly great Negro artist, the one who is not afraid to be himself. Whereas the better-class Negro would tell the artist what to do, the people at least let him alone when he does appear. And they are not ashamed of him—if they know he exists at all. And they accept what beauty is their own without question.

Certainly there is, for the American Negro artist who can escape the restrictions the more advanced among his own group would put upon him,

a great field of unused material ready for his art. Without going outside his race, and even among the better classes with their "white" culture and conscious American manners, but still Negro enough to be different, there is sufficient matter to furnish a black artist with a lifetime of creative work. And when he chooses to touch on the relations between Negroes and whites in this country with their innumerable overtones and undertones, surely, and especially for literature and the drama, there is an inexhaustible supply of themes at hand. To these the Negro artist can give his racial individuality, his heritage of rhythm and warmth, and his incongruous humor that so often, as in the Blues, becomes ironic laughter mixed with tears. But let us look again at the mountain.

A prominent Negro clubwoman in Philadelphia paid eleven dollars to hear Raquel Meller sing Andalusian popular songs. But she told me a few weeks before she would not think of going to hear "that woman," Clara Smith, a great black artist, sing Negro folksongs. And many an upper-class Negro church, even now, would not dream of employing a spiritual in its services. The drab melodies in white folks' hymnbooks are much to be preferred. "We want to worship the Lord correctly and quietly. We don't believe in 'shouting.' "Let's be dull like the Nordics," they say, in effect.

The road for the serious black artist, then, who would produce a racial art is most certainly rocky and the mountain is high. Until recently he received almost no encouragement for his work from either white or colored people. The fine novels of Chesnutt go out of print with neither race noticing their passing. The quaint charm and humor of Dunbar's dialect verse brought to him, in his day, largely the same kind of encouragement one would give a side-show freak (A colored man writing poetry! How odd!) or a clown (How amusing!).

The present vogue in things Negro, although it may do as much harm as good for the budding colored artist, has at least done this: it has brought him forcibly to the attention of his own people among whom for so long, unless the other race had noticed him beforehand, he was a prophet with little honor. I understand that Charles Gilpin acted for years in Negro theaters without any special acclaim from his own, but when Broadway gave him eight curtain calls, Negroes, too, began to beat a tin pan in his honor. I know a young colored writer, a manual worker by day, who had been writing well for the colored magazines for some years, but it was not until he recently broke into the white publications and his first book was accepted by a prominent New York publisher that the "best" Negroes in his city took the trouble to discover that he lived there. Then almost immediately they decided to give a grand dinner for him. But the society ladies were careful to whisper to his mother that perhaps she'd better not come. They were not sure she would have an evening gown.

The Negro artist works against an undertow of sharp criticism and misunderstanding from his own group and unintentional bribes from the whites. "O, be respectable, write about nice people, show how good we are," say the Negroes. "Be stereotyped, don't go too far, don't shatter our illusions about you, don't amuse us too seriously. We will pay you," say the whites. Both would have told Jean Toomer not to write Cane. The colored people did not praise it. The white people did not buy it. Most of the colored people who did read Cane hate it. They are afraid of it.

Although the critics gave it good reviews the public remained indifferent. Yet (excepting the work of DuBois) Cane contains the finest prose written by a Negro in America. And like the singing of Robeson, it is truly racial.

But in spite of the Nordicized Negro intelligentsia and the desires of some white editors, we have an honest American Negro literature already with us. Now await the rise of the Negro theater. Our folk music, having achieved world-wide fame, offers itself to the genius of the great individual American Negro composer who is to come. And within the next decade I expect to see the work of a growing school of colored artists who paint and model the beauty of dark faces and create with new technique the expressions of their own soul-world. And the Negro dancers who will dance like flame and the singers who will continue to carry out songs to all who listen—they will be with us in even greater numbers tomorrow.

Most of my own poems are racial in theme and treatment, derived from the life I know. In many of them I try to grasp and hold some of the meanings and rhythms of jazz. I am sincere as I know how to be in these poems and yet after every reading I answer questions like these from my own people: Do you think Negroes should always write about Negroes? I wish you wouldn't read some of your poems to white folks. How do you find anything interesting in a place like a cabaret? Why do you write about black people? You aren't black. What makes you do so many jazz poems?

But jazz to me is one of the inherent expressions of Negro life in America: the eternal tom-tom beating in the Negro soul—the tom-tom of revolt against weariness in a white world, a world of subway trains, and work, work, work; the tom-tom of joy and laughter, and pain swallowed in a smile. Yet the Philadelphia club-woman is ashamed to say that her race created it and she does not like me to write about it. The old subconscious "white is best" runs through her mind. Years of study under white teachers, a lifetime of white books, pictures, and papers, and white manners, morals, and Puritan standards made her dislike the spirituals. And now she turns up her nose at jazz and all its manifestations—likewise almost everything else distinctly racial. She doesn't care for the Winold Reiss portraits of Negroes because they are "too Negro." She does not want a true picture of herself from anybody. She wants the artist to flatter her, to make the white world believe that all Negroes are as smug and as near white in soul as she wants to be. But, to my mind, it is the duty of the younger Negro artist, if he accepts any duties at all from outsiders, to change through the force of his art that old whispering "I want to be white," hidden in the aspirations of his people, to "Why should I want to be white? I am a Negro—and beautiful!"

So I am ashamed for the black poet who says, "I want to be a poet, not a Negro poet," as though his own racial world were not as interesting as any other world. I am ashamed, too, for the colored artist who runs from the painting of Negro faces to the painting of sunsets after the manner of the academicians because he fears the strange un-whiteness of his own features. An artist must be free to choose what he does, certainly, but he must also never be afraid to do what he might choose.

Let the blare of Negro jazz bands and the bellowing voice of Bessie Smith singing Blues penetrate the closed ears of the colored near-intellectuals until they listen and perhaps understand. Let Paul Robeson singing Water Boy, and Rudolph Fisher writing about the streets of Harlem, and Jean Toomer holding the heart of Georgia in his hands, and Aaron Douglas drawing strange black fantasies cause the smug Negro middle class to turn from their white, respectable, ordinary books and papers to catch a glimmer of their own beauty. We younger Negro artists who create now intend to express our individual dark-skinned selves without fear or shame. If white people are pleased we are glad. If they are not, it doesn't matter. We know we are beautiful. And ugly too. The tom-tom cries and the tom-tom laughs. If colored people are pleased we are glad. If they are not, their displeasure doesn't matter either. We build our temples for tomorrow, strong as we know how, and we stand on top of the mountain, free within ourselves.

◇ ◇ ◇

To Negro Writers

LANGSTON HUGHES

There are certain practical things American Negro writers can do through their work.

We can reveal to the Negro masses, from which we come, our potential power to transform the now ugly face of the Southland into a region of peace and plenty.

We can reveal to the white masses those Negro qualities which go beyond the mere ability to laugh and sing and dance and make music, and which are a part of the useful heritage that we place at the disposal of a future free America.

Negro writers can seek to unite blacks and whites in our country, not on the nebulous basis of an interracial meeting, or the shifting sands of religious brotherhood, but on the *solid* ground of the daily working-class struggle to wipe out, now and forever, all the old inequalities of the past.

Furthermore, by way of exposure, Negro writers can reveal in their novels, stories, poems, and articles:

The lovely grinning face of Philanthropy—which gives a million dollars to a Jim Crow school, but not one job to a graduate of that school; which builds a Negro hospital with second-rate equipment, then commands black patients and student-doctors to go there whether they will or no; or which, out of the kindness of its heart, erects yet another separate, segregated, shut-off, Jim Crow Y.M.C.A.

Negro writers can expose those white labor leaders who keep their unions closed against Negro workers and prevent the betterment of all workers.

We can expose, too, the sick-sweet smile of organized religion—which lies about what it doesn't know, and about what it *does* know. And the half-voodoo, half-clown, face of revivalism, dulling the mind with the clap of its empty hands.

Expose, also, the false leadership that besets the Negro people—bought and paid for leadership, owned by capital, afraid to open its mouth except in the old conciliatory way so advantageous to the exploiters.

And all the economic roots of race hatred and race fear.

And the Contentment Tradition of the O-lovely-Negroes school of American fiction, which makes an ignorant black face and a Carolina head filled with superstition, appear more desirable than a crown of gold; the jazz-band; and the O-so-gay writers who make of the Negro's poverty and misery a dusky funny paper.

And expose war. And the old My-Country-'Tis-of-Thee lie. And the colored American Legion posts strutting around talking about the privilege of dying for the nobel Red, White and Blue, when they aren't even permitted the privilege of living for it. Or voting for it in Texas. Or working for it in the diplomatic service. Or even rising, like every other good little boy, from the log cabin to the White House.

White House is right!

Dear colored American Legion, you can swing from a lynching tree, uniform and all, with pleasure—and nobody'll fight for you. Don't you know that? Nobody even salutes you down South, dead or alive, medals or no medals, chevrons or not, no matter how many wars you've fought in.

Let Negro writers write about the irony and pathos of the *colored* American Legion.

"*Salute, Mr. White Man!*"
"Salute, hell! . . . You're a nigger."

Or would you rather write about the moon?

Sure, the moon still shines over Harlem. Shines over Scottsboro. Shines over Birmingham, too, I reckon. Shines over Cordie Cheek's grave, down South.

Write about the moon if you want to. Go ahead. This is a free country.

But there are certain very practical things American Negro writers can do. And must do. There's a song that says, "the time ain't long." That song is right. Something has got to change in America—and change soon. We must help that change to come.

The moon's still shining as poetically as ever, but all the stars on the flag are dull. (And the stripes, too.)

We want a new and better America, where there won't be any poor, where there won't be any more Jim Crow, where there won't be any lynchings, where there won't be any munition makers, where we won't need philanthropy, nor charity, nor the New Deal, nor Home Relief.

We want an America that will be ours, a world that will be ours—we Negro workers and white workers! Black writers and white! We'll make that world!

◆ ◇ ◆

My Adventures as a Social Poet

LANGSTON HUGHES

Poets who write mostly about love, roses and moonlight, sunsets and snow, must lead a very quiet life. Seldom, I imagine, does their poetry get them into difficulties. Beauty and lyricism are really related to another world, to ivory towers, to your head in the clouds, feet floating off the earth.

Unfortunately, having been born poor—and also colored—in Missouri, I was stuck in the mud from the beginning. Try as I might to float off into the clouds, poverty and Jim Crow would grab me by the heels, and right back on earth I would land. A third-floor furnished room is the nearest thing I have ever had to an ivory tower.

Some of my earliest poems were social poems in that they were about people's problems—whole groups of people's problems—rather than my own personal difficulties. Sometimes, though, certain aspects of my personal problems happened to be also common to many other people. And certainly, racially speaking, my own problems of adjustment to American life were the same as those of millions of other segregated Negroes. The moon belongs to everybody, but not this American earth of ours. That is perhaps why poems about the moon perturb no one, but poems about color and poverty do perturb many citizens. Social forces pull backwards or forwards, right or left, and social poems get caught in the pulling and hauling. Sometimes the poet himself gets pulled and hauled—even hauled off to jail.

I have never been in jail but I have been detained by the Japanese police in Tokyo and by the immigration authorities in Cuba—in custody, to put it politely—due, no doubt, to their interest in my written words. These authorities would hardly have detained me had I been a writer of the roses and moonlight school. I have never known the police of any country to show an interest in lyric poetry as such. But when poems stop talking about the moon and begin to mention poverty, trade unions, color lines, and colonies, somebody tells the police. The history of world literature has many examples of poets fleeing into exile to escape persecution, of poets in jail, even of poets killed like Placido or, more recently, Lorca in Spain.

My adventures as a social poet are mild indeed compared to the body-breaking, soul-searing experiences of poets in the recent Fascist countries or of the resistance poets of the Nazi-invaded lands during the war. For that reason, I can use so light a word as "adventure" in regard to my own skirmishes with reaction and censorship.

My adventures as a social poet began in a colored church in Atlantic City shortly after my first book, *The Weary Blues,* was published in 1926. I had been invited to come down to the shore from Lincoln University where I was a student, to give a program of my poems in the church. During the course of my program I read several of my poems in the form of the Negro folk songs, including some blues poems about hard luck and hard work. As I read I noticed a deacon approach the pulpit with a note which he placed on the rostrum beside me, but I did not stop to open the note until I had finished and had acknowledged the applause of a cordial audience. The note read, "Do not read any more blues in my pulpit." It was signed by the minister. That was my first experience with censorship.

The kind and generous woman who sponsored my writing for a few years after my college days did not come to the point quite so directly as did the minister who disliked blues. Perhaps, had it not been in the midst of the great depression of the late '20's and '30's, the kind of poems that I am afraid helped to end her patronage might not have been written. But it was impossible for me to travel from hungry Harlem to the lovely homes on Park Avenue without feeling in my soul the great gulf between the very poor and the very rich in our society. In those days, on the way to visit this kind lady I would see the homeless sleeping in subways and the hungry begging in doorways on sleet-stung winter days. It was then that I wrote a poem called "Advertisement for the Waldorf-Astoria," satirizing the slick-paper magazine advertisements of the opening of that de luxe hotel. Also I wrote:

PARK BENCH

I live on a park bench,
You, Park Avenue.
Hell of a distance
Between us two.

I beg a dime for dinner—
You got a butler and maid.
But I'm wakin' up!
Say, ain't you afraid

That I might, just maybe,
In a year or two,
Move on over
To Park Avenue?

In a little while I did not have a patron any more.

But that year I won a prize, the Harmon Gold Award for Literature, which consisted of a medal and four hundred dollars. With the four hundred dollars I went to Haiti. On the way I stopped in Cuba and I was cordially received by the writers and artists. I had written poems about the exploitation of Cuba by the sugar barons and I had translated many poems of Nicolás Guillén such as:

CANE

Negro
In the cane fields.
White man
Above the cane fields
Earth
Beneath the cane fields.
Blood
That flows from us.

This was during the days of the dictatorial Machado regime. Perhaps someone called his attention to these poems and translations because, when I came back from Haiti weeks later, I was not allowed to land in Cuba, but was detained by the immigration authorities at Santiago and put on an island until the American consul came, after three days, to get me off with the provision that I cross the country to Havana and leave Cuban soil at once.

That was my first time being put out of any place. But since that time I have been put out of or barred from quite a number of places, all because of my poetry—not the roses and moonlight poems (which I write, too) but because of poems about poverty, oppression, and segregation. Nine Negro boys in Alabama were on trial for their lives when I got back from Cuba and Haiti. The famous Scottsboro "rape" case was in full session. I visited those boys in the death house at Kilby Prison, and I wrote many poems about them. One of these poems was:

CHRIST IN ALABAMA

Christ is a Nigger,
Beaten and black—
O, bare your back.

Mary is His Mother—
Mammy of the South,
Silence your mouth.

God's His Father—
White Master above,
Grant us your love.

Most holy bastard
Of the bleeding mouth:
Nigger Christ
On the cross of the South.

Contempo, a publication of some of the students at the University of North Carolina, published the poem on its front page on the very day that I was being presented in a program of my poems at the University in Chapel Hill. That evening there were police outside the building in which I spoke, and in the air the rising tension of race that is peculiar to the South. It had been rumored that some of the local citizenry were saying that I should be run out of town, and that one of the sheriffs agreed, saying, "Sure, he ought to be run out! It's bad enough to call Christ a *bastard*. But when he calls him a *nigger*, he's gone too far!"

The next morning a third of my fee was missing when I was handed my check. One of the departments of the university jointly sponsoring my program had refused to come through with its portion of the money. Nevertheless, I remember with pleasure the courtesy and kindness of many of the students and faculty at Chapel Hill and their lack of agreement with the anti-Negro elements of the town. There I began to learn at the University of North Carolina how hard it is to be a white liberal in the South.

It was not until I had been to Russia and around the world as a writer and journalist that censorship and opposition to my poems reached the point of completely preventing me from appearing in public programs on a few occasions. It happened first in Los Angeles shortly after my return from the Soviet Union. I was to have been one of several speakers on a memorial program to be held at the colored branch Y.M.C.A. for a young Negro journalist of the community. At the behest of white higher-ups, no doubt, some reactionary Negro politicians informed the Negro Y.M.C.A. that I was a Communist. The secretary of the Negro Branch Y then informed the committee of young people in charge of the memorial that they could have their program only if I did not appear.

I have never been a Communist, but I soon learned that anyone visiting the Soviet Union and speaking with favor of it upon returning is liable to be so labeled. Indeed when Mrs. Roosevelt, Walter White, and so Christian a lady as Mrs. Bethune who has never been in Moscow, are so labeled, I should hardly be surprised! I wasn't surprised. And the young people's committee informed the Y secretary that since the Y was a public community center which they helped to support, they saw no reason why it should censor their memorial program to the extent of eliminating any speaker.

Since I had been allotted but a few moments on the program, it was my intention simply to read this short poem of mine:

Dear lovely death
That taketh all things under wing,
Never to kill,
Only to change into some other
    thing
This suffering flesh—
To make it either more or less
But not again the same,
Dear lovely death,
Change is thy other name.

But the Negro branch Y, egged on by the reactionary politicians (whose incomes, incidentally, were allegedly derived largely from gambling houses and other underworld activities), informed the young people's committee that the police would be at the door to prevent my entering the Y on the afternoon of the scheduled program. So when the crowd gathered, the memorial was not held that Sunday. The young people simply informed the audience of the situation and said that the memorial would be postponed until a place could be found where all the participants could be heard. The program was held elsewhere a few Sundays later.

Somebody with malice aforethought (probably the Negro politicians of Uncle Tom vintage) gave the highly publicized California evangelist, Aimee Semple McPherson, a copy of a poem of mine, "Goodbye, Christ." This poem was one of my least successful efforts at poetic communication, in that many persons have misinterpreted it as an anti-Christian poem. I intended it to be just the opposite. Satirical, even ironic, in style, I meant it to be a poem against those whom I felt were misusing religion for worldly or

profitable purposes. In the poem I mentioned Aimee Semple McPherson. This apparently made her angry. From her Angelus Temple pulpit she preached against me, saying, "There are many devils among us, but the most dangerous of all is the red devil. And now there comes among us a red devil *in a black skin!*"

She gathered her followers together and sent them to swoop down upon me one afternoon at an unsuspecting and innocent literary luncheon in Pasadena's Vista del Arroyo Hotel. Robert Nathan, I believe, was one of the speakers, along with a number of other authors. I was to have five minutes on the program to read a few poems from my latest collection of folk verses, *Shakespeare in Harlem,* hardly a radical book.

When I arrived at the hotel by car from Los Angeles, I noticed quite a crowd in the streets where the traffic seemed to be tangled. So I got out some distance from the front of the hotel and walked through the grounds to the entrance, requesting my car to return at three o'clock. When I asked in the lobby for the location of the luncheon, I was told to wait until the desk clerk sent for the chairman, George Palmer Putnam. Mr. Putnam arrived with the manager, both visibly excited. They informed me that the followers of Aimee McPherson were vehemently picketing the hotel because of my appearance there. The manager added with an aggrieved look that he could not have such a commotion in front of his hotel. Either I would have to go or he would cancel the entire luncheon.

Mr. Putnam put it up to me. I said that rather than inconvenience several hundred guests and a half dozen authors, I would withdraw—except that I did not know where my car had gone, so would someone be kind enough to drive me to the station. Just then a doorman came in to inform the manager that traffic was completely blocked in front of the hotel. Frantically the manager rushed out. About that time a group of Foursquare Gospel members poured into the lobby in uniforms and armbands and surrounded me and George Palmer Putnam demanding to know if we were Christians. Before I could say anything, Mr. Putnam lit into them angrily, saying it was none of their business and stating that under our Constitution a man could have any religion he chose, as well as freedom to express himself.

Just then an old gentleman [of] about seventy-two who was one of the organizers of the literary luncheon came up, saying he had been asked to drive me to the station and get me out of there so they could start the luncheon. Shaking hands with Mr. Putnam, I accompanied the old gentleman to the street. There Aimee's sound truck has been backed across the roadway blocking all passage so that limousines, trucks, and taxis were tangled up in all directions. The sound truck was playing "God Bless America" while hundreds of pickets milled about with signs denouncing Langston Hughes—atheistic Red. Rich old ladies on the arms of their chauffeurs were trying to get through the crowd to the luncheon. Reporters were dashing about.

None of the people recognized me, but in the excitement the old gentleman could not find his car. Finally he hailed a taxi and nervously thrust a dollar into the driver's hand with the request that I be driven to the station. He asked to be excused himself in order to get back to the luncheon. Just as I reached out the door to shake hands in farewell, three large white ladies with banners rushed up to the cab. One of them screamed, "We don't shake hands with niggers where we come from!"

The thought came over me that the picketing might turn into a race riot, in which case I did not wish to be caught in a cab in a traffic jam alone. I did not turn loose the old gentleman's hand. Instead of shaking it in farewell, I simply pulled him into the taxi with me, saying, "I thought you were going to the station, too."

As the pickets snarled outside, I slammed the door. The driver started off, but we were caught in the traffic blocked by the sound truck lustily playing "God Bless America." The old gentleman trembled beside me, until finally we got clear of the mob. As we backed down a side street and turned to head for the station, the sirens of approaching police cars were heard in the distance.

Later I learned from the afternoon papers that the whole demonstration had been organized by Aimee McPherson's publicity man, and that when the police arrived he had been arrested for refusing to give up the keys to the sound truck stalled midway in the street to block the traffic. This simply proved the point I had tried to make in the poem—that the church might as well bid Christ goodbye if His gospel were left in the hands of such people.

Four years later I was to picketed again in Detroit by Gerald L. K. Smith's Mothers of America—for ever since the Foursquare Gospel demonstration in California, reactionary groups have copied, used and distributed this poem. Always they have been groups like Smith's, never known to help the fight for democratic Negro rights in America, but rather to use their energies to foment riots such as that before Detroit's Sojourner Truth housing project where the Klanminded tried to prevent colored citizens from occupying government homes built for them.

I have had one threatening communication signed *A Klansman*. And many scurrilous anonymous anti-Negro letters from persons whose writing did not always indicate illiteracy. On a few occasions, reactionary elements have forced liberal sponsors to cancel their plans to present me in a reading of my poems. I recall that in Gary, Indiana, some years ago the colored teachers were threatened with the loss of their jobs if I accepted their invitation to appear at one of the public schools. In another city a white high school principal, made apprehensive by a small group of reactionary parents, told me that he communicated with the F.B.I. at Washington to find out if I were a member of the Communist party. Assured that I was not, with the approval of his school board, he presented me to his study body. To further fortify his respectability, that morning at assembly, he had invited all of the Negro ministers and civic leaders of the town to sit on the stage in a semi-circle behind me. To the students it must have looked like a kind of modern minstrel show, as it was the first time any Negroes at all had been invited to their assembly.

So goes the life of social poet. I am sure none of these things would ever have happened to me had I limited the subject matter of my poems to roses and moonlight. But, unfortunately, I was born poor—and colored—and almost all the prettiest roses I have seen have been in rich white people's yards—not in mine. That is why I cannot write exclusively about roses and moonlight—for sometimes in the moonlight my brothers see a fiery cross and a circle of Klansmen's hoods. Sometimes in the moonlight a dark body sways from a lynching tree—but for his funeral there are no roses.

◇ ◇ ◇

Langston Hughes Speaks

LANGSTON HUGHES

During a period in my life coinciding roughly with the beginning of the Scottsboro Case and the depression of the 1930's and running through to the Nazi-Soviet Pact, I wrote a number of poems which reflected my then deep sympathies with certain of the aims and objectives of the leftist philosophies and the interests of the Soviet Union in the problem of poverty, minorities, colonial peoples, and particularly of Negroes and Jim Crow. Most of these poems appeared only in booklet form and have long been out of print. I was amazed to learn that some of these out-dated examples of my work are today being circulated in our State Department's overseas libraries. Written, some of them, partially in leftist terminology with the red flag as a symbol of freedom, they could hardly serve to present a contemporary picture of American ideals or of my personal ones.

I am not now and have never been a member of the Communist party, and have so stated over the years in my speeches and writings. But there is in my family a long history of participation in social struggle—from my grandfather who went to prison for helping slaves to freedom and another relative who died with John Brown at Harper's Ferry to my great uncle, John M. Langston, only Negro Representative in Congress from Virginia following the Reconstruction, and who had supported Abraham Lincoln in his recruiting Negro troops, and spoken for freedom on the same platform with Garrison and Phillips. In my own youth, faced with the problems of both poverty and color, and penniless at the beginning of the depression, I was strongly attracted by some of the promises of Communism, but always with the reservations, among others, of a creative writer wishing to preserve my own freedom of action and expression—and as an American Negro desiring full integration into our body politic. These two reservations—particularly (since I could never accept the totalitarian regimentation of the artist nor the Communist theory of a Negro state for the Black Belt)—were among other reasons why I never contemplated joining the Communist party, although various aspects of Communist interests were for some years reflected in the emotional content of my writing. But I was shocked at the Nazi-Soviet Pact, just as I am shocked now by the reported persecution of the Jewish people. And I was disturbed by the complete lack of freedom of press and publication I observed in the USSR. In our own country I have been greatly heartened in recent years by the progress being made in race-relations, by the recent Supreme Court decisions relative to Negro education, restrictive covenants, the ballot, and travel. My work of the war years, and my latest books have reflected this change of emphasis and development in my own thinking and orientation. This is, I think, clearly and simply shown in the last paragraph of my latest book [*The First Book of Negroes*]:

Our country has many problems still to solve, but America is young, big, strong, and beautiful. And we are trying very hard to be, as the flag says, 'one nation, indivisible, with liberty and justice for all.' Here people are free to vote and work out their problems. In some countries people are governed by rulers, and ordinary folks can't do a thing about it. But here all of us are a part of democracy. By taking an interest in our government, and by treating our neighbors as we would like to be treated, each one of us can help make our country the most wonderful country in the world.

◊ ◊ ◊

Swinging High

LANGSTON HUGHES

"A meat ball by any other name is still a meat ball just the same," said Simple. "My wife, Joyce, is a fiend for foreign foods. Almost every time she drags me downtown to a show, she wants to go eat in some new kind of restaurant, Spanish, French, Greek, or who knows what? Last night we had something writ on the menu in a Philippine restaurant in big letters as Bola-Bolas. They returned out to be nothing but meat balls."

"*Bola* probably means 'ball' in their language," I said. "But I am like Joyce. I sort of go for foreign foods, too—something different once in a while, you know."

"Me, I like plain old down-home victuals, soul food with corn bread," said Simple, "spare ribs, pork chops, and things like that. Ham hock, string beans, salt pork and cabbage."

"All good foods," I said, "but for a change, why not try chicken curry and rootie next time you take Joyce out."

"What is that?" asked Simple.

"An East Indian dish, chicken stewed in curry sauce."

"I am not West Indian nor East," said Simple.

"You don't have to be foreign to like foreign food," I said.

"Left to me, I would go to Jenny Lou's up yonder on Seventh Avenue across from Small's Paradise. Jenny Lou's is where all the down-home folks eat when they is visiting Harlem. They knows good home-like food a mile away by the way it smells."

"A restaurant is not supposed to smell," I said. "The scent of cooking is supposed to be kept in the kitchen."

"Jenny Lou's kitchen is in the dining room," said Simple. "When I were a single man, I et there often. Them low prices suited my pocket."

"How about Frank's?" I asked. "Now Negro-owned."

"That's where Joyce takes her society friends like Mrs. Maxwell-Reeves," said Simple. "The menu is as big as newspaper. So many things on it, it is hard to know what to pick out. I like to just say 'pork chops' and be done with it. I don't want soup, neither salad. And who wants rice pudding for dessert? Leave off them things, also olives. Just give me pork chops."

"Is that all?"

"I'll take the gravy," Simple said.

"Pork chops, bread, and gravy," I shook my head. "As *country* as you can be!"

"If that is what you call *country*," said Simple. "still gimme pork chops. Pork chops and fried apples maybe, if they is on the menu. I love fried apples, and my Uncle Tige had an apple tree in his back yard. When I was a little small boy, I used to set in a rope swing behind my Uncle Tige's house. The swing were attached to that apple

tree which were a very old apple tree, and big for an apple tree, and a good tree for a swing for boys and girls. It were nice to set in this swing when I was yet a wee small boy and be pushed by the bigger children because I was still too small for my feet to touch the ground, and I did not know how to pump myself up into the air. Later I could. Later I could stand up in that swing and pump myself way up into the air, almost as high as the limb on which the swing were tied. Oh, I remember very well that swing and that apple tree when I were a child.

"It looks to me life is like a swing," continued Simple. "When young, somebody else must push you because your feet are too short to touch the ground and start the swing in motion. But later you go for yourself. By and by, you can stand up and swing high, swing high, way high up, and you are on your own. How wonderful it is to stand up in the swing, pumping all by yourself! But suppose the rope was to break, the tree limb snap off when you have pumped yourself up so high? Suppose it dies? You will be the one to fall, nobody else, just you yourself. Yes, life is like a swing! But in spite of all and everything, it is good to swing. Oh, yes! The swing of life is wonderful, but if you are a colored swinger, you have to have a stout heart, pump hard, and hold tight to get even a few feet above the ground. And be careful that your neighbor next door, white, has not cut your rope, so that just when you are swinging highest, it will break and throw you to the ground. 'Look at the Negro swinging! But he done fell!' they say. But someday we gonna swing right up to the very top of the tree and not fall. Yes, someday we will."

"Integrated, I hope," I said.

"Yes, integrated, I reckon," said Simple. "But some folks is getting so wrapped up in this integration thing, white and colored, that I do believe some of them is going stone-cold crazy. You see how here in New York peoples is talking to themselves on buses and in the subways, whirling around in the middle of the street, mumbling and grumbling all by themselves to nobody on park benches, dumping garbage on bridges, slicing up subway seats with knives and nail files, running out of gas on crowded highways on purpose and liable to get smashed up in traffic jams. Oh, I do not know what has come over the human race—like that nice young white minister in Cleveland laying down *behind* a rolling bulldozer, *not* in front of it—where the driver could see him and maybe stop in time before the man got crushed to death. He were protesting Jim Crow—but sometimes the protest is worse than the Crow."

"That earnest white man, no doubt, was trying to call attention to the urgency of the civil rights," I said. "He wanted to keep the movement on the front pages of the newspapers."

"It has been on the front pages of the newspapers for ten years," said Simple, "and if everybody does not know by now something needs to be done about civil rights, they will never know. After so many Freedom Rides and sit-ins and picketings and head bustings and police dogs and bombings and little children blowed up, and teenagers in jail by the thousands up to now, and big headlines across the newspapers, colored and white, why did that good white minister in Cleveland with his glasses on have to lay down *behind* a bulldozer?"

"I gather there are some things you would not do for a cause," I said.

"I would not lay down behind a bulldozer going backwards. How would my dying help anything—and my wife, Joyce, would be left a widow? It is not that I might be dying in a good cause, but let me die on my own two feet, knowing where, when, and why, and maybe making a speech telling off the world—not in a wreck because somebody has stalled a car whilst traffic is speeding. To me that is crazy! Whoever drives them stalled cars might be smashed up and killed too."

"They would consider themselves martyrs," I said.

"They should not make a martyr out of me in another car who do not even know them," said Simple. "Let me make a martyr out of myself, if I want to, but don't make me one under other peoples' cars. I do not want to be a martyr on nobody else's time. And don't roll no bulldozer over me unless I am standing in front, not behind it when it rolls. If I have got to look death in the face ahead of time, at least let me know who is driving. Also don't take me by surprise before I have paid my next year's dues to the NAACP. Anyhow, a car or a bulldozer is a dangerous thing to fool around with, as is any kind of moving machinery. You remember that old joke about the washer-woman who bent over too far and got both her breasts caught in the wringer? There is such a thing as bending over too far—even to get your clothes clean. Certainly there is plenty of dirty linen in this U.S.A., but I do not advise nobody to get their breast caught in a wringer. Machines do not have no sense."

"A cynic might say the same thing about martyrs," I said. "Except sometimes it takes an awful lot of sense to have no sense."

"Maybe you are right," said Simple, "just like it takes a mighty lot of pumping to swing high in the swing of life."

◊ ◊ ◊

The Origins of Poetry in Langston Hughes

ARNOLD RAMPERSAD

In his study *The Life of the Poet: Beginning and Ending Poetic Careers* (1981) Lawrence Lipking asks three main questions, one of which concerns me here in the case of Langston Hughes: "How does an aspiring author of verses become a poet?" In the case of John Keats, for example, how did the poet arrive at "On First Looking Into Chapman's Homer," that great leap in creative ability in which Keats, sweeping from the legend of "the realms of gold" toward modern history, "catches sight not of someone else's dream but of his own reality? He stares at his future, and surmises that he may be a poet. The sense of possibility is thrilling, the moment truly awesome. Keats has discovered Keats." Or in the well-known words of Keats himself: "The Genius of Poetry must work out its own salvation in a man: It cannot be matured by law & precept, but by sensation & watchfulness in itself—That which is creative must create itself."

Can one ask a similar question about the origins of poetry in Langston Hughes, who in June 1921, at the age of nineteen, began a celebrated career when he published his own landmark poem "The Negro Speaks of Rivers" in W.E.B. Du Bois' *Crisis* magazine? Like Keats before "Chapman's Homer," Hughes had written poems before "The Negro Speaks of Rivers." Much of the poetry before "Rivers" is available for examination, since Hughes published steadily in the monthly magazine of his high school in Cleveland, Ohio. Certain aspects of this verse are noteworthy. It has nothing to do with race; it is dominated by images of the poet not as a teenager but as a little child; and, in Hughes's junior year, he published his first poem in free verse, one that showed the clear influence of Walt Whitman for the first (but not the last) time. Revealing an increase in skill, Hughes's early poetry nevertheless gives no sign of a major poetic talent in the making. At some point in his development, however, something happened to Hughes that was as mysterious and as wonderful, in its own way, as the miracle that overtook John Keats after the watchful night spent with his friend Charles Cowden Clarke and a copy of Chapman's translation. With "The Negro Speaks of Rivers" the creativity in Langston Hughes, hitherto unexpressed, suddenly created itself.

In writing thus about Hughes, are we taking him too seriously? With a few exceptions, literary critics have resisted offering even a modestly complicated theory concerning his creativity. His relentless affability and charm, his deep, open love of the black masses, his devotion to their folk forms, and his insistence on writing poetry that they could understand, all have contributed to the notion that Langston Hughes was intellectually and emotionally shallow. One wonders, then, at the source of the creative energy that drove him from 1921 to 1967 to write so many poems, novels, short stories, plays, operas, popular histories, children's books, and assorted other work. As a poet, Hughes virtually reinvented Afro-American poetry with his pioneering use of the blues and other folk forms; as Howard Mumford Jones marveled in a 1927 review, Hughes added the verse form of the blues to poetry in English (a form that continues to attract the best black poets, including Michael Harper, Sherley Anne Williams, and Raymond Patterson). One wonders, too, in his aspect as a poet, why this apparently happy, apparently shallow man defined his creativity in terms of unhappiness. "I felt bad for the next three or four years," he would write in *The Big Sea* about the period beginning more or less with the publication of "The Negro Speaks of Rivers," and "those were the years when I wrote most of my poetry. (For my best poems were all written when I felt the worst. When I was happy, I didn't write anything)."

Hughes actively promoted the image of geniality to which I have alluded. Wanting and needing to be loved, he scrubbed and polished his personality until there was no abrasive side, no jagged edge that might wound another human being. Publicly and privately, his manner belied the commonly held belief that creativity and madness are allied, that neuroses and a degree of malevolence are the fair price of art. His autobiographies, *The Big Sea* (1940) and *I Wonder As I Wander* (1956), made no enemies; to many readers, Hughes's mastery of that form consists in his ability to cross its chill deep by paddling nonchalantly on its surface. And yet in two places, no doubt deliberately, Hughes allows the reader a glimpse of inner turmoil. Both appear in the earlier book, *The Big Sea*. Both involve personal and emotional conflicts so intense that they led to physical illness. Because of their extreme rarity, as well as their strategic location in the context of his creativity, these passages deserve close scrutiny if we hope to glimpse the roots of Hughes's originality as a poet.

The first of these two illnesses took place in the summer of 1919, when Hughes (at seventeen) saw his father for the first time in a dozen years. In 1903, James Hughes had gone to Mexico, where he would become a prosperous property owner. In a lonely, impoverished, passed-around childhood in the Midwest, his son had fantasized about the man "as a kind of strong, bronze cowboy, in a big Mexican hat, going back and forth from his business in the city to his ranch in the mountains, free—in a land where there were no white folks to draw the color line, and no tenements with rent always due—just mountains and cacti: Mexico!" Elated to be invited suddenly to Mexico in 1919 at the end of his junior year in high school, Langston left the United States with high hopes for his visit.

The summer was a disaster. James Hughes proved to be an unfeeling, domineering, and materialistic man, scornful of Indians and blacks (he was himself black) and the poor in general; and contemptuous of his son's gentler pace and artistic temperament. One day, Langston could take no more: "Suddenly my stomach began to turn over and over. And I could not swallow another mouthful. Waves of heat engulfed me. My eyes burned. My body shook. I wanted more than anything on earth to hit my father, but instead I got up from the table and went back to bed. The bed went round and round and the room turned dark. Anger clotted in every vein, and my tongue tasted like dry blood." But the boy, ill for a long time, never confessed the true cause of his affliction. Having been moved to Mexico City, he declined to help his doctors: "I never told them . . . that I was sick because I hated my father." He recovered only when it was time to return to the United States.

Hughes's second major illness came eleven years later. By this time he had finished high school, returned to Mexico to live with his father for a year, attended Columbia University for one year (supported grudgingly by James Hughes), dropped out of school, and served as a messman on voyages to Africa and to Europe, where he spent several months in 1924 as a dishwasher. All the while, however, Hughes was publishing poetry in a variety of places, especially in important black journals. This activity culminated in books of verse published in 1926 (*The Weary Blues*) and 1927 (*Fine Clothes to the Jew*) that established him, with Countee Cullen, as one of two major black poets of the decade. In 1929, he graduated after three and a half years at black Lincoln University, Pennsylvania. In 1930, Hughes published his first novel, *Not Without Laughter*.

This book had been virtually dragged out of him by his patron of the preceding three years, "Godmother" (as she wished to be called), an old, white, very generous but eccentric woman who ruled Hughes with a benevolent despotism inspired by her volatile beliefs in African spirituality, folk culture, mental telepathy, and the potential of his genius. But the result of her largesse was a paradox: the more comfortable he grew, the less Hughes was inclined to create. Estranged by his apparent languor, his patron finally seized on an episode of conflict to banish him once and for all. Hughes was devastated. Surviving drafts of his letters to "Godmother" reveal him deep in self-abasement before a woman with whom he was clearly in love. Ten years later, he confessed in *The Big Sea:* "I cannot write here about that last half-hour in the big bright drawing-room high above Park Avenue . . .

because when I think about it, even now, something happens in the pit of my stomach that makes me ill. That beautiful room . . . suddenly became like a trap closing in, faster and faster, the room darker and darker, until the light went out with a sudden crash in the dark, and everything became like . . . that morning in Mexico when I suddenly hated my father.

"I was violently and physically ill, with my stomach turning over and over. . . . And there was no rationalizing anything. I couldn't." For several months, according to my research (Hughes erroneously presents a far briefer time frame in *The Big Sea*), he waited in excruciating hope for a reconciliation. As in Mexico, he wasted time and money on doctors without revealing to them the source of his chronic illness (which one very ingenious Harlem physician diagnosed as a Japanese tapeworm). Rather than break his silence, Hughes even agreed to have his tonsils removed. Gradually it became clear that reconciliation was impossible. Winning a prize of four hundred dollars for his novel, Hughes fled to seclusion in hot, remote Haiti. When his money ran out some months later, he returned home, healed at last but badly scarred.

Although they occurred more than a decade apart, the two illnesses were similar. Both showed a normally placid Hughes driven into deep rage by an opponent, a rage which he was unable to ventilate because the easy expression of personal anger and indignation was anathema to him. In both cases, he developed physical symptoms of hyperventilation and, eventually, anemia. More importantly, both were triggered in a period of relatively low poetic creativity (as when he was still a juvenile poet) or outright poetic inactivity (as with his patron). In each instance, Hughes had become satisfied with this low creativity or inactivity. At both times, a certain powerful figure, first his father, then "Godmother," had opposed his right to be content. His father had opposed any poetic activity at all; "Godmother" had opposed his right to enjoy the poetical state without true poetical action, or writing. In other words, a powerful will presented itself in forceful opposition to what was, in one sense, a vacuum of expressive will on Hughes's part. (Needless to say, the *apparent* absence of will in an individual can easily be a token of the presence of a very powerful will.) The result on both occasions, which was extraordinary, was first Hughes's endurance of, then his violent rebellion against, a force of will that challenged his deepest vision of the poetic life.

I use the term "will" knowing that to many people it is an obsolete concept, in spite of the revival of interest in Otto Rank, or continuing critiques of Freud's use of the term as, for example, Harold Bloom's excellent essay "Freud's Concepts of Defense and the Poetic Will." But I am referring here mainly, though not exclusively, to the will as a function of consciousness, as in the case of "Godmother's" will, or that of Hughes's father, or—far less demonstrably—Hughes's own volition. And what do I mean by Hughes's "vision of poetic life"? I refer to what one might call unshaped or amorphous poetic consciousness, poetry not concretized or written down, but the crucial element (when combined with poetic "material") out of which written or oral poetry is made. In an old-fashioned but still significant way, the poet Richard Eberhart has written of "Will and Psyche in Poetry" (in Don Cameron Allen's *The Moment of Poetry,* 1962). Poems of the will value

the body, activity, struggle, and the things of this world; poems of the psyche endorse spirit, "an uncontaminated grace," and the "elusive, passive, imaginative quality" of the world beyond this world. A poem of will, such as Marvell's "To His Coy Mistress," might involve a man calling a woman to bed; for an exemplary poem of psyche, Eberhart chose Poe's "To Helen," where desire leads directly away from sexuality toward spirit.

The notorious placidity of surface in Hughes, as I see it, bespeaks the extent to which he was a poet who preferred his poems unwritten—a poet, like his great mentor Walt Whitman, who saw his life itself as a poem greater than any poem he could possibly write. Hughes's greatest poetical instinct was to preserve his unformed or dormant poetic consciousness as the highest form of poetry. Such an instinct may suggest infantilism; one remembers Freud's unfortunate words about the link between creative writing and daydreaming. Infantilism would be wrong as an explanation. But, in Hughes's case, I suspect, the instinct had something to do with the youthfulness of the self he clearly regarded as his authentic, or most cherished self. Placidity of surface, anxiety to please and to be loved, apparent asexuality (the most consistent conclusion—rather than that of homosexuality, for which there is no evidence—about his libido among people who knew him well), and the compulsion against concretized or written poetry reflect a sense of self as prepubescent, or apubescent; in other words, a sense of self as an eternal child. At some level, Hughes saw himself ideally as a child—a dreamy genius child, a perfect child, a princely child, a loving child, even a mothering and maternal child—but first and foremost as a child (almost never is he the destructively rebellious child, in spite of his radical poetry).

It must be stressed that such a sense of self, although it modulates art (as does every other factor of comparable importance), is by no means an inherent handicap to a creative person. In any event, Hughes teetered between a sense of confidence (a sense of being loved by a particular person to whom he was emotionally mortgaged) and a rival, harrowing sense, born in his own childhood, of abandonment and despair. The latter was closer to the origins of his poetry. Release Hughes as an artist from the stabilizing social context and he flies almost immediately toward themes of nihilism and death. For example, take his poem "Border Line":

> I used to wonder
> About living and dying—
> I think the difference lies
> Between tears and crying.

> I used to wonder
> About here and there—
> I think the distance
> Is nowhere.

Or "Genius Child":

> . . . *Nobody loves a genius child.*

> Can you love an eagle,
> Tame or wild?

> Wild or tame,
> Can you love a monster
> Of frightening name?

> *Nobody loves a genius child.*

> *Kill him*—and let his soul run wild!

Or "End":

> There are
> No clocks on the wall,
> And no time,
> No shadows that move

> From dawn to dusk
> Across the floor.

> There is neither light
> Nor dark
> Outside the door.

> *There is no door!*

In Hughes's writing, there is precious little middle ground between such verse and that for which he is far better known (and deservedly so), the poems steeped in race and other social concerns. Nature as flora and fauna bored the man who preferred Harlem in hot summer to the cool New England woods, as he once joked, because "I prefer wild people to wild animals." Hughes understood wherein his salvation rested.

This bleakness, almost always ignored in critical treatments of Hughes, evolved out of the saturation of his dormant poetical consciousness by the powerful will toward death stimulated in him by his loneliness as a child. But Hughes did not surrender passively to the force of his father and "Godmother" when they turned against him. These attacks, in fact, elicited in him a massive retaliatory display of willfulness, at first (while he was ill) as uncontrolled and uncontrollable as the right to the passive poetic consciousness it defended. The invocation of will in such massive degree could easily have remained as toxic as it was while he was sick with his silent rage. Only the modification of will, a compromise between passive poetic consciousness and the purposefulness needed to defend that consciousness, could prevent the consummation of poetry (amorphous or concrete) by rage. And only an appeal to a third force that was neither Hughes nor his enemy could allow him to fashion a balance between will and his unformed poetical consciousness.

Both in the experience with his father in Mexico and in the struggle with "Godmother," the third force was represented by the black race. Hughes's attitude to the black masses is too complicated to detail here. But my argument depends on the crucial understanding that Hughes was virtually unique among major black writers not so much because of the considerable depth of his love of black people, but because of *the depth of his psychological dependence on them.* Hughes became dependent because of a relatively complicated set of circumstances in his youth, when he was reared by his poor but very proud grandmother, the aged, wrinkled, and laconic Mary Langston, whose first husband had died at Harpers Ferry with John Brown. But Mary Langston's zeal to defend the rights of her race was offset for her grandson by her personal remoteness both from him and the race, and by the severity of her pride—a pride compounded by her very light skin, her Indian rather than predominantly African features, her Oberlin education, and her high-toned religion, which all kept her distant from the black masses. She did not attend black churches, did not sing black spirituals (much less the blues); she spoke in a clipped manner, rather than a folksy drawl, and she detested popular culture—as Hughes spelled out partially in *The Big Sea,* but more completely in an unpublished portrait prepared in 1943.

What Mary Langston offered in the abstract, however, was made wonderfully concrete to young Hughes by two persons with whom he lived from time to time (when his grandmother was forced to rent out her house, and after she died) and whom he described in an Arcadian paragraph in *The Big Sea*—"Uncle" and "Auntie" Reed. "Uncle" James Reed, who dug ditches for the city, smoked his pipe and stayed home on Sundays. "Auntie" Reed (later Mrs. Mary J. Reed Campbell) took Langston to St. Luke's A.M.E. church (a church apparently not good enough for his grandmother) and taught the Sunday School there in which the boy was the brightest star. Through the childless Reeds, who clearly adored the boy, he learned how to love the race, its church ways and folk ways, and its dreams and aspirations, of which the handsome, scrubbed, light brown boy, the grandson of "Colonel" Charles Langston (whose brother John Mercer Langston had served in the U.S. Congress and as an ambassador of the U.S.) was the shining embodiment. And it was a lie he told to the Reeds (that Jesus had come to Hughes at a revival meeting, after "Auntie" Reed had prayed that this would happen) that led to the major trauma of his childhood, as related in *The Big Sea*—a long weeping into the night (the second to last time he cried, Hughes wrote) because he had waited for Jesus, who had never come, then had lied to the people who loved him most. In *The Big Sea* Hughes would admit to hating his father; he would partly ridicule his mother; he would admit that he did not cry when his grandmother died. The Reeds, however, were different: "For me, there have never been any better people in the world. I loved them very much."

In his bitter struggles with his father and "Godmother," Hughes turned to the black race for direction. But one needs to remember that this appeal in itself hardly gave Hughes distinction as a poet; what made Hughes distinct was the highly original manner in which he internalized the Afro-American racial dilemma and expressed it in poems such as "When Sue Wears Red," "The Negro Speaks of Rivers," "Mother to Son,"

"Dream Variations," and "The Weary Blues," poems of Hughes's young manhood on which his career would rest. Of these, the most important was "The Negro Speaks of Rivers."

> I've known rivers.
> I've known rivers ancient as the
>   world and older than the flow of
>   human blood in human veins.
>
> My soul has grown deep like the
>   rivers.
>
> I bathed in the Euphrates when
>   dawns were young.
> I built my hut near the Congo and
>   it lulled me to sleep.
> I looked upon the Nile and raised
>   the pyramids above it.
> I heard the singing of the
>   Mississippi when Abe Lincoln
>   went down to New Orleans, and
>   I've seen its muddy bosom turn
>   all golden in the sunset.
>
> I've known rivers:
> Ancient, dusky rivers.
>
> My soul has grown deep like the
>   rivers.

Here, the persona moves steadily from dimly starred personal memory ("I've known rivers") toward a rendezvous with modern history (Lincoln going down the Mississippi and seeing the horror of slavery that, according to legend, would make him one day free the slaves). The death wish, benign but suffusing, of its images of rivers older than human blood, of souls grown as deep as these rivers, gives way steadily to an altering, ennobling vision whose final effect gleams in the evocation of the Mississippi's "muddy bosom" turning at last "all golden in the sunset." Personal anguish has been alchemized by the poet into a gracious meditation on his race, whose despised ("muddy") culture and history, irradiated by the poet's vision, changes within the poem from mud into gold. This is a classic example of the essential process of creativity in Hughes.

The poem came to him, according to Hughes (accurately, it seems clear) about ten months after his Mexican illness, when he was riding a train from Cleveland to Mexico to rejoin his father. The time was sundown, the place the Mississippi outside St. Louis. "All day on the train I had been thinking of my father," he would write in *The Big Sea*. "Now it was just sunset and we crossed the Mississippi, slowly, over a long bridge. I looked out of the window of the Pullman at the great muddy river flowing down toward the heart of the South, and I began to think what that river, the old Mississippi, had meant to Negroes in the past—how to be sold down the river was the worst fate that could overtake a slave in bondage. Then I remembered reading how Abraham Lincoln had made a trip down the Mississippi on a raft, and how he had seen slavery at its worst, and had decided within himself that it should be removed from American life. Then I began to think of other rivers in our past—the Congo, and the Niger, and the Nile in Africa—and the thought came to me: 'I've known rivers,' and I put it down on the back of an envelope I had in my pocket, and within the space of ten or fifteen minutes, as the train gathered speed in the dusk, I had written this poem."

Here, starting with anguish over his father, Hughes discovered the compressed ritual of passivity, challenge, turmoil, and transcendence he would probably have to re-create, doubtless in variant forms, during the great poetic trysts of his life. Even after he became a successful, published poet, the basic process remained the same, because his psychology remained largely the same even though he had become technically expert. In his second major illness, caused by his patron "Godmother," Hughes wrote poetry as he struggled for a transcendence that would be long in coming. The nature of that interim poetry is telling. When he sent some poems to a friend for a little book to be printed privately, she noticed at once that many spoke of death—"Dear lovely Death/That taketh all things under wing—/Never to kill. . . ." She called the booklet *Dear Lovely Death*. In "Afro-American Fragment," unlike in "The Negro Speaks of Rivers," Africa is seen plaintively:

> . . . Subdued and time-lost
> Are the drums—and yet
> Through some vast mist of race
> There comes this song
> I do not understand,
> This song of atavistic land,
> Of bitter yearnings lost
> Without a place—
> So long,
> So far away
> Is Africa's
> Dark face.

But when Hughes returned home, scarred but healed, after months in seclusion in Haiti, he no longer thought of loss and death. Instead, he plunged directly into the life of the black masses with a seven-month tour of the South in which he read his poetry in their churches and schools. Then he set out for the Soviet Union, where he would spend more than a year. Hughes then reached the zenith of his revolutionary ardor with poems (or verse) such as "Good Morning Revolution," "Goodbye Christ," and "Put One More 'S' in the USA."

"Good Morning Revolution," for example, and "The Negro Speaks of Rivers" are very different poems. The former is the polar opposite of the poetry of nihilism; the latter blends aspects of existential gloom with the life-affirming spirit of the black race. Together, the poems illustrate the wide range of possibility in the mixture of will and passivity which characterizes Hughes's art (although one can argue that "Good Morning Revolution"—by far the lesser poem— marks an overreaction of will, and thus is not truly representative of Hughes's poetic temperament in that it contains no element of passivity). But the creative process has remained the same. The right to amorphous poetic consciousness is challenged. The will is aroused in defense of that consciousness. Illness (an extreme version of Wallace Stevens' "blessed rage for order"?) marks the struggle of will against opposing will. The long-endured illness, in silence, gradually allows the mutual fertilization of will and poetic consciousness that is needed for concrete art. Illness ends when that ratio is achieved or perceived, and writing begins. Creativity, in Keats's term, has created itself. A poet, or a poem, is born.

To some extent, this process is nothing more than Wordsworth's definition of poetry as the final recollection "in tranquility" (a phrase often underplayed or even ignored in quoting Wordsworth's definition) of emotion that had once spontaneously overflowed. What is different, of course, is that Wordsworth (and Keats and Stevens) did not have to contend with race as a factor of his creativity. For many writers, perhaps even most, race is a distracting, demoralizing force. Hughes's genius, or his good fortune, consisted in his ability to accommodate race harmoniously within the scheme of creativity common to all major poets, and to turn it from an anomaly into an intimate advantage.

◆ ◆ ◆

"Midnight Ruffles of Cat-Gut Lace": The Boogie Poems of Langston Hughes

STEVEN C. TRACY

The influence of the blues tradition on Langston Hughes' poetry is by now an oft-discussed and readily accepted fact, although the depth and breadth of his employment of the tradition has not often been discussed with a similar depth and breadth. A close examination of a related sequence of Hughes' blues poems offers the opportunity to explore his fusion of oral and written traditions and to examine his tremendous skills as a literary-jazz improviser. That is not to suggest that Hughes' poems are spontaneous creations. Improvisation is normally thought of as a spontaneous act, but the jazz or blues musician's improvisations are in fact bounded by several things: the musician's "vocabulary"—style, patterns, techniques, and riffs; the accepted conventions of the specific genre (even if those conventions are deliberately violated, they are, in a large sense, at work); and the boundaries of the individual piece being performed. For example, boogie-woogie pianist Pete Johnson, in his 1947 version of "Swanee River Boogie," performs the melody of the song to a boogie-woogie beat, thereafter improvising solos built around the song's chord changes, the boogie-woogie beat, and variations on the melody of the piece, combined with his arsenal of boogie-woogie riffs and performed in his inimitable style.[1] Hughes, in his 1951 collection, *Montage of a Dream Deferred,* generated a set or sequence of six "boogie" poems—"Dream Boogie," "Easy Boogie," "Boogie 1 a.m.," "Lady's Boogie," "Nightmare Boogie," and

"Dream Boogie: Variation"—that have in common much more than the "boogie" of the titles. The poems comprise an intricate series of interwoven "improvisations" over a set boogie-woogie rhythm, with Hughes modulating and modifying rhythm, words, imagery, moods, and themes, and constructing a complex interrelationship between music, the musical instrument, the performance, and a set of attitudes exemplified by them.

Structurally, Hughes' six boogie poems share the exciting, rushing rhythms of boogie-woogie: Hughes at work on his poems, pounding out rhythms on his typewriter keyboard. Briefly, boogie-woogie is a form of Afro-American music, normally performed on the piano, that emerged as a recognizable genre in the 1920s. As blues researcher Karl Gert zur Heide points out, "the theme of boogie is the blues, some features derive from ragtime, and the rhythmic interplay of both hands can be traced back to African roots."[2] In boogie-woogie, the improvisations executed by the pianist's right hand on the treble keys of the piano are set off against the ostinato or repeated phrases of the left hand on the bass keys. Characteristically boogie-woogie follows the twelve-bar blues chord change pattern—in the key of C, CFC GFC—employing a repeated bass pattern recognizable most often for its eight beats to the bar and performed at a medium-to-fast tempo that builds an explosive drive and swing appropriate to the dance step after which it was named. Besides identifying a dance step and a type of music, however, the term "boogie" functions in other contexts: to boogie is to raise a ruckus or act wildly or uninhibitedly; it also has sexual connotations:

> I'm gonna pull off my pants and
> keep on my shirt,
> I'm gonna get so low you think I'm
> in the dirt.
> I'm gonna pitch a boogie-woogie,
> Gonna boogie-woogie all night
> long.[3]

In this tune, singer Big Bill Broonzy has taken a boogie-woogie beat suitable for dancing and provided both the "wild acting" and sexual connotations that go with it. In the tradition, the word carried these connotations, and typically Hughes tried to capture the ambience of the tradition.

Hughes demonstrated his knowledge of boogie-woogie in *The First Book of Jazz,* in which he and his coauthors identified among the outstanding exponents of boogie-woogie "Pinetop" Smith, Jimmy Yancy, Meade Lux Lewis, Albert Ammons, and Pete Johnson—all important and generally recognized masters.[4] It was the spirited, exuberant, danceable, and often rhythmically complex and intricate music of performers like those men that provided the basis for Hughes' boogie poem rhythms and the connotations of the word and the tradition that he tried to capture in his poems.

Hughes obviously wanted us to hear the boogie rhythms in these poems: the first four poems in the boogie sequence ("Dream," "Easy," "1 a.m.," and "Lady's") are very "aural"; the words "hear" and "heard" are employed repeatedly, both in a question—

> Ain't you heard
> The boogie-woogie rumble
> Of a dream deferred?[5]

and an assertion—

> I know you've heard
> The boogie-woogie rumble
> Of a dream deferred. ("Boogie 1
> a.m.," p. 250)

The incessant rhythm and rumbling of boogie-woogie becomes in the poems symbolic of the dream he had delineated in his earlier poem "Dream Variations":

> To fling my arms wide
> In some place of the sun,
> To whirl and to dance
> Till the white day is done.
> Then rest at cool evening
> Beneath a tall tree
> While night comes on gently,
> Dark like me—
> That is my dream! ("Dream
> Variations," p. 14)

Hughes is trying to get black people to recognize that the deferment of that dream is a large part of their lives, both by questioning and by asserting the "obvious." If they hadn't heard that boogie-woogie rumble, they could certainly hear it in the rhythms of Hughes' poems; for example, if one were to treat "Dream Boogie," the first poem of the sequence and therefore a prototype for the other poems in the sequence, as if it were a lyric to be sung to boogie-woogie music, and identify the beats and chord changes as they relate to the words, the annotation would look as follows:

> C
> 1 2 34 567 8
> Good morning, daddy!
>
> 1 2 34 5 6 7
> Ain't you heard
>
> 8   12   34   56
> The boogie-woogie rumble
>
> 7 8 12 34 56   7 8
> Of a dream deferred?

F
1234 567
Listen closely:

  8 12 34 5 6 7 8
You'll hear their feet

  C
 1 2 3 4 5 6 7 8
Beating out and beating out a—
You think
It's a happy beat?

G
1 2 3 4 5 6 7 8
Listen to it closely:

F
1 2 3 4 5 6 78
Ain't you heard

  C
 1 2 3 4 5 6 7 8
Something underneath like a—

What did I say?

Sure,
I'm happy!
Take it away!

Hey pop!
Re-bop!
Mop!

Y-e-a-h! ("Dream Boogie," p. 221)

What Hughes had done is create a twelve-line, twelve-bar boogie-woogie poem, annexing an exclamatory "tag" ending like those occasionally employed in music. Here, though, Hughes has manipulated the form and rhythm: stanzas two and three are jarred by the dramatic insertion of disturbing questions that achieve their impact by rewording the line we would expect in the normal rhythm and progression of thoughts into a question. Thus, in stanza two, "Beating out and beating out a happy beat" becomes:

Beating out and beating out—

You think
It's a happy beat?

Just as Hughes shifts to the interrogative and separates those questions from their normal stanzaic group, he just as surely upsets the boogie-woogie rhythm, eventually violating even the rhyming pattern in stanza three. This is significant because stanza three draws on the first two stanzas for a repetition of important lines: "Listen closely" of stanza two becomes "Listen to it closely" (Hughes employs a common characteristic of blues lyrics, building slightly modulated lines around loose formulaic patterns) in stanza three, while "Ain't you heard" of stanza one is lifted verbatim. Stanza three, however, becomes deliberately vague—"Something underneath"—in order to force the audience to answer the subsequent question, "What did I say?" By upsetting the rhythm and asking the questions, Hughes highlights the disparity between the rumbling seriousness of the deferred dream and the superficial happiness of the beat or performance. To this masterful maneuvering of the idiom Hughes annexes the "tag" ending—in jazz and blues a four-bar section appended to the end of a tune that repeats a phrase, offers a final comment, or indicates that the performance is about to end—often for those dancing to the performance. Hughes' seven-line ending contrasts once again the happiness of the words/music performance with the underlying problem. In light of the dramatic irony with which Hughes dealt with the subject earlier, this return to the facade of carefree happiness adds psychological complexity to the poem. Hughes felt that blacks needed to recognize the reality of deferred dreams, as he has forced in stanza three, but in stanza four he emphasizes the need to retain the spirit of cultural expression and the usefulness of the elaborate role-playing that provided blacks with the opportunity for advances, while whites concentrate on the superficial happy roles that blacks played.

The boogie rhythms extend to other poems in the sequence, although the twelve-bar progression is not necessarily present in any of them. "Easy Boogie," "Nightmare Boogie," and "Dream Boogie: Variation" could theoretically fit into the twelve-bar pattern annotated with the variations above. One indication that they may not have been intended to fit into the twelve-bar pattern is the presence, in "Easy Boogie," of the line "Riffs, smears, breaks" between stanzas two and three, which seems to indicate an instrumental break that would not be characteristic in a standard twelve-bar blues—the breaks would come between the twelve-bar verses. This underscores the importance of "hearing" the boogie-woogie rhythm and spirit of the performance as opposed to following a predetermined structure. "Lady's Boogie" and "Boogie 1 a.m." reemphasize the distinction, each of them eight-line poems (with an additional mock-jive exclamation in the former) in boogie rhythm. These poems, then, are tied together by the rhythm and spirit of boogie-woogie—a rhythm and spirit that Hughes clearly intended for us to hear.

The poems, of course, have other features in common besides boogie-woogie rhythm. The first four poems in the sequence all employ black jive slang: in "Dream Boogie" he uses "Daddy!" and "Hey pop! Re-bop! Mop! Y-e-a-h!"; in "Easy Boogie" he uses "Hey, Lawdy Mama!"; in ""Boogie 1 a.m." he uses "Daddy!"; and in "Lady's Boogie" he employs the phrase "Be-Bach!" Coupled with the boogie rhythms this plying of black speech demonstrates the influence of oral culture on Hughes' work, giving the distinctively black flavor to the poems necessary to suggest encoded messages appropriate to a segregated group of people. Music critic John McDonough has pointed out the usefulness of slang code words:

> There is a fraternal link that always seems to bond together those who would challenge or otherwise separate themselves from the mainstream of social custom. Sometimes the trappings and devices of such brotherhood are enjoyed for their own sake—a sort of college game without substance. But more commonly, they have a very specific and necessary function. In a hostile and crowded world, such devices identify each member to the other. It may be a handshake, a secret word or phrase, gesture or symbol. In short, a lexicon of code words that separate the true believers from the indifferent or unfriendly.[6]

Hughes doesn't employ code words that whites are unlikely to understand, but the words are readily identifiable with black culture, and by doing so he intimates that his message is directed at blacks and, to a great measure, originates with them.

This slang also helps call attention to the similarities and contrasts of the poems. Both "Dream Boogie" and "Boogie 1 a.m.," for example, are narrated by women, as indicated by the address "Daddy." This address, along with "Papa," is common in the blues songs of females and in black culture in general, but the term of address would not be used by a male; "Daddy-o" would be used, but not simply "Daddy." This use of a female speaker, which is also prevalent in Hughes' blues poems, is important in that it indicates that the ideas are not necessarily identifiable with a single viewpoint: that of the black male Hughes. The suggestion is that the problems of blacks connected with deferred dreams is not simply an intricate artistic stance of the author, but the representative stance of sensitive blacks, both male and female, who, especially in terms of the sexual theme of the poems, will be creating future generations.

"Dream Boogie" is a poem of beginnings: besides being the first poem of the sequence, it is the poem that greets at the beginning of the day and poses the nagging and disconcerting questions dealt with repeatedly in the other poems. It is appropriate that this is the first poem in the sequence, since upon awakening one would have the best chance of recalling dreams, and awakening from the fantasy/dream world to reality would accentuate the disparity between those two worlds. In "Dream Boogie" the speaker asks questions, in contrast to "Boogie 1 a.m.," a poem of conclusion that addresses the listener at day's end— "Good evening, Daddy"—and asserts that the listener is aware of the rumblings of the dream deferred, presumable after day-long contact with the white-controlled world.

Similarly, "Easy Boogie," the second poem of the sequence, and "Lady's Boogie," the fourth, are related. In contrast to "Dream Boogie," in "Easy Boogie" a man addresses a woman—"Hey, Lawdy Mama!" The speaker associates the recognition of the steady beat of the dream deferred with the vitality of the sexual act:

> Hey, Lawdy Mama!
> Do you hear what I said?
> Easy like I rock it
> In my bed! ("Easy Boogie,"
>   pp. 229–30)

This sexual vitality, implicit in the word "boogie," as already pointed out, is also linked with the soul's aspirations through the repetition of sentence construction:

> Down in the bass
> That easy roll
> Rolling like I like it
> In my soul.

The souls' dreams are seen as vital, lively, and life-giving. Thus through the repetition of phrases and structures, Hughes expands the importance of his words beyond their initial and superficial meanings.

"Lady's Boogie" exposes the superficial concerns of a posturing "lady" who

> ain't got boogie-woogie
> On her mind. ("Lady's Boogie,"
>   p. 251)

Viewed in comparison to "Easy Boogie," the sexual connotation is at work here, suggesting a sexually ineffectual or inhibited person and connecting that to the inability to hear the beat of the dream deferred. Hughes suggests that the "Lady" has not listened, and could be successful if she did:

> But if she was to listen
> I bet she'd hear
> Way up in the treble
> The tingle of a tear.

However, the final exclamation ("Be-Bach!") suggests that her pretense makes a mockery of her own people's language in combining the phrase be-bop with the classical composer from another culture, mocking the pretension of her position and making it seem ludicrous.

"Easy Boogie" and "Lady's Boogie" also begin to deal with the relationships between the performer/creator, his instrument, and his creation, as they relate to the underlying desires and feelings of blacks. Although the "boogie-woogie rumble of a dream deferred" played "underneath" on the bass keys of a piano had already been introduced in "Dream Boogie,"

"Easy Boogie" further connects the bass rumble with something "down," something "underneath," something sexual, something elemental. It is the walking bass of solidarity.

> Down in the bass
> That steady beat
> Walking, walking, walking
> Like marching feet. ("Easy Boogie,"
>   pp. 229–30)

This solidarity is connected, through repetition and parallel sentence structure, with the feeling of the soul:

> Down in the bass
> that steady roll
> Rolling like I like it
> In my soul.

Conversely, "Lady's Boogie" deals with the speaker's attitude toward a woman who has allowed the pretensions of "society" to interfere with her realizations about the problems of her people. This woman's mind is linked to the notes played in the treble on the piano:

> See that lady
> Dressed so fine
> She ain't got boogie-woogie
> On her mind—

> But if she was to listen
> I bet she'd hear
> Way up in the treble
> The tingle of a tear. ("Lady's
>   Boogie," p. 251)

Once again the lines relate through their parallel structures: the lady whose pretensions prevent her from "hearing," being aware; who concentrates on appearances rather than sounds, messages; who doesn't listen to the agent that would "enlighten" her, the treble improvisations; whose mind refuses her emotional involvement with the boogie-woogie message. Hughes is, in effect, replicating the amazing dexterity and remarkable

rhythmic diversity of the boogie-woogie pianist: he is combining the rumbling, infectious bass beat and rhythm with treble variations and improvisations, relating the former to the "soul" and action, and the latter to the mind and thought of the "movement" to foster awareness of the problems of black people in terms of the deferred dream. The staccato alliteration is particularly effective in "Lady's Boogie," "Boogie 1 a.m." ("trilling the treble"), and "Dream Boogie: Variation" ("tinkling treble"), particularly when picked out over the momentum of the rolling bass.

These treble and bass patterns are used to introduce and indeed are a part of the compelling unifying image of the poems:

> Trilling the treble
> And twining the bass
> Into midnight ruffles
> of cat-gut lace. ("Boogie 1 a.m.,"
>   p. 250)

Here the right-hand treble notes and the left-hand bass notes are united in performance, just as the mind and soul or thought and feeling of blacks are meant to be united in a common cause: the recognition of the dream deferred and the organization into a unified front to confront the problems of blacks in America. Hughes did not want to overemphasize the bass/sex/soul of the second poem of the sequence, "Easy Boogie"; neither did he want to concentrate exclusively on the treble/inhibitions/mind of the fourth poem, "Lady's Boogie." It was the poem in between, "Boogie 1 a.m.," that presented the "unified sensibility" for which Hughes aimed and that combined the bass and treble into a single compelling image.

The image itself at once suggests several things: ruffles and lace both suggest the delicate trimming of clothing; however, to be ruffled is to become disturbed, and to ruffle is to cause disturbances, as in water; the lace becomes something to hold things together in light of the "cat-gut" prefix. All these combine to suggest a decorative appearance tied to an underlying disquietedness. The "midnight" of "midnight ruffles" identifies the revelation as a black one and places the revelation of nighttime— the time of dreams and nightmares.

A variation of the image returns in "Nightmare Boogie," which follows "Lady's Boogie" and, with "Dream Boogie: Variation," helps emphasize the dream theme at the end of the-sequence. "Nightmare Boogie" deals with the collective loss of black identity:

> I had a dream
> and I could see
> a million faces
> black as me!
>
> A nightmare dream:
> *Quicker than light*
> *All them faces*
> *Turned dead white!* ("Nightmare
>   Boogie," p. 258)

This sentiment is a magnification of the problem recognized in "Lady's Boogie," where the "lady" has lost the ability to hear and understand cultural messages. In "Nightmare" Hughes identifies the instantaneous loss of black identity as a phenomenon that occurred more quickly than it could be recognized, more quickly than it could be exposed, thus stressing the urgency of black identity, pride, and unity. What is important here is that the first four lines have a direct parallel relationship to lines five through eight: the dream of line one is the nightmare of line five; the seeing of line two is the revelation of line six; the faces of lines three and seven and the colors of lines four and

eight define whether the event was a dream or a nightmare. At the climax of the metamorphosis from black to white, from dream to nightmare, Hughes eschews a smooth transition, generating a "whirling" midnight incantation, as if awakening to a real solution:

> Boogie-woogie,
> Rolling bass,
> Whirling treble
> Of cat-gut lace. ("Nightmare
>   Boogie," p. 258)

This variation on the lines of "Boogie 1 a.m." labels the dream deferred as a nightmare that leads to a racial identity, resolvable only by hearing and understanding the "message" of boogie-woogie.

In contrast to the nightmare of the dream deferred, the black pride/identity "movement," the marching, walking feet of "Dream Boogie" and "Easy Boogie," is a whirling awakening to a new dream, which forms a very natural sequence to "Dream Boogie: Variation"—the final poem of the entire sequence—and a counterpoint to "Dream Boogie," the first. Whereas "Dream Boogie" is an upbeat, urgent poem, "Variation" is much more sad and subdued: the portrait of the boogie-woogie pianist, performing his music, his piano screaming for him under his lone stomping feet, his eyes misting at the prospect of having missed his chance at freedom. Here, however, the "midnight ruffles of/cat-gut lace" of the "Boogie 1 a.m." quatrain, and the "Whirling treble/ of cat-gut lace" of the "Nightmare Boogie" quatrain become "High noon teeth/In a midnight face," identifying the central idea and image of the poems with the actual facial features and identity of the performer, the creator, the one closest to the music itself. Hughes is emphasizing here how easy it is for an individual to fail to recognize the dream deferred, the nightmare as it relates to the individual himself. The final image is not the jive-talking, energetic persona of "Dream Boogie"; it is the embodiment of the boogie-woogie tradition, alone and too late, playing the wistful boogie of freedom deferred.

By varying and manipulating the rhythm, words, imagery, moods, and themes of these poems, Hughes has illuminated the issue of the dream deferred from different emotional perspectives. By employing folk culture so well, he in effect gives his poems traditional authority, makes them unadulteratedly black, and establishes a continuity that makes them seem to express the ideas of the people for the people.

NOTES

1 Pete Johnson, "Swanee River Boogie," *Boogie Woogie Trio,* Storyville SLP 4006, 1976.

2 Karl Gert zur Heide, *Deep South Piano* (London: Studio Vista, 1970), p. 11.

3 Big Bill Broonzy, "Let's Reel and Rock," Melotone, 7-06-64, 1936, 78 R.P.M. recording.

4 Langston Hughes, Cliff Roberts, and David Martin, *The First Book of Jazz* (New York: Franklin Watts, Inc., 1955).

5 Langston Hughes, *Selected Poems* (New York: Vintage Books, 1974), p. 221. All further references to Hughes' poems will be followed in the text by page numbers from this work.

6 John McDonoough, Jacket Notes, *Tea Pad Songs, Vol. 2,* Stash Records ST-104, n.d.

◇ ◇ ◇

Do Right to Write Right: Langston Hughes's Aesthetics of Simplicity

KAREN JACKSON FORD

The one thing most readers of twentieth-century American poetry can say about Langston Hughes is that he has known rivers. "The Negro Speaks of Rivers" has become memorable for its lofty, oratorical tone, mythic scope, and powerful rhythmic repetitions.

> I've known rivers:
> I've known rivers ancient as the
>   world and older than the flow of
>   human blood in human veins.
>
> (1656)

But however beautiful its cadences, the poem is remembered primarily because it is Hughes's most frequently anthologized work. The fact is, "The Negro Speaks of Rivers" is one of Hughes's most uncharacteristic poems, and yet it has defined his reputation, along with a small but constant selection of other poems included in anthologies. "A Negro Speaks of Rivers," "A House in Taos," "The Weary Blues," "Montage of a Dream Deferred," "Theme for English B," "Refugee in America," and "I, Too"—these poems invariably comprise his anthology repertoire despite the fact that none of them typifies his writing. What makes these poems atypical is exactly what makes them appealing and intelligible to the scholars who edit anthologies—their complexity. True, anthologies produced in the current market, which is hospitable to the African-American tradition and to canon reform, now include a brief selection of poems in black folk forms. But even though Hughes has fared better in anthologies that most African-American writers, only a small and predictable segment of his poetry has been preserved. A look back through the original volumes of poetry, and even through the severely redrawn *Selected Poems*, reveals a wealth of simpler poems we ought to be reading.[1]

Admittedly, an account of Hughes's poetic simplicity requires some qualification. Most obvious is the fact that he wrote poems that are not simple. "A Negro Speaks of Rivers" is oracular; "The Weary Blues" concludes enigmatically; "A House in Taos" is classically modernist in both its fragmented form and its decadent sensibility. Even more to the point, many of the poems that have been deemed simple are only ironically so. "The Black Christ," for example, is a little jingle that invokes monstrous cultural complexity. Likewise, two later books, *Ask Your Mama* (1961) and *The Panther and the Lash* (1967), contain an intricate vision of American history beneath their simple surfaces.[2] Nevertheless, the overwhelming proportion of poems in the Hughes canon consists of work in the simpler style, and even those poems that can yield complexities make use of simplicity in ways that ought not to be ignored.

The repression of the great bulk of Hughes's poems is the result of chronic critical scorn for their simplicity. Throughout his long career, but especially after his first two volumes of poetry (readers were at first willing to assume that a youthful poet might grow to be more complex), his books received their harshest reviews for a variety of "flaws" that all originate in an aesthetics of simplicity. From his first book, *The Weary Blues* (1926), to his last one, *The Panther and the Lash* (1967), the reviews invoke a litany of faults: the poems are superficial, infantile, silly, small, unpoetic, common, jejune, iterative, and, of course, simple.[3] Even his admirers reluctantly conclude

that Hughes's poetics failed. Saunders Redding flatly opposes simplicity and artfulness. "While Hughes's rejection of his own growth shows an admirable loyalty to his self-commitment as the poet of the 'simple, Negro commonfolk' . . . it does a disservice to his art" (Mullen 74). James Baldwin, who recognizes the potential of simplicity as an artistic principle, faults the poems for "tak[ing] refuge . . . in a fake simplicity in order to avoid the very difficult simplicity of the experience" (Mullen 85).

Despite a lifetime of critical disappointments, then, Hughes remained loyal to the aesthetic program he had outlined in 1926 in his decisive poetic treatise, "The Negro Artist and the Racial Mountain." There he had predicted that the common people would "give to this world its truly great Negro artist, the one who is not afraid to be himself," a poet who would explore the "great field of unused [folk] material ready for his art" and recognize that this source would provide "sufficient matter to furnish a black artist with a lifetime of creative work" (692). This is clearly a portrait of the poet Hughes would become, and he maintained his fidelity to this ideal at great cost to his literary reputation.

In what follows I will look at some of that forgotten poetry and propose a way to read it that refutes the criticism that most of Hughes's poetry is too simple for serious consideration. I will first reconstruct Hughes's conception of the poet by looking at one of his prose characters who embodies his poetics; and, second, I will turn to a reading of *Shakespeare in Harlem* (1942), a volume of poetry that typifies Hughes's aesthetic program.

In his column in the *Chicago Defender* on February 13, 1943, Hughes first introduced the prototype of the humorous and beloved fictional character Jesse B. Semple, nicknamed by his Harlem friends "Simple." For the next twenty-three years Hughes would continue to publish Simple stories both in the *Defender* and in several volumes of collected and edited pieces.[4] Hughes called Simple his "ace-boy," and it is surely not coincidental that the Simple stories span the years, the 1940s to the 1960s, when Langston Hughes needed a literary ace in the hole.[5] The success of the Simple stories was an important consolation of the writer's later years, when his poetry was reviewed with disappointment, his autobiography dismissed as "chit-chat," his plays refused on Broadway, and his fiction diminished in importance next to Richard Wright's *Native Son* (1940) and Ralph Ellison's *Invisible Man* (1952).[6]

It seems obvious, however, that in the long association with his ace-boy Hughes found more than popularity and financial success. In fact, his prefatory sketches of Simple attest to the character's importance, in the sheer number of times Hughes sets out to explain him and in the specific details these explanations provide.[7] All of them depict Simple as an African American Everyman, the authentic—even unmediated—voice of the community that engendered him. For instance, in "Who Is Simple?" Hughes emphasizes the authenticity of his creation: "[Simple's] first words came directly out of the mouth of a young man who lived just down the block from me" (*Best* vii). Here and elsewhere Hughes asserts a vital connection between the fictional character and the people he represents: "If there were not a lot of genial souls in Harlem as talkative as Simple, I would never have these tales to write down that are 'just like him'" (*Best* viii). The author's dedication to Simple is surely rooted in his conviction that Simple embodies and speaks for the very people to whom Hughes

had committed himself back in the 1920s. But Hughes's affinity with Simple is more complete than this.

Commentators on the Simple stories have concentrated on two points: theme, "Hughes's handling of the race issue" (Mullen 20); and genre, "the generic nature of these prose sketches" (Mullen 20).[8] It is exclusively Hughes as prose artist we have acknowledged when considering these tales. However, I will argue that the Simple stories reveal a great deal about Hughes's poetic genius as well. Casting Simple as the figure of the poet illuminates Hughes's poetic program and explains his powerful affinity with his prose creation.

Crucial in tracing Simple's significance are the "Character Notes" to the 1957 musical comedy *Simply Heavenly*, which describe Simple in terms that stress his contradictions:

> Simple is a Chaplinesque character, slight of build, awkwardly graceful, given to flights of fancy, and positive statements of opinion—stemming from a not so positive soul. He is dark with a likable smile, ordinarily dressed, except for rather flamboyant summer sports shirts. Simple tries hard to succeed, but the chips seldom fall just right. Yet he bounces like a rubber ball. He may go down, but he always bounds back up. (*Plays* 115)

The parallel to Charlie Chaplin, an icon of contradiction, is telling. Like Chaplin, whose physical appearance announces internal tensions (his hat is too small, his shoes too large, his vest too tight, his pants too loose), Simple is awkward yet graceful, ordinary yet flamboyant. And, again as with Chaplin, these external tensions reveal deeper ones; he is obstinate yet fanciful, decent yet flawed, and—perhaps most poignant for Hughes—optimistic despite failure.

Simple is a compelling figure for Hughes precisely because of these tensions. For these contraries—even the apparently internal ones—hang about Simple like a fool's motley. The fool's motley, of course, traditionally implies chaos; yet while his multicolored costume reflects the intricacies and contradictions around him, the fool himself may often be a perfect simpleton. This is also true of Hughes's character: though his appearance and even to some extent his character express contradiction, his fundamental nature is unequivocally simple. Obstinate, positivistic, and optimistic, Simple is able to register contradictions without finally resolving them and therefore has special significance for Hughes's poetic project. Hughes, after all, claims that "where life is simple, truth and reality are one" (*Big Sea* 311). Yet where in America is life simple for African Americans? The "where" Hughes invokes is not a place but a state of mind. The terms of his formulation—simplicity, truth, reality—are broad and vague because they are nearly synonymous to him. If one recognizes the simple facts of life, one will be able to see the truth; if one lives by the truth, one's reality will match one's ideals. Simplicity *is* truth in Hughes's vision.

Simple is the personification of such a poetics, a philosophy of composition that resorts to simplicity, not in response to singleness or triviality, but, ironically, in response to almost unspeakable contradiction. This is why he appears surrounded by complexities—his culture, his friends, even his clothing registering the confusion of the world around him. To shift the metaphor, simpleness, in both the character and the poetry, functions as a brick wall against which complexities collide. In its artless, uncomprehending re-

fusal to incorporate contradictions, it exacerbates them. For a poet who equates simplicity with truth, cultivating a thematics and aesthetics of simplicity is essential—poetically and politically. Simplicity resists the pernicious subtleties and complexities of integrationist thought. Further, it reveals the inadequacies of such thought. But more important, it achieves these aims by reinstating the truth.

Let me turn to some examples. In "There Ought to Be a Law," Simple tells his friend Boyd that Congress ought to pass a law "setting up a few Game Preserves for Negroes" (*Reader* 181). Having seen a short movie about wildlife preserves, where "buffaloes roams and nobody can shoot a single one of them" (181), Simple concludes that "Congress ought to set aside some place where we can go and nobody can jump on us and beat us, neither lynch us nor Jim Crow us every day. Colored folks rate as much protection as a buffalo, or a deer" (181). Boyd, Simple's educated integrationist foil, first faults the plan for drawing a parallel between animals and humans: "Negroes are not wild," he asserts confidently. Yet in observing Simple's logical flaw, he misses Simple's important point. Precisely because blacks are human beings, they should be treated better than animals. Boyd admits, "You have a point there" (181), but immediately discerns another shortcoming in Simple's argument. When Simple says that one of the things he would like about living on a preserve is that he could "fight in peace and not get fined them high fines" (182), Boyd recoils: "You disgust me. I thought you were talking about a place where you could be quiet and compose your mind" (182). Again Boyd reacts against the racist stereotype that black men are physically aggressive.

In fact, however, the freedom to fight was suggested to Simple by a scene in the movie showing two elks locking horns. While Boyd would replace one behavioral cliché (black men fighting) with another (men meditating in nature), he fails to see that both prescriptions curtail freedom. Once again, Simple makes the more substantial point: "I would like a place where I could do both" (182). While Simple's ideas always sound regressive at first, he ultimately articulates a far more radical position than Boyd's; and he does so by rejecting the falsifying complexities Boyd raises. Boyd's willingness to view all racial issues as hopelessly intricate finally renders him ineffective and conservative. Simple's obstinacy, on the other hand, enables him to view all issues in black and white, so to speak. Indeed, "There Ought to Be a Law" introduces, in a back-handed way, a black separatist position that Simple holds throughout the stories. Far from capitulating to white racist stereotypes about African Americans, Simple advocates a complete break with the white world and, thus, a thorough rejection of white racist assumptions.[9]

When Simple tries his hand at poetry in two stories, we can begin to see how he embodies Hughes's conception of the poet. Ironically, in "Wooing the Muse" Simple is first inspired to compose poetry when he leaves the city to spend his vacation on the beach. Though the natural setting is a conventional pretext for poetry, Simple's verses ignore the romantic idealization of nature in favor of his characteristic realism regarding a subject that interests him more, human nature:

> Sitting under the trees
> With the birds and the bees
> Watching the girls go by. (*Best* 28)

In fact, he gently mocks Romantic clichés like "the birds and the bees" by incorporating such phrases into his irreverent lines. But it is precisely their status as clichés that Simple exploits, tossing off such lines as empty gestures toward figuration to contrast the way his poems barrel unmetaphorically toward their artless points (though his prose is highly figurative). And, of course, that second line is not just any cliché but a euphemism for sexual relations, and thus it receives a double reproof when Simple follows it with his blunt restatement, "Watching the girls go by."

Predictably, Boyd misses the poem's own logic and faults the verse for its failure to realize conventional Anglo-American form: "You ought to have another rhyme. *By* ought to rhyme with *sky* or something" (28). Boyd cannot read the poem on its own terms but views it only as an unfinished quatrain composed (ideally) of two rhymed (aa/bb) couplets. Simple, on the other hand, sees no reason why form should exceed meaning: "I was not looking at no sky, as I told you in the poem. I was looking at the girls" (30).

Simple's second poem is a free-verse composition about racism; "This next one is a killer," he tells Boyd. "It's serious" (30). In it he compares the treatment of non-black immigrants in the United States with the mistreatment of African Americans:

> I wonder how it can be
> That Greeks, Germans, Jews,
> Italians, Mexicans,
> And everybody but me
> Down South can ride in the trains,
> Streetcars and busses
> Without any fusses.
> But when I come along—
> Pure American—
> They got a sign up
> For me to ride behind:

COLORED
My folks and my folks' folkses
And their folkses before
Have been here 300 years or more—
Yet any foreigner from Polish to
      Dutch
Rides anywhere he want to
And is not subject to such
Treatments as my fellow-men give
      me
In this Land of the Free. (30)

Again the poem is evaluated in terms of conventional literary standards when Joyce, Simple's fiancée, wants him "to change *folkses* to say *peoples*" in order to elevate its diction (31). But since Simple doesn't have an eraser, his original phrasing is preserved. This suggests another constituent feature of Simple's poetry: it is improvisational. Even when he writes poems, they are subject to the pressures of the immediate moment and cannot be polished or refined.

While the lack of an eraser might suggest the opposite, that the poem is fixed and unchangeable, it actually indicates that the process of composition—rather than the product (which is another matter and might receive revision at another time)—is spontaneous and improvisational. In fact, Simple thinks this poem should be longer, but he has to conclude it where he does because Joyce interrupts him during composition. And his sense that the poem should have been longer derives not from some external formal measure but from the integral relationship of structure and meaning. Boyd, on the other hand, thinks "It's long enough" because he doubts the poem's worth; but Simple asserts, "It's not as long as Jim Crow" (31).

After a lengthy discussion with Boyd about why he does not write more nature poems, Simple recites a third piece—a ten-stanza toast in the "counting rhymes" genre, structured in tercets (until the final stanza which is five lines) rhyming aab, like a blues stanza. The "b" line in each stanza is also a refrain line throughout, as in a ballad:

When I get to be ninety-one
And my running days is done,
Then I will do better. (33)

Simple has concocted this toast as a retort to people who tell him, as Boyd has just done, "You should be old enough to know better." Simple distinguishes between "knowing" and "doing":

"I might be old enough to know better, but I am not old enough to *do* better," said Simple. "Come on in the bar and I will say you a toast I made up the last time somebody told me just what you are saying now about doing better. . . . That's right bartender, two beers for two steers. . . . Thank you! . . . Pay for them, chum! . . . Now, here goes. Listen fluently." (33)

Several points in this passage bear upon Simple's poetic practice. Most important is the assertion that recognizing (knowing) social or literary conventions need not result in enacting them (doing). When Simple orders "two beers for two steers," he playfully supports this by infusing the poetical (by virtue of the rhymes) into the mundane as easily as he has infused the mundane into the poetical. Finally, when Simple cautions Boyd to "Listen fluently," he coins a phrase that will appear again and again in the stories, whenever Simple suspects that habitual ways of "reading" will obstruct the proper reception of his compositions. The odd phrase pulls artist and audience together, insisting that writer and reader accompany each other in a new literacy. "Listen fluently" also introduces orality, and appropriately so, since it precedes the toast, an oral composition, and thus widens the scope of poetry. As we have seen, many of Simple's poetic models are African-American folk forms—ballads, blues, toasts—genres that can claim written *and* oral status. Certainly Hughes, like Simple, "knows" about literary convention but chooses to "do" things his own way.

The opposition of correctness as knowledge and correctness as action (in the context of poetry, "action" means writing truthfully) is central to "Grammar and Goodness," another story that treats Simple's poetic production. Simple's formulation of this borders on the nonsensical, like many of his wise sayings: "It is better to *do* right than to write right" (*Stakes* 182). Simple reads two poems to the narrator (who in this story is apparently not Boyd). The first is one that Joyce and Boyd have edited. Its conclusion uneasily renders Boyd's accommodationist perspective in Simple's belligerent style:

> Now, listen, white folks:
> In line with Rev. King
> Down in Montgomery—
> Also because the Bible
> Says I must—
> In spite of bombs and buses,
> *I'm gonna love you.*
> I say, I'm gonna LOVE you—
> White folks, OR BUST! (181)

The "authorities"—Reverend King and the Bible (and behind them, certainly, Joyce and Boyd)—want Simple's poem to advocate loving the enemy.

However, this conciliatory theme is gainsaid by the imperative construction, the screaming capital letters, the allusions to white violence, and the threatening last line (which comes off as a warning to whites to *be* lovable rather than as a promise on Simple's part to love them "in

spite" of themselves). Despite these obvious contradictions, the narrator extricates a coherent "message" from the piece by ignoring its style, and doubts whether Simple could have written such a poem: "You never wrote a poem that logical all by yourself in life" (181). Simple admits this freely and offers another, unedited, poem in its place; it is no surprise when it completely contradicts the first one. It begins,

> In the North
> The Jim Crow line
> Ain't clear—
> But it's here!

and ends,

> Up North Jim Crow
> Wears an angel's grin—
> But still he sin.
> I swear he do!
> Don't you? (181)

Though the narrator agrees with the sentiment of this poem, he chides Simple "for the grammar" (182). Simple once again rejects the notion that poems must meet normal standards, claiming, "If I get the sense right . . . the grammar can take care of itself" (182). Both "Wooing the Muse" and "Grammar and Goodness" repudiate the aesthetics of traditional poetry, especially adherence to conventional forms, elevation of diction, preference for written rather than oral forms, the necessity of polish and finish, and the subordination of content to form.

Simple is thus a folk poet in the African and African-American traditions. His poems are communal, colloquial, and often improvisational. When he uses existing verse forms, he chooses ballads, blues, toasts, and spirituals. Moreover, his speech is rendered lyrical through a high content of figuration and internal rhyme.[10] In addition to his status as folk poet, however, Simple is the embodiment of—and, considering his life span, perhaps the defender of—Langston Hughes's aesthetic program. His name, an epigrammatic poem in its own right, captures this aspect of the character.

In "Family History" Simple explains his highly suggestive name:

> "Grandpa's name was Jess, too. So I am Jesse B. Semple.
> "What does the *B* stand for?"
> "Nothing. I just put it there myself since they didn't give me no initial when I was born. I am really Jess Semple." (*Speaks* 179)

Simple's name invokes his family history, a heritage that the story reveals is multi-racial. His name, then, links him to a diverse cultural past and thereby at least superficially legitimates him as a representative figure. A second interesting feature of his name is the self-defining middle initial "B." He says the "B" stands for nothing, but knowing him, we wonder if it doesn't signify "black." Or, it may derive from another story, "Bop," in which he explains to Boyd that the difference between the prefixes "*Re* and *Be*" (in "Re-Bop" and "Be-Bop") is that the "*Be*" signifies "the real thing like the colored boys play" (*Wife* 56). In such a reading, the middle initial "B" might indicate the integrity of self-authorship, a prerequisite for being an authentic representative of his larger culture. Even more suggestive are the puns involved in Simple's names. By giving himself the middle initial he transforms his given name from a negative description of himself—Jess Semple ("just simple")—into an imperative statement—Jess B. Semple ("just be simple"). The revised name, then, issues a commanding motto for Hughes's poetic program. And finally, "Semple" may also be an ironic appropriation of the middle name of

Aimee Semple McPherson, the evangelist, who became a vicious and outspoken opponent of Hughes during the early forties.[11] It would be sweet revenge to name his irreverent, black-nationalist bard after a white evangelist who tried to censor and, failing that, excoriated Hughes's poetry.

Simple's provocative name, his rich and original use of language, his obstinate literalism, his radical politics, and his eccentric appearance distinguish him as a poet figure and associate him with a long line of poetic simpletons—most important, with Shakespeare's fools. This is especially obvious in a story like "Cocktail Sip," where Boyd says Simple sounds like an Elizabethan poet, or "Midsummer Madness," in which Simple composes pithy proverbs. Like a Shakespearean fool, the Hughesian bard often encodes wisdom in nonsense.[12] Indeed, the cardinal point of the Simple stories is the wisdom of simplicity—a precept that, when applied to poetry, demands a daring aesthetic program.

Shakespeare in Harlem (1942), roughly contemporary with the Simple period, self-consciously engages in wooing Simple's muse. The volume is exemplary for two reasons: first, because it declares itself to be "A book of light verse," and second, because it has been largely overlooked by critics (the latter point undoubtedly due to the former). That is, its outspoken aesthetic recalcitrance has almost certainly doomed it to critical neglect. To read *Shakespeare in Harlem* we need an interpretative practice that accommodates these poems on their own terms, one that strives, as Simple would say, to "listen fluently."

From the prefatory note at the front of the book,

> A book of light verse. Afro-Americana in the blues mood. Poems

syncopated and variegated in the colors of Harlem, Beale Street, West Dallas, and Chicago's South Side.

Blues, ballads, and reels to be read aloud, crooned, shouted, recited, and sung. Some with gestures, some not—as you like. None with a far-away voice (viii)

to "A Note on the Type" on the last page of the book,

The headings are set in Vogue Extra-Bold, a typeface designed in our time with the aim to express the utmost simplicity (125)

Shakespeare in Harlem equates the poetic with the simple. It declares itself to contain merely "light verse," "Afro-*Americana*"—a collection of folk materials—rather than high art. Like much of Hughes's canon, this book will employ folk forms—"blues, ballads, and reels"—that common readers are already familiar with from the oral culture. Indeed, the poet encourages readers to make the poems their own: they should be "read aloud, crooned, shouted, recited, and sung." Further, they can be acted out, "Some with gestures, some not." The preface, then, casts readers in the role of performers who will interpret the poems "as [they] like." The allusion to *As You Like It* is the first oblique reference to the namesake of the book. Yet this Shakespeare, *in Harlem,* is near at hand, colloquial, folksy; he does not speak with the "far-away voice" of Elizabethan England or literary convention or classical poetry. Even his typeface expresses the "utmost simplicity."

But the appropriation of Shakespeare into simplicity in Harlem is not merely an adjustment undertaken for the audience, nor is it entirely a political maneuver. When Shakespeare goes to Harlem, he faces a crisis of language that is figured forth in extreme sim-

plicity. The material and psychological conditions of Harlem as depicted here (elsewhere Hughes emphasizes its many positive aspects)—poverty, hunger, violence, lack of opportunity, unfathomable despair—render him almost speechless; it is only through the fool, conventionally a voice of simplicity amid overwhelming complexity, that the poet maintains expression. Like Virginia Woolf's imaginative "reconstruction" of the life of Julia Shakespeare in *A Room of One's Own,* in which she tries to imagine what would have been the fate of Shakespeare's sister (that is, of a talented female poet in the sixteenth century), Hughes is to some extent exploring what Shakespeare's fate would be were he an unemployed African American in twentieth-century Harlem.

Little wonder, then, that the title poem—in which we first hear how Shakespeare sounds in Harlem—is half nonsense:

Hey ninny neigh!
And a hey nonny noe!
Where, oh, where
Did my sweet mama go?

Hey ninny neigh
With a tra-la-la-la!
They say your sweet mama
Went home to her ma. (111)

The poem's nonsense syllables, as might be expected, echo a song from *As You Like It* which two pages sing in honor of the fool's engagement:

It was a lover and his lass,
    With a hey, and a ho, and a hey
    nonino,
That o'er the green cornfield did
    pass
    In springtime, the only pretty
    ringtime,
When birds do sing, hey ding a
    ding, ding.
Sweet lovers love the spring.
    (V.iii.15–20)

Shakespeare in Harlem reverses this song: love cannot be idealized through images of springtime and green fields. *As You Like It* itself ridicules romantic equations about love, nature, and the simple life, and the nonsense syllables in the pages' song suggest the fatuousness of those idealized formulations. In the Hughes poem, by contrast, the allusion to Shakespeare seems to marshal the linguistic resources of the fool. Here the nonsense, rather than echoing the mindless babble of the clichéd lyrics, disrupts the portentousness of the lines that communicate the loss of love. Indeed, the first two lines of nonsense in each quatrain seem almost to make possible the utterance of the final two lines that admit loss.

The structure of the stanzas, then, which move from nonsense to sense, suggests that the incantatory energy of the nonsense—deriving from rhymes, alliteration, exclamation marks, and most of all from the liberating effects of non-referential language—is necessary in order to accommodate the painful reality of the sense lines. The word "ninny" in Hughes's stanzas can thus be read simultaneously as a nonsense utterance and a direct address to the fool, "Hey, Ninny." In both cases the special capacities of foolishness are invoked. Similarly, the literal "no" that is released in the nonsensical "nonny noe" provides an aural negation of the otherwise ineluctable misfortune of the sense lines.

And though the poem sounds somewhat whimsical, lost love is not a comic subject in *Shakespeare in Harlem*. The "un-sonnet sequence" that opens the book (another revision of Shakespeare), "Seven Moments of Love," demonstrates what the rest of the book will reiterate: that to be abandoned by a lover is to be cast deeper into poverty. "Supper Time" moves from poverty as an image of loneliness to poverty as the literal result of being alone:

> I look in the kettle, the kettle is dry.
> Look in the bread box, nothing but
>   a fly.
> Turn on the light and look real
>   good!
> I would make a fire but there ain't
>   no wood.
> Look at that water dripping in the
>   sink.
> Listen to my heartbeats trying to
>   think.
> Listen at my footprints walking on
>   the floor.
> That place where your trunk was,
>   ain't no trunk no more.
> Place where your clothes hung's
>   empty and bare.
> Stay away if your want to, and see if
>   I care!
> If I had a fire I'd make me some tea
> And set down and drink it, myself
>   and me.
> Lawd! I got to find me a woman for
>   the WPA—
> Cause if I don't they'll cut down my
>   pay.

The un-sonnet sequence, indeed the entire book, treats love as a social rather than merely a private problem. Abandoned lovers are exposed to hunger and cold, to diminished wages and status. Details like the dry kettle, the empty breadbox, and the lack of firewood function simultaneously as metaphors for the speaker's isolation and as factual examples of the hardships he will face living on one income.

The title poem begins a process of recontextualization of private life that the rest of the book develops. In "Shakespeare in Harlem" a speaker registers his loss of love in the first quatrain and another person answers him with the reports of still other people ("they say") in the second quatrain. The poem, in a section of the book called "Lenox Avenue," obviously invokes the voices of the people living along the street. A man arrives home, discovers his partner is gone, asks where she went, and is answered by a crowd of neighbors that she went home to her mother. The communal nature of the event is further registered in the appellation "sweet mama" and in the lover's retreat to her own "ma." This is clearly a family affair, not the isolated nuclear family of suburbia but the extended family of a population that is shifting from the rural south to the urban north. (The Harlem resident's responsibility to aid even remote family members who move north is a repeated theme of the Simple stories.) Romance in this context is not the usual stuff of sonnets but a relationship modeled on the family, as the similarity between the terms "sweet mama" and "ma" indicates. The speaker's "sweet mama" has not left for independence or romance but has retreated to another community, where she will receive care: to her family. There can be little doubt that she is shrinking from the kind of hardships that the "Supper Time" speaker faces.

The poem's simplicity, then, has a great deal of work to do. The nonsense lines allude to a tradition of empty love sentiments even as they also tap the special verbal resources of the fool. The plurality of voices situates love as a public issue. The appellations "sweet mama" and "ma" suggest a paradigm of need and dependence that love can support but not conquer. Though the speaker may to some extent employ nonsense in an effort at "laughing to keep from crying," this cannot wholly account for the poem. After all, this is Shakespeare, a master of the oxymoron and paradox; that he resorts to nonsense and repetition indicates that

his relocation to Harlem has taken a heavy linguistic toll.

"Shakespeare in Harlem" probably has echoes of another fool's song. King Lear's Fool advises that nonsense is an appropriate response (it is the sign, in fact, of some vestige of sense) to the extreme emotional and physical hardships that Lear and the Fool experience on the stormy heath:

> He that has and a little tiny wit,
>   With a heigh-ho, the wind and
>   the rain,
> Must make content with his
>   fortunes fit,
>   For the rain it raineth every day.
>   (III.ii.74–77)

The logic of the Fool's song turns on the double use of "little tiny wit": it argues that he who has a shred of sense left will employ a bit of humor to accept his situation, no matter how horrible it seems. The association of the fool's perspective with wisdom is here and elsewhere abbreviated in the word "wit" that refers at once to humor, to knowledge, and, most important, to a quality that humor and knowledge combined may inspire: ingenuity. In *As You Like It* Rosalind tells Touchstone what is true for nearly all of Shakespeare's fools at one time or another, "Thou speak'st wiser than thou art ware of" (II.iv.55). Hughes's simpletons are blood brothers to Shakespeare's fools.

The wisdom and ingenuity of the Ninny become apparent when we contrast two of the poems in *Shakespeare in Harlem*. In "Kid Sleepy" the title character, like Melville's Bartleby the Scrivener, prefers not to participate in life. To all of the speaker's efforts at imaginatively resuscitating him, Kid Sleepy responds, "I don't care":

> Listen, Kid Sleepy,
> Don't you want to get up
>
> And go to work down-

Town somewhere
At six dollars a week
For lunches and car fare?

Kid Sleepy said,
I don't care. (24)

The prospect of working for a pit-tance, of earning just enough money to continue going to work, does not inspire Kid Sleepy. The speaker of "*If-ing,*" on the other hand, is brimming with optimism and energy, though he has no more material resources than Kid Sleepy does. He has, instead, verbal ones:

If I had some small change
I'd buy me a mule,
Get on that mule and
Ride like a fool.

If I had some greenbacks
I'd buy me a Packard,
Fill it up with gas and
Drive that baby backward.

If I had a million
I'd get me a plane
And everybody in America'd
Think I was insane.

But I ain't got a million.
Fact is, ain't got a dime—
So just by *if*-ing
I have a good time! (32)

The difference between Kid Sleepy and this speaker is that the second speaker, as he proudly admits in stanza one, is a fool. He can acknowl-edge that he "ain't got a dime," but that "fact" is countered by another, more important, fact: he has had a good time.

Kid Sleepy, as his name indicates, has utterly succumbed to hardship, while the "*If-ing*" speaker has turned nonsense into a survival strategy. And notably that strategy is a linguis-tic game that finds new uses for even the most apparently unavailing words. The very contingency of the word "if" renders it susceptible to transformation. The fool Touchstone in *As You Like It* recognizes a similar indeterminacy in the word. Touch-stone explains that quarrels can be resolved not by determining the truth or falsity of conflicting claims but by rejecting these inflexible categories:

All these [quarrels] you may avoid but the Lie Direct, and you may avoid that too, with an If. I knew when seven justices could not take up a quarrel, but when the parties were met themselves, one of them thought but of an If: as, "If you said so, then I said so"; and they shook hands and swore brothers. Your If is the only peacemaker. Much virtue in If. (V.iv.96–103)

Hughes's speaker also has discov-ered the virtue in "if," and he ex-ploits its contingency in order to imagine a better life.[13] Further, the speaker's word game employs rhyme, alliteration, metaphor, and rhetorical extravagance in order to conjure lin-guistic wealth. Kid Sleepy's response to poverty and unproductive work is more sensible than the second speaker's, but it is killing him. His name tells us he is on the brink of unconsciousness, he drowses in the harmful sun throughout the poem, and, most troubling, he has almost no language. His final utterance, the one that ends the poem and probably finishes off Kid Sleepy himself, lacks a subject and verb—lacks, that is, subjectivity and thus the capacity to act: "*Rather just/stay here*" (25). The "*If-ing*" speaker, by contrast, uses "I" nine times in his short poem and not only employs a range of action verbs but creates the most crucial one him-self. Indeed, "coining" the word "*if-ing*" is another way he amasses his imaginary fortune.

These two poems suggest that the simpleton's penchant for verbal play saves him because it makes linguistic production possible. When Shakespeare gets to Harlem, he is dumbstruck. Having recourse to the voice of the fool is how he continues to write poetry. What I have been calling his crisis of language is an important theme in these and other poems. It is also, however, a structural principle in the volume. The book consists of eight sections of poetry, four of which have generic designations that are anticipated in the preface: "Blues for Men," "Mammy Songs," "Ballads," and "Blues for Ladies." Two other titles emphasize locale rather than genre: "Death in Harlem" and "Lenox Avenue" (the street where Simple's hangout is located). All these sections answer to the interests of simplicity in their folk forms, common speakers, colloquial diction, everyday concerns, and uncomplicated ideas. Even more interesting are the first two sections: "Seven Moments of Love: An Un-Sonnet Sequence in Blues" and "Declarations" identify forms that are far simpler than ballads and blues: "moments," "declarations," a "statement," and one "little lyric." These new designations all emphasize brevity, bluntness, and simplicity, and they all take the thematics of simplicity to the structural level. As we will see, the poems themselves function like little elemental chunks of poetry that resist complication and elaboration. If we can find ways to read these atomic lyrics, we will have begun to achieve fluency in Hughes's poetry of simplicity.

I will conclude, then, by looking at several such poems in the "Declarations" section. The section title warns that these poems are not meditative or subtle in content, not figurative or lyrical in form. Instead, they are blurtings that make poetry out of the obvious or even the obtuse. "Hope," for example, reveals that the speaker's

sense of possibility depends in an ironic way on her or his impoverished mental and linguistic resources:

> Sometimes when I'm lonely,
> Don't know why,
> Keep thinkin' I won't be lonely
> By and by. (16)

It is precisely the speaker's not knowing that makes hope possible. To know more, to think this out more thoroughly would surely mean the eradication of all hope. The speaker's language supports the sense that inarticulateness is bliss; the last line, "By and by," is a phrase from spirituals and hymns, songs that turn from misery toward hope by positing another time when suffering will be alleviated and even rewarded.

The speaker seems not to know where this formulation originates, but it is nevertheless part of her or his severely limited verbal repertoire. The exhaustion and vagueness of "by and by," ironically, make it efficacious. Two insubstantial words create hope by putting the concreteness of a harsh reality (now) into relation with the abstractness of a better future time (then); and in the process the phrase conjures up an in-between realm of relation even though it cannot visualize hope in more decisive terms. Further, "by" is a homonym for the "bye" in "goodbye" and lends a sense of finality that shuts down further thought and thus staves off despair. "Hope" is achieved, then, by dwelling in an intellectual and linguistic limbo, by waiting in some state that is neither "here" nor "there"—a provisional state characterized by verbal simplicity. "By and by" defers all the mental and linguistic processes that would inevitably lead to the negation of hope.

"Statement" announces its simplicity in its title. And, true to its name, it offers only this bare fact:

Down on '33rd Street
They cut you
Every way they is. (28)

The speaker making this statement has no time for pondering the by-and-by, subject as he is to the perils of the present moment. The knife-wielding, anonymous "they" are not just the perpetrators of street violence but also other evils—hunger, poverty, unemployment, disappointment—that produce physical violence (as the dialect "they" for "there" suggests). The ubiquitousness of "they" and "every way" demands the full attention of this speaker, who can only state or declare the bald truth about life on 133rd Street. The conditions of his existence prevent him from analyzing, lyricizing, or elaborating his plight. The reader, of course, can do these things; in fact, to listen fluently *is* to analyze these brief utterances and elaborate recognitions and insights that move beyond them. But "Statement" itself remains a hard fact and thus an obstinate form that articulates the exigencies of Harlem.

Finally, "Little Lyric" self-consciously demonstrates the way that poetry will be altered when Shakespeare gets to Harlem: The poem's epigraph insists parenthetically that this little lyric is *"Of Great Importance"*:

I wish the rent
Was heaven sent. (21)

What is lost in reproducing the poem here is the way the tiny couplet is engulfed by the rest of the page. The white space that ominously surrounds it is as crucial to a reading of the poem as its two lines are. "Little Lyric" says visually that the sigh of desire expressed in the poem has been nearly extinguished by the vast emptiness around it. The visual hopelessness and fragility of the poem on the page are translated into language in the poem proper. Like "by and by," the idiomatic phrase "heaven sent" does not express a real confidence in divinity to pay the rent miraculously but rather employs the unavailing concept of heaven to figure forth dumb luck. Since there is obviously no heaven (as the hardships and injustices of Harlem seem to indicate), or at least no heaven that is willing to intervene, wishing "the rent/Was heaven sent" is merely an ironic way to acknowledge that the rent will not be paid. Again the brevity of the poem, the sufficiency of its perfect rhymes, and the elemental simplicity of its point are features that defy further elaboration within the poem.

The "Little Lyric" enacts the near loss of language. It reveals in an extreme form what all the other poems in the volume suggest—that utter simplicity is the only adequate response to a dislocated life in an urban ghetto in a racist country. Simplicity, as we have seen, sometimes takes the form of nonsense and foolishness and sometimes takes the form of brevity and obviousness. Both manifestations of Hughes's aesthetics of simplicity forgo the complexities of "great poetry" in order to express something that is "of great importance." Such poems would rather do right than write right.

NOTES

1 Easily ninety per cent of the poems in Hughes's canon are of the sort that I am describing as simple.

2 Jemie, Hudson, and Miller, among others, have persuasively demonstrated the intricacies of Hughes's jazz structures in these two late books.

³ Reviews in which these epithets appear are collected in Mullen.

⁴ The stories are collected in five volumes, *The Best of Simple, Simple Speaks His Mind, Simple Stakes a Claim, Simple Takes a Wife,* and *Simple's Uncle Sam.* Additionally, Hughes takes Simple to the stage with *Simply Heavenly,* a comedy about Simple's marriage.

⁵ In "Who Is Simple?"—the foreword to *The Best of Simple*—Hughes concludes, "He is my ace-boy, Simple. I hope you like him, too" (viii).

⁶ For a chronicle of Hughes's disappointments during these years, see Rampersad, especially chapter 8 of the second volume "In Warm Manure: 1951 to 1953." Ellison characterized *The Big Sea* as a "chit-chat" book during an interview with Rampersad in 1983 (202).

⁷ Hughes wrote at least four explanations of Simple: "The Happy Journey of 'Simply Heavenly,'" "Simple and Me," "Who Is Simple?" and the "Character Notes" to *Simply Heavenly.*

⁸ In his Introduction Mullen surveys the scholarship on the Simple stories; all the works he cites discuss either their racial politics or their prose structures.

⁹ One might wonder how a character described as an "Everyman" or a "black separatist"—that is, as a stereotype—can break stereotypes. That is, how can black separatism resist stereotypes when it, *by definition,* carries racist stereotypes with it? This is a subtlety that would not interest Simple, who accepts the necessity of his own racism and rejects the idea that African Americans should "overcome" black nationalist stereotypes. As long as white racism prevails, he will resist in kind. See "Color on the Brain" (*Stakes* 106–110) for one of many exchanges between Simple and Boyd about this issue.

¹⁰ In "Cocktail Sip," for example, Boyd's quotations of Elizabethan poetry are juxtaposed with Simple's rhyming prose: "Zarita is strictly a after-hours gal—great when the hour is late, the wine is fine, and mellow whiskey has made you frisky" (*Wife* 47).

¹¹ Rampersad explains McPherson's antagonism to Hughes in chapter 14 of his second volume: "McPherson had a specific reason to harass Hughes. She was one of the allegedly fraudulent ministers of religion mentioned by name in his 'Goodbye Christ'" (390).

¹² For discussions of the fool that emphasize the wisdom of his simplicity, see Welsford, Willeford, Weimann, and Goldsmith.

¹³ In his chapter on *Henry IV, Part I,* Holland makes a similar point, describing Falstaff's way of using "if" as a habit of speech that liberates him from the world of responsibilities and permits him to enter a "world of imaginings" (119).

WORKS CITED

Baldwin, James. "Sermon and Blues." Mullen 85–87.

Goldsmith, R.H. *Wise Fools in Shakespeare.* East Lansing: Michigan State UP, 1955.

Hollands, Norman N. *The Shakespearean Imagination: A Critical Introduction.* Bloomington: Indiana UP, 1964.

Hudson, Theodore R. "Technical Aspects of the Poetry of Langston Hughes." *Black World* (1973): 24–45.

Hughes, Langston. *The Best of Simple.* New York: Hill, 1961.

———. *The Big Sea: An Autobiography.* New York: Knopf, 1940.

———. *Five Plays by Langston Hughes.* Bloomington: Indiana UP, 1968.

———. "The Happy Journey of 'Simply Heavenly.'" *New York Herald-Tribune* 18 Aug. 1957, sec. 4: 1+.

———. *The Langston Hughes Reader.* New York: Braziller, 1958.

———. "The Negro Artist and the Racial Mountain." *The Nation* CXXII (1926): 692–94.

———. "The Negro Speaks of Rivers." *The Norton Anthology of American Literature.* Ed. Nina Baym et al. 2nd ed. New York: Norton, 1985.

————. *Selected Poems of Langston Hughes*. New York: Vintage, 1974.

————. *Shakespeare in Harlem*. New York: Knopf, 1942.

————. "Simple and Me." *Phylon 6* (1945): 349–52.

————. *Simple Speaks His Mind*. New York: Simon, 1950.

————. *Simple Stakes a Claim*. New York: Rinehart, 1953.

————. *Simple's Uncle Sam*. New York: Hill, 1965.

————. *Simple Takes a Wife*. New York: Simon, 1953.

————. *Simply Heavenly. Five Plays by Langston Hughes*. Bloomington: Indiana UP, 1968.

————. "Who Is Simple?" *The Best of Simple*. New York: Hill, 1961. vii–viii.

Jemie, Onwuchekwa. *Langston Hughes: An Introduction to the Poetry*. New York: Columbia UP, 1976.

Miller, R. Baxter. *The Art and Imagination of Langston Hughes*. Lexington: UP of Kentucky, 1989.

Mullen, Edward J. *Critical Essays on Langston Hughes*. Boston: Hall, 1986.

Rampersad, Arnold. *The Life of Langston Hughes, Volume II: 1941–1967*. New York: Oxford UP, 1988.

Redding, Saunders. "Old Form, Old Rhythms, New Words." Mullen 73–74.

Welsford, Enid. *The Fool: His Social and Literary History*. London: Faber, 1935.

Wiemann, Robert. *Shakespeare and the Popular Tradition in the Theater: Studies in the Social Dimension of Dramatic Form and Function*. Baltimore: Johns Hopkins UP, 1978.

Willeford, William. *The Fool and His Scepter: A Study in Clowns, Jesters, and Their Audiences*. Evanston: Northwestern UP, 1969.

◆ ◆ ◆

Dead Rocks and Sleeping Men: Aurality in the Aesthetic of Langston Hughes

HERMAN BEAVERS

In his 1940 autobiography, *The Big Sea*, Langston Hughes discusses the circumstances that lead him, at the puerile age of 19, to the creation of his poem, "The Negro Speaks of Rivers." The poem came into being during a trip to Mexico, Hughes writes, "when [he] was feeling very bad."[1] Thus, he connects poetic inspiration and emotional turbulence, both of which stemmed from his attempt to understand his father's self-hatred. He relates, "All day on the train I had been thinking about my father and his strange dislike of his own people. I didn't understand it because I was a Negro, and I liked Negroes very much" (54). What is striking about the end of this passage is that one finds Hughes adopting a posture both inside and outside the race: he does not make a statement of self-love (e.g. I like myself), rather he indicates through a kind of reflexivity, that he has self-worth. In short, he is unable to articulate self-valuation, he can only construct his positionality as the mirror opposite of his father's racial feeling. But then Hughes shifts the subject and recalls that "one of the happiest jobs [he] ever had," was the time he spent working behind the soda fountain of a refreshment parlor, in "the heart of the colored neighborhood" in Cleveland. He offers this description:

> People just up from the South used to come in for ice cream and sodas and watermelon. And I never tired of

hearing their talk, *listening* to thunderclaps of their laughter, to their troubles, to their discussions of the war and the men who had gone to Europe from the Jim Crow South, their complaints over the high rent and the long overtime hours that brought what seemed big checks, until the weekly bills were paid. (54, my emphasis)

I quote this passage at length to point to the disjointed quality Hughes's narrative assumes. In one chapter, we find the self-hatred of his father, his own admiration for the recuperative powers of newly arrived Southern blacks, and the act of composing a famous poem. The elements that form Hughes's account can be read, at least on a cursory level, as an attempt to demonstrate that his "best poems were written when [he] felt the worst" (54). This notwithstanding, what I would like to propose is that we can place the poem into an aesthetic frame that brings these three disparate elements into a more geometrical alignment.

Hughes's autobiographical account can be found in the middle of a chapter entitled, "I've Known Rivers." Having established his father as someone he neither understands nor wishes to emulate, the autobiography paints the older man as an outsider, not only geographically, but spiritually as well. That Hughes would discuss his father in relation to such an important poem, alludes to body travel of a different sort than that which he undertakes in this chapter of his autobiography. Moving further away from Cleveland, the geographical space where he encountered the individuals he describes as "the gayest and bravest people possible . . ." (54), Hughes elides the distance his father has put between himself and other blacks. He resists the

impulses that lead to the latter's self-imposed exile: he is immersed in a vernacular moment and simultaneously peripheral to that moment. What differentiates the younger Hughes is that he listens to the voices of the folk and is "empowered rather than debilitated" by what he hears.[2]

In composing the poem, Hughes looks at "the great muddy river flowing down toward the heart of the South" (*The Big Sea* 55). While he suggests that it is his gaze—looking out of the train window at the Mississippi—that initiates composition, I would assert that what catalyzes his act of writing is the act of recovering the spoken word. A point emphasized, moreover, by the fact that he recounts a moment where he is listener rather than speaker.

Later in the autobiography, Hughes relates, in much less detail, the events which lead to his poem, "The Weary Blues." There, he states, simply: "That winter, I wrote a poem called "The Weary Blues," about a piano-player I heard in Harlem . . ." (92). Again, Hughes's poetic composition moves forward from an aural moment where, as with "The Negro Speaks of Rivers," he is an outsider. Arnold Rampersad alludes to this when he observes:

> . . . [I]n his willingness to stand back and record, with minimal intervention as a craftsman, aspects of the drama of black religion or black music, Hughes had clearly shown already that he saw his *own art as inferior* [my emphasis] to that of either black musicians or religionists. . . . At the heart of his sense of inferiority . . . was the knowledge that he stood to a great extent *outside* the culture he worshipped.[3]

Rampersad concludes that Hughes's sense of alienation resulted from the fact that "his life had been spent away from consistent, normal involvement with the black masses whose affection and regard he craved" (64–5).

This trajectory repeats itself in "The Weary Blues." Rampersad intimates as much in his description of the poem's inception: "And then one night in March [of 1922], in a little cabaret in Harlem, he finally *wrote himself and his awkward position accurately into a poem* [my emphasis]" (65). This assessment calls our attention to an important consideration, namely, that Hughes's aural aesthetic employs the externality he felt in the African American community. That he was a writer and not a musician, preacher, or dancer meant that his artistic project was to record artistic expression, to amplify the African American vernacular speech event for the rest of the world to hear. Further, Hughes's sense that his literary representation of the folk was inferior, mere imitation, in turn means that he was positioned, as artist, as a distance from the "real source," almost as if he were a loudspeaker serving as a medium through which sound travels, rather than the source itself. In becoming comfortable with this role, Hughes traversed repeatedly the conceptual distance necessary to create authentic representations of black speech. Hence, as he achieved a greater place among the African American intellectual elite, the distance increased between him and the masses he sought to portray. Nonetheless, as his aesthetic sensibility crystallized, his conceptual movement was *toward* them.

This is evidenced by the fact that Hughes's Simple character resulted from a conversation he shared with a factory worker and his girlfriend in a Harlem bar in 1943. Intrigued as he listened to the exchange, Hughes used the qualities he discerned from the conversation to create the character, who first appeared in his column for *The Chicago Defender.*[4] Constructed as a dialogue between a narrator speaking in standard English and Jesse B. Semple (or Simple), who spoke in a more colorful, Southern idiom, the columns work out Hughes's passionate desire to honor the self-redemptive power found in the African American community. Thus, Simple became a vehicle for giving voice to the nature of his artistic project; indeed, it is he who articulates the necessity, as if it were a constant reminder to Hughes, to listen "eloquently."

If the ability to "listen eloquently" characterizes Hughes's attempts to celebrate "the folk," one also finds him creating stories that illustrate the ways that African American culture is objectified because people, particularly whites, fail to understand what African American voices articulate. In Hughes's collection of stories, *The Ways of White Folks,* for example, we find stories like "Slaves on the Block," where the Carraways are described as "people who went in for Negroes." When their maid's nephew, Luther, arrives at their home, they are immediately attracted to him as the ultimate exotic. Michael Carraway, as one who thinks "in terms of music," exclaims, "He's 'I Couldn't Hear Nobody Pray.'" Not only does Hughes suggest that Carraway confuses physicality and spirituality, but the song title signals his lack of aural dexterity as well.

In "The Blues I'm Playing," Mrs. Ellsworth takes on the role of benefactress for Oceola, a young black woman who is a gifted pianist. However, the investment leads her to believe that she can dictate what her protégé will play. Indeed, she can only "hear" Oceola when she plays classical music, despite the fact that she also plays the blues and spirituals.

Tension develops between the two when the older woman, "really [begins] to hate jazz, especially on a grand piano." In short, Oceola is mute unless she capitulates to Mrs. Ellsworth's belief that classical music is "superior" to vernacular musical expression.

What both these stories suggest, through their dramatization of white aural incompetence, is that African American culture is self-constituted, discursive, and regenerative. In each, Hughes is positioned at the nexus of the two cultures to mediate the events, to encode what one reads in the stories as aural incompetence. At the end of "The Blues I'm Playing," Mrs. Ellsworth claims that marriage will "take all the music" out of Oceola. The latter responds by playing the blues, which symbolizes her rejection of what Hughes suggests is the bourgeoisie's inclination to compartmentalize experience in order to create art.

Herein lies an important consideration: that Hughes's aesthetic works out a trope that brings internality and externality into a state of opposition. One sees an example of how this unfolds in "The Weary Blues." The speaker in the poem documents the experience of listening to a piano player in Harlem play the blues. Steven Tracy's compelling argument asserts that the piano player and speaker are united by the performance.[5]

I would like to argue to the contrary however. In my view, the poem works out Hughes's apprehension, his feeling that his ability to understand the emotions that generated this form of artistic expression was not on a par with the expression itself. This is indicated by the last line of the poem, where the speaker notes that the piano player "slept like a rock or a man that's dead." The key word here is "or," for it denotes the imprecision of the speaker's understanding. What the blues articulates is the simultaneous presence of the "tragic and comic aspects of the human condition."[6] Thus, the blues in the poem is not the conventional "either/or" condition configured within the Cartesian construct. Rather, the piano player, by metaphorizing loneliness has already chosen self-recovery.[7] The poem's last line, then, ignores the blues performer's ability to articulate pain and likewise to subsume it. That the speaker and the piano player never meet, or as Tracy asserts, "strike up a conversation, share a drink, or anything else," suggests that the experience does not rupture the speaker's externality. He never enters that space whereby the piano player is speaking for him, giving utterance to his loneliness. Finally, at no point in time does the speaker in the poem insert himself into the lyrics.[8]

What this implies is that "The Weary Blues" can also be read as an anti-Jazz Age poem. That is, a case can be made in which we need not equate the speaker in the poem with Hughes at all. While Hughes obviously had a strong desire to "link the lowly blues to formal poetry," locking him into the poem ignores its efficacy as cultural commentary. Given the increasing number of whites travelling to Harlem to be entertained in clubs like The Cotton Club, the poem can be seen as an attempt on Hughes's part to warn the community that African American expression was being appropriated by mainstream culture.[9]

The poem's structure enables this reading, if only because the speaker "quotes" the lyrics, but never allows his own voice to give way to them. Moreover, the speaker is "Down on Lenox Avenue . . ." which also, interestingly enough, marks the location of the Cotton Club and thus implies travel from downtown Manhattan. The I/he dichotomy Hughes establishes never collapses, which means that we can read the exteriority of the speaker as that which pertains to someone being entertained, who will leave Harlem after the performance is over. In this respect, the "or" in the last line calls our attention to the slippage that occurs when an understanding of the blues is lacking. That the speaker utters the possibility that the piano player has killed himself illustrates his failure to realize that the blues is performed reflection and not a preface to suicidal behavior.

If we return to the moment in his autobiography where Hughes is headed to Mexico towards his father, what is clear is that he circumvents his father's hatred of blacks by reconstituting the aural joy he feels in their midst. In short, Hughes's aesthetic rests on his need to assure his readership that if his writing spoke, both to and for them, it was because he took great pains to hear them. In his multivarious roles as poet, fiction writer, autobiographer, and columnist, Langston Hughes relates to the African American community as a speaker to be sure, but here the term is dualistic: the term alludes to the act of writing as both composition and amplification. As the Rampersad biography makes very clear, Hughes never elevated books over spoken forms of eloquence and his passion for writing flowed naturally from the fact that he seized every opportunity to posit himself as a listener. *The Big Sea* begins, after all, with Hughes standing on the deck of the *S.S. Malone* (his pseudonym for the freighter, *West Hesseltine*) and throwing books into the sea (3).[10] "[B]ooks had been happening to me," he writes, "I was glad they were gone" (4). What this suggests is that Hughes never wanted to subordinate experience to literacy; books could not replace the value of improvisation. Although their disappearance from his life was temporary, one can imagine that that movement, like so many others in Hughes's life, led him towards what he so dearly loved to do: put his ear to the wind and serve as a witness for all there was to hear.

NOTES

[1] Langston Hughes, *The Big Sea* (1940; New York: Hill and Wang, 1963) 54. All subsequent references to this text are from this volume.

[2] Arnold Rampersad, *The Life of Langston Hughes, Volume I: 1902–1941: I, Too, Sing America*, 2 vols. (New York: Oxford UP, 1986) 1: 64.

[3] Rampersad 64–65. My emphasis.

[4] Rampersad, *The Life of Langston Hughes, Volume II: 1941–1967: I Dream a World*, 2 vols. (New York: Oxford UP, 1988) 2: 61–62.

[5] Steven Tracy, *Langston Hughes and the Blues*. (Urbana: U of Illinois P, 1988) 222–23.

[6] Ralph Ellison, "Blues People," *Shadow and Act* (New York: Vintage, 1972) 256. Consider also Ellison's definition of the blues, found in his essay, "Richard Wright's Blues," where he notes: "The blues is an impulse to keep the painful details and episodes of a brutal experience alive in one's aching consciousness, to finger its jagged grain, and to transcend it, not by the consolation of philosophy but by squeezing from it a near-tragic, near-comic lyricism. As a form, the blues is an autobiographical chronicle of personal catastrophe expressed lyrically." Ellison's definition allows me to invalidate Hughes's "or" at the end of "The Weary Blues," and to move towards the notion that he intentionally "misreads" the silence that comes in the poem when the piano player has "stopped playing and [gone] to bed." That he conjectures about the dualistic nature of the blues suggests that he is still outside, he does not move into the "zone of the sacred" that the blues represents.

[7] In her seminal essay, "The Blues Roots of Poetry," Sherley Anne Williams argues: "The internal strategy of the blues is action rather than contemplation; for the song itself is the creation of reflection." Michael S. Harper and Robert B. Stepto, eds. *Chant of Saints* (Urbana: U of Illinois P, 1979) 125.

[8] This would represent what Michael S. Harper refers to in his liner notes to the album, "John Coltrane" as "the communal nature of the relationship between blues singer and audience . . . which assumes 'we' even though the blues singer sings 'I.'" Williams 124.

[9] Hughes asserts this point when he observes: "White people began to come to Harlem in droves. For several years they packed the expensive Cotton Club on Lenox Avenue. But I was never there, because the Cotton Club was a Jim Crow club for gangsters and monied whites." If we refer back to the poem, then, it is clear that Hughes's speaker could easily have been one of that hoard. One might also consider that this poem anticipates a later Hughes poem in which he laments: "you've taken my blues and gone—/You sing 'em on Broadway/and you sing 'em in the Hollywood Bowl. . . . " *The Big Sea* 224–225.

[10] In throwing books from Columbia into the sea, Hughes was likewise acting out the final break from his father, who had paid for him to attend. That the elder Hughes wanted Langston to "[acquire] a good business head," (*The Big Sea* 45) only drove him further towards being an artist.

◆ ◆ ◆

Langston Hughes and the "Other" Whitman

GEORGE B. HUTCHINSON

By the "other" Whitman in my title I have in mind two distinct but related concepts. One comes from the title of an article published by Leandro Wolfson in 1978, "The Other Whitman in Spanish America," in which Wolfson criticizes the continued adoration of Whitman in Latin America, pointing out the inaccuracies in the Hispanic view of the North American poet. This "other" Whitman has been debunked and/or repressed (depending upon how you look at it) in the United States since the 1950s as part of the effort to bring his poetry into the academy during an era of formalism, hostility to political writing or propaganda, and emphasis upon confessional aspects of poetry. It was felt that Whitman had to be saved from his disciples as well as from the criticism of scholars who found his work to lack "form."

The second concept I have in mind is closer to Borges's, that of Whitman as a poetic "other" to all of us for the very reason that he is each one of us when we respond to his call, a ubiquitous signifier always slipping in and out of our embrace, an ecstatic moving always outside our attempts to fix a position for him. This "other" Whitman will always elude us because his otherness is fundamental to his own textual production. It is this more radical and mercurial otherness that has made him the most diversely appropriated American poet. For some reason, in Whitman's mirror many "others" to white, patriarchal American culture have seen themselves; the process of translating his voice has helped them to find their own. Langston Hughes certainly attested to this effect in his own career.

The association of Hughes with Whitman, I suspect, is less than obvious to most readers. If Whitman is often singled out as the archetypal (white male) American poet, Hughes's experiments with black-based idioms and aesthetic principles rooted in blues, ballads, and spirituals have had an incalculable effect upon the development of a distinctive African-American poetics. Yet, like Sterling Brown after him, even in writing his "folk" poems Hughes considered himself to be following out the implications of Whitman's poetic theory (Rampersad, 1:146). At various points in his long career, Hughes put together no fewer than three separate anthologies of Whitman's poetry (one of them for children), included several Whitman poems in an anthology on *The Poetry of the Negro,* wrote a poem entitled "Old Walt" for the one hundredth anniversary of *Leaves of Grass,* and repeatedly—in lectures, newspaper columns, and introductions—encouraged black Americans to read his work. He called Whitman "America's greatest poet" and spoke of *Leaves of Grass* as the greatest expression of "the real meaning of democracy ever made on our shores." Feeling that Whitman had been ignored and, in current parlance, marginalized by the custodians of culture, Hughes indeed attempted in his own way to canonize the poet he considered "the Lincoln of our Letters" (*Chicago Defender,* July 4, 1953).

The poems Hughes most liked are not the ones most taught today. For example, "Ethiopia Saluting the Colors," which has been called racist in content and hackneyed in form, Hughes praised as "the most beautiful poem in our language concerning a Negro subject," and he included it in *Poetry of the Negro.* His collaborator Harry T. Burleigh (an important black composer) even set the poem to music. "Song of the Open Road" and "Song of the Answerer" were two of his other favorites. Hughes admired the public poems that dramatized the singer's egalitarian ubiquity, his ability to permeat social boundaries, and his role of multiversal "answerer," which accounted, in Hughes's view, for Whitman's ability to portray black people realistically.

In "Song of the Answerer"—a poem that has rarely attracted the notice of scholars—the answerer knows that "Every existence has its idiom, every thing has an idiom and tongue . . . /He says indifferently and alike *How are you friend?* to the President at his levee,/And he says *Good-day my brother,* to Cudge that hoes in the sugar-field,/And both understand him and know that his speech is right" (31, 34–36). The egalitarian message and the specific reference to the black field-worker would have attracted Hughes at once. But two other characteristics also stand out. First is the importance of respecting the "idiom" of each existence. The answerer is able to resolve this idiom into his own tongue, which he then bestows upon people, who then translate that tongue back into their own even as they translate the answerer himself. "The English believe he comes of their English stock,/A Jew to the Jew he seems, a Russ to the Russ, usual and near, removed from none" (45–46). Whitman also allows for the possibility of multiple translations and thereby answers the objections of those, such as Doris Sommer, who claim that he tries to make us all equal by making us all mirror images of himself. On the contrary he demands that each of us make him a mirror image of *our* selves. As Hughes saw it, "his poems contain us all. The reader cannot help but see his own better self therein" (Perlman et al., 98). Whitman's specular answerer acts as a mediator between plural identities, reconciling pluralism with union—"One part does not counteract another part, he is the joiner, he sees how they join" (33). Hughes insisted that, in his masked performances, Whitman was able to project a voice, ventriloquistically, outside his own socially constructed role within American culture, a voice that resonated in the sensibilities of a tremendous range of writers throughout the world (*Chicago Defender*, Aug. 1, 1953).

Though precipitated by the specific ideological and social conflicts in which Whitman was immersed in the years leading up to the Civil War, the evident drive in the poems toward a resolution of those conflicts opens up a liminal, antistructural arena in which the very self is dismembered as it escapes all formulae. This semiotic shattering of the unity of the self in the process of textual production is matched by the exceedingly multivalent quality of Whitman's poetic language, the quality which helps account for its "translations" into so many different social contexts. On top of even these factors is the function of the unnamed second person within the very type of poems Hughes most admired—those like "Song of the Answerer" and "Song of the Open Road."

One reason Whitman's poetry has resonated in the sensibilities of black American writers is that in certain of his poems he uses the condition of the slave as representative of the condition of his audience. The "you" of his songs, if it is to apply to *all* readers, must apply to slaves, those most graphically denied the right to self-determination. The poem "To You (Whoever You Are)" at times seems directly addressed to a slave:

> None has done justice to you, you
> have not done justice to yourself,
> None but has found you imperfect, I
> only find no imperfection in
> you,

> None but would subordinate you, I
> only am he who will never
> consent to subordinate you,
> I only am he who places over you
> no master, owner, better, God,
> beyond what waits intrinsically
> in yourself. (14–17)

Arguably, Whitman here distills the specific oppression of black people in the antebellum United States into a metaphor for the hidden condition of all people—"you, whoever you are." But his slave is not just any slave—his slave is the *most* enslaved, the one rejected by all others and even by himself or herself. Eschewing pity for admiration and love, the poet projects upon his reader, as by a shamanistic charm, a spiritual freedom that will ensure self-fulfillment: "The hopples fall from your ankles, you find an unfailing sufficiency,/Old or young, male or female, rude, low, rejected by the rest, whatever you are promulges itself" (44–45). A poem such as this virtually begs for appropriation to an African American frame of reference.

Hence, Hughes was not simply in *the* Whitman tradition (although he may have been happy with such a characterization); rather, he practiced an African-American–based poetic syncretism that Whitman's answerer explicitly invited: "The words of the true poems give you more than poems,/They give you to form for yourself poems, religions, politics, war, peace, behavior, histories, essays, daily life, and every thing else,/They balance ranks, colors, races, creeds, and the sexes" (75–77). The very nature of Hughes's absorption of Whitman was inevitably shaped by his "racial" identity and historical placement. In fact, it appears that by moving him toward an appreciation of the poetry of the common people, insisting on self-trust, and teaching "straying" from the teacher-poet himself, Hughes's demonic Whitman encouraged black cultural self-identification.

The very years in which Hughes grew close to the urban black community (having grown up largely removed from it) while determining to make his living as a poet were those in which he was most intensely under the spell of Whitman, as Arnold Rampersad's biography shows. Moreover, at a critical point in his life, when leaving the United States for Europe and Africa on a merchant ship, he threw overboard every book he owned except *Leaves of Grass*. "I had no intention of throwing that one away," he wrote in a passage from his autobiography (Rampersad, 1:72). But the time he returned to America, Hughes had determined what his vocation would be. His absorption of Whitman was as thorough as that of any other North American poet of his generation. Even in describing the blues to Carl Van Vechten to help him with a preface to *The Weary Blues*, Hughes would slip effortlessly into a cadence, a mixture of idioms, and even the exact phrasing of "old Walt," stealing Whitman's evocation of sexual desire: "In the Gulf Coast Blues one can feel the cold northern snows, the memory of the melancholy mists of the Louisianna [sic] low-lands, the shack that is home, the worthless lovers with hands full of gimme, mouths full of much oblige, the eternal unsatisfied longings."

Hughes was the first African-American poet to sense the affinity between the inclusive "I" of Whitman (which Whitman claimed as his most important innovation—"the quite changed attitude of the ego, the one chanting or talking, towards himself and towards his fellow humanity" ("A Backward Glance," 564) and the "I" of the blues and even of the spirituals. The result of Hughes's

appropriation of this triply descended "I" is amply demonstrated in one of his first published poems, "The Negro Speaks of Rivers":

> I've known rivers ancient as the world and old as the flow of human blood in human veins.
>
> My soul has grown deep like the rivers.
>
> I bathed in the Euphrates when dawns were young.
> I built my hut near the Congo and it lulled me to sleep.
> I looked upon the Nile and raised the pyramids above it.
> I heard the singing of the Mississippi when Abe Lincoln went down to New Orleans, and I've seen its muddy bosom turn all golden in the sunset. (*Weary Blues*, 51)

Though Hughes would later, for the most part, turn away from the Whitmanesque style of free verse, the example of Whitman's break with traditional definitions of the poetic, his attempts to achieve an orally based poetics with the cadence and diction of the voice on the street, at the pond-side, or at the pulpit, provided a partial model for the young black poet looking for a way to sing his own song, which would be at the same time a song of his people.

Furthermore, Whitman's conception of the relationship between poet and community was fundamentally that in which Hughes came to believe: "In vain," Whitman had written, "will America seek successfully to tune any superb national song unless the heartstrings of the people start it from their own breasts—to be return'd and echoed there again." Hughes would not have to wait for the people to start the song from their breasts; it was ready-formed in the spirituals and blues, which he could justly regard as the most American of song genres available to modern poets. Moreover, these forms embodied the very sort of call-and-response pattern for which Whitman seemed to be asking. It would take Hughes's example (and later that of Zora Neale Hurston and Sterling Brown) to transform the dialect tradition into an uncompromising revelation of the folk-based African-American expressive arts, with a range, a flexibility, and a precision that had not yet found their way into poetry.

The "Epilogue" (later entitled "I, Too") of Hughes's first book, *The Weary Blues,* can be read in part as a signifying riff on "old Walt's" songs, forthrightly challenging American rituals of incorporation and exclusion while more subtly playing off of Whitman's "I Hear America Singing" with a dark minor chord.

> I, too, sing America
> I am the darker brother.
> They send me to eat in the kitchen
> When company comes . . . (109)

In the American family home, the "darker brother," disowned by white siblings, has been cast out of the common room to servants' space, where he nonetheless grows strong. The poem prophesies the transforming force of the black singer's particular challenge—on the basis of his own aesthetic standards—for the humanization of the white American audience: "They'll see how beautiful I am/And be ashamed,—/I, too, am America." In this epilogue to his first collection—a poem with which he often concluded his poetry readings—Hughes registers his own distinctive poetic identity as both black and American. Simultaneously, he protests a *community*—even *family*—relationship with those across the color line and makes his claim as an heir to Whitman.

His second volume, *Fine Clothes to the Jew,* would show an even more radical break than *The Weary Blues* with past "literary" models by relying more exclusively upon the blues matrix for its aesthetic. Ironically, while the book was being blasted in the black press on genteel grounds and such intellectuals as Benjamin Brawley speculated that Hughes was pandering to the prurient interests of white folks, Hughes was invited to speak to the Walt Whitman Foundation about his poetry. Here, according to his biographer, he described "modern free verse, and his own work, as descending from Whitman's great example" (Rampersad, 1:146), an admission T. S. Eliot and Amy Lowell declined to make. At the same time, he emphasized his reliance upon the black folk tradition, which he characterized as the source of some of America's most distinctive aesthetic achievements. His very descent from Whitman demands difference from him, but difference within an American field. Hughes's liminal status—between white and black intellectual communities—freed him to explore new African-American literary forms.

Hughes had come to Whitman by way of such midwestern rebels as Carl Sandburg prior to the twenties. His was in most respects the democratic "transnationalist" and socialist Whitman pushed by Horace Traubel and other early disciples in the United States, followed by such influential figures as the French unanimist Léon Bazalgette, whose hagiographical study, *Walt Whitman,* had an enormous impact throughout Europe and Latin America, finally reacting back upon left-wing "cultural nationalists" in the United States. *Whitmanisme,* as the French called it, was a pervasive intercultural phenomenon (Betsy Erkkila) that embraced anti-imperialists in Europe (Romain Rolland) and the United States (*The Seven Arts* circle), as well as India (Rabindranath Tagore) and Latin America (José Martí, Rubén Dario) (see Grünzweig). The Hispanic reception of Whitman deserves particular attention here, for Hughes's connections with writers in the Caribbean and Latin America (and in Spain during its Civil War) were important in his career.

Whitman's influence upon such influential poets and revolutionaries as José Martí and Pablo Neruda is generally well known. Even as these socially engaged writers fought imperialism, they looked toward Whitman as a great New World forebear, the champion of democracy, social justice, and national self-determination. Fernando Alegría's account of the image of Whitman he'd had as a student at the University of Chile before World War II is broadly representative: "Whitman was the defender of liberty and the spirit, the enemy of prejudice, the proud sustainer of the purity and excellence of the artistic work, the chanter of youth, of life in contact with nature, the older brother of the workers, the romantic apostle of the persecuted and exploited" (9–10). Such views of Whitman have remained very strong to this day and have even come back to influence North American writers such as June Jordan, who has recently championed him as a "white father" whom reactionary college professors in the United States have repressed.

Jordan's view is quite similar in this respect to Hughes's, as his 1946 essay "The Ceaseless Rings of Walt Whitman" makes clear: "Many timid poetry lovers over the years have been frightened away from his *Leaves of Grass* . . . because of his simplicity. Perhaps, too, because his all embracing words lock arms with workers and farmers, Negroes and whites, Asiatics and Europeans, serfs and free men, beaming democracy to all, many academic-minded intellectual isolationists in America have had little use for Whitman, and have impeded his handclasp with today by keeping him imprisoned in silence on library shelves" (96–97). Knowing that Whitman's name had been invoked in movements for social change, Hughes claimed that *Leaves of Grass* had literally helped millions of people struggling against oppression around the world.

North American critics have generally dismissed Latin American interpretations of Whitman as naïve, overly politicized, or insufficiently attuned to Whitman's craftsmanship. These dismissals can be attributed not only to the North Americans' more accurate knowledge of the poet's life but also to the ways in which critical trends within the United States have shaped the academic readings of *Leaves of Grass* and to the way in which literature has been institutionalized. In the revaluation of Whitman which coincided with his rising status within English departments, the earlier left-wing, populist, politically engaged, prophetic, and "public" Whitman (espoused by such figures as Eugene Debs, Clarence Darrow, and Emma Goldman when Hughes was young) was debunked along with his disciples, while the private, relatively apolitical poet was discovered beneath the yawping pose. Whitman's academic reputation grew as the work of critics such as Gay Wilson Allen, James E. Miller, and Edwin Haviland Miller in the 1950s and 1960s succeeded in differentiating the weaker, supposedly more prophetic verse from the stronger, more aesthetically satisfying "poetry." The interpretive shift contributed significantly to the developing appreciation of Whitman's work but had the effect of devaluing, even suppressing, many of those elements of *Leaves of Grass* which had done most to gain Whitman a broad international following and which had most appealed to Hughes. This may partly account for our difficulty in recognizing the close relationship between Whitman and African-American poetry. Precisely the elements that scholars found in Whitman as they established him in university curricula were the elements Hughes deprecated in other modern poets: linguistic "difficulty" or apparently willful obscurity, literary allusiveness, and private confession—qualities professors love to explore but that often alienate "common" readers (and that one rarely finds in Hughes's work).

The legendary Whitman Hughes encountered in Latin America was also ubiquitous among writers in Spain during its civil war; Whitman was a heroic personage to such poets as Federico García Lorca and Miguel de Unamuno, not to mention Neruda, who also fought for the antifascist cause. These are all people whom Hughes knew in Spain. García Lorca became one of Hughes's favorite poets; indeed, Hughes translated the play *Bodas de Sangre* and some of the gypsy ballads, and he intended to translate *The Poet in New York* at one point. The "Ode to Walt Whitman" in this book-long poem functions as what one translator calls "a synthesis, climax, and solution to the underlying theme of the book" (Jaen, 81). But what is more intriguing about *The Poet in New York* is the connection it draws between the spirit of Whitman and black American culture. In this poem, black people emerge as those who, still expressing the elemental passions and desires of humanity, hold out the hope of realizing Whitman's dream.

At the end of "Ode to Walt Whitman," Whitman's spirit is to be carried on by a black American child who will "announce to the whites of the gold/the coming of the reign of the wheat," a veiled allusion to *Leaves of Grass* (as quoted in Craige, 79). Indeed, throughout *The Poet in New York,* the suggested revolt of African-Americans against an oppressive, dehumanizing, and mechanistic civilization seems the only hope of realizing the sort of society of which Whitman had dreamed. A host of themes and images interrelate Whitman and the black people of Harlem: the ability to dream (one of Hughes's constant themes), the power of "blood," erotic energy, closeness to nature, water and beach imagery, a valuing of community, and a subversive threat to socio-economic oppression. The "Ode to Whitman" initiates a turn in the poem as a whole toward the speaker's reconnection with nature, accompanied by a growing sense of hope and community. This shift is signified in part by the increasingly musical and incantatory style, which reaches its apogee in the optimistic closing section, "*Son* of the Negroes in Cuba." The poem must have hit Hughes with great force, for he had earlier convinced Nicolás Guillén of Cuba to use folk-based *son* lyrics as a basis for poetry. Of course, by the mid-thirties the main thrust of Hughes's poetry had already been determined, but what I would like to emphasize is an intertextual field connecting Whitman, Hughes, García Lorca, and such Latin American poets as Guillén, a field which considerably alters our vision of "American" poetry and the relationships between its "black" and "white" avatars. As late as 1965, when the separatist Black Arts Movement was gaining steam, Hughes wrote a show called "Tell It to Telstar" in which he combined excerpts from Whitman with songs and spirituals of black America.

The nature and history of Langston Hughes's relationship to Whitman complicate the project of developing sweeping theoretical models for the complex interplay between what at any given time might be constituted as particular radical traditions in the United States, for the centers of these traditions do not hold. Authors are not unitary figures inhabiting fixed cultural coordinates but are often liminal voyagers upon open roads, transgressors of even our latest pieties. This is not necessarily because they were in living fact freer than we give them credit for, nor because of some timeless, transcendent property but because of the subversive, multivalent quality of poetic signification itself, because of the tendency of artists to straddle thresholds of social difference, which may be fundamental to their roles, and because of the multiple ways in which authors have been received on their textual journeys.

WORKS CITED

Alegría, Fernando. *Walt Whitman en Hispanoamerica*. Mexico City: Ediciones Stadium, 1954.

Craige, Betty Jean. *Lorca's Poet in New York: The Fall into Consciousness*. Lexington: University of Kentucky Press, 1977.

Grünzweig, Walter. "Whitmania as an Intercultural Phenomenon." *Walt Whitman Quarterly Review* 5(1988): 16–26.

Hughes, Langston. *The Weary Blues*. New York: Knopf, 1926.

———. "The Ceaseless Rings of Walt Whitman." In Perlman, et al.

Hughes, Langston, and Arna Bontemps, eds. *Poetry of the Negro, 1746–1949*. Garden City, NY: Doubleday, 1949.

Jaen, Didier Tisdel, trans and ed. *Homage to Walt Whitman: A Collection of Poems from the Spanish*. Tuscaloosa: University of Alabama, 1969.

Perlman, Jim, Ed Folsom, and Dan Campion, eds. *Walt Whitman: The Measure of His Song*. Minneapolis: Holy Cow! Press, 1981.

Rampersad, Arnold. *The Life of Langston Hughes*. 2 Vols. New York: Oxford, 1986.

Whitman, Walt. *Leaves of Grass: Comprehensive Reader's Edition*. Edited by Harold W. Blodgett and Sculley Bradley. New York: NYU Press, 1965.

READING AND REACTING

◇ ◇ ◇

1. How do historical and geographic allusions contribute to the power of "The Negro Speaks of Rivers"?
2. How does Hughes use music and musical allusions? Are they "background" to the poems? Are the poems themselves meant to be musical?
3. Which poems strike you as being poems of protest? Do any seem to place social or political goals above literary concerns?

4. Is the question of identity (and especially racial identity) handled differently in "The Negro Speaks of Rivers" and "Theme for English B"? Explain.

5. How would you characterize Hughes's attitude to America as expressed in poems like "Let America Be America Again" and "I, Too"? Do you see these poems as patriotic?

6. Hughes is often celebrated for his ability to communicate complex human dilemmas in accessible language and forms. Evalute his accomplishment in this regard in "Harlem" (p. 808).

7. Given the horror of the event that precipitated the poem "Birmingham Sunday," why does Hughes include indirect statements about Chinese mythology and history? What does his obliqueness accomplish?

8. Is the "dream" in "Harlem" (p. 808) the same as the one in "Dream Boogie"? Do you think the poems were meant to be read side by side? Do they shed light on each other, or do they represent significantly different approaches to a similar problem?

9. In which poems do you think the first person voice is explicitly autobiographical? In which poems is Hughes simply creating a dramatic speaker?

10. What do you think Hughes expects of readers of his poetry? Action? Reflection? A change of heart?

11. **JOURNAL ENTRY** Are Langston Hughes's poems relevant only to African-Americans, or do they also have relevance for other Americans—or for readers in other countries?

12. **CRITICAL PERSPECTIVE** In his essay "The Negro Artist and the Racial Mountain," Hughes states his respect for the "common people," those he admires for their lack of self-importance:

> But then there are the low-down folks, the so-called common element, and they are the majority—may the Lord be praised! The people who have their nip of gin on Saturday nights are not too important to themselves or the community, or too well fed, or too learned to watch the lazy world go round. They live on Seventh Street in Washington or State Street in Chicago, and they do not particularly care whether they are like white folks or anybody else [. . .] They furnish a wealth of colorful, distinctive material for any artist because they still hold their own individuality in the face of American standardizations.

How does Hughes depict the "common people" in his poetry? What are their concerns? How have America's "standardizations" attempted to shape and change the common people, and what has been the result of those attempts?

Related Works: "Big Black Good Man" (p. 207), "Photograph of My Father in His Twenty-Second Year" (p. 675), "The Unknown Citizen" (p. 750), "Ballad of Birmingham" (p. 755), "We Real Cool" (p. 782), "Sadie and Maud" (p. 835), *Florence* (p. 1183), *Aspects of Negro Life* (color insert)

RESEARCH QUESTIONS
◇ ◇ ◇

1. As Hughes's own essays in this volume suggest, much of his life was spent actively campaigning for various causes. Research the nature of his commitments and their effect on his poetry. How was his social and political work different in 1935 and in 1955?
2. Investigate the ways in which Hughes's poetry was inspired by the accomplishments of African-American musicians. For example, how did the different musical forms of, say, the female blues singers of the 1920s and the bebop musicians of the 1940s inspire Hughes?
3. Hughes was a primary inspiration for the artistic movement known as "negritude." Poets and writers like Nicolás Guillén, Jacques Roumain, Aimé Cesaire, and Leopold Senghor all acknowledged Hughes's influence. Find out what the "negritude" poets stood for, and consider why Hughes was so important to their development.
4. Hughes's work was distinct from that of his two most important contemporaries, Gwendolyn Brooks and Robert Hayden, who were influenced by modernism. Using a dictionary or an encyclopedia of literary criticism, find out what modernist poetry is. Is "modernism" a useful term in discussing what distinguishes Brooks and Hayden from Hughes? Why might Hughes be skeptical about some aspects of modernism? Find a collection of the work of either of these writers, and compare some of their poems to those of Hughes.
5. George Hutchinson's article in this casebook talks about the influence of Walt Whitman on Hughes. Read some of the Whitman poems that Hutchinson argues were important to Hughes, and develop your own conclusions about what

Hughes might have learned from Whitman. What do you think Hughes might have rejected in Whitman's work?

6. Read a collection of Hughes's "Simple Stories," newspaper columns that were later collected in book form. What is he able to do in fiction that he is unable to do in poetry? What is he able to do in poetry that he is unable to do in fiction?

Alston 1

Grace R. Alston

Professor Hall

African-American Literature

September 15, 1999

Challenging the Father/Challenging the Self:

Langston Hughes's "The Negro Speaks of Rivers"

Langston Hughes's career as a poet began with the publication of "The Negro Speaks of Rivers" in the June 1921 issue of <u>The Crisis</u>. Hughes wrote this poem during a trip to Mexico to visit his father, African-American businessman James Hughes. James Hughes, an "unfeeling, domineering, and materialistic man, scornful of Indians and blacks and the poor in general, and contemptuous of his son's gentler pace and artistic temperament" (Rampersad 1066), had purposefully removed himself from African-American life in the United States. Throughout the trip Langston Hughes dreaded the confrontation he knew he would have with his father about his desire to become a writer. He was very anxious, even depressed, but as he wrote, "my best poems were all written when I felt the worst. When I was happy, I didn't write anything" (Rampersad 1066).

Herman Beavers argues that the emotionally distant relationship between Hughes and his father influenced the younger Hughes to adopt "a posture both inside and outside the race" (1095), a kind of double consciousness. According to Beavers, Hughes's position nside the race was to affirm blackness, counter to his father's racial beliefs. Hughes's position outside the race was to maintain objectivity and artistic distance

Alston 2

while simultaneously displaying an artist's passion
(Beavers 1097). Ironically, then, Hughes's desire to
celebrate blackness--with a kind of passionate objec-
tivity--was born out of the dysfunctional relationship
he had with his father. In Hughes's case we can see
typical adolescent rebellion connected to the unusual
task of confronting racism. Not only did Hughes reject
his father's feelings about race, but he also insisted
on becoming a writer even though his father saw writing as impractical and somehow not quite manly.

The specific form of "The Negro Speaks of Rivers"
reveals Hughes's struggle with this double consciousness. In this poem, Hughes actively engages his father's racism, but he also develops a voice that
allows him to do more than just affirm blackness. The
poem also celebrates the role of African-Americans in
the universal human community.

Hughes understood early in life the peculiarities of this double consciousness, and investigated
ways it could be managed in poetry. Hughes understood
this concept of "double consciousness" as early as
high school; he believed that the role of class poet
was thrust upon him at Cleveland's Central High because he was black, and supposed to have "rhythm." The
idea that his individuality was not recognized--that
he was seen in terms of racial stereotypes--caused
him great anxiety, an anxiety heightened by his father's questioning of African-American character. In
the face of so much conflict, it is not surprising

Alston 3

that double consciousness became one of Hughes's poetic themes.

In "The Negro Artist and the Racial Mountain," Hughes argues that "white" is the standard to which blacks have to measure up (1051). Against this standard, he suggested that the Negro artist would have a high mountain to climb in order to discover the self and the community. Hughes was able to climb this mountain, but at what emotional cost? (If some of Hughes's best poems were written when he felt most pessimistic about the prospects for black people, the number of poems reflecting this pessimism suggests he was frequently under stress.) He was able, however, to transform negative emotions into strong, accessible poems. He experienced great pain while writing "The Negro Speaks of Rivers," but was able to put this emotion aside as he glanced out of a train window and became fascinated by the Mississippi River. As the image of the river engulfed him, he transformed his desire to rebel against his father's disapproval into a poem that Karen Jackson Ford notes is uncharacteristic because of its strong "oratorical tone" (1080). In the poem, Hughes writes these lines:

> I've known rivers:
> I've known rivers ancient as the world and
> older than the flow of human blood in
> human veins.
> My soul has grown deep like the rivers.
> (1-5)

Alston 4

The words "I've known rivers" are universal--and ironic
given the rest of the poem. The words uplift and inspire
because they remind us of shared experience. "Knowing"
and "rivers" are not extraordinary; they suggest shared
feelings, and in this sharing we begin a process by
which readers come to appreciate blackness.

Hughes's tone in "The Negro Speaks of Rivers" is
marked by struggle and, despite the poem's affirmation, by anger. The "I" of the poem says that he has
"known rivers ancient as human blood" and that his
"soul has grown deep like the rivers." (Hughes also
once wrote of the time with his father that "Anger
clotted in every vein, and my tongue tasted like dry
blood" [Rampersad 1066].) With this use of blood,
Hughes identifies a common human denominator: our bi-
ology, or bloodline. The poem also recalls a time in
America when if a person had "one drop" of "Negro
blood" he or she was not entitled to full citizenship.
The separateness Hughes felt as an American was the
same separateness he felt as a son. The "bloodline"
was their only tie.

In focusing on the following lines, Karen Jackson
Ford suggests the poem's "mythic scope" (1080):

> I bathed in the Euphrates when dawns were
> young.
> I built my hut near the Congo and it lulled
> me to sleep.
> I looked upon the Nile and raised the pyra-
> mids above it.

Alston 5

> I heard the singing of the Mississippi when
>   Abe Lincoln went down to New Orleans,
>   and I've seen its muddy bosom turn all
>   golden in the sunset.
>
> I've known rivers:
> Ancient dusky rivers.
>
>   My soul has grown deep like the rivers.
>   (5-13)

The scope here is perhaps as much historic as mythic. Although Hughes depicts certain conventions of black culture in an imaginative and symbolic way, his choice of rivers suggests a very particular history. The Congo and Nile illustrate the beauty of blackness and its accomplishments; they appear "naturally" alongside the Euphrates, and with it suggest the beginnings of civilization. In this way, Hughes makes clear to his father--and to the nation--the nobility of an African past. Moreover, his use of the Mississippi not only places the American river in a continuous historical relationship with the Euphrates but also introduces the question of slavery. Once again, Hughes is able to perform the double task of confronting both American culture and his father. The image of defenseless slaves being sold up and down the Mississippi River's "muddy bosom" may have reminded him of his own defenseless position in his relationship with his father. And as the "muddy bosom" turning "golden in the sunset" suggests freedom for slaves, it may have also meant for Hughes freedom from his father.

Alston 6

Repetition also contributes to the poem's effect. Because the poem promotes healing and liberation, Hughes uses words implying motion, such as "built," "bathed," "looked," "raised," and "singing," emphasizing ritual and religion. "Rivers," of course, works in a slightly different manner, but it may be the most effective means by which Hughes communicates his feeling of displacement. Like a kind of chant, creation of this complex rhythm is the most striking way he rises to his double challenge, but the success of this "rhythm" is based in readers' collective experience, and not upon racial stereotype.

Hughes believed that black writers had a responsibility to reveal to whites that blacks could do more than sing, dance, laugh, and make music. He believed black writers had a role to play in racial reconciliation (Hughes, "To Negro Writers" 1055), and his ability to affirm blackness without stereotyping is what earns him his distinction as a poet. That the source of his racial identity is, at least partially, his troubled relationship with his father is striking. His passion for "blackness" increased as he resisted his black father, while his ability to develop a poetic persona emerged from his awareness of his own "double position."

Alston 7

Works Cited

Beavers, Herman. "Dead Rocks and Sleeping Men: Aural-
     ity in the Aesthetic of Langston Hughes."
     Kirszner and Mandell 1095–1100.

Ford, Karen Jackson. "Do Right to Write Right:
     Langston Hughes's Aesthetics of Simplicity."
     Kirszner and Mandell 1080–1095.

Hughes, Langston. "The Negro Artist and the Racial
     Mountain." Kirszner and Mandell 1051–1054.

---. "The Negro Speaks of Rivers." Kirszner and Man-
     dell 1043.

---. "To Negro Writers." Kirszner and Mandell
     1054–1056.

Kirszner, Laurie G., and Stephen R. Mandell, eds. Lit-
     erature: Reading, Reacting, Writing. 4th ed.
     Fort Worth: Harcourt, 2001.

Rampersad, Arnold. "The Origins of Poetry in Langston
     Hughes." Kirszner and Mandell 1065–1072.

DRAMA

CHAPTER 20

Understanding Drama

DRAMATIC LITERATURE
◇ ◇ ◇

The distinctive appearance of a script, with its stage directions, character parts, and divisions into acts and scenes, identifies **drama** as a unique form of literature. A play is written to be performed in front of an audience by actors who take on the roles of the characters and who present the story through dialogue and action. (An exception is **closet drama,** which is meant to be read, not performed.) Indeed, the term *theater* comes from the Greek word *theasthai,* which means "to view" or "to see." Thus, drama is different from novels and short stories, which are meant to be read.

Dramatic works differ from other prose works in a number of other ways as well. Unlike novels and short stories, plays do not usually have narrators to tell the audience what a character is thinking or what happened in the past; the audience knows only what the characters reveal. Drama develops primarily by means of **dialogue,** the lines spoken by the characters. The plot and the action of drama unfold on the stage as the characters interact. Playwrights employ various techniques to compensate for the absence of a narrator. For example, playwrights use **monologues**—extended speeches by one character. (A monologue in which a character expresses private thoughts while alone on the stage is called a **soliloquy.**) Playwrights can also use **asides**—brief comments by an actor who addresses the audience but is not heard by the other characters—to reveal the thoughts of the speaker. Like the observations of a narrator, these dramatic techniques give the audience insight into a character's motives and attitudes. In addition, makeup, costumes, scenery, and lighting enhance a dramatic performance, as do actors' and directors' interpretations of dialogue and stage directions.

THE ORIGINS OF THE MODERN THEATER
◆ ◆ ◆

THE ANCIENT GREEK THEATER

The dramatic presentations of ancient Greece developed out of religious rites performed to honor gods or to mark the coming of spring. Playwrights such as Aeschylus (525–456 B.C.), Sophocles (496–406 B.C.), and Euripides (480?–406 B.C.) composed plays to be performed and judged at competitions held during the yearly Dionysian festivals. Works were chosen by a selection board and evaluated by a panel of judges. To compete in the contest, authors had to submit three tragedies, which could be either based on a common theme or unrelated, and one comedy. Unfortunately, relatively few of these ancient Greek plays survive today.

The open-air semicircular ancient Greek theater, built into the side of a hill, looked much like a primitive version of a modern sports stadium. Some Greek theaters, such as the Athenian theater, could seat almost seventeen thousand spectators. Sitting in tiered seats, the audience would look down on the *orchestra,* or "dancing place," occupied by the **chorus**— originally a group of men (led by an individual called the *choragos*) who danced and chanted and later a group of onlookers who commented on the drama. Raised a few steps above the orchestra was a platform on which

◆ **The Theater of Dionysus at Athens.** Redrawn from a drawing by R. C. Flickinger, *The Greek Theater and Its Drama* (Chicago: U of Chicago P, 1918).

the actors performed, behind which was a *skene,* or building, that originally served as a resting place or dressing room. (The modern term *scene* is derived from the Greek *skene.*) Behind the skene was a line of pillars called a *colonnade,* which was covered by a roof. Actors used the skene for entrances and exits; beginning with the plays of Sophocles, painted backdrops were hung there. These backdrops, however, were most likely more decorative than realistic. Historians believe that realistic props and scenery were probably absent from the ancient Greek theater. Instead, the setting was suggested by the play's dialogue, and the audience had to imagine the specific physical details of a scene.

Two mechanical devices were used. One, a rolling cart or platform, was sometimes employed to introduce action that had occurred offstage. For example, actors frozen in position could be rolled onto the roof of the skene to illustrate an event such as the killing of Oedipus's father, which occurred before the play began. Another mechanical device, a small crane, was used to show gods ascending to or descending from heaven. Such devices enabled playwrights to dramatize many of the myths that were celebrated at the Dionysian festivals.

The ancient Greek theater was designed to enhance acoustics. The flat stone wall of the skene reflected the sound from the orchestra and the stage, and the curved shape of the amphitheater captured the sound, enabling the audience to hear the lines spoken by the actors. Each actor wore a stylized mask, or **persona,** to convey to the audience the personality traits of the particular character being portrayed—a king, a soldier, a wise old man, a young girl (female roles were played by men). The mouths of these masks were probably constructed so they amplified the voice and projected it into the audience. In addition, the actors wore *kothorni,* high shoes that elevated them above the stage, perhaps also helping to project their voices. Due to the excellent acoustics, audiences who see plays performed in these ancient theaters today can hear clearly without microphones or speaker systems.

Because actors wore masks and because males played the parts of women and gods as well as men, acting methods in the ancient Greek theater were probably not realistic. In their masks, high shoes, and full-length tunics (called *chiton*), actors could not hope to appear natural or to mimic the attitudes of everyday life. Instead, they probably recited their lines while standing in stylized poses, with emotions conveyed more by gesture and tone than by action. Typically, three actors had all the speaking roles. One actor—the **protagonist**—would play the central role and have the largest speaking part. Two other actors would divide the remaining lines between them. Although other characters would come on and off the stage, they would usually not have speaking roles.

Ancient Greek tragedies were typically divided into five parts. First came the *prologos,* or prologue, in which an actor gave the background or explanations that the audience needed to follow the rest of the drama. Then came the *párodos,* in which the chorus entered and commented on the events presented in the prologue. Following this were several *episodia,* or episodes, in which characters spoke to one another on the stage and developed the central conflict of the play. Alternating with episodes were *stasimon* (choral odes), in which the chorus commented on the exchanges that had taken place during the preceding episode. Frequently the choral odes were divided into *strophes,* or stanzas, that were recited or sung as the chorus moved across the orchestra in one direction, and *antistrophes* that were recited as it moved in the opposite direction. (Interestingly, the chorus stood between the audience and the actors, often functioning as an additional audience, expressing the political, social, and moral views of the community.) Finally came the *exodos,* the last scene of the play, during which the conflict was resolved and the actors left the stage.

Using music, dance, and verse—as well as a variety of architectural and technical innovations—the ancient Greek theater was able to convey traditional themes of tragedy. Thus, the theater powerfully expressed ideas that were central to the religious festivals in which they first appeared: the reverence for the cycles of life and death, the unavoidable dictates of the gods, and the inscrutable workings of fate.

THE ELIZABETHAN THEATER

The Elizabethan theater, influenced by the classical traditions of Roman and Greek dramatists, traces its roots back to local religious pageants performed at medieval festivals during the twelfth and thirteenth centuries. Town guilds, organizations of craftsmen who worked in the same profession, reenacted Old and New Testament stories: the fall of man, Noah and the flood, David and Goliath, and the crucifixion of Christ, for example. Church fathers encouraged these plays because they brought the Bible to a largely illiterate audience. Sometimes these spectacles, called **mystery plays,** were presented in the market square or on the church steps, and at other times actors appeared on movable stages or wagons called *pageants,* which could be wheeled to a given location. (Some of these wagons were quite elaborate, with trapdoors and pulleys and an upper tier that simulated heaven.) As mystery plays became more popular, they were performed in series over several days, presenting an entire cycle of a holiday—the death and resurrection of Christ during Easter, for example.

Related to mystery plays are **morality plays,** which developed in the fourteenth and fifteenth centuries. Unlike mystery plays, which depict scenes from the Bible, morality plays allegorize the Christian way of life. Typically, characters representing various virtues and vices struggle or debate over the soul of man. *Everyman* (1500), the best known of these plays, dramatizes the good and bad qualities of Everyman and shows his struggle to determine what is of value to him as he journeys toward death.

By the middle of the sixteenth century, mystery and morality plays had lost ground to a new secular drama. One reason for this decline was that mystery and morality plays were associated with Catholicism and consequently discouraged by the Protestant clergy. In addition, newly discovered plays of ancient Greece and Rome introduced a dramatic tradition that supplanted the traditions of religious drama. English plays that followed the classic model were sensational and bombastic, often dealing with murder, revenge, and blood retribution. Appealing to privileged classes and commoners alike, these plays were extremely popular. (One source estimates that between 20,000 and 25,000 people attended the London theaters each week.) Companies of professional actors performed works such as Christopher Marlowe's *Tamburlaine* and Thomas Kyd's *The Spanish Tragedy* in tavern courtyards and then eventually in theaters. According to scholars, the structure of the Elizabethan theater evolved from these tavern courtyards.

The Globe Theater (a corner of which was unearthed in 1989), where Shakespeare's plays were performed, consisted of a large main stage that extended out into the open-air *yard* where the *groundlings,* or common people, stood. Spectators who paid more sat on small stools in two or three levels of galleries that extended in front of and around the stage. (The theater could probably seat almost two thousand people at a performance.) Most of the play's action occurred on the stage, which had no curtain and could be seen from three sides. Beneath the stage was a space called the *hell,* which could be reached when the floorboards were removed. This space enabled actors to "disappear" or descend into a hole or grave when the play called for such action. Above the stage was a roof called the *heavens,* which protected the actors from the weather and contained ropes and pulleys used to lower props or to create special effects.

At the rear of the stage was a narrow alcove covered by a curtain that could be open or closed. This curtain, often painted, functioned as a decorative rather than a realistic backdrop. The main function of this alcove was to enable actors to hide when the script called for them to do so. Some Elizabethan theaters contained a rear stage instead of an alcove. Because the rear stage was concealed by a curtain, props could be arranged on it ahead of time. When the action on the rear stage was finished, the curtain would be drawn and the action would continue on the front stage.

On either side of the rear stage was a door through which the actors could enter and exit the front stage. Above the rear stage was an upper, curtained stage called the *chamber,* which functioned as a balcony or as any other setting located above the action taking place on the stage below. On either side of the chamber were casement windows, which actors could use when a play called for a conversation with someone leaning out a window or standing on a balcony. Above the chamber was the *music gallery,* a balcony that housed the musicians who provided musical interludes throughout the play (and that doubled as a stage if the play required it). The *huts,* windows located above the music gallery, could be used by characters playing lookouts or sentries. Because of the many acting sites, more than one action could take place simultaneously. For example, lookouts

The Globe Playhouse,

1599-1613

A CONJECTURAL

RECONSTRUCTION

KEY

AA   Main entrance
B   The Yard
CC   Entrances to lowest gallery
D   Entrances to staircase and upper
       galleries
E   Corridor serving the different sections
       of the middle gallery
F   Middle gallery ('Twopenny Rooms')
G   'Gentlemen's Rooms' or 'Lords' Rooms'
H   The stage

J   The hanging being put up round the
       stage
K   The 'Hell' under the stage
L   The stage trap, leading down to the
       Hell
MM Stage doors
N   Curtained 'place behind the stage'
O   Gallery above the stage, used as re-
       quired sometimes by musicians, some-
       times by spectators, and often as part
       of the play
P   Back-stage area (the tiring-house)
Q   Tiring-house door
R   Dressing-rooms
S   Wardrobe and storage
T   The hut housing the machine for
       lowering enthroned gods, etc., to the
       stage
U   The 'Heavens'
W   Hoisting the playhouse flag

◆ **The Globe Playhouse.** 1599–1613; a conjectural reconstruction. From C. Walter Hodges, *The Globe Restored*.

could stand in the towers of Hamlet's castle while Hamlet and Horatio walked the walls below.

During Shakespeare's time, the theater had many limitations that challenged the audience's imagination. Because women did not perform on the stage, young boys—usually between the ages of ten and twelve—played all the women's parts. In addition, there was no artificial lighting, so plays had to be performed in daylight. Rain, wind, or clouds could disrupt a performance or ruin an image—such as "the morn in russet mantle clad"— that the audience was asked to imagine. Finally, because few sets and props were used, the audience had to visualize the high walls of a castle or the trees of a forest. The plays themselves were performed without intermission, except for musical interludes that occurred at various points. Thus, the experience of seeing one of Shakespeare's plays staged in the Elizabethan theater was different from seeing it staged today in a modern theater.

THE MODERN THEATER

Unlike the theaters of ancient Greece and Elizabethan England, seventeenth- and eighteenth-century theaters—such as the Palais Royal, where the great French playwright Molière presented many of his plays—were covered by a roof, beautifully decorated, and illuminated by candles so that plays could be performed at night. The theater remained brightly lit even during performances, partly because there was no easy way to extinguish hundreds of candles and partly because people went to the theater as much to see each other as to see the play. A curtain opened and closed between acts. The audience of about five hundred spectators sat in a long room and viewed the play on a **picture-frame stage.** This type of stage contained the action within a **proscenium arch** that surrounded the opening through which the audience viewed the performance. Thus, the action seemed to take place in an adjoining room with one of its walls cut away. Painted scenery (some of it quite elaborate), intricately detailed costumes, and stage makeup were commonplace, and for the first time women performed female roles. Because the theaters were small, audiences were relatively close to the stage, so actors could use subtle movements and facial expressions to enhance their performances.

Many of the first innovations in the theater were quite basic. For example, the first stage lighting was produced by candles lining the front of the stage. This method of lighting was not only ineffective—actors were lit from below and had to step forward to be fully illuminated—but also dangerous. Costumes and even entire theaters could and did accidentally catch fire. Later, covered lanterns with reflectors provided more light. In the nineteenth century a device that used an oxyhydrogen flame directed on a cylinder of lime created extremely bright illumination that could, with the aid of a lens, be concentrated into a spotlight. (It is from this method of stage lighting that we get the expression *to be in the limelight.*)

Eventually, in the twentieth century, electric lights provided a dependable and safe way of lighting the stage. Electric spotlights, footlights, and ceiling light bars made the actors clearly visible and enabled playwrights to create special effects. In Arthur Miller's *Death of a Salesman* (p. 1410), for example, lighting focuses attention on action in certain areas of the stage while leaving other areas in complete darkness.

Along with electric lighting came other innovations, such as electronic amplification. Microphones made it possible for actors to speak conversationally and to avoid using unnaturally loud "stage diction" to project their voices to the rear of the theater. Microphones placed at various points around the stage enabled actors and actresses to interact naturally and to deliver their lines audibly even without facing the audience. More recently, small wireless microphones eliminated the unwieldy wires and the "dead spaces" left between upright or hanging microphones, allowing characters to move freely around the stage.

The true revolutions in staging came with the advent of **realism** in the middle of the nineteenth century. Until this time, scenery was painted on canvas backdrops that trembled visibly, especially when they were intersected by doors through which actors and actresses entered. With realism came settings that were accurate down to the smallest detail. (Improved lighting, which revealed the inadequacies of painted backdrops, made such realistic stage settings necessary.) Backdrops were replaced by the **box set,** three flat panels arranged to form connected walls, with the fourth wall removed so the audience had the illusion of looking into a room. The room itself was decorated with real furniture, plants, and pictures on the walls; the door of one room might connect to another completely furnished room, or a window might open to a garden filled with realistic foliage. In addition, new methods of changing scenery were employed. Elevator stages, hydraulic lifts, and moving platforms enabled directors to make complicated changes in scenery out of the audience's view.

During the late nineteenth and early twentieth centuries, however, some playwrights reacted against what they saw as the excesses of realism. They introduced **surrealistic** stage settings, in which color and scenery mirrored the uncontrolled images of dreams, and **expressionistic** stage settings, in which costumes and scenery were exaggerated and distorted to reflect the workings of a troubled, even unbalanced mind. In addition, playwrights used lighting to create areas of light, shadow, and color that reinforced the themes of the play or reflected the emotions of the protagonist. In *The Emperor Jones,* for example, Eugene O'Neill used a series of expressionistic scenes to show the mental state of the terrified protagonist.

Sets in contemporary plays run the gamut from realistic to fantastic, from a detailed re-creation of a room in a production of Tennessee Williams's *The Glass Menagerie* (p. 1805) to a dreamlike set for Edward Albee's *The Sandbox* (p. 1610). Motorized devices, such as revolving turntables, and *wagons*—scenery mounted on wheels—make possible rapid changes of scenery. The Broadway musical *Les Miserables,* for example, requires scores of elaborate sets—Parisian slums, barricades, walled gardens—to be shifted as the audience watches. A gigantic barricade constructed on stage at one point in the play is later rotated to show the carnage that has taken place on both sides of a battle. Light, sound, and smoke are used to heighten the impact of the scene.

Today, as dramatists attempt to break down the barriers that separate audiences from the action they are viewing, plays are not limited to the picture-frame stage; in fact, they are performed on many different kinds of stages. Some plays, for example, take place on a **thrust stage,** which has an area that projects out into the audience. Others are performed on an **arena stage,** with the audience surrounding the actors. This kind of performance is often called **theater in the round.** In addition, experiments have been done with *environmental staging,* in which the stage surrounds the audience or several stages are situated at various locations throughout the audience. Plays may also be performed outdoors, in settings ranging from parks to city streets. Some playwrights even try to blur the line that divides the audience from the stage by having actors move through or sit in the audience—or even by eliminating the stage entirely. For example, *Tony 'n Tina's Wedding,* a "participatory drama" created in 1988 by the theater group Artificial Intelligence, takes place not in a theater but at a church where a wedding is performed and then at a catering hall where the wedding reception is held. Throughout the play the members of the audience function as guests, joining in the wedding celebration

◊ **Thrust-Stage Theater.** With seats on three sides of the stage area, the thrust stage and its background can assume many forms other than the conventional living-room interior in the illustration. Entrances can be made from the aisles, from the sides, through the stage floor, and from the back.

◆ **Arena Theater.** The audience surrounds the stage area, which may or may not be raised. Use of scenery is limited—perhaps to a single piece of scenery standing alone in the middle of the stage.

and mingling with the actors, who improvise freely. More recent examples of such "interactive" drama include *Grandma Sylvia's Funeral* and *Off the Wall,* in which audiences "attend" an art auction. Today, no single architectural form defines the theater. The modern stage is a flexible space suited to the many varieties of contemporary theatrical production.

KINDS OF DRAMA

◆ ◆ ◆

TRAGEDY

In his *Poetics,* Aristotle (384–322 B.C.) sums up ancient Greek thinking about drama when he writes that a **tragedy** is a drama treating a serious subject and involving persons of significance. According to Aristotle, when the members of an audience see a tragedy, they should feel both pity (and thus closeness to the protagonist) and fear (and thus revulsion) because they recognize in themselves the potential for similar reactions. The purging of these emotions that the audience experiences as they see the dramatic action unfold is called **catharsis.** For this catharsis to occur, the protagonist of a tragedy must be worthy of the audience's attention and sympathy. Because of his or her exalted position, the fall of a tragic protagonist is greater than that of an average person; therefore, it arouses more pity and fear in the audience. Often the entire society suffers as a result of the actions of the protagonist. Before the action of Sophocles' *Oedipus the King* (p. 1509), for example, Oedipus has freed Thebes from the deadly grasp of the Sphinx by answering her riddle and, as a result, he has been welcomed as king. But because of his sins, Oedipus is an affront to the gods and brings famine and pestilence to the city. When his fall finally comes, it is sudden and absolute.

According to Aristotle, the protagonist of a tragedy is neither all good nor all evil, but a mixture of the two. He is like the rest of us—only more exalted and possessing some weakness or flaw **(hamartia).** This tragic flaw—perhaps narrowness of vision or overwhelming pride **(hubris)**—is typically the element that creates the conditions for tragedy. Shakespeare's Romeo and Juliet, for example, are so much in love they think they can ignore the blood feud that rages between their two families. However, their naive efforts to sustain their love despite the feud lead them to their tragic deaths. Similarly, Richard III's blind ambition to gain the throne causes him to murder all those who stand in his way. His unscrupulousness sets into motion the forces that eventually cause his death.

Irony is central to tragedy. **Dramatic irony** (also called **tragic irony**) emerges from a situation in which the audience knows more about the dramatic situation than a character does. As a result, the character's words and actions may be consistent with what he or she expects but at odds with what the audience knows will happen. Thus, a character may say or do something that causes the audience to infer a meaning beyond what the character intends or realizes. The dramatic irony is clear, for example, when Oedipus announces that whoever has disobeyed the dictates of the gods will be exiled. The audience knows, although Oedipus does not, that he has just condemned himself. **Cosmic irony,** also called **irony of fate,** occurs when God, fate, or some larger, uncontrollable force seems to be intentionally deceiving characters into believing they can escape their fate. Too late, they realize that trying to avoid their destiny is futile. Years before Oedipus was born, for example, the oracle of Apollo foretold that Oedipus would kill his parents. Naturally, his parents attempted to thwart the prophecy, but ironically, their actions ensured that the prophecy would be fulfilled.

At some point in a tragedy—usually after the climax—the protagonist recognizes the reasons for his or her downfall. It is this recognition (and the accompanying acceptance) that elevates tragic protagonists to grandeur and gives their suffering meaning. Without this recognition there would be no tragedy, just **pathos**—suffering that exists simply to satisfy the sentimental or morbid sensibilities of the audience. In spite of the death of the protagonist, then, tragedy enables the audience to see the nobility of the character and thus to experience a sense of elation. In Shakespeare's *King Lear,* for example, a king at the height of his powers decides to divide his kingdom among his three daughters. Too late, he realizes that without his power, he is just a bothersome old man to his ambitious children. Only after going mad does he understand the vanity of his former existence; he dies a humbled but enlightened man.

According to Aristotle, a tragedy achieves the illusion of reality only when it has *unity of action*—that is, when the play contains only those actions that lead to its tragic outcome. Later critics interpreted this to mean that including subplots or mixing tragic and comic elements would destroy this unity. To the concept of unity of action, these later critics added two other requirements: *unity of place*—the requirement that the play have a single setting—and *unity of time*—the requirement that the events depicted by the play take no longer than the actual duration of the play (or, at most, a single day).

The three unities have had a long and rather uneven history. In some of his plays—*The Tempest* and *The Comedy of Errors,* for example—Shakespeare observed the unities. Shakespeare, however, had no compunctions about writing plays with subplots and frequent changes of location. He also wrote **tragicomedies,** such as *The Merchant of Venice,* that have a serious theme appropriate for tragedy but end happily, usually because of a sudden turn of events. During the eighteenth century, with its emphasis on classic form, the unities were adhered to quite strictly, but in the late eighteenth and early nineteenth centuries, with the onset of romanticism and its emphasis on the natural, interest in the unities of place and time waned. Even though some modern dramatists occasionally observe the unities—*'night, Mother* (p. 1708), for instance, has a single setting and takes place during a period of time that corresponds to the length of the play—few adhere to them strictly.

Ideas about appropriate subjects for tragedy have also changed. For Aristotle, the protagonist of a tragedy had to be exceptional—a king, for example. The protagonists of Greek tragedies were usually historical or mythical figures. Shakespeare often used kings and princes as protagonists—Richard II and Hamlet, for example—but he also used people of lesser rank, as in *Romeo and Juliet* and *A Midsummer Night's Dream* (p. 1551). In our times, interest in the lives of monarchs has been overshadowed by involvement in the lives of ordinary people. Modern tragedies—*Death of a Salesman,* for example—are more likely to focus on a traveling salesman than on a king.

With the rise of the middle class in the nineteenth century, ideas about the nature of tragedy changed. Responding to the age's desire for sentimentality, playwrights produced **melodramas,** sensational plays that appealed mainly to the emotions. Melodramas contain many of the elements of tragedy but end happily and often rely on conventional plots and stock characters. Because the protagonists in melodramas—often totally virtuous heroines suffering at the hands of impossibly wicked villains—helplessly endure their tribulations without ever gaining insight or enlightenment, they never achieve tragic status. As a result, they remain cardboard cutouts who exist only to exploit the emotions of the audience. Melodrama survives today in many films and in television soap operas.

Realism, which arose in the late nineteenth century as a response to the artificiality of melodrama, presented serious (and sometimes tragic) themes and believable characters in the context of everyday contemporary life. Writers of realistic drama used their plays to educate their audiences about the problems of the society in which they lived. For this reason, realistic drama focuses on the commonplace and eliminates the unlikely coincidences and excessive sentimentality of melodrama. Dramatists like Henrik Ibsen scrutinize the lives of ordinary people, not larger-than-life characters. After great suffering, these characters rise above the limitations of their mediocre lives and exhibit courage or emotional strength. The insight they gain often focuses attention on a social problem—the restrictive social conventions that define the behavior of women in nineteenth-century marriages, for example. Realistic drama also features settings and props similar to those used in people's daily lives and includes dialogue that reflects the way people actually speak.

Developing alongside realism was another literary movement called **naturalism.** Like realism, naturalism rejected the unrealistic plots and sentimentality of melodrama, but unlike realism, naturalism sought to explore the depths of the human condition. Influenced by Charles Darwin's ideas about evolution and natural selection and Karl Marx's ideas about economic forces that shape people's lives, naturalism is a pessimistic philosophy that presents a world which at worst is hostile and at best is indifferent to human concerns. It pictures human beings as higher-order animals who are driven by basic instincts—especially hunger, fear, and sexuality—and who are subject to economic, social, and biological forces beyond their understanding or control. It is, therefore, well suited to tragic themes.

The nineteenth-century French writer Émile Zola did much to develop the theory of naturalism, and later so did the American writers Stephen Crane, Frank Norris, and Theodore Dreiser. Naturalism also finds its way into the work of contemporary dramatists, such as Arthur Miller. Unlike other tragic protagonists, the protagonists of naturalist works are crushed not by the gods or by fate, but by poverty, animal drives, or social class. Willy Loman in *Death of a Salesman,* for example, is subject to the economic forces of a society that does not value its workers and discards those it no longer finds useful.

COMEDY

A **comedy** is a dramatic work that treats themes and characters with humor and typically has a happy ending. Whereas tragedy focuses on the hidden dimensions of the tragic hero's character, comedy focuses on the public persona, the protagonist as a social being. Tragic figures are typically seen in isolation, questioning the meaning of their lives and trying to comprehend their suffering. Hamlet—draped in sable, longing for death, and self-consciously contemplating his duty—epitomizes the isolation of the tragic hero.

Unlike tragic heroes, comic figures are seen in the public arena, where people intentionally assume the masks of pretension and self-importance. The purpose of comedy is to strip away these masks and expose human beings for what they are. Whereas tragedy reveals the nobility of the human condition, comedy reveals its inherent folly, portraying human beings as selfish, hypocritical, vain, weak, irrational, and capable of self-delusion. Thus, the basic function of comedy is critical—to tell people that things are not what they seem and that appearances are not necessarily reality. In the comic world nothing is solid or predictable, and accidents and coincidences are more important to the plot than reason. Many of Shakespeare's come-dies, for example, depend on exchanged or confused identities. The word-play and verbal nonsense of comedy add to this general confusion.

Comedies typically rely on certain familiar plot devices. Many come-dies begin with a startling or unusual situation that attracts the audience's attention. In Shakespeare's *A Midsummer Night's Dream,* for example, The-seus, the duke of Athens, rules that Hermia will either marry the man her father has chosen for her or be put to death. Such an event could lead to tragedy if comedy did not intervene to save the day.

Comedy often depends on obstacles and hindrances to further its plot: the more difficult the problems the lovers face, the more satisfying their eventual triumph will be. For this reason, the plot of a comedy is usually more complex than the plot of a tragedy. Compare the rather straight-forward plot of *Hamlet* (p. 1307)—a prince ordered to avenge his murdered father's death is driven mad with indecision and, after finally acting deci-sively, is killed himself—with the mix-ups, mistaken identities, and gen-eral confusion of *A Midsummer Night's Dream.*

Finally, comedies have happy endings. Whereas tragedy ends with death, comedy ends with an affirmation of life. Eventually the confusion and misunderstandings reach a point where some resolution must be achieved: the difficulties of the lovers are overcome, the villains are ban-ished, and the lovers marry—or at least express their intention to do so. In this way the lovers establish their connection with the rest of society, and its values are affirmed.

The first comedies, written in Greece in the fifth century B.C., heavily satirized the religious and social issues of the day. In the fourth and third centuries B.C., this **Old Comedy** gave way to **New Comedy,** a comedy of romance with stock characters—lovers and untrustworthy servants, for example—and conventional settings. Lacking the bitter satire and bawdi-ness of Old Comedy, New Comedy depends on outrageous plots, mistaken identities, young lovers, interfering parents, and conniving servants. Ulti-mately the young lovers outwit all those who stand between them and in so doing affirm the primacy of youth and love over old age and death.

Old and New Comedy represent two distinct lines of humor that ex-tend to modern times. Old Comedy depends on **satire**—bitter humor that diminishes a person, idea, or institution by ridiculing it or holding it up to scorn. Unlike comedy, which exists simply to make people laugh, satire is social criticism, deriding hypocrisy, pretension, and vanity or condemn-ing vice. At its best, satire appeals to the intellect, has a serious purpose, and arouses thoughtful laughter. New Comedy may also be satiric, but it frequently contains elements of **farce,** comedy in which stereotypical characters engage in boisterous horseplay and slapstick humor, all the while making jokes and sexual innuendoes—as they do in Anton Chek-hov's *The Brute* (p. 1266).

English comedy got its start in the sixth century A.D. in the form of farcical episodes that appeared in morality plays. During the Renaissance, comedy developed rapidly, beginning in 1533 with Nicholas Udall's *Ralph*

Roister Doister and eventually evolving into Shakespeare's **romantic comedy**—such as *A Midsummer Night's Dream,* in which love is the main subject and idealized heroines and lovers endure great difficulties until the inevitable happy ending is reached.

Also during the Renaissance, particularly in the latter part of the sixteenth century, writers like Ben Jonson experimented with a different type of comedy—the **comedy of humours,** which focused on characters whose behavior was controlled by a characteristic trait, or *humour.* During the Renaissance a person's temperament was thought to be determined by the mix of fluids, or humours, in the body. When one humour dominated, a certain type of disposition resulted. Playwrights capitalized on this belief, writing comedies in which characters are motivated by stereotypical behaviors that result from the imbalance of the humours. In comedies such as Jonson's *Volpone* and *The Alchemist,* characters such as the suspicious husband and the miser can be manipulated by others because of their predictable dispositions.

Closely related to the comedy of humours is the satiric **comedy of manners,** which developed during the sixteenth century and achieved great popularity in the nineteenth century. This form focuses on the manners and customs of society and directs its satire against characters who violate social conventions and rules of behavior. These plays tend to be memorable more for their witty dialogue than for their development of characters or setting. Oliver Goldsmith's *She Stoops to Conquer,* George Bernard Shaw's *Pygmalion,* and even some television sitcoms are examples of this type of comedy.

In the eighteenth century, a reaction against the perceived immorality of the comedy of manners led to **sentimental comedy,** which eventually achieved great popularity. This kind of comedy relies on sentimental emotion rather than on wit or humor to move an audience. It also dwells on the virtues rather than on the vices of life. The heroes of sentimental comedy are unimpeachably noble, moral, and honorable; the pure, virtuous, middle-class heroines suffer trials and tribulations calculated to move the audience to tears rather than laughter. Eventually, the distress of the hero and heroine is resolved in a sometimes contrived (but always happy) ending.

In his 1877 essay *The Idea of Comedy,* novelist and critic George Meredith suggests that comedy that appeals to the intellect should be called **high comedy.** Shakespeare's *As You Like It* and Shaw's *Pygmalion* can be characterized in this way. When comedy has little or no intellectual appeal, according to Meredith, it is **low comedy.** Low comedy appears in parts of Shakespeare's *The Taming of the Shrew* and as comic relief in *Macbeth.*

The twentieth century has developed its own characteristic comic forms. Most reflect the uncertainty and pessimism of a century that has seen two world wars, the Holocaust, and nuclear destruction, as well as threats posed by environmental pollution and ethnic and racial conflict. Combining laughter and hints of tragedy, these modern tragicomedies feature **antiheroes,** characters who, instead of manifesting dignity and power, are ineffectual or petty. Their plight frequently elicits laughter, not pity and fear, from the audience. **Black** or **dark comedies,** for example, rely for their comedy on the morbid and the absurd. These works are usually so satiric and bitter that they threaten to slip over the edge into tragedy. The screenplay of Joseph Heller's novel *Catch-22,* which ends with a character dropping bombs on his own men, is a classic example of such comedy. **Theater of the absurd,** which includes comedies such as Edward Albee's *The Sandbox,* begins with the assumption that the human condition is irrational. Typically, this type of drama does not have a discernible plot; instead, it presents a series of apparently unrelated images and illogical exchanges of dialogue meant to reinforce the idea that human beings live in a remote, confusing, and often incomprehensible universe. Absurdist dramas seem to go in circles, never progressing to a climax or achieving a resolution, reinforcing the theme of the endless and meaningless repetition that characterizes modern life.

A NOTE ON TRANSLATIONS
◆ ◆ ◆

Many dramatic works that we read or see are translations. For example, Ibsen wrote in Norwegian, Sophocles in Greek, Molière in French, and Chekhov in Russian. Before English-speaking viewers or readers can evaluate the language of a translated play, they must understand that the language they hear or read is the translator's interpretation of what the playwright intended to communicate. Translation is interpretation, not just a search for literal equivalents; as a result, a translation is always different from the original. Moreover, different translations are different from one another. During the course of Henrik Ibsen's 1879 play *A Doll House* (p. 1196), for instance, Nora, the main character, refers several times to a symbolic gesture of support she expects from her husband Torvald. In the translation in this text, that gesture is translated as "the miracle"; in another translation, it is translated as "the wonderful." Not only is *miracle* more consistent with idiomatic English usage, but also it is a more absolute, and therefore a more forceful, term.

The choices translators make can be very different. Compare these two versions of an exchange of dialogue from two different translations of the same Chekhov play, called *The Brute* in the translation which begins on page 1266 and *The Bear* in the alternate version.

—From *The Brute:*

> **SMIRNOV:** You'd like me to come simpering to you in French, I suppose. *'Enchanté, madame! Merci beaucoup* for not paying zee money, *madame! Pardonnez-moi* if I 'ave disturbed you, *madame!* How *charmante* you look in mourning, *madame!'*

> **Mrs. Popov:** Now you're being silly, Mr. Smirnov.
>
> **Smirnov:** *(mimicking)* 'Now you're being silly, Mr. Smirnov.' 'You don't know how to talk to a lady, Mr. Smirnov.' Look here, Mrs. Popov. I've known more women than you've known pussy cats. I've fought three duels on their account. I've jilted twelve, and been jilted by nine others. Oh, yes, Mrs. Popov, I've played the fool in my time, whispered sweet nothings, bowed and scraped and endeavoured to please. Don't tell me I don't know what it is to love, to pine away with longing, to have the blues, to melt like butter, to be weak as water. I was full of tender emotion. I was carried away with passion. I squandered half my fortune on the sex. I chattered about women's emancipation. But there's an end to everything, dear madam.

—From *The Bear:*

> **Smirnov:** Ach, it's astonishing! How would you like me to talk to you? In French, perhaps? *(Lisps in anger.) Madame, je vous prie. . . . how happy I am that you're not paying me the money. . . . Ah, pardon, I've made you uneasy! Such lovely weather we're having today! And you look so becoming in your mourning dress. (Bows and scrapes.)*
>
> **Mrs. Popov:** That's rude and not very clever!
>
> **Smirnov:** *(teasing)* Rude and not very clever! I don't know how to behave in the company of ladies. Madam, in my time I've seen far more women than you've seen sparrows. Three times I've fought duels over women; I've jilted twelve women, nine have jilted me! Yes! There was a time when I played the fool; I became sentimental over women, used honeyed words, fawned on them, bowed and scraped. . . . I loved, suffered, sighed at the moon; I became limp, melted, shivered . . . I loved passionately, madly, every which way, devil take me, I chattered away like a magpie about the emancipation of women, ran through half my fortune as a result of my tender feelings; but now, if you will excuse me, I'm on to your ways! I've had enough!

Although both translations convey Smirnov's anger and frustration, they use different words (with different connotations), different phrasing—and even different stage directions. In *The Bear,* for instance, only one French phrase is used, whereas *The Brute* uses several and specifies a French accent as well; other differences between the two translations include *The Bear*'s use of "teasing," "sparrows," and "I've had enough!" where *The Brute* uses "mimicking," "pussy cats," and "But there's an end to everything, dear madam." (Elsewhere in the play *The Bear* uses profanity while *The Brute* uses more polite language.) Many words and idiomatic expressions used in daily speech cannot be translated exactly from one language to another; as a result, the two translators made different choices.

CHAPTER 21

Reading and Writing
about Drama

READING DRAMA

When you read a play, you will notice features it shares with works of fiction—for instance, its use of language and symbols, the interaction among its characters, and its development of a theme or themes. In addition, you will notice features that distinguish it from fiction—for example, the presence of stage directions and the division into acts and scenes.

The following guidelines, designed to help you explore works of dramatic literature, focus on issues that will be examined in depth in chapters to come.

◇ Trace the play's **plot.** What conflicts are present? Where does the rising action reach a climax? Where does the falling action begin? What techniques move the action along? (See Chapter 22.)

◇ Analyze the play's **characters.** Who are the central characters? What are their most distinctive traits? How do you learn about their personalities, backgrounds, appearances, and strengths and weaknesses? (See Chapter 23.)

◇ Examine the play's language. How does dialogue reveal characters' emotions, conflicts, opinions, and motivation? (See Chapter 23.)

◇ Does the play include soliloquies or asides? What do they contribute to your knowledge of the play's characters and events? (See Chapter 23.)

◇ How do the characters interact with one another? Do the characters change and grow in response to the play's events, or do they remain essentially unchanged? (See Chapter 23.)

◇ Read the play's stage directions. What do you learn from the descriptions of the characters, including their dress, gestures, and facial expressions? (See Chapter 23.) What information do you gain from studying the playwright's descriptions of the play's setting? Do the stage directions include information about lighting, props, music, or sound effects? (See Chapter 24.)

◇ Consider the play's **staging.** Where and when does the action take place? What techniques are used to convey a sense of time and place to the audience? (See Chapter 24.)

◇ Try to interpret the play's **themes.** What main idea does the play communicate? What additional themes are explored? (See Chapter 25.)

◇ Identify any symbolic elements in the play. How do such symbols enhance the play's themes? (See Chapter 25.)

ACTIVE READING

As you read a play about which you plan to write, you follow the same process that guides you when you read any work of literature: you read actively, marking the text as you proceed. Then, you go on to select a topic and generate ideas about it, decide on a thesis, prepare an outline, and write and revise several drafts.

Kimberly Allison, a student in an introduction to literature course, was given the following assignment:

> Without consulting any outside sources, write a three- to five-page essay about any play in our literature anthology. You may focus on action, character, staging, or theme, or you may consider more than one of these elements.

Previewing

Kim decided to write her paper on Susan Glaspell's play *Trifles,* which begins on page 1163. She began by previewing *Trifles,* noting its brief length, its one-act structure, its list of characters, and its setting in John Wright's farm house. Kim noticed immediately that John Wright does not appear in the play, and this aroused her curiosity.

Highlighting and Annotating

As Kim read *Trifles,* she highlighted the dialogue and stage directions she thought she might want to examine closely, identified possible links among ideas and patterns of action and language, and jotted down questions and observations. She found herself especially interested in the female and male characters' different reactions to the objects discovered in the house and in the interaction between women and men.

The following highlighted and annotated passage illustrates some of her responses to the play.

The men laugh; the women looked abashed. **Why do the men and women react so differently?**

COUNTY ATTORNEY: (*rubbing his hands over the stove*) Frank's fire didn't

do much up there, did it? Well, let's go out to the barn and get that

cleared up.

The men go outside.

MRS. HALE: (*resentfully*) I don't know as there's anything so strange, our

taken' up our time with little things while we're waiting for them to

get the evidence. (*She sits down at the big table smoothing out a block with*

decision.) I don't see as it's anything to laugh about.

Why do the men go and the women stay?

MRS. PETERS: (*apologetically*) Of course they've got awful important

things on their minds. **Like what? Why does she make excuses for the men?**

Pulls up a chair and joins Mrs. Hale at the table.

Most of Kim's highlighting and annotations, like the preceding notes, focused on the play's characters, suggesting some interesting possibilities
for her essay.

WRITING ABOUT DRAMA

◊ ◊ ◊

PLANNING AN ESSAY

After Kim decided to write about the play's characters, she knew she had
to narrow her focus. Her notes suggested that gender roles in general, and
the role of the women in particular, would make an interesting topic, so
she decided to explore this idea further.

Choosing a Topic

To help her decide on a direction for her paper, Kim wrote the following
entry in her journal:

```
What is the role of the women in this play? Although the
women have gone with their husbands to get some items for
Mrs. Wright, they seem to be primarily interested in why
Mrs. Wright would leave her house in such disarray. They
find several objects that suggest that Mrs. Wright was
lonely and that she was dominated by her husband. But
```

these women are left on their own and seem to band
together. Their guilt about not visiting Mrs. Wright also
seems to connect them with the murder suspect. Mrs. Hale
even begins to empathize with Mrs. Wright's loss of her
bird. The women find the details, or "trifles," of Mrs.
Wright's life interesting and learn from them the facts
surrounding the murder while the men wander aimlessly
around the house and yard. The real clue to the murder
appears to be Mrs. Wright's untended house, but the men do
not seem to understand the implications of the disorder.
The women appear to have an understanding that comes from
their own experiences as women, which the men are unable
to tap into.

At this point, Kim concluded that the idea of the role of the women in
Trifles would be the best focus for her paper. As she went on to gather ideas
to write about, she also planned to examine the women characters' interaction with the men.

Finding Something to Say

Brainstorming   Kim's next step was to generate the specific ideas she would
discuss in her paper. She reread the play and her annotations, brainstorming about her topic and jotting down ideas about men and women as she
proceeded. Some of her brainstorming notes appear below:

Sheriff Peters says there is nothing in the kitchen
but kitchen stuff; he thinks Mrs. Wright is a typical
woman, worried about her preserves while imprisoned for
murder.
Mrs. Hale feels animosity toward the men for laughing
about the women's interest in the quilt; she regrets not
visiting Mrs. Wright; she feels sorry for Mrs. Wright
because she had no children.
Mr. Henderson eventually sides with the other two
men, claiming that women's worries are trifles.
Mr. Hale mentions Mr. Wright's cheapness; he seems to
know Mr. Wright best.
Men think women are shallow and worry only about
trifles.
Women empathize with Mrs. Wright because they
understand her treatment.

Mrs. Peters (wife of Sheriff) empathizes with Mrs. Wright's loss of bird; notes that keeping house was Mrs. Wright's duty.

Mrs. Wright restricted by husband; never leaves the house; loses control after her bird is killed.

John Wright strips wife of her identity; controls her every move; stops her from singing, which she enjoys; kills canary.

When she reread her notes, the first thing Kim noticed was that the women and men have two entirely different attitudes about women's lives and concerns: the men think their work is much more important than that of the women, which they see as trivial; the women realize they are not much different from Mrs. Wright. Now Kim saw that in order to discuss the role of women in the play, she must first define that role in relation to the role of the men. To do so, she needed to find a logical arrangement for her ideas that would enable her to clarify the differences between the men's role and the women's.

Seeing Connections

Listing At this point, Kim decided that listing ideas under the heads *Men* and *Women* could help her clarify the differences between men's and women's roles:

Men's Role	Women's Role
working outside the home	making preserves
making decisions about financial expenditures	cleaning house
	making quilts
think women should do just housework	raising children
	going to ladies' clubs for socializing
create and enforce law	
dictate wives' actions	must follow laws that men create and enforce
have separate identities and power	subordinate to their husbands
actions are accepted by society	must act defiantly to break boundaries set by social role

Listing enabled Kim to confirm her idea that the men's and the women's roles are portrayed very differently in *Trifles*. Both men and women seem to agree that they have different responsibilities, and both seem to understand and accept the fact that power and freedom are unevenly distributed between the two genders.

Deciding on a Thesis

Kim's listing clarified her understanding of the limited role women have in the society portrayed in *Trifles*. This in turn enabled her to develop the following tentative thesis statement, which she could use to help guide her essay's first draft:

> The central focus of <u>Trifles</u> is not on finding out who
> killed Mr. Wright, but on the limited, even subservient,
> role of women like Mrs. Wright.

Preparing an Outline

Guided by her thesis statement and the information she had collected in her notes, Kim made a scratch outline, arranging her supporting details in a logical order under appropriate headings:

<u>Mrs. Hale and Mrs. Peters had limited roles</u>
    --Subservient to husbands
    --Do domestic chores
    --Confined to kitchen
    --Identify with Minnie Wright's loneliness
<u>Minnie Wright had limited role</u>
    --Did what husband told her to do
    --Had no link with outside world
    --Couldn't sing
    --Had no friends
    --Had no identity

DRAFTING AN ESSAY

Following her scratch outline, Kim wrote the following first draft of her essay. Before she began, she reviewed her highlighting to look for details that would illustrate and support her generalizations about the play.

first draft

The Women's Role in Trifles

Susan Glaspell's Trifles seems to focus on the murder of John Wright. Mr. Wright had little concern for his wife's opinions. Mr. Hale suggested that Minnie Wright was powerless against her husband, and Sheriff Henry Peters questioned whether Minnie was allowed to quilt her log cabin pattern. Perhaps, because Mr. Wright did not spend his money freely, he would have made Minnie knot the quilt because it cost less. Minnie was controlled by her husband. He forced her to perform repetitive domestic chores. The central focus of Trifles is not on who killed Mr. Wright, but on the limited, even subservient role of women like Mrs. Wright.

Mrs. Peters and Mrs. Hale were similar to Minnie. Mrs. Peters and Mrs. Hale also performed domestic chores and had to do what their husbands wanted them to do, and they too were confined to Mrs. Wright's kitchen. The kitchen was the focal point of the play. Mrs. Peters and Mrs. Hale remained confined to the kitchen while their husbands exercised their freedom to enter and exit the house at will. This mirrored Minnie's life because she stayed home while her husband went to work and into town. The two women discussed Minnie's isolation. Beginning to identify with Minnie's loneliness, Mrs. Peters and Mrs. Hale recognized that while they were busy in their own homes, they had, in fact, participated in isolating and confining Minnie.

Eventually, the women found that the kitchen held the clues to Mrs. Wright's loneliness and to the details of the murder. The two women discovered that Minnie's only connection to the outside world was her bird. Minnie too was a caged bird because she was kept from singing and communicating with others by her husband. And piecing together the evidence, the women came to believe that John Wright had broken the bird's neck.

At the same time, Mrs. Peters and Mrs. Hale discovered the connection between the dead canary and Minnie's situation, and they began to recognize that they had to band together in order to exert their strength against the men. They realized that Minnie's independence and identity were crushed by her husband and that their own husbands believed women's lives were trivial and unimportant. The revelation that Mrs. Peters and Mrs. Hale experienced urged them to commit an act as rebellious as the one that got Minnie in trouble: they concealed their discovery from their husbands and from the law.

Because Mrs. Hale and Mrs. Peters empathized with Minnie's condition, they suppressed the evidence they found and endured the men's insults rather than confronting their husbands. And through this, the women attempted to break through the boundaries of their social roles, just as Minnie had done before them.

First Draft: Commentary

Kim's peer review group suggested that she develop her paper, especially paragraph 3, further. They also agreed that her paper's sentences seemed choppy—many needed to be linked with transitional words and phrases— and that her introduction was unfocused.

When Kim reread her first draft, she realized that she had gone beyond the scope of her tentative thesis statement and scratch outline. She had considered not just the women's subservient role but also the actions they take to break free of this role. She decided to revise her thesis statement to reflect this new emphasis—and, then, to expand her paper to develop this aspect of her thesis more fully.

When she met with her instructor to discuss her new ideas, he encouraged her to expand her paper's focus and to use quotations and specific examples to support her ideas. He also reminded her to use the present tense in her paper—not "Mrs. Peters and Mrs. Hale *were* similar to Minnie" but "Mrs. Peters and Mrs. Hale *are* similar to Minnie." (He explained that only events that occurred *before* the time in which the play takes place— for example, the murder itself or Minnie's girlhood experiences—should be described in past tense.)

After her meeting with her instructor, Kim made a new scratch outline to guide her as she continued to revise:

Subservient role of women
    --Minnie's husband didn't respect her opinion
    --Didn't let her sing
    --Could perform only domestic chores
Confinement of women in home
    --Mrs. Hale and Mrs. Peters are confined to kitchen
    --Minnie didn't belong to Ladies Aid
    --Minnie was lonely at home because she had no children
    --Minnie was a caged bird
Women's defiance
    --Mrs. Hale and Mrs. Peters solve "mystery"
    --Realize they must band together
    --Take action
    --Defy men's law

REVISING AND EDITING AN ESSAY

Before she wrote her next draft, Kim reviewed the suggestions she had recorded in meetings with classmates and with her instructor. Then she incorporated this material, along with her own new ideas, into her second draft, which appears on pages 1146–1149.

(second draft)

Confinement and Rebellion in Trifles

Susan Glaspell's play Trifles involves the solving of a murder. Two women, Mrs. Peters and Mrs. Hale, discover that Mrs. Wright, who remains in jail throughout the play, has indeed murdered her husband. Interestingly, the women make this discovery through the examination of evidence in Mrs. Wright's kitchen, which their husbands, Sheriff Henry Peters and farmer Lewis Hale, along with the county attorney, Mr. Henderson, dismiss as women's "trifles." The focus of Trifles, however, is not on the murder of John Wright but on the subservient role of women, the confinement of the wife in the home, and the desperate measures women had to take to achieve autonomy.

The role of Minnie Foster (Mrs. Wright) becomes evident in the first few minutes of the play, when Mr. Hale declares, "I didn't know as what his wife wanted made much difference to John--" (1164). Minnie's powerlessness is revealed further when the women discuss how Mr. Wright forced Minnie to give up the thing she loved--singing. Both of these observations suggest that Minnie's every action was controlled and stifled by her husband. She was not allowed to make decisions or be an individual; instead, she was permitted to perform only domestic chores.

Doing domestic chores was the only part of life that Minnie was allowed to exert some power over, a condition that is shared by Mrs. Peters and Mrs. Hale, especially because these two women can be assumed to work only in the home and because their behavior as wives is also determined by their husbands.

The men are free to walk throughout the house and outside of it while the women are, not surprisingly, confined to the kitchen, just as Minnie had been confined to the house. Early in the play, Mrs. Hale refers to Minnie's isolation, saying she "kept so much to herself. She didn't even belong to the Ladies Aid" (1168). Mrs. Hale goes on to mention Minnie's lack of nice clothing, which further suggests her confinement in the home: if she never left her home, she wouldn't need to look nice, and why would she want to leave home if she had no nice clothes? Minnie's isolation is further revealed when Mrs. Hale contemplates Minnie's lack of children: "Not having children makes less work--but it makes a quiet house, and Wright out to work all day, and no company when he did come in" (1171). As a result, Minnie's only connection to the outside world was her bird, which becomes the symbol of Minnie's confinement, because Minnie herself was a caged bird. In a sense, Mr. Wright strangled her, as he did the bird, by preventing her from talking to other people in the community. Unlike the men, Mrs. Peters and Mrs. Hale realize the connection between the dead canary and Minnie's situation as "<u>Their eyes meet</u>" and they share "<u>A look of growing comprehension, of horror</u>" (1172).

The comprehension that Mrs. Peters and Mrs. Hale experience urges them to rebel by concealing their discovery from their husbands and from the law. Mrs. Peters does concede that "the law is the law," but she also understands that because Mr. Wright treated his wife badly, treating her as a domestic slave and isolating her from the world, Minnie is justified in killing him. And even if Minnie had been able to communicate the abuse she suffered, the law would not take the abuse into account because the men on the jury would not be sympathetic to a woman's complaints about how her husband treated her.

The dialogue in <u>Trifles</u> reveals a huge difference in how women and men view their experiences. From the opening of the play, the gulf between the men and women emerges, and as the play progresses, the polarization of the male and female characters becomes clearer. Once the men leave the kitchen to find what they consider to be significant criminal evidence, the men and women are divided physically as well as emotionally. The men create their own community, as do the women, leading them to separate according to gender. With the women alone in the kitchen, the focus of the dialogue is on the female experience. The women discuss the preserves, the quilt, and the disarray in the kitchen, emphasizing that Mrs. Wright would not leave her home in disorder unless she was distracted by some more pressing situation.

Women accept servitude voluntarily, making the work in the home their main interest, and this role keeps them subservient. But the men further trivialize Mrs. Wright's and other women's significance when they criticize her role as homemaker. The county attorney condemns Minnie, sarcastically observing, "I shouldn't say she had the homemaking instinct" (1166). Minnie has attempted to keep her home clean and do her chores, but the lack of heat has exploded her preserves, and her husband has dirtied the towels. What has caused Minnie to neglect her chores is something of great importance: her desire for independence and freedom from the servitude she once accepted voluntarily.

What makes this play most interesting is that the women come to realize that they too have volunteered to be subservient to their husbands. They even accept the fact that their husbands will trivialize their discovery about the murder, as the men earlier trivialized their discussions of Minnie's daily tasks. Therefore, the women band together and conceal the information, breaking through their subservient roles as wives. And in the end, they find their own independence and significance in society.

Second Draft: Commentary

When she read her second draft, Kim had mixed feelings. She thought it was an improvement over her first draft, primarily because she had expanded the focus of her thesis and added specific details and quotations to support her points. She also believed her essay was now clearer, with smoother transitions.

Even though she knew what she wanted to say, however, Kim thought her paper's logic was somewhat difficult to follow, and she thought clearer topic sentences might correct this problem by guiding readers more smoothly through her essay. She also thought her organization, which did not follow her revised scratch outline, was somewhat confusing. (For example, she discussed the women's subservient role in two different parts of her essay—paragraphs 2 and 7.) In addition, Kim thought her third paragraph could be developed further, and she still believed her essay could use additional supporting details and quotations throughout. After rereading her notes, she wrote her final draft, which appears on the following pages.

Allison 1

Kimberly Allison

English 1013

Professor Johnson

1 March 2000

Desperate Measures: Acts of

Defiance in <u>Trifles</u>

Susan Glaspell wrote her best-known play, <u>Trifles</u>, in 1916, at a time when women were beginning to challenge their socially defined roles, realizing that their identities as wives and domestics kept them in a subordinate position in society. Because women were demanding more autonomy, traditional institutions such as marriage, which confined women to the home and made them mere extensions of their husbands, were beginning to be reexamined.

As a married woman, Glaspell was evidently touched by these concerns, perhaps because when she wrote <u>Trifles</u> she was at the mercy of her husband's wishes and encountered barriers in pursuing her career as a writer because she was a woman. But for whatever reason, Glaspell chose as the play's protagonist a married woman, Minnie Foster (Mrs. Wright), who has challenged society's expectations in a very extreme way: by murdering her husband. Minnie's defiant act has occurred before the action begins, and as the play unfolds two women, Mrs. Peters and Mrs. Hale, who accompany their husbands on an investigation of the murder scene, piece together the details of the situation surrounding the murder. As the events unfold, however, it becomes clear that the focus of <u>Trifles</u> is not on

Double-space.

Opening
sentence
identifies
author and
work.

Introduction
places play in
historical
context.

Allison 2

Thesis statement

who killed John Wright, but on the themes of the subordinate role of women, the confinement of the wife in the home, and the experiences all women share; through these themes, Glaspell shows her audience the desperate measures women had to take to achieve autonomy.

Topic sentence identifies first point paper will discuss: women's subordinate role.

The subordinate role of women, particularly Minnie's role in her marriage, becomes evident in the first few minutes of the play when Mr. Hale observes that the victim, John Wright, had little concern for his wife's opinions: "I didn't know as what his wife wanted made much difference to John" (1164). Here Mr. Hale suggests that Minnie was powerless against the wishes of her husband. Indeed, as these characters imply, Minnie's every act and thought were controlled by her husband, who tried to break her spirit by forcing her to perform repetitive domestic chores alone in the home. Minnie's only power in the household remained her kitchen work, a situation that Mrs. Peters and Mrs. Hale understand because each of these women's behavior is determined by her husband. Therefore, when Sheriff Peters makes fun of Minnie's concern about her preserves, saying, "Well, can you beat the woman! Held for murder and worrying about her preserves" (1166), he is, in a sense, criticizing all three of the women for worrying about domestic matters rather than about the murder that has been committed. Indeed, the sheriff's comment suggests that he assumes women's lives are trivial, an assumption that influences the thoughts and speech of all three men.

Allison 3

Mrs. Peters and Mrs. Hale are similar to Minnie in another way as well: throughout the play, they are confined to the kitchen of the Wrights' house. As a result, the kitchen becomes the focal point of the play. The women find that the kitchen holds the clues to Mrs. Wright's loneliness and to the details of the murder. Mrs. Peters and Mrs. Hale remain confined to the kitchen while their husbands enter and exit the house at will. This scenario mirrors Minnie's daily life, as she remained in the home while her husband went to work and into town. The two women discuss Minnie's isolation in being housebound: "Not having children makes less work--but it makes a quiet house, and Wright out to work all day, and no company when he did come in" (1171). Beginning to identify with Minnie's loneliness, Mrs. Peters and Mrs. Hale recognize that, busy in their own homes, they have, in fact, participated in isolating and confining Minnie. Mrs. Hale declares, "Oh, I <u>wish</u> I'd come over here once in a while! That was a crime! That was a crime! Who's going to punish that? [. . .] I might have known she needed help!" (1173).

Soon the two women discover that Minnie's only connection to the outside world was her bird, the symbol of her confinement; Minnie was a caged bird who was kept from singing and communicating with others because of her restrictive husband. And piecing together the evidence--the disorderly kitchen, the mis-stitched quilt pieces, and the dead canary--the women come to believe that John Wright broke the bird's neck just as he had broken Minnie's spirit. At this point,

Topic sentence introduces second point paper will discuss: women's confinement.

Transitional paragraph discusses women's observations and conclusions.

Allison 4

Mrs. Peters and Mrs. Hale figure out the connection between the dead canary and Minnie's situation. The stage directions describe the moment when the women become aware of the truth behind the murder: "<u>Their eyes meet</u>," and the women share "<u>A look of growing comprehension, of horror</u>" (1172).

Topic sentence introduces third point paper will discuss: commonality of women's experiences.

Through their observations and discussions in Mrs. Wright's kitchen, Mrs. Hale and Mrs. Peters come to understand the commonality of women's experiences. Mrs. Hale speaks for both of them when she says, "I know how things can be--for women. [. . .] We all go through the same things--it's all just a different kind of the same thing" (1173). And, once the two women realize the experiences they share, they begin to recognize that they must join together in order to challenge a male-oriented society; although their experiences may seem trivial to the men, the "trifles" of their lives are significant to them. They realize that Minnie's independence and identity were crushed by her husband and that their own husbands have asserted that women's lives are trivial and unimportant as well. This realization leads them to commit an act as defiant as the one that has gotten Minnie into trouble: they conceal their discovery from their husbands and from the law.

Significantly, Mrs. Peters does acknowledge that "the law is the law," yet she understands that because Mr. Wright treated his wife badly, Minnie is justified in killing him. They also realize, however, that for men the law is black and white and that an all-male jury will not take into account the extenuating circumstances

Allison 5

that prompted Minnie to kill her husband. And even if Minnie were allowed to communicate to the all-male court the psychological abuse she has suffered, the law would undoubtedly view her experience as trivial because a woman who complained about how her husband treated her would be seen as ungrateful.

Nevertheless, because Mrs. Hale and Mrs. Peters empathize with Minnie's condition, they suppress the evidence they find, enduring their husbands' conde-scension rather than standing up to them. And, through this desperate action, the women break through the boundaries of their social role, just as Minnie has done. Although Minnie is imprisoned for her crime, she has freed herself; and, although Mrs. Peters and Mrs. Hale conceal their knowledge, fearing the men will laugh at them, these women are really challenging so-ciety and freeing themselves as well.

In <u>Trifles</u>, Susan Glaspell addresses many of the problems shared by early twentieth-century women, in-cluding their subordinate status and their confinement in the home. In order to emphasize the pervasiveness of these problems and the desperate measures women had to take to break out of restrictive social roles, Glaspell does more than focus on the plight of a woman who has ended her isolation and loneliness by committing a heinous crime against society. By presenting three male and two female characters who demonstrate the vast dif-ferences between male and female experience, she illus-trates how men define the roles of women and how women can challenge these roles in search of their own sig-nificance in society and their eventual independence.

Conclusion places play in historical context.

Final Draft: Commentary

Kim made many changes in her final draft. Although her focus is much the same as it was in her previous draft, she has expanded her paper considerably. Most important, she added a discussion of the commonality of women's experience in paragraph 6 and elsewhere, and this material helps to explain what motivates Mrs. Hale and Mrs. Peters to conceal evidence from their husbands.

As she expanded her essay, Kim added illustrative explanations, details, and quotations, taking care to provide accurate page numbers in parentheses after each quotation. (Because students were required to use only a play from this anthology, and no outside sources, Kim's instructor did not require a Works Cited page.) She also worked hard to make her topic sentences clearer, and she used information from her class notes to help her write a new introduction and conclusion that discussed the status of women at the time in which *Trifles* was written. Finally, she added a new title and revised her thesis statement to emphasize the focus of her essay on the "desperate measures" all three women are driven to in response to their subjugation and confinement.

CHAPTER 22

Plot

◇ ◇ ◇

We assume that, for the finest form of tragedy, the plot must be not simple but complex; and further, that it must imitate actions arousing fear and pity, since that is the distinctive function of this kind of imitation. It follows, therefore, that there are three forms of plot to be avoided. (1) A good man must not be seen passing from happiness to misery, or (2) a bad man from misery to happiness. The first situation is not fear-inspiring or piteous, but simply odious to us. The second is the most untragic that can be; it has not one of the requisites of tragedy; it does not appeal either to the human feeling in us, or to our pity, or to our fears. Nor, on the other hand, should (3) an extremely bad man be seen falling from happiness into misery. Such a story may arouse the human feeling in us, but it will not move us to either pity or fear; pity is occasioned by undeserved misfortune, and fear by that of one like ourselves; so that there will be nothing either piteous or fear-inspiring in the situation [. . .].

ARISTOTLE, *Poetics*, trans. Ingram Bywater

Great character creation is a fine thing in a drama, but the sum of all its characters is the story that they enact. Aristotle puts the plot at the head of the dramatic elements; of all these he thinks plot the most difficult and the most expressive. And he is right.

STARK YOUNG, *The Theatre*

How many times in my years of teaching have I stood before the blackboard guiding the abhorrent chalk carefully along a 30-degree incline to explain Freytag's triangle, that indispensable construct for mapping the ideal course of the classic novel: complications of character and situation creating a "rising action" that culminates in a climactic moment, which is followed in turn by the afterglow of denouement, the tying up of threads.

But other roads do diverge in the [. . .] yellow wood, one of them representing a structure quite different, in which the climactic event [. . .] takes place right at the outset, and the essential action can be described as "falling."

SVEN BIRKERTS, in *New York Times Book Review*

◇ ◇ ◇

Plot denotes the way events are arranged in a work of literature. Although the accepted conventions of drama require that the plot of a play be presented somewhat differently from the plot of a short story, the same components of plot are present in both. Plot in a dramatic work, like plot in a short story, presents conflicts that are revealed, intensified, and resolved during the course of the play through the characters' actions. (See Chapter 4 for a discussion of **conflict.**)

PLOT STRUCTURE
◇ ◇ ◇

In 1863, the German critic Gustav Freytag devised a pyramid to represent a prototype for the plot of a dramatic work. According to Freytag, a play typically begins with **exposition,** which presents characters and setting and introduces the basic situation in which the characters are involved. Then, during the **rising action,** complications develop, conflicts emerge, suspense builds, and crises occur. The rising action culminates in a **climax,** at which point the plot's tension peaks. Finally, during the **falling action,** the intensity subsides, eventually winding down to a **resolution,** or **denouement,** in which all loose ends are tied up.

The familiar plot of a detective story follows Freytag's concept of plot: the exposition section includes the introduction of the detective and the explanation of the crime; the rising action develops as the investigation of the crime proceeds, with suspense increasing as the solution approaches; the high point of the action, the climax, comes with the revelation of the crime's solution; and the falling action presents the explanation of the solution. The story concludes with a resolution typically characterized by the capture of the criminal and the restoration of order.

The action of Susan Glaspell's one-act play *Trifles* (p. 1163), which in many ways resembles a detective story, might be diagrammed as follows:

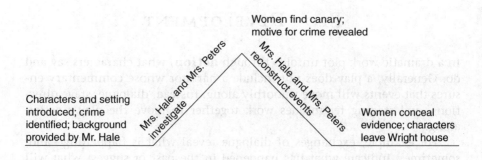

Women find canary; motive for crime revealed

Mrs. Hale and Mrs. Peters investigate

Mrs. Hale and Mrs. Peters reconstruct events

Characters and setting introduced; crime identified; background provided by Mr. Hale

Women conceal evidence; characters leave Wright house

Of course, the plot of a complex dramatic work rarely conforms to the neat pattern represented by Freytag's pyramid. In fact, a play can lack exposition or resolution entirely, and the climax can occur at the beginning. Because long stretches of exposition can be dull, a playwright may arouse audience interest by moving directly into conflict. *Oedipus the King* (p. 1509), for example, begins with the conflict, and so does *The Cuban Swimmer* (p. 1495). Similarly, because audiences tend to lose interest after the play's climax is reached, a playwright may choose to dispense with extended falling action. Thus, after Hamlet's death, the play ends abruptly.

PLOT AND SUBPLOT

While the main plot is developing, another, parallel plot, called a **subplot,** may be developing alongside it. This structural device is common in the works of Shakespeare and in many other plays as well.

The subplot's function may not immediately be clear, so at first it may seem to draw attention away from the main plot. Eventually, however, the subplot reinforces elements of the primary plot. In Henrik Ibsen's *A Doll House* (p. 1196), for example, the threat of Dr. Rank's impending death parallels the threat of Nora's approaching exposure; for both of them, time is running out. In Shakespeare's *King Lear,* a more elaborate subplot involves the earl of Gloucester who, like Lear, misjudges his children, favoring a deceitful son who does not deserve his support and overlooking a more deserving one. Both families suffer greatly as a result of the fathers' misplaced loyalties. Thus, the parallel plot places additional emphasis on Lear's poor judgment and magnifies the consequences of his misguided acts: both fathers, and all but one of the five children, are dead by the play's end. A subplot can also set up a contrast—as it does in *Hamlet,* where Fortinbras acts decisively to avenge his father, an action that underscores Hamlet's hesitation and procrastination when faced with a comparable challenge.

Plot Development

◊ ◊ ◊

In a dramatic work plot unfolds through **action,** what characters say and do. Generally, a play does not include a narrator whose commentary ensures that events will move smoothly along. Instead, dialogue, stage directions, and staging techniques work together to move the play's action along.

For example, exchanges of dialogue reveal what is happening—and, sometimes, indicate what has happened in the past or suggest what will happen in the future. Characters can recount past events to other characters, announce an intention to take some action in the future, or summarize events that are occurring offstage. In such cases, dialogue takes the place of formal narrative. On the printed page, stage directions efficiently move readers from one location and time period to another by specifying entrances and exits and identifying the play's structural divisions—acts and scenes—and their accompanying changes of setting.

Staging techniques can also advance a play's action. A change in lighting, for instance, can shift the focus to another part of the stage—and thus to another place and time. Similarly, an adjustment of **scenery** or **props**—for instance, a breakfast table, complete with morning paper, replacing a bedtime setting—can indicate that the action has moved forward in time, as can a change of costumes. In Tennessee Williams's *The Glass Menagerie* (p.1805) various staging devices—such as words projected on a screen that preview words to be spoken by a character and visual images on screen that predict scenes to follow—help to keep the action moving. For example, a screen image of blue roses leads into a scene in which Laura tells her mother how Jim gave her the nickname "Blue Roses."

Music can also move a play's action along, predicting excitement or doom or a romantic interlude—or a particular character's entrance. In scene 5 of *The Glass Menagerie,* for example, stage directions announce "The Dance-Hall Music Changes to a Tango That Has a Minor and Somewhat Ominous Tone"; a "music legend" repeated throughout the play serves as a signature in scenes focusing on Laura.

Less often, a narrator advances the action. In Thornton Wilder's 1938 play *Our Town,* for example, a character known as the Stage Manager functions as a narrator, not only describing the play's setting and introducing the characters to the audience, but also soliciting questions from characters scattered around the audience, prompting characters, and interrupting dialogue. In *The Glass Menagerie* the protagonist, Tom Wingfield, also serves as a narrator, summarizing what has happened and moving readers on to the next scene: "After the fiasco at Rubicam's Business College, the idea of getting a gentleman caller for Laura began to play a more important part in Mother's calculations" (scene 3).

FLASHBACKS

Many plays—such as *The Glass Menagerie* and Arthur Miller's *Death of a Salesman* (p. 1410)—include **flashbacks,** which depict events that occurred before the play's main action. In addition, dialogue can overcome the limitations set by the chronological action on stage by recounting events that occurred earlier. Thus, Mr. Hale in *Trifles* tells the other characters how he discovered John Wright's murder, and Nora in *A Doll House* confides her secret past to her friend Kristine. As characters on stage are brought up to date, the audience is also given necessary information—facts that are essential to an understanding of the characters' motivation. Naturally, characters must have plausible reasons for explaining past events. In *Trifles,* Mr. Hale is the only character who has witnessed the events he describes, and in *A Doll House,* Kristine, formerly Nora's friend and confidante, has not seen her in years. Thus, a character's need for information provides playwrights with a convenient excuse for supplying readers with necessary background. In less realistic dramas, however, no such excuse is necessary: characters can interrupt the action to deliver long monologues or soliloquies that fill in background details—or even address the audience directly, as Tom does in *The Glass Menagerie.*

FORESHADOWING

In addition to revealing past events, dialogue can **foreshadow,** or look ahead to, future action. In many cases, seemingly unimportant comments have significance that becomes clear as the play develops. For example, in act 3 of *A Doll House* Torvald Helmer says to Kristine, "An exit should always be effective, Mrs. Linde, but that's what I can't get Nora to grasp." At the end of the play, Nora's exit is not only effective, but also memorable.

Elements of staging can also suggest events to come. In *The Glass Menagerie,* for instance, the ever-present photograph of the absent father—who, Tom tells the audience, may be seen as a symbol of "the long delayed but always expected something that we live for"—foreshadows Tom's escape. Various bits of **stage business**—gestures or movements designed to attract the audience's attention—may also foreshadow future events. In *A Doll House,* for instance, Nora's sneaking forbidden macaroons seems at first to suggest her fear of her husband, but her actions actually foreshadow her eventual defiance of his authority.

CHECKLIST: WRITING ABOUT PLOT

✓ Summarize the play's events.

✓ What is the play's central conflict? How is it resolved? What other conflicts are present?

✓ What section of the play constitutes its rising action?

✓ Where does the play's climax occur?

✓ What crises can you identify?

✓ How is suspense created?

✓ What section of the play constitutes its falling action?

✓ Does the play contain a subplot? What is its purpose? How is it related to the main plot?

✓ Does the play have flashbacks? Does the play's dialogue contain summaries of past events or references to events in the future? How does the use of flashbacks or foreshadowing advance the play's plot?

✓ Does the play include a narrator?

✓ How does the dialogue advance the play's plot?

✓ How do characters' actions advance the play's plot?

✓ How do stage directions advance the play's plot?

✓ How does staging advance the play's plot?

✓ Does the play use any other devices to advance the plot?

◆ **SUSAN GLASPELL** (1882–1948) was born in Davenport, Iowa, and graduated from Drake University in 1899. First a reporter and then a freelance writer, she lived in Chicago (where she was part of the Chicago Renaissance that included poet Carl Sandburg and novelist Theodore Dreiser) and later in Greenwich Village. Her works include two plays in addition to *Trifles*, *The Verge* (1921) and *Alison's House* (1930), and several novels, including *Fidelity* (1915) and *The Morning Is Near Us* (1939). With her husband, George Cram Cook, she founded the Provincetown Players, which became the staging ground for innovative plays by Eugene O'Neill, among others.

Glaspell herself wrote plays for the Provincetown Players, beginning with *Trifles*, which she created for the 1916 season although she had never previously written a drama. The play opened on August 8, 1916, with Glaspell and her husband in the cast. Glaspell said she wrote *Trifles* in one afternoon, sitting in the empty theater and looking at the bare stage: "After a time, the stage became a kitchen—a kitchen there all by itself."

She remembered a murder trial she had covered in Iowa in her days as a reporter, and the story began to play itself out on the stage as she gazed. Throughout her revisions, she said, she returned to look at the stage to see whether the events she was recording came to life on it. Although Glaspell later rewrote *Trifles* in the form of a short story called "A Jury of Her Peers," the play remains her most successful and memorable work.

CULTURAL CONTEXT ◇ In 1916, when *Trifles* was first produced, women were not allowed to serve on juries in most states. Even in the 1920s, only about half the states allowed women to serve on juries, while other states resisted for decades. For example, it was not until 1937 that the state of New York passed a law allowing women to serve on juries.

◇ ◇ ◇

SUSAN GLASPELL

Trifles
(1916)

CHARACTERS

GEORGE HENDERSON, *county attorney*
HENRY PETERS, *sheriff*
LEWIS HALE, *a neighboring farmer*
MRS. PETERS
MRS. HALE

SCENE

The kitchen in the now abandoned farmhouse of John Wright, a gloomy kitchen, and left without having been put in order—unwashed pans under the sink, a loaf of bread outside the breadbox, a dish towel on the table—other signs of incompleted work. At the rear the outer door opens and the Sheriff comes in followed by the County Attorney and Hale. The Sheriff and Hale are men in middle life, the County Attorney is a young man; all are much bundled up and go at once to the stove. They are followed by two women—the Sheriff's wife first; she is a slight wiry woman, a thin nervous face. Mrs. Hale is larger and would ordinarily be called more comfortable looking, but she is disturbed now and looks fearfully about as she enters. The women have come in slowly, and stand close together near the door.

COUNTY ATTORNEY: *(rubbing his hands)* This feels good. Come up to the fire, ladies.

MRS. PETERS: *(after taking a step forward)* I'm not—cold.

SHERIFF: *(unbuttoning his overcoat and stepping away from the stove as if to mark the beginning of official business)* Now, Mr. Hale, before we move things about, you explain to Mr. Henderson just what you saw when you came here yesterday morning.

COUNTY ATTORNEY: By the way, has anything been moved? Are things just as you left them yesterday?

5   SHERIFF: *(looking about)* It's just the same. When it dropped below zero last night I thought I'd better send Frank out this morning to make a fire for us—no use getting pneumonia with a big case on, but I told him not to touch anything except the stove—and you know Frank.

COUNTY ATTORNEY: Somebody should have been left here yesterday.

SHERIFF: Oh—yesterday. When I had to send Frank to Morris Center for that man who went crazy—I want you to know I had my hands full yesterday. I knew you could get back from Omaha by today and as long as I went over everything here myself—

COUNTY ATTORNEY: Well, Mr. Hale, tell just what happened when you came here yesterday morning.

HALE: Harry and I had started to town with a load of potatoes. We came along the road from my place and as I got here I said, "I'm going to see if I can't get John Wright to go in with me on a party telephone." I spoke to Wright about it once before and he put me off, saying folks talked too much anyway, and all he asked was peace and quiet—I guess you know about how much he talked himself; but I thought maybe if I went to the house and talked about it before his wife, though I said to Harry that I didn't know as what his wife wanted made much difference to John—

10   COUNTY ATTORNEY: Let's talk about that later, Mr. Hale. I do want to talk about that, but tell now just what happened when you got to the house.

HALE: I didn't hear or see anything; I knocked at the door, and still it was all quiet inside. I knew they must be up, it was past eight o'clock. So I knocked again, and I thought I heard somebody say, "Come in." I wasn't sure, I'm not sure yet, but I opened the door—this door *(indicating the door by which the two women are still standing)* and there in that rocker—*(pointing to it)* sat Mrs. Wright.

They all look at the rocker.

COUNTY ATTORNEY: What—was she doing?

HALE: She was rockin' back and forth. She had her apron in her hand and was kind of—pleating it.

COUNTY ATTORNEY: And how did she—look?

15   HALE: Well, she looked queer.

COUNTY ATTORNEY: How do you mean—queer?

HALE: Well, as if she didn't know what she was going to do next. And kind of done up.

COUNTY ATTORNEY: How did she seem to feel about your coming?

HALE: Why, I don't think she minded—one way or other. She didn't pay much attention. I said, "How do, Mrs. Wright, it's cold, ain't it?" And she said, "Is it?"—and went on kind of pleating at her apron. Well, I was surprised; she didn't ask me to come up to the stove, or to set down, but just sat there, not even looking at me, so I said, "I want to see John." And then she—laughed. I guess you would call it a laugh. I thought of Harry and the team outside, so I said a little sharp: "Can't I see John?" "No," she says, kind o' dull like. "Ain't he home?" says I. "Yes," says she, "he's home." "Then why can't I see him?" I asked her, out of patience. "'Cause he's dead," says she. "*Dead?*" says I. She just nodded her head, not getting a bit excited, but rockin' back and forth. "Why—where is he?" says I, not knowing what to say. She just pointed upstairs—like that. *(Himself pointing to the room above.)* I got up, with the idea of going up there. I walked from there to here—then I says, "Why, what did he die of?" "He died of a rope round his neck," says she, and just went on pleatin' at her apron. Well, I went out and called Harry. I thought I might—need help. We went upstairs and there he was lyin'—

20 COUNTY ATTORNEY: I think I'd rather have you go into that upstairs, where you can point it all out. Just go on now with the rest of the story.

HALE: Well, my first thought was to get that rope off. It looked . . . *(stops, his face twitches)* . . . but Harry, he went up to him, and he said, "No, he's dead all right, and we'd better not touch anything." So we went back down stairs. She was still sitting that same way. "Has anybody been notified?" I asked. "No," says she, unconcerned. "Who did this, Mrs. Wright?" said Harry. He said it businesslike—and she stopped pleatin' of her apron. "I don't know," she says. "You don't *know?*" says Harry. "No," says she. "Weren't you sleepin' in the bed with him?" says Harry. "Yes," says she, "but I was on the inside." "Somebody slipped a rope round his neck and strangled him and you didn't wake up?" says Harry. "I didn't wake up," she said after him. We must 'a looked as if we didn't see how that could be, for after a minute she said, "I sleep sound." Harry was going to ask her more questions but I said maybe we ought to let her tell her story first to the coroner, or the sheriff, so Harry went fast as he could to Rivers' place, where there's a telephone.

COUNTY ATTORNEY: And what did Mrs. Wright do when she knew that you had gone for the coroner?

HALE: She moved from that chair to this one over here *(pointing to a small chair in the corner)* and just sat there with her hands held together and looking down. I got a feeling that I ought to make some conversation, so I said I had come in to see if John wanted to put in a telephone, and at that she started to laugh, and then she stopped and looked at me—scared. *(The County Attorney, who has had his notebook out, makes a note.)* I dunno, maybe it wasn't scared. I wouldn't like to say it was. Soon Harry got back, and then Dr. Lloyd came, and you, Mr. Peters, and so I guess that's all I know that you don't.

COUNTY ATTORNEY: *(looking around)* I guess we'll go upstairs first—and then out to the barn and around there. *(To the Sheriff.)* You're

convinced that there was nothing important here—nothing that
would point to any motive.

25 SHERIFF: Nothing here but kitchen things.

*The County Attorney, after again looking around the kitchen, opens the door of
a cupboard closet. He gets up on a chair and looks on a shelf. Pulls his hand
away, sticky.*

COUNTY ATTORNEY: Here's a nice mess.

The women draw nearer.

MRS. PETERS: *(to the other woman)* Oh, her fruit; it did freeze. *(To the
County Attorney.)* She worried about that when it turned so cold. She
said the fire'd go out and her jars would break.

SHERIFF: Well, can you beat the woman! Held for murder and worryin'
about her preserves.

COUNTY ATTORNEY: I guess before we're through she may have something
more serious than preserves to worry about.

30 HALE: Well, women are used to worrying over trifles.

The two women move a little closer together.

COUNTY ATTORNEY: *(with the gallantry of a young politician)* And yet, for all
their worries, what would we do without the ladies? *(The women do
not unbend. He goes to the sink, takes a dipperful of water from the pail
and pouring it into a basin, washes his hands. Starts to wipe them on the
roller towel, turns it for a cleaner place.)* Dirty towels! *(Kicks his foot
against the pans under the sink.)* Not much of a housekeeper, would
you say, ladies?

MRS. HALE: *(stiffly)* There's a great deal of work to be done on a farm.

COUNTY ATTORNEY: To be sure. And yet *(with a little bow to her)* I know
there are some Dickson county farmhouses which do not have such
roller towels.

He gives it a pull to expose its full length again.

MRS. HALE: Those towels get dirty awful quick. Men's hands aren't
always as clean as they might be.

35 COUNTY ATTORNEY: Ah, loyal to your sex, I see. But you and Mrs. Wright
were neighbors. I suppose you were friends, too.

MRS. HALE: *(shaking her head)* I've not seen much of her of late years. I've
not been in this house—it's more than a year.

COUNTY ATTORNEY: And why was that? You didn't like her?

MRS. HALE: I liked her all well enough. Farmers' wives have their hands
full, Mr. Henderson. And then—

COUNTY ATTORNEY: Yes—?

40 MRS. HALE: *(looking about)* It never seemed a very cheerful place.

COUNTY ATTORNEY: No—it's not cheerful. I shouldn't say she had the
homemaking instinct.

MRS. HALE: Well, I don't know as Wright had, either.

COUNTY ATTORNEY: You mean that they didn't get on very well?

MRS. HALE: No, I don't mean anything. But I don't think a place'd be any cheerfuller for John Wright's being in it.

45 **COUNTY ATTORNEY:** I'd like to talk more of that a little later. I want to get the lay of things upstairs now.

He goes to the left, where three steps lead to a stair door.

SHERIFF: I suppose anything Mrs. Peters does'll be all right. She was to take in some clothes for her, you know, and a few little things. We left in such a hurry yesterday.

COUNTY ATTORNEY: Yes, but I would like to see what you take, Mrs. Peters, and keep an eye out for anything that might be of use to us.

MRS. PETERS: Yes, Mr. Henderson.

The women listen to the men's steps on the stairs, then look about the kitchen.

MRS. HALE: I'd hate to have men coming into my kitchen, snooping around and criticizing.

She arranges the pans under sink which the County Attorney had shoved out of place.

50 **MRS. PETERS:** Of course it's no more than their duty.

MRS. HALE: Duty's all right, but I guess that deputy sheriff that came out to make the fire might have got a little of this on. *(Gives the roller towel a pull.)* Wish I'd thought of that sooner. Seems mean to talk about her for not having things slicked up when she had to come away in such a hurry.

MRS. PETERS: *(who has gone to a small table in the left rear corner of the room, and lifted one end of a towel that covers a pan)* She had bread set.

Stands still.

MRS. HALE: *(eyes fixed on a loaf of bread beside the breadbox, which is on a low shelf at the other side of the room. Moves slowly toward it.)* She was going to put this in there. *(Picks up loaf, then abruptly drops it. In a manner of returning to familiar things.)* It's a shame about her fruit. I wonder if it's all gone. *(Gets up on the chair and looks.)* I think there's some here that's all right, Mrs. Peters. Yes—here; *(holding it toward the window)* this is cherries, too. *(Looking again.)* I declare I believe that's the only one. *(Gets down, bottle in her hand. Goes to the sink and wipes it off on the outside.)* She'll feel awful bad after all her hard work in the hot weather. I remember the afternoon I put up my cherries last summer.

She puts the bottle on the big kitchen table, center of the room. With a sigh, is about to sit down in the rocking-chair. Before she is seated realizes what chair it is; with a slow look at it, steps back. The chair which she has touched rocks back and forth.

MRS. PETERS: Well, I must get those things from the front room closet. *(She goes to the door at the right, but after looking into the other room, steps back.)* You coming with me, Mrs. Hale? You could help me carry them.

They go in the other room; reappear, Mrs. Peters carrying a dress and skirt, Mrs. Hale following with a pair of shoes.

55 MRS. PETERS: My, it's cold in there.

She puts the clothes on the big table, and hurries to the stove.

MRS. HALE: *(examining her skirt)* Wright was close. I think maybe that's why she kept so much to herself. She didn't even belong to the Ladies Aid. I suppose she felt she couldn't do her part, and then you don't enjoy things when you feel shabby. She used to wear pretty clothes and be lively, when she was Minnie Foster, one of the town girls singing in the choir. But that—oh, that was thirty years ago. This all you was to take in?

MRS. PETERS: She said she wanted an apron. Funny thing to want, for there isn't much to get you dirty in jail, goodness knows. But I suppose just to make her feel more natural. She said they was in the top drawer in this cupboard. Yes, here. And then her little shawl that always hung behind the door. *(Opens stair door and looks.)* Yes, here it is.

Quickly shuts door leading upstairs.

MRS. HALE: *(abruptly moving toward her)* Mrs. Peters?
MRS. PETERS: Yes, Mrs. Hale?
60 MRS. HALE: Do you think she did it?
MRS. PETERS: *(in a frightened voice)* Oh, I don't know.
MRS. HALE: Well, I don't think she did. Asking for an apron and her little shawl. Worrying about her fruit.
MRS. PETERS: *(starts to speak, glances up, where footsteps are heard in the room above. In a low voice.)* Mr. Peters says it looks bad for her. Mr. Henderson is awful sarcastic in a speech and he'll make fun of her sayin' she didn't wake up.
MRS. HALE: Well, I guess John Wright didn't wake when they was slipping that rope under his neck.
65 MRS. PETERS: No, it's strange. It must have been done awful crafty and still. They say it was such a—funny way to kill a man, rigging it all up like that.
MRS. HALE: That's just what Mr. Hale said. There was a gun in the house. He says that's what he can't understand.
MRS. PETERS: Mr. Henderson said coming out that what was needed for the case was a motive; something to show anger, or—sudden feeling.

MRS. HALE: *(who is standing by the table)* Well, I don't see any signs of anger around here. *(She puts her hand on the dish towel which lies on the table, stands looking down at table, one half of which is clean, the other half messy.)* It's wiped to here. *(Makes a move as if to finish work, then turns and looks at loaf of bread outside the breadbox. Drops towel. In that voice of coming back to familiar things.)* Wonder how they are finding things upstairs. I hope she had it a little more red-up[1] up there. You know, it seems kind of *sneaking*. Locking her up in town and then coming out here and trying to get her own house to turn against her!

MRS. PETERS: But Mrs. Hale, the law is the law.

70 MRS. HALE: I s'pose 'tis. *(Unbuttoning her coat.)* Better loosen up your things, Mrs. Peters. You won't feel them when you go out.

Mrs. Peters takes off her fur tippet, goes to hang it on hook at back of room, stands looking at the under part of the small corner table.

MRS. PETERS: She was piecing a quilt.

She brings the large sewing basket and they look at the bright pieces.

MRS. HALE: It's log cabin pattern. Pretty, isn't it? I wonder if she was goin' to quilt it or just knot it?

Footsteps have been heard coming down the stairs. The Sheriff enters followed by Hale and the County Attorney.

SHERIFF: They wonder if she was going to quilt it or just knot it!

The men laugh; the women look abashed.

COUNTY ATTORNEY: *(rubbing his hands over the stove)* Frank's fire didn't do much up there, did it? Well, let's go out to the barn and get that cleared up.

The men go outside.

75 MRS. HALE: *(resentfully)* I don't know as there's anything so strange, our takin' up our time with little things while we're waiting for them to get the evidence. *(She sits down at the big table smoothing out a block with decision.)* I don't see as it's anything to laugh about.

MRS. PETERS: *(apologetically)* Of course they've got awful important things on their minds.

Pulls up a chair and joins Mrs. Hale at the table.

MRS. HALE: *(examining another block)* Mrs. Peters, look at this one. Here, this is the one she was working on, and look at the sewing! All the rest of it has been so nice and even. And look at this! It's all over the place! Why, it looks as if she didn't know what she was about!

---

[1] Spruced up. (slang)

After she has said this they look at each other, then start to glance back at the door. After an instant Mrs. Hale has pulled at a knot and ripped the sewing.

Mrs. Peters: Oh, what are you doing, Mrs. Hale?

Mrs. Hale: *(mildly)* Just pulling out a stitch or two that's not sewed very good. *(Threading a needle.)* Bad sewing always made me fidgety.

80 **Mrs. Peters:** *(nervously)* I don't think we ought to touch things.

Mrs. Hale: I'll just finish up this end. *(Suddenly stopping and leaning forward.)* Mrs. Peters?

Mrs. Peters: Yes, Mrs. Hale?

Mrs. Hale: What do you suppose she was so nervous about?

Mrs. Peters: Oh—I don't know. I don't know as she was nervous. I sometimes sew awful queer when I'm just tired. *(Mrs. Hale starts to say something, looks at Mrs. Peters, then goes on sewing.)* Well, I must get these things wrapped up. They may be through sooner than we think. *(Putting apron and other things together.)* I wonder where I can find a piece of paper, and string.

85 **Mrs. Hale:** In that cupboard, maybe.

Mrs. Peters: *(looking in cupboard)* Why, here's a birdcage. *(Holds it up.)* Did she have a bird, Mrs. Hale?

Mrs. Hale: Why, I don't know whether she did or not—I've not been here for so long. There was a man around last year selling canaries cheap, but I don't know as she took one; maybe she did. She used to sing real pretty herself.

Mrs. Peters: *(glancing around)* Seems funny to think of a bird here. But she must have had one, or why would she have a cage? I wonder what happened to it.

Mrs. Hale: I s'pose maybe the cat got it.

90 **Mrs. Peters:** No, she didn't have a cat. She's got that feeling some people have about cats—being afraid of them. My cat got in her room and she was real upset and asked me to take it out.

Mrs. Hale: My sister Bessie was like that. Queer, ain't it?

Mrs. Peters: *(examining the cage)* Why, look at this door. It's broke. One hinge is pulled apart.

Mrs. Hale: *(looking too)* Looks as if someone must have been rough with it.

Mrs. Peters: Why, yes.

She brings the cage forward and puts it on the table.

95 **Mrs. Hale:** I wish if they're going to find any evidence they'd be about it. I don't like this place.

Mrs. Peters: But I'm awful glad you came with me, Mrs. Hale. It would be lonesome for me sitting here alone.

Mrs. Hale: It would, wouldn't it? *(Dropping her sewing.)* But I tell you what I do wish, Mrs. Peters. I wish I had come over sometimes when *she* was here. I—*(looking around the room)*—wish I had.

MRS. PETERS: But of course you were awful busy, Mrs. Hale—your house
and your children.

MRS. HALE: I could've come. I stayed away because it weren't cheerful—
and that's why I ought to have come. I—I've never liked this place.
Maybe because it's down in a hollow and you don't see the road. I
dunno what it is but it's a lonesome place and always was. I wish I
had come over to see Minnie Foster sometimes. I can see now—

Shakes her head.

100 MRS. PETERS: Well, you mustn't reproach yourself, Mrs. Hale. Somehow we
just don't see how it is with other folks until—something comes up.

MRS. HALE: Not having children makes less work—but it makes a quiet
house, and Wright out to work all day, and no company when he did
come in. Did you know John Wright, Mrs. Peters?

MRS. PETERS: Not to know him; I've seen him in town. They say he was a
good man.

MRS. HALE: Yes—good; he didn't drink, and kept his word as well as
most, I guess, and paid his debts. But he was a hard man, Mrs. Peters.
Just to pass the time of day with him—*(Shivers.)* Like a raw wind that
gets to the bone. *(Pauses, her eye falling on the cage.)* I should think she
would 'a wanted a bird. But what do you suppose went with it?

MRS. PETERS: I don't know, unless it got sick and died.

*She reaches over and swings the broken door, swings it again. Both women
watch it.*

105 MRS. HALE: You weren't raised round here, were you? *(Mrs. Peters shakes
her head.)* You didn't know—her?

MRS. PETERS: Not till they brought her yesterday.

MRS. HALE: She—come to think of it, she was kind of like a bird herself—
real sweet and pretty, but kind of timid and—fluttery. How—she—
did—change. *(Silence; then as if struck by a happy thought and relieved to
get back to everyday things.)* Tell you what, Mrs. Peters, why don't you
take the quilt in with you? It might take up her mind.

MRS. PETERS: Why, I think that's a real nice idea, Mrs. Hale. There
couldn't possibly be any objection to it, could there? Now, just what
would I take? I wonder if her patches are in here—and her things.

They look in the sewing basket.

MRS. HALE: Here's some red. I expect this has got sewing things in it.
(Brings out a fancy box.) What a pretty box. Looks like something
somebody would give you. Maybe her scissors are in here. *(Opens box.
Suddenly puts her hand to her nose.)* Why—*(Mrs. Peters bends nearer,
then turns her face away.)* There's something wrapped up in this piece
of silk.

110 MRS. PETERS: Why, this isn't her scissors.

MRS. HALE: *(lifting the silk)* Oh, Mrs. Peters—it's—

Mrs. Peters bends closer.

MRS. PETERS: It's the bird.

MRS. HALE: *(jumping up)* But, Mrs. Peters—look at it! Its neck! Look at its neck! It's all—other side *to.*

MRS. PETERS: Somebody—wrung—its—neck.

Their eyes meet. A look of growing comprehension, of horror. Steps are heard outside. Mrs. Hale slips box under quilt pieces, and sinks into her chair. Enter Sheriff and County Attorney. Mrs. Peters rises.

115 COUNTY ATTORNEY: *(as one turning from serious things to little pleasantries)* Well, ladies, have you decided whether she was going to quilt it or knot it?

MRS. PETERS: We think she was going to—knot it.

COUNTY ATTORNEY: Well, that's interesting, I'm sure. *(Seeing the birdcage.)* Has the bird flown?

MRS. HALE: *(putting more quilt pieces over the box)* We think the—cat got it.

COUNTY ATTORNEY: *(preoccupied)* Is there a cat?

Mrs. Hale glances in a quick covert way at Mrs. Peters.

120 MRS. PETERS: Well, not *now.* They're superstitious, you know. They leave.

COUNTY ATTORNEY: *(to Sheriff Peters, continuing an interrupted conversation)* No sign at all of anyone having come from the outside. Their own rope. Now let's go up again and go over it piece by piece. *(They start upstairs.)* It would have to have been someone who knew just the—

Mrs. Peters sits down. The two women sit there not looking at one another, but as if peering into something and at the same time holding back. When they talk now it is in the manner of feeling their way over strange ground, as if afraid of what they are saying, but as if they can not help saying it.

MRS. HALE: She liked the bird. She was going to bury it in that pretty box.

MRS. PETERS: *(in a whisper)* When I was a girl—my kitten—there was a boy took a hatchet, and before my eyes—and before I could get there—*(Covers her face an instant.)* If they hadn't held me back I would have—*(catches herself, looks upstairs where steps are heard, falters weakly)*—hurt him.

MRS. HALE: *(with a slow look around her)* I wonder how it would seem never to have had any children around. *(Pause.)* No, Wright wouldn't like the bird—a thing that sang. She used to sing. He killed that, too.

125 MRS. PETERS: *(moving uneasily)* We don't know who killed the bird.

MRS. HALE: I knew John Wright.

MRS. PETERS: It was an awful thing was done in this house that night, Mrs. Hale. Killing a man while he slept, slipping a rope around his neck that choked the life out of him.

MRS. HALE: His neck. Choked the life out of him.

Her hand goes out and rests on the birdcage.

MRS. PETERS: *(with rising voice)* We don't know who killed him. We don't know.

130 MRS. HALE: *(her own feeling not interrupted)* If there'd been years and years of nothing, then a bird to sing to you, it would be awful—still, after the bird was still.

MRS. PETERS: *(something within her speaking)* I know what stillness is. When we homesteaded in Dakota, and my first baby died—after he was two years old, and me with no other then—

MRS. HALE: *(moving)* How soon do you suppose they'll be through, looking for the evidence?

MRS. PETERS: I know what stillness is. *(Pulling herself back.)* The law has got to punish crime, Mrs. Hale.

MRS. HALE: *(not as if answering that)* I wish you'd seen Minnie Foster when she wore a white dress with blue ribbons and stood up there in the choir and sang. *(A look around the room.)* Oh, I *wish* I'd come over here once in a while! That was a crime! That was a crime! Who's going to punish that?

135 MRS. PETERS: *(looking upstairs)* We mustn't—take on.

MRS. HALE: I might have known she needed help! I know how things can be—for women. I tell you, it's queer, Mrs. Peters. We live close together and we live far apart. We all go through the same things— it's all just a different kind of the same thing. *(Brushes her eyes; noticing the bottle of fruit, reaches out for it.)* If I was you I wouldn't tell her her fruit was gone. Tell her it *ain't.* Tell her it's all right. Take this in to prove it to her. She—she may never know whether it was broke or not.

MRS. PETERS: *(takes the bottle, looks about for something to wrap it in; takes petticoat from the clothes brought from the other room, very nervously begins winding this around the bottle. In a false voice)* My, it's a good thing the men couldn't hear us. Wouldn't they just laugh! Getting all stirred up over a little thing like a—dead canary. As if that could have anything to do with—with—wouldn't they *laugh!*

The men are heard coming down stairs.

MRS. HALE: *(under her breath)* Maybe they would—maybe they wouldn't.

COUNTY ATTORNEY: No, Peters, it's all perfectly clear except a reason for doing it. But you know juries when it comes to women. If there was some definite thing. Something to show—something to make a story about—a thing that would connect up with this strange way of doing it—

The women's eyes meet for an instant. Enter Hale from outer door.

140 HALE: Well, I've got the team around. Pretty cold out there.

COUNTY ATTORNEY: I'm going to stay here a while by myself. *(To the Sheriff.)* You can send Frank out for me, can't you? I want to go over everything. I'm not satisfied that we can't do better.

SHERIFF: Do you want to see what Mrs. Peters is going to take in?

The County Attorney goes to the table, picks up the apron, laughs.

COUNTY ATTORNEY: Oh, I guess they're not very dangerous things the ladies have picked out. *(Moves a few things about, disturbing the quilt pieces which cover the box. Steps back.)* No, Mrs. Peters doesn't need supervising. For that matter, a sheriff's wife is married to the law. Ever think of it that way, Mrs. Peters?

MRS. PETERS: Not—just that way.

145 SHERIFF: *(chuckling)* Married to the law. *(Moves toward the other room.)* I just want you to come in here a minute, George. We ought to take a look at these windows.

COUNTY ATTORNEY: *(scoffingly)* Oh, windows!

SHERIFF: We'll be right out, Mr. Hale.

Hale goes outside. The Sheriff follows the County Attorney into the other room. Then Mrs. Hale rises, hands tight together, looking intensely at Mrs. Peters, whose eyes make a slow turn, finally meeting Mrs. Hale's. A moment Mrs. Hale holds her, then her own eyes point the way to where the box is concealed. Suddenly Mrs. Peters throws back quilt pieces and tries to put the box in the bag she is wearing. It is too big. She opens box, starts to take bird out, cannot touch it, goes to pieces, stands there helpless. Sound of a knob turning in the other room. Mrs. Hale snatches the box and puts it in the pocket of her big coat. Enter County Attorney and Sheriff.

COUNTY ATTORNEY: *(facetiously)* Well, Henry, at least we found out that she was not going to quilt it. She was going to—what is it you call it, ladies?

MRS. HALE: *(her hand against her pocket)* We call it—knot it, Mr. Henderson.

READING AND REACTING

1. What key events have occurred before the play begins? Why do you suppose these events are not presented in the play itself?
2. What are the "trifles" to which the title refers? How do these "trifles" advance the play's plot?
3. Glaspell's short story version of *Trifles* is called "A Jury of Her Peers." Who are Mrs. Wright's peers? What do you suppose the verdict would be if she were tried for her crime in 1916, when only men were permitted to serve on juries? If the trial were held today, do you think the jury might reach a different verdict?

4. *Trifles* is a one-act play, and all its action occurs in the Wrights' kitchen. Does this static setting slow down the flow of the plot? Are there any advantages to this setting? Explain.

5. All background information about Mrs. Wright is provided by Mrs. Hale. Do you consider her to be a reliable source of information? Why or why not?

6. Mr. Hale's summary of his conversation with Mrs. Wright is the reader's only chance to hear her version of events. How would Mrs. Wright's presence change the play?

7. *Trifles* is a relatively slow-moving, "talky" play, with very little physical action. Is this a weakness of the play, or is the slow development consistent with the effect Glaspell is trying to achieve? Explain.

8. How does each of the following events advance the play's action: the men's departure from the kitchen, the discovery of the quilt pieces, the discovery of the dead bird?

9. How do the county attorney's sarcastic comments and his patronizing attitude toward Mrs. Hale and Mrs. Peters advance the play's action?

10. How do Mrs. Peters's memories of her own life advance the action?

11. What assumptions about women do the male characters make? In what ways do the female characters conform to or depart from these assumptions?

12. In what sense is the process of making a quilt an appropriate metaphor for the plot of *Trifles*?

13. **JOURNAL ENTRY** Do you think Mrs. Hale and Mrs. Peters do the right thing by concealing evidence?

14. **CRITICAL PERSPECTIVE** Gary A. Richardson writes in *American Drama from the Colonial Period through World War I* that in *Trifles*, Glaspell "developed a new structure for her action [. . .].":

> While action in the traditional sense is minimal, Glaspell is nevertheless able to rivet attention on the two women, wed the audience to their perspective, and make a compelling case for the fairness of their actions. Existing on the margins of their society, Mrs. Peters and Mrs. Hale become emotional surrogates for the jailed Minnie Wright, effectively exonerating her action as "justifiable homicide."
> *Trifles* is carefully crafted to match Glaspell's subject matter—the action meanders, without a clearly delineated beginning, middle, or end [. . .].

Exactly how does Glaspell "rivet attention on" Mrs. Hale and Mrs. Peters? Do you agree that the play's action "meanders, without a clearly delineated beginning, middle, and end"? If so, do you too see this "meandering" as appropriate for Glaspell's subject matter?

Related Works: "I Stand Here Ironing" (p. 160), "The Cask of Amontillado" (p. 219), "Everyday Use" (p. 324), "The Disappearance" (p. 419), "Fleur" (p. 426), "Eveline" (p. 470)

✦ **August Strindberg** (1849–1912) was born in Stockholm, Sweden, the child of a shipping merchant and his former maid. He studied at Uppsala University but left the university without a degree. By 1872, he had moved into the artistic circles in Stockholm and had begun work as a journalist.

In 1874, Strindberg was appointed assistant librarian at the Royal Library in Stockholm. Beginning the first of several stormy marriages, Strindberg struggled over the next few years; in 1879, he declared bankruptcy. During the same period, however, he wrote the novel that marked his breakthrough as a writer, *The Red Room* (1879). In 1881, he left the Royal Library to devote himself to writing, and in 1883, he left Sweden to join an artists' colony near Paris. His restlessness continued, however, and he soon moved to Switzerland, later living in Denmark, Berlin, and Austria, before returning at last to Stockholm.

Strindberg was a prolific artist, and his work includes novels, plays, poetry, and painting. He is considered one of the most influential dramatists in literature. His troubled life ended in 1912.

Strindberg's *The Stronger* has been called a monodrama, a dramatic monologue, and a battle of brains in one scene. *The Stronger* was the kind of experimental work being encouraged in the late nineteenth century at the Théâtre Libre in Paris, for which Strindberg wrote several plays while hoping to form his own experimental theater in Stockholm. Though written in 1889, *The Stronger* did not premiere on stage until 1907.

Cultural Context ✦ The explicit nature of Strindberg's subject matter (*The Stronger,* for example, is about a meeting between an actress and her husband's mistress) shocked and sometimes scandalized the sensibilities of his nineteenth-century contemporaries. As a result, he had difficulty getting his plays performed in commercial theaters. For this reason, Strindberg and other playwrights became involved with the independent theatre movement. By producing plays outside the control of official censors, they were able to get an audience for their work.

❖ ❖ ❖

AUGUST STRINDBERG

The Stronger
(1889)

Translated by Elizabeth Sprigge

CHARACTERS

MRS. X., *actress, married*
MISS Y., *actress, unmarried*
A WAITRESS

SCENE*
A corner of a ladies' café [in Stockholm in the eighteen eighties]. Two small wrought-iron tables, a red plush settee and a few chairs.

Miss Y. is sitting with a half-empty bottle of beer on the table before her, reading an illustrated weekly which from time to time she exchanges for another.

Mrs. X. enters, wearing a winter hat and coat and carrying a decorative Japanese basket.

MRS. X: Why, Millie, my dear, how are you? Sitting here all alone on Christmas Eve like some poor bachelor.

Miss Y. looks up from her magazine, nods, and continues to read.

MRS. X: You know it makes me feel really sad to see you. Alone. Alone in a café and on Christmas Eve of all times. It makes me feel as sad as when once in Paris I saw a wedding party at a restaurant. The bride was reading a comic paper and the bridegroom playing billiards with the witnesses. Ah me, I said to myself, with such a beginning how will it go, and how will it end? He was playing billiards on his wedding day! And she, you were going to say, was reading a comic paper on hers. But that's not quite the same.

A waitress brings a cup of chocolate to Mrs X. and goes out.

MRS. X: Do you know, Amelia, I really believe now you would have done better to stick to him. Don't forget I was the first who told you to forgive him. Do you remember? Then you would be married now and have a home. Think how happy you were that Christmas when you stayed with your finance's people in the country. How warmly you spoke of domestic happiness! You really quite longed to be out of the theatre. Yes, Amelia dear, home is best—next best to the stage, and as for children—but you couldn't know anything about that.

---

*Note: Translator's addition to scene bracketed. First mention of Miss Y. and Mrs. X. reversed.

Miss Y.'s expression is disdainful. Mrs. X. sips a few spoonfuls of chocolate, then opens her basket and displays some Christmas presents.

MRS. X: Now you must see what I have bought for my little chicks. *(Takes out a doll.)* Look at this. That's for Lisa. Do you see how she can roll her eyes and turn her head. Isn't she lovely? And here's a toy pistol for Maja.[1] *(She loads the pistol and shoots it at Miss Y. who appears frightened.)*

5 MRS. X: Were you scared? Did you think I was going to shoot you? Really, I didn't think you'd believe that of me. Now if *you* were to shoot *me* it wouldn't be so surprising, for after all I did get in your way, and I know you never forget it—although I was entirely innocent. You still think I intrigued to get you out of the Grand Theatre, but I didn't. I didn't, however much you think I did. Well, it's no good talking, you will believe it was me . . . *(Takes out a pair of embroidered slippers.)* And these are for my old man, with tulips on them that I embroidered myself. As a matter of fact I hate tulips, but he has to have tulips on everything.

Miss Y. looks up, irony and curiosity in her face.

MRS. X: *(putting one hand in each slipper)* Look what small feet Bob has, hasn't he? And you ought to see the charming way he walks—you've never seen him in slippers, have you?

Miss Y. laughs.

MRS. X: Look, I'll show you. *(She makes the slippers walk across the table, and Miss Y. laughs again.)*

MRS. X: But when he gets angry, look, he stamps his foot like this. "Those damn girls who can never learn to make coffee! Blast! That silly idiot hasn't trimmed the lamp properly!" Then there's a draught under the door and his feet get cold. "Hell, it's freezing, and the damn fools can't even keep the stove going!" *(She rubs the sole of one slipper against the instep of the other. Miss Y roars with laughter.)*

MRS. X: And then he comes home and has to hunt for his slippers, which Mary has pushed under the bureau . . . Well, perhaps it's not right to make fun of one's husband like this. He's sweet anyhow, and a good, dear husband. You ought to have had a husband like him, Amelia. What are you laughing at? What is it? Eh? And, you see, I know he is faithful to me. Yes, I know it. He told me himself—what *are* you giggling at?—that while I was on tour in Norway that horrible Frederica came and tried to seduce him. Can you imagine anything more abominable? *(Pause.)* I'd have scratched her eyes out if she had come around while I was at home. *(Pause.)* I'm glad Bob told me about it himself, so I didn't just hear it from gossip. *(Pause.)* And, as a matter of fact, Frederica wasn't the only one. I can't think why, but

---

[1] Pronounced Maja.

all the women in the Company[2] seem to be crazy about my husband.
They must think his position gives him some say in who is engaged
at the Theatre. Perhaps you have run after him yourself? I don't trust
you very far, but I know he has never been attracted by you, and you
always seemed to have some sort of grudge against him, or so I felt.
(Pause. They look at one another guardedly.)

10 MRS. X: Do come and spend Christmas Eve with us tonight, Amelia—just
to show that you're not offended with us, or anyhow not with me. I
don't know why, but it seems specially unpleasant not to be friends
with you. Perhaps it's because I did get in your way that time . . .
(slowly) or—I don't know—really, I don't know at all why it is.

Pause. Miss Y. gazes curiously at Mrs. X.

MRS. X: *(thoughtfully)* It was so strange when we were getting to know
one another. Do you know, when we first met, I was frightened of
you, so frightened I didn't dare let you out of my sight. I arranged all
my goings and comings to be near you. I dared not be your enemy, so
I became your friend. But when you came to our home, I always had
an uneasy feeling, because I saw my husband didn't like you, and
that irritated me—like when a dress doesn't fit. I did all I could to
make him be nice to you, but it was no good—until you went and got
engaged. Then you became such tremendous friends that at first it
looked as if you only dared show your real feelings then—when you
were safe. And then, let me see, how was it after that? I wasn't
jealous—that's queer. And I remember at the christening, when you
were the godmother, I told him to kiss you. He did, and you were so
upset . . . As a matter of fact I didn't notice that then . . . I didn't
think about it afterwards either . . . I've never thought about it—until
now! (Rises abruptly.) Why don't you say something? You haven't said
a word all this time. You've just let me go on talking. You have sat
there with your eyes drawing all these thoughts out of me—they were
there in me like silk in a cocoon—thoughts . . . Mistaken thoughts?
Let me think. Why did you break off your engagement? Why did you
never come to our house after that? Why don't you want to come to
us tonight?

Miss Y. makes a motion, as if about to speak.

MRS. X: No. You don't need to say anything, for now I see it all. That was
why—and why—and why. Yes. Yes, that's why it was. Yes, yes, all the
pieces fit together now. That's it. I won't sit at the same table as you.
(Moves her things to the other table.) That's why I have to embroider
tulips, which I loathe, on his slippers—because you liked tulips.
(Throws the slippers on the floor.) That's why we have to spend the

---

[2] "In the Company" translator's addition.

summer on the lake—because you couldn't bear the seaside. That's why my son had to be called Eskil—because it was your father's name. That's why I had to wear your colours, read your books, eat the dishes you liked, drink your drinks—your chocolate, for instance. That's why—oh my God, it's terrible to think of, terrible! Everything, everything came to me from you—even your passions. Your soul bored into mine like a worm into an apple, and ate and ate and burrowed and burrowed, till nothing was left but the skin and a little black mould. I wanted to fly from you, but I couldn't. You were there like a snake, your black eyes fascinating me. When I spread my wings, they only dragged me down. I lay in the water with my feet tied together, and the harder I worked my arms, the deeper I sank—down, down, till I reached the bottom, where you lay in waiting like a giant crab to catch me in your claws—and now here I am. Oh how I hate you! I hate you, I hate you! And you just go on sitting there, silent, calm, indifferent, not caring whether the moon is new or full, if it's Christmas or New Year, if other people are happy or unhappy. You don't know how to hate or to love. You just sit there without moving—like a cat[3] at a mouse-hole. You can't drag your prey out, you can't chase it, but you can out-stay it. Here you sit in your corner—you know they call it the rat-trap after you—reading the papers to see if anyone's ruined or wretched or been thrown out of the Company. Here you sit sizing up your victims and weighing your chances—like a pilot his shipwrecks for the salvage. *(Pause.)* Poor Amelia! Do you know, I couldn't be more sorry for you. I know you are miserable, miserable like some wounded creature, and vicious because you are wounded. I can't be angry with you. I should like to be, but after all you are the small one—and as for your affair with Bob, that doesn't worry me in the least. Why should it matter to me? And if you, or somebody else taught me to drink chocolate, what's the difference? *(Drinks a spoonful. Smugly.)* Chocolate is very wholesome anyhow. And if I learnt from you how to dress, *tant mieux!*—that only gave me a stronger hold over my husband, and you have lost what I gained. Yes, to judge from various signs, I think you have now lost him. Of course, you meant me to walk out, as you once did, and which you're now regretting. But I won't do that, you may be sure. One shouldn't be narrow-minded, you know. And why should nobody else want what I have? *(Pause.)* Perhaps, my dear, taking everything into consideration, at this moment it is I who am the stronger. You never got anything from me, you just gave away—from yourself. And now, like the thief in the night, when you woke up I had what you had lost. Why was it then that everything you

---

[3] In Swedish, "stork."

touched became worthless and sterile? You couldn't keep a man's love—for all your tulips and your passions—but I could. You couldn't learn the art of living from your books—but I learnt it. You bore no little Eskil, although that was your father's name. *(Pause.)* And why is it you are silent—everywhere, always silent? Yes, I used to think this was strength, but perhaps it was because you hadn't anything to say, because you couldn't think of anything. *(Rises and picks up the slippers.)* Now I am going home, taking the tulips with me—*your* tulips. You couldn't learn from others, you couldn't bend, and so you broke like a dry stick. I did not. Thank you, Amelia, for all your good lessons. Thank you for teaching my husband how to love. Now I am going home—to love him.

Exit.

READING AND REACTING

1. Summarize the plot of *The Stronger*. What actually happens during the course of the play? What events have already occurred before the play's opening?
2. Explain the nature of the conflict between Mrs. X and Miss Y. Is it largely personal or professional?
3. Why do you suppose Strindberg chose to make this play a **monologue** rather than have Miss Y speak? Would exchanges of dialogue strengthen the play? What do you suppose Miss Y would like to tell Mrs. X?
4. In the absence of exchanges of dialogue, what devices advance the play's action?
5. Where does the play's climax occur?
6. List all the play's props—for example, the toy gun and the slippers. What function does each prop serve? Are they all necessary?
7. What does the audience learn about Bob, Mrs. X's husband, during the course of the play? What more can we infer about him?
8. Both Miss Y and Mrs. X are actresses. What significance, if any, do you see in this fact?
9. As she continues to speak, Mrs. X's **similes**—for example, "Your soul bored into mine like a worm into an apple"—grow increasingly vivid. Identify as many similes as you can. How do they advance the play's action?
10. During the course of the play, Mrs. X seems to gain knowledge and self-awareness. Does she actually do so, or is she deceiving herself?
11. **JOURNAL ENTRY** Which of the two women do you see as "the stronger"? Explain your position.
12. **CRITICAL PERSPECTIVE** Strindberg often experimented with avant-garde staging, using it, at times, to draw attention to gender issues. Although *The Stronger* is a monologue, it involves

two characters (both of whom are female). How does Strindberg use staging to comment on gender issues?

Related Works: "The Story of an Hour" (p. 77), "Big Black Good Man" (p. 207), "A Clean, Well-Lighted Place" (p. 261)

 ◆ **ALICE CHILDRESS** (1920–1994) was born in Charleston, South Carolina, but she moved to Harlem at age nine. She studied drama at the American Negro Theatre in the 1940s, where she wrote, directed, and starred in her first play, *Florence* (1949). She went on to become a leading African-American playwright, novelist, and actress, and she is best known for her portrayal of the spirit of survival and endurance of African-Americans. Other works by Childress include *Trouble in Mind* (produced in 1955 and revised and published in 1971), *Wedding Band* (produced in 1966), *String* (produced in 1969), *Wine in the Wilderness* (produced in 1969), *Just a Little Simple* (produced in 1950), *Gold through the Trees* (produced in 1952), *The African Garden* (produced in 1971), *Gullah* (produced in 1984), and *Moms* (produced in 1987). She was also a noted children's writer, and her novels for children include *A Hero Ain't Nothin' but a Sandwich* (1973), which was made into a film in 1978, and *Rainbow Jordan* (1981). Her plays for juveniles include *When the Rattlesnake Sounds* (1975) and *Let's Hear It for the Queen* (1976).

Florence, set in the 1940s, is about a black woman who meets an insensitive white actress in a railway station waiting room. Through the interchange with the woman, she gains respect for her own daughter's pursuit of an acting career.

CULTURAL CONTEXT ◆ In the 1940s in the South, when *Florence* is set, there were separate public restrooms and water fountains for blacks and whites, and African-Americans were not permitted in most restaurants where whites dined. The civil rights movement, which would lead to the end of segregation, would not begin until 1955 when Rosa Parks refused to give up her seat to a white man on a segregated Montgomery, Alabama, bus. Her arrest resulted in a year-long boycott of the Montgomery bus system by African-Americans and the emergence of Martin Luther King, Jr., as a leading figure in the civil rights movement.

◊ ◊ ◊

A L I C E   C H I L D R E S S

Florence
(1949)

CHARACTERS

MARGE
MAMA
PORTER
MRS. CARTER

PLACE
A very small town in the South.

TIME
The late 1940s.

SCENE
A railway station waiting room. The room is divided in two sections by a low railing. Upstage center is a double door which serves as an entrance to both sides of the room. Over the doorway stage right is a sign "Colored," over the doorway stage left is another sign "White." Stage right are two doors . . . one marked "Colored men" . . . the other "Colored women." Stage left two other doorways are "White ladies" and "White gentlemen." There are two benches, one on each side. The room is drab and empty looking. Through the double doors upstage center can be seen a gray lighting which gives the effect of an early evening and open platform.

At rise of curtain the stage remains empty for about twenty seconds . . . A middle aged Negro woman enters, looks offstage . . . then crosses to the "Colored" side and sits on the bench. A moment later she is followed by a young Negro woman about twenty-one years old. She is carrying a large new cardboard suitcase and a wrapped shoebox. She is wearing a shoulder strap bag and a newspaper protrudes from the flap. She crosses to the "Colored" side and rests the suitcase at her feet as she looks at her mother with mild annoyance.

MARGE: You didn't have to get here so early, Mama. Now you got to wait!
MAMA: If I'm goin' someplace . . . I like to get there in plenty time. You
    don't have to stay.
MARGE: You shouldn't wait 'round here alone.
MAMA: I ain't scared. Ain't a soul going to bother me.
5 MARGE: I got to get back to Ted. He don't like to be in the house by
    himself. *(She picks up the bag and places it on the bench by Mama.)*
MAMA: You'd best go back. *(Smiles.)* You know he misses Florence.
MARGE: He's just a little fellow. He needs his mother. You make her come
    home! She shouldn't be way up there in Harlem. She ain't got nobody
    there.
MAMA: You know Florence don't like the South.

MARGE: It ain't what we like in this world! You tell her that.

10 MAMA: If Mr. Jack ask about the rent, you tell him we gonna be a little late on account of the trip.

MARGE: I'll talk with him. Don't worry so about everything. *(Places suitcase on floor.)* What you carryin', Mama . . . bricks?

MAMA: If Mr. Jack won't wait . . . write to Rudley. He oughta send a little somethin'.

MARGE: Mama . . . Rudley ain't got nothin' fo himself. I hate to ask him to give us.

MAMA: That's your brother! If push come to shove, we got to ask.

15 MARGE: *(places box on bench)* Don't forget to eat your lunch . . . and try to get a seat near the window so you can lean on your elbow and get a little rest.

MAMA: Hmmmm . . . mmmph. Yes.

MARGE: Buy yourself some coffee when the man comes through. You'll need something hot and you can't go to the diner.

MAMA: I know that. You talk like I'm a northern greenhorn.

MARGE: You got handkerchiefs?

20 MAMA: I got everything, Marge.

MARGE: *(wanders upstage to the railing division line)* I know Florence is real bad off or she wouldn't call on us for money. Make her come home. She ain't gonna get rich up there and we can't afford to do for her.

MAMA: We talked all of that before.

MARGE: *(touches rail)* Well, you got to be strict on her. She got notions a Negro woman don't need.

MAMA: But she was in a real play. Didn't she send us twenty-five dollars a week?

25 MARGE: For two weeks.

MAMA: Well the play was over.

MARGE: *(crosses to Mama and sits beside her)* It's not money, Mama. Sarah wrote us about it. You know what she said Florence was doin'. Sweepin' the stage!

MAMA: She was *in* the play!

MARGE: Sure she was in it! Sweepin'! Them folks ain't gonna let her be no actress. You tell her to wake up.

30 MAMA: I . . . I . . . think.

MARGE: Listen, Mama . . . She won't wanna come. We know that . . . but she gotta!

MAMA: Maybe we shoulda told her to expect me. It's kind of mean to just walk in like this.

MARGE: I bet she's livin' terrible. What's the matter with her? Don't she know we're keepin' her son?

MAMA: Florence don't feel right 'bout down here since Jim got killed.

35 MARGE: Who does? I should be the one goin' to get her. You tell her she ain't gonna feel right in no place. Mama, honestly! She must think she's white!

MAMA: Florence is brownskin.

MARGE: I don't mean that. I'm talkin' about her attitude. Didn't she go to Strumley's down here and ask to be a salesgirl? *(Rises.)* Now ain't that somethin'? They don't hire no Colored folks.

MAMA: Others beside Florence been talkin' about their rights.

MARGE: I know it . . . but there's things we can't do cause they ain't gonna let us. *(She wanders over to the "White" side of the stage.)* Don't feel a damn bit different over here than it does on our side. *(Silence.)*

40 MAMA: Maybe we shoulda just sent her the money this time. This one time.

MARGE: *(coming back to the "Colored" side)* Mama! Don't you let her cash that check for nothin' but to bring her back home.

MAMA: I know.

MARGE: *(restless . . . fidgets with her hair . . . patting it in place)* I oughta go now.

MAMA: You best get back to Ted. He might play with the lamp.

45 MARGE: He better not let me catch him! If you got to go to the ladies' room take your grip.

MAMA: I'll be alright. Make Ted get up on time for school.

MARGE: *(kisses her quickly and gives her the newspaper)* Here's something to read. So long, Mama.

MAMA: G'bye, Margie baby.

MARGE: *(goes to door . . . stops and turns to her mother)* You got your smelling salts?

50 MAMA: In my pocketbook.

MARGE: *(wistfully)* Tell Florence I love her and miss her too.

PORTER: *(can be heard singing in the distance)*

MAMA: Sure.

MARGE: *(reluctant to leave)* Pin that check in your bosom, Mama. You might fall asleep and somebody'll rob you.

55 MAMA: I got it pinned to me. *(Feels for the check which is in her blouse.)*

MARGE: *(almost pathetic)* Bye, Ma.

MAMA: *(Sits for a moment looking at her surroundings. She opens the paper and begins to read.)*

PORTER: *(offstage)* Hello, Marge. What you doin' down here?

MARGE: I came to see Mama off.

60 PORTER: Where's she going?

MARGE: She's in there; she'll tell you. I got to get back to Ted.

PORTER: Bye now . . . Say, wait a minute, Marge.

MARGE: Yes?

PORTER: I told Ted he could have some of my peaches and he brought all them Brandford boys and they picked 'em all. I wouldn't lay a hand on him but I told him I was gonna tell you.

65 MARGE: I'm gonna give it to him!

PORTER: *(Enters and crosses to white side of waiting room. He carries a pail of water and a mop. He is about fifty years old. He is obviously tired but not lazy.)* Every peach off my tree!

MAMA: There wasn't but six peaches on that tree.

PORTER: *(smiles . . . glances at Mama as he crosses to the "White" side and begins to mop)* How d'ye do, Mrs. Whitney . . . you going on a trip?

MAMA: Fine, I thank you. I'm going to New York.

70 PORTER: Wish it was me. You gonna stay?

MAMA: No, Mr. Brown. I'm bringing Florence . . . I'm visiting Florence.

PORTER: Tell her I said hello. She's a fine girl.

MAMA: Thank you.

PORTER: My brother Bynum's in Georgia now.

75 MAMA: Well now, that's nice.

PORTER: Atlanta.

MAMA: He goin' to school?

PORTER: Yes'm. He saw Florence in a Colored picture. A moving picture.

MAMA: Do tell! She didn't say a word about it.

80 PORTER: They got Colored moving picture theaters in Atlanta.

MAMA: Yes. Your brother going to be a doctor?

PORTER: *(with pride)* No. He writes things.

MAMA: Oh.

PORTER: My son is goin' back to Howard next year.

85 MAMA: Takes an awful lot of goin' to school to be anything. Lot of money leastways.

PORTER: *(thoughtfully)* Yes'm, it sure do.

MAMA: That sure was a nice church sociable the other night.

PORTER: Yes'm. We raised 87 dollars.

MAMA: That's real nice.

90 PORTER: I won your cake at the bazaar.

MAMA: The chocolate one?

PORTER: *(as he wrings mop)* Yes'm . . . was light as a feather. That old train is gonna be late this evenin'. It's number 42.

MAMA: I don't mind waitin'.

PORTER: *(Lifts pail, tucks mop handle under his arm. He looks about in order to make certain no one is around and leans over and addresses Mama in a confidential tone.)* Did you buy your ticket from that Mr. Daly?

95 MAMA: *(in a low tone)* No. Marge bought it yesterday.

PORTER: *(leaning against railing)* That's good. That man is real mean. Especially if he thinks you're goin' north. *(He starts to leave . . . then turns back to Mama.)* If you go to the rest room, use the Colored men's . . . the other one is out of order.

MAMA: Thank you, sir.

MRS. CARTER: *(A white woman . . . well dressed, wearing furs and carrying a small, expensive overnight bag breezes in . . . breathless . . . flustered and smiling. She addresses the Porter as she almost collides with him.)* Boy! My bags are out there. There taxi driver just dropped them. Will they be safe?

PORTER: Yes, mam. I'll see after them.

100 **MRS. CARTER:** I thought I'd missed the train.

PORTER: It's late, mam.

MRS. CARTER: *(crosses to bench on the "White" side and rests her bag)* Fine! You come back here and get me when it comes. There'll be a tip in it for you.

PORTER: Thank you, mam. I'll be here. *(As he leaves.)* Miss Whitney, I'll take care of your bag too.

MAMA: Thank you, sir.

105 **MRS. CARTER:** *(wheels around . . . notices Mama)* Oh . . . Hello there . . .

MAMA: Howdy, mam. *(She opens her newspaper and begins to read.)*

MRS. CARTER: *(Paces up and down rather nervously. She takes a cigarette from her purse, lights it and takes a deep draw. She looks at her watch and then speaks to Mama across the railing.)* Have you any idea how late the train will be?

MAMA: No, mam. *(Starts to read again.)*

MRS. CARTER: I can't leave this place fast enough. Two days of it and I'm bored to tears. Do you live here?

110 **MAMA:** *(rests paper on her lap)* Yes, mam.

MRS. CARTER: Where are you going?

MAMA: New York City, mam.

MRS. CARTER: Good for you! You can stop "maming" me. My name is Mrs. Carter. I'm not a southerner really. *(Takes a handkerchief from her purse and covers her nose for a moment.)* My God! Disinfectant! This is a frightful place. My brother's here writing a book. Wants atmosphere. Well, he's got it. I'll never come back here ever.

MAMA: That's too bad, mam . . . Mrs. Carter.

115 **MRS. CARTER:** That's good. I'd die in this place. Really die. Jeff . . . Mr. Wiley . . . my brother . . . He's tied in knots, a bundle of problems . . . positively in knots.

MAMA: *(amazed)* That so, mam?

MRS. CARTER: You don't have to call me mam. It's so southern. Mrs. Carter! These people are still fighting the Civil War. I'm really a New Yorker now. Of course, I was born here . . . in the South I mean. Memphis. Listen . . . am I annoying you? I've simply got to talk to someone.

MAMA: *(places her newspaper on the bench)* No, Mrs. Carter. It's perfectly alright.

MRS. CARTER: Fine! You see Jeff has ceased writing. Stopped! Just like that! *(Snaps fingers.)*

120 **MAMA:** *(turns to her)* That so?

MRS. CARTER: Yes. The reviews came out on his last book. Poor fellow.

MAMA: I'm sorry, mam . . . Mrs. Carter. They didn't like his book?

MRS. CARTER: Well enough . . . but Jeff's . . . well, Mr. Wiley is a genius. He says they missed the point! Lost the whole message! Did you read . . . do you . . . have you heard of *Lost My Lonely Way?*

MAMA: No, mam. I can't say I have.

125 MRS. CARTER: Well, it doesn't matter. It's profound. Real . . . you know. *(Stands at the railing upstage.)* It's about your people.

MAMA: That's nice.

MRS. CARTER: Jeff poured his complete self into it. Really delved into the heart of the problem, pulled no punches! He hardly stopped for his meals . . . And of course I wasn't here to see that he didn't overdo. He suffers so with his characters.

MAMA: I guess he wants to do his best.

MRS. CARTER: Zelma! . . . That's his heroine . . . Zelma! A perfect character.

130 MAMA: *(interested . . . coming out of her shell eagerly)* She was colored, mam?

MRS. CARTER: Oh yes! . . . But of course you don't know what it's about do you?

MAMA: No, miss . . . Would you tell me?

MRS. CARTER: *(leaning on the railing)* Well . . . she's almost white, see? Really you can't tell except in small ways. She wants to be a lawyer . . . and . . . and . . . well, there she is full of complexes and this deep shame you know.

MAMA: *(excitedly but with curiosity)* Do tell! What shame has she got?

135 MRS. CARTER: *(takes off her fur neckpiece and places it on bench with overnight bag)* It's obvious! This lovely creature . . . intelligent, ambitious, and well . . . she's a Negro!

MAMA: *(waiting eagerly)* Yes'm, you said that . . .

MRS. CARTER: Surely you understand? She's constantly hating herself. Just before she dies she says it! . . . Right on the bridge . . .

MAMA: *(genuinely moved)* How sad. Ain't it a shame she had to die?

MRS. CARTER: It was inevitable . . . . couldn't be any other way!

140 MAMA: What did she say on the bridge?

MRS. CARTER: Well . . . just before she jumped . . .

MAMA: *(slowly straightening)* You mean she killed *herself?*

MRS. CARTER: Of course. Close your eyes and picture it!

MAMA: *(turns front and closes her eyes tightly with enthusiasm)* Yes'm.

145 MRS. CARTER: *(center stage on "White" side)* Now . . . ! She's standing on the bridge in the moonlight . . . Out of her shabby purse she takes a mirror . . . and by the light of the moon she looks at her reflection in the glass.

MAMA: *(clasps her hands together gently)* I can see her just as plain.

MRS. CARTER: *(sincerely)* Tears roll down her cheeks as she says . . . almost! almost white . . . but I'm black! I'm a Negro! and then . . . *(Turns to Mama.)* she jumps and drowns herself!

MAMA: *(opens her eyes and speaks quietly)* Why?

MRS. CARTER: She can't face it! Living in a world where she almost belongs but not quite. *(Drifts upstage.)* Oh it's so . . . so . . . tragic.

150 MAMA: *(Carried away by her convictions . . . not anger . . . she feels challenged. She rises.)* That ain't so! Not one bit it ain't!

MRS. CARTER: *(surprised)* But it is!

MAMA: *(during the following she works her way around the railing until she crosses over about one foot to the "White" side and is face to face with Mrs. Carter)* I know it ain't! Don't my friend Essie Kitredge daughter look just like a German or somethin'? She didn't kill herself! She's teachin' the third grade in the colored school right here. Even the bus drivers ask her to sit in the front seats cause they think she's white! . . . an' . . . an' . . . she just says as clear as you please . . . "I'm sittin' where my people got to sit by law. I'm a Negro woman!"

MRS. CARTER: *(uncomfortable and not knowing why)* . . . But there you have it. The exception makes the rule. That's proof!

MAMA: No such thing! My cousin Hemsly's as white as you! . . . an' . . . an' he never . . .

155 MRS. CARTER: *(flushed with anger . . . yet lost . . . because she doesn't know why)* Are you losing your temper? *(Weakly.)* Are you angry with me?

MAMA: *(Stands silently trembling as she looks down and notices she is on the wrong side of the railing. She looks up at the "White Ladies room" sign and slowly works her way back to the "Colored" side. She feels completely lost.)* No, *mam.* Excuse me please. *(With bitterness.)* I just meant Hemsly works in the colored section of the shoe store . . . He never once wanted to kill his self! *(She sits down on the bench and fumbles for her newspaper. Silence.)*

MRS. CARTER: *(caught between anger and reason . . . she laughs nervously)* Well! Let's not be upset by this. It's entirely my fault you know. This whole thing is a completely controversial subject. *(Silence.)* If it's too much for Jeff . . . well naturally I shouldn't discuss it with you. *(Approaching railing.)* I'm sorry. Let *me* apologize.

MAMA: *(keeps her eyes on the paper)* No need for that, mam. *(Silence.)*

MRS. CARTER: *(painfully uncomfortable)* I've drifted away from . . . What started all of this?

160 MAMA: *(no comedy intended or allowed on this line)* Your brother, mam.

MRS. CARTER: *(trying valiantly to brush away the tension)* Yes . . . Well, I had to come down and sort of hold his hand over the reviews. He just thinks too much . . . and studies. He knows the Negro so well that sometimes our friends tease him and say he almost *seems* like . . . well you know . . .

MAMA: *(tightly)* Yes'm.

MRS. CARTER: *(slowly walks over the "Colored" side near the top of the rail)* You know I try but it's really difficult to understand you people. However . . . I keep trying.

MAMA: *(still tight)* Thank you, mam.

165 MRS. CARTER: *(retreats back to "White" side and begins to prove herself)* Last week . . . Why do you know what I did? I sent a thousand dollars to a Negro college for scholarships.

MAMA: That was right kind of you.

MRS. CARTER: *(almost pleading)* I know what's going on in your
    mind . . . and what you're thinking is wrong. I've . . . I've . . . eaten
    with Negroes.

MAMA: Yes, mam.

MRS. CARTER: *(trying to find a straw)* . . . And there's Malcolm! If it
    weren't for the guidance of Jeff he'd never written his poems.
    Malcolm is a Negro.

170 MAMA: *(freezing)* Yes, mam.

MRS. CARTER: *(Gives up, crosses to her bench, opens her overnight bag and
    takes out a book and begins to read. She glances at Mama from time to
    time. Mama is deeply absorbed in her newspaper. Mrs. Carter closes her
    book with a bang . . . determined to penetrate the wall Mama has built
    around her.)* Why are you going to New York?

MAMA: *(almost accusingly)* I got a daughter there.

MRS. CARTER: I lost my son in the war. *(Silence . . . Mama is ill at ease.)*
    Your daughter . . . what is she doing . . . studying?

MAMA: No'm, she's trying to get on stage.

175 MRS. CARTER: *(pleasantly)* Oh . . . a singer?

MAMA: No, mam. She's . . .

MRS. CARTER: *(warmly)* You people have such a gift. I love
    spirituals . . . "Steal Away," "Swing Low, Sweet Chariot."

MAMA: They are right nice. But Florence wants to act. Just say things in
    plays.

MRS. CARTER: A dramatic actress?

180 MAMA: Yes, that's what it is. She been in a colored moving picture, and a
    big show for two weeks on Broadway.

MRS. CARTER: The dear, precious child! . . . But this is funny . . . no! it's
    pathetic. She must be bitter . . . *really* bitter. Do you know what I do?

MAMA: I can't rightly say.

MRS. CARTER: I'm an actress! A dramatic actress . . . And I haven't really
    worked in six months . . . And I'm pretty well-known . . . And
    everyone knows Jeff. I'd like to work. Of course, there are my
    committees, but you see, they don't need me. No really . . . not even
    Jeff.

MAMA: Now that's a shame.

185 MRS. CARTER: Now your daughter . . . you must make her stop before she's
    completely unhappy. Make her stop!

MAMA: Yes'm . . . why?

MRS. CARTER: I have the best of contacts and *I've* only done a few
    broadcasts lately. Of course, I'm not counting the things I just
    wouldn't do. Your daughter . . . make her stop.

MAMA: A drama teacher told her she has real talent.

MRS. CARTER: A drama teacher! My dear woman, there are loads
    of unscrupulous whites up there that just hand out opinions for . . .

190 MAMA: This was a colored gentleman down here.

MRS. CARTER: Oh well! . . . And she went up there on the strength of that? This makes me very unhappy. *(Puts book away in case, and snaps lock, silence.)*

MAMA: *(getting an idea)* Do you really, truly feel that way, mam?

MRS. CARTER: I do. Please . . . I want you to believe me.

MAMA: Could I ask you something?

195 MRS. CARTER: Anything.

MAMA: You won't be angry, mam?

MRS. CARTER: *(remembering)* I won't. I promise you.

MAMA: *(gathering courage)* Florence is proud . . . but she's having it hard.

MRS. CARTER: I'm sure she is.

200 MAMA: Could you help her out some, mam? Knowing all the folks you do . . . maybe . . .

MRS. CARTER: *(rubs the outside of the case)* Well . . . it isn't that simple . . . but . . . you're very sweet. If only I could . . .

MAMA: Anything you did, I feel grateful. I don't like to tell it, but she can't even pay her rent and things. And she's used to my cooking for her . . . I believe my girl goes hungry sometime up there . . . and yet she'd like to stay so bad.

MRS. CARTER: *(looks up, resting case on her knees)* How can I refuse? You seem like a good woman.

MAMA: Always lived as best I knew how and raised my children up right. We got a fine family, mam.

205 MRS. CARTER: And I've no family at all. I've got to! It's clearly my duty. Jeff's books . . . guiding Malcolm's poetry . . . It isn't enough . . . oh I know it isn't. Have you ever heard of Melba Rugby?

MAMA: No, mam. I don't know anybody much . . . except right here.

MRS. CARTER: *(brightening)* She's in California, but she's moving East again . . . hates California.

MAMA: Yes'm.

MRS. CARTER: A most versatile woman. Writes, directs, acts . . . everything!

210 MAMA: That's nice, mam.

MRS. CARTER: Well, she's uprooting herself and coming back to her first home . . . New York . . . to direct "Love Flowers" . . . it's a musical.

MAMA: Yes'm.

MRS. CARTER: She's grand . . . helped so many people . . . and I'm sure she'll help your . . . what's her name.

MAMA: Florence.

215 MRS. CARTER: *(turns back to bench, opens bag, takes out a pencil and an address book)* Yes, Florence. She'll have to *make* a place for her.

MAMA: Bless you, mam.

MRS. CARTER: *(holds handbag steady on rail as she uses it to write on)* Now let's see . . . the best thing to do would be to give you the telephone number . . . since you're going there.

Mama: Yes'm.

Mrs. Carter: *(writing address on paper)* Your daughter will love
her . . . and if she's a deserving girl . . .

220 Mama: *(looking down as Mrs. Carter writes)* She's a good girl. Never a bit of
trouble. Except about her husband, and neither one of them could
help that.

Mrs. Carter: *(stops writing, raises her head questioning)* Oh?

Mama: He got killed at voting time. He was a good man.

Mrs. Carter: *(embarrassed)* I guess that's worse than losing him in the
war.

Mama: We all got our troubles passing through here.

225 Mrs. Carter: *(gives her the address)* Tell your dear girl to call this number
about a week from now.

Mama: Yes, mam.

Mrs. Carter: Her experience won't matter with Melba. I know she'll
understand. I'll call her too.

Mama: Thank you, mam.

Mrs. Carter: I'll just tell her . . . no heavy washing or ironing . . . just
light cleaning and a little cooking . . . does she cook?

230 Mama: Mam? *(Slowly backs away from Mrs. Carter and sits down on bench.)*

Mrs. Carter: Don't worry, that won't matter to Melba. *(Silence, moves
around the rail to "Colored" side, leans over Mama.)* I'd take your
daughter myself, but I've got Binnie. She's been with me for years,
and I just can't let her go . . . can I?

Mama: *(looks at Mrs. Carter closely)* No, mam.

Mrs. Carter: Of course she must be steady. I couldn't ask Melba to take a
fly-by-night. *(Touches Mama's arm.)* But she'll have her own room and
bath, and above all . . . security.

Mama: *(reaches out, clutches Mrs. Carter's wrist almost pulling her off
balance)* Child!

235 Mrs. Carter: *(frightened)* You're hurting my wrist.

Mama: *(looks down, realizes how tight she's clutching her, and releases her
wrist)* I mustn't hurt you, must I.

Mrs. Carter: *(backing away rubbing her wrist)* It's all right.

Mama: *(rises)* You better get over on the other side of that rail. It's against
the law for you to be over here with me.

Mrs. Carter: *(frightened and uncomfortable)* If you think so.

240 Mama: I don't want to break the law.

Mrs. Carter: *(keeps her eye on Mama as she drifts around railing to bench on
her side, gathers overnight bag)* I know I must look a fright. The train
should be along soon. When it comes, I won't see you until New
York. These silly laws. *(Silence.)* I'm going to powder my nose. *(Exits
into "White ladies" room.)*

Porter: *(singing offstage)*

Mama: *(Sits quietly, staring in front of her . . . then looks at the address for a
moment . . . tears the paper into little bits and lets them flutter to the*

floor. *She opens the suitcase, takes out notebook, an envelope and a pencil.* *She writes a few words on the paper.)*

PORTER: *(enters with broom and dust pan)* Number 42 will be coming along in nine minutes. *(When Mama doesn't answer him, he looks up and watches her. She reaches in her bosom, unpins the check, smooths it out, places it in the envelope with the letter. She closes the suitcase.)* I said the train's coming. Where's the lady?

245 MAMA: She's in the *ladies'* room. You got a stamp?

PORTER: No. But I can get one out of the machine. Three for a dime.

MAMA: *(hands him the letter)* Put one on here and mail it for me.

PORTER: *(looks at it)* Gee . . . you writing Florence when you're going to see her?

MAMA: *(picks up the shoebox and puts it back on the bench)* You want a good lunch? It's chicken and fruit.

250 PORTER: Sure . . . thank you . . . but you won't . . .

MAMA: *(rises, paces up and down)* I ain't gonna see Florence for a long time. Might be never.

PORTER: How's that, Mrs. Whitney?

MAMA: She can be anything in the world she wants to be! That's her right. Marge can't make her turn back, Mrs. Carter can't make her turn back. *Lost My Lonely Way!* That's a book! People killing theyselves 'cause they look white but be black. They just don't know do they, Mr. Brown?

PORTER: Whatever happened don't you fret none. Life is too short.

255 MAMA: Oh, I'm gonna fret plenty! You know what I wrote Florence?

PORTER: No, mam. But you don't have to tell me.

MAMA: I said "Keep trying." . . . Oh, I'm going home.

PORTER: I'll take your bag. *(Picks up bag and starts out.)* Come on Mrs. Whitney. *(Porter exits.)*

Mama moves around to "White" side, stares at sign over door. She starts to knock on "White Ladies" door, but changes her mind. As she turns to leave, her eye catches the railing; she approaches it gently, touches it, turns, exits. Stage is empty for about six or seven seconds. Sound of train whistle is heard in the distance. Slow curtain.

Curtain

READING AND REACTING

1. What actually happens in *Florence*? Can you identify the play's exposition, major conflict, climax, and resolution?
2. *Florence* takes place in a train station. What is the significance of this setting?
3. In the waiting room, a railing separates whites from blacks; signs over the entrances and over the doors of the restrooms denote the

white and black facilities. In what way do these elements reinforce the major themes of the play?

4. *Florence* is set in the South during the late 1940s. How might the play be different if it were set in the North? If it were set today?

5. In line 17, Marge tells Mama that she had better buy some food because she "can't go to the diner." Then again in line 23, Marge says that Florence has "notions a Negro woman don't need." What situation is Marge alluding to? Find other references to this "situation" in the play.

6. Does Mrs. Carter think of herself as a racist? Do you agree with her assessment of herself?

7. What causes Mama to disagree with Mrs. Carter about her brother's book? What does this disagreement tell the audience about both characters?

8. Does Mama's view of Mrs. Carter change or remain the same as the plot develops? Why does Mama ask Mrs. Carter to help Florence? What does she learn that causes her to reject the "help" that Mrs. Carter offers?

9. What is Mama's opinion of her daughter at the beginning of the play? How does this view change by the end? In what way is Mrs. Carter responsible for this change?

10. Although the play bears her name, Florence never appears on stage. In what sense is Florence nevertheless a character in the play? Why do you think Childress names the play for her?

11. **Journal Entry** Should Mama have confronted Mrs. Carter directly? What do you think would have happened had she done so?

12. **Critical Perspective** In an analysis of Alice Childress's work, Jeanne-Marie A. Miller says, "To Childress, however, the black woman is the most heroic figure to emerge in America." At the heart of Childress's plays, Miller notes, is an ordinary woman "whose life is uneventful until circumstances force her to rise to the fullness of her strength." According to Miller, "the black woman not only transcends her own predicaments but often functions as a catalyst for change in those whose lives she touches." How does Mama fit this characterization?

Related Works: "How to Talk to Your Mother (Notes)" (p. 96), "Like a Winding Sheet" (p. 125), "Everyday Use" (p. 324), "Shopping" (p. 559), "Negro" (p. 727), "The Ballad of Rudolph Reed" (p. 932), *Fences* (p. 1745)

◊ **HENRIK IBSEN** (1828–1906) is Norway's foremost dramatist. He was born in Skien, Norway, into a prosperous family, but his father lost his fortune when Ibsen was six; when Ibsen was fifteen, he was apprenticed to an apothecary away from home and was permanently estranged from his family. He studied to enter the university and wrote plays during his apprenticeship; though he did not pass the university entrance exam, his second play, *The Warrior's Barrow*, was produced by the Christiania Theatre in 1850. He began a life in the theater, writing plays and serving as artistic director of a theatrical company. Disillusioned by the public's lack of interest in theater, he left Norway, living in Italy and Germany with his wife and son between 1864 and 1891. By the time he returned to Norway, he was famous and revered. Ibsen's most notable plays include *Brand* (1865), *Peer Gynt* (1867), *A Doll House* (1879), *Ghosts* (1881), *An Enemy of the People* (1882), *The Wild Duck* (1884), *Hedda Gabler* (1890), and *When We Dead Awaken* (1899).

A Doll House marks the beginning of Ibsen's successful realist period, during which he explored the ordinary lives of small-town people—in this case, what he called "a modern tragedy." Ibsen based the play on a true story, which closely paralleled the main events of the play: a wife borrows money to finance a trip for an ailing husband, repayment is demanded, she forges a check and is discovered. (In the real-life story, however, the husband demanded a divorce, and the wife had a nervous breakdown and was committed to a mental institution.) The issue in *A Doll House,* he said, is that there are "two kinds of moral law, [. . .] one in man and a completely different one in woman. They do not understand each other [. . .]. " Nora and Helmer destroy their marriage because they cannot comprehend or accept their differences. Though the play begins conventionally, it does not fulfill its audience's expectations for a tidy resolution; as a result, the play was not very successful when first performed. Nevertheless, the publication of *A Doll House* made Ibsen internationally famous.

CULTURAL CONTEXT ◊ During the nineteenth century, the law treated women only a little better than it did children. Not only couldn't a woman vote, but she was also considered unable to handle her own financial affairs. As a result, a woman could not borrow money in her own name, and when she married, her finances were put in the care of her husband. Moreover, for a middle-class woman, working outside the home was out of the question. Therefore, if a woman were to leave her husband, she most likely would have no way of supporting herself.

◇ ◇ ◇

HENRIK IBSEN

A Doll House

(1879)

Translated by Rolf Fjelde

CHARACTERS

TORVALD HELMER, *a lawyer*

NORA, *his wife*

DR. RANK

MRS. LINDE

A DELIVERY BOY

NILS KROGSTAD, *a bank clerk*

THE HELMERS' THREE SMALL

    CHILDREN

ANNE-MARIE, *their nurse*

HELENE, *a maid*

The action takes place in Helmer's residence.

ACT I

A comfortable room, tastefully but not expensively furnished. A door to the right in the back wall leads to the entryway; another to the left leads to Helmer's study. Between these doors, a piano. Midway in the left-hand wall a door, and further back a window. Near the window a round table with an armchair and a small sofa. In the right-hand wall, toward the rear, a door, and nearer the foreground a porcelain stove with two armchairs and a rocking chair beside it. Between the stove and the side door, a small table. Engravings on the walls. An étagère with china figures and other small art objects; a small bookcase with richly bound books; the floor carpeted; a fire burning in the stove. It is a winter day.

A bell rings in the entryway; shortly after we hear the door being unlocked. Nora comes into the room, humming happily to herself; she is wearing street clothes and carries an armload of packages, which she puts down on the table to the right. She has left the hall door open; and through it a Delivery Boy is seen, holding a Christmas tree and a basket, which he gives to the Maid who let them in.

NORA: Hide the tree well, Helene. The children mustn't get a glimpse of it till this evening, after it's trimmed. *(To the Delivery Boy, taking out her purse.)* How much?

DELIVERY BOY: Fifty, ma'am.

NORA: There's a crown. No, keep the change. *(The Boy thanks her and leaves. Nora shuts the door. She laughs softly to herself while taking off her street things. Drawing a bag of macaroons from her pocket, she eats a couple, then steals over and listens at her husband's study door.)* Yes, he's home. *(Hums again as she moves to the table right.)*

HELMER: *(from the study)* Is that my little lark twittering out there?

5   NORA: *(busy opening some packages)* Yes, it is.

HELMER: Is that my squirrel rummaging around?

NORA: Yes!

HELMER: When did my squirrel get in?

NORA: Just now. *(Putting the macaroon bag in her pocket and wiping her mouth.)* Do come in, Torvald, and see what I've bought.

10 HELMER: Can't be disturbed. *(After a moment he opens the door and peers in, pen in hand.)* Bought, you say? All that there? Has the little spendthrift been out throwing money around again?

NORA: Oh, but Torvald, this year we really should let ourselves go a bit. It's the first Christmas we haven't had to economize.

HELMER: But you know we can't go squandering.

NORA: Oh yes, Torvald, we can squander a little now. Can't we? Just a tiny, wee bit. Now that you've got a big salary and are going to make piles and piles of money.

HELMER: Yes—starting New Year's. But then it's a full three months till the raise comes through.

15 NORA: Pooh! We can borrow that long.

HELMER: Nora! *(Goes over and playfully takes her by the ear.)* Are your scatterbrains off again? What if today I borrowed a thousand crowns, and you squandered them over Christmas week, and then on New Year's Eve a roof tile fell on my head, and I lay there—

NORA: *(putting her hand on his mouth)* Oh! Don't say such things!

HELMER: Yes, but what if it happened—then what?

NORA: If anything so awful happened, then it just wouldn't matter if I had debts or not.

20 HELMER: Well, but the people I'd borrowed from?

NORA: Them? Who cares about them! They're strangers.

HELMER: Nora, Nora, how like a woman! No, but seriously, Nora, you know what I think about that. No debts! Never borrow! Something of freedom's lost—and something of beauty, too—from a home that's founded on borrowing and debt. We've made a brave stand up to now, the two of us; and we'll go right on like that the little while we have to.

NORA: *(going toward the stove)* Yes, whatever you say, Torvald.

HELMER: *(following her)* Now, now, the little lark's wings mustn't droop. Come on, don't be a sulky squirrel. *(Taking out his wallet.)* Nora, guess what I have here.

25 NORA: *(turning quickly)* Money!

HELMER: There, see. *(Hands her some notes.)* Good grief, I know how costs go up in a house at Christmastime.

NORA: Ten—twenty—thirty—forty. Oh, thank you, Torvald; I can manage no end on this.

HELMER: You really will have to.

NORA: Oh yes, I promise I will! But come here so I can show you everything I bought. And so cheap! Look, new clothes for Ivar here—and a sword. Here a horse and a trumpet for Bob. And a doll and a doll's bed here for Emmy; they're nothing much, but she'll tear them to bits in no time anyway. And here I have dress material and handkerchiefs for the maids. Old Anne-Marie really deserves something more.

30 HELMER: And what's in that package there?

NORA: (with a cry) Torvald, no! You can't see that till tonight!

HELMER: I see. But tell me now, you little prodigal, what have you thought of for yourself?

NORA: For myself? Oh, I don't want anything at all.

HELMER: Of course you do. Tell me just what—within reason—you'd most like to have.

35 NORA: I honestly don't know. Oh, listen, Torvald—

HELMER: Well?

NORA: (fumbling at his coat buttons, without looking at him) If you want to give me something, then maybe you could—you could—

HELMER: Come on, out with it.

NORA: (hurriedly) You could give me money, Torvald. No more than you think you can spare; then one of these days I'll buy something with it.

40 HELMER: But Nora—

NORA: Oh, please, Torvald darling, do that! I beg you, please. Then I could hang the bills in pretty gilt paper on the Christmas tree. Wouldn't that be fun?

HELMER: What are those little birds called that always fly through their fortunes?

NORA: Oh yes, spendthrifts; I know all that. But let's do as I say, Torvald; then I'll have time to decide what I really need most. That's very sensible, isn't it?

HELMER: (smiling) Yes, very—that is, if you actually hung onto the money I give you, and you actually used it to buy yourself something. But it goes for the house and for all sorts of foolish things, and then I only have to lay out some more.

45 NORA: Oh, but Torvald—

HELMER: Don't deny it, my dear little Nora. (Putting his arm around her waist.) Spendthrifts are sweet, but they use up a frightful amount of money. It's incredible what it costs a man to feed such birds.

NORA: Oh, how can you say that! Really, I save everything I can.

HELMER: (laughing) Yes, that's the truth. Everything you can. But that's nothing at all.

NORA: (humming, with a smile of quiet satisfaction) Hm, if you only knew what expenses we larks and squirrels have, Torvald.

50 HELMER: You're an odd little one. Exactly the way your father was. You're never at a loss for scaring up money; but the moment you have it, it runs right out through your fingers; you never know what you've done with it. Well, one takes you as you are. It's deep in your blood. Yes, these things are hereditary, Nora.

NORA: Ah, I could wish I'd inherited many of Papa's qualities.

HELMER: And I couldn't wish you anything but just what you are, my sweet little lark. But wait; it seems to me you have a very—what should I call it?—a very suspicious look today—

NORA: I do?

HELMER: You certainly do. Look me straight in the eye.

55 NORA: *(looking at him)* Well?

HELMER: *(shaking an admonitory finger)* Surely my sweet tooth hasn't been running riot in town today, has she?

NORA: No. Why do you imagine that?

HELMER: My sweet tooth really didn't make a little detour through the confectioner's?

NORA: No, I assure you, Torvald—

60 HELMER: Hasn't nibbled some pastry?

NORA: No, not at all.

HELMER: Nor even munched a macaroon or two?

NORA: No, Torvald, I assure you, really—

HELMER: There, there now. Of course I'm only joking.

65 NORA: *(going to the table, right)* You know I could never think of going against you.

HELMER: No, I understand that; and you *have* given me your word. *(Going over to her.)* Well, you keep your little Christmas secrets to yourself, Nora darling. I expect they'll come to light this evening, when the tree is lit.

NORA: Did you remember to ask Dr. Rank?

HELMER: No. But there's no need for that; it's assumed he'll be dining with us. All the same, I'll ask him when he stops by here this morning. I've ordered some fine wine. Nora, you can't imagine how I'm looking forward to this evening.

NORA: So am I. And what fun for the children, Torvald!

70 HELMER: Ah, it's so gratifying to know that one's gotten a safe, secure job, and with a comfortable salary. It's a great satisfaction, isn't it?

NORA: Oh, it's wonderful!

HELMER: Remember last Christmas? Three whole weeks before, you shut yourself in every evening till long after midnight, making flowers for the Christmas tree, and all the other decorations to surprise us. Ugh, that was the dullest time I've ever lived through.

NORA: It wasn't at all dull for me.

HELMER: *(smiling)* But the outcome *was* pretty sorry, Nora.

75 NORA: Oh, don't tease me with that again. How could I help it that the cat came in and tore everything to shreds.

HELMER: No, poor thing, you certainly couldn't. You wanted so much to please us all, and that's what counts. But it's just as well that the hard times are past.

NORA: Yes, it's really wonderful.

HELMER: Now I don't have to sit here alone, boring myself, and you don't have to tire your precious eyes and your fair little delicate hands—

NORA: *(clapping her hands)* No, is it really true, Torvald, I don't have to? Oh, how wonderfully lovely to hear! *(Taking his arm.)* Now I'll tell you just how I've thought we should plan things. Right after Christmas— *(The doorbell rings.)* Oh, the bell. *(Straightening the room up a bit.)* Somebody would have to come. What a bore!

80 HELMER: I'm not at home to visitors, don't forget.

MAID: *(from the hall doorway)* Ma'am, a lady to see you—

NORA: All right, let her come in.

MAID: *(to Helmer)* And the doctor's just come too.

HELMER: Did he go right to my study?

85 MAID: Yes, he did.

Helmer goes into his room. The Maid shows in Mrs. Linde, dressed in traveling clothes, and shuts the door after her.

MRS. LINDE: *(in a dispirited and somewhat hesitant voice)* Hello, Nora.

NORA: *(uncertain)* Hello—

MRS. LINDE: You don't recognize me.

NORA: No, I don't know—but wait, I think—*(Exclaiming.)* What! Kristine! Is it really you?

90 MRS. LINDE: Yes, it's me.

NORA: *Kristine!* To think I didn't recognize you. But then, how could I? *(More quietly.)* How you've changed, Kristine!

MRS. LINDE: Yes, no doubt I have. In nine—ten long years.

NORA: Is it so long since we met! Yes, it's all of that. Oh, these last eight years have been a happy time, believe me. And so now you've come in to town, too. Made the long trip in the winter. That took courage.

MRS. LINDE: I just got here by ship this morning.

95 NORA: To enjoy yourself over Christmas, of course. Oh, how lovely! Yes, enjoy ourselves, we'll do that. But take your coat off. You're not still cold? *(Helping her.)* There now, let's get cozy here by the stove. No, the easy chair there! I'll take the rocker here. *(Seizing her hands.)* Yes, now you have your old look again; it was only in that first moment. You're a bit more pale, Kristine—and maybe a bit thinner.

MRS. LINDE: And much, much older, Nora.

NORA: Yes, perhaps a bit older; a tiny, tiny bit; not much at all. *(Stopping short; suddenly serious.)* Oh, but thoughtless me, to sit here, chattering away. Sweet, good Kristine, can you forgive me?

MRS. LINDE: What do you mean, Nora?

NORA: *(softly)* Poor Kristine, you've become a widow.

100 MRS. LINDE: Yes, three years ago.

NORA: Oh, I knew it, of course; I read it in the papers. Oh, Kristine, you must believe me; I often thought of writing you then, but I kept postponing it, and something always interfered.

MRS. LINDE: Nora dear, I understand completely.

NORA: No, it was awful of me, Kristine. You poor thing, how much you must have gone through. And he left you nothing?

MRS. LINDE: No.

105 NORA: And no children?

MRS. LINDE: No.

NORA: Nothing at all, then?

MRS. LINDE: Not even a sense of loss to feed on.

NORA: *(looking incredulously at her)* But Kristine, how could that be?

110 MRS. LINDE: *(smiling wearily and smoothing her hair)* Oh, sometimes it happens, Nora.

NORA: So completely alone. How terribly hard that must be for you. I have three lovely children. You can't see them now; they're out with the maid. But now you must tell me everything—

MRS. LINDE: No, no, no, tell me about yourself.

NORA: No, you begin. Today I don't want to be selfish. I want to think only of you today. But there *is* something I must tell you. Did you hear of the wonderful luck we had recently?

MRS. LINDE: No, what's that?

115 NORA: My husband's been made manager in the bank, just think!

MRS. LINDE: Your husband? How marvelous!

NORA: Isn't it? Being a lawyer is such an uncertain living, you know, especially if one won't touch any cases that aren't clean and decent. And of course Torvald would never do that, and I'm with him completely there. Oh, we're simply delighted, believe me! He'll join the bank right after New Year's and start getting a huge salary and lots of commissions. From now on we can live quite differently—just as we want. Oh, Kristine, I feel so light and happy! Won't it be lovely to have stacks of money and not a care in the world?

MRS. LINDE: Well, anyway, it would be lovely to have enough for necessities.

NORA: No, not just for necessities, but stacks and stacks of money!

120 MRS. LINDE: *(smiling)* Nora, Nora, aren't you sensible yet? Back in school you were such a free spender.

NORA: *(with a quiet laugh)* Yes, that's what Torvald still says. *(Shaking her finger.)* But "Nora, Nora" isn't as silly as you all think. Really, we've been in no position for me to go squandering. We've had to work, both of us.

MRS. LINDE: You too?

NORA: Yes, at odd jobs—needlework, crocheting, embroidery, and such— *(casually)* and other things too. You remember that Torvald left the department when we were married? There was no chance of promotion in his office, and of course he needed to earn more money. But that first year he drove himself terribly. He took on all kinds of extra work that kept him going morning and night. It wore him down, and then he fell deathly ill. The doctors said it was essential for him to travel south.

MRS. LINDE: Yes, didn't you spend a whole year in Italy?

125   **Nora:** That's right. It wasn't easy to get away, you know. Ivar had just been born. But of course we had to go. Oh, that was a beautiful trip, and it saved Torvald's life. But it cost a frightful sum, Kristine.

    Mrs. Linde: I can well imagine.

    Nora: Four thousand, eight hundred crowns it cost. That's really a lot of money.

    Mrs. Linde: But it's lucky you had it when you needed it.

    Nora: Well, as it was, we got it from Papa.

130   **Mrs. Linde:** I see. It was just about the time your father died.

    Nora: Yes, just about then. And, you know, I couldn't make that trip out to nurse him. I had to stay here, expecting Ivar any moment, and with my poor sick Torvald to care for. Dearest Papa, I never saw him again, Kristine. Oh, that was the worst time I've known in all my marriage.

    Mrs. Linde: I know how you loved him. And then you went off to Italy?

    Nora: Yes. We had the means now, and the doctors urged us. So we left a month after.

    Mrs. Linde: And your husband came back completely cured?

135   **Nora:** Sound as a drum!

    Mrs. Linde: But—the doctor?

    Nora: Who?

    Mrs. Linde: I thought the maid said he was a doctor, the man who came in with me.

    Nora: Yes, that was Dr. Rank—but he's not making a sick call. He's our closest friend, and he stops by at least once a day. No, Torvald hasn't had a sick moment since, and the children are fit and strong, and I am, too. *(Jumping up and clapping her hands.)* Oh, dear God, Kristine, what a lovely thing to live and be happy! But how disgusting of me— I'm talking of nothing but my own affairs. *(Sits on a stool close by Kristine, arms resting across her knees.)* Oh, don't be angry with me! Tell me, is it really true that you weren't in love with your husband? Why did you marry him, then?

140   **Mrs. Linde:** My mother was still alive, but bedridden and helpless—and I had my two younger brothers to look after. In all conscience, I didn't think I could turn him down.

    Nora: No, you were right there. But was he rich at the time?

    Mrs. Linde: He was very well off, I'd say. But the business was shaky, Nora. When he died, it all fell apart, and nothing was left.

    Nora: And then—?

    Mrs. Linde: Yes, so I had to scrape up a living with a little shop and a little teaching and whatever else I could find. The last three years have been like one endless workday without a rest for me. Now it's over, Nora. My poor mother doesn't need me, for she's passed on. Nor the boys, either; they're working now and can take care of themselves.

145   **Nora:** How free you must feel—

    Mrs. Linde: No—only unspeakably empty. Nothing to live for now. *(Standing up anxiously.)* That's why I couldn't take it any longer out in that desolate hole. Maybe here it'll be easier to find something to do and keep my mind occupied. If I could only be lucky enough to get a steady job, some office work—

NORA: Oh, but Kristine, that's so dreadfully tiring, and you already look so tired. It would be much better for you if you could go off to a bathing resort.

MRS. LINDE: *(going toward the window)* I have no father to give me travel money, Nora.

NORA: *(rising)* Oh, don't be angry with me.

150 MRS. LINDE: *(going to her)* Nora dear, don't you be angry with me. The worst of my kind of situation is all the bitterness that's stored away. No one to work for, and yet you're always having to snap up your opportunities. You have to live; and so you grow selfish. When you told me the happy change in your lot, do you know I was delighted less for your sakes than for mine?

NORA: How so? Oh, I see. You think Torvald could do something for you.

MRS. LINDE: Yes, that's what I thought.

NORA: And he will, Kristine! Just leave it to me; I'll bring it up so delicately—find something attractive to humor him with. Oh, I'm so eager to help you.

MRS. LINDE: How very kind of you, Nora, to be so concerned over me—doubly kind, considering you really know so little of life's burdens yourself.

155 NORA: I—? I know so little—?

MRS. LINDE: *(smiling)* Well my heavens—a little needlework and such— Nora, you're just a child.

NORA: *(tossing her head and pacing the floor)* You don't have to act so superior.

MRS. LINDE: Oh?

NORA: You're just like the others. You all think I'm incapable of anything serious—

160 MRS. LINDE: Come now—

NORA: That I've never had to face the raw world.

MRS. LINDE: Nora dear, you've just been telling me all your troubles.

NORA: Hm! Trivial! *(Quietly.)* I haven't told you the big thing.

MRS. LINDE: Big thing? What do you mean?

165 NORA: You look down on me so, Kristine, but you shouldn't. You're proud that you worked so long and hard for your mother.

MRS. LINDE: I don't look down on a soul. But it *is* true: I'm proud—and happy, too—to think it was given to me to make my mother's last days almost free of care.

NORA: And you're also proud thinking of what you've done for your brothers.

MRS. LINDE: I feel I've a right to be.

NORA: I agree. But listen to this, Kristine—I've also got something to be proud and happy for.

170 MRS. LINDE: I don't doubt it. But whatever do you mean?

Nora: Not so loud. What if Torvald heard! He mustn't, not for anything in the world. Nobody must know, Kristine. No one but you.

Mrs. Linde: But what is it, then?

Nora: Come here. *(Drawing her down beside her on the sofa.)* It's true—I've also got something to be proud and happy for. I'm the one who saved Torvald's life.

Mrs. Linde: Saved—? Saved how?

175 Nora: I told you about the trip to Italy. Torvald never would have lived if he hadn't gone south—

Mrs. Linde: Of course; your father gave you the means—

Nora: *(smiling)* That's what Torvald and all the rest think, but—

Mrs. Linde: But—?

Nora: Papa didn't give us a pin. I was the one who raised the money.

180 Mrs. Linde: You? That whole amount?

Nora: Four thousand, eight hundred crowns. What do you say to that?

Mrs. Linde: But Nora, how was it possible? Did you win the lottery?

Nora: *(disdainfully)* The lottery? Pooh! No art to that.

Mrs. Linde: But where did you get it from then?

185 Nora: *(humming, with a mysterious smile)* Hmm, tra-la-la-la.

Mrs. Linde: Because you couldn't have borrowed it.

Nora: No? Why not?

Mrs. Linde: A wife can't borrow without her husband's consent.

Nora: *(tossing her head)* Oh, but a wife with a little business sense, a wife who knows how to manage—

190 Mrs. Linde: Nora, I simply don't understand—

Nora: You don't have to. Whoever said I *borrowed* the money? I could have gotten it other ways. *(Throwing herself back on the sofa.)* I could have gotten it from some admirer or other. After all, a girl with my ravishing appeal—

Mrs. Linde: You lunatic.

Nora: I'll bet you're eaten up with curiosity, Kristine.

Mrs. Linde: Now listen here, Nora—you haven't done something indiscreet?

195 Nora: *(sitting up again)* Is it indiscreet to save your husband's life?

Mrs. Linde: I think it's indiscreet that without his knowledge you—

Nora: But that's the point: he mustn't know! My Lord, can't you understand? He mustn't ever know the close call he had. It was to *me* the doctors came to say his life was in danger—that nothing could save him but a stay in the south. Didn't I try strategy then! I began talking about how lovely it would be for me to travel abroad like other young wives; I begged and I cried; I told him please to remember my condition, to be kind and indulge me; and then I dropped a hint that he could easily take out a loan. But at that, Kristine, he nearly exploded. He said I was frivolous, and it was his duty as man of the house not to indulge me in whims and fancies—as I think he called them. Aha, I thought, now you'll just have to be saved—and that's when I saw my chance.

MRS. LINDE: And your father never told Torvald the money wasn't from him?

NORA: No, never. Papa died right about then. I'd considered bringing him into my secret and begging him never to tell. But he was too sick at the time—and then, sadly, it didn't matter.

200 MRS. LINDE: And you've never confided in your husband since?

NORA: For heaven's sake, no! Are you serious? He's so strict on that subject. Besides—Torvald, with all his masculine pride—how painfully humiliating for him if he ever found out he was in debt to me. That would just ruin our relationship. Our beautiful, happy home would never be the same.

MRS. LINDE: Won't you ever tell him?

NORA: *(thoughtfully, half smiling)* Yes—maybe sometime, years from now, when I'm no longer so attractive. Don't laugh! I only mean when Torvald loves me less than now, when he stops enjoying my dancing and dressing up and reciting for him. Then it might be wise to have something in reserve—*(Breaking off.)* How ridiculous! That'll never happen—Well, Kristine, what do you think of my big secret? I'm capable of something too, hm? You can imagine, of course, how this thing hangs over me. It really hasn't been easy meeting the payments on time. In the business world there's what they call quarterly interest and what they call amortization, and these are always so terribly hard to manage. I've had to skimp a little here and there, wherever I could, you know. I could hardly spare anything from my house allowance, because Torvald has to live well. I couldn't let the children go poorly dressed; whatever I got for them, I felt I had to use up completely—the darlings!

MRS. LINDE: Poor Nora, so it had to come out of your own budget, then?

205 NORA: Yes, of course. But I was the one most responsible, too. Every time Torvald gave me money for new clothes and such, I never used more than half; always bought the simplest, cheapest outfits. It was a godsend that everything looks so well on me that Torvald never noticed. But it did weigh me down at times, Kristine. It *is* such a joy to wear fine things. You understand.

MRS. LINDE: Oh, of course.

NORA: And then I found other ways of making money. Last winter I was lucky enough to get a lot of copying to do. I locked myself in and sat writing every evening till late in the night. Ah, I was tired so often, dead tired. But still it was wonderful fun, sitting and working like that, earning money. It was almost like being a man.

MRS. LINDE: But how much have you paid off this way so far?

NORA: That's hard to say, exactly. These accounts, you know, aren't easy to figure. I only know that I've paid out all I could scrape together. Time and again I haven't known where to turn. *(Smiling.)* Then I'd sit here dreaming of a rich old gentleman who had fallen in love with me—

210 MRS. LINDE: What! Who is he?

NORA: Oh, really! And that he'd died, and when his will was opened, there in big letters it said, "All my fortune shall be paid over in cash, immediately, to that enchanting Mrs. Nora Helmer."

MRS. LINDE: But Nora dear—who *was* this gentleman?

NORA: Good grief, can't you understand? The old man never existed; that was only something I'd dream up time and again whenever I was at my wits' end for money. But it makes no difference now; the old fossil can go where he pleases for all I care; I don't need him or his will— because now I'm free. *(Jumping up.)* Oh, how lovely to think of that, Kristine! Carefree! To know you're carefree, utterly carefree; to be able to romp and play with the children, and to keep up a beautiful, charming home—everything just the way Torvald likes it! And think, spring is coming, with big blue skies. Maybe we can travel a little then. Maybe I'll see the ocean again. Oh yes, it *is* so marvelous to live and be happy!

The front doorbell rings.

MRS. LINDE: *(rising)* There's the bell. It's probably best that I go.

215 NORA: No, stay. No one's expected. It must be for Torvald.

MAID: *(from the hall doorway)* Excuse me, ma'am—there's a gentleman here to see Mr. Helmer, but I didn't know—since the doctor's with him—

NORA: Who is the gentleman?

KROGSTAD: *(from the doorway)* It's me, Mrs. Helmer.

Mrs. Linde starts and turns away toward the window.

NORA: *(stepping toward him, tense, her voice a whisper)* You? What is it? Why do you want to speak to my husband?

220 KROGSTAD: Bank business—after a fashion. I have a small job in the investment bank, and I hear now your husband is going to be our chief—

NORA: In other words, it's—

KROGSTAD: Just dry business, Mrs. Helmer. Nothing but that.

NORA: Yes, then please be good enough to step into the study. *(She nods indifferently as she sees him out by the hall door, then returns and begins stirring up the stove.)*

MRS. LINDE: Nora—who was that man?

225 NORA: That was a Mr. Krogstad—a lawyer.

MRS. LINDE: Then it really was him.

NORA: Do you know that person?

MRS. LINDE: I did once—many years ago. For a time he was a law clerk in our town.

NORA: Yes, he's been that.

230 MRS. LINDE: How he's changed.

NORA: I understand he had a very unhappy marriage.

MRS. LINDE: He's a widower now.

NORA: With a number of children. There now, it's burning. *(She closes the stove door and moves the rocker a bit to one side.)*

MRS. LINDE: They say he has a hand in all kinds of business.

235 NORA: Oh? That may be true: I wouldn't know. But let's not think about business. It's so dull.

Dr. Rank enters from Helmer's study.

RANK: *(still in the doorway)* No, no, really—I don't want to intrude, I'd just as soon talk a little while with your wife. *(Shuts the door, then notices Mrs. Linde.)* Oh, beg pardon. I'm intruding here too.

NORA: No, not at all. *(Introducing him.)* Dr. Rank, Mrs. Linde.

RANK: Well now, that's a name much heard in this house. I believe I passed the lady on the stairs as I came.

MRS. LINDE: Yes, I take the stairs very slowly. They're rather hard on me.

240 RANK: Uh-hm, some touch of internal weakness?

MRS. LINDE: More overexertion, I'd say.

RANK: Nothing else? Then you're probably here in town to rest up in a round of parties?

MRS. LINDE: I'm here to look for work.

RANK: Is that the best cure for overexertion?

245 MRS. LINDE: One has to live, Doctor.

RANK: Yes, there's a common prejudice to that effect.

NORA: Oh, come on, Dr. Rank—you really do want to live yourself.

RANK: Yes, I really do. Wretched as I am, I'll gladly prolong my torment indefinitely. All my patients feel like that. And it's quite the same, too, with the morally sick. Right at this moment there's one of those moral invalids in there with Helmer—

MRS. LINDE: *(softly)* Ah!

250 NORA: Who do you mean?

RANK: Oh, it's a lawyer, Krogstad, a type you wouldn't know. His character is rotten to the root—but even he began chattering all-importantly about how he had to *live.*

NORA: Oh? What did he want to talk to Torvald about?

RANK: I really don't know. I only heard something about the bank.

NORA: I didn't know that Krog—that this man Krogstad had anything to do with the bank.

255 RANK: Yes, he's gotten some kind of berth down there. *(To Mrs. Linde.)* I don't know if you also have, in your neck of the woods, a type of person who scuttles about breathlessly, sniffing out hints of moral corruption, and then maneuvers his victim into some sort of key position where he can keep an eye on him. It's the healthy these days that are out in the cold.

MRS. LINDE: All the same, it's the sick who most need to be taken in.

RANK: *(with a shrug)* Yes, there we have it. That's the concept that's turning society into a sanatorium.

Nora, lost in her thoughts, breaks out into quiet laughter and claps her hands.

RANK: Why do you laugh at that? Do you have any real idea of what society is?

NORA: What do I care about dreary old society? I was laughing at something quite different—something terribly funny. Tell me, Doctor—is everyone who works in the bank dependent now on Torvald?

260 RANK: Is that what you find so terribly funny?

NORA: *(smiling and humming)* Never mind, never mind! *(Pacing the floor.)* Yes, that's really immensely amusing: that we—that Torvald has so much power now over all those people. *(Taking the bag out of her pocket.)* Dr. Rank, a little macaroon on that?

RANK: See here, macaroons! I thought they were contraband here.

NORA: Yes, but these are some that Kristine gave me.

MRS. LINDE: What? I—?

265 NORA: Now, now, don't be afraid. You couldn't possibly know that Torvald had forbidden them. You see, he's worried they'll ruin my teeth. But hmp! Just this once! Isn't that so, Dr. Rank? Help yourself! *(Puts a macaroon in his mouth.)* And you too, Kristine. And I'll also have one, only a little one—or two, at the most. *(Walking about again.)* Now I'm really tremendously happy. Now there's just one last thing in the world that I have an enormous desire to do.

RANK: Well! And what's that?

NORA: It's something I have such a consuming desire to say so Torvald could hear.

RANK: And why can't you say it?

NORA: I don't dare. It's quite shocking.

270 MRS. LINDE: Shocking?

RANK: Well, then it isn't advisable. But in front of us you certainly can. What do you have such a desire to say so Torvald could hear?

NORA: I have such a huge desire to say—to hell and be damned!

RANK: Are you crazy?

MRS. LINDE: My goodness, Nora!

275 RANK: Go on, say it. Here he is.

NORA: *(hiding the macaroon bag)* Shh, shh, shh!

Helmer comes in from his study, hat in hand, overcoat over his arm.

NORA: *(going toward him)* Well, Torvald dear, are you through with him?

HELMER: Yes, he just left.

NORA: Let me introduce you—this is Kristine, who's arrived here in town.

280 HELMER: Kristine—? I'm sorry, but I don't know—

NORA: Mrs. Linde, Torvald dear. Mrs. Kristine Linde.

HELMER: Of course. A childhood friend of my wife's, no doubt?

MRS. LINDE: Yes, we knew each other in those days.

NORA: And just think, she made the long trip down here in order to talk with you.

285 HELMER: What's this?

MRS. LINDE: Well, not exactly—

NORA: You see, Kristine is remarkably clever in office work, and so she's terribly eager to come under a capable man's supervision and add more to what she already knows—

HELMER: Very wise, Mrs. Linde.

NORA: And then when she heard that you'd become a bank manager—the story was wired out to the papers—then she came in as fast as she could and—Really, Torvald, for my sake you can do a little something for Kristine, can't you?

290 HELMER: Yes, it's not at all impossible. Mrs. Linde, I suppose you're a widow?

MRS. LINDE: Yes.

HELMER: Any experience in office work?

MRS. LINDE: Yes, a good deal.

HELMER: Well, it's quite likely that I can make an opening for you—

295 NORA: *(clapping her hands)* You see, you see!

HELMER: You've come at a lucky moment, Mrs. Linde.

MRS. LINDE: Oh, how can I thank you?

HELMER: Not necessary. *(Putting his overcoat on.)* But today you'll have to excuse me—

RANK: Wait, I'll go with you. *(He fetches his coat from the hall and warms it at the stove.)*

300 NORA: Don't stay out long, dear.

HELMER: An hour; no more.

NORA: Are you going too, Kristine?

MRS. LINDE: *(putting on her winter garments)* Yes, I have to see about a room now.

HELMER: Then perhaps we can all walk together.

305 NORA: *(helping her)* What a shame we're so cramped here, but it's quite impossible for us to—

MRS. LINDE: Oh, don't even think of it! Good-bye, Nora dear, and thanks for everything.

NORA: Good-bye for now. Of course you'll be back this evening. And you too, Dr. Rank. What? If you're well enough? Oh, you've got to be! Wrap up tight now.

In a ripple of small talk the company moves out into the hall; children's voices are heard outside on the steps.

NORA: There they are! There they are! *(She runs to open the door. The children come in with their nurse, Anne-Marie.)* Come in, come in! *(Bends down and kisses them.)* Oh, you darlings—! Look at them, Kristine. Aren't they lovely!

Rank: No loitering in the draft here.

310 Helmer: Come, Mrs. Linde—this place is unbearable now for anyone but
mothers.

*Dr. Rank, Helmer, and Mrs. Linde go down the stairs. Anne-Marie goes into the
living room with the children. Nora follows, after closing the hall door.*

Nora: How fresh and strong you look. Oh, such red cheeks you have! Like
apples and roses. *(The children interrupt her throughout the following.)*
And it was so much fun? That's wonderful. Really? You pulled both
Emmy and Bob on the sled? Imagine, all together! Yes, you're a clever
boy, Ivar. Oh, let me hold her a bit, Anne-Marie. My sweet little doll
baby! *(Takes the smallest from the nurse and dances with her.)* Yes, yes,
Mama will dance with Bob as well. What? Did you throw snowballs?
Oh, if I'd only been there! No, don't bother, Anne-Marie—I'll undress
them myself. Oh yes, let me. It's such fun. Go in and rest; you look
half frozen. There's hot coffee waiting for you on the stove. *(The
nurse goes into the room to the left. Nora takes the children's winter things
off, throwing them about, while the children talk to her all at once.)* Is that
so? A big dog chased you? But it didn't bite? No, dogs never bite
little, lovely doll babies. Don't peek in the packages, Ivar! What is it?
Yes, wouldn't you like to know. No, no, it's an ugly something. Well?
Shall we play? What shall we play? Hide-and-seek? Yes, let's play
hide-and-seek. Bob must hide first. I must? Yes, let me hide first.
*(Laughing and shouting, she and the children play in and out of the living
room and the adjoining room to the right. At last Nora hides under the
table. The children come storming in, search, but cannot find her, then
hear her muffled laughter, dash over to the table, lift the cloth up and
find her. Wild shouting. She creeps forward as if to scare them. More
shouts. Meanwhile, a knock at the hall door; no one has noticed it. Now
the door half opens, and Krogstad appears. He waits a moment; the game
goes on.)*

Krogstad: Beg pardon, Mrs. Helmer—

Nora: *(with a strangled cry, turning and scrambling to her knees)* Oh! What
do you want?

Krogstad: Excuse me. The outer door was ajar; it must be someone forgot
to shut it—

315 Nora: *(rising)* My husband isn't home, Mr. Krogstad.

Krogstad: I know that.

Nora: Yes—then what do you want here?

Krogstad: A word with you.

Nora: With—? *(To the children, quietly.)* Go in to Anne-Marie. What? No,
the strange man won't hurt Mama. When he's gone, we'll play some
more. *(She leads the children into the room to the left and shuts the door
after them. Then, tense and nervous.)* You want to speak to me?

320 Krogstad: Yes, I want to.

Nora: Today? But it's not yet the first of the month—

KROGSTAD: No, it's Christmas Eve. It's going to be up to you how merry a
  Christmas you have.

NORA: What is it you want? Today I absolutely can't—

KROGSTAD: We won't talk about that till later. This is something else. You
  do have a moment to spare, I suppose?

325 NORA: Oh yes, of course—I do, except—

KROGSTAD: Good. I was sitting over at Olsen's Restaurant when I saw your
  husband go down the street—

NORA: Yes?

KROGSTAD: With a lady.

NORA: Yes. So?

330 KROGSTAD: If you'll pardon my asking: wasn't that lady a Mrs. Linde?

NORA: Yes.

KROGSTAD: Just now come into town?

NORA: Yes, today.

KROGSTAD: She's a good friend of yours?

335 NORA: Yes, she is. But I don't see—

KROGSTAD: I also knew her once.

NORA: I'm aware of that.

KROGSTAD: Oh? You know all about it. I thought so. Well, then let me ask
  you short and sweet: is Mrs. Linde getting a job in the bank?

NORA: What makes you think you can cross-examine me, Mr. Krogstad—
  you, one of my husband's employees? But since you ask, you might as
  well know—yes, Mrs. Linde's going to be taken on at the bank. And
  I'm the one who spoke for her, Mr. Krogstad. Now you know.

340 KROGSTAD: So I guessed right.

NORA: (pacing up and down) Oh, one does have a tiny bit of influence, I
  should hope. Just because I am a woman, don't think it means that—
  When one has a subordinate position, Mr. Krogstad, one really ought
  to be careful about pushing somebody who—hm—

KROGSTAD: Who has influence?

NORA: That's right.

KROGSTAD: (in a different tone) Mrs. Helmer, would you be good enough to
  use your influence on my behalf?

345 NORA: What? What do you mean?

KROGSTAD: Would you please make sure that I keep my subordinate
  position in the bank?

NORA: What does that mean? Who's thinking of taking away your
  position?

KROGSTAD: Oh, don't play the innocent with me. I'm quite aware that
  your friend would hardly relish the chance of running into me again;
  and I'm also aware now whom I can thank for being turned out.

NORA: But I promise you—

350 KROGSTAD: Yes, yes, yes, to the point: there's still time, and I'm advising
  you to use your influence to prevent it.

NORA: But Mr. Krogstad, I have absolutely no influence.

KROGSTAD: You haven't? I thought you were just saying—

NORA: You shouldn't take me so literally. I! How can you believe that I have any such influence over my husband?

KROGSTAD: Oh, I've known your husband from our student days. I don't think the great bank manager's more steadfast than any other married man.

355 NORA: You speak insolently about my husband, and I'll show you the door.

KROGSTAD: The lady has spirit.

NORA: I'm not afraid of you any longer. After New Year's, I'll soon be done with the whole business.

KROGSTAD: *(restraining himself)* Now listen to me, Mrs. Helmer. If necessary, I'll fight for my little job in the bank as if it were life itself.

NORA: Yes, so it seems.

360 KROGSTAD: It's not just a matter of income; that's the least of it. It's something else—All right, out with it! Look, this is the thing. You know, just like all the others, of course, that once, a good many years ago, I did something rather rash.

NORA: I've heard rumors to that effect.

KROGSTAD: The case never got into court; but all the same, every door was closed in my face from then on. So I took up those various activities you know about. I had to grab hold somewhere; and I dare say I haven't been among the worst. But now I want to drop all that. My boys are growing up. For their sakes, I'll have to win back as much respect as possible here in town. That job in the bank was like the first rung in my ladder. And now your husband wants to kick me right back down in the mud again.

NORA: But for heaven's sake, Mr. Krogstad, it's simply not in my power to help you.

KROGSTAD: That's because you haven't the will to—but I have the means to make you.

365 NORA: You certainly won't tell my husband that I owe you money?

KROGSTAD: Hm—what if I told him that?

NORA: That would be shameful of you. *(Nearly in tears.)* This secret—my joy and my pride—that he should learn it in such a crude and disgusting way—learn it from you. You'd expose me to the most horrible unpleasantness—

KROGSTAD: Only unpleasantness?

NORA: *(vehemently)* But go on and try. It'll turn out the worse for you, because then my husband will really see what a crook you are, and then you'll *never* be able to hold your job.

370 KROGSTAD: I asked if it was just domestic unpleasantness you were afraid of.

NORA: If my husband finds out, then of course he'll pay what I owe at once, and then we'd be through with you for good.

KROGSTAD: *(a step closer)* Listen, Mrs. Helmer—you've either got a very bad memory, or else no head at all for business. I'd better put you a little more in touch with the facts.

NORA: What do you mean?

KROGSTAD: When your husband was sick, you came to me for a loan of four thousand, eight hundred crowns.

375 NORA: Where else could I go?

KROGSTAD: I promised to get you that sum—

NORA: And you got it.

KROGSTAD: I promised to get you that sum, on certain conditions. You were so involved in your husband's illness, and so eager to finance your trip, that I guess you didn't think out all the details. It might just be a good idea to remind you. I promised you the money on the strength of a note I drew up.

NORA: Yes, and that I signed.

380 KROGSTAD: Right. But at the bottom I added some lines for your father to guarantee the loan. He was supposed to sign down there.

NORA: Supposed to? He did sign.

KROGSTAD: I left the date blank. In other words, your father would have dated his signature himself. Do you remember that?

NORA: Yes, I think—

KROGSTAD: Then I gave you the note for you to mail to your father. Isn't that so?

385 NORA: Yes.

KROGSTAD: And naturally you sent it at once—because only some five, six days later you brought me the note, properly signed. And with that, the money was yours.

NORA: Well, then; I've made my payments regularly, haven't I?

KROGSTAD: More or less. But—getting back to the point—those were hard times for you then, Mrs. Helmer.

NORA: Yes, they were.

390 KROGSTAD: Your father was very ill, I believe.

NORA: He was near the end.

KROGSTAD: He died soon after?

NORA: Yes.

KROGSTAD: Tell me, Mrs. Helmer, do you happen to recall the date of your father's death? The day of the month, I mean.

395 NORA: Papa died the twenty-ninth of September.

KROGSTAD: That's quite correct; I've already looked into that. And now we come to a curious thing—*(taking out a paper)* which I simply cannot comprehend.

NORA: Curious thing? I don't know—

KROGSTAD: This is the curious thing: that your father co-signed the note for your loan three days after his death.

NORA: How—? I don't understand.

400 KROGSTAD: Your father died the twenty-ninth of September. But look. Here your father dated his signature October second. Isn't that curious, Mrs. Helmer? *(Nora is silent.)* Can you explain it to me? *(Nora remains silent.)* It's also remarkable that the words "October second" and the year aren't written in your father's hand, but rather in one

that I think I know. Well, it's easy to understand. Your father forgot perhaps to date his signature, and then someone or other added it, a bit sloppily, before anyone knew of his death. There's nothing wrong in that. It all comes down to the signature. And there's no question about *that,* Mrs. Helmer. It really *was* your father who signed his own name here, wasn't it?

NORA: *(after a short silence, throwing her head back and looking squarely at him)* No, it wasn't. *I* signed Papa's name.

KROGSTAD: Wait, now—are you fully aware that this is a dangerous confession?

NORA: Why? You'll soon get your money.

KROGSTAD: Let me ask you a question—why didn't you send the paper to your father?

405 NORA: That was impossible. Papa was so sick. If I'd asked him for his signature, I also would have had to tell him what the money was for. But I couldn't tell him, sick as he was, that my husband's life was in danger. That was just impossible.

KROGSTAD: Then it would have been better if you'd given up the trip abroad.

NORA: I couldn't possibly. The trip was to save my husband's life. I couldn't give that up.

KROGSTAD: But didn't you ever consider that this was a fraud against me?

NORA: I couldn't let myself be bothered by that. You weren't any concern of mine. I couldn't stand you, with all those cold complications you made, even though you knew how badly off my husband was.

410 KROGSTAD: Mrs. Helmer, obviously you haven't the vaguest idea of what you've involved yourself in. But I can tell you this: it was nothing more and nothing worse than I once did—and it wrecked my whole reputation.

NORA: You? Do you expect me to believe that you ever acted bravely to save your wife's life?

KROGSTAD: Laws don't inquire into motives.

NORA: Then they must be very poor laws.

KROGSTAD: Poor or not—if I introduce this paper in court, you'll be judged according to law.

415 NORA: This I refuse to believe. A daughter hasn't a right to protect her dying father from anxiety and care? A wife hasn't a right to save her husband's life? I don't know much about laws, but I'm sure that somewhere in the books these things are allowed. And you don't know anything about it—you who practice the law? You must be an awful lawyer, Mr. Krogstad.

KROGSTAD: Could be. But business—the kind of business we two mixed up in—don't you think I know about that? All right. Do what you want now. But I'm telling you *this:* if I get shoved down a second time, you're going to keep me company. *(He bows and goes out through the hall.)*

NORA: *(pensive for a moment, then tossing her head)* Oh, really! Trying to frighten me! I'm not so silly as all that. *(Begins gathering up the children's clothes, but soon stops.)* But—? No, but that's impossible! I did it out of love.

THE CHILDREN: *(in the doorway, left)* Mama, that strange man's gone out the door.

NORA: Yes, yes, I know it. But don't tell anyone about the strange man. Do you hear? Not even Papa!

420 THE CHILDREN: No, Mama. But now will you play again?

NORA: No, not now.

THE CHILDREN: Oh, but Mama, you promised.

NORA: Yes, but I can't now. Go inside; I have too much to do. Go in, go in, my sweet darlings. *(She herds them gently back in the room and shuts the door after them. Settling on the sofa, she takes up a piece of embroidery and makes some stitches, but soon stops abruptly.)* No! *(Throws the work aside, rises, goes to the hall door and calls out.)* Helene! Let me have the tree in here. *(Goes to the table, left, opens the table drawer, and stops again.)* No, but that's utterly impossible!

MAID: *(with the Christmas tree)* Where should I put it, ma'am?

425 NORA: There. The middle of the floor.

MAID: Should I bring anything else?

NORA: No, thanks. I have what I need.

The Maid, who has set the tree down, goes out.

NORA: *(absorbed in trimming the tree)* Candles here—and flowers here. That terrible creature! Talk, talk, talk! There's nothing to it at all. The tree's going to be lovely. I'll do anything to please you, Torvald. I'll sing for you, dance for you—

Helmer comes in from the hall, with a sheaf of papers under his arm.

NORA: Oh! You're back so soon?

430 HELMER: Yes. Has anyone been here?

NORA: Here? No.

HELMER: That's odd. I saw Krogstad leaving the front door.

NORA: So? Oh yes, that's true. Krogstad was here a moment.

HELMER: Nora, I can see by your face that he's been here, begging you to put in a good word for him.

435 NORA: Yes.

HELMER: And it was supposed to seem like your own idea? You were to hide it from me that he'd been here. He asked you that, too, didn't he?

NORA: Yes, Torvald, but—

HELMER: Nora, Nora, and you could fall for that? Talk with that sort of person and promise him anything? And then in the bargain, tell me an untruth.

NORA: An untruth—?

440 HELMER: Didn't you say that no one had been here? *(Wagging his finger.)*
   My little songbird must never do that again. A songbird needs a clean
   beak to warble with. No false notes. *(Putting his arm about her waist.)*
   That's the way it should be, isn't it? Yes, I'm sure of it. *(Releasing her.)*
   And so, enough of that. *(Sitting by the stove.)* Ah, how snug and cozy
   it is here. *(Leafing among his papers.)*

NORA: *(busy with the tree, after a short pause)* Torvald!

HELMER: Yes.

NORA: I'm so much looking forward to the Stenborgs' costume party, day
   after tomorrow.

HELMER: And I can't wait to see what you'll surprise me with.

445 NORA: Oh, that stupid business!

HELMER: What?

NORA: I can't find anything that's right. Everything seems so ridiculous,
   so inane.

HELMER: So my little Nora's come to *that* recognition?

NORA: *(going behind his chair, her arms resting on its back)* Are you very
   busy, Torvald?

450 HELMER: Oh—

NORA: What papers are those?

HELMER: Bank matters.

NORA: Already?

HELMER: I've gotten full authority from the retiring management to make
   all necessary changes in personnel and procedure. I'll need Christmas
   week for that. I want to have everything in order by New Year's.

455 NORA: So that was the reason this poor Krogstad—

HELMER: Hm.

NORA: *(still leaning on the chair and slowly stroking the nape of his neck)* If
   you weren't so very busy, I would have asked you an enormous favor,
   Torvald.

HELMER: Let's hear. What is it?

NORA: You know, there isn't anyone who has your good taste—and I want
   so much to look well at the costume party. Torvald, couldn't you take
   over and decide what I should be and plan my costume?

460 HELMER: Ah, is my stubborn little creature calling for a lifeguard?

NORA: Yes, Torvald, I can't get anywhere without your help.

HELMER: All right—I'll think it over. We'll hit on something.

NORA: Oh, how sweet of you. *(Goes to the tree again. Pause.)* Aren't the red
   flowers pretty—? But tell me, was it really such a crime that this
   Krogstad committed?

HELMER: Forgery. Do you have any idea what that means?

465 NORA: Couldn't he have done it out of need?

HELMER: Yes, or thoughtlessness, like so many others. I'm not so heartless
   that I'd condemn a man categorically for just one mistake.

NORA: No, of course not, Torvald!

HELMER: Plenty of men have redeemed themselves by openly confessing their crimes and taking their punishment.

NORA: Punishment—?

470 HELMER: But now Krogstad didn't go that way. He got himself out by sharp practices, and that's the real cause of his moral breakdown.

NORA: Do you really think that would—?

HELMER: Just imagine how a man with that sort of guilt in him has to lie and cheat and deceive on all sides, has to wear a mask even with the nearest and dearest he has, even with his own wife and children. And with the children, Nora—that's where it's most horrible.

NORA: Why?

HELMER: Because that kind of atmosphere of lies infects the whole life of a home. Every breath the children take in is filled with the germs of something degenerate.

475 NORA: *(coming closer behind him)* Are you sure of that?

HELMER: Oh, I've seen it often enough as a lawyer. Almost everyone who goes bad early in life has a mother who's a chronic liar.

NORA: Why just—the mother?

HELMER: It's usually the mother's influence that's dominant, but the father's works in the same way, of course. Every lawyer is quite familiar with it. And still this Krogstad's been going home year in, year out, poisoning his own children with lies and pretense; that's why I call him morally lost. *(Reaching his hands out toward her.)* So my sweet little Nora must promise me never to plead his cause. Your hand on it. Come, come, what's this? Give me your hand. There, now. All settled. I can tell you it'd be impossible for me to work alongside of him. I literally feel physically revolted when I'm anywhere near such a person.

NORA: *(withdraws her hand and goes to the other side of the Christmas tree)* How hot it is here! And I've got so much to do.

480 HELMER: *(getting up and gathering his papers)* Yes, and I have to think about getting some of these read through before dinner. I'll think about your costume, too. And something to hang on the tree in gilt paper, I may even see about that. *(Putting his hand on her head.)* Oh you, my darling little songbird. *(He goes into his study and closes the door after him.)*

NORA: *(softly, after a silence)* Oh, really! It isn't so. It's impossible. It must be impossible.

ANNE-MARIE: *(in the doorway, left)* The children are begging so hard to come in to Mama.

NORA: No, no, no, don't let them in to me! You stay with them, Anne-Marie.

ANNE-MARIE: Of course, ma'am. *(Closes the door.)*

485 NORA: *(pale with terror)* Hurt my children—! Poison my home? *(A moment's pause; then she tosses her head.)* That's not true. Never. Never in all the world.

ACT II

*Same room. Beside the piano the Christmas tree now stands stripped of orna-
ments, burned-down candle stubs on its ragged branches. Nora's street clothes lie
on the sofa. Nora, alone in the room, moves restlessly about; at last she stops at
the sofa and picks up her coat.*

NORA: *(dropping the coat again)* Someone's coming! *(Goes toward the door,
listens.)* No—there's no one. Of course—nobody's coming today,
Christmas Day—or tomorrow, either. But maybe—*(Opens the door and
looks out.)* No, nothing in the mailbox. Quite empty. *(Coming
forward.)* What nonsense! He won't do anything serious. Nothing
terrible could happen. It's impossible. Why, I have three small
children.

Anne-Marie, with a large carton, comes in from the room to the left.

ANNE-MARIE: Well, at last I found the box with the masquerade clothes.
NORA: Thanks. Put it on the table.
ANNE-MARIE: *(does so)* But they're all pretty much of a mess.
5 NORA: Ahh! I'd love to rip them in a million pieces!
ANNE-MARIE: Oh, mercy, they can be fixed right up. Just a little patience.
NORA: Yes, I'll go get Mrs. Linde to help me.
ANNE-MARIE: Out again now? In this nasty weather? Miss Nora will catch
cold—get sick.
NORA: Oh, worse things could happen—How are the children?
10 ANNE-MARIE: The poor mites are playing with their Christmas presents,
but—
NORA: Do they ask for me much?
ANNE-MARIE: They're so used to having Mama around, you know.
NORA: Yes. But Anne-Marie, I *can't* be together with them as much as I was.
ANNE-MARIE: Well, small children get used to anything.
15 NORA: You think so? Do you think they'd forget their mother if she was
gone for good?
ANNE-MARIE: Oh, mercy—gone for good!
NORA: Wait, tell me, Anne-Marie—I've wondered so often—how could
you ever have the heart to give your child over to strangers?
ANNE-MARIE: But I had to, you know, to become little Nora's nurse.
NORA: Yes, but how could you *do* it?
20 ANNE-MARIE: When I could get such a good place? A girl who's poor and
who's gotten in trouble is glad enough for that. Because that slippery
fish, he didn't do a thing for me, you know.
NORA: But your daughter's surely forgotten you.
ANNE-MARIE: Oh, she certainly has not. She's written to me, both when
she was confirmed and when she was married.
NORA: *(clasping her about the neck)* You old Anne-Marie, you were a good
mother for me when I was little.
ANNE-MARIE: Poor little Nora, with no other mother but me.

25 NORA: And if the babies didn't have one, then I know that you'd—What silly talk! *(Opening the carton.)* Go in to them. Now I'll have to— Tomorrow you can see how lovely I'll look.

ANNE-MARIE: Oh, there won't be anyone at the party as lovely as Miss Nora. *(She goes off into the room, left.)*

NORA: *(begins unpacking the box, but soon throws it aside)* Oh, if I dared to go out. If only nobody would come. If only nothing would happen here while I'm out. What craziness—nobody's coming. Just don't think. This muff—needs a brushing. Beautiful gloves, beautiful gloves. Let it go. Let it go! One, two, three, four, five, six—*(With a cry.)* Oh, there they are! *(Poises to move toward the door, but remains irresolutely standing. Mrs. Linde enters from the hall, where she has removed her street clothes.)*

NORA: Oh, it's you, Kristine. There's no one else out there? How good that you've come.

MRS. LINDE: I hear you were up asking for me.

30 NORA: Yes, I just stopped by. There's something you really can help me with. Let's get settled on the sofa. Look, there's going to be a costume party tomorrow evening at the Stenborgs' right above us, and now Torvald wants me to go as a Neapolitan peasant girl and dance the tarantella that I learned in Capri.

MRS. LINDE: Really, are you giving a whole performance?

NORA: Torvald says yes, I should. See, here's the dress. Torvald had it made for me down there; but now it's all so tattered that I just don't know—

MRS. LINDE: Oh, we'll fix that up in no time. It's nothing more than the trimmings—they're a bit loose here and there. Needle and thread? Good, now we have what we need.

NORA: Oh, how sweet of you!

35 MRS. LINDE: *(sewing)* So you'll be in disguise tomorrow, Nora. You know what? I'll stop by then for a moment and have a look at you all dressed up. But listen, I've absolutely forgotten to thank you for that pleasant evening yesterday.

NORA: *(getting up and walking about)* I don't think it was as pleasant as usual yesterday. You should have come to town a bit sooner, Kristine—Yes, Torvald really knows how to give a home elegance and charm.

MRS. LINDE: And you do, too, if you ask me. You're not your father's daughter for nothing. But tell me, is Dr. Rank always so down in the mouth as yesterday?

NORA: No, that was quite an exception. But he goes around critically ill all the time—tuberculosis of the spine, poor man. You know, his father was a disgusting thing who kept mistresses and so on—and that's why the son's been sickly from birth.

MRS. LINDE: *(lets her sewing fall to her lap)* But my dearest Nora, how do you know about such things?

40   **Nora:** *(walking more jauntily)* Hmp! When you've had three children, then you've had a few visits from—from women who know something of medicine, and they tell you this and that.

    Mrs. Linde: *(resumes sewing; a short pause)* Does Dr. Rank come here every day?

    Nora: Every blessed day. He's Torvald's best friend from childhood, and *my* good friend, too. Dr. Rank almost belongs to this house.

    Mrs. Linde: But tell me—is he quite sincere? I mean, doesn't he rather enjoy flattering people?

    Nora: Just the opposite. Why do you think that?

45   **Mrs. Linde:** When you introduced us yesterday, he was proclaiming that he'd often heard my name in this house; but later I noticed that your husband hadn't the slightest idea who I really was. So how could Dr. Rank—?

    Nora: But it's all true, Kristine. You see, Torvald loves me beyond words, and, as he puts it, he'd like to keep me all to himself. For a long time he'd almost be jealous if I even mentioned any of my old friends back home. So of course I dropped that. But with Dr. Rank I talk a lot about such things, because he likes hearing about them.

    Mrs. Linde: Now listen, Nora; in many ways you're still like a child. I'm a good deal older than you, with a little more experience. I'll tell you something: you ought to put an end to all this with Dr. Rank.

    Nora: What should I put an end to?

    Mrs. Linde: Both parts of it, I think. Yesterday you said something about a rich admirer who'd provide you with money—

50   **Nora:** Yes, one who doesn't exist—worse luck. So?

    Mrs. Linde: Is Dr. Rank well off?

    Nora: Yes, he is.

    Mrs. Linde: With no dependents?

    Nora: No, no one. But—

55   **Mrs. Linde:** And he's over here every day?

    Nora: Yes, I told you that.

    Mrs. Linde: How can a man of such refinement be so grasping?

    Nora: I don't follow you at all.

    Mrs. Linde: Now don't try to hide it, Nora. You think I can't guess who loaned you the forty-eight hundred crowns?

60   **Nora:** Are you out of your mind? How could you think such a thing! A friend of ours, who comes here every single day. What an intolerable situation that would have been!

    Mrs. Linde: Then it really wasn't him.

    Nora: No, absolutely not. It never even crossed my mind for a moment— And he had nothing to lend in those days; his inheritance came later.

    Mrs. Linde: Well, I think that was a stroke of luck for you, Nora dear.

    Nora: No, it never would have occurred to me to ask Dr. Rank—Still, I'm quite sure that if I had asked him—

65   **Mrs. Linde:** Which you won't, of course.

NORA: No, of course not. I can't see that I'd ever need to. But I'm quite positive that if I talked to Dr. Rank—

MRS. LINDE: Behind your husband's back?

NORA: I've got to clear up this other thing; *that's* also behind his back. I've *got* to clear it all up.

MRS. LINDE: Yes, I was saying that yesterday, but—

70 NORA: *(pacing up and down)* A man handles these problems so much better than a woman—

MRS. LINDE: One's husband does, yes.

NORA: Nonsense. *(Stopping.)* When you pay everything you owe, then you get your note back, right?

MRS. LINDE: Yes, naturally.

NORA: And can rip it into a million pieces and burn it up—that filthy scrap of paper!

75 MRS. LINDE: *(looking hard at her, laying her sewing aside, and rising slowly)* Nora, you're hiding something from me.

NORA: You can see it in my face?

MRS. LINDE: Something's happened to you since yesterday morning. Nora, what is it?

NORA: *(hurrying toward her)* Kristine! *(Listening.)* Shh! Torvald's home. Look, go in with the children a while. Torvald can't bear all this snipping and stitching. Let Anne-Marie help you.

MRS. LINDE: *(gathering up some of the things)* All right, but I'm not leaving here until we've talked this out. *(She disappears into the room, left, as Torvald enters from the hall.)*

80 NORA: Oh, how I've been waiting for you, Torvald dear.

HELMER: Was that the dressmaker?

NORA: No, that was Kristine. She's helping me fix up my costume. You know, it's going to be quite attractive.

HELMER: Yes, wasn't that a bright idea I had?

NORA: Brilliant! But then wasn't I good as well to give in to you?

85 HELMER: Good—because you give in to your husband's judgment? All right, you little goose, I know you didn't mean it like that. But I won't disturb you. You'll want to have a fitting, I suppose.

NORA: And you'll be working?

HELMER: Yes. *(Indicating a bundle of papers.)* See. I've been down to the bank. *(Starts toward his study.)*

NORA: Torvald.

HELMER: *(stops)* Yes.

90 NORA: If your little squirrel begged you, with all her heart and soul, for something—?

HELMER: What's that?

NORA: Then would you do it?

HELMER: First, naturally, I'd have to know what it was.

NORA: Your squirrel would scamper about and do tricks, if you'd only be sweet and give in.

95 Helmer: Out with it.

Nora: Your lark would be singing high and low in every room—

Helmer: Come on, she does that anyway.

Nora: I'd be a wood nymph and dance for you in the moonlight.

Helmer: Nora—don't tell me it's that same business from this morning?

100 Nora: *(coming closer)* Yes, Torvald, I beg you, please!

Helmer: And you actually have the nerve to drag that up again?

Nora: Yes, yes, you've got to give in to me; you *have* to let Krogstad keep his job in the bank.

Helmer: My dear Nora, I've slated his job for Mrs. Linde.

Nora: That's awfully kind of you. But you could just fire another clerk instead of Krogstad.

105 Helmer: This is the most incredible stubbornness! Because you go and give an impulsive promise to speak up for him, I'm expected to—

Nora: That's not the reason, Torvald. It's for your own sake. That man does writing for the worst papers; you said it yourself. He could do you any amount of harm. I'm scared to death of him—

Helmer: Ah, I understand. It's the old memories haunting you.

Nora: What do you mean by that?

Helmer: Of course, you're thinking about your father.

110 Nora: Yes, all right. Just remember how those nasty gossips wrote in the papers about Papa and slandered him so cruelly. I think they'd have had him dismissed if the department hadn't sent you up to investigate, and if you hadn't been so kind and open-minded toward him.

Helmer: My dear Nora, there's a notable difference between your father and me. Your father's official career was hardly above reproach. But mine is; and I hope it'll stay that way as long as I hold my position.

Nora: Oh, who can ever tell what vicious minds can invent? We could be so snug and happy now in our quiet, carefree home—you and I and the children, Torvald! That's why I'm pleading with you so—

Helmer: And just by pleading for him you make it impossible for me to keep him on. It's already known at the bank that I'm firing Krogstad. What if it's rumored around now that the new bank manager was vetoed by his wife—

Nora: Yes, what then—?

115 Helmer: Oh yes—as long as our little bundle of stubbornness gets her way—! I should go and make myself ridiculous in front of the whole office—give people the idea I can be swayed by all kinds of outside pressure. Oh, you can bet I'd feel the effects of that soon enough! Besides—there's something that rules Krogstad right out at the bank as long as I'm the manager.

Nora: What's that?

Helmer: His moral failings I could maybe overlook if I had to—

Nora: Yes, Torvald, why not?

HELMER: And I hear he's quite efficient on the job. But he was a crony of mine back in my teens—one of those rash friendships that crop up again and again to embarrass you later in life. Well, I might as well say it straight out: we're on a first-name basis. And that tactless fool makes no effort at all to hide it in front of others. Quite the contrary—he thinks that entitles him to take a familiar air around me, and so every other second he comes booming out with his "Yes, Torvald!" and "Sure thing, Torvald!" I tell you, it's been excruciating for me. He's out to make my place in the bank unbearable.

120 NORA: Torvald, you can't be serious about all this.

HELMER: Oh no? Why not?

NORA: Because these are such petty considerations.

HELMER: What are you saying? Petty? You think I'm petty!

NORA: No, just the opposite, Torvald dear. That's exactly why—

125 HELMER: Never mind. You call my motives petty; then I might as well be just that. Petty! All right! We'll put a stop to this for good. (*Goes to the hall door and calls.*) Helene!

NORA: What do you want?

HELMER: (*searching among his papers*) A decision. (*The Maid comes in.*) Look here; take this letter; go out with it at once. Get hold of a messenger and have him deliver it. Quick now. It's already addressed. Wait, here's some money.

MAID: Yes, sir. (*She leaves with the letter.*)

HELMER: (*straightening his papers*) There, now, little Miss Willful.

130 NORA: (*breathlessly*) Torvald, what was that letter?

HELMER: Krogstad's notice.

NORA: Call it back, Torvald! There's still time. Oh, Torvald, call it back! Do it for my sake—for your sake, for the children's sake! Do you hear, Torvald; do it! You don't know how this can harm us.

HELMER: Too late.

NORA: Yes, too late.

135 HELMER: Nora dear, I can forgive you this panic, even though basically you're insulting me. Yes, you are! Or isn't it an insult to think that *I* should be afraid of a courtroom hack's revenge? But I forgive you anyway, because this shows so beautifully how much you love me. (*Takes her in his arms.*) This is the way it should be, my darling Nora. Whatever comes, you'll see: when it really counts, I have strength and courage enough as a man to take on the whole weight myself.

NORA: (*terrified*) What do you mean by that?

HELMER: The whole weight, I said.

NORA: (*resolutely*) No, never in all the world.

HELMER: Good. So we'll share it, Nora, as man and wife. That's as it should be. (*Fondling her.*) Are you happy now? There, there, there—not these frightened dove's eyes. It's nothing at all but empty fantasies—Now you should run through your tarantella and practice your tambourine. I'll go to the inner office and shut both doors, so I won't hear a thing; you can make all the noise you like. *(Turning in the doorway.)* And when Rank comes, just tell him where he can find me. *(He nods to her and goes with his papers into the study, closing the door.)*

140 NORA: *(standing as though rooted, dazed with fright, in a whisper)* He really could do it. He will do it. He'll do it in spite of everything. No, not that, never, never! Anything but that! Escape! A way out—*(The doorbell rings.)* Dr. Rank! Anything but that! *Anything,* whatever it is! *(Her hands pass over her face, smoothing it; she pulls herself together, goes over and opens the hall door. Dr. Rank stands outside, hanging his fur coat up. During the following scene, it begins getting dark.)*

NORA: Hello, Dr. Rank. I recognized your ring. But you mustn't go in to Torvald yet; I believe he's working.

RANK: And you?

NORA: For you, I always have an hour to spare—you know that. *(He has entered, and she shuts the door after him.)*

RANK: Many thanks. I'll make use of these hours while I can.

145 NORA: What do you mean by that? While you can?

RANK: Does that disturb you?

NORA: Well, it's such an odd phrase. Is anything going to happen?

RANK: What's going to happen is what I've been expecting so long—but I honestly didn't think it would come so soon.

NORA: *(gripping his arm)* What is it you've found out? Dr. Rank, you have to tell me!

150 RANK: *(sitting by the stove)* It's all over with me. There's nothing to be done about it.

NORA: *(breathing easier)* Is it you—then—?

RANK: Who else? There's no point in lying to one's self. I'm the most miserable of all my patients, Mrs. Helmer. These past few days I've been auditing my internal accounts. Bankrupt! Within a month I'll probably be laid out and rotting in the churchyard.

NORA: Oh, what a horrible thing to say.

RANK: The thing itself is horrible. But the worst of it is all the other horror before it's over. There's only one final examination left; when I'm finished with that, I'll know about when my disintegration will begin. There's something I want to say. Helmer with his sensitivity has such a sharp distaste for anything ugly. I don't want him near my sickroom.

155 NORA: Oh, but Dr. Rank—

RANK: I won't have him in there. Under no condition. I'll lock my door to him—As soon as I'm completely sure of the worst, I'll send you my calling card marked with a black cross, and you'll know then the wreck has started to come apart.

NORA: No, today you're completely unreasonable. And I wanted you so much to be in a really good humor.

RANK: With death up my sleeve? And then to suffer this way for
somebody else's sins. Is there any justice in that? And in every single
family, in some way or another, this inevitable retribution of nature
goes on—

NORA: *(her hands pressed over her ears)* Oh, stuff! Cheer up! Please—be gay!

160 RANK: Yes, I'd just as soon laugh at it all. My poor, innocent spine,
serving time for my father's gay army days.

NORA: *(by the table, left)* He was so infatuated with asparagus tips and *pâté
de foie gras,* wasn't that it?

RANK: Yes—and with truffles.

NORA: Truffles, yes. And then with oysters, I suppose?

RANK: Yes, tons of oysters, naturally.

165 NORA: And then the port and champagne to go with it. It's so sad that all
these delectable things have to strike at our bones.

RANK: Especially when they strike at the unhappy bones that never
shared in the fun.

NORA: Ah, that's the saddest of all.

RANK: *(looks searchingly at her)* Hm.

NORA: *(after a moment)* Why did you smile?

170 RANK: No, it was you who laughed.

NORA: No, it was you who smiled, Dr. Rank!

RANK: *(getting up)* You're even a bigger tease than I'd thought.

NORA: I'm full of wild ideas today.

RANK: That's obvious.

175 NORA: *(putting both hands on his shoulders)* Dear, dear Dr. Rank, you'll
never die for Torvald and me.

RANK: Oh, that loss you'll easily get over. Those who go away are soon
forgotten.

NORA: *(looks fearfully at him)* You believe that?

RANK: One makes new connections, and then—

NORA: Who makes new connections?

180 RANK: Both you and Torvald will when I'm gone. I'd say you're well under
way already. What was that Mrs. Linde doing here last evening?

NORA: Oh, come—you can't be jealous of poor Kristine?

RANK: Oh yes, I am. She'll be my successor here in the house. When I'm
down under, that woman will probably—

NORA: Shh! Not so loud. She's right in there.

RANK: Today as well. So you see.

185 NORA: Only to sew on my dress. Good gracious, how unreasonable you
are. *(Sitting on the sofa.)* Be nice now, Dr. Rank. Tomorrow you'll see
how beautifully I'll dance; and you can imagine then that I'm
dancing only for you—yes, and of course for Torvald, too—that's
understood. *(Takes various items out of the carton.)* Dr. Rank, sit over
here and I'll show you something.

RANK: *(sitting)* What's that?

NORA: Look here. Look.

RANK: Silk stockings.

NORA: Flesh-colored. Aren't they lovely? Now it's so dark here, but tomorrow—No, no, no, just look at the feet. Oh well, you might as well look at the rest.

190 RANK: Hm—

NORA: Why do you look so critical? Don't you believe they'll fit?

RANK: I've never had any chance to form an opinion on that.

NORA: *(glancing at him a moment)* Shame on you. *(Hits him lightly on the ear with the stockings.)* That's for you. *(Puts them away again.)*

RANK: And what other splendors am I going to see now?

195 NORA: Not the least bit more, because you've been naughty. *(She hums a little and rummages among her things.)*

RANK: *(after a short silence)* When I sit here together with you like this, completely easy and open, then I don't know—I simply can't imagine—whatever would have become of me if I'd never come into this house.

NORA: *(smiling)* Yes, I really think you feel completely at ease with us.

RANK: *(more quietly, staring straight ahead)* And then to have to go away from it all—

NORA: Nonsense, you're not going away.

200 RANK: *(his voice unchanged)*—and not even be able to leave some poor show of gratitude behind, scarcely a fleeting regret—no more than a vacant place that anyone can fill.

NORA: And if I asked you now for—? No—

RANK: For what?

NORA: For a great proof of your friendship—

RANK: Yes, yes?

205 NORA: No, I mean—for an exceptionally big favor—

RANK: Would you really, for once, make me so happy?

NORA: Oh, you haven't the vaguest idea what it is.

RANK: All right, then tell me.

NORA: No, but I can't, Dr. Rank—it's all out of reason. It's advice and help, too—and a favor—

210 RANK: So much the better. I can't fathom what you're hinting at. Just speak out. Don't you trust me?

NORA: Of course. More than anyone else. You're my best and truest friend, I'm sure. That's why I want to talk to you. All right, then, Dr. Rank: there's something you can help me prevent. You know how deeply, how inexpressibly dearly Torvald loves me; he'd never hesitate a second to give up his life for me.

RANK: *(leaning close to her)* Nora—do you think he's the only one—

NORA: *(with a slight start)* Who—?

RANK: Who'd gladly give up his life for you.

215 NORA: *(heavily)* I see.

RANK: I swore to myself you should know this before I'm gone. I'll never find a better chance. Yes, Nora, now you know. And also you know now that you can trust me beyond anyone else.

NORA: *(rising, natural and calm)* Let me by.

RANK: *(making room for her, but still sitting)* Nora—

NORA: *(in the hall doorway)* Helene, bring the lamp in. *(Goes over to the stove.)* Ah, dear Dr. Rank, that was really mean of you.

220 RANK: *(getting up)* That I've loved you just as deeply as somebody else? Was *that* mean?

NORA: No, but that you came out and told me. That was quite unnecessary—

RANK: What do you mean? Have you known—?

The Maid comes in with the lamp, sets it on the table, and goes out again.

RANK: Nora—Mrs. Helmer—I'm asking you: have you known about it?

NORA: Oh, how can I tell what I know or don't know? Really, I don't know what to say—Why did you have to be so clumsy, Dr. Rank! Everything was so good.

225 RANK: Well, in any case, you now have the knowledge that my body and soul are at your command. So won't you speak out?

NORA: *(looking at him)* After that?

RANK: Please, just let me know what it is.

NORA: You can't know anything now.

RANK: I have to. You mustn't punish me like this. Give me the chance to do whatever is humanly possible for you.

230 NORA: Now there's nothing you can do for me. Besides, actually, I don't need any help. You'll see—it's only my fantasies. That's what it is. Of course! *(Sits in the rocker, looks at him, and smiles.)* What a nice one you are, Dr. Rank. Aren't you a little bit ashamed, now that the lamp is here?

RANK: No, not exactly. But perhaps I'd better go—for good?

NORA: No, you certainly can't do that. You must come here just as you always have. You know Torvald can't do without you.

RANK: Yes, but *you*?

NORA: You know how much I enjoy it when you're here.

235 RANK: That's precisely what threw me off. You're a mystery to me. So many times I've felt you'd almost rather be with me than with Helmer.

NORA: Yes—you see, there are some people that one loves most and other people that one would almost prefer being with.

RANK: Yes, there's something to that.

NORA: When I was back home, of course I loved Papa most. But I always thought it was so much fun when I could sneak down to the maids' quarters, because they never tried to improve me, and it was always so amusing, the way they talked to each other.

RANK: Aha, so it's *their* place that I've filled.

240 NORA: *(jumping up and going to him)* Oh, dear, sweet Dr. Rank, that's not what I mean at all. But you can understand that with Torvald it's just the same as with Papa—

The Maid enters from the hall.

MAID: Ma'am—please! *(She whispers to Nora and hands her a calling card.)*

NORA: *(glancing at the card)* Ah! *(Slips it into her pocket.)*

RANK: Anything wrong?

NORA: No, no, not at all. It's only some—it's my new dress—

245 RANK: Really? But—there's your dress.

NORA: Oh, that. But this is another one—I ordered it—Torvald mustn't know—

RANK: Ah, now we have the big secret.

NORA: That's right. Just go in with him—he's back in the inner study. Keep him there as long as—

RANK: Don't worry. He won't get away. *(Goes into the study.)*

250 NORA: *(to the Maid)* And he's standing waiting in the kitchen?

MAID: Yes, he came up by the back stairs.

NORA: But didn't you tell him somebody was here?

MAID: Yes, but that didn't do any good.

NORA: He won't leave?

255 MAID: No, he won't go till he's talked with you, ma'am.

NORA: Let him come in, then—but quietly. Helene, don't breathe a word about this. It's a surprise for my husband.

MAID: Yes, yes, I understand—*(Goes out.)*

NORA: This horror—it's going to happen. No, no, no, it can't happen, it mustn't. *(She goes and bolts Helmer's door. The Maid opens the hall door for Krogstad and shuts it behind him. He is dressed for travel in a fur coat, boots, and a fur cap.)*

NORA: *(going toward him)* Talk softly. My husband's home.

260 KROGSTAD: Well, good for him.

NORA: What do you want?

KROGSTAD: Some information.

NORA: Hurry up, then. What is it?

KROGSTAD: You know, of course, that I got my notice.

265 NORA: I couldn't prevent it, Mr. Krogstad. I fought for you to the bitter end, but nothing worked.

KROGSTAD: Does your husband's love for you run so thin? He knows everything I can expose you to, and all the same he dares to—

NORA: How can you imagine he knows anything about this?

KROGSTAD: Ah, no—I can't imagine it either, now. It's not at all like my fine Torvald Helmer to have so much guts—

NORA: Mr. Krogstad, I demand respect for my husband!

270 KROGSTAD: Why, of course—all due respect. But since the lady's keeping it so carefully hidden, may I presume to ask if you're also a bit better informed than yesterday about what you've actually done?

NORA: More than you ever could teach me.

KROGSTAD: Yes, I *am* such an awful lawyer.

NORA: What is it you want from me?

KROGSTAD: Just a glimpse of how you are, Mrs. Helmer. I've been thinking about you all day long. A cashier, a night-court scribbler, a—well, a type like me also has a little of what they call a heart, you know.

275 NORA: Then show it. Think of my children.

KROGSTAD: Did you or your husband ever think of mine? But never mind. I simply wanted to tell you that you don't need to take this thing too seriously. For the present, I'm not proceeding with any action.

NORA: Oh no, really! Well—I knew that.

KROGSTAD: Everything can be settled in a friendly spirit. It doesn't have to get around town at all; it can stay just among us three.

NORA: My husband must never know anything of this.

280 KROGSTAD: How can you manage that? Perhaps you can pay me the balance?

NORA: No, not right now.

KROGSTAD: Or you know some way of raising the money in a day or two?

NORA: No way that I'm willing to use.

KROGSTAD: Well, it wouldn't have done you any good, anyway. If you stood in front of me with a fistful of bills, you still couldn't buy your signature back.

285 NORA: Then tell me what you're going to do with it.

KROGSTAD: I'll just hold onto it—keep it on file. There's no outsider who'll even get wind of it. So if you've been thinking of taking some desperate step—

NORA: I have.

KROGSTAD: Been thinking of running away from home—

NORA: I have!

290 KROGSTAD: Or even of something worse—

NORA: How could you guess that?

KROGSTAD: You can drop those thoughts.

NORA: How could you guess I was thinking of *that*?

KROGSTAD: Most of us think about *that* at first. I thought about it too, but I discovered I hadn't the courage—

295 NORA: *(lifelessly)* I don't either.

KROGSTAD: *(relieved)* That's true, you haven't the courage? You too?

NORA: I don't have it—I don't have it.

KROGSTAD: It would be terribly stupid, anyway. After that first storm at home blows out, why, then—I have here in my pocket a letter for your husband—

NORA: Telling everything?

300 KROGSTAD: As charitably as possible.

NORA: *(quickly)* He mustn't ever get that letter. Tear it up. I'll find some way to get money.

KROGSTAD: Beg pardon, Mrs. Helmer, but I think I just told you—

NORA: Oh, I don't mean the money I owe you. Let me know how much you want from my husband, and I'll manage it.

KROGSTAD: I don't want any money from your husband.

305 NORA: What do you want, then?

Krogstad: I'll tell you what. I want to recoup, Mrs. Helmer; I want to get on in the world—and there's where your husband can help me. For a year and a half I've kept myself clean of anything disreputable—all that time struggling with the worst conditions; but I was satisfied, working my way up step by step. Now I've been written right off, and I'm just not in the mood to come crawling back. I tell you, I want to move on. I want to get back in the bank—in a better position. Your husband can set up a job for me—

Nora: He'll never do that!

Krogstad: He'll do it. I know him. He won't dare breathe a word of protest. And once I'm in there together with him, you just wait and see! Inside of a year, I'll be the manager's right-hand man. It'll be Nils Krogstad, not Torvald Helmer, who runs the bank.

Nora: You'll never see the day!

310 Krogstad: Maybe you think you can—

Nora: I have the courage now—for *that*.

Krogstad: Oh, you don't scare me. A smart, spoiled lady like you—

Nora: You'll see; you'll see!

Krogstad: Under the ice, maybe? Down in the freezing, coal-black water? There, till you float up in the spring, ugly, unrecognizable, with your hair falling out—

315 Nora: You don't frighten me.

Krogstad: Nor do you frighten me. One doesn't do these things, Mrs. Helmer. Besides, what good would it be? I'd still have him safe in my pocket.

Nora: Afterwards? When I'm no longer—?

Krogstad: Are you forgetting that *I'll* be in control then over your final reputation? *(Nora stands speechless, staring at him.)* Good; now I've warned you. Don't do anything stupid. When Helmer's read my letter, I'll be waiting for his reply. And bear in mind that it's your husband himself who's forced me back to my old ways. I'll never forgive him for that. Good-bye, Mrs. Helmer. *(He goes out through the hall.)*

Nora: *(goes to the hall door, opens it a crack, and listens)* He's gone. Didn't leave the letter. Oh no, no, that's impossible too! *(Opening the door more and more.)* What's that? He's standing outside—not going downstairs. He's thinking it over? Maybe he'll—? *(A letter falls in the mailbox; then Krogstad's footsteps are heard, dying away down a flight of stairs. Nora gives a muffled cry and runs over toward the sofa table. A short pause.)* In the mailbox. *(Slips warily over to the hall door.)* It's lying there. Torvald, Torvald—now we're lost!

320 Mrs. Linde: *(entering with the costume from the room, left)* There now, I can't see anything else to mend. Perhaps you'd like to try—

Nora: *(in a hoarse whisper)* Kristine, come here.

Mrs. Linde: *(tossing the dress on the sofa)* What's wrong? You look upset.

Nora: Come here. See that letter? *There!* Look—through the glass in the mailbox.

MRS. LINDE: Yes, yes, I see it.

325 NORA: That letter's from Krogstad—

MRS. LINDE: Nora—it's Krogstad who loaned you the money!

NORA: Yes, and now Torvald will find out everything.

MRS. LINDE: Believe me, Nora, it's best for both of you.

NORA: There's more you don't know. I forged a name.

330 MRS. LINDE: But for heaven's sake—?

NORA: I only want to tell you that, Kristine, so that you can be my witness.

MRS. LINDE: Witness? Why should I—?

NORA: If I should go out of my mind—it could easily happen—

MRS. LINDE: Nora!

335 NORA: Or anything else occurred—so I couldn't be present here—

MRS. LINDE: Nora, Nora, you aren't yourself at all!

NORA: And someone should try to take on the whole weight, all of the guilt, you follow me—

MRS. LINDE: Yes, of course, but why do you think—?

NORA: Then you're the witness that it isn't true, Kristine. I'm very much myself; my mind right now is perfectly clear; and I'm telling you: nobody else has known about this; I alone did everything. Remember that.

340 MRS. LINDE: I will. But I don't understand all this.

NORA: Oh, how could you ever understand it? It's the miracle now that's going to take place.

MRS. LINDE: The miracle?

NORA: Yes, the miracle. But it's so awful, Kristine. It mustn't take place, not for anything in the world.

MRS. LINDE: I'm going right over and talk with Krogstad.

345 NORA: Don't go near him; he'll do you some terrible harm!

MRS. LINDE: There was a time once when he'd gladly have done anything for me.

NORA: He?

MRS. LINDE: Where does he live?

NORA: Oh, how do I know? Yes. (Searches in her pocket.) Here's his card. But the letter, the letter—!

350 HELMER: (from the study, knocking on the door) Nora!

NORA: (with a cry of fear) Oh! What is it? What do you want?

HELMER: Now, now, don't be so frightened. We're not coming in. You locked the door—are you trying on the dress?

NORA: Yes, I'm trying it. I'll look just beautiful, Torvald.

MRS. LINDE: (who has read the card) He's living right around the corner.

355 NORA: Yes, but what's the use? We're lost. The letter's in the box.

MRS. LINDE: And your husband has the key?

NORA: Yes, always.

MRS. LINDE: Krogstad can ask for his letter back unread; he can find some excuse—

NORA: But it's just this time that Torvald usually—

360 MRS. LINDE: Stall him. Keep him in there. I'll be back as quick as I can.
(She hurries out through the hall entrance.)

NORA: *(goes to Helmer's door, opens it, and peers in)* Torvald!

HELMER: *(from the inner study)* Well—does one dare set foot in one's own
living room at last? Come on, Rank, now we'll get a look—*(In the
doorway.)* But what's this?

NORA: What, Torvald dear?

HELMER: Rank had me expecting some grand masquerade.

365 RANK: *(in the doorway)* That was my impression, but I must have been
wrong.

NORA: No one can admire me in my splendor—not till tomorrow.

HELMER: But Nora dear, you look so exhausted. Have you practiced too
hard?

NORA: No, I haven't practiced at all yet.

HELMER: You know, it's necessary—

370 NORA: Oh, it's absolutely necessary, Torvald. But I can't get anywhere
without your help. I've forgotten the whole thing completely.

HELMER: Ah, we'll soon take care of that.

NORA: Yes, take care of me, Torvald, please! Promise me that? Oh, I'm so
nervous. That big party—You must give up everything this evening
for me. No business—don't even touch your pen. Yes? Dear Torvald,
promise?

HELMER: It's a promise. Tonight I'm totally at your service—you little
helpless thing. Hm—but first there's one thing I want to—*(Goes
toward the hall door.)*

NORA: What are you looking for?

375 HELMER: Just to see if there's any mail.

NORA: No, no, don't do that, Torvald!

HELMER: Now what?

NORA: Torvald, please. There isn't any.

HELMER: Let me look, though. *(Starts out. Nora, at the piano, strikes the
first notes of the tarantella. Helmer, at the door, stops.)* Aha!

380 NORA: I can't dance tomorrow if I don't practice with you.

HELMER: *(going over to her)* Nora dear, are you really so frightened?

NORA: Yes, so terribly frightened. Let me practice right now; there's still
time before dinner. Oh, sit down and play for me, Torvald. Direct me.
Teach me, the way you always have.

HELMER: Gladly, if it's what you want. *(Sits at the piano.)*

NORA: *(snatches the tambourine up from the box, then a long, varicolored
shawl, which she throws around herself, whereupon she springs forward
and cries out)* Play for me now! Now I'll dance!

*Helmer plays and Nora dances. Rank stands behind Helmer at the piano and
looks on.*

385 HELMER: *(as he plays)* Slower. Slow down.

NORA: Can't change it.

HELMER: Not so violent, Nora!

NORA: Has to be just like this.

HELMER: *(stopping)* No, no, that won't do at all.

390 NORA: *(laughing and swinging her tambourine)* Isn't that what I told you?

RANK: Let me play for her.

HELMER: *(getting up)* Yes, go on. I can teach her more easily then.

Rank sits at the piano and plays; Nora dances more and more wildly. Helmer has stationed himself by the stove and repeatedly gives her directions; she seems not to hear them; her hair loosens and falls over her shoulders; she does not notice, but goes on dancing. Mrs. Linde enters.

MRS. LINDE: *(standing dumbfounded at the door)* Ah—!

NORA: *(still dancing)* See what fun, Kristine!

395 HELMER: But Nora darling, you dance as if your life were at stake.

NORA: And it is.

HELMER: Rank, stop! This is pure madness. Stop it, I say!

Rank breaks off playing, and Nora halts abruptly.

HELMER: *(going over to her)* I never would have believed it. You've
   forgotten everything I taught you.

NORA: *(throwing away the tambourine)* You see for yourself.

400 HELMER: Well, there's certainly room for instruction here.

NORA: Yes, you see how important it is. You've got to teach me to the very
   last minute. Promise me that, Torvald?

HELMER: You can bet on it.

NORA: You mustn't, either today or tomorrow, think about anything else
   but me; you mustn't open any letters—or the mailbox—

HELMER: Ah, it's still the fear of that man—

405 NORA: Oh yes, yes, that too.

HELMER: Nora, it's written all over you—there's already a letter from him
   out there.

NORA: I don't know. I guess so. But you mustn't read such things now;
   there mustn't be anything ugly between us before it's all over.

RANK: *(quietly to Helmer)* You shouldn't deny her.

HELMER: *(putting his arm around her)* The child can have her way. But
   tomorrow night, after you've danced—

410 NORA: Then you'll be free.

MAID: *(in the doorway, right)* Ma'am, dinner is served.

NORA: We'll be wanting champagne, Helene.

MAID: Very good, ma'am. *(Goes out.)*

HELMER: So—a regular banquet, hm?

415 NORA: Yes, a banquet—champagne till daybreak! *(Calling out.)* And some
   macaroons, Helene. Heaps of them—just this once.

HELMER: *(taking her hands)* Now, now, now—no hysterics. Be my own
   little lark again.

NORA: Oh, I will soon enough. But go on in—and you, Dr. Rank. Kristine, help me put up my hair.

RANK: *(whispering, as they go)* There's nothing wrong—really wrong, is there?

HELMER: Oh, of course not. It's nothing more than this childish anxiety I was telling you about. *(They go out, right.)*

420 NORA: Well?

MRS. LINDE: Left town.

NORA: I could see by your face.

MRS. LINDE: He'll be home tomorrow evening. I wrote him a note.

NORA: You shouldn't have. Don't try to stop anything now. After all, it's a wonderful joy, this waiting here for the miracle.

425 MRS. LINDE: What is it you're waiting for?

NORA: Oh, you can't understand that. Go in to them: I'll be along in a moment.

Mrs. Linde goes into the dining room. Nora stands a short while as if composing herself; then she looks at her watch.

NORA: Five. Seven hours to midnight. Twenty-four hours to the midnight after, and then the tarantella's done. Seven and twenty-four? Thirty-one hours to live.

HELMER: *(in the doorway, right)* What's become of the little lark?

NORA: *(going toward him with open arms)* Here's your lark!

ACT III

Same scene. The table, with chairs around it, has been moved to the center of the room. A lamp on the table is lit. The hall door stands open. Dance music drifts down from the floor above. Mrs. Linde sits at the table, absently paging through a book, trying to read, but apparently unable to focus her thoughts. Once or twice she pauses, tensely listening for a sound at the outer entrance.

MRS. LINDE: *(glancing at her watch)* Not yet—and there's hardly any time left. If only he's not—(Listening again.) Ah, there he is. *(She goes out in the hall and cautiously opens the outer door. Quiet footsteps are heard on the stairs. She whispers:)* Come in. Nobody's here.

KROGSTAD: *(in the doorway)* I found a note from you at home. What's back of all this?

MRS. LINDE: I just *had* to talk to you.

KROGSTAD: Oh? And it just *had* to be here in this house?

5 MRS. LINDE: At my place it was impossible; my room hasn't a private entrance. Come in; we're all alone. The maid's asleep, and the Helmers are at the dance upstairs.

KROGSTAD: *(entering the room)* Well, well, the Helmers are dancing tonight? Really?

MRS. LINDE: Yes, why not?

KROGSTAD: How true—why not?

MRS. LINDE: All right, Krogstad, let's talk.

10 KROGSTAD: Do we two have anything more to talk about?

MRS. LINDE: We have a great deal to talk about.

KROGSTAD: I wouldn't have thought so.

MRS. LINDE: No, because you've never understood me, really.

KROGSTAD: Was there anything more to understand—except what's all too common in life? A calculating woman throws over a man the moment a better catch comes by.

15 MRS. LINDE: You think I'm so thoroughly calculating? You think I broke it off lightly?

KROGSTAD: Didn't you?

MRS. LINDE: Nils—is that what you really thought?

KROGSTAD: If you cared, then why did you write me the way you did?

MRS. LINDE: What else could I do? If I had to break off with you, then it was my job as well to root out everything you felt for me.

20 KROGSTAD: *(wringing his hands)* So that was it. And this—all this, simply for money!

MRS. LINDE: Don't forget I had a helpless mother and two small brothers. We couldn't wait for you, Nils; you had such a long road ahead of you then.

KROGSTAD: That may be; but you still hadn't the right to abandon me for somebody else's sake.

MRS. LINDE: Yes—I don't know. So many, many times I've asked myself if I did have that right.

KROGSTAD: *(more softly)* When I lost you, it was as if all the solid ground dissolved from under my feet. Look at me; I'm a half-drowned man now, hanging onto a wreck.

25 MRS. LINDE: Help may be near.

KROGSTAD: It was near—but then you came and blocked it off.

MRS. LINDE: Without my knowing it, Nils. Today for the first time I learned that it's you I'm replacing at the bank.

KROGSTAD: All right—I believe you. But now that you know, will you step aside?

MRS. LINDE: No, because that wouldn't benefit you in the slightest.

30 KROGSTAD: Not "benefit" me, hm! I'd step aside anyway.

MRS. LINDE: I've learned to be realistic. Life and hard, bitter necessity have taught me that.

KROGSTAD: And life's taught me never to trust fine phrases.

MRS. LINDE: Then life's taught you a very sound thing. But you do have to trust in actions, don't you?

KROGSTAD: What does that mean?

35 MRS. LINDE: You said you were hanging on like a half-drowned man to a wreck.

KROGSTAD: I've good reason to say that.

Mrs. Linde: I'm also like a half-drowned woman on a wreck. No one to
    suffer with; no one to care for.

Krogstad: You made your choice.

Mrs. Linde: There wasn't any choice then.

40 Krogstad: So—what of it?

Mrs. Linde: Nils, if only we two shipwrecked people could reach across
    to each other.

Krogstad: What are you saying?

Mrs. Linde: Two on one wreck are at least better off than each on his own.

Krogstad: Kristine!

45 Mrs. Linde: Why do you think I came into town?

Krogstad: Did you really have some thought of me?

Mrs. Linde: I have to work to go on living. All my born days, as long as I
    can remember, I've worked, and it's been my best and my only joy.
    But now I'm completely alone in the world; it frightens me to be so
    empty and lost. To work for yourself—there's no joy in that. Nils, give
    me something—someone to work for.

Krogstad: I don't believe all this. It's just some hysterical feminine urge
    to go out and make a noble sacrifice.

Mrs. Linde: Have you ever found me to be hysterical?

50 Krogstad: Can you honestly mean this? Tell me—do you know
    everything about my past?

Mrs. Linde: Yes.

Krogstad: And you know what they think I'm worth around here.

Mrs. Linde: From what you were saying before, it would seem that with
    me you could have been another person.

Krogstad: I'm positive of that.

55 Mrs. Linde: Couldn't it happen still?

Krogstad: Kristine—you're saying this in all seriousness? Yes, you are! I
    can see it in you. And do you really have the courage, then—?

Mrs. Linde: I need to have someone to care for; and your children need a
    mother. We both need each other. Nils, I have faith that you're good
    at heart—I'll risk everything together with you.

Krogstad: *(gripping her hands)* Kristine, thank you, thank you—Now I
    know I can win back a place in their eyes. Yes—but I forgot—

Mrs. Linde: *(listening)* Shh! The tarantella. Go now! Go on!

60 Krogstad: Why? What is it?

Mrs. Linde: Hear the dance up there? When that's over, they'll be
    coming down.

Krogstad: Oh, then I'll go. But—it's all pointless. Of course, you don't
    know the move I made against the Helmers.

Mrs. Linde: Yes, Nils, I know.

Krogstad: And all the same, you have the courage to—?

65 Mrs. Linde: I know how far despair can drive a man like you.

Krogstad: Oh, if I only could take it all back.

Mrs. Linde: You easily could—your letter's still lying in the mailbox.

KROGSTAD: Are you sure of that?

MRS. LINDE: Positive. But—

70 KROGSTAD: *(looks at her searchingly)* Is that the meaning of it, then? You'll save your friend at any price. Tell me straight out. Is that it?

MRS. LINDE: Nils—anyone who's sold herself for somebody else once isn't going to do it again.

KROGSTAD: I'll demand my letter back.

MRS. LINDE: No, no.

KROGSTAD: Yes, of course. I'll stay here till Helmer comes down; I'll tell him to give me my letter again—that it only involves my dismissal— that he shouldn't read it—

75 MRS. LINDE: No, Nils, don't call the letter back.

KROGSTAD: But wasn't that exactly why you wrote me to come here?

MRS. LINDE: Yes, in that first panic. But it's been a whole day and night since then, and in that time I've seen such incredible things in this house. Helmer's got to learn everything; this dreadful secret has to be aired; those two have to come to a full understanding; all these lies and evasions can't go on.

KROGSTAD: Well, then, if you want to chance it. But at least there's one thing I can do, and do right away—

MRS. LINDE: *(listening)* Go now, go, quick! The dance is over. We're not safe another second.

80 KROGSTAD: I'll wait for you downstairs.

MRS. LINDE: Yes, please do; take me home.

KROGSTAD: I can't believe it; I've never been so happy. *(He leaves by way of the outer door; the door between the room and the hall stays open.)*

MRS. LINDE: *(straightening up a bit and getting together her street clothes)* How different now! How different! Someone to work for, to live for— a home to build. Well, it is worth the try! Oh, if they'd only come! *(Listening.)* Ah, there they are. Bundle up. *(She picks up her hat and coat. Nora's and Helmer's voices can be heard outside; a key turns in the lock, and Helmer brings Nora into the hall almost by force. She is wearing the Italian costume with a large black shawl about her; he has on evening dress, with a black domino open over it.)*

NORA: *(struggling in the doorway)* No, no, no, not inside! I'm going up again. I don't want to leave so soon.

85 HELMER: But Nora dear—

NORA: Oh, I beg you, please, Torvald. From the bottom of my heart, *please*—only an hour more!

HELMER: Not a single minute, Nora darling. You know our agreement. Come on, in we go; you'll catch cold out here. *(In spite of her resistance, he gently draws her into the room.)*

MRS. LINDE: Good evening.

NORA: Kristine!

90 HELMER: Why, Mrs. Linde—are you here so late?

MRS. LINDE: Yes, I'm sorry, but I did want to see Nora in costume.

NORA: Have you been sitting here, waiting for me?

MRS. LINDE: Yes. I didn't come early enough; you were all upstairs; and then I thought I really couldn't leave without seeing you.

HELMER: *(removing Nora's shawl)* Yes, take a good look. She's worth looking at, I can tell you that, Mrs. Linde. Isn't she lovely?

95 MRS. LINDE: Yes, I should say—

HELMER: A dream of loveliness, isn't she? That's what everyone thought at the party, too. But she's horribly stubborn—this sweet little thing. What's to be done with her? Can you imagine, I almost had to use force to pry her away.

NORA: Oh, Torvald, you're going to regret you didn't indulge me, even for just a half hour more.

HELMER: There, you see. She danced her tarantella and got a tumultuous hand—which was well earned, although the performance may have been a bit too naturalistic—I mean it rather overstepped the proprieties of art. But never mind—what's important is, she made a success, an overwhelming success. You think I could let her stay on after that and spoil the effect? Oh no; I took my lovely little Capri girl—my capricious little Capri girl, I should say—took her under my arm; one quick tour of the ballroom, a curtsy to every side, and then—as they say in novels—the beautiful vision disappeared. An exit should always be effective, Mrs. Linde, but that's what I can't get Nora to grasp. Phew, it's hot in here. *(Flings the domino on a chair and opens the door to his room.)* Why's it dark in here? Oh yes, of course. Excuse me. *(He goes in and lights a couple of candles.)*

NORA: *(in a sharp, breathless whisper)* So?

100 MRS. LINDE: *(quietly)* I talked with him.

NORA: And—?

MRS. LINDE: Nora—you must tell your husband everything.

NORA: *(dully)* I knew it.

MRS. LINDE: You've got nothing to fear from Krogstad, but you have to speak out.

105 NORA: I won't tell.

MRS. LINDE: Then the letter will.

NORA: Thanks, Kristine. I know now what's to be done. Shh!

HELMER: *(reentering)* Well, then, Mrs. Linde—have you admired her?

MRS. LINDE: Yes, and now I'll say good night.

110 HELMER: Oh, come, so soon? Is this yours, this knitting?

MRS. LINDE: Yes, thanks. I nearly forgot it.

HELMER: Do you knit, then?

MRS. LINDE: Oh yes.

HELMER: You know what? You should embroider instead.

115 MRS. LINDE: Really? Why?

HELMER: Yes, because it's a lot prettier. See here, one holds the embroidery so, in the left hand, and then one guides the needle with the right—so—in an easy, sweeping curve—right?

MRS. LINDE: Yes, I guess that's—

HELMER: But, on the other hand, knitting—it can never be anything but ugly. Look, see here, the arms tucked in, the knitting needles going up and down—there's something Chinese about it. Ah, that was really a glorious champagne they served.

MRS. LINDE: Yes, good night, Nora, and don't be stubborn any more.

120 HELMER: Well put, Mrs. Linde!

MRS. LINDE: Good night, Mr. Helmer.

HELMER: *(accompanying her to the door)* Good night, good night. I hope you get home all right. I'd be very happy to—but you don't have far to go. Good night, good night. *(She leaves. He shuts the door after her and returns.)* There, now, at last we got her out the door. She's a deadly bore, that creature.

NORA: Aren't you pretty tired, Torvald?

HELMER: No, not a bit.

125 NORA: You're not sleepy?

HELMER: Not at all. On the contrary, I'm feeling quite exhilarated. But you? Yes, you really look tired and sleepy.

NORA: Yes, I'm very tired. Soon now I'll sleep.

HELMER: See! You see! I was right all along that we shouldn't stay longer.

NORA: Whatever you do is always right.

130 HELMER: *(kissing her brow)* Now my little lark talks sense. Say, did you notice what a time Rank was having tonight?

NORA: Oh, was he? I didn't get to speak with him.

HELMER: I scarcely did either, but it's a long time since I've seen him in such high spirits. *(Gazes at her a moment, then comes nearer her.)* Hm— it's marvelous, though, to be back home again—to be completely alone with you. Oh, you bewitchingly lovely young woman!

NORA: Torvald, don't look at me like that!

HELMER: Can't I look at my richest treasure? At all that beauty that's mine, mine alone—completely and utterly.

135 NORA: *(moving around to the other side of the table)* You mustn't talk to me that way tonight.

HELMER: *(following her)* The tarantella is still in your blood, I can see— and it makes you even more enticing. Listen. The guests are beginning to go. *(Dropping his voice.)* Nora—it'll soon be quiet through this whole house.

NORA: Yes, I hope so.

HELMER: You do, don't you, my love? Do you realize—when I'm out at a party like this with you—do you know why I talk to you so little, and keep such a distance away; just send you a stolen look now and then—you know why I do it? It's because I'm imagining then that you're my secret darling, my secret young bride-to-be, and that no one suspects there's anything between us.

NORA: Yes, yes; oh, yes, I know you're always thinking of me.

140 HELMER: And then when we leave and I place the shawl over those fine young rounded shoulders—over that wonderful curving neck—then I pretend that you're my young bride, that we're just coming from the

wedding, that for the first time I'm bringing you into my house—that for the first time I'm alone with you—completely alone with you, your trembling young beauty! All this evening I've longed for nothing but you. When I saw you turn and sway in the tarantella—my blood was pounding till I couldn't stand it—that's why I brought you down here so early—

NORA: Go away, Torvald! Leave me alone. I don't want all this.

HELMER: What do you mean? Nora, you're teasing me. You will, won't you? Aren't I your husband—?

A knock at the outside door.

NORA: *(startled)* What's that?

HELMER: *(going toward the hall)* Who is it?

145 RANK: *(outside)* It's me. May I come in a moment?

HELMER: *(with quiet irritation)* Oh, what does he want now? *(Aloud.)* Hold on. *(Goes and opens the door.)* Oh, how nice that you didn't just pass us by!

RANK: I thought I heard your voice, and then I wanted so badly to have a look in. *(Lightly glancing about.)* Ah, me, these old familiar haunts. You have it snug and cozy in here, you two.

HELMER: You seemed to be having it pretty cozy upstairs, too.

RANK: Absolutely. Why shouldn't I? Why not take in everything in life? As much as you can, anyway, and as long as you can. The wine was superb—

150 HELMER: The champagne especially.

RANK: You noticed that too? It's amazing how much I could guzzle down.

NORA: Torvald also drank a lot of champagne this evening.

RANK: Oh?

NORA: Yes, and that always makes him so entertaining.

155 RANK: Well, why shouldn't one have a pleasant evening after a well spent day?

HELMER: Well spent? I'm afraid I can't claim that.

RANK: *(slapping him on the back)* But I can, you see!

NORA: Dr. Rank, you must have done some scientific research today.

RANK: Quite so.

160 HELMER: Come now—little Nora talking about scientific research!

NORA: And can I congratulate you on the results?

RANK: Indeed you may.

NORA: Then they were good?

RANK: The best possible for both doctor and patient—certainty.

165 NORA: *(quickly and searchingly)* Certainty?

RANK: Complete certainty. So don't I owe myself a gay evening afterwards?

NORA: Yes, you're right, Dr. Rank.

HELMER: I'm with you—just so long as you don't have to suffer for it in the morning.

RANK: Well, one never gets something for nothing in life.

170 NORA: Dr. Rank—are you very fond of masquerade parties?

RANK: Yes, if there's a good array of odd disguises—

NORA: Tell me, what should we two go as at the next masquerade?

HELMER: You little featherhead—already thinking of the next!

RANK: We two? I'll tell you what: you must go as Charmed Life—

175 HELMER: Yes, but find a costume for *that!*

RANK: Your wife can appear just as she looks every day.

HELMER: That was nicely put. But don't you know what you're going to be?

RANK: Yes, Helmer, I've made up my mind.

HELMER: Well?

180 RANK: At the next masquerade I'm going to be invisible.

HELMER: That's a funny idea.

RANK: They say there's a hat—black, huge—have you never heard of the hat that makes you invisible? You put it on, and then no one on earth can see you.

HELMER: *(suppressing a smile)* Ah, of course.

RANK: But I'm quite forgetting what I came for. Helmer, give me a cigar, one of the dark Havanas.

185 HELMER: With the greatest of pleasure. *(Holds out his case.)*

RANK: Thanks. *(Takes one and cuts off the tip.)*

NORA: *(striking a match)* Let me give you a light.

RANK: Thank you. *(She holds the match for him; he lights the cigar.)* And now good-bye.

HELMER: Good-bye, good-bye, old friend.

190 NORA: Sleep well, Doctor.

RANK: Thanks for that wish.

NORA: Wish me the same.

RANK: You? All right, if you like—Sleep well. And thanks for the light. *(He nods to them both and leaves.)*

HELMER: *(his voice subdued)* He's been drinking heavily.

195 NORA: *(absently)* Could be. *(Helmer takes his keys from his pocket and goes out in the hall.)* Torvald—what are you after?

HELMER: Got to empty the mailbox; it's nearly full. There won't be room for the morning papers.

NORA: Are you working tonight?

HELMER: You know I'm not. Why—what's this? Someone's been at the lock.

NORA: At the lock—?

200 HELMER: Yes, I'm positive. What do you suppose—? I can't imagine one of the maids—? Here's a broken hairpin. Nora, it's yours—

NORA: *(quickly)* Then it must be the children—

HELMER: You'd better break them of that. Hm, hm—well, opened it after all. *(Takes the contents out and calls into the kitchen.)* Helene! Helene, would you put out the lamp in the hall. *(He returns to the room, shutting the hall door, then displays the handful of mail.)* Look how it's piled up. *(Sorting through them.)* Now what's this?

NORA: *(at the window)* The letter! Oh, Torvald, no!

HELMER: Two calling cards—from Rank.

205 NORA: From Dr. Rank?

HELMER: *(examining them)* "Dr. Rank, Consulting Physician." They were on top. He must have dropped them in as he left.

NORA: Is there anything on them?

HELMER: There's a black cross over the name. See? That's a gruesome notion. He could almost be announcing his own death.

NORA: That's just what he's doing.

210 HELMER: What! You've heard something? Something he's told you?

NORA: Yes. That when those cards came, he'd be taking his leave of us. He'll shut himself in now and die.

HELMER: Ah, my poor friend! Of course I knew he wouldn't be here much longer. But so soon—And then to hide himself away like a wounded animal.

NORA: If it has to happen, then it's best it happens in silence—don't you think so, Torvald?

HELMER: *(pacing up and down)* He'd grown right into our lives. I simply can't imagine him gone. He with his suffering and loneliness—like a dark cloud setting off our sunlit happiness. Well, maybe it's best this way. For him, at least. *(Standing still.)* And maybe for us too, Nora. Now we're thrown back on each other, completely. *(Embracing her.)* Oh you, my darling wife, how can I hold you close enough? You know what, Nora—time and again I've wished you were in some terrible danger, just so I could stake my life and soul and everything, for your sake.

215 NORA: *(tearing herself away, her voice firm and decisive)* Now you must read your mail, Torvald.

HELMER: No, no, not tonight. I want to stay with you, dearest.

NORA: With a dying friend on your mind?

HELMER: You're right. We've both had a shock. There's ugliness between us—these thoughts of death and corruption. We'll have to get free of them first. Until then—we'll stay apart.

NORA: *(clinging about his neck)* Torvald—good night! Good night!

220 HELMER: *(kissing her on the cheek)* Good night, little songbird. Sleep well, Nora. I'll be reading my mail now. *(He takes the letters into his room and shuts the door after him.)*

NORA: *(with bewildered glances, groping about, seizing Helmer's domino, throwing it around her, and speaking in short, hoarse, broken whispers)* Never see him again. Never, never. *(Putting her shawl over her head.)* Never see the children either—them, too. Never, never. Oh, the freezing black water! The depths—down—Oh, I wish it were over—He has it now; he's reading it—now. Oh no, no, not yet. Torvald, good-bye, you and the children—(She starts for the hall; as she does, Helmer throws open his door and stands with an open letter in his hand.)*

HELMER: Nora!

NORA: *(screams)* Oh—!

HELMER: What is this? You know what's in this letter?

225 NORA: Yes, I know. Let me go! Let me out!

HELMER: *(holding her back)* Where are you going?

NORA: *(struggling to break loose)* You can't save me, Torvald!

HELMER: *(slumping back)* True! Then it's true what he writes? How horrible! No, no, it's impossible—it can't be true.

NORA: It *is* true. I've loved you more than all this world.

230 HELMER: Ah, none of your slippery tricks.

NORA: *(taking one step toward him)* Torvald—!

HELMER: What *is* this you've blundered into!

NORA: Just let me loose. You're not going to suffer for my sake. You're not going to take on my guilt.

HELMER: No more playacting. *(Locks the hall door.)* You stay right here and give me a reckoning. You understand what you've done? Answer! You understand?

235 NORA: *(looking squarely at him, her face hardening)* Yes. I'm beginning to understand everything now.

HELMER: *(striding about)* Oh, what an awful awakening! In all these eight years—she who was my pride and joy—a hypocrite, a liar—worse, worse—a criminal! How infinitely disgusting it all is! The shame! *(Nora says nothing and goes on looking straight at him. He stops in front of her.)* I should have suspected something of the kind. I should have known. All your father's flimsy values—Be still! All your father's flimsy values have come out in you. No religion, no morals, no sense of duty—Oh, how I'm punished for letting him off! I did it for your sake, and you repay me like this.

NORA: Yes, like this.

HELMER: Now you've wrecked all my happiness—ruined my whole future. Oh, it's awful to think of. I'm in a cheap little grafter's hands; he can do anything he wants with me, ask for anything, play with me like a puppet—and I can't breathe a word. I'll be swept down miserably into the depths on account of a featherbrained woman.

NORA: When I'm gone from this world, you'll be free.

240 HELMER: Oh, quit posing. Your father had a mess of those speeches too. What good would that ever do me if you were gone from this world, as you say? Not the slightest. He can still make the whole thing known; and if he does, I could be falsely suspected as your accomplice. They might even think that I was behind it—that I put you up to it. And all that I can thank you for—you that I've coddled the whole of our marriage. Can you see now what you've done to me?

NORA: *(icily calm)* Yes.

HELMER: It's so incredible, I just can't grasp it. But we'll have to patch up whatever we can. Take off the shawl. I said, take if off! I've got to appease him somehow or other. The thing has to be hushed up at any cost. And as for you and me, it's got to seem like everything between us is just as it was—to the outside world, that is. You'll go right on living in this house, of course. But you can't be allowed to bring up the children; I don't dare trust you with them—Oh, to have to say this to someone I've loved so much! Well, that's done with. From now on happiness doesn't matter; all that matters is saving the bits and pieces, the appearance—*(The doorbell rings. Helmer starts.)* What's that? And so late. Maybe the worst—? You think he'd—? Hide, Nora! Say you're sick. *(Nora remains standing motionless. Helmer goes and opens the door.)*

MAID: *(half dressed, in the hall)* A letter for Mrs. Helmer.

HELMER: I'll take it. *(Snatches the letter and shuts the door.)* Yes, it's from him. You don't get it; I'm reading it myself.

245 NORA: Then read it.

HELMER: *(by the lamp)* I hardly dare. We may be ruined, you and I. But—I've got to know. *(Rips open the letter, skims through a few lines, glances at an enclosure, then cries out joyfully.)* Nora! *(Nora looks inquiringly at him.)* Nora! Wait—better check it again—Yes, yes, it's true. I'm saved. Nora, I'm saved!

NORA: And I?

HELMER: You too, of course. We're both saved, both of us. Look. He's sent back your note. He says he's sorry and ashamed—that a happy development in his life—oh, who cares what he says! Nora, we're saved! No one can hurt you. Oh, Nora, Nora—but first, this ugliness all has to go. Let me see—*(Takes a look at the note.)* No, I don't want to see it; I want the whole thing to fade like a dream. *(Tears the note and both letters to pieces, throws them into the stove and watches them burn.)* There—now there's nothing left—He wrote that since Christmas Eve you—Oh, they must have been three terrible days for you, Nora.

NORA: I fought a hard fight.

250 HELMER: And suffered pain and saw no escape but—No, we're not going to dwell on anything unpleasant. We'll just be grateful and keep on repeating: it's over now, it's over! You hear me, Nora? You don't seem to realize—it's over. What's it mean—that frozen look? Oh, poor little Nora, I understand. You can't believe I've forgiven you. But I have, Nora; I swear I have. I know that what you did, you did out of love for me.

NORA: That's true.

HELMER: You loved me the way a wife ought to love her husband. It's simply the means that you couldn't judge. But you think I love you any the less for not knowing how to handle your affairs? No, no—just lean on me; I'll guide you and teach you. I wouldn't be a man if this feminine helplessness didn't make you twice as attractive to me. You mustn't mind those sharp words I said—that was all in the first confusion of thinking my world had collapsed. I've forgiven you, Nora; I swear I've forgiven you.

NORA: My thanks for your forgiveness. *(She goes out through the door, right.)*

HELMER: No, wait—*(Peers in.)* What are you doing in there?

255 NORA: *(inside)* Getting out of my costume.

HELMER: *(by the open door)* Yes, do that. Try to calm yourself and collect your thoughts again, my frightened little songbird. You can rest easy now; I've got wide wings to shelter you with. *(Walking about close by the door.)* How snug and nice our home is, Nora. You're safe here; I'll keep you like a hunted dove I've rescued out of a hawk's claws. I'll bring peace to your poor, shuddering heart. Gradually it'll happen, Nora; you'll see. Tomorrow all this will look different to you; then everything will be as it was. I won't have to go on repeating I forgive you; you'll feel it for yourself. How can you imagine I'd ever conceivably want to disown you—or even blame you in any way? Ah, you don't know a man's heart, Nora. For a man there's something indescribably sweet and satisfying in knowing he's forgiven his wife— and forgiven her out of a full and open heart. It's as if she belongs to him in two ways now: in a sense he's given her fresh into the world again, and she's become his wife and his child as well. From now on that's what you'll be to me—you little, bewildered, helpless thing. Don't be afraid of anything, Nora; just open your heart to me, and I'll be conscience and will to you both—*(Nora enters in her regular clothes.)* What's this? Not in bed? You've changed your dress?

NORA: Yes, Torvald, I've changed my dress.

HELMER: But why now, so late?

NORA: Tonight I'm not sleeping.

260 HELMER: But Nora dear—

NORA: *(looking at her watch)* It's still not so very late. Sit down, Torvald; we have a lot to talk over. *(She sits at one side of the table.)*

HELMER: Nora—what is this? That hard expression—

NORA: Sit down. This'll take some time. I have a lot to say.

HELMER: *(sitting at the table directly opposite her)* You worry me, Nora. And I don't understand you.

265 NORA: No, that's exactly it. You don't understand me. And I've never understood you either—until tonight. No, don't interrupt. You can just listen to what I say. We're closing out accounts, Torvald.

HELMER: How do you mean that?

NORA: *(after a short pause)* Doesn't anything strike you about our sitting here like this?

HELMER: What's that?

NORA: We've been married now eight years. Doesn't it occur to you that this is the first time we two, you and I, man and wife, have ever talked seriously together?

270 HELMER: What do you mean—seriously?

NORA: In eight whole years—longer even—right from our first acquaintance, we've never exchanged a serious word on any serious thing.

HELMER: You mean I should constantly go and involve you in problems you couldn't possibly help me with?

NORA: I'm not talking of problems. I'm saying that we've never sat down seriously together and tried to get to the bottom of anything.

HELMER: But dearest, what good would that ever do you?

275 NORA: That's the point right there: you've never understood me. I've been wronged greatly, Torvald—first by Papa, and then by you.

HELMER: What! By us—the two people who've loved you more than anyone else?

NORA: *(shaking her head)* You never loved me. You've thought it fun to be in love with me, that's all.

HELMER: Nora, what a thing to say!

NORA: Yes, it's true now, Torvald. When I lived at home with Papa, he told me all his opinions, so I had the same ones too; or if they were different I hid them, since he wouldn't have cared for that. He used to call me his doll-child, and he played with me the way I played with my dolls. Then I came into your house—

280 HELMER: How can you speak of our marriage like that?

NORA: *(unperturbed)* I mean, then I went from Papa's hands into yours. You arranged everything to your own taste, and so I got the same taste as you—or I pretended to; I can't remember. I guess a little of both, first one, then the other. Now when I look back, it seems as if I'd lived here like a beggar—just from hand to mouth. I've lived by doing tricks for you, Torvald. But that's the way you wanted it. It's a great sin what you and Papa did to me. You're to blame that nothing's become of me.

HELMER: Nora, how unfair and ungrateful you are! Haven't you been happy here?

NORA: No, never. I thought so—but I never have.

HELMER: Not—not happy!

285 NORA: No, only lighthearted. And you've always been so kind to me. But our home's been nothing but a playpen. I've been your doll-wife here, just as at home I was Papa's doll-child. And in turn the children have been my dolls. I thought it was fun when you played with me, just as they thought it fun when I played with them. That's been our marriage, Torvald.

HELMER: There's some truth in what you're saying—under all the raving exaggeration. But it'll all be different after this. Playtime's over; now for the schooling.

NORA: Whose schooling—mine or the children's?

HELMER: Both yours and the children's, dearest.

NORA: Oh, Torvald, you're not the man to teach me to be a good wife to you.

290 HELMER: And you can say that?

NORA: And I—how am I equipped to bring up children?

HELMER: Nora!

NORA: Didn't you say a moment ago that that was no job to trust me with?

HELMER: In a flare of temper! Why fasten on that?

295 NORA: Yes, but you were so very right. I'm not up to the job. There's another job I have to do first. I have to try to educate myself. You can't help me with that. I've got to do it alone. And that's why I'm leaving you now.

HELMER: *(jumping up)* What's that?

NORA: I have to stand completely alone, if I'm ever going to discover myself and the world out there. So I can't go on living with you.

HELMER: Nora, Nora!

NORA: I want to leave right away. Kristine should put me up for the night—

300 HELMER: You're insane! You've no right! I forbid you!

NORA: From here on, there's no use forbidding me anything. I'll take with me whatever is mine. I don't want a thing from you, either now or later.

HELMER: What kind of madness is this!

NORA: Tomorrow I'm going home—I mean, home where I came from. It'll be easier up there to find something to do.

HELMER: Oh, you blind, incompetent child!

305 NORA: I must learn to be competent, Torvald.

HELMER: Abandon your home, your husband, your children! And you're not even thinking what people will say.

NORA: I can't be concerned about that. I only know how essential this is.

HELMER: Oh, it's outrageous. So you'll run out like this on your most sacred vows.

NORA: What do you think are my most sacred vows?

310 HELMER: And I have to tell you that! Aren't they your duties to your husband and children?

NORA: I have other duties equally sacred.

HELMER: That isn't true. What duties are they?

NORA: Duties to myself.

HELMER: Before all else, you're a wife and a mother.

315 NORA: I don't believe in that any more. I believe that, before all else, I'm a human being, no less than you—or anyway, I ought to try to become one. I know the majority thinks you're right, Torvald, and plenty of books agree with you, too. But I can't go on believing what the majority says, or what's written in books. I have to think over these things myself and try to understand them.

HELMER: Why can't you understand your place in your own home? On a point like that, isn't there one everlasting guide you can turn to? Where's your religion?

NORA: Oh, Torvald, I'm really not sure what religion is.

HELMER: What—?

NORA: I only know what the minister said when I was confirmed. He told me religion was this thing and that. When I get clear and away by myself, I'll go into that problem too. I'll see if what the minister said was right, or, in any case, if it's right for me.

320 HELMER: A young woman your age shouldn't talk like that. If religion can't move you, I can try to rouse your conscience. You do have some moral feeling? Or, tell me—has that gone too?

NORA: It's not easy to answer that, Torvald. I simply don't know. I'm all confused about these things. I just know I see them so differently from you. I find out, for one thing, that the law's not at all what I'd thought—but I can't get it through my head that the law is fair. A woman hasn't a right to protect her dying father or save her husband's life! I can't believe that.

HELMER: You talk like a child. You don't know anything of the world you live in.

NORA: No, I don't. But now I'll begin to learn for myself. I'll try to discover who's right, the world or I.

HELMER: Nora, you're sick; you've got a fever. I almost think you're out of your head.

325 NORA: I've never felt more clearheaded and sure in my life.

HELMER: And—clearheaded and sure—you're leaving your husband and children?

NORA: Yes.

HELMER: Then there's only one possible reason.

NORA: What?

330 HELMER: You no longer love me.

NORA: No. That's exactly it.

HELMER: Nora! You can't be serious!

NORA: Oh, this is so hard, Torvald—you've been so kind to me always. But I can't help it. I don't love you any more.

HELMER: (struggling for composure) Are you also clearheaded and sure about that?

335 NORA: Yes, completely. That's why I can't go on staying here.

HELMER: Can you tell me what I did to lose your love?

NORA: Yes, I can tell you. It was this evening when the miraculous thing didn't come—then I knew you weren't the man I'd imagined.

HELMER: Be more explicit; I don't follow you.

NORA: I've waited now so patiently eight long years—for, my Lord, I know miracles don't come every day. Then this crisis broke over me, and such a certainty filled me: *now* the miraculous event would occur. While Krogstad's letter was lying out there, I never for an instant dreamed that you could give in to his terms. I was so utterly sure you'd say to him: go on, tell your tale to the whole wide world. And when he'd done that—

340 HELMER: Yes, what then? When I'd delivered my own wife into shame and disgrace—!

NORA: When he'd done that, I was so utterly sure that you'd step forward, take the blame on yourself and say: I am the guilty one.

HELMER: Nora—!

NORA: You're thinking I'd never accept such a sacrifice from you? No, of course not. But what good would my protests be against you? That was the miracle I was waiting for, in terror and hope. And to stave that off, I would have taken my life.

HELMER: I'd gladly work for you day and night, Nora—and take on pain and deprivation. But there's no one who gives up honor for love.

345 NORA: Millions of women have done just that.

HELMER: Oh, you think and talk like a silly child.

NORA: Perhaps. But you neither think nor talk like the man I could join myself to. When your big fright was over—and it wasn't from any threat against me, only for what might damage you—when all the danger was past, for you it was just as if nothing had happened. I was exactly the same, your little lark, your doll, that you'd have to handle with double care now that I'd turned out so brittle and frail. *(Gets up.)* Torvald—in that instant it dawned on me that for eight years I've been living here with a stranger, and that I'd even conceived three children—oh, I can't stand the thought of it! I could tear myself to bits.

HELMER: *(heavily)* I see. There's a gulf that's opened between us—that's clear. Oh, but Nora, can't we bridge it somehow?

NORA: The way I am now, I'm no wife for you.

350 HELMER: I have the strength to make myself over.

NORA: Maybe—if your doll gets taken away.

HELMER: But to part! To part from you! No, Nora, no—I can't imagine it.

NORA: *(going out, right)* All the more reason why it has to be. *(She reenters with her coat and a small overnight bag, which she puts on a chair by the table.)*

HELMER: Nora, Nora, not now! Wait till tomorrow.

355 NORA: I can't spend the night in a strange man's room.

HELMER: But couldn't we live here like brother and sister—

NORA: You know very well how long that would last. *(Throws her shawl about her.)* Good-bye, Torvald. I won't look in on the children. I know they're in better hands than mine. The way I am now, I'm no use to them.

HELMER: But someday, Nora—someday—?

NORA: How can I tell? I haven't the least idea what'll become of me.

360 HELMER: But you're my wife, now and wherever you go.

NORA: Listen, Torvald—I've heard that when a wife deserts her husband's house just as I'm doing, then the law frees him from all responsibility. In any case, I'm freeing you from being responsible. Don't feel yourself bound, any more than I will. There has to be absolute freedom for us both. Here, take your ring back. Give me mine.

HELMER: That too?

NORA: That too.

HELMER: There it is.

365 NORA: Good. Well, now it's all over. I'm putting the keys here. The maids know all about keeping up the house—better than I do. Tomorrow, after I've left town, Kristine will stop by to pack up everything that's mine from home. I'd like those things shipped up to me.

HELMER: Over! All over! Nora, won't you ever think about me?

NORA: I'm sure I'll think of you often, and about the children and the house here.

HELMER: May I write you?

NORA: No—never. You're not to do that.

370 HELMER: Oh, but let me send you—

NORA: Nothing. Nothing.

HELMER: Or help you if you need it.

NORA: No. I accept nothing from strangers.

HELMER: Nora—can I never be more than a stranger to you?

375 NORA: *(picking up the overnight bag)* Ah, Torvald—it would take the greatest miracle of all—

HELMER: Tell me the greatest miracle!

NORA: You and I both would have to transform ourselves to the point that—Oh, Torvald, I've stopped believing in miracles.

HELMER: But I'll believe. Tell me! Transform ourselves to the point that—?

NORA: That our living together could be a true marriage. *(She goes out down the hall.)*

380 HELMER: *(sinks down on a chair by the door, face buried in his hands)* Nora! Nora! *(Looking about and rising.)* Empty. She's gone. *(A sudden hope leaps in him.)* The greatest miracle—?

From below, the sound of a door slamming shut.

READING AND REACTING

1. What is your attitude toward Nora at the beginning of the play? How does your attitude toward her change as the play progresses? What actions and/or lines of dialogue change your assessment of her?

2. List the key events that occur before the play begins. How do we learn of each event?

3. In act 1, how do the various references to macaroons in the stage directions reinforce plot developments?

4. Explain the role of each of the following in advancing the play's action: the Christmas tree, the locked mailbox, the telegram Dr. Rank receives, Dr. Rank's calling cards.

5. In act 2, Torvald says, "Whatever comes, you'll see: when it really counts, I have strength and courage enough as a man to take on the whole weight myself." How does this statement influence Nora's subsequent actions?

6. How do the upcoming costume party and Nora's dance influence the development of the play's plot? Where does the play's climax occur?

7. Explain how the following foreshadow events that will occur later in the play: Torvald's comments about Krogstad's children (act 1); Torvald's attitude toward Nora's father (act 2); Krogstad's suggestions about suicide (act 2).

8. In addition to the play's main plot—which concerns the blackmail of Nora by Krogstad and her attempts to keep her crime secret from Torvald—the play contains several subplots, some of which have developed before the play begins and some of which unfold alongside the main plot. Identify these subplots. How do they advance the themes of survival, debt, sacrifice, and duty that run through the play?

9. Is Kristine Linde essential to the play? How might the play be different without her?

10. Is Mrs. Linde as much of a "modern woman" as Nora? Is she actually *more* of a modern woman? Explain.

11. Do you think *A Doll House* is primarily about the struggle between the needs of the individual and the needs of society, or about the conflict between women's roles in the family and in the larger society? Explain.

12. **JOURNAL ENTRY** Nora makes a drastic decision at the end of the play. Do you think she overreacts? What other options does she have? What other options might she have today?

13. **CRITICAL PERSPECTIVE** Since its earliest performances, there has been much comment on the conclusion of *A Doll House*. Many viewers have found the play's ending unrealistically harsh. In fact, a famous German actress refused to play the scene as written because she insisted she would never leave her children. (Ibsen reluctantly rewrote the ending for her; in this version, Helmer forces Nora to the doorway of the children's bedroom, and she sinks to the floor as the curtain falls.) Moreover, many critics have found it hard to accept Nora's transformation from, in Elizabeth Hardwick's words, "the girlish, charming wife to the radical, courageous heroine setting out alone" ("Ibsen's Women" in *Seduction and Betrayal*).

    What is your response to the play's ending? Do you think it makes sense in light of what we have learned about Nora and her marriage? Or do you, for example, agree with Hardwick that Nora's abandonment of her children is not only implausible but also a "rather casual" gesture that "drops a stain on our admiration of Nora"?

Related Works: "The Story of an Hour" (p. 77), "The Chrysanthemums" (p. 333), "The Rocking-Horse Winner" (p. 362), "The Birthmark" (p. 450), "Girl" (p. 509), "Barbie Doll" (p. 980)

◇ **WRITING SUGGESTIONS: PLOT**

1. Central to the plots of both *Trifles* and *A Doll House* is a woman who commits a crime. Compare and contrast the reactions of the two plays' other characters, particularly each woman's friends, to her crime.

2. Write an essay in which you compare the influence of Nora's father on the plot of *A Doll House* to the role of the father in another play in this text, such as *The Glass Menagerie* (p. 1805) or *Hamlet* (p. 1307).

3. In both *Trifles* and *A Doll House,* the plot depends to some extent on the fact that male characters misjudge—and perhaps underestimate—women. Write an essay in which you compare and contrast the attitudes the men in these plays hold toward women, the ways in which they reveal these attitudes, and the ways in which the women react.

4. Three of the four plays in this chapter deal with troubled marriages. Suppose you were a marriage counselor and one of the couples came to you for help. What would you say to them? Write an essay in which you give the troubled couple advice for saving their marriage.

5. Write a monologue for Miss Y, including everything you think she would like to tell Mrs. X. Or write a monologue for *Florence,* including everything she would like to tell her mother.

6. **WEB ACTIVITY** The following Web site contains information about Henrik Ibsen:

   http://www.hf.uio.no/ibsensenteret/index_eng.html

   According to this Web site from the University of Oslo, Ibsen is considered the father of modern drama. Locate a Web site that gives a thorough definition of "modernism." Write an essay about how *A Doll House* exhibits the characteristics of modernism.

CHAPTER 23

Character

◊ ◊ ◊

Character in a play is like a blank check which a dramatist accords to the actor for him to fill in—not entirely blank, for a number of indications of individuality are already there, but to a far less definite and absolute degree than in the novel.

THORNTON WILDER, "Some Thoughts on Playwriting"

A character living onstage is a union of the creative talents of the actor and the dramatist. Any argument over which of the two is more important is futile because they are completely interdependent. The actor requires the character created by the dramatist to provide the initial and vital stimulus. The dramatist requires the embodiment of the character by the actor to bring his creation to fulfillment. The result of this collaboration is the finished performance to which both the actor and the dramatist have made a unique contribution. The result can be neither Shakespeare's Macbeth nor the actor's Macbeth. It must be the actor *as* Shakespeare's Macbeth.

CHARLES McGRAW, *Acting Is Believing*, 2d ed.

Shakespeare is above all writers, at least above all modern writers, the poet of nature: the poet that holds up to his readers a faithful mirror of manners and life. His characters are not modified by the customs of particular places, unpracticed by the rest of the world; by the peculiarities of studies or professions, which can operate but upon small numbers; or by the accidents of transient fashions or temporary opinions: they are the genuine progeny of common humanity, such as the world will always supply, and observation will always find.

From the Preface to Samuel Johnson's Edition of Shakespeare

A sensible playwright would write a play with three or four people. Three is best. A man and his dog is even better.

TOM STOPPARD, quoted in the *New York Times*

◊ ◊ ◊

In Tennessee Williams's 1945 play *The Glass Menagerie* (p. 1805) the protagonist, Tom Wingfield, functions as the play's narrator. Stepping out of his role as a character and speaking directly to the audience, he directs the play's action, music, lighting, and other elements. In addition, he summarizes characters' actions, explains their motivation, and discusses the significance of their behavior in the context of the play—commenting on his own character's actions as well. As narrator, Tom also presents useful background information about the characters. For instance, when he introduces his coworker, Jim, he prepares readers for Jim's entrance and helps them to understand his subsequent actions:

> In high school Jim was a hero. He had tremendous Irish good nature and vitality with the scrubbed and polished look of white chinaware. He seemed to move in a continual spotlight. [. . .] But Jim apparently ran into more interference after his graduation. [. . .] His speed had definitely slowed. Six years after he left high school he was holding a job that wasn't much better than mine.

Most plays, however, do not include narrators who present background. Instead, readers learn about characters from their own words and from comments by others about them, as well as from the characters' actions and from the playwright's stage directions. At a performance, the audience has the added advantage of seeing the actors' interpretations of the characters.

Characters in plays, like characters in novels and short stories, may be **round** or **flat, static** or **dynamic.** Generally speaking, major characters are likely to be round, whereas minor characters are likely to be flat. Through the language and the actions of the characters, audiences learn whether the characters are multidimensional, skimpily developed, or perhaps merely **foils,** players whose main purpose is to shed light on more important characters. Audiences also learn about the emotions, attitudes, and values that help to shape the characters—their hopes and fears, their strengths and weaknesses. In addition, by comparing characters' early words and actions with later ones, audiences learn from the play whether or not characters grow and change emotionally.

CHARACTERS' WORDS
❖ ❖ ❖

Characters' words reveal the most about their attitudes, feelings, beliefs, and values. Sometimes information is communicated (to other characters as well as to the audience) in a **monologue**—an extended speech by one character. This device is used with great success in August Strindberg's *The Stronger* (p. 1177). A **soliloquy**—a monologue revealing a character's thoughts and feelings, directed at the audience and presumed not to be heard by other characters—can also convey information about a character. For example, Hamlet's well-known soliloquy that begins "To be or not to be" eloquently communicates his distraught mental state—his resentment of his mother and uncle, his confusion about what course of action to take, his suicidal thoughts. Finally, **dialogue**—an exchange of words between two characters—can reveal misunderstanding or conflict between them, or it can show their agreement, mutual support, or similar beliefs.

In Henrik Ibsen's *A Doll House* (p. 1196), dialogue reveals a good deal about the characters. Nora Helmer, the spoiled young wife, has broken the law and kept her crime secret from her husband. Through her words, we learn about her motivation, her emotions, and her reactions to other characters and to her potentially dangerous situation. We learn, for instance, that she is flirtatious—"If your little squirrel begged you, with all her heart and soul [. . .]" (act 2)—and that she is childishly unrealistic about the consequences of her actions. When her husband, Torvald, asks what she would do if he was seriously injured, leaving her in debt, she says, "If anything so awful happened, then it just wouldn't matter if I had debts or not" (act 1). When Torvald presses, "Well, but the people I'd borrowed from?" she dismisses them: "Them? Who cares about them! They're strangers." As the play progresses, Nora's lack of understanding of the power of the law becomes more and more significant as she struggles with her moral and ethical dilemma.

The inability of both Nora and Torvald to confront ugly truths is also revealed through their words. When, in act 1, Nora tells Krogstad, her blackmailer, that his revealing her secret could expose her to "the most horrible unpleasantness," he responds, "Only unpleasantness?" Yet later on, in act 3, Torvald uses the same word, fastidiously dismissing the horror with, "No, we're not going to dwell on anything unpleasant."

The ease with which Torvald is able to dismiss his dying friend Dr. Rank in act 3 ("He with his suffering and loneliness—like a dark cloud setting off our sunlit happiness. Well, maybe it's best this way.") exposes his egocentrism and foreshadows the lack of support he will give Nora immediately thereafter. Especially revealing is his use of *I* and *my* and *me,* which convey his self-centeredness:

> Now you've wrecked all my happiness—ruined my whole future. Oh, it's awful to think of. I'm in a cheap little grafter's hands; he can do anything he wants with me, ask for anything, play with me like a puppet—and I can't breathe a word. I'll be swept down miserably into the depths on account of a featherbrained woman.

Just as Torvald's words reveal that he has not been changed by the play's events, Nora's words show that she has changed significantly. Her dialogue near the end of act 3 shows that she has become a responsible, determined woman—one who understands her situation and her options and is no longer blithely oblivious to her duties. When she says, "I've never felt more clearheaded and sure in my life," she is calm and decisive; when she says, "Our home's been nothing but a playpen. I've been your doll-wife here, just as at home I was Papa's doll-child," she reveals her newly found self-awareness. When she confronts her husband, she displays complete honesty—perhaps for the first time in her relationship with Torvald.

Sometimes what other characters say to or about a character can reveal more to an audience than the character's own words. (Keep in mind, however, that you should measure the accuracy of characters' comments against what you already know about them.) For instance, in act 2 of *A Doll House,* when the dying Dr. Rank says, apparently without malice, "[Torvald] Helmer with his sensitivity has such a sharp distaste for anything ugly," readers not only think ill of the man who is too "sensitive" to visit his sick friend but also question his ability to withstand situations that may be emotionally or morally "ugly" as well.

When a character is offstage for much (or even all) of the action, the audience must rely on other characters' assessments of the absent character. In Susan Glaspell's *Trifles* (p. 1163) the play's focus is on an absent character, Minnie Wright, who is described solely through other characters' remarks. The evidence suggests that Mrs. Wright has killed her husband, and only Mrs. Hale's and Mrs. Peters's comments about Mrs. Wright's dreary life can delineate her character and suggest a likely motive for the murder. Although we never meet Mrs. Wright, we learn essential information from the other women: that as a young girl she liked to sing and that more recently she was so distraught about the lack of beauty in her life that even her sewing revealed her distress. Similarly, the father in *The Glass Menagerie* never appears (and therefore never speaks), but the play's other characters describe him as "A telephone man who—fell in love with long-distance" (scene 6)—the absent husband and father who symbolizes abandonment and instability to Laura and Amanda and the possibility of freedom and escape to Tom.

Whether they are in the form of a monologue, a soliloquy, or dialogue, and whether they reveal information about the character who is speaking or about someone else, a character's words are always revealing. Explicitly or implicitly, they convey a character's nature, attitudes, and relationships with other characters. A character may, for instance, use learned words, foreign words, elaborate figurative language, irony or sarcasm, regionalisms, slang, jargon, clichés, or profanity. Words can also be used to indicate tone—for example, to express irony. Any of these uses of language may communicate vital information to the audience about a character's background, attitudes, and motivation. And, of course, a character's language may change as a play progresses, and this change too may be revealing.

FORMAL AND INFORMAL LANGUAGE

One character in a dramatic work may be very formal and aloof, using absolutely correct grammar, a learned vocabulary, and long, complex sentences; another may be informal, using conversational speech, collo-quialisms, and slang. At times, two characters with different levels of language may be set in opposition for dramatic effect, as they are in Irish playwright George Bernard Shaw's 1912 play *Pygmalion,* which updates the ancient Greek myth of a sculptor who creates (and falls in love with) a statue of a woman. In Shaw's version, a linguistics professor sets out to teach "proper" speech and manners to a lowly flower seller. Throughout the play, the contrasting language of Henry Higgins, the professor, and Eliza Doolittle, the flower seller, indicates their differing social standing:

> **LIZA:** I ain't got no mother. Her that turned me out was my sixth stepmother. But I done without them. And I'm a good girl, I am.
> **HIGGINS:** Very well, then, what on earth is all this fuss about?

A character's accent or dialect may also be significant. In comedies of manners, for instance, rustic or provincial characters, identified by their speech, were often objects of humor. In *Pygmalion* Eliza Doolittle uses cockney dialect, the dialect spoken in the East End of London. At first, her colorful, distinctive language (complete with expressions like *Nah-ow, garn,* and *ah-ah-ah-ow-ow-ow-oo*) and her nonstandard grammatical con-structions make her an object of ridicule; later, the transformation of her speech parallels the dramatic changes in her character.

PLAIN AND ELABORATE STYLE

A character's speech can be simple and straightforward or complex and convoluted; it can be plain and unadorned, or it can be embellished with elaborate **figures of speech.** The relative complexity or lack of complex-ity of a character's speech can have different effects on the audience. For example, a character whose language is simple and unsophisticated may seem to be unintelligent, unenlightened, gullible, or naive—especially if he or she also uses slang, dialect, or colloquial expressions. Conversely, a character's plain, down-to-earth language can convey common sense or intelligence. Plain language can also be quite emotionally powerful. Thus, Willy Loman's speech in act 2 of *Death of a Salesman* (p. 1410), about an eighty-four-year-old salesman named Dave Singleman, moves the audience with its sincerity and directness:

> Do you know? When he died—and by the way he died the death of a salesman, in his green velvet slippers in the smoker of the New York, New Haven and Hartford, going into Boston—when he died, hundreds of salesmen and buyers were at his funeral. Things were sad on a lotta trains for months after that.

Like plain speech, elaborate language may have different effects in different contexts. Sometimes, use of figurative language can make a character seem to have depth and insight and analytical skills absent in other characters. In the following excerpt from a soliloquy from *Hamlet*, for example, complex language reveals the depth of Hamlet's anguished self-analysis:

> **HAMLET:** O, that this too too solid flesh would melt,
> Thaw, and resolve itself into a dew!
> Or that the Everlasting had not fix'd
> His canon 'gainst self-slaughter! O God! O God!
> How weary, stale, flat, and unprofitable
> Seem to me all the uses of this world!
> Fie on't, O fie, 'tis an unweeded garden,
> That grows to seed[. . .]. (1.2.129–36)

In the preceding lines, Hamlet compares the world to a garden gone to seed. His use of imagery and figurative language vividly communicates his feelings about the world and his internal struggle against the temptation to commit suicide.

Sometimes, however, elaborate figurative language may make a character seem pompous or untrustworthy. In the following passages from Shakespeare's *King Lear*, for example, Goneril and Regan, the deceitful daughters, use elaborate language to conceal their true feelings from their father, King Lear. However, Cordelia—the loyal, loving daughter—uses simple, straightforward prose that suggests her sincerity and lack of artifice. Compare the three speeches:

> **GONERIL:** Sir, I love you more than words can wield the matter;
> Dearer than eyesight, space, and liberty;
> Beyond what can be valued, rich or rare;
> No less than life, with grace, health, beauty, honour;
> As much as child e'er lov'd, or father found;
> A love that makes breath poor, and speech unable.
> Beyond all manner of so much I love you. (1.1.56–62)

> **REGAN:** Sir, I am made
> Of the selfsame metal that my sister is,
> And prize me at her worth. In my true heart
> I find she names my very deed of love;
> Only she comes too short, that I profess
> Myself an enemy to all other joys
> Which the most precious square of sense possesses,
> And find I am alone felicitate
> In your dear Highness' love. (1.1.70–78)

> **CORDELIA:** Unhappy that I am, I cannot heave
> My heart into my mouth. I love your Majesty
> According to my bond; no more no less. (1.1.93–95)

Cordelia's unwillingness, even when she is prodded by Lear, to exaggerate her feelings or misrepresent her love through inflated language shows the audience her honesty and nobility. The contrast between her language and that of her sisters makes their very different motives clear to the audience.

TONE

Tone reveals a character's mood or attitude. Tone can be flat or hysterical, bitter or accepting, affectionate or aloof, anxious or calm. Contrasts in tone can indicate differences in outlook or emotional state between two characters; changes in tone from one point in the play to another can suggest corresponding changes within a character. At the end of *A Doll House,* for instance, Nora is resigned to what she must do, and her language is appropriately controlled. Her husband, however, is desperate to change her mind, and his language reflects this desperation. The following exchanges from act 3 of the play illustrate their contrasting emotional states:

> **HELMER:** But to part! To part from you! No, Nora, no—I can't imagine it.
> **NORA:** *(going out, right)* All the more reason why it has to be.

> **HELMER:** Over! All over! Nora, won't you ever think about me?
> **NORA:** I'm sure I'll think of you often, and about the children and the house here.

In earlier scenes between the two characters, Nora is emotional—at times, hysterical—and her husband is considerably more controlled. As the preceding dialogue indicates, both Nora and Torvald Helmer change drastically during the course of the play.

IRONY

Irony, a contradiction or discrepancy between two different levels of meaning, can reveal a great deal about character. **Verbal irony**—a contradiction between what a character says and what he or she means—is very important in drama, where the verbal interplay between characters carries the weight of the play. For example, when Nora and Dr. Rank discuss the latest news about his health in *A Doll House,* there is deep irony in his use of the phrase "complete certainty." Although the phrase usually suggests reassuring news, here it is meant to suggest death, and both Nora and Dr. Rank understand this.

Dramatic irony depends on the audience's knowing something that a character has not yet realized, or on one character's knowing something that other characters do not know. In some cases, dramatic irony is created by an audience's awareness of historical background or events of which characters are unaware. (Familiar with the story of Oedipus, for instance, the audience knows that the man who has caused all the problems in Thebes—the man Oedipus vows to find and take revenge on—is Oedipus himself.) In other cases, dramatic irony emerges when the audience learns something—something the characters do not yet know or comprehend— from a play's unfolding action. The central irony in *A Doll House,* for example, is that the family's "happy home" rests on a foundation of secrets, lies, and deception. Torvald does not know about the secrets, and Nora does not understand how they have poisoned her marriage. The audience, however, quickly becomes aware of the atmosphere of deceit—and aware of how it threatens the family's happiness.

Dramatic irony may also be conveyed through dialogue. Typically, dramatic irony is revealed when a character, in conversation, delivers lines that give the audience information that other characters, offstage at the time, do not know. In *A Doll House,* the audience knows—because Nora has explained her situation to Kristine—that Nora has spent the previous Christmas season hard at work, earning money to pay her secret debt. Torvald, however, remains unaware of her activities and believes her story that she was using the time to make holiday decorations, which the cat destroyed. This belief is consistent with his impression of her as an irresponsible child, yet the audience has quite a different impression of Nora. This discrepancy, one of many contradictions between the audience's view of Nora and Torvald's view of her, helps to create dramatic tension in the play.

Finally, **asides** can create dramatic irony by undercutting dialogue, providing ironic contrast between what the characters on stage know and what the audience knows. In Anton Chekhov's *The Brute* (p. 1266), for example, the audience knows that Mr. Smirnov is succumbing to Mrs. Popov's charms because he says, in an aside, "My god, what eyes she has! They're setting me on fire." Mrs. Popov, however, is not yet aware of his infatuation. The discrepancy between the audience's awareness and the character's adds to the play's humor.

CHARACTERS' ACTIONS
❖ ❖ ❖

Through their actions, characters convey their values and attitudes to the audience. Actions also reveal aspects of a character's personality. When Laura Wingfield, a character in *The Glass Menagerie,* hides rather than face the "gentleman caller," readers see just how shy she is; when Nora in *A Doll House* plays hide-and-seek with her children, eats forbidden macaroons, and takes childish joy in Christmas, her immaturity is apparent.

Readers also learn about characters from what they do *not* do. Thus, Nora's failure to remain in touch with her friend Kristine, who has had a hard life, reveals her selfishness, and the failure of Mrs. Peters and Mrs. Hale in *Trifles* to communicate their evidence to the sheriff indicates their support for Mrs. Wright and their understanding of what motivated her to take such drastic action.

Audiences also learn a good deal about characters by observing how they interact with other characters. In William Shakespeare's *Othello*, Iago is the embodiment of evil, and as the play's action unfolds, we discover his true nature. He reveals the secret marriage of Othello and Desdemona to her father; he schemes to arouse Othello's jealousy, making him believe Desdemona has been unfaithful with his lieutenant, Cassio; he persuades Cassio to ask Desdemona to plead his case with Othello, knowing this act will further arouse Othello's suspicions; he encourages Othello to be suspicious of Desdemona's defense of Cassio; he plants Desdemona's handkerchief in Cassio's room; and, finally, he persuades Othello to kill Desdemona and then kills his own wife, Emilia, to prevent her from exposing his role in the intrigue. As the play progresses, then, Iago's dealings with others consistently reveal him to be evil and corrupt.

STAGE DIRECTIONS

◊ ◊ ◊

When we read a play, we also read the playwright's italicized **stage directions,** the notes that concern **staging**—the scenery, props, lighting, music, sound effects, costumes, and other elements that contribute to the way the play looks and sounds to an audience (Chapter 24). In addition to commenting on staging, stage directions may supply physical details about the characters, suggesting their age, appearance, movements, gestures, relative positions, and facial expressions. These details may in turn convey additional information about characters: appearance may reveal social position or economic status, expressions may reveal attitudes, and so on. Stage directions may also indicate the manner in which a line of dialogue is to be delivered—haltingly, confidently, hesitantly, or loudly, for instance. The way a line is spoken may reveal a character to be excited, upset, angry, shy, or disappointed. Finally, stage directions may indicate *changes* in characters—for instance, a character whose speech is described as timid in early scenes may deliver lines emphatically and forcefully later on in the play.

Some plays' stage directions provide a good deal of detail about character; others do little more than list characters' names. Arthur Miller is one playwright who often chooses to provide detailed information about character through stage directions. In *Death of a Salesman,* for instance, Miller's stage directions characterize Willy Loman immediately and specifically:

He is past sixty years of age, dressed quietly. Even as he crosses the stage to the doorway of the house, his exhaustion is apparent. He unlocks the door, comes into the kitchen, and thankfully lets his burden down, feeling the soreness of his palms. A word-sigh escapes his lips—

Subsequent stage directions indicate how lines are to be spoken. For example, in the play's opening lines, Willy's wife Linda calls out to him *"with some trepidation"*; Linda speaks *"very carefully, delicately,"* and Willy speaks *"with casual irritation."* These instructions to readers (and actors) are meant to suggest the strained relationship between the two characters.

George Bernard Shaw is notorious for the full character description in his stage directions. In these directions—seen by readers of the play but not heard by audiences—he communicates complex information about characters' attitudes and values, strengths and weaknesses, motivation and reactions, and relationships with other characters. In doing so Shaw functions as a narrator, explicitly communicating his own attitudes toward various characters. (Unlike the voice of Tom Wingfield in *The Glass Menagerie*, however, the voice in Shaw's stage directions is not also the voice of a character in the play; it is the voice of the playwright.) Shaw's stage directions for *Pygmalion* initially describe Eliza Doolittle as follows:

She is not at all an attractive person. She is perhaps eighteen, perhaps twenty, hardly older. She wears a little sailor hat of black straw that has long been exposed to the dust and soot of London and has seldom if ever been brushed. Her hair needs washing rather badly; its mousy color can hardly be natural. She wears a shoddy black coat that reaches nearly to her knees and is shaped to her waist. She has a brown skirt with a coarse apron. Her boots are much the worse for wear. She is no doubt as clean as she can afford to be; but compared to the ladies she is very dirty. Her features are no worse than theirs; but their condition leaves something to be desired; and she needs the services of a dentist.

Rather than providing an objective summary of the character's most notable physical attributes, Shaw injects subjective comments *("seldom if ever brushed"; "color can hardly be natural"; "no doubt as clean as she can afford to be")* that reveal his attitude toward Eliza. This initially supercilious attitude, which he shares with Professor Higgins, is tempered considerably by the end of the play, helping to make Eliza's transformation more obvious to readers than it would be if measured by her words and actions alone. By act 5 the tone of the stage directions characterizing Eliza has changed to admiration: *"Eliza enters, sunny, self-possessed, and giving a staggeringly convincing exhibition of ease of manner."*

Stage directions in *Hamlet* are not nearly as comprehensive. Characters are introduced with only the barest identifying tags: "Claudius, *King of Denmark*"; "Hamlet, *Son to the former, and nephew to the present King*"; "Gertrude, *Queen of Denmark, mother to Hamlet.*" Most stage directions do little more than chronicle the various characters' entrances and exits or specify particular physical actions: *"Enter Ghost"; "Spreads his arms";*

"Ghost beckons Hamlet"; "He kneels"; "Sheathes his sword"; "Leaps in the grave." Occasionally, stage directions specify a prop *("Puts down the skull");* a sound effect *("A noise within");* or a costume *("Enter the ghost in his nightgown").* Such brevity is typical of Shakespeare's plays, in which characters are delineated almost solely by their words—and, not incidentally, by the way actors have interpreted the characters over the years. In fact, because Shakespeare's stage directions only suggest characters' gestures, physical reactions, movements, and facial expressions, actors have been left quite free to experiment, reading various interpretations into Shakespeare's characters.

ACTORS' INTERPRETATIONS
◆ ◆ ◆

When we watch a play, we gain insight into a character not merely through what the character says and does or how other characters react, but also through the way an actor interprets the role. If a playwright does not specify a character's mannerisms, gestures, or movements, or does not indicate how a line is to be delivered (and sometimes even if he or she does), an actor is free to interpret the role as he or she believes it should be played. Even when a playwright *does* specify such actions, the actor has a good deal of freedom to decide which gestures or expressions will convey a certain emotion.

In "Some Thoughts on Playwriting," American dramatist Thornton Wilder argues that "the theatre is an art which reposes upon the work of many collaborators" rather than on "one governing selecting will." Citing examples from Shakespeare and Ibsen, Wilder illustrates the great degree of "intervention" that may occur in dramatic productions. For instance, Wilder observes, Shakespeare's Shylock has been portrayed by two different actors as "noble, wronged and indignant" and as "a vengeful and hysterical buffoon"—and both performances were considered positive contributions to the theater. As noted earlier, the absence of detailed stage directions in Shakespeare's plays makes possible (and perhaps even encourages) such widely diverging interpretations. However, as Wilder notes, even when playing roles created by a dramatist such as Ibsen, whose stage directions are typically quite specific, actors and directors have a good deal of leeway. Thus, actress Janet McTeer, who played the part of Ibsen's Nora in the 1997 London production of *A Doll House,* saw Nora and Torvald, despite their many problems, as "the perfect couple," deeply in love and involved in a passionate marriage. "You have to make that marriage sexually credible," McTeer told the *New York Times,* "to imagine they have a wonderful time in bed, so there becomes something to lose. If you play them as already past it or no longer attracted to each other, then there is no play." This interpretation is not inconsistent with the play, but it does go beyond what Ibsen actually wrote. In a sense, then, the playwright's words on the page are just the beginning of the character's lives.

Irish playwright Samuel Beckett devotes a good deal of attention to indicating actors' movements and gestures and their physical reactions to one another. In his 1952 play *Waiting for Godot*, for example, Beckett seems to choreograph every gesture, every emotion, every intention, with stage directions such as the following:

◊ *(he looks at them ostentatiously in turn to make it clear they are both meant)*

◊ *Vladimir seizes Lucky's hat. Silence of Lucky. He falls. Silence. Panting of the victors.*

◊ *Estragon hands him the boot. Vladimir inspects it, throws it down angrily.*

◊ *Estragon pulls, stumbles, falls. Long silence.*

◊ *He goes feverishly to and fro, halts finally at extreme left, broods.*

Clearly, Beckett provides full and obviously carefully thought-out stage directions and, in so doing, attempts to retain a good deal of control over his characters. Still, in a 1988 production of *Godot*, director Mike Nichols and comic actors Robin Williams and Steve Martin felt free to improvise, adding gestures and movements not specified or even hinted at—and most critics believed that this production managed to remain true to the tragicomic spirit of Beckett's existentialist play.

✳ Checklist: Writing about Character

✓ Does any character serve as a narrator? If so, what information does this narrator supply about the other characters? How reliable is the narrator?

✓ Are the major characters fully developed?

✓ Do the major characters change and grow during the course of the play, or do they remain essentially unchanged?

✓ What function does each of the minor characters serve in the play?

✓ What elements reveal changes in the characters?

✓ What is revealed about the characters through their words?

✓ Do characters use foreign words, regionalisms, slang, jargon, clichés, or profanity? What does such use of language reveal about characters? About theme?

✓ Is the language formal or informal?

✓ Do characters speak in dialect? Do they have accents?

✓ Is the language elaborate or plain?

✓ Do different characters exhibit contrasting styles or levels of language? What is the significance of these differences?

✓ In what way does language reveal characters' emotional states?

✓ Does the tone or style of any character's language change significantly as the play progresses? What does this change reveal?

✓ Does the play include verbal irony? Dramatic irony? How is irony conveyed? What purpose does irony achieve?

✓ What is revealed about the characters through what others say about them?

✓ Is the audience encouraged to react sympathetically to the character?

✓ What is revealed about the characters through their actions?

✓ What is revealed about the characters through the playwright's stage directions?

✓ How might different actors' interpretations change an audience's understanding of the characters?

◈ **ANTON CHEKHOV** (1860–1904) is the major nineteenth-century Russian playwright and short story writer. He became a doctor and, as a young adult, supported the rest of his family following his father's bankruptcy. After his early adult years in Moscow, Chekhov spent the rest of his life in the country, moving to Yalta, a resort town in Crimea, for his health (he suffered from tuberculosis). He continued to write plays, mostly for the Moscow Art Theatre, although he could not supervise their production as he would have wished. His plays include *The Seagull* (1896), *Uncle Vanya* (1898), *The Three Sisters* (1901), and *The Cherry Orchard* (1904).

The Brute, or *The Bear* (1888), is one of a number of one-act farces Chekhov wrote just before his major plays. It is based on a French farce (*Les Jurons de Cadillac* by Pierre Breton) about a man who cannot refrain from swearing. The woman he loves offers to marry him if he can avoid swearing for one hour; though he can't do it, he fails so charmingly that she agrees to marry him anyway.

CULTURAL CONTEXT ◈ Did you know that Chekhov is considered one of the founding fathers of the modern short story? In 1888, his short story "The Steppe" won the Pushkin Prize. He wrote hundreds of stories in his lifetime, and his influences on the modern story are still evident today.

◆ ◆ ◆

ANTON CHEKHOV

The Brute

A Joke in One Act

(1888)

English Version by Eric Bentley

Characters

Mrs. Popov, *widow and landowner,*   Gardener
small, with dimpled cheeks   Coachman
Mr. Grigory S. Smirnov,   Hired Men
gentleman farmer, middle-aged
Luka, *Mrs. Popov's footman, an old*
man

Scene

The drawing room of a country house. Mrs. Popov, in deep mourning, is staring
hard at a photograph. Luka is with her.

Luka: It's not right, ma'am, you're killing yourself. The cook has gone
off with the maid to pick berries. The cat's having a high old time in
the yard catching birds. Every living thing is happy. But you stay
moping here in the house like it was a convent, taking no pleasure in
nothing. I mean it, ma'am! It must be a full year since you set foot
out of doors.

Mrs. Popov: I must never set foot out of doors again, Luka. Never! I have
nothing to set foot out of doors *for*. My life is done. *He* is in his
grave. I have buried myself alive in this house. We are *both* in our
graves.

Luka: You're off again, ma'am. I just won't listen to you no more. Mr.
Popov is dead, but what can we do about that? It's God's doing. God's
will be done. You've cried over him, you've done your share of
mourning, haven't you? There's a limit to everything. You can't go
on weeping and wailing forever. My old lady died, for that matter,
and I wept and wailed over her a whole month long. Well, that was it.
I couldn't weep and wail all my life. She just wasn't worth it. *(He
sighs.)* As for the neighbors, you've forgotten all about them, ma'am.
You don't visit them and you don't let them visit you. You and I are
like a pair of spiders—excuse the expression, ma'am—here we are in
this house like a pair of spiders, we never see the light of day. And it
isn't like there was no nice people around either. The whole county's
swarming with 'em. There's a regiment quartered at Riblov, and the
officers are so good-looking! The girls can't take their eyes off them—
There's a ball at the camp every Friday—The military band plays most
every day of the week—What do you say, ma'am? You're young,

you're pretty, you could enjoy yourself! Ten years from now you may want to strut and show your feathers to the officers, and it'll be too late.

MRS. POPOV: *(firmly)* You must never bring this subject up again, Luka. Since Popov died, life has been an empty dream to me, you know that. *You* may think I am alive. Poor ignorant Luka! You are wrong. I am dead. I'm in my grave. Never more shall I see the light of day, never strip from my body this . . . raiment of death! Are you listening, Luka? Let his ghost learn how I love him! Yes, *I* know, and *you* know, he was often unfair to me, he was cruel to me, and he was unfaithful to me. What of it? *I* shall be faithful to *him*, that's all. I will show him how *I* can love. Hereafter, in a better world than this, he will welcome me back, the same loyal girl I always was—

5 LUKA: Instead of carrying on this way, ma'am, you should go out in the garden and take a bit of a walk, ma'am. Or why not harness Toby and take a drive? Call on a couple of the neighbours, ma'am?

MRS. POPOV: *(breaking down)* Oh, Luka!

LUKA: Yes, ma'am? What have I said, ma'am? Oh, dear!

MRS. POPOV: Toby! You said Toby! He adored that horse. When he drove me out to the Korchagins and the Vlasovs, it was always with Toby! He was a wonderful driver, do you remember, Luka? So graceful! So strong! I can see him now, pulling at those reins with all his might and main! Toby! Luka, tell them to give Toby an extra portion of oats today.

LUKA: Yes, ma'am.

A bell rings.

10 MRS. POPOV: Who is that? Tell them I'm not at home.

LUKA: Very good, ma'am. *(Exit.)*

MRS. POPOV: *(gazing again at the photograph)* You shall see, my Popov, how a wife can love and forgive. Till death do us part. Longer than that. Till death re-unite us forever! *(Suddenly a titter breaks through her tears.)* Aren't you ashamed of yourself, Popov? Here's your little wife, being good, being faithful, so faithful she's locked up here waiting for her own funeral, while you—doesn't it make you ashamed, you naughty boy? You were terrible, you know. You were unfaithful, and you made those awful scenes about it, you stormed out and left me alone for weeks—

Enter Luka.

LUKA: *(upset)* There's someone asking for you, ma'am. Says he must—

MRS. POPOV: I suppose you told him that since my husband's death I see no one?

15 LUKA: Yes, ma'am. I did, ma'am. But he wouldn't listen, ma'am. He says it's urgent.

MRS. POPOV: *(shrilly)* I see no one!!

Luka: He won't take no for an answer, ma'am. He just curses and swears and comes in anyway. He's a perfect monster, ma'am. He's in the dining room right now.

Mrs. Popov: In the dining room, is he? I'll give him his come-uppance. Bring him in here this minute.

Exit Luka.

(*Suddenly sad again.*) Why do they do this to me? Why? Insulting my grief, intruding on my solitude? (*She sighs.*) I'm afraid I'll have to enter a convent. I will, I *must* enter a convent!

Enter Mr. Smirnov and Luka.

Smirnov: (*to Luka*) Dolt! Idiot! You talk too much! (*Seeing Mrs. Popov. With dignity.*) May I have the honor of introducing myself, madam? Grigory S. Smirnov, landowner and lieutenant of artillery, retired. Forgive me, madam, if I disturb your peace and quiet, but my business is both urgent and weighty.

20 Mrs. Popov: (*declining to offer him her hand*) What is it you wish, sir?

Smirnov: At the time of his death, your late husband—with whom I had the honor to be acquainted, ma'am—was in my debt to the tune of twelve hundred rubles. I have two notes to prove it. Tomorrow, ma'am, I must pay the interest on a bank loan. I have therefore no alternative, ma'am, but to ask you to pay me the money today.

Mrs. Popov: Twelve hundred rubles? But what did my husband owe it to you for?

Smirnov: He used to buy his oats from me, madam.

Mrs. Popov: (*to Luka, with a sigh*) Remember what I said, Luka: tell them to give Toby an extra portion of oats today!

Exit Luka.

My dear Mr.—what was the name again?

25 Smirnov: Smirnov, ma'am.

Mrs. Popov: My dear Mr. Smirnov, if Mr. Popov owed you money, you shall be paid—to the last ruble, to the last kopeck. But today—you must excuse me, Mr.—what was it?

Smirnov: Smirnov, ma'am.

Mrs. Popov: Today, Mr. Smirnov, I have no ready cash in the house. (*Smirnov starts to speak.*) Tomorrow, Mr. Smirnov, no, the day after tomorrow, all will be well. My steward will be back from town. I shall see that he pays what is owing. Today, no. In any case, today is exactly seven months from Mr. Popov's death. On such a day you will understand that I am in no mood to think of money.

Smirnov: Madam, if you don't pay up now, you can carry me out feet foremost. They'll seize my estate.

30 Mrs. Popov: You can have your money. (*He starts to thank her.*) Tomorrow. (*He again starts to speak.*) That is: the day after tomorrow.

SMIRNOV: I don't need the money the day after tomorrow. I need it today.

MRS. POPOV: I'm sorry, Mr.—

SMIRNOV: *(shouting)* Smirnov!

MRS. POPOV: *(sweetly)* Yes, of course. But you can't have it today.

35 SMIRNOV: But I can't wait for it any longer!

MRS. POPOV: Be sensible, Mr. Smirnov. How can I pay you if I don't
 have it?

SMIRNOV: You don't have it?

MRS. POPOV: I don't have it.

SMIRNOV: Sure?

40 MRS. POPOV: Positive.

SMIRNOV: Very well. I'll make a note to that effect. *(Shrugging.)* And then
 they want me to keep cool. I meet the tax commissioner on the street,
 and he says, "Why are you always in such a bad humor, Smirnov?"
 Bad humor! How can I help it, in God's name? I need money, I need
 it desperately. Take yesterday: I leave home at the crack of dawn, I call
 on all my debtors. Not a one of them pays up. Footsore and weary. I
 creep at midnight into some little dive, and try to snatch a few winks
 of sleep on the floor by the vodka barrel. Then today, I come here,
 fifty miles from home, saying to myself, "At last, at last, I can be sure
 of something," and you're not in the mood! You give me a mood!
 Christ, how can I help getting all worked up?

MRS. POPOV: I thought I'd made it clear, Mr. Smirnov, that you'll get your
 money the minute my steward is back from town.

SMIRNOV: What the hell do I care about your steward? Pardon the
 expression, ma'am. But it was you I came to see.

MRS. POPOV: What language! What a tone to take to a lady! I refuse to
 hear another word. *(Quickly, exit.)*

45 SMIRNOV: Not in the mood, huh? "Exactly seven months since Popov's
 death," huh? How about me? *(Shouting after her.)* Is there this interest
 to pay, or isn't there? I'm asking you a question: is there this interest
 to pay, or isn't there? So your husband died, and you're not in the
 mood, and your steward's gone off some place, and so forth and so
 on, but what can *I* do about all that, huh? What do *you* think I should
 do? Take a running jump and shove my head through the wall? Take
 off in a balloon? You don't know my *other* debtors. I call on Gruzdeff.
 Not at home. I look for Yaroshevitch. He's hiding out. I find
 Kooritsin. He kicks up a row, and I have to throw him through the
 window. I work my way right down the list. Not a kopeck. Then I
 come to you, and God damn it to hell, if you'll pardon the
 expression, you're not in the mood! *(Quietly, as he realizes he's talking
 to air.)* I've spoiled them all, that's what, I've let them play me for a
 sucker. Well, I'll show them. I'll show this one. I'll stay right here till
 she pays up. Ugh! *(He shudders with rage.)* I'm in a rage! I'm in a
 positively towering rage! Every nerve in my body is trembling at forty
 to the dozen! I can't breathe, I feel ill, I think I'm going to faint, hey,
 you there!

Enter Luka.

Luka: Yes, sir? Is there anything you wish, sir?
Smirnov: Water! Water! No, make it vodka.

Exit Luka.

> Consider the logic of it. A fellow creature is desperately in need of
> cash, so desperately in need that he has to seriously contemplate
> hanging himself, and this woman, this mere chit of a girl, won't pay
> up, and why not? Because, forsooth, she isn't in the mood! Oh, the
> logic of women! Come to that, I never have liked them, I could do
> without the whole sex. Talk to a woman? I'd rather sit on a barrel of
> dynamite, the very thought gives me gooseflesh. Women! Creatures
> of poetry and romance! Just to see one in the distance gets me mad.
> My legs start twitching with rage. I feel like yelling for help.

Enter Luka, handing Smirnov a glass of water.

Luka: Mrs. Popov is indisposed, sir. She is seeing no one.
Smirnov: Get out.

Exit Luka.

> Indisposed, is she? Seeing no one, huh? Well, she can see me or not,
> but I'll be here, I'll be right here till she pays up. If you're sick for a
> week, I'll be here for a week. If you're sick for a year, I'll be here for a
> year. You won't get around *me* with your widow's weeds and your
> schoolgirl dimples. I know all about dimples. *(Shouting through the
> window.)* Semyon, let the horses out of those shafts, we're not leaving,
> we're staying, and tell them to give the horses some oats, yes, oats,
> you fool, what do you think? *(Walking away from the window.)* What a
> mess, what an unholy mess! I didn't sleep last night, the heat is
> terrific today, not a damn one of 'em has paid up, and here's this—
> this skirt in mourning that's not in the mood! My head aches,
> where's that—*(He drinks from the glass.)* Water, ugh! You there!

Enter Luka.

50 Luka: Yes, sir. You wish for something, sir?
Smirnov: Where's that confounded vodka I asked for?

Exit Luka.

> *(Smirnov sits and looks himself over.)* Oof! A fine figure of a man *I* am!
> Unwashed, uncombed, unshaven, straw on my vest, dust all over me.
> The little woman must've taken me for a highwayman. *(Yawns.)* I
> suppose it wouldn't be considered polite to barge into a drawing
> room in this state, but who cares? I'm not a visitor, I'm a creditor—
> most unwelcome of guests, second only to Death.

Enter Luka.

LUKA: *(handing him the vodka)* If I may say so, sir, you take too many liberties, sir.

SMIRNOV: What?!

LUKA: Oh, nothing, sir, nothing.

55 SMIRNOV: Who in hell do you think you're talking to? Shut your mouth!

LUKA: *(aside)* There's an evil spirit abroad. The Devil must have sent him. Oh! *(Exit Luka.)*

SMIRNOV: What a rage I'm in! I'll grind the whole world to powder. Oh, I feel ill again. You there!

Enter Mrs. Popov.

MRS. POPOV: *(looking at the floor)* In the solitude of my rural retreat, Mr. Smirnov, I've long since grown unaccustomed to the sound of the human voice. Above all, I cannot bear shouting. I must beg you not to break the silence.

SMIRNOV: Very well. Pay me my money and I'll go.

60 MRS. POPOV: I told you before, and I tell you again, Mr. Smirnov. I have no cash, you'll have to wait till the day after tomorrow. Can I express myself more plainly?

SMIRNOV: And *I* told *you* before, and *I* tell *you* again, that I need the money today, that the day after tomorrow is too late, and that if you don't pay, and pay now, I'll have to hang myself in the morning!

MRS. POPOV: But I have no cash. This is quite a puzzle.

SMIRNOV: You won't pay, huh?

MRS. POPOV: I *can't* pay, Mr. Smirnov.

65 SMIRNOV: In that case, I'm going to sit here and wait. *(Sits down.)* You'll pay up the day after tomorrow? Very good. Till the day after tomorrow, here I sit. *(Pause. He jumps up.)* Now look, do I have to pay that interest tomorrow, or don't I? Or do you think I'm joking?

MRS. POPOV: I must ask you not to raise your voice, Mr. Smirnov. This is not a stable.

SMIRNOV: Who said it was? Do I have to pay the interest tomorrow or not?

MRS. POPOV: Mr. Smirnov, do you know how to behave in the presence of a lady?

SMIRNOV: No, madam, I do not know how to behave in the presence of a lady.

70 MRS. POPOV: Just what I thought. I look at you, and I say: ugh! I hear you talk, and I say to myself: "That man doesn't know how to talk to a lady."

SMIRNOV: You'd like me to come simpering to you in French, I suppose. *"Enchanté, madame! Merci beaucoup* for not paying zee money, *madame! Pardonnez-moi* if I 'ave disturbed you, *madame!* How *charmante* you look in mourning, *madame!"*

MRS. POPOV: Now you're being silly, Mr. Smirnov.

SMIRNOV: *(mimicking)* "Now you're being silly, Mr. Smirnov." "You don't know how to talk to a lady, Mr. Smirnov." Look here, Mrs. Popov, I've known more women than you've known pussy cats. I've fought three duels on their account. I've jilted twelve, and been jilted by nine others. Oh, yes, Mrs. Popov, I've played the fool in my time, whispered sweet nothings, bowed and scraped and endeavored to please. Don't tell me I don't know what it is to love, to pine away with longing, to have the blues, to melt like butter, to be weak as water. I was full of tender emotion. I was carried away with passion. I squandered half my fortune on the sex. I chattered about women's emancipation. But there's an end to everything, dear madam. Burning eyes, dark eyelashes, ripe, red lips, dimpled cheeks, heaving bosoms, soft whisperings, the moon above; the lake below—I don't give a rap for that sort of nonsense any more, Mrs. Popov. I've found out about women. Present company excepted, they're liars. Their behavior is mere play acting; their conversation is sheer gossip. Yes, dear lady, women, young or old, are false, petty, vain, cruel, malicious, unreasonable. As for intelligence, any sparrow could give them points. Appearances, I admit, can be deceptive. In appearance, a woman may be all poetry and romance, goddess and angel, muslin and fluff. To look at her exterior is to be transported to heaven. But I have looked at her interior, Mrs. Popov, and what did I find there—in her very soul? A crocodile. *(He has gripped the back of the chair so firmly that it snaps.)* And, what is more revolting, a crocodile with an illusion, a crocodile that imagines tender sentiments are its own special province, a crocodile that thinks itself queen of the realm of love! Whereas, in sober fact, dear madam, if a woman can love anything except a lapdog you can hang me by the feet on that nail. For a man, love is suffering, love is sacrifice. A woman just swishes her train around and tightens her grip on your nose. Now, you're a woman, aren't you, Mrs. Popov? You must be an expert on some of this. Tell me, quite frankly, did you ever know a woman to be— faithful, for instance? Or even sincere? Only old hags, huh? Though some women are old hags from birth. But as for the others? You're right: a faithful woman is a freak of nature—like a cat with horns.

MRS. POPOV: Who *is* faithful, then? Who *have* you cast for the faithful lover? Not man?

75 SMIRNOV: Right first time, Mrs. Popov: man.

MRS. POPOV: *(going off into a peal of bitter laughter)* Man! Man is faithful! that's a new one! *(Fiercely.)* What right do you have to say this, Mr. Smirnov? Men faithful? Let me tell you something. Of all the men I have ever known my late husband Popov was the best. I loved him, and there are women who know how to love, Mr. Smirnov. I gave him my youth, my happiness, my life, my fortune. I worshipped the ground he trod on—and what happened? The best of men was unfaithful to me, Mr. Smirnov. Not once in a while. All the time. After he died, I found his desk drawer full of love letters. While he was alive, he was always going away for the week-end. He squandered my money. He made love to other women before my very eyes. But, in spite of all, Mr. Smirnov, *I* was faithful. Unto death. And beyond. I am *still* faithful, Mr. Smirnov! Buried alive in this house, I shall wear mourning till the day I, too, am called to my eternal rest.

SMIRNOV: *(laughing scornfully)* Expect me to believe that? As if I couldn't see through all this hocus-pocus. Buried alive! Till you're called to your eternal rest! Till when? Till some little poet—or some little subaltern with his first moustache—comes riding by and asks: "Can that be the house of the mysterious Tamara who for love of her late husband has buried herself alive, vowing to see no man?" Ha!

MRS. POPOV: *(flaring up)* How dare you? How dare you insinuate—?

SMIRNOV: You may have buried yourself alive, Mrs. Popov, but you haven't forgotten to powder your nose.

80 MRS. POPOV: *(incoherent)* How dare you? How—?

SMIRNOV: Who's raising his voice now? Just because I call a spade a spade. Because I shoot straight from the shoulder. Well, don't shout at me, I'm not your steward.

MRS. POPOV: I'm not shouting, you're shouting! Oh, leave me alone!

SMIRNOV: Pay me the money, and I will.

MRS. POPOV: You'll get no money out of me!

85 SMIRNOV: Oh, so that's it!

MRS. POPOV: Not a ruble, not a kopeck. Get out! Leave me alone!

SMIRNOV: Not being your husband, I must ask you not to make scenes with me. *(He sits.)* I don't like scenes.

MRS. POPOV: *(choking with rage)* You're sitting down?

SMIRNOV: Correct, I'm sitting down.

90 MRS. POPOV: I asked you to leave!

SMIRNOV: Then give me the money. *(Aside.)* Oh, what a rage I'm in, what a rage!

MRS. POPOV: The impudence of the man! I won't talk to you a moment longer. Get out. *(Pause.)* Are you going?

SMIRNOV: No.

MRS. POPOV: No?!

95 SMIRNOV: No.

MRS. POPOV: On your head be it. Luka!

Enter Luka.

Show the gentleman out, Luka.

LUKA: *(approaching)* I'm afraid, sir, I'll have to ask you, um, to leave, sir, now, um—

SMIRNOV: *(jumping up)* Shut your mouth, you old idiot! Who do you think you're talking to? I'll make mincemeat of you.

LUKA: *(clutching his heart)* Mercy on us! Holy saints above! *(He falls into an armchair.)* I'm taken sick! I can't breathe!!

100 MRS. POPOV: Then where's Dasha? Dasha! Dasha! Come here at once! *(She rings.)*

LUKA: They gone picking berries, ma'am, I'm alone here—Water, water, I'm taken sick!

MRS. POPOV: *(to Smirnov)* Get out, you!

SMIRNOV: Can't you even be polite with me, Mrs. Popov?

MRS. POPOV: *(clenching her fists and stamping her feet)* With you? You're a wild animal, you were never house-broken!

105 SMIRNOV: What? What did you say?

MRS. POPOV: I said you were a wild animal, you were never house-broken.

SMIRNOV: *(advancing upon her)* And what right do you have to talk to me like that?

MRS. POPOV: Like what?

SMIRNOV: You have insulted me, madam.

110 MRS. POPOV: What of it? Do you think I'm scared of you?

SMIRNOV: So you think you can get away with it because you're a woman. A creature of poetry and romance, huh? Well, it doesn't go down with me. I hereby challenge you to a duel.

LUKA: Mercy on us! Holy saints alive! Water!

SMIRNOV: I propose we shoot it out.

MRS. POPOV: Trying to scare me again? Just because you have big fists and a voice like a bull? You're a brute.

115 SMIRNOV: No one insults Grigory S. Smirnov with impunity! And I don't care if you *are* a female.

MRS. POPOV: *(trying to outshout him)* Brute, brute, brute!

SMIRNOV: The sexes are equal, are they? Fine: then it's just prejudice to expect men alone to pay for insults. I hereby challenge—

MRS. POPOV: *(screaming)* All right! You want to shoot it out? All right! Let's shoot it out!

SMIRNOV: And let it be here and now!

120 MRS. POPOV: Here and now! All right! I'll have Popov's pistols here in one minute! *(Walks away, then turns.)* Putting one of Popov's bullets through your silly head will be a pleasure! Au revoir. *(Exit.)*

SMIRNOV: I'll bring her down like a duck, a sitting duck. I'm not one of your little poets, I'm no little subaltern with his first moustache. No, sir, there's no weaker sex where I'm concerned!

LUKA: Sir! Master! *(He goes down on his knees.)* Take pity on a poor old man, and do me a favor: go away. It was bad enough before, you nearly scared me to death. But a duel—!

SMIRNOV: *(ignoring him)* A duel! That's equality of the sexes for you! That's women's emancipation! Just as a matter of principle I'll bring her down like a duck. But what a woman! "Putting one of Popov's bullets through your silly head . . ." Her cheeks were flushed, her eyes were gleaming! And, by God, she's accepted the challenge! I never knew a woman like this before!

LUKA: Sir! Master! Please go away! I'll always pray for you!

125 SMIRNOV: *(again ignoring him)* What a woman! Phew!! *She's* no sour puss, *she's* no cry baby. She's fire and brimstone. She's a human cannon ball. What a shame I have to kill her!

LUKA: *(weeping)* Please, kind sir, please, go away!

SMIRNOV: *(as before)* I like her, isn't that funny? With those dimples and all? I like her. I'm even prepared to consider letting her off that debt. And where's my rage? It's gone. I never knew a woman like this before.

Enter Mrs. Popov with pistols.

MRS. POPOV: *(boldly)* Pistols, Mr. Smirnov! *(Matter of fact.)* But before we start, you'd better show me how it's done. I'm not too familiar with these things. In fact I never gave a pistol a second look.

LUKA: Lord, have mercy on us, I must go hunt up the gardener and the coachman. Why has this catastrophe fallen upon us, O Lord? *(Exit.)*

130 SMIRNOV: *(examining the pistols)* Well, it's like this. There are several makes: one is the Mortimer, with capsules, especially constructed for dueling. What you have here are Smith and Wesson triple-action revolvers, with extractor, first-rate job, worth ninety rubles at the very least. You hold it this way. *(Aside.)* My God, what eyes she has! They're setting me on fire.

MRS. POPOV: This way?

SMIRNOV: Yes, that's right. You cock the trigger, take aim like this, head up, arm out like this. Then you just press with this finger here, and it's all over. The main thing is, keep cool, take slow aim, and don't let your arm jump.

MRS. POPOV: I see. And if it's inconvenient to do the job here, we can go out in the garden.

SMIRNOV: Very good. Of course, I should warn you: I'll be firing in the air.

135 MRS. POPOV: What? This is the end. Why?

SMIRNOV: Oh, well—because—for private reasons.

MRS. POPOV: Scared, huh? *(She laughs heartily.)* Now don't you try to get out of it, Mr. Smirnov. My blood is up. I won't be happy till I've drilled a hole through that skull of yours. Follow me. What's the matter? Scared?

SMIRNOV: That's right. I'm scared.

MRS. POPOV: Oh, come on, what's the matter with you?

140 SMIRNOV: Well, um, Mrs. Popov, I, um, I like you.

MRS. POPOV: *(laughing bitterly)* Good God! He likes me, does he? The gall of the man. *(Showing him the door.)* You may leave, Mr. Smirnov.

SMIRNOV: *(Quietly puts the gun down, takes his hat, and walks to the door. Then he stops and the pair look at each other without a word. Then, approaching gingerly.)* Listen, Mrs. Popov. Are you still mad at me? I'm in the devil of a temper myself, of course. But then, you see—what I mean is—it's this way—the fact is—(Roaring.) Well, is it my fault, damn it, if I like you? *(Clutches the back of a chair. It breaks.)* Christ, what fragile furniture you have here. I like you. Know what I mean? I could fall in love with you.

MRS. POPOV: I hate you. Get out!

Smirnov: What a woman! I never saw anything like it. Oh, I'm lost, I'm done for, I'm a mouse in a trap.

145 Mrs. Popov: Leave this house, or I shoot!

Smirnov: Shoot away! What bliss to die of a shot that was fired by that little velvet hand! To die gazing into those enchanting eyes. I'm out of my mind. I know: you must decide at once. Think for one second, then decide. Because if I leave now, I'll never be back. Decide! I'm a pretty decent chap. Landed gentleman, I should say. Ten thousand a year. Good stable. Throw a kopeck up in the air, and I'll put a bullet through it. Will you marry me?

Mrs. Popov: *(indignant, brandishing the gun)* We'll shoot it out! Get going! Take your pistol!

Smirnov: I'm out of my mind. I don't understand anything any more. *(Shouting.)* You there! That vodka!

Mrs. Popov: No excuses! No delays! We'll shoot it out!

150 Smirnov: I'm out of my mind. I'm falling in love. I *have* fallen in love. *(He takes her hand vigorously; she squeals.)* I love you. *(He goes down on his knees.)* I love you as I've never loved before. I jilted twelve, and was jilted by nine others. But I didn't love a one of them as I love you. I'm full of tender emotion. I'm melting like butter. I'm weak as water. I'm on my knees like a fool, and I offer you my hand. It's a shame, it's a disgrace. I haven't been in love in five years. I took a vow against it. And now, all of a sudden, to be swept off my feet, it's a scandal. I offer you my hand, dear lady. Will you or won't you? You won't? Then don't! *(He rises and walks toward the door.)*

Mrs. Popov: I didn't say anything.

Smirnov: *(stopping)* What?

Mrs. Popov: Oh, nothing, you can go. Well, no, just a minute. No, you can go. Go! I detest you! But, just a moment. Oh, if you knew how furious I feel! *(Throws the gun on the table.)* My fingers have gone to sleep holding that horrid thing. *(She is tearing her handkerchief to shreds.)* And what are you standing around for? Get out of here!

Smirnov: Goodbye.

155 Mrs. Popov: Go, go, go! *(Shouting.)* Where are you going? Wait a minute! No, no, it's all right, just go. I'm fighting mad. Don't come near me, don't come near me!

Smirnov: *(who is coming near her)* I'm pretty disgusted with myself— falling in love like a kid, going down on my knees like some moongazing whippersnapper, the very thought gives me gooseflesh. *(Rudely.)* I love you. But it doesn't make sense. Tomorrow, I have to pay that interest, and we've already started mowing. *(He puts his arm about her waist.)* I shall never forgive myself for this.

Mrs. Popov: Take your hands off me, I hate you! Let's shoot it out!

A long kiss. Enter Luka with an axe, the Gardener with a rake, the coachman with a pitchfork, hired men with sticks.

LUKA: *(seeing the kiss)* Mercy on us! Holy saints above!

MRS. POPOV: *(dropping her eyes)* Luka, tell them in the stable that Toby is *not* to have any oats today.

READING AND REACTING

1. Are Mr. Smirnov and Mrs. Popov round or flat characters? Are they static or dynamic?

2. Which of the two characters do you think has the upper hand in their relationship?

3. Although Mrs. Popov's husband is dead, he is, in a sense, an important character in *The Brute*. What do we know about him? How does he influence the play's two main characters?

4. Why are Mrs. Popov and Mr. Smirnov distrustful of members of the opposite sex? How is this distrust revealed to the audience?

5. Do you think this play reinforces gender stereotypes or challenges them? Explain.

6. Because *The Brute* is a **farce,** Chekhov's characters frequently exaggerate for comic effect. For instance, Smirnov tells Mrs. Popov, "I've known more women than you've known pussy cats. I've fought three duels on their account. I've jilted twelve, and been jilted by nine others." Give some additional examples of such broadly exaggerated language, and explain its function.

7. Give some examples of physical actions used to reinforce emotions or attitudes in *The Brute*.

8. Explain and illustrate how the characters' words reveal each of the following moods: Mrs. Popov's anger at Mr. Smirnov, Mrs. Popov's ambivalence toward her late husband, Mr. Smirnov's impatience with Mrs. Popov, Mr. Smirnov's stubbornness.

9. As the play progresses, Mrs. Popov's changing language communicates her changing attitude toward her husband. Give some examples that illustrate this change in attitude.

10. What can you infer about Mrs. Popov's relationship with Luka from the language she uses when she addresses him? From the language he uses with her? What function does Luka serve in the play?

11. At what point in the play does Mr. Smirnov's speech become more elaborate? What does his use of figurative language suggest?

12. Where in the play does dramatic irony occur? Is verbal irony also present?

13. Identify all the asides in the play. What is their function?

14. **JOURNAL ENTRY** If you had to take a side in the dispute between Mrs. Popov and Mr. Smirnov, whose side would you be on? Why?

15. **CRITICAL PERSPECTIVE** Critic Harvey Pilcher characterizes
The Brute, like Chekhov's other one-act "farce-vaudevilles," as a
"comedy of situation":

> Although they contain an assortment of comic ingredients—
> parody, slapstick, misunderstandings, the absurd, the gro-
> tesque, irony, and social satire—the vaudevilles still belong to
> the genre of "comedy of situation." This is because [. . .] the
> emphasis for an audience is 'not on mystery and surprise, but
> on the working-out of a known situation . . . not so much on
> what will happen next as to how it will happen.' In the best
> of the comedy of situation stories, the situation itself opens
> the door to comedy of characterization. There is a comic psy-
> chological inevitability about the way Smirnov [. . .] fails to
> live up to his misogynistic principles and [Mrs. Popov] aban-
> dons the role of the faithful widow [. . .].

In what way is the "comedy of situation" Pilcher describes
similar to today's television "situation comedies" (sitcoms)?

Related Works: "Big Black Good Man" (p. 207), "The Cask of Amontillado" (p. 219), "Popular Mechanics" (p. 412), "General Review of the Sex
Situation" (p. 687), "You Fit into Me" (p. 828), "Women" (p. 891)

 ◆ **PADDY CHAYEFSKY** (1923–1981) was born Sidney Chayefsky in The Bronx, New York. He attended
City College of New York, and he served in the U.S.
Army during World War II. It was in the Army that
he earned the nickname "Paddy" after requesting
permission to attend mass in an attempt to avoid KP
duty. (His lieutenant, skeptical about his request since
Chayefsky was Jewish, gave him the Irish-Catholic
nickname.) Returning to New York after serving in
the Army, Chayefsky worked as a printer's apprentice
and began writing radio adaptations and mystery dramas for television
series. His first full-length television play was *Holiday Song* (1952), but he
won true success with *Marty* (1953), a television play which was later
made into an Oscar award–winning motion picture. Another of his television dramas, *The Middle of the Night* (1954), was rewritten and expanded to
become his first stage play in 1956. His next two stage plays, *The Tenth
Man* (1959) and *Gideon* (1961), were based on religious themes, and *The
Passion of Josef D.* (1964) was based on Stalin and the Russian Revolution.
Chayefsky also wrote screenplays, and his writing was honored with Academy Awards for *The Hospital* (1971) and *Network* (1976), as well as for the
film versoin of *Marty.*

Marty, about the awakening of love between two ordinary people, a shy
butcher and a plain teacher, proved television's capability to produce powerful drama. The 1955 film version of *Marty* won four Academy Awards (including Best Picture) in 1956 and the Golden Palm of the Cannes Festival.

CULTURAL CONTEXT ◆ *Marty* was first broadcast as a live television play. During the 1950s, the so-called Golden Age of television, live dramas were performed weekly on such programs as *Playhouse 90* and *Studio One*. Virtually all of today's television shows are videotaped and can be edited to delete flubbed lines or unexpected occurrences.

◆ ◆ ◆

PADDY CHAYEFSKY

Marty
(1955)

CHARACTERS

MARTY PILLETTI	BARTENDER
CLARA DAVIS	TWENTY-YEAR-OLD
ANGIE	ITALIAN WOMAN
MOTHER	SHORT GIRL
AUNT CATHERINE	GIRL
VIRGINIA	YOUNG MOTHER
THOMAS	STAG
YOUNG MAN	FORTY-YEAR-OLD
CRITIC	

ACT I

FADE-IN: *A butcher shop in the Italian district of New York City. Actually, we fade in on a close-up of a butcher's saw being carefully worked through a side of beef, and we dolly back to show the butcher at work, and then the whole shop. The butcher is a mild-mannered, stout, short, balding young man of thirty-six. His charm lies in an almost indestructible good-natured amiability.*

The shop contains three women customers. One is a Young Mother with a baby carriage. She is chatting with a second woman of about forty at the door. The customer being waited on at the moment is a stout, elderly Italian Woman who is standing on tiptoe, peering over the white display counter, checking the butcher as he saws away.

ITALIAN WOMAN: Your kid brother got married last Sunday, eh, Marty?
MARTY: *(absorbed in his work)* That's right, Missus Fusari. It was a very nice affair.
ITALIAN WOMAN: That's the big tall one, the fellow with the mustache.
MARTY: *(sawing away)* No, that's my other brother Freddie. My other brother Freddie, he's been married four years already. He lives down on Quincy Street. The one who got married Sunday, that was my little brother Nickie.
5 ITALIAN WOMAN: I thought he was a big, tall, fat fellow. Didn't I meet him here one time? Big, tall, fat fellow, he tried to sell me life insurance?
MARTY: *(sets the cut of meat on the scale, watches its weight register)* No, that's my sister Margaret's husband Frank. My sister Margaret, she's married

to the insurance salesman. My sister Rose, she married a contractor. They moved to Detroit last year. And my other sister, Frances, she got married about two and a half years ago in Saint John's Church on Adams Boulevard. Oh, that was a big affair. Well, Missus Fusari, that'll be three dollars, ninety-four cents. How's that with you?

The Italian Woman produces an old leather change purse from her pocketbook and painfully extracts three single dollar bills and ninety-four cents to the penny and lays the money piece by piece on the counter.

YOUNG MOTHER: *(calling from the door)* Hey, Marty, I'm inna hurry.
MARTY: *(wrapping the meat, calls amiably back)* You're next right now, Missus Canduso.

The old Italian Woman has been regarding Marty *with a baleful scowl.*

ITALIAN WOMAN: Well, Marty, when you gonna get married? You should be ashamed. All your brothers and sisters, they all younger than you, and they married, and they got children. I just saw your mother inna fruit shop, and she says to me: "Hey, you know a nice girl for my boy Marty?" Watsa matter with you? That's no way. Watsa matter with you? Now, you get married, you hear me what I say?
10 MARTY: *(amiably)* I hear you, Missus Fusari.

The old lady takes her parcel of meat, but apparently feels she still hasn't quite made her point.

ITALIAN WOMAN: My son Frank, he was married when he was nineteen years old. Watsa matter with you?
MARTY: Missus Fusari, Missus Canduso over there, she's inna big hurry, and . . .
ITALIAN WOMAN: You be ashamed of yourself.

She takes her package of meat, turns, and shuffles to the door and exits. Marty *gathers up the money on the counter, turns to the cash register behind him to ring up the sale.*

YOUNG MOTHER: Marty, I want a nice big fat pullet, about four pounds. I hear your kid brother got married last Sunday.
15 MARTY: Yeah, it was a very nice affair, Missus Canduso.
YOUNG MOTHER: Marty, you oughtta be ashamed. All you kid brothers and sisters, married and have children. When you gonna get married?

CLOSE-UP: *Marty. He sends a glance of weary exasperation up to the ceiling. With a gesture of mild irritation, he pushes the plunger of the cash register. It makes a sharp ping.*

DISSOLVE TO: *Close-up of television set. A baseball game is in progress. Camera pulls back to show we are in a typical neighborhood bar—red leatherette booths—a jukebox, some phone booths. About half the bar stools are occupied by neighborhood folk.* Marty *enters, pads amiably to one of the booths where a young man of about thirty-odd already sits. This is Angie. Marty slides into the booth across from Angie. Angie is a little wasp of a fellow. He has a newspaper spread out before him to the sports pages. Marty reaches over and pulls one of the pages over for himself to read. For a moment the two friends sit across from each other, reading the sports pages. Then Angie, without looking up, speaks.*

ANGIE: Well, what do you feel like doing tonight?

MARTY: I don't know, Angie. What do you feel like doing?

ANGIE: Well, we oughtta do something. It's Saturday night. I don't wanna go bowling like last Saturday. How about calling up that big girl we picked up inna movies about a month ago in the RKO Chester?

20 MARTY: *(not very interested)* Which one was that?

ANGIE: That big girl that was sitting in front of us with the skinny friend.

MARTY: Oh, yeah.

ANGIE: We took them home alla way out in Brooklyn. Her name was Mary Feeney. What do you say? You think I oughtta give her a ring? I'll take the skinny one.

MARTY: It's five o'clock already, Angie. She's probably got a date by now.

25 ANGIE: Well, let's call her up. What can we lose?

MARTY: I didn't like her, Angie. I don't feel like calling her up.

ANGIE: Well, what do you feel like doing tonight?

MARTY: I don't know. What do you feel like doing?

ANGIE: Well, we're back to that, huh? I say to you: "What do you feel like doing tonight?" And you say to me: "I don't know, what do you feel like doing?" And then we wind up sitting around your house with a couple of cans of beer, watching Sid Caesar on television. Well, I tell you what I feel like doing. I feel like calling up this Mary Feeney. She likes you.

Marty looks up quickly at this.

30 MARTY: What makes you say that?

ANGIE: I could see she likes you.

MARTY: Yeah, sure.

ANGIE: *(half rising in his seat)* I'll call her up.

MARTY: You call her up for yourself, Angie. I don't feel like calling her up.

Angie sits down again. They both return to reading the paper for a moment. Then Angie looks up again.

35 ANGIE: Boy, you're getting to be a real drag, you know that?

MARTY: Angie, I'm thirty-six years old. I been looking for a girl every Saturday night of my life. I'm a little, short, fat fellow, and girls don't go for me, that's all. I'm not like you. I mean, you joke around, and they laugh at you, and you get along fine. I just stand around like a bug. What's the sense of kidding myself? Everybody's always telling me to get married. Get married. Get married. Don't you think I wanna get married? I wanna get married. They drive me crazy. Now, I don't wanna wreck your Saturday night for you, Angie. You wanna go somewhere, you go ahead. I don't wanna go.

ANGIE: Boy, they drive me crazy too. My old lady, every word outta her mouth, when you gonna get married?

MARTY: My mother, boy, she drives me crazy.

Angie leans back in his seat, scowls at the paper-napkin container. Marty returns to the sports page. For a moment a silence hangs between them. Then . . .

ANGIE: So what do you feel like doing tonight?

40 MARTY: *(without looking up)* I don't know. What do you feel like doing?

They both just sit, Angie frowning at the napkin container, Marty at the sports page.

The camera slowly moves away from the booth, looks down the length of the bar, up the wall, past the clock—which reads ten to five—and over to the television screen, where the baseball game is still going on.

DISSOLVE SLOWLY TO: *The television screen, now blank. The clock now reads a quarter to six.*

Back in the booth, Marty now sits alone. In front of him are three empty beer bottles and a beer glass, half filled. He is sitting there, his face expressionless, but his eyes troubled. Then he pushes himself slowly out of the booth and shuffles to the phone booth; he goes inside, closing the booth door carefully after him. For a moment Marty just sits squatly. Then with some exertion—due to the cramped quarters—he contrives to get a small address book out of his rear pants pocket. He slowly flips through it, finds the page he wants, and studies it, scowling; then he takes a dime from the change he has just received, plunks it into the proper slot, waits for a dail tone . . . then carefully dials a number. . . . He waits. He is beginning to sweat a bit in the hot little booth, and his chest begins to rise and fall deeply.

MARTY: *(with a vague pretense at good diction)* Hello, is this Mary Feeney? . . . Could I please speak to Miss Mary Feeney? . . . Just tell her an old friend . . . *(He waits again. With his free hand he wipes the gathering sweat from his brow.)* . . . Oh, hello there, is this Mary Feeney? Hello there, this is Marty Pilletti. I wonder if you recall me . . . Well, I'm kind of a stocky guy. The last time we met was inna movies, the RKO Chester. You was with another girl, and I was with a friend of mine name Angie. This was about a month ago . . .

The girl apparently doesn't remember him. A sort of panic begins to seize Marty. His voice rises a little.

The RKO Chester on Payne Boulevard. You was sitting in front of us, and we was annoying you, and you got mad, and . . . I'm the fellow who works inna butcher shop . . . come on, you know who I am! . . . hat's right, we went to Howard Johnson's and we had hamburgers. You hadda milk shake . . . Yeah, that's right. I'm the stocky one, the heavy-set fellow. . . . Well, I'm glad you recall me, because I hadda swell time that night, and I was just wondering how everything was with you. How's everything? . . . That's swell . . . Yeah, well, I'll tell you why I called . . . I was figuring on taking in a movie tonight, and I was wondering if you and your friend would care to see a movie tonight with me and my friend . . . *(His eyes are closed now.)* Yeah, tonight. I know it's pretty late to call for a date, but I didn't know myself till . . . Yeah, I know, well how about . . . Yeah, I know, well maybe next Saturday night. You free next Saturday night? . . . Well, how about the Saturday after that? . . . Yeah, I know . . . Yeah . . . Yeah . . . Oh, I understand, I mean . . .

He just sits now, his eyes closed, not really listening. After a moment he returns the receiver to its cradle and sits, his shoulders slack, his hands resting listlessly in the lap of his spotted white apron. . . . Then he opens his eyes, straightens himself, pushes the booth door open, and advances out into the bar. He perches on a stool across the bar from the Bartender, who looks up from his magazine.

BARTENDER: I hear your kid brother got married last week, Marty.
MARTY: *(looking down at his hands on the bar)* Yeah, it was a very nice affair.
BARTENDER: Well, Marty, when you gonna get married?

Marty tenders the bartender a quick scowl, gets off his perch, and starts for the door—untying his apron as he goes.

45 MARTY: If my mother calls up, Lou, tell her I'm on my way home.

DISSOLVE TO: *Marty's Mother and a young couple sitting around the table in the dining room of Marty's home. The young couple—we will soon find out—are Thomas, Marty's cousin, and his wife, Virginia. They have apparently just been telling the mother some sad news, and the three are sitting around frowning.*

The dining room is a crowded room filled with chairs and lamps, pictures and little statues, perhaps even a small grotto of little vigil lamps. To the right of the dining room is the kitchen, old-fashioned, Italian, steaming, and overcrowded. To the left of the dining room is the living room, furnished in same fashion as the dining room. Just off the living room is a small bedroom, which is Marty's. This bedroom and the living room have windows looking out on front. The dining room has windows looking out to side alleyway. A stairway in the dining room leads to the second floor. The Mother is a round, dark, effusive little woman.

MOTHER: *(after a pause)* Well, Thomas, I knew sooner or later this was gonna happen. I told Marty, I said: "Marty, you watch. There's gonna be real trouble over there in your cousin Thomas' house." Because your mother was here, Thomas, you know?
THOMAS: When was this, Aunt Theresa?
MOTHER: This was one, two, three days ago. Wednesday. Because I went to the fruit shop on Wednesday, and I came home. And I come arounna back and there's your mother sitting onna steps onna porch. And I

said: "Catherine, my sister, wadda you doing here?" And she look
uppa me, and she beganna cry.

THOMAS: *(to his wife)* Wednesday. That was the day you threw the milk
bottle.

50 MOTHER: That's right. Because I said to her: "Catherine, watsa matter?"
And she said to me: "Theresa, my daughter-in-law, Virginia, she just
threw the milk bottle at me."

VIRGINIA: Well, you see what happen, Aunt Theresa . . .

MOTHER: I know, I know . . .

VIRGINIA: She comes inna kitchen, and she begins poking her head over
my shoulder here and poking her head over my shoulder there . . .

MOTHER: I know, I know . . .

55 VIRGINIA: And she begins complaining about this, and she begins
complaining about that. And she got me so nervous, I spilled some
milk I was making for the baby. You see, I was making some food for
the baby, and . . .

MOTHER: So I said to her, "Catherine . . ."

VIRGINIA: So, she got me so nervous I spilled some milk. So she said:
"You're spilling the milk." She says: "Milk costs twenty-four cents a
bottle. Wadda you, a banker?" So I said: "Mama, leave me alone,
please. You're making me nervous. Go on in the other room and turn
on the television set." So then she began telling me how I waste
money, and how I can't cook, and how I'm raising my baby all wrong,
and she kept talking about these couple of drops of milk I spilt, and I
got so mad, I said: "Mama, you wanna see me really spill some milk?"
So I took the bottle and threw it against the door. I didn't throw it at
her. That's just something she made up. I didn't throw it anywheres
near her. Well, of course, alla milk went all over the floor. The whole
twenty-four cents. Well, I was sorry right away, you know, but she ran
outta the house.

Pause.

MOTHER: Well, I don't know what you want me to do, Virginia. If you
want me, I'll go talk to her tonight.

*Thomas and Virginia suddenly frown and look down at their hands as if of one
mind.*

THOMAS: Well, I'll tell you, Aunt Theresa . . .

60 VIRGINIA: Lemme tell it, Tommy.

THOMAS: Okay.

VIRGINIA: *(leaning forward to the Mother)* We want you to do a very big
favor for us, Aunt Theresa.

MOTHER: Sure.

VIRGINIA: Aunt Theresa, you got this big house here. You got four
bedrooms upstairs. I mean, you got this big house just for you and
Marty. All your other kids are married and got their own homes. And

I thought maybe Tommy's mother could come here and live with you and Marty.

65 MOTHER: Well . . .

VIRGINIA: She's miserable living with Tommy and me, and you're the only one that gets along with her. Because I called up Tommy's brother, Joe, and I said: "Joe, she's driving me crazy. Why don't you take her for a couple of years?" And he said: "Oh, no!" I know I sound like a terrible woman . . .

MOTHER: No, Virginia, I know how you feel. My husband, may God bless his memory, his mother, she lived with us for a long time, and I know how you feel.

VIRGINIA: *(practically on the verge of tears)* I just can't stand it no more! Every minute of the day! Do this! Do that! I don't have ten minutes alone with my husband! We can't even have a fight! We don't have no privacy! Everybody's miserable in our house!

THOMAS: All right, Ginnie, don't get so excited.

70 MOTHER: She's right. She's right. Young husband and wife, they should have their own home. And my sister, Catherine, she's my sister, but I gotta admit, she's an old goat. And plenny-a times in my life I feel like throwing the milk bottle at her myself. And I tell you now, as far as I'm concerned, if Catherine wantsa come live here with me and Marty, it's all right with me.

Virginia promptly bursts into tears.

THOMAS: *(not far from tears himself, lowers his face)* That's very nice-a you, Aunt Theresa.

MOTHER: We gotta ask Marty, of course, because this is his house too. But he's gonna come home any minute now.

VIRGINIA: *(having mastered her tears)* That's very nice-a you, Aunt Theresa.

MOTHER: *(rising)* Now, you just sit here. I'm just gonna turn onna small fire under the food. *(She exits into the kitchen.)*

75 VIRGINIA: *(calling after her)* We gotta go right away because I promised the baby sitter we'd be home by six, and it's after six now . . .

She kind of fades out. A moment of silence. Thomas takes out a cigarette and lights it.

THOMAS: *(calling to his aunt in the kitchen)* How's Marty been lately, Aunt Theresa?

MOTHER: *(off in kitchen)* Oh, he's fine. You know a nice girl he can marry? *(She comes back into the dining room, wiping her hands on a kitchen towel.)* I'm worried about him, you know? He's thirty-six years old, gonna be thirty-seven in January.

THOMAS: Oh, he'll get married, don't worry, Aunt Theresa.

MOTHER: *(sitting down again)* Well, I don't know. You know a place where he can go where he can find a bride?

80 THOMAS: The Waverly Ballroom. That's a good place to meet girls, Aunt
Theresa. That's a kind of big dance hall, Aunt Theresa. Every Saturday
night, it's just loaded with girls. It's a nice place to go. You pay
seventy-seven cents. It used to be seventy-seven cents. It must be
about a buck and a half now. And you go in and you ask some girl to
dance. That's how I met Virginia. Nice, respectable place to meet
girls. You tell Marty, Aunt Theresa, you tell him: "Go to the Waverly
Ballroom. It's loaded with tomatoes."
MOTHER: *(committing the line to memory)* The Waverly Ballroom. It's
loaded with tomatoes.
THOMAS: Right.
VIRGINIA: You tell him, go to the Waverly Ballroom.

*There is the sound of a door being unlatched off through the kitchen. The Mother
promptly rises.*

MOTHER: He's here.

*She hurries into the kitchen. At the porch entrance to the kitchen, Marty has just
come in. He is closing the door behind him. He carries his butcher's apron in a
bundle under his arm.*

MARTY: Hello, Ma.

She comes up to him, lowers her voice to a whisper.

MOTHER: *(whispers)* Marty, Thomas and Virginia are here. They had
another big fight with your Aunt Catherine. So they ask me, would it
be all right if Catherine come to live with us. So I said, all right with
me, but we have to ask you. Marty, she's a lonely old lady. Nobody
wants her. Everybody's throwing her outta their house. . . .
MARTY: Sure, Ma, it's okay with me.

*The Mother's face breaks into a fond smile. She reaches up and pats his cheek
with genuine affection.*

MOTHER: You gotta good heart. *(Turning and leading the way back to the
dining room. Thomas has risen.)* He says okay, it's all right Catherine
comes here.
THOMAS: Oh, Marty, thanks a lot. That really takes a load offa my mind.
90 MARTY: Oh, we got plenty-a room here.
MOTHER: Sure! Sure! It's gonna be nice! It's gonna be nice! I'll come over
tonight to your house, and I talk to Catherine, and you see,
everything is gonna work out all right.
THOMAS: I just wanna thank you people again because the situation was
just becoming impossible.
MOTHER: Siddown, Thomas, siddown. All right, Marty, siddown. . . .

She exits into the kitchen.

Marty has taken his seat at the head of the table and is waiting to be served. Thomas takes a seat around the corner of the table from him and leans across to him.

THOMAS: You see, Marty, the kinda thing that's been happening in our house is Virginia was inna kitchen making some food for the baby. Well, my mother comes in, and she gets Virginia so nervous, she spills a couple-a drops . . .

95 VIRGINIA: *(tugging at her husband)* Tommy, we gotta go. I promise the baby sitter six o'clock.

THOMAS: *(rising without interrupting his narrative)* So she starts yelling at Virginia, waddaya spilling the milk for. So Virginia gets mad . . .

His wife is slowly pulling him to the kitchen door.

She says, "You wanna really see me spill milk?" So Virginia takes the bottle and she throws it against the wall. She's got a real Italian temper, my wife, you know that . . .

He has been tugged to the kitchen door by now.

VIRGINIA: Marty, I don't have to tell you how much we appreciate what your mother and you are doing for us.

THOMAS: All right, Marty, I'll see you some other time . . . I'll tell you all about it.

MARTY: I'll see you, Tommy.

Thomas disappears into the kitchen after his wife.

100 VIRGINIA: *(off, calling)* Good-by, Marty!

Close in on Marty, sitting at table.

MARTY: Good-by, Virginia! See you soon!

He folds his hands on the table before him and waits to be served.
The Mother enters from the kitchen. She sets the meat plate down in front of him and herself takes a chair around the corner of the table from him. Marty without a word takes up his knife and fork and attacks the mountain of food in front of him. His mother sits quietly, her hands a little nervous on the table before her, watching him eat. Then . . .

MOTHER: So what are you gonna do tonight, Marty?

MARTY: I don't know, Ma. I'm all knocked out. I may just hang arounna house.

The Mother nods a couple of times. There is a moment of silence. Then . . .

MOTHER: Why don't you go to the Waverly Ballroom?

This gives Marty pause. He looks up.

105 MARTY: What?

MOTHER: I say, why don't you go to the Waverly Ballroom? It's loaded with tomatoes.

Marty regards his mother for a moment.

MARTY: It's loaded with what?

MOTHER: Tomatoes.

MARTY: *(snorts)* Ha! Who told you about the Waverly Ballroom?

110 MOTHER: Thomas, he told me it was a very nice place.

MARTY: Oh, Thomas. Ma, it's just a big dance hall, and that's all it is. I been there a hundred times. Loaded with tomatoes. Boy, you're funny, Ma.

MOTHER: Marty, I don't want you hang arounna house tonight. I want you to go take a shave and go out and dance.

MARTY: Ma, when are you gonna give up? You gotta bachelor on your hands. I ain't never gonna get married.

MOTHER: You gonna get married.

115 MARTY: Sooner or later, there comes a point in a man's life when he gotta face some facts, and one fact I gotta face is that whatever it is that women like, I ain't got it. I chased enough girls in my life. I went to enough dances. I got hurt enough. I don't wanna get hurt no more. I just called a girl this afternoon, and I got a real brush-off, boy. I figured I was past the point of being hurt, but that hurt. Some stupid woman who I didn't even wanna call up. She gave me the brush. That's the history of my life. I don't wanna go to the Waverly Ballroom because all that ever happened to me there was girls made me feel like I was a bug. I got feelings, you know. I had enough pain. No, thank you.

MOTHER: Marty . . .

MARTY: Ma, I'm gonna stay home and watch Sid Caesar.

MOTHER: You gonna die without a son.

MARTY: So I'll die without a son.

120 MOTHER: Put on your blue suit . . .

MARTY: Blue suit, gray suit, I'm still a fat little man. A fat little ugly man.

MOTHER: You not ugly.

MARTY: *(his voice rising)* I'm ugly . . . I'm ugly! . . . I'm UGLY!

MOTHER: Marty . . .

125 MARTY: *(crying aloud, more in anguish than in anger)* Ma! Leave me alone! . . . *(He stands abruptly, his face pained and drawn. He makes half-formed gestures to his mother, but he can't find words at the moment. He turns and marches a few paces away, turns to his mother again.)* Ma, waddaya want from me?! Waddaya want from me?! I'm miserable enough at it is! Leave me alone! I'll go to the Waverly Ballroom! I'll put onna blue suit and I'll go! And you know what I'm gonna get for my trouble? Heartache! A big night of heartache! *(He sullenly marches back to his seat, sits down, picks up his fork, plunges it into the lasagna, and stuffs a mouthful into his mouth; he chews vigorously for a moment.*

It is impossible to remain angry for long. After a while he is shaking his head and muttering.) Loaded with tomatoes . . . boy, that's rich . . .

He plunges his fork in again. Camera pulls slowly away from him and his mother, who is seated—watching him
    Fade out

Act II

FADE IN: *Exterior, three-story building. Pan up to second floor . . . bright neon lights reading "Waverly Ballroom" . . . The large, dirty windows are open; and the sound of a fair-to-middling swing band whooping it up comes out.*
    DISSOLVE TO: *Interior, Waverly Ballroom—large dance floor crowded with jitterbugging couples, eight-piece combination hitting a loud kick. Ballroom is vaguely dark, made so by papier-mâché over the chandeliers to create alleged romantic effect. The walls are lined with stags and waiting girls, singly and in small murmuring groups. Noise and mumble and drone.*
    DISSOLVE TO: *Live shot—a row of stags along a wall. Camera is looking lengthwise down the row. Camera dollies slowly past each face, each staring out at the dance floor, watching in his own manner of hungry eagerness. Short, fat, tall, thin stags. Some pretend diffidence. Some exhibit patent hunger.*
    Near the end of the line, we find Marty and Angie, freshly shaved and groomed. They are leaning against the wall, smoking, watching their more fortunate brethren out on the floor.

ANGIE: Not a bad crowd tonight, you know?
MARTY: There was one nice-looking one there in a black dress and beads, but she was a little tall for me.
ANGIE: *(looking down past Marty along the wall right into the camera)* There's a nice-looking little short one for you right now.
MARTY: *(following his gaze)* Where?
5 ANGIE: Down there. That little one there.

The camera cuts about eight faces down, to where the girls are now standing. Two are against the wall. One is facing them, with her back to the dance floor. This last is the one Angie has in mind. She is a cute little kid, about twenty, and she has a bright little smile on—as if the other two girls are just amusing her to death.

MARTY: Yeah, she looks all right from here.
ANGIE: Well, go on over and ask her. You don't hurry up, somebody else'll grab her.

Marty scowls, shrugs.

MARTY: Okay, let's go.

They slouch along past the eight stags, a picture of nonchalant unconcern. The three girls, aware of their approach, stiffen, and their chatter comes to a halt. Angie advances to one of the girls along the wall.

ANGIE: Waddaya say, you wanna dance?

The girl looks surprised—as if this were an extraordinary invitation to receive in this place—looks confounded at her two friends, shrugs, detaches herself from the group, moves to the outer fringe of the pack of dancers, raises her hand languidly to dancing position, and awaits Angie with ineffable boredom. Marty, smiling shyly, addresses the short girl.

10 MARTY: Excuse me, would you care for this dance?

The short girl gives Marty a quick glance of appraisal, then looks quickly at her remaining friend.

SHORT GIRL: *(not unpleasantly)* Sorry. I just don't feel like dancing just yet.
MARTY: Sure.

He turns and moves back past the eight stags, all of whom have covertly watched his attempt. He finds his old niche by the wall, leans there. A moment later he looks guardedly down to where the short girl and her friend are. A young, dapper boy is approaching the short girl. He asks her to dance. The short girl smiles, excuses herself to her friend, and follows the boy out onto the floor. Marty turns back to watching the dancers bleakly. A moment later he is aware that someone on his right is talking to him. . . . He turns his head. It is a young man of about twenty-eight.

MARTY: You say something to me?
YOUNG MAN: Yeah. I was just asking you if you was here stag or with a
    girl.
15 MARTY: I'm stag.
YOUNG MAN: Well, I'll tell you. I got stuck onna blind date with a dog,
    and I just picked up a nice chick, and I was wondering how I'm gonna
    get ridda the dog. Somebody to take her home, you know what I mean?
    I be glad to pay you five bucks if you take the dog home for me.
MARTY: *(a little confused)* What?
YOUNG MAN: I'll take you over, and I'll introduce you as an old army
    buddy of mine, and then I'll cut out. Because I got this chick waiting
    for me out by the hatcheck, and I'll pay you five bucks.
MARTY: *(stares at the Young Man)* Are you kidding?
20 YOUNG MAN: No, I'm not kidding.
MARTY: You can't just walk off onna girl like that.

The Young Man grimaces impatiently and moves down the line of stags. . . . Marty watches him, still a little shocked at the proposition. Abut two stags down, the Young Man broaches his plan to another Stag. This Stag, frowning and pursing his lips, seems more receptive to the idea. . . . The Young Man takes out a wallet and gives the Stag a five-dollar bill. The Stag detaches himself from the wall and, a little ill at ease, follows the Young Man back past Marty and into the lounge. Marty pauses a moment and then, concerned, walks to the archway that separates the lounge from the ballroom and looks in.

The lounge is a narrow room with a bar and booths. In contrast to the ball-room, it is brightly lighted—causing Marty to squint.

In the second booth from the archway sits a Girl, about twenty-eight. De-spite the careful grooming that she has put into her cosmetics, she is blatantly plain. The Young Man and the Stag are standing, talking to her. She is looking up at the Young Man, her hands nervously gripping her Coca-Cola glass. We cannot hear what the Young Man is saying, but it is apparent that he is introducing his new-found army buddy and is going through some cock-and-bull story about being called away on an emergency. The Stag is presented to her escort-to-be, who will see to it that she gets home safely. The Girl apparently is not taken in at all by this, though she is trying hard not to seem affected.

She politely rejects the Stag's company and will get home by herself, thanks for asking anyway. The Young Man makes a few mild protestations, and then he and the Stag leave the booth and come back to the archway from where Marty has been watching the scene. As they pass Marty, we overhear a snatch of dialogue.

YOUNG MAN: . . . In that case, as long as she's going home alone, give me the five bucks back . . .

STAG: . . . Look, Mac, you paid me five bucks. I was willing. It's my five bucks. . . .

They pass on. Marty returns his attention to the Girl. She is still sitting as she was, gripping and ungripping the glass of Coca-Cola in front of her. Her eyes are closed. Then, with a little nervous shake of her head, she gets out of the booth and stands—momentarily at a loss for what to do next. The open fire doors lead-ing out onto the large fire escape catch her eye. She crosses to the fire escape, ner-vous, frowning, and disappears outside.

Marty stares after her, then slowly shuffles to the open fire-escape doorway. It is a large fire escape, almost the size of a small balcony. The Girl is standing by the railing, her back to the doorway, her head slunk on her bosom. For a mo-ment Marty is unaware that she is crying. Then he notices the shivering tremors running through her body and the quivering shoulders. He moves a step onto the fire escape. He tries to think of something to say.

MARTY: Excuse me, Miss. Would you care to dance?

The Girl slowly turns to him, her face streaked with tears, her lip trembling. Then, in one of those peculiar moments of simultaneous impulse, she lurches to Marty with a sob, and Marty takes her to him. For a moment they stand in an awkward embrace, Marty a little embarrassed, looking out through the doors to the lounge, wondering if anybody is seeing them. Reaching back with one hand, he closes the fire doors, and then, replacing the hand around her shoulder, he stands stiffly, allowing her to cry on his chest.

DISSOLVE TO: *Exterior, apartment door. The Mother is standing, in a black coat and a hat with a little feather, waiting for her ring to be answered. The door opens, Virginia stands framed in the doorway.*

25 **VIRGINIA:** Hello, Aunt Theresa, come in.

The Mother goes into the small foyer. Virginia closes the door.

MOTHER: *(in a low voice, as she pulls her coat off)* Is Catherine here?

VIRGINIA: *(helps her off with coat, nods—also in a low voice)* We didn't tell her nothing yet. We thought we'd leave it to you. We thought you'd put it like how you were lonely, and why don't she come to live with you. Because that way it looks like she's doing you a favor, insteada we're throwing her out, and it won't be so cruel on her. Thomas is downstairs with the neighbors . . . I'll go call him.

MOTHER: You go downstairs to the neighbors and stay there with Thomas.

VIRGINIA: Wouldn't it be better if we were here?

30 MOTHER: You go downstairs. I talk to Catherine alone. Otherwise, she's gonna start a fight with you.

A shrill, imperious woman's voice from an offstage room suddenly breaks into the muttered conference in the foyer.

AUNT: *(off)* Who's there?! Who's there?!

The Mother heads up the foyer to the living room, followed by Virginia, holding the Mother's coat.

MOTHER: *(calls back)* It's me, Catherine! How you feel?

At the end of the foyer, the two sisters meet. The Aunt is a spare, gaunt woman with a face carved out of granite. Tough, embittered, deeply hurt type of face.

AUNT: Hey! What are you doing here?

MOTHER: I came to see you. *(The two sisters quickly embrace and release each other.)* How you feel?

35 AUNT: I gotta pain in my left side and my leg throbs like a drum.

MOTHER: I been getting pains in my shoulder.

AUNT: I got pains in my shoulder, too. I have a pain in my hip, and my right arm aches so much I can't sleep. It's a curse to be old. How you feel?

MOTHER: I feel fine.

AUNT: That's nice.

Now that the standard greetings are over, Aunt Catherine abruptly turns and goes back to her chair. It is obviously her chair. It is an old, heavy oaken chair with thick armrests. The rest of the apartment is furnished in what is known as "modern"—a piece from House Beautiful *here, a piece from* Better Homes and Gardens *there. Aunt Catherine sits, erect, and forbidding, in her chair. The Mother seats herself with a sigh in a neighboring chair. Virginia, having hung the Mother's coat, now turns to the two older women. A pause.*

40 VIRGINIA: I'm going downstairs to the Cappacini's. I'll be up inna little while.

Aunt Catherine nods expressionlessly. Virginia looks at her for a moment, then impulsively crosses to her mother-in-law.

Virginia: You feel all right?

The old lady looks up warily, suspicious of this sudden solicitude.

Aunt: I'm all right.

Virginia nods and goes off to the foyer. The two old sisters sit, unmoving, waiting for the door to close behind Virginia. Then the Mother addresses herself to Aunt Catherine.

Mother: We gotta post card from my son, Nickie, and his bride this
morning. They're in Florida inna big hotel. Everything is very nice.
Aunt: That's nice.
45 Mother: Catherine, I want you come live with me in my house with
Marty and me. In my house, you have your own room. You don't
have to sleep onna couch inna living room like here.

The Aunt looks slowly and directly at the Mother.

Catherine, your son is married. He got his own home. Leave him in
peace. He wants to be alone with his wife. They don't want no old
lady sitting inna balcony. Come and live with me. We will cook in
the kitchen and talk like when we were girls. You are dear to me, and
you are dear to Marty. We are pleased for you to come.
Aunt: Did they come to see you?
Mother: Yes.
Aunt: Did my son Thomas come with her?
Mother: Your son Thomas was there.
50 Aunt: Did he also say he wishes to cast his mother from his house?
Mother: Catherine, don't make an opera outta this. The three-a you
anna baby live in three skinny rooms. You are an old goat, and she
has an Italian temper. She is a good girl, but you drive her crazy.
Leave them alone. They have their own life.

*The old Aunt turns her head slowly and looks her sister square in the face. Then
she rises slowly from her chair.*

Aunt: *(coldly)* Get outta here. This is my son's house. This is where I live.
I am not to be cast out inna street like a newspaper.

The Mother likewise rises. The two old women face each other directly.

Mother: Catherine, you are very dear to me. We have cried many times
together. When my husband died, I would have gone insane if it were
not for you. I ask you to come to my house because I can make you
happy. Please come to my house.

*The two sisters regard each other. Then Aunt Catherine sits again in her oaken
chair, and the Mother returns to her seat. The hardened muscles in the old
Aunt's face suddenly slacken, and she turns to her sister.*

Aunt: Theresa, what shall become of me?

55 Mother: Catherine . . .

Aunt: It's gonna happen to you. Mark it well. These terrible years. I'm afraida look inna mirror. I'm afraid I'm gonna see an old lady with white hair, like the old ladies inna park, little bundles inna black shawl, waiting for the coffin. I'm fifty-six years old. What am I to do with myself? I have strength in my hands. I wanna cook. I wanna clean. I wanna make dinner for my children. I wanna be of use to somebody. Am I an old dog to lie in fronta the fire till my eyes close? These are terrible years, Theresa! Terrible years!

Mother: Catherine, my sister . . .

The old Aunt stares, distraught, at the Mother.

Aunt: It's gonna happen to you! It's gonna happen to you! What will you do if Marty gets married?! What will you cook?! What happen to alla children tumbling in alla rooms?! Where is the noise?! It is a curse to be a widow! A curse! What will you do if Marty gets married?! What will you do?!

She stares at the Mother—her deep, gaunt eyes haggard and pained. The Mother stares back for a moment, then her own eyes close. The Aunt has hit home. The Aunt sinks back onto her chair, sitting stiffly, her arms on the thick armrests. The Mother sits hunched a little forward, her hands nervously folded in her lap.

(Quietly) I will put my clothes inna bag and I will come to you tomorrow.

The camera slowly dollies back from the two somber sisters.

SLOW FADE-OUT.

CUT TO: *Close-up, intimate, Marty and the Girl dancing cheek to cheek. Occasionally the heads of other couples slowly waft across the camera view, temporarily blocking our view of Marty and the Girl. Camera stays with them as the slow dance carries them around the floor. Tender scene . . .*

Girl: . . . The last time I was here the same sort of thing happened.

60 Marty: Yeah?

Girl: Well, not exactly the same thing. The last time I was up here about four months ago. Do you see that girl in the gray dress sitting over there?

Marty: Yeah.

Girl: That's where I sat. I sat there for an hour and a half without moving a muscle. Now and then, some fellow would sort of walk up to me and then change his mind. I just sat there, my hands in my lap. Well, about ten o'clock, a bunch of kids came in swaggering. They weren't more than seventeen, eighteen years old. Well, they swaggered down along the wall, leering at all the girls. I thought they were kind of cute . . . and as they passed me, I smiled at them. One of the kids looked at me and said: "Forget it, ugly, you ain't gotta chance." I burst out crying. I'm a big crier, you know.

MARTY: So am I.

65 GIRL: And another time when I was in college . . .

MARTY: I cry alla time. Any little thing. I can recognize pain a mile away. My brothers, my brother-in-laws, they're always telling me what a goodhearted guy I am. Well, you don't get goodhearted by accident. You get kicked around long enough you get to be a real professor of pain. I know exactly how you feel. And I also want you to know I'm having a very good time with you now and really enjoying myself. So you see, you're not such a dog as you think you are.

GIRL: I'm having a very good time too.

MARTY: So there you are. So I guess I'm not such a dog as I think I am.

GIRL: You're a very nice guy, and I don't know why some girl hasn't grabbed you off long ago.

70 MARTY: I don't know either. I think I'm a very nice guy. I also think I'm a pretty smart guy in my own way.

GIRL: I think you are.

MARTY: I'll tell you some of my wisdom which I thunk up on those nights when I got stood up, and nights like that, and you walk home thinking: "Watsa matter with me? I can't be that ugly." Well, I figure, two people get married, and they gonna live together forty, fifty years. So it's just gotta be more than whether they're good-looking or not. My father was a real ugly man, but my mother adored him. She told me that she used to get so miserable sometimes, like everybody, you know? And she says my father always tried to understand. I used to see them sometimes when I was a kid, sitting in the living room, talking and talking, and I used to adore my old man because he was so kind. That's one of the most beautiful things I have in my life, the way my father and mother were. And my father was a real ugly man. So it don't matter if you look like a gorilla. So you see, dogs like us, we ain't such dogs as we think we are.

They dance silently for a moment, cheeks pressed against each other. Close-ups of each face . . .

GIRL: I'm twenty-nine years old. How old are you?

MARTY: Thirty-six.

They dance silently, closely. Occasionally the heads of other couples sway in front of the camera, blocking our view of Marty and the Girl. Slow, sweet dissolve.

    DISSOLVE TO: *Interior, kitchen, Marty's home. Later that night. It is dark. Nobody is home. The rear porch door now opens, and the silhouettes of Marty and the Girl appear—blocking up the doorway.*

75 MARTY: Wait a minute. Lemme find the light.

He finds the light. The kitchen is suddenly brightly lit. The two of them stand squinting to adjust to the sudden glare.

> I guess my mother ain't home yet. I figure my cousin Thomas and Virginia musta gone to the movies, so they won't get back till one o'clock, at least.

The Girl has advanced into the kitchen, a little ill at ease, and is looking around. Marty closes the porch door.

> This is the kitchen.

GIRL: Yes, I know.

Marty leads the way into the dining room.

MARTY: Come on inna dining room. *(He turns on the light in there as he goes. The Girl follows him in.)* Siddown, take off your coat. You want something to eat? We gotta whole halfa chicken left over from yesterday.

GIRL: *(perching tentatively on the edge of a chair)* No, thank you. I don't think I should stay very long.

MARTY: Sure. Just take off your coat a minute.

He helps her off with her coat and stands for a moment behind her, looking down at her. Conscious of his scrutiny, she sits uncomfortably, her breasts rising and falling unevenly. Marty takes her coat into the dark living room. The Girl sits patiently, nervously. Marty comes back, sits down on another chair. Awkward silence . . .

> So I was telling you, my kid brother Nickie got married last Sunday . . . That was a very nice affair. And they had this statue of some woman, and they had whisky spouting outta her mouth. I never saw anything so grand in my life. *(The silence falls between them again.)* And watta meal. I'm a butcher, so I know a good hunka steak when I see one. That was choice filet, right off the toppa the chuck. A buck-eighty a pound. Of course, if you wanna cheaper cut, get rib steak. That gotta lotta waste on it, but it comes to about a buck and a quarter a pound, if it's trimmed. Listen, Clara, make yourself comfortable. You're all tense.

80 GIRL: Oh, I'm fine.

MARTY: You want me to take you home, I'll take you home.

GIRL: Maybe that would be a good idea.

She stands. He stands, frowning, a little angry—turns sullenly and goes back into the living room for her coat. She stands unhappily. He comes back and wordlessly starts to help her into her coat. He stands behind her, his hands on her shoulders. He suddenly seizes her, begins kissing her on the neck. Camera comes up quickly to intensely intimate close-up, nothing but the heads. The dialogue drops to quick, hushed whispers.

No, Marty, please . . .
MARTY: I like you, I like you, I been telling you all night I like you . . .
GIRL: Marty . . .
85 MARTY: I just wanna kiss, that's all . . .

He tries to turn her face to him. She resists.

GIRL: No . . .
MARTY: Please . . .
GIRL: No . . .
MARTY: Please . . .
90 GIRL: Marty . . .

He suddenly releases her, turns away violently.

MARTY: *(crying out)* All right! I'll take you home! All right! *(He marches a few angry paces away, deeply disturbed. Turns to her.)* All I wanted was a lousy kiss! What am I, a leper or something?!

He turns and goes off into the living room to hide the flush of hot tears threatening to fill his eyes. The Girl stands, herself on the verge of tears.

GIRL: *(mutters, more to herself than to him)* I just don't feel like it, that's all.

She moves slowly to the archway leading to the living room. Marty is sitting on the couch, hands in his lap, looking straight ahead. The room is dark except for the overcast of the dining-room light reaching in. The Girl goes to the couch, perches on the edge beside him. He doesn't look at her.

MARTY: Well, that's the history of my life. I'm a little, short, fat, ugly guy. Comes New Year's Eve, everybody starts arranging parties, I'm the guy they gotta dig up a date for. I'm old enough to know better. Let me get a packa cigarettes, and I'll take you home.

He starts to rise, but doesn't . . . sinks back onto the couch, looking straight ahead. The Girl looks at him, her face peculiarly soft and compassionate.

GIRL: I'd like to see you again, very much. The reason I didn't let you kiss me was because I just didn't know how to handle the situation. You're the kindest man I ever met. The reason I tell you this is because I want to see you again very much. Maybe, I'm just so desperate to fall in love that I'm trying too hard. But I know that when you take me home, I'm going to just lie on my bed and think about you. I want very much to see you again.

Marty stares down at his hands in his lap.

95 MARTY: *(without looking at her)* Waddaya doing tomorrow night?
GIRL: Nothing.
MARTY: I'll call you up tomorrow morning. Maybe we'll go see a movie.
GIRL: I'd like that very much.

MARTY: The reason I can't be definite about it now is my Aunt Catherine is probably coming over tomorrow, and I may have to help out.

100 GIRL: I'll wait for your call.

MARTY: We better get started to your house because the buses only run about one an hour now.

GIRL: All right.

She stands.

MARTY: I'll just get a packa cigarettes.

He goes into his bedroom. We can see him through the doorway, opening his bureau drawer and extracting a pack of cigarettes. He comes out again and looks at the girl for the first time. They start to walk to the dining room. In the archway, Marty pauses, turns to the Girl.

Waddaya doing New Year's Eve?

GIRL: Nothing.

They quietly slip into each other's arms and kiss. Slowly their faces part, and Marty's head sinks down upon her shoulder. He is crying. His shoulders shake slightly. The Girl presses her cheek against the back of his head. They stand . . . there is the sound of the rear porch door being unlatched. They both start from their embrace. A moment later the Mother's voice is heard off in the kitchen.

105 MOTHER: Hallo! Hallo, Marty? *(She comes into the dining room, stops at the sight of the Girl.)* Hallo, Marty, when you come home?

MARTY: We just got here about fifteen minutes ago, Ma. Ma, I want you to meet Miss Clara Davis. She's a graduate of New York University. She teaches history in Benjamin Franklin High School.

This seems to impress the Mother.

MOTHER: Siddown, siddown. You want some chicken? We got some chicken in the icebox.

GIRL: No, Mrs. Pilletti, we were just going home. Thank you very much anyway.

MOTHER: Well, siddown a minute. I just come inna house. I'll take off my coat. Siddown a minute. *(She pulls her coat off.)*

110 MARTY: How'd you come home, Ma? Thomas give you a ride?

The Mother nods.

MOTHER: Oh, it's a sad business, a sad business.

She sits down on a dining-room chair, holding her coat in her lap. She turns to the Girl, who likewise sits.

My sister Catherine, she don't get along with her daughter-in-law, so she's gonna come live with us.

MARTY: Oh, she's coming, eh, Ma?

MOTHER: Oh, sure. *(To the Girl.)* It's a very sad thing. A woman, fifty-six years old, all her life, she had her own home. Now, she's just an old lady, sleeping on her daughter-in-law's couch. It's a curse to be a mother, I tell you. Your children grow up and then what is left for you to do? What is a mother's life but her children? It is a very cruel thing when your son has no place for you in his home.

GIRL: Couldn't she find some sort of hobby to fill out her time?

115 MOTHER: Hobby! What can she do? She cooks and she cleans. You gotta have a house to clean. You gotta have children to cook for. These are the terrible years for a woman, the terrible years.

GIRL: You mustn't feel too harshly against her daughter-in-law. She also wants to have a house to clean and a family to cook for.

The Mother darts a quick, sharp look at the Girl—then looks back to her hands which are beginning to twist nervously.

MOTHER: You don't think my sister Catherine should live in her daughter-in-law's house?

GIRL: Well, I don't know the people, of course, but, as a rule, I don't think a mother-in-law should live with a young couple.

MOTHER: Where do you think a mother-in-law should go?

120 GIRL: I don't think a mother should depend so much upon her children for her rewards in life.

MOTHER: That's what it says in the book in New York University. You wait till you are a mother. It don't work out that way.

GIRL: Well, it's silly for me to argue about it. I don't know the people involved.

MARTY: Ma, I'm gonna take her home now. It's getting late, and the buses only run about one an hour.

MOTHER: *(standing)* Sure.

The Girl stands.

125 GIRL: It was very nice meeting you, Mrs. Pilletti. I hope I'll see you again.

MOTHER: Sure.

Marty and the Girl move to the kitchen.

MARTY: All right, Ma. I'll be back in about an hour.

MOTHER: Sure.

GIRL: Good night, Mrs. Pilletti.

130 MOTHER: Good night.

Marty and the Girl exit into the kitchen. The Mother stands, expressionless, by her chair watching them go. She remains standing rigidly even after the porch door can be heard being opened and shut. The camera moves up to a close-up of the Mother. Her eyes are wide. She is staring straight ahead. There is fear in her eyes.

Fade out.

<u>**Act III**</u>

FADE-IN: *Film—close-up of church bells clanging away. Pan down church to see typical Sunday morning, people going up the steps of a church and entering. It is a beautiful June morning.*

DISSOLVE TO: *Interior, Marty's bedroom—sun fairly streaming through the curtains. Marty is standing in front of his bureau, slipping his arms into a clean white shirt. He is freshly shaved and groomed. Through the doorway of his bedroom we can see the Mother in the dining room, in a coat and hat, all set to go to Mass, taking the last breakfast plates away and carrying them into the kitchen. The camera moves across the living room into the dining room. The Mother comes out of the kitchen with a paper napkin and begins crumbing the table.*

There is a knock on the rear porch door. The Mother leaves her crumbing and goes into the kitchen. Camera goes with her. She opens the rear door to admit Aunt Catherine, holding a worn old European carpetbag. The Aunt starts to go deeper into the kitchen, but the Mother stays her with her hand.

MOTHER: *(in low, conspiratorial voice)* Hey, I come home from your house last night, Marty was here with a girl.
AUNT: Who?
MOTHER: Marty.
AUNT: Your son Marty?
5 MOTHER: Well, what Marty you think is gonna be here in this house with a girl?
AUNT: Were the lights on?
MOTHER: Oh, sure. *(Frowns suddenly at her sister.)* The girl is a college graduate.
AUNT: They're the worst. College girls are one step from the streets. They smoke like men inna saloon.

The Aunt puts her carpetbag down and sits on one of the wooden kitchen chairs. The Mother sits on another.

MOTHER: That's the first time Marty ever brought a girl to this house. She seems like a nice girl. I think he has a feeling for this girl.

At this moment a burst of spirited whistling emanates from Marty's bedroom.
    CUT TO: *Marty's bedroom—Marty standing in front of his mirror, buttoning his shirt or adjusting his tie, whistling a gay tune.*
    CUT BACK TO: *The two sisters, both their faces turned in the direction of the whistling. The whistling abruptly stops. The two sisters look at each other. The Aunt shrugs.*

He been whistling like that all morning.

The Aunt nods bleakly.

10 AUNT: He is bewitched. You will see. Today, tomorrow, inna week, he's gonna say to you: "Hey, Ma, it's no good being a single man. I'm

tired running around." Then he's gonna say: "Hey, Ma, wadda we need this old house? Why don't we sell this old house, move into a nicer parta town? A nice little apartment?"

MOTHER: I don't sell this house, I tell you that. This is my husband's house, and I had six children in this house.

AUNT: You will see. A couple-a months, you gonna be an old lady, sleeping onna couch in your daughter-in-law's house.

MOTHER: Catherine, you are a blanket of gloom. Wherever you go, the rain follows. Some day, you gonna smile, and we gonna declare a holiday.

Another burst of spirited whistling comes from Marty, off. It comes closer, and Marty now enters in splendid spirits, whistling away. He is slipping into his jacket.

MARTY: *(ebulliently)* Hello, Aunt Catherine! How are you? You going to Mass with us?

15 AUNT: I was at Mass two hours ago.

MARTY: Well, make yourself at home. The refrigerator is loaded with food. Go upstairs, take any room you want. It's beautiful outside, ain't it?

AUNT: There's a chill. Watch out, you catch a good cold and pneumonia.

MOTHER: My sister Catherine, she can't even admit it's a beautiful day.

Marty—now at the sink, getting himself a glass of water—is examining a piece of plaster that has fallen from the ceiling.

MARTY: *(examining the chunk of plaster in his palm)* Boy, this place is really coming to pieces. *(Turns to Mother.)* You know, Ma, I think, sometime we oughtta sell this place. The plumbing is rusty—everything. I'm gonna have to replaster that whole ceiling now. I think we oughtta get a little apartment somewheres in a nicer parta town. . . . You all set, Ma?

20 MOTHER: I'm all set.

She starts for the porch door. She slowly turns and looks at Marty, and then at Aunt Catherine—who returns her look. Mother and Marty exit.

DISSOLVE TO: *Church. The Mother comes out of the doors and down a few steps to where Marty is standing, enjoying the clearness of the June morning.*

MOTHER: In a couple-a minutes nine o'clock Mass is gonna start—in a couple-a minutes . . . *(to passers-by off)* hallo, hallo . . . *(To Marty.)* Well, that was a nice girl last night, Marty. That was a nice girl.

MARTY: Yeah.

MOTHER: She wasn't a very good-looking girl, but she look like a nice girl. I said, she wasn't a very good-looking girl, not very pretty.

MARTY: I heard you, Ma.

25 MOTHER: She look a little old for you, about thirty-five, forty years old?

MARTY: She's twenty-nine, Ma.

MOTHER: She's more than twenny-nine years old, Marty. That's what she tells you. She looks thirty-five, forty. She didn't look Italian to me. I said, is she an Italian girl?

MARTY: I don't know. I don't think so.

MOTHER: She don't look like Italian to me. What kinda family she come from? There was something about her I don't like. It seem funny, the first time you meet her she comes to your empty house alone. These college girls, they all one step from the streets.

Marty turns, frowning, to his Mother.

30 MARTY: What are you talkin' about? She's a nice girl.

MOTHER: I don't like her.

MARTY: You don't like her? You only met her for two minutes.

MOTHER: Don't bring her to the house no more.

MARTY: What didn't you like about her?

35 MOTHER: I don't know! She don't look like Italian to me, plenty nice Italian girls around.

MARTY: Well, let's not get into a fight about it, Ma. I just met the girl. I probably won't see her again.

Marty leaves frame.

MOTHER: Eh, I'm no better than my sister Catherine.

DISSOLVE TO: *Interior, the bar . . . about an hour later. The after-Mass crowd is there, about six men ranging from twenty to forty. A couple of women in the booths. One woman is holding a glass of beer in one hand and is gently rocking a baby carriage with the other.*

Sitting in the booth of Act One are Angie and three other fellows, ages twenty, thirty, and forty. One of the fellows, aged thirty-two, is giving a critical resumé of a recent work of literature by Mickey Spillane.

CRITIC: . . . So the whole book winds up, Mike Hammer, he's inna room there with this doll. So he says: "You rat, you are the murderer." So she begins to con him, you know? She tells him she loves him. And then Bam! He shoots her in the stomach. So she's laying there, gasping for breath, and she says: "How could you do that?" And he says: "It was easy."

TWENTY-YEAR-OLD: Boy, that Mickey Spillane. Boy, he can write.

40 ANGIE: *(leaning out of the booth and looking down the length of the bar, says with some irritation)* What's keeping Marty?

CRITIC: What I like about Mickey Spillane is he knows how to handle women. In one book, he picks up a tomato who gets hit with a car, and she throws a pass at him. And then he meets two beautiful twins, and they throw passes at him. And then he meets some beautiful society leader, and she throws a pass at him, and . . .

TWENTY-YEAR-OLD: Boy, that Mickey Spillane, he sure can write . . .

ANGIE: *(looking out, down the bar again)* I don't know watsa matter with Marty.

FORTY-YEAR-OLD: Boy, Angie, what would you do if Marty ever died? You'd die right with him. A couple-a old bachelors hanging to each other like barnacles. There's Marty now.

Angie leans out of the booth.

45 ANGIE: *(calling out)* Hello, Marty, where you been?

CUT TO: *Front end of the bar. Marty has just come in. He waves back to Angie, acknowledges another hello from a man by the bar, goes over to the bar, and gets the bartender's attention.*

MARTY: Hello, Lou, gimme change of a half and put a dime in it for a telephone call.

The Bartender takes the half dollar, reaches into his apron pocket for the change.

BARTENDER: I hear you was at the Waverly Ballroom last night.

MARTY: Yeah. Angie tell you?

BARTENDER: *(picking out change from palm full of silver)* Yeah, I hear you really got stuck with a dog.

Marty looks at him.

50 MARTY: She wasn't so bad.

BARTENDER: *(extending the change)* Angie says she was a real scrawny-looking thing. Well, you can't have good luck alla time.

Marty takes the change slowly and frowns down at it. He moves down the bar and would make for the telephone booth, but Angie hails him from the booth.

ANGIE: Who you gonna call, Marty?

MARTY: I was gonna call that girl from last night, take her to a movie tonight.

ANGIE: Are you kidding?

55 MARTY: She was a nice girl. I kinda liked her.

ANGIE: *(indicating the spot in the booth vacated by the Forty-Year-Old)* Siddown. You can call her later.

Marty pauses, frowning, and then shuffles to the booth where Angie and the other two sit. The Critic moves over for Marty. There is an exchange of hellos.

TWENTY-YEAR-OLD: I gotta girl, she's always asking me to marry her. So I look at that face, and I say to myself: "Could I stand looking at that face for the resta my life?"

CRITIC: Hey, Marty, you ever read a book called *I, the Jury,* by Mickey Spillane?

MARTY: No.

60 ANGIE: Listen, Marty, I gotta good place for us to go tonight. The kid
here, he says, he was downna bazaar at Our Lady of Angels last night
and . . .

MARTY: I don't feel like going to the bazaar, Angie. I thought I'd take this
girl to a movie.

ANGIE: Boy, you really musta made out good last night.

MARTY: We just talked.

ANGIE: Boy, she must be some talker. She musta been about fifty years
old.

65 CRITIC: I always figger a guy oughtta marry a girl who's twenny years
younger than he is, so that when he's forty, his wife is a real nice-
looking doll.

TWENTY-YEAR-OLD: That means he'd have to marry the girl when she was
one year old.

CRITIC: I never thoughta that.

MARTY: I didn't think she was so bad-looking.

ANGIE: She musta kept you inna shadows all night.

70 CRITIC: Marty, you don't wanna hang around with dogs. It gives you a
bad reputation.

ANGIE: Marty, let's go downna bazaar.

MARTY: I told this dog I was gonna call her today.

ANGIE: Brush her.

Marty looks questioningly at Angie.

MARTY: You didn't like her at all?

75 ANGIE: A nothing. A real nothing.

*Marty looks down at the dime he has been nervously turning between two fin-
gers and then, frowning, he slips it into his jacket pocket. He lowers his face and
looks down, scowling at his thoughts. Around him, the voices clip along.*

CRITIC: What's playing on Fordham Road? I think there's a good picture
in the Loew's Paradise.

ANGIE: Let's go down to Forty-second Street and walk around. We're sure
to wind up with something.

Slowly Marty begins to look up again. He looks from face to face as each speaks.

CRITIC: I'll never forgive La Guardia for cutting burlesque outta New York
City.

TWENTY-YEAR-OLD: There's burlesque over in Union City. Let's go to
Union City. . . .

80 ANGIE: Ah, they're always crowded on Sunday night.

CRITIC: So wadda you figure on doing tonight, Angie?

ANGIE: I don't know. Wadda you figure on doing?

CRITIC: I don't know. *(Turns to the Twenty-Year-Old.)* Wadda you figure on
doing?

The Twenty-Year-Old shrugs.

Suddenly Marty brings his fist down on the booth table with a crash. The others turn, startled, toward him. Marty rises in his seat.

MARTY: "What are you doing tonight?" "I don't know, what are you doing?" Burlesque! Loew's Paradise! Miserable and lonely! Miserable and lonely and stupid! What am I, crazy or something?! I got something good! What am I hanging around with you guys for?!

He has said this in tones so loud that it attracts the attention of everyone in the bar. A little embarrassed, Marty turns and moves quickly to the phone booth, pausing outside the door to find his dime again. Angie is out of his seat immediately and hurries after him.

85 ANGIE: *(a little shocked at Marty's outburst)* Watsa matter with you?

MARTY: *(in a low, intense voice)* You don't like her. My mother don't like her. She's a dog, and I'm a fat, ugly little man. All I know is I had a good time last night. I'm gonna have a good time tonight. If we have enough good times together, I'm going down on my knees and beg that girl to marry me. If we make a party again this New Year's, I gotta date for the party. You don't like her, that's too bad. *(He moves into the booth, sits, turns again to Angie, smiles.)* When you gonna get married, Angie? You're thirty-four years old. All your kid brothers are married. You oughtta be ashamed of yourself.

Still smiling at his private joke, he puts the dime into the slot and then—with a determined finger—he begins to dial.

Fade out.

READING AND REACTING

1. The main plot of the play focuses on Marty; the subplot focuses on Aunt Catherine. How are Marty's and Aunt Catherine's situations alike?
2. Although Marty is in his mid-thirties, he acts as if he is much younger. In what respects is he like an adolescent (or an even younger child)?
3. A number of key phrases are repeated throughout the play. Identify several of these phrases, and explain what they contribute to the development of plot and character.
4. In several revealing speeches, Marty confronts some unpleasant truths about himself and his life. How do you react to this kind of self-scrutiny? Does it make you more or less sympathetic to him?
5. What function does Virginia serve in the play? How is she different from Marty? How would the play be different without Virginia and Thomas?

6. What factors motivate Marty to "rescue" Clara at the dance? Is this gesture consistent with his character? How does it foreshadow the play's ending?
7. What do Marty and Clara have in common? Is this enough for a lasting relationship?
8. Is Angie a flat character or a round character? What is his role in the play?
9. Do you think Marty's relationship with his mother is a healthy one? Explain.
10. Given what you know about Marty and his world, is the play's ending believable?
11. **JOURNAL ENTRY** What obstacles (besides Marty's mother and aunt) do you think will stand in the way of Marty and Clara's future happiness?
12. **CRITICAL PERSPECTIVE** According to the critic Thomas T. Apple, Chayefsky is thought of today as an historical figure. Except among historians of television's Golden Age, however, his work for the theater is almost unknown. Apple goes on to characterize Marty as sentimental realism. On the basis of your reading of this play, do you think it deserves to be dismissed as simply "sentimental realism"?

Related Works: "How to Talk to Your Mother (Notes)" (p. 96), "Eveline" (p. 470), "Two Kinds" (p. 594), "Ex-Basketball Player" (p. 813)

✧ **WILLIAM SHAKESPEARE** (1564–1616) was born in Stratford-on-Avon, England, and raised his family there, although he spent most of his adult life in London. Though relatively little is known of his daily life, he was deeply involved in all aspects of the theater: he was an actor who joined the Lord Chamberlain's Men (an acting company) in 1594; a shareholder in that company; a part owner of the Globe Theater from 1599; and, most significantly, the author of at least thirty-six plays. Most of his plays were not published during his lifetime; his friends issued the first legitimate version of his collected plays, the First Folio edition, in 1623.

It is difficult to date many of Shakespeare's plays exactly because they must be dated by records of their first performance (often hard to come by) and topical references in the text. We do know from an entry in the *Stationers' Register* that a play called the *Revenge of Hamlett Prince Denmarke* was presented around July 26, 1602, though Shakespeare's company probably first staged the play at the Globe Theater in 1600 or 1601. Some scholars believe the play was composed as early as 1598, though no earlier, because it was not among Shakespeare's plays listed in Francis Meres's *Palladis Tamis*, published in 1598.

CULTURAL CONTEXT ◆ *Hamlet* was based on a real event that was widely known in Shakespeare's time. In 1538, the Duke of Urbino, a famous military and political leader, was found dead. Later, his barber surgeon confessed to the killing, saying that a political rival had paid him to put poison in the Duke's ears. Shakespeare was impressed enough by this notorious crime to adapt it to his own use in *Hamlet* where Hamlet's father is killed by the same unusual means.

◆ ◆ ◆

WILLIAM SHAKESPEARE

Hamlet
PRINCE OF DENMARK*
(c. 1600)

CHARACTERS

CLAUDIUS, *King of Denmark*
HAMLET, *son to the former and
   nephew to the present King*
POLONIUS, *Lord Chamberlain*
HORATIO, *friend to Hamlet*
LAERTES, *son to Polonius*
VOLTIMAND
CORNELIUS
ROSENCRANTZ } *courtiers*
GUILDENSTERN
OSRIC
A GENTLEMAN
A PRIEST
FRANCISCO, *a soldier*
MARCELLUS } *officers*
BERNARDO

REYNALDO, *servant to Polonius*
PLAYERS
TWO CLOWNS, *grave-diggers*
FORTINBRAS, *Prince of Norway*
A CAPTAIN
ENGLISH AMBASSADORS
GHOST OF HAMLET'S FATHER
GERTRUDE, *Queen of Denmark and
   mother of Hamlet*
OPHELIA, *daughter to Polonius*
LORDS, LADIES, OFFICERS,
SOLDIERS, SAILORS
MESSENGERS, AND OTHER
ATTENDANTS

ACT I
SCENE 1

Elsinore. A platform before the castle.

(Francisco at his post. Enter to him Bernardo.)

BERNARDO: Who's there?
FRANCISCO: Nay, answer me: stand, and unfold yourself.
BERNARDO: Long live the king!
FRANCISCO: Bernardo?
5 BERNARDO: He.
FRANCISCO: You come most carefully upon your hour.

_____

* Note that individual lines are numbered in the following play. When a line is shared
  by two or more characters, it is counted as one line.

BERNARDO: 'Tis now struck twelve; get thee to bed, Francisco.

FRANCISCO: For this relief much thanks: 'tis bitter cold,
And I am sick at heart.

10 BERNARDO: Have you had quiet guard?

FRANCISCO: Not a mouse stirring.

BERNARDO: Well, good-night.
If you do meet Horatio and Marcellus,
The rivals of my watch, bid them make haste.

FRANCISCO: I think I hear them.—Stand, ho! Who is there?

(Enter Horatio and Marcellus.)

15 HORATIO: Friends to this ground.

MARCELLUS: And liegemen to the Dane.

FRANCISCO: Give you good-night.

MARCELLUS: O, farewell, honest soldier:
Who hath reliev'd you?

FRANCISCO: Bernardo has my place.
Give you good-night.

(Exit.)

MARCELLUS: Holla! Bernardo!

BERNARDO: Say.
What, is Horatio there?

HORATIO: A piece of him.

20 BERNARDO: Welcome, Horatio:—welcome, good Marcellus.

MARCELLUS: What, has this thing appear'd again to-night?

BERNARDO: I have seen nothing.

MARCELLUS: Horatio says 'tis but our fantasy,
And will not let belief take hold of him

25   Touching this dreaded sight, twice seen of us:
Therefore I have entreated him along
With us to watch the minutes of this night;
That, if again this apparition come
He may approve our eyes and speak to it.

30 HORATIO: Tush, tush, 'twill not appear.

BERNARDO: Sit down awhile,
And let us once again assail your ears,
That are so fortified against our story,
What we two nights have seen.

HORATIO: Well, sit we down,
And let us hear Bernardo speak of this.

35 BERNARDO: Last night of all,
When yon same star that's westward from the pole
Had made his course to illume that part of heaven
Where now it burns, Marcellus and myself,
The bell then beating one,—

40 MARCELLUS: Peace, break thee off; look where it comes again!

(Enter Ghost, armed.)

BERNARDO: In the same figure, like the king that's dead.

MARCELLUS: Thou art a scholar; speak to it, Horatio.

BERNARDO: Looks it not like the king? mark it, Horatio.

HORATIO: Most like:—it harrows me with fear and wonder.

45 BERNARDO: It would be spoke to.

MARCELLUS: Question it, Horatio.

HORATIO: What art thou, that usurp'st this time of night,
    Together with that fair and warlike form
    In which the majesty of buried Denmark
    Did sometimes march? by heaven I charge thee, speak!

50 MARCELLUS: It is offended.

BERNARDO: See, it stalks away!

HORATIO: Stay! speak, speak! I charge thee, speak!

(Exit Ghost.)

MARCELLUS: 'Tis gone, and will not answer.

BERNARDO: How now, Horatio! you tremble and look pale:
    Is not this something more than fantasy?

55   What think you on't?

HORATIO: Before my God, I might not this believe
    Without the sensible and true avouch
    Of mine own eyes.

MARCELLUS: Is it not like the king?

HORATIO: As thou art to thyself:

60   Such was the very armor he had on
    When he the ambitious Norway combated;
    So frown'd he once when, in an angry parle,[1]
    He smote the sledded Polacks on the ice.
    'Tis strange.

65 MARCELLUS: Thus twice before, and just at this dead hour,
    With martial stalk hath he gone by our watch.

HORATIO: In what particular thought to work I know not;
    But, in the gross and scope of my opinion,
    This bodes some strange eruption to our state.

70 MARCELLUS: Good now, sit down, and tell me, he that knows,
    Why this same strict and most observant watch
    So nightly toils the subject of the land;
    And why such daily cast of brazen cannon,
    And foreign mart for implements of war;

75   Why such impress of shipwrights, whose sore task
    Does not divide the Sunday from the week;

---

[1] *parle:* parley, or conference.

What might be toward, that this sweaty haste
Doth make the night joint-laborer with the day:
Who is't that can inform me?

HORATIO: That can I;
80 At least, the whisper goes so. Our last king,
Whose image even but now appear'd to us,
Was, as you know, by Fortinbras of Norway,
Thereto prick'd on by a most emulate pride,
Dar'd to the combat; in which our valiant Hamlet,—
85 For so this side of our known world esteem'd him,—
Did slay this Fortinbras; who, by a seal'd compact,
Well ratified by law and heraldry,
Did forfeit, with his life, all those his lands.
Which he stood seiz'd of,[2] to the conqueror:
90 Against the which, a moiety competent[3]
Was gagéd[4] by our king; which had return'd
To the inheritance of Fortinbras,
Had he been vanquisher; as by the same cov'nant,
And carriage of the article design'd,
95 His fell to Hamlet. Now, sir, young Fortinbras,
Of unimproved mettle hot and full,
Hath in the skirts of Norway, here and there,
Shark'd up a list of landless resolutes,
For food and diet, to some enterprise
100 That hath a stomach in't: which is no other,—
As it doth well appear unto our state,—
But to recover of us by strong hand,
And terms compulsatory, those foresaid lands
So by his father lost: and this, I take it,
105 Is the main motive of our preparations,
The source of this our watch, and the chief head
Of this post-haste and romage[5] in the land.

BERNARDO: I think it be no other, but e'en so:
Well may it sort that this portentous figure
110 Comes armed through our watch; so like the king
That was and is the question of these wars.

HORATIO: A mote it is to trouble the mind's eye.
In the most high and palmy state of Rome,
A little ere the mightiest Julius fell,
115 The graves stood tenantless, and the sheeted dead
Did squeak and gibber in the Roman streets:
As, stars with trains of fire and dews of blood,

---

[2] *seiz'd of:* possessed.   [3] *moiety competent:* a sufficient portion of his lands.   [4] *gagéd:* engaged or pledged.   [5] *post-haste and romage:* general activity.

Disasters in the sun; and the moist star,
Upon whose influence Neptune's empire stands,
120 Was sick almost to doomsday with eclipse:
And even the like precurse of fierce events,—
As harbingers preceding still the fates,
And prologue to the omen coming on,—
Have heaven and earth together demonstrated
125 Unto our climature and countrymen.—
But, soft, behold! lo, where it comes again!

(Re-enter Ghost.)

I'll cross it, though it blast me.—Stay, illusion!
If thou hast any sound or use of voice,
Speak to me:
130 If there be any good thing to be done,
That may to thee do ease, and grace to me,
Speak to me:
If thou art privy to thy country's fate,
Which, happily,[6] foreknowing may avoid,
135 O, speak!
Or if thou has uphoarded in thy life
Extorted treasure in the womb of earth,
For which, they say, you spirits oft walk in death,

(Cock crows.)

Speak of it:—stay, and speak!—Stop it, Marcellus.
140 MARCELLUS: Shall I strike at it with my partisan?[7]
HORATIO: Do, if it will not stand.
BERNARDO: 'Tis here!
HORATIO: 'Tis here!
MARCELLUS: 'Tis gone!

(Exit Ghost.)

We do it wrong, being so majestical,
To offer it the show of violence;
145 For it is, as the air, invulnerable,
And our vain blows malicious mockery.
BERNARDO: It was about to speak when the cock crew.
HORATIO: And then it started like a guilty thing
Upon a fearful summons. I have heard,
150 The cock, that is the trumpet to the morn,
Doth with his lofty and shrill-sounding throat
Awake the god of day; and at his warning,

---

[6] *happily:* haply, or perhaps.   [7] *partisan:* pike.

Whether in sea or fire, in earth or air,
The extravagant and erring spirit hies
155   To his confine: and of the truth herein
This present object made probation.[8]
MARCELLUS: It faded on the crowing of the cock.
Some say that ever 'gainst that season comes
Wherein our Saviour's birth is celebrated,
160   The bird of dawning singeth all night long:
And then, they say, no spirit can walk abroad;
The nights are wholesome; then no planets strike,
No fairy takes, nor witch hath power to charm;
So hallow'd and so gracious is the time.
165 HORATIO: So have I heard, and do in part believe.
But, look, the morn, in russet mantle clad,
Walks o'er the dew of yon high eastern hill:
Break we our watch up: and, by my advice,
Let us impart what we have seen to-night
170   Unto young Hamlet; for, upon my life,
This spirit, dumb to us, will speak to him:
Do you consent we shall acquaint him with it,
As needful in our loves, fitting our duty?
MARCELLUS: Let's do't, I pray; and I this morning know
175   Where we shall find him most conveniently.

(Exeunt.)

SCENE 2

Elsinore. A room of state in the castle.

(Enter the King, Queen, Hamlet, Polonius, Laertes, Voltimand, Cornelius, Lords, and Attendants.)

KING: Though yet of Hamlet our dear brother's death
The memory be green; and that it us befitted
To bear our hearts in grief, and our whole kingdom
To be contracted in one brow of woe;
5   Yet so far hath discretion fought with nature
That we with wisest sorrow think on him,
Together with remembrance of ourselves.
Therefore our sometime sister, now our queen,
The imperial jointress of this warlike state,
10   Have we, as 'twere with defeated joy,—
With one auspicious and one dropping eye,
With mirth and funeral, and with dirge in marriage,
In equal scale weighing delight and dole,—

---

[8] *probation:* proof.

Taken to wife: nor have we herein barr'd
15 Your better wisdoms, which have freely gone
With this affair along:—for all, our thanks.
Now follows that you know, young Fortinbras,
Holding a weak supposal of our worth,
Or thinking by our late dear brother's death
20 Our state to be disjoint and out of frame,
Colleagued with the dream of his advantage,
He hath not fail'd to pester us with message,
Importing the surrender of those lands
Lost by his father, with all bonds of law,
25 To our most valiant brother. So much for him.—
Now for ourself, and for this time of meeting:
Thus much the business is:—we have here writ
To Norway, uncle of young Fortinbras,—
Who, impotent and bed-rid, scarcely hears
30 Of this his nephew's purpose,—to suppress
His further gait herein; in that the levies,
The lists, and full proportions, are all made
Out of his subject:—and we here despatch
You, good Cornelius, and you, Voltimand,
35 For bearers of this greeting to old Norway;
Giving to you no further personal power
To business with the king more than the scope
Of these dilated articles allow.
Farewell; and let your haste commend your duty.
40 CORNELIUS and VOLTIMAND: In that and all things will we show our duty.
KING: We doubt it nothing: heartily farewell.

(Exeunt Voltimand and Cornelius.)

And now, Laertes, what's the news with you?
You told us of some suit; what is't, Laertes?
You cannot speak of reason to the Dane,
45 And lose your voice: what wouldst thou beg, Laertes,
That shall not be my offer, nor thy asking?
The head is not more native to the heart,
The hand more instrumental to the mouth,
Than is the throne of Denmark to thy father.
50 What wouldst thou have, Laertes?
LAERTES: Dread my lord,
Your leave and favor to return to France;
From whence though willingly I came to Denmark,
To show my duty in your coronation;
Yet now, I must confess, that duty done,
55 My thoughts and wishes bend again toward France.
And bow them to your gracious leave and pardon.

KING: Have you your father's leave? What says Polonius?

POLONIUS: He hath, my lord, wrung from me my slow leave
   By laborsome petition; and at last
60 Upon his will I seal'd my hard consent:
   I do beseech you, give him leave to go.

KING: Take thy fair hour, Laertes; time be thine,
   And thy best graces spend it at thy will!—
   But now, my cousin Hamlet, and my son,—

65 HAMLET: *(Aside)* A little more than kin, and less than kind.

KING: How is it that the clouds still hang on you?

HAMLET: Not so, my lord; I am too much i' the sun.

QUEEN: Good Hamlet, cast thy nighted color off,
   And let thine eye look like a friend on Denmark.
70 Do not for ever with thy vailed[1] lids
   Seek for thy noble father in the dust:
   Thou know'st 'tis common,—all that live must die,
   Passing through nature to eternity.

HAMLET: Ay, madam, it is common.

QUEEN: If it be,
75 Why seems it so particular with thee?

HAMLET: Seems, madam! nay, it is; I know not seems.
   'Tis not alone my inky cloak, good mother,
   Nor customary suits of solemn black,
   Nor windy suspiration of forc'd breath,
80 No, nor the fruitful river in the eye,
   Nor the dejected 'havior of the visage,
   Together with all forms, moods, shows of grief,
   That can denote me truly: these, indeed, seem;
   For they are actions that a man might play:
85 But I have that within which passeth show;
   These but the trappings and the suits of woe.

KING: 'Tis sweet and cómmendable in your nature, Hamlet,
   To give these mourning duties to your father:
   But, you must know, your father lost a father;
90 That father lost, lost his; and the survivor bound,
   In filial obligation, for some term
   To do obsequious sorrow: but to persever[2]
   In obstinate condolement is a course
   Of impious stubbornness; 'tis unmanly grief:
95 It shows a will most incorrect to heaven;
   A heart unfortified, a mind impatient;
   An understanding simple and unschool'd:
   For what we know must be, and is as common

---

[1] *vailed:* downcast.   [2] *persever:* persevere.

As any the most vulgar thing to sense,[3]
100 Why should we, in our peevish opposition,
Take it to heart? Fie! 'tis a fault to heaven,
A fault against the dead, a fault to nature,
To reason most absurd; whose common theme
Is death of fathers, and who still[4] hath cried,
105 From the first corse till he that died to-day,
This must be so. We pray you, throw to earth
This unprevailing woe; and think of us
As of a father: for let the world take note
You are the most immediate to our throne;
110 And with no less nobility of love
Than that which dearest father bears his son
Do I impart toward you. For your intent
In going back to school in Wittenberg,
It is most retrograde to our desire:
115 And we beseech you bend you to remain
Here, in the cheer and comfort of our eye,
Our chiefest courtier, cousin, and our son.
QUEEN: Let not thy mother lose her prayers, Hamlet:
I pray thee, stay with us; go not to Wittenberg.
120 HAMLET: I shall in all my best obey you, madam.
KING: Why, 'tis a loving and a fair reply:
Be as ourself in Denmark.—Madam, come;
This gentle and unforc'd accord of Hamlet
Sits smiling to my heart: in grace whereof,
125 No jocund health that Denmark drinks to-day
But the great cannon to the clouds shall tell;
And the king's rouse[5] the heavens shall bruit[6] again,
Re-speaking earthly thunder. Come away.

(Exeunt all but Hamlet.)

HAMLET: O, that this too too solid flesh would melt,
130 Thaw, and resolve itself into a dew!
Or that the Everlasting had not fix'd
His canon 'gainst self-slaughter! O God! O God!
How weary, stale, flat, and unprofitable
Seem to me all the uses of this world!
135 Fie on't! O fie! 'tis an unweeded garden,
That grows to seed; things rank and gross in nature
Possess it merely. That it should come to this!
But two months dead!—nay, not so much, not two:
So excellent a king; that was, to this,

---

[3] *any . . . sense:* anything that is very commonly seen or heard. [4] *still:* ever, or always.
[5] *rouse:* drink. [6] *bruit:* echo.

140 Hyperion[7] to a satyr: so loving to my mother,
  That he might not beteem the winds of heaven
  Visit her face too roughly. Heaven and earth!
  Must I remember? why, she would hang on him
  As if increase of appetite had grown
145 By what it fed on: and yet, within a month,—
  Let me not think on't,—Frailty, thy name is woman!—
  A little month; or ere those shoes were old
  With which she follow'd my poor father's body
  Like Niobe, all tears;—why she, even she,—
150 O God! a beast, that wants discourse of reason,
  Would have mourn'd longer,—married with mine uncle,
  My father's brother; but no more like my father
  Than I to Hercules: within a month;
  Ere yet the salt of most unrighteous tears
155 Had left the flushing in her galled eyes,
  She married:—O, most wicked speed, to post
  With such dexterity to incestuous sheets!
  It is not, nor it cannot come to good;
  But break, my heart,—for I must hold my tongue!

(Enter Horatio, Marcellus, and Bernardo.)

160 **Horatio:** Hail to your lordship!
  Hamlet: I am glad to see you well:
   Horatio,—or I do forget myself.
  Horatio: The same, my lord, and your poor servant ever.
  Hamlet: Sir, my good friend; I'll change that name with you:
   And what make you from Wittenberg, Horatio?—Marcellus?
165 **Marcellus:** My good lord,—
  Hamlet: I am very glad to see you.—Good even, sir.—
   But what, in faith, make you from Wittenberg?
  Horatio: A truant disposition, good my lord.
  Hamlet: I would not hear your enemy say so;
170 Nor shall you do mine ear that violence,
  To make it truster of your own report
  Against yourself: I know you are no truant.
  But what is your affair in Elsinore?
  We'll teach you to drink deep ere you depart.
175 **Horatio:** My lord, I came to see your father's funeral.
  Hamlet: I pray thee, do not mock me, fellow-student;
   I think it was to see my mother's wedding.
  Horatio: Indeed, my lord, it follow'd hard upon.
  Hamlet: Thrift, thrift, Horatio! the funeral-bak'd meats
180 Did coldly furnish forth the marriage tables.

---

[7] *Hyperion:* the Greek sun god, the brightest and most beautiful of the gods.

Would I had met my dearest foe[8] in heaven
Ere I had ever seen that day, Horatio!—
My father,—methinks I see my father.

HORATIO: Where, my lord?

HAMLET: In my mind's eye, Horatio.

185 HORATIO: I saw him once; he was a goodly[9] king.

HAMLET: He was a man, take him for all in all,
I shall not look upon his like again.

HORATIO: My lord, I think I saw him yester-night.

HAMLET: Saw who?

190 HORATIO: My lord, the king your father.

HAMLET: The king my father!

HORATIO: Season your admiration[10] for awhile
With an attent ear, till I may deliver,
Upon the witness of these gentlemen,
This marvel to you.

HAMLET: For God's love, let me hear.

195 HORATIO: Two nights together had these gentlemen,
Marcellus and Bernardo, in their watch,
In the dead vast and middle of the night,
Been thus encounter'd. A figure like your father,
Arm'd at all points exactly, cap-a-pe,[11]

200   Appears before them, and with solemn march
Goes slow and stately by them: thrice he walk'd
By their oppress'd[12] and fear-surprised eyes,
Within his truncheon's length; whilst they, distill'd
Almost to jelly with the act of fear,

205   Stand dumb, and speak not to him. This to me
In dreadful secrecy impart they did;
And I with them the third night kept the watch:
Where, as they had deliver'd, both in time,
Form of the thing, each word made true and good,

210   The apparition comes: I knew your father;
These hands are not more like.

HAMLET: But where was this?

MARCELLUS: My lord, upon the platform where we watch'd.

HAMLET: Did you not speak to it?

HORATIO: My lord, I did;
But answer made it none: yet once methought

215   It lifted up its head, and did address
Itself to motion, like as it would speak:
But even then the morning cock crew loud,
And at the sound it shrunk in haste away,
And vanish'd from our sight.

---

[8] *dearest foe:* worst enemy.   [9] *goodly:* handsome.   [10] *admiration:* astonishment.   [11] *cap-a-pe:* from head to toe.   [12] *oppress'd:* overwhelmed.

HAMLET: 'Tis very strange.

220 HORATIO: As I do live, my honor'd lord, 'tis true;
        And we did think it writ down in our duty
        To let you know of it.

HAMLET: Indeed, indeed, sirs, but this troubles me.
        Hold you the watch to-night?

225 MARCELLUS and BERNARDO: We do, my lord.

HAMLET: Arm'd, say you?

MARCELLUS and BERNARDO: Arm'd, my lord.

HAMLET: From top to toe?

MARCELLUS and BERNARDO: My lord, from head to foot.

230 HAMLET: Then saw you not his face?

HORATIO: O yes, my lord; he wore his beaver up.

HAMLET: What, look'd he frowningly?

HORATIO: A countenance more in sorrow than in anger.

HAMLET: Pale or red?

235 HORATIO: Nay, very pale.

HAMLET: And fix'd his eyes upon you?

HORATIO: Most constantly.

HAMLET: I would I had been there.

HORATIO: It would have much amaz'd you.

HAMLET: Very like, very like. Stay'd it long?

HORATIO: While one with moderate haste might tell[13] a hundred.

240 MARCELLUS and BERNARDO: Longer, longer.

HORATIO: Not when I saw't.

HAMLET: His beard was grizzled,—no?

HORATIO: It was, as I have seen it in his life,
        A sable silver'd.

HAMLET: I will watch to-night;
        Perchance 'twill walk again.

HORATIO: I warrant it will.

245 HAMLET: If it assume my noble father's person
        I'll speak to it, though hell itself should gape
        And bid me hold my peace. I pray you all,
        If you have hitherto conceal'd this sight,
        Let it be tenable in your silence still;

250   And whatsoever else shall hap to-night,
        Give it an understanding, but no tongue:
        I will requite your loves. So, fare ye well:
        Upon the platform, 'twixt eleven and twelve,
        I'll visit you.

ALL: Our duty to your honor.

255 HAMLET: Your loves, as mine to you: farewell.

---

[13] *tell:* count.

(Exeunt Horatio, Marcellus, and Bernardo.)

> My father's spirit in arms; all is not well;
> I doubt some foul play: would the night were come!
> Till then sit still, my soul: foul deeds will rise,
> Though all the earth o'erwhelm them, to men's eyes.

(Exit.)

SCENE 3

A room in Polonius' house.

(Enter Laertes and Ophelia.)

LAERTES: My necessaries are embark'd: farewell:
> And, sister, as the winds give benefit,
> And convoy¹ is assistant, do not sleep,
> But let me hear from you.

OPHELIA: Do you doubt that?

5 **LAERTES:** For Hamlet, and the trifling of his favor,
> Hold it a fashion and a toy in blood:
> A violet in the youth of primy nature,
> Forward, not permanent, sweet, not lasting,
> The perfume and suppliance of a minute;

10   No more.

OPHELIA: No more but so?

LAERTES: Think it no more:
> For nature, crescent,² does not grow alone
> In thews and bulk; but as this temple³ waxes,
> The inward service of the mind and soul
> Grows wide withal. Perhaps he loves you now;

15 And now no soil nor cautel⁴ doth besmirch
> The virtue of his will: but you must fear,
> His greatness weigh'd, his will is not his own;
> For he himself is subject to his birth:
> He may not, as unvalu'd persons do,

20   Carve for himself; for on his choice depends
> The safety and the health of the whole state;
> And therefore must his choice be circumscrib'd
> Unto the voice and yielding of that body
> Whereof he is the head. Then if he says he loves you,

25   It fits your wisdom so far to believe it
> As he in his particular act and place
> May give his saying deed; which is no further

---

¹ *convoy:* means of conveyance.   ² *crescent:* growing.   ³ *temple:* body.   ⁴ *cautel:* deceit.

Than the main[5] voice of Denmark goes withal.
Then weigh what loss your honor may sustain
30   If with too credent ear you list his songs,
Or lose your heart, or your chaste treasure open
To his unmaster'd importunity.
Fear it, Ophelia, fear it, my dear sister;
And keep within the rear of your affection,
35   Out of the shot and danger of desire.
The chariest maid is prodigal enough
If she unmask her beauty to the moon:
Virtue itself scrapes not calumnious strokes:
The canker galls the infants of the spring
40   Too oft before their buttons be disclos'd;
And in the morn and liquid dew of youth
Contagious blastments are most imminent.
Be wary, then; best safety lies in fear:
Youth to itself rebels, though none else near.
45 OPHELIA: I shall the effect of this good lesson keep
As watchman to my heart. But, good my brother,
Do not, as some ungracious pastors do,
Show me the steep and thorny way to heaven;
Whilst like a puff'd and reckless libertine,
50   Himself the primrose path of dalliance treads,
And recks not his own rede.[6]
LAERTES: O, fear me not.
I stay too long:—but here my father comes.

(Enter Polonius.)

A double blessing is a double grace;
Occasion smiles upon a second leave.
55 POLONIUS: Yet here, Laertes! aboard, aboard, for shame!
The wind sits in the shoulder of your sail,
And you are stay'd for. There,—my blessing with you!

(Laying his hand on Laertes' head.)

And these few precepts in thy memory
See thou character.[7] Give thy thoughts no tongue,
60   Nor any unproportion'd thought his act.
Be thou familiar, but by no means vulgar.
The friends thou hast, and their adoption tried,
Grapple them to thy soul with hoops of steel;
But do not dull thy palm with entertainment
65   Of each new-hatch'd, unfledg'd comrade. Beware

---

[5] *main:* strong, or mighty.   [6] *rede:* counsel.   [7] *in . . . character:* engrave in your mind.

Of entrance to a quarrel; but, being in,
Bear't that the opposèd may beware of thee.
Give every man thine ear, but few thy voice:
Take each man's censure,[8] but reserve thy judgment.
70 Costly thy habit as thy purse can buy,
But not express'd in fancy; rich, not gaudy:
For the apparel oft proclaims the man;
And they in France of the best rank and station
Are most select and generous chief in that.
75 Neither a borrower nor a lender be:
For a loan oft loses both itself and friend;
And borrowing dulls the edge of husbandry.
This above all,—to thine own self be true;
And it must follow, as the night the day,
80 Thou canst not then be false to any man.
Farewell: my blessing season this in thee!
LAERTES: Most humbly do I take my leave, my lord.
POLONIUS: The time invites you; go, your servants tend.[9]
LAERTES: Farewell, Ophelia; and remember well
85 What I have said to you.
OPHELIA: 'Tis in my memory lock'd,
And you yourself shall keep the key of it.
LAERTES: Farewell. (Exit.)
POLONIUS: What is't, Ophelia, he hath said to you?
OPHELIA: So please you, something touching the Lord Hamlet.
90 POLONIUS: Marry, well bethought:
'Tis told me he hath very oft of late
Given private time to you; and you yourself
Have of your audience been most free and bounteous:
If it be so,—as so 'tis put on me,
95 And that in way of caution,—I must tell you,
You do not understand yourself so clearly
As it behoves my daughter and your honor.
What is between you? give me up the truth.
OPHELIA: He hath, my lord, of late made many tenders
100 Of his affection to me.
POLONIUS: Affection! pooh! you speak like a green girl,
Unsifted in such perilous circumstance.
Do you believe his tenders,[10] as you call them?
OPHELIA: I do not know, my lord, what I should think.
105 POLONIUS: Marry, I'll teach you: think yourself a baby;
That you have ta'en these tenders for true pay,
Which are not sterling. Tender yourself more dearly;

---

[8] *censure:* opinion.   [9] *tend:* wait.   [10] *tenders:* offers.

Or,—not to crack the wind of the poor phrase,
Wronging it thus,—you'll tender me a fool.

110 OPHELIA: My lord, he hath impórtun'd me with love
In honorable fashion.

POLONIUS: Ay, fashion you may call it; go to, go to.

OPHELIA: And hath given countenance to his speech, my lord,
With almost all the holy vows of heaven.

115 POLONIUS: Ay, springes to catch woodcocks. I do know,
When the blood burns, how prodigal the soul
Lends the tongue vows: these blazes, daughter,
Giving more light than heat,—extinct in both,
Even in their promise, as it is a-making,—

120 You must not take for fire. From this time
Be somewhat scanter of your maiden presence;
Set your entreatments at a higher rate
Than a command to parley. For Lord Hamlet,
Believe so much in him, that he is young;

125 And with a larger tether may he walk
Than may be given you: in few, Ophelia,
Do not believe his vows; for they are brokers,[11]—
Not of that die which their investments show,
But mere implorators of unholy suits,

130 Breathing like sanctified and pious bawds,
The better to beguile. This is for all,—
I would not, in plain terms, from this time forth,
Have you so slander any moment leisure
As to give words or talk with the Lord Hamlet.

135 Look to't, I charge you; come your ways.

OPHELIA: I shall obey, my lord.

(Exeunt.)

SCENE 4

The platform.

(Enter Hamlet, Horatio, and Marcellus.)

HAMLET: The air bites shrewdly; it is very cold.

HORATIO: It is a nipping and an eager air.

HAMLET: What hour now?

HORATIO: I think it lacks of twelve.

MARCELLUS: No, it is struck.

5 HORATIO: Indeed? I heard it not: then it draws near the season
Wherein the spirit held his wont to walk.

---

[11] *brokers:* procurers.

(A flourish of trumpets, and ordnance shot off within.)

    What does this mean, my lord?

HAMLET: The king doth wake to-night, and takes his rouse,
    Keeps wassail, and the swaggering upspring[1] reels;

10   And, as he drains his draughts of Rhenish down,
    The kettle-drum and trumpet thus bray out
    The triumph of his pledge.[2]

HORATIO: Is it a custom?

HAMLET: Ay, marry, is't:
    But to my mind,—though I am native here,

15   And to the manner born,—it is a custom
    More honor'd in the breach than the observance.
    This heavy-headed revel east and west
    Makes us traduc'd and tax'd of other nations:
    They clepe us drunkards, and with swinish phrase

20   Soil our addition;[3] and, indeed, it takes
    From our achievements, though perform'd at height,
    The pith and marrow of our attribute.
    So oft it chances in particular men
    That, for some vicious mole of nature in them,

25   As in their birth,—wherein they are not guilty,
    Since nature cannot choose his origin,—
    By the o'ergrowth of some complexion,
    Oft breaking down the pales and forts of reason;
    Or by some habit, that too much o'erleavens

30   The form of plausive[4] manners;—that these men,—
    Carrying, I say, the stamp of one defect,
    Being nature's livery or fortune's star,—
    Their virtues else,—be they as pure as grace,
    As infinite as man may undergo,—

35   Shall in the general censure take corruption
    From that particular fault: the dram of evil
    Doth all the noble substance of a doubt
    To his own scandal.

HORATIO: Look, my lord, it comes!

(Enter Ghost.)

HAMLET: Angels and ministers of grace defend us!—

40   Be thou a spirit of health or goblin damn'd,
    Bring with thee airs from heaven or blasts from hell,
    Be thy intents wicked or charitable,
    Thou com'st in such a questionable shape

---

[1] *upspring:* a dance.   [2] *triumph . . . pledge:* the glory of his toasts.   [3] *addition:* reputation.   [4] *plausive:* pleasing.

That I will speak to thee: I'll call thee Hamlet,
45 King, father, royal Dane: O, answer me!
Let me not burst in ignorance; but tell
Why thy canóniz'd bones, hearsèd in death,
Have burst their cerements; why the sepulchre,
Wherein we saw thee quietly in-urn'd,
50 Hath op'd his ponderous and marble jaws
To cast thee up again! What may this mean,
That thou, dead corse, again in còmplete steel,
Revisit'st thus the glimpses of the moon,
Making night hideous and we[5] fools of nature
55 So horridly to shake our disposition
With thoughts beyond the reaches of our souls?
Say, why is this? wherefore? what should we do?

(Ghost beckons Hamlet.)

Horatio: It beckons you to go away with it,
    As if it some impartment did desire
60   To you alone.
Marcellus: Look, with what courteous action
    It waves you to a more removed ground:
    But do not go with it.
Horatio: No, by no means.
Hamlet: It will not speak; then will I follow it.
Horatio: Do not, my lord.
Hamlet: Why, what should be the fear?
65   I do not set my life at a pin's fee;
    And for my soul, what can it do to that,
    Being a thing immortal as itself?
    It waves me forth again;—I'll follow it.
Horatio: What if it tempt you toward the flood, my lord.
70   Or to the dreadful summit of the cliff
    That beetles o'er his base into the sea,
    And there assume some other horrible form,
    Which might deprive your sovereignty of reason,
    And draw you into madness? think of it:
75   The very place puts toys of desperation,
    Without more motive, into every brain
    That looks so many fathoms to the sea
    And hears it roar beneath.
Hamlet: It waves me still.—
    Go on; I'll follow thee.
80 Marcellus: You shall not go, my lord.

---

[5] *we:* us.

HAMLET: Hold off your hands.
HORATIO: Be rul'd; you shall not go.
HAMLET: My fate cries out,
   And makes each petty artery in this body
   As hardy as the Némean lion's[6] nerve.—

(Ghost beckons.)

   Still am I call'd;—unhand me, gentlemen;—*(Breaking from them)*
85   By heaven, I'll make a ghost of him that lets[7] me.
   I say, away!—Go on; I'll follow thee.

(Exeunt Ghost and Hamlet.)

HORATIO: He waxes desperate with imagination.
MARCELLUS: Let's follow; 'tis not fit thus to obey him.
HORATIO: Have after.—To what issue will this come?
90 MARCELLUS: Something is rotten in the state of Denmark.
HORATIO: Heaven will direct it.
MARCELLUS: Nay, let's follow him.

(Exeunt.)

SCENE 5

A more remote part of the platform.

(Enter Ghost and Hamlet.)

HAMLET: Where wilt thou lead me? speak, I'll go no further.
GHOST: Mark me.
HAMLET: I will.
GHOST: My hour is almost come,
   When I to sulphurous and tormenting flames
   Must render up myself.
HAMLET: Alas, poor ghost!
5 GHOST: Pity me not, but lend thy serious hearing
   To what I shall unfold.
HAMLET: Speak; I am bound to hear.
GHOST: So art thou to revenge, when thou shalt hear.
HAMLET: What?
GHOST: I am thy father's spirit;
10   Doom'd for a certain term to walk the night,
   And, for the day, confin'd to waste in fires
   Till the foul crimes[1] done in my days of nature
   Are burnt and purg'd away. But that I am forbid
   To tell the secrets of my prison-house,

---

[6] *Némean lion's:* the fierce lion that Hercules was called upon to slay as one of his "twelve labors." [7] *lets:* hinders.

[1] *foul crimes:* rather, sins or faults.

15   I could a tale unfold whose lightest word
    Would harrow up thy soul; freeze thy young blood;
    Make thy two eyes, like stars, start from their spheres;
    Thy knotted and combined locks to part,
    And each particular hair to stand on end,
20   Like quills upon the fretful porcupine:
    But this eternal blazon[2] must not be
    To ears of flesh and blood.—List, list, O, list!—
    If thou didst ever thy dear father love,—
HAMLET: O God!
25 GHOST: Revenge his foul and most unnatural murder.
HAMLET: Murder!
GHOST: Murder—most foul, as in the best it is;
    But this most foul, strange, and unnatural.
HAMLET: Haste me to know't, that I, with wings as swift
30   As meditation or the thoughts of love,
    May sweep to my revenge.
GHOST: I find thee apt;
    And duller shouldst thou be than the fat weed
    That rots itself in ease on Lethe[3] wharf,
    Wouldst thou not stir in this. Now, Hamlet,
35   'Tis given out that, sleeping in mine orchard,
    A serpent stung me; so the whole ear of Denmark
    Is by a forged process of my death
    Rankly abus'd: but know, thou noble youth,
    The serpent that did sting thy father's life
40   Now wears his crown.
HAMLET: O my prophetic soul! mine uncle!
GHOST: Ay, that incestuous, that adulterate beast,
    With witchcraft of his wit, with traitorous gifts,—
    O wicked wit and gifts that have the power
    So to seduce!—won to his shameful lust
45   The will of my most seeming virtuous queen:
    O Hamlet, what a falling-off was there!
    From me, whose love was of that dignity
    That it went hand in hand even with the vow
    I made to her in marriage: and to decline
50   Upon a wretch whose natural gifts were poor
    To those of mine!
    But virtue, as it never will be mov'd,
    Though lewdness court it in a shape of heaven;
    So lust, though to a radiant angel link'd,

---

[2] *eternal blazon:* disclosure of information concerning the other world.   [3] *Lethe:* the river of forgetfulness of the past, out of which the dead drink.

55   Will sate itself in a celestial bed
        And prey on garbage.
        But, soft! methinks I scent the morning air;
        Brief let me be.—Sleeping within mine orchard,
        My custom always in the afternoon,
60   Upon my sécure hour thy uncle stole,
        With juice of cursed hebenon[4] in a vial,
        And in the porches of mine ears did pour
        The leperous distilment; whose effect
        Holds such an enmity with blood of man
65   That, swift as quicksilver, it courses through
        The natural gates and alleys of the body;
        And with a sudden vigor it doth posset[5]
        And curd, like eager[6] droppings into milk,
        The thin and wholesome blood: so did it mine;
70   And a most instant tetter bark'd about,
        Most lazar-like,[7] with vile and loathsome crust,
        All my smooth body.
        Thus was I, sleeping, by a brother's hand,
        Of life, of crown, of queen, at once despatch'd:
75   Cut off even in the blossoms of my sin,
        Unhousel'd, unanointed, unanel'd;
        No reckoning made, but sent to my account
        With all my imperfections on my head:
        O, horrible! O, horrible! most horrible!
80   If thou hast nature in thee, bear it not;
        Let not the royal bed of Denmark be
        A couch for luxury[8] and damned incest.
        But, howsoever thou pursu'st this act,
        Taint not thy mind, nor let thy soul contrive
85   Against thy mother aught: leave her to heaven,
        And to those thorns that in her bosom lodge,
        To prick and sting her. Fare thee well at once!
        The glowworm shows the matin to be near,
        And 'gins to pale his uneffectual fire:
90   Adieu, adieu! Hamlet, remember me. *(Exit.)*
    HAMLET: O all you host of heaven! O earth! what else?
        And shall I couple hell?—O, fie!—Hold, my heart;
        And you, my sinews, grow not instant old,
        But bear me stiffly up.—Remember thee!
95   Ay, thou poor ghost, while memory holds a seat
        In this distracted globe. Remember thee!

---

[4] *hebenon:* ebony.   [5] *posset:* coagulate.   [6] *eager:* acid.   [7] *lazar-like:* like a leper, whose skin is rough.   [8] *luxury:* lechery.

Yea, from the table of my memory
I'll wipe away all trivial fond[9] recórds,
All saws of books, all forms, all pressures past,
100 That youth and observation copied there;
And thy commandment all alone shall live
Within the book and volume of my brain,
Unmix'd with baser matter: yes, by heaven.—
O most pernicious woman!
105 O villain, villain, smiling, damned villain!
My tables,—meet it is I set it down,
That one may smile, and smile, and be a villain;
At least, I am sure, it may be so in Denmark:

(Writing.)

So, uncle, there you are. Now to my word;
110 It is, *Adieu, adieu! remember me:*
I have sworn't.
HORATIO: *(Within)* My lord, my lord,—
MARCELLUS: *(Within)*   Lord Hamlet,—
HORATIO: *(Within)*   Heaven secure him!
MARCELLUS: *(Within)* So be it!
HORATIO: *(Within)* Illo, ho, ho, my lord!
HAMLET: Hillo, ho, ho, boy! come, bird, come.[10]

(Enter Horatio and Marcellus.)

115 MARCELLUS: How is't, my noble lord?
HORATIO: What news, my lord?
HAMLET: O, wonderful!
HORATIO: Good my lord, tell it.
HAMLET: No; you'll reveal it.
HORATIO: Not I, my lord, by heaven.
MARCELLUS: Nor I, my lord.
HAMLET: How say you, then; would heart of man once think it?—
120 But you'll be secret?
HORATIO and MARCELLUS: Ay, by heaven, my lord.
HAMLET: There's ne'er a villain dwelling in all Denmark
But he's an arrant knave.
HORATIO: There needs no ghost, my lord, come from the grave
125 To tell us this.
HAMLET: Why, right; you are i' the right;
And so, without more circumstance at all,

---

[9] *fond:* foolish.   [10] *bird:* Hamlet uses the word "bird" because this is a falconer's call.

I hold it fit that we shake hands and part:
You, as your business and desire shall point you,—
130   For every man has business and desire,
Such as it is;—and for mine own poor part,
Look you, I'll go pray.
HORATIO: These are but wild and whirling words, my lord.
HAMLET: I'm sorry they offend you, heartily;
135   Yes, faith, heartily.
HORATIO: There's no offence, my lord.
HAMLET: Yes, by Saint Patrick, but there is, Horatio,
And much offence too. Touching this vision here,—
It is an honest ghost, that let me tell you:
For you desire to know what is between us,
140   O'ermaster't as you may. And now, good friends,
As you are friends, scholars, and soldiers,
Give me one poor request.
HORATIO: What is't, my lord? we will.
HAMLET: Never make known what you have seen to-night.
145 HORATIO and MARCELLUS: My lord, we will not.
HAMLET: Nay, but swear't.
HORATIO: In faith,
My lord, not I.
MARCELLUS: Nor I, my lord, in faith.
HAMLET: Upon my sword.
MARCELLUS: We have sworn, my lord, already.
HAMLET: Indeed, upon my sword, indeed.
GHOST: *(Beneath)* Swear.
150 HAMLET: Ha, ha, boy! say'st thou so? art thou there, truepenny?—
Come on,—you hear this fellow in the cellarage,—
Consent to swear.
HORATIO: Propose the oath, my lord.
HAMLET: Never to speak of this that you have seen,
Swear by my sword.
155 GHOST: *(Beneath)* Swear.
HAMLET: *Hic et ubique?*[11] then we'll shift our ground.—
Come hither, gentlemen,
And lay your hands again upon my sword:
Never to speak of this that you have heard,
160   Swear by my sword.
GHOST: *(Beneath)* Swear.
HAMLET: Well said! old mole! canst work i' the earth so fast?
A worthy pioneer![12]—Once more remove, good friends.
HORATIO: O day and night, but this is wondrous strange!

---

[11] *Hic et ubique:* here and everywhere?   [12] *pioneer:* a soldier who digs trenches and undermines fortresses.

165 Hamlet: And therefore as a stranger give it welcome.
There are more things in heaven and earth, Horatio,
Than are dreamt of in your philosophy.
But come;—
Here, as before, never, so help you mercy,
170 How strange or odd soe'er I bear myself,—
As I, perchance, hereafter shall think meet
To put an antic disposition on,—
That you, at such times seeing me, never shall,
With arms encumber'd[13] thus, or this headshake,
175 Or by pronouncing of some doubtful phrase,
As, *Well, well, we know;*—or, *We could, an if we would;*—
Or, *If we list to speak;*—or, *There be, an if they might;*—
Or such ambiguous giving out, to note
That you know aught of me:—this not to do,
180 So grace and mercy at your most need help you,
Swear.
Ghost: *(Beneath)* Swear.
Hamlet: Rest, rest, perturbed spirit!—So, gentlemen,
With all my love I do commend to you:
185 And what so poor a man as Hamlet is
May do, to express his love and friending to you,
God willing, shall not lack. Let us go in together;
And still your fingers on your lips, I pray.
The time is out of joint:—O cursed spite,
190 That ever I was born to set it right!—
Nay, come, let's go together.

(Exeunt.)

Act II
Scene 1

A room in Polonius' house.

(Enter Polonius and Reynaldo.)

Polonius: Give him this money and these notes, Reynaldo.
Reynaldo: I will, my lord.
Polonius: You shall do marvelous wisely, good Reynaldo,
Before you visit him, to make inquiry
5 On his behavior.
Reynaldo: My lord, I did intend it.
Polonius: Marry, well said; very well said. Look you, sir,
Inquire me first what Danskers[1] are in Paris;

---

[13] *encumber'd:* folded.

---

[1] *Danskers:* Danes.

And how, and who, what means, and where they keep,
What company, at what expense; and finding,
10 By this encompassment and drift of question,
That they do know my son, come you more nearer
Than your particular demands will touch it:
Take you, as 'twere, some distant knowledge of him;
As thus, *I know his father and his friends,*
15 *And in part him;*—do you mark this, Reynaldo?

REYNALDO: Ay, very well, my lord.

POLONIUS: *And in part him;*—but, you may say, *not well:*
But if't be he I mean, he's very wild;
Addicted so and so; and there put on him
20 What forgeries you please; marry, none so rank
As may dishonor him; take heed of that;
But, sir, such wanton, wild, and usual slips
As are companions noted and most known
To youth and liberty.

REYNALDO: As gaming, my lord.

25 POLONIUS: Ay, or drinking, fencing, swearing, quarreling,
Drabbing:[2]—you may go so far.

REYNALDO: My lord, that would dishonor him.

POLONIUS: Faith, no; as you may season it in the charge.
You must not put another scandal on him,
30 That he is open to incontinency;
That's not my meaning: but breathe his faults so quaintly
That they may seem the taints of liberty;
The flash and outbreak of a fiery mind;
A savageness in unreclaimed blood,
35 Of general assault.

REYNALDO: But, my good lord,—

POLONIUS: Wherefore should you do this?

REYNALDO: Ay, my lord,
I would know that.

POLONIUS: Marry, sir, here's my drift;
And I believe it is a fetch of warrant:[3]
You laying these slight sullies on my son.
40 As 'twere a thing a little soil'd i' the working,
Mark you,
Your party in converse, him you would sound,
Having ever seen in the prenominate crimes
The youth you breathe of guilty, be assur'd
45 He closes with you in this consequence;
Good sir, or so; or *friend,* or *gentleman,*—

---

[2] *Drabbing:* going about with loose women.   [3] *fetch of warrant:* a good device.

According to the phrase or the addition[4]
Of man and country.

REYNALDO: Very good, my lord.

POLONIUS: And then, sir, does he this,—he does,—
50   What was I about to say?—By the mass, I was
        About to say something:—where did I leave?

REYNALDO: At *closes in the consequence,*
        At *friend or so,* and *gentleman.*

POLONIUS: At—closes in the consequence,—ay, marry;
55   He closes with you thus:—*I know the gentleman;*
        I saw him yesterday, or t'other day,
        Or then, or then; with such, or such; and, as you say,
        There was he gaming; there o'ertook in's rouse;
        There falling out at tennis: or perchance,
60   *I saw him enter such a house of sale,—*
        Videlicet, a brothel,—or so forth.—
        See you now;
        Your bait of falsehood takes this carp of truth:
        And thus do we of wisdom and of reach,
65   With windlasses, and with assays of bias,
        By indirections find directions out:
        So, by my former lecture and advice,
        Shall you my son. You have me, have you not?

REYNALDO: My lord, I have.

POLONIUS: God b' wi' you; fare you well.
70 REYNALDO: Good my lord!

POLONIUS: Observe his inclination in yourself.

REYNALDO: I shall, my lord.

POLONIUS: And let him ply his music.

REYNALDO: Well, my lord.

POLONIUS: Farewell!

(Exit Reynaldo.)

(Enter Ophelia.)

75   How now, Ophelia! what's the matter?

OPHELIA: Alas, my lord, I have been so affrighted.

POLONIUS: With what, i' the name of God?

OPHELIA: My lord, as I was sewing in my chamber,
        Lord Hamlet,—with his doublet all unbrac'd;
80   No hat upon his head; his stockings foul'd,
        Ungarter'd, and down-gyved[5] to his ankle;
        Pale as his shirt; his knees knocking each other;
        And with a look so piteous in purport

---

[4] *addition:* form of address. [5] *down-gyved:* dangling like chains.

As if he had been loosed out of hell
85   To speak of horrors,—he comes before me.
POLONIUS: Mad for thy love?
OPHELIA: My lord, I do not know;
    But truly I do fear it.
POLONIUS: What said he?
OPHELIA: He took me by the wrist, and held me hard;
    Then goes he to the length of all his arm;
90   And with his other hand thus o'er his brow,
    He falls to such perusal of my face
    As he would draw it. Long stay'd he so;
    At last,—a little shaking of mine arm,
    And thrice his head thus waving up and down,—
95   He rais'd a sigh so piteous and profound
    That it did seem to shatter all his bulk
    And end his being; that done, he lets me go:
    And, with his head over his shoulder turn'd,
    He seem'd to find his way without his eyes;
100   For out o' doors he went without their help,
    And to the last bended their light on me.
POLONIUS: Come, go with me: I will go seek the king.
    This is the very ecstasy[6] of love;
    Whose violent property fordoes itself,[7]
105   And leads the will to desperate undertakings,
    As oft as any passion under heaven
    That does afflict our nature. I am sorry,—
    What, have you given him any hard words of late?
OPHELIA: No, my good lord; but, as you did command,
110   I did repel his letters, and denied
    His access to me.
POLONIUS: That hath made him mad.
    I am sorry that with better heed and judgment
    I had not quoted him: I fear'd he did but trifle,
    And meant to wreck thee; but, beshrew my jealousy!
115   It seems it is as proper to our age
    To cast beyond ourselves in our opinions
    As it is common for the younger sort
    To lack discretion. Come, go we to the king:
    This must be known; which, being kept close, might move
120   More grief to hide than hate to utter love.

(Exeunt.)

---

[6] *ecstasy:* madness.   [7] *fordoes itself:* destroys itself.

Scene 2

A room in the castle.

(Enter King, Queen, Rosencrantz, Guildenstern, and Attendants.)

KING: Welcome, dear Rosencrantz and Guildenstern!
    Moreover that we much did long to see you,
    The need we have to use you did provoke
    Our hasty sending. Something have you heard
5   Of Hamlet's transformation; so I call it,
    Since nor the exterior nor the inward man
    Resembles that it was. What it should be,
    More than his father's death, that thus hath put him
    So much from the understanding of himself,
10   I cannot dream of: I entreat you both,
    That being of so young days brought up with him,
    And since so neighbor'd to his youth and humor,
    That you vouchsafe your rest here in our court
    Some little time: so by your companies
15   To draw him on to pleasures, and to gather,
    So much as from occasion you may glean,
    Whether aught, to us unknown, afflicts him thus,
    That, open'd, lies within our remedy.
QUEEN: Good gentlemen, he hath much talk'd of you;
20   And sure I am two men there are not living
    To whom he more adheres. If it will please you
    To show us so much gentry and good-will
    As to expend your time with us awhile,
    For the supply and profit of our hope,
25   Your visitation shall receive such thanks
    As fits a king's remembrance.
ROSENCRANTZ: Both your majesties
    Might, by the sovereign power you have of us,
    Put your dread pleasures more into command
    Than to entreaty.
GUILDENSTERN: We both obey,
30   And here give up ourselves, in the full bent,
    To lay our service freely at your feet,
    To be commanded.
KING: Thanks, Rosencrantz and gentle Guildenstern.
QUEEN: Thanks, Guildenstern and gentle Rosencrantz:
35   And I beseech you instantly to visit
    My too-much-changed son.—Go, some of you,
    And bring these gentlemen where Hamlet is.
GUILDENSTERN: Heavens make our presence and our practices
    Pleasant and helpful to him!
QUEEN: Ay, amen!

(Exeunt Rosencrantz, Guildenstern, and some Attendants.)

(Enter Polonius.)

40 POLONIUS: The ambassadors from Norway, my good lord,
　　Are joyfully return'd.
KING: Thou still has been the father of good news.
POLONIUS: Have I, my lord? Assure you, my good liege,
　　I hold my duty, as I hold my soul,
45　　Both to my God and to my gracious king:
　　And I do think,—or else this brain of mine
　　Hunts not the trail of policy[1] so sure
　　As it hath us'd to do,—that I have found
　　The very cause of Hamlet's lunacy.
50 KING: O, speak of that; that do I long to hear.
POLONIUS: Give first admittance to the ambassadors;
　　My news shall be the fruit to that great feast.
KING: Thyself do grace to them, and bring them in.

(Exit Polonius.)

　　He tells me, my sweet queen, that he hath found
55　　The head and source of all your son's distemper.
QUEEN: I doubt it is no other but the main,—
　　His father's death and our o'erhasty marriage.
KING: Well, we shall sift him.

(Re-enter Polonius, with Voltimand and Cornelius.)

　　　　　　　　　　　　Welcome, my good friends!
　　Say, Voltimand, what from our brother Norway?
60 VOLTIMAND: Most fair return of greetings and desires.
　　Upon our first, he sent out to suppress
　　His nephew's levies; which to him appear'd
　　To be a preparation 'gainst the Polack;
　　But, better look'd into, he truly found
65　　It was against your highness: whereat griev'd,—
　　That so his sickness, age, and impotence
　　Was falsely borne in hand,—sends out arrests
　　On Fortinbras; which he, in brief, obeys;
　　Receives rebuke from Norway; and, in fine,
70　　Makes vows before his uncle never more
　　To give the assay of arms against your majesty.
　　Whereon old Norway, overcome with joy,
　　Gives him three thousand crowns in annual fee;
　　And his commission to employ those soldiers,
75　　So levied as before, against the Polack:

---

[1] *trail of policy:* statecraft.

With an entreaty, herein further shown, *(gives a paper)*
That it might please you to give quiet pass
Through your dominions for this enterprise,
On such regards of safety and allowance

80   As therein are set down.

King: It likes us well;
And at our more consider'd time we'll read,
Answer, and think upon this business.
Meantime we thank you for your well-took labor:
Go to your rest; at night we'll feast together:

85   Most welcome home!

(Exeunt Voltimand and Cornelius.)

Polonius: This business is well ended.—
My liege, and madam,—to expostulate
What majesty should be, what duty is,
Why day is day, night night, and time is time,
Were nothing but to waste night, day, and time.

90   Therefore, since brevity is the soul of wit,
And tediousness the limbs and outward flourishes,
I will be brief:—your noble son is mad:
Mad call I it; for to define true madness,
What is't but to be nothing else but mad?

95   But let that go.

Queen: More matter with less art.

Polonius: Madam, I swear I use no art at all.
That he is mad, 'tis true 'tis pity;
And pity 'tis 'tis true: a foolish figure;
But farewell it, for I will use no art.

100   Mad let us grant him, then: and now remains
That we find out the cause of this effect;
Or rather say, the cause of this defect,
For this effect defective comes by cause:
Thus it remains, and the remainder thus.

105   Perpend.
I have a daughter,—have whilst she is mine,—
Who, in her duty and obedience, mark,
Hath given me this: now gather, and surmise

(Reads)

To the celestial, and my soul's idol, the most beautified Ophelia,—

110   That's an ill phrase, a vile phrase,—*beautified* is a vile phrase: but
          you shall hear. Thus:

(Reads)

In her excellent white bosom, these, &c.

QUEEN: Came this from Hamlet to her?
POLONIUS: Good madam, stay a while; I will be faithful.

(Reads)

115   *Doubt thou the stars are fire;*
                  Doubt that the sun doth move;
                  Doubt truth to be a liar;
                  But never doubt I love.

      O dear Ophelia, I am ill at these numbers, I have not art to reckon
120   *my roans: but that I love thee best, O most best, believe it.*
      Adieu.
          Thine evermore, most dear lady, whilst this machine is to him, Hamlet

This, in obedience, hath my daughter show'd me:
And more above, hath his solicitings,
125 As they fell out by time, by means, and place,
All given to mine ear.
KING: But how hath she
Receiv'd his love?
POLONIUS: What do you think of me?
KING: As of a man faithful and honorable.
POLONIUS: I would fain prove so. But what might you think,
130 When I had seen this hot love on the wing,—
As I perceiv'd it, I must tell you that,
Before my daughter told me,—what might you,
Or my dear majesty your queen here, think,
If I had play'd the desk or table-book;[2]
135 Or given my heart a winking, mute and dumb;
Or look'd upon this love with idle sight;—
What might you think? No, I went round to work,
And my young mistress thus I did bespeak:
Lord Hamlet is a prince out of thy sphere;
140 *This must not be:* and then I precepts gave her,
That she should lock herself from his resort,
Admit no messengers, receive no tokens.
Which done, she took the fruits of my advice;
And he, repulsed,—a short tale to make,—
145 Fell into a sadness; then into a fast;
Thence to a watch; thence into a weakness;
Thence to a lightness; and, by this declension,
Into the madness wherein now he raves
And all we wail for.
KING: Do you think 'tis this?
150 QUEEN: It may be, very likely.

---

[2] *table-book:* memorandum pad.

POLONIUS: Hath there been such a time,—I'd fain know that,—
      That I have positively said, *'Tis so,*
      When it prov'd otherwise?
KING: Not that I know.
POLONIUS: Take this from this, if this be otherwise: *(Pointing to his head*
      and shoulder)
155   If circumstances lead me, I will find
      Where truth is hid, though it were hid indeed
      Within the center.
KING: How may we try it further?
POLONIUS: You know, sometimes he walks for hours together
      Here in the lobby.
QUEEN: So he does, indeed.
160 POLONIUS: At such a time I'll loose my daughter to him:
      Be you and I behind an arras³ then;
      Mark the encounter: if he love her not,
      And be not from his reason fall'n thereon,
      Let me be no assistant for a state,
165   But keep a farm and carters.
KING: We will try it.
QUEEN: But look, where sadly the poor wretch comes reading.
POLONIUS: Away, I do beseech you, both away:
      I'll board⁴ him presently:—O, give me leave.

(Exeunt King, Queen, and Attendants.)

(Enter Hamlet, reading.)

      How does my good Lord Hamlet?
170 HAMLET: Well, God-a-mercy.
POLONIUS: Do you know me, my lord?
HAMLET: Excellent, excellent well; you're a fishmonger.
POLONIUS: Not I, my lord.
HAMLET: Then I would you were so honest a man.
175 POLONIUS: Honest, my lord!
HAMLET: Ay, sir; to be honest, as this world goes, is to be one man
      picked out of ten thousand.
POLONIUS: That's very true, my lord.
HAMLET: For if the sun breed maggots in a dead dog, being a god
180   kissing carrion,—Have you a daughter?
POLONIUS: I have, my lord.
HAMLET: Let her not walk i' the sun: conception is a blessing; but not
      as your daughter may conceive:—friend, look to't.
POLONIUS: How say you by that?—*(Aside)* Still harping on my
185   daughter:—yet he knew me not at first; he said I was a fishmonger:

---

³ *arras:* tapestry, hung some distance away from a wall.   ⁴ *board:* address.

he is far gone, far gone: and truly in my youth I suffered much
extremity for love; very near this. I'll speak to him again.—What do
you read, my lord?

HAMLET: Words, words, words.

190 POLONIUS: What is the matter, my lord?

HAMLET: Between who?

POLONIUS: I mean, the matter that you read, my lord.

HAMLET: Slanders, sir: for the satirical slave says here that old men
have gray beards; that their faces are wrinkled; their eyes purging
195 thick amber and plum-tree gum; and that they have a plentiful
lack of wit, together with most weak hams: all which, sir, though I
most powerfully and potently believe, yet I hold it not honesty to
have it thus set down; for you yourself, sir, should be old as I am,
if, like a crab, you could go backward.

200 POLONIUS: *(Aside)* Though this be madness, yet there is method in't.—
ill you walk out of the air, my lord?

HAMLET: Into my grave?

POLONIUS: Indeed, that is out o' the air.—*(Aside)* How pregnant[5]
sometimes his replies are! a happiness that often madness hits on,
205 which reason and sanity could not so prosperously be delivered of.
I will leave him, and suddenly contrive the means of meeting
between him and my daughter.—More honorable lord, I will most
humbly take my leave of you.

HAMLET: You cannot, sir, take from me anything that I will more
210 willingly part withal,—except my life, except my life, except my life.

POLONIUS: Fare you well, my lord.

HAMLET: These tedious old fools!

(Enter Rosencrantz and Guildenstern.)

POLONIUS: You go to seek the Lord Hamlet; there he is.

ROSENCRANTZ: *(To Polonius)* God save you, sir!

(Exit Polonius.)

215 GUILDENSTERN: Mine honored lord!

ROSENCRANTZ: My most dear lord!

HAMLET: My excellent good friends! How dost thou, Guildenstern?
Ah, Rosencrantz? Good lads, how do ye both?

ROSENCRANTZ: As the indifferent children of the earth.

220 GUILDENSTERN: Happy in that we are not overhappy; on fortune's cap
we are not the very button.

HAMLET: Nor the soles of her shoe?

ROSENCRANTZ: Neither, my lord.

HAMLET: Then you live about her waist, or in the middle of her favors?

225 GUILDENSTERN: Faith, her privates we.

---

[5] *pregnant:* ready, and clever.

HAMLET: In the secret parts of fortune? O, most true; she is a strumpet. What's the news?

ROSENCRANTZ: None, my lord, but that the world's grown honest.

HAMLET: Then is doomsday near: but your news is not true. Let me
230   question more in particular: what have you, my good friends, deserved at the hands of fortune, that she sends you to prison hither?

GUILDENSTERN: Prison, my lord!

HAMLET: Denmark's a prison.

235 ROSENCRANTZ: Then is the world one.

HAMLET: A goodly one; in which there are many confines, wards, and dungeons, Denmark being one o' the worst.

ROSENCRANTZ: We think not so, my lord.

HAMLET: Why, then, 'tis none to you; for there is nothing either good
240   or bad, but thinking makes it so: to me it is a prison.

ROSENCRANTZ: Why, then, your ambition makes it one; 'tis too narrow for your mind.

HAMLET: O God, I could be bounded in a nutshell, and count myself a king of infinite space, were it not that I have bad dreams.

245 GUILDENSTERN: Which dreams, indeed, are ambition; for the very substance of the ambitious is merely the shadow of a dream.

HAMLET: A dream itself is but a shadow.

ROSENCRANTZ: Truly, and I hold ambition of so airy and light a quality that it is but a shadow's shadow.

250 HAMLET: Then are our beggars bodies, and our monarchs and outstretched heroes the beggars' shadows. Shall we to the court? for, by my fay, I cannot reason.

ROSENCRANTZ and GUILDENSTERN: We'll wait upon you.

HAMLET: No such matter: I will not sort you with the rest of my
255   servants, for, to speak to you like an honest man, I am most dreadfully attended. But, in the beaten way of friendship, what make you at Elsinore?

ROSENCRANTZ: To visit you, my lord; no other occasion.

HAMLET: Beggar that I am, I am even poor in thanks; but I thank you:
260   and sure, dear friends, my thanks are too dear a halfpenny. Were you not sent for? Is it your own inclining? Is it a free visitation? Come, deal justly with me: come, come; nay, speak.

GUILDENSTERN: What should we say, my lord?

HAMLET: Why, anything—but to the purpose. You were sent for; and
265   there is a kind of confession in your looks, which your modesties have not craft enough to color: I know the good king and queen have sent for you.

ROSENCRANTZ: To what end, my lord?

HAMLET: That you must teach me. But let me conjure you, by the rights
270   of our fellowship, by the consonancy of our youth, by the obligation of our ever-preserved love, and by what more dear a better proposer

could charge you withal, be even and direct with me, whether you
were sent for or no?

ROSENCRANTZ: What say you? *(To Guildenstern)*

275 HAMLET: *(Aside)* Nay, then, I have an eye of you.—If you love me,
hold not off.

GUILDENSTERN: My lord, we were sent for.

HAMLET: I will tell you why; so shall my anticipation prevent your
discovery, and your secrecy to the king and queen moult no
280 feather. I have of late,—but wherefore I know not,—lost all my
mirth, forgone all custom of exercises; and, indeed, it goes so
heavily with my disposition that this goodly frame, the earth,
seems to me a sterile promontory; this most excellent canopy, the
air, look you, this brave o'erhanging firmament, this majestical
285 roof fretted[6] with golden fire,—why, it appears no other thing to
me than a foul and pestilent congregation of vapors. What a piece
of work is man! How noble in reason! how infinite in faculties! in
form and moving, how express and admirable! in action, how like
an angel! in apprehension, how like a god! the beauty of the world!
290 the paragon of animals! And yet, to me, what is this quintessence
of dust? man delights not me; no, nor woman neither, though by
your smiling you seem to say so.

ROSENCRANTZ: My lord, there was no such stuff in my thoughts.

HAMLET: Why did you laugh, then, when I said, *Man delights not me*?

295 ROSENCRANTZ: To think, my lord, if you delight not in man, what
lenten entertainment[7] the players shall receive from you: we coted[8]
them on the way; and hither are they coming, to offer you service.

HAMLET: He that plays the king shall be welcome,—his majesty shall
have tribute of me; the adventurous knight shall use his foil and
300 target; the lover shall not sigh gratis; the humorous[9] man shall end
his part in peace; the clown shall make those laugh whose lungs
are tickled o' the sere;[10] and the lady shall say her mind freely, or
the blank verse shall halt[11] for't.—What players are they?

ROSENCRANTZ: Even those you were wont to take delight in,—the
305 tragedians of the city.

HAMLET: How chances it they travel? their residence, both in reputation
and profit, was better both ways.

ROSENCRANTZ: I think their inhibition[12] comes by the means of the
late innovation.

310 HAMLET: Do they hold the same estimation they did when I was in
the city? Are they so followed?

ROSENCRANTZ: No, indeed, they are not.

HAMLET: How comes it? do they grow rusty?

---

[6] *roof fretted:* a roof with fretwork. [7] *lenten entertainment:* poor reception. [8] *coted:*
passed. [9] *humorous:* eccentric. [10] *whose . . . sere:* whose lungs, for laughter, are easily
tickled. [11] *halt:* limp. [12] *inhibition:* difficulty, preventing them from remaining in
the capital.

ROSENCRANTZ: Nay, their endeavor keeps in the wonted pace; but there
315   is, sir, an aery[13] of children, little eyases,[14] that cry out on the top of
    question, and are most tyrannically clapped for't: these are now the
    fashion; and so berattle the common stages,—so they call them,—
    that many wearing rapiers are afraid of goose-quills, and dare scarce
    come thither.
320 HAMLET: What, are they children? who maintains 'em? how are they
    escoted?[15] Will they pursue the quality[16] no longer than they can
    sing? will they not say afterwards, if they should grow themselves
    to common players,—as it is most like, if their means are no better,
    —their writers do them wrong, to make them exclaim against
325   their own succession?
ROSENCRANTZ: Faith, there has been much to do on both sides; and
    the nation holds it no sin to tarre[17] them to controversy: there was
    for awhile no money bid for argument, unless the poet and the
    player went to cuffs in the question.
330 HAMLET: Is't possible?
GUILDENSTERN: O, there has been much throwing about of brains.
HAMLET: Do the boys carry it away?
ROSENCRANTZ: Ay, that they do, my lord; Hercules and his load[18] too.
HAMLET: It is not strange; for mine uncle is king of Denmark, and those
335   that would make mouths at him while my father lived, give twenty,
    forty, fifty, an hundred ducats a-piece for his picture in little.
    'Sblood, there is something in this more than natural, if philosophy
    could find it out.

(Flourish of trumpets within.)

GUILDENSTERN: There are the players.
340 HAMLET: Gentlemen, you are welcome to Elsinore. Your hands, come:
    the appurtenance of welcome is fashion and ceremony: let me comply
    with you in this garb; lest my extent[19] to the players, which, I
    tell you, must show fairly outward, should more appear like
    entertainment[20] than yours. You are welcome: but my uncle-father
345   and aunt-mother are deceived.
GUILDENSTERN: In what, my dear lord?
HAMLET: I am but mad north-north-west: when the wind is southerly
    I know a hawk from a handsaw.

(Enter Polonius.)

POLONIUS: Well be with you, gentlemen!
350 HAMLET: Hark you, Guildenstern;—and you too;—at each ear a hearer:
    that great baby you see there is not yet out of his swathing-clouts.

---

[13] *aery:* brood of birds of prey. [14] *little eyases:* young hawks; a reference to the boys' companies that became popular rivals of Shakespeare's company of players. [15] *escoted:* financially supported. [16] *quality:* profession. [17] *tarre:* egg them on. [18] *load:* the globe, or the world. [19] *extent:* show of friendliness. [20] *entertainment:* welcome.

ROSENCRANTZ: Happily he's the second time come to them; for they
    say an old man is twice a child.
HAMLET: I will prophesy he comes to tell me of the players; mark it.
355   You say right, sir: o' Monday morning; 'twas so indeed.
POLONIUS: My lord, I have news to tell you.
HAMLET: My lord, I have news to tell you. When Roscius was an actor
    in Rome,—
POLONIUS: The actors are come hither, my lord.
360 HAMLET: Buzz, buzz!
POLONIUS: Upon mine honor,—
HAMLET: Then came each actor on his ass,—
POLONIUS: The best actors in the world, either for tragedy, comedy,
    history, pastoral, pastoral-comical, historical-pastoral, tragical-
365   historical, tragical-comical-historical-pastoral, scene individable,[21]
    or poem unlimited:[22] Seneca cannot be too heavy nor Plautus too
    light. For the law of writ and the liberty,[23] these are the only men.
HAMLET: O Jephthah, judge of Israel, what a treasure hadst thou!
POLONIUS: What a treasure had he, my lord?
370 HAMLET: Why—

        One fair daughter, and no more,
        The which he loved passing well.

POLONIUS: (Aside) Still on my daughter.
HAMLET: Am I not i' the right, old Jephthah?
375 POLONIUS: If you call me Jephthah, my lord, I have a daughter that I
    love passing well.
HAMLET: Nay, that follows not.
POLONIUS: What follows, then, my lord?
HAMLET: Why—

380   As by lot, God wot,

and then, you know,

        It came to pass, as most like it was,

the first row of the pious chanson will show you more; for look
where my abridgement comes.

(Enter four or five Players.)

385   You are welcome, masters; welcome, all:—I am glad to see thee
    well:—welcome, good friends.—O, my old friend! Thy face is
    valanced since I saw thee last; comest thou to beard me in

---

[21] *scene individable:* a play that observes the unities of time and place. [22] *poem unlimited:* a typical multiscened Elizabethan type of drama, not restricted by the unities; examples are *Hamlet, Macbeth, King Lear,* and virtually any other play by Shakespeare. [23] *For . . . liberty:* for the laws of the unities and for playwriting that is not so restricted.

Denmark?—What, my young lady and mistress! By'r lady, your
ladyship is nearer heaven than when I saw you last, by the altitude

390 of a chopine.[24] Pray God, your voice, like a piece of uncurrent gold,
be not cracked within the ring.—Masters, you are all welcome.
We'll e'en to't like French falconers, fly at anything we see: we'll
have a speech straight: come, give us a taste of your quality; come,
a passionate speech.

395 1ST PLAYER: What speech, my lord?

HAMLET: I heard thee speak me a speech once,—but it was never
acted; or, if it was, not above once; for the play, I remember,
pleased not the million; 'twas caviare to the general: but it was,—
as I received it, and others whose judgments in such matters cried

400 in the top of mine,—an excellent play, well digested in the scenes,
set down with as much modesty as cunning. I remember, one said
there were no sallets in the lines to make the matter savory, nor no
matter in the phrase that might indite the author of affectation;
but called it an honest method, as wholesome as sweet, and by

405 very much more handsome than fine. One speech in it I chiefly
loved: 'twas Aeneas' tale to Dido; and thereabout of it especially
where he speaks of Priam's slaughter: if it live in your memory,
begin at this line;—let me see, let me see:—

The rugged Pyrrhus, like the Hyrcanian beast,[25]

410 —it is not so:—it begins with Pyrrhus:—

The rugged Pyrrhus,—he whose sable arms,
Black as his purpose, did the night resemble
When he lay couched in the ominous horse,—
Hath now this dread and black complexion smear'd

415 With heraldry more dismal; head to foot
Now is he total gules; horridly trick'd
With blood of fathers, mothers, daughters, sons,
Bak'd and impasted with the parching streets,
That lend a tyrannous and damned light

420 To their vile murders: roasted in wrath and fire,
And thus o'er-sized with coagulate gore,
With eyes like carbuncles, the hellish Pyrrhus
Old grandsire Priam seeks.—

So proceed you.

425 POLONIUS: 'Fore God, my lord, well spoken, with good accent and
good discretion.

1ST PLAYER: Anon he finds him

---

[24] *chopine:* a wooden stilt more than a foot high used under a woman's shoe; a Venetian
fashion introduced into England.   [25] *The rugged . . . :* this speech is an example of the
declamatory style of drama, which Shakespeare surely must have considered outmoded.

Striking too short at Greeks; his antique sword,
Rebellious to his arm, lies where it falls,
430   Repugnant to command: unequal match'd,
Pyrrhus at Priam drives; in rage strikes wide;
But with the whiff and wind of his fell sword
The unnerved father falls. Then senseless Ilium,
Seeming to feel this blow, with flaming top
435   Stoops to his base; and with a hideous crash
Takes prisoner Pyrrhus' ear: for, lo! his sword,
Which was declining on the milky head
Of reverend Priam, seem'd i' the air to stick:
So, as a painted tyrant, Pyrrhus stood;
440   And, like a neutral to his will and matter,
Did nothing.
But as we often see, against some storm,
A silence in the heavens, the rack stand still,
The blood winds speechless, and the orb below
445   As hush as death, anon the dreadful thunder
Doth rend the region; so, after Pyrrhus' pause,
A roused vengeance sets him new a-work;
And never did the Cyclops' hammers fall
On Mars his armor, forg'd for proof eterne,
450   With less remorse than Pyrrhus' bleeding sword
Now falls on Priam.—
Out, out, thou strumpet, Fortune! All you gods,
In general synod, take away her power;
Break all the spokes and fellies from her wheel,
455   And bowl the round knave down the hill of heaven,
As low as to the fiends!

POLONIUS: This is too long.

HAMLET: It shall to the barber's, with your beard.—Pr'ythee, say
on.—He's for a jig, or a tale of bawdry, or he sleeps:—say on; come
460   to Hecuba.

1ST PLAYER: But who, O, who had seen the mobled queen,—

HAMLET: *The mobled queen?*

POLONIUS: That's good; *mobled queen* is good.

1ST PLAYER: Run barefoot up and down, threatening the flames
465   With bissom rheum; a clout upon that head
Where late the diadem stood; and, for a robe,
About her lank and all o'er-teemed loins,
A blanket, in the alarm of fear caught up;—
Who this had seen, with tongue in venom steep'd,
470   'Gainst Fortune's state would treason have pronounc'd:
But if the gods themselves did see her then,
When she saw Pyrrhus make malicious sport
In mincing with his sword her husband's limbs,

The instant burst of clamor that she made,—
475   Unless things mortal move them not at all,—
Would have made milch the burning eyes of heaven,
And passion in the gods.

POLONIUS: Look, whether he has not turn'd his color, and has tears in's eyes.—Pray you, no more.

480 HAMLET: 'Tis well; I'll have thee speak out the rest soon.—Good my lord, will you see the players well bestowed? Do you hear, let them be well used; for they are the abstracts and brief chronicles of the time; after your death you were better have a bad epitaph than their ill report while you live.

485 POLONIUS: My lord, I will use them according to their desert.

HAMLET: God's bodykins,[26] man, better: use every man after his desert, and who should 'scape whipping? Use them after your own honor and dignity: the less they deserve the more merit is in your bounty. Take them in.

490 POLONIUS: Come, sirs.

HAMLET: Follow him, friends: we'll hear a play to-morrow.

(Exit Polonius with all the Players but the First.)

Dost thou hear me, old friend; can you play the Murder of Gonzago?

1ST PLAYER: Ay, my lord.

HAMLET: We'll ha't to-morrow night. You could, for a need, study a
495   speech of some dozen or sixteen lines which I would set down and insert in't? could you not?

1ST PLAYER: Ay, my lord.

HAMLET: Very well.—Follow that lord; and look you mock him not.

(Exit First Player.)

—My good friends, *(to Rosencrantz and Guildenstern)* I'll leave you
500   till night: you are welcome to Elsinore.

ROSENCRANTZ: Good my lord!

(Exeunt Rosencrantz and Guildenstern.)

HAMLET: Ay, so God b' wi' ye!—Now I am alone.
O, what a rogue[27] and peasant slave am I!
Is it not monstrous that this player here,
505   But in a fiction, in a dream of passion,
Could force his soul so to his own conceit[28]
That from her working all his visage wan'd;
Tears in his eyes, distraction in's aspéct,
A broken voice, and his whole function suiting

---

[26] *God's bodykins:* by God's little body.   [27] *rogue:* wretched creature.   [28] *conceit:* conception.

510 With forms to his conceit? And all for nothing!
For Hecuba?
What's Hecuba to him or he to Hecuba,
That he should weep for her? What would he do,
Had he the motive and the cue for passion
515 That I have? He would drown the stage with tears,
And cleave the general ear with horrid speech;
Make mad the guilty, and appal the free;
Confound the ignorant, and amaze, indeed,
The very faculties of eyes and ears.
520 Yet I,
A dull and muddy-mettled rascal, peak,
Like John-a-dreams, unpregnant of my cause,
And can say nothing; no, not for a king
Upon whose property and most dear life
525 A damn'd defeat was made. Am I a coward?
Who calls me villain? breaks my pate across?
Plucks off my beard and blows it in my face?
Tweaks me by the nose? gives me the lie i' the throat,
As deep as to the lungs? who does me this, ha?
530 'Swounds, I should take it: for it cannot be
But I am pigeon-liver'd, and lack gall
To make oppression bitter; or ere this
I should have fatted all the region kites
With this slave's offal:—bloody, bawdy villain!
535 Remorseless, treacherous, lecherous, kindless villain!
O, vengeance!
Why, what an ass am I! This is most brave,
That I, the son of a dear father murder'd,
Prompted to my revenge by heaven and hell,
540 Must, like a whore, unpack my heart with words,
And fall a-cursing like a very drab,
A scullion!
Fie upon't! foh!—About, my brain! I have heard
That guilty creatures, sitting at a play,
545 Have by the very cunning of the scene
Been struck so to the soul that presently
They have proclaim'd their malefactions;
For murder, though it have no tongue, will speak
With most miraculous organ. I'll have these players
550 Play something like the murder of my father
Before mine uncle: I'll observe his looks;
I'll tent[29] him to the quick: if he but blench,
I know my course. The spirit that I have seen

---

[29] *tent:* probe.

May be the devil: and the devil hath power
555 To assume a pleasing shape; yea, and perhaps
Out of my weakness and my melancholy,—
As he is very potent with such spirits,—
Abuses me to damn me: I'll have grounds
More relative than this:—the play's the thing
560 Wherein I'll catch the conscience of the king. *(Exit.)*

ACT III
SCENE 1

A room in the castle.

(Enter King, Queen, Polonius, Ophelia, Rosencrantz, and Guildenstern.)

KING: And can you, by no drift of circumstance,
Get from him why he puts on this confusion,
Grating so harshly all his days of quiet
With turbulent and dangerous lunacy?
5 ROSENCRANTZ: He does confess he feels himself distracted;
But from what cause he will by no means speak.
GUILDENSTERN: Nor do we find him forward to be sounded;
But, with a crafty madness, keeps aloof
When we would bring him on to some confession
10 Of his true state.
QUEEN: Did he receive you well?
ROSENCRANTZ: Most like a gentleman.
GUILDENSTERN: But with much forcing of his disposition.
ROSENCRANTZ: Niggard of question; but, of our demands,
Most free in his reply.
QUEEN: Did you assay him
15 To any pastime?
ROSENCRANTZ: Madam, it so fell out that certain players
We o'er-raught on the way: of these we told him;
And there did seem in him a kind of joy
To hear of it: they are about the court;
20 And, as I think, they have already order
This night to play before him.
POLONIUS: 'Tis most true:
And he beseech'd me to entreat your majesties
To hear and see the matter.
KING: With all my heart; and it doth much content me
25 To hear him so inclin'd.
Good gentlemen, give him a further edge,
And drive his purpose on to these delights.
ROSENCRANTZ: We shall, my lord.

(Exeunt Rosencrantz and Guildenstern.)

KING: Sweet Gertrude, leave us too;
         For we have closely sent for Hamlet hither
30   That he, as 'twere by accident, may here
         Affront Ophelia:
         Her father and myself,—lawful espials,[1]—
         Will so bestow ourselves that, seeing, unseen,
         We may of their encounter frankly judge;
35   And gather by him, as he is behav'd,
         If't be the affliction of his love or no
         That thus he suffers for.
QUEEN: I shall obey you:—
         And for your part, Ophelia, I do wish
         That your good beauties be the happy cause
40   Of Hamlet's wildness: so shall I hope your virtues
         Will bring him to his wonted way again,
         To both your honors.
OPHELIA: Madam, I wish it may.

(Exit Queen.)

POLONIUS: Ophelia, walk you here.—Gracious, so please you,
         We will bestow ourselves.—*(To Ophelia)* Read on this book;
45   That show of such an exercise may color
         Your loneliness.—We are oft to blame in this,—
         'Tis too much prov'd,—that with devotion's visage
         And pious action we do sugar o'er
         The devil himself.
KING: *(Aside)*   O, 'tis too true!
50   How smart a lash that speech doth give my conscience!
         The harlot's cheek, beautied with plastering art,
         Is not more ugly to the thing that helps it
         Than is my deed to my most painted word:
         O heavy burden!
55 POLONIUS: I hear him coming: let's withdraw, my lord.

(Exeunt King and Polonius.)

(Enter Hamlet.)

HAMLET: To be, or not to be,—that is the question:
         Whether 'tis nobler in the mind to suffer
         The slings and arrows of outrageous fortune,
         Or to take arms against a sea of troubles,
60   And by opposing end them?—To die,—to sleep,—
         No more; and by a sleep to say we end
         The heart-ache and the thousand natural shocks

---

[1] *espials:* spies.

That flesh is heir to,—'tis a consummation
Devoutly to be wish'd. To die,—to sleep;—
65 To sleep! perchance to dream:—ay, there's the rub;
For in that sleep of death what dreams may come,
When we have shuffled off this mortal coil,
Must give us pause: there's the respect
That makes a calamity of so long life;
70 For who would bear the whips and scorns of time,
The oppressor's wrong, the proud man's contumely,
The pangs of déspis'd love, the law's delay,
The insolence of office, and the spurns
That patient merit of the unworthy takes,
75 When he himself might his quietus make
With a bare bodkin?[2] who would fardels[3] bear,
To grunt[4] and sweat under a weary life,
But that the dread of something after death,—
The undiscover'd country, from whose bourn[5]
80 No traveler returns,—puzzles the will,
And makes us rather bear those ills we have
Than to fly to others that we know not of?
Thus conscience does make cowards of us all;
And thus the native hue of resolution
85 Is sicklied o'er with the pale cast of thought;
And enterprises of great pith and moment,
With this regard, their currents turn awry,
And lose the name of action.—Soft you now!
The fair Ophelia.—Nymph, in thy orisons[6]
90 Be all my sins remember'd.
OPHELIA: Good my lord,
How does your honor for this many a day?
HAMLET: I humbly thank you; well, well, well.
OPHELIA: My lord, I have remembrances of yours,
That I have longed long to re-deliver;
95 I pray you, now receive them.
HAMLET: No, not I;
I never gave you aught.
OPHELIA: My honor'd lord, you know right well you did;
And with them, words of so sweet breath compos'd
As made the things more rich: their perfume lost,
100 Take these again; for to the noble mind
Rich gifts wax poor when givers prove unkind.
There, my lord.
HAMLET: Ha, ha! are you honest?

---

[2] *bodkin:* stiletto. [3] *fardels:* burdens. [4] *grunt:* groan. [5] *bourn:* boundary. [6] *orisons:* prayers.

OPHELIA: My lord?

105 HAMLET: Are you fair?

OPHELIA: What means your lordship?

HAMLET: That if you be honest and fair, your honesty should admit
no discourse to your beauty.

OPHELIA: Could beauty, my lord, have better commerce than with
110 honesty?

HAMLET: Ay, truly; for the power of beauty will sooner transform
honesty from what it is to a bawd than the force of honesty can
translate beauty into his likeness: this was sometime a paradox,
but now the time gives it proof. I did love you once.

115 OPHELIA: Indeed, my lord, you made me believe so.

HAMLET: You should not have believed me; for virtue cannot so
inoculate our old stock but we shall relish of it: I loved you not.

OPHELIA: I was the more deceived.

HAMLET: Get thee to a nunnery: why wouldst thou be a breeder of
120 sinners? I am myself indifferent[7] honest; but yet I could accuse me
of such things that it were better my mother had not borne me: I
am very proud, revengeful, ambitious; with more offences at my
beck than I have thoughts to put them in, imagination to give
them shape, or time to act them in. What should such fellows as I
125 do crawling between heaven and earth? We are arrant knaves, all;
believe none of us. Go thy ways to a nunnery. Where's your father?

OPHELIA: At home, my lord.

HAMLET: Let the doors be shut upon him, that he may play the fool
nowhere but in's own house. Farewell.

130 OPHELIA: O, help him, you sweet heavens!

HAMLET: If thou dost marry, I'll give thee this plague for thy
dowry,—be thou as chaste as ice, as pure as snow, thou shalt not
escape calumny. Get thee to a nunnery, go: farewell. Or, if thou
wilt needs marry, marry a fool; for wise men know well enough
135 what monsters you make of them. To a nunnery, go; and quickly
too. Farewell.

OPHELIA: O heavenly powers, restore him!

HAMLET: I have heard of your paintings too, well enough; God has
given you one face and you make yourselves another: you jig, you
140 amble, and you lisp, and nickname God's creatures, and make your
wantonness your ignorance. Go to, I'll no more on't; it hath made
me mad. I say, we will have no more marriages: those that are
married already, all but one, shall live; the rest shall keep as they are.
To a nunnery, go. (*Exit.*)

145 OPHELIA: O, what a noble mind is here o'erthrown!
The courtier's, soldier's, scholar's eye, tongue, sword:

---

[7] *indifferent:* tolerably.

The expectancy and rose of the fair state,
The glass of fashion and the mould of form,
The observ'd of all observers,—quite, quite down!
150 And I, of ladies most deject and wretched
That suck'd the honey of his music vows,
Now see that noble and most sovereign reason,
Like sweet bells jangled, out of tune and harsh;
That unmatch'd form and feature of blown[8] youth
155 Blasted with ecstasy: O, woe is me,
To have seen what I have seen, see what I see!

(Re-enter King and Polonius.)

KING: Love! his affections do not that way tend;
Nor what he spake, though it lack'd form a little,
Was not like madness. There's something in his soul
160 O'er which his melancholy sits on brood;
And I do doubt[9] the hatch and the disclose
Will be some danger: which for to prevent,
I have in quick determination
Thus set it down:—he shall with speed to England
165 For the demand of our neglected tribute:
Haply, the seas and countries different,
With variable objects, shall expel
This something-settled matter in his heart;
Whereon his brains still beating puts him thus
170 From fashion of himself. What think you on't?
POLONIUS: It shall do well: but yet do I believe
The origin and commencement of his grief
Sprung from neglected love.—How now, Ophelia!
You need not tell us what Lord Hamlet said;
175 We heard it all.—My lord, do as you please;
But if you hold it fit, after the play,
Let his queen mother all alone entreat him
To show his grief: let her be round with him;
And I'll be plac'd, so please you, in the ear
180 Of all their conference. If she finds him not,[10]
To England send him; or confine him where
Your wisdom best shall think.
KING: It shall be so:
Madness in great ones must not unwatch'd go.

(Exeunt.)

---

[8] *blown:* full-blown.   [9] *doubt:* fear.   [10] *she . . . not:* does not find him out.

SCENE 2

A hall in the castle.

(Enter Hamlet and certain Players.)

HAMLET: Speak the speech, I pray you, as I pronounced it to you,
trippingly on the tongue: but if you mouth it, as many of your
players do, I had as lief the town-crier spoke my lines. Nor do not
saw the air too much with your hand, thus; but use all gently: for
5   in the very torrent, tempest, and, as I may say, the whirlwind of
passion, you must acquire and beget a temperance that may give it
smoothness. O, it offends me to the soul, to hear a robustious
periwigpated fellow tear a passion to tatters, to very rags, to split
the ears of the groundlings, who, for the most part, are capable of
10   nothing but inexplicable dumb shows and noise: I could have such
a fellow whipped for o'erdoing Termagant;[1] it out-herods Herod:[2]
pray you, avoid it.

1ST PLAYER: I warrant your honor.

HAMLET: Be not too tame neither, but let your own discretion be
15   your tutor; suit the action to the word, the word to the action;
with this special observance, that you o'erstep not the modesty of
nature: for anything so overdone is from the purpose of playing,
whose end, both at the first and now, was and is, to hold, as
'twere, the mirror up to nature; to show virtue her own feature,
20   scorn her own image, and the very age and body of the time his
form and pressure. Now, this overdone or come tardy off, though it
make the unskilful laugh, cannot but make the judicious grieve;
the censure of the which one must, in your allowance, o'erweigh
a whole theater of others. O, there be players that I have seen
25   play,—and heard others praise, and that highly,—not to speak it
profanely, that, neither having the accent of Christians, nor the
gait of Christian, pagan, nor man, have so strutted and bellowed
that I have thought some of nature's journeymen had made men,
and not made them well, they imitated humanity so abominably.

30 1ST PLAYER: I hope we have reformed that indifferently with us, sir.

HAMLET: O, reform it altogether. And let those that play your clowns
speak no more than is set down for them: for there be of them that
will themselves laugh, to set on some quantity of barren spectators
to laugh too; though, in the meantime, some necessary question of
35   the play be then to be considered: that's villainous, and shows a
most pitiful ambition in the fool that uses it. Go, make you ready.

(Exeunt Players.)

---

[1] *Termagant:* a violent pagan deity, supposedly Mohammedan.   [2] *out-herods Herod:* out-rants the ranting Herod, who figures in medieval drama.

(Enter Polonius, Rosencrantz, and Guildenstern.)

How now, my lord! will the king hear this piece of work?

POLONIUS: And the queen, too, and that presently.

HAMLET: Bid the players make haste.

(Exit Polonius.)

40 Will you two help to hasten them?

ROSENCRANTZ and GUILDENSTERN: We will, my lord. *(Exeunt.)*

HAMLET: What, ho, Horatio!

(Enter Horatio.)

HORATIO: Here, sweet lord, at your service.

HAMLET: Horatio, thou art e'en as just a man

45 As e'er my conversation cop'd withal.

HORATIO: O, my dear lord,—

HAMLET: Nay, do not think I flatter;

For what advancement may I hope from thee,

That no revénue hast, but thy good spirits,

To feed and clothe thee? Why should the poor be flatter'd?

50 No, let the candied tongue lick ábsurd pomp;

And crook the pregnant hinges of the knee

Where thrift may follow fawning. Dost thou hear?

Since my dear soul was mistress of her choice,

And could of men distinguish, her election

55 Hath seal'd thee for herself: for thou hast been

As one, in suffering all, that suffers nothing;

A man that Fortune's buffets and rewards

Hast ta'en with equal thanks: and bless'd are those

Whose blood and judgment are so well commingled

60 That they are not a pipe for Fortune's finger

To sound what stop she please. Give me that man

That is not passion's slave, and I will wear him

In my heart's core, ay, in my heart of heart,

As I do thee.—Something too much of this.—

65 There is a play to-night before the king;

One scene of it comes near the circumstance

Which I have told thee of my father's death:

I pr'ythee, when thou see'st that act a-foot,

Even with the very comment of thy soul

70 Observe mine uncle: if this his occulted guilt

Do not itself unkennel in one speech,

It is a damned ghost that we have seen;

And my imaginations are as foul

As Vulcan's stithy.³ Give him heedful note:

---

³ *stithy:* smithy.

75   For I mine eyes will rivet to his face;
    And, after, we will both our judgments join
    In censure of his seeming.
  HORATIO: Well, my lord:
    If he steal aught the whilst this play is playing,
    And 'scape detecting, I will pay the theft.
80 HAMLET: They are coming to the play; I must be idle:[4]
    Get you a place.

(Danish march. A flourish. Enter King, Queen, Polonius, Ophelia, Rosencrantz, Guildenstern, and others.)

KING: How fares our cousin Hamlet?
HAMLET: Excellent, i'faith; of the chameleon's dish:[5] I eat the air, promise-crammed: you cannot feed capons so.
85 KING: I have nothing with this answer, Hamlet; these words are not mine.
HAMLET: No, nor mine now. *(To Polonius)* My lord, you played once i'the university, you say?
POLONIUS: That did I, my lord, and was accounted a good actor.
90 HAMLET: And what did you enact?
POLONIUS: I did enact Julius Caesar: I was killed i' the Capitol; Brutus killed me.
HAMLET: It was a brute part of him to kill so capital a calf there.—Be the players ready.
95 ROSENCRANTZ: Ay, my lord; they stay upon your patience.
QUEEN: Come hither, my good Hamlet, sit by me.
HAMLET: No, good mother, here's metal more attractive.
POLONIUS: O, ho! do you mark that? *(To the King)*
HAMLET: Lady, shall I lie in your lap? *(Lying down at Ophelia's feet)*
100 OPHELIA: No, my lord.
HAMLET: I mean, my head upon your lap?
OPHELIA: Ay, my lord.
HAMLET: Do you think I meant country matters?
OPHELIA: I think nothing, my lord.
105 HAMLET: That's a fair thought to lie between maids' legs.
OPHELIA: What is, my lord?
HAMLET: Nothing.
OPHELIA: You are merry, my lord.
HAMLET: Who, I?
110 OPHELIA: Ay, my lord.
HAMLET: O, your only jig-maker. What should a man do but be merry? for, look you, how cheerfully my mother looks, and my father died within's two hours.
OPHELIA: Nay, 'tis twice two months, my lord.

---

[4] *idle:* foolish.   [5] *chameleon's dish:* Chameleons were supposed to live on air.

115   HAMLET: So long? Nay, then, let the devil wear black, for I'll have a
       suit of sables. O heavens! die two months ago, and not forgotten
       yet? Then there's hope a great man's memory may outlive his life
       half a year: but, by'r lady, he must build churches, then; or else shall
       he suffer not thinking on, with the hobby-horse, whose epitaph is,
120   *For, O, for, O, the hobby-horse is forgot.*

(Trumpets sound. The dumb show enters.)

*(Enter a King and a Queen, very lovingly; the Queen embracing him and he her.
She kneels, and makes show of protestation unto him. He takes her up, and declines his head upon her neck: lays him down upon a bank of flowers: she, seeing
him asleep, leaves him. Anon comes in a fellow, takes off his crown, kisses it,
and pours poison in the King's ears, and exit. The Queen returns; finds the King
dead, and makes passionate action. The Poisoner, with some two or three Mutes,
comes in again, seeming to lament with her. The dead body is carried away. The
Poisoner woos the Queen with gifts: she seems loth and unwilling awhile, but in
the end accepts his love.)*

(Exeunt.)

OPHELIA: What means this, my lord?
HAMLET: Marry, this is miching mallecho;[6] it means mischief.
OPHELIA: Belike this show imports the argument of the play.

(Enter Prologue.)

HAMLET: We shall know by this fellow: the players cannot keep counsel;
125   they'll tell all.
OPHELIA: Will he tell us what this show meant?
HAMLET: Ay, or any show that you'll show him: be not you ashamed
       to show, he'll not shame to tell you what it means.
OPHELIA: You are naught, you are naught: I'll mark the play.
130 PROLOGUE:

> For us, and for our tragedy,
> Here stooping to your clemency,
> We beg your hearing patiently.

HAMLET: Is this a prologue, or the posy[7] of a ring?
OPHELIA: 'Tis brief, my lord.
135 HAMLET: As woman's love.

(Enter a King and a Queen.)

PROLOGUE KING: Full thirty times hath Phoebus' cart gone round
       Neptune's salt wash and Tellus' orbed ground,[8]
       And thirty dozen moons with borrow'd sheen
       About the world have times twelve thirties been,

---

[6]*miching mallecho:* a sneaking misdeed. [7]*posy:* motto or inscription. [8]*Nep-tune's . . . ground:* the globe.

140 Since love our hearts, and Hymen did our hands
   Unite commutual in most sacred bands.
  PROLOGUE QUEEN: So many journeys may the sun and moon
   Make us again count o'er ere love be done!
   But, woe is me, you are so sick of late,
145 So far from cheer and from your former state
   That I distrust you.[9] Yet, though I distrust,
   Discomfort you, my lord, it nothing must:
   For women's fear and love holds quantity,[10]
   In neither aught, or in extremity.
150 Now, what my love is, proof hath made you know;
   And as my love is siz'd, my fear is so:
   Where love is great, the littlest doubts are fear;
   Where little fears grow great, great love grows there.
  PROLOGUE KING: Faith, I must leave thee, love, and shortly too;
155 My operant powers their functions leave[11] to do:
   And thou shalt live in this fair world behind,
   Honor'd, belov'd; and haply one as kind
   For husband shalt thou,—
  PROLOGUE QUEEN: O, confound the rest!
   Such love must needs be treason in my breast:
160 In second husband let me be accurst!
   None wed the second but who kill'd the first.
  HAMLET: *(Aside)* Wormwood, wormwood.
  PROLOGUE QUEEN: The instances that second marriage move
   Are base respects of thrift, but none of love:
165 A second time I kill my husband, dead,
   When second husband kisses me in bed.
  PROLOGUE KING: I do believe you think what now you speak;
   But what we do determine oft we break.
   Purpose is but the slave to memory;
170 Of violent birth, but poor validity:
   Which now, like fruit unripe, sticks on the tree;
   But fall unshaken when they mellow be.
   Most necessary 'tis that we forget
   To pay ourselves what to ourselves is debt:
175 What to ourselves in passion we propose,
   The passion ending, doth the purpose lose.
   The violence of either grief or joy
   Their own enactures with themselves destroy:
   Where joy most revels grief doth most lament;
180 Grief joys, joy grieves, on slender accident.
   This world is not for aye; nor 'tis not strange

---

[9] *distrust you:* worry about you. [10] *holds quantity:* correspond in degree. [11] *leave:* cease.

That even our loves should with our fortunes change;
For 'tis a question left us yet to prove
Whether love lead fortune or else fortune love.

185 The great man down, you mark his favorite flies;
The poor advanc'd makes friends of enemies.
And hitherto doth love on fortune tend:
For who not needs shall never lack a friend;
And who in want a hollow friend doth try,

190 Directly seasons him his enemy.
But, orderly to end where I begun,—
Our wills and fates do so contrary run
That our devices still are overthrown;
Our thoughts are ours, their ends none of our own:

195 So think thou wilt no second husband wed;
But die thy thoughts when thy first lord is dead.

PROLOGUE QUEEN: Nor earth to me give food, nor heaven light!
Sport and repose lock from me day and night!
To desperation turn my trust and hope!

200 An anchor's[12] cheer in prison be my scope!
Each opposite, that blanks the face of joy,
Meet what I would have well, and it destroy!
Both here and hence, pursue me lasting strife,
If, once a widow, ever I be wife!

205 HAMLET: If she should break it now! *(To Ophelia)*

PROLOGUE KING: 'Tis deeply sworn. Sweet, leave me here awhile;
My spirits grow dull, and fain I would beguile
The tedious day with sleep. *(Sleeps)*

PROLOGUE QUEEN: Sleep rock thy brain,
And never come mischance between us twain! *(Exit.)*

210 HAMLET: Madam, how like you this play?

QUEEN: The lady doth protest too much, methinks.

HAMLET: O, but she'll keep her word.

KING: Have you heard the argument? Is there no offence in't?

HAMLET: No, no, they do but jest, poison in jest; no offence i' the
215 world.

KING: What do you call the play?

HAMLET: The Mouse-trap. Marry, how? Tropically.[13] This play is the
image of a murder done in Vienna: Gonzago is the duke's name:
his wife, Baptista: you shall see anon; 'tis a knavish piece of work:
220 but what o' that? your majesty, and we that have free souls, it
touches us not: let the galled jade wince, our withers are unwrung.

(Enter Lucianus.)

---

[12] *anchor's:* anchorite's, or hermit's.   [13] *Tropically:* figuratively, or metaphorically; by
means of a "trope."

This is one Lucianus, nephew to the king.

OPHELIA: You are a good chorus, my lord.

HAMLET: I could interpret between you and your love, if I could see
225 the puppets dallying.

OPHELIA: You are keen, my lord, you are keen.

HAMLET: It would cost you a groaning to take off my edge.

OPHELIA: Still better, and worse.

HAMLET: So you must take your husbands.—Begin, murderer; pox,
230 leave thy damnable faces and begin. Come:—*The croaking raven
doth bellow for revenge.*

LUCIANUS: Thoughts black, hands apt, drugs fit, and time agreeing;
Confederate season, else no creature seeing;
Thou mixture rank, of midnight weeds collected,
235 With Hecate's ban[14] thrice blasted, thrice infected,
Thy natural magic and dire property
On wholesome life usurp immediately.

(Pours the poison into the sleeper's ears.)

HAMLET: He poisons him i' the garden for's estate. His name's Gonzago:
the story is extant, and writ in choice Italian: you shall see anon how
240 the murderer gets the love of Gonzago's wife.

OPHELIA: The king rises.

HAMLET: What, frighted with false fire!

QUEEN: How fares my lord?

POLONIUS: Give o'er the play.

245 KING: Give me some light:—away!

ALL: Lights, lights, lights!

(Exeunt all but Hamlet and Horatio.)

HAMLET:

Why, let the stricken deer go weep,
The hart ungalled play;
For some must watch, while some must sleep:
250   So runs the world away.—

Would not this, sir, and a forest of feathers, if the rest of my fortunes
turn Turk with me, with two Provencial roses on my razed shoes, get
me a fellowship in a cry[15] of players, sir?

HORATIO: Half a share.

255 HAMLET: A whole one, I.

For thou dost know, O Damon dear,
This realm dismantled was

---

[14] *Hecate's ban:* the spell of the goddess of witchcraft.   [15] *cry:* company.

          Of Jove himself; and now reigns here
          A very, very—pajock.[16]

260 HORATIO: You might have rhymed.

HAMLET: O good Horatio, I'll take the ghost's word for a thousand
    pound. Didst perceive?

HORATIO: Very well, my lord.

HAMLET: Upon the talk of the poisoning,—

265 HORATIO: I did very well note him.

HAMLET: Ah, ha!—Come, some music! come, the recorders!—

          For if the king like not the comedy,
          Why, then, belike,—he likes it not, perdy.

Come, some music!

(Re-enter Rosencrantz and Guildenstern.)

270 GUILDENSTERN: Good my lord, vouchsafe me a word with you.

HAMLET: Sir, a whole history.

GUILDENSTERN: The king, sir,—

HAMLET: Ay, sir, what of him?

GUILDENSTERN: Is, in his retirement, marvelous distempered.

275 HAMLET: With drink, sir?

GUILDENSTERN: No, my lord, rather with choler.

HAMLET: Your wisdom should show itself more richer to signify this
    to his doctor; for, for me to put him to his purgation would perhaps
    plunge him into far more choler.

280 GUILDENSTERN: Good my lord, put your discourse into some frame,
    and start not so wildly from my affair.

HAMLET: I am tame, sir:—pronounce.

GUILDENSTERN: The queen, your mother, in most great affliction of
    spirit, hath sent me to you.

285 HAMLET: You are welcome.

GUILDENSTERN: Nay, good my lord, this courtesy is not of the right
    breed. If it shall please you to make me a wholesome answer, I will
    do you mother's commandment: if not, your pardon and my return
    shall be the end of my business.

290 HAMLET: Sir, I cannot.

GUILDENSTERN: What, my lord?

HAMLET: Make you a wholesome answer; my wit's diseas'd: but, sir,
    such answer as I can make, you shall command; or, rather, as you
    say, my mother: therefore no more, but to the matter: my mother,

295   you say,—

ROSENCRANTZ: Then thus she says: your behavior hath struck her into
    amazement and admiration.

---

[16] *pajock:* peacock.

HAMLET: O wonderful son, that can so astonish a mother!—But is there no sequel at the heels of this mother's admiration?

300 ROSENCRANTZ: She desires to speak with you in her closet[17] ere you go to bed.

HAMLET: We shall obey, were she ten times our mother. Have you any further trade with us?

ROSENCRANTZ: My lord, you once did love me.

305 HAMLET: So I do still, by these pickers and stealers.[18]

ROSENCRANTZ: Good, my lord, what is your cause of distemper? you do, surely, bar the door upon your own liberty if you deny your griefs to your friend.

HAMLET: Sir, I lack advancement.

310 ROSENCRANTZ: How can that be, when you have the voice of the king himself for your succession in Denmark?

HAMLET: Ay, but *While the grass grows,*—the proverb is something musty.

(Re-enter the Players, with recorders.)

O, the recorders:—let me see one.—To withdraw with you:—why
315 do you go about to recover the wind of me, as if you would drive me into a toil?

GUILDENSTERN: O, my lord, if my duty be too bold, my love is too unmannerly.

HAMLET: I do not well understand that. Will you play upon this pipe?

320 GUILDENSTERN: My lord, I cannot.

HAMLET: I pray you.

GUILDENSTERN: Believe me, I cannot.

HAMLET: I do beseech you.

GUILDENSTERN: I know no touch of it, my lord.

325 HAMLET: 'Tis as easy as lying: govern these ventages[19] with your finger and thumb, give it breath with your mouth, and it will discourse most eloquent music. Look you, these are the stops.

GUILDENSTERN: But these cannot I command to any utterance of harmony; I have not the skill.

330 HAMLET: Why, look you now, how unworthy a thing you make of me! You would play upon me; you would seem to know my stops; you would pluck out the heart of my mystery; you would sound me from my lowest note to the top of my compass: and there is much music, excellent voice, in this little organ; yet cannot you make it
335 speak. 'Sblood, do you think that I am easier to be played on than a pipe? Call me what instrument you will, though you can fret me you cannot play upon me.

---

[17] *closet:* boudoir.   [18] *pickers and stealers:* fingers.   [19] *ventages:* holes.

(Enter Polonius.)

    God bless you, sir!

Polonius: My lord, the queen would speak with you, and
340   presently.

Hamlet: Do you see yonder cloud that's almost in shape of a camel?

Polonius: By the mass, and 'tis like a camel indeed.

Hamlet: Methinks it is like a weasel.

Polonius: It is backed like a weasel.

345 Hamlet: Or like a whale?

Polonius: Very like a whale.

Hamlet: Then will I come to my mother by and by.—They fool me
    to the top of my bent.—I will come by and by.

Polonius: I will say so.

350 Hamlet: By and by is easily said.

(Exit Polonius.)

    Leave me, friends.

(Exeunt Rosencrantz, Guildenstern, Horatio, and Players.)

    'Tis now the very witching time of night,
    When churchyards yawn, and hell itself breathes out
    Contagion to this world: now could I drink hot blood,
355   And do such bitter business as the day
    Would quake to look on. Soft! now to my mother.—
    O heart, lose not thy nature; let not ever
    The soul of Nero[20] enter this firm bosom:
    Let me be cruel, not unnatural:
360   I will speak daggers to her, but use none;
    My tongue and soul in this be hypocrites,—
    How in my words soever she be shent,
    To give them seals never, my soul, consent! *(Exit.)*

Scene 3

A room in the castle.

(Enter King, Rosencrantz, and Guildenstern.)

King: I like him not; nor stands it safe with us
    To let his madness range. Therefore prepare you;
    I your commission with forthwith despatch,
    And he to England shall along with you:
5   The terms of our estate may not endure

---

[20] *soul of Nero:* Nero killed his mother, a crime of which Hamlet does not want to be guilty.

Hazard so dangerous as doth hourly grow
Out of his lunacies.
GUILDENSTERN: We will ourselves provide:
Most holy and religious fear it is
To keep those many many bodies safe
10   That live and feed upon your majesty.
ROSENCRANTZ: The single and peculiar life is bound,
With all the strength and armor of the mind,
To keep itself from 'noyance; but much more
That spirit upon whose weal depend and rest
15   The lives of many. The cease of majesty
Dies not alone; but like a gulf doth draw
What's near it with it: it is a massy wheel,
Fix'd on the summit of the highest mount,
To whose huge spokes ten thousand lesser things
20   Are mortis'd and adjoin'd; which, when it falls,
Each small annexment, petty consequence,
Attends the boisterous ruin. Never alone
Did the king sigh, but with a general groan.
KING: Arm you, I pray you, to this speedy voyage;
25   For we will fetters put upon this fear,
Which now goes too free-footed.
ROSENCRANTZ and GUILDENSTERN: We will haste us.

(Exeunt Rosencrantz and Guildenstern.)

(Enter Polonius.)

POLONIUS: My lord, he's going to his mother's closet:
Behind the arras I'll convey myself
To hear the process; I'll warrant she'll tax him home:[1]
30   And, as you said, and wisely was it said,
'Tis meet that some more audience than a mother,
Since nature makes them partial, should o'erhear
The speech, of vantage. Fare you well, my liege:
I'll call upon you ere you go to bed,
35   And tell you what I know.
KING: Thanks, dear my lord.

(Exit Polonius.)

O, my offence is rank, it smells to heaven;
It hath the primal eldest curse upon't,—
A brother's murder!—Pray can I not,
Though inclination be as sharp as will:
40   My stronger guilt defeats my strong intent;

---

[1] *tax him home:* reprove him properly.

And, like a man to double business bound,
I stand in pause where I shall first begin,
And both neglect. What if this cursed hand
Were thicker than itself with brother's blood,—
45   Is there not rain enough in the sweet heavens
To wash it white as snow? Whereto serves mercy
But to confront the visage of offence?
And what's in prayer but this twofold force,—
To be forestalled ere we come to fall,
50   Or pardon'd being down? Then I'll look up;
My fault is past. But, O, what form of prayer
Can serve my turn? Forgive me my foul murder?—
That cannot be; since I am still possess'd
Of those effects for which I did the murder,—
55   My crown, mine own ambition, and my queen.
May one be pardon'd and retain the offence?[2]
In the corrupted currents of this world
Offence's gilded hand may shove by justice;
And oft 'tis seen the wicked prize itself
60   Buys out the law: but 'tis not so above;
There is no shuffling,—there the action lies
In his true nature; and we ourselves compell'd,
Even to the teeth and forehead of our faults,
To give in evidence. What then? what rests?[3]
65   Try what repentance can: what can it not?
Yet what can it when one can not repent?
O wretched state! O bosom black as death!
O limed[4] soul, that, struggling to be free,
Art more engag'd! Help, angels! make assay:
70   Bow, stubborn knees; and, heart, with strings of steel,
Be soft as sinews of the new-born babe!
All may be well. *(Retires and kneels)*

(Enter Hamlet.)

HAMLET: Now might I do it pat, now he is praying;
And now I'll do't—and so he goes to heaven;
75   And so am I reveng'd:—that would be scann'd:
A villain kills my father; and for that,
I, his sole son, do this same villain send
To heaven.
O, this is hire and salary, not revenge.
80   He took my father grossly, full of bread;
With all his crimes broad blown, as flush as May;

---

[2] *offence:* that is, the gains won by the offense.   [3] *rests:* remains.   [4] *limed:* snared.

And how his audit stands who knows save heaven?
But in our circumstance and course of thought
'Tis heavy with him: and am I, then, reveng'd,
85 To take him in the purging of his soul,
When he is fit and season'd for his passage?
No.
Up, sword; and know thou a more horrid hent:[5]
When he is drunk, asleep, or in his rage;
90 Or in the incestuous pleasure of his bed;
At gaming, swearing; or about some act
That has no relish of salvation in't;—
Then trip him, that his heels may kick at heaven;
And that his soul may be as damn'd and black
95 As hell, whereto it goes. My mother stays:
This physic but prolongs thy sickly days. *(Exit.)*

(The King rises and advances.)

KING: My words fly up, my thoughts remain below:
Words without thoughts never to heaven go. *(Exit.)*

SCENE 4

Another room in the castle.

(Enter Queen and Polonius.)

POLONIUS: He will come straight. Look you lay home to him:
Tell him his pranks have been too broad to bear with,
And that your grace hath screen'd and stood between
Much heat and him. I'll silence me e'en here.
5 Pray you, be round with him.
HAMLET: *(Within)* Mother, mother, mother!
QUEEN: I'll warrant you:
Fear me not:—withdraw, I hear him coming.

(Polonius goes behind the arras.)

(Enter Hamlet.)

HAMLET: Now, mother, what's the matter?
QUEEN: Hamlet, thou hast thy father much offended.
10 HAMLET: Mother, you have my father much offended.
QUEEN: Come, come, you answer with an idle tongue.
HAMLET: Go, go, you question with a wicked tongue.
QUEEN: Why, how now, Hamlet!
HAMLET: What's the matter now?

---

[5] *hent:* opportunity.

QUEEN: Have you forgot me?

HAMLET: No, by the rood, not so:

15   You are the queen, your husband's brother's wife;
        And,—would it were not so!—you are my mother.

QUEEN: Nay, then, I'll set those to you that can speak.

HAMLET: Come, come, and sit you down; you shall not budge;
        You go not till I set you up a glass

20   Where you may see the inmost part of you.

QUEEN: What wilt thou do? thou wilt not murder me?—
        Help, help, ho!

POLONIUS: *(Behind)* What, ho! help, help, help!

HAMLET: How now! a rat? *(Draws)*
        Dead, for a ducat, dead! *(Makes a pass through the arras)*

25 POLONIUS: *(Behind)* O, I am slain! *(Falls and dies.)*

QUEEN: O me, what hast thou done?

HAMLET: Nay, I know not:
        Is it the king? *(Draws forth Polonius)*

QUEEN: O, what a rash and bloody deed is this!

HAMLET: A bloody deed!—almost as bad, good mother,

30   As kill a king and marry with his brother.

QUEEN: As kill a king!

HAMLET: Ay, lady, 'twas my word.—
        Thou wretched, rash, intruding fool, farewell! *(To Polonius)*
        I took thee for thy better: take thy fortune;
        Thou find'st to be too busy is some danger.—

35   Leave wringing of your hands: peace; sit you down,
        And let me wring your heart: for so I shall,
        If it be made of penetrable stuff;
        If damned custom have not braz'd it so
        That it is proof and bulwark against sense.

40 QUEEN: What have I done, that thou dar'st wag thy tongue
        In noise so rude against me?

HAMLET: Such an act
        That blurs the grace and blush of modesty;
        Calls virtue hypocrite; takes off the rose
        From the fair forehead of an innocent love,

45   And sets a blister there; makes marriage-vows
        As false as dicers' oaths: O, such a deed
        As from the body of contraction plucks
        The very soul, and sweet religion makes
        A rhapsody of words: heaven's face doth glow;

50   Yea, this solidity and compound mass,
        With tristful[1] visage, as against the doom,
        Is thought-sick at the act.

---

[1] *tristful:* gloomy.

QUEEN: Ah me, what act,
That roars so loud, and thunders in the index?
HAMLET: Look here upon this picture and on this,—
55   The counterfeit presentment of two brothers.
See what grace was seated on this brow;
Hyperion's curls; the front of Jove himself;
An eye like Mars, to threaten and command;
A station like the herald Mercury
60   New-lighted on a heaven-kissing hill;
A combination and a form, indeed,
Where every god did seem to set his seal,
To give the world assurance of a man:
This was your husband.—Look you now, what follows:
65   Here is your husband, like a mildew'd ear
Blasting his wholesome brother. Have you eyes?
Could you on this fair mountain leave to feed,
And batten on this moor? Ha! have you eyes?
You cannot call it love; for at your age
70   The hey-day in the blood is tame, it's humble,
And waits upon the judgment: and what judgment
Would step from this to this? Sense, sure, you have,
Else could you not have motion: but sure that sense
Is apoplex'd: for madness would not err;
75   Nor sense to ecstasy was ne'er so thrill'd
But it reserv'd some quantity of choice
To serve in such a difference. What devil was't
That thus hath cozen'd you at hoodman-blind?[2]
Eyes without feeling, feeling without sight,
80   Ears without hand or eyes, smelling sans all,
Or but a sickly part of one true sense
Could not so mope.
O shame! where is thy blush! Rebellious hell,
If thou canst mutine in a matron's bones,
85   To flaming youth let virtue be as wax,
And melt in her own fire: proclaim no shame
When the compulsive ardor gives the charge,
Since frost itself as actively doth burn,
And reason panders[3] will.
QUEEN: O Hamlet, speak no more:
90   Thou turn'st mine eyes into my very soul;
And there I see such black and grained spots
As will not leave their tinct.[4]

---

[2] *cozen'd . . . hoodman-blind:* tricked you at blindman's bluff.   [3] *panders:* becomes subservient to.   [4] *As . . . tinct:* as will not yield up their color.

HAMLET: Nay, but to live
        In the rank sweat of an enseamed bed,
        Stew'd in corruption, honeying and making love
95   Over the nasty sty,—
QUEEN: O, speak to me no more;
        These words like daggers enter in mine ears;
        No more, sweet Hamlet.
HAMLET: A murderer and a villain;
        A slave that is not twentieth part the tithe
        Of your precedent lord; a vice of kings;[5]
100   A cutpurse of the empire and the rule,
        That from a shelf the precious diadem stole,
        And put it in his pocket!
QUEEN: No more.
HAMLET: A king of shreds and patches,—

(Enter Ghost.)

        Save me, and hover o'er me with your wings,
105   You heavenly guards!—What would your gracious figure?
QUEEN: Alas, he's mad!
HAMLET: Do you not come your tardy son to chide,
        That, laps'd in time and passion, lets go by
        The important acting of your dread command?
110   O, say!
GHOST: Do not forget: this visitation
        Is but to whet thy almost blunted purpose.
        But, look, amazement on thy mother sits:
        O, step between her and her fighting soul,—
115   Conceit in weakest bodies strongest works,—
        Speak to her, Hamlet.
HAMLET: How is it with you, lady?
QUEEN: Alas, how is't with you,
        That you do bend your eye on vacancy,
        And with the incorporal air do hold discourse?
120   Forth at your eyes your spirits wildly peep;
        And, as the sleeping soldiers in the alarm,
        Your bedded hair, like life in excrements,[6]
        Starts up and stands on end. O gentle son,
        Upon the heat and flame of thy distemper
125   Sprinkle cool patience. Whereon do you look?
HAMLET: On him, on him! Look you, how pale he glares!
        His form and cause conjoin'd, preaching to stones,

---

[5] *a vice of kings:* a buffoon among kings; the "Vice" in morality plays.   [6] *excrements:* in outgrowths or extremities.

Would make them capable.—Do not look upon me;
Lest with this piteous action you convert
130   My stern effects: then what I have to do
Will want true color; tears perchance for blood.
QUEEN: To whom do you speak this?
HAMLET: Do you see nothing there?
QUEEN: Nothing at all; yet all that is I see.
HAMLET: Nor did you nothing hear?
135 QUEEN: No, nothing but ourselves.
HAMLET: Why, look you there! look, how it steals away!
My father, in his habit as he liv'd!
Look, where he goes, even now, out at the portal!

(Exit Ghost.)

QUEEN: This is the very coinage of your brain:
140   This bodiless creation ecstasy
Is very cunning in.
HAMLET: Ecstasy!
My pulse, as yours, doth temperately keep time.
And makes as healthful music: it is not madness
That I have utter'd: bring me to the test,
145   And I the matter will re-word; which madness
Would gambol from. Mother, for love of grace,
Lay not that flattering unction to your soul,
That not your trespass, but my madness speaks:
It will but skin and film the ulcerous place,
150   Whilst rank corruption, mining all within,
Infects unseen. Confess yourself to Heaven;
Repent what's past; avoid what is to come;
And do not spread the compost on the weeds,
To make them ranker. Forgive me this my virtue;
155   For in the fatness[7] of these pursy times
Virtue itself of vice must pardon beg,
Yea, curb and woo for leave to do him good.
QUEEN: O Hamlet, thou hast cleft my heart in twain.
HAMLET: O, throw away the worser part of it,
160   And live the purer with the other half.
Good-night: but go not to mine uncle's bed;
Assume a virtue, if you have it not.
That monster custom, who all sense doth eat,
Of habits devil, is angel yet in this,—
165   That to the use of actions fair and good
He likewise gives a frock or livery

---

[7] *fatness:* corruption.

That aptly is put on. Refrain to-night;
And that shall lend a kind of easiness
To the next abstinence: the next more easy;
170 For use almost can change the stamp of nature,
And either curb the devil, or throw him out
With wondrous potency. Once more, good-night:
And when you are desirous to be bless'd,
I'll blessing beg of you.—For this same lord *(Pointing to Polonius)*
175 I do repent: but Heaven hath pleas'd it so,
To punish me with this, and this with me,
That I must be their[8] scourge and minister.
I will bestow him, and will answer well
The death I gave him. So, again, good-night.—
180 I must be cruel only to be kind:
Thus bad begins and worse remains behind.—
One word more, good lady.
QUEEN: What shall I do?
HAMLET: Not this, by no means, that I bid you do:
Let the bloat king tempt you again to bed;
185 Pinch wanton on your cheek; call you his mouse;
And let him, for a pair of reechy kisses,
Or paddling in your neck with his damn'd fingers,
Make you to ravel all this matter out,
That I essentially am not in madness,
190 But mad in craft. 'Twere good you let him know;
For who that's but a queen, fair, sober, wise,
Would from a paddock,[9] from a bat, a gib,[10]
Such dear concernings hide? who would do so?
No, in despite of sense and secrecy,
195 Unpeg the basket on the house's top,
Let the birds fly, and, like the famous ape,
To try conclusions, in the basket creep,
And break your own neck down.
QUEEN: Be thou assur'd, if words be made of breath
200 And breath of life, I have not life to breathe
What thou hast said to me.
HAMLET: I must to England; you know that?
QUEEN: Alack,
I had forgot: 'tis so concluded on.
HAMLET: There's letters seal'd: and my two school-fellows,—
205 Whom I will trust as I will adders fang'd,
They bear the mandate; they must sweep my way,
And marshal me to knavery. Let it work;

---

[8] *their:* Heaven's, or the heavens'.   [9] *paddock:* toad.   [10] *gib:* tomcat.

For 'tis the sport to have the éngineer
Hoist with his own petard: and't shall go hard
210   But I will delve one yard below their mines,
And blow them at the moon: O, 'tis most sweet,
When in one line two crafts directly meet.—
This man shall set me packing:
I'll lug the guts into the neighbor room.—
215   Mother, good-night.—Indeed, this counsellor
Is now most still, most secret, and most grave,
Who was in life a foolish prating knave.
Come, sir, to draw toward an end with you:—
Good-night, mother.

(Exeunt severally; Hamlet dragging out Polonius.)

ACT IV
SCENE 1

A room in the castle.

(Enter King, Queen, Rosencrantz, and Guildenstern.)

KING: There's matter in these sighs, these prófound heaves:
You must translate: 'tis fit we understand them.
Where is your son?
QUEEN: Bestow this place on us a little while. *(To Rosencrantz and
Guildenstern, who go out)*
5   Ah, my good lord, what have I seen to-night!
KING: What, Gertrude? How does Hamlet?
QUEEN: Mad as the sea and wind, when both contend
Which is the mightier: in his lawless fit,
Behind the arras hearing something stir,
10   He whips his rapier out, and cries, *A rat, a rat!*
And, in this brainish apprehension,[1] kills
The unseen good old man.
KING: O heavy deed!
It had been so with us had we been there:
His liberty is full of threats to all;
15   To you yourself, to us, to every one.
Alas, how shall this bloody deed be answer'd?
It will be laid to us, whose providence
Should have kept short, restrain'd, and out of haunt
This mad young man: but so much was our love,
20   We would not understand what was most fit;
But, like the owner of a foul disease,

----

[1] *brainish apprehension:* mad notion.

  To keep it from divulging, let it feed
  Even on the pith of life. Where is he gone?
QUEEN: To draw apart the body he hath kill'd:
25 O'er whom his very madness, like some ore
  Among a mineral of metals base,
  Shows itself pure; he weeps for what is done.
KING: O Gertrude, come away!
  The sun no sooner shall the mountains touch
30 But we will ship him hence: and this vile deed
  We must, with all our majesty and skill,
  Both countenance and excuse.—Ho, Guildenstern!

(Enter Rosencrantz and Guildenstern.)

  Friends both, go join you with some further aid:
  Hamlet in madness hath Polonius slain,
35 And from his mother's closet hath he dragg'd him:
  Go seek him out; speak fair, and bring the body
  Into the chapel. I pray you, haste in this.

(Exeunt Rosencrantz and Guildenstern.)

  Come, Gertrude, we'll call up our wisest friends;
  And let them know both what we mean to do
40 And what's untimely done: so haply slander,—
  Whose whisper o'er the world's diameter,
  As level as the cannon to his blank,
  Transports his poison'd shot,—may amiss our name,
  And hit the woundless air.—O, come away!
45 My soul is full of discord and dismay.

(Exeunt.)

SCENE 2

Another room in the castle.

(Enter Hamlet.)

HAMLET: Safely stowed.
ROSENCRANTZ and GUILDENSTERN: *(Within)* Hamlet! Lord Hamlet!
HAMLET: What noise? who calls on Hamlet? O, here they come.

(Enter Rosencrantz and Guildenstern.)

ROSENCRANTZ: What have you done, my lord, with the dead body?
5 HAMLET: Compounded it with dust, whereto 'tis kin.
ROSENCRANTZ: Tell us where 'tis, that we may take it thence,
  And bear it to the chapel.
HAMLET: Do not believe it.
ROSENCRANTZ: Believe what?

10 HAMLET: That I can keep your counsel, and not mine own. Besides, to
be demanded of a sponge!—what replication should be made by the
son of a king?

ROSENCRANTZ: Take you me for a sponge, my lord?

HAMLET: Ay, sir; that soaks up the king's countenance, his rewards,
15 his authorities. But such officers do the king best service in the
end: he keeps them, like an ape, in the corner of his jaw; first
mouthed, to be last swallowed: when he needs what you have
gleaned, it is but squeezing you, and, sponge, you shall be dry
again.

20 ROSENCRANTZ: I understand you not, my lord.

HAMLET: I am glad of it: a knavish speech sleeps in a foolish ear.

ROSENCRANTZ: My lord, you must tell us where the body is, and go
with us to the king.

HAMLET: The body is with the king, but the king is not with the
25 body. The king is a thing,—

GUILDENSTERN: A thing, my lord!

HAMLET: Of nothing: bring me to him. Hide fox, and all after.

(Exeunt.)

SCENE 3

Another room in the castle.

(Enter King, attended.)

KING: I have sent to seek him, and to find the body.
How dangerous is it that this man goes loose!
Yet must not we put the strong law on him:
He's lov'd of the distracted multitude,
5 Who like not in their judgment, but their eyes;
And where 'tis so, the offender's scourge is weigh'd,
But never the offence. To bear all smooth and even,
This sudden sending him away must seem
Deliberate pause: diseases desperate grown
10 By desperate appliance are reliev'd,
Or not at all.

(Enter Rosencrantz.)

How now! what hath befallen!

ROSENCRANTZ: Where the dead body is bestow'd, my lord,
We cannot get from him.

KING: But where is he?

ROSENCRANTZ: Without, my lord; guarded, to know your pleasure.

15 KING: Bring him before us.

ROSENCRANTZ: Ho, Guildenstern! bring in my lord.

(Enter Hamlet and Guildenstern.)

KING: Now, Hamlet, where's Polonius?

HAMLET: At supper.

KING: At supper! where?

HAMLET: Not where he eats, but where he is eaten: a certain
20   convocation of politic worms are e'en at him. Your worm is your
    only emperor for diet: we fat all creatures else to fat us, and we fat
    ourselves for maggots: your fat king and your lean beggar is but
    variable service,—two dishes, but to one table: that's the end.

KING: Alas, alas!

25 HAMLET: A man may fish with the worm that hath eat of a king, and
    eat of the fish that hath fed of that worm.

KING: What does thou mean by this?

HAMLET: Nothing but to show you how a king may go a progress
    through the guts of a beggar.

30 KING: Where is Polonius?

HAMLET: In heaven; send thither to see: if your messenger find him
    not there, seek him i' the other place yourself. But, indeed, if you
    find him not within this month, you shall nose him as you go up
    the stairs into the lobby.

35 KING: Go seek him there. *(To some Attendants)*

HAMLET: He will stay till ye come.

(Exeunt Attendants.)

KING: Hamlet, this deed, for thine especial safety,—
    Which we do tender, as we dearly grieve
    For that which thou hast done,—must send thee hence
40   With fiery quickness: therefore prepare thyself;
    The bark is ready, and the wind at help,
    The associates tend, and everything is bent
    For England.

HAMLET: For England!

KING: Ay, Hamlet.

HAMLET: Good.

KING: So is it, if thou knew'st our purposes.

45 HAMLET: I see a cherub that sees them.—But, come; for England!—
    Farewell, dear mother.

KING: Thy loving father, Hamlet.

HAMLET: My mother: father and mother is man and wife; man and
    wife is one flesh; and so, my mother.—Come, for England! *(Exit.)*

50 KING: Follow him at foot; tempt him with speed aboard;
    Delay it not; I'll have him hence to-night:
    Away! for everything is seal'd and done
    That else leans on the affair, pray you, make haste.

(Exeunt Rosencrantz and Guildenstern.)

And, England, if my love thou hold'st at aught,—
55   As my great power thereof may give thee sense,
Since yet thy cicatrice looks raw and red
After the Danish sword, and thy free awe
Pays homage to us,—thou mayst not coldly set
Our sovereign process; which imports at full,
60   By letters conjuring to that effect,
The present death of Hamlet. Do it, England;
For like the hectic in my blood he rages,
And thou must cure me: till I know 'tis done,
Howe'er my haps, my joys will ne'er begin. *(Exit.)*

Scene 4

A plain in Denmark.

(Enter Fortinbras, and Forces marching.)

FORTINBRAS: Go, from me greet the Danish king:
Tell him that, by his license, Fortinbras
Craves the conveyance of a promis'd march
Over his kingdom. You know the rendezvous,
5   If that his majesty would aught with us,
We shall express our duty in his eye,
And let him know so.
CAPTAIN: I will do't, my lord.
FORTINBRAS: Go softly on.

(Exeunt Fortinbras and Forces.)

(Enter Hamlet, Rosencrantz, Guildenstern, &c.)

HAMLET: Good sir, whose powers are these?
10 CAPTAIN: They are of Norway, sir.
HAMLET: How purpos'd, sir, I pray you?
CAPTAIN: Against some part of Poland.
HAMLET: Who commands them, sir?
CAPTAIN: The nephew to old Norway, Fortinbras.
15 HAMLET: Goes it against the main of Poland, sir,
Or for some frontier?
CAPTAIN: Truly to speak, and with no addition,
We go to gain a little patch of ground
That hath in it no profit but the name.
20   To pay five ducats, five, I would not farm it;
Nor will it yield to Norway or the Pole
A ranker[1] rate should it be sold in fee.

---

[1] *ranker:* dearer.

HAMLET: Why, then the Polack never will defend it.
CAPTAIN: Yes, it is already garrison'd.
25 HAMLET: Two thousand souls and twenty thousand ducats
    Will not debate the question of this straw:
    This is the imposthume² of much wealth and peace,
    That inward breaks, and shows no cause without
    Why the man dies.—I humbly thank you, sir.
30 CAPTAIN: God b' wi' you, sir. *(Exit.)*
ROSENCRANTZ: Will't please you go, my lord?
HAMLET: I'll be with you straight. Go a little before.

(Exeunt all but Hamlet.)

    How all occasions do inform against me,
    And spur my dull revenge! What is a man,
35 If his chief good and market of his time
    Be but to sleep and feed? a beast, no more.
    Sure he that made us with such large discourse,³
    Looking before and after, gave us not
    That capability and godlike reason
40 To fust⁴ in us unus'd. Now, whether it be
    Bestial oblivion or some craven scruple
    Of thinking too precisely on the event,—
    A thought which, quarter'd, hath but one part wisdom
    And ever three parts coward,—I do not know
45 Why yet I live to say, *This thing's to do;*
    Sith⁵ I have cause, and will, and strength, and means
    To do't. Examples, gross as earth, exhort me:
    Witness this army, of such mass and charge,
    Led by a delicate and tender prince;
50 Whose spirit, with divine ambition puff'd,
    Makes mouths at the invisible event;
    Exposing what is mortal and unsure
    To all that fortune, death, and danger dare,
    Even for an egg-shell. Rightly to be great
55 Is not to stir without great argument,
    But greatly to find quarrel in a straw
    When honor's at the stake. How stand I, then,
    That have a father kill'd, a mother stain'd,
    Excitements of my reason and my blood,
60 And let all sleep? while, to my shame, I see
    The imminent death of twenty thousand men,
    That, for a fantasy and trick of fame,
    Go to their graves like beds; fight for a plot

---

²*imposthume:* ulcer.   ³*discourse:* reasoning faculty.   ⁴*fust:* grow musty.   ⁵*Sith:* since.

Whereon the numbers cannot try the cause,
65   Which is not tomb enough and continent[6]
To hide the slain?—O, from this time forth,
My thoughts be bloody, or be nothing worth! *(Exit.)*

SCENE 5

Elsinore. A room in the castle.

(Enter Queen and Horatio.)

QUEEN: I will not speak with her.
HORATIO: She is importunate; indeed, distract:
    Her mood will needs be pitied.
QUEEN: What would she have?
HORATIO: She speaks much of her father; says she hears
5   There's tricks i' the world; and hems, and beats her heart;
    Spurns enviously at straws; speaks things in doubt,
    That carry but half sense: her speech is nothing,
    Yet the unshapéd use of it doth move
    The hearers to collection; they aim at it,
10   And botch the words up fit to their own thoughts;
    Which, as her winks, and nods, and gestures yield them,
    Indeed would make one think there might be thought,
    Though nothing sure, yet much unhappily.
    'Twere good she were spoken with; for she may strew
15   Dangerous conjectures in ill-breeding minds.
QUEEN: Let her come in.

(Exit Horatio.)

    To my sick soul, as sin's true nature is,
    Each toy seems prologue to some great amiss:
    So full of artless jealousy is guilt,
20   It spills itself in fearing to be spilt.

(Re-enter Horatio and Ophelia.)

OPHELIA: Where is the beauteous majesty of Denmark?
QUEEN: How now, Ophelia!
OPHELIA: *(Sings)*

How should I your true love know
From another one?
25   By his cockle hat and staff,
And his sandal shoon.

QUEEN: Alas, sweet lady, what imports this song?
OPHELIA: Say you? nay, pray you, mark.

---

[6]*continent:* container.

(Sings)

He is dead and gone, lady,
        He is dead and gone;
At his head a grass green turf,
        At his heels a stone.

QUEEN: Nay, but, Ophelia,—
OPHELIA: Pray you, mark.

(Sings)

White his shroud as the mountain snow,

(Enter King.)

35 QUEEN: Alas, look here, my lord.
OPHELIA: *(Sings)*

                Larded with sweet flowers;
Which bewept to the grave did go
        With true-love showers.

KING: How do you, pretty lady?
40 OPHELIA: Well, God 'ild[1] you! They say the owl was a baker's daughter.
    Lord, we know what we are, but know not what we may be.
    God be at your table!
KING: Conceit upon her father.
OPHELIA: Pray you, let's have no words of this; but when they ask
45   you what it means, say you this:

(Sings.)

To-morrow is Saint Valentine's day
    All in the morning betime,
And I a maid at your window,
    To be your Valentine.

50 Then up he rose, and donn'd his clothes,
        And dupp'd the chamber-door;
    Let in the maid, that out a maid
        Never departed more.

KING: Pretty Ophelia!
55 OPHELIA: Indeed, la, without an oath, I'll make an end on't;

(Sings)

By Gis[2] and by Saint Charity,
    Alack, and fie for shame!
Young men will do't, if they come to't;
    By cock, they are to blame.

---

[1] *'ild:* yield you—that is, reward you.   [2] *By Gis:* a contraction for "by Jesus."

60   Quoth she, before you tumbled me,
             You promis'd me to wed.
         So would I ha' done, by yonder sun,
             An thou hadst not come to my bed.

KING: How long hath she been thus?

65 OPHELIA: I hope all will be well. We must be patient: but I cannot
        choose but weep, to think they should lay him i' the cold ground.
        My brother shall know of it: and so I thank you; for your good
        counsel.—Come, my coach!—Good-night, ladies; good-night,
        sweet ladies; good-night, good-night. *(Exit.)*

70 KING: Follow her close; give her good watch, I pray you.

(Exit Horatio.)

     O, this is the poison of deep grief; it springs
     All from her father's death. O Gertrude, Gertrude,
     When sorrows come, they come not single spies,
     But in battalions! First, her father slain:
75   Next, your son gone; and he most violent author
     Of his own just remove: the people muddied,
     Thick and unwholesome in their thoughts and whispers
     For good Polonius' death; and we have done but greenly
     In hugger-mugger[3] to inter him: poor Ophelia
80   Divided from herself and her fair judgment,
     Without the which we are pictures, or mere beasts:
     Last, and as much containing as all these,
     Her brother is in secret come from France;
     Feeds on his wonder, keeps himself in clouds,
85   And wants not buzzers to infect his ear
     With pestilent speeches of his father's death;
     Wherein necessity, of matter beggar'd,
     Will nothing stick our person to arraign
     In ear and ear. O my dear Gertrude, this,
90   Like to a murdering piece,[4] in many places
     Gives me superfluous death.

(A noise within.)

QUEEN: Alack, what noise is this?
KING: Where are my Switzers?[5] let them guard the door.

(Enter a Gentleman.)

     What is the matter?

---

[3] *In hugger-mugger:* in great secrecy and haste. [4] *piece:* a cannon. [5] *Switzers:* bodyguard of Swiss mercenaries.

GENTLEMAN: Save yourself, my lord:
The ocean, overpeering of his list,
95   Eats not the flats with more impetuous haste
Than young Laertes, in a riotous head,
O'erbears your officers. The rabble call him lord;
And, as the world were now but to begin,
Antiquity forgot, custom not known,
100   The ratifiers and props of every word,
They cry, *Choose we, Laertes shall be king!*
Caps, hands, and tongues applaud it to the clouds,
Laertes shall be king, Laertes king!
QUEEN: How cheerfully on the false trail they cry!
105   O, this is counter, you false Danish dogs!
KING: The doors are broke.

(Noise within.)

(Enter Laertes armed; Danes following.)

LAERTES: Where is this king?—Sirs, stand you all without.
DANES: No, let's come in.
LAERTES: I pray you, give me leave.
DANES: We will, we will. *(They retire without the door.)*
110 LAERTES: I thank you:—keep the door.—O thou vile king,
Give me my father!
QUEEN: Calmly, good Laertes.
LAERTES: That drop of blood that's calm proclaims me bastard;
Cries cuckold to my father; brands the harlot
Even here, between the chaste unsmirched brow
115   Of my true mother.
KING: What is the cause, Laertes,
That thy rebellion looks so giant-like?—
Let him go, Gertrude; do not fear our person:
There's such divinity doth hedge a king,
That treason can but peep to what it would,
120   Acts little of his will.—Tell me, Laertes,
Why thou art thus incens'd.—Let him go, Gertrude:—
Speak, man.
LAERTES: Where is my father?
KING: Dead.
QUEEN: But not by him.
KING: Let him demand his fill.
125 LAERTES: How came he dead? I'll not be juggled with:
To hell, allegiance! vows, to the blackest devil!
Conscience and grace, to the profoundest pit!
I dare damnation:—to this point I stand,—
That both the worlds I give to negligence,

130   Let come what comes; only I'll be reveng'd
       Most thoroughly for my father.
KING: Who shall stay you?
LAERTES: My will, not all the world:
       And for my means, I'll husband them so well,
       They shall go far with little.
KING: Good Laertes,
135   If you desire to know the certainty
       Of your dear father's death, is't writ in your revenge
       That, sweepstake, you will draw both friend and foe,
       Winner or loser?
LAERTES: None but his enemies.
KING: Will you know them, then?
140 LAERTES: To his good friends thus wide I'll ope my arms;
       And, like the kind life-rendering pelican,[6]
       Repast them with my blood.
KING: Why, now you speak
       Like a good child and a true gentleman.
       That I am guiltless of your father's death,
145   And am most sensible in grief for it,
       It shall as level to your judgment pierce
       As day does to your eye.
DANES: *(Within)*   Let her come in.
LAERTES: How now! what noise is that?

(Re-enter Ophelia, fantastically dressed with straws and flowers.)

       O heat, dry up my brains! tears seven times salt
150   Burn out the sense and virtue of mine eyes!—
       By heaven, thy madness shall be paid by weight
       Till our scale turn the beam. O rose of May!
       Dear maid, kind sister, sweet Ophelia!—
       O heavens! is't possible a young maid's wits
155   Should be as mortal as an old man's life!
       Nature is fine in love; and where 'tis fine
       It sends some precious instance of itself
       After the thing it loves.
OPHELIA: *(Sings)*

                They bore him barefac'd on the bier;
160   Hey no nonny, nonny, hey nonny;
                And on his grave rain'd many a tear,—
                  Fare you well, my dove!

---

[6] *life-rendering pelican:* the pelican mother was believed to draw blood from itself to feed its young.

LAERTES: Hadst thou thy wits, and didst persuade revenge,
      It could not move thus.

165 OPHELIA: You must sing, *Down-a-down, an you call him a-down-a.* O,
      how the wheel becomes it! It is the false steward, that stole his
      master's daughter.

LAERTES: This nothing's more than matter.

OPHELIA: There's rosemary, that's for remembrance; pray, love,
170   remember: and there is pansies that's for thoughts.

LAERTES: A document in madness,—thoughts and remembrance fitted.

OPHELIA: There's fennel for you, and columbines:—there's rue for
      you; and here's some for me:—we may call it herb-grace o' Sundays:—
      O, you must wear your rue with a difference.—There's a
175   daisy:—I would give you some violets, but they withered all when
      my father died:—they say, he made a good end,—

(Sings)

      For bonny sweet Robin is all my joy,—

LAERTES: Thoughts and affliction, passion, hell itself,
      She turns to favor and to prettiness.

OPHELIA: *(Sings)*
180   And will he not come again?
                    And will he not come again?
                         No, no, he is dead,
                         Go to thy death-bed,
                    He never will come again.

185   His beard was as white as snow
                    All flaxen was his poll:
                         He is gone, he is gone,
                         And we cast away moan:
                    God ha' mercy on his soul!

190   And of all Christian souls, I pray God.—God b' wi' ye. *(Exit.)*

LAERTES: Do you see this, O God?

KING: Laertes, I must commune with your grief,
      Or you deny me right. Go but apart,
      Make choice of whom your wisest friends you will,
195   And they shall hear and judge 'twixt you and me:
      If by direct or by collateral hand
      They find us touch'd, we will our kingdom give,
      Our crown, our life, and all that we call ours,
      To you in satisfaction; but if not,
200   Be you content to lend your patience to us,
      And we shall jointly labor with your soul
      To give it due content.

LAERTES: Let this be so;
His means of death, his obscure burial,—
No trophy, sword, nor hatchment[7] o'er his bones
205 No noble rite nor formal ostentation,—
Cry to be heard, as 'twere from heaven to earth,
That I must call't in question.
KING: So you shall;
And where the offence is, let the great axe fall.
I pray you, go with me.

(Exeunt.)

SCENE 6

Another room in the castle.

(Enter Horatio and a Servant.)

HORATIO: What are they that would speak with me?
SERVANT: Sailors, sir: they say they have letters for you.
HORATIO: Let them come in.—

(Exit Servant.)

I do not know from what part of the world
5 I should be greeted, if not from Lord Hamlet.

(Enter Sailors.)

1ST SAILOR: God bless you, sir.
HORATIO: Let him bless thee too.
1ST SAILOR: He shall, sir, an't please him. There's a letter for you, sir;
it comes from the ambassador that was bound for England; if your
10 name be Horatio, as I am let to know it is.
HORATIO: *(Reads) Horatio, when thou shalt have overlooked this, give these
fellows some means to the king: they have letters for him. Ere we were
two days old at sea, a pirate of very warlike appointment gave us chase.
Finding ourselves too slow of sail, we put on a compelled valor; and in
15 he grapple I boarded them; on the instant they got clear of our ship; so I
alone became their prisoner. They have dealt with me like thieves of
mercy: but they knew what they did; I am to do a good turn for them.
Let the king have the letters I have sent; and repair thou to me with as
much haste as thou wouldst fly death. I have words to speak in thine ear
20 will make thee dumb; yet are they much too light for the bore of the
matter. These good fellows will bring thee where I am. Rosencrantz and
Guildenstern hold their course for England: of them I have much to tell
thee. Farewell. He that thou knowest thine.* Hamlet

---

[7] *hatchment:* a tablet with coat of arms.

Come, I will give you way for these your letters;
25   And do't the speedier, that you may direct me
        To him from whom you brought them.

(Exeunt.)

Another room in the castle.

(Enter King and Laertes.)

KING: Now must your conscience my acquittance seal,
        And you must put me in your heart for friend,
        Sith you have heard, and with a knowing ear,
        That he which hath your noble father slain
5   Pursu'd my life.
LAERTES: It well appears:—but tell me
        Why you proceeded not against these feats,
        So crimeful and so capital in nature.
        As by your safety, wisdom, all things else,
        You mainly were stirr'd up.
KING: O, for two special reasons;
10   Which may to you, perhaps, seem much unsinew'd,
        But yet to me they are strong. The queen his mother
        Lives almost by his looks; and for myself,—
        My virtue or my plague, be it either which,—
        She's so conjunctive to my life and soul,
15   That, as the star moves not but in his sphere,
        I could not but by her. The other motive,
        Why to a public count I might not go,
        Is the great love the general gender bear him;
        Who, dipping all his faults in their affection,
20   Would, like the spring that turneth wood to stone,
        Convert his gyves to graces; so that my arrows,
        Too slightly timber'd for so loud a wind,
        Would have reverted to my bow again,
        And not where I had aim'd them.
25 LAERTES: And so have I a noble father lost;
        A sister driven into desperate terms,—
        Whose worth, if praises may go back again,
        Stood challenger on mount of all the age
        For her perfections:—but my revenge will come.
30 KING: Break not your sleeps for that: you must not think
        That we are made of stuff so flat and dull
        That we can let our beard be shook with danger,
        And think it pastime. You shortly shall hear more:

I lov'd your father, and we love ourself;
35 And that, I hope, will teach you to imagine,—

(Enter a Messenger.)

How now! what news?
MESSENGER: Letters, my lord, from Hamlet:
This to your majesty; this to the queen.
KING: From Hamlet! Who brought them?
MESSENGER: Sailors, my lord, they say; I saw them not:
40 They were given me by Claudio,—he receiv'd them
Of him that brought them.
KING: Laertes, you shall hear them.—Leave us.

(Exit Messenger.)

(Reads) High and mighty,—You shall know I am set naked on your
kingdom. To-morrow shall I beg leave to see your kingly eyes: when I shall,
45 *first asking your pardon thereunto, recount the occasions of my sudden*
and more strange return. Hamlet
What should this mean? Are all the rest come back?
Or is it some abuse,[1] and no such thing?
LAERTES: Know you the hand?
50 KING: 'Tis Hamlet's character:[2]—*Naked,*—
And in a postscript here, he says, *alone.*
Can you advise me?
LAERTES: I am lost in it, my lord. But let him come;
It warms the very sickness in my heart,
55 That I shall live, and tell him to his teeth,
Thus diddest thou.
KING: If it be so, Laertes,—
As how should it be so? how otherwise?—
Will you be rul'd by me?
LAERTES: Ay, my lord:
So you will not o'errule me to a peace.
60 KING: To thine own peace. If he be now return'd,—
As checking at his voyage, and that he means
No more to undertake it,—I will work him
To an exploit, now ripe in my device,
Under the which he shall not choose but fall:
65 And for his death no wind of blame shall breathe;
But even his mother shall uncharge the practice
And call it accident.

---

[1] *abuse:* ruse.   [2] *character:* handwriting.

LAERTES: My lord, I will be rul'd;
          The rather if you could devise it so
          That I might be the organ.
KING: It falls right.
70   You have been talk'd of since your travel much,
          And that in Hamlet's hearing, for a quality
          Wherein they say you shine: your sum of parts
          Did not together pluck such envy from him
          As did that one; and that, in my regard,
75   Of the unworthiest siege.
LAERTES: What part is that, my lord?
KING: A very riband in the cap of youth,
          Yet needful too; for youth no less becomes
          The light and careless livery that it wears
          Than settled age his sables and his weeds,
80   Importing health and graveness.—Two months since,
          Here was a gentleman of Normandy,—
          I've seen myself, and serv'd against, the French,
          And they can well on horseback: but this gallant
          Had witchcraft in't; he grew unto his seat;
85   And to such wondrous doing brought his horse,
          As he had been incorps'd and demi-natur'd[3]
          With the brave beast: so far he topp'd my thought,
          That I, in forgery of shapes and tricks,[4]
          Come short of what he did.
LAERTES: A Norman was't?
90 KING: A Norman.
LAERTES: Upon my life, Lamond.
KING: The very same.
LAERTES: I know him well: he is the brooch, indeed,
          And gem of all the nation.
KING: He made confession of you;
95   And gave you such a masterly report
          For art and exercise in your defence,
          And for your rapier most especially,
          That he cried out, 'twould be a sight indeed
          If one could match you: the scrimers[5] of their nation,
100   He swore, had neither motion, guard, nor eye,
          If you oppos'd them. Sir, this report of his
          Did Hamlet so envenom with his envy,
          That he could nothing do but wish and beg
          Your sudden coming o'er, to play with him.
105   Now, out of this,—

---

[3] *incorps'd and demi-natur'd:* made as one body and formed into half man, half horse—
or centaur.   [4] *in . . . tricks:* in imagining tricks of horsemanship.   [5] *scrimers:* fencers.

LAERTES: What out of this, my lord?
KING: Laertes, was your father dear to you?
     Or are you like the painting of a sorrow,
     A face without a heart?
LAERTES: Why ask you this?
KING: Not that I think you did not love your father;
110   But that I know love is begun by time;
     And that I see, in passages of proof,[6]
     Time qualifies the spark and fire of it.
     There lives within the very flame of love
     A kind of wick or snuff that will abate it;
115   And nothing is at a like goodness still;
     For goodness, growing to a pleurisy,[7]
     Dies in his own too much: that we would do
     We should do when we would; for this *would* changes,
     And hath abatements and delays as many
120   As there are tongues, or hands, or accidents;
     And then this *should* is like a spendthrift sigh
     That hurts by easing. But to the quick o' the ulcer:
     Hamlet comes back: what would you undertake
     To show yourself your father's son in deed
125   More than in words?
LAERTES: To cut his throat i' the church.
KING: No place, indeed, should murder sanctuarize;
     Revenge should have no bounds. But, good Laertes,
     Will you do this, keep close within your chamber.
     Hamlet return'd shall know you are come home:
130   We'll put on those shall praise your excellence,
     And set a double varnish on the fame
     The Frenchman gave you; bring you, in fine, together,
     And wager on your heads: he, being remiss,[8]
     Most generous, and free from all contriving,
135   Will not peruse the foils; so that, with ease,
     Or with a little shuffling, you may choose
     A sword unbated, and, in a pass of practice,
     Requite him for your father.
LAERTES: I will do't it:
     And, for that purpose, I'll anoint my sword.
140   I bought an unction of a mountebank,
     So mortal that but dip a knife in it,
     Where it draws blood no cataplasm so rare,[9]
     Collected from all simples that have virtue

---

[6] *passages of proof:* the evidence of experience.   [7] *pleurisy:* plethora, an excess of blood.
[8] *remiss:* unguarded and free from suspicion.   [9] *Where . . . rare:* no poultice, however remarkably efficacious.

Under the moon, can save the thing from death
145   That is but scratch'd withal: I'll touch my point
With this contagion, that, if I gall him slightly,
It may be death.

KING: Let's further think of this;
Weigh what convenience both of time and means
May fit us to our shape: if this should fail,
150   And that our drift look through our bad performance,
'Twere better not assay'd: therefore this project
Should have a back or second, that might hold
If this should blast in proof. Soft! let me see:—
We'll make a solemn wager on your cunnings,—
155   I ha't:
When in your motion you are hot and dry,—
As make your bouts more violent to that end,—
And that he calls for drink, I'll have prepar'd him
A chalice for the nonce;[10] whereon but sipping,
160   If he by chance escape your venom'd stuck
Our purpose may hold there.

(Enter Queen.)

How now, sweet queen!
QUEEN: One woe doth tread upon another's heel,
So fast they follow:—your sister's drown'd, Laertes.
LAERTES: Drown'd! O, where?
165   QUEEN: There is a willow grows aslant a brook,
That shows his hoar leaves in the glassy stream;
There with fantastic garlands did she come
Of crowflowers, nettles, daisies, and long purples,
That liberal shepherds give a grosser name,
170   But our cold maids do dead men's fingers call them.
There, on the pendant boughs her coronet weeds
Clambering to hang, an envious[11] sliver broke;
When down her weedy trophies and herself
Fell in the weeping brook. Her clothes spread wide;
175   And, mermaid-like, awhile they bore her up:
Which time she chanted snatches of old tunes;
As one incapable of her own distress,
Or like a creature native and indu'd
Unto that element: but long it could not be
180   Till that her garments, heavy with their drink,
Pull'd the poor wretch from her melodious lay
To muddy death.
LAERTES: Alas, then, she is drown'd?

---

[10] *nonce:* purpose.   [11] *envious:* malicious.

QUEEN: Drown'd, drown'd.

LAERTES: Too much of water hast thou, poor Ophelia,

185   And therefore I forbid my tears: but yet
      It is our trick; nature her custom holds,
      Let shame say what it will: when these are gone,
      The woman will be out.[12]—Adieu, my lord:
      I have a speech of fire, that fain would blaze,
190   But that this folly douts it.[13] *(Exit.)*

KING: Let's follow, Gertrude;
      How much I had to do to calm his rage!
      Now fear I this will give it start again;
      Therefore let's follow.

(Exeunt.)

ACT V
SCENE 1

A churchyard.

(Enter two Clowns[1] with spades, &c.)

1ST CLOWN: Is she to be buried in Christian burial that wilfully seeks
   her own salvation?

2ND CLOWN: I tell thee she is; and therefore make her grave straight:
   the crowner[2] hath sat on her, and finds it Christian burial.

5 1ST CLOWN: How can that be, unless she drowned herself in her own
   defence?

2ND CLOWN: Why, 'tis found so.

1ST CLOWN: It must be *se offendendo*,[3] it cannot be else. For here lies
   the point: if I drown myself wittingly, it argues an act: and an act
10   hath three branches; it is to act, to do, and to perform: argal,[4] she
   drowned herself wittingly.

2ND CLOWN: Nay, but hear you, goodman delver,—

1ST CLOWN: Give me leave. Here lies the water; good: here stands the
   man; good: if the man go to this water and drown himself, it is,
15   will he, nill he, he goes,—mark you that: but if the water come to
   him and drown him, he drowns not himself: argal, he that is not
   guilty of his own death shortens not his own life.

2ND CLOWN: But is this law?

1ST CLOWN: Ay, marry, is't; crowner's quest law.

20 2ND CLOWN: Will you ha' the truth on't? If this had not been a
   gentlewoman she should have been buried out of Christian burial.

---

[12] *The . . . out:* that is, "I shall be ruthless."   [13] *douts it:* drowns it.

---

[1] *Clowns:* rustic fellows.   [2] *crowner:* coroner.   [3] *se offendendo:* in self-offense; he means
se defendendo, in self-defense.   [4] *argal:* he means *ergo,* therefore.

1ST CLOWN: Why, there thou say'st: and the more pity that great folks
should have countenance in this world to drown or hang themselves
more than their even-Christian.[5]—Come, my spade. There is
25 no ancient gentlemen but gardeners, ditchers, and grave-makers;
they hold up Adam's profession.

2ND CLOWN: Was he a gentleman?

1ST CLOWN: He was the first that ever bore arms.

2ND CLOWN: Why, he had none.

30 1ST CLOWN: What, art a heathen? How dost thou understand the
Scripture? The Scripture says, Adam digged: could he dig without
arms? I'll put another question to thee: if thou answerest me not
to the purpose, confess thyself,[6]—

2ND CLOWN: Go to.

35 1ST CLOWN: What is he that builds stronger than either the mason,
the shipwright, or the carpenter?

2ND CLOWN: The gallows-maker; for that frame outlives a thousand
tenants.

1ST CLOWN: I like thy wit well, in good faith: the gallows does well;
40 but how does it well? it does well to those that do ill: now thou
dost ill to say the gallows is built stronger than the church: argal,
the gallows may do well to thee. To't again, come.

2ND CLOWN: Who builds stronger than a mason, a shipwright, or a
carpenter?

45 1ST CLOWN: Ay, tell me that, and unyoke.

2ND CLOWN: Marry, now I can tell.

1ST CLOWN: To't.

2ND CLOWN: Mass, I cannot tell.

(Enter Hamlet and Horatio, at a distance.)

1ST CLOWN: Cudgel thy brains no more about it, for your dull ass will
50 not mend his pace with beating; and when you are asked this
question next, say a grave-maker; the houses that he makes last till
doomsday. Go, get thee to Yaughan: fetch me a stoup of liquor.

(Exit Second Clown.)

(Digs and sings.)

> In youth, when I did love, did love,
> Methought it was very sweet,
55 > To contract, O, the time, for, ah, my behove,[7]
> O, methought there was nothing meet.

HAMLET: Has this fellow no feeling of his business, that he sings at
grave-making?

---

[5] *even-Christian:* fellow Christian.   [6] *confess thyself:* "Confess thyself an ass," perhaps.
[7] *behove:* behoof, or advantage.

HORATIO: Custom hath made it in him a property of easiness.

60 HAMLET: 'Tis e'en so: the hand of little employment hath the daintier sense.

1ST CLOWN: *(Sings)*

> But age, with his stealing steps,
> Hath claw'd me in his clutch,
> And hath shipp'd me intil the land,
65 > As if I had never been such.

(Throws up a skull)

HAMLET: That skull had a tongue in it, and could sing once: how the knave joels[8] it to the ground, as if it were Cain's jawbone, that did the first murder! This might be the pate of a politician, which this ass now o'erreaches; one that would circumvent God, might it not?

70 HORATIO: It might, my lord.

HAMLET: Or of a courtier; which could say, *Good-morrow, sweet lord! How dost thou, good lord?* This might be my lord such-a-one, that praised my lord such-a-one's horse, when he meant to beg it,— might it not?

75 HORATIO: Ay, my lord.

HAMLET: Why, e'en so: and now my Lady Worm's; chapless,[9] and knocked about the mazard[10] with a sexton's spade: here's fine revolution, an we had the trick to see't. Did these bones cost no more the breeding but to play at loggats[11] with 'em? Mine ache
80 to think on't.

1ST CLOWN: *(Sings)*

> A pick-axe and a spade, a spade,
> For and a shrouding sheet:
> O, a pit of clay for to be made
> For such a guest is meet.

(Throws up another.)

85 HAMLET: There's another: why may not that be the skull of a lawyer? Where be his quiddits[12] now, his quillets,[13] his cases, his tenures, and his tricks? why does he suffer this rude knave now to knock him about the sconce with a dirty shovel, and will not tell him of his action of battery? Hum! This fellow might be in's time a great
90 buyer of land, with his statutes, his recognizances, his fines, his double vouchers, his recoveries: is this the fine of his fines, and the recovery of his recoveries, to have his fine pate full of fine dirt? will his vouchers vouch him no more of his purchases, and double ones too, than the length and breadth of a pair of indentures? The

---

[8]*joels:* throws.　[9]*chapless:* without a lower jaw.　[10]*mazard:* head.　[11]*loggats:* a game in which small pieces of wood are hurled at a stake.　[12]*quiddits:* "whatnesses"—that is, hair-splittings.　[13]*quillets:* quibbling distinctions.

95   very conveyances of his lands will hardly lie in this box; and must
    the inheritor himself have no more, ha?

HORATIO: Not a jot more, my lord.

HAMLET: Is not parchment made of sheep-skins?

HORATIO: Ay, my lord, and of calf-skins too.

100 HAMLET: They are sheep and calves which seek out assurance in that.
    I will speak to this fellow.—Whose grave's this, sir?

1ST CLOWN: Mine, sir.—*(Sings)*

> O, a pit of clay for to be made
> For such a guest is meet.

105 HAMLET: I think it be thine indeed; for thou liest in't.

1ST CLOWN: You lie out on't, sir, and therefore it is not yours: for my
    part, I do not lie in't, and yet it is mine.

HAMLET: Thou dost lie in't, to be in't, and say it is thine: 'tis for the
    dead, not for the quick; therefore thou liest.

110 1ST CLOWN: 'Tis a quick lie, sir: 'twill away again from me to you.

HAMLET: What man dost thou dig it for?

1ST CLOWN: For no man, sir.

HAMLET: What woman, then?

1ST CLOWN: For none, neither.

115 HAMLET: Who is to be buried in't?

1ST CLOWN: One that was a woman, sir; but, rest her soul, she's dead.

HAMLET: How absolute the knave is! we must speak by the card, or
    equivocation will undo us. By the Lord, Horatio, these three years I
    have taken note of it; the age is grown so picked[14] that the toe of
120   the peasant comes so near the heel of the courtier, he galls his
    kibe.[15]—How long hast thou been a grave-maker?

1ST CLOWN: Of all the days i' the year, I came to't that day that our
    last King Hamlet o'ercame Fortinbras.

HAMLET: How long is that since?

125 1ST CLOWN: Cannot you tell that? every fool can tell that: it was the
    very day that young Hamlet was born,—he that is mad, and sent
    into England.

HAMLET: Ay, marry, why was he sent into England?

1ST CLOWN: Why, because he was mad: he shall recover his wits there;
130   or, if he do not, it's no great matter there.

HAMLET: Why?

1ST CLOWN: 'Twill not be seen in him there; there the men are as mad
    as he.

HAMLET: How came he mad?

135 1ST CLOWN: Very strangely, they say.

HAMLET: How strangely?

---

[14] *picked:* refined or educated.   [15] *he . . . kibe:* rubs and irritates the chilblain sore on
the courtier's heel.

1ST CLOWN: Faith, e'en with losing his wits.

HAMLET: Upon what ground?

1ST CLOWN: Why, here in Denmark: I have been sexton here, man
and boy, thirty years.

HAMLET: How long will a man lie i' the earth ere he rot?

1ST CLOWN: Faith, if he be not rotten before he die,—as we have many
pocky corses now-a-days, that will scarce hold the laying in,—he
will last you some eight year or nine year: a tanner will last you nine
year.

HAMLET: Why he more than another?

1ST CLOWN: Why, sir, his hide is so tanned with his trade that he will
keep out water a great while; and your water is a sore decayer of
your whoreson dead body. Here's a skull now; this skull has lain in
the earth three-and-twenty years.

HAMLET: Whose was it?

1ST CLOWN: A whoreson mad fellow's it was: whose do you think
it was?

HAMLET: Nay, I know not.

1ST CLOWN: A pestilence on him for a mad rogue! 'a poured a flagon
of Rhenish on my head once. This same skull, sir, was Yorick's
skull, the king's jester.

HAMLET: This?

1ST CLOWN: E'en that.

HAMLET: Let me see. *(Takes the skull)*—Alas, poor Yorick!—I knew
him, Horatio; a fellow of infinite jest, of most excellent fancy: he
hath borne me on his back a thousand times; and now, how abhorred
in my imagination it is! my gorge rises at it. Here hung
those lips that I have kissed I know not how oft. Where be your
gibes now? your gambols? your songs? your flashes of merriment,
that were wont to set the table on a roar? Not one now, to mock
your own grinning? quite chap-fallen? Now get you to my lady's
chamber, and tell her, let her paint an inch thick, to this favor[16]
she must come; make her laugh at that.—Pr'ythee, Horatio, tell me
one thing.

HORATIO: What's that, my lord?

HAMLET: Dost thou think Alexander looked o' this fashion i' the earth?

HORATIO: E'en so.

HAMLET: And smelt so? pah! *(Throws down the skull)*

HORATIO: E'en so, my lord.

HAMLET: To what base uses we may return, Horatio! Why may not
imagination trace the noble dust of Alexander till he find it stopping
a bung-hole?

HORATIO: 'Twere to consider too curiously to consider so.

---

[16] *favor:* face.

180 HAMLET: No, faith, not a jot; but to follow him thither with modesty
enough, and likelihood to lead it: as thus; Alexander died, Alexander
was buried, Alexander returneth into dust; the dust is earth; of earth
we make loam; and why of that loam whereto he was converted
might they not stop a beer-barrel?

185   Imperious Caesar, dead and turn'd to clay,
          Might stop a hole to keep the wind away:
        O, that that earth which kept the world in awe
          Should patch a wall to expel the winter's flaw!—

But soft! but soft! aside.—Here comes the king.

*(Enter Priests, &c., in procession; the corpse of Ophelia, Laertes and Mourners
following; King, Queen, their Trains, &c.)*

190   The queen, the courtiers: who is that they follow?
    And with such maimed rites? This doth betoken
    The corse they follow did with desperate hand
    Fordo its own life: 'twas of some estate.
    Couch we awhile and mark. *(Retiring with Horatio)*
195 LAERTES: What ceremony else?
HAMLET: That is Laertes,
    A very noble youth: mark.
LAERTES: What ceremony else?
1ST PRIEST: Her obsequies have been as far enlarg'd
    As we have warrantise: her death was doubtful,
200   And, but that great command o'ersways the order,
    She should in ground unsanctified have lodg'd
    Till the last trumpet; for charitable prayers,
    Shards, flints, and pebbles, should be thrown on her,
    Yet here she is allowed her virgin rites,
205   Her maiden strewments, and the bringing home
    Of bell and burial.
LAERTES: Must there no more be done?
1ST PRIEST: No more be done:
    We should profane the service of the dead
    To sing a *requiem,* and such rest to her
210   As to peace-parted souls.
LAERTES: Lay her i' the earth;—
    And from her fair and unpolluted flesh
    May violets spring!—I tell thee, churlish priest,
    A ministering angel shall my sister be
    When thou liest howling.
HAMLET: What, the fair Ophelia!
215 QUEEN: Sweets to the sweet: farewell! *(Scattering flowers)*
    I hop'd thou shouldst have been my Hamlet's wife;
    I thought thy bride-bed to have deck'd, sweet maid,
    And not have strew'd thy grave.

LAERTES: O, treble woe
  Fall ten times treble on that cursed head
220 Whose wicked deed thy most ingenious sense
  Depriv'd thee of!—Hold off the earth awhile,
  Till I have caught her once more in mine arms:

(Leaps into the grave.)

  Now pile your dust upon the quick and dead,
  Till of this flat a mountain you have made,
225 To o'er-top old Pelion[17] or the skyish head
  Of blue Olympus.

HAMLET: *(Advancing)* What is he whose grief
  Bears such an emphasis? whose phrase of sorrow
  Conjures the wandering stars, and makes them stand
230 Like wonder-wounded hearers? this is I, Hamlet the
  Dane. *(Leaps into the grave)*

LAERTES: The devil take thy soul! *(Grappling with him)*

HAMLET: Thou pray'st not well.
  I pr'ythee, take thy fingers from my throat;
235 For, though I am not splenitive[18] and rash,
  Yet have I in me something dangerous,
  Which let thy wiseness fear: away thy hand.

KING: Pluck them asunder.

QUEEN: Hamlet! Hamlet!

ALL: Gentlemen,—

HORATIO: Good my lord, be quiet.

(The Attendants part them, and they come out of the grave.)

240 HAMLET: Why, I will fight with him upon this theme
  Until my eyelids will no longer wag.

QUEEN: O my son, what theme?

HAMLET: I lov'd Ophelia; forty thousand brothers
  Could not, with all their quantity of love,
245 Make up my sum.—What wilt thou do for her?

KING: O, he is mad, Laertes.

QUEEN: For love of God, forbear him.

HAMLET: 'Swounds, show me what thou'lt do:
  Woul't weep? woul't fight? woul't fast? woul't tear thyself?
250 Woul't drink up eisel?[19] eat a crocodile?
  I'll do't.—Dost thou come here to whine?
  To outface me with leaping in her grave?
  Be buried quick[20] with her, and so will I:
  And, if thou prate of mountains, let them throw
255 Millions of acres on us, till our ground,

---

[17] *Pelion:* a mountain in Greece. [18] *splenitive:* hot-tempered. [19] *eisel:* vinegar. [20] *quick:* alive.

Singeing his pate against the burning zone,[21]
Make Ossa[22] like a wart! Nay, an thou'lt mouth,
I'll rant as well as thou.

QUEEN: This is mere madness:
And thus awhile the fit will work on him;
260   Anon, as patient as the female dove,
When that her golden couplets are disclos'd,[23]
His silence will sit drooping.

HAMLET: Hear you, sir;
What is the reason that you use me thus?
I lov'd you ever: but it is no matter;
265   Let Hercules himself do what he may,
The cat will mew, and dog will have his day. *(Exit.)*

KING: I pray thee, good Horatio, wait upon him.—

(Exit Horatio.)

(To Laertes) Strengthen your patience in our last night's speech;
We'll put the matter to the present push.—
270   Good Gertrude, set some watch over your son.—
This grave shall have a living monument:
An hour of quiet shortly shall we see;
Till then, in patience our proceeding be.

(Exeunt.)

SCENE 2

A hall in the castle.

(Enter Hamlet and Horatio.)

HAMLET: So much for this, sir: now let me see the other;
You do remember all the circumstance?

HORATIO: Remember it, my lord!

HAMLET: Sir, in my heart there was a kind of fighting
5   That would not let me sleep: methought I lay
Worse than the mutines in the bilboes.[1] Rashly,
And prais'd be rashness for it,—let us know,
Our indiscretion sometimes serves us well,
When our deep plots do fail: and that should teach us
10   There's a divinity that shapes our ends,
Rough-hew them how we will.

HORATIO: This is most certain.

---

[21] *burning zone:* the fiery zone of the celestial sphere.   [22] *Ossa:* a high mountain in Greece.   [23] *golden . . . disclos'd:* when the golden twins are hatched.

[1] *bilboes:* mutineers in the iron stocks on board ship.

HAMLET: Up from my cabin,
    My sea-gown scarf'd about me, in the dark
    Grop'd I to find out them: had my desire;
15   Finger'd their packet; and, in fine, withdrew
    To mine own room again: making so bold,
    My fears forgetting manners, to unseal
    Their grand commission; where I found, Horatio,
    O royal knavery! an exact command,—
20   Larded with many several sorts of reasons,
    Importing Denmark's health and England's too,
    With, ho! such bugs[2] and goblins in my life,—
    That, on the supervise, no leisure bated,
    No, not to stay the grinding of the axe,
25   My head should be struck off.
HORATIO: Is't possible?
HAMLET: Here's the commission: read it at more leisure.
    But wilt thou hear me how I did proceed?
HORATIO: I beseech you.
HAMLET: Being thus benetted round with villainies,—
30   Ere I could make a prologue to my brains,
    They had begun the play,—I sat me down;
    Devis'd a new commission; wrote it fair:
    I once did hold it, as our statists do,
    A baseness to write fair, and labor'd much
35   How to forget that learning; but, sir, now
    It did me yeoman's service. Wilt thou know
    The effect of what I wrote?
HORATIO: Ay, good my lord.
HAMLET: An earnest conjuration from the king,—
    As England was his faithful tributary;
40   As love between them like the palm might flourish;
    As peace should still her wheaten garland wear
    And stand a comma[3] 'tween their amities;
    And many such like as's of great charge,—
    That, on the view and know of these contents,
45   Without debatement further, more or less,
    He should the bearers put to sudden death,
    Not shriving-time allow'd.
HORATIO: How was this seal'd?
HAMLET: Why, even in that was heaven ordinant.
    I had my father's signet in my purse,
50   Which was the model of that Danish seal:
    Folded the writ up in form of the other;

---

[2] *bugs:* bugbears.   [3] *comma:* link.

Subscrib'd it; gav't the impression; plac'd it safely,
The changeling never known. Now, the next day
Was our sea-fight; and what to this was sequent
55   Thou know'st already.
HORATIO: So Guildenstern and Rosencrantz go to't.
HAMLET: Why, man, they did make love to this employment;
They are not near my conscience; their defeat
Does by their own insinuation[4] grow:
60   'Tis dangerous when the baser nature[5] comes
Between the pass and fell[6] incensed points
Of mighty opposites.
HORATIO: Why, what a king is this!
HAMLET: Does it not, think'st thee, stand me now upon,[7]
He that hath kill'd my king and whor'd my mother;
65   Popp'd in between the election and my hopes;
Thrown out his angle for my proper life,
And with such cozenage,[8]—is't not perfect conscience
To quit him with this arm? and is't not to be damn'd,
To let this canker of our nature come
70   In further evil?
HORATIO: It must be shortly known to him from England
What is the issue of the business there.
HAMLET: It will be short: the interim is mine;
And a man's life's no more than to say One.
75   But I am very sorry, good Horatio,
That to Laertes I forgot myself;
For by the image of my cause I see
The portraiture of his: I'll court his favors:
But, sure, the bravery[9] of his grief did put me
Into a towering passion.
80 HORATIO: Peace; who comes here?

(Enter Osric.)

OSRIC: Your lordship is right welcome back to Denmark.
HAMLET: I humbly thank you, sir.—Dost know this water-fly?
HORATIO: No, my good lord.
HAMLET: Thy state is the more gracious; for 'tis a vice to know him.
85   He hath much land, and fertile: let a beast be lord of beasts, and
his crib shall stand at the king's mess: 'tis a chough;[10] but, as I say,
spacious in the possession of dirt.

---

[4] *Does . . . insinuation:* by their own "sticking their noses" into the business.   [5] *baser
nature:* men of lower rank.   [6] *fell:* fierce.   [7] *Does . . . upon:* that is, "Don't you think it
is my duty?"   [8] *cozenage:* deceit.   [9] *bravery:* ostentation.   [10] *his . . . chough:* He shall
have his trough at the king's table: he is a chattering fool.

OSRIC: Sweet lord, if your lordship were at leisure, I should impart a
    thing to you from his majesty.
90 HAMLET: I will receive it with all diligence of spirit. Put your bonnet
    to his right use; 'tis for the head.
OSRIC: I thank your lordship, 'tis very hot.
HAMLET: No, believe me, 'tis very cold; the wind is northerly.
OSRIC: It is indifferent cold, my lord, indeed.
95 HAMLET: Methinks it is very sultry and hot for my complexion.
OSRIC: Exceedingly, my lord; it is very sultry,—as't were,—I cannot
    tell how.—But, my lord, his majesty bade me signify to you that he
    has laid a great wager on your head. Sir, this is the matter,—
HAMLET: I beseech you, remember,—

(Hamlet moves him to put on his hat.)

100 OSRIC: Nay, in good faith; for mine ease, in good faith. Sir, here is
    newly come to court Laertes; believe me, an absolute gentleman, full
    of most excellent differences, of very soft society and great showing:
    indeed, to speak feelingly of him, he is the card or calendar of gentry,
    for you shall find in him the continent of what part a gentleman
105   would see.
HAMLET: Sir, his definement suffers no perdition in you;—though, I
    know, to divide him inventorially would dizzy the arithmetic of
    memory, and yet but yaw neither, in respect of his quick sail. But,
    in the verity of extolment, I take him to be a soul of great article;
110   and his infusion of such dearth[11] and rareness as, to make true
    diction of him, his semblable is his mirror; and who else would
    trace him, his umbrage,[12] nothing more.
OSRIC: Your lordship speaks most infallibly of him.
HAMLET: The concernancy, sir? why do we wrap the gentleman in our
115   more rawer breath?
OSRIC: Sir?
HORATIO: Is't not possible to understand in another tongue? You will
    do't sir, really.
HAMLET: What imports the nomination[13] of this gentleman?
120 OSRIC: Of Laertes?
HORATIO: His purse is empty already; all's golden words are spent.
HAMLET: Of him, sir.
OSRIC: I know, you are not ignorant,—
HAMLET: I would you did, sir; yet, in faith, if you did, it would not
125   much approve me.[14]—Well, sir.
OSRIC: You are not ignorant of what excellence Laertes is,—

---

[11] *dearth:* rareness, or excellence. [12] *umbrage:* shadow. [13] *nomination:* naming.
[14] *I . . . me:* If you, who are a fool, thought me not ignorant, that would not be particularly to my credit.

HAMLET: I dare not confess that, lest I should compare with him in
    excellence; but to know a man well were to know himself.

OSRIC: I mean, sir, for his weapon; but in the imputation laid on him
130   by them, in his meed he's unfellowed.[15]

HAMLET: What's his weapon?

OSRIC: Rapier and dagger.

HAMLET: That's two of his weapons: but, well.

OSRIC: The king, sir, hath wagered with him six Barbary horses:
135   against the which he has imponed,[16] as I take it, six French rapiers
    and poniards, with their assigns, as girdle, hangers, and so: three
    of the carriages, in faith, are very dear to fancy, very responsive to
    the hilts, most delicate carriages, and of very liberal conceit.

HAMLET: What call you the carriages?

140 HORATIO: I knew you must be edified by the margent ere you had
    done.[17]

OSRIC: The carriages, sir, are the hangers.

HAMLET: The phrase would be more germane to the matter if we could
    carry cannon by our sides: I would it might be hangers till then.
145   But, on: six Barbary horses against six French swords, their assigns,
    and three liberal conceited carriages; that's the French bet against
    the Danish: why is this imponed, as you call it?

OSRIC: The king, sir, hath laid, that in a dozen passes between you
    and him he shall not exceed you three hits: he hath laid on twelve
150   for nine; and it would come to immediate trial if your lordship
    would vouchsafe the answer.

HAMLET: How if I answer no?

OSRIC: I mean, my lord, the opposition of your person in trial.[18]

HAMLET: Sir, I will walk here in the hall: if it please his majesty, it is
155   the breathing time of day with me: let the foils be brought, the
    gentleman willing, and the king hold his purpose, I will win for him
    if I can; if not, I will gain nothing but my shame and the odd hits.

OSRIC: Shall I re-deliver you[19] e'en so?

HAMLET: To this effect, sir; after what flourish your nature will.

160 OSRIC: I commend my duty to your lordship.

HAMLET: Yours, yours.

(Exit Osric.)

    He does well to commend it himself; there are no tongues else for's
    turn.

HORATIO: This lapwing runs away with the shell on his head.[20]

---

[15] *in . . . unfellowed:* In his worth he has no equal. [16] *imponed:* staked. [17] *edified . . . done:* informed by a note in the margin of your instructions. [18] *I . . . trial:* that is, the presence of your person as Laertes' opponent in the fencing contest. [19] *redeliver you:* carry back your answer. [20] *This . . . head:* This precocious fellow is like a lapwing that starts running when it is barely out of the shell.

165 HAMLET: He did comply with his dug before he sucked it.[21] Thus has
he,—and many more of the same bevy, that I know the drossy age
dotes on,—only got the tune of the time, and outward habit of
encounter; a kind of yesty collection,[22] which carries them through
and through the most fanned and winnowed opinions; and do but
blow them to their trial, the bubbles are out.

(Enter a Lord.)

LORD: My lord, his majesty commended him to you by young Osric,
who brings back to him that you attend him in the hall: he sends
to know if your pleasure hold to play with Laertes, or that you will
take longer time.

175 HAMLET: I am constant to my purposes; they follow the king's pleasure:
if his fitness speaks, mine is ready; now or whensoever, provided I be
so able as now.

LORD: The king and queen and all are coming down.

HAMLET: In happy time.

180 LORD: The queen desires you to use some gentle entertainment to
Laertes before you fall to play.

HAMLET: She well instructs me.

(Exit Lord.)

HORATIO: You will lose this wager, my lord.

HAMLET: I do not think so; since he went into France I have been in
185 continual practice: I shall win at the odds. But thou wouldst not
think how ill all's here about my heart: but it is no matter.

HORATIO: Nay, good my lord,—

HAMLET: It is but foolery; but it is such a kind of gain-giving[23] as
would perhaps trouble a woman.

190 HORATIO: If your mind dislike anything, obey it: I will forestall their
repair hither, and say you are not fit.

HAMLET: Not a whit, we defy augury: there's a special providence in
the fall of a sparrow. If it be now, 'tis not to come; if it be not to
come, it will be now; if it be not now, yet it will come: the readiness
195 is all. Since no man has aught of what he leaves, what is't to leave
betimes?[24]

(Enter King, Queen, Laertes, Lords, Osric, and Attendants with foils, &c.)

KING: Come, Hamlet, come, and take this hand from me.

(The King puts Laertes' hand into Hamlet's.)

---

[21] *He . . . it:* He paid compliments to his mother's breast before he sucked it.   [22] *yesty collection:* yeasty or frothy affair.   [23] *gain-giving:* misgiving.   [24] *What . . . betimes?:* What does an early death matter?

HAMLET: Give me your pardon, sir: I have done you wrong:
    But pardon't, as you are a gentleman.
200   This presence knows, and you must needs have heard,
    How I am punish'd with sore distraction.
    What I have done,
    That might your nature, honor, and exception
    Roughly awake, I here proclaim was madness.
205   Was't Hamlet wrong'd Laertes? Never Hamlet:
    If Hamlet from himself be ta'en away,
    And when he's not himself does wrong Laertes,
    Then Hamlet does it not, Hamlet denies it.
    Who does it, then? His madness: if't be so,
210   Hamlet is of the faction that is wrong'd;
    His madness is poor Hamlet's enemy.
    Sir, in this audience,
    Let my disclaiming from a purpos'd evil
    Free me so far in your most generous thoughts
215   That I have shot mine arrow o'er the house
    And hurt my brother.
LAERTES: I am satisfied in nature,
    Whose motive, in this case, should stir me most
    To my revenge: but in my terms of honor
    I stand aloof; and will no reconcilement
220   Till by some elder masters of known honor
    I have a voice and precedent of peace
    To keep my name ungor'd. But till that time
    I do receive your offer'd love like love,
    And will not wrong it.
HAMLET: I embrace it freely;
225   And will this brother's wager frankly play.[25]—
    Give us the foils; come on.
LAERTES: Come, one for me.
HAMLET: I'll be your foil, Laertes; in mine ignorance
    Your skill shall, like a star in the darkest night,
    Stick fiery off indeed.
LAERTES: You mock me, sir.
230 HAMLET: No, by this hand.
KING: Give them the foils, young Osric.
    Cousin Hamlet,
    You know the wager?
HAMLET: Very well, my lord;
    Your grace hath laid the odds o' the weaker side.
235 KING: I do not fear it; I have seen you both;
    But since he's better'd, we have therefore odds.

---

[25] *And . . . play:* fence with a heart free from resentment.

LAERTES: This is too heavy, let me see another.

HAMLET: This likes me well. These foils have all a length?

(They prepare to play.)

OSRIC: Ay, my good lord.

240 KING: Set me the stoups of wine upon that table,—
    If Hamlet give the first or second hit,
    Or quit in answer of the third exchange,
    Let all the battlements their ordnance fire;
    The king shall drink to Hamlet's better breath;
245   And in the cup an union[26] shall he throw,
    Richer than that which four successive kings
    In Denmark's crown have worn. Give me the cups;
    And let the kettle[27] to the trumpet speak,
    The trumpet to the cannoneer without,
250   The cannons to the heavens, the heavens to earth,
    Now the king drinks to Hamlet.—Come, begin;—
    And you, the judges, bear a wary eye.

HAMLET: Come on, sir.

LAERTES: Come, my lord.

(They play.)

HAMLET: One.

LAERTES: No.

HAMLET: Judgment.

OSRIC: A hit, a very palpable hit.

LAERTES: Well;—again.

255 KING: Stay, give me a drink.—Hamlet, this pearl is thine;
    Here's to thy health.—

(Trumpets sound, and cannon shot off within.)

    Give him the cup.

HAMLET: I'll play this bout first; set it by awhile.—
    Come.—Another hit; what say you?

(They play.)

260 LAERTES: A touch, a touch, I do confess.

KING: Our son shall win.

QUEEN: He's fat, and scant of breath.—
    Here, Hamlet, take my napkin, rub thy brows:
    The queen carouses to thy fortune, Hamlet.

HAMLET: Good madam!

KING: Gertrude, do not drink.

265 QUEEN: I will, my lord; I pray you, pardon me.

---

[26] *an union:* a pearl.   [27] *kettle:* kettledrum.

King: *(Aside)* It is the poison'd cup; it is too late.

Hamlet: I dare not drink yet, madam; by and by.

Queen: Come, let me wipe thy face.

Laertes: My lord, I'll hit him now.

King: I do not think't.

270 Laertes: *(Aside)* And yet 'tis almost 'gainst my conscience.

Hamlet: Come, for the third, Laertes: you but dally;
    I pray you, pass with your best violence:
    I am afeard you make a wanton of me.

Laertes: Say you so? come on.

(They play.)

275 Osric: Nothing, neither way.

Laertes: Have at you now!

(Laertes wounds Hamlet; then, in scuffling, they change rapiers, and Hamlet wounds Laertes.)

King: Part them; they are incens'd.

Hamlet: Nay, come, again.

(The Queen falls.)

Osric: Look to the queen there, ho!

Horatio: They bleed on both sides.—How is it, my lord?

Osric: How is't, Laertes?

280 Laertes: Why, as a woodcock to my own springe, Osric;
    I am justly kill'd with mine own treachery.

Hamlet: How does the queen?

King: She swoons to see them bleed.

Queen: No, no, the drink, the drink,—O my dear Hamlet,—
    The drink, the drink!—I am poison'd. *(Dies.)*

285 Hamlet: O villainy!—Ho! let the door be lock'd:
    Treachery! seek it out.

(Laertes falls.)

Laertes: It is here, Hamlet: Hamlet, thou art slain;
    No medicine in the world can do thee good;
    In thee there is not half an hour of life;
290   The treacherous instrument is in thy hand,
    Unbated and envenom'd: the foul practice
    Hath turn'd itself on me; lo, here I lie,
    Never to rise again: thy mother's poison'd:
    I can no more:—the king, the king's to blame.

295 Hamlet: The point envenom'd too!—
    Then venom to thy work. *(Stabs the King)*

Osric and Lords: Treason! treason!

King: O, yet defend me, friends; I am but hurt.

HAMLET: Here, thou incestuous, murderous, damned Dane,

300   Drink off this potion.—Is thy union here?

     Follow my mother.

(King dies.)

LAERTES: He is justly serv'd;

     It is a poison temper'd by himself.—

     Exchange forgiveness with me, noble Hamlet:

305   Mine and my father's death come not upon thee,

     Nor thine on me! *(Dies.)*

HAMLET: Heaven make thee free of it! I follow thee.—

     I am dead, Horatio.—Wretched queen, adieu!—

     You that look pale and tremble at this chance,

310   That art but mutes or audience to this act,

     Had I but time,—as this fell sergeant, death,

     Is strict in his arrest,—O, I could tell you,—

     But let it be.—Horatio, I am dead;

     Thou liv'st; report me and my cause aright

315   To the unsatisfied.[28]

HORATIO: Never believe it:

     I am more an antique Roman than a Dane,—

     Here's yet some liquor left.

HAMLET: As thou'rt a man,

     Give me the cup; let go; by heaven, I'll have't.—

     O good Horatio, what a wounded name,

320   Things standing thus unknown, shall live behind me!

     If thou didst ever hold me in thy heart,

     Absent thee from felicity awhile,

     And in this harsh world draw thy breath in pain,

     To tell my story.—

(March afar off, and shot within.)

           What warlike noise is this?

325 **OSRIC:** Young Fortinbras, with conquest come from Poland,

     To the ambassadors of England gives

     This warlike volley.

HAMLET: O, I die, Horatio;

     The potent poison quite o'er-crows my spirit:

     I cannot live to hear the news from England;

330   But I do prophesy the election lights

     On Fortinbras: he has my dying voice;

     So tell him, with the occurrents, more and less,

     Which have solicited.[29]—The rest is silence. *(Dies)*

---

[28] *unsatisfied:* the uninformed.   [29] *So . . . solicited:* So tell him, together with the events, more or less, that have brought on this tragic affair.

Horatio: Now cracks a noble heart.—Good-night, sweet prince,
335   And flights of angels sing thee to thy rest!
     Why does the drum come hither?

(March within. Enter Fortinbras, the English Ambassadors, and others.)

Fortinbras: Where is this sight?
Horatio: What is it you would see?
     If aught of woe or wonder, cease your search.
Fortinbras: This quarry cries on havoc.[30]—O proud death,
340   What feast is toward in thine eternal cell,
     That thou so many princes at a shot
     So bloodily hast struck?
1st Ambassador: The sight is dismal;
     And our affairs from England come too late:
     The ears are senseless that should give us hearing,
345   To tell him his commandment is fulfill'd,
     That Rosencrantz and Guildenstern are dead:
     Where should we have our thanks?
Horatio: Not from his mouth,
     Had it the ability of life to thank you:
     He never gave commandment for their death.
350   But since, so jump[31] upon this bloody question,
     You from the Polack wars, and you from England,
     Are here arriv'd, give order that these bodies
     High on a stage be placed to the view;
     And let me speak to the yet unknowing world
355   How these things came about: so shall you hear
     Of carnal, bloody, and unnatural acts;
     Of accidental judgments, casual slaughters;
     Of deaths put on by cunning and forc'd cause;
     And, in this upshot, purposes mistook
360   Fall'n on the inventors' heads: all this can I
     Truly deliver.
Fortinbras: Let us haste to hear it,
     And call the noblest to the audience.
     For me, with sorrow I embrace my fortune:
     I have some rights of memory in this kingdom,[32]
365   Which now to claim my vantage doth invite me.
Horatio: Of that I shall have also cause to speak,
     And from his mouth whose voice will draw on more:
     But let this same be presently perform'd,
     Even while men's minds are wild: lest more mischance
370   On plots and errors happen.

---

[30] *This . . . havoc:* This collection of dead bodies cries out havoc.   [31] *jump:* opportunely.
[32] *I . . . kingdom:* I have some unforgotten rights to this kingdom.

FORTINBRAS: Let four captains
    Bear Hamlet like a soldier to the stage;
    For he was likely, had he been put on,[33]
    To have prov'd most royally: and, for his passage,
    The soldier's music and the rites of war
375   Speak loudly for him.—
    . Take up the bodies.—Such a sight as this
    Becomes the field, but here shows much amiss.
    Go, bid the soldiers shoot.

(A dead march)

(Exeunt, bearing off the dead bodies: after which a peal of ordnance is shot off.)

READING AND REACTING

1. What are Hamlet's most notable character traits?
2. Review each of Hamlet's **soliloquies.** Judging from his own words, do you believe his assessments of his own problems are accurate? Are his assessments of other characters' behavior accurate? Point to examples from the soliloquies that reveal Hamlet's insight (or lack of insight).
3. Is Hamlet a sympathetic character? Where (if anywhere) do you find yourself growing impatient with him or disagreeing with him?
4. What is the emotional impact on the audience of having Hamlet behave so cruelly toward Ophelia after his "To be or not to be" soliloquy?
5. What do other characters' comments reveal about Hamlet's character *before* the key events in the play begin to unfold? For example, in what way has he changed since he returned to the castle and found out about his father's death?
6. Claudius is presented as the play's villain. Is he all bad, or does he have any redeeming qualities?
7. List those in the play whom you believe to be **flat characters.** Why do you characterize each individual in this way? What does each of these flat characters contribute to the play?
8. Is Fortinbras simply Hamlet's **foil,** or does he have another essential role? Explain.
9. Each of the play's major characters has one or more character flaws that influence plot development. What specific weaknesses do you see in Claudius, Gertrude, Polonius, Laertes, Ophelia, and in Hamlet himself? Through what words or actions is each weakness revealed? How does each weakness contribute to the play's action?

---

[33] *had . . . on:* tested by succession to the throne.

10. Why doesn't Hamlet kill Claudius as soon as the Ghost tells him what Claudius did? Why doesn't he kill him when he has the chance in act 3? What words or actions reveal his motivation for hesitating? What are the implications of his failure to act?

11. Why does Hamlet pretend to be insane? Why does he arrange for the "play within a play" to be performed? Why does he agree to the duel with Laertes? In each case, what words or actions reveal his motivation to the audience?

12. Is the Ghost an essential character, or could the information he reveals and the reactions he arouses come from another source? Explain. (Keep in mind that the ghost is a **stock character** in Elizabethan drama.)

13. Describe Hamlet's relationship with his mother. Do you consider this a typical mother/son relationship? Why or why not?

14. In the graveyard scene (act 5, scene 1), the gravediggers make many ironic comments. In what way do these comments shed light on the events taking place in the play?

15. **JOURNAL ENTRY** Both Gertrude and Ophelia are usually seen as weak women, firmly under the influence of the men in their lives. Do you think this characterization of them as passive and dependent is accurate? Explain.

16. **CRITICAL PERSPECTIVE** In a 1951 book, *The Meaning of Shakespeare*, Harold Goddard reads *Hamlet* as, in part, a play about war, with a grimly ironic conclusion in that "all the Elder Hamlet's conquests have been for nothing—for less than nothing. Fortinbras, his former enemy, is to inherit the kingdom! Such is the end to which the Ghost's thirst for vengeance has led." He goes on to describe the play's ending:

> The dead Hamlet is borne out "like a soldier" and the last rites over his body are to be the rites of war. The final word of the text is "shoot." The last sounds we hear are a dead march and the reverberations of ordnance being shot off. The end crowns the whole. The sarcasm of fate could go no further. Hamlet, who aspired to nobler things, is treated at death as if he were the mere image of his father: a warrior. Shakespeare knew what he was about in making the conclusion of his play martial. Its theme has been war as well as revenge. It is the story of the Minotaur over again, of that monster who from the beginning of human strife has exacted his annual tribute of youth. No sacrifice ever offered to it was more precious than Hamlet. But he was not the last.
>
> If ever a play seems expressly written for the twentieth century, it is *Hamlet*. It should be unnecessary to underscore its pertinence to an age in which, twice within three

decades, the older generation has called on the younger generation to settle a quarrel with the making of which it had nothing to do. So taken, *Hamlet* is an allegory of our time. Imagination or violence, Shakespeare seems to say, there is no other alternative.

Can you find other evidence in the play to support the idea that one of its major themes is war? Do you agree that the play is "an allegory of our time"?

Related Works: "The Cask of Amontillado" (p. 219), "Young Goodman Brown" (p. 304), *Oedipus the King* (p. 1509), *The Glass Menagerie* (p. 1805)

♦ **ARTHUR MILLER** (1915–   ) was born in New York City and graduated in 1938 from the University of Michigan, where he began to write plays. His first big success, which won the New York Drama Critics Circle Award, was *All My Sons* (1947), about a man who has knowingly manufactured faulty airplane parts. Other significant plays are *The Crucible* (1953), based on the Salem witch trials of 1692, which Miller saw as parallel to contemporary investigations by the House Un-American Activities Committee; *A View from the Bridge* (1955); and *After the Fall* (1955). He was married for a time to actress Marilyn Monroe and wrote the screenplay for her movie *The Misfits* (1961). His play *The Last Yankee* opened off-Broadway in 1993, and *Broken Glass* was both published and performed in 1994.

Death of a Salesman is his most significant work, a play that quickly became an American classic. Miller has said he is very much influenced by the structure of Greek tragedy, and in his play he shows that a tragedy can also be the story of an ordinary person told in realistic terms. The play is frequently produced, and Miller continues to be involved in new productions because, as he says, with each production he learns to see the play differently. When he directed *Death of a Salesman* in China in 1983, audiences perceived it as primarily the story of the mother, and in the 1983 Broadway production Miller himself realized "at a certain point that it was far more the story of Biff, the son, than it was of Willy Loman, the salesman of the title."

CULTURAL CONTEXT ♦ At the time *Death of a Salesman* was written in 1949, the United States was experiencing the largest economic expansion in its history. Businesses were consolidating, and large, impersonal corporations were replacing the mom-and-pop stores that once dominated the American business scene. At the same time, the first Levittown, completed in 1946, anticipated the mass movement of population from older urban neighborhoods to the suburbs. Both these trends are evident in Miller's play.

◆ ◆ ◆

ARTHUR MILLER

Death of a Salesman

CERTAIN PRIVATE CONVERSATIONS IN
TWO ACTS AND A REQUIEM
(1949)

CHARACTERS

WILLY LOMAN	THE WOMAN
LINDA, *his wife*	HOWARD WAGNER
BIFF } *his sons*	JENNY
HAPPY } *his sons*	STANLEY
UNCLE BEN	MISS FORSYTHE
CHARLEY	LETTA
BERNARD	

The action takes place in Willy Loman's house and yard and in various places he visits in the New York and Boston of today.

Throughout the play, in the stage directions, left and right mean stage left and stage right.

ACT I

A melody is heard, played upon a flute. It is small and fine, telling of grass and trees and the horizon. The curtain rises.

Before us is the Salesman's house. We are aware of towering, angular shapes behind it, surrounding it on all sides. Only the blue light of the sky falls upon the house and forestage; the surrounding area shows an angry glow of orange. As more light appears, we see a solid vault of apartment houses around the small, fragile-seeming home. An air of the dream clings to the place, a dream rising out of reality. The kitchen at center seems actual enough, for there is a kitchen table with three chairs, and a refrigerator. But no other fixtures are seen. At the back of the kitchen there is a draped entrance, which leads to the livingroom. To the right of the kitchen, on a level raised two feet, is a bedroom furnished only with a brass bedstead and a straight chair. On a shelf over the bed a silver athletic trophy stands. A window opens onto the apartment house at the side.

Behind the kitchen, on a level raised six and a half feet, is the boys' bedroom, at present barely visible. Two beds are dimly seen, and at the back of the room a dormer window. (This bedroom is above the unseen livingroom.) At the left a stairway curves up to it from the kitchen.

The entire setting is wholly or, in some places, partially transparent. The roofline of the house is one-dimensional; under and over it we see the apartment buildings. Before the house lies an apron, curving beyond the forestage into the orchestra. This forward area serves as the back yard as well as the locale of all Willy's imaginings and of his city scenes. Whenever the action is in the present the actors observe the imaginary wall-lines, entering the house only through the door at the left. But in the scenes of the past these boundaries are broken, and characters enter or leave a room by stepping "through" a wall onto the forestage.

From the right, Willy Loman, the Salesman, enters, carrying two large sample cases. The flute plays on. He hears but is not aware of it. He is past sixty years of age, dressed quietly. Even as he crosses the stage to the doorway of the house, his exhaustion is apparent. He unlocks the door, comes into the kitchen, and thankfully lets his burden down, feeling the soreness of his palms. A word-sigh escapes his lips—it might be "Oh, boy, oh, boy." He closes the door, then carries his cases out into the livingroom, through the draped kitchen doorway.

Linda, his wife, has stirred in her bed at the right. She gets out and puts on a robe, listening. Most often jovial, she has developed an iron repression of her exceptions to Willy's behavior—she more than loves him, she admires him, as though his mercurial nature, his temper, his massive dreams and little cruelties, served her only as sharp reminders of the turbulent longings within him, longings which she shares but lacks the temperament to utter and follow to their end.

LINDA: *(hearing Willy outside the bedroom, calls with some trepidation)* Willy!

WILLY: It's all right. I came back.

LINDA: Why? What happened? *(Sight pause.)* Did something happen, Willy?

WILLY: No, nothing happened.

5 LINDA: You didn't smash the car, did you?

WILLY: *(with casual irritation)* I said nothing happened. Didn't you hear me?

LINDA: Don't you feel well?

WILLY: I am tired to the death. *(The flute has faded away. He sits on the bed beside her, a little numb.)* I couldn't make it. I just couldn't make it, Linda.

LINDA: *(very carefully, delicately)* Where were you all day? You look terrible.

10 WILLY: I got as far as a little above Yonkers. I stopped for a cup of coffee. Maybe it was the coffee.

LINDA: What?

WILLY: *(after a pause)* I suddenly couldn't drive any more. The car kept going onto the shoulder, y'know?

LINDA: *(helpfully)* Oh. Maybe it was the steering again. I don't think Angelo knows the Studebaker.

WILLY: No, it's me, it's me. Suddenly I realize I'm goin' sixty miles an hour and I don't remember the last five minutes. I'm—I can't seem to—keep my mind to it.

15 LINDA: Maybe it's your glasses. You never went for your new glasses.

WILLY: No, I see everything. I came back ten miles an hour. It took me nearly four hours from Yonkers.

LINDA: *(resigned)* Well, you'll just have to take a rest, Willy, you can't continue this way.

Willy: I just got back from Florida.

Linda: But you didn't rest your mind. Your mind is overactive, and the mind is what counts, dear.

20 Willy: I'll start out in the morning. Maybe I'll feel better in the morning. *(She is taking off his shoes.)* These goddam arch supports are killing me.

Linda: Take an aspirin. Should I get you an aspirin? It'll soothe you.

Willy: *(with wonder)* I was driving along, you understand? And I was fine. I was even observing the scenery. You can imagine, me looking at scenery, on the road every week of my life. But it's so beautiful up there, Linda, the trees are so thick, and the sun is warm. I opened the windshield and just let the warm air bathe over me. And then all of a sudden I'm goin' off the road! I'm tellin' ya, I absolutely forgot I was driving. If I'd've gone the other way over the white line I might've killed somebody. So I went on again—and five minutes later I'm dreamin' again, and I nearly—*(He presses two fingers against his eyes.)* I have such thoughts, I have such strange thoughts.

Linda: Willy, dear. Talk to them again. There's no reason why you can't work in New York.

Willy: They don't need me in New York. I'm the New England man. I'm vital in New England.

25 Linda: But you're sixty years old. They can't expect you to keep traveling every week.

Willy: I'll have to send a wire to Portland. I'm supposed to see Brown and Morrison tomorrow morning at ten o'clock to show the line. Goddammit, I could sell them! *(He starts putting on his jacket.)*

Linda: *(taking the jacket from him)* Why don't you go down to the place tomorrow and tell Howard you've simply got to work in New York? You're too accommodating, dear.

Willy: If old man Wagner was alive I'd a been in charge of New York now! That man was a prince, he was a masterful man. But that boy of his, that Howard, he don't appreciate. When I went north the first time, the Wagner Company didn't know where New England was!

Linda: Why don't you tell those things to Howard, dear?

30 Willy: *(encouraged)* I will, I definitely will. Is there any cheese?

Linda: I'll make you a sandwich.

Willy: No, go to sleep. I'll take some milk. I'll be up right away. The boys in?

Linda: They're sleeping. Happy took Biff on a date tonight.

Willy: *(interested)* That so?

35 Linda: It was so nice to see them shaving together, one behind the other, in the bathroom. And going out together. You notice? The whole house smells of shaving lotion.

Willy: Figure it out. Work a lifetime to pay off a house. You finally own it, and there's nobody to live in it.

Linda: Well, dear, life is a casting off. It's always that way.

WILLY: No, no, some people—some people accomplish something. Did Biff say anything after I went this morning?

LINDA: You shouldn't have criticized him, Willy, especially after he just got off the train. You mustn't lose your temper with him.

40 WILLY: When the hell did I lose my temper? I simply asked him if he was making any money. Is that a criticism?

LINDA: But, dear, how could he make any money?

WILLY: *(worried and angered)* There's such an undercurrent in him. He became a moody man. Did he apologize when I left this morning?

LINDA: He was crestfallen, Willy. You know how he admires you. I think if he finds himself, then you'll both be happier and not fight any more.

WILLY: How can he find himself on a farm? Is that a life? A farmhand? In the beginning, when he was young, I thought, well, a young man, it's good for him to tramp around, take a lot of different jobs. But it's more than ten years now and he has yet to make thirty-five dollars a week!

45 LINDA: He's finding himself, Willy.

WILLY: Not finding yourself at the age of thirty-four is a disgrace!

LINDA: Shh!

WILLY: The trouble is he's lazy, goddammit!

LINDA: Willy, please!

50 WILLY: Biff is a lazy bum!

LINDA: They're sleeping. Get something to eat. Go on down.

WILLY: Why did he come home? I would like to know what brought him home.

LINDA: I don't know. I think he's still lost, Willy. I think he's very lost.

WILLY: Biff Loman is lost. In the greatest country in the world a young man with such—personal attractiveness, gets lost. And such a hard worker. There's one thing about Biff—he's not lazy.

55 LINDA: Never.

WILLY: *(with pity and resolve)* I'll see him in the morning; I'll have a nice talk with him. I'll get him a job selling. He could be big in no time. My God! Remember how they used to follow him around in high school? When he smiled at one of them their faces lit up. When he walked down the street . . . *(He loses himself in reminiscences.)*

LINDA: *(trying to bring him out of it)* Willy, dear, I got a new kind of American-type cheese today. It's whipped.

WILLY: Why do you get American when I like Swiss?

LINDA: I just thought you'd like a change—

60 WILLY: I don't want a change! I want Swiss cheese. Why am I always being contradicted?

LINDA: *(with a covering laugh)* I thought it would be a surprise.

WILLY: Why don't you open a window in here, for God's sake?

LINDA: *(with infinite patience)* They're all open, dear.

Willy: The way they boxed us in here. Bricks and windows, windows and bricks.

65 Linda: We should've bought the land next door.

Willy: The street is lined with cars. There's not a breath of fresh air in the neighborhood. The grass don't grow any more, you can't raise a carrot in the back yard. They should've had a law against apartment houses. Remember those two beautiful elm trees out there? When I and Biff hung the swing between them?

Linda: Yeah, like being a million miles from the city.

Willy: They should've arrested the builder for cutting those down. They massacred the neighborhood. *(Lost.)* More and more I think of those days, Linda. This time of year it was lilac and wisteria. And then the peonies would come out, and the daffodils. What fragrance in this room!

Linda: Well, after all, people had to move somewhere.

70 Willy: No, there's more people now.

Linda: I don't think there's more people. I think—

Willy: There's more people! That's what's ruining this country! Population is getting out of control. The competition is maddening! Smell the stink from that apartment house! And another on the other side . . . How can they whip cheese?

On Willy's last line, Biff and Happy raise themselves up in their beds, listening.

Linda: Go down, try it. And be quiet.

Willy: *(turning to Linda, guiltily)* You're not worried about me, are you, sweetheart?

75 Biff: What's the matter?

Happy: Listen!

Linda: You've got too much on the ball to worry about.

Willy: You're my foundation and my support, Linda.

Linda: Just try to relax, dear. You make mountains out of molehills.

80 Willy: I won't fight with him any more. If he wants to go back to Texas, let him go.

Linda: He'll find his way.

Willy: Sure. Certain men just don't get started till later in life. Like Thomas Edison, I think. Or B. F. Goodrich. One of them was deaf. *(He starts for the bedroom doorway.)* I'll put my money on Biff.

Linda: And Willy—if it's warm Sunday we'll drive in the country. And we'll open the windshield, and take lunch.

Willy: No, the windshields don't open on the new cars.

85 Linda: But you opened it today.

Willy: Me? I didn't. *(He stops.)* Now isn't that peculiar! Isn't that remarkable—*(He breaks off in amazement and fright as the flute is heard distantly.)*

Linda: What, darling?

Willy: That is the most remarkable thing.

LINDA: What, dear?

90 WILLY: I was thinking of the Chevvy. *(Slight pause.)* Nineteen twenty-eight . . . when I had that red Chevvy—*(Breaks off.)* That funny? I coulda sworn I was driving that Chevvy today.

LINDA: Well, that's nothing. Something must've reminded you.

WILLY: Remarkable. Ts. Remember those days? The way Biff used to simonize that car? The dealer refused to believe there was eighty thousand miles on it. *(He shakes his head.)* Heh! *(To Linda.)* Close your eyes, I'll be right up. *(He walks out of the bedroom.)*

HAPPY: *(to Biff)* Jesus, maybe he smashed up the car again!

LINDA: *(calling after Willy)* Be careful on the stairs, dear! The cheese is on the middle shelf! *(She turns, goes over to the bed, takes his jacket, and goes out of the bedroom.)*

Light has risen on the boys' room. Unseen, Willy is heard talking to himself, "Eighty thousand miles," and a little laugh. Biff gets out of bed, comes downstage a bit, and stands attentively. Biff is two years older than his brother Happy, well built, but in these days bears a worn air and seems less self-assured. He has succeeded less, and his dreams are stronger and less acceptable than Happy's. Happy is tall, powerfully made. Sexuality is like a visible color on him, or a scent that many women have discovered. He, like his brother, is lost, but in a different way, for he has never allowed himself to turn his face toward defeat and is thus more confused and hard-skinned, although seemingly more content.

95 HAPPY: *(getting out of bed)* He's going to get his license taken away if he keeps that up. I'm getting nervous about him, y'know, Biff?

BIFF: His eyes are going.

HAPPY: No, I've driven with him. He sees all right. He just doesn't keep his mind on it. I drove into the city with him last week. He stops at a green light and then it turns red and he goes. *(He laughs.)*

BIFF: Maybe he's color-blind.

HAPPY: Pop? Why he's got the finest eye for color in the business. You know that.

100 BIFF: *(sitting down on his bed)* I'm going to sleep.

HAPPY: You're not still sour on Dad, are you, Biff?

BIFF: He's all right, I guess.

WILLY: *(underneath them, in the livingroom)* Yes, sir, eighty thousand miles—eighty-two thousand!

BIFF: You smoking?

105 HAPPY: *(holding out a pack of cigarettes)* Want one?

BIFF: *(taking a cigarette)* I can never sleep when I smell it.

WILLY: What a simonizing job, heh!

HAPPY: *(with deep sentiment)* Funny, Biff, y'know? Us sleeping in here again? The old beds. *(He pats his bed affectionately.)* All the talk that went across those two beds, huh? Our whole lives.

BIFF: Yeah. Lotta dreams and plans.

110 HAPPY: *(with a deep and masculine laugh)* About five hundred women
would like to know what was said in this room.

They share a soft laugh.

BIFF: Remember that big Betsy something—what the hell was her name—
over on Bushwick Avenue?

HAPPY: *(combing his hair)* With the collie dog!

BIFF: That's the one. I got you in there, remember?

HAPPY: Yeah, that was my first time—I think. Boy, there was a pig! *(They
laugh, almost crudely.)* You taught me everything I know about
women. Don't forget that.

115 BIFF: I bet you forgot how bashful you used to be. Especially with girls.

HAPPY: Oh, I still am, Biff.

BIFF: Oh, go on.

HAPPY: I just control it, that's all. I think I got less bashful and you got
more so. What happened, Biff? Where's the old humor, the old
confidence? *(He shakes Biff's knee. Biff gets up and moves restlessly
about the room.)* What's the matter?

BIFF: Why does Dad mock me all the time?

120 HAPPY: He's not mocking you, he—

BIFF: Everything I say there's a twist of mockery on his face. I can't get
near him.

HAPPY: He just wants you to make good, that's all. I wanted to talk to you
about Dad for a long time, Biff. Something's—happening to him.
He—talks to himself.

BIFF: I noticed that this morning. But he always mumbled.

HAPPY: But not so noticeable. It got so embarrassing I sent him to Florida.
And you know something? Most of the time he's talking to you.

125 BIFF: What's he say about me?

HAPPY: I can't make it out.

BIFF: What's he say about me?

HAPPY: I think the fact that you're not settled, that you're still kind of up
in the air . . .

BIFF: There's one or two other things depressing him, Happy.

130 HAPPY: What do you mean?

BIFF: Never mind. Just don't lay it all to me.

HAPPY: But I think if you just got started—I mean—is there any future for
you out there?

BIFF: I tell ya, Hap, I don't know what the future is. I don't know—what
I'm supposed to want.

HAPPY: What do you mean?

135 BIFF: Well, I spent six or seven years after high school trying to work
myself up. Shipping clerk, salesman, business of one kind or
another. And it's a measly manner of existence. To get on that
subway on the hot mornings in summer. To devote your whole life
to keeping stock, or making phone calls, or selling or buying. To

suffer fifty weeks of the year for the sake of a two-week vacation, when all you really desire is to be outdoors, with your shirt off. And always to have to get ahead of the next fella. And still—that's how you build a future.

HAPPY: Well, you really enjoy it on a farm? Are you content out there?

BIFF: *(with rising agitation)* Hap, I've had twenty or thirty different kinds of jobs since I left home before the war, and it always turns out the same. I just realized it lately. In Nebraska when I herded cattle, and the Dakotas, and Arizona, and now in Texas. It's why I came home now, I guess, because I realized it. This farm I work on, it's spring there now, see? And they've got about fifteen new colts. There's nothing more inspiring or—beautiful than the sight of a mare and a new colt. And it's cool there now, see? Texas is cool now, and it's spring. And whenever spring comes to where I am, I suddenly get the feeling, my God, I'm not gettin' anywhere! What the hell am I doing, playing around with horses, twenty-eight dollars a week! I'm thirty-four years old, I oughta be makin' my future. That's when I come running home. And now, I get here, and I don't know what to do with myself. *(After a pause.)* I've always made a point of not wasting my life, and every time I come back here I know that all I've done is to waste my life.

HAPPY: You're a poet, you know that, Biff? You're a—you're an idealist!

BIFF: No, I'm mixed up very bad. Maybe I oughta get married. Maybe I oughta get stuck into something. Maybe that's my trouble. I'm like a boy. I'm not married, I'm not in business, I just—I'm like a boy. Are you content, Hap? You're a success, aren't you? Are you content?

140 HAPPY: Hell, no!

BIFF: Why? You're making money, aren't you?

HAPPY: *(moving about with energy, expressiveness)* All I can do now is wait for the merchandise manager to die. And suppose I get to be merchandise manager? He's a good friend of mine, and he just built a terrific estate on Long Island. And he lived there about two months and sold it, and now he's building another one. He can't enjoy it once it's finished. And I know that's just what I would do. I don't know what the hell I'm workin' for. Sometimes I sit in my apartment—all alone. And I think of the rent I'm paying. And it's crazy. But then, it's what I always wanted. My own apartment, a car, and plenty of women. And still, goddammit, I'm lonely.

BIFF: *(with enthusiasm)* Listen, why don't you come out West with me?

HAPPY: You and I, heh?

145 BIFF: Sure, maybe we could buy a ranch. Raise cattle, use our muscles. Men built like we are should be working out in the open.

HAPPY: *(avidly)* The Loman Brothers, heh?

BIFF: *(with vast affection)* Sure, we'd be known all over the counties!

HAPPY: *(enthralled)* That's what I dream about, Biff. Sometimes I want to just rip my clothes off in the middle of the store and outbox that goddam merchandise manager. I mean I can outbox, outrun, and outlift anybody in that store, and I have to take orders from those common, petty sons-of-bitches till I can't stand it any more.

BIFF: I'm telln' you, kid, if you were with me I'd be happy out there.

150 HAPPY: *(enthused)* See, Biff, everybody around me is so false that I'm constantly lowering my ideals . . . .

BIFF: Baby, together we'd stand up for one another, we'd have someone to trust.

HAPPY: If I were around you—

BIFF: Hap, the trouble is we weren't brought up to grub for money. I don't know how to do it.

HAPPY: Neither can I!

155 BIFF: Then let's go!

HAPPY: The only thing is—what can you make out there?

BIFF: But look at your friend. Builds an estate and then hasn't the peace of mind to live in it.

HAPPY: Yeah, but when he walks into the store the waves part in front of him. That's fifty-two thousand dollars a year coming through the revolving door, and I got more in my pinky finger than he's got in his head.

BIFF: Yeah, but you just said—

160 HAPPY: I gotta show some of those pompous, self-important executives over there that Hap Loman can make the grade. I want to walk into the store the way he walks in. Then I'll go with you, Biff. We'll be together yet, I swear. But take those two we had tonight. Now weren't they gorgeous creatures?

BIFF: Yeah, yeah, most gorgeous I've had in years.

HAPPY: I get that any time I want, Biff. Whenever I feel disgusted. The only trouble is, it gets like bowling or something. I just keep knockin' them over and it doesn't mean anything. You still run around a lot?

BIFF: Naa. I'd like to find a girl—steady, somebody with substance.

HAPPY: That's what I long for.

165 BIFF: Go on! You'd never come home.

HAPPY: I would! Somebody with character, with resistance! Like Mom, y'know? You're gonna call me a bastard when I tell you this. That girl Charlotte I was with tonight is engaged to be married in five weeks. *(He tries on his new hat.)*

BIFF: No kiddin'!

HAPPY: Sure, the guy's in line for the vice-presidency of the store. I don't know what gets into me, maybe I just have an overdeveloped sense of competition or something, but I went and ruined her, and furthermore I can't get rid of her. And he's the third executive I've done that to. Isn't that a crummy characteristic? And to top it all, I go to their weddings! *(Indignantly, but laughing.)* Like I'm not supposed to take bribes. Manufacturers offer me a hundred-dollar bill now and then to throw an order their way. You know how honest I am, but it's like this girl, see. I hate myself for it. Because I don't want the girl, and, still, I take it and—I love it!

BIFF: Let's go to sleep.

170 HAPPY: I guess we didn't settle anything, heh?

BIFF: I just got one idea that I think I'm going to try.

HAPPY: What's that?

BIFF: Remember Bill Oliver?

HAPPY: Sure, Oliver is very big now. You want to work for him again?

175 BIFF: No, but when I quit he said something to me. He put his arm on my shoulder, and he said, "Biff, if you ever need anything, come to me."

HAPPY: I remember that. That sounds good.

BIFF: I think I'll go to see him. If I could get ten thousand or even seven or eight thousand dollars I could buy a beautiful ranch.

HAPPY: I bet he'd back you. 'Cause he thought highly of you, Biff, I mean, they all do. You're well liked, Biff. That's why I say to come back here, and we both have the apartment. And I'm telln' you, Biff, any babe you want . . .

BIFF: No, with a ranch I could do the work I like and still be something. I just wonder though. I wonder if Oliver still thinks I stole that carton of basketballs.

180 HAPPY: Oh, he probably forgot that long ago. It's almost ten years. You're too sensitive. Anyway, he didn't really fire you.

BIFF: Well, I think he was going to. I think that's why I quit. I was never sure whether he knew or not. I know he thought the world of me, though. I was the only one he'd let lock up the place.

WILLY: *(below)* You gonna wash the engine, Biff?

HAPPY: Shh!

Biff looks at Happy, who is gazing down, listening. Willy is mumbling in the parlor.

HAPPY: You hear that?

They listen. Willy laughs warmly.

185 BIFF: *(growing angry)* Doesn't he know Mom can hear that?

WILLY: Don't get your sweater dirty, Biff!

A look of pain crosses Biff's face.

HAPPY: Isn't that terrible? Don't leave again, will you? You'll find a job here. You gotta stick around. I don't know what to do about him, it's getting embarrassing.

WILLY: What a simonizing job!

BIFF: Mom's hearing that!

190 WILLY: No kiddin', Biff, you got a date? Wonderful!

HAPPY: Go on to sleep. But talk to him in the morning, will you?

BIFF: *(reluctantly getting into bed)* With her in the house. Brother!

HAPPY: *(getting into bed)* I wish you'd have a good talk with him.

The light on their room begins to fade.

BIFF: *(to himself in bed)* That selfish, stupid . . .

195 HAPPY: Sh . . . Sleep, Biff.

Their light is out. Well before they have finished speaking, Willy's form is dimly seen below in the darkened kitchen. He opens the refrigerator, searches in there, and takes out a bottle of milk. The apartment houses are fading out, and the entire house and surroundings become covered with leaves. Music insinuates itself as the leaves appear.

WILLY: Just wanna be careful with those girls, Biff, that's all. Don't make any promises. No promises of any kind. Because a girl, y'know, they always believe what you tell'em, and you're very young, Biff, you're too young to be talking seriously to girls.

Light rises on the kitchen. Willy, talking, shuts the refrigerator door and comes downstage to the kitchen table. He pours milk into a glass. He is totally immersed in himself, smiling faintly.

WILLY: Too young entirely, Biff. You want to watch your schooling first. Then when you're all set, there'll be plenty of girls for a boy like you. *(He smiles broadly at a kitchen chair.)* That so? The girls pay for you? *(He laughs.)* Boy, you must really be makin' a hit.

Willy is gradually addressing—physically—a point offstage, speaking through the wall of the kitchen, and his voice has been rising in volume to that of a normal conversation.

WILLY: I been wondering why you polish the car so careful. Ha! Don't leave the hubcaps, boys. Get the chamois to the hubcaps. Happy, use newspaper on the windows, it's the easiest thing. Show him how to do it, Biff! You see, Happy? Pad it up, use it like a pad. That's it, that's it, good work. You're doin' all right, Hap. *(He pauses, then nods in approbation for a few seconds, then looks upward.)* Biff, first thing we gotta do when we get time is clip that big branch over the house. Afraid it's gonna fall in a storm and hit the roof. Tell you what. We get a rope and sling her around, and then we climb up there with a couple of saws and take her down. Soon as you finish the car, boys, I wanna see ya. I got a surprise for you, boys.

BIFF: *(offstage)* Whatta ya got, Dad?

200 WILLY: No, you finish first. Never leave a job till you're finished— remember that. *(Looking toward the "big trees.")* Biff, up in Albany I saw a beautiful hammock. I think I'll buy it next trip, and we'll hang it right between those two elms. Wouldn't that be something? Just swingin' there under those branches. Boy, that would be . . .

Young Biff and Young Happy appear from the direction Willy was addressing. Happy carries rags and a pail of water. Biff, wearing a sweater with a block "S," carries a football.

BIFF: *(pointing in the direction of the car offstage)* How's that, Pop, professional?
WILLY: Terrific. Terrific job, boys. Good work, Biff.
HAPPY: Where's the surprise, Pop?
WILLY: In the back seat of the car.
205 HAPPY: Boy! *(He runs off.)*
BIFF: What is it, Dad? Tell me, what'd you buy?
WILLY: *(laughing, cuffs him)* Never mind, something I want you to have.
BIFF: *(turns and starts off)* What is it, Hap?
HAPPY: *(offstage)* It's a punching bag!
210 BIFF: Oh, Pop!
WILLY: It's got Gene Tunney's[1] signature on it!

Happy runs onstage with a punching bag.

BIFF: Gee, how'd you know we wanted a punching bag?
WILLY: Well, it's the finest thing for the timing.
HAPPY: *(lies down on his back and pedals with his feet)* I'm losing weight, you notice, Pop?
215 WILLY: *(to Happy)* Jumping rope is good too.
BIFF: Did you see the new football I got?
WILLY: *(examining the ball)* Where'd you get a new ball?
BIFF: The coach told me to practice my passing.
WILLY: That so? And he gave you the ball, heh?
220 BIFF: Well, I borrowed it from the locker room. *(He laughs confidentially.)*
WILLY: *(laughing with him at the theft)* I want you to return that.
HAPPY: I told you he wouldn't like it!
BIFF: *(angrily)* Well, I'm bringing it back!
WILLY: *(stopping the incipient argument, to Happy)* Sure, he's gotta practice with a regulation ball, doesn't he? *(To Biff.)* Coach'll probably congratulate you on your initiative!
225 BIFF: Oh, he keeps congratulating my initiative all the time, Pop.
WILLY: That's because he likes you. If somebody else took that ball there'd be an uproar. So what's the report, boys, what's the report?
BIFF: Where'd you go this time, Dad? Gee we were lonesome for you.
WILLY: *(pleased, puts an arm around each boy and they come down to the apron)* Lonesome, heh?
BIFF: Missed you every minute.

---

[1] Gene (James Joseph) Tunney (1897–1978)—U.S. boxer, heavyweight champion from his defeat of Jack Dempsey in 1926 until his retirement in 1928.

230 WILLY: Don't say? Tell you a secret, boys. Don't breathe it to a soul.
Someday I'll have my own business, and I'll never have to leave home
any more.

HAPPY: Like Uncle Charley, heh?

WILLY: Bigger than Uncle Charley! Because Charley is not—liked. He's
liked, but he's not—well liked.

BIFF: Where'd you go this time, Dad?

WILLY: Well, I got on the road, and I went north to Providence. Met the
Mayor.

235 BIFF: The Mayor of Providence!

WILLY: He was sitting in the hotel lobby.

BIFF: What'd he say?

WILLY: He said, "Morning!" And I said, "You've got a fine city here,
Mayor." And then he had coffee with me. And then I went to
Waterbury. Waterbury is a fine city. Big clock city, the famous
Waterbury clock. Sold a nice bill there. And then Boston—Boston is
the cradle of the Revolution. A fine city. And a couple of other towns
in Mass., and on to Portland and Bangor and straight home!

BIFF: Gee, I'd love to go with you sometime, Dad.

240 WILLY: Soon as summer comes.

HAPPY: Promise?

WILLY: You and Hap and I, and I'll show you all the towns. America is full
of beautiful towns and fine, upstanding people. And they know me,
boys, they know me up and down New England. The finest people.
And when I bring you fellas up, there'll be open sesame for all of us,
'cause one thing, boys: I have friends. I can park my car in any street
in New England, and the cops protect it like their own. This summer,
heh?

BIFF and HAPPY: (together) Yeah! You bet!

WILLY: We'll take our bathing suits.

245 HAPPY: We'll carry your bags, Pop!

WILLY: Oh, won't that be something! Me comin' into the Boston store
with you boys carryin' my bags. What a sensation!

Biff is prancing around, practicing passing the ball.

WILLY: You nervous, Biff, about the game?

BIFF: Not if you're gonna be there.

WILLY: What do they say about you in school, now that they made you
captain?

250 HAPPY: There's a crowd of girls behind him everytime the classes change.

BIFF: (taking Willy's hand) This Saturday, Pop, this Saturday—just for you,
I'm going to break through for a touchdown.

HAPPY: You're supposed to pass.

BIFF: I'm takin' one play for Pop. You watch me, Pop, and when I take off
my helmet, that means I'm breakin' out. Then you watch me crash
through that line!

WILLY: *(kisses Biff)* Oh, wait'll I tell this in Boston!

Bernard enters in knickers. He is younger than Biff, earnest and loyal, a worried boy.

255 BERNARD: Biff, where are you? You're supposed to study with me today.
WILLY: Hey, looka Bernard. What're you lookin' so anemic about, Bernard?
BERNARD: He's gotta study, Uncle Willy. He's got Regents next week.
HAPPY: *(tauntingly, spinning Bernard around)* Let's box, Bernard!
BERNARD: Biff! *(He gets away from Happy.)* Listen, Biff, I heard Mr. Birnbaum say that if you don't start studyin' math he's gonna flunk you, and you won't graduate. I heard him!
260 WILLY: You better study with him, Biff. Go ahead now.
BERNARD: I heard him!
BIFF: Oh, Pop, you didn't see my sneakers! *(He holds up a foot for Willy to look at.)*
WILLY: Hey, that's a beautiful job of printing!
BERNARD: *(wiping his glasses)* Just because he printed University of Virginia on his sneakers doesn't mean they've got to graduate him, Uncle Willy!
265 WILLY: *(angrily)* What're you talking about? With scholarships to three universities they're gonna flunk him?
BERNARD: But I heard Mr. Birnbaum say—
WILLY: Don't be a pest, Bernard! *(To his boys.)* What an anemic!
BERNARD: Okay, I'm waiting for you in my house, Biff.

Bernard goes off. The Lomans laugh.

WILLY: Bernard is not well liked, is he?
270 BIFF: He's liked, but he's not well liked.
HAPPY: That's right, Pop.
WILLY: That's just what I mean. Bernard can get the best marks in school, y'understand, but when he gets out in the business world, y'understand, you are going to be five times ahead of him. That's why I thank Almighty God you're both built like Adonises. Because the man who makes an appearance in the business world, the man who creates personal interest, is the man who gets ahead. Be liked and you will never want. You take me, for instance. I never have to wait in line to see a buyer. "Willy Loman is here!" That's all they have to know, and I go right through.
BIFF: Did you knock them dead, Pop?
WILLY: Knocked 'em cold in Providence, slaughtered 'em in Boston.
275 HAPPY: *(on his back, pedaling again)* I'm losing weight, you notice, Pop?

Linda enters, as of old, a ribbon in her hair, carrying a basket of washing.

LINDA: *(with youthful energy)* Hello, dear!
WILLY: Sweetheart!

LINDA: How'd the Chevvy run?

WILLY: Chevrolet, Linda, is the greatest car ever built. *(To the boys.)* Since when do you let your mother carry wash up the stairs?

280 BIFF: Grab hold there, boy!

HAPPY: Where to, Mom?

LINDA: Hang them up on the line. And you better go down to your friends, Biff. The cellar is full of boys. They don't know what to do with themselves.

BIFF: Ah, when Pop comes home they can wait!

WILLY: *(laughs appreciatively)* You better go down and tell them what to do, Biff.

285 BIFF: I think I'll have them sweep out the furnace room.

WILLY: Good work, Biff.

BIFF: *(goes through wall-line of kitchen to doorway at back and calls down)* Fellas! Everybody sweep out the furnace room! I'll be right down!

VOICES: All right! Okay, Biff.

BIFF: George and Sam and Frank, come out back! We're hangin' up the wash! Come on, Hap, on the double! *(He and Happy carry out the basket.)*

290 LINDA: The way they obey him!

WILLY: Well, that's training, the training. I'm tellin' you, I was sellin' thousands and thousands, but I had to come home.

LINDA: Oh, the whole block'll be at that game. Did you sell anything?

WILLY: I did five hundred gross in Providence and seven hundred gross in Boston.

LINDA: No! Wait a minute, I've got a pencil. *(She pulls pencil and paper out of her apron pocket.)* That makes your commission . . . Two hundred— my God! Two hundred and twelve dollars!

295 WILLY: Well, I didn't figure it yet, but . . .

LINDA: How much did you do?

WILLY: Well, I—I did—about a hundred and eighty gross in Providence. Well, no—it came to—roughly two hundred gross on the whole trip.

LINDA: *(without hesitation)* Two hundred gross. That's . . . *(She figures.)*

WILLY: The trouble was that three of the stores were half closed for inventory in Boston. Otherwise I woulda broke records.

300 LINDA: Well, it makes seventy dollars and some pennies. That's very good.

WILLY: What do we owe?

LINDA: Well, on the first there's sixteen dollars on the refrigerator—

WILLY: Why sixteen?

LINDA: Well, the fan belt broke, so it was a dollar eighty.

305 WILLY: But it's brand new.

LINDA: Well, the man said that's the way it is. Till they work themselves in, y'know.

They move through the wall-line into the kitchen.

WILLY: I hope we didn't get stuck on that machine.

LINDA: They got the biggest ads of any of them!

WILLY: I know, it's a fine machine. What else?

310 LINDA: Well, there's nine-sixty for the washing machine. And for the vacuum cleaner there's three and a half due on the fifteenth. Then the roof, you got twenty-one dollars remaining.

WILLY: It don't leak, does it?

LINDA: No, they did a wonderful job. Then you owe Frank for the carburetor.

WILLY: I'm not going to pay that man! That goddam Chevrolet, they ought to prohibit the manufacture of that car!

LINDA: Well, you owe him three and a half. And odds and ends, comes to around a hundred and twenty dollars by the fifteenth.

315 WILLY: A hundred and twenty dollars! My God, if business don't pick up I don't know what I'm gonna do!

LINDA: Well, next week you'll do better.

WILLY: Oh, I'll knock them dead next week. I'll go to Hartford. I'm very well liked in Hartford. You know, the trouble is, Linda, people don't seem to take to me.

They move onto the forestage.

LINDA: Oh, don't be foolish.

WILLY: I know it when I walk in. They seem to laugh at me.

320 LINDA: Why? Why would they laugh at you? Don't talk that way, Willy.

Willy moves to the edge of the stage. Linda goes into the kitchen and starts to darn stockings.

WILLY: I don't know the reason for it, but they just pass me by. I'm not noticed.

LINDA: But you're doing wonderful, dear. You're making seventy to a hundred dollars a week.

WILLY: But I gotta be at it ten, twelve hours a day. Other men—I don't know—they do it easier. I don't know why—I can't stop myself—I talk too much. A man oughta come in with a few words. One thing about Charley. He's a man of few words, and they respect him.

LINDA: You don't talk too much, you're just lively.

325 WILLY: *(smiling)* Well, I figure, what the hell, life is short, a couple of jokes. *(To himself.)* I joke too much! *(The smile goes.)*

LINDA: Why? You're—

WILLY: I'm fat. I'm very—foolish to look at, Linda. I didn't tell you, but Christmas time I happened to be calling on F. H. Stewarts, and a salesman I know, as I was going in to see the buyer I heard him say something about—walrus. And I—I cracked him right across the face. I won't take that. I simply will not take that. But they do laugh at me. I know that.

LINDA: Darling . . .

WILLY: I gotta overcome it. I know I gotta overcome it. I'm not dressing to advantage, maybe.

330 LINDA: Willy, darling, you're the handsomest man in the world—
WILLY: Oh, no, Linda.
LINDA: To me you are. *(Slight pause.)* The handsomest.

From the darkness is heard the laughter of a woman. Willy doesn't turn to it, but it continues through Linda's lines.

LINDA: And the boys, Willy. Few men are idolized by their children the way you are.

Music is heard as behind a scrim, to the left of the house, The Woman, dimly seen, is dressing.

WILLY: *(with great feeling)* You're the best there is, Linda, you're a pal, you know that? On the road—on the road I want to grab you sometimes and just kiss the life outa you.

The laughter is loud now, and he moves into a brightening area at the left, where The Woman has come from behind the scrim and is standing, putting on her hat, looking into a "mirror" and laughing.

335 WILLY: 'Cause I get so lonely—especially when business is bad and there's nobody to talk to. I get the feeling that I'll never sell anything again, that I won't make a living for you, or a business, a business for the boys. *(He talks through The Woman's subsiding laughter; The Woman primps at the "mirror.")* There's so much I want to make for—
THE WOMAN: Me? You didn't make me, Willy. I picked you.
WILLY: *(pleased)* You picked me?
THE WOMAN: *(who is quite proper-looking, Willy's age)* I did. I've been sitting at that desk watching all the salesmen go by, day in, day out. But you've got such a sense of humor, and we do have such a good time together, don't we?
WILLY: Sure, sure. *(He takes her in his arms.)* Why do you have to go now?
340 THE WOMAN: It's two o'clock . . .
WILLY: No, come on in! *(He pulls her.)*
THE WOMAN: . . . my sisters'll be scandalized. When'll you be back?
WILLY: Oh, two weeks about. Will you come up again?
THE WOMAN: Sure thing. You do make me laugh. It's good for me. *(She squeezes his arm, kisses him.)* And I think you're a wonderful man.
345 WILLY: You picked me, heh?
THE WOMAN: Sure. Because you're so sweet. And such a kidder.
WILLY: Well, I'll see you next time I'm in Boston.
THE WOMAN: I'll put you right through to the buyers.
WILLY: *(slapping her bottom)* Right. Well, bottoms up!
350 THE WOMAN: *(slaps him gently and laughs)* You just kill me, Willy. *(He suddenly grabs her and kisses her roughly.)* You kill me. And thanks for the stockings. I love a lot of stockings. Well, good night.
WILLY: Good night. And keep your pores open!
THE WOMAN: Oh, Willy!

The Woman bursts out laughing, and Linda's laughter blends in. The Woman disappears into the dark. Now the area at the kitchen table brightens. Linda is sitting where she was at the kitchen table, but now is mending a pair of silk stockings.

LINDA: You are, Willy. The handsomest man. You've got no reason to feel that—

WILLY: *(coming out of The Woman's dimming area and going over to Linda)* I'll make it all up to you, Linda, I'll—

355 LINDA: There's nothing to make up, dear. You're doing fine, better than—

WILLY: *(noticing her mending)* What's that?

LINDA: Just mending my stockings. They're so expensive—

WILLY: *(angrily, taking them from her)* I won't have you mending stockings in this house! Now throw them out!

Linda puts the stockings in her pocket.

BERNARD: *(entering on the run)* Where is he? If he doesn't study!

360 WILLY: *(moving to the forestage, with great agitation)* You'll give him the answers!

BERNARD: I do, but I can't on a Regents! That's a state exam! They're liable to arrest me!

WILLY: Where is he? I'll whip him, I'll whip him!

LINDA: And he'd better give back that football, Willy, it's not nice.

WILLY: Biff! Where is he? Why is he taking everything?

365 LINDA: He's too tough with the girls, Willy. All the mothers are afraid of him!

WILLY: I'll whip him!

BERNARD: He's driving the car without a license!

The Woman's laugh is heard.

WILLY: Shut up!

LINDA: All the mothers—

370 WILLY: Shut up!

BERNARD: *(backing quietly away and out)* Mr. Birnbaum says he's stuck up.

WILLY: Get outa here!

BERNARD: If he doesn't buckle down he'll flunk math! *(He goes off.)*

LINDA: He's right, Willy, you've gotta—

375 WILLY: *(exploding at her)* There's nothing the matter with him! You want him to be a worm like Bernard? He's got spirit, personality . . .

As he speaks, Linda, almost in tears, exits into the livingroom. Willy is alone in the kitchen, wilting and staring. The leaves are gone. It is night again, and the apartment houses look down from behind.

WILLY: Loaded with it. Loaded! What is he stealing? He's giving it back, isn't he? Why is he stealing? What did I tell him? I never in my life told him anything but decent things.

Happy in pajamas has come down the stairs; Willy suddenly becomes aware of Happy's presence.

HAPPY: Let's go now, come on.

WILLY: *(sitting down at the kitchen table)* Huh! Why did she have to wax the floors herself? Everytime she waxes the floors she keels over. She knows that!

HAPPY: Shh! Take it easy. What brought you back tonight?

380 WILLY: I got an awful scare. Nearly hit a kid in Yonkers. God! Why didn't I go to Alaska with my brother Ben that time! Ben! That man was a genius, that man was success incarnate! What a mistake! He begged me to go.

HAPPY: Well, there's no use in—

WILLY: You guys! There was a man started with the clothes on his back and ended up with diamond mines!

HAPPY: Boy, someday I'd like to know how he did it.

WILLY: What's the mystery? The man knew what he wanted and went out and got it! Walked into a jungle, and comes out, the age of twenty-one, and he's rich! The world is an oyster, but you don't crack it open on a mattress!

385 HAPPY: Pop, I told you I'm gonna retire you for life.

WILLY: You'll retire me for life on seventy goddam dollars a week? And your women and your car and your apartment, and you'll retire me for life! Christ's sake, I couldn't get past Yonkers today! Where are you guys, where are you? The woods are burning! I can't drive a car!

Charley has appeared in the doorway. He is a large man, slow of speech, laconic, immovable. In all he says, despite what he says, there is pity, and now, trepidation. He has a robe over his pajamas, slippers on his feet. He enters the kitchen.

CHARLEY: Everything all right?

HAPPY: Yeah, Charley, everything's . . .

WILLY: What's the matter?

390 CHARLEY: I heard some noise. I thought something happened. Can't we do something about the walls? You sneeze in here, and in my house hats blow off.

HAPPY: Let's go to bed, Dad. Come on.

Charley signals to Happy to go.

WILLY: You go ahead, I'm not tired at the moment.

HAPPY: *(to Willy)* Take it easy, huh? *(He exits.)*

WILLY: What're you doin' up?

395 CHARLEY: *(sitting down at the kitchen table opposite Willy)* Couldn't sleep good. I had a heartburn.

WILLY: Well, you don't know how to eat.

CHARLEY: I eat with my mouth.

WILLY: No, you're ignorant. You gotta know about vitamins and things like that.

CHARLEY: Come on, let's shoot. Tire you out a little.

400 WILLY: *(hesitantly)* All right. You got cards?

CHARLEY: *(taking a deck from his pocket)* Yeah, I got them. Someplace. What is it with those vitamins?

WILLY: *(dealing)* They build up your bones. Chemistry.

CHARLEY: Yeah, but there's no bones in a heartburn.

WILLY: What are you talkin' about? Do you know the first thing about it?

405 CHARLEY: Don't get insulted.

WILLY: Don't talk about something you don't know anything about.

They are playing. Pause.

CHARLEY: What're you doin' home?

WILLY: A little trouble with the car.

CHARLEY: Oh. *(Pause.)* I'd like to take a trip to California.

410 WILLY: Don't say.

CHARLEY: You want a job?

WILLY: I got a job, I told you that. *(After a slight pause.)* What the hell are you offering me a job for?

CHARLEY: Don't get insulted.

WILLY: Don't insult me.

415 CHARLEY: I don't see no sense in it. You don't have to go on this way.

WILLY: I got a good job. *(Slight pause.)* What do you keep comin' in here for?

CHARLEY: You want me to go?

WILLY: *(after a pause, withering)* I can't understand it. He's going back to Texas again. What the hell is that?

CHARLEY: Let him go.

420 WILLY: I got nothin' to give him, Charley, I'm clean, I'm clean.

CHARLEY: He won't starve. None a them starve. Forget about him.

WILLY: Then what have I got to remember?

CHARLEY: You take it too hard. To hell with it. When a deposit bottle is broken you don't get your nickel back.

WILLY: That's easy enough for you to say.

425 CHARLEY: That ain't easy for me to say.

WILLY: Did you see the ceiling I put up in the livingroom?

CHARLEY: Yeah, that's a piece of work. To put up a ceiling is a mystery to me. How do you do it?

WILLY: What's the difference?

CHARLEY: Well, talk about it.

430 WILLY: You gonna put up a ceiling?

CHARLEY: How could I put up a ceiling?

WILLY: Then what the hell are you bothering me for?

CHARLEY: You're insulted again.

WILLY: A man who can't handle tools is not a man. You're disgusting.

435 CHARLEY: Don't call me disgusting, Willy.

Uncle Ben, carrying a valise and an umbrella, enters the forestage from around the right corner of the house. He is a stolid man, in his sixties, with a mustache and an authoritative air. He is utterly certain of his destiny, and there is an aura of far places about him. He enters exactly as Willy speaks.

WILLY: I'm getting awfully tired, Ben.

Ben's music is heard. Ben looks around at everything.

CHARLEY: Good, keep playing; you'll sleep better. Did you call me Ben?

Ben looks at his watch.

WILLY: That's funny. For a second there you reminded me of my brother Ben.

BEN: I have only a few minutes. *(He strolls, inspecting the place. Willy and Charley continue playing.)*

440 CHARLEY: You never heard from him again, heh? Since that time?

WILLY: Didn't Linda tell you? Couple of weeks ago we got a letter from his wife in Africa. He died.

CHARLEY: That so.

BEN: *(chuckling)* So this is Brooklyn, eh?

CHARLEY: Maybe you're in for some of his money.

445 WILLY: Naa, he had seven sons. There's just one opportunity I had with that man . . .

BEN: I must make a train, William. There are several properties I'm looking at in Alaska.

WILLY: Sure, sure! If I'd gone with him to Alaska that time, everything would've been totally different.

CHARLEY: Go on, you'd froze to death up there.

WILLY: What're you talking about?

450 BEN: Opportunity is tremendous in Alaska, William. Surprised you're not up there.

WILLY: Sure, tremendous.

CHARLEY: Heh?

WILLY: There was the only man I ever met who knew the answers.

CHARLEY: Who?

455 BEN: How are you all?

WILLY: *(taking a pot, smiling)* Fine, fine.

CHARLEY: Pretty sharp tonight.

BEN: Is Mother living with you?

WILLY: No, she died a long time ago.

460 CHARLEY: Who?

BEN: That's too bad. Fine specimen of a lady, Mother.

WILLY: *(to Charley)* Heh?

BEN: I'd hoped to see the old girl.

CHARLEY: Who died?

465 BEN: Heard anything from Father, have you?

WILLY: *(unnerved)* What do you mean, who died?

CHARLEY: *(taking a pot)* What're you talkin' about?

BEN: *(looking at his watch)* William, it's half-past eight!

WILLY: *(as though to dispel his confusion he angrily stops Charley's hand)* That's my build!

470 CHARLEY: I put the ace—

WILLY: If you don't know how to play the game I'm not gonna throw my money away on you!

CHARLEY: *(rising)* It was my ace, for God's sake!

WILLY: I'm through, I'm through!

BEN: When did Mother die?

475 WILLY: Long ago. Since the beginning you never knew how to play cards.

CHARLEY: *(picks up the cards and goes to the door)* All right! Next time I'll bring a deck with five aces.

WILLY: I don't play that kind of game!

CHARLEY: *(turning to him)* You should be ashamed of yourself!

WILLY: Yeah?

480 CHARLEY: Yeah! *(He goes out.)*

WILLY: *(slamming the door after him)* Ignoramus!

BEN: *(as Willy comes toward him through the wall-line of the kitchen)* So you're William.

WILLY: *(shaking Ben's hand)* Ben! I've been waiting for you so long! What's the answer? How did you do it?

BEN: Oh, there's a story in that.

Linda enters the forestage, as of old, carrying the wash basket.

485 LINDA: Is this Ben?

BEN: *(gallantly)* How do you do, my dear.

LINDA: Where've you been all these years? Willy's always wondered why you—

WILLY: *(pulling Ben away from her impatiently)* Where is Dad? Didn't you follow him? How did you get started?

BEN: Well, I don't know how much you remember.

490 WILLY: Well, I was just a baby, of course, only three or four years old—

BEN: Three years and eleven months.

WILLY: What a memory, Ben!

BEN: I have many enterprises, William, and I have never kept books.

WILLY: I remember I was sitting under the wagon in—was it Nebraska?

495 BEN: It was South Dakota, and I gave you a bunch of wild flowers.

WILLY: I remember you walking away down some open road.

BEN: *(laughing)* I was going to find Father in Alaska.

WILLY: Where is he?

BEN: At that age I had a very faulty view of geography, William. I discovered after a few days that I was heading due south, so instead of Alaska, I ended up in Africa.

500 LINDA: Africa!

WILLY: The Gold Coast!

BEN: Principally, diamond mines.

LINDA: Diamond mines!

BEN: Yes, my dear. But I've only a few minutes—

505 WILLY: No! Boys! Boys! *(Young Biff and Happy appear.)* Listen to this. This is your Uncle Ben, a great man! Tell my boys, Ben!

BEN: Why, boys, when I was seventeen I walked into the jungle, and when I was twenty-one I walked out. *(He laughs.)* And by God I was rich.

WILLY: *(to the boys)* You see what I been talking about? The greatest things can happen!

BEN: *(glancing at his watch)* I have an appointment in Ketchikan Tuesday week.

WILLY: No, Ben! Please tell about Dad. I want my boys to hear. I want them to know the kind of stock they spring from. All I remember is a man with a big beard, and I was in Mamma's lap, sitting around a fire, and some kind of high music.

510 BEN: His flute. He played the flute.

WILLY: Sure, the flute, that's right!

New music is heard, a high, rollicking tune.

BEN: Father was a very great and a very wild-hearted man. We would start in Boston, and he'd toss the whole family into the wagon, and then he'd drive the team right across the country; through Ohio, and Indiana, Michigan, Illinois, and all the Western states. And we'd stop in the towns and sell the flutes that he'd made on the way. Great inventor, Father. With one gadget he made more in a week than a man like you could make in a lifetime.

WILLY: That's just the way I'm bringing them up, Ben—rugged, well liked, all-around.

BEN: Yeah? *(To Biff.)* Hit that, boy—hard as you can. *(He pounds his stomach.)*

515 BIFF: Oh, no, sir!

BEN: *(taking boxing stance)* Come on, get to me! *(He laughs.)*

WILLY: Go to it, Biff! Go ahead, show him!

BIFF: Okay! *(He cocks his fist and starts in.)*

LINDA: *(to Willy)* Why must he fight, dear?

520 BEN: *(sparring with Biff)* Good boy! Good boy!

WILLY: How's that, Ben, heh?

HAPPY: Give him the left, Biff!

LINDA: Why are you fighting?

BEN: Good boy! *(Suddenly comes in, trips Biff, and stands over him, the point of his umbrella poised over Biff's eye.)*

525 LINDA: Look out, Biff!

BIFF: Gee!

BEN: *(patting Biff's knee)* Never fight fair with a stranger, boy. You'll never get out of the jungle that way. *(Taking Linda's hand and bowing.)* It was an honor and a pleasure to meet you, Linda.

LINDA: *(withdrawing her hand coldly, frightened)* Have a nice—trip.

BEN: *(to Willy)* And good luck with your—what do you do?

530 WILLY: Selling.

BEN: Yes. Well . . . *(He raises his hand in farewell to all.)*

WILLY: No, Ben, I don't want you to think . . . *(He takes Ben's arm to show him.)* It's Brooklyn, I know, but we hunt too.

BEN: Really, now.

WILLY: Oh, sure, there's snakes and rabbits and—that's why I moved out here. Why, Biff can fell any one of these trees in no time! Boys! Go right over to where they're building the apartment house and get some sand. We're gonna rebuild the entire front stoop right now! Watch this, Ben!

535 BIFF: Yes, sir! On the double, Hap!

HAPPY: *(as he and Biff run off)* I lost weight, Pop, you notice?

Charley enters in knickers, even before the boys are gone.

CHARLEY: Listen, if they steal any more from that building the watchman'll put the cops on them!

LINDA: *(to Willy)* Don't let Biff . . .

Ben laughs lustily.

WILLY: You shoulda seen the lumber they brought home last week. At least a dozen six-by-tens worth all kinds of money.

540 CHARLEY: Listen, if that watchman—

WILLY: I gave them hell, understand. But I got a couple of fearless characters there.

CHARLEY: Willy, the jails are full of fearless characters.

BEN: *(clapping Willy on the back, with a laugh at Charley)* And the stock exchange, friend!

WILLY: *(joining in Ben's laughter)* Where are the rest of your pants?

545 CHARLEY: My wife bought them.

WILLY: Now all you need is a golf club and you can go upstairs and go to sleep. *(To Ben.)* Great athlete! Between him and his son Bernard they can't hammer a nail!

BERNARD: *(rushing in)* The watchman's chasing Biff!

WILLY: *(angrily)* Shut up! He's not stealing anything!

LINDA: *(alarmed, hurrying off left)* Where is he? Biff, dear! *(She exits.)*

550 WILLY: *(moving toward the left, away from Ben)* There's nothing wrong. What's the matter with you?

Ben: Nervy boy. Good!

Willy: *(laughing)* Oh, nerves of iron, that Biff!

Charley: Don't know what it is. My New England man comes back and he's bleedin', they murdered him up there.

Willy: It's contacts, Charley, I got important contacts!

555 Charley: *(sarcastically)* Glad to hear it, Willy. Come in later, we'll shoot a little casino. I'll take some of your Portland money. *(He laughs at Willy and exits.)*

Willy: *(turning to Ben)* Business is bad, it's murderous. But not for me, of course.

Ben: I'll stop by on my way back to Africa.

Willy: *(longingly)* Can't you stay a few days? You're just what I need, Ben, because I—I have a fine position here, but I—well, Dad left when I was such a baby and I never had a chance to talk to him and I still feel—kind of temporary about myself.

Ben: I'll be late for my train.

They are at opposite ends of the stage.

560 Willy: Ben, my boys—can't we talk? They'd go into the jaws of hell for me, see, but I—

Ben: William, you're being first-rate with your boys. Outstanding, manly chaps!

Willy: *(hanging on to his words)* Oh, Ben, that's good to hear! Because sometimes I'm afraid that I'm not teaching them the right kind of— Ben, how should I teach them?

Ben: *(giving great weight to each word, and with a certain vicious audacity)* William, when I walked into the jungle, I was seventeen. When I walked out I was twenty-one. And, by God, I was rich! *(He goes off into darkness around the right corner of the house.)*

Willy: . . . was rich! That's just the spirit I want to imbue them with! To walk into a jungle! I was right! I was right! I was right!

Ben is gone, but Willy is still speaking to him as Linda, in nightgown and robe, enters the kitchen, glances around for Willy, then goes to the door of the house, looks out and sees him. Comes down to his left. He looks at her.

565 Linda: Willy, dear? Willy?

Willy: I was right!

Linda: Did you have some cheese? *(He can't answer.)* It's very late, darling. Come to bed, heh?

Willy: *(looking straight up)* Gotta break your neck to see a star in this yard.

Linda: You coming in?

570 Willy: What ever happened to that diamond watch fob? Remember? When Ben came from Africa that time? Didn't he give me a watch fob with a diamond in it?

LINDA: You pawned it, dear. Twelve, thirteen years ago. For Biff's radio
correspondence course.

WILLY: Gee, that was a beautiful thing. I'll take a walk.

LINDA: But you're in your slippers.

WILLY: *(starting to go around the house at the left)* I was right! I was! *(Half to
Linda, as he goes, shaking his head.)* What a man! There was a man
worth talking to. I was right!

575 LINDA: *(calling after Willy)* But in your slippers, Willy!

*Willy is almost gone when Biff, in his pajamas, comes down the stairs and en-
ters the kitchen.*

BIFF: What is he doing out there?

LINDA: Sh!

BIFF: God Almighty, Mom, how long has he been doing this?

LINDA: Don't, he'll hear you.

580 BIFF: What the hell is the matter with him?

LINDA: It'll pass by morning.

BIFF: Shouldn't we do anything?

LINDA: Oh, my dear, you should do a lot of things, but there's nothing to
do, so go to sleep.

Happy comes down the stairs and sits on the steps.

HAPPY: I never heard him so loud, Mom.

585 LINDA: Well, come around more often; you'll hear him. *(She sits down at
the table and mends the lining of Willy's jacket.)*

BIFF: Why didn't you ever write me about this, Mom?

LINDA: How would I write to you? For over three months you had no
address.

BIFF: I was on the move. But you know I thought of you all the time. You
know that, don't you, pal?

LINDA: I know, dear, I know. But he likes to have a letter. Just to know
that there's still a possibility for better things.

590 BIFF: He's not like this all the time, is he?

LINDA: It's when you come home he's always the worst.

BIFF: When I come home?

LINDA: When you write you're coming, he's all smiles, and talks about
the future, and—he's just wonderful. And then the closer you seem to
come, the more shaky he gets, and then, by the time you get here,
he's arguing, and he seems angry at you. I think it's just that maybe
he can't bring himself to—to open up to you. Why are you so hateful
to each other? Why is that?

BIFF: *(evasively)* I'm not hateful, Mom.

595 LINDA: But you no sooner come in the door than you're fighting!

BIFF: I don't know why. I mean to change. I'm tryin', Mom, you
understand?

LINDA: Are you home to stay now?

BIFF: I don't know. I want to look around, see what's doin'.

LINDA: Biff, you can't look around all your life, can you?

600 BIFF: I just can't take hold, Mom. I can't take hold of some kind of a life.

LINDA: Biff, a man is not a bird, to come and go with the springtime.

BIFF: Your hair . . . *(He touches her hair.)* Your hair got so gray.

LINDA: Oh, it's been gray since you were in high school. I just stopped dyeing it, that's all.

BIFF: Dye it again, will ya? I don't want my pal looking old. *(He smiles.)*

605 LINDA: You're such a boy! You think you can go away for a year and . . . You've got to get it into your head now that one day you'll knock on this door and there'll be strange people here—

BIFF: What are you talking about? You're not even sixty, Mom.

LINDA: But what about your father?

BIFF: *(lamely)* Well, I meant him too.

HAPPY: He admires Pop.

610 LINDA: Biff, dear, if you don't have any feeling for him, then you can't have any feeling for me.

BIFF: Sure I can, Mom.

LINDA: No. You can't just come to see me, because I love him. *(With a threat, but only a threat, of tears.)* He's the dearest man in the world to me, and I won't have anyone making him feel unwanted and low and blue. You've got to make up your mind now, darling, there's no leeway any more. Either he's your father and you pay him that respect, or else you're not to come here. I know he's not easy to get along with—nobody knows that better than me—but . . .

WILLY: *(from the left, with a laugh)* Hey, hey, Biffo!

BIFF: *(starting to go out after Willy)* What the hell is the matter with him? *(Happy stops him.)*

615 LINDA: Don't—don't go near him!

BIFF: Stop making excuses for him! He always, always wiped the floor with you. Never had an ounce of respect for you.

HAPPY: He's always had respect for—

BIFF: What the hell do you know about it?

HAPPY: *(surlily)* Just don't call him crazy!

620 BIFF: He's got no character—Charley wouldn't do this. Not in his own house—spewing out that vomit from his mind.

HAPPY: Charley never had to cope with what he's got to.

BIFF: People are worse off than Willy Loman. Believe me, I've seen them!

LINDA: Then make Charley your father, Biff. You can't do that, can you? I don't say he's a great man. Willy Loman never made a lot of money. His name was never in the paper. He's not the finest character that ever lived. But he's a human being, and a terrible thing is happening to him. So attention must be paid. He's not to be allowed to fall into his grave like an old dog. Attention, attention must be finally paid to such a person. You called him crazy—

BIFF: I didn't mean—

625 LINDA: No, a lot of people think he's lost his—balance. But you don't
   have to be very smart to know what his trouble is. The man is
   exhausted.

HAPPY: Sure!

LINDA: A small man can be just as exhausted as a great man. He works for
   a company thirty-six years this March, opens up unheard-of-
   territories to their trademark, and now in his old age they take his
   salary away.

HAPPY: *(indignantly)* I didn't know that, Mom.

LINDA: You never asked, my dear! Now that you get your spending money
   someplace else you don't trouble your mind with him.

630 HAPPY: But I gave you money last—

LINDA: Christmas time, fifty dollars! To fix the hot water it cost ninety-
   seven fifty! For five weeks he's been on straight commission, like a
   beginner, an unknown!

BIFF: Those ungrateful bastards!

LINDA: Are they any worse than his sons? When he brought them
   business, when he was young, they were glad to see him. But now his
   old friends, the old buyers that loved him so and always found some
   order to hand him in a pinch—they're all dead, retired. He used to
   be able to make six, seven calls a day in Boston. Now he takes his
   valises out of the car and puts them back and takes them out again
   and he's exhausted. Instead of walking he talks now. He drives seven
   hundred miles, and when he gets there no one knows him any more,
   no one welcomes him. And what goes through a man's mind,
   driving seven hundred miles home without having earned a cent?
   Why shouldn't he talk to himself? Why? When he has to go to
   Charley and borrow fifty dollars a week and pretend to me that it's
   his pay? How long can that go on? How long? You see what I'm
   sitting here and waiting for? And you tell me he has no character?
   The man who never worked a day but for your benefit? When does
   he get the medal for that? Is this his reward—to turn around at the
   age of sixty-three and find his sons, who he loved better than his
   life, one a philandering bum—

HAPPY: Mom!

635 LINDA: That's all you are, my baby! *(To Biff.)* And you! What happened to
   the love you had for him? You were such pals! How you used to talk
   to him on the phone every night! How lonely he was till he could
   come home to you!

BIFF: All right, Mom. I'll live here in my room, and I'll get a job. I'll keep
   away from him, that's all.

LINDA: No, Biff. You can't stay here and fight all the time.

BIFF: He threw me out of this house, remember that.

LINDA: Why did he do that? I never knew why.

640 BIFF: Because I know he's a fake and he doesn't like anybody around who
   knows!

LINDA: Why a fake? In what way? What do you mean?

BIFF: Just don't lay it all at my feet. It's between me and him—that's all I have to say. I'll chip in from now on. He'll settle for half my pay check. He'll be all right. I'm going to bed. *(He starts for the stairs.)*

LINDA: He won't be all right.

BIFF: *(turning on the stairs, furiously)* I hate this city and I'll stay here. Now what do you want?

645 LINDA: He's dying, Biff.

Happy turns quickly to her, shocked.

BIFF: *(after a pause)* Why is he dying?

LINDA: He's been trying to kill himself.

BIFF: *(with great horror)* How?

LINDA: I live from day to day.

650 BIFF: What're you talking about?

LINDA: Remember I wrote you that he smashed up the car again? In February?

BIFF: Well?

LINDA: The insurance inspector came. He said that they have evidence. That all these accidents in the last year—weren't—weren't—accidents.

HAPPY: How can they tell that? That's a lie.

655 LINDA: It seems there's a woman . . . *(She takes a breath as—)*

BIFF: *(sharply but contained)*   What woman?

LINDA: *(simultaneously)*   . . . and this woman . . .

LINDA: What?

BIFF: Nothing. Go ahead.

660 LINDA: What did you say?

BIFF: Nothing. I just said what woman?

HAPPY: What about her?

LINDA: Well, it seems she was walking down the road and saw his car. She says that he wasn't driving fast at all, and that he didn't skid. She says he came to that little bridge, and then deliberately smashed into the railing, and it was only the shallowness of the water that saved him.

BIFF: Oh, no, he probably just fell asleep again.

665 LINDA: I don't think he fell asleep.

BIFF: Why not?

LINDA: Last month . . . *(With great difficulty.)* Oh, boys, it's so hard to say a thing like this! He's just a big stupid man to you, but I tell you there's more good in him than in many other people. *(She chokes, wipes her eyes.)* I was looking for a fuse. The lights blew out, and I went down the cellar. And behind the fuse box—it happened to fall out—was a length of rubber pipe—just short.

HAPPY: No kidding?

LINDA: There's a little attachment on the end of it. I knew right away. And sure enough, on the bottom of the water heater there's a new little nipple on the gas pipe.

670 HAPPY: *(angrily)* That—jerk.

BIFF: Did you have it taken off?

LINDA: I'm—I'm ashamed to. How can I mention it to him? Every day I go down and take away that little rubber pipe. But, when he comes home, I put it back where it was. How can I insult him that way? I don't know what to do. I live from day to day, boys. I tell you, I know every thought in his mind. It sounds so old-fashioned and silly, but I tell you he put his whole life into you and you've turned your backs on him. *(She is bent over in the chair, weeping, her face in her hands.)* Biff, I swear to God! Biff, his life is in your hands!

HAPPY: *(to Biff)* How do you like that damned fool!

BIFF: *(kissing her)* All right, pal, all right. It's all settled now. I've been remiss. I know that, Mom, but now I'll stay, and I swear to you, I'll apply myself. *(Kneeling in front of her, in a fever of self-reproach.)* It's just—you see, Mom, I don't fit in business. Not that I won't try. I'll try, and I'll make good.

675 HAPPY: Sure you will. The trouble with you in business was you never tried to please people.

BIFF: I know, I—

HAPPY: Like when you worked for Harrison's. Bob Harrison said you were tops, and then you go and do some damn fool thing like whistling whole songs in the elevator like a comedian.

BIFF: *(against Happy)* So what? I like to whistle sometimes.

HAPPY: You don't raise a guy to a responsible job who whistles in the elevator!

680 LINDA: Well, don't argue about it now.

HAPPY: Like when you'd go off and swim in the middle of the day instead of taking the line around.

BIFF: *(his resentment rising)* Well, don't you run off? You take off sometimes, don't you? On a nice summer day?

HAPPY: Yeah, but I cover myself!

LINDA: Boys!

685 HAPPY: If I'm going to take a fade the boss can call any number where I'm supposed to be and they'll swear to him that I just left. I'll tell you something that I hate to say, Biff, but in the business world some of them think you're crazy.

BIFF: *(angered)* Screw the business world!

HAPPY: All right, screw it! Great, but cover yourself!

LINDA: Hap, Hap!

BIFF: I don't care what they think! They've laughed at Dad for years, and you know why? Because we don't belong in this nut-house of a city! We should be mixing cement on some open plain, or—or carpenters. A carpenter is allowed to whistle!

Willy walks in from the entrance of the house, at left.

690 WILLY: Even your grandfather was better than a carpenter. *(Pause. They watch him.)* You never grew up. Bernard does not whistle in the elevator, I assure you.

Biff: *(as though to laugh Willy out of it)* Yeah, but you do, Pop.

Willy: I never in my life whistled in an elevator! And who in the business world thinks I'm crazy?

Biff: I didn't mean it like that, Pop. Now don't make a whole thing out of it, will ya?

Willy: Go back to the West! Be a carpenter, a cowboy, enjoy yourself!

695 Linda: Willy, he was just saying—

Willy: I heard what he said!

Happy: *(trying to quiet Willy)* Hey, Pop, come on now . . .

Willy: *(continuing over Happy's line)* They laugh at me, heh? Go to Filene's, go to the Hub, go to Slattery's, Boston. Call out the name Willy Loman and see what happens! Big shot!

Biff: All right, Pop.

700 Willy: Big!

Biff: All right!

Willy: Why do you always insult me?

Biff: I didn't say a word. *(To Linda.)* Did I say a word?

Linda: He didn't say anything, Willy.

705 Willy: *(going to the doorway of the livingroom)* All right, good night, good night.

Linda: Willy, dear, he just decided . . .

Willy: *(to Biff)* If you get tired hanging around tomorrow, paint the ceiling I put up in the livingroom.

Biff: I'm leaving early tomorrow.

Happy: He's going to see Bill Oliver, Pop.

710 Willy: *(interestedly)* Oliver? For what?

Biff: *(with reserve, but trying, trying)* He always said he'd stake me. I'd like to go into business, so maybe I can take him up on it.

Linda: Isn't that wonderful?

Willy: Don't interrupt. What's wonderful about it? There's fifty men in the City of New York who'd stake him. *(To Biff.)* Sporting goods?

Biff: I guess so. I know something about it and—

715 Willy: He knows something about it! You know sporting goods better than Spalding, for God's sake! How much is he giving you?

Biff: I don't know, I didn't even see him yet, but—

Willy: Then what're you talkin' about?

Biff: *(getting angry)* Well, all I said was I'm gonna see him, that's all!

Willy: *(turning away)* Ah, you're counting your chickens again.

720 Biff: *(starting left for the stairs)* Oh, Jesus, I'm going to sleep!

Willy: *(calling after him)* Don't curse in this house!

Biff: *(turning)* Since when did you get so clean!

Happy: *(trying to stop them)* Wait a . . .

Willy: Don't use that language to me! I won't have it!

725 Happy: *(grabbing Biff, shouts)* Wait a minute! I got an idea. I got a feasible idea. Come here, Biff, let's talk this over now, let's talk some sense here. When I was down in Florida last time, I thought of a great idea

to sell sporting goods. It just came back to me. You and I, Biff—we have a line, the Loman Line. We train a couple of weeks, and put on a couple of exhibitions, see?

WILLY: That's an idea!

HAPPY: Wait! We form two basketball teams, see? Two water-polo teams. We play each other. It's a million dollars' worth of publicity. Two brothers, see? The Loman Brothers. Displays in the Royal Palms—all the hotels. And banners over the ring and the basketball court: "Loman Brothers." Baby, we could sell sporting goods!

WILLY: That is a one-million-dollar idea.

LINDA: Marvelous!

730 BIFF: I'm in great shape as far as that's concerned.

HAPPY: And the beauty of it is, Biff, it wouldn't be like a business. We'd be out playin' ball again . . .

BIFF: (enthused) Yeah, that's . . .

WILLY: Million-dollar . . .

HAPPY: And you wouldn't get fed up with it, Biff. It'd be the family again. There'd be the old honor, and comradeship, and if you wanted to go off for a swim or somethin'—well, you'd do it! Without some smart cooky gettin' up ahead of you!

735 WILLY: Lick the world! You guys together could absolutely lick the civilized world.

BIFF: I'll see Oliver tomorrow. Hap, if we could work that out . . .

LINDA: Maybe things are beginning to—

WILLY: (wildly enthused, to Linda) Stop interrupting! (To Biff.) But don't wear sport jacket and slacks when you see Oliver.

BIFF: No, I'll—

740 WILLY: A business suit, and talk as little as possible, and don't crack any jokes.

BIFF: He did like me. Always liked me.

LINDA: He loved you!

WILLY: (to Linda) Will you stop! (To Biff.) Walk in very serious. You are not applying for a boy's job. Money is to pass. Be quiet, fine, and serious. Everybody likes a kidder, but nobody lends him money.

HAPPY: I'll try to get some myself, Biff. I'm sure I can.

745 WILLY: I can see great things for you, kids, I think your troubles are over. But remember, start big and you'll end big. Ask for fifteen. How much you gonna ask for?

BIFF: Gee, I don't know—

WILLY: And don't say "Gee." "Gee" is a boy's word. A man walking in for fifteen thousand dollars does not say "Gee!"

BIFF: Ten, I think, would be top though.

WILLY: Don't be so modest. You always started too low. Walk in with a big laugh. Don't look worried. Start off with a couple of your good stories to lighten things up. It's not what you say, it's how you say it—because personality always wins the day.

750   LINDA: Oliver always thought the highest of him—
       WILLY: Will you let me talk?
       BIFF: Don't yell at her, Pop, will ya?
       WILLY: *(angrily)* I was talking, wasn't I!
       BIFF: I don't like you yelling at her all the time, and I'm tellin' you, that's all.
755   WILLY: What're you, takin' over this house?
       LINDA: Willy—
       WILLY: *(turning on her)* Don't take his side all the time, goddammit!
       BIFF: *(furiously)* Stop yelling at her!
       WILLY: *(suddenly pulling on his cheek, beaten down, guilt ridden)* Give my best to Bill Oliver—he may remember me. *(He exits through the livingroom doorway.)*
760   LINDA: *(her voice subdued)* What'd you have to start that for? *(Biff turns away.)* You see how sweet he was as soon as you talked hopefully? *(She goes over to Biff.)* Come up and say good night to him. Don't let him go to bed that way.
       HAPPY: Come on, Biff, let's buck him up.
       LINDA: Please, dear. Just say good night. It takes so little to make him happy. Come. *(She goes through the livingroom doorway, calling upstairs from within the livingroom.)* Your pajamas are hanging in the bathroom. Willy!
       HAPPY: *(looking toward where Linda went out)* What a woman! They broke the mold when they made her. You know that, Biff?
       BIFF: He's off salary. My God, working on commission!
765   HAPPY: Well, let's face it: he's no hot-shot selling man. Except that sometimes, you have to admit, he's a sweet personality.
       BIFF: *(deciding)* Lend me ten bucks, will ya? I want to buy some new ties.
       HAPPY: I'll take you to a place I know. Beautiful stuff. Wear one of my striped shirts tomorrow.
       BIFF: She got gray. Mom got awful old. Gee, I'm gonna go in to Oliver tomorrow and knock him for a—
       HAPPY: Come on up. Tell that to Dad. Let's give him a whirl. Come on.
770   BIFF: *(steamed up)* You know, with ten thousand bucks, boy!
       HAPPY: *(as they go into the livingroom)* That's the talk, Biff, that's the first time I've heard the old confidence out of you! *(From within the livingroom, fading off.)* You're gonna live with me, kid, and any babe you want you just say the word . . . *(The last lines are hardly heard. They are mounting the stairs to their parents' bedroom.)*
       LINDA: *(entering her bedroom and addressing Willy, who is in the bathroom. She is straightening the bed for him)* Can you do anything about the shower? It drips.
       WILLY: *(from the bathroom)* All of a sudden everything falls to pieces! Goddam plumbing, oughta be sued, those people. I hardly finished putting it in and the thing . . . *(His words rumble off.)*

LINDA: I'm just wondering if Oliver will remember him. You think he might?

775 WILLY: *(coming out of the bathroom in his pajamas)* Remember him? What's the matter with you, you crazy? If he'd've stayed with Oliver he'd be on top by now! Wait'll Oliver gets a look at him. You don't know the average caliber any more. The average young man today—*(he is getting into bed)*—is got a caliber of zero. Greatest thing in the world for him was to bum around.

Biff and Happy enter the bedroom. Slight pause.

WILLY: *(stops short, looking at Biff)* Glad to hear it, boy.

HAPPY: He wanted to say good night to you, sport.

WILLY: *(to Biff)* Yeah. Knock him dead, boy. What'd you want to tell me?

BIFF: Just take it easy, Pop. Good night. *(He turns to go.)*

780 WILLY: *(unable to resist)* And if anything falls off the desk while you're talking to him—like a package or something—don't you pick it up. They have office boys for that.

LINDA: I'll make a big breakfast—

WILLY: Will you let me finish? *(To Biff.)* Tell him you were in the business in the West. Not farm work.

BIFF: All right, Dad.

LINDA: I think everything—

785 WILLY: *(going right through her speech)* And don't undersell yourself. No less than fifteen thousand dollars.

BIFF: *(unable to bear him)* Okay. Good night, Mom. *(He starts moving.)*

WILLY: Because you got a greatness in you, Biff, remember that. You got all kinds a greatness . . . *(He lies back, exhausted. Biff walks out.)*

LINDA: *(calling after Biff)* Sleep well, darling!

HAPPY: I'm gonna get married, Mom. I wanted to tell you.

790 LINDA: Go to sleep, dear.

HAPPY: *(going)* I just wanted to tell you.

WILLY: Keep up the good work. *(Happy exits.)* God . . . remember that Ebbets Field game? The championship of the city?

LINDA: Just rest. Should I sing to you?

WILLY: Yeah. Sing to me. *(Linda hums a soft lullaby.)* When that team came out—he was the tallest, remember?

795 LINDA: Oh, yes. And in gold.

Biff enters the darkened kitchen, takes a cigarette, and leaves the house. He comes downstage into a golden pool of light. He smokes, staring at the night.

WILLY: Like a young god. Hercules—something like that. And the sun, the sun all around him. Remember how he waved to me? Right up from the field, with the representatives of three colleges standing by? And the buyers I brought, and the cheers when he came out—Loman,

Loman, Loman! God Almighty, he'll be great yet. A star like that, magnificent, can never really fade away!

The light on Willy is fading. The gas heater begins to glow through the kitchen wall, near the stairs, a blue flame beneath red coils.

LINDA: *(timidly)* Willy, dear, what has he got against you?
WILLY: I'm so tired. Don't talk any more.

Biff slowly returns to the kitchen. He stops, stares toward the heater.

LINDA: Will you ask Howard to let you work in New York?
800   WILLY: First thing in the morning. Everything'll be all right.

Biff reaches behind the heater and draws out a length of rubber tubing. He is horrified and turns his head toward Willy's room, still dimly lit, from which the strains of Linda's desperate but monotonous humming rise.

WILLY: *(staring through the window into the moonlight)* Gee, look at the moon moving between the buildings!

Biff wraps the tubing around his hand and quickly goes up the stairs. Curtain.

ACT II

Music is heard, gay and bright. The curtain rises as the music fades away. Willy, in shirt sleeves, is sitting at the kitchen table, sipping coffee, his hat in his lap. Linda is filling his cup when she can.

WILLY: Wonderful coffee. Meal in itself.
LINDA: Can I make you some eggs?
WILLY: No. Take a breath.
LINDA: You look so rested, dear.
5   WILLY: I slept like a dead one. First time in months. Imagine, sleeping till ten on a Tuesday morning. Boys left nice and early, heh?
LINDA: They were out of here by eight o'clock.
WILLY: Good work!
LINDA: It was so thrilling to see them leaving together. I can't get over the shaving lotion in this house.
WILLY: *(smiling)* Mmm—
10   LINDA: Biff was very changed this morning. His whole attitude seemed to be hopeful. He couldn't wait to get downtown to see Oliver.
WILLY: He's heading for a change. There's no question, there simply are certain men that take longer to get—solidified. How did he dress?
LINDA: His blue suit. He's so handsome in that suit. He could be a— anything in that suit!

Willy gets up from the table. Linda holds his jacket for him.

WILLY: There's no question, no question at all. Gee, on the way home tonight I'd like to buy some seeds.

LINDA: *(laughing)* That'd be wonderful. But not enough sun gets back there. Nothing'll grow any more.

15 WILLY: You wait, kid, before it's all over we're gonna get a little place out in the country, and I'll raise some vegetables, a couple of chickens . . .

LINDA: You'll do it yet, dear.

Willy walks out of his jacket. Linda follows him.

WILLY: And they'll get married, and come for a weekend. I'd build a little guest house. 'Cause I got so many fine tools, all I'd need would be a little lumber and some peace of mind.

LINDA: *(joyfully)* I sewed the lining . . .

WILLY: I could build two guest houses, so they'd both come. Did he decide how much he's going to ask Oliver for?

20 LINDA: *(getting him into the jacket)* He didn't mention it, but I imagine ten or fifteen thousand. You going to talk to Howard today?

WILLY: Yeah. I'll put it to him straight and simple. He'll just have to take me off the road.

LINDA: And Willy, don't forget to ask for a little advance, because we've got the insurance premium. It's the grace period now.

WILLY: That's a hundred . . . ?

LINDA: A hundred and eight, sixty-eight. Because we're a little short again.

25 WILLY: Why are we short?

LINDA: Well, you had the motor job on the car . . .

WILLY: That goddam Studebaker!

LINDA: And you got one more payment on the refrigerator . . .

WILLY: But it just broke again!

30 LINDA: Well, it's old, dear.

WILLY: I told you we should've bought a well-advertised machine. Charley bought a General Electric and it's twenty years old and it's still good, that son-of-a-bitch.

LINDA: But, Willy—

WILLY: Whoever heard of a Hastings refrigerator? Once in my life I would like to own something outright before it's broken! I'm always in a race with the junkyard! I just finished paying for the car and it's on its last legs. The refrigerator consumes belts like a goddam maniac. They time those things. They time them so when you finally paid for them, they're used up.

LINDA: *(buttoning up his jacket as he unbuttons it)* All told, about two hundred dollars would carry us, dear. But that includes the last payment on the mortgage. After this payment, Willy, the house belongs to us.

35 WILLY: It's twenty-five years!

LINDA: Biff was nine years old when we bought it.

WILLY: Well, that's a great thing. To weather a twenty-five year mortgage is—

LINDA: It's an accomplishment.

WILLY: All the cement, the lumber, the reconstruction I put in this house! There ain't a crack to be found in it any more.

40 LINDA: Well, it served its purpose.

WILLY: What purpose? Some stranger'll come along, move in, and that's that. If only Biff would take this house, and raise a family . . . *(He starts to go.)* Good-by, I'm late.

LINDA: *(suddenly remembering)* Oh, I forgot! You're supposed to meet them for dinner.

WILLY: Me?

LINDA: At Frank's Chop House on Forty-eighth near Sixth Avenue.

45 WILLY: Is that so! How about you?

LINDA: No, just the three of you. They're gonna blow you to a big meal!

WILLY: Don't say! Who thought of that?

LINDA: Biff came to me this morning, Willy, and he said, "Tell Dad, we want to blow him to a big meal." Be there six o'clock. You and your two boys are going to have dinner.

WILLY: Gee whiz! That's really somethin'. I'm gonna knock Howard for a loop, kid. I'll get an advance, and I'll come home with a New York job. Goddammit, now I'm gonna do it!

50 LINDA: Oh, that's the spirit, Willy!

WILLY: I will never get behind a wheel the rest of my life!

LINDA: It's changing, Willy, I can feel it changing!

WILLY: Beyond a question. G'by, I'm late. *(He starts to go again.)*

LINDA: *(calling after him as she runs to the kitchen table for a handkerchief)* You got your glasses?

55 WILLY: *(feels for them, then comes back in)* Yeah, yeah, got my glasses.

LINDA: *(giving him the handkerchief)* And a handkerchief.

WILLY: Yeah, handkerchief.

LINDA: And your saccharine?

WILLY: Yeah, my saccharine.

60 LINDA: Be careful on the subway stairs.

She kisses him, and a silk stocking is seen hanging from her hand. Willy notices it.

WILLY: Will you stop mending stockings? At least while I'm in the house. It gets me nervous. I can't tell you. Please.

Linda hides the stocking in her hand as she follows Willy across the forestage in front of the house.

LINDA: Remember, Frank's Chop House.

WILLY: *(passing the apron)* Maybe beets would grow out there.

LINDA: *(laughing)* But you tried so many times.

65 WILLY: Yeah. Well, don't work hard today. *(He disappears around the right corner of the house.)*

LINDA: Be careful!

As Willy vanishes, Linda waves to him. Suddenly the phone rings. She runs across the stage and into the kitchen and lifts it.

LINDA: Hello? Oh, Biff! I'm so glad you called, I just . . . Yes, sure, I just told him. Yes, he'll be there for dinner at six o'clock, I didn't forget. Listen, I was just dying to tell you. You know that little rubber pipe I told you about? That he connected to the gas heater? I finally decided to go down the cellar this morning and take it away and destroy it. But it's gone! Imagine? He took it away himself, it isn't there! *(She listens.)* When? Oh, then you took it. Oh—nothing, it's just that I'd hoped he'd taken it away himself. Oh, I'm not worried, darling, because this morning he left in such high spirits, it was like the old days! I'm not afraid any more. Did Mr. Oliver see you? . . . Well, you wait there then. And make a nice impression on him, darling. Just don't perspire too much before you see him. And have a nice time with Dad. He may have big news too! . . . That's right, a New York job. And be sweet to him tonight, dear. Be loving to him. Because he's only a little boat looking for a harbor. *(She is trembling with sorrow and joy.)* Oh, that's wonderful, Biff, you'll save his life. Thanks, darling. Just put your arm around him when he comes into the restaurant. Give him a smile. That's the boy . . . Good-by, dear. . . . You got your comb? . . . That's fine. Good-by, Biff dear.

In the middle of her speech, Howard Wagner, thirty-six, wheels in a small type-writer table on which is a wire-recording machine and proceeds to plug it in. This is on the left forestage. Light slowly fades on Linda as it rises on Howard. Howard is intent on threading the machine and only glances over his shoulder as Willy appears.

WILLY: Pst! Pst!

HOWARD: Hello, Willy, come in.

70 WILLY: Like to have a little talk with you, Howard.

HOWARD: Sorry to keep you waiting. I'll be with you in a minute.

WILLY: What's that, Howard?

HOWARD: Didn't you ever see one of these? Wire recorder.

WILLY: Oh. Can we talk a minute?

75 HOWARD: Records things. Just got delivery yesterday. Been driving me crazy, the most terrific machine I ever saw in my life. I was up all night with it.

WILLY: What do you do with it?

HOWARD: I bought it for dictation, but you can do anything with it. Listen to this. I had it home last night. Listen to what I picked up. The first one is my daughter. Get this. *(He flicks the switch and "Roll out the Barrel" is heard being whistled.)* Listen to that kid whistle.

WILLY: That is lifelike, isn't it?

HOWARD: Seven years old. Get that tone.

80 WILLY: Ts, ts. Like to ask a little favor if you . . .

The whistling breaks off, and the voice of Howard's Daughter is heard.

His Daughter: "Now you, Daddy."
Howard: She's crazy for me! *(Again the same song is whistled.)* That's me! Ha! *(He winks.)*
WILLY: You're very good!

The whistling breaks off again. The machine runs silent for a moment.

Howard: Sh! Get this now, this is my son.
85 His Son: "The capital of Alabama is Montgomery; the capital of Arizona is Phoenix; the capital of Arkansas is Little Rock; the capital of California is Sacramento . . ." *(And on, and on.)*
Howard: *(holding up five fingers)* Five years old, Willy!
WILLY: He'll make an announcer some day!
His Son: *(continuing)* "The capital . . ."
Howard: Get that—alphabetical order! *(The machine breaks off suddenly.)* Wait a minute. The maid kicked the plug out.
90 WILLY: It certainly is a—
Howard: Sh, for God's sake!
His Son: "It's nine o'clock, Bulova watch time. So I have to go to sleep."
WILLY: That really is—
Howard: Wait a minute! The next is my wife.

They wait.

95 Howard's Voice: "Go on, say something." *(Pause.)* "Well, you gonna talk?"
His Wife: "I can't think of anything."
Howard's Voice: "Well, talk—it's turning."
His Wife: *(shyly, beaten)* "Hello." *(Silence.)* "Oh, Howard, I can't talk into this . . ."
Howard: *(snapping the machine off)* That was my wife.
100 WILLY: That is a wonderful machine. Can we—
Howard: I tell you, Willy, I'm gonna take my camera, and my bandsaw, and all my hobbies, and out they go. This is the most fascinating relaxation I ever found.
WILLY: I think I'll get one myself.
Howard: Sure, they're only a hundred and a half. You can't do without it. Supposing you wanna hear Jack Benny, see? But you can't be at home at that hour. So you tell the maid to turn the radio on when Jack Benny comes on, and this automatically goes on with the radio . . .
WILLY: And when you come home you . . .
105 Howard: You can come home twelve o'clock, one o'clock, any time you like, and you get yourself a Coke and sit yourself down, throw the switch, and there's Jack Benny's program in the middle of the night!

WILLY: I'm definitely going to get one. Because lots of time I'm on the road, and I think to myself, what I must be missing on the radio!

HOWARD: Don't you have a radio in the car?

WILLY: Well, yeah, but who ever thinks of turning it on?

HOWARD: Say, aren't you supposed to be in Boston?

110 WILLY: That's what I want to talk to you about, Howard. You got a minute?

He draws a chair in from the wing.

HOWARD: What happened? What're you doing here?

WILLY: Well . . .

HOWARD: You didn't crack up again, did you?

WILLY: Oh, no. No . . .

115 HOWARD: Geez, you had me worried there for a minute. What's the trouble?

WILLY: Well, to tell you the truth, Howard, I've come to the decision that I'd rather not travel any more.

HOWARD: Not travel! Well, what'll you do?

WILLY: Remember, Christmas time, when you had the party here? You said you'd try to think of some spot for me here in town.

HOWARD: With us?

120 WILLY: Well, sure.

HOWARD: Oh, yeah, yeah. I remember. Well, I couldn't think of anything for you, Willy.

WILLY: I tell ya, Howard. The kids are all grown up, y'know. I don't need much any more. If I could take home—well, sixty-five dollars a week, I could swing it.

HOWARD: Yeah, but Willy, see I—

WILLY: I tell ya why, Howard. Speaking frankly and between the two of us, y'know—I'm just a little tired.

125 HOWARD: Oh, I could understand that, Willy. But you're a road man, Willy, and we do a road business. We've only got a half-dozen salesmen on the floor here.

WILLY: God knows, Howard, I never asked a favor of any man. But I was with the firm when your father used to carry you in here in his arms.

HOWARD: I know that, Willy, but—

WILLY: Your father came to me the day you were born and asked me what I thought of the name of Howard, may he rest in peace.

HOWARD: I appreciate that, Willy, but there just is no spot here for you. If I had a spot I'd slam you right in, but I just don't have a single, solitary spot.

He looks for his lighter. Willy has picked it up and gives it to him. Pause.

130 WILLY: *(with increasing anger)* Howard, all I need to set my table is fifty dollars a week.

HOWARD: But where am I going to put you, kid?

WILLY: Look, it isn't a question of whether I can sell merchandise, is it?

HOWARD: No, but it's a business, kid, and everybody's gotta pull his own weight.

WILLY: *(desperately)* Just let me tell you a story, Howard—

135 HOWARD: 'Cause you gotta admit, business is business.

WILLY: *(angrily)* Business is definitely business, but just listen for a minute. You don't understand this. When I was a boy—eighteen, nineteen—I was already on the road. And there was a question in my mind as to whether selling had a future for me. Because in those days I had a yearning to go to Alaska. See, there were three gold strikes in one month in Alaska, and I felt like going out. Just for the ride, you might say.

HOWARD: *(barely interested)* Don't say.

WILLY: Oh, yeah, my father lived many years in Alaska. He was an adventurous man. We've got quite a little streak of self-reliance in our family. I thought I'd go out with my older brother and try to locate him, and maybe settle in the North with the old man. And I was almost decided to go, when I met a salesman in the Parker House. His name was Dave Singleman. And he was eighty-four years old, and he'd drummed merchandise in thirty-one states. And old Dave, he'd go up to his room, y'understand, put on his green velvet slippers—I'll never forget—and pick up his phone and call the buyers, and without ever leaving his room, at the age of eighty-four, he made his living. And when I saw that, I realized that selling was the greatest career a man could want. 'Cause what could be more satisfying than to be able to go, at the age of eighty-four, into twenty or thirty different cities, and pick up a phone, and be remembered and loved and helped by so many different people? Do you know? when he died—and by the way he died the death of a salesman, in his green velvet slippers in the smoker of the New York, New Haven and Hartford, going into Boston—when he died, hundreds of salesmen and buyers were at his funeral. Things were sad on a lotta trains for months after that. *(He stands up. Howard has not looked at him.)* In those days there was personality in it, Howard. There was respect, and comradeship, and gratitude in it. Today, it's all cut and dried, and there's no chance for bringing friendship to bear—or personality. You see what I mean? They don't know me any more.

HOWARD: *(moving away, to the right)* That's just the thing, Willy.

140 WILLY: If I had forty dollars a week—that's all I'd need. Forty dollars, Howard.

HOWARD: Kid, I can't take blood from a stone, I—

WILLY: *(desperation is on him now)* Howard, the year Al Smith was nominated, your father came to me and—

HOWARD: *(starting to go off)* I've got to see some people, kid.

WILLY: *(stopping him)* I'm talking about your father! There were promises made across this desk! You mustn't tell me you've got people to see—I put thirty-four years into this firm, Howard, and now I can't pay my insurance! You can't eat the orange and throw the peel away—a man is not a piece of fruit! *(After a pause.)* Now pay attention. Your father—in 1928 I had a big year. I averaged a hundred and seventy dollars a week in commissions.

145 HOWARD: *(impatiently)* Now, Willy, you never averaged—

WILLY: *(banging his hand on the desk)* I averaged a hundred and seventy dollars a week in the year of 1928! And your father came to me—or rather, I was in the office here—it was right over this desk—and he put his hand on my shoulder—

HOWARD: *(getting up)* You'll have to excuse me, Willy, I gotta see some people. Pull yourself together. *(Going out.)* I'll be back in a little while.

On Howard's exit, the light on his chair grows very bright and strange.

WILLY: Pull myself together! What the hell did I say to him? My God, I was yelling at him! How could I! *(Willy breaks off, staring at the light, which occupies the chair, animating it. He approaches this chair, standing across the desk from it.)* Frank, Frank, don't you remember what you told me that time? How you put your hand on my shoulder, and Frank . . . *(He leans on the desk and as he speaks the dead man's name he accidentally switches on the recorder, and instantly—)*

HOWARD'S SON: ". . . of New York is Albany. The capital of Ohio is Cincinnati, the capital of Rhode Island is . . ." *(The recitation continues.)*

150 WILLY: *(leaping away with fright, shouting)* Ha! Howard! Howard! Howard!

HOWARD: *(rushing in)* What happened?

WILLY: *(pointing at the machine, which continues nasally, childishly, with the capital cities)* Shut it off! Shut it off!

HOWARD: *(pulling the plug out)* Look, Willy . . .

WILLY: *(pressing his hands to his eyes)* I gotta get myself some coffee. I'll get some coffee . . .

Willy starts to walk out. Howard stops him.

155 HOWARD: *(rolling up the cord)* Willy, look . . .

WILLY: I'll go to Boston.

HOWARD: Willy, you can't go to Boston for us.

WILLY: Why can't I go?

HOWARD: I don't want you to represent us. I've been meaning to tell you for a long time now.

160 WILLY: Howard, are you firing me?

HOWARD: I think you need a good long rest, Willy.

WILLY: Howard—

HOWARD: And when you feel better, come back, and we'll see if we can work something out.

WILLY: But I gotta earn money, Howard. I'm in no position—

165 HOWARD: Where are your sons? Why don't your sons give you a hand?
WILLY: They're working on a very big deal.
HOWARD: This is no time for false pride, Willy. You go to your sons and
tell them that you're tired. You've got two great boys, haven't you?
WILLY: Oh, no question, no question, but in the meantime . . .
HOWARD: Then that's that, heh?
170 WILLY: All right, I'll go to Boston tomorrow.
HOWARD: No, no.
WILLY: I can't throw myself on my sons. I'm not a cripple!
HOWARD: Look, kid, I'm busy this morning.
WILLY: *(grasping Howard's arm)* Howard, you've got to let me go to Boston!
175 HOWARD: *(hard, keeping himself under control)* I've got a line of people to
see this morning. Sit down, take five minutes, and pull yourself
together, and then go home, will ya? I need the office, Willy. *(He
starts to go, turns, remembering the recorder, starts to push off the table
holding the recorder.)* Oh, yeah. Whenever you can this week, stop by
and drop off the samples. You'll feel better, Willy, and then come
back and we'll talk. Pull yourself together, kid, there's people outside.

*Howard exits, pushing the table off left. Willy stares into space, exhausted. Now
the music is heard—Ben's music—first distantly, then closer, closer. As Willy
speaks, Ben enters from the right. He carries valise and umbrella.*

WILLY: Oh, Ben, how did you do it? What is the answer? Did you wind up
the Alaska deal already?
BEN: Doesn't take much time if you know what you're doing. Just a short
business trip. Boarding ship in an hour. Wanted to say good-by.
WILLY: Ben, I've got to talk to you.
BEN: *(glancing at his watch)* Haven't the time, William.
180 WILLY: *(crossing the apron to Ben)* Ben, nothing's working out. I don't
know what to do.
BEN: Now, look here, William. I've bought timberland in Alaska and I
need a man to look after things for me.
WILLY: God, timberland! Me and my boys in those grand outdoors!
BEN: You've a new continent at your doorstep, William. Get out of these
cities, they're full of talk and time payments and courts of law. Screw
on your fists and you can fight for a fortune up there.
WILLY: Yes, yes! Linda! Linda!

Linda enters as of old, with the wash.

185 LINDA: Oh, you're back?
BEN: I haven't much time.
WILLY: No, wait! Linda, he's got a proposition for me in Alaska.
LINDA: But you've got—*(To Ben.)* He's got a beautiful job here.
WILLY: But in Alaska, kid, I could—
190 LINDA: You're doing well enough, Willy!

BEN: *(to Linda)* Enough for what, my dear?

LINDA: *(frightened of Ben and angry at him)* Don't say those things to him! Enough to be happy right here, right now. *(To Willy, while Ben laughs.)* Why must everybody conquer the world? You're well liked, and the boys love you, and someday—*(to Ben)*—why, old man Wagner told him just the other day that if he keeps it up he'll be a member of the firm, didn't he, Willy?

WILLY: Sure, sure. I am building something with this firm, Ben, and if a man is building something he must be on the right track, mustn't he?

BEN: What are you building? Lay your hand on it. Where is it?

195 WILLY: *(hesitantly)* That's true, Linda, there's nothing.

LINDA: Why? *(To Ben.)* There's a man eighty-four years old—

WILLY: That's right, Ben, that's right. When I look at that man I say, what is there to worry about?

BEN: Bah!

WILLY: It's true, Ben. All he has to do is go into any city, pick up the phone, and he's making his living and you know why?

200 BEN: *(picking up his valise)* I've got to go.

WILLY: *(holding Ben back)* Look at this boy!

Biff, in his high school sweater, enters carrying suitcase. Happy carries Biff's shoulder guards, gold helmet, and football pants.

WILLY: Without a penny to his name, three great universities are begging for him, and from there the sky's the limit, because it's not what you do, Ben. It's who you know and the smile on your face! It's contacts, Ben, contacts! The whole wealth of Alaska passes over the lunch table at the Commodore Hotel, and that's the wonder, the wonder of this country, that a man can end with diamonds here on the basis of being liked! *(He turns to Biff.)* And that's why when you get out on that field today it's important. Because thousands of people will be rooting for you and loving you. *(To Ben, who has again begun to leave.)* And Ben! when he walks into a business office his name will sound out like a bell and all the doors will open to him! I've seen it, Ben, I've seen it a thousand times! You can't feel it with your hand like timber, but it's there!

BEN: Good-by, William.

WILLY: Ben, am I right? Don't you think I'm right? I value your advice.

205 BEN: There's a new continent at your doorstep, William. You could walk out rich. Rich. *(He is gone.)*

WILLY: We'll do it here, Ben! You hear me? We're gonna do it here!

Young Bernard rushes in. The gay music of the boys is heard.

BERNARD: Oh, gee, I was afraid you left already!

WILLY: Why? What time is it?

BERNARD: It's half-past one!

210 WILLY: Well, come on, everybody! Ebbets Field[2] next stop! Where's the pennants? *(He rushes through the wall-line of the kitchen and out into the livingroom.)*

LINDA: *(to Biff)* Did you pack fresh underwear?

BIFF: *(who has been limbering up)* I want to go!

BERNARD: Biff, I'm carrying your helmet, ain't I?

HAPPY: No, I'm carrying the helmet.

215 BERNARD: Oh, Biff, you promised me.

HAPPY: I'm carrying the helmet.

BERNARD: How am I going to get in the locker room?

LINDA: Let him carry the shoulder guards. *(She puts her coat and hat on in the kitchen.)*

BERNARD: Can I, Biff? 'Cause I told everybody I'm going to be in the locker room.

220 HAPPY: In Ebbets Field it's the clubhouse.

BERNARD: I meant the clubhouse. Biff!

HAPPY: Biff!

BIFF: *(grandly, after a slight pause)* Let him carry the shoulder guards.

HAPPY: *(as he gives Bernard the shoulder guards)* Stay close to us now.

Willy rushes in with the pennants.

225 WILLY: *(handing them out)* Everybody wave when Biff comes out on the field. *(Happy and Bernard run off.)* You set now, boy?

The music has died away.

BIFF: Ready to go, Pop. Every muscle is ready.

WILLY: *(at the edge of the apron)* You realize what this means?

BIFF: That's right, Pop.

WILLY: *(feeling Biff's muscles)* You're comin' home this afternoon captain of the All-Scholastic Championship Team of the City of New York.

230 BIFF: I got it, Pop. And remember, pal, when I take off my helmet, that touchdown is for you.

WILLY: Let's go! *(He is starting out, with his arm around Biff, when Charley enters, as of old, in knickers.)* I got no room for you, Charley.

CHARLEY: Room? For what?

WILLY: In the car.

CHARLEY: You goin' for a ride? I wanted to shoot some casino.

235 WILLY: *(furiously)* Casino! *(Incredulously.)* Don't you realize what today is?

LINDA: Oh, he knows, Willy. He's just kidding you.

WILLY: That's nothing to kid about!

CHARLEY: No, Linda, what's goin' on?

LINDA: He's playing in Ebbets Field.

240 CHARLEY: Baseball in this weather?

---

[2] The home park of the Brooklyn Dodgers.

WILLY: Don't talk to him. Come on, come on! *(He is pushing them out.)*
CHARLEY: Wait a minute, didn't you hear the news?
WILLY: What?
CHARLEY: Don't you listen to the radio? Ebbets Field just blew up.
245 WILLY: You go to hell! *(Charley laughs. Pushing them out.)* Come on, come on! We're late.
CHARLEY: *(as they go)* Knock a homer, Biff, knock a homer!
WILLY: *(the last to leave, turning to Charley)* I don't think that was funny, Charley. This is the greatest day of his life.
CHARLEY: Willy, when are you going to grow up?
WILLY: Yeah, heh? When this game is over, Charley, you'll be laughing out of the other side of your face. They'll be calling him another Red Grange.[3] Twenty-five thousand a year.
250 CHARLEY: *(kidding)* Is that so?
WILLY: Yeah, that's so.
CHARLEY: Well, then, I'm sorry, Willy. But tell me something.
WILLY: What?
CHARLEY: Who is Red Grange?
255 WILLY: Put up your hands. Goddam you, put up your hands!

Charley, chuckling, shakes his head and walks away, around the left corner of the stage. Willy follows him. The music rises to a mocking frenzy.

WILLY: Who the hell do you think you are, better than everybody else? You don't know everything, you big, ignorant, stupid . . . Put up your hands!

Light rises, on the right side of the forestage, on a small table in the reception room of Charley's office. Traffic sounds are heard. Bernard, now mature, sits whistling to himself. A pair of tennis rackets and an overnight bag are on the floor beside him.

WILLY: *(offstage)* What are you walking away for? Don't walk away! If you're going to say something say it to my face! I know you laugh at me behind my back. You'll laugh out of the other side of your goddam face after this game. Touchdown! Touchdown! Eighty thousand people! Touchdown! Right between the goal posts.

Bernard is a quiet, earnest, but self-assured young man. Willy's voice is coming from right upstage now. Bernard lowers his feet off the table and listens. Jenny, his father's secretary, enters.

JENNY: *(distressed)* Say, Bernard, will you go out in the hall?
BERNARD: What is that noise? Who is it?
260 JENNY: Mr. Loman. He just got off the elevator.

---

[3] Red (Harold Edward) Grange (b. 1903)—U.S. football player. A running back for the New York Yankees football team and the Chicago Bears, Grange was elected to the Football Hall of Fame in 1963.

BERNARD: *(getting up)* Who's he arguing with?

JENNY: Nobody. There's nobody with him. I can't deal with him any more, and your father gets all upset everytime he comes. I've got a lot of typing to do, and your father's waiting to sign it. Will you see him?

WILLY: *(entering)* Touchdown! Touch—*(He sees Jenny.)* Jenny, Jenny, good to see you. How're ya? Workin'? Or still honest?

JENNY: Fine. How've you been feeling?

265 WILLY: Not much any more, Jenny. Ha, ha! *(He is surprised to see the rackets.)*

BERNARD: Hello, Uncle Willy.

WILLY: *(almost shocked)* Bernard! Well, look who's here! *(He comes quickly, guiltily, to Bernard and warmly shakes his hand.)*

BERNARD: How are you? Good to see you.

WILLY: What are you doing here?

270 BERNARD: Oh, just stopped by to see Pop. Get off my feet till my train leaves. I'm going to Washington in a few minutes.

WILLY: Is he in?

BERNARD: Yes, he's in his office with the accountant. Sit down.

WILLY: *(sitting down)* What're you going to do in Washington?

BERNARD: Oh, just a case I've got there, Willy.

275 WILLY: That so? *(indicating the rackets)* You going to play tennis there?

BERNARD: I'm staying with a friend who's got a court.

WILLY: Don't say. His own tennis court. Must be fine people, I bet.

BERNARD: They are, very nice. Dad tells me Biff's in town.

WILLY: *(with a big smile)* Yeah, Biff's in. Working on a very big deal, Bernard.

280 BERNARD: What's Biff doing?

WILLY: Well, he's been doing very big things in the West. But he decided to establish himself here. Very big. We're having dinner. Did I hear your wife had a boy?

BERNARD: That's right. Our second.

WILLY: Two boys! What do you know!

BERNARD: What kind of a deal has Biff got?

285 WILLY: Well, Bill Oliver—very big sporting-goods man—he wants Biff very badly. Called him in from the West. Long distance, carte blanche, special deliveries. Your friends have their own private tennis court?

BERNARD: You still with the old firm, Willy?

WILLY: *(after a pause)* I'm—I'm overjoyed to see how you made the grade, Bernard, overjoyed. It's an encouraging thing to see a young man really—really—Looks very good for Biff—very—*(He breaks off, then.)* Bernard—*(He is so full of emotion, he breaks off again.)*

BERNARD: What is it, Willy?

WILLY: *(small and alone)* What—what's the secret?

290   **Bernard:** What secret?

      Willy: How—how did you? Why didn't he ever catch on?

      Bernard: I wouldn't know that, Willy.

      Willy: *(confidentially, desperately)* You were his friend, his boyhood
friend. There's something I don't understand about it. His life ended
after that Ebbets Field game. From the age of seventeen nothing good
ever happened to him.

      Bernard: He never trained himself for anything.

295   **Willy:** But he did, he did. After high school he took so many
correspondence courses. Radio mechanics; television; God knows
what, and never made the slightest mark.

      Bernard: *(taking off his glasses)* Willy, do you want to talk candidly?

      Willy: *(rising, faces Bernard)* I regard you as a very brilliant man, Bernard.
I value your advice.

      Bernard: Oh, the hell with the advice, Willy. I couldn't advise you.
There's just one thing I've always wanted to ask you. When he was
supposed to graduate, and the math teacher flunked him—

      Willy: Oh, that son-of-a-bitch ruined his life.

300   **Bernard:** Yeah, but, Willy, all he had to do was go to summer school and
make up that subject.

      Willy: That's right, that's right.

      Bernard: Did you tell him not to go to summer school?

      Willy: Me? I begged him to go. I ordered him to go!

      Bernard: Then why wouldn't he go?

305   **Willy:** Why? Why! Bernard, that question has been trailing me like a
ghost for the last fifteen years. He flunked the subject, and laid down
and died like a hammer hit him!

      Bernard: Take it easy, kid.

      Willy: Let me talk to you—I got nobody to talk to. Bernard, Bernard, was
it my fault? Y'see? It keeps going around in my mind, maybe I did
something to him. I got nothing to give him.

      Bernard: Don't take it so hard.

      Willy: Why did he lay down? What is the story there? You were his
friend!

310   **Bernard:** Willy, I remember, it was June, and our grades came out. And
he'd flunked math.

      Willy: That son-of-a-bitch!

      Bernard: No, it wasn't right then. Biff just got very angry, I remember,
and he was ready to enroll in summer school.

      Willy: *(surprised)* He was?

      Bernard: He wasn't beaten by it at all. But then, Willy, he disappeared
from the block for almost a month. And I got the idea that he'd gone
up to New England to see you. Did he have a talk with you then?

Willy stares in silence.

315   BERNARD: Willy?

    WILLY: *(with a strong edge of resentment in his voice)* Yeah, he came to
        Boston. What about it?

    BERNARD: Well, just that when he came back—I'll never forget this, it
        always mystifies me. Because I'd thought so well of Biff, even though
        he'd always taken advantage of me. I loved him, Willy, y'know? And
        he came back after that month and took his sneakers—remember
        those sneakers with "University of Virginia" printed on them? He
        was so proud of those, wore them every day. And he took them down
        in the cellar, and burned them up in the furnace. We had a fist fight.
        It lasted at least half an hour. Just the two of us, punching each other
        down the cellar, and crying right through it. I've often thought of
        how strange it was that I knew he'd given up his life. What happened
        in Boston, Willy?

Willy looks at him as at an intruder.

    BERNARD: I just bring it up because you asked me.

    WILLY: *(angrily)* Nothing. What do you mean, "What happened?" What's
        that got to do with anything?

320   BERNARD: Well, don't get sore.

    WILLY: What are you trying to do, blame it on me? If a boy lays down is
        that my fault?

    BERNARD: Now, Willy, don't get—

    WILLY: Well, don't—don't talk to me that way! What does that mean,
        "What happened?"

Charley enters. He is in his vest, and he carries a bottle of bourbon.

    CHARLEY: Hey, you're going to miss that train. *(He waves the bottle.)*

325   BERNARD: Yeah, I'm going. *(He takes the bottle.)* Thanks, Pop. *(He picks up
        his rackets and bag.)* Good-by, Willy, and don't worry about it. You
        know, "If at first you don't succeed . . ."

    WILLY: Yes, I believe in that.

    BERNARD: But sometimes, Willy, it's better for a man just to walk away.

    WILLY: Walk away?

    BERNARD: That's right.

330   WILLY: But if you can't walk away?

    BERNARD: *(after a slight pause)* I guess that's when it's tough. *(Extending
        his hand.)* Good-by, Willy.

    WILLY: *(shaking Bernard's hand)* Good-by, boy.

    CHARLEY: *(an arm on Bernard's shoulder)* How do you like this kid? Gonna
        argue a case in front of the Supreme Court.

    BERNARD: *(protesting)* Pop!

335   WILLY: *(genuinely shocked, pained, and happy)* No! The Supreme Court!

    BERNARD: I gotta run, 'By, Dad!

    CHARLEY: Knock 'em dead, Bernard!

Bernard goes off.

WILLY: *(as Charley takes out his wallet)* The Supreme Court! And he didn't even mention it!

CHARLEY: *(counting out money on the desk)* He don't have to—he's gonna do it.

340 WILLY: And you never told him what to do, did you? You never took any interest in him.

CHARLEY: My salvation is that I never took any interest in anything. There's some money—fifty dollars. I got an accountant inside.

WILLY: Charley, look . . . *(With difficulty.)* I got my insurance to pay. If you can manage it—I need a hundred and ten dollars.

Charley doesn't reply for a moment; merely stops moving.

WILLY: I'd draw it from my bank but Linda would know, and I . . .

CHARLEY: Sit down, Willy.

345 WILLY: *(moving toward the chair)* I'm keeping an account of everything, remember. I'll pay every penny back. *(He sits.)*

CHARLEY: Now listen to me, Willy.

WILLY: I want you to know I appreciate . . .

CHARLEY: *(sitting down on the table)* Willy, what're you doin'? What the hell is goin' on in your head?

WILLY: Why? I'm simply . . .

350 CHARLEY: I offered you a job. You can make fifty dollars a week. And I won't send you on the road.

WILLY: I've got a job.

CHARLEY: Without pay? What kind of a job is a job without pay? *(He rises.)* Now, look, kid, enough is enough. I'm no genius but I know when I'm being insulted.

WILLY: Insulted!

CHARLEY: Why don't you want to work for me?

355 WILLY: What's the matter with you? I've got a job.

CHARLEY: Then what're you walkin' in here every week for?

WILLY: *(getting up)* Well, if you don't want me to walk in here—

CHARLEY: I am offering you a job.

WILLY: I don't want your goddam job!

360 CHARLEY: When the hell are you going to grow up?

WILLY: *(furiously)* You big ignoramus, if you say that to me again I'll rap you one! I don't care how big you are! *(He's ready to fight.)*

Pause.

CHARLEY: *(kindly, going to him)* How much do you need, Willy?

WILLY: Charley, I'm strapped. I'm strapped. I don't know what to do. I was just fired.

CHARLEY: Howard fired you?

365 WILLY: That snotnose. Imagine that? I named him. I named him Howard.

CHARLEY: Willy, when're you gonna realize that them things don't mean anything? You named him Howard, but you can't sell that. The only thing you got in this world is what you can sell. And the funny thing is that you're a salesman, and you don't know that.

WILLY: I've always tried to think otherwise, I guess. I always felt that if a man was impressive, and well liked, that nothing—

CHARLEY: Why must everybody like you? Who liked J. P. Morgan?[4] Was he impressive? In a Turkish bath he'd look like a butcher. But with his pockets on he was very well liked. Now listen, Willy, I know you don't like me, and nobody can say I'm in love with you, but I'll give you a job because—just for the hell of it, put it that way. Now what do you say?

WILLY: I—I just can't work for you, Charley.

370 CHARLEY: What're you, jealous of me?

WILLY: I can't work for you, that's all, don't ask me why.

CHARLEY: (angered, takes out more bills) You been jealous of me all your life, you damned fool! Here, pay your insurance. (He puts the money in Willy's hand.)

WILLY: I'm keeping strict accounts.

CHARLEY: I've got some work to do. Take care of yourself. And pay your insurance.

375 WILLY: (moving to the right) Funny, y'know? After all the highways, and the trains, and the appointments, and the years, you end up worth more dead than alive.

CHARLEY: Willy, nobody's worth nothin' dead. (After a slight pause.) Did you hear what I said?

Willy stands still, dreaming.

CHARLEY: Willy!

WILLY: Apologize to Bernard for me when you see him. I didn't mean to argue with him. He's a fine boy. They're all fine boys, and they'll end up big—all of them. Someday they'll all play tennis together. Wish me luck, Charley. He saw Bill Oliver today.

CHARLEY: Good luck.

380 WILLY: (on the verge of tears) Charley, you're the only friend I got. Isn't that a remarkable thing? (He goes out.)

CHARLEY: Jesus!

Charley stares after him a moment and follows. All light blacks out. Suddenly raucous music is heard, and a red glow rises behind the screen at right. Stanley, a young waiter, appears, carrying a table, followed by Happy, who is carrying two chairs.

---

[4] John Pierpont Morgan (1837–1913)—U.S. financier.

STANLEY: *(putting the table down)* That's all right, Mr. Loman, I can handle it myself. *(He turns and takes the chairs from Happy and places them at the table.)*

HAPPY: *(glancing around)* Oh, this is better.

STANLEY: Sure, in the front there you're in the middle of all kinds a noise. Whenever you got a party, Mr. Loman, you just tell me and I'll put you back here. Y'know, there's a lotta people they don't like it private, because when they go out they like to see a lotta action around them because they're sick and tired to stay in the house by theirself. But I know you, you ain't from Hackensack. You know what I mean?

385 HAPPY: *(sitting down)* So, how's it coming, Stanley?

STANLEY: Ah, it's a dog's life. I only wish during the war they'd a took me in the Army. I coulda been dead by now.

HAPPY: My brother's back, Stanley.

STANLEY: Oh, he come back, heh? From the Far West.

HAPPY: Yeah, big cattle man, my brother, so treat him right. And my father's coming too.

390 STANLEY: Oh, your father too!

HAPPY: You got a couple of nice lobsters?

STANLEY: Hundred per cent, big.

HAPPY: I want them with the claws.

STANLEY: Don't worry, I don't give you no mice. *(Happy laughs.)* How about some wine? It'll put a head on the meal.

395 HAPPY: No. You remember, Stanley, that recipe I brought you from overseas? With the champagne in it?

STANLEY: Oh, yeah, sure. I still got it tacked up yet in the kitchen. But that'll have to cost a buck apiece anyways.

HAPPY: That's all right.

STANLEY: What'd you, hit a number or somethin'?

HAPPY: No, it's a little celebration. My brother is—I think he pulled off a big deal today. I think we're going into business together.

400 STANLEY: Great! That's the best for you. Because a family business, you know what I mean?—that's the best.

HAPPY: That's what I think.

STANLEY: 'Cause what's the difference? Somebody steals? It's in the family. Know what I mean? *(Sotto voce.)* Like this bartender here. The boss is goin' crazy what kinda leak he's got in the cash register. You put it in but it don't come out.

HAPPY: *(raising his head)* Sh!

STANLEY: What?

405 HAPPY: You notice I wasn't lookin' right or left, was I?

STANLEY: No.

HAPPY: And my eyes are closed.

STANLEY: So what's the—

HAPPY: Strudel's comin'.

410 STANLEY: *(catching on, looks around)* Ah, no, there's no—

He breaks off as a furred, lavishly dressed Girl enters and sits at the next table. Both follow her with their eyes.

STANLEY: Geez, how'd ya know?

HAPPY: I got radar or something. *(Staring directly at her profile.)* Ooooooo . . . Stanley.

STANLEY: I think that's for you, Mr. Loman.

HAPPY: Look at that mouth. Oh, God. And the binoculars.

415 STANLEY: Geez, you got a life, Mr. Loman.

HAPPY: Wait on her.

STANLEY: *(going to The Girl's table)* Would you like a menu, ma'am?

GIRL: I'm expecting someone, but I'd like a—

HAPPY: Why don't you bring her—excuse me, miss, do you mind? I sell champagne, and I'd like you to try my brand. Bring her a champagne, Stanley.

420 GIRL: That's awfully nice of you.

HAPPY: Don't mention it. It's all company money. *(He laughs.)*

GIRL: That's a charming product to be selling, isn't it?

HAPPY: Oh, gets to be like everything else. Selling is selling, y'know.

GIRL: I suppose.

425 HAPPY: You don't happen to sell, do you?

GIRL: No, I don't sell.

HAPPY: Would you object to a compliment from a stranger? You ought to be on a magazine cover.

GIRL: *(looking at him a little archly)* I have been.

Stanley comes in with a glass of champagne.

HAPPY: What'd I say before, Stanley? You see? She's a cover girl.

430 STANLEY: Oh, I could see, I could see.

HAPPY: *(to The Girl)* What magazine?

GIRL: Oh, a lot of them. *(She takes the drink.)* Thank you.

HAPPY: You know what they say in France, don't you? "Champagne is the drink of the complexion"—Hya, Biff!

Biff has entered and sits with Happy.

BIFF: Hello, kid. Sorry I'm late.

435 HAPPY: I just got here. Uh, Miss—?

GIRL: Forsythe.

HAPPY: Miss Forsythe, this is my brother.

BIFF: Is Dad here?

HAPPY: His name is Biff. You might've heard of him. Great football player.

440 GIRL: Really? What team?

HAPPY: Are you familiar with football?

GIRL: No, I'm afraid I'm not.

HAPPY: Biff is quarterback with the New York Giants.

GIRL: Well, that is nice, isn't it? *(She drinks.)*

445 HAPPY: Good health.

GIRL: I'm happy to meet you.

HAPPY: That's my name. Hap. It's really Harold, but at West Point they called me Happy.

GIRL: *(now really impressed)* Oh, I see. How do you do? *(She turns her profile.)*

BIFF: Isn't Dad coming?

450 HAPPY: You want her?

BIFF: Oh, I could never make that.

HAPPY: I remember the time that idea would never come into your head. Where's the old confidence, Biff?

BIFF: I just saw Oliver—

HAPPY: Wait a minute. I've got to see that old confidence again. Do you want her? She's on call.

455 BIFF: Oh, no. *(He turns to look at The Girl.)*

HAPPY: I'm telling you. Watch this. *(Turning to The Girl.)* Honey? *(She turns to him.)* Are you busy?

GIRL: Well, I am . . . but I could make a phone call.

HAPPY: Do that, will you, honey? And see if you can get a friend. We'll be here for a while. Biff is one of the greatest football players in the country.

GIRL: *(standing up)* Well, I'm certainly happy to meet you.

460 HAPPY: Come back soon.

GIRL: I'll try.

HAPPY: Don't try, honey, try hard.

The Girl exits. Stanley follows, shaking his head in bewildered admiration.

HAPPY: Isn't that a shame now? A beautiful girl like that? That's why I can't get married. There's not a good woman in a thousand. New York is loaded with them, kid!

BIFF: Hap, look—

465 HAPPY: I told you she was on call!

BIFF: *(strangely unnerved)* Cut it out, will ya? I want to say something to you.

HAPPY: Did you see Oliver?

BIFF: I saw him all right. Now look, I want to tell Dad a couple of things and I want you to help me.

HAPPY: What? Is he going to back you?

470 BIFF: Are you crazy? You're out of your goddam head, you know that?

HAPPY: Why? What happened?

BIFF: *(breathlessly)* I did a terrible thing today, Hap. It's been the strangest day I ever went through. I'm all numb, I swear.

Happy: You mean he wouldn't see you?

Biff: Well, I waited six hours for him, see? All day. Kept sending my name in. Even tried to date his secretary so she'd get me to him, but no soap.

475 Happy: Because you're not showin' the old confidence, Biff. He remembered you, didn't he?

Biff: *(stopping Happy with a gesture)* Finally, about five o'clock, he comes out. Didn't remember who I was or anything. I felt like such an idiot, Hap.

Happy: Did you tell him my Florida idea?

Biff: He walked away. I saw him for one minute. I got so mad I could've torn the walls down! How the hell did I ever get the idea I was a salesman there? I even believed myself that I'd been a salesman for him! And then he gave me one look and—I realized what a ridiculous lie my whole life has been! We've been talking in a dream for fifteen years. I was a shipping clerk.

Happy: What'd you do?

480 Biff: *(with great tension and wonder)* Well, he left, see. And the secretary went out. I was all alone in the waiting-room. I don't know what came over me, Hap. The next thing I know I'm in his office—paneled walls, everything. I can't explain it. I—Hap, I took his fountain pen.

Happy: Geez, did he catch you?

Biff: I ran out. I ran down all eleven flights. I ran and ran and ran.

Happy: That was an awful dumb—what'd you do that for?

Biff: *(agonized)* I don't know, I just—wanted to take something, I don't know. You gotta help me, Hap. I'm gonna tell Pop.

485 Happy: You crazy? What for?

Biff: Hap, he's got to understand that I'm not the man somebody lends that kind of money to. He thinks I've been spiting him all these years and it's eating him up.

Happy: That's just it. You tell him something nice.

Biff: I can't.

Happy: Say you got a lunch date with Oliver tomorrow.

490 Biff: So what do I do tomorrow?

Happy: You leave the house tomorrow and come back at night and say Oliver is thinking it over. And he thinks it over for a couple of weeks, and gradually it fades away and nobody's the worse.

Biff: But it'll go on forever!

Happy: Dad is never so happy as when he's looking forward to something!

Willy enters.

Happy: Hello, scout!

495 Willy: Gee, I haven't been here in years!

Stanley has followed Willy in and sets a chair for him. Stanley starts off but Happy stops him.

HAPPY: Stanley!

Stanley stands by, waiting for an order.

BIFF: *(going to Willy with guilt, as to an invalid)* Sit down, Pop. You want a
drink?

WILLY: Sure, I don't mind.

BIFF: Let's get a load on.

500 WILLY: You look worried.

BIFF: N-no. *(To Stanley.)* Scotch all around. Make it doubles.

STANLEY: Doubles, right. *(He goes.)*

WILLY: You had a couple already, didn't you?

BIFF: Just a couple, yeah.

505 WILLY: Well, what happened, boy? *(Nodding affirmatively, with a smile.)*
Everything go all right?

BIFF: *(takes a breath, then reaches out and grasps Willy's hand)* Pal . . . *(He is
smiling bravely, and Willy is smiling too.)* I had an experience today.

HAPPY: Terrific, Pop.

WILLY: That so? What happened?

BIFF: *(high, slightly alcoholic, above the earth)* I'm going to tell you
everything from first to last. It's been a strange day. *(Silence. He looks
around, composes himself as best he can, but his breath keeps breaking the
rhythm of his voice.)* I had to wait quite a while for him, and—

510 WILLY: Oliver?

BIFF: Yeah, Oliver. All day, as a matter of cold fact. And a lot of—
instances—facts, Pop, facts about my life came back to me. Who was
it, Pop? Who ever said I was a salesman with Oliver?

WILLY: Well, you were.

BIFF: No, Dad, I was a shipping clerk.

WILLY: But you were practically—

515 BIFF: *(with determination)* Dad, I don't know who said it first, but I was
never a salesman for Bill Oliver.

WILLY: What're you talking about?

BIFF: Let's hold on to the facts tonight, Pop. We're not going to get
anywhere bullin' around. I was a shipping clerk.

WILLY: *(angrily)* All right, now listen to me—

BIFF: Why don't you let me finish?

520 WILLY: I'm not interested in stories about the past or any crap of that
kind because the woods are burning, boys, you understand? There's a
big blaze going on all around. I was fired today.

BIFF: *(shocked)* How could you be?

WILLY: I was fired, and I'm looking for a little good news to tell your
mother, because the woman has waited and the woman has suffered.
The gist of it is that I haven't got a story left in my head, Biff. So
don't give me a lecture about facts and aspects. I am not interested.
Now what've you got to say to me?

Stanley enters with three drinks. They wait until he leaves.

WILLY: Did you see Oliver?

BIFF: Jesus, Dad!

525 WILLY: You mean you didn't go up there?

HAPPY: Sure he went up there.

BIFF: I did. I—saw him. How could they fire you?

WILLY: *(on the edge of his chair)* What kind of a welcome did he give you?

BIFF: He won't even let you work on commission?

530 WILLY: I'm out! *(Driving.)* So tell me, he gave you a warm welcome?

HAPPY: Sure, Pop, sure!

BIFF: *(driven)* Well, it was kind of—

WILLY: I was wondering if he'd remember you. *(To Happy.)* Imagine, man doesn't see him for ten, twelve years and gives him that kind of a welcome!

HAPPY: Damn right!

535 BIFF: *(trying to return to the offensive)* Pop, look—

WILLY: You know why he remembered you, don't you? Because you impressed him in those days.

BIFF: Let's talk quietly and get this down to the facts, huh?

WILLY: *(as though Biff had been interrupting)* Well, what happened? It's great news, Biff. Did he take you into his office or'd you talk in the waiting-room?

BIFF: Well, he came in, see, and—

540 WILLY: *(with a big smile)* What'd he say? Betcha he threw his arm around you.

BIFF: Well, he kinda—

WILLY: He's a fine man. *(To Happy.)* Very hard man to see, y'know.

HAPPY: *(agreeing)* Oh, I know.

WILLY: *(to Biff)* Is that where you had the drinks?

545 BIFF: Yeah, he gave me a couple of—no, no!

HAPPY: *(cutting in)* He told him my Florida idea.

WILLY: Don't interrupt. *(To Biff.)* How'd he react to the Florida idea?

BIFF: Dad, will you give me a minute to explain?

WILLY: I've been waiting for you to explain since I sat down here! What happened? He took you into his office and what?

550 BIFF: Well—I talked. And—and he listened, see.

WILLY: Famous for the way he listens, y'know. What was his answer?

BIFF: His answer was—*(He breaks off, suddenly angry.)* Dad, you're not letting me tell you what I want to tell you!

WILLY: *(accusing, angered)* You didn't see him, did you?

BIFF: I did see him!

555 WILLY: What'd you insult him or something? You insulted him, didn't you?

BIFF: Listen, will you let me out of it, will you just let me out of it!

HAPPY: What the hell!

WILLY: Tell me what happened!

BIFF: *(to Happy)* I can't talk to him!

A single trumpet note jars the ear. The light of green leaves stains the house, which holds the air of night and a dream. Young Bernard enters and knocks on the door of the house.

560 **YOUNG BERNARD:** *(frantically)* Mrs. Loman, Mrs. Loman!

HAPPY: Tell him what happened!

BIFF: *(to Happy)* Shut up and leave me alone!

WILLY: No, no! You had to go and flunk math!

BIFF: What math? What're you talking about?

565 **YOUNG BERNARD:** Mrs. Loman, Mrs. Loman!

Linda appears in the house, as of old.

WILLY: *(wildly)* Math, math, math!

BIFF: Take it easy, Pop!

YOUNG BERNARD: Mrs. Loman!

WILLY: *(furiously)* If you hadn't flunked you'd've been set by now!

570 **BIFF:** Now, look, I'm gonna tell you what happened, and you're going to
listen to me.

YOUNG BERNARD: Mrs. Loman!

BIFF: I waited six hours—

HAPPY: What the hell are you saying?

BIFF: I kept sending in my name but he wouldn't see me. So finally
he . . . *(He continues unheard as light fades low on the restaurant.)*

575 **YOUNG BERNARD:** Biff flunked math!

LINDA: No!

YOUNG BERNARD: Birnbaum flunked him! They won't graduate him!

LINDA: But they have to. He's gotta go to the university. Where is he?
Biff! Biff!

YOUNG BERNARD: No, he left. He went to Grand Central.

580 **LINDA:** Grand—You mean he went to Boston!

YOUNG BERNARD: Is Uncle Willy in Boston?

LINDA: Oh, maybe Willy can talk to the teacher. Oh, the poor, poor boy!

Light on house area snaps out.

BIFF: *(at the table, now audible, holding up a gold fountain pen)* . . . so I'm
washed up with Oliver, you understand? Are you listening to me?

WILLY: *(at a loss)* Yeah, sure. If you hadn't flunked—

585 **BIFF:** Flunked what? What're you talking about?

WILLY: Don't blame everything on me! I didn't flunk math—you did!
What pen?

HAPPY: That was awful dumb, Biff, a pen like that is worth—

WILLY: *(seeing the pen for the first time)* You took Oliver's pen?

BIFF: *(weakening)* Dad, I just explained it to you.

590 **WILLY:** You stole Bill Oliver's fountain pen!

BIFF: I didn't exactly steal it! That's just what I've been explaining to you!

HAPPY: He had it in his hand and just then Oliver walked in, so he got nervous and stuck it in his pocket!

WILLY: My God, Biff!

BIFF: I never intended to do it, Dad!

595 OPERATOR'S VOICE: Standish Arms, good evening!

WILLY: *(shouting)* I'm not in my room!

BIFF: *(frightened)* Dad, what's the matter? *(He and Happy stand up.)*

OPERATOR: Ringing Mr. Loman for you!

WILLY: I'm not there, stop it!

600 BIFF: *(horrified, gets down on one knee before Willy)* Dad, I'll make good, I'll make good. *(Willy tries to get to his feet. Biff holds him down.)* Sit down now.

WILLY: No, you're no good, you're no good for anything.

BIFF: I am, Dad, I'll find something else, you understand? Now don't worry about anything. *(He holds up Willy's face.)* Talk to me, Dad.

OPERATOR: Mr. Loman does not answer. Shall I page him?

WILLY: *(attempting to stand, as though to rush and silence the Operator)* No, no, no!

605 HAPPY: He'll strike something, Pop.

WILLY: No, no . . .

BIFF: *(desperately, standing over Willy)* Pop, listen! Listen to me! I'm telling you something good. Oliver talked to his partner about the Florida idea. You listening? He—he talked to his partner, and he came to me . . . I'm going to be all right, you hear? Dad, listen to me, he said it was just a question of the amount!

WILLY: Then you . . . got it?

HAPPY: He's gonna be terrific, Pop!

610 WILLY: *(trying to stand)* Then you got it, haven't you? You got it! You got it!

BIFF: *(agonized, holds Willy down)* No, no. Look, Pop. I'm supposed to have lunch with them tomorrow. I'm just telling you this so you'll know that I can still make an impression, Pop. And I'll make good somewhere, but I can't go tomorrow, see?

WILLY: Why not? You simply—

BIFF: But the pen, Pop!

WILLY: You give it to him and tell him it was an oversight!

615 HAPPY: Sure, have lunch tomorrow!

BIFF: I can't say that—

WILLY: You were doing a crossword puzzle and accidentally used his pen!

BIFF: Listen, kid, I took those balls years ago, now I walk in with his fountain pen? That clinches it, don't you see? I can't face him like that! I'll try elsewhere.

PAGE'S VOICE: Paging Mr. Loman!

620 WILLY: Don't you want to be anything?

BIFF: Pop, how can I go back?

WILLY: You don't want to be anything, is that what's behind it?

BIFF: *(now angry at Willy for not crediting his sympathy)* Don't take it that way! You think it was easy walking into that office after what I'd done to him? A team of horses couldn't have dragged me back to Bill Oliver!

WILLY: Then why'd you go?

625 BIFF: Why did I go? Why did I go? Look at you! Look at what's become of you!

Off left, The Woman laughs.

WILLY: Biff, you're going to go to that lunch tomorrow, or—

BIFF: I can't go. I've got no appointment!

HAPPY: Biff, for . . . !

WILLY: Are you spiting me?

630 BIFF: Don't take it that way! Goddammit!

WILLY: *(strikes Biff and falters away from the table)* You rotten little louse! Are you spiting me?

THE WOMAN: Someone's at the door, Willy!

BIFF: I'm no good, can't you see what I am?

HAPPY: *(separating them)* Hey, you're in a restaurant! Now cut it out, both of you! *(The Girls enter.)* Hello, girls, sit down.

The Woman laughs, off left.

635 MISS FORSYTHE: I guess we might as well. This is Letta.

THE WOMAN: Willy, are you going to wake up?

BIFF: *(ignoring Willy)* How're ya, miss, sit down. What do you drink?

MISS FORSYTHE: Letta might not be able to stay long.

LETTA: I gotta get up very early tomorrow. I got jury duty. I'm so excited! Were you fellows ever on a jury?

640 BIFF: No, but I been in front of them! *(The Girls laugh.)* This is my father.

LETTA: Isn't he cute? Sit down with us, Pop.

HAPPY: Sit him down, Biff!

BIFF: *(going to him)* Come on, slugger, drink us under the table. To hell with it! Come on, sit down, pal.

On Biff's last insistence, Willy is about to sit.

THE WOMAN: *(now urgently)* Willy, are you going to answer the door!

The Woman's call pulls Willy back. He starts right, befuddled.

645 BIFF: Hey, where are you going?

WILLY: Open the door.

BIFF: The door?

WILLY: The washroom . . . the door . . . where's the door?

BIFF: *(leading Willy to the left)* Just go straight down.

Willy moves left.

650 The Woman: Willy, Willy, are you going to get up, get up, get up, get up?

Willy exits left.

Letta: I think it's sweet you bring your daddy along.

Miss Forsythe: Oh, he isn't really your father!

Biff: *(at left, turning to her resentfully)* Miss Forsythe, you've just seen a prince walk by. A fine, troubled prince. A hard-working, unappreciated prince. A pal, understand? A good companion. Always for his boys.

Letta: That's so sweet.

655 Happy: Well, girls, what's the program? We're wasting time. Come on, Biff. Gather round. Where would you like to go?

Biff: Why don't you do something for him?

Happy: Me!

Biff: Don't you give a damn for him, Hap?

Happy: What're you talking about? I'm the one who—

660 Biff: I sense it, you don't give a good goddam about him. *(He takes the rolled-up hose from his pocket and puts it on the table in front of Happy.)* Look what I found in the cellar, for Christ's sake. How can you bear to let it go on?

Happy: Me? Who goes away? Who runs off and—

Biff: Yeah, but he doesn't mean anything to you. You could help him—I can't! Don't you understand what I'm talking about? He's going to kill himself, don't you know that?

Happy: Don't I know it! Me!

Biff: Hap, help him! Jesus . . . help him . . . Help me, help me, I can't bear to look at his face! *(Ready to weep, he hurries out, up right.)*

665 Happy: *(starting after him)* Where are you going?

Miss Forsythe: What's he so mad about?

Happy: Come on, girls, we'll catch up with him.

Miss Forsythe: *(as Happy pushes her out)* Say, I don't like that temper of his!

Happy: He's just a little overstrung, he'll be all right!

670 Willy: *(off left, as The Woman laughs)* Don't answer! Don't answer!

Letta: Don't you want to tell your father—

Happy: No, that's not my father. He's just a guy. Come on, we'll catch Biff, and, honey, we're going to paint this town! Stanley, where's the check! Hey, Stanley!

They exit. Stanley looks toward left.

Stanley: *(calling to Happy indignantly)* Mr. Loman! Mr. Loman!

Stanley picks up a chair and follows them off. Knocking is heard off left. The Woman enters, laughing. Willy follows her. She is in a black slip; he is buttoning his shirt. Raw, sensuous music accompanies their speech.

WILLY: Will you stop laughing? Will you stop?

675 THE WOMAN: Aren't you going to answer the door? He'll wake the whole hotel.

WILLY: I'm not expecting anybody.

THE WOMAN: Whyn't you have another drink, honey, and stop being so damn self-centered?

WILLY: I'm so lonely.

THE WOMAN: You know you ruined me, Willy? From now on, whenever you come to the office, I'll see that you go right through to the buyers. No waiting at my desk any more, Willy. You ruined me.

680 WILLY: That's nice of you to say that.

THE WOMAN: Gee, you are self-centered! Why so sad? You are the saddest self-centeredest soul I ever did see-saw. *(She laughs. He kisses her.)* Come on inside, drummer boy. It's silly to be dressing in the middle of the night. *(As knocking is heard.)* Aren't you going to answer the door?

WILLY: They're knocking on the wrong door.

THE WOMAN: But I felt the knocking. And he heard us talking in here. Maybe the hotel's on fire!

WILLY: *(his terror rising)* It's a mistake.

685 THE WOMAN: Then tell him to go away!

WILLY: There's nobody there.

THE WOMAN: It's getting on my nerves, Willy. There's somebody standing out there and it's getting on my nerves!

WILLY: *(pushing her away from him)* All right, stay in the bathroom here, and don't come out. I think there's a law in Massachusetts about it, so don't come out. It may be that new room clerk. He looked very mean. So don't come out. It's a mistake, there's no fire.

The knocking is heard again. He takes a few steps away from her, and she vanishes into the wing. The light follows him, and now he is facing Young Biff, who carries a suitcase. Biff steps toward him. The music is gone.

BIFF: Why didn't you answer?

690 WILLY: Biff! What are you doing in Boston?

BIFF: Why didn't you answer? I've been knocking for five minutes, I called you on the phone—

WILLY: I just heard you. I was in the bathroom and had the door shut. Did anything happen home?

BIFF: Dad—I let you down.

WILLY: What do you mean?

695 BIFF: Dad . . .

WILLY: Biffo, what's this about? *(Putting his arm around Biff.)* Come on, let's go downstairs and get you a malted.

BIFF: Dad, I flunked math.

WILLY: Not for the term?

BIFF: The term. I haven't got enough credits to graduate.

700 WILLY: You mean to say Bernard wouldn't give you the answers?

BIFF: He did, he tried, but I only got a sixty-one.

WILLY: And they wouldn't give you four points?

BIFF: Birnbaum refused absolutely. I begged him, Pop, but he won't give me those points. You gotta talk to him before they close the school. Because if he saw the kind of man you are, and you just talked to him in your way, I'm sure he'd come through for me. The class came right before practice, see, and I didn't go enough. Would you talk to him? He'd like you, Pop. You know the way you could talk.

WILLY: You're on. We'll drive right back.

705 BIFF: Oh, Dad, good work! I'm sure he'll change it for you!

WILLY: Go downstairs and tell the clerk I'm checkin' out. Go right down.

BIFF: Yes, Sir! See, the reason he hates me, Pop—one day he was late for class so I got up at the blackboard and imitated him. I crossed my eyes and talked with a lithp.

WILLY: *(laughing)* You did? The kids like it?

BIFF: They nearly died laughing!

710 WILLY: Yeah? What'd you do?

BIFF: The thquare root of thixthy twee is . . . *(Willy bursts out laughing; Biff joins him.)* And in the middle of it he walked in!

Willy laughs and The Woman joins in offstage.

WILLY: *(without hesitating)* Hurry downstairs and—

BIFF: Somebody in there?

WILLY: No, that was next door.

The Woman laughs offstage.

715 BIFF: Somebody got in your bathroom!

WILLY: No, it's the next room, there's a party—

THE WOMAN: *(enters, laughing. She lisps this)* Can I come in? There's something in the bathtub, Willy, and it's moving!

Willy looks at Biff, who is staring open-mouthed and horrified at The Woman.

WILLY: Ah—you better go back to your room. They must be finished painting by now. They're painting her room so I let her take a shower here. Go back, go back . . . *(He pushes her.)*

THE WOMAN: *(resisting)* But I've got to get dressed, Willy, I can't—

720 WILLY: Get out of here! Go back, go back . . . *(Suddenly striving for the ordinary.)* This is Miss Francis, Biff, she's a buyer. They're painting her room. Go back, Miss Francis, go back . . .

THE WOMAN: But my clothes, I can't go out naked in the hall!

WILLY: *(pushing her offstage)* Get outa here! Go back, go back!

Biff slowly sits down on his suitcase as the argument continues offstage.

THE WOMAN: Where's my stockings? You promised me stockings, Willy!

WILLY: I have no stockings here!

725 THE WOMAN: You had two boxes of size nine sheers for me, and I want them!

WILLY: Here, for God's sake, will you get outa here!

THE WOMAN: *(enters holding a box of stockings)* I just hope there's nobody in the hall. That's all I hope. *(To Biff.)* Are you football or baseball?

BIFF: Football.

THE WOMAN: *(angry, humiliated)* That's me too. G'night. *(She snatches her clothes from Willy, and walks out.)*

730 WILLY: *(after a pause)* Well, better get going. I want to get to the school first thing in the morning. Get my suits out of the closet. I'll get my valise. *(Biff doesn't move.)* What's the matter? *(Biff remains motionless, tears falling.)* She's a buyer. Buys for J. H. Simmons. She lives down the hall—they're painting. You don't imagine—*(He breaks off. After a pause.)* Now listen, pal, she's just a buyer. She sees merchandise in her room and they have to keep it looking just so . . . *(Pause. Assuming command.)* All right, get my suits. *(Biff doesn't move.)* Now stop crying and do as I say. I gave you an order. Biff, I gave you an order! Is that what you do when I give you an order? How dare you cry! *(Putting his arm around Biff.)* Now look, Biff, when you grow up you'll understand about these things. You mustn't—you mustn't overemphasize a thing like this. I'll see Birnbaum first thing in the morning.

BIFF: Never mind.

WILLY: *(getting down beside Biff)* Never mind! He's going to give you those points. I'll see to it.

BIFF: He wouldn't listen to you.

WILLY: He certainly will listen to me. You need those points for the U. of Virginia.

735 BIFF: I'm not going there.

WILLY: Heh? If I can't get him to change that mark you'll make it up in summer school. You've got all summer to—

BIFF: *(his weeping breaking from him)* Dad . . .

WILLY: *(infected by it)* Oh, my boy . . .

BIFF: Dad . . .

740 WILLY: She's nothing to me, Biff. I was lonely, I was terribly lonely.

BIFF: You—you gave her Mama's stockings! *(His tears break through and he rises to go.)*

WILLY: *(grabbing for Biff)* I gave you an order!

BIFF: Don't touch me, you—liar!

WILLY: Apologize for that!

745 BIFF: You fake! You phony little fake! You fake! *(Overcome, he turns quickly and weeping fully goes out with his suitcase. Willy is left on the floor on his knees.)*

WILLY: I gave you an order! Biff, come back here or I'll beat you! Come back here! I'll whip you!

Stanley comes quickly in from the right and stands in front of Willy.

WILLY: *(shouts at Stanley)* I gave you an order . . .

STANLEY: Hey, let's pick it up, pick it up, Mr. Loman. *(He helps Willy to his feet.)* Your boys left with the chippies. They said they'll see you home.

A second waiter watches some distance away.

WILLY: But we were supposed to have dinner together.

Music is heard, Willy's theme.

750 STANLEY: Can you make it?

WILLY: I'll—sure, I can make it. *(Suddenly concerned about his clothes.)* Do I—I look all right?

STANLEY: Sure, you look all right. *(He flicks a speck off Willy's lapel.)*

WILLY: Here—here's a dollar.

STANLEY: Oh, your son paid me. It's all right.

755 WILLY: *(putting it in Stanley's hand)* No, take it. You're a good boy.

STANLEY: Oh, no, you don't have to . . .

WILLY: Here—here's some more, I don't need it any more. *(After a slight pause.)* Tell me—is there a seed store in the neighborhood?

STANLEY: Seeds? You mean like to plant?

As Willy turns, Stanley slips the money back into his jacket pocket.

WILLY: Yes. Carrots, peas . . .

760 STANLEY: Well, there's hardware stores on Sixth Avenue, but it may be too late now.

WILLY: *(anxiously)* Oh, I'd better hurry. I've got to get some seeds. *(He starts off to the right.)* I've got to get some seeds, right away. Nothing's planted. I don't have a thing in the ground.

Willy hurries out as the light goes down. Stanley moves over to the right after him, watches him off. The other waiter has been staring at Willy.

STANLEY: *(to the waiter)* Well, whatta you looking at?

The waiter picks up the chairs and moves off right. Stanley takes the table and follows him. The light fades on this area. There is a long pause, the sound of the flute coming over. The light gradually rises on the kitchen, which is empty. Happy appears at the door of the house, followed by Biff. Happy is carrying a large bunch of long-stemmed roses. He enters the kitchen, looks around for Linda. Not seeing her, he turns to Biff, who is just outside the house door, and makes a gesture with his hands, indicating "Not here, I guess." He looks into the livingroom and freezes. Inside, Linda, unseen, is seated, Willy's coat on her lap. She rises ominously and quietly and moves toward Happy, who backs up into the kitchen, afraid.

HAPPY: Hey, what're you doing up? *(Linda says nothing but moves toward him implacably.)* Where's Pop? *(He keeps backing to the right, and now Linda is in full view in the doorway to the livingroom.)* Is he sleeping?

LINDA: Where were you?

765 HAPPY: *(trying to laugh it off)* We met two girls, Mom, very fine types. Here, we brought you some flowers. *(Offering them to her.)* Put them in your room, Ma.

She knocks them to the floor at Biff's feet. He has now come inside and closed the door behind him. She stares at Biff, silent.

HAPPY: Now what'd you do that for? Mom, I want you to have some flowers—

LINDA: *(cutting Happy off, violently to Biff)* Don't you care whether he lives or dies?

HAPPY: *(going to the stairs)* Come upstairs, Biff.

BIFF: *(with a flare of disgust, to Happy)* Go away from me! *(To Linda.)* What do you mean, lives or dies? Nobody's dying around here, pal.

770 LINDA: Get out of my sight! Get out of here!

BIFF: I wanna see the boss.

LINDA: You're not going near him!

BIFF: Where is he? *(He moves into the livingroom and Linda follows.)*

LINDA: *(shouting after Biff)* You invite him for dinner. He looks forward to it all day—*(Biff appears in his parents' bedroom, looks around, and exits)*—and then you desert him there. There's no stranger you'd do that to!

775 HAPPY: Why? He had a swell time with us. Listen, when I—*(Linda comes back into the kitchen)*—desert him I hope I don't outlive the day!

LINDA: Get out of here!

HAPPY: Now look, Mom . . .

LINDA: Did you have to go to women tonight? You and your lousy rotten whores!

Biff re-enters the kitchen.

HAPPY: Mom, all we did was follow Biff around trying to cheer him up! *(To Biff.)* Boy, what a night you gave me!

780 LINDA: Get out of here, both of you, and don't come back! I don't want you tormenting him any more. Go on now, get your things together! *(To Biff.)* You can sleep in his apartment. *(She starts to pick up the flowers and stops herself.)* Pick up this stuff, I'm not your maid any more. Pick it up, you bum, you!

Happy turns his back to her in refusal. Biff slowly moves over and gets down on his knees, picking up the flowers.

LINDA: You're a pair of animals! Not one, not another living soul would have had the cruelty to walk out on that man in a restaurant!

BIFF: *(not looking at her)* Is that what he said?

LINDA: He didn't have to say anything. He was so humiliated he nearly limped when he came in.

HAPPY: But, Mom he had a great time with us—

785 BIFF: *(cutting him off violently)* Shut up!

Without another word, Happy goes upstairs.

LINDA: You! You didn't even go in to see if he was all right!

BIFF: *(still on the floor in front of Linda, the flowers in his hand; with self-loathing)* No. Didn't. Didn't do a damned thing. How do you like that, heh? Left him babbling in a toilet.

LINDA: You louse. You . . .

BIFF: Now you hit it on the nose! *(He gets up, throws the flowers in the wastebasket.)* The scum of the earth, and you're looking at him!

790 LINDA: Get out of here!

BIFF: I gotta talk to the boss, Mom. Where is he?

LINDA: You're not going near him. Get out of this house!

BIFF: *(with absolute assurance, determination)* No. We're gonna have an abrupt conversation, him and me.

LINDA: You're not talking to him!

Hammering is heard from outside the house, off right. Biff turns toward the noise.

795 LINDA: *(suddenly pleading)* Will you please leave him alone?

BIFF: What's he doing out there?

LINDA: He's planting the garden!

BIFF: *(quietly)* Now? Oh, my God!

Biff moves outside, Linda following. The light dies down on them and comes up on the center of the apron as Willy walks into it. He is carrying a flashlight, a hoe and a handful of seed packets. He raps the top of the hoe sharply to fix it firmly, and then moves to the left, measuring off the distance with his foot. He holds the flashlight to look at the seed packets, reading off the instructions. He is in the blue of night.

WILLY: Carrots . . . quarter-inch apart. Rows . . . one-foot rows. *(He measures it off.)* One foot. *(He puts down a package and measures off.)* Beets. *(He puts down another package and measures again.)* Lettuce. *(He reads the package, puts it down.)* One foot—*(He breaks off as Ben appears at the right and moves slowly down to him.)* What a proposition, ts, ts. Terrific, terrific. 'Cause she's suffered, Ben, the woman has suffered. You understand me? A man can't go out the way he came in, Ben, a man has got to add up to something. You can't, you can't—*(Ben moves toward him as though to interrupt.)* You gotta consider, now. Don't answer so quick. Remember, it's a guaranteed twenty-thousand-dollar proposition. Now look, Ben, I want you to go through the ins and outs of this thing with me. I've got nobody to talk to, Ben, and the woman has suffered, you hear me?

800 BEN: *(standing still, considering)* What's the proposition?

WILLY: It's twenty thousand dollars on the barrelhead. Guaranteed, gilt-edged, you understand?

BEN: You don't want to make a fool of yourself. They might not honor the policy.

WILLY: How can they dare refuse? Didn't I work like a coolie to meet every premium on the nose? And now they don't pay off? Impossible!

BEN: It's called a cowardly thing, William.

805 WILLY: Why? Does it take more guts to stand here the rest of my life ringing up a zero?

BEN: *(yielding)* That's a point, William. *(He moves, thinking, turns.)* And twenty thousand—that *is* something one can feel with the hand, it is there.

WILLY: *(now assured, with rising power)* Oh, Ben, that's the whole beauty of it! I see it like a diamond, shining in the dark, hard and rough, that I can pick up and touch in my hand. Not like—like an appointment! This would not be another damned-fool appointment, Ben, and it changes all the aspects. Because he thinks I'm nothing, see, and so he spites me. But the funeral—*(Straightening up.)* Ben, that funeral will be massive! They'll come from Maine, Massachusetts, Vermont, New Hampshire! All the old-timers with the strange license plates—that boy will be thunder-struck, Ben, because he never realized—I am known! Rhode Island, New York, New Jersey—I am known, Ben, and he'll see it with his eyes once and for all. He'll see what I am, Ben! He's in for a shock, that boy!

BEN: *(coming down to the edge of the garden)* He'll call you a coward.

WILLY: *(suddenly fearful)* No, that would be terrible.

810 BEN: Yes. And a damned fool.

WILLY: No, no, he mustn't, I won't have that! *(He is broken and desperate.)*

BEN: He'll hate you, William.

The gay music of the boys is heard.

WILLY: Oh, Ben, how do we get back to all the great times? Used to be so full of light, and comradeship, the sleigh-riding in winter, and the ruddiness on his cheeks. And always some kind of good news coming up, always something nice coming up ahead. And never even let me carry the valises in the house, and simonizing, simonizing that little red car! Why, why can't I give him something and not have him hate me?

BEN: Let me think about it. *(He glances at his watch.)* I still have a little time. Remarkable proposition, but you've got to be sure you're not making a fool of yourself.

Ben drifts off upstage and goes out of sight. Biff comes down from the left.

815 WILLY: *(suddenly conscious of Biff, turns and looks up at him, then begins picking up the packages of seeds in confusion)* Where the hell is that seed? *(Indignantly.)* You can't see nothing out here! They boxed in the whole goddam neighborhood!

BIFF: There are people all around here. Don't you realize that?

WILLY: I'm busy. Don't bother me.

BIFF: *(taking the hoe from Willy)* I'm saying good-by to you, Pop. *(Willy looks at him, silent, unable to move.)* I'm not coming back any more.

WILLY: You're not going to see Oliver tomorrow?

820 BIFF: I've got no appointment, Dad.

WILLY: He put his arm around you, and you've got no appointment?

BIFF: Pop, get this now, will you? Everytime I've left it's been a fight that sent me out of here. Today I realized something about myself and I tried to explain it to you and I—I think I'm just not smart enough to make any sense out of it for you. To hell with whose fault it is or anything like that. *(He takes Willy's arm.)* Let's just wrap it up, heh? Come on in, we'll tell Mom. *(He gently tries to pull Willy to the left.)*

WILLY: *(frozen, immobile, with guilt in his voice)* No, I don't want to see her.

BIFF: Come on! *(He pulls again, and Willy tries to pull away.)*

825 WILLY: *(highly nervous)* No, no, I don't want to see her.

BIFF: *(tries to look into Willy's face, as if to find the answer there)* Why don't you want to see her?

WILLY: *(more harshly now)* Don't bother me, will you?

BIFF: What do you mean, you don't want to see her? You don't want them calling you yellow, do you? This isn't your fault; it's me, I'm a bum. Now come inside! *(Willy strains to get away.)* Did you hear what I said to you?

Willy pulls away and quickly goes by himself into the house. Biff follows.

LINDA: *(to Willy)* Did you plant, dear?

830 BIFF: *(at the door, to Linda)* All right, we had it out. I'm going and I'm not writing any more.

LINDA: *(going to Willy in the kitchen)* I think that's the best way, dear. 'Cause there's no use drawing it out, you'll just never get along.

Willy doesn't respond.

BIFF: People ask where I am and what I'm doing, you don't know, and you don't care. That way it'll be off your mind and you can start brightening up again. All right? That clears it, doesn't it? *(Willy is silent, and Biff goes to him.)* You gonna wish me luck, scout? *(He extends his hand.)* What do you say?

LINDA: Shake his hand, Willy.

WILLY: *(turning to her, seething with hurt)* There's no necessity to mention the pen at all, y'know.

835 BIFF: *(gently)* I've got no appointment, Dad.

WILLY: *(erupting fiercely)* He put his arm around . . . ?

BIFF: Dad, you're never going to see what I am, so what's the use of arguing? If I strike oil I'll send you a check. Meantime forget I'm alive.

WILLY: *(to Linda)* Spite, see?

BIFF: Shake hands, Dad.

840 WILLY: Not my hand.

BIFF: I was hoping not to go this way.

WILLY: Well, this is the way you're going. Good-by.

Biff looks at him a moment, then turns sharply and goes to the stairs.

WILLY: *(stops him with)* May you rot in hell if you leave this house!

BIFF: *(turning)* Exactly what is it that you want from me?

845 WILLY: I want you to know, on the train, in the mountains, in the valleys, wherever you go, that you cut down your life for spite!

BIFF: No, no.

WILLY: Spite, spite, is the word of your undoing! And when you're down and out, remember what did it. When you're rotting somewhere beside the railroad tracks, remember, and don't you dare blame it on me!

BIFF: I'm not blaming it on you!

WILLY: I won't take the rap for this, you hear?

Happy comes down the stairs and stands on the bottom step, watching.

850 BIFF: That's just what I'm telling you!

WILLY: *(sinking into a chair at the table, with full accusation)* You're trying to put a knife in me—don't think I don't know what you're doing!

BIFF: All right, phony! Then let's lay it on the line. *(He whips the rubber tube out of his pocket and puts it on the table.)*

HAPPY: You crazy—

LINDA: Biff! *(She moves to grab the hose, but Biff holds it down with his hand.)*

855 BIFF: Leave it there! Don't move it!

WILLY: *(not looking at it)* What is that?

BIFF: You know goddam well what that is.

WILLY: *(caged, wanting to escape)* I never saw that.

BIFF: You saw it. The mice didn't bring it into the cellar! What is this supposed to do, make a hero out of you? This supposed to make me sorry for you?

860 WILLY: Never heard of it.

BIFF: There'll be no pity for you, you hear it? No pity!

WILLY: *(to Linda)* You hear the spite!

BIFF: No, you're going to hear the truth—what you are and what I am!

LINDA: Stop it!

865 WILLY: Spite!

HAPPY: *(coming down toward Biff)* You cut it now!

BIFF: *(to Happy)* The man don't know who we are! The man is gonna know! *(To Willy.)* We never told the truth for ten minutes in this house!

HAPPY: We always told the truth!

BIFF: *(turning on him)* You big blow, are you the assistant buyer? You're one of the two assistants to the assistant, aren't you?

870 HAPPY: Well, I'm practically—

BIFF: You're practically full of it! We all are! And I'm through with it. *(To Willy.)* Now hear this, Willy, this is me.

WILLY: I know you!

BIFF: You know why I had no address for three months? I stole a suit in Kansas City and I was in jail. *(To Linda, who is sobbing.)* Stop crying. I'm through with it.

Linda turns away from them, her hands covering her face.

WILLY: I suppose that's my fault!

875 BIFF: I stole myself out of every good job since high school!

WILLY: And whose fault is that?

BIFF: And I never got anywhere because you blew me so full of hot air I could never stand taking orders from anybody! That's whose fault it is!

WILLY: I hear that!

LINDA: Don't, Biff!

880 BIFF: It's goddam time you heard that! I had to be boss big shot in two weeks, and I'm through with it!

WILLY: Then hang yourself! For spite, hang yourself!

BIFF: No! Nobody's hanging himself, Willy! I ran down eleven flights with a pen in my hand today. And suddenly I stopped, you hear me? And in the middle of that office building, do you hear this? I stopped in the middle of that building and I saw—the sky. I saw the things that I love in this world. The work and the food and time to sit and smoke. And I looked at the pen and said to myself, what the hell am I grabbing this for? Why am I trying to become what I don't want to be? What am I doing in an office, making a contemptuous, begging fool of myself, when all I want is out there, waiting for me the minute I say I know who I am! Why can't I say that, Willy? *(He tries to make Willy face him, but Willy pulls away and moves to the left.)*

WILLY: *(with hatred, threateningly)* The door of your life is wide open!

BIFF: Pop! I'm a dime a dozen, and so are you!

885 WILLY: *(turning on him now in an uncontrolled outburst)* I am not a dime a dozen! I am Willy Loman, and you are Biff Loman!

Biff starts for Willy, but is blocked by Happy. In his fury, Biff seems on the verge of attacking his father.

BIFF: I am not a leader of men, Willy, and neither are you. You were never anything but a hard-working drummer who landed in the ash can like all the rest of them! I'm one dollar an hour, Willy! I tried seven states and couldn't raise it. A buck an hour! Do you gather my meaning? I'm not bringing home any prizes any more, and you're going to stop waiting for me to bring them home!

WILLY: *(directly to Biff)* You vengeful, spiteful mutt!

Biff breaks from Happy. Willy, in fright, starts up the stairs. Biff grabs him.

BIFF: *(at the peak of his fury)* Pop, I'm nothing! I'm nothing, Pop. Can't you understand that? There's no spite in it any more. I'm just what I am, that's all.

Biff's fury has spent itself, and he breaks down, sobbing, holding on to Willy, who dumbly fumbles for Biff's face.

WILLY: *(astonished)* What're you doing? What're you doing? *(To Linda.)* Why is he crying?

890 BIFF: *(crying, broken)* Will you let me go, for Christ's sake? Will you take that phony dream and burn it before something happens? *(Struggling to contain himself, he pulls away and moves to the stairs.)* I'll go in the morning. Put him—put him to bed. *(Exhausted, Biff moves up the stairs to his room.)*

WILLY: *(after a long pause, astonished, elevated)* Isn't that remarkable? Biff— he likes me!

LINDA: He loves you, Willy!

HAPPY: *(deeply moved)* Always did, Pop.

WILLY: Oh, Biff! *(Staring wildly.)* He cried! Cried to me! *(He is choking with his love, and now cries out his promise.)* That boy—that boy is going to be magnificent!

Ben appears in the light just outside the kitchen.

895 BEN: Yes, outstanding, with twenty thousand behind him.

LINDA: *(sensing the racing of his mind, fearfully, carefully)* Now come to bed, Willy. It's all settled now.

WILLY: *(finding it difficult not to rush out of the house)* Yes, we'll sleep. Come on. Go to sleep, Hap.

BEN: And it does take a great kind of man to crack the jungle.

In accents of dread, Ben's idyllic music starts up.

HAPPY: *(his arm around Linda)* I'm getting married, Pop, don't forget it. I'm changing everything. I'm gonna run that department before the year is up. You'll see, Mom. *(He kisses her.)*

900 BEN: The jungle is dark but full of diamonds, Willy.

Willy turns, moves, listening to Ben.

LINDA: Be good. You're both good boys, just act that way, that's all.

HAPPY: 'Night, Pop. *(He goes upstairs.)*

LINDA: *(to Willy)* Come, dear.

BEN: *(with greater force)* One must go in to fetch a diamond out.

905 WILLY: *(to Linda, as he moves slowly along the edge of the kitchen, toward the door)* I just want to get settled down, Linda. Let me sit alone for a little.

LINDA: *(almost uttering her fear)* I want you upstairs.

WILLY: *(taking her in his arms)* In a few minutes, Linda. I couldn't sleep right now. Go on, you look awful tired. *(He kisses her.)*

BEN: Not like an appointment at all. A diamond is rough and hard to the touch.

WILLY: Go on now. I'll be right up.

910 LINDA: I think this is the only way, Willy.

WILLY: Sure, it's the best thing.

BEN: Best thing!

WILLY: The only way. Everything is gonna be—go on, kid, get to bed. You look so tired.

LINDA: Come right up.

915 WILLY: Two minutes.

Linda goes into the livingroom, then reappears in her bedroom. Willy moves just outside the kitchen door.

WILLY: Loves me. *(Wonderingly.)* Always loved me. Isn't that a remarkable thing? Ben, he'll worship me for it!

BEN: *(with promise)* It's dark there, but full of diamonds.

WILLY: Can you imagine that magnificence with twenty thousand dollars in his pocket?

LINDA: *(calling from her room)* Willy! Come up!

920 WILLY: *(calling from the kitchen)* Yes! Yes! Coming! It's very smart, you realize that, don't you, sweetheart? Even Ben sees it. I gotta go, baby. 'By! By! *(Going over to Ben, almost dancing.)* Imagine? When the mail comes he'll be ahead of Bernard again!

BEN: A perfect proposition all around.

WILLY: Did you see how he cried to me? Oh, if I could kiss him, Ben!

BEN: Time, William, time!

WILLY: Oh, Ben, I always knew one way or another we were gonna make it, Biff and I!

925 BEN: *(looking at his watch)* The boat. We'll be late. *(He moves slowly off into the darkness.)*

WILLY: *(elegiacally, turning to the house)* Now when you kick off, boy, I want a seventy-yard boot, and get right down the field under the ball, and when you hit, hit low and hit hard, because it's important, boy. *(He swings around and faces the audience.)* There's all kinds of important people in the stands, and the first thing you know . . . *(Suddenly realizing he is alone.)* Ben! Ben, where do I . . . ? *(He makes a sudden movement of search.)* Ben, how do I . . . ?

LINDA: *(calling)* Willy, you coming up?

WILLY: *(uttering a gasp of fear, whirling about as if to quiet her)* Sh! *(He turns around as if to find his way; sounds, faces, voices, seem to be swarming in upon him and he flicks at them, crying.)* Sh! Sh! *(Suddenly music, faint and high, stops him. It rises in intensity, almost to an unbearable scream. He goes up and down on his toes, and rushes off around the house.)* Shhh!

LINDA: Willy?

There is no answer. Linda waits. Biff gets up off his bed. He is still in his clothes. Happy sits up. Biff stands listening.

930 LINDA: *(with real fear)* Willy, answer me! Willy!

There is the sound of a car starting and moving away at full speed.

LINDA: No!
BIFF: *(rushing down the stairs)* Pop!

As the car speeds off, the music crashes down in a frenzy of sound, which becomes the soft pulsation of a single cello string. Biff slowly returns to his bedroom. He and Happy gravely don their jackets. Linda slowly walks out of her room. The music has developed into a dead march. The leaves of day are appearing over everything. Charley and Bernard, somberly dressed, appear and knock on the kitchen door. Biff and Happy slowly descend the stairs to the kitchen as Charley and Bernard enter. All stop a moment when Linda, in clothes of mourning, bearing a little bunch of roses, comes through the draped doorway into the kitchen. She goes to Charley and takes his arm. Now all move toward the audience, through the wall-line of the kitchen. At the limit of the apron, Linda lays down the flowers, kneels, and sits back on her heels. All stare down at the grave.

REQUIEM

CHARLEY: It's getting dark, Linda.

Linda doesn't react. She stares at the grave.

BIFF: How about it, Mom? Better get some rest, heh? They'll be closing
   the gate soon.

Linda makes no move. Pause.

HAPPY: *(deeply angered)* He had no right to do that! There was no necessity
   for it. We would've helped him.
CHARLEY: *(grunting)* Hmmm.
5 BIFF: Come along, Mom.
LINDA: Why didn't anybody come?
CHARLEY: It was a very nice funeral.
LINDA: But where are all the people he knew? Maybe they blame him.
CHARLEY: Naa. It's a rough world, Linda. They wouldn't blame him.
10 LINDA: I can't understand it. At this time especially. First time in thirty-
   five years we were just about free and clear. He only needed a little
   salary. He was even finished with the dentist.
CHARLEY: No man only needs a little salary.
LINDA: I can't understand it.
BIFF: There were a lot of nice days. When he'd come home from a trip; or
   on Sundays, making the stoop; finishing the cellar; putting on the
   new porch; when he built the extra bathroom; and put up the garage.
   You know something, Charley, there's more of him in that front
   stoop than in all the sales he ever made.
CHARLEY: Yeah. He was a happy man with a batch of cement.
15 LINDA: He was so wonderful with his hands.

Biff: He had the wrong dreams. All, all, wrong.

Happy: *(almost ready to fight Biff)* Don't say that!

Biff: He never knew who he was.

Charley: *(stopping Happy's movement and reply. To Biff.)* Nobody dast blame this man. You don't understand: Willy was a salesman. And for a salesman, there is no rock bottom to the life. He don't put a bolt to a nut, he don't tell you the law or give you medicine. He's a man out there in the blue, riding on a smile and a shoeshine. And when they start not smiling back—that's an earthquake. And then you get yourself a couple of spots on your hat, and you're finished. Nobody dast blame this man. A salesman is got to dream, boy. It comes with the territory.

20 Biff: Charley, the man didn't know who he was.

Happy: *(infuriated)* Don't say that!

Biff: Why don't you come with me, Happy?

Happy: I'm not licked that easily. I'm staying right in this city, and I'm gonna beat this racket! *(He looks at Biff, his chin set.)* The Loman Brothers!

Biff: I know who I am, kid.

25 Happy: All right, boy. I'm gonna show you and everybody else that Willy Loman did not die in vain. He had a good dream. It's the only dream you can have—to come out number-one man. He fought it out here, and this is where I'm gonna win it for him.

Biff: *(with a hopeless glance at Happy, bends toward his mother)* Let's go, Mom.

Linda: I'll be with you in a minute. Go on, Charley. *(He hesitates.)* I want to, just for a minute. I never had a chance to say good-by.

Charley moves away, followed by Happy. Biff remains a slight distance up and left of Linda. She sits there, summoning herself. The flute begins, not far away, playing behind her speech.

Linda: Forgive me, dear. I can't cry. I don't know what it is, but I can't cry. I don't understand it. Why did you ever do that? Help me, Willy, I can't cry. It seems to me that you're just on another trip. I keep expecting you. Willy, dear, I can't cry. Why did you do it? I search and search and I search, and I can't understand it, Willy. I made the last payment on the house today. Today, dear. And there'll be nobody home. *(A sob rises in her throat.)* We're free and clear. *(Sobbing more fully, released.)* We're free. *(Biff comes slowly toward her.)* We're free . . . We're free . . .

Biff lifts her to her feet and moves out up right with her in his arms. Linda sobs quietly. Bernard and Charley come together and follow them, followed by Happy. Only the music of the flute is left on the darkening stage as over the house the hard towers of the apartment buildings rise into sharp focus, and—

The Curtain Falls

READING AND REACTING

1. With which character in the play do you most identify? Why?
2. Is Willy a likeable character? What words and actions—both Willy's and those of other characters—help you form your conclusion?
3. How does the existence of The Woman affect your overall impression of Willy? What does she reveal about his character?
4. What does Willy's attitude toward his sons indicate about his character? How is this attitude revealed?
5. Does this play have a hero? A villain? Explain.
6. In the absence of a narrator, what devices does Miller use to provide exposition—basic information about character and setting?
7. The conversation between Biff and Happy in act 1 reveals many of their differences. List some of the differences between these two characters.
8. In numerous remarks, Willy expresses his philosophy of business. Summarize some of his key ideas about the business world. How realistic do you think these ideas are? How do these ideas help to delineate his character?
9. In act 1 Linda tells Willy, "Few men are idolized by their children the way you are." Is she sincere, is she being ironic, or is she just trying to make Willy feel better?
10. How do the frequent flashbacks help to explain what motivates Willy? How else could this background information have been presented in the play? Are there advantages to using flashbacks instead of the alternative you suggest?
11. Is Linda simply a stereotype of the long-suffering wife, or is she an individualized, multidimensional character? Explain.
12. Willy Loman lives in Brooklyn, New York; his "territory" is New England. What is the significance to him of the "faraway places"—Africa, Alaska, California, Texas, and the like—mentioned in the play?
13. Explain the function of Bernard in the play.
14. The play concludes with a requiem. What is a requiem? What information about each of the major characters is supplied in this brief section? Is this information essential to your understanding or appreciation of the play, or would the play have been equally effective without the requiem? Explain.
15. **JOURNAL ENTRY** Do you believe Willy Loman is an innocent victim of the society in which he lives, or do you believe there are flaws in his character that make him at least partially responsible for his own misfortune? Explain.
16. **CRITICAL PERSPECTIVE** In his 1949 essay "Tragedy and the Common Man," Arthur Miller attempts to define modern tragedy:

There is a misconception of tragedy with which I have been struck in review after review, and in many conversations with writers and readers alike. It is the idea that tragedy is of necessity allied to pessimism. Even the dictionary says nothing more about the word than that it means a story with a sad or unhappy ending. This impression is so firmly fixed that I almost hesitate to claim that in truth tragedy implies more optimism in its author than does comedy, and that its final result ought to be the reinforcement of the onlooker's brightest opinions of the human animal. [. . .]

Pathos truly is the mode for the pessimist. But tragedy requires a nicer balance between what is possible and what is impossible. And it is curious, although edifying, that the plays we revere, century after century, are the tragedies. In them, and in them alone, lies the belief—optimistic, if you will, in the perfectibility of man.

Death of a Salesman, like other tragedies, is certainly "a story with a sad or unhappy ending." Do you find the play at all optimistic?

Related Works: "Do Not Go Gentle into That Good Night" (p. 677), "Those Winter Sundays" (p. 703), "The Love Song of J. Alfred Prufrock" (p. 950), *Oedipus the King* (p. 1509), *Fences* (p. 1745)

◊ WRITING SUGGESTIONS: CHARACTER

1. In *Death of a Salesman,* each character pursues his or her version of the American Dream. Choose two characters, define their idea of the American Dream, and explain how each tries to make the dream a reality. In each case, consider the obstacles the character encounters, and try to account for their success or lack of success. If you like, you may consider other works in which the American Dream is central—for example, "Two Kinds" (p. 594) or *Fences* (p. 1745).

2. Many of the female characters in this chapter's plays—for example, Mrs. Popov, Marty's mother and Aunt Catherine, Gertrude, Ophelia, and Linda—are, in one way or another, in conflict with men. Focusing on the women in two different plays, define each conflict, and consider whether or not it is resolved in the play. (If you like, you may discuss a female character in one of the plays in another chapter.)

3. Minor characters are often flat characters; in many cases, their sole function is to advance the plot or to highlight a particular trait in a major character. Sometimes, however, minor characters may be of more than minor importance. Choose one minor character from *Marty, Hamlet,* or *Death of a Salesman* (or from a play in another chapter), and write a paper in which you discuss how the play would be different without this character.

4. Watch two or three film versions of one of the plays in this chapter (for example, *Death of a Salesman* with Lee J. Cobb, Dustin Hoffman, or Brian Dennehy as Willy Loman). Based on your understanding of the play, which actor's interpretation seems most accurate? Explain your conclusion in an essay.

5. Review the explanation of tragedy in Chapter 20, "Understanding Drama." Using the discussion of the tragic hero as your guide, write an essay in which you discuss either Willy Loman or Hamlet as a tragic hero.

6. **WEB ACTIVITY** The following Web site contains information about Arthur Miller:

> http://www.deathofasalesman.com/rev-49-nytimes3.htm

In Miller's essay "Tragedy and the Common Man," he states, "I believe that the common man is as apt a subject for tragedy in its highest sense as kings were." He goes on to further define the tragic hero:

> I think the tragic feeling is evoked in us when we are in the presence of a character who is ready to lay down his life, if need be, to secure one thing—his sense of personal dignity. From Orestes to Hamlet, Medea to Macbeth, the underlying struggle is that of the individual attempting to gain his "rightful" position in his society.

After reading "Tragedy and the Common Man," locate a Web site that explains Aristotle's definition of tragedy. Write an essay in which you examine Willy Loman as a modern-day tragic hero, considering Aristotle's definition of tragedy as well as Miller's.

CHAPTER 24

Staging

◇ ◇ ◇

In reading a play rather than witnessing it on stage, we [. . .] have to imagine what it might look like in performance, projecting in our mind's eye an image of the setting and the props, as well as the movements, gestures, facial expressions, and vocal intonations of the characters. [. . .] And we—like the director, designers, and actors—must develop our understanding of the play and our idea of the play in performance primarily from a careful reading of the dialogue, as well as from whatever stage directions and other information the dramatist might provide about the characters and the setting.

CARL H. KLAUS, MIRIAM GILBERT, AND BRAFORD S. FIELD, JR., *Stages of Drama*

The playwright as playwright is in part a director. If he is truly a man of the theatre (some playwrights only suffer the theatre but do not feel they belong to it) the playwright "sees" the play on the stage as he writes. His dialogue as well as his notations of stage behavior suggest movement and part of the total physical life that the script is to acquire when it is produced.

HAROLD CLURMON, *On Directing*

Whether the director sees [. . .] a play as tragedy, comedy or even farce will have an immediate and very practical effect on his handling of the production: it will influence his casting, the design of the set and costumes, the tone, rhythm and pacing of the performance. And, above all, the style in which it is to be acted.

MARTIN ESSLIN, *An Anatomy of Drama*

The argument is sometimes advanced that the complete verisimilitude of the movies is more enjoyable than the necessarily limited illusionism of the live theater. Hollywood producers evidently believe the public in general holds such an opinion. Yet accepting conventions can be a source of pleasure for its own sake, just as children have always had fun putting on shows in the cellar by ignoring the steampipe or else turning it into the Brooklyn Bridge.

THELMA ALTSHULER AND RICHARD PAUL JENARO, *Responses to Drama*

◇ ◇ ◇

Staging refers to the elements of a play's production that determine how the play looks and sounds to an audience. It encompasses the **stage settings,** or **sets**—scenery and props—as well as the costumes, lighting, sound effects, and music that bring the play to life on the stage. In short, staging is everything that goes into making a written script a play.

Most contemporary staging in the West has concentrated on re-creating the outside world. This concept of staging, which has dominated Western theatrical productions for centuries, would seem alien in many non-Western theaters. Japanese kabuki dramas and No plays, for example, depend on staging conventions that make no attempt to mirror reality or everyday speech. Scenery and costumes are largely symbolic, and often actors wear highly stylized makeup or masks. Although some European and American playwrights have been strongly influenced by non-Western staging, the majority of plays being produced in the West still try to create the illusion of reality.

STAGE DIRECTIONS

✧ ✧ ✧

Usually a playwright presents instructions for the staging of a play in **stage directions**—notes that comment on the scenery, the movements of the performers, the lighting, and the placement of props. (In the absence of detailed stage directions, dialogue can provide information about staging.) Sometimes these stage directions are quite simple, leaving much to the imagination of the director. Consider how little specific information about the setting of the play is provided in these stage directions from Samuel Beckett's 1952 absurdist play *Waiting for Godot:*

ACT I

A country road. A tree. Evening.

Often, however, playwrights furnish much more detailed information about staging. Consider these notes from Anton Chekhov's *The Cherry Orchard:*

ACT I

A room, which has always been called the nursery. One of the doors leads into Anya's room. Dawn, sun rises during the scene. May, the cherry trees in flower, but it is cold in the garden with the frost of the early morning. Windows closed.

Enter Dunyasha with a candle and Lopahin with a book in his hand.

These comments indicate that the first act takes place in a room with more than one door and that several windows reveal cherry trees in bloom. They also specify that the lighting should simulate the sun rising at dawn and that certain characters should enter carrying particular props. Still,

Chekhov leaves it up to those staging the play to decide on the costumes for the characters and on the furniture that will be placed around the room.

Some stage directions are even more specific. George Bernard Shaw's long, complex stage directions are legendary in the theater. Note the degree of detail he provides in these stage directions from his comedy *The Doctor's Dilemma:*

> *The consulting-room has two windows looking on Queen Anne Street. Between the two is a marble-topped console, with haunched gilt legs ending in sphinx claws. The huge pier-glass [a long narrow mirror that fits between two windows] which surmounts it is mostly disabled from reflection by elaborate painting on its surface of palms, ferns, lilies, tulips, and sunflowers. The adjoining wall contains the fireplace, with two arm-chairs before it. As we happen to face the corner we see nothing of the other two walls. On the right of the fireplace, or rather on the right of any person facing the fireplace, is the door. On the left is the writing-table at which Redpenny [a medical student] sits. It is an untidy table with a microscope, several test tubes, and a spirit lamp [an alcohol burner] standing up through its litter of papers. There is a couch in the middle of the room, at right angles to the console, and parallel to the fireplace. A chair stands between the couch and the window. Another in the corner. Another at the other end of the windowed wall. [. . .] The wallpaper and carpets are mostly green. [. . .] The house, in fact, was so well furnished in the middle of the XIXth century that it stands unaltered to this day and is still quite presentable.*

Not only does Shaw describe the furniture to be placed on stage, but he also includes a good deal of detail—specifying, for example, "gilt legs ending in sphinx claws" and "test tubes and a spirit lamp" that clutter the writing table. In addition, he defines furniture placement and specifies color.

Regardless of how detailed the stage directions are, they do not eliminate the need for creative interpretations on the part of the producer, director, set designers, and actors (See "Actors' Interpretations," p. 1263). Stage directions—and, for that matter, the entire script—are the foundation on which to construct the play that the audience finally sees. Many directors, in fact, see stage directions as suggestions, not requirements, and some even consider them more confusing than helpful. Therefore, directors may choose to interpret a play's stage directions quite loosely—or even to ignore them entirely.

The Uses of Staging

❖ ❖ ❖

Staging is a key element of drama, and details that the audience sees and hears—such as costumes, props, scenery, lighting, and music and sound effects—communicate important information about characters and their motivation as well as about the play's theme.

COSTUMES

Costumes not only establish the historical period in which a play is set but also provide insight into the character who wears them. When he first appears, Hamlet is profoundly disillusioned and quite melancholy. This fact was immediately apparent to Shakespeare's audience because Hamlet is dressed in sable, which to the Elizabethans signified a melancholy nature. In Tennessee Williams's *The Glass Menagerie* (p. 1805), Laura's dress of soft violet material and her hair ribbon reflect her delicate, childlike innocence. In contrast, her mother's "imitation velvety-looking cloth coat with imitation fur collar" and her "enormous black patent-leather pocketbook" reveal her somewhat pathetic attempt to achieve respectability. Later in the play, awaiting the "gentleman caller," Laura's mother wears a dress that is both outdated and inappropriately youthful, suggesting both her need to relive her own past and her increasingly desperate desire to marry off her daughter.

PROPS

Props (short for *properties*)—pictures, furnishings, objects, and the like— can also help audiences to interpret a play's characters and themes. For example, the handkerchief in Shakespeare's *Othello* gains significance as the play progresses. It begins as an innocent object and ends as the piece of evidence that convinces Othello his wife is committing adultery. Sometimes props can have symbolic significance. During the Renaissance, for example, flowers had symbolic meaning. In act 4 of *Hamlet,* Ophelia, who is mad, gives flowers to various characters. In a note to the play the critic Thomas Parrott points out the symbolic significance of her gifts: to Claudius, the murderer of Hamlet's father, she gives fennel and columbines, which signify flattery and ingratitude; to the Queen, she gives rue and daisies, which symbolize sadness and unfaithfulness. Although modern audiences probably do not understand the full implications of the flowers, many people in Shakespeare's Elizabethan audience would have been aware of their meaning.

The furnishings in a room can also reveal a lot about a play's characters and themes. Willy Loman's house in Arthur Miller's *Death of a Salesman* (p. 1410) is sparsely furnished, revealing the declining financial status of the family. The kitchen contains a table and three chairs, and the bedroom is furnished with only a brass bed and a straight chair. Over the bed on a shelf is Biff's silver athletic trophy, which is a constant reminder of his loss of status. Like Willy Loman's house, the Wingfield apartment in *The Glass Menagerie* reflects its inhabitants' modest economic circumstances. For example, the living room, which contains a sofa that unfolds into a bed, also serves as a bedroom for Laura. In addition, one piece of furniture highlights a central theme of the play: an old-fashioned cabinet in the living room displays a collection of transparent glass animals which, like Laura, are too fragile to be removed from their surroundings.

SCENERY AND LIGHTING

Playwrights often use scenery and lighting to create imaginative stage settings. In *Death of a Salesman* the house is surrounded by "towering angular shapes" of apartment houses that emphasize the "small, fragile-seeming home." Arthur Miller calls for a set that is "wholly, or in some places, transparent." Whenever the action is in the present, the actors observe the imaginary boundaries that separate rooms or mark the exterior walls of the house. But when the characters reenact past events, they walk over the boundaries and come to the front of the stage. By lighting up and darkening different parts of the stage, Miller shifts from the present to the past and back again.

The set of *The Glass Menagerie* is also innovative, combining imaginative backdrops with subtle lighting. As the curtain rises, the audience sees the dark rear wall of the Wingfield tenement, which is flanked on both sides by alleys lined with clotheslines, garbage cans, and fire escapes. After Tom delivers his opening narrative, the tenement wall becomes transparent, revealing the interior of the Wingfield apartment. To create this effect, Williams uses a **scrim,** a curtain that when illuminated from the front appears solid but when illuminated from the back becomes transparent. For Williams, such "atmospheric touches" represented a new direction in theater that contrasted with the theater of "realistic conventions."

Contemporary playwrights often use sets that combine realistic and nonrealistic elements. In his 1988 Tony Award–winning play *M. Butterfly,* for example, David Henry Hwang employs not only scrims but also a large red lacquered ramp that runs from the bottom to the top of the stage. The action takes place beneath, on, and above the ramp, creating an effect not unlike that created by Shakespeare's multiple stages. At several points in the play, a character who acts as the narrator sits beneath the ramp, addressing the audience, while at the same time a character on top of the ramp acts out the narrator's words.

MUSIC AND SOUND EFFECTS

Staging involves more than visual elements such as costumes and scenery; it also involves music and sound effects. The stage directions for *Death of a Salesman,* for example, begin, *"A melody is heard, played upon a flute."* Although not specifically identified, the music is described as *"small and fine, telling of grass and trees and the horizon."* Interestingly, this music stands in stark contrast to the claustrophobic urban setting of the play. Music also has a major role in *The Glass Menagerie,* where a single recurring tune, like circus music, weaves in and out of the play. This musical motif gives emotional impact to certain lines and suggests the fantasy world into which Laura has retreated.

Sound effects play an important part in Henrik Ibsen's *A Doll House* (p. 1196). At the end of the play, after his wife has left him, Torvald Helmer sits alone on the stage. Notice in the following stage directions how the final sound effect cuts short Helmer's attempt at self-deluding optimism:

HELMER: *(sinks down on a chair by the door, face buried in his hands)* Nora! Nora! *(Looking about and rising.)* Empty. She's gone. *(A sudden hope leaps in him.)* The greatest miracle—?

From below, the sound of a door slamming shut.

When you read a play, it may be difficult to appreciate the effect that staging can have on a performance. As you read, pay particular attention to the stage directions, and use your imagination to visualize the scenes the playwright describes. In addition, try to imagine the play's sights and sounds, and consider the options for staging that are suggested as characters speak to one another. Although even such careful reading cannot substitute for actually seeing a play performed, it can help you imagine the play as it might appear on the stage.

A FINAL NOTE

◊ ◊ ◊

Because of a play's limited performance time, and because of space and financial limitations, not every action or event can be represented on stage. Frequently, incidents that would involve many actors or require elaborate scenery are only suggested. For example, a violent political riot may be suggested by a single scuffle, a full-scale wedding by the kiss between bride and groom, a gala evening at the opera by a well-dressed group in box seats, and a trip to an exotic locale by a departure scene. Other events are simply said to occur offstage, with the roar of a crowd suggesting an athletic event, for instance.

✹ **CHECKLIST: WRITING ABOUT STAGING**

- ✓ What information about staging is contained in the stage directions of the play?
- ✓ What information about staging is suggested by the play's dialogue?
- ✓ What information about staging is left to the imagination?
- ✓ How might different decisions about staging change the play?
- ✓ Do the stage directions provide information about how characters are supposed to look or behave?
- ✓ What costumes are specified? In what ways do costumes give insight into the characters who wear them?
- ✓ What props play an important part in the play? Do these props have symbolic meaning?

✓ Is the scenery used in the play special or unusual in any way?

✓ What kind of lighting is specified by the stage directions? In what way does this lighting affect your reaction to the play?

✓ In what ways are music and sound effects used in the play? Are musical themes associated with any characters? Do music and sound effects heighten the emotional impact of certain lines?

✓ How does staging help to communicate the play's themes?

✓ What events occur offstage? Why? How are they suggested?

◆ **Milcha Sanchez-Scott*** (1949 or 1950–   ) is a Los Angeles–based writer of plays that include *Dog Lady* and *The Cuban Swimmer,* both one-act plays (1984); *Roosters,* published in *On New Ground: Contemporary Hispanic American Plays* (1987); and *Stone Wedding,* produced at the Los Angeles Theater Center (1988). Also produced by the Los Angeles Theater Center was her play *Carmen,* adapted from Georges Bizet's opera of the same title.

Sanchez-Scott, born in Bali, is the daughter of an Indonesian mother and a Colombian-Mexican father. Her early childhood was spent in Mexico, South America, and Britain, before her family moved to San Diego when she was fourteen. Since then, she has worked as an actress, as a maid, and at an employment agency.

Writing in *Time* magazine, William A. Henry observes that the visionary or hallucinatory elements in Sanchez-Scott's plays derive from the Latin American "magic realism" tradition of Jorge Luis Borges and Gabriel García Márquez. In *Roosters,* Henry notes that what seems "a straightforward depiction of the life of farmlands gives way to mysterious visitations, symbolic cockfights enacted by dancers, virginal girls wearing wings, archetypal confrontations between father and son."

In 1984, the New York production of *The Cuban Swimmer* was noteworthy for an ingeniously designed set that realistically re-created on stage Pacific Ocean waves, a helicopter, and a boat. According to the *New York Times,* "The audience can almost feel the resisting tides and the California oil slick that are represented by a watery-blue floor and curtain." Jeannette Mirabel, as the Cuban swimmer, made an "auspicious" debut in the play, according to the *Times;* "In a tour de force of balletic movements, she [kept] her arms fluttering in the imaginary waters throughout the play."

Cultural Context ◆ Under the terms of the Cuban Migration Accords, an agreement between the United States and the Cuban government, the United States can now admit up to twenty thousand Cuban defectors each year.

---

*No photograph available for this author.

◊ ◊ ◊

MILCHA SANCHEZ-SCOTT

The Cuban Swimmer
(1984)

CHARACTERS

MARGARITA SUÁREZ, *the swimmer*
EDUARDO SUÁREZ, *her father,*
the coach
SIMÓN SUÁREZ, *her brother*
AÍDA SUÁREZ, *her mother*

ABUELA, *her grandmother*
VOICE OF MEL MUNSON
VOICE OF MARY BETH WHITE
VOICE OF RADIO OPERATOR

SETTING
The Pacific Ocean between San Pedro and Catalina Island.

TIME
Summer.

Live conga drums can be used to punctuate the action of the play.

SCENE 1

Pacific Ocean. Midday. On the horizon, in perspective, a small boat enters upstage left, crosses to upstage right, and exits. Pause. Lower on the horizon, the same boat, in larger perspective, enters upstage right, crosses and exits upstage left. Blackout.

SCENE 2

Pacific Ocean. Midday. The swimmer, Margarita Suárez, is swimming. On the boat following behind her are her father, Eduardo Suárez, holding a megaphone, and Simón, her brother, sitting on top of the cabin with his shirt off, punk sunglasses on, binoculars hanging on his chest.

EDUARDO: *(leaning forward, shouting in time to Margarita's swimming)* Uno, dos, uno, dos. Y uno, dos . . . keep your shoulders parallel to the water.
SIMÓN: I'm gonna take these glasses off and look straight into the sun.
EDUARDO: *(through megaphone)* Muy bien, muy bien . . . but punch those arms in, baby.
SIMÓN: *(looking directly at the sun through binoculars)* Come on, come on, zap me. Show me something. *(He looks behind at the shoreline and ahead at the sea.)* Stop! Stop, *Papi!* Stop!

Aída Suárez and Abuela, the swimmer's mother and grandmother, enter running from the back of the boat.

5 AÍDA and ABUELA: *Qué? Qué es?*
AÍDA: *Es un* shark?
EDUARDO: Eh?

ABUELA: *Que es un* shark *dicen?*

Eduardo blows whistle. Margarita looks up at the boat.

SIMÓN: No, *Papi,* no shark, no shark. We've reached the halfway mark.

10 ABUELA: *(looking into the water) A dónde está?*

AÍDA: It's not in the water.

ABUELA: Oh, no? Oh, no?

AÍDA: No! *A poco* do you think they're gonna have signs in the water to say you are halfway to Santa Catalina? No. It's done very scientific. *A ver, hijo,* explain it to your grandma.

SIMÓN: Well, you see, Abuela—*(He points behind.)* There's San Pedro. *(He points ahead.)* And there's Santa Catalina. Looks halfway to me.

Abuela shakes her head and is looking back and forth, trying to make the decision, when suddenly the sound of a helicopter is heard.

15 ABUELA: *(looking up)* Virgencita de la Caridad del Cobre. *Qué es eso?*

Sound of helicopter gets closer. Margarita looks up.

MARGARITA: *Papi, Papi!*

A small commotion on the boat, with Everybody pointing at the helicopter above. Shadows of the helicopter fall on the boat. Simón looks up at it through binoculars.

Papi—qué es? What is it?

EDUARDO: *(through megaphone)* Uh . . . uh . . . uh, *un momentico . . . mi hija. . . .* Your *papi's* got everything under control, understand? Uh . . . you just keep stroking. And stay . . . uh . . . close to the boat.

SIMÓN: Wow, *Papi!* We're on TV, man! Holy Christ, we're all over the fucking U.S.A.! It's Mel Munson and Mary Beth White!

AÍDA: *Por Dios!* Simón, don't swear. And put on your shirt.

Aída fluffs her hair, puts on her sunglasses and waves to the helicopter. Simón leans over the side of the boat and yells to Margarita.

20 SIMÓN: Yo, Margo! You're on TV, man.

EDUARDO: Leave your sister alone. Turn on the radio.

MARGARITA: *Papi! Qué está pasando?*

ABUELA: *Que es la televisión dicen? (She shakes her head.) Porque como yo no puedo ver nada sin mis espejuelos.*

Abuela rummages through the boat, looking for her glasses. Voices of Mel Munson and Mary Beth White are heard over the boat's radio.

MEL'S VOICE: As we take a closer look at the gallant crew of *La Havana . . .* and there . . . yes, there she is . . . the little Cuban swimmer from Long Beach, California, nineteen-year-old Margarita Suárez. The unknown swimmer is our Cinderella entry . . . a bundle of tenacity,

battling her way through the choppy, murky waters of the cold
Pacific to reach the Island of Romance . . . Santa Catalina . . . where
should she be the first to arrive, two thousand dollars and a gold cup
will be waiting for her.

25 AÍDA: Doesn't even cover our expenses.

ABUELA: *Qué dice?*

EDUARDO: Shhhh!

MARY BETH'S VOICE: This is really a family effort, Mel, and—

MEL'S VOICE: Indeed it is. Her trainer, her coach, her mentor, is her
father, Eduardo Suárez. Not a swimmer himself, it says here, Mr.
Suárez is head usher of the Holy Name Society and the owner-
operator of Suárez Treasures of the Sea and Salvage Yard. I guess it's
one of those places—

30 MARY BETH'S VOICE: If I might interject a fact here, Mel, assisting in this
swim is Mrs. Suárez, who is a former Miss Cuba.

MEL'S VOICE: And a beautiful woman in her own right. Let's try and get
a closer look.

Helicopter sound gets louder. Margarita, frightened, looks up again.

MARGARITA: *Papi!*

EDUARDO: *(through megaphone) Mi hija,* don't get nervous . . . it's the press.
I'm handling it.

AÍDA: I see how you're handling it.

35 EDUARDO: *(through megaphone)* Do you hear? Everything is under control.
Get back into your rhythm. Keep your elbows high and kick and kick
and kick and kick . . .

ABUELA: *(finds her glasses and puts them on) Ay sí, es la televisión* . . . *(She
points to helicopter.) Qué lindo mira* . . . *(She fluffs her hair, gives a big
wave.) Aló América! Viva mi Margarita, viva todo los Cubanos en los
Estados Unidos!*

AÍDA: *Ay por Dios,* Cecilia, the man didn't come all this way in his
helicopter to look at you jumping up and down, making a fool of
yourself.

ABUELA: I don't care. I'm proud.

AÍDA: He can't understand you anyway.

40 ABUELA: *Viva* . . . *(She stops.) Simón, comó se dice viva?*

SIMÓN: Hurray.

ABUELA: Hurray for *mi Margarita y* for all the Cubans living *en* the United
States, *y un abrazo* . . . *Simón, abrazo* . . .

SIMÓN: A big hug.

ABUELA: *Sí,* a big hug to all my friends in Miami, Long Beach, Union
City, except for my son Carlos, who lives in New York in sin! He
lives . . . *(she crosses herself)* in Brooklyn with a Puerto Rican woman
in sin! *No decente* . . .

45 SIMÓN: Decent.

ABUELA: Carlos, *no decente*. This family, *decente*.

AÍDA: Cecilia, *por Dios*.

MEL'S VOICE: Look at that enthusiasm. The whole family has turned out to cheer little Margarita on to victory! I hope they won't be too disappointed.

MARY BETH'S VOICE: She seems to be making good time, Mel.

50 MEL'S VOICE: Yes, it takes all kinds to make a race. And it's a testimonial to the all-encompassing fairness . . . the greatness of this, the Wrigley Invitational Women's Swim to Catalina, where among all the professionals there is still room for the amateurs . . . like these, the simple people we see below us on the ragtag *La Havana,* taking their long-shot chance to victory. *Vaya con Dios!*

Helicopter sound fading as family, including Margarita, watch silently. Static as Simón turns radio off. Eduardo walks to bow of boat, looks out on the horizon.

EDUARDO: *(to himself)* Amateurs.

AÍDA: Eduardo, that person insulted us. Did you hear, Eduardo? That he called us a simple people in a ragtag boat? Did you hear . . . ?

ABUELA: *(clenching her fist at departing helicopter)* Mal-Rayo los parta!

SIMÓN: *(same gesture)* Asshole!

Aída follows Eduardo as he goes to side of boat and stares at Margarita.

55 AÍDA: This person comes in his helicopter to insult your wife, your family, your daughter . . .

MARGARITA: *(pops her head out of the water)* Papi?

AÍDA: Do you hear me, Eduardo? I am not simple.

ABUELA: *Sí.*

AÍDA: I am complicated.

60 ABUELA: *Sí, demasiada complicada.*

AÍDA: Me and my family are not so simple.

SIMÓN: Mom, the guy's an asshole.

ABUELA: *(shaking her fist at helicopter)* Asshole!

AÍDA: If my daughter was simple, she would not be in that water swimming.

65 MARGARITA: Simple? *Papi* . . . ?

AÍDA: *Ahora,* Eduardo, this is what I want you to do. When we get to Santa Catalina, I want you to call the TV station and demand an apology.

EDUARDO: *Cállete mujer! Aquí mando yo.* I will decide what is to be done.

MARGARITA: *Papi,* tell me what's going on.

EDUARDO: Do you understand what I am saying to you, Aída?

70 SIMÓN: *(leaning over side of boat, to Margarita)* Yo Margo! You know that Mel Munson guy on TV? He called you a simple amateur and said you didn't have a chance.

ABUELA: *(leaning directly behind Simón.)* Mi hija, insultó a la familia. Desgraciado!

AÍDA: *(leaning in behind Abuela)* He called us peasants! And your father is not doing anything about it. He just knows how to yell at me.

EDUARDO: *(through megaphone)* Shut up! All of you! Do you want to break her concentration? Is that what you are after? Eh?

Abuela, Aída, and Simón shrink back. Eduardo paces before them.

> Swimming is rhythm and concentration. You win a race *aquí.* *(Pointing to his head.)* Now . . . *(to Simón)* you, take care of the boat, Aída *y Mama* . . . do something. Anything. Something practical.

Abuela and Aída get on knees and pray in Spanish.

> Hija, give it everything, eh? . . . *por la familia. Uno . . . dos.* . . . You must win.

Simón goes into cabin. The prayers continue as lights change to indicate bright sunlight, later in the afternoon.

SCENE 3

Tableau for a couple of beats. Eduardo on bow with timer in one hand as he counts strokes per minute. Simón is in the cabin steering, wearing his sunglasses, baseball cap on backward. Abuela and Aída are at the side of the boat, heads down, hands folded, still muttering prayers in Spanish.

AÍDA and ABUELA: *(crossing themselves) En el nombre del Padre, del Hijo y del Espíritu Santo amén.*

75 EDUARDO: *(through megaphone)* You're stroking seventy-two!

SIMÓN: *(singing)* Mama's stroking, Mama's stroking seventy-two. . . .

EDUARDO: *(through megaphone)* You comfortable with it?

SIMÓN: *(singing)* Seventy-two, seventy-two, seventy-two for you.

AÍDA: *(looking at the heavens) Ay,* Eduardo, *ven acá,* we should be grateful that *Nuestro Señor* gave us such a beautiful day.

80 ABUELA: *(crosses herself) Si, gracias a Dios.*

EDUARDO: She's stroking seventy-two, with no problem. *(He throws a kiss to the sky.)* It's a beautiful day to win.

AÍDA: *Qué hermoso!* So clear and bright. Not a cloud in the sky. *Mira! Mira!* Even rainbows on the water . . . a sign from God.

SIMÓN: *(singing)* Rainbows on the water . . . you in my arms . . .

ABUELA and EDUARDO: *(Looking the wrong way.) Dónde?*

85 AÍDA: *(pointing toward Margarita)* There, dancing in front of Margarita, leading her on . . .

EDUARDO: Rainbows on . . . *Ay coño!* It's an oil slick! You . . . you . . . *(To Simón.)* Stop the boat. *(Runs to bow, yelling.)* Margarita! Margarita!

On the next stroke, Margarita comes up all covered in black oil.

MARGARITA: *Papi! Papi . . . !*

Everybody goes to the side and stares at Margarita, who stares back. Eduardo freezes.

Aída: *Apúrate,* Eduardo, move . . . what's wrong with you . . . *no me oíste,* get my daughter out of the water.

Eduardo: *(softly)* We can't touch her. If we touch her, she's disqualified.

90 Aída: But I'm her mother.

Eduardo: Not even by her own mother. Especially by her own mother. . . . You always want the rules to be different for you, you always want to be the exception. *(To Simón.)* And you . . . you didn't see it, eh? You were playing again?

Simón: *Papi,* I was watching . . .

Aída: *(interrupting) Pues,* do something Eduardo. You are the big coach, the monitor.

Simón: Mentor! Mentor!

95 Eduardo: How can a person think around you? *(He walks off to bow, puts head in hands.)*

Abuela: *(looking over side) Mira como todos los* little birds are dead. *(She crosses herself.)*

Aída: Their little wings are glued to their sides.

Simón: Christ, this is like the La Brea tar pits.

Aída: They can't move their little wings.

100 Abuela: *Esa niña tiene que moverse.*

Simón: Yeah, Margo, you gotta move, man.

Abuela and Simón gesture for Margarita to move. Aída gestures for her to swim.

Abuela: *Anda niña, muévete.*

Aída: Swim, *hija,* swim or the *aceite* will stick to your wings.

Margarita: *Papi?*

105 Abuela: *(taking megaphone)* Your *papi* say "move it!"

Margarita with difficulty starts moving.

Abuela, Aída and Simón: *(laboriously counting) Uno, dos . . . uno, dos . . . anda . . . uno, dos.*

Eduardo: *(running to take megaphone from Abuela) Uno, dos . . .*

Simón races into cabin and starts the engine. Abuela, Aída and Eduardo count together.

Simón: *(looking ahead) Papi,* it's over there!

Eduardo: Eh?

110 Simón: *(pointing ahead and to the right)* It's getting clearer over there.

Eduardo: *(through megaphone)* Now pay attention to me. Go to the right.

Simón, Abuela, Aída and Eduardo all lean over side. They point ahead and to the right, except Abuela, who points to the left.

Family: *(shouting together) Para yá! Para yá!*

Lights go down on boat. A special light on Margarita, swimming through the oil,
and on Abuela, watching her.

ABUELA: *Sangre de mi sangre,* you will be another to save us. En Bolondron,
where your great-grandmother Luz Suárez was born, they say one day
it rained blood. All the people, they run into their houses. They cry,
they pray, *pero* your great-grandmother Luz she had *cojones* like a
man. She run outside. She look straight at the sky. She shake her fist.
And she say to the evil one, *"Mira . . . (beating her chest) coño, Diablo,*
aquí estoy si me quieres." And she open her mouth, and she drunk the
blood.

Blackout

SCENE 4

Lights up on boat. Aída and Eduardo are on deck watching Margarita swim. We
hear the gentle, rhythmic lap, lap, lap of the water, then the sound of inhaling
and exhaling as Margarita's breathing becomes louder. Then Margarita's heart-
beat is heard, with the lapping of the water and the breathing under it. These
sounds continue beneath the dialogue to the end of the scene.

AÍDA: *Dios mío.* Look how she moves through the water. . . .
115 EDUARDO: You see, it's very simple. It is a matter of concentration.
AÍDA: The first time I put her in water she came to life, she grew before
my eyes. She moved, she smiled, she loved it more than me. She
didn't want my breast any longer. She wanted the water.
EDUARDO: And of course, the rhythm. The rhythm takes away the pain
and helps the concentration.

Pause. Aída and Eduardo watch Margarita.

AÍDA: Is that my child or a seal. . . .
EDUARDO: Ah, a seal, the reason for that is that she's keeping her arms
very close to her body. She cups her hands, and then she reaches and
digs, reaches and digs.
120 AÍDA: To think that a daughter of mine . . .
EDUARDO: It's the training, the hours in the water. I used to tie weights
around her little wrists and ankles.
AÍDA: A spirit, an ocean spirit, must have entered my body when I was
carrying her.
EDUARDO: *(to Margarita)* Your stroke is slowing down.

Pause. We hear Margarita's heartbeat with the breathing under, faster now.

AÍDA: Eduardo, that night, the night on the boat . . .
125 EDUARDO: Ah, the night on the boat again . . . the moon was . . .
AÍDA: The moon was full. We were coming to America. . . . *Qué romantico.*

Heartbeat and breathing continue.

EDUARDO: We were cold, afraid, with no money, and on top of everything, you were hysterical, yelling at me, tearing at me with your nails. *(Opens his shirt, points to the base of his neck.)* Look, I still bear the scars . . . telling me that I didn't know what I was doing . . . saying that we were going to die. . . .

AÍDA: You took me, you stole me from my home . . . you didn't give me a chance to prepare. You just said we have to go now, now! Now, you said. You didn't let me take anything. I left everything behind. . . . I left everything behind.

EDUARDO: Saying that I wasn't good enough, that your father didn't raise you so that I could drown you in the sea.

130 AÍDA: You didn't let me say even a good-bye. You took me, you stole me, you tore me from my home.

EDUARDO: I took you so we could be married.

AÍDA: That was in Miami. But that night on the boat, Eduardo. . . . We were not married, that night on the boat.

EDUARDO: *No pasó nada!* Once and for all get it out of your head, it was cold, you hated me, and we were afraid. . . .

AÍDA: *Mentiroso!*

135 EDUARDO: A man can't do it when he is afraid.

AÍDA: Liar! You did it very well.

EDUARDO: I did?

AÍDA: *Sí.* Gentle. You were so gentle and then strong . . . my passion for you so deep. Standing next to you . . . I would ache . . . looking at your hands I would forget to breathe, you were irresistible.

EDUARDO: I was?

140 AÍDA: You took me into your arms, you touched my face with your fingertips . . . you kissed my eyes . . . *la esquina de la boca y* . . .

EDUARDO: *Sí, sí,* and then . . .

AÍDA: I look at your face on top of mine, and I see the lights of Havana in your eyes. That's when you seduced me.

EDUARDO: Shhh, they're gonna hear you.

Lights go down. Special on Aída.

AÍDA: That was the night. A woman doesn't forget those things . . . and later that night was the dream . . . the dream of a big country with fields of fertile land and big, giant things growing. And there by a green, slimy pond I found a giant pea pod and when I opened it, it was full of little, tiny baby frogs.

Aída crosses herself as she watches Margarita. We hear louder breathing and heartbeat.

145 MARGARITA: Santa Teresa. Little Flower of God, pray for me. San Martín de Porres, pray for me. Santa Rosa de Lima, *Virgencita de la Caridad del Cobre,* pray for me. . . . Mother pray for me.

SCENE 5

Loud howling of wind is heard, as lights change to indicate unstable weather, fog and mist. Family on deck, braced and huddled against the wind. Simón is at the helm.

AÍDA: *Ay Dios mío, qué viento.*

EDUARDO: *(through megaphone)* Don't drift out . . . that wind is pushing you out. *(To Simón.)* You! Slow down. Can't you see your sister is drifting out?

SIMÓN: It's the wind, *Papi.*

AÍDA: Baby, don't go so far. . . .

150 ABUELA: *(to heaven) Ay Gran Poder de Dios, quita este maldito viento.*

SIMÓN: Margo! Margo! Stay close to the boat.

EDUARDO: Dig in. Dig in hard. . . . Reach down from your guts and dig in.

ABUELA: *(to heaven) Ay Virgen de la Caridad del Cobre, por lo más tú quieres a pararla.*

AÍDA: *(putting her hand out, reaching for Margarita)* Baby, don't go far.

Abuela crosses herself. Action freezes. Lights get dimmer, special on Margarita. She keeps swimming, stops, starts again, stops, then, finally exhausted, stops altogether. The boat stops moving.

155 EDUARDO: What's going on here? Why are we stopping?

SIMÓN: *Papi,* she's not moving! Yo Margo!

The family all run to the side.

EDUARDO: *Hija!* . . . *Hijita!* You're tired, eh?

AÍDA: *Por supuesto* she's tired. I like to see you get in the water, waving your arms and legs from San Pedro to Santa Catalina. A person isn't a machine, a person has to rest.

SIMÓN: Yo, Mama! Cool out, it ain't fucking brain surgery.

160 EDUARDO: *(to Simón)* Shut up, you. *(Louder to Margarita.)* I guess your mother's right for once, huh? . . . I guess you had to stop, eh? . . . Give your brother, the idiot . . . a chance to catch up with you.

SIMÓN: *(clowning like Mortimer Snerd)* Dum dee dum dee dum ooops, ah shucks . . .

EDUARDO: I don't think he's Cuban.

SIMÓN: *(like Ricky Ricardo) Oye,* Lucy! I'm home! Ba ba lu!

EDUARDO: *(joins in clowning, grabbing Simón in a headlock)* What am I gonna do with this idiot, eh? I don't understand this idiot. He's not like us, Margarita. *(Laughing.)* You think if we put him into your bathing suit with a cap on his head . . . *(He laughs hysterically.)* You think anyone would know . . . huh? Do you think anyone would know? *(Laughs.)*

165 SIMÓN: *(vamping) Ay, mi amor.* Anybody looking for tits would know.

Eduardo slaps Simón across the face, knocking him down. Aída runs to Simón's aid. Abuela holds Eduardo back.

Margarita: *Mía culpa! Mía culpa!*

Abuela: *Qué dices hija?*

Margarita: *Papi,* it's my fault, it's all my fault. . . . I'm so cold, I can't
move. . . . I put my face in the water . . . and I hear them
whispering . . . laughing at me. . . .

Aída: Who is laughing at you?

170 Margarita: The fish are all biting me . . . they hate me . . . they whisper
about me. She can't swim, they say. She can't glide. She has no
grace. . . . Yellowtails, bonita, tuna, man-o'-war, snub-nose sharks, *los
baracudas* . . . they all hate me . . . only the dolphins care . . . and
sometimes I hear the whales crying . . . she is lost, she is dead. I'm so
numb, I can't feel. *Papi! Papi!* Am I dead?

Eduardo: *Vamos,* baby, punch those arms in. Come on . . . do you
hear me?

Margarita: *Papi . . . Papi . . .* forgive me. . . .

*All is silent on the boat. Eduardo drops his megaphone, his head bent down in
dejection. Abuela, Aída, Simón, all leaning over the side of the boat. Simón
slowly walks away.*

Aída: *Mi hija, qué tienes?*

Simón: Oh, Christ, don't make her say it. Please don't make her say it.

175 Abuela: Say what? *Qué cosa?*

Simón: She wants to quit, can't you see she's had enough?

Abuela: *Mira, para eso. Esta niña* is turning blue.

Aída: *Oyeme, mi hija.* Do you want to come out of the water?

Margarita: *Papi?*

180 Simón: *(to Eduardo)* She won't come out until *you* tell her.

Aída: Eduardo . . . answer your daughter.

Eduardo: *Le dije* to concentrate . . . concentrate on your rhythm. Then
the rhythm would carry her . . . ay, it's a beautiful thing, Aída. It's
like yoga, like meditation, the mind over matter . . . the mind
controlling the body . . . that's how the great things in the world
have been done. I wish you . . . I wish my wife could understand.

Margarita: *Papi?*

Simón: *(to Margarita)* Forget him.

185 Aída: *(imploring)* Eduardo, *por favor.*

Eduardo: *(walking in circles)* Why didn't you let her concentrate? Don't
you understand, the concentration, the rhythm is everything. But no,
you wouldn't listen. *(Screaming to the ocean.)* Goddamn Cubans, why,
God, why do you make us go everywhere with our families? *(He goes
to back of boat.)*

Aída: *(opening her arms) Mi hija, ven,* come to *Mami. (Rocking.)* Your *mami*
knows.

*Abuela has taken the training bottle, puts it in a net. She and Simón lower it to
Margarita.*

SIMÓN: Take this. Drink it. *(As Margarita drinks, Abuela crosses herself.)*
ABUELA: *Sangre de mi sangre.*

Music comes up softly. Margarita drinks, gives the bottle back, stretches out her arms, as if on a cross. Floats on her back. She begins a graceful backstroke. Lights fade on boat as special lights come up on Margarita. She stops. Slowly turns over and starts to swim, gradually picking up speed. Suddenly as if in pain she stops, tries again, then stops in pain again. She becomes disoriented and falls to the bottom of the sea. Special on Margarita at the bottom of the sea.

190 MARGARITA: *Ya no puedo* . . . I can't. . . . A person isn't a machine . . . *es mi culpa* . . . Father forgive me . . . *Papi! Papi!* One, two. *Uno, dos. (Pause.) Papi! A dónde estás? (Pause.)* One, two, one, two. *Papi! Ay, Papi!* Where are you . . . ? Don't leave me. . . . Why don't you answer me? *(Pause. She starts to swim, slowly.) Uno, dos, uno, dos.* Dig in, dig in. *(Stops swimming.) Por favor, Papi! (Starts to swim again.)* One, two, one, two. Kick from your hip, kick from your hip. *(Stops swimming. Starts to cry.)* Oh God, please. . . . *(Pause.)* Hail Mary, full of grace . . . dig in, dig in . . . the Lord is with thee. . . . *(She swims to the rhythm of her Hail Mary.)* Hail Mary, full of grace . . . dig in, dig in . . . the Lord is with thee . . . dig in, dig in. . . . Blessed art thou among women. . . . *Mami,* it hurts. You let go of my hand. I'm lost. . . . And blessed is the fruit of thy womb, now and at the hour of our death. Amen. I don't want to die, I don't want to die.

Margarita is still swimming. Blackout. She is gone.

SCENE 6

Lights up on boat, we hear radio static. There is a heavy mist. On deck we see only black outline of Abuela with shawl over her head. We hear the voices of Eduardo, Aída, and Radio Operator.

EDUARDO'S VOICE: *La Havana!* Coming from San Pedro. Over.
RADIO OPERATOR'S VOICE: Right, DT6-6, you say you've lost a swimmer.
AÍDA'S VOICE: Our child, our only daughter . . . listen to me. Her name is Margarita Inez Suárez, she is wearing a black one-piece bathing suit cut high in the legs with a white racing stripe down the sides, a white bathing cap with goggles and her whole body covered with a . . . with a . . .
EDUARDO'S VOICE: With lanolin and paraffin.
195 AÍDA'S VOICE: *Sí . . . con lanolin and paraffin.*

More radio static. Special on Simón, on the edge of the boat.

SIMÓN: Margo! Yo Margo! *(Pause.)* Man don't do this. *(Pause.)* Come on. . . . Come on. . . . *(Pause.)* God, why does everything have to be so hard? *(Pause.)* Stupid. You know you're not supposed to die for this. Stupid. It's his dream and he can't even swim. *(Pause.)* Punch those arms in. Come home. Come home. I'm your little brother. Don't forget what Mama said. You're not supposed to leave me behind. *Vamos*, Margarita, take your little brother, hold his hand tight when you cross the street. He's so little. *(Pause.)* Oh, Christ, give us a sign. . . . I know! I know! Margo, I'll send you a message . . . like mental telepathy. I'll hold my breath, close my eyes, and I'll bring you home. *(He takes a deep breath; a few beats.)* This time I'll beep . . . I'll send out sonar signals like a dolphin. *(He imitates dolphin sounds.)*

The sound of real dolphins takes over from Simón, then fades into sound of Abuela saying the Hail Mary in Spanish, as full lights come up slowly.

SCENE 7

Eduardo coming out of cabin, sobbing, Aída holding him. Simón anxiously scanning the horizon. Abuela looking calmly ahead.

EDUARDO: *Es mi culpa, sí, es mi culpa. (He hits his chest.)*
AÍDA: *Ya, ya viejo* . . . it was my sin . . . I left my home.
EDUARDO: Forgive me, forgive me. I've lost our daughter, our sister, our granddaughter, *mi carne, mi sangre, mis ilusiones. (To heaven.) Dios mío,* take me . . . take me, I say . . . Goddammit, take me!
200 SIMÓN: I'm going in.
AÍDA and EDUARDO: No!
EDUARDO: *(grabbing and holding Simón, speaking to heaven)* God, take me, not my children. They are my dreams, my illusions . . . and not this one, this one is my mystery . . . he has my secret dreams. In him are the parts of me I cannot see.

Eduardo embraces Simón. Radio static becomes louder.

AÍDA: I . . . I think I see her.
SIMÓN: No, it's just a seal.
205 ABUELA: *(looking out with binoculars) Mi nietacita, dónde estás? (She feels her heart.)* I don't feel the knife in my heart . . . my little fish is not lost.

Radio crackles with static. As lights dim on boat, Voices of Mel and Mary Beth are heard over the radio.

MEL'S VOICE: Tragedy has marred the face of the Wrigley Invitational Women's Race to Catalina. The Cuban swimmer, little Margarita Suárez, has reportedly been lost at sea. Coast Guard and divers are looking for her as we speak. Yet in spite of this tragedy the race must go on because . . .
MARY BETH'S VOICE: *(interrupting loudly)* Mel!
MEL'S VOICE: *(startled)* What!
MARY BETH'S VOICE: Ah . . . excuse me, Mel . . . we have a winner. We've just received word from Catalina that one of the swimmers is just fifty yards from the breakers . . . it's, oh, it's . . . Margarita Suárez!

Special on family in cabin listening to radio.

210 **MEL'S VOICE:** What? I thought she died!

Special on Margarita, taking off bathing cap, trophy in hand, walking on the water.

MARY BETH'S VOICE: Ahh . . . unless . . . unless this is a tragic . . . No . . . there she is, Mel. Margarita Suárez! The only one in the race wearing a black bathing suit cut high in the legs with a racing stripe down the side.

Family cheering, embracing.

SIMÓN: *(screaming)* Way to go, Margo!

MEL'S VOICE: This is indeed a miracle! It's a resurrection! Margarita Suárez, with a flotilla of boats to meet her, is now walking on the waters, through the breakers . . . onto the beach, with crowds of people cheering her on. What a jubilation! This is a miracle!

Sound of crowds cheering. Lights and cheering sounds fade.

Blackout

READING AND REACTING

1. *The Cuban Swimmer* is a short play with a single setting. In what additional locations could Sanchez-Scott have set the play's action? What might she have gained or lost by using these additional settings?
2. What lighting and sound effects does the play call for? In what way do these effects advance the action of the play? In what way—if any—do they help to communicate the play's theme?
3. Although most of the play is in English, the characters frequently speak Spanish. What are the advantages of this use of Spanish? Are there any drawbacks?
4. What function do the voices of Mel and Mary Beth serve in the play?
5. What conflicts develop among the family members as the play proceeds? In what way might these conflicts represent the problems of other immigrants to the United States?
6. In what sense is Mel's final comment "This is a miracle!" ironic?
7. Do you think this play comments on the position of women in American culture? In Cuban-American culture?
8. Could this play be seen as an **allegory?** What is the value of seeing it in this way?
9. Throughout much of the play Margarita is swimming in full view of the audience. Devise three ways in which a director

could achieve this effect on stage. Which one would you choose if you were directing the play?

10. As the headnote that precedes the play explains, the 1984 New York production of *The Cuban Swimmer* had an extremely realistic set. Could the play be staged unrealistically, with the characters on a raised platform in make-believe water? How do you think this kind of set would affect the audience?

11. **Journal Entry** Are you able to empathize with Margarita's struggle? What elements of the play make it easy or difficult for you to do so?

12. **Critical Perspective** In a 1998 article in the *New York Times,* theater critic Brooks Atkinson said, "Nothing is better for good actors than a stage with no scenery." Do you think this remark could be applied to the staging of *The Cuban Swimmer?*

Related Works: "Two Kinds" (p. 594), "Africa" (p. 924), "Ellis Island" (p. 936), "Black Hair" (p. 995)

❖ **Sophocles** (496–406 B.C.), along with Aeschylus and Euripides, is one of the three great Greek tragic dramatists. He lived during the great flowering and subsequent decline of fifth-century Athens—the high point of Greek civilization. Born as Greece struggled against the Persian empire and moved to adopt democracy, he lived as an adult under Pericles in the Golden Age of Athens and died as it became clear that Athens would lose the Peloponnesian War. Sophocles was an active participant in the public life of Athens, serving as a collector of tribute from Athenian subjects and later as a general. Though he wrote at least one hundred and twenty plays, only seven have survived, including three plays about Oedipus: *Oedipus the King* (c. 430 B.C.), *Oedipus at Colonus* (411? B.C.), and *Antigone* (441 B.C.).

Oedipus the King, or *Oedipus Rex* (sometimes called *Oedipus the Tyrant*), was performed shortly after a great plague in Athens (probably in 429 or 425 B.C.) and as Athens was falling into decline; the play opens with the account of a plague in Thebes, Oedipus's kingdom. Over the years, *Oedipus the King* has attracted impressive critical attention, from Aristotle's use of it as a model for his definition of tragedy to Freud's use of its power as evidence of the validity of the so-called Oedipus complex.

Cultural Context ❖ Between 431–404 B.C., the Peloponnesian War raged in ancient Greece between Athens and Sparta. A Spartan army invaded Attica in 431 B.C., after which Athenians hid behind the walls of their city while the Athenian fleet began raids. Between 430–428 B.C., a plague wiped out at least a quarter of the Athenian population.

❖ ❖ ❖

SOPHOCLES

Oedipus the King*
(C. 430 B.C.)

Translated by Thomas Gould

CHARACTERS

OEDIPUS,[1] *the King of Thebes*
PRIEST OF ZEUS, *leader of the*
   suppliants
CREON, *Oedipus's brother-in-law*
CHORUS, *a group of Theban elders*
CHORAGOS, *spokesman of the*
   Chorus

TIRESIAS, *a blind seer or prophet*
JOCASTA, *the queen of Thebes*
MESSENGER, *from Corinth, once a*
   shepherd
HERDSMAN, *once a servant of Laius*
SECOND MESSENGER, *a servant of*
   Oedipus

MUTES

SUPPLIANTS, *Thebans seeking Oedipus's help*
ATTENDANTS, *for the Royal Family*
SERVANTS, *to lead Tiresias and Oedipus*
ANTIGONE, *daughter of Oedipus and Jocasta*
ISMENE, *daughter of Oedipus and Jocasta*

The action takes place during the day in front of the royal palace in Thebes. There are two altars (left and right) on the proscenium and several steps leading down to the orchestra. As the play opens, Thebans of various ages who have come to beg Oedipus for help are sitting on these steps and in part of the orchestra. These suppliants are holding branches of laurel or olive which have strips of wool[2] wrapped around them. Oedipus enters from the palace (the central door of the skene).

PROLOGUE[3]

OEDIPUS: My children, ancient Cadmus'[4] newest care,
   why have you hurried to those seats, your boughs
   wound with the emblems of the suppliant?
   The city is weighed down with fragrant smoke,
5   with hymns to the Healer[5] and the cries of mourners.

---

*Note that individual lines are numbered in the following play. When a line is shared by two or more characters, it is counted as one line.

---

[1] *Oedipus:* The name means "swollen foot." It refers to the mutilation of Oedipus's feet done by his father, Laius, before the infant was sent to Mount Cithaeron to be put to death by exposure. [2] *wool:* Branches wrapped with wool are traditional symbols of prayer or supplication. [3] *Prologue:* portion of the play containing the exposition, or explanation, of what has gone before and what is now happening. [4] *Cadmus:* Oedipus's great great grandfather (although he does not know this) and the founder of Thebes. [5] *Healer:* Apollo, god of prophecy, light, healing, justice, purification, and destruction.

I thought it wrong, my sons, to hear your words
through emissaries, and have come out myself,
I, Oedipus, a name that all men know.

(Oedipus addresses the Priest.)

Old man—for it is fitting that you speak
10   for all—what is your mood as you entreat me,
fear or trust? You may be confident
that I'll do anything. How hard of heart
if an appeal like this did not rouse my pity!
Priest: You, Oedipus, who hold the power here,
15   you see our several ages, we who sit
before your altars—some not strong enough
to take long flight, some heavy in old age,
the priests, as I of Zeus,[6] and from our youths
a chosen band. The rest sit with their windings
20   in the markets, at the twin shrines of Pallas,[7]
and the prophetic embers of Ismēnos.[8]
Our city, as you see yourself, is tossed
too much, and can no longer lift its head
above the troughs of billows red with death.
25   It dies in the fruitful flowers of the soil,
it dies in its pastured herds, and in its women's
barren pangs. And the fire-bearing god[9]
has swooped upon the city, hateful plague,
and he has left the house of Cadmus empty.
30   Black Hades[10] is made rich with moans and weeping.
Not judging you an equal of the gods,
do I and the children sit here at your hearth,
but as the first of men, in troubled times
and in encounters with divinities.
35   You came to Cadmus' city and unbound
the tax we had to pay to the harsh singer,[11]
did it without a helpful word from us,

---

[6] *Zeus:* father and king of the gods.   [7] *Pallas:* Athena, goddess of wisdom, arts, crafts, and war.   [8] *Ismēnos:* a reference to the temple of Apollo near the river Ismēnos in Thebes. Prophecies were made here by "reading" the ashes of the altar fires.   [9] *fire-bearing god:* contagious fever viewed as a god.   [10] *Black Hades:* refers to both the underworld where the spirits of the dead go and the god of the underworld.   [11] *harsh singer:* the Sphinx, a monster with a woman's head, a lion's body, and wings. The "tax" that Oedipus freed Thebes from was the destruction of all the young men who failed to solve the Sphinx's riddle and were subsequently devoured. The Sphinx always asked the same riddle: "What goes on four legs in the morning, two legs at noon, and three legs in the evening, and yet is weakest when supported by the largest number of feet?" Oedipus discovered the correct answer—man, who crawls in infancy, walks in his prime, and uses a stick in old age—and thus ended the Sphinx's reign of terror. The Sphinx destroyed herself when Oedipus answered the riddle. Oedipus's reward for freeing Thebes of the Sphinx was the throne and the hand of the recently widowed Jocasta.

with no instruction; with a god's assistance
you raised up our life, so we believe.
40 Again now Oedipus, our greatest power,
we plead with you, as suppliants, all of us,
to find us strength, whether from a god's response,
or learned in some way from another man.
I know that the experienced among men
45 give counsels that will prosper best of all.
Noblest of men, lift up our land again!
Think also of yourself; since now the land
calls you its Savior for your zeal of old,
oh let us never look back at your rule
50 as men helped up only to fall again!
Do not stumble! Put our land on firm feet!
The bird of omen was auspicious then,
when you brought that luck; be that same man again!
The power is yours; if you will rule our country,
55 rule over men, not in an empty land.
A towered city or a ship is nothing
if desolate and no man lives within.
OEDIPUS: Pitiable children, oh I know, I know
the yearnings that have brought you. Yes, I know
60 that you are sick. And yet, though you are sick,
there is not one of you so sick as I.
For your affliction comes to each alone,
for him and no one else, but my soul mourns
for me and for you, too, and for the city.
65 You do not waken me as from a sleep,
for I have wept, bitterly and long,
tried many paths in the wanderings of thought,
and the single cure I found by careful search
I've acted on: I sent Menoeceus' son,
70 Creon, brother of my wife, to the Pythian
halls of Phoebus,[12] so that I might learn
what I must do or say to save this city.
Already, when I think what day this is,
I wonder anxiously what he is doing.
75 Too long, more than is right, he's been away.
But when he comes, then I shall be a traitor
if I do not do all that the god reveals.
PRIEST: Welcome words! But look, those men have signaled
that it is Creon who is now approaching!
80 OEDIPUS: Lord Apollo! May he bring Savior Luck,
a Luck as brilliant as his eyes are now!

---

[12] *Pythian . . . Phoebus:* the temple of Phoebus Apollo's oracle or prophet at Delphi.

PRIEST: His news is happy, it appears. He comes,
    forehead crowned with thickly berried laurel.[13]
OEDIPUS: We'll know, for he is near enough to hear us.

(Enter Creon along one of the parados.)

85   Lord, brother in marriage, son of Menoeceus!
    What is the god's pronouncement that you bring?
CREON: It's good. For even troubles, if they chance
    to turn out well, I always count as lucky.
OEDIPUS: But what was the response? You seem to say
90   I'm not to fear—but not to take heart either.
CREON: If you will hear me with these men present,
    I'm ready to report—or go inside.

(Creon moves up the steps toward the palace.)

OEDIPUS: Speak out to all! The grief that burdens me
    concerns these men more than it does my life.
95   CREON: Then I shall tell you what I heard from the god.
    The task Lord Phoebus sets for us is clear:
    drive out pollution sheltered in our land,
    and do not shelter what is incurable.
OEDIPUS: What is our trouble? How shall we cleanse ourselves?
100   CREON: We must banish or murder to free ourselves
    from a murder that blows storms through the city.
OEDIPUS: What man's bad luck does he accuse in this?
CREON: My Lord, a king named Laius ruled our land
    before you came to steer the city straight.
105   OEDIPUS: I know. So I was told—I never saw him.
CREON: Since he was murdered, you must raise your hand
    against the men who killed him with their hands.
OEDIPUS: Where are they now? And how can we ever find
    the track of ancient guilt now hard to read?
110   CREON: In our own land, he said. What we pursue,
    that can be caught; but not what we neglect.
OEDIPUS: Was Laius home, or in the countryside—
    or was he murdered in some foreign land?
CREON: He left to see a sacred rite, he said;
115   He left, but never came home from his journey.
OEDIPUS: Did none of his party see it and report—
    someone we might profitably question?
CREON: They were all killed but one, who fled in fear,
    and he could tell us only one clear fact.
120   OEDIPUS: What fact? One thing could lead us on to more
    if we could get a small start on our hope.

---

[13] *laurel:* Creon is wearing a garland of laurel leaves, sacred to Apollo.

CREON: He said that bandits chanced on them and killed him—
    with the force of many hands, not one alone.
OEDIPUS: How could a bandit dare so great an act—
125   unless this was a plot paid off from here!
CREON: We thought of that, but when Laius was killed,
    we had no one to help us in our troubles.
OEDIPUS: It was your very kingship that was killed!
    What kind of trouble blocked you from a search?
130 CREON: The subtle-singing Sphinx asked us to turn
    from the obscure to what lay at our feet.
OEDIPUS: Then I shall begin again and make it plain.
    It was quite worthy of Phoebus, and worthy of you,
    to turn our thoughts back to the murdered man,
135   and right that you should see me join the battle
    for justice to our land and to the god.
    Not on behalf of any distant kinships,
    it's for myself I will dispel this stain.
    Whoever murdered him may also wish
140   to punish me—and with the selfsame hand.
    In helping him I also serve myself.
    Now quickly, children: up from the altar steps,
    and raise the branches of the suppliant!
    Let someone go and summon Cadmus' people:
145   say I'll do anything.

(Exit an Attendant along one of the parados.)

                        Our luck will prosper
    if the god is with us, or we have already fallen.
PRIEST: Rise, my children; that for which we came,
    he has himself proclaimed he will accomplish.
    May Phoebus, who announced this, also come
150   as Savior and reliever from the plague.

(Exit Oedipus and Creon into the palace. The Priest and the Suppliants exit left and right along the parados. After a brief pause, the Chorus (including the Choragos) enters the orchestra from the parados.)

PARADOS[14]

STROPHE 1[15]

CHORUS: Voice from Zeus,[16] sweetly spoken, what are you
    that have arrived from golden
    Pytho[17] to our shining

---

[14] *Parados*: a song sung by the chorus on the first entering.   [15] *Strophe, Antistrophe*: probably refer to the direction in which the Chorus danced while reciting specific stanzas. Strophe may have indicated dance steps to stage left, antistrophe to stage right.   [16] *Voice from Zeus*: a reference to Apollo's prophecy. Zeus taught Apollo how to prophesy.   [17] *Pytho*: Delphi.

Thebes? I am on the rack, terror
155   shakes my soul.
Delian Healer,[18] summoned by "iē!"
I await in holy dread what obligation, something new
or something back once more with the revolving years,
          you'll bring about for me.
160   Oh tell me, child of golden Hope,
          deathless Response!

ANTISTROPHE 1

I appeal to you first, daughter of Zeus,
          deathless Athena,
and to your sister who protects this land,
165   Artemis,[19] whose famous throne is the whole circle
          of the marketplace,
and Phoebus, who shoots from afar: iō!
Three-fold defenders against death, appear!
If ever in the past, to stop blind ruin
170   sent against the city,
you banished utterly the fires of suffering,
          come now again!

STROPHE 2

Ah! Ah! Unnumbered are the miseries
I bear. The plague claims all
175   our comrades. Nor has thought found yet a spear
by which a man shall be protected. What our glorious
earth gives birth to does not grow. Without a birth
from cries of labor
          do the women rise.
180   One person after another
          you may see, like flying birds,
faster than indomitable fire, sped
to the shore of the god that is the sunset.[20]

ANTISTROPHE 2

And with their deaths unnumbered dies the city.
185   Her children lie unpitied on the ground,
spreading death, unmourned.
Meanwhile young wives, and gray-haired mothers with them,
on the shores of the altars, from this side and that,
suppliants from mournful trouble,
190   cry out their grief.

---

[18] *Delian Healer:* Apollo.   [19] *Artemis:* goddess of virginity, childbirth, and hunting.
[20] *god . . . sunset:* Hades, god of the underworld.

A hymn to the Healer shines,
    the flute a mourner's voice.
Against which, golden goddess, daughter of Zeus,
    send lovely Strength.

STROPHE 3

195 Causing raging Ares[21]—who,
    armed now with no shield of bronze,
burns me, coming on amid loud cries—
to turn his back and run from my land,
with a fair wind behind, to the great
200   hall of Amphitritē,[22]
or to the anchorage that welcomes no one,
Thrace's troubled sea!
If night lets something get away at last,
    it comes by day.
205 Fire-bearing god . . .
    you who dispense the might of lightning,
Zeus! Father! Destroy him with your thunderbolt!

(Enter Oedipus from the palace.)

ANTISTROPHE 3

Lycēan Lord![23] From your looped
    bowstring, twisted gold,
210 I wish indomitable missiles might be scattered
and stand forward, our protectors; also fire-bearing
radiance of Artemis, with which
    she darts across the Lycian mountains.
I call the god whose head is bound in gold,
215 with whom this country shares its name,
Bacchus,[24] wine-flushed, summoned by "euoi!,"
    Maenads' comrade,
to approach ablaze
    with gleaming . . .
220 pine, opposed to that god-hated god.

EPISODE 1[25]

OEDIPUS: I hear your prayer. Submit to what I say
and to the labors that the plague demands
and you'll get help and a relief from evils.
I'll make the proclamation, though a stranger
225 to the report and to the deed. Alone,

---

[21] *Ares:* god of war and destruction.   [22] *Amphitritē:* the Atlantic Ocean.   [23] *Lycēan Lord:* Apollo.   [24] *Bacchus:* Dionysus, god of fertility and wine.   [24] *Episode:* the portion of ancient Greek plays that appears between choric songs.

had I no key, I would soon lose the track.
Since it was only later that I joined you,
to all the sons of Cadmus I say this:
whoever has clear knowledge of the man
230   who murdered Laius, son of Labdacus,
I command him to reveal it all to me—
nor fear if, to remove the charge, he must
accuse himself: his fate will not be cruel—
he will depart unstumbling into exile.
235   But if you know another, or a stranger,
to be the one whose hand is guilty, speak:
I shall reward you and remember you.
But if you keep your peace because of fear,
and shield yourself or kin from my command,
240   hear you what I shall do in that event:
I charge all in this land where I have throne
and power, shut out that man—no matter who—
both from your shelter and all spoken words,
nor in your prayers or sacrifices make
245   him partner, nor allot him lustral[26] water.
All men shall drive him from their homes: for he
is the pollution that the god-sent Pythian
response has only now revealed to me.
In this way I ally myself in war
250   with the divinity and the deceased.[27]
And this curse, too, against the one who did it,
whether alone in secrecy, or with others:
may he wear out his life unblest and evil!
I pray this, too: if he is at my hearth
255   and in my home, and I have knowledge of him,
may the curse pronounced on others come to me.
All this I lay to you to execute,
for my sake, for the god's, and for this land
now ruined, barren, abandoned by the gods.
260   Even if no god had driven you to it,
you ought not to have left this stain uncleansed,
the murdered man a nobleman, a king!
You should have looked! But now, since, as it happens,
It's I who have the power that he had once,
265   and have his bed, and a wife who shares our seed,
and common bond had we had common children
(had not his hope of offspring had bad luck—
but as it happened, luck lunged at his head);

---

[26] *lustral:* purifying.   [27] *the deceased:* Laius.

because of this, as if for my own father,
270   I'll fight for him, I'll leave no means untried,
to catch the one who did it with his hand,
for the son of Labdacus, of Polydōrus,
of Cadmus before him, and of Agēnor.[28]
This prayer against all those who disobey:
275   the gods send out no harvest from their soil,
nor children from their wives. Oh, let them die
victims of this plague, or of something worse.
Yet for the rest of us, people of Cadmus,
we the obedient, may Justice, our ally,
280   and all the gods, be always on our side!

Cʜᴏʀᴀɢᴏs:[29] I speak because I feel the grip of your curse:
the killer is not I. Nor can I point
to him. The one who set us to this search,
Phoebus, should also name the guilty man.

285 Oᴇᴅɪᴘᴜs: Quite right, but to compel unwilling gods—
no man has ever had that kind of power.

Cʜᴏʀᴀɢᴏs: May I suggest to you a second way?

Oᴇᴅɪᴘᴜs: A second or a third—pass over nothing!

Cʜᴏʀᴀɢᴏs: I know of no one who sees more of what
290   Lord Phoebus sees than Lord Tiresias.
My Lord, one might learn brilliantly from him.

Oᴇᴅɪᴘᴜs: Nor is this something I have been slow to do.
At Creon's word I sent an escort—twice now!
I am astonished that he has not come.

295 Cʜᴏʀᴀɢᴏs: The old account is useless. It told us nothing.

Oᴇᴅɪᴘᴜs: But tell it to me. I'll scrutinize all stories.

Cʜᴏʀᴀɢᴏs: He is said to have been killed by travelers.

Oᴇᴅɪᴘᴜs: I have heard, but the one who did it no one sees.

Cʜᴏʀᴀɢᴏs: If there is any fear in him at all,
300   he won't stay here once he has heard that curse.

Oᴇᴅɪᴘᴜs: He won't fear words: he had no fear when he did it.

(Enter Tiresias from the right, led by a Servant and two of Oedipus's Attendants.)

Cʜᴏʀᴀɢᴏs: Look there! There is the man who will convict him!
It's the god's prophet they are leading here,
one gifted with the truth as no one else.

305 Oᴇᴅɪᴘᴜs: Tiresias, master of all omens—
public and secret, in the sky and on the earth—
your mind, if not your eyes, sees how the city
lives with a plague, against which Thebes can find

---

[28]*Son . . . Agēnor:* refers to Laius by citing his genealogy.   [29]*Choragos:* leader of the Chorus and principal commentator on the play's action.

no Saviour or protector, Lord, but you.
310 For Phoebus, as the attendants surely told you,
returned this answer to us: liberation
from the disease would never come unless
we learned without a doubt who murdered Laius—
put them to death, or sent them into exile.
315 Do not begrudge us what you may learn from birds
or any other prophet's path you know!
Care for yourself, the city, care for me,
care for the whole pollution of the dead!
We're in your hands. To do all that he can
320 to help another is man's noblest labor.
Tiresias: How terrible to understand and get
no profit from the knowledge! I knew this,
but I forgot, or I had never come.
Oedipus: What's this? You've come with very little zeal.
325 Tiresias: Let me go home! If you will listen to me,
You will endure your troubles better—and I mine.
Oedipus: A strange request, not very kind to the land
that cared for you—to hold back this oracle!
Tiresias: I see your understanding comes to you
330 inopportunely. So that won't happen to me . . .
Oedipus: Oh, by the gods, if you understand about this,
don't turn away! We're on our knees to you.
Tiresias: None of you understands! I'll never bring
my grief to light—I will not speak of yours.
335 Oedipus: You know and won't declare it! Is your purpose
to betray us and to destroy this land!
Tiresias: I will grieve neither of us. Stop this futile
cross-examination. I'll tell you nothing!
Oedipus: Nothing? You vile traitor! You could provoke
340 a stone to anger! You still refuse to tell?
Can nothing soften you, nothing convince you?
Tiresias: You blamed anger in me—you haven't seen.
The kind that lives with you, so you blame me.
Oedipus: Who wouldn't fill with anger, listening
345 to words like yours which now disgrace this city?
Tiresias: It will come, even if my silence hides it.
Oedipus: If it will come, then why won't you declare it?
Tiresias: I'd rather say no more. Now if you wish,
respond to that with all your fiercest anger!
350 Oedipus: Now I am angry enough to come right out
with this conjecture: you, I think, helped plot
the deed; you did it—even if your hand,
cannot have struck the blow. If you could see,
I should have said the deed was yours alone.

355 TIRESIAS: Is that right! Then I charge you to abide
     by the decree you have announced: from this day
     say no word to either these or me,
     for you are the vile polluter of this land!
  OEDIPUS: Aren't you appalled to let a charge like that
360   come bounding forth? How will you get away?
  TIRESIAS: You cannot catch me. I have the strength of truth.
  OEDIPUS: Who taught you this? Not your prophetic craft!
  TIRESIAS: You did. You made me say it. I didn't want to.
  OEDIPUS: Say what? Repeat it so I'll understand.
365 TIRESIAS: I made no sense? Or are you trying me?
  OEDIPUS: No sense I understood. Say it again!
  TIRESIAS: I say you are the murderer you seek.
  OEDIPUS: Again that horror! You'll wish you hadn't said that.
  TIRESIAS: Shall I say more, and raise your anger higher?
370 OEDIPUS: Anything you like! Your words are powerless.
  TIRESIAS: You live, unknowing, with those nearest to you
     in the greatest shame. You do not see the evil.
  OEDIPUS: You won't go on like that and never pay!
  TIRESIAS: I can if there is any strength in truth.
375 OEDIPUS: In truth, but not in you! You have no strength,
     blind in your ears, your reason, and your eyes.
  TIRESIAS: Unhappy man! Those jeers you hurl at me
     before long all these men will hurl at you.
  OEDIPUS: You are the child of endless night; it's not
380   for me or anyone who sees to hurt you.
  TIRESIAS: It's not my fate to be struck down by you.
     Apollo is enough. That's his concern.
  OEDIPUS: Are these inventions Creon's or your own?
  TIRESIAS: No, your affliction is yourself, not Creon.
385 OEDIPUS: Oh success!—in wealth, kingship, artistry,
     in any life that wins much admiration—
     the envious ill will stored up for you!
     to get at my command, a gift I did not
     seek, which the city put into my hands,
390   my loyal Creon, colleague from the start,
     longs to sneak up in secret and dethrone me.
     So he's suborned this fortuneteller—schemer!
     deceitful beggar-priest!—who has good eyes
     for gains alone, though in his craft he's blind.
395   Where were your prophet's powers ever proved?
     Why, when the dog who chanted verse[30] was here,
     did you not speak and liberate this city?
     Her riddle wasn't for a man chancing by

---

[30] *dog . . . verse:* the Sphinx.

	to interpret; prophetic art was needed,
400	but you had none, it seems—learned from birds
	or from a god. I came along, yes I,
	Oedipus the ignorant, and stopped her—
	by using thought, not augury from birds.
	And it is I whom you now wish to banish,
405	so you'll be close to the Creontian throne.
	You—and the plot's concocter—will drive out
	pollution to your grief: you look quite old
	or you would be the victim of that plot!

CHORAGOS: It seems to us that this man's words were said
410   in anger, Oedipus, and yours as well.
    Insight, not angry words, is what we need,
    the best solution to the god's response.

TIRESIAS: You are the king, and yet I am your equal
    in my right to speak. In that I too am Lord.
415   for I belong to Loxias,[31] not you.
    I am not Creon's man. He's nothing to me.
    Hear this, since you have thrown my blindness at me:
    Your eyes can't see the evil to which you've come,
    nor where you live, nor who is in your house.
420   Do you know your parents? Not knowing, you are
    their enemy, in the underworld and here.
    A mother's and a father's double-lashing
    terrible-footed curse will soon drive you out.
    Now you can see, then you will stare into darkness.
425   What place will not be harbor to your cry,
    or what Cithaeron[32] not reverberate
    when you have heard the bride-song in your palace
    to which you sailed? Fair wind to evil harbor!
    Nor do you see how many other woes
430   will level you to yourself and to your children.
    So, at my message, and at Creon, too,
    splatter muck! There will never be a man
    ground into wretchedness as you will be.

OEDIPUS: Am I to listen to such things from him!
435   May you be damned! Get out of here at once!
    Go! Leave my palace! Turn around and go!

(Tiresias begins to move away from Oedipus.)

TIRESIAS: I wouldn't have come had you not sent for me.
OEDIPUS: I did not know you'd talk stupidity,
    or I wouldn't have rushed to bring you to my house.

---

[31] *Loxias:* Apollo.   [32] *Cithaeron:* reference to the mountain on which Oedipus was to be exposed as an infant.

440 Tiresias: Stupid I seem to you, yet to your parents
   who gave you natural birth I seemed quite shrewd.
   Oedipus: Who? Wait! Who is the one who gave me birth?
   Tiresias: This day will give you birth,[33] and ruin too.
   Oedipus: What murky, riddling things you always say!
445 Tiresias: Don't you surpass us all at finding out?
   Oedipus: You sneer at what you'll find has brought me greatness.
   Tiresias: And that's the very luck that ruined you.
   Oedipus: I wouldn't care, just so I saved the city.
   Tiresias: In that case I shall go. Boy, lead the way!
450 Oedipus: Yes, let him lead you off. Here, underfoot,
   you irk me. Gone, you'll cause no further pain.
   Tiresias: I'll go when I have said what I was sent for.
   Your face won't scare me. You can't ruin me.
   I say to you, the man whom you have looked for
455 as you pronounced your curses, your decrees
   on the bloody death of Laius—he is here!
   A seeming stranger, he shall be shown to be
   a Theban born, though he'll take no delight
   in that solution. Blind, who once could see,
460 a beggar who was rich, through foreign lands
   he'll go and point before him with a stick.
   To his beloved children, he'll be shown
   a father who is also brother; to the one
   who bore him, son and husband; to his father,
465 his seed-fellow and killer. Go in
   and think this out; and if you find I've lied,
   say then I have no prophet's understanding!

(Exit Tiresias, led by a Servant. Oedipus exits into the palace with his Attendants.)

Stasimon 1[34]

Strophe 1
Chorus: Who is the man of whom the inspired
         rock of Delphi[35] said
470 he has committed the unspeakable
         with blood-stained hands?
   Time for him to ply a foot
   mightier than those of the horses
         of the storm in his escape;
475 upon him mounts and plunges the weaponed
   son of Zeus,[36] with fire and thunderbolts,
   and in his train the dreaded goddesses
   of Death, who never miss.

---

[33] *give you birth:* that is, identify your parents. [34] *Stasimon:* Greek choral ode between episodes. [35] *rock of Delphi:* Apollo's oracle at Delphi. [36] *son of Zeus:* Apollo.

ANTISTROPHE 1

The message has just blazed,
480   gleaming from the snows
of Mount Parnassus: we must track
everywhere the unseen man.
He wanders, hidden by wild
forests, up through caves
485   and rocks, like a bull,
anxious, with an anxious foot, forlorn.
He puts away from him the mantic[37] words come from earth's
navel,[38] at its center, yet these live
forever and still hover round him.

STROPHE 2

490 Terribly he troubles me,
the skilled interpreter of birds![39]
I can't assent, nor speak against him.
Both paths are closed to me.
I hover on the wings of doubt,
495   not seeing what is here nor what's to come.
What quarrel started in the house of Labdacus[40]
or in the house of Polybus,[41]
either ever in the past
or now, I never
500 heard, so that . . . with this fact for my touchstone
I could attack the public
fame of Oedipus, by the side of the Labdaceans
an ally, against the dark assassination.

ANTISTROPHE 2

No, Zeus and Apollo
505   understand and know things
mortal; but that another man
can do more as a prophet than I can—
for that there is no certain test,
though, skill to skill,
510 one man might overtake another.
No, never, not until
I see the charges proved,
when someone blames him shall I nod assent.
For once, as we all saw, the winged maiden[42] came
515 against him: he was seen then to be skilled,

---

[37] *mantic:* prophetic. [38] *earth's navel:* Delphi. [39] *interpreter of birds:* Tiresias. The Chorus is troubled by his accusations. [40] *house of Labdacus:* the line of Laius. [41] *Polybus:* Oedipus's foster father. [42] *winged maiden:* the Sphinx.

proved, by that touchstone, dear to the people. So,
never will my mind convict him of the evil.

EPISODE 2

(Enter Creon from the right door of the skene and speaks to the Chorus.)

CREON: Citizens, I hear that a fearful charge
  is made against me by King Oedipus!
520   I had to come. If, in this crisis,
  he thinks that he has suffered injury
  from anything that I have said or done,
  I have no appetite for a long life—
  bearing a blame like that! It's no slight blow
525   the punishment I'd take from what he said:
  it's the ultimate hurt to be called traitor
  by the city, by you, by my own people!
CHORAGOS: The thing that forced that accusation out
  could have been anger, not the power of thought.
530 CREON: But who persuaded him that thoughts of mine
  had led the prophet into telling lies?
CHORAGOS: I do not know the thought behind his words.
CREON: But did he look straight at you? Was his mind right
  when he said that I was guilty of this charge?
535 CHORAGOS: I have no eyes to see what rulers do.
  But here he comes himself out of the house.

(Enter Oedipus from the palace.)

OEDIPUS: What? You here? And can you really have
  the face and daring to approach my house
  when you're exposed as its master's murderer
540   and caught, too, as the robber of my kingship?
  Did you see cowardice in me, by the gods,
  or foolishness, when you began this plot?
  Did you suppose that I would not detect
  your stealthy moves, or that I'd not fight back?
545   It's your attempt that's folly, isn't it—
  tracking without followers or connections,
  kingship which is caught with wealth and numbers?
CREON: Now wait! Give me as long to answer back!
  Judge me for yourself when you have heard me!
550 OEDIPUS: You're eloquent, but I'd be slow to learn
  from you, now that I've seen your malice toward me.
CREON: That I deny. Hear what I have to say.
OEDIPUS: Don't you deny it! You are the traitor here!
CREON: If you consider mindless willfulness
555   a prized possession, you are not thinking sense.

OEDIPUS: If you think you can wrong a relative
    and get off free, you are not thinking sense.
CREON: Perfectly just, I won't say no. And yet
    what is this injury you say I did you?
560 OEDIPUS: Did you persuade me, yes or no, to send
    someone to bring that solemn prophet here?
CREON: And I still hold to the advice I gave.
OEDIPUS: How many years ago did your King Laius . . .
CREON: Laius! Do what? Now I don't understand.
565 OEDIPUS: Vanish—victim of a murderous violence?
CREON: That is a long count back into the past.
OEDIPUS: Well, was this seer then practicing his art?
CREON: Yes, skilled and honored just as he is today.
OEDIPUS: Did he, back then, ever refer to me?
570 CREON: He did not do so in my presence ever.
OEDIPUS: You did inquire into the murder then.
CREON: We had to, surely, though we discovered nothing.
OEDIPUS: But the "skilled" one did not say this then? Why not?
CREON: I never talk when I am ignorant.
575 OEDIPUS: But you're not ignorant of your own part.
CREON: What do you mean? I'll tell you if I know.
OEDIPUS: Just this: if he had not conferred with you
    he'd not have told about my murdering Laius.
CREON: If he said that, you are the one who knows.
580   But now it's fair that you should answer me.
OEDIPUS: Ask on! You won't convict me as the killer.
CREON: Well then, answer. My sister is your wife?
OEDIPUS: Now there's a statement that I can't deny.
CREON: You two have equal power in this country?
585 OEDIPUS: She gets from me whatever she desires.
CREON: And I'm a third? The three of us are equals?
OEDIPUS: That's where you're treacherous to your kinsman!
CREON: But think about this rationally, as I do.
    First look at this: do you think anyone
590   prefers the anxieties of being king
    to untroubled sleep—if he has equal power?
    I'm not the kind of man who falls in love
    with kingship. I am content with a king's power.
    And so would any man who's wise and prudent.
595   I get all things from you, with no distress;
    as king I would have onerous duties, too.
    How could the kingship bring me more delight
    than this untroubled power and influence?
    I'm not misguided yet to such a point
600   that profitable honors aren't enough.
    As it is, all wish me well and all salute;

those begging you for something have me summoned,
for their success depends on that alone.
Why should I lose all this to become king?
605 A prudent mind is never traitorous.
Treason's a thought I'm not enamored of;
nor could I join a man who acted so.
In proof of this, first go yourself to Pytho[43]
and ask if I brought back the true response.
610 Then, if you find I plotted with that portent
reader,[44] don't have me put to death by your vote
only—I'll vote myself for my conviction.
Don't let an unsupported thought convict me!
It's not right mindlessly to take the bad
615 for good or to suppose the good are traitors.
Rejecting a relation who is loyal
is like rejecting life, our greatest love.
In time you'll know securely without stumbling,
for time alone can prove a just man just,
620 though you can know a bad man in a day.
CHORAGOS: Well said, to one who's anxious not to fall.
Swift thinkers, Lord, are never safe from stumbling.
OEDIPUS: But when a swift and secret plotter moves
against me, I must make swift counterplot.
625 If I lie quiet and await his move,
he'll have achieved his aims and I'll have missed.
CREON: You surely cannot mean you want me exiled!
OEDIPUS: Not exiled, no. Your death is what I want!
CREON: If you would first define what envy is . . .
630 OEDIPUS: Are you still stubborn? Still disobedient?
CREON: I see you cannot think!
OEDIPUS: For me I can.
CREON: You should for me as well!
OEDIPUS: But you're a traitor!
CREON: What if you're wrong?
OEDIPUS: Authority must be maintained.
CREON: Not if the ruler's evil.
OEDIPUS: Hear that, Thebes!
635 CREON: It is my city too, not yours alone!
CHORAGOS: Please don't, my Lords! Ah, just in time, I see
Jocasta there, coming from the palace.
With her help you must settle your quarrel.

(Enter Jocasta from the palace.)

---

[43] *Pytho:* Delphi.   [44] *portent reader:* Apollo's oracle or prophet.

JOCASTA: Wretched men! What has provoked this ill-
640   advised dispute? Have you no sense of shame,
         with Thebes so sick, to stir up private troubles?
         Now go inside! And Creon, you go home!
         Don't make a general anguish out of nothing!
CREON: My sister, Oedipus your husband here
645   sees fit to do one of two hideous things:
         to have me banished from the land—or killed!
OEDIPUS: That's right: I caught him, Lady, plotting harm
         against my person—with a malignant science.
CREON: May my life fail, may I die cursed, if I
650   did any of the things you said I did!
JOCASTA: Believe his words, for the god's sake, Oedipus,
         in deference above all to his oath
         to the gods. Also for me, and for these men!

KOMMOS[45]

STROPHE 1

CHORUS: Consent, with will and mind,
655   my king, I beg of you!
OEDIPUS: What do you wish me to surrender?
CHORUS: Show deference to him who was not feeble in time past
         and is now great in the power of his oath!
OEDIPUS: Do you know what you're asking?
CHORUS: Yes.
OEDIPUS: Tell me then.
660 CHORUS: Never to cast into dishonored guilt, with an unproved
         assumption, a kinsman who has bound himself by curse.
OEDIPUS: Now you must understand, when you ask this,
         you ask my death or banishment from the land.

STROPHE 2

CHORUS: No, by the god who is the foremost of all gods,
665   the Sun! No! Godless,
              friendless, whatever death is worst of all,
         let that be my destruction, if this
              thought ever moved me!
         But my ill-fated soul
670   this dying land
         wears out—the more if to these older troubles
         she adds new troubles from the two of you!
OEDIPUS: Then let him go, though it must mean my death,
         or else disgrace and exile from the land.

---

[45] *Kommos:* a dirge or lament sung by the Chorus and one or more of the chief characters.

675 My pity is moved by your words, not by his—
he'll only have my hate, wherever he goes.
CREON: You're sullen as you yield; you'll be depressed
when you've passed through this anger. Natures like yours
are hardest on themselves. That's as it should be.
680 OEDIPUS: Then won't you go and let me be?
CREON: I'll go.
Though you're unreasonable, they know I'm righteous.

(Exit Creon.)

ANTISTROPHE 1
CHORUS: Why are you waiting, Lady?
Conduct him back into the palace!
JOCASTA: I will, when I have heard what chanced.
685 CHORUS: Conjectures—words alone, and nothing based on thought.
But even an injustice can devour a man.
JOCASTA: Did the words come from both sides?
CHORUS: Yes.
JOCASTA: What was said?
CHORUS: To me it seems enough! enough! the land already troubled,
that this should rest where it has stopped.
690 OEDIPUS: See what you've come to in your honest thought,
in seeking to relax and blunt my heart?

ANTISTROPHE 2
CHORUS: I have not said this only once, my Lord.
That I had lost my sanity,
without a path in thinking—
695 be sure this would be clear
if I put you away
who, when my cherished land
wandered crazed
with suffering, brought her back on course.
700 Now, too, be a lucky helmsman!
JOCASTA: Please, for the god's sake, Lord, explain to me
the reason why you have conceived this wrath?
OEDIPUS: I honor you, not them,[46] and I'll explain
to you how Creon has conspired against me.
705 JOCASTA: All right, if that will explain how the quarrel started.
OEDIPUS: He says I am the murderer of Laius!
JOCASTA: Did he claim knowledge or that someone told him?
OEDIPUS: Here's what he did: he sent that vicious seer
so he could keep his own mouth innocent.

---

[46] *them:* the Chorus.

710 JOCASTA: Ah then, absolve yourself of what he charges!
　　Listen to this and you'll agree, no mortal
　　is ever given skill in prophecy.
　　I'll prove this quickly with one incident.
　　It was foretold to Laius—I shall not say
715　by Phoebus himself, but by his ministers—
　　that when his fate arrived he would be killed
　　by a son who would be born to him and me.
　　And yet, so it is told, foreign robbers
　　murdered him, at a place where three roads meet.
720　As for the child I bore him, not three days passed
　　before he yoked the ball-joints of its feet,[47]
　　then cast it, by others' hands, on a trackless mountain.
　　That time Apollo did not make our child
　　a patricide, or bring about what Laius
725　feared, that he be killed by his own son.
　　That's how prophetic words determined things!
　　Forget them. The things a god must track
　　he will himself painlessly reveal.
　　OEDIPUS: Just now, as I was listening to you, Lady,
730　what a profound distraction seized my mind!
　　JOCASTA: What made you turn around so anxiously?
　　OEDIPUS: I thought you said that Laius was attacked
　　　and butchered at a place where three roads meet.
　　JOCASTA: That is the story, and it is told so still.
735 OEDIPUS: Where is the place where this was done to him?
　　JOCASTA: The land's called Phocis, where a two-forked road
　　　comes in from Delphi and from Daulia.
　　OEDIPUS: And how much time has passed since these events?
　　JOCASTA: Just prior to your presentation here
740　as king this news was published to the city.
　　OEDIPUS: Oh, Zeus, what have you willed to do to me?
　　JOCASTA: Oedipus, what makes your heart so heavy?
　　OEDIPUS: No, tell me first of Laius' appearance,
　　　what peak of youthful vigor he had reached.
745 JOCASTA: A tall man, showing his first growth of white.
　　He had a figure not unlike your own.
　　OEDIPUS: Alas! It seems that in my ignorance
　　　I laid those fearful curses on myself.
　　JOCASTA: What is it, Lord? I flinch to see your face.
750 OEDIPUS: I'm dreadfully afraid the prophet sees.
　　But I'll know better with one more detail.
　　JOCASTA: I'm frightened too. But ask: I'll answer you.

---

[47] *ball-joints of its feet:* the ankles.

OEDIPUS: Was his retinue small, or did he travel
    with a great troop, as would befit a prince?
755 JOCASTA: There were just five in all, one a herald.
    There was a carriage, too, bearing Laius.
    OEDIPUS: Alas! Now I see it! But who was it,
    Lady, who told you what you know about this?
    JOCASTA: A servant who alone was saved unharmed.
760 OEDIPUS: By chance, could he be now in the palace?
    JOCASTA: No, he is not. When he returned and saw
    you had the power of the murdered Laius,
    he touched my hand and begged me formally
    to send him to the fields and to the pastures,
765   so he'd be out of sight, far from the city.
    I did. Although a slave, he well deserved
    to win this favor, and indeed far more.
    OEDIPUS: Let's have him called back in immediately.
    JOCASTA: That can be done, but why do you desire it?
770 OEDIPUS: I fear, Lady, I have already said
    too much. That's why I wish to see him now.
    JOCASTA: Then he shall come; but it is right somehow
    that I, too, Lord, should know what troubles you.
    OEDIPUS: I've gone so deep into the things I feared
775   I'll tell you everything. Who has a right
    greater than yours, while I cross through this chance?
    Polybus of Corinth was my father,
    my mother was the Dorian Meropē.
    I was first citizen, until this chance
780   attacked me—striking enough, to be sure,
    but not worth all the gravity I gave it.
    This: at a feast a man who'd drunk too much
    denied, at the wine, I was my father's son.
    I was depressed and all that day I barely
785   held it in. Next day I put the question
    to my mother and father. They were enraged
    at the man who'd let this fiction fly at me.
    I was much cheered by them. And yet it kept
    grinding into me. His words kept coming back.
790   Without my mother's or my father's knowledge
    I went to Pytho. But Phoebus sent me away
    dishonoring my demand. Instead, other
    wretched horrors he flashed forth in speech.
    He said that I would be my mother's lover,
795   show offspring to mankind they could not look at,
    and be his murderer whose seed I am.[48]

---

[48] *be . . . am:* that is, murder my father.

When I heard this, and ever since, I gauged
the way to Corinth by the stars alone,
running to a place where I would never see
800   the disgrace in the oracle's words come true.
But I soon came to the exact location
where, as you tell of it, the king was killed.
Lady, here is the truth. As I went on,
when I was just approaching those three roads,
805   a herald and a man like him you spoke of
came on, riding a carriage drawn by colts.
Both the man out front and the old man himself[49]
tried violently to force me off the road.
The driver, when he tried to push me off,
810   I struck in anger. The old man saw this, watched
me approach, then leaned out and lunged down
with twin prongs[50] at the middle of my head!
He got more than he gave. Abruptly—struck
once by the staff in this my hand—he tumbled
815   out, head first, from the middle of the carriage.
And then I killed them all. But if there is
a kinship between Laius and this stranger,
who is more wretched than the man you see?
Who was there born more hated by the gods?
820   For neither citizen nor foreigner
may take me in his home or speak to me.
No, they must drive me off. And it is I
who have pronounced these curses on myself!
I stain the dead man's bed with these my hands,
825   by which he died. Is not my nature vile?
Unclean?—if I am banished and even
in exile I may not see my own parents,
or set foot in my homeland, or else be yoked
in marriage to my mother, and kill my father,
830   Polybus, who raised me and gave me birth?
If someone judged a cruel divinity
did this to me, would he not speak the truth?
You pure and awful gods, may I not ever
see that day, may I be swept away
835   from men before I see so great and so
calamitous a stain fixed on my person!
CHORAGOS: These things seem fearful to us, Lord, and yet,
until you hear it from the witness, keep hope!

---

[49] *old man himself:* Laius.   [50] *lunged . . . prongs:* Laius strikes Oedipus with a two-pronged horse goad, or whip.

OEDIPUS: That is the single hope that's left to me,
840   to wait for him, that herdsman—until he comes.
JOCASTA: When he appears, what are you eager for?
OEDIPUS: Just this: if his account agrees with yours
         then I shall have escaped this misery.
JOCASTA: But what was it that struck you in my story?
845 OEDIPUS: You said he spoke of robbers as the ones
         who killed him. Now: if he continues still
         to speak of many, then I could not have killed him.
         One man and many men just do not jibe.
         But if he says one belted man, the doubt
850   is gone. The balance tips toward me. I did it.
JOCASTA: No! He told it as I told you. Be certain.
         He can't reject that and reverse himself.
         The city heard these things, not I alone.
         But even if he swerves from what he said,
855   he'll never show that Laius' murder, Lord,
         occurred just as predicted. For Loxias
         expressly said my son was doomed to kill him.
         The boy—poor boy—he never had a chance
         to cut him down, for he was cut down first.
860   Never again, just for some oracle
         will I shoot frightened glances right and left.
OEDIPUS: That's full of sense. Nonetheless, send a man
         to bring that farm hand here. Will you do it?
JOCASTA: I'll send one right away. But let's go in.
865   Would I do anything against your wishes?

(Exit Oedipus and Jocasta through the central door into the palace.)

STASIMON 2

STROPHE 1
CHORUS: May there accompany me
         the fate to keep a reverential purity in what I say,
         in all I do, for which the laws have been set forth
         and walk on high, born to traverse the brightest,
870   highest upper air; Olympus[51] only
         is their father, nor was it
         mortal nature
         that fathered them, and never will
         oblivion lull them into sleep;
875   the god in them is great and never ages.

---

[51] *Olympus:* Mount Olympus, home of the gods, treated as a god.

ANTISTROPHE 1

The will to violate, seed of the tyrant,
if it has drunk mindlessly of wealth and power,
without a sense of time or true advantage,
mounts to a peak, then
880 plunges to an abrupt . . . destiny,
where the useful foot
is of no use. But the kind
of struggling that is good for the city
I ask the god never to abolish.
885 The god is my protector: never will I give that up.

STROPHE 2

But if a man proceeds disdainfully
in deeds of hand or word
and has no fear of Justice
or reverence for shrines of the divinities
890 (may a bad fate catch him
for his luckless wantonness!),
if he'll not gain what he gains with justice
and deny himself what is unholy,
or if he clings, in foolishness, to the untouchable
895 (what man, finally, in such an action, will have strength
enough to fend off passion's arrows from his soul?),
if, I say, this kind of
deed is held in honor—
why should I join the sacred dance?

ANTISTROPHE 2

900 No longer shall I visit and revere
Earth's navel,[52] the untouchable,
nor visit Abae's[53] temple,
or Olympia,[54]
if the prophecies are not matched by events
905 for all the world to point to.
No, you who hold the power, if you are rightly called
Zeus the king of all, let this matter not escape you
and your ever-deathless rule,
for the prophecies to Laius fade . . .
910 and men already disregard them;
nor is Apollo anywhere
glorified with honors.
Religion slips away.

---

[52] *Earth's navel:* Delphi.   [53] *Abae:* a town in Phocis where there was another oracle of
Apollo.   [54] *Olympia:* site of the oracle of Zeus.

EPISODE 3

(Enter Jocasta from the palace carrying a branch wound with wool and a jar of incense. She is attended by two women.)

JOCASTA: Lords of the realm, the thought has come to me
915   to visit shrines of the divinities
        with suppliant's branch in hand and fragrant smoke.
        For Oedipus excites his soul too much
        with alarms of all kinds. He will not judge
        the present by the past, like a man of sense.
920   He's at the mercy of all terror-mongers.

(Jocasta approaches the altar on the right and kneels.)

        Since I can do no good by counseling,
        Apollo the Lycēan!—you are the closest—
        I come a suppliant, with these my vows,
        for a cleansing that will not pollute him.
925   For when we see him shaken we are all
        afraid, like people looking at their helmsman.

(Enter a Messenger along one of the parados. He sees Jocasta at the altar and then addresses the Chorus.)

MESSENGER: I would be pleased if you would help me, stranger.
        Where is the palace of King Oedipus?
        Or tell me where he is himself, if you know.
930 CHORUS: This is his house, stranger. He is within.
        This is his wife and mother of his children.
MESSENGER: May she and her family find prosperity,
        if, as you say, her marriage is fulfilled.
JOCASTA: You also, stranger, for you deserve as much
935   for your gracious words. But tell me why you've come.
        What do you wish? Or what have you to tell us?
MESSENGER: Good news, my Lady, both for your house and husband.
JOCASTA: What is your news? And who has sent you to us?
MESSENGER: I come from Corinth. When you have heard my news
940   you will rejoice, I'm sure—and grieve perhaps.
JOCASTA: What is it? How can it have this double power?
MESSENGER: They will establish him their king, so say
        the people of the land of Isthmia.[55]
JOCASTA: But is old Polybus not still in power?
945 MESSENGER: He's not, for death has clasped him in the tomb.
JOCASTA: What's this? Has Oedipus' father died?
MESSENGER: If I have lied then I deserve to die.

---

[55] *land of Isthmia:* Corinth, which was on an isthmus.

JOCASTA: Attendant! Go quickly to your master,
and tell him this.

(Exit an Attendant into the palace.)

Oracles of the gods!
950   Where are you now? The man whom Oedipus
fled long ago, for fear that he should kill him—
he's been destroyed by chance and not by him!

(Enter Oedipus from the palace.)

OEDIPUS: Darling Jocasta, my beloved wife,
Why have you called me from the palace?
955 JOCASTA: First hear what this man has to say. Then see
what the god's grave oracle has come to now!
OEDIPUS: Where is he from? What is this news he brings me?
JOCASTA: From Corinth. He brings news about your father:
that Polybus is no more! that he is dead!
960 OEDIPUS: What's this, old man? I want to hear you say it.
MESSENGER: If this is what must first be clarified,
please be assured that he is dead and gone.
OEDIPUS: By treachery or by the touch of sickness?
MESSENGER: Light pressures tip agéd frames into their sleep.
965 OEDIPUS: You mean the poor man died of some disease.
MESSENGER: And of the length of years that he had tallied.
OEDIPUS: Aha! Then why should we look to Pytho's vapors,[56]
or to the birds that scream above our heads?[57]
If we could really take those things for guides,
970   I would have killed my father. But he's dead!
He is beneath the earth, and here am I,
who never touched a spear. Unless he died
of longing for me and I "killed" him that way!
No, in this case, Polybus, by dying, took
975   the worthless oracle to Hades with him.
JOCASTA: And wasn't I telling you that just now?
OEDIPUS: You were indeed. I was misled by fear.
JOCASTA: You should not care about this anymore.
OEDIPUS: I must care. I must stay clear of my mother's bed.
980 JOCASTA: What's there for man to fear? The realm of chance
prevails. True foresight isn't possible.
His life is best who lives without a plan.
This marriage with your mother—don't fear it.
How many times have men in dreams, too, slept

---

[56] *Pytho's vapors:* the prophecies of the oracle at Delphi. [57] *birds . . . heads:* the prophecies derived from interpreting the flights of birds.

985   with their own mothers! Those who believe such things
       mean nothing endure their lives most easily.
    OEDIPUS: A fine, bold speech, and you are right, perhaps,
       except that my mother is still living,
       so I must fear her, however well you argue.
990 JOCASTA: And yet your father's tomb is a great eye.
    OEDIPUS: Illuminating, yes. But I still fear the living.
    MESSENGER: Who is the woman who inspires this fear?
    OEDIPUS: Meropē, Polybus' wife, old man.
    MESSENGER: And what is there about her that alarms you?
995 OEDIPUS: An oracle, god-sent and fearful, stranger.
    MESSENGER: Is it permitted that another know?
    OEDIPUS: It is. Loxias once said to me
       I must have intercourse with my own mother
       and take my father's blood with these my hands.
1000   So I have long lived far away from Corinth.
       This has indeed brought much good luck, and yet,
       to see one's parents' eyes is happiest.
    MESSENGER: Was it for this that you have lived in exile?
    OEDIPUS: So I'd not be my father's killer, sir.
1005 MESSENGER: Had I not better free you from this fear,
       my Lord? That's why I came—to do you service.
    OEDIPUS: Indeed, what a reward you'd get for that!
    MESSENGER: Indeed, this is the main point of my trip,
       to be rewarded when you get back home.
1010 OEDIPUS: I'll never rejoin the givers of my seed![58]
    MESSENGER: My son, clearly you don't know what you're doing.
    OEDIPUS: But how is that, old man? For the gods' sake, tell me!
    MESSENGER: If it's because of them you won't go home.
    OEDIPUS: I fear that Phoebus will have told the truth.
1015 MESSENGER: Pollution from the ones who gave you seed?
    OEDIPUS: That is the thing, old man, I always fear.
    MESSENGER: Your fear is groundless. Understand that.
    OEDIPUS: Groundless? Not if I was born their son.
    MESSENGER: But Polybus is not related to you.
1020 OEDIPUS: Do you mean Polybus was not my father?
    MESSENGER: No more than I. We're both the same to you.
    OEDIPUS: Same? One who begot me and one who didn't?
    MESSENGER: He didn't beget you any more than I did.
    OEDIPUS: But then, why did he say I was his son?
1025 MESSENGER: He got you as a gift from my own hands.

---

[58] *givers of my seed:* that is, my parents. Oedipus still thinks Meropē and Polybus are his parents.

OEDIPUS: He loved me so, though from another's hands?

MESSENGER: His former childlessness persuaded him.

OEDIPUS: But had you bought me, or begotten me?

MESSENGER: Found you. In the forest hallows of Cithaeron.

1030 OEDIPUS: What were you doing traveling in that region?

MESSENGER: I was in charge of flocks which grazed those mountains.

OEDIPUS: A wanderer who worked the flocks for hire?

MESSENGER: Ah, but that day I was your savior, son.

OEDIPUS: From what? What was my trouble when you took me?

1035 MESSENGER: The ball-joints of your feet might testify.

OEDIPUS: What's that? What makes you name that ancient trouble?

MESSENGER: Your feet were pierced and I am your rescuer.

OEDIPUS: A fearful rebuke those tokens left for me!

MESSENGER: That was the chance that names you who you are.

1040 OEDIPUS: By the gods, did my mother or my father do this?

MESSENGER: That I don't know. He might who gave you to me.

OEDIPUS: From someone else? You didn't chance on me?

MESSENGER: Another shepherd handed you to me.

OEDIPUS: Who was he? Do you know? Will you explain!

1045 MESSENGER: They called him one of the men of—was it Laius?

OEDIPUS: The one who once was king here long ago?

MESSENGER: That is the one! The man was shepherd to him.

OEDIPUS: And is he still alive so I can see him?

MESSENGER: But you who live here ought to know that best.

1050 OEDIPUS: Does any one of you now present know
    about the shepherd whom this man has named?
    Have you seen him in town or in the fields? Speak out!
    The time has come for the discovery!

CHORAGOS: The man he speaks of, I believe, is the same
1055   as the field hand you have already asked to see.
    But it's Jocasta who would know this best.

OEDIPUS: Lady, do you remember the man we just
    now sent for—is that the man he speaks of?

JOCASTA: What? The man he spoke of? Pay no attention!
1060   His words are not worth thinking about. It's nothing.

OEDIPUS: With clues like this within my grasp, give up?
    Fail to solve the mystery of my birth?

JOCASTA: For the love of the gods, and if you love your life,
    give up this search! My sickness is enough.

1065 OEDIPUS: Come! Though my mothers for three generations
    were in slavery, you'd not be lowborn!

JOCASTA: No, listen to me! Please! Don't do this thing!

OEDIPUS: I will not listen; I will search out the truth.

JOCASTA: My thinking is for you—it would be best.

1070 OEDIPUS: This "best" of yours is starting to annoy me.

JOCASTA: Doomed man! Never find out who you are!

OEDIPUS: Will someone go and bring that shepherd here?
Leave her to glory in her wealthy birth!

JOCASTA: Man of misery! No other name
1075   shall I address you by, ever again.

(Exit Jocasta into the palace after a long pause.)

CHORAGOS: Why has your lady left, Oedipus,
hurled by a savage grief? I am afraid
disaster will come bursting from this silence.

OEDIPUS: Let it burst forth! However low this seed
1080   of mine may be, yet I desire to see it.
She, perhaps—she has a woman's pride—
is mortified by my base origins.
But I who count myself the child of Chance,
the giver of good, shall never know dishonor.
1085   She is my mother,[59] and the months my brothers
who first marked out my lowness, then my greatness.
I shall not prove untrue to such a nature
by giving up the search for my own birth.

STASIMON 3

STROPHE

CHORUS: If I have mantic power
1090   and excellence in thought,
by Olympus,
    you shall not, Cithaeron, at tomorrow's
full moon,
fail to hear us celebrate you as the countryman
1095   of Oedipus, his nurse and mother,
or fail to be the subject of our dance,
    since you have given pleasure
to our king.
Phoebus, whom we summon by "iē!,"
1100   may this be pleasing to you!

ANTISTROPHE

Who was your mother, son?
which of the long-lived nymphs
after lying with Pan,[60]
    the mountain roaming . . . Or was it a bride
1105   of Loxias?[61]

---

[59] *She . . . mother:* Chance is my mother.   [60] *Pan:* god of shepherds and woodlands, half
man and half goat.   [61] *Loxias:* Apollo.

For dear to him are all the upland pastures.
Or was it Mount Cyllēnē's lord,[62]
or the Bacchic god,[63]
        dweller of the mountain peaks,
1110   who received you as a joyous find
from one of the nymphs of Helicon,
the favorite sharers of his sport?

EPISODE 4

OEDIPUS: If someone like myself, who never met him,
        may calculate—elders, I think I see
1115   the very herdsman we've been waiting for.
His many years would fit that man's age,
and those who bring him on, if I am right,
are my own men. And yet, in real knowledge,
you can outstrip me, surely: you've seen him.

(Enter the old Herdsman escorted by two of Oedipus's Attendants. At first, the Herdsman will not look at Oedipus.)

1120   CHORAGOS: I know him, yes, a man of the house of Laius,
        a trusty herdsman if he ever had one.
OEDIPUS: I ask you first, the stranger come from Corinth:
        is this the man you spoke of?
MESSENGER: That's he you see.
OEDIPUS: Then you, old man. First look at me! Now answer:
1125   did you belong to Laius' household once?
HERDSMAN: I did. Not a purchased slave but raised in the palace.
OEDIPUS: How have you spent your life? What is your work?
HERDSMAN: Most of my life now I have tended sheep.
OEDIPUS: Where is the usual place you stay with them?
1130   HERDSMAN: On Mount Cithaeron. Or in that district.
OEDIPUS: Do you recall observing this man there?
HERDSMAN: Doing what? Which is the man you mean?
OEDIPUS: This man right here. Have you had dealings with him?
HERDSMAN: I can't say right away. I don't remember.
1135   MESSENGER: No wonder, master. I'll bring clear memory
        to his ignorance. I'm absolutely sure
he can recall it, the district was Cithaeron,
he with a double flock, and I, with one,
lived close to him, for three entire seasons,
1140   six months along, from spring right to Arcturus.[64]
Then for the winter I'd drive mine to my fold,

---

[52] *Mount Cyllēnē's lord:* Hermes, messenger of the gods.   [63] *Bacchic god:* Dionysus.
[64] *Arcturus:* a star that is first seen in September in the Grecian sky.

and he'd drive his to Laius' pen again.
Did any of the things I say take place?
HERDSMAN: You speak the truth, though it's from long ago.
1145 MESSENGER: Do you remember giving me, back then,
a boy I was to care for as my own?
HERDSMAN: What are you saying? Why do you ask me that?
MESSENGER: There, sir, is the man who was that boy!
HERDSMAN: Damn you! Shut your mouth! Keep your silence!
1150 OEDIPUS: Stop! Don't you rebuke his words.
Your words ask for rebuke far more than his.
HERDSMAN: But what have I done wrong, most royal master?
OEDIPUS: Not telling of the boy of whom he asked.
HERDSMAN: He's ignorant and blundering toward ruin.
1155 OEDIPUS: Tell it willingly—or under torture.
HERDSMAN: Oh god! Don't—I am old—don't torture me!
OEDIPUS: Here! Someone put his hands behind his back!
HERDSMAN: But why? What else would you find out, poor man?
OEDIPUS: Did you give him the child he asks about?
1160 HERDSMAN: I did. I wish that I had died that day!
OEDIPUS: You'll come to that if you don't speak the truth.
HERDSMAN: It's if I speak that I shall be destroyed.
OEDIPUS: I think this fellow struggles for delay.
HERDSMAN: No, no! I said already that I gave him.
1165 OEDIPUS: From your own home, or got from someone else?
HERDSMAN: Not from my own. I got him from another.
OEDIPUS: Which of these citizens? What sort of house?
HERDSMAN: Don't—by the gods!—don't, master, ask me more!
OEDIPUS: It means your death if I must ask again.
1170 HERDSMAN: One of the children of the house of Laius.
OEDIPUS: A slave—or born into the family?
HERDSMAN: I have come to the dreaded thing, and I shall say it.
OEDIPUS: And I to hearing it, but hear I must.
HERDSMAN: He was reported to have been—his son.
1175   Your lady in the house could tell you best.
OEDIPUS: Because she gave him to you?
HERDSMAN: Yes, my lord.
OEDIPUS: What was her purpose?
HERDSMAN: I was to kill the boy.
OEDIPUS: The child she bore?
HERDSMAN: She dreaded prophecies.
OEDIPUS: What were they?
HERDSMAN: The word was that he'd kill his parents.
1180 OEDIPUS: Then why did you give him up to this old man?
HERDSMAN: In pity, master—so he would take him home,
to another land. But what he did was save him
for this supreme disaster. If you are the one
he speaks of—know your evil birth and fate!

1185 OEDIPUS: Ah! All of it was destined to be true!
Oh light, now may I look my last upon you,
shown monstrous in my birth, in marriage monstrous,
a murderer monstrous in those I killed.

(Exit Oedipus, running into the palace.)

STASIMON 4

STROPHE 1

CHORUS: Oh generations of mortal men,
1190   while you are living, I will
appraise your lives at zero!
What man
comes closer to seizing lasting blessedness
than merely to seize its semblance,
1195   and after living in this semblance, to plunge?
With your example before us,
with your destiny, yours,
suffering Oedipus, no mortal
can I judge fortunate.

ANTISTROPHE 1

1200   For he,[65] outranging everybody,
shot his arrow[66] and became the lord
of wide prosperity and blessedness,
oh Zeus, after destroying
the virgin with the crooked talons,[67]
1205   singer of oracles; and against death,
in my land, he arose a tower of defense.
From which time you were called my king
and granted privileges supreme—in mighty
Thebes the ruling lord.

STROPHE 2

1210   But now—whose story is more sorrowful than yours?
Who is more intimate with fierce calamities,
with labors, now that your life is altered?
Alas, my Oedipus, whom all men know:
one great harbor[68]—
1215   one alone sufficed for you,
as son and father,
when you tumbled,[69] plowman[70] of the woman's chamber.

---

[65] *he:* Oedipus.   [66] *shot his arrow:* took his chances; made a guess at the Sphinx's riddle.
[67] *virgin . . . talons:* the Sphinx.   [68] *one great harbor:* metaphorical allusion to Jocasta's
body.   [69] *tumbled:* were born and had sex.   [70] *plowman:* plowing is used here as a sexual metaphor.

How, how could your paternal
    furrows, wretched man,
1220   endure you silently so long.

ANTISTROPHE 2
Time, all-seeing, surprised you living an unwilled life
and sits from of old in judgment on the marriage, not a marriage,
where the begetter is the begot as well.
Ah, son of Laius . . . ,
1225   would that—oh, would that
I had never seen you!
I wail, my scream climbing beyond itself
from my whole power of voice. To say it straight:
    from you I got new breath—
1230   but I also lulled my eye to sleep.[71]

EXODOS[72]

(Enter the Second Messenger from the palace.)

SECOND MESSENGER: You who are first among the citizens,
    what deeds you are about to hear and see!
    What grief you'll carry, if, true to your birth,
    you still respect the house of Labdacus!
1235   Neither the Ister nor the Phasis river
    could purify this house, such suffering
    does it conceal, or soon must bring to light—
    willed this time, not unwilled. Griefs hurt worst
    which we perceive to be self-chosen ones.
1240 CHORAGOS: They were sufficient, the things we knew before,
    to make us grieve. What can you add to those?
SECOND MESSENGER: The thing that's quickest said and quickest heard:
    our own, our royal one, Jocasta's dead.
CHORAGOS: Unhappy queen! What was responsible?
1245 SECOND MESSENGER: Herself. The bitterest of these events
    is not for you, you were not there to see,
    but yet, exactly as I can recall it,
    you'll hear what happened to that wretched lady.
    She came in anger through the outer hall,
1250   and then she ran straight to her marriage bed,
    tearing her hair with the fingers of both hands.
    Then, slamming shut the doors when she was in,
    she called to Laius, dead so many years,
    remembering the ancient seed which caused

---

[71] *I . . . sleep:* I failed to see the corruption you brought.   [72] *Exodus:* the final scene, containing the play's resolution.

1255   his death, leaving the mother to the son
              to breed again an ill-born progeny.
              She mourned the bed where she, alas, bred double—
              husband by husband, children by her child.
              From this point on I don't know how she died,
1260   for Oedipus then burst in with a cry,
              and did not let us watch her final evil.
              Our eyes were fixed on him. Wildly he ran
              to each of us, asking for his spear
              and for his wife—no wife: where he might find
1265   the double mother-field, his and his children's.
              He raved, and some divinity then showed him—
              for none of us did so who stood close by.
              With a dreadful shout—as if some guide were leading—
              he lunged through the double doors; he bent the hollow
1270   bolts from the sockets, burst into the room,
              and there we saw her, hanging from above,
              entangled in some twisted hanging strands.
              He saw, was stricken, and with a wild roar
              ripped down the dangling noose. When she, poor woman,
1275   lay on the ground, there came a fearful sight:
              he snatched the pins of worked gold from her dress,
              with which her clothes were fastened: these he raised
              and struck into the ball-joints of his eyes.[73]
              He shouted that they would no longer see
1280   the evils he had suffered or had done,
               see in the dark those he should not have seen,
              and know no more those he once sought to know.
              While chanting this, not once but many times
              he raised his hand and struck into his eyes.
1285   Blood from his wounded eyes poured down his chin,
              not freed in moistening drops, but all at once
              a stormy rain of black blood burst like hail.
              These evils, coupling them, making them one,
              have broken loose upon both man and wife.
1290   The old prosperity that they had once
              was true prosperity, and yet today,
              mourning, ruin, death, disgrace, and every
              evil you could name—not one is absent.
      CHORAGOS: Has he allowed himself some peace from all this grief?
1295 SECOND MESSENGER: He shouts that someone slide the bolts and show
              to all the Cadmeians the patricide,

---

[73] *ball-joints of his eyes:* his eyeballs. Oedipus blinds himself in both eyes at the same time.

his mother's—I can't say it, it's unholy—
so he can cast himself out of the land,
not stay and curse his house by his own curse.
1300   He lacks the strength, though, and he needs a guide,
for his is a sickness that's too great to bear.
Now you yourself will see: the bolts of the doors
are opening. You are about to see
a vision even one who hates must pity.

(Enter the blinded Oedipus from the palace, led in by a household Servant.)

1305 CHORAGOS: Terrifying suffering for men to see,
more terrifying than any I've ever
come upon. Oh man of pain
what madness reached you? Which god from far off,
surpassing in range his longest spring,
1310   struck hard against your god-abandoned fate?
Oh man of pain,
I cannot look upon you—though there's so much
I would ask you, so much to hear,
so much that holds my eyes—
1315   such is the shudder you produce in me.
   OEDIPUS: Ah! Ah! I am a man of misery.
Where am I carried? Pity me! Where
is my voice scattered abroad on wings?
      Divinity, where has your lunge transported me?
1320 CHORAGOS: To something horrible, not to be heard or seen.

KOMMOS

STROPHE 1
OEDIPUS: Oh, my cloud
of darkness, abominable, unspeakable as it attacks me,
not to be turned away, brought by an evil wind!
Alas!
1325   Again alas! Both enter me at once:
the sting of the prongs,[74] the memory of evils!
   CHORUS: I do not marvel that in these afflictions
you carry double griefs and double evils.

ANTISTROPHE 1
OEDIPUS: Ah, friend,
1330   so you at least are there, resolute servant!

---

[74] *prongs:* refers to both the whip that Laius used and the two gold pins Oedipus used to blind himself.

Still with a heart to care for me, the blind man.
Oh! Oh!
I know that you are there. I recognize
even inside my darkness, that voice of yours.

1335   CHORUS: Doer of horror, how did you bear to quench
your vision? What divinity raised your hand?

STROPHE 2

OEDIPUS: It was Apollo there, Apollo, friends,
   who brought my sorrows, vile sorrows to their perfection,
     these evils that were done to me.

1340   But the one who struck them with his hand,
     that one was none but I, in wretchedness.
   For why was I to see
   when nothing I could see would bring me joy?
  CHORUS: Yes, that is how it was.

1345   OEDIPUS: What could I see, indeed,
   or what enjoy—what greeting
   is there I could hear with pleasure, friends?
   Conduct me out of the land
     as quickly as you can!

1350   Conduct me out, my friends,
     the man utterly ruined,
   supremely cursed,
     the man who is by gods
   the most detested of all men!

1355   CHORUS: Wretched in disaster and in knowledge:
   oh, I could wish you'd never come to know!

ANTISTROPHE 2

OEDIPUS: May he be destroyed, whoever freed the savage shackles
   from my feet when I'd been sent to the wild pasture,
     whoever rescued me from murder

1360   and became my savior—
     a bitter gift:
   if I had died then,
   I'd not have been such grief to self and kin.
  CHORUS: I also would have had it so.

1365   OEDIPUS: I'd not have returned to be my father's
   murderer; I'd not be called by men
   my mother's bridegroom.
   Now I'm without a god,
     child of a polluted parent,

1370   fellow progenitor with him
     who gave me birth in misery.

If there's an evil that
    surpasses evils, that
has fallen to the lot of Oedipus.

1375 CHORAGOS: How can I say that you have counseled well?
Better not to be than live a blind man.

OEDIPUS: That this was not the best thing I could do—
don't tell me that, or advise me any more!
Should I descend to Hades and endure
1380 to see my father with these eyes? Or see
my poor unhappy mother? For I have done,
to both of these, things too great for hanging.
Or is the sight of children to be yearned for,
to see new shoots that sprouted as these did?
1385 Never, never with these eyes of mine!
Nor city, nor tower, nor holy images
of the divinities! For I, all-wretched,
most nobly raised—as no one else in Thebes—
deprived myself of these when I ordained
1390 that all expel the impious one—god-shown
to be polluted, and the dead king's son![75]
Once I exposed this great stain upon me,
could I have looked on these with steady eyes?
No! No! And if there were a way to block
1395 the source of hearing in my ears, I'd gladly
have locked up my pitiable body,
so I'd be blind and deaf. Evils shut out—
that way my mind could live in sweetness.
Alas, Cithaeron,[76] why did you receive me?
1400 Or when you had me, not killed me instantly?
I'd not have had to show my birth to mankind.
Polybus, Corinth, halls—ancestral,
they told me—how beautiful was your ward,
a scar that held back festering disease!
1405 Evil my nature, evil my origin.
You, three roads, and you, secret ravine,
you oak grove, narrow place of those three paths
that drank my blood[77] from these hands, from him
who fathered me, do you remember still
1410 the things I did to you? When I'd come here,

---

[75] *I . . . son:* Oedipus refers to his own curse against the murderer as well as his sins of patricide and incest. [76] *Cithaeron:* the mountain on which the infant Oedipus was supposed to be exposed. [77] *my blood:* that is, the blood of my father, Laius.

what I then did once more? Oh marriages! Marriages!
You gave us life and when you'd planted us
you sent the same seed up, and then revealed
fathers, brothers, sons, and kinsman's blood,
1415   and brides, and wives, and mothers, all the most
atrocious things that happen to mankind!
One should not name what never should have been.
Somewhere out there, then, quickly, by the gods,
cover me up, or murder me, or throw me
1420   to the ocean where you will never see me more!

(Oedipus moves toward the Chorus and they back away from him.)

    Come! Don't shrink to touch this wretched man!
    Believe me, do not be frightened! I alone
    of all mankind can carry these afflictions.

(Enter Creon from the palace with Attendants.)

CHORAGOS: Tell Creon what you wish for. Just when we need him
1425   he's here. He can act, he can advise you.
    He's now the land's sole guardian in your place.
OEDIPUS: Ah! Are there words that I can speak to him?
    What ground for trust can I present? It's proved
    that I was false to him in everything.
1430 CREON: I have not come to mock you, Oedipus,
    nor to reproach you for your former falseness.
    You men, if you have no respect for sons
    of mortals, let your awe for the all-feeding
    flames of lordy Hēlius[78] prevent
1435   your showing unconcealed so great a stain,
    abhorred by earth and sacred rain and light.
    Escort him quickly back into the house!
    If blood kin only see and hear their own
    afflictions, we'll have no impious defilement.
1440 OEDIPUS: By the gods, you've freed me from one terrible fear,
    so nobly meeting my unworthiness:
    grant me something—not for me; for you!
CREON: What do you want that you should beg me so?
OEDIPUS: To drive me from the land at once, to a place
1445   where there will be no man to speak to me!
CREON: I would have done just that—had I not wished
    to ask first of the god what I should do.

---

[78] *Hēlius:* the sun.

OEDIPUS: His answer was revealed in full—that I,
　　the patricide, unholy, be destroyed.
1450 CREON: He said that, but our need is so extreme,
　　it's best to have sure knowledge what must be done.
OEDIPUS: You'll ask about a wretched man like me?
CREON: Is it not time you put your trust in the god?
OEDIPUS: But I bid you as well, and shall entreat you.
1455　　Give her who is within what burial
　　you will—you'll give your own her proper rites;
　　but me—do not condemn my fathers' land
　　to have me dwelling here while I'm alive,
　　but let me live on mountains—on Cithaeron
1460　　famed as mine, for my mother and my father,
　　while they yet lived, made it my destined tomb,
　　and I'll be killed by those who wished my ruin!
　　And yet I know: no sickness will destroy me,
　　nothing will: I'd never have been saved
1465　　when left to die unless for some dread evil.
　　Then let my fate continue where it will!
　　As for my children, Creon, take no pains
　　for my sons—they're men and they will never lack
　　the means to live, wherever they may be—
1470　　but my two wretched, pitiable girls,
　　who never ate but at my table, never
　　were without me—everything that I
　　would touch, they'd always have a share of it—
　　please care for them! Above all, let me touch
1475　　them with my hands and weep aloud my woes!
　　Please, my Lord!
　　Please, noble heart! Touching with my hands,
　　I'd think I held them as when I could see.

(Enter Antigone and Ismene from the palace with Attendants.)

　　What's this?
1480　　Oh gods! Do I hear, somewhere, my two dear ones
　　sobbing? Has Creon really pitied me
　　and sent to me my dearest ones, my children?
　　Is that it?
CREON: Yes, I prepared this for you, for I knew
1485　　you'd feel this joy, as you have always done.
OEDIPUS: Good fortune, then, and, for your care, be guarded
　　far better by divinity than I was!
　　Where are you, children? Come to me! Come here
　　to these my hands, hands of your brother, hands
1490　　of him who gave you seed, hands that made
　　these once bright eyes to see now in this fashion.

(Oedipus embraces his daughters.)

> He, children, seeing nothing, knowing nothing,
> he fathered you where his own seed was plowed.
> I weep for you as well, though I can't see you,
> 1495   imagining your bitter life to come,
> the life you will be forced by men to live.
> What gatherings of townsmen will you join,
> what festivals, without returning home
> in tears instead of watching holy rites?
> 1500   And when you've reached the time for marrying,
> where, children, is the man who'll run the risk
> of taking on himself the infamy
> that will wound you as it did my parents?
> What evil is not here? Your father killed
> 1505   his father, plowed the one who gave him birth,
> and from the place where he was sown, from there
> he got you, from the place he too was born.
> These are the wounds: then who will marry you?
> No man, my children. No, it's clear that you
> 1510   must wither in dry barrenness, unmarried.

(Oedipus addresses Creon.)

> Son of Menoeceus! You are the only father
> left to them—we two who gave them seed
> are both destroyed: watch that they don't become
> poor, wanderers, unmarried—they are your kin.
> 1515   Let not my ruin be their ruin, too!
> No, pity them! You see how young they are,
> bereft of everyone, except for you.
> Consent, kind heart, and touch me with your hand!

(Creon grasps Oedipus's right hand.)

> You, children, if you had reached an age of sense,
> 1520   I would have counseled much. Now, pray you may live
> always where it's allowed, finding a life
> better than his was, who gave you seed.

CREON: Stop this now. Quiet your weeping. Move away, into the house.

OEDIPUS: Bitter words, but I obey them.

CREON: There's an end to all things.

1525 OEDIPUS: I have first this request.

CREON: Tell me. I shall judge when I will hear it.

OEDIPUS: Banish me from my homeland.

CREON: You must ask that of the god.

OEDIPUS: But I am the gods' most hated man!

CREON: Then you will soon get what
    you want.

OEDIPUS: Do you consent?

CREON: I never promise when, as now, I'm ignorant.

OEDIPUS: Then lead me in.

CREON: Come. But let your hold fall from your
    children.

1530 OEDIPUS: Do not take them from me, ever!

CREON: Do not wish to keep all of the
    power.
    You had power, but that power did not follow you through life.

(Oedipus's daughters are taken from him and led into the palace by Attendants. Oedipus is led into the palace by a Servant. Creon and the other Attendants follow. Only the Chorus remains.)

CHORUS: People of Thebes, my country, see: here is that Oedipus—
    he who "knew" the famous riddle, and attained the highest power,
    whom all citizens admired, even envying his luck!

1535   See the billows of wild troubles which he has entered now!
    Here is the truth of each man's life: we must wait, and see his end,
    scrutinize his dying day, and refuse to call him happy
    till he has crossed the border of his life without pain.

(Exit the Chorus along each of the parados.)

READING AND REACTING

1. The ancient Greeks used no scenery in their theatrical productions. In the absence of scenery, how is the setting established at the beginning of *Oedipus the King*?
2. In order not to detract from the language of *Oedipus the King*, some contemporary productions use very simple costumes. Do you agree with this decision? If so, why? If not, what kind of costumes would you use?
3. In some recent productions of *Oedipus the King*, actors wear copies of ancient Greek masks. What are the advantages and disadvantages of using such masks in a contemporary production of the play?
4. In the ancient Greek theater, the *strophe* and *antistrophe* were sung or chanted by the chorus as it danced back and forth across the stage. If you were staging the play today, would you retain the chorus or do away with it entirely? What would be gained or lost with each alternative?

5. Why does Sophocles have Oedipus blind himself offstage? What would be the effect of having Oedipus perform this act in full view of the audience?

6. In what ways does Sophocles observe the unities of time, place, and action described on pages 1130–31? How does Sophocles manage to present information about what happened years before the action of the play while still maintaining the three unities?

7. The ancient Greek audience that viewed *Oedipus the King* was familiar with the plot of the play. Given this situation, how does Sophocles create suspense? What are the advantages and disadvantages of using a story that the audience already knows?

8. At the end of the play, what has Oedipus learned about himself? About the gods? About the quest for truth? Is he a tragic or a pathetic figure? (See pages 1129–30 for a discussion of *tragedy* and *pathos*.)

9. Today, some directors employ *color-blind casting*—that is, they cast an actor in a role without regard to his or her race. Do you think this practice could be used in casting *Oedipus the King?* How, for example, would you react to an African-American as Oedipus or to an Asian-American as Creon?

10. **JOURNAL ENTRY** Do you think Oedipus deserves his fate? Why or why not?

11. **CRITICAL PERSPECTIVE** In "On Misunderstanding the *Oedipus Rex*," F. R. Dodds argues that Sophocles did not intend that Oedipus's tragedy be seen as rising from a "grave moral flaw." Neither, says Dodds, was Oedipus a "mere puppet" of the gods. Rather, "what fascinates us is the spectacle of a man freely choosing, from the highest motives, a series of actions which lead to his own ruin":

   > Oedipus is great, not in virtue of a great worldly position—
   > for his worldly position is an illusion which will vanish like
   > a dream—but in virtue of his inner strength: strength to
   > pursue the truth at whatever personal cost, and strength to
   > accept and endure it when found.[. . .] Oedipus is great be-
   > cause he accepts the responsibility for *all* his acts, including
   > those which are objectively most horrible, though subjec-
   > tively innocent.

   Do you agree with Dodd's arguments? Do you see Oedipus as someone who has inner strength or as a morally flawed victim of the gods?

Related Works: "Barn Burning" (p. 226), " 'Out, Out—' " (p. 826), "Ulysses" (p. 999), *Hamlet* (p. 1307), *Antigone* (p. 1631)

◆ **WILLIAM SHAKESPEARE** (1564–1616). (picture and biography on p. 1306) *A Midsummer Night's Dream* was first performed in celebration of an aristocratic marriage, either in January of 1595 or February of 1596; its three levels of love stories, all worked out by the end, make it a suitable wedding entertainment. Uncharacteristically for Shakespeare, there is no central earlier source for the story, though parts of it probably come from Chaucer, Ovid, and English folk legends. The play has always been popular with audiences and has frequently been adapted into other forms, such as ballet and opera. In Seattle in 1979, a musical adaptation used popular songs from the 1950s: Puck sang, "Why Do Fools Fall in Love?" and Oberon entered on a motorcycle and sang "Love Potion Number Nine."

CULTURAL CONTEXT ◆ During the Renaissance, it was common for artists (and sometimes writers) to have patrons—aristocrats who financed the work of the given artist. Though Shakespeare wrote for a professional theater group, some of Shakespeare's plays were written for nobility. Many critics believe that *A Midsummer Night's Dream* was written for Robert Stanley, earl of Derby, and Elizabeth Vere, daughter of Lord Burleigh.

◆ ◆ ◆

WILLIAM SHAKESPEARE

A Midsummer Night's Dream*
(c. 1595)

CHARACTERS

THESEUS, *Duke of Athens*
EGEUS, *father of Hermia*
LYSANDER, *beloved of Hermia*
DEMETRIUS, *in love with Hermia, favoured by Egeus*
PHILOSTRATE, *Master of the Revels to Theseus*
PETER QUINCE, *a carpenter (Prologue)*
NICK BOTTOM, *a weaver (Pyramus)*
FRANCIS FLUTE, *a bellows-mender (Thisby)*
TOM SNOUT, *a tinker (Wall)*
SNUG, *a joiner (Lion)*
ROBIN STARVELING, *a tailor (Moonshine)*

HIPPOLYTA, *Queen of the Amazons, betrothed to Theseus*
HERMIA, *daughter of Egeus, in love with Lysander*
HELENA, *in love with Demetrius*
OBERON, *King of the Fairies*
TITANIA, *Queen of the Fairies*
PUCK, *or Robin Goodfellow*
PEASEBLOSSOM
COBWEB
MOTH   } *Fairies*
MUSTARDSEED
OTHER FAIRIES *attending Oberon and Titania. Attendants on Theseus and Hippolyta.*

---

*Note that individual lines are numbered in the following play. When a line is shared by two or more characters, it is counted as one line.

Act I
Scene 1

Athens. The palace of Theseus.

(Enter Theseus, Hippolyta, Philostrate, and Attendants.)

THESEUS: Now, fair Hippolyta,[1] our nuptial hour
    Draws on apace;[2] four happy days bring in
    Another moon. But oh, methinks, how slow
    This old moon wanes! She lingers[3] my desires,
5   Like to a stepdame, or a dowager,
    Long withering out a young man's revenue.[4]
HIPPOLYTA: Four days will quickly steep[5] themselves in night,
    Four nights will quickly dream away the time,
    And then the moon, like to a silver bow
10   New-bent in heaven, shall behold the night
    Of our solemnities.
THESEUS: Go, Philostrate,
    Stir up the Athenian youth to merriments,
    Awake the pert[6] and nimble spirit of mirth.
    Turn melancholy forth to funerals.
15   The pale companion[7] is not for our pomp.

(Exit Philostrate.)

    Hippolyta, I wooed thee with my sword,
    And won thy love, doing thee injuries;
    But I will wed thee in another key,
    With pomp, with triumph, and with reveling.

(Enter Egeus, Hermia, Lysander, and Demetrius.)

20 EGEUS: Happy be Theseus, our renownèd Duke!
THESEUS: Thanks, good Egëus. What's the news with thee?
EGEUS: Full of vexation come I, with complaint
    Against my child, my daughter Hermia.
    Stand forth, Demetrius. My noble lord,
25   This man hath my consent to marry her.
    Stand forth, Lysander. And, my gracious Duke,
    This man hath bewitched the bosom of my child.
    Thou, thou, Lysander, thou hast given her rhymes,
    And interchanged love tokens with my child.
30   Thou hast by moonlight at her window sung,

---

[1] *Hippolyta:* Queen of the Amazons, a legendary race of female warriors who lived in South Russia. Theseus had defeated them in battle.   [2] *apace:* quickly.   [3] *lingers:* delays.   [4] *Like . . . revenue:* i.e., like a stepmother or a widowed mother *(dowager)* who has to be provided with an annuity. withring out: making to dwindle   [5] *steep:* turn into.   [6] *pert:* lively.   [7] *pale companion:* i.e., melancholy. companion: fellow.

With feigning[8] voice, verses of feigning love;
And stolen the impression of her fantasy[9]
With bracelets of they hair, rings, gawds,[10] conceits,[11]
Knacks,[12] trifles, nosegays,[13] sweetmeats, messengers
35 Of strong prevailment in unhardened youth.
With cunning hast thou filched my daughter's heart,
Turned her obedience, which is due to me,
To stubborn harsheness. And, my gracious Duke,
Be it so[14] she will not here before your Grace
40 Consent to marry with Demetrius,
I beg the ancient privilege of Athens,
As she is mine, I may dispose of her—
Which shall be either to this gentleman
Or to her death, according to our law
45 Immediately[15] provided in that case.
THESEUS: What say you, Hermia? Be advised,[16] fair maid,
To you your father should be as a god,
One that composed[17] your beauties—yea, and one
To whom you are but as a form[18] in wax
50 By him imprinted and within his power
To leave the figure or disfigure it.
Demetrius is a worthy gentleman.
HERMIA: So is Lysander.
THESEUS: In himself he is;
But in this kind,[19] wanting[20] your father's voice,
55 The other must be held the worthier.
HERMIA: I would my father looked but with my eyes.
THESEUS: Rather your eyes must with his judgment look.
HERMIA: I do entreat your Grace to pardon me.
I know not by what power I am made bold,
60 Nor how it may concern my modesty,[21]
In such a presence here to plead my thoughts;
But I beseech your Grace that I may know
The worst that may befall me in this case
If I refuse to wed Demetrius.
65 THESEUS: Either to die the death,[22] or to abjure
Forever the society of men.
Therefore, fair Hermia, question your desires.

---

[8] *feigning:* deceptive.   [9] *stolen . . . fantasy:* made a false impression on her imagination.   [10] *gawds:* trifles.   [11] *conceits:* pretty compliments.   [12] *Knacks:* knick-knacks.   [13] *nosegays:* bunches of flowers.   [14] *Be it so:* if.   [15] *Immediately:* expressly.   [16] *Be advised:* consider.   [17] *composed:* formed.   [18] *form:* shape.   [19] *in . . . kind:* in this case; i.e., the marriage.   [20] *wanting:* being without.   [21] *how . . . modesty:* whether it may make me appear immodest.   [22] *die . . . death:* to be put to death by the law.

Know of[23] your youth, examine well your blood,
Whether, if you yield not to your father's choice,
70 You can endure the livery of a nun—
For aye[24] to be in shady cloister mewed,[25]
To live a barren sister all your life,
Chanting faint hymns to the old fruitless moon.[26]
Thrice blessèd they that master so their blood,
75 To undergo such maiden pilgrimage;
But earthlier happy[27] is the rose distilled,[28]
Than that which, withering on the virgin thorn,
Grows, lives, and dies in single blessedness.
HERMIA: So will I grow, so live, so die, my lord,
80 Ere I will yield my virgin patent[29] up
Unto his lordship, whose unwishèd yoke
My soul consents not to give sovereignty.
THESEUS: Take time to pause; and by the next new moon—
The sealing day betwixt my love and me,
85 For everlasting bond of fellowship[30]—
Upon that day either prepare to die
For disobedience to your father's will,
Or else to wed Demetrius, as he would,
Or on Diana's altar to protest[31]
90 For aye austerity and single life.
DEMETRIUS: Relent, sweet Hermia. And, Lysander, yield
Thy crazèd title[32] to my certain right.
LYSANDER: You have her father's love, Demetrius,
Let me have Hermia's. Do you marry him.
95 EGEUS: Scornful Lysander! True, he hath my love,
And what is mine my love shall render[33] him.
And she is mine, and all my right of her
I do estate[34] unto Demetrius.
LYSANDER: I am, my lord, as well derived as he,
100 As well possessed;[35] my love is more than his;
My fortunes every way as fairly ranked,
If not with vantage,[36] as Demetrius'.
And, which is more than all these boasts can be,
I am beloved of beauteous Hermia.
105 Why should not I then prosecute my right?
Demetrius, I'll avouch it to his head,[37]

---

[23] *Know of:* remember.   [24] *aye:* ever.   [25] *mewed:* caged.   [26] *moon:* i.e., Diana, goddess of chastity and single life.   [27] *earthlier happy:* happier on earth.   [28] *distilled:* which sheds its essence on another.   [29] *virgin patent:* privilege of my virginity.   [30] *sealing . . . fellowship:* the day when we conclude our marriage.   [31] *protest:* vow.   [32] *crazed title:* flawed claim.   [33] *render:* give up to.   [34] *estate:* transfer.   [35] *derived . . . possessed:* of as good birth and wealth.   [36] *vantage:* advantage, superiority.   [37] *avouch . . . head:* declare it to his face.

Made love to Nedar's daughter, Helena,
And won her soul, and she, sweet lady, dotes,
Devoutly dotes, dotes in idolatry,
110   Upon this spotted[38] and inconstant man.
Theseus: I must confess that I have heard so much,
    And with Demetrius thought to have spoke thereof;
    But, being overfull of self-affairs,
    My mind did lose it. But, Demetrius, come,
115   And come, Egëus. You shall go with me.
    I have some private schooling[39] for you both.
    For you, fair Hermia, look you arm yourself
    To fit your fancies[40] to your father's will,
    Or else the law of Athens yields you up—
120   Which by no means we may extenuate—
    To death, or to a vow of single life.
    Come, my Hippolyta. What cheer, my love?
    Demetrius and Egëus, go along.
    I must employ you in some business.
125   Against[41] our nuptial, and confer with you
    Of something nearly[42] that concerns yourselves.
Egeus: With duty and desire we follow you.

(Exeunt all but Lysander and Hermia.)

Lysander: How now, my love! Why is your cheek so pale?
    How chance the roses there do fade so fast?
130 Hermia: Belike for want of rain, which I could well
    Beteem[43] them from the tempest of my eyes.
Lysander: Aye me! for aught that I could ever read,
    Could ever hear by tale or history,
    The course of true love never did run smooth,
135   But either it was different in blood——
Hermia: Oh, cross![44] Too high to be enthralled[45] to low.[46]
Lysander: Or else misgraffèd[47] in respect of years——
Hermia: Oh, spite! Too old to be engaged to young.
Lysander: Or else it stood upon the choice of friends——
140 Hermia: Oh, Hell! To choose love by another's eyes.
Lysander: Or, if there were a sympathy in choice,
    War, death, or sickness did lay siege to it,
    Making it momentany[48] as a sound,
    Swift as a shadow, short as any dream;
145   Brief as the lightning is the collied[49] night,

---

[38] *spotted:* stained.   [39] *schooling:* advice.   [40] *fit . . . fancies:* suit your ideas of love.
[41] *Against:* in anticipation of.   [42] *nearly:* closely.   [43] *Beteem:* bring forth.
[44] *cross:* perversity.   [45] *enthralled:* made servant to.   [46] *low:* one of low birth.
[47] *misgraffed:* ill-grafted.   [48] *momentany:* momentary.   [49] *collied:* coal-black.

That, in a spleen,[50] unfolds both heaven and earth,
And ere a man hath power to say "Behold!"
The jaws of darkness do devour it up.
So quick bright things come to confusion.[51]

150 HERMIA: If then true lovers have been ever crossed,[52]
It stands as an edíct in destiny.[53]
Then let us teach our trial patience,
Because it is a customary cross,
As due to love as thoughts and dreams and sighs,
155 Wishes and tears, poor fancy's[54] followers.

LYSANDER: A good persuasion. Therefore hear me, Hermia.
I have a widow aunt, a dowager
Of great revénue, and she hath no child.
From Athens is her house remote seven leagues;[55]
160 And she respects[56] me as her only son.
There, gentle Hermia, may I marry thee,
And to that place the sharp Athenian law
Cannot pursue us. If thou lovest me, then,
Steal forth thy father's house tomorrow night,
165 And in the wood, a league without the town,
Where I did meet thee once with Helena
To do observance to a morn of May,[57]
There will I stay for thee.

HERMIA: My good Lysander!
I swear to thee, by Cupid's strongest bow,
170 By his best arrow with the golden head,[58]
By the simplicity of Venus' doves,[59]
By that which knitteth souls and prospers loves,
And by that fire which burned the Carthage Queen[60]
When the false Troyan under sail was seen—
175 By all the vows that ever men have broke,
In number more than ever women spoke,
In that same place thou hast appointed me,
Tomorrow truly will I meet with thee.

LYSANDER: Keep promise, love. Look, here comes Helena.

(Enter Helena.)

180 HERMIA: Godspeed, fair Helena! Whither away?

---

[50] *spleen:* flash of wrath.   [51] *confusion:* pronounced as four syllables.   [52] *crossed:* thwarted.   [53] *edict in destiny:* decree of fate.   [54] *fancy:* love.   [55] *league:* three miles.   [56] *respects:* regards.   [57] *do . . . May:* observe May Day.   [58] *golden head:* Cupid has two kinds of arrows, the leaden causes dislike, the golden, love.   [59] *Venus' doves:* Doves were sacred to Venus, the goddess of love.   [60] *Carthage Queen:* Dido, Queen of Carthage, fell in love with Aeneas when he visited her after his escape from Troy. Aeneas deserted her, whereupon she mounted a funeral pyre and killed herself in the flames.

HELENA: Call you me fair? That fair again unsay.
    Demetrius loves your fair. O happy fair!
    Your eyes are lodestars,[61] and your tongue's sweet air
    More tunable than lark to shepherd's ear
185   When wheat is green, when hawthorn buds appear.
    Sickness is catching. Oh, were favor[62] so,
    Yours would I catch, fair Hermia, ere I go.
    My ear should catch your voice, my eye your eye,
    My tongue should catch your tongue's sweet melody.
190   Were the world mine, Demetrius being bated,[63]
    The rest I'd give to be to you translated.[64]
    Oh, teach me how you look, and with what art
    You sway the motion[65] of Demetrius' heart!
HERMIA: I frown upon him, yet he loves me still.
195 HELENA: Oh, that your frowns would teach my smiles such skill!
HERMIA: I give him curses, yet he gives me love.
HELENA: Oh, that my prayers could such affection move!
HERMIA: The more I hate, the more he follows me.
HELENA: The more I love, the more he hateth me.
200 HERMIA: His folly, Helena, is no fault of mine.
HELENA: None but your beauty. Would that fault were mine!
HERMIA: Take comfort. He no more shall see my face.
    Lysander and myself will fly this place.
    Before the time I did Lysander see,
205   Seemed Athens as a paradise to me.
    Oh then, what graces in my love do dwell,
    That he hath turned a Heven unto a Hell!
LYSANDER: Helen, to you our minds we will unfold.
    Tomorrow night, when Phoebe[66] doth behold
210   Her silver visage in the watery glass,[67]
    Decking with liquid pearl the bladed grass,
    A time that lovers' flights doth still[68] conceal,
    Through Athens' gates have we devised to steal.
HERMIA: And in the wood, where often you and I
215   Upon faint primrose beds were wont to lie,
    Emptying our bosoms of their counsel sweet,
    There my Lysander and myself shall meet,
    And thence from Athens turn away our eyes,
    To seek new friends and stranger companies.
220   Farewell, sweet playfellow. Pray thou for us,
    And good luck grant thee thy Demetrius!

---

[61] *lodestars:* guiding stars.   [62] *favor:* with double meaning, "beauty" and "affection."
[63] *bated:* excepted.   [64] *translated:* transformed.   [65] *motion:* inclination.   [66] *Phoebe:*
Diana, the moon.   [67] *watery glass:* i.e., reflected in the water.   [68] *still:* always.

Keep word, Lysander. We must starve our sight
From lovers' food till morrow deep midnight.
LYSANDER: I will, my Hermia. *(Exit Hermia.)* Helena, adieu.
225   As you on him, Demetrius dote on you! *(Exit.)*
HELENA: How happy some o'er other some[69] can be!
    Through Athens I am thought as fair as she.
    But what of that? Demetrius thinks not so,
    He will not know what all but he do know.
230   And as he errs, doting on Hermia's eyes,
    So I, admiring of his qualities.
    Things base and vile, holding no quantity,[70]
    Love can transpose to form and dignity.
    Love looks not with the eyes, but with the mind;
235   And therefore is winged Cupid painted blind.
    Nor hath Love's mind of any judgment taste;[71]
    Wings, and no eyes, figure unheedy haste.
    And therefore is Love said to be a child,
    Because in choice he is so oft beguiled.
240   As waggish[72] boys in game themselves forswear,
    So the boy Love is perjured everywhere:
    For ere Demetrius looked on Hermia's eyne,[73]
    He hailed down oaths that he was only mine;
    And when this hail some heat from Hermia felt,
245   So he dissolved, and showers of oaths did melt.
    I will go tell him of fair Hermia's flight.
    Then to the wood will he tomorrow night
    Pursue her; and for this intelligence[74]
    If I have thanks, it is a dear expense.[75]
250   But herein mean I to enrich[76] my pain,
    To have his sight thither and back again. *(Exit.)*

SCENE 2

The same. Quince's house.

(Enter Quince, Snug, Bottom, Flute, Snout, and Starveling.)

QUINCE: Is all our company here?
BOTTOM: You were best to call them generally,[1] man by man, according to
    the scrip.[2]

---

[69] *o'er . . . some:* compared with some others.   [70] *quantity:* proportion.   [71] *Nor . . .
taste:* i.e., Love has no judgment.   [72] *waggish:* frolicsome.   [73] *eyne:* eyes.   [74] *intelligence:* information.   [75] *dear expense:* something that costs one dear.   [76] *enrich:*
make rich—by the pleasure of seeing him.

---

[1] *generally:* Bottom loves a long word, but usually gets it wrong. Here he means "severally"; i.e., separately.   [2] *scrip:* list.

QUINCE: Here is the scroll of every man's name which is thought fit,
5   through all Athens, to play in our interlude[3] before the Duke and the
    Duchess on his wedding day at night.

BOTTOM: First, good Peter Quince, say what the play treats on. Then read
    the names of the actors, and so grow to a point.[4]

QUINCE: Marry,[5] our play is, *The most lamentable comedy, and most cruel*
10   *death of Pyramus and Thisby.*

BOTTOM: A very good piece of work, I assure you, and a merry. Now, good
    Peter Quince, call forth your actors by the scroll. Masters, spread
    yourselves.

QUINCE: Answer as I call you. Nick Bottom, the weaver.

15 BOTTOM: Ready. Name what part I am for, and proceed.

QUINCE: You, Nick Bottom, are set down for Pyramus.

BOTTOM: What is Pyramus? A lover, or a tyrant?

QUINCE: A lover, that kills himself most gallant for love.

BOTTOM: That will ask some tears in the true performing of it. If I do it,
20   let the audience look to their eyes, I will move storms, I will condole[6]
    in some measure. To the rest. Yet my chief humor[7] is for a tyrant. I
    could play Ercles[8] rarely, or a part to tear a cat[9] in, to make all split.

> "The raging rocks
> And shivering shocks
25   > Shall break the locks
> Of prison gates.
> And Phibbus'[10] car[11]
> Shall shine from far,
> And make and mar
30   > The foolish Fates."

    This was lofty! Now name the rest of the players. This is Ercles' vein,
    a tyrant's vein. A lover is more condoling.

QUINCE: Francis Flute, the bellows-mender.

FLUTE: Here, Peter Quince.

35 QUINCE: Flute, you must take Thisby on you.

FLUTE: What is Thisby? A wandering knight?

QUINCE: It is the lady that Pyramus must love.

FLUTE: Nay, faith, let not me play a woman. I have a beard coming.

QUINCE: That's all one. You shall play it in a mask, and you may speak as
40   small[12] as you will.

BOTTOM: An[13] I may hide my face, let me play Thisby too. I'll speak in a
    monstrous little voice, "Thisne, Thisne." "Ah Pyramus, my lover dear!
    Thy Thisby dear, and lady dear!"

---

[3] *interlude:* play.   [4] *grow . . . point:* come to a conclusion.   [5] *Marry:* Mary, by the
Virgin.   [6] *condole:* lit., sympathize; Bottom means "lament."   [7] *humor:* whim.
[8] *Ercles:* Hercules, a roaring figure in the old drama.   [9] *tear a cat:* proverbial expression for ham acting.   [10] *Phibbus:* for "Phoebus."   [11] *car:* chariot.   [12] *small:*
shrilly.   [13] *An:* if.

QUINCE: No, no. You must play Pyramus, and Flute, you Thisby.

45 BOTTOM: Well, proceed.

QUINCE: Robin Starveling, the tailor.

STARVELING: Here, Peter Quince.

QUINCE: Robin Starveling, you must play Thisby's mother. Tom Snout, the tinker.

50 SNOUT: Here, Peter Quince.

QUINCE: You, Pyramus' father. Myself, Thisby's father. Snug, the joiner, you, the lion's part. And, I hope, here is a play fitted.

SNUG: Have you the lion's part written? Pray you, if it be, give it me, for I am slow of study.

55 QUINCE: You may do it extempore, for it is nothing but roaring.

BOTTOM: Let me play the lion too. I will roar that I will do any man's heart good to hear me; I will roar that I will make the Duke say, "Let him roar again, let him roar again."

QUINCE: An you should do it too terribly, you would fright the Duchess
60 and the ladies, that they would shriek; and that were enough to hang us all.

ALL: That would hang us, every mother's son.

BOTTOM: I grant you, friends, if you should fright the ladies out of their wits, they would have no more discretion but to hang us. But I will
65 aggravate[14] my voice so that I will roar you as gently as any sucking dove, I will roar you an 'twere any nightingale.

QUINCE: You can play no part but Pyramus; for Pyramus is a sweet-faced man, a proper[15] man as one shall see in a summer's day, a most lovely, gentlemanlike man. Therefore you must needs play Pyramus.

70 BOTTOM: Well, I will undertake it. What beard were I best to play it in?

QUINCE: Why, what you will.

BOTTOM: I will discharge it in either your straw-color beard, your orange-tawny beard, your purple-in-grain[16] beard, or your French-crown-color beard, your perfect yellow.

75 QUINCE: Some of your French crowns have no hair at all,[17] and then you will play barefaced. But, masters, here are your parts. And I am to entreat you, request you, and desire you, to con[18] them by tomorrow night; and meet me in the palace wood, a mile without the town, by moonlight. There will we rehearse, for if we meet in the city, we shall
80 be dogged with company, and our devices known. In the meantime I will draw a bill of properties such as our play wants. I pray you, fail me not.

BOTTOM: We will meet, and there we may rehearse most obscenely[19] and courageously. Take pains, be perfect. Adieu.

---

[14] *aggravate:* for "moderate."   [15] *proper:* handsome.   [16] *purple-in-grain:* dyed purple.
[17] *French . . . all:* Loss of hair was one of the results of venereal or "French" disease.
[18] *con:* learn by heart.   [19] *obscenely:* for "obscurely."

85 QUINCE: At the Duke's Oak we meet.
BOTTOM: Enough. Hold or cut bowstrings.[20]

(Exeunt.)

ACT II
SCENE 1

A wood near Athens.

(Enter, from opposite sides, a Fairy, and Puck.)

PUCK: How now, spirit! Whither wander you?
FAIRY:

    Over hill, over dale,
     Thorough[1] bush, thorough brier,
    Over park, over pale,[2]
5   Thorough flood, thorough fire,
    I do wander everywhere,
    Swifter than the moon's sphere.
    And I serve the Fairy Queen,
    To dew her orbs[3] upon the green.
10   The cowslips[4] tall her pensioners[5] be.
    In their gold coats spots you see;
    Those be rubies, fairy favors,
    In those freckles live their savors.

  I must go seek some dewdrops here,
15 And hang a pearl in every cowslip's ear.
  Farewell, thou lob[6] of spirits, I'll be gone.
  Our Queen and all her elves come here anon.
PUCK: The King doth keep his revels here tonight.
  Take heed the Queen come not within his sight;
20 For Oberon is passing[7] fell[8] and wrath,
  Because that she as her attendant hath
  A lovely boy, stolen from an Indian king.
  She never had so sweet a changeling,[9]
  And jealous Oberon would have the child
25 Knight of his train,[10] to trace[11] the forests wild;

---

[20] *Hold . . . bowstrings:* a proverbial phrase, of which the origin is not satisfactorily explained, meaning come what may.

---

[1] *Thorough:* through. [2] *pale:* fence. [3] *orbs:* fairy rings; circles of dark grass common in English meadows. [4] *cowslips:* a wild plant which grows in meadows, with clusters of small yellow-orange flowers on a stem about eight to nine inches tall. [5] *pensioners:* the Queen's personal bodyguard, all young men of fine physique and good family. [6] *lob:* lubber, lout. [7] *passing:* exceedingly. [8] *fell:* fierce. [9] *changeling:* child exchanged by fairies. It was a country superstition that the fairies sometimes stole a beautiful child and left an ugly one in its place; here the changeling is the stolen child. [10] *train:* following. [11] *trace:* follow the tracks in.

But she perforce withholds the lovèd boy,
Crowns him with flowers, and makes him all her joy.
And now they never meet in grove or green,
By fountain clear or spangled starlight sheen,
30 But they do square,[12] that all their elves for fear
Creep into acorn cups and hide them there.
FAIRY: Either I mistake your shape and making quite,
Or else you are that shrewd and knavish sprite
Called Robin Goodfellow.[13] Are not you he
35 That frights the maidens of the villagery;
Skim milk, and somtimes labor in the quern,[14]
And bootless[15] make the breathless housewife churn;
And sometimes make the drink to bear no barm;[16]
Mislead night wanderers, laughing at their harm?
40 Those that Hobgoblin call you, and sweet Puck,
You do their work, and they shall have good luck.
Are not you he?
PUCK: Thou speak'st aright.
I am that merry wanderer of the night.
I jest to Oberon, and make him smile,
45 When I a fat and bean-fed horse beguile,
Neighing in likeness of a filly foal.
And sometime lurk I in a gossip's[17] bowl,
In very likeness of a roasted crab;[18]
And when she drinks, against her lips I bob
50 And on her withered dewlap[19] pour the ale.
The wisest aunt, telling the saddest tale,
Sometime for three-foot stool mistaketh me;
Then slip I from her bum, down topples she,
And "tailor"[20] cries, and falls into a cough,
55 And then the whole quire[21] hold their hips and laugh,
And waxen in their mirth, and neeze,[22] and swear
A merrier hour was never wasted there.
But, room, fairy! Here comes Oberon.
FAIRY: And here my mistress. Would that he were gone!

(Enter, from one side, Oberon, with his train; from the other, Titania, with hers.)

60 OBERON: Ill met by moonlight,[23] proud Titania.

---

[12] *square:* quarrel.   [13] *Robin Goodfellow:* the more common name for Puck, the mischief-maker.   [14] *quern:* handmill for grinding wheat.   [15] *bootless:* vainly.
[16] *barm:* yeast.   [17] *gossip:* goodwife (by nature given to gossiping).   [18] *crab:* crab apple. Roasted apples were sometimes floated in drinks to give flavor.   [19] *dewlap:* loose skin under the chin.   [20] *tailor:* Nobody has as yet explained convincingly why she should cry "tailor."   [21] *quire:* company.   [22] *neeze:* sneeze.   [23] *moonlight:* The constant suggestion of moonlight throughout Acts 2, 3, and 4 is worth noting.

TITANIA: What, jealous Oberon! Fairies, skip hence.
    I have forsworn[24] his bed and company.
OBERON: Tarry, rash wanton. Am not I thy lord?
TITANIA: Then I must be thy lady. But I know
65   When thou hast stolen away from fairyland,
    And in the shape of Corin sat all day,
    Playing on pipes of corn,[25] and versing love
    To amorous Phillida.[26] Why art thou here,
    Come from the farthest steppe of India
70   But that, forsooth, the bouncing Amazon,
    Your buskined[27] mistress and your warrior love,
    To Theseus must be wedded, and you come
    To give their bed joy and prosperity?
OBERON: How canst thou thus for shame, Titania,
75   Glance at my credit[28] with Hippolyta,
    Knowing I know thy love to Theseus?
    Didst thou not lead him through the glimmering night
    From Perigenia, whom he ravishèd?
    And make him with fair Aegle break his faith,
80   With Ariadne and Antiopa?[29]
TITANIA: These are the forgeries[30] of jealousy.
    And never, since the middle summer's spring,
    Met we on hill, in dale, forest, or mead,
    By pavèd fountain or by rushy brook,
85   Or in the beachèd margent[31] of the sea,
    To dance our ringlets[32] to the whistling wind,
    But with thy brawls thou hast disturbed our sport.
    Therefore[33] the winds, piping to us in vain,
    As in revenge, have sucked up from the sea
90   Contagious fogs, which, falling in the land,
    Have every pelting[34] river made so proud
    That they have overborne their continents.[35]
    The ox hath therefore stretched his yoke in vain,
    The plowman lost his sweat, and the green corn[36]
95   Hath rotted ere his youth attained a beard.
    The fold[37] stands empty in the drownèd field,
    And crows are fatted with the murrion[38] flock.

---

[24] *forsworn:* sworn to avoid.   [25] *pipes of corn:* oaten straws, a favorite musical instrument of pastoral shepherds.   [26] *shape . . . Phillida:* i.e., becoming an idle shepherd making love to a shepherdess. Corin and Phillida are typical names in pastoral verse. [27] *buskined:* wearing hunting boots.   [28] *credit:* reputation.   [29] *Perigenia . . . Antiopa:* These details of Theseus's love life Shakespeare found in Plutarch.   [30] *forgeries:* false inventions.   [31] *margent:* margin.   [32] *ringlets:* round dances.   [33] *Therefore . . . which:* passage perhaps inspired by the extreme weather of the summer of 1594.   [34] *pelting:* paltry.   [35] *continents:* banks.   [36] *corn:* wheat, oats, barley, rye, but *not* maize.   [37] *fold:* sheep-pen.   [38] *murrion:* plague-stricken.

The nine men's morris[39] is filled up with mud;
And the quaint[40] mazes[41] in the wanton[42] green,
100   For lack of tread, are undistinguishable.
The human mortals want[43] their winter here.
No night is now with hymn or carol blest.
Therefore the moon, the governess of floods,
Pale in her anger, washes all the air,
105   That rhéumatic diseases do abound.
And thorough this distemperature[44] we see
The seasons alter. Hoary-headed frosts
Fall in the fresh lap of the crimson rose,
And on old Hiems[45] thin and icy crown
110   An odorous chaplet of sweet summer buds
Is, as in mockery, set. The spring, the summer,
The childing[46] autumn, angry winter, change
Their wonted liveries, and the mazed[47] world,
By their increase, now knows not which is which.
115   And this same progeny of evils comes
From our debate, from our dissension.
We are their parents and original.
OBERON: Do you amend it, then. It lies in you.
Why should Titania cross her Oberon?
120   I do but beg a little changeling boy,
To be my henchman.[48]
TITANIA: Set your heart at rest.
The fairyland buys not the child of me.
His mother was a votaress[49] of my order.
And in the spicèd Indian air, by night,
125   Full often hath she gossiped by my side;
And sat with me on Neptune's yellow sands,
Marking the embarkèd traders[50] on the flood,
When we have laughed to see the sails conceive
And grow big-bellied with the wanton wind,
130   Which she, with pretty and with swimming gait
Following—her womb then rich with my young squire—
Would imitate, and sail upon the land,
To fetch me trifles, and return again

---

[39] *nine . . . morris:* popular Elizabethan game.   [40] *quaint:* curious.   [41] *maze:* a set of elaborate and intricate paths leading (or misleading) to a center. Those who know the secret can find their way; those who do not are baffled at every turn. To preserve the pattern in a village green, the paths must be re-trod every year. At Hampton Court there is an ancient maze with high yew hedges in which it is easy to be lost for hours.   [42] *wanton:* luxuriant.   [43] *want:* lack; i.e., are without the usual winter feasting.   [44] *distemperature:* disorder in nature.   [45] *Hiems:* Winter.   [46] *childing:* pregnant, fertile.   [47] *mazed:* bewildered.   [48] *henchman:* servant.   [49] *votaress:* devoted follower.   [50] *embarked traders:* merchant ships.

As from a voyage, rich with merchandise.
135　But she, being mortal, of that boy did die,
　　And for her sake do I rear up her boy,
　　And for her sake I will not part with him.
　　OBERON: How long within this wood intend you stay?
　　TITANIA: Perchance till after Theseus' wedding day.
140　If you will patiently dance in our round,
　　And see our moonlight revels, go with us;
　　If not, shun me, and I will spare[51] your haunts.
　　OBERON: Give me that boy, and I will go with thee.
　　TITANIA: Not for thy fairy kingdom. Fairies, away!
145　We shall chide downright, if I longer stay.

(Exit Titania with her train.)

　　OBERON: Well, go thy way. Thou shalt not from this grove
　　Till I torment thee for this injury.
　　My gentle Puck, come hither. Thou rememberest
　　Since once I sat upon a promontory
150　And heard a mermaid,[52] on a dolphin's back,
　　Uttering such dulcet and harmonious breath
　　That the rude sea grew civil at her song,
　　And certain stars shot madly from their spheres[53]
　　To hear the sea maid's music.
　　PUCK:　　　　　　　　　　　　I remember.
155　OBERON: That very time I saw, but thou couldst not,
　　Flying between the cold moon and the earth,
　　Cupid all armed. A certain aim he took
　　At a fair[54] vestal[55] thronèd by the west,
　　And loosed his love shaft smartly from his bow,
160　As it should pierce a hundred thousand hearts.
　　But I might see young Cupid's fiery shaft
　　Quenched in the chaste beams of the watery moon,
　　And the imperial votaress[56] passed on,
　　In maiden meditation, fancy-free.[57]
165　Yet marked I where the bolt[58] of Cupid fell.
　　It fell upon a little western flower,
　　Before milk-white, now purple with love's wound,
　　And maidens call it love-in-idleness.[59]
　　Fetch me that flower, the herb I showed thee once.
170　The juice of it on sleeping eyelids laid

---

[51] *spare:* avoid.　[52] *heard a mermaid:* probably an allusion to one of the elaborate entertainments prepared for Queen Elizabeth.　[53] *spheres:* courses.　[54] *fair . . . fancy-free:* a tactful and complimentary allusion to Queen Elizabeth, the Virgin Queen, whose bosom was impenetrable to Cupid's arrows.　[55] *vestal:* one vowed to virginity.　[56] *votaress:* one who has made a vow.　[57] *fancy-free:* not caught by love.　[58] *bolt:* arrow.　[59] *love-in-idleness:* wild pansy.

Will make or man or woman madly dote
Upon the next live creature that it sees.
Fetch me this herb, and be thou here again
Ere the leviathan[60] can swim a league.

175 Puck: I'll put a girdle round about the earth[61]
In forty minutes. *(Exit.)*

Oberon: Having once this juice,
I'll watch Titania when she is asleep
And drop the liquor of it in her eyes.
The next thing then she waking looks upon,
180 Be it on lion, bear, or wolf, or bull,
On meddling monkey or on busy ape,
She shall pursue it with the soul of love.
And ere I take this charm from off her sight,
As I can take it with another herb,
185 I'll make her render up her page to me.
But who comes here? I am invisible,[62]
And I will overhear their conference.

(Enter Demetrius, Helena following him.)

Demetrius: I love thee not, therefore pursue me not.
Where is Lysander and fair Hermia?
190 The one I'll slay, the other slayeth me.
Thou told'st me they were stolen unto this wood,
And here am I, and wode[63] within this wood,
Because I cannot meet my Hermia.
Hence, get thee gone, and follow me no more.

195 Helena: You draw me, you hardhearted adamant.[64]
But yet you draw not iron, for my heart
Is true as steel. Leave you[65] your power to draw,
And I shall have no power to follow you.

Demetrius: Do I entice you? Do I speak you fair?
200 Or, rather, do I not in plainest truth
Tell you I do not nor I cannot love you?

Helena: And even for that do I love you the more.
I am your spaniel, and, Demetrius,
The more you beat me, I will fawn on you.
205 Use me but as your spaniel, spurn me, strike me,
Neglect me, lose me—only give me leave,
Unworthy as I am, to follow you.

---

[60] *leviathan:* whale.   [61] *I'll . . . earth:* I'll fly round the earth.   [62] *I am invisible:* Presumably Oberon here puts on a cloak to symbolize invisibility. Henslowe in his *Diary* noted that the Admiral's Men in 1598 bought "a robe for to go invisible."   [63] *wode:* mad.   [64] *adamant:* lodestone, a very hard magnetic stone.   [65] *Leave you:* if you will leave off.

What worser place can I beg in your love—
And yet a place of high respect with me—
210   Than to be usèd as you use your dog?
DEMETRIUS: Tempt not too much the hatred of my spirit,
    For I am sick when I do look on thee.
HELENA: And I am sick when I look not on you.
DEMETRIUS: You do impeach[66] your modesty too much,
215   To leave the city, and commit yourself
    Into the hands of one that loves you not;
    To trust the opportunity of night
    And the ill counsel of a desert place
    With the rich worth of your virginity.
220 HELENA: Your virtue is my privilege. For that
    It is not night when I do see your face,
    Therefore I think I am not in the night.
    Nor doth this wood lack worlds of company,
    For you in my respect[67] are all the world.
225   Then how can it be said I am alone
    When all the world is here to look on me?
DEMETRIUS: I'll run from thee and hide me in the brakes,[68]
    And leave thee to the mercy of wild beasts.
HELENA: The wildest hath not such a heart as you.
230   Run when you will, the story shall be changed.
    Apollo flies, and Daphne holds the chase;[69]
    The dove pursues the griffin;[70] the mild hind
    Makes speed to catch the tiger—bootless[71] speed
    When cowardice pursues, and valor flies.
235 DEMETRIUS: I will not stay thy questions, let me go.
    Or, if thou follows me, do not believe
    But I shall do thee mischief in the wood.
HELENA: Aye, in the temple, in the town, the field,
    You do me mischief. Fie, Demetrius!
240   Your wrongs do set a scandal on my sex.
    We cannot fight for love, as men may do;
    We should be wooed, and were not made to woo.

(Exit Demetrius.)

    I'll follow thee, and make a Heaven of Hell,
    To die upon the hand I love so well. *(Exit.)*
245 OBERON: Fare thee well, nymph. Ere he do leave this grove,
    Thou shalt fly him, and he shall seek thy love.

---

[66] *impeach:* discredit.   [67] *respect:* estimation.   [68] *brakes:* bushes.   [69] *Apollo . . . chase:* The natural order is reversed; the meek pursues the strong. According to the legend, Apollo pursued Daphne, who was turned into a laurel bush.   [70] *griffin:* a fabulous beast, eagle in front and lion behind.   [71] *bootless:* vain.

(Re-enter Puck.)

      Hast thou the flower there? Welcome, wanderer.

Puck: Aye, there it is.

Oberson: I pray thee, give it me.

      I know a bank where the wild thyme blows,

250   Where oxlips[72] and the nodding violet grows;

      Quite overcanopied with luscious woodbine,[73]

      With sweet musk roses, and with eglantine.[74]

      There sleeps Titania sometime of the night,

      Lulled in these flowers with dances and delight.

255   And there the snake throws her enameled[75] skin,

      Weed[76] wide enough to wrap a fairy in.

      And with the juice of this I'll streak her eyes,

      And make her full of hateful fantasies.

      Take thou some of it, and seek through this grove.

260   A sweet Athenian lady is in love

      With a disdainful youth. Anoint his eyes;

      But do it when the next thing he espies

      May be the lady. Thou shalt know the man

      By the Athenian garments he hath on.

265   Effect it with some care, that he may prove

      More fond[77] on her than she upon her love.

      And look thou meet me ere the first cock crow.

Puck: Fear not, my lord, your servant shall do so.

(Exeunt.)

Scene 2

Another part of the wood.

(Enter Titania, with her train.)

Titania: Come, now a roundel[1] and a fairy song,

      Then, for the third part of a minute, hence—

      Some to kill cankers[2] in the musk-rose buds,

      Some war with reremice[3] for their leathern wings,

5   To make my small elves coats, and some keep back

      The clamorous owl that nightly hoots and wonders

      At our quaint spirits. Sing me now asleep,

      Then to your offices, and let me rest.

(The fairies sing.)

---

[72] *oxlips:* cross between the primrose and the cowslip.   [73] *woodbine:* honeysuckle.
[74] *eglantine:* sweetbrier.   [75] *enameled:* shiny.   [76] *Weed:* garment.   [77] *fond:* foolishly doting.

---

[1] *roundel:* round dance.   [2] *cankers:* cankerworms.   [3] *reremice:* bats.

1ST FAIRY: You spotted snakes with double tongue,
10   Thorny hedgehogs, be not seen.
                  Newts and blindworms,[4] do no wrong,
                  Come not near our fairy Queen.
CHORUS: Philomel,[5] with melody
                  Sing in our sweet lullaby;
15   Lulla, lulla, lullaby, lulla, lulla, lullaby.
                      Never harm,
                      Nor spell, nor charm,
                  Come our lovely lady nigh.
                  So, good night, with lullaby.
20 1ST FAIRY: Weaving spiders, come not here.
                  Hence, you long-legged spinners, hence!
                  Beetles black, approach not near.
                  Worm nor snail, do no offense.
CHORUS: Philomel, with melody
25   Sing in our sweet lullaby;
                  Lulla, lulla, lullaby, lulla, lulla, lullaby.
                      Never harm,
                      Nor spell, nor charm,
                  Come our lovely lady nigh.
30   So, good night, with lullaby.

2ND FAIRY: Hence, away! Now all is well.
    One aloof stand sentinel.

(Exeunt Fairies. Titania sleeps.)

(Enter Oberon, and squeezes the flower on Titania's eyelids.)

OBERON: What thou seest when thou dost wake,
    Do it for thy truelove take,
35   Love and languish for his sake.
    Be it ounce,[6] or cat, or bear,
    Pard,[7] or boar with bristled hair,
    In thy eye that shall appear
    When thou wakest, it is thy dear.
40   Wake when some vile thing is near. *(Exit.)*

(Enter Lysander and Hermia.)

LYSANDER: Fair love, you faint with wandering in the wood,
    And to speak troth, I have forgot our way.
    We'll rest us, Hermia, if you think it good,
    And tarry for the comfort of the day.

---

[4] *blindworm:* slow worm, a small harmless snakelike creature (actually a legless lizard), common in the English countryside.   [5] *Philomel:* the nightingale.   [6] *ounce:* lynx. [7] *Pard:* leopard.

45   HERMIA: Be it so, Lysander. Find you out a bed,
      For I upon this bank will rest my head.
  LYSANDER: One turf shall serve as pillow for us both—
      One heart, one bed, two bosoms, and one troth.[8]
  HERMIA: Nay, good Lysander, for my sake, my dear,
50   Lie further off yet, do not lie so near.
  LYSANDER: Oh, take the sense, sweet, of my innocence!
      Love takes the meaning in love's conference.
      I mean that my heart unto yours is knit
      So that but one heart we can make of it.
55   Two bosoms interchainèd with an oath,
      So then two bosoms and a single troth.
      Then by your side no bedroom me deny
      For lying so, Hermia, I do not lie.
  HERMIA: Lyander riddles very prettily.
60   Now much beshrew[9] my manners and my pride,
      If Hermia meant to say Lysander lied.
      But, gentle friend, for love and courtesy
      Lie further off; in human modesty,
      Such separation as may well be said
65   Becomes a virtuous bachelor and a maid,
      So far be distant. And good night, sweet friend.
      Thy love ne'er alter till thy sweet life end!
  LYSANDER: Amen, amen, to that fair prayer say I,
      And then end life when I end loyalty!
70   Here is my bed. Sleep give thee all his rest!
  HERMIA: With half that wish the wisher's eye be pressed! *(They sleep.)*

(Enter Puck.)

  PUCK: Through the forest have I gone,
      But Athenian found I none
      On whose eyes I might approve[10]
75   This flower's force in stirring love.
      Night and silence.—Who is here?
      Weeds of Athens he doth wear.
      This is he, my master said,
      Despisèd the Athenian maid,
80   And here the maiden, sleeping sound
      On the dank and dirty ground.
      Pretty soul! She durst not lie
      Near this lacklove, this kill-courtesy.
      Churl,[11] upon thy eyes I throw
85   All the power this charm doth owe.

---

[8] *troth:* truth.   [9] *beshrew:* plague on.   [10] *approve:* test.   [11]*Churl:* boor.

When thou wakest, let love forbid
Sleep his seat on thy eyelid.
So awake when I am gone,
For I must now to Oberon. *(Exit.)*

(Enter Demetrius and Helena, running.)

90 HELENA: Stay, though thou kill me, sweet Demetrius.
DEMETRIUS: I charge thee, hence, and do not haunt me thus.
HELENA: Oh, wilt thou darkling[12] leave me? Do not so.
DEMETRIUS: Stay, on thy peril.[13] I alone will go. *(Exit.)*
HELENA: Oh, I am out of breath in this fond[14] chase!
95   The more my prayer, the lesser is my grace.
    Happy is Hermia, whereso'er she lies,
    For she hath blessèd and attractive eyes.
    How came her eyes so bright? Not with salt tears;
    If so, my eyes are oftener washed than hers.
100   No, no, I am as ugly as a bear,
    For beasts that meet me run away for fear.
    Therefore no marvel though Demetrius
    Do, as a monster, fly my presence thus.
    What wicked and dissembling[15] glass of mine
105   Made me compare with Hermia's sphery[16] eyne?
    But who is here? Lysander! On the ground!
    Dead? Or asleep? I see no blood, no wound.
    Lysander, if you live, good sir, awake.
LYSANDER: *(Awaking)* And run through fire I will for thy sweet sake.
110   Transparent[17] Helena! Nature shows art,
    That through thy bosom makes me see thy heart.
    Where is Demetrius? Oh, how fit a word
    Is that vile name to perish on my sword!
HELENA: Do not say so, Lysander, say not so.
115   What though he love your Hermia? Lord, what though?
    Yet Hermia still loves you. Then be content.
LYSANDER: Content with Hermia! No, I do repent
    The tedious minutes I with her have spent.
    Not Hermia but Helena I love.
120   Who will not change a raven for a dove?
    The will of man is by his reason swayed,
    And reason says you are the worthier maid.
    Things growing are not ripe until their season.

---

[12] *darkling:* in the dark.   [13] *on . . . peril:* i.e., or harm will come to you.   [14] *fond:* foolish.   [15] *dissembling:* deceiving.   [16] *sphery:* starlike.   [17] *Transparent:* i.e., because her heart is visible.

So I, being young, till now ripe not to reason;
125 And touching now the point[18] of human skill,
Reason becomes the marshal[19] to my will,[20]
And leads me to your eyes, where I o'erlook
Love's stories, written in love's richest book.

Helena: Wherefore was I to this keen mockery born?
130 When at your hands did I deserve this scorn?
Is't not enough, is't not enough, young man,
That I did never, no, nor never can,
Deserve a sweet look from Demetrius' eye,
But you must flout my insufficiency?
135 Good troth, you do me wrong, good sooth,[21] you do,
In such disdainful manner me to woo.
But fare you well. Perforce I must confess
I thought you lord of more true gentleness.
Oh, that a lady, of one man refused,
140 Should of another therefore be abused! *(Exit.)*

Lysander: She sees not Hermia. Hermia, sleep thou there.
And never mayst thou come Lysander near!
For as a surfeit of the sweetest things
The deepest loathing to the stomach brings,
145 Or as the heresies that men do leave
Are hated most of those they did deceive,
So thou, my surfeit and my heresy,
Of all be hated, but the most of me!
And, all my powers, address your love and might
150 To honor Helen and to be her knight! *(Exit.)*

Hermia: *(Awaking)* Help me, Lysander, help me! Do thy best
To pluck this crawling serpent from my breast!
Aye me, for pity! What a dream was here!
Lysander, look how I do quake with fear.
155 Methought a serpent eat my heart away,
And you sat smiling at his cruel prey.
Lysander! What, removed? Lysander! Lord!
What, out of hearing? Gone? No sound, no word?
Alack, where are you? Speak, an if you hear,
160 Speak, of all loves! I swoon almost with fear.
No? Then I well perceive you are not nigh.
Either death or you I'll find immediately. *(Exit.)*

---

[18] *point:* high spot.   [19] *marshal:* director.   [20] *will:* passion.   [21] *sooth:* truth.

ACT III
SCENE 1

The wood. Titania lying asleep.

(Enter Quince, Snug, Bottom, Flute, Snout, and Starveling.)

BOTTOM: Are we all met?

QUINCE: Pat, pat, and here's a marvelous convenient place for our rehearsal. This green plot shall be our stage, this hawthorn brake[1] our tiring-house;[2] and we will do it in action as we will do it before the
5   Duke.

BOTTOM: Peter Quince——

QUINCE: What sayest thou, bully Bottom?

BOTTOM: There are things in this comedy of Pyramus and Thisby that will never please. First, Pyramus must draw a sword to kill himself,
10   which the ladies cannot abide. How answer you that?

SNOUT: By'r lakin,[3] a parlous fear.

STARVELING: I believe we must leave the killing out, when all is done.

BOTTOM: Not a whit. I have a device to make all well. Write me a prologue, and let the prologue seem to say we will do no harm with
15   our swords, and that I Pyramus is not killed indeed. And, for the more better assurance, tell them that Pyramus am not Pyramus, but Bottom the weaver. This will put them out of fear.

QUINCE: Well, we will have such a prologue, and it shall be written in eight and six.[4]

20 BOTTOM: No, make it two more. Let it be written in eight and eight.

SNOUT: Will not the ladies be afeard of the lion?

STARVELING: I fear it, I promise you.

BOTTOM: Masters, you ought to consider with yourselves. To bring in— God shield us!—a lion among ladies[5] is a most dreadful thing; for
25   there is not a more fearful wildfowl than your lion living, and we ought to look to 't.

SNOUT: Therefore another prologue must tell he is not a lion.

BOTTOM: Nay, you must name his name, and half his face must be seen through the lion's neck. And he himself must speak through, saying
30   thus, or to the same defect[6]—"Ladies"—or "Fair ladies—I would wish you"—or "I would request you"—or "I would entreat you—not to fear, not to tremble. My life for yours. If you think I come hither as a lion, it were pity of my life. No, I am no such thing, I am a man as other men are." And there indeed let him name his name, and tell
35   them plainly he is Snug the joiner.

---

[1] *brake:* thicket.   [2] *tiring-house:* dressing room.   [3] *By'r lakin:* by our little lady; i.e., the Virgin Mary.   [4] *eight . . . six:* the common ballad meter of alternate lines of six and eight syllables.   [5] *lion . . . ladies:* allusion to a pamphlet of the time describing the baptismal ceremony for the infant son of King James VI of Scotland.   [6] *defect:* for "effect."

QUINCE: Well, it shall be so. But there is two hard things: that is, to bring the moonlight into a chamber, for you know Pyramus and Thisby meet by moonlight.

SNOUT: Doth the moon shine that night we play our play?

40 BOTTOM: A calendar, a calendar! Look in the almanac. Find out moonshine, find out moonshine.

QUINCE: Yes, it doth shine that night.

BOTTOM: Why, then may you leave a casement[7] of the great-chamber[8] window, where we play, open, and the moon may shine in at the
45   casement.

QUINCE: Aye, or else one must come in with a bush of thorns and a lantern,[9] and say he comes to disfigure,[10] or to present, the person of moonshine. Then, there is another thing. We must have a wall in the great chamber, for Pyramus and Thisby, says the story, did talk
50   through the chink of a wall.

SNOUT: You can never bring in a wall. What say you, Bottom?

BOTTOM: Some man or other must present wall. And let him have some plaster, or some loam,[11] or some roughcast[12] about him, to signify wall. And let him hold his fingers thus, and through that cranny
55   shall Pyramus and Thisby whisper.

QUINCE: If that may be, then all is well. Come, sit down, every mother's son, and rehearse your parts. Pyramus, you begin. When you have spoken your speech, enter into that brake. And so every one according to his cue.

(Enter Puck behind.)

60 PUCK: What hempen homespuns[13] have we swaggering here,
        So near the cradle of the Fairy Queen?
        What, a play toward![14] I'll be an auditor—
        An actor too perhaps, if I see cause.

QUINCE: Speak, Pyramus. Thisby, stand forth.

65 BOTTOM: "Thisby, the flowers of odious savors sweet——"

QUINCE: Odors, odors.

BOTTOM: "——odors savors sweet.
        So hath thy breath, my dearest Thisby dear.
        But hark, a voice! Stay thou but here awhile,
70   And by and by I will to thee appear." *(Exit.)*

PUCK: A stranger Pyramus than e'er played here. *(Exit.)*

FLUTE: Must I speak now?

---

[7] *casement:* window opening on a hinge.   [8] *great-chamber:* hall of a great house.
[9] *bush . . . lantern:* supposedly carried by the man in the moon.   [10] *disfigure:* for "prefigure."   [11] *loam:* preparation of clay used for covering wall.   [12] *roughcast:* rough plaster.   [13] *hempen homespuns:* coarse clothing spun at home; i.e., country clowns.   [14] *toward:* in hand.

QUINCE: Aye, marry must you, for you must understand he goes but to see
a noise that he heard, and is to come again.

75 FLUTE: "Most radiant Pyramus, most lily-white of hue,
Of color like the red rose on triumphant brier,
Most briskly juvenal,[15] and eke most lovely Jew,
As true as truest horse, that yet would never tire,
I'll meet thee, Pyramus, at Ninny's tomb."

80 QUINCE: "Ninus' tomb," man. Why, you must not speak that yet. That
you answer to Pyramus. You speak all your part at once, cues and all.
Pyramus enter. Your cue is past. It is "never tire."

FLUTE: Oh—"As true as truest horse, that yet would never tire."

(Re-enter Puck, and Bottom with an ass's head.)

BOTTOM: "If I were fair, Thisby, I were only thine."

85 QUINCE: Oh, monstrous! Oh, strange! We are haunted. Pray, masters! Fly,
masters! Help!

(Exeunt Quince, Snug, Flute, Snout, and Starveling.)

PUCK: I'll follow you, I'll lead you about a round,[16]
Through bog, through bush, through brake, through brier.
Sometime a horse I'll be, sometime a hound,
90 A hog, a headless bear, sometime a fire,
And neigh, and bark, and grunt, and roar, and burn,
Like horse, hound, hog, bear, fire, at every turn. *(Exit.)*

BOTTOM: Why do they run away? This is a knavery of them to make me
afeard.

(Re-enter Snout.)

95 SNOUT: O Bottom, thou art changed! What do I see on thee?

BOTTOM: What do you see? You see an asshead of your own, do you?

(Exit Snout.)

(Re-enter Quince.)

QUINCE: Bless thee, Bottom! Bless thee! Thou art translated.[17] *(Exit.)*

BOTTOM: I see their knavery. This is to make an ass of me, to fright me, if
they could. But I will not stir from this place, do what they can. I will
100 walk up and down here, and I will sing, that they shall hear I am not
afraid.

(Sings.)

"The ousel[18] cock so black of hue,
With orange-tawny bill,

---

[15] *juvenal:* youth, eke: also.   [16] *about a round:* roundabout.   [17] *translated:* transformed.   [18] *ousel:* blackbird.

The throstle[19] with his note so true,
105   The wren[20] with little quill;[21]

TITANIA: *(Awaking)* What angel wakes me from my flower bed?
BOTTOM: *(Sings.)*
            "The finch, the sparrow, and the lark,
                The plainsong[22] cuckoo gray,
110   Whose note full many a man doth mark,
                And dares not answer nay—"
for indeed who would set his wit to[23] so foolish a bird? Who would
give a bird the lie, though he cry "cuckoo" never so?
TITANIA: I pray thee, gentle mortal, sing again.
115   Mine ear is much enamored of thy note,
So is mine eye enthrallèd[24] to thy shape.
And thy fair virtue's force perforce doth move me
On the first view to say, to swear, I love thee.
BOTTOM: Methinks, mistress, you should have little reason for that. And
120   yet, to say the truth, reason and love keep little company together
nowadays; the more the pity, that some honest neighbors will not
make them friends. Nay, I can gleek[25] upon occasion.
TITANIA: Thou art as wise as thou art beautiful.
BOTTOM: Not so, neither. But if I had wit enough to get out of this wood,
125   I have enough to serve mine own turn.
TITANIA: Out of this wood do not desire to go.
Thou shalt remain here, whether thou wilt or no.
I am a spirit of no common rate.
The summer still[26] doth tend[27] upon my state;
130   And I do love thee. Therefore go with me.
I'll give thee fairies to attend on thee,
And they shall fetch thee jewels from the deep,
And sing while thou on pressèd flowers dost sleep.
And I will purge thy mortal grossness so
135   That thou shalt like an airy spirit go.
Peaseblossom! Cobweb! Moth! And Mustardseed!

(Enter Peaseblossom, Cobweb, Moth, and Mustardseed.)

1ST FAIRY: Ready.
2ND FAIRY: And I.
3RD FAIRY: And I.
4TH FAIRY: And I.
ALL: Where shall we go?
TITANIA: Be kind and courteous to this gentleman.
    Hop in his walks, and gambol[28] in his eyes.

---

[19] *throstle:* thrush.   [20] *wren:* the smallest of English birds.   [21] *throstle quill:* feather.
[22] *plainsong:* singing a simple melody.   [23] *set . . . to:* try to answer.   [24] *enthralled:*
enslaved.   [25] *gleek:* wisecrack.   [26] *still:* always.   [27] *tend:* attend.   [28] *gambol:*
caper.

140   Feed him with apricocks[29] and dewberries,[30]
      With purple grapes, green figs, and mulberries.
      The honey bags steal from the humblebees,
      And for night tapers crop their waxen thighs,
      And light them at the fiery glowworm's eyes,
145   To have my love to bed and to arise.
      And pluck the wings from painted butterflies,
      To fan the moonbeams from his sleeping eyes.
      Nod to him, elves, and do him courtesies.
      1ST FAIRY: Hail, mortal!
150   2ND FAIRY: Hail!
      3RD FAIRY: Hail!
      4TH FAIRY: Hail!
      BOTTOM: I cry your Worship's mercy,[31] heartily. I beseech your Worship's
      name.
155   COBWEB: Cobweb.
      BOTTOM: I shall desire you of more acquaintance, good Master Cobweb. If
      I cut my finger, I shall make bold with you.[32] You name, honest
      gentleman?
      PEASEBLOSSOM: Peaseblossom.[33]
160   BOTTOM: I pray you, commend me to Mistress Squash,[34] your mother, and
      to Master Peascod,[35] your father. Good Master Peaseblossom, I shall
      desire you of more acquaintance too. Your name, I beseech you, sir?
      MUSTARDSEED: Mustardseed.
      BOTTOM: Good Master Mustardseed, I know your patience well. That
165   same cowardly, giantlike ox beef hath devoured many a gentleman of
      your house. I promise you your kindred hath made my eyes water ere
      now. I desire your more acquaintance, good Master Mustardseed.
      TITANIA: Come, wait upon him; lead him to my bower.
      The moon methinks looks with a watery eye,
170   And when she weeps, weeps every little flower,
      Lamenting some enforcèd chastity.
      Tie up my love's tongue, bring him silently.

(Exeunt.)

SCENE 2

Another part of the wood.

(Enter Oberon.)

OBERON: I wonder if Titania be awaked,
      Then, what it was that next came in her eye,
      Which she must dote on in extremity.

---

[29] *apricocks:* apricots.   [30] *dewberries:* blackberries.   [31] *I . . . mercy:* I beg your pardon.   [32] *Cobweb . . . you:* an ancient means of first aid for a cut finger.   [33] *Peaseblossom:* the blossom of a garden pea.   [34] *Squash:* the unripe peapod.   [35] *Peascod:* the full pod.

(Enter Puck.)

How now, mad spirit!
              Here comes my messenger.
5   What night rule[1] now about this haunted grove?
Puck: My mistress with a monster is in love.
     Near to her close and consecrated bower,
     While she was in her dull and sleeping hour,
     A crew of patches,[2] rude mechanicals,[3]
10   That work for bread upon Athenian stalls,[4]
     Were met together to rehearse a play,
     Intended for great Theseus' nuptial day.
     The shallowest thickskin of that barren[5] sort,
     Who Pyramus presented,[6] in their sport
15   Forsook his scene, and entered in a brake,
     When I did him at this advantage take,
     An ass's nole[7] I fixèd on his head.
     Anon his Thisbe must be answerèd,
     And forth my mimic[8] comes. When they him spy,
20   As wild geese that the creeping fowler eye,
     Or russet-pated choughs,[9] many in sort,
     Rising and cawing at the gun's report,
     Sever themselves and madly sweep the sky,
     So at his sight away his fellows fly.
25   And, at our stamp, here o'er and o'er one falls,
     He murder cries, and help from Athens calls.
     Their sense thus weak, lost with their fears thus strong,
     Made senseless things begin to do them wrong;
     For briers and thorns at their apparel snatch,
30   Some sleeves, some hats, from yielders all things catch.
     I led them on in this distracted fear,
     And left sweet Pyramus translated there,
     When in that moment, so it came to pass,
     Titania waked, and straightway loved an ass.
35 Oberon: This falls out better than I could devise.
     But hast thou yet latched[10] the Athenian's eyes
     With the love juice, as I did bid thee do?
Puck: I took him sleeping—that is finished too—
     And the Athenian woman by his side,
40   That, when he waked, of force she must be eyed.

(Enter Hermia and Demetrius.)

---

[1] *night rule:* mischief.   [2] *patches:* clowns.   [3] *mechanicals:* workingmen.   [4] *stalls:* shops.   [5] *barren:* empty-headed.   [6] *presented:* represented.   [7] *nole:* noddle, head.   [8] *mimic:* actor.   [9] *russet-pated choughs:* gray-headed jackdaws.   [10] *latched:* caught; i.e., charmed.

OBERON: Stand close. This is the same Athenian.

PUCK: This is the woman, but not this the man.

DEMETRIUS: Oh, why rebuke you him that loves you so?
Lay breath so bitter on your bitter foe.

45 HERMIA: Now I but chide, but I should use thee worse,
For thou, I fear, hast given me cause to curse.
If thou hast slain Lysander in his sleep,
Being o'er shoes in blood, plunge in the deep,
And kill me too.

50 The sun was not so true unto the day
As he to me. Would he have stolen away
From sleeping Hermia? I'll believe as soon
This whole earth may be bored, and that the moon
May through the center[11] creep, and so displease

55 Her brother's noontide with the Antipodes.[12]
It cannot be but thou hast murdered him.
So should a murderer look, so dead,[13] so grim.

DEMETRIUS: So should the murdered look, and so should I,
Pierced through the heart with your stern cruelty.

60 Yet you, the murderer, look as bright, as clear,
As yonder Venus[14] in her glimmering sphere.

HERMIA: What's this to my Lysander? Where is he?
Ah, good Demetrius, wilt thou give him me?

DEMETRIUS: I had rather give his carcass to my hounds.

65 HERMIA: Out, dog! Out, cur! Thou drivest me past the bounds
Of maiden's patience. Hast thou slain him, then?
Henceforth be never numbered among men!
Oh, once tell true, tell true, even for my sake!
Durst thou have looked upon him being awake.

70 And hast thou killed him sleeping? Oh, brave touch.[15]
Could not a worm, an adder, do so much?
An adder did it, for with doubler tongue
Than thine, thou serpent, never adder stung.

DEMETRIUS: You spend your passion on a misprised[16] mood.

75 I am not guilty of Lysander's blood,
Nor is he dead, for aught that I can tell.

HERMIA: I pray thee, tell me then that he is well.

DEMETRIUS: An if I could, what should I get therefore?

HERMIA: A privilege never to see me more.

80 And from thy hated presence part I so.
See me no more, whether he be dead or so. *(Exit.)*

---

[11] *center:* i.e., of the earth.   [12] *so . . . Antipodes:* i.e., the moon will pass through the earth and appear at the other side, to the annoyance of the sun who is shining there.   [13] *dead:* deadly.   [14] *Venus:* i.e., the star.   [15] *touch:* feat.   [16] *misprised:* mistaken.

DEMETRIUS: There is no following her in this fierce vein.
    Here therefore for a while I will remain.
    So sorrow's heaviness doth heavier grow
85   For debt that bankrupt sleep doth sorrow owe,[17]
    Which now in some slight measure it will pay
    If for his tender[18] here I make some stay. *(Lies down and sleeps)*
OBERON: What hast thou done? Thou hast mistaken quite,
    And laid the love juice on some truelove's sight,
90   Of thy misprision[19] must perforce ensue
    Some true love turned, and not a false turned true.
PUCK: Then fate o'errules, that, one man holding troth,
    A million fail, confounding oath on oath.[20]
OBERON: About the wood go swifter than the wind,
95   And Helena of Athens look thou find.
    All fancy-sick[21] she is and pale of cheer,[22]
    With sighs of love that costs the fresh blood[23] dear.
    By some illusion[24] see thou bring her here.
    I'll charm his eyes against[25] she do appear.
100 PUCK: I go, I go, look how I go,
    Swifter than arrow from the Tartar's[26] bow. *(Exit.)*
OBERON: Flower of this purple dye,
    Hit with Cupid's archery,
    Sink in apple of his eye.
105   When his love he doth espy,
    Let her shine as gloriously
    As the Venus of the sky.
    When thou wakest, if she be by,
    Beg of her for remedy.

(Re-enter Puck.)

110 PUCK: Captain of our fairy band,
    Helena is here at hand,
    And the youth, mistook by me,
    Pleading for a lover's fee.
    Shall we their fond pageant see?
115   Lord, what fools these mortals be!
OBERON: Stand aside. The noise they make
    Will cause Demetrius to awake.
PUCK: Then will two at once woo one,
    That must needs be sport alone.

---

[17] *So . . . owe:* a man in sorrow cannot sleep; sleep's debt to sorrow thus becomes heavier.   [18] *tender:* offer; i.e., sleep.   [19] *misprision:* mistake.   [20] *Then . . . oath:* then fate overrules my efforts, for one man true in love, a million are false, breaking oath after oath.   [21] *fancy-sick:* lovesick.   [22] *cheer:* face.   [23] *sighs . . . blood:* It was believed that sighs consumed the heart's blood.   [24] *illusion:* deception.   [25] *against:* by the time that.   [26] *Tartar:* the Tartars, who live in Siberia, were famous bowmen.

120   And those things do best please me
          That befall preposterously.

(Enter Lysander and Helena.)

LYSANDER: Why should you think that I should woo in scorn?
          Scorn and derision never come in tears.
          Look, when I vow, I weep, and vows so born
125   In their nativity all truth appears.
          How can these things in me seem scorn to you,
          Bearing the badge of faith to prove them true?
HELENA: You do advance your cunning more and more.
          When truth kills truth, oh, devilish-holy fray!
130   These vows are Hermia's. Will you give her o'er?
          Weigh oath with oath, and you will nothing weigh.
          Your vows to her and me, put in two scales,
          Will even weigh—and both as light as tales.
LYSANDER: I had no judgment when to her I swore.
135 HELENA: Nor none, in my mind, now you give her o'er.
LYSANDER: Demetrius loves her, and he loves not you.
DEMETRIUS: *(Awaking)* O Helen, goddess, nymph, perfect, divine!
          To what, my love, shall I compare thine eyne?
          Crystal is muddy. Oh, how ripe in show
140   Thy lips, those kissing cherries, tempting grow!
          That pure congealèd white, high Taurus'[27] snow,
          Fanned with the eastern wind, turns to a crow
          When thou hold'st up thy hand. Oh, let me kiss
          This princess of pure white, this seal[28] of bliss!
145 HELENA: Oh, spite! Oh, Hell! I see you all are bent
          To set against me for your merriment.
          If you were civil and knew courtesy,
          You would not do me thus much injury.
          Can you not hate me, as I know you do,
150   But you must join in souls to mock me too?
          If you were men, as men you are in show,
          You would not use a gentle lady so—
          To vow, and swear, and superpraise my parts,
          When I am sure you hate me with your hearts.
155   You both are rivals, and love Hermia,
          And now both rivals, to mock Helena.
          A trim[29] exploit, a manly enterprise,
          To conjure tears up in a poor maid's eyes
          With your derision! None of noble sort
160   Would so offend a virgin, and extort
          A poor soul's patience, all to make you sport.

---

[27] *Taurus:* a range of mountains in Asia Minor.   [28] *seal:* guarantee.   [29] *trim:* fine.

LYSANDER: You are unkind, Demetrius. Be not so;
    For you love Hermia—this you know I know.
    And here, with all goodwill, with all my heart,
165   In Hermia's love I yield you up my part.
    And yours of Helena to me bequeath,
    Whom I do love, and will do till my death.
HELENA: Never did mockers waste more idle breath.
DEMETRIUS: Lysander, keep thy Hermia. I will none.
170   If e'er I loved her, all that love is gone.
    My heart to her but as guest-wise sojourned,[30]
    And now to Helen is it home returned,
    There to remain.
LYSANDER: Helen, it is not so.
DEMETRIUS: Disparage not the faith thou dost not know,
175   Lest, to thy peril, thou aby[31] it dear.
    Look where thy love comes—yonder is thy dear.

(Re-enter Hermia.)

HERMIA: Dark night, that from the eye his function takes,
    The ear more quick of apprehension makes.
    Wherein it doth impair the seeing sense,
180   It pays the hearing double recompense.
    Thou art not by mine eye, Lysander, found;
    Mine ear, I thank it, brought me to thy sound.
    But why unkindly didst thou leave me so?
LYSANDER: Why should he stay whom love doth press to go?
185 HERMIA: What love could press Lysander from my side?
LYSANDER: Lysander's love, that would not let him bide
    Fair Helena, who more engilds the night
    Than all yon fiery oes[32] and eyes of light.
    Why seek'st thou me? Could not this make thee know,
190   The hate I bare thee made me leave thee so?
HERMIA: You speak not as you think. It cannot be.
HELENA: Lo, she is one of this confederacy!
    Now I perceive they have conjoined all three
    To fashion this false sport, in spite of me.[33]
195   Injurious Hermia! Most ungrateful maid!
    Have you conspired, have you with these contrived[34]
    To bait[35] me with this foul derision?
    Is all the counsel that we two have shared,
    The sister's vows, the hours that we have spent,

---

[30] *guest-wise sojourned:* made a short stay.   [31] *aby:* abide, pay for.   [32] *oes:* circles; i.e., stars, with a pun on "o" and "i."   [33] *in . . . me:* to spite me.   [34] *contrived:* devised, plotted.   [35] *bait:* taunt.

200   When we have chid the hasty-footed time
    For parting us—Oh, is it all forgot?
    All school days' friendship, childhood innocence?
    We, Hermia, like two artificial[36] gods,
    Have with our needles created both one flower,
205   Both on one sampler,[37] sitting on one cushion,
    Both warbling of one song, both in one key—
    As if our hands, our sides, voices, and minds
    Had been incorporate.[38] So we grew together,
    Like to a double cherry, seeming parted
210   But yet a union in partition—
    Two lovely berries molded on one stem.
    So, with two seeming bodies, but one heart,
    Two of the first, like coats in heraldry,
    Due but to one, and crownèd with one crest.[39]
215   And will you rent our ancient love asunder,
    To join with men in scorning your poor friend?
    It is not friendly, 'tis not maidenly.
    Our sex, as well as I, may chide you for it,
    Though I alone do feel the injury.
220 **HERMIA:** I am amazèd at your passionate words.
    I scorn you not. It seems that you scorn me.
    HELENA: Have you not set Lysander, as in scorn,
    To follow me and praise my eyes and face?
    And made your other love, Demetrius,
225   Who even but now did spurn me with his foot,
    To call me goddess, nymph, divine and rare,
    Precious, celestial! Wherefore speaks he this
    To her he hates? And wherefore doth Lysander
    Deny your love, so rich within his soul,
230   And tender me, forsooth, affection,
    But by your setting on, by your consent?
    What though I be not so in grace as you,
    So hung upon with love, so fortunate,
    But miserable most, to love unloved?
235   This you should pity rather than despise.
    HERMIA: I understand not what you mean by this.
    HELENA: Aye, do, persever,[40] counterfeit sad looks,
    Make mouths upon me when I turn my back,
    Wink each at other, hold the sweet jest up.

---

[36] *artificial:* creative.   [37] *sampler:* piece of embroidery.   [38] *incorporate:* in one body.
[39] *Two . . . crest:* i.e., two bodies with a single heart—an elaborate mataphor from heraldry. After marriage the coats of arms of husband and wife are united in one coat under one crest.   [40] *persever:* keep it up.

240   This sport, well carried, shall be chronicled.[41]
         If you have any pity, grace, or manners,
         You would not make me such an argument.[42]
         But fare ye well. 'Tis partly my own fault,
         Which death or absence soon shall remedy.
245 Lysander: Stay, gentle Helena, hear my excuse.
         My love, my life, my soul, fair Helena!
    Helena: Oh, excellent!
    Hermia: Sweet, do not scorn her so.
    Demetrius: If she cannot entreat, I can compel.
    Lysander: Thou canst compel no more than she entreat.
250   Thy threats have no more strength than her weak prayers.
         Helen, I love thee, by my life, I do.
         I swear by that which I will lose for thee,
         To prove him false that says I love thee not.
    Demetrius: I say I love thee more than he can do.
255 Lysander: If thou say so, withdraw, and prove it too.
    Demetrius: Quick, come!
    Hermia: Lysander, whereto tends all this?
    Lysander: Away, you Ethiope![43]
    Demetrius: No, no, he'll——
         Seem to break loose,[44] take on as you would follow,
         But yet come not. You are a tame man, go!
260 Lysander: Hang off, thou cat, thou bur! Vile thing, let loose,
         Or I will shake thee from me like a serpent!
    Hermia: Why are you grown so rude? What change is this?
         Sweet love——
    Lysander: Thy love! Out, tawny[45] Tartar, out!
         Out, loathèd medicine! Hated potion, hence!
265 Hermia: Do you not jest?
    Helena: Yes, sooth, and so do you.
    Lysander: Demetrius, I will keep my word with thee.
    Demetrius: I would I had your bond,[46] for I perceive
         A weak bond[47] holds you. I'll not trust your word.
    Lysander: What, should I hurt her, strike her, kill her dead?
270   Although I hate her, I'll not harm her so.
    Hermia: What, can you do me greater harm than hate?
         Hate me! Wherefore? Oh, me! What news, my love!

---

[41] *chronicled:* recorded in the history book.   [42] *argument:* subject for a story.
[43] *Ethiope:* Ethiopian. From the number of references to the dark complexion of different women in Shakespeare's plays it is evident that one of the boy actors was dark-skinned.   [44] *No . . . loose:* There is a difficulty of reading here. Q1 reads "No, no: heele, Seeme to breake loose." The Folio reads: "No, no, Sir, seem to breake loose." This makes sense. Hermia is clutching Lysander; Demetrius taunts him saying that he pretends to want a fight, but is in reality willing enough to be held back by a woman. [45] *tawny:* dark-skinned.   [46] *bond:* written agreement.   [47] *weak bond:* i.e., Hermia.

Am not I Hermia? Are not you Lysander?
I am as fair now as I was erewhile.[48]
275 Since night you loved me, yet since night you left me.
Why, then you left me—Oh, the gods forbid—
In earnest, shall I say?
LYSANDER: Aye, by my life,
And never did desire to see thee more.
Therefore be out of hope, of question, of doubt;
280 Be certain, nothing truer. 'Tis no jest
That I do hate thee, and love Helena.
HERMIA: Oh, me! You juggler! You canker blossom![49]
You thief of love! What, have you come by night
And stolen my love's heart from him?
HELENA: Fine, i'faith!
285 Have you no modesty, no maiden shame,
No touch of bashfulness? What, will you tear
Impatient answers from my gentle tongue?
Fie, fie! You counterfeit, you puppet,[50] you!
HERMIA: Puppet? Why so? Aye, that way goes the game.
290 Now I perceive that she hath made compare
Between our statures, she hath urged her height.
And with her personage, her tall personage,
Her height, forsooth, she hath prevailed with him.
And are you grown so high in his esteem
295 Because I am so dwarfish and so low?
How low am I, thou painted maypole?[51] Speak—
How long am I? I am not yet so low
But that my nails can reach unto thine eyes.
HELENA: I pray you, though you mock me, gentlemen,
300 Let her not hurt me. I was never curst,[52]
I have no gift at all in shrewishness.
I am a right maid[53] for my cowardice.
Let her not strike me. You perhaps may think,
Because she is something lower than myself,
305 That I can match her.
HERMIA: Lower! Hark again.
HELENA: Good Hermia, do not be so bitter with me.
I evermore did love you, Hermia,
Did ever keep your counsels, never wronged you,
Save that, in love unto Demetrius,
310 I told him of your stealth unto this wood.
He followed you, for love I followed him;

---

[48] *erewhile:* a short while ago.   [49] *canker blossom:* worm in the bud.   [50] *puppet:* doll.
[51] *maypole:* because compared to Hermia she is tall and thin.   [52] *curst:* bad-tempered.
[53] *right maid:* truly feminine.

But he hath chid[54] me hence, and threatened me
To strike me, spurn me, nay, to kill me too.
And now, so you will let me quiet go,
315 To Athens will I bear my folly back,
And follow you no further. Let me go.
You see how simple and how fond I am.
HERMIA: Why, get you gone. Who is't that hinders you?
HELENA: A foolish heart, that I leave here behind.
320 HERMIA: What, with Lysander?
HELENA: With Demetrius.
LYSANDER: Be not afraid. She shall not harm thee, Helena.
DEMETRIUS: No, sir, she shall not, though you take her part.
HELENA: Oh, when she's angry, she is keen and shrewd!
She was a vixen when she went to school,
325 And though she be but little, she is fierce.
HERMIA: Little again! Nothing but low and little!
Why will you suffer her to flout me thus?
Let me come to her.
LYSANDER: Get you gone, you dwarf,
You minimus,[56] of hindering knotgrass[57] made,
330 You bead, you acorn.
DEMETRIUS: You are too officious
In her behalf that scorns your services.
Let her alone. Speak not of Helena,
Take not her part; for it thou dost intend
Never so little show of love to her,
335 Thou shalt aby it.
LYSANDER: Now she holds me not.
Now follow, if thou darest, to try whose right,
Of thine or mine, is most in Helena.
DEMETRIUS: Follow! Nay, I'll go with thee, cheek by jole.[58]

(Exeunt Lysander and Demetrius.)

HERMIA: You, mistress, all this coil[59] is 'long of you.
340 Nay, go not back.
HELENA: I will not trust you, I,
Nor longer stay in your curst company.
Your hands than mine are quicker for a fray,
My legs are longer though, to run away. *(Exit.)*
HERMIA: I am amazed, and know not what to say. *(Exit.)*
345 OBERON: This is thy negligence. Still thou mistakest,
Or else committ'st thy knaveries willfully.

---

[54] *chid:* scolded.   [55] *shrewd:* a shrew.   [56] *minimus:* littlest thing.   [57] *hindering knotgrass:* believed to stunt growth; it is a clinging weed.   [58] *cheek by jole:* lit., cheek by jaw.   [59] *coil:* tumult.

PUCK: Believe me, King of Shadows, I mistook.
Did not you tell me I should know the man
By the Athenian garments he had on?
350 And so far blameless proves my enterprise
That I have 'nointed an Athenian's eyes.
And so far am I glad it so did sort,
As this their jangling[60] I esteem a sport.
OBERON: Thou see'st these lovers seek a place to fight.
355 Hie[61] therefore, Robin, overcast the night.
The starry welkin[62] cover thou anon[63]
With drooping fog, as black as Acheron,[64]
And lead these testy rivals to astray
As one come not within another's way.
360 Like to Lysander sometime frame thy tongue,
Then stir Demetrius up with bitter wrong.
And sometime rail thou like Demetrius,
And from each other look thou lead them thus
Till o'er their brows death-counterfeiting sleep
365 With leaden[65] legs and batty wings doth creep.
Then crush this herb into Lysander's eye,
Whose liquor hath this virtuous property,
To take from thence all error with his might,
And make his eyeballs roll with wonted sight.
370 When they next wake, all this derision[66]
Shall seem a dream and fruitless vision,
And back to Athens shall the lovers wend,
With league whose date till death shall never end.[67]
Whiles I in this affair do thee employ,
375 I'll to my Queen and beg her Indian boy.
And then I will her charmèd eye release
From monster's view, and all things shall be peace.
PUCK: My fairy lord, this must be done with haste,
For night's swift dragons[68] cut the clouds full fast,
380 And yonder shines Aurora's[69] harbinger,[70]
At whose approach, ghosts, wandering here and there,
Troop home to churchyards. Damnèd spirits all,
That in crossways[71] and floods have burial,
Already to their wormy beds are gone.
385 For fear lest day should look their shames upon,

---

[60] *jangling:* wrangling.   [61] *Hie:* hasten.   [62] *welkin:* sky.   [63] *anon:* at once.
[64] *Acheron:* river of the underworld.   [65] *leaden:* heavy.   [66] *derision:* mockery.
[67] *With . . . end:* united everlastingly.   [68] *night's . . . dragons:* the dragons which draw
the chariot of Night.   [69] *Aurora:* the dawn.   [70] *harbinger:* forerunner.   [71] *cross-ways:* suicides were buried at crossroads.

They willfully themselves exíle from light,
And must for aye[72] consort with black-browed night.
OBERON: But we are spirits of another sort.[73]
I with the morning's love have oft made sport,
390   And, like a forester, the groves may tread
Even till the eastern gate, all fiery-red,
Opening on Neptune with fair blessèd beams,
Turns into yellow gold his salt green streams.
But, notwithstanding, haste. Make no delay.
395   We may effect this business yet ere day. *(Exit.)*
PUCK: Up and down, up and down,
I will lead them up and down.
I am feared in field and town.
Goblin, lead them up and down.
400   Here comes one.

(Re-enter Lysander.)

LYSANDER: Where art thou, proud Demetrius? Speak thou now.
PUCK: Here, villain, drawn[74] and ready. Where art thou?
LYSANDER: I will be with thee straight.
PUCK: Follow me, then,
To plainer[75] ground.

(Exit Lysander, as following the voice.)

(Re-enter Demetrius.)

DEMETRIUS: Lysander! Speak again.
405   Thou runaway, thou coward, art thou fled?
Speak! In some bush? Where does thou hide thy head?
PUCK: Thou coward, art thou bragging to the stars,
Telling the bushes that thou look'st for wars,
And wilt not come? Come, recreant.[76] Come, thou child,
410   I'll whip thee with a rod. He is defiled
That draws a sword on thee.
DEMETRIUS: Yea, art thou there?
PUCK: Follow my voice. We'll try no manhood here.[77]

(Exeunt.)

(Re-enter Lysander.)

LYSANDER: He goes before me and still dares me on.
When I come where he calls, then he is gone.
415   The villain is much lighter-heeled than I,

---

[72] *aye:* ever.   [73] *another sort:* i.e., not damned or infernal, and so able to endure day-light.   [74] *drawn:* with a sword drawn.   [75] *plainer:* flatter.   [76] *recreant:* traitor.
[77] *We'll . . . here:* we will not make trial of your courage here.

I followed fast, but faster he did fly,
That fallen am I in dark uneven way,
And here will rest me. *(Lies down.)* Come, thou gentle day!
For if but once thou show me thy gray light,
420   I'll find Demetrius, and revenge this spite. *(Sleeps.)*

(Re-enter Puck and Demetrius.)

PUCK: Ho, ho, ho! Coward, why comest thou not?
DEMETRIUS: Abide[78] me, if thou darest, for well I wot[79]
    Thou runn'st before me, shifting every place,
    And darest not stand, nor look me in the face.
425   Where art thou now?
PUCK: Come hither. I am here.
DEMETRIUS: Nay, then, thou mock'st me. Thou shalt buy this dear
    If ever I thy face by daylight see.
    Now, go thy way. Faintness constaineth me
    To measure out my length on this cold bed.
430   By day's approach look to be visited. *(Lies down and sleeps)*

(Re-enter Helena.)

HELENA:
          O weary night, O long and tedious night,
          Abate[80] thy hours! Shine comforts from the east,
       That I may back to Athens by daylight,
          From these that my poor company detest.
435   And sleep, that sometimes shuts up sorrow's eye,
       Steal me awhile from mine own company. *(Lies down and sleeps)*
PUCK: Yet but three? Come one more,
    Two of both kinds makes up four.
    Here she comes, curst and sad.
440   Cupid is a knavish lad,
    Thus to make poor females mad.

(Re-enter Hermia.)

HERMIA:
          Never so weary, never so in woe,
          Bedabbled with the dew, and torn with briers,
       I can no further crawl, no further go,
445   My legs can keep no pace with my desires.
       Here will I rest me till the break of day.
       Heavens shield Lysnder, if they mean a fray! *(Lies down and
       sleeps)*

---

[78] *Abide:* wait for.   [79] *wot:* know.   [80] *Abate:* shorten.

PUCK: On the ground
                 Sleep sound.
450   I'll apply
                 To your eye,
                 Gentle lover, remedy.

(Squeezing the juice on Lysander's eye.)

                 When thou wakest,
                 Thou takest
455   True delight
                 In the sight
                 Of thy former lady's eye.
                 And the country proverb known,
                 That every man should take his own,
460   In your waking shall be shown.
                 Jack shall have Jill,
                 Nought shall go ill,

The man shall have his mare again, and all shall be well. *(Exit.)*

ACT IV
<u>SCENE 1</u>

The same. Lysander, Demetrius, Helena, and Hermia, lying asleep.

(Enter Titania and Bottom; Peaseblossom, Cobweb, Moth, Mustardseed, and other Fairies attending; Oberon behind unseen.)

TITANIA: Come, sit thee down upon this flowery bed,
    While I thy amiable cheeks do coy,[1]
    And stick musk roses in thy sleek smooth head,
      And kiss thy fair large ears, my gentle joy.
5 BOTTOM: Where's Peaseblossom?
PEASEBLOSSOM: Ready.
BOTTOM: Scratch my head, Peaseblossom. Where's Mounsieur Cobweb?
COBWEB: Ready.
BOTTOM: Mounsieur Cobweb, good mounsieur, get you your weapons in
10   your hand, and kill me a red-hipped humblebee on the top of a
    thistle, and, good mounsieur, bring me the honey bag. Do not fret
    yourself too much in the action, mounsieur, and, good mounsieur,
    have a care the honey bag break not. I would be loath to have
    you overflown with a honey bag, signior. Where's Mounsieur
15   Mustardseed?
MUSTARDSEED: Ready.
BOTTOM: Give me your neaf,[2] Mounsieur Mustardseed. Pray you, leave
    your courtesy,[3] good mounsieur.

---

[1] *coy:* caress.   [2] *neaf:* fist.   [3] *leave . . . courtesy:* i.e., there's no need to bow.

MUSTARDSEED: What's your will?

20 BOTTOM: Nothing, good mounsieur, but to help Cavalery[4] Cobweb to
scratch. I must to the barber's, mounsieur, for methinks I am
marvelous hairy about the face, and I am such a tender ass, if my hair
do but tickle me, I must scratch.

TITANIA What, wilt thou hear some music, my sweet love?

25 BOTTOM: I have a reasonable good ear in music.
Let's have the tongs and the bones.

TITANIA: Or say, sweet love, what thou desirest to eat.

BOTTOM: Truly, a peck of provender. I could munch your good dry oats.
Methinks I have a great desire to a bottle[5] of hay. Good hay, sweet
30 hay, hath no fellow.[6]

TITANIA: I have a venturous fairy that shall seek the squirrel's hoard, and
fetch thee new nuts.

BOTTOM: I had rather have a handful or two of dried peas. But I pray you
let none of your people stir me. I have an exposition[7] of sleep come
35 upon me.

TITANIA: Sleep thou, and I will wind thee in my arms. Fairies, be gone,
and be all ways away.

(Exeunt Fairies.)

So doth the woodbine the sweet honeysuckle
Gently entwist, the female ivy so
40 Enrings the barky fingers of the elm.
Oh, how I love thee! How I dote on thee!

(They sleep.)

(Enter Puck.)

OBERON: *(Advancing)* Welcome, good Robin. See'st thou this sweet sight?
Her dotage now I do begin to pity.
For, meeting her of late behind the wood,
45 Seeking sweet favors for this hateful fool,
I did upbraid her, and fall out with her;
For she his hairy temples then had rounded
With coronet of fresh and fragrant flowers,
And that same dew, which sometime on the buds
50 Was wont to swell, like round and orient pearls,
Stood now within the pretty flowerets' eyes
Like tears that did their own disgrace bewail.
When I had at my pleasure taunted her,
And she in mild terms begged my patience,
55 I then did ask of her her changeling child,

---

[4] *Cavalery:* cavaleiro, a gallant soldier.   [5] *bottle:* bundle.   [6] *fellow:* equal.   [7] *exposition:* for "disposition."

Which straight she gave me, and her fairy sent
To bear him to my bower in fairyland.
And now I have the boy, I will undo
This hateful imperfection of her eyes.
60 And, gentle Puck, take this transformèd scalp
From off the head of this Athenian swain,
That, he awaking when the other do,
May all to Athens back again repair,[8]
And think no more of this night's accidents
65 But as the fierce vexation of a dream.
But first I will release the Fairy Queen.
  Be as thou wast wont to be,
  See as thou wast wont to see.
  Dian's[9] bud o'er Cupid's flower
70   Hath such force and blessèd power.
Now, my Titania, wake you, my sweet Queen.
TITANIA: My Oberon! What visions have I seen!
Methought I was enamored of an ass.
OBERON: There lies your love.
TITANIA: How came these things to pass?
75 Oh, how mine eyes do loathe his visage now!
OBERON: Silence awhile. Robin, take off this head.
Titania, music call, and strike more dead
Than common sleep of all these five[10] the sense.[11]
TITANIA: Music, ho! Music, such as charmeth sleep!

(Music, still.)

80 PUCK: Now, when thou wakest, with thine own fool's eyes peep.
OBERON: Sound, music! Come, my Queen, take hands with me,
And rock the ground whereon these sleepers be.
Now thou and I are new in amity,
And will tomorrow midnight solemnly
85 Dance in Duke Theseus' house triumphantly,
And bless it to all fair prosperity.
There shall the pairs of faithful lovers be
Wedded, with Theseus, all in jollity.
PUCK: Fairy King, attend, and mark.
90 I do hear the morning lark.
OBERON: Then, my Queen, in silence sad,[12]
Trip we after night's shade.
We the globe can compass soon,
Swifter than the wandering moon.

---

[8] *repair:* return.   [9] *Dian:* Diana. See I.i.73.   [10] *strike . . . sense:* make them more dead asleep than normal.   [11] *these five:* i.e., Bottom, Demetrius, Lysander, Hermia, and Helena.   [12] *sad:* serious.

95 TITANIA: Come, my lord, and in our flight,
     Tell me how it came this night
     That I sleeping here was found
     With these mortals on the ground.

(Exeunt.)

(Horns winded[13] within. Enter Theseus, Hippolyta, Egeus, and train.)

THESEUS: Go, one of you, find out the forester,
100   For now our observation[14] is performed.
        And since we have the vaward[15] of the day,
        My love shall hear the music of my hounds.
        Uncouple in the western valley, let them go.
        Dispatch, I say, and find the forester.

(Exit an Attendant.)

105   We will, fair Queen, up to the mountain's top,
        And mark the musical confusion
        Of hounds and echo in conjunction.
     HIPPOLYTA: I was with Hercules and Cadmus once
        When in a wood of Crete they bayed[16] the bear
110   With hounds of Sparta. Never did I hear
        Such gallant chiding;[17] for, besides the groves,
        The skies, the fountains, every region near
        Seemed all one mutual cry. I never heard
        So musical a discord, such sweet thunder.
115 THESEUS: My hounds are bred out of the Spartan kind,
        So flewed,[18] so sanded;[19] and their heads are hung
        With ears that sweep away the morning dew;
        Crook-kneed, and dewlapped[20] like Thessalian bulls;
        Slow in pursuit, but matched in mouth like bells,[21]
120   Each under each.[22] A cry[23] more tunable
        Was never holloed to, nor cheered with horn,
        In Crete, in Sparta, nor in Thessaly.
        Judge when you hear. But, soft! What nymphs are these?
     EGEUS: My lord, this is my daughter here asleep.
125   And this, Lysander. This Demetrius is,
        This Helena, old Nedar's Helena.
        I wonder of their being here together.

---

[13] *winded:* sounded.   [14] *observation:* i.e., the rites of May. See 1.1.167.   [15] *vaward:* forepart.   [16] *bayed:* brought to bay.   [17] *chiding:* barking.   [18] *flewed:* with hanging cheeks.   [19] *sanded:* sandy colored.   [20] *dewlapped:* the dewlap is a flap of loose skin hanging down from the throats of cattle and certain kinds of dog and hound.
[21] *matched . . . bells:* In a perfect pack of hounds each hound uttered a different note, the whole effect being a harmony.   [22] *Each . . . each:* one a note lower than the other.   [23] *cry:* pack of hounds.

THESEUS: No doubt they rose up early to observe
    The rite of May, and, hearing our intent,
130   Came here in grace of[24] our solemnity.[25]
    But speak, Egëus, is not this the day
    That Hermia should give answer of her choice?
EGEUS: It is, my lord.
THESEUS: Go, bid the huntsmen wake them with their horns.

(Horns and shout within.[26] Lysander, Demetrius, Helena, and Hermia, wake and start up.)

135   Good morrow, friends. Saint Valentine[27] is past.
    Begin these wood birds but to couple now?
LYSANDER: Pardon, my lord.
THESEUS: I pray you all, stand up.
    I know you two are rival enemies.
    How comes this gentle concord in the world,
140   That hatred is so far from jealousy,
    To sleep by hate, and fear no enmity?
LYSANDER: My lord, I shall reply amazedly,
    Half sleep, half waking. But as yet, I swear,
    I cannot truly say how I came here,
145   But, as I think—for truly would I speak,
    And now I do bethink me, so it is—
    I came with Hermia hither. Our intent
    Was to be gone from Athens, where we might,
    Without the peril[28] of the Athenian law—
150 EGEUS: Enough, enough, my lord, you have enough.
    I beg the law, the law, upon his head.
    They would have stolen away. They would, Demetrius,
    Thereby to have defeated you and me,
    You of your wife and me of my consent—
155   Of my consent that she should be your wife.
DEMETRIUS: My lord, fair Helen told me of their stealth,
    Of this their purpose hither to this wood.
    And I in fury hither followed them,
    Fair Helena in fancy[29] following me.
160   But, my good lord, I wot not by what power—
    But by some power it is—my love to Hermia,
    Melted as the snow, seems to me now
    As the remembrance of an idle gaud[30]
    Which in my childhood I did dote upon.
165   And all the faith, the virtue of my heart,

---

[24] *in . . . of:* in compliment to.   [25] *solemnity:* celebration.   [26] *within:* off stage.
[27] *Saint Valentine:* the day on which birds were supposed to mate.   [28] *With-out . . . peril:* beyond danger.   [29] *fancy:* love.   [30] *gaud:* trifle.

The object and the pleasure of mine eye,
Is only Helena. To her, my lord,
Was I betrothed ere I saw Hermia.
But, like in sickness, did I loathe this food,
170 But, as in health, come to my natural taste,
Now I do wish it, love it, long for it,
And will forevermore be true to it.
THESEUS: Fair lovers, you are fortunately met.
Of this discourse we more will hear anon.
175 Egëus, I will overbear your will,
For in the temple, by and by, with us
These couples shall eternally be knit.
And, for[31] the morning now is something worn,
Our purposed hunting shall be set aside.
180 Away with us to Athens! Three and three,[32]
We'll hold a feast in great solemnity.
Come, Hippolyta.

(Exeunt Theseus, Hippolyta, Egeus, and train.)

DEMETRIUS: These things seem small and undistinguishable,
Like far-off mountains turnèd into clouds.
185 HERMIA: Methinks I see these things with parted eye,
When everything seems double.
HELENA: So methinks.
And I have found Demetrius like a jewel,
Mine own, and not mine own.
DEMETRIUS: Are you sure
That we are awake? It seems to me
190 That yet we sleep, we dream. Do not you think
The Duke was here, and bid us follow him?
HERMIA: Yea, and my father.
HELENA: And Hippolyta.
LYSANDER: And he did bid us follow to the temple.
DEMETRIUS: Why, then, we are awake. Let's follow him,
195 And by the way let us recount our dreams.

(Exeunt.)

BOTTOM: *(Awaking)* When my cue comes, call me, and I will answer. My
next is "Most fair Pyramus." Heigh-ho! Peter Quince! Flute, the
bellows-mender! Snout, the tinker! Starveling! God's my life, stolen
hence, and left me asleep! I have had a most rare vision. I have had a
200 dream past the wit of man to say what dream it was. Man is but an
ass if he go about to expound this dream. Methought I was—there is
no man can tell what. Methought I was—and methought I had—but

---

[31] *for:* since.   [32] *Three . . . three:* i.e., a triple wedding.

man is but a patched[33] fool if he will offer to say what methought I
had. The eye of man hath not heard, the ear of man hath not seen,
205 man's hand is not able to taste, his tongue to conceive, nor his heart
to report, what my dream was. I will get Peter Quince to write a
ballad of this dream. It shall be called Bottom's Dream, because it
hath no bottom, and I will sing it in the latter end of a play, before
the Duke. Peradventure,[34] to make it the more gracious, I shall sing it
210 at her death.[35] *(Exit.)*

SCENE 2

Athens. Quince's house.

(Enter Quince, Flute, Snout, and Starveling.)

QUINCE: Have you sent to Bottom's house? Is he come home yet?
STARVELING: He cannot be heard of. Out of doubt he is transported.[1]
FLUTE: If he come not, then the play is marred. It goes not forward,
doth it?
5 QUINCE: It is not possible. You have not a man in all Athens able to
discharge Pyramus but he.
FLUTE: No, he hath simply the best wit of any handicraft man in Athens.
QUINCE: Yea, and the best person too, and he is a very paramour for a
sweet voice.
10 FLUTE: You must say "paragon." A paramour is, God bless us, a thing of
naught.[2]

(Enter Snug.)

SNUG: Masters, the Duke is coming from the temple, and there is two or
three lords and ladies more married. If our sport had gone forward,
we had all been made men.
15 FLUTE: Oh, sweet bully Bottom! Thus hath he lost sixpence a day during
his life;[3] he could not have scaped sixpence a day. An the Duke had
not given him sixpence a day for playing Pyramus, I'll be hanged. He
would have deserved it. Sixpence a day in Pyramus, or nothing.

(Enter Bottom.)

BOTTOM: Where are these lads? Where are these hearts?
20 QUINCE: Bottom! Oh, most courageous day! Oh, most happy hour!
BOTTOM: Masters, I am to discourse wonders. But ask me not what, for if I
tell you I am no true Athenian. I will tell you everything, right as it
fell out.

---

[33] *patched:* wearing a particolored coat, the regular costume of a professional fool.
[34] *Peradventure:* perchance.   [35] *at . . . death:* i.e., Thisby's at the end of the play.

---

[1] *transported:* carried off.   [2] *naught:* wickedness.   [3] *sixpence . . . life:* i.e., a royal
pension of sixpence a day for life.

QUINCE: Let us hear, sweet Bottom.

25 BOTTOM: Not a word of me. All that I will tell you is that the Duke hath
dined. Get your apparel together, good strings[4] to your beards, new
ribbons to your pumps.[5] Meet presently[6] at the palace. Every man
look o'er his part, for the short and the long is, our play is preferred.[7]
In any case, let Thisby have clean linen, and let not him that plays
30 the lion pare his nails, for they shall hang out for the lion's claws.
And, most dear actors, eat no onions nor garlic, for we are to utter
sweet breath, and I do not doubt but to hear them say it is a sweet
comedy. No more words. Away! Go, away!

(Exeunt.)

ACT V
SCENE 1

Athens. The palace of Theseus.

(Enter Theseus, Hippolyta, Philostrate, Lords, and Attendants.)

HIPPOLYTA: 'Tis strange, my Theseus, that these lovers speak of.
THESEUS: More strange than true. I never may believe
These antique fables, nor these fairy toys.[1]
Lovers and madmen have such seething brains,
5   Such shaping fantasies,[2] that apprehend
More than cool reason ever comprehends.
The lunatic, the lover, and the poet
Are of imagination all compact.[3]
One sees more devils than vast Hell can hold,
10   That is the madman. The lover, all as frantic,
Sees Helen's beauty in a brow of Egypt.[4]
The poet's eye, in a fine frenzy rolling,
Doth glance from heaven to earth, from earth to heaven,
And as imagination bodies forth
15   The forms of things unknown, the poet's pen
Turns them to shapes, and gives to airy nothing
A local habitation and a name.
Such tricks hath strong imagination
That if it would but apprehend some joy,
20   It comprehends some bringer of that joy;

---

[4] *strings:* i.e., for tying them on.   [5] *pumps:* shoes.   [6] *presently:* immediately.
[7] *preferred:* accepted.

---

[1] *fairy toys:* trifling tales about fairies.   [2] *fantasies:* fancies.   [3] *Are . . . compact:*
wholly composed of imagination—which in Shakespeare's time meant the "power of
seeing things."   [4] *Sees . . . Egypt:* i.e., to the lover a gypsy is as beautiful as Helen of
Troy. Gypsies were supposed to be Egyptians.

Or in the night, imagining some fear,
How easy is a bush supposed a bear!
HIPPOLYTA: But all the story of the night told over,
And all their minds transfigured[5] so together,

25   More witnesseth than fancy's images,
And grows to something of great constancy,[6]
But, howsoever, strange and admirable.[7]
THESEUS: Here come the lovers, full of joy and mirth.

(Enter Lysander, Demetrius, Hermia, and Helena.)

Joy, gentle friends! Joy and fresh days of love

30   Accompany your hearts!
LYSANDER: More than to us
Wait in your royal walks, your board, your bed!
THESEUS: Come now, what masques,[8] what dances shall we have
To wear away this long age of three hours
Between our after-supper and bedtime?

35   Where is our usual manager of mirth?
What revels are in hand? Is there no play
To ease the anguish of a torturing hour?
Call Philostrate.
PHILOSTRATE: Here, mighty Theseus.
THESEUS: Say, what abridgment[9] have you for this evening?

40   What masque? What music? How shall we beguile
The lazy time, if not with some delight?
PHILOSTRATE: There is a brief[10] how many sports are ripe.[11]
Make choice of which your Highness will see first. *(Giving a paper)*
THESEUS: *(Reads.)* "The battle with the Centaurs,[12] to be sung

45   By an Athenian eunuch to the harp."
We'll none of that. That have I told my love,
In glory of my kinsman Hercules.
"The riot of the tipsy Bacchanals,
Tearing the Thracian singer in their rage."[13]

50   That is an old device, and it was played
When I from Thebes came last a conqueror.
"The thrice three Muses mourning for the death
Of Learning,[14] late deceased in beggary."

---

[5] *transfigured:* excited.   [6] *constancy:* consistency; i.e., the fact that they are all ex-cited shows that something strange has happened to them.   [7] *admirable:* marvelous.
[8] *masques:* courtly entertainments.   [9] *abridgment:* pastime, entertainment.   [10] *brief:* list.   [11] *ripe:* ready.   [12] *Centaurs:* creatures half man, half horse.   [13] *riot . . . rage:* the story of how Orpheus the singer was torn in pieces by the frenzied women wor-shippers of Bacchus.   [14] *death . . . learning:* Depending on when this portion of the play was last revised, the words most likely refer to the death of either the English poet and dramatist Robert Greene (1592) or the English poet Edmund Spenser (1599).

That is some satire, keen and critical,
55   Not sorting with a nuptial ceremony.
        "A tedious brief scene of young Pyramus
        And his love Thisbe, very tragical mirth."
        Merry and tragical! Tedious and brief!
        That is, hot ice and wondrous strange snow.
60   How shall we find the concord of this discord?
    PHILOSTRATE: A play there is, my lord, some ten words long,
        Which is as brief as I have known a play.
        But by ten words, my lord, it is too long,
        Which makes it tedious; for in all the play
65   There is not one word apt, one player fitted.
        And tragical, my noble lord, it is,
        For Pyramus therein doth kill himself.
        Which, when I saw rehearsed, I must confess
        Made mine eyes water, but more merry tears
70   The passion of loud laughter never shed.
    THESEUS: What are they that do play it?
    PHILOSTRATE: Hardhanded men that work in Athens here,
        Which never labored in their minds till now,
        And now have toiled their unbreathed[15] memories
75   With this same play, against[16] your nuptial.
    THESEUS: And we will hear it.
    PHILOSTRATE: No, my noble lord,
        It is not for you. I have heard it over,
        And it is nothing, nothing in the world—
        Unless you can find sport in their intents,[17]
80   Extremely stretched[18] and conned with cruel pain,[19]
        To do you service.
    THESEUS: I will hear that play,
        For never anything can be amiss,
        When simpleness and duty tender it.
        Go, bring them in, and take your places, ladies.

    (Exit Philostrate.)

85 HIPPOLYTA: I love not to see wretchedness o'ercharged,[20]
        And duty in his service perishing.[21]
    THESEUS: Why, gentle sweet, you shall see no such thing.
    HIPPOLYTA: He says they can do nothing in this kind.[22]
    THESEUS: The kinder we, to give them thanks for nothing.
90   Our sport shall be to take what they mistake.

---

[15] *unbreathed:* unpracticed.   [16] *against:* in anticipation of.   [17] *intents:* intentions.
[18] *Extremely stretched:* overreaching themselves.   [19] *pain:* labor.   [20] *wretchedness o'ercharged:* poor men trying to do too much.   [21] *duty . . . perishing:* a subject ruining himself through excess of zeal.   [22] *kind:* i.e., acting.

And what poor duty cannot do, noble respect
Takes it in might, not merit.[23]
Where I have come, great clerks[24] have purposed
To greet me with premeditated welcomes,
95   Where I have seen them shiver and look pale,
Make periods in the midst of sentences,
Throttle their practiced accent in their fears,
And, in conclusion, dumbly have broke off,
Nor paying me a welcome. Trust me, sweet,
100   Out of this silence yet I picked a welcome,
And in the modesty of fearful[25] duty
I read as much as from the rattling tongue
Of saucy and audacious eloquence.
Love, therefore, and tongue-tied simplicity
105   In least speak most, to my capacity.[26]

(Re-enter Philostrate.)

PHILOSTRATE: So please your Grace, the Prologue is addressed.[27]
THESEUS: Let him approach.

(Flourish of trumpets. Enter Quince for the Prologue.)

PROLOGUE: If[28] we offend, it is with our goodwill.
     That you should think, we come not to offend,
110   But with goodwill. To show our simple skill,
     That is the true beginning of our end.
Consider, then, we come but in despite.[29]
     We do not come, as minding to content you,
Our true intent is. All for your delight,
115   We are not here. That you should here repent you,
The actors are at hand, and, by their show,
You shall know all, that you are like to know.
THESEUS: This fellow doth not stand upon points.[30]
LYSANDER: He hath rid his prologue like a rough colt, he knows not the
120   stop. A good moral, my lord. It is not enough to speak, but to speak
     true.
HIPPOLYTA: Indeed he hath played on his prologue like a child on a
     recorder[31]—a sound, but not in government.[32]
THESEUS: His speech was like a tangled chain—nothing impaired, but all
125   disordered. Who is next?

(Enter Pyramus and Thisbe. Wall, Moonshine, and Lion.)

---

[23] *noble . . . merit:* i.e., a noble mind accepts the good intention for the bad performance.   [24] *great clerks:* learned scholars.   [25] *fearful:* full of fear.   [26] *capacity:*
understanding.   [27] *addressed:* ready.   [28] *If . . . know:* Quince, by mistaking his
punctuation, makes woeful sense of his words.   [29] *despite:* ill will.   [30] *stand
. . . points:* observe his punctuation marks.   [31] *recorder:* musical instrument.
[32] *government:* control.

PROLOGUE: Gentles, perchance you wonder at this show,
    But wonder on, till truth make all things plain.
This man is Pyramus, if you would know.
This beauteous lady Thisby is certáin.
130 This man, with lime and roughcast, doth present
    Wall, that vile Wall which did these lovers sunder,
And through Wall's chink, poor souls, they are content
    To whisper. At the which let no man wonder.
This man, with lanthorn,[33] dog, and bush of thorn,
135   Presenteth Moonshine; for, if you will know,
By moonshine did these lovers think no scorn
    To meet at Ninus' tomb, there, there to woo.
This grisly beast, which Lion hight[34] by name,
    The trusty Thisby, coming first by night,
140 Did scare away, or rather did affright.
    And, as she fled, her mantle she did fall,[35]
    Which Lion vile with bloody mouth did stain.
Anon comes Pyramus, sweet youth and tall,
    And finds his trusty Thisby's mantle slain.
145 Whereat, with blade, with bloody blameful blade,
    He bravely broached his boiling bloody breast.
And Thisby, tarrying in mulberry shade,
    His dagger drew, and died. For all the rest,
Let Lion, Moonshine, Wall, and lovers twain
150   At large discourse, while here they do remain.

(Exeunt Prologue, Pyramus, Thisbe, Lion, and Moonshine.)

THESEUS: I wonder if the lion be to speak.
DEMETRIUS: No wonder, my lord. One lion may when many asses do.
WALL: In this same interlude it doth befall
    That I, one Snout by name, present a wall,
155 And such a wall, as I would have you think,
    That had in it a crannied[36] hole or chink,
Through which the lovers, Pyramus and Thisby,
    Did whisper often very secretly.
This loam, this roughcast, and this stone doth show
160 That I am that same wall. The truth is so.
    And this the cranny is, right and siníster,[37]
Through which the fearful lovers are to whisper.
THESEUS: Would you desire lime and hair to speak better?
DEMETRIUS: It is the wittiest partition that ever I heard discourse, my
165   lord.
THESEUS: Pyramus draws near the wall. Silence!

---

[33] *lanthorn:* lantern with horn sides.   [34] *hight:* called.   [35] *fall:* let fall.   [36] *crannied:* cracked.   [37] *sinister:* left-handed.

(Re-enter Pyramus.)

PYRAMUS: O grim-looked night! O night with hue so black!
　　　O night, which ever art when day is not!
　　　O night, O night! alack, alack, alack,
170　　I fear my Thisby's promise is forgot!
　　　And thou, O wall, O sweet, O lovely wall,
　　　That stand'st between her father's ground and mine!
　　　Thou wall, O wall, O sweet and lovely wall,
　　　Show me thy chink, to blink through with mine eyne!

(Wall holds up his fingers.)

175　　Thanks, courteous wall. Jove shield thee well for this!
　　　But what see I? No Thisby do I see.
　　　O wicked wall, through whom I see no bliss!
　　　Cursed be thy stones for thus deceiving me!
THESEUS: The wall, methinks, being sensible,[38] should curse again.
180 PYRAMUS: No, in truth, sir, he should not. "Deceiving me" is Thisby's
　　　cue. She is to enter now, and I am to spy her through the wall. You
　　　shall see, it will fall pat as I told you. Yonder she comes.

(Re-enter Thisbe.)

THISBE: O wall, full often hast thou heard my moans,
　　　For parting my fair Pyramus and me!
185　　My cherry lips have often kissed thy stones,
　　　Thy stones with lime and hair knit up in thee.
PYRAMUS: I see a voice. Now will I to the chink,
　　　To spy an I can hear my Thisby's face.
　　　Thisby!
190 THISBE: My love thou art, my love I think.
PYRAMUS: Think what thou wilt, I am thy lover's grace;
　　　And, like Limander,[39] am I trusty still.
THISBE: And I like Helen,[40] till the Fates me kill.
PYRAMUS: Not Shafalus to Procrus[41] was so true.
195 THISBE: As Shafalus to Procrus, I to you.
PYRAMUS: Oh, kiss me through the hole of this vile wall!
THISBE: I kiss the wall's hole, not your lips at all.
PYRAMUS: Wilt thou at Ninny's tomb meet me straight way?
THISBE: 'Tide life, 'tide death, I come without delay.

(Exeunt Pyramus and Thisbe.)

200 WALL: Thus have I, wall, my part dischargèd so;
　　　And, being done, thus wall away doth go. *(Exit.)*

---

[38] *being sensible:* having feeling.　[39] *Limander:* for "Leander."　[40] *Helen:* for "Hero,"
Leander's love.　[41] *Shafalus to Procrus:* Cephalus to Procris.

THESEUS: Now is the mural[42] down between the two neighbors.

DEMETRIUS: No remedy, my lord, when walls are so willful to hear without warning.

205 HIPPOLYTA: This is the silliest stuff that ever I heard.

THESEUS: The best in this kind are but shadows,[43] and the worst are no worse if imagination amend them.

HIPPOLYTA: It must be your imagination, then, and not theirs.

THESEUS: If we imagine no worse of them than they of themselves, they

210 may pass for excellent men. Here come two noble beasts in, a man and a lion.

(Re-enter Lion and Moonshine.)

LION: You, ladies, you, whose gentle hearts do fear
    The smallest monstrous mouse that creeps on floor,
    May now perchance both quake and tremble here,
215   When lion rough in wildest rage doth roar.
    Then know that I, one Snug the joiner, am
    A lion fell,[44] nor else no lion's dam;
    For, if I should as lion come in strife
    Into this place, 'twere pity on my life.[45]

220 THESEUS: A very gentle beast, and of a good conscience.

DEMETRIUS: The very best at a beast, my lord, that e'er I saw.

LYSANDER: This lion is a very fox for his valor.

THESEUS: True, and a goose for his discretion.

DEMETRIUS: Not so, my lord, for his valor cannot carry his discretion, and

225 the fox carries the goose.

THESEUS: His discretion, I am sure, cannot carry his valor, for the goose carries not the fox. It is well. Leave it to his discretion, and let us listen to the moon.

MOONSHINE: This lanthorn doth the hornèd moon present——

230 DEMETRIUS: He should have worn the horns on his head.

THESEUS: He is no crescent, and his horns are invisible within the circumference.

MOONSHINE: This lanthorn doth the hornèd moon present,
    Myself the man i' the moon do seem to be.

235 THESEUS: This is the greatest error of all the rest. The man should be put into the lantern. How is it else the man i' the moon?

DEMETRIUS: He dares not come there for the candle, for you see it is already in snuff.[46]

HIPPOLYTA: I am aweary of this moon. Would he would change!

---

[42] *mural:* wall.   [43] *shadows:* things of no substance.   [44] *fell:* fierce.   [45] *pity . . . life:* i.e., I should be hanged for it.   [46] *in snuff:* smoking. Before self-consuming wicks were invented for candles, wicks had to be snuffed (cut) constantly or they would smoke foully.

240 THESEUS: It appears, by his small light of discretion, that he is in the
wane. But yet, in courtesy, in all reason, we must stay the time.[47]

LYSANDER: Proceed, Moon.

MOONSHINE: All that I have to say is, to tell you that the lanthorn is the
moon; I, the man i' the moon; this thornbush, my thornbush; and
245 this dog, my dog.

DEMETRIUS: Why, all these should be in the lantern, for all these are in
the moon. But, silence! Here comes Thisbe.

(Re-enter Thisbe.)

THISBE This is old Ninny's tomb. Where is my love?

LION: *(Roaring)* Oh——

(Thisbe runs off.)

250 DEMETRIUS: Well roared, Lion.

THESEUS: Well run, Thisbe.

HIPPOLYTA: Well shone, Moon. Truly, the moon shines with a good grace.

(The Lion shakes Thisbe's mantle, and exit.)

THESEUS: Well moused,[48] Lion.

LYSANDER: And so the lion vanished.

255 DEMETRIUS: And then came Pyramus.

(Re-enter Pyramus.)

PYRAMUS: Sweet Moon, I thank thee for thy sunny beams,
I thank thee, Moon, for shining now so bright.
For, by thy gracious, golden, glittering gleams,
I trust to take of truest Thisby sight.
260 But stay, oh, spite!
But mark, poor knight,
What dreadful dole[49] is here!
Eyes, do you see?
How can it be?
265 Oh, dainty duck! Oh, dear!
Thy mantle good,
What, stained with blood!
Approach, ye Furies fell!
O Fates, come, come,
270 Cut thread and thrum,[50]
Quail,[51] crush, conclude, and quell![52]

THESEUS: This passion, and the death of a dear friend, would go near to
make a man look sad.

---

[47] *stay . . . time:* see it out.　　[48] *moused:* torn as a cat tears a mouse.　　[49] *dole:* dolor,
grief.　　[50] *thrum:* lit., the end of the thread in a piece of weaving. So *cut thread and
thrum* means "destroy everything."　　[51] *Quail:* overwhelm.　　[52] *quell:* slay.

HIPPOLYTA: Beshrew my heart, but I pity the man.
275 PYRAMUS: O wherefore, Nature, didst thou lions frame?
    Since lion vile hath here deflowered my dear,
    Which is—no, no—which was the fairest dame
    That lived, that loved, that liked, that looked with cheer.
       Come, tears, confound.
280   Out, sword, and wound
    The pap of Pyramus.
       Aye, that let pap,
       Where heart doth hop.

(Stabs himself.)

    Thus die I, thus, thus, thus.
285   Now am I dead,
       Now am I fled,
    My soul is in the sky.
       Tongue, lose thy light,
       Moon, take thy flight,

(Exit Moonshine.)

290   Now die, die, die, die, die. *(Dies.)*
DEMETRIUS: No die, but an ace,[53] for him,[54] for he is but one.
LYSANDER: Less than an ace, man, for he is dead, he is nothing.
THESEUS: With the help of a surgeon he might yet recover, and prove an
    ass.
295 HIPPOLYTA: How chance Moonshine is gone before Thisbe comes back and
    finds her lover?
THESEUS: She will find him by starlight. Here she comes, and her passion
    ends the play.

(Re-enter Thisbe.)

HIPPOLYTA: Methinks she should not use a long one for such a Pyramus. I
300   hope she will be brief.
DEMETRIUS: A mote[55] will turn the balance, which Pyramus, which
    Thisbe, is the better—he for a man, God warrant us, she for a woman,
    God bless us.
LYSANDER: She hath spied him already with those sweet eyes.
305 DEMETRIUS: And thus she means, videlicet:[56]
THISBE: Asleep, my love?
                    What, dead, my dove?
                    O Pyramus, arise!
                    Speak, speak. Quite dumb?
310   Dead, dead? A tomb

---

[53]*ace:* throw of one.   [54]*No . . . him:* Demetrius makes a poor pun on *die* (perish) and *die* (singular of "dice").   [55]*mote:* speck of dust.   [56]*videlicet:* namely, "viz."

Must cover thy sweet eyes.
　These lily lips,
　This cherry nose,
These yellow cowslip cheeks,
315　　　　Are gone, are gone.
　Lovers, make moan.
His eyes were green as leeks.
　O Sisters Three,[57]
　Come, come to me,
320　With hands as pale as milk,
　Lay them in gore,
　Since you have shore
With shears his thread of silk.
　Tongue, not a word.
325　　　Come, trusty sword,
Come, blade, my breast imbrue.[58]

(Stabs herself.)

And, farewell, friends.
Thus Thisby ends.
Adieu, adieu, adieu. *(Dies)*

330 THESEUS: Moonshine and Lion are left to bury the dead.
DEMETRIUS: Aye, and Wall too.
BOTTOM: *(Starting up)* No, I assure you the wall is down that parted
　　their fathers. Will it please you to see the epilogue, or to hear a
　　Bergomask[59] dance between two of our company?
335 THESEUS: No epilogue, I pray you, for your play needs no excuse. Never
　　excuse, for when the players are all dead, there need none to be
　　blamed. Marry, if he that writ it had played Pyramus and hanged
　　himself in Thisbe's garter, it would have been a fine tragedy. And so
　　it is, truly, and very notably discharged. But, come, your Bergomask.
340　　Let your epilogue alone.

(A dance.)

The iron tongue of midnight hath told twelve.
Lovers, to bed, 'tis almost fairy time.
I fear we shall outsleep the coming morn
As much as we this night have overwatched.
345 This palpable-gross[60] play hath well beguiled
The heavy gait of night. Sweet friends, to bed.
A fortnight hold we this solemnity,
In nightly revels and new jollity.

---

[57] *Sisters Three:* the three Fates who sit spinning man's destiny.　　[58] *imbrue:* make
bloody.　　[59] *Bergomask:* a rough country-dance, named after the province of Bergamo
in Italy, whose people were noted for their rustic manners.　　[60] *palpable-gross:* crudely
gross.

(Exeunt.)

(Enter Puck.)

PUCK: Now the hungry lion roars,
350   And the wolf behowls the moon,
Whilst the heavy plowman snores,
    All with weary task fordone.[61]
Now the wasted brands[62] do glow,
    Whilst the screech owl, screeching loud,
355 Puts the wretch that lies in woe
    In remembrance of a shroud.
Now it is the time of night
    That the graves, all gaping wide,
Every one lets forth his sprite,
360   In the churchway paths to glide.
And we fairies, that do run
    By the triple Hecate's[63] team,
From the presence of the sun,
    Following darkness like a dream,
365 Now are frolic. Not a mouse
Shall disturb this hallowed house.
I am sent with broom before,
To sweep the dust behind the door.

(Enter Oberon and Titania with their train.)

OBERON: Through the house give glimmering light,
370   By the dead and drowsy fire.
Every elf and fairy sprite
    Hop as light as bird from brier,
And this ditty, after me,
Sing, and dance it trippingly.
375 TITANIA: First, rehearse your song by rote,
To each word a warbling note.
Hand in hand, with fairy grace,
Will we sing, and bless this place.

(Song and dance.)

OBERON: Now, until the break of day,
380   Through this house each fairy stray.
To the best bridebed will we,
Which by us shall blessèd be,

---

[61] *fordone:* overcome.   [62] *brands:* fire-brands.   [63] *triple Hecate:* The goddess Diana is sometimes referred to as three-formed, because she was worshiped as Luna (or Cynthia), the Moon, in Heaven; Diana on earth; and Proserpine (or *Hecate*) in Hades.

And the issue there create
Ever shall be fortunate.
385 So shall all the couples three
Ever true in loving be,
And the blots of Nature's hand
Shall not in their issue stand—
Never mole, harelip, nor scar,
390 Nor mark prodigious,[64] such as are
Despisèd in nativity,
Shall upon their children be.
With this field dew consecrate,
Every fairy take his gait,
395 And each several[65] chamber bless,
Through this palace, with sweet peace,
And the owner of it blest,
Ever shall in safety rest.
Trip away, make no stay,
400 Meet me all by break of day.

(Exeunt Oberon, Titania, and train.)

PUCK: If we shadows have offended,
Think but this, and all is mended,
That you have but slumbered here
While these visions did appear,
405 And this weak and idle theme,
No more yielding but a dream,
Gentles, do not reprehend.
If you pardon, we will mend.
And, as I am an honest Puck,
410 If we have unearnèd luck
Now to scape the serpent's tongue,[66]
We will make amends ere long,
Else the Puck a liar call.
So, good night unto you all.
415 Give me your hands,[67] if we be friends,
And Robin shall restore amends. *(Exit.)*

READING AND REACTING

1. What are the two settings of *A Midsummer Night's Dream*? How do they help to define the action of the play?
2. This play contains very few stage directions. How does Shakespeare establish the settings of the play? How does he indicate the actions of the various characters?

---

[64] *prodigious:* unnatural.   [65] *several:* separate.   [66] *serpent's tongue:* i.e., hissing.
[67] *Give . . . hands:* clap.

3. What costumes might highligh the most distinctive character traits of the following characters: Theseus, Hermia, Bottom, Hippolyta, Oberon, and Puck?

4. Musical interludes occur throughout *A Midsummer Night's Dream* (see act 2, scene 3, for example). How does music help to establish the mood of the play? In what way does it underscore the play's themes?

5. What is the significance of Oberon's flower? What kind of prop would you design to represent it?

6. Would you use a realistic ass's head on Bottom, or would some other alternative be more effective? Explain your answer.

7. The role of Puck is frequently played by a female. How might you explain this casting decision? How would you cast Puck?

8. Theseus's final speech is interrupted by a dance of clowns. What do you think the purpose of this dance is? If you were directing the play, would you include or delete this interlude?

9. How would you use lighting to establish the mood of act 3?

10. **JOURNAL ENTRY** A critic has observed that *A Midsummer Night's Dream* "does not read as well as it plays." What do you think he means? What, if anything does one lose by reading this play instead of seeing it?

11. **CRITICAL PERSPECTIVE** In his commentary on *A Midsummer Night's Dream,* Charles Boyce says, "Scholars generally agree that *A Midsummer Night's Dream* was written to be performed at an aristocratic wedding. Everything in the play is related to the theme of marriage." What elements of the play do you think are related to "the theme of marriage"? What "message" does Shakespeare's play have for those who are about to be married?

Related Works: "Sleepy Time Gal" (p. 242), "Araby" (p. 254), "Young Goodman Brown" (p. 304), "The Passionate Shepherd to His Love" (p. 682), "La Belle Dame sans Merci" (p. 969), *The Brute* (p. 1266)

◊ **EDWARD ALBEE** (1928–   ) was abandoned by his parents as an infant and adopted by a wealthy couple, Reed and Frances Albee. He was always a writer, producing two unpublished novels in his teens, but did not turn to playwriting until his thirtieth birthday. A rebellious teenager, he was expelled from several schools and then lasted only a year at Trinity College. Now one of America's foremost and most controversial playwrights in the theater of the absurd, his most famous plays are *The Zoo Story* (1958), *The American Dream* (1961), *Who's Afraid of Virginia Woolf?* (1962), *The Marriage Play* (1992), and *Three Tall Women* (1994), which won Albee his third Pulitzer

Prize. *The Sandbox* (1960), a one-act play, is closely related to *The American Dream*. Not only are the plays related thematically, but they also share the same characters. In 1985 Albee was playwright-in-residence at the University of Houston, where he wrote *Sand*, a collection of thematically related plays including *The Sandbox*, only fifteen minutes long. "With the possible exception of the little play *The Sandbox* [. . .] I don't think anything I've done has worked out to perfection," he said in an interview in 1966. In 1975, when an interviewer asked him which was his favorite play, he replied, "I'm terribly fond of *The Sandbox*. I think it's an absolutely beautiful, lovely little play."

CULTURAL CONTEXT ◊   *The Sandbox* is a criticism of the American nuclear family as it existed in the 1960s. During this time, many critics—including feminists such as Betty Friedan, author of the book *The Feminine Mystique*—saw the nuclear family as a power structure that exploited its members. Albee himself saw it as a materialistic entity concerned with satisfying its own selfish needs.

◊ ◊ ◊

EDWARD ALBEE

The Sandbox
(1960)

A Brief Play, in Memory of My Grandmother (1876–1959)

CHARACTERS

THE YOUNG MAN 25, *a good-looking, well-built boy in a bathing suit*
MOMMY 55, *a well-dressed, imposing woman*
DADDY 60, *a small man; gray, thin*
GRANDMA 86, *a tiny, wizened woman with bright eyes*
THE MUSICIAN *no particular age, but young would be nice*

NOTE
When, in the course of the play, Mommy and Daddy call each other by these names, there should be no suggestion of regionalism. These names are of empty affection and point up the pre-senility and vacuity of their characters.

THE SCENE
A bare stage, with only the following: Near the footlights, far stage-right, two simple chairs set side by side, facing the audience; near the footlights, far stage-left, a chair facing stage-right with a music stand before it; farther back, and stage-center, slightly elevated and raked, a large child's sandbox with a toy pail and shovel; the background is the sky, which alters from brightest day to deepest night.

   At the beginning, it is brightest day; the Young Man is alone on stage to the rear of the sandbox, and to one side. He is doing calisthenics; he does

calisthenics until quite at the very end of the play. These calisthenics, employing the arms only, should suggest the beating and fluttering of wings. The Young Man is, after all, the Angel of Death.
    Mommy and Daddy enter from stage-left, Mommy first.

MOMMY: *(motioning to Daddy)* Well, here we are; this is the beach.
DADDY: *(whining)* I'm cold.
MOMMY: *(dismissing him with a little laugh)* Don't be silly; it's as warm as toast. Look at that nice young man over there: *he* doesn't think it's cold. *(Waves to the Young Man)* Hello.
YOUNG MAN: *(with an endearing smile)* Hi!
5 MOMMY: *(looking about)* This will do perfectly . . . don't you think so, Daddy? There's sand there . . . and the water beyond. What do you think, Daddy?
DADDY: *(vaguely)* Whatever you say, Mommy.
MOMMY: *(with the same little laugh)* Well, of course . . . whatever I say. Then, it's settled, is it?
DADDY: *(shrugs)* She's *your* mother, not mine.
MOMMY: *I* know she's my mother. What do you take me for? *(A pause)* All right, now; let's get on with it. *(She shouts into the wings, stage-left.)* You! Out there! You can come in now. *(The Musician enters, seats himself in the chair, stage-left, places music on the music stand, is ready to play. Mommy nods approvingly.)* Very nice; very nice. Are you ready, Daddy? Let's go get Grandma.
10 DADDY: Whatever you say, Mommy.
MOMMY: *(leading the way out, stage-left)* Of course, whatever I say. *(To the Musician.)* You can begin now. *(The Musician begins playing; Mommy and Daddy exit; the Musician, all the while playing, nods to the Young Man.)*
YOUNG MAN: *(with the same endearing smile)* Hi! *(After a moment, Mommy and Daddy re-enter, carrying Grandma. She is borne in by their hands under her armpits; she is quite rigid; her legs are drawn up; her feet do not touch the ground; the expression on her ancient face is that of puzzlement and fear.)*
DADDY: Where do we put her?
MOMMY: *(the same little laugh)* Wherever I say, of course. Let me see . . . well . . . all right, over there . . . in the sandbox. *(Pause.)* Well, what are you waiting for, Daddy? . . . The sandbox! *(Together they carry Grandma over to the sandbox and more or less dump her in.)*
15 GRANDMA: *(righting herself to a sitting position; her voice a cross between a baby's laugh and cry)* Ahhhhhh! Graaaaa!
DADDY: *(dusting himself)* What do we do now?
MOMMY: *(to the Musician)* You can stop now. *(The Musician stops.)* *(Back to Daddy.)* What do you mean, what do we do now? We go over there and sit down, of course. *(To the Young Man.)* Hello there.
YOUNG MAN: *(again smiling)* Hi! *(Mommy and Daddy move to the chairs, stage-right, and sit down. A pause.)*

GRANDMA: *(same as before)* Ahhhhhh! Ah-haaaaaa! Graaaaaa!

20 DADDY: Do you think . . . do you think she's . . . comfortable?

MOMMY: *(impatiently)* How would I know?

DADDY: *(pause)* What do we do now?

MOMMY: *(as if remembering)* We . . . wait. We . . . sit here . . . and we wait
. . . that's what we do.

DADDY: *(after a pause)* Shall we talk to each other?

25 MOMMY: *(with that little laugh; picking something off her dress)* Well, *you* can
talk, if you want to . . . if you can think of anything to say . . . if you
can think of anything *new.*

DADDY: *(thinks)* No . . . I suppose not.

MOMMY: *(with a triumphant laugh)* Of course not!

GRANDMA: *(banging the toy shovel against the pail)* Haaaaaa! Ah-ha-aaaaa!

MOMMY: *(out over the audience)* Be quiet, Grandma . . . just be quiet, and
wait. *(Grandma throws a shovelful of sand at Mommy. Still out over the
audience.)* She's throwing sand at me! You stop that, Grandma; you
stop throwing sand at Mommy! *(To Daddy.)* She's throwing sand at
me. *(Daddy looks around at Grandma, who screams at him.)*

30 GRANDMA: GRAAAAA!

MOMMY: Don't look at her. Just . . . sit here . . . be very still . . . and wait.
(To the Musician.) You . . . uh . . . you go ahead and do whatever it is
you do. *(The Musician plays. Mommy and Daddy are fixed, staring out
beyond the audience. Grandma looks at them, looks at the Musician, looks
at the sandbox, throws down the shovel.)*

GRANDMA: Ah-haaaaaa! Graaaaaa! *(Looks for reaction; gets none. Now . . .
directly to the audience.)* Honestly! What a way to treat an old woman!
Drag her out of the house . . . stick her in a car . . . bring her out here
from the city . . . dump her in a pile of sand . . . and leave her here to
set. I'm eighty-six years old! I was married when I was seventeen. To
a farmer. He died when I was thirty. *(To the Musician.)* Will you stop
that, please? *(The Musician stops playing.)* I'm a feeble old woman . . .
how do you expect anybody to hear me over that peep! peep! peep!
(To herself.) There's no respect around here. *(To the Young Man.)*
There's no respect around here!

YOUNG MAN: *(same smile)* Hi!

GRANDMA: *(after a pause, a mild double-take, continues, to the audience)* My
husband died when I was thirty *(indicates Mommy)*, and I had to raise
that big cow over there all by my lonesome. You can imagine what
that was like. Lordy! *(To the Young Man.)* Where'd they get *you?*

35 YOUNG MAN: Oh . . . I've been around for a while.

GRANDMA: I'll bet you have! Heh, heh, heh. Will you look at you!

YOUNG MAN: *(flexing his muscles)* Isn't that something? *(Continues his
calisthenics.)*

GRANDMA: Boy, oh boy; I'll say. Pretty good.

YOUNG MAN: *(sweetly)* I'll say.

40 GRANDMA: Where ya from?

YOUNG MAN: Southern California.

GRANDMA: *(nodding)* Figgers; figgers. What's your name, honey?

YOUNG MAN: I don't know . . .

GRANDMA: *(to the audience)* Bright, too!

45 YOUNG MAN: I mean . . . I mean, they haven't given me one yet . . . the studio . . .

GRANDMA: *(giving him the once-over)* You don't say . . . you don't say. Well . . . uh, I've got to talk some more . . . don't you go 'way.

YOUNG MAN: Oh, no.

GRANDMA: *(turning her attention back to the audience)* Fine; fine. *(Then, once more, back to the Young Man.)* You're . . . you're an actor, hunh?

YOUNG MAN: *(beaming)* Yes. I am.

50 GRANDMA: *(to the audience again, shrugs)* I'm smart that way. *Anyhow,* I had to raise . . . *that* over there all by my lonesome; and what's next to her there . . . that's what she married. Rich? I tell you . . . money, money, money. They took me off the *farm* . . . which was real decent of them . . . and they moved me into the big town house with *them* . . . fixed a nice place for me under the stove . . . gave me an army blanket . . . and my own dish . . . my very own dish! So, what have I got to complain about? Nothing, of course. I'm not complaining. *(She looks up at the sky, shouts to someone off stage.)* Shouldn't it be getting dark now, dear? *(The lights dim, night comes on. The Musician begins to play; it becomes deepest night. There are spots on all the players, including the Young Man, who is, of course, continuing his calisthenics.)*

DADDY: *(stirring)* It's nighttime.

MOMMY: Shhhh. Be still . . . wait.

DADDY: *(whining)* It's so hot.

MOMMY: Shhhhhh. Be still . . . wait.

55 GRANDMA: *(to herself)* That's better. Night. *(To the Musician.)* Honey, do you play all through this part? *(The Musician nods.)* Well, keep it nice and soft; that's a good boy. *(The Musician nods again; plays softly.)* That's nice. *(There is an off-stage rumble.)*

DADDY: *(starting)* What was that?

MOMMY: *(beginning to weep)* It was nothing.

DADDY: It was . . . it was . . . thunder . . . or a wave breaking . . . or something.

MOMMY: *(whispering, through her tears)* It was an off-stage rumble . . . and you know what *that* means . . .

60 DADDY: I forget . . .

MOMMY: *(barely able to talk)* It means the time has come for poor Grandma . . . and I can't bear it!

DADDY: *(vacantly)* I . . . I suppose you've got to be brave.

GRANDMA: *(mocking)* That's right, kid; be brave. You'll bear up; you'll get over it. *(Another off-stage rumble . . . louder.)*

MOMMY: Ohhhhhhhhhh . . . poor Grandma . . . poor Grandma . . .

65 GRANDMA: *(to Mommy)* I'm fine! I'm all right! It hasn't happened yet! *(A violent off-stage rumble. All the lights go out, save the spot on the Young Man; the Musician stops playing.)*

MOMMY: Ohhhhhhhhh . . . Ohhhhhhhhhh . . . *(Silence.)*

GRANDMA: Don't put the lights up yet . . . I'm not ready; I'm not quite ready. *(Silence)* All right, dear . . . I'm about done. *(The lights come up again, to brightest day; the Musician begins to play. Grandma is discovered, still in the sandbox, lying on her side, propped up on an elbow, half covered, busily shoveling sand over herself.)*

GRANDMA: *(muttering)* I don't know how I'm supposed to do anything with this goddam toy shovel . . .

DADDY: Mommy! It's daylight!

70 MOMMY: *(brightly)* So it is! Well! Our long night is over. We must put away our tears, take off our mourning . . . and face the future. It's our duty.

GRANDMA: *(still shoveling; mimicking)* . . . take off our mourning . . . face the future . . . Lordy! *(Mommy and Daddy rise, stretch. Mommy waves to the Young Man.)*

YOUNG MAN: *(with that smile)* Hi! *(Grandma plays dead. [!] Mommy and Daddy go over to look at her; she is a little more than half buried in the sand; the toy shovel is in her hands, which are crossed on her breast.)*

MOMMY: *(before the sandbox; shaking her head)* Lovely! It's . . . it's hard to be sad . . . she looks . . . so happy. *(With pride and conviction.)* It pays to do things well. *(To the Musician.)* All right, you can stop now, if you want to. I mean, stay around for a swim, or something; it's all right with us. *(She sighs heavily.)* Well, Daddy . . . off we go.

DADDY: Brave Mommy!

75 MOMMY: Brave Daddy! *(They exit, stage left.)*

GRANDMA: *(after they leave; lying quite still)* It pays to do things well . . . Boy, oh boy! *(She tries to sit up)* . . . well, kids . . . *(but she finds she can't)* . . . I . . . I can't get up. I . . . I can't move . . . *(The Young Man stops his calisthenics, nods to the Musician, walks over to Grandma, kneels down by the sandbox.)*

GRANDMA: I . . . can't move . . .

YOUNG MAN: Shhhhh . . . be very still . . .

GRANDMA: I . . . I can't move . . .

80 YOUNG MAN: Uh . . . ma'am; I . . . I have a line here.

GRANDMA: Oh, I'm sorry, sweetie; you go right ahead.

YOUNG MAN: I am . . . uh . . .

GRANDMA: Take your time, dear.

YOUNG MAN: *(prepares; delivers the line like a real amateur)* I am the Angel of Death. I am . . . uh . . . I am come for you.

85 GRANDMA: What . . . wha . . . *(then, with resignation)* . . . ohhhh . . . ohhhh, I see. *(The Young Man bends over, kisses Grandma gently on the forehead.)*

GRANDMA: *(her eyes closed, her hands folded on her breast again, the shovel between her hands, a sweet smile on her face)* Well . . . that was very nice, dear . . .

YOUNG MAN: *(still kneeling)* Shhhhh . . . be still . . .

GRANDMA: What I meant was . . . you did that very well, dear . . .

YOUNG MAN: *(blushing)* . . . oh . . .

90 GRANDMA: No; I mean it. You've got that . . . you've got a quality.

YOUNG MAN: *(with his endearing smile)* Oh . . . thank you; thank you very much . . . ma'am.

GRANDMA: *(slowly; softly—as the Young Man puts his hands on top of Grandma's)* You're . . . you're welcome . . . dear.

(Tableau. The Musician continues to play as the curtain slowly comes down.)

READING AND REACTING

1. Albee's characters are two-dimensional. What does he gain by creating such flat characters? What does he lose?

2. Albee says that there should be "no suggestion of regionalism" in the speech of Mommy and Daddy. What do you believe he is trying to achieve with this stage direction?

3. Why do you think Albee recommends a bare stage with just a few props?

4. What purpose is served by each of the following props: the music stand, the sandbox, the toy pail and shovel? Do you think any of these props has symbolic significance?

5. In what way do changes in lighting affect the mood of the play?

6. What do costumes reveal about each character in the play? Why, for example, is The Young Man dressed in a bathing suit?

7. What function is served by the musician playing? By the offstage rumble?

8. Why does Grandma bury herself with sand? How would you stage this event?

9. At various points Grandma directly addresses the audience, gives lighting directions, and signals the musician. At one point, The Young Man interrupts her, saying, "I have a line here." How do you react to these characters' calling attention to the fact that they are actors in a play?

10. **JOURNAL ENTRY** What does *The Sandbox* seem to be saying about the American family? Do you think the play's assessment of the family is accurate?

11. **CRITICAL PERSPECTIVE** Critic Mickey Pearlman has argued that Albee's women "epitomize the worst stereotypes of American females—Mommy is the evil, all-powerful emasculator [. . .] and Grandma is the pathetic, ill-used, and nameless saint figure." Do you agree? Or do you believe Pearlman is overstating his case?

Related Works: "Once upon a Time" (p. 81), "A Good Man Is Hard to Find" (p. 266), "My Grandmother Would Rock Quietly and Hum" (p. 725), "The Meal" (p. 796), *Marty* (p. 1279)

◆ WRITING SUGGESTIONS: STAGING

1. Choose either *Oedipus the King* or *A Midsummer Night's Dream* and discuss the problems its original staging poses for contemporary audiences.
2. Write an essay in which you discuss what staging elements of *The Sandbox* strike you as "absurd" (see p. 1135 for a definition of **theater of the absurd**). How do these absurd elements help to communicate the play's ideas?
3. Discuss and analyze the staging techniques used in a play that is not in this chapter—for example, *Trifles* or *'night, Mother.*
4. Choose a short story that appears in this anthology, and explain how you would stage it if it were a play. What props, costumes, lighting, and sound effects would you choose? What events would occur offstage? Possible subjects for this paper might include "A&P" (p. 113), "The Story of an Hour" (p. 77), or "The Storm" (p. 154).
5. Suppose you were asked to update the staging of either *Oedipus the King* or *A Midsummer Night's Dream* for a contemporary production. What scenery, props, and costumes would you use to transform the setting to a contemporary drama?
6. **WEB ACTIVITY** The following Web site contains information about Sophocles and Greek Tragedy:

   http://depthome.brooklyn.cuny.edu/classics/tragedy.htm

   On the Web page, Roger Dunkle writes, in "An Introduction to Greek Tragedy," that while many tragedies end in misery, "there are also tragedies in which a satisfactory solution of the tragic situation is attained."

   Read Dunkle's article, and write an essay discussing whether there is a "satisfactory solution" in *Oedipus*. In your essay, focus on the consequences of the tragedy and how the society is affected by it.

CHAPTER 25

Theme

◊ ◊ ◊

Plays are like doors to me. They can be as massive and ornate as cathedrals or as small and intimate as keyholes. They can be as real as the kitchen sink or as ephemeral as dreams. When we read them in the quiet or sit in a darkened theatre space and listen we step over the threshold of the door that the playwright has opened for us. We walk into their secret garden or jungle and hopefully we are taken on an adventurous odyssey.

MARSHA MASON, *Women Playwrights*

[D]rama is one of the things that makes possible a solution to the problem of socializing people. In other words, we are born private, and we die private, but we live of necessity in direct relation to other people, even if we live alone. And dramatic conflict of significance always verges on and deals with the way men live together. And this is incomprehensible to Man as a private person. He is always trying to find out where he stands in his society, whether he uses those terms or not. He always wants to know whether his life has a meaning, and that meaning is always in relation to others. It is always in relation to his society, it's always in relation to his choices, to the absence of his choices, which are dominated by other people. I think that when we speak of dramatic significance we're really talking about, either openly or unknowingly, about the dilemma of living together, of living a social existence, and the conflict is endless between Man and his fellows and between his own instincts and the social necessity.

ARTHUR MILLER, *The Playwrights Speak*

I can't even count how many times I've heard the line, "Where did the idea for this play come from?" [. . .] Ideas emerge from plays—not the other way around. [. . .] I think explanation destroys [a play] and makes it less than it is.

SAM SHEPARD, *Fool for Love and Other Plays*

◊ ◊ ◊

Like a short story or a novel, a play is open to interpretation. Readers' reactions are influenced by the language of the text, and audiences' reactions are influenced by the performance on stage. Just as in fiction, every element of a play—its title, its conflicts, its dialogue, its characters, and its staging, for instance—can shed light on its themes.

TITLES

◊ ◊ ◊

The title of a play can provide insight into themes. The ironic title of Susan Glaspell's *Trifles* (p. 1163), for example, suggests that women's concern with "trifles" may get to the heart of the matter more effectively than the preoccupations of self-important men do. Wendy Wasserstein's *Tender Offer* (p. 1623) is another title that offers clues to a theme of the play. It not only suggests the father's preoccupation with business (a company makes a *tender offer* when it wants to buy another company), but also makes the point that parents need to take the time to relate (make tender offers) to their children. Likewise, the title of Edward Albee's *The Sandbox* (p. 1610) offers clues to a theme of the play, suggesting that individuals in modern society are like children in a sandbox, concerned only with satisfying their physical and material needs. Finally, Anton Chekhov's *The Brute* (p. 1266) effectively calls attention to the play's ideas about male-female relationships. The title may refer to Smirnov, who says that he has never liked women—whom he characterizes as "creatures of poetry and romance." Or it may refer to Mrs. Popov's late husband, to whose memory she has dedicated her life despite the fact that he was repeatedly unfaithful. Either alternative reinforces the play's tongue-in-cheek characterization of men as "brutes."

CONFLICTS

◊ ◊ ◊

The unfolding plot of a play—especially the conflicts that develop—can also reveal the play's themes. In Henrik Ibsen's *A Doll House* (p. 1196), for example, at least three major conflicts are present: one between Nora and her husband Torvald, one between Nora and Krogstad (an old acquaintance), and one between Nora and society. Each of these conflicts sheds light on the themes of the play.

Through Nora's conflict with Torvald, Ibsen examines the constraints placed on women and men by marriage in the nineteenth century. Both Nora and Torvald are imprisoned within their respective roles: Nora must be passive and childlike, and Torvald must be proper and always in control. Nora, therefore, expects her husband to be noble and generous and, in a crisis, to sacrifice himself for her. When he fails to live up to her expectations, she is profoundly disillusioned.

Nora's conflict with Krogstad underscores Ibsen's criticisms of the class system in nineteenth-century Norway. At the beginning of the play, Nora finds it "immensely amusing: that we—that Torvald has so much power over [. . .] people." Krogstad, a bank clerk who is in the employ of Torvald, visits Nora in act 1 to enlist her aid in saving his job. It is clear that she sees him as her social inferior. When Krogstad questions her about a woman with whom he has seen her, she replies, "What makes you think you can cross-examine me, Mr. Krogstad—you, one of my husband's employees?" Nora does not realize that she and Krogstad are, ironically, very much alike: both occupy subordinate positions and therefore have no power to determine their own destinies.

Finally, through Nora's conflict with society Ibsen examines an important theme of his play: the destructive nature of the forces that subjugate women. Nineteenth-century society was male-dominated. Married women could not borrow money without their husband's signatures, own real estate in their own names, or enter into contracts. In addition, all their assets—including inheritances and trust funds—automatically became the property of their husbands at the time of marriage. As a result of her sheltered life, Nora at the beginning of the play is completely innocent of the consequences of her actions. Most readers share Dr. Rank's confusion when he asks Nora, "Why do you laugh at that? Do you have any idea of what society is?" It is Nora's disillusionment at finding out that Torvald and the rest of society are not what she has been led to believe they are that ultimately causes her to rebel. By walking out the door at the end of the play, Nora rejects not only her husband and her children (to whom, incidentally, she has no legal right once she leaves), but also society and its laws.

These conflicts, then, underscore many of the themes that dominate *A Doll House.* First, the conflicts show that marriage in the nineteenth century imprisons both men and women in narrow, constricting roles. Next, the conflicts show that middle-class Norwegian society is narrow, smug, and judgmental. (Krogstad, for example, is looked down upon for a crime years after he committed it, and Nora is looked down upon because she borrows money to save her husband's life.) Finally, the conflicts show that society does not offer individuals—especially women—the freedom to lead happy and fulfilling lives. Only when the social and economic conditions that govern society change, Ibsen suggests, can women and men live together in mutual esteem.

DIALOGUE
◊ ◊ ◊

The dialogue of a play can also give insight into its themes. Sometimes a character will suggest—or even explicitly state—a theme. In act 3 of *A Doll House,* for example, Nora's friend, Mrs. Linde, comes as close as any character to expressing a central concern of the play when she says, "Helmer's got to learn everything; this dreadful secret has to be aired; those two have to come to a full understanding; all these lies can't go on." As the play goes on to demonstrate, the lies that exist both in marriage and in society are obstacles to love and happiness.

One of the main themes of Arthur Miller's *Death of a Salesman* (p. 1410)—the questionable validity of the American Dream, given the nation's social, political, and economic realities—is suggested by the play's dialogue. As his son Biff points out, Willy Loman's stubborn belief in upward mobility and material success is based more on fantasy than on fact:

> **WILLY:** *(with hatred, threatening)* The door of your life is wide open!
> **BIFF:** Pop! I am a dime a dozen, and so are you!
> **WILLY:** *(turning on him now in an uncontrolled outburst)* I am not a dime a dozen! I am Willy Loman, and you are Biff Loman!
>
> *Biff starts for Willy, but is blocked by Happy. In his fury, Biff seems on the verge of attacking his father.*
>
> **BIFF:** I am not a leader of men, Willy, and neither are you. You were never anything but a hard-working drummer who landed in the ash can like all the rest of them! I'm one dollar an hour, Willy! I tried seven states and couldn't raise it. A buck an hour! Do you gather my meaning? I'm not bringing home any prizes any more, and you're going to stop waiting for me to bring them home!

Although not explicitly stating the theme of the play, this exchange strongly suggests that Biff rejects the materialistic values to which Willy clings.

CHARACTERS

◊ ◊ ◊

Because a dramatic work focuses on a central character, or protagonist, the development of this character can shed light on a play's themes. Willy Loman in *Death of a Salesman,* for example, is developed in great detail. At the beginning of the play, he feels trapped, exhausted, and estranged from his surroundings. As Willy gradually sinks from depression into despair, the action of the play shifts from the present to the past, showing the events that shaped Willy's life. His attitudes, beliefs, dreams, and dashed hopes reveal him to be an embodiment of the major theme of the play— that an unquestioning belief in the American Dream of success and upward mobility is unrealistic and possibly destructive.

Nora, the main character in *A Doll House,* changes a great deal during the course of the play. At the beginning of the play, she is more her husband's possession than an adult capable of determining her own destiny. Nora's status becomes apparent in the first act when Torvald gently scolds his "little spendthrift" and refers to her as his "little lark" and his "squirrel." She is reduced to childish deceptions, such as hiding her macaroons from her husband when he enters the room. After Krogstad accuses her of committing forgery and threatens to expose her, she expects her husband to rise to the occasion and take the blame for her. When Torvald instead accuses her of being a hypocrite, a liar, and a criminal, Nora's neat little world comes crashing down. As a result of this experience, Nora changes; no longer is she the submissive and obedient wife. Instead, she becomes confident and assertive, ultimately telling Torvald that their marriage is a sham and that she can no longer stay with him. This abrupt shift in Nora's personality gives the audience a clear understanding of the major themes of the play.

Unlike Willy and Nora, Laura in Tennessee Williams's *The Glass Menagerie* (p. 1805) is a character who changes very little during the course of the play. Laura suffers from such pathological shyness that she is unable to attend typing class, let alone talk to a potential suitor. Although the "gentleman caller" does draw Laura out of her shell for a short time, she soon withdraws again. Laura's inability to change reinforces the play's theme that contemporary society, with its emphasis on progress, has no place for people like Laura who live in private worlds "of glass animals and old, worn-out phonograph records."

STAGING
◊ ◊ ◊

Scenery and props may also convey the themes of a play. As the stage directions of *The Sandbox* indicate, the stage is relatively bare. Containing only two chairs and a sandbox, this bare stage suggests the play's frightening emptiness, a quality Albee believes characterizes the lives of all human beings. In *Death of a Salesman*, Biff's trophy, which is constantly in the audience's view, ironically underscores the futility of Willy's efforts to achieve success. Similarly, the miniature animals in *The Glass Menagerie* reflect the fragility of Laura's character and the futility of her efforts to fit into the modern world.

Special lighting effects and music can also suggest a play's themes. Throughout *The Glass Menagerie,* for example, words and pictures are projected onto a section of the set between the front room and dining room walls. In scene 1 of the play, as Tom's mother, Amanda, tells him about her experiences with her "gentlemen callers," an image of her as a girl greeting callers appears on the screen. As Amanda continues, the words *"Où sont Les Neiges"*—"Where are the snows [of yesteryear]?"—appear on the screen. Later in the play, when Laura and her mother discuss a boy Laura knew, his picture is projected on the screen, showing him as a high school hero carrying a silver cup. In addition to the slides, Williams uses music— a recurring tune, dance music, and "Ave Maria"—to increase the emotional impact of certain scenes. Williams also uses shafts of light focused on selected areas or characters to create a dreamlike atmosphere for the play. Collectively, the slides, the music, and the lighting reinforce the theme that those who retreat obsessively into the past eventually become estranged from the present.

A FINAL NOTE

◊ ◊ ◊

As you read, your values and beliefs will influence your interpretation of a play's themes. For instance, your interest in feminism could lead you to focus your attention on the submissive, almost passive, role of Willy's wife, Linda, in *Death of a Salesman*. As a result, you could conclude that the play shows how, in the post–World War II United States, women like Linda often sacrificed their own happiness for their husbands. Remember, however, that the details of a play, not just your own feelings or assumptions, must support your interpretation.

 ## CHECKLIST: WRITING ABOUT THEME

✓ What is the central theme of the play?

✓ What other themes can you identify?

✓ Does the title of the play suggest a theme?

✓ What conflicts exist in the play? In what way do they shed light on the themes of the play?

✓ Do any characters' statements express or imply a theme of the play?

✓ Do any characters change during the play? How do these changes suggest the play's themes?

✓ Do certain characters resist change? How does their failure to change suggest a theme of the play?

✓ Do scenery and props help to communicate the play's themes?

✓ Does music reinforce certain ideas in the play?

✓ Does lighting underscore the themes of the play?

 ◊ **WENDY WASSERSTEIN** (1950–   ) was born in Brooklyn, New York. She failed to gain entry into law school and business school, but she went on to become a Tony Award– and Pulitzer Prize–winning dramatist known for plays about educated women and the challenges they face. The characters in her plays often struggle to define themselves in relation to (and sometimes in opposition to) the stereotypical roles of wife, mother, and career woman.

Her plays include *Uncommon Women and Others* (1977), her Yale School of Drama thesis; *Isn't It Romantic* (1983), the story of a budding writer; and *The Heidi Chronicles* (1988), for which she won both a Tony Award and a Pulitzer Prize. Her first book of essays, *Bachelor Girls* (1991), is openly autobiographical, and her recent novel, *An American Daughter* (1998), chronicles a woman's struggles with politics and fame. In plays, essays, and prose fiction, Wasserstein's work conveys its themes through realistic dialogue, through realistic situations, and, most of all, through humor.

CULTURAL CONTEXT ◆ During the 1980s and 1990s, most new drama was being undertaken away from Broadway. For example, Wendy Wasserstein's career began in regional theater. As a matter of fact, three of the 1980s Pulitzer Prize winners began in regional theater, including Wasserstein's *The Heidi Chronicles*.

◆ ◆ ◆

WENDY WASSERSTEIN

Tender Offer
(1983)

CHARACTERS

LISA
PAUL

A girl of around nine is alone in a dance studio. She is dressed in traditional leotards and tights. She begins singing to herself, "Nothing Could be Finer Than to Be in Carolina." She maps out a dance routine, including parts for the chorus. She builds to a finale. A man, Paul, around thirty-five, walks in. He has a sweet, though distant, demeanor. As he walks in, Lisa notices him and stops.

PAUL: You don't have to stop, sweetheart.
LISA: That's okay.
PAUL: Looked very good.
LISA: Thanks.
5 PAUL: Don't I get a kiss hello?
LISA: Sure.
PAUL: *(embraces her)* Hi, Tiger.
LISA: Hi, Dad.
PAUL: I'm sorry I'm late.
10 LISA: That's okay.
PAUL: How'd it go?
LISA: Good.
PAUL: Just good?
LISA: Pretty good.
15 PAUL: "Pretty good." You mean you got a lot of applause or "pretty good" you could have done better.

LISA: Well, Courtney Palumbo's mother thought I was pretty good. But you know the part of the middle when everybody's supposed to freeze and the big girl comes out. Well, I think I moved a little bit.

PAUL: I thought what you were doing looked very good.

LISA: Daddy, that's not what I was doing. That was tap-dancing. I made that up.

PAUL: Oh. Well it looked good. Kind of sexy.

20 LISA: Yuch!

PAUL: What do you mean "yuch"?

LISA: Just yuch!

PAUL: You don't want to be sexy?

LISA: I don't care.

25 PAUL: Let's go Tiger. I promised your mother I'd get you home in time for dinner.

LISA: I can't find my leg warmers.

PAUL: You can't find your what?

LISA: Leg warmers. I can't go home till I find my leg warmers.

PAUL: I don't see you looking for them.

30 LISA: I was waiting for you.

PAUL: Oh.

LISA: Daddy.

PAUL: What?

LISA: Nothing.

35 PAUL: Where do you think you left them?

LISA: Somewhere around here. I can't remember.

PAUL: Well, try to remember, Lisa. We don't have all night.

LISA: I told you. I think somewhere around here.

PAUL: I don't see them. Let's go home now. You'll call the dancing school tomorrow.

40 LISA: Daddy, I can't go home till I find them. Miss Judy says it's not professional to leave things.

PAUL: Who's Miss Judy?

LISA: She's my ballet teacher. She once danced the lead in *Swan Lake,* and she was a June Taylor dancer.

PAUL: Well, then, I'm sure she'll understand about the leg warmers.

LISA: Daddy, Miss Judy wanted to know why you were late today.

45 PAUL: Hmmmmmmmm?

LISA: Why were you late?

PAUL: I was in a meeting. Business. I'm sorry.

LISA: Why did you tell Mommy you'd come instead of her if you knew you had business?

PAUL: Honey, something just came up. I thought I'd be able to be here. I was looking forward to it.

50 LISA: I wish you wouldn't make appointments to see me.

PAUL: Hmmmmmmmm.

LISA: You shouldn't make appointments to see me unless you know you're going to come.

PAUL: Of course I'm going to come.

LISA: No, you're not. Talia Robbins told me she's much happier living without her father in the house. Her father used to come home late and go to sleep early.

55 PAUL: Lisa, stop it. Let's go.

LISA: I can't find my leg warmers.

PAUL: Forget your leg warmers.

LISA: Daddy.

PAUL: What is it?

60 LISA: I saw this show on television, I think it was WPIX Channel 11. Well, the father was crying about his daughter.

PAUL: Why was he crying? Was she sick?

LISA: No. She was at school. And he was at business. And he just missed her, so he started to cry.

PAUL: What was the name of this show?

LISA: I don't know. I came in in the middle.

65 PAUL: Well, Lisa, I certainly would cry if you were sick or far away, but I know that you're well and you're home. So no reason to get maudlin.

LISA: What's maudlin?

PAUL: Sentimental, soppy. Frequently used by children who make things up to get attention.

LISA: I am sick! I am sick! I have Hodgkin's disease and a bad itch on my leg.

PAUL: What do you mean you have Hodgkin's disease? Don't say things like that.

70 LISA: Swoosie Kurtz, she had Hodgkin's disease on a TV movie last year, but she got better and now she's on *Love Sidney*.

PAUL: Who is Swoosie Kurtz?

LISA: She's an actress named after an airplane. I saw her on *Live at Five*.

PAUL: You watch too much television; you should do your homework. Now, put your coat on.

LISA: Daddy, I really do have a bad itch on my leg. Would you scratch it?

75 PAUL: Lisa, you're procrastinating.

LISA: Why do you use words I don't understand? I hate it. You're like Daria Feldman's mother. She always talks in Yiddish to her husband so Daria won't understand.

PAUL: Procrastinating is not Yiddish.

LISA: Well, I don't know what it is.

PAUL: Procrastinating means you don't want to go about your business.

80 LISA: I don't go to business. I go to school.

PAUL: What I mean is you want to hang around here until you and I are late for dinner and your mother's angry and it's too late for you to do your homework.

Lisa: I do not.

Paul: Well, it sure looks that way. Now put your coat on and let's go.

Lisa: Daddy.

85 Paul: Honey, I'm tired. Really, later.

Lisa: Why don't you want to talk to me?

Paul: I do want to talk to you. I promise when we get home we'll have a nice talk.

Lisa: No, we won't. You'll read the paper and fall asleep in front of the news.

Paul: Honey, we'll talk on the weekend, I promise. Aren't I taking you to the theater this weekend? Let me look. *(He takes out an appointment book.)* Yes. Sunday. *Joseph and the Amazing Technicolor Raincoat* with Lisa. Okay, Tiger?

90 Lisa: Sure. It's Dreamcoat.

Paul: What?

Lisa: Nothing. I think I see my leg warmers. *(She goes to pick them up, and an odd-looking trophy.)*

Paul: What's that?

Lisa: It's stupid. I was second best at the dance recital, so they gave me this thing. It's stupid.

95 Paul: Lisa.

Lisa: What?

Paul: What did you want to talk about?

Lisa: Nothing.

Paul: Was it about my missing your recital? I'm really sorry, Tiger. I would have liked to have been here.

100 Lisa: That's okay.

Paul: Honest?

Lisa: Daddy, you're prostrastinating.

Paul: I'm procrastinating. Sit down. Let's talk. How's school?

Lisa: Fine.

105 Paul: You like it?

Lisa: Yup.

Paul: You looking forward to camp this summer?

Lisa: Yup.

Paul: Is Daria Feldman going back?

110 Lisa: Nope.

Paul: Why not?

Lisa: I don't know. We can go home now. Honest, my foot doesn't itch anymore.

Paul: Lisa, you know what you do in business when it seems like there's nothing left to say? That's when you really start talking. Put a bid on the table.

Lisa: What's a bid?

115 Paul: You tell me what you want and I'll tell you what I've got to offer. Like Monopoly. You want Boardwalk, but I'm only willing to give you

the Railroads. Now, because you are my daughter I'd throw in Water
Works and Electricity. Understand, Tiger?

LISA: No. I don't like board games. You know, Daddy, we could get Space
Invaders for our home for thirty-five dollars. In fact, we could get an
Osborne System for two thousand. Daria Feldman's parents . . .

PAUL: Daria Feldman's parents refuse to talk to Daria, so they bought a
computer to keep Daria busy so they won't have to speak in Yiddish.
Daria will probably grow up to be a homicidal maniac lesbian
prostitute.

LISA: I know what the word prostitute means.

PAUL: Good. *(Pause.)* You still haven't told me about school. Do you still
like your teacher?

120 LISA: She's okay.

PAUL: Lisa, if we're talking try to answer me.

LISA: I am answering you. Can we go home now, please?

PAUL: Damn it, Lisa, if you want to talk to me . . . Talk to me!

LISA: I can't wait till I'm old enough so I can make my own money and
never have to see you again. Maybe I'll become a prostitute.

125 PAUL: Young lady, that's enough.

LISA: I hate you, Daddy! I hate you! *(She throws her trophy into the
trash bin.)*

PAUL: What'd you do that for?

LISA: It's stupid.

PAUL: Maybe I wanted it.

130 LISA: What for?

PAUL: Maybe I wanted to put it where I keep your dinosaur and the
picture you made of Mrs. Kimbel with the chicken pox.

LISA: You got mad at me when I made that picture. You told me I had to
respect Mrs. Kimbel because she was my teacher.

PAUL: That's true. But she wasn't my teacher. I liked her better with the
chicken pox. *(Pause.)* Lisa, I'm sorry. I was very wrong to miss your
recital, and you don't have to become a prostitute. That's not the
type of profession Miss Judy has in mind for you.

LISA: *(mumbles)* No.

135 PAUL: No. *(Pause.)* So Talia Robbins is really happy her father moved out?

LISA: Talia Robbins picks open the eighth-grade lockers during gym
period. But she did that before her father moved out.

PAUL: You can't always judge someone by what they do or what they
don't do. Sometimes you come home from dancing school and run
upstairs and shut the door, and when I finally get to talk to you,
everything is "okay" or "fine." Yup or nope?

LISA: Yup.

PAUL: Sometimes, a lot of times, I come home and fall asleep in front of
the television. So you and I spend a lot of time being a little scared of
each other. Maybe?

140 LISA: Maybe.

PAUL: Tell you what. I'll make you a tender offer.

LISA: What?

PAUL: I'll make you a tender offer. That's when one company publishes in the newspaper that they want to buy another company. And the company that publishes is called the Black Knight because they want to gobble up the poor little company. So the poor little company needs to be rescued. And then a White Knight comes along and makes a bigger and better offer so the shareholders won't have to tender shares to the Big Black Knight. You with me?

LISA: Sort of.

145 PAUL: I'll make you a tender offer like the White Knight. But I don't want to own you. I just want to make a much better offer. Okay?

LISA: *(sort of understanding)* Okay. *(Pause. They sit for a moment.)* Sort of, Daddy, what do you think about? I mean, like when you're quiet what do you think about?

PAUL: Oh, business usually. If I think I made a mistake or if I think I'm doing okay. Sometimes I think about what I'll be doing five years from now and if it's what I hoped it would be five years ago. Sometimes I think about what your life will be like, if Mount Saint Helen's will erupt again. What you'll become if you'll study penmanship or word processing. If you speak kindly of me to your psychiatrist when you are in graduate school. And how the hell I'll pay for your graduate school. And sometimes I try and think what it was I thought about when I was your age.

LISA: Do you ever look out your window at the clouds and try to see which kinds of shapes they are? Like one time, honest, I saw the head of Walter Cronkite in a flower vase. Really! Like look don't those kinda look like if you turn it upside down, two big elbows or two elephant trunks dancing?

PAUL: Actually still looks like Walter Cronkite in a flower vase to me. But look up a little. See the one that's still moving? That sorts looks like a whale on a thimble.

150 LISA: Where?

PAUL: Look up to your right.

LISA: I don't see it. Where?

PAUL: The other way.

LISA: Oh, yeah! There's the head and there's the stomach. Yeah! *(Lisa picks up her trophy.)* Hey, Daddy.

155 PAUL: Hey, Lisa.

LISA: You can have this thing if you want it. But you have to put it like this, because if you put it like that it is gross.

PAUL: You know what I'd like? So I can tell people who come into my office why I have this gross stupid thing on my shelf, I'd like it if you could show me your dance recital.

LISA: Now?

PAUL: We've got time. Mother said she won't be home till late.

160 LISA: Well, Daddy, during a lot of it I freeze and the big girl in front
  dances.
PAUL: Well, how 'bout the number you were doing when I walked in?
LISA: Well, see, I have parts for a lot of people in that one, too.
PAUL: I'll dance the other parts.
LISA: You can't dance.
165 PAUL: Young lady, I played Yvette Mimieux in a *Hasty Pudding Show.*[1]
LISA: Who's Yvette Mimieux?
PAUL: Watch more television. You'll find out. *(Paul stands up.)* So I'm
  ready. *(He begins singing.)* "Nothing could be finer than to be in
  Carolina."
LISA: Now I go. In the morning. And now you go. Dum-da.
PAUL: *(obviously not a tap dancer)* Da-da-dum.
170 LISA: *(whines)* Daddy!
PAUL: *(mimics her)* Lisa! Nothing could be finer . . .
LISA: That looks dumb.
PAUL: Oh, yeah? You think they do this better in *The Amazing Minkcoat?*
  No way! Now you go—da da da dum.
LISA: Da da da dum.
175 PAUL: If I had Aladdin's lamp for only a day, I'd make a wish . . .
LISA: Daddy, that's maudlin!
PAUL: I know it's maudlin. And here's what I'd say:
LISA and PAUL: I'd say that "nothing could be finer than to be in
  Carolina in the moooooooooooornin'."

READING AND REACTING

1. How would you describe the relationship between Paul and his
   daughter? Does this relationship change during the course of the
   play?
2. How would you characterize Paul? Would you describe him as
   loving? Arrogant? Distant? Preoccupied? Or would you describe
   him in some other way?
3. During the first half of the play, Lisa wants to have a
   conversation, and her father doesn't. At what point does the
   situation change? What do you think causes this change?
4. Do you find any of Paul's comments to Lisa—for example, his
   telling her that her tap dance looked "kind of sexy"—
   inappropriate or unusual? How would you explain these remarks?
5. What is the main point of this play? What other points are
   developed?

---

[1] Shows put on by the Hasty Pudding Club of Harvard University at the Hasty Pudding
Theatre in Harvard Square. A 150-year-old tradition, the shows are famous for their
use of a completely male cast, with female roles being played by men dressed as
women.

6. At one point in the play, Paul says that he performed in a Hasty Pudding Club show, suggesting that he attended Harvard University. This, along with his preoccupation with business, would seem to suggest that he and his family are privileged. What else suggests the family's social status? Does the main point of this play apply primarily to affluent families, or can it apply to all families, regardless of income level?

7. What is the significance of the play's title? In what way does it express the play's main theme?

8. Do any of the characters change during the course of the play? If so, what is the significance of these changes?

9. What is the central conflict of the play? In what way is it resolved?

10. The play, which begins with Lisa dancing alone, ends with Paul and Lisa dancing together. What is the significance of this ending? Can you think of another ending that would be more effective?

11. **JOURNAL ENTRY** Do you think the relationship between Paul and Lisa will be better in the future? Or, after all is said and done, will it remain the same?

12. **CRITICAL PERSPECTIVE** According to playwright Arthur Miller, "drama is one of the things that makes possible a solution to the problem of socializing people." In other words, drama addresses the "dilemma of living together" and helps people resolve the conflict between their "own instincts and the social necessity."

   In what way does *Tender Offer* address the conflict between instincts and social necessity? Is this conflict resolved?

Related Works: "Doe Season" (p. 349), "Eveline" (p. 470), "My Father in the Navy: A Childhood Memory" (p. 676), "Daddy" (p. 818), *The Cuban Swimmer* (p. 1495)

◆ **SOPHOCLES** (496–406 B.C.) (picture and biography on p. 1508) Even though it was written long before *Oedipus the King*, *Antigone* traces the events that befall Oedipus's younger daughter after his banishment from Thebes. Antigone, caught between the laws of the gods and the edict of her uncle the king, follows her conscience despite the fatal consequences to herself. In the 1960s, the story of Antigone was especially meaningful to Americans who practiced civil disobedience in struggles for civil rights and against the war in Vietnam.

CULTURAL CONTEXT ◆ Sophocles was one of nine generals elected for a military campaign against Samos, a portion of Greece that was in revolt against Athens. Sophocles' election was due at least in part to the popularity of his play *Antigone*. Greek plays often centered on problems of the city-state, and the theater was in many ways the center of the state's religious and political life.

◊ ◊ ◊

SOPHOCLES*

Antigone
(441 B.C.)

An English Version by Dudley Fitts and Robert Fitzgerald

CHARACTERS

ANTIGONE	TEIRESIAS
ISMENE	A SENTRY
EURYDICE	A MESSENGER
CREON	CHORUS
HAIMON	

SCENE
Before the palace of Creon, King of Thebes. A central double door, and two lateral doors. A platform extends the length of the façade, and from this platform three steps lead down into the "orchestra," or chorus-ground.

TIME
Dawn of the day after the repulse of the Argive army from the assault on Thebes.

PROLOGUE[1]

(Antigone and Ismene enter from the central door of the palace.)

ANTIGONE: Ismene, dear sister,
   You would think that we had already suffered enough
   For the curse on Oedipus.[2]
   I cannot imagine any grief

---

* Note that individual lines are numbered in the following play. When a line is shared by two or more characters, it is counted as one line.

---

[1] *Prologue:* Portion of the play containing the exposition, or explanation, of what has gone before and what is now happening.   [2] *the curse on Oedipus:* As Sophocles tells in *Oedipus the King*, the King of Thebes discovered that he had lived his life under a curse. Unknowingly, he had slain his father and married his mother. On realizing this terrible truth, Oedipus put out his own eyes and departed into exile. Now, years later, as *Antigone* opens, Antigone and Ismene, daughters of Oedipus, are recalling how their two brothers died. After the abdication of their father, the brothers had ruled Thebes together. But they fell to quarreling. When Eteocles expelled Polyneices, the latter returned with an army and attacked the city. The two brothers killed each other in combat, leaving the throne to Creon. The new king of Thebes has buried Eteocles with full honors, but, calling Polyneices a traitor, has decreed that his body shall be left to the crows—an especially terrible decree, for a rotting corpse might offend Zeus, bring down plague, blight, and barrenness upon Thebes, and prevent the soul of a dead hero from entering the Elysian Fields, abode of those favored by the gods.

5   That you and I have not gone through. And now—
     Have they told you of the new decree of our King Creon?
ISMENE: I have heard nothing: I know
     That two sisters lost two brothers, a double death
     In a single hour; and I know that the Argive army
10   Fled in the night; but beyond this, nothing.
ANTIGONE: I thought so. And that is why I wanted you
     To come out here with me. There is something we must do.
ISMENE: Why do you speak so strangely?
ANTIGONE: Listen, Ismene:
15   Creon buried our brother Eteocles
     With military honors, gave him a soldier's funeral,
     And it was right that he should; but Polyneices,
     Who fought as bravely and died as miserably,—
     They say that Creon has sworn
20   No one shall bury him, no one mourn for him,
     But his body must lie in the fields, a sweet treasure
     For carrion birds to find as they search for food.
     That is what they say, and our good Creon is coming here
     To announce it publicly; and the penalty—
25   Stoning to death in the public square!
                                    There it is,
     And now you can prove what you are:
     A true sister, or a traitor to your family.
ISMENE: Antigone, you are mad! What could I possibly do?
ANTIGONE: You must decide whether you will help me or not.
30 ISMENE: I do not understand you. Help you in what?
ANTIGONE: Ismene, I am going to bury him. Will you come?
ISMENE: Bury him! You have just said the new law forbids it.
ANTIGONE: He is my brother. And he is your brother, too.
ISMENE: But think of the danger! Think what Creon will do!
35 ANTIGONE: Creon is not strong enough to stand in my way.
ISMENE: Ah sister!
     Oedipus died, everyone hating him
     For what his own search brought to light, his eyes
     Ripped out by his own hand; and Jocasta died,
40   His mother and wife at once: she twisted the cords
     That strangled her life; and our two brothers died,
     Each killed by the other's sword. And we are left:
     But oh, Antigone,
     Think how much more terrible than these
45   Our own death would be if we should go against Creon
     And do what he has forbidden! We are only women,
     We cannot fight with men, Antigone!
     The law is strong, we must give in to the law

In this thing, and in worse. I beg the Dead
50   To forgive me, but I am helpless: I must yield
To those in authority. And I think it is dangerous business
To be always meddling.

ANTIGONE: If that is what you think,
I should not want you, even if you asked to come.
You have made your choice, you can be what you want to be.
55   But I will bury him; and if I must die,
I say that this crime is holy: I shall lie down
With him in death, and I shall be as dear
To him as he to me.
                 It is the dead,
Not the living, who make the longest demands:
60   We die for ever . . .
                 You may do as you like,
Since apparently the laws of the gods mean nothing to you.

ISMENE: They mean a great deal to me; but I have no strength
To break laws that were made for the public good.

ANTIGONE: That must be your excuse, I suppose. But as for me,
65   I will bury the brother I love.

ISMENE: Antigone,
I am so afraid for you!

ANTIGONE: You need not be:
You have yourself to consider, after all.

ISMENE: But no one must hear of this, you must tell no one!
I will keep it a secret, I promise!

ANTIGONE: O tell it! Tell everyone!
70   Think how they'll hate you when it all comes out
If they learn that you knew about it all the time!

ISMENE: So fiery! You should be cold with fear.

ANTIGONE: Perhaps. But I am doing only what I must.

ISMENE: But can you do it? I say that you cannot.

75 ANTIGONE: Very well: when my strength gives out,
I shall do no more.

ISMENE: Impossible things should not be tried at all.

ANTIGONE: Go away, Ismene:
I shall be hating you soon, and the dead will too,
80   For your words are hateful. Leave me my foolish plan:
I am not afraid of the danger; if it means death,
It will not be the worst of deaths—death without honor.

ISMENE: Go then, if you feel that you must.
You are unwise,
85   But a loyal friend indeed to those who love you.

(Exit into the palace. Antigone goes off, left. Enter the Chorus.)

PARADOS[3]

STROPHE 1

CHORUS: Now the long blade of the sun, lying
    Level east to west, touches with glory
    Thebes of the Seven Gates. Open, unlidded
    Eye of golden day! O marching light
90   Across the eddy and rush of Dirce's stream,[4]
    Striking the white shields of the enemy
    Thrown headlong backward from the blaze of morning!
CHORAGOS:[5] Polyneices their commander
    Roused them with windy phrases,
95   He the wild eagle screaming
    Insults above our land,
    His wings their shields of snow,
    His crest their marshalled helms.

ANTISTROPHE 1

CHORUS: Against our seven gates in a yawning ring
100   The famished spears came onward in the night;
    But before his jaws were sated with our blood,
    Or pinefire took the garland of our towers,
    He was thrown back; and as he turned, great Thebes—
    No tender victim for his noisy power—
105   Rose like a dragon behind him, shouting war.
CHORAGOS: For God hates utterly
    The bray of bragging tongues;
    And when he beheld their smiling,
    Their swagger of golden helms,
110   The frown of his thunder blasted
    Their first man from our walls.

STROPHE 2

CHORUS: We heard his shout of triumph high in the air
    Turn to a scream; far out in a flaming arc
    He fell with his windy torch, and the earth struck him.
115   And others storming in fury no less than his
    Found shock of death in the dusty joy of battle.

---

[3] *Parados:* a song sung by the chorus on the first entering. Its *strophe* (according to scholarly theory) was sung while the chorus danced from stage right to stage left; its *antistrophe,* while they danced back again. Another parados follows the prologue of *Oedipus the King.*   [4] *Dirce's stream:* river near Thebes.   [5] *Choragos:* leader of the Chorus and principal commentator on the play's action.

CHORAGOS: Seven captains at seven gates
    Yielded their clanging arms to the god
    That bends the battle-line and breaks it.
120   These two only, brothers in blood,
    Face to face in matchless rage,
    Mirroring each the other's death,
    Clashed in long combat.

ANTISTROPHE 2

CHORUS: But now in the beautiful morning of victory
125   Let Thebes of the many chariots sing for joy!
    With hearts for dancing we'll take leave of war:
    Our temples shall be sweet with hymns of praise,
    And the long nights shall echo with our chorus.

SCENE 1

CHORAGOS: But now at last our new King is coming:
130   Creon of Thebes, Menoeceus' son.
    In this auspicious dawn of his reign
    What are the new complexities
    That shifting Fate has woven for him?
    What is his counsel? Why has he summoned
135   The old men to hear him?

(Enter Creon from the palace, center. He addresses the Chorus from the top step.)

CREON: Gentlemen: I have the honor to inform you that our Ship of
    State, which recent storms have threatened to destroy, has come
    safely to harbor at last, guided by the merciful wisdom of Heaven.
    I have summoned you here this morning because I know that I can
140   depend upon you: your devotion to King Laius was absolute; you
    never hesitated in your duty to our late ruler Oedipus; and when
    Oedipus died, your loyalty was transferred to his children.
    Unfortunately, as you know, his two sons, the princes Eteocles and
    Polyneices, have killed each other in battle; and I, as the next in
145   blood, have succeeded to the full power of the throne.
        I am aware, of course, that no Ruler can expect complete loyalty
    from his subjects until he has been tested in office. Nevertheless, I
    say to you at the very outset that I have nothing but contempt for the
    kind of Governor who is afraid, for whatever reason, to follow the
150   course that he knows is best for the State; and as for the man who
    sets private friendship above the public welfare,—I have no use for
    him, either. I call God to witness that I saw my country headed for
    ruin, I should not be afraid to speak out plainly; and I need hardly
    remind you that I would never have any dealings with an enemy of
155   the people. No one values friendship more highly than I; but we must

remember that friends made at the risk of wrecking our Ship are not real friends at all.

These are my principles, at any rate, and that is why I have made the following decision concerning the sons of Oedipus: Eteocles, who
160 died as a man should die, fighting for his country, is to be buried with full military honors, with all the ceremony that is usual when the greatest heroes die; but his brother Polyneices, who broke his exile to come back with fire and sword against his native city and the shrines of his fathers' gods, whose one idea was to spill the blood of
165 his blood and sell his own people into slavery—Polyneices, I say, is to have no burial: no man is to touch him or say the least prayer for him; he shall lie on the plain, unburied; and the birds and the scavenging dogs can do with him whatever they like.

This is my command, and you can see the wisdom behind it.
170 As long as I am King, no traitor is going to be honored with the loyal man. But whoever shows by word and deed that he is on the side of the State,—he shall have my respect while he is living and my reverence when he is dead.
Choragos: If that is your will, Creon son of Menoeceus,
175 You have the right to enforce it: we are yours.
Creon: That is my will. Take care that you do your part.
Choragos: We are old men: let the younger ones carry it out.
Creon: I do not mean that: the sentries have been appointed.
Choragos: Then what is it that you would have us do?
180 Creon: You will give no support to whoever breaks this law.
Choragos: Only a crazy man is in love with death!
Creon: And death it is; yet money talks, and the wisest
Have sometimes been known to count a few coins too many.

(Enter Sentry from left.)

Sentry: I'll not say that I'm out of breath from running, King, because
185 every time I stopped to think about what I have to tell you, I felt like going back. And all the time a voice kept saying, "You fool, don't you know you're walking straight into trouble?"; and then another voice: "Yes, but if you let somebody else get the news to Creon first, it will be even worse than that for you!" But good sense won out, at least I
190 hope it was good sense, and here I am with a story that makes no sense at all; but I'll tell it anyhow, because, as they say, what's going to happen's going to happen and—
Creon: Come to the point. What have you to say?
Sentry: I did not do it. I did not see who did it. You must not punish
195 me for what someone else has done.
Creon: A comprehensive defense! More effective, perhaps,
If I knew its purpose. Come: what is it?
Sentry: A dreadful thing . . . I don't know how to put it—
Creon: Out with it!

SENTRY: Well, then;
200   The dead man—
              Polyneices—

(Pause. The Sentry is overcome, fumbles for words. Creon waits impassively.)

                      out there—
                              someone,—
       New dust on the slimy flesh!

(Pause. No sign from Creon.)

       Someone has given it burial that way, and
       Gone . . .

(Long pause. Creon finally speaks with deadly control.)

CREON: And the man who dared do this?
SENTRY: I swear I
205   Do not know! You must believe me!
                              Listen:
       The ground was dry, not a sign of digging, no,
       Not a wheeltrack in the dust, no trace of anyone.
       It was when they relieved us this morning: and one of them,
       The corporal, pointed to it.
                      There it was,
210   The strangest—
              Look:
       The body, just mounded over with light dust: you see?
       Not buried really, but as if they'd covered it
       Just enough for the ghost's peace. And no sign
       Of dogs or any wild animal that had been there.
215   And then what a scene there was! Every man of us
       Accusing the other: we all proved the other man did it,
       We all had proof that we could not have done it.
       We were ready to take hot iron in our hands,
       Walk through fire, swear by all the gods,
220   *It was not I!*
       I do not know who it was, but it was not I!

*(Creon's rage has been mounting steadily, but the Sentry is too intent upon his
story to notice it.)*

       And then, when this came to nothing, someone said
       A thing that silenced us and made us stare
       Down at the ground: you had to be told the news,
225   And one of us had to do it! We threw the dice,
       And the bad luck fell to me. So here I am,
       No happier to be here than you are to have me:
       Nobody likes the man who brings bad news.

CHORAGOS: I have been wondering, King: can it be that the gods have
230   done this?
CREON: *(Furiously)* Stop!
        Must you doddering wrecks
        Go out of your heads entirely? "The gods"!
        Intolerable!
235   The gods favor this corpse? Why? How had he served them?
        Tried to loot their temples, burn their images,
        Yes, and the whole State, and its laws with it!
        Is it your senile opinion that the gods love to honor bad men?
        A pious thought!—
                              No, from the very beginning
240   There have been those who have whispered together,
        Stiff-necked anarchists, putting their heads together,
        Scheming against me in alleys. These are the men,
        And they have bribed my own guard to do this thing.
        (Sententiously) Money!
245   There's nothing in the world so demoralizing as money.
        Down go your cities,
        Homes gone, men gone, honest hearts corrupted,
        Crookedness of all kinds, and all for money!
        (To Sentry)   But you—
        I swear by God and by the throne of God,
250   The man who has done this thing shall pay for it!
        Find that man, bring him here to me, or your death
        Will be the least of your problems: I'll string you up
        Alive, and there will be certain ways to make you
        Discover your employer before you die;
255   And the process may teach you a lesson you seem to have missed:
        The dearest profit is sometimes all too dear:
        That depends on the source. Do you understand me?
        A fortune won is often misfortune.
SENTRY: King, may I speak?
CREON: Your very voice distresses me.
260 SENTRY: Are you sure that it is my voice, and not your conscience?
CREON: By God, he wants to analyze me now!
SENTRY: It is not what I say, but what has been done, that hurts you.
CREON: You talk too much.
SENTRY: Maybe; but I've done nothing.
CREON: Sold your soul for some silver: that's all you've done.
265 SENTRY: How dreadful it is when the right judge judges wrong!
CREON: Your figures of speech
        May entertain you now; but unless you bring me the man,
        You will get little profit from them in the end.

(Exit Creon into the palace.)

SENTRY: "Bring me the man"—!
270   I'd like nothing better than bringing him the man!
      But bring him or not, you have seen the last of me here.
      At any rate, I am safe!

(Exit Sentry.)

ODE 1[6]

STROPHE 1

CHORUS: Numberless are the world's wonders, but none
        More wonderful than man; the stormgray sea
275   Yields to his prows, the huge crests bear him high;
        Earth, holy and inexhaustible, is graven
        With shining furrows where his plows have gone
        Year after year, the timeless labor of stallions.

ANTISTROPHE 1

        The lightboned birds and beasts that cling to cover,
280   The lithe fish lighting their reaches of dim water,
        All are taken, tamed in the net of his mind;
        The lion on the hill, the wild horse windy-maned,
        Resign to him; and his blunt yoke has broken
        The sultry shoulders of the mountain bull.

STROPHE 2

285   Words also, and thought as rapid as air,
        He fashions to his good use; statecraft is his,
        And his the skill that deflects the arrows of snow,
        The spears of winter rain: from every wind
        He has made himself secure—from all but one:
290   In the late wind of death he cannot stand.

ANTISTROPHE 2

        O clear intelligence, force beyond all measure!
        O fate of man, working both good and evil!
        When the laws are kept, how proudly his city stands!
        When the laws are broken, what of his city then?
295   Never may the anárchic man find rest at my hearth,
        Never be it said that my thoughts are his thoughts.

---

[6] *Ode 1:* first song sung by the Chorus, who at the same time danced. Here again, as in
the parados, *strophe* and *antistrophe* probably divide the song into two movements of
the dance: right-to-left, then left-to-right.

SCENE 2

(Reenter Sentry leading Antigone.)

CHORAGOS: What does this mean? Surely this captive woman
    Is the Princess, Antigone. Why should she be taken?
SENTRY: Here is the one who did it! We caught her
300   In the very act of burying him.—Where is Creon?
CHORAGOS: Just coming from the house.

(Enter Creon, center.)

CREON: What has happened?
    Why have you come back so soon?
SENTRY: *(Expansively)*   O King,
    A man should never be too sure of anything:
    I would have sworn
305   That you'd not see me here again: your anger
    Frightened me so, and the things you threatened me with;
    But how could I tell then
    That I'd be able to solve the case so soon?
    No dice-throwing this time: I was only too glad to come!
310   Here is this woman. She is the guilty one:
    We found her trying to bury him.
    Take her, then; question her; judge her as you will.
    I am through with the whole thing now, and glad of it.
CREON: But this is Antigone! Why have you brought her here?
315 SENTRY: She was burying him, I tell you!
CREON: *(Severely)*   Is this the truth?
SENTRY: I saw her with my own eyes. Can I say more?
CREON: The details: come, tell me quickly!
SENTRY: It was like this:
    After those terrible threats of yours, King,
    We went back and brushed the dust away from the body.
320   The flesh was soft by now, and stinking,
    So we sat on a hill to windward and kept guard.
    No napping this time! We kept each other awake.
    But nothing happened until the white round sun
    Whirled in the center of the round sky over us:
325   Then, suddenly,
    A storm of dust roared up from the earth, and the sky
    Went out, the plain vanished with all its tress
    In the stinging dark. We closed our eyes and endured it.
    The whirlwind lasted a long time, but it passed;
330   And then we looked, and there was Antigone!
    I have seen
    A mother bird come back to a stripped nest, heard

Her crying bitterly a broken note or two
For the young ones stolen. Just so, when this girl
335 Found the bare corpse, and all her love's work wasted,
She wept, and cried on heaven to damn the hands
That had done this thing.
                              And then she brought more dust
And sprinkled wine three times for her brother's ghost.
We ran and took her at once. She was not afraid,
340 Not even when we charged her with what she had done.
She denied nothing.
                              And this was a comfort to me,
And some uneasiness: for it is a good thing
To escape from death, but it is no great pleasure
To bring death to a friend.
                              Yet I always say
345 There is nothing so comfortable as your own safe skin!
CREON: *(Slowly, dangerously)* And you, Antigone,
You with your head hanging,—do you confess this thing?
ANTIGONE: I do. I deny nothing.
CREON: *(To Sentry)*   You may go.

(Exit Sentry.)

(To Antigone.) Tell me, tell me briefly:
350 Had you heard my proclamation touching this matter?
ANTIGONE: It was public. Could I help hearing it?
CREON: And yet you dared defy the law.
ANTIGONE: I dared.
It was not God's proclamation. That final Justice
That rules the world below makes no such laws.
355 Your edict, King, was strong,
But all your strength is weakness itself against
The immortal unrecorded laws of God.
They are not merely now: they were, and shall be,
Operative for ever, beyond man utterly.
360 I knew I must die, even without your decree:
I am only mortal. And if I must die
Now, before it is my time to die,
Surely this is no hardship: can anyone
Living, as I live, with evil all about me,
365 Think Death less than a friend? This death of mine
Is of no importance; but if I had left my brother
Lying in death unburied, I should have suffered.
Now I do not.
                              You smile at me. Ah Creon,
Think me a fool, if you like; but it may well be
370 That a fool convicts me of folly.

CHORAGOS: Like father, like daughter: both headstrong, deaf to reason!
   She has never learned to yield:

CREON: She has much to learn.
   The inflexible heart breaks first, the toughest iron
   Cracks first, and the wildest horses bend their necks

375   At the pull of the smallest curb.
                                   Pride? In a slave?
   This girl is guilty of a double insolence,
   Breaking the given laws and boasting of it.
   Who is the man here,
   She or I, if this crime goes unpunished?

380   Sister's child, or more than sister's child,
   Or closer yet in blood—she and her sister
   Win bitter death for this!
   (To Servants)   Go, some of you,
   Arrest Ismene. I accuse her equally.
   Bring her: you will find her sniffling in the house there.

385   Her mind's a traitor: crimes kept in the dark
   Cry for light, and the guardian brain shudders;
   But how much worse than this
   Is brazen boasting of barefaced anarchy!

ANTIGONE: Creon, what more do you want than my death?

CREON: Nothing.

390   That gives me everything.

ANTIGONE: Then I beg you: kill me.
   This talking is a great weariness: your words
   Are distasteful to me, and I am sure that mine
   Seem so to you. And yet they should not seem so:
   I should have praise and honor for what I have done.

395   All these men here would praise me
   Were their lips not frozen shut with fear of you.
   (Bitterly) Ah the good fortune of kings,
   Licensed to say and do whatever they please!

CREON: You are alone here in that opinion.

400 ANTIGONE: No, they are with me. But they keep their tongues in leash.

CREON: Maybe. But you are guilty, and they are not.

ANTIGONE: There is no guilt in reverence for the dead.

CREON: But Eteocles—was he not your brother too?

ANTIGONE: My brother too.

CREON: And you insult his memory?

405 ANTIGONE: *(Softly)* The dead man would not say that I insult it.

CREON: He would: for you honor a traitor as much as him.

ANTIGONE: His own brother, traitor or not, and equal in blood.

CREON: He made war on his country. Eteocles defended it.

ANTIGONE: Nevertheless, there are honors due all the dead.

410 CREON: But not the same for the wicked as for the just.
ANTIGONE: Ah Creon, Creon
Which of us can say what the gods hold wicked?
CREON: An enemy is an enemy, even dead.
ANTIGONE: It is my nature to join in love, not hate.
415 CREON: *(Finally losing patience)* Go join them then; if you must have
your love,
Find it in hell!
CHORAGOS: But see, Ismene comes:

(Enter Ismene, guarded.)

Those tears are sisterly, the cloud
That shadows her eyes rains down gentle sorrow.
420 CREON: You too, Ismene,
Snake in my ordered house, sucking my blood
Stealthily—and all the time I never knew
That these two sisters were aiming at my throne!
Ismene,
Do you confess your share in this crime, or deny it?
425 Answer me.
ISMENE: Yes, if she will let me say so. I am guilty.
ANTIGONE: *(Coldly)* No, Ismene. You have no right to say so.
You would not help me, and I will not have you help me.
ISMENE: But now I know what you meant; and I am here
430 To join you, to take my share of punishment.
ANTIGONE: The dead man and the gods who rule the dead
Know whose act this was. Words are not friends.
ISMENE: Do you refuse me, Antigone? I want to die with you:
I too have a duty that I must discharge to the dead.
435 ANTIGONE: You shall not lessen my death by sharing it.
ISMENE: What do I care for life when you are dead?
ANTIGONE: Ask Creon. You're always hanging on his opinions.
ISMENE: You are laughing at me. Why, Antigone?
ANTIGONE: It's a joyless laughter, Ismene.
ISMENE: But can I do nothing?
440 ANTIGONE: Yes. Save yourself. I shall not envy you.
There are those who will praise you; I shall have honor, too.
ISMENE: But we are equally guilty!
ANTIGONE: No more, Ismene.
You are alive, but I belong to Death.
CREON: *(to the Chorus)* Gentlemen, I beg you to observe these girls:
445 One has just now lost her mind; the other
It seems, has never had a mind at all.
ISMENE: Grief teaches the steadiest minds to waver, King.
CREON: Yours certainly did, when you assumed guilt with the guilty!

ISMENE: But how could I go on living without her?

CREON: You are.

450   She is already dead.

ISMENE: But your own son's bride!

CREON: There are places enough for him to push his plow.
      I want no wicked women for my sons!

ISMENE: O dearest Haimon, how your father wrongs you!

CREON: I've had enough of your childish talk of marriage!

455   CHORAGOS: Do you really intend to steal this girl from your son?

CREON: No; Death will do that for me.

CHORAGOS: Then she must die?

CREON: (Ironically) You dazzle me.

                              —But enough of this talk!
      (To Guards) You, there, take them away and guard them well:
      For they are but women, and even brave men run

460   When they see Death coming.

(Exeunt Ismene, Antigone, and Guards.)

ODE 2

STROPHE 1

CHORUS: Fortunate is the man who has never tasted God's vengeance!
      Where once the anger of heaven has struck, that house is shaken
      For ever: damnation rises behind each child
      Like a wave cresting out of the black northeast,

465   When the long darkness under sea roars up
      And bursts drumming death upon the windwhipped sand.

ANTISTROPHE 1

      I have seen this gathering sorrow from time long past
      Loom upon Oedipus' children: generation from generation
      Takes the compulsive rage of the enemy god.

470   So lately this last flower of Oedipus' line
      Drank the sunlight! but now a passionate word
      And a handful of dust have closed up all its beauty.

STROPHE 2

      What mortal arrogance
      Transcends the wrath of Zeus?

475   Sleep cannot lull him nor the effortless long months
      Of the timeless gods: but he is young for ever,
      And his house is the shining day of high Olympos.
            All that is and shall be,
            And all the past, is his.

480   No pride on earth is free of the curse of heaven.

ANTISTROPHE 2
    The straying dreams of men
        May bring them ghosts of joy:
    But as they drowse, the waking embers burn them;
    Or they walk with fixed eyes, as blind men walk.
485   But the ancient wisdom speaks for our own time:
        Fate works most for woe
        With Folly's fairest show.
    Man's little pleasure is the spring of sorrow.

SCENE 3

CHORAGOS: But here is Haimon, King, the last of all your sons.
490   Is it grief for Antigone that brings him here,
    And bitterness at being robbed of his bride?

(Enter Haimon.)

CREON: We shall soon see, and no need of diviners.
                                                —Son,
    You have heard my final judgment on that girl:
    Have you come here hating me, or have you come
495   With deference and with love, whatever I do?
HAIMON: I am your son, father. You are my guide.
    You make things clear for me, and I obey you.
    No marriage means more to me than your continuing wisdom.
CREON: Good. That is the way to behave: subordinate
500   Everything else, my son, to your father's will.
    This is what a man prays for, that he may get
    Sons attentive and dutiful in his house,
    Each one hating his father's enemies,
    Honoring his father's friends. But if his sons
505   Fail him, if they turn out unprofitably,
    What has he fathered but trouble for himself
    And amusement for the malicious?
                                        So you are right
    Not to lose your head over this woman.
    Your pleasure with her would soon grow cold, Haimon,
510   And then you'd have a hellcat in bed and elsewhere.
    Let her find her husband in Hell!
    Of all the people in this city, only she
    Has had contempt for my law and broken it.
    Do you want me to show myself weak before the people?
515   Or to break my sworn word? No, and I will not.
    The woman dies.
    I suppose she'll plead "family ties." Well, let her.
    If I permit my own family to rebel,

How shall I earn the world's obedience?
520   Show me the man who keeps his house in hand,
He's fit for public authority.
                                        I'll have no dealings
With lawbreakers, critics of the government:
Whoever is chosen to govern should be obeyed—
Must be obeyed, in all things, great and small,
525   Just and unjust! O Haimon,
The man who knows how to obey, and that man only,
Knows how to give commands when the time comes.
You can depend on him, no matter how fast
The spears come: he's a good soldier, he'll stick it out.

530   Anarchy, anarchy! Show me a greater evil!
This is why cities tumble and the great houses rain down,
This is what scatters armies!
No, no: good lives are made so by discipline.
We keep the laws then, and the lawmakers,
535   And no woman shall seduce us. If we must lose,
Let's lose to a man, at least! Is a woman stronger than we?
CHORAGOS: Unless time has rusted my wits,
What you say, King, is said with point and dignity.
HAIMON: *(Boyishly earnest)* Father:
540   Reason is God's crowning gift to man, and you are right
To warn me against losing mine. I cannot say—
I hope that I shall never want to say!—that you
Have reasoned badly. Yet there are other men
Who can reason, too; and their opinions might be helpful.
545   You are not in a position to know everything
That people say or do, or what they feel:
Your temper terrifies—everyone
Will tell you only what you like to hear.
But I, at any rate, can listen; and I have heard them
550   Muttering and whispering in the dark about this girl.
They say no woman has ever, so unreasonably,
Died so shameful a death for a generous act:
"She covered her brother's body. Is this indecent?
She kept him from dogs and vultures. Is this a crime?
555   Death?—She should have all the honor that we can give her!"

This is the way they talk out there in the city.

You must believe me:
Nothing is closer to me than your happiness.
What could be closer? Must not any son
560   Value his father's fortune as his father does his?
I beg you, do not be unchangeable:
Do not believe that you alone can be right.

The man who thinks that,
The man who maintains that only he has the power
565   To reason correctly, the gift to speak, the soul—
A man like that, when you know him, turns out empty.
It is not reason never to yield to reason!

In flood time you can see how some trees bend,
And because they bend, even their twigs are safe,
570   While stubborn trees are torn up, roots and all.
And the same thing happens in sailing:
Make your sheet fast, never slacken,—and over you go,
Head over heels and under: and there's your voyage.
Forget you are angry! Let yourself be moved!
575   I know I am young; but please let me say this:
The ideal condition
Would be, I admit, that men should be right by instinct;
But since we are all too likely to go astray,
The reasonable thing is to learn from those who can teach.
580 CHORAGOS: You will do well to listen to him, King,
If what he says is sensible. And you, Haimon,
Must listen to your father.—Both speak well.
CREON: You consider it right for a man of my years and experience
To go to school to a boy?
HAIMON: It is not right
585   If I am wrong. But if I am young, and right,
What does my age matter?
CREON: You think it right to stand up for an anarchist?
HAIMON: Not at all. I pay no respect to criminals.
CREON: Then she is not a criminal?
590 HAIMON: The City would deny it, to a man.
CREON: And the City proposes to teach me how to rule?
HAIMON: Ah. Who is it that's talking like a boy now?
CREON: My voice is the one voice giving orders in this City!
HAIMON: It is no City if it takes orders from one voice.
595 CREON: The State is the King!
HAIMON: Yes, if the State is a desert.

(Pause.)

CREON: This boy, it seems, has sold out to a woman.
HAIMON: If you are a woman: my concern is only for you.
CREON: So? Your "concern"! In a public brawl with your father!
HAIMON: How about you, in a public brawl with justice?
600 CREON: With justice, when all that I do is within my rights?
HAIMON: You have no right to trample on God's right.
CREON: *(Completely out of control)* Fool, adolescent fool! Taken in by a
woman!

HAIMON: You'll never see me taken in by anything vile.

CREON: Every word you say is for her!

HAIMON: *(Quietly, darkly)*   And for you.

605   And for me. And for the gods under the earth.

CREON: You'll never marry her while she lives.

HAIMON: Then she must die.—But her death will cause another.

CREON: Another?

        Have you lost your senses? Is this an open threat?

610   HAIMON: There is no threat in speaking to emptiness.

CREON: I swear you'll regret this superior tone of yours!

        You are the empty one!

HAIMON: If you were not my father,

        I'd say you were perverse.

CREON: You girl-struck fool, don't play at words with me!

615   HAIMON: I am sorry. You prefer silence.

CREON: Now, by God—

        I swear, by all the gods in heaven above us,

        You'll watch it, I swear you shall!

        (To the Servants)   Bring her out!

        Bring the woman out! Let her die before his eyes!

        Here, this instant, with her bridegroom beside her!

620   HAIMON: Not here, no; she will not die here, King.

        And you will never see my face again.

        Go on raving as long as you've a friend to endure you.

(Exit Haimon.)

CHORAGOS: Gone, gone.

        Creon, a young man in a rage is dangerous!

625   CREON: Let him do, or dream to do, more than a man can.

        He shall not save these girls from death.

CHORAGOS: These girls?

        You have sentenced them both?

CREON: No, you are right.

        I will not kill the one whose hands are clean.

CHORAGOS: But Antigone?

CREON: *(Somberly)*   I will carry her far away

630   Out there in the wilderness, and lock her

        Living in a vault of stone. She shall have food,

        As the custom is, to absolve the State of her death.

        And there let her pray to the gods of hell:

        They are her only gods:

635   Perhaps they will show her an escape from death,

        Or she may learn,

                        though late,

        That piety shown the dead is pity in vain.

(Exit Creon.)

ODE 3

STROPHE

CHORUS: Love, unconquerable
  Waster of rich men, keeper
640 Of warm lights and all-night vigil
  In the soft face of a girl:
  Sea-wanderer, forest-visitor!
  Even the pure Immortals cannot escape you,
  And mortal man, in his one day's dusk,
645 Trembles before your glory.

ANTISTROPHE

  Surely you swerve upon ruin
  The just man's consenting heart,
  As here you have made bright anger
  Strike between father and son—
650 And none has conquered but Love!
  A girl's glánce wórking the will of heaven:
  Pleasure to her alone who mocks us,
  Merciless Aphrodite.[7]

SCENE 4

CHORAGOS: *(As Antigone enters guarded)* But I can no longer stand in
  awe of this,
655 Nor, seeing what I see, keep back my tears.
  Here is Antigone, passing to that chamber
  Where all find sleep at last.

STROPHE 1

ANTIGONE: Look upon me, friends, and pity me
  Turning back at the night's edge to say
660 Good-by to the sun that shines for me no longer;
  Now sleepy Death
  Summons me down to Acheron,[8] that cold shore:
  There is no bridesong there, nor any music.
CHORUS: Yet not unpraised, not without a kind of honor,
665 You walk at last into the underworld;
  Untouched by sickness, broken by no sword.
  What woman has ever found your way to death?

---

[7] *Aphrodite:* goddess of love and beauty.   [8] *Acheron:* river in Hades, domain of the dead.

ANTISTROPHE 1

ANTIGONE: How often I have heard the story of Niobe,[9]
    Tantalos' wretched daughter, how the stone
670   Clung fast about her, ivy-close: and they say
    The rain falls endlessly
    And sifting soft snow; her tears are never done.
    I feel the loneliness of her death in mine.
CHORUS: But she was born of heaven, and you
675   Are woman, woman-born. If her death is yours,
    A mortal woman's, is this not for you
    Glory in our world and in the world beyond?

STROPHE 2

ANTIGONE: You laugh at me. Ah, friends, friends,
    Can you not wait until I am dead? O Thebes,
680   O men many-charioted, in love with Fortune,
    Dear springs of Dirce, sacred Theban grove,
    Be witnesses for me, denied all pity,
    Unjustly judged! and think a word of love
    For her whose path turns
685   Under dark earth, where there are no more tears.
CHORUS: You have passed beyond human daring and come at last
    Into a place of stone where Justice sits.
    I cannot tell
    What shape of your father's guilt appears in this.

ANTISTROPHE 2

690 ANTIGONE: You have touched it at last: that bridal bed
    Unspeakable, horror of son and mother mingling:
    Their crime, infection of all our family!
    O Oedipus, father and brother!
    Your marriage strikes from the grave to murder mine.
695   I have been a stranger here in my own land:
    All my life
    The blasphemy of my birth has followed me.
CHORUS: Reverence is a virtue, but strength
    Lives in established law: that must prevail.
700   You have made your choice,
    Your death is the doing of your conscious hand.

---

[9] *story of Niobe:* in which this mother, when her fourteen children were slain, wept so copiously that she was transformed to a stone on Mount Sipylus. Her tears became the mountain's streams.

EPODE

ANTIGONE: Then let me go, since all your words are bitter,
And the very light of the sun is cold to me.
Lead me to my vigil, where I must have
705   Neither love nor lamentation; no song, but silence.

(Creon interrupts impatiently.)

CREON: If dirges and planned lamentations could put off death,
Men would be singing for ever.
(To the Servants)   Take her, go!
You know your orders: take her to the vault
And leave her alone there. And if she lives or dies,
710   That's her affair, not ours: our hands are clean.
ANTIGONE: O tomb, vaulted bride-bed in eternal rock,
Soon I shall be with my own again
Where Persephone[10] welcomes the thin ghosts underground:
And I shall see my father again, and you, mother,
715   And dearest Polyneices—
                    dearest indeed
To me, since it was my hand
That washed him clean and poured the ritual wine:
And my reward is death before my time!

And yet, as men's hearts know, I have done no wrong,
720   I have not sinned before God. Or if I have,
I shall know the truth in death. But if the guilt
Lies upon Creon who judged me, then, I pray,
May his punishment equal my own.
CHORAGOS: O passionate heart,
Unyielding, tormented still by the same winds!
725 CREON: Her guards shall have good cause to regret their delaying.
ANTIGONE: Ah! That voice is like the voice of death!
CREON: I can give you no reason to think you are mistaken.
ANTIGONE: Thebes, and you my fathers' gods,
And rulers of Thebes, you see me now, the last
730   Unhappy daughter of a line of kings,
Your kings, led away to death. You will remember
What things I suffer, and at what men's hands,
Because I would not transgress the laws of heaven.
(To the Guards, simply) Come: let us wait no longer.

(Exit Antigone, left, guarded.)

---

[10] *Persephone:* whom Pluto, god of the underworld, abducted to be his queen.

ODE 4

STROPHE 1

735 CHORUS: All Danae's beauty was locked away
In a brazen cell where the sunlight could not come:
A small room still as any grave, enclosed her.
Yet she was a princess too,
And Zeus in a rain of gold poured love upon her.[11]
740 O child, child,
No power in wealth or war
Or tough sea-blackened ships
Can prevail against untiring Destiny!

ANTISTROPHE 1

And Dryas' son[12] also, that furious king,
745 Bore the god's prisoning anger for his pride:
Sealed up by Dionysos in deaf stone,
His madness died among echoes.
So at the last he learned what dreadful power
His tongue had mocked:
750 For he had profaned the revels,
And fired the wrath of the nine
Implacable Sisters[13] that love the sound of the flute.

STROPHE 2

And old men tell a half-remembered tale
Of horror[14] where a dark ledge splits the sea
755 And a double surf beats on the gráy shóres:
How a king's new woman, sick
With hatred for the queen he had imprisoned,
Ripped out his two sons' eyes with her bloody hands
While grinning Ares watched the shuttle plunge
760 Four times: four blind wounds crying for revenge,

---

[11] *All Danae's beauty . . . poured love upon her:* In legend, when an oracle told Acrisius, king of Argos, that his daughter Danae would bear a son who would grow up to slay him, he locked the princess into a chamber made of bronze, lest any man impregnate her. But Zeus, father of the gods, entered Danae's prison in a shower of gold. The resultant child, the hero Perseus, was accidentally to fulfill the prophecy by killing Acrisius with an ill-aimed discus throw.   [12] *Dryas' son:* King Lycurgus of Thrace, whom Dionysos, god of wine, caused to be stricken with madness.   [13] *Sisters:* the Muses, nine sister goddesses who presided over poetry and music, arts and sciences. [14] *a half-remembered tale of horror:* As the Chorus recalls in the rest of this song, the point of this tale is that being nobly born will not save one from disaster. King Phineas cast off his first wife Cleopatra (not the later Egyptian queen, but the daughter of Boreas, god of the north wind) and imprisoned her in a cave. Out of hatred for Cleopatra, the cruel Eidothea, second wife of the king, blinded her stepsons. Ares, god of war, was said to gloat over bloodshed.

ANTISTROPHE 2
>   Crying, tears and blood mingled.—Piteously born,
>   Those sons whose mother was of heavenly birth!
>   Her father was the god of the North Wind
>   And she was cradled by gales,
> 765 She raced with young colts on the glittering hills
>   And walked untrammeled in the open light:
>   But in her marriage deathless Fate found means
>   To build a tomb like yours for all her joy.

SCENE 5

(Enter blind Teiresias, led by a boy. The opening speeches of Teiresias should be in singsong contrast to the realistic lines of Creon.)

TEIRESIAS: This is the way the blind man comes, Princes, Princes,
770   Lockstep, two heads lit by the eyes of one.
CREON: What new thing have you to tell us, old Teiresias?
TEIRESIAS: I have much to tell you: listen to the prophet, Creon.
CREON: I am not aware that I have ever failed to listen.
TEIRESIAS: Then you have done wisely, King, and ruled well.
775 CREON: I admit my debt to you. But what have you to say?
TEIRESIAS: This, Creon: you stand once more on the edge of fate.
CREON: What do you mean? Your words are a kind of dread.
TEIRESIAS: Listen, Creon:
>   I was sitting in my chair of augury, at the place
> 780 Where the birds gather about me. They were all a-chatter,
>   As is their habit, when suddenly I heard
>   A strange note in their jangling, a scream, a
>   Whirring fury; I knew that they were fighting,
>   Tearing each other, dying
> 785 In a whirlwind of wings clashing. And I was afraid.
>   I began the rites of burnt-offering at the altar,
>   But Hephaistos[15] failed me: instead of bright flame,
>   There was only the sputtering slime of the fat thigh-flesh
>   Melting: the entrails dissolved in gray smoke,
> 790 The bare bone burst from the welter. And no blaze!

>   This was a sign from heaven. My boy described it,
>   Seeing for me as I see for others.

>   I tell you, Creon, you yourself have brought
>   This new calamity upon us. Our hearths and altars
> 795 Are stained with the corruption of dogs and carrion birds
>   That glut themselves on the corpse of Oedipus' son.

---

[15] *Hephaistos:* god of fire.

The gods are deaf when we pray to them, their fire
Recoils from our offering, their birds of omen
Have no cry of comfort, for they are gorged
800   With the thick blood of the dead.

                           O my son,
These are no trifles! Think: all men make mistakes,
But a good man yields when he knows his course is wrong,
And repairs the evil. The only crime is pride.
Give in to the dead man, then: do not fight with a corpse—
805   What glory is it to kill a man who is dead?
Think, I beg you:
It is for your own good that I speak as I do.
You should be able to yield for your own good.
CREON: It seems that prophets have made me their especial province.
810   All my life long
I have been a kind of butt for the dull arrows
Of doddering fortune-tellers!

                      No, Teiresias:
If your birds—if the great eagles of God himself
Should carry him stinking bit by bit to heaven,
815   I would not yield. I am not afraid of pollution:
No man can defile the gods.

                 Do what you will,
Go into business, make money, speculate
An India gold or that synthetic gold from Sardis,
Get rich otherwise than by my consent to bury him.
820   Teiresias, it is a sorry thing when a wise man
Sells his wisdom, lets out his words for hire!
TEIRESIAS: Ah Creon! Is there no man left in the world—
CREON: To do what?—Come, let's have the aphorism!
TEIRESIAS: No man who knows that wisdom outweighs any wealth?
825 CREON: As surely as bribes are baser than any baseness.
TEIRESIAS: You are sick, Creon! You are deathly sick!
CREON: As you say: it is not my place to challenge a prophet.
TEIRESIAS: Yet you have said my prophecy is for sale.
CREON: The generation of prophets has always loved gold.
830 TEIRESIAS: The generation of kings has always loved brass.
CREON: You forget yourself! You are speaking to your King.
TEIRESIAS: I know it. You are a king because of me.
CREON: You have a certain skill; but you have sold out.
TEIRESIAS: King, you will drive me to words that—
CREON: Say them, say them!
835   Only remember: I will not pay you for them.
TEIRESIAS: No, you will find them too costly.
CREON: No doubt. Speak:
Whatever you say, you will not change my will.

TEIRESIAS: Then take this, and take it to heart!
　　　The time is not far off when you shall pay back
840　　Corpse for corpse, flesh of your own flesh.
　　　You have thrust the child of this world into living night,
　　　You have kept from the gods below the child that is theirs:
　　　The one in a grave before her death, the other,
　　　Dead, denied the grave. This is your crime:
845　　And the Furies and the dark gods of Hell
　　　Are swift with terrible punishment for you.

　　　Do you want to buy me now, Creon?
　　　　　　　　　　　　　　　　　　　　Not many days,
　　　And your house will be full of men and women weeping,
　　　And curses will be hurled at you from far
850　　Cities grieving for sons unburied, left to rot
　　　Before the walls of Thebes.
　　　There are my arrows, Creon: they are all for you.

　　　(To Boy) But come, child: lead me home.
　　　Let him waste his fine anger upon younger men.
855　　Maybe he will learn at last
　　　To control a wiser tongue in a better head.

(Exit Teiresias.)

CHORAGOS: The old man has gone, King, but his words
　　　Remain to plague us. I am old, too,
　　　But I cannot remember that he was ever false.
860　CREON: That is true. . . . It troubles me.
　　　Oh it is hard to give in! but it is worse
　　　To risk everything for stubborn pride.
CHORAGOS: Creon: take my advice.
CREON:　　　　　　　　　　　　What shall I do?
CHORAGOS: Go quickly: free Antigone from her vault
865　　And build a tomb for the body of Polyneices.
CREON: You would have me do this!
CHORAGOS:　　　　　　　　　　　　Creon, yes!
　　　And it must be done at once: God moves
　　　Swiftly to cancel the folly of stubborn men.
CREON: It is hard to deny the heart! But I
870　　Will do it: I will not fight with destiny.
CHORAGOS: You must go yourself, you cannot leave it to others.
CREON: I will go.
　　　　　　　—Bring axes, servants:
　　　Come with me to the tomb. I buried her, I
　　　Will set her free.
　　　　　　　　　　Oh quickly!

875   My mind misgives—
          The laws of the gods are mighty, and a man must serve them
          To the last day of his life!

(Exit Creon.)

PAEAN[16]

Strophe 1
Choragos: God of many names
Chorus: O Iacchos
                                                          son
    of Kadmeian Sémele
                              O born of the Thunder!
880   Guardian of the West
                              Regent
    Of Eleusis' plain
                    O Prince of maenad Thebes
    and the Dragon Field by rippling Ismenós:[17]

Antistrophe 1
Choragos: God of many names
Chorus: the flame of torches
    flares on our hills
                    the nymphs of Iacchos
885   dance at the spring of Castalia:[18]
    from the vine-close mountain
                                        come ah come in ivy:
    Evohé evohé! [19] sings through the streets of Thebes

---

[16] *Paean:* a song of praise or prayer, here to Dionysos, god of wine.   [17] *God of many names . . . Dragon Field by rippling Ismenós:* Dionysos was also called Iacchos (or, by the Romans, Bacchus). He was the son of Zeus ("the Thunderer") and of Sémele, daughter of Kadmos (or Cadmus), legendary founder of Thebes. "Regent of Eleusis' plain" is another name for Dionysos, honored in secret rites at Eleusis, a town northwest of Athens. "Prince of maenad Thebes" is yet another: The Maenads were women of Thebes said to worship Dionysos with wild orgiastic rites. Kadmos, so the story goes, sowed dragon's teeth in a field beside the river Ismenós. Up sprang a crop of fierce warriors who fought among themselves until only five remained. These victors became the first Thebans.   [18] *Castalia:* a spring on Mount Parnassus, named for a maiden who drowned herself in it to avoid rape by the god Apollo. She became a nymph, or nature spirit, dwelling in its waters. In the temple of Delphi, at the mountain's foot, priestesses of Dionysos (the "nymphs of Iacchos") used the spring's waters in rites of purification.   [19] *Evohé evohé!:* cry of the Maenads in supplicating Dionysos: "Come forth, come forth!"

STROPHE 2
CHORAGOS: God of many names
CHORUS: Iacchos of Thebes
        heavenly Child
                of Sémele bride of the Thunderer!
890   The shadow of plague is upon us:
                                        come
        with clement feet
                        oh come from Parnasos
        down the long slopes
                        across the lamenting water

ANTISTROPHE 2
CHORAGOS: Io[20] Fire! Chorister of the throbbing stars!
        O purest among the voices of the night!
895   Thou son of God, blaze for us!
CHORUS: Come with choric rapture of circling Maenads
        Who cry *Iô Iacche!*
                        God of many names!

EXODUS[21]

(Enter Messenger from left.)

MESSENGER: Men of the line of Kadmos, you who live
        Near Amphion's citadel,[22]
                        I cannot say
900   Of any condition of human life "This is fixed,
        This is clearly good, or bad." Fate raises up,
        And Fate casts down the happy and unhappy alike:
        No man can foretell his Fate.
                        Take the case of Creon:
        Creon was happy once, as I count happiness:
905   Victorious in battle, sole governor of the land,
        Fortunate father of children nobly born.
        And now it has all gone from him! Who can say
        That a man is still alive when his life's joy fails?
        He is a walking dead man. Grant him rich,
910   Let him live like a king in his great house:
        If his pleasure is gone, I would not give
        So much as the shadow of smoke for all he owns.

---

[20] *Io:* "Hail" or "Praise be to. . . ."   [21] *Exodus:* the final scene, containing the play's resolution.   [22] *Amphion's citadel:* a name for Thebes. Amphion, son of Zeus, had built a wall around the city by playing so beautifully on his lyre that the charmed stones leaped into their slots.

CHORAGOS: Your words hint at sorrow: what is your news for us?

MESSENGER: They are dead. The living are guilty of their death.

915 CHORAGOS: Who is guilty? Who is dead? Speak!

MESSENGER: Haimon.

    Haimon is dead; and the hand that killed him

    Is his own hand.

CHORAGOS: His father's? or his own?

MESSENGER: His own, driven mad by the murder his father had done.

CHORAGOS: Teiresias, Teiresias, how clearly you saw it all!

920 MESSENGER: This is my news: you must draw what conclusions you can

    from it.

CHORAGOS: But look: Eurydice, our Queen:

    Has she overheard us?

(Enter Eurydice from the palace, center.)

EURYDICE: I have heard something, friends:

925   As I was unlocking the gate of Pallas'[23] shrine,

    For I needed her help today, I heard a voice

    Telling of some new sorrow. And I fainted

    There at the temple with all my maidens about me.

    But speak again: whatever it is, I can bear it:

930   Grief and I are no strangers.

MESSENGER: Dearest Lady,

    I will tell you plainly all that I have seen.

    I shall not try to comfort you: what is the use,

    Since comfort could lie only in what is not true?

    The truth is always best.

                      I went with Creon

935   To the outer plain where Polyneices was lying,

    No friend to pity him, his body shredded by dogs.

    We made our prayers in that place to Hecate

    And Pluto,[24] that they would be merciful. And we bathed

    The corpse with holy water, and we brought

940   Fresh-broken branches to burn what was left of it,

    And upon the urn we heaped up a towering barrow

    Of the earth of his own land.

                    When we were done, we ran

    To the vault where Antigone lay on her couch of stone.

    One of the servants had gone ahead,

945   And while he was yet far off he heard a voice

    Grieving within the chamber, and he came back

    And told Creon. And as the King went closer,

---

[23] *Pallas:* Pallas Athene, goddess of wisdom, and hence an excellent source of advice.
[24] *Hecate and Pluto:* two fearful divinities—the goddess of witchcraft and sorcery and the king of Hades, underworld of the dead.

The air was full of wailing, the words lost,
And he begged us to make all haste. "Am I a prophet?"
950 He said, weeping, "And must I walk this road,
The saddest of all that I have gone before?
My son's voice calls me on. Oh quickly, quickly!
Look through the crevice there, and tell me
If it is Haimon, or some deception of the gods!"

955 We obeyed; and in the cavern's farthest corner
We saw her lying:
She had made a noose of her fine linen veil
And hanged herself. Haimon lay beside her,
His arms about her waist, lamenting her,
960 His love lost under ground, crying out
That his father had stolen her away from him.

When Creon saw him the tears rushed to his eyes
And he called to him: "What have you done, child? Speak to me.
What are you thinking that makes your eyes so strange?
965 O my son, my son, I come to you on my knees!"
But Haimon spat in his face. He said not a word,
Staring—
   And suddenly drew his sword
And lunged. Creon shrank back, the blade missed; and the boy,
Desperate against himself, drove it half its length
970 Into his own side, and fell. And as he died
He gathered Antigone close in his arms again,
Choking, his blood bright red on her white cheek.
And now he lies dead with the dead, and she is his
At last, his bride in the house of the dead.

(Exit Eurydice into the palace.)

975 CHORAGOS: She has left us without a word. What can this mean?
MESSENGER: It troubles me, too; yet she knows what is best,
Her grief is too great for public lamentation,
And doubtless she has gone to her chamber to weep
For her dead son, leading her maidens in his dirge.

(Pause.)

980 CHORAGOS: It may be so: but I fear this deep silence.
MESSENGER: I will see what she is doing. I will go in.

(Exit Messenger into the palace.)

(Enter Creon with attendants, bearing Haimon's body.)

CHORAGOS: But here is the king himself: oh look at him,
  Bearing his own damnation in his arms.

CREON: Nothing you say can touch me any more.

985   My own blind heart has brought me
       From darkness to final darkness. Here you see
       The father murdering, the murdered son—
       And all my civic wisdom!

       Haimon my son, so young, so young to die,
990   I was the fool, not you; and you died for me.
CHORAGOS: That is the truth; but you were late in learning it.
CREON: This truth is hard to bear. Surely a god
       Has crushed me beneath the hugest weight of heaven,
       And driven me headlong a barbaric way
995   To trample out the thing I held most dear.

       The pains that men will take to come to pain!

(Enter Messenger from the palace.)

MESSENGER: The burden you carry in your hands is heavy,
       But it is not all: you will find more in your house.
CREON: What burden worse than this shall I find there?
1000 MESSENGER: The Queen is dead.
CREON: O port of death, deaf world,
       Is there no pity for me? And you, Angel of evil,
       I was dead, and your words are death again.
       Is it true, boy? Can it be true?
1005   Is my wife dead? Has death bred death?
MESSENGER: You can see for yourself.

(The doors are opened and the body of Eurydice is disclosed within.)

CREON: Oh pity!
       All true, all true, and more than I can bear!
       O my wife, my son!
1010 MESSENGER: She stood before the altar, and her heart
       Welcomed the knife her own hand guided,
       And a great cry burst from her lips for Megareus[25] dead,
       And for Haimon dead, her sons; and her last breath
       Was a curse for their father, the murderer of her sons.
1015   And she fell, and the dark flowed in through her closing eyes.
CREON: O God, I am sick with fear.
       Are there no swords here? Has no one a blow for me?
MESSENGER: Her curse is upon you for the deaths of both.
CREON: It is right that it should be. I alone am guilty.
1020   I know it, and I say it. Lead me in,

---

[25] *Megareus:* Son of Creon and brother of Haimon, Megareus was slain in the unsuccessful attack on Thebes.

Quickly, friends.
I have neither life nor substance. Lead me in.
CHORAGOS: You are right, if there can be right in so much wrong.
The briefest way is best in a world of sorrow.
1025 CREON: Let it come,
Let death come quickly, and be kind to me.
I would not ever see the sun again.
CHORAGOS: All that will come when it will; but we, meanwhile,
1030 Have much to do. Leave the future to itself.
CREON: All my heart was in that prayer!
CHORAGOS: Then do not pray any more: the sky is deaf.
CREON: Lead me away. I have been rash and foolish.
I have killed my son and my wife.
I look for comfort; my comfort lies here dead.
1035 Whatever my hands have touched has come to nothing.
Fate has brought all my pride to a thought of dust.

(As Creon is being led into the house, the Choragos advances and speaks directly to the audience.)

CHORAGOS: There is no happiness where there is no wisdom;
No wisdom but in submission to the gods.
Big words are always punished,
1040 And proud men in old age learn to be wise.

READING AND REACTING

1. What ideas does *Antigone* express about duty? About obedience? In what ways do these ideas conform (or fail to conform) to your own concepts of duty and obedience?
2. The chorus expresses the values of the community. According to the chorus, is Antigone a danger to the community? How far do you believe a community should go to protect its values?
3. Both Creon and Antigone defend rights that they believe are sacred. What rights are in conflict? Is there any room for compromise?
4. Do you sympathize with Antigone or with Creon? What characteristics of each do you find noble? Do you ever lose patience with either of them? Explain.
5. Aristotle believed that to be effective, tragic heroes must have elements of both good and evil. To what extent does Antigone conform to Aristotle's requirements?
6. What is Antigone's fatal flaw? How does this flaw lead to the tragic resolution of the play?
7. As the play progresses, do Creon and Antigone change, or do they remain essentially unchanged by events?

8. What lines of dialogue do you believe best express the play's central theme?

9. At the end of *Antigone* the chorus says, "Big words are always punished, / And proud men in old age learn to be wise." Do you think Creon has gained wisdom from his experiences? Why or why not?

10. In what way does Antigone's gender affect her actions? In what way does it determine how she is treated? Are the play's attitudes toward women consistent with those of contemporary American society? Explain.

11. **Journal Entry** If you were Antigone, would you have stuck to your principles, or would you have given in? Explain your reasoning.

12. **Critical Perspective** In *Sophocles the Playwright*, S. M. Adams argues that, to the ancient Greek audience, Antigone and Creon were both tragic heroes. Do you agree? If so, do you see the fact that the play has *two* tragic heroes as a problem?

Related Works: "A Worn Path" (p. 388), "Bartleby the Scrivener" (p. 520), "The Colonel" (p. 889), *Hamlet* (p. 1307), *Oedipus the King* (p. 1509), *Another Antigone* (p. 1663)

 ◊ **A. R. (Arthur Ramsdell) "Pete" Gurney** (1930–   ) stakes out dramatic territory occupied in fiction by writers such as John Updike and John Cheever, examining what the *Village Voice* once called "the dying lifestyle of wealthy WASPdom." Born to an affluent Buffalo family who "had sat in the same pew for a hundred years," Gurney was educated at St. Paul's prep school, Williams College, and Yale, where he wrote the first musical produced there.

Gurney's breakthrough came in 1971 with a Lincoln Center production of his play *Scenes from American Life*—a success followed by a string of others, including *Children* (1974), *Who Killed Richard Cory?* (1976), *Entertaining Strangers* (1977) and three plays produced during the 1982–1983 season: *The Middle Ages, What I Did Last Summer,* and *The Dining Room. Sweet Sue* was published in 1987; *The Cocktail Hour, Perfect Party,* and *Another Antigone* in 1989; and *Love Letters* and *The Golden Age* in 1990. Gurney writes, says one reviewer, "with an interweaving detachment and no small sense of nostalgia intricately crafted scenes of a Protestant culture challenged by Jews, blacks, women, and others seeking a share of the American pie." His more recent plays include *Later Life* (1993), *A Cheever Evening* (1994), *Sylvia* (1995), and *Overtime* (1996), a sequel to Shakespeare's *The Merchant of Venice*.

Gurney's *Another Antigone* (1988), notes *New York Times* critic Jeremy Gerard, is a significant departure for a playwright noted for his light, satiric touch. Like Sophocles' *Antigone*, the play deals with the cost of adhering to values.

CULTURAL CONTEXT ◆ Numerous twentieth-century plays are based on Greek tragedies. Three other plays besides Gurney's which were based on Sophocles' *Antigone* are Bertold Brecht's *Antigone*, Jean Anouilh's *Antigone*, and Tom Paulin's *The Riot Act: A Version of Sophocles's Antigone*. At least seven twentieth-century plays are based on *Oedipus*.

◆ ◆ ◆

A. R. GURNEY, JR.

Another Antigone
(1989)

To John Tillinger

CHARACTERS

HENRY HARPER, *Professor of Classics*
JUDY MILLER, *a student*
DIANA EBERHART, *Dean of Humane Studies*
DAVID APPLETON, *a student*

The play takes place in a university in Boston during the latter half of the spring term.

It is designed, as Sophocles' Antigone *was, to be performed without an intermission. If one is deemed essential, however, it should occur after Dave's last line on page 1687.*

The general effect of the set should evoke the Greek Revival architecture of a typical New England college. There should be columns and steps and benches. Somewhere in the center there should be a slightly abstracted desk and two chairs, indicating both Henry's and Diana's office. Near it is a bookcase, a filing cabinet, on which is an old hotplate, a possibly tin coffee pot, and a couple of cracked mugs. The general effect should be multi-scenic, fluid and shifting, indoors and out, and vaguely Greek.

AT RISE: Henry sits at his desk, perusing a typewritten paper. Judy sits in the other chair. She watches intently. He is middle aged and conservatively dressed. She, in her early twenties, is casually dressed in whatever students are currently wearing.

HENRY: *(finally, putting the document down neatly on the desk between them)*
    Another Antigone.
JUDY: Did someone else write one?

HENRY: Sophocles[1] wrote one.

JUDY: No, I mean someone in *class*.

5 HENRY: Aeschylus[2] wrote one, which is lost. Euripides[3] we *think* wrote one. Seneca[4] tried to write one. Voltaire[5] tried not to. Jean Anouilh[6] wrote a rather peculiar one in 1944, during the Nazi occupation of Paris.

JUDY: But I'm the only one in *class* who wrote one.

HENRY: *(weak smile)* That's right. *(Pause.)* This year.

JUDY: You mean, other students wrote them in other years?

HENRY: Oh yes.

10 JUDY: Really?

HENRY: Of course. *(Henry goes to the filing cabinet. He pulls out a drawer.)* Let's see . . . *Antigone* . . . *Antigone* . . . *(He thumbs through a file of old folders and records.)* Here we are. *Antigone. (He takes out a particular folder.)* Now. I have a record of one in 1955, written during the McCarthy hearings. And another, by a student who I recall was black, about the Civil Rights movement in 1963. And of course there were two, no, three, which cropped up during the Vietnam war.

JUDY: Did anyone ever deal with the Nuclear Arms Race before?

HENRY: No. As far as I know, you are the first to apply the Antigone myth to that particular topic.

JUDY: The story really turned me on.

15 HENRY: I'm glad it did. It is one of the great works of Western literature. Antigone herself is the classic rebel, the ancestor to such figures as Saint Joan or Martin Luther.

JUDY: Oh yes. I see that.

HENRY: And Creon[7] is the ultimate image of uncompromising political authority.

JUDY: I got that, too.

HENRY: Their clash is inevitable and tragic.

20 JUDY: I understand. *(Indicating her manuscript.)* I tried to make them like Jane Fonda and Ronald Reagan.

HENRY: I know what you tried to do, Miss . . . uh . . . Miss . . . *(He glances at her title page.)* Miller. I read all . . . *(He glances at the last page.)* twelve pages of it, in preparation for this conference. *(He slides the*

---

[1] Sophocles (c. 496–406 B.C.)—Greek dramatist. Sophocles, Aeschylus, and Euripides are considered the greatest Athenian tragic dramatists.

[2] Aeschylus (c. 525–456 B.C.)—Greek dramatist.

[3] Euripides (c. 480–406 B.C.)—Greek dramatist.

[4] Seneca (Lucius Annacus Seneca; c. 3 B.C.–A.D. 65)—Roman philosopher, statesman, and dramatist.

[5] François Marie Arouet de Voltaire (1674–1778)—French philosopher and writer.

[6] Jean Anouilh (1910–1987)—French dramatist. His version is also entitled *Antigone*.

[7] The antagonist in *Antigone*. Antigone opposes Creon's law.

*script across the desk to her. She takes it, looks at the title page, flips
through it, looks at the last page, then looks at him.)*

JUDY: You didn't mark it.

HENRY: I most certainly did. I underlined several run-on sentences, and I
circled a rather startling number of misspelled words.

JUDY: No, I mean you didn't *grade* it.

25 HENRY: No I didn't.

JUDY: Why not?

HENRY: Because this course is about Greek tragedy, and your paper isn't.

JUDY: Did you grade those other *Antigone's?*

HENRY: I most certainly did not. I simply keep a record of them on file,
the way the Pope keeps a file on various heresies.

30 JUDY: Well mine isn't a heresy!

HENRY: It is, to me.

JUDY: Don't you believe in nuclear disarmament?

HENRY: Of course I do. I think the arms race is madness.

JUDY: Then don't you think these things should be said?

35 HENRY: Absolutely. And I believe I said them, back in February, when I was
discussing the political background of Greek drama. Then, if you'll
remember, I compared Athens and Sparta, and pointed out rather
frightening analogies to the United States and the Soviet Union.

JUDY: I had mono in February.

HENRY: Mono?

JUDY: Nucleosis. I kept falling asleep at the Film Festival, even during
Psycho.

HENRY: I'm sorry to hear that. You must get the notes, then, from a fellow
student. You might need them when you write your term paper.

40 JUDY: But this *is* my term paper.

HENRY: It's not on an assigned topic.

JUDY: It's on *Antigone.*

HENRY: But it's not on Sophocles.

JUDY: But I spent two weeks working on it.

45 HENRY: Sophocles spent two years.

JUDY: But I'm taking other courses!

HENRY: And Sophocles didn't—I grant you.

JUDY: Yes, but . . .

HENRY: Miss Miller: At the beginning of the semester, I handed out a list
of assigned topics. I stated specifically that any departures from these
topics should be cleared through me. Now suddenly, long before the
term is over, I discover this odd effort, stuffed under my door, with
no previous permission whatsoever.

50 JUDY: I had to try it first. To see if it worked.

HENRY: Well, you did. And it didn't.

JUDY: So what do I do?

HENRY: You read the texts carefully. You attend class religiously. And in
the middle of May, you hand in a fifteen-page, coherently organized,

typewritten paper, with adequate margins and appropriate footnotes, on the main issues of this course.

JUDY: Couldn't you give me partial credit? For the idea?

55 HENRY: Miss Miller, how can I? It's misguided. It's wrong. You have taken one of the world's great plays, and reduced it to a juvenile polemic on current events.

JUDY: Juvenile?

HENRY: I'm sorry.

JUDY: Of course that's your opinion.

HENRY: I'm afraid my opinion is the one that counts.

60 JUDY: But what if I put it on?

HENRY: On?

JUDY: In front of the class—just reading it out loud.

HENRY: Miss Miller: we have only so much time before the end of the term. We have yet to absorb the very difficult concept of Greek tragedy. I doubt if there's time in class to play show-and-tell.

JUDY: Then I'll do it somewhere else.

65 HENRY: I'd spend my time on a paper.

JUDY: I'll do my play instead. You could come and see.

HENRY: I'm afraid I'd see a great gap in your education, Miss Miller. As well as in my list of grades.

JUDY: You mean I'd fail?

HENRY: You'd receive an incomplete.

70 JUDY: Which means, since I'm a senior, that I'd fail. I wouldn't graduate, Professor Harper.

HENRY: Which means you'd better not spend these last valuable days of your academic life on amateur theatrics. *(He gets up, begins organizing his books and notes.)* And now I have to teach a class. And I strongly suspect you have to go to one. *(Judy gets up, too.)*

JUDY: Professor Harper, I don't want to sound conceited or anything, but you should know that after I graduate, I've been accepted for a special training program in investment banking at Morgan Guaranty Trust in New York City.

HENRY: My congratulations.

JUDY: Well, in my interview, they were particularly impressed by my leadership qualities, my creativity, and my personal sense of commitment. They wrote me that in a letter, Professor Harper.

75 HENRY: Congratulations again.

JUDY: I also heard, from someone who works there, that I'm only the second Jewish woman to be brought into that program at that level since its inception.

HENRY: I am virtually overwhelmed.

JUDY: Yes, well, I believe in my abilities, Professor Harper. I plan to apply them. I'm going to put this play *on.* I wrote it, and I like it, and I'm committed to what it says. And if it's no good now, I'll work to make it better. And I'll bet, by the end of the term, you'll be able to give me a straight A.

HENRY: *(Turning, as if at the door.)* Miss Miller: After such a magnificent display of American optimism and industry, I'm tempted to give you a straight A right now.

80 **JUDY:** Thank you.

HENRY: And I believe I would if this were a course on comedy. But alas, it is not. It's a course on tragedy. And you have just demonstrated that you have no conception of tragedy at all! *(He goes off, with his books and notes. Judy looks at him, and looks at her paper. She goes off, reading it aloud.)*

JUDY:

> People of this land, we suffer under a yoke.
> *(She begins to realize a new pertinence.)*
> A tyrant rules our city, and unjust laws
> Now squelch all forms of perfectly plausible protest . . .

She goes off. As she goes off, Diana comes on to address the audience. She is a harassed, nervous, middle-aged woman, dressed efficiently. She speaks to the audience as if it were a group of concerned students. She might speak from note cards.

DIANA: Good morning . . . I spoke to you as freshmen. I speak to you now as seniors and what we hope will be very generous alumni . . . The topic of today's meeting is "Preparing for the Future." I'll be brief, since I know all of you are waiting to hear from the Placement people about the world beyond these walls. I do want to make a quick comment on our curriculum, however. A number of you have recently complained about the traditional courses which are still required. Why, you ask, with tuitions so high and the search for jobs so increasingly competitive, are you forced to take such impractical courses? You may be sure, by the way, that the recruiting offices at I.B.M. and General Electric are asking the same question: Why must you take these things? After all, they are concerned only with some book, some poem, some old play. "Only some work," as my special favorite Jane Austen[8] once said, "in which the best powers of the mind are displayed, in the best chosen language." Well, there you are. They're the best. And we need no reason beyond that to justify, for example, Professor Harper's course on Greek tragedy. It deals with the best. It exists. It is there. And will remain there, among several other valuable requirements, for what we hope is a very long time. *(She glances offstage.)* And now, Alice Zimmerman, from Placement, will talk to you about . . . *(She glances at her note card.)* "The Job Market Jungle versus the Graduate School Grind." Those of you who are tardy now be seated. *(The late members of the audience may be seated here.)* Have a good morning. *(She goes off as Dave comes on from another direction. He reads aloud from a typewritten script.)*

---

[8] Jane Austen (1775–1817)—English novelist.

DAVE:
"No, Antigone, no. Please reconsider.
Do not take on this dangerous enterprise.
The risks are too great, the payoff insignificant."

(Judy comes on, as if down the steps of the library, carrying a stack of books.)

85 JUDY: *(breathlessly)* Look what I got. *(Reads off the titles.)* The Nuclear
Insanity . . . A World Beyond War . . . Our Debt to the Future . . . I'm
going to put all this in.
DAVE: You're racking up a lot of time on this thing.
JUDY: Well I want to make it good. Did you read the first scene?
DAVE: *(reciting by heart)*
"No, Antigone, no. Please reconsider."
JUDY: What do you think? *(Pause.)*
90 DAVE: You're in blank verse.
JUDY: I know that.
DAVE: Every line.
(Accentuates it.)
"Do *not* take *on* this *dang'*rous *enter*prise."
JUDY: I know.
DAVE: How come?
95 JUDY: *(accenting it)* I *just* got *into* it and *couldn't stop.*
DAVE: *(dramatically, as if it were Shakespeare)*
"The risks are too great, the payoff insignificant."
JUDY: Want to do this?
DAVE: Me?
JUDY: Want to?
100 DAVE: *(looking at script)* This is a woman's part. This is her sister talking
here.
JUDY: I've changed it. I've made it her lover.
DAVE: Get someone from Drama.
JUDY: I already did. Drama people are doing all the other roles. Please,
Dave. Do it.
DAVE: *(melodramatically)*
"No, Antigone, no. Please reconsider."
(Pause.) I better not, Judy.
105 JUDY: I need company.
DAVE: No thanks.
JUDY: I thought you liked Greek stuff.
DAVE: I do.
JUDY: You even talked me into taking the course.
110 DAVE: I know, I know.
JUDY: You're always borrowing the books . . .
DAVE: Yeah, but I don't have time for anything anymore. I've got a
double lab in my major this term. And a brutal schedule in track
every weekend. And, as you know, I'm not doing too well in
either.

JUDY: You're doing fine. You're just a slow starter. *(Slyly.)* Which is part of your charm.

DAVE: All I know is, you get straight A's, you've got a great job waiting for you on the outside, you can afford to fool around with drama. Me? I've only had one interview so far, and I blew it.

115 JUDY: You didn't *blow* it, Dave. You just overslept.

DAVE: Yeah well, how can we live together next year if I can't nail down a job in New York? I've got to get my grades up, Jude.

JUDY: All right, Dave. That's cool. I'll look for someone else. *(She takes her own copy of her script out of her backpack, looks at it, looks at him.)* Would you at least read it with me?

DAVE: Sure.

JUDY: From the top?

120 DAVE: Sure. Why not? *(Reading.)*

> "Hello, Antigone. And what brings you here,
> Worried and out of sorts on this spring morning?
> You look like you've got something on—

(Pause.)

> —your mind."

JUDY: *(reading)*

> "My friend Lysander—"

DAVE: *(looking at his script)* Lysander? I have "Beloved sister."

JUDY: That's what I changed. I changed it to Lysander.

DAVE: Lysander? That's Shakespeare. It's from *Midsummer Night's Dream*.

125 JUDY: It's also Greek. I looked it up.

DAVE: But it primarily—

JUDY: *(reads, with feeling)*

> "My friend Lysander, will you join with me
> In picketing and protesting the bomb
> At several local military bases
> Where nuclear arms are stored? And would you be willing,
> O my loyal Lysander—"

DAVE: Lysander. Sounds like a disinfectant.

JUDY: *(insistently)*

> "Would you be willing, O my loyal Lysander
> Even to chain yourself to a chain-link fence
> Or lie down in the road in front of a gate
> And so prevent all types of vehicular access?"

130 DAVE: I do.

JUDY:

> "And if the state police or National Guard,
> Accompanied by snarling German shepherds,
> Attempted to dislodge us from our task,
> Would you be willing, my lover and my friend . . .
> To go to jail with me, and there remain
> At least till our parents post appropriate bail."

(Pause.)

DAVE: Who'll you get for Lysander if I don't do it?

JUDY: Oh probably that blond fraternity type who lifts weights and
played the lead in *Fool for Love.*[9]

DAVE: Mark Shapiro? *(Judy nods.)* I'll do Lysander.

135 JUDY: Now don't if you don't want to.

DAVE: So I get another C in another course.

JUDY: Now think positively, Dave.

DAVE: So I mess up another interview.

JUDY: *(handing him her script)* I'll buy you a new alarm clock. Read from
here.

140 DAVE: *(looking at it)* This is all new.

JUDY: I rewrote it last night. With you in mind.

DAVE: You knew I'd do it.

JUDY: I hoped you would. *(Henry reenters his office, settles into a chair to
read a book.)*

DAVE: *(kissing her)*
"Antigone . . .
(Then reading.)
Much as I've loved you, even since freshman year,
And lived with you since the second semester of sophomore,
Built you a loft for our bed in off-campus housing,
Prepared your pasta, shared your stereo,
Still I have fears about what you've just proposed.
The risks are too great, the payoff insignificant."

145 JUDY: What do you think?

DAVE: I love it.

JUDY: You do?

DAVE: I love you.

JUDY: *(taking the script back)* I don't like it.

150 DAVE: What's the matter?

JUDY: It sounds wrong. I'm going to rewrite it.

DAVE: Again?

JUDY: *(gathering up her books and bag)* I'll make it better.

DAVE: What if you cut Lysander?

155 JUDY: Why? You're good. I'm going to build up his part.

DAVE: *(following her)*
"No, Antigone, no. Please reconsider."
(They go off as Diana appears in the doorway to Henry's office.)

DIANA: Henry?

HENRY: Yes? Come in. *(He sees her and jumps to his feet.)* Ah. Our Dean.
Empress of all Humanities, including Remedial Reading. *(He gives her
an elaborately courtly salute and bow.)*

DIANA: Knock if off, Henry.

---

[9] A 1983 play by American playwright/actor Sam Shepard.

160 HENRY: You look particularly lovely today, Diana. What is it? New hairdo? New blouse? New something.

DIANA: It's the same old me, Henry.

HENRY: No, no. There's something different. Maybe it's your eyes. They blaze like beacons 'cross The Hellespont.[10]

DIANA: And it's the same old you, Henry. You've been saying things like that for twenty years.

HENRY: And meaning them, Diana.

165 DIANA: I used to think you meant them. Now I know different.

HENRY: Dear lady . . .

DIANA: Now I know that you just say these things by rote, Henry. You say them to the librarian in the reserve book room, and you say them to the Xerox woman, and you say them to the cashier in the cafeteria. You say them to keep us all at a distance, so you won't have to say anything else. If any of us *did* have a new blouse, you wouldn't notice it at all.

HENRY: Now, Diana . . .

DIANA: Let's change the channel, shall we, Henry? Something's come up.

170 HENRY: What dark words seek to escape through the gate of thy teeth?

DIANA: Judy Miller.

HENRY: Judy . . . ?

DIANA: Miller. *(Pause.)*

HENRY: Ah. Miss Miller. *(French accent.)* L'affaire Antigone.

175 DIANA: You know that's why I'm here, Henry.

HENRY: I swear I didn't. I have a number of students, a number of courses.

DIANA: You teach two courses, Henry. And you have relatively few students in each. Now let's focus, please, on the issue.

HENRY: Administration has made you cruel as Clytemnestra.[11]

DIANA: Henry, *please. (Pause.)*

180 HENRY: All right. Judy Miller.

DIANA: I understand—

HENRY: Would you like some coffee? *(He crosses to pour her some.)*

DIANA: Yes, please—I understand she brought in a rewritten version.

HENRY: She brought in *two* rewritten versions.

185 DIANA: Well she brought one to me, as well.

HENRY: The first? Or the second?

---

[10] Ancient name for the Dardanelles, a strait dividing European and Asian Turkey, and connecting the Sea of Marmara with the Aegean Sea. British poet George Gordon, Lord Byron, swam the Hellespont (May 3, 1810) and later wrote a poem about it, "Written after Swimming from Sestos to Abydos." It is interesting—perhaps ironic—that Henry, a classicist, makes such a decidedly Romantic allusion.

[11] In Greek legend, the daughter of the King of Sparta and wife to Agamemnon. She murders her husband and is in turn killed by her son, Orestes.

DIANA: A third.

HENRY: I said I wouldn't read that one.

DIANA: It's not bad, Henry. It's longer, it's getting better. It's now at least a play.

190 HENRY: It's hopeless.

DIANA: Give her a B for effort.

HENRY: A *B?* I won't give her any grade at all.

DIANA: A student takes our course, becomes inspired by an old play, writes a modern version . . .

HENRY: And demonstrates thereby that she knows nothing about Sophocles, nothing about the Greeks, nothing about tragedy.

195 DIANA: Henry, she tried.

HENRY: And failed. A B? A B means good. A B means very good. I am not so far lost in the current inflation of grades as to litter the campus with disposable Bs.

DIANA: Oh, Henry . . .

HENRY: I'm sorry. If I gave her a grade for that nonsense, Diana, it would make the whole course meaningless. *(Pause.)* It would make *me* meaningless. *(Pause. Diana lights a cigarette.)* Still smoking, I see.

DIANA: Sometimes.

200 HENRY: Don't.

DIANA: I smoke, Henry, when I find myself caught in the middle of something. Which seems to be the case a good deal lately with this job.

HENRY: Ah hah. Second thoughts from our Dean. You asked for that job, Diana. You agitated for it. All the chatter about the need for more women at the administrative level. Well, now you've sunk to that level and it's leveling you. Come back to the classroom where you belong.

DIANA: Sometimes I wish I could.

HENRY: *(taking an ashtray out of a desk drawer, holding it out to her)* At least put out that cigarette. Life is tragic enough without your contributing to it.

205 DIANA: Let me enjoy it, Henry.

HENRY: Your lungs or mine, Diana. *(He holds out the ashtray.)* Put it out.

DIANA: You win. *(She puts it out; he cleans out the ashtray, puts it away.)* Now let me win one.

HENRY: No.

DIANA: How about partial credit?

210 HENRY: No.

DIANA: She's a senior. She needs to graduate.

HENRY: I'm sorry. *(Pause.)*

DIANA: She's putting it on, you know.

HENRY: The play?

215 DIANA: She's putting it on.

HENRY: Reading it? In some dining hall?

DIANA: Staging it. She asked my permission to use Spingler Auditorium.

HENRY: You said No.

DIANA: I said Yes.

220 HENRY: You gave her permission?

DIANA: Of course I gave it to her. I had to give it to her. *(Pause.)* I wanted to give it to her.

HENRY: Traitor. Or is it, Traitress?

DIANA: Well, I'm sorry, Henry. But there seems to be a lot of interest cropping up for this thing. Several of the student antinuclear groups want to sponsor it. Bill Silverstein is writing some incidental music on the Moog Synthesizer. And someone over in Art has agreed to do simple neoclassic scenery. They plan to present it on the Friday night before graduation. For parents. And alumni. And friends.

HENRY: Poor Sophocles . . .

225 DIANA: Oh now.

HENRY: Set to the tune of a Moog Synthesizer.

DIANA: Yes well, it should create quite a stir.

HENRY: Quite a stir! That's it, exactly, Diana! Quite a stir! It will stir up a lot of cheap liberal guilt and a lot of fake liberal piety and a lot of easy liberal anger at the poor Creons of this world who are really working on this nuclear thing, and frantically trying to keep the world from blowing itself up!

DIANA: Oh, Henry . . .

230 HENRY: Do you know what tragedy is, Diana?

DIANA: I think I do, yes.

HENRY: I don't think you do, Diana. I don't think anyone in this happy-ending country really does. Tragedy means the universe is unjust and unfair, Diana. It means we are hedged about by darkness, doom, and death. It means the good, the just, and well-intentioned don't always *win,* Diana. That's what tragedy means. And if we can learn that, if I can teach that, if I can give these bright, beady-eyed students at least a glimmer of that, then perhaps someday we will be able to join hands with our enemies across the water, or our neighbors down below, or the outcasts in our own back*yard,* and create a common community against this darkness. That's what I believe, Diana. And that's what Sophocles believed in 443 B.C. when he wrote *Antigone.* That's what Shakespeare believed when he wrote *King Lear.* Tragedy keeps us honest, keeps us real, keeps us human. All great nations should have a tragic vision, Diana, and we have none. And that is why I cannot endorse what this woman, no, this *girl,* is doing when she puts on her strident little travesty for the passing parade in Spingler Auditorium on graduation weekend. That is not tragedy, Diana. That is just trouble-making. And I cannot give her credit for it. *(Pause.)*

DIANA: May I have the ashtray back, please?

HENRY: No.

235 DIANA: I want it *back,* Henry. I don't want to tap ashes all over your floor.

HENRY: *(handing it to her)* Here. *(Gets up.)* I'll open the door.

DIANA: I'd leave the door closed, Henry. Open the window if you want. This is private. *(She smokes.)*

HENRY: *(not opening anything)* Private?

DIANA: Have you given any thoughts to your low enrollments, Henry?

240 HENRY: Thought? Of course I've given thought. In a world of television and Punk Rock, it's a little difficult to maintain—

DIANA: The Provost thinks there might be another reason, Henry.

HENRY: The Provost?

DIANA: He brought it up last fall, when he saw the registration figures.

HENRY: And what does the Provost think?

245 DIANA: Apparently . . . over the years . . . there've been complaints about you, Henry.

HENRY: Oh I'm sure. That I take attendance. That I take off for misspellings. That I actually *call* on people in class.

DIANA: No, it's something else, Henry. Some students . . . over the years . . . have complained that you're . . . biased.

HENRY: Biased?

DIANA: Prejudiced.

250 HENRY: *Prejudiced?*

DIANA: Anti-Semitic, Henry. *(Pause.)*

HENRY: Say that again.

DIANA: There's been a pattern of complaints.

HENRY: But on what *grounds?*

255 DIANA: Apparently the administration thinks you make certain remarks in the classroom. Which students pass on. And cause others to stay away. *(Pause.)*

HENRY: This is ridiculous.

DIANA: I agree.

HENRY: And outrageous.

DIANA: I think so, too.

260 HENRY: It's slander! I'm going to see the Provost right now!

DIANA: Hold on, Henry!

HENRY: I mean this is unconscionable. It's like the time five years ago when poor Bob Klein was accused of some late night unpleasantness in the lab by that little temptress in a T-shirt. He had to resign.

DIANA: He resigned because he was *guilty,* Henry.

HENRY: Well I'm not guilty of anti-Semitism. Or do you think I am?

265 DIANA: I think you . . . make remarks, Henry.

HENRY: Remarks?

DIANA: For example, in the curriculum meeting last fall . . .

HENRY: What did I say?

DIANA: You told that joke.

270 HENRY: It was a good joke. I got that joke from Jack Nathanson.

DIANA: Well no one laughed when *you* told it, Henry. And no one laughed when you delivered that diatribe against Israel last week at lunch.

HENRY: That wasn't supposed to be funny.

DIANA: Well it certainly wasn't.

HENRY: I mean, when you think how we let one small country so totally dominate our foreign policy . . .

275 DIANA: Henry!

HENRY: Well I mean it's insane! It's suicidal! Pericles[12] warned us about it in 426 B.C.: "Beware of entanglements in Asia Minor," he said.

DIANA: Henry, Dick Livingston was sitting right across the *table* when you said those things!

HENRY: Is Dick Jewish?

DIANA: *I'm* Jewish, Henry.

280 HENRY: *You're* Jewish?

DIANA: Half Jewish. My mother was an Austrian Jew.

HENRY: I didn't know that.

DIANA: Well I am. And Judy Miller is Jewish. *(Pause.)*

HENRY: Has she complained that I'm prejudiced?

285 DIANA: No. *She* hasn't . . .

HENRY: But you still think I'm some raving neo-Nazi who is pumping anti-Semitic propaganda into his courses three times a week?

DIANA: *(quietly)* No. I think you're a passionate teacher and scholar, whose lectures are loaded with extravagant analogies which are occasionally misinterpreted by sensitive Jewish students.

HENRY: And the Provost?

DIANA: The Provost thinks it's an issue which should never even arise. Seeing as how we're in the middle of a major fund drive. And more and more, it seems to be Jewish generosity that's keeping us all afloat.

290 HENRY: *(thinking)* I do the Auerbach[13] thing at the beginning of the term.

DIANA: The Auerbach thing?

HENRY: A great scholar. Jewish, Diana. And superb! He sees two fundamental themes in Western culture. The Greek and the Hebraic. Odysseus versus Abraham. Public honor versus private conscience.

DIANA: Well maybe that starts you off on the wrong foot.

HENRY: No, no. It works marvelously. I carry it further. I build to the basic contrast between Athens and Jerusalem.

295 DIANA: Well maybe those generalizations could be taken the wrong way.

HENRY: Do you think so?

DIANA: Henry: This is a free country. And academic life is even more so. You may write four-letter words all over the blackboard. You may denounce the government, blaspheme God, take off your clothes . . .

HENRY: Good Heavens, Diana . . .

DIANA: You may do all of these things in here, and most of them out there. But there is one thing, here and there, you may not do. You

---

[12] Pericles (c. 495–429 B.C.)—Greek statesman. He dominated Athens for over thirty years, and was noted for his skill at oratory, his leadership, and his honesty.

[13] Erich Auerbach, noted literary scholar, whose work includes *Mimesis*. Before his death in 1957, Auerbach was a professor at Yale University.

may *not* be insensitive about the Jews. That is taboo. The twentieth century is still with us, Henry. We live in the shadow of the Holocaust. Remember that, please. And be warned. *(Pause.)*

300   **Henry:** I hear you, Diana.

  Diana: Thank you.

  Henry: I'll stay simply with the Greeks. I'll lash myself to the mast, and avoid the Bible. I'll even avoid the Book of Job.[14]

  Diana: Thank you, Henry.

  Henry: I must say, Diana, I've never really understood the Old Testament anyway. All that brooding, internal self-laceration. And the sense of a special contract with God. The sense of being chosen. The sense of sure salvation somewhere on down the line. Have you ever felt that? I haven't. But the Jews must feel it. Even after Auschwitz,[15] they feel it. Perhaps because of Auschwitz, they feel it all the more. I suppose that's why they put so much stock in their children. They spoil them, you know. The children are generally spoiled. They bring them to dinner parties. They teach them to feel—what is that word?— "entitled." Perhaps that's why this girl, excuse me, this woman, this Miss Miller, feels so strongly she deserves special treatment.

305   **Diana:** Henry.

  Henry: My children don't feel that way. I taught my children to toe the mark. To take their turn. To submit to authority. Of course, that hasn't worked out so well either. I mean, I don't hear from my children much anymore. The Jews hear from their children. Their children telephone them all the time. *(Turns to her.)* I'm painting myself into a corner, aren't I?

  Diana: Yes you are, Henry.

  Henry: Yes. Well. You're right. All this could be . . . misinterpreted. I'll try to be more careful.

  Diana: Yes, I would, Henry. Because the Provost is talking about cutting back.

310   **Henry:** Cutting back?

  Diana: On courses that are—undersubscribed.

  Henry: My course on tragedy is required!

  Diana: Your course is on a *list* of *several* required courses. And the Provost can take it off that list any time.

  Henry: What? Tear from the Tree of Knowledge one of the last golden apples that still remain? A course that survived the ghastly chaos of the sixties? A course that—

315   **Diana:** Henry, he can do it.

---

[14] The Book of Job recounts the sufferings of Job, who despite the trials and hardships God bestows on him, persists in his faith.

[15] Notorious World War II Nazi concentration camp, where many of the Holocaust victims died.

HENRY: I'll be more careful . . . "Whom the Gods would destroy,[16] they first drive mad."

DIANA: Yes, well, and it might be a good idea, Henry—just to avoid any misunderstanding—to give Judy Miller a grade for what she's done. *(Pause.)*

HENRY: You *think* so?

DIANA: Yes I do. Otherwise you might come out of this whole thing looking very much like Creon in that damn play.

320 HENRY: This is not a tragedy by Sophocles, Diana. It is a comedy by Aristophanes,[17] at best. I am not Creon, and that little Jewish princess is not Antigone, Princess of Thebes.

DIANA: Cool it, Henry!

HENRY: *(with great reluctance)* I'll give her a D. For Determination.

DIANA: Henry . . .

HENRY: *(angrily)* All right. A C, then. For Commitment.

325 DIANA: I don't think she'll accept a C.

HENRY: Won't *accept?*

DIANA: She feels she deserves a good grade.

HENRY: She'll get a good grade when she shows me some small awareness of what tragedy is. Lord knows she's shown me what it isn't. *(Judy comes out now. She sits on some steps or a bench D., takes a spiral notebook out of her backpack, and writes in it, concentratedly. Diana sighs and gets up.)*

DIANA: If I were you, Henry, I'd head for the hills of New Hampshire after your last class. I wouldn't want to be around when the grades go in and that play goes on and that girl doesn't graduate. Go up to your cottage, chop wood, disconnect the telephone.

330 HENRY: I don't like to go up there alone.

DIANA: Oh dear. Trouble again?

HENRY: Elsa's moved out. Again.

DIANA: She'll be back.

HENRY: I don't think so. She says now the children have gone, I'm impossible to live with.

335 DIANA: Now where did she get an idea like that? *(She goes out. Henry exits, after a moment, another way. The lights come up more fully on Judy, hard at her writing on the steps in the sun. Dave comes on carrying a paperback book.)*

DAVE: Hi.

---

[16] Publius Syrus, in his Maxim 911, says "Fortune" rather than "the Gods." The line as recalled by Henry is a paraphrased version from British poet John Dryden (1631–1700).

[17] Aristophanes (c. 450–385 B.C.)—Greek comic dramatist. Note that when Henry says "that little Jewish princess," he is using a pejorative term. This usage is in ironic contrast to "Antigone, Princess of Thebes."

Judy: *(looking up from her work)* Hey, aren't you supposed to be in
  Chemistry?

Dave: Missed it. Lost track of the time.

Judy: But you flunked the last quiz.

340 Dave: I got hung up reading one of your books.

Judy: Which one?

Dave: *(showing her)* Sophocles . . . *Antigone.*

Judy: Oh. *(Pause.)*

Dave: It's good.

345 Judy: It's fair.

Dave: It's awesome.

Judy: It's good.

Dave: Maybe we should do that version.

Judy: What about mine?

350 Dave: Maybe you'd get your A if you did Sophocles.

Judy: I've thought about that, Dave: In Sophocles, all she wants to do is
  bury one dead brother.

Dave: True.

Judy: In mine, she sees everyone in the *world* as her brother, and she's
  fighting to keep them all *alive.*

Dave: O.K., Jude. *(He sits down beside her, takes out a banana.)* Want some?

355 Judy: No thanks.

Dave: *(as he eats)* While I was reading, your dad called.

Judy: Again?

Dave: From the hospital. Between patients.

Judy: What did he want?

360 Dave: He wants you to graduate.

Judy: I'll graduate.

Dave: He wants to be sure.

Judy: Did you tell him I'm appealing to the Grievance Committee? Did
  you say that the Dean herself is presenting my case?

Dave: He said committees make him nervous.

365 Judy: Well, parents make *me* nervous.

Dave: He said he hasn't spent thirty years in the lower intestine just so
  his daughter could flunk college.

Judy: Sounds familiar.

Dave: He said write the paper. Get the degree. Argue with the professor
  after.

Judy: That's my father.

370 Dave: That's everyone's father.

Judy: Actually, I got a letter from my mother today.

Dave: Coordinated attack, huh.

Judy: She wrote from her office. On her "Department of Mental Health"
  stationery. Saying I was just acting out my guilt for being so lucky in
  life.

DAVE: You are lucky.

375 JUDY: I know and I know they've worked hard to keep it that way. Moving to Westport, so I could grow up in a "healthy suburban environment." Sending me to Andover, so I could frolic in preppy heaven. Europe last summer, so I could learn how to use a credit card. Hell, four years *here*, for God's sake. And now they're offering to pay a psychiatrist two hundred dollars a week so I can blame it all on them.

DAVE: You're kidding!

JUDY: My mother even enclosed a note from my grandmother saying that Jewish people should bend over backwards not to make waves.

DAVE: Got you surrounded, huh?

JUDY: Sure have.

380 DAVE: They all just want you to do well.

JUDY: I know that. I appreciate that.

DAVE: Look. Why not hedge your bets? Do the play *and* write the paper.

JUDY: I *can't,* Dave. I've tried and I can't. It all comes out fake and phony and not me.

DAVE: Then take the C. The Dean says Harper will give you that. Take it, and run.

385 JUDY: I can't do that either.

DAVE: Why *not?*

JUDY: I don't know, Dave. Here I am working with a bunch of really dedicated people . . . trying to reach out to the local community . . . on a subject which deals with the survival of the entire planet . . . don't you think that's worth a tad more than a C, Dave?

DAVE: Sure it is.

JUDY: Then let me go for it.

390 DAVE: O.K. Let's rehearse. (*He tosses the banana peel into a trash can with a basketball leap.*)

JUDY: Thanks, Dave. (*She hugs him.*) Listen to this new stuff. (*She reads what she has just written.*)
  "Lately I'm feeling very much alone.
  Even you, Lysander, seem to be backing off,
  Advising caution, counseling compromise."

DAVE: (*reading over her shoulder*)
  "I just don't want to see you get in trouble.
  Just think what they could do to you, Antigone:
  They could throw you in jail, there to be beaten up
  By roving gangs of angry lesbians.
  Or worse:
  They could banish you, and send you off
  With no degree to grace your resume
  To fritter away essential earning years
  In waitressing or joining a typing pool."

Judy: *(reading)*
    "Still, my conscience tells me I am right.
    And if I am to suffer—"
    (She stops; looks at him.)
Dave: What's the matter?

395 Judy: Maybe I *am* just being a brat.
Dave: No, no . . .
Judy: A spoiled little JAP, playing sixties-type games as a last gasp before
    facing up to the real world . . .
Dave: Naaa . . .
Judy: Maybe I should just take a massive all-nighter in the library, and
    grunt out one of those boring, studenty papers with a title like
    "Tragic Irony in Sophocles" or some such thing.

400 Dave: Sounds good to me. Want me to help?
Judy: You don't have time. *(Looking at her notebook; reading.)*
    "And yet this stupid arms race still goes on.
    Oh it appalls me! God, it makes me mad!
    (She begins to gather steam.)
    It's as if the United States and Soviet Russia
    Were two small boys comparing penises
    With the fate of the world dependent on the outcome!"
Dave: *(covering his crotch)* Right on, Antigone!
Judy: *(cranking up)*
    "Oh men, men, men!
    Why are you all—with only a few exceptions—
    (A glance at Dave.)
    So miserably hung up on competition?
    The Air Force General, the Corporation Executive,
    The College Professor tyrannizing his students . . ."
Dave: *(looking over her shoulder)* Hey! Where's that line? I don't see that.

405 Judy: I'm improvising! I'm winging it!
    "The College Professor tyrannizing his students,
    It seems the entire world is under the thumb
    Of self-important men. I fear, Lysander,
    That one of these days, one of these little men
    Will reach across his desk and push the button
    Which will destroy us all!"
Dave: Now that's pretty good.
Judy: *(gathering up her stuff)* No it isn't. And you know it isn't. But I'll
    make it better. *(She starts off.)*
Dave: *(starting after her)* I'll give you a hand.
Judy: You better make up that chemistry. There's no reason for you to
    flunk out, even if I do. *(She goes.)*

410 Dave: *(calling after her)* But I really want to—*(He looks at the Sophocles still
    in his hand, gets an idea, concludes quietly.)* Help. *(He goes off the
    opposite way as Henry enters to teach his class. He carries an old, worn*

leather book, stuffed with scraps of paper. He might use half-lens reading glasses, so that he can peer out at the audience as necessary.)

HENRY: It might be particularly appropriate at this point in the course to let Sophocles speak for himself. I will try to translate for you—directly from the Greek—portions of the great choral ode from the *Antigone*. I will attempt to make it speak as immediately as I can. And I hope, as you hear it, you will compare it to other local efforts on this subject that may have come to your attention in recent weeks. *(Opening his book, finding his place, translating with great feeling.)*

"There are many wondrous things in the world,
But nothing is more wondrous than Man."

(Looks up.) Deinos . . . "wondrous" . . . the other day I heard one of you use the word "awesome." All right. Let's try *awesome. (Returns to text.)*

"Nothing is more awesome than Man."

(Looks up; sighs.) Or yes. All right. Today: woman. The point is nothing is more awesome than the human being. Here I used to contrast this awesome view with the rather abject and quarrelsome vision of man emerging in the Old Testament. But I won't do that now. Rather, returning to the text . . . *(He does.)* I will simply call your attention to the series of magnificent images on the taming of nature: ships, plows, fishnets, ox-yokes . . . *(Looks up.)* Today planes, rockets, computers, laser beams . . . *(Returns to text.)*

"which man has created through his uncanny technology."

(Looks up.) And then come our social inventions, those things we have invented to tame ourselves . . . *(Translates.)* "language which leads to thought" . . . "laws" . . . "medicine" . . . "religion" . . . "cities" . . . *(Looks up.)* There it is. The city. The *polis*. The human community. The result of all this creative activity. We'll come back to that. *(Translates.)*

"Man—or woman—is resourceful in everything, and proudly
prepares for the future. *But . . .*"

(Looks up.) There is a big But here . . . *But . . . (Translates.)*

"There is one thing he can't tame, can't control: and that is
Death."

(Looks up.) All right now, death was terrifying—the Greeks loved life—but Sophocles goes on to mention something *worse* than death. *(Looks at text.)* And here comes the crack of the whip: *(Translates grimly.)*

"Yet if, for the sake of pride, he . . ."

(Looks up; is glad to use the feminine this time.) Or she . . . *(Returns to text.)*

"Goes too far, then he becomes an exile . . ."

(Looks up.) Which to the Greek was far, far worse than death. *(Translates.)*

"An exile without a country,

Lost and alone,
    Homeless and outlawed forever."
You see? Sophocles joyfully celebrates the lawful human community,
the Greek *polis*, but then threatens those who defy it with a death
beyond death—exile, banishment, ostracism. *(Returns to the text.)*
    "Lost and alone.
    Homeless and outlawed forever."
(Looks up.) Last year, I compared these grim lines to the Hebrews'
lamentations in the Psalms. This year, I will try to conjure up other
images of profound alienation: *(He thinks.)* The haunted Orestes . . .
Napoleon dying his slow death on the desolate island of Saint
Helena . . . some lost astronaut severed forever from the good, green
earth . . . *(Returns to the text.)*
    "Homeless and outlawed forever."
(Pause.) Those words were written over two thousand years ago. I
have read and taught them countless times. I get shivers up and down
my spine every time I do. *(The bell rings. He closes his book.)* I think
even Sophocles would commend my theatrical timing. For the next
session, read *The Trojan Women* by Euripides. Feminists will appreciate
his sympathetic portrayal of women. Pacifists will admire his bitter
attack on war. Classicists, however, prefer to reach beyond such
limited responses. Thank you, and good afternoon. *(He gathers his
books as Dave approaches him.)*
Dave: Professor Harper?
Henry: *(turning)* Yes?
Dave: I'm a friend of Judy's.
415 Henry: Judy?
Dave: Miss Miller.
Henry: Ah.
Dave: *(holding out envelope)* She asked me to give you this.
Henry: "Has she sent poison or some other implement of dark death?"
420 Dave: Excuse me?
Henry: A line from *Medea*.[18]
Dave: It's just her term paper.
Henry: She should be in class. She should hand it in herself.
Dave: I think she's—a little mad at you, sir.
425 Henry: Mad? At me? Because I want her to learn? Oh dear. Would you
    tell her, please, that the quest for truth and beauty is a slow and
    painful climb, and she shouldn't bite the hand that leads her. *(His
    little pun.)*
Dave: I'll—tell her something.
Henry: Good. Meanwhile, I'll take that paper, in hopes she soon will
    return to the fold.

---

[18] By Euripides (431).

DAVE: Thank you, sir.

HENRY: *(opening the envelope, sliding the paper out far enough to read the title)* "Tragic Irony in Sophocles' *Antigone.*" A good, no-nonsense title.

430 DAVE: I'll tell her, sir. *(He starts off.)*

HENRY: *(pulling the paper out of the envelope)* Lovely looking paper . . . Well typed.

DAVE: Mmm.

HENRY: Is this an electric typewriter?

DAVE: No actually, it's a word processor.

435 HENRY: She can't come to class, but she seems to have found time to form a relationship with a computer.

DAVE: Actually, I did the typing, sir.

HENRY: Well let's hope the contents are as attractive as the form. *(He starts to thumb through the papers.)*

DAVE: I'll be going, then. *(He starts off.)*

HENRY: *(as he reads; calling out)* Oh, ah, Mr.—

440 DAVE: *(stopping, turning)* Dave.

HENRY: Do you have a moment?

DAVE: Well I—

HENRY: Would you be so kind as to accompany me to my office?

DAVE: Me?

445 HENRY: If you would.

DAVE: Now?

HENRY: If you'd be so kind. *(He turns and crosses slowly toward his office, still reading the paper. Dave hesitates a moment, and then follows. Henry enters his office, and sits at his desk, still reading. Dave stands in the doorway. As he reads, gesturing vaguely.)* Please sit down, Mr. . . . ah . . .

DAVE: Dave.

HENRY: Sit down, please.

450 DAVE: Thank you. *(He sits on the edge of the chair. Henry continues to read. Dave watches him.)*

HENRY: *(as he reads)* This . . . appears to be . . . an excellent paper.

DAVE: Is it?

HENRY: *(thumbing through to the end)* Even a cursory glance tells me it's first-rate.

DAVE: I'll tell her, sir.

455 HENRY: I've been around a long time. I've taught this course a good many years. I know a good paper when I see one, and I see one here.

DAVE: *(almost at the door)* That's great, sir.

HENRY: *(quietly)* Who wrote this?

DAVE: Huh?

HENRY: Who wrote this paper?

460 DAVE: Judy wrote it.

HENRY: No she didn't. I've also been around long enough to know that. She wrote a promising little essay for me at the start of the semester. She wrote a rather breathless hour exam. But she did not write this. She is not yet capable of the care and commitment I see emerging here.

Dave: Maybe she's changed, sir.

Henry: Ah. Then I would like to discuss this paper with her. Would you get her, please?

Dave: I think she's rehearsing, sir.

465 Henry: Then I must ask you to seek her out. Tell her I am passionate to engage in an intensive discussion with a kindred classicist.

Dave: Sir . . .

Henry: You might also tell her, *en passant*,[19] that I think this is plagiarism, pure and simple. She has tried to pass off as her own the work of somebody else. This is an offense punishable, according to the rules, by . . . *(He has found the college rule book and is already thumbing through it. He finds his place.)* "Automatic failure of the course involved."

Dave: Sir . . .

Henry: *(reading)* "And, after due deliberation by the Discipline Committee, possible expulsion from the University." *(Pause. He looks at Dave.)*

470 Dave: *(quietly)* Oh boy.

Henry: You might also be interested in the fact that . . . *(He reads again from the book.)* "persons aiding or contributing to a plagiaristic act will similarly be charged and punished." *(Looks up.)* You personally might be interested in that, Mr.—?

Dave: Appleton.

Henry: Well I'm not going to press charges against you, Mr. Appleton.

Dave: Sir—

475 Henry: Nor am I going to press charges against Miss Miller. Believe it or not, I would hate to prevent her from graduating. I would simply ask you to tell her to make an appointment at her earliest convenience, so that I may explain to her why, in the world of scholarship and learning, plagiarism is a dark and bloody crime. *(Dave stands at the door.)* That's all I have to say. You may go.

Dave: She didn't write it.

Henry: *(infinitely patient)* Yes I know. That's what I've been saying.

Dave: No, I mean she doesn't even know about it.

Henry: Doesn't know?

480 Dave: She still wants her play to be her paper. *(Pause.)*

Henry: Then who wrote this?

Dave: I did.

Henry: Unbeknownst to her?

Dave: Yes, sir.

485 Henry: Hoping I'd give it a good grade, and she'd go along with it, and the problem would be solved?

---

[19] In passing.

DAVE: I don't know what I hoped. *(Pause.)*

HENRY: *(looking at paper again)* And where did you get this paper? From some other student at some other college? From one of those companies who accept money and do your research?

DAVE: No! I wrote it myself.

HENRY: I don't believe that.

490 DAVE: Well I did.

HENRY: How could you? You're not in my course.

DAVE: I still wrote it. *(Pause. Henry looks at the paper, looks at Dave.)*

HENRY: Sit down, please. *(Dave does. Henry is now all business.)* Name three plays by Sophocles beside the *Antigone*.

DAVE: *Oedipus Rex, Oedipus at Colonnus . . . Ajax.*

495 HENRY: Describe Antigone's genealogy.

DAVE: Her father was Oedipus. Her mother, Jocasta. Her sister was Ismene. She had two brothers, Eteocles and Polyneices. *(Pause.)* Who killed each other. *(Pause.)* Fighting. *(Pause.)* For the throne. *(Pause.)* Of Thebes. *(Pause.)*

HENRY: And what, briefly, do you think *is* the "Tragic Irony in Sophocles' *Antigone*"?

DAVE: I don't think it's Antigone's tragedy at all. I think it's Creon's.

HENRY: And why do you think that?

500 DAVE: Because she at least wins her point in the end.

HENRY: She dies.

DAVE: But she wins. He loses. Everything. The Gods are much more unfair to him. *(Pause.)*

HENRY: You're very good.

DAVE: Thank you.

505 HENRY: Where did you learn all this?

DAVE: I read the play.

HENRY: *(indicating paper)* No. There's more here than just that.

DAVE: My grandfather liked the Greeks.

HENRY: Was he an academic?

510 DAVE: No. He just liked the classics. He spent most of his spare time in the library, reading the Greeks.

HENRY: And he taught you?

DAVE: Right. And I kept it up when I had time.

HENRY: I could never get my own son to read anything but science fiction.

DAVE: That's what my dad reads. *(They laugh together.)*

515 HENRY: Why have you never taken a course from me?

DAVE: I couldn't fit it into my schedule.

HENRY: What's your major?

DAVE: Chemistry.

HENRY: Better worlds through chemistry, eh.

520 DAVE: Actually, my grades aren't too good.

HENRY: They'd be good in the classics.

DAVE: Not many jobs out there in that.

HENRY: Still, you should take my course.

DAVE: I wish I could.

525 HENRY: We could do a special seminar together. Study one play in depth. I'm fascinated with the *Antigone*. We could really dig in, you and I, next fall.

DAVE: I'm supposed to graduate this spring, sir.

HENRY: Oh dear . . . Then perhaps we might meet in the afternoon, from here on in. A small tutorial.

DAVE: I can't, sir. I'm on the track team.

HENRY: The track team? Splendid! The Greeks invented competitive sport!

530 DAVE: I know.

HENRY: *Hygies psyche meta somatos hygious.*

DAVE: Excuse me?

HENRY: We'll shift to Latin: *Mens sana in corpore sano.*

DAVE: *(trying to translate)* Sane mind . . .

535 HENRY: Sound mind in a sound body. The Tenth Satire by Juvenal.[20]

DAVE: Juvenal . . . Tenth . . .

HENRY: You don't by any chance throw the discus, do you? No, that would be too much.

DAVE: I just run the Four Hundred.

HENRY: Ah. Fleet of foot. A true Greek. "Skilled in all ways of contending."

540 DAVE: Thank you, sir.

HENRY: Well, then, I wonder if I might keep this fine paper long enough for Mrs. Murphy to make a Xerox copy.

DAVE: Sure. *(He gets up to leave.)*

HENRY: Just to remind me occasionally of what a good student can do.

DAVE: Sure. *(He starts for the door. At this point, Judy enters at another part of the stage. She sits on a bench, and waits impatiently, as if in a waiting room.)*

545 HENRY: You must be very fond of Miss Miller.

DAVE: I am.

HENRY: To have written this for her.

DAVE: I liked writing it.

HENRY: Will you be seeing her soon?

550 DAVE: I think so.

HENRY: Would you remind her that she and I have yet to resolve our difficulties?

DAVE: She's stubborn, sir.

HENRY: I give you permission to help her. Be her tutor. See that she gets some small awareness of Greek tragedy.

DAVE: She thinks she already has, sir.

---

[20] Juvenal (Decimus Junius Juvenalis; c. A.D. 60–130)—Roman satirist.

555 HENRY: But she *hasn't!* She sees answers, solutions, revisions. Tell her there are things beyond the world of management which are profoundly unmanageable!

DAVE: She wouldn't listen, sir.

HENRY: Then she and I are on a collision course.

DAVE: I'm afraid so, sir. *(Dave starts for the door again.)*

HENRY: One more minute, please *(Dave stops.)* Appleton, you said your name was?

560 DAVE: That's right.

HENRY: English, I suppose.

DAVE: Originally.

HENRY: The English love the classics.

DAVE: Yes.

565 HENRY: And Miss Miller's Jewish.

DAVE: That's right.

HENRY: May I speak classicist to classicist?

DAVE: Yeah. Sure.

HENRY: What you are witnessing here, Mr. Appleton, is once again the age-old clash between Athens and Jerusalem.

570 DAVE: I don't get you, sir.

HENRY: Read Tertullian.[21] Third century, A.D. "What is Athens to Jerusalem, or Jerusalem to Athens?" There it all is. The private conscience versus the communal obligation. Jew versus Greek. Miss Miller versus me.

DAVE: You think so?

HENRY: I do, but they tell me I shouldn't.

DAVE: It seems a little . . . exaggerated, sir.

575 HENRY: You're probably right. *(Henry gets up; takes his arm.)* Come, I'll walk with you down the hall. Plato and Aristotle, strolling through the colonnades of academe. We'll discuss simply Sophocles.

DAVE: O.K.

HENRY: *(as they go)* And I hope Miss Miller appreciates this grand gesture you made on her behalf.

DAVE: God, I hope she never finds out about it. *(They go out as Diana comes on, carrying a folder. Judy gets up expectantly.)*

JUDY: Well?

580 DIANA: The meeting's over.

JUDY: And?

DIANA: *(deep breath)* The Grievance Committee voted against you, Judy.

JUDY: Against?

DIANA: I'm sorry. *(They move into her office.)*

585 JUDY: Did the students on the committee vote against me?

---

21 Tertullian (Quintus Septimius Florens Tertullianus; c. A.D. 160–225)—African Father of the Church, born in Carthage.

DIANA: I can't reveal the specific vote.

JUDY: How about you? How did you vote?

DIANA: I abstained, of course. Since I was presenting your case.

JUDY: How would you have voted? If you could have? *(Pause.)*

590 DIANA: Against.

JUDY: What?!

DIANA: I put your case as fairly as I could, Judy. Really. But your argument simply didn't hold. The committee felt you were asking them to violate the integrity of the classroom. You want them to intrude on a principle that goes back to the Middle Ages.

JUDY: But other people do it all the time! There's a guy in Geology who got partial credit for skiing down Mount Washington!

DIANA: I know . . .

595 JUDY: And there's a girl who passed her Chemistry lab by cooking a crabmeat casserole.

DIANA: I know that, and I think it's disgraceful. But those are other instructors. We cannot dictate standards to *any* professor. You signed up for Greek tragedy. You bought the books. You read the syllabus. You agreed in effect to submit to the rules. There it is.

JUDY: There it is. Everyone seems to be backing off these days. You, my family, now the committee.

DIANA: Oh, Judy . . .

JUDY: *(almost in tears)* I guess I'm doomed to be alone.

600 DIANA: What about all those people working on your play?

JUDY: It's just extra curricular to them. I'm the one who's really on the line.

DIANA: Well what about that boy you go with?

JUDY: Oh, he just loves me, that's all.

DIANA: *(lighting a cigarette)* Well I'm sorry, Judy. I did what I could.

605 JUDY: Please don't smoke!

DIANA: I'm sorry.

JUDY: I think I'm allergic to it.

DIANA: All right, Judy.

JUDY: And it violates my air space.

610 DIANA: *(putting cigarettes away)* All right, all right. *(Pause.)*

JUDY: So what do I do?

DIANA: I told you: he's offered a C.

JUDY: I'm beyond a C.

DIANA: Beyond?

615 JUDY: I can't settle for a C.

DIANA: Then you won't graduate.

JUDY: Not in June. No.

DIANA: That's ridiculous!

JUDY: I'll make it up in summer school with that course on comedy where all they do is study *Annie Hall*. You can mail me my degree in September.

620 DIANA: That makes me a little angry, Judy. You told me you wanted to
    stand up with your class.

JUDY: I'm standing up, all right.

DIANA: But you'll lose your job! It depends on your graduating.

JUDY: I'll find another.

DIANA: That's not so easy these days.

625 JUDY: What's a job anyway? Is it the most important thing in the world? I
    suppose this is a hopelessly middle-class thing to say, but
    am I supposed to live and die over a job? Do you? You've been here a
    long time, worked your way up, now you're Dean of the whole
    department. Is that *it*? Are you in heaven now? Aren't there other
    things in your life beside your job?

DIANA: *(taken aback)* Of course there are, Judy . . .

JUDY: I mean, that's all I cared about, once upon a time. A *job*. I couldn't
    wait until I was scampering up and down Wall Street in my gray and
    white Adidas and a new suit from Saks, with my little leather
    briefcase swinging by my side. Meeting men for lunch and women for
    dinner, and both in the Health Club afterwards. A co-op on the East
    Side with a VCR and an answering machine with a funny message.
    Weekends at Sugarbush and Vineyard. Vacations in the Bahamas and
    France. Nailing down forty or fifty thou per annum within three
    years. Moving onward and upward through the corridors of power
    until I get an office with a corner view where I can look down on
    millions of women scampering up and down Wall Street in their gray
    and white Adidas.

DIANA: That's not the worst thing in the world!

JUDY: Isn't it? I'm not so sure. I'm beginning to think it's a con deal. All
    us women now killing ourselves to do those things that a lot of men
    decided not to do twenty years ago. I mean, here we are, the
    organization women, punching the clock, flashing the credit card,
    smoking our lungs out, while the really smart men are off making
    furniture or playing the clarinet or something. Look at you. Do you
    really want to be Dean, or are you just making some sort of feminist
    statement?

630 DIANA: Let's leave me out of this, please.

JUDY: Well all I know is I'm not so hung up on "The Job" anymore. It just
    seems like more of the same. More of what I did at Andover and at
    Westport Junior High before that. More of what I've done every
    summer, with my creative camps and Internships and my Special
    Summer Projects. Touching all the bases, following all the rules, ever
    since I can remember. And now here I am, about to graduate, or
    rather *not* graduate, because I've come up with the first vaguely
    unselfish idea I've ever had in my life, and this place, this
    institution—in which my family has invested at least seventy
    thousand dollars—won't give me credit for it.

DIANA: A C is a decent grade, Judy. We used to call it a gentleman's C.

JUDY: Well I'm no gentleman. *(She starts out.)*

DIANA: Judy . . . One more thing. *(Judy stops, turns.)*

635 JUDY: What?

DIANA: The Provost sat in on the Grievance Committee meeting.

JUDY: And?

DIANA: After it was over, he took me aside. He asked me to ask you a
question.

JUDY: Go ahead.

640 DIANA: . . . the Provost wondered if your difficulty with Professor Harper
has anything to do with . . . ethnic issues.

JUDY: Say again?

DIANA: A student has recently complained that Professor Harper is
anti-Semitic?

JUDY: Anti-Semitic?

DIANA: That's the complaint.

645 JUDY: Anti-Semitic? It's probably that Talmudic type who sits in the front
row and argues about everything. I bet he wears his yarmulke even in
the shower.

DIANA: Ah, but you don't feel that way?

JUDY: No way.

DIANA: Oh, Judy, I'm so glad to hear it.

JUDY: I never even thought of it.

650 DIANA: Good. Then I'll tell the Provost.

JUDY: I mean should I worry about that? My grandmother says you have
to watch out for that sort of thing at all times.

DIANA: Yes, well, times change.

JUDY: Unless it's there, and I didn't see it.

DIANA: No, no . . .

655 JUDY: I mean, maybe I'm so assimilated into white-bread middle-class
America that it passed me right by. Maybe I should reexamine this
whole issue with that in mind. Thanks a lot, Dean! *(She goes out.)*

DIANA: *(calling after her)* Judy! Judy! . . . Oh God! *(She makes up her mind,
opens a desk drawer, takes out a small tape recorder which she slams onto
the desk. She pushes the buttons determinedly and then begins to dictate,
pacing around her office as she smokes. Dictating.)* Monica, please type a
letter to the Provost . . . Dear Walter . . . I herewith submit my
resignation as Dean, to be effective at the end of this school year. I
find I long to return to the clear lines and concrete issues of the
classroom. I especially yearn to resume my studies of Jane Austen,
and the subordinate role of women in the 18th century. I will miss, of
course, the sense of bustle and activity I've found here in
Administration. There's something to be said, after all, for the
friendships which come from working closely with other people
during regular hours—among which I count my friendship with the
other Deans, and you, Walter, and Monica, my fine assistant . . .

Indeed, in some ways, I dread retreating to the hermetic world of bickering colleagues, sullen students, hopeless meetings, long hours of preparation . . . *(She slows down.)* . . . the loneliness of the library . . . the meals alone . . . the sense that something more important is going on everywhere else in the world . . . *(Long pause.)* Just type a rough draft of this, Monica. I'll look at it tomorrow. *(She clicks off the tape recorder, puts it back in her desk. Dave enters in a track suit, starts doing stretch exercises. Diana crosses to doorway, calls off.)* Monica, see if you can locate Professor Harper . . . *(Then she takes some computer printout sheets out of her briefcase and begins to go over them at her desk as the lights dim on her. The lights come up more fully on Dave, doing stretch exercises. We hear the distant sounds of students cheering. Judy comes on. It is by now late enough in the spring so she doesn't wear a jacket.)*

JUDY: Dave . . . *(She hugs him from behind.)*

DAVE: *(through his stretches; pantingly)* Hi . . .

JUDY: Am I bothering you?

660 DAVE: *(grunting; stretching)* Yes . . . But that's O.K.

JUDY: I just want to tell you something, David.

DAVE: *(still exercising)* Uh oh. When it's David, it's serious.

JUDY: I just want to tell you not to memorize any more of those speeches.

DAVE: Thank God.

665 JUDY: I'm changing everything.

DAVE: Again?

JUDY: I'm starting all over. From scratch.

DAVE: Why?

JUDY: I didn't like what we had. I can do better.

670 DAVE: Yeah?

JUDY: Now I'm on a totally different track. I mean, it's still *Antigone.* But I'm adding a whole new dimension.

DAVE: Are you throwing in acid rain?

JUDY: *(laughing)* No. I'm onto something much deeper. *(A whistle is heard offstage. Dave starts off.)*

DAVE: There's the Four Hundred. I've got to go.

675 JUDY: So throw away the old stuff.

DAVE: Is there a lot new to learn?

JUDY: Mostly for me.

DAVE: Can you tell me where you're taking it?

JUDY: Well I'm striving for a more natural style.

680 DAVE: Way to go.

JUDY: And I'm connecting my attack on nuclear armaments with the issue of meaningful work.

DAVE: Excellent.

JUDY: And I'm making Antigone Jewish. *(She goes off. Another whistle from offstage. He looks after her, then runs off the opposite way as . . . the lights come up on Diana, who is still at her desk, working on printout sheets. After a moment, Henry appears in the doorway. He watches her affectionately for a moment.)*

HENRY: *(finally)* Woman at her work. I am reminded of Penelope at her loom.

685 DIANA: *(looking up; quickly putting away the sheets)* Come in, Henry.

HENRY: *(coming in)* What a magnificent office, Diana! What corporate dimensions! *(As Diana puts her cigarette out.)* Thank you . . . A view of the Charles! The spires of Harvard dimly seen up the river! How different it is from the monkish cells assigned to those of us who teach.

DIANA: You've been here before, Henry.

HENRY: Never. I've scrupulously avoided all official contact with the bureaucracy, except on my own turf. I wouldn't be here now, dear Diana, but for a series of rather frantic telephone messages left under my door. *(He takes a stack of pink slips out of his pocket, reads.)* Call the Dean . . . See the Dean . . . Please call or see the Dean.

DIANA: Sit down, Henry.

690 HENRY: *(sitting)* I will, but I must warn you I have very little time. We are now deep in the last plays of Euripides, particularly the *Bacchae*, which I continually find to be one of the more profoundly disturbing works of man. He has an even darker vision than Sophocles.

DIANA: Well maybe I've got some news that will cheer you up, Henry.

HENRY: Beware of Deans bearing gifts.

DIANA: Remember that grant you applied for two years ago?

HENRY: Ah yes. To go to Greece. To see the restorations at Epidaurus.[22] *(Pause.)* And to restore a ruin or two in my own life.

695 DIANA: Well you've got that grant now, Henry.

HENRY: Now?

DIANA: I've been talking to the Provost. He's giving you next year off. All year. At full pay.

HENRY: Are you serious?

DIANA: I'm always serious, Henry. That's my problem, in case you ever notice. *(Pause.)*

700 HENRY: Why suddenly now?

DIANA: Ours not to reason why, Henry.

HENRY: I begged for that leave two years ago. I practically fell to my knees and supplicated the Provost like old Priam before Achilles.[23] I thought if Elsa and I could just get away . . .

DIANA: Call her. Tell her you've lucked out, at long last.

---

[22] Or Epidauros, an ancient city-state in Greece. The fourth-century B.C. theater there is preserved and still used for plays.

[23] In Greek legend, Priam, the last King of Troy, lost most of his sons in the Trojan War and was forced to beg Achilles for the body of Hector.

HENRY: It's too late. She's . . . found someone. Apparently they sit and
hold hands and watch television. Anyway, she wants a divorce.

705 DIANA: I am sorry.

HENRY: No, no, it's good. It's very good. The other shoe has dropped.
Finally.

DIANA: Take one of your children then. Give them a trip.

HENRY: They wouldn't come. *(Pause.)* They have their own lives. *(Pause.)*
Such as they are. *(Quietly.)* I'll go alone. *(Pause; he looks at her.)* Unless
you'd come with me.

DIANA: Henry!

710 HENRY: Why not? Take a sabbatical. You're overdue.

DIANA: You mean, just—blip out into the blue Aegean?

HENRY: Exactly! Spend a naughty year abroad with an old satyr. Tell you
what, I'd even let you smoke.

DIANA: I think I'd give it up if I went abroad.

HENRY: Then there we are!

715 DIANA: Oh gosh! To get away! To see something else besides these—walls!
Just think, Henry . . . *(She stops.)* Just think. *(Pause. Sadly.)* It wouldn't
work, Henry.

HENRY: It might.

DIANA: It already didn't, Henry. On that strange weekend in that gloomy
hotel during the M.L.A. conference.

HENRY: That was a lovely weekend.

DIANA: It was not.

720 HENRY: Dido and Aeneas in their enchanted cave . . .

DIANA: Oh Henry, *please!*

HENRY: What's the matter?

DIANA: Dido, Penelope,[24] Clytemnestra! I am not a *myth,* Henry! I am not
a *meta*phor!

HENRY: My dear lady . . .

725 DIANA: No, no, I'm *me,* Henry! I live and breathe in my own right! Do
you know anything about my *life?* Do you know where I live? Do you
know I have a daughter in Junior High?

HENRY: Of course I know you have . . .

DIANA: What's her name, Henry? What's my daughter's *name?* It's not
Electra and it's not Athena and it's not . . .

HENRY: Let me think . . .

DIANA: You don't *know,* Henry. And you don't know that my mother died
last semester, and you don't know that I used to play the French
horn. You don't *see* me, Henry. You don't see anyone. In your mind,

---

[24] In Greek legend, Dido fled to Africa after her husband was murdered and founded
Carthage. In one version of the myth she throws herself on a funeral pyre to avoid
marriage to Iarras of Numidia; in Virgil's *Aeneid,* she kills herself after being abandoned by Aeneas, her lover. Penelope is the faithful wife of Odysseus (Ulysses), who
rejected suitors and patiently awaited his return from his years of adventuring.

everything is an example of something else! I suppose it's called
stereotyping, but whatever it is, I don't like it, Henry! It makes me
feel insignificant and unreal.

730 HENRY: Diana, dear friend . . . *(He moves toward her.)*

DIANA: No, now stay away from me, Henry. Don't touch me. Go to *Greece,*
for God's sake! Find some young woman—excuse me, some sea
nymph—who will throw herself into your arms on the topless shores
of Mykonos. Really. Just go. *(Pause.)*

HENRY: Tell the Provost I'll take a raincheck.

DIANA: A raincheck?

HENRY: Maybe in a year or two. When my life is more in order.

735 DIANA: It doesn't work that way, Henry. It's now or not at all.

HENRY: Then I'll have to forgo it.

DIANA: Oh Henry . . .

HENRY: At this point in my life, I need my classes. Strange as that may
seem. *(He starts out.)* And now, if you'll excuse me, the *Bacchae* call
me to the dance.

DIANA: Henry! *(He stops.)* Other things go on in this university at the end
of the school year besides discussions of the *Bacchae.*

740 HENRY: *(stopping, turning)* Such as?

DIANA: *(taking the computer printouts from her desk)* Well, for example,
Henry, there's something called preregistration, when students give
an indication of what courses they'd like to take next fall.

HENRY: The annual body count.

DIANA: *(indicating sheets)* Exactly, Henry. And we in the Humanities are
down.

HENRY: We are always down. We are doomed to be down. We live in an
age where a book—a good book—is as obsolete as an Aeolian harp.[25]
All the more reason to keep standards *up.*

745 DIANA: You, particularly, are down, Henry. *(Pause.)*

HENRY: How many did I get?

DIANA: Two.

HENRY: Two? Two next fall? Two students to take through the entire rise
and fall of the Roman Empire.

DIANA: Two, Henry.

750 HENRY: How many for my elective on Plato?

DIANA: Four.

HENRY: Four. Two for Rome, four for Plato. Six students, next fall, out of
over four thousand, have shown some interest in the classical
tradition. This, in a country founded by Washington and Jefferson
and Madison precisely to reestablish that tradition.

DIANA: Shakespeare, on the other hand, is up.

---

[25] Ancient instrument.

HENRY: I must say, Diana, I fail to understand why students choose what they do. They land on courses like starlings on a telephone wire. It seems totally random.

755 DIANA: The Provost is cancelling all undergraduate courses with an enrollment of less than five, Henry.

HENRY: What?

DIANA: The Provost is cancelling your courses.

HENRY: He has no right!

DIANA: He has every right. It's a budgetary thing. There are clear rules about it. Jack Edwards's seminar on Racine goes. Sally Weiskopf's section on Keats.[26] The history department lost the entire seventeenth century.

760 HENRY: I'll talk to him. These things can change. Students can sign up in the fall.

DIANA: He's laid down the law, Henry. Jack Edwards has already gone up and been refused. *(Pause.)*

HENRY: Then I'll teach something else.

DIANA: Such as what, Henry?

HENRY: Dante. I'll teach Dante. I'm beginning to get a new understanding of Hell.

765 DIANA: Bill Brindisi's got Dante.

HENRY: Shakespeare, then. I'll do a section of Shakespeare.

DIANA: You don't like Shakespeare.

HENRY: Of course I like Shakespeare. He's just a bit . . . messy, that's all. And a bit over-picked. I refuse to spend an entire class focusing on the button image in *King Lear*. I'll do the Roman plays: *Julius Caesar, Coriolanus* . . .

DIANA: Jane Tillotson's got Shakespeare, Henry. All of him.

770 HENRY: All right then, what? Tolstoy? Joyce? I'm an educated man. I can do anything. Give me the freshman course—Introduction to Literature. I'll take it over. I'll muster that motley crew of junior instructors who teach it. We'll begin with the *Iliad*, and stride down the centuries, concluding with Conrad.

DIANA: I think they *start* with Conrad in that course, Henry.

HENRY: Oh really? Well, we'll change that. We'll—

DIANA: Henry. *(Pause.)* The Provost doesn't want you to teach. At all.

HENRY: Why not?

775 DIANA: He thinks your courses are becoming . . . problematic, Henry.

HENRY: The *Antigone* thing?

DIANA: And the anti-Semitic thing.

HENRY: I have scrupulously avoided anything controversial in my class.

DIANA: Apparently she hasn't, in her play. I hear it's more and more about being Jewish, and more and more about you.

---

[26] Jean Racine (1639–1699)—French dramatist; John Keats (1795–1821)—British poet.

780 HENRY: *(quietly, with increasing anger)* There is a law as old as Solon which allows a man to confront his accusers. I want to meet her, right now, in front of the Provost, and you, and Ariel Sharon, if he wants to be there!

DIANA: The Provost already met with her, Henry.

HENRY: And what did she say?

DIANA: Nothing! Everything! I don't know! He said it was all very general . . . He said you both deserve each other. He said if he didn't have the alumni breathing down his neck, he'd turn you both loose in the ring, and the hell with it. But right now, all he wants to do is get her graduated and you out of the country, so that things can simmer *down.* Now go to *Greece,* Henry, and enjoy it!

HENRY: And when I come back, he'll suggest early retirement.

785 DIANA: He might.

HENRY: He'll sweeten the pot. Buy me off with a few impressive benefits.

DIANA: You've been here a long time, Henry. I think they'd be very generous.

HENRY: I want to teach, Diana.

DIANA: I know.

790 HENRY: I need to teach.

DIANA: I know, I know . . .

HENRY: It's what I do.

DIANA: Henry, my old colleague . . .

HENRY: I am a classical scholar. I trained at Harvard. I have written three good books. I know a great deal, and I have to teach what I know, and I'm only good when I'm teaching it! My wife has left me, my children have scattered, I have nothing else but this! I have to teach, Diana. Have to. Or I'm dead.

795 DIANA: You need students, Henry.

HENRY: Then I'll have to get them, won't I? *(He goes off. Diana sits there for a moment, then opens her purse, takes out a pack of cigarettes. She shakes it, but it's empty. She gets up, and begins to walk toward the wings, calling out sweetly as she goes.)*

DIANA: Monica? . . . Did you bring any cigarettes in today? . . . Because if you did, even though you're down to your last one, I intend to get it, Monica. I intend to wrestle you to the ground! *(She goes off, as Judy comes on. She leans against a pillar in a rather theatrical pose and recites her lines, referring only occasionally to a script she carries, in her hand.)*

JUDY: "So Creon has determined I go to jail. I wonder if this is happening because I'm Jewish. I don't mean simply that Creon's prejudiced—though he probably is. I mean more because of me. Maybe it's built into my Jewish blood to rise up against the Creons of this world. All I know is for the first time in my life I've felt in tune with something larger than myself. I've been to the library lately. I've studied my roots. And I've learned how often we Jews have stood our ground against injustice. Pharaoh and Philistine, Hittite and Herod have fallen before us. Roman generals and Spanish Inquisitors, Venetian businessmen and Russian Cossacks, Nazis, Arabs, McCarthyites—all the arrogant authorities of this world have tried to subdue us. And when we protest, they throw us into jail. Well, what's jail these days? Maybe this is a jail right here. This so-called ivory tower. This labyrinth of curricular obligations. This festering nest of overpaid administrators. This rotten pit of dry and exhausted pedants. This winter camp which capitalism creates to keep its children off the job market. What job market? Where are the jobs? Where is there decent work in an economy so devoted to nonessential goods and destructive weapons?" *(Dave comes on.)*

DAVE: Judy—

800 JUDY: Wait. I'm almost done. *(She continues to recite.)* "Or maybe this whole damn country is a jail. Maybe we're all prisoners. Prisoners of these oppressive corporations, who capture us with their advertising, chain us to their products, and work us forever in meaningless jobs to pay for things we shouldn't even want."

DAVE: Judy. It's important.

JUDY: Hold it. *(She takes a deep breath.)* "And to protect this prison, this fortress America, this so-called way of life, we arm ourselves with weapons which, if they're used, could ten times over destroy the world, blot out the past, and turn the future into a desolate blank. Are we so sure we're right? Is life in these United States so great? Would the homeless hordes on the streets of New York agree? Would the hungry blacks in the South? Would the migrant workers breaking their backs to feed us go along with it? Oh God, Lysander, this might be a terrible thing to say, but I don't think our country is worth dying for any more. The world at large is worth dying for, not just us."

DAVE: Wow! That's tremendous.

JUDY: Thank you. *(Pause.)*

805 DAVE: *(quietly)* He wants to see you.

JUDY: The Provost? I know. I have a meeting with him in half an hour.

DAVE: No, *Harper! Harper* wants to see you.

JUDY: Harper?

DAVE: He called me at the lab.

810 JUDY: How come he called *you?*

DAVE: I don't know . . . I guess he knew I knew you. Anyway, he said he watched the rehearsal last night.

JUDY: *What?*

DAVE: He was there. And he wants to talk to you about it.

JUDY: Oh God. What did he think?

815 DAVE: Didn't say. *(The lights begin to come up on Henry's office, as Henry comes in, settles his desk.)*

JUDY: Oh Lord, he must have hated it. All that Creon stuff I put in. Well, maybe it'll do him good.

DAVE: He said he'd be in his office all afternoon. You better see him.

JUDY: *(putting on lip gloss)* I might. Then again I might not. First, of course, I have a major meeting with the Provost. *(She starts out.)*

DAVE: *(calling after Judy)* Hey, you're quite the Queen Bee around here these days.

820 JUDY: I'm another Antigone.

DAVE: Antigone dies in the end, remember.

JUDY: That's the old version. Mine ends happily ever after. *(She goes off.)*

DAVE: *(calling after her)* Ever hear of *hubris,* Judy? Know what that word means . . . *(He sees she's gone, speaks to himself.)* Pride. Overweening pride. For example, take a man whose father gives him a chemistry set when he's eight years old. This man takes Chemistry in high school, and majors in it in college. What makes this man think he can graduate if he doesn't study? What makes this man think he can find a job if he doesn't graduate? What makes this man stand around, talking to himself, when his final exam in Chemistry starts in five minutes, and he doesn't know the stuff at *all?* Pride, that's what. *Hubris.* Which leads to tragedy every time. *(He goes off grimly as the lights come up on Henry in his office. After a moment, Judy comes in.)*

JUDY: You wanted to see me, Professor Harper?

825 HENRY: *(jumping up)* Ah. Miss Miller. Yes. *(Indicates a chair.)* Please. *(Judy comes in.)* How well you look.

JUDY: Thank you.

HENRY: I am reminded of a line from the *Andromache:* "I now wear different robes."

JUDY: I don't know that one.

HENRY: No matter. You look lovely. Life on the wicked stage becomes you.

830 JUDY: Thanks. *(She sits.)*

HENRY: Yes, well, now I have recently had the opportunity to watch you practice your play.

JUDY: You mean, re*hearse.*

HENRY: Yes. Rehearse. Last night, in fact. I happen to know old Bill, who's the custodian of the Spingler Auditorium, and he took me up to the back of the balcony and let me sit there unobtrusively and watch you rehearse your play.

JUDY: I heard.

835 HENRY: Oh yes? Well that's where I was. All evening. *(Pause.)* I found it . . . *(This is tough for him.)* Interesting. *(Pause.)* Quite interesting. *(Pause.)* The crude poetry, the naive theatricality . . .

JUDY: Thank you.

HENRY: Your work also demonstrated an earnestness and commitment which I found . . . refreshing, in a world which seems too often concerned only with the meaning of meaning.

JUDY: You mean, you *liked* it? *(Pause.)*

HENRY: I . . . admired it.

840 JUDY: Well thank you very much! I appreciate that.

HENRY: I have decided it may substitute after all for your term paper.

JUDY: That's great!

HENRY: Miss Miller, you might be interested to know that Sophocles
himself was a practical man of the theatre. Not only did he write his
plays, but he directed most of them, and sometimes acted in them as
well, just as you are doing.

JUDY: Really?

845 HENRY: Absolutely. And according to Aristotle—this might amuse you—
he actually danced in a lost play of his called *Nausicaa*. He danced.
He danced the part of a young woman playing ball.

JUDY: No kidding! That makes me feel very proud!

HENRY: Then I wonder if you would play ball with *me*, Miss Miller.

JUDY: What do you mean?

HENRY: Well now, last night, I noticed a number of people scurrying
about, assisting with your production.

850 JUDY: Yes . . .

HENRY: Good, practical souls, hard at work. I mean, not only did I notice
your personal and particular friend . . .

JUDY: Dave . . .

HENRY: Yes, Dave. A fine, stalwart young man. I noticed him. But I also
noticed other actors, and that odd cluster of people pretending to be
the chorus.

JUDY: Right . . .

855 HENRY: And then I hear there's to be an orchestra . . .

JUDY: A group. A combo, really . . .

HENRY: Well how many do you think are involved, in toto?

JUDY: In toto?

HENRY: Altogether.

860 JUDY: Oh . . . maybe . . . thirty-five.

HENRY: And of course not all of them will graduate this year, will they?

JUDY: No. Some. Not all.

HENRY: Miss Miller, I wonder if you would announce to everyone in your
production that I'm planning to give a special seminar next fall.

JUDY: Special seminar?

865 HENRY: On the Greeks. And since these students have all been working on
your *Antigone*, I'll give them the inside track. They *must*, however—
you must tell them this—they *must* let the Dean's office know they're
interested, so we'll have some indication of preenrollment.

JUDY: Professor Harper, I'm not sure they'd want to—

HENRY: Oh yes they would. Tell them this course will be—how shall I put
it?—"project-oriented." They can put on plays. They can make
models of the Parthenon. They can draw maps of the Peloponnesian
Peninsula, I don't care!

JUDY: That doesn't sound like you, Professor Harper.

HENRY: Oh yes, yes. And tell them I'll grade it Pass/Fail, if they want. And
I'll have very few papers. No papers at all, really, if that's what they
want. Because the important thing is not papers, is it, it's the Greeks!

We'll be studying the Greeks next year, that's the thing! We'll still be reading and discussing those fine old plays. We'll still be holding onto the heart of Western Civilization. That's what we'll be doing, Miss Miller, and you will have helped us do it! *(Pause.)*

870 JUDY: You mean you want students next year.

HENRY: Yes, frankly, I do. *(Pause.)*

JUDY: Wow!

HENRY: There it is.

JUDY: I always thought we had to go through you. I never thought you had to go through *us.*

875 HENRY: Well we do.

JUDY: You really *need* us, don't you? You have to have us.

HENRY: Without you, we'd die.

JUDY: I never knew that before.

HENRY: Now you do. *(Pause.)* So will you tell them about the course?

880 JUDY: Yes I will.

HENRY: And you'll encourage them to come?

JUDY: I'll tell them, Professor Harper. I'll let them choose.

HENRY: But you won't . . . undercut me?

JUDY: No, I won't do that.

885 HENRY: And you'll remind them to sign up immediately. So the administration will know.

JUDY: I'll do all that, sir. I mean, you have a right to live, too, after all.

HENRY: You're magnanimous in victory, Miss Miller.

JUDY: Thank you, sir.

HENRY: Now, before we turn to the crass topic of grades, suppose we celebrate the conclusion of these negotiations. *(Opens his drawer again, takes out a sherry bottle and two murky glasses.)* I keep this sherry around for those rare occasions when a fellow scholar stops by.

890 JUDY: Oh I don't—

HENRY: *(pouring)* Please. It's important. Old Odysseus and the nymph Calypso, in Book Five of the *Odyssey,*[27] sharing a glass before they say goodbye. *(He hands her her glass, raises his in a toast.)* To peace and reconciliation. *(They click glasses and drink.)* Doesn't that hit the spot?

JUDY: Actually, it does.

HENRY: Have some more.

JUDY: Oh, well. No. I mean, all right. *(He pours her more, and a touch more for himself. Judy gets up.)* You know, I was just thinking, Professor Harper . . .

895 HENRY: *(his little joke)* That's always a good sign.

---

[27] In Homer's *Odyssey,* the nymph Calypso holds Odysseus captive for seven years; she treats him well, but he longs for his homeland and family. Finally, Zeus, prompted by Athena's intervention, orders Odysseus released. Calypso obeys, outfitting him with food and drink.

JUDY: No, seriously, I was thinking that you and I are basically very much
    alike.

HENRY: Ah? And how so?

JUDY: I mean we both see too big a picture.

HENRY: Elucidate, please.

900 JUDY: Sure. I mean, there you are, always talking about the Greeks versus
    the Jews, and here I am, talking about the Jews versus all authority.

HENRY: I see.

JUDY: Maybe we should both scale things down.

HENRY: Maybe we should. *(Settling back in his chair.)* In any case, I think
    you can count on receiving a B in my course, Miss Miller.

JUDY: A B.

905 HENRY: A strong B. A solid B. A B which leans longingly toward a B plus.

JUDY: I was kind of hoping I'd get an A.

HENRY: I don't think your work quite warrants an A, Miss Miller.

JUDY: You don't think so?

HENRY: Let's reserve the A's for Sophocles, shall we? It gives us something
    to go for. *(Pause.)*

910 JUDY: That's cool.

HENRY: I take it you agree.

JUDY: I guess a B from you is like an A from anyone else.

HENRY: Well, thank you, Miss Miller.

JUDY: *(getting up)* Besides, I don't really believe in grades anymore.

915 HENRY: Good for you.

JUDY: I think I've grown beyond them.

HENRY: Unfortunately we live in a world which seems to require them.
    We have to toss them, like bones, to a ravenous administration.

JUDY: Oh God, I know. *They* even wanted me to take an A.

HENRY: And where did they propose you find that A?

920 JUDY: A professor in Drama saw a rehearsal, and offered to give me a
    straight A.

HENRY: Ah, but of course that wouldn't count.

JUDY: Oh sure. He said I could register it under Special Topics.

HENRY: Well then, I'm afraid I'd have to go to the Provost. To protest this
    blatant interference in my course.

JUDY: I just came from the Provost. It was his idea, actually. *(Pause.)*

925 HENRY: You mean you don't need a grade in my course to graduate.

JUDY: Not any more.

HENRY: You don't really need me at all.

JUDY: Technically, no.

HENRY: Why did you bother to come?

930 JUDY: I wanted your opinion of my *play!* I wanted to hear what you
    thought.

HENRY: And I told you: B.

JUDY: Right. Fine. And I'm accepting your B. I'll tell the Registrar. *(She
    starts out.)*

HENRY: Miss Miller. *(She stops.)* This professor who offered to intrude. Who was he?

JUDY: Who?

935 HENRY: Do I know him?

JUDY: He's new this year.

HENRY: What's his name?

JUDY: Bob Birnbaum.

HENRY: Bob—?

940 JUDY: Birnbaum. *(Pause.)*

HENRY: Of course.

JUDY: What do you mean?

HENRY: Once again Athens is forced to bow to Jerusalem.

JUDY: Explain that, please.

945 HENRY: I mean the Chosen People always choose to intrude.

JUDY: That's what I thought you meant. *(She strides for the door, then wheels on him.)* All bets are off, Professor Harper. I wouldn't recommend this course to a Nazi! And I'll take a good, solid, Jewish A from Birnbaum! *(She storms out.)*

HENRY: *(quietly; to himself as he sits)* Good God. What have I done? *(The lights dim on him as he sits at his desk. Diana crosses the stage hurriedly, carrying a stack of folders. Dave is following her.)*

DAVE: Dean . . . ? *(She turns.)* Could I speak to you for a minute, please?

DIANA: I'm sorry, but I'm late for an important meeting.

950 DAVE: The Committee on Academic Performance, right?

DIANA: That's the one.

DAVE: That's what I've got to speak to you about. *(She stops, looks at him.)*

DIANA: Aren't you that friend of Judy Miller's?

DAVE: David Appleton. My name's coming up before the committee today. I flunked the Chemistry final. I'm not graduating.

955 DIANA: Chemistry will take care of you. There's infinite salvation: makeup exams, summer school, degrees given out in the fall . . .

DAVE: I don't want any of that. I want to switch to your department and be here all next year.

DIANA: Studying what?

DAVE: The Greeks.

DIANA: But we don't have a Classics Department anymore.

960 DAVE: You have Professor Harper.

DIANA: He may be on sabbatical next year.

DAVE: Oh. Then I'll make up my general requirements till he returns and take Ancient Greek on my own.

DIANA: *(starting out)* If you'd make an appointment with Monica, my assistant, we'll discuss all this.

DAVE: No, I've thought it through. I just need your approval.

965 DIANA: You're talking about another year's tuition.

DAVE: I know. And my dad's cutting me off. But I've gotten a double shift in the cafeteria. I'll get my degree next June, and apply for postgraduate studies with Professor Harper. *(Pause.)*

Diana: I'll tell the committee you're staying on.

Dave: Thank you.

Diana: I envy you.

970 Dave: For studying with Harper?

Diana: For being so sure. *(Judy enters.)*

Judy: What's going on, Dave?

Dave: I'm changing my life.

Diana: Make an appointment if you want to change it back! *(She goes out.)*

975 Judy: We have a rehearsal, remember? I'm putting in the final rewrites.

Dave: Can't make it. Got a class.

Judy: At this hour? What class?

Dave: Harper's actually.

Judy: *Harper's? My* Harper?

980 Dave: I've been auditing it for the past three weeks.

Judy: Why?

Dave: I like him. I like the subject. I like myself when I'm working on it.

Judy: You never told me that.

Dave: I knew it would freak you out.

985 Judy: Damn right! He's a bigot, Dave.

Dave: I don't think so.

Judy: He's an anti-Semite.

Dave: I don't think so, Judy.

Judy: I *know* so! *Personally!* He made an anti-Semitic *slur!*

990 Dave: He just generalizes, Judy. It's his tragic flaw.

Judy: I don't buy that, Dave.

Dave: All right, so he made a crack? So what? People make ethnic digs all the time in this country. We all get it in the neck—the Poles, the Italians, now the Wasps.

Judy: The Jews are different! All through history—

Dave: So I keep hearing. Still, seems to me you're people, like everyone else. I think this Jewish thing is getting out of hand. Suddenly nothing counts except you're Jewish!

995 Judy: Dave . . .

Dave: No, let me finish, for once in my life! I didn't fall in love with a Jewish Revolutionary, I fell in love with *you!* I fell in love with a particular person who liked Springsteen and Moo Sho Pork and staying in bed all day on Sunday. What happened to all that? What happens to us next *year?* These are the important things—not that you're Jewish, for God's sake!

Judy: I think we're in a little hot water here.

Dave: I guess we are. *(A bell rings.)* Saved by the bell. *(He starts off.)*

Judy: Dave. *(He stops.)* We have a rehearsal now.

1000 Dave: Work around me.

Judy: It's too late for that.

Dave: Look, it's his last class. The whole school knows about this. Everyone wants to see what he's going to say.

Judy: Not if they're with *Antigone.*

DAVE: Give me an hour.

1005 JUDY: No! It's him or me, Dave. You choose.

DAVE: Be serious.

JUDY: I am. I'll put in Mark Shapiro. I'll replace you. Totally. *(Pause.)*

DAVE: Fair enough. *(He starts off again.)*

JUDY: *(calling after him)* Then it's true, what my grandmother said! You people always turn your backs when the chips are down! *(He turns, glares at her, then exits. She speaks softly, to herself.)* Oh Lord. I'm as bad as Harper. *(She goes off slowly the opposite way. The lights come up on Henry as he comes D., addressing the audience once again as if it were his class. Dave enters, to sit on the side and listen, as if he were in class.)*

1010 HENRY: *(to audience)* This has been a course on tragedy. That is what this course is supposed to be about. *(Pause.)* First, let me remind you what tragedy is *not*. Tragedy has nothing to do with choice. If you can choose, it is not tragic. There are some people who think that our arms race with the Russians is tragic. It is not. It is not, because we have the choice, they have the choice, to say No, to stop, to disarm, to embrace each other in the name of peace at any time. So it is not tragic. It is stupid, yes. It is insane, it is suicidal, it is pathetic, but it is not—repeat Not—tragic, in the true Greek sense of the word. *(Pause.)* Tragedy occurs when you cannot choose, when you have no choice at all. This is hard for Americans to understand. Because most of us are free, or think we are. Nowhere else in the world, and never before in history, have so many people been so free to choose so many destinies. Perhaps, because of this freedom, it is impossible for us to sense what the Greeks called tragedy. We have no oracles, no gods, no real sense of ultimate authority to insist that if we do one thing, another will inevitably follow. We are free. *(Pause.)* On the other hand, there might come a time to some of us, to one or two, *(He glances at Dave.)* when we get an inkling, a glimmer, a faint shadow of a shadow of what it might have been like for the Greeks when they sat in a theatre and saw the universe close in on a man, or woman, because of some flaw, some excess, some overshooting of the mark . . . *(Pause.)* Then the net tightens, and as he struggles, tightens further, until he is crushed by forces total and absurd. *(Pause.)* Then we might be touching the outer borders of tragedy, as the Greeks once knew it. *(Pause. He takes up his book of Antigone.)* But I've just discovered something else about tragedy, or at least about Sophoclean tragedy. Something I thought I knew, but didn't understand till now. And that is what the tragic heroes do after the net has closed around them. What they do, even in the teeth of disaster, is accept responsibility, assert their own destiny, and mete out proudly their own punishments. This is what Oedipus does when he puts out his eyes. This is what Antigone does, when she hangs herself. And this is what Creon does, at the end of the same play. He has lost his wife, his children, all he holds dear. And he realizes why: that in his commitment to abstract and dehumanizing laws, he has neglected the very heart of life. And so he banishes himself from his own city. His Polis. He goes. He disappears. He leaves the stage, forever doomed now to wander far from the only community he knows, self-exiled and alone. *(Pause.)* I'll expect all papers under my door by five o'clock this evening. You may retrieve them, graded and with appropriate comments, from the Departmental office next Monday. Enjoy your summer. Read good books. Go to good plays. Think of the Greeks. Thank you and goodbye. *(He sees Dave go, then crosses to his desk, where he leaves his book of* Antigone. *Then he exits, as graduation music comes up loudly: an optimistic piece, played by a brass ensemble. Diana comes out in gown and colorful academic hood. She reads from a formal-looking document.)*

DIANA: Our final award is the Peabody Prize . . . *(Reads from card.)* "Offered annually to that student who best combines academic excellence with extracurricular commitment . . ." *(To audience.)* It is awarded this year to Judith Rachel Miller, of the graduating class, for her exceptional academic record as well as for her fascinating contemporary version of Sophocles' *Antigone. (Applause and cheers. Judy comes on, in academic robes. She accepts an envelope from Diana, who gives her a kiss.)* Congratulations, Judy . . . And now refreshments will be—

JUDY: May I say something, please?

DIANA: *(very reluctantly)* All right.

JUDY: *(to audience)* First, I want to thank everyone involved for making our play possible. *(Looks at envelope.)* And I want to thank the Peabody Foundation for making this prize possible. *(Looks out.)* And I want to thank my parents for making *me* possible. *(Diana tries to step in.)* I'm not finished. *(Diana steps back. To audience.)* Lately I've been doing some thinking, and as someone once told me, that's always a good sign. I've been thinking about this prize, for example. I guess it stands for everything I used to believe in: personal ambition . . . success . . . *(She peeks into the envelope.)* And sure, why not? money . . . I mean, these are the things they tell us make our country great . . . *(Diana looks worried.)* Trouble is, I'm beginning to think these things aren't so important. Maybe my play hasn't influenced anyone else, but it sure has influenced me. I don't feel good about my life anymore. I don't feel good about my country. I can't accept all this *stuff* that's going on these days. I can't accept it. No, I'm sorry, but I just can't accept it. *(She hands the envelope back to Diana and hurries off.)*

1015 DIANA: Judy! *(She hurries off after Judy, as the lights come up on Henry's office. Dave enters, carrying a note. He finds Henry's book on the desk. He picks it up, looks at it, and starts deciphering the title.)*

DAVE: Alpha . . . Nu . . . Tau . . . Iota . . . Gamma . . . Omicron . . . Nu . . . Eta . . . *Antigone. (Diana enters, no longer in her robes, but still carrying the prize envelope.)*

DIANA: Mr. Appleton? Monica told me you got a note from Professor Harper.

DAVE: *(indicating the book)* He said he was leaving me his book.

DIANA: But did he say where he'd *be?* We can't locate him anywhere.

1020 DAVE: He just mentions the book.

DIANA: Oh dear.

DAVE: I'll find him. I'll track him down. Like Telemachus.[28] In the *Odyssey.*

DIANA: You're beginning to sound a little like him.

DAVE: Maybe. In some ways.

1025 DIANA: I suppose you heard about Judy.

DAVE: Saw it. From the sidelines.

DIANA: That girl seems to be interested in systematically hanging herself.

DAVE: She likes to go for broke.

DIANA: This prize is a sizable check. Do you know any cause she'd want to donate it to?

1030 DAVE: Tell you what: I'll ask her. It'll give me an excuse to open diplomatic relations.

DIANA: I have a feeling we may have lost them both forever.

DAVE: Oh God, I hope not.

DIANA: So do I . . . Meanwhile, I have no idea how to summarize all this for the Departmental report. What does Sophocles say at the end of that damn play?

DAVE: Well, he says that wisdom and reverence lead to happiness . . .

1035 DIANA: Oh good. I'll go along with that! Thank you. *(Dave starts out, then stops, turns back.)*

DAVE: But then he goes on to say that we only learn this when we're too old for it to make much difference.

DIANA: Then heaven help us all. *(They look at each other. Blackout.)*

The End

READING AND REACTING

1. The play introduces a number of opposing forces:
   ◊ anarchy versus tyranny
   ◊ individual versus community rights
   ◊ Greek versus Hebraic sensibility

   Identify as many additional opposing forces as you can, and consider how each pair expresses the themes of the play.
2. What various meanings does the title of the play suggest? Is it necessary to be familiar with Sophocles' *Antigone* before reading *Another Antigone?* Explain.

---

[28] Odysseus's son, who searches for his father.

3. In what way is Professor Harper like Creon? How is Judy like Antigone? In what ways are they different from their counterparts?

4. Is Professor Harper an effective teacher? What do his students and his colleagues think of him? What do you think of him?

5. In an interview, A. R. Gurney said that the tendency to abstract or generalize dehumanizes the people who are placed in categories. What do you suppose Gurney meant by this statement? In what sense do Judy and Professor Harper dehumanize each other?

6. What power does Professor Harper have? What power does Judy have? At what point does the balance of power shift?

7. Why does Diana, Professor Harper's dean, warn him that he must not be insensitive about the Jews? What does she mean when she says, "The 20th century is still with us, Henry. We live in the shadow of the Holocaust. Remember that, please, and be warned"? Do you think Professor Harper is anti-Semitic?

8. Why is Professor Harper unable to keep his opinions to himself? Should he be censured for his remarks, or should he be able to express any opinion he wants to?

9. What is Dave's function in the play? Why does Dave choose Professor Harper over Judy? What does he realize about Harper that Judy fails to understand? Do you agree with his assessment of Professor Harper?

10. After accusing Dave of deserting her, Judy says to herself, "Oh Lord. I'm as bad as Harper." Do you think she is correct? What does this remark show about her?

11. At the end of the play, Professor Harper points out that the essence of tragedy lies in the fact that tragic figures have no choice. "If you can choose," he says, "it is not tragic." According to Harper's definition, which of the characters in *Another Antigone* (if any) are tragic? Explain.

12. Is it significant that Judy is female and Professor Harper is male? Would the conflict have occurred if their roles had been reversed or if both Judy and Professor Harper were of the same gender?

13. **JOURNAL ENTRY** Given all the problems confronting higher education today, do you think Judy's battle is worth fighting?

14. **CRITICAL PERSPECTIVE** In a review of the New York production of *Another Antigone*, Robert Feldberg observes that although neither Judy nor Professor Harper is a sympathetic character, Gurney favors Harper:

> In most ways Harper is a fool. But there is a sense that Gurney, who shares a similar social background and is himself a teacher, has a feeling for the man. [. . .] Gurney may be

trying to be evenhanded, but in his battle of the bores, the professor—and his values—easily win the sympathy vote.

Do you think Gurney's depiction of the two central characters is "evenhanded," or do you agree that he seems to favor Harper?

Related Works: "The German Refugee" (p. 511), "For the Student Strikers" (p. 777), "Daddy" (p. 818), "Ethics" (p. 979), "Barbie Doll" (p. 980), *Antigone* (p. 1631)

◆ **Marsha Norman** (1947–   ) is a writer who finds drama in ordinary settings. She was born and grew up in Louisville, Kentucky, where her father sold insurance and her mother was a housewife fascinated by revivalist religion.

Norman often writes about the world of poor Southerners without resorting to stereotypical clichés. Her most famous play, *'night, Mother* (1982) won the 1983 Pulitzer Prize. Her first work of collected plays, *Marsha Norman: Collected Plays* (1998) includes the plays *Getting Out, Third and Oak, Circus Valentine,* and *Traveler in the Dark.* Her Tony Award–winning musical *The Secret Garden* (1992), based on the novel by Frances Hodgson Burnett (1911), is an adaptation of Burnett's classic tale about the healing power of love.

Cultural Context ◆ Suicide is the ninth-leading cause of death in the United States. In fact, more people die from suicide than from homicide. Suicide is the third-leading cause of death for people between the ages of fifteen and twenty-four, five thousand of whom commit suicide each year.

◆ ◆ ◆

MARSHA NORMAN

'night, Mother
(1982)

CHARACTERS

Jessie Cates, *in her late thirties or early forties, is pale and vaguely unsteady physically. It is only in the last year that Jessie has gained control of her mind and body, and tonight she is determined to hold on to that control. She wears pants and a long black sweater with deep pockets, which contain scraps of paper, and there may be a pencil behind her ear or a pen clipped to one of the pockets of the sweater.*

As a rule, Jessie doesn't feel much like talking. Other people have rarely found her quirky sense of humor amusing. She has a peaceful energy on this night, a sense of purpose, but is clearly aware of the time passing moment by moment. Oddly enough, Jessie has never been as communicative or as enjoyable as she is on this evening, but we must know she has not always been this way. There is a familiarity between these two women that comes from having lived together for a long time. There is a shorthand to the talk and a sense of routine comfort in the way they relate to each other physically. Naturally, there are also routine aggravations.

THELMA CATES, *"Mama," is Jessie's mother, in her late fifties or early sixties. She has begun to feel her age and so takes it easy when she can, or when it serves her purpose to let someone help her. But she speaks quickly and enjoys talking. She believes that things* are *what she says they are. Her sturdiness is more a mental quality than a physical one, finally. She is chatty and nosy, and this is* her *house.*

The play takes place in a relatively new house built way out on a country road, with a living room and connecting kitchen, and a center hall that leads off to the bedrooms. A pull cord in the hall ceiling releases a ladder which leads to the attic. One of these bedrooms opens directly onto the hall, and its entry should be visible to everyone in the audience. It should be, in fact, the focal point of the entire set, and the lighting should make it disappear completely at times and draw the entire set into it at others. It is a point of both threat and promise. It is an ordinary door that opens onto absolute nothingness. That door is the point of all the action, and the utmost care should be given to its design and construction.

The living room is cluttered with magazines and needlework catalogues, ashtrays and candy dishes. Examples of Mama's needlework are everywhere— pillows, afghans, and quilts, doilies and rugs, and they are quite nice examples. The house is more comfortable than messy, but there is quite a lot to keep in place here. It is more personal than charming. It is not quaint. Under no circumstances should the set and its dressing make a judgment about the intelligence or taste of Jessie and Mama. It should simply indicate that they are very specific real people who happen to live in a particular part of the country. Heavy accents, which would further distance the audience from Jessie and Mama, are also wrong.

The time is the present, with the action beginning about 8:15. Clocks onstage in the kitchen and on a table in the living room should run throughout the performance and be visible to the audience.

There will be no intermission.

Mama stretches to reach the cupcakes in a cabinet in the kitchen. She can't see them, but she can feel around for them, and she's eager to have one, so she's working pretty hard at it. This may be the most serious exercise Mama ever gets. She finds a cupcake, the coconut-covered, raspberry-and-marshmallow-filled kind known as a snowball, but sees that there's one missing from the package. She calls to Jessie, who is apparently somewhere else in the house.

MAMA: *(unwrapping the cupcake)* Jessie, it's the last snowball, sugar. Put it on the list, O.K.? And we're out of Hershey bars, and where's that peanut brittle? I think maybe Dawson's been in it again. I ought to put a big mirror on the refrigerator door. That'll keep him out of my treats, won't it? You hear me, honey? *(Then more to herself.)* I hate it when the coconut falls off. Why does the coconut fall off?

Jessie enters from her bedroom, carrying a stack of newspapers.

JESSIE: We got any old towels?

MAMA: There you are!

JESSIE: *(holding a towel that was on the stack of newspapers)* Towels you don't want anymore. *(Picking up Mama's snowball wrapper.)* How about this swimming towel Loretta gave us? Beach towel, that's the name of it. You want it? *(Mama shakes her head no.)*

5 MAMA: What have you been doing in there?

JESSIE: And a big piece of plastic like a rubber sheet or something. Garbage bags would do if there's enough.

MAMA: Don't go making a big mess, Jessie. It's eight o'clock already.

JESSIE: Maybe an old blanket or towels we got in a soap box sometime?

MAMA: I said don't make a mess. Your hair is black enough, hon.

10 JESSIE: *(continuing to search the kitchen cabinets, finding two or three more towels to add to her stack)* It's not for my hair, Mama. What about some old pillows anywhere, or a foam cushion out of a yard chair would be real good.

MAMA: You haven't forgot what night it is, have you? *(Holding up her fingernails.)* They're all chipped, see? I've been waiting all week, Jess. It's Saturday night, sugar.

JESSIE: I know. I got it on the schedule.

MAMA: *(crossing to the living room)* You want me to wash 'em now or are you making your mess first? *(Looking at the snowball.)* We're out of these. Did I say that already?

JESSIE: There's more coming tomorrow. I ordered you a whole case.

15 MAMA: *(checking the* TV Guide*)* A whole case will go stale, Jessie.

JESSIE: They can go in the freezer till you're ready for them. Where's Daddy's gun?

MAMA: In the attic.

JESSIE: Where in the attic? I looked your whole nap and couldn't find it anywhere.

MAMA: One of his shoeboxes, I think.

20 JESSIE: Full of shoes. I looked already.

MAMA: Well, you didn't look good enough, then. There's that box from the ones he wore to the hospital. When he died, they told me I could have them back, but I never did like those shoes.

JESSIE: *(pulling them out of her pocket)* I found the bullets. They were in an old milk can.

MAMA: *(as Jessie starts for the hall)* Dawson took the shotgun, didn't he? Hand me that basket, hon.

JESSIE: *(getting the basket for her)* Dawson better not've taken that pistol.

25 MAMA: *(stopping her again)* Now my glasses, please. *(Jessie returns to get the glasses.)* I told him to take those rubber boots, too, but he said they were for fishing. I told him to take up fishing.

Jessie reaches for the cleaning spray, and cleans Mama's glasses for her.

JESSIE: He's just too lazy to climb up there, Mama. Or maybe he's just being smart. That floor's not very steady.

MAMA: *(getting out a piece of knitting)* It's not a floor at all, hon, it's a board now and then. Measure this for me. I need six inches.

JESSIE: *(as she measures)* Dawson could probably use some of those clothes up there. Somebody should have them. You ought to call the Salvation Army before the whole thing falls in on you. Six inches exactly.

MAMA: It's plenty safe! As long as you don't go up there.

30 JESSIE: *(turning to go again)* I'm careful.

MAMA: What do you want the gun for, Jess?

JESSIE: *(not returning this time. Opening the ladder in the hall)* Protection. *(She steadies the ladder as Mama talks.)*

MAMA: You take the TV way too serious, hon. I've never seen a criminal in my life. This is way too far to come for what's out here to steal. Never seen a one.

JESSIE: *(taking her first step up)* Except for Ricky.

35 MAMA: Ricky is mixed up. That's not a crime.

JESSIE: Get your hands washed. I'll be right back. And get 'em real dry. You dry your hands till I get back or it's no go, all right?

MAMA: I thought Dawson told you not to go up those stairs.

JESSIE: *(going up)* He did.

MAMA: I don't like the idea of a gun, Jess.

40 JESSIE: *(calling down from the attic)* Which shoebox, do you remember?

MAMA: Black.

JESSIE: The box was black?

MAMA: The shoes were black.

JESSIE: That doesn't help much, Mother.

45 MAMA: I'm not trying to help, sugar. *(No answer.)* We don't have anything anybody'd want, Jessie. I mean, I don't even want what we got, Jessie.

JESSIE: Neither do I. Wash your hands. *(Mama gets up and crosses to stand under the ladder.)*

MAMA: You come down from there before you have a fit. I can't come up and get you, you know.

JESSIE: I know.

MAMA: We'll just hand it over to them when they come, how's that? Whatever they want, the criminals.

50 JESSIE: That's a good idea, Mama.

MAMA: Ricky will grow out of this and be a real fine boy, Jess. But I have to tell you, I wouldn't want Ricky to know we had a gun in the house.

JESSIE: Here it is. I found it.

MAMA: It's just something Ricky's going through. Maybe he's in with some bad people. He just needs some time, sugar. He'll get back in school or get a job or one day you'll get a call and he'll say he's sorry for all the trouble he's caused and invite you out for supper someplace dress-up.

JESSIE: *(coming back down the steps)* Don't worry. It's not for him, it's for me.

55 MAMA: I didn't think you would shoot your own boy, Jessie. I know you've felt like it, well, we've all felt like shooting somebody, but we don't do it. I just don't think we need . . .

JESSIE: *(interrupting)* Your hands aren't washed. Do you want a manicure or not?

MAMA: Yes, I do, but . . .

JESSIE: *(crossing to the chair)* Then wash your hands and don't talk to me any more about Ricky. Those two rings he took were the last valuable thing *I* had, so now he's started in on other people, door to door. I hope they put him away sometime. I'd turn him in myself if I knew where he was.

MAMA: You don't mean that.

60 JESSIE: Every word. Wash your hands and that's the last time I'm telling you.

Jessie sits down with the gun and starts cleaning it, pushing the cylinder out, checking to see that the chambers and barrel are empty, then putting some oil on a small patch of cloth and pushing it through the barrel with the push rod that was in the box. Mama goes to the kitchen and washes her hands, as instructed, trying not to show her concern about the gun.

MAMA: I shoulda got you to bring down that milk can. Agnes Fletcher sold hers to somebody with a flea market for forty dollars apiece.

JESSIE: I'll go back and get it in a minute. There's a wagon wheel up there, too. There's even a churn. I'll get it all if you want.

MAMA: *(coming over, now, taking over now)* What are you doing?

JESSIE: The barrel has to be clean, Mama. Old powder, dust gets in it . . .

65 MAMA: What for?

JESSIE: I told you.

MAMA: *(reaching for the gun)* And I told you, we don't get criminals out here.

JESSIE: *(quickly pulling it to her)* And I told you . . . *(Then trying to be calm.)* The gun is for me.

MAMA: Well, you can have it if you want. When I die, you'll get it all, anyway.

70 JESSIE: I'm going to kill myself, Mama.

MAMA: *(returning to the sofa)* Very funny. Very funny.

JESSIE: I am.

MAMA: You are not! Don't even say such a thing, Jessie.

JESSIE: How would you know if I didn't say it? You want it to be a surprise? You're lying there in your bed or maybe you're just brushing your teeth and you hear this . . . noise down the hall?

75 MAMA: Kill yourself.

JESSIE: Shoot myself. In a couple of hours.

MAMA: It must be time for your medicine.

JESSIE: Took it already.

MAMA: What's the matter with you?

80 JESSIE: Not a thing. Feel fine.

MAMA: You feel fine. You're just going to kill yourself.

JESSIE: Waited until I felt good enough, in fact.

MAMA: Don't make jokes, Jessie. I'm too old for jokes.

JESSIE: It's not a joke, Mama.

Mama watches for a moment in silence.

85 MAMA: That gun's no good, you know. He broke it right before he died. He dropped it in the mud one day.

JESSIE: Seems O.K. *(She spins the chamber, cocks the pistol, and pulls the trigger. The gun is not yet loaded, so all we hear is the click, but it will definitely work. It's also obvious that Jessie knows her way around a gun. Mama cannot speak.)* I had Cecil's all ready in there, just in case I couldn't find this one, but I'd rather use Daddy's.

MAMA: Those bullets are at least fifteen years old.

JESSIE: *(pulling out another box)* These are from last week.

MAMA: Where did you get those?

90 JESSIE: Feed store Dawson told me about.

MAMA: Dawson!

JESSIE: I told him I was worried about prowlers. He said he thought it was a good idea. He told me what kind to ask for.

MAMA: If he had any idea . . .

JESSIE: He took it as a compliment. He thought I might be taking an interest in things. He got through telling me all about the bullets and then he said we ought to talk like this more often.

95 MAMA: And where was I while this was going on?

JESSIE: On the phone with Agnes. About the milk can, I guess. Anyway, I asked Dawson if he thought they'd send me some bullets and he said he'd just call for me, because he knew they'd send them if he told them to. And he was absolutely right. Here they are.

MAMA: How could he do that?

JESSIE: Just trying to help, Mama.

MAMA: And then I told you where the gun was.

100 JESSIE: *(smiling, enjoying this joke)* See? Everybody's doing what they can.

MAMA: You told me it was for protection!

JESSIE: It *is!* I'm still doing your nails, though. Want to try that new Chinaberry color?

MAMA: Well, I'm calling Dawson right now. We'll just see what he has to say about this little stunt.

JESSIE: Dawson doesn't have any more to do with this.

105 MAMA: He's your brother.

JESSIE: And that's all.

MAMA: *(stands up, moves toward the phone)* Dawson will put a stop to this. Yes he will. He'll take the gun away.

JESSIE: If you call him, I'll just have to do it before he gets here. Soon as you hang up the phone, I'll just walk in the bedroom and lock the door. Dawson will get here just in time to help you clean up. Go ahead, call him. Then call the police. Then call the funeral home. Then call Loretta and see if *she'll* do your nails.

MAMA: You will not! This is crazy talk, Jessie!

Mama goes directly to the telephone and starts to dial, but Jessie is fast, coming up behind her and taking the receiver out of her hand, putting it back down.

110 JESSIE: *(firm and quiet)* I said no. This is private. Dawson is not invited.

MAMA: Just me.

JESSIE: I don't want anybody else over here. Just you and me. If Dawson comes over, it'll make me feel stupid for not doing it ten yeas ago.

MAMA: I think we better call the doctor. Or how about the ambulance. You like that one driver, I know. What's his name, Timmy? Get you somebody to talk to.

JESSIE: *(going back to her chair)* I'm through talking, Mama. You're it. No more.

115 MAMA: We're just going to sit around like every other night in the world and then you're going to kill yourself? *(Jessie doesn't answer.)* You'll miss. *(Again there is no response.)* You'll just wind up a vegetable. How would you like that? Shoot your ear off? You know what the doctor said about getting excited. You'll cock the pistol and have a fit.

JESSIE: I think I can kill myself, Mama.

MAMA: You're not going to kill yourself, Jessie. You're not even upset! *(Jessie smiles, or laughs quietly, and Mama tries a different approach.)* People don't really kill themselves, Jessie. No, mam, doesn't make sense, unless you're retarded or deranged, and you're as normal as they come, Jessie, for the most part. We're all *afraid* to die.

JESSIE: I'm not, Mama. I'm cold all the time, anyway.

MAMA: That's ridiculous.

120 JESSIE: It's exactly what I want. It's dark and quiet.

MAMA: So is the back yard, Jessie! Close your eyes. Stuff cotton in your ears. Take a nap! It's quiet in your room. I'll leave the TV off all night.

JESSIE: So quiet I don't know it's quiet. So nobody can get me.

MAMA: You don't know what dead is like. It might not be quiet at all. What if it's like an alarm clock and you can't wake up so you can't shut it off. Ever.

JESSIE: Dead is everybody and everything I ever knew, gone. Dead is dead quiet.

125 MAMA: It's a sin. You'll go to hell.

JESSIE: Uh-huh.

MAMA: You will!

JESSIE: Jesus was a suicide, if you ask me.

MAMA: You'll go to hell just for saying that. Jessie!

130 JESSIE: *(with genuine surprise)* I didn't know I thought that.

MAMA: Jessie!

Jessie doesn't answer. She puts the now-loaded gun back in the box and crosses to the kitchen. But Mama is afraid she's headed for the bedroom.

MAMA: *(in a panic)* You can't use my towels! They're my towels. I've had
    them for a long time. I like my towels.

JESSIE: I asked you if you wanted that swimming towel and you said you
    didn't.

MAMA: And you can't use your father's gun, either. It's mine now, too.
    And you can't do it in my house.

135 JESSIE: Oh, come on.

MAMA: No. You can't do it. I won't let you. The house is in my name.

JESSIE: I have to go in the bedroom and lock the door behind me so they
    won't arrest you for killing me. They'll probably test your hands for
    gunpowder, anyway, but you'll pass.

MAMA: Not in my house!

JESSIE: If I'd known you were going to act like this, I wouldn't have told
    you.

140 MAMA: How am I supposed to act? Tell you to go ahead? O.K. by me,
    sugar? Might try it myself. What took you so long?

JESSIE: There's just no point in fighting me over it, that's all. Want some
    coffee?

MAMA: Your birthday's coming up, Jessie. Don't you want to know what
    we got you?

JESSIE: You got me dusting powder, Loretta got me a new housecoat, pink
    probably, and Dawson got me new slippers, too small, but they go
    with the robe, he'll say. *(Mama cannot speak.)* Right? *(Apparently Jessie
    is right.)* Be back in a minute.

Jessie takes the gun box, puts it on top of the stack of towels and garbage bags, and takes them into her bedroom. Mama, alone for a moment, goes to the phone, picks up the receiver, looks toward the bedroom, starts to dial, and then replaces the receiver in its cradle as Jessie walks back into the room. Jessie wonders, silently. They have lived together for so long there is very rarely any reason for one to ask what the other was about to do.

MAMA: I started to, but I didn't. I didn't call him.

145 JESSIE: Good. Thank you.

MAMA: *(starting over, a new approach)* What's this all about, Jessie?

JESSIE: About?

Jessie now begins the next task she had "on the schedule," which is refilling all the candy jars, taking the empty papers out of the boxes of chocolates, etc. Mama generally snitches when Jessie does this. Not tonight, though. Nevertheless, Jessie offers.

MAMA: What did I do?

JESSIE: Nothing. Want a caramel?

150 MAMA: *(ignoring the candy)* You're mad at me.

JESSIE: Not a bit. I am worried about you, but I'm going to do what I can before I go. We're not just going to sit around tonight. I made a list of things.

MAMA: What things?

JESSIE: How the washer works. Things like that.

MAMA: I know how the washer works. You put the clothes in. You put the soap in. You turn it on. You wait.

155 JESSIE: You do something else. You don't just wait.

MAMA: Whatever else you find to do, you're still mainly waiting. The waiting's the worst part of it. The waiting's what you pay somebody else to do, if you can.

JESSIE: *(nodding)* O.K. Where do we keep the soap?

MAMA: I could find it.

JESSIE: See?

160 MAMA: If you're mad about doing the wash, we can get Loretta to do it.

JESSIE: Oh now, that might be worth staying to see.

MAMA: She'd never in her life, would she?

JESSIE: Nope.

MAMA: What's the matter with her?

165 JESSIE: She thinks she's better than we are. She's not.

MAMA: Maybe if she didn't wear that yellow all the time.

JESSIE: The washer repair number is on a little card taped to the side of the machine.

MAMA: Loretta doesn't ever have to come over here again. Dawson can just leave her at home when he comes. And we don't ever have to see Dawson either if he bothers you. Does he bother you?

JESSIE: Sure he does. Be sure you clean out the lint tray every time you use the dryer. But don't ever put your house shoes in, it'll melt the soles.

170 MAMA: What does Dawson do, that bothers you?

JESSIE: He just calls me Jess like he knows who he's talking to. He's always wondering what I do all day. I mean, I wonder that myself, but it's my day, so it's mine to wonder about, not his.

MAMA: Family is just accident, Jessie. It's nothing personal, hon. They don't mean to get on your nerves. They don't even mean to be your family, they just are.

JESSIE: They know too much.

MAMA: About what?

175 JESSIE: They know things about you, and they learned it before you had a chance to say whether you wanted them to know it or not. They were there when it happened and it don't belong to them, it belongs to you, only they got it. Like my mail-order bra got delivered to their house.

MAMA: By accident!

JESSIE: All the same . . . they opened it. They saw the little rosebuds on it. *(Offering her another candy.)* Chewy mint?

MAMA: *(shaking her head no)* What do they know about you? I'll tell them never to talk about it again. Is it Ricky or Cecil or your fits or your hair is falling out or you drink too much coffee or you never go out of the house or what?

JESSIE: I just don't like their talk. The account at the grocery is in Dawson's name when you call. The number's on a whole list of numbers on the back cover of the phone book.

180 MAMA: Well! Now we're getting somewhere. They're none of them ever setting foot in this house again.

JESSIE: It's not them, Mother. I wouldn't kill myself just to get away from them.

MAMA: You leave the room when they come over, anyway.

JESSIE: I stay as long as I can. Besides, it's you they come to see.

MAMA: That's because I stay in the room when they come.

185 JESSIE: It's not them.

MAMA: Then what is it?

JESSIE: *(checking the list on her note pad)* The grocery won't deliver on Saturday anymore. And if you want your order the same day, you have to call before ten. And they won't deliver less than fifteen dollars' worth. What I do is tell them what we need and tell them to add on cigarettes until it gets to fifteen dollars.

MAMA: It's Ricky. You're trying to get through to him.

JESSIE: If I thought I could do that, I would stay.

190 MAMA: Make him sorry he hurt you, then. That's it, isn't it?

JESSIE: He's hurt me, I've hurt him. We're about even.

MAMA: You'll be telling him killing is O.K. with you, you know. Want him to start killing next? Nothing wrong with it. Mom did it.

JESSIE: Only a matter of time, anyway, Mama. When the call comes, you let Dawson handle it.

MAMA: Honey, nothing says those calls are always going to be some new trouble he's into. You could get one that he's got a job, that he's getting married, or how about he's joined the army, wouldn't that be nice?

195 JESSIE: If you call the Sweet Tooth before you call the grocery, that Susie will take your fudge next door to the grocery and it'll all come out together. Be sure you talk to Susie, though. She won't let them put it in the bottom of a sack like that one time, remember?

MAMA: Ricky could come over, you know. What if he calls us?

JESSIE: It's not Ricky, Mama.

MAMA: Or anybody could call us, Jessie.

JESSIE: Not on Saturday night, Mama.

200 MAMA: Then what is it? Are you sick? If your gums are swelling again, we can get you to the dentist in the morning.

JESSIE: No. Can you order your medicine or do you want Dawson to? I've got a note to him. I'll add that to it if you want.

MAMA: Your eyes don't look right. I thought so yesterday.

JESSIE: That was just the ragweed. I'm not sick.

MAMA: Epilepsy is sick, Jessie.

205 JESSIE: It won't kill me. *(Pause.)* If it would, I wouldn't have to.

MAMA: You don't *have* to.

JESSIE: No, I don't. That's what I like about it.

MAMA: Well, I won't let you!

JESSIE: It's not up to you.

210 MAMA: Jessie!

JESSIE: I want to hang a big sign around my neck, like Daddy's on the barn. GONE FISHING.

MAMA: You don't like it here.

JESSIE: *(smiling)* Exactly.

MAMA: I meant here in my house.

215 JESSIE: I know you did.

MAMA: You never should have moved back in here with me. If you'd kept your little house or found another place when Cecil left you, you'd have made some new friends at least. Had a life to lead. Had your own things around you. Give Ricky a place to come see you. You never should've come here.

JESSIE: Maybe.

MAMA: But I didn't force you, did I?

JESSIE: If it was a mistake, we made it together. You took me in. I appreciate that.

220 MAMA: You didn't have any business being by yourself right then, but I can see how you might want a place of your own. A grown woman should . . .

JESSIE: Mama . . . I'm just not having a very good time and I don't have any reason to think it'll get anything but worse. I'm tired. I'm hurt. I'm sad. I feel used.

MAMA: Tired of what?

JESSIE: It all.

MAMA: What does that mean?

225 JESSIE: I can't say it any better.

MAMA: Well, you'll have to say it better because I'm not letting you alone till you do. What were those other things? Hurt . . . *(Before Jessie can answer.)* You had this all ready to say to me, didn't you? Did you write this down? How long have you been thinking about this?

JESSIE: Off and on, ten years. On all the time, since Christmas.

MAMA: What happened at Christmas?

JESSIE: Nothing.

230 MAMA: So why Christmas?

JESSIE: That's it. On the nose.

A pause. Mama knows exactly what Jessie means. She was there, too, after all.

JESSIE: *(putting the candy sacks away)* See where all this is? Red hots up front, sour balls and horehound mixed together in this one sack. New packages of toffee and licorice right in back there.

MAMA: Go back to your list. You're hurt by what?

JESSIE: *(Mama knows perfectly well)* Mama . . .

235 MAMA: O.K. Sad about what? There's nothing real sad going on right now. If it was after your divorce or something that would make sense.

JESSIE: *(looking at her list, then opening the drawer)* Now, this drawer has everything in it that there's no better place for. Extension cords, batteries for the radio, extra lighters, sandpaper, masking tape, Elmer's glue, thumbtacks, that kind of stuff. The mousetraps are under the sink, but you call Dawson if you've got one and let him do it.

MAMA: Sad about what?

JESSIE: The way things are.

MAMA: Not good enough. What things?

240 JESSIE: Oh, everything from you and me to Red China.

MAMA: I think we can leave the Chinese out of this.

JESSIE: *(crosses back into the living room)* There's extra light bulbs in a box in the hall closet. And we've got a couple of packages of fuses in the fuse box. There's candles and matches in the top of the broom closet, but if the lights go out, just call Dawson and sit tight. But don't open the refrigerator door. Things will stay cool in there as long as you keep the door shut.

MAMA: I asked you a question.

JESSIE: I read the paper. I don't like how things are. And they're not any better out there than they are in here.

245 MAMA: If you're doing this because of the newspapers, I can sure fix that!

JESSIE: There's just more of it on TV.

MAMA: *(kicking the television set)* Take it out, then!

JESSIE: You wouldn't do that.

MAMA: Watch me.

250 JESSIE: What would you do all day?

MAMA: *(desperately)* Sing. *(Jessie laughs.)* I would, too. You want to watch? I'll sing till morning to keep you alive, Jessie, please!

JESSIE: No. *(Then affectionately.)* It's a funny idea, though. What do you sing?

MAMA: *(has no idea how to answer this)* We've got a good life here!

JESSIE: *(going back into the kitchen)* I called this morning and canceled the papers, except for Sunday, for your puzzles; you'll still get that one.

255 MAMA: Let's get another dog, Jessie! You like a big dog, now, didn't you? That King dog, didn't you?

JESSIE: *(washing her hands)* I did like that King dog, yes.

MAMA: I'm so dumb. He's the one run under the tractor.

JESSIE: That makes him dumb, not you.

MAMA: For bringing it up.

260 JESSIE: It's O.K. Handi-Wipes and sponges under the sink.

MAMA: We could get a new dog and keep him in the house. Dogs are cheap!

JESSIE: *(getting big pill jars out of the cabinet)* No.

Mama: Something for you to take care of.

Jessie: I've had you, Mama.

265 Mama: *(frantically starting to fill pill bottles)* You do too much for me. I can fill pill bottles all day, Jessie, and change the shelf paper and wash the floor when I get through. You just watch me. You don't have to do another thing in this house if you don't want to. You don't have to take care of me, Jessie.

Jessie: I know that. You've just been letting me do it so I'll have something to do, haven't you?

Mama: *(realizing this was a mistake)* I don't do it as well as you. I just meant if it tires you out or makes you feel used . . .

Jessie: Mama, I know you used to ride the bus. Riding the bus and it's hot and bumpy and crowded and too noisy and more than anything in the world you want to get off and the only reason in the world you don't get off is it's still fifty blocks from where you're going? Well, I can get off right now if I want to, because even if I ride fifty more years and get off then, it's the same place when I step down to it. Whenever I feel like it, I can get off. As soon as I've had enough, it's my stop. I've had enough.

Mama: You're feeling sorry for yourself!

270 Jessie: The plumber's helper is under the sink, too.

Mama: You're not having a good time! Whoever promised you a good time? Do you think I've had a good time?

Jessie: I think you're pretty happy, yeah. You have things you like to do.

Mama: Like what?

Jessie: Like crochet.

275 Mama: I'll teach you to crochet.

Jessie: I can't do any of that nice work, Mama.

Mama: Good time don't come looking for you, Jessie. You could work some puzzles or put in a garden or go to the store. Let's call a taxi and go to the A&P!

Jessie: I shopped you up for about two weeks already. You're not going to need toilet paper till Thanksgiving.

Mama: *(interrupting)* You're acting like some little brat, Jessie. You're mad and everybody's boring and you don't have anything to do and you don't like me and you don't like going out and you don't like staying in and you never talk on the phone and you don't watch TV and you're miserable and it's your own sweet fault.

280 Jessie: And it's time I did something about it.

Mama: Not something like killing yourself. Something like . . . buying us all new dishes! I'd like that. Or maybe the doctor would let you get a driver's license now, or I know what let's do right this minute, let's rearrange the furniture.

Jessie: I'll do that. If you want. I always thought if the TV was somewhere else, you wouldn't get such a glare on it during the day. I'll do whatever you want before I go.

Mama: *(badly frightened by those words)* You could get a job!

JESSIE: I took that telephone sales job and I didn't even make enough money to pay the phone bill, and I tried to work at the gift shop at the hospital and they said I made people real uncomfortable smiling at them the way I did.

285 MAMA: You could keep books. You kept your dad's books.

JESSIE: But nobody ever checked them.

MAMA: When he died, they checked them.

JESSIE: And that's when they took the books away from me.

MAMA: That's because without him there wasn't any business, Jessie!

290 JESSIE: (putting the pill bottles away) You know I couldn't work. I can't do anything. I've never been around people my whole life except when I went to the hospital. I could have a seizure any time. What good would a job do? The kind of job I could get would make me feel worse.

MAMA: Jessie!

JESSIE: It's true!

MAMA: It's what you think is true!

JESSIE: (struck by the clarity of that) That's right. It's what I think is true.

295 MAMA: (hysterically) But I can't do anything about that!

JESSIE: (quietly) No. You can't. (Mama slumps, if not physically, at least emotionally.) And I can't do anything either, about my life, to change it, make it better, make me feel better about it. Like it better, make it work. But I can stop it. Shut it down, turn if off like the radio when there's nothing on I want to listen to. It's all I really have that belongs to me and I'm going to say what happens to it. And it's going to stop. And I'm going to stop it. So. Let's just have a good time.

MAMA: Have a good time.

JESSIE: We can't go on fussing all night. I mean, I could ask you things I always wanted to know and you could make me some hot chocolate. The old way.

MAMA: (in despair) It takes cocoa, Jessie.

300 JESSIE: (gets it out of the cabinet) I bought cocoa, Mama. And I'd like to have a caramel apple and do your nails.

MAMA: You didn't eat a bit of supper.

JESSIE: Does that mean I can't have a caramel apple?

MAMA: Of course not. I mean . . . (Smiling a little.) Of course you can have a caramel apple.

JESSIE: I thought I could.

305 MAMA: I make the best caramel apples in the world.

JESSIE: I know you do.

MAMA: Or used to. And you don't get cocoa like mine anywhere anymore.

JESSIE: It takes time, I know, but . . .

MAMA: The salt is the trick.

310 JESSIE: Trouble and everything.

MAMA: (backing away toward the stove) It's no trouble. What trouble? You put it in the pan and stir it up. All right. Fine. Caramel apples. Cocoa. O.K.

Jessie walks to the counter to retrieve her cigarettes as Mama looks for the right pan. There are brief near-smiles, and maybe Mama clears her throat. We have a truce, for the moment. A genuine but nevertheless uneasy one. Jessie, who has been in constant motion since the beginning, now seems content to sit.

Mama starts looking for a pan to make the cocoa, getting out all the pans in the cabinets in the process. It looks like she's making a mess on purpose so Jessie will have to put them all away again. Mama is buying time, or trying to, and entertaining.

JESSIE: You talk to Agnes today?

MAMA: She's calling me from a pay phone this week. God only knows why. She has a perfectly good Trimline at home.

JESSIE: *(laughing)* Well, how is she?

315 MAMA: How is she every day, Jessie? Nuts.

JESSIE: Is she really crazy or just silly?

MAMA: No, she's really crazy. She was probably using the pay phone because she had another little fire problem at home.

JESSIE: Mother . . .

MAMA: I'm serious! Agnes Fletcher's burned down every house she ever lived in. Eight fires, and she's due for a new one any day now.

320 JESSIE: *(laughing)* No!

MAMA: Wouldn't surprise me a bit.

JESSIE: *(laughing)* Why didn't you tell me this before? Why isn't she locked up somewhere?

MAMA: 'Cause nobody ever got hurt, I guess. Agnes woke everybody up to watch the fires as soon as she set 'em. One time she set out porch chairs and served lemonade.

JESSIE: *(shaking her head)* Real lemonade?

325 MAMA: The houses they lived in, you knew they were going to fall down anyway, so why wait for it, is all I could ever make out about it. Agnes likes a feeling of accomplishment.

JESSIE: Good for her.

MAMA: *(finding the pan she wants)* Why are you asking about Agnes? One cup or two?

JESSIE: One. She's your friend. No marshmallows.

MAMA: *(getting the milk, etc.)* You have to have marshmallows. That's the old way, Jessie. Two or three? Three is better.

330 JESSIE: Three, then. Her whole house burns up? Her clothes and pillows and everything? I'm not sure I believe this.

MAMA: When she was a girl, Jess, not now. Long time ago. But she's still got it in her, I'm sure of it.

JESSIE: She wouldn't burn her house down now. Where would she go? She can't get Buster to build her a new one, he's dead. How could she burn it up?

MAMA: Be exciting, though, if she did. You never know.

JESSIE: You do too know, Mama. She wouldn't do it.

335 MAMA: *(forced to admit, but reluctant)* I guess not.

JESSIE: What else? Why does she wear all those whistles around her neck?

MAMA: Why does she have a house full of birds?

JESSIE: I didn't know she had a house full of birds!

MAMA: Well, she does. And she says they just follow her home. Well, I know for a fact she's still paying on the last parrot she bought. You gotta keep your life filled up, she says. She says a lot of stupid things. *(Jessie laughs, Mama continues, convinced she's getting somewhere.)* It's all that okra she eats. You can't just willy-nilly eat okra two meals a day and expect to get away with it. Made her crazy.

340 JESSIE: She really eats okra twice a day? Where does she get it in the winter?

MAMA: Well, she eats it a lot. Maybe not two meals, but . . .

JESSIE: More than the average person.

MAMA: *(beginning to get irritated)* I don't know how much okra the average person eats.

JESSIE: Do you know how much okra Agnes eats?

345 MAMA: No.

JESSIE: How many birds does she have?

MAMA: Two.

JESSIE: Then what are the whistles for?

MAMA: They're not real whistles. Just little plastic ones on a necklace she won playing Bingo, and I only told you about it because I thought I might get a laugh out of you for once even if it wasn't the truth, Jessie. Things don't have to be true to talk about 'em, you know.

350 JESSIE: Why won't she come over here?

Mama is suddenly quiet, but the cocoa and milk are in the pan now, so she lights the stove and starts stirring.

MAMA: Well now, what a good idea. We should've had more cocoa. Cocoa is perfect.

JESSIE: Except you don't like milk.

MAMA: *(another attempt, but not as energetic)* I hate milk. Coats your throat as bad as okra. Something just downright disgusting about it.

JESSIE: It's because of me, isn't it?

355 MAMA: No, Jess.

JESSIE: Yes, Mama.

MAMA: O.K. Yes, then, but she's crazy. She's as crazy as they come. She's a lunatic.

JESSIE: What is it exactly? Did I say something, sometime? Or did she see me have a fit and's afraid I might have another one if she came over, or what?

MAMA: I guess.

360 JESSIE: You guess what? What's she ever said? She must've given you some reason.

Mama: Your hands are cold.

Jessie: What difference does that make?

Mama: "Like a corpse," she says, "and I'm gonna be one soon enough as it is."

Jessie: That's crazy.

365 Mama: That's Agnes. "Jessie's shook the hand of death and I can't take the chance it's catching, Thelma, so I ain't comin' over, and you can understand or not, but I ain't comin'. I'll come up the driveway, but that's as far as I go."

Jessie: *(laughing, relieved)* I thought she didn't like me! She's scared of me! How about that! Scared of me.

Mama: I could make her come over here, Jessie. I could call her up right now and she could bring the birds and come visit. I didn't know you ever thought about her at all. I'll tell her she just has to come and she'll come, all right. She owes me one.

Jessie: No, that's all right. I just wondered about it. When I'm in the hospital, does she come over here?

Mama: Her kitchen is just a tiny thing. When she comes over here, she feels like . . . *(Toning it down a little.)* Well, we all like a change of scene, don't we?

370 Jessie: *(playing along)* Sure we do. Plus there's no birds diving around.

Mama: I hate those birds. She says I don't understand them. What's there to understand about birds?

Jessie: Why Agnes likes them, for one thing. Why they stay with her when they could be outside with the other birds. What their singing means. How they fly. What they think Agnes is.

Mama: Why do you have to know so much about things, Jessie? There's just not that much *to* things that I could ever see.

Jessie: That you could ever *tell,* you mean. You didn't have to lie to me about Agnes.

375 Mama: I didn't lie. You never asked before!

Jessie: You lied about setting fire to all those houses and about how many birds she has and how much okra she eats and why she won't come over here. If I have to keep dragging the truth out of you, this is going to take all night.

Mama: That's fine with me. I'm not a bit sleepy.

Jessie: Mama . . .

Mama: All right. Ask me whatever you want. Here.

They come to an awkward stop, as the cocoa is ready and Mama pours it into the cups Jessie has set on the table.

380 Jessie: *(as Mama takes her first sip)* Did you love Daddy?

Mama: No.

Jessie: *(pleased that Mama understands the rules better now)* I didn't think so. Were you really fifteen when you married him?

Mama: The way he told it? I'm sitting in the mud, he comes along, drags me in the kitchen, "She's been there ever since"?

JESSIE: Yes.

385 MAMA: No. It was a big fat lie, the whole thing. He just thought it was funnier that way. God, this milk in here.

JESSIE: The cocoa helps.

MAMA: *(pleased that they agree on this, at least)* Not enough, though, does it? You can still taste it, can't you?

JESSIE: Yeah, it's pretty bad. I thought it was my memory that was bad, but it's not. It's the milk, all right.

MAMA: It's a real waste of chocolate. You don't have to finish it.

390 JESSIE: *(putting her cup down)* Thanks, though.

MAMA: I should've known not to make it. I knew you wouldn't like it. You never did like it.

JESSIE: You didn't ever love him, or he did something and you stopped loving him, or what?

MAMA: He felt sorry for me. He wanted a plain country woman and that's what he married, and then he held it against me the rest of my life like I was supposed to change and surprise him somehow. Like I remember this one day he was standing on the porch and I told him to get a shirt on and he went in and got one and then he said, real peaceful, but to the point, "You're right, Thelma. If God had meant for people to go around without any clothes on, they'd have been born that way."

JESSIE: *(sees Mama's hurt)* He didn't mean anything by that, Mama.

395 MAMA: He never said a word he didn't have to, Jessie. That was probably all he'd said to me all day, Jessie. So if he said it, there was something to it, but I never did figure that one out. What did that mean?

JESSIE: I don't know. I liked him better than you did, but I didn't know him any better.

MAMA: How could I love him, Jessie. I didn't have a thing he wanted. *(Jessie doesn't answer.)* He got his share, though. You loved him enough for both of us. You followed him around like some . . . Jessie, all the man ever did was farm and sit . . . and try to think of somebody to sell the farm to.

JESSIE: Or make me a boyfriend out of pipe cleaners and sit back and smile like the stick man was about to dance and wasn't I going to get a kick out of that. Or sit up with a sick cow all night and leave me a chain of sleepy stick elephants on my bed in the morning.

MAMA: Or just sit.

400 JESSIE: I liked him sitting. Big old faded blue man in the chair. Quiet.

MAMA: Agnes gets more talk out of her birds than I got from the two of you. He could've had that GONE FISHING sign around his neck in that chair. I saw him stare off at the water. I saw him look at the weather rolling in. I got where I could practically see that boat myself. But you, you knew what he was thinking about and you're going to tell me.

JESSIE: I don't know, Mama! His life, I guess. His corn. His boots. Us. Things. You know.

MAMA: No, I don't know, Jessie! You had those quiet little conversations after supper every night. What were you whispering about?

JESSIE: We weren't whispering, you were just across the room.

405 MAMA: What did you talk about?

JESSIE: We talked about why black socks are warmer than blue socks. Is that something to go tell Mother? You were just jealous because I'd rather talk to him than wash the dishes with you.

MAMA: I was jealous because you'd rather talk to him than anything! *(Jessie reaches across the table for the small clock and starts to wind it.)* If I had died instead of him, he wouldn't have taken you in like I did.

JESSIE: I wouldn't have expected him to.

MAMA: Then what would you have done?

410 JESSIE: Come visit.

MAMA: Oh, I see. He died and left you stuck with me and you're mad about it.

JESSIE: *(getting up from the table)* Not anymore. He didn't mean to. I didn't have to come here. We've been through this.

MAMA: He felt sorry for you, too, Jessie, don't kid yourself about that. He said you were a runt and he said it from the day you were born and he said you didn't have a chance.

JESSIE: *(getting the canister of sugar and starting to refill the sugar bowl)* I know he loved me.

415 MAMA: What if he did? It didn't change anything.

JESSIE: It didn't have to. I miss him.

MAMA: He never really went fishing, you know. Never once. His tackle box was full of chewing tobacco and all he ever did was drive out to the lake and sit in his car. Dawson told me. And Bennie at the bait shop, he told Dawson. They all laughed about it. And he'd come back from fishing and all he'd have to show for it was a . . . a whole pipe cleaner *family*—chickens, pigs, a dog with a bad leg—it was creepy strange. It made me sick to look at them and I hid his pipe cleaners a couple of times but he always had more somewhere.

JESSIE: I thought it might be better for you after he died. You'd get interested in things. Breathe better. Change somehow.

MAMA: Into what? The Queen? A clerk in a shoe store? Why should I? Because he said to? Because you said to? *(Jessie shakes her head.)* Well I wasn't here for his entertainment and I'm not here for yours either, Jessie. I don't know what I'm here for, but then I don't think about it. *(Realizing what all this means.)* But I bet you wouldn't be killing yourself if he were still alive. That's a fine thing to figure out, isn't it?

420 JESSIE: *(filling the honey jar now)* That's not true.

MAMA: Oh no? Then what were you asking about him for? Why did you want to know if I loved him?

JESSIE: I didn't think you did, that's all.

MAMA: Fine then. You were right. Do you feel better now?

JESSIE: *(cleaning the honey jar carefully)* It feels good to be right about it.

425 MAMA: It didn't matter whether I loved him. It didn't matter to me and it didn't matter to him. And it didn't mean we didn't get along. It wasn't important. We didn't talk about it. *(Sweeping the pots off the cabinet.)* Take all these pots out to the porch!

JESSIE: What for?

MAMA: Just leave me this one pan. *(She jerks the silverware drawer open.)* Get me one knife, one fork, one big spoon, and the can opener, and put them out where I can get them. *(Starts throwing knives and forks in one of the pans.)*

JESSIE: Don't do that! I just straightened that drawer!

MAMA: *(throwing the pan in the sink)* And throw out all the plates and cups. I'll use paper. Loretta can have what she wants and Dawson can sell the rest.

430 JESSIE: *(calmly)* What are you doing?

MAMA: I'm not going to cook. I never like it, anyway. I like candy. Wrapped in plastic or coming in sacks. And tuna. I'll eat tuna, thank you.

JESSIE: *(taking the pan out of the sink)* What if you want to make apple butter? You can't make apple butter in that little pan. What if you leave carrots on cooking and burn up that pan?

MAMA: I don't like carrots.

JESSIE: What if the strawberries are good this year and you want to go picking with Agnes.

435 MAMA: I'll tell her to bring a pan. You said you would do whatever I wanted! I don't want a bunch of pans cluttering up my cabinets I can't get down to, anyway. Throw them out. Every last one.

JESSIE: *(gathering up the pots)* I'm putting them all back in. I'm not taking them to the porch. If you want them, they'll be here. You'll bend down and get them, like you got the one for the cocoa. And if somebody else comes over here to cook, they'll have something to cook in, and that's the end of it!

MAMA: Who's going to come cook here?

JESSIE: Agnes.

MAMA: In my pots. Not on your life.

440 JESSIE: There's no reason why the two of you couldn't just live here together. Be cheaper for both of you and somebody to talk to. And if the birds bothered you, well, one day when Agnes is out getting her hair done, you could take them all for a walk!

MAMA: *(as Jessie straightens the silverware)* So that's why you're pestering me about Agnes. You think you can rest easy if you get me a new babysitter? Well, I don't want to live with Agnes. I barely want to talk with Agnes. She's just around. We go back, that's all. I'm not letting Agnes near this place. You don't get off as easy as that, child.

JESSIE: O.K., then. It's just something to think about.

MAMA: I don't like things to think about. I like things to go on.

JESSIE: *(closing the silverware drawer)* I want to know what Daddy said to you the night he died. You came storming out of his room and said I could wait it out with him if I wanted to, but you were going to watch *Gunsmoke*. What did he say to you?

445 MAMA: He didn't have *anything* to say to me, Jessie. That's why I left. He didn't say a thing. It was his last chance not to talk to me and he took full advantage of it.

JESSIE: *(after a moment)* I'm sorry you didn't love him. Sorry for you, I mean. He seemed like a nice man.

MAMA: *(as Jessie walks to the refrigerator)* Ready for your apple now?

JESSIE: Soon as I'm through here, Mama.

MAMA: You won't like the apple, either. It'll be just like the cocoa. You never liked eating at all, did you? Any of it! What have you been living on all these years, toothpaste?

450 JESSIE: *(as she starts to clean out the refrigerator)* Now, you know the milkman comes on Wednesdays and Saturdays, and he leaves the order blank in an egg box, and you give the bills to Dawson once a month.

MAMA: Do they still make that orangeade?

JESSIE: It's not orangeade, it's just orange.

MAMA: I'm going to get some. I thought they stopped making it. You just stopped ordering it.

JESSIE: You should drink milk.

455 MAMA: Not anymore, I'm not. That hot chocolate was the last. Hooray.

JESSIE: *(getting the garbage can from under the sink)* I told them to keep delivering a quart a week no matter what you said. I told them you'd run out of Cokes and you'd have to drink it. I told them I knew you wouldn't pour it on the ground . . .

MAMA: *(finishing her sentence)* And you told them you weren't going to be ordering anymore?

JESSIE: I told them I was taking a little holiday and to look after you.

MAMA: And they didn't think something was funny about that? You who doesn't go to the front steps? You, who only sees the driveway looking down from a stretcher passed out cold?

460 JESSIE: *(enjoying this, but not laughing)* They said it was about time, but why didn't I take you with me? And I said I didn't think you'd want to go, and they said, "Yeah, everybody's got their own idea of vacation."

MAMA: I guess you think that's funny.

JESSIE: *(pulling jars out of the refrigerator)* You know there never was any reason to call the ambulance for me. All they ever did for me in the emergency room was let me wake up. I could've done that here. Now, I'll just call them out and you say yes or no. I know you like pickles. Ketchup?

MAMA: Keep it.

JESSIE: We've had this since last Fourth of July.

465 MAMA: Keep the ketchup. Keep it all.

JESSIE: Are you going to drink ketchup from the bottle or what? How can you want your food and not want your pots to cook it in? This stuff will all spoil in here, Mother.

MAMA: Nothing I ever did was good enough for you and I want to know why.

JESSIE: That's not true.

MAMA: And I want to know why you've lived here this long feeling the way you do.

470 JESSIE: You have no earthly idea how I feel.

MAMA: Well, how could I? You're real far back there, Jessie.

JESSIE: Back where?

MAMA: What's it like over there, where you are? Do people always say the right thing or get whatever they want, or what?

JESSIE: What are you talking about?

475 MAMA: Why do you read the newspaper? Why don't you wear that sweater I made for you? Do you remember how I used to look, or am I just any old woman now? When you have a fit, do you see stars or what? How did you fall off the horse, really? Why did Cecil leave you? Where did you put my old glasses?

JESSIE: *(stunned by Mama's intensity)* They're in the bottom drawer of your dresser in an old Milk of Magnesia box. Cecil left me because he made me choose between him and smoking.

MAMA: Jessie, I know he wasn't that dumb.

JESSIE: I never understood why he hated it so much when it's so good. Smoking is the only thing I know that's always just what you think it's going to be. Just like it was the last time, right there when you want it and real quiet.

MAMA: Your fits made him sick and you know it.

480 JESSIE: Say seizures, not fits. Seizures.

MAMA: It's the same thing. A seizure in the hospital is a fit at home.

JESSIE: They didn't bother him at all. Except he did feel responsible for it. It *was* his idea to go horseback riding that day. It was his idea I could do *anything* if I just made up my mind to. I fell off the horse because I didn't know how to hold on. Cecil left for pretty much the same reason.

MAMA: He had a girl, Jessie. I walked right in on them in the toolshed.

JESSIE: *(after a moment)* O.K. That's fair. *(Lighting another cigarette.)* Was she very pretty?

485 MAMA: She was Agnes's girl, Carlene. Judge for yourself.

JESSIE: *(as she walks to the living room)* I guess you and Agnes had a good talk about that, huh?

MAMA: I never thought he was good enough for you. They moved here from Tennessee, you know.

JESSIE: What are you talking about? You liked him better than I did. You flirted him out here to build your porch or I'd never even met him at all. You thought maybe he'd help you out around the place, come in and get some coffee and talk to you. God knows what you thought. All that curly hair.

MAMA: He's the best carpenter I ever saw. That little house of yours will still be standing at the end of the world, Jessie.

490 JESSIE: You didn't need a porch, Mama.

MAMA: All right! I wanted you to have a husband.

JESSIE: And I couldn't get one on my own, of course.

MAMA: How were you going to get a husband never opening your mouth to a living soul?

JESSIE: So I was quiet about it, so what?

495 MAMA: So I should have let you just sit here? Sit like your daddy? Sit here?

JESSIE: Maybe.

MAMA: Well, I didn't think so.

JESSIE: Well, what did you know?

MAMA: I never said I knew much. How was I supposed to learn anything living out here? I didn't know enough to do half the things I did in my life. Things happen. You do what you can about them and you see what happens next. I married you off to the wrong man, I admit that. So I took you in when he left, I'm sorry.

500 JESSIE: He wasn't the wrong man.

MAMA: He didn't love you, Jessie, or he wouldn't have left.

JESSIE: He wasn't the wrong man, Mama. I loved Cecil so much. And I tried to get more exercise and I tried to stay awake. I tried to learn to ride a horse. And I tried to stay outside with him, but he always knew I was trying, so it didn't work.

MAMA: He was a selfish man. He told me once he hated to see people move into his houses after he built them. He knew they'd mess them up.

JESSIE: I loved that bridge he built over the creek in back of the house. It didn't have to be anything special, a couple of boards would have been just fine, but he used that yellow pine and rubbed it so smooth . . .

505 MAMA: He had responsibilities here. He had a wife and son here and he failed you.

JESSIE: Or that baby bed he built for Ricky. I told him he didn't have to spend so much time on it, but he said it had to last, and the thing ended up weighing two hundred pounds and I couldn't move it. I said, "How long does a baby bed have to last, anyway?" But maybe he thought if it was strong enough, it might keep Ricky a baby.

MAMA: Ricky is too much like Cecil.

JESSIE: He is not. Ricky is as much like me as it's possible for any human to be. We even wear the same size pants. These are his, I think.

MAMA: That's just the same size. That's not you're the same person.

510 JESSIE: I see it on his face. I hear it when he talks. We look out at the world and we see the same thing: Not Fair. And the only difference

between us is Ricky's out there trying to get even. And he knows not to trust anybody and he got it straight from me. And he knows not to try to get work, and guess where he got that. He walks around like there's loose boards in the floor, and you know who laid that floor, I did.

MAMA: Ricky isn't through yet. You don't know how he'll turn out!

JESSIE: *(going back to the kitchen)* Yes I do and so did Cecil. Ricky is the two of us together for all time in too small a space. And we're tearing each other apart, like always, inside that boy, and if you don't see it, then you're just blind.

MAMA: Give him time, Jess.

JESSIE: Oh, he'll have plenty of that. Five years for forgery, ten years for armed assault . . .

515 MAMA: *(furious)* Stop that! *(Then pleading.)* Jessie, Cecil might be ready to try it again, honey, that happens sometimes. Go downtown. Find him. Talk to him. He didn't know what he had in you. Maybe he sees things different now, but you're not going to know that till you see him. Or call him up! Right now! He might be home.

JESSIE: And say what? Nothing's changed, Cecil, I'd just like to look at you, if you don't mind? No. He loved me, Mama. He just didn't know how things fall down around me like they do. I think he did the right thing. He gave himself another chance, that's all. But I did beg him to take me with him. I did tell him I would leave Ricky and you and everything I loved out here if only he would take me with him, but he couldn't and I understood that. *(Pause.)* I wrote that note I showed you. I wrote it. Not Cecil. I said "I'm sorry, Jessie, I can't fix it all for you." I said I'd always love me, not Cecil. But that's how he felt.

MAMA: Then he should've taken you with him!

JESSIE: *(picking up the garbage bag she has filled)* Mama, you don't pack your garbage when you move.

MAMA: You will not call yourself garbage, Jessie.

520 JESSIE: *(taking the bag to the big garbage can near the back door)* Just a way of saying it, Mama. Thinking about my list, that's all. *(Opening the can, putting the garbage in, then securing the lid.)* Well, a little more than that. I was trying to say it's all right that Cecil left. It was . . . a relief in a way. I never was what he wanted to see, so it was better when he wasn't looking at me all the time.

MAMA: I'll make your apple now.

JESSIE: No thanks. You get the manicure stuff and I'll be right there.

Jessie ties up the big garbage bag in the can and replaces the small garbage bag under the sink, all the time trying desperately to regain her calm. Mama watches, from a distance, her hand reaching unconsciously for the phone. Then she has a better idea. Or rather she thinks of the only other thing left and is willing to try it. Maybe she is even convinced it will work.

MAMA: Jessie, I think your daddy had little . . .

JESSIE: *(interrupting her)* Garbage night is Tuesday. Put it out as late as you can. The Davis's dogs get in it if you don't. *(Replacing the garbage bag in the can under the sink.)* And keep ordering the heavy black bags. It doesn't pay to buy the cheap ones. And I've got all the ties here with the hammers and all. Take them out of the box as soon as you open a new one and put them in this drawer. They'll get lost if you don't, and rubber bands or something else won't work.

525 MAMA: I think your daddy had fits, too. I think he sat in his chair and had little fits. I read this a long time ago in a magazine, how little fits go, just little blackouts where maybe their eyes don't even close and people just call them "thinking spells."

JESSIE: *(getting the slipcover out of the laundry basket)* I don't think you want this manicure we've been looking forward to. I washed this cover for the sofa, but it'll take both of us to get it back on.

MAMA: I watched his eyes. I know that's what it was. The magazine said some people don't even know they've had one.

JESSIE: Daddy would've known if he'd had fits, Mama.

MAMA: The lady in this story had kept track of hers and she'd had eighty thousand of them in the last eleven years.

530 JESSIE: Next time you wash this cover, it'll dry better if you put it on wet.

MAMA: Jessie, listen to what I'm telling you. This lady had anywhere between five and five hundred fits a day and they lasted maybe fifteen seconds apiece, so that out of her life, she'd only lost about two weeks altogether, and she had a full-time secretary job and an IQ of 120.

JESSIE: *(amused by Mama's approach)* You want to talk about the fits, is that it?

MAMA: Yes. I do. I want to say . . .

JESSIE: *(interrupting)* Most of the time I wouldn't even know I'd had one, except I wake up with different clothes on, feeling like I've been run over. Sometimes I feel my heart start to turn around or hear myself scream. And sometimes there *is* this dizzy stupid feeling a little before it, but if the TV's on, well, it's easy to miss.

As Jessie and Mama replace the slipcover on the sofa and the afghan on the chair, the physical struggle somehow mirrors the emotional one in the conversation.

535 MAMA: I can tell when you're about to have one. Your eyes get this big! But, Jessie, you haven't . . .

JESSIE: *(taking charge of this)* What do they look like? The seizures.

MAMA: *(reluctant)* Different each time, Jess.

JESSIE: O.K. Pick one, then. A good one. I think I want to know now.

MAMA: There's not much to tell. You just . . . crumple, in a heap, like a puppet and somebody cut the strings all at once, or like the firing squad in some Mexican movie, you just slide down the wall, you know. You don't know what happens? How can you not know what happens?

540 JESSIE: I'm busy.

MAMA: That's not funny.

JESSIE: I'm not laughing. My head turns around and I fall down and then what?

MAMA: Well, your chest squeezes in and out, and you sound like you're gagging, sucking air in and out like you can't breathe.

JESSIE: Do it for me. Make the sound for me.

545 MAMA: I will not. It's awful-sounding.

JESSIE: Yeah. It felt like it might be. What's next?

MAMA: Your mouth bites down and I have to get your tongue out of the way fast, so you don't bite yourself.

JESSIE: Or you. I bite you, too, don't I?

MAMA: You got me once real good. I had to get a tetanus! But I know what to watch for now. And then you turn blue and the jerks start up. Like I'm standing there poking you with a cattle prod or you're sticking your finger in a light socket as fast as you can . . .

550 JESSIE: Foaming like a mad dog the whole time.

MAMA: It's bubbling, Jess, not foam like the washer overflowed, for God's sake; it's bubbling like a baby spitting up. I go get a wet washcloth, that's all. And then the jerks slow down and you wet yourself and it's over. Two minutes tops.

JESSIE: How do I get to bed?

MAMA: How do you think?

JESSIE: I'm too heavy for you now. How do you do it?

555 MAMA: I call Dawson. But I get you cleaned up before he gets here and I make him leave before you wake up.

JESSIE: You could just leave me on the floor.

MAMA: I want you to wake up someplace nice, O.K.? *(Then making a real effort.)* But, Jessie, and this is the reason I even brought this up! You haven't had a seizure for a solid year. A whole year, do you realize that?

JESSIE: Yeah, the phenobarb's about right now, I guess.

MAMA: You bet it is. You might never have another one, ever! You might be through with it for all time!

560 JESSIE: Could be.

MAMA: You are. I know you are!

JESSIE: I sure am feeling good. I really am. The double vision's gone and my gums aren't swelling. No rashes or anything. I'm feeling as good as I ever felt in my life. I'm even feeling like worrying or getting mad and I'm not afraid it will start a fit if I do, I just go ahead.

MAMA: Of course you do! You can even scream at me, if you want to. I can take it. You don't have to act like you're just visiting here, Jessie. This is your house, too.

JESSIE: The best part is, my memory's back.

565 MAMA: Your memory's always been good. When couldn't you remember things? You're always reminding me what . . .

JESSIE: Because I've made lists for everything. But now I remember what things mean on my lists. I see "dish towels," and I used to wonder whether I was supposed to wash them, buy them, or look for them because I wouldn't remember where I put them after I washed them, but now I know it means wrap them up, they're a present for Loretta's birthday.

MAMA: *(finished with the sofa now)* You used to go looking for your lists, too, I've noticed that. You always know where they are now! *(Then suddenly worried.)* Loretta's birthday isn't coming up, is it?

JESSIE: I made a list of all the birthdays for you. I even put yours on it. *(A small smile.)* So you can call Loretta and remind her.

MAMA: Let's take Loretta to Howard Johnson's and have those fried clams. I *know* you love that clam roll.

570 JESSIE: *(slight pause)* I won't be here, Mama.

MAMA: What have we just been talking about? You'll be here. You're well, Jessie. You're starting all over. You said it yourself. You're remembering things and . . .

JESSIE: I won't be here. If I'd ever had a year like this, to think straight and all, before now, I'd be gone already.

MAMA: *(not pleading, commanding)* No, Jessie.

JESSIE: *(folding the rest of the laundry)* Yes, Mama. Once I started remembering, I could see what it all added up to.

575 MAMA: The fits are over!

JESSIE: It's not the fits, Mama.

MAMA: Then it's me for giving them to you, but I didn't do it!

JESSIE: It's not the fits! You said it yourself, the medicine takes care of the fits.

MAMA: *(interrupting)* Your daddy gave you those fits, Jessie. He passed it down to you like your green eyes, and your straight hair. It's not my fault!

580 JESSIE: So what if he had little fits? It's not inherited. I fell off the horse. It was an accident.

MAMA: The horse wasn't the first time, Jessie. You had a fit when you were five years old.

JESSIE: I did not.

MAMA: You did! You were eating a popsicle and down you went. He gave it to you. It's *his* fault, not mine.

JESSIE: Well, you took your time telling me.

585 MAMA: How do you tell that to a five-year-old?

JESSIE: What did the doctor say?

MAMA: He said kids have them all the time. He said there wasn't anything to do but wait for another one.

JESSIE: But I didn't have another one.

Now there is a real silence.

JESSIE: You mean to tell me I had fits all the time as a kid and you just told me I fell down or something and it wasn't till I had the fit when

Cecil was looking that anybody bothered to find out what was the matter with me?

590 MAMA: It wasn't *all the time*, Jessie. And they changed when you started to school. More like your daddy's. Oh, that was some swell time, sitting here with the two of you turning off and on like light bulbs some nights.

JESSIE: How many fits did I have?

MAMA: You never hurt yourself. I never let you out of my sight. I caught you every time.

JESSIE: But you didn't tell anybody.

MAMA: It was none of their business.

595 JESSIE: You were ashamed.

MAMA: I didn't want anybody to know. Least of all you.

JESSIE: Least of all me. Oh, right. That was mine to know, Mama, not yours. Did Daddy know?

MAMA: He thought you were . . . you fell down a lot. That's what he thought. You were careless. Or maybe he thought I beat you. I don't know what he thought. He didn't think about it.

JESSIE: Because you didn't tell him!

600 MAMA: If I told him about you, I'd have to tell him about him!

JESSIE: I don't like this. I don't like this one bit.

MAMA: I didn't think you'd like it. That's why I didn't tell you.

JESSIE: If I'd known I was an epileptic, Mama, I wouldn't have ridden any horses.

MAMA: Make you feel like a freak, is that what I should have done?

605 JESSIE: Just get the manicure tray and sit down!

MAMA: *(throwing it to the floor)* I don't want a manicure!

JESSIE: Doesn't look like you do, no.

MAMA: Maybe I did drop you, you don't know.

JESSIE: If you say you didn't, you didn't.

610 MAMA: *(beginning to break down)* Maybe I fed you the wrong thing. Maybe you had a fever sometime and I didn't know it soon enough. Maybe it's a punishment.

JESSIE: For what?

MAMA: I don't know. Because of how I felt about your father. Because I didn't want any more children. Because I smoked too much or didn't eat right when I was carrying you. It has to be something I did.

JESSIE: It does not. It's just a sickness, not a curse. Epilepsy doesn't mean anything. It just is.

MAMA: I'm not talking about the fits here, Jessie! I'm talking about this killing yourself. It has to be me that's the matter here. You wouldn't be doing this if it wasn't. I didn't tell you things or I married you off to the wrong man or I took you in and let your life get away from you or all of it put together. I don't know what I did, but I did it, I know. This is all my fault, Jessie, but I don't know what to do about it now?

615 JESSIE: *(exasperated at having to say this again)* It doesn't have anything to do with you!

MAMA: Everything you do has to do with me, Jessie. You can't do *anything,* wash your face or cut your finger, without doing it to me. That's right! You might as well kill me as you, Jessie, it's the same thing. This has to do with me, Jessie.

JESSIE: Then what if it does! What if it has everything to do with you! What if you are all I have and you're not enough? What if I could take all the rest of it if only I didn't have you here? What if the only way I can get away from you for good is to kill myself? What if it is? I can *still* do it!

MAMA: *(in desperate tears)* Don't leave me, Jessie! *(Jessie stands for a moment, then turns for the bedroom.)* No! *(She grabs Jessie's arm.)*

JESSIE: *(carefully taking her arm away)* I have a box of things I want people to have. I'm just going to go get it for you. You . . . just rest a minute.

Jessie is gone. Mama heads for the telephone, but she can't even pick up the receiver this time and, instead, stoops to clean up the bottles that have spilled out of the manicure tray.

Jessie returns, carrying a box that groceries were delivered in. It probably says Hershey Kisses or StarKist Tuna. Mama is still down on the floor cleaning up, hoping that maybe if she just makes it look nice enough, Jessie will stay.

620 MAMA: Jessie, how can I live here without you? I need you! You're supposed to tell me to stand up straight and say how nice I look in my pink dress, and drink my milk. You're supposed to go around and lock up so I know we're safe for the night, and when I wake up, you're supposed to be out there making the coffee and watching me get older every day, and you're supposed to help me die when the time comes. I can't do that by myself, Jessie. I'm not like you, Jessie. I hate the quiet and I don't want to die and I don't want you to go, Jessie. How can I . . . *(Has to stop a moment.)* How can I get up every day knowing you had to kill yourself to make it stop hurting and I was here all the time and I never even saw it. And then you gave me this chance to make it better, convince you to stay alive, and I couldn't do it. How can I live with myself after this, Jessie?

JESSIE: I only told you so I could explain it, so you wouldn't blame yourself, so you wouldn't feel bad. There wasn't anything you could say to change my mind. I didn't want you to save me. I just wanted you to know.

MAMA: Stay with me just a little longer. Just a few more years. I don't have that many more to go, Jessie. And as soon as I'm dead, you can do whatever you want. Maybe with me gone, you'll have all the quiet you want, right here in the house. And maybe one day you'll put in some begonias up the walk and get just the right rain for them all summer. And Ricky will be married by then and he'll bring your grandbabies over and you can sneak them a piece of candy when their daddy's not looking and then be real glad when they've gone home and left you to your quiet again.

JESSIE: Don't you see, Mama, everything I do winds up like this. How could I think you would understand? How could I think you would want a manicure? We could hold hands for an hour and then I could go shoot myself? I'm sorry about tonight, Mama, but it's exactly why I'm doing it.

MAMA: If you've got the guts to kill yourself, Jessie, you've got the guts to stay alive.

625 JESSIE: I know that. So it's really just a matter of where I'd rather be.

MAMA: Look, maybe I can't think of what you should do, but that doesn't mean there isn't something that would help. *You* find it. *You* think of it. You can keep trying. You can get brave and try some more. You don't have to give up!

JESSIE: I'm *not* giving up! This *is* the other thing I'm trying. And I'm sure there are some other things that might work, but *might* work isn't good enough anymore. I need something that *will* work. *This* will work. That's why I picked it.

MAMA: But something might happen. Something that could change everything. Who knows what it might be, but it might be worth waiting for! *(Jessie doesn't respond.)* Try it for two more weeks. We could have more talks like tonight.

JESSIE: No, Mama.

630 MAMA: I'll pay more attention to you. Tell the truth when you ask me. Let you have your say.

JESSIE: No, Mama! We wouldn't have more talks like tonight, because it's this next part that's made this last part so good, Mama. No, Mama. *This* is how I have my say. This is how I say what I thought about it *all* and I say no. To Dawson and Loretta and the Red Chinese and epilepsy and Ricky and Cecil and you. And me. And hope. I say no! *(Then going to Mama on the sofa.)* Just let me go easy, Mama.

MAMA: How can I let you go?

JESSIE: You can because you have to. It's what you've always done.

MAMA: You are my child!

635 JESSIE: I am what became of your child. *(Mama cannot answer.)* I found an old baby picture of me. And it was somebody else, not me. It was somebody pink and fat who never heard of sick or lonely, somebody who cried and got fed, and reached up and got held and kicked but didn't hurt anybody, and slept whenever she wanted to, just by closing her eyes. Somebody who mainly just laid there and laughed at the colors waving around over her head and chewed on a polka-dot whale and woke up knowing some new trick nearly every day, and rolled over and drooled on the sheet and felt your hand pulling my quilt back up over me. That's who I started out and this is who is left. *(There is no self-pity here.)* That's what this is about. It's somebody I lost, all right, it's my own self. Who I never was. Or who I tried to be and never got there. Somebody I waited for who never came. And never will. So, see, it doesn't much matter what else happens in the world or in this

house, even. I'm what was worth waiting for and I didn't make it.
Me . . . who might have made a difference to me . . . I'm not going to
show up, so there's no reason to stay, except to keep you company . . .
not reason enough because I'm not . . . very good company. *(Pause.)*
Am I?

MAMA: *(knowing she must tell the truth)* No. And neither am I.

JESSIE: I had this strange little thought, well, maybe it's not so strange.
Anyway, after Christmas, after I decided to do this, I would wonder,
sometimes, what might keep me here, what might be worth staying
for, and you know what it was? It was maybe if there was something I
really liked, like maybe if I really liked rice pudding or cornflakes for
breakfast or something, that might be enough.

MAMA: Rice pudding is good.

JESSIE: Not to me.

640 MAMA: And you're not afraid?

JESSIE: Afraid of what?

MAMA: I'm afraid of it, for me, I mean. When my time comes. I know it's
coming, but . . .

JESSIE: You don't know when. Like in a scary movie.

MAMA: Yeah, sneaking up on me like some killer on the loose, hiding out
in the back yard just waiting for me to have my hands full someday
and how am I supposed to protect myself anyhow when I don't know
what he looks like and I don't know how he sounds coming up
behind me like that or if it will hurt or take very long or what I don't
get done before it happens.

645 JESSIE: You've got plenty of time left.

MAMA: I forget what for, right now.

JESSIE: For whatever happens, I don't know. For the rest of your life. For
Agnes burning down one more house or Dawson losing his hair or . . .

MAMA: *(quickly)* Jessie. I can't just sit here and say O.K., kill yourself if
you want to.

JESSIE: Sure you can. You just did. Say it again.

650 MAMA: *(really startled)* Jessie! *(Quiet horror.)* How dare you! *(Furious.)* How
dare you! You think you can just leave whenever you want, like you're
watching television here? No, you can't, Jessie. You make me feel like
a fool for being alive, child, and you are so wrong! I like it here, and I
will stay here until they make me go, until they drag me screaming
and I mean screeching into my grave, and you're real smart to get
away before then because, I mean, honey, you've never heard noise
like that in your life. *(Jessie turns away.)* Who am I talking to? You're
gone already, aren't you? I'm looking right through you! I can't stop
you because you're already gone! I guess you think they'll all have to
talk about you now! I guess you think this will really confuse them.
Oh yes, ever since Christmas you've been laughing to yourself and
thinking, "Boy, are they all in for a surprise." Well, nobody's going

to be a bit surprised, sweetheart. This is just like you. Do it the hard
way, that's my girl, all right. *(Jessie gets up and goes into the kitchen,
but Mama follows her.)* You know who they're going to feel sorry for?
Me! How about that! Not you, me! They're going to be *ashamed* of
you. Yes. *Ashamed!* If somebody asks Dawson about it, he'll change the
subject as fast as he can. He'll talk about how much he has to pay to
park his car these days.

JESSIE: Leave me alone.

MAMA: It's the truth!

JESSIE: I should've just left you a note!

MAMA: *(screaming)* Yes! *(Then suddenly understanding what she has said,
nearly paralyzed by the thought of it, she turns slowly to face Jessie, nearly
whispering.)* No. No. I . . . might not have thought of all the things
you've said.

655 JESSIE: It's O.K., Mama.

*Mama is nearly unconscious from the emotional devastation of these last few
moments. She sits down at the kitchen table, hurt and angry and desperately
afraid. But she looks almost numb. She is so far beyond what is known as pain
that she is virtually unreachable and Jessie knows this, and talks quietly, watching for signs of recovery.*

JESSIE: *(washes her hands in the sink)* I remember you liked that preacher
who did Daddy's, so if you want to ask him to do the service, that's
O.K. with me.

MAMA: *(not an answer, just a word)* What.

JESSIE: *(putting on hand lotion as she talks)* And pick some songs you like or
let Agnes pick, she'll know exactly which ones. Oh, and I had your
dress cleaned that you wore to Daddy's. You looked real good in that.

MAMA: I don't remember, hon.

660 JESSIE: And it won't be so bad once your friends start coming to the
funeral home. You'll probably see people you haven't seen for years,
but I thought about what you should say to get you over that nervous
part when they first come in.

MAMA: *(simply repeating)* Come in.

JESSIE: Take them up to see their flowers, they'd like that. And when they
say, "I'm so sorry, Thelma," you just say, "I appreciate your coming,
Connie." And then ask how their garden was this summer or what
they're doing for Thanksgiving or how their children . . .

MAMA: I don't think I should ask about their children. I'll talk about what
they have on, that's always good. And I'll have some crochet work
with me.

JESSIE: And Agnes will be there, so you might not have to talk at all.

665 MAMA: Maybe if Connie Richards does come, I can get her to tell me
where she gets that Irish yarn, she calls it. I know it doesn't come
from Ireland. I think it just comes with a green wrapper.

JESSIE: And be sure to invite enough people home afterwards so you get enough food to feed them all and have some left for you. But don't let anybody take anything home, especially Loretta.

MAMA: Loretta will get all the food set up, honey. It's only fair to let her have some macaroni or something.

JESSIE: No, Mama. You have to be more selfish from now on. *(Sitting at the table with Mama.)* Now, somebody's bound to ask you why I did it and you just say you don't know. That you loved me and you know I loved you and we just sat around tonight like every other night of our lives, and then I came over and kissed you and said, "'Night, Mother," and you heard me close my bedroom door and the next thing you heard was the shot. And whatever reasons I had, well, you guess I just took them with me.

MAMA: *(quietly)* It was something personal.

670 JESSIE: Good. That's good, Mama.

MAMA: That's what I'll say, then.

JESSIE: Personal. Yeah.

MAMA: Is that what I tell Dawson and Loretta, too? We sat around, you kissed me, "'Night, Mother"? They'll want to know more, Jessie. They won't believe it.

JESSIE: Well, then, tell them what we did. I filled up the candy jars. I cleaned out the refrigerator. We made some hot chocolate and put the cover back on the sofa. You had no idea. All right? I really think it's better that way. If they know we talked about it, they really won't understand how you let me go.

675 MAMA: I guess not.

JESSIE: It's private. Tonight is private, yours and mine, and I don't want anybody else to have any of it.

MAMA: O.K., then.

JESSIE: *(standing behind Mama now, holding her shoulders)* Now, when you hear the shot, I don't want you to come in. First of all, you won't be able to get in by yourself, but I don't want you trying. Call Dawson, then call the police, and then call Agnes. And then you'll need something to do till somebody gets here, so wash the hot-chocolate pan. You wash that pan till you hear the doorbell ring and I don't care if it's an hour, you keep washing that pan.

MAMA: I'll make my calls and then I'll just sit. I won't need something to do. What will the police say?

680 JESSIE: They'll do that gunpowder test, I guess, and ask you what happened, and by that time, the ambulance will be here and they'll come in and get me and you know how that goes. You stay out here with Dawson and Loretta. You keep Dawson out here. I want the police in the room first, not Dawson, O.K.?

MAMA: What if Dawson and Loretta want me to go home with them?

JESSIE: *(returning to the living room)* That's up to you.

MAMA: I think I'll stay here. All they've got is Sanka.

JESSIE: Maybe Agnes could come stay with you for a few days.

685 MAMA: *(standing up, looking into the living room)* I'd rather be by myself, I think. *(Walking toward the box Jessie brought in earlier.)* You want me to give people those things?

JESSIE: *(they sit down on the sofa, Jessie holding the box on her lap)* I want Loretta to have my little calculator. Dawson bought it for himself, you know, but then he saw one he liked better and he couldn't bring both of them home with Loretta counting every penny the way she does, so he gave the first one to me. Be funny for her to have it now, don't you think? And all my house slippers are in a sack for her in my closet. Tell her I know they'll fit and I've never worn any of them, and make sure Dawson hears you tell her that. I'm glad he loves Loretta so much, but I wish he knew not everybody has her size feet.

MAMA: *(taking the calculator)* O.K.

JESSIE: *(reaching into the box again)* This letter is for Dawson, but it's mostly about you, so read it if you want. There's a list of presents for you for at least twenty more Christmases and birthdays, so if you want anything special you better add it to this list before you give it to him. Or if you want to be surprised, just don't read that page. This Christmas, you're getting mostly stuff for the house, like a new rug in your bathroom and needlework, but next Christmas, you're really going to cost him next Christmas. I think you'll like it a lot and you'd never think of it.

MAMA: And you think he'll go for it?

690 JESSIE: I think he'll feel like a real jerk if he doesn't. Me telling him, to, like this and all. Now, this number's where you call Cecil. I called it last week and he answered, so I know he still lives there.

MAMA: What do you want me to tell him?

JESSIE: Tell him we talked about him and I only had good things to say about him, but mainly tell him to find Ricky and tell him what I did, and tell Ricky you have something for him, out here, from me, and to come get it. *(Pulls a sack out of the box.)*

MAMA: *(the sack feels empty)* What is it?

JESSIE: *(taking it off)* My watch. *(Putting it in the sack and taking a ribbon out of the sack to tie around the top of it.)*

695 MAMA: He'll sell it!

JESSIE: That's the idea. I appreciate him not stealing it already. I'd like to buy him a good meal.

MAMA: He'll buy dope with it!

JESSIE: Well, then, I hope he gets some good dope with it, Mama. And the rest of this is for you. *(Handing Mama the box now. Mama picks up the things and looks at them.)*

MAMA: *(surprised and pleased)* When did you do all this? During my naps, I guess.

700 JESSIE: I guess. I tried to be quiet about it. *(As Mama is puzzled by the presents.)* Those are just little presents. For whenever you need one.

They're not bought presents, just things I thought you might like to look at, pictures or things you think you've lost. Things you didn't know you had, even. You'll see.

MAMA: I'm not sure I want them. They'll make me think of you.

JESSIE: No they won't. They're just things, like a free tube of toothpaste I found hanging on the door one day.

MAMA: Oh. All right, then.

JESSIE: Well, maybe there's one nice present in there somewhere. It's Granny's ring she gave me and I thought you might like to have it, but I didn't think you'd wear it if I gave it to you right now.

705 MAMA: *(taking the box to a table nearby)* No. Probably not. *(Turning back to face him.)* I'm ready for my manicure, I guess. Want me to wash my hands again?

JESSIE: *(standing up)* It's time for me to go, Mama.

MAMA: *(starting for her)* No, Jessie, you've got all night!

JESSIE: *(as Mama grabs her)* No, Mama.

MAMA: It's not even ten o'clock.

710 JESSIE: *(very calm)* Let me go, Mama.

MAMA: I can't. You can't go. You can't do this. You didn't say it would be so soon, Jessie. I'm scared. I love you.

JESSIE: *(takes her hands away)* Let go of me, Mama. I've said everything I had to say.

MAMA: *(standing still a minute)* You said you wanted to do my nails.

JESSIE: *(taking a small step backward)* I can't. It's too late.

715 MAMA: It's not too late!

JESSIE: I don't want you to wake Dawson and Loretta when you call. I want them to still be up and dressed so they can get right over.

MAMA: *(as Jessie backs up, Mama moves in on her, but carefully)* They wake up fast, Jessie, if they have to. They don't matter here, Jessie. You do. I do. We're not through yet. We've got a lot of things to take care of here. I don't know where my prescriptions are and you didn't tell me what to tell Dr. Davis when he calls or how much you want me to tell Ricky or who I call to rake the leaves or . . .

JESSIE: Don't try and stop me, Mama, you can't do it.

MAMA: *(grabbing her again, this time hard)* I can too! I'll stand in front of this hall and you can't get past me. *(They struggle.)* You'll have to knock me down to get away from me, Jessie. I'm not about to let you . . .

Mama struggles with Jessie at the door and in the struggle Jessie gets away from her and—

720 JESSIE: *(almost a whisper)* 'Night, Mother. *(She vanishes into her bedroom and we hear the door lock just as Mama gets to it.)*

MAMA: *(screams)* Jessie! *(Pounding on the door.)* Jessie, you let me in there. Don't you do this, Jessie. I'm not going to stop screaming until you open this door, Jessie. Jessie! Jessie! What if I don't do any of the things you told me to do! I'll tell Cecil what a miserable man he was to make you feel the way he did and I'll give Ricky's watch to Dawson if I feel like it and the only way you can make sure I do what you want is you come out here and make me, Jessie! *(Pounding again.)* Jessie! Stop this! I didn't know! I was here with you all the time. How could I know you were so alone?

And Mama stops for a moment, breathless and frantic, putting her ear to the door, and when she doesn't hear anything, she stands up straight again and screams once more.

Jessie! Please!

And we hear the shot, and it sounds like an answer, it sounds like No.
Mama collapses against the door, tears streaming down her face, but not screaming anymore. In shock now.

Jessie, Jessie, child . . . Forgive me. *(Pause.)* I thought you were mine.

And she leaves the door and makes her way through the living room, around the furniture, as though she didn't know where it was, not knowing what to do. Finally, she goes to the stove in the kitchen and picks up the hot-chocolate pan and carries it with her to the telephone, and holds on to it while she dials the number. She looks down at the pan, holding it tight like her life depended on it. She hears Loretta answer.

MAMA: Loretta, let me talk to Dawson, honey.

READING AND REACTING

1. *'night, Mother* begins with lengthy and rather detailed stage directions—specifying, for example, the time that should appear on the clock and the appearance of the bedroom doorway. How do these stage directions help Norman communicate her theme?
2. In what way would you describe the relationship between Mama and Jessie? For example, is it loving? Cordial? Antagonistic?
3. Identify some examples of foreshadowing at the beginning of the play. What future events in the play does this foreshadowing suggest?
4. What is the significance of the play's title? How does it shed light on the play's theme?
5. In one sense, *'night, Mother* is about relationships—between Jessie and Mama, Jessie and Dawson, and Mama and her dead husband, for example. What do these relationships, and others discussed in the play, reveal about Mama and Jessie as individuals?
6. Throughout the play, Mama mentions incidents from Jessie's life—for instance, hospitalization, seizures, a fall from a horse. What do these incidents tell the audience about Jessie? In what way do they help to explain Jessie's suicide?

7. Do you consider Jessie a tragic figure or someone who is simply ineffectual and petty? Explain.

8. What characters are mentioned in the play but never appear onstage? What function do they serve? How would the play have been different if one or two of them had appeared in the play?

9. At one point in the play, Jessie says to her mother, "I should've just left you a note!" Why does she choose not to? Why do you think she decides to tell her mother that she intends to kills herself?

10. At the end of the play, after Jessie has shot herself, Mama says, "Jessie, Jessie, child . . . Forgive me. *(Pause.)* I thought you were mine." What does Mama mean? In what way does this statement communicate the main theme of the play?

11. **JOURNAL ENTRY** What reasons does Jessie give for wanting to kill herself? Can you think of any reasons that she has neglected to mention?

12. **CRITICAL PERSPECTIVE** In an interview, Marsha Norman says *'night, Mother* "exists because Jessie wants something from Mama" while at the same time "Mama wants Jessie to stay." Norman goes on to explain, "So you have two conflicting goals. And at that point it is a real struggle. It might as well be armed warfare. Only very late in the piece do they realize that both goals are achievable given some moderation."

   If, as Norman says, compromise is possible, why does Jessie kill herself?

Related Works: "I Stand Here Ironing" (p. 160), "A Clean, Well-Lighted Place" (p. 261), "Suicide Note" (p. 733), "Dreams of Suicide" (p. 910), *The Glass Menagerie* (p. 1805)

◆ **AUGUST WILSON** (1945–   ) was born in Pittsburgh, Pennsylvania, and lived in the African-American neighborhood known as the Hill. After leaving school at fifteen, he participated in the Black Arts movement in Pittsburgh, submitting poems to local African-American publications. In 1969, Wilson and his friend Rob Penny founded the Black Horizons Theatre Company, for which Wilson produced and directed plays. Although Wilson wrote plays while living in Pittsburgh, his work began to gain recognition only after 1978, when he moved to St. Paul, Minnesota. There, in 1982, Lloyd Richards, dean of the Yale School of Drama and artistic director of the Yale Repertory Company, staged a performance of Wilson's *Ma Rainey's Black Bottom.*

Wilson's plays give powerful voice to the African-American experience by exploring the historical and metaphysical roots of African-American culture and by reflecting the rhythmic patterns of African-American storytelling. In addition to *Ma Rainey's Black Bottom,* a Tony Award winner, Wilson's plays include *Fences* (1985), which won a Pulitzer Prize in 1987; *Joe Turner's Come and Gone* (1986); *Two Trains Running* (1989), which won Wilson his fifth New York Drama Critics Circle Award; *The Piano Lesson* (1987), which won a second Pulitzer Prize for Wilson in 1990; and *Seven Guitars* (1996).

Fences explores how the long-upheld color barrier in professional baseball affects the main character, Troy, who struggles with the pain of never realizing his dream of becoming a big-league player. Throughout the play Troy retreats behind literal and figurative barriers that impair his relations with his family.

CULTURAL CONTEXT ◆ Jackie Robinson was the first African-American to play in the modern baseball major leagues. As a member of the Brooklyn Dodgers, he played his first game on April 15, 1947, against the Boston Braves. Robinson was a 28-year-old first baseman when he broke baseball's color barrier.

◆ ◆ ◆

AUGUST WILSON

Fences
(1985)

CHARACTERS

TROY MAXSON
JIM BONO, *Troy's friend*
ROSE, *Troy's wife*
LYONS, *Troy's oldest son by previous marriage*

GABRIEL, *Troy's brother*
CORY, *Troy and Rose's son*
RAYNELL, *Troy's daughter*

SETTING

The setting is the yard which fronts the only entrance to the Maxson household, an ancient two-story brick house set back off a small alley in a big-city neighborhood. The entrance to the house is gained by two or three steps leading to a wooden porch badly in need of paint.

A relatively recent addition to the house and running its full width, the porch lacks congruence. It is a sturdy porch with a flat roof. One or two chairs of dubious value sit at one end where the kitchen window opens onto the porch. An old-fashioned icebox stands silent guard at the opposite end.

The yard is a small dirt yard, partially fenced, except for the last scene, with a wooden sawhorse, a pile of lumber, and other fence-building equipment set off to the side. Opposite is a tree from which hangs a ball made of rags. A baseball bat leans against the tree. Two oil drums serve as garbage receptacles and sit near the house at right to complete the setting.

The Play

Near the turn of the century, the destitute of Europe sprang on the city with tenacious claws and an honest and solid dream. The city devoured them. They swelled its belly until it burst into a thousand furnaces and sewing machines, a thousand butcher shops and bakers' ovens, a thousand churches and hospitals and funeral parlors and money-lenders. The city grew. It nourished itself and offered each man a partnership limited only by his talent, his guile, and his willingness and capacity for hard work. For the immigrants of Europe, a dream dared and won true.

The descendants of African slaves were offered no such welcome or participation. They came from places called the Carolinas and the Virginias, Georgia, Alabama, Mississippi, and Tennessee. They came strong, eager, searching. The city rejected them and they fled and settled along the riverbanks and under bridges in shallow, ramshackle houses made of sticks and tarpaper. They collected rags and wood. They sold the use of their muscles and their bodies. They cleaned houses and washed clothes, they shined shoes, and in quiet desperation and vengeful pride, they stole, and lived in pursuit of their own dream. That they could breathe free, finally, and stand to meet life with the force of dignity and whatever eloquence the heart could call upon.

By 1957, the hard-won victories of the European immigrants had solidified the industrial might of America. War had been confronted and won with new energies that used loyalty and patriotism as its fuel. Life was rich, full, and flourishing. The Milwaukee Braves won the World Series, and the hot winds of change that would make the sixties a turbulent, racing, dangerous, and provocative decade had not yet begun to blow full.

Act I
Scene 1

It is 1957. Troy and Bono enter the yard, engaged in conversation. Troy is fifty-three years old, a large man with thick, heavy hands; it is this largeness that he strives to fill out and make an accommodation with. Together with his blackness, his largeness informs his sensibilities and the choices he has made in his life.

Of the two men, Bono is obviously the follower. His commitment to their friendship of thirty-odd years is rooted in his admiration of Troy's honesty, capacity for hard work, and his strength, which Bono seeks to emulate.

It is Friday night, payday, and the one night of the week the two men engage in a ritual of talk and drink. Troy is usually the most talkative and at times he can be crude and almost vulgar, though he is capable of rising to profound heights of expression. The men carry lunch buckets and wear or carry burlap aprons and are dressed in clothes suitable to their jobs as garbage collectors.

Bono: Troy, you ought to stop that lying!

Troy: I ain't lying! The nigger had a watermelon this big. *(He indicates with his hands.)* Talking about . . . "What watermelon, Mr. Rand?" I

liked to fell out! "What watermelon, Mr. Rand?" . . . And it sitting
there big as life.

BONO: What did Mr. Rand say?

TROY: Ain't said nothing. Figure if the nigger too dumb to know he
carrying a watermelon, he wasn't gonna get much sense out of him.
Trying to hide that great big old watermelon under his coat. Afraid to
let the white man see him carry it home.

5 BONO: I'm like you . . . I ain't got no time for them kind of people.

TROY: Now what he look like getting mad 'cause he see the man from the
union talking to Mr. Rand?

BONO: He come to me talking about . . . "Maxson gonna get us fired." I
told him to get away from me with that. He walked away from me
calling you a troublemaker. What Mr. Rand say?

TROY: Ain't said nothing. He told me to go down the Commissioner's
office next Friday. They called me down there to see them.

BONO: Well, as long as you got your complaint filed, they can't fire you.
That's what one of them white fellows tell me.

10 TROY: I ain't worried about them firing me. They gonna fire me 'cause I
asked a question? That's all I did. I went to Mr. Rand and asked him,
"Why? Why you got the white mens driving and the colored
lifting?" Told him, "what's the matter, don't I count? You think
only white fellows got sense enough to drive a truck. That ain't no
paper job! Hell, anybody can drive a truck. How come you got all
whites driving and the colored lifting?" He told me "take it to the
union." Well, hell, that's what I done! Now they wanna come up
with this pack of lies.

BONO: I told Brownie if the man come and ask him any questions . . . just
tell the truth! It ain't nothing but something they done trumped up
on you 'cause you filed a complaint on them.

TROY: Brownie don't understand nothing. All I want them to do is change
the job description. Give everybody a chance to drive the truck.
Brownie can't see that. He ain't got that much sense.

BONO: How you figure he be making out with that gal be up at Taylors'
all the time . . . that Alberta gal?

TROY: Same as you and me. Getting just as much as we is. Which is to say
nothing.

15 BONO: It is, huh? I figure you doing a little better than me . . . and I ain't
saying what I'm doing.

TROY: Aw, nigger, look here . . . I know you. If you had got anywhere
near that gal, twenty minutes later you be looking to tell somebody.
And the first one you gonna tell . . . that you gonna want to brag
to . . . is me.

BONO: I ain't saying that. I see where you be eyeing her.

TROY: I eye all the women. I don't miss nothing. Don't never let nobody
tell you Troy Maxson don't eye the women.

BONO: You been doing more than eyeing her. You done bought her a
    drink or two.

20 TROY: Hell yeah, I bought her a drink! What that mean? I bought you
    one, too. What that mean 'cause I buy her a drink? I'm just being
    polite.

BONO: It's all right to buy her one drink. That's what you call being
    polite. But when you wanna be buying two or three . . . that's what
    you call eyeing her.

TROY: Look here, as long as you known me . . . you ever known me to
    chase after women?

BONO: Hell yeah! Long as I done known you. You forgetting I knew you
    when.

TROY: Naw, I'm talking about since I been married to Rose?

25 BONO: Oh, not since you been married to Rose. Now, that's the truth,
    there. I can say that.

TROY: All right then! Case closed.

BONO: I see you be walking up around Alberta's house. You supposed to
    be at Taylors' and you be walking up around there.

TROY: What you watching where I'm walking for? I ain't watching after
    you.

BONO: I seen you walking around there more than once.

30 TROY: Hell, you liable to see me walking anywhere! That don't mean
    nothing cause you see me walking around there.

BONO: Where she come from anyway? She just kinda showed up one day.

TROY: Tallahassee. You can look at her and tell she one of them Florida
    gals. They got some big healthy women down there. Grow them right
    up out the ground. Got a little bit of Indian in her. Most of them
    niggers down in Florida got some Indian in them.

BONO: I don't know about that Indian part. But she damn sure big and
    healthy. Woman wear some big stockings. Got them great big old legs
    and hips as wide as the Mississippi River.

TROY: Legs don't mean nothing. You don't do nothing but push them out
    of the way. But them hips cushion the ride!

35 BONO: Troy, you ain't got no sense.

TROY: It's the truth! Like you riding on Goodyears!

*Rose enters from the house. She is ten years younger than Troy, her devotion to
him stems from her recognition of the possibilities of her life without him: a succession of abusive men and their babies, a life of partying and running the
streets, the Church, or aloneness with its attendant pain and frustration. She
recognizes Troy's spirit as a fine and illuminating one and she either ignores or
forgives his faults, only some of which she recognizes. Though she doesn't drink,
her presence is an integral part of the Friday night rituals. She alternates between the porch and the kitchen, where supper preparations are under way.*

ROSE: What you all out here getting into?

TROY: What you worried about what we getting into for? This is men talk, woman.

ROSE: What I care what you all talking about? Bono, you gonna stay for supper?

40 BONO: No, I thank you, Rose. But Lucille say she cooking up a pot of pigfeet.

TROY: Pigfeet! Hell, I'm going home with you! Might even stay the night if you got some pigfeet. You got something in there to top them pigfeet, Rose?

ROSE: I'm cooking up some chicken. I got some chicken and collard greens.[1]

TROY: Well, go on back in the house and let me and Bono finish what we was talking about. This is men talk. I got some talk for you later. You know what kind of talk I mean. You go on and powder it up.

ROSE: Troy Maxson, don't you start that now!

45 TROY: *(puts his arm around her)* Aw, woman . . . come here. Look here, Bono . . . when I met this woman . . . I got out that place, say, "Hitch up my pony, saddle up my mare . . . there's a woman out there for me somewhere. I looked here. Looked there. Saw Rose and latched on to her." I latched on to her and told her—I'm gonna tell you the truth—I told her, "Baby, I don't wanna marry, I just wanna be your man." Rose told me . . . tell him what you told me, Rose.

ROSE: I told him if he wasn't the marrying kind, then move out the way so the marrying kind could find me.

TROY: That's what she told me. "Nigger, you in my way. You blocking the view! Move out the way so I can find me a husband." I thought it over two or three days. Come back—

ROSE: Ain't no two or three days nothing. You was back the same night.

TROY: Come back, told her . . . "Okay, baby . . . but I'm gonna buy me a banty rooster and put him out there in the backyard . . . and when he see a stranger come, he'll flap his wings and crow . . ." Look here, Bono, I could watch the front door by myself . . . it was that back door I was worried about.

50 ROSE: Troy, you ought not talk like that. Troy ain't doing nothing but telling a lie.

TROY: Only thing is . . . when we first got married . . . forget the rooster . . . we ain't had no yard!

BONO: I hear you tell it. Me and Lucille was staying down there on Logan Street. Had two rooms with the outhouse in the back. I ain't mind the outhouse none. But when that goddamn wind blow through there in the winter . . . that's what I'm talking about! To this day I wonder why in the hell I ever stayed down there for six long years. But see, I

---

[1] A leafy green vegetable.

didn't know I could do no better. I thought only white folks had inside toilets and things.

Rose: There's a lot of people don't know they can do no better than they doing now. That's just something you got to learn. A lot of folks still shop at Bella's.

Troy: Ain't nothing wrong with shopping at Bella's. She got fresh food.

55 Rose: I ain't said nothing about if she got fresh food. I'm talking about what she charge. She charge ten cents more than the A&P.

Troy: The A&P ain't never done nothing for me. I spends my money where I'm treated right. I go down to Bella, say, "I need a loaf of bread, I'll pay you Friday." She give it to me. What sense that make when I got money to go and spend it somewhere else and ignore the person who done right by me? That ain't in the Bible.

Rose: We ain't talking about what's in the Bible. What sense it make to shop there when she overcharge?

Troy: You shop where you want to. I'll do my shopping where the people been good to me.

Rose: Well, I don't think it's right for her to overcharge. That's all I was saying.

60 Bono: Look here . . . I got to get on. Lucille going be raising all kind of hell.

Troy: Where you going, nigger? We ain't finished this pint. Come here, finish this pint.

Bono: Well, hell, I am . . . if you ever turn the bottle loose.

Troy: *(hands him the bottle)* The only thing I say about the A&P is I'm glad Cory got that job down there. Help him take care of his school clothes and things. Gabe done moved out and things getting tight around here. He got that job . . . He can start to look out for himself.

Rose: Cory done went and got recruited by a college football team.

65 Troy: I told that boy about that football stuff. The white man ain't gonna let him get nowhere with that football. I told him when he first come to me with it. Now you come telling me he done went and got more tied up in it. He ought to go and get recruited in how to fix cars or something where he can make a living.

Rose: He ain't talking about making no living playing football. It's just something the boys in school do. They gonna send a recruiter by to talk to you. He'll tell you he ain't talking about making no living playing football. It's a honor to be recruited.

Troy: It ain't gonna get him nowhere. Bono'll tell you that.

Bono: If he be like you in the sports . . . he's gonna be all right. Ain't but two men ever played baseball as good as you. That's Babe Ruth[2] and

---

[2] George Herman Ruth (1895–1948), American baseball player most prominent as a New York Yankee during the 1910's and 20's; known for his homerun hitting and his flamboyant lifestyle.

Josh Gibson.[3] Them's the only two men ever hit more home runs than you.

TROY: What it ever get me? Ain't got a pot to piss in or a window to throw it out of.

70 ROSE: Times have changed since you was playing baseball, Troy. That was before the war. Times have changed a lot since then.

TROY: How in hell they done changed?

ROSE: They got lots of colored boys playing ball now. Baseball and football.

BONO: You right about that, Rose. Times have changed, Troy. You just come along too early.

TROY: There ought not never have been no time called too early! Now you take that fellow . . . what's that fellow they had playing right field for the Yankees back then? You know who I'm talking about, Bono. Used to play right field for the Yankees.

75 ROSE: Selkirk?

TROY: Selkirk! That's it! Man batting .269, understand? .269. What kind of sense that make? I was hitting .432 with thirty-seven home runs! Man batting .269 and playing right field for the Yankees! I saw Josh Gibson's daughter yesterday. She walking around with raggedy shoes on her feet. Now I bet you Selkirk's daughter ain't walking around with raggedy shoes on her feet! I bet you that!

ROSE: They got a lot of colored baseball players now. Jackie Robinson[4] was the first. Folks had to wait for Jackie Robinson.

TROY: I done seen a hundred niggers play baseball better than Jackie Robinson. Hell, I know some teams Jackie Robinson couldn't even make! What you talking about Jackie Robinson. Jackie Robinson wasn't nobody. I'm talking about if you could play ball then they ought to have let you play. Don't care what color you were. Come telling me I come along too early. If you could play . . . then they ought to have let you play.

Troy takes a long drink from the bottle.

ROSE: You gonna drink yourself to death. You don't need to be drinking like that.

80 TROY: Death ain't nothing. I done seen him. Done wrassled with him. You can't tell me nothing about death. Death ain't nothing but a fastball on the outside corner. And you know what I'll do to that! Lookee here, Bono . . . am I lying? You get one of them fastballs, about waist high, over the outside corner of the plate where you can

---

[3] (1911–1947), American baseball player in the Negro Leagues of the 1920's, 30's, and 40's; known as "the Negro Babe Ruth"; barred from Major League baseball by an unwritten rule against black players.

[4] John Roosevelt Robinson (1919–1972), first black player to enter Major League baseball; joined the Brooklyn Dodgers in 1947.

get the meat of the bat on it . . . and good god! You can kiss it goodbye. Now, am I lying?

BONO: Naw, you telling the truth there. I seen you do it.

TROY: If I'm lying . . . that 450 feet worth of lying! *(Pause.)* That's all death is to me. A fastball on the outside corner.

ROSE: I don't know why you want to get on talking about death.

TROY: Ain't nothing wrong with talking about death. That's part of life. Everybody gonna die. You gonna die, I'm gonna die. Bono's gonna die. Hell, we all gonna die.

85 ROSE: But you ain't got to talk about it. I don't like to talk about it.

TROY: You the one brought it up. Me and Bono was talking about baseball . . . you tell me I'm gonna drink myself to death. Ain't that right, Bono? You know I don't drink this but one night out of the week. That's Friday night. I'm gonna drink just enough to where I can handle it. Then I cuts it loose. I leave it alone. So don't you worry about me drinking myself to death. 'Cause I ain't worried about Death. I done seen him. I done wrestled with him.

Look here, Bono . . . I looked up one day and Death was marching straight at me. Like Soldiers on Parade! The Army of Death was marching straight at me. The middle of July, 1941. It got real cold just like it be winter. It seem like Death himself reached out and touched me on the shoulder. He touch me just like I touch you. I got cold as ice and Death standing there grinning at me.

ROSE: Troy, why don't you hush that talk.

TROY: I say . . . what you want, Mr. Death? You be wanting me? You done brought your army to be getting me? I looked him dead in the eye. I wasn't fearing nothing. I was ready to tangle. Just like I'm ready to tangle now. The Bible say be ever vigilant. That's why I don't get but so drunk. I got to keep watch.

ROSE: Troy was right down there in Mercy Hospital. You remember he had pneumonia? Laying there with a fever talking plumb out of his head.

90 TROY: Death standing there staring at me . . . carrying that sickle in his hand. Finally he say, "You want bound over for another year?" See, just like that . . . "You want bound over for another year?" I told him, "Bound over hell! Let's settle this now!"

It seem like he kinda fell back when I said that, and all the cold went out of me. I reached down and grabbed that sickle and threw it just as far as I could throw it . . . and me and him commenced to wrestling.

We wrestled for three days and three nights. I can't say where I found the strength from. Every time it seemed like he was gonna get the best of me, I'd reach way down deep inside myself and find the strength to do him one better.

ROSE: Every time Troy tell that story he find different ways to tell it. Different things to make up about it.

TROY: I ain't making up nothing. I'm telling you the facts of what happened. I wrestled with Death for three days and three nights and I'm standing here to tell you about it. *(Pause.)* All right. At the end of the third night we done weakened each other to where we can't hardly move. Death stood up, throwed on his robe . . . had him a white robe with a hood on it. He throwed on that robe and went off to look for his sickle. Say, "I'll be back." Just like that. "I'll be back." I told him, say, "Yeah, but . . . you gonna have to find me!" I wasn't no fool. I wan't going looking for him. Death ain't nothing to play with. And I know he's gonna get me. I know I got to join his army . . . his camp followers. But as long as I keep my strength and see him coming . . . as long as I keep up my vigilance . . . he's gonna have to fight to get me. I ain't going easy.

BONO: Well, look here, since you got to keep up your vigilance . . . let me have the bottle.

TROY: Aw hell, I shouldn't have told you that part. I should have left out that part.

95 ROSE: Troy be talking that stuff and half the time don't even know what he be talking about.

TROY: Bono know me better than that.

BONO: That's right. I know you. I know you got some Uncle Remus[5] in your blood. You got more stories than the devil got sinners.

TROY: Aw hell, I done seen him too! Done talked with the devil.

ROSE: Troy, don't nobody wanna be hearing all that stuff.

Lyons enters the yard from the street. Thirty-four years old, Troy's son by a previous marriage, he sports a neatly trimmed goatee, sport coat, white shirt, tieless and buttoned at the collar. Though he fancies himself a musician, he is more caught up in the rituals and "idea" of being a musician than in the actual practice of the music. He has come to borrow money from Troy, and while he knows he will be successful, he is uncertain as to what extent his lifestyle will be held up to scrutiny and ridicule.

100 LYONS: Hey, Pop.

TROY: What you come "Hey, Popping" me for?

LYONS: How you doing, Rose? *(He kisses her.)* Mr. Bono. How you doing?

BONO: Hey, Lyons . . . how you been?

TROY: He must have been doing all right. I ain't seen him around here last week.

105 ROSE: Troy, leave your boy alone. He come by to see you and you wanna start all that nonsense.

---

[5] Narrator of *Uncle Remus: His Songs and His Sayings* (1880) and a number of sequels by Joel Chandler Harris; tells tales about characters such as Brer Rabbit and the Tarbaby in exaggerated dialect, now widely considered to be a derogatory representation of African Americans.

TROY: I ain't bothering Lyons. *(Offers him the bottle.)* Here . . . get you a drink. We got an understanding. I know why he come by to see me and he know I know.

LYONS: Come on, Pop . . . I just stopped by to say hi . . . see how you was doing.

TROY: You ain't stopped by yesterday.

ROSE: You gonna stay for supper, Lyons? I got some chicken cooking in the oven.

110 LYONS: No, Rose . . . thanks. I was just in the neighborhood and thought I'd stop by for a minute.

TROY: You was in the neighborhood all right, nigger. You telling the truth there. You was in the neighborhood cause it's my payday.

LYONS: Well, hell, since you mentioned it . . . let me have ten dollars.

TROY: I'll be damned! I'll die and go to hell and play blackjack with the devil before I give you ten dollars.

BONO: That's what I wanna know about . . . that devil you done seen.

115 LYONS: What . . . Pop done seen the devil? You too much, Pops.

TROY: Yeah, I done seen him. Talked to him too!

ROSE: You ain't seen no devil. I done told you that man ain't had nothing to do with the devil. Anything you can't understand, you want to call it the devil.

TROY: Look here, Bono . . . I went down to see Hertzberger about some furniture. Got three rooms for two-ninety-eight. That what it say on the radio. "Three rooms . . . two-ninety-eight." Even made up a little song about it. Go down there . . . man tell me I can't get no credit. I'm working every day and can't get no credit. What to do? I got an empty house with some raggedy furniture in it. Cory ain't got no bed. He's sleeping on a pile of rags on the floor. Working every day and can't get no credit. Come back here—Rose'll tell you—madder than hell. Sit down . . . try to figure what I'm gonna do. Come a knock on the door. Ain't been living here but three days. Who know I'm here? Open the door . . . devil standing there bigger than life. White fellow . . . white fellow . . . got on good clothes and everything. Standing there with a clipboard in his hand. I ain't had to say nothing. First words come out of his mouth was . . . "I understand you need some furniture and can't get no credit." I liked to fell over. He say, "I'll give you all the credit you want, but you got to pay the interest on it." I told him, "Give me three rooms worth and charge whatever you want." Next day a truck pulled up here and two men unloaded them three rooms. Man what drove the truck give me a book. Say send ten dollars, first of every month to the address in the book and everything will be all right. Say if I miss a payment the devil was coming back and it'll be hell to pay. That was fifteen years ago. To this day . . . the first of the month I send my ten dollars, Rose'll tell you.

ROSE: Troy lying.

120 TROY: I ain't never seen that man since. Now you tell me who else that could have been but the devil? I ain't sold my soul or nothing like that, you understand. Naw, I wouldn't have truck with the devil about nothing like that. I got my furniture and pays my ten dollars the first of the month just like clockwork.

BONO: How long you say you been paying this ten dollars a month?

TROY: Fifteen years!

BONO: Hell, ain't you finished paying for it yet? How much the man done charged you?

TROY: Ah hell, I done paid for it. I done paid for it ten times over! The fact is I'm scared to stop paying it.

125 ROSE: Troy lying. We got that furniture from Mr. Glickman. He ain't paying no ten dollars a month to nobody.

TROY: Aw hell, woman. Bono know I ain't that big a fool.

LYONS: I was just getting ready to say . . . I know where there's a bridge for sale.

TROY: Look here, I'll tell you this . . . it don't matter to me if he was the devil. It don't matter if the devil give credit. Somebody has got to give it.

ROSE: It ought to matter. You going around talking about having truck with the devil . . . God's the one you gonna have to answer to. He's the one gonna be at the Judgment.

130 LYONS: Yeah, well, look here, Pop . . . let me have that ten dollars. I'll give it back to you. Bonnie got a job working at the hospital.

TROY: What I tell you, Bono? The only time I see this nigger is when he wants something. That's the only time I see him.

LYONS: Come on, Pop, Mr. Bono don't want to hear all that. Let me have the ten dollars. I told you Bonnie working.

TROY: What that mean to me? "Bonnie working." I don't care if she working. Go ask her for the ten dollars if she working. Talking about "Bonnie working." Why ain't you working?

LYONS: Aw, Pop, you know I can't find no decent job. Where am I gonna get a job at? You know I can't get no job.

135 TROY: I told you I know some people down there. I can get you on the rubbish if you want to work. I told you that the last time you came by here asking me for something.

LYONS: Naw, Pop . . . thanks. That ain't for me. I don't wanna be carrying nobody's rubbish. I don't wanna be punching nobody's time clock.

TROY: What's the matter, you too good to carry people's rubbish? Where you think that ten dollars you talking about come from? I'm just supposed to haul people's rubbish and give my money to you 'cause you too lazy to work. You too lazy to work and wanna know why you ain't got what I got.

ROSE: What hospital Bonnie working at? Mercy?

LYONS: She's down at Passavant working in the laundry.

140 TROY: I ain't got nothing as it is. I give you that ten dollars and I got to eat beans the rest of the week. Naw . . . you ain't getting no ten dollars here.

LYONS: You ain't got to be eating no beans. I don't know why you wanna say that.

TROY: I ain't got no extra money. Gabe done moved over to Miss Pearl's paying her the rent and things done got tight around here. I can't afford to be giving you every payday.

LYONS: I ain't asked you to give me nothing. I asked you to loan me ten dollars. I know you got ten dollars.

TROY: Yeah, I got it. You know why I got it? 'Cause I don't throw my money away out there in the streets. You living the fast life . . . wanna be a musician . . . running around in them clubs and things . . . then, you learn to take care of yourself. You ain't gonna find me going and asking nobody for nothing. I done spent too many years without.

145 LYONS: You and me is two different people, Pop.

TROY: I done learned my mistake and learned to do what's right by it. You still trying to get something for nothing. Life don't owe you nothing. You owe it to yourself. Ask Bono. He'll tell you I'm right.

LYONS: You got your way of dealing with the world . . . I got mine. The only thing that matters to me is the music.

TROY: Yeah, I can see that! It don't matter how you gonna eat . . . where your next dollar is coming from. You telling the truth there.

LYONS: I know I got to eat. But I got to live too. I need something that gonna help me to get out of the bed in the morning. Make me feel like I belong in the world. I don't bother nobody. I just stay with the music 'cause that's the only way I can find to live in the world. Otherwise there ain't no telling what I might do. Now I don't come criticizing you and how you live. I just come by to ask you for ten dollars. I don't wanna hear all that about how I live.

150 TROY: Boy, your mama did a hell of a job raising you.

LYONS: You can't change me, Pop. I'm thirty-four years old. If you wanted to change me, you should have been there when I was growing up. I come by to see you . . . ask for ten dollars and you want to talk about how I was raised. You don't know nothing about how I was raised.

ROSE: Let the boy have ten dollars, Troy.

TROY: *(to Lyons)* What the hell you looking at me for? I ain't got no ten dollars. You know what I do with my money. *(To Rose.)* Give him ten dollars if you want him to have it.

ROSE: I will. Just as soon as you turn it loose.

155 TROY: *(handing Rose the money)* There it is. Seventy-six dollars and forty-two cents. You see this, Bono? Now, I ain't gonna get but six of that back.

ROSE: You ought to stop telling that lie. Here, Lyons. *(She hands him the money.)*

LYONS: Thanks, Rose. Look . . . I got to run . . . I'll see you later.

TROY: Wait a minute. You gonna say "thanks, Rose" and ain't gonna look to see where she got that ten dollars from? See how they do me, Bono?

LYONS: I know she got it from you, Pop. Thanks. I'll give it back to you.

160 **TROY:** There he go telling another lie. Time I see that ten dollars . . . he'll be owing me thirty more.

LYONS: See you, Mr. Bono.

BONO: Take care, Lyons!

LYONS: Thanks, Pop. I'll see you again.

Lyons exits the yard.

TROY: I don't know why he don't go and get him a decent job and take care of that woman he got.

165 **BONO:** He'll be all right, Troy. The boy is still young.

TROY: The *boy* is thirty-four years old.

ROSE: Let's not get off into all that.

BONO: Look here . . . I got to be going. I got to be getting on. Lucille gonna be waiting.

TROY: *(puts his arm around Rose)* See this woman, Bono? I love this woman. I love this woman so much it hurts. I love her so much . . . I done run out of ways of loving her. So I got to go back to basics. Don't you come by my house Monday morning talking about time to go to work . . . 'cause I'm still gonna be stroking!

170 **ROSE:** Troy! Stop it now!

BONO: I ain't paying him no mind, Rose. That ain't nothing but gin-talk. Go on, Troy. I'll see you Monday.

TROY: Don't you come by my house, nigger! I done told you what I'm gonna be doing.

The lights go down to black.

SCENE 2

The lights come up on Rose hanging up clothes. She hums and sings softly to herself. It is the following morning.

ROSE: *(sings)*

> Jesus, be a fence all around me every day
> Jesus, I want you to protect me as I travel on my way.
> Jesus, be a fence all around me every day.

Troy enters from the house.

> Jesus, I want you to protect me
> As I travel on my way.

(To Troy.) 'Morning, You ready for breakfast? I can fix it soon as I finish hanging up these clothes?

Troy: I got the coffee on. That'll be all right. I'll just drink some of that this morning.

175 Rose: That 651 hit yesterday. That's the second time this month. Miss Pearl hit for a dollar . . . seem like those that need the least always get lucky. Poor folks can't get nothing.

Troy: Them numbers don't know nobody. I don't know why you fool with them. You and Lyons both.

Rose: It's something to do.

Troy: You ain't doing nothing but throwing your money away.

Rose: Troy, you know I don't play foolishly. I just play a nickel here and a nickel there.

180 Troy: That's two nickels you done thrown away.

Rose: Now I hit sometimes . . . that makes up for it. It always comes in handy when I do hit. I don't hear you complaining then.

Troy: I ain't complaining now. I just say it's foolish. Trying to guess out of six hundred ways which way the number gonna come. If I had all the money niggers, these Negroes, throw away on numbers for one week—just one week—I'd be a rich man.

Rose: Well, you wishing and calling it foolish ain't gonna stop folks from playing numbers. That's one thing for sure. Besides . . . some good things come from playing numbers. Look where Pope done bought him that restaurant off of numbers.

Troy: I can't stand niggers like that. Man ain't had two dimes to rub together. He walking around with his shoes all run over bumming money for cigarettes. All right. Got lucky there and hit the numbers . . .

185 Rose: Troy, I know all about it.

Troy: Had good sense, I'll say that for him. He ain't throwing his money away. I seen niggers hit the numbers and go through two thousand dollars in four days. Man bought him that restaurant down there . . . fixed it up real nice . . . and then didn't want nobody to come in it! A Negro go in there and can't get no kind of service. I seen a white fellow come in there and order a bowl of stew. Pope picked all the meat out the pot for him. Man ain't had nothing but a bowl of meat! Negro come behind him and ain't got nothing but the potatoes and carrots. Talking about what numbers do for people, you picked a wrong example. Ain't done nothing but make a worser fool out of him than he was before.

Rose: Troy, you ought to stop worrying about what happened at work yesterday.

Troy: I ain't worried. Just told me to be down there at the Commissioner's office on Friday. Everybody think they gonna fire me. I ain't worried about them firing me. You ain't got to worry about that. *(Pause.)* Where's Cory? Cory in the house? *(Calls.)* Cory?

ROSE: He gone out.

190 TROY: Out, huh? He gone out 'cause he know I want him to help me with
this fence. I know how he is. That boy scared of work.

*Gabriel enters. He comes halfway down the alley and, hearing Troy's voice,
stops.*

TROY: *(continues)* He ain't done a lick of work in his life.

ROSE: He had to go to football practice. Coach wanted them to get in a
little extra practice before the season start.

TROY: I got his practice . . . running out of here before he get his chores
done.

ROSE: Troy, what is wrong with you this morning? Don't nothing set
right with you. Go on back in there and go to bed . . . get up on the
other side.

195 TROY: Why something got to be wrong with me? I ain't said nothing
wrong with me.

ROSE: You got something to say about everything. First it's the
numbers . . . then it's the way the man runs his restaurant . . . then
you done got on Cory. What's it gonna be next? Take a look up there
and see if the weather suits you . . . or is it gonna be how you gonna
put up the fence with the clothes hanging in the yard.

TROY: You hit the nail on the head then.

ROSE: I know you like I know the back of my hand. Go on in there and
get you some coffee . . . see if that straighten you up. 'Cause you ain't
right this morning.

*Troy starts into the house and sees Gabriel. Gabriel starts singing. Troy's brother,
he is seven years younger than Troy. Injured in World War II, he has a metal plate
in his head. He carries an old trumpet tied around his waist and believes with
every fiber of his being that he is the Archangel Gabriel.[6] He carries a chipped
basket with an assortment of discarded fruits and vegetables he has picked up in
the strip district and which he attempts to sell.*

GABRIEL: *(singing)*

> Yes, ma'am, I got plums
> You ask me how I sell them
> Oh ten cents apiece
> Three for a quarter
> Come and buy now
> 'Cause I'm here today
> And tomorrow I'll be gone

Gabriel enters.

Hey, Rose!

---

[6] The Archangel Gabriel, a messenger of God.

200 ROSE: How you doing, Gabe?

GABRIEL: There's Troy . . . Hey, Troy!

TROY: Hey, Gabe.

Exit into kitchen.

ROSE: *(to Gabriel)* What you got there?

GABRIEL: You know what I got, Rose. I got fruits and vegetables.

205 ROSE: *(looking in basket)* Where's all these plums you talking about?

GABRIEL: I ain't got no plums today, Rose. I was just singing that. Have
some tomorrow. Put me in a big order for plums. Have enough plums
tomorrow for St. Peter and everybody.

Troy reenters from kitchen, crosses to steps.

(To Rose.) Troy's mad at me.

TROY: I ain't mad at you. What I got to be mad at you about? You ain't
done nothing to me.

GABRIEL: I just moved over to Miss Pearl's to keep out from in your way.
I ain't mean no harm by it.

TROY: Who said anything about that? I ain't said anything about that.

210 GABRIEL: You ain't mad at me, is you?

TROY: Naw . . . I ain't mad at you, Gabe. If I was mad at you I'd tell you
about it.

GABRIEL: Got me two rooms. In the basement. Got my own door too.
Wanna see my key? *(He holds up a key.)* That's my own key! Ain't
nobody else got a key like that. That's my key! My two rooms!

TROY: Well, that's good, Gabe. You got your own key . . . that's good.

ROSE: You hungry, Gabe? I was just fixing to cook Troy his breakfast.

215 GABRIEL: I'll take some biscuits. You got some biscuits? Did you know
when I was in heaven . . . every morning me and St. Peter[7] would sit
down by the gate and eat some big fat biscuits? Oh, yeah! We had us a
good time. We'd sit there and eat us them biscuits and then St. Peter
would go off to sleep and tell me to wake him up when it's time to
open the gates for the judgment.

ROSE: Well, come on . . . I'll make up a batch of biscuits.

Rose exits into the house.

GABRIEL: Troy . . . St. Peter got your name in the book. I seen it. It
say . . . Troy Maxson. I say . . . I know him! He got the same name
like what I got. That's my brother!

TROY: How many times you gonna tell me that, Gabe?

GABRIEL: Ain't got my name in the book. Don't have to have my name. I
done died and went to heaven. He got your name though. One
morning St. Peter was looking at his book . . . marking it up for the
judgment . . . and he let me see your name. Got it in there under M.

---

[7] Disciple of Christ, believed to be the guard at the gates of heaven.

Got Rose's name . . . I ain't seen it like I seen yours . . . but I know it's in there. He got a great big book. Got everybody's name what was ever been born. That's what he told me. But I seen your name. Seen it with my own eyes.

220 TROY: Go on in the house there. Rose going to fix you something to eat.

GABRIEL: Oh, I ain't hungry. I done had breakfast with Aunt Jemima. She come by and cooked me up a whole mess of flapjacks. Remember how we used to eat them flapjacks?

TROY: Go on in the house and get you something to eat now.

GABRIEL: I got to sell my plums. I done sold some tomatoes. Got me two quarters. Wanna see? *(He shows Troy his quarters.)* I'm gonna save them and buy me a new horn so St. Peter can hear me when it's time to open the gates. *(Gabriel stops suddenly. Listens.)* Hear that? That's the hellhounds. I got to chase them out of here. Go on get out of here! Get out!

Gabriel exits singing.

> Better get ready for the Judgment
> Better get ready for the Judgment
> My Lord is coming down

Rose enters from the house.

TROY: He's gone off somewhere.

225 GABRIEL: *(offstage)*

> Better get ready for the Judgment
> Better get ready for the Judgment morning
> Better get ready for the Judgment
> My God is coming down

ROSE: He ain't eating right. Miss Pearl say she can't get him to eat nothing.

TROY: What you want me to do about it, Rose? I done did everything I can for the man. I can't make him get well. Man got half his head blown away . . . what you expect?

ROSE: Seem like something ought to be done to help him.

TROY: Man don't bother nobody. He just mixed up from that metal plate he got in his head. Ain't no sense for him to go back into the hospital.

230 ROSE: Least he be eating right. They can help him take care of himself.

TROY: Don't nobody wanna be locked up, Rose. What you wanna lock him up for? Man go over there and fight the war . . . messin' around with them Japs, get half his head blown off . . . and they give him a lousy three thousand dollars. And I had to swoop down on that.

ROSE: Is you fixing to go into that again?

TROY: That's the only way I got a roof over my head . . . 'cause of that metal plate.

Rose: Ain't no sense you blaming yourself for nothing. Gabe wasn't in no condition to manage that money. You done what was right by him. Can't nobody say you ain't done what was right by him. Look how long you took care of him . . . till he wanted to have his own place and moved over there with Miss Pearl.

235 Troy: That ain't what I'm saying, woman! I'm just stating the facts. If my brother didn't have that metal plate in his head . . . I wouldn't have a pot to piss in or a window to throw it out of. And I'm fifty-three years old. Now see if you can understand that!

Troy gets up from the porch and starts to exit the yard.

Rose: Where you going off to? You been running out of here every Saturday for weeks. I thought you was gonna work on this fence?

Troy: I'm gonna walk down to Taylors'. Listen to the ball game. I'll be back in a bit. I'll work on it when I get back.

He exits the yard. The lights go to black.

Scene 3

The lights come up on the yard. It is four hours later. Rose is taking down the clothes from the line. Cory enters carrying his football equipment.

Rose: Your daddy like to had a fit with you running out of here this morning without doing your chores.

Cory: I told you I had to go to practice.

240 Rose: He say you were supposed to help him with this fence.

Cory: He been saying that the last four or five Saturdays, and then he don't never do nothing, but go down to Taylors'. Did you tell him about the recruiter?

Rose: Yeah, I told him.

Cory: What he say?

Rose: He ain't said nothing too much. You get in there and get started on your chores before he gets back. Go on and scrub down them steps before he gets back here hollering and carrying on.

245 Cory: I'm hungry. What you got to eat, Mama?

Rose: Go on and get started on your chores. I got some meat loaf in there. Go on and make you a sandwich . . . and don't leave no mess in there.

Cory exits into the house. Rose continues to take down the clothes. Troy enters the yard and sneaks up and grabs her from behind.

Troy! Go on, now. You liked to scared me to death. What was the score of the game? Lucille had me on the phone and I couldn't keep up with it.

Troy: What I care about the game? Come here, woman. *(He tries to kiss her.)*

Rose: I thought you went down Taylors' to listen to the game. Go on, Troy! You supposed to be putting up this fence.

TROY: *(attempting to kiss her again)* I'll put it up when I finish with what is at hand.
250 ROSE: Go on, Troy. I ain't studying you.
TROY: *(chasing after her)* I'm studying you . . . fixing to do my homework!
ROSE: Troy, you better leave me alone.
TROY: Where's Cory? That boy brought his butt home yet?
ROSE: He's in the house doing his chores.
255 TROY: *(calling)* Cory! Get your butt out here, boy!

Rose exits into the house with the laundry. Troy goes over to the pile of wood, picks up a board, and starts sawing. Cory enters from the house.

TROY: You just now coming in here from leaving this morning?
CORY: Yeah, I had to go to football practice.
TROY: Yeah, what?
CORY: Yessir.
260 TROY: I ain't but two seconds off you noway. The garbage sitting in there overflowing . . . you ain't done none of your chores . . . and you come in here talking about "Yeah."
CORY: I was just getting ready to do my chores now, Pop . . .
TROY: Your first chore is to help me with this fence on Saturday. Everything else come after that. Now get that saw and cut them boards.

Cory takes the saw and begins cutting the boards. Troy continues working. There is a long pause.

CORY: Hey, Pop . . . why don't you buy a TV?
TROY: What I want with a TV? What I want one of them for?
265 CORY: Everybody got one. Earl, Ba Bra . . . Jesse!
TROY: I ain't asked you who had one. I say what I want with one?
CORY: So you can watch it. They got lots of things on TV. Baseball games and everything. We could watch the World Series.
TROY: Yeah . . . and how much this TV cost?
CORY: I don't know. They got them on sale for around two hundred dollars.
270 TROY: Two hundred dollars, huh?
CORY: That ain't that much, Pop.
TROY: Naw, it's just two hundred dollars. See that roof you got over your head at night? Let me tell you something about that roof. It's been over ten years since that roof was last tarred. See now . . . the snow comes this winter and sit up there on that roof like it is . . . and it's gonna seep inside. It's just gonna be a little bit . . . ain't gonna hardly notice it. Then the next thing you know, it's gonna be leaking all over the house. Then the wood rot from all that water and you gonna need a whole new roof. Now, how much you think it cost to get that roof tarred?
CORY: I don't know.

Troy: Two hundred and sixty-four dollars . . . cash money. While you thinking about a TV, I got to be thinking about the roof . . . and whatever else go wrong here. Now if you had two hundred dollars, what would you do . . . fix the roof or buy a TV?

275 Cory: I'd buy a TV. Then when the roof started to leak . . . when it needed fixing . . . I'd fix it.

Troy: Where you gonna get the money from? You done spent it for a TV. You gonna sit up and watch the water run all over your brand new TV.

Cory: Aw, Pop. You got money. I know you do.

Troy: Where I got it at, huh?

Cory: You got it in the bank.

280 Troy: You wanna see my bankbook? You wanna see that seventy-three dollars and twenty-two cents I got sitting up in there.

Cory: You ain't got to pay for it all at one time. You can put a down payment on it and carry it on home with you.

Troy: Not me. I ain't gonna owe nobody nothing if I can help it. Miss a payment and they come and snatch it right out your house. Then what you got? Now, soon as I get two hundred dollars clear, then I'll buy a TV. Right now, as soon as I get two hundred and sixty-four dollars, I'm gonna have this roof tarred.

Cory: Aw . . . Pop!

Troy: You go on and get you two hundred and buy one if ya want it. I got better things to do with my money.

285 Cory: I can't get no two hundred dollars. I ain't never seen two hundred dollars.

Troy: I'll tell you what . . . you get you a hundred dollars and I'll put the other hundred with it.

Cory: All right, I'm gonna show you.

Troy: You gonna show me how you can cut them boards right now.

Cory begins to cut the boards. There is a long pause.

Cory: The Pirates won today. That makes five in a row.

290 Troy: I ain't thinking about the Pirates. Got an all-white team. Got that boy . . . that Puerto Rican boy . . . Clemente. Don't even half-play him. That boy could be something if they give him a chance. Play him one day and sit him on the bench the next.

Cory: He gets a lot of chances to play.

Troy: I'm talking about playing regular. Playing every day so you can get your timing. That's what I'm talking about.

Cory: They got some white guys on the team that don't play every day. You can't play everybody at the same time.

Troy: If they got a white fellow sitting on the bench . . . you can bet your last dollar he can't play! The colored guy got to be twice as good before he get on the team. That's why I don't want you to get all tied up in them sports. Man on the team and what it get him? They got colored on the team and don't use them. Same as not having them. All them teams the same.

295 CORY: The Braves got Hank Aaron and Wes Covington. Hank Aaron hit two home runs today. That makes forty-three.

TROY: Hank Aaron ain't nobody. That what you supposed to do. That's how you supposed to play the game. Ain't nothing to it. It's just a matter of timing . . . getting the right follow-through. Hell, I can hit forty-three home runs right now!

CORY: Not off no major-league pitching, you couldn't.

TROY: We had better pitching in the Negro leagues. I hit seven home runs off of Satchel Paige.[8] You can't get no better than that!

CORY: Sandy Koufax.[9] He's leading the league in strikeouts.

300 TROY: I ain't thinking of no Sandy Koufax.

CORY: You got Warren Spahn[10] and Lew Burdette.[11] I bet you couldn't hit no home runs off of Warren Spahn.

TROY: I'm through with it now. You go on and cut them boards. *(Pause.)* Your mama tell me you done got recruited by a college football team? Is that right?

CORY: Yeah. Coach Zellman say the recruiter gonna be coming by to talk to you. Get you to sign the permission papers.

TROY: I thought you supposed to be working down there at the A&P. Ain't you suppose to be working down there after school?

305 CORY: Mr. Stawicki say he gonna hold my job for me until after the football season. Say starting next week I can work weekends.

TROY: I thought we had an understanding about this football stuff? You suppose to keep up with your chores and hold that job down at the A&P. Ain't been around here all day on a Saturday. Ain't none of your chores done . . . and now you telling me you done quit your job.

CORY: I'm going to be working weekends.

TROY: You damn right you are! And ain't no need for nobody coming around here to talk to me about signing nothing.

CORY: Hey, Pop . . . you can't do that. He's coming all the way from North Carolina.

---

[8] Leroy Robert Paige (1906–1982), American baseball player in the Negro Leagues from the 1920's until 1948, when he joined the Cleveland Indians; reportedly pitched 55 no-hit games during his career; called by Joe DiMaggio "the best pitcher I have ever faced."

[9] Sanford Koufax (1935–   ), left-handed pitcher who won 129 games and lost only 47 for the Los Angeles Dodgers in the six seasons between 1961 and 1966; won three Cy Young Awards; pitched four no-hit games, the last of which (1965) was a perfect game.

[10] (1921–   ), left-handed pitcher who at the time of his retirement in 1966 held the National League record of 363 wins; won twenty or more games in four consecutive seasons (1947–1950) and in several other seasons during the 1950's.

[11] Selva Lewis Burdette (1926–   ), American baseball player who pitched and won three games for the Milwaukee Braves against the New York Yankees in the 1957 World Series; ERA of .067 for that Series.

310 TROY: I don't care where he coming from. The white man ain't gonna let you get nowhere with that football noway. You go on and get your book-learning so you can work yourself up in that A&P or learn how to fix cars or build houses or something, get you a trade. That way you have something can't nobody take away from you. You go on and learn how to put your hands to some good use. Besides hauling people's garbage.

CORY: I get good grades, Pop. That's why the recruiter wants to talk with you. You got to keep up your grades to get recruited. This way I'll be going to college. I'll get a chance . . .

TROY: First you gonna get your butt down there to the A&P and get your job back.

CORY: Mr. Stawicki done already hired somebody else 'cause I told him I was playing football.

TROY: You a bigger fool than I thought . . . to let somebody take away your job so you can play some football. Where you gonna get your money to take out your girlfriend and whatnot? What kind of foolishness is that to let somebody take away your job?

315 CORY: I'm still gonna be working weekends.

TROY: Naw . . . naw. You getting your butt out of here and finding you another job.

CORY: Come on, Pop! I got to practice. I can't work after school and play football too. The team needs me. That's what Coach Zellman say . . .

TROY: I don't care what nobody else say. I'm the boss . . . you understand? I'm the boss around here. I do the only saying what counts.

CORY: Come on, Pop!

320 TROY: I asked you . . . did you understand?

CORY: Yeah . . .

TROY: What?!

CORY: Yessir.

TROY: You go on down there to that A&P and see if you can get your job back. If you can't do both . . . then you quit the football team. You've got to take the crookeds with the straights.

325 CORY: Yessir. *(Pause.)* Can I ask you a question?

TROY: What the hell you wanna ask me? Mr. Stawicki the one you got the questions for.

CORY: How come you ain't never liked me?

TROY: Liked you? Who the hell say I got to like you? What law is there say I got to like you? Wanna stand up in my face and ask a damn fool-ass question like that. Talking about liking somebody. Come here, boy, when I talk to you.

Cory comes over to where Troy is working. He stands slouched over and Troy shoves him on his shoulder.

Straighten up, goddammit! I asked you a question . . . what law is there say I got to like you?

CORY: None.

330 TROY: Well, all right then! Don't you eat every day? *(Pause.)* Answer me when I talk to you! Don't you eat every day?

CORY: Yeah.

TROY: Nigger, as long as you in my house, you put that sir on the end of it when you talk to me!

CORY: Yes . . . sir.

TROY: You eat every day.

335 CORY: Yessir!

TROY: Got a roof over your head.

CORY: Yessir!

TROY: Got clothes on your back.

CORY: Yessir.

340 TROY: Why you think that is?

CORY: 'Cause of you.

TROY: Ah, hell I know it's 'cause of me . . . but why do you think that is?

CORY: *(hesitant)* 'Cause you like me.

TROY: Like you? I go out of here every morning . . . bust my butt . . . putting up with them crackers[12] every day . . . 'cause I like you? You are the biggest fool I ever saw. *(Pause.)* It's my job. It's my responsibility! You understand that? A man got to take care of his family. You live in my house . . . sleep you behind on my bedclothes . . . fill you belly up with my food . . . 'cause you my son. You my flesh and blood. Not 'cause I like you! 'Cause it's my duty to take care of you. I owe a responsibility to you! Let's get this straight right here . . . before it go along any further . . . I ain't got to like you. Mr. Rand don't give me my money come payday cause he likes me. He give me 'cause he owe me. I done give you everything I had to give you. I gave you your life! Me and your mama worked that out between us. And liking your black ass wasn't part of the bargain. Don't you try and go through life worrying about if somebody like you or not. You best be making sure they doing right by you. You understand what I'm saying, boy?

345 CORY: Yessir.

TROY: Then get the hell out of my face, and get on down to that A&P.

Rose has been standing behind the screen door for much of the scene. She enters as Cory exits.

ROSE: Why don't you let the boy go ahead and play football, Troy? Ain't no harm in that. He's just trying to be like you with the sports.

TROY: I don't want him to be like me! I want him to move as far away from my life as he can get. You the only decent thing that ever happened to me. I wish him that. But I don't wish him a thing else from my life. I decided seventeen years ago that boy wasn't getting involved in no sports. Not after what they did to me in the sports.

---

[12] Derogatory term for white people, generally poor Southern whites.

Rose: Troy, why don't you admit you was too old to play in the major leagues? For once . . . why don't you admit that?

350 Troy: What do you mean too old? Don't come telling me I was too old. I just wasn't the right color. Hell, I'm fifty-three years old and can do better than Selkirk's .269 right now!

Rose: How's was you gonna play ball when you were over forty? Sometimes I can't go no sense out of you.

Troy: I got good sense, woman. I got sense enough not to let my boy get hurt over playing no sports. You been mothering that boy too much. Worried about if people like him.

Rose: Everything that boy do . . . he do for you. He wants you to say "Good job, son." That's all.

Troy: Rose, I ain't got time for that. He's alive. He's healthy. He's got to make his own way. I made mine. Ain't nobody gonna hold his hand when he get out there in that world.

355 Rose: Times have changed from when you was young, Troy. People change. The world's changing around you and you can't even see it.

Troy: *(slow, methodical)* Woman . . . I do the best I can do. I come in here every Friday. I carry a sack of potatoes and a bucket of lard. You all line up at the door with your hands out. I give you the lint from my pockets. I give you my sweat and my blood. I ain't got no tears. I done spent them. We go upstairs in that room at night . . . and I fall down on you and try to blast a hole into forever. I get up Monday morning . . . find my lunch on the table. I go out. Make my way. Find my strength to carry me through to the next Friday. *(Pause.)* That's all I got, Rose. That's all I got to give. I can't give nothing else.

Troy exits into the house. The lights go down to black.

Scene 4

It is Friday. Two weeks later. Cory starts out of the house with his football equipment. The phone rings.

Cory: *(calling)* I got it! *(He answers the phone and stands in the screen door talking.)* Hello? Hey, Jesse. Naw . . . I was just getting ready to leave now.

Rose: *(calling)* Cory!

Cory: I told you, man, them spikes[13] is all tore up. You can use them if you want, but they ain't no good. Earl got some spikes.

360 Rose: *(calling)* Cory!

Cory: *(calling to Rose)* Mam? I'm talking to Jesse. *(Into phone.)* When she say that? *(Pause.)* Aw, you lying, man. I'm gonna tell her you said that.

Rose: *(calling)* Cory, don't you go nowhere!

---

13 Athletic shoes with sharp metal grips set into the soles.

CORY: I got to go to the game, Ma! *(Into the phone.)* Yeah, hey, look, I'll talk to you later. Yeah, I'll meet you over Earl's house. Later. Bye, Ma.

Cory exits the house and starts out the yard.

ROSE: Cory, where you going off to? You got that stuff all pulled out and thrown all over your room.

365 CORY: *(in the yard)* I was looking for my spikes. Jesse wanted to borrow my spikes.

ROSE: Get up there and get that cleaned up before your daddy get back in here.

CORY: I got to go to the game! I'll clean it up *when I get back.*

Cory exits.

ROSE: That's all he need to do is see that room all messed up.

Rose exits into the house. Troy and Bono enter the yard. Troy is dressed in clothes other than his work clothes.

BONO: He told him the same thing he told you. Take it to the union.

370 TROY: Brownie ain't got that much sense. Man wasn't thinking about nothing. He wait until I confront them on it . . . then he wanna come crying seniority. *(Calls.)* Hey, Rose!

BONO: I wish I could have seen Mr. Rand's face when he told you.

TROY: He couldn't get it out of his mouth! Liked to bit his tongue! When they called me down there to the Commissioner's office . . . he thought they was gonna fire me. Like everybody else.

BONO: I didn't think they was gonna fire you. I thought they was gonna put you on the warning paper.

TROY: Hey, Rose! *(To Bono.)* Yeah, Mr. Rand like to bit his tongue.

Troy breaks the seal on the bottle, takes a drink, and hands it to Bono.

375 BONO: I see you run right down to Taylors' and told that Alberta gal.

TROY: *(calling)* Hey, Rose! *(To Bono.)* I told everybody. Hey, Rose! I went down there to cash my check.

ROSE: *(entering from the house)* Hush all that hollering, man! I know you out here. What they say down there at the Commissioner's office?

TROY: You supposed to come when I call you, woman. Bono'll tell you that. *(To Bono.)* Don't Lucille come when you call her?

ROSE: Man, hush your mouth, I ain't no dog . . . talk about "come when you call me."

380 TROY: *(puts his arm around Rose)* You hear this, Bono? I had me an old dog used to get uppity like that. You say, "C'mere, Blue!" . . . and he just lay there and look at you. End up getting a stick and chasing him away trying to make him come.

ROSE: I ain't studying you and your dog. I remember you used to sing that old song.

TROY: *(he sings)*

> Hear it ring! Hear it ring!
> I had a dog his name was Blue.

ROSE: Don't nobody wanna hear you sing that old song.
TROY: *(sings)*

> You know Blue was mighty true.

385 ROSE: Used to have Cory running around here singing that song.
BONO: Hell, I remember that song myself.
TROY: *(sings)*

> You know Blue was a good old dog.
> Blue treed a possum in a hollow log.

That was my daddy's song. My daddy made up that song.
ROSE: I don't care who made it up. Don't nobody wanna hear you sing it.
TROY: *(makes a song like calling a dog)* Come here, woman.
390 ROSE: You come in here carrying on, I reckon they ain't fired you. What
they say down there at the Commissioner's office?
TROY: Look here, Rose . . . Mr. Rand called me into his office today when
I got back from talking to them people down there . . . it come from
up top . . . he called me in and told me they was making me a driver.
ROSE: Troy, you kidding!
TROY: No I ain't. Ask Bono.
ROSE: Well, that's great, Troy. Now you don't have to hassle them people
no more.

Lyons enters from the street.

395 TROY: Aw hell, I wasn't looking to see you today. I thought you was in
jail. Got it all over the front page of the *Courier* about them raiding
Sefus's place . . . where you be hanging out with all them thugs.
LYONS: Hey, Pop . . . that ain't got nothing to do with me. I don't go
down there gambling. I go down there to sit in with the band. I ain't
got nothing to do with the gambling part. They got some good music
down there.
TROY: They got some rogues . . . is what they got.
LYONS: How you been, Mr. Bono? Hi, Rose.
BONO: I see where you playing down at the Crawford Grill tonight.
400 ROSE: How come you ain't brought Bonnie like I told you? You should
have brought Bonnie with you, she ain't been over in a month of
Sundays.
LYONS: I was just in the neighborhood . . . thought I'd stop by.
TROY: Here he come . . .
BONO: Your daddy got a promotion on the rubbish. He's gonna be the
first colored driver. Ain't got to do nothing but sit up there and read
the paper like them white fellows.

LYONS: Hey, Pop . . . if you knew how to read you'd be all right.

405 BONO: Naw . . . naw . . . you mean if the nigger knew how to *drive* he'd be all right. Been fighting with them people about driving and ain't even got a license. Mr. Rand know you ain't got no driver's license?

TROY: Driving ain't nothing. All you do is point the truck where you want it to go. Driving ain't nothing.

BONO: Do Mr. Rand know you ain't got no driver's license? That's what I'm talking about. I ain't asked if driving was easy. I asked if Mr. Rand know you ain't got no driver's license.

TROY: He ain't got to know. The man ain't got to know my business. Time he find out, I have two or three driver's licenses.

LYONS: *(going into his pocket)* Say, look here, Pop . . .

410 TROY: I knew it was coming. Didn't I tell you, Bono? I know what kind of "Look here, Pop" that was. The nigger fixing to ask me for some money. It's Friday night. It's my payday. All them rogues down there on the avenue . . . the ones that ain't in jail . . . and Lyons is hopping in his shoes to get down there with them.

LYONS: See, Pop . . . if you give somebody else a chance to talk sometimes, you'd see that I was fixing to pay you back your ten dollars like I told you. Here . . . I told you I'd pay you when Bonnie got paid.

TROY: Naw . . . you go ahead and keep that ten dollars. Put it in the bank. The next time you feel like you wanna come by here and ask me for something . . . you go on down there and get that.

LYONS: Here's your ten dollars, Pop. I told you I don't want you to give me nothing. I just wanted to borrow ten dollars.

TROY: Naw . . . you go on and keep that for the next time you want to ask me.

415 LYONS: Come on, Pop . . . here go your ten dollars.

ROSE: Why don't you go on and let the boy pay you back, Troy?

LYONS: Here you go, Rose. If you don't take it I'm gonna have to hear about it for the next six months. *(He hands her the money.)*

ROSE: You can hand yours over here too, Troy.

TROY: You see this, Bono. You see how they do me.

420 BONO: Yeah, Lucille do me the same way.

Gabriel is heard singing offstage. He enters.

GABRIEL: Better get ready for the Judgment! Better get ready for . . . Hey! . . . Hey! . . . There's Troy's boy!

LYONS: How are you doing, Uncle Gabe?

GABRIEL: Lyons . . . The King of the Jungle! Rose . . . hey, Rose. Got a flower for you. *(He takes a rose from his pocket.)* Picked it myself. That's the same rose like you is!

ROSE: That's right nice of you, Gabe.

425 LYONS: What you been doing, Uncle Gabe?

GABRIEL: Oh, I been chasing hellhounds and waiting on the time to tell St. Peter to open the gates.

LYONS: You been chasing hellhounds, huh? Well . . . you doing the right thing, Uncle Gabe. Somebody got to chase them.

GABRIEL: Oh, yeah . . . I know it. The devil's strong. The devil ain't no pushover. Hellhounds snipping at everybody's heels. But I got my trumpet waiting on the judgment time.

LYONS: Waiting on the Battle of Armageddon, huh?

430 GABRIEL: Ain't gonna be too much of a battle when God get to waving that Judgment sword. But the people's gonna have a hell of a time trying to get into heaven if them gates ain't open.

LYONS: *(putting his arm around Gabriel)* You hear this, Pop. Uncle Gabe, you all right!

GABRIEL: *(laughing with Lyons)* Lyons! King of the Jungle.

ROSE: You gonna stay for supper, Gabe? Want me to fix you a plate?

GABRIEL: I'll take a sandwich, Rose. Don't want no plate. Just wanna eat with my hands. I'll take a sandwich.

435 ROSE: How about you, Lyons? You staying? Got some short ribs cooking.

LYONS: Naw, I won't eat nothing till after we finished playing. *(Pause.)* You ought to come down and listen to me play, Pop.

TROY: I don't like that Chinese music. All that noise.

ROSE: Go on in the house and wash up, Gabe . . . I'll fix you a sandwich.

GABRIEL: *(to Lyons, as he exits)* Troy's mad at me.

440 LYONS: What you mad at Uncle Gabe for, Pop?

ROSE: He thinks Troy's mad at him cause he moved over to Miss Pearl's.

TROY: I ain't mad at the man. He can live where he want to live at.

LYONS: What he move over there for? Miss Pearl don't like nobody.

ROSE: She don't mind him none. She treats him real nice. She just don't allow all that singing.

445 TROY: She don't mind that rent he be paying . . . that's what she don't mind.

ROSE: Troy, I ain't going through that with you no more. He's over there cause he want to have his own place. He can come and go as he please.

TROY: Hell, he could come and go as he please here. I wasn't stopping him. I ain't put no rules on him.

ROSE: It ain't the same thing, Troy. And you know it.

Gabriel comes to the door.

Now, that's the last I wanna hear about that. I don't wanna hear nothing else about Gabe and Miss Pearl. And next week . . .

GABRIEL: I'm ready for my sandwich, Rose.

450 ROSE: And next week . . . when that recruiter come from that school . . . I want you to sign that paper and go on and let Cory play football. Then that'll be the last I have to hear about that.

TROY: *(to Rose as she exits into the house)* I ain't thinking about Cory nothing.

LYONS: What . . . Cory got recruited? What school he going to?

TROY: That boy walking around here smelling his piss . . . thinking he's grown. Thinking he's gonna do what he want, irrespective of what I say. Look here, Bono . . . I left the Commissioner's office and went down to the A&P . . . that boy ain't working down there. He lying to me. Telling me he got his job back . . . telling me he working weekends . . . telling me he working after school . . . Mr. Stawicki tell me he ain't working down there at all!

LYONS: Cory just growing up. He's just busting at the seams trying to fill out your shoes.

455 TROY: I don't care what he's doing. When he get to the point where he wanna disobey me . . . then it's time for him to move on. Bono'll tell you that. I bet he ain't never disobeyed his daddy without paying the consequences.

BONO: I ain't never had a chance. My daddy came on through . . . but I ain't never knew him to see him . . . or what he had on his mind or where he went. Just moving on through. Searching out the New Land. That's what the old folks used to call it. See a fellow moving around from place to place . . . woman to woman . . . called it searching out the New Land. I can't say if he ever found it. I come along, didn't want no kids. Didn't know if I was gonna be in one place long enough to fix on them right as their daddy. I figured I was going searching too. As it turned out I been hooked up with Lucille near about as long as your daddy been with Rose. Going on sixteen years.

TROY: Sometimes I wish I hadn't known my daddy. He ain't cared nothing about no kids. A kid to him wasn't nothing. All he wanted was for you to learn how to walk so he could start you to working. When it come time for eating . . . he ate first. If there was anything left over, that's what you got. Man would sit down and eat two chickens and give you the wing.

LYONS: You ought to stop that, Pop. Everybody feed their kids. No matter how hard times is . . . everybody care about their kids. Make sure they have something to eat.

TROY: The only thing my daddy cared about was getting them bales of cotton in to Mr. Lubin. That's the only thing that mattered to him. Sometimes I used to wonder why he was living. Wonder why the devil hadn't come and got him. "Get them bales of cotton in to Mr. Lubin" and find out he owe him money . . .

460 LYONS: He should have just went on and left when he saw he couldn't get nowhere. That's what I would have done.

TROY: How he gonna leave with eleven kids? And where he gonna go? He ain't knew how to do nothing but farm. No, he was trapped and I think he knew it. But I'll say this for him . . . he felt a responsibility toward us. Maybe he ain't treated us the way I felt he should have . . . but without that responsibility he could have walked off and left us . . . made his own way.

BONO: A lot of them did. Back in those days what you talking about . . . they walk out their front door and just take on down one road or another and keep on walking.

LYONS: There you go? That's what I'm talking about.

BONO: Just keep on walking till you come to something else. Ain't you never heard of nobody having the walking blues? Well, that's what you call it when you just take off like that.

465 TROY: My daddy ain't had them walking blues! What you talking about? He stayed right there with his family. But he was just as evil as he could be. My mama couldn't stand him. Couldn't stand that evilness. She run off when I was about eight. She sneaked off one night after he had gone to sleep. Told me she was coming back for me. I ain't never seen her no more. All his women run off and left him. He wasn't good for nobody.

When my turn come to head out, I was fourteen and got to sniffing around Joe Canewell's daughter. Had us an old mule we called Greyboy. My daddy sent me out to do some plowing and tied up Greyboy and went to fooling around with Joe Canewell's daughter. We done found us a nice little spot, got real cozy with each other. She about thirteen and we done figured we was grown anyway . . . so we down there enjoying ourselves . . . ain't thinking about nothing. We didn't know Greyboy had got loose and wandered back to the house and my daddy was looking for me. We down there by the creek enjoying ourselves when my daddy come up on us. Surprised us. He had them leather straps off the mule and commenced to whupping me like there was no tomorrow. I jumped up, mad and embarrassed. I was scared of my daddy. When he commenced to whupping on me . . . quite naturally I run to get out of the way. *(Pause.)* Now I thought he was mad 'cause I ain't done my work. But I see where he was chasing me off so he could have that gal for himself. When I see what the matter of it was, I lost all fear of my daddy. Right there is where I become a man . . . at fourteen years of age. *(Pause.)* Now it was my turn to run him off. I picked up them same reins that he had used on me. I picked up them reins and commenced to whupping on him. The gal jumped up and run off . . . and when my daddy turned to face me, I could see why the devil had never come to get him . . . cause he was the devil himself. I don't know what happened. When I woke up, I was laying right there by the creek, and Blue . . . this old dog we had . . . was licking my face. I thought I was blind. I couldn't see nothing. Both my eyes were swollen shut. I laid there and cried. I didn't know what I was gonna do. The only thing I knew was the time had come for me to leave my daddy's house. And right there the world suddenly got big. And it was a long time before I could cut it down to where I could handle it.

Part of that cutting down was when I got to the place where I could feel him kicking in my blood and knew that the only thing that separated us was the matter of a few years.

Gabriel enters from the house with a sandwich.

LYONS: What you got there, Uncle Gabe?

GABRIEL: Got me a ham sandwich. Rose gave me a ham sandwich.

TROY: I don't know what happened to him. I done lost touch with everybody except Gabriel. But I hope he's dead. I hope he found some peace.

LYONS: That's a heavy story, Pop. I didn't know you left home when you was fourteen.

470 TROY: And didn't know nothing. The only part of the world I knew was the forty-two acres of Mr. Lubin's land. That's all I knew about life.

LYONS: Fourteen's kinda young to be out on your own. *(Phone rings.)* I don't even think I was ready to be out on my own at fourteen. I don't know what I would have done.

TROY: I got up from the creek and walked on down to Mobile.[14] I was through with farming. Figured I could do better in the city. So I walked the two hundred miles to Mobile.

LYONS: Wait a minute . . . you ain't walked no two hundred miles, Pop. Ain't nobody gonna walk no two hundred miles. You talking about some walking there.

BONO: That's the only way you got anywhere back in them days.

475 LYONS: Shhh. Damn if I wouldn't have hitched a ride with somebody!

TROY: Who you gonna hitch it with? They ain't got no cars and things like they got now. We talking about 1918.

ROSE: *(entering)* What you all out here getting into?

TROY: *(to Rose)* I'm telling Lyons how good he got it. He don't know nothing about this I'm talking.

ROSE: Lyons, that was Bonnie on the phone. She say you supposed to pick her up.

480 LYONS: Yeah, okay, Rose.

TROY: I walked on down to Mobile and hitched up with some of them fellows that was heading this way. Got up here and found out . . . not only couldn't you get a job . . . you couldn't find no place to live. I thought I was in freedom. Shhh. Colored folks living down there on the riverbanks in whatever kind of shelter they could find for themselves. Right down there under the Brady Street Bridge. Living in shacks made of sticks and tarpaper. Messed around there and went from bad to worse. Started stealing. First it was food. Then I figured, hell, if I steal money I can buy me some food. Buy me some shoes too! One thing led to another. Met your mama. I was young and anxious to be a man. Met your mama and had you. What I do that for? Now I got to worry about feeding you and her. Got to steal three times as much. Went out one day looking for somebody to rob . . . that's what I was, a robber. I'll tell you the truth. I'm ashamed of it today. But it's the truth. Went to rob this fellow . . . pulled out my

---

[14] City and seaport in southwestern Alabama.

knife . . . and he pulled out a gun. Shot me in the chest. I felt just like somebody had taken a hot branding iron and laid it on me. When he shot me I jumped at him with my knife. They told me I killed him and they put me in the penitentiary and locked me up for fifteen years. That's where I met Bono. That's where I learned how to play baseball. Got out that place and your mama had taken you and went on to make life without me. Fifteen years was a long time for her to wait. But that fifteen years cured me of that robbing stuff. Rose'll tell you. She asked me when I met her if I had gotten all that foolishness out of my system. And I told her, "Baby, it's you and baseball all what count with me." You hear me, Bono? I meant it too. She say, "Which one comes first?" I told her, "Baby, ain't no doubt it's baseball . . . but you stick and get old with me and we'll both outlive this baseball." Am I right, Rose? And it's true.

ROSE: Man, hush your mouth. You ain't said no such thing. Talking about "Baby, you know you'll always be number one with me." That's what you was talking.

TROY: You hear that, Bono. That's why I love her.

BONO: Rose'll keep you straight. You get off the track, she'll straighten you up.

485 ROSE: Lyons, you better get on up and get Bonnie. She waiting on you.

LYONS: *(gets up to go)* Hey, Pop, why don't you come on down to the Grill and hear me play?

TROY: I ain't going down there. I'm too old to be sitting around in them clubs.

BONO: You got to be good to play down at the Grill.

LYONS: Come on, Pop . . .

490 TROY: I got to get up in the morning.

LYONS: You ain't got to stay long.

TROY: Naw, I'm gonna get my supper and go on to bed.

LYONS: Well, I got to go. I'll see you again.

TROY: Don't you come around my house on my payday.

495 ROSE: Pick up the phone and let somebody know you coming. And bring Bonnie with you. You know I'm always glad to see her.

LYONS: Yeah, I'll do that, Rose. You take care now. See you, Pop. See you, Mr. Bono. See you, Uncle Gabe.

GABRIEL: Lyons! King of the Jungle!

Lyons exits.

TROY: Is supper ready, woman? Me and you got some business to take care of. I'm gonna tear it up too.

ROSE: Troy, I done told you now!

500 TROY: *(puts his arm around Bono)* Aw hell, woman . . . this is Bono. Bono like family. I done known this nigger since . . . how long I done know you?

BONO: It's been a long time.

TROY: I done know this nigger since Skippy was a pup. Me and him done been through some times.

BONO: You sure right about that.

TROY: Hell, I done know him longer than I known you. And we still standing shoulder to shoulder. Hey, look here, Bono . . . a man can't ask for no more than that. *(Drinks to him.)* I love you, nigger.

505 BONO: Hell, I love you too . . . I got to get home see my woman. You got yours in hand. I got to go get mine.

Bono starts to exit as Cory enters the yard, dressed in his football uniform. He gives Troy a hard, uncompromising look.

CORY: What you do that for, Pop?

He throws his helmet down in the direction of Troy.

ROSE: What's the matter? Cory . . . what's the matter?

CORY: Papa done went up to the school and told Coach Zellman I can't play football no more. Wouldn't even let me play the game. Told him to tell the recruiter not to come.

ROSE: Troy . . .

510 TROY: What you Troying me for. Yeah, I did it. And the boy know why I did it.

CORY: Why you wanna do that to me? That was the one chance I had.

ROSE: Ain't nothing wrong with Cory playing football, Troy.

TROY: The boy lied to me. I told the nigger if he wanna play football . . . to keep up his chores and hold down that job at the A&P. That was the conditions. Stopped down there to see Mr. Stawicki . . .

CORY: I can't work after school during the football season, Pop! I tried to tell you that Mr. Stawicki's holding my job for me. You don't never want to listen to nobody. And then you wanna go and do this to me!

515 TROY: I ain't done nothing to you. You done it to yourself.

CORY: Just cause you didn't have a chance! You just scared I'm gonna be better than you, that's all.

TROY: Come here.

ROSE: Troy . . .

Cory reluctantly crosses over to Troy.

TROY: All right! See. You done made a mistake.

520 CORY: I didn't even do nothing!

TROY: I'm gonna tell you what your mistake was. See . . . you swung at the ball and didn't hit it. That's strike one. See, you in the batter's box now. You swung and you missed. That's strike one. Don't you strike out!

Lights fade to black.

ACT II

SCENE 1

The following morning. Cory is at the tree hitting the ball with the bat. He tries to mimic Troy, but his swing is awkward, less sure. Rose enters from the house.

ROSE: Cory, I want you to help me with this cupboard.

CORY: I ain't quitting the team. I don't care what Poppa say.

ROSE: I'll talk to him when he gets back. He had to go see about your Uncle Gabe. The police done arrested him. Say he was disturbing the peace. He'll be back directly. Come on in here and help me clean out the top of this cupboard.

Cory exits into the house. Rose sees Troy and Bono coming down the alley.

Troy . . . what they say down there?

TROY: Ain't said nothing. I give them fifty dollars and they let him go. I'll talk to you about it. Where's Cory?

5 ROSE: He's in there helping me clean out these cupboards.

TROY: Tell him to get his butt out here.

Troy and Bono go over to the pile of wood. Bono picks up the saw and begins sawing.

TROY: *(to Bono)* All they want is the money. That makes six or seven times I done went down there and got him. See me coming they stick out their *hands*.

BONO: Yeah. I know what you mean. That's all they care about . . . that money. They don't care about what's right. *(Pause.)* Nigger, why you got to go and get some hard wood? You ain't doing nothing but building a little old fence. Get you some soft pine wood. That's all you need.

TROY: I know what I'm doing. This is outside wood. You put pine wood inside the house. Pine wood is inside wood. This here is outside wood. Now you tell me where the fence is gonna be?

10 BONO: You don't need this wood. You can put it up with pine wood and it'll stand as long as you gonna be here looking at it.

TROY: How you know how long I'm gonna be here, nigger? Hell, I might just live forever. Live longer than old man Horsely.

BONO: That's what Magee used to say.

TROY: Magee's a damn fool. Now you tell me who you ever heard of gonna pull their own teeth with a pair of rusty pliers.

BONO: The old folks . . . my granddaddy used to pull his teeth with pliers. They ain't had no dentists for the colored folks back then.

15 TROY: Get clean pliers! You understand? Clean pliers! Sterilize them! Besides we ain't living back then. All Magee had to do was walk over to Doc Goldblum's.

BONO: I see where you and that Tallahassee gal . . . that Alberta . . . I see where you all done got tight.

TROY: What you mean "got tight"?

BONO: I see where you be laughing and joking with her all the time.

TROY: I laughs and jokes with all of them, Bono. You know me.

20 BONO: That ain't the kind of laughing and joking I'm talking about.

Cory enters from the house.

CORY: How you doing, Mr. Bono?

TROY: Cory? Get that saw from Bono and cut some wood. He talking about the wood's too hard to cut. Stand back there, Jim, and let that young boy show you how it's done.

BONO: He's sure welcome to it.

Cory takes the saw and begins to cut the wood.

Whew-e-e! Look at that. Big old strong boy. Look like Joe Louis.[15] Hell, must be getting old the way I'm watching that boy whip through that wood.

CORY: I don't see why Mama want a fence around the yard noways.

25 TROY: Damn if I know either. What the hell she keeping out with it? She ain't got nothing nobody want.

BONO: Some people build fences to keep people out . . . and other people build fences to keep people in. Rose wants to hold on to you all. She loves you.

TROY: Hell, nigger, I don't need nobody to tell me my wife loves me.

Cory . . . go on in the house and see if you can find that other saw.

CORY: Where's it at?

TROY: I said find it! Look for it till you find it!

Cory exits into the house.

What's that supposed to mean? Wanna keep us in?

30 BONO: Troy . . . I done known you seem like damn near my whole life. You and Rose both. I done know both of you all for a long time. I remember when you met Rose. When you was hitting them baseballs out the park. A lot of them gals was after you then. You had the pick of the litter. When you picked Rose, I was happy for you. That was the first time I knew you had any sense. I said . . . My man Troy knows what he's doing . . . I'm gonna follow this nigger . . . he might take me somewhere. I been following you too. I done learned a whole heap of things about life watching you. I done learned how to tell where the shit lies. How to tell it from the alfalfa. You done learned me a lot of things. You showed me how to not make the same mistakes . . . to take life as it comes along and keep putting one foot in front of the other. *(Pause.)* Rose a good woman, Troy.

---

[15] Joseph Louis Barrow (1914–1981), known as "the Brown Bomber"; in 1937 became the youngest boxer ever to win the Heavyweight Championship, which he defended twenty-five times; retired undefeated in 1949.

Troy: Hell, nigger, I know she a good woman. I been married to her for eighteen years. What you got on your mind, Bono?

Bono: I just say she a good woman. Just like I say anything. I ain't got to have nothing on my mind.

Troy: You just gonna say she a good woman and leave it hanging out there like that? Why you telling me she a good woman?

Bono: She loves you, Troy. Rose loves you.

35 Troy: You saying I don't measure up. That's what you trying to say. I don't measure up 'cause I'm seeing this other gal. I know what you trying to say.

Bono: I know what Rose means to you, Troy. I'm just trying to say I don't want to see you mess up.

Troy: Yeah, I appreciate that, Bono. If you was messing around on Lucille I'd be telling you the same thing.

Bono: Well, that's all I got to say. I just say that because I love you both.

Troy: Hell, you know me . . . I wasn't out there looking for nothing. You can't find a better woman than Rose. I know that. But seems like this woman just stuck onto me where I can't shake her loose. I done wrestled with it, tried to throw her off me . . . but she just stuck on tighter. Now she's stuck on for good.

40 Bono: You's in control . . . that's what you tell me all the time. You responsible for what you do.

Troy: I ain't ducking the responsibility of it. As long as it sets right in my heart . . . then I'm okay. 'Cause that's all I listen to. It'll tell me right from wrong every time. And I ain't talking about doing Rose no bad turn. I love Rose. She done carried me a long ways and I love and respect her for that.

Bono: I know you do. That's why I don't want to see you hurt her. But what you gonna do when she find out? What you got then? If you try and juggle both of them . . . sooner or later you gonna drop one of them. That's common sense.

Troy: Yeah, I hear what you saying, Bono. I been trying to figure a way to work it out.

Bono: Work it out right, Troy. I don't want to be getting all up between you and Rose's business . . . but work it so it come out right.

45 Troy: Ah hell, I get all up between you and Lucille's business. When you gonna get that woman that refrigerator she been wanting? Don't tell me you ain't got no money now. I know who your banker is. Mellon don't need that money bad as Lucille want that refrigerator. I'll tell you that.

Bono: Tell you what I'll do . . . when you finish building this fence for Rose . . . I'll buy Lucille that refrigerator.

Troy: You done stuck your foot in your mouth now!

Troy grabs up a board and begins to saw. Bono starts to walk out the yard.

Hey, nigger . . . where you going?

BONO: I'm going home. I know you don't expect me to help you now. I'm protecting my money. I wanna see you put that fence up by yourself. That's what I want to see. You'll be here another six months without me.

TROY: Nigger, you ain't right.

50 BONO: When it comes to my money . . . I'm right as fireworks on the Fourth of July.

TROY: All right, we gonna see now. You better get out your bankbook.

Bono exits, and Troy continues to work. Rose enters from the house.

ROSE: What they say down there? What's happening with Gabe?

TROY: I went down there and got him out. Cost me fifty dollars. Say he was disturbing the peace. Judge set up a hearing for him in three weeks. Say to show 'cause why he shouldn't be recommitted.

ROSE: What was he doing that 'cause them to arrest him?

55 TROY: Some kids were teasing him and he run them off home. Say he was howling and carrying on. Some folks seen him and called the police. That's all it was.

ROSE: Well, what's you say? What'd you tell the judge?

TROY: Told him I'd look after him. It didn't make no sense to recommit the man. He stuck out his big greasy palm and told me to give him fifty dollars and take him on home.

ROSE: Where's he at now? Where'd he go off to?

TROY: He's gone about his business. He don't need nobody to hold his hand.

60 ROSE: Well, I don't know. Seem like that would be the best place for him if they did put him into the hospital. I know what you're gonna say. But that's what I think would be best.

TROY: The man done had his life ruined fighting for what? And they wanna take and lock him up. Let him be free. He don't bother nobody.

ROSE: Well, everybody got their own way of looking at it I guess. Come on and get your lunch. I got a bowl of lima beans and some cornbread in the oven. Come and get something to eat. Ain't no sense you fretting over Gabe.

Rose turns to go into the house.

TROY: Rose . . . got something to tell you.

ROSE: Well, come on . . . wait till I get this food on the table.

65 TROY: Rose!

She stops and turns around.

I don't know how to say this. *(Pause.)* I can't explain it none. It just sort of grows on you till it gets out of hand. It starts out like a little bush . . . and the next thing you know it's a whole forest.

ROSE: Troy . . . what is you talking about?

TROY: I'm talking, woman, let me talk. I'm trying to find a way to tell
you . . . I'm gonna be a daddy. I'm gonna be somebody's daddy.

ROSE: Troy . . . you're not telling me this? You're gonna be . . . what?

TROY: Rose . . . now . . . see . . .

70 ROSE: You telling me you gonna be somebody's daddy? You telling your
wife this?

Gabriel enters from the street. He carries a rose in his hand.

GABRIEL: Hey, Troy! Hey, Rose!

ROSE: I have to wait eighteen years to hear something like this.

GABRIEL: Hey, Rose . . . I got a flower for you. *(He hands it to her.)* That's a
rose. Same rose like you is.

ROSE: Thanks, Gabe.

75 GABRIEL: Troy, you ain't mad at me is you? Them bad mens come and put
me away. You ain't mad at me is you?

TROY: Naw, Gabe, I ain't mad at you.

ROSE: Eighteen years and you wanna come with this.

GABRIEL: *(takes a quarter out of his pocket)* See what I got? Got a brand new
quarter.

TROY: Rose . . . it's just . . .

80 ROSE: Ain't nothing you can say, Troy. Ain't no way of explaining that.

GABRIEL: Fellow that give me this quarter had a whole mess of them. I'm
gonna keep this quarter till it stop shining.

ROSE: Gabe, go on in the house there. I got some watermelon in the
Frigidaire. Go on and get you a piece.

GABRIEL: Say, Rose . . . you know I was chasing hellhounds and them bad
mens come and get me and take me away. Troy helped me. He come
down there and told them they better let me go before he beat them
up. Yeah, he did!

ROSE: You go on and get you a piece of watermelon, Gabe. Them bad
mens is gone now.

85 GABRIEL: Okay, Rose . . . gonna get me some watermelon. The kind with
the stripes on it.

Gabriel exits into the house.

ROSE: Why, Troy? Why? After all these years to come dragging this in to
me now. It don't make no sense at your age. I could have expected
this ten or fifteen years ago, but not now.

TROY: Age ain't got nothing to do with it, Rose.

ROSE: I done tried to be everything a wife should be. Everything a wife
could be. Been married eighteen years and I got to live to see the day
you tell me you been seeing another woman and done fathered a
child by her. And you know I ain't never wanted no half nothing in
my family. My whole family is half. Everybody got different fathers
and mothers . . . my two sisters and my brother. Can't hardly tell

who's who. Can't never sit down and talk about Papa and Mama. It's
your papa and your mama and my papa and my mama . . .

TROY: Rose . . . stop it now.

90 ROSE: I ain't never wanted that for none of my children. And now you
wanna drag your behind in here and tell me something like this.

TROY: You ought to know. It's time for you to know.

ROSE: Well, I don't want to know, goddamn it!

TROY: I can't just make it go away. It's done now. I can't wish the
circumstance of the thing away.

ROSE: And you don't want to either. Maybe you want to wish me and my
boy away. Maybe that's what you want? Well, you can't wish us away.
I've got eighteen years of my life invested in you. You ought to have
stayed upstairs in my bed where you belong.

95 TROY: Rose . . . now listen to me . . . we can get a handle on this thing.
We can talk this out . . . come to an understanding.

ROSE: All of a sudden it's "we." Where was "we" at when you was down
there rolling around with some godforsaken woman? "We" should
have come to an understanding before you started making a damn
fool of yourself. You're a day late and a dollar short when it comes to
an understanding with me.

TROY: It's just . . . She gives me a different idea . . . a different
understanding about myself. I can step out of this house and get away
from the pressures and problems . . . be a different man. I ain't got to
wonder how I'm gonna pay the bills or get the roof fixed. I can just
be a part of myself that I ain't never been.

ROSE: What I want to know . . . is do you plan to continue seeing her.
That's all you can say to me.

TROY: I can sit up in her house and laugh. Do you understand what I'm
saying. I can laugh out loud . . . and it feels good. It reaches all the
way down to the bottom of my shoes. *(Pause.)* Rose, I can't give
that up.

100 ROSE: Maybe you ought to go on and stay down there with her . . . if she's
a better woman than me.

TROY: It ain't about nobody being a better woman or nothing. Rose, you
ain't the blame. A man couldn't ask for no woman to be a better wife
than you've been. I'm responsible for it. I done locked myself into a
pattern trying to take care of you all that I forgot about myself.

ROSE: What the hell was I there for? That was my job, not somebody else's.

TROY: Rose, I done tried all my life to live decent . . . to live a clean . . .
hard . . . useful life. I tried to be a good husband to you. In every way
I knew how. Maybe I come into the world backwards, I don't know.
But . . . you born with two strikes on you before you come to the
plate. You got to guard it closely . . . always looking for the curve ball
on the inside corner. You can't afford to let none get past you. You
can't afford a call strike. If you going down . . . you going down

swinging. Everything lined up against you. What you gonna do. I fooled them, Rose. I bunted. When I found you and Cory and a halfway decent job . . . I was safe. Couldn't nothing touch me. I wasn't gonna strike out no more. I wasn't going back to the penitentiary. I wasn't gonna lay in the streets with a bottle of wine. I was safe. I had me a family. A job. I wasn't gonna get that last strike. I was on first looking for one of them boys to knock me in. To get me home.

ROSE: You should have stayed in my bed, Troy.

105 TROY: Then when I saw that gal . . . she firmed up my backbone. And I got to thinking that if I tried . . . I just might be able to steal second. Do you understand after eighteen years I wanted to steal second.

ROSE: You should have held me tight. You should have grabbed me and held on.

TROY: I stood on first base for eighteen years and I thought . . . well, goddamn it . . . go on for it!

ROSE: We're not talking about baseball! We're talking about you going off to lay in bed with another woman . . . and then bring it home to me. That's what we're talking about. We ain't talking about no baseball.

TROY: Rose, you're not listening to me. I'm trying the best I can to explain it to you. It's not easy for me to admit that I been standing in the same place for eighteen years.

110 ROSE: I been standing with you! I been right here with you, Troy. I got a life too. I gave eighteen years of my life to stand in the same spot with you. Don't you think I ever wanted other things? Don't you think I had dreams and hopes? What about my life? What about me. Don't you think it ever crossed my mind to want to know other men? That I wanted to lay up somewhere and forget about my responsibilities? That I wanted someone to make me laugh so I could feel good? You not the only one who's got wants and needs. But I held on to you, Troy. I took all my feelings, my wants and needs, my dreams . . . and I buried them inside you. I planted a seed and watched and prayed over it. I planted myself inside you and waited to bloom. And it didn't take me no eighteen years to find out the soil was hard and rocky and it wasn't never gonna bloom.

But I held on to you, Troy. I held you tighter. You was my husband. I owed you everything I had. Every part of me I could find to give you. And upstairs in that room . . . with the darkness falling in on me . . . I gave everything I had to try and erase the doubt that you wasn't the finest man in the world. And wherever you was going . . . I wanted to be there with you. 'Cause you was my husband. 'Cause that's the only way I was gonna survive as your wife. You always talking about what you give . . . and what you don't have to give. But you take too. You take . . . and don't even know nobody's giving!

Rose turns to exit into the house; Troy grabs her arm.

TROY: You say I take and don't give!

ROSE: Troy! You're hurting me!

TROY: You say I take and don't give!

ROSE: Troy . . . you're hurting my arm! Let go!

115 TROY: I done give you everything I got. Don't you tell that lie on me.

ROSE: Troy!

TROY: Don't you tell that lie on me!

Cory enters from the house.

CORY: Mama!

ROSE: Troy. You're hurting me.

120 TROY: Don't you tell me about no taking and giving.

Cory comes up behind Troy and grabs him. Troy, surprised, is thrown off balance just as Cory throws a glancing blow that catches him on the chest and knocks him down. Troy is stunned, as is Cory.

ROSE: Troy. Troy. No!

Troy gets to his feet and starts at Cory.

Troy . . . no. Please! Troy!

Rose pulls on Troy to hold him back. Troy stops himself.

TROY: *(to Cory)* All right. That's strike two. You stay away from around me, boy. Don't you strike out. You living with a full count. Don't you strike out.

Troy exits out the yard as the lights go down.

SCENE 2

It is six months later, early afternoon. Troy enters from the house and starts to exit the yard. Rose enters from the house.

ROSE: Troy, I want to talk to you.

TROY: All of a sudden, after all this time, you want to talk to me, huh? You ain't wanted to talk to me for months. You ain't wanted to talk to me last night. You ain't wanted no part of me then. What you wanna talk to me about now?

125 ROSE: Tomorrow's Friday.

TROY: I know what day tomorrow is. You think I don't know tomorrow's Friday? My whole life I ain't done nothing but look to see Friday coming and you got to tell me it's Friday.

ROSE: I want to know if you're coming home.

TROY: I always come home, Rose. You know that. There ain't never been a night I ain't come home.

Rose: That ain't what I mean . . . and you know it. I want to know if you're coming straight home after work.

130 **Troy:** I figure I'd cash my check . . . hang out at Taylors' with the boys . . . maybe play a game of checkers . . .

Rose: Troy, I can't live like this. I won't live like this. You livin' on borrowed time with me. It's been going on six months now you ain't been coming home.

Troy: I be here every Friday. Every night of the year. That's 365 days.

Rose: I want you to come home tomorrow after work.

Troy: Rose . . . I don't mess up my pay. You know that now. I take my pay and I give it to you. I don't have no money but what you give me back. I just want to have a little time to myself . . . a little time to enjoy life.

135 **Rose:** What about me? When's my time to enjoy life?

Troy: I don't know what to tell you, Rose. I'm doing the best I can.

Rose: You ain't been home from work but time enough to change your clothes and run out . . . and you wanna call that the best you can do?

Troy: I'm going over to the hospital to see Alberta. She went into the hospital this afternoon. Look like she might have the baby early. I won't be gone long.

Rose: Well, you ought to know. They went over to Miss Pearl's and got Gabe today. She said you told them to go ahead and lock him up.

140 **Troy:** I ain't said no such thing. Whoever told you that is telling a lie. Pearl ain't doing nothing but telling a big fat lie.

Rose: She ain't had to tell me. I read it on the papers.

Troy: I ain't told them nothing of the kind.

Rose: I saw it right there on the papers.

Troy: What it say, huh?

145 **Rose:** It said you told them to take him.

Troy: Then they screwed that up, just the way they screw up everything. I ain't worried about what they got on the paper.

Rose: Say the government send part of his check to the hospital and the other part to you.

Troy: I ain't got nothing to do with that if that's the way it works. I ain't made up the rules about how it work.

Rose: You did Gabe just like you did Cory. You wouldn't sign the paper for Cory . . . but you signed for Gabe. You signed that paper.

The telephone is heard ringing inside the house.

150 **Troy:** I told you I ain't signed nothing, woman! The only thing I signed was the release form. Hell, I can't read. I don't know what they had on that paper! I ain't signed nothing about sending Gabe away.

Rose: I said send him to the hospital . . . you said let him be free . . . now you done went down there and signed him to the hospital for half his money. You went back on yourself, Troy. You gonna have to answer for that.

TROY: See now . . . you been over there talking to Miss Pearl. She done got mad cause she ain't getting Gabe's rent money. That's all it is. She's liable to say anything.

ROSE: Troy, I seen where you signed the paper.

TROY: You ain't seen nothing I signed. What she doing got papers on my brother anyway? Miss Pearl telling a big fat lie. And I'm gonna tell her about it too! You ain't seen nothing I signed. Say . . . you ain't seen nothing I signed.

Rose exits into the house to answer the telephone. Presently she returns.

155 ROSE: Troy . . . that was the hospital. Alberta had the baby.

TROY: What she have? What is it?

ROSE: It's a girl.

TROY: I better get on down to the hospital to see her.

ROSE: Troy . . .

160 TROY: Rose . . . I got to go see her now. That's only right . . . what's the matter . . . the baby's all right, ain't it?

ROSE: Alberta died having the baby.

TROY: Died . . . you say she's dead? Alberta's dead?

ROSE: They said they done all they could. They couldn't do nothing for her.

TROY: The baby? How's the baby?

165 ROSE: They say it's healthy. I wonder who's gonna bury her.

TROY: She had family, Rose. She wasn't living in the world by herself.

ROSE: I know she wasn't living in the world by herself.

TROY: Next thing you gonna want to know if she had any insurance.

ROSE: Troy, you ain't got to talk like that.

170 TROY: That's the first thing that jumped out your mouth. "Who's gonna bury her?" Like I'm fixing to take on that task for myself.

ROSE: I am your wife. Don't push me away.

TROY: I ain't pushing nobody away. Just give me some space. That's all. Just give me some room to breathe.

Rose exits into the house. Troy walks about the yard.

TROY: *(with a quiet rage that threatens to consume him)* All right . . . Mr. Death. See now . . . I'm gonna tell you what I'm gonna do. I'm gonna take and build me a fence around this yard. See? I'm gonna build me a fence around what belongs to me. And then I want you to stay on the other side. See? You stay over there until you're ready for me. Then you come on. Bring your army. Bring your sickle. Bring your wrestling clothes. I ain't gonna fall down on my vigilance this time. You ain't gonna sneak up on me no more. When you ready for me . . . when the top of your list say Troy Maxson . . . that's when you come around here. You come up and knock on the front door. Ain't nobody else got nothing to do with this. This is between you and me. Man to man. You stay on the other side of the fence until you ready for me. Then you come up and knock on the front door. Anytime you want. I'll be ready for you.

The lights go down to black.

<u>Scene 3</u>

The lights come up on the porch. It is late evening three days later. Rose sits listening to the ball game waiting for Troy. The final out of the game is made and Rose switches off the radio. Troy enters the yard carrying an infant wrapped in blankets. He stands back from the house and calls.

Rose enters and stands on the porch. There is a long, awkward silence, the weight of which grows heavier with each passing second.

Troy: Rose . . . I'm standing here with my daughter in my arms. She ain't but a wee bittie little old thing. She don't know nothing about grownups' business. She innocent . . . and she ain't got no mama.

175 Rose: What you telling me for, Troy?

She turns and exits into the house.

Troy: Well . . . I guess we'll just sit out here on the porch.

He sits down on the porch. There is an awkward indelicateness about the way he handles the baby. His largeness engulfs and seems to swallow it. He speaks loud enough for Rose to hear.

A man's got to do what's right for him. I ain't sorry for nothing I done. It felt right in my heart. *(To the baby.)* What you smiling at? Your daddy's a big man. Got these great big old hands. But sometimes he's scared. And right now your daddy's scared 'cause we sitting out here and ain't got no home. Oh, I been homeless before. I ain't had no little baby with me. But I been homeless. You just be out on the road by your lonesome and you see one of them trains coming and you just kinda go like this . . .

He sings a lullaby.

Please, Mr. Engineer let a man ride the line
Please, Mr. Engineer let a man ride the line
I ain't got no ticket please let me ride the blinds

Rose enters from the house. Troy, hearing her steps behind him, stands and faces her.

She's my daughter, Rose. My own flesh and blood. I can't deny her no more than I can deny them boys. *(Pause.)* You and them boys is my family. You and them and this child is all I got in the world. So I guess what I'm saying is . . . I'd appreciate it if you'd help me take care of her.

Rose: Okay, Troy . . . you're right. I'll take care of your baby for you . . . 'cause . . . like you say . . . she's innocent . . . and you can't visit the sins of the father upon the child. A motherless child has got a hard time. *(She takes the baby from him.)* From right now . . . this child got a mother. But you a womanless man.

Rose turns and exits into the house with the baby. Lights go down to black.

SCENE 4

It is two months later. Lyons enters from the street. He knocks on the door and calls.

LYONS: Hey, Rose! *(Pause.)* Rose!

ROSE: *(from inside the house)* Stop that yelling. You gonna wake up Raynell. I just got her to sleep.

180 LYONS: I just stopped by to pay Papa this twenty dollars I owe him. Where's Papa at?

ROSE: He should be here in a minute. I'm getting ready to go down to the church. Sit down and wait on him.

LYONS: I got to go pick up Bonnie over her mother's house.

ROSE: Well, sit it down there on the table. He'll get it.

LYONS: *(enters the house and sets the money on the table)* Tell Papa I said thanks. I'll see you again.

185 ROSE: All right, Lyons. We'll see you.

Lyons starts to exit as Cory enters.

CORY: Hey, Lyons.

LYONS: What's happening, Cory? Say man, I'm sorry I missed your graduation. You know I had a gig and couldn't get away. Otherwise, I would have been there, man. So what you doing?

CORY: I'm trying to find a job.

LYONS: Yeah I know how that go, man. It's rough out there. Jobs are scarce.

190 CORY: Yeah, I know.

LYONS: Look here, I got to run. Talk to Papa . . . he know some people. He'll be able to help get you a job. Talk to him . . . see what he say.

CORY: Yeah . . . all right, Lyons.

LYONS: You take care. I'll talk to you soon. We'll find some time to talk.

Lyons exits the yard. Cory wanders over to the tree, picks up the bat, and assumes a batting stance. He studies an imaginary pitcher and swings. Dissatisfied with the result, he tries again. Troy enters. They eye each other for a beat. Cory puts the bat down and exits the yard. Troy starts into the house as Rose exits with Raynell. She is carrying a cake.

TROY: I'm coming in and everybody's going out.

195 ROSE: I'm taking this cake down to the church for the bake sale. Lyons was by to see you. He stopped by to pay you your twenty dollars. It's laying in there on the table.

TROY: *(going into his pocket)* Well . . . here go this money.

ROSE: Put it in there on the table, Troy. I'll get it.

TROY: What time you coming back?

ROSE: Ain't no use in you studying me. It don't matter what time I come back.

200 TROY: I just asked you a question, woman. What's the matter . . . can't I ask you a question?

ROSE: Troy, I don't want to go into it. Your dinner's in there on the stove. All I got to do is heat it up. And don't you be eating the rest of them cakes in there. I'm coming back for them. We having a bake sale at the church tomorrow.

Rose exits the yard. Troy sits down on the steps, takes a pint bottle from his pocket, opens it, and drinks. He begins to sing.

TROY:

> Hear it ring! Hear it ring!
> Had an old dog his name was Blue
> You know Blue was mighty true
> You know Blue was a good old dog
> Blue treed a possum in a hollow log
> You know from that he was a good old dog

Bono enters the yard.

BONO: Hey, Troy.

TROY: Hey, what's happening, Bono?

205 BONO: I just thought I'd stop by to see you.

TROY: What you stop by and see me for? You ain't stopped by in a month of Sundays. Hell, I must owe you money or something.

BONO: Since you got your promotion I can't keep up with you. Used to see you every day. Now I don't even know what route you working.

TROY: They keep switching me around. Got me out in Greentree now . . . hauling white folks' garbage.

BONO: Greentree, huh? You lucky, at least you ain't got to be lifting them barrels. Damn if they ain't getting heavier. I'm gonna put in my two years and call it quits.

210 TROY: I'm thinking about retiring myself.

BONO: You got it easy. You can *drive* for another five years.

TROY: It ain't the same, Bono. It ain't like working the back of the truck. Ain't got nobody to talk to . . . feel like you working by yourself. Naw, I'm thinking about retiring. How's Lucille?

BONO: She all right. Her arthritis get to acting up on her sometime. Saw Rose on my way in. She going down to the church, huh?

TROY: Yeah, she took up going down there. All them preachers looking for somebody to fatten their pockets. *(Pause.)* Got some gin here.

215 BONO: Naw, thanks. I just stopped by to say hello.

TROY: Hell, nigger . . . you can take a drink. I ain't never known you to say no to a drink. You ain't got to work tomorrow.

BONO: I just stopped by. I'm fixing to go over to Skinner's. We got us a domino game going over his house every Friday.

TROY: Nigger, you can't play no dominoes. I used to whup you four games out of five.

BONO: Well, that learned me. I'm getting better.

220 TROY: Yeah? Well, that's all right.

BONO: Look here . . . I got to be getting on. Stop by sometime, huh?

TROY: Yeah, I'll do that, Bono. Lucille told Rose you bought her a new refrigerator.

BONO: Yeah, Rose told Lucille you had finally built your fence . . . so I figured we'd call it even.

TROY: I knew you would.

225 BONO: Yeah . . . okay. I'll be talking to you.

TROY: Yeah, take care, Bono. Good to see you. I'm gonna stop over.

BONO: Yeah. Okay, Troy.

Bono exits. Troy drinks from the bottle.

TROY:

> Old Blue died and I dig his grave
> Let him down with a golden chain
> Every night when I hear old Blue bark
> I know Blue treed a possum in Noah's Ark.
> Hear it ring! Hear it ring!

Cory enters the yard. They eye each other for a beat. Troy is sitting in the middle of the steps. Cory walks over.

CORY: I got to get by.

230 TROY: Say what? What's you say?

CORY: You in my way. I got to get by.

TROY: You got to get by where? This is my house. Bought and paid for. In full. Took me fifteen years. And if you wanna go in my house and I'm sitting on the steps . . . you say excuse me. Like your mama taught you.

CORY: Come on, Pop . . . I got to get by.

Cory starts to maneuver his way past Troy. Troy grabs his leg and shoves him back.

TROY: You just gonna walk over top of me?

235 CORY: I live here too!

TROY: *(advancing toward him)* You just gonna walk over top of me in my own house?

CORY: I ain't scared of you.

TROY: I ain't asked if you was scared of me. I asked you if you was fixing to walk over top of me in my own house? That's the question. You ain't gonna say excuse me? You just gonna walk over top of me?

CORY: If you wanna put it like that.

240 TROY: How else am I gonna put it?

CORY: I was walking by you to go into the house 'cause you sitting on the steps drunk, singing to yourself. You can put it like that.

TROY: Without saying excuse me???

Cory doesn't respond.

I asked you a question. Without saying excuse me???

CORY: I ain't got to say excuse me to you. You don't count around here no more.

TROY: Oh, I see . . . I don't count around here no more. You ain't got to say excuse me to your daddy. All of a sudden you done got so grown that your daddy don't count around here no more . . . Around here in his own house and yard that he done paid for with the sweat of his brow. You done got so grown to where you gonna take over. You gonna take over my house. Is that right? You gonna wear my pants. You gonna go in there and stretch out on my bed. You ain't got to say excuse me 'cause I don't count around here no more. Is that right?

245 CORY: That's right. You always talking this dumb stuff. Now, why don't you just get out my way?

TROY: I guess you got someplace to sleep and something to put in your belly. You got that, huh? You got that? That's what you need. You got that, huh?

CORY: You don't know what I got. You ain't got to worry about what I got.

TROY: You right! You one hundred percent right! I done spent the last seventeen years worrying about what you got. Now it's your turn, see? I'll tell you what to do. You grown . . . we done established that. You a man. Now, let's see you act like one. Turn your behind around and walk out this yard. And when you get out there in the alley . . . you can forget about this house. See? 'Cause this is my house. You go on and be a man and get your own house. You can forget about this. 'Cause this is mine. You go on and get yours 'cause I'm through with doing for you.

CORY: You talking about what you did for me . . . what'd you ever give me?

250 TROY: Them feet and bones! That pumping heart, nigger! I give you more than anybody else is ever gonna give you.

CORY: You ain't never gave me nothing! You ain't never done nothing but hold me back. Afraid I was gonna be better than you. All you ever did was try and make me scared of you. I used to tremble every time you called my name. Every time I heard your footsteps in the house. Wondering all the time . . . what's Papa gonna say if I do this? . . . What's he gonna say if I do that? . . . What's Papa gonna say if I turn on the radio? And Mama, too . . . she tries . . . but she's scared of you.

TROY: You leave your mama out of this. She ain't got nothing to do with this.

CORY: I don't know how she stand you . . . after what you did to her.

TROY: I told you to leave your mama out of this!

He advances toward Cory.

255 CORY: What you gonna do . . . give me a whupping? You can't whup me
no more. You're too old. You just an old man.

TROY: *(shoves him on his shoulder)* Nigger! That's what you are. You just
another nigger on the street to me!

CORY: You crazy! You know that?

TROY: Go on now! You got the devil in you. Get on away from me!

CORY: You just a crazy old man . . . talking about I got the devil in me.

260 TROY: Yeah, I'm crazy! If you don't get on the other side of that yard . . .
I'm gonna show you how crazy I am! Go on . . . get the hell out of
my yard.

CORY: It ain't your yard. You took Uncle Gabe's money he got from the
army to buy this house and then you put him out.

TROY: *(advances on Cory)* Get your black ass out of my yard!

Troy's advance backs Cory up against the tree. Cory grabs up the bat.

CORY: I ain't going nowhere! Come on . . . put me out! I ain't scared of
you.

TROY: That's my bat!

265 CORY: Come on!

TROY: Put my bat down!

CORY: Come on, put me out.

Cory swings at Troy, who backs across the yard.

What's the matter? You so bad . . . put me out!

Troy advances toward Cory.

CORY: *(backing up)* Come on! Come on!

TROY: You're gonna have to use it! You wanna draw that bat back on
me . . . you're gonna have to use it.

270 CORY: Come on! . . . Come on!

*Cory swings the bat at Troy a second time. He misses. Troy continues to advance
toward him.*

TROY: You're gonna have to kill me! You wanna draw that bat back on me.
You're gonna have to kill me.

*Cory, backed up against the tree, can go no farther. Troy taunts him. He sticks
out his head and offers him a target.*

Come on! Come on!

Cory is unable to swing the bat. Troy grabs it.

TROY: Then I'll show you.

*Cory and Troy struggle over the bat. The struggle is fierce and fully engaged.
Troy ultimately is the stronger and takes the bat away from Cory and stands
over him ready to swing. He stops himself.*

Go on and get away from around my house.

Cory, stung by his defeat, picks himself up, walks slowly out of the yard and up the alley.

CORY: Tell Mama I'll be back for my things.
TROY: They'll be on the other side of that fence.

Cory exits.

275 TROY: I can't taste nothing. Helluljah! I can't taste nothing no more. *(Troy assumes a batting posture and begins to taunt Death, the fastball on the outside corner.)* Come on! It's between you and me now! Come on! Anytime you want! Come on! I be ready for you . . . but I ain't gonna be easy.

The lights go down on the scene.

SCENE 5

The time is 1965. The lights come up in the yard. It is the morning of Troy's funeral. A funeral plaque with a light hangs beside the door. There is a small garden plot off to the side. There is noise and activity in the house as Rose, Gabriel, and Bono have gathered. The door opens and Raynell, seven years old, enters dressed in a flannel nightgown. She crosses to the garden and pokes around with a stick. Rose calls from the house.

ROSE: Raynell!
RAYNELL: Mam?
ROSE: What you doing out there?
RAYNELL: Nothing.

Rose comes to the door.

280 ROSE: Girl, get in here and get dressed. What you doing?
RAYNELL: Seeing if my garden growed.
ROSE: I told you it ain't gonna grow overnight. You got to wait.
RAYNELL: It don't look like it never gonna grow. Dag!
ROSE: I told you a watched pot never boils. Get in here and get dressed.
285 RAYNELL: This ain't even no pot, Mama.
ROSE: You just have to give it a chance. It'll grow. Now you come on and do what I told you. We got to be getting ready. This ain't no morning to be playing around. You hear me?
RAYNELL: Yes, mam.

Rose exits into the house. Raynell continues to poke at her garden with a stick. Cory enters. He is dressed in a Marine corporal's uniform, and carries a duffel bag. His posture is that of a military man, and his speech has a clipped sternness.

CORY: *(to Raynell)* Hi. *(Pause.)* I bet your name is Raynell.
RAYNELL: Uh huh.
290 CORY: Is your mama home?

Raynell runs up on the porch and calls through the screen door.

RAYNELL: Mama . . . there's some man out here. Mama?

Rose comes to the door.

ROSE: Cory? Lord have mercy! Look here, you all!

Rose and Cory embrace in a tearful reunion as Bono and Lyons enter from the house dressed in funeral clothes.

BONO: Aw, looka here . . .
ROSE: Done got all grown up!
295 CORY: Don't cry, Mama. What you crying about?
ROSE: I'm just so glad you made it.
CORY: Hey Lyons. How you doing, Mr. Bono.

Lyons goes to embrace Cory.

LYONS: Look at you, man. Look at you. Don't he look good, Rose. Got
   them Corporal stripes.
ROSE: What took you so long?
300 CORY: You know how the Marines are, Mama. They got to get all their
   paperwork straight before they let you do anything.
ROSE: Well, I'm sure glad you made it. They let Lyons come. Your Uncle
   Gabe's still in the hospital. They don't know if they gonna let him
   out or not. I just talked to them a little while ago.
LYONS: A Corporal in the United States Marines.
BONO: Your daddy knew you had it in you. He used to tell me all the
   time.
LYONS: Don't he look good, Mr. Bono?
305 BONO: Yeah, he remind me of Troy when I first met him. *(Pause.)* Say,
   Rose, Lucille's down at the church with the choir. I'm gonna go down
   and get the pallbearers lined up. I'll be back to get you all.
ROSE: Thanks, Jim.
CORY: See you, Mr. Bono.
LYONS: *(with his arm around Raynell)* Cory . . . look at Raynell. Ain't she
   precious? She gonna break a whole lot of hearts.
ROSE: Raynell, come and say hello to your brother. This is your brother,
   Cory. You remember Cory.
310 RAYNELL: No, Mam.
CORY: She don't remember me, Mama.
ROSE: Well, we talk about you. She heard us talk about you. *(To Raynell.)*
   This is your brother, Cory. Come on and say hello.
RAYNELL: Hi.
CORY: Hi. So you're Raynell. Mama told me a lot about you.
315 ROSE: You all come on into the house and let me fix you some breakfast.
   Keep up your strength.
CORY: I ain't hungry, Mama.
LYONS: You can fix me something, Rose. I'll be in there in a minute.

Rose: Cory, you sure you don't want nothing? I know they ain't feeding you right.

Cory: No, Mama . . . thanks. I don't feel like eating. I'll get something later.

320 Rose: Raynell . . . get on upstairs and get that dress on like I told you.

Rose and Raynell exit into the house.

Lyons: So . . . I hear you thinking about getting married.

Cory: Yeah, I done found the right one, Lyons. It's about time.

Lyons: Me and Bonnie been split up about four years now. About the time Papa retired. I guess she just got tired of all them changes I was putting her through. *(Pause.)* I always knew you was gonna make something out yourself. Your head was always in the right direction. So . . . you gonna stay in . . . make it a career . . . put in your twenty years?

Cory: I don't know. I got six already, I think that's enough.

325 Lyons: Stick with Uncle Sam and retire early. Ain't nothing out here. I guess Rose told you what happened with me. They got me down the workhouse. I thought I was being slick cashing other people's checks.

Cory: How much time you doing?

Lyons: They give me three years. I got that beat now. I ain't got but nine more months. It ain't so bad. You learn to deal with it like anything else. You got to take the crookeds with the straights. That's what Papa used to say. He used to say that when he struck out. I seen him strike out three times in a row . . . and the next time up he hit the ball over the grandstand. Right out there in Homestead Field. He wasn't satisfied hitting in the seats . . . he want to hit it over everything! After the game he had two hundred people standing around waiting to shake his hand. You got to take the crookeds with the straights. Yeah, Papa was something else.

Cory: You still playing?

Lyons: Cory . . . you know I'm gonna do that. There's some fellows down there we got us a band . . . we gonna try and stay together when we get out . . . but yeah, I'm still playing. It still helps me to get out of bed in the morning. As long as it do that I'm gonna be right there playing and trying to make some sense out of it.

330 Rose: *(calling)* Lyons, I got these eggs in the pan.

Lyons: Let me go on and get these eggs, man. Get ready to go bury Papa. *(Pause.)* How you doing? You doing all right?

Cory nods. Lyons touches him on the shoulder and they share a moment of silent grief. Lyons exits into the house. Cory wanders about the yard. Raynell enters.

Raynell: Hi.

Cory: Hi.

RAYNELL: Did you used to sleep in my room?

335 CORY: Yeah . . . that used to be my room.

RAYNELL: That's what Papa call it. "Cory's room." It got your football in the closet.

Rose comes to the door.

ROSE: Raynell, get in there and get them good shoes on.

RAYNELL: Mama, can't I wear these? Them other ones hurt my feet.

ROSE: Well, they just gonna have to hurt your feet for a while. You ain't said they hurt your feet when you went down to the store and got them.

340 RAYNELL: They didn't hurt then. My feet done got bigger.

ROSE: Don't you give me no backtalk now. You get in there and get them shoes on.

Raynell exits into the house.

Ain't too much changed. He still got that piece of rag tied to that tree. He was out here swinging that bat. I was just ready to go back in the house. He swung that bat and then he just fell over. Seem like he swung it and stood there with this grin on his face . . . and then he just fell over. They carried him on down to the hospital, but I knew there wasn't no need . . . why don't you come on in the house?

CORY: Mama . . . I got something to tell you. I don't know how to tell you this . . . but I've got to tell you . . . I'm not going to Papa's funeral.

ROSE: Boy, hush your mouth. That's your daddy you talking about. I don't want hear that kind of talk this morning. I done raised you to come to this? You standing there all healthy and grown talking about you ain't going to your daddy's funeral?

CORY: Mama . . . listen . . .

345 ROSE: I don't want to hear it, Cory. You just get that thought out of your head.

CORY: I can't drag Papa with me everywhere I go. I've got to say no to him. One time in my life I've got to say no.

ROSE: Don't nobody have to listen to nothing like that. I know you and your daddy ain't seen eye to eye, but I ain't got to listen to that kind of talk this morning. Whatever was between you and your daddy . . . the time has come to put it aside. Just take it and set it over there on the shelf and forget about it. Disrespecting your daddy ain't gonna make you a man, Cory. You got to find a way to come to that on your own. Not going to your daddy's funeral ain't gonna make you a man.

CORY: The whole time I was growing up . . . living in his house . . . Papa was like a shadow that followed you everywhere. It weighed on you and sunk into your flesh. It would wrap around you and lay there until you couldn't tell which one was you anymore. That shadow digging in your flesh. Trying to crawl in. Trying to live through you. Everywhere I looked, Troy Maxson was staring back at me . . . hiding under the bed . . . in the closet. I'm just saying I've got to find a way to get rid of that shadow, Mama.

ROSE: You just like him. You got him in you good.

350 CORY: Don't tell me that, Mama.

ROSE: You Troy Maxson all over again.

CORY: I don't want to be Troy Maxson. I want to be me.

ROSE: You can't be nobody but who you are, Cory. That shadow wasn't nothing but you growing into yourself. You either got to grow into it or cut it down to fit you. But that's all you got to make life with. That's all you got to measure yourself against that world out there. Your daddy wanted you to be everything he wasn't . . . and at the same time he tried to make you into everything he was. I don't know if he was right or wrong . . . but I do know he meant to do more good than he meant to do harm. He wasn't always right. Sometimes when he touched he bruised. And sometimes when he took me in his arms he cut.

When I first met your daddy I thought . . . Here is a man I can lay down with and make a baby. That's the first thing I thought when I seen him. I was thirty years old and had done seen my share of men. But when he walked up to me and said, "I can dance a waltz that'll make you dizzy." I thought, Rose Lee, here is a man that you can open yourself up to and be filled to bursting. Here is a man that can fill all them empty spaces you been tipping around the edges of. One of them empty spaces was being somebody's mother.

I married your daddy and settled down to cooking his supper and keeping clean sheets on the bed. When your daddy walked through the house he was so big he filled it up. That was my first mistake. Not to make him leave some room for me. For my part in the matter. But at that time I wanted that. I wanted a house that I could sing in. And that's what your daddy gave me. I didn't know to keep up his strength I had to give up little pieces of mine. I did that. I took on his life as mine and mixed up the pieces so that you couldn't hardly tell which was which anymore. It was my choice. It was my life and I didn't have to live it like that. But that's what life offered me in the way of being a woman and I took it. I grabbed hold of it with both hands.

By the time Raynell came into the house, me and your daddy had done lost touch with one another. I didn't want to make my blessing off of nobody's misfortune . . . but I took on to Raynell like she was all them babies I had wanted and never had.

The phone rings.

Like I'd been blessed to relive a part of my life. And if the Lord see fit to keep up my strength . . . I'm gonna do her just like your daddy did you . . . I'm gonna give her the best of what's in me.

RAYNELL: *(entering, still with her old shoes)* Mama . . . Reverend Tollivier on the phone.

Rose exits into the house.

355 RAYNELL: Hi.
CORY: Hi.
RAYNELL: You in the Army or the Marines?
CORY: Marines.
RAYNELL: Papa said it was the Army. Did you know Blue?
360 CORY: Blue? Who's Blue?
RAYNELL: Papa's dog what he sing about all the time.
CORY: *(singing)*

> Hear it ring! Hear it ring!
> I had a dog his name was Blue
> You know Blue was mighty true
> You know Blue was a good old dog
> Blue treed a possum in a hollow log
> You know from that he was a good old dog.
> Hear it ring! Hear it ring!

Raynell joins in singing.

CORY and RAYNELL:

> Blue treed a possum out on a limb
> Blue looked at me and I looked at him
> Grabbed that possum and put him in a sack
> Blue stayed there till I came back
> Old Blue's feets was big and round
> Never allowed a possum to touch the ground.
>
> Old Blue died and I dug his grave
> I dug his grave with a silver spade
> Let him down with a golden chain
> And every night I call his name
> Go on Blue, you good dog you
> Go on Blue, you good dog you

RAYNELL:

> Blue laid down and died like a man
> Blue laid down and died . . .

365 BOTH:

> Blue laid down and died like a man
> Now he's treeing possums in the Promised Land
> I'm gonna tell you this to let you know
> Blue's gone where the good dogs go
> When I hear old Blue bark
> When I hear old Blue bark

Blue treed a possum in Noah's Ark[16]
Blue treed a possum in Noah's Ark.

Rose comes to the screen door.

Rose: Cory, we gonna be ready to go in a minute.
Cory: *(to Raynell)* You go on in the house and change them shoes like Mama told you so we can go to Papa's funeral.
Raynell: Okay, I'll be back.

Raynell exits into the house. Cory gets up and crosses over to the tree. Rose stands in the screen door watching him. Gabriel enters from the alley.

Gabriel: *(calling)* Hey, Rose!
370 **Rose:** Gabe?
Gabriel: I'm here, Rose. Hey Rose, I'm here!

Rose enters from the house.

Rose: Lord . . . Look here, Lyons!
Lyons: See, I told you, Rose . . . I told you they'd let him come.
Cory: How you doing, Uncle Gabe?
375 **Lyons:** How you doing, Uncle Gabe?
Gabriel: Hey, Rose. It's time. It's time to tell St. Peter to open the gates. Troy, you ready? You ready, Troy. I'm gonna tell St. Peter to open the gates. You get ready now.

Gabriel, with great fanfare, braces himself to blow. The trumpet is without a mouthpiece. He puts the end of it into his mouth and blows with great force, like a man who has been waiting some twenty-odd years for this single moment. No sound comes out of the trumpet. He braces himself and blows again with the same result. A third time he blows. There is a weight of impossible description that falls away and leaves him bare and exposed to a frightful realization. It is a trauma that a sane and normal mind would be unable to withstand. He begins to dance. A slow, strange dance, eerie and life-giving. A dance of atavistic signature and ritual. Lyons attempts to embrace him. Gabriel pushes Lyons away. He begins to howl in what is an attempt at song, or perhaps a song turning back into itself in an attempt at speech. He finishes his dance and the gates of heaven stand open as wide as God's closet.

That's the way that go!

Reading and Reacting

1. Obviously, fences are a central metaphor of the play. To what different kinds of fences does the play's title refer?

---

[16] See Genesis 6: 14–20.

2. In what ways are the fathers and sons in the play alike? In what ways are they different? Does the play imply that sons must inevitably follow in their fathers' footsteps?

3. What purpose does the section of the stage directions entitled "The Play" serve? How does it prepare readers for the events to follow?

4. What is the significance of the fact that the play is set in 1957? Given the racial climate of the country at that time, how realistic are Cory's ambitions? How reasonable are his father's criticisms?

5. In what ways has Troy's character been shaped by his contact with the white world?

6. Is Troy a tragic hero? If so, what is his flaw?

7. Which of the play's characters, if any, do you consider to be stereotypes? What comment do you think the play makes about stereotypes?

8. In what ways does the conflict between Troy and his son reflect conflicts within the African-American community? Does the play suggest any possibilities for compromise?

9. Which characters do you like? Which do you dislike? Why?

10. Do you consider this play to be optimistic or pessimistic? Why?

11. **JOURNAL ENTRY** How would the play be different if all the characters in the play were white? What would be the same?

12. **CRITICAL PERSPECTIVE** Robert Brustein, theater critic and artistic director of Harvard's American Repertory Theater, has criticized Wilson on the ground that "his recurrent theme is the familiar American charge of victimization"; in *Fences,* he argues, "Wilson's larger purpose depends on his conviction that Troy's potential was stunted not [by] 'his own behavior' but by centuries of racist oppression."

    Do you agree with Brustein's characterization of Wilson's theme? Or do you think there is another theme that Brustein misses?

Related Works: "Big Black Good Man" (p. 207), "Ex-Basketball Player" (p. 813), "Yet Do I Marvel" (p. 913), "The *Chicago Defender* Sends a Man to Little Rock" (p. 933) *Death of a Salesman* (p. 1410)

◆ WRITING SUGGESTIONS: THEME

1. Both *Antigone* and *Another Antigone* deal with the theme of obedience to authority: Antigone is executed for defying Creon's orders, and Judy is punished for refusing to rewrite a term paper for a course. Write an essay in which you discuss whether or not Antigone and Judy should have compromised their principles. Be specific and use examples from the two plays to support your points.

2. In an interview, John Tillinger, who directed *Another Antigone,* said that Gurney "worried that some theatergoers might . . . see the heroine as simply a stereotype of an aggressive young Jewish-American woman." Write an essay in which you discuss whether or not Gurney's concerns are justified.

3. Write an essay in which you analyze the function of baseball images in *Fences*. How do the references to baseball help develop the play's themes?

4. One of the themes of *Fences* is the dream a family has for its children. Compare the development of this theme in *Fences* and in another play in this book—for example, *The Cuban Swimmer* (p. 1495) or *The Glass Menagerie* (p. 1805).

5. At one point in *'night, Mother* Jessie says that her killing herself is not a lack of courage but a matter of personal choice. Do you agree? Does Jessie's act show personal courage or cowardice?

6. Write an essay in which you compare the relationship between the father and daughter in *Tender Offer* to the relationship between fathers and daughters in two or three other works in this anthology—"Doe Season" (p. 349), "My Father's Wars" (p. 681), or "Daddy" (p. 818), for example.

7. **Web Activity** The following Web site contains information about August Wilson:

http://www.humboldt.edu/~ah/wilson/reviews/index.html

From the Web page, link to the review "Theater: Family Ties In Wilson's 'Fences'," by Frank Rich. In it, the author states:

> The struggle between father and son over conflicting visions of black identity, aspirations and values is the play's narrative fulcrum, and a paradigm of violent divisions that would later tear apart a society. As written, the conflict is also a didactic one, reminiscent of old-fashioned plays, black and white, about disputes between first-generation American parents and their rebellious children.

Write an essay exploring the struggle between father and son in *Fences*, concentrating on how the struggle is fueled by "visions of black identity" and the conflict between all "first-generation American parents and their rebellious children."

Drama Casebook

This section contains the play *The Glass Menagerie* by Tennessee Williams, a collection of source materials,* questions to stimulate discussion and writing, and a student paper.

SOURCE MATERIALS

❖ ❖ ❖

---

* Note that the Scanlan article does not use the parenthetical documentation style recommended by the most recent guidelines set by the Modern Language Association and explained in Appendix A of this text.

Each of these sources offers insights into *The Glass Menagerie* that
can help you to understand, enjoy, and perhaps write about it. Other
kinds of sources can also enrich your understanding of Williams's
accomplishments—for example, other plays by Williams, biographical
data about the author, or works of imaginative literature by other
writers dealing with similar themes. In addition, the following Web
sites devoted to Williams can offer insights into his work: <http://
www.olemiss.edu/depts/english/ms-writers/dir/williams_tennessee/>;
<http://www.csustan.edu/english/reuben/pal/chap8/williams.html>;
<http://www.cc.columbia.edu/cu/record/record2026.14.html>; <http://
hipp.gator.net/glass_menagerie_perspectives_dramaturg.html>.

In preparation for writing an essay on a topic of your choice about *The
Glass Menagerie,* read the play and the accompanying source materials.
After doing so, explore—in your journal, in group discussions, or in brainstorming notes—the possibilities suggested by the Reading and Reacting
questions on pages 1890–91. Keep in mind the ideas expressed in the critical articles, memoirs, short story, and interviews as well as those in the
play itself. Your goal is to decide on a topic you can develop in a three- to
six-page essay. Remember to document any words or ideas that you borrow
from the play or from any other source. See the Appendix for information
about documentation style. For guidelines on evaluating literary criticism,
see page 15; for guidelines on using source materials, see page 34.

A student paper, "Laura's Gentleman Caller," based on the source materials in this Casebook, begins on page 1893.

◆ **TENNESSEE WILLIAMS** (1911–1983) was born in Columbus, Mississippi, but moved to St. Louis, the setting of *The Glass Menagerie*, when he was eight. He became interested in playwriting while at college, eventually graduating from the University of Iowa in 1938. Christened Thomas Lanier Williams, he began to publish under the name Tennessee in 1939. His plays include *A Streetcar Named Desire* (1947), *Cat on a Hot Tin Roof* (1955), *Night of the Iguana* (1961), and *Sweet Bird of Youth* (1959). An early play, *Not about Nightingales*, was recently discovered; it was staged in New York in 1999.

The Glass Menagerie (1945) was his first major success, winning the New York Drama Critics Circle Award and freeing him to write plays fulltime. *The Glass Menagerie* was written partly at Provincetown, Massachusetts, the site of Susan Glaspell's theater company, and partly at Hollywood while Williams was working as a screenwriter. Williams saw the play as somewhat autobiographical: he said his sister Rose had a collection of glass animals in her room in St. Louis, and he gives his real first name to Tom, Laura's brother in the play. When the first movie version of the play was made, it was altered to include a second, more promising Gentleman Caller at its conclusion, giving it a happy ending; to the end of his life, Williams strongly disliked the change.

◆　◆　◆

TENNESSEE WILLIAMS

The Glass Menagerie
(1945)

Nobody, not even the rain, has such small hands.
E. E. Cummings

CHARACTERS

AMANDA WINGFIELD, *the mother. A little woman of great but confused vitality clinging frantically to another time and place. Her characterization must be carefully created, not copied from type. She is not paranoiac, but her life is paranoia. There is much to admire in Amanda, and as much to love and pity as there is to laugh at. Certainly she has endurance and a kind of heroism, and though her foolishness makes her unwittingly cruel at times, there is tenderness in her slight person.*

Laura Wingfield, *her daughter. Amanda, having failed to establish contact with reality, continues to live vitally in her illusions, but Laura's situation is even graver. A childhood illness has left her crippled, one leg slightly shorter than the other, and held in a brace. This defect need not be more than suggested on the stage. Stemming from this, Laura's separation increases till she is like a piece of her own glass collection, too exquisitely fragile to move from the shelf.*

Tom Wingfield, *her son. And the narrator of the play. A poet with a job in a warehouse. His nature is not remorseless, but to escape from a trap he has to act without pity.*

Jim O'Connor, *the gentleman caller. A nice, ordinary, young man.*

Scene
An alley in St. Louis.

Part I
Preparation for a Gentleman Caller.

Part II
The Gentleman Calls.

Time
Now and the Past.

Scene 1

The Wingfield apartment is in the rear of the building, one of those vast hive-like conglomerations of cellular living-units that flower as warty growths in overcrowded urban centers of lower middle-class population and are sympto-matic of the impulse of this largest and fundamentally enslaved section of American society to avoid fluidity and differentiation and to exist and function as one interfused mass of automatism.

The apartment faces an alley and is entered by a fire-escape, a structure whose name is a touch of accidental poetic truth, for all of these huge buildings are always burning with the slow and implacable fires of human desperation. The fire-escape is included in the set—that is, the landing of it and steps descending from it.

The scene is memory and is therefore nonrealistic. Memory takes a lot of poetic license. It omits some details; others are exaggerated, according to the emotional value of the articles it touches, for memory is seated predominantly in the heart. The interior is therefore rather dim and poetic.

At the rise of the curtain, the audience is faced with the dark, grim rear wall of the Wingfield tenement. This building, which runs parallel to the footlights, is flanked on both sides by dark, narrow alleys which run into murky canyons of tangled clotheslines, garbage cans and the sinister latticework of neighboring fire-escapes. It is up and down these side alleys that exterior entrances and exits are made, during the play. At the end of Tom's opening commentary, the dark tenement wall slowly reveals (by means of a transparency) the interior of the ground floor Wingfield apartment.

Downstage is the living room, which also serves as a sleeping room for Laura, the sofa unfolding to make her bed. Upstage, center, and divided by a wide arch or second proscenium with transparent faded portieres (or second curtain), is the dining room. In an old-fashioned what-not in the living room are seen scores of transparent glass animals. A blown-up photograph of the father hangs on the wall of the living room, facing the audience, to the left of the arch-way. It is the face of a very handsome young man in a doughboy's First World War cap. He is gallantly smiling, ineluctably smiling, as if to say, "I will be smiling forever."

The audience hears and sees the opening scene in the dining room through both the transparent fourth wall of the building and the transparent gauze portieres of the dining-room arch. It is during this revealing scene that the fourth wall slowly ascends, out of sight. This transparent exterior wall is not brought down again until the very end of the play, during Tom's final speech.

The narrator is an undisguised convention of the play. He takes whatever license with dramatic convention as is convenient to his purposes.

Tom enters dressed as a merchant sailor from the alley, stage left, and strolls across the front of the stage to the fire-escape. There he stops and lights a cigarette. He addresses the audience.

TOM: Yes, I have tricks in my pocket, I have things up my sleeve. But I am the opposite of a stage magician. He gives you illusion that has the appearance of truth. I give you truth in the pleasant disguise of illusion. To begin with, I turn back time. I reverse it to that quaint period, the thirties, when the huge middle class of America was matriculating in a school for the blind. Their eyes had failed them, or they had failed their eyes, and so they were having their fingers pressed forcibly down on the fiery Braille alphabet of a dissolving economy. In Spain there was revolution.[1] Here there was only shouting and confusion. In Spain there was Guernica.[2] Here there were disturbances of labor, sometimes pretty violent, in otherwise peaceful cities such as Chicago, Cleveland, Saint Louis. . . . This is the social background of the play.

(Music.)

The play is memory. Being a memory play, it is dimly lighted, it is sentimental, it is not realistic. In memory everything seems to happen to music. That explains the fiddle in the wings. I am the narrator of the play, and also a character in it. The other characters are my mother, Amanda, my sister, Laura, and a gentleman caller who appears in the final scenes. He is the most realistic character in the play, being an emissary from a

---

[1] The Spanish Civil War (1936–1939).

[2] A Basque town in northern Spain, bombed and virtually destroyed on April 27, 1937 by German planes aiding fascist General Francisco Franco's Nationalists. The destruction is depicted in one of Pablo Picasso's most famous paintings, *Guernica* (1937).

world of reality that we were somehow set apart from. But since I have a
poet's weakness for symbols, I am using this character also as a symbol; he
is the long delayed but always expected something that we live for. There
is a fifth character in the play who doesn't appear except in this larger-
than-life photograph over the mantel. This is our father who left us a long
time ago. He was a telephone man who fell in love with long distances; he
gave up his job with the telephone company and skipped the light
fantastic out of town . . . The last we heard of him was a picture post-card
from Mazatlan, on the Pacific coast of Mexico, containing a message of
two words—"Hello—Good-bye!" and an address. I think the rest of the
play will explain itself. . . .

Amanda's voice becomes audible through the portieres.

(Legend On Screen: "Où Sont Les Neiges.")[3]

He divides the portieres and enters the upstage area.
   *Amanda and Laura are seated at a drop-leaf table. Eating is indicated by
gestures without food or utensils. Amanda faces the audience. Tom and Laura
are seated in profile.*
   *The interior has lit up softly and through the scrim we see Amanda and
Laura seated at the table in the upstage area.*

AMANDA: *(calling)* Tom?
TOM: Yes, Mother.
AMANDA: We can't say grace until you come to the table!
5 **TOM:** Coming, Mother. *(He bows slightly and withdraws, reappearing a few
   moments later in his place at the table.)*
AMANDA: *(to her son)* Honey, don't *push* with your *fingers.* If you have to push
   with something, the thing to push with is a crust of bread. And chew—
   chew! Animals have sections in their stomachs which enable them to
   digest food without mastication, but human beings are supposed to chew
   their food before they swallow it down. Eat food leisurely, son, and really
   enjoy it. A well-cooked meal has lots of delicate flavors that have to be
   held in the mouth for appreciation. So chew your food and give your
   salivary glands a chance to function!

*Tom deliberately lays his imaginary fork down and pushes his chair back from
the table.*

TOM: I haven't enjoyed one bite of this dinner because of your constant
   directions on how to eat it. It's you that makes me rush through meals with
   your hawk-like attention to every bite I take. Sickening—spoils my
   appetite—all this discussion of animals' secretion—salivary glands—
   mastication!

---
[3] "Where are the snows [of yesteryear]." A famous line by French poet François Villon (1431–1463?).

AMANDA: *(lightly)* Temperament like a Metropolitan star! *(He rises and crosses downstage.)* You're not excused from the table.

TOM: I am getting a cigarette.

10 AMANDA: You smoke too much.

Laura rises.

LAURA: I'll bring in the blanc mange.

He remains standing with his cigarette by the portieres during the following.

AMANDA: *(rising)* No, sister, no, sister—you be the lady this time and I'll be the darky.

LAURA: I'm already up.

AMANDA: Resume your seat, little sister—I want you to stay fresh and pretty—for gentlemen callers!

15 LAURA: I'm not expecting any gentlemen callers.

AMANDA: *(crossing out to kitchenette. Airily)* Sometimes they come when they are least expected! Why, I remember one Sunday afternoon in Blue Mountain—*(Enters kitchenette.)*

TOM: I know what's coming!

LAURA: Yes. But let her tell it.

TOM: Again?

20 LAURA: She loves to tell it.

Amanda returns with bowl of dessert.

AMANDA: One Sunday afternoon in Blue Mountain—your mother received—seventeen!—gentlemen callers! Why, sometimes there weren't chairs enough to accommodate them all. We had to send the nigger over to bring in folding chairs from the parish house.

TOM: *(remaining at portieres)* How did you entertain those gentlemen callers?

AMANDA: I understood the art of conversation!

TOM: I bet you could talk.

25 AMANDA: Girls in those days *knew* how to talk, I can tell you.

TOM: Yes?

(Image: Amanda As A Girl On A Porch Greeting Callers.)

AMANDA: They knew how to entertain their gentlemen callers. It wasn't enough for a girl to be possessed of a pretty face and a graceful figure—although I wasn't slighted in either respect. She also needed to have a nimble wit and a tongue to meet all occasions.

TOM: What did you talk about?

AMANDA: Things of importance going on in the world! Never anything coarse or common or vulgar. *(She addresses Tom as though he were seated in the vacant chair at the table though he remains by portieres. He plays this scene as though he held the book.)* My callers were gentlemen—all! Among my callers were some of the most prominent young planters of the Mississippi Delta—planters and sons of planters!

Tom motions for music and a spot of light on Amanda. Her eyes lift, her face glows, her voice becomes rich and elegiac.

(Screen Legend: "Où Sont Les Neiges.")

> There was young Champ Laughlin who later became vice-president of the Delta Planters Bank. Hadley Stevenson who was drowned in Moon Lake and left his widow one hundred and fifty thousand in Government bonds. There were the Cutrere brothers, Wesley and Bates. Bates was one of my bright particular beaux! He got in a quarrel with that wild Wainright boy. They shot it out on the floor of Moon Lake Casino. Bates was shot through the stomach. Died in the ambulance on his way to Memphis. His widow was also well-provided for, came into eight or ten thousand acres, that's all. She married him on the rebound—never loved her—carried my picture on him the night he died! And there was that boy that every girl in the Delta had set her cap for! That beautiful, brilliant young Fitzhugh boy from Green County!

30 **Tom:** What did he leave his widow?

Amanda: He never married! Gracious, you talk as though all of my old admirers had turned up their toes to the daisies!

Tom: Isn't this the first you mentioned that still survives?

Amanda: That Fitzhugh boy went North and made a fortune—came to be known as the Wolf of Wall Street! He had the Midas touch, whatever he touched turned to gold! And I could have been Mrs. Duncan J. Fitzhugh, mind you! But—I picked your *father!*

Laura: *(rising)* Mother, let me clear the table.

35 **Amanda:** No dear, you go in front and study your typewriter chart. Or practice your shorthand a little. Stay fresh and pretty!—It's almost time for our gentlemen callers to start arriving. *(She flounces girlishly toward the kitchenette.)* How many do you suppose we're going to entertain this afternoon?

Tom throws down the paper and jumps up with a groan.

Laura: *(alone in the dining room)* I don't believe we're going to receive any, Mother.

Amanda: *(reappearing, airily)* What? No one—not one? You must be joking! *(Laura nervously echoes her laugh. She slips in a fugitive manner through the half-open portieres and draws them gently behind her. A shaft of very clear light is thrown on her face against the faded tapestry of the curtains.) (Music: "The Glass Menagerie" under faintly.) (Lightly.)* Not one gentleman caller? It can't be true! There must be a flood, there must have been a tornado!

Laura: It isn't a flood, it's not a tornado, Mother. I'm just not popular like you were in Blue Mountain. . . . *(Tom utters another groan. Laura glances at him with a faint, apologetic smile. Her voice catching a little.)* Mother's afraid I'm going to be an old maid.

(The Scene Dims Out With "Glass Menagerie" Music.)

SCENE 2

"Laura, Haven't You Ever Liked Some Boy?"

On the dark stage the screen is lighted with the image of blue roses.
Gradually Laura's figure becomes apparent and the screen goes out.
The music subsides.
Laura is seated in the delicate ivory chair at the small clawfoot table.
She wears a dress of soft violet material for a kimono—her hair tied back
from her forehead with a ribbon.
She is washing and polishing her collection of glass.
Amanda appears on the fire-escape steps. At the sound of her ascent, Laura
catches her breath, thrusts the bowl of ornaments away and seats herself stiffly
before the diagram of the typewriter keyboard as though it held her spellbound.
Something has happened to Amanda. It is written in her face as she climbs to
the landing: a look that is grim and hopeless and a little absurd.
She has on one of those cheap or imitation velvety-looking cloth coats with
imitation fur collar. Her hat is five or six years old, one of those dreadful cloche
hats that were worn in the late twenties, and she is clasping an enormous black
patent-leather pocketbook with nickel clasp and initials. This is her fulldress out-
fit, the one she usually wears to the D.A.R.[4]
Before entering she looks through the door.
She purses her lips, opens her eyes wide, rolls them upward and shakes her
head.
Then she slowly lets herself in the door. Seeing her mother's expression
Laura touches her lips with a nervous gesture.

LAURA: Hello, Mother, I was—*(She makes a nervous gesture toward the chart*
  on the wall. Amanda leans against the shut door and stares at Laura with a
  martyred look.)

AMANDA: Deception? Deception? *(She slowly removes her hat and gloves,*
  continuing the swift suffering stare. She lets the hat and gloves fall on the
  floor—a bit of acting.)

LAURA: *(shakily)* How was the D.A.R. meeting? *(Amanda slowly opens her*
  purse and removes a dainty white handkerchief which she shakes out
  delicately and delicately touches to her lips and nostrils.) Didn't you go to
  the D.A.R. meeting, Mother?

AMANDA: *(faintly, almost inaudibly)*—No.—No. *(Then more forcibly.)* I did not
  have the strength—to go the D.A.R. In fact, I did not have the courage! I
  wanted to find a hole in the ground and hide myself in it forever! *(She*
  crosses slowly to the wall and removes the diagram of the typewriter
  keyboard. She holds it in front of her for a second, staring at it sweetly and
  sorrowfully—then bites her lips and tears it in two pieces.)

5 **LAURA:** *(faintly)* Why did you do that, Mother? *(Amanda repeats the same*
  procedure with the chart of the Gregg Alphabet.) Why are you—

---

[4] The Daughters of the American Revolution, an organization for female descendants of
participants in the American Revolution, founded in 1890. That Amanda is a member
says much about her concern with the past, as well as about her pride and affectations.

Amanda: Why? Why? How old are you, Laura?

Laura: Mother, you know my age.

Amanda: I thought that you were an adult; it seems that I was mistaken. *(She crosses slowly to the sofa and sinks down and stares at Laura.)*

Laura: Please don't stare at me, Mother.

Amanda closes her eyes and lowers her head. Count ten.

10 **Amanda:** What are we going to do, what is going to become of us, what is the future?

Count ten.

Laura: Has something happened, Mother? *(Amanda draws a long breath and takes out the handkerchief again. Dabbing process.)* Mother, has— something happened?

Amanda: I'll be all right in a minute. I'm just bewildered—*(count five)*—by life. . . .

Laura: Mother, I wish that you would tell me what's happened.

Amanda: As you know, I was supposed to be inducted into my office at the D.A.R. this afternoon. *(Image: A Swarm Of Typewriters.)* But I stopped off at Rubicam's Business College to speak to your teachers about your having a cold and ask them what progress they thought you were making down there.

15 **Laura:** Oh. . . .

Amanda: I went to the typing instructor and introduced myself as your mother. She didn't know who you were. Wingfield, she said. We don't have any such student enrolled at the school! I assured her she did, that you had been going to classes since early in January. "I wonder," she said, "if you could be talking about that terribly shy little girl who dropped out of school after only a few days' attendance?" "No," I said, "Laura, my daughter, has been going to school every day for the past six weeks!" "Excuse me," she said. She took the attendance book out and there was your name, unmistakably printed, and all the dates you were absent until they decided that you had dropped out of school. I still said, "No, there must have been some mistake! There must have been some mix-up in the records!" And she said, "No—I remember her perfectly now. Her hand shook so that she couldn't hit the right keys! The first time we gave a speed-test, she broke down completely—was sick at the stomach and almost had to be carried into the wash-room! After that morning she never showed up any more. We phoned the house but never got any answer"—while I was working at Famous and Barr, I suppose, demonstrating those—Oh! I felt so weak I could barely keep on my feet. I had to sit down while they got me a glass of water! Fifty dollars' tuition, all of our plans—my hopes and ambitions for you—just gone up the spout, just gone up the spout like that. *(Laura draws a long breath and gets awkwardly to her feet. She crosses to the Victrola and winds it up.)* What are you doing?

Laura: Oh! *(She releases the handle and returns to her seat.)*
Amanda: Laura, where have you been going when you've gone out pretending that you were going to business college?
Laura: I've just been going out walking.
20 **Amanda:** That's not true.
Laura: It is. I just went walking.
Amanda: Walking? Walking? In winter? Deliberately courting pneumonia in that light coat? Where did you walk to, Laura?
Laura: It was the lesser of two evils, Mother. *(Image: Winter Scene In Park.)* I couldn't go back up. I—threw up—on the floor!
Amanda: From half past seven till after five every day you mean to tell me you walked around in the park, because you wanted to make me think that you were still going to Rubicam's Business College?
25 **Laura:** It wasn't as bad as it sounds. I went inside places to get warmed up.
Amanda: Inside where?
Laura: I went in the art museum and the bird-houses at the Zoo. I visited the penguins every day! Sometimes I did without lunch and went to the movies. Lately I've been spending most of my afternoons in the Jewel-box, that big glass house where they raise the tropical flowers.
Amanda: You did all this to deceive me, just for the deception? *(Laura looks down.)* Why?
Laura: Mother, when you're disappointed, you get that awful suffering look on your face, like the picture of Jesus' mother in the museum!
30 **Amanda:** Hush!
Laura: I couldn't face it.

Pause. A whisper of strings.

(Legend: "The Crust Of Humility.")

Amanda: *(hopelessly fingering the huge pocketbook)* So what are we going to do the rest of our lives? Stay home and watch the parades go by? Amuse ourselves with the glass menagerie, darling? Eternally play those worn-out phonograph records your father left as a painful reminder of him? We won't have a business career—we've given that up because it gave us nervous indigestion! *(Laughs wearily.)* What is there left but dependency all our lives? I know so well what becomes of unmarried women who aren't prepared to occupy a position. I've seen such pitiful cases in the South—barely tolerated spinsters living upon the grudging patronage of sister's husband or brother's wife!—stuck away in some little mouse-trap of a room—encouraged by one in-law to visit another—little birdlike women without any nest—eating the crust of humility all their life! Is that the future that we've mapped out for ourselves? I swear it's the only alternative I can think of! It isn't a very pleasant alternative, is it? Of course—some girls *do marry. (Laura twists her hands nervously.)* Haven't you ever liked some boy?
Laura: Yes I liked one once. *(Rises.)* I came across his picture a while ago.

AMANDA: *(with some interest)* He gave you his picture?

35 **LAURA:** No, it's in the year-book.

AMANDA: *(disappointed)* Oh—a high-school boy.

(Screen Image: Jim As A High-School Hero Bearing A Silver Cup.)

LAURA: Yes. His name was Jim. *(Laura lifts the heavy annual from the clawfoot table.)* Here he is in *The Pirates of Penzance*.[5]

AMANDA: *(absently)* The what?

LAURA: The operetta the senior class put on. He had a wonderful voice and we sat across the aisle from each other Mondays, Wednesdays and Fridays in the Aud. Here he is with the silver cup for debating! See his grin?

40 **AMANDA:** *(absently)* He must have had a jolly disposition.

LAURA: He used to call me—Blue Roses.

(Image: Blue Roses.)

AMANDA: Why did he call you such a name as that?

LAURA: When I had that attack of pleurosis—he asked me what was the matter when I came back. I said pleurosis—he thought that I said Blue Roses! So that's what he always called me after that. Whenever he saw me, he'd holler, "Hello, Blue Roses!" I didn't care for the girl that he went out with. Emily Meisenbach. Emily was the best-dressed girl at Soldan. She never struck me, though, as being sincere ... It says in the Personal Section— they're engaged. That's—six years ago! They must be married by now.

AMANDA: Girls that aren't cut out for business careers usually wind up married to some nice man. *(Gets up with a spark of revival.)* Sister, that's what you'll do!

Laura utters a startled, doubtful laugh. She reaches quickly for a piece of glass.

45 **LAURA:** But, Mother—

AMANDA: Yes? *(Crossing to photograph.)*

LAURA: *(in a tone of frightened apology)* I'm—crippled!

(Image: Screen.)

AMANDA: Nonsense! Laura, I've told you never, never to use that word. Why, you're not crippled, you just have a little defect—hardly noticeable, even! When people have some slight disadvantage like that, they cultivate other things to make up for it—develop charm—and vivacity—and—*charm!* That's all you have to do! *(She turns again to the photograph.)* One thing your father had *plenty* of—was *charm!*

Tom motions to the fiddle in the wings.

(The Scene Fades Out With Music.)

---

[5] A musical by Gilbert and Sullivan.

SCENE 3

(Legend On The Screen: "After The Fiasco—")

Tom speaks from the fire-escape landing.

TOM: After the fiasco at Rubicam's Business College, the idea of getting a gentleman caller for Laura began to play a more important part in Mother's calculations. It became an obsession. Like some archetype of the universal unconscious, the image of the gentleman caller haunted our small apartment. . . . *(Image: Young Man At Door With Flowers.)* An evening at home rarely passed without some allusion to this image, this spectre, this hope. . . . Even when he wasn't mentioned, his presence hung in Mother's preoccupied look and in my sister's frightened, apologetic manner—hung like a sentence passed upon the Wingfields! Mother was a woman of action as well as words. She began to take logical steps in the planned direction. Late that winter and in the early spring—realizing that extra money would be needed to properly feather the nest and plume the bird—she conducted a vigorous campaign on the telephone, roping in subscribers to one of those magazines for matrons called *The Home-maker's Companion,* the type of journal that features the serialized sublimations of ladies of letters who think in terms of delicate cup-like breasts, slim, tapering waists, rich, creamy thighs, eyes like wood-smoke in autumn, fingers that soothe and caress like strains of music, bodies as powerful as Etruscan sculpture.

(Screen Image: A Glamour Magazine Cover.)

Amanda enters with phone on long extension cord. She is spotted in the dim stage.

AMANDA: Ida Scott? This is Amanda Wingfield! We *missed* you at the D.A.R. last Monday! I said to myself: She's probably suffering with that sinus condition! How is that sinus condition? Horrors! Heaven have mercy!—You're a Christian martyr, yes, that's what you are, a Christian martyr! Well, I just now happened to notice that your subscription to the *Companion's* about to expire! Yes, it expires with the next issue, honey!—just when that wonderful new serial by Bessie Mae Hopper is getting off to such an exciting start. Oh, honey, it's something that you can't miss! You remember how *Gone With the Wind* took everybody by storm? You simply couldn't go out if you hadn't read it. All everybody *talked* was Scarlett O'Hara. Well, this is a book that critics already compare to *Gone With the Wind.* It's the *Gone With the Wind* of the post-World War generation!—What?—Burning?—Oh, honey, don't let them burn, go take a look in the oven and I'll hold the wire! Heavens—I think she's hung up!

(Dim Out.)

(Legend On Screen: "You Think I'm In Love With Continental Shoemakers?")

Before the stage is lighted, the violent voices of Tom and Amanda are heard. They are quarreling behind the portieres. In front of them stands Laura with clenched hands and panicky expression.

A clear pool of light on her figure throughout this scene.

TOM: What in Christ's name am I—
AMANDA: *(shrilly)* Don't you use that—
5 **TOM:** Supposed to do!
AMANDA: Expression! Not in my—
TOM: Ohhh!
AMANDA: Presence! Have you gone out of your senses?
TOM: I have, that's true, *driven* out!
10 **AMANDA:** What is the matter with you, you—big—big—IDIOT!
TOM: Look—I've got *no thing,* no single thing—
AMANDA: Lower your voice!
TOM: In my life here that I can call my OWN! Everything is—
AMANDA: Stop that shouting!
15 **TOM:** Yesterday you confiscated my books! You had the nerve to—
AMANDA: I took that horrible novel back to the library—yes! That hideous book by that insane Mr. Lawrence. *(Tom laughs wildly.)* I cannot control the output of diseased minds or people who cater to them—*(Tom laughs still more wildly.)* BUT I WON'T ALLOW SUCH FILTH BROUGHT INTO MY HOUSE! No, no, no, no, no!
TOM: House, house! Who pays rent on it, who makes a slave of himself to—
AMANDA: *(fairly screeching)* Don't you DARE to—
TOM: No, no, *I* mustn't say things! *I've* got to just—
20 **AMANDA:** Let me tell you—
TOM: I don't want to hear any more! *(He tears the portieres open. The upstage area is lit with a turgid smoky red glow.)*

Amanda's hair is in metal curlers and she wears a very old bathrobe, much too large for her slight figure, a relic of the faithless Mr. Wingfield.

An upright typewriter and a wild disarray of manuscripts are on the drop-leaf table. The quarrel was probably precipitated by Amanda's interruption of his creative labor. A chair lying overthrown on the floor.

Their gesticulating shadows are cast on the ceiling by the fiery glow.

AMANDA: You *will* hear more, you—
TOM: No, I won't hear more, I'm going out!
AMANDA: You come right back in—
25 **TOM:** Out, out out! Because I'm—
AMANDA: Come back here, Tom Wingfield! I'm not through talking to you!
TOM: Oh, go—
LAURA: *(desperately)* Tom!
AMANDA: You're going to listen, and no more insolence from you! I'm at the end of my patience! *(He comes back toward her.)*

30 **Tom:** What do you think I'm at? Aren't I supposed to have any patience to reach the end of, Mother? I know, I know. It seems unimportant to you, what I'm *doing*—what I *want* to do—having a little *difference* between them! You don't think that—

Amanda: I think you've been doing things that you're ashamed of. That's why you act like this. I don't believe that you go every night to the movies. Nobody goes to the movies night after night. Nobody in their right mind goes to the movies as often as you pretend to. People don't go to the movies at nearly midnight, and movies don't let out at two A.M. Come in stumbling. Muttering to yourself like a maniac! You get three hours' sleep and then go to work. Oh, I can picture the way you're doing down there. Moping, doping, because you're in no condition.

Tom: *(wildly)* No, I'm in no condition!

Amanda: What right have you got to jeopardize your job? Jeopardize the security of us all? How do you think we'd manage if you were—

Tom: Listen! You think I'm crazy *about* the *warehouse? (He bends fiercely toward her slight figure.)* You think I'm in love with the Continental Shoemakers? You think I want to spend fifty-five *years* down there in that—*celotex interior!* with—*fluorescent—tubes!* Look! I'd rather somebody picked up a crowbar and battered out my brains—than go back mornings! I *go!* Every time you come in yelling that God damn *"Rise and Shine!" "Rise and Shine!"* I say to myself "How *lucky dead* people are!" But I get up. I *go!* For sixty-five dollars a month I give up all that I dream of doing and being *ever!* And you say self—*self's* all I ever think of. Why, listen, if self is what I thought of, Mother, I'd be where he is— Gone! *(Pointing to father's picture.)* As far as the system of transportation reaches! *(He starts past her. She grabs his arm.)* Don't grab at me, Mother!

35 **Amanda:** Where are you going?

Tom: I'm going to the *movies!*

Amanda: I don't believe that lie!

Tom: *(crouching toward her, overtowering her tiny figure. She backs away, gasping)* I'm going to opium dens! Yes, opium dens, dens of vice and criminals' hang-outs, Mother. I've joined the Hogan gang, I'm a hired assassin, I carry a tommy-gun in a violin case! I run a string of cat-houses in the Valley! They call me Killer, Killer Wingfield, I'm leading a double-life, a simple, honest warehouse worker by day, by night a dynamic *czar of the underworld, Mother.* I go to gambling casinos, I spin away fortunes on the roulette table! I wear a patch over one eye and a false mustache, sometimes I put on green whiskers. On those occasions they call me—*El Diablo!* Oh, I could tell you things to make you sleepless! My enemies plan to dynamite this place. They're going to blow us all sky-high some night! I'll be glad, very happy, and so will you! You'll go up, up on a broomstick, over Blue Mountain with seventeen gentlemen callers! You ugly—babbling old—*witch.* . . . *(He goes through a series of violent, clumsy movements,* *seizing his overcoat, lunging to the door, pulling it fiercely open. The women watch him, aghast. His arm catches in the sleeve of the coat as he struggles to pull it on. For a moment he is pinioned by the bulky garment. With an outraged groan he tears the coat off again, splitting the shoulders of it, and hurls it across the room. It strikes against the shelf of Laura's glass collection, there is a tinkle of shattering glass. Laura cries out as if wounded.)*

(Music Legend: "The Glass Menagerie.")

LAURA: *My glass!*—menagerie. . . . *(She covers her face and turns away.)*

But Amanda is still stunned and stupefied by the "ugly witch" so that she barely notices this occurrence. Now she recovers her speech.

40 **AMANDA:** *(in an awful voice)* I won't speak to you—until you apologize! *(She crosses through portieres and draws them together behind her. Tom is left with Laura. Laura clings weakly to the mantel with her face averted. Tom stares at her stupidly for a moment. Then he crosses to shelf. Drops awkwardly to his knees to collect the fallen glass, glancing at Laura as if he would speak but couldn't.)*

"The Glass Menagerie" steals in as

(The Scene Dims Out.)

SCENE 4

The interior is dark. Faint in the alley.

A deep-voiced bell in a church is tolling the hour of five as the scene commences.

Tom appears at the top of the alley. After each solemn boom of the bell in the tower, he shakes a little noise-maker or rattle as if to express the tiny spasm of man in contrast to the sustained power and dignity of the Almighty. This and the unsteadiness of his advance make it evident that he has been drinking.

As he climbs the few steps to the fire-escape landing light steals up inside. Laura appears in night-dress, observing Tom's empty bed in the front room.

Tom fishes in his pockets for the door-key, removing a motley assortment of articles in the search, including a perfect shower of movie-ticket stubs and an empty bottle. At last he finds the key, but just as he is about to insert it, it slips from his fingers. He strikes a match and crouches below the door.

TOM: *(bitterly)* One crack—and it falls through!

Laura opens the door.

LAURA: Tom! Tom, what are you doing?
TOM: Looking for a door-key.
LAURA: Where have you been all this time?
5 **TOM:** I have been to the movies.
LAURA: All this time at the movies?

Tom: There was a very long program. There was a Garbo picture and a Mickey Mouse and a travelogue and a newsreel and a preview of coming attractions. And there was an organ solo and a collection for the milk-fund—simultaneously—which ended up in a terrible fight between a fat lady and an usher!

Laura: *(innocently)* Did you have to stay through everything?

Tom: Of course! And, oh, I forgot! There was a big stage show! The headliner on this stage show was Malvolio the Magician. He performed wonderful tricks, many of them, such as pouring water back and forth between pitchers. First it turned to wine and then it turned to beer and then it turned to whiskey. I know it was whiskey it finally turned into because he needed somebody to come up out of the audience to help him, and I came up—both shows! It was Kentucky Straight Bourbon. A very generous fellow, he gave souvenirs. *(He pulls from his back pocket a shimmering rainbow-colored scarf.)* He gave me this. This is his magic scarf. You can have it, Laura. You wave it over a canary cage and you get a bowl of gold-fish. You wave it over the gold-fish bowl and they fly away canaries. . . . But the wonderfullest trick of all was the coffin trick. We nailed him into a coffin and he got out of the coffin without removing one nail. *(He has come inside.)* There is a trick that would come in handy for me—get me out of this 2 by 4 situation! *(Flops onto bed and starts removing shoes.)*

10 **Laura:** Tom—Shhh!

Tom: What you shushing me for?

Laura: You'll wake up Mother.

Tom: Goody, goody! Pay 'er back for all those "Rise an' Shines." *(Lies down, groaning.)* You know it don't take much intelligence to get yourself into a nailed-up coffin, Laura. But who in hell ever got himself out of one without removing one nail?

As if in answer, the father's grinning photograph lights up.

(Scene Dims Out.)

Immediately following: The church bell is heard striking six. At the sixth stroke the alarm clock goes off in Amanda's room, and after a few moments we hear her calling: "Rise and Shine! Rise and Shine! Laura, go tell your brother to rise and shine!"

Tom: *(sitting up slowly)* I'll rise—but I won't shine.

The light increases.

15 **Amanda:** Laura, tell your brother his coffee is ready.

Laura slips into front room.

Laura: Tom! it's nearly seven. Don't make Mother nervous. *(He stares at her stupidly. Beseechingly.)* Tom, speak to Mother this morning. Make up with her, apologize, speak to her!

Tom: She won't to me. It's her that started not speaking.

Laura: If you just say you're sorry she'll start speaking.

Tom: Her not speaking—is that such a tragedy?

20 Laura: Please—please!

Amanda: *(calling from kitchenette)* Laura, are you going to do what I asked you to do, or do I have to get dressed and go out myself?

Laura: Going, going—soon as I get on my coat! *(She pulls on a shapeless felt hat with nervous, jerky movement, pleadingly glancing at Tom. Rushes awkwardly for coat. The coat is one of Amanda's inaccurately made-over, the sleeves too short for Laura.)* Butter and what else?

Amanda: *(entering upstage)* Just butter. Tell them to charge it.

Laura: Mother, they make such faces when I do that.

25 Amanda: Sticks and stones may break my bones, but the expression on Mr. Garfinkel's face won't harm us! Tell your brother his coffee is getting cold.

Laura: *(at door)* Do what I asked you, will you, will you, Tom?

He looks sullenly away.

Amanda: Laura, go now or just don't go at all!

Laura: *(rushing out)* Going—going! *(A second later she cries out. Tom springs up and crosses to the door. Amanda rushes anxiously in. Tom opens the door.)*

Tom: Laura?

30 Laura: I'm all right. I slipped, but I'm all right.

Amanda: *(peering anxiously after her)* If anyone breaks a leg on those fire-escape steps, the landlord ought to be sued for every cent he possesses! *(She shuts door. Remembers she isn't speaking and returns to other room.)*

As Tom enters listlessly for his coffee, she turns her back to him and stands rigidly facing the window on the gloomy gray vault of the areaway. Its light on her face with its aged but childish features is cruelly sharp, satirical as a Daumier print.

(Music Under: "Ave Maria.")

Tom glances sheepishly but sullenly at her averted figure and slumps at the table. The coffee is scalding hot; he sips it and gasps and spits it back in the cup. At his gasp, Amanda catches her breath and half turns. Then catches herself and turns back to window.

Tom blows on his coffee, glancing sidewise at his mother. She clears her throat. Tom clears his. He starts to rise. Sinks back down again, scratches his head, clears his throat again. Amanda coughs. Tom raises his cup in both hands to blow on it, his eyes staring over the rim of it at his mother for several moments. Then he slowly sets the cup down and awkwardly and hesitantly rises from the chair.

Tom: *(hoarsely)* Mother. I—I apologize. Mother. *(Amanda draws a quick, shuddering breath. Her face works grotesquely. She breaks into childlike tears.)* I'm sorry for what I said, for everything that I said, I didn't mean it.

AMANDA: *(sobbingly)* My devotion has made me a witch and so I make myself hateful to my children!

TOM: No, you *don't*.

35 **AMANDA:** I worry so much, don't sleep, it makes me nervous!

TOM: *(gently)* I understand that.

AMANDA: I've had to put up a solitary battle all these years. But you're my right-hand bower! Don't fall down, don't fail!

TOM: *(gently)* I try, Mother.

AMANDA: *(with great enthusiasm)* Try and you will SUCCEED! *(The notion makes her breathless.)* Why, you—you're just *full* of natural endowments! Both of my children—they're *unusual* children! Don't you think I know it? I'm so—proud! Happy and—feel I've—so much to be thankful for but—Promise me one thing, son!

40 **TOM:** What, Mother?

AMANDA: Promise, son, you'll—never be a drunkard!

TOM: *(turns to her grinning)* I will never be a drunkard, Mother.

AMANDA: That's what frightened me so, that you'd be drinking! Eat a bowl of Purina!

TOM: Just coffee, Mother.

45 **AMANDA:** Shredded wheat biscuit?

TOM: No. No, Mother, just coffee.

AMANDA: You can't put in a day's work on an empty stomach. You've got ten minutes—don't gulp! Drinking too-hot liquids makes cancer of the stomach. . . . Put cream in.

TOM: No, thank you.

AMANDA: To cool it.

50 **TOM:** No! No, thank you, I want it black.

AMANDA: I know, but it's not good for you. We have to do all that we can to build ourselves up. In these trying times we live in, all that we have to cling to is—each other. . . . That's why it's so important to—Tom, I—I sent out your sister so I could discuss something with you. If you hadn't spoken I would have spoken to you. *(Sits down.)*

TOM: *(gently)* What is it, Mother, that you want to discuss?

AMANDA: Laura!

Tom puts his cup down slowly.

(Legend On Screen: "Laura.")

(Music: "The Glass Menagerie.")

TOM: —Oh.—Laura . . .

55 **AMANDA:** *(touching his sleeve)* You know how Laura is. So quiet but—still water runs deep! She notices things and I think she—broods about them. *(Tom looks up.)* A few days ago I came in and she was crying.

TOM: What about?

AMANDA: You.

TOM: Me?

AMANDA: She has an idea that you're not happy here.

60 **Tom:** What gave her that idea?

Amanda: What gives her any idea? However, you do act strangely. I—I'm not criticizing, understand *that!* I know your ambitions do not lie in the warehouse, that like everybody in the whole wide world—you've had to—make sacrifices, but—Tom—Tom—life's not easy, it calls for—Spartan endurance! There's so many things in my heart that I cannot describe to you! I've never told you but I—*loved* your father....

Tom: (gently) I know that, Mother.

Amanda: And you—when I see you taking after his ways! Staying out late—and—well, you *had* been drinking the night you were in that—terrifying condition! Laura says that you hate the apartment and that you go out nights to get away from it! Is that true, Tom?

Tom: No. You say there's so much in your heart that you can't describe to me. That's true of me, too. There's so much in my heart that I can't describe to *you!* So let's respect each other's—

65 **Amanda:** But, why—*why,* Tom—are you always so *restless?* Where do you go to, nights?

Tom: I—go to the movies.

Amanda: Why do you go to the movies so much, Tom?

Tom: I go to the movies because—I like adventure. Adventure is something I don't have much of at work, so I go to the movies.

Amanda: But, Tom, you go to the movies *entirely* too *much!*

70 **Tom:** I like a lot of adventure.

Amanda looks baffled, then hurt. As the familiar inquisition resumes he becomes hard and impatient again. Amanda slips back into her querulous attitude toward him.

(Image On Screen: Sailing Vessel With Jolly Roger.)

Amanda: Most young men find adventure in their careers.

Tom: Then most young men are not employed in a warehouse.

Amanda: The world is full of young men employed in warehouses and offices and factories.

Tom: Do all of them find adventure in their careers?

75 **Amanda:** They do or they do without it! Not everybody has a craze for adventure.

Tom: Man is by instinct a lover, a hunter, a fighter, and none of those instincts are given much play at the warehouse!

Amanda: Man is by instinct! Don't quote instinct to me! Instinct is something that people have got away from! It belongs to animals! Christian adults don't want it!

Tom: What do Christian adults want, then, Mother?

Amanda: Superior things! Things of the mind and the spirit! Only animals have to satisfy instincts! Surely your aims are somewhat higher than theirs! Than monkeys—pigs—

80 **Tom:** I reckon they're not.

AMANDA: You're joking. However, that isn't what I wanted to discuss.

TOM: *(rising)* I haven't much time.

AMANDA: *(pushing his shoulders)* Sit down.

TOM: You want me to punch in red at the warehouse, Mother?

85 **AMANDA:** You have five minutes. I want to talk about Laura.

(Legend: "Plans And Provisions.")

TOM: All right! What about Laura?

AMANDA: We have to be making plans and provisions for her. She's older than you, two years, and nothing has happened. She just drifts along doing nothing. It frightens me terribly how she just drifts along.

TOM: I guess she's the type that people call home-girls.

AMANDA: There's no such type, and if there is, it's a pity! That is unless the home is hers, with a husband!

90 **TOM:** What?

AMANDA: Oh, I can see the handwriting on the wall as plain as I see the nose in front of my face! It's terrifying! More and more you remind me of your father! He was out all hours without explanation—Then *left! Good-bye!* And me with the bag to hold. I saw that letter you got from the Merchant Marine. I know what you're dreaming of. I'm not standing here blindfolded. Very well, then. Then *do* it! But not till there's somebody to take your place.

TOM: What do you mean?

AMANDA: I mean that as soon as Laura has got somebody to take care of her, married, a home of her own, independent—why, then you'll be free to go wherever you please, on land, on sea, whichever way the wind blows! But until that time you've got to look out for your sister. I don't say me because I'm old and don't matter! I say for your sister because she's young and dependent. I put her in business college—a dismal failure! Frightened her so it made her sick to her stomach. I took her over to the Young People's League at the church. Another fiasco. She spoke to nobody, nobody spoke to her. Now all she does is fool with those pieces of glass and play those worn-out records. What kind of a life is that for a girl to lead!

TOM: What can I do about it?

95 **AMANDA:** Overcome selfishness! Self, self, self is all that you ever think of! *(Tom springs up and crosses to get his coat. It is ugly and bulky. He pulls on a cap with earmuffs.)* Where is your muffler? Put your wool muffler on! *(He snatches it angrily from the closet and tosses it around his neck and pulls both ends tight.)* Tom! I haven't said what I had in mind to ask you.

TOM: I'm too late to—

AMANDA: *(catching his arms—very importunately. Then shyly)* Down at the warehouse, aren't there some—nice young men?

TOM: No!

AMANDA: There *must* be—*some* . . .

100 **TOM:** Mother—

Gesture.

AMANDA: Find out one that's clean-living—doesn't drink and—ask him out for sister!

TOM: What?

AMANDA: For *sister!* To *meet!* Get *acquainted!*

TOM: *(stamping to door)* Oh, my *go-osh!*

105 **AMANDA:** Will you? *(He opens door. Imploringly.)* Will you? *(He starts down.)* Will you? *Will* you, dear?

TOM: *(calling back)* YES!

Amanda closes the door hesitantly and with a troubled but faintly hopeful expression.

(Screen Image: A Glamour Magazine Cover.)

Spot Amanda at phone.

AMANDA: Ella Cartwright? This is Amanda Wingfield! How are you, honey? How is that kidney condition? *(Count five.)* Horrors! *(Count five.)* You're a Christian martyr, yes, honey, that's what you are, a Christian martyr! Well, I just happened to notice in my little red book that your subscription to the *Companion* has just run out! I knew that you wouldn't want to miss out on the wonderful serial starting in this new issue. It's by Bessie Mae Hopper, the first thing she's written since *Honeymoon for Three.* Wasn't that a strange and interesting story? Well, this one is even lovelier, I believe. It has a sophisticated society background. It's all about the horsey set on Long Island!

(Fade Out.)

SCENE 5

(Legend On Screen: "Annunciation.") Fade with music.

It is early dusk of a spring evening. Supper has just been finished in the Wingfield apartment. Amanda and Laura in light colored dresses are removing dishes from the table, in the upstage area, which is shadowy, their movements formalized almost as a dance or ritual, their moving forms as pale and silent as moths.

Tom, in white shirt and trousers, rises from the table and crosses toward the fire-escape.

AMANDA: *(as he passes her)* Son, will you do me a favor?

TOM: What?

AMANDA: Comb your hair! You look so pretty when your hair is combed! *(Tom slouches on sofa with evening paper. Enormous caption "Franco Triumphs.")* There is only one respect in which I would like you to emulate your father.

TOM: What respect is that?

5 **AMANDA:** The care he always took of his appearance. He never allowed himself
    to look untidy. *(He throws down the paper and crosses to fire-escape.)*
    Where are you going?

TOM: I'm going out to smoke.

AMANDA: You smoke too much. A pack a day at fifteen cents a pack. How
    much would that amount to in a month? Thirty times fifteen is how much,
    Tom? Figure it out and you will be astounded at what you could save.
    Enough to give you a night-school course in accounting at Washington U!
    Just think what a wonderful thing that would be for you, son!

Tom is unmoved by the thought.

TOM: I'd rather smoke. *(He steps out on landing, letting the screen door slam.)*

AMANDA: *(sharply)* I know! That's the tragedy of it. . . . *(Alone, she turns to
    look at her husband's picture.)*

(Dance Music: "All The World Is Waiting For The Sunrise!")

10 **TOM:** *(to the audience)* Across the alley from us was the Paradise Dance Hall.
    On evenings in spring the windows and doors were open and the music
    came outdoors. Sometimes the lights were turned out except for a large
    glass sphere that hung from the ceiling. It would turn slowly about and
    filter the dusk with delicate rainbow colors. Then the orchestra played a
    waltz or a tango, something that had a slow and sensuous rhythm.
    Couples would come outside, to the relative privacy of the alley. You
    could see them kissing behind ash-pits and telephone poles. This was the
    compensation for lives that passed like mine, without any change or
    adventure. Adventure and change were imminent in this year. They were
    waiting around the corner for all these kids. Suspended in the mist over
    Berchtesgaden,[6] caught in the folds of Chamberlain's[7] umbrella—In Spain
    there was Guernica! But here there was only hot swing music and liquor,
    dance halls, bars, and movies, and sex that hung in the gloom like a
    chandelier and flooded the world with brief, deceptive rainbows. . . . All
    the world was waiting for bombardments!

Amanda turns from the picture and comes outside.

AMANDA: *(sighing)* A fire-escape landing's a poor excuse for a porch. *(She
    spreads a newspaper on a step and sits down, gracefully and demurely as
    if she were settling into a swing on a Mississippi veranda.)* What are you
    looking at?

TOM: The moon.

AMANDA: Is there a moon this evening?

---

[6] A resort in West Germany, in the Bavarian Alps, site of Hitler's fortified retreat, the
Berghof.

[7] (Arthur) Neville Chamberlain (1869–1940)—Conservative party Prime Minister of
England (1937–1940) who advocated a policy of appeasement toward Hitler.

TOM: It's rising over Garfinkel's Delicatessen.

15 AMANDA: So it is! A little silver slipper of a moon. Have you made a wish on it yet?

TOM: Um-hum.

AMANDA: What did you wish for?

TOM: That's a secret.

AMANDA: A secret, huh? Well, I won't tell mine either. I will be just as mysterious as you.

20 TOM: I bet I can guess what yours is.

AMANDA: Is my head so transparent?

TOM: You're not a sphinx.

AMANDA: No, I don't have secrets. I'll tell you what I wished for on the moon. Success and happiness for my precious children! I wish for that whenever there's a moon, and when there isn't a moon, I wish for it, too.

TOM: I thought perhaps you wished for a gentleman caller.

25 AMANDA: Why do you say that?

TOM: Don't you remember asking me to fetch one?

AMANDA: I remember suggesting that it would be nice for your sister if you brought home some nice young man from the warehouse. I think I've made that suggestion more than once.

TOM: Yes, you have made it repeatedly.

AMANDA: Well?

30 TOM: We are going to have one.

AMANDA: What?

TOM: A gentleman caller!

(The Annunciation Is Celebrated With Music.)

Amanda rises.

(Image On Screen: Caller With Bouquet.)

AMANDA: You mean you have asked some nice young man to come over?

TOM: Yep. I've asked him to dinner.

35 AMANDA: You really did?

TOM: I did!

AMANDA: You did, and did he—*accept*?

TOM: He did!

AMANDA: Well, well—well, well! That's—lovely!

40 TOM: I thought that you would be pleased.

AMANDA: It's definite, then?

TOM: Very definite.

AMANDA: Soon?

TOM: Very soon.

45 AMANDA: For heaven's sake, stop putting on and tell me some things, will you?

TOM: What things do you want me to tell you?

AMANDA: Naturally I would like to know when he's *coming!*

TOM: He's coming tomorrow.

AMANDA: *Tomorrow?*

50 **TOM:** Yep. Tomorrow.

AMANDA: But, Tom!

TOM: Yes, Mother?

AMANDA: Tomorrow gives me no time!

TOM: Time for what?

55 **AMANDA:** Preparations! Why didn't you phone me at once, as soon as you asked him, the minute that he accepted? Then, don't you see, I could have been getting ready!

TOM: You don't have to make any fuss.

AMANDA: Oh, Tom, Tom, Tom, of course I have to make a fuss! I want things nice, not sloppy! Not thrown together. I'll certainly have to do some fast thinking, won't I?

TOM: I don't see why you have to think at all.

AMANDA: You just don't know. We can't have a gentleman caller in a pig-sty! All my wedding silver has to be polished, the monogrammed table linen ought to be laundered! The windows have to be washed and fresh curtains put up. And how about clothes? We have to *wear* something, don't we?

60 **TOM:** Mother, this boy is no one to make a fuss over!

AMANDA: Do you realize he's the first young man we've introduced to your sister? It's terrible, dreadful, disgraceful that poor little sister has never received a single gentleman caller! Tom, come inside! *(She opens the screen door.)*

TOM: What for?

AMANDA: I want to ask you some things.

TOM: If you're going to make such a fuss, I'll call it off, I'll tell him not to come.

65 **AMANDA:** You certainly won't do anything of the kind. Nothing offends people worse than broken engagements. It simply means I'll have to work like a Turk! We won't be brilliant, but we'll pass inspection. Come on inside. *(Tom follows, groaning.)* Sit down.

TOM: Any particular place you would like me to sit?

AMANDA: Thank heavens I've got that new sofa! I'm also making payments on a floor lamp I'll have sent out! And put the chintz covers on, they'll brighten things up! Of course I'd hoped to have these walls re-papered. . . . What is the young man's name?

TOM: His name is O'Connor.

AMANDA: That, of course, means fish—tomorrow is Friday! I'll have that salmon loaf—with Durkee's dressing! What does he do? He works at the warehouse?

70 **TOM:** Of course! How else would I—

AMANDA: Tom, he—doesn't drink?

TOM: Why do you ask me that?

AMANDA: Your father *did!*

TOM: Don't get started on that!

75 **Amanda:** He *does* drink, then?

Tom: Not that I know of!

Amanda: Make sure, be certain! The last thing I want for my daughter's a boy who drinks!

Tom: Aren't you being a little premature? Mr. O'Connor has not yet appeared on the scene!

Amanda: But will tomorrow. To meet your sister, and what do I know about his character? Nothing! Old maids are better off than wives of drunkards!

80 **Tom:** Oh, my God!

Amanda: Be still!

Tom: *(leaning forward to whisper)* Lots of fellows meet girls whom they don't marry!

Amanda: Oh, talk sensibly, Tom—and don't be sarcastic! *(She has gotten a hairbrush.)*

Tom: What are you doing?

85 **Amanda:** I'm brushing that cow-lick down! What is this young man's position at the warehouse?

Tom: *(submitting grimly to the brush and the interrogation)* This young man's position is that of a shipping clerk, Mother.

Amanda: Sounds to me like a fairly responsible job, the sort of a job *you* would be in if you just had more *get-up.* What is his salary? Have you got any idea?

Tom: I would judge it to be approximately eighty-five dollars a month.

Amanda: Well—not princely, but—

90 **Tom:** Twenty more than I make.

Amanda: Yes, how well I know! But for a family man, eighty-five dollars a month is not much more than you can just get by on. . . .

Tom: Yes, but Mr. O'Connor is not a family man.

Amanda: He might be, mightn't he? Some time in the future?

Tom: I see. Plans and provisions.

95 **Amanda:** You are the only young man that I know of who ignores the fact that the future becomes the present, the present the past, and the past turns into everlasting regret if you don't plan for it!

Tom: I will think that over and see what I can make of it.

Amanda: Don't be supercilious with your mother! Tell me some more about this—what do you call him?

Tom: James D. O'Connor. The D. is for Delaney.

Amanda: Irish on *both* sides! *Gracious!* And doesn't drink?

100 **Tom:** Shall I call him up and ask him right this minute?

Amanda: The only way to find out about those things is to make discreet inquiries at the proper moment. When I was a girl in Blue Mountain and it was suspected that a young man drank, the girl whose attentions he had been receiving, if any girl *was,* would sometimes speak to the minister of his church, or rather her father would if her father was living, and sort of feel him out on the young man's character. That is the way such things are discreetly handled to keep a young woman from making a tragic mistake!

TOM: Then how did you happen to make a tragic mistake?

AMANDA: That innocent look of your father's had everyone fooled! He *smiled*— the world was *enchanted!* No girl can do worse than put herself at the mercy of a handsome appearance! I hope that Mr. O'Connor is not too good-looking.

TOM: No, he's not too good-looking. He's covered with freckles and hasn't too much of a nose.

105 **AMANDA:** He's not right-down homely, though?

TOM: Not right-down homely. Just medium homely, I'd say.

AMANDA: Character's what to look for in a man.

TOM: That's what I've always said, Mother.

AMANDA: You've never said anything of the kind and I suspect you would never give it a thought.

110 **TOM:** Don't be suspicious of me.

AMANDA: At least I hope he's the type that's up and coming.

TOM: I think he really goes in for self-improvement.

AMANDA: What reason have you to think so?

TOM: He goes to night school.

115 **AMANDA:** *(beaming)* Splendid! What does he do, I mean study?

TOM: Radio engineering and public speaking!

AMANDA: Then he has visions of being advanced in the world! Any young man who studies public speaking is aiming to have an executive job some day! And radio engineering? A thing for the future! Both of these facts are very illuminating. Those are the sort of things that a mother should know concerning any young man who comes to call on her daughter. Seriously or—not.

TOM: One little warning. He doesn't know about Laura. I didn't let on that we had dark ulterior motives. I just said, why don't you come have dinner with us? He said okay and that was the whole conversation.

AMANDA: I bet it was! You're eloquent as an oyster. However, he'll know about Laura when he gets here. When he sees how lovely and sweet and pretty she is, he'll thank his lucky stars he was asked to dinner.

120 **TOM:** Mother, you mustn't expect too much of Laura.

AMANDA: What do you mean?

TOM: Laura seems all those things to you and me because she's ours and we love her. We don't even notice she's crippled any more.

AMANDA: Don't say crippled! You know that I never allow that word to be used!

TOM: But face facts, Mother. She is and—that's not all—

125 **AMANDA:** What do you mean "not all"?

TOM: Laura is very different from other girls.

AMANDA: I think the difference is all to her advantage.

TOM: Not quite all—in the eyes of others—strangers—she's terribly shy and lives in a world of her own and those things make her seem a little peculiar to people outside the house.

AMANDA: Don't say peculiar.

130 **Tom:** Face the facts. She is.

(The Dance-Hall Music Changes To A Tango That Has A Minor And Somewhat Ominous Tone.)

Amanda: In what way is she peculiar—may I ask?

Tom: *(gently)* She lives in a world of her own—a world of—little glass ornaments, Mother. . . . *(Gets up. Amanda remains holding brush, looking at him, troubled.)* She plays old phonograph records and—that's about all—*(He glances at himself in the mirror and crosses to door.)*

Amanda: *(sharply)* Where are you going?

Tom: I'm going to the movies. *(Out screen door.)*

135 **Amanda:** Not to the movies, every night to the movies! *(Follows quickly to screen door.)* I don't believe you always go to the movies! *(He is gone. Amanda looks worriedly after him for a moment. Then vitality and optimism return and she turns from the door. Crossing to portieres.)* Laura! Laura! *(Laura answers from kitchenette.)*

Laura: Yes, Mother.

Amanda: Let those dishes go and come in front! *(Laura appears with dish towel. Gaily.)* Laura, come here and make a wish on the moon!

Laura: *(entering)* Moon—moon?

Amanda: A little silver slipper of a moon. Look over your left shoulder, Laura, and make a wish! *(Laura looks faintly puzzled as if called out of sleep. Amanda seizes her shoulders and turns her at an angle by the door.)* Now! Now, darling, *wish!*

140 **Laura:** What shall I wish for, Mother?

Amanda: *(her voice trembling and her eyes suddenly filling with tears)* Happiness! Good Fortune!

The violin rises and the stage dims out.

Scene 6

(Image: High-School Hero.)

Tom: And so the following evening I brought Jim home to dinner. I had known Jim slightly in high school. In high school Jim was a hero. He had tremendous Irish good nature and vitality with the scrubbed and polished look of white chinaware. He seemed to move in a continual spotlight. He was a star in basketball, captain of the debating club, president of the senior class and the glee club and he sang the male lead in the annual light operas. He was always running or bounding, never just walking. He seemed always at the point of defeating the law of gravity. He was shooting with such velocity through his adolescence that you would logically expect him to arrive at nothing short of the White House by the time he was thirty. But Jim apparently ran into more interference after his graduation from Soldan. His speed had definitely slowed. Six years after he left high school he was holding a job that wasn't much better than mine.

(Image: Clerk.)

He was the only one at the warehouse with whom I was on friendly terms. I was valuable to him as someone who could remember his former glory, who had seen him win basketball games and the silver cup in debating. He knew of my secret practice of retiring to a cabinet of the washroom to work on poems when business was slack in the warehouse. He called me Shakespeare. And while the other boys in the warehouse regarded me with suspicious hostility, Jim took a humorous attitude toward me. Gradually his attitude affected the others, their hostility wore off and they also began to smile at me as people smile at an oddly fashioned dog who trots across their path at some distance.

I knew that Jim and Laura had known each other at Soldan, and I had heard Laura speak admiringly of his voice. I didn't know if Jim remembered her or not. In high school Laura had been as unobtrusive as Jim had been astonishing. If he did remember Laura, it was not as my sister, for when I asked him to dinner, he grinned and said, "You know, Shakespeare, I never thought of you as having folks!" He was about to discover that I did. . . .

(Light Up Stage.)

(Legend On Screen: "The Accent Of A Coming Foot.")

Friday evening. It is about five o'clock of a late spring evening which comes "scattering poems in the sky."

A delicate lemony light is in the Wingfield apartment.

Amanda has worked like a Turk in preparation for the gentleman caller. The results are astonishing. The new floor lamp with its rose-silk shade is in place, a colored paper lantern conceals the broken light fixture in the ceiling, new billowing white curtains are at the windows, chintz covers are on chairs and sofa, a pair of new sofa pillows make their initial appearance.

Open boxes and tissue paper are scattered on the floor.

Laura stands in the middle with lifted arms while Amanda crouches before her, adjusting the hem of the new dress, devout and ritualistic. The dress is colored and designed by memory. The arrangement of Laura's hair is changed; it is softer and more becoming. A fragile, unearthly prettiness has come out in Laura: she is like a piece of translucent glass touched by light, given a momentary radiance, not actual, not lasting.

AMANDA: *(impatiently)* Why are you trembling?
LAURA: Mother, you've made me so nervous!
AMANDA: How have I made you nervous?
5 **LAURA:** By all this fuss! You make it seem so important!
AMANDA: I don't understand you, Laura. You couldn't be satisfied with just sitting home, and yet whenever I try to arrange something for you, you seem to resist it. *(She gets up.)* Now take a look at yourself. No, wait! Wait just a moment—I have an idea!

Laura: What is it now?

Amanda produces two powder puffs which she wraps in handkerchiefs and stuffs in Laura's bosom.

Laura: Mother, what are you doing?
Amanda: They call them "Gay Deceivers"!
10 **Laura:** I won't wear them!
Amanda: You will!
Laura: Why should I?
Amanda: Because, to be painfully honest, your chest is flat.
Laura: You make it seem like we were setting a trap.
15 **Amanda:** All pretty girls are a trap, a pretty trap, and men expect them to be. *(Legend: "A Pretty Trap.")* Now look at yourself, young lady. This is the prettiest you will ever be! I've got to fix myself now! You're going to be surprised by your mother's appearance! *(She crosses through portieres, humming gaily.)*

Laura moves slowly to the long mirror and stares solemnly at herself.
A wind blows the white curtains inward in a slow, graceful motion and with a faint, sorrowful sighing.

Amanda: *(offstage)* It isn't dark enough yet. *(She turns slowly before the mirror with a troubled look.)*

(Legend On Screen: "This Is My Sister: Celebrate Her With Strings!" Music.)

Amanda: *(laughing, off)* I'm going to show you something. I'm going to make a spectacular appearance!
Laura: What is it, Mother?
Amanda: Possess your soul in patience—you will see! Something I've resurrected from that old trunk! Styles haven't changed so terribly much after all. . . . *(She parts the portieres.)* Now just look at your mother! *(She wears a girlish frock of yellowed voile with a blue silk sash. She carries a bunch of jonquils—the legend of her youth is nearly revived. Feverishly.)* This is the dress in which I led the cotillion. Won the cakewalk twice at Sunset Hill, wore one spring to the Governor's ball in Jackson! See how I sashayed around the ballroom, Laura? *(She raises her skirt and does a mincing step around the room.)* I wore it on Sundays for my gentlemen callers! I had it on the day I met your father—I had malaria fever all that spring. The change of climate from East Tennessee to the Delta— weakened resistance—I had a little temperature all the time—not enough to be serious—just enough to make me restless and giddy! Invitations poured in—parties all over the Delta!—"Stay in bed," said Mother, "you have fever!"—but I just wouldn't.—I took quinine but kept on going, going!—Evenings, dances!—Afternoons, long, long rides! Picnics— lovely!—So lovely, that country in May. All lacy with dogwood, literally flooded with jonquils!—That was the spring I had the craze for jonquils.

Jonquils became an absolute obsession. Mother said, "Honey, there's no more room for jonquils." And still I kept bringing in more jonquils. Whenever, wherever I saw them, I'd say, "Stop! Stop! I see jonquils!" I made the young men help me gather the jonquils! It was a joke, Amanda and her jonquils! Finally there were no more vases to hold them, every available space was filled with jonquils. No vases to hold them? All right, I'll hold them myself! And then I—*(She stops in front of the picture.)* *(Music)* met your father! Malaria fever and jonquils and then—this— boy. . . . *(She switches on the rose-colored lamp.)* I hope they get here before it starts to rain. *(She crosses upstage and places the jonquils in bowl on table.)* I gave your brother a little extra change so he and Mr. O'Connor could take the service car home.

20 **LAURA:** *(with altered look)* What did you say his name was?

AMANDA: O'Connor.

LAURA: What is his first name?

AMANDA: I don't remember. Oh, yes, I do. It was—Jim!

Laura sways slightly and catches hold of a chair.

(Legend On Screen: "Not Jim!")

LAURA: *(faintly)* Not—Jim!

25 **AMANDA:** Yes, that was it, it was Jim! I've never known a Jim that wasn't nice!

(Music: Ominous.)

LAURA: Are you sure his name is Jim O'Connor?

AMANDA: Yes. Why?

LAURA: Is he the one that Tom used to know in high school?

AMANDA: He didn't say so. I think he just got to know him at the warehouse.

30 **LAURA:** There was a Jim O'Connor we both knew in high school—*(Then, with effort.)* If that is the one that Tom is bringing to dinner—you'll have to excuse me, I won't come to the table.

AMANDA: What sort of nonsense is this?

LAURA: You asked me once if I'd ever liked a boy. Don't you remember I showed you this boy's picture?

AMANDA: You mean the boy you showed me in the year book?

LAURA: Yes, that boy.

35 **AMANDA:** Laura, Laura, were you in love with that boy?

LAURA: I don't know, Mother. All I know is I couldn't sit at the table if it was him!

AMANDA: It won't be him! It isn't the least bit likely. But whether it is or not, you will come to the table. You will not be excused.

LAURA: I'll have to be, Mother.

AMANDA: I don't intend to humor your silliness, Laura. I've had too much from you and your brother, both! So just sit down and compose yourself till they come. Tom has forgotten his key so you'll have to let them in, when they arrive.

40 LAURA: *(panicky)* Oh, Mother—*you* answer the door!

AMANDA: *(lightly)* I'll be in the kitchen—busy!

LAURA: Oh, Mother, please answer the door, don't make me do it!

AMANDA: *(crossing into kitchenette)* I've got to fix the dressing for the salmon. Fuss, fuss—silliness!—over a gentleman caller!

Door swings shut. Laura is left alone.

(Legend: "Terror!")

She utters a low moan and turns off the lamp—sits stiffly on the edge of the sofa, knotting her fingers together.

(Legend On Screen: "The Opening Of A Door!")

Tom and Jim appear on the fire-escape steps and climb to landing. Hearing their approach, Laura rises with a panicky gesture. She retreats to the portieres.
The doorbell. Laura catches her breath and touches her throat. Low drums.

AMANDA: *(calling)* Laura, sweetheart! The door!

Laura stares at it without moving.

45 JIM: I think we just beat the rain.

TOM: Uh-huh. *(He rings again, nervously. Jim whistles and fishes for a cigarette.)*

AMANDA: *(very, very gaily)* Laura, that is your brother and Mr. O'Connor! Will you let them in, darling?

Laura crosses toward kitchenette door.

LAURA: *(breathlessly)* Mother—you go to the door!

Amanda steps out of kitchenette and stares furiously at Laura. She points imperiously at the door.

LAURA: Please, please!

50 AMANDA: *(in a fierce whisper)* What is the matter with you, you silly thing?

LAURA: *(desperately)* Please, you answer it, *please!*

AMANDA: I told you I wasn't going to humor you, Laura. Why have you chosen this moment to lose your mind?

LAURA: Please, please, please, you go!

AMANDA: You'll have to go to the door because I can't!

55 LAURA: *(despairingly)* I can't either!

AMANDA: Why?

LAURA: I'm *sick!*

AMANDA: I'm sick, too—of your nonsense! Why can't you and your brother be normal people? Fantastic whims and behavior! *(Tom gives a long ring.)* Preposterous goings on! Can you give me one reason—*(Calls out lyrically.)* COMING! JUST ONE SECOND!—why should you be afraid to open a door? Now you answer it, Laura!

LAURA: Oh, oh, oh . . . *(She returns through the portieres. Darts to the Victrola and winds it frantically and turns it on.)*

60 **AMANDA:** Laura Wingfield, you march right to that door!

LAURA: Yes—yes, Mother!

A faraway, scratchy rendition of "Dardanella" softens the air and gives her strength to move through it. She slips to the door and draws it cautiously open. Tom enters with the caller, Jim O'Connor.

TOM: Laura, this is Jim. Jim, this is my sister, Laura.

JIM: *(stepping inside)* I didn't know that Shakespeare had a sister!

LAURA: *(retreating stiff and trembling from the door)* How—how do you do?

65 **JIM:** *(heartily extending his hand)* Okay!

Laura touches it hesitantly with hers.

JIM: Your hand's *cold,* Laura!

LAURA: Yes, well—I've been playing the Victrola. . . .

JIM: Must have been playing classical music on it! You ought to play a little hot swing music to warm you up!

LAURA: Excuse me—I haven't finished playing the Victrola. . . .

She turns awkwardly and hurries into the front room. She pauses a second by the Victrola. Then catches her breath and darts through the portieres like a frightened deer.

70 **JIM:** *(grinning)* What was the matter?

TOM: Oh—with Laura? Laura is—terribly shy.

JIM: Shy, huh? It's unusual to meet a shy girl nowadays. I don't believe you ever mentioned you had a sister.

TOM: Well, now you know. I have one. Here is the *Post Dispatch.* You want a piece of it?

JIM: Uh-huh.

75 **TOM:** What piece? The comics?

JIM: Sports! *(Glances at it.)* Ole Dizzy Dean is on his bad behavior.

TOM: *(disinterested)* Yeah? *(Lights cigarette and crosses back to fire-escape door.)*

JIM: Where are *you* going?

TOM: I'm going out on the terrace.

80 **JIM:** *(goes after him)* You know, Shakespeare—I'm going to sell you a bill of goods!

TOM: What goods?

JIM: A course I'm taking.

TOM: Huh?

JIM: In public speaking! You and me, we're not the warehouse type.

85 **TOM:** Thanks—that's good news. But what has public speaking got to do with it?

JIM: It fits you for—executive positions!

TOM: Awww.

JIM: I tell you it's done a helluva lot for me.

(Image: Executive At Desk.)

TOM: In what respect?

90 **JIM:** In every! Ask yourself what is the difference between you an' me and men in the office down front? Brains?—No!—Ability?—No! Then what? Just one little thing—

TOM: What is that one little thing?

JIM: Primarily it amounts to—social poise! Being able to square up to people and hold your own on any social level!

AMANDA: *(offstage)* Tom?

TOM: Yes, Mother?

95 **AMANDA:** Is that you and Mr. O'Connor?

TOM: Yes, Mother.

AMANDA: Well, you just make yourselves comfortable in there.

TOM: Yes, Mother.

AMANDA: Ask Mr. O'Connor if he would like to wash his hands.

100 **JIM:** Aw—no—thank you—I took care of that at the warehouse. Tom—

TOM: Yes?

JIM: Mr. Mendoza was speaking to me about you.

TOM: Favorably?

JIM: What do you think?

105 **TOM:** Well—

JIM: You're going to be out of a job if you don't wake up.

TOM: I am waking up—

JIM: You show no signs.

TOM: The signs are interior.

(Image On Screen: The Sailing Vessel With Jolly Roger Again.)

110 **TOM:** I'm planning to change. *(He leans over the rail speaking with quiet exhilaration. The incandescent marquees and signs of the first-run movie houses light his face from across the alley. He looks like a voyager.)* I'm right at the point of committing myself to a future that doesn't include the warehouse and Mr. Mendoza or even a night-school course in public speaking.

JIM: What are you gassing about?

TOM: I'm tired of the movies.

JIM: Movies!

TOM: Yes, movies! Look at them—*(A wave toward the marvels of Grand Avenue.)* All of those glamorous people—having adventures—hogging it all, gobbling the whole thing up! You know what happens? People go to the *movies* instead of *moving!* Hollywood characters are supposed to have all the adventures for everybody in America, while everybody in America sits in a dark room and watches them have them! Yes, until there's a war.

That's when adventure becomes available to the masses! *Everyone's* dish, not only Gable's! Then the people in the dark room come out of the dark room to have some adventures themselves—Goody, goody—It's our turn now, to go to the South Sea Island—to make a safari—to be exotic, far-off—But I'm not patient. I don't want to wait till then. I'm tired of the *movies* and I am *about* to *move!*

115 **JIM:** *(incredulously)* Move?

TOM: Yes.

JIM: When?

TOM: Soon!

JIM: Where? Where?

Theme three music seems to answer the question, while Tom thinks it over. He searches among his pockets.

120 **TOM:** I'm starting to boil inside. I know I seem dreary, but inside—well, I'm boiling! Whenever I pick up a shoe, I shudder a little thinking how short life is and what I am doing!—Whatever that means. I know it doesn't mean shoes—except as something to wear on a traveler's feet! *(Finds paper.)* Look—

JIM: What?

TOM: I'm a member.

JIM: *(reading)* The Union of Merchant Seamen.

TOM: I paid my dues this month, instead of the light bill.

125 **JIM:** You will regret it when they turn the lights off.

TOM: I won't be here.

JIM: How about your mother?

TOM: I'm like my father. The bastard son of a bastard! See how he grins? And he's been absent going on sixteen years!

JIM: You're just talking, you drip. How does your mother feel about it?

130 **TOM:** Shhh—Here comes Mother! Mother is not acquainted with my plans!

AMANDA: *(enters portieres)* Where are you all?

TOM: On the terrace, Mother.

They start inside. She advances to them. Tom is distinctly shocked at her appearance. Even Jim blinks a little. He is making his first contact with girlish Southern vivacity and in spite of the night-school course in public speaking is somewhat thrown off the beam by the unexpected outlay of social charm.

Certain responses are attempted by Jim but are swept aside by Amanda's gay laughter and chatter. Tom is embarrassed but after the first shock Jim reacts very warmly. Grins and chuckles, is altogether won over.

(Image: Amanda As A Girl.)

AMANDA: *(coyly smiling, shaking her girlish ringlets)* Well, well, well, so this is Mr. O'Connor. Introductions entirely unnecessary. I've heard so much about you from my boy. I finally said to him, Tom—good gracious!—why don't you bring this paragon to supper? I'd like to meet this nice young man at the warehouse!—Instead of just hearing him sing your praises so much! I don't know why my son is so stand-offish—that's not Southern behavior! Let's sit down and—I think we could stand a little more air in here! Tom, leave the door open. I felt a nice fresh breeze a moment ago. Where has it gone? Mmm, so warm already! And not quite summer, even. We're going to burn up when summer really gets started. However, we're having—we're having a very light supper. I think light things are better fo' this time of year. The same as light clothes are. Light clothes an' light food are what warm weather calls fo'. You know our blood gets so thick during th' winter—it takes a while fo' us to *adjust* ou'selves!—when the season changes . . . It's come so quick this year. I wasn't prepared. All of a sudden—heavens! Already summer!—I ran to the trunk an' pulled out this light dress—Terribly old! Historical almost! But feels so good—so good an' co-ol, y'know. . . .

Tom: Mother—

135 **Amanda:** Yes, honey?

Tom: How about—supper?

Amanda: Honey, you go ask Sister if supper is ready! You know that Sister is in full charge of supper! Tell her you hungry boys are waiting for it. *(To Jim.)* Have you met Laura?

Jim: She—

Amanda: Let you in? Oh, good, you've met already! It's rare for a girl as sweet an' pretty as Laura to be domestic! But Laura is, thank heavens, not only pretty but also very domestic. I'm not at all. I never was a bit. I never could make a thing but angel-food cake. Well, in the South we had so many servants. Gone, gone, gone. All vestiges of gracious living! Gone completely! I wasn't prepared for what the future brought me. All of my gentlemen callers were sons of planters and so of course I assumed that I would be married to one and raise my family on a large piece of land with plenty of servants. But man proposes—and woman accepts the proposal!—To vary that old, old saying a little bit—I married no planter! I married a man who worked for the telephone company!—that gallantly smiling gentleman over there! *(Points to the picture.)* A telephone man who—fell in love with long-distance!—Now he travels and I don't even know where!—But what am I going on for about my—tribulations? Tell me yours—I hope you don't have any! Tom?

140 **Tom:** *(returning)* Yes, Mother?

Amanda: Is supper nearly ready?

Tom: It looks to me like supper is on the table.

Amanda: Let me look—*(She rises prettily and looks through portieres.)* Oh, lovely—But where is Sister?

Tom: Laura is not feeling well and says that she thinks she'd better not come to the table.

145 **Amanda:** What?—Nonsense!—Laura? Oh, Laura!

Laura: *(offstage, faintly)* Yes, Mother.

AMANDA: You really must come to the table. We won't be seated until you come to the table! Come in, Mr. O'Connor. You sit over there and I'll— Laura? Laura Wingfield! You're keeping us waiting, honey! We can't say grace until you come to the table!

The back door is pushed weakly open and Laura comes in. She is obviously quite faint, her lips trembling, her eyes wide and staring. She moves unsteadily toward the table.

(Legend: "Terror!")

Outside a summer storm is coming abruptly. The white curtains billow inward at the windows and there is a sorrowful murmur and deep blue dusk.
     Laura suddenly stumbles—She catches at a chair with a faint moan.

TOM: Laura!
AMANDA: Laura! *(There is a clap of thunder.) (Legend: "Ah!") (Despairingly.)* Why, Laura, you *are* sick, darling! Tom, help your sister into the living room, dear! Sit in the living room, Laura—rest on the sofa. Well! *(To the gentleman caller.)* Standing over the hot stove made her ill!—I told her that it was just too warm this evening, but—*(Tom comes back in. Laura is on the sofa.)* Is Laura all right now?
150 TOM: Yes.
AMANDA: What *is* that? Rain? A nice cool rain has come up! *(She gives the gentleman caller a frightened look.)* I think we may—have grace— now . . . *(Tom looks at her stupidly.)* Tom, honey—you say grace!
TOM: Oh . . . "For these and all thy mercies—" *(They bow their heads, Amanda stealing a nervous glance at Jim. In the living room Laura, stretched on the sofa, clenches her hand to her lips, to hold back a shuddering sob.)* God's Holy Name be praised—

(The Scene Dims Out.)

SCENE 7

(A Souvenir.)

Half an hour later. Dinner is just being finished in the upstage area which is concealed by the drawn portieres.
     As the curtain rises Laura is still huddled upon the sofa, her feet drawn under her, her head resting on a pale blue pillow, her eyes wide and mysteriously watchful. The new floor lamp with its shade of rose-colored silk gives a soft, becoming light to her face, bringing out the fragile, unearthly prettiness which usually escapes attention. There is a steady murmur of rain, but it is slackening and stops soon after the scene begins; the air outside becomes pale and luminous as the moon breaks out.
     A moment after the curtain rises, the lights in both rooms flicker and go out.

JIM: Hey, there, Mr. Light Bulb!

Amanda laughs nervously.

(Legend: "Suspension Of A Public Service.")

Amanda: Where was Moses when the lights went out? Ha-ha. Do you know the answer to that one, Mr. O'Connor?

Jim: No, Ma'am, what's the answer?

Amanda: In the dark! *(Jim laughs appreciatively.)* Everybody sit still. I'll light the candles. Isn't it lucky we have them on the table? Where's a match? Which of you gentlemen can provide a match?

5   **Jim:** Here.

Amanda: Thank you, sir.

Jim: Not at all, Ma'am!

Amanda: I guess the fuse has burnt out. Mr. O'Connor, can you tell a burnt-out fuse? I know I can't and Tom is a total loss when it comes to mechanics. *(Sound: Getting Up: Voices Recede A Little To Kitchenette.)* Oh, be careful you don't bump into something. We don't want our gentleman caller to break his neck. Now wouldn't that be a fine howdy-do?

Jim: Ha-ha! Where is the fuse-box?

10   **Amanda:** Right here next to the stove. Can you see anything?

Jim: Just a minute.

Amanda: Isn't electricity a mysterious thing? Wasn't it Benjamin Franklin who tied a key to a kite? We live in such a mysterious universe, don't we? Some people say that science clears up all the mysteries for us. In my opinion it only creates more! Have you found it yet?

Jim: No, Ma'am. All these fuses look okay to me.

Amanda: Tom!

15   **Tom:** Yes, Mother?

Amanda: That light bill I gave you several days ago. The one I told you we got the notices about?

Tom: Oh.—Yeah.

(Legend: "Ha!")

Amanda: You didn't neglect to pay it by any chance?

Tom: Why, I—

20   **Amanda:** Didn't! I might have known it!

Jim: Shakespeare probably wrote a poem on that light bill, Mrs. Wingfield.

Amanda: I might have known better than to trust him with it! There's such a high price for negligence in this world!

Jim: Maybe the poem will win a ten-dollar prize.

Amanda: We'll just have to spend the remainder of the evening in the nineteenth century, before Mr. Edison made the Mazda lamp!

25   **Jim:** Candlelight is my favorite kind of light.

Amanda: That shows you're romantic! But that's no excuse for Tom. Well, we got through dinner. Very considerate of them to let us get through dinner before they plunged us into everlasting darkness, wasn't it, Mr. O'Connor?

JIM: Ha-ha!

AMANDA: Tom, as a penalty for your carelessness you can help me with the dishes.

JIM: Let me give you a hand.

30 **AMANDA:** Indeed you will not!

JIM: I ought to be good for something.

AMANDA: Good for something? *(Her tone is rhapsodic.) You?* Why, Mr. O'Connor, nobody, *nobody's* given me this much entertainment in years— as you have!

JIM: Aw, now, Mrs. Wingfield!

AMANDA: I'm not exaggerating, not one bit! But Sister is all by her lonesome. You go keep her company in the parlor! I'll give you this lovely old candelabrum that used to be on the altar at the church of the Heavenly Rest. It was melted a little out of shape when the church burnt down. Lightning struck it one spring. Gypsy Jones was holding a revival at the time and he intimated that the church was destroyed because the Episcopalians gave card parties.

35 **JIM:** Ha-ha.

AMANDA: And how about coaxing Sister to drink a little wine? I think it would be good for her! Can you carry both at once?

JIM: Sure. I'm Superman!

AMANDA: Now, Thomas, get into this apron!

The door of kitchenette swings closed on Amanda's gay laughter; the flickering light approaches the portieres.

Laura sits up nervously as he enters. Her speech at first is low and breathless from the almost intolerable strain of being alone with a stranger.

(The Legend: "I Don't Suppose You Remember Me At All!")

In her first speeches in this scene, before Jim's warmth overcomes her paralyzing shyness, Laura's voice is thin and breathless as though she has run up a steep flight of stairs.

Jim's attitude is gently humorous. In playing this scene it should be stressed that while the incident is apparently unimportant, it is to Laura the climax of her secret life.

JIM: Hello, there, Laura.

40 **LAURA:** *(faintly)* Hello. *(She clears her throat.)*

JIM: How are you feeling now? Better?

LAURA: Yes. Yes, thank you.

JIM: This is for you. A little dandelion wine. *(He extends it toward her with extravagant gallantry.)*

LAURA: Thank you.

45 **JIM:** Drink it—but don't get drunk! *(He laughs heartily. Laura takes the glass uncertainly; laughs shyly.)* Where shall I set the candles?

LAURA: Oh—oh, anywhere ...

Jim: How about here on the floor? Any objections?

Laura: No.

Jim: I'll spread a newspaper under to catch the drippings. I like to sit on the floor. Mind if I do?

50 **Laura:** Oh, no.

Jim: Give me a pillow?

Laura: What?

Jim: A pillow!

Laura: Oh . . . *(Hands him one quickly.)*

55 **Jim:** How about you? Don't you like to sit on the floor?

Laura: Oh—yes.

Jim: Why don't you, then?

Laura: I—will.

Jim: Take a pillow! *(Laura does. Sits on the other side of the candelabrum. Jim crosses his legs and smiles engagingly at her.)* I can't hardly see you sitting way over there.

60 **Laura:** I can—see you.

Jim: I know, but that's not fair, I'm in the limelight. *(Laura moves her pillow closer.)* Good! Now I can see you! Comfortable?

Laura: Yes.

Jim: So am I. Comfortable as a cow. Will you have some gum?

Laura: No, thank you.

65 **Jim:** I think that I will indulge, with your permission. *(Musingly unwraps it and holds it up.)* Think of the fortune made by the guy that invented the first piece of chewing gum. Amazing, huh? The Wrigley Building is one of the sights of Chicago.—I saw it summer before last when I went up to the Century of Progress. Did you take in the Century of Progress?

Laura: No, I didn't.

Jim: Well, it was quite a wonderful exposition. What impressed me most was the Hall of Science. Gives you an idea of what the future will be in America, even more wonderful than the present time is! *(Pause. Smiling at her.)* Your brother tells me you're shy. Is that right, Laura?

Laura: I—don't know.

Jim: I judge you to be an old-fashioned type of girl. Well, I think that's a pretty good type to be. Hope you don't think I'm being too personal—do you?

70 **Laura:** *(hastily, out of embarrassment)* I believe I *will* take a piece of gum, if you—don't mind. *(Clearing her throat.)* Mr. O'Connor, have you—kept up with your singing?

Jim: Singing? Me?

Laura: Yes. I remember what a beautiful voice you had.

Jim: When did you hear me sing?

(Voice Offstage In The Pause.)

Voice (offstage):

> O blow, ye winds, heigh-ho,
> A-roving I will go!

I'm off to my love
With a boxing glove—

Ten thousand miles away!

JIM: You say you've heard me sing?

75 **LAURA:** Oh, yes! Yes, very often . . . I—don't suppose you remember me—at all?

JIM: *(smiling doubtfully)* You know I have an idea I've seen you before. I had that idea soon as you opened the door. It seemed almost like I was about to remember your name. But the name that I started to call you—wasn't a name! And so I stopped myself before I said it.

LAURA: Wasn't it—Blue Roses?

JIM: *(springs up, grinning)* Blue Roses! My gosh, yes—Blue Roses! That's what I had on my tongue when you opened the door! Isn't it funny what tricks your memory plays? I didn't connect you with the high school somehow or other. But that's where it was; it was high school. I didn't even know you were Shakespeare's sister! Gosh, I'm sorry.

LAURA: I didn't expect you to. You—barely knew me!

80 **JIM:** But we did have a speaking acquaintance, huh?

LAURA: Yes, we—spoke to each other.

JIM: When did you recognize me?

LAURA: Oh, right away!

JIM: Soon as I came in the door?

85 **LAURA:** When I heard your name I thought it was probably you. I knew that Tom used to know you a little in high school. So when you came in the door—Well, then I was—sure.

JIM: Why didn't you *say* something, then?

LAURA: *(breathlessly)* I didn't know what to say, I was—too surprised!

JIM: For goodness' sakes! You know, this sure is funny!

LAURA: Yes! Yes, isn't it, though . . .

90 **JIM:** Didn't we have a class in something together?

LAURA: Yes, we did.

JIM: What class was that?

LAURA: It was—singing—Chorus!

JIM: Aw!

95 **LAURA:** I sat across the aisle from you in the Aud.

JIM: Aw.

LAURA: Mondays, Wednesdays and Fridays.

JIM: Now I remember—you always came in late.

LAURA: Yes, it was so hard for me, getting upstairs. I had that brace on my leg—it clumped so loud!

100 **JIM:** I never heard any clumping.

LAURA: *(wincing at the recollection)* To me it sounded like—thunder!

JIM: Well, well, well. I never even noticed.

LAURA: And everybody was seated before I came in. I had to walk in front of all those people. My seat was in the back row. I had to go clumping all the way up the aisle with everyone watching!

Jim: You shouldn't have been self-conscious.

105 **Laura:** I know, but I was. It was always such a relief when the singing started.

Jim: Aw, yes, I've placed you now! I used to call you Blue Roses. How was it that I got started calling you that?

Laura: I was out of school a little while with pleurosis. When I came back you asked me what was the matter. I said I had pleurosis—you thought I said Blue Roses. That's what you always called me after that!

Jim: I hope you didn't mind.

Laura: Oh, no—I liked it. You see, I wasn't acquainted with many—people. . . .

110 **Jim:** As I remember you sort of stuck by yourself.

Laura: I—I—never had much luck at—making friends.

Jim: I don't see why you wouldn't.

Laura: Well, I—started out badly.

Jim: You mean being—

115 **Laura:** Yes, it sort of—stood between me—

Jim: You shouldn't have let it!

Laura: I know, but it did, and—

Jim: You were shy with people!

Laura: I tried not to be but never could—

120 **Jim:** Overcome it?

Laura: No, I—I never could!

Jim: I guess being shy is something you have to work out of kind of gradually.

Laura: *(sorrowfully)* Yes—I guess it—

Jim: Takes time!

125 **Laura:** Yes—

Jim: People are not so dreadful when you know them. That's what you have to remember! And everybody has problems, not just you, but practically everybody has got some problems. You think of yourself as having the only problems, as being the only one who is disappointed. But just look around you and you will see lots of people as disappointed as you are. For instance, I hoped when I was going to high school that I would be further along at this time, six years later, than I am now—You remember that wonderful write-up I had in *The Torch?*

Laura: Yes! *(She rises and crosses to table.)*

Jim: It said I was bound to succeed in anything I went into! *(Laura returns with the annual.)* Holy Jeez! *The Torch!* *(He accepts it reverently. They smile across it with mutual wonder. Laura crouches beside him and they begin to turn through it. Laura's shyness is dissolving in his warmth.)*

Laura: Here you are in *Pirates of Penzance!*

130 **Jim:** *(wistfully)* I sang the baritone lead in that operetta.

Laura: *(rapidly)* So—*beautifully!*

Jim: *(protesting)* Aw—

Laura: Yes, yes—beautifully—beautifully!

Jim: You heard me?

135 **LAURA:** All three times!

JIM: No!

LAURA: Yes!

JIM: All three performances?

LAURA: *(looking down)* Yes.

140 **JIM:** Why?

LAURA: I—wanted to ask you to—autograph my program.

JIM: Why didn't you ask me to?

LAURA: You were always surrounded by your own friends so much that I never had a chance to.

JIM: You should have just—

145 **LAURA:** Well, I—thought you might think I was—

JIM: Thought I might think you was—what?

LAURA: Oh—

JIM: *(with reflective relish)* I was beleaguered by females in those days.

LAURA: You were terribly popular!

150 **JIM:** Yeah—

LAURA: You had such a—friendly way—

JIM: I was spoiled in high school.

LAURA: Everybody—liked you!

JIM: Including you?

155 **LAURA:** I—yes, I—I did, too—*(She gently closes the book in her lap.)*

JIM: Well, well, well!—Give me that program, Laura. *(She hands it to him. He signs it with a flourish.)* There you are—better late than never!

LAURA: Oh, I—what a—surprise!

JIM: My signature isn't worth very much right now. But some day—maybe—it will increase in value! Being disappointed is one thing and being discouraged is something else. I am disappointed but I'm not discouraged. I'm twenty-three years old. How old are you?

LAURA: I'll be twenty-four in June.

160 **JIM:** That's not old age!

LAURA: No, but—

JIM: You finished high school?

LAURA: *(with difficulty)* I didn't go back.

JIM: You mean you dropped out?

165 **LAURA:** I made bad grades in my final examinations. *(She rises and replaces the book and the program. Her voice strained.)* How is—Emily Meisenbach getting along?

JIM: Oh, that kraut-head!

LAURA: Why do you call her that?

JIM: That's what she was.

LAURA: You're not still—going with her?

170 **JIM:** I never see her.

LAURA: It said in the Personal Section that you were—engaged!

JIM: I know, but I wasn't impressed by that—propaganda!

Laura: It wasn't—the truth?

Jim: Only in Emily's optimistic opinion!

175 Laura: Oh—

(Legend: "What Have You Done Since High School?")

Jim lights a cigarette and leans indolently back on his elbows smiling at Laura with a warmth and charm which light her inwardly with altar candles. She remains by the table and turns in her hands a piece of glass to cover her tumult.

Jim: *(after several reflective puffs on a cigarette)* What have you done since high school? *(She seems not to hear him.)* Huh? *(Laura looks up.)* I said what have you done since high school, Laura?

Laura: Nothing much.

Jim: You must have been doing something these six long years.

Laura: Yes.

180 Jim: Well, then, such as what?

Laura: I took a business course at business college—

Jim: How did that work out?

Laura: Well, not very—well—I had to drop out, it gave me—indigestion—

Jim laughs gently.

Jim: What are you doing now?

185 Laura: I don't do anything—much. Oh, please don't think I sit around doing nothing! My glass collection takes up a good deal of my time. Glass is something you have to take good care of.

Jim: What did you say—about glass?

Laura: Collection I said—I have one—*(She clears her throat and turns away again, acutely shy.)*

Jim: *(abruptly)* You know what I judge to be the trouble with you? Inferiority complex! Know what that is? That's what they call it when someone low-rates himself! I understand it because I had it, too. Although my case was not so aggravated as yours seems to be. I had it until I took up public speaking, developed my voice, and learned that I had an aptitude for science. Before that time I never thought of myself as being outstanding in any way whatsoever! Now I've never made a regular study of it, but I have a friend who says I can analyze people better than doctors that make a profession of it. I don't claim that to be necessarily true, but I can sure guess a person's psychology, Laura! *(Takes out his gum.)* Excuse me, Laura. I always take it out when the flavor is gone. I'll use this scrap of paper to wrap it in. I know how it is to get it stuck on a shoe. Yep—that's what I judge to be your principal trouble. A lack of confidence in yourself as a person. You don't have the proper amount of faith in yourself. I'm basing that fact on a number of your remarks and also on certain observations I've made. For instance that clumping you thought was so awful in high school. You say that you even dreaded to walk into class. You see what you did? You dropped out of school, you gave up an education because of a clump, which as far as I know was practically nonexistent! A little physical defect is what you have. Hardly noticeable even! Magnified thousands of times by imagination! You know what my strong advice to you is? Think of yourself as *superior* in some way!

Laura: In what way would I think?

190 **Jim:** Why, man alive, Laura! Just look about you a little. What do you see? A world full of common people! All of 'em born and all of 'em going to die! Which of them has one-tenth of your good points! Or mine! Or anyone else's, as far as that goes—Gosh! Everybody excels in some one thing. Some in many! *(Unconsciously glances at himself in the mirror.)* All you've got to do is discover in *what!* Take me, for instance. *(He adjusts his tie at the mirror.)* My interest happens to lie in electro-dynamics. I'm taking a course in radio engineering at night school, Laura, on top of a fairly responsible job at the warehouse. I'm taking that course and studying public speaking.

Laura: Ohhhh.

Jim: Because I believe in the future of television! *(Turning back to her.)* I wish to be ready to go up right along with it. Therefore I'm planning to get in on the ground floor. In fact, I've already made the right connections and all that remains is for the industry itself to get underway! Full steam—*(His eyes are starry.)* Knowledge—Zzzzzp! *Money*—Zzzzzzp!—*Power!* That's the cycle democracy is built on! *(His attitude is convincingly dynamic. Laura stares at him, even her shyness eclipsed in her absolute wonder. He suddenly grins.)* I guess you think I think a lot of myself!

Laura: No—o-o-o, I—

Jim: Now how about you? Isn't there something you take more interest in than anything else?

195 **Laura:** Well, I do—as I said—have my—glass collection—

A peal of girlish laughter from the kitchen.

Jim: I'm not right sure I know what you're talking about. What kind of glass is it?

Laura: Little articles of it, they're ornaments mostly! Most of them are little animals made out of glass, the tiniest little animals in the world. Mother calls them a glass menagerie! Here's an example of one, if you'd like to see it! This one is one of the oldest. It's nearly thirteen. *(He stretches out his hand.)* *(Music: "The Glass Menagerie.")* Oh, be careful—if you breathe, it breaks!

Jim: I'd better not take it. I'm pretty clumsy with things.

Laura: Go on, I trust you with him! *(Places it in his palm.)* There now—you're holding him gently! Hold him over the light, he loves the light! You see how the light shines through him?

200 **Jim:** It sure does shine!

Laura: I shouldn't be partial, but he is my favorite one.

Jim: What kind of a thing is this one supposed to be?

Laura: Haven't you noticed the single horn on his forehead?

Jim: A unicorn, huh?

205 **Laura:** Mmm-hmmm!

Jim: Unicorns, aren't they extinct in the modern world?

Laura: I know!

Jim: Poor little fellow, he must feel sort of lonesome.

Laura: *(smiling)* Well, if he does he doesn't complain about it. He stays on a shelf with some horses that don't have horns and all of them seem to get along nicely together.

210 **Jim:** How do you know?

Laura: *(lightly)* I haven't heard any arguments among them!

Jim: *(grinning)* No arguments, huh? Well, that's a pretty good sign! Where shall I set him?

Laura: Put him on the table. They all like a change of scenery once in a while!

Jim: *(stretching)* Well, well, well, well—Look how big my shadow is when I stretch!

215 **Laura:** Oh, oh, yes—it stretches across the ceiling!

Jim: *(crossing to door)* I think it's stopped raining. *(Opens fire-escape door.)* Where does the music come from?

Laura: From the Paradise Dance Hall across the alley.

Jim: How about cutting the rug a little, Miss Wingfield?

Laura: Oh, I—

220 **Jim:** Or is your program filled up? Let me have a look at it. *(Grasps imaginary card.)* Why, every dance is taken! I'll just have to scratch some out. *(Waltz Music: "La Golondrina.")* Ahhh, a waltz! *(He executes some sweeping turns by himself, then holds his arms toward Laura.)*

Laura: *(breathlessly)* I—can't dance!

Jim: There you go, that inferiority stuff!

Laura: I've never danced in my life!

Jim: Come on, try!

225 **Laura:** Oh, but I'd step on you!

Jim: I'm not made out of glass.

Laura: How—how—how do we start?

Jim: Just leave it to me. You hold your arms out a little.

Laura: Like this?

230 **Jim:** A little bit higher. Right. Now don't tighten up, that's the main thing about it—relax.

Laura: *(laughing breathlessly)* It's hard not to.

Jim: Okay.

Laura: I'm afraid you can't budge me.

Jim: What do you bet I can't? *(He swings her into motion.)*

235 **Laura:** Goodness, yes, you can!

Jim: Let yourself go, now, Laura, just let yourself go.

Laura: I'm—

Jim: Come on!

Laura: Trying!

240 **JIM:** Not so stiff—Easy does it!

LAURA: I know but I'm—

JIM: Loosen th' backbone! There now, that's a lot better.

LAURA: Am I?

JIM: Lots, lots better! *(He moves her about the room in a clumsy waltz.)*

245 **LAURA:** Oh, my!

JIM: Ha-ha!

LAURA: Goodness, yes you can!

JIM: Ha-ha-ha! *(They suddenly bump into the table, Jim stops.)* What did we hit on?

LAURA: Table.

250 **JIM:** Did something fall off it? I think—

LAURA: Yes.

JIM: I hope that it wasn't the little glass horse with the horn!

LAURA: Yes.

JIM: Aw, aw, aw. Is it broken?

255 **LAURA:** Now it is just like all the other horses.

JIM: It's lost its—

LAURA: Horn! It doesn't matter. Maybe it's a blessing in disguise.

JIM: You'll never forgive me. I bet that that was your favorite piece of glass.

LAURA: I don't have favorites much. It's no tragedy, Freckles. Glass breaks so easily. No matter how careful you are. The traffic jars the shelves and things fall off them.

260 **JIM:** Still I'm awfully sorry that I was the cause.

LAURA: *(smiling)* I'll just imagine he had an operation. The horn was removed to make him feel less—freakish! *(They both laugh.)* Now he will feel more at home with the other horses, the ones that don't have horns . . .

JIM: Ha-ha, that's very funny! *(Suddenly serious.)* I'm glad to see that you have a sense of humor. You know—you're—well—very different! Surprisingly different from anyone else I know! *(His voice becomes soft and hesitant with a genuine feeling.)* Do you mind me telling you that? *(Laura is abashed beyond speech.)* You make me feel sort of—I don't know how to put it! I'm usually pretty good at expressing things, but—This is something that I don't know how to say! *(Laura touches her throat and clears it— turns the broken unicorn in her hands.) (Even softer.)* Has anyone ever told you that you were pretty? *(Pause: Music.) (Laura looks up slowly, with wonder, and shakes her head.)* Well, you are! In a very different way from anyone else. And all the nicer because of the difference, too. *(His voice becomes low and husky. Laura turns away, nearly faint with the novelty of her emotions.)* I wish you were my sister. I'd teach you to have some confidence in yourself. The different people are not like other people, but being different is nothing to be ashamed of. Because other people are not such wonderful people. They're one hundred times one thousand. You're one times one! They walk all over the earth. You just stay here. They're common as—weeds, but—you—well, you're—*Blue Roses!*

(Image On Screen: Blue Roses.)

(Music Changes.)

LAURA: But blue is wrong for—roses . . .

JIM: It's right for you—You're—pretty!

265 **LAURA:** In what respect am I pretty?

JIM: In all respects—believe me! Your eyes—your hair—are pretty! Your hands are pretty! *(He catches hold of her hand.)* You think I'm making this up because I'm invited to dinner and have to be nice. Oh, I could do that! I could put on an act for you, Laura, and say lots of things without being very sincere. But this time I am. I'm talking to you sincerely. I happened to notice you had this inferiority complex that keeps you from feeling comfortable with people. Somebody needs to build your confidence up and make you proud instead of shy and turning away and—blushing— Somebody ought to—ought to—*kiss* you, Laura! *(His hand slips slowly up her arm to her shoulder.) (Music Swells Tumultuously.) (He suddenly turns her about and kisses her on the lips. When he releases her Laura sinks on the sofa with a bright, dazed look. Jim backs away and fishes in his pocket for a cigarette.) (Legend On Screen: "Souvenir.")* Stumble-john! *(He lights the cigarette, avoiding her look. There is a peal of girlish laughter from Amanda in the kitchen. Laura slowly raises and opens her hand. It still contains the little broken glass animal. She looks at it with a tender, bewildered expression.)* Stumble-john! I shouldn't have done that—That was way off the beam. You don't smoke, do you? *(She looks up, smiling, not hearing the question. He sits beside her a little gingerly. She looks at him speechlessly—waiting. He coughs decorously and moves a little farther aside as he considers the situation and senses her feelings, dimly, with perturbation. Gently.)* Would you—care for a—mint? *(She doesn't seem to hear him but her look grows brighter even.)* Peppermint—Life Saver? My pocket's a regular drug store—wherever I go . . . *(He pops a mint in his mouth. Then gulps and decides to make a clean breast of it. He speaks slowly and gingerly.)* Laura, you know, if I had a sister like you, I'd do the same thing as Tom, I'd bring out fellows—introduce her to them. The right type of boys of a type to—appreciate her. Only—well—he made a mistake about me. Maybe I've got no call to be saying this. That may not have been the idea in having me over. But what if it was? There's nothing wrong about that. The only trouble is that in my case—I'm not in a situation to do the right thing. I can't take down your number and say I'll phone. I can't call up next week and—ask for a date. I thought I had better explain the situation in case you misunderstood it and—hurt your feelings. . . . *(Pause. Slowly, very slowly, Laura's look changes, her eyes returning slowly from his to the ornament in her palm.)*

Amanda utters another gay laugh in the kitchen.

LAURA: *(faintly)* You—won't—call again?

JIM: No, Laura. I can't. *(He rises from the sofa.)* As I was just explaining, I've— got strings on me, Laura, I've—been going steady! I go out all the time with a girl named Betty. She's a home-girl like you, and Catholic, and Irish, and in a great many ways we—get along fine. I met her last summer on a moonlight boat trip up the river to Alton, on the *Majestic.* Well—right away from the start it was—love! *(Legend: Love!) (Laura sways slightly forward and grips the arm of the sofa. He fails to notice, now enrapt in his own comfortable being.)* Being in love has made a new man of me! *(Leaning stiffly forward, clutching the arm of the sofa, Laura struggles visibly with her storm. But Jim is oblivious, she is a long way off.)* The power of love is really pretty tremendous! Love is something that—changes the whole world, Laura! *(The storm abates a little and Laura leans back. He notices her again.)* It happened that Betty's aunt took sick, she got a wire and had to go to Centralia. So Tom—when he asked me to dinner—I naturally just accepted the invitation, not knowing that you—that he—that I—*(He stops awkwardly.)* Huh—I'm a stumble-john! *(He flops back on the sofa. The holy candles in the altar of Laura's face have been snuffed out! There is a look of almost infinite desolation. Jim glances at her uneasily.)* I wish that you would—say something. *(She bites her lip which was trembling and then bravely smiles. She opens her hand again on the broken glass ornament. Then she gently takes his hand and raises it level with her own. She carefully places the unicorn in the palm of his hand, then pushes his fingers closed upon it.)* What are you—doing that for? You want me to have him?—Laura? *(She nods.)* What for?

LAURA: A—souvenir . . .

She rises unsteadily and crouches beside the Victrola to wind it up.

(Legend On Screen: "Things Have A Way Of Turning Out So Badly.")

(Or Image: "Gentleman Caller Waving Good-bye!—Gaily.")

At this moment Amanda rushes brightly back in the front room. She bears a pitcher of fruit punch in an old-fashioned cut-glass pitcher and a plate of maca-roons. The plate has a gold border and poppies painted on it.

270 **AMANDA:** Well, well, well! Isn't the air delightful after the shower? I've made you children a little liquid refreshment. *(Turns gaily to the gentleman caller.)* Jim, do you know that song about lemonade?

> "Lemonade, lemonade
> Made in the shade and stirred with a spade—
> Good enough for any old maid!"

JIM: *(uneasily)* Ha-ha! No—I never heard it.

AMANDA: Why, Laura! You look so serious!

JIM: We were having a serious conversation.

AMANDA: Good! Now you're better acquainted!

275 **JIM:** *(uncertainly)* Ha-ha! Yes.

AMANDA: You modern young people are much more serious-minded than my generation. I was so gay as a girl!

JIM: You haven't changed, Mrs. Wingfield.

AMANDA: Tonight I'm rejuvenated! The gaiety of the occasion, Mr. O'Connor! *(She tosses her head with a peal of laughter. Spills lemonade.)* Oooo! I'm baptizing myself!

JIM: Here—let me—

280 **AMANDA:** *(setting the pitcher down)* There now. I discovered we had some maraschino cherries. I dumped them in, juice and all!

JIM: You shouldn't have gone to that trouble. Mrs. Wingfield.

AMANDA: Trouble, trouble? Why it was loads of fun! Didn't you hear me cutting up in the kitchen? I bet your ears were burning! I told Tom how outdone with him I was for keeping you to himself so long a time! He should have brought you over much, much sooner! Well, now that you've found your way, I want you to be a very frequent caller! Not just occasional but all the time. Oh, we're going to have a lot of gay times together! I see them coming! Mmm, just breathe that air! So fresh, and the moon's so pretty! I'll skip back out—I know where my place is when young folks are having a—serious conversation!

JIM: Oh, don't go out, Mrs. Wingfield. The fact of the matter is I've got to be going.

AMANDA: Going, now? You're joking! Why, it's only the shank of the evening, Mr. O'Connor!

285 **JIM:** Well, you know how it is.

AMANDA: You mean you're a young workingman and have to keep workingmen's hours. We'll let you off early tonight. But only on the condition that next time you stay later. What's the best night for you? Isn't Saturday night the best night for you workingmen?

JIM: I have a couple of time-clocks to punch, Mrs. Wingfield. One at morning, another one at night!

AMANDA: My, but you *are* ambitious! You work at night, too?

JIM: No, Ma'am, not work but—Betty! *(He crosses deliberately to pick up his hat. The band at the Paradise Dance Hall goes into a tender waltz.)*

290 **AMANDA:** Betty? Betty? Who's Betty! *(There is an ominous cracking sound in the sky.)*

JIM: Oh, just a girl. The girl I go steady with! *(He smiles charmingly. The sky falls.)*

(Legend: "The Sky Falls.")

AMANDA: *(a long-drawn exhalation)* Ohhhh . . . Is it a serious romance Mr. O'Connor?

JIM: We're going to be married the second Sunday in June.

AMANDA: Ohhhh—how nice! Tom didn't mention that you were engaged to be married.

295 **JIM:** The cat's not out of the bag at the warehouse yet. You know how they are. They call you Romeo and stuff like that. *(He stops at the oval mirror*

to put on his hat. He carefully shapes the brim and the crown to give a discreetly dashing effect.) It's been a wonderful evening, Mrs. Wingfield. I guess this is what they mean by Southern hospitality.

AMANDA: It really wasn't anything at all.

JIM: I hope it don't seem like I'm rushing off. But I promised Betty I'd pick her up at the Wabash depot, an' by the time I get my jalopy down there her train'll be in. Some women are pretty upset if you keep 'em waiting.

AMANDA: Yes, I know—The tyranny of women! *(Extends her hand.)* Good-bye, Mr. O'Connor. I wish you luck—and happiness—and success! All three of them, and so does Laura!—Don't you, Laura?

LAURA: Yes!

300 JIM: *(taking her hand)* Good-bye, Laura. I'm certainly going to treasure that souvenir. And don't you forget the good advice I gave you. *(Raises his voice to a cheery shout.)* So long, Shakespeare! Thanks again, ladies— Good night!

He grins and ducks jauntily out.
   Still bravely grimacing, Amanda closes the door on the gentleman caller. Then she turns back to the room with a puzzled expression. She and Laura don't dare to face each other. Laura crouches beside the Victrola to wind it.

AMANDA: *(faintly)* Things have a way of turning out so badly. I don't believe that I would play the Victrola. Well, well—well—Our gentleman caller was engaged to be married! Tom!

TOM: *(from back)* Yes, Mother?

AMANDA: Come in here a minute. I want to tell you something awfully funny.

TOM: *(enters with macaroon and a glass of the lemonade)* Has the gentleman caller gotten away already?

305 AMANDA: The gentleman caller has made an early departure. What a wonderful joke you played on us!

TOM: How do you mean?

AMANDA: You didn't mention that he was engaged to be married.

TOM: Jim? Engaged?

AMANDA: That's what he just informed us.

310 TOM: I'll be jiggered! I didn't know about that.

AMANDA: That seems very peculiar.

TOM: What's peculiar about it?

AMANDA: Didn't you call him your best friend down at the warehouse?

TOM: He is, but how did I know?

315 AMANDA: It seems extremely peculiar that you wouldn't know your best friend was going to be married!

TOM: The warehouse is where I work, not where I know things about people!

AMANDA: You don't know things anywhere! You live in a dream; you manufacture illusions! *(He crosses to door.)* Where are you going?

TOM: I'm going to the movies.

AMANDA: That's right, now that you've had us make such fools of ourselves. The effort, the preparations, all the expense! The new floor lamp, the rug, the clothes for Laura! All for what? To entertain some other girl's fiancé! Go to the movies, go! Don't think about us, a mother deserted, an unmarried sister who's crippled and has no job! Don't let anything interfere with your selfish pleasure! Just go, go, go—to the movies!

320 **TOM:** All right, I will! The more you shout about my selfishness to me the quicker I'll go, and I won't go to the movies!

AMANDA: Go, then! Then go to the moon—you selfish dreamer!

Tom smashes his glass on the floor. He plunges out on the fire-escape, slamming the door. Laura screams—cut by door.

Dance-hall music up. Tom goes to the rail and grips it desperately, lifting his face in the chill white moonlight penetrating the narrow abyss of the alley.

(Legend On Screen: "And So Good-bye . . . ")

Tom's closing speech is timed with the interior pantomime. The interior scene is played as though viewed through sound-proof glass. Amanda appears to be making a comforting speech to Laura who is huddled upon the sofa. Now that we cannot hear the mother's speech, her silliness is gone and she has dignity and tragic beauty. Laura's dark hair hides her face until at the end of the speech she lifts it to smile at her mother. Amanda's gestures are slow and graceful, almost dancelike, as she comforts the daughter. At the end of her speech she glances a moment at the father's picture—then withdraws through the portieres. At close of Tom's speech, Laura blows out the candles, ending the play.

TOM: I didn't go to the moon, I went much further—for time is the longest distance between two places—Not long after that I was fired for writing a poem on the lid of a shoe-box. I left Saint Louis. I descended the steps of this fire-escape for a last time and followed, from then on, in my father's footsteps, attempting to find in motion what was lost in space—I traveled around a great deal. The cities swept about me like dead leaves, leaves that were brightly colored but torn away from the branches. I would have stopped, but was pursued by something. It always came upon me unawares, taking me altogether by surprise. Perhaps it was a familiar bit of music. Perhaps it was only a piece of transparent glass. Perhaps I am walking along a street at night, in some strange city, before I have found companions. I pass the lighted window of a shop where perfume is sold. The window is filled with pieces of colored glass, tiny transparent bottles in delicate colors, like bits of a shattered rainbow. Then all at once my sister touches my shoulder. I turn around and look into her eyes . . . Oh, Laura, Laura, I tried to leave you behind me, but I am more faithful than I intended to be! I reach for a cigarette, I cross the street, I run into the movies or a bar, I buy a drink, I speak to the nearest stranger—anything that can blow your candles out! *(Laura bends over the candles.)*—for nowadays the world is lit by lightning! Blow out your candles, Laura—and so good-bye . . .

She blows the candles out.

(The Scene Dissolves.)

❖ ❖ ❖

Author's Production Notes

(PREFACE TO THE PUBLISHED EDITION)

Being a "memory play," The Glass Menagerie can be presented with unusual freedom of convention. Because of its considerably delicate or tenuous material, atmospheric touches and subtleties of direction play a particularly important part. Expressionism and all other unconventional techniques in drama have only one valid aim, and that is a closer approach to truth. When a play employs unconventional techniques, it is not, or certainly shouldn't be, trying to escape its responsibility of dealing with reality, or interpreting experience, but is actually or should be attempting to find a closer approach, a more penetrating and vivid expression of things as they are. The straight realistic play with its genuine Frigidaire and authentic ice-cubes, its characters that speak exactly as its audience speaks, corresponds to the academic landscape and has the same virtue of a photographic likeness. Everyone should know nowadays the unimportance of the photographic in art: that truth, life, or reality is an organic thing which the poetic imagination can represent or suggest, in essence, only through transformation, through changing into other forms than those which were merely present in appearance.

These remarks are not meant as a preface only to this particular play. They have to do with a conception of a new, plastic theatre which must take the place of the exhausted theater of realistic conventions if the theatre is to resume vitality as a part of our culture.

The Screen Device: There is *only one important difference between the original and acting version of the play* and that is the *omission* in the latter of the device which I tentatively included in my *original* script. This device was the use of a screen on which were projected magic-lantern slides bearing images or titles. I do not regret the omission of this device from the present Broadway production. The extraordinary power of Miss Taylor's performance made it suitable to have the utmost simplicity in the physical production. But I think it may be interesting to some readers to see how this device was conceived. So I am putting it into the published manuscript. These images and legends, projected from behind, were cast on a section of wall between the front-room and dining-room areas, which should be indistinguishable from the rest when not in use.

The purpose of this will probably be apparent. It is to give accent to certain values in each scene. Each scene contains a particular point (or several) which is structurally the most important. In an episodic play, such as this, the basic structure or narrative line may be obscured from the audience; the effect may seem fragmentary rather than architectural. This may not be the fault of the play so much as a lack of attention in the audience. The legend or image upon the screen will strengthen the effect of what is merely allusion in the writing and allow the primary point to be made more simply and lightly than if the entire responsibility were on the spoken lines. Aside from this structural value, I think the screen will have a definite emotional appeal, less definable but just as important. An imaginative producer or director may invent many other uses for this device than those indicated in the present script. In fact the possibilities of the device seem much larger to me than the instance of this play can possibly utilize.

The Music: Another extra-literary accent in this play is provided by the use of music. A single recurring tune, "The Glass Menagerie," is used to give emotional emphasis to suitable passages. This tune is like circus music, not when you are on the grounds or in the immediate vicinity of the parade, but when you are at some distance and very likely thinking of something else. It seems under those circumstances to continue almost interminably and it weaves in and out of the preoccupied consciousness; then it is the lightest, most delicate music in the world and perhaps the saddest. It expresses the surface vivacity of life with the underlying strain of immutable and inexpressible sorrow. When you look at a piece of delicately spun glass you think of two things: how beautiful it is and how easily it can be broken. Both of those ideas should be woven into the recurring tune, which dips in and out of the play as if it were carried on a wind that changes. It serves as a thread of connection and allusion between the narrator with his separate point in time and space and the subject of his story. Between each episode it returns as reference to the emotion, nostalgia, which is the first

condition of the play. It is primarily Laura's music and therefore comes out most clearly when the play focuses upon her and the lovely fragility of glass which is her image.

The Lighting: The lighting in the play is not realistic. In keeping with the atmosphere of memory, the stage is dim. Shafts of light are focused on selected areas or actors, sometimes in contradistinction to what is the apparent center. For instance, in the quarrel scene between Tom and Amanda, in which Laura has no active part, the clearest pool of light is on her figure. This is also true of the supper scene, when her silent figure on the sofa should remain the visual center. The light upon Laura should be distinct from the others, having a peculiar pristine clarity such as light used in early religious portraits of female saints or madonnas. A certain correspondence to light in religious paintings, such as El Greco's, where the figures are radiant in atmosphere that is relatively dusky, could be effectively used throughout the play. (It will also permit a more effective use of the screen.) A free, imaginative use of light can be of enormous value in giving a mobile, plastic quality to plays of a more or less static nature.

T. W.

Excerpts from Three Memoirs

(1) TENNESSEE WILLIAMS'S MOTHER
(EDWINA DAKIN WILLIAMS)

I had not read *Menagerie*, knew nothing of its story except the snatches I glimpsed at rehearsals. After the curtain went up, I became lost in the magic of the words and the superb performance of its four players. You

couldn't call Laurette or Julie pretty but they imbued their parts with a strong spiritual quality.

This was the first of Tom's plays I had seen, . . . and I was thrilled to think he had created a play without a wasted word and one in which every moment added drama. I don't think there's been a play like it, before or since.

The audience, too, seemed spellbound throughout and particularly when Mr. Dowling stood to one side of the stage and uttered the words, "I didn't go to the moon, I went much further—for time is the longest distance between two places. . . . Oh, Laura, Laura, I tried to leave you behind me, but I am more faithful than I intended to be! I reach for a cigarette, I cross the street, I run into the movies or a bar, I buy a drink, I speak to the nearest stranger—anything that can blow your candles out!"

At this moment, in the center of the stage behind a thin veil of a curtain, Julie bent low over the candles in her tenement home as Mr. Dowling said sadly, "—for nowadays the world is lit by lightning! Blow out your candles, Laura—and so good-bye. . . . "

And the curtain dropped slowly on the world premiere of *The Glass Menagerie*.

At first it was so quiet I thought the audience didn't like the play. A young woman behind me clapped wildly, as though to make up for the lack of applause, and I heard her remark indignantly, "These Chicago audiences make me mad! This is a beautiful play."

Then, all of a sudden, a tumultuous clapping of hands broke out. The audience had been recovering from the mood into which the play had plunged it. Gratefully I turned to the young woman, who I later found out was a student of English at the University of Chicago, and asked, "Would you like to meet the author? I'm his mother." When Tom arrived to take me backstage, I introduced the young woman, breathless with excitement, and we invited her to go behind the scenes with us.

I wanted to congratulate Laurette, who had brought down the house with her amazing performance as Amanda Wingfield, the faded, fretful, dominating mother lost in the dream world of her past, bullying her son into finding a gentleman caller for his abnormally shy sister.

I entered Laurette's dressing room, not knowing what to expect, for she was sometimes quite eccentric. She was sitting with her feet propped up on the radiator, trying to keep warm. Before I had a chance to get out a word, she greeted me.

"Well, how did you like you'seff, Miz' Williams?" she asked.

I was so shocked I didn't know what to say. It had not occurred to me as I watched Tom's play that *I* was Amanda. But I recovered quickly.

"You were magnificent," I said quietly to Laurette.

Someone mentioned to Tom the opposite receptions given *Angels* and *Menagerie* and he explained this by saying, "You can't mix sex and religion . . . but you can always write safely about mothers."

To which I say, "Ah, can you, Tom?"

Over the years both subtly and not so subtly, I have often been reminded that the character of Amanda was rooted in me, and this is not generally meant as a compliment. The critics have described Amanda in such inelegant words as "an old witch riding a broomstick," "a raddled belle of the old South, sunk deep in frustration," "the scuffed, rundown slipper that outlived the ball," "a simple, sanely insane, horrible Mother, pathetic and terribly human and terribly real" and "a bit of a scold, a bit of a snob."

Tom's own description of Amanda as stated in the play held that she was "a little woman of great but confused vitality clinging frantically to another time and place. Her characterization must be carefully created, not copied from type. She is not paranoiac, but her life is paranoia. There is much to admire in Amanda, and as much to love and pity as there is to laugh at. Certainly she has endurance and a kind of heroism, and though her foolishness makes her unwittingly cruel at times, there is tenderness in her slight person."

Tom has contradicted himself when asked if the play were based on his life. Once he told a reporter it was a "memory play," adding, "My mother and sister will never forgive me for that." Another time he said, "It was derived from years of living." Then again, he denied it was autobiographical, calling it "a dream or fantasy play. The gentleman caller is meant to be the symbol of the world and its attitude toward the unrealistic dreamers who are three characters of the play."

I think it is high time the ghost of Amanda was laid. I am *not* Amanda. I'm sure if Tom stops to think, he realizes I am not. The only resemblance I have to Amanda is that we both like jonquils.

(2) T E N N E S S E E   W I L L I A M S

Rose was a popular girl in high school but only for a brief while. Her beauty was mainly in her expressive green-gray eyes and in her curly auburn hair. She was too narrow-shouldered and her state of anxiety when in male company inclined her to hunch them so they looked even narrower; this made her strong-featured, very Williams head seem too large for her thin, small-breasted body. She also, when she was on a date, would talk with an almost hysterical animation which few young men knew how to take.

The first real breakdown occurred shortly after I had suffered the heart attack that ended my career as a clerk-errand boy at the shoe company.

My first night back from St. Vincent's, as I mentioned, Rose came walking like a somnambulist into my tiny bedroom and said, "We must all die together."

I can assure you that the idea did not offer to me an irresistible appeal. Being now released at last from my three years as a clerk-typist at Continental, God damn it I was in no mood to consider group suicide with the family, not even at Rose's suggestion—however appropriate the suggestion may have been.

For several days Rose was demented. One afternoon she put a kitchen knife in her purse and started to leave for her psychiatrist's office with apparent intent of murder.

The knife was noticed by Mother and snatched away.

Then a day or so later this first onset of dementia praecox passed off and Rose was, at least on the surface, her usual (now very quiet) self again.

A few days later I departed for Memphis to recuperate at my grandparents' little house on Snowden Avenue near Southwestern University in Memphis.

I think it was about this time that our wise old family doctor told Mother that Rose's physical and mental health depended upon what struck Miss Edwina as a monstrous thing—an arranged, a sort of "therapeutic" marriage. Obviously old Doc Alexander had hit upon the true seat of Rose's afflictions. She was a very normal—but highly sexed—girl who was tearing herself apart mentally and physically by those repressions imposed upon her by Miss Edwina's monolithic Puritanism.

I may have inadvertently omitted a good deal of material about the unusually close relations between Rose and me. Some perceptive critic of the theatre made the observation that the true theme of my work is "incest." My sister and I had a close relationship, quite unsullied by any carnal knowledge. As a matter of fact, we were rather shy of each other, physically, there was no casual physical intimacy of the sort that one observes among the Mediterranean people in their family relations. And yet our love was, and is, the deepest in our lives and was, perhaps, very pertinent to our withdrawal from extra-familial attachments.

There were years when I was in the shoe company and summers when I was a student at the State University of Missouri when my sister and I spent nearly all our evenings together aside from those which I spent with Hazel.

What did we do those evenings, Rose and I? Well, we strolled about the business streets of University City. It was a sort of ritual with a pathos that I assure you was never caught in *Menagerie* nor in my story "Portrait of Girl in Glass," on which *Menagerie* was based.

I think it was Delmar—that long, long street which probably began near the Mississippi River in downtown St. Louis and continued through University City and on out into the country—that Rose and I strolled along in the evenings. There was a root-beer stand at which we always stopped. Rose was inordinately fond of root-beer, especially on warm summer evenings. And before and after our root-beer stop, we would window-shop. Rose's passion, as well as Blanche's, was clothes. And all along that part of Delmar that cut through University City were little shops with lighted windows at night in which were displayed dresses and accessories for women. Rose did not have much of a wardrobe and so her window-shopping on Delmar was like a hungry child's gazing through the window-fronts of restaurants. Her taste in clothes was excellent.

"How about *that* dress, Rose?"

"Oh no, that's tacky. But this one here's very nice."

The evening excursions lasted about an hour and a half, and although, as I've noted, we had a physical shyness of each other, never even touching hands except when dancing together in the Enright apartment, I'd usually follow her into her bedroom when we came home, to continue our warmly desultory chats. I felt most at home in that room, which was furnished with the white ivory bedroom set that had been acquired with the family's "furnished apartment" on Westminster Place when we first moved to St. Louis in 1918.

It was the only attractive room in the apartment—or did it seem so because it was my sister's?

I have mentioned our dancing together.

Rose taught me to dance to the almost aboriginal standing (nonhorned) Victrola that had been acquired in Mississippi and shipped to St. Louis at the time of the disastrous family move there.

• • •

As I drifted away from my sister, during this period, she drew close to our little Boston terrier Jiggs. She was constantly holding and hugging him and now and then Miss Edwina would say:

"Miss Florence, I'm afraid that you forget we have neighbors and Mrs. Ebbs upstairs sometimes complains when Cornelius[1] raises his voice."

Miss Florence would be likely to reply something to the effect that Mrs. Ebbs upstairs could go to hell, for all it mattered to her . . .

The last time I was in St. Louis, for a visit at Christmas, I had my brother Dakin drive me about all the old places where we had lived in my childhood. It was a melancholy tour. Westminster Place and Forest Park Boulevard had lost all semblance of their charm in the twenties. The big old residences had been converted into sleazy rooming-houses or torn down for nondescript duplexes and small apartment buildings.

The Kramer residence was gone: in fact, all of the family, including dear Hazel, were by then dead.

This can only serve as a preamble, in this "thing," to the story of my great love for Hazel, and not at all an adequate one at that . . .

In my adolescence in St. Louis, at the age of sixteen, several important events in my life occurred. It was in the sixteenth year that I wrote "The Vengeance of Nitocris" and received my first publication in a magazine and the magazine was *Weird Tales*. The story wasn't published till June of 1928. That same year my grandfather Dakin took me with him on a tour of Europe with a large party of Episcopalian ladies from the Mississippi Delta. . . . And, it was in my sixteenth year that my deep nervous problems approached what might well have been a crisis as shattering as that which broke my sister's mind, lastingly, when she was in her twenties.

I was at sixteen a student at University City High School in St. Louis and the family was living in a cramped apartment at 6254 Enright Avenue.

University City was not a fashionable suburb of St. Louis and our neighborhood, while a cut better than that of the Wingfields in *Menagerie,* was only a little cut better: it was an ugly region of hive-like apartment buildings, for the most part, and fire escapes and pathetic little patches of green among concrete driveways.

My younger brother, Dakin, always an indomitable enthusiast at whatever he got into, had turned our little patch of green behind the apartment on Enright into quite an astonishing little vegetable garden. If there were flowers in it, they were, alas, obscured by the profuse growth of squash, pumpkins, and other edible flora.

I would, of course, have preempted all the space with rosebushes but I doubt they would have borne roses. The impracticalities, let's say the fantastic impracticalities, of my adolescence were not at all inclined to successful ends: and I can recall no roses in all the years that I spent in St. Louis and its environs except the two living Roses in my life, my grandmother, Rose O. Dakin, and, of course, my sister, Rose Isabel.

My adolescent problems took their most violent form in a shyness of a pathological degree. Few people realize, now, that I have always been and even remain in my years as a crocodile an extremely shy creature—in my crocodile years I compensate for this shyness by the typical Williams heartiness and bluster and sometimes explosive fury of behavior. In my

---

[1] Cornelius Coffin—father of Tennessee Williams.

high school days I had no disguise, no façade. And it was at University City High School that I developed the habit of blushing whenever anyone looked me in the eyes, as if I harbored behind them some quite dreadful or abominable secret.

(3) TENNESSEE WILLIAMS'S BROTHER AND A FRIEND (DAKIN WILLIAMS AND SHEPHERD MEADE)

While they were at the Webster Groves house a minor episode occurred that Tom might have made into a one-act play. All the actors were strictly in character. Dakin remembers it well. It was a Saturday midnight in August and still very hot. Tom telephoned. He was in his old Scatterbolt jalopy out on Sappington Road, and had run out of gas. (Very much in character. Tom never did and never would remember to put either oil or gas in cars.) "What *can* we do?" cried Rose frantically. (And in character.)

"Well," said Edwina, organizing things (in character), "your father has the car—and it's Saturday, so *he* won't be home until dawn." (Cornelius in character, and Edwina in character for putting it that way.)

Edwina decided that Rose and Dakin should get a taxi, stop for a can of gas and find Tom. They followed his directions, and there he was, standing with Scatterbolt beside a closed gas station.

"Oh, where have you been, Tom?" said Rose.

Tom answered, "To the movies."

"Mother won't believe that," said Rose, who didn't believe it either, knowing that Tom always said that as a cover story when he'd been with anybody his mother didn't approve of, which was practically everybody.

And that was what happened. When they reached home, Edwina was wearing her standard look of advanced suffering, like Amanda's in *The Glass Menagerie*.

"I was at the movies, mother," Tom said.

"I don't believe that lie!" Edwina said, in character.

"Well, you can go to hell then!" said Tom, going a bit beyond his character.

And then, Dakin remembers, "Mother's eyes shot up in their sockets toward the ceiling. She staggered backward as if struck by a physical blow. Cunningly she glanced behind her to be sure there was an overstuffed chair in the correct position, and proceeded to fall backward in a well-planned and frequently performed faint."

"Oh, my God!" gasped Rose (in character). "Tom, look what you've done! You've killed our mother!"

But Dakin wasn't worried. He had seen his mother "pull this on a monthly basis when arguing with dad over bills." He was, however, impressed by the performance, which he thought was better than usual.

If there'd only been a gentleman caller around, the whole scene might have come right out of one of Tom's plays.

❖ ❖ ❖

Excerpts from Two Interviews with Williams

(1) JEAN EVANS (1945)

I'd read four of Mr. Williams's one-act plays. All but one had been about poverty-stricken people whose situations seemed hopeless. I asked Mr. Williams if he always wrote about unhappy, trapped, hopeless people. He'd been half-reclining against a pillow on his bed, but he sat up now.

"I hadn't thought of them as being hopeless," he said. "That's not really what I was writing about. It's human valor that moves me. The one dominant theme in most of my writings, the most magnificent thing in all human nature, is valor—and endurance.

"The mother's valor is the core of *The Glass Menagerie*," he went on. "She's confused, pathetic, even stupid, but everything has *got* to be all right. She fights to make it that way in the only way she knows how."

We talked a little about his other plays and then, a trifle anxiously, he asked if I had found them without humor. I said no. There was a great deal of humor in them if he meant the wry kind that sprang out of incredibly miserable situations, the kind that made an audience want to cry while it was laughing. He nodded.

"George Jean Nathan, in his review of *Menagerie*, said I was *deficient* in humor," Williams remarked. [*New York Journal American*, 9 April 1945, 11—Editor] His manner was casual, but there was an edge of annoyance in his voice. "He said that all the humor had been embroidered into the play by Mr. Dowling." (Dowling is co-producer of the play, plays the narrator, and the son, Tom) "I'd love for somebody who knows my other work to refute him."

He paused, and then went on defensively, "Not one line of *Glass Menagerie* was changed after the final draft came back from the typist. A scene was inserted, the drunk scene. That was Mr. Dowling's idea, but entirely of my authorship. And one line by Mr. Dowling, was added. The last line, where he says to the audience, 'Here's where memory stops and your imagination begins.'" He paused. "Mr. Dowling did a great job. A magnificent job. But there was humor *contained* in the play. I had that in mind, along with the rest, when I was writing it."

Mr. Nathan had also written that the play, as originally written, was *freakish*. I wanted to know if Mr. Williams liked writing plays unconventional in form.

"If you mean unconventional in that my plays are light on plot and heavy on characterization, yes. But not in structure. *Glass Menagerie* is not at all freakish in structure.

"Have you read Saroyan's *Get Away, Old Man*?" Williams gave a peal of gay, sudden laughter that rang through the room. "There's a play that would give Mr. Nathan pause. The curtain goes up and down, up and down, all through the play."

He said he liked Saroyan very much, "his short stories perhaps, more than his plays."

I said I'd like Saroyan better if he were able to admit there was evil under the sun. Mr. Williams smiled. "His point of view—his attitude—I suppose you could say, is childish," he said. "Saroyan's characters are all little Saroyans. He multiplies himself like rabbits. But he is himself so interesting, that he usually gets away with writing only about himself."

How did he think the human situation could be improved? I asked. He looked as though the question had startled him.

"It's a social and economic problem, of course," he said, "not something mystical. I don't think there will be any equity in American life until at least 90 percent of our population are living under different circumstances. The white collar worker, for instance. Most people consider him pretty well off. I think his situation is horrible.

"I'd like to see people getting a lot more for what they invest in the way of effort and time. It's insane for human beings to work their whole lives away at dull, stupid, routine, anesthetizing jobs for just a little more than the necessities of life. There should be time—and money— for development. For living."

(2) W A L T E R   W A G E R   (1 9 6 7)

Albee said to me that he writes a play when it becomes more painful not to write it than to write it.

WILLIAMS: That's a very good way of putting it, you know.

Then the subject literally forces itself out?

WILLIAMS: Yes, some people accuse you of being too personal, you know, in your writing. The truth of the matter is—I don't think you can escape being personal in your writing.

Impossible.

WILLIAMS: That doesn't mean that you are one of the characters in the play. What it means simply is that the dynamics of the characters in the play, the tensions correspond to something that you are personally going through—the concerns of the play and the tensions of the play and your own concerns and tensions at the time you wrote it. I have always found that to be true.

◇ ◇ ◇

The Glass Menagerie

ROGER BOXILL

The play is cradled in the playwright's recall of the Depression years when he worked in the warehouse of the International Shoe Company by day and wrote by night. The faded belle as doting mother derives from Miss Edwina. The absent father who fell in love with long distance alludes to C. C. during his happy days as a Delta drummer. Rose Williams's short-lived business studies, disappointing relationships and withdrawal from life inform the character of Laura as the predestined spinster with a lost love. Even the title refers to the collection of little glass animals that Rose and Tom kept in her room in St. Louis, tiny figurines that came to represent for him all the softest emotions that belong to the remembrance of things past.

The theme of this gentle confessional work is aspiration and disappointment. The action is contained in the dashing of Laura's hope for romance, anticipated in the break-up of Amanda's marriage, and echoed in the failure of Tom's effort to become a writer. The plot centers on Laura's non-Cinderella story. A shy, crippled girl encounters in the flesh the very man she loves, who leads her on and quickly lets her down. The exposition of Amanda's ideal girlhood in Blue Mountain and unfortunate middle age in St. Louis is like an organ point that sounds the play's nostalgic note. She was once the belle of the ball, surrounded by suitors and is now a deserted housewife, struggling for survival. As the disillusioned narrator, Tom looks back to a time when adventure and success seemed possible. Even Jim, although not discouraged, finds life after adolescence disappointing.

The historical setting provides an enveloping action that ironically reflects the play's theme. The economic recovery following the Great Depression came with the Second World War. The optimistic phrases in which Jim forecasts his future—*"Knowledge—Zzzzp! Money—Zzzzp!—Power!"*—hint at the sounds of battle. The customers of the Paradise Dance Hall across the alley from the Wingfield apartment house find an end to boredom in a hell on earth. Tom gets his wish to live the life of a hero in an adventure movie through his role as a merchant seaman in a world lit by lightning.

The full historical background extends from the Second World War, in which Tom serves, to the First World War, in which his father served before him, and even to the American Civil War, which ended in the fall of the Old South, to whose vestiges of gracious living his mother still so desperately clings. Amanda Wingfield is an anachronism in the St. Louis of the 1930s and may even have been one in the Blue Mountain of her girlhood. Besides the story of her failed marriage, she brings to the play the sense of a world that, like herself, has long since faded. Her expectation that she would marry a wealthy planter and settle down to raise her family on a large plantation with many servants is a *belle rêve* of Southern aristocratic life in antebellum times. Her reminiscences are a confusion of wish and reality consistent with the play's premise that memory is primarily seated in the heart.

The Glass Menagerie is a dramatic elegy that plays within three concentric spheres of time: the time of the Second World War, in which Tom speaks to the audience as a merchant seaman; the time of the Depression, in which Tom lived with his mother and his sister in St. Louis; and the time that Amanda thinks of as a vanished golden age—her girlhood in the rural South before the Great War. Like Tom's, the memory of her cherished past is partly enacted when she appears for the evening of the dinner party with a bunch of jonquils on her arm and skips coquettishly around the living-room, dressed in the girlish frock of yellowed voile with blue silk sash in which she led the cotillion long ago, won the cakewalk twice at Sunset Hill, and went to the Governor's Ball in Jackson.

The primary conditions of Amanda's poignant resurrection of her youth—spring and courtship—conform to the conventions of pastoral romance. Invitations poured in from all over the Delta that enchanted season when she had her craze for jonquils. In the evenings there were dances, and in the afternoons picnics and long carriage rides through the countryside, lacy with dogwood in May, and flooded with the jonquils that she made her young men help gather for her. On a single Sunday afternoon in Blue Mountain, she had seventeen gentleman callers, and extra chairs had to be brought in from the parish house to accommodate them. She could have become the wife of the brilliant Duncan J. Fitzhugh or of the dashing Bates Cutrere, who married another after Amanda refused him but carried her picture on him until he died. Amanda's arias on the lost dreams of her youth echo spring rites and tall tales of princesses wooed by many suitors. Tom's memory of his mother's memory modulates easily into legend because it is twice removed from reality, recessed within the play's innermost sphere of time.

The Christian symbolism with which *Menagerie* is filled suggests that the time of Amanda's youth, the time of the Depression and the time of the Second World War are analogues, respectively, of Paradise, Purgatory and Hell. From the midst of global conflagration Tom looks back to the years of trial in St. Louis that followed the disappearance of the Edenic South his mother remembers. The idea of the gentleman caller as saviour is clear from the "Annunciation" to Amanda by her son that Jim is coming to dinner. One night at the movies Tom sees a stage magician turn water into wine and escape from a coffin. Amanda exhorts her children to "rise and shine" and calls her ailing magazine-subscribers "Christian martyrs." In an atmosphere that is relatively dusky, the light on Laura has a pristine clarity reminiscent of that on saints in medieval paintings. The qualities of intimacy and reverence combine in her scene with Jim, the only light for which is provided by a candelabrum that once stood on the altar of a church.

As the gentleman caller does not fulfill his role as redeemer, the altar candles in Laura's heart are soon extinguished. The play's central image—light playing on a broken surface—suggests the ephemeral nature of life, beauty and human feeling.

Joyful moments flicker only for an instant within the surrounding darkness of eternity, as when Jim and Laura look at the little glass unicorn together by candlelight, Amanda wishes on the moon, or couples find brief comfort in fleeting intimacy at the nearby dance hall, whose glass sphere, revolving slowly at the ceiling, filters the surrounding shadows with delicate rainbow colours. In the dim poetic interior of the Wingfield living-room, the picture of the absent father with smiling doughboy face is intermittently illuminated, while outside, beyond the dark alleyways and murky canyons of tangled clotheslines, garbage cans, and neighbouring fire escapes, the running lights of movie marquees blink and beckon in the distance. The movies themselves are no more than images of light that pass quickly into oblivion like cut jonquils or spring showers. For even art in *The Glass Menagerie* is presented as a feeble consolation for the sorry transience of life—fragile glass, scratchy phonograph records, scraps of poetry scribbled on shoe boxes.

Like the spotty, shadowy lighting, other extra-literary effects, drawn principally from film, emphasise the first condition of the play, which is nostalgia, and help to project the sense of an insubstantial world, wispy as memory itself. Transparent gauze scrims, one representing the outside wall of the tenement, another the portieres in the archway or second proscenium between the living-room and dining-room upstage, not only make scene transitions cinematic in their fluidity but also create a stage within a stage within a stage—a use of space which relates to the idea of containing time within time within time. After Tom's introductory speech, the grim wall of the building before which he has stood fades out as the Wingfield living-room fades in behind it. In turn, the portieres upstage dissolve and separate like a second curtain or inner veil of memory as soft lighting slowly reveals the family seated at the dining-table. The first scene is played without food or utensils. The last is played without words. During Tom's closing speech, Amanda appears to comfort Laura as if behind sound proof glass, her studied gestures reminiscent of the silent screen.

Music from three sources weaves through the scenes, bridging the spheres of time. On the on-stage Victrola Laura plays the music of her parents' youth, records her father left behind. The dance hall mixes the hot swing of the thirties with the slow tangos of the twenties and the tender waltzes of Amanda's girlhood. The music to which Jim and Laura dance, "La Golondrina," is the same Mexican waltz that Alma Winemiller sings on Independence Day 1916 in *Summer and Smoke*. Most prominent is the recurring theme that comes out of nowhere and fades away again in accordance with film convention, like the images in a reverie. It is primarily Laura's *Leitmotiv* and suggests her fragile beauty as does the spun glass with which she is also identified. Williams's idea of barely audible circus music is consistent with his central image of light glimmering sporadically in the void. The immutable sorrow of life persists under the superficial gaiety of the passing moment. The distant calliope, with its associations of sad clowns, trapeze acts and performing animals, is an invitation occasionally to escape into a garish, itinerant world of make-believe. Human creativity is once more presented in the most pathetic terms. Indeed the circus animals are continuous with the figurines of Laura's menagerie, whose tiny size on stage corresponds to the remoteness of the fairground.

In the course of this memory play, some forty projections of images, speeches or titles associate the graphic with the verbal in the sometimes whimsical manner of the mind when in the relatively free condition of sleep or reverie. Williams's explanation notwithstanding, the projections do not make structural points but instead spoof the sentiment of the scenes in which they appear. A pirate ship, a magazine cover, or the gentleman caller waving goodbye are pictures that undermine the pathos of the play like the farcical moments in Chekhov. Since the first production, directors have almost without exception cut the device as an expressionist intrusion upon an essentially naturalistic work. Perhaps they are right. Yet the projections are indebted less to the German theatre than to the silent screen. Such lines as "Ah!" or "Not Jim!" and such titles as "The Annunciation," "The Accent of a Coming Foot" or "The Sky Falls" appear to derive, like so much else in *Menagerie,* from the playwright's frequent movie-going in childhood.

The call in Williams's production notes for "a new, plastic theatre" to replace the outworn theatre of conventional realism is essentially a manifesto of the cinematic stage. The writer is to become more visual. He is to use lighting to suggest mood and assert relationships—such as the clear pool of light in which the fragile and unearthly Laura sits while Jim, Tom and Amanda are having supper upstage. He is to bring in music from out of the blue or flash images on a screen in order to give a plastic, mobile quality to plays that are relatively actionless. The lyric naturalism of the twentieth-century play of sensibility depends for its theatrical expression upon the writer's imaginative use of the methods and resources with which motion pictures have enriched theatrical art.

This explains why the American theatre became more of a director's medium, like film, in the time of Williams. When Elia Kazan founded the Actors Studio in 1947, three years after *Menagerie,* it was for the purpose of training actors to give film-size performances. His successor, Lee Strasberg, would later train them in the requisite docility. Actors were to become more compliant, more "plastic," like the scenery and the lighting through which the all-powerful director would express his predetermined "concept." The neo-Stanislavskyan American Method repudiates "projection consciousness" as leading to oversized mannerisms put out of date by the microphone and camera.

It is partly the convention of film, although chiefly that of the short story, from which the episodic structure of *Menagerie* derives. The play is an adaptation of a film script *(The Gentleman Caller)* based on a short story ("Portrait of a Girl in Glass"). The seven scenes mingle with allusive narrative speeches to convey a casual sense of order that accords with the nature of memory. In neither the story nor the play is the tiny plot the point. It is the revelation of characters locked in time. This explains why nothing much happens in *Menagerie.* Its lyrical, non-linear form is rooted in the gently exfoliative "Portrait of a Girl in Glass." It is also rooted in a particular character's point of view, a technique common enough in fiction but atypical of drama. Since that character happens to be an aspiring poet in both the story and the play, an inclination to lyricism is obligatory.

"Portrait" is essentially a character sketch of Laura, as its title from the static art of sculpture implies. Her brother, Tom, remembers her from the time they lived in St. Louis with their mother and he worked in a warehouse. Their father had long ago deserted them. Laura was a frightened, reclusive girl who appeared to exist in a world of make-believe. While decorating the tree one Christmas, she picked up the star that went on top and asked Tom if stars really had five points. She spent most of the time listening to her father's old records, polishing her collection of glass figurines, and rereading Gene Stratton Porter's *Freckles,* with whose hero, a young one-armed lumberjack, she carried on an imaginary relationship. He would drop by her room for an occasional visit just as her brother habitually did. When she was twenty, she was unable to face the demands of secretarial school. When she turned twenty-three, her mother asked Tom to bring a friend home to dinner in order to meet her. He turned out to be a hearty and befreckled fellow employee (Jim Delaney), with whom Laura, much to her family's amazement, got along famously because she confused him in her mind with the hero of the much-read book. Unfortunately, he was already engaged. Not long after Jim's visit, Tom lost his job at the warehouse, left St. Louis and took to wandering. He became independent and succeeded in forgetting his home, although from time to time he thinks of his sister.

The revelation that Jim is already engaged becomes more pathetic in the play because Williams makes the gentleman caller into Laura's real rather than her imaginary love. Her abnormality is less mental but more physical. Instead of the obsession to reread the same book, she has the more playable handicap of a slight limp. It is particularly effective when she and Jim dance together by candle-light (they are never alone in "Por-trait") and accidentally break the glass unicorn's horn—a piece of busi-ness, missing from the story, that uses the play's titular symbol and suggests, among other things, the sudden collapse of male ardour upon the removal of maidenly defence.

"Portrait" is a wistful memory, *Menagerie* a moving elegy. The play gains power from an intensification of theme and a strengthening of logic in the progression of events. The three years that pass in the story be-tween the mother's discovery of her daughter's truancy and the appear-ance of the gentleman caller are re-duced to three months in the play, long enough considering Amanda's determination to find Laura a hus-band if she is not to be a secretary. In the story, Tom's departure is peremp-tory because it is not preceded by a climactic quarrel with his mother. Jim Delaney makes no thematic con-tribution of his own because he is not a former high-school hero like Jim O'Connor. The mother is a minor character with neither reminiscences nor a name. Nor are the Wingfields specifically from the South.

The Glass Menagerie combines Williams's two archetypal actions. The climax of the outer play is the spoiled occasion, the climax of the inner play the eviction or loss of home. Laura does not sit at table with Jim. The gentleman caller, having de-clined his hostess's offer of lemon-ade, leaves early to meet his fiancée. After all the preparation, Amanda's party is ruined. Tom's curtain speech reminds us that everything has hap-pened within his memory, and we may be sure that it will do so again and again. Whether the two belles, one faded, one never having bloomed, manage to keep their home after his departure we can only guess; but it

is clear that the wanderer has none apart from them.

In the play's last moments, Tom's two roles, narrator and participant, coalesce. Dressed as a merchant sea-man, the one who broke free to seek adventure stands before the audience and admits that he is a haunted fugi-tive. He calls out to Laura that he has tried but not been able to forget her. The many cities to which he has sailed seem to sweep about him like dead leaves torn loose from their branches. A strain of familiar music, a display of perfumes in a store win-dow, or simply a fragment of trans-parent glass is enough to remind him of what he has lost. Up stage, behind the gauze scrim which marks the out-side wall of the St. Louis tenement that was once his home, the mother and sister he left behind enact a scene without words, like silent ghosts, vis-ible only to the eye of memory. Still facing the audience, he tells Laura to blow out the candles which light the dim interior. She does so, he says goodbye, but on his exit the elusive, nostalgic music that has dipped in and out of the scenes from the begin-ning breaks off without resolution. Tom's climactic realisation that he will play out his "memory play" for the rest of his days is like the "epiphany" in a short story by Joyce. His confession throws all of the events that have preceded it into a different light; or, more precisely, it casts them into a greater elegiac darkness.

The problem of playing *The Glass Menagerie* arises from the fact that, whereas from a dramatic critic's point of view it is Tom's play, from an actor's it is Amanda's. . . .

In 1973 Thomas L. King published a valuable article arguing that *Me-nagerie* belongs to Tom, who tricks the audience into shouldering the pain he exorcises by creating his memory play. In 1975 Rip Torn, cast opposite Maureen Stapleton's second Amanda, made the only all-out effort to read the narrations from character. The curtain speech was the key to his portrait. The result was a wild, brooding, quirky, homosexual Tom who flung his words at the house like accusations. Torn's performance did not receive a unanimous welcome; but neither was it damned with faint praise. Those who attacked it were inclined to do so without reserve; others were as absolute in their esteem. Barnes of the *New York Times* was reminded of a Greek tragic hero, Kalem of *Time* thought it "just right," and Watt of the *New York Daily News* made the telling observation that Torn was at his best in "the beautifully written narrative sections."

◆ ◆ ◆

Irony and Distance in
The Glass Menagerie

THOMAS L. KING

Tennessee Williams's *The Glass Menagerie*, though it has achieved a firmly established position in the canon of American plays, is often distorted, if not misunderstood, by readers, directors, and audiences. The distortion results from an overemphasis on the scenes involving Laura and Amanda and their plight, so that the play becomes a sentimental tract on the trapped misery of two women in St. Louis. This leads to the neglect of Tom's soliloquies—speeches that can be ignored or discounted only at great peril, since they occupy such a prominent position in the play. When not largely ignored, they are in danger of being treated as nostalgic yearnings for a former time. But they are not sentimental excursions into the past, paralleling Amanda's, for while they contain sentiment and nostalgia, they also evince a pervasive humor and irony and, indeed, form and contain the entire play.

Judging from the reviews, the distortion of the play began with the original production. The reviews deal almost wholly with Laurette Taylor's performance, making Amanda seem to be the principal character, and nearly ignore the soliloquies. Even the passage of time has failed to correct this tendency, for many later writers also force the play out of focus by pushing Amanda forward. Among the original reviewers, Stark Young was one of the few who recognized that the play is Tom's when he said: "The story . . . all happens in the son's mind long afterward." He also recognized that the production and Laurette Taylor tended to obscure the script, for, after a lengthy discussion of Miss Taylor, he said, "But true as all this may be of Miss Taylor, we must not let that blind us to the case of the play itself and of the whole occasion." Young blamed on Eddie Dowling the failure of the narration noted by others: "He speaks his Narrator scenes plainly and serviceably by which, I think, they are made to seem to be a mistake on the playwright's part, a mistake to include them at all; for they seem extraneous and tiresome in the midst of the play's emotional current. If these speeches were spoken with variety, impulse and intensity . . . the whole thing would be another matter, truly a part of the story." Young indicates that while the reviewers tended to neglect Tom and the soliloquies to concentrate on Laurette Taylor, they were encouraged to do so by a production which made the play Amanda's.

The play, however, is not Amanda's. Amanda is a striking and a powerful character, but the play is Tom's. Tom opens the play and he closes it; he also opens the second act and two further scenes in the first act—his is the first word and the last. Indeed, Amanda, Laura, and the Gentleman Caller do not appear in the play at all as separate characters. In a sense, as Stark Young noted, Tom is the only character in the play, for we see not the characters but Tom's memory of them—Amanda and the rest are merely aspects of Tom's consciousness. Tom's St. Louis is not an objective one, but a solipsist's created by Tom, the artist-magician, and containing Amanda, Laura, and the Gentleman Caller. Tom is the Prospero of *The Glass Menagerie,* and its world is the world of Tom's mind even more than *Death of a Salesman*'s is the world of Willy Loman's mind. The play is warped and distorted when any influence gives Amanda, Laura, or the glass menagerie any undue prominence. If Amanda looms large, she looms large in Tom's mind, not in her own right: though of course the image that finally dominates Tom's mind is that of Laura and the glass menagerie.

The full meaning of the scenes between the soliloquies lies not in themselves alone but also in the commentary provided by Tom standing outside the scenes and speaking with reasonable candor to the audience and reader. Moreover, the comment that the soliloquies makes is not a sentimental one; that is, they are not only expressions of a wistful nostalgia for the lost, doomed world of Amanda, Laura, and the glass menagerie but also contain a good deal of irony and humor which work in the opposite direction. They reveal Tom as an artist figure whose utterances show how the artist creates, using the raw material of his own life.

The nature of the narrator's role as artist figure is indicated by Tom's behavior in the scenes. He protects himself from the savage in-fighting in the apartment by maintaining distance between himself and the pain of the situation through irony. For example, when he gets into a fight with Amanda in the third scene and launches into a long, ironic, and even humorous tirade—about how he "runs a string of cat-houses in the valley," how they call him "Killer, Killer Wingfield," how, on some occasions, he wears green whiskers—the irony is heavy and propels him out of the painful situation, out of the argument, and ultimately to the movies. Significantly, this scene begins with Tom writing, Tom the artist, and in it we see how the artistic sensibility turns a painful situation into "art" by using distance. In his verbal assault on his mother, Tom "creates" Killer Wingfield. Tom's ability to distance his experience, to protect himself from the debilitating atmosphere of the apartment makes him different from Laura. Laura does not have this refuge; she is unable to detach herself completely from the situation and she is destroyed by it. She does, of course, retreat to the glass menagerie and the Victrola, but this is the behavior of a severely disturbed woman. Her method of dealing with the situation, retreating into a "world of her own," does indeed, as Tom says, make her seem "just a little bit peculiar." Tom's method is more acceptable; he makes art.

The kind of contrast that exists between Laura and Tom is illustrated by a comment Jung made about James Joyce and his daughter, Lucia. Lucia had had a history of severe mental problems and, in 1934, she was put under the care of Jung. Discussing his patient and her famous father in a letter, Jung wrote: "His [Joyce's] 'psychological' style is definitely schizophrenic, with the difference, however, that the ordinary patient cannot help himself talking and thinking in such a way, while Joyce willed it and moreover developed it with all his creative forces, which incidentally explains why he himself did not go over the border. But his daughter did, because she was not a genius like her father, but merely a victim of her disease." On another occasion Jung said that the father and daughter "were like two people going to the bottom of a river, one falling and the other diving." We see here a psychoanalyst's perception of the problem of artist and non-artist which is much the same as the problem of Tom and Laura. Tennessee Williams's real-life sister, Rose, has also suffered from mental disturbances.

That an author's early play should contain a highly autobiographical character who shows the mechanism by which art is made out of the material of one's life is not particularly surprising, but it is a generally unnoted feature of *The Glass Menagerie* which is inextricably linked to the irony of the soliloquies. For the artist, irony is a device that protects him from the pain of his experience so that he may use it objectively in his art. We may suppose that Swift's irony shielded him from the dark view that he had of the world and that the failure of that irony brought on the madness that affected him at the end of his life. The artist needs his distance from the material of his art so that he may handle it objectively, and the soliloquies of *The Glass Menagerie,* in part, reveal the nature of that distance and how it is maintained.

Generally, each soliloquy oscillates between a sentimental memory of the past, which draws the narrator into it, and a wry irony which keeps him from being fully engulfed and controlled by it. This tension is found in all the soliloquies, though it is not always handled in the same way: sometimes the fond memory is predominant and sometimes the irony, but both are always present. At times, Tom seems almost deliberately to court disaster by creating for himself and the audience a memory so lovely and poignant that the pain of giving it up to return to reality is too much to bear, but return he does with mockery and a kind of wit that interrupts the witchery of memory just short of a withdrawn madness surrounded by soft music and a mind filled with "delicate rainbow colors." In short, Tom toys with the same madness in which his sister Laura is trapped but saves himself with irony.

The opening soliloquy begins on an ironic note. Tom says:

> Yes, I have tricks in my pocket, I have things up my sleeve. But I am the opposite of a stage magician. He gives you illusion that has the appearance of truth. I give you truth in the pleasant disguise of illusion.

These opening lines have a cocky tone—"I will trick you," Tom says, "I'll tell you that I'm going to trick you and I'll still do it even after you've been warned. Besides," he says with perhaps just a touch of derision, "you prefer trickery to the naked truth." Tom begins in the attitude of Whitman on the facing page of the first edition of *Leaves of Grass*—head thrown back, mocking, insolent, but not cruel.

Tom continues in the same mode by saying:

> To begin with, I turn back time. I reverse it to that quaint period, the thirties, when the huge middle class of America was matriculating in a school for the blind. Their eyes had failed them, or they had failed their eyes, and so they were having their fingers pressed forcibly down on the fiery Braille alphabet of a dissolving economy.
>
> In Spain there was revolution. Here there was only shouting and confusion. In Spain there was Guernica. Here there were disturbances of labor, sometimes pretty violent, in otherwise peaceful cities such as Chicago, Cleveland, Saint Louis . . .

To this point in the speech, Tom's principal mode is ironic, but as he moves on, though the irony remains, a stronger element of sentiment, of poignant memory creeps in. He begins to speak of memory and to enumerate the characters in the play:

> The play is memory. Being a memory play, it is dimly lighted, it is sentimental, it is not realistic. In memory everything seems to happen to music. That explains the fiddle in the wings.
>
> I am the narrator of the play, and also a character in it. The other characters are my mother, Amanda, my sister, Laura, and a gentleman caller who appears in the final scenes.

The only break in this poignant mood is the phrase "that explains the fiddle in the wings"—an unfortunate phrase, but demonstrative of the tension, of the rhythmic swing back and forth between sweet nostalgia and bitter irony. The play may be sentimental rather than realistic, but

"that explains the fiddle in the wings" breaks the sentiment.

Tom continues by saying:

> He [the gentleman caller] is the most realistic character in the play, being an emissary from a world of reality that we were somehow set apart from. But since I have a poet's weakness for symbols, I am using this character also as a symbol; he is the long delayed but always expected something that we live for.

With these words, the narrator drops his ironic detachment and enters into the mood of memory. The words can hardly be delivered but as in a reverie, in a deep reflection, the voice coming out of a man who, after frankly acknowledging the audience at the beginning of the speech, has now sunk far into himself so that the audience seems to overhear his thoughts. He then shakes off the mood with a return to irony and makes a kind of joke:

> There is a fifth character in the play who doesn't appear except in this larger-than-life-size photograph over the mantel. This is our father who left us a long time ago. He was a telephone man who fell in love with long distances; he gave up his job with the telephone company and skipped the light fantastic out of town . . .
>
> The last we heard of him was a picture post-card from Mazatlan, on the Pacific coast of Mexico, containing a message of two words— "Hello—Good-bye!" and no address.

There is humor here—not sentiment and not sentimental humor. Tom speaks fondly of his mother and sister and remembers their lost lives and the gentleman caller who symbolizes the loss and the failure, and we can imagine that his gaze becomes distant and withdrawn as he allows himself to be carried away into the memory, but then he remembers another member of the family, the father, and that hurts too much to give in to so he shakes off the reverie and returns once more to irony. The irony is no longer the playful irony of the interlocutor before the audience, but an irony which protects him from the painful memories of the past, that allows him to rise superior to the "father who left us" and to get a laugh from the audience, for the audience should and will chuckle at the end of the opening soliloquy as the light fades on Tom and he leaves his seaman's post. The chuckle may be good-natured, but the humor is not; it is gallows humor in which the condemned man asserts himself before a crowd in relation to which he is horribly disadvantaged by making it laugh. Tom is in control of his memory and already he is beginning to endeavor to work his trick by manipulating the audience's mood.

The opening soliloquy, then, reveals a number of elements that are to be important in the play: it establishes a tension between sentimental nostalgia and detached irony as well as a narrator who is to function as stage magician. The narrator disavows this, but we cannot take him at his word. He says that he is the opposite of a stage magician, but only because his truth looks like illusion rather than the other way round; he is still the magician who creates the play. He says that the play is sentimental rather than realistic, but that is a half truth, for while it contains large doses of sentiment, for the narrator at least, irony sometimes quenches the sentiment. Indeed, Irving Babbit's phrase describing romantic irony is appropriate here: "Hot baths of sentiment . . . followed by cold douches of irony."

The dominant note of the second soliloquy, at the beginning of the third scene, is irony. In the first soliloquy, Tom has provided the audience with a poignant picture of Laura and Amanda cut off from the world "that we were somehow set apart from." In the second soliloquy, irony almost completely obliterates the poignance as we see Amanda at work trying to find a gentleman caller for Laura, a gentleman caller who is "like some archetype of the universal unconscious." Tom continues the irony as he says:

She began to take logical steps in the planned direction.

Late that winter and in the early spring—realizing that extra money would be needed to properly feather the nest and plume the bird—she conducted a vigorous campaign on the telephone, roping in subscribers to one of those magazines for matrons called *The Home-maker's Companion,* the type of journal that features the serialized sublimations of ladies of letters who think in terms of delicate cup-like breasts, slim, tapering waists, rich, creamy thighs, eyes like wood-smoke in autumn, fingers that soothe and caress like strains of music, bodies as powerful as Etruscan sculpture.

The mocking humor in this is revealed by the derisive alliteration, the hyperbolic language, and in the humorous, parodying evocation of all the clichés of these stories. The speech makes fun of the literary equivalents of Amanda's memories of gentleman callers in the mythical South. This is not to say that Amanda is savagely attacked with a kind of Swiftian irony; nevertheless, the attack is there, though the irony is balanced somewhat by one irruption of the nostalgic, pitying mode of discourse when Tom says that even when the gentleman caller was not mentioned "his presence hung in mother's preoccupied look and in my sister's frightened, apologetic manner." The irony is also humorous and gets a laugh from audiences if it is performed as irony—especially at the end of the speech where, just as the first soliloquy breaks into a mild humor at the end, Tom humorously parodies the magazine stories.

The first soliloquy strikes a balance between irony and nostalgia, the second is primarily ironic, and the third is primarily nostalgic. The third soliloquy begins with the Paradise Dance Hall:

> Across the alley from us was the Paradise Dance Hall. On evenings in spring the windows and doors were open and the music came outdoors. Sometimes the lights were turned out except for a large glass sphere that hung from the ceiling. It would turn slowly about and filter the dusk with delicate rainbow colors.

Rainbow colors, in fact, fill much of the play: in the scene with Laura, late at light, after Tom has returned from the movies, the magic scarf he produces is rainbow-colored—this is one of the few scenes in which Tom and Laura relate tenderly to one another; the Paradise Dance Hall filters the dusk with "delicate rainbow colors"; sex hangs "in the gloom like a chandelier" and floods the world with "brief, deceptive rainbows"; and, in the last soliloquy Tom says that he sometimes passes the window of a shop where perfume is sold—"The window is filled with pieces of colored glass, tiny transparent bottles in delicate colors like bits of a shattered rainbow." In the third soliloquy, the Paradise Dance Hall provides the

rainbow colors that fill and transform the alley. The irony breaks through in only a few places: when Tom disrupts the mood of magic by pointing out that you could see the young couples "kissing behind ash-pits and telephone poles," and, as usual at the end when he says, "All the world was waiting for bombardments."

All three soliloquies in the first act work together to help define its movement. The first soliloquy is fairly well balanced between nostalgia and irony. The detached irony of the second soliloquy foreshadows Tom's struggle to detach himself from his situation; after it Tom fights with his mother and leaves to go to the movies. The third soliloquy asserts the nostalgic mode, and the scene following this, in which Tom and Amanda talk of the gentleman caller, is a tender, loving one. We see a playful, warm scene between Tom and his mother out on the fire escape which shows how, in spite of their quarrels, Tom and Amanda could also have their warm, understanding moments. By the end of the first act, the audience should be taken in by Tom's trick, drawn into the rainbow-colored world and the pleasant memory of past times. The pain of Tom's memory has been repudiated in the second soliloquy with irony, and, after the fight, when Tom runs off to the movies, with the delicate nostalgia of the third soliloquy, flooding the stage with rainbow light. The trick is working—we begin to think that Tom and his mother will get along after all, that a gentleman caller will come to rescue them, but it remains a trick wrought by the magic of the rainbow which is broken, whose colors are "deceptive."

The second act begins with a soliloquy which, like the first, strikes something of a balance between irony and nostalgia. Tom begins with a description of Jim in language that indicates that he has a genuine kind of amazed liking for this Irish boy. Only gentle irony is present in the following words:

> In high school, Jim was a hero. He had tremendous Irish good nature and vitality with the scrubbed and polished look of white chinaware. He seemed to move in a continual spotlight. He was a star in basketball, captain of the debating club, president of the senior class and the glee club, and he sang the male lead in the annual light operas. He was always running or bounding, never just walking. He seemed always at the point of defeating the law of gravity.

Jim is made light of by the phrases "white chinaware" and "defeating the law of gravity," but the mockery is mild, though it becomes stronger as the speech continues:

> He was shooting with such velocity through his adolescence that you would logically expect him to arrive at nothing short of the White House by the time he was thirty. But Jim apparently ran into more interference after his graduation from Soldan. His speed had definitely slowed. Six years after he left high school he was holding a job that wasn't much better than mine.

The irony begins to break through even more strongly after these words, for Tom was "valuable to him as someone who could remember his former glory, who had seen him win basketball games and the silver cup in debating." And the irony even cuts against Tom: "He knew of my secret practice of retiring to a cabinet of the wash-room to work on poems whenever business was slack in the warehouse." A degree of bitterness begins to emerge when Tom says that, with the example of Jim, the other boys began to smile at him too, "as people smile at some oddly fashioned dog that trots across their path at some distance." The bitterness is quickly moderated, however, when Tom sympathetically remembers his sister in high school: "In high school Laura was as unobtrusive as Jim was astonishing." Finally, as always in these soliloquies, the speech ends with an ironic barb that can often draw a laugh from the audience. Tom says that when he asked Jim home to dinner, "he grinned and said, 'You know, Shakespeare, I never thought of you as having folks!' He was about to discover that I did . . ."

The culmination of all the soliloquies and of the tension between irony and nostalgia that is carefully developed in them, is in the final one. Tom's last speech contains just two touches of ironic detachment, but these are critical and are the foci on which this speech and, indeed, for Tom, the whole play turns. The speech begins with a touch of ironic humor. In the preceding scene, Amanda has told Tom to go to the moon. He begins his final speech with "I didn't go to the moon." This is a decidedly humorous line, indicating that Tom still has access to his detachment, but the audience is not laughing anymore, its detachment has been broken down. The speech then quickly moves into a tone of lyric regret:

> I didn't go to the moon, I went much further—for time is the longest distance between two places. Not long after that I was fired for writing a poem on the lid of a shoe-box. I left Saint Louis. I descended the steps of this fire-escape for a last time and followed, from then on, in my father's footsteps, attempting to find in motion what was lost in space. I traveled around a great deal. The cities swept about me like dead leaves, leaves

that were brightly colored but torn away from the branches. I would have stopped, but I was pursued by something. It always came upon me unawares, taking me altogether by surprise. Perhaps it was a familiar bit of music. Perhaps it was only a piece of transparent glass. Perhaps I am walking along a street at night, in some strange city, before I have found companions. I pass the lighted window of a shop where perfume is sold. The window is filled with pieces of colored glass, tiny transparent bottles in delicate colors, like bits of a shattered rainbow. Then all at once my sister touches my shoulder. I turn around and look into her eyes. Oh, Laura, Laura, I tried to leave you behind me, but I am more faithful than I intended to be! I reach for a cigarette, I cross the street, I run into the movies or a bar, I buy a drink, I speak to the nearest stranger—anything that can blow your candles out!

For nowadays the world is lit by lightning! Blow out your candles, Laura—and so good-bye.

The irony in this passage is no longer humorous. When Tom says "I didn't go to the moon," no one is laughing, and the final, ironic "and so good-bye"

is not even potentially humorous. Tom seems to have been captured by the memory and the audience has almost certainly been captured, but Tom, in the end, still has his detachment. Laura's candles go out and Tom is relieved of his burden, uttering a final, flip farewell, but the audience has been more faithful than it intended to be; they are left behind, tricked by Tom who is free for the moment while they must face their grief, their cruelty, for they are the world that the Wingfields were somehow set apart from, they are the ones who shattered the rainbow.

The soliloquies, then, are of a piece: they all alternate between sentiment and irony, between mockery and nostalgic regret, and they all end with an ironic tag, which, in most cases, is potentially humorous. They show us the artist manipulating his audience, seeming to be manipulated himself to draw them in, but in the end resuming once more his detached stance. When Tom departs, the audience is left with Laura and Amanda alone before the dead, smoking candles, and Tom escapes into his artist's detachment having exorcized the pain with the creation of the play. This is the trick that Tom has in his pocket.

◇   ◇   ◇

from *Family, Drama, and American Dreams*

TOM SCANLAN

The major dilemmas of family life are imbedded in the dramatic action of Williams's plays, and the ideal that haunts his characters is family-related. Moreover, those plays which have been most successful artistically have been those mostly about the family. . . .

In the earlier plays Williams dramatized the family world in a state of collapse; in later ones family collapse is antecedent to the action. These two situations are combined in *The Glass Menagerie,* Williams's first successful play (and probably his most popular one[1]). The play is a perfect fusion of the two subjects and so is a figure for Williams's entire career. In it the family is long lost and, also, we witness its struggle before it is lost. Williams captures the poignancy of family memories in a way all his own, without sacrificing the core of dramatic conflict which makes such memories less static.

The play is a prime example of Williams's artistry in establishing the relation between his own dramatic world and the conventions of realistic domestic drama to which his audience owes great allegiance, as he well knew. The play occurs in the mind of Tom Wingfield, who drifts in and out of the action both as narrator and participant in a peculiarly appropriate way. From the moment at the beginning when the scrim of the tenement wall dissolves and we enter the Wingfields' apartment, we are reminded of the household of so many family plays. The realistic convention of the fourth wall is evoked as Tom remembers his family.

Tom's evocation is self-conscious, for as "stage manager" he has control over the setting. But Tom is also at the mercy of his memories and irresistibly must relive them. The play keeps us poised between these two styles, these two times, throughout. This is, in fact, its strongest and most subtle conflict. Like Tom, we are continually tempted into the world of a realistic family struggle, but never allowed to enter it completely. The projections and lighting keep the effect slightly stylized during the scenes, the fragmented structure blocks us from too long an absorption in the action, and the re-appearance of Tom as narrator forces us back to the present. It is Tom's final reappearance in this role, when the action of the memory play is completed, which releases the tension created between the two styles and dramatizes, in a final rush of emotion, the irretrievable loss of the family which Tom can never escape.

Tom cannot shake the memory of his family from his mind; the dissolution of time and space in the play—that is, in his consciousness—heightens the importance of what he is remembering to make it the most significant thing about his existence. What he remembers—the bulk of the play—centers around two lines of action. The first is his desire to escape from his family just as his father had done before him: "He was a telephone man who fell in love with long distances."[2] Tom, a would-be writer, is caught between a domineering mother and a stultifying warehouse job. He escapes to the porch, to the movies, to the saloon. And finally, in the end, we learn that he has followed his father out into long distances. The second line of action, the principal one, concerns his mother, Amanda, and her attempts to establish some kind of life for Tom's crippled sister, Laura. Amanda pins her hopes on getting "sister" married, after Laura fails because of painful shyness to continue in business school. A "gentleman caller" is found, Jim O'Connor, "an emissary from the world of reality," but all of Amanda's hopes are crushed as he turns out to be already engaged.

The plot is slight stuff, as Williams himself knew.[3] The effect of the play derives in part from the contrast between its two lines of action. Amanda is given over to memories of her past life of happiness as a young southern debutante in Blue Mountain, Mississippi, where on one incredible Sunday she had seventeen gentlemen callers. She imitates the manners and graciousness of those days, a faintly ludicrous parody of southern gentility, the played-out tradition of the antebellum South and its family of security. But she has spirit, too, and responds to the problems of raising two children in a St. Louis tenement during the Depression. Her practicality is what gives her dignity; as she cares for Laura we realize how much Amanda herself needs to be cared for. Her refusal to give in to her nostalgia, even while she indulges in it, enhances her character and makes us susceptible to her longing.

Tom is smothered by such a woman. He fights with her, in part, because she continually tells him what to do: how to eat; how to sleep; how to get ahead. But he fights, also, because her standards represent the conventionality of family responsibility:

AMANDA: Where are you going?
TOM: I'm going to the *movies!*
AMANDA: I don't believe that lie!

(Tom crouches toward her, overtowering her tiny figure. She backs away, gasping.)

TOM: I'm going to opium dens! Yes, opium dens, dens of vice and criminals, hang-outs, Mother. I've joined the Hogan Gang, I'm a hired assassin, I carry a tommy-gun in a violin case! I run a string of cat-houses in the Valley! They call me Killer, Killer Wingfield, I'm leading a double-life, a simple, honest warehouse worker by day, by night a dynamic *czar* of the *underworld, Mother.* I go to gambling casinos, I spin away fortunes on the roulette table! I wear a patch over one eye and a false mustache, sometimes I put on green whiskers. On those occasions they call me—*El Diablo!* Oh, I could tell you things to make you sleepless! My enemies plan to dynamite this place. They're going to blow us all

sky-high some night! I'll be glad, very happy, and so will you! You'll go up, on a broomstick, over Blue Mountain with seventeen gentlemen callers! You ugly—babbling old—*witch.* . . .[4]

He can no more accept her memories of genteel home life in Blue Mountain than he can the spirit with which she has managed to carry on. Both suffocate him. The dead family world of the past is as stultifying as the present. Tom feels the need to escape both:

You know it don't take much intelligence to get yourself into a nailed-up coffin, Laura. But who in hell ever got himself out of one without removing one nail?

(As if in answer, the father's grinning photograph lights up. The scene dims out.)[5]

The absent father, who still represents the memory of romantic family love to Amanda, is the possibility of romantic escape from family to Tom.[6] He loves his sister Laura, yet he will not accept the responsibility for her which Amanda demands of him. The Wingfields are only a ghost of the family of security, but even this demand to be close-knit repels the restless Tom.

Tom's love for Laura needs to be emphasized, I think, not only because it is one part of the final image of the play—the moment of revelation toward which the action tends—but because it shows Williams's interest in the special qualities of those whom the world has hurt. They are the delicate and fragile people, too sensitive to be able to withstand the crude and harsh necessities by which life drives us along. They have an extraordinary awareness of hidden, almost mystical, qualities of spiritual beauty; and this openness dooms them to be crushed or perverted by the animal vigor of the world.

Laura's specialness is seen largely in contrast with Jim, her gentleman caller. He is, by all odds, the kindest of Williams's emissaries from reality, perhaps because his faith in the American dream of self-improvement and success is so complete as to be itself a touching illusion:

> JIM: *(goes after him)* You know, Shakespeare—I'm going to sell you a bill of goods!
> TOM: What goods?
> JIM: A course I'm taking.
> TOM: Huh?
> JIM: In public speaking! You and me, we're not the warehouse type.
> TOM: Thanks—that's good news. But what has public speaking got to do with it?
> JIM: It fits you for—executive positions!
> TOM: Awww.
> JIM: I tell you it's done a helluva lot for me.

> *(Image On Screen: Executive At His Desk.)*[7]

Williams mocks Jim just enough in the use of the slide projection so that we need not take him seriously, yet he makes Jim's naïveté spring from high spirits and an openheartedness which is endearing. He is healthy, happy, and full of hope, but set next to Laura and her needs he is crude, clumsy, and shallow:

> You know what I judge to be the trouble with you? Inferiority complex! Know what that is? That's what they call it when someone low-rates himself![8]

So much for the intricacies of the human personality. To Jim, Laura's problems are easily solved and he sets about, in his well-intentioned way, to cure her. First, he persuades her to dance; and then, caught up himself in the romance of the moment, he kisses her. But Laura needs more than a kiss, more in fact than Jim could ever give her. She needs a tenderness and love that she will never find. Her needs are so great that to satisfy them would mean altering the real world to fit her, changing it into a world like that inhabited by her glass animals, full of delicacy, beauty, and tender harmony.

When this incompatible couple waltzes into the glass menagerie, they begin to destroy it. At first, Laura does not mind. She is too thrilled with the prospect of being normal to care whether her glass unicorn has lost its distinctive horn. But the accident warns us of what Jim awkwardly confesses after the kiss—that he has made a mistake and will see her no more:

> I wish that you would—say something.

> *(She bites her lip which was trembling and then bravely smiles. She opens her hand again on the broken glass ornament. Then she gently takes his hand and raises it level with her own. She carefully places the unicorn in the palm of his hand, then pushes his fingers closed upon it.)*

> What are you—doing that for? You want me to have him?—Laura?

> *(She nods.)*

> What for?
> LAURA: A—souvenir. . . .[9]

Laura now knows that she belongs to a different world from Jim. He wandered into a zoo of exotic animals, but that was on his day off and he must return to the workaday world.

There will be no normal love of marriage and family for Laura nor for any of the Wingfields. Laura is too tender, too special, too fragile like her glass menagerie. It is Tom's painful sensitivity to Laura's predicament which makes him love her and which drives him from her. But he cannot escape Laura. The necessity of leaving her and the guilt over doing so, haunt him:

> Oh, Laura, Laura, I tried to leave you behind me, but I am more faithful than I intended to be! I reach for a cigarette, I cross the street, I run into the movies or a bar, I buy a drink, I speak to the nearest stranger—anything that can blow your candles out!

> *(Laura bends over the candles.)*

> For nowadays the world is lit by lightning! Blow out your candles, Laura—and so good-bye....

> *(She blows the candles out.)*[10]

Laura's painful encounter with the world's lightning represents all of the Wingfields. Amanda's last glance at her husband's picture reveals as much of her as does Tom's final speech of him. The family is the supreme case of love trying to struggle against the world, and the family fails. Fundamentally romantic, Williams evokes the beauty of failure, the beauty which must fail.

While family life is impossibly difficult, Williams does not actually reject it. Instead, he allows his characters—and his audience—the full "pleasures" of family nostalgia and suffering. It is Williams's peculiar ability to do so without bathos. We can savor the situation because, like Amanda, we are never lost in it uninterruptedly. Williams insures his family memories against outright sentimentality by a delightful (and convenient) comic touch. He does not really create a comic perspective, which would change the meaning of his vision and would suggest the sanity of compromise. Rather, he edges the serious matter of his plays with humor. For example, early in *Orpheus Descending* one of the minor characters declares that most people find hate in marriage and an outlet in money. Her laughter at this observation is a perfect Williams moment. It conveys his temporary emotional defense against the painful truth. *Streetcar* is framed in the same way, with a dirty joke at the beginning and an ironic double entendre at the end: "This game is seven-card stud." Williams seldom maintains his comic view, however, since it is for him, and for his strongest characters, a temporary way of keeping the world at bay. When he waxes "true," his characters speak directly, often lyrically, and the ironic edge disappears. Maggie, in *Cat*, has this edge, this style as part of her character. For her, it is a defense against the suffocating world of her in-laws. At private moments she may drop this defense; the curtain parts, and we see the loneliness, the isolation, and the gentleness within her. The painful inner lives of his characters remain as desperate as ever, only we are given alternate moments of rest from the hurt.

The distancing in *The Glass Menagerie* is fully and artfully done. In Tom's opening speech, for example, the touch of social comment which appears mocks the world of the middle class as well as itself:

> In Spain there was revolution. Here there was only shouting and confusion. . . . This is the social background of the play.[11]

Later, when this motif reappears, it is directly associated with the dilemmas of the Wingfield family. Their private world looks out on the social world in the same way that their windows look out on the alley. Tom says to the audience:

> Couples would come outside, to the relative privacy of the alley. You could see them kissing behind ash-pits and telephone poles. This was the compensation for lives that passed like mine, without any change or adventure. . . .
> In Spain there was Guernica![12]

And immediately Amanda unwittingly provides the mocking counterpoint:

> A fire-escape landing's a poor excuse for a porch. *(She spreads a newspaper on a step and sits down, gracefully and demurely as if she were settling into a swing on a Mississippi veranda.)* What are you looking at?[13]

A more often used technique in *The Glass Menagerie* to provide a comic edge is the projection of legends or images onto a wall in the Wingfield apartment, an element which is frequently dropped in production.[14] The published editions of the play continue to retain them. Williams argues that their use is important to maintain a sense of the play's structure beneath its episodic surface.[15] A number of the projections do seem to have only this architectural function: legends such as "After the Fiasco," "You Think I'm in Love with Continental Shoemaker's?," "High School Hero;" images such as typewriters or a wintry scene in the park. But many are obviously funny, sardonic, or ironic as well. Amanda's memories of Blue Mountain are introduced with "Où Sont Les Neiges d'Antan?" Tom's desire for adventure brings forth the image of a sailing vessel with a Jolly Roger. Music, too, is used to evoke straightforward emotion. "Between each episode it [the theme tune] returns as a reference to the emotion,

nostalgia, which is the first condition of the play."[16] But music also mocks the characters as when Amanda's self-pitying reproach to Tom's rudeness is introduced with "Ave Maria."

Perhaps the most complex use of these alternating effects is near the end of the play. Laura and Jim waltz to "La Golondrina." Their kiss is preceded by the symbol of Laura's freakish beauty—a projected image of blue roses—and swelling music. Then, having given us the emotional luxury of this melodrama, the legend becomes slightly ambiguous—"Souvenir" anticipates the broken glass figure Laura will give to Jim, and it also comes directly after the kiss and may refer to it as well. There is less doubt about the next legend. Jim's cliché explanation of his feelings for another girl brings forth the mock-enthusiastic "Love!" on the screen, and Laura's tender gesture with the broken unicorn ends with a choice of the legend "Things Have a Way of Turning Out So Badly" or the harsh image "Gentleman Caller Waving Good-bye—Gaily." Finally, when Jim tells Amanda he is engaged to another girl, we read the sardonic "The Sky Falls."

Williams tries to have his sentiment and mock it, too, using these devices both to intensify the family drama and to pull back from it. These "plastic" elements, then, are Williams's way of using the realistic situation while not being exclusively bound to it. The core of the play is the attempt by Amanda to find a family and the desire by Tom to escape from family. This surface action is alternately heightened and diminished by these nonrealistic devices. We are asked to embrace the characters and to laugh at them, to empathize and then to sympathize. Much of the same strategy can be seen in the dialogue, once we are alerted to it. Amanda's telephone campaign to sell subscriptions to the magazine *Companion* is filled with this juxtaposition of tears and laughter. More poignantly, her memories of her home life in Blue Mountain are made up of a dramatic alternation between vivid nostalgia and shrewd practicality:

> Finally there were no more vases to hold them, every available space was filled with jonquils. No vases to hold them? All right, I'll hold them myself! And then I—*[She stops in front of the picture. Music plays.]* met your father! Malaria fever and jonquils and then—this—boy. . . . *[She switches on the rose-colored lamp.]*
>
> I hope they get here before it starts to rain.[17]

Nearly lost in the intensity of her memory, Amanda begins to speak as though the past were the present, only to be brought up short by the reality of her situation. The rose-colored lamp is both a reprise of her vulnerability to charm and an instance of her coping, in the only way she knows how, with the situation in which that vulnerability has placed her: she puts a good light on harsh truths, and she dresses up the faded room to catch the gentleman caller for sister. And one might even say that all the Wingfields get caught out in the rain, away from the warm safety of home. Thus, the drama is embodied in the rhetoric and through its sequential movement each emotionally resonant element is followed by a flat deflation.

Williams uses a similar technique to add a more complex texture to the raw emotions of the Wingfields' family battles. Tom's angry speech denouncing his mother as a witch is slightly muted by his satiric, fanciful tone. But if the direct emotion is reduced in volume, it can also be said that the sense of calculation which Tom's imagery implies makes the hurt Amanda receives all the keener for having been so carefully de-

signed. And in the rare moments when mother and son can talk to, rather than at, each other, Williams manages this shift in tone with greatest delicacy:

> AMANDA: When I was a girl in Blue Mountain and it was suspected that a young man drank, the girl whose attentions he had been receiving, if any girl *was,* would sometimes speak to the minister of his church, or rather her father would if her father was living, and sort of feel him out on the young man's character. That is the way such things are discreetly handled to keep a young woman from making a tragic mistake!
>
> TOM: Then how did you happen to make a tragic mistake?
>
> AMANDA: That innocent look of your father's had everyone fooled! He *smiled*—the world was *enchanted!* No girl can do worse than put herself at the mercy of a handsome appearance! I hope that Mr. O'Connor is not too good-looking.
>
> TOM: No, he's not too good-looking. He's covered with freckles and hasn't too much of a nose.
>
> AMANDA: He's not right-down homely, though?
>
> TOM: Not right-down homely. Just medium homely, I'd say.[18]

The lines play first between Amanda's nostalgia and Tom's blunt irony, and then between her ecstatic memories (with the painful lesson they teach) and Tom's more gentle teasing. At moments such as these, the play's tone becomes a mode of encounter between characters, its surface ingenuity a way of revealing inner lives. The Wingfields exist most vividly when they appear to us caught between moments of direct revelation of their psyches and moments of indirect relief from that painful confrontation. In *The Glass Menagerie* the longing for the family of security is mocked but never abandoned, indulged even as it is shown up.

In *The Glass Menagerie* Williams consciously manipulated his subject matter and his tone, playing off the oppressiveness of the family of security against a teasing stylized realism. He did not grapple with the assumptions beneath the conflicting claims of personal freedom and security, nor did he construct a dramatic action which defined them. Rather, he relied on the evocative power of family strife, running the risk of being merely agitated and pathos-filled as in the soap opera. His family victims are at their most vivid at those points where they are both caught up in their lyrical self-indulgence and at the same time aware of the difficulty in communicating to those around them what they truly feel.

Williams does not test the family attitudes which are his subject. He has evoked family fears and frustrations without probing them. But it is important to recognize the genuine, if limited, appeal of Williams's strategy. He has asked us to see his plays as artifice and as reports on reality. And he has used the artificial, "plastic" elements both to intensify and to relieve the intensity of the family struggles. This paradox is a most intriguing one. He has counted on our familiarity with the family drama, reminded us of it, and then eluded its more rigid restrictions. He has been a realist, if only in part, to refresh our response to the dilemmas of family life. His best plays remind us of our quest for relatedness and independence and so depend on, and contribute to, the very tradition of American domestic drama which he proposed to escape.

NOTES

[1] Jackson, *Broken World*, p. viii, note 1.

[2] Williams, *Menagerie*, p. 145.

[3] "A free, imaginative use of light can be of enormous value in giving a mobile, plastic quality to plays of a more or less static nature." Williams, "Production Notes," *Menagerie*, p. 134.

[4] Ibid., pp. 163–164.

[5] Ibid., pp. 167–168.

[6] Tischler, *Williams*, p. 97.

[7] Williams, *Menagerie*, p. 199.

[8] Ibid., p. 220.

[9] Ibid., pp. 230–231.

[10] Ibid., p. 237.

[11] Ibid., p. 145.

[12] Ibid., p. 179.

[13] Ibid., p. 180.

[14] The original New York production and the recent revival both omitted the projections. Without them the play is moved even closer to the conventional realism of domestic drama, a tendency which can also be seen in the Broadway productions of *Streetcar,* which have deemphasized the expressionist elements in such scenes as those presenting symbolic images of Blanche's mental state.

[15] Williams, "Production Notes," p. 132.

[16] Ibid., p. 133.

[17] Ibid., p. 194.

[18] Ibid., p. 186.

◊ ◊ ◊

Portrait of a Girl in Glass

TENNESSEE WILLIAMS

We lived in a third floor apartment on Maple Street in Saint Louis, on a block which also contained the Ever-ready Garage, a Chinese laundry, and a bookie shop disguised as a cigar store.

Mine was an anomalous character, one that appeared to be slated for radical change or disaster, for I was a poet who had a job in a warehouse. As for my sister Laura, she could be classified even less readily than I. She made no positive motion toward the world but stood at the edge of the water, so to speak, with feet that anticipated too much cold to move. She'd never have budged an inch, I'm pretty sure, if my mother who was a relatively aggressive sort of woman had not shoved her roughly forward, when Laura was twenty years old, by enrolling her as a student in a nearby business college. Out of her "magazine money" (she sold subscriptions to women's magazines), Mother had paid my sister's tuition for a term of six months. It did not work out. Laura tried to memorize the typewriter keyboard, she had a chart at home, she used to sit silently in front of it for hours, staring at it while she cleaned and polished her infinite number of little glass ornaments. She did this every evening after dinner. Mother would caution me to be very quiet. "Sister is looking at her typewriter chart!" I felt somehow that it would do her no good, and I was right. She would seem to know the positions of the keys until the weekly speed drill got underway, and then they would fly from her mind like a bunch of startled birds.

At last she couldn't bring herself to enter the school any more. She kept this failure a secret for a while.

She left the house each morning as before and spent six hours walking around the park. This was in February, and all the walking outdoors regardless of weather brought on influenza. She was in bed for a couple of weeks with a curiously happy little smile on her face. Of course Mother phoned the business college to let them know she was ill. Whoever was talking on the other end of the line had some trouble, it seems, in remembering who Laura was, which annoyed my mother and she spoke up pretty sharply. "Laura has been attending that school of yours for two months, you certainly ought to recognize her name!" Then came the stunning disclosure. The person sharply retorted, after a moment or two, that now she *did* remember the Wingfield girl, and that she had not been at the business college *once* in about a month. Mother's voice became strident. Another person was brought to the phone to verify the statement of the first. Mother hung up and went to Laura's bedroom where she lay with a tense and frightened look in place of the faint little smile. Yes, admitted my sister, what they said was true. "I couldn't go any longer, it scared me too much, it made me sick at the stomach!"

After this fiasco, my sister stayed at home and kept in her bedroom mostly. This was a narrow room that had two windows on a dusky areaway between two wings of the building. We called this areaway Death Valley for a reason that seems worth telling. There were a great many alley cats in the neighborhood and one particularly vicious dirty white Chow who stalked them continually. In the open or on the fire escapes they could usually elude him but now and again he cleverly contrived to run some youngster among them into the cul-de-sac of this narrow areaway at the far end of which, directly beneath my sister's bedroom windows, they made the blinding discovery that what had appeared to be an avenue of escape was really a locked arena, a gloomy vault of concrete and brick with walls too high for any cat to spring, in which they must suddenly turn to spit at their death until it was hurled upon them. Hardly a week went by without a repetition of this violent drama. The areaway had grown to be hateful to Laura because she could not look out on it without recalling the screams and the snarls of killing. She kept the shades drawn down, and as Mother would not permit the use of electric current except when needed, her days were spent almost in perpetual twilight. There were three pieces of dingy ivory furniture in the room, a bed, a bureau, a chair. Over the bed was a remarkably bad religious painting, a very effeminate head of Christ with teardrops visible just below the eyes. The charm of the room was produced by my sister's collection of glass. She loved colored glass and had covered the walls with shelves of little glass articles, all of them light and delicate in color. These she washed and polished with endless care. When you entered the room there was always this soft, transparent radiance in it which came from the glass absorbing whatever faint light came through the shades on Death Valley. I have no idea how many articles there were of this delicate glass. There must have been hundreds of them. But Laura could tell you exactly. She loved each one.

She lived in a world of glass and also a world of music. The music came from a 1920 Victrola and a bunch of records that dated from about the same period, pieces such as "Whispering" or "The Love Nest" or "Dardanella." These records were souvenirs of our father, a man whom we barely remembered, whose name was spoken rarely. Before his sudden and unexplained disappearance from our lives, he had made this gift to the household, the phonograph and the records, whose music remained as a sort of apology for him. Once in a while, on payday at the warehouse, I would bring home a new record. But Laura seldom cared for these new records, maybe because they reminded her too much of the noisy tragedies in Death Valley or the speed drills at the business college. The tunes she loved were the ones she had always heard. Often she sang to herself at night in her bedroom. Her voice was thin, it usually wandered off-key. Yet it had a curious childlike sweetness. At eight o'clock in the evening I sat down to write in my own mousetrap of a room. Through the closed doors, through the walls, I would hear my sister singing to herself, a piece like "Whispering" or "I Love You" or "Sleepy Time Gal," losing the tune now and then but always preserving the minor atmosphere of the music. I think that was why I always wrote such strange and sorrowful poems in those days. Because I had in my ears the wispy sound of my sister serenading her pieces of colored glass, washing them while she sang or merely looking down at them with her vague blue eyes until the points of gem-like radiance in them gently drew the arching particles of reality from her mind and finally produced a state of hypnotic calm in which she even stopped singing or washing the glass and merely sat without motion until my mother knocked at the door and warned her against the waste of electric current.

I don't believe that my sister was actually foolish. I think the petals of her mind had simply closed through fear, and it's no telling how much they had closed upon in the way of secret wisdom. She never talked very much, not even to me, but once in a while she did pop out with something that took you by surprise.

After work at the warehouse or after I'd finished my writing in the evening, I'd drop in her room for a little visit because she had a restful and soothing effect on nerves that were worn rather thin from trying to ride two horses simultaneously in two opposite directions.

I usually found her seated in the straight-back ivory chair with a piece of glass cupped tenderly in her palm.

"What are you doing? Talking to it?" I asked.

"No," she answered gravely, "I was just looking at it."

On the bureau were two pieces of fiction which she had received as Christmas or birthday presents. One was a novel called the *Rose-Garden Husband* by someone whose name escapes me. The other was *Freckles* by Gene Stratton Porter. I never saw her reading the *Rose-Garden Husband,* but the other book was one that she actually lived with. It had probably never occurred to Laura that a book was something you read straight through and then laid aside as finished. The character Freckles, a one-armed orphan youth who worked in a lumber camp, was someone that she invited into her bedroom now and then for a friendly visit just as she did me. When I came in and found this novel open upon her lap, she would gravely remark that Freckles was having some trouble with the foreman of the lumber camp or that he had just received an injury to his spine when a tree fell on him. She frowned with genuine sorrow when she reported these misadventures of her storybook hero, possibly not recalling how successfully he came through them all, that the injury to the spine fortuitously resulted in the discovery of rich parents and that the bad-tempered foreman has a heart of gold at the end of the book. Freckles became involved in romance with a girl he called The Angel, but my sister usually stopped reading when this girl became too prominent in the story. She closed the book or turned back to the lonelier periods in the orphan's story. I only remember her making one reference to this heroine of the novel. "The Angel is nice," she said, "but seems to be kind of conceited about her looks."

Then one time at Christmas, while she was trimming the artificial tree, she picked up the Star of Bethlehem that went on the topmost branch and held it gravely toward the chandelier.

"Do stars have five points really?" she enquired.

This was the sort of thing that you didn't believe and that made you stare at Laura with sorrow and confusion.

"No," I told her, seeing she really meant it, "they're round like the earth and most of them much bigger."

She was gently surprised by this new information. She went to the window to look up at the sky which was, as usual during Saint Louis winters, completely shrouded by smoke.

"It's hard to tell," she said, and returned to the tree.

So time passed on till my sister was twenty-three. Old enough to be married, but the fact of the matter was she had never even had a date with a boy. I don't believe this seemed as awful to her as it did to Mother.

At breakfast one morning Mother said to me, "Why don't you cultivate some nice young friends? How about down at the warehouse? Aren't there some young men down there you could ask to dinner?"

This suggestion surprised me because there was seldom quite enough food on her table to satisfy three people. My mother was a terribly stringent housekeeper, God knows we were poor enough in actuality, but my mother had an almost obsessive dread of becoming even poorer. A not unreasonable fear since the man of the house was a poet who worked in a warehouse, but one which I thought played too important a part in all her calculations.

Almost immediately Mother explained herself.

"I think it might be nice," she said, "for your sister."

I brought Jim home to dinner a few nights later. Jim was a big red-haired Irishman who had the scrubbed and polished look of well-kept chinaware. His big square hands seemed to have a direct and very innocent hunger for touching his friends. He was always clapping them on your arms or shoulders and they burned through the cloth of your shirt like plates taken out of an oven. He was the best-liked man in the warehouse and oddly enough he was the only one that I was on good terms with. He found me agreeably ridiculous I think. He knew of my secret practice of retiring to a cabinet in the lavatory and working on rhyme schemes when work was slack in the warehouse, and of sneaking up on the roof now and then to smoke my cigarette with a view across the river at the undulant open country of Illinois. No doubt I was classified as screwy in Jim's mind as much as in the others', but while their attitude was suspicious and hostile when they first knew me, Jim's was warmly tolerant from the beginning. He

called me Slim, and gradually his cordial acceptance drew the others around, and while he remained the only one who actually had anything to do with me, the others had now begun to smile when they saw me as people smile at an oddly fashioned dog who crosses their path at some distance.

Nevertheless it took some courage for me to invite Jim to dinner. I thought about it all week and delayed the action till Friday noon, the last possible moment, as the dinner was set for that evening.

"What are you doing tonight?" I finally asked him.

"Not a God damn thing," said Jim. "I had a date but her Aunt took sick and she's hauled her freight to Centralia!"

"Well," I said, "why don't you come over for dinner?"

"Sure!" said Jim. He grinned with astonishing brightness.

I went outside to phone the news to Mother.

Her voice that was never tired responded with an energy that made the wires crackle.

"I suppose he's Catholic?" she said

"Yes," I told her, remembering the tiny silver cross on his freckled chest.

"Good!" she said. "I'll bake a salmon loaf!"

And so we rode home together in his jalopy.

I had a curious feeling of guilt and apprehension as I led the lamb-like Irishman up three flights of cracked marble steps to the door of Apartment F, which was not thick enough to hold inside it the odor of baking salmon.

Never having a key, I pressed the bell.

"Laura!" came Mother's voice. "That's Tom and Mr. Delaney! Let them in!"

There was a long, long pause.

"Laura?" she called again. "I'm busy in the kitchen, you answer the door!"

Then at last I heard my sister's footsteps. They went right past the door at which we were standing and into the parlor. I heard the creaking noise of the phonograph crank. Music commenced. One of the oldest records, a march of Sousa's, put on to give her the courage to let in a stranger.

The door came timidly open and there she stood in a dress from Mother's wardrobe, a black chiffon ankle-length and high-heeled slippers on which she balanced uncertainly like a tipsy crane of melancholy plumage. Her eyes stared back at us with a glass brightness and her delicate wing-like shoulders were hunched with nervousness.

"Hello!" said Jim, before I could introduce him.

He stretched out his hand. My sister touched it only for a second.

"Excuse me!" she whispered, and turned with a breathless rustle back to her bedroom door, the sanctuary beyond it briefly revealing itself with the tinkling, muted radiance of glass before the door closed rapidly but gently on her wraithlike figure.

Jim seemed to be incapable of surprise.

"Your sister?" he asked.

"Yes, that was her," I admitted. "She's terribly shy with strangers."

"She looks like you," said Jim, "except she's pretty."

Laura did not reappear till called to dinner. Her place was next to Jim at the drop-leaf table and all through the meal her figure was slightly tilted away from his. Her face was feverishly bright and one eyelid, the one on the side toward Jim, had developed a nervous wink. Three times in the course of the dinner she dropped her fork on her plate with a terrible clatter and she was continually raising the water glass to her lips for hasty little gulps. She went on doing this even after the water was gone from the glass. And her handling of the silver became more awkward and hurried all the time.

I thought of nothing to say.

To Mother belonged the conversational honors, such as they were. She asked the caller about his home and family. She was delighted to learn that his father had a business of his own, a retail shoe store somewhere in Wyoming. The news that he went to night school to study accounting was still more edifying. What was his heart set on beside the warehouse? Radio-engineering? My, my, my! It was easy to see that here was a very up-and-coming young man who was certainly going to make his place in the world!

Then she started to talk about her children. Laura, she said, was not cut out for business. She was domestic, however, and making a home was really a girl's best bet.

Jim agreed with all this and seemed not to sense the ghost of an implication. I suffered through it dumbly, trying not to see Laura trembling more and more beneath the incredible unawareness of Mother.

And bad as it was, excruciating in fact, I thought with dread of the moment when dinner was going to be over, for then the diversion of food would be taken away, we would have to go into the little steam-heated parlor. I fancied the four of us having run out of talk, even Mother's seemingly endless store of questions about Jim's home and his job all used up finally—the four of us, then, just sitting there in the parlor, listening to the hiss of the radiator and nervously clearing our throats in the kind of self-consciousness that gets to be suffocating.

But when the blancmange was finished, a miracle happened.

Mother got up to clear the dishes away. Jim gave me a clap on the shoulders and said, "Hey, slim, let's go have a look at those old records in there!"

He sauntered carelessly into the front room and flopped down on the floor beside the Victrola. He began sorting through the collection of worn-out records and reading their titles aloud in a voice so hearty that it shot like beams of sunlight through the vapors of self-consciousness engulfing my sister and me.

He was sitting directly under the floor-lamp and all at once my sister jumped up and said to him, "Oh— you have freckles!"

Jim grinned. "Sure that's what my folks call me—Freckles!"

"Freckles?" Laura repeated. She looked toward me as if for the confirmation of some too wonderful hope. I looked away quickly, not knowing whether to feel relieved or alarmed at the turn that things were taking.

Jim had wound the Victrola and put on *Dardanella*.

He grinned at Laura.

"How about you an' me cutting the rug a little?"

"What?" said Laura breathlessly, smiling and smiling.

"Dance!" he said, drawing her into his arms.

As far as I knew she had never danced in her life. But to my everlasting wonder she slipped quite naturally into those huge arms of Jim's, and they danced round and around the small steam-heated parlor, bumping against the sofa and chairs and laughing loudly and happily together. Something opened up in my sister's face. To say it was love is not too

hasty a judgment, for after all he had freckles and that was what his folks called him. Yes, he had undoubtedly assumed the identity—for all practical purposes—of the one-armed orphan youth who lived in the Limberlost, that tall and misty region to which she retreated whenever the walls of Apartment F became too close to endure.

Mother came back in with some lemonade. She stopped short as she entered the portieres.

"Good heavens! Laura? Dancing?"

Her look was absurdly grateful as well as startled.

"But isn't she stepping all over you, Mr. Delaney?"

"What if she does?" said Jim, with bearish gallantry. "I'm not made of eggs!"

"Well, well, well!" said Mother, senselessly beaming.

"She's light as a feather!" said Jim. "With a little more practice she'd dance as good as Betty!"

There was a little pause of silence.

"Betty?" said Mother.

"The girl I go out with!" said Jim.

"Oh!" said Mother.

She set the pitcher of lemonade carefully down and with her back to the caller and her eyes on me, she asked him just how often he and the lucky young lady went out together.

"Steady!" said Jim.

Mother's look, remaining on my face, turned into a glare of fury.

"Tom didn't mention that you went out with a girl!"

"Nope," said Jim. "I didn't mean to let the cat out of the bag. The boys at the warehouse'll kid me to death when Slim gives the news away."

He laughed heartily but his laughter dropped heavily and awkwardly away as even his dull senses were gradually penetrated by the unpleasant sensation the news of Betty had made.

"Are you thinking of getting married?" said Mother.

"First of next month!" he told her.

It took her several moments to pull herself together. Then she said in a dismal tone, "How nice! If Tom had only told us we could have asked you *both!*"

Jim had picked up his coat.

"Must you be going?" said Mother.

"I hope it don't seem like I'm rushing off," said Jim, "but Betty's gonna get back on the eight o'clock train an' by the time I get my jalopy down to the Wabash depot—"

"Oh, then, we mustn't keep you."

Soon as he'd left, we all sat down, looking dazed.

Laura was the first to speak.

"Wasn't he nice?" she asked. "And all those freckles!"

"Yes," said Mother. Then she turned to me.

"You didn't mention that he was engaged to be married!"

"Well, how did I know that he was engaged to be married?"

"I thought you called him your best friend down at the warehouse?"

"Yes, but I didn't know he was going to be married!"

"How peculiar!" said Mother. "How very peculiar!"

"No," said Laura gently, getting up from the sofa. "There's nothing peculiar about it."

She picked up one of the records and blew on its surface a little as if it were dusty, then set it softly back down.

"People in love," she said, "take everything for granted."

What did she mean by that? I never knew.

She slipped quietly back to her room and closed the door.

Not very long after that I lost my job at the warehouse. I was fired for writing a poem on the lid of a shoebox. I left Saint Louis and took to moving around. The cities swept about me like dead leaves, leaves that were brightly colored but torn away from the branches. My nature changed. I grew to be firm and sufficient.

In five years' time I had nearly forgotten home. I had to forget it, I couldn't carry it with me. But once in a while, usually in a strange town before I have found companions, the shell of deliberate hardness is broken through. A door comes softly and irresistibly open. I hear the tired old music my unknown father left in the place he abandoned as faithlessly as I. I see the faint and sorrowful radiance of the glass, hundreds of little transparent pieces of it in very delicate colors. I hold my breath, for if my sister's face appears among them—the night is hers!

June 1943 (Published 1948)

READING AND REACTING

◊ ◊ ◊

1. Who is this play really about—Tom, Laura, or Amanda?
2. What is the function of the absent father in the play?
3. Besides serving as a possible suitor for Laura, what other roles does Jim play?

4. Identify references to historical events occurring at the time of the play's action. How are these events related to the play's central theme?

5. Is Tom's primary role in the play actor, character, playwright, or narrator?

6. How do the music, the lighting, and the words and pictures projected on slides—which Tennessee Williams called "extra-literary accents"—contribute to the play's action? Are they essential? (Note that at the urging of the director, Williams eliminated these "accents" when the play opened on Broadway.)

7. Tennessee Williams called *The Glass Menagerie* a "memory play." What events are presented as memories?

8. Discuss how props help to develop the play. For example, consider the picture of the father, the Victrola, the fire escape, the telephone, the alarm clock, the high school yearbook, the unicorn, the candles.

9. What events and dialogue foreshadow Tom's escape?

10. Do Amanda and Laura change as the play proceeds? What do you think will happen to them after the action of the play is over? What is the significance of Laura's blowing out the candles at the end of the play?

11. Identify several examples of religious imagery in the play—for example, the Paradise Dance Hall. What is the significance of this imagery? In what way does it relate to the major theme of the play?

12. **JOURNAL ENTRY** Do you think Tom's decision to leave his family is a sign of strength or of weakness?

13. **CRITICAL PERSPECTIVE** At one point in his discussion of the play (p. 1863), Roger Boxill contrasts the short story "Portrait of a Girl in Glass" and *The Glass Menagerie*. According to Boxill, "'Portrait' is a wistful memory, *Menagerie* is a moving elegy."

    Do you agree with Boxill's assessment of these two works? What do you think are the major differences between the short story and the play that developed out of it?

Related Works: "A&P" (p. 113), "Barn Burning" (p. 226), "Eveline" (p. 470), "The Soul Selects Her Own Society" (p. 943), "The Road Not Taken" (p. 959), *Marty* (p. 1279), *'night, Mother* (p. 1708)

RESEARCH QUESTIONS
✧ ✧ ✧

1. *The Glass Menagerie* is set in St. Louis. Find out whether natives of St. Louis consider themselves Southerners. To what extent are the characters and themes of the play regional and to what extent are they universal?

2. In the Jean Evans interview from "Excerpts from Two Interviews with Williams" (p. 1862), Williams responds to the question of his use of "plays unconventional in form." In his response, he states that his plays are "light on plot and heavy on characterization." How does such an emphasis benefit *The Glass Menagerie?* What other plays most represent this method?

3. Roger Boxill (p. 1863) states that the Christian symbolism in *The Glass Menagerie* suggests that "the time of Amanda's youth, the time of the Depression and the time of the Second World War are analogues, respectively, of Paradise, Purgatory and Hell." Do you agree? If so, how are the analogies filled out and detailed?

4. In Scanlan's essay (p. 1876) from "Family, Drama, and American Dreams," he states that Williams "consciously manipulated his subject matter and his tone, playing off the oppressiveness of the family of security against a teasing stylized realism." Do you agree? How does Williams use realism in the play? How does this affect the subject matter?

5. Williams has called himself a "moral symbolist" in the tradition of Nathaniel Hawthorne. Williams, however, has made sexuality's mystery one of his central metaphors. How has he portrayed sexuality in his plays? What is his moral message? How has his portrayal both resembled and differed from Hawthorne's in such works as *The Scarlet Letter*, "Young Goodman Brown" (p. 304), and "Rappaccini's Daughter"?

6. Williams writes about his characters' attempt to escape their reality, and most often their reality is one of loneliness. What methods do his characters use to try to escape their loneliness? Do any of his characters succeed in their attempt? When they do not succeed, what causes their failure? Are the successes and failures of Williams's lonely characters similar to or different from those of Chayefsky's *Marty* (p. 1279)?

Heather Jenkins

English 202

Professor Spand

April 17, 2000

Laura's Gentleman Caller

One of the major points of debate about Tennessee Williams's play <u>The Glass Menagerie</u> centers on the character Jim O'Connor, "the gentleman caller." Jim is an outgoing young man who approaches life lightheartedly, and his friendliness and charm make him a good suitor for Laura. But beside being Laura's suitor, what role does Jim play in the drama? Is Jim merely another character lost in the world of illusion, or is he something more? The answers to these questions become clear when we examine Jim's behavior and his influence on the other characters.

One possible interpretation of Jim's role is that he is simply another character living in a world of illusion. Jim's vision of the future is a grand one. He dreams of becoming part of the newly formed television industry, and throughout his appearance on stage, he rambles on about himself and his plans for the future:

> Because I believe in the future of television! <u>(Turning back to her.)</u> I wish to be ready to go up right along with it. Therefore I'm planning to get in on the ground floor. In fact, I've already made the right connections and all that remains is for the industry itself to get underway! Full steam--<u>(His eyes are starry.)</u> Knowledge--

Jenkins 2

Zzzzzp! <u>Money</u>--Zzzzzp!--<u>Power</u>! That's the cycle democracy is built on! <u>(His attitude is convincingly dynamic. Laura stares at him, even her shyness eclipsed in her ab-solute wonder. He suddenly grins.)</u> I guess you think I think a lot of myself! (1847)

Jim is so enthralled with his own self-importance that when Amanda asks Jim to persuade Laura to drink some wine, he refers to himself as "Superman." This reference suggests that Jim believes his training in public speaking has given him the strength to overcome any obstacle. Jim's delusions define his view of real-ity to such an extent that he considers his view of life to be the only appropriate one. As a result, he continually compares his perspective to that of oth-ers, expecting to convince them that his views and his views alone are correct.

Because Jim believes that he has discovered the one true path to success, he considers Tom's dream of being a poet to be unrealistic. Likewise, Jim regards Tom's plan to join the Merchant Marine, to live the glamorous and adventurous life depicted in the movies, as a delusion. To "save" Tom, Jim tries to persuade him to take a public speaking course that will make him fit for "executive positions." All of Jim's prod-ding, however, only reinforces Tom's desire to proceed with his plan to join the Merchant Marine. Indeed, when Jim tells Tom that he had better wake up, Jim to-tally misses the irony of Tom's reply, "I am waking up--" (1836).

Jenkins 3

Jim's fantasies about the future play into and reinforce Amanda's romantic fantasies. Amanda's plans to
find Laura a husband surface long before Jim enters the
Wingfield house. As Tom observes early in the play,
Amanda's desire to find a suitor for Laura is "an obsession"; according to Tom, "[T]he image of the gentleman
caller haunted our small apartment" (1815). When Amanda
learns that Jim will attend their dinner, her dream of
entertaining gentlemen callers in the Southern tradition
becomes a reality. As a result, she begins to have unrealistically high expectations for Jim's visit. When Jim
charms Amanda and attempts to impress her with his
dreams of success, he unknowingly fulfills her fantasy.

Another possible interpretation of Jim's role is
that he acts as a savior. In his article "The Glass
Menagerie," Roger Boxill explains that Jim's role as
savior is inherent in the play's Christian symbolism,
which first appears when Tom announces Jim's plans to
come to dinner. Boxill asserts that along with Tom's
"Annunciation" of Jim's visit, Tom is alluding to
Transubstantiation and the Resurrection when he discusses a movie in which "a stage magician turn[s]
water to wine and escape[s] from a coffin" (1819). In
simpler terms, Jim's role as possible savior for the
family is suggested by his ability to reach out to
Laura and encourage her to enjoy the pleasures of the
real world--dancing and romance.

Jim's role as Laura's savior can be seen in the
short story "Portrait of a Girl in Glass," from which
the play evolved, as well as in the play itself. In

the story, Jim and Laura begin to dance almost immediately after they are left alone. Although their encounter in the story is less intimate than the one in the play, Laura responds to Jim with joy and hope. In the play, Laura's visit with Jim evokes a similar response: Laura enjoys the feeling of being valued and accepted. Thus, when Jim announces his departure and his engagement, Laura realizes what she has lost and is overwhelmed with emotion.

Ironically, just as Jim offers Laura a way to escape her world of illusions, he abandons her, leaving her trapped in her own world. For this reason, Jim fails as a savior. One might argue that he consciously rejects his role as a savior; but we must remember that Jim enters the play unaware of the family's expectations; he views the visit purely as an opportunity to pass the time and to meet his friend's family, not as a prelude to romance. Jim's perception of his visit is made clear in "Portrait of a Girl in Glass," where he agrees to visit the Wingfields only because he has nothing else to do:

> "What are you doing tonight?" I finally asked him.
>
> "Not a God damn thing," said Jim. "I had a date but her Aunt took sick and she's hauled her freight to Centralia!"
>
> "Well," I said, "why don't you come over for dinner?"
>
> "Sure!" said Jim. He grinned with astonishing brightness. (1887)

Jenkins 5

Although both these interpretations of Jim's role offer insights into the play, neither adequately explains Jim's function. Perhaps the best explanation of Jim's role comes from the play itself, where Jim is called "an emissary from a world of reality" (1807–08). In this sense, his solid presence in the play emphasizes the fragility of the other characters. As an emissary of reality, Jim lives in the real world and realizes the importance of striving for a better life. He attends public speaking and radio engineering classes so that he can advance beyond his low-level job at the warehouse. He scolds Tom for wanting to be a poet, an impractical goal for anyone living during the economic depression of the 1930s. Likewise, Jim challenges Laura to relinquish her feelings of deformity and difference; he does not understand why Laura has given up hope and isolated herself. The contrast between Jim and Laura emphasizes not only Laura's vulnerability, but also her family's consuming and ultimately debilitating delusions.

Because Jim lives in a world of reality, he is the only character who escapes the illusions that engulf the Wingfields. Jim's connection with reality allows him to continue to search for a better life, something that none of the Wingfields will ever attain (King 1876). Even though Tom escapes the confines of the apartment, he is unable to leave behind the imaginary world his mother and his sister have created. Moreover, like his father, Tom leaves not to seek reality but to escape from one dream world into another, one that is little different from the movies in which he has lost himself. As the play ends, Tom delivers a monologue about how he has been unable to leave the memory of his sister behind. And we are reminded of Jim, the happy and healthy gentleman caller, who has moved on.

Although Jim is referred to as the gentleman caller, his role in the play is much more complex. In one sense, Jim is detached from reality, enchanted by his own egotistical vision of how people should behave. In another sense, he is a kind of savior who reaches out to Laura, conveying the warmth and compassion of a saint. But these two conflicting images are overshadowed by Jim's role as an emissary from the real world who journeys to the seductive world of fantasy and whose presence there emphasizes the destructive power of dreams that have become delusions. In this role, Jim is "the kindest of Williams's emissaries from reality, perhaps because his faith in the American dream of self-improvement and success is so complete as to be itself a touching illusion" (Scanlan 1879).

Works Cited

Boxill, Roger. "The Glass Menagerie." Kirszner and
    Mandell 1863-69.

King, Thomas L. "Irony and Distance in The Glass
    Menagerie." Kirszner and Mandell 1869-76.

Kirszner, Laurie G., and Stephen R. Mandell, eds.
    Literature: Reading, Reacting, Writing. 4th ed.
    Fort Worth: Harcourt, 2001.

Scanlan, Tom. From Family, Drama, and American Dreams.
    Kirszner and Mandell 1876-83.

Williams, Tennessee. The Glass Menagerie. Kirszner and
    Mandell 1805-54.

---. "Portrait of a Girl in Glass." Kirszner and
    Mandell 1884-90.

APPENDIX A

◇ ◇ ◇

Writing a Research Paper

When you write a paper about a literary topic, you often supplement your own observations and interpretations with information from other sources. These sources may include works of literature as well as books and journal articles by literary critics (see p. 15). You may get this information from print sources, from electronic databases, or from the Internet. You should not, however, let the task of gathering information make you forget all you have learned about writing a paper on a literary topic. Remember, your primary task is to present your ideas clearly and convincingly. For this reason, you will have a much easier time writing a literary research paper if you follow the process discussed below.

CHOOSING A TOPIC

◇ ◇ ◇

Your instructor may assign a topic or may allow you to choose one. If you choose a topic, make sure your topic is neither too broad nor too narrow for the paper's length, the amount of time you have to write it, and the number of sources your instructor expects you to use.

Daniel Collins, a student in an introduction to literature course, was given six weeks to write a five- to seven-page research paper on one of the short stories the class had read. Daniel chose to write about Eudora Welty's "A Worn Path" because he liked the story and because the main character, Phoenix Jackson, interested him. He knew, however, that he would have to narrow his topic before he could begin. In class, Daniel's instructor had posed some provocative questions about the significance of Phoenix Jackson's journey. Daniel thought that this topic might work well because he could explore it in five pages and could complete it within the six-week time limit.

LOOKING FOR SOURCES

◇ ◇ ◇

To see whether you will be able to find enough material about your topic, do a quick survey of your library's resources. (Before you start, arrange a meeting with a reference librarian, who can save you time by pointing you to the most useful resources.)

Begin your survey by consulting your library's online central information system. Frequently, this system includes the library's catalog as well as a number of bibliographic databases, such as *Readers' Guide to Periodical Literature* and *Humanities Index*. Then, consult general reference works like encyclopedias and specialized dictionaries to get an overview of your subject.

Daniel's quick look at the library's central information system showed him that his library's holdings included several books and numerous articles on Eudora Welty.

Narrowing Your Topic

♦ ♦ ♦

As you survey the resources of your library, the titles of books and articles as well as the subject headings of the catalog should help you to further narrow your topic.

Daniel found two critical articles that discussed the significance of Phoenix Jackson's journey, and he hoped they would enable him to figure our why Phoenix Jackson continued her journey despite all the hardships she encountered. Daniel knew that he would have to do more than just summarize the articles; he would have to make a point about the journey, one that he could support with examples from the story as well as from his research.

Doing Research

♦ ♦ ♦

Once you have narrowed your topic, you are ready to look for the specific information you will need to develop your ideas. Go back to the library and check out any books you think will be useful. Then, consult reference works—indexes and bibliographies, for example—to find relevant articles. If you find articles in print form, use the copy machines in the library to photocopy them (and be sure to copy down the publication information you will need to document these sources). Also search electronic databases (either CD-ROM or online), such as *InfoTrac* or *Lexis/Nexis,* to find relevant articles. Usually, you can download information from these databases to a diskette or print out a hard copy. Finally, browse the World Wide Web, beginning at a site such as *Voice of the Shuttle: Web Page for Humanities Research* (http://vos.ucsb.edu/index.html) and following the links to other relevant sites.

Daniel was lucky enough to find everything he needed in his college library. He retrieved two articles about the Welty story, and he found two more listed in *Humanities Index*. Finally, a careful search of his library's online central information system revealed that among the library's holdings was a videocassette of "A Worn Path" that included an interview with the author.

TAKING NOTES

◇ ◇ ◇

Once you have located your sources, write down the information you think will be useful for your paper. There is no single correct way to take notes; different writers take notes differently. Some writers keep their notes on 3 × 5 index cards, while others store information in a computer file that they have created for this purpose. Whatever system you use, be sure to keep a record of the author's full name as well as complete publication information. You will need this information later on to compile your Works Cited list (see p. 1911).

When you take notes from a source, you have three options: you can *paraphrase, summarize,* or *quote.*

When you **paraphrase,** you put the author's ideas into your own words, keeping the order and emphasis of the original. You paraphrase when you want to make a difficult or complex discussion accessible to readers. (Keep in mind that you are conveying the author's ideas, not your own.) Here is a passage from Roland Bartel's article "Life and Death in Eudora Welty's 'A Worn Path,'" followed by Daniel's paraphrase.

Original

> The assumption that the grandson is dead helps explain Phoenix Jackson's stoical behavior in the doctor's office. She displays a "ceremonial stiffness" as she sits "bolt upright" staring "straight ahead, her face solemn and withdrawn into rigidity." This passiveness suggests her psychological dilemma—she cannot explain why she made the journey. Her attempt to blame the lapse of memory on her illiteracy is unconvincing. Her lack of education is hardly an excuse for forgetting her grandson, but it goes a long way toward explaining her inability to articulate her subconscious motives for her journey.

Paraphrase

> As Roland Bartel points out in "Life and Death in Eudora Welty's 'A Worn Path,'" Phoenix Jackson's lack of response at the doctor's office makes sense if we assume that her grandson is dead. She sits still, without showing any emotion, and she does not answer people's questions.

```
Although she says her forgetfulness is because of her lack
of education, this excuse doesn't seem believable to
Bartel, who observes that although her lack of education
doesn't explain why she forgets about her grandson, it
might account for her failure to understand why she makes
the trip to the city.
```

When you write a **summary,** you also put an author's ideas into your own words. A summary, however, presents just the general point of a passage. For this reason, a summary is always shorter than the original. Here is Daniel's summary of the passage from the article quoted above.

Summary

```
        As Roland Bartel points out in "Life and Death in
Eudora Welty's 'A Worn Path,'" Phoenix Jackson's actions
at the doctor's office make sense only if we assume that
her grandson is dead and that she does not understand her
reasons for making her trip.
```

When you *quote,* you reproduce a passage exactly, word for word and punctuation mark for punctuation mark, enclosing the entire passage in quotation marks. Because too many quotations can distract readers, use a quotation only when you think that the author's words will add something—memorable wording, for example—to your paper.

INTEGRATING SOURCES
◆ ◆ ◆

To integrate a summary, paraphrase, or quotation smoothly into your paper, use a phrase that introduces your source and its author—*Bartel points out, according to Bartel, Bartel claims,* or *Bartel says,* for example. You can place this identifying phrase at various points in a sentence.

```
According to Roland Bartel, "The assumption that the
grandson is dead helps explain Phoenix Jackson's stoical
behavior in the doctor's office."
```

```
"The assumption that the grandson is dead helps explain
Phoenix Jackson's stoical behavior in the doctor's
office," observes Roland Bartel in his article "Life and
Death in Eudora Welty's 'A Worn Path.'"
```

```
"The assumption that the grandson is dead," says the
literary critic Roland Bartel, "helps explain Phoenix
Jackson's stoical behavior in the doctor's office."
```

AVOIDING PLAGIARISM

Plagiarism is taking credit for ideas or words that are not your own. Sometimes plagiarism is intentional, but often it is unintentional—occurring, for example, when you paste a quoted passage from your computer file directly into a paper and forget to use quotation marks and documentation. The best way to avoid plagiarism is to keep careful notes, to distinguish between your ideas and those of your sources, and to give credit to your sources with **documentation.** For literary research, documentation consists of in-text citations and a list of works cited (see page 1908).

In general, you document words and ideas borrowed from your sources. (This rule applies to both print and electronic sources.) Of course, there are certain items that don't need to be documented: common knowledge (information every reader will probably know), facts available from a variety of reference sources, familiar sayings and well-known quotations, and your own original research (interviews and surveys you conduct, for example).

You can avoid the possibility of plagiarism if you remember exactly what types of information require documentation.

◇ *Document all word-for-word quotations from a source.* Whenever you use a writer's exact words, document them. Even if you only quote a word or two within a paraphrase or summary, you must document the quoted words separately, after the final quotation marks.

◇ *Document ideas from a source that you put into your own words.* Be sure to document all paraphrases or summaries of a source, including an author's judgments, conclusions, and arguable assertions.

◇ *Document all tables, charts, graphs, or statistics from a source.* Because tables and graphs are almost always the product of someone's original research, they must be documented. (If you compile your own table using data from a source, you must still credit the source.)

NOTE: Plagiarism can also occur when a paraphrase or summary too closely follows the wording and sentence structure of the original. Even if you do not use the exact words of the original and even if you provide documentation, you commit plagiarism if you simply use synonyms and follow the sentence structure of your source. Acceptable paraphrases and summaries do more than change words; they use original wording and syntax to convey the source's meaning.

Drafting a Thesis Statement

❖ ❖ ❖

After you have taken notes, review the information you have gathered, and draft a thesis statement. This **thesis statement,** a single sentence that tells readers what direction you will take in your paper, should make a point that you will support with a combination of your own ideas and the ideas you have drawn from your research.

After reviewing his notes, Daniel developed this thesis statement about Eudora Welty's "A Worn Path."

Thesis statement

> The main focus of "A Worn Path" is Phoenix Jackson's
> character and her act of making her journey.

As you draft and revise your paper, your thesis statement will probably change. Still, it gives your ideas focus and enables you to organize them into an outline.

Making an Outline

❖ ❖ ❖

Once you have drafted a thesis statement, you can construct an outline from your notes. Write your thesis statement at the top of the page. Then, review your notes, and arrange them in the order in which you plan to use them. As you construct your outline, arrange these points under appropriate headings. When it is completed, your outline will show you how much support you have for each of your points, and it will be your guide when you write a draft of your paper. Your outline, which covers the body paragraphs of your essay, can be a *sentence outline,* in which each idea is expressed as a sentence, or a *topic outline,* in which each idea is expressed in a word or a short phrase.

After reviewing his notes, Daniel constructed the following topic outline. Notice that he uses roman numerals for first-level headings, capital letters for second-level headings, and arabic numerals for third-level headings. Notice too that all points in the outline are presented in parallel structure.

> **Thesis Statement:** The main focus of "A Worn Path" is
> Phoenix Jackson's character and her act of making her
> journey.

I. Critical interpretations of "A Worn Path"
   A. Heroic act of sacrifice
   B. Journey of life
   C. Religious pilgrimage
II. Focus on journey
   A. Little information about Jackson and her grandson
   B. Nurse's question
   C. Jackson's reply
III. Jackson's character
   A. Interaction between Jackson's character and journey
      1. Significance of Jackson's first name
      2. Jackson as a complex character
   B. Jackson's physical problems
      1. Failing eyesight
      2. Difficulty walking
IV. Jackson's spiritual strength
   A. Belief in God
   B. Child of nature
V. Jackson's emotional strength
   A. Love for grandson
   B. Fearlessness and selflessness
   C. Determination

WRITING YOUR PAPER

◊ ◊ ◊

Once you have constructed your outline, you can begin to draft your paper. Follow your outline as you write, using your notes as the need arises.

Your paper's **introduction** will usually be a single paragraph. In addition to identifying the work or works you are writing about and stating your thesis, the introduction to a literary research paper can present an overview of your topic, a survey of critical opinion, or necessary background information.

The body of your paper supports your thesis statement, with each of your paragraphs developing a single point. Support your points with examples from the literary work you are discussing or with summaries, paraphrases, and quotations from your sources. You can also include your own observations and inferences.

Your paper's **conclusion,** usually a single paragraph (but sometimes more), restates your main points and reinforces your thesis statement.

Remember, the purpose of your first draft is to get ideas down on paper so that you can react to them. You should expect to revise, possibly writing several drafts.

The final draft of Daniel Collins's paper on Eudora Welty's "A Worn Path" appears on p. 1919.

DOCUMENTING YOUR SOURCES
◇ ◇ ◇

Documentation is the acknowledgement of information from an outside source that you use in your paper. Students writing about literature use the documentation style recommended by the Modern Language Association (MLA), a professional organization of more than 25,000 teachers and students of English and other languages. This style of documentation has three parts: *parenthetical references* in the text, a *Works Cited* list at the end of the paper, and *explanatory notes.**

PARENTHETICAL REFERENCES IN THE TEXT

MLA documentation style uses parenthetical references within the text that refer to an alphabetical list of works cited at the end of the paper. A parenthetical reference should contain just enough information to guide readers to your Works Cited list. A typical parenthetical reference consists of the author's last name and a page number.

> Gwendolyn Brooks uses the sonnet form to create poems that have a wide social and aesthetic range (Williams 972).

If you use more than one source by the same author, include a shortened title in the parenthetical reference.

> Brooks knows not only Shakespeare, Spenser, and Milton, but also the full range of African-American poetry (Williams, "Brooks's Way" 972).

If you mention the author's name or the title of the work in your paper, only a page reference is needed.

> According to Gladys Margaret Williams in "Gwendolyn Brooks's Way with the Sonnet," Brooks combines a sensitivity to poetic forms with a depth of emotion appropriate for her subject matter (972–73).

---

* For more information see the *MLA Handbook for Writers of Research Papers,* 5th ed. (New York: MLA, 1999). You can also consult the MLA Web site at <http://www.mla.org>.

GUIDELINES FOR PUNCTUATING PARENTHETICAL REFERENCES

◇ *Paraphrases and summaries*

Place the parenthetical reference after the last word of the sentence and before the final punctuation:

In her works, Brooks combines the pessimism of Modernist poetry with the optimism of the Harlem Renaissance (Smith 978).

◇ *Direct quotations run in with the text*

Place the parenthetical reference after the quotation marks and before the final punctuation:

According to Gary Smith, Brooks's <u>A Street in Bronzeville</u> "conveys the primacy of suffering in the lives of poor Black women" (980).

According to Gary Smith, the poems in <u>A Street in Bronzeville</u> "served notice that Brooks had learned her craft [. . .]" (978).

Along with Thompson we must ask, "Why did it take so long for critics to acknowledge that Gwendolyn Brooks is an important voice in twentieth-century American poetry" (123)?

◇ *Quotations set off from the text*

Omit the quotation marks and place the parenthetical reference one space after the final punctuation. (For guidelines for setting off long quotations, see p. 34.)

For Gary Smith, the identity of Brooks's African-American women is inextricably linked with their sense of race and poverty:

> For Brooks, unlike the Renaissance poets, the victimization of poor Black women becomes not simply a minor chord but a predominant theme of <u>A Street in Bronzeville</u>. Few, if any, of her female characters are able to free themselves from a web of poverty that threatens to strangle their lives. (980)

SAMPLE REFERENCES

An entire work

> August Wilson's play <u>Fences</u> treats many themes frequently
> expressed in modern drama.

When citing an entire work, state the name of the author in your paper instead of in a parenthetical reference.

A work by two or three authors

> Myths cut across boundaries and cultural spheres and reappear in strikingly similar forms from country to country (Feldman and Richardson 124).

> The effect of a work of literature depends on the audience's predispositions that derive from membership in various social groups (Hovland, Janis, and Kelley 87).

A work by more than three authors

> Hawthorne's short stories frequently use a combination of allegorical and symbolic methods (Guerin et al. 91).

The abbreviation *et al.* is Latin for "and others."

A work in an anthology

> In his essay "Flat and Round Characters" E. M. Forster distinguishes between one-dimensional characters and those that are well developed (Stevick 223–31).

The parenthetical reference cites the anthology (edited by Stevick) that contains Forster's essay; full information about the anthology appears in the list of works cited.

A work with volume and page numbers

> Critics consider <u>The Zoo Story</u> to be one of Albee's best plays (Eagleton 2:17).

An indirect source

> Wagner observed that myth and history stood before him "with opposing claims" (qtd. in Winkler 10).

The abbreviation *qtd. in* (quoted in) indicates that the quoted material was not taken from the original source.

A play with numbered lines

> "Give thy thoughts no tongue," says Polonius, "Nor any
> unproportioned thought his act" (<u>Ham.</u> 1.3.59-60).

The parentheses contain the act, scene, and line numbers, separated by periods. When included in parenthetical references, titles of the books of the Bible and well-known literary works are often abbreviated—*Gen.* for *Genesis* and *Ado* for *Much Ado about Nothing,* for example.

A poem

> "I muse my life-long hate, and without flinch / I bear it
> nobly as I live my part," says Claude McKay in his
> bitterly ironic poem "The White City" (3-4).

Notice that a slash (/) is used to separate lines of poetry run in with the text. The parenthetical reference cites the lines quoted.

THE LIST OF WORKS CITED

Parenthetical references refer to a **Works Cited** list that includes all the sources you refer to in your paper. Begin the Works Cited list on a new page, continuing the page numbers of the paper. For example, if the text of the paper ends on page 6, the Works Cited section will begin on page 7.

INFORMAL DOCUMENTATION

Sometimes, when you are writing a paper that includes quotations from a single source that the entire class has read or if all your sources are from your textbook, your instructor may give you permission to use *informal documentation*. Because both the instructor and the class are familiar with the sources, you supply the authors' last names and page numbers in parentheses and omit a works cited list.

Center the title *Works Cited* one inch from the top of the page. (If your list includes all the works consulted, whether you cite them or not, use the title *Works Consulted.*) Arrange entries alphabetically, according to the last name of each author (or the first word of the title if the author is unknown). Articles—*a, an,* and *the*—at the beginning of a title are not considered first words. In order to conserve space, publishers' names are abbreviated—for example, *Harcourt* for Harcourt Brace College Publishers. Double-space the entire Works Cited list between and within entries. Begin typing each entry at the left margin, and indent subsequent lines five spaces, or one-half inch. Each Works Cited entry has three divisions—author, title, and publishing information—separated by periods.*

A book by a single author

> Kingston, Maxine Hong. <u>The Woman Warrior: Memoirs of a Girlhood among Ghosts</u>. New York: Knopf, 1976.

A book by two or three authors

> Feldman, Burton, and Robert D. Richardson. <u>The Rise of Modern Mythology</u>. Bloomington: Indiana UP, 1972.

Notice that only the *first* author's name is in reverse order.

A book by more than three authors

> Guerin, Wilfred, et al., eds. <u>A Handbook of Critical Approaches to Literature</u>. 3rd. ed. New York: Harper, 1992.

Instead of using *et al.,* you may list all the authors' names in the order in which they appear on the title page.

Two or more works by the same author

> Novoa, Juan-Bruce. <u>Chicano Authors: Inquiry by Interview</u>. Austin: U of Texas P, 1980.
> ---. "Themes in Rudolfo Anaya's Work." Address given at New Mexico State University, Las Cruces. 11 Apr. 1987.

List two or more works by the same author in alphabetical order by title. Include the author's full name in the first entry; use three unspaced hyphens followed by a period to take the place of the author's name in second and subsequent entries.

An edited book

> Oosthuizen, Ann, ed. <u>Sometimes When It Rains: Writings by South African Women</u>. New York: Pandora, 1987.

Notice that the abbreviation *ed.* stands for *editor.*

A book with a volume number

> Eagleton, T. Allston. <u>A History of the New York Stage</u>. Vol. 2. Englewood Cliffs: Prentice, 1987.

---

* The *MLA Handbook for Writers of Research Papers* shows a single space after all end punctuation.

All three volumes have the same title.

> Durant, Will, and Ariel Durant. <u>The Age of Napoleon: A</u>
> <u>History of European Civilization from 1789 to 1815</u>.
> New York: Simon, 1975.

Each volume has a different title. *The Age of Napoleon* is volume 2 of *The Story of Civilization*.

A short story, poem, or play in a collection of the author's work

> Gordimer, Nadine. "Once upon a Time." <u>"Jump" and Other</u>
> <u>Stories</u>. New York: Farrar, 1991. 23-30.

A short story in an anthology

> Salinas, Marta. "The Scholarship Jacket." <u>Nosotros: Latina</u>
> <u>Literature Today</u>. Ed. Maria del Carmen Boza, Beverly
> Silva, and Carmen Valle. Binghamton: Bilingual, 1986.
> 68-70.

The inclusive page numbers follow the year of publication. Note that here the abbreviation *Ed.* stands for *Edited by*.

A poem in an anthology

> Simmerman, Jim. "Child's Grave, Hale County, Alabama." <u>The</u>
> <u>Pushcart Prize, X: Best of the Small Presses</u>. Ed.
> Bill Henderson. New York: Penguin, 1986. 198-99.

A play in an anthology

> Hughes, Langston. <u>Mother and Child</u>. <u>Black Drama Anthology</u>.
> Ed. Woodie King and Ron Miller. New York: NAL, 1986.
> 399-406.

An article in an anthology

> Forster, E. M. "Flat and Round Characters." <u>The Theory of</u>
> <u>the Novel</u>. Ed. Philip Stevick. New York: Free, 1980.
> 223-31.

More than one selection from the same anthology

If you are using more than one selection from an anthology, cite the anthology in a separate entry. Also, list each individual selection separately, including the author and title of the selection, the anthology editor's last name, and the inclusive page numbers.

Kirszner, Laurie G., and Stephen R. Mandell, eds. <u>Literature: Reading, Reacting, Writing</u>. 4th ed. Fort Worth: Harcourt, 2001.

Rich, Adrienne. "Diving into the Wreck." Kirszner and Mandell. 905–07.

A translation

Carpentier, Alejo. <u>Reasons of State</u>. Trans. Francis Partridge. New York: Norton, 1976.

An article in a journal with continuous pagination in each issue

LeGuin, Ursula K. "American Science Fiction and the Other." <u>Science Fiction Studies</u> 2 (1975): 208–10.

An article with separate pagination in each issue

Grossman, Robert. "The Grotesque in Faulkner's 'A Rose for Emily.'" <u>Mosaic</u> 20.3 (1987): 40–55.

[*20.3* signifies volume 20, issue 3.]

An article in a magazine

Milosz, Czeslaw. "A Lecture." <u>The New Yorker</u> 22 June 1992: 32.

"Solzhenitsyn: An Artist Becomes an Exile." <u>Time</u> 25 Feb. 1974: 34+.

34+ indicates that the article appears on pages that are not consecutive; in this case, the article begins on page 34 and then continues on page 37. An article with no listed author is entered by title on the works cited list.

An article in a daily newspaper

Oates, Joyce Carol. "When Characters from the Page Are Made Flesh on the Screen." <u>New York Times</u> 23 Mar. 1986, late ed.: C1+.

C1+ indicates that the article begins on page 1 of Section C and continues on a subsequent page.

An article in a reference book

"Dance Theatre of Harlem." <u>The New Encyclopaedia Britannica: Micropaedia</u>. 15th ed. 1987.

You do not need to include publication information for well-known reference books.

Grimstead, David. "Fuller, Margaret Sarah." <u>Encyclopedia
of American Biography</u>. Ed. John A. Garraty. New York:
Harper, 1974.

You must include publication information when citing reference books
that are not well known.

A film or videocassette

"<u>A Worn Path</u>." By Eudora Welty. Dir. John Reid and Claudia
Velasco. Perf. Cora Lee Day and Conchita Ferrell.
Videocassette. Harcourt, 1994.

An interview

Brooks, Gwendolyn. "An Interview with Gwendolyn Brooks."
<u>Triquarterly</u> 60 (1984): 405–10.

A lecture or an address

Novoa, Juan-Bruce. "Themes in Rudolfo Anaya's Work."
Literature Colloquium. New Mexico State University.
Las Cruces. 11 Apr. 1987.

An online source: A scholarly project or information database

<u>Philadelphia Writers Project</u>. Ed. Miriam Kotzen Green. May
1998. Drexel U. 12 June 1999 <http://www.Drexel.edu/
letrs/wwp/>.

When citing Internet sources appearing on the World Wide Web, include
both the date of the electronic publication (if available) and the date you
accessed the source. In addition, include the URL (electronic address) in
angle brackets.

An online source: A document within a scholarly project or information database

"D-Day: June 7th, 1944" <u>The History Channel Online</u>. 1999.
History Channel. 7 June 1999
<http://historychannel.com/thisday/today/997690.html>.

An online source: A personal site

Yerkes, James. <u>Chiron's Forum: John Updike Home Page</u>. 23
June 1999. 30 June 1999
<http://www.users.fast.net/~joyerkers/item9.html>.

An online source: A book

Douglass, Frederick. <u>My Bondage and My Freedom</u>. Boston:
1855. 8 June 1999
<gopher://gopher.vt.edu:10024/22/178/3>.

An online source: An article in a scholarly journal

> Dekoven, Marianne. "Utopias Limited: Post-Sixties and
>   Postmodern American Fiction." <u>Modern Fiction Studies</u>
>   41.1 (1995): 13 pp. 17 Mar. 1999 <http://muse.jhu.edu/
>   journals/mfs.v041/41.1dwkovwn.html>.

When you cite information from the print version of an online source, include the publication information for the printed source, the number of pages or paragraphs (if available), and the date of access.

An online source: An article in an encyclopedia

> "Hawthorne, Nathaniel." <u>Britannica Online</u>. Vers. 98.2.
>   Apr. 1998. Encyclopedia Britannica. 16 May 1998
>   <http://www.eb/com/:220>.

An online source: An article in a newspaper

> Lohr, Steve. "Microsoft Goes to Court." <u>New York Times on
>   the Web</u> 19 Oct. 1998. 29 Apr. 1999
>   <http://www.nytimes.com/web/docroot/library.cyber/
>   week/1019business.html>.

An online source: An article in a magazine

> Weiser, Jay. "The Tyranny of Informality." <u>Time</u> 26 Feb.
>   1996. 1 Mar. 1999.<http://www.enews.com/
>   magazines.tnr/current/022696.3.html>.

An online source: A work from an online service

> "Kafka, Franz." <u>Compton's Encyclopedia Online</u>. Vers. 2.0.
>   1997. American Online. 8 June 1998. Key Word:
>   Compton's.

Frequently, online services like America Online and Lexis-Nexis enable you to access material without providing a URL. If you access such material by using a keyword, provide the keyword (following the date of access) at the end of the entry.

> "Elizabeth Adams." <u>History Resources</u>. 11 Nov. 1997.
>   America Online. 28 June 1999. Path: Research;
>   Biography; Women in Science; Biographies.

If, instead of using a keyword, you follow a series of paths, list the paths separated by semicolons.

A CD-ROM: A nonperiodical publication

> "Windhover." <u>The Oxford English Dictionary</u>. 2nd ed. CD-
>   ROM. Oxford: Oxford UP, 1992.

A CD-ROM: A periodical publication

> Zurbach, Kate. "The Linguistic Roots of Three Terms."
> Linguistic Quarterly 37 (1994): 12–47. InfoTrac:
> Magazine Index Plus. CD-ROM. Information Access. Jan.
> 1996.

Other electronic sources: A painting or photograph

> Lange, Dorothea. Looking at Pictures. 1936. Museum of Mod.
> Art, New York. 28 June 1999
> <http://moma.org/exhibitions/lookingatphotographs/
> lang-fr.html>.

Other electronic sources: An e-mail

> Adkins, Camille. E-mail to the author. 28 June 1999.

Other electronic sources: An online posting

> Gilford, Mary. "Dog Heroes in Children's Literature."
> Online posting. 17 Mar. 1999. 12 Apr. 1999 <news:
> alt.animals.dogs>.
> Schiller, James. "Paper Cost and Publishing Costs." Online
> posting. 24 Apr. 1999. Book Forum. 11 May 1999
> <www.nytimes.com/webin/webx?13A^41356@.ee765e/0>.

WARNING: Using information from an Internet source—especially newsgroups and online forums—is risky. Contributors are not necessarily experts, and they frequently are incorrect and misinformed. Unless you can be certain that the information you are obtaining from these sources is reliable, don't use it. You can check the reliability of an Internet source by asking your instructor or librarian for guidance.

Content Notes

Use **content notes,** indicated by a superscript (a raised number) in the text, to cite several sources at once or to provide commentary or explanations that do not fit smoothly into your paper. The full text of these notes appears on the first numbered page following the last page of the paper. (If your paper has no content notes, the Works Cited page follows the last page of the paper.) Like Works Cited entries, content notes are double-spaced within and between entries. However, the first line of each explanatory note is indented five spaces (or one-half inch), with subsequent lines flush with the left-hand margin.

TO CITE SEVERAL SOURCES

In the paper

> Surprising as it may seem, there have been many attempts to define literature.[1]

In the note

> [1] For an overview of critical opinion, see Arnold 72; Eagleton 1-2; Howe 43-44; and Abrams 232-34.

TO PROVIDE EXPLANATIONS

In the paper

> In recent years, gothic novels have achieved great popularity.[3]

In the note

> [3] Gothic novels, works written in imitation of medieval romances, originally relied on supernatural occurrences. They flourished in the late eighteenth and early nineteenth centuries.

SAMPLE LITERATURE PAPERS WITH MLA DOCUMENTATION

The two literature papers that follow, written for introduction to literature courses, use MLA documentation style. The first was written by Daniel Collins, whose writing process you have been following throughout this appendix. The second, written by Tim Westmoreland, uses electronic sources.

Collins 1

Daniel Collins

English 201

Professor Smith

31 January 2000

And Again She Makes the Journey: Character
and Act in Eudora Welty's "A Worn Path"

Over the past fifty years, Eudora Welty's "A Worn
Path," the tale of an elderly black woman, Phoenix
Jackson, traveling to the city to obtain medicine for
her sick grandson, has been the subject of much critical interpretation. Critics have speculated on the
meaning of the many death and rebirth symbols, including the scarecrow, which the old woman believes is a
ghost; the buzzard who watches her travel; the skele-
ton-like branches that reach out to slow her; and her
first name, Phoenix. From the study of these symbols,
various critics have concluded that "A Worn Path" represents either a "heroic act of sacrifice," "a parable
for the journey of life," or "a religious pilgrimage"
(Keys 354). It is certainly true, as these interpretations imply, that during her journey Phoenix Jackson
struggles through difficult terrain and encounters
many dangers and that despite these obstacles, she
does not abandon her quest. However, it is neither the
symbols associated with the quest nor the quest itself
that is the story's primary focus; what is most important is Phoenix Jackson's character and her act of
making the journey.

Eudora Welty discusses the characterization of
Phoenix Jackson in a videotaped interview. Here, Welty

acknowledges that Jackson's first name refers to a mythical bird that dies and is reborn every five hundred years. She explains, however, that despite her character's symbolic name, Phoenix Jackson is a complex being with human frailties and emotions (Henley).

Phoenix Jackson has a number of physical problems that challenge her ability to perform daily tasks. Because of her age, she has failing eyesight, which distorts her perception of the objects she encounters during her journey. For instance, Phoenix mistakes a patch of thorns for "a pretty little green bush," and she believes a scarecrow is the ghost of a man (Welty 389-90). Likewise, she has difficulty walking, so she must use a cane; at one point, she is unable to bend and tie her own shoes. Because of these physical disabilities, readers might expect her to fail in her attempt to reach town, because "the journey is long; the path, though worn, is difficult" (Keys 354). So what gives Phoenix Jackson the energy and endurance for the journey? The question can best be answered by looking at the inner qualities of the woman: although Jackson's body is weak, she has great spiritual and emotional strength.

Phoenix Jackson's spiritual strength comes from her oneness with nature and her belief in God. This oneness with nature, claims James Saunders, helps her overcome the challenges that she encounters (67). Because Phoenix Jackson is "a child of nature," her impaired vision, although it slows her journey, does not stop it, because as Saunders explains, "mere human

Collins 3

vision would not have been sufficient for the journey"
(67). Instead of allowing her failing vision to restrict her actions, Phoenix Jackson relies on her spiritual connection with nature; thus, she warns various
animals to "Keep out from under these feet" (Welty
389). Additionally, her spiritual strength comes from
her belief in God--a quality seen when she refers to
God watching her steal the hunter's nickel.

Phoenix Jackson's spiritual strength is comple-
mented by her emotional strength. Her love for her
grandson compels her to endure any difficulty and to
defy any personal danger. Thus, throughout her journey, she demonstrates fearlessness and selflessness.
For example, when the hunter threatens her with his
gun, she tells him that she has faced worse dangers.
Even after stealing and accepting nickels, she does
not consider replacing her own worn shoes, but instead
remains intent upon buying a paper windmill for her
grandson.

In her video interview, Eudora Welty explains how
she came to create the paradoxical Phoenix Jackson--
outwardly frail and inwardly strong. Welty tells how
she noticed an "old lady" slowly making her way across
a "silent horizon,"[1] driven by an overwhelming determination to reach her destination; as Welty says, "she
had a purpose" (Henley). Welty created Phoenix Jackson
in the image of this determined woman. In order to
emphasize the character's strength, Welty had her
make the journey to Natchez to get medication for
her grandson. Because the act had to be performed

Collins 4

repeatedly, the journey became a ritual that had to be completed at all costs. Thus, as Welty explains in her interview, the act of making the journey is the most important element in the story (Henley).

In order to convey the significance of the journey, Welty focuses her story on the process of the journey. For this reason, readers receive little information about the daily life of the boy and his grandmother or about the illness for which the boy is being treated. Regardless of the boy's condition--or even whether he is alive or dead--Jackson must complete her journey (Henley). The nurse's statement--"The doctor said as long as you came to get it [the medicine], you could have it" (Welty 394)--reinforces the ritualistic nature of Jackson's journey, a journey that Bartel suggests is a "subconscious" act (289). Thus, Phoenix Jackson cannot answer the nurse's questions because she does not consciously know what compels her to make the journey. According to Welty, the character's silence and disorientation can also be attributed to her relief and disillusionment upon completing the ritualistic journey (Henley). Nevertheless, next Saturday, Phoenix Jackson will again walk "miles and miles, and will continue to do so, regardless of the difficulties facing her, along the worn path that leads through the wilderness of the Natchez Trace, cheerfully performing her labor of love" (Howard 84).

Clearly, the interaction of character (Phoenix Jackson) and act (the ritual journey in search of medication) is the most important element of Welty's

Collins 5

story. By relying heavily on the characterization of Phoenix Jackson and by describing her difficult encounters during her ritual journey to town, Welty emphasizes how spiritual and emotional strength can overcome physical frailty and how determination and fearlessness can overcome any danger. These moral messages become clear by the time Phoenix reaches the doctor's office. The image of the elderly woman determinedly walking across the horizon, the image that prompted Welty's writing of the story, remains in the minds of the readers, and significantly, it is the final image of the videotaped version of "A Worn Path."

Collins 6

Note

[1] Unlike the written version of "A Worn Path,"
the video of the short story ends not at the doctor's
office but with a vision similar to the one that inspired Welty to write the story--the elderly black
woman silently walking along the horizon at dusk.

Collins 7

Works Cited

Bartel, Roland. "Life and Death in Eudora Welty's 'A Worn Path.'" <u>Studies in Short Fiction</u> 14 (1977): 288-90.

Henley, Beth. <u>Interview with Eudora Welty</u>. Dir. John Reid and Claudia Velasco. Videocassette. Harcourt, 1994.

Howard, Zelma Turner. <u>The Rhetoric of Eudora Welty's Short Stories</u>. Jackson: UP of Mississippi, 1973.

Keys, Marilyn. "'A Worn Path': The Way of Dispossession." <u>Studies in Short Fiction</u> 16 (1979): 354-56.

Saunders, James Robert. "'A Worn Path': The Eternal Quest of Welty's Phoenix Jackson." <u>Southern Literary Journal</u> 25.1 (Fall 1992): 62-73.

Welty, Eudora. "A Worn Path." <u>Literature: Reading, Reacting, Writing</u>. 4th ed. Ed. Laurie G. Kirszner and Stephen R Mandell. Fort Worth: Harcourt, 2001. 388-95.

<u>"A Worn Path."</u> By Eudora Welty. Dir. John Reid and Claudia Velasco. Perf. Cora Lee Day and Conchita Ferrell. Videocassette. Harcourt, 1994.

Tim Westmoreland

Professor Adkins

Literature 2101

5 April 2001

"A&P": A Class Act

John Updike's "A&P," like many of his other works, is a "profoundly American" story about social inequality and an attempt to bridge the gap between social classes (Steiner 105). The story is told by an eighteen-year-old boy who is working as a check-out clerk in an A&P in a small New England town five miles from the beach. The narrative is delivered in a slangy, colloquial voice that tells of a brief but powerful encounter with a "beautiful but inaccessible girl" from another social and economic level (Wells). Sammy, the narrator, is working his cash register on a slow Thursday afternoon when, as he says, "In walks these three girls in nothing but bathing suits" ("A&P" 113). Lengel, the store's manager--a Sunday school teacher and "self appointed moral policeman"--confronts the girls, telling them that they should be decently dressed (Wells). It is a moment of embarrassment and insight for all parties concerned, and in an apparently impulsive act, Sammy quits his job. Although the plot is simple, what is at the heart of this story is more complex: a noble gesture that serves as a futile attempt to cross social and economic boundaries that are all but unbridgeable.

Through Sammy's eyes, we see the class conflict that defines the story. The privileged young girls in bathing suits are in sharp contrast to the few

Westmoreland 2

customers who are shopping in the store. Sammy refers to the customers as "sheep" and describes one of them as "a witch about fifty with rouge on her cheekbones and no eyebrows" ("A&P" 113). Other customers are characterized in equally negative terms--for example, "houseslaves in pin curlers" ("A&P" 114) and "an old party in baggy gray pants" ("A&P" 115). Unlike the other customers, the leader of the three girls is described as a "queen":

> She came down a little hard on her heels, as if she didn't walk in her bare feet that much, putting down her heels and then letting the weight move along to her toes as if she was testing the floor with every step, putting a little deliberate extra action to it. ("A&P" 113-14).

The mere fact that "Queenie" does not seem to have walked barefoot much seems to hint at a social gap between the girls and the other customers. However, it seems clear that Sammy realizes that Queenie and her friends come from farther away than just the beach. They have come to test the floors of the less well-off and do it openly, in defiance of social rules. In a sense, they are "slumming."

Queenie, whose name suggests her superior status, clearly understands her position in social as well as sexual terms. She has come to the A&P to purchase "Kingfish Fancy Herring Snacks in Pure Sour Cream" for her parents, while Sammy has to spend the summer working. Even the choice of the exotic and

Westmoreland 3

expensive herring snacks hints at their different backgrounds. Regardless, the two act in ways that are not all that different. Both are self-consciously trying out new roles, with Sammy trying to rise above his station in life and Queenie trying to move below hers. As Queenie arrives at the register, Sammy observes, "Now her hands are empty, not a ring or a bracelet, bare as God made them, and I wonder where the money's coming from. Still with that prim look she lifts a folded dollar bill out of the hollow at the center of her nubbled pink top" ("A&P" 116). With this gesture, she not only tests her own sexual powers but also sinks to the level of the supermarket and its workers and customers. Despite her act, though, Sammy knows how different Queenie's world is from his:

> I slid down her voice into her living room. Her father and the other men were standing around in ice-cream coats and bow ties and women were in sandals picking up herring snacks on toothpicks off a big glass plate and they were holding drinks the color of water with olives and sprigs of mint in them. When my parents have somebody over they get lemonade and if it's a real racy affair Schlitz in tall glasses with "They'll Do It Every Time" cartoons stencilled on. ("A&P" 116)

As Updike says in a 1996 interview, "[Sammy] is a blue-collar kid longing for a white-collar girl" (Murray, e-mail).

At this point in the story, as Sammy says, "everybody's luck begins to run out" ("A&P" 116).

Westmoreland 4

Lengel, the store manager (who, according to Updike, was named after a strict boss for whom his mother once worked) represents "the cruel and unethical" rules that govern matters of social etiquette (Murray, <u>Interview</u>). In the story he confronts the girls, telling them that they are indecently dressed. "'We <u>are</u> decent,' Queenie says suddenly, her lower lip pushing, getting sore now that she remembers her place, a place from which the crowd that runs the A&P must look pretty crummy. Fancy Herring Snacks flashed in her very blue eyes" ("A&P" 116). Suddenly, Sammy can no longer be a detached observer and, in a gesture of defiance, he quits. The real question here is <u>why</u> he quits. Updike himself says, "I wonder to what extent his gesture of quitting has to do with the fact that she is rich and he is poor" (Murray, <u>Interview</u>).

By quitting, Sammy challenges social inequality, but is his response heroic posturing or an action that expresses his longstanding frustration? In other words, does Sammy quit because of what Updike calls a "misunderstanding of how the world is put together" (Murray, <u>Interview</u>) or because he is "a boy who's tried to reach out of his immediate environment towards something bigger and better" (Updike, "Still Afraid" 55)? Although Sammy's action may be simply impulsive--Sammy even states it would be fatal not to go through with his initial gesture--it seems likely that he is taking a deliberate stand against what he sees as social injustice. Unlike Queenie's act of defiance, Sammy's gesture will have long-term consequences (Oates).

Westmoreland 5

As Updike points out, in Sammy's small town everyone will find out what he has done, and he may be "known [. . .] as a quitter" (Murray, Interview). Sammy's understanding and acceptance of these consequences ("'You'll feel this for the rest of your life,' Lengel says, and I know that's true"), and of the limitations his social class imposes upon him, constitute his initiation into adulthood ("A&P" 118). Whether quitting is Sammy's first step toward overcoming these limitations or a romantic gesture he will live to regret remains to be seen.[1] As Updike says, "How blind we are, as we awkwardly push outward into the world!" (Updike, "Still Afraid" 57).

Although it is true that both Queenie and Sammy attempt to cross social boundaries, the reasons for their actions are different. Queenie's provocative gesture is well thought out; she deliberately relinquishes her trappings, her clothes and jewelry. If only for a few minutes, she concedes her dignity and wealth in order to flaunt her sexuality and her power. In contrast, Sammy chooses impulsively, in what Updike calls a "hot flash," a "moment of manly decisiveness," to take action and, ultimately, gives up both his dignity and his power (Murray, Interview). He gains only a brief moment of glory before he finds himself alone in the parking lot. In this instant, he confronts the social inequality and the unspeakable frustration it represents. According to Updike, Sammy cannot win, though in a "noble surrender of his position," he gains an understanding of the weight he must bear (Murray, Interview).

Westmoreland 6

Note

[1] In a recent e-mail message, Donald Murray agrees that Sammy's quitting will have implications for him that it will not have for Queenie and her friends. He goes on to say, however, that it is also possible that the young women will remain "imprisoned in their class," while Sammy may have a chance of escaping the limitations of his.

Westmoreland 7

Works Cited

Murray, Donald. E-mail to the author. 2 April 1999.

---. <u>Interview with John Updike</u>. Dir. Bruce Schwartz. Videocassette. Harcourt, 1997.

Oates, Joyce Carol. "John Updike's American Comedies." <u>Joyce Carol Oates on John Updike</u>. 5 Apr. 1998. 28 June 1999 <http://www.usfca.edu/fac-staff/southerr/ Onupdike.html>.

Steiner, George. "Supreme Fiction: America Is in the Details." <u>The New Yorker</u> 11 Mar. 1996. America On-line. 20 Mar. 1999. Keyword: New Yorker Magazine.

Updike, John. "A&P." <u>Literature: Reading, Reacting, Writing</u>. 4th ed. Ed. Laurie G. Kirszner and Stephen R. Mandell. Fort Worth: Harcourt, 2001. 113–18.

---. "Still Afraid of Being Caught." <u>New York Times</u> 8 Oct. 1995, late ed., sec. 6: 55+. <u>New York Times Ondisc</u>. CD-ROM. UMI-Proquest. Jan. 1999.

Wells, Walter. "John Updike's 'A&P': A Return Visit to Araby." <u>Studies in Short Fiction</u> 30.2 (Spring 1993): 15 pars. <u>Infotrac: Magazine Index Plus</u>. CD-ROM. Information Access. Mar. 1999.

◆ ◆ ◆

Literary History: Aristotle to the Twentieth Century

The standard literary *canon* (the works of authors commonly read and taught) has been, until very recently, mainly male, white, upper-class, and European—with some American influence. Most readers are not aware, however, that the fiction, drama, and poetry now designated "classics" represent a series of choices about literary worth made over a long period of time. During the past twenty-five years or so, many challenges to the traditional canon have been made. To understand both the development of the traditional canon and the challenges to that canon, it is important to understand the history of Western literary criticism.

BEGINNINGS: THE GREEKS AND ROMANS (C. 450 B.C.–A.D. 400)

◆ ◆ ◆

The Western critical tradition begins with the Greeks. In the *Republic* Plato (427–347 B.C.) described the ideal state as well as the role of philosophers and poets. His pupil, Aristotle (384–322 B.C.), was by far the most significant classical influence on Europeans of the Middle Ages and the Renaissance. Even today drama critics and students pay careful attention to the theories presented in Aristotle's *Poetics* about how literature imitates life, how an audience responds with pity and fear to a tragedy, and how a well-written play is constructed.

The Romans contributed works on what would now be called "loftiness of style" (*On the Sublime*, Longinus, first century A.D.) and a treatise on the art of poetry (*Ars Poetica*, Horace, 65–8 B.C.). These writers were typically more interested in the craft of poetry—in how one might construct a poem that would have a pleasing effect on a reader—than in the power of the poet. In contrast to the Greek philosophical approach, Roman literary criticism was more like a practical handbook.

THE MIDDLE AGES
(C. A.D. 400–1500)

◇ ◇ ◇

After the fall of the Western Roman Empire in the fifth century A.D., Christianity became the unifying force of Western culture. The literature of the European Middle Ages was intended to demonstrate moral virtue in the hopes that people would follow the behavior patterns it praised. Much literature of this period took the form of morality and mystery plays, both of which had religious themes. Worldly art was discouraged because the clergy who kept learning alive during these hard times believed that the role of literature was to instruct people in the way to lead a virtuous life. Significant departures from moralistic literature appeared in the French romances, which depicted adventures undertaken in the cause of love, and in Chaucer's *Canterbury Tales,* which drew on English, French, and Italian sources. These served as antidotes to the traditional cautionary plays and tales. It is not surprising, given the strong moral purpose of most literature of the Middle Ages, that literary criticism was not a priority of the intellectual life of the period.

THE RENAISSANCE
(C. 1500–1660)

◇ ◇ ◇

During the fourteenth and fifteenth centuries, Europe emerged from the church-centered Middle Ages with a rebirth (*renaissance* is French for "rebirth") of learning. Renewed access to Greek and Roman writers led Renaissance humanists to a broad interest in intellectual considerations. Sir Philip Sidney's (1554–1586) *The Defense of Poesy* (c. 1580) is usually considered the most important work of literary criticism from this period. In his *Defense* Sidney argues that poetry must not simply give pleasure, but also contribute positively to the life of society. Unlike the writers of medieval allegories, however, Sidney believed that literature could—and should—have a moral impact without being didactic or prescriptive. Despite Sidney's contributions, Aristotle continued to be the undisputed arbiter of critical questions, although his role was complicated by the emergence of William Shakespeare (1564–1616) as a dramatist of exceptional talent.

Shakespeare's work posed a problem because many critics realized that he was a fine playwright despite his frequent disregard for Aristotle's rules governing well-constructed plays. As a result, a major concern of criticism up to the eighteenth century became the reconciling of Aristotle's standards with the challenges of contemporary playwriting.

THE ENLIGHTENMENT
(1660–1798)

◊ ◊ ◊

Samuel Johnson (1709–1784), who devoted much of the preface of his edition of Shakespeare's plays to the question of the bard's departures from Aristotle's rules, was a major critical figure of the Enlightenment, a period of neoclassicism characterized by a revitalized interest in the values and ideas of the classical world, particularly of the Romans. Along with Johnson, poets John Dryden (1631–1700) and Alexander Pope (1688–1744), as well as philosopher Edmund Burke (1729–1797), compared contemporary practice with the ideas of their Roman forebears. Burke, for instance, addressed the subject of Longinus's *On the Sublime* in his own treatise, *The Origin of Our Ideas of the Sublime and the Beautiful* (1757). Eighteenth-century critics stressed the value of reason and what they called "common sense." Their architectural style, familiar to us in structures like the Capitol building in Washington, D.C., provides a visual example of what they sought in literature: clarity, symmetry, discipline. They demanded that a play or poem be tightly constructed and favored the heroic couplet (two lines of rhymed iambic pentameter) as the perfect building block with which to construct didactic poems such as Pope's famous *Essay on Criticism* (1711), a scathing statement of neoclassical literary principles.

Thomas Paine's *Common Sense: Addressed to the Inhabitants of America* (1776) inspired his fellow Americans to revolution, and his *Rights of Man* (1791, 1792) made a stirring case for freedom as the right of every individual. The literature of the American Revolutionary Age, when Paine, Thomas Jefferson, Alexander Hamilton, Philip Freneau, and Joel Barlow were writing, reflected the patriotic concerns of the infant democracy.

THE ROMANTIC PERIOD
(1798–1837)

◊ ◊ ◊

Perhaps as an inevitable counterreaction to the Enlightenment came the Romantics. They believed that poetry was *not* an objective construction like a building with a precise and unchanging meaning but, instead, a subjective creation whose meaning depends on the poet's emotional state and a reader's personal response. Romantic poet William Blake (1757–1827) illustrated the conflict between romanticism and neoclassicism through his criticism of the opinions of Enlightenment artist Joshua Reynolds. In his notes on Reynolds's views, Blake observed that the emphasis on materialism and on physical evidence (empiricism) impoverishes art. Blake believed that the neoclassicists denied both imagination and subjective experience their preeminent role in the creative process. He thought that the artist must begin from the most concrete and minute sensory experience in order to reach the truth. Unlike most eighteenth-century writers, Blake and his fellow Romantics believed in the importance of the individual example rather than the general principle.

Like Blake, Samuel Taylor Coleridge (1772–1834) and William Wordsworth (1770–1850) placed value on the mysterious and on the significance of the common person's experience. Wordsworth in particular stressed the importance of concrete, simple language and offered, in his preface to the second edition of *Lyrical Ballads* (1800), a definition of poetry that has since become famous. A poem, Wordsworth says, should originate in "the spontaneous overflow of powerful feelings" whose energy comes from "emotion recollected in tranquility." George Gordon, Lord Byron (1788–1824), who himself lived a flamboyant life of publicly expressed powerful emotions, created in his poetry the melancholy Romantic hero, defiant and haunted by secret guilt. Percy Bysshe Shelley (1792–1822) makes perhaps the greatest claims for the poet's power and obligation to society in "A Defense of Poetry" (1821), where he argues that the "great instrument of moral good is the imagination."

The difference in attitude between neoclassicists and Romantics can also be seen through a comparison of the Shakespearean criticism of Samuel Johnson and Samuel Taylor Coleridge. In his *Preface to Shakespeare* (1765) Johnson argues that Shakespeare's faults include being much more concerned with pleasing an audience than with teaching it morals; he observes that often virtue is not rewarded, nor wickedness suitably punished. Additionally, Johnson notes, Shakespeare's diction is too elevated, and he lets the characters in the tragedies talk too much without advancing the action.

Coleridge, on the other hand, sees in the tragic character of Hamlet the prototype of the Romantic hero and argues in his lecture "Shakespeare's Judgment Equal to his Genius" (1836) that Shakespeare knew exactly what he was doing in describing how people actually behave rather than how they ought to behave.

John Keats (1795–1821), another Romantic poet, continued Coleridge's defense of Shakespeare. Keats believed that Shakespeare's intensity, particularly evident in the tragedies, moved his work onto another level altogether, where the work itself takes on life through its relationship with "beauty and truth" rather than with teaching proper patterns of behavior.

The Romantics in general, both in Britain and in the United States, saw the poet as particularly close to God and nature. The American philosopher Ralph Waldo Emerson (1803–1882) thought nature offered to the poet a mystical symbolism, while Henry David Thoreau (1817–1862) extolled the view that man should live close to nature and follow his personal conscience rather than the dictates of society. Mary Shelley

(1797–1851) and Edgar Allan Poe (1809–1849) were influential in another strand of romanticism: the macabre, melancholy, and mysterious.

THE VICTORIAN PERIOD
(1837–1901)
❖ ❖ ❖

The literary problem facing the post-Romantic generation of critics was dealing with a world where sublime isolation and communing with nature were less and less possible, even as ideals. During the Victorian era rapid industrialization, poverty, population growth, and mass transportation contributed to a general sense that the world was changing rapidly, and people had difficulty coping with these changes. In England critics like poet Matthew Arnold (1822–1888) argued that literature could help anchor people to their world and that literary criticism, as an occupation, should be a "disinterested endeavor" whose responsibility was to minister to a modern society that had lost its faith in other things, particularly religion. Although Arnold differed in many ways from the Romantics, he too believed in the ability of poetry to help us live productive, satisfying lives.

Just before the turn of the nineteenth century, the pendulum swung back from the Arnoldian view that poetry has moral utility—and that the best of it is serious and elevating—to the view that art should exist for its own sake. The dichotomy seen by the Romantics between intellect and feeling became in the 1890s the split between art and science. Oscar Wilde (1854–1900), Stéphane Mallarmé (1842–1898), and Charles Baudelaire (1821–1867) all dealt with this dichotomy by retreating altogether into the world of art and denying connection with anything else. These members of the symbolist movement valued suggestion, private symbols, and evocative references in their poetry. They attempted to connect their writing with a spiritual world they believed existed but knew was not accessible by the rational methods of science.

Charles Darwin (1809–1882) presented his theory of natural selection in his landmark *Origin of Species* (1859), and his ideas influenced novels and poetry of the latter part of the century. Those who believed natural selection contradicted the Bible were outraged, and others interpreted his theories as evidence of latent bestiality in humans. The certainty that mankind was the center of the universe was undermined, as was the conviction that the universe had been intelligently planned for a good purpose.

American writers of the late nineteenth century, including William Dean Howells and Henry James, were noted for realism; others, including naturalists Frank Norris and Theodore Dreiser, built on Darwin's views, exploring the idea of individuals being at the mercy of their instinctual drives and of external sociological forces.

THE MODERN PERIOD
(1901–PRESENT)

◆ ◆ ◆

In the next major attempt to demonstrate some objective significance to poetry, T. S. Eliot (1888–1965) argued against the lingering Romantic idea that a poem is the original child of a poet's inspiration. Instead, he proposed in "Tradition and the Individual Talent" (1917) that the poem supersedes the poet, who is merely the agent of its creation. Eliot argues that Wordsworth is wrong to put the poet in the central role of life-experiencer and recreator. According to Eliot, the poem itself will join the tradition, and it will be up to the *critic* to make sense of that tradition. To continue with the example of Shakespeare, Eliot's analysis of *Hamlet* focuses neither on the character of Hamlet and his personal agony (as did the Romantics) nor on the moral tone of the play (as did the neoclassicists), but rather on the story of Hamlet as treated by dramatists before Shakespeare. Eliot concludes that the problems with Shakespeare's play come about because he cannot successfully balance the early source materials with his own desire to write a play about the effect of Gertrude's guilt on her son. Thus, Eliot judges Shakespeare within a literary and historical tradition rather than within a moral or personal context.

The twentieth century has produced many important critics and theoreticians of literature who built upon the legacy of the past, though some only to the extent that they attempt to contradict earlier approaches. The dominant critical views, which are discussed more fully in Appendix C, can be divided into three categories: *formal,* those concerned with the structure or form of texts (formalism, structuralism, deconstruction); *social,* those concerned with texts in relation to social contexts (new historicism, feminism, Marxism); and *personal,* those concerned with the interaction of the individual (author or reader) and texts (reader-response criticism, psychoanalytic criticism). Each of these theoretical approaches can be traced to the writings of authors in the early part of the twentieth century or before.

Formalism, which acquired prominence in English and American criticism in the middle part of the century, actually began in the early part of the century in Moscow and Petrograd, and was initially a term used in a negative fashion because the techniques focused on patterns and devices in a work of literature and ignored the subject matter. Soon, however, formalism's logical appeal took hold, and it was advocated by Victor Shklovsky, Boris Eichenbaum, and Roman Jakobson in the 1920s. Though many literary theorists since Aristotle have stressed the importance of structure, the roots of structuralist criticism can be traced more directly to Russian formalists and French anthropologist Claude Levi-Strauss (1908–   ), who posited that all cultural phenomena have an underlying structural system. Deconstruction both reacts against the tenets of structuralism and builds upon the theories of German philosophers Friedrich Nietzsche (1844–1900) and Martin Heidegger (1889–1976), who questioned the validity and verifiability of "truth," "knowledge," and other basic philosophical concepts.

Social criticism also had precursors in pre–twentieth-century writing. For example, Mary Wollstonecraft's *A Vindication of the Rights of Women* (1792) was an early forerunner of feminism. Virginia Woolf's *A Room of One's Own* (1929) anticipated feminist criticism by addressing the effects upon women of the patriarchal Western society and identifying deeply entrenched attitudes of male-oriented society that hindered women in the pursuit of their creative possibilities. Similarly, Marxist criticism is based on the writings of Karl Marx and Friedrich Engels; they borrowed their key term *ideology* from French philosophers of the late eighteenth century who used it to label the study of how sense perceptions develop into concepts. The term Marxism itself was used in the same period to mean a rigidly held set of political ideas. Marx and Engels adapted and changed the terms, investing them with new meaning that built upon meanings already present in the culture. New historicism is an even more recent mode of literary study, beginning in the 1980s, that reacts to formalism, structuralism, and deconstruction, arguing that the historical context is an integral part of a literary work and that the text cannot be considered in isolation.

Personal criticism too has its origins in earlier writing. For instance, the roots of psychoanalytic criticism can be traced to the psychological criticism of the early nineteenth century. Thomas Carlyle suggested in 1827 that the best criticism of the day was psychological, deriving meaning from a poem by analyzing the mental state and personality structure of the author. Finally, reader-response criticism, a late-twentieth-century approach begun in the 1960s, focuses on the reader and the reader's process and experience, rather than on the text or the text and its historical context.

The theoretical positions and techniques of each of these approaches to the study of literature are considered in detail in Appendix C.

APPENDIX C

◇ ◇ ◇

Twentieth-Century Literary Theories

As you become aware of various schools of literary criticism, you see new ways to think about fiction, poetry, and drama. Just as you value the opinions of your peers and your professors, you will also find that the ideas of literary critics can enrich your own reactions and evaluations of literature. Keep in mind that no single literary theory offers the "right" way of approaching what you read; no single critic provides the definitive analysis of any short story, poem, or play. As you become aware of the richly varied possibilities of twentieth-century criticism, you will begin to ask new questions and discover new insights about the works you read.

FORMALISM

◇ ◇ ◇

Formalism stresses the importance of literary form in determining the meaning of a work. Each work of literature is considered in isolation. Formalist scholars consider biographical, historical, and social questions to be irrelevant to the real meaning of a play, short story, novel, or poem. For example, a formalist would see the relationship between Adam and Eve in *Paradise Lost* as entirely unrelated to Milton's own marital concerns, and theological themes in the same work would be viewed as entirely separate from Milton's deep involvement with the Puritan religious and political cause in seventeenth-century England. Milton's intentions and readers' responses to the famous epic poem would also be regarded by formalists as irrelevant. Instead, formalists would read the text closely, paying attention to organization and structure, to verbal nuances (suggested by word choice and use of figurative language), and to multiple meanings (often created through the writer's use of paradox and irony). The formalist critic tries to reconcile the tensions and oppositions inherent in the text in order to develop a unified reading.

The formalist movement in English language criticism began in England with I. A. Richards's *Practical Criticism* (1929). To explain and introduce his theory, Richards asked students to interpret famous poems without telling them the poet's names. This strategy encouraged close reading of the text rather than reliance on a poet's reputation, biographical data, or historical context. The American formalist movement, called *new criticism,* was made popular largely by college instructors who realized that formalist criticism provided a useful way for students to work along with an instructor in interpreting a literary work rather than passively listening to a lecture on biographical, literary, and historical influences. In fact, the new critical theorists Cleanth Brooks and Robert Penn Warren put together a series of textbooks (*Understanding Poetry, Understanding Fiction,* and *Understanding Drama,* first published in the late 1930s) used in colleges for years. After the 1950s, many new critics began to reevaluate their theories and to broaden their approaches. Although few scholars currently maintain a strictly formalist approach, nearly every critical movement of this century, including feminist, Marxist, psychoanalytic, structuralist, and deconstructionist criticism, owes a debt to the close reading techniques introduced by the formalists.

A FORMALIST READING: KATE CHOPIN'S "THE STORM" (P. 154)

A formalist critic reading Chopin's "The Storm," might begin by noting the story's three distinctive sections. What relationship do the sections bear to one another? What do we learn from the word choice, the figures of speech, and the symbols in these sections? And, most important, how do these considerations lead readers to a unified view of the story?

In the first section of "The Storm," readers meet Bobinôt and his son Bibi. The description of the approaching clouds as "sombre," "sinister," and "sullen" suggests an atmosphere of foreboding, yet the alliteration of these words also introduces a poetic tone. The conversation between father and son in the final part of this section contrasts, yet does not conflict with, the rather formal language of the introduction. Both Bobinôt and Bibi speak in Cajun dialect, suggesting their humble origins, yet their words have a rhythm that echoes the poetic notes struck in the description of the storm. As the section closes, Bobinôt, thinking of his wife, Calixta, at home, buys a can of the shrimp he knows she likes and holds the treasure "stolidly," ironically suggesting the protection he cannot offer his wife in his separation from her during the coming storm.

The long second section brings readers to the story's central action. Calixta, as she watches the rain, sees her former lover, Alcée, riding up to seek shelter. Just as in the first section, the language of the narrator is somewhat formal and always poetic, filled with sensuous diction and images. For instance, we see Calixta "unfasten[ing] her white sacque at the throat" and, later, Alcée envisions her lips "as red and moist as pomegranate seed." Again, paralleling the first section, the conversation of the characters is carried on in dialect, suggesting their lack of sophistication and their connection to the powerful natural forces that surround them. The lovemaking that follows, then, seems both natural and poetic. There is nothing sordid about this interlude and, as the final sections of the story suggest through their rather ordinary, matter-of-fact language, nothing has been harmed by Calixta and Alcée's yielding to passion.

In Section 3, Bobinôt brings home the shrimp, symbol of his love for Calixta, and, although we recognize the tension between Bobinôt's shy, gentle approach and Alcée's passion, readers can accept the final sentence as literal rather than ironic. The "storms" (both the rain and the storm of passion) have passed, and no one has been hurt. The threat suggested in the opening sentences has been diffused; both the power and the danger evoked by the poetic diction of the first two sections have disappeared, to be replaced entirely by the rhythms of daily life and speech.

FOR FURTHER READING: FORMALISM

Brooks, Cleanth. *The Well Wrought Urn.* 1947.
Empson, William. *Seven Types of Ambiguity.* 1930.
Hartman, Geoffrey H. *Beyond Formalism.* 1970.
Stallman, Robert W. *Critiques and Essays in Criticism. 1920–1948.* 1949.
Wellek, René. *A History of Modern Criticism.* Vol. 6. 1986.
Wimsatt, W. K. *The Verbal Icon.* 1954.

READER-RESPONSE CRITICISM
❖ ❖ ❖

Reader-response criticism suggests a critical view that opposes formalism, seeing the reader's interaction with the text as central to interpretation. Unlike formalists, reader-response critics do not believe that a work of literature exists as a separate, closed entity. Instead, they consider the reader's contribution to the text as essential. A poem, short story, novel, or play is not a solid piece of fabric, but rather a series of threads separated by gaps that readers must fill in, drawing on their own experiences and knowledge.

As we read realistic fiction (where the world of the text closely resembles what we call reality), we may not notice that we are contributing our interpretation. As we read one sentence and then the next, we develop expectations; and, in realistic stories, these expectations are generally met. Nevertheless, nearly every reader supplies personal meanings and observations, making each reader's experience with a work unique and distinctive from every other reader's experience with the same work. For example, imagine Shakespeare's *Romeo and Juliet* as it might be read by a fourteen-year-old high school student and by her father. The young woman, whose age is the same as Juliet's, is almost certain to identify closely with the female protagonist and to "read" Lord Capulet, Juliet's father, as overbearing and rigid. The young reader's father, however, may be drawn to the poignant passage where Capulet talks with a prospective suitor, urging that he wait while Juliet has time to enjoy her youth. Capulet describes the loss of his other children and calls Juliet "the hopeful lady of my earth." Although the young woman reading this line may interpret it as yet another indication of Capulet's possessiveness, her father may see it as a sign of love and even generosity. The twentieth-century father may "read" Capulet as a man willing to risk offending a friend in order to keep his daughter safe from the rigors of early marriage (and early childbearing). Whose interpretation is correct? Reader-response theorists would say that both readings are entirely possible and, therefore, equally "right."

The differing interpretations produced by different readers can be seen as simply the effect of the different personalities (and personal histories) involved in constructing meaning from the same series of clues. Not only does the reader "create" the work of literature, in large part, but the literature itself may work on the reader as he or she reads, altering the reader's experience, and thus the reader's interpretation. For example, the father reading *Romeo and Juliet* may alter his sympathetic view of Capulet as he continues through the play and observes the old Lord's later, angry exchanges with Juliet.

Reader-response theorists believe in the importance of *recursive reading*—that is, reading and rereading with the idea that no interpretation is carved in stone. A second or third interaction with the text may well produce a new interpretation. This changing view is particularly likely when the rereading takes place significantly later than the initial reading. For example, if the young woman just described reread *Romeo and Juliet* when she was middle-aged and herself the mother of teenage children, her reaction to Capulet would quite likely be different from her reaction when she read the work at age fourteen.

In one particular application of reader-response theory, called *reception theory,* the idea of developing readings is applied to the general reading public rather than to individual readers. Reception theory, as proposed by Hans Robert Jauss ("Literary History as a Challenge to Literary Theory" in *New Literary History,*" Vol. 2. 1970–71), suggests that each new generation reads the same works of literature differently. Because each generation of readers has experienced different historical events, read different books, and been aware of different critical theories, each generation will view the same works very differently from its predecessors. Certainly a quick look back at the summary of literary history in Appendix B will support this idea. (Consider, for example, the changing views toward Shakespeare from the seventeenth to the twentieth centuries.)

Reader-response criticism has received serious attention since the 1960s, with Norman Holland's *The Dynamics of Literary Response* (1968) formulating the theory. The German critic Wolfgang Iser (*The Implied Reader,* 1974) argued that in order to be an effective reader, one must be familiar with the conventions and "codes" of writing. This, then, is one reason for studying literature in a classroom, not to produce only approved interpretations, but to develop strategies and information that will make sense of a text. Stanley Fish, an American critic, goes even further, arguing that there may not be any "objective" text at all (*Is There a Text in This Class?*, 1980). Fish says that no two readers read the same book, though readers can be trained to have relatively similar responses to a text if they have had relatively similar experiences. For instance, if readers have gone to college and taken an introduction to literature course, where they have learned to respond to the various elements of literature such as character, theme, irony, and figurative language, they are likely to have similar responses to a text.

Reader-Response Readings: Kate Chopin's "The Storm" (p. 154)

To demonstrate possible reader-response readings, we can look at the same story previously considered from a formalist perspective. (Of course, if several formalist critics read the story, they too would each write a somewhat different interpretation.)

Written by a 25-year-old man; has studied American literature

> In Kate Chopin's "The Storm," attention must be paid to the two adult male characters, Bobinôt and Alcée. Usually in a love triangle situation one man is portrayed more sympathetically than the other. But Chopin provides us with a dilemma. Alcée is not merely the cavalier seducer; he genuinely cares for Calixta. Neither is he the brooding hero. There is nothing gruff or angry about Alcée, and he returns to his family home with no apparent harm done following the passionate interlude. On the other hand, Bobinôt is not a cruel or abusive husband. We can see no clear reason for Calixta's affair except for her desire to fulfill a sexual longing for Alcée.

Written by an 18-year-old man; first-year literature course

> Bibi doesn't seem to be a very important character in the story, but we should pay attention to him as a reflection of his father. At the beginning of the story, Bibi worries about his mother and he expresses his concern to his father. Bobinôt tries to reassure his son, but he gets up and buys a treat for Calixta as much to comfort himself as to get something for her. Then Bibi sits with his father, and it seems as if he has transferred all his worries to Bobinôt. In the third section of the story, after Calixta and Alcée have had their love affair, Bibi and Bobinôt come home. They both seem like children, worried about how Calixta will react. She, of course, is nice to them because she feels so guilty. At the end of Section 3, both father and son are happy and enjoying themselves. You can't help but feel great sympathy for them both because they are so loving and simple and because they have been betrayed by Calixta, who has not behaved the way a loving mother and wife should.

Written by a 45-year-old woman; has studied Kate Chopin's life and work

A decade after the controversial novel *The Awakening* was published in 1899, one critic protested, "To think of Kate Chopin, who once contented herself with mild yarns about genteel Creole life [. . .] blowing us a hot blast like that!" (qtd. in Gilbert and Gubar 981). This literary observer was shocked, as one might expect from an early-twentieth-century reader, by Chopin's frank picture of sexual relations, and particularly of the sexual feelings of the novel's heroine. One cannot help but wonder, however, whether the scandalized reader was really widely acquainted with Chopin.

Certainly he could not have read "The Storm." This short story is surprising for many reasons, but primarily because it defies the sexual mores of the late nineteenth century by showing a woman who is neither evil nor doomed enjoying, even glorying in, her sexuality. Calixta is presented as a good wife and loving mother, concerned about her husband and son who are away from home during the storm. Yet her connection to Bobinôt and Bibi does not keep her from passionately enjoying her interlude with Alcée. She goes to his arms unhesitatingly, with no false modesty or guilt (feigned or real) to hold her back. Somehow, this scenario does not seem to fit the definition of "a mild yarn about genteel Creole life."

FOR FURTHER READING: READER-RESPONSE CRITICISM

Bleich, David. *Subjective Criticism.* 1978.
Fish, Stanley. *Is There a Text in This Class?* 1980.
Holland, Norman. *The Dynamics of Literary Response.* 1968.
Iser, Wolfgang. *The Implied Reader.* 1974; *The Act of Reading: A Theory of Aesthetic Response.* 1978.
Rosenblatt, Louise. *The Reader, the Text, the Poem.* 1978.
Sulleiman, Susan, and Inge Crosman, eds. *The Reader in the Text.* 1980.
Tomkins, Jane P., ed. *Reader-Response Criticism.* 1980.

SOCIOLOGICAL CRITICISM

◇ ◇ ◇

Like reader-response criticism, **sociological criticism** takes issue with formalism. Sociological theorists maintain that the literary work cannot be separated from the social context in which it was created, insisting that literature reflects society and derives its essential existence and significance from the social situations to which it responds. Sociological critics speculate about why a particular work might have been written and explore the ways in which it reacts to a specific situation.

For instance, a sociological literary scholar might note with interest that Shakespeare's history plays about Richard II, Henry IV, and Henry V deal with the consequences of uncertain royal succession and usurpation.

These dramas were written during the final reigning years of Queen Elizabeth I, a monarch who had not produced an heir and refused to designate one. Although the plays cited were set considerably before Elizabeth's time, a sociological critic might conclude that they reflect the English concern about the threat of monarchic chaos should Elizabeth die with no clear line of succession.

In the twentieth century two strong arms of sociological criticism have emerged as dominant: feminist criticism and Marxist criticism. They are particularly forceful theories because most of their practitioners have a strong commitment to these ideologies, which they apply as they read literature. Feminism and Marxism share a concern with segments of society that have been underrepresented and often ignored. These views are, of course, supported by modern critical theories such as the reader-response idea of gaps in the text that must be filled in through the reader's own experience and knowledge. In addition, the techniques of New Criticism (in particular, close reading of the text), psychoanalysis, and structuralism have allowed sociological critics to focus on what had been overlooked or skewed in traditional readings and to analyze how the experience of marginal and minority groups has been represented in literature.

FEMINIST CRITICISM

Throughout the nineteenth century, women such as the Brontë sisters, George Eliot (Mary Ann Evans), Elizabeth Barrett Browning, and Christina Rossetti struggled for the right to be taken as seriously as their male counterparts. In addition, in 1929 Virginia Woolf, an experimental novelist and literary critic, published *A Room of One's Own*, which described the difficulties that women writers faced and defined a tradition of literature written by women.

Feminist criticism emerged as a defined approach to literature in the late 1960s. Modern feminist criticism began with works such as Mary Ellman's *Thinking About Women* (1968), which focuses on the negative female stereotypes in books authored by men and points out alternative feminine characteristics suggested by women authors. Another pioneering feminist work was Kate Millet's *Sexual Politics* (1969), which analyzes the societal mechanisms that perpetuate male domination of women. Since that time feminist writings, though not unified in one theory or methodology, have appeared in ever growing numbers. Some feminist critics have adapted psychoanalytic, Marxist, or other post-structuralist theories, and others have broken new ground. In general, feminist critics take the view that our culture—and by extension our literature—is primarily patriarchal (controlled by males).

According to feminist critics, what is at issue is not anatomical sex, but gender. As Simone de Beauvoir explained, a person is not born feminine, as our society defines it, but rather becomes so because of cultural conditioning. According to feminist critics, paternalist Western culture has defined the feminine as "other" to the male, as passive and emotional in opposition to the masculine as dominating and rational.

Feminist critics claim that paternalist cultural stereotypes pervade works of literature in the canon. Feminists point out that, until very recently, the canon has consisted of works almost exclusively written by males and has focused on male experiences. Female characters, when they do appear, are often subordinate to male characters. A female reader of these works must either identify with the male protagonist or accept a marginalized role.

One response of feminist critics is to reinterpret works in the traditional canon. As Judith Fetterley explains in *The Resisting Reader* (1978), the reader "revisions" the text, focusing on the covert sexual bias in a literary work. For example, a feminist scholar might study Shakespeare's *Macbeth*, looking closely at the role played by Lady Macbeth and arguing that she was not, in fact, simply a cold-hearted villain. Instead, a feminist might see her as a victim of the circumstances of her time: Women were not permitted to follow their own ambitions but were relegated to supporting roles, living their lives through achievements of their husbands and sons.

A second focus of feminist scholars has been the redefinition of the canon. By seeking out, analyzing, and evaluating little-known works by women, feminist scholars have rediscovered women writers who were ignored or shunned by the reading public and by critics of their own times. Thus, writers such as Kate Chopin (whose short story "The Storm" has been discussed above) and Charlotte Perkins Gilman (see "The Yellow Wall-Paper," p. 168), who wrote during the late nineteenth and early twentieth centuries, are now recognized as worthy of study and consideration.

A FEMINIST READING: TILLIE OLSEN'S "I STAND HERE IRONING" (P. 160)

To approach Tillie Olsen's "I Stand Here Ironing," feminist scholars might focus on the passages in which the narrator describes her relationships and encounters with men.

> Some readings of Tillie Olsen's "I Stand Here Ironing" suggest that the narrator makes choices that doom her older daughter to a life of confusion. If we look at the narrator's relationships with the men in her life, however, we can see that she herself is the story's primary victim.
>
> At nineteen the narrator is a mother, abandoned by her husband who leaves her a note saying that he "could no longer endure sharing want" with his wife and infant daughter. This is the first desertion we hear about in the narrator's life, and although she agonizingly describes her painful decisions and the mistakes she makes with her daughter Emily, we cannot help but recognize that she is the one who stays and tries to make things right.

Her actions contrast sharply with those of her husband, who runs away, implying that his wife and daughter are burdens too great for him to bear.

The second abandonment is more subtle than the first but no less devastating. After the narrator has remarried, she is once again left alone to cope with a growing family while her second husband goes off to war. True, this desertion comes for a "noble" purpose and is probably not voluntary, but the narrator must, nevertheless, seek one of the low-paying jobs available to women to supplement her allotment checks. This time she is again forced to leave her children because her husband must serve the needs of the male-dominated military establishment.

The narrator is alone at crucial points in Emily's life and must turn away from her daughter simply in order to survive. Although she has been brought up in a world that teaches women to depend on men, she learns that she is ultimately alone. Although the desertions she endures are not always intentional, she must bear the brunt of circumstances that are not her choice but are, rather, foisted on her by the patriarchal society in which she lives.

FOR FURTHER READING: FEMINIST CRITICISM

Benstock, Shari, ed. *Feminist Issues in Literary Scholarship*. 1987.
Eagleton, Mary, ed. *Feminist Issues in Literary Theory: A Reader*. 1986.
Gilbert, Sandra, and Susan Gubar. *The Madwoman in the Attic*. 1979.
————. *No Man's Land*. 3 vols. 1988, 1989, 1994.
————, eds. *The Norton Anthology of Literature by Women*. 1985.
Heilbrun, Carolyn G. *Hamlet's Mother and Other Women*. 1990.
Jacobus, Mary. *Reading Woman: Essays in Feminist Criticism*. 1986.
Miller, Nancy, K., ed. *The Poetics of Gender*. 1986.
————. *Subject to Change*. 1988.
Showalter, Elaine. *A Literature of Their Own*. 1977.
————. *Sisters Choice: Tradition and Change in American Women's Writing*. 1991.

MARXIST CRITICISM

Scholars influenced by Marxist criticism base their readings of literature on the social and economic theories of Karl Marx (*Das Kapital*, 1867–94) and his colleague and coauthor Friedrich Engels (*The Communist Manifesto*, 1884). Marx and Engels believed that the dominant capitalist middle class would eventually be challenged and overthrown by the working class. In the meantime, however, middle-class capitalists exploit the working class, who produce excess products and profits yet do not share in the benefits of their labor. Marx and Engels further regarded all parts of the society in which they lived—religious, legal, educational, governmental—as tainted by what they saw as the corrupt values of middle-class capitalists.

Marxist critics apply these views to their readings of poetry, fiction, and drama. They tend to analyze the literary works of any historical era as products of the ideology, or network of concepts, that supports the interests of the cultural elite and suppresses those of the working class. Some Marxist critics see all Western literature as distorted by the privileged views of the elite class, but most believe that at least some creative writers reject the distorted views of their society and instead see clearly the wrongs to which working-class people have been subjected. For example, George Lukacs, a Hungarian Marxist critic, proposed that great works of literature create their own worlds, which reflect life with clarity. These great works, though not written by Marxists, can be studied for their revealing examples of class conflict and other Marxist concerns. A Marxist critic would certainly look with favor on Charles Dickens, who in nearly every novel pointed out inequities in the political, legal, and educational establishments of his time. Those who remember Oliver Twist's pitiful plea for "more" workhouse porridge (refused by evil Mr. Bumble, who skims money from funds intended to feed the impoverished inmates) cannot help but see fertile ground for the Marxist critic, who would certainly applaud Dickens's scathing criticism of Victorian social and economic inequality.

Although Marxist criticism developed in the 1920s and 1930s in Germany and the Soviet Union, British and American Marxism has received greatest attention since 1960 with works such as Raymond Williams's *Culture and Society, 1780–1950* (1960) and Terry Eagleton's *Criticism and Ideology* (1976).

A MARXIST READING: TILLIE OLSEN'S "I STAND HERE IRONING" (P. 160)

The Marxist theorist reading Tillie Olsen's "I Stand Here Ironing" might concentrate on the events that demonstrate how both the narrator's and Emily's fates have been directly affected by the capitalist society of the United States.

> Tillie Olsen's "I Stand Here Ironing" stands as a powerful indictment of the capitalist system. The narrator and her daughter Emily are repeatedly exploited and defeated by the pressures of the economic system in which they live.
>
> The narrator's first child, Emily, is born into the world of the 1930s depression—an economic disaster brought on by the excesses and greed of Wall Street. When the young mother is deserted by her husband, there are no government programs in place to help her. She says it was the "pre-relief, pre-WPA world of the depression" that forced her away from her child and into "a job hashing at night." Although she is willing to work, she is paid so poorly that she must finally send Emily to live with her husband's family. Raising the money to bring Emily back takes a long time, and after this incident Emily's health, both physical and emotional, is precarious.
>
> When Emily gets the measles, we get a hard look at what the few social programs that existed during the Depression were like. The child is sent—at

the urging of a government social worker—to a convalescent home. The narrator notes bitterly, "They still send children to that place. I see pictures on the society page of sleek young women planning affairs to raise money for it, or dancing at the affairs, or decorating Easter eggs or filling Christmas stockings for the children." The privileged class basks in the artificial glow of their charity work for the poor, yet the newspapers never show pictures of the hospitalized children who are kept isolated from anyone they loved and forced to eat "runny eggs [. . .] or mush with lumps." Here again the mother is separated from her daughter by a system that discriminates against the poor. Because the family cannot afford private treatment, Emily is forced to undergo treatment in a public institution that not only denies her any contact with her family, but also cruelly forbids her to save the letters she receives from home. Normal family relationships are severely disrupted by an uncaring economic structure that only grudgingly offers aid to the poor.

It is clear that the division between mother and daughter is created and exacerbated by the social conditions in which they live. Because they are poor, they are separated at crucial times and, therefore, never get to know each other fully. Thus, neither can truly understand the ordeals the other has been forced to endure.

For Further Reading: Marxist Criticism

Agger, Ben. *The Discourse of Domination.* 1992.
Bullock, Chris, and David Peck, eds. *Guide to Marxist Literary Criticism.* 1980.
Eagleton, Terry. *Marxism and Literary Criticism.* 1976.
Frow, John. *Marxism and Literary History.* 1986.
Holub, Renate and Antonio Gramsci. *Beyond Marxism and Postmodernism.* 1992.
Jameson, Fredric. *Marxism and Form.* 1971.
Lentricchia, Frank. *Criticism and Social Change.* 1983.
Ohmann, Richard M. *Politics of Letters.* 1987.
Strelka, Joseph P., ed., *Literary Criticism and Sociology.* 1973.
Williams, Raymond. *Culture and Society, 1780–1950.* 1960; *Marxism and Literature.* 1977.

New Historicism
✦ ✦ ✦

New historicist critics focus on a text in relation to the historical and cultural contexts of the period in which it was created and the periods in which it was critically evaluated. These contexts are not considered simply as "background" but as integral parts of a text. According to new historicists, history is not an objective fact; rather, like literature, history is interpreted and reinterpreted depending on the power structure of a society.

Louis Althusser, for example, suggests that ideology intrudes in the discourse of an era, subjecting readers to the interests of the ruling establishment. Michel Foucault reflects that the discourse of an era defines the nature of "truth" and what behaviors are acceptable, sane, or criminal. "Truth," for Foucault, is produced by the interaction of power and the systems in which the power flows, and it changes as society changes. Mikhail Bakhtin suggests that all discourse is dialogic, containing within it many independent and sometimes conflicting voices.

Literature, in new historical criticism, does not exist outside time and place and cannot be interpreted without reference to the era in which it was written. Criticism likewise cannot be evaluated without reference to the time and place in which it was written. A fallacy of much criticism, according to new historicists, is to consider a literary text as an organic whole, ignoring the diversity of conflicting voices in a text or in the cultural context in which a text is embedded. Indeed, Stephen Greenblatt prefers the term "cultural poetics" to new historicism because it acknowledges the integral role literature and art play in the culture of any era of history. Works of art and literature, according to Greenblatt, actively foster subversive elements or voices but somehow "contain" those forces in ways that defuse challenges to the dominant culture.

New historicists also point out that readers, like texts, are influenced and shaped by the cultural context of their eras. A thoroughly objective "reading" of a text is, then, impossible. All readers to some degree "appropriate" a text. Acknowledging this problem, some new historicists present their criticism of texts as "negotiations" between past and present contexts. Thus, criticism of a particular work of literature would involve both the cultural contexts of the era in which the text was written and the critic's present cultural context; and the critic would acknowledge how the latter context influences the interpretation of the former.

Beginning in the early 1970s, feminist critics adopted some new historicist positions, focusing on male-female power conflicts. And critics interested in multicultural texts stressed the role of the dominant white culture in suppressing or marginalizing the texts of nonwhites. Marxist critics, including Raymond Williams, have adopted the term "cultural materialism" in discussing their mode of new historicism, which focuses on the political significance of a literary text.

A NEW HISTORICIST READING: CHARLOTTE PERKINS GILMAN'S "THE YELLOW WALL-PAPER" (P. 168)

A new historicist scholar might write an essay about "The Yellow Wall-Paper" as an illustration of the destructive effects of the patriarchical culture of the late nineteenth century upon women. This reading would be vastly different from that of most nineteenth-century critics, who interpreted the story as a harrowing case study of female mental illness. Even some earlier twentieth-century readings have considered the narrator's mental illness caused by her individual psychological problems. New historicist critics, however, might focus on the social conventions of the time, which produced conflicting discourses that drove the narrator to madness.

The female narrator of "The Yellow Wall-Paper," who is writing in her private journal (which is the text of the short story), explains that her husband, a physician, has diagnosed her as having a "temporary nervous depression—a slight hysterical tendency." She says she should believe such a "physician of high standing" and cooperate with his treatment, which is to confine her to a room in an isolated country estate and compel her to rest and have no visitors and not to write. The "cure" is intended to reduce her nervousness, she further explains. But as the story unfolds, the narrator reveals that she suspects the treatment will not cure her because it leaves her alone with her thoughts without even her writing to occupy her mind. Her husband's "cure" forces her into a passive role and eliminates any possibility of asserting her own personality. However, she guiltily suggests that her own lack of confidence in her husband's diagnosis may be what is preventing her cure.

The text of "The Yellow Wall-Paper" can, then, be divided into at least two conflicting discourses: (1) the husband, who has the authority both of a highly respected physician and of a husband, two positions reinforced by the patriarchical culture of the time; and (2) the narrator, whose own hesitant personal female voice contradicts the masculine voice or discourse but undermines itself because it keeps reminding her that women should obey their husbands and their physicians.

A third discourse underlies the two dominant ones—that of the gothic horror tale, a popular genre of the late nineteenth century. The narrator in "The Yellow Wall-Paper" is isolated against her will in a room with barred windows in an almost deserted palatial country mansion she describes as "the most beautiful place"; she is at the mercy of her captor, in this case her husband; she is not sure whether she is hallucinating and thinks the mansion may be haunted; she does not know whom to trust, not being sure whether her husband really wants to "cure" her or to punish her for expressing her rebellion.

The narrator learns to hide her awareness of the conflicting discourses. She avoids mentioning her thoughts and fears about her illness or her fancies about the house being haunted, and she hides her writing. She speaks reasonably and in "a very quiet voice." But this inability to speak freely to anyone is a kind of torture, and alone in her room with the barred windows, she takes up discourse with the wallpaper. At first she describes it as "one of those sprawling flamboyant patterns committing every artistic sin." But she is fascinated by the pattern, which has been distorted by mildew and by portions that have been torn away. The narrator begins to strip off the wallpaper to free a woman she thinks is trapped inside; and, eventually, she visualizes herself as that woman, trapped, yet freed by the destruction of the wallpaper. The narrator retreats, or escapes into madness, driven there by the multiple discourses she cannot resolve.

FOR FURTHER READING:
NEW HISTORICIST CRITICISM

Brook, Thomas. *The New Historicism and Other Old Fashioned Topics*. 1991.
Coates, Christopher. "What Was the new Historicism?" *Centennial Review* 32.2 (Spring 1993): 267–80.
Geertz, Clifford. "Thick Description: Toward an Interpretive Theory of Culture," in *The Interpretation of Cultures*. 1973.
Greenblatt, Stephen, ed. *Representing the English Renaissance*. 1988.
Levin, David. "American Historicism: Old and New." *American Literary History* 6.3 (Fall 1994): 527–38.
Rabinov, Paul, ed. *The Foucault Reader*. 1986.
Veeser, H. Aram, ed. *The New Historicism*. 1989.

PSYCHOANALYTIC CRITICISM
◆ ◆ ◆

Psychoanalytic criticism focuses on a work of literature as an expression in fictional form of the inner workings of the human mind. The premises and procedures used in psychoanalytic criticism were developed by Sigmund Freud (1846–1939), though some critics disagree strongly with his conclusions and their therapeutic and literary applications. Feminists, for example, take issue with Freud's notion that women are inherently masochistic. Some of the major points of Freud's theories depend on the idea that much of what is most significant to us does not take place in our conscious life. Freud believed that we have been forced (mostly by the rigors of having to live in harmony with other people) to repress much of our experience and many of our desires in order to coexist peacefully with others.

Some of this repressed experience Freud saw as available to us through dreams and other unconscious structures. He believed that literature could often be interpreted as the reflection of our unconscious life. Freud himself was among the first psychoanalytic critics, often using the techniques developed for interpreting dreams to interpret literature. Among other analyses, he wrote an insightful study of Dostoevsky's *The Brothers Karamazov* as well as brief commentaries on several of Shakespeare's plays, including *A Midsummer Night's Dream, Macbeth, King Lear,* and *Hamlet.* The latter study may have inspired a classic of psychoanalytic criticism: Ernest Jones's *Hamlet and Oedipus* (1949), in which Jones explains Hamlet's strange reluctance to act against his Uncle Claudius as resulting from Hamlet's unresolved longings for his mother and subsequent drive to eliminate his father. Since Hamlet's own father is dead, Jones argues, Claudius becomes, in the young man's subconscious mind, a father substitute. Hamlet, then, cannot make up his mind to kill his uncle because he does not see a simple case of revenge (for Claudius's murder of his father) but rather a complex web that includes incestuous desire for his own mother (now wed to Claudius). Jones extends his analysis to include the suggestion that Shakespeare himself experienced such a conflict and reflected his own Oedipal feelings in *Hamlet*.

A French psychoanalyst, Jacques Lacan (1901–1981), combined Freudian theories with structuralist literary theories to argue that the essential alienating experience of the human psyche is the acquisition of language. Lacan believed that once you can name yourself and distinguish yourself from others, you have entered the difficult social world that requires you to repress your instincts. Like Lacan, who modified and adapted psychoanalytic criticism to connect it to structuralism, many twentieth-century literary scholars, including Marxists and feminists, have found useful approaches in psychoanalytic literary theory (see, for example, Mary Jacobus's *Reading Woman: Essays in Feminist Criticism*, 1986).

PSYCHOANALYTIC TERMS

To fully appreciate psychoanalytic criticism, you should understand the following terms:

◇ *id*—The part of the mind that determines sexual drives and other unconscious compulsions that urge individuals to unthinking gratification.

◇ *ego*—The conscious mind that strives to deal with the demands of the id and to balance its needs with messages from the superego.

◇ *superego*—The part of the unconscious that seeks to repress the demands of the id and to prevent gratification of basic physical appetites. The superego, then, is a sort of censor that represents the prohibitions of society, religion, family beliefs, and so on.

◇ *condensation*—A process that takes place in dreams (and in literature) when several elements from the repressed unconscious are linked together to form a new, yet disguised, whole.

◇ *symbolism*—Use of representative objects to stand for forbidden (often sexual) objects. This process takes place in dreams and in literature. For instance, a pole, knife, or gun may stand for the penis.

◇ *displacement*—Substitution of a socially acceptable desire for a desire that is not acceptable. Again, this process may take place in dreams or in literature. For example, a woman who experiences sexual desires for her son may instead dream of being intimate with a neighbor who has the same first name as (or who looks like) her son.

◇ *Oedipus complex*—Repressed desire of a son to unite sexually with his mother and kill his father. According to Freud, all young boys go through this stage, but most resolve these conflicts before puberty.

◇ *projection*—Defense mechanism in which people mistakenly see in others antisocial impulses they fail to recognize in themselves.

A Psychoanalytic Reading: Edgar Allan Poe's "The Cask of Amontillado" (p. 219)

Since Edgar Allan Poe died in 1849, six years before Freud was born, Poe could not possibly have known Freud's work. Nevertheless, psychoanalytic critics argue that the principles discovered by Freud and those who followed are inherent in human nature. Therefore, they believe it is perfectly plausible to use modern psychiatric terms when analyzing a work that was written before their invention.

Montresor, the protagonist of Poe's "The Cask of Amontillado," has long fascinated readers who have puzzled over his motives for the story's climactic action when he imprisons his rival, Fortunato, and leaves him to die. Montresor claims that Fortunato has insulted him and has dealt him a "thousand injuries." Yet when we meet Fortunato, although he appears something of a pompous fool, none of his actions—or even his comments—seems powerful enough to motivate Montresor's thirst for revenge.

If, however, we consider a defense mechanism, first named "projection" and described by Sigmund Freud, we gain a clearer picture of Montresor. Those who employ projection are often people who experience antisocial impulses yet are not conscious of these impulses. It seems highly likely that Fortunato has not persecuted Montresor; rather, Montresor himself has experienced the impulse to act in a hostile manner toward Fortunato. We know, for instance, that Fortunato belongs to the exclusive order of masons because he gives Montresor the secret masonic sign. Montresor's failure to recognize the sign shows that he is only a mason in the grimmest literal sense. Montresor clearly resents Fortunato's high standing and projects onto Fortunato all of his own hostility toward those who (he thinks) have more or know more than he does. Thus he imagines that Fortunato's main business in life is to persecute and insult him.

Montresor's obsessive behavior further indicates his pathology. He plans Fortunato's punishment with the cunning one might ordinarily reserve for a major battle, cleverly figuring out a way to keep his servants from the house and to lure the ironically named Fortunato to his death. Each step of the revenge is carefully plotted. This is no sudden crime of passion, but rather the diabolically planned act of a deeply disturbed mind.

If we understand Montresor's need to take all of the hatred and anger that is inside himself and to rid himself of those socially unacceptable emotions by projecting them on to someone else, then we can see how he rationalizes a crime that seems otherwise nearly unmotivated. By killing Fortunato, Montresor symbolically kills the evil in himself. It is interesting to note that the final lines of the story support this reading. Montresor observes that "for half of a century no mortal has disturbed" the bones. In other words, these unacceptable emotions have not again been aroused. His last words, a Latin phrase from the mass for the dead meaning "rest in peace," suggest that only through his heinous crime has he found release from the torment of his own hatred.

For Further Reading:
Psychoanalytic Criticism

Freud, Sigmund. *The Interpretation of Dreams.* 1900.

Gardner, Shirley N., ed. *The (M)other Tongue: Essays in Feminist Psychoanalytic Interpretation.* 1985.

Hartman, Geoffrey H., ed. *Psychoanalysis and the Question of the Text.* 1979.

Kris, Ernst. *Psychoanalytic Explorations in Art.* 1952.

Kristeva, Julia. *Desire in Language.* 1980.

Nelson, Benjamin, ed. *Sigmund Freud on Creativity and the Unconscious.* 1958.

Wright, Elizabeth. *Psychoanalytic Criticism: Theory in Practice.* 1984.

Structuralism
◇ ◇ ◇

Structuralism is a literary movement with roots in linguistics and anthropology that concentrates on literature as a system of signs that have no inherent meaning except in their agreed-upon or conventional relation to one another. Structuralism is usually described by its proponents not as a new way to interpret literary works, but rather as a way to understand how works of literature come to have meaning for us. Because structuralism developed from linguistic theory, some structuralists use linguistic approaches to literature. That is, they talk about literary texts using terms employed by linguists (such as *morpheme* and *phoneme*) as they study the nature of language. Many structuralists, however, use the linguistic model as an analogy. To understand the analogy, then, you need to know a bit of linguistic theory.

The French linguist Ferdinand de Saussure (*Course in General Linguistics,* 1915) suggested that the relationship between an object and the name we use to designate it is purely arbitrary. What, for example, makes "C-A-T" signify a small, furry animal with pointed ears and whiskers? It is only our learned expectation that makes us associate "cat" with the family feline pet. Had we grown up in France, we would make the same association with *chat,* or in Mexico with *gato.* Therefore, the words we use to designate objects (linguists call these words *signs*) make sense only within the large context of our entire language system and would not be understood as meaningful by someone who did not know that language system. Further, Saussure pointed out, signs become truly useful only when we use them to designate difference. For instance, "cat" becomes useful when we want to differentiate a small furry animal that meows from a small furry animal that barks. Saussure was interested in how language, as a structure of conventions, worked. He asked intriguing questions about the underlying rules that allowed this made-up structure of signs to work, and, as a result, his pioneering study caught the interest of scholars in many fields.

Many literary scholars saw linguistic structuralism as analogous to the study of literary works. Literary structuralism leads readers to think of poems, short stories, novels, and plays not as self-contained and individual entities that have some kind of inherent meaning, but rather as part of a larger literary system. In order to fully appreciate and analyze the work, then, the reader must understand the system within which it operates. Like linguistic structuralism, literary structuralism focuses on the importance of difference. We must, for example, understand the difference between the structure of poetry and the structure of prose before we can make sense of a sentence like this:

> so much depends
> upon
> a red wheel
> barrow
>
> WILLIAM CARLOS WILLIAMS, "Red Wheelbarrow," p. 794

◊　◊　◊

Readers unacquainted with the conventions of poetry would find these lines meaningless and confusing, although if they knew the conventions of prose they would readily understand this sentence:

> So much depends upon a red wheelbarrow.

The way we interpret any group of "signs," then, depends on how they are structured and on the way we understand the system that governs their structure.

Structuralists believe that literature is basically artificial because although it uses the same "signs" as our everyday language, whose purpose is to give information, the purpose of literature is *not* primarily to relay data. For example, a poem like Dylan Thomas's "Do Not Go Gentle into That Good Night" (p. 677) is written in the linguistic form of a series of commands, yet the poem goes much further than that. Its meaning is created not only by our understanding the lines as a series of commands, but also by our recognition of the poetic form, the rhyming conventions, and the figures of speech Thomas uses. We can only fully discuss the poem within the larger context of our literary knowledge.

A STRUCTURALIST READING: WILLIAM FAULKNER'S "BARN BURNING" (P. 226)

A structuralist reading tries to bring to light some of the assumptions about language and form that we are likely to take for granted. Looking at the opening paragraph of Faulkner's "Barn Burning," a structuralist critic might first look at an interpretation that reads the passage as a stream of Sarty's thoughts. The structuralist critic might then consider the assumptions a reader would have to make to see what Faulkner has written as the thoughts of an illiterate child. Next, the structuralist might look at evidence to suggest the language in this section operates outside the system of language that would be available to Sarty and that, therefore, "Barn Burning" opens not with a simple recounting of the main character's thoughts but rather with something far more complex.

> The opening paragraph of William Faulkner's "Barn Burning" is often read as an excursion into the mind of Sarty, the story's young protagonist. When we read the passage closely, however, we note that a supposedly simple consciousness is represented in a highly complex way. For Sarty—uneducated and illiterate—the "scarlet devils" and "silver curve of fish" on the labels of food tins serve as direct signs appealing to his hunger. It is unlikely, however, that Sarty could consciously understand what he sees and express it as metaphor. We cannot, then, read this opening passage as a recounting of the thoughts that pass through Sarty's mind. Instead, these complex sentences and images offer possibilities that reach beyond the limits of Sarty's linguistic system.
>
> Because our own knowledge is wider than Sarty's, the visual images the narrator describes take on meanings for us that are unavailable to the young boy. For example, like Sarty, we know that the "scarlet devils" stand for preserved ham. Yet the devils also carry another possible connotation. They may indicate evil and thus serve to emphasize the despair and grief Sarty feels are ever-present. So, then, we are given images that flash through the mind of an illiterate young boy, apparently intended to suggest his poverty and ignorance (he cannot read the words on the labels), yet we are led to see a highly complicated set of meanings. When we encounter later in the passage Sarty's articulated thought, "our enemy [. . .] ourn! mine and hisn both! [. . .]," his down-to-earth dialect shows clearly the sharp distinction between the system of language the narrator uses to describe Sarty's view of the store shelves and the system of language Sarty uses to describe what he sees and feels.

FOR FURTHER READING: STRUCTURALISM

Barthes, Roland. *Critical Essays*. 1964.
Culler, Jonathan. *Structuralist Poetics*. 1975.
Greimas, A. J. *Structured Semantics: An Attempt at a Method*. Trans. McDowell, Schleifer, and Velie. 1983.
Hawkes, Terence. *Structuralism and Semiotics*. 1977.
Lentricchia, Frank. *After the New Criticism*. 1980.
Pettit, Philip. *The Concept of Structuralism: A Critical Analysis*. 1975.
Scholes, Robert. *Structuralism in Literature: An Introduction*. 1974.

DECONSTRUCTION
⟡ ⟡ ⟡

Deconstruction is a literary movement developed from structuralism. It argues that every text contains within it some ingredient undermining its purported system of meaning. In other words, the structure that seems to hold the text together is unstable because it depends on the conclusions of a particular ideology (for instance, the idea that women are inferior to men or that peasants are content with their lowly position in life), conclusions that are not really as natural or inevitable as the text may pretend. The practice of finding the point at which the text falls apart because of these internal inconsistencies is called deconstruction.

Deconstructive theorists share with formalists and structuralists a concern for the work itself rather than for biographical, historical, or ideological influences. Like formalists, deconstructionists focus on possibilities for multiple meanings within texts. However, while formalists seek to explain paradox by discovering tensions and ironies that can lead to a unified reading, deconstructionists insist on the primacy of multiple possibilities. Any given text is capable of yielding many divergent readings, all of which are equally valid and yet all of which may in some way undermine and oppose one another.

Like structuralists, deconstructionists see literary texts as part of larger systems of discourse. A key structuralist technique is identifying opposites in an attempt to show the structure of language used in a work. Having identified the opposites, the structuralist rests the case. Deconstructionists, however, go further. Jacques Derrida, a French philosopher, noticed that these oppositions do not simply reflect linguistic structures but are the linguistic response to the way people deal with their beliefs (their ideologies). For instance, if you believe strongly that democracy is the best possible form of government, you tend to lump other forms of government into the category of nondemocracies. If a government is nondemocratic, that—not its other distinguishing characteristics—would be significant to you. This typical ideological response operates in all kinds of areas of belief, even ones we are not aware of. Deconstructionists contend that texts tend to give away their ideological basis by means of this opposition.

Derrida called this distinction between "A" and "Not-A" (rather than "A" and "B") *différance,* a word he coined to suggest a concept represented by the French verb *différer,* which has two meanings: "to be different" and "to defer." (Note that in Derrida's new term an "a" is substituted for an "e"—a distinction that can be seen in writing, but not heard in speaking.) When a deconstructionist uncovers *différance* through careful examination of a text, he or she also finds an (often unwitting) ideological bias. Deconstructionists argue that the reader must transcend such ideological biases and must instead acknowledge contradictory possibilities as equally worthy of consideration. No one meaning can or should be designated as correct.

Deconstruction, then, is not really a system of criticism (and, in fact, deconstructionists resist being labeled as a school of criticism). Rather, deconstruction offers a way to take apart a literary text and thereby reveal its separate layers. Deconstructionists often focus on the metaphorical nature of language, claiming that all language is basically metaphoric because the sign we use to designate any given object or action stands apart from the object itself. In fact, deconstructionists believe that all writing is essentially literary and metaphorical because language, by its very nature, can only *stand for* what we call reality or truth; it cannot *be* reality or truth.

A major contribution of deconstructive critics lies in their playful approach to language and to literary criticism. They refuse to accept as absolute any one way of reading poetry, fiction, or drama, and they guard against what they see as the fixed conclusions and arbitrary operating assumptions of many schools of criticism.

A Deconstructionist Reading: Flannery O'Connor's "A Good Man Is Hard to Find (p. 266)

A deconstructionist reading of Flannery O'Connor's "A Good Man Is Hard to Find" might challenge the essentially religious interpretations the author offered of her own stories in essays and letters. A deconstructionist critic might argue that the author's reading of the story is no more valid than anyone else's, and that the story can just as legitimately be read as an investigation of the functions of irony in language.

Flannery O'Connor has explained that the grotesque and violent aspects of her stories are intended to shock the reader into recognizing the inhospitable nature of the world and thereby the universal human need for divine grace. The last sentence of "A Good Man Is Hard to Find" is spoken by The Misfit, who has just murdered a family of travelers: "It's no real pleasure in life."

However, the language of O'Connor's stories is extremely ironic. That is, her narrators and characters often say one thing but mean another. So it is possible that their statements are not empirically true but are representations of a persona or elements of a story they have created using language.

The Grandmother, for example, lives almost entirely in fictions—newspaper clippings, stories for the grandchildren, her belief that The Misfit is a good man. On the other hand, The Misfit is more literal than the Grandmother in his perception of reality. He knows, for example, whether the car has turned over once or twice. But he too is posing, at first as the tough guy who rejects religious and societal norms by saying, "It's nothing for you to do but enjoy the few minutes you got left the best way you can—by killing somebody or burning down his house or doing some other meanness to him. No pleasure but meanness." Finally, he poses as the pessimist—or, according to O'Connor's reading, the Christian—who claims, "It's no real pleasure in life." The contradictions in The Misfit's language make it impossible to tell which of these façades is "real."

FOR FURTHER READING: DECONSTRUCTION

Abrams, M. H. "Rationality and the Imagination in Cultural History." *Critical Inquiry* 2 (1976): 447–64. (Abrams claims deconstructionists are parasites who depend on other critics to come up with interpretations that can be deconstructed.)

Arac, Jonathan, Wlad Godzich, and Wallace Martin, eds. *The Yale Critics: Deconstruction in America.* 1983.

Berman, Art. *From the New Criticism to Deconstruction.* 1988.

Culler, Jonathan. *On Deconstruction: Theory and Criticism After Structuralism.* 1982.

Jefferson, Ann. "Structuralism and Post-Structuralism." *Modern Literary Theory: A Comparative Introduction.* 1982.

Johnson, Barbara. *The Critical Difference: Essays in the Contemporary Rhetoric of Reading.* 1980.

Leitsch, Vincent B. *Deconstructive Theory and Practice.* 1982.

Lynn, Steven. "A Passage into Critical Theory." *College English* 52 (1990): 258–271.

Miller, J. Hillis. "The Critic as Host." *In Deconstruction and Criticism.* Ed. Harold Bloom, et al. 1979. (response to Abrams article above)

Norris, Christopher. *Deconstruction: Theory and Practice.* 1982.

Writing Essay Exams about Literature

Taking exams is a skill, one you have been developing throughout your life as a student. Although both short-answer and essay exams require you to study, to recall what you know, and to budget your time carefully as you write your answers, only essay questions ask you to synthesize information and to arrange ideas in a series of clear, logically connected sentences and paragraphs. To write an essay exam, or even a paragraph-length answer, you must do more than memorize facts; you must see the relationships among them. In other words, you must think critically about your subject.

PLANNING AN ESSAY EXAM ANSWER

◇ ◇ ◇

Because you are under pressure during an exam and tend to write quickly, you may be tempted to skip the planning and revision stages of the writing process. But if you write in a frenzy and hand in your exam without a second glance, you are likely to produce a disorganized or even incoherent answer. With careful planning and editing, you can write an answer that demonstrates your understanding of the material.

REVIEW YOUR MATERIAL

Be sure you know beforehand the scope and format of the exam. How much of your text and class notes will the exam cover—the entire semester's work or only the material covered since the last test? Will you have to answer every question, or will you be able to choose among alternatives? Will the exam test your ability to recall specific facts, or will it require you to demonstrate your understanding of the course material by drawing conclusions?

Exams challenge you to recall and express in writing what you already know—what you have read, what you have heard in class, what you have reviewed in your notes. Before you even begin any exam, then, you must study: reread your text and class notes, highlight key points, and perhaps outline particularly important sections of your notes. When you prepare for a short-answer exam, you may memorize facts without analyzing their relationship to one another or their relationship to a body of knowledge as a whole: the definition of romanticism, the date of Queen Victoria's death, two examples of irony, four characteristics of a villanelle. When you prepare for an essay exam, however, you must do more than remember bits of information; you must also make connections among ideas.

When you are sure you know what to expect, see if you can anticipate the essay questions your instructor might ask. Try out likely questions on classmates, and see whether you can do some collaborative brainstorming to outline answers to possible questions. If you have time, you might even practice answering one or two in writing.

CONSIDER YOUR AUDIENCE AND PURPOSE

The audience for any exam is the instructor who prepared it. As you read the questions, think about what your instructor has emphasized in class. Although you may certainly arrange material in a new way or use it to make an original point, keep in mind that your purpose is to demonstrate that you understand the material, not to make clever remarks or introduce irrelevant information. In addition, you should make every effort to use the vocabulary of the discipline for which you are writing and to follow the conventions for writing about literature (pp. 35–36).

READ THROUGH THE ENTIRE EXAM

Your time is usually limited when you take an exam, so plan carefully. How long should a "one-paragraph" or "essay-length" answer be? How much time should you devote to answering each question? The exam question itself may specify the time allotted for each answer, so look for that information. More often the point value of each question or the number of questions on the exam will indicate how much time to spend on each answer. If an essay question is worth 50 out of 100 points, for example, you will probably have to spend at least half of your time planning, writing, and proofreading your answer.

Before you begin to write, read the entire exam carefully to determine your priorities and your strategy. First, be sure that your copy of the test is complete and that you understand exactly what each question requires. If you need clarification, ask your instructor or proctor for help. Then, decide where to start. If there is more than one question on the exam, responding first to the one you feel most confident to answer is usually a good strategy. This approach ensures that you will not become bogged down responding to a question that baffles you and left with too little time to write a strong answer to a question you understand well. Moreover, starting with the question you are sure of can help build your confidence.

READ THE QUESTION CAREFULLY

To write an effective answer, you need to understand the question. As you read any essay question, you may find it helpful to underline key words and important terms.

Summarize in detail the contributions of American writers of the Harlem Renaissance, briefly outlining the contributions of artists and musicians.

Now, look carefully at the question's wording. If the question calls for a comparison and contrast of two works of literature, a description or analysis of one work, no matter how comprehensive, will not be acceptable. If a question asks for causes *and* effects, a discussion of causes alone will be insufficient.

KEY WORDS IN EXAM QUESTIONS

◊ Explain   ◊ Clarify   ◊ Classify
◊ Compare   ◊ Relate   ◊ Identify
◊ Contrast ◊ Justify   ◊ Illustrate
◊ Trace   ◊ Analyze   ◊ Define
◊ Evaluate ◊ Interpret ◊ Support
◊ Discuss   ◊ Describe ◊ Summarize

As its key words indicate, the question below requires a very specific kind of response. The response that follows it, which simply *identifies* three characteristics of *one* kind of detective story, is not acceptable.

Question

Identify three differences between the hard-boiled detective story and the classical detective story.

Unacceptable answer

The hard-boiled detective story, popularized in Black Mask magazine in the 1930s and 1940s, is very different from the classical detective stories of Edgar Allan Poe or Agatha Christie. The hard-boiled stories feature a down-on-his-luck detective who is constantly tempted and betrayed. His world is dark and chaotic, and the crimes he tries to solve are not out-of-the-ordinary occurrences; they are the norm. These stories have no happy endings; even when the crime is solved, the world is still corrupt.

The following answer, which *contrasts* the two kinds of detective stories, is acceptable.

Acceptable answer

> The hard-boiled detective story differs from the classical detective story in its characters, its setting, and its plot. The classical detective is usually well educated and well off; he is aloof from the other characters and therefore can remain in total control of the situation. The hard-boiled detective, on the other hand, is typically a decent but down-on-his-luck man who is drawn into the chaos around him, constantly tempted and betrayed. In the orderly world of the classical detective, the crime is a temporary disruption. In the hard-boiled detective's dark and chaotic world, the crimes he tries to solve are not out-of-the-ordinary occurrences; they are the norm. In the classical detective story, order is restored at the end, but hard-boiled stories have no happy endings; even when the crime is solved, the world is still corrupt.

BRAINSTORM TO FIND IDEAS

Once your understand the question, you need to find something to say. Begin by **brainstorming,** quickly listing all the relevant ideas you can remember. Then, identify the most important points on your list, and delete the others. A quick review of the exam question and your supporting ideas should lead you toward a workable thesis for your essay answer.

SHAPING AN ESSAY EXAM ANSWER
◆ ◆ ◆

STATING A THESIS

Often, you can rephrase the exam question as a **thesis statement.** For example, the question "Summarize in detail the contributions of American writers of the Harlem Renaissance, briefly outlining the contributions of artists and musicians" suggests the following thesis statement.

Effective thesis statement

> Writers of the Harlem Renaissance--notably Richard Wright, Gwendolyn Brooks, Zora Neale Hurston, and Langston Hughes-- made significant contributions to American literature; artists and musicians of the movement also left an important legacy.

An effective thesis statement addresses all aspects of the question but highlights only relevant concerns. The following thesis statements are not effective.

Vague thesis statement

> The Harlem Renaissance produced many important writers, artists, and musicians.

Incomplete thesis statement

> The Harlem Renaissance's writers, such as Richard Wright, Gwendolyn Brooks, Zora Neale Hurston, and Langston Hughes, made significant contributions to American literature.

Irrelevant thesis statement

> The writers of the Harlem Renaissance had a greater impact on American literature than the writers of the Beat generation, such as Jack Kerouac.

Making a Scratch Outline

Because time is limited, you should plan your answer before you write it. Therefore, once you have decided on a suitable thesis, you should make a **scratch outline** of your major points.

On the inside cover of your exam book, arrange your supporting points in the order in which you plan to discuss them. Once you have completed your outline, check it against the exam question to make certain it covers everything the question calls for—and *only* what the question calls for.

A scratch outline for an answer to the question "Summarize in detail the contributions of American writers of the Harlem Renaissance, briefly outlining the contributions of artists and musicians" might look like this.

Thesis statement

> Writers of the Harlem Renaissance--notably Richard Wright, Gwendolyn Brooks, Zora Neale Hurston, and Langston Hughes-- made significant contributions to American literature; artists and musicians of the movement also left an important legacy.

Supporting points

> Writers
> Wright--<u>Uncle Tom's Children</u>, <u>Black Boy</u>, <u>Native Son</u>
> Brooks--poetry (classical forms; social issues)
> Hurston--<u>Their Eyes Were Watching God</u>, essays, autobiography
> Hughes--poetry (ballads, blues); "Simple stories"
> <u>Artists and Musicians</u>: Henry Tanner, Duke Ellington

DRAFTING AND
REVISING AN
ESSAY EXAM ANSWER
◊ ◊ ◊

Referring to your outline, you can now begin to draft your answer. Don't bother crafting an elaborate or unusual **introduction;** your time is precious, and so is your reader's. A simple statement of your thesis that summarizes your answer is your best introductory strategy: this approach is efficient, and it reminds you to address the question directly.

To develop the body of the essay, follow your outline point by point, using clear topic sentences and transitions to indicate your progression and to help your instructor see that you are answering the question in full. Such signals, along with parallel sentence structure and repeated key words, make your answer easy to follow.

The most effective **conclusion** for an essay exam is a clear, simple restatement of the thesis or a summary of the essay's main points.

Essay answers should be complete and detailed, but they should not contain irrelevant material. Every unnecessary fact or opinion increases your chance of error, so don't repeat yourself or volunteer unrequested information, and don't express your own feelings or opinions unless such information is specifically called for. In addition, be sure to support all your general statements with specific examples.

Leave enough time to reread and revise what you have written. Try to view your answer from a fresh perspective. Is your thesis statement clearly worded? Does your essay support your thesis and answer the question? Are your facts correct, and are your ideas presented in a logical order? Review your topic sentences and transitions. Check sentence structure and word choice, spelling and punctuation. If a sentence—or even a whole paragraph—seems irrelevant, cross it out. If you suddenly remember something you want to add, you can insert a few additional words with a caret (^). Neatly insert a longer addition at the end of your answer, box it, and label it so your instructor will know where it belongs. Finally, be sure that you have written legibly and that you have not inadvertently left out any words.

The following one-hour essay answer was written in response to the question that follows.

Question

Fictional characters (like real people) do not always behave as others wish or expect them to. Sometimes, in fact, they rebel against these expectations and act quite differently. In a clearly written and supported essay, explain how the specific actions of any four characters in works we have read this semester defy the expectations of those around them. Then, briefly consider the consequences of each character's decision to rebel.

Sample Exam Answer

Introduction rephrases exam question and introduces four characters to be discussed.

Many characters we have read about this semester do not behave as others believe they should behave. This is apparent in the actions of Connie in "Where Are You Going, Where Have You Been?" Nora in <u>A Doll House</u>, Marty in <u>Marty</u>, and the narrator in "Boys and Girls." For each of these characters, rebellion comes with a significant sacrifice.

Thesis Statement

First character's actions explained

Connie's rebellion is somewhat typical for a teenager: she rebels against the constraints her parents put on her to be a "good girl" by being a "bad girl" (at least in their terms). The makeup and style of clothing that Connie wears when she is away from home reinforce this "bad girl" image. Her behavior-- staying out late, lying about where she is going, having "trashy daydreams"--creates a problem for her parents because she is not conforming to their standards, and she is not conducting herself in a manner they consider appropriate. Her actions also put a strain on the relationship between her and her sister, who is the perfect example of a "good girl." Her determination to rebel ultimately makes her stay home from the family outing, and this in turn leaves her alone and vulnerable to Arnold's advances. Thus, her rebellious actions lead to probable violence (she goes with Arnold, who we know has frightening plans for her). The ending of the story is ambiguous. We don't know it she ever comes back; possibly, her innocent rebellion leads to her death.

Consequences of actions

Second character's actions explained.

Nora in <u>A Doll House</u> rebels only after she understands the conflict between the duty to herself to be a "real" person and the duty to her husband and children. Throughout the play, we see this conflict escalating until Nora has no choice but to act to resolve it, choosing to go against the norms of society and against how others think she should act. This behavior creates a problem for Torvald because of the image it presents to others. Torvald's greatest fear is that society will not accept him, and when Nora admits what she has done, he panics. At the end of the play, Nora chooses to be true to herself even though the person closest to her does not approve--and even though she will lose her children. She will be a stronger person because she had the courage to stand up for herself.

Marty's rebellious act is simply his decision to call Clara even though his friends and his mother do not approve. Although Marty is an adult, he is very much still a teenager in some ways. He has not yet broken away from his mother, and he continues to seek approval from her (and from his friends). He struggles to please his mother—by going to the dance, by allowing Aunt Catherine to move in--even when her desires are in conflict with his own. Marty's action at the play's end--calling Clara--will create a problem for his mother and his friends, who fear his growing independence and fight his decision to pursue a relationship with Clara. But Marty, like Nora, chooses to be true to himself and to do what he thinks is the right thing for him, rather than what others force upon him. He risks hurting his mother, alienating his friends, and losing the only life he knows. But for Marty, the potential gains seem worth the risk.

Consequences of actions

Third character's actions explained

Consequences of actions

Transitional
paragraph

      Connie, Nora, and Marty all break with society; all struggle to be independent. For all three, this independence has a cost. Connie may lose her life, Nora gives up her marriage and her children, and Marty leaves behind the comforting, secure existence he has known. The narrator of "Boys and Girls," however, is a special case.

Fourth
character's
actions
explained

      Although the protagonist of "Boys and Girls" is in conflict with society's expectations at the beginning of the story, the ending shows that she no longer wants to be involved in the conflict between the men's roles and women's roles. While at the beginning of the story she enjoys being outside with her father, by the end she is resigned to being considered a woman. She makes one grand rebellious gesture--freeing Flora from captivity--but she knows it is useless, and she is re-

Consequences
of actions

signed to her fate. At the story's end, there is no longer a conflict between what she wants and what society wants her to be. She has resolved the conflict between herself and society because now what society wants from her has become what she wants also: to be and act like a woman.

Conclusion

      Although each character deals with conflict and rebellion in a different way, all four struggle within themselves when decisions they must make are in conflict with the norms and expectations of society. The choice all of us must make for ourselves is how much influence society will have on us as we face similar decisions, and how we will handle the consequences should we choose to defy what society wishes us to be.

Notice that the student writer does not include any irrelevant information. She does not, for example, provide unnecessary plot summary or discuss more than four characters; she covers only what the question asks for. Guided by the question's key words—explain and briefly consider—she explains how each character's actions are defiant and outlines the consequences of those actions.

Glossary

Action   What happens in a drama.

Alexandrine   Iambic hexameter, a common form in French poetry but relatively rare in English poetry.

Allegorical figure or **framework**   See **Allegory.**

Allegory   Story with two parallel and consistent levels of meaning, one literal and one figurative, in which the figurative level offers a moral or political lesson; John Bunyan's *The Pilgrim's Progress* and Nathaniel Hawthorne's "Young Goodman Brown" are examples of moral allegory. An **allegorical figure** has only one meaning (for instance, it may represent good or evil), as opposed to a **symbol,** which may suggest a complex network of meanings. An **allegorical framework** is the system of ideas that conveys the allegory's message.

Alliteration   Repetition of initial sounds in a series of words, as in Blake's "The Chimney Sweeper": "So your chimneys I sweep, and in soot I sleep." Alliteration may be reinforced by repeated sounds within and at the ends of words.

Allusion   Reference, often to literature, history, mythology, or the Bible, that is unacknowledged in the text but that the author expects a reader to recognize. An example of allusion in a title is Charles Baxter's "Gryphon" (a mythical beast). Some modern writers, notably T.S. Eliot and James Joyce, use allusions drawn from their private reading, expecting few readers to understand them.

Ambiguity   Device in which authors intentionally evoke a number of possible meanings of a word or grammatical structure by leaving unclear which meaning they intend.

Anapest   See **Meter.**

Antagonist   Character who is in conflict with or opposition to the protagonist; the villain. Sometimes the antagonist may be a force or situation (war or poverty) rather than a person.

Antihero   Modern character who possesses the opposite attributes of a hero. Rather than being dignified and powerful, the antihero tends to be passive and ineffectual. Willy Loman, the main character in *Death of a Salesman,* is an antihero.

Apostrophe   Figure of speech in which an absent character or a personified force or object is addressed directly, as if it were present or could comprehend: "O Rose, thou art sick!"

Archetype   Image or symbol that is so common or significant to a culture that it seems to have a universal importance. The psychologist Carl Jung believed that because archetypes are an inherent part of psyches, we recognize them subconsciously when we encounter them and therefore give them a greater meaning than they would otherwise possess. Many archetypes appear in classical myths (for example, a journey to the underworld).

Arena stage Stage on which the actors are surrounded by the audience; also called *theater in the round*.

Aside Brief comment spoken by the actor to the audience (such as, "Here she comes. I'll play a fine trick on her now!") and assumed not to be heard by the other characters. Chekhov's *The Brute* includes asides.

Assonance Repetition of vowel sounds in a series of words: "cr<u>ee</u>p thr<u>ee</u> f<u>ee</u>t."

Atmosphere Tone or mood of a literary work, often established by the setting and language. Atmosphere is the emotional aura that determines readers' expectations about a work—for example, the sense of doom established at the beginning of Shakespeare's *Macbeth*.

Aubade Poem about morning, usually celebrating the dawn—for example, Philip Larkin's "Aubade."

Ballad Narrative poem, rooted in an oral tradition, usually arranged in quatrains rhyming *abcb* and containing a refrain.

Ballad stanza See **Stanza.**

Beast fable Short tale, usually including a moral, in which animals assume human characteristics—for example, Aesop's "The Tortoise and the Hare."

Beginning rhyme See **Rhyme.**

Black comedy Comedy that relies on the morbid and absurd. Often black comedies are so satiric that they become ironic and tragic; examples are Joseph Heller's novel *Catch 22* and Edward Albee's play *The Sandbox*.

Blank verse Lines of unrhymed iambic pentameter in no particular stanzaic form. Because iambic pentameter resembles the rhythms of ordinary English speech, blank verse is often unobtrusive; for instance, Shakespeare's noble characters usually use it, though they may seem to us at first reading to be speaking in prose. See **Meter.**

Blocking Decisions about how characters move and where they stand on stage in a dramatic production.

Box set A stage setting that gives the audience the illusion of looking into a room.

Cacophony Harsh or unpleasant spoken sound created by clashing consonants: "squawking chipmunks."

Caesura Strong or long pause in the middle of a poetic line, created by punctuation or by the sense of the poem, as in Yeats's "Leda and the Swan": "And Agamemnon dead. Being so caught up [. . .]."

Carpe diem "Seize the day"; the philosophy that gave its name to a kind of seventeenth-century poetry arguing that one should enjoy life today before it passes one by, as seen in Herrick's "To the Virgins, to Make Much of Time."

Catastrophe Traditionally, the moment in a tragedy after the climax, when the rising action has ended and the falling action has begun, when the protagonist begins to understand the implications of events that will lead to his or her downfall, and when such events begin to occur.

Catharsis Aristotle's term for the emotional reaction or "purgation" that takes place in an audience watching a tragedy. Aristotle theorized that when we see a good tragedy, we feel both pity (and thus closeness to the protagonist) and fear (or revulsion from the actions taking place on stage) because we recognize in ourselves the potential for similar action. The purging of these emotions we experience by seeing the dramatic action unfold before us is **catharsis.**

Character Fictional representation of a person, usually but not necessarily in a psychologically realistic way. E. M. Forster classified characters as **round** (well developed, closely involved in the action and responsive to it) or **flat** (static, stereotypical, or operating as **foils** for the protagonist). Characters can also be classified as **dynamic** (growing and changing in the course of the action) or **static** (remaining unchanged). Also, a brief satirical sketch illustrating a type of personality, popular in eighteenth-century England.

Characterization Way in which writers develop their characters and reveal those characters' traits to readers.

Choragos See **Chorus.**

Chorus Group of actors in classical Greek drama who comment in unison on the action and the hero; they are led by the **Choragos.**

Classicism Attitude toward art that values symmetry, clarity, discipline, and objectivity. Neoclassicism, such as that practiced in eighteenth-century Europe, appreciated those qualities as found in Greek and Roman art and culture; Alexander Pope's poetry follows neoclassical principles.

Cliché Overused phrase or expression.

Climax Point of greatest tension or importance, where the decisive action of a play or story takes place.

Closed form Type of poetic structure that has a recognizable rhyme scheme, meter, or stanzaic pattern; also called *fixed form.*

Closet drama Play meant to be read instead of performed—for example, Shelley's *Prometheus Unbound.*

Comedy Any literary work, but especially a play, in which events end happily, a character's fortunes are reversed for the better, and a community is drawn more closely together, often by the marriage of one or more protagonists at the end.

Comedy of humours Comedy that focuses on characters whose behavior is controlled by a characteristic trait, or humour, such as *Volpone* (1606) by Ben Jonson, who popularized the form.

Comedy of manners Satiric comedy that developed during the sixteenth century and achieved great popularity in the nineteenth century. This form focuses on the manners and customs of society and directs its satire against the characters who violate its social conventions and norms. *The Importance of Being Earnest* by Oscar Wilde is a comedy of manners.

Common measure See **Stanza.**

Conceit Extended or complicated metaphor, common in the Renaissance, that is impressive largely because it shows off an author's power to manipulate and sustain a striking comparison between two dissimilar items; John Donne's use of the compass metaphor in "A Valediction: Forbidding Mourning" is an example.

Concrete poem   Poem whose typographical appearance on the page reenforces its theme, as with George Herbert's "Easter Wings."

Conflict   Struggle between opposing forces (protagonist and antagonist) in a work of literature.

Connotation   Meaning that a word suggests beyond its literal, explicit meaning, carrying emotional associations, judgments, or opinions. Connotations can be positive, neutral, or negative. For example, *family* has a positive connotation when it describes a group of loving relatives; a neutral connotation when it describes a biological category; and a negative connotation when it describes an organization of criminals.

Convention   See **Literary convention.**

Conventional symbol   See **Symbol.**

Cosmic irony   See **Irony.**

Couplet   See **Stanza.**

Crisis   Peak or moment of tension in the action of a story; the point of greatest tension is the **climax.**

Dactyl   See **Meter.**

Denotation   Dictionary meaning of a word; its explicit, literal meaning.

Denouement   See **Resolution.**

Deus ex machina   "The god from the machine": any improbable resolution of plot involving the intervention of some force or agent hitherto extraneous to the story.

Dialect   Particular regional variety of language, which may differ from the more widely used standard or written language in its pronunciation, grammar, or vocabulary. Eliza Doolittle's cockney dialect in the George Bernard Shaw play *Pygmalion* is an example.

Dialogue   Conversation between two or more characters.

Diction   Word choice of an author, which determines the level of language used in a piece of literature. **Formal diction** is lofty and elaborate (typical of Shakespearean nobility); **informal diction** is idiomatic and relaxed (like the dialogue in John Updike's "A&P"). **Jargon** is the specialized diction of a professional or occupational group (such as computer hackers). **Idioms** are the colloquial expressions, including slang, of a particular group or society.

Didactic poetry   Poetry whose purpose is to make a point or teach a lesson, particularly common in the eighteenth century.

Double entendre   Phrase or word with a deliberate double meaning, one of which is usually sexual.

Double plot   See **Plot.**

Drama   Literature written to be performed.

Dramatic irony   See **Irony.**

Dramatic monologue   Type of poem perfected by Robert Browning that consists of a single speaker talking to one or more listeners and often revealing much more about the speaker than he or she seems to intend; Browning's "My Last Duchess" is the best known example of this form.

Dramatis personae   Characters in a play.

Dynamic character See **Character.**

Elegy Poem commemorating someone's death, usually in a reflective or mournful tone, such as A. E. Housman's "To an Athlete Dying Young."

Elision Leaving out an unstressed syllable or vowel, usually in order to keep a regular meter in a line of poetry ("o'er" instead of "over," for example).

End rhyme See **Rhyme.**

End-stopped line Line of poetry that has a full pause at the end, typically indicated by a period or semicolon.

Enjambment See **Run-on line.**

Envoi Three-line conclusion to a sestina that includes all six of the poem's key words, three placed at the ends of lines and three within the lines. See **Sestina.**

Epic Long narrative poem, such as the *Iliad* or the *Aeneid*, recounting the adventures of heroes on whose actions depend the fate of a nation or race. Frequently the gods or other supernatural beings take active interest in the events presented in the epic.

Epigram Short witty poem or phrase that makes a pointed statement—for example, Dorothy Parker's comment on an actress's performance, "She runs the gamut of emotions from A to B."

Epiphany Term first applied to literature by James Joyce and now used generally to describe a sudden moment of revelation about the deep meaning inherent in common things, such as the boy's realization at the end of "Araby."

Euphemism Word consciously chosen for its pleasant **Connota-** tions; often used for subjects like sex and death whose frank discussion is somewhat taboo in our society. For example, a euphemism for "to die" is "to pass away" or "to go to one's reward."

Euphony Pleasant spoken sound created by smooth consonants such as "ripple" or "pleasure."

Exposition First stage of a plot, where the author presents the information a reader or viewer will need to understand the characters and subsequent action.

Expressionism Artistic and literary movement that attempts to portray inner experience. It moves away from realistic portrayals of life and is characterized by violent exaggeration of objective reality and extremes of mood and feeling. In drama, expressionistic stage sets mirror the inner states of the character.

Extended metaphor See **Metaphor.**

Extended simile See **Metaphor.** Also see **Conceit.**

Eye rhyme See **Rhyme.**

Fable Short didactic story, often involving animals or supernatural beings and stressing plot above character development, whose object is to teach a pragmatic or moral lesson. See **Beast fable.**

Fairy tale See **Folktale.**

Falling action Stage in a play's plot during which the intensity of the climax subsides.

Falling meter Trochaic and dactylic meters, so called because they move from stressed to unstressed syllables. See **Rising meter.**

Fantasy Nonrealistic piece of literature that depends on whimsical plot, supernatural or mythical characters, and implausible actions, usually with a happy ending.

Farce   Comedy in which stereotypical characters engage in boisterous horseplay and slapstick humor, as in Chekhov's *The Brute*.

Feminine rhyme   See **Rhyme.**

Fiction   Form of narrative that is primarily imaginative, though its form may resemble that of factual writing like history and biography.

Figures of speech   Expressions—such as **hyperbole, metaphor, metonymy, personification, simile, synechdoche,** and **understatement**—that use words to achieve effects beyond ordinary language.

Flashback   Variation on chronological order that presents an event or situation that occurred before the time in which the story's action takes place.

Flat character   See **Character.**

Foil   Minor character whose role is to highlight the main character by presenting a contrast with him or her. In a modern comedic team, the "straight man" can be seen as a foil for the other performer.

Folktale   Contemporary version of an old, even ancient, oral tale that can be traced back centuries through many different cultures. Folktales include fairy tales, myths, and fables.

Foot   See **Meter.**

Foreshadowing   Presentation early in a story of situations, characters, or objects that seem to have no special importance but in fact are later revealed to have great significance. For example, a casual mention of a character's unusually accurate memory for faces may become significant only when his or her fate turns out to hinge on recognizing a person from the distant past.

Form   Structure or shape of a literary work; the way a work's parts fit together to form a whole. In poetry, form is described in terms of the presence (or absence) in a particular work of elements like rhyme, meter, and stanzaic pattern. See **Open form** and **Closed form.**

Formal diction   See **Diction.**

Free verse   See **Open form.**

Freytag's pyramid   The five parts of classic dramatic plots: exposition, complication (the introduction of elements that will lead to conflict and ultimately crisis), climax, catastrophe, and resolution. In his *Technique of the Drama* (1863) Gustav Freytag suggested that this pattern resembles a pyramid, with rising action leading to the climax and giving way to falling action.

Genre   Category of literature. Fiction, drama, and poetry are the three major genres; subgenres include the novel, the farce, and the lyric poem.

Haiku   Seventeen-syllable, three-line form of Japanese verse that almost always uses concrete imagery and deals with the natural world.

Hamartia   Aristotle's term for the "tragic flaw" in characters that eventually causes their downfall in Greek tragedy.

Hermeneutics   Traditionally, the use of the Bible to interpret other historical or current events; in current critical theory, the principles and procedures followed to determine the meaning of a text.

Heroic couplet   See **Stanza.**

High comedy   Term introduced in 1877 by George Meredith to denote comedy that appeals to the intellect, such as Shakespeare's *As You Like It*. See **Low comedy.**

Hubris   Tragic flaw of overwhelming pride that exists in the protagonist of a tragedy.

Hyperbole   Figurative language that depends on intentional overstatement; Mark Twain often used it to create humor; Jonathan Swift used it for **satire.**

Iamb   See **Meter.**

Imagery   Words and phrases that describe the concrete experience of the five senses, most often sight. A **pattern of imagery** is a group of related images developed throughout a work. **Synesthesia** is a form of imagery that mixes the experience of the senses (hearing something visual, smelling something audible, and so on): "He smelled the blue fumes of her scent." **Static imagery** freezes the moment to give it the timeless quality of painting or sculpture. **Kinetic imagery** attempts to show motion or change.

Imagism   Movement in modern poetry much influenced by **haiku,** stressing terseness and concrete imagery. Imagists were a group of American poets in the early twentieth century, such as Ezra Pound, William Carlos Williams, and Amy Lowell, who completely dispensed with traditional principles of English versification, creating new rhythms and meters.

Imperfect rhyme   See **Rhyme.**

In medias res   Latin phrase describing works like Homer's *Iliad* that begin in the middle of the action in order to catch a reader's interest.

Informal diction   See **Diction.**

Internal rhyme   See **Rhyme.**

Irony   Literary device or situation that depends on the existence of at least two separate and contrasting levels of meaning or experience. **Dramatic** or **tragic irony,** such as that found in *Oedipus the King,* depends on the audience's knowing something the protagonist has not yet realized (and thus experiencing simultaneously its own interpretation of the events and that of the protagonist). **Situational irony** exists when what happens is at odds with what the story's situation leads readers to expect will happen, as in Browning's "Porphyria's Lover." **Cosmic irony** (or irony of fate) exists when fate frustrates any effort a character might make to control or reverse his or her destiny. **Verbal irony** occurs when what is said is in contrast with what is meant. It can be expressed as **understatement, hyperbole,** or **sarcasm.**

Jargon   Specialized language associated with a particular trade or profession.

Kinetic imagery   Imagery that attempts to show motion or change. See, for example, William Carlos Williams's "The Great Figure."

Literary canon   Group of literary works generally acknowledged by critics and teachers to be the best and most significant to have emerged from our history. Until recently, the canon tended to be conservative (it was difficult to add to or remove works from it), and it reflected ideological positions that were not universally accepted. Many contemporary teachers and critics have attempted to expand the canon to include works by women and by writers of color.

Literary convention Something whose meaning is so widely understood within a society that authors can expect their audiences to accept and comprehend it unquestioningly—for example, the division of plays into acts or the fact that stepmothers in fairy tales are likely to be wicked.

Literary criticism Descriptions, analyses, interpretations, or evaluations of works of literature by experts in the field.

Literary symbol See **Symbol.**

Low comedy Introduced by George Meredith, it refers to comedy with little or no intellectual appeal. Low comedy is used as comic relief in *Macbeth.* See **High comedy.**

Lyric Form of poetry, usually brief and intense, that expresses a poet's subjective response to the world. In classical times, lyrics were set to music. The Romantic poets, particularly Keats, often wrote lyrics about love, death, and nature.

Masculine rhyme See **Rhyme.**

Meditation Lyric poem that focuses on a physical object—for example, Keats's "Ode on a Grecian Urn"—using this object as a vehicle for considering larger issues.

Melodrama Sensational play that appeals shamelessly to the emotions, contains elements of tragedy but ends happily, and often relies on set plots and stock characters.

Metaphor Concise form of comparison equating two things that may at first seem completely dissimilar, often an abstraction and a concrete image—for example, "My love's a fortress." Some people consider metaphor to be the essential element of poetry. An *extended metaphor,* or **conceit,** is a comparison used throughout a work; in Tillie Olsen's "I Stand Here Ironing," the mother compares her daughter to a dress waiting to be ironed, thus conveying her daughter's passivity and vulnerability. See **Simile.**

Meter Regular pattern of stressed and unstressed syllables, each repeated unit of which is called a **foot:** an **anapest** has three syllables, two unstressed and the third stressed; a **dactyl** has three syllables, the first stressed and the subsequent ones unstressed. An **iamb** has two syllables, unstressed followed by stressed; a **trochee** has a stressed syllable followed by an unstressed one; a **spondee** has two stressed syllables; and a **pyrrhic** has two unstressed syllables. A poem's meter is described in terms of the kind of foot (anapest, for example) and the number of feet found in each line. The number of feet is designated by the Greek prefix for the number, so one foot per line is called *monometer,* two feet is *dimeter,* followed by *trimeter,* tetrameter, pentameter, hexameter, and so on. The most common meter in English is *iambic pentameter.* See also **Rising meter** and **Falling meter.**

Metonymy Figure of speech in which the term for one thing can be applied to another with which it is closely associated—for example, using "defend the flag" to mean "defend the nation."

Mimesis Aristotle's term for the purpose of literature, which he felt was "imitation" of life; literature represents the essence of life and we are affected by it because we recognize (perhaps in another form) elements of our own experiences.

Monologue Extended speech by one character.

Mood Atmosphere created by the elements of a literary work (setting, characterization, imagery, tone, and so on).

Morality play Medieval Christian allegory.

Motivation Reasons behind a character's behavior that make us accept or believe that character.

Mystery play Medieval play depicting biblical scenes.

Myth Anonymous story reflecting the religious and social values of a culture or explaining natural phenomena, often involving gods and heroes.

Narrative The "storytelling" of a piece of fiction; the forward-moving recounting of episode and description. When an event that occurred earlier is told during a later sequence of events, it is called a **flashback;** suggesting earlier in a narration something that will occur later on is called **foreshadowing.**

Narrator Person who tells the story. See **Point of view.**

Naturalism Nineteenth-century movement whose followers believed that life should not be idealized when depicted in literature. Rather, literature should show that human experience is a continual (and for the most part losing) struggle against the natural

world. Émile Zola, Jack London, and Stephen Crane are important practitioners of naturalism.

New Comedy Greek comedies of the fourth and third centuries B.C. that followed the Old Comedies. They were comedies of romance with stock characters and conventional settings. They lacked the satire, abusive language, and bawdiness of Old Comedies. New Comedy originated in the works of the Greek dramatist Meander and was further developed by the Roman dramatists Plautus and Terence. See **Old Comedy.**

Novel Fictional narrative, traditionally realistic, relating a series of events or following the history of a character or group of characters through a period of time.

Novella Extended short story, usually concentrated in episode and action (like a short story) but involving greater character development (like a novel); Franz Kafka's "The Metamorphosis" is a novella.

Octave See **Sonnet.**

Ode Relatively long lyric poem, common in antiquity and adapted by the Romantic poets, for whom it was a serious poem of formal diction, often addressed to some significant object (such as a nightingale or the west wind) that has stimulated the poet's imagination.

Old Comedy The first comedies, written in Greece in the fifth century B.C., which heavily satirized the religious and social issues of the day. The chief practitioner of Old Comedy was Aristophanes. See **New Comedy.**

Onomatopoeia Word whose sound resembles what it describes:

"snap, crackle, pop." Lewis Carroll's "Jabberwocky" uses onomatopoeia.

Open form Sometimes called *free verse* or *vers libre*, open form poetry makes use of varying line lengths, abandoning stanzaic divisions, breaking lines in unexpected places, and even dispensing with any pretense of formal structure. See **Form.**

Ottava rima See **Stanza.**

Oxymoron Phrase combining two seemingly incompatible elements: "crashing silence."

Parable Story that uses analogy to make a moral point, such as the parable of the prodigal son in the New Testament.

Paradox Seemingly contradictory situation. Adrienne Rich's "A Woman Mourned by Daughters" uses paradox.

Parody "Take-off" or exaggerated imitation of a serious piece of literature for humorous effect. Shakespeare's "My Mistress' Eyes are Nothing Like the Sun" is a parody of traditional Renaissance love poetry.

Pastoral Literary work, such as Christopher Marlowe's lyric poem "The Passionate Shepherd to His Love," that deals nostalgically and usually unrealistically with a simple, preindustrial rural life; the name comes from the fact that traditionally pastorals feature shepherds.

Pastoral romance Prose tale set in an idealized rural world; popular in Renaissance England.

Pathos Suffering that exists simply to satisfy the sentimental or morbid sensibilities of the audience.

Pattern of imagery See **Imagery.**

Perfect rhyme See **Rhyme.**

Persona Narrator or speaker of a poem or story; in Greek tragedy, a persona was a mask worn by an actor.

Personification Endowing inanimate objects or abstract ideas with life or human characteristics: "the river wept."

Petrarchan sonnet See **Sonnet.**

Picaresque Episodic, often satirical work about a rogue or rascal—for example, Cervantes's *Don Quixote.* The form emerged in sixteenth-century Spain.

Picture-frame stage Stage that looks like a room with a missing fourth wall through which the audience views the play. The **proscenium arch** separates the audience from the play.

Plot Way in which the events of the story are arranged. When there are two stories of more or less equal importance, the work has a **double plot;** when there is more than one story but one string of events is clearly the most significant, the other stories are called **subplots.** Plot in fiction often follows the pattern of action in drama, rising to a **climax** and then falling to a resolution.

Poetic rhythm See **Rhythm.**

Point of view Perspective from which a story is told. The storyteller may be a character in the story (*first-person narrator*) or someone who does not figure in the action (*third-person narrator*), in which case he or she may know the actions and internal doings of everyone in the story (*omniscient narrator*) or some part of these (*limited omniscient narrator*). Rarely, there may be a *second-person narrator* who uses "you" and the imperative mood throughout the story.

The narrator may be an *observer* or a *participant*. If he or she is untrustworthy (stupid or bad, for instance), one has an *unreliable narrator;* narrators who are unreliable because they do not understand what they are reporting (children, for instance) are called *naive narrators.* If the perspective on the events is the same as one would get by simply watching the action unfold on stage, the point of view is *dramatic* or *objective.*

Popular fiction   Works aimed at a mass audience.

Prologue   First part of a play (originally of a Greek tragedy) in which the actor gives the background or explanations that the audience needs to follow the rest of the drama.

Props (short for properties)   Pictures, furnishings, and so on that decorate the stage for a play.

Proscenium arch   Arch that surrounds the opening in a **picture-frame stage;** through this arch the audience views the performances.

Prose poem   Open form poem whose long lines appear to be prose set in paragraphs—for example, Walt Whitman's "Cavalry Crossing a Ford."

Protagonist   Principal character of a drama or fiction; the hero. The *tragic* hero is the noble protagonist in classical Greek drama who falls because of a tragic flaw.

Pyrrhic   See **Meter.**

Quatrain   See **Stanza.**

Realism   Writing that stresses careful description of setting and the trappings of daily life, psychological probability, and the lives of ordinary people. Its practitioners believe they are presenting life "as it really is"; Ibsen's *A Doll House* is an example.

Resolution   Also called the **denouement,** this is the final stage in the plot of a drama or work of fiction. Here the action comes to an end and remaining loose ends are tied up.

Rhetoric   Organization, strategy, and development of literary works, guided by an eye to how such elements will further the writer's intended effect on the reader.

Rhyme   Repetition of concluding sounds in different words, often intentionally used at the ends of poetic lines. In **masculine rhyme** (also called **rising rhyme**) single syllables correspond. In **feminine rhyme** (also called **double rhyme** or **falling rhyme**) two syllables correspond, the second of which is stressed. In **triple rhyme,** three syllables correspond. **Eye rhyme** occurs when words look as though they should rhyme but are pronounced differently ("cough/tough"). In **perfect rhyme** the corresponding vowel and consonant sounds of accented syllables must be preceded by different consonants— for example, the *b* and *h* in "born" and "horn." **Imperfect rhyme,** also called *near rhyme, off rhyme,* or *slant rhyme,* occurs when consonants in two words are the same but intervening vowels are different—for example, "pick/pack," "lads/lids." The most common type of rhyme within a poem is **end rhyme,** where the rhyming syllables are placed at the end of a rhyme. **Internal rhyme** consists of rhyming words found within a line of poetry. **Beginning rhyme** occurs in the first syllable or syllables of the line.

Rhyme royal   See **Stanza.**

Rhythm   Regular recurrence of sounds in a poem. Ordinarily rhythm is determined by the arrangement of metrical feet in a line, but sometimes an alternate form of "sprung" rhythm, introduced by Gerard Manley Hopkins, is used. In this type of rhythm the number of strong stresses in a line determines the rhythm, regardless of how many weak stresses there might be.

Rising action   Stage in a play's plot during which the action builds in intensity. See **Freytag's pyramid.**

Romance   Type of narrative that deals with love and adventure in a nonrealistic way, most popular in the Middle Ages but sometimes used by more modern authors, such as Hawthorne, to separate themselves from the drabness of ordinary life.

Romantic comedy   Comedy such as Shakespeare's *Much Ado about Nothing* in which love is the main subject and idealized lovers endure great difficulties until the inevitable happy ending is reached.

Romanticism   Eighteenth- and nineteenth-century literary movement that valued subjectivity, individuality, the imagination, nature, excess, the exotic, and the mysterious.

Round character   See **Character.**

Run-on line   Line of poetry that ends with no punctuation or natural pause and consequently runs over into the next line; also called *enjambment.*

Sarcasm   Form of irony in which apparent praise is used to convey strong, bitter criticism.

Satire   Literary attack on folly or vanity by means of ridicule; usually intended to improve society.

Scansion   Process of determining the meter of a poem by analyzing the strong and weak stresses in a line to find the unit of **meter** (each recurring pattern of stresses) and the number of these units (or **feet**) in each line.

Scrim   Curtain that when illuminated from the front appears solid but when lit from the back becomes transparent.

Sentimental comedy   Reaction against the **comedy of manners.** This type of comedy relies on sentimental emotion rather than on wit or humor to move an audience and dwells on the virtues of life.

Sestet   See **Sonnet.**

Sestina   Poem composed of six six-line stanzas and a three-line conclusion called an **envoi.** Each line ends with one of six key words. The alternation of these six words in different positions—but always at the ends of lines—in the poem's six stanzas creates a rhythmic verbal pattern that unifies the poem.

Setting   Background against which the action of a piece of literature takes place: the historical time, locale, season, time of day, interior decoration, and so on. See **Context.**

Shakespearean sonnet   See **Sonnet.**

Short story   Fictional narrative centered on one climatic event and usually developing only a single character in depth; its scope is narrower than that of the **novel,** and it often uses setting and characterization more directly to make its theme clear.

Simile Comparison of two seemingly unlike things using the words *like* or *as:* "My love is like an arrow through my heart." See **Metaphor.**

Situational irony See **Irony.**

Soliloquy Convention of drama in which a character speaks directly to the audience, revealing thoughts and feelings which other characters present on stage are assumed not to hear. By convention, a soliloquy is taken to reflect a character's sincere feelings and beliefs.

Sonnet Fourteen-line poem, usually a **lyric** in *iambic pentameter* (see **Meter**). It has a strict rhyme scheme in one of two forms: the *Italian,* or **Petrarchan sonnet** (an octave rhymed *abba/abba* with a sestet rhymed *cdc/cdc* or a variation) and the *English,* or **Shakespearean sonnet** (three quatrains rhymed *abab/cdcd/efef* with a concluding couplet rhymed *gg*). The English sonnet developed partly because the Italian rhyme scheme was so difficult to achieve in English, where end rhymes are less frequent than they are in Italian. Modern poets often exploit the rigorous sonnet form by contrasting its restraints with violent content or imagery, as in Yeats's "Leda and the Swan."

Speaker See **Persona.**

Spenserian stanza See **Stanza.**

Spondee See **Meter.**

Stage business Actions or movements of an actor onstage—for example, lighting a cigarette, leaning on a mantel, straightening a picture.

Stage directions Words in a play that describe an actor's role apart from the dialogue, dealing with movements, attitudes, and so on.

Stage setting (set) In the production of a play, scenery and props. In *expressionist* stage settings, scenery and props are exaggerated and distorted to reflect the workings of a troubled, even abnormal mind. *Surrealistic* stage settings are designed to mirror the uncontrolled images of dreams or nightmares. See **Staging.**

Staging Overall production of a play in performance: the sets, costumes, lighting, sound, music, and so on.

Stanza Group of lines in a poem that forms a metrical or thematic unit. Each stanza is usually separated from others by a blank space on the page. Some common stanzaic forms are the **couplet** (two lines), **tercet** (three lines), **quatrain** (four lines), **sestet** (six lines), and **octave** (eight lines). The **heroic couplet,** first used by Chaucer and especially popular throughout the eighteenth century, as in Alexander Pope's poetry, consists of two rhymed lines of iambic pentameter, with a weak pause after the first line and a strong pause after the second. **Terza rima,** a form used by Dante, has a rhyme scheme (*aba, bcb, ded*) that creates an interlocking series of stanzas. The **ballad stanza** alternates lines of eight and six syllables. Typically only the second and fourth lines rhyme. **Common measure** is a four-line stanzaic pattern closely related to the ballad stanza. It differs in that its rhyme scheme is *abab* rather than *abcb*. **Rhyme royal** is a seven-line stanza (*abab-bcc*) set in iambic pentameter. **Ottava rima** is an eight-line stanza (*abababcc*) set in iambic pentameter. The **Spenserian stanza** is a nine-line form (*ababbcbcc*) with the first eight lines in iambic pentameter and the last line in iambic hexameter.

Static character See **Character.**

Static imagery Imagery that freezes a moment to give it the timeless quality of painting or sculpture. Much visual imagery is static.

Stock character Stereotypical character who behaves consistently and whom the audience of a play can recognize and classify instantly: the town drunk, the nerd, and so on.

Stream of consciousness Form of narration controlled not by external events but by the thoughts and subjective impressions of the narrator, commonly found in modern literature, such as the work of Virginia Woolf and James Joyce.

Stress Accent or emphasis, either strong or weak, given to each syllable in a piece of writing, as determined by conventional pronunciation (cárpĕt, not cărpét) and intended emphasis ("going dówn, dówn, dówn tŏ thĕ bóttŏm ŏf thĕ ócĕan"). Strong stresses are marked with a ´ and weak ones with a ˇ; stress can be an important clue in helping to determine a poet's intended emphasis.

Structure Formal pattern or arrangement of elements to form a whole in a piece of literature.

Style Way an author selects and arranges words to express ideas and, ultimately, theme.

Subplot See **Plot.**

Surrealism Literary movement that allows unconventional use of syntax; chronology; juxtaposition; and bizarre, dreamlike images in prose and poetry.

Symbol Person, object, action, or idea whose meaning transcends its literal or denotative sense in a complex way. For instance, if someone wears a rose in a lapel to a dance, the rose may simply be a decoration, but in Blake's "The Sick Rose" it becomes a symbol because it takes on a range of paradoxical and complementary meanings. A symbol is invested with significance beyond what it could carry on its own: A swastika, for instance, is a powerful and frightening symbol as a result of Hitler's Nazism. **Universal symbols,** such as the grim reaper, may be called **archetypes; conventional symbols,** such as national flags, evoke a general and agreed-upon response from most people. There are also **private symbols,** such as the "gyre" created by Yeats, which the poet himself invested with extraordinary significance.

Synechdoche Figure of speech in which a part of something is used to represent the whole—for example, "hired hand" represents a laborer.

Synesthesia See **Imagery.**

Tale Short story often involving mysterious atmosphere and supernatural or inexplicable events, such as "The Black Cat" by Edgar Allan Poe.

Tercet See **Stanza.**

Terza rima See **Stanza.**

Theater in the round See **Arena stage.**

Theater of the absurd Type of drama that discards conventions of plot, character, and motivation in order to depict a world in which nothing makes sense. Albee's *The Sandbox* is an example.

Theme Central or dominant idea of a piece of literature, made concrete by the details and emphasis in the work itself.

Thrust stage Stage that juts out into the audience so the action may be viewed from three sides.

Tone Attitude of the speaker or author of a work toward the subject itself or the audience, as can be determined from the word choice and arrangement of the piece.

Tragedy Literary work, especially a play, that recounts the downfall of an individual. Greek tragedy demanded a noble protagonist whose fall could be traced to a tragic personal flaw. Shakespearean tragedy also treats noble figures, but the reasons for their tragedies may be less clear-cut than in Greek drama. Domestic or modern tragedy tends to deal with the fates of ordinary people.

Tragic irony See **Irony.**

Tragicomedy Type of Elizabethan and Jacobean drama that uses elements of both tragedy and comedy.

Triple rhyme See **Rhyme.**

Trochee See **Meter.**

Understatement Intentional downplaying of a situation's significance, often for ironic or humorous effect, as in Mark Twain's famous comment on reading his own obituary, "The reports of my death are greatly exaggerated."

Unities Rules that require a dramatic work to be unified in terms of its time, place, and action. *Oedipus the King* illustrates the three unities.

Universal symbol See **Symbol.**

Verbal irony See **Irony.**

Villanelle First introduced in France in the Middle Ages, a nineteen-line poem composed of five tercets and a concluding quatrain; its rhyme scheme is *aba aba aba aba aba abaa*. Two different lines are systematically repeated in the poem: line 1 appears again in lines 6, 12, and 18, and line 3 reappears as lines 9, 15, and 19. Thus each tercet concludes with an exact (or close) duplication of either line 1 or line 3, and the final quatrain concludes by repeating both line 1 and line 3.

Wagons Sets mounted on wheels, which make possible rapid changes of scenery.

Auden. Copyright 1940 and renewed © 1968 by W. H. Auden. Reprinted by permission of Random House, Inc.

MATSUO BASHO, "Four Haiku" from *The Penguin Book of Japanese Verse,* translated by Geoffrey Bownas and Anthony Thwaite. Copyright © 1964 by Geoffrey Bownas and Anthony Thwaite. Reprinted by permission of Penguin Books, Ltd.

CHARLES BAXTER, "Gryphon" from *Through the Safety Net* by Charles Baxter. Copyright © 1985 by Charles Baxter. Reprinted by permission of Vintage Books, a division of Random House, Inc.

HERMAN BEAVERS, "Dead Rocks and Sleeping Men: Aurality in the Aesthetic of Langston Hughes" by Herman Beavers from *Langston Hughes Review* 11.1 (Spring 1992). Reprinted by permission of the Langston Hughes Society.

SUZANNE E. BERGER, "The Meal" from *Legacies* by Suzanne E. Berger. Originally published by Alice James Books, then again in *Tendrill.* Copyright © 1984 by and reprinted by permission of Suzanne E. Berger.

ELIZABETH BISHOP, "Sestina" from *The Complete Poems 1927–1979* by Elizabeth Bishop. Copyright © 1979, 1983 by Alice Helen Methfessel. Reprinted by permission of Farrar, Straus & Giroux, Inc.

ROGER BOXILL, *"The Glass Menagerie"* by Roger Boxill from *Tennessee Williams.* Copyright © 1987, 1989 by Roger Boxill. Reprinted by permission of St. Martin's Press, Inc., and the author.

T. CORAGHESSAN BOYLE, "Greasy Lake" from *Greasy Lake and Other Stories* by T. Coraghessan Boyle. Copyright © 1979, 1981, 1982, 1983, 1984, 1985 by T. Coraghessan Boyle. Used by permission of Viking Penguin, a division of Penguin Putnam, Inc.

RICHARD BRAUTIGAN, "Widow's Lament" from *The Pill versus the Springhill Mine Disaster* by Richard Brautigan. Copyright © 1968 by Richard Brautigan. Reprinted by permission of Houghton Mifflin Company. All rights reserved.

GWENDOLYN BROOKS, "We Real Cool," "The Ballad of Rudolph Reed," "First Fight. Then Fiddle," "The *Chicago Defender* Sends a Man to Little Rock," "Medgar Evers," and "Sadie and Maud" from *Blacks* by Gwendolyn Brooks. Copyright © 1991. Published by Third World Press. No portion of this text may be reprinted without permission of Gwendolyn Brooks.

JOSEPH BRUCHAC, "Ellis Island." from *The Remembered Earth* (Albuquerque, NM: Red Earth Press, 1979). Reprinted by permission of the author.

CHARLES BUKOWSKI, "Dog Fight." Copyright © 1984 by Charles Bukowski. Reprinted by permission of Black Sparrow Press.

RAYMOND CARVER, "Popular Mechanics" from *What We Talk about When We Talk about Love* by Raymond Carver. Copyright © 1981 by Raymond Carver. Reprinted by permission of Alfred A. Knopf, Inc. "Photograph of My Father in His Twenty-Second Year" from *Fires* by Raymond Carver. Copyright © 1983 by Raymond Carver. Reprinted by permission of Capra Press, Santa Barbara.

PADDY CHAYEFSKY, *Marty* from *Collected Works of Paddy Chayefsky: The TV Plays* by Paddy Chayefsky. Copyright © 1994 Applause Books. Reprinted by permission.

ANTON CHEKHOV, *The Brute* from *The Brute and Other Farces,* edited by Eric Bentley. Copyright © 1958, with kind permission of Applause Theatre Books.

ALICE CHILDRESS, *Florence.* Copyright 1950. Renewed © 1978 by Alice Childress. Used by permission of Flora Roberts, Inc.

SANDRA CISNEROS, "Barbie-Q" from *Woman Hollering Creek* by Sandra Cisneros. Copyright © 1991 by Sandra Cisneros. Published by Vintage Books, a division of Random House, Inc., New York, and originally in hardcover by Random House, Inc. Reprinted by permission of Susan Bergholz Literary Services, New York. All rights reserved.

LUCILLE CLIFTON, "My Mama Moved among the Days." Copyright © 1987 by Lucille Clifton. Reprinted from *Good Woman: Poems and a Memoir 1969–1980* with the permission of BOA Editions, Ltd., 260 East Avenue, Rochester, NY, 14604.

recitation, lecturing, public reading, radio broadcasting, television, video or sound recording, all other forms of mechanical or electronic reproduction, such as CD-ROM, CD-I, information storage and retrieval systems and photocopying, and the rights of translation into foreign languages, are strictly reserved. Particular emphasis is laid upon the matter of readings, permission for which must be secured from the author's agent in writing. Inquiries concerning rights should be addressed to: William Morris Agency, Inc., 1325 Avenue of the Americas, New York, New York 10019, Attn: Gilbert Parker.

H. D., "Helen" and "Heat, Part II of Garden" from *Collected Poems, 1912–1944* by H. D. Doolittle. Copyright © 1982 by the Estate of Hilda Doolittle. Reprinted by permission of New Directions Publishing Corporation.

DONALD HALL, "My Son, My Executioner" from *Old and New Poems* by Donald Hall. Copyright © 1990 by Donald Hall. Reprinted by permission of Ticknor & Fields/Houghton Mifflin Company. All rights reserved.

ROBERT HAYDEN, "Those Winter Sundays." Copyright © 1966 by Robert Hayden. "Monet's 'Waterlilies'." Copyright © 1970 by Robert Hayden. "Homage to the Empress of the Blues." Copyright © 1966 by Robert Hayden. From *Collected Poems of Robert Hayden* by Robert Hayden, edited by Frederick Glaysher. Reprinted by permission of Liveright Publishing Corporation.

SEAMUS HEANEY, "Digging" and "Lightenings viii" from *Opened Ground: Selected Poems 1966–1996* by Seamus Heaney. Copyright © 1998 by Seamus Heaney. Reprinted by permission of Farrar, Straus & Giroux, Inc., and Faber & Faber.

ERNEST HEMINGWAY, "A Clean, Well-Lighted Place" from *Winner Take Nothing* by Ernest Hemingway. Copyright 1933 by Charles Scribner's Sons and renewed © 1961 by Mary Hemingway. Reprinted with permission of Scribner, a division of Simon & Schuster, Inc.

DAVID HUDDLE, "Holes Commence Falling" from *Paper Boy* by David Huddle. Reprinted by permission of the author.

ROBERT HUFF, "Rainbow." May not be further reproduced without permission.

LANGSTON HUGHES, "Negro," "Island," "The Negro Speaks of Rivers," "Theme for English B," and "Harlem" ("Dream Deferred") from *Collected Poems* by Langston Hughes. Copyright © 1994 by the Estate of Langston Hughes. Reprinted by permission of Alfred A. Knopf, Inc. "The Negro Artist and the Racial Mountain." Reprinted with permission from the June 23, 1926 issue of the *Nation*. "The Weary Blues," "Let America be America Again," "I, Too," "Ballad of the Landlord," "Dream Boogie," and "Birmingham Sunday (September 15, 1963)" from *Collected Poems* by Langston Hughes. Copyright © 1994 by the Estate of Langston Hughes. Reprinted by permission of Alfred A. Knopf, a Division of Random House, Inc. "To Negro Writers." Copyright 1935. Reprinted by permission of Harold Ober Associates, Inc. "My Adventures as a Social Poet." Copyright 1947. Reprinted by permission of Harold Ober Associates, Inc. "Swinging High" from *Simple's Uncle Same* by Langston Hughes. Copyright © 1965 by Langston Hughes. Copyright renewed © 1993 by Arnold Rampersad and Ramona Bass. Reprinted by permission of Hill & Wang, a division of Farrar, Straus & Giroux, LLC. "Langston Hughes Speaks" by Langston Hughes from the *Crisis*, 1953. The authors wish to thank the Crisis Publishing Co., Inc., the publisher of the magazine of the National Association for the Advancement of Colored People, for authorizing the use of this work.

TED HUGHES, "A Pink Wool Knitted Dress" from *Birthday Letters* by Ted Hughes. Copyright © 1998 by Ted Hughes. Reprinted by permission of Farrar, Straus & Giroux, Inc., and Faber & Faber, Ltd. "Visit" from *Birthday Letters* by Ted Hughes. Copyright © 1998 by Ted Hughes. Reprinted by permission of Farrar, Straus & Giroux, LLC, and Faber & Faber, Ltd.

GEORGE B. HUTCHINSON, "Langston Hughes and the 'Other' Whitman" from *The Continuing Presence of Walt Whitman: The Life after the Life,* edited by Robert K. Martin. Reprinted by permission of the University of Iowa Press. Copyright © 1992.

HENRIK IBSEN, *A Doll's House* from *The Complete Major Prose Plays of Henrik Ibsen* by Henrik Ibsen, translated by Rolf Fjelde. Translation copyright © 1965, 1970, 1978 by Rolf Fjelde. Used by permission of Dutton Signet, a division of Penguin Putnam, Inc.

SHIRLEY JACKSON, "The Lottery" from *The Lottery* by Shirley Jackson. Copyright 1948, 1949 by Shirley Jackson renewed © 1976, 1977 by Laurence Hyman, Barry Hyman, Mrs. Sarah Webster, and Mrs. Joanne Schnurer. Reprinted by permission of Farrar, Straus & Giroux, Inc. "The Possibility of Evil" from *Just an Ordinary Life: The Uncollected Stories* by Shirley Jackson. Copyright © 1965 by Stanley Edgar Hyman. Used by permission of Bantam Books, a division of Random House, Inc.

RANDALL JARRELL, "The Death of the Ball Turret Gunner" from *The Complete Poems* by Randall Jarrell. Copyright © 1969 and renewed 1997 by Mary von S. Jarrell. Reprinted by permission of Farrar, Straus & Giroux, Inc.

BILLY JOEL, "Goodnight Saigon." Copyright © 1981 by Joelsongs. All rights reserved. Used by permission.

JAMES JOYCE, "Araby" and "Eveline" from *Dubliners* by James Joyce. Copyright 1916 by B. W. Heubsch. Definitive text: copyright © 1967 by the Estate of James Joyce. Used by permission of Viking Penguin, a division of Penguin Putnam, Inc.

FRANZ KAFKA, "Metamorphosis" from *The Metamorphosis, the Penal Colony, and Other Stories* by Franz Kafka, translated by Willa and Edwin Muir. Copyright 1948 and renewed © 1975 by Schocken Books. Reprinted by permission of Schocken Books, distributed by Pantheon Books, a division of Random House, Inc.

DAVID MICHAEL KAPLAN, "Doe Season" from *Comfort* by David Michael Kaplan. Published by Viking Penguin, Inc. First appeared in the *Atlantic Monthly*. Also appeared in *Best American Short Stories 1986*. Copyright © 1987 by David Michael Kaplan. Reprinted by permission of Brand & Brandt Literary Agents, Inc.

FAYE KICKNOSWAY, "Gracie" from *All These Voices* by Faye Kicknosway. Reprinted by permission of Morgan Blair a.k.a. Faye Kicknosway.

JAMAICA KINCAID, "Girl" from *At the Bottom of the River* by Jamaica Kincaid. Copyright © 1983 by Jamaica Kincaid. Reprinted by permission of Farrar, Straus & Giroux, LLC.

THOMAS L. KING, "Irony and Distance in *The Glass Menagerie*" from *Educational Theatre Journal*. No portion of this text may be reprinted without permission.

CAROLYN KIZER, "After Basho" from *Yin: New Poems* by Carolyn Kizer. Copyright © 1984 by Carolyn Kizer. Reprinted with the permission of BOA Editions, Ltd., 260 East Avenue, Rochester, NY 14604.

ETHERIDGE KNIGHT, "For Malcolm, a Year After" from *The Essential Etheridge Knight* by Etheridge Knight. Copyright © 1986. Reprinted by permission of the University of Pittsburgh Press.

YUSEF KOMUNYAKAA, "Facing It" from *Neon Vernacular* by Yusef Komunyakaa. Copyright © 1993 by Yusef Komunyakaa. Reprinted by permission of Wesleyan University Press.

PHILIP LARKIN, "Aubade" from *Collected Poems* by Philip Larkin. Copyright © 1988, 1989 by the Estate of Philip Larkin. Reprinted by permission of Farrar, Straus & Giroux, Inc., and Faber & Faber.

D. H. LAWRENCE, "The Rocking-Horse Winner." Copyright 1933 by the Estate of D. H. Lawrence and renewed © 1961 by Angelo Ravagli and C. M. Weekley, Executors of the Estate of Frieda Lawrence. Reprinted from *Complete Short Stories of D. H. Lawrence* by D. H. Lawrence. Used by permission of Viking Penguin, a division of Penguin Putnam, Inc.

DENISE LEVERTOV, "What Were They Like" from *Poems 1960–1967* by Denise Levertov. Copyright © 1966 by Denise Levertov. Reprinted by permission of New Directions Publishing Corporation.

AUDRE LORDE, "Rooming Houses Are Old Women." Copyright © 1973, 1970, 1968 by Audre Lorde. Reprinted from *Chosen Poems: Old and New* by Audre Lorde. Used by permission of W. W. Norton & Company, Inc.

ROBERT LOWELL, "For the Union Dead" from *For the Union Dead* by Robert Lowell. Copyright © 1959 by Robert Lowell and renewed 1987 by Harriet Lowell, Caroline Lowell, and Sheridan Lowell. Reprinted by permission of Farrar, Straus & Giroux, Inc.

DICK POTHIER AND THOMAS J. GIBBONS, JR., "A Woman's Wintry Death Leads to a Long-Dead Friend" from the *Philadelphia Inquirer,* 30 January 1987. Reprinted by permission.

EZRA POUND, "In A Station of the Metro" and "The River-Merchant's Wife: A Letter" from *Personae* by Ezra Pound. Copyright 1926 by Ezra Pound. Reprinted by permission of New Directions Publishing Corporation.

ARNOLD RAMPERSAD, "The Origins of Poetry in Langston Hughes" from *Southern Review* 21.3 (1985): 695–705. Reprinted by permission of the author.

DUDLEY RANDALL, "Ballad of Birmingham." Copyright © by and reprinted by permission of Dudley Randall.

JOHN CROWE RANSOM, "Bells for John Whiteside's Daughter" from *Selected Poems* by John Crowe Ransom. Copyright 1924 by Alfred A. Knopf, Inc., and renewed 1952 by John Crowe Ransom. Reprinted by permission of the publisher.

HENRY REED, "Naming of Parts." Copyright 1946 by Henry Reed. Reprinted by permission of Literary Executor of the Estate of Henry Reed, John Tydemann.

ADRIENNE RICH, "A Woman Mourned by Daughters," "Living in Sin," "Aunt Jennifer's Tigers," and "Diving into the Wreck" from *The Fact of a Doorframe: Poems Selected and New, 1950–1984* by Adrienne Rich. Copyright © 1984 by Adrienne Rich. Copyright © 1975, 1978 by W. W. Norton & Company, Inc. Copyright © 1981 by Adrienne Rich. Reprinted by permission of W. W. Norton & Company, Inc.

ALBERTO ALVARO RÍOS, "Nani" (1982) from *Whispering to Fool the Wind.* Reprinted by permission of the author. "The Secret Lion" from *The Iguana Killer: Twelve Stories of the Heart* by Alberto Alvaro Ríos. Copyright © 1984 by Alberto Alvaro Ríos. Reprinted by permission of Lewis & Clark College.

THEODORE ROETHKE, "My Papa's Waltz." Copyright 1942 by Hearst Magazines, Inc. "I Knew a Woman." Copyright 1954 by Theodore Roethke. "The Waking." Copyright 1953 by Theodore Roethke. "Night Crow." Copyright 1944 by Saturday Review Association, Inc. Reprinted from *The Collected Poems of Theodore Roethke* by Theodore Roethke. Used by permission of Doubleday, a division of Random House, Inc.

JIM SAGEL, "Baca Grande" from *Hispanics in the U.S.: An Anthology of Creative Literature* 2 (1982). Reprinted by permission of Bilingual Press/Editorial Bilingue (Arizona State University, Tempe, AZ).

SONIA SANCHEZ, "On Passing thru Morgantown, PA" from *Homegirls and Handgrenades* by Sonia Sanchez. Copyright © 1984 by and reprinted by permission of Sonia Sanchez.

MILCHA SANCHEZ-SCOTT, *The Cuban Swimmer.* Copyright © 1994 by Milcha Sanchez-Scott. All rights reserved. Reprinted by permission of William Morris Agency, Inc., on behalf of the author. CAUTION: Professionals and amateurs are hereby warned that *The Cuban Swimmer* is subject to a royalty. It is fully protected under the copyright laws of the United States of America and of all countries covered under the copyright laws of the United States of America and of all countries covered by the International Copyright Union (including the Dominion of Canada and the rest of the British Commonwealth), the Berne Convention, the Pan-American Copyright Convention and the Universal Copyright Convention as well as all countries with which the United States has reciprocal copyright relations. All rights, including professional/amateur stage rights, motion picture, recitation, lecturing, public reading, radio broadcasting, television, video or sound recording, all other forms of mechanical or electronic reproduction, such as CD-ROM, CD-I, information storage and retrieval systems and photocopying, and the rights of translation into foreign languages, are strictly reserved. Particular emphasis is laid upon the matter of readings, permission for which must be secured from the author's agent in writing. Inquiries concerning rights should be addressed to: William Morris Agency, Inc., 1325 Avenue of the Americas, New York, NY 10019, Attn: George Lane. Originally produced in New York City by INTAR Hispanic American Arts Center.

CARL SANDBURG, "Chicago" and "Fog" from *Chicago Poems* by Carl Sandburg. Copyright 1916 by Holt, Rinehart & Winston and renewed 1944 by Carl Sandburg. Reprinted by permission of Harcourt Brace & Company.

ЪЪЪЪ

Margaret Walker, "Lineage" from *This Is My Sensory* by Margaret Walker. Copyright 1942 by Margaret Walker. Reprinted by permission of Margaret Walker.

Wendy Wasserstein, *Tender Offer.* Reprinted by permission of International Creative Management.

Joyce M. Wegs, "Don't You Know Who I Am? The Grotesque in Oates's 'Where Are You Going, Where Have You Been?'" from the *Journal of Narrative Techniques* 5 (1975). Copyright © by Joyce M. Wegs. Reprinted by permission of Joyce M. Wegs.

James Welch, "The Man from Washington" from *Riding the Earthboy 40* by James Welch. Copyright © 1971 by James Welch. Reprinted by permission of Elaine Markson Literary Agency.

Eudora Welty, "A Worn Path" from *A Curtain of Green and Other Stories* by Eudora Welty. Copyright 1941 and renewed © 1969 by Eudora Welty. Reprinted by permission of Harcourt Brace & Company.

Richard Wilbur, "For the Student Strikers" from *The Mind-Reader.* Copyright © 1971 by Richard Wilbur. Reprinted by permission of Harcourt Brace & Company. "A Sketch" from *The Mind-Reader.* Copyright © 1975 by Richard Wilbur. Reprinted by permission of Harcourt Brace & Company. "Sleepless at Crown Point" from *The Mind-Reader.* Copyright © 1973 by Richard Wilbur. Reprinted by permission of Harcourt Brace & Company.

Dakin Williams and Sheperd Meade, excerpt from *Tennessee Williams: An Intimate Biography.* No portion of this text may be reprinted without further permission of Arbor House (NY).

Edwina Dakin Williams, *Remember Me to Tom,* 1963. Published by the Putnam Publishing Group. No portion of this text may be reprinted without permission.

Tennessee Williams, *The Glass Menagerie.* Copyright 1945 by Tennessee Williams and Edwina D. Williams and renewed © 1973 by Tennessee Williams. Reprinted by permission of Random House, Inc. Excerpt from *Tennessee Williams: Memoirs* by Tennessee Williams. Copyright © 1972, 1975 by Tennessee Williams. Used by permission of Doubleday, a division of Random House, Inc. "Portrait of a Girl in Glass" from *The Collected Stories of Tennessee Williams* by Tennessee Williams. Copyright 1948 by Tennessee Williams. Reprinted by permission of New Directions Publishing Corporation. "Production Notes" from *The Glass Menagerie* by Tennessee Williams. Copyright 1945 by Tennessee Williams and Edwin D. Williams and renewed © 1973 by Tennessee Williams. Reprinted by permission of Random House, Inc.

William Carlos Williams, "The Great Figure," "Spring and All," and "The Red Wheelbarrow" from *Collected Poems: 1909–1939,* Vol. 1, by William Carlos Williams. Copyright 1938 by New Directions Publishing Corporation. Reprinted by permission of New Directions Publishing Corporation. "The Dance" from *Collected Poems: 1909–1939,* Vol. 1, by William Carlos Williams. Copyright 1944, 1945 by New Directions Publishing Corporation. Reprinted by permission of New Directions Publishing Corporation.

August Wilson, *Fences.* Copyright © 1986 by August Wilson. Used by permission of Dutton Signet, a division of Penguin Putnam, Inc.

James Wright, "Autumn Begins in Martins Ferry, Ohio" and "A Blessing" from *Above the River: The Complete Poems.* Copyright © 1990 by Anne Wright, Wesleyan University Press. Reprinted by permission of University Press of New England.

Richard Wright, "Hokku Poems" from *Richard Wright Reader* by Richard Wright. Copyright © 1959 by Richard Wright. Published by Arcade Publishing, Inc., New York, NY. Reprinted by permission. "Big Black Good Man" from *Eight Men* by Richard Wright. Copyright 1940, © 1961 by Richard Wright and renewed 1989 by Ellen Wright. Reprinted by permission of HarperCollins Publishers, Inc.

Hisaye Yamamoto, "Seventeen Syllables" from *Seventeen Syllables and Other Stories* by Hisaye Yamamoto DeSoto. Copyright by Partisan Review, November 1949. Copyright © renewed 1976. Hisaye Yamamoto DeSoto. Kitchen Table: Women of Color Press, 1988. Rutgers University Press, 1998. Reprinted by permission of Rutgers University Press.

William Butler Yeats, "Leda and the Swan," "Crazy Jane Talks with the Bishop," and "Sailing to Byzantium" reprinted with the permission of Simon & Schuster from *The*

Poems of W. B. Yeats: A New Edition, edited by Richard J. Finneran. Copyright 1928 by Macmillan Publishing Company and renewed © 1956 by Georgie Yeats. "The Lake Isle of Innisfee" and "An Irish Airman Foresees His Death" reprinted with the permission of Simon & Schuster from *The Poems of W. B. Yeats: A New Edition,* edited by Richard J. Finneran (New York: Macmillan, 1989). "The Second Coming" reprinted with the permission of Simon & Schuster from *The Poems of W. B. Yeats: A New Edition,* edited by Richard J. Finneran. Copyright 1924 by Macmillan Publishing Company and renewed 1952 by Bertha Georgie Yeats.

Louis Zukofsky, "I Walk in the Old Street" from *Complete Short Poetry* by Louis Zukofsky. Copyright © 1991 by and reprinted by permission of Louis Zukofsky and the Johns Hopkins University Press, Baltimore, London.

PHOTO CREDITS

◈ ◈ ◈

p. 48, Courtesy of Alberto Ríos.

p. 76, Courtesy of Louisiana State University Press.

p. 80, Wide World Photos, Inc.

p. 86, Wide World Photos, Inc.

p. 96, Copyright © Marion Ettlinger/Corbis Outline.

p. 112, Copyright © 1988 Wilbur Funches/AP/Wide World Photos, Inc.

p. 119, UPI/Bettmann.

p. 124, AP/Wide World Photos, Inc.

p. 133, Copyright © 1993 Wyatt Counts/AP/Wide World Photos, Inc.

p. 159, Copyright © AP/Wide World Photos, Inc.

p. 167, The Granger Collection, New York

p. 182, Photo by Rex Rystedt.

p. 206, AP/Wide World Photos, Inc.

p. 218, AP/Wide World Photos, Inc.

p. 241, Courtesy of Gary Gildner.

p. 254, AP/Wide World Photos, Inc.

p. 260, AP/Wide World Photos, Inc.

p. 265, AP/Wide World Photos, Inc.

p. 279, AP/Wide World Photos, Inc.

p. 303, The Bettmann Archive.

p. 315, AP/Wide World Photos, Inc.

p. 323, Wide World Photos, Inc.

p. 332, AP/Wide World Photos, Inc.

p. 348, Courtesy of David Michael Kaplan.

p. 362, Copyright © Murray/Corbis-Bettmann.

p. 376, Courtesy of Hisaye Yamamoto.

p. 388, Wide World Photos, Inc.

p. 613, Photo by Norman Seeff.

p. 1015, top, AP/Wide World Photos, Inc.

p. 1015, bottom, Copyright © Wyatt Counts/AP/Wide World Photos, Inc.

p. 1016, top, AP/Wide World Photos, Inc.

p. 1016, bottom, Photo by Bill Tague.

p. 1017, top, Copyright © 1988 Marion Ettlinger/AP/Wide World Photos, Inc.

p. 1017, bottom, Courtesy of St. Mary's College of Maryland.

p. 1018, top, AP/Wide World Photos, Inc.

p. 1018, bottom, The Bettmann Archive.

p. 1019, top, Copyright © AP/Wide World Photos, Inc.

p. 1019, bottom, AP/Wide World Photos, Inc.

p. 1020, top, Copyright © 1993 Michael Dorris.

p. 1020, bottom, AP/Wide World Photos, Inc.

p. 1021, top, The Bettmann Archive.

p. 1021, bottom, Copyright © 1992 AP/Wide World Photos, Inc.

p. 1022, top, AP/Wide World Photos, Inc.

p. 1022, bottom, AP/Wide World Photos, Inc.

p. 1023, top, The Bettmann Archive.

p. 1023, bottom, Copyright © Simon Walker/Rex USA, Ltd.

p. 1024, top, The Granger Collection, New York.

p. 1024, bottom, Pencil drawing by Francis Dodd, 1935, Bettmann Archive.

p. 1025, top, Copyright © AFP/Corbis.

Index of Authors, Titles, and First Lines of Poetry